D1381525

The
Textbook of Adult Nursing

The
Textbook of Adult Nursing

Lillian Sholtis Brunner and Doris Smith Suddarth

Adapted and edited for the UK from the
Lippincott *Textbook of Medical–Surgical Nursing* (Sixth edition)
by
Brian Gilchrist, Catherine M. Robertson,
Christine Webb and Stephen Wright

CHAPMAN & HALL
London · New York · Tokyo · Melbourne · Madras

Published by Chapman & Hall, 2–6 Boundary Row, London SE1 8HN

Chapman & Hall, 2–6 Boundary Row, London SE1 8HN, UK

Chapman & Hall, 29 West 35th Street, New York, NY10001, USA

Chapman & Hall, Japan, Thomson Publishing Japan, Hirakawacho Nemoto Building, 6F, 1-7-11 Hirakawa-cho, Chiyoda-ku, Tokyo 102, Japan

Chapman & Hall Australia, Thomas Nelson Australia, 102 Dodds Street, South Melbourne, Victoria 3205, Australia

Chapman & Hall India, R. Seshadri, 32 Second Main Road, CIT East, Madras 600 035, India

First edition 1992

© 1992 Chapman & Hall

Adapted from *Textbook of Medical–Surgical Nursing*, Sixth edition. Copyright © 1988 by J. B. Lippincott Company. Copyright © 1984, 1980, 1975, 1970, 1964 by J.B. Lippincott Company.
Adapted by arrangement with J. B. Lippincott Company, 227 East Washington Square, Philadelphia, PA 19106–3780, USA

Typeset in 9½/11 Times by Tradespools Ltd., Frome, Somerset
Printed and bound in Hong Kong

ISBN 0 412 43980 8

CONTENTS

Contents

PREFACE

We welcome this opportunity to introduce to readers this new British adaptation of the American *Lippincott Textbook of Medical–Surgical Nursing*. We aim to meet the needs of students on diploma and degree courses for a comprehensive text that will last throughout their course. The book should also be a valuable source of reference and updating for qualified nurses and those in continuing education.

Production of an anglicized edition of the Textbook was needed not only to make its language more accessible to British readers, but also to adapt some of the information so that it is appropriate to our different health care system.

But the British version is not merely an anglicized version. The editorial team was keen to adopt an approach that built on the reputation established by the American text, and that reflected a humane and sensitive approach to nursing care. We wanted the new version to be based on our personal philosophies of care in a rapidly changing multicultural society. Our aim has been to show, through a nursing process approach, how patients and clients have rights to individualized care that respect their own unique needs as members of particular social groupings based on cultural, gender, race, religion and individual preference.

Therefore, we have tried to provide advice about how to give nursing care, rather than being prescriptive, and to give references and bibliographies so that readers have access to the rationales behind what is suggested. Just as we believe that patients and clients should be treated as thinking, feeling beings, so we have tried to use an approach that offers the same respect to nurses.

To achieve these aims, we have rewritten Unit 1 completely to reflect the fundamental ideas and principles that we feel should underpin nursing care in Britain in the 1990s. We have tried to use a style that reflects our philosophy, avoiding culturally specific terms and using gender-neutral language. We decided not to use models of nursing as bases for the care plans, both because there are now many good books on models available and because we did not want to impose particular models on our readers. Nurses should be able to adapt the care plans in the book for use with the philosophy or model adopted in their own practice settings.

Many care plans are included and, as far as possible, these address individuals rather than adopting a standard care plan approach. Nevertheless, these care plans are intended to convey the comprehensive care needed by patients with particular health deviations. Patient-centred problems are identified, together with their causes. Expected outcomes are patient-centred and measurable wherever possible. Nursing interventions are worded concisely and set out clearly. Care is also discussed in the text to back up and elaborate on the care plans.

We hope that the energy and enthusiasm invested by contributors, the publishing team and ourselves have paid off. We have tried to produce an up-to-date, comprehensive and attractive textbook that helps readers to deliver high quality, soundly based nursing care in an understanding way. This has been a long-term effort for all of us, but if we have achieved our aims then the project will have been worthwhile.

Brian Gilchrist
Catherine M. Robertson
Christine Webb
Stephen Wright

CONTRIBUTORS

Brian Gilchrist BSc MSc RGN
Lecturer, Department of Nursing Studies, King's
College, London

Catherine M. Robertson BA PhD RGN SCM RCNT RNT
Director of Centre for Nursing Studies, Dundee Institute
of Technology

Christine Webb BA MSc PhD SRN RSCN RNT
Professor, Department of Nursing Studies, University of
Manchester

Stephen Wright RGN DipN RCNT DANS RNT MSc
Consultant Nurse, The Nursing Development Unit,
Tameside General Hospital

WITH

Rachel Baughan RGN DipN
Formerly Senior Nurse, Surgical Unit, University
College Hospital

Ann Brown RMN RGN BSc
Charge Nurse, Royal Victoria Hospital, Edinburgh

Irene Callahan BSc RGN SCM DipN RCNT
Clinical Teacher, Tayside College of Nursing and
Midwifery

Mark Collier SEN SRN ONC RCNT
Lecturer, Bloomsbury College of Nurse Education,
Royal National Orthopaedic Hospital

Jessica Corner BSc PhD RGN
Senior Macmillan Lecturer, Academic Nursing Unit,
Institute of Cancer Research, Royal Marsden Hospital

Linda Corrin RGN BA OND RCNT RNT
Tutor, Ophthalmic Nursing School, South West
Manchester College of Nursing, Manchester Royal Eye
Hospital

Carol Dealey RGN RCNT
Clinical Nurse Specialist in Tissue Viability, Queen
Elizabeth Hospital; and Mosley Hall Hospital

Jo Duncan RGN
Formerly Clinical Nurse Teacher, Royal National
Throat, Nose and Ear Hospital

Alistair Farley BSc RMN DipN
Clinical Teacher, Tayside College of Nursing and
Midwifery

Caroline Fincham Gee SRN OND Derm Cert RCNT Cert Ed
RNT
Tutor, Department of Academic Standards, The
Nightingale School and Guy College

Carolyn Galpin RGN RCNT RNT DipN
Tutor, Department of Academic Studies, The
Nightingale School

Isobel M. Gibson RGN SCM RCNT
Clinical Nurse Teacher, Lothian College of Nursing and
Midwifery (North Division), Edinburgh

Dinah Gould BSc MPhil RGN DipN Cert Ed
Lecturer in Nursing Studies, King's College

Morag Gray RGN RCNT DipCNE RNT MN
Nurse Teacher, Lothian College of Nursing and
Midwifery (South Division)

Janice Henderson RGN RMN BSc
Sister, Medical Unit, Stracathro Hospital by Brechin
Angus, Scotland

Susan Holmes BSc (Hons) PhD SRN FRSH
Director of Postgraduate Studies, Department of Nursing
and Midwifery, University of Surrey

Pamela Jackson BSc (Hons) RGN RHV RCNT
Lecturer in Nursing Studies, Department of Nursing and
Midwifery, University of Surrey

Jan Maycock RGN RM
Senior Manager, District Nursing; and Consultant in
Rheumatology Nursing, Waltham Forest Community
Health Services, London

James Millar RGN
Charge Nurse, Western General Hospital, Edinburgh

Linda Moore RGN
Sister, Accident and Emergency Department, Royal
Victoria Hospital, Belfast

Alexander Nesbitt BA(Hons) RGN
Charge Nurse, The Middlesex Hospital

Barbara Parfitt RGN SCM RNT MCommH MSC FNP ALBC
Head of Department, Advanced Nursing Studies, North
East Wales Institute

Robert J. Pratt BA MSC RGN RNT DipN (London)
Vice Principal and Head of Faculty, Faculty of
Vocational and Professional Practice, Riverside College
of Nursing, London

Noel Scanlon RGN ONC FETC
Senior Charge Nurse, Bath Cancer Unit, Royal United
Hospital; formerly Charge Nurse, Haematology Unit,
Southmead Hospital

Lynette Stone BA RGN RM(NSW) DMS
Clinical Nurse Manager, Dermatology, St John's
Dermatology Centre, St Thomas' Hospital, London

Lynda Taylor RGN RM
Infection Control Nurse, Division of Hospital Infection,
Central Public Health Laboratory

Diane Thomlinson BSc(Hons) RGN ONC
Infection Control Nurse, Worcester Health Authority,
Worcester Royal Infirmary

David R. Thompson BSc PhD RGN RMN ONC
Clinical Nurse Specialist, Coronary Care Unit, Leicester
General Hospital

Ann E. Topping RGN BSc(Hons) Cert Ed
Senior Lecturer in Nursing/Health Studies, Huddersfield
Polytechnic

Linda Veitch RGN DipCE
Clinical Teacher, Post Basic Department, Lothian
College of Nursing and Midwifery (South Division)

Rosemary A. Webster BSC RGN
Sister, Coronary Care Unit, Leicester General Hospital

CONTRIBUTORS TO THE US EDITION

EDITORS

Lillian Sholtis Brunner RN MSN ScD LittD FAAN
Vice-Chairman (Education and Research) Board of
Trustees; Consultant in Nursing, Presbyterian-University
of Pennsylvania Medical Center, Philadelphia,
Pennsylvania

Member, Board of Overseers, School of Nursing,
University of Pennsylvania, Philadelphia, Pennsylvania

Formerly Assistant Professor of Nursing, Yale
University School of Nursing, New Haven, Connecticut

Doris Smith Suddarth RN BSNE MSN
Formerly Coordinator of the Curriculum, The
Alexandria Hospital School of Nursing, Alexandria,
Virginia

CONTRIBUTORS

Brenda G. Bare RN MSN
Director of Medical–Surgical Nursing, The Alexandria
Hospital, Alexandria, Virginia

Elizabeth W. Bayley RN MS
Assistant Professor, Burn, Emergency, and Trauma
Nursing, Widener University, Chester, Pennsylvania

Ellen K. Boyda RN MS CCRN
Pulmonary Rehabilitation Program Coordinator, Taylor
Hospital, Ridley Park, Pennsylvania

Mary Jo Boyer RN MSN
Professor of Nursing, Nursing Program Coordinator,
Delaware County Community College, Media,
Pennsylvania

Contributors to the US Edition

David B.P. Goodman MD PhD
Professor and Department Chief, Department of
Pathology and Laboratory Medicine, Hospital of the
University of Pennsylvania, Philadelphia, Pennsylvania

Gail P. Hamilton RN MSN DSW
Associate Professor of Nursing, Department of Nursing,
College of Allied Health Professions, Temple
University, Philadelphia, Pennsylvania

Lois M. Hoskins RN PhD
Dean and Associate Professor of Nursing, School of
Nursing, The Catholic University of America,
Washington, DC

Dorothy B. Liddel RN MSN
Curriculum Coordinator, The Alexandria Hospital
School of Nursing, Alexandria, Virginia

Norma Milligan Metheny RN PhD
Professor and Coordinator, Graduate Medical–Surgical
Nursing Major, St Louis University, St Louis, Missouri

Rita Nemchik RN MS
Director, Centre for Continuing Education, University of
Pennsylvania School of Nursing, Philadelphia,
Pennsylvania

Kathryn A. Pollon RNC MSN
Mental Health Specialist, Mt Vernon Hospital,
Alexandria, Virginia

Susan A. Rokita RN MS
Oncology Clinical Nurse Specialist, The Thomas
Jefferson University Hospital, Philadelphia,
Pennsylvania

Mona B. Shevlin MA PhD
Licensed Psychologist, Professor, The Catholic
University of America, Washington, DC; Director,
Counseling Center for Greater Washington, McLean,
Virginia

Suzanne C. O'Connell Smeltzer RN MS EdD
Assistant Professor, Rutgers University College of
Nursing, Newark, New Jersey

Loretta Spittle RN MS CCRN
Director of Critical Care Services, The Fairfax Hospital,
Falls Church, Virginia

Cindy L. Stern RN MSN
Oncology Clinical Nurse Specialist, The Thomas
Jefferson University Hospital, Philadelphia,
Pennsylvania

*Contributors to the fifth edition whose work appeared in
the sixth edition are listed below.*

Silvia Prodan Lange
Margo McCaffery
Diane Deegan McCrann
Josephine Messer
Ruth Mrozek
Kyriake Valassi

Unit 1

INTRODUCTION

chapter *1*

ILLNESS AND THE HOSPITAL EXPERIENCE—A NURSING PERSPECTIVE

INTRODUCTION

The focus of this text is on the nurse's role in helping people who have clearly defined medical or surgical problems. By and large, such problems tend to necessitate treatment and care in a hospital setting. Illness alone can be a highly stressful event for both body and mind. A wide range of physical sensations (the effects of nausea, pain or a high temperature, for example) are coupled with fears and uncertainties over their meaning ('Is it serious?', 'Does the pain get worse?', 'How will I cope?', 'Am I dying?'). The stress extends beyond concern for the self, into anxieties about others who are 'cared about' in the person's life, as well as affecting those who 'care for' that person. When all this is added to the enforced relocation of the individual from safe, familiar surroundings to the unknown and often frightening hospital setting, then it is not surprising that an admission to hospital can be a terrifying experience. Illness and admission to hospital, together with the accompanying fear of their effects upon personal relationships, finances, employment and so on, rank high in the list of the 'stress inventory' (Cooper, Cooper and Eaten, 1988). Most individuals are well adapted to cope with the stresses and strains of everyday life; however, those that accumulate around illness and hospitalization require a keen awareness by nurses of their nature and consequences, and of what nurses can best do to alleviate them.

STRESS AND COPING

Considerable evidence is now available to suggest that stress is an important component in illness. It affects the person's perception of the illness and how it can be responded to, and can adversely affect healing and recovery rates (Bailey and Clarke, 1985; Benner and Wrubel, 1989; Boore, 1978). Undoubtedly, understanding the nature of stress and its effects upon patients and nurses is essential to effective nursing.

A variety of approaches to defining stress have been taken. Some models appear to adopt a mechanistic view, in which something outside the individual in the environment (the stressor or stimulus) produces a change in the individual's behaviour (either physical or psychological). These are called stimulus–response models. For example, a blow from a stick causes bruising and pain, or the loss of a loved one causes depression. Such models of stress tend to be based on a linear cause–effect approach. While this may account for some of the response of human beings to illness, it seems to underestimate the capacity of different individuals to respond differently to similar stresses. Individuals are also able to adjust their responses to a particular stress through their own ways of coping (Elsdorfer, Cohen, Kleinman and Maxim, 1981; Welford, 1974).

Approaches to the stimulus–response syndromes (such as Selye, 1976) have tended to focus on the physiological response of the person to the stressor. Elsdorfer, Cohen, Kleinman and Maxim (1981) and Lazarus and Folkman (1984) have argued that this underestimates the ability of different individuals to deal with different stresses. Psychological effects and abilities are often underestimated. Bailey and Clarke (1985) have developed Lazarus's work to describe the cognitive–phenomenological–transactional view of stress and coping.

This approach suggests that individuals can respond to stressors (including various forms of illness) in ways that are more complex than simple stimulus–response mechanisms. Thinking and memory (cognitive) can affect our response to stress (e.g., by reducing the fear of the effects of surgery after meeting others who have successfully recovered from the same operation). At the same time, the individual's response is highly idiosyncratic and may vary from time to time (phenomenological). For example, some patients may perceive the presence of a monitor as comforting because 'something is being done', while others may find them frightening. Later, that same patient may interpret the presence of the monitor as discomfiting and inconvenient. The other aspect of this model recognizes that there is an interaction by the individual with the environment and the people in it. This transaction enables the individual to appraise each situation and evaluate how much threat or harm is perceived. For example, one patient sees entering hospital as terrifying and life threatening, while another may feel fortunate and glad that help is at hand to solve the problem.

Thus the individual's own understanding of illness, what it means to that individual and the context in which it occurs add complex dimensions that affects how each person responds. Human beings are more than mere identical stress-adaptors. The response by each person to their illness experience is unique: 'Illness is always an interruption, and one of the major things it interrupts is an ongoing life course' (Benner and Wrubel, 1989). The interruption

in life that sickness brings, when combined with hospitalization, produces a varied catalogue of stress:

Mrs Swiatczak, sweating, pale and tearful, was assisted into bed as she was admitted to the surgical ward in the early hours of the morning. Her clothes were soiled with vomit and she clutched at her abdomen. Her words and phrases lurched from English into Polish, and back again. At 67, this was her first experience of hospital. Her doctor had told her that she must be admitted for surgery to deal with a suspected strangulated femoral hernia. She was alone and repeatedly asked if her husband was well—he was bedfast at home and she was his principal carer. Despite the pain and nausea, she repeatedly asked to go home; she did not want to die in hospital. A review of this individual's situation illustrates the complexities of the stress she was experiencing and its effects upon her. Some key points may be summarized thus:

- Worry about her husband. How would he manage alone? Would the general practitioner keep his promise to make sure that the district nurse and relatives would be called in to help him?
- Loneliness and separation. She and her husband had never been parted in 35 years.
- The physical effects—pain, nausea, sweating, vomiting, and a racing heartbeat—terrified her. The effects were a normal response to the underlying disease, and were not in themselves life threatening, but to her they signalled impending death. At the same time she tried to convince herself that the pain was easing, and told her nurse and doctor so in the hope that they would send her home.
- She was surrounded by unfamiliar faces, strange sounds, smells and objects. The meaning of many were uncertain. Trays and trolleys were filled with innocent instruments in the eyes of the nurse. To Mrs Swiatczak they seemed fearsome, dangerous, pain-inducing.
- For days she had felt unwell, unable to eat, and her normal sleep pattern had been disturbed. She was uncertain if it was day or night, or indeed what day it was.
- The staff seemed to speak quickly and she did not always understand. The words they used seemed unfamiliar, and their attitude remote. The hands that touched her, moved her, felt strange. They were strangers' hands that took off her clothes and touched her body. The doctor was a young man—she felt exposed and vulnerable—she had never let such a person see her body before.
- She felt confused and frightened. Her body was behaving in ways she did not understand. She did not really understand what a hernia was or what it was doing to her. With her fear her pulse raced, and the pain worsened. Would she get better, would she get out of this place, would she die here?

● She felt unable to make herself understood; waves of panic overtook her and she seemed unable to speak clearly. Her language became muddled. The staff tried to explain things to her, but she could not take in all that was being said.

This is a brief summary of one person's response to the stress of illness and admission to hospital. The interaction of physical and psychological responses, overlaid with its complex images, ideas and expectations provides an illustration of the unique meaning these events hold for one particular person.

The stress and senses of threat and anxiety that may accompany illness and hospitalization are addressed by a wide range of coping strategies, designed to minimize the danger and restore body integrity. Some of these take the form of basic physiological responses, which are largely automatic in nature. Selye (1980) has described the General Adaptation Syndrome. For example, a wide range of physiological responses takes place to maintain the blood pressure and cerebral function (e.g., rising pulse and respiratory rates, glucogenesis, release of stored red cells, arterial contractions and so on) in the event of a major haemorrhage. Similarly, the Local Adaptation Syndrome occurs in a specific part of the body in response to injury, e.g., a minor cut sets of an inflammatory process to seal the wound, destroy infection, remove dead cells and replace damaged tissue. A complex interplay of body defence mechanisms such as the autonomic nervous system, the endocrine and immune response systems, is set in motion to escape from stresses, limit the damage and restore body integrity. Specific details of these issues will be dealt with separately under the various diagnoses in subsequent chapters.

However, coping mechanisms to deal with stress have components other than physiological interventions, and relate to the response of the person as a whole.

Bailey and Clarke (1985) described three other methods of coping, based on the work of Lazarus and Launier (in Pervin and Lewis (eds), 1978). These can be summarized briefly as follows:

1. Direct coping—the person attempts to change the situation to reduce or avoid the stresses and their effects. For example, a smoker perceives the threat of cancer and takes action to reduce or give up smoking.
2. Indirect coping—often the individual is unable to change the source and effects of the stresses. For example, a patient dying from a terminal illness is unable to change its nature. However, what the individual might do is either:
   a. Change the perception of the threat by seeing it as a release from life and an opportunity to move on to something better, or
   b. Use methods that actually change the individual's experience of their stresses. In this case, the threat of death may be alleviated by adopting relaxation or meditation techniques, or concentrating on 'living life to the full', or 'taking each day as it comes'.
3. Palliative coping—in this case the individual takes steps that help by offering temporary relief, but which may not, in the long term, remove the threat. Indeed, they may eventually lead to greater stress at a later date. Bailey and Clarke (1985) cite examples such as:
   a. Eating snacks when bored and depressed. This may relieve depression in the short term, but may later exacerbate it when weight is gained.
   b. A doctor tells a patient she has a serious breast problem and must see a consultant. The patient avoids telling anyone and fails to keep the appointment. In the short term she may forget the problem, but later develops an extensive carcinoma.

A variety of coping mechanisms, both physical and psychological, can be used to restore a sense of personal and bodily control and integrity. It is clear, however, that the use of these coping mechanisms is extremely complex and in many instances requires resources that are beyond the capacity of the individual. For example, a major haemorrhage may require blood transfusion and the help of nurses and doctors to maintain life and restore health; giving up smoking may require expert teaching and counselling from others. Understanding the nature of stress and coping, and how help might be given, places these subjects very much within the concern of nursing.

In order that nurses may help patients to cope with the stress of illness and to manage their own health, they need to understand the variety of social factors that provide people with different types and levels of resources for coping. These social factors include those related to social class, including income, employment, financial security and educational background, as well as experiences throughout childhood and adult life that have led individuals to have their own unique personalities and ways of coping. The following sections will consider these social influences as a preparation for discussing how nurses may help patients to manage health and illness.

SOCIAL CLASS, HEALTH AND ILLNESS

Defining and Measuring Social Class

Social class is a difficult concept to define because it used with different meanings in varying circumstances, and because it has emotional overtones. While some people think it is unnecessarily divisive to talk about social class in Britain today, signs of class divisions confront us everywhere we look. They do this nowhere more vividly than in our work as nurses, and therefore it is important to have an understanding of class and the enormous influence that social inequalities have in determining people's health and illness experiences.

In Britain, social class is almost always defined and measured using the Registrar General's classification, which breaks down into the following categories:

I   Professional (e.g., lawyer, doctor).
II   Intermediate (e.g., nurse, teacher).
IIIN Skilled nonmanual (e.g., shop assistant, typist).
IIIM Skilled manual (e.g., miner, bus driver).
IV   Partly skilled manual (e.g., farm worker, bus conductor).
V   Unskilled manual (e.g., cleaner, labourer).

This scheme is based on the census, and it is useful to understand how it is drawn up in order to be aware of the problems involved in using this form of social categorization. The original intention was to have a system based solely on occupational skill and job content, but there is clearly more to the present scheme than this. For example, all 'nurses' are placed in social class II by the Registrar General, regardless of whether they possess a statutory qualification. Thus registered and enrolled nurses are grouped together with nursing auxiliaries.

Plainly, the idea of relative social prestige is being used by the compilers as well as notions of skill. Stevenson, the originator of the scheme, was clearly aware of this, for he is reported as saying that ranking people by income alone would produce 'such obviously bizarre results as a publican ranking above a clergyman'. This would be bizarre, because of the differences in 'culture' associated with the two jobs (Burgess, 1986). There is a bizarreness, too, for nurses in the way they are categorized, and within the scheme other workers would doubtless find similar anomalies.

'Snob value' seems to form part of the Registrar General's scheme, but the reality behind this does have an effect in everyday life. Being an electrician is a different kind of occupation from being a teacher even though the salaries might be similar. However, when different ways of measuring social class are considered, these different lifestyle factors still have an influence. For example, using educational level, car ownership, housing tenure (owner occupation versus renting in the private or public sectors) and ownership of various kinds of consumer durables parallels very closely social class. Predicting health and illness status using these alternative measures gives remarkably similar results (Whitehead, 1988) and therefore there are real differences being measured when social class is considered.

Nevertheless, measuring social class is not without its difficulties. If assessment is based on employment, how can we know the social class of retired, unemployed people and housewives? Retired and unemployed people are often assigned the class of their last job or the one they held for the majority of their working lives. But this may not reflect their current economic position because pensions and unemployment benefits are substantially lower than their previous income. And what about the increasing numbers of unemployed people who have never had a job—how are they to be classified?

Women and Social Class

Assessing women's social class is fraught with even greater difficulties, and ways of getting round the problems that were used in the past are becoming impractical and socially unacceptable. At a very basic level, women increasingly find the link of the housewife role with the unemployed status offensive. Clearly, being a housewife is very demanding, both physically and emotionally (Oakley, 1981), and involves the skills of childcare, nursing, catering, laundering, budgeting and planning, counselling and many others. Women therefore feel insulted that their role as 'housewife' is undervalued by being regarded as a form of unemployment.

The previous convention of assessing a household by the occupation of its head—usually identified as the male—is both socially unacceptable as well as very misleading. The combined incomes of a two-worker household will obviously provide greater purchasing power than if only one member is in paid employment. Today the majority of women work outside the home even when they have young children, and the traditional household consisting of a male 'breadwinner', a wife who stays at home and their (two) children is in the minority.

As far as health is concerned, income is a very important influence. However, educational level is also a factor, and it is common for women to marry a man of lower social class than themselves. This arises partly from the vagaries of the classification system, where manual jobs are classed as lower than nonmanual jobs. For example, a bus driver in social class IIIM may be married to a typist in IIIM or a nursing auxiliary in class II. The educational level of the woman, who is likely to have the more influential role in relation to family health, may be a more important consideration than the occupational class of the male head of household. For this reason, a more rounded approach is to consider more than one measure of social class.

For example, in a study of women recovering from hysterectomy, Webb and Wilson-Barnett (1983) assessed recovery using husband's occupation, woman's own occupation (including housewife as a distinct status) and woman's educational level (O-levels, A-levels, postschool education). In this example, the various factors measured could have had a different influence on recovery. Occupation of both partners would condition their material standard of living, and whether equipment like washing machines, freezers and vacuum cleaners would be available to ease recovery. People in higher social class jobs would also be more likely to be able to take time off work without loss of pay or loss of the job itself. The woman's own educational level might influence both her understanding of how her body worked and the likelihood of her seeking out books and leaflets about hysterectomy that could help her.

Inequalities and Health

No matter how social class is measured, its influence on people's health and illness is crucial. Both in the Black report (Townsend and Davidson, 1982) and the more recent publication by Whitehead (1988), higher social class was strongly associated with better health, and lower social class was accompanied by poorer health. Just as differing ways of assessing social class led to the same result, so did different ways of measuring health and illness status. Thus, rates of stillbirth, infant mortality, morbidity (illness) and mortality among adults and life expectancy all showed exactly the same trend.

All causes of illness and death gave similar results. Whether consideration is given to the leading causes of death, including lung cancer, coronary heart disease and cerebrovascular disease, or rates of alcoholism and depression, the results are the same. The only condition that occurs more commonly in richer people is malignant melanoma, which is caused by over-exposure to the sun—clearly an activity indulged in more often by wealthier people (Whitehead, 1988).

Unemployment and Health

Unemployed people have worse health than those in work, including higher suicide and attempted suicide rates (Brenner, 1979; Platt and Kreitman, 1984). Unemployed women also have higher sickness rates, but the highest rates for women occur in those who are married. Studies of mental health consistently show that married men have the best mental health, followed by single men and women, with married women being worst off. This has been linked with the fact that these women often have two jobs (paid worker and housewife), are chiefly responsible for the burdens of running the home and bringing up children and may lack emotional support from their partner or another person in whom they can confide (Brown and Harries, 1978; Oakley 1981). Studies have also shown that the wives and children of unemployed men suffer psychologically as well as materially (Fagin and Little, 1984). Unemployed people and their families also consult their general practitioners more and have more outpatient consultations than the employed.

Regional Inequalities

Geographical location also has a strong influence on health and illness status. Death rates are lower in England and Wales in comparison with Scotland. Within these countries, different regions also have varying mortality statistics. For example, East Anglia has the lowest death rate, followed by the South East and South West of England. High death rates in North West and North East England are only surpassed by those in Strathclyde and Clydeside (Whitehead, 1988). Furthermore, the same inequalities are repeated within each region. For example, in Greater Manchester, certain electoral wards have mortality rates as low as those in the South East and South West, and others have rates equalling those in the highest areas (Manchester Joint Consultative Committee).

Ethnicity and Health

Ethnic origin is another factor closely linked with health, although not in a straightforward manner. For example, tuberculosis rates are high in immigrants from India, and in those from Ireland, the Caribbean and Africa. Conversely, cancer of the stomach, large intestine and breast have low rates of mortality among Indians. Obstructive lung disease is low in all immigrants in comparison with those born in England and Wales, but violence and accidents are high in all immigrant groups (Whitehead, 1988). Undoubtedly, lifestyle factors such as smoking, alcohol consumption and nutritional patterns interact with poverty and unemployment in these groups just as they do in all populations. This highlights the importance of considering groups separately and examining the particular factors relevant to their health, rather than lumping together everyone who is part of an 'ethnic minority'.

Health and Illness Behaviour

'Victim-blaming' explanations of inequalities in health and illness lay the blame for poor health on individual lifestyles. According to this way of thinking, people who are better educated and have more money choose to use their resources and to live in a way that leads to a more healthy lifestyle and greater life expectancy. They smoke less, take more exercise and are more likely to limit their family size. They are also more likely to seek professional help in relation to their health and, having sought help, are more likely to follow the advice given. On the other hand, poorer and less well educated people choose different lifestyles. They are less concerned with healthy eating, smoke and drink more and choose to adopt more dangerous habits that involve them in more accidents.

While it is certainly true that middle class people use the health services more (Whitehead, 1980), this individual lifestyle explanation is seriously deficient. It presupposes that everyone has the freedom to turn their choices into actions. This is easier for the better off, but poorer people cannot be said to choose to live in damp and badly heated homes, to eat 'junk' foods that are high in refined carbohydrates and saturated fats, and low in protein and fibre. Certain choices are simply not available to them because of financial limitations. Similarly, they do not elect to enter more dangerous occupations: in order to avoid unemployment they are forced to do more dangerous work down mines, on building sites and in manufacturing industries where there are recognized or unrecognized industrial hazards that may lead to pulmonary diseases or various cancers (Townsend and Davidson, 1982).

Individual lifestyle theories may also adopt a condescending approach to the way less well off people think about and act on health and illness issues. The assumption that poorer people are feckless and do not understand how to live healthy lives is contradicted by many studies. Blaxter (in Cox, Blaxter, Buckle *et al.*, 1987) reports that middle class people define health in terms of positive fitness and feel that they have more control over their health. In an earlier report, Blaxter (1983) showed that women from social classes IV and V distinguish between illness and disease. They see illness as weakness, and as giving in to being unwell. Diseases, however, are actually diagnoses of the same type as doctors use, and include concepts such as infection, environmental agents and heredity, as well as the idea that bad housing, working conditions and pollution can render a person more susceptible to diseases. There is no evidence here that poorer and less educated people have less sophisticated understandings of health and illness than middle class people. Oakley's work on smoking in pregnancy (Oakley, 1988) confirms these findings by showing that pregnant women have a good knowledge of the harmful effects of smoking on fetal development and the subsequent growth and performance of children. However, they also know that smoking is a valuable aid to them in coping with their stressful lives, and they balance the advantages and disadvantages when deciding whether to continue smoking or to take tranquillizers, for example.

All this evidence suggests that structural or materialist explanations of health and illness, which concentrate of the structure of society and the material conditions of people's lives, offer more convincing explanations of social class differences than claims that if you 'look after yourself' you will achieve better standards.

Social Class and Nursing Care

It is vital for nurses to understand the profound links between social class and health and illness. Without an awareness of the relationship between poverty and illness, nurses could fall into the same trap as the victim-blaming theorists described earlier. It would be worse then useless, for example, to give excellent nutritional education to a person who could not afford to buy the kinds of foods recommended. Similarly, to advise a depressed, working class woman with young children to get out and meet more people by joining an evening class would be likely to arouse hostility rather than have a positive effect.

These examples, of course, bring out the pessimistic side of the way in which the health service functions.

Because nurses work in isolation from social and employment services and housing agencies, they are strictly limited in the kind of nursing care that is possible. This can be very frustrating, when nurses know the root causes of people's problems but feel powerless to deal with these fundamental issues.

But by having a thorough understanding of social influences on health and illness and by assessing each patient or client as an individual with a unique social background and with particular health resources and needs, nurses can assist people to cope as well as possible within the limitations they face. Nurses can also be aware of other agencies to which they can be referred for help with problems beyond their remit, for example social workers, disablement resettlement officers and voluntary action groups.

Bowers (1980) discusses Becker's health belief model and identifies five major influences on people's willingness to take health-related action. These are as follows:

1. They must believe that they are susceptible to a disease.
2. They must also believe that the disease would have serious consequences on some component of their lives.
3. They must be convinced that the proposed action would be beneficial in reducing their susceptibility to disease.
4. Barriers to the action must be surmountable, and the proposed health action must be a truly feasible option for the individual.
5. There must be a cue to taking the health action.

Keeping these five points in mind can aid carrying out a nursing assessment, and in planning and giving individualized care. Point 4, that barriers to health action must be surmountable and feasible, is particularly relevant when thinking about social class and health. It ties in closely with explanations of illness as being poverty-linked, and reminds nurses of the need both for individualized assessment and care planning, and to discuss and plan care in conjunction with patients and clients so that nurses can devise feasible care with them.

LIFE CYCLES, CRISES OR TRANSITIONS?

Life cycle, life crisis, *rites de passage* and stressful life events are all terms which have been used to describe changes happening at different times in a person's life. Achieving adulthood after adolescence is the first of these after childhood in our culture. However, the fact that these events are handled very differently in other cultures immediately suggests that there is nothing inevitable about the way people experience these times in their lives.

Aries' study describes the very different ways in which

children have been reared in the past, and concludes that the particular way children are treated is a recent development (1962). In many societies in the past, children were not seen as being so very different from adults. They were not dressed differently, did not eat different kinds of food and they spent their time with adults, often sharing in the family's work in the home and in agriculture. It is only recently that the 'cult of childhood' has developed.

Still today in many rural societies, the transition from childhood to adulthood occurs at puberty, when special rites or ceremonies mark the passage to adult status. The equivalent of a 'teenage' phase exists either not at all or to a much lesser extent. The ceremonies marking this transition, like others such as marriage and acceptance into a group of respected elders, are called a *rites de passage*. This example illustrates the fact that there is nothing inevitable about the timing of life transitions or the form that they take.

Psychologists writing about these events have imposed on them a regularity that seldom occurs in real life. Sometimes psychologists' definitions have become self-fulfilling prophecies, making people expect and anticipate that they will have difficulties at a particular stage. It is then only too easy for the expectation to become the reality, as for example in the case of the menopause, as will be seen below.

The idea of a life cycle is rejected by Rossi (1980) because this only makes sense if there are repeated cycles, such as the trade cycle with its phases of economic prosperity and depression. Since humans have only one life cycle, Rossi prefers to talk of 'life course'.

Writers such as Erickson (1959) assume that there is a basic ground plan to all human development. These psychologists are interested in psychological qualities such as inner strength, repression of emotions and achievements. Rossi (1980) criticizes these 'timing of events' approaches because they focus on supposed stages of development leading to changes to which *everyone* has difficulty in adjusting. She points out that it is *unanticipated* events rather than anticipated ones that are likely to cause trauma. For example, events such as children leaving home and job success or failure do not occur at the same time in life for everyone.

Research focusing on 'life events' suggests that it is when a number of negative events occur together that stress is likely to result (Dohrenwend and Dohrenwend, 1974). This can occur at any stage in life, and is not restricted to particular times.

Furthermore, it has been clearly demonstrated that how someone reacts to a stressful life event is strongly linked with the quality and quantity of support available to them at the time. Pregnant women undergoing stress, for example, develop fewer symptoms when they have good support (Nuckalls, Cassel and Kaplan, 1972). Similarly, depression and physical illness rates are lower when unemployed people are supported by their families and friends (Gore, 1978).

In other words, it is necessary to consider not only the

events occurring at various times in people's lives, but also the resources they have available to help them cope. When support resources are available—whether they are the emotional or moral support of family and friends or the material support of unemployment and sickness benefits and social services—people are able to work out coping strategies to deal with what is happening to them.

This way of thinking about stress and coping seems more useful because it sees people as unique individuals facing their lives with different resources. They exercise some choice and are not simply at the whim of events beyond their control.

The idea of coping strategies also seems more useful than the term 'mental defence mechanisms'. 'Mental' gives the impression either that it is 'all in the mind', or that people have to cope as individuals and make a mental adjustment when it may be that something wrong in society is contributing to their problems. Unemployment is a good illustration of this. If social changes mean that workers are made redundant, then this is a real problem outside their own immediate individual control.

'Mechanisms' suggests that people respond mechanically or automatically in a 'knee-jerk' kind of way, whereas the coping resources idea implies that they can think about and work out what to do in the light of the help available to them. Again, this is a more individualized way of thinking about people as unique beings.

A final problem with the life crisis kind of approach is that it sees everything that happens to people as a result of their biology. Ageing, sexual maturity or loss of reproductive functions are the focus, whereas it is psychosocial factors that influence people's responses to their biology (Kearl and Hoag, 1984).

An Example: The Menopause

Consider the menopause as an example of the life crisis kind of approach to understanding changes and how people respond to them.

The menopause is defined as the ending of menstruation and it is marked by the last episode of menstrual bleeding (Voda and George, 1986). The climacterium is the period from about the age of 40 to 55 when a woman is passing from the reproductive to the nonreproductive phase of her life. The premenopause is a time of irregular menstruation before menopause, and the postmenopause is the stage of shrinking of the ovaries.

The only symptoms that can be linked definitely with the menopause are hot flushes and sweating (Greene, 1980). Other so-called menopausal symptoms occur mainly before the menopause, and tiredness, palpitations, dizzy spells, poor concentration, insomnia, irritability, anxiety, depression and decreased libido (sexual interest) are general complaints that may accompany an enormous variety of physical and psychological disorders.

These symptoms occur more often in women in the

lower social classes, those with no job outside the home and those with few social contacts (Greene, 1980; Hallstrom and Samuelsson, 1985). Studies of women in different cultures show a wide variation in attitudes and responses to the menopause. For example, Arabs and Israelis have few symptoms and do not perceive the menopause as a crisis. In the United States, Cuban women show more negative attitudes than Jewish women towards the menopause (Greene, 1980).

With regard to sexual activity, again, research findings are contradictory. Some writers report that postmenopausal women are less satisfied with their partners as lovers, have fewer sexual thoughts or fantasies, and suffer more from lack of vaginal lubrication during sex. However, others report no decline in sexual interest, and it may be that the quality of the marital relationship is more important than menopausal changes in influencing sex life at the time of menopause (McCoy and Davidson, 1985).

In fact, the 'normal' menopause has not been written about very much. This may be due to the fact that the 'experts' on the subject—gynaecologists and psychologists—have mainly been men. They are trained to deal with abnormalities rather than the normal, and they have never had similar experiences themselves. As Kahana and Kahana (1982) say,

> One explanation for this may be that society's labelling of menopause as a highly stressful event is based on stereotyped notions offered by persons who have not experienced this event. Middle aged women are far more likely to provide positive evaluations of middle age changes than are persons in younger age groups. The majority of middle-aged women ... believe that the woman herself has some control over her symptoms ... and rate menopause as requiring little adjustment when compared with other life events.

The menopause may coincide with children leaving home and mothers feeling that their main role has been taken away. This has been called the 'empty nest syndrome' and has been linked with symptoms of depression. However, other research has found that women are pleased and relieved when their children leave home, and that there are higher levels of depression in those whose children remain at home after the time when they are expected to leave (Barnett and Baruch, 1978). This is more likely to occur in times when it is hard to get a job. Divorced and childless women and those from lower social classes have more psychiatric disorders at this time.

These reports suggest that children bring stress and negative life events, but that they are also a source of social support that helps women to cope in difficult times. Positive influences that help with adjustment include a good relationship with one's children and new opportunities opening out when childcare responsibilities decrease.

In other words, with the menopause, as with other life transitions, age and biological changes seem to play a minor role in comparison with social influences. It is social factors, too, that help to identify those at risk as well as the support resources that lessen the risk of distress.

All this is not meant to suggest that menopausal symptoms are 'all in the mind'. On the contrary, it is essential to see each individual woman as a unique person and to take seriously her experiences at the time of the menopause. It is a mistake to assume that because a symptom cannot be explained as part of the biological menopause, there is nothing 'really' wrong. First, if a person *feels* distressed then they *are* distressed and need help. Second, if there are no ready explanations for a symptom then investigations need to be done to ensure that serious disease is not being missed. This is particularly the case with postmenopausal bleeding, which may be a sign of endometrial cancer. (See Chapter 22 for further discussion of the menopause.)

Life Changes and Nursing Care

Once again, a similar message emerges for nurses. It is a mistake to see people as falling into particular 'boxes' or stereotypes. Some people may experience distress or even illness at certain times in life, but others may not. Alternatively, a person may sail through one period but not have sufficient support to cope with a different change.

If nurses are aware of the possibilities of these kinds of reactions, they can be alert for them when assessing care needs and can respond appropriately. They may do this simply by using listening skills, or by giving straightforward explanations about what may be happening to the person concerned. They will also be alerted to those patients who are at greater risk of distress, for example, due to coming from a lower social class group, having no employment outside the home or lacking good quality or quantity of support from family and friends.

Nurses must also be able to assess when a person needs more skilled help than they are able to offer, and seek a referral to a specialist practitioner such as a psychiatrist or social worker. This is a situation in which self-help or voluntary organizations may be able to offer support to someone having difficulty in coping with a life transition.

Just as life does not follow a prearranged pattern, and people do not react to stress in predictable or mechanical ways, so there are no readily available solutions for nurses. Individualized patient care remains the key to an effective, helping relationship.

SEXUALITY, HEALTH AND ILLNESS

Defining Sexuality

Like social class, sexuality is a complex idea to define. Most writers agree that there are biological, psychological and social aspects to how a person learns about and expresses sexuality, but they vary in the emphasis given to each facet.

Traditionally, more attention has been paid in nursing textbooks to the biological side of sexuality—or what is more commonly termed 'sex'. Thus, a nursing assessment guide will include questions about intercourse, menstruation, childbearing history, contraception and related matters and problems. However, this is a very limited approach for Savage (1987) reminds us that human sex is much more of a psychosocial than a physical act.

In fact, the saying that 'the whole is greater than the sum of the parts' is perhaps nowhere so relevant as in relation to sexuality.

Psychological aspects of sexuality include body image and self-concept, or the mental picture people have of themselves. Sexual or gender identity forms another component, and refers to the way people define their own sexuality. Thus some people see themselves as heterosexual, others as homosexual or bisexual. Gender preference, or the sexuality of desired sexual partners, is yet another aspect.

But how do people come to have these mental pictures or self-concepts of sexuality? The kind of anatomy and physiology people are born with simply gives them the potential for sexual development. From the moment of birth, babies are treated differently according to their biological sex and people's expectations and standards of appropriate behaviour. One of the very first acts of the midwife may be to label the baby with a pink or blue name band, and from then on socialization takes over from biology and babies learn how to behave. Very young children are able to tell the difference between 'appropriate' behaviour for girls and boys—and realize that nursing is a job for women, while being a doctor is a masculine activity.

This socialization is carried on by the media, with its images of soft, feminine women and manly 'hunks' in advertisements, and as part of a 'hidden curriculum' in schools. While it is possible nowadays for girls to study craft, design and technology and for boys to take domestic science, in practice sexual divisions persist. Girls are more likely to take arts and modern languages, and to drop science and mathematics subjects earlier than boys. This separation in schools then cuts girls and boys off from a whole range of career choices because they do not have the necessary school leaving qualifications (Deem, 1978).

Socialization is the route by which people develop what have been called 'sex role stereotypes' or views of women as essentially emotional, non-intellectual and fragile, and of men as psychologically 'strong', unemotional, rational and assertive. However, psychologists have shown that these sex or gender stereotypes can have profound and disadvantageous effects for both women and men (Bem, 1974). 'Typical' or 'super-feminine' women tend to have poor self-esteem and to lack confidence and a sense of independence. 'Typical' or 'macho' men may have difficulty living up to expectations of masculine behaviour too. As a result, levels of anxiety and depression are considerably higher in women than men, while on the other hand men indulge in more violence against themselves and others in the form of suicides, alcoholism and crime (Oakley, 1981). It seems that the most 'healthy' outcome is a balance of both supposedly feminine and masculine attributes, or what Bem has called an androgynous personality.

Sexuality, Illnesses and Treatment

There is probably no illness or medical treatment that is without implications for sexuality. At the simplest level, anyone who feels unwell experiences falls in energy levels and is therefore less able to continue all their usual activities. Paying attention to personal appearance, moods, maintaining relationships at home, work and in leisure activities, as well as sexual activity itself, are all likely to be affected.

Each particular state of ill health and each individual treatment will also bring particular effects as well as these general ones. For example, a person who has an acute or chronic respiratory condition may not be able to work or be independent in their activities of living. Communication may be interrupted by breathlessness, cough and sputum production, and the person may be unhappy with themselves, let alone feel positive about themselves as a companion or sexual partner. Or someone with painful arthritis that restricts their movements and alters appearance will experience the stigma of disability and an altered body image. All activities, including sexual activity, may be affected and the wearing effect of chronic pain may lead to depression and loss of libido (sexual interest).

Drug treatments can have a wide range of side-effects that impair sexual functioning, and this is true of many commonly used preparations. Antihypertensive drugs can cause impotence in men (inability to have an erection), and make the taker feel depressed and lethargic, with inevitable implications for activities and relationships. Common side-effects of medications include skin rashes and nausea, which are both debilitating and damaging to body image.

There is insufficient space here to discuss the enormous variety of conditions and treatments that affect sexuality in all its aspects, but nurses can look up information relevant to their own work in the growing number of books about sexuality and nursing. Some suitable titles are listed at the end of this chapter under Further Reading.

Sexuality and Nursing Care

This brief discussion of human sexuality makes it clear that nurses need to have a holistic view of sexuality as a basis for individualized nursing care. Only if a nursing assessment takes the vital influence of sexuality into account, can care be comprehensive.

Sexuality can be a difficult area to consider during a nursing assessment, and several writers have offered guidelines for how to approach the topic (Webb, 1985). Woods (1984) suggests asking two very simple questions:

1. Has anything (such as illness or pregnancy) changed the way you feel about yourself as (a woman, mother, man, father)?
2. Has anything (for example, disease, surgery) affected your sex life?

An advantage of this simple format is that no assumptions are made about whether the patient is homo- or heterosexual, is or is not sexually active, does or does not use contraception, and so on. On the basis of the responses received, nurses can use their interpersonal skills to follow up in a nondirective way cues that are given in answer to these and other questions. A form of questioning that can be helpful in this situation is that which 'gives permission' to respondents to give information or to ask questions that may feel risky to them. For example, a nurse might say, 'It is quite common for people with your illness to experience. ... Has anything like this happened to you?' or 'Many people have questions they would like to ask about. ... Would you like to ask me anything?'

A nursing assessment and care plan should be able to identify and respond to issues of sexuality within the competence of the nurse involved. For example, nurses should be aware of the possible effects upon sexuality of the health and illness states and treatments they encounter regularly in their own work. At the same time, they should be able to detect more complex problems beyond their immediate competence, be able to judge their own level of skill and refer patients to the appropriate specialist who can help them. Sex therapy, for example, is a complex subject requiring long training and is not an activity for all nurses. However, basic patient teaching and health education are the business of all nurses, especially as they become increasingly aware of the linkages between health, illness and sexuality.

RACE AND CULTURE

Britain is a multi-racial, multi-cultural society. Nursing in Britain is itself a multi-racial and multi-cultural occupation. Learning to nurse within this changing society requires awareness of the key issues concerned with nursing people with diverse value systems. These issues focus on how different ethnic groups respond to both health and illness, and the effects of racism and ethnocentrism in care given both by individual workers and by health care institutions.

A definition of terms is given in this section, followed by a discussion of the health problems affecting various ethnic groups. Nursing care for those from different ethnic groups is also discussed.

Race
This is a term used to group people according to their physical characteristics.

Ethnicity
Ethnic groups are groups of people or communities that share the same cultural and social heritage.

Racism
Racism occurs when one group of people is able to combine prejudice with power over another group because of colour or ethnic differences. Racism can be personal or institutional. Personal racism is easily recognized, often taking the form of both verbal and physical abuse between individuals or groups of people. Institutional racism is incorporated into the practices and policies of organizations that reflect the value systems of the dominant ethnic group within a society.

Ethnocentrism
This occurs when any one group believes that its own culture is superior to others. The group sees its own standards and ideals as highly desirable and they are always used as a standard for measurement when making comparisons with other groups. All racial and cultural groups are subject to ethnocentrism, which in itself is neither good nor bad. An example of unacceptable ethnocentrism is nurses viewing the health care beliefs of their own cultural group as 'right' and others as 'wrong'. This demonstrates a complete lack of awareness of ethnic and cultural differences that may make positive contributions to the wellbeing of those they are caring for, and can be interpreted as a form of racism.

Culture
Culture is a learned system of behaviour shared by a group, and it consists of a set of beliefs and values that are passed from one generation to another through the process of learning from parents, mass media, educational and religious activities, and so on. Culture is socially, not biologically, transmitted.

In reviewing these definitions it becomes apparent that not all people of the same race belong to the same ethnic group and not everyone from one ethnic group has the same culture. If all people of the same race are treated as if they are from the same ethnic group and the same culture, then there is a danger of stereotyping them.

Stereotyping
When an individual is labelled with certain characteristics, assumptions are made about them on the basis of their race, ethnic group or culture. It is assumed that all

people within a single group are the same. A common example of stereotyping is to assume that all black people of Afro-Caribbean origin come from Jamaica and play in steel bands. In reality, they may have been born in England of black British parents and have no musical ability.

British society is made up of many diverse ethnic groups. Throughout the history of these islands, many races have settled here. These include people from Europe, Asia, Africa and America. Many of these groups of people have long been integrated into the mainstream of the British population. Others, for a variety of reasons, have maintained their cultural identity. The differing cultural values and beliefs of groups of people go beyond simple distinctions of black and white. Regional and national differences within Britain highlight the diversity within this society.

Some key areas to take into account when considering the cultural beliefs of a particular person or group of people are the social structures within the group (including male and female roles and relationships, family structures and lines of authority), common language and communication systems, work and educational patterns, food and eating habits, and religious and spiritual customs and behaviours.

Health and Illness

There are common health and illness problems in any population group. These may be associated with disadvantaged ethnic groups (Whitehead, 1988). Environmental and social factors may be causing the problem rather than genetic factors, for example, poverty with low income, and inadequate health care facilities with poor access to health care institutions and expertise. These difficulties may be compounded by language and cultural misunderstandings. The health problems remain essentially universal but the ethnic group is highly susceptible.

In addition to health problems associated with environmental factors, there are also health problems to which different ethnic groups are particularly susceptible. These are probably due to a combination of genetic factors and social environment (Brownlee, 1978). Some examples are now discussed.

Hypertension
People of Afro-Caribbean origin are between four and six times more likely to suffer from hypertension as those from other races (Whitehead, 1988). Hypertension can lead to renal damage, heart failure and cerebrovascular accidents (see Chapter 9).

Heart Disease
In Britain there is a higher incidence of heart disease among Asian and Afro-Caribbean populations compared with the white British population.

Perinatal and Infant Mortality
These are very high among children born of Asian and Afro-Caribbean parents. Among Asians they vary according to social class and the mother's marital status (*Training In Health and Race*, 1978).

Inherited Conditions
Some conditions that occur among Afro-Caribbean and Asian ethnic groups are genetic and so are inherited, for example, sickle cell disease and thalassaemia (see Chapter 10).

Nursing Care For People From Varying Ethnic Backgrounds

The nursing process offers an effective tool for enabling appropriate nursing care for patients from differing ethnic backgrounds to be delivered. It does so by requiring nurses to assess, plan, implement and evaluate care for each individual person whom they are attending. Whatever their background, every person has their own individual needs and preferences that must be taken into account when nursing care is given.

Assessment

To aid nurses in this assessment a variety of assessment tools has been developed (Tripp-Reimer, Brink and Saunders, 1984). The most appropriate for people in Britain is probably that developed by Baxter (Mares, Larbie and Baxter, 1987). Baxter points out that it is unnecessary to ask every question of every patient or client. As with any nursing assessment, there must be a rationale for asking a particular question, and an individual judgement is needed to decide its relevance in each unique situation.

The areas considered for assessment in Baxter's scheme are:

1. Religious beliefs: any beliefs that the person holds and any important practices or rituals they wish to follow.
2. Food and diet: dietary rules for everyday life, including fasting, as well as those necessary during illness, and individual needs that can be met by relatives.
3. Hygiene and grooming: the importance of jewellery, head and body coverings, the appropriateness of shaving of head and body hair, care of the skin and hair, clothes and ideas of modesty, reactions to care from nurses of the opposite sex, toilet practices, left and right hand practices for hygiene.
4. Hospital procedures: identification of hospital procedures that might cause offence, reactions to medications and treatments.
5. Death and bereavement: care of the family through

death and bereavement, an understanding of family roles, customs and ceremonies, preferences about where the person wishes to die, wishes with regard to postmortem examination, cremation and burial. Arrangements for last offices, and ways in which relatives wish to express grief and mourning.

Identification of Patient Problems

Kozier, Erb and McKay-Bufalino (1989) identify the following possible problems with patients who have different ethnic backgrounds:

1. Difficulty in communicating. This has been related directly to language difficulties. For example, women from Asian and Chinese groups may be unable to speak English and so need to express their needs through an interpreter. Link workers have been identified in many hospitals who can translate, and a list of staff is maintained so that a patient with a language difficulty can be readily helped.

   These efforts on the part of the institution do not exempt nurses from trying to improve communication. Some suggestions are as follows:
   a. The person should be given plenty of time to talk to the nurse.
   b. The nurse should use nonverbal skills to communicate interest and concern.
   c. The nurse should communicate information through pictures, drawings or other visual means.
   d. It is helpful if the nurse learns the names of the people being looked after, and practises the pronunciation correctly.
   e. Nurses should introduce themselves so that they are known.
   f. The nurse should carry out an assessment with a relative or a link worker present who can act as interpreter so that information can be exchanged. This will help the nurse to know the person better, and allay some of the anxieties the patient is experiencing.
   g. The nurse should learn some key phrases and sentences of the non-host language most commonly encountered.
2. Effective individual and family coping. Many people from ethnic groups suffer from the effects of racism and social injustice that they have experienced over a long period of time. This may have left them reluctant or unable to take part in decision-making. They may appear apathetic and resigned to situations, with little motivation to change. This may be less the result of their religious and cultural beliefs than the effect of their current social situation. In some ethnic groups there is dependence on extended family ties and a reliance on family leadership. If the family structure breaks down, then coping may be difficult (Carpenito, 1987).

Giving Nursing Care

According to Kozier, Erb and McKay-Bufalino (1989), key issues for nurses in the maintenance of therapeutic interactions between themselves and people from different ethnic groups include:

A good working knowledge of particular ethnic groups most commonly encountered.
Awareness of differences in nonverbal and verbal communication between different ethnic groups and the nurses' own ethnic groups.
A recognition by nurses of their own personal attitudes, beliefs, biases and prejudices.
Knowledge of religious and spiritual practices, symbols or expressions.
Facilitation of cultural practices that may bring comfort and support to the patient and significant others.
Awareness of inappropriate practices that may cause offence to the patient and significant others.
Understanding of the variety of views about health, illness and grieving.
Openness and readiness to learn from others from a different background.

Evaluation and Expected Outcomes of Nursing Care

Two major outcomes need to be achieved. The first is to try to meet the needs of a particular person within their own culture. The second is to develop a level of interaction between nurses and people needing care that will enable their needs to be met effectively.

Nurses who have had the opportunity to care for people from different ethnic groups can evaluate their care by asking themselves if they have cared for that person with a sensitivity that incorporates feelings of respect and recognition of others. Second, they can ask themselves if they have acknowledged the validity of alternative ways of meeting people's needs.

PEOPLE WITH PHYSICAL DIFFERENCES

Questions of Definition

The World Health Organisation (1980) model of disablement contains four levels of definition, as shown in Figure 1.1. In this scheme, impairment refers to loss or abnormality of psychological, physiological or anatomical structure or function. Disability is any restriction or lack of ability to perform an activity in the manner or within the range considered normal, as a result of the impairment. Handicap is the disadvantage that results from an impairment of disability, that limits or prevents the ful-

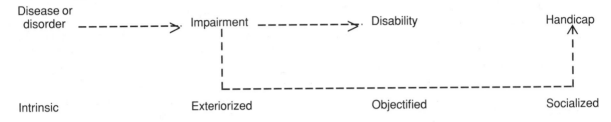

Figure 1.1 The WHO model of disablement. (Reproduced and adapted, by permission, from *International Classification of Impairments, Disabilities and Handicaps. A Manual of Classification Relating to the Consequences of Disease*, World Health Organisation (1980), Geneva, p. 30 (reprinted 1985, 1989).)

filment of a role that is normal for that individual. For example, a person may suffer from a bone neoplasm, which is treated by amputation of a lower limb. The resulting absence of a limb is an impairment that leads to the disability of being unable to walk without a prosthesis. Handicap may follow as a result of inadequate arrangements made in society for easy access to buildings, suitable work and leisure opportunities, and so on, and from the negative attitudes of other people who judge the amputee as inadequate and defective as a person as a result of the impairment.

This social handicapping has been discussed by Goffman (1963) in terms of stigma. Sometimes people attribute blame to an individual for causing their own problem, for example, women requesting abortion, those who have lung cancer or people who are diagnosed positive for infection with human immunodeficiency virus (HIV positive). Even when a victim-blaming attitude is not taken, people with physical differences may experience social rejection as a result of their condition. Mental handicap is a clear example of this, but still today the same response may occur to people with epilepsy, cerebral palsy, skin conditions or deafness, to name but a few of many possible examples.

When this happens, the physical difference overrides all other attributes in the eyes of stigmatizers, and they react to the person as though no other aspect of their personhood is relevant. This is much the same process as occurs with racial stereotyping, prejudice and discrimination. Because of all these possible 'knock-on effects' of impairment, it is preferable to use a less 'loaded' description such as 'people with physical differences' in order to avoid the negative associations of terms like handicap and disability.

Caring For People With Physical Differences

Stewart (1985) reminds us that people with physical differences are 'not a clinical condition' and that care is more likely to be successful if the people and their relatives 'are fully committed to what is happening by being encouraged to be active partners and not passive recipients of a programme'.

A full discussion of rehabilitation is beyond the scope of this book, and the aim in this chapter is to give some pointers for care of people with physical differences who coincidentally become patients when they are ill.

Perhaps the most useful approach to nursing them is to use an activities of living model such as that of Roper, Logan and Tierney (1986). Nursing assessment based on this model requires nurses to discover patients' usual routines, what they can and cannot do independently and how they cope with their activities of living. Once again, an individualized approach to care is the key to meeting needs and trying to ensure that an episode of illness and treatment causes as little disruption as possible in a person's life. While this is important for all patients, it is even more so for those who have evolved their own unique ways of coping with their different ways of functioning.

People who use wheelchairs are a case in point. They are taught to use their wheelchair in particular ways—to transfer in and out of beds, chairs, baths, and so on. They also learn the importance of using their arms to do regular small lifts to relieve pressure on vulnerable skin areas (Redfern, 1986). It is vital that they retain the use of their own wheelchair if they are in hospital so that they can continue to use their coping strategies. Nurses should resist the temptation to ask relatives to take the chair home for safe keeping or to use hospital wheelchairs—or even worse to nurse the person in bed or a hospital chair. Such action would be likely to lead to pressure sore formation in a person who might have managed their own skin care for years without mishap.

Hearing impairment can easily lead to social isolation and depression, and in a busy and noisy hospital ward it can be exceedingly difficult to use a hearing aid because of background noise. By remembering some simple guidelines, nurses can improve their communication with people who are hard of hearing. Everyone relies to some extent on lip-reading to hear, and deaf people do this to a much greater extent. Martin (in Simpson and Levitt (eds), 1981) advises those who communicate with hearing-impaired people as follows:

1. Position yourself so that the light is on your face.
2. Do not stand with your back to the light.

3. Make sure the person knows what you are talking about; do not change subject without warning.
4. Keep your hands away from your mouth and face.
5. Speak a little slower but do not overemphasize the way you produce words.
6. Do not smoke a pipe or cigarette while talking.

It should be remembered that beards make lip-reading more difficult, and those who have them will need to make an extra effort to ensure that they are understood. Gilhomme Herbst (in Redfern, 1986) adds additional guidelines to those given above by recommending that deaf people are encouraged to wear their spectacles if appropriate, that shouting should be avoided, familiar words and phrases should be used, slower speech may be helpful and an atmosphere of kindness and sympathy should be created to reduce stress, using laughter to defuse the situation if difficulties arise.

Nurses should encourage people to use their hearing aids, referring them to a hearing therapist for checks and adjustments if necessary, and for consideration for additional aids such as modified telephones, alarm lights to replace door bells and adaptations to television sets (Martin, in Simpson and Levitt (eds), 1981).

Visual handicap may vary from slight impairment corrected by spectacles, through partial sightedness to blindness. Nurses should help visually handicapped people to get the most function they can from their limitations by ensuring that a good light is available and that spectacles are used appropriately. Visually impaired people should be reassured, if necessary, that their residual sight cannot be damaged by use. Therefore, a high level of illumination may be used, curtains should be well drawn back and holding objects close to the eyes to facilitate vision is not harmful. If reading is possible by holding print very close to the eyes, no damage can be done and there is no objection to doing this (Simpson and Levitt, 1981).

As a sighted person approaches someone who is visually handicapped, they should introduce themselves so as not to surprise the person, and should take particular care to explain what is going on and to anticipate what is going to happen so that this can be passed on. When guiding visually handicapped people about, they should not be led by the hand. The guide should stand slightly in front and to the side, and the blind person should grasp the guide's upper arm. When approaching stairs the guide should warn whether the stairs go up or down. When seating a visually handicapped person, the guide should place their hand on the back of the chair and indicate in which direction the seat is.

Aids used to facilitate independence should always be allowed into hospital and used freely, and relatives and friends should be offered as free an access as possible for visiting and helping with the patient's care. Nurses may feel frustrated at their seeming ignorance and lack of skills in helping people with physical differences who are in their care. But while this is an understandable reaction, it should not be allowed to get in the way of effective help. It should be remembered that patients themselves are a valuable source of readily available information. They will have built up a wide repertoire of skills and coping strategies over the years, and will almost certainly be very eager to pass these on—both for their own benefit and so that nurses may help others in the future. There is no substitute for talking to people and finding out directly from them how best they would like to be helped.

This last point also acts as a reminder that there is an increasing number of self-help and voluntary organizations that can offer assistance both to clients and nurses (see Useful Addresses, p. xxx). It is important that people with physical differences know about the existence of these groups and are put in touch with them by nurses if this is their wish. Social work staff or the local general or nursing libraries will be able to help locate appropriate contacts.

HOW NURSES CAN HELP

Henderson's (1966) classic definition of nursing suggests that nursing has a key role to play in helping people when illness strikes. It is concerned with helping patients to retain and restore personal control of their health, to promote health, healing and rehabilitation. The nurse in effect becomes a coping mechanism, with the aim of helping the patient to restore maximum physical and psychological integrity and to be as free of dependence on nurses as possible. At the same time, it is recognized that the nurse may support the patient when inevitable death approaches. Much earlier, Nightingale (1860) saw nursing as 'putting the patient in the best condition for nature to act'—alluding to the work of nurses in promoting health through good diet and personal hygiene and helping the sick to heal. Ultimately, the sign of effective nursing was that it was no longer needed—because the person, in mind and body, was in control of their own life. The person must be healthy enough to resist stressors such as disease, or to adapt them with minimal damage. When these failed, then it was the role of the nurse to step in.

However, it would be simplistic to suggest that the nurse's role is entirely that of an external instrument of coping. The interaction between nurse and patient is laden with subtle influences and effects. Campbell (1984), for example, has argued that nurse may gain as much from the nurse–patient relationship as patients themselves. In giving care, the nurse derives satisfaction from fulfilment of the need to feel needed. It seems that the helping relationship between nurse and patient is not exclusively one way from nurse to patient, but a mutual meeting of needs.

Recent years have seen greater emphasis being placed on the nature of the relationship between nurse and patient. The drift away from the image of handmaiden to the doctor has been concurrent with the recognition of the nurse as 'partner' (Pearson, 1988; Wright, 1986) or 'companion' (Campbell, 1984) in care. Partnership and companionship appear to have many similar qualities, and these concepts have now been endorsed as the main plank of official documents in a strategy for nursing for the future (Department of Health, 1989).

Some key concepts are addressed in Campbell's discussion of companionship:

A closeness which is not sexually stereotyped; it implies movement and change; it expressed mutuality, and it requires commitment but within defined limits ... companionship describes a closeness which is neither sexual union nor deep personal friendship. It is a bodily presence which accompanies the other for a while. The image of the journey springs to mind when we think of the companions.

Companionship often arises from a chance meeting and it is terminated when the joint purpose which keeps companions together no longer obtains. The good companion is someone who shares freely, but does not impose, allowing others to make their own journey.

Partnership and companionship imply an almost contractual relationship between the two parties, in which the nurse provides a given set of services to meet the needs of the patient. In some circumstances, patients may have a dominant role in choosing the quality of that service, which is based largely on their level of independence and knowledge. For example, in some circumstances women have begun to exercise considerable control over the manner in which they will give birth. At the other extreme, the role of patients may be one of complete dependence where they are unable or unwilling (e.g., comatose, disorientated or severely mentally handicapped) to make choices in care. In such cases, nurses use their judgement to act in the patient's best interests, and are held accountable for doing so (United Kingdom Central Council for Nursing, Midwifery and Health Visitors, 1987).

As Lazarus and Folkman (1984), Selye (in Klaus and Bailey, 1980) and Cooper, Cooper and Eaten (1988) have shown, the combination of illness and relocation into hospital, with their attendant fears and uncertainties, are highly stressful events. The effects of stress on body and mind can inhibit or be counterproductive to the process of healing. If nurses, working in partnership with patients, have a role in reducing and reversing these stresses, then what principles must guide their actions?

While coming into hospital can be a stressful event, it provides an opportunity for nurses and others to form a helping relationship with the patient. Unfortunately, nurses in many settings have historically failed to deliver what the patient wants. Martin, for example, cites many settings where the health care system has failed and in which the aim of helping patients has been distorted:

'How is it that institutions established to care for the sick and helpless can have allowed them to be neglected, treated with callousness and even deliberate cruelty?' (Martin, 1984). Whether it be the application of rigid routines on the medical ward, or regimented and irrational methods of preparation on the surgical ward, restrictions on visiting in the hospital or the absence of opportunities for parents to stay with children—whatever the case, nursing still seems filled with myriad rituals and routines that seem to serve only to control the health system and depersonalize patient care. In part, Menzies (1961; in Menzies-Lyth, 1988) has argued that such a system of care serves to protect the nurse, ill-equipped with self-awareness and interpersonal skills, from the anxiety of 'being involved' with the patient.

Yet, as has been suggested earlier, nurses are being urged to 'get involved' from many quarters, and to adopt styles of practice that are more personal and patient-centred. Martin (1984) goes on to suggest that to prevent 'the perversion of individual motives' it is necessary to examine both the context in which caring is taking place as well as the individuals who are doing the caring. Thus it is important to look at:

1. The attitudes and values that nurses possess about themselves and their patients—which are derived not just from being socialized as a nurse, but from society as a whole.
2. The style of leadership that provides creative caring and the management climate that supports it and encourages staff involvement in decision-making.
3. The resources—buildings, equipment, salaries and so on that are assigned to the setting.
4. The way the staff are developed, the knowledge they are given and the way they are encouraged to apply it.

If nurses are developing patient-centred practices across the spectrum, then it is clear that this approach lies beyond the work of nurses alone. The 'new nursing' (Salvage, 1990) requires an active programme of nursing development (Salvage, 1990; Wright, 1990). It requires a management style that seeks to support its staff, actively fights for resources and encourages them, rather than seeking merely to control them. At the same time there is the need for public and political will at local and national level, to ensure that staff have the resources they need (Dean, 1988); Price Waterhouse, 1988). When such circumstances come together, then there is evidence to show that considerable progress can be made in producing forms of practice that both patients and nurses find more satisfying, and have both long- and short-term benefits for patient wellbeing and staff recruitment and retention (Bamber, Johnson, Purdy and Wright, 1989; Bond, Fall and Thomas, 1990; Pearson, Durand and Punton, 1989).

When adequately supported and developed, nurses are able to develop modes of practice, based on the concepts of partnership or companionship, that appear to be more patient-centred. When patients become ill and are admitted to the hospital setting, then there is much evidence to show that nurses have a key role in alleviating stress and promoting healing (Cassée, in Cox and Mead, 1975; Franklin, 1974; Wilson-Barnett and Carrigy, 1978; Wong, 1979). The following summary covers some of the key issues (Cassée, in Cox and Mead, 1975):

> *The way the hospital staff behave towards their patients has an important part to play in the healing process. Successful 'therapeutic behaviour' is facilitated when an open two-way communication process takes place; the staff must keep the patient informed about the nature of his illness and treatment, but also encourage him to express his fears and anxieties ... if the nurse is to perform satisfactorily this element of her therapeutic role, she will be encouraged to do this if she is a member of a group which is open and within which she can express her own feelings and anxieties, which will in turn enable her to cope with closer emotional contact with her patient.*

Open relationships between nurses and patients, and nurses and each other are characterized by a number of salient features:

1. Offering information—working as partners with the patients, nurses share information with patients, who want it, about their illness, care, progress and so on. In some settings, this might mean more than verbal updates, and extend into giving patients access to nursing and medical notes with an opportunity to contribute to them if they wish (Wright, 1990). Methods of planning and evaluating care are chosen that involve patients who so wish.
2. Rights—patients are made aware of their rights as patients, perhaps in writing in the form of an information book or leaflet. An example might be that produced by the Association of Community Health Councils (1986) or the following abstract from a patients' information book (Tameside and Glossop Health Authority, 1988):

As a patient on the ward you have a right to:

- *Skilled care, by all members of the hospital team, to meet your needs.*
- *Know how and why you are being treated and what is being done to help you, and what alternatives are available.*
- *Be given enough information and skill to be as independent as possible.*
- *Have choice in your care and be given enough knowledge so that you can make an informed decision.*
- *Be treated as an individual and accorded respect, dignity and equal quality of care, regardless of age, sex, religion, race or beliefs.*

- *Have total support with the nurse and other members of the team acting on your behalf and in your best interests, when you are unable to make choices for yourself.*

3. Standards of care—these are defined and, where possible, made available to patients before they enter the hospital setting.
4. Compliments and complaints procedures—when patients wish to comment on their care, clear guidelines are available to enable them to do so. When standards are not being met, for example, or when rights are being infringed, then there needs to be a simple mechanism which enables the issues to be addressed quickly and easily.
5. Advocacy—when patients are unwilling or unable to make choices for themselves, then the professionals themselves are clearly working 'on the patient's side'. This is a role commonly seen as appropriate to nurses, although most others would lay claim to being patients' advocates as well. However, nurses, because of their level of contact with patients and the nature of their relationships, are well placed to act as patients' advocates. At a simple level, it might be a case of seeking some aspect of information on a patient's behalf. Nurses enter more uncertain territory when they seek to express a view on behalf of the patient which may conflict with the wishes and activities of other health care workers.

Acting as the patient's advocate is an extension of the concept of partnership and may call into question the traditional roles of patient and nurse. Parsons's (1951) classic descriptions of the 'sick role'—the patient must wish to recover as quickly as possible and seek professional advice and follow treatment, in order to have the privilege of being relieved from normal tasks and accorded sympathy and support—seems too limiting for nurses and patients working in partnership. Patients who did not fall into the classic 'sick role' mode were often labelled as unpopular (Stockwell, 1972) and failed to receive therapeutic nursing as a result. The concept of nurses working *with* patients (rather than *on* them) to provide healing and health challenges the traditional view of the nurse–patient relationship. New roles for each partner come into play where negotiation, information-giving, trust-building and sharing caring are essential factors.

PARTICIPATION AND CONSENT

The nurse's role as advocate is closely related to the willingness of the patient to participate in treatment, and to the patient's level of understanding. In British law, if a patient does not give consent for treatment performed, the member of staff concerned and the employing authority could be 'liable for assault and battery, and find themselves being sued in court for damages' (Young, 1981). For this reason, most major treatments in hospital (such as those requiring an anaesthetic) require the patient's written consent beforehand (or the consent of the parent or guardian when the patient is under 16 years of age).

However, the patient may also give consent in other ways. For example, there is implied consent. Patients, except in rare situations, enter hospital voluntarily and this implies that they are prepared to undergo various treatments and investigations, without written consent being needed for each one. Patients may also imply consent by their actions, for example, 'the nurse approaching the patient with an injection will assume the patient consents when she sees him roll over in readiness' (Young, 1981).

At other times, the patient's consent may also be given (or refused) orally, for example, when a doctor or nurse asks the patient's permission before carrying out a particular procedure, e.g., giving an injection or taking a blood sample.

While the consent of the patient is a straightforward issue in most circumstances, there is no doubting the very real conflicts that can arise for nurses, as Rumbold (1986) has suggested. In many respects, it may be difficult for patients not to comply with the wishes of powerful professionals (see the 'sick role', above) whom they hope and assume will act in their best interests. While much of the legal responsibility for gaining consent lies with the doctor, it may be to the nurse that the patient confides doubts and reservations. Can the nurse, then acting as the patient's advocate, represent the patient's views, even if they conflict with the will of the doctor?

Consent can also be less clear-cut in circumstances where more than one person is involved in giving the consent. This is a requirement, for example, in operations concerning abortion or sterilization. Under such circumstances, consent of the partner is more a matter of courtesy than of legal requirement although, as Young (1981) points out, in certain cultures 'the ability of the wife to bear children may have serious repercussions on the marriage and the husband's consent may then become legally more important'.

If consent is withheld by a partner, this may not prohibit an operation in the above circumstances, but the issue is much more uncertain when parents or guardians withhold consent for treatment of those under 16 years old. How are nurses to react when a child does not wish to pursue a course of treatment to which the parents have agreed? How will the nurse respond when parents have refused treatment (for example, blood transfusions) to a child in their care who may otherwise die?

In such circumstances, nurses have to draw upon more than legal direction, but also upon their own moral and ethical values, and the framework provided by professional codes of conduct (Melia, 1989; Vaughan, 1990).

Two key principles, however, are helpful to nurses in making decisions on these issues.

The first is that the patient should give informed consent. This requires that the nurse is both able and willing to give the required information upon which the patient can make a rational decision. The nurse's role is often that of ensuring that the patient has understood what others, especially medical staff, have explained to them. As Young (1981) points out 'sometimes the doctor may have used words which the patient may not understand', or the patient is in 'too much awe of the medical establishment to question'. It might be argued that such circumstances should not arise if the medical profession addressed itself to this area of weakness in the doctor–patient relationship. However, the reality is that it is to nurses that patients often turn for the information they seek, and it is here that nurses can fully apply their concepts of partnership and advocacy. It may be the nurse who helps clarify information to the patient, or acts as advocate on the patient's behalf and asks the doctor to discuss issues with the patient again. If the patient has any queries, the doctor has a legal duty to answer them.

The second issue relates to the role of the nurse in having a first duty to patients. The nurse is with the patient from the time consent is given until the actual procedure takes place. Therefore, nurses need to know how to deal with the situation if the patient has a change of mind or expresses reservations. The nurse has a clear duty to act on the individual patient's behalf, and to keep written records of what transpires.

THERAPEUTIC NURSING

A number of the above issues have touched on the nature of the nurse–patient relationship. Such a relationship has been described as professional friendship (Peplau, 1952), as 'partnership' (Pearson, 1988; Wright, 1986) and 'companionship' (Campbell, 1984). It is concerned not so much with the things that nurses do, but rather with the way that they do them. In combining skills that are instrumental (practical, technical skills and so on) with those that are expressive (caring, comforting, explaining, teaching), nursing actions can actually be therapeutic or healing. Benner (1985) has described the concept of 'presencing'—the ability to 'be with' patients, to deal with them as whole people, and to draw upon an enormous range of complex manual and psychological skills to produce a pattern of caring that enables patients to feel 'better'. Such caring emphasizes, for example, the sharing of information to inform and involve patients when they wish. In so doing, nurses adopt a different approach from that of traditional professionalism—one that moves away from the paternalistic model and which seeks instead to work with patients, sharing knowledge and skills and not remaining aloof and remote. Therapeutic 'presencing' in nursing also involves, for example, the sensitive use of touch in its many forms to promote healing and comforting. This may range from a contact gesture to express concern, as in the holding of hands, or as a planned intervention in nursing therapy (Autton, 1989; Krieger, 1979).

If nursing is to fulfil its true role as a therapy, not only nurses themselves have to recognize its potential. Nurses need a wider organization that supports and encourages them to develop in ways that promote patient-centred practice.

ORGANIZING CARE

So far it has been suggested that the values that nurses hold, and the way they choose to work with patients, can have fundamental effects upon the patient's experience of hospital and illness. If, as has been argued, nurses work as partners in care and deal with the patient as a whole individual to promote healing and minimize stress, then how can nurses best organize their care? How can they put themselves in the best position for therapeutic nursing to act?

Nursing Models and the Nursing Process

Much discussion and debate has ranged around nursing models since they began to receive wider coverage in the UK during the 1980s. A full discussion of these issues is beyond the scope of this text, and because of the variety available, no particular model has been advocated.

Every nurse carries in their head an 'image' (Reilly, 1975) of what nursing is. The 'informal' model, built up of the nurse's knowledge, values and experiences, determines what each nurse thinks about nursing. It has important implications, for it determines the way in which the nurse acts out nursing in practice. For example, the nurse's beliefs about the elderly, whether as hopeless cases or as individuals with potential for rehabilitation, will affect the way in which the nurse works with those patients.

A large number of texts are now available to British nurses that give guidance on nursing models (Kershaw and Salvage, 1986; Pearson and Vaughan, 1986; Salvage and Kershaw, 1990). This may range from the use of nurses' own informal models (Luker, 1988) or the local development of a nursing model (Wright, 1986), through to the application of more formal well-documented approaches (for example, Orem, 1980; Roper, Logan and Tierney, 1983; or Riehl and Roy, 1980). Whichever approach to nursing models is taken, there appears to be general agreement that the next step is to decide how to translate the thoughts into practice.

While models may provide the theoretical framework for practice, a problem-solving approach (nursing process) is widely adopted to help plan what help is needed. The nursing process might simply be described as the process by which nursing is thought through. Thus, by assessing the patient, deciding what help is needed (planning) and actually getting on with it (implementing), while at the same time making sure it is effective (evaluating), the process cycle is established.

Nurses are able to carry out this problem-solving approach in their heads. However, to ensure that what they are doing can be passed on to others and that a record is kept, a wide range of documentation has been designed by nurses.

Various forms are used to provide written details in the form of care plans. The pattern that will be used in this text includes four key elements, as shown in Table 1.1.

It is worth noting at this stage that the care plan pattern used includes a 'rationale' column. This is to provide the reader with additional background information to the decision-making process. Educational care plans of this nature should be distinguished from working care plans used in the clinical area. The latter rarely include a 'rationale' column. In part, this is because of the time that would be involved to complete it. However, it might also be argued that nurses should not be prescribing care unless they are certain of the sound rationale behind it.

Methods of Organizing Care

If nursing models are used to help organize nurses' thinking and actions, and care plans devised to give directions to the care, then a third issue is also important. This is the way that nurses choose to put their thinking and plans into action. If it is accepted that the values of holistic, therapeutic, individualized care are desirable, how can nurses

Table 1.1 *Care plan pattern*

Problem	Expected outcomes	Nursing care	Rationale
Statement of the patient's problem identified after assessment, e.g. lack of movement producing risk of pressure sore formation on sacrum	What the results of nursing care are expected to achieve, e.g. skin to remain intact, no pressure sores to develop	Actions required by the nurse, e.g. two nurses to adjust patient's position every two hours	Reasons behind the choice of nursing care, with references where appropriate, e.g. change of position will relieve pressure on the skin and permit adequate blood flow

organize their work to ensure that patients are treated as individuals, holistically and therapeutically?

Four common methods occur in the hospital setting, as described here.

Task Allocation

The patient's care is divided into a series of tasks to be completed by different levels of nurse, e.g., one nurse gives medicines, another checks blood pressure, a third tests urine samples and so on. A large body of literature suggests that this 'production line concept of care' (*Report of the Committee on Nursing*, 1972) is fundamentally dissatisfying to both patients and nurses. Yet it remains a common phenomenon as a means of getting through the work, and in some respects serves to defend nurses from the anxiety of patient involvement (Menzies-Lyth, 1988).

Team Nursing

This is the 'allocation of a small group of nurses (team) to a group of patients, for whose care they are responsible' (Waters, 1985). The general aim is to make use of different levels of staff within the team to meet the needs of the patient. A team leader guides a small group of nurses to co-ordinate the care of a group of patients.

Patient Allocation

Patients are allocated to individual nurses who are responsible for carrying out their care, with some degree of continuity. This may be for several shifts or perhaps longer (Marks-Maran, 1978).

Primary Nursing

A qualified nurse is responsible and accountable for the care of a patient from admission through to discharge. Other nurses may help with the care when the primary nurse is off duty, but the primary nurse remains responsible for overall co-ordination of the patient's care (Wright, 1990).

A full explanation of the methods of organizing care is not possible within the scope of this text, but clearly a number of alternatives are on offer to nurses. Given that most nurses would espouse the values of individualized patient care in their nursing model, the question arises as to which method they will choose to meet that goal. Several points need to be taken into consideration.

1. What method would be best suited to the existing staffing levels, qualities and skill mix?
2. If one method is used now, but another preferred, what can be done in the longer term to make the change?
3. Does the method used offer the best possible opportunity for individualized, patient-centred practice, and if not, what changes need to be made?

The answer to these questions will vary from one setting to another, and primary nursing has emerged in recent years as a dominant theme to provide patient-centred care. In other methods, there remain the risks of hierarchies developing among the staff, patient care being fragmented into tasks and accountability being lost when there is little continuity in the relationship between nurse and patient.

Nurses and patients appear to achieve more satisfaction with care when fewer nurses have responsibility for fewer patients. Nursing itself becomes more effective and efficient when individual nurses have their responsibilities to particular patients more clearly defined. Overall, continuity of care appears to improve when nurses choose methods of organization that ensure that fewer nurses look after a limited number of patients for the longest possible time.

The Nurse as Part of a Team

The work in nursing is not carried out in isolation and, in dealing with the multiplicity of health problems the patient encounters, it takes more than the skills of one person to achieve solutions.

While nurses work with people from a variety of occupations—social workers, dieticians, physiotherapists, doctors—relatively little work has been undertaken on evaluating multidisciplinary teams. Does the ideal of a team of equals, with each contributing to the patients' needs according to skills (rather than one professional ruling overall on the basis of authority), work in reality?

To participate as equals in the team, nurses must possess the necessary skills, information and training to meet the expectations of their role by others in the team (Baker, 1976). The concept of the multidisciplinary team means the bringing together of groups of colleagues involved in the care and treatment of an individual patient (Royal Commission, 1979). McFarlane (1980) claims that the narrow disease orientation of the NHS, coupled with undue emphasis on medical function, have served to concentrate attention on the role of the doctor and minimize the contribution and potential of other health workers. The level to which doctors will relinquish their traditionally dominant role in the team is debatable. Kyes and Hoffling (1977) see the development of a health climate where there is a minimum of negative competition, hostility and resentment as being the primary move to the development of positive clinical relationships. The success of the team depends upon the freedom of each member to use their professional skills independently in an atmosphere of mutual respect.

The Nurse as Educator

Working with the patient—guiding, helping, explaining—underpins the whole process of nursing activity towards rehabilitation. If patients are to move through illness to a stage where they are no longer dependent on nursing, then involving patients in their own care, at appropriate times, is part of the nurse's teaching and rehabilitation role. As Kershaw points out (in Wright, 1988):

In order for patients to manage their own care, and thus control their lifestyle, they need knowledge about, and insight into, their health difficulties ... most patients are capable of understanding what they must do to maintain health and to improve it provided they are adequately and professionally taught.

Teaching patients, relatives and other carers is a highly skilful act. The Nurses' Rules laid down in the Nurses, Midwives and Health Visitors Act (1979) state that nurses are the most important health educators in the multidisciplinary team and that they have a duty to develop this aspect of their role.

Wilson-Barnett (1983) emphasizes that all patients benefit from understanding their disease and treatment and by having explanations of how they can best co-operate with the nursing care plan. The inclusion of patient (and relatives and friends) in education should be an integral part of care planning.

Discovering their patients' abilities to achieve realistic health outcomes is part of an overall assessment within the nursing process. The patient's willingness and readiness to learn can be estimated, and it is helpful also to discover when they last made an attempt to learn anything new. Teaching patients, once their learning needs have been assessed, is a highly complex activity. Learning to become an effective educator is an integral part of every nurse's development, in order for them to fulfil their role effectively (Redman, 1980; Wilson-Barnett, 1983).

A full exploration of this role is found in numerous texts, some of which are listed at the end of this chapter, and the reader is urged to read some of these to contribute to improving expertise in patient teaching. Meanwhile, a number of key points that are directly relevant to nurses include developing skills in the following:

- Communicating with patients in an appropriate language (considering intellect, language, culture, class, values and so on).
- Recognizing that patients learn at different rates.
- Taking account of factors that affect learning ability, such as age, physiological changes in the brain.
- Using reinforcement and opportunity for the patient to practise when being taught.
- Accepting that not everyone wishes to learn or accept responsibility for their own care.
- Recognizing that effective teaching is based on an open, friendly and trusting relationship with the nurse.
- Identifying for the patients the benefits that education in health and managing their care can bring.

- Relieving barriers to learning (anxiety, stress, pain, sleeplessness and confusion) before attempting to teach.
- Teaching the patient in privacy, and ensuring patient is comfortable and feeling ready to learn.
- Using group teaching, explanations or referral to self-help groups.

This list indicates the complexity of teaching in the nurse–patient relationship, and suggests that nurses have to develop considerable knowledge and skill to be effective teachers. A careful assessment of the patient beforehand is necessary before any teaching can be undertaken, and plans of care that include teaching can form part of the patient's total nursing care plan. The practice is very similar to the nursing process—assessing the patient's learning ability and what needs to be learned, planning what is to be taught and recognizing how carrying out the teaching gives opportunities for questions, practice and reinforcement, and then evaluating and modifying the programme accordingly.

Thus it is possible to develop teaching plans that incorporate an assessment, planning, implementation and evaluation strategy. Teaching and informing patients may be formally organized in this way. However, it has to be recognized that great areas of what happens between nurse and patient are a learning experience for both partners and cannot be compared with a formal teaching plan. These are well suited where formal teaching on a specific issue is required. At other times, the nurse's awareness and use of less formal arrangements is also essential. In the day-to-day delivery of nursing care, nurses act as teachers, advisers and role models in far more subtle ways than can be described in formal teaching plans.

BEYOND THE HOSPITAL

Most patients, for whom death is not inevitable, anticipate return to their own homes after the experience of illness and hospital. If nurses are to achieve their expected outcome of enabling the patient to do this, with minimal dependence on nursing, then it is necessary to accept that rehabilitation and preparation for discharge might begin at the moment the patient is admitted. These may take the form at an early stage of outlining the care to be given, the objectives to be achieved, and offering a sense of hope and possibility.

The then Department of Health and Social Security (1988) produced a document requiring that all wards and departments have clear procedures for patients' discharge and that appropriate arrangements be made for the patient's return home. It is clear throughout this document that planning for discharge 'should begin on admission and that lack of planning can lead to blocked beds and unnecessary readmission' (DHSS, 1988). Four main failures were outlined with regard to discharge planning:

1. Lack of information and reassurance about the care of the patient on discharge.
2. Failure to check on the day that the patient is fit to leave hospital.
3. Failure to inform the general practitioner, district nurses and social services of the patient's potential needs.
4. Failure to carry out an assessment before discharge to ensure that facilities available in the patient's home are appropriate to meet the patient's needs.

People who live alone, the very frail, the very old and the very young were found to be particularly at risk of these failures.

To minimize risks to the patient on discharge, a planned approach is essential. Many patients will return home to be cared for by their family. However, nurses must bear in mind the fact that not everyone has family members willing and/or able to participate in their care. Indeed, a large minority of people do not live in a family situation at all. Government statistics show that 24 per cent of households consist of only one person, and 9 per cent of the population live in a one-person 'household'. Five per cent of households consist of a lone parent with dependent children, and only 30 per cent of households are made up of the 'traditional' married couple with dependent children (Central Statistical Office, 1985). The fact that this 'normal' family makes up less than one third of present families is the reason why statistics relate to 'households' and not 'families'. Almost one third of people over the age of 65, and half of the over-85s, live alone or with unrelated people, although some of these will be in residential care. Ninety per cent of retired people live near enough to one of their children to see them weekly. The converse of this is that 10 per cent of elderly people do not easily have the support of their children (Leonard and Speakman, in Beechey and Whitelegg, 1986).

It is clear, therefore, that nurses need to make an individual assessment of each patient's personal situation in order to identify whether they have family members, friends or other carers who will support them when they are discharged. For those who do not have this type of support, it will be necessary to arrange the appropriate community services to ensure that they have the necessary care at home.

Jupp and Sims (1986) state that the aims of discharge planning are to:

- Prepare the patient, family or other carers physically and psychologically for the transfer home.
- Promote the highest possible level of independence.
- Provide continuity of care from hospital to community.
- Ensure the smooth transfer from hospital to community.

Heywood-Jones (1988) points out that nurses have to base their main focus on nursing care in the hospital. However, nurses cannot 'afford to function in isolation in a hospital, blind to what goes on beyond their walls'. Nurses have a 'responsibility to become acquainted with outside services and to reach out to link a partnership' with other agencies at work in the community. Nurses need to be aware of what services are on offer beyond the hospital and then to liaise with them.

Bowling and Betts (1984) suggest that a formal documented structure for the discharge process is needed. Waters (1987) argues for thorough assessment for discharge as soon as possible after admission. Many settings have now adopted a range of assessment and discharge forms to aid communication.

Other points to consider include:

- Multidisciplinary meetings should be held to assess each patient's potential for discharge and what role each health care worker will play.
- Community and hospital staff should have a means (written and oral) of sharing information about the patient.
- Patients, relatives and other carers should be taught any necessary skills to help with care.
- One person should be responsible for co-ordinating the discharge so that all concerned know to whom to turn for assistance.
- The use of medicines, their dosages, purpose and side-effects should be taught before discharge (and written back-up information given).
- Clear oral and written advice should be given to patients and other carers about the patient's condition and care at home.
- Patients, families and other carers should be given the ward/hospital telephone numbers.
- Necessary referrals should be made fully and accurately beforehand, including members of the health care team and specialist support groups.
- All equipment should be ready on the day of discharge (oxygen equipment, catheters and so on) where relevant.

With these points in mind, it is possible to ensure adequate planning before discharge, which will reduce the risk of readmission, and of failure by patients to participate in treatment and care. Patients will also feel more secure after discharge and more satisfied with the quality of care given. Preparing the patient for discharge remains very much within the remit of nurses, and success depends a great deal upon how well they fulfil this role. In general, to overcome the current weaknesses in discharge planning, a major attitudinal change is needed. That is, staff at all levels need to be aware of, and act upon, the importance of discharge planning.

CONCLUSION

An illness that requires medical or surgical intervention, and that necessitates admission to hospital, can be a stressful event for any patient. For some it can be a time of great fear and pain, compounded by the dislocation from the normal flow of life. The patient enters a world where control of mind and body can be lost to others, a place filled with strange sights and sounds, where hopes and expectations are challenged by the uncertain and the unpredictable. This chapter has suggested that nurses have a key role to play as companions to the patient through the journey of illness.

Nurses can do far more than assist with treatments or dole out medicines on the patient's road towards health. They can work sensitively with patients, accepting them as whole people, and can pursue the unique form of helping that each patient needs. By using the kind of principles discussed so far, they can have a wide knowledge base to help them understand all kinds of people and their varied responses to illness. Nurses can do far more than merely help diagnose and treat a disease. By understanding the complex physical, psychological and social dimensions of health and illness, and applying creative and thoughtful caring techniques, they can transform the patient's experience in hospital. Nurses can help patients cope with stress, adjust their lifestyles, manage disability, promote care or ease the path towards death. It is possible for nurses to help the whole person, and make nursing a therapeutic act. The way each nurse works with each patient can be, of itself, healing and comforting. Therein lies the value of nursing to the individual and to society.

BIBLIOGRAPHY

Aries, P. (1962) *Centuries Of Childhood*, Cape, London.

Association of Community Health Councils (1986) *Patients' Charter*, Association of Community Health Councils, London.

Autton, N. (1989) *Touch—An Exploration*, Darton, Longman and Todd, London.

Bailey, R. and Clarke, M. (1985) *Stress and Coping in Nursing*, Chapman and Hall, London.

Baker, E. (ed.) (1976) Modern development in psychiatric nursing care, C. J. Harries in *Comprehensive Psychiatric Care*, Blackwell Scientific, Oxford.

Bamber, T., Johnson, M. L., Purdy, E. and Wright, S. G. (1989) The Tameside experience, *Nursing Standard*, Vol. 22, No. 3, p. 26.

Barnett, R. C. and Baruch, G. (1978) Women in the middle years: a critique of research and theory, *Psychology of Women Quarterly*, Vol. 32, No. 2, pp. 187–97.

Beechey, V. and Whitelegg, E. (eds) (1986) Women in the family: companions or caretakers?, D. Leonard and M. A. Speakman in *Women in Britain Today*, Open University, Milton Keynes.

Bem, S. (1974) The measurement of psychological androgyny, *Journal of Clinical and Consulting Psychology*, Vol. 42, pp. 155–62.

Benner, P. (1985) *From Novice To Expert*, Addison Wesley, New York.

Benner, P. and Wrubel, J. (1989) *The Primacy of Caring: Stress and Coping in Health and Illness*, Addison-Wesley, Menlo Park, California.

Blaxter, M. (1983) The causes of disease. Women talking, *Social Science and Medicine*, Vol. 17, No. 2, pp. 59–69.

Bond, S., Fall, F. and Thomas, L. (1990) *A Summary Report of a Study of Primary Nursing and Primary Medical Care: a Comparative Study in Community Hospitals*, Report No. 39, Health Care Research Unit, University of Newcastle upon Tyne.

Boore, J. (1978) *Prescription for Recovery*, Royal College of Nursing, London.

Bowers, K. A. (1980) Explaining health behaviour: the health belief model, *Nursing Administration Quarterly*, Vol. 4, No. 2, pp. 47–54.

Bowling, A. and Betts, G. (1984) Communication discharge, *Nursing Times*, Vol. 80, No. 32, pp. 31–3 and Vol. 80, No. 33, pp. 44–6.

Brenner, M. H. (1979) Mortality and the national economy: a review and the experience of England and Wales 1936–1976, *Lancet*, Vol. ii, pp. 568–73.

Brown, G. W. and Harries, T. (1978) *The Social Origins of Depression*, Tavistock, London.

Brownlee, A. (1978) *Community, Culture and Care*, C. V. Mosby, St Louis.

Burgess, R. G. (ed.) (1986) Social class and occupation, C. Marsh in *Key Variables in Social Investigation*, Routledge & Kegan Paul, London.

Campbell, A. V. (1984) *Moderated Love*, SPCK, London.

Carpenito, L. J. (1987) *Nursing Diagnosis* (2nd edition), J. B. Lippincott, Philadelphia.

Central Statistical Office (1985) *Social Trends No. 15*, HMSO, London.

Claus, K. E. and Bailey, J. T. (1980) *Living with Stress and Promoting Well-being*, C. V. Mosby, St Louis.

Cooper, C., Cooper, R. and Eaten, L. (1988) *Living with Stress*, Penguin, Harmondsworth.

Cox, B. D., Blaxter, M., Buckle, A. L. J. *et al.* (eds) (1987) Attitudes to health, M. Blaxter in *The Health and Lifestyle Survey*, Health Promotion Trust, London.

Cox, C. and Mead, A. (eds) (1975) Therapeutic behaviour, hospital culture and communication, E. Cassée in *A Sociology of Medical Practice*, Collier-MacMillan, London.

Dean, D. (1988) *Manpower Solutions*, Royal College of Nursing, London.

Deem, R. (1978) *Women and Schooling*, Routledge and Kegan Paul, London.

Department of Health (Nursing Division) (1989) *A Strategy for Nursing*, Department of Health, London.

Department of Health and Social Security (1980) *Discharge of Patients from Hospital*, HMSO, London.

Dohrenwend, B. S. and Dohrenwend, B. P. (1974) *Stressful life Events*, Wiley, New York.

Elsdorfer, C., Cohen, A., Kleinman, A. and Maxim, P. (eds) (1981) The stress and coping paradigm, R. Lazarus in *Theoretical Bases for Psychopathology*, Spectrum, New York.

Erikson, E. H. (1959) Identity and the life cycle, *Psychological Issues*, Vol. 1.

Fagin, L. and Little, M. (1984) *The Forsaken Families*, Penguin, Harmondsworth.

Franklin, B. L. (1974) *Patient Anxiety on Admission to Hospital*, Royal College of Nursing, London.

Goffman, E. (1963) *Stigma: Notes on the Management of Spoiled Identity*, Prentice Hall, Englewood Cliffs, New Jersey.

Gore, S. (1978) The effect of social support in moderating the health consequences of unemployment, *Journal of Health and Social Behavior*, Vol. 19, pp. 157–65.

Greene, J. G. (1980) Stress in the Phyllosan years, *New Society*, Vol. 54, pp. 944–5.

Hallstrom, T. and Samuelsson, S. (1985) Mental health in the climacteric, *Acta Obstetrica Gynecologica Scandinavica*, Suppl. 130, pp. 13–18.

Henderson, V. (1966) *The Nature of Nursing*, Macmillan, New York.

Heywood-Jones, I. (1988) Beyond the walls, *Nursing Times*, Vol. 84, No. 16, p. 45.

Jupp, M. and Sims, S. (1986) Going home, *Nursing Times*, 1 October, Vol. 82, No. 40, pp. 40–2.

Kahana, B. and Kahana, E. (1982) Clinical issues of middle age and later life, *Annals of the American Academy of Political and Social Science*, Vol. 464, pp. 140–61.

Kearl, M. C. and Hoag, L. J. (1984) The social construction of the midlife crisis, *Sociological Inquiry*, Vol. 54, No. 3, pp. 279–300.

Kershaw, B. and Salvage, J. (eds) (1986) *Models for Nursing*, John Wiley, Chichester.

Klaus, K. E. and Bailey, J. T. (eds) (1980) Stress and a holistic view of health for the nursing profession, H. Selye in *Living With Stress and Promoting Well-Being*, C. V. Mosby, St Louis.

Kozier, B., Erb, G. and McKay-Bufalino, P. (1989) Ethnicity and culture, *An Introduction to Nursing*, Addison Wesley, California.

Krieger, D. (1979) *Therapeutic Touch*, Prentice Hall, London.

Kyes, J. and Hoffling, M. D. (1977) *Basic Psychiatric Concepts in Nursing*, J. B. Lippincott, Philadelphia.

Lazarus, R. S. and Folkman, S. (1984) *Stress, Appraisal and Coping*, Springer, New York.

Luker, K. (1988) Do models work? *Nursing Times*, Vol. 84, No. 5, pp. 27–9.

Manchester Joint Consultative Committee, *Health Inequalities and Manchester*.

Mares, P., Larbie, J. and Baxter, C. (1987) *Training in Health and Race*, National Extension College, Cambridge.

Marks-Maran, D. (1978) Patient allocation and task allocation in relation to the nursing process, *Nursing Times*, Vol. 74, No. 10, pp. 413–16.

Martin, J.P. (1984) *Hospitals in Trouble*, Blackwell Scientific, London.

McCoy, N. L. and Davidson, J. M. (1985) A longitudinal study of the effect of menopause on sexuality, *Maturitas*, Vol. 7, pp. 203–10.

McFarlane, J. K. (1980) *Multidisciplinary Clinical Teams*, Kings' Fund, London.

Melia, K. M. (1989) *Everyday Nursing Ethics*, MacMillan, London.

Menzies-Lyth, I. (reprinted 1988) The functioning of the social system as a defence against anxiety, I. Menzies (1961) in *Containing Anxiety in Institutions*, Free Association Books, London.

Nightingale, F. (1860; reprinted 1980) *Notes On Nursing: What It Is and What It Is Not*, Churchill Livingstone, Edinburgh.

Nuckalls, C. B., Cassel, J. and Kaplan, B. H. (1972) Psychosocial assets, life crises and the prognosis of pregnancy, *American Journal of Epidemiology*, Vol. 95, pp. 431–4.

Nurses, Midwives and Health Visitors Act (1979) HMSO, London.

Oakley, A. (1981) *Subject Women*, Fontana, Glasgow.

Oakley, A. (1988) Smoking in pregnancy: smokescreen or risk factor? Towards a materialist analysis, *Sociology of Health and Illness*, Vol. 11, No. 4, pp. 311–35.

Orem, E. E. (1980) *Nursing: Concepts of Practice*, McGraw-Hill, New York.

Parsons, T. (1951) *The Social System*, Routledge & Kegan Paul, London.

Pearson, A. (ed.) (1988) *Primary Nursing*, Croom Helm, London.

Pearson, A., Durand, I. and Punton, S. (1988) *Therapeutic Nursing: An Evaluation of an Experimental Nursing Unit in the British National Health Service*, Burford and Oxford Nursing Development Unit, Oxford.

Pearson, A. and Vaughan, B. (1986) *Nursing Models for Practice*, Heinemann, London.

Peplau, H. E. (1952) *Interpersonal Relationships In Nursing*, Putnam, New York.

Pervin, M. and Lewis, M. (1978) Stress related transactions between person and the environment, R. S. Lazarus and R. Launier in *Perspectives in Interactional Psychology*, Plenum Press, New York.

Platt, S. and Kreitmann, N. (1984) Unemployment and parasuicide in Edinburgh 1968–1982, *British Medical Journal*, Vol. 289, pp. 1029–32.

Price Waterhouse (1988) *Nurse Retention and Recruitment*, Price Waterhouse, London.

Redfern, S. J. (ed.) (1986) *Nursing Elderly People*, Churchill Livingstone, Edinburgh.

Redfern, S. J. (ed.) (1986) Hearing, K. Gilhomme Herbst in *Nursing Elderly People*, Churchill Livingstone, Edinburgh.

Redman, B. (1980) *The Process of Patient Teaching in Nursing*, C. V. Mosby, St Louis.

Reilly, D. (1975) Why a conceptual framework? *Nursing Outlook*, Vol. 23, No. 9, pp. 14–22.

Report of the Committee on Nursing (Brigg Report) (1972) HMSO, London.

Riehl, J. P. and Roy, C. (eds) (1980) The Roy adaptation model, C. Roy in *Conceptual Models For Nursing Practice*, Appleton-Century-Crofts, New York.

Roper, N., Logan, W. and Tierney, A. (1983) *Using A Model For Nursing*, Churchill Livingstone, Edinburgh.

Roper, N., Logan, W. and Tierney, A. (1986) *The Elements of Nursing*, Churchill Livingstone, Edinburgh.

Rossi, A. S. (1980) Lifespan theories and women's lives, *Signs*, Vol. 6, No. 1, pp. 4–32.

Royal Commission (1979) *Royal Commission on the National Health Service*, HMSO, London.

Rumbold, G. (1986) *Ethics in Nursing Practice*, Baillière Tindall, London.

Savage, J. (1987) *Nurses, Gender and Sexuality*, Heinemann, London.

Salvage, J. (1990) The theory and practice of the 'new nursing', *Nursing Times*, Vol. 84, No. 4, pp. 42–5.

Salvage, J. and Kershaw, B. (1990) *Models For Nursing (2)*, Scutari, London.

Selye, H. (1976) *Stress in Health and Disease*, Butterworths, London.

Simpson, J. E. P. and Levitt, R. (eds) (1981) Visual disability, M. A. Ford in *Going Home*, Churchill Livingstone, Edinburgh.

Simpson, J. E. P. and Levitt, R. (eds) (1981) The hearing impaired, M. C. Martin in *Going Home*, Churchill Livingstone, Edinburgh.

Stewart, W. (1985) *Counselling in Rehabilitation*, Croom Helm, London.

Stockwell, F. (1972) *The Unpopular Patient*, Royal College of Nursing, London.

Tameside and Glossop Health Authority, Nursing Development Unit (1988) *Information for Patients and Visitors*, Tameside and Glossop Health Authority.

Townsend, P. and Davidson, N. (1982) *Inequalities in Health*, Penguin, Harmondsworth.

Tripp-Reimer, T., Brink, P. J. and Saunders, J. M. (1984) Cultural assessment. Content and process, *Nursing Outlook*, Vol. 32, pp. 78–82.

United Kingdom Central Council for Nursing, Midwifery and Health Visitors (1983) *Code of Professional Conduct for the Nurse, Midwife and Health Visitor*, UKCC, London.

Vaughan, B. (ed.) (1990) *Managing Nursing Work*, Scutari, London.

Voda, A. M. and George, T. (1986) Menopause, *Annual Review of Nursing Research*, Vol. 4, pp. 55–75.

Waters, K. (1985) Team nursing, *Nursing Practice*, Vol. 1, No. 1, pp. 7–15.

Waters, K. (1987) Discharge planning: an exploratory study, *Journal of Advanced Nursing*, Vol. 12, No. 1, pp. 71–83.

Webb, C. and Wilson-Barnett, J. (1983) Coping with hysterectomy, *Journal of Advanced Nursing*, Vol. 8, No. 3, pp. 311–19.

Webb, C. (1985) *Sexuality, Nursing and Health*, John Wiley, Chichester.

Welford, A. T. (ed.) (1974) *Man Under Stress*, Taylor and Francis, London.

Whitehead, M. (1988) *The Health Divide*, Penguin, Harmondsworth.

Wilson-Barnett, J. (1983) *Patient Teaching*, Churchill Livingstone, Edinburgh.

Wilson-Barnett, J. and Carrigy, A. (1978) Factors affecting patients' responses to hospitalisation, *Journal of Advanced Nursing*, Vol. 3, pp. 221–8.

Wong, J. (1979) An exploration of a patient-centred nursing approach in the admission of selected surgical patients: a replicated study, *Journal of Advanced Nursing*, Vol. 4, No. 6, pp. 611–19.

Woods, N. (1984) *Human Sexuality in Health and Illness*, C. V. Mosby, St Louis.

World Health Organisation (1980) *International Classification of Impairments, Disabilities and Handicaps*, WHO, Geneva.

Wright, S. G. (1986) *Building and Using a Model of Nursing*, Edward Arnold, London.

Wright, S. G. (1988) Learning, B. Kershaw in *Nursing the Older Patient*, Harper & Row, London.

Wright, S. G. (1990) *My Patient, My Nurse: Primary Nursing in Practice*, Scutari, London.

Young, A. P. (1981) *Legal Problems in Nursing Practice*, Harper & Row, London.

FURTHER READING

Books

Sexuality and Nursing

Godow, A. G. (1982) *Human Sexuality*, C. V. Mosby, New York.

Hogan, R. (1980) *Human Sexuality. A Nursing Perspective*, Appleton-Century-Crofts, New York.

Lion, E. M. (1982) *Human Sexuality In the Nursing Process*, John Wiley, New York.

Poorman, S. G. (1988) *Human Sexuality and the Nursing Process*, Appleton & Lange, Norwalk, Ct.

Savage, J. (1987) *Nurses, Gender and Sexuality*, Heinemann, London.

Webb, C. (1985) *Sexuality, Nursing and Health*, John Wiley, Chichester.

Woods, N. (1984) *Human Sexuality in Health and Illness*, C. V. Mosby, St Louis.

chapter 2

ISSUES AND CONCEPTS IN MEDICAL–SURGICAL NURSING

NUTRITION

Nutrition plays an important role in maintaining health and preventing disease. When illness or injury occur, nutrition is an essential factor in promoting healing and reinforcing resistance to infection. Assessment of nutritional status provides information on obesity, undernutrition, weight loss, deficiencies in specific nutrients, metabolic abnormalities and the special problems of hospitalized patients.

In other words, food is essential for life and, whatever the nature of the presenting illness, all patients require adequate food of the right kind presented in the most acceptable way (i.e., adequate nutrition). If this is to be achieved successfully, it is essential that all those involved in patient care understand the fundamentals of nutrition and are able to apply them when providing food for the sick. Nurses, through their continued contact with the patient, are in the best position to liaise between patients and other health care professionals and so have an important role in nutritional care. To be effective in this role, they must understand the basic principles of nutrition and be able to apply these to the patients in their care.

Basic Principles of Nutrition

The body is composed of many different substances, all of which are derived either from the air that is breathed or the food that is eaten. Thus, there is considerable truth in the saying that 'you are what you eat'.

Nutrients, the substances needed for normal body function, are provided by food, although it is important to recognize that not all food components are nutrients (e.g., food additives) (Holmes, 1986a).

Nutrients can be considered in two broad categories: macronutrients and micronutrients. Macronutrients include: carbohydrate, protein and fat and also those minerals required in amounts greater than 100 mg/day. Micronutrients, including the vitamins and minerals, are required in very small amounts (usually only a few milligrams day).

Energy Production

A person's major nutritional need is for energy (calories). Daily energy requirements vary and are determined by two major factors: the basal metabolic rate and the level of physical activity. Thus, like food intake, energy demand varies daily depending on workload, physiological status, age and level of activity. However, because regulatory mechanisms maintain homeostasis, body weight remains remarkably constant, and normal functions continue despite wide variations in food consumption. This means that the body need not be in energy balance each day as physiological mechanisms generally control the energy intake so that, over time, intake equals output.

There are four forms of energy in the body: chemical, electrical, thermal and mechanical. Chemical energy, derived from the catabolism of nutrients, is the only form of energy that can support the function of body cells. Once formed, chemical energy can be used immediately, stored or, through an irreversible reaction, transformed into other forms of energy. However, although mechanical, thermal or electrical energy can be formed from chemical energy, the reverse process cannot occur.

Digestive processes (Chapter 11) convert foods to glucose (and other monosaccharides), amino acids and fatty acids, which are taken up by body cells. Here they are oxidized by a complex reaction in which they react with oxygen (O_2) to produce carbon dioxide (CO_2), water (H_2O) and energy. This is achieved through the tricarboxylic acid cycle, the final common pathway of metabolism (Figure 2.1), and is concerned primarily with the conversion of chemical energy into adenosine triphosphate (ATP), a high-energy storage compound. When broken down, adenosine triphosphate releases energy, most of which is chemical, although some 'escapes' as heat, helping to maintain body temperature.

Adenosine triphosphate releases energy rapidly it is often described as the 'energy currency' of the body. Its breakdown and synthesis are continuous and depend on regular provision of energy from food or from the breakdown of body tissues.

Carbohydrates

Most dietary energy is derived from carbohydrates (CHO; starches and sugars) in which carbon atoms are linked with water. Their basic structure is $C_6(H_2O)_6$ (i.e., six atoms of carbon and six molecules of water). A carbohydrate containing one such unit is known as a monosaccharide (e.g., glucose), one with two units is a disaccharide (e.g., sucrose) and one with many units as described as a polysaccharide (complex carbohydrate, e.g., starch).

Dietary disaccharides, and those produced by digestion of polysaccharides (see below), are taken up by the intestinal mucosal cells where they are broken down by enzymic action to form monosaccharides. These are absorbed by active transport, enter the portal circulation and are transported to the liver and other tissues, where they are metabolized to provide energy. Excess glucose is used to form glycogen, the storage form of carbohydrate, and is released by the liver when needed to maintain optimal blood glucose concentration. Muscle tissue (e.g., skeletal muscle) can also store glycogen, using it to provide energy for its metabolism. However, as the body can store only limited amounts of glycogen, excess glucose is also converted into fat and stored in adipose tissue. Thus excess energy consumption results in fat deposition and weight gain. Conversely, when carbohydrates are not available to provide energy, the liver can synthesize glucose using parts of amino acids and fats; body components (e.g., protein and adipose tissue) may be broken down to provide energy.

Polysaccharides

Starch is a glucose storage molecule found extensively in grains, cereals, legumes, root vegetables and tubers (e.g., potatoes). As starches derived from different sources differ both in the number of glucose molecules they contain and in their physical properties, those derived from different foods are digested at different rates (Crapo, Reaven and Olefsky, 1977). However, all starches need a longer period of digestion than disaccharides, so the glucose they provide becomes available to the body at a relatively slow rate.

Indigestible polysaccharides include cellulose, which resembles starch, comprising many glucose molecules. However, the molecules are linked differently so that it is indigestible and passes through the intestine essentially unchanged. Noncellulose polysaccharides contain not only glucose but also other monosaccharides, and include substances like hemicellulose, pectin, mucilages, gums and lignin. Like cellulose, hemicellulose and pectin are found in plant cell walls. Mucilages and gums are found in plant secretions and seeds, while lignin is present in the woody part of plants. All indigestible polysaccharides are components of dietary fibre and help to maintain normal bowel function by absorbing water, increasing faecal bulk, and increasing the movement of the intestinal content along the gastrointestinal tract thereby preventing constipation.

Fats (Lipids)

The term lipids refers to a large number of fat-like and waxy compounds that are insoluble in water but soluble in organic solvents. In dietary terms, 'fat' generally refers to fats and oils and, nutritionally, it is the triglycerides that are the most important. Triglycerides are composed of one molecule of glycerol linked to three molecules of fatty acid (Figure 2.2A); different triglycerides result from the presence of different fatty acids. When the three fatty acids are identical, a simple triglyceride is produced: when at least two different fatty acids are present, the fat is

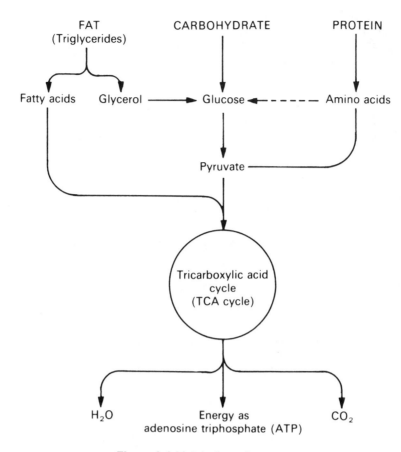

Figure 2.1 Metabolism of energy.

known as a mixed triglyceride. Most natural fats contain a mixture of two or more different triglycerides.

Saturated and Unsaturated Fatty Acids

As part of triglycerides, fatty acids are the major components of food fats and are often discussed in terms of their degree of saturation. The terms saturated and unsaturated refer to the number of hydrogen atoms present in the fatty acid molecule, each of which is comprised of a chain of carbon atoms linked to hydrogen atoms. When a fat does not contain a full complement of hydrogen atoms a double bond exists between adjacent carbon atoms, producing an unsaturated fat; more than one double bond results in a polyunsaturated fat (Figure 2.2B).

Saturated fatty acids are chemically stable; triglycerides containing them are solid at room temperature and so are known as 'hard' fats (e.g., meat fat and hydrogenated vegetable fats). Unsaturated fats are less chemically stable and are more susceptible to oxidation and rancidity. They are liquid at room temperature. Examples include corn, soya and fish oils.

In the intestine, ingested fats are emulsified by bile making them accessible to the pancreatic enzymes, which release fatty acids from glycerol. This enables them to aggregate with bile and be transported to the intestinal mucosal cells where fat diffuses through the membranes into the cells. Bile salts are reabsorbed, transported to the liver and reused.

Within the cells, most fatty acid are converted into new triglycerides before entering the lymphatic system and, from there, passing into the systemic circulation through the thoracic duct. Fats are taken up from the circulation within a few hours by either the liver or the adipose tissue. In the liver, lipids may be metabolized, stored or converted to a suitable form for transport to other tissues where they are used to provide energy.

Proteins

Proteins are part of all body cells. Since body proteins depend on dietary protein for their formation and maintenance, protein is a dietary essential. All proteins are comprised of amino acids, often described as the 'building blocks' of protein. Individual proteins contain a unique sequence of amino acids that makes them adopt a particular conformation, the native state. Proteins cannot be digested in this state and must first be denatured. Denaturation, resulting from either cooking or the action of gastric acid, enables the digestive enzymes to break down protein releasing individual amino acids that can subsequently be absorbed. Free amino acids cross the mucosa by active transport, entering the portal circulation from where they are taken up by body cells, primarily the liver.

Twenty-two amino acids are recognized as constituents of most proteins (Table 2.1); eight of these (nine in children) are described as essential since the body cannot synthesize them in adequate amounts; they must be provided by the diet. Although both essential and nonessential amino acids are needed for protein synthesis, non-essential amino acids can be synthesized from other dietary components (e.g., carbohydrate, other amino acids).

The nutritional value of individual proteins is determined by the relationship between their amino acid content and body requirements. A useful nutritional classification is based on their 'completeness'. An 'ideal'

A. General structure

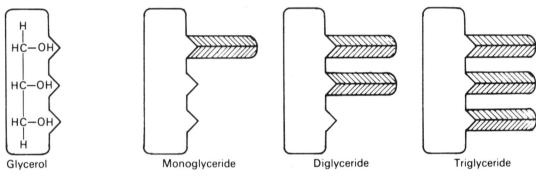

B. Saturated, monounsaturated and polyunsaturated fatty acids

Saturated fatty acid (stearic acid)

Monounsaturated fatty acid (oleic acid)

Polyunsaturated fatty acid (linoleic acid)

Figure 2.2 Structure of triglycerides and fatty acids.

Table 2.1 *Amino acids*

Non-essential	Essential
Glycine	Valine
Alanine	Lysine
Serine	Threonine
Cystine	Leucine
Tyrosine	Isoleucine
Aspartic acid	Tryptophan
Glutamic acid	Phenylalanine
Proline	Methionine
Hydroxyproline	Histidine – in children
Citrulline	
Arginine	
Norleucine	
Hydroxyglutamic acid	

(complete) protein contains all the essential amino acids in amounts sufficient to support growth and maintain body tissues: one failing to supply essential amino acids in appropriate amounts is partially complete and cannot support growth when eaten as the sole protein source. Animal proteins (e.g., meat, milk, eggs, fish, poultry) are complete proteins; peas, beans and nuts are examples of partially complete proteins. Incomplete proteins are deficient in one or more essential amino acid and so will neither support growth nor maintain life; examples include bread, cereals and vegetables. The biological value of a protein can be high or low depending on its completeness.

Animal proteins are complete and, therefore, of high biological value. Some vegetable proteins are only partially complete and others are incomplete. This is important because, ideally, essential amino acids are consumed together so that they are presented to the gut, circulation and, ultimately, body cells in the correct ratio to enable protein synthesis to occur. If this is not so, some essential amino acids are metabolized and used to provide energy and so lost to the body for protein synthesis. This does not, however, mean that partially complete or incomplete proteins cannot be useful, since combining protein sources can provide a desirable proportion of essential amino acids by making use of the complementary effects of individual proteins so that the resulting combination is of higher biological value than when either is eaten alone. Thus, combining proteins with complementary effects can significantly increase protein quality.

Other Essential Compounds

Water. After oxygen, water is the most important constituent for the maintenance of life. Although it is possible to live for several weeks without food, life without water can last only a few days. A 10 per cent loss of body water results in severe disorders; a 20 per cent loss results in death.

Water is derived not only from drinks but also from food: metabolic water, produced in the body, is a less obvious source. Water is the solvent in which all metabolic reactions occur and, as the transport medium for nutrients and other substances, it is involved in digestion, absorption, excretion and the circulation, helping to maintain fluid and electrolyte balance and body temperature. Water also plays a central role in the maintenance of homeostasis and in the control of acid–base balance, electrolyte concentration and osmotic pressure.

Vitamins. Vitamins are essential substances required for normal growth and maintenance and to ensure the normal metabolism of other nutrients. Since humans cannot synthesize most vitamins they must be obtained through food. Individual vitamins vary greatly both in chemical composition and in functions (Table 2.2). In general, only very small amounts are needed as their functions are primarily catalytic, as components of enzyme systems involved in metabolic reactions (Table 2.3). However, although most foods contain a variety of vitamins, no single food contains all the vitamins required: this is why a diet drawn from a wide range of food is recommended.

Inorganic elements are also necessary (Tables 2.4 and 2.5). Although not all elements are essential to life, almost all have been found in living cells. Oxygen, carbon, hydrogen and nitrogen account for 96 per cent of the body weight. Of this, over 50 per cent is oxygen which, combined with hydrogen to form water, makes up 65 per cent of the body weight.

The remainder of the body weight is comprised of essential elements (minerals), which are categorized according to the amount present. Those comprising 0.01 per cent (or more) body weight are the macroelements, of which calcium and phosphorus account for 75 per cent of the average mineral content. Trace elements comprise less than 0.01 per cent of body weight.

Minerals perform many important functions as components of body tissues, fluids and many specialized substances, such as hormones, enzymes and transport molecules. They are essential in the regulation of water and acid–base balance, in the transmission of nerve impulses and many other processes.

Achieving Good Nutrition

Most of the diets found worldwide can meet man's complex nutritional needs provided they are consumed in adequate amounts. Since requirements vary considerably between individuals, an ideal diet does not exist. Nonetheless, nutritional standards have been formulated that are designed to meet the known needs of most healthy people (Department of Health, 1991) (Table 2.6). They do not, however, take account of the special needs arising in illness and/or disease. Similarly, they make no recommendations with regard to the composition of the diet (see below).

Table 2.2 *The vitamins*

Vitamin	Major functions	Deficiency and toxicity	Main dietary sources
Fat soluble Vitamin A (retinol)	Repair and maintenance of epithelial tissues, resistance to infection, growth of bone, development of the central nervous system, synthesis of RNA, vision	*Deficiency:* Frequent infections affecting eye or mouth, loss of night vision, rough, dry scaly skin, sinus problems *Toxicity:* Desquammation or dryness of the skin, hair loss, bone pain, hepatomegaly, splenomegaly, headache	Green, leafy vegetables, fish, milk and milk products
Vitamin D (calciferol)	Use and metabolism of both calcium and phosphorus; regulation of serum calcium; mineralization of bones and teeth	*Deficiency:* Diarrhoea, myopia, insomnia, nervousness, softening of bones and teeth, rickets (infants/children), osteomalacia (adults)) *Toxicity:* Nocturia, polyuria, muscle weakness, loss of night vision. Nausea and vomiting, diarrhoea, anorexia. If severe leads to calcification of soft tissues	Egg yolk, organ meat, butter, fatty fish. *Note:* Can be synthesized in body following exposure to sunlight (ultraviolet light)*
Vitamin E (tocopherol)	Exerts antioxidant functions, which protect cellular membranes; prevents haemolysis of erythrocytes (effects on sexual potency and maintenance of fertility are as yet unproven)	*Deficiency:* Haemolysis of erythrocytes; dull, dry hair; muscle wasting, alopecia; oedema and skin lesions in infants *Toxicity:* Disturbances of utilization of vitamins A and K; weakness of skeletal muscles; gastrointestinal disturbances	Butter, dark, green leafy vegetables, fruits, nuts, whole grains and cereals
Vitamin K (menadione)	Synthesis of prothrombin and other clotting factors (in liver)	*Deficiency* (rare): Disturbances in coagulation, epistaxis, miscarriage *Toxicity* (most common in infants): Kernicterus	Green, leafy vegetables, yoghurt (live), liver, safflower oil. *(Note: Intestinal synthesis is also important)*
Water soluble Vitamin C (ascorbic acid)	Formation of collagen, bones, teeth and red blood cells; healing. Resistance to infection, iron absorption, endogenous synthesis of corticosteroids	*Deficiency* (scurvy): Bleeding gums, easy bruising, dental decay, anorexia, fatigue; muscle/joint pains, petechiae; low resistance to infection *Toxicity* (rare): Gastrointestinal disturbance, excessive absorption of iron, renal calculi	Fresh fruits, especially citrus fruits, and vegetables

*Vitamin D: For those exposed to adequate sunlight, a dietary source is not essential.

Table 2.2 *Continued*

Vitamin	Major functions	Deficiency and toxicity	Main dietary sources
Vitamin B$_1$ (thiamin)	Carbohydrate, protein and fat metabolism; energy production; maintenance of central nervous system function	*Deficiency* (beriberi): anorexia, dyspnoea, weakness, constipation, myocardial pain, memory loss, nervousness and irritability; parasthesiae, ataxia *Toxicity:* Tremors, sweating, oedema, tachycardia, hypotension	Meat, fish, poultry, yeast, brown rice, whole and enriched cereals and grains, wheat germ
Vitamin B$_2$ (riboflavin)	Erythrocyte and antibody formation; production of energy; maintenance of epithelial tissues	*Deficiency:* Cheilosis, dizziness, itching or burning of eyes, oily skin, glossitis *Toxicity:* None known	Fish, meat, poultry, milk, yeast, eggs, fruit, whole grains, green, leafy vegetables
Vitamin B$_3$ (nicotinic acid)	Carbohydrate, fat and protein metabolism, energy production, production of sex hormones, synthesis of glycogen	*Deficiency:* Diarrhoea, dermatitis, depression, anorexia, fatigue, headaches, indigestion, impaired memory and muscle weakness	Lean and organ meats, seafood, whole grains and cereals
Vitamin B$_6$ (pyridoxine)	Digestion; formation of DNA and RNA, antibodies and haemoglobin; metabolism of protein and fat, sodium and potassium balance, maintenance of central nervous system	*Deficiency:* Seborrhoeic dermatitis, glossitis, cheilosis, depression, alopecia; acne, arthritis, learning disabilities, generalized weakness *Toxicity:* Rare – occurs only at very high doses and causes central nervous system effects, including peripheral neuropathy	Meat, poultry, yeast, fish, green, leafy vegetables, peanuts, raisins, whole grains and wheat germ
Folic acid	Erythrocyte and leucocyte formation; formation of DNA and RNA	*Deficiency:* Microcytic or megaloblastic anaemia; fatigue and weakness, digestive disturbances, glossitis, impaired memory, insomnia *Toxicity:* No known effects	Eggs, green, leafy vegetables, citrus fruits, milk/milk products, seafood, organ meats, whole grains and cereals
Vitamin B$_{12}$ (cyanocobalamin)	Intracellular metabolism, maturation of erythrocytes, absorption of iron, tissue growth, maintenance of nerve cells and formation of myelin	*Deficiency* (most likely in vegans or vegetarians): Fatigue, memory loss, depression, confusion, reduced reflex responses; glossitis, headache, pernicious anaemia *Toxicity:* No known effects	Meat, particularly organ meats, beef, pork and fish
Pantothenic acid	Carbohydrate, fat and protein metabolism; cortisone production; formation of antibodies; cholesterol synthesis	*Deficiency* (rare): Diarrhoea, eczema, alopecia, muscle cramps, fatigue *Toxicity:* None known	Eggs, mushrooms, organ meats, whole grains, wheat germ, yeast, fresh vegetables

Table 2.3 *Reference Nutrient Intakes for vitamins*

Age	Thiamin	Riboflavin	Niacin (nicotinic acid equivalent)	Vitamin B$_6$	Vitamin B$_{12}$	Folate	Vitamin C	Vitamin A	Vitamin D
	mg/d	mg/d	mg/d	mg/d†	µg/d	µg/d	mg/d	µg/d	µg/d
0–3 months	0.2	0.4	3	0.2	0.3	50	25	350	8.5
4–6 months	0.2	0.4	3	0.2	0.3	50	25	350	8.5
7–9 months	0.2	0.4	4	0.3	0.4	50	25	350	7
10–12 months	0.3	0.4	5	0.4	0.4	50	25	350	7
1–3 years	0.5	0.6	8	0.7	0.5	70	30	400	7
4–6 years	0.7	0.8	11	0.9	0.8	100	30	500	—
7–10 years	0.7	1.0	12	1.0	1.0	150	30	500	—
Males									
11–14 years	0.9	1.2	15	1.2	1.2	200	35	600	—
15–18 years	1.1	1.3	18	1.5	1.5	200	40	700	—
19–50 years	1.0	1.3	17	1.4	1.5	200	40	700	—
50+ years	0.9	1.3	16	1.4	1.5	200	40	700	**
Females									
11–14 years	0.7	1.1	12	1.0	1.2	200	35	600	—
15–18 years	0.8	1.1	14	1.2	1.5	200	40	600	—
19–50 years	0.8	1.1	13	1.2	1.5	200	40	600	—
50+ years	0.8	1.1	12	1.2	1.5	200	40	600	**
Pregnancy	+0.1***	+0.3	*	*	*	+100	+10	+100	10
Lactation:									
0–4 months	+0.2	+0.5	+2	*	+0.5	+60	+30	+350	10
4+ months	+0.2	+0.5	+2	*	+0.5	+60	+30	+350	10

*No increment
**After age 65 the Reference Nutrient Intake is 10 µg/d for men and women
***For last trimester only
†Based on protein providing 14.7 per cent of Estimated Average Requirement for energy
(From Department of Health (1991) Report on Health and Social Subjects No. 41, Dietary Reference Values for Food Energy and Nutrients for the United Kingdom, HMSO, London. Reproduced with the permission of the Controller of Her Majesty's Stationery Office.)

Table 2.4 *Minerals and trace elements*

Mineral	Major functions	Deficiency and toxicity	Main food sources
Macroelements			
Calcium	Formation of bones and teeth; haemostasis; regulation of cardiac function and muscle contraction, transmission of nerve impulses	*Deficiency* (hypocalcaemia): Parasthesiae, palpitations, muscle cramps, tetany, rickets osteoporosis, osteomalacia *Toxicity* (hypercalcaemia): Lethargy, drowsiness, nausea and vomiting, constipation, polyuria and polydispsia, pathological fractures	Milk, cheese, yoghurt, whole grains, nuts, legumes, leafy, green vegetables
Sodium	Component of extracellular fluid, osmotic pressure, muscle contraction, maintenance of acid–base balance, transmission of nerve impulses	*Deficiency* (hyponatraemia): Nausea, vomiting, anorexia, muscle atrophy, hypotension, dryness of the mucosa *Toxicity* (hypernatraemia): Hypertension, thirst, dry mucous membranes, irritability, weight gain	Milk/milk products, seafood
Potassium	Maintenance of cardiac rhythm, muscle contraction, transmission of nerve impulses; distribution of fluid, osmotic pressure, acid–base balance	*Deficiency* (hypokalaemia): Arrhythmias, muscular weakness, leg cramps, nervousness, irritability, anorexia, vomiting, bradycardia, weak reflexes *Toxicity* (hyperkalaemia): Bradycardia, apathy, confusion, flaccid muscle weakness, oliguria, anuria	Seafood, bananas, peaches, oranges, raisins, nuts
Phosphorus	Formation of bones and teeth, growth/repair of body cells; carbohydrate, protein and fat metabolism; contraction of the myocardium, activity of nerves and muscles, acid–base balance	*Deficiency* (hypophosphataemia): Anorexia, fatigue, irregular respiration, ataxia, parasthesiae, muscle weakness *Toxicity* (hyperphosphataemia): Tetany, soft tissue calcification	Eggs, fish, meat, poultry, grains, milk/milk products
Chloride	Maintenance of electrolyte, fluid, acid–base balance and osmotic pressure	*Deficiency* (rare): Hypochloraemic alkalosis *Toxicity:* No known effects	Fruit and vegetables, table salt
Sulphur	Synthesis of collagen and mucopolysaccharides, intracellular metabolism, haemostasis	*Deficiency/toxicity:* No known effects	Milk, meat, fish, poultry, eggs, pulses, legumes
Trace elements			
Chromium	Carbohydrate and fat metabolism, maintenance of blood glucose concentration	*Deficiency:* Glucose intolerance, particularly in diabetics No known toxic effects	Meat, cheese, corn oil, whole grains, yeast

▶

Table 2.4 *Continued*

Mineral	Major functions	Deficiency and toxicity	Main food sources
Cobalt	Formation of vitamin B (cyanocobalamin)	*Deficiency:* Manifests as vitamin B deficiency No known toxic effects	Eggs, fish, beef, pork, milk products, organ meats
Copper	Formation of bones and haemoglobin, erythrocytes and enzymes; utilization of iron	*Deficiency:* General weakness, malformation of bones, skin sores, impaired respiratory functions; diarrhoea (infants) *Toxicity:* Weakness, heartburn, nausea, vomiting, diarrhoea, Wilson's disease	Organ meats, seafood, nuts, raisins
Fluorine	Formation of bones and teeth	*Deficiency:* Dental caries *Toxicity* (fluorosis): Mottled or discoloured tooth enamel; increased calcification/density of bone	Drinking water
Iodine	Production of thyroid hormones; regulation of basal metabolic rate and cellular metabolism	*Deficiency:* Cold hands and feet, dry hair, irritability, obesity *Toxicity:* No known effects	Seaweed, iodized salt, seafood
Iron	Haemoglobin production, oxygen transport, energy production, regulation of chemical and biological reactions, resistance to disease	*Deficiency:* Brittle nails, constipation, dyspnoea, glossitis, anaemia, pallor of mucous membranes, fatigue *Toxicity* (haemochromatosis): Abdominal pain/cramps, nausea and vomiting, haemosiderosis	Meats (particularly organ meats), poultry, green vegetables, wheat germ, fortified breads and cereals
Manganese	Carbohydrate, protein and fat metabolism, activation of enzymes; production of sex hormones; utilization of vitamin E	*Deficiency:* Hearing disturbances, dizziness, ataxia *Toxicity:* Parkinsonian-like effects	Egg yolk, bananas, green, leafy vegetables, liver, nuts, whole grains, tea and coffee
Molybdenum	Metabolic processes	No known effects from either deficiency or toxicity	Legumes, organ meats, whole grains
Selenium	Immunocompetence, ATP synthesis, fat metabolism, antioxidant effects	No known deficiency or toxic effects	Meat, seafood, some vegetables
Zinc	Wound healing, digestion and metabolism of carbohydrate, fat and protein; prostatic and reproductive function; growth/development of reproductive organs; maintenance of normal taste and smell sensation	*Deficiency:* Hypogonadism and delayed sexual maturity, loss of taste and smell; delayed wound healing; retarded growth *Toxicity:* Diarrhoea, vomiting, pancreatitis	Seafood, spinach, meat, mushrooms

Table 2.5 *Reference Nutrient Intakes for minerals*

Age	Calcium mg/d	Phosphorus[1] mg/d	Magnesium mg/d	Sodium mg/d[2]	Potassium mg/d[3]	Chloride[4] mg/d	Iron mg/d	Zinc mg/d	Copper mg/d	Selenium µg/d	Iodine µg/d
0–3 months	525	400	55	210	800	320	1.7	4.0	0.2	10	50
4–6 months	525	400	60	280	850	400	4.3	4.0	0.3	13	60
7–9 months	525	400	75	320	700	500	7.8	5.0	0.3	10	60
10–12 months	525	400	80	350	700	500	7.8	5.0	0.3	10	60
1–3 years	350	270	85	500	800	800	6.9	5.0	0.4	15	70
4–6 years	450	350	120	700	1,100	1,100	6.1	6.5	0.6	20	100
7–10 years	550	450	200	1,200	2,000	1,800	8.7	7.0	0.7	30	110
Males											
11–14 years	1,000	775	280	1,600	3,100	2,500	11.3	9.0	0.8	45	130
15–18 years	1,000	775	300	1,600	3,500	2,500	11.3	9.5	1.0	70	140
19–50 years	700	550	300	1,600	3,500	2,500	8.7	9.5	1.2	75	140
50+ years	700	550	300	1,600	3,500	2,500	8.7	9.5	1.2	75	140
Females											
11–14 years	800	625	280	1,600	3,100	2,500	14.8[5]	9.0	0.8	45	130
15–18 years	800	625	300	1,600	3,500	2,500	14.8[5]	7.0	1.0	60	140
19–50 years	700	550	270	1,600	3,500	2,500	14.8[5]	7.0	1.2	60	140
50+ years	700	550	270	1,600	3,500	2,500	8.7	7.0	1.2	60	140
Pregnancy	*	*	*	*	*	*	*	*	*	*	*
Lactation:											
0–4 months	+550	+440	+ 50	*	*	*	*	+6.0	+0.3	+15	*
4+ months	+550	+440	+ 50	*	*	*	*	+2.5	+0.3	+15	*

*No increment
[1] Phosphorus Reference Nutrient Intake is set equal to calcium in molar terms
[2] 1 mmol sodium=23 mg
[3] 1 mmol potassium=39 mg
[4] Corresponds to sodium 1 mmol=35.5 mg
[5] Insufficient for women with high menstrual losses where the most practical way of meeting iron requirements is to take iron supplements
(From Department of Health (1991) Report on Health and Social Subjects No. 41, Dietary Reference Values for Food Energy and Nutrients for the United Kingdom, HMSO, London. Reproduced with the permission of the Controller of Her Majesty's Stationery Office.)

Table 2.6 *Summary: current dietary recommendations*

National Advisory Committee on Nutrition Education (NACNE) (1983)	Committee on Medical Aspects of Food Policy (COMA) (1984)
Energy Intake must be appropriate to maintain optimal weight for height and should be combined with adquate exercise	Intake should be appropriate to prevent obesity. Control diet and take the appropriate amount of exercise
Fat Total fat should represent 30% of the total energy intake	Should represent an average of 35% of total energy intake (*not* in the under-5s)
Saturated fat should supply only 10% of total energy derived from fat	Should supply only 15% of total fat
Polyunsaturated fat: Adherence to the other recommendations should ensure an increase in the ratio of polyunsaturated to saturated fat so that no further recommendation is made	Increase the ratio of polyunsaturated to saturated fat
Dietary fibre Increase daily fibre intake to 30 g. Increase consumption of wholegrain cereals, pulses, fruit and vegetables	Increase intake of high fibre, complex carbohydrates
Sucrose Reduce intake to 12% total energy	Try to decrease intake; do *not* increase
Salt Decrease salt intake to about 11 g/day	Do *not* increase; try to decrease
Alcohol Should comprise only 4% of total daily energy consumption	No recommendation
Vitamins/minerals Should match current British dietary guidelines	No recommendation
Food labelling Should be further improved in terms of both health education and fulfilment of regulatory functions	Improve so that fat content is clear

Current dietary recommendations (Department of Health and Social Security, 1984; National Advisory Committee on Nutrition Education (NACNE), 1983) are based on the belief that many diseases (e.g., cardiovascular and cerebrovascular disease, obesity, diverticulitis, dental caries) are diet-related, so that their incidence could be reduced by dietary change. Since the diet in the United Kingdom is high in total fat, sugar and salt, and low in dietary fibre, the recommendations (Table 2.6) centre on a diet that is high in dietary fibre and low in fat, particularly saturated fat, sugar and salt. However, Bradley and Theobald (1988) have attempted to achieve the required dietary changes in a normal population and have identified significant difficulties, particularly with regard to consumption of adequate energy, dietary fibre, vitamins and minerals. This raises many questions, not least of which is that of the applicability of such recommendations in the hospital setting, where it is known that nutrient needs are often

increased, and where malnutrition is not uncommon (British Dietetic Association, 1988; Hill, Blackett and Pickford *et al.*, 1977).

The provision of nutritious meals depends on the inclusion of all essential nutrients in optimal amounts and an adequate supply of energy. However, any nutrient, even when supplied in the recommended amount, is valuable only if the requirement for all other nutrients is met; this what is meant by the term dietary balance (Holmes, 1986b). At the same time, since the requirement for some essential nutrients, particularly trace elements, has not yet been established, it is essential that the diet is not overly restricted and a wide variety of foods is consumed; this will provide for such uncertainties.

However, during illness, food intake is often reduced as a result of the illness itself, its treatment or dietary modification. This may compromise nutritional status and, in turn, the response to treatment.

Many different factors interact to affect food intake and utilization (Figure 2.3), and the effects of food on health are multiple. Nutrition must be seen as an integral part of the total care of all patients, each of whom is an individual with personal likes and dislikes: these must be taken into account when care is planned.

Food also provides both social and psychological support. Thus familiar foods presented in an acceptable fashion will contribute to the patient's sense of security. Therefore, nutritional care must be regarded as a positive contribution to the patient's care and treatment.

Methods of Food Preparation and Service

Since a wide variety of methods are employed both to prepare the patient's food and to transport it from the kitchen to the bedside, it is not possible to cover these in any depth. An awareness of the general principles may aid in understanding the factors involved.

Menus are planned by the caterer and the dietician, who advises on both its nutritional content and its suitability for therapeutic or modified diets. Such menus are usually cyclic, running for two to six weeks, and generally offer patients at least some choice over each meal; many dishes are also suitable for the common therapeutic diets (e.g., reducing, low fat) so that they can be used to demonstrate to patients requiring dietary modification that they can eat at least some 'normal' dishes.

Food is usually produced in bulk in central kitchens using one of a variety of methods including large-scale, 'home-style', traditional techniques, cook-freeze or cook-chill methods (Glew, 1973). The latter have a number of advantages as they enable foods to be purchased in bulk and save on staff time and, therefore, costs. Similarly, they can reduce wastage and, it is suggested, the nutritional content is superior (DHSS, 1980; Glew, 1973).

Many different methods of food transportation and service are employed within the NHS—only the major methods are discussed here.

Bulk Service

Bulk service was the original method of serving meals and, in some institutions, remains in use. Catering staff estimate the quantity of individual items required by each ward, loading these into bulk containers in a trolley with both hot and cold compartments to store food at the appropriate temperature. The trolleys are delivered to the wards, where nurses are generally responsible for serving meals to the patients. Bulk service has both advantages and disadvantages. Its principle advantage is that, since nurses themselves serve the meals, portion size can be adjusted to meet the needs of individual patients and, at the same time, nurses can observe their nutrient intake. However, although flexibility in portion size is advantageous in caring for the individual, erratic control can mean either that food is wasted or, alter-

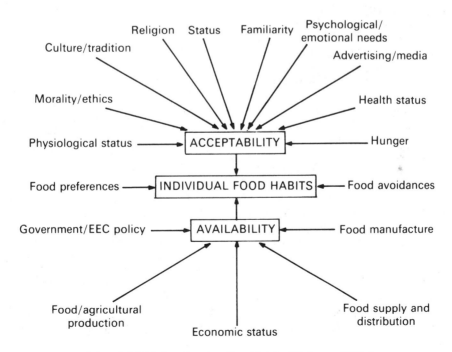

Figure 2.3 Determinants of food intake (Holmes, 1986d).

natively, that more must be obtained from the kitchen. This has significant financial implications; it is largely for this reason that alternative methods have been sought.

Plated Meal Services

The principle underlying the use of plated meal services is that catering personnel are responsible for serving food onto plates which are then transported to the wards. A number of techniques may be employed to keep food at the appropriate temperature. First, food may be served onto dishes/plates, covered and stacked in a trolley with both hot and cold compartments. On the ward, the patient's meals are placed on a tray and served. Alternatively, plated meals may be covered and placed either on a heated base container that retains heat for the required period of time, or in a double-lined vacuum container (usually reserved for desserts). The complete meal is then assembled on a tray, loaded into a trolley and transported to the ward, where labelled trays can then be delivered to named patients. As the meals are kept hot by the containers they need not be transported in heated trolleys but, once on the ward, must be delivered rapidly to the patient.

As each meal is labelled, plated techniques are less time-consuming at ward level and have removed responsibility for meal delivery from nurses, who need not be involved directly. However, nurses must make a conscious effort to observe what, and how much, is consumed by individual patients since, as has been shown, adequate food consumption is essential if nutritional status is to be maintained. Clearly, the patient who repeatedly rejects food, or who eats inadequate amounts, will be at considerable nutritional risk. Observation of the quantity and quality of food consumed is an essential part of the nutritional assessment of hospitalized patients.

Although it is more than 15 years since the prevalence of malnutrition among hospital patients was first identified (Bistrian, Blackburn, Hallowell *et al.*, 1974; Bistrian, Blackburn, Vitale *et al.*, 1976; Butterworth, 1974; Butterworth and Blackburn, 1975; Hill *et al.*, 1977), such malnutrition still occurs (BDA, 1988). While the failure to identify and treat malnourished patients is often attributed to the lack of doctor-awareness (Anon., 1988; Roubenoff, Roubenoff, Preto *et al.*, 1977), the role of nurses is often overlooked. Yet nurses play a central role in patient feeding and in monitoring and evaluating the patient's response to treatment. Inadequate food consumption, particularly when combined with illness, leads to a decline in nutritional status and, in turn, to a reduced response to therapy, prolonged convalescence and a reduced quality of life (Holmes, 1986c). However, although nutritional care is clearly essential in the total care of all patients, it is often considered only after the patient has already become undernourished.

It can be difficult for hospitalized patients to maintain their nutritional status. First, the act of hospitalization may have adverse effects on food consumption since, for example, disruption of usual eating patterns, unfamiliar food(s) and unusual, or simply different, timing of meals may disturb the normal routine. Under normal circumstances meal times are social occasions: in hospital, however, there may not be a common eating place, and patients are left to eat in isolation either in bed or at the bedside. This significantly reduces social interaction and may markedly affect food consumption. At the same time, particularly when a plated meal service is employed, meals are served in large portions or in individual containers that are impersonal and often appear to take little note of individual requests or needs. Clearly, it is difficult to allow for individual likes and dislikes when catering for large numbers, but a flexible and apparently individual approach is essential if food intake is to be maintained. Interest from nurses may help significantly. They can, for example, help patients to select their meals and ensure that they are well presented and to their liking. When a meal is unacceptable, nurses can arrange for an alternative to be provided.

The physical and emotional effects of illness may also affect food consumption. Fear, anxiety and depression, for instance, can markedly reduce the desire for food; similarly, pain and discomfort may also adversely affect the appetite. The interaction of all these factors can make it difficult for patients to maintain their nutritional status. Since the first step in ensuring that a patient's nutritional needs are met is assessment of nutritional status, this clearly highlights the need for regular nutritional assessment.

Assessment of Nutritional Status

Assessment of nutritional status is designed to establish the degree to which the need for nutrients is met by the nutrient intake and may be defined as 'the interpretation of information obtained from dietary, biochemical, anthropometric and clinical studies' (Gibson, 1990). It is carried out for a number of reasons, as follows:

1. To establish the likelihood of potential or existing problems.
2. To identify the cause of existing problems.
3. To provide a database against which future changes can be judged.
4. To enable evaluation of the response to dietary intervention and/or nutritional support.

Nutritional status can be evaluated by one or more of the following methods:

- Clinical examination and observation.
- Anthropometric techniques.
- Assessment/evaluation of dietary intake.
- Biochemical tests.

Clinical Examination

Although nutritional status is reflected by the patient's appearance, certain signs and symptoms suggestive of nutritional deficiency are nonspecific (Table 2.7) and may be the result of other unrelated factors (e.g., poor hygiene, exposure to the sun or systemic disorders, such as endocrine disturbances, infectious disease or disorders of digestion/absorption, excretion or storage of nutrients in the body).

Thus a clinical examination, which includes observation of the patient's general condition and a complete physical examination, will reflect overall nutritional status. However, a physical sign suggestive of nutritional abnormality should be considered a clue rather than a diagnosis and, as such, should be pursued further. Although the most obvious physical sign of good nutrition is a normal body weight with respect to height and age (see below), other body sites can serve as indicators of nutritional status. These include: the skin, hair, mouth, teeth, gums, mucous membranes and skeletal muscle tone (Table 2.7). Psychosocial factors to be considered include

Table 2.7 *Physical signs indicative of nutritional status*

Body area	Signs of good nutrition	Signs of poor nutrition
Hair	Shiny, lustrous; firm, healthy scalp	Dull and dry, brittle, depigmented, easily plucked
Face	Skin colour uniform; healthy appearance	Skin dark over cheeks and under eyes, skin flaky, face swollen
Eyes	Bright, clear, moist	Eye membranes pale, dry (xerophthalmia); Bitot's spots, increased vascularity, cornea soft (keratomalacia)
Lips	Good colour (pink), smooth	Swollen and puffy (cheilosis), angular lesion at corners of mouth (angular fissures)
Tongue	Deep red in appearance; surface papillae present	Smooth appearance, swollen, beefy red, sores, atrophic papillae
Teeth	Straight, no crowding, no cavities, bright	Cavities, mottled appearance (fluorosis), malpositioned
Gums	Firm, good colour (pink)	Spongy, bleed easily, marginal redness, recession
Glands	No enlargement of the thyroid	Thyroid enlargement (simple goitre)
Skin	Smooth, good colour, moist	Rough, dry, flaky, swollen, pale, pigmented; lack of fat under skin
Nails	Firm, pink	Spoon shaped, ridged
Skeleton	Good posture, no malformation	Poor posture, beading of ribs, bowed legs or knock knees
Muscles	Well developed, firm	Flaccid, poor tone, wasted, underdeveloped
Extremities	No tenderness	Weak and tender, presence of oedema
Abdomen	Flat	Swollen
Nervous system	Normal reflexes	Decrease in or loss of ankle and knee reflexes

the presence of anxiety, fear or depression, all of which may potentiate anorexia.

Although a careful dietary history is required, much of this data should be provided by a thorough nursing assessment (Table 2.8). Discussion with family and friends may provide valuable additional information. Current drug therapy should also be identified, including any prescribed medication and other drugs, vitamins and over-the-counter medicines and 'recreational' drugs.

Anthropometric data should form an important part of the physical examination although it must be admitted that, despite their importance, they are not often used in clinical practice. This is unfortunate since anthropometry can provide valuable information. Anthropometric techniques involve physical measurements that reflect the nutritional condition (Table 2.9) and include height, weight and the circumferences of the upper arm and arm muscle. Some, such as height, reflect past or chronic nutritional status, while others, such as weight, mid-arm circumference and skinfold thickness, reflect the present condition and are used to assess skeletal energy reserves. It should be noted that although such measurements focus on undernutrition, they also detect obesity.

When anthropometric measurements are gathered as part of data collection, standardized equipment and procedure are used, as well as standard reference tables.

The following anthropometric measurements should be used in the nutritional assessment of the hospitalized patient:

- Weight/height.
- Triceps and infold thickness.
- Mid-arm muscle circumference.

Weight loss is always an important nutritional indicator that reflects an inadequate calorie intake. In the semi-

Table 2.8 *Components of a dietary history*

		Comments
Socioeconomic data	Is patient in regular employment? Receiving benefit?	Can patient afford to eat adequately?
	Amount of money available for food? Has the situation changed due to illness?	Can patient meet the needs of a modified diet?
	Other influences (e.g., religious beliefs) on eating habits	Do these affect range/types of foods available to the individual?
	Who does shopping and cooking? Ability of patient to shop/prepare food What facilities available for storing/ cooking?	Can this continue or does the patient now need help?
Physical and clinical data	Type and frequency of occupation Type and frequency of exercise	Indicate level of energy expenditure
	Is appetite good or poor? Has this changed?	May help to identify factors affecting the appetite
	Sensation of taste and smell. Have these changed? Dental/oral health	May influence appetite and affect types of food available to the patient; aids in identifying foods that are acceptable or unacceptable to the individual
	Gastrointestinal changes, e.g. heartburn or indigestion, flatulence, diarrhoea, nausea and vomiting	All are factors that may affect food intake
	Frequency of problems – remedies used	Can these be applied to the current situation?
	Chronic disease – treatment; medications – including over-the-counter remedies	Illness *per se*, or methods of treatment may affect nutritional needs
	Recent weight change – loss or gain, time period over which changes have occurred. Were/are the changes intentional?	
Allergies, intolerances, food avoidances and preferences	Why are specific foods preferred/ avoided?	May indicate nutritional problems – extent depends on the nature of the food(s) involved

starved (inadequately nourished) patient, weight loss indicates a loss of protein from the body cell mass. To determine the degree and rapidity of weight loss, the percentage of usual body weight is calculated and the time scale over which this has occurred is noted.

However, body weight may be inappropriate even in the absence of recent change (loss or gain). This is estimated by means of the height:weight ratio and relies on accurate measurement of both height and weight.

Height is measured using a stadiometer firmly fixed to a solid surface. The patient should be barefoot, or wearing only socks/stockings, the feet should be together and the heels against the wall. The patient should be standing erect and looking straight ahead. The horizontal bar is lowered to rest flat against the top of the head and height is read to the nearest 0.5 cm.

If weight is to be obtained accurately, the patient should be weighed in the morning, before breakfast

Table 2.9 *Summary of anthropometric measurements used in nutritional assessment*

	Purpose	Technique
Body weight	Represents the sum of all body constituents so that repeated measures will indicate changes. Provides the basis for other anthropometric measures	Use same scale, clothing and time of day. Empty bladder before weighing
Height	Represents past (chronic) nutritional status. Used with weight to calculate ideal body weight	See text
Ideal body weight (IBW)	Provides an indication of nutritional status. A current weight 70–80% IBW indicates moderate malnutrition; less than 70% IBW = severe malnutrition	Calculated from height and weight (using standard text)
Usual body weight (UBW)	Provides an indication of weight changes	$\%\ UBW = \dfrac{Current\ weight\ (kg)}{UBW\ (kg)} \times 100$
Weight change	Calculated from UBW	$\%\ weight\ change = \dfrac{UBW\ (kg) - current\ weight\ (kg)}{UBW\ (kg)} \times 100$
Mid-arm circumference (MAC)	Measurement reflects body protein and fat content	Measure circumference of arm at midpoint between acromial process of scapula and olecranon process of the ulna; must use a 'non-stretchable' tape measure (Figure 2.5)
Triceps skin-fold thickness (TSF)	Enables estimation of subcutaneous fat and energy reserves	Measure at same point as MAC using calipers. Take an average of three readings. Be sure to lift skin and fat clear of the underlying tissue before measurement
Mid-arm muscle circumference (MAMC)		Estimated indirectly from MAC and TSF $MAMC\ (cm) = MAC\ (cm) - (3.142 \times TSF(cm))$
Arm muscle area (AMA)		$AMA\ (cm) = \dfrac{(MAMC - 3.142 \times TSF)^2}{4 \times 3.142} - 6.25$ (females) $AMA\ (cm) = \dfrac{(MAMC - 3.142 \times TSF)^2}{4 \times 3.142} - 10.0$ (males)

Note: Anthropometric measurements provide an approximate guide to changes in energy reserves. They are most valuable when used to monitor patients over a period of time.

Table 2.10 *Ideal weights derived from life insurance tables*

Men				Women			
Weight (kg)				Weight (kg)			
Height (cm)	Small frame	Medium frame	Large frame	Height (cm)	Small frame	Medium frame	Large frame
157.5	58.2–60.9	59.5–64.1	62.7–68.2	147.3	46.3–50.5	49.5–55.0	53.6–59.5
160.0	59.1–61.8	60.5–65.0	63.6–69.5	149.9	46.8–51.4	50.5–55.9	54.6–60.9
162.6	60.0–62.7	61.4–65.9	64.6–70.9	152.4	44.9–52.3	51.4–57.3	55.5–62.3
165.1	60.9–63.6	62.3–67.3	65.5–72.7	154.9	48.2–53.6	52.3–58.6	56.8–63.6
167.6	61.8–64.5	63.2–68.6	66.4–74.4	157.3	49.1–55.0	53.6–60.0	58.2–65.0
170.2	62.7–65.9	64.5–70.0	67.7–76.4	160.0	50.5–56.4	55.0–61.4	59.6–66.8
172.7	63.6–67.3	65.9–71.4	69.1–78.2	162.6	51.8–57.7	56.4–62.7	60.9–68.6
175.3	64.6–68.6	67.3–72.7	70.5–80.0	165.1	53.2–59.1	57.7–64.1	62.3–70.5
177.8	65.5–70.0	68.6–74.1	71.9–81.8	167.6	54.5–60.5	59.1–65.5	63.6–72.3
180.3	66.4–71.4	70.0–75.5	73.2–83.6	170.2	55.9–61.8	60.5–66.8	65.0–74.1
182.9	67.7–72.7	71.4–77.3	74.6–85.5	172.7	57.3–63.2	61.8–68.2	66.4–75.9
185.4	69.1–74.5	72.4–79.1	76.4–87.3	175.3	58.6–64.5	63.2–69.6	67.7–77.3
188.0	70.5–76.4	74.6–80.9	78.2–89.5	177.8	60.0–65.9	64.5–70.9	69.1–78.6
190.5	71.8–78.2	75.9–82.7	80.0–91.8	180.3	61.4–66.3	65.9–72.3	70.5–80.0
193.5	73.6–80.0	77.9–85.0	82.3–94.1	182.9	62.7–68.6	67.3–73.6	71.8–81.4

Use of frame size approximation table

Extend arm and bend upward at 90° angle. Keep fingers straight and turn inside of the wrist towards the body. Use a caliper to measure the distance between the two prominent bones on either side of the elbow. Without a caliper measure the space between prominences using finger and thumb; measure the space between the fingers with a ruler or tape measure.

Compare the measurement obtained with the table for medium-framed individuals.

Measurements below those given indicate a small frame size; higher measurements indicate a large frame.

Men		Women	
Height (cm)	Elbow breadth (cm)	Height (cm)	Elbow breadth (cm)
154.9–157.5	6.4–7.3	144.8–147.3	5.7–6.4
160.0–167.6	6.7–7.3	149.9–157.5	5.7–6.4
170.2–177.8	7.0–7.6	160.0–167.6	6.0–6.7
180.3–188.0	7.0–7.9	170.2–177.8	6.0–6.7
>190.5	7.3–8.2	>180.3	6.4–7.0

(Based on height-weight tables derived from life insurance statistics prepared by the Metropolitan Life Insurance Company: men and women. Copyright 1983, Metropolitan Life Insurance Company.)

and with an empty bladder, using accurate scales: the same clothes should be worn each time the patient is weighed.

To determine whether the patient's weight is appropriate for height (ideal body weight), a comparison is made with standard tables, the most common of which are the Metropolitan Life Insurance Tables (1983): these provide weight ranges for both men and women at different heights and at three body frame sizes (Table 2.10).

It is important to realize that the recorded body weight may be distorted in the presence of oedema, lymphoedema, ascites or a tumour mass. In affected patients body weight *per se* may be of little clinical value, although a weight loss is always of clinical importance. Similarly, it must be remembered that, although a patient's height: weight ratio may be in the normal range, this may still be considerably below or above their ideal body weight. Thus comparison of the current weight with the usual weight is a valuable parameter for use in nutritional

assessment. Furthermore, the required dose of many drugs is calculated for individual patients on the basis of the body surface area. This is calculated from the patient's height (in centimetres) and weight (in kilograms) using the following formula:

$$M^2 = W^{0.425} \times H^{0.725} \times 71.84, \text{ where}$$
$$M^2 = \text{surface area in square metres}$$
$$H = \text{height in centimetres}$$
$$W = \text{weight in kilograms}$$

Thus, accurate recording of height and weight is of considerable clinical importance although, because this is not always recognized, they are often measured carelessly and inaccurately.

Of the remaining anthropometric indices, the best available indicators of protein-calorie malnutrition are triceps skinfold thickness and mid-arm muscle circumference.

Triceps skinfold thickness measures subcutaneous fat

thus providing an indication of fat stores (Figure 2.4). Once measured, it is compared with reference standard tables (see Goodinson, 1987a) (Table 2.11). Since the amount of fat located in the subcutaneous tissues varies with both age and sex, the standards used must be age- and sex-specific.

Mid-arm muscle circumference is measured halfway between the acromium process of the scapula and the ulnar tip of the elbow, and indicates the state of muscle protein (Figure 2.5). Again, this is compared to reference standards (Table 2.11) (see Goodinson, 1987a).

When triceps skinfold thickness and mid-arm muscle circumference are considered together it is possible to calculate arm muscle and fat area, thus obtaining an indication of lean body mass and, therefore, skeletal protein reserves and body fat (energy reserves); serial measurements are, therefore, particularly valuable in assessment of the hospitalized patient (Wright and Heymsfield. 1985).

Anthropometric techniques are simple, safe and noninvasive procedures (Heymsfield and Casper, 1987) and are inexpensive to perform. When performed by trained personnel, they can provide precise and accurate data (Gibson, 1990), thus assisting in identification of malnourished patients, particularly when serial measurements are obtained. However, they cannot alone identify specific nutrient deficiencies; additional data is required.

Assessment of Food Intake

Appraisal of food intake includes both the quantity and quality of the diet, and may also include an assessment of

Table 2.11 *Anthropometric measurements: standard values at various deficiency levels*

(mm)	90% Standard	80% Standard	70% Standard	60% Standard
Triceps skinfold (adult)				
Male 12.5	11.3	10.0	8.8	7.5
Female 16.5	14.9	13.2	11.6	9.9
Arm circumference (adult)				
Male 29.3	26.3	23.4	20.5	17.6
Female 28.5	25.7	22.8	20.0	17.1
Muscle circumference (adult)				
Male 25.3	22.8	20.2	17.7	15.2
Female 23.2	20.9	18.6	16.2	13.9

(Adapted from Butterworth, C.E. and Blackburn, G.L. (1975) Hospital malnutrition, Nutrition Today, March/April, Vol. 10, No. 2, pp. 11–12.)

the frequency of consumption of certain food items in order to determine the current, or customary, intake of nutrients. Food intake can be evaluated in a variety of ways (Table 2.12); the method selected must be carefully explained to the patient.

Food Records

Food records (diary) are commonly used in assessing nutritional status. The person is asked to keep a record of food and beverages actually consumed over a period of time, varying from three to seven days, including at least one weekend day to allow for potential day-of-the-week

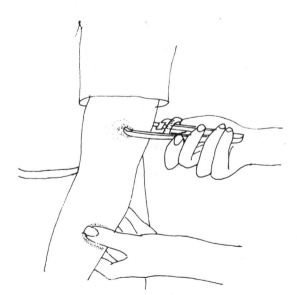

Figure 2.4 Skinfold calipers for measurement of skinfold thickness.

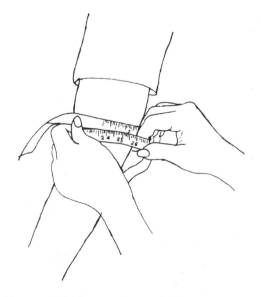

Figure 2.5 Measurement of mid-arm muscle circumference.

effects on food consumption (Gibson, 1990). This is an accurate method but depends on the subject's integrity and ability to estimate quantity; weighing all food can help to improve the accuracy but makes greater demands on the individual.

24-Hour Recall

24-hour recall relies on recall of food intake over a 24-hour period. The patient is asked to recall all the food eaten during the previous day and to estimate the quantity. Since the previous day's diet is not always representative of the usual intake, the patient must be asked if this was a typical day. To obtain supplementary information about the usual diet, the patient should also be asked about the frequency of consumption of individual foods. This can validate data obtained through recall.

Evaluating Dietary Information

Once dietary information has been obtained, it must be evaluated for its nutritive value. This can be achieved by two main methods, the first of which relies on the use of tables, such as McCance and Widdowson's *The Composition of Foods* (Paul and Southgate, 1978), from labels on manufactured food products and from information provided by manufacturers on the nutrient composition of their products.

Table 2.12 *Methods used to record food intake*

	Method	Comment
24-hour recall	Interview/questionnaire designed to establish everything eaten/drunk during previous 24 hours and to provide an estimate of quantity	Contains inherent sources of error since it relies on memory and it is difficult to remember accurately all that has been consumed in preceding 24 hours. At same time, the previous day's intake may not be typical; the individual may not be telling the truth. Finally, it is difficult to estimate quantity with any accuracy
Food frequency questionnaire	Gives information about the frequency of consumption of individual foods, e.g., how often it is eaten per day, week, month	Can be used to validate the 24-hour recall, clarifying the real food consumption. Can be selective, looking only at areas believed to be deficient, or more general to identify unsuspected areas of concern
Food diary	Patient asked to maintain record of all food/drink consumed over defined time period – usually 3 to 4 days, including both weekend and week days. Can also provide information about lifestyle by recording companions and atmosphere in which meals are eaten	Requires more time, understanding and motivation on the patient's behalf but, if recorded immediately after eating, gives complete and accurate data. Problems include nonco-operation, inaccuracy when not all the intake is recorded or when the intake on recording days is atypical and does not represent usual food consumption
Direct observation	Enables accurate recording of food presented and amount actually consumed. Should, wherever possible, be achieved by non-intrusive means. Most easily achieved when patient's meals are provided – as in hospital. Precision can be improved when weighed quantities of food are presented and amount of uneaten food is reweighed; the difference represents the amount consumed	The most time-consuming, expensive and difficult way of obtaining dietary data and, when weighed intakes are required, can cause difficulties with patient co-operation

Once the nutrient composition of the various dietary components has been established, the total nutrient intake can be calculated and compared with the dietary reference values (Department of Health, 1991) (Table 2.13): nutritional adequacy is expressed in terms of percentage of adequacy for each nutrient. However, it must be remembered that individuals have unique needs and that recommended intakes are intended only as guidelines for evaluating nutritional adequacy. They make no allowance for ill health. Thus dietary reference values must not be applied indiscriminately, but should take account of individual needs.

A second method of dietary evaluation is comparison of dietary data with recommendations based on the four food groups (Table 2.14). Although this is, undoubtedly, the simplest and quickest means of evaluating food intake data, it provides only a crude measure of the nutrient intake. However, it will enable gross nutrient deficiencies or excesses to be detected.

If one is interested in the intake of specific nutrients, such as vitamin A, iron or calcium, the food record method is appropriate, enabling the intake to be analysed

by reference to food tables (e.g., Paul and Southgate, 1978).

Interpreting the 24-Hour Recall

An example of a 24-hour recall is shown in Table 2.15, which gives dietary information about Mrs Brown, a 25-year-old housewife, indicating the different kinds of foods she consumed, the times of day when they were consumed and the quantities consumed, measured in household units. The data indicate that the diet is adequate with respect to the bread and cereals group and foods rich in vitamin A; it is low in sources of calcium and vitamin C, and slightly lacking in protein. On the other hand, the record shows an excessive intake of high-calorie foods from the miscellaneous group. This pattern of consumption is reflected in her body weight, which is 19 per cent over acceptable normal standards.

A plan of nutritional care, based on the dietary assessment and on clinical/anthropometric data suggests a need for:

Table 2.13 *Summary: dietary reference values (Department of Health, 1991)*

	Estimated Average Requirement (kcal)		Population average CH0 (as % energy)	Fat (as % energy)	Reference Nutrient Intake protein	
	Male	*Female*				
0– 3 months	545	515			12.5	
4– 6 months	690	645			12.7	
7– 9 months	825	765			13.7	
10–12 months	920	865			14.9	
1– 3 years	1,230	1,165			14.5	
4– 6 years	1,715	1,545			19.7	
7–10 years	1,970	1,740			28.3	
					Males	*Females*
11–14 years	2,220	1,845			42.1	41.2
15–18 years	2,755	2,110			55.2	45.0
19–50 years	2,550	1,940	47	33	55.5	45.0
51–59 years	2,550	1,900	47	33	53.3	46.5
60–64 years	2,380	1,900	47	33	53.3	46.5
65–75 years	2,330	1,900	47	33	53.3	46.5
75+ years	2,100	1,810	47	33	53.3	46.5
Pregnancy		+0.80				+ 6
Lactation	1 month	+1.90				+11
	2 months	+2.20				+11
	3 months	+2.40				+11

Estimated Average Requirement *(EAR)*—an estimate of the average requirement of any nutrient. As with any average value, some will need more and others less.
Reference Nutrient Intake *(RNI)*—the amount of any nutrient which is sufficient to meet the needs of almost every individual even when the need is increased. In general, individuals consuming the RNI of any nutrient are unlikely to be deficient in that nutrient. Will meet the needs of 97.5% of the healthy population.
Lower Reference Nutrient Intake *(LRNI)*—this term is used to represent the amount of nutrient which will meet the needs of those with a low requirement for that nutrient. Most people should eat more than the LRNI if they are not to become deficient.
Dietary Reference Values—a generic term used to describe all the above figures, i.e. the range of nutrient requirements. These ranges apply only to the healthy population and make no allowance for illness.
In practical terms, Reference Nutrient Intake is that used to describe the level of vitamin and mineral intake sufficient to meet the needs of practically all healthy people in a population.

- Appropriate food selection for a balanced diet.
- Appropriate food intake for weight control.

Therefore, planned care requires development of a teaching plan designed to help Mrs Brown to modify her eating so that her diet is a balanced one that will, at first, help her to achieve weight loss. This approach will help her to modify her eating habits so that, once weight has reached a desirable level, she will be able to select a diet that will maintain both her body weight and her nutritional status.

Biochemical Analyses

Biochemical analyses (Table 2.16) are important in nutritional assessment and provide additional information when taken in conjunction with other measures of nutritional status. For example, low serum albumin and transferrin levels are useful measures of visceral protein status; serum transferrin also reflects body protein synthesis. Thus, both can be used as indicators of the degree of malnutrition; serial measurements are used to monitor the success of nutritional therapy. The total lymphocyte count reflects immunocompetence as well as visceral protein stores, while a reduced leucocyte count is associated with impaired cellular immunity; recall skin antigen testing can be used to reflect T-cell-mediated immunity. Urinary urea nitrogen reflects somatic protein mass. An excellent discussion of the biochemical assessment of nutritional status is to be found in Goodinson (1987b).

Information about electrolyte balance provides an assessment of renal function as well as the metabolic response to trauma, illness or infused electrolytes. The creatinine:height index, calculated over a 24-hour period, provides an assessment of metabolically active tissue and, by comparison of the expected body mass for height with the actual body cell mass, indicates the degree of protein depletion.

Table 2.14 *Basic four food groups: the daily guide to good eating*

Food groups	Recommended amounts	
Milk group	*6-ounce portions:*	
Milk, cottage cheese, ice cream, yogurt	Children under 9	2 to 3 portions
	Children 9–12	3 to 4 portions
	Adolescents	4 or more portions
	Adults	2 or more portions
	Pregnant women	3 or more portions
	Nursing mothers	4 or more portions
Meat group	2- to 3-ounce serving; cooked, without bone; 2 servings total	
Lean beef, veal, pork, lamb, poultry, fish		
Alternatives:		
Dried beans, peas, lentils	1- to 6-ounce serving, cooked	
Peanut butter	4-tablespoon serving	
Eggs	2	
Vegetables, fruits	3-ounce serving, 1 piece fruit; 4 servings total	
Dark green or yellow	1 serving, vitamin A rich	
Citrus fruit or vegetable	1 serving, vitamin C Rich – or 2 servings of a fair source	
Other vegetables and fruits	2 or more servings	
Breads and cereals	4 servings total	
Bread, rolls, biscuits, muffins	1 slice or small piece	
Ready-to-eat cereals	1-ounce serving	
Cooked cereal, macaroni, noodles, rice, spaghetti	3- to 4.5-ounce serving, cooked	
Miscellaneous group		
Cream, bacon, butter, margarine, oil, salad dressing, olives, jam, jelly, sugar, sweets, cake, pie, carbonated beverages, relishes, alcoholic beverages, snack foods, crisps	Provide mostly calories for the day's total intake	

Table 2.15 *24-Hour recall questionnaire for adults*

Name: *Mrs Brown* Age: *24 years* Height: *160 cm*	Date of recall: *3/4* Male _____ Weight: *67.3 kg*	Day of recall: *Tuesday* Female *✓* Ideal weight: *56.3 kg*	Occupation: *Housewife* % of ideal: *119 per cent*		
Ingestion period	**Kinds of food and description**	**Amount in household units**	**Frequency of consumption of various foods**	**Times per day-week-month**	
				×D	×W	×M

Ingestion period	Kinds of food and description	Amount in household units	Frequency of consumption of various foods	×D	×W	×M
6 a.m.	Coffee	1 cup	Milk, whole		4	
	Sugar	1 tsp	Milk, skim			
	Cream	2 tbsp	Yogurt		3	
8 a.m.	Cornflakes	1 ounce	Cheese		3	
	Milk, whole	½ cup	Ice cream		5	
			Beef		4	
12 noon	Sandwich		Pork			1
	Bread, white	2 slices	Lamb			1
	Peanut butter	2 tbsp	Fish		1	
	Apple	1 small	Poultry		3	
	Coffee	1 cup	Eggs		5	
	Sugar	1 tsp	Cream	3		
	Cream	2 tbsp	Butter		3	
			Margarine	3		
3 p.m.	Cola drink	1 (12-ounce can)	Oil	1		
	Chocolate bar	1½ ounces	Salad dressings	1		
			Vegetables			
6.30 p.m.	Fried fillet of sole	3 ounces	Green-yellow	1		
	Green beans	3 ounces	Citrus fruits		3	
	Boiled potato	1 medium	Legumes			
	Lettuce salad	6 ounces	Beans		1	
	French dressing	2 tbsp	Chick peas			1
	Muffin	1 small	Lentils			
	Coffee	1 cup	Potatoes	1		
	Sugar	1 tsp	Breads	3		
	Cream	2 tbsp	Pastas		4	
10.30 p.m.	Chocolate cake (20 cm diam.)	1/16 cake	Rice			
			Cakes	1		
	Cola drink	1 12-ounce can)	Pies		4	
			Sweets	1		
			Jams/jellies		5	
			Sugar	3		
			Alcoholic beverage			
			Carbonated beverage	3		
			Coffee, tea	3		
			Snack foods	1		
			Vitamin supplement			
			Mineral supplement			

Diagnosis of Malnutrition

Once the nutritional assessment data has been collected it is possible to determine whether or not the patient is malnourished. Table 2.17 shows a classification of malnutrition. Once the data relating to individual patients has been evaluated, it becomes possible to plan an effective regime through which to provide nutritional support.

Summary

This section has shown that hospital patients are at considerable nutritional risk for a variety of reasons, and has highlighted the ways in which their nutritional status can be monitored. The nurse can play a central role in nutritional screening. Regular monitoring of nutritional status can enable identification of patients at risk of nutritional depletion in order that a more intensive nutritional evaluation can be carried out. The importance of

Table 2.16 *Suggested guide to interpretation of blood data**

	Deficient	Low	Acceptable	High
Total plasma protein: g/dl	<6.0	6.0–6.4	6.5–6.9	≥7.0
Serum albumin (electrophoretic method): g/dl	<2.80	2.80–3.51	3.52–4.24	≥4.25
Serum globulin (percentage of serum protein):				
α_1			4–7	
α_2			9–11	
β			11–15	
γ			12–16	
Haemoglobin, g/dl:				
Men	<12.0	12.0–13.9	14.0–14.9	≥15.0
Women (nonpregnant, nonlactating; ≥ 13 years)	<10.0	10.0–10.9	11.0–14.4	≥14.5
Children (3–12 years)	<10.0	10.0–10.9	11.0–12.4	≥12.5
Haematocrit (PCV), percent:				
Men	<36	36–41	42–44	≥45
Women (nonpregnant, nonlactating; ≥ 13 years)	<30	30–37	38–42	≥43
Children (3–12 years)	<30.0	30.0–33.9	34.0–36.9	≥37.0
Plasma ascorbic acid: mg/dl	<0.10	0.10–0.19	0.20–0.39	≥0.40
Plasma vitamin A: µg/dl	<10	10–19	20–49	≥50
Plasma carotene: µg/dl	3	20–39	40–99	≥100
Red cell riboflavin: µg/dl – red blood cells	<10.0	10.0–14.9	15.0–19.9	≥20

*Except for the particulates in blood, serum levels of nutrients in children do not differ appreciably beyond infancy from those of adults. Similarly, with the exception of haemoglobin and haematocrit, the serum levels of blood constituents in women of childbearing age are comparable to those of men. (Interdepartmental Committee on Nutrition for National Defense Manual for Nutrition Surveys (2nd edition).)

Table 2.17 *Malnutritional status classification*

Standards		Mild	Moderate	Severe
Albumin (g/dl)		3.5–3.0	<3.0–2.5	<2.5
Transferrin (g/dl)		200–180	<180–160	<160
Lymphocyte count		1,800–1,500	<1,500–900	<900
Triceps skinfold	% deficit			
Mid-arm circumference	% deficit	>5%–15%	>15%–30%	>30%
Arm muscle circumference	% deficit			

(Adapted from Kaminski, M.V. and Winborn, A.L. (1978) Nutritional Assessment Guide, Midwest Nutrition, Education and Research Foundation Inc.)

the nurses' role cannot be overemphasized since they can liaise between the patient and other health care professionals. The nurse's findings must be communicated to the dietician and the rest of the health care team so that appropriate clinical interventions can be employed.

SLEEP

Sleep is a vital aspect of life. Without it, people become irritable and irrational, and recuperation may be delayed (Willis, 1989). Sleep generally occurs at night-time, although this is not necessarily so (Fordham, in Wilson-Barnett and Batchup, 1988). The amount of sleep each person needs varies: a baby will require as many as 17 hours in every 24, while an adult will sleep for seven or eight hours each night. Indeed, an elderly person may sleep for only five or six hours a night, but may nap during the day as well. Other factors that affect the normal sleep pattern include gender, diet, temperature, position, anxiety and genetic links (Bouton, 1986; Closs, 1988a, b).

Sleep is an active process controlled by the hypothalamus in the brain. Human sleep patterns are thought to be determined by circadian rhythms over a 24- or 25-hour period, although this time span is disputed (Roper, Logan and Tierney, 1985). Changes in the pattern of brain activity during sleep can be identified and compared using electroencephalography (Morgan, 1987), and the significance of the differing levels of consciousness, restlessness and dreaming can be studied.

Sleep occurs in five stages:

- Stage 1—drowsiness.
- Stage 2—light sleep, when wakening can occur easily.
- Stages 3 and 4—deep sleep.
- Stage 5—rapid eye movement: physiological changes occur, such as an increase in respiration, pulse, blood pressure and oxygen intake. This is the dreaming stage, before which body muscles relax.

Progression from each stage is haphazard and varies in each individual. Each sleep cycle lasts for 90 to 100 minutes.

Sleep Problems

Problems with sleep may be due to disturbances of the circadian rhythms that affect this internal control mechanism, for example, when normal sleeping and waking times are changed, or when people are unable to adapt to the natural change of reduction in sleeping time as they age. Problems can also be due to external factors such as changes in the environment, noise and light levels, bedding and personal habits.

More serious problems in the form of insomnia can be differentiated into difficulty in getting off to sleep, and wakefulness during the night and early in the morning. These problems can be caused by anxiety, pain, physical illness and depression. Most people sleep poorly when in hospital, irrespective of the reason for their admission (Willis, 1989).

No reliable measurement of sleep performance has yet been devised. A subjective appraisal must be made by the nurse to assess the patient's sleep pattern on admission to hospital; it can then be reviewed by observation by the night nursing staff. Any problem with sleep should be identified on admission to enable the nurse to take steps to prevent further problems, such as increased anxiety. The patient's personal habits, such as retiring time or the taking of hot drinks before bedtime, should be taken into account and allowed to continue, if possible.

Nurses should try to ensure that the environment is as sleep-inducing as possible. Lighting levels should be reduced, bedclothes should be unrestricting and warm, and patients should be free from pain and anxiety as far as possible. Fear of incontinence or of surgery can provoke anxiety and keep patients awake. Any hypnotic and other medications should be given as prescribed by the doctor, and their effectiveness should be recorded. The nurse should encourage the patient to relax, thus relieving anxiety and aiding sleep.

Drugs

The use of hypnotic drugs, which induce and maintain sleep, should be avoided as much as possible. Barbiturates used to be popular but are rarely used nowadays because they cause dependency. Sleeping tablets can be misused and can be dangerous, especially to the elderly, who may not realize how potent they are.

Hypnotic drugs or sleeping tablets of choice today are the benzodiazepines (Neal, 1987, p. 50), although even these impair psychomotor activity and drowsiness, with dependence occurring after a period of more than two months of regular use (Lyall, 1989; Trevelyan, 1988). Patients who take benzodiazepines to aid sleeping often develop a tolerance to them after a short period of time, and complain of headaches on wakening. These drugs should be prescribed only for a period of two to three weeks.

Nurses should not underestimate the importance of the need for sleep. A thorough assessment of sleep problems should be undertaken, and the patient's problem with sleep taken seriously. There is a great deal the nurse can do to alleviate any sleep problems that patients might have, even without resorting to drug therapy (Gournay, 1988).

HYGIENE

While they are in hospital, patients should be encouraged to carry out, as far as possible, their own normal daily hygiene routines, such as washing, shaving, foot and nail care, and care of the mouth and hair. This will help to reduce the risk of infection, and will also increase their self-esteem. However, even when patients are relatively independent, each individual's hygiene should be assessed so that assistance can be given if necessary (Webster, Thompson, Bourmay *et al.*, 1988). When nursing help is required, nurses should not dictate the care given unless the patient is unable to express a preference. Even with the very ill or helpless patient, individual preferences should be taken into account, and as much privacy as possible should be provided.

If a bedbath is required, the nurse should ensure that the patient has enough assistance, without being intrusive. Gooch (1987) and Greaves (1985) argue that nurses create more infection hazards and discomfort with this activity than is necessary. Therefore, it is important to ensure that all items used, such as the basin and washcloths, are cleaned thoroughly after use to avoid the hazard of cross-infection.

The patient's hair should be kept clean and tidy. Regular washing, even if the patient is in bed, can really boost morale. Similarly, men should be given the opportunity to shave, or be shaved, regularly.

It is important that the patient's feet are washed and dried thoroughly, and that the nails are trimmed—remembering that the poor circulation associated with diabetes makes this a particularly important and hazardous procedure. A visit from the chiropodist is advisable for diabetic, elderly and longstay patients.

Oral hygiene is particularly important. Neglect of the

mouth can lead to bad breath, anorexia, parotitis, thrush and dental decay. Regular oral fluids help to ensure that the mouth is kept clean, moist, free of infection and comfortable to the patient.

If a patient's physical or mental state is such that a nurse must perform the patient's mouth care, then this should be undertaken frequently and thoroughly, and should include attention to the teeth or dentures and the giving of oral fluids if they are permitted. Dentures should be removed and brushed as regularly as required, and soaked overnight in an appropriate sterilizing solution (Harrison, 1987).

Some drug regimes, such as cytotoxic drugs and antibiotics, can have harmful effects on the mouth (Crosby, 1989), and therefore thorough assessments should be undertaken to prevent complications. The use of cleansing agents and practices for cleaning the patient's mouth vary, and research has shown that some well-used techniques and the substances applied are actually harmful to the mouth (Shepherd, Page and Sammon, 1987).

Roth and Creason (1986) identified practices in oral hygiene where nursing care is needed. Nursing researchers studied the significance of frequent brushing and flossing for plaque removal (Alderman, 1988; Meckstroth, 1989). Firm bristles and horizontal strokes were found to cause gum inflammation and laceration, especially in older people. Studies showed that foamsticks were ineffective in plaque removal, and in one group of 22 subjects, only 20 per cent preferred the foamstick (Harris, 1980).

Antimicrobial mouthwashes have been accepted as adjuncts to brushing and flossing. However, in one nursing study, the alkaline mouthwash was found to be less effective than hydrogen peroxide (Gooch, 1985).

Studies of lemon and glycerol solutions have failed to show a significant correlation between their use and effective cleansing and moisturizing. Additionally, local dehydrating effects are well documented in the nursing literature.

Studies indicated that the frequency of oral hygiene should be increased when the patient is exposed to dehydrating stressors such as nasal oxygen, mouth-breathing, continuous suctioning and restricted oral intake of food and fluid. Some research indicates that mouth care given at four-hourly intervals is insufficient to maintain comfort; two-hourly intervals are recommended.

Patients should be reminded to brush twice daily with a soft-bristled toothbrush and floss after each brushing. This should be done for those patients who are unable to provide their own care.

During any hygiene activity, the opportunity should be taken to observe the patient with a view to assessing both the physical and psychological state. This ensures that potential and actual problems are noted as soon as possible, allowing steps to be taken to prevent deterioration in the patient's condition.

FLUID AND ELECTROLYTE BALANCE

Fundamental Concepts

Amount and Composition of Body Fluids

The proportion of body fluid found in humans is influenced by age, sex and body fat content. As a general rule, younger people have a higher percentage of body fluid than do older people, and men have proportionately more body fluid than do women (Table 2.18). Obese people have less fluid than thin people because fat cells contain little water.

The typical adult is composed of approximately 60 per cent fluid (water and electrolytes) by weight. Approximately two thirds of the body fluid in adults exists in the intracellular space (primarily in the skeletal muscle mass). The remaining one third is found in the extracellular space, between the cells and in the plasma.

Electrolytes

Electrolytes in body fluids are active chemicals (anions and cations) that unite in varying combinations. Electrolyte concentration in the body is now expressed in terms of millimoles per litre (mmol/l).

Electrolyte concentrations in intracellular fluid differ from those in extracellular fluid. Because special techniques are required to measure electrolyte concentrations in the intracellular fluid, it is customary to measure the electrolytes in the most accessible portion of body fluids, namely, the plasma.

Sodium ions in the extracellular fluid far outnumber other extracellular cations (Table 2.19). About 90 per cent of the extracellular fluid osmolality is determined by the sodium concentration. As a result, sodium is important in the regulation of body fluid volume. Retention of sodium is associated with fluid retention; conversely, excessive

Table 2.18 *Approximate values of total body fluid as a percentage of body weight in relation to age and sex*

Age		Total body fluid (% body weight)
Full-term newborn		70–80
1 year		64
Puberty to 39 years	Men:	60
	Women:	52
40 to 60 years	Men:	55
	Women:	47
More than 60 years	Men:	52
	Women:	46

(Metheny, N. (1984) Quick Reference to Fluid Balance, J.B. Lippincott, Philadelphia.)

sodium loss is usually associated with decreased body fluid volume.

As shown in Table 2.20, the major electrolytes in the intracellular fluid are potassium and phosphate. As the extracellular fluid can tolerate only small potassium concentrations (approximately 5 mmol/l), release of large stores of intracellular potassium by trauma can be extremely dangerous. The body expends a great deal of energy maintaining the extracellular preponderance of sodium and the intracellular preponderance of potassium. The extracellular fluid transports other substances, such as enzymes and hormones. It also carries blood components, such as red and white blood cells, throughout the body.

Regulation of Body Fluid Compartments

Osmosis

When two different solutions are separated by a membrane impermeable to the dissolved substances, a shift of water occurs through the membrane from the region of low solute concentration to the region of high solute concentration until the solutions are of equal concentration (Figure 2.6). The magnitude of this force depends on the number of particles dissolved in the solutions and not on their weights. The number of dissolved particles contained in a unit of water determines the osmolality of a solution.

Diffusion

Diffusion is defined as the natural tendency of a substance to move from an area of higher concentration to one of lower concentration. It occurs through the random movement of ions and molecules. An example of diffusion is the exchange of oxygen and carbon dioxide between the pulmonary capillaries and alveoli.

Filtration

Hydrostatic pressure in the capillaries tends to filter fluid out of the vascular compartment into the interstitial fluid. An example of filtration is the passage of water and electrolytes from the arterial capillary bed to the interstitial fluid; in this instance, the hydrostatic pressure is furnished by the pumping action of the heart.

Sodium–Potassium Pump

As stated earlier, sodium concentration is greater in extracellular fluid than in intracellular fluid; because of this, there is a tendency for sodium to enter the cell by diffusion. This tendency is offset by the sodium–potassium pump, which is located in the cell membrane and actively moves sodium from the cell into the extracellular fluid. Conversely, the high intracellular potassium concentration is maintained by pumping of potassium into the cell.

By definition, active transport implies that there must be energy expenditure for the movement to occur against a concentration gradient.

Table 2.19 *Plasma electrolytes*

Electrolytes	mmol/l
Cations	
Sodium	140
Potassium	4
Calcium	2.5
Magnesium	1
Anions	
Chloride	102
Bicarbonate	27
Phosphate	1
Sulphate	0.5
Protein	2
Organic anions	3

(Wade, A. (ed.) (1988) Pharmaceutical Handbook *(19th edition), The Pharmaceutical Press, London.)*

Table 2.20 *Intracellular electrolytes*

Electrolytes	mmol/l
Cations	
Sodium	10
Potassium	155
Calcium	1
Magnesium	15
Anions	
Chloride	5
Bicarbonate	10
Phosphate	50
Sulphate	10
Protein	8
Organic anions	2

(Wade, A. (ed.) (1988) Pharmaceutical Handbook *(19th edition), The Pharmaceutical Press, London.)*

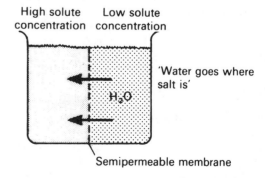

Figure 2.6 Osmosis. ('Water goes where salt is.') (Metheny, N. (1987) *Fluid and Electrolyte Balance: Nursing Considerations*, J. B. Lippincott, Philadelphia.)

Routes of Gains and Losses

Water and electrolytes are gained in various ways. In health, one gains fluids by drinking and eating. In some types of illness, fluids may be gained by the parenteral route (intravenously or subcutaneously) or by means of an enteral feeding tube in the stomach or intestine. When fluid balance is critical, all routes of gain and all routes of loss must be recorded and the volumes compared. Organs of fluid loss include the kidneys, skin, lungs and gastrointestinal tract.

Kidneys

The usual urine volume produced in the adult is between one and two litres each day. A general rule is that the output is approximately 1 ml of urine per kilogram of body weight per hour (1 ml/kg/hr) in all age-groups.

Skin

Sensible perspiration refers to visible water and electrolyte loss through the skin by way of sweating. The chief solutes in sweat are sodium chloride and potassium. Actual sweat losses can vary from 0 to 1,000 ml or more every hour, depending on the environmental temperature. Continuous water loss by evaporation (approximately 600 ml/day) occurs through the skin as insensible perspiration, a nonvisible form of water loss. Fever greatly increases insensible water loss through the lungs and the skin, as does loss of the natural skin barrier through major burns.

Lungs

The lungs normally eliminate water vapour (insensible loss) at a rate of 300 to 400 ml every day. The loss is much greater with increased respiratory rate or depth, or both.

Gastrointestinal Tract

The usual loss through the gastrointestinal tract is only 100 to 200 ml every day, even though approximately 8 litres of fluid circulate through the gastrointestinal system every 24 hours (called the 'gastrointestinal circulation'). Since the bulk of fluid is reabsorbed in the small intestine, it is obvious that large losses can be incurred from the gastrointestinal tract if diarrhoea or fistulae occur.

In healthy people the 24-hour average intake and output of water are approximately equal (Table 2.21).

Homeostatic Mechanisms

The body is equipped with homeostatic mechanisms to keep the composition and volume of body fluid within the narrow limits of normal. Organs involved in homeostasis include the kidneys, lungs, heart, adrenal glands, parathyroid glands and pituitary mechanism.

Kidneys

Vital to the regulation of fluid and electrolyte balance, the kidneys normally filter 170 litres of plasma every day in the adult, while excreting only 1.5 litres of urine. They act both autonomously and in response to blood-borne messengers, such as aldosterone and antidiuretic hormone. Major functions of the kidneys in fluid balance homeostasis include the following:

- Regulation of extracellular fluid volume and osmolality by selective retention and excretion of body fluids.
- Regulation of electrolyte levels in the extracellular fluid by selective retention of needed substances and excretion of unneeded substances.
- Regulation of pH of extracellular fluid by excretion or retention of hydrogen ions.
- Excretion of metabolic wastes and toxic substances.

It is therefore readily apparent that renal failure will result in multiple fluid and electrolyte problems.

Heart and Blood Vessels

The pumping action of the heart circulates blood through the kidneys under sufficient pressure for urine to form. Failure of this pumping action interferes with renal perfusion and thus with water and electrolyte regulation.

Lungs

The lungs are also vital in maintaining homeostasis. The lungs remove approximately 300 ml of water daily through exhalation in the normal adult. Abnormal conditions such as hyperpnoea or continuous coughing increase this loss; mechanical ventilation with excessive moisture decreases it. The lungs also have a major role in maintenance of acid–base balance, which is discussed later in this chapter.

Pituitary Gland

The hypothalamus manufactures a substance known as antidiuretic hormone, which is stored in the posterior pituitary gland and released as needed. Sometimes referred to as the 'water conserving hormone', antidiuretic hormone makes the body retain water. Functions of antidiuretic hormone include maintenance of osmotic pressure of the cells by controlling renal water retention or excretion, and control of blood volume (Figure 2.7).

Table 2.21 *Average intake and output in an adult for a 24-hour period (ml)*

Intake		Output	
Oral liquids	1,300	Urine	1,500
Water in food	1,000	Stool	200
Water produced by			
metabolism	300	*Insensible*	
Total	2,600	Lungs	300
		Skin	600
		Total	2,600

(Metheny, N. (1987) Fluid and Electrolyte Balance: Nursing Considerations, J.B. Lippincott, Philadelphia.)

Adrenal Glands

Aldosterone, a mineralocorticoid secreted by the zona glomerulosa (outer zone) of the adrenal cortex, has a profound effect on fluid balance. Increased secretion of aldosterone causes sodium retention (and thus water retention) and potassium loss. Conversely, a decreased secretion of aldosterone causes sodium and water loss and potassium retention. Cortisol, another adrenocortical hormone, has only a fraction of the mineralocorticoid potency of aldosterone. However, when secreted in large quantities, it can also produce sodium and fluid retention and potassium deficit.

Parathyroid Glands

The parathyroid glands, embedded in the corners of the thyroid gland, regulate calcium and phosphate balance by means of parathyroid hormone. Parathyroid hormone influences bone resorption, calcium absorption from the intestines and calcium reabsorption from the renal tubules.

Fluid Volume Disturbances

Fluid Volume Deficit

Definition and Aetiology

Fluid volume deficit results when water and electrolytes are lost in the same proportion as they exist in normal body fluids, so that the ratio of serum electrolytes to water remains the same. It should not be confused with the term dehydration, which refers to loss of water alone with increased serum sodium levels. Fluid volume deficit may occur alone or in combination with other imbalances. Unless other imbalances are present concurrently, serum electrolyte levels remain essentially unchanged.

Fluid volume deficit results from loss of body fluids and occurs more rapidly when coupled with decreased fluid intake. It is possible to develop fluid volume deficit on the basis of inadequate intake alone if the decreased intake is prolonged. Causes of fluid volume deficit include abnormal fluid losses, such as those resulting from vomiting, diarrhoea, gastrointestinal suction and sweating, and decreased intake, as in the presence of nausea or inability to gain access to fluids. Third-space fluid shifts or the movement of fluid from the vascular system to other body spaces (i.e., with oedema formation in burns or ascites with liver dysfunction) also produces fluid volume deficit.

Clinical Features

Fluid volume deficit can develop rapidly and can be mild, moderate or severe, depending on the degree of fluid loss. Important characteristics of fluid volume deficit include acute weight loss, decreased skin turgor, oliguria, concentrated urine, postural hypotension and a weak, rapid pulse.

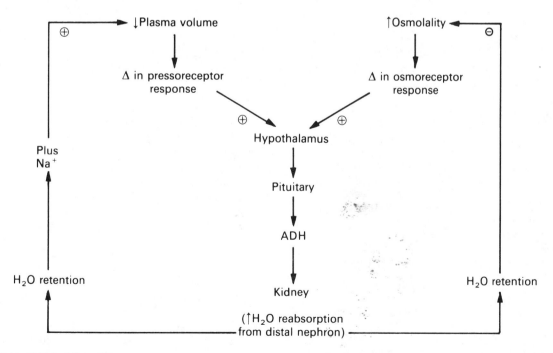

Figure 2.7 Antidiuretic hormone-induced water retention. The major stimulus for antidiuretic hormone secretion is increased serum osmolality. A secondary stimulus is a severe decrease in extracellular volume. (Underhill, S. L. *et al.* (eds) (1982) Fluid and electrolyte balance, J. S. Rokosky and J. Shaver in *Cardiac Nursing*, J. B. Lippincott, Philadelphia, p. 90.)

Diagnosis

Laboratory data useful in evaluating fluid volume status include the blood urea level and its relationship with the serum creatinine concentration. A volume-depleted patient has a blood urea level out of proportion to the serum creatinine level (>10:1). Also, the haematocrit level is greater than normal as the red blood cells become suspended in a decreased plasma volume. Normal values for these tests are listed in Table 2.22.

Management

In planning correction of fluid loss for the patient with fluid volume deficit, usual maintenance requirements and other factors (such as fever) that can influence fluid needs, are considered. When the deficit is not severe, the oral route is preferred, provided the patient is able to drink. However, when fluid losses are acute or severe, the intravenous route is required. Isotonic electrolyte solutions, such as Ringer's lactate (Hartmann's solution) or 0.9 per cent sodium chloride, are frequently used to treat the hypotensive patient with fluid volume deficit since such fluids expand plasma volume. These, and additional fluids, are summarized in Table 2.23.

If the patient with severe fluid volume deficit is oliguric, it must be determined whether the depressed renal

Table 2.22 *Laboratory tests used to evaluate fluid, electrolyte and acid–base status*

Test	SI units
Serum sodium	135–145 mmol/l
Serum potassium	3.5–5.5 mmol/l
Serum calcium	2.1–2.6 mmol/l
Serum magnesium	0.80–1.2 mmol/l
Serum phosphorus	0.80–1.5 mmol/l
Serum chloride	100–106 mmol/l
Carbon dioxide content	24–30 mmol/l
Serum osmolality	280–295 nmol/l
Blood urea	3.5–7 mmol/l
Serum creatinine	60–130 µmol/l
Haematocrit	Volume fraction: 0.44–0.52 (male)
	Volume fraction: 0.39–0.47 (female)
Serum glucose	3.9–6.1 mmol/l
Arterial blood gases	
pH	7.35–7.45
$PaCO_2$	38–42 mmHg
HCO_3^-	22–26 mmol/l
Urinary sodium	80–180 mmol/d
Urinary potassium	40–80 mmol/d
Urinary chloride	110–250 mmol/d
Urinary specific gravity	1.003–1.035
Urine osmolality	
Extreme range:	50–1,400 mmol/kg
Typical urine:	500–800 mmol/kg
Urinary pH	4.5–8.0
Typical urine:	<6.6

function is the result of reduced renal blood flow secondary to fluid volume deficit (prerenal azotaemia) or, more seriously, to acute tubular necrosis due to prolonged fluid volume deficit. The therapeutic test used in this situation is referred to as a fluid challenge test. Prompt treatment of fluid volume deficit is imperative to prevent renal damage.

► NURSING PROCESS
► THE PATIENT WITH FLUID VOLUME DEFICIT

► *Assessment*

To assess for the presence of fluid volume deficit, fluid intake and output are measured and evaluated at least at eight-hourly intervals; sometimes, hourly measurements are indicated. As fluid volume deficit is developing, body fluid losses exceed fluid intake. This loss may be in the form of polyuria, diarrhoea, vomiting and so on. Later, after fluid volume deficit has fully developed, the kidneys attempt to conserve needed body fluids, leading to a urinary output less than 30 ml/hr in an adult; urine in this instance is concentrated and represents a healthy renal response. Daily body weight measurements are monitored, keeping in mind that an acute weight loss of 0.5 kg represents a fluid loss of approximately 500 ml. (One litre of fluid weighs approximately 1 kg.)

The vital signs are closely monitored. The nurse should be particularly alert for a weak, rapid pulse and postural hypotension (i.e., a drop in the systolic pressure greater than 10 mmHg when changed from a lying to a sitting position). A decrease in body temperature often accompanies fluid volume deficit, unless there is a concurrent infection.

Skin and tongue turgor are monitored regularly. In a normal person, pinched skin will immediately fall back to its normal position when released. This elastic property, referred to as turgor, is partially dependent on interstitial fluid volume. In a person with fluid volume deficit, the skin flattens more slowly after the pinch is released; when the fluid volume deficit is severe, the skin may remain elevated for many seconds. Tissue turgor is best measured by pinching the skin over the sternum, inner aspects of the thighs or forehead. The skin turgor test is not as valid in elderly people as in younger people since skin elasticity is affected by age. Evaluation of tongue turgor, which is not affected by age may be more valid than evaluation of skin turgor. In a normal person, the tongue has one longitudinal furrow. In the person with fluid volume deficit there are additional longitudinal furrows and the tongue is smaller, owing to fluid loss. The degree of oral mucous membrane moisture is also assessed; a dry mouth may indicate either fluid volume deficit or mouth breathing.

The specific gravity of urine is monitored. In a

Table 2.23 *Selected water and electrolyte solutions*

Solution	Comments
0.9% NaCl (isotonic saline) Na$^+$ 150 mmol/l Cl$^-$ 150 mmol/l Also available with varying concentrations of dextrose (the most frequently used is a 5% dextrose concentration)	• An isotonic solution that expands the extracellular fluid volume, used in hypovolaemic states • Supplies an excess of Na$^+$ and Cl$^-$; can cause fluid volume excess and hyperchloraemic acidosis if used in excessive volumes, particularly in patients with compromised renal function • Not desirable as a routine maintenance solution since it provides only Na$^+$ and Cl$^-$ (and these are provided in excessive amounts) • Sometimes used to correct mild Na$^+$ deficit • When mixed with 5% dextrose, the resulting solution becomes hypertonic in relation to plasma and, in addition to the above described electrolytes, provides 170 calories per litre
0.45% NaCl (half-strength saline) Na$^+$ 77 mmol/l Cl$^-$ 77 mmol/l Also available with varying concentrations of dextrose (the most common is a 5% concentration)	• A hypotonic solution that provides Na$^+$, Cl$^-$ and free water • Free water is desirable to aid the kidneys in elimination of solute • Lacking in electrolytes other than Na$^+$ and Cl$^-$ • When mixed with 5% dextrose, the solution becomes slightly hypertonic to plasma and in addition to the above-described electrolytes provides 170 calories
Ringer's lactate solution (Hartmann's solution) Na$^+$ 131 mmol/l K$^+$ 5 mmol/l Ca^{2+} 2 mmol/l Cl$^-$ 111 mmol/l Lactate (metabolized to bicarbonate) 29 mmol/l Also available with varying concentrations of dextrose (the most common is 5% dextrose)	• An isotonic solution that contains multiple electrolytes in roughly the same concentration as found in plasma (note that solution is lacking in Mg^{2+}) • Used in the treatment of hypovolaemia, burns and fluid lost as bile or diarrhoea • Does not supply free water for renal excretory purposes; excessive use without provision for free water (as with 5% dextrose in water or hypotonic electrolyte solutions) can cause elevation of the serum sodium level in people not deficient in sodium • When mixed with 5% dextrose, the resulting solution becomes hypertonic to plasma and provides 170 calories per litre. Of course, the electrolyte concentration remains constant
5% dextrose in water No electrolytes 50 g of dextrose/l	• An isotonic solution that supplies 170 calories per litre and free water to aid in renal excretion of solutes • Should not be used in excessive volumes in the early postoperative period (when antidiuretic hormone secretion is increased due to stress reaction) • Should not be used solely in treatment of fluid volume deficit since it dilutes plasma electrolyte concentrations
3% NaCl (hypertonic saline) Na$^+$ 500 mmol/l Cl$^-$ 500 mmol/l (1,026 mOsm/kg)	• Grossly hypertonic solution used only in critical situations to treat hyponatraemia

volume-depleted patient, the urinary specific gravity should be above 1.020 (indicating healthy renal conservation of fluid).

Severe volume depletion eventually affects the sensorium by decreasing cerebral perfusion. Decreased peripheral perfusion can result in cold extremities. In patients with relatively normal cardiopulmonary function, a low central venous pressure is indicative of hypovolaemia. Patients with acute cardiopulmonary decompensation require more extensive haemodynamic monitoring with a device that measures pressures in both sides of the heart.

▶ Patient's Problems

The nursing assessment and identification of patients at risk for this disturbance lead to identification of the patient's problems, in this case one of fluid volume deficit. For example, in a patient with volume depletion secondary to uncontrolled diabetes mellitus, the problem may be stated as fluid volume deficit related to osmotic diuresis.

▶ Planning and Implementation
▶ Expected Outcomes

The main expected outcome is the prevention of this common disturbance. Once the imbalance has developed, the aim is to correct the abnormal fluid volume status before renal damage results. More precise expected outcomes vary with the cause of fluid volume deficit and individual patient characteristics.

Nursing Care

Prevention of Fluid Volume Deficit

In order to prevent fluid volume deficit, the nurse must be aware of at-risk patients and take measures to minimize fluid losses. For example, if the patient has diarrhoea, measures should be implemented to control the diarrhoea while replacing fluids. This may include the administration of antidiarrhoeal medications and small volumes of oral fluids at frequent intervals.

Correction of Fluid Volume Deficit

When possible, oral fluids are given to help correct fluid volume deficit, keeping in mind the patient's likes and dislikes. Also, the type of fluid the patient has lost is considered and attempts are made to select fluids most likely to replace the lost electrolytes. If the patient is reluctant to drink because of oral discomfort, frequent mouth care is given and fluids that do not irritate the mucosa are provided. It is often helpful to offer small volumes of fluids at frequent intervals rather than a large volume all at once. If nausea is present, antiemetics may be needed before oral fluid replacement can be tolerated.

If the patient is unable to eat and drink, the doctor may consider an alternative route (enteral or parenteral) for fluid intake. This care is important to prevent renal damage related to prolonged fluid volume deficit.

▶ Evaluation
▶ Expected Outcomes

1. Patient exhibits normal turgor of skin and tongue.
2. Excretes increased amount of urine with normal specific gravity.
3. Exhibits return of pulse and blood pressure to normal.
4. Exhibits clear sensorium; is oriented to time, person and place.
5. Drinks fluids as prescribed.
6. Exhibits absence of precipitating risk factors (e.g., excessive fluid loss, decreased fluid intake).

Fluid Volume Excess

Definition and Aetiology

Fluid volume excess refers to an isotonic expansion of the extracellular fluid caused by the abnormal retention of water and sodium in approximately the same proportions in which they normally exist in the extracellular fluid. It is always secondary to an increase in the total body sodium content, which, in turn, leads to an increase in total body water. Because there is isotonic retention of body substances, the serum sodium concentration remains essentially normal.

Fluid volume excess may be caused by simple fluid overloading or by diminished function of the homeostatic mechanisms responsible for regulating fluid balance. Aetiological factors can include congestive heart failure, renal failure and cirrhosis of the liver. Over-zealous administration of sodium-containing fluids to people with impaired regulatory mechanisms particularly predisposes to serious fluid volume excess. Excessive ingestion of table salt (sodium chloride) or other sodium salts also predisposes to fluid overload.

Clinical Features

The clinical features of fluid volume excess stem from expansion of the extracellular fluid compartment and include oedema, distended veins, increased venous pressure, bounding pulse and crackles in the skin when it is touched.

Diagnosis

Laboratory data useful in the diagnosis of fluid volume excess include the blood urea and haematocrit levels. In the presence of fluid volume excess, both of these values may be decreased owing to plasma dilution. Other causes of abnormalities in these values include low protein intake and anaemia.

Management

Management of fluid volume excess is directed towards the causative factors. Symptomatic treatment consists of administration of diuretics, restriction of fluids, or both. When the fluid excess is related to excessive administration of sodium-containing fluids, discontinuing the infusion may be all that is needed. Treatment almost always involves sodium restriction in the diet, and concepts related to sodium-restricted diets are discussed below.

Sodium-Restricted Diets. An average daily diet not restricted in sodium contains 6–15 g of salt, whereas low-sodium diets can range from a mild restriction to as low as 250 mg of sodium per day, depending on the patient's needs. A mild sodium-restricted diet allows only light salting of food (about half the amount as usual) in cooking and at the table, and no addition of salt to commercially prepared foods that are already seasoned. Of course, foods high in sodium must be avoided. Because about half of ingested sodium is in the form of seasoning, use of substitute seasonings plays a major role in decreasing sodium intake. Lemon juice, onion and garlic are excellent substitute flavouring agents; however, some patients prefer salt substitutes. Most salt substitutes contain potassium and should be used cautiously by those patients taking potassium-sparing diuretics (e.g., spironolactone, triamterene and amiloride). They should not be used at all in patients with conditions associated with potassium retention, such as advanced renal disease. Salt substitutes containing ammonium chloride can be harmful to patients with liver damage.

In certain communities, the drinking water may contain too much sodium for a sodium-restricted diet. Depending on its source, water may contain as little as 1 mg or more than 1,500 mg per litre. It may be necessary for patients to use distilled water when the local water supply is very high in sodium. Also, patients on sodium-restricted diets should be cautioned to avoid 'water softeners' which add sodium to water in exchange for other ions, such as calcium.

► NURSING PROCESS
► THE PATIENT WITH FLUID VOLUME EXCESS

► Assessment

To assess for fluid volume excess, the fluid intake and output are measured at regular intervals for indications of excessive fluid retention. The patient is weighed daily, and acute weight gain is noted. (An acute weight gain of 0.9 kg represents a gain of approximately 1 litre of fluid.)

It is important to assess breath sounds at regular intervals in at-risk patients, particularly when parenteral fluids are being administered. The nurse monitors the degree of oedema in the most dependent parts of the body, such as the feet and ankles in ambulatory patients and the sacral region in bedridden patients. The degree of pitting oedema is assessed and the extent of peripheral oedema is measured with a tape marked in millimetres.

► Patient's Problems

Based on the nursing assessment and identification of the patient at risk for this disturbance, the patient's main problem is fluid volume excess. For example, in a patient with congestive heart failure, the problem might be stated as follows: fluid volume excess related to compromised regulatory mechanism (cardiac failure).

► Planning and Implementation
► Expected Outcomes

The main expected outcome is the prevention of fluid volume excess in patients at risk. If prevention is not possible, the presence of fluid volume excess must be detected early so that therapeutic care can be implemented before the condition becomes severe. Specific outcomes vary with individual patients and their clinical conditions.

Nursing Care

Prevention of Fluid Volume Excess

Specific care varies somewhat with the underlying pathological condition and the degree of fluid volume excess. However, most patients require sodium-restricted diets in some form. Therefore, adherence to the prescribed diet is encouraged. The patient is instructed to avoid 'over-the-counter' drugs without first checking with the chemist because these substances may contain sodium. When fluid retention persists despite adherence to a prescribed diet, hidden sources of sodium, such as the water supply or use of water softeners, should be considered.

Detection and Control of Fluid Volume Excess

It is important to detect fluid volume excess before the condition becomes critical. Care includes providing rest, sodium restriction, close monitoring of parenteral fluid therapy and administration of appropriate medications. Some patients benefit from regular rest periods because bedrest favours excretion of oedema fluid. Sodium and fluid restriction should be instituted as indicated. Because most patients with fluid volume excess require diuretics, the patient's response to these drugs is monitored. The rate of parenteral fluids and the patient's response to the fluids are also closely monitored. If dyspnoea or orthopnoea is present, the patient should assume an upright position to favour lung expansion. The patient is turned and positioned at regular intervals since oedematous tissue is more prone to skin breakdown than normal tissue.

Because conditions predisposing to fluid volume excess are likely to be chronic, patients are taught how to monitor their own responses to therapy by recording and evaluating fluid intake and output and body weight changes. The importance of adherence to the medical regime is emphasized.

► *Evaluation*
► **Expected Outcomes**

1. Patient exhibits normal skin turgor and the absence of oedema.
2. Excretes increased amount of urine.
3. Demonstrates return of body weight to normal.
4. Demonstrates no distension of jugular veins.
5. Adheres to diet with prescribed sodium intake.
6. States rationale for dietary prescription.
7. Exhibits normal breath sounds without adventitious sounds (crackles, rhonchi, wheezes).
8. Maintains bedrest when prescribed.
9. Exhibits absence of precipitating risk factors (e.g., fluid overload, high sodium intake).

Considerations for the Elderly

Elderly people have special nursing care needs because of their increased risk of developing fluid and electrolyte problems. Fluid balance in the elderly is often marginal at best because of physiological changes associated with the ageing process. Some of these changes include reduction in total body water (associated with increased body fat content and decreased muscle mass), reduction in renal function resulting in decreased ability to concentrate urine, decreased cardiovascular and respiratory function, and disturbances in hormonal regulatory functions. Although these changes are regarded as normal in the ageing process, they must be considered when the elderly person becomes ill because they predispose to fluid and electrolyte imbalances.

Assessment of the elderly patient should be modified somewhat from that of younger adults. For example, skin turgor is less valid as an assessment tool in the elderly since their skin has lost some of its elasticity; therefore, other assessment measures, such as slowness in filling of veins of the hands and feet, become more important in detecting fluid volume deficit. When skin turgor is tested in the elderly, it is best tested over the forehead or the sternum because alterations in skin elasticity are less marked in these areas. As in any patient, skin turgor should be monitored serially to detect subtle changes.

The nurse should perform a functional assessment of the elderly person's ability to determine the need for and to obtain adequate food and fluid intake. For example, is the patient mentally alert? Is mobilization possible? Can the arms and hands be used to reach fluids and foods? Is swallowing possible? All of these questions have direct bearing on how the patient will be able to manage the need for fluids and food. The nurse must, of course, provide for such patients when they are unable to provide for themselves.

Sodium Imbalances

Disturbances in sodium balance occur frequently in clinical practice and can develop under simple and complex circumstances. Before discussion of disruptions in sodium balance, important facts about the role of sodium in physiological activities are reviewed.

Functions of Sodium

Sodium is the most abundant electrolyte in the extracellular fluid; its concentration ranges from 135 to 145 mmol/l. Because of this, it is the primary determinant of extracellular fluid concentration. The fact that sodium does not easily cross the cell-wall membrane, with its dominance in quantity, accounts for its primary role in controlling water distribution throughout the body. In addition, sodium is the primary regulator of extracellular fluid volume. A loss or gain of sodium is usually accompanied by a loss or gain of water. Sodium also functions in the establishment of the electrochemical state necessary for muscle contraction and the transmission of nerve impulses.

Sodium Deficit (Hyponatraemia)

Definition and Aetiology
Hyponatraemia refers to a serum sodium level that is below normal (less than 135 mmol/l). It may be due to an excessive loss of sodium or an excessive gain of water; in either event, it results in a relatively greater concentration of water than of sodium. This imbalance should not be confused with fluid volume deficit, which refers to an isotonic or equivalent loss of sodium and water, resulting in an essentially normal serum sodium level. A hyponatraemic state can, however, be superimposed on an existing fluid volume deficit or fluid volume excess.

Sodium may be lost by way of vomiting, diarrhoea, fistulae or sweating, or it may be associated with diuretics, particularly in combination with a low-salt diet. A deficiency of aldosterone, such as occurs in adrenal insufficiency, also predisposes the patient to sodium deficiency.

Water may be gained abnormally by the excessive parenteral administration of dextrose and water solutions, particularly during periods of stress. It may also be gained by compulsive water drinking (psychogenic polydipsia).

Clinical Features
Clinical features of hyponatraemia depend on the cause, magnitude and rapidity of onset. Although nausea and

abdominal cramping occur, most of the symptoms are neuropsychiatric and are probably related to the cellular swelling and cerebral oedema associated with hyponatraemia. As the extracellular sodium level decreases, the cellular fluid becomes relatively more concentrated and 'pulls' water into the cells (Figure 2.8). In general, those patients having acute decline in serum sodium levels have more severe symptoms and higher mortality rates than do those with more slowly developing hyponatraemia.

Features of hyponatraemia associated with sodium loss and water gain include anorexia, muscle cramps and a feeling of exhaustion. When the serum sodium level drops below 115 mmol/l, signs of increasing intracranial pressure, such as lethargy, confusion, muscular twitching, focal weakness, hemiparaesis, papilloedema and convulsions, may occur.

Diagnosis

Regardless of the cause of hyponatraemia, the serum sodium level is less than 135 mmol/l; it may be as low as 100 mmol/l or less. When hyponatraemia is due primarily to sodium loss, the urinary sodium content is less than 10 mmol/l and the specific gravity is low.

Management

The obvious treatment for hyponatraemia is careful administration of sodium. This may be accomplished orally, by nasogastric tube or parenterally. For patients who are able to eat and drink, sodium replacement is easily accomplished because sodium is plentiful in a normal diet. For those unable to take sodium orally, Ringer's lactate solution or isotonic saline (0.9 per cent sodium chloride) may be prescribed (see Table 2.23). The usual daily sodium requirement in adults is approximately 100 mmol, provided there are no abnormal losses.

When hyponatraemia is present in a patient with nor-

movolaemia or hypervolaemia, the treatment of choice is water restriction. This is far safer than sodium administration and is usually quite effective. However, when neurological symptoms are present, it may be necessary to administer small volumes of a hypertonic sodium solution, such as 3 or 5 per cent sodium chloride. Incorrect use of these fluids is extremely dangerous; this is understandable when one considers that a litre of 3 per cent sodium chloride solution contains 500 mmol of sodium, and a litre of 5 per cent sodium chloride solution contains 833 mmol of sodium. Grossly hypertonic sodium solutions (3 and 5 per cent sodium chloride) should be administered only in intensive care settings under close observation because only small volumes are needed to elevate the serum sodium level from a dangerously low value. These fluids are administered slowly, and in small volumes, while the patient is monitored closely for fluid overload.

► NURSING PROCESS
► THE PATIENT WITH SODIUM DEFICIT

► *Assessment*

It is important to identify patients at risk for hyponatraemia so that they can be monitored. Early detection and treatment of this disorder are necessary to prevent serious consequences. For patients at risk, the nurse monitors fluid intake and output as well as daily body weight. Abnormal losses of sodium and/or gains of water are noted. Gastrointestinal features, such as anorexia, nausea, vomiting and abdominal cramping, are also noted. The nurse should be particularly alert for central nervous system changes, such as lethargy, confusion, muscular twitching and convulsions. In general, more severe neurological signs are associated with very low sodium levels that have fallen rapidly owing to water overloading. It is most important to monitor serum sodium

Explains why hyponatraemic patients may develop brain swelling

Explains why hypernatraemic patients may develop brain contraction

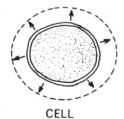

CELL

Hyponatraemia
Na less than 130 mmol/l

CELL

Hypernatraemia
Na greater than 150 mmol/l

Figure 2.8 Effect of extracellular sodium levels on cell size. (Metheny, N. (1987) *Fluid and Electrolyte Balance: Nursing Considerations*, J. B. Lippincott, Philadelphia.)

levels in patients at risk for hyponatraemia. When indicated, urinary sodium levels and specific gravity are also monitored.

▶ *Patient's Problems*

The nursing assessment and the presence of clinical features associated with hyponatraemia in a patient at risk lead to the identification of the patient's problem. For example, in a patient with diarrhoea who drinks large amounts of tap water to relieve thirst, the diagnosis might be stated as follows: alteration in sodium balance (hyponatraemia) related to excessive sodium loss and water gain. Once the aetiological factors have been identified, therapeutic measures can be taken to deal with the disturbance. Some of the nursing care for this imbalance is independent (such as increasing dietary sodium or limiting free water intake, as tolerated). Often, however, the nursing care is associated with that of other disciplines, such as the safe parenteral administration of fluids containing sodium.

▶ *Planning and Implementation*
▶ Expected Outcomes

The main expected outcome is the early detection of hyponatraemia so that care can be implemented before the condition becomes severe. Once hyponatraemia has developed, the expected outcome is a safe return of the serum sodium level to normal. How quickly this can be accomplished depends on a number of variables, such as the cause and severity of the imbalance.

Nursing Care

Early Detection and Control of Hyponatraemia

The nurse should be aware of patients at risk for hyponatraemia and initiate measures to detect the disturbance before it becomes severe. Patients suffering abnormal losses of sodium, yet able to consume a general diet, should be provided with foods and fluids with a high sodium content. For example, broth made with one beef cube contains approximately 900 mg of sodium, and 225 ml of tomato juice contains approximately 700 mg of sodium.

It is important to be familiar with the sodium content of parenteral fluids (see Table 2.23). When administering fluids to patients with cardiovascular disease, the nurse should monitor the patient for signs of circulatory overload, such as crackles with auscultation of the lungs. As was stated earlier, extreme care is essential when administering grossly hypertonic sodium fluids (such as 3 or 5 per cent sodium chloride), because these fluids can be lethal if they are infused carelessly.

If patients are taking lithium, the nurse should be alert for lithium toxicity when sodium is lost by an abnormal route. In such instances, supplemental salt and fluid are administered. Because diuretics promote sodium loss, patients taking lithium are instructed not to use diuretics unless under close medical supervision. All patients on lithium therapy should have an adequate salt intake.

Excess water supplements are avoided in patients receiving isotonic or hypotonic tube feedings, particularly if routes of abnormal sodium loss are present or water is being abnormally retained. Actual fluid needs are determined by evaluating the intake and output, urinary specific gravity and serum sodium levels.

Safe Return of Serum Sodium Level to Normal

When the primary problem is water retention, it is safer to restrict fluid intake than to administer sodium. Administration of sodium to a patient with normovolaemia or hypervolaemia predisposes to fluid volume overload. As was stated previously, patients with cardiovascular disease receiving fluids containing sodium should be monitored very closely for signs of circulatory overload. In severe hyponatraemia, the expected outcome of therapy is to elevate the serum sodium level only enough to alleviate neurological signs.

▶ *Evaluation*
▶ Expected Outcomes

1. Patient is oriented to time, place and person.
2. Reports decreased muscle cramping and muscle twitching.
3. Exhibits normal strength of upper and lower extremities.
4. Reports decreased level of fatigue, exhaustion and lethargy.
5. Achieves normal body weight.
6. Excretes normal urine volume with normal concentration and specific gravity.
7. Demonstrates no seizure activity.
8. Consumes food and fluids within prescribed fluid and sodium intake.
9. Exhibits absence of precipitating risk factors (e.g., gastrointestinal loss of sodium, diuretic therapy, excessive intake of electrolyte-free fluid).

Sodium Excess (Hypernatraemia)

Definition and Aetiology

Hypernatraemia refers to a greater than normal serum sodium level, that is, a serum level greater than 145 mmol/l. It can be caused by a gain of sodium in excess of water or by a loss of water in excess of sodium. It can occur in patients with normal fluid volume or in those with fluid volume deficit or fluid volume excess. Those most often affected are the very old, very young and cognitively impaired patients who are unable to communicate their thirst. Another common cause of hypernatraemia is deprivation of water in unconscious patients, who are unable to perceive or respond to thirst. Administration of hypertonic tube feeds without adequate water supplements also leads to hypernatraemia, as does watery diarrhoea and greatly increased insensible water loss (e.g., in hyperventilation or denuding effects of burns). Diabetes insipidus leads to hypernatraemia if the patient does not experience, or cannot respond to, thirst or if fluids are excessively restricted.

Clinical Features

The clinical features of hypernatraemia are primarily neurological and are presumably the consequence of cellular dehydration. Hypernatraemia results in a relatively concentrated extracellular fluid, causing water to be pulled from the cells (see Figure 2.8). Clinically, these changes may be manifested by restlessness and weakness in moderate hypernatraemia and by disorientation, delusions and hallucinations in severe cases. If hypernatraemia is severe, permanent brain damage can occur (especially in children). Brain damage is apparently due to subarachnoid haemorrhages that result from brain contraction.

A primary characteristic of hypernatraemia is thirst. Thirst is so strong a defender of serum sodium levels in normal people that hypernatraemia never occurs unless the person is unconscious or is denied access to water; unfortunately, ill people may have an impaired thirst mechanism. Other signs include dry, swollen tongue and sticky mucous membranes. A mild elevation in body temperature may occur, but on correction of the hypernatraemia the body temperature should return to normal.

Diagnosis

In hypernatraemia the serum sodium level is greater than 145 mmol/l and the serum osmolality is greater than 295 mmol/l. The urinary specific gravity is greater than 1.015 as the kidneys attempt to conserve water (provided the water loss is from a route other than the kidneys).

Management

Treatment of hypernatraemia consists of a gradual lowering of the serum sodium level by the infusion of a hypotonic electrolyte solution (such as 0.3 per cent sodium chloride). A hypotonic sodium solution is considered safer than 5 per cent dextrose in water because it allows a gradual reduction in the serum sodium level and thus decreases the risk of cerebral oedema. A rapid reduction in the serum sodium level temporarily decreases the plasma osmolality below that of the fluid in the brain tissue, causing dangerous cerebral oedema.

▶ NURSING PROCESS
▶ THE PATIENT WITH SODIUM EXCESS

▶ *Assessment*

Fluid losses and gains are carefully monitored in patients at risk for hypernatraemia. One should look for abnormal losses of water or low water intake and for large gains of sodium, as might occur with ingestion of proprietary drugs with a high sodium content. It is also important to obtain a drug history because some prescription drugs have a high sodium content.

The presence of thirst or an elevated body temperature is noted and evaluated in relation to other clinical signs. The patient is monitored for changes in behaviour, such as restlessness, disorientation and lethargy.

▶ *Patient's Problems*

The nursing assessment and identification of the presence of clinical features associated with hypernatraemia in patients at risk for this disorder should lead to identification of the patient's problems. For example, in an elderly patient receiving a hyperosmolar tube feeding solution with no additional water, the problem might be alteration in sodium balance (hypernatraemia) related to hypertonic tube feeding and inadequate water supplementation.

▶ *Planning and Implementation*
▶ Expected Outcomes

The main expected outcome is to prevent hypernatraemia in patients at risk. Once hypernatraemia has developed, the primary outcome is to return the serum sodium level to normal gradually, thus avoiding further cerebral changes.

Nursing Care

Prevention of Hypernatraemia

The nurse attempts to prevent hypernatraemia by offering fluids at regular intervals, particularly in debilitated patients unable to perceive or respond to thirst. If fluid intake remains inadequate, the nurse consults with the doctor to plan an alternate route for intake, either by tube feeds or by the parenteral route. If tube feeds are used, sufficient water should be given to keep the serum sodium and blood urea levels within normal limits. As a general rule, the higher the osmolality of the tube feed, the greater the need for water supplementation.

Safe Correction of Hypernatraemia

When hypernatraemia is present and parenteral fluids are necessary for its management, the nurse monitors the patient's response to the fluids by observing for changes in neurological signs. The medical staff review serum sodium levels. The neurological signs should improve with a gradual decrease in the serum sodium level.

▶ *Evaluation*
▶ **Expected Outcomes**

1. Patient is oriented to time, place and person.
2. Exhibits absence of delusions, hallucinations and restlessness.
3. Reports normal thirst.
4. Exhibits moist skin and mucous membranes.
5. Demonstrates normal body temperature.
6. Excretes normal urinary volume with normal specific gravity.
7. Consumes adequate fluid and adheres to low-sodium diet.
8. States rationale for adequate fluid intake and sodium restriction.
9. Reports decreased lethargy.
10. Exhibits normal serum and urinary sodium levels.
11. Exhibits absence of precipitating risk factors (e.g., excessive fluid restriction, ingestion of hypertonic tube feeds).

Potassium Imbalances

Disturbances in potassium balance are common because they are associated with a number of disease and injury states. Unfortunately, they may also be induced by medications such as diuretics, laxatives and certain antibiotics, as well as by therapies such as total parenteral nutrition and chemotherapy.

Functions of Potassium

Potassium is the major intracellular electrolyte; in fact, 98 per cent of the body's potassium is inside the cells. The remaining 2 per cent is in the extracellular fluid; it is this 2 per cent that is all important in neuromuscular function. Potassium influences both skeletal and cardiac muscle activity. For example, alterations in its concentration change myocardial irritability and rhythm. Potassium is constantly moving in and out of cells according to the body's needs, under the influence of the sodium–potassium pump. The normal serum potassium concentration ranges from 3.5 to 5.5 mmol/l, and even minor variations are significant. Normal renal function is necessary for maintenance of potassium balance, since 80 per cent of the potassium is excreted daily from the body by way of the kidneys. The other 20 per cent is lost through the bowel and sweat glands.

Potassium Deficit (Hypokalaemia)

Definition and Aetiology
Hypokalaemia refers to a below-normal serum potass-

ium concentration. It usually indicates a real deficit in total potassium stores; however, it may occur in patients with normal potassium stores when alkalosis is present, since alkalosis causes a temporary shift of serum potassium into the cells. (See pp. 76–7 for a discussion of alkalosis.)

Gastrointestinal loss of potassium is probably the most common cause of potassium depletion. Vomiting and gastric suction frequently lead to hypokalaemia, partly because of actual potassium loss in gastric fluid but largely because of increased renal potassium loss associated with metabolic alkalosis. Relatively large amounts of potassium are contained in intestinal fluids; for example, diarrhoeal fluid may contain as much as 30 mmol/l. Therefore, potassium deficit occurs frequently with diarrhoea, prolonged intestinal suction, recent ileostomy and villous adenoma (a tumour of the intestinal tract characterized by excretion of potassium-rich mucus).

Alterations in acid–base balance have a significant effect on potassium distribution. The mechanism involves shifts of hydrogen ions and potassium ions between the cells and extracellular fluid. Hypokalaemia can cause alkalosis, and alkalosis can cause hypokalaemia. For example, hydrogen ions move out of the cells in alkalotic states to help correct the high pH, and potassium ions move in to maintain electroneutrality. (See p. 75 for a discussion of acid–base balance).

Hyperaldosteronism increases renal potassium wasting and can lead to severe potassium depletion. Primary hyperaldosteronism is seen in patients with adrenal adenomas. Secondary hyperaldosteronism occurs in patients with cirrhosis, nephrotic syndrome, congestive heart failure and malignant hypertension. Potassium-losing diuretics, such as frusemide, the thiazides and ethacrynic acid, can induce hypokalaemia, particularly when given in large doses to patients with poor potassium intake. Other medications that can lead to hypokalaemia include steroids, sodium penicillin, carbenicillin and amphotericin.

Entry of potassium into skeletal muscle and hepatic cells is promoted by insulin. Thus, patients with persistent insulin hypersecretion may experience hypokalaemia; this is often seen in patients receiving high-carbohydrate parenteral fluids (as in total parenteral nutrition).

Patients unable or unwilling to eat a normal diet for a prolonged period may become hypokalaemic, e.g., debilitated elderly people, alcoholics and patients with anorexia nervosa. In addition to poor intake, people with bulaemia frequently suffer increased potassium loss through self-induced vomiting and laxative and diuretic abuse.

Clinical Features
Potassium deficiency can have widespread effects on physiological function. Most importantly, severe hypokalaemia can result in death through cardiac or respiratory arrest. Clinical signs rarely develop before the serum potassium level has fallen below 3 mmol/l unless the rate

of fall has been rapid. Features of hypokalaemia include fatigue, anorexia, nausea, vomiting, muscle weakness, decreased bowel motility, paraesthesias, arrhythmias and increased sensitivity to digitalis. If prolonged, hypokalaemia can lead to impaired renal concentrating ability, causing dilute urine, polyuria, nocturia and polydipsia.

Diagnosis

In hypokalaemia the serum potassium concentration is less than the lower limit of normal. Electrocardiographic changes can include flat T waves and ST segment depression (Figure 2.9). Hypokalaemia increases sensitivity to digitalis, predisposing to digitalis toxicity at lower digitalis levels. Metabolic alkalosis is frequently associated with hypokalaemia (see section on acid–base balance, pp. 75–8).

Management

The best treatment of hypokalaemia is prevention. Potassium loss must be corrected daily; administration of 40 to 60 mmol/l/day of potassium is adequate in the adult if there are no abnormal losses of potassium. For patients at risk, a diet containing sufficient potassium should be provided; dietary intake of potassium in the average adult is 50 to 100 mmol/l/day. Foods high in potassium include raisins, bananas, apricots, oranges, avocados, beans and potatoes. When dietary intake is inadequate for any reason, the doctor may prescribe potassium supplements. Many salt substitutes contain 50 to 60 mmol of potassium per teaspoon and that may be all the patient needs to supplement potassium intake.

When oral administration of potassium is not feasible, the intravenous route is indicated. Indeed, the intravenous route is mandatory for patients with severe hypokalaemia (such as a serum level of 2 mmol/l).

▶ **NURSING PROCESS**
▶ **THE PATIENT WITH POTASSIUM DEFICIT**

▶ *Assessment*

Because hypokalaemia can be life threatening, it is important to monitor for its early presence in patients at risk. Fatigue, anorexia, muscle weakness, decreased bowel motility, paraesthesias or arrhythmias may all be signs of serum potassium imbalance. When available, electrocardiograms may provide useful information. Patients receiving digitalis are at risk for potassium deficiency and should be monitored closely for signs of digitalis toxicity because hypokalaemia potentiates the action of digitalis. For this reason, some medical staff prefer to keep the serum potassium levels above 3.5 mmol/l in digitalized patients.

▶ *Patient's Problems*

The nursing assessment and identification of patients at

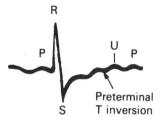

Figure 2.9 Electrocardiogram in hypokalaemia. Note increased height of U wave.

risk for hypokalaemia lead to identification of the patient's problems. For example, in a patient with diarrhoea, the diagnosis might be stated as follows: alteration in potassium imbalance (hypokalaemia) related to excessive potassium loss in diarrhoeal fluid. Once the aetiological factors have been identified, therapeutic measures are taken to deal with the imbalance.

▶ **Expected Outcomes**

The main expected outcome is the prevention of hypokalaemia. Once it has developed, the goal of nursing care is to help to correct the condition safely before serious derangements in cardiac or respiratory function occur.

Nursing Care

Prevention of Hypokalaemia

Measures are taken to prevent hypokalaemia when possible. Prevention may take the form of encouraging extra potassium intake for the patient at risk (when the diet allows). When hypokalaemia is due to abuse of laxatives or diuretics, patient education may help alleviate the problem. Part of the nursing history and assessment should be directed towards identifying problems amenable to prevention through education.

Safe Correction of Hypokalaemia

Great care should be exercised when administering potassium intravenously. It should be administered only after adequate urine flow has been established. A decrease in urine volume to less than 20 ml/hr for two consecutive hours is an indication to stop potassium infusion until the situation is evaluated. Potassium is excreted primarily by the kidneys; therefore, when oliguria is present, administration of potassium can cause the serum potassium concentration to rise to dangerous levels.

▶ *Evaluation*
▶ **Expected Outcomes**

1. Patient exhibits normal cardiac function with regular pulse rate, normal electrocardiogram and absence of arrhythmias.

2. Demonstrates normal muscle strength of upper and lower extremities.
3. Exhibits normal bowel sounds and gastrointestinal function.
4. Reports decreased level of fatigue.
5. Reports normal appetite without nausea or vomiting.
6. Consumes prescribed foods high in potassium and potassium supplements.
7. Excretes adequate urine volume.
8. Exhibits absence of precipitating risk factors (e.g., diarrhoea, vomiting, laxative and diuretic abuse).

Potassium Excess (Hyperkalaemia)

Definition and Aetiology

Hyperkalaemia refers to a greater than normal serum potassium concentration. It seldom occurs in patients with normal renal function. Like hypokalaemia, it is often due to iatrogenic (treatment-induced) causes. Although less common than hypokalaemia, it is usually more dangerous since cardiac arrest is more frequently associated with high serum potassium levels.

The major cause of hyperkalaemia is decreased renal excretion of potassium. Thus, significant hyperkalaemia is commonly seen in untreated patients with renal failure, particularly when potassium is being liberated from cells during infectious processes or exogenous sources of potassium are excessive, as in diet or medications. A deficiency of adrenal steroids causes sodium loss and potassium retention; thus, hypoaldosteronism and Addison's disease predispose to hyperkalaemia.

Although a high intake of potassium can cause severe hyperkalaemia in patients with impaired renal function, the disorder rarely occurs in people with normal renal function. However, for all patients, improper use of potassium supplements predisposes to hyperkalaemia, especially when salt substitutes are used. It should be remembered that not all patients receiving potassium-losing diuretics require potassium supplements. Certainly, those patients receiving potassium-conserving diuretics should not receive supplements. Potassium supplements are extremely dangerous when patients have impaired renal function and thus decreased ability to excrete potassium. Even more dangerous is the intravenous administration of potassium to such patients since serum levels can rise very quickly. Old blood should not be given to patients with impaired renal function because the serum concentration of stored blood increases as storage time increases, a result of red blood cell deterioration. It is possible to exceed the renal tolerance of any patient with rapid intravenous potassium administration, as well as when large amounts of oral potassium supplements are ingested.

In the presence of acidosis, potassium leaks out of the cells into the extracellular fluid. This occurs as hydrogen ions enter the cells, a process that buffers the pH of the extracellular fluid. (See pp. 75–8 for further discussion of acidosis.) An elevated extracellular potassium level should be anticipated when extensive tissue trauma has occurred, as in burns, crushing injuries, or severe infections. Similarly, it can occur with lysis of malignant cells after chemotherapy.

Clinical Features

By far the most clinically important effect of hyperkalaemia is its effect on the myocardium. Cardiac effects of an elevated serum potassium level are usually not significant below a concentration of 7 mmol/L, but they are almost always present when the level is 8 mmol/L or greater. As the plasma potassium concentration is increased, disturbances in cardiac conduction occur. The earliest changes, often occurring at a serum potassium level greater than 6 mmol/L, are peaked narrow T waves and a shortened QT interval. If the serum potassium level continues to rise, the PR interval becomes prolonged and is followed by disappearance of the P waves. Finally, there is decomposition and prolongation of the QRS complex (Figure 2.10). Ventricular arrhythmias and cardiac arrest may occur at any point in this progression.

Severe hyperkalaemia causes muscle weakness and even paralysis, related to a depolarization block in muscle. Similarly, ventricular conduction is slowed. Although hyperkalaemia has marked effects on the peripheral neuromuscular system, it has little effect on the central nervous system. Rapidly ascending muscular weakness leading to flaccid quadriplegia has been reported in patients with very high serum potassium levels. Paralysis of respiratory muscles and those required for phonation can also occur.

Gastrointestinal features, such as nausea, intermittent intestinal colic, and diarrhoea, usually occur in hyperkalaemic patients.

Diagnosis

Serum potassium levels and electrocardiographic changes are crucial to the diagnosis of hyperkalaemia. See the discussion of clinical features.

Management

In nonacute situations, restriction of dietary potassium

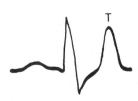

Figure 2.10 Electrocardiogram in hyperkalaemia, showing widening QRS complex, decreased amplitude of P wave and peaked T wave.

and potassium-containing medications may suffice. For example, eliminating the use of potassium-containing salt substitutes in the patient taking a potassium-conserving diuretic may be all that is needed to deal with mild hyperkalaemia. Prevention of serious hyperkalaemia by the administration of ion exchange resins (polystyrene sulphonate resins), e.g., calcium resonium and resonium A, may be necessary in renal patients.

Emergency Measures. In an emergency, it may be necessary to administer calcium gluconate intravenously. Within minutes after administration, calcium antagonizes the action of hyperkalaemia on the heart. The ECG should be monitored continuously during administration; the appearance of bradycardia is an indication to stop the infusion. The myocardial protective effects of calcium are transient, lasting about 30 minutes. Extra caution is required if the patient has been digitalized, because parenteral administration of calcium sensitizes the heart to digitalis and may precipitate digitalis toxicity.

Intravenous administration of sodium bicarbonate may be necessary to alkalinize the plasma and cause a temporary shift of potassium into the cells. Also, sodium bicarbonate furnishes sodium to antagonize the cardiac effects of potassium. Effects of this therapy begin within 30 to 60 minutes and may persist for hours, although they are only temporary.

Intravenous administration of regular insulin and hypertonic dextrose causes a temporary shift of potassium into the cells. Glucose and insulin therapy has an onset of action within 30 minutes and lasts for several hours.

The above measures only temporarily protect the patient from hyperkalaemia. If the hyperkalaemic condition is not transient, actual removal of potassium from the body is required; this may be accomplished by using ion exchange resins, peritoneal dialysis or haemodialysis.

► NURSING PROCESS
► THE PATIENT WITH POTASSIUM EXCESS

► *Assessment*

Patients at risk for potassium excess should be identified so that they can be monitored for signs of hyperkalaemia. The nurse observes for signs of muscular weakness and arrhythmias. The presence of paraesthesias is noted, as are gastrointestinal symptoms such as nausea and intestinal colic. For patients at risk, serum potassium levels are measured periodically.

► *Patient's Problems*

The nursing assessment is used to identify the patient at risk for this disturbance. For example, for a patient with oliguric renal failure, the problem might be stated as alteration in potassium balance (hyperkalaemia) related to decreased potassium excretion.

► *Planning and Implementation*
► **Expected Outcomes**

The main expected outcome in the care of patients at risk for hyperkalaemia is prevention of the disorder. If the imbalance cannot be prevented, it must be detected early so that therapeutic care can be undertaken to safely restore potassium balance and prevent life-threatening effects such as cardiac arrest.

Nursing Care

Prevention of Hyperkalaemia

Measures are taken to prevent hyperkalaemia in patients at risk, when possible, by encouraging the patient to adhere to the prescribed potassium restriction. Foods high in potassium to be avoided include coffee, cocoa, tea, dried fruits, dried beans and whole grain breads. Milk and eggs also contain substantial amounts of potassium. Conversely, foods with minimal potassium content include butter, margarine, cranberry juice or sauce, ginger ale, gumdrops or jellybeans, lollipops, sugar and honey.

Safe Restoration of Potassium Balance

As stated earlier, it is possible to exceed the tolerance for potassium in any person if the substance is administered rapidly by the intravenous route. Therefore, great care should be taken to monitor potassium solutions closely, paying careful attention to the solution's concentration and rate of administration.

It is important to caution patients to use salt substitutes sparingly if they are taking other supplementary forms of potassium or potassium-conserving diuretics. Also, potassium-conserving diuretics (such as spironolactone, triamterene and amiloride), potassium supplements, and salt substitutes should not be administered to patients with renal dysfunction.

► *Evaluation*
► **Expected Outcomes**

1. Patient exhibits normal cardiac function with normal pulse rate and no arrhythmias on ECG.
2. Excretes adequate urine volume.
3. Exhibits normal thoracic excursion and normal respiratory function.
4. Reports normal gastrointestinal function without diarrhoea or abdominal cramping.
5. Consumes foods low in potassium and avoids use of salt substitutes.
6. States rationale for low-potassium diet.
7. Exhibits normal serum potassium level.

8. Exhibits absence of precipitating risk factors (e.g., decreased renal function, excessive intake of potassium, extensive tissue trauma as in burns or crushing injuries).

Calcium Imbalances

Because many factors affect calcium regulation, both hypocalcaemia and hypercalcaemia are relatively common disturbances.

Functions of Calcium

Over 99 per cent of the body's calcium is concentrated in the skeletal system, where it is a major component of strong, durable bones and teeth. About 1 per cent of skeletal calcium is rapidly exchangeable with blood calcium; the rest is more stable and only slowly exchanged. The small amount of calcium located outside the bone circulates in the serum. Calcium helps to hold body cells together. It also exerts a sedative action on nerve cells and thus plays a major role in the transmission of nerve impulses. It helps to regulate muscle contraction and relaxation, including normal heartbeat. Calcium is instrumental in activating enzymes that stimulate many essential chemical reactions in the body and it also plays a role in blood coagulation.

The normal total serum calcium level is 2.2 to 2.6 mmol/l. About 50 per cent of the serum calcium exists in an ionized form that is physiologically active and important for neuromuscular activity. The remainder of serum calcium exists bound to serum proteins, primarily albumin.

Calcium Deficit (Hypocalcaemia)

Definition and Aetiology
Hypocalcaemia refers to a lower than normal serum concentration of calcium, which occurs in a variety of clinical situations. A patient, however, may have a total body calcium deficit (as in osteoporosis) and a normal serum calcium level.

A number of factors can cause hypocalcaemia, including primary hypoparathyroidism, surgical hypoparathyroidism, parathyroid operations and radical neck dissection, when it is most likely in the first 24 to 48 hours after surgery.

Inflammation of the pancreas causes release of proteolytic and lipolytic enzymes; it is thought that calcium ions combine with the fatty acids released by lipolysis, forming soaps. As a result of this process, hypocalcaemia is common in pancreatitis. It has also been suggested that hypocalcaemia may be related to excessive secretion of glucagon from the inflamed pancreas, resulting in increased secretion of calcitonin (a hormone that lowers serum calcium).

Hypocalcaemia is common in patients with renal failure because these patients frequently have elevated serum phosphate levels. Hyperphosphataemia usually causes a reciprocal drop in the serum calcium level. Other causes of hypocalcaemia can include inadequate vitamin D consumption, magnesium deficiency, medullary thyroid carcinoma, low serum albumin levels and alkalosis. Drugs predisposing to hypocalcaemia can include aluminium-containing antacids, aminoglycosides, caffeine, cisplatin, corticosteroids, mithramycin, phosphates, isoniazid and loop diuretics.

Osteoporosis, which affects many women, is associated with prolonged low intake of calcium and represents a total body calcium deficit, even though serum calcium levels are usually normal. It is characterized by loss of bone mass, causing bones to become porous and brittle and, therefore, susceptible to fracture. (See Chapter 37.)

Clinical Features
Tetany is the most characteristic feature of hypocalcaemia. Tetany refers to the complex of symptoms induced by increased neural excitability. These symptoms are due to spontaneous discharges of both sensory and motor fibres in peripheral nerves. Sensations of tingling may occur in the tips of the fingers, around the mouth and, less commonly, in the feet. Spasms of the muscles of the extremities and face may occur. Pain may develop as a result of these spasms.

Trousseau's sign (Figure 2.11) can be elicited by inflating a blood pressure cuff on the upper arm to about 20 mmHg above systolic pressure; within two to five minutes carpal spasm will occur as ischaemia of the ulnar

Figure 2.11 Trousseau's sign. Carpopedal spasm with hypocalcaemia. (Ezrin, C., Godden, J. O., Volpe, R. and Wilson, R. (1979) *Systematic Endocrinology* (2nd edition), Harper & Row, Hagerstown, Maryland, p. 1510.)

nerve develops. Chvostek's sign consists of twitching of muscles supplied by the facial nerve when the nerve is tapped about 2 cm anterior to the earlobe, just below the zygomatic arch.

Seizures may result because hypocalcaemia increases irritability of the central nervous system as well as of the peripheral nerves. Other changes associated with hypocalcaemia include an increased QT interval and mental changes such as emotional depression, impairment of memory, confusion, delirium and even hallucinations. Chronic hypocalcaemia in children can retard growth and lower the IQ.

Diagnosis

When evaluating serum calcium levels, the medical staff must also consider several other variables, such as serum protein levels and arterial pH. Clinically, it is important to correlate the serum calcium concentration with the serum albumin level. As the serum albumin level falls or rises, so too does the calcium concentration fall or rise. Because of this, the medical staff may ignore a low serum calcium level in the presence of a similarly low serum albumin level. The ionized calcium level is usually normal in patients with reduced total serum calcium levels and concomitant hypoalbuminaemia.

When the arterial pH increases (alkalosis), more calcium becomes bound to protein. As a result, the ionized portion decreases. Symptoms of hypocalcaemia often occur in the presence of alkalosis. Acidosis (low pH) has the opposite effect, that is, less calcium is bound to protein and thus more exists in the ionized form. Rarely will signs of hypocalcaemia develop in the presence of acidosis, even when the total serum calcium level is lower than normal.

In the absence of a routine test for measuring the ionised serum calcium, the total serum calcium is usually measured and 'corrected' to take into account serum albumin concentration. This 'corrected calcium' level correlates well with the ionised calcium measurement.

Management

Acute symptomatic hypocalcaemia is a medical emergency, requiring prompt intravenous administration of calcium, mainly in the form of calcium gluconate. Too rapid intravenous administration of calcium can induce cardiac arrest, preceded by bradycardia. Intravenous calcium administration is particularly dangerous in digitalized patients because calcium ions exert an effect similar to that of digitalis and can cause digitalis toxicity with adverse cardiac effects.

Nursing Care

It is important to observe for hypocalcaemia in patients at risk and to be aware of the dangers of seizures when hypocalcaemia is severe. The condition of the airway is closely monitored because laryngeal stridor can occur. Safety precautions are taken, as indicated, if confusion is present. People at high risk for osteoporosis are instructed about the need for adequate dietary calcium intake; if not consumed in the diet, calcium supplements should be considered. Also, the value of regular exercise in decreasing bone loss should be emphasized.

Calcium Excess (Hypercalcaemia)

Definition and Aetiology

Hypercalcaemia refers to an excess of calcium in the plasma. It is a dangerous imbalance when severe; in fact, hypercalcaemic crisis can have a mortality as high as 50 per cent if it is not treated promptly.

The most common causes of hypercalcaemia are malignant neoplastic diseases, e.g., multiple myeloma, and hyperparathyroidism. Malignant tumours can produce hypercalcaemia by a variety of mechanisms. The excessive parathyroid hormone secretion associated with hyperparathyroidism causes increased bony release of calcium and increased intestinal and renal absorption of calcium.

Bone mineral is lost during immobilization, sometimes causing elevation of total (and especially ionized) calcium in the bloodstream. Symptomatic hypercalcaemia from immobilization, however, is rare; when it does occur it is virtually limited to people with high calcium turnover rates (such as adolescents during a growth spurt). Most cases of hypercalcaemia secondary to immobility occur after severe or multiple fractures or after extensive traumatic paralysis.

Thiazide diuretics may cause a slight elevation in serum calcium levels because they potentiate the action of parathyroid hormone on the kidneys, reducing urinary calcium excretion. The milk-alkali syndrome can occur in patients with peptic ulcer treated for a prolonged period with milk and alkaline antacids, particularly calcium carbonate.

Clinical Features

As a rule, the symptoms of hypercalcaemia are proportional to the degree of elevation of the serum calcium level. Hypercalcaemia reduces neuromuscular excitability since it acts as a sedative at the myoneural junction. Symptoms such as muscular weakness, inco-ordination, anorexia and constipation may be due to decreased tone in smooth and striated muscle.

Anorexia, nausea, vomiting and constipation are common symptoms of hypercalcaemia. Abdominal pain may also be present and at times may be so severe as to be mistaken for an acute abdominal emergency. Abdominal distension and ileus may complicate severe hypercalcaemic crisis. Severe thirst may occur, secondary to the polyuria caused by the high solute (calcium) load. Patients with chronic hypercalcaemia may develop symptoms similar to those of peptic ulcer since hypercalcaemia increases the secretion of acid and pepsin by the stomach.

Mental confusion, impairment of memory, slurred speech, lethargy, acute psychotic behaviour or coma may occur. The more severe symptoms tend to appear when the serum calcium level is approximately 4 mmol/l or above. However, some patients may become profoundly disturbed with serum calcium levels of only 3 mmol/l.

Polyuria due to disturbed renal tubular function produced by hypercalcaemia may be present. Cardiac standstill can occur when the serum calcium is about 4.5 mmol/l. The inotropic effect of digitalis is enhanced by calcium; therefore, digitalis toxicity is aggravated by hypercalcaemia.

Hypercalcaemic crisis refers to an acute rise in the serum calcium level to 4.25 mmol/l or higher. Severe thirst and polyuria are characteristically present. Other findings may include muscular weakness, intractable nausea, abdominal cramps, obstipation (very severe constipation) or diarrhoea, peptic ulcer symptoms and bone pain. Lethargy, mental confusion and coma may also occur. This condition is very dangerous and may result in cardiac arrest.

Diagnosis

The serum calcium level is greater than 2.6 mmol/l. Cardiovascular changes may include a variety of arrhythmias and shortening of the QT interval.

Management

Therapeutic aims in hypercalcaemia include decreasing the serum calcium level and reversing the process causing hypercalcaemia. General measures include administering fluids to dilute serum calcium and promote its renal excretion, mobilizing the patient and dietary calcium restriction. Administration of 0.45 per cent sodium chloride or 0.9 per cent sodium chloride solutions intravenously dilutes the serum calcium level and increases urinary calcium excretion by inhibiting tubular reabsorption of calcium. Frusemide is often used in conjunction with saline administration; in addition to causing diuresis, frusemide increases calcium excretion. Calcitonin can be used to lower the serum calcium level and is particularly useful for patients with heart disease or renal failure who cannot tolerate large sodium loads.

For patients with malignant disease, treatment is directed at controlling the condition by surgery, chemotherapy or radiotherapy. Corticosteroids may be used to decrease bone turnover and tubular reabsorption for patients with sarcoidosis, myelomas, lymphomas and leukaemias; patients with solid tumours are less responsive. Mithramycin, a cytotoxic antibiotic, inhibits bone resorption and thus lowers the serum calcium levels. This drug must be used cautiously because it has significant side-effects, including thrombocytopenia, nephrotoxicity and hepatotoxicity. Inorganic phosphate salts can be given

orally or by nasogastric tube (in the form of sodium cellulose phosphate) or intravenously. Intravenous phosphate therapy is used with extreme caution in the treatment of hypercalcaemia since it can cause severe calcification in various tissues, including the vein through which it is given.

Nursing Care

It is important to monitor for the occurrence of hypercalcaemia in patients at risk for this disorder. Initiation of care, such as increasing patient mobility and encouraging fluids, can help prevent hypercalcaemia, or at least minimize its severity. Hospitalized patients at risk for hypercalcaemia should be allowed to mobilize as soon as possible, and outpatients should be told the importance of frequent mobilization. Sodium-containing fluids should be given, unless contraindicated by other conditions, because sodium favours calcium excretion. Patients are encouraged to drink three to four litres of fluid daily, if possible. Adequate bulk should be provided in the diet to offset the tendency for constipation. Safety precautions are taken, as necessary, when mental symptoms of hypercalcaemia are present. The patient and home carers are informed that these mental changes are reversible with treatment.

Magnesium Imbalances

Functions of Magnesium

Next to potassium, magnesium is the most abundant intracellular cation. It acts as an activator for many intracellular enzyme systems and plays a role in both carbohydrate and protein metabolism. Magnesium balance is important in neuromuscular function. Because magnesium acts directly on the myoneural junction, variations in its serum concentration affect neuromuscular irritability and contractility. For example, an excess of magnesium diminishes excitability of the muscle cells while a deficit increases neuromuscular irritability and contractility. Magnesium produces its sedative effect at the neuromuscular junction, probably by inhibiting the release of the neurotransmitter acetylcholine. It also increases the stimulus threshold in nerve fibres.

Magnesium exerts effects on the cardiovascular system, acting peripherally to produce vasodilatation. Magnesium is thought to have a direct effect on peripheral arteries and arterioles, which results in a decreased total peripheral resistance.

Magnesium Deficit (Hypomagnesaemia)

Definition and Aetiology

Hypomagnesaemia refers to a below normal serum magnesium concentration. The normal serum magnesium level is 0.75 to 1.25 mmol/l. Approximately one third of serum magnesium is bound to protein; the remaining two thirds exists as free cations (Mg^2pl). Like calcium, it is the ionized fraction that is involved primarily in neuromuscular activity and other physiological processes.

Hypomagnesaemia is a common imbalance in critically ill patients, yet it is frequently overlooked. Magnesium deficit also occurs in less acutely ill patients, such as those experiencing withdrawal from alcohol and those receiving nourishment after a period of starvation, as in tube feeds or total parenteral nutrition.

An important route for magnesium loss is the gastrointestinal tract. Losses may take the form of drainage from nasogastric suction, diarrhoea or fistulae. Since fluid from the lower gastrointestinal tract is richer in magnesium (5 to 7 mmol/l) than is fluid from the upper tract (0.5 to 1 mmol/l), losses from diarrhoea and intestinal fistulae are more likely to induce magnesium deficit than are those from gastric suction. Although magnesium losses are relatively small in nasogastric suction, hypomagnesaemia will occur if losses are prolonged and parenteral fluids are magnesium free. Because the distal small bowel is the major site of magnesium absorption, any disruption in small bowel function, as in intestinal resection or inflammatory bowel disease, can lead to hypomagnesaemia.

Alcoholism is a common cause of symptomatic hypomagnesaemia in the United Kingdom. It is particularly troublesome during treatment of alcohol withdrawal. Because of this, it is recommended that the serum magnesium level be measured every two or three days in hospitalized patients going through withdrawal from alcohol. While the serum magnesium level may be normal on admission, it can fall as a result of metabolic changes associated with therapy, such as the intracellular shift of magnesium associated with intravenous glucose administration.

During nutritional repletion, the major cellular electrolytes are taken from the serum and deposited in newly synthesized cells. Thus, if the enteral or parenteral feed formula is deficient in magnesium content, serious hypomagnesaemia will occur. Because of this, serum levels of these primarily intracellular ions should be measured at regular intervals during the administration of total parenteral nutrition and even during enteral feeds, especially to patients who have undergone a period of starvation.

Other causes of hypomagnesaemia include the administration of gentamicin and cisplatin and the rapid administration of citrated blood, especially to patients with renal or hepatic disease. Magnesium deficiency is often seen in patients with diabetic ketoacidosis; it is primarily the result of increased renal excretion of magnesium during osmotic diuresis and shifting of magnesium into the cells with insulin therapy.

Clinical Features
Clinical features of hypomagnesaemia are largely con-

fined to the neuromuscular system. Some of the effects are due directly to the low serum magnesium level; others are due to secondary changes in potassium and calcium metabolism. Symptoms do not usually occur until the serum magnesium level is less than 0.5 mmol/l).

Among the neuromuscular changes are hyperexcitability with muscular weakness, tremors and athetoid movements (slow, involuntary twisting and writhing movements). Others include tetany, generalized tonic-clonic or focal seizures, laryngeal stridor and positive Chvostek's and Trousseau's signs (see discussion on p. 68).

Magnesium deficiency predisposes to cardiac arrhythmias, such as premature ventricular contractions, supraventricular tachycardia and ventricular fibrillation. Increased susceptibility to digitalis toxicity is associated with low serum magnesium levels. This is an important consideration because patients receiving digoxin are also likely to be on diuretic therapy, predisposing to renal loss of magnesium.

Hypomagnesaemia may be accompanied by marked alterations in mood. Apathy, depression, apprehension or extreme agitation have been noted, as well as ataxia, vertigo and a confusional state. At times, delirium and frank psychoses may occur, as may auditory or visual hallucinations.

Diagnosis
On laboratory analysis, the serum magnesium level is less than 0.75 mmol/l.

Management
Mild magnesium deficiency can be corrected by diet alone. Principal dietary sources of magnesium are green vegetables, nuts and legumes, and fruits such as bananas, grapefruits and oranges. Magnesium is also plentiful in peanut butter and chocolate. When necessary, magnesium salts can be given orally to replace continuous excessive losses. Patients receiving total parenteral nutrition require magnesium in the solution to prevent the development of hypomagnesaemia.

Overt symptoms of hypomagnesaemia are treated with parenteral administration of magnesium. Magnesium sulphate is the most commonly used magnesium salt. Serial magnesium concentrations can be used to regulate the dosage.

Nursing Care
The nurse should be aware of patients at risk for hypomagnesaemia and observe for its presence. Patients on digitalis are monitored closely because a deficit of magnesium predisposes to digitalis toxicity. When hypomagnesaemia is severe, there is a danger of seizures and precautions are required. Other safety precautions are instituted if there is confusion.

Because difficulty in swallowing may occur in magnesium-depleted patients, the ability to swallow should be tested with water before oral medications or foods are offered. Dysphagia is probably related to the athetoid or choreiform (rapid, involuntary and irregular jerky) movements associated with magnesium deficit.

When magnesium deficit is due to abuse of diuretics or laxatives, patient education may help to alleviate the problem. For patients on a general diet who are experiencing abnormal magnesium losses, the intake of magnesium-rich foods (e.g., green vegetables, nuts and legumes, bananas and oranges) should be encouraged.

Magnesium Excess (Hypermagnesaemia)

Definition and Aetiology
Hypermagnesaemia refers to a greater than normal serum concentration of magnesium. The most common cause of hypermagnesaemia is renal failure. In fact, most patients with advanced renal failure have at least a modest elevation in serum magnesium levels. This condition is aggravated when such patients are given magnesium to control convulsions or inadvertently receive one of the many commercial antacids that contain magnesium salts. Patients with renal failure may also receive an exogenous magnesium load during haemodialysis, either because of inadvertent use of hard water or an error in manufacture of the concentrate used for preparing the dialysate.

Hypermagnesaemia can occur in a patient with untreated diabetic ketoacidosis when catabolism causes release of cellular magnesium that cannot be excreted because of profound fluid volume depletion and resulting oliguria.

Clinical Features
Acute elevation of the serum magnesium level depresses the central nervous system as well as the peripheral neuromuscular junction. At mildly elevated levels, there is a tendency for lowered blood pressure because of peripheral vasodilatation. Facial flushing and hypotension may occur, as well as sensations of warmth. At higher elevations, lethargy, dysarthria and drowsiness can appear. Deep tendon reflexes are lost, and muscular weakness and paralysis may supervene. The respiratory centre is depressed when serum magnesium levels exceed 5 mmol/l. Coma and cardiac arrest can occur when the serum magnesium level is greatly elevated.

Diagnosis
On laboratory analysis, the serum magnesium level is greater than 1.25 mmol/l.

Management
The best treatment for hypermagnesaemia is prevention. This can be accomplished by avoiding magnesium administration to patients with renal failure and by careful vigilance when magnesium salts are administered to seriously ill patients. In the presence of severe hypermagnesaemia, all parenteral and oral magnesium salts are discontinued. When respiratory depression or defective cardiac conduction is present, emergency measures such as ventilatory support and intravenous administration of calcium are indicated. Haemodialysis with a magnesium-free dialysate is an effective treatment that should produce a safe serum magnesium level within hours.

Nursing Care
Patients at risk for hypermagnesaemia are identified and assessed. When hypermagnesaemia is suspected, the nurse should monitor the vital signs, noting the presence of hypotension and shallow respirations, and check for decreased patellar reflexes and changes in the level of consciousness. Care should be taken to avoid giving magnesium-containing medications to patients with renal failure or compromised renal function. Similarly, one should caution patients with renal failure to check with their health care providers before taking over-the-counter medications. Care should also be used when magnesium fluids are administered parenterally.

Phosphorus Imbalances

Functions of Phosphorus

Phosphorus is a critical constituent of all the body's tissues. It is essential to the function of muscle, red blood cells and the nervous system, and to the intermediary metabolism of carbohydrate, protein and fat. The normal serum phosphorus level ranges between 0.8 to 1.5 mmol/l and may be as high as 1.94 mmol/l in infants and children. Serum phosphorus levels are presumably greater in children because of the high rate of skeletal growth.

Phosphorus Deficit (Hypophosphataemia)

Definition and Aetiology
Hypophosphataemia is defined as a below-normal serum concentration of inorganic phosphorus. Although it often indicates phosphorus deficiency, it may occur under a variety of circumstances in which total body phosphorus stores are normal. Conversely, phosphorus deficiency refers to an abnormally low content of phosphorus in lean tissues and may exist in the absence of hypophosphataemia. Hypophosphataemia may occur during the treatment of patients with severe protein-calorie malnutrition with simple carbohydrates (such as patients with anorexia nervosa, alcoholism or elderly, debilitated patients who are unable to eat).

Marked hypophosphataemia may develop in malnourished patients receiving total parenteral nutrition if correction of phosphorus loss is inadequate. Other causes of hypophosphataemia include prolonged intense hyperventilation, alcohol withdrawal, poor dietary intake, diabetic ketoacidosis and major thermal burns.

Clinical Features

Most of the signs and symptoms of phosphorus deficiency appear to result from deficiency of adenosine triphosphate, of 2,3-diphosphoglycerate or of both. The former impairs cellular energy resources and the latter impairs oxygen delivery to tissues.

A wide range of neurological symptoms may occur, such as irritability, apprehension, weakness, numbness, paraesthesias, confusion, seizures and coma. Low levels of 2,3-diphosphoglycerate may reduce the delivery of oxygen to peripheral tissues, resulting in tissue anoxia.

It is thought that hypophosphataemia predisposes to infection. In laboratory animals, hypophosphataemia has been noted to produce depression of the chemotactic, phagocytic and bacterial activity of granulocytes.

Muscle damage may develop as the adenosine triphosphate level in the muscle tissue declines. This is manifested clinically by muscle weakness, muscle pain and, at times, acute rhabdomyolysis (disintegration of striated muscle). Weakness of respiratory muscles may greatly impair ventilation. Also, hypophosphataemia may predispose to an insulin-resistant state, and thus hyperglycaemia.

Diagnosis

On laboratory analysis, the serum phosphorus level will be less than 0.80 mmol/l in adults. It is important to remember that glucose administration causes a slight decrease in the serum phosphorus level.

Management

As in any electrolyte imbalance, the best treatment is prevention. In patients at risk for hypophosphataemia, serum phosphate levels should be closely monitored and correction initiated before deficits become severe. Adequate amounts of phosphorus should be added to total parenteral nutrition solutions, and attention should also be paid to phosphorus levels in enteral feed solutions.

Severe hypophosphataemia is dangerous and requires prompt attention. Aggressive intravenous phosphorus repair is usually limited to patients with serum phosphorus levels below 0.3 mmol/l. Possible dangers of intravenous administration of phosphorus include hypocalcaemia and metastatic calcification from hyperphosphataemia. In less acute situations, oral phosphorus replacement is satisfactory.

Nursing Care

The nurse should identify patients at risk for hypophosphataemia and monitor for its presence. Since malnourished patients receiving total parenteral nutrition are at risk when calories are introduced too rapidly, prevention can take the form of gradual introduction of the feed solution to avoid rapid shifts of phosphorus into the cells.

For patients with documented hypophosphataemia, careful attention should be paid to preventing infection because hypophosphataemia may produce changes in the granulocytes. For patients requiring correction of phosphorus losses, frequent monitoring of the serum phosphorus levels is indicated to augment clinical assessment.

Phosphorus Excess (Hyperphosphataemia)

Definition and Aetiology

Hyperphosphataemia refers to a serum phosphorus level greater than normal. A variety of conditions can lead to this imbalance.

The most common cause of hyperphosphataemia is decreased renal phosphorus excretion in renal failure. Other causes include chemotherapy for neoplastic disease, high phosphate intake, profound muscle necrosis and increased phosphorus absorption.

Clinical Features

An elevated serum phosphorus level causes little in the way of symptoms. The most important long-term consequence is soft tissue calcification, which occurs mainly in patients with reduced glomerular filtration rates; the most important short-term consequence is tetany. High levels of serum inorganic phosphorus are harmful because they promote precipitation of calcium phosphate in non-osseous sites. Because of the reciprocal relationship between phosphorus and calcium, a high serum phosphorus level tends to cause a low calcium concentration in the serum. Tetany can result and can present as sensations of tingling in the tips of the fingers and around the mouth.

Diagnosis

On laboratory analysis, the serum phosphorus level is greater than 1.5 mmol/l in adults. Serum phosphorus levels are normally higher in children, presumably because of the high rate of skeletal growth.

Management

When possible, treatment is directed at the underlying disorder. For example, hyperphosphataemia related to tumour cell lysis may be lessened by prior administration of allopurinol to prevent urate nephropathy. For patients with renal failure, measures to decrease the serum phosphate level are indicated; these include the administration of phosphate-binding gels, dietary phosphate restriction and dialysis.

Table 2.24 *Summary of major fluid and electrolyte imbalances*

Imbalance	Causes	Clinical signs and symptoms
Fluid volume deficit	Loss of water and electrolytes, as in vomiting, diarrhoea, fistulae, gastrointestinal suction and third-space fluid shifts; and decreased intake, as in anorexia, nausea and inability to gain access to fluid	Acute weight loss, decreased skin and tongue turgor, oliguria, concentrated urine, weak rapid pulse and low central venous pressure
Fluid volume excess	Compromised regulatory mechanisms, such as renal failure, congestive heart failure and cirrhosis; and overzealous administration of sodium-containing fluids	Acute weight gain, oedema distended veins, crackles and elevated central venous pressure
Sodium deficit (hyponatraemia)	Loss of sodium, as in use of diuretics, loss of gastrointestinal fluids and adrenal insufficiency; gain of water, as in excessive administration of 5% dextrose in water and excessive water supplements for patients receiving hypotonic tube feedings; and pharmacological agents associated with water retention such as oxytocin and certain tranquillizers	Anorexia, nausea and vomiting, lethargy, confusion, muscle cramps, muscular twitching, seizures, papilloedema, serum sodium < 145 mmol/l
Sodium excess (hypernatraemia)	Water deprivation in patients unable to drink at will, hypertonic tube feeds without adequate water supplements, diabetes insipidus, heatstroke, hyperventilation and watery diarrhoea	Thirst, elevated body temperature, swollen dry tongue and sticky mucous membranes, hallucinations, lethargy, irritability, focal or grand mal seizures, serum sodium > 145 mmol/l
Potassium deficit (hypokalaemia)	Diarrhoea, vomiting, gastric suction, steroid administration, hyperaldosteronism, carbenicillin, amphotericin, bulimia and osmotic diuresis	Fatigue, anorexia, nausea and vomiting, muscle weakness, decreased bowel motility, arrhythmias, paraesthesias, serum potassium < 3.5 mmol/l and flat T waves on ECG
Potassium excess (hyperkalaemia)	Oliguric renal failure, use of potassium-conserving diuretics in patients with renal insufficiency, acidosis	Vague muscular weakness, bradycardia, arrhythmias, flaccid paralysis, paraesthesias, intestinal colic, tall tented T waves on ECG, serum potassium > 5.8 mmol/l
Calcium deficit (hypocalcaemia)	Hypoparathyroidism, surgical hypoparathyroidism (may follow thyroid surgery or radical neck dissection), malabsorption, pancreatitis and alkalosis	Numbness, tingling of fingers, toes and circumoral region; Trousseau's sign; Chvostek's sign; convulsions; and serum calcium < 2.2 mmol/l or ionised calcium < 50 per cent
Calcium excess (hypercalcaemia)	Hyperparathyroidism, malignant neoplastic disease, prolonged immobilization, and overuse of calcium supplements	Muscular weakness, constipation, anorexia, nausea and vomiting, polyuria and polydipsia, neurotic behaviour, cardiac arrhythmias and serum calcium > 2.6 mmol/l

Table 2.24 *Continued*

Imbalance	Causes	Clinical signs and symptoms
Magnesium deficit (hypomagnesaemia)	Chronic alcoholism, malabsorptive disorders, diabetic ketoacidosis, refeeding after starvation and certain pharmacological agents (such as gentamicin and cisplatin)	Neuromuscular irritability, arrhythmias, disorientation, serum magnesaemia > 0.75 mmol/l
Magnesium excess (hypermagnesaemia)	Renal failure (particularly when magnesium-containing medications are administered), adrenal insufficiency, excessive magnesium administration	Flushing, hypotension, drowsiness, hypoactive reflexes, depressed respirations, cardiac arrest, coma and serum Mg > 1.25 mmol/l
Phosphorus deficit (hypophosphataemia)	Refeeding after starvation, alcohol withdrawal, diabetic ketoacidosis, respiratory alkalosis	Paraesthesias, muscle weakness, muscle pain and tenderness, mental changes, cardiomyopathy, respiratory failure
Phosphorus excess (hyperphosphataemia)	Renal failure, excessive intake of phosphorus (as in phosphorus supplements and phosphate-containing laxatives)	Short-term consequences (symptoms of tetany, such as tingling of fingertips and around mouth); long-term consequences (precipitation of calcium phosphate in non-osseous sites)

Nursing Care

The nurse should be aware of patients at risk for hyperphosphataemia and monitor for its presence. When a low-phosphorus diet is prescribed, the patient should be instructed to avoid foods high in phosphorus content. Such foods include hard cheese; cream; nuts; whole grain cereals; dried fruits; dried vegetables; special meats, such as kidneys, sardines and sweetbreads; and desserts made with milk. When appropriate, the nurse instructs the patient to avoid phosphate-containing substances, such as phosphate-containing laxatives and enemas.

Summary of Fluid and Electrolyte Imbalances

Major fluid and electrolyte imbalances are summarized in Table 2.24.

Acid–Base Disturbances

Regulation of Acid–Base Balance

There are four types of acid–base imbalance: metabolic acidosis and alkalosis and respiratory acidosis and alkalosis.

A number of homeostatic mechanisms exist to maintain plasma pH within the narrow normal range of 7.35 to 7.45. These consist of chemical buffering mechanisms, the kidneys, and the lungs. The pH is defined as H^+ concentration; the more hydrogen ions, the more acidic is the solution. The pH range compatible with life (6.8 to 7.8) represents a tenfold difference in hydrogen ion concentration in plasma.

Chemical Buffers

Chemical buffers are substances that prevent major changes in the pH of body fluids by removing or releasing hydrogen ions; they can act quickly to prevent excessive changes in hydrogen ion concentration. The body's major buffer system is the bicarbonate–carbonic acid (HCO_3^-–H_2CO_3) buffer system. Normally, there are 20 parts of bicarbonate to one part of carbonic acid. If this ratio is altered, the pH will change. It is the ratio that is important in maintaining pH, not the absolute values. It must be remembered that carbon dioxide (CO_2) is a potential acid; when CO_2 is dissolved in water, it becomes carbonic acid ($CO_2 + H_2O = H_2CO_3$). Thus, when carbon dioxide is increased, the carbonic acid content is also increased and vice versa. If either bicarbonate or carbonic acid is increased or decreased so that the 20:1 ratio is no longer maintained, acid–base imbalance results.

Other less important buffer systems in the extracellular fluid include the inorganic phosphates and the plasma proteins. Intracellular buffers include proteins, organic and inorganic phosphates and, in red blood cells, haemoglobin.

Kidneys

The kidneys regulate the bicarbonate level in extracellular fluid; they are able to regenerate bicarbonate ions as well as reabsorb them from the renal tubular cells. In the presence of respiratory acidosis, and most cases of metabolic acidosis, the kidneys excrete hydrogen ions and conserve bicarbonate ions to help to restore balance. In the presence of respiratory and metabolic alkalosis, the kidneys retain hydrogen ions and excrete bicarbonate ions to help to restore balance. The kidneys obviously cannot compensate for the metabolic acidosis created by renal failure. Renal compensation for imbalances is relatively slow (a matter of hours or days).

Lungs
The lungs, under the control of the medulla, control the carbon dioxide, and thus carbonic acid content of extracellular fluid. They do so by adjusting ventilation in response to the amount of carbon dioxide in the blood. A rise in the partial pressure of carbon dioxide in arterial blood ($PaCO_2$) is a powerful stimulant to respiration. Of course, the partial pressure of oxygen in arterial blood (PaO_2) also influences respiration. However, normally, its effect is not as marked as that produced by the $PaCO_2$. (By contrast, in chronic obstructive airways disease, the $PaCO_2$ is the main stimulus.)

In the presence of metabolic acidosis, the respiratory rate is increased, causing greater elimination of carbon dioxide (to reduce the acid load). In the presence of metabolic alkalosis, the respiratory rate is decreased, causing carbon dioxide to be retained (to increase the acid load).

Metabolic Acidosis (Base Bicarbonate Deficit)

Definition and Aetiology
Metabolic acidosis is a clinical disturbance characterized by a low pH (increased hydrogen concentration) and a low plasma bicarbonate concentration. It can be produced by a gain of hydrogen ion or a loss of bicarbonate. It can be divided clinically into two forms according to the values of the serum anion gap (AG): high anion gap acidosis and normal anion gap acidosis. Anion gap refers to the difference of anions (negatively charged electrolytes) and cations (electrolytes with a positive charge). The anion gap can be calculated by subtracting the sum of the serum chloride and bicarbonate concentrations (anions, or negatively charged electrolytes) from the serum sodium level (a cation, or positively charged electrolyte): $AG = Na^+ - (Cl^- + HCO_3^-)$. There are some unmeasured anions in the serum, such as sulphates, ketones and lactic acid, that normally account for less than 16 mmol/l of the anion production. An anion gap greater than 16 mmol/l suggests excessive accumulation of unmeasured anions.

High anion gap acidosis results from excessive accumulation of fixed acid. It occurs in ketoacidosis, lactic acidosis, late phase of salicylate poisoning, uraemia, methanol or ethylene glycol toxicity and ketoacidosis with starvation. In all of these instances, abnormally high levels of anions flood the system, increasing the anion gap above normal limits.

Normal anion gap acidosis results from direct loss of bicarbonate, as in diarrhoea and intestinal fistulae or from excessive gain of chloride, as in the administration of large quantities of isotonic saline or ammonium chloride.

Clinical Features
Signs and symptoms of metabolic acidosis vary with the severity of metabolic acidosis. They may include headache, confusion, drowsiness, increased respiratory rate and depth, nausea and vomiting. Peripheral vasodilatation and decreased cardiac output occur when the pH falls below 7.

Diagnosis
Arterial blood gas measurements are valuable in the diagnosis of metabolic acidosis. Expected changes include a low bicarbonate level (less than 22 mmol/l) and a low pH (less than 7.35). Hyperkalaemia may accompany metabolic acidosis, as a result of shift of potassium out of the cells. Hyperventilation decreases the carbon dioxide level as a compensatory action. Calculation of the anion gap is helpful in determining the cause of metabolic acidosis.

Management
Treatment is directed at correcting the metabolic defect. If the cause of the problem is excessive intake of chloride, treatment is elimination of the source of the chloride. When necessary, bicarbonate is administered.

Metabolic Alkalosis (Base Bicarbonate Excess)

Definition and Aetiology
Metabolic alkalosis is a clinical disturbance characterized by a high pH (decreased hydrogen ion concentration) and a high plasma bicarbonate concentration. It can be produced by a gain of bicarbonate or a loss of hydrogen ions.

Probably the most common cause of metabolic alkalosis is vomiting or gastric suction, leading to loss of hydrogen and chloride ions; this is a particular problem in pyloric stenosis because only gastric fluid is lost in this disorder. Gastric fluid has an acid pH (usually 1 to 3); therefore, loss of this highly acidic fluid increases alkalinity of body fluids. Other situations predisposing to metabolic alkalosis include those associated with loss of potassium, such as taking potassium-losing diuretics (e.g., thiazides, frusemide and ethacrynic acid) and excessive adrenalcorticoid hormones (as in hyperaldosteronism and Cushing's syndrome). Hypokalaemia produces alkalosis in two ways: (1) the kidneys conserve potassium and thus hydrogen ion excretion is increased; and (2) cellular potassium moves out of the cells into the extracellular fluid in an attempt to maintain near-normal serum levels (as potassium ions (K^+) leave the cells, hydrogen ions must enter to maintain electroneutrality). Excessive alkali ingestion, as of bicarbonate-containing antacids or sodium bicarbonate during cardiopulmonary resuscitation, can also cause metabolic alkalosis.

Clinical Features

Alkalosis is manifested primarily by symptoms related to decreased calcium ionization, such as tingling of the fingers and toes, dizziness and hypertonic muscles. The ionized fraction of serum calcium decreases in the presence of alkalosis as more calcium combines with serum proteins. Because it is the ionized fraction of calcium that influences neuromuscular activity, it is understandable that symptoms of hypocalcaemia are often the predominant symptoms of alkalosis. Respirations are depressed as a compensatory action by the lungs.

Diagnosis

Evaluation of arterial blood gases reveals a pH greater than 7.45 and a serum bicarbonate concentration greater than 32 mmol/l. The partial pressure of carbon dioxide will increase as the lungs attempt to compensate for the excess bicarbonate by retaining carbon dioxide. This hypoventilation is more pronounced in semiconscious, unconscious or debilitated patients than in alert patients. The former may develop marked hypoxaemia as a result of hypoventilation. Hypokalaemia may accompany metabolic alkalosis.

Management

Treatment is aimed at reversal of the underlying disorder. Sufficient chloride must be supplied for the kidney to absorb sodium with chloride (allowing the excretion of excess bicarbonate). Treatment also includes restoration of normal fluid volume by administration of sodium chloride fluids (because continued volume depletion serves to maintain the alkalosis).

Respiratory Acidosis (Carbonic Acid Excess)

Definition and Aetiology

Respiratory acidosis is a clinical disorder in which the pH is less than 7.35 and the $PaCO_2$ is greater than 42 mmHg. It may be either acute or chronic.

Respiratory acidosis is always due to inadequate excretion of carbon dioxide with inadequate ventilation, resulting in elevated plasma carbon dioxide levels and thus elevated carbonic acid levels. In addition to an elevated $PaCO_2$, hypoventilation usually causes a decrease in PaO_2. Acute respiratory acidosis occurs in emergency situations, such as acute pulmonary oedema, aspiration of a foreign object, atelectasis, pneumothorax, overdosage of sedatives and severe pneumonia. Chronic respiratory acidosis is associated with chronic disorders such as emphysema, bronchiectasis and bronchial asthma.

Clinical Features

Clinical signs are variable in acute and chronic respiratory acidosis. Sudden hypercapnia (elevated $PaCO_2$) can cause increased pulse and respiratory rate, increased blood pressure, mental cloudiness and feelings of fullness in the head. An elevated $PaCO_2$ causes cerebrovascular vasodilatation and increased cerebral blood flow, particularly when it is higher than 60 mmHg. Ventricular fibrillation may be the first sign of respiratory acidosis in anaesthetized patients.

A patient with chronic respiratory acidosis may complain of weakness, dull headache and symptoms of the underlying disease process. Patients with chronic obstructive pulmonary disease who gradually accumulate carbon dioxide over a prolonged period (days to months) may not develop symptoms of hypercapnia because there has been time for compensatory renal changes.

● When the $PaCO_2$ is chronically above 50 mmHg, the respiratory centre becomes relatively insensitive to carbon dioxide as a respiratory stimulant, leaving hypoxaemia as the major drive for respiration. Excessive oxygen administration removes the stimulus of hypoxaemia, and the patient develops 'carbon dioxide narcosis' unless the situation is quickly reversed.

Diagnosis

Arterial blood gas evaluation reveals a pH less than 7.35 and a $PaCO_2$ greater than 42 mmHg in acute respiratory acidosis. When there has been full compensation (renal retention of bicarbonate), the arterial pH may be within the lower limits of normal.

Management

Treatment is directed at improving ventilation; exact measures vary with the cause of inadequate ventilation. For example, bronchodilators help to reduce bronchial spasm; antibiotics are used for respiratory infections. Pulmonary hygiene measures are employed, when necessary, to rid the respiratory tract of mucus and purulent drainage. Adequate hydration (two to three litres/day) is indicated to keep the mucous membranes moist and thereby facilitate removal of secretions. Supplemental oxygen is used as necessary. A mechanical ventilator, used cautiously, may improve pulmonary ventilation. Overzealous use of a mechanical ventilator may cause such rapid excretion of carbon dioxide that the kidneys will be unable to eliminate excess bicarbonate sufficiently quickly to prevent alkalosis and convulsions. For this reason, the elevated $PaCO_2$ must be decreased slowly.

Respiratory Alkalosis (Carbonic Acid Deficit)

Definition and Aetiology
Respiratory alkalosis is a clinical condition in which the arterial pH is greater than 7.45 and the $PaCO_2$ is less than 38 mmHg. As with respiratory acidosis, acute and chronic conditions can occur in respiratory alkalosis.

Respiratory alkalosis is always due to hyperventilation, which causes excessive 'blowing off' of carbon dioxide and, hence, a decrease in plasma carbonic acid content. Causes can include extreme anxiety, hypoxaemia, the early phase of salicylate intoxication, gram-negative bacteraemia and excessive ventilation by mechanical ventilators.

Diagnosis
Analysis of arterial blood gases is needed to diagnose respiratory alkalosis. In the acute state, the pH is elevated above normal as a result of a low $PaCO_2$ and a normal bicarbonate level. (The kidneys cannot alter the bicarbonate level quickly.) In the compensated state, the kidneys have had sufficient time to lower the bicarbonate level to a suitable level.

Clinical Features
Clinical signs consist of lightheadedness due to vaso-constriction and decreased cerebral blood flow, inability to concentrate, numbness and tingling due to decreased calcium ionization, tinnitus and at times loss of consciousness.

Management
Treatment depends on the underlying cause of respiratory alkalosis. If it is due to anxiety, the patient should be made aware that the abnormal breathing pattern is responsible for the symptoms. Instructing the patient to breathe more slowly to cause accumulation of CO_2 or to breathe into a closed system (such as a paper bag) is helpful. Usually a sedative is required to relieve hyperventilation in very anxious patients. Treatment for other causes of respiratory alkalosis is directed at correcting the underlying problem.

Parenteral Fluid Therapy

Purpose

The choice of an intravenous solution depends on the specific purpose for which it is intended. Generally, intravenous fluids are administered to achieve one or more of the following expected outcomes:

● To provide water, electrolytes and nutrients to meet daily requirements.
● To replace water and correct electrolyte deficits.
● To provide a medium for intravenous drug administration.

Intravenous solutions contain dextrose or electrolytes mixed in various proportions with water. Pure or 'free' water can never be administered intravenously because it rapidly enters red blood cells and causes them to burst.

Types of Intravenous Solutions

Solutions are often categorized as isotonic, hypotonic or hypertonic, according to whether their total osmolality is the same as, less than or greater than that of blood.

Some common water and electrolyte solutions are listed in Table 2.23 with comments about their use. Electrolyte solutions are considered to be isotonic if the total electrolyte content (anions plus cations) approximates to 300 mmol/l. They are considered hypotonic if the total electrolyte content is less than this, and hypertonic if the total electrolyte content exceeds this.

When administering parenteral fluids, it is important to monitor the patient's response to the fluids. The nurse should consider the fluid volume, the content of the fluid and the patient's clinical state.

Isotonic Fluids
Fluids which are classified as isotonic have a total osmolality close to that of extracellular fluid and do not cause red blood cells to shrink or swell. The composition of these fluids may or may not approximate that of extracellular fluid.

A solution of 5 per cent dextrose in water once administered is rapidly metabolized; this initially isotonic solution then disperses as a hypotonic fluid, one third extracellular and two thirds intracellular. Therefore, 5 per cent dextrose in water is mainly used to supply water and to correct an increased serum osmolality. One litre of 5 per cent dextrose in water provides less than 200 kcal and is a minor source of calories for the body's daily requirements.

Because the osmolality of normal saline (0.9 per cent sodium chloride) is entirely contributed by electrolytes, the solution remains within the extracellular compartment. For this reason, normal saline is often used to treat an extracellular volume deficit. Although referred to as normal, it contains only sodium and chloride and does not actually simulate extracellular fluid.

Several other solutions in addition to sodium and chloride contain ions, and are somewhat more similar to extracellular fluid in composition. Ringer's solution contains potassium and calcium in addition to sodium chloride. Ringer's lactate solution contains bicarbonate precursors as well. These solutions are marketed, with slight variations, under a variety of trade names.

Hypotonic Fluids

One purpose of giving hypotonic solutions is to replace cellular fluid, because it is hypotonic as compared with plasma. Another purpose is to provide free water for excretion of body wastes. At times, hypotonic sodium solutions are used to treat hypernatraemia and other hyperosmolar conditions. Half-normal saline (0.45 per cent sodium chloride) is frequently used. Multiple-electrolyte solutions are also available.

Hypertonic Fluids

When 5 per cent dextrose is added to normal saline or Ringer's lactate solution, the total osmolality exceeds that of extracellular fluid. The dextrose is quickly metabolized, however, and only the isotonic solution remains. Therefore, any effect on the intracellular compartment is temporary: Similarly, 5 per cent dextrose is usually added to hypotonic multiple-electrolyte solutions. Once the dextrose is metabolized, these solutions disperse as hypotonic fluids.

Higher concentrations of dextrose, such as 50 per cent dextrose in water, are given to help to meet calorie requirements. These solutions are strongly hypertonic and must be administered into central veins so that they can be diluted by rapid blood flow.

Saline solutions are also available in osmolar concentrations greater than that of extracellular fluid. These solutions draw water from the intracellular compartment to the extracellular compartment and cause cells to shrink. If given rapidly or in quantity, they may cause an extracellular volume excess and precipitate pulmonary oedema. For this reason, these solutions are given cautiously and usually only when the serum osmolality has decreased to dangerously low levels.

Other Substances Given Intravenously

When the gastrointestinal tract cannot accept food, nutrition can be provided intravenously. Parenteral administration may include high concentrations of glucose, protein or fat to meet nutritional requirements.

Many drugs are also delivered intravenously, either by infusion or directly into the vein. Because intravenous medications circulate rapidly, administration by this route is potentially very hazardous. Administration rates and recommended dilutions for individual drugs are available in specialized texts pertaining to intravenous medications.

Nursing Care of Patients Receiving Intravenous Therapy

Informing the Patient

Except in an emergency, a patient should be prepared in advance for having an intravenous infusion. A brief description of the venepuncture process, information about the expected length of infusion and restrictions on activities are important topics. An opportunity should also be given for the patient to express anxieties. For example, some patients believe they will die if small bubbles in the tubing enter their veins. After acknowledging this fear, the nurse can explain that usually only relatively large quantities of air administered rapidly are fatal.

Preparation of Site

Because infection is the major complication of intravenous therapy, strict asepsis is essential during venepuncture. In addition to hand washing and the use of sterile materials, careful preparation of the site is important: it should be cleansed with appropriate antiseptic solution.

Monitoring Intravenous Therapy

Maintenance of an existing intravenous infusion is a nursing responsibility that demands knowledge of the solutions being administered and the principles of flow. In addition, patients must be assessed carefully for both local and systemic complications.

Factors Affecting the Flow of Intravenous Fluids

The flow of an intravenous infusion is subject to the same principles that govern fluid movement in general.

- *Flow is directly proportional to the height of the liquid column.* Raising the height of the infusion container will sometimes improve a sluggish flow.
- *Flow is directly proportional to the diameter of the tubing.* The clamp on intravenous tubing regulates the flow by changing the tubing diameter. In addition, the flow will be faster through a large-gauge cannula than through a small-gauge one.
- *Flow is inversely proportional to the length of the tubing.* Adding extension tubing to an intravenous line will decrease the flow.
- *Flow is inversely proportional to the viscosity of a fluid.* Viscous intravenous solutions, like blood, require a larger cannula than do water or saline solutions.

Monitoring the Flow

Because so many factors influence the flow, a solution does not necessarily continue to run at the speed originally set. Therefore, intravenous infusions must be monitored frequently to ensure that the fluid is flowing at the intended rate. The intravenous bottle or bag may be marked with tape to indicate at a glance whether the correct amount has infused. The flow rate should be calculated when the solution is originally hung, then rechecked at least hourly. To calculate the flow rate, the number of drops delivered per millilitre must be ascertained. This number varies with the equipment and is usually printed on the solution set packaging. A formula that can be used to calculate the drop rate follows:

drops/ml of giving set ÷ 60 (min in hr) × total hourly volume = drops/min

A variety of infusion pumps is available to assist in intravenous fluid delivery. These pumps are particularly useful when potent medications, such as heparin, are being infused. They do not, however, eliminate the need for frequent monitoring of the infusion.

Discontinuing an Infusion

The removal of an intravenous cannula is associated with two possible dangers: haemorrhage and catheter embolism. To prevent excessive bleeding, a dry, sterile sponge should be held over the site as the cannula is removed. Firm pressure should then be applied until all bleeding has stopped. If a plastic intravenous catheter is severed, it can travel to the right ventricle and block the blood flow. To prevent this complication during cannula removal, the type and length of the cannula should be ascertained before the intravenous infusion is discontinued. Plastic catheters should be withdrawn carefully and their length measured to make certain that no fragment has broken off.

Complications Associated with Parenteral Fluid Therapy

Unfortunately, intravenous therapy predisposes to a number of both local and systemic complications. Systemic complications occur less frequently but are often more serious than local complications and include circulatory overload, air embolism, febrile reaction and infection.

Systemic Complications

Overloading the circulatory system with excessive intravenous fluids will cause increased blood pressure and central venous pressure and even severe dyspnoea and cyanosis. This is particularly likely to happen in patients with cardiac disease and is referred to as circulatory overload.

The danger of air embolism is always present, even though it does not occur frequently. It is most often associated with cannulation of central veins. The presence of air embolism may be manifested by dyspnoea and cyanosis, hypotension, weak rapid pulse and loss of consciousness. The amount of air necessary to induce death in humans is not known. Some sources state that as little as 10 ml of air may be fatal in seriously ill patients. The rate of entry may be as important as the actual volume of air.

The presence of pyrogenic substances in either the infusion solution or the administration set can induce a febrile reaction. With such a reaction, one might observe an abrupt elevation in temperature shortly after the infusion is started, with backache, headache, general malaise and, if severe, vascular collapse.

Infection ranges in severity from local involvement of the insertion site to systemic dissemination of organisms through the bloodstream. Measures to prevent infection are essential at the time of insertion and throughout the entire period of infusion. Some of these include the following:

- Careful hand washing before every contact with any part of the infusion system or patient.
- Examination of bottles or bags for cracks, leaks or cloudiness, which may indicate a contaminated solution.
- Strict asepsis.
- Firm anchoring of the intravenous cannula to prevent to-and-fro motion.
- Daily intravenous site inspection and replacement of sterile dressing (application of an antimicrobial ointment to the insertion site may confer a slight additional benefit).
- Removal of the intravenous cannula at the first sign of local inflammation.
- Replacement of the intravenous cannula every 48 hours.
- Replacement of the intravenous cannula inserted during an emergency (with questionable asepsis) as soon as possible.
- Replacement of the bottle or bag every 24 hours and the entire administration set at least every 48 hours, and every 24 hours when blood or lipid products are being infused.

Local Complications

Local complications of intravenous therapy include infiltration, phlebitis and thrombophlebitis.

Dislodging of a needle and local infiltration of the solution into subcutaneous tissues is not uncommon. Infiltration is characterized by oedema at the site of the injection, pain and discomfort in the area of infiltration and significant decrease in the flow rate. When the solution is particularly irritating, sloughing of tissue may result. Close monitoring of the insertion site is necessary to detect infiltration before it becomes severe. Infiltration is easily recognized if the insertion area is larger than an identical region in the opposite extremity. However, infiltration is not always so obvious. A common misconception is that a backflow of blood into the tubing proves that the cannula is properly placed within the vein. However, if the catheter tip has pierced the wall of the vessel, intravenous fluid will seep into tissues as well as flow into the vein. A more reliable means of confirming infiltration is to apply a tourniquet above or proximal to the infusion site and tighten it enough to restrict venous flow. If the infusion continues to drip despite the venous obstruction, infiltration is present.

Phlebitis is defined as inflammation of a vein and is evidenced by heat, redness and swelling at the injection site. The incidence of phlebitis increases with the length of time the intravenous line is in place. Thrombophlebitis refers to the presence of a clot and inflammation in the vein. It is evidenced by localized heat, redness, swelling and hardness of the vein.

Summary

The administration of intravenous fluids is frequently managed by nurses. Although it is a common and extremely important form of treatment, intravenous therapy is associated with several serious hazards. These potential risks include infection, embolism and fluid and electrolyte imbalances. By the use of aseptic technique during every contact with the apparatus, application of principles of flow and frequent patient assessment, the nurse can reduce the likelihood of any of these complications.

TEMPERATURE CONTROL

In humans, body temperature is controlled by a thermoregulatory centre in the hypothalamus, which is often compared to a thermostat. Homeostasis is achieved when thermoregulatory processes balance heat loss against heat gain. Near the surface of the tissues, the temperature can vary on different occasions and between one location and another, but deep in the body it remains remarkably constant at or near 37°C (Edholm, 1978). Deviations detected by receptor cells in the skin and possibly in the viscera are relayed to the hypothalamus via sensory nerve fibres (Figure 2.12). If the temperature falls below 37°C, heat conservation results: skin arterioles constrict, diverting blood more deeply into the tissues, reducing

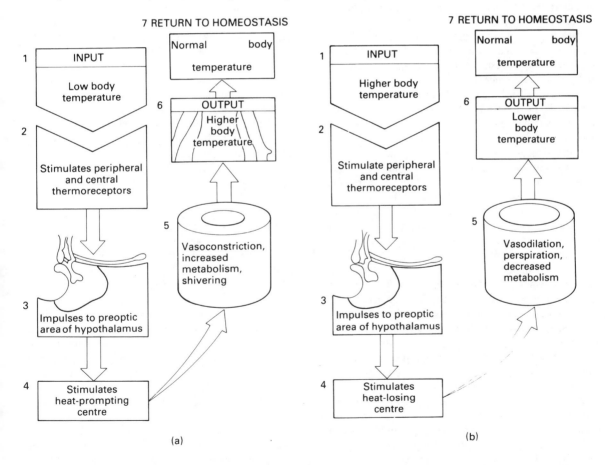

Figure 2.12 Regulation of body temperature by the hypothalamus. (A) Responses to low body temperature. (B) Responses to high body temperature. (From Tortora, G.J. and Anagnostakos, N.P. (1990) *Principles of Anatomy and Physiology* (6th edition), Harper & Row, New York.)

heat loss by conduction and convection via the skin. When the temperature falls very low, additional heat can be generated by the rapid muscular contractions and relaxations recognized as shivering. Piloerection (the contraction of muscles attached to the shafts of hair follicles, causing them to 'stand on end' and producing 'gooseflesh' in order to trap a layer of warm air next to the skin) is of much less importance in man than in other mammals.

If the temperature exceeds 37°C, the hypothalamus relays impulses that promote heat loss. Arterioles in the skin dilate, permitting heat loss by conduction and convection. The hairs lie flat against the surface of the skin. Evaporation of sweat has an additional cooling effect.

Pyrexia (fever) is a systemic reaction of the body to infection, provoked by bacteria, viruses and their toxins. When infection supervenes, antigens present on the surface of micro-organisms cause the hypothalamic thermostat to 'reset' at a higher temperature until they have been eliminated successfully from the tissues. Research indicates that release of chemicals from neutrophils during the inflammatory response is responsible for altering the thermostat, but the physiological advantage of this is unknown. It has been suggested that higher temperatures enable the body to destroy foreign substances more rapidly by generally increasing metabolic rate. For the patient, pyrexia has little in its favour.

Once the thermostat is set above 37°C, the body responds by vasoconstriction, shivering and an increase in metabolic rate to achieve the new level. These effects can be exhausting: for every 1°C increase, the adult pulse increases by approximately 20 beats per minute, and the respiratory by about seven inspirations per minute. Despite the increase, the patient feels chilled. Efforts to reduce the temperature by removing bedclothes, supplying a fan or tepid sponging are not appreciated and will remain futile until the thermostat has reset. Once body temperature has stabilized at the new level, it will be maintained until all the foreign antigens have been neutralized or removed from the body. As the infection subsides, either in response to the body's own defences or to antibiotics, the temperature returns gradually to 37°C. It is at this stage, when losing heat, that the patient feels hot and sweaty. Nursing actions such as providing a single, clean cotton covering, a fan and tepid sponging can provide comfort and allow the temperature to return to normal more quickly.

Pyrexia is a problem because the added metabolic demands it places on the body deplete glycogen stores, leading to nitrogen wastage as proteins are used instead of carbohydrate to provide energy. The patient who cannot eat because of unconsciousness or nausea, is placed at risk of malnutrition and poor tissue repair. Dehydration occurs rapidly, especially if there is profuse sweating. Other unwanted effects of fever include rigors—uncontrollable and exhausting attacks of shivering in adults, or febrile convulsions in infants and young children.

Severe infection (e.g., meningitis) is often accompanied by unconsciousness or confusion and restlessness. The patient must be observed carefully at all times. This may be difficult to achieve if nursing is carried out in isolation because of an infectious condition.

IATROGENIC EFFECTS OF BEING IN HOSPITAL

Hospitals can be dangerous places, both for patients and staff. To begin with, the way in which a building is constructed can have detrimental effects on health—they come in all shapes and sizes, some are airy, others dreary. Lighting and space are particularly important (Dopson, 1986). Too little of either can cause headaches and isolation.

Then there are the problems that can occur from the actual care given in hospitals. Bedrest can lead to complications such as pressure sores, pneumonia or the development of deep venous thrombosis. Even some equipment used because it was thought to be beneficial has been found to be detrimental to patients' health (Kennedy, 1989). Drug therapy can cause many side-effects, which can be distressing and even dangerous, for example, anaphylactic shock (an allergic reaction to an antigen), in which the effects are quick and life threatening. However, the patient's ability to understand advice and guidelines may reduce the risk of serious side-effects remaining undetected (Bradshaw, 1987).

Infection

Infection can be introduced in many ways, for example, via a urinary catheter (Hartley, 1988; Wright, 1988), or when cleaning a wound (Thomlinson, 1987). This problem is a great worry with the emergence of the methicillin-resistant bacteria *Staphylococcus aureus* (Sadler, 1987). This is an extremely dangerous and deadly strain of bacteria, which has evolved due to a build-up of resistance to certain antibiotics. Nurses can carry this organism in their noses and on their hands. Hygiene is of the utmost importance to reduce the risk of spreading this unwanted organism, which could reach epidemic proportions unless infection control measures are adhered to strictly (Whipp, 1987).

Another main source of infection is the linen used on hospital beds. Most hospitals seem to favour the use of duvets as it is known that the number of organisms present in the air from conventional linen is much higher than that from duvets (Overton, 1988; Webster, Cowan and Allen, 1986).

Despite hygiene procedures, nurses have been found to be infection carriers, especially with their hands. It has been suggested (Campbell, 1988) that nurses' attitudes towards hand hygiene does not live up to their actions, and that facilities for this important activity can be far from adequate (Gidley, 1987; Williams and Buckles, 1988).

Hospital Meals

Hospitals are infamous for promoting poor sleeping habits and serving poor quality food—indeed, the amount of money the National Health Service, for example, spends on patients' food has decreased (Taylor, 1988). This is further compounded by the fact that some patients are found to be undernourished on admission. This does not aid recovery, particularly after surgery and treatments such as chemotherapy (Levin, 1985). The changes in legislation, with the lifting of Crown Immunity from hospitals, have had a great effect and can be more of a hindrance than help. Bringing food in by relatives was stopped because of the risk of introducing infection. This makes eating a less enjoyable activity than it already is for the ill or handicapped person (Darbyshire, 1987).

Other Considerations

Hospital managements are at times inconsiderate to their staff—increasing their workload and making them fallible to human error, such as poor lifting technique that leads to backache, and needlestick injuries through resheathing needles (Symington, 1987).

A hospital can be a lonely and confusing place for patients, particularly for those nursed in isolation to reduce the spread of infection or to protect them from such risk. Even the fact that staff are busy with their own priorities reinforces the feeling of isolation, which can lead to patients suffering from depression, sensory deprivation and hallucinations, and the nurse may be unaware of how patients are feeling. These feelings may be exacerbated if the patient is confined to bed (Grazier, 1988).

BEDREST

Although bedrest may be a therapeutic intervention for an illness such as myocardial infarction, a fractured limb or cerebrovascular accident, it is associated with a number of complications. Therefore, the amount of time required for bedrest varies according to the illness, the patient's ability to recover and whether or not there are any complications of the illness.

Bedrest alters a person's centre of gravity, thus changing the pressure exerted on the musculoskeletal and cardiovascular system. Muscles lose their tone, leading to eventual atrophy, and connective tissue can shorten as it becomes dense due to lack of appropriate motion. The person becomes weak and can develop contractures of the hands and/or feet. Reversal of these pro-

blems can be lengthy and so prevention is best achieved by way of active and passive exercises while the patient is in bed.

Skin breakdown and other effects of pressure due to bedrest can be serious problems and are to be avoided. However, they can happen, depending on the patient's physical state. They may occur on the patient's sacrum, heels and shoulders, as well as the elbows and ears.

The patient can develop constipation due to decreased activity and reduced fluid and food intake, associated with anorexia and poor appetite.

The patient confined to bed can also develop depression due to isolation or as a reaction to the illness. In addition, changes in sleep patterns are common, with patients usually sleeping less.

Cardiovascular Complications

The distribution of blood within the cardiovascular system is altered due to bedrest, with a large volume of blood staying within the thorax. This increases the volume of the blood to the heart, and ultimately increases its workload. A problem with orthostatic hypotension can occur due to these changes, causing the patient to feel dizzy and nauseated. Development of a deep venous thrombosis is possible due to stasis of blood flow within the limbs, especially since the patient on bedrest loses fluid as bedrest continues (Rubin, 1988), and the veins are compressed due to position. Full expansion of the lungs is not achieved, again due to position, causing the muscles to work less efficiently. This is compounded by extra pressure from the abdominal contents pressing against the diaphragm. The patient tends to breathe less deeply, causing secretions to lie and increasing the risk of a chest infection developing.

Bone Demineralization

Bedrest also increases the risk of demineralization of the bones, which changes bone strength and appearance; the danger of fractures occurring is real, depending on other factors such as previous health and nutritional state. The increase of calcium (hypercalcaemia) in the blood can cause renal calculi to develop as calcium is excreted by via the kidneys. Hypercalcaemia can also cause cardiac problems (Green, 1978, p. 10) and neuronal depression; it also causes vomiting and eventual dehydration. There is the possibility or urinary tract infections, and even incontinence of urine, due to the high levels of calcium. However, this could depend on the patient's age and condition: an elderly or very ill person might be more at-risk of incontinence occurring (Milne, 1989).

The person who is confined to bed is more susceptible to infection because the body's defence mechanisms are lowered and because the patient is in an environment where pathogenic organisms are present.

AMBULATION

Philosophy of Rehabilitation

Rehabilitation is a process that enables an ill or disabled person to achieve the greatest possible level of physical, psychological, mental, social and economic functioning. Modern rehabilitation is a process whereby a patient adjusts to a disability by learning how to integrate all of the available resources and to concentrate more on existing abilities than on the permanent disabilities that must be lived with.

It is important that such people are helped to develop a satisfying way of life that preserves individuality. They gain an inner strength from their own resources that makes it possible for them to partake of the joys and meet the problems of life in a meaningful way.

The trend in rehabilitation is to include not only the physically, mentally and emotionally handicapped (including those suffering from cancer), but also the aged and those who are disadvantaged because of poverty or social deprivation. Because the ageing population is increasing and advances in technology are saving the lives of the seriously ill and disabled, more people will require rehabilitation services in the future.

Rehabilitation begins during the first contact with patients. The emphasis is on restoring them to independence or helping them regain their pre-illness/predisability level of function in as short a period as possible.

In the health care setting, patients and their problems are assessed, mutual goals are set and a care plan is set up to enable them to achieve self-sufficiency up to the level of their capabilities. Abilities are stressed rather than disabilities. Since each patient has a different level of capability, the care plan is individualized. The ultimate goal is to obtain optimal function in the patient's daily routine— that is, the activities of daily living (Roper, Logan and Tierney, 1983). Rehabilitation goals must be realistic, taking into consideration the patient's ability (the most important factor) and then the disability.

The Rehabilitation Team

Rehabilitation is a process that requires a multidisciplinary approach for a common goal, with each health professional making a unique contribution. They meet in group sessions at frequent intervals to evaluate the patient's progress and collaborate in a dynamic process of modifying goals and enhancing functional performance.

Patients are the key members of the rehabilitation team because they are the ones who determine the final outcome. They participate in the setting of expected outcomes, and in learning and working on their rehabilitation care plans, so that they can eventually take control of their own lives.

The patient's family and/or significant others are in-corporated into the team, giving ongoing support and participating in problem-solving and care.

The rehabilitation nurse is responsible for developing a patient care plan directed towards defined, expected outcomes for the patient, and for co-ordinating the actions of other team members towards these outcomes. Additional outcomes include the prevention of complications and the restoration and maintenance of optimal physical and psychosocial health. The nurse establishes a therapeutic relationship with the patient and applies the nursing process in skin care, positioning, transfer techniques, bladder and bowel management, nutrition, psychosocial support and patient and family education.

The psychologist may be requested to assess the patient's mental state, if the patient's mental condition warrants this.

The physiotherapist teaches and supervises the patient through a prescribed exercise programme designed to strengthen weak muscles and prevent deformities. The physiotherapist also teaches new ways of mobilization and daily activities.

The occupational therapist assists the disabled person in adapting to challenges of daily living and interacting successfully with the environment. The occupational therapist recommends aids and teaches energy conservation and work simplification.

The social worker assesses the patient's social environment (lifestyle, coping patterns, resources, support system) and socioeconomic status and assists the patient and home carers in adjusting to the home and community. The social worker advises on financial matters and disability benefits.

Other specialists may join the team depending on the needs of individual patients.

Rehabilitation is an integral part of nursing. It should begin with the initial contact with the patient. Every major illness carries with it the threat of disability. If the patient is hospitalized with a burn and develops a contracture deformity, recovery time will be greatly delayed. Disabilities are not static but tend to become worse, and some complications of inactivity can give the patient more pain and discomfort than the initial injury or disease.

Although all hospitals do not have departments of physical medicine and rehabilitation, the principles of rehabilitation are basic to the care of all patients, and the discussion that follows indicates how the nurse applies them.

Psychological Implications of a Disability

A physical disability often has a deep psychological significance to patients. It has a direct impact on their body image and can cause a state of conflict. Physically, a part of their body has deteriorated. Patients may have the shattering realization that they can do less than they did formerly. Their shape and posture may have changed, as may their state of mind. Even their position in society may be altered, as well as their social interaction with others. They perceive themselves as second-class citizens, as devalued people. In short, they feel that they are different.

Disability may mean hardship or even tragedy to the individual, depending on the premorbid personality, occupation, cultural background and social status, and on the support received from significant others.

A person usually goes through a series of emotional reactions to a newly acquired disability (Kubler Ross, 1970). The first reaction may be confusion, disorganization and denial. The patient is in a state of conflict and has to cope with problems of forced dependence, loss of self-esteem and feelings that personal and family integrity are threatened. The patient may refuse to accept the new limitations and at times has an unjustified over-confidence in speedy recovery. False hopes lead the patient to hear only what is wanted. The patient is likely to be self-centred and even childlike in the demands made. The mechanism of denial is useful up to a certain point, but eventually the reality of the situation must be accepted.

Patients may progress to a stage of grief and depression in which they appear to mourn for their lost function or missing body part. (Depression may also be caused by sensory deprivation and restricted environmental stimulation.) There may be behavioural changes, particularly regression. This stage of grief appears to be a necessary phase in adapting to the disability. Mourning is part of the process of working through the meaning of the losses and is part of the emotional work of rehabilitation. Therefore, the patient should not merely be encouraged blithely to 'cheer up'. Such an approach can evoke extreme hostility and provoke behaviour that will result in a 'problem patient' (Stockwell, 1972). Listening to the patient talk about the loss is important for healing.

The patient may go through a stage of anger in which blame is projected on others. This behaviour frequently alienates family, friends and medical and nursing staff, who may either capitulate to the patient's demands or withdraw.

Following the stages of depression, grief and anger, there is generally a period of adaptation and adjustment. In time, patients become more familiar with their condition and are able to tolerate it better. As they revise their body image and modify their former picture of themselves, patients redirect their energies towards coping with physical functioning.

They are able to accept a degree of dependency and not resent being 'waited on'. They begin to realize that hopelessness is futile and know that they must adapt to the permanent aspects of the disability and modify their goals.

The acceptance of the limitations imposed by the dis-

ability and the total investment of patients in their rehabilitation programmes are basic to adjustment. It is from this point in rehabilitation that patients begin to look ahead and develop realistic goals for their future.

At the same time, it is important to realize that not every patient will progress in orderly fashion through the stages of grieving. Many frequently fluctuate between acceptance and grief, so that angry outbursts and depression may continue long after the usual period of mourning has supposedly passed. Each new situation (going home, starting vocational rehabilitation, entering a new relationship) reminds the patient anew of the limitations, the changed body image and the reality of the permanence of the situation. Thus, even though the disabled person makes progress and increases independence, the grief process and the need to grow throughout life must be dealt with continuously.

At the other end of the spectrum are those patients who do not accept their disability but instead waste emotional energy in futile rebellion against unalterable damage. Or, there are those patients who ignore the disability and refuse to put forth any effort to adapt to everyday living. Still others may overreact and build a false reputation for being 'cheerful and courageous'. Although 'ignoring' may seem healthy, often it involves a total rejection of the disability, which keeps patients from doing the things that will be helpful to them. When people fail to react at the appropriate time, it may indicate that they are not coping adequately. These patients may require assistance from either a psychologist or a psychiatrist.

Diagnosis

A team of health professionals (see The Rehabilitation Team, p. 84) is required to evaluate the patient's physical condition and assess cognitive, emotional, social and psychological functioning. The clinical examination also includes a history, physical examination and evaluation of functional abilities. Functional ability depends on good joint motion, muscle strength and an intact neurological system. Disabilities most likely to produce loss of function are those involving the musculoskeletal, neurological and cardiovascular systems. In addition, secondary problems related to the disability, such as muscle atrophy and deconditioning, and the residual strengths unaffected by the disease or disability are assessed.

Nursing Assessment and Management

The nurse's responsibility is to find out how patients, their families and significant others perceive the change in body function or structure. No two people react in the same way to a disability. Nurses need to listen and help patients identify their feelings towards their disability, treatment and those involved in rehabilitation.

The nursing assessment also focuses on the functional effects of the patient's disability or disease with particular attention paid to self-care and mobility. Assessment of functioning is best done by observing the patient perform an activity (eating, dressing) and noting the degree of independence/dependence, the time taken and the amount of assistance required. The patient's degree of co-ordination and endurance are noted, as these can alert the nurse to a patient's potential for falls.

In general, the expected outcomes of rehabilitation for the patient and nurse are to facilitate independence ultimately in the home and community settings, where possible.

The nurse continues to work with the patient, always emphasizing the patient's assets and remaining strengths, while at the same time listening, encouraging and sharing in any triumphs as the patient progresses in the care plan. The patient is praised for efforts to improve self-concept and self-care abilities. The nurse helps the patient to identify strengths and past successes and develop new goals. Participation in the ongoing rehabilitation regime, achieving satisfactory experiences and engaging in social activities will be helpful in renewing a positive self-concept.

Principles and Practices of Rehabilitation Nursing

The most common complications that threaten a patient with a prolonged illness or disability are contractures, pressure sores and bladder and bowel problems.

Contractures result when muscles are not used or joints are not put through their full range of motion. A contracture is actually a shortening of the muscle, which leads to deformity. Contractures increase the energy expenditure for movement, produce pain and limit joint mobility. They are prevented by continuing assessment, passive and active exercise of all joints, particularly those affected by the patient's disability, and proper positioning.

When tissues do not receive adequate nourishment, circulation and exercise, they tend to deteriorate and atrophy. Initiating deliberate and proper measures can combat and prevent tissue damage and pressure sores.

Bladder and bowel difficulties may result from disease, injury or shock. In many patients, refunctioning can be accomplished through individualized teaching and persistent attention to the establishment of regular function.

The major expected outcomes for the nurse in rehabilitation are as follows:

1. To prevent deformities and complications.
2. To motivate, teach and support the patient (and significant others) during the daily activities of living, which include self-care.
3. To refer the patient for proper follow-up care and supervision.

Considerations for Elderly Patients

In restoring older people to their fullest functional capacity, the nursing assessment focuses not only on information about pathological processes and disability but also on how the impairment is affecting their ability to move about, communicate, live at home and engage in social activities. Rehabilitation of the elderly person is directed towards the maintenance of wellbeing and the support of independent living for as long as possible. Fear of dependency is the greatest anxiety of the aged. Doing even simple activities may be very important to the frail, elderly person (Robertson, 1986).

The rehabilitation management and care are similar to those of the young: treatment of underlying disease or disability, prevention of secondary disabilities, restoration of physical and mental capabilities and adaptation in managing persisting disability. High priority is given to performing standing exercises, maintenance of balance and walking. Certain modifications have to be made when there is multiple pathology along with impairments of mobility and balance, as well as mental status changes. Extra time will be needed to learn to manage the components of the programme. The very old require a more extensive support system.

Prevention of Deformities and Complications

Positioning

Deformities and complications of illness or injury can often be prevented by proper positioning in bed, frequent changes of position and exercise. Turning and positioning the patient correctly can relieve pressure on a body area, prevent contractures, stimulate circulation, help prevent oedema and promote lung expansion and drainage of respiratory secretions.

Assuming and maintaining correct body alignment while in bed is essential regardless of the position selected. The nurse observes the patient's position during every patient contact. While carrying out other nursing activities, the nurse suggests and helps patients to make changes that will place them in alignment. The nurse observes the appearance of the body parts in the positions that the patient commonly assumes. The most common positions that a patient assumes in bed are the dorsal, or supine; the side-lying, or lateral; and the prone positions. The essential principles of body alignment applied in maintaining these positions are as follows:

Dorsal or Supine Position

1. The head is in line with the spine, both laterally and anteroposteriorly.

2. The trunk is positioned so that flexion of the hips is minimized.
3. The arms are flexed at the elbow with the hands resting against the lateral abdomen.
4. The legs are extended.
5. The heels are suspended in a space between the mattress and the footboard.
6. The toes are pointed straight up.

Side-Lying or Lateral Position

1. The head is in line with the spine.
2. The uppermost hip joint is slightly forward and supported in a position of slight abduction by a pillow.
3. A pillow supports the arm, which is flexed at both the elbow and the shoulder joints.

Prone Position (on Abdomen)

1. The head is turned laterally and is in alignment with the rest of the body.
2. The arms are abducted and externally rotated at the shoulder joint; the elbows are flexed.
3. A small, flat support is placed under the pelvis, extending from the level of the umbilicus to the upper third of the thigh.
4. The lower extremities remain in a neutral position.
5. The toes are suspended over the edge of the mattress.

Therapeutic Exercises

Exercise involves the function of muscles, nerves, bones and joints as well as the cardiovascular and respiratory systems. Return to function is dependent on the strength of the musculature that controls the joints. The therapeutic exercises are performed with the assistance and guidance of a physiotherapist or nurse.

Before a therapeutic exercise programme is started, a functional evaluation is made by the physiotherapist. Included are posture assessment, goniometric measurements (use of a protractor for measurement of joint motion), manual muscle testing, range of motion testing and flexibility and endurance testing. A neurological assessment for motor weakness and change in sensation may be indicated.

The nurse observes the patient's activities throughout the day (and night) to determine how the patient moves and, indeed, willingness to move. Important also is the nurse's assessment of how the patient perceives the symptoms and coping methods.

Patient Education
The patient should have a clear understanding of what the prescribed exercise is to accomplish. Providing written instructions setting forth the frequency, duration and number of repetitions as well as simple line drawings of the exercise will help transfer this learning to the home setting.

Exercises, when correctly done, assist in (1) maintaining and building muscle strength, (2) maintaining joint function, (3) preventing deformity, (4) stimulating circulation, (5) building strength and endurance and (6) promoting relaxation. Exercise is also valuable in helping restore the motivation and wellbeing of the patient. There are five types of exercise: passive, active assistive, active, resistive and isometric. The description, purpose and action of each of these exercises are summarized in Table 2.25.

Range of Motion Exercises

Range of motion is the movement of a joint through its full range in all appropriate planes, such as flexion, where the joint is bent so that the angle of the joint diminishes. The opposite of this is extension—the return movement of the joint—which increases the angle of the joint. Rotation of a joint also determines its range of motion; this is the turning or movement of a part around its axis. Usually, range of motion testing is done by the physiotherapist to determine the movement that exists at the joint areas. Testing helps set positive and realistic goals. Standardized testing procedures may be used. Goniometric measurements can be made to obtain a baseline of range of motion and flexibility.

Each joint of the body has a normal range of motion. In many musculoskeletal and neurological conditions, the joints may lose their normal range, stiffen and produce a permanent disability. If the range of motion is limited, the functions of the joint and of the muscle that moves the joint are impaired. In order to prevent painful deformities, range of motion activities are carried out when permitted, to either maintain or increase the maximal motion of a joint and to prevent deterioration.

These exercises should begin as soon as the patient's clinical condition allows. The range of motion exercises are planned for the individual to accommodate the wide variation in the degrees of motion that people of varying body build and age-groups can attain.

Preventing External Rotation of the Hip

Patients who are in bed for periods of time may develop external rotation deformity of the hip. The hip is a ball-and-socket joint and has a tendency to rotate outwards when the patient lies on the back. A trochanter roll extending from the crest of the ilium to the midthigh will prevent this deformity. With correct placement, the trochanter roll serves as a mechanical wedge under the projection of the greater trochanter.

Preventing Footdrop (Plantar Flexion)

Footdrop is a deformity in which the foot is plantar flexed (the ankle bends in the direction of the sole of the foot). If

Table 2.25 *Therapeutic exercises*

Exercise	Description	Purposes	Action
Passive	An exercise carried out by the physiotherapist or the nurse without assistance from the patient	To retain as much joint range of motion as possible, to maintain circulation	Stabilize the proximal joint, and support the distal part. Move the joint smoothly, slowly and gently through its full range of motion. Avoid producing pain
Active assistive	An exercise carried out by the patient with the assistance of the physiotherapist or the nurse	To encourage normal muscle function	Support the distal part, and encourage the patient to take the joint actively through its range of motion. Give no more assistance than is necessary to accomplish the action. Short periods of activity should be followed by adequate rest periods
Active	An exercise accomplished by the patient without assistance, activities include turning from side to side and from back to abdomen and moving up and down in bed	To increase muscle strength	When possible, active exercise should be done against gravity. The joint is moved through full range of motion without assistance. (Nurse should ensure that the patient does not substitute another joint movement for the one intended)
Resistive	An active exercise carried out by the patient working against resistance produced by either manual or mechanical means	To provide resistance in order to increase muscle power	The patient moves the joint through its range of motion while the physiotherapist resists slightly at first and then with progressively increasing resistance. Sandbags and weights can be used and are applied at the distal point of the involved joint. The movements should be done smoothly
Isometric or muscle setting	Alternatively contracting and relaxing a muscle while keeping the part in a fixed position; this exercise is performed by the patient	To maintain strength when a joint is immobilized	Contract or tighten the muscle as much as possible without moving the joint, hold for several seconds, then 'let go' and relax. Breathe deeply

the condition continues without correction, the patient will not be able to hold the foot in a normal position and will walk on the toes without touching the ground with the heel of the foot. The deformity is caused by contracture of both the gastrocnemius and the soleus muscles. It may also be produced by loss of flexibility of the Achilles tendon.

● Prolonged bedrest, lack of exercise, incorrect positioning in bed and the weight of the bedding, forcing the toes into plantar flexion, are factors that contribute to footdrop.

To prevent this crippling deformity, a footboard or pillows are used to keep the feet at right angles to the legs when the patient is in a supine position. The feet are positioned so that both plantar surfaces are firmly against the footboard or pillows. A trochanter roll(s) is used to maintain the leg(s) in a neutral position. The patient is encouraged to flex and then to extend (curl and stretch) the feet and toes frequently. The ankles should be moved clockwise and counterclockwise in a rotary motion several times each hour.

Assisting the Patient with Ambulation

Assessment

Preparation for ambulation begins with maintaining joint range of motion, preventing contractures and achieving bed mobility. Muscle-strengthening exercises are started while patients are still in bed. As soon as they can tolerate it, patients are assisted to sit up on the side of the bed and taught to transfer from the bed to the chair (if this is necessary) and then to walk.

During these activities, assessment focuses on the patient's abilities, the extent of the disability and the residual capacity for physiological adaptation. The nurse observes for signs and symptoms of fatigue and orthostatic hypotension and for pallor, sweating, nausea and tachycardia. If these occur, the activity should be stopped and the patient encouraged to rest.

Transfer Activities

A transfer is the movement of the patient from one piece of furniture or equipment to another (i.e., from bed to chair or bed to wheelchair).

As soon as the patient is allowed out of bed, transfer activities are started. While still confined to bed, it is important that the patient should practise 'push-up' exercises to strengthen the arm and shoulder extensors. It is desirable that the patient be able to raise and move the body in different directions by means of these push-up exercises.

Because nurses are so frequently concerned with getting weak and incapacitated patients out of bed, it is important to be familiar with the techniques of moving patients to the edge of the bed, sitting them on the edge of the bed and assisting them to stand. Nurses should adhere to local policy regarding lifting techniques and perform them safely.

Before patients are taught to transfer, they are evaluated to determine their ability to transfer from one area to another. The nurse should always encourage patients to move towards their stronger side.

Use of a Transfer or Sliding Board

If the muscles which patients use to lift themselves off the bed are not strong enough to overcome the resistance of body weight, a polished, lightweight board may be used to bridge the gap between the bed and the chair, while they slide across on it. This board (or bench) also may be used to transfer the patient from the chair to the toilet or the bathtub.

● Place one end of the transfer board under the patient's buttocks and the other end on the surface to which the transfer is being made (i.e., the chair).
● Ask the patient to push up with the hands to shift the buttocks and then to slide across the board to the other surface.

Patient Education for Transfers at Home

In the home setting, getting in and out of bed and performing chair, toilet and bath transfers for people with weak musculature and loss of hip, knee and ankle motion are difficult. A rope attached to the headboard of the bed helps patients to pull themselves towards the centre of the bed, and the use of a rope attached to the footboard facilitates getting in and out of bed. The height of a chair can be raised with blocks placed under the chair legs or with cushions on the seat. Bars can be attached to the wall near the toilet and bath to provide leverage and stability.

Preparation for Ambulation

Regaining the ability to walk is a prime morale builder. To be prepared for ambulation—whether with brace, frame, cane or crutches—the patient must be strengthened and conditioned. Exercise is the foundation of preparation. By performing mat and parallel bar exercises, the patient develops balance and co-ordination and strengthens the muscles. These exercises are supervised by the physiotherapist, who assesses which exercises are required.

Mobility Aids

Crutch Walking

In the treatment of various forms of arthritis and of most fractures of the lower extremity, and after operations on the leg—especially after amputation—crutches provide a support and balance and a convenient method of getting from one place to another. Because crutch walking is not an inherited skill, it must be taught, and this learning process must begin early. Crutch walking requires a high energy expenditure and considerable cardiovascular stress. Older people with reduced exercise capacity, arm strength and problems with balance due to age and multiple diseases may be unable to meet the energy demands of crutch walking.

One of the first prerequisites is to develop power in the shoulder girdle and upper arm muscles, which will bear the patient's weight while crutch walking. Exercise to increase the strength and co-ordination of these muscle groups should be started before the patient is walking and then should progress to balancing exercises between parallel bars.

Of equal importance is psychological preparation, which can be developed long before the physical need is present. The individual needs of each patient must be considered and the methods of approach directed to them. The patient's age, interests and future intentions, as well as the prognosis, are essential factors.

Crutch Stance. The tripod position is the basic crutch stance. The crutches rest approximately 20 to 25 cm in front and to the side of the patient's toes. This gives the strongest and most balanced support (see Figure 2.13). Because, to provide stability, a greater height requires a broader base, a taller patient needs a wider base and a shorter patient a narrower base.

The patient must be taught to support the weight on the hand piece. If the weight is borne on the axilla, the pressure of the crutch can damage the brachial plexus nerves and produce 'crutch paralysis'. A foam-rubber pad on the underarm piece will relieve pressure on the upper arm and the thoracic cage.

Ability to shift body weight is the next step. The crutch gait selected depends on the nature of the patient's disability. The nurse must know how much (if any) weight can be placed on the affected side and whether the crutches are being used for balance or support.

Crutch Gaits. The selection of the crutch gait depends on the type and severity of the disability and on the patient's physical condition, arm and trunk strength and body balance. The patient should be taught two gaits so that changes can be made from one to another. Shifting crutch gaits relieves fatigue since each gait requires the use of a different combination of muscles. (If a muscle is forced to contract steadily without relaxing, the circulation of the blood to the part is reduced.) A faster gait can be used for making speed, whereas a slower one is used in crowded places.

All gaits begin in the tripod position. The more common gaits are the 4-point, the 2-point, the 3-point, and the swinging-to and swinging-through gaits.

Patients should not practise crutch walking for too

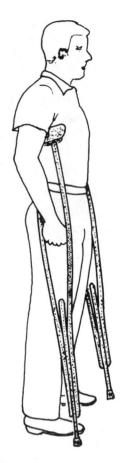

Figure 2.13 Crutch stance.

long, especially if they have been in bed for a prolonged period. Such signs as sweating or shortness of breath should be indications that the lesson on crutches should be stopped and the patient permitted to rest or go back to bed.

Use of a Walking Frame

A walking frame provides more support than a cane or crutches for the patient who has poor balance and cannot use crutches. It gives stability but it does not permit a natural reciprocal walking pattern. The following sequence should be taught:

1. Lift the walking frame, placing it in front of you while leaning your body slightly forward.
2. Take a step or two into the walking frame.
3. Lift the walking frame and place it is front of you again.

Ambulation with a Cane

A cane is used to help the patient walk with greater balance and support and with less fatigue. It also relieves the pressure on weight-bearing joints and prevents undue pressure and use of the unaffected extremity.

Cane–Foot Sequence

1. Hold the cane in the hand opposite to the affected extremity (i.e., the cane should be used on the good side. In normal walking, the opposite leg and arm move together; thus, holding the cane opposite the involved side widens the base of support and reduces stress on the involved extremity).
2. Advance the cane at the same time the affected leg is moved forward.
3. Keep the cane fairly close to the body to prevent leaning, and bear down on the cane when the unaffected extremity begins the swing phase.
4. If for some reason the patient is unable to use the cane in the opposite hand, the cane may be carried on the same side and advanced when the affected leg is advanced.

To Go Up and Down Stairs Using the Cane–Foot Sequence

1. Step up on the unaffected extremity.
2. Then place the cane and affected extremity up on the step.
3. Reverse this procedure for descending steps. (Strong leg goes up first and comes down last).

Supporting the Patient with an Orthotic or a Prosthetic Appliance

Orthotic Devices

An orthosis is an external appliance used to provide support and alignment, prevent or correct deformities, and improve the function of the body. This includes braces, splints, collars, corsets, supports or calipers that may be designed and produced by an orthotist. An orthosis may be static (no moving parts) or dynamic (with moving parts). Static orthoses are used to stabilize joints and prevent contractures, while dynamic orthoses are flexible and used to improve functioning by assisting weak muscles.

Patient Education. The nurse reinforces the orthotist's instructions concerning care of the skin under an orthotic device because skin problems/pressure sores may develop if the device is applied too tightly. The patient should be taught to examine the orthosis periodically to see that it has not slipped out of position or become distorted, and that the padding distributes the pressure evenly.

Prosthetic Devices

A prosthesis is a replacement for a missing part of the body (e.g., extremity, joint, eye, breast, tooth). A prosthetist is a limb maker or a maker of other prostheses, and is responsible for fabricating the prosthesis, fitting it and training the patient to use the device.

Nursing Care. The nurse performs an essential func-

tion in the preprosthetic phase of the patients' care by helping them to develop an attitude of realistic hopefulness and by preventing deformities, so that the time between the healing of the tissues and the fitting of the prosthesis is kept to a minimum. In the amputation of an extremity, the nurse is responsible for bandaging the stump (or the residual extremity) correctly, so that proper shrinkage and shaping occur, and the patient can be fitted more effectively with a prosthesis.

PREVENTION AND TREATMENT OF PRESSURE SORES

Definition

A pressure sore (bed sore, decubitus ulcer) is a localized area of damaged tissue caused by pressure, shear, friction or a combination of any of these.

Aetiology

Pressure

Any external pressure over the skin surface that is greater than capillary pressure (approximately 32 mmHg) will cause the collapse of vessel walls. Long periods of pressure will result in the build up of waste products, tissue anoxia and ultimately necrosis.

The normal body response is called reactive hyperaemia. A red flush or erythema appears on the skin surface when pressure is removed. This is because capillary dilatation brings oxygen and nutrients and removes waste products. Reactive hyperaemia can be demonstrated very simply by pressing the thumb firmly on the back of the opposite hand for several minutes. After removing the pressure, a white patch can be seen. This area gradually becomes bright red. The skin will return to its normal colour within a short time. This protective mechanism becomes ineffective after long periods of unrelieved pressure.

Shear

As the patient slides down the bed or chair, the skin may remain in contact with the supporting surface while the skeleton slides over it. This causes the stretching and tearing of tissues and blood vessels, thus disrupting the underlying microcirculation.

Friction

When a patient is handled incorrectly, the resultant dragging can lead to a friction burn.

Other Contributing Factors

Many factors that can contribute to pressure sore development must be taken into consideration when assessing the patient.

Reduced Mobility. The problem of reduced mobility can be the result of many causes, such as disorders of the locomotor system, major surgery, trauma or sedation. Whatever the cause, the patient is unable to make the normal spontaneous pressure-relieving movements that are made in health.

Loss of Sensation. Patients suffering from a loss of sensation are unaware of any feelings of discomfort that normally encourage movements to relieve pressure.

Incontinence. Incontinence has been shown to be a significant problem in those patients with pressure sores (Exton-Smith, 1987). Urine can cause maceration of the skin, and the frequent washing to remove it also removes normal skin oils and increases the risk of friction.

Poor Nutrition. A reduced nutritional status reduces the elasticity of the skin and increases the risk of sore formation. Deficiencies of protein, vitamin C and zinc have been shown to be the most important factors (Tweedle, 1978).

Age. The association between the development of pressure sores and age is well documented (David, Chapman, Chapman *et al.*, 1983). The ageing skin has diminished epidermal thickness, dermal collagen and tissue elasticity. In addition, there is an increased likelihood of disease and/or poor nutrition.

Disease. Many diseases can result in the development of the above factors. Others, such as diabetes mellitus, can increase the risk of infection, thus either precipitating the development of sores, or delaying healing.

Drugs. Many drugs can increase the risk of pressure sore development. Steroids can make the skin very thin; sedatives reduce spontaneous movements. Other drugs can cause a loss of appetite, for example, digoxin.

Weight. Extremes of weight can also cause problems. Obesity may lead to a reduced mobility, poor positioning or dragging when being moved. Emaciated patients have little subcutaneous fat to provide padding over bony prominences.

Pressure Areas

Some parts of the body are more prone to pressure sores than others. They are known as the pressure areas. In particular, they are the weight-bearing, bony prominences that are covered only with skin and a small amount of subcutaneous fat, and where tissues are compressed easily between the supporting surface and the bone. The most important pressure areas are over the sacrum, ischial tuberosities and the greater trochanters, especially in patients who sit for long periods of time (Figure 2.14). Other bony areas susceptible to pressure sore development are the knees, medial condyles of the tibia, fibular head, malleoli, heels and elbows.

► NURSING PROCESS
► THE PATIENT AT RISK OF PRESSURE SORES

► *Assessment*

It is very important to identify those patients at risk of pressure sore development so that appropriate preventive measures can be taken. There are several risk assessment scores available to assist in the identification of vulnerable patients. The best known is the Norton score (Figure 2.15) (Norton, Exton-Smith and McLaren, 1975). The patient is given a score in each of the following five categories: physical condition, mental con-

Major pressure sites

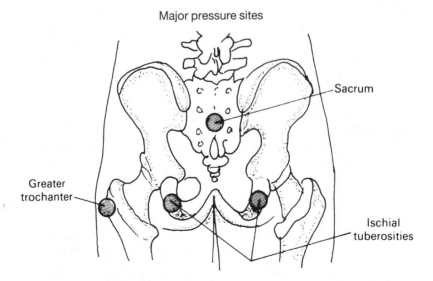

Figure 2.14 Areas of major pressure sites where pressure sores can develop.

NORTON SCALE ASSESSMENT:

SCORING SYSTEM KEY: TOTAL SCORE OF 14 or below – 'AT RISK'				
A Physical Condition	**B** Mental Condition	**C** Activity	**D** Mobility	**E** Incontinent
Good — 4	Alert — 4	Ambulent — 4	Full — 4	Not — 4
Fair — 3	Apathetic — 3	Walk/Help — 3	Slightly Limited — 3	Occasion- ally — 3
Poor — 2	Confused — 2	Chairbound — 2	Very Limited — 2	Usually Urine — 2
Very bad — 1	Stuporous — 1	Bedfast — 1	Immobile — 1	Doubly — 1

Figure 2.15 The Norton score (reprinted from Norton, D., Exton-Smith, A. N. and McLaren, R. (1975) *An Investigation of Geriatric Nursing Problems in Hospital*, by kind permission of Churchill Livingstone).

dition, activity, mobility and incontinence. These are then added together to give a total score (maximum of 20). Patients scoring 14 or less are deemed to be at risk. However, the Norton scale has been seen to be less effective outside the area of caring for the elderly, where it was developed (Barratt, 1988). More recently, other scoring systems have been developed to make good this deficiency. They include the Douglas Pressure Sore Risk Calculator (Table 2.26) (Pritchard, 1986), the Pressure Sore Prediction Score (Figure 2.16) (Lowthian, 1987) and

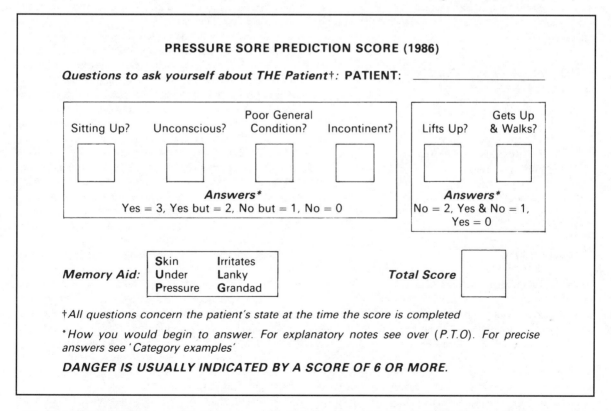

PRESSURE SORE PREDICTION SCORE (1986)

Questions to ask yourself about THE Patient†: **PATIENT:** _____

Sitting Up? Unconscious? Poor General Condition? Incontinent? ☐ ☐ ☐ ☐

Answers*
Yes = 3, Yes but = 2, No but = 1, No = 0

Lifts Up? Gets Up & Walks? ☐ ☐

Answers*
No = 2, Yes & No = 1, Yes = 0

Memory Aid:
Skin	Irritates
Under	Lanky
Pressure	Grandad

Total Score ☐

†*All questions concern the patient's state at the time the score is completed*

**How you would begin to answer. For explanatory notes see over (P.T.O). For precise answers see 'Category examples'*

DANGER IS USUALLY INDICATED BY A SCORE OF 6 OR MORE.

Figure 2.16 The pressure sore prediction score (reprinted from Lowthian, P. T. (1987) The practical assessment of pressure sore risk, *Care—Science and Practice*, Vol. 5, No. 4, pp. 3–7).

Table 2.26 *Douglas Pressure Sore Risk Calculator – total score 18 and below are 'at risk'*

Nutritional state /Hb	Activity	Incontinence	Pain	Skin state	Mental state
Well-balanced diet 4	Fully mobile 4	Continent 4	Pain free 4	Intact 4	Alert 4
Inadequate diet 3	Walk with difficulty 3	Occasionally 3	Fear of pain 3	Dry/red/thin 3	Apathetic 3
Fluids only 2	Chairbound 2	Urine 2	Periodic 2	Superficial break 2	Stuporous/ sedated 2
Peripheral/par-enteral feeding 1	Bedfast 1	Doubly 1	Pain on movement 1	Full tissue thickness or cavity 1	Unco-operative 1
Low haemoglobin below 10, 1			Continual discomfort 0		Comatose 0

Special risk factors – deduct 2 for each factor
 Steroid therapy
 Diabetes
 Cytotoxic therapy
 Dyspnoea

the Waterlow Score (Figure 2.17) (Waterlow, 1985). Whatever system is being used, it should be repeated regularly and systematically, especially when the patient's condition changes.

Physical assessment should include careful observation of all the pressure areas for signs of redness (erythema). If there is any redness in an unusual position, the cause should be sought and eliminated, if possible. Causative factors can include poor posture or badly fitting appliances.

► *Planning and Implementation*
► Expected Outcomes
The main outcomes for the patient may include the following:

1. The relief or removal of pressure.
2. The avoidance of shearing or friction.
3. The promotion of nutrition.
4. Improved continence.
5. Improved mobility.
6. Patient education.

Nursing Care

Relief or Removal of Pressure
The traditional method of relieving pressure is to regularly change the patient's position. This is usually carried out every two to four hours. Patients are turned from side to side, or from side to back to side. The 'turning clock' (Lowthian, 1979) is a device developed to help nurses plan a systematic turning programme throughout a 24-hour period, regardless of shift changes. It also takes into consideration the times when a patient may need to sit up, such as for meals.

More recently, it has been recognized that two-hourly turning is very disruptive to the patient, as it reduces periods of uninterrupted rest and sleep. If patients are being cared for in the community, it is unreasonable to expect that the carers can continue such a regime for any length of time. It should also be noted that, by placing a patient on the side and with the legs flexed, there is an increased risk of both the development of pressure sores over the greater trochanter and contractures of the legs in the immobile patient.

Preston (1988) has described the use in a Younger Disabled Unit of an alternative method known as the '30 degree tilt'. It involves placing patients so that the bulk of their weight is over the buttocks, which is usually an area that is better padded than the sacrum or the greater trochanters. Judicious placing of three pillows will tilt the patient to 30 degrees (Figure 2.18) (note that other pillows are still required to go under the patient's head). The patient is turned by removing the pillow under the buttock and placing it under the other buttock. This is a fairly simple but effective method of pressure relief. Preston reports that patients can be left in this position for up to six hours. However, there should be a very careful initial observation of the patient's skin, and the time the patient is left on each side should be increased gradually from two hours up to the number of hours the patient can tolerate without the skin becoming reddened or uncomfortable.

Another method of pressure relief is the use of pressure-relieving devices, hereafter referred to as support systems. They can be very simple or extremely sophisticated. Most support systems can be found in the ward area, but patients also need pressure relief if they are lying on trolleys or operating tables for any length of time. Support systems may include beds, mattresses, pads, cushions or padding for specific areas.

To make effective use of support systems, it is helpful to divide patients into low-, medium- or high-risk categories by means of a scoring system, e.g., Waterlow

WATERLOW PRESSURE SORE PREVENTION/TREATMENT POLICY
RING SCORES IN TABLE, ADD TOTAL. SEVERAL SCORES PER CATEGORY CAN BE USED

BUILD/WEIGHT FOR HEIGHT	★	SKIN TYPE VISUAL RISK AREAS	★	SEX AGE	★	SPECIAL RISKS	★
AVERAGE	0	HEALTHY	0	MALE	1	**TISSUE MALNUTRITION**	★
ABOVE AVERAGE	1	TISSUE PAPER	1	FEMALE	2		
OBESE	2	DRY	1	14–49	1	e.g.: TERMINAL CACHEXIA	8
BELOW AVERAGE	3	OEDEMATOUS	1	50–64	2	CARDIAC FAILURE	5
		CLAMMY(TEMP ↑)	1	65–74	3	PERIPHERAL VASCULAR	
CONTINENCE	★	DISCOLOURED	2	75–80	4	DISEASE	5
		BROKEN SPOT	3	81 +	5	ANAEMIA	2
COMPLETE						SMOKING	1
CATHETERISED	0	**MOBILITY**	★	**APPETITE**	★		
OCCASION INCONT.	1					**NEUROLOGICAL DEFICIT**	★
CATH. INCONTINENT		FULLY	0	AVERAGE	0		
OF FAECES	2	RESTLESS FIDGETY	1	POOR	1	e.g.: DIABETES, M.S., CVA,	
DOUBLY INCONT.	3	APATHETIC	2	N.G. TUBE/		MOTOR/SENSORY,	
		RESTRICTED	3	FLUIDS ONLY	2	PARAPLEGIA	4 6
		INERT/TRACTION	4	NBM/ANOREXIC	3		
(J. Waterlow 1988		CHAIRBOUND	5			**MAJOR SURGERY/TRAUMA**	★
						ORTHOPAEDIC	
						BELOW WAIST, SPINAL	5
SCORE: 10 + AT RISK 15 + HIGH RISK 20 + VERY HIGH RISK						ON TABLE >2 HOURS	5
						MEDICATION	★
						STEROIDS, CYTOTOXICS, HIGH DOSE ANTI-INFLAMMATORY	4

Figure 2.17 The Waterlow score (by kind permission of *Nursing Times*, where these figures first appeared: Waterlow, J. (1985) A risk assessment card, Vol. 81, No. 48, pp. 49–55).

score. The available equipment can then be categorized in the same way. Thus, selection of an appropriate support system depends on the degree of risk of the patient and individual choice. For example, a hollow-core fibre pad is ideal for the low-risk patient, especially one who feels the cold; another patient may prefer to use a foam topper, which does not retain so much heat. Table 2.27 lists the range of available support systems and indicates their most appropriate use.

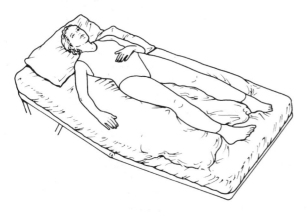

Figure 2.18 The 30 degree tilt.

A more rigorous approach is needed if a patient is going to be permanently at risk. An appropriate mattress and cushion may have to be selected with the patient, nurse and physiotherapist or occupational therapist working as a team. Factors to be taken into consideration include adequate pressure relief, comfort, maintenance of good posture and assistance in maintaining the maximum possible mobility. Assessment of pressure relief can be measured by using a pressure measuring device. This can help in eliminating those support systems giving an excessively high pressure reading. The patient then needs to test the chosen equipment for a few days so that the skin can be observed for red areas. During this time, it will also be possible to decide if the cushion or mattress causes any problems in maintaining posture or mobility. For example, a patient may discover that, although a cushion provides good posture initially, after a time it causes slumping. Another example might be of a mattress where the edge is not firm enough to support a patient when transferring from bed to chair.

Patients sitting in wheelchairs for long periods should not only be assessed for seating, but should also always have the footplates positioned correctly. Badly positioned footplates affect posture and distort the seating pressures.

Table 2.27 *The range of support systems currently available*

Support systems	Type*	Comments	Suggested usage
Alternating air	M C	Cells of air that inflate and deflate alternatively	Medium risk
Double layer alternating	M	Two layers of cells, as above	Medium risk
Air fluidized	B	Patient 'suspended' in dry fluid, which evenly distributes pressure at approx. 11 mmHg. Suitable for ITU or burns unit	High risk
Air floatation	M C	Patient sits in mattress or cushion Widely used by spinal injury patients	High risk
Air wave	M	A double layer of air cells that work in 'threes' – 1 inflated, 1 partially inflated and 1 deflated	High risk
Low air loss	B	Large air cells whose pressures can be adjusted according to patient's weight; electric controls assist movement in bed	High risk
Bead topper	MT C	Polystyrene beads help to spread and even out pressure	Low risk
Foam	M MT C	Foams of different depths or density reduce pressure by weight distribution	Low/medium risk
Gel sheets	C	Absorb pressure, so spreading the load	Low risk
Gell cell	M C	Gel cells supported by foam redistribute pressure	Medium risk
Hollow core/ sillicore fibre	MT C P	Padding that reduces pressure Ideal for bony patients who feel cold; too hot for some	Low risk
Sheepskin	P	Reduces shear but not pressure Absorbs moisture	Low risk
Water bed	B	Patient floats on surface; difficult to move patient; bed very heavy	High risk
Water cells	B	Cells of water supported by foam Movement difficult on mattress	Medium risk

*B= bed
M= mattress
MT= mattress topper
C= cushion
P= padding

Avoidance of Shear or Friction

Nurses need to be aware of the factors that can cause a patient to slip in either a bed or chair. Raising the head of the bed by even a few centimetres increases shearing over the sacral area. Use of the backrest also increases the likelihood of a patient sliding down the bed. Thus the semi-reclining position is best avoided for the at-risk patient. The use of sheepskin pads either under the sacrum and buttocks or under the heels can effectively reduce the risk of shear or friction. Sheepskins do not reduce pressure, but they absorb moisture and allow the circulation of air. Pads can be applied to elbows, heels

Figure 2.19 Bad posture leading to shearing.

and knees. They help to prevent friction as patients move in the bed.

Many hospital chairs may encourage patients to sit in an inappropriate posture, which leads to slumping (Figure 2.19). The physiotherapist can advise about more appropriate seating.

Great care must be taken when moving patients. Extra help must be sought and the use of hoists encouraged if a patient is particularly heavy.

Promotion of Nutrition

Poor nutrition is often unrecognized. Several studies have shown that hospital malnutrition is a common occurrence that could frequently be avoided (Dickerson, 1987; Hill, Blackett and Pickford, 1977). The dietary intake of all patients should be monitored, and the reason for any loss of appetite sought. The dietician can give advice about patients requiring special diets. (See also the section on nutrition, pages 26 to 51.)

The patient's nutritional status and a positive nitrogen balance must be maintained. Pressure sores develop more quickly and are more resistant to treatment in patients suffering from nutritional disorders. A high-protein diet with protein supplements may be helpful. Iron preparations and whole blood transfusions may be necessary to raise the haemoglobin levels above 1.86 mmol/l, so that tissue oxygen levels will be maintained within acceptable limits. Supplements of zinc and vitamin C may be required if the diet provides inadequate amounts.

Improved Continence

Incontinence is a very distressing problem for any patient. It is addressed in detail in Unit 6. Regular toileting can be beneficial, particularly for the elderly. It has the added advantage of providing a change of position and so relieving pressure. The use of pads can help to keep the skin dry, as urine will soak to the outer side. This can help reduce the number of times the skin must be washed. When the skin is wet it should be washed and dried carefully. There is no evidence to support the use of creams other than a barrier cream if there is persistent incontinence.

Improved Mobility

Impaired mobility can be temporary or longterm. Passive exercises can help to maintain muscle tone if the patient is unable to move unaided. They also prevent contractures of the limbs, which make positioning very difficult, and limit the activities of the patient. Exercises can be part of the programme of care when turning a patient.

Patients should be encouraged to use their full range of movements. Sometimes this requires great patience on the part of the nurse as a patient struggles to achieve some simple goal. The patient should understand the rationale for the need to move frequently and regularly, so that full co-operation can be obtained.

Patient Education

Providing the patient with information about the potential problem of pressure sores is important for any patient at risk. It is vital that any such patient and/or the carers should have a full understanding of the causes of pressure sores and the relevant predisposing factors. The educational programme should also include advice about methods of pressure relief, such as turning, repositioning and shifts of weight. For example, paraplegic patients can be taught how to raise themselves in their chairs at regular intervals. Patients who are unable to achieve this can learn how to make small shifts of weight by leaning slightly first in one direction and then another. It is helpful to provide patients and their carers with written information. It allows time for a quiet review of what has been taught, and provides a reference if problems arise at a later date.

▶ *Evaluation*
▶ **Expected Outcomes**

Patient prevents pressure sores from occurring.

1. Avoids pressure.
   a. Changes position regularly.
   b. Uses the 30 degree tilt if possible.
   c. Relieves pressure when sitting by lifting up body, or making small movements.
2. Avoids shearing forces or friction.
   a. Avoids semi-recumbent position.
   b. Uses sheepskin pad/heel protectors when appropriate.
3. Attains/maintains adequate nutritional intake.
   a. Understands the importance of protein and vitamin C in the diet.
   b. Selects foods high in protein and vitamin C.

c. Haemoglobin level is maintained within normal limits.

d. Supplements are given if required.

4. Continence is maintained.
    a. Regular toileting is carried out, if appropriate.
    b. Pads are used to keep the skin dry.

5. Promotion of mobility.
    a. Patient understands the importance of regular exercises.
    b. Maintains exercise regime.

6. Completes patient education programme.
    a. Describes the causes of pressure sores and the relevant predisposing factors.
    b. Demonstrates how to relieve pressure.
    c. With the help of the carer, is able to follow the turning and positioning programme.

Care of a Patient With Pressure Sores

Clinical Features

The first sign of a pressure sore is the appearance of an area of erythema that does not fade. Initially, the erythema will blanche under light pressure, but will not do so once damage has occurred to the microcirculation. Blistering and a superficial break in the skin follow. The lesion may extend gradually to involve deeper soft tissues, muscles, tendons and even bone. A skin lesion may represent only the 'tip of the iceberg', since a small surface sore may overlie a large, undermining defect below.

If the sore is longstanding and has repeatedly broken and healed, secondary induration (hardening of tissue) develops and the blood supply to the area is compromised by underlying scar tissue. Deep pockets of infection are often present.

The complications of pressure sores can be life-threatening, and include sepsis, osteomyelitis, pyarthrosis (pus formation within a joint cavity) and joint disarticulation (separation at the joint).

The nursing assessment provides an objective record of progress if the sore is graded regularly according to depth. Various grading systems are available; one example is shown in Table 2.28.

The expected outcomes of nursing care include:

1. Elimination of pressure.
2. Maintenance of nutritional status.
3. Appropriate wound care.

Elimination of Pressure

The sore cannot heal unless pressure is removed. An appropriate turning regime, including use of the 30 degree tilt, should be established. Use of support systems can also improve pressure relief. It may be best to confine a young, disabled person to bed until the sore is healed. This may

Table 2.28 *Classification of pressure sores based on Torrance (1983)*

	Pressure sore assessment
Grade 1	Redness that blanches under light finger pressure, indicating micro-circulation is intact
Grade 2	Redness remains, even when light finger pressure is applied; blistering and the breakdown of superficial skin will follow
Grade 3	Full thickness ulceration through to junction with subcutaneous tissue
Grade 4	Sore extends into subcutaneous fat with lateral extension
Grade 5	Sore extends through the deep fascia with destruction of muscle tissue; may even be bony involvement

(From Torrance, C. (1983) Pressure Sores: Actiology, Provention and Treatment, *Croom Helm, Beckenham.)*

not be suitable for an elderly patient because mobility may be impaired permanently.

Maintenance of Nutritional Status

A heavily exuding sore can lose large amounts of protein that will further debilitate the patient. Any protein deficiency must be corrected in order to heal the sore. Carbohydrates are necessary to 'spare' protein and provide an energy source as well as resistance to infection. Wound healing is also dependent on collagen. In turn, ascorbic acid (vitamin C) is necessary for collagen formation. Zinc is also required.

Wound Management

See the section on wound care (page 142).

INFECTION CONTROL

The Challenge of Hospital-acquired Infection

In addition to the impact of infectious diseases on the people of the planet (Chapter 38), there is another, silent epidemic that is estimated to affect about one million people on any given day. This epidemic is hospital-acquired, or nosocomial, infection. This figure is extrapolated from data gathered from a World Health Organisation prevalence study in 55 hospitals in 14 countries, which found a mean infection rate of 8.7 per cent (range 3 to 20.7 per cent.) The most prevalent hospital-acquired infection was surgical wound infection (25 per cent of the total), followed by urinary tract infection (22 per cent) and respiratory infection (20.5 per cent) (WHO, 1990).

The final results of the United States' study on the efficacy of nosocomial infection control were published in 1985 (Haley, Culver, White, *et al.*). The main aim of the study was to determine the impact of hospital infection control programmes on infection rates in a representative sample of United States hospitals between 1970 and 1975/76. It found that the essential components of effective programmes were organized surveillance and control activities; having a trained effectual infection control physician; an infection control nurse per 250 beds and a system for reporting infection rates to practising surgeons. Hospitals with these components reduced their infection rates by 32 per cent; those without experienced an increase of 18 per cent.

In 1986, Haley compared deaths wholly or partly attributable to hospital-acquired infection with national figures for mortality from other causes, e.g. road traffic accidents and heart disease, and found it to be in the top 10 of causes of death in the United States. Similar figures are not available for the United Kingdom. The last United Kingdom national prevalence study, (Meers, Ayliffe, Emmerson, *et al.*, 1981) found a prevalence of hospital-acquired infection of 9.2 per cent in the acute care hospitals studied. Urinary tract infection accounted for 2.8 per cent of this figure, wound infection 1.7 per cent and respiratory tract infection 1.8 per cent.

Thus it can be seen that the silent epidemic is a worldwide phenomenon and that the proportions of the major types of infections are relatively constant. However, the patients infected and the infecting organisms vary according to the average income of the population, the sophistication of medical services and intrinsic patient factors (see Chapter 26).

The Chain of Infection

A chain of events is necessary for the continual spread of an infectious disease, whether it is one of those described in Chapter 38 (e.g., bacteraemia, septic shock, staphylococcal infection, typhoid fever and so on) or whether it is a hospital-acquired infection. This chain of events includes the following (Figure 2.20):

● A causative agent (source).
● A reservoir.
● A portal of exit or mode of escape.
● A mode of transmission.
● A portal of entry.
● A susceptible host.

Causative Agent
The chain begins with a causative agent or invading

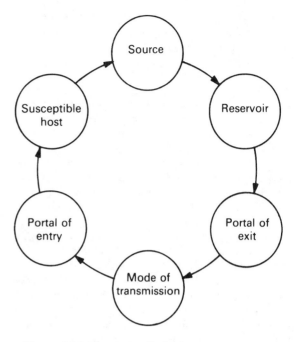

Figure 2.20 The chain of infection.

organism, which may be bacterial, viral, rickettsial, protozoal, fungal or helminthic. Infection by each type of organism gives rise to specific reactions in the infected person. Relatively few agents are pathogenic. Many bacteria, described as commensals, colonize the skin and mucous membranes and form one of the body's defences against disease, either by secreting substances that are lethal to other organisms or by competitive colonization, in which the resident organisms reach a state of dynamic equilibrium with each other and with the host, thus allowing no niche in which an invading organism can gain a foothold.

Reservoir
The second link in the chain is a reservoir, a place for the invading organism to live and multiply. The reservoir is the environment in which the agent is found, whether it is human, arthropod, plant, soil or inanimate matter; for example, humans are the reservoir for syphilis, soil is the reservoir for tetanus and animals the reservoir for brucellosis. In humans, infectious diseases and hospital-acquired infection most often arise from contact with infected or colonized people and, to a lesser extent, with contaminated objects.

Portal of Exit
The next link is the portal of exit (mode of escape) from the reservoir. Organisms may exit through various body systems, such as the respiratory tract (most common when the reservoir is the human respiratory tract), intestinal tract and genitourinary tract, or through skin lesions. In

addition, the agent may escape from the bloodstream or tissues of the host by means of insect bites, hypodermic needles or surgical instruments.

Mode of Transmission

After the infectious organism has escaped from its reservoir, it is dangerous only if it finds a way of reaching a host. This mode of transmission (the next link) may be direct (person-to-person contact, exposure to animal bite, exposure to droplet spray) or indirect (transfer without close contact, usually from an intermediate vehicle such as water, serum or contaminated fomites). Examples of organisms spread by indirect transmission are the typhoid bacillus, which is able to survive for a long period of time outside the body provided it is protected (e.g., within food), and *Staphylococcus aureus*, the organism causing the most hospital-acquired infection, which can survive unprotected in the environment for weeks. Disease may be transmitted by the vehicle route (contaminated food, water, drugs or blood), by air (droplets) or by vector (arthropods). While the majority of hospital-acquired infection is endogenous, the most common mode of transmission of other hospital-acquired infection is by contact. The major contact route is via the hands of health care providers.

Portal of Entry

The fifth link in the chain is the portal of entry of organisms into the body. This corresponds somewhat to the mode of escape and includes the respiratory tract, gastrointestinal tract, direct infection of mucous membranes or infection through a break in the skin.

Susceptible Host

The sixth link in the chain is a susceptible host. The presence of an infectious agent does not inevitably produce disease. Whether or not the person becomes ill following the entrance of infectious organisms into the body depends on numerous factors. These include: the number of organisms to which the host is exposed; the duration of the exposure; the person's age and general physical, mental and emotional health; the person's nutritional state; the status of the haematopoietic system; the absence of immunoglobulins (or the presence of abnormal immunoglobulins); and the number of T-lymphocytes and their ability to function. This introduces the important concept of the infecting dose of an agent in relation to host susceptibility, and it will be referred to again.

Removing one link in the chain of the infectious process controls infections. See Table 2.29 for a glossary of infectious disease terms.

Preventing and Controlling Infection in the Hospital

In Chapter 38 methods of controlling the spread of specific infectious diseases are described, including those caused by organisms of particular importance in the hospital setting—staphylococci and Gram-negative bacteria. Assessment of the patient and of the method of spread of the organism leads to a plan of care that aims to block the route of spread using proven techniques (Bowell in Caddow, 1989). The development of a care plan is based on the idea of identifying an appropriate point (or points) where the chain of infection can be broken.

This may be a simple or a difficult and complex process. The patient is admitted for a course of treatment that may be unrelated to an existing infectious process, so there is no specific organism around which to plan. Many diagnostic and therapeutic interventions carry a risk of infection, either by invading normally sterile body tissues or cavities, or by their potential to move normal flora or commensals from an area of harmless colonization to an area where they have the potential to cause disease. Each patient has unique risk factors for hospital-acquired infection, which interact in complex and poorly understood ways. These include age and general physical, mental and emotional health and nutritional state, together with the condition for which the patient is receiving treatment. Nursing care designed to support patients and help them return to health may itself carry infection risks.

The patient is then nursed with others who are similarly vulnerable and who may also be carrying, or infected by, a transmissible organism. The most vulnerable are further segregated into, for example, intensive care units or oncology units.

All patients receive services in common: catering, housekeeping, laundry, pharmacy, products from a sterilization and decontamination unit. Further removed from the patient, but critical to the efficiency of the support services, are engineering and other maintenance services which deal with, for example, operating theatre ventilation, water supply and air conditioning (Department of Health, 1986a).

Most important of all in preventing infection are health care providers who finally deliver care and treatment, both in the way care is provided and in the health of the provider.

These complex relationships can be divided broadly into two groups: external systems over which the health care provider has little control, and direct care where the health care provider has most control. Both groups are usually covered by hospital policies, some of which are based on national guidelines or regulations.

Infection Control Policies

These are commonly found in the ward handbook on nursing practices or in the hospital's infection control manual. Occasionally policies of particular importance are issued separately, e.g. catering.

Table 2.29 *Glossary of infectious disease terms*

Antigen – agent that is capable of producing antibodies when introduced into the body of a susceptible person

Antiserum – a serum containing antibodies given to provide immunity against a specific disease; usually regarded as temporary protection

Antitoxin – an antibody that neutralizes a bacterial toxin

Attenuation – the weakening of the toxicity or virulence of an infectious agent

Bacteraemia – presence of bacteria in the circulating blood

Bactericidal – lethal or killing to bacteria

Bacteriostatic – inhibiting or slowing growth

Carrier – one who harbours an infectious agent causing a specific disease, although giving no evidence of having the disease

Case – a particular instance of disease

Colonize – presence of organisms without an adverse host response

Commensal – an organism that lives on another without causing harm

Communicable – transmissible from person to person, directly or indirectly

Contact – a person known or believed to have been exposed to an infectious disease

Contact spread – transmission of infection by the direct route (person-to-person, droplet spray, animal bite)

Contaminated – objects that have come in contact with infectious agents

Disinfection – removal or destruction of microbes, but not necessarily bacterial spores

Endemic – a disease occurring habitually within a given geographical area, location or community

Endogenous infection – infection caused by microbes derived from the host's own flora

Epidemic – a disease attacking many people in a community simultaneously

Epidemiology – study of the occurrence and distribution of disease

Exanthem – an eruption on the skin

Exogenous infection – infection caused by microbes derived from outside the host

Fomites – inanimate vehicles other than food, milk, water and air that may harbour or be the means of transmission of organisms

Hospital-acquired infection – infection occurring during hospitalization, not present or incubating at the time of admission

Immune – protected against disease

Incidence – number of new cases of a disease (or event) occurring in a specified time

Incubation period – the development of an infection from the time it gains entry into the body until the appearance of the first signs and symptoms

Infection – deposition and growth of an organism with an associated host reaction

Infectious – capable of causing infection or disease

Infestation – invasion of body by arthropods, including insects, mites, mosquitoes and ticks, and by helminths

In vitro – within the test tube

In vivo – within a living body

Morbidity rate – the number of illnesses compared to the population; the rate may be measured in incidence or prevalence

Mortality rate – the number of deaths compared to the population

Normal flora – indigenous organisms living on or in healthy people

Nosocomial infection – hospital-acquired infection

Opportunistic pathogen – an organism that does not normally cause disease, but can do so when host defences are impaired

Pandemic – disease affecting a large portion of the population; extensive epidemic

Pathogenic – disease-producing

Prevalence – ratio of the total number of all individuals who have a disease at a particular time to the population at risk of having the disease

Prodromal – symptoms occurring at the beginning stage of the disease

Prophylaxis – measures taken to prevent disease

Sterilization – complete destruction or removal of all microbes

Surveillance – dynamic system of collecting, tabulating, analyzing and reporting data on the occurrence and distribution of disease

Toxin – a poisonous substance produced by bacterial action

Toxoid – a modified toxin capable of stimulating the production of antibodies

Vaccine – a suspension of attenuated or killed micro-organisms or their components given to build up an active immunity against an infectious disease

Policies should reflect current knowledge and be based on evidence that has been subjected to peer review, and published in the nursing and medical literature. Nevertheless, policies on the same subject vary from one hospital to another. There are several reasons for this phenomenon. Policies can take many months to prepare and be approved by various committees, and they may be in force for years. In this time new knowledge can emerge that makes the policy obsolete. More commonly, policies are soundly based on currently accepted principles, but the principles are given different priorities by different hospitals. An illustration of this is given by enteric isolation precautions for patients who have a diarrhoeal disease that spreads by the faecal–oral route. The principles to be applied here are blocking the faecal–oral route of spread and avoiding environmental contamination. Some hospitals achieve this by single room isolation, requiring the patient to use a commode in the room and hand washing afterwards. Other hospitals will also use single room isolation, but consider that patients who are able to use a flush toilet should do so, since flushing cleans the toilet bowl adequately (Newsom, 1972), the seat can be cleaned as readily as a commode seat if it becomes contaminated and patients can wash their hands afterwards.

Less commonly, a hospital may have experience of a particular disease that leads it to adopt a different policy from other hospitals. An example of this is given by methicillin-resistant *Staphylococcus aureus* (MRSA). Where this organism has caused problems (outbreaks, extensive colonization of patients and staff, and infections), the policy for its control is likely to be more stringent than in a hospital which rarely sees methicillin-resistant *Staphylococcus aureus*.

All the policies considered here are intended to minimize the risk of patients developing hospital-acquired infection and limit the spread of infection within hospitals. The first group of policies are the general ones that affect most patients. They are often dictated by legislation, and compliance may not be optional. The second group includes policies concerned with direct patient care. These are the policies from which nurses construct a shield to protect patients from hospital-acquired infection. They are not totally inflexible and provided the principles are understood, the detail can be adapted to provide innovative and sensitive care for individual patients.

Food Handling

An outbreak of food poisoning in 1984 in a large hospital for care of the elderly resulted in illness in many patients and several deaths (Department of Health, 1986b). Subsequently, Crown Immunity (protection from prosecution) was lifted from NHS premises and hospitals must now comply with the various regulations governing the preparation and handling of food, and more recently, with the Food Act (1990).

The major principles are (Ayliffe, Collins and Taylor, 1990 p.109):

1. Good separation of naturally contaminated food from food already cooked or likely to be eaten without cooking.
2. Adequate cooking to destroy causative organisms and some of the more heat-labile toxins.
3. Storage at a temperature likely to prevent the multiplication of microbes.
4. High standards of catering and personal hygiene promoted by adequate training and enforced by constant supervision.

Nurses are designated food handlers and require specific training. Hand washing is the most important measure, in particular before handling food, including enteral feeds. Enteral feeds are a particularly rich environment for microbes and may hang for several hours at room temperature. Patients have been infected in this way (Casewell and Phillips, 1978) and by inadequate cleaning of a blender used to make up feeds (Kiddy, Josse and Griffin, 1987).

Outbreaks of food-poisoning are seldom traced to a carrier. Incorrect food handling is the most usual cause (Roberts, 1990). However, the carrier route remains a possibility if a nurse or household contact has food-poisoning. As food handlers, nurses are required to report this, usually to the occupational health service, so that appropriate action can be taken, for example, microbiological sampling, advice on hand hygiene, counselling and sick leave while symptoms persist.

Laundry Arrangements

Guidance on laundry arrangements is given by the Department of Health in HC(87)30 (1987). This defines the categories of used linen and the colour of the bag into which it should be put:

- Used (soiled and fouled)—containers should be coloured white or off-white.
- Infected linen from patients with or suspected of suffering from enteric fever, other salmonella infections, dysentery, hepatitis cases and carriers, open pulmonary tuberculosis, human immunodeficiency virus (HIV) infection, notifiable diseases and other infections specified by the infection control officer as hazardous to staff—containers should be red or predominantly red.
- Heat-labile linen that would be damaged by a heat disinfection process—containers should be coloured white with an orange stripe.

These is some controversy about the used and infected linen categories, and to some extent the guidelines have been overtaken by the introduction of universal infection control precautions. Most hospitals follow the colour code, but vary the definitions, for example, fouled linen is often treated as infected linen. The underlying principle is that linen that may present a hazard to porters and laundry workers is safely contained and not handled until it has been heat disinfected.

Heat-labile linen is usually personalized patient clothing or children's clothing. Many hospitals choose to launder the latter in domestic washing machines on the ward or unit. In that case the laundry process should aim to achieve the same standards of disinfection as set out in the guidelines. Clean and dirty linen should be kept apart to avoid cross-contamination, and either the washing temperature or the tumble dryer should achieve heat disinfection.

Used linen should be handled with care to avoid increasing the number of bacteria in the air (Overton, 1988). Particles generated in this way are quite heavy and resettle rapidly. It is generally recommended that wounds are not exposed within 15 minutes of bed-making, but this is seldom possible when individualized patient care is practised. The practical solution, if a ventilated treatment room is not available, is to avoid making a bed in the immediate vicinity when a wound is being dressed.

Many foreign objects are found in laundry bags, including sharp instruments and needles, which present a hazard to laundry handlers. Other objects of more significance to patients are also found, for example, hearing aids and spectacles (Taylor, 1988).

Waste Disposal

Waste disposal is also the subject of national guidelines (Department of Health, 1982), which are likely to become more stringent as regulations enacted under the Environmental Protection Act (1990) come into force. There are presently three categories of waste of importance in the clinical areas.

1. Clinical waste includes all materials used on patients or for cleaning up spillages and must be placed in a yellow plastic bag for incineration.
2. Sharps, needles and broken glass must be placed in a sharps disposal container, also for incineration.
3. The remaining waste is designated as household waste. It is placed in black plastic bags and generally goes to landfill. (Both bags and sharps containers should be sealed and discarded when two-thirds full. If overfilled, the tops cannot be sealed securely.)

The definition of clinical waste is controversial since the majority of it presents little risk to handlers. It is aesthetically unacceptable to the general public and waste handlers and so must be segregated and incinerated.

There is little controversy about the need to dispose of sharps safely. Twenty-one different infections have been recorded as being acquired by a needlestick injury, including hepatitis B and human immunodeficiency virus

(HIV) (Collins and Kennedy, 1987). Injuries have been reported in workers who would not expect to handle sharps, such as domestic staff and porters removing bags of household waste. Even if disease does not result, the injury can cause emotional distress that could have been avoided. The safe handling of sharps is described under Universal Precautions (p. 106).

Cleaning

Hospital cleaning is a specialized task, quite different to household cleaning. Different techniques are used and some equipment is different, for example, vacuum cleaners have three filters to collect dust and an exhaust diffuser to prevent the jet of exhaust air hitting the floor, whereas a household vacuum generally has one filter and limited diffusion.

Cleaning techniques are designed to remove and not redistribute soil or microbes, as can be the case in household cleaning. As an illustration of this, most households have a dishcloth in the kitchen which may be in use for some days and which is used for wiping surfaces. Any item that becomes wet and stays wet provides an environment in which Gram-negative bacteria can grow. Thus the cloth used to wipe surfaces leaves them looking clean, but heavily contaminated. Fortunately, the organisms die as the surface dries.

Nurses are responsible for some cleaning, depending on hospital policy: for example, patient wash bowls (Greaves, 1985), mattresses (Fujita, Lilly and Ayliffe, 1981) and pillows. Efficient cleaning reduces microbial contamination by the physical removal of substances that support their growth or attach them to the surface. It is usually sufficient for low-risk items, that is, any item that does not come into close contact with patients, and where there is no reason to suspect contamination by infectious material. Efficient cleaning is a requirement before disinfection or sterilization. The usual cleaning agent is general purpose detergent and hot water. This has good 'wetting' properties and emulsifies protein. The principles underlying good cleaning practice are summarized in the following outline policy adapted from Ayliffe *et al.* (1990, page 97):

1. A fresh solution for each task should be prepared in a clean, dry container. Hot water cleans better than cold.
2. A new wipe should be used for each task. If a mop or brush is used, it should be clean and preferably dry.
3. The solution should be applied evenly to all surfaces, using as little fluid as necessary. This avoids seepage into cracks, shrinkage of materials and difficulties in subsequent removal.
4. The solution should be changed frequently to prevent a build-up of soil or microbes in the solution that would recontaminate the surface.

5. The cleaning solution should be rinsed off when practical to avoid a build-up of detergent film.
6. Used cleaning solutions should be disposed of promptly in the dirty utility area, not in wash-basins or clinical sinks where environmental contamination could occur.
7. The cleaned surface should be dried as much as possible, as a dry surface is a hostile environment for many bacteria.
8. The equipment used should be cleaned and dried, and used wipes discarded.
9. Hands should be washed before carrying out any other duties.

Disinfection

Disinfection involves the destruction of microbes, but not necessarily bacterial spores. Heat is the preferred method, such as in a bedpan washer or washer-disinfector, since it is more reliable and easier to control than most liquid disinfectants. Other heat disinfection processes are available in hospital sterilization and disinfection units, and this service is usually preferable to disinfection in the clinical areas.

In some circumstances, liquid disinfectants have to be used, but their effectiveness depends on several factors, as follows:

● Contact—the fluid must come into contact with the contaminated surface; therefore, the surface must first be cleaned of grease film, protein or soil.
● Neutralization—a wide range of substances, including soaps, detergents and some plastics used in the manufacture of cleaning equipment, may neutralize the disinfectant.
● Concentration—a solution that is too weak may not be effective and some disinfectants, such as alcohol, may be less efficient if the concentration is too high. Dilutions must be accurate.
● Stability—disinfectants may become unstable when diluted and may deteriorate with storage.
● Speed of action—disinfectants vary in their speed of action; therefore, the contact time is critical.
● Range of action—disinfectants are not usually equally effective against the whole range of organisms likely to be present (Ayliffe *et al.*, 1990, page 90).

For these reasons, disinfectant policies are generally quite rigorously controlled. Other reasons include human toxicity and cost. As a guide, disinfectants suitable for use on skin or mucous membranes are unsuitable for disinfecting equipment or the environment (alcohol is an exception). Disinfection is required for intermediate risk items such as equipment that comes into contact with intact skin or mucous membranes, and for cleaning spillages of blood or body fluids.

Sterilization

Sterilisation is usually defined as complete destruction or removal of all microbes, including spores. It can be achieved by heat, chemicals, irradiation and filtration.

Heat is most commonly used in hospital sterilization and disinfection units, either with an autoclave or a hot air oven. An autoclave has been described as a sophisticated pressure cooker (Ayliffe *et al.*, 1990). The simpler downward displacement autoclaves, including the table-top autoclaves sometimes found in clinics, are used for unwrapped instruments and other metal or plastic equipment that do not have to be maintained in a sterile condition. Wrapped instruments and soft packs, such as theatre clothing and dressing packs, are sterilized in a porous load autoclave, which ensures that the equipment is dry at the end of the process.

Hot air ovens are used for heat-resistant instruments that will not withstand the pressures used in autoclaving. Irradiation is used by commercial manufacturers. Filtration is used for some liquids and pharmaceutical preparations. Some hospitals have ethylene oxide gas sterilizers for heat-sensitive equipment, but the process is more commonly used by industry. The chemical usually used to sterilize or disinfect heat-sensitive equipment is glutaraldehyde. Under controlled conditions, it is a reliable disinfectant, but sterilization is more difficult to achieve. It is most useful for high-level disinfection of endoscopes. Its use in other circumstances has declined since the introduction of the Control of Substances Hazardous to Health Regulations (1988), as it is potentially toxic and allergenic.

Sterilization is generally regarded as an absolute term, but as it is difficult to test whether an object is sterile, control of the process of sterilization is necessary to ensure a high probability of sterilization taking place (Kelsey, 1972). This is best achieved in a hospital sterilization and disinfection unit.

When sterile products have been delivered to the clinical area, the users then have the responsibility of ensuring that sterility is maintained. This is achieved by storing the packs in conditions that protect them from damage and moisture. The final check immediately before use should ensure that the autoclave indicator tape or panel has changed colour and that the pack is dry and undamaged. Single-use products supplied by industry, such as syringes, should be treated in a similar manner. The integrity of these packs is best maintained by storing them in the shelf pack supplied by the manufacturer, rather than decanting them into another container where damage is more likely to occur.

Patient Care

The preceding paragraphs have listed some of the ways in which patients are protected from the hospital environment. Application of these policies offers only limited protection. Bearing in mind that each patient has a unique inherent risk of acquiring infection, the most significant protection the patient has is the way in which the health care provider actually provides care.

Hospitals tend to have procedures for all manner of nursing practices: insertion and management of indwelling urinary catheters and management of intravenous lines, among many others. With the reservations discussed earlier about policies in general, these provide a reasonable framework around which to construct a plan of care. However, there are two further problems. First, there are the circumstances not covered by a policy or covered by a nonspecific policy. An example is hand washing. There may be no policy on hand washing in general, although it is contained within specific procedures; or the policy may be a list of events which should be preceded or followed by a hand wash. This can be difficult to remember, and some of it may not make much sense.

In essence, if policies are to have their desired outcome, it is necessary for health care providers to learn to 'see' microbes and react accordingly, rather than follow policies or regard each policy in isolation from all others.

Hand Washing

Hand hygiene is the most important measure in preventing infection (Larson, 1988). Broughall, Marsham, Jackson *et al.* (1984) asked nurses to estimate the frequency of hand washing per shift and then measured the frequency with an automatic device. The mean claimed frequency of hand washing was 24 in the first period of study and 21 in the second. The monitored frequency was 10 in the first period and 5 in the second.

Opinion remains divided as to whether a disinfectant/ detergent hand washing preparation is needed (Ayliffe, Babb, Davies, *et al.* 1988; Webster and Faoagali, 1989). There is agreement that such preparations are a valuable element of the surgical scrub, but the evidence for their value in other areas is mixed. Some authorities recommend that disinfectant/detergents are used in high-risk areas, such as neonatal and adult intensive care units and isolation units. Others recommend liquid soap for all areas, with an alcohol-based disinfectant available for aseptic procedures and in high-risk areas. In any event the most important points are how the preparation is used and when.

An efficient hand wash involves thorough lathering of all hand surfaces, rinsing under running water and careful drying on a paper towel (Caddow, 1989). Soap helps to loosen and emulsify adherent protein or soil; rinsing removes the protein or soil and residual soap that can cause drying of the skin; careful drying completes the removal process and helps to avoid sore hands.

An alternative method of hand hygiene is the application of an alcohol-based solution to physically clean hands and rubbing to dryness. Care has to be taken to apply the solution to all hand surfaces as the alcohol can only kill the organisms it touches (Taylor, 1978).

Studies indicate that nurses wash their hands as required by specific procedures, but are less certain when to wash their hands outside this framework (Taylor, 1978). This study was done when task allocation was commonly practised. One observation was that nurses would empty several urine drainage bags before washing their hands. It is difficult to know what thoughts lay behind this practice, since the drainage taps are the distal end of a tube that enters a sterile body cavity. Interestingly, a similar study in 1984, when task allocation had largely disappeared, produced similar findings (Sedgwick, 1984).

A list of when hands should be washed may be incomplete, and in any event has little meaning when divorced from the reality of clinical activity. Approaching these difficulties from another angle, deciding whether or not to wash hands outside the framework of a defined procedure is one of the few independent decisions nurses at the start of their careers are allowed to take. It is an important decision in terms of exposing patients to infection. If the wrong decision is taken, it has been taken without the patients' knowledge or consent. Patients may well feel that their opinion should be sought before a risk is taken on their behalf.

It is difficult to define a decision pathway that takes account of the varied nature of clinical activity, but two questions give a reasonable clue as to whether a hand wash is needed. Was the last, or last-but-one, task likely to have contaminated the hands? If so, is the next task likely to place a patient at risk? An alternative question the nurse could ask presupposes a degree of knowledge of food hygiene: 'If the next thing I was about to do was eat a sandwich, would I wash my hands?'

Universal Precautions

The concept of universal precautions arose from concern about transmission of human immunodeficiency virus (HIV) to health care providers (Centers for Disease Control, 1985). It combines blood and body fluid isolation precautions (wearing gloves for contact with these substances) with increased care in handling sharps, in particular not resheathing needles unless there is a safe method of so doing. In 1984 (anonymous), the first recorded case of transmission of HIV to a health care provider by a needlestick injury was reported. The nurse received a microinjection of blood when resheathing a needle used to take blood from a patient with acquired immunodeficiency syndrome (AIDS). The incident appeared to confirm that the principal risk to health care providers was by inoculation.

Opinion began to be modified as the AIDS epidemic spread and it was clear that the concept of risk groups for

AIDS was becoming increasingly inaccurate. When three health care providers became HIV-antibody-positive following blood contamination of non-intact skin, universal precautions were modified and extended (Centers for Disease Control, 1987). Some uncertainties still remained about which body fluids constituted a risk, but those have now been clarified by the Centers for Disease Control and by the United Kingdom Expert Advisory Group on AIDS (1990).

The premise of universal precautions is that it is seldom possible to recognize the patient who may be carrying a blood-borne disease. Therefore measures to protect health care providers must be applied universally to all patients. An additional advantage for patients is that it is non-judgemental and non-discriminatory, and respects the patient's right to confidentiality. Each health care provider makes a decision on the appropriate protective clothing to wear based on anticipated contact with blood or with body fluids, which should be treated with the same precautions as blood. These fluids include the following (Expert Advisory Group on AIDS, 1990):

1. Cerebrospinal fluid, peritoneal fluid, pleural fluid, pericardial fluid, synovial fluid, amniotic fluid, semen, vaginal secretions.
2. Any other body fluid containing visible blood.
3. Saliva in association with dentistry.
4. Unfixed tissues or organs.

The amount of protective clothing used increases as the likelihood of contact or splashing increases (Table 2.30). Some additional precautions are also necessary, as follows (see also Table 2.31):

- Good basic hygiene with regular hand washing is required.
- Gloves should be worn when cleaning equipment before sterilization or disinfection, when handling chemical disinfectants and when cleaning up spillages of blood or body fluids.
- Existing wounds or skin lesions should be covered with a waterproof dressing and replaced as often as necessary.
- Care should be taken in the handling and disposal of sharps; in particular, needles should not be resheathed unless there is a method of doing so without directing the needle towards an unprotected hand.
- Spillages of blood or body fluids should be cleared up promptly and surfaces disinfected.

The use of universal precautions is controversial (Speller, Shanson, Ayliffe *et al.*, 1990). It can be argued that where the prevalence of human immunodeficiency virus in the community is low, universal precautions are unnecessary. Additional measures need only be used when providing care for someone at increased risk of having human immunodeficiency virus infection. Others argue that the HIV-antibody-positive person cannot be easily recog-

nized and, although HIV causes most concern, other viruses spread by the blood-borne route (e.g., hepatitis B and the newly recognized hepatitis C) present a risk to staff, and the patients who have these viruses also cannot be easily recognized (Centers for Diseases Control, 1987; Lynch, Jackson, Cummings, *et al.*, 1987; Wilson and Breedon, 1990).

Universal precautions are designed to protect health care providers, but Lynch *et al.* (1987) saw an extension of these precautions as a way of protecting patients from hospital-acquired infection. They call this method 'body substance isolation'. It is an attractive idea as it blocks most of the routes by which infection spreads and minimizes the need to isolate patients. The authors argue that the value of traditional isolation methods is largely unproven, and that it is illogical to use one set of standards when a patient does not appear to have an infection and another set of standards when the infection is diagnosed some time after admission. They also point out that some infections, such as some of the childhood fevers, are most infectious before there is evidence of infection. Moreover, isolation precautions are 'diagnosis driven' and thus of limited value in preventing the majority of hospital-acquired infections.

Table 2.30 *Patient contact and protective clothing required*

No contact with blood or body fluids	No protective clothing
Contact probable, but splashing unlikely	Gloves to be worn
Contact and some splashing probable	Gloves and plastic apron to be worn; masks/protective eyewear or visor to be available
High risk of splashing	Gloves, waterproof gown, mask/protective eyewear or visor to be worn

Table 2.31 *Universal precautions*

1. Wear appropriate protection
2. Always wash your hands
3. Wear gloves for direct contact with:
   a. Blood/body fluids
   b. Broken skin or mucous membranes
4. Discard sharps safely:
   a. NEVER resheath needles
   b. Place all sharps directly into a sharps bin
   c. Discard bin when two-thirds full
5. Keep cuts and abrasions covered
6. Disinfect blood/body fluid spillages

The essence of body substance isolation is that all body substances, including excreta, are treated in the same way as in universal precautions and that only those nurses with known immunity care for patients with infectious diseases such as measles, mumps, rubella and chickenpox. Single rooms are required only for some diseases spread in whole or part by the airborne route, or for patients who soil articles in the environment with body substances.

The concept has been described in the United Kingdom by Wilson and Breedon (1990) as universal infection control precautions, and they anticipate that many expensive rituals that surround the management of infected patients can be discontinued. They also point out that patients appear to find the principle of protection for handling body fluids entirely acceptable, and that patients often express a greater concern for hygiene than do health care providers.

There is some emerging evidence that body substance isolation reduces the transmission of some bacteria and viruses in hospitals (Leclair, Freeman, Sullivan, *et al.*, 1987; Lynch, Cummings, Roberts, *et al.*, 1990). Other evidence, not yet published, attributes the spread of hospital-acquired infection to body substance isolation. It appears that nurses were not changing their gloves after each patient contact.

Body substance isolation or universal infection control precautions should be seen as a partnership between carer and patient in protecting each person from infection. This partnership is further emphasized by the recent report of probable transmission of human immunodeficiency virus from a health care provider to two, and possibly three, patients (Centers for Disease Control, 1991).

Hospital Infection Control

Management of the hospital infection control service includes a multidisciplinary infection control committee and a small infection control team: the infection control doctor (usually a medical microbiologist), one or more infection control nurses and sometimes a medical laboratory scientific officer (Department of Health, 1988; Scottish Home and Health Department, 1988). The committee devises and monitors the overall infection control programme. The team provides expert advice to the committee and to hospital staff. Together, they prepare policies and monitor their effectiveness, monitor infections with a view to improving practice, deal with outbreaks, undertake research and teach. The team is a resource for all health care providers. The infection control nurse, in particular, works closely with nursing colleagues and is available in person or by telephone or 'pager' whenever information or advice is needed. Infection control nurses have wide professional experience and have generally undertaken a one-year course of specialist preparation.

PERIOPERATIVE CARE

Surgical Indications and Classifications

Surgery may be classified as elective or emergency. An elective operation is one that has been planned beforehand, allowing adequate time for the patient to be prepared. An example of elective surgery may be removal of superficial cysts or ligation of varicose veins. An emergency operation is one that is carried out unexpectedly and without delay, in a life-threatening situation, e.g., to treat intestinal obstruction or gunshot or stab wounds. The patient may have had little or no time to prepare for admission to hospital and surgery.

Concept of the Patient Undergoing Surgery

For the patient undergoing surgery, the total experience (perioperative nursing care) can be divided into three phases:

1. Preoperative phase—from the time that the decision is made for operative intervention to the transfer of the patient to the operating theatre.
2. Intraoperative phase—from the time that the patient is received in theatre until admission to the recovery room.
3. Postoperative phase—from the time of admission to the recovery room to the follow-up clinic and evaluation.

Psychological Preparation of the Patient For Surgery

Any surgical procedure is always preceded by some type of emotional reaction in a patient, whether it is obvious or hidden, normal or abnormal. Preoperative anxiety is an anticipatory response to an experience that patients may view as a threat to their customary role in life, body integrity or even life itself. A mind that is not at peace directly influences the functioning of the body. Therefore, it is imperative to know what anxieties the patient is experiencing.

By taking a careful nursing history, the nurse may elicit patient concerns that can have a direct bearing on the course of the surgical experience. Undoubtedly, a patient facing surgery is beset by fears: fears of the unknown, of death, of anaesthesia, of cancer. Add to that worries about the possible loss of a job, the need to support a family or the possibility of permanent incapacity and one can get a sense of the enormous emotional strain created by the prospect of surgery. Consequently, the nurse needs to be tolerant and understanding.

Psychological preparation of the patient begins as soon

as it is known that surgery will be required. The patient's reaction to surgery is dependent on many factors. Sufficient time must be taken to explain to the patient in simple, understandable terms what is going to happen in order to identify any fears the patient may have and to answer any questions. In Hayward's study (1973), therapeutic discussion to reduce preoperative anxiety was rated by 33 per cent of patients as the most comforting and reassuring factor. It is important that the patient is given information regarding the type of surgery to be performed, what effect it is likely to have on the patient's life and lifestyle, and how long the recovery period can be expected to be. Anxieties may be expressed in many ways (Gray, 1989), and nurses need to be sensitive to the features of anxiety, which may range from overtalkativeness to silence, and from submission to aggression. Ignorance of what is about to happen usually causes more fear and mental stress than does being kept informed. Involvement of the patient's family and/or significant others is important, and will help the patient's rehabilitation. Fear is expressed in different ways by different people.

Fear of Pain

Fear of pain, and how the patient will react to it, is very relevant. The patient may have bad memories of pain following surgery, and be afraid that the same thing will happen again. The patient may be afraid of a 'loss of face' if pain is admitted to, and believe that it should be withstood stoically. Explanations regarding the steps that will be taken to relieve pain are important in allaying the patient's anxieties.

Family Worries

Many patients have family worries, perhaps about small children or elderly, dependent relatives, or perhaps the head of the household is afraid that this role will no longer be fulfilled after surgery. It may be necessary to organize help via the social work department in order to give the patient peace of mind.

Fear of the Unknown

Fear of the unknown tends to be more threatening than the known. It may stem partly from a belief on the patient's part that not everything has been told about the diagnosis and illness. The patient may never have been in hospital before, and may not know what to expect. The nurse may do much to allay these fears by finding out exactly what the patient does know, and informing the nurse in charge and the surgeon about these anxieties.

Fear of Anaesthesia

Many patients are frightened that they will not be 'asleep' when the operation takes place. Some are frightened that they will not awaken at the end, and others with previous experience fear that they will vomit and have further pain. Normally, before surgery, patients are visited by the anaesthetist, and careful explanation is given about what type of anaesthetic will be given, and its after-effects. If the nurse has identified any particular fears that the patient may have, it is important that this information is passed on to the anaesthetist. Visits to the ward by anaesthetists and theatre nursing staff help to establish a rapport with the patient and makes the arrival in the anaesthetic room less traumatic.

Financial Worry

Financial problems may cause the patient great anxiety when surgery is necessary. Single-parent families may face financial loss if the parent is unable to work. The hospital may be some distance from the patient's home, thus involving travelling expenses, which may cause financial hardship. The type of surgery being carried out may necessitate the end of a career or the loss of a job. The social work department may be involved in helping to sort out any financial worries that the patient may have.

Fear of Death

This is a real fear, and cannot be dismissed lightly. The nurse must explore why the patient fears death, and pass on this information to the nurse in charge and the surgeon. Good rapport between the patient and nurse, together with tact on the part of the nurse, may help the patient to realize that this fear is magnified. Such fears may also be allayed by counselling from the patient's religious advisor.

The significance of spiritual therapy must not be forgotten. Regardless of the religious affiliation of the patient, the nurse recognizes that faith in a 'higher power' can be as therapeutic as medication. Every attempt must be made to help the patient obtain the desired spiritual help. This may be accomplished by participating in prayer, by reading passages from the Scriptures or by contacting an appropriate religious advisor. Faith has great sustaining power; thus, the beliefs of each individual patient should be respected and supported.

The preparation of the patient for theatre depends on a team approach from those involved in patient care and other support; each member has a role to play in relieving the patient's anxieties.

Physical Preparation of Patient For Surgery

Physical Assessment

During the admission procedure, the nurse should observe and note any problems that the patient may have and which ones may complicate the condition and interfere with progress. Any abnormalities should be reported to the doctor: for example, elevation of temperature, alteration of pulse rate or blood pressure, skin rash, cough or symptoms of a cold, mouth ulcers or gum changes, onset of menstruation, diarrhoea, nausea or vomiting, evidence of dehydration (dry tongue, reduced skin turgor, sunken eyes) or pressure sores. Knowledge of a past history of allergies, especially to drugs or dressings, is very important if problems are to be avoided. A record of the patient's medication is noted. Urinalysis, usually with dipsticks, can screen for many disease, especially diabetes mellitus, jaundice, kidney diseases or infections.

The medical examination and the specific assessment of the disease process will also evaluate cardiac and pulmonary function, and measure blood pressure. Chest X-rays may be taken, and blood is drawn for haematological and biochemical tests, as well as for grouping and cross-matching in case transfusion is required. It is important to recognize the existence of hypertension, a previous history of heart disease, deep venous thrombosis or pulmonary embolism, metabolic diseases, particularly diabetes mellitus and other conditions such as pregnancy. An electrocardiogram (ECG) may be carried out, particularly for older patients or those with pre-existing risk factors, to examine for evidence of cardiac ischaemia, hypertrophy or rhythm disorders. Fluid and electrolyte balance and nutritional state are assessed.

These preliminary contacts with the staff during the taking of the nursing history, physical examination and diagnostic tests provide patients with opportunities to ask questions and to get acquainted with those who will be caring for them. In their efforts to establish rapport with the patient, the doctor and nurse must respect the patient's feelings and needs.

Nutritional State

(See also Nutrition, p. 26.) Protein and vitamin C are essential for the promotion of healing, and a malnourished patient will not respond well to surgery. Deficiencies delay healing and decrease resistance to infection because antibodies are formed more slowly. Vitamin C is necessary for the synthesis of collagen, and hence wound healing is delayed with vitamin C deficiency. Carbohydrate deficiency reduces liver glycogen, so that the release of glucose from stored glycogen may be impaired. This, in turn, will inhibit recovery during a period when the body particularly requires energy. Postoperatively, the body catabolizes energy sources, and food intake is often very limited at this time.

Patient education regarding postoperative nutrition is important, and the patient is more likely to co-operate if the facts are understood. Identifying the patient's likes and dislikes will also enhance co-operation. Any dental problems or poor oral hygiene should be corrected during the preoperative stage. If oral intake is insufficient or impossible, it may be necessary to give intravenous carbohydrate, lipid or protein solutions.

Obesity

If the patient is overweight, and if preoperative time permits, the patient should be started on a reduction diet, usually 800 to 1,000 Kcal a day to reduce the risks of surgery. Obesity greatly increases the severity of complications, as fatty tissues are poorly resistant to infection, and wound infection and dehiscence are more common. Other problems include chest infections and phlebitis, as the patient finds it more difficult to move. Such patients have a higher incidence of cerebrovascular, endocrine, hepatic and biliary disease.

Respiratory State

The expected outcome for potential surgical patients is to have optimum respiratory function. All patients are urged to stop smoking four to six weeks before an operation; those undergoing upper abdominal and chest surgery are taught breathing exercises.

Since it is necessary to maintain adequate ventilation during all phases of surgical treatment, surgery is usually contraindicated when the patient has a respiratory infection. Respiratory difficulties increase the possibility of atelectasis, bronchopneumonia and respiratory failure when anaesthetics are superimposed. Patients with pulmonary problems are evaluated by testing pulmonary function and determining blood gas values to note the extent of respiratory insufficiency. Antibiotics may be given for infections.

Cardiovascular State

The expected outcome in preparing any patient for surgery is to have a well-functioning cardiovascular system to meet the oxygen, fluid and nutritional needs throughout the perioperative period.

Since the margin of safety is lessened when a patient exhibits signs of cardiovascular disease, this condition demands greater than usual diligence during all phases of management and care. Depending on the severity of symptoms, surgery may be deferred until maximal benefits have been obtained from medical treatment. At times, surgical treatment can be modified to meet the likely tolerance of the patient. For example, in an obese patient with acute obstructive cholecystitis and possible diabetes and coronary artery disease, simple gallbladder drainage with removal of calculi may be done rather than a more extensive operation.

Of particular significance in the patient with cardiovascular disease is the necessity to avoid sudden changes of position, prolonged immobilization, hypotension or hypoxia and overloading of the body with fluids or blood.

Hepatic and Renal Function

The expected outcome is to have maximum functioning of

the liver and urinary systems so that drugs, anaesthetic agents and body waste and toxins are adequately removed from the body.

The liver is important in the biotransformation of anaesthetic compounds. Therefore, any disease of the liver has an effect on anaesthetic intake. Because acute liver disease is associated with a high surgical death rate, preoperative improvement in liver function is desirable. Careful assessment is made using various liver function tests (see Chapter 16).

The kidney is involved in the excretion of anaesthetic drugs and their metabolites. Acid–base and water metabolism are also important considerations in anaesthetic administration. Surgery is contraindicated when a patient has acute glomerulonephritis, acute renal insufficiency with oliguria or anuria, or other acute renal problems, unless the surgery is a lifesaving measure or is necessary to improve urinary function, as in an obstructive uropathy.

Endocrine Function

In uncontrolled diabetes, the chief life-threatening hazard is that of hypoglycaemia, which may develop during anaesthesia or postoperatively. It results from inadequate intake of carbohydrates or from insulin overdosage. Other hazards that threaten but occur less rapidly are acidosis and glucosuria.

In general, the surgical risk of the patient with controlled diabetes is no greater than that of the nondiabetic patient (see Chapter 18).

Immunological Function

An important nursing outcome is to identify any history of allergy, including previous allergic reactions. It is particularly important to note any sensitivities to drugs and past adverse reactions to medication. The nurse should obtain a list of offending agents and document how the allergy was manifested. The nurse should also ask about blood transfusion reactions in the past. Any affirmative responses should be recorded, along with current drug therapy. A history of bronchial asthma is reported to the anaesthetist.

Immunosuppression is now common with steroid therapy, renal transplantation, cancer radiotherapy and chemotherapy, therefore strict asepsis must be practised to prevent infection. The mildest symptoms or slightest elevation of temperature need to be investigated.

Immuno-incompetence as a result of infection by the human immunodeficiency virus (HIV) is becoming more frequent. At present, assessment of HIV antibody status requires patient consent.

Prior Drug Therapy

Attention should be given to the history of drug usage by the patient. Potent medications have an effect on physiological functions and interactions of such drugs with anaesthetic agents can cause serious problems, such as arterial hypotension and circulatory collapse or depression.

The potential effects of prior drug therapy are evaluated by the anaesthetist, who considers the length of time the patient has used the drugs, the patient's condition and the nature of the proposed surgery. Drugs that cause particular concern are the following:

1. Adrenal steroids. It is advisable to continue corticosteroids before surgery. Because the sudden termination of therapy may cause cardiovascular collapse if steroid therapy has been used for a chronic problem over a period of time, it is usually advisable to give a 'burst' of high-dose steroid immediately before and after surgery.
2. Diuretics, in particular the thiazide drugs, may cause excessive respiratory depression during anaesthesia; this results from an electrolyte imbalance.
3. Phenothiazine drugs may increase the hypotensive action of anaesthetics.
4. Antidepressants, in particular monoamine oxidase inhibitors, increase the hypotensive effects of anaesthetics.
5. Tranquillizers, e.g., barbiturates, diazepam and chlordiazepoxide, are medications that can cause anxiety, tension and even seizures if withdrawn suddenly.
6. Insulin: interaction between anaesthetics and insulin must be considered when a diabetic patient is undergoing surgery.
7. Antibiotics: 'mycin' drugs such as neomycin, kanamycin and, less frequently, streptomycin may present problems; when these drugs are combined with a curariform muscle relaxant, nerve transmission is interrupted and apnoea due to respiratory paralysis may result. For the reasons cited, it is imperative that the patient's drug history be assessed by the nurse and anaesthetist.

Considerations For the Elderly Patient

An older person facing an operation usually has a combination of medical problems in addition to the specific one for which surgery is indicated. Elderly people frequently do not report symptoms, perhaps because they fear that a serious illness may be diagnosed or because they accept such symptoms as part of growing old. A high level of awareness of subtle clues will alert the nurse to underlying problems.

In general, the elderly are considered to be poorer surgical risks than younger patients. Cardiac reserves are lower, renal and hepatic functions are depressed and gastrointestinal activity is likely to be reduced. Dehydration, constipation and malnutrition may be evident.

Sensory limitations such as dimming vision, impaired hearing and reduced sensitivity of touch are often the reasons for accidents, injuries and burns. Therefore the nurse must be alert to maintaining a safe environment. Arthritis is common in older people and may affect mobility, making it difficult for the patient to turn from one side to the other without discomfort. Protective measures include adequate padding for tender areas, moving the patient slowly, protecting bony prominences against prolonged pressure and providing gentle massage to promote adequate circulation.

It is important to assess the condition of the mouth to identify any dental caries, dentures and partial plates.

The loss of sweat glands leads to dry, itchy skin. Such fragile skin is easily abraded, so added precautions are taken in moving an elderly person. The loss of subcutaneous fat makes older people less resistant to temperature changes. A lightweight cotton blanket is a desirable cover when an elderly patient is moved to and from the operating theatre.

Elderly people have had innumerable experiences in their lifetime. They have been exposed to personal illness and life-threatening illnesses of friends and family. Consequently, they have fears about their own futures that may not be obvious, but nonetheless are there. Taking time to talk with them may elicit any fears, and make possible the relaxation and acceptance needed.

The optimum goal is to have as many positive factors as possible. Every attempt is made to stabilize those conditions that otherwise hinder a smooth recovery.

Informed Consent

Before any operative procedure, a consent form is signed by the patient, giving the surgeon permission to perform the operation. This is a medico-legal document, and the full implications of the surgery must be explained by the doctor before the consent form is signed. The signing is also witnessed by the doctor. The document protects the patient against any unauthorized procedures, and protects the surgeon and the hospital against legal action by the patient, who might otherwise claim that an unauthorized procedure had been carried out. Every surgical procedure requires its own consent form.

If the patient is unable to write, an 'X' to indicate a signature is acceptable provided there are two signed witnesses to the mark.

Consent in the Adolescent Patient or in Emergencies

In the United Kingdom, the age of medical consent is taken to be 16 years. In the absence of a parent, guardian or next of kin, or where consent is unobtainable for any reason, it may be given by the consultant in charge in an emergency. The completed consent form should be placed in the patient's notes, and checked by the theatre nursing staff and surgeon.

Preoperative Patient Education

The value of preoperative advice to the patient has long been recognized. Information and advice should be directed at the individual patient's needs, hopes and fears. Swindale (1989) states that it is well recognized that patients who are anxious remember little information if it is given verbally; in fact, 50 to 60 per cent of information given in this way is forgotten. Initially, it is likely that the patient will be able to recall only seven items, unless repetition or overlearning occurs (Franklin, 1974; Summers, 1984). This may be due to the reticular activating centre, which, as part of the central nervous system, is unable to sort out and filter incoming information as a result of the patient's preoccupation with anxiety. Groen (1971), Hildgard and Atkinson (1979), Hayward (1973) and Boore (1978) demonstrated that the provision of information before surgery lowers anxiety levels, reduces stress, decreases pain and promotes a better and quicker recovery. It is also important that the patient is advised of the sensations that will be experienced. For example, saying that preoperative medication will relax the patient before the operation is not as effective as informing the patient that the medication will cause lightheadedness and sleepiness. Once the patient knows what to expect, these reactions will be anticipated and thus a higher degree of relaxation should be attained.

Deep Breathing, Coughing and Relaxation Skills

One goal of preoperative nursing care is to show the patient how to promote lung ventilation and blood oxygenation following general anaesthesia. This is done by demonstrating to the patient how to take a deep, slow breath (maximal sustained inspiration) and how to exhale slowly. The patient is placed in a sitting position to provide maximum lung expansion. After practising deep breathing several times, the patient is instructed to breathe deeply, exhale through the mouth, take a short breath and cough from deep in the lungs (Figure 2.21). In addition to enhancing respiration, these exercises make the patient more relaxed.

If there is to be a thoracic or abdominal incision, the nurse can demonstrate how the incision line can be supported so that pressure is minimized and pain is controlled. The patient should put the palms of the hands together, interlacing the fingers snugly. Placing the hands across the incisional site acts as an effective support when coughing. The patient also needs to know that medication will be given to control pain.

The expected outcome in promoting coughing is to loosen secretions so that they can be removed. When a deep breath is taken before coughing, the cough reflex is stimulated. If coughing is not encouraged, hypostatic pneumonia and other lung complications may occur.

Turning and Active Body Movement

The expected outcomes of promoting deliberate body movement postoperatively are to improve the patient's circulation, to prevent venous stasis and to contribute to optimal respiratory exchange.

The patient is shown how to turn from side to side and how to assume the lateral position. This position will be used postoperatively (even before the patient is conscious) and should be assumed every second hour.

Exercises of the extremities include extension and flexion of the knee and hip joints (similar to bicycle-riding while lying on the side). The foot is rotated as though tracing the largest possible circle with the great toe (Figure 2.22). The elbow and shoulder are also put through the range of motion. At first the patient will be assisted and reminded to do these exercises, but later is encouraged to do them alone.

The nurse is reminded to use proper body mechanics and to instruct the patient to do the same. When the patient is placed in any position, the body is to be maintained in proper alignment. Muscle tone is maintained so that ambulation will be made easier.

Pain Control and Medications

The patient is told that premedication will be given to encourage relaxation and perhaps make the patient feel sleepy. The patient is also informed that it may make the mouth dry. Postoperatively, the patient can expect medications to maintain comfort but they will not prevent the patient from regaining activity and maintaining an adequate air exchange.

Prophylactic antibiotics may be prescribed in specific instances.

Other Information

Patients feel more at ease when they know at what point postoperatively they can expect a visit from family or friends. It helps them to know that loved ones will be kept informed about the acute phases of the surgical experience. They may also appreciate knowing that a spiritual adviser will be available, if required.

If patients know beforehand that they will be on assisted breathing and that drainage tubes will be in place along with any special equipment required, they are more

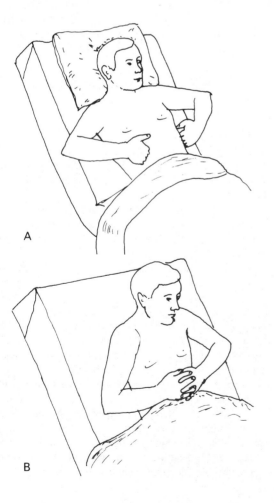

A

B

Figure 2.21 A. Diaphragmatic breathing: refers to a flattening of the dome of the diaphragm during inspiration with resulting enlargement of the upper abdomen as air rushes in. During expiration, the abdominal muscles contract. (1) The patient should practise in the same position assumed in bed following surgery, i.e. a semi-recumbent position, propped in bed with the back and shoulders well supported with pillows; (2) with the hands in a loose-fist position, the patient should allow the hands to rest lightly on the front of the lower ribs—fingernails against lower chest to feel the movement; (3) the patient should breathe out gently and fully as the ribs sink down and inwards towards the middle line; (4) then the patient should take a deep breath through the nose and mouth, and let the abdomen rise as the lungs fill with air; (5) this breath should be held for a count of five; (6) the patient should exhale and let out all the air through the nose and mouth; (7) this should be repeated 15 times, with a short rest after each group of five; (8) the procedure should be practised twice a day preoperatively.
B. Coughing: (1) the patient should lean forward slightly from a sitting position in bed, interlace the fingers together and place the hands across the incisional site to act as a support when coughing; (2) diaphragmatic breathing should take place, as described above; (3) with the mouth slightly open, the patient should breathe in fully; (4) then the patient should 'hack' out sharply for three short breaths; (5) keeping the mouth open, the patient should then take in a quick, deep breath and immediately give a strong cough once or twice. This will help clear secretions from the chest; it may cause some discomfort, but will not harm the incision.

likely to accept them postoperatively, thus reducing anxiety levels.

Preoperative Fasting

Nutrition and Fluids

When the operation is scheduled for the morning, the meal on the preceding evening may be an ordinary light diet. Dehydrated patients, particularly the elderly, may require intravenous fluids preoperatively. Fluids may be administered intravenously to patients to whom fluids cannot be given by mouth. If the operation is scheduled to take place in the afternoon and does not involve any part of the gastrointestinal tract, the patient may be given a soft diet for breakfast.

The expected outcome in withholding food before surgery is to prevent aspiration. Aspiration occurs when food or fluid is regurgitated from the stomach and inhaled into the pulmonary system. Such inhaled material acts as a foreign substance, is irritating and causes an inflammatory reaction, and at the same time interferes with and even intercepts adequate air exchange. Aspiration is a serious problem, as is reflected in a high mortality rate (60 to 70 per cent) when it occurs, and to prevent it, food and fluid intake is restricted for 8 to 10 hours preoperatively. However, Walsh and Ford (1989) investigated the 'ritual' of preoperative fasting, which ranged from between 8 to 20 hours preoperatively. They were concerned about the damaging physiological effects from this lengthy period of starvation. Citing Nimmo (1983), Bateman and Whittingham (1982) and Summerskill (1976), Walsh and Ford suggested that a four-hour period of starvation is the maximum required for any patient. They also suggested that although a day without food causes the patient no harm, a day without fluid would certainly be harmful, particularly to elderly patients who may be dehydrated by the time they reach theatre. Apart from causing avoidable physiological harm for patients, unnecessary fasting has been suggested as a contributory factor to preoperative stress. Thomas (1987) found that 76 per cent of patients were unaware why, and 62 per cent for how long, they were fasted. It is therefore important for nurses to explain to patients how long they are to fasted, and why.

Bowel Preparation

A warm cleansing enema or suppositories may be given the evening before an operation and may be repeated if ineffectual. This is to prevent defaecation during anaesthesia and to prevent accidental surgical trauma during abdominal surgery. Unless the patient's condition presents some contraindication, the toilet, and not the bedpan, is used in evacuating the enema. In addition, antibiotics may be prescribed to alter intestinal flora.

Depending on the type of surgery, and the surgeon's wishes, a low-residue diet for three to five days preoperatively may be advised. In bowel surgery, some surgeons request a colonic lavage on the morning of the operation.

Preoperative Skin Preparation

When there is time, such as in elective surgery, the patient may use a soap containing a detergent–germicide to

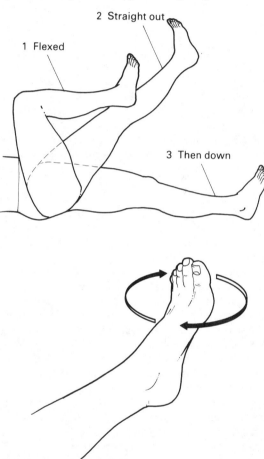

Figure 2.22 Leg exercises: (1) the patient should lie in a semi-recumbent position and perform the following simple exercises to improve circulation; (2) the knee should be bent, the foot raised and the position held for a few seconds, after which the leg should be extended and lowered to the bed; (3) this should be performed about five times with one leg and then the other; (4) the patient should then trace circles with the feet by bending them down, in towards each other and then out; (5) this should be repeated five times.
Turning to the side: (1) the patient should turn onto the side with the uppermost leg flexed most and supported on a pillow; (2) the side rail should be grasped as an aid to manoeuvre to the side; (3) diaphragmatic breathing and coughing should be practised while the patient is lying on the side.

cleanse the skin area for several days before surgery in order to reduce the number of skin organisms.

Before surgery, the patient should take a warm, relaxing bath or shower, using an antiseptic skin cleanser or medicated soap. Although it is preferable that this be done on the day of surgery, the timetable may mean that the shower has to be taken the night before. The reason for recommending that the cleansing shower be taken as close to surgery as possible is to reduce the risk of skin contamination of the surgical wound. A shampoo the day before the operation is advisable unless the patient's condition does not make this feasible.

It is preferred that the skin at and around the operative site is not shaved. However, the use of a depilatory to remove skin hair is acceptable. If the hair on the skin is shaved, the skin may be injured by the razor and provide a portal of entry for bacteria; this injured tissue may act as a substrate for bacterial growth. In addition, *the longer the interval between the shave and the operation, the higher the rate of postoperative wound infection.* Skin that is well cleansed but unshaven is less often implicated in wound infections than shaved skin. Some surgeons prefer that hair be removed in and around the operative site. One approach is to use electrical clippers to remove hair to within 1 mm to 2 mm of the skin; in this way, skin is not abraded.

If the surgeon asks for the skin be shaved, the patient is told about the shaving procedure, placed in a comfortable position and is not exposed unduly. Any adhesive or grease may be readily removed with a sponge moistened in benzene or ether, if the odour and cold temperature are not objectionable to the patient.

The expected outcome is to remove the hair without injuring the skin. There are several options. One is to use an electric clipper that can be thoroughly cleaned after use. Another is to use a sharp disposable razor with a recessed blade. A third method is to use scissors to remove hair that is 3 mm or longer in length. A fourth option is to use a depilatory cream (see below).

Skin shaving may be done by the nurse assigned to the patient or by a member of the operating theatre team. An antimicrobial detergent can be used to raise a lather that makes hair easier to remove. The skin should be held taut and shaved in the direction of hair growth. The nurse should use long, continuous strokes. Scratches should be avoided, and any potential sites of infection reported. All actions and findings should be documented. Winfield (1986) found that 22 per cent of shaved patients had cuts or significant skin abrasions after preoperative shaving.

Depilatory Cream

Chemical compounds (creams to remove hair) are safe for preparing the skin of the surgical patient. If there is any question about the possibility of an allergic reaction, a test patch can be tried first. As an economy measure, long hairs may be cut before the cream is applied in order to reduce the amount of cream used.

The depilatory cream usually comes in a collapsible tube and is expressed on the body surface. The cream is spread in a smooth layer of about 1.25 cm in depth over the entire operative site. A wooden tongue blade or a gloved hand can be used to apply the cream. After the cream has been allowed to remain on the skin for 10 minutes, it is scraped off gently with the tongue blade or multiple moistened gauze sponges. When all cream and hair have been removed, the skin is then washed with soap and water and patted dry.

There are several advantages in using a depilatory cream for preoperative skin preparation. The end result is a clean, smooth and intact skin. Scrapes, abrasions, cuts and inadequate hair removal are eliminated. It is more comfortable for patients, because they are less apprehensive and often find this method relaxing. There is even the possibility of patients preparing themselves in selected operative procedures. Depilatory creams are more effective and safer for use on unco-operative or agitated patients. This method is no more expensive than other methods. A disadvantage is that a few patients have had some transient skin reactions if depilatory cream is used near the rectal and scrotal areas. Depending on local policy, skin cleansing with an antibactericidal agent may be requested, particularly in orthopaedic surgery. Care must also be taken to ensure that all make-up and nail varnish are removed.

Preparation For Theatre

The nurse dresses the patient in the regulation short gown, leaving it untied and open at the back. Any hairpins are removed, and the head and the hair are entirely covered with a disposable paper cap, depending on local policy. The mouth must be inspected and dentures or plates are removed prior to the administration of the anaesthetic. If left in the mouth, these items could easily fall to the back of the throat during induction of anaesthesia and cause respiratory obstruction. If the patient wears contact lenses, they should be removed to a place of safety until the patient returns from theatre.

All jewellery should be removed before transfer to the operating theatre, and the wedding ring, if retained, should be secured to the patient's finger with adhesive tape. All articles of value, including dentures and prosthetic devices, are labelled clearly with the patient's name and stored in a safe place according to local policy.

The nurse checks that the patient is wearing an identity band clearly labelled with the patient's name, ward, unit number and name of operating consultant. This is checked with the patient before the premedication is given.

All patients should void urine immediately before going to the operating theatre to maintain continence during low abdominal surgery and to make abdominal organs more accessible. Catheterization should not be resorted to, except in an emergency or when it is desirable to have an indwelling catheter in place to ensure an empty bladder. In this instance, such a catheter would be connected to a closed drainage system. The urine voided is measured, and the amount and the time of voiding may need to be recorded on the preoperative checklist.

Medication

It is important that medications are given as prescribed, even if the patient is otherwise fasting. Patients using respiratory inhalers should be given these just before transfer to theatre. In particular, cardiac drugs such as beta-blockers should be given, otherwise arrhythmias may occur. In the case of the diabetic patient, insulin would normally be continued perioperatively, perhaps by infusion, along with dextrose to guard against hypoglycaemia; however, oral hypoglycaemics are discontinued on the day before surgery. Drugs that interfere with clotting, namely oral contraceptives and anticoagulants, should be stopped some days before surgery. In the case of some oral contraceptives, the recommendation is for a four-week minimum break, while patients on warfarin will need a few days' transference onto a heparin regime (the effects of heparin can be reversed with protamine sulphate; warfarin more slowly by vitamin K).

The anaesthetist must be aware of all medications the patient is receiving, as certain drugs may interfere with those used in anaesthesia.

Premedication

Premedication is given for the following reasons:

● To make the patient feel calm and to relieve apprehension.
● To provide some degree of amnesia, and to shorten the appreciation of time.
● To diminish bronchial and salivary secretions by interfering with vagal tone, and to reduce excess vagal effects on the heart (particularly important in children).
● To make induction and maintenance of anaesthesia easier.
● To provide some basal anaesthesia and sedation for the immediate postoperative period.

Premedication is prescribed by the anaesthetist, to be given either orally or intramuscularly, one to two hours before the anticipated operation time. A sleeping tablet, or early-morning sedative, may also be prescribed to ensure that the patient rests well before surgery. The best premedication is considered to be the reassuring visit by the anaesthetist during the ward assessment. In addition, a number of units have anaesthetic or recovery room nurses who also conduct preoperative visits.

Premedication Drugs

For some procedures, such as day surgery, premedications may not be used, as long-acting sedatives may be contraindicated. Oral sedatives, usually benzodiazepines in adults (e.g., temazepam 10 mg) and trimeprazine in children, are usually given two to four hours before surgery.

Classically, an intramuscular injection of an opiate (e.g., pethidine or papaveretum) and an antisecretory drug (promethazine or scopolamine) is given one-and-a-half to two-and-a-half hours preoperatively. In the elderly patient, scopolamine may cause confusion and all premedicant drugs may delay recovery.

Preoperative Checklist

A preoperative checklist is shown in Figure 2.23. The completed chart accompanies the patient to the operating room. The informed consent is also attached, as are all laboratory reports and nurses' records. Any unusual last-minute observations that may have a bearing on the anaesthesia or surgery should be put at the front of the chart in a prominent place.

Transfer of the Patient to the Operating Theatre

The patient is transferred as gently as possible, either on a trolley or in a bed. It is helpful if a nurse who is known to the patient can escort the patient to theatre. All records, X-rays and charts accompany the patient. The nurse is responsible for safety during transfer, so the patient's arms and elbows, for example, should be tucked in to avoid injury while going through doorways. If intravenous fluids or a blood transfusion are *in situ*, care should be taken to avoid disturbing them when handing over the patient to the anaesthetic nurse. The information given to the anaesthetic nurse should include: the patient's full name, the ward number, the operation which is to be done, what premedication has been given, and when— and what—other drugs may have been given to the patient, e.g., insulin in the case of a diabetic patient. Pharo (1989) states that it is from the premedication to the induction of anaesthesia that a patient is most in need of nursing support or 'high touch' care. She identifies the stressors as:

● Fear of the unknown, coupled with removal from a familiar background.
● Lack of privacy.
● Loss of dignity.
● Loss of control over events.

The accompanying nurse has a vital role. An appropriate response to the patient's needs requires empathy with the individual, and good counselling and communication skills.

A. *Theatre request sheet*   Theatre no ....

Patient's surname .... Forenames ....

Surgeon .... Ward ....

Anticipated operation ....

Please bring to theatre at .... a.m./p.m. on ....

                                        Signature ....

B. The following should be checked before the patient leaves the ward and on reception in theatre:-

	Tick ✔	WARD	THEATRE
1. Consent form is signed			
2. Patient's identity against identity band and Case Records			
3. Dentures, contact lens, etc., have been removed			
4. Premedication given			
5. Any further prescribed pre-operative care has been given			
6. Case notes/Kardex/X-rays			
7. Allergies			
8.			
Signature			

C. *Postoperative instructions*

1. Operation performed ....
2. Drains ....
3. Catheter ....
4. Special remarks ....

....

                                        Signature ....

Figure 2.23 Preoperative checklist.

Care of the Patient in the Anaesthetic Room

The role of the nurse in the anaesthetic room is to stay with the patient while the anaesthetic is being given, and to assist the anaesthetist in the induction. In the case of a child, a parent may be present to provide support and to allay anxiety.

In assisting the anaesthetist, the nurse will help to establish intravenous access, aid in achieving a smooth induction of anaesthesia and be prepared to assist should an unexpected complication occur.

Considerations For Elderly Patients

Elderly patients face higher risks from anaesthesia and surgery than do younger people, partly due to physiological changes associated with the ageing process and partly due to the increased incidence of pre-existing medical conditions. Increasing numbers of old people are now being accepted for surgery, and a great deal of research has gone into their altered response to the anaesthesia they receive: they require less anaesthetic to produce the desired effect and take longer to eliminate the drugs from their bodies.

As people age, the amount of fatty tissue steadily increases, from about 20 to 30 per cent at the age of 20, to 35 to 45 per cent in the 60 to 70 age group. Anaesthetic agents have an affinity for fatty tissue and will concentrate in body fat and the brain, perhaps to prolong recovery. In addition, there is a shrinkage of body tissues that are made up predominantly of water and those with a rich blood supply, such as skeletal muscle, liver and kidney. Reduction in size of the liver means that the rate at which it can inactivate many anaesthetics slows down.

With ageing, the heart and blood vessels decrease in their ability to respond to stress. Brain cells are reduced. The function of kidney cells is decreased, which means that waste products and anaesthetics are not excreted as readily as in a younger person.

Excessive or over-rapid infusions may cause pulmonary oedema. Blood pressure that takes a sudden or prolonged drop may lead to circulatory insufficiency, which in turn may cause cerebral ischaemia, thrombosis, embolism, infarction and anoxaemia. Consequently, continuous and careful monitoring with rapid interventions when needed are essential for those in the older age group.

Types of Anaesthesia

Anaesthesia is a state of narcosis, analgesia, relaxation and reflex loss.

Anaesthetics are divided into two classes according to whether they suspend sensation (1) in the whole body (general anaesthesia) or (2) in parts of the body (local or regional anaesthesia). Inhalation anaesthesia is the most popular because of its controllability. The intake and elimination of the agent is in large measure affected by pulmonary ventilation. Greater depth or plane of anaesthesia requires greater concentration of the agent and *vice versa*.

General Anaesthesia

General anaesthesia is whole-body anaesthesia, and implies loss of consciousness as the brain is exposed to controlled concentrations of reversible 'poisons', administered either by the inhalational route or intravenously. The intravenous route is the usual choice for the *induction* of anaesthesia, because the patient can be quickly and safely taken to a deep level of unconsciousness within one arm–brain circulation time. Sometimes, in young children or where there are airway problems, the anaesthetist may choose an inhalational induction, but then the patient will pass through a stage of excitation first described with early ether anaesthesia: ringing in the ears, heightened sensations, warmth, dizziness and increased activity characterized by struggling. Only then will the patient descend into the plane of restful surgical anaesthesia, or *maintenance* phase, when surgery can take place.

Although computer-controlled intravenous anaesthesia is being increasingly utilized for the maintenance of anaesthesia during surgery, traditional inhalational anaesthesia remains the more popular because of its controllability. The intake and elimination of the agent is in large measure affected by pulmonary ventilation, and greater depth is achieved by increasing the concentration of the agent. Overdosage can lead to the so-called fourth stage of anaesthesia, with respiratory and cardiovascular collapse, but the anaesthetist will be familiar with recognizing the signs (pulse, respiration, pupil size and reactivity), and keep the patient at a safe level of anaesthesia throughout surgery.

In earlier times, when a single agent such as ether or chloroform was used, the correct plane of anaesthesia was difficult to achieve for surgery without moving close to overdosage. Today, several groups of drugs may well be used together in a balanced anaesthetic to provide the three components required: sleep, analgesia and muscle relaxation. The advent of muscle relaxants derived from the South American arrow poison, curare, has done most to decrease the mortality from surgery, as they produce perfect muscle relaxation, without the need to deepen the anaesthesia too greatly. Powerful opiates and nitrous oxide provide analgesia, and either inhaled vapours (halothane, enflurane or isoflurane), or intravenous infusions (of an anaesthetic like propofol) keep the patient asleep.

In simple operations not requiring profound relaxation, anaesthesia may proceed by mask inhalation and muscle relaxants are not given. If deeper relaxation is required, the patient is paralyzed with a curare-like drug and will then require ventilation: the airway being secured by the insertion of an endotracheal tube, and ventilation maintained by a mechanical respirator.

At the end of the operation, the levels of all anaesthetic agents are allowed to fall until the patient can be roused quickly and regain airway integrity and respiratory effort, yet retain adequate analgesia. Residual relaxant effects are reversed specifically with the anticholinesterase neostigmine (which is always given with atropine, to counteract the unwanted effects of bradycardia and bronchoconstriction). Prolonged recovery time may be due to an increased sensitivity to opiates, which can be reversed with naloxone, an opiate antagonist; respiratory depression can be countered by a respiratory stimulant such as doxapram, which does not reverse the opiate's analgesic effects.

Regional Anaesthesia

Regional anaesthesia preserves consciousness, and involves the injection of a local anaesthetic to interrupt transmission of impulses through sensory nerves. This may be a one-nerve infiltration, a plexus block (such as a brachial plexus block for upper limb surgery) or at a spinal level, either extradurally (epidural anaesthesia) or intrathecally (spinal anaesthesia).

All three components of nerves are affected, motor, sensory and autonomic. Motor nerves are affected least, due to their large size and thicker myelin sheathing; the sensory fibres are specifically targeted with the appropriate dose and concentration of local anaesthetic to block the transmission of pain sensations to the central

nervous system; but the smallest diameter fibres belonging to the autonomic nervous system, which control blood pressure homeostasis, are also interrupted. Therefore, patients receiving a spinal or epidural anaesthetic must have their blood pressures monitored carefully while the block is operational, and must have an intravenous line to receive intravenous fluids to restore the effective circulating blood volume and, perhaps, a vasopressor (such as ephedrine) should the blood pressure fall too low.

Patients considered for regional anaesthesia include:

● Those too frail for general anaesthesia, but who may be considered fit for regional anaesthesia.
● Those with serious limb injuries who have recently eaten or drunk.
● Those attending centres where there is enthusiasm for the benefits of this technique (drier surgical field, decreased blood loss, reduced incidence of deep venous thrombosis).

Patients who do not wish to be awake during surgery may be offered an additional sedative to keep them asleep and to render them amnesic; they would have to fast preoperatively, as for a general anaesthetic.

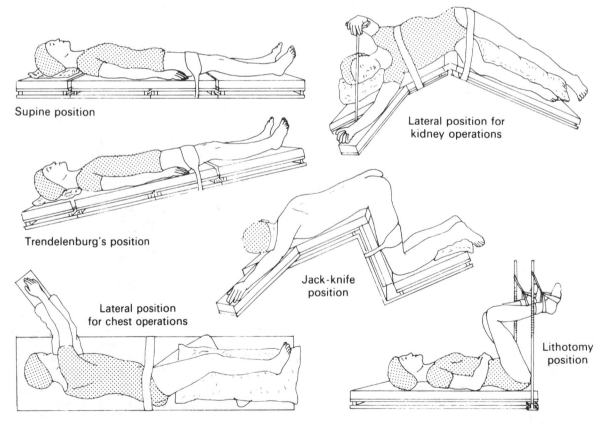

Figure 2.24 Positioning the patient for surgery. (From Pugh, J. and Millar, B. (1989) Mobility in the perioperative phase, *Surgical Nurse*, Vol. 2, No. 4, pp. 11–15.)

There are very few drawbacks or dangers from spinal or epidural anaesthesia, provided the technique is performed scrupulously and the patient is properly managed and monitored throughout. Postoperative headache has always been a drawback of spinal anaesthesia due to cerebrospinal fluid leakage. Now, however, with more sophisticated needle technology, the use of fine 25 to 27 gauge needles and proper attention to intravenous fluid balance, the incidence of postoperative headache can be reduced to less than 1 per cent. Prolonged immobilization in bed for 24 hours is probably unnecessary, but full mobilization is inadvisable immediately (Carbatt and Van Crevel, 1981).

Epidural anaesthesia is slightly more difficult to perform, and there is delay before anaesthesia is complete across the required segment. Inadvertent dural puncture with the much larger (18 gauge) needle will cause a considerable leakage of cerebrospinal fluid, often leading to headache, but it has the advantage that a catheter may be left in the epidural space for 'top-ups', every two to three hours, continued for up to 48 hours if required. This has proved to be extremely useful in the management of pain after major surgery, and in the analgesic care of women in labour. If a forceps or caesarean delivery proves to be necessary, the mother and baby will have been spared a risky general anaesthetic, and the mother may also be awake to share in the experience of the birth of her baby.

Care of the Patient in Theatre

Pugh and Millar (1989a, b, c) identified the importance of correct positioning of the patient on the operating table to prevent the occurrence of complications. They suggested that the ideal position is one that gives optimal exposure for the surgeon, allows the best access for monitoring the patient and is physiologically safe for the patient. Peripheral nerve damage may occur as a result of occlusion of the blood supply to a nerve, resulting in ischaemia, with a loss in sensory and/or motor function. Pressure sores may also result from poor positioning: those at risk are patients whose surgery lasts more than two hours, the elderly, critically ill patients, obese patients and very thin patients.

Patients with a previous history of vascular disease or deep vein thromboses may have passive exercises to the calf muscles prophylactically during the operation.

The position in which the patient is placed on the operating table depends on the operation to be performed as well as on the physical condition of the patient (Figure 2.24). Factors to consider include the following:

- The patient should be in as comfortable a position as possible, whether asleep or awake.
- The operative area must be adequately exposed.

- Circulation should not be obstructed by an awkward position or undue pressure on a part.
- There should be no interference with the patient's respiration as a result of pressure of the arms on the chest or constriction of the neck or chest caused by a gown.
- Nerves must be protected from undue pressure. Improper positioning of the arms, hands, legs or feet may cause serious injury or paralysis. Shoulder braces must be well padded to prevent irreparable nerve injury, especially when the Trendelenburg position is necessary.
- Concerns for the patient as an individual must be practised, particularly with the very thin, the elderly or the obese patient.
- Every patient needs gentle restraint before induction, in case of excitement.

Dorsal Recumbent Position. The usual position is flat on the back; one arm at the side of the table, with the hand placed palm down; the other carefully positioned on an armboard for intravenous infusion.

The dorsal recumbent position is used for most abdominal operations, except for those upon the gallbladder and the pelvis, and for the operations described below.

Trendelenburg Position. The Trendelenburg position (Figure 2.24) is usually employed for operations on the lower abdomen and the pelvis in order to obtain good exposure by displacing the intestines into the upper abdomen.

In this position the head and body are lowered so that the plane of the body meets the horizontal at an angle. The knees are flexed by 'breaking' the table, and the patient is held in position by padded shoulder braces.

Lithotomy Position. In the lithotomy position the patient lies on the back with the legs and thighs flexed at right angles. The position is maintained by placing the feet in stirrups. Nearly all perineal, rectal and vaginal operations require this posture.

Sims's Position. The patient is placed on the unaffected side with an air pillow 12.5 to 15 cm thick under the loin, or placed on a table with a kidney or back lift (Figure 2.24).

For Chest and Abdominothoracic Operations. The position varies with the operation to be performed. The surgeon and the anaesthetist place the patient on the operating table in the desired position.

Operations on the Neck. Neck operations—for example, those involving the thyroid—are performed with the patient lying on the back, the neck extended somewhat by a pillow beneath the shoulders, and the head and chest elevated in order to reduce venous pressure.

Operations on the Skull and the Brain. Such procedures demand special positions and apparatus, usually adjusted by the surgeon.

Artificial Hypotension During the Operation

There are times during surgery when it is desirable to lower blood pressure in order to reduce bleeding at the operative site, because this allows for more rapid surgery with less blood loss. Artificially induced hypotension has been used in operations such as brain surgery, radical neck dissection and radical pelvic surgery.

Deliberate hypotension is accomplished by inhalation or intravenous injection of drugs that affect the sympathetic nervous system and peripheral smooth muscle. Halothane is the inhalational anaesthetic agent commonly used. This anaesthetic is supplemented with other measures to lower blood pressure, such as a head-up position, positive pressure applied to the airway and administration of a ganglionic blocking drug such as pentolinium, sodium nitroprusside or other vasodilator drugs.

Transfer of the Patient to the Recovery Room

Care of the Patient in the Recovery Room

On completion of the operation, the patient is transferred to the recovery room. Most hospitals now have a fully equipped and staffed anaesthetic recovery room close to theatre, with emergency equipment always available. The advantage of this is that an anaesthetist will be readily available should there be a problem.

The patient is transferred to a warm bed, and each bed area is equipped with piped oxygen, suction and power points for any equipment required.

The responsibility of the recovery room staff is to monitor the patient's condition until it is stable and the patient is able to return to the ward. Where there is no recovery room, the patient is returned directly to the ward. In this case, the accompanying nurse should be at the patient's head, maintaining the airway, if necessary, by keeping the lower jaw extended to prevent the tongue falling backwards. A Guedel's airway may be used to keep the airway open and to allow free access for oropharyngeal aspiration.

The patient is put in the recovery position unless there are contraindications to this, for example, thoracotomy, spinal operations that require the patient to lie on the back and certain orthopaedic procedures.

● Attention must be paid at all times to ensure that the airway is open.

A full report on the operation performed, the patient's condition, the presence of drains and catheters, and anything to which the recovery room staff must be alerted, is given on transfer to the recovery room.

Immediate Postoperative Assessment

The recovery room nurse who receives the patient reviews the following with the anaesthetist:

1. Medical diagnosis and type of surgery performed.
2. Patient's age and general condition: airway patency, vital signs, blood pressure.
3. Anaesthetic and other medications used: narcotics, muscle relaxant, antibiotics.
4. Any untoward problems that occurred in the operating room that might influence postoperative care (e.g., extensive haemorrhage, shock, cardiac arrest).
5. Pathology encountered (if malignancy, whether the patient or family has been informed).
6. Fluid administered, blood loss and replacement.
7. Any tubing, drains, catheters or other supportive aids.
8. Specific information about which the surgeon or anaesthetist wishes to be notified.

This joint preliminary assessment of the patient includes an evaluation of pulse volume and regularity, depth and nature of respirations, skin colour, level of consciousness and the ability of the patient to respond to commands. The operative site is checked for evidence of haemorrhage or drainage and for tubing that needs to be connected to a drainage receptacle.

It is also essential for the nurse to know anything pertinent in the preoperative history that may be significant at this time (e.g., patient is hard of hearing, epileptic, diabetic, allergic to certain medications). This information may have been acquired in a preoperative visit with the patient.

Immediate Postoperative Care

Once the patient has been transferred safely and is positioned comfortably in bed, a set of baseline observations, including vital signs, is established as quickly as possible. A nurse remains with the patient at all times. Observations are then made regularly, usually every 15 minutes, and are recorded on the patient's chart. These include airway status and whether or not an artificial airway is *in situ*.

The patient's blood pressure is monitored, and should compare favourably with preoperative blood pressure levels, although some anaesthetic agents do lower the blood pressure somewhat. Therefore, it is important for the recovery room staff to be informed if these agents have been used.

The pulse rate is also monitored, and any rise in pulse must be reported to the anaesthetist, particularly if it is accompanied by increasing pallor and falling blood pressure as *this may indicate haemorrhage* (see sections on Shock and Haemorrhage). Any alteration in the rhythm of the pulse should be noted and reported.

The patient's respirations should be observed for rate,

rhythm and depth, and the patient's colour noted for pallor or cyanosis. Temperature is recorded two-hourly unless there is hypothermia or pyrexia.

The patient's level of consciousness is monitored, and should be seen to be improving. There should be a gradual return of reflexes until the patient is conscious. Observations should be made of response to painful stimuli, level of consciousness and any signs of confusion. If an airway is *in situ* it should *never* be removed by the nurse. When the gag reflex returns, the patient will reject the airway spontaneously.

Before patients are returned to the ward, they should be able to respond to simple commands and to answer to their name. If the patient does not appear to be recovering consciousness, then the anaesthetist should be informed.

Observation of the Wound

The wound must be checked during the postoperative observations, and any oozing of blood noted: if it is excessive, it should be reported to the nurse in charge, who will report it to the surgeon. Unless otherwise specified, the wound dressing is not removed, as this may interfere with the healing process and introduce infection. Sterile gauze dressings are applied, with added padding, until the bleeding stops.

Drainage Systems

All tubes and drains must be checked regularly to monitor the amount of drainage, and to ensure that the drains are patent. If an intravenous infusion of fluids or blood is *in situ*, then the intravenous site must be checked, and fluids must be kept running to time and recorded on the patient's fluid balance chart.

Where there is an indwelling catheter, the amount of urine is monitored, and the catheter checked to ensure free drainage.

Analgesia

In most cases, the anaesthetist will prescribe analgesia for the patient, and may administer it in theatre before the patient is transferred to the recovery room. However, restlessness in the patient may indicate sensations of pain, so further analgesia may be required to ensure that the return to the ward will be comfortable and as pain-free as possible.

The time that the patient spends in the recovery room varies with the type of operation performed and the type of anaesthetic given, and can vary from 30 minutes to several hours. Return to the ward is generally dependent on the level of consciousness: the patient is usually awake, the cough reflex is present and the vital signs are stable.

An accurate record of observations, drugs administered and intravenous fluids and analgesics given should accompany the patient back to the ward.

Transfer of the Patient to the Ward

Ideally, the patient should be breathing without the aid of an artificial airway when transferred from the recovery room to the ward. The accompanying nurse must be at the patient's head to ensure that a clear airway is maintained. If the patient is on a theatre trolley, transfer to the bed should be very gentle to minimize pain and discomfort, and to ensure that any drains are not dislodged. The bed should be warm, with no pillows, and a cotton cellular blanket should be tucked around patient to maintain warmth and prevent shivering. Excessive shivering, which may be caused by some anaesthetic drugs as well as by coldness, can be exhausting and painful.

If there is any doubt about the airway status, the patient is nursed in the recovery position; otherwise, if the patient is fully alert, the most comfortable position is adopted unless there are specific contraindications.

In reporting the patient's return from the recovery room, the nurse informs the nurse in charge about the operation performed, the vital signs, the existence of tubes, drains, intravenous infusions or blood transfusions, and when analgesia was last given.

The observations of vital signs normally continue every half-an-hour, for two to three hours, and then hourly until stable. It usually takes approximately four hours for the body to excrete anaesthetic drugs. The charge nurse will decide at what interval the observations will be continued, and when they are to be discontinued. At the same time, observations should be made of the wound and drains, and of the intravenous fluids, ensuring that they are running to time. The anaesthetist may want the patient to continue on oxygen therapy for several hours, and this should be carried out bearing in mind the appropriate precautions.

The patient will be helped to assume an upright position with the aid of pillows as consciousness and alertness return. This should be done gradually to prevent a hypotensive attack. It is important to maintain this position to prevent chest complications, particularly for elderly patients, the obese and those who smoke heavily.

Assistance with deep-breathing exercises will help to expand the lungs and improve lung ventilation. This will be achieved better with good analgesic cover, and with wound support, as taught to the patient in the preoperative period.

General Comfort of the Patient

One of the most uncomfortable problems for the postoperative patient is a dry mouth and halitosis following an anaesthetic. As soon as the patient is able, a mouth wash or the facility to clean the teeth should be offered. Dentures, if worn, should be returned to the patient. The face and hands should be washed, the theatre gown should be removed, if the patient is able, and ordinary pyjamas or nightdress put on. This improves the patient's morale, particularly if visitors are expected. Care should be taken to inspect pressure areas, and the patient's position in bed should be changed two-hourly to prevent problems.

Pain Relief

Analgesia should be given as prescribed, bearing in mind that not only is pain relief achieved, but pain is controlled. Narcotic pain relief should be given every three to four hours following surgery in the first 24 to 72 hours, depending on how long the patient requires it. Some 'minor' operations can be extremely painful in the short term, and pain relief should not be withheld merely because the patient has had only 'minor' surgery. Walsh and Ford (1989a, b) urge the change from giving pain relief at fixed times (e.g., the drug round), to planned analgesia in advance of when pain is felt. It is unreasonable to keep a patient waiting for half-an-hour simply because the next injection is not due until then.

Pain is a unique experience for each patient: 'Pain is what the patient says it is, and exists when the patient says it exists' (McCaffery, 1983). Nurses' fears of causing addiction have frequently been shown to be a reason for withholding analgesia, but these fears are unfounded in the case of the postoperative patient in hospital.

When planning analgesia, factors such as physiotherapy, the changing of dressings or moving patients for investigations such as X-rays should be considered. Analgesia given in advance can make these procedures pain free and will enable the patient to co-operate more readily. It is also important that the nurse recognizes that some analgesic drugs cause vomiting, which can be very painful for the patient, and so narcotics are best given in conjunction with an antiemetic.

Physiotherapy

The patient is encouraged to do deep-breathing and leg exercises as soon as possible. This prevents the accumulation of secretions at the bases of the lungs, which may lead to chest infections. Leg exercises will prevent the formation of deep venous thrombosis. The patient should be discouraged from crossing the legs while in bed or when sitting in a chair. This puts unnecessary pressure in the calf muscles and may predispose to deep venous thrombosis. Depending on the type of operation performed, the physiotherapist will continue specific exercises, which are reinforced by the nursing staff.

Oral Hygiene

In the days following surgery, care must be paid to fluid intake, nutrition and elimination. If foods and fluids are withheld, then particular attention must be paid to oral hygiene to prevent complications such as mouth ulcers and parotitis.

Wound Care

Wound care will be carried out according to local policy (see Wound Care and Wound Healing, p. 142). Depending on ward policy and the type of operation performed, sutures may be removed between five and ten days after the operation.

Care of Drainage Tubes

Drains are normally inserted through a stab wound and anchored by a suture, and therefore asepsis must be maintained when dressing the wound site to prevent infection.

Where there is an indwelling urinary catheter, care of the catheter is carried out twice daily, or when the patient has a bowel movement. The care involves cleaning around the urethral meatus, taking care to avoid tension on the catheter, and cleaning away from the urethral meatus to avoid ascending infection. Urine bags should not be allowed to become too full, as this causes unnecessary tension on the catheter.

Vital Signs

Observations of blood pressure, temperature, pulse and respiration are continued until the dangers of shock and infection have passed.

Personal Hygiene

It may be necessary to bed-bath the patient for the first few days following surgery. Each patient should be assessed individually, according to the operation performed and how well the patient can manage. It is advisable that analgesia is given before bed-bathing, to make the experience more comfortable for the patient. Gradually, as mobility improves, the patient may be able to take a shower or immersion bath. Until patients are able to be independent, a nurse should accompany them to the bathroom or shower.

Common Postoperative Problems

Restlessness

Restlessness is a postoperative symptom which must be treated seriously. The most common cause is probably general discomfort from the operation owing to the patient lying in one position on the operating table, the surgeon's handling of tissues and the body's reaction to recovering from the anaesthetic. These discomforts may be relieved by giving the prescribed postoperative sedation and changing the patient's position frequently. At the same time, the nurse assesses other possible contributing causes, such as tight, drainage-soaked bandages. Reinforcing or changing the dressing completely will make the patient more comfortable. Urinary output is noted and the patient is observed for urinary retention. Overdistension of the bladder is to be avoided. If possible, the patient should be helped to assume as normal a position as possible for voiding. Various techniques are tried to encourage voiding before resorting to catheterization.

Nausea and Vomiting

With the advent of newer anaesthetic agents and antiemetic drugs, vomiting has become a less common postoperative phenomenon, although inadequate ventilation during anaesthesia can increase the incidence of vomiting. The vomiting that occurs as the patient comes out of anaesthesia is frequently an attempt to relieve the stomach of the mucus and saliva swallowed during the anaesthetic period.

Other causes of postoperative vomiting include an accumulation of fluid in the stomach, inflation of the stomach and the ingestion of food and fluid before peristalsis returns. Psychological factors also may play a role; the patient who expects to vomit postoperatively usually will. Thus, helpful preoperative instruction can reduce the probability of vomiting after surgery.

After surgery, simple symptomatic therapy is usually all that is required. Many authorities believe that most antiemetic drugs (usually derivatives of phenothiazine) promote more undesirable effects, such as hypotension and respiratory depression. If a medication is required, short-acting barbiturates are often prescribed. Cyclizine or prochlorperazine may be prescribed for intravenous or intramuscular use to produce tranquillization and reduce the incidence of nausea and vomiting. If the drug is given preoperatively and during surgery, its effects may carry over into the postoperative period.

● Following the slightest indication of nausea, the patient is turned completely on one side to increase mouth drainage.
● The most important nursing care required when vomiting occurs is to prevent aspiration of vomit, which can cause asphyxiation and death.

When vomiting is likely because of the nature of surgery, a nasogastric tube is passed preoperatively and remains in place throughout the operative procedure and the immediate postoperative period.

Vomiting requires no special treatment beyond rinsing out the mouth and withholding fluids for a few hours. The main danger, as already indicated, is from aspiration of the vomit. Thus, precautions are necessary even before the patient begins to vomit.

In an emergency situation, a patient may be brought to the operating room with food in the stomach. Some anaesthetists administer preoperative oral antacids to counteract the acid-aspiration syndrome. Otherwise, if acid from the vomit is inhaled into the lungs it causes an asthma-like attack, with severe bronchial spasms and wheezing. Patients can subsequently develop pneumonitis and pulmonary oedema and become extremely hypoxic.

Increasing medical attention is being paid to silent regurgitation of gastric contents because it occurs more frequently than was previously realized. The importance of pH in the aetiology of acid aspiration is being studied, as is the value of administering an H_2-receptor antagonist such as cimetidine preoperatively.

Abdominal Distension

Postoperative distension of the abdomen results from the accumulation of gas in the intestinal tract. Manipulation of the abdominal organs during the operation may produce a loss of normal peristalsis for 24 to 48 hours, depending on the type and the extent of surgery. Although nothing is given by mouth, swallowed air and gastrointestinal secretions enter the stomach and the intestines; if not propelled by peristaltic activity, they collect in the intestinal coils, producing distension and causing the patient to complain of fullness or pain in the abdomen. Most often the gas collects in the colon, hence passing a rectal tube or catheter may give relief.

After major abdominal surgery, distension may be avoided by encouraging the patient to turn frequently, exercise and, when permissible, mobilize. Distension may be anticipated preoperatively and therefore a nasogastric tube may be inserted before surgery. Swallowing of air (often done by patients as part of an anxiety reaction) provides most of the gas that produces distension. The nasogastric tube may be retained until full peristaltic activity (passage of flatus) has resumed.

Another nursing action to relieve distension is as follows. Due to the anatomical structure of the colon, a gas bubble will move from the lower right side upward to the hepatic flexure, and then proceed to the left splenic flexure and down the left side to the rectum. Gas movement can be facilitated by getting the patient to lie on the back with the legs extended and a pillow placed under the knees. The right leg is slowly flexed at the knee, and the knee is pulled toward the abdomen. The patient holds the knee on the abdomen for 10 seconds before slowly lowering and extending the leg. After three or four deep breaths, the exercise is repeated with the other leg. After doing this three or four times, the patient rests. This may be repeated several times. With this exercise, gas has a tendency to be moved and expelled. Another method that is often helpful is to gently massage the abdomen in the same direction as gas moves in the colon.

Relief of Hiccoughs

Hiccough is produced by intermittent spasms of the

diaphragm and is manifested by a coarse sound (an audible 'hic'), a result of the vibration of the closed vocal cords as the air rushes suddenly into the lungs. The cause of the diaphragmatic spasm may be any irritation of the phrenic nerve from its centre in the spinal cord to its terminal ramifications on the undersurface of the diaphragm. This irritation may be: (1) direct—such as stimulation of the nerve itself by a distended stomach, peritonitis or subdiaphragmatic abscess, abdominal distension, pleurisy or tumours in the chest pressing on the nerves; (2) indirect—such as from toxaemia or uraemia that stimulates the centre; or (3) reflexive—such as irritation from a drainage tube, exposure to cold, drinking very hot or very cold fluids or obstruction of the intestines.

Hiccough occurs occasionally after abdominal operations. Often it occurs in mild transitory attacks that cease spontaneously or with very simple treatment. When hiccoughs persist, they may produce considerable distress and serious effects, such as vomiting, acid–base and fluid imbalance, malnutrition, exhaustion and possibly wound dehiscence.

The multitude of remedies suggested for the relief of this condition is proof that no one treatment is effective in every situation. The best remedy is to eliminate causes, for example, by not administering fluids that are too hot or too cold. Probably the most efficient of the older and simpler remedies is to hold the breath while taking large swallows of water. Prescription of phenothiazine drugs has been helpful on occasion. Another method is finger pressure on the eyeballs, applied through closed lids for several minutes. Induced vomiting has helped in some instances. If these are not successful, more drastic medical measures may need to be tried.

Injury

A patient coming out of anaesthesia may display restless behaviour. If at all possible, the patient should not be restrained, but must be protected from self-injury or from interfering with intravenous therapy, tubes and monitoring equipment. Analgesics and sedatives are administered as prescribed. Attention is given to possible causes of discomfort that can affect subconscious cognition, such as dressings that are too tight, pressure on a nerve due to improper positioning, irritating drainage or leakage of intravenous fluids. Through careful monitoring as the patient emerges from the anaesthetic, the nurse can detect problems before they can cause injury. This helps to prevent subsequent litigation, since the nurse can be held accountable for patient injuries due to negligence.

Maintenance of Adequate Fluid Volume

A considerable loss of body fluids occurs with surgery as a result of increased perspiration, increased mucus secretion in the lungs and loss of blood. To combat the loss of fluids, solutions are given intravenously for the first few hours after operation. Even though an adequate amount of fluid is taken by this method, often it does not relieve thirst. Thirst is also a troublesome symptom after many general anaesthetics, and even after local anaesthesia. It stems largely from the dryness of the mouth and the pharynx caused by the inhibition of mucus secretion after the usual preoperative medication of atropine. Many patients operated on under local anaesthesia complain of thirst during the operation.

Because a sticky, dry mouth demands moisture, fluids may be given to most patients as soon as the postoperative nausea and vomiting have passed. Sips of hot tea with lemon juice help to dissolve the mucus better than cold water, and small pieces of ice to suck relieve thirst better than drinks of water. As soon as the patient can take water by mouth in sufficient quantities, parenteral administration is discontinued.

Maintenance of Normal Body Temperature

Patients who have been anaesthetized are susceptible to chills and drafts. If the patient has undergone prolonged exposure to cold in the operating theatre and has received large amounts of intravenous infusions, the nurse should monitor for potential hypothermia. Signs of hypothermia should be reported to the doctor. A comfortable room temperature should be maintained and blankets provided as needed to prevent chilling.

Maintenance of Nutritional Balance

Following surgery, the more rapidly the patient can accept a normal diet, the more quickly will normal gastrointestinal function resume. The best way for the postoperative patient to take food is by mouth. This stimulates digestive juices and promotes gastric function and intestinal peristalsis. Exercise in bed or early ambulation also assists the digestive process and prevents such problems as distension and constipation. Chewing of food prevents parotitis (inflammation of the parotid glands), formerly a common postoperative problem that occurred in dehydrated patients whose oral hygiene was poor.

The return to a normal dietary pattern should proceed at the pace set by the individual patient. Of course, the nature of surgery and the type of anaesthesia directly affect the rate of return. Once the patient has completely recovered from the effects of anaesthesia and is no longer nauseated, steps may be taken to resume a normal diet.

Liquids are usually the first substances desired and tolerated by the patient after operation. Water, fruit juices and tea with lemon and sugar may be given in increasing amounts if vomiting does not occur. The fluids administered should be cool, not ice cold or tepid.

A well-balanced diet is provided and includes foods

that have been selected and preferred by the patient. Usually it takes two to three days for appetite to return, so the attractive presentation of food should be a therapeutic consideration.

● When surgery has been carried out on the gastrointestinal tract, fluids and food are not given until peristalsis returns.

Usually, a nasogastric or gastrointestinal tube is in place for the first 24 to 48 hours following gastrointestinal surgery. Such decompression tubes remove flatus and secretions. Attention is given to the maintenance of proper fluid and electrolyte balance, and an attempt is made with parenteral fluids, and where necessary, total parenteral nutrition to achieve this nutritional level.

When nothing is given by mouth postoperatively, regular oral hygiene is required. A clean, refreshed mouth encourages eating and reduces nausea.

Return of Normal Urinary Function

The length of time a patient may be permitted to go without passing urine after operation varies considerably with the type of operation performed.

● Generally, every effort must be made to avoid the use of a catheter.

All known methods to aid the patient in passing urine should be tried, for example, running water, applying heat to the perineum. A patient should never be given a cold bedpan. When a patient complains of not being able to use the bedpan, it may be permissible to use a commode rather than resort to catheterization. Male patients are often permitted to sit up or stand beside the bed, but safeguards should be taken to prevent falling or fainting.

● All urine, whether voided or catheterized, must be measured and the amount noted on the fluid balance chart.
● An intake and output chart is kept on all patients following urological or complex operative procedures and on all elderly patients.
● A urine output of less than 30 ml for each of two consecutive hours should be reported.

Resumption of Usual Pattern of Bowel Elimination

Preoperative bowel preparation, immobility, intestinal manipulation during surgery and reduced oral intake can all affect bowel function. Increased fluid intake and early ambulation can facilitate the return of bowel sounds and peristalsis.

Paralytic ileus is a complication that may occur after intestinal or abdominal surgery. It is characterized by the absence of bowel sounds (no peristalsis) and discomfort and distension of the abdomen (denoted by increased abdominal girth). The condition may even result in reverse peristalsis, which causes nausea and vomiting, and possibly the vomiting of faecal material. A nasogastric tube is inserted as prescribed, and preparations made for intravenous feeding.

Constipation

The causes of constipation after operation may be minor or serious. Irritation and trauma to the bowel at the time of the operation may inhibit intestinal movement for several days, but usually peristaltic function returns after the third day, following the combined effect of early ambulation, perhaps a simple enema and an increase in diet. Local inflammation, peritonitis or abscess may cause constipation, in which case treatment of the causal condition is indicated.

● Constipation may be a symptom of complete intestinal obstruction.

It must be borne in mind, also, that many people are constipated habitually and often give a history of having taken some form of laxative drug every day for years. Attempts should be made to correct their bowel habits as soon as is practical. However, in some instances, especially with elderly patients, these attempts may not be feasible. Enemas are usually effective in evacuating the lower bowel.

● Cathartic drugs should not be given unless prescribed by the doctor.

Avoidance of Infection and Maintenance of Skin Integrity

Between 10 and 15 per cent of surgical patients will develop nosocomial (hospital-acquired) infections. Most of these will be in one of four anatomical sites: surgical wound, urinary tract, bloodstream or respiratory tract. The infections occur for several reasons:

1. Intact skin and mucous membranes have been invaded by tubes and catheters, by the disease process or by the surgical operation.
2. The effects of anaesthesia and surgery reduce the resistance of the body.
3. The patient environment is made up of many people who have complicating and often chronic medical problems; consequently, the patient may be exposed to infection.
4. The organisms that are found in hospital infections are widespread and sometimes resistant: e.g., *Staphylococcus aureus*, *Escherichia coli*, *Serratia marcescens*, *Pseudomonas, Klebsiella pneumoniae* and *Proteus*.
5. Poor hand washing practices and careless techniques are practised (Gidley, 1983).

When postoperative infections occur, healing is delayed, convalescence is prolonged, functional recovery may be impaired and death may occur. These complications impose serious burdens on the patient, the family and other patients.

Each hospital must make a determined effort to control infections by an intensive education programme involving every employee. Usually an active infection control committee (including an epidemiologist) can be effective in establishing policies and procedures and monitoring practice.

Effective infection control is carried out postoperatively by encouraging the patient to cough, by frequent turning and by deep breathing. These measures will prevent secretions from being retained and possibly causing atelectasis, lung congestion and pneumonia. Use of sterile equipment (needles, cannulae, dressings), including equipment for respiratory management, will prevent transmission of pathogenic organisms. Antibiotics may be prescribed prophylactically by the doctor when infected areas are encountered, and antimicrobials may be prescribed for specific identified organisms in established infections. *The nurse plays a key role in infection control by practising strict aseptic techniques and by conscientiously monitoring and instructing others.*

● Conscientious hand washing is essential for every person who comes in contact with patients and moves from one patient to the next.

Dressings are inspected periodically to detect signs of undue haemorrhage or abnormal drainage. When incisions are on the anterior part of the body, the posterior area is checked for signs of bleeding, since gravity enables seepage to accumulate in an area quite removed from the incision. Dressings should be reinforced if necessary, and the time noted on the care plan. (Dressings and care of the incision are discussed in detail in the Section entitled, Wound Care and Wound Healing, p. 142).

Restoration of Mobility

As a result of dressings, splints or drainage apparatus, the patient is frequently unable to shift position. Lying constantly in the same position may lead to pressure sores, hypostatic pneumonia or deep venous thrombosis.

● The helpless patient must be turned from side to side at least every two hours, and the position must be changed as soon as the patient becomes uncomfortable.

Positioning

Following surgery, the patient may be placed in a variety of positions (depending on the nature of the operation) to promote comfort and ease pain.

Supine Position. The patient lies on the back without

elevation of the head. In most cases this is the position in which the patient is placed immediately after operation. Bed covers should not restrict the movement of the patient's toes and feet.

Lateral Position. The patient lies on either side with the upper arm forward. The underleg is slightly flexed, while the upper leg is flexed at the thigh and the knee. The head is supported on a pillow, and a second pillow is placed longitudinally between the legs. This position is used when it is desirable to have the patient change position frequently, to aid in the drainage of cavities, such as chest and abdomen, and to prevent postoperative pulmonary, respiratory, and circulatory complications.

Recumbent Position.

Of all the positions prescribed for a patient, perhaps the most common, as well as the most difficult to maintain, is the recumbent position. The difficulty in most instances lies in trying to make the patient fit the bed rather than having the bed conform to the needs of the patient. The patient's trunk is raised to form an angle of from 60 to 70 with the horizontal plane. This is a comfortable sitting position. Patients with abdominal drainage are usually put in the recumbent position as soon as they have recovered consciousness, but great caution must be observed in raising the bed.

● It is not unusual for a patient to feel faint after the head of the bed is raised; for this reason, a close watch must be kept on pulse rate and colour. If the patient complains of any dizziness, the bed must be slowly lowered. If the dizziness disappears, the head of the bed may be raised within one to two hours.

The nurse must determine whether the patient is in the correct position and comfortable. Often, very short people are most uncomfortable in the ordinary hospital bed and must be supported by pillows. It is advisable to place a support against the feet to prevent the patient from slipping down in bed, to prevent foot drop and to make the patient feel more secure.

It is the nurse's responsibility to see that the recumbent position is maintained. No matter how correctly placed or how well supported by pillows, the patient will slip down in the course of time. Thus it will be necessary to move the patient up in bed frequently and to readjust the pillows.

Ambulation

Most surgical patients are encouraged to be out of bed as soon as it is safe. This is determined by the stability of a patient's cardiovascular and neuromuscular systems, the usual level of physical activity and the nature of the surgery performed. Following minor surgery and day surgery, the patient can be up and about the same day.

● The advantage of early ambulation is that it reduces postoperative complications such as atelectasis, hypostatic pneumonia, gastrointestinal discomfort and circulatory problems.

Atelectasis and hypostatic pneumonia are relatively infrequent when the patient is ambulatory, since ambulation increases respiratory exchange and aids in preventing stasis of bronchial secretions within the lung. Ambulation also reduces the possibility of postoperative abdominal distension because it helps to increase the tone of the gastrointestinal tract and the abdominal wall.

Thrombophlebitis occurs less frequently because ambulation, by increasing the rate of circulation in the extremities, prevents stasis of venous blood. Clinical as well as experimental evidence shows that the rate of healing in abdominal wounds is more rapid when ambulation is started early, and the occurrence of postoperative evisceration in a series of cases actually was less frequent when patients were allowed to be out of bed soon after operation. Statistics also indicate that pain is decreased when early ambulation is allowed. Comparative records show that the pulse rate and the temperature return to normal sooner when the patient attempts to regain normal preoperative activity as quickly as possible. Finally, there is the further advantage to the patient of a shorter stay in the hospital.

However, early ambulation should not be overdone. The condition of the patient must be the deciding factor, and a progression of steps must be followed in getting the patient out of bed.

1. First of all, with nursing support and encouragement, and with safety as the main concern, the patient moves gradually from the lying position to the sitting position until any evidence of dizziness has passed. This position can be obtained by raising the head of the bed.
2. Then the patient may be helped to sit completely upright and turned so that both legs hang over the edge of the bed.
3. After this preparation, the patient may be helped to stand beside the bed.

When accustomed to the upright position, the patient may start to walk. The nurse should be at the patient's side to give physical support and encouragement. Care must be taken not to tire the patient, and the extent of the first few periods of ambulation will vary with the type of operation and the patient's physical condition and age.

Bed Exercises

When early ambulation is not feasible because of circumstances already mentioned, bed exercises may go some way towards achieving the same desirable results. General exercises should begin as soon after operation as possible —preferably within the first 24 hours—and are carried out under supervision to ensure their adequacy. These exercises are done to promote circulation and prevent the development of contractures and other deformities as well as to permit the patient the fullest return of physiological functions. Such exercises include the following:

- Deep-breathing exercises for complete lung expansion.
- Arm exercises through full range of motion, with specific attention to abduction and external rotation of the shoulder.
- Hand and finger exercises.
- Foot exercises to prevent foot drop and toe deformities and to aid in maintaining good circulation.
- Exercises to prepare the patient for ambulation activities.
- Abdominal and gluteal contraction exercises.

Psychological Care

Almost all postoperative patients need psychological support during the immediate postoperative period. When the patient's condition permits, a close member of the family or friend may see the patient for a few moments. Thus loved ones are reassured and the patient feels more secure.

The questions posed by an awakening patient often indicate the deep feelings and thoughts. Perhaps there is concern about the outcome of the operation or about the future—whatever the patient's questions, the nurse should be in a position to answer them reassuringly without going into a discussion of details. The immediate postoperative period is not the time for discussion of operative findings or prognosis. On the other hand, these questions ought not to be dismissed lightly because they may offer clues which suggest the method to select in directing future treatment and rehabilitation.

As patients move through the early postoperative phases, measures are implemented to provide feelings of stability. This is accomplished by assuring patients that a nurse is available to talk with them, to reinforce the explanations of the doctor and to correct any misconceptions they may have. Patients are advised about relaxation techniques and diversional activities. Significant others are included in instructional sessions to assist patients when they leave the hospital. Projections are made about their adjustments and needs when they leave the hospital. The nurse encourages patients to talk about their concerns about the recovery phase and their increasing assumption of self-care.

Considerations For Elderly Patients

Transfer of the elderly patient from the operating room table to the bed is done slowly and gently while monitoring the effects of this action on blood pressure, observing facial expression (if the patient is awake) and watching for evidence of hypoxia. Special attention is given to keeping the patient warm, since body temperature in the elderly is labile. The patient's position is changed frequently, not only for comfort, because lying in one position can be painful, but to stimulate respirations and circulation.

Immediate postoperative care for the older adult is the same as that for any surgical patient, but additional support is given if there is impaired function of the cardiovascular, pulmonary or renal systems.

With invasive monitoring, it is possible to detect cardiopulmonary deficit before obvious signs and symptoms are apparent. As a result of monitoring and better preoperative preparation, many older adults are tolerating surgery and recovering well.

Confusion is one of the most common experiences of an older postoperative patient. This is aggravated by social isolation, restraints and sensory deprivation. It is important to recognize that night-time confusion can be reduced by frequent nursing attention and caution in the use of drugs, especially narcotic analgesics and sedatives.

Early mobilization is instituted to prevent pneumonia, the most frequent respiratory complication in the elderly. Keeping the patient active also prevents atelectasis, irritation of pressure areas, deep venous thrombosis and undue weakness. Sitting positions that promote venous stasis in the lower extremities are to be avoided. Ambulation means that the patient walks about, rather than merely sitting in a chair. Adequate assistance is required to prevent bumping into things and falling.

Urinary incontinence can be prevented by providing easy access to the call bell, the commode and the toilet. Early ambulation and familiarity with the ward help the patient to become self-sufficient. Postoperative distension, reduced peristalsis and faecal impaction can be prevented by promoting adequate hydration and activity.

During the early postoperative days the patient may complain of painful muscles. This is common and is usually due to maintaining confined positions during the operation. Massaging aching parts gently and providing support with pillows can ease the discomfort.

Fluids and electrolytes are monitored to avoid the extremes of fluid overload and dehydration. The nurse compares previous documentation with current records to note changes in fluid balance and weight. It may be necessary to recommend physiotherapy and intensive rehabilitation for patients undergoing prolonged convalescence.

Encouragement and positive thinking should always be offered. The nurse gently challenges the older adult to recognize that participation in all activities can enhance recovery and prevent complications.

Postoperative Complications

The danger inherent in surgery involves not only the risk of the operative procedure, but also the very definite hazard of postoperative complications which may prolong convalescence or even adversely affect the surgical outcome. The nurse plays an important part in the prevention of these complications and in their early treatment, should they arise. The signs and symptoms of the more common postoperative complications are discussed below. In each instance the most effective method of prevention and the usual treatment are emphasized.

It should constantly be borne in mind that attention must be paid to the patient as an individual as well as to the particular surgical condition.

Shock

One of the most serious postoperative complications is shock, which occurs when there is inadequate cellular perfusion and oxygenation, leading to a build-up of waste (usually acidic) products of metabolism. This can be caused by many disorders, such as haemorrhage, major illness, fluid loss, burns, infection and heart disease.

The blood pressure is related to cardiac output and peripheral resistance, so shock may be caused by problems leading to failure of the pump action of the heart, a fall in the peripheral resistance or loss of blood volume.

Altered Physiology

As a response to shock, various hormones, particularly catecholamines (adrenaline and noradrenaline), are released. Catecholamines increase the blood flow to the vital organs, such as the heart, liver and brain, and decrease blood flow to nonvital organs such as the skin, gut and kidneys, by selective vasodilatation and vasoconstriction.

The heart output is increased by increasing the heart rate and contractility, and the blood volume is increased by the renin–angiotensin–aldosterone system, triggered by reduced renal perfusion. This expands the extracellular compartment by retaining sodium (mineralocorticoid [aldosterone] and prostaglandin activity), and by vasoconstriction of the veins in the splanchnic bed (mainly in the liver and gut, which contain 30 per cent of total blood volume). This is mediated by angiotensin II, the most potent vasoconstrictor known.

The release of glucocorticoids, which increase blood sugar levels by stimulating the release of glycogen and its conversion to glucose, is stimulated by shock, due to an increase in adrenocorticotrophic hormone from the anterior pituitary. Glucagon levels, mainly from the pancreas, are elevated via the anti-insulin activity, leading to higher blood sugar levels; and antidiuretic hormone levels are high, leading to an expansion of extracellular volume due to the diminution of water loss via the distal renal tubules and the vasoconstrictor activity of antidiuretic hormone (vasopressin).

Pathophysiological Consequences of Shock

The microcirculation (arterioles, capillaries and venules) sustains the greatest impact in shock. Initially, the capillary blood flow is reduced, so that tissue fluid moves back into the capillaries and re-expands the blood volume. However, the reduced blood flow, if prolonged, reduces available oxygen for the tissues, leading to anaerobic metabolism in the tissues supplied by these capillaries (particularly those of the peripheral circulation: skin, lungs, gastrointestinal tract and kidneys). As a result, acidic waste products of metabolism build up in the cells and capillary beds, leading, if protracted, to cellular and capillary damage. Ultimately, if the processes resulting in shock are not corrected before decompensation sets in, the cellular and vascular changes become irreversible and fatal.

In septicaemic ('warm') shock, particularly, the damage to the microcirculation may result in the formation of widely disseminated thrombi in the capillaries—disseminated intravascular coagulopathy—where all of the clotting factors are used up. As a result, the patient exhibits a marked bleeding tendency, with severe bruising and bleeding from puncture sites.

The net effect of the various hormonal changes is a stimulation of catabolism, but the increased heart rate and poor tissue perfusion lead to a decrease in oxygen utilization.

Classification

Shock may be classified as hypovolaemic (oligaemic), cardiogenic, neurogenic or septic. The differences are noted below as each is described. Both neurogenic and septic shock cause dilatation of the vascular bed, leading to reduction in peripheral resistance.

Hypovolaemic Shock. Hypovolaemic shock is caused by decreased fluid volume owing to loss of blood or plasma, or even fluid losses from prolonged vomiting or diarrhoea. Fluid volume is frequently decreased after surgery for a number of reasons. In particular, more blood may be lost at operation than is realized, and the handling of body tissues may cause local trauma and loss of blood and plasma from the circulation, thereby creating a decrease in the circulating blood volume. Hypovolaemic shock is characterized by a fall in venous pressure, a rise in peripheral resistance and tachycardia (Table 2.32).

Cardiogenic Shock. Cardiogenic shock results from cardiac failure or an interference with heart function (poor heart-pump function, causing diminished cardiac output), as in myocardial infarction, arrhythmias, tamponade, pulmonary embolism, advanced (late) hypovolaemia or epidural and general anaesthesia. The signs are increased pressure in the venous bed and an increase in peripheral resistance.

Neurogenic Shock. Neurogenic shock occurs as a result of a failure of arterial resistance (such as may be caused by spinal anaesthesia, quadriplegia). It is characterized by a fall in blood pressure owing to pooling of blood in dilated capacitance vessels (those with the ability to change volume capacity). Heart activity increases and thus maintains a normal output (stroke volume); this helps to fill the dilated vascular system as it attempts to preserve perfusion pressure.

Septic Shock. Septic shock results most frequently from gram-negative septicaemia (infection, peritonitis). At first the patient may exhibit a fever with a rapid, strong pulse, rapid respirations and normal or slightly decreased

Table 2.32 *Correlation of magnitude of shock to volume deficit and clinical presentation*

Approximate deficit	Decrease in blood volume	Shock	
		Degree	Signs
ml	per cent		
0–500	0–10	None	None
500–1,200	10–25	Mild (compensated)	Slight tachycardia Mild hypotension Mild peripheral vasoconstriction
1,200–1,800	25–35	Moderate	Thready pulse, 100–120 beats/min Blood pressure, 90–100 mmHg systolic Marked vasoconstriction Sweating Anxiety, restlessness Decreased urinary output
1,800–2,500	35–50	Severe	Thready pulse, 120 beats/min Blood pressure, 60 mmHg systolic Marked vasoconstriction Marked sweating No urinary output

Source: *Wilkins, E. W. Jr (ed.) (1989)* MGH Textbook of Emergency Medicine *(3rd edition), Williams & Wilkins, Baltimore, p. 40. By permission of Williams & Wilkins.*

blood pressure. The skin is flushed, warm and dry. However, if infection continues untreated, hypovolaemic shock develops. These two phases may be referred to as hyperdynamic septic shock (the former) and hypodynamic shock (the latter, which is similar to hypovolaemic shock). Hypovolaemia develops along with depressed cardiac function.

Clinical Features

The classical signs of shock *from any cause* are as follows:

- Increasing pallor—due to diversion of the blood supply from the peripheral to the central circulation, usually associated with cold, clammy skin due to catecholamine release.
- Increasing heart rate—further perfusion defect requires an increased heart rate to compensate for falling effective blood volume.
- Falling blood pressure—due to the progressive failure of the various compensatory mechanisms.
- Rapid respiration—'air hunger', due to a decrease in haemoglobin and a reduction in tissue oxygenation.
- Oliguria—the renal circulation is reduced during shock, leading to a reduction of urinary output (oliguria); rarely anuria.

Assessment of Shock

The expected outcome of the initial assessment is to determine the cause of volume loss and the status of the airway. Only then can treatment be instituted promptly and intelligently. The initial assessment should include the following:

1. Respirations—hyperventilation is an early sign of septic shock.
2. Skin—a cold, pale, moist skin indicates vasoconstriction with increased arteriolar resistance and is suggestive of hypovolaemic shock. Warm, red skin indicates a decrease in arteriolar resistance and may be seen in septic and neurogenic shock.
3. Pulse and blood pressure—alone, pulse and blood pressure may not be reliable guides to the severity of shock, but their progressive pattern is significant. A rising pulse rate, followed by a falling blood pressure, is indicative of shock. A useful 'rule of thumb' is that a pulse rate exceeding 100 beats per minute, followed by a fall in systolic blood pressure to less than 100 mm Hg (in a nonhypertensive patient), indicates a significant degree of shock. The greater the pulse rate and the lower the blood pressure, the greater the degree of shock. Cardiogenic shock indicates a damaged heart, usually due to a myocardial infarction, and is often complicated by arrhythmias of various types.
4. Urinary output—because the output of urine is one of the most valuable indices of adequacy of vital organ

perfusion, an indwelling catheter is recommended for any patient susceptible to shock. A drop in renal artery pressure and flow produces renal artery vasoconstriction and results in decreased glomerular filtration and decreased urine output. Normal urine flow is 50 ml/hr. An output of 30 ml/hr or less (oliguria or anuria) is suggestive of cardiac failure or inadequate volume replacement.

5. Central venous pressure—this is the pressure within the right atrium or in the great veins within the thorax. It is a valuable guide to vascular volume replacement when other parameters are also considered, e.g., vital signs and cardiopulmonary status. A reading near zero may indicate hypovolaemia (if the patient improves with rapid intravenous infusion, the patient was hypovolaemic). Readings over 15 cm water may suggest hypervolaemia, vasoconstriction or congestive heart failure. Pulmonary artery pressure and pulmonary capillary wedge pressure are more accurate indications of the pumping ability of the left side of the heart (see Chapter 6).
6. Levels of consciousness—consciousness levels may range from alert in mild shock to mental cloudiness in moderate shock. As the condition worsens, the patient becomes lethargic and reacts only to noxious stimuli. Irreversible shock is noted when the patient fails to react to stimuli.

Nursing Care

Prevention. The best treatment for shock is prophylaxis. This consists of adequate preparation of the patient for surgery, mentally as well as physically, and anticipation of any complication that may arise during or after the operation. Special equipment for the treatment of shock, including blood and blood substitutes, must be readily available. Blood loss should be accurately measured or intelligently estimated.

- If the amount of blood loss exceeds 500 ml (especially if it is rapid), replacement is usually indicated.

The individual patient and the particular circumstances must be considered in determining replacement therapy. An older patient may require replacement therapy when a younger patient in generally good health does not; but older patients may have a poor myocardial reserve, so that the rate of replacement may need to be slow.

Operative trauma should be kept at a minimum as the first step in avoiding shock. After operation, factors that may promote shock should receive attention. Pain can be controlled by making the patient as comfortable as possible and by using narcotics judiciously. Exposure should be avoided, and lightweight, unheated covers can be used to prevent vasodilatation. In the recovery room the patient should be observed and cared for by nurses trained especially in the recovery of patients from anaesthesia. In addition, a quiet room helps to reduce mental trauma. Any moving of the patient should be done gently. The supine position is preferred to facilitate circulation. Monitoring of vital signs should be continued until the patient's recovery indicates that shock is unlikely.

Treatment. The patient is kept warm, but overheating should be avoided to prevent cutaneous vasodilatation, which could reduce blood flow to the vital organs. Intravenous fluids should be administered as prescribed by the medical staff.

The patient should be positioned as shown in Figure 2.25, with the trunk flat and the legs elevated. The Trendelenberg (head-low) position should be avoided as the initial benefit is lost rapidly by reflex vasoconstriction (reducing blood supply to vital organs) and pressure of the viscera against the diaphragm (which reduces cardiac filling and hence output, and ventilation). The patient's respiratory and circulatory status should be monitored every 15 minutes, with recordings of heart rate, blood pressure and respiration, and central venous pressure measurements if a central recording line is *in situ*. Urinary output should be monitored by means of an indwelling catheter. The patient's level of consciousness should be observed closely.

● The basic approach to the treatment of shock is to determine its cause and correct it if possible.

1. Ensure adequacy of airway. When the patient is ventilating adequately, blood gas determinations are made to determine adequacy of pulmonary function, and the patient is given oxygen if required.
2. Restore blood/fluid volume. The kind of fluid and blood replacement depends upon the kind and amount lost as well as the condition of the patient. Fluids are administered intravenously immediately; when the nature of loss is determined, fluid replacement is modified accordingly. Of the total blood volume, under normal conditions 20 per cent is in the capillaries, 10 per cent in the arterial system, and the balance in the veins and heart. In shock there is dilatation of the capillary beds, so a considerable volume of blood can be accommodated. Two kinds of fluids are used: crystalloids and colloids. Crystalloids are electrolyte solutions that diffuse into interstitial spaces. An example is Ringer's lactate injection, a buffering solution in which lactate is metabolized and excess hydrogen ions are neutralized. Three parts of crystalloids are lost to extra vascular space for every one part that remains in the vascular system. This means that for every 2,000 ml given, 500 ml increases the vascular volume. For haemorrhagic shock, crystalloids are given initially to lower blood viscosity and aid in microcirculation. Colloids are blood, artificial blood, blood substitutes, plasma, serum albumin and plasma substitutes, such as dextran; these remain in the intravascular compartment. Blood of the same type as the patient's should be administered in preference to the generally used group O rhesus negative blood. Burn shock requires large amounts of colloid replacement.
3. Drug therapy: vasodilators are prescribed to reduce peripheral resistance, which in turn decreases the work of the heart and increases cardiac output and tissue perfusion. Some authorities believe that hypovolaemic shock should not be treated with vasoactive drugs. Their effect is to increase vascular resistance and decrease tissue perfusion, thus aggravating the effects of shock.

Nursing staff should be aware of the effects of the drugs prescribed by the medical staff, and care for the patient accordingly. For example, if a vasodilator drug is prescribed, the patient's blood pressure will need to be monitored carefully, and the drug dosage and supportive treatment adjusted as necessary.

The nursing care of the patient will involve both general supportive measures and specific nursing observations.

● The patient's ventilation will need to be maintained. This requires that the airway be kept clear, and humidified oxygen is administered by a face mask, as prescribed.
● Oral hygiene should be performed regularly, to keep the patient comfortable and to prevent infection.
● Fluid balance records should be maintained, so that the risks of over- or underhydration might be minimized.
● The patient should be turned regularly every two hours to prevent complications such as pressure sores, deep venous thrombosis and pulmonary embolism.
● Psychological support is best provided by explaining to the (conscious) patient what is happening, and the reasons for the measures being taken. *Pain relief should be effective*, since pain may exacerbate shock. Family members and significant others have an invaluable supportive role, and they should be advised of the patient's condition whenever possible.

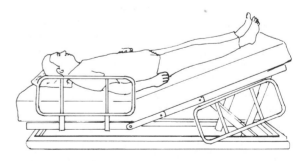

Figure 2.25 Correct positioning of the patient showing signs of shock. The lower extremities are elevated to an angle of about 20°; knees are straight, trunk is horizontal and head is slightly elevated.

Haemorrhage

Classification

Haemorrhage is classified as: (1) primary, when it occurs at the time of the operation; (2) intermediary or reactionary, when it occurs within the first few hours after an operation, because of the return of blood pressure to its normal level and the consequent washing out of the insecure clots from untied vessels; and (3) secondary, when it occurs some time after the operation, as a result of the slipping of a ligature because of infection, insecure tying or erosion of a vessel by a drainage tube.

A further classification frequently is made according to the kind of vessel that is bleeding. Capillary haemorrhage is characterized by a slow, general ooze; venous haemorrhage bubbles out quickly and is darkly coloured; arterial haemorrhage is brightly coloured and appears in spurts with each heartbeat.

When the bleeding is on the surface and can be seen, it is described as being evident or external; when it cannot be seen, as in the peritoneal cavity, it is described as being concealed or internal.

Clinical Features

Haemorrhage presents a more or less well-defined syndrome, depending on the amount of blood lost and the rapidity of its escape. The patient is apprehensive and restless, moves continually and is thirsty; the skin is cold, moist and pale. The pulse rate increases, the temperature falls and respirations are rapid and deep, often of the gasping type described as 'air hunger'. As the haemorrhage progresses, cardiac output decreases, arterial and venous blood pressure and the haemoglobin of the blood fall rapidly, the lips and the conjunctivae become pallid, spots appear before the eyes, a ringing is heard in the ears and the patient grows weaker but remains conscious until near death.

Nursing Care

Care should be taken to alleviate and not to exacerbate the patient's anxiety. For all types of bleeding, the treatment is essentially similar. The wound should be inspected, and the haemorrhage managed by direct pressure and application of a sterile dressing pad or bandage. General measures should be taken, such as placing the patient in the shock position (Figure 2.25), and elevating the bleeding part wherever possible. If the bleeding is arterial, and the blood loss heavy, a proximal artery may need to be compressed as an initial measure.

Medical Management

The medical staff should be contacted as soon as possible. Blood replacement should be with appropriately grouped and cross-matched blood, but, in an emergency, group O rhesus negative ('universal donor') blood may be given. Plasma expanders and colloid solutions may be used to maintain plasma volume until the blood is available. Too large a volume replacement, or too rapid a transfusion, may expand the blood volume and pressure and lead to rebleeding. Sedation or a narcotic may be prescribed as appropriate.

Where the haemorrhage is concealed, the patient will be transferred to the operating theatre so that the haemorrhage may be controlled surgically.

Deep Venous Thrombosis

Deep venous thrombosis is the formation of a thrombus (clot) in deep veins, usually in the saphenous, femoral, iliac or (rarely) the inferior vena cava. It may be a life-threatening complication after surgery if a portion of the thrombus breaks off and floats through the great veins to the lungs, where a pulmonary embolism may ensue. This may be massive and fatal, or associated with pain and morbidity.

Incidence

Postoperatively, those at greatest risk for deep venous thrombosis have been identified as follows:

- Orthopaedic patients having hip surgery, knee reconstruction and elective lower extremity surgery.
- Urological patients having transvesical prostatectomy, and older patients having urological surgery.
- General surgical patients over the age of 40, obese, with malignancy or having had prior deep venous thrombosis or pulmonary embolism, or those having extensive complicated surgical procedures.
- Gynaecological (and obstetric) patients over the age of 40 with added risk factors (varicose veins, previous venous thrombosis, infection, malignancy, obesity).
- Neurosurgical patients, similar to other surgical high risk groups. (In stroke, for example, the risk of deep venous thrombosis in the paralyzed leg is as high as 75 per cent.)

Altered Physiology

Inflammation of the vein occurs in association with the clotting of the blood, which occurs from an interplay of factors: (1) alteration (usually obstruction) in blood flow; (2) alteration in clotting factors (particularly after surgery); and (3) alteration in vessel wall (local injury from any cause) (Virchow's triad). There is a particular hazard when patients are in plaster of Paris, particularly if the plaster ends at mid-thigh level.

The complication may result from a number of causes, including injury to the vein by tight straps or leg-holders at the time of operation, pressure from a blanket-roll under the knees, concentration of blood by loss of fluid or dehydration or, more commonly, the slowing of the blood flow in the extremity owing to a lowered metabolism and depression of the circulation after operation. It is probable that several of these factors act together to produce thrombosis. The left leg is affected more frequently.

Clinical Features

The first symptom of deep vein thrombosis may be a pain or a cramp in the calf (Figure 2.26), although in many cases it is asymptomatic. Pressure in the calf gives pain, and a day or so later there is painful swelling of the entire leg, often associated with a slight fever and sometimes with chills and perspiration. The swelling is due to a soft oedema that pits easily on pressure. There is marked tenderness over the anteromedial surface of the thigh.

A milder form of the same disease is termed phlebothrombosis, to indicate intravascular clotting without marked inflammation of the vein. The clotting occurs usually in the veins of the calf, often with few symptoms except slight soreness of the calf. The danger from this type of thrombosis is that the clot may be dislodged, producing an embolus. It is believed that most pulmonary emboli arise from this source (Figure 2.26).

Investigation

Where the presence of a deep venous thrombosis is suspected, the diagnosis may be confirmed by radiological studies, using venography, where dye is injected into the distal veins of the affected limb. Other techniques use ultrasound, where the thrombosed vein is noncompressible, and Doppler ultrasound, which studies the flow through vessels (reduced in deep venous thrombosis).

Nursing Care

The treatments of thrombophlebitis and deep venous thrombosis may be considered as (1) preventive and (2) active. In any situation where a patient may be confined to bed or is at risk of developing a deep venous thrombosis, nursing care should emphasize prevention. Such measures include preoperative patient education, when leg exercises may be taught. Passive exercises may be carried out by the nurse or physiotherapist, when patients cannot do this for themselves. The crossing of legs, either in bed or when sitting, should be discouraged. In the operating theatre, passive exercises to the calf muscles may be carried out by the theatre staff prophylactically during lengthy operating procedures.

Where there is a previous history of deep venous thrombosis, low-dose heparin may be used preoperatively. This is administered in prescribed units subcutaneously. External pneumatic compression, with gradient elastic stockings, can be used alone or in combination with low-dose heparin. These stockings prevent swelling and stagnation of venous flow in the legs, and do much to relieve limb pain, particularly in older patients.

Early ambulation postoperatively and adequate hydration will also prevent the development of a deep venous thrombosis. It is important to avoid the use of blanket rolls, pillow rolls or any form of elevation that will cause constriction under the knees. Even the practice of allowing the patient to dangle the legs while sitting on the edge of the bed may be dangerous, and is not recommended because pressure under the knees can impede circulation.

When a patient has developed a deep venous throm-

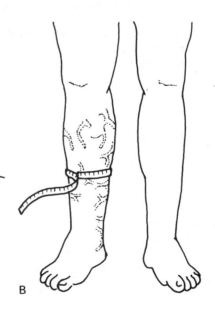

Figure 2.26 Assessment of signs and symptoms of deep venous thrombosis. (A) With the knee flexed, the patient may complain of pain in the calf on dorsiflexion of the foot (Homans's sign)—this is considered an unmistakable sign of early and subclinical thrombosis; it may or may not be present. Gentle compression reveals tenderness of the calf muscles (note arrows). This must be performed gently as it could dislodge a thrombus. (B) The affected leg may swell; veins are more prominent and may be palpated easily. (From Brunner, L. S. and Suddarth, D. S. (1986) *The Lippincott Manual of Nursing Practice* (4th edition), J. B. Lippincott, Philadelphia.)

bosis, the emphasis must be on controlling the extension of the thrombus, with analgesia, anticoagulants and prevention of complications. Measures include: elevating the affected limb and bedrest; ensuring adequate hydration; and the application of elastic compression stockings of the graduated compression type to aid venous return.

The patient is confined to bed for approximately 5 to 10 days, to permit the symptoms to settle and to allow the thrombus to organize and become less friable, thus reducing the probability of a pulmonary embolism. During this time, the affected leg is rested but the patient should be encouraged to exercise the unaffected leg to prevent the formation of further thrombi and muscle wasting (see Chapter 9).

Medical Management

Medical management may include either anticoagulant therapy, such as heparin or warfarin, or, occasionally, thrombolytic therapy, such as streptokinase or tissue plasminogen activator. Anticoagulant therapy with heparin is normally administered intravenously, and may also be administered subcutaneously, but local bruising is often troublesome. Continuing anticoagulant therapy with oral agents such as warfarin requires careful dose monitoring, using the patient's prothrombin time to regulate the dose required. This therapy is often continued for several months, occasionally longterm. Patients must be advised of the major risk of bleeding, such as epistaxis, bruising, haematuria or any injury where bleeding is prolonged.

Thrombolytic therapy may be used for either deep venous thrombosis or the severe complication of pulmonary embolism. These agents interfere with the clotting mechanism, and streptokinase is antigenic, so patients should be monitored closely, preferably in an intensive care unit (see also Chapter 9).

Pulmonary Embolism

An embolus is a foreign body in the bloodstream, usually formed by a blood clot that becomes dislodged from its original site and is carried along in the blood.

When the clot is carried to the heart it is forced by the blood into the pulmonary artery, where it plugs the main artery or one of its branches. The symptoms produced may be among the most sudden and startling in surgical practice. A patient experiencing an apparently normal convalescence suddenly cries out with sharp, stabbing pains in the chest and becomes breathless, cyanotic and anxious. The pupils dilate, cold perspiration appears, the pulse becomes rapid, irregular and then imperceptible, and death usually results. If death does not occur within 30 minutes there is a chance of recovery.

Fortunately, pulmonary embolism is usually a less dramatic event than that described above and may be

heralded by no more than mild dyspnoea, arrhythmia or seemingly innocent chest pain. Alertness on the part of the nurse is necessary to detect these subtle emboli in order that early treatment may be initiated and further embolization avoided.

● One of the many reasons for getting the patient out of bed as soon after surgery as possible is to avoid a pulmonary embolism.

Respiratory Complications

Respiratory complications are among the most frequent and serious problems that confront the surgical team (Table 2.33).

Experience has shown that such complications may be avoided in large measure by careful preoperative observation and teaching, and by taking every precaution during and after the operation. It is well known that patients who have some respiratory disease before operation are more

Table 2.33 *Risk factors affecting postoperative pulmonary complications*

Type of surgery	Greater incidence following all forms of abdominal surgery when compared with peripheral surgery
Location of incision	The closer the incision to the diaphragm, the higher the incidence of pulmonary complications
Preoperative respiratory complications	
Age	Greater risk over the age of 40
Sepsis	
Obesity	Weight greater than 110% of ideal body weight
Prolonged bedrest	
Duration of operation	Over 3 hours
Aspiration	
Dehydration	
Malnutrition	
Hypotension and shock	

apt to develop serious complications after operation. The refore, only emergency operations are performed when acute disease of the respiratory tract exists. The nurse reports any symptom, such as cough, sneezing, inflamed conjunctivae and nasal discharge, to the surgeon and anaesthetist before the operation.

During and immediately after the operation every effort should be made to prevent chilling. Aspiration of the nasopharynx in the recovery room removes secretions that would otherwise cause respiratory problems in the postoperative period. In very debilitated patients in whom retained secretions are a complicating factor, a tracheostomy may be performed so that aspiration of the trachea is done directly through the tube as necessary.

Atelectasis

When the mucus plug closes one of the bronchi entirely, there is a collapse of the pulmonary tissue beyond, and a massive atelectasis is said to result. (See Chapter 3.)

Bronchitis

Bronchitis may appear at any time after operation, usually within the first five to six days. The symptoms vary according to the disease. A simple bronchitis is characterized by a cough that produces considerable mucopurulent sputum, but without marked temperature or pulse elevation.

Bronchopneumonia

Bronchopneumonia is perhaps the second most frequent pulmonary complication. Along with a productive cough, there may be considerable elevation of temperature and an increase in pulse and respiratory rates.

Lobar Pneumonia

Lobar pneumonia is a less frequent complication after operation. Usually, it begins with a chill, followed by high temperature and pulse and respiration rates. There may be little or no cough, but the respiratory embarrassment, flushed cheeks and evident illness of the patient make a combination of clinical signs that is distinctive. The disease runs its usual course with the added complication of the operative wound.

Hypostatic Pulmonary Congestion

Hypostatic pulmonary congestion is a condition that may develop in elderly or very weak patients. Its cause is a weakened heart and vascular system that permit stagnation of secretions at the base of both lungs. It occurs most frequently in elderly patients who are not mobilized effectively. The symptoms often are not marked for a time— perhaps a slight elevation of temperature, pulse and respiratory rate and a slight cough. However, physical examination reveals dullness and crackles at the base of the lungs. If the condition goes untreated the outcome may be fatal.

Pleurisy

Pleurisy is not an uncommon development after operation. Its chief symptom is an acute, knifelike pain in the chest on the affected side that is particularly excruciating when the patient takes a deep breath. There is usually some slight rise in temperature and pulse, and respirations are rapid and more shallow than normal.

Management

A most effective method of treating bronchitis is the inhalation of cool mist or steam, which may be administered by electric vaporizers as prescribed. The apparatus must be kept filled with water, and precautions should be taken to prevent the patient from being burned.

In lobar pneumonia and bronchopneumonia, the patient is encouraged to take fluids; expectorant and antibiotic drugs are also prescribed. Distension is observed for and prevented, if possible, so as to avoid added respiratory or cardiac embarrassment.

For pleurisy, analgesics may be prescribed, or the doctor may carry out an intercostal block to provide symptomatic relief. A search is made to detect any possible underlying disease (pneumonia, infarction).

Pleurisy with effusion may develop secondary to a primary pleurisy. In these patients aspiration of the pleural space is frequently necessary.

In many cases, the pulmonary complication of hypostatic pulmonary congestion becomes more serious than the original surgical condition, in which case the prime objective of therapeutic management is to treat the hypostatic pneumonia.

Because the reduced aeration in many of these pulmonary complications means that less oxygen reaches the blood and therefore the tissues, oxygen therapy is often prescribed.

Superinfections

Superinfections can occur when antimicrobial agents change the bacterial flora of the respiratory tract. Susceptible bacteria are killed and resistant bacteria multiply. These infections must be treated aggressively.

Nursing Care

Awareness of the many possible respiratory complications enables the nurse to initiate the preventive measures cited in the previous discussion on preoperative patient education (p. 111). Timely recognition of signs and symptoms allows the nurse to direct efforts toward combating specific respiratory difficulties. Not only is the first postoperative day one of concern, but the first postoperative week of the patient's recovery requires careful management. The early signs of elevations in temperature, and pulse and respiration rates are significant. Chest pain, dyspnoea and cough may or may not accompany these signs; however, the patient may seem to be restless and apprehensive. Such indications are important and should be reported and documented.

Measures to Promote the Full Aeration of the Lungs. The prophylactic treatment of respiratory complications includes measures to promote full aeration of the lungs. The nurse instructs the patient to take at least 10 deep inhalations every hour. Turning the patient from side to side sometimes results in coughing, with expulsion of a mucus plug and increased aeration of the lungs.

The increased metabolism, more complete pulmonary aeration and general improvement of all body functions incidental to getting the patient up out of bed is one of the best prophylactic measures for pulmonary complications. When the wound or other condition permits, the patient is usually allowed to get out of bed on the first or second day after surgery, and frequently on the day of the operation. This practice is especially valuable in preventing pulmonary complications in older patients.

Urinary Retention

Urinary retention may follow any operation, but it occurs most frequently after operations on the rectum, the anus and the vagina, and after herniorrhaphies and operations on the lower abdomen. The cause is thought to be a spasm of the bladder sphincter.

Nursing Care

Quite often patients are unable to void urine while lying in bed, but they do so without difficulty when allowed to sit or stand up. When standing or sitting does not interfere with the operative result, male patients may be allowed to stand by the side of the bed and female patients to sit on the edge of the bed with their feet on a chair or a stool. However, some patients cannot be permitted this activity, and other means of encouraging urination must be tried. Some people cannot pass urine with another person in the room. These patients should be left alone for a time after being provided with a warm bedpan or urinal.

Frequently the sound or sight of running water relaxes the spasm of the bladder sphincter. Using a bedpan containing warm water or irrigating the perineum with warm water frequently initiates urination for female patients. A small, warm enema is often of value under medical supervision. If urinary retention continues for some hours and the patient complains of considerable pain in the lower abdomen, the bladder can frequently be palpated and seen in outline distending the lower anterior abdominal wall.

When all conservative measures have failed, catheterization becomes necessary. If the patient has voided just before operation, this procedure may be delayed for 12 to 18 hours. There are two reasons for wanting to avoid catheterization: (1) there is the possibility of infecting the bladder and producing a cystitis, and (2) experience has

shown that once a patient has been catheterized, often subsequent catheterizations are needed.

Many patients exhibit a palpable bladder, with lower abdominal discomfort, and still void small amounts of urine at frequent intervals. The alert nurse does not mistake this for normal functioning of the bladder. This voiding of 30 to 60 ml of urine at intervals of 15 to 30 minutes is a sign of an overdistended bladder, the very distension being sufficient to allow the escape of small amounts of urine at intervals. The condition is described as 'retention with overflow'. Catheterization usually relieves the patient by draining from 600 to 900 ml of urine from the bladder. No more than 1,000 ml of urine are removed at a time, unless otherwise advised. 'Incontinence of retention' may be evidenced by a constant dribble of urine while the bladder remains overdistended. Because distension injures the bladder, catheterization is indicated. There may be a psychological element in urinary retention.

The surgeon may anticipate voiding difficulties following extensive surgery, and an indwelling catheter is inserted before the patient emerges from anaesthesia. Usually, the surgeon will want to be notified if an amount less than 30 ml of urine per hour is collected.

Gastrointestinal Complications

Nutritional Considerations

Surgery of the gastrointestinal tract frequently disrupts the normal physiological processes of digestion and absorption. Complications arising from this disruption may take several forms, depending on the location and extent of surgery. For example, oral surgery may present problems of chewing and swallowing, requiring that the diet be modified to accommodate the difficulty. Other surgical procedures, such as gastrectomy, small bowel resection, ileostomy and colostomy, have a more drastic effect on the gastrointestinal system and require more extensive dietary considerations, as indicated in Table 2.34.

Intestinal Obstruction

Intestinal obstruction is a complication that may follow abdominal operations. It occurs most often after operations on the lower abdomen and the pelvis, and especially after operations in which drainage has been necessary. The symptoms usually appear between the third and fifth days, but may occur at any time, even years after the operation. The cause is some obstruction of the intestinal current—frequently a loop of intestine that has become kinked because of inflammatory adhesions or is involved with peritonitis or generalized irritation of the peritoneal surface.

Usually there is no elevation of temperature or pulse rate. At first the pains are localized, a point that should be noted by the nurse because the localization of the early pains identifies in a general way the loop of intestine that is just above the obstruction.

Usually the patient continues to have abdominal pains, with shorter and shorter intervals between waves of pain. When a stethoscope is placed on the abdomen, sounds that give evidence of extremely active intestinal movements may be heard, especially during an attack of pain. The intestinal contents, being unable to move forward, distend the intestinal coils, are carried backward to the stomach and are vomited. Thus, vomiting and increasing distension gradually become more prominent symptoms. Hiccough often precedes the vomiting. Defaecation does not occur, and enemas return nearly clear, showing that a very small amount of the intestinal contents has reached the large bowel. Unless the obstruction is relieved, the patient continues to vomit, distension becomes more pronounced, the pulse becomes rapid and the outcome is death.

Management. Sometimes the distension of the intestine above the obstruction can be prevented by the use of constant-suction drainage through a nasogastric tube, in which case the inflammatory reaction of the bowel at the site of the obstruction may subside and the obstruction is relieved. However, it may necessary to relieve the obstruction surgically. Intravenous infusions of prescribed solutions are usually given as well. (See the section on intestinal obstruction for a more complete discussion of the treatment and postoperative care, Chapter 15.)

Postoperative Psychosis

Postoperative psychosis (mental aberrations) may be physiological or psychological in origin. Cerebral hypoxia, thromboembolism and fluid–electrolyte imbalances are recognized physical factors in postoperative central nervous system impairment and stress. Emotional factors such as fear, pain and disorientation can contribute to postoperative depression and anxiety.

Older patients, particularly those with cerebrovascular atherosclerosis, are most susceptible to psychological disturbances. Usually they manage fairly well until they have been subjected to the anaesthetic and operation. Post-

Table 2.34 *Dietary support of common complications in surgical treatment*

Procedure	Complications	Dietary support
Radical oropharyngeal surgery	Difficulty in mastication and swallowing	*Diet:* Liquid consistency – tube feeds Fluid by mouth; fruit juices as tolerated Coffee, tea, gelatin, ice cream
Gastrectomy	*Small pouch* 'Dumping syndrome' Epigastric fullness, distension; pallor, sweating, tachycardia, hypotension, diarrhoea	Low-carbohydrate Moderate-fat High-protein Small, frequent feeds Periodic injections of vitamin B_{12}
Small bowel resection	Poor absorption Weight loss (absorptive capacity improves with time)	*Immediate support after surgery:* Long-term parenteral nutrition Later: oral intake of high protein, high-calorie, low-fat diet Medium-chain triglycerides
Ileostomy/colostomy	Initial loss of water and electrolytes	Daily replacement of electrolytes, full liquid diet, high in protein
Bypass surgery	For relief of pain and obstruction Malabsorption syndrome Maldigestion, diarrhoea	Feedings by natural route High-protein, high-vitamin C Adequate vitamins and minerals

(Source: Valassi, K. Nutritional management of cancer patients in a variety of therapeutic regimens, *Arch. Phys. Med. Rehab.,* Vol. 58.)

operatively, they may become very disturbed and disorientated.

Disfiguring surgery and operations for cancer also predispose to intense emotional problems. Dressings that obscure vision or confinement in a plaster of Paris can result in behavioural changes because of the reduced sensory input.

A high incidence of psychotic sequelae appears to occur in patients who have had open-heart surgery. Several factors seem significantly related to neurological damage: age (the older, the more likely), length of extracorporeal circulation (the longer, the greater the likelihood), mean arterial pressure of less than 50 mmHg during perfusion and the possibility of air emboli. Even the sensory overload of the intensive care unit is believed to contribute to postcardiotomy delirium.

Preoperative and Postoperative Nursing Care

The patient should be well informed before the operation about what to expect after surgery. Opportunities need to be provided for the patient to express thoughts and fears; misinformation can be corrected and reassurance provided. High-risk patients, as described above, may require special attention and support. Judicious use of narcotics can also reduce confusion and disorientation.

Orientating patients to time, day and place can help them to accept unfamiliar surroundings. Studies have indicated that thorough preoperative briefing of both patient and family or significant others can usually counteract many of the potential postoperative psychological stresses. In addition, a positive attitude conveyed by all staff who come into contact with the patient will foster positive feelings.

For overt psychosis, the patient may require major tranquillizers and consultation and therapy with mental health professionals. Since postoperative psychosis does occur, it is helpful when discussing this with patients to indicate that it is transient. A patient with illusions or hallucinations is often reassured to know that these aberrations are occasionally experienced and do not reflect on the patient's sanity.

Restraint. In the postoperative care of patients with psychological disturbances, it is prudent for the nurse to explain the necessity for the patient to remain in bed. Often, patients prefer to get out of bed to pass urine or to get a drink of water rather than bother the nurse. This may lead to serious complications that a brief explanation can prevent. However, some patients, especially older patients and those who are disorientated, may find this impossible to grasp. For such patients, the simplest form of restraint is the use of beds with side rails or side protection. This permits patients to move about in bed but prevents them from getting out of bed easily and injuring themselves.

To protect both patient and nurse, it may become necessary to apply some form of restraint in cases of delirium. The psychological effect of being restrained can be severe; therefore, any form of restraint is applied only as a last resort. All other means of quietening the patient are tried first. If possible, the patient should be isolated from other patients. Any potentially harmful article in the vicinity is removed.

When restraints are used, the patient should be in a comfortable and natural position, and care must be taken that no part is so constricted as to interfere with the circulation. Restraint to the chest is avoided, if possible. The appearance of cyanosis of the hand or foot indicates that an appliance is too tight. The appliances are padded carefully and placed so as to prevent chafing or pressure sores. The skin underneath them is inspected frequently, bathed carefully and massaged at least every two to three hours. Even though restraints are applied, the patient is never left unwatched. Any patient requiring restraint should have constant and careful nursing attention. Consideration is given to respecting the patient as a person; as someone who is experiencing changes in body image and self-esteem, and who needs understanding and support.

Delirium

Postoperative delirium occurs occasionally in several groups of patients. The most common types of delirium are toxic, traumatic and alcoholic (delirium tremens).

Toxic Delirium. Toxic delirium occurs in conjunction with the signs and symptoms of a general toxaemia. The patient with toxic delirium is very ill, usually with a high temperature and pulse rate. The face is flushed, and the eyes are bright and roving. The patient moves incessantly, often attempting to get out of bed and disarranging the bedcothes continually. A marked degree of mental confusion is present. These states are seen most often in patients with general peritonitis or other septic conditions.

In such patients, elimination is promoted by encouraging the intake of fluids and the causative condition is treated by antimicrobial therapy. At times, however, the condition is fatal.

Traumatic Delirium. Traumatic delirium is a mental state resulting from sudden trauma of any sort, especially in highly nervous people. The malady may take the form of wild, maniacal excitement, simple confusion with hallucinations and delusions or depression. Treatment involves the use of sedative drugs. Usually, the state begins and ends suddenly.

Delirium Tremens. Individuals who have used alcohol habitually over a long period of time are poor surgical risks. Not only is their resistance lower than normal, but the effects of alcohol may have damaged practically every organ. In addition, these patients take anaesthesia poorly.

After operation, such patients may do well for a few days, but the prolonged abstinence from alcohol causes restlessness, nervousness and irritation at the slightest little thing. Facial expressions may change entirely. Sleep is poor and often disturbed by unreal dreams. When approached by the doctor or the nurse, such patients appear to wake suddenly, ask ''Who are you?'' and, when told where they are, appear to be fairly normal for a short time. These symptoms should be looked for in patients who have been alcoholics; by active treatment at this stage, the more violent delirium may be avoided.

Active delirium tremens may come on suddenly or gradually. After a period of restless, nervous semi-delirium, the patients finally lose control of their mental functions and 'horrors reign supreme'. Their minds are a chaos of ever-changing ideas. They talk incessantly and try to get out of bed to get away from the hallucinations of fear and persecution that torment them continually. If attempts are made to restrain them, they may fight maniacally and often injure themselves and others. In this stage the patients are obviously sick. They are sleepless, perspire freely and display a marked tremor in the extremities. Finally, after many hours of torture, the patients become stuporous.

Medical and Nursing Care. When possible, the treatment of patients with delirium tremens should begin two or three days before operation with an increased fluid intake to encourage elimination from the kidneys, the bowels and the skin. These measures should be continued after operation, especially if any of the early signs of the condition develop. Sedative drugs or tranquillizers should be given to keep the patient quiet. The chief cause of the symptoms in patients with chronic alcoholism has been shown to be a depletion of the carbohydrate stores of the body and an inadequate ingestion of vitamins. Therefore, glucose is given intravenously and vitamins are administered in concentrated form by mouth and by injection.

Day Surgery

Admitting patients for day surgery is becoming increasingly common. Patients are normally admitted fasting in the morning and, provided there are no complications, are allowed home the same day.

The advantages of this type of surgery are that there is a greater turnover of patients, thus reducing the waiting lists, and that the patient spends less time in hospital, which, in turn, reduces hospital costs. Infection risks are also lessened, and patient recovery is more rapid. However, the disadvantages are that there is less time to assess and evaluate the patient, and to establish rapport between the patient and health care staff. In addition, the immediate discharge of the patient will not permit assessment of late postoperative complications.

It must not be forgotten that merely because the surgery is 'minor', and patients are in hospital for only one day, they still experience just as much anxiety as the patient who is admitted for several days (Autton, 1968). Swindale (1989) identifies the importance of the nurse's role in giving preoperative advice to reduce anxiety in patients admitted to hospital for elective minor surgery.

Wilson-Barnett (1981) defines anxiety as 'fear of the unknown', and Cochran (1984) suggests that, regardless of disease, hospitalization provokes anxiety. Therefore, it is necessary for the nurse to recognize that the patient will be anxious and will feel threatened by admission to hospital. According to Autton (1968), 'there is no such thing as a minor operation for the patient'.

Boore (1978) and Hayward (1973) show that providing information before surgery lowers anxiety levels, reduces stress, decreases pain and promotes a better and quicker recovery. Therefore, information regarding anaesthesia, time of operation and what the patient may feel afterwards will help to reduce anxiety levels (see section on psychological care, p. 107).

A point worth noting is that some anaesthetic agents have amnesic properties and some patients may have no recollection postoperatively of information given by the surgeon. It is therefore important to ensure that patients are fully alert and able to understand what they are being told regarding the outcome of surgery.

Types of Procedures Handled as Day Surgery

Day surgery procedures are usually of short duration, from 15 to 90 minutes, in which minimal bleeding and minor physiological disturbance are anticipated, as in the following examples:

1. General surgery—hernia repair, excision of small lumps or tumours.
2. Gynaecology—dilatation and curettage (D & C), tubal ligation, pregnancy termination, cervical diagnostic laparoscopy, biopsy and conization.
3. Dermatology—excision of warts and condylomata.
4. Ophthalmology—cataract extraction, minor eye operations.
5. Ear, nose and throat—myringotomy, adenoidectomy, tonsillectomy, nasal polypectomy, oral surgery.
6. Cardiac surgery—cardioversion, insertion and replacement of pacemakers.
7. Orthopaedic surgery—carpal tunnel surgery, ganglionectomy.
8. Vasectomy.

Patient Selection

The patient should be in stable medical condition and be free of infection. It may be more practical for the person with a mild systemic disease to have a surgical procedure in this short-term facility than to be exposed to the greater risk of hospitalization. Usually age is not a factor; however, premature infants are usually not considered because of potential problems. It is desirable that, psychologically, the patient is willing to accept this treatment.

Nursing Care

The admission procedure to the day ward should identify any problems the patient has which may have to be reported to the surgeon. The doctor will discuss the consent form with the patient, and witness the patient's signature. The patient's general condition is assessed, and anxiety levels noted. Any allergies are identified and recorded in the patient's notes, and current medication is reported to the doctor. Baseline recordings of temperature, pulse, blood pressure and respirations are taken and recorded in the patient's chart, and any history of previous major illnesses or severe headaches are noted.

All make-up and nail varnish are removed. Patients are advised not to bring jewellery or money with them, but a wedding ring may be taped to the finger to avoid loss when the patient is anaesthetized.

Urine is tested routinely for glucose, blood and protein, and any abnormality is reported. It is important that the nurse checks when the patient last had something to eat or drink.

Preparation For Theatre

An identity band is attached to the patient's wrist to ensure correct identification. The patient is asked to empty the bladder. Any dentures are removed and placed in a named container, and the anaesthetist is informed about any dental prosthesis. The patient is dressed in an operating gown.

Not all day surgery patients are given premedication, but any that is prescribed is given at the correct time. The patient is transferred to the operating theatre with the correct notes and X-rays.

Postoperative Care

The patient is transferred to the recovery room from the operating theatre (see section on the care of the patient in the recovery room, p. 120), and vital signs are checked regularly until stable. If an airway is *in situ*, a nurse stays with the patient until the gag reflex has returned and the patient is breathing normally. The head of the bed is gradually elevated. When the observations are stable and the patient is fully conscious and alert, oral fluids or tea and toast may be allowed.

Before the patient is allowed home, it is important that the nursing staff check that the vital signs are stable, that the patient can stand without feeling dizzy or nauseated, and is able to walk. The patient should be orientated to time, place and person, and should be comfortable and free from excessive pain. In order to avoid retention of urine, the patient should be able to empty the bladder before leaving hospital.

Any advice to the patient regarding ongoing care should be given in writing, bearing in mind the amnesic effect of some anaesthetic drugs. Clear advice as to when to return to the outpatient clinic, or what to do should any problems arise, should be given to the patient or home carers.

INFLAMMATION

Cells or tissues of the body may be injured or killed by many agents (physical, chemical, infectious). When this happens there is a naturally occurring response in the healthy tissues adjacent to the site of injury. This is called the inflammatory response, or inflammation. It is a non-specific defensive reaction, which serves to neutralize, control and/or eliminate the offending agent and to prepare the site for repair. For example, inflammation may be observed at the site of a bee sting, a sore throat, a surgical incision or a burn. Inflammation also occurs where there is more serious cell injury such as in strokes and heart attacks.

It is important to distinguish between inflammation and infection. An infectious agent is only one of several agents that may trigger an inflammatory response. An infection exists when the infectious agent is living, growing and multiplying in the tissues and is able to overcome the body's normal defences.

Regardless of the cause, there is a general sequence of events that can be described as the local inflammatory response. This sequence involves changes in the microcirculation in the area of the injury that include vasodilatation, increased vascular permeability and leucocytic cellular infiltration. As these changes take place, five cardinal signs of inflammation are produced: redness, heat, swelling, pain and loss of function.

A transient vasoconstriction that occurs immediately after injury is followed by vasodilatation and an increased rate of blood flow through the microcirculation. Local heat and redness result. Next, vascular permeability increases, and plasma fluids (including proteins and solutes) leak into the inflamed tissues, producing swelling. The pain produced is attributed to the pressure of fluids (swelling) on nerve endings and, possibly, to direct irritation of nerve endings by chemical mediators released at the site. Bradykinin is one of the chemical mediators suspected of causing pain. Loss of function is most likely related to the pain and swelling, but the exact mechanism has not been explained.

As the blood flow increases and fluid leaks into the surrounding tissues, the formed elements (red blood cells, white blood cells and platelets) are left and the blood becomes more viscous and sluggish. Leucocytes (white blood cells) collect in the vessels, exit and migrate to the site of injury to engulf offending organisms and to remove cellular debris in a process called phagocytosis. Fibrinogen in the leaked plasma fluid coagulates, forming fibrin for clot formation that serves to wall off the injured area and prevent the spread of infection.

Chemical Mediators

Injury initiates the inflammatory response, but chemical substances released at the site induce the vascular changes. Foremost among these are histamine and the kinins. Histamine is present in many tissues of the body but is concentrated in mast cells. It is released when injury occurs and is responsible for the early changes in vasodilatation and vascular permeability. Kinins increase vasodilatation and vascular permeability; they also attract neutrophils to the area. Prostaglandins, another group of chemical substances, are also suspected of causing increased permeability.

The process described is complex. Although it has phases, once started they may all be occurring at the same time. The process may be modified by different variables, the most important of which are (1) the nature and intensity of the injury, (2) the site and tissue affected and (3) the resistance of the host.

The inflammatory response may be confined to the site, and produce local signs only. On the other hand, systemic responses may also occur. Fever is the most common sign of a systemic response to injury. It is most likely caused by endogenous pyrogens released from neutrophils and macrophages (specialized forms of leucocytes), which reset the hypothalamic thermostat controlling body temperature. Leucocytosis, an increase in the synthesis and release of neutrophils from bone marrow, may occur. Constitutional symptoms may develop, including malaise, loss of appetite, aching and weakness.

Types of Inflammation

Inflammation is categorized primarily by duration and the type of exudate produced. It may be acute, subacute or chronic. A typical case of acute inflammation is characterized by the local vascular and exudative changes described above and usually lasts for less than two weeks. An acute inflammatory response is immediate, and it serves a protective function. When the injurious agent is removed, the inflammation subsides and healing takes place with the return of normal or near-normal structure and function.

Chronic inflammation develops when the injurious agent persists and the acute response is perpetuated. Symptoms may appear for many months or years. Chronic inflammation may also begin insidiously and never have an acute phase. The chronic response does not serve a beneficial and protective function but, on the contrary, is debilitating and may produce long-lasting effects in the person. As the inflammation becomes chronic, changes occur at the site of injury and the nature of the exudate becomes proliferative. There is a continuing cycle of cellular infiltration, necrosis and fibrosis (repair and breakdown go on side by side). Considerable scarring may occur, resulting in permanent damage to tissues.

Subacute inflammation falls in between acute and chronic inflammation. There are elements of the active exudative phase of the acute response, and simultaneously there is also some repair occurring as in the chronic response. The term is not widely used.

Repair

The reparative process begins at approximately the same time as the injury and is indeed interwoven with inflammation. Healing proceeds after the inflammatory debris is removed. Healing may be by regeneration, in which there is gradual repair of the defect by proliferation of cells of the same type as those destroyed. Or, it may be by replacement with cells of another type, usually connective tissue, resulting in scar formation.

Healing by Regeneration

The ability of cells to regenerate depends on whether they are labile, stable or permanent. Labile cells include those that multiply constantly to replace cells worn out by normal physiological processes; these include epithelial cells of the skin and those lining the gastrointestinal tract. Permanent cells include neurons—the nerve cell bodies, not their axons. Destruction of a neuron is a permanent loss, but axons may regenerate. If normal activity is to return, tissue regeneration must occur in a functional pattern, especially in the growth of several axons. Stable cells have a latent ability to regenerate. Under normal physiological processes, they are not shed and do not need replacement, but if they are damaged or destroyed, they are able to regenerate. These include functional cells of the kidney, liver, pancreas and other glands of the body.

Healing by Replacement

Healing may be by primary intention or secondary intention. In primary intention healing, the wound is clean and dry and the edges are approximated, such as may occur in a surgical wound. Little scar formation occurs, and the wound is usually healed in a week. In secondary intention healing, the wound or defect is larger and gaping and has more necrotic material. The wound fills from the bottom upward with granulation tissue. The process of repair takes longer and results in more scar formation with loss of specialized function. People who have recovered from myocardial infarcts will have abnormal electrocardiographic tracings because the electrical signal cannot be conducted through the connective tissue that replaces the defect.

WOUND CARE AND WOUND HEALING

Care of the Wound

A wound may be described as a disruption in the continuity of cells; it follows, then, that wound healing is the restoration of that continuity.

When wounds occur, a variety of effects may result: (1) immediate loss of all or part of the function of an organ, (2) sympathetic stress response, (3) bleeding and blood clotting, (4) bacterial contamination and (5) death of cells.

Wound Classification

Wounds may be classified in two different ways: according to the manner in which they were made, and according to the likelihood and degree of wound contamination at the time of surgery.

Mechanism of Injury

Wounds may be described as incised, contused, lacerated or puncture.

- Incised wounds are made by a clean cut with a sharp instrument—for example, those made by the surgeon in most operations. Clean wounds (those made aseptically) are usually closed by sutures after all bleeding vessels have been carefully ligated.
- Contused wounds are made by blunt force and are characterized by considerable injury to the soft parts, haemorrhage and swelling.
- Lacerated wounds are those with jagged, irregular edges, such as would be made by glass or barbed wire.
- Puncture wounds result in small openings in the skin—for example, those made by bullets or knife stabs.

Degree of Contamination

Wounds may be described as clean, clean-contaminated, contaminated, or dirty or infected.

- Clean wounds are uninfected surgical wounds in which there is no inflammation and the respiratory, alimentary, genital or uninfected urinary tracts are not entered. Clean wounds are closed by primary closure; if necessary, they are drained with closed drainage. The relative probability of wound infection is 1 to 5 per cent.
- Clean-contaminated wounds are surgical wounds in which the respiratory, alimentary, genital or urinary tract is entered under controlled conditions; there is no

unusual contamination. The relative probability of wound infection is 3 to 11 per cent.
- Contaminated wounds include open, fresh, accidental wounds, and operations with major breaks in aseptic technique or gross spillage from the gastrointestinal tract; in this category are also incisions in which there is acute, nonpurulent inflammation. The relative probability of wound infection is 10 to 17 per cent.
- Dirty or infected wounds are those in which the organisms that cause postoperative infection are present in the operative field before surgery. These include old traumatic wounds with retained devitalized tissue and those which involve existing clinical infections or perforated viscera. The relative probability of wound infection is over 27 per cent. (See Wound Sepsis, p. 149.)

Treatment. Prophylactic antibiotics may be administered when bacterial contamination is expected, or for the patient with a clean wound in which a prosthetic device is being inserted.

When wounds are potentially infected, they cannot be closed until every effort has been made to remove all devitalized and infected tissue. Therefore, a formal operation is performed for the purpose of cutting out the infected and devitalized tissue. This operation is called debridement. Often a small drain is inserted before the wound is sutured to prevent lymph and blood from collecting and retarding the healing process.

Physiology of Wound Healing

Various continuous and overlapping cellular processes contribute to the restoration of a wound: cell regeneration, cell proliferation, and collagen production. The response of tissue to injury goes through several phases: inflammatory, destructive, proliferative and maturation (Table 2.35).

Inflammatory Phase

This phase begins within a few minutes of injury and lasts for about three days. When tissue is disrupted and blood vessels are injured, there is reflex constriction of the smooth muscle of the tunica media; in small blood vessels, this may close the lumen and prevent further blood loss. Larger blood vessels will not close completely but the flow of blood will be slowed down. Blood platelets and fibrin (protein molecules) plug the bleeding vessel

Table 2.35 *Phases of wound healing*

Phase	Length of time
Traumatic inflammation	0–3 days
Destructive phase	1–6 days
Proliferative phase	3–24 days
Maturation	24 days–1 year

and cause the blood to clot. The injured blood vessels then thrombose and the bleeding stops. The damaged tissue and mast cells (basophils) release histamine and other enzymes that cause vasodilation of the local surrounding blood vessels and an increased flow of blood through the damaged tissue. The capillary walls become more permeable, allowing serum, white blood cells, antibodies and a few red blood cells to infiltrate the surrounding tissues and the wound itself. These local responses are typical following tissue disruption and give rise to the signs of inflammation—redness, heat, swelling and pain.

At this stage, two important types of cells arrive at the site of the wound. First are the polymorphonuclear leucocytes (polymorphs) and then the macrophages, whose numbers continue to increase throughout this inflammatory phase. These cells begin the important phase of clearing the area of foreign bodies, unwanted and damaged material and the blood clot, and initiate the body's defence mechanisms against invading bacteria.

Destructive Phase

During the destructive phase, the polymorphs and macrophages clear the area of all unwanted material. Many of the polymorphs are broken down (lysed), releasing their contents into the wound. Phagocytosis is carried out mainly by the macrophages, which engulf foreign material and transport it away from the wound. The macrophages also attract and recruit fibroblasts into the area. Fibroblasts are cells that synthesize collagen—the principal body-building protein.

Proliferative Phase

During the proliferative phase, the fibroblasts follow behind the macrophages and begin to 'weave' strands of collagen. This early collagen is very delicate and its continued growth is dependent upon a good supply of oxygenated blood.

An adequate supply of vitamin C is essential for the continued synthesis of collagen. Because vitamin C is water soluble, an adequate nutritional intake is required; if necessary, vitamin C supplements can be given.

Cellular and chemical activities lead to the formation of granulation tissue, which at this stage, although being delicate, adds to the tensile strength of the wound. Movement at the wound site should be minimized in order to protect this delicate tissue. Blood vessels continue to grow into the wound from its edges. After two weeks, the wound has only 3 to 5 per cent of the original skin strength; by the end of four weeks, only 35 to 59 per cent of wound strength has been reached.

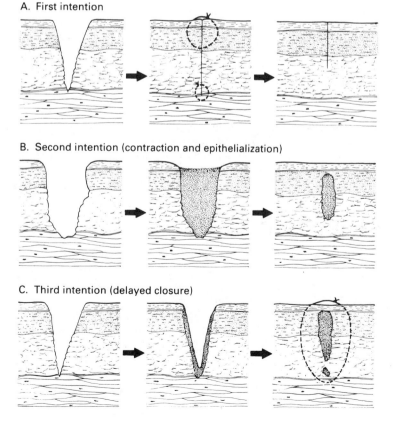

Figure 2.27 Classification of wound healing. (A) First intention—a clean incision is made with primary closure; there is minimal scarring. (B) Second intention (contraction and epithelialization)—the wound is left open to granulate in with resultant large scab and abnormal dermal–epidermal junction. (C) Third intention (delayed closure)—the wound is left open and closed secondarily when there is no evidence of infection. (Hardy, J. D. (1983) *Hardy's Textbook of Surgery*, J. B. Lippincott, Philadelphia, p. 109.)

A. First intention

B. Second intention (contraction and epithelialization)

C. Third intention (delayed closure)

Maturation Phase

During the maturation phase, fibroblasts begin to leave the wound. The scar originally appears large, but collagen fibres reorganize into tighter positions. This, along with dehydration, reduces the scar but adds to its tensile strength. Such tissue maturation continues over the weeks, adding to the strength of the wounded tissue, but it never regains more than 70 to 80 per cent of its original strength.

Forms of Healing

In the surgical management of wound healing, wounds are described as healing by first, second or third intention.

Healing by First Intention (Primary Union)

Wounds made aseptically, with a minimum of tissue destruction and where the skin edges are brought together, as with sutures or clips, heal with very little tissue reaction 'by first intention' (Figure 2.27). When wounds heal by first intention, granulation tissue is invisible and scar formation is minimal.

Healing by Second Intention (Granulation)

Here, the wound edges are not brought together surgically, and the wound gradually fills with granulation tissue. Granulation tissue is formed from macrophages and fibroblasts, which surround the newly developed capillary loops. This tissue is red, soft, sensitive and bleeds very easily. The granulation tissue slowly fills the wound, and healing is complete when skin cells (epithelium) grow over these granulations. This form of healing occurs in pressure sores, leg ulcers and open excisions.

Healing by Third Intention (Secondary Suture)

If a deep wound either has not been sutured immediately or breaks down and is then resutured later, two apposing granulation surfaces are brought together. This results in a deeper, wider and more pronounced scar.

Factors Affecting Wound Healing

Patient's Age

The older the patient, the less resilient the tissues, and the more likely the patient is to have systemic or malignant disease which can interfere with tissue healing. The inflammatory and immune responses may not be as effective as in the younger patient and vascularity may be impaired generally.

Handling of Tissues

All tissues must be handled carefully and evenly because rough handling can cause injury and delayed healing.

Haemorrhage

Accumulation of blood creates dead spaces as well as dead cells, which must be removed. The area can quickly become a culture medium for infection. The nurse should monitor the patient's vital signs, and observe for pyrexia. The incision site should be observed for evidence of bleeding.

Hypovolaemia

Insufficient blood volume leads to vasoconstriction and reduced oxygen and nutrients being available for wound healing. Thus the nurse should monitor for circulatory volume deficit, and any deficiencies should be corrected by fluid replacement therapy, as prescribed.

Infection

Wound infection discourages fibroblast activity. The pathogens compete with body cells for available oxygen and nutrients. The inflammatory response is less able to attend to the wound and wound healing, and abscesses may form in the wound (see Wound Complications, p. 149).

Wound Dressings

The choice of wound dressing and its manner of application and removal can affect wound healing. Traditional fibre-based dressings allow the wound to dry out and thus delay healing. 'Strike through' (soaking to the outer layer by wound exudate) can occur quickly, and micro-organisms can travel down through the saturated dressing when this happens (Colebrook and Hood, 1948). Adherence to the wound can occur as the serous exudate dries out onto the dressing, thus causing trauma as the dressing is removed.

These and other problems can be overcome by the use of some of the new synthetic dressings. (See Types of Dressings, p. 146.)

Nutritional State

Undernourishment leads to delayed wound healing due to a reduction in collagen synthesis. The injured patient, facing prolonged fasting, may use up plasma proteins to satisfy energy requirements in place of depleted carbohydrate, and thus less protein is available for tissue repair.

Vitamin C is essential for collagen synthesis, and it has been demonstrated that there is a decrease in plasma vitamin C levels following injury, which may necessitate the administration of large doses of vitamin C intravenously following surgery (Westaby, 1981). Other vitamins and minerals, such as vitamin A, copper and zinc, have also been shown to influence wound healing, and therefore the patient's nutritional state should be assessed on admission and throughout the stay in hospital. Provision of a balanced nutritional supply, which can be 'topped up' by supplements, is required. Early involvement by the dietician for patients at risk will reduce nutritional deficits.

Foreign Bodies

The presence of foreign bodies in the wound can encourage wound infection, and adversely affect wound healing. Traumatic wounds require meticulous cleaning and removal of foreign bodies. All wounds should be kept free of dressing threads, talcum powder and starch from gloves.

Oxygen Deficit

An adequate supply of oxygen reaching the wound is essential for satisfactory wound healing to occur because the phagocytes cannot function effectively if there is oxygen deficiency.

Inadequate oxygen may be due to inadequate lung and cardiovascular function, excessive blood loss and localized vasoconstriction. Respiratory and cardiovascular function should be assessed and any deficiencies treated. Blood volume will have to be restored if it is depleted. Deep breathing exercises will help to make more oxygenated blood available to the tissues.

Drainage Collection

Functioning wound drains prevent secretions from gathering within the wound and therefore prevent haematoma formation. Drains must be kept patent and the vacuum must be maintained if suction is required.

Drugs

1. Steroids may mask the presence of infection by impairing the normal inflammatory response to injury.
2. Anticoagulants may cause haemorrhage.
3. Cytotoxic drugs suppress the immune response and thus the patient may be more susceptible to infections.
4. Antibiotics are most effective when given immediately before surgery for specific pathology of bacterial contamination.

Temperature

In order to maintain biological processes such as mitosis and enzyme activity at an optimal level, it is necessary to maintain a constant temperature of 37°C. A fall in temperature of only 2°C is sufficient to affect the rate of cell division significantly (Johnson, 1988a). This can also inhibit leucocyte activity for up to two hours while the temperature loss is reversed (Barton and Barton, 1981).

During dressing changes, long exposures of wet wounds can reduce surface temperature to as little as 12°C, with the recovery of full mitotic activity taking up to three hours (Turner, 1982).

Dressings should not be removed until the nurse is ready to redress the wound; the dressing used should maintain thermal insulation or be supplemented by secondary dressings that have this property.

Systemic Disorders

If the patient is anaemic, the supply of oxygen to the wound may be reduced because of the decreased oxygen-carrying capacity of the blood. The underlying cause of the anaemia should be treated appropriately.

Diabetic patients, particularly those who are not well controlled, have an increased susceptibility to infection and may also have poor peripheral circulation. This can lead to prolonged and difficult wound healing. The diabetes itself must therefore be brought under control.

Immunosuppressive Therapy

The patient undergoing immunosuppressive therapy is more vulnerable to bacterial and viral infection, as the body's defence mechanisms are compromised.

Communication and Information

Good communication between nurse and patient should be established early on in the relationship. Accurate information about the patient's condition and the sensations likely to be experienced can decrease the amount of anxiety and distress the patient experiences (Samson and Spielberger, 1976). Improved psychological care can reduce the incidence of postoperative wound infection and assist in wound healing (Boore, 1978), as well as improve the patient's general postoperative condition (Schmitt and Wooldridge, 1973). Therefore, nurses must improve their communication skills and give accurate information to patients. This can be time consuming, but the nurse must find the time to do it and be prepared to repeat the information or write it down for the patient if necessary.

Staff Attitudes

A positive approach by nursing staff towards patients and their care may have an influence on how patients respond to treatment. A double-blind placebo study by Fernie and Dornan (in Kenedi and Cowden, 1976) demonstrated that when staff held a positive attitude towards treatment, patients themselves felt optimistic about it, which in turn was thought to have a significant effect on healing.

Wound Dressings

There are many dressings which can be used in the care of a patient's wound. Before deciding on which to use, the nurse must have a sound knowledge of the physiology of wound healing, the factors that delay or advance healing, and the types of dressings available, including their advantages and disadvantages. During treatment, it is important to keep the patient informed of how the dressing will assist wound healing, and of how the patient can help in this process.

Turner (1982) suggested that the ideal wound dressing should: (1) maintain a high humidity between the dressing and the wound surface; (2) remove excess exudate; (3) allow gaseous exchange; (4) provide thermal insulation; (5) be impermeable to micro-organisms; (6) be free from particle and toxic wound contaminants; and (7) on removal, prevent secondary trauma caused by dressing adherence to the wound. However, no single dressing can claim to be the optimum one for every type of wound. All wounds demand different strategies of care—the type of dressing used on a clean, surgical wound may be quite inappropriate on a sloughy, infected, 'traumatic' wound.

The decision to use a particular type of wound dressing must be taken only after careful assessment of the wound, taking into consideration the general condition of the patient. Habit and tradition should no longer dictate how wounds are cared for, but rather a sound knowledge of wound healing and of the products available, which have been tried and tested in clinical trials and proven to be effective through research.

As knowledge of wound healing and how wound dressings affect it has increased, so too have the number and types of wound dressings available. Dressing materials that encourage the drying of wounds have now been replaced by materials which allow the wound to heal in a moist environment. Wound exudate, rather than being the nuisance it was once thought to be, has been shown to contain not only nutrients essential for wound healing, but also antibodies, polymorphs and macrophages; it therefore plays a major role in tissue healing. Bathing the wound in this exudate prevents surrounding cells from drying out and dying, and tissue healing and epithelial migration occur much more readily than in dry conditions (Winter, 1978). Cells are supplied with the essential nutrients required for tissue growth and repair. The moist environment helps to maintain wound temperature, which in turn encourages rapid tissue growth; the presence of phagocytic cells reduces the risk of wound infection.

However, different wounds require different types of dressings if the optimum microenvironment for the promotion of rapid wound healing is to be encouraged. Indeed, it may be necessary to change the type of dressing as the wound's needs change in order to maintain optimum conditions.

Types of Dressings

Absorbent Dressings

These dressings are highly absorbent, permeable to oxygen, insulating and provide protection from accidental knocks. However, they allow exudate to dry on the wound, become adhesive and cause trauma on removal (Wood, 1976). Absorbent dressings can shed particles into the wound, which may stimulate a foreign body response, thus prolonging the inflammatory response during healing. They do not provide a moist wound environment, as exudate is absorbed, and once the exudate reaches the top layer of the dressing, a 'track' is formed along which micro-organisms can gain access to the wound surface ('strike through'). Thus, if absorbent dressings are used, they may require to be changed frequently if adhesion and trauma on removal, leakage and strike through of exudate are to be avoided. This can be costly in terms of nursing time and materials used.

Nonadherent Dressings

Nonadherent dressings consist of an absorbent cotton backing with a wound contact surface of perforated polymeric film, which is claimed to be nonadherent. However, these surfaces have been found to be adherent, to shed particles into the wound (Draper, 1985), to allow dehydration of the wound (Barnett and Varley, 1986) and strike through can occur quickly. Again, frequent dressing changes may be required.

Tulle Gras

Tulle gras dressings consist of cotton gauze tulle impregnated with soft paraffin, and they may also be medicated. They are often used in conjunction with an absorbent dressing. They help to retain moisture, are permeable to oxygen and are said to be nonadherent. When medicated, they can be effective against a wide range of bacteria. However, they are permeable to bacteria, often adhere to the wound unless changed at frequent intervals and the medication, when used, is absorbed into the top dressing rather than into the wound (Turner, 1983). When impregnated with antibiotics, tulle gras dressings can encourage the emergence of resistant strains of bacteria.

Wet Dressings

Wet dressings consist of gauze or gauze ribbon soaked in antiseptic, hypochlorite solutions or normal saline. They may be used to keep the wound surface bathed in the appropriate solution or to pack wound cavities. However, they can dry out if they are not changed regularly, harbour bacteria and traumatize the wound on removal. The use of antiseptics and hypochlorites in wound care is now being questioned (see section on wound cleansing, p. 148).

Semipermeable Polymeric Film Dressings

These are transparent, conformable, polyurethane films that allow the wound to be bathed in exudate, thus encouraging moist wound healing. Such dressings are permeable to air and water vapour, but impermeable to bacteria and water. They can be left in place for several days, depending on the characteristics of the wound. This type of film dressing is often used for treating clean, superficial wounds, burns and decubitus ulcers. They should not be used on infected wounds; Draper (1985) recommends taking a wound swab before applying film dressings. Exudate underneath the dressing can build up to intolerable levels, but this can be aspirated easily without interfering with the wound; the puncture hole is covered by a fresh piece of film dressing after the procedure.

Foam Dressings

Foam dressings are gas- and water vapour-permeable. Their absorbency properties vary according to their structure. They are conformable and are good thermal insulators. A gel of exudate, which encourages rapid tissue healing, is produced at the wound surface.

Silastic foam is a liquid dressing that sets into a spongy plug when mixed and poured (in liquid form) into the wound. It moulds itself into the exact shape of the wound. It is often used in the treatment of noninfected, deep, granulating wounds. It is inert and absorbent but nonadherent, and it can be used instead of traditional gauze packings. It should be removed daily for cleaning in a suitable antiseptic solution, and rinsed with normal saline before being replaced (Turner, 1987). As the wound heals and its size decreases, smaller plugs should be made and used. Cutting and Harding (1990) report successful use of a hydrophilic polyurethane dressing containing foam chips which are enclosed in a polymer envelope, when used to treat cavity wounds. Wound exudate is absorbed into the foam chips, which are able to absorb up to 14 times their own weight in fluid. They have used this dressing with success in pilonidal sinus excisions, pressure sores and abdominal wounds.

Hydrogel Dressings

Hydrogel dressings are gas- and water vapour-permeable, absorbent and nonadherent. They are suitable for dressing superficial wounds, donor sites, narrow sinuses and hard necrotic eschars. Bale and Harding (1990) recommend the use of a semipermeable film on top of the hydrogel when used on necrotic eschars. This not only keeps the gel in place, it also keeps the area moist, which allows the necrotic tissue to liquify and separate.

Hydrocolloid Dressings

Hydrocolloid dressings are adhesive, waterproof dressings, most of which have an inner layer that converts to a gel on the wound surface when it comes into contact with wound exudate. Most are backed with a continuous plastic film, which prevents entry of bacteria and which is impermeable to liquids. This impermeability to liquids and bacteria has been used to prevent the spread of epidemic methicillin-resistant *Staphylococcus aureus* from infected wounds (Wilson, Burroughs and Dunn, 1988).

Hydrocolloid dressings can be left in place for up to one week, depending on the characteristics of the wound. Most hydrocolloid dressings produce an anaerobic wound environment, which has been shown to stimulate angiogenesis and contribute towards pain relief at the wound site (Johnson, 1988b). Such dressings can be used to remove sloughy and necrotic tissue as they allow both to rehydrate; autolysis can then occur at an enhanced rate. The use of hydrocolloid dressings is not recommended when infection is present. They are widely available in sheet form, and some brands are also available as granules and pastes.

Dextranomers

Dextranomers are hydrophilic agents, which form a hydrophilic paste when in contact with wound exudate. They create a moist wound environment that can rehydrate eschar and necrotic debris. Johnson (1988c) recommends the use of polyurethane foam over the paste in order to maintain a moist environment. The resulting gel absorbs exudate and progressively removes dead cells and bacteria from the surface of the wound, thus cleansing and debriding it. Dextranomers can be of particular use in infected, sloughy, exuding wounds.

Alginates

Alginates are manufactured from calcium alginate (brown seaweed) and are formed as nonwoven pads or as alginate 'rope' to be used in cavity wounds. The pad is placed directly onto the wound and held in place by a secondary dressing, for example, film dressing or nonadherent dressing. The alginate rope is used to pack cavity wounds lightly. A gel is formed on contact with wound exudate, which creates a moist environment and prevents wound dehydration. Alginates are suitable for use in heavily exuding and sloughy wounds, but are of little value in dry, necrotic wounds or those having little exudate (*The Dressing Times*, 1989).

The gel is washed away when the wound is irrigated with normal saline. Any remaining fibres are eventually broken down into simple sugars, which are then absorbed (Johnson, 1988b). The frequency of dressing changes is determined by the condition of the wound. Heavily exuding wounds and infected wounds require daily changes, reducing to twice weekly changes as the infection subsides, exudation decreases and the wound heals.

Enzymatic Agents

This type of dressing contains enzymes that can break down fibrin, blood clots and necrotic tissue. The wound surface must not be allowed to dry out when these agents are used (Hellgren, 1983).

Wound Cleansing

There are a number of solutions that can be used to clean wounds during dressing changes. Before deciding which solution to use, the nurse should understand the purpose of wound cleansing, the nature of the solutions available and their advantages and disadvantages in wound care. The nurse should also have a sound knowledge of wound healing. The purpose of wound cleansing includes physical removal of excess exudate and debris in order to provide the best possible local environment before the wound dressing is applied; the wound dressing should then provide the optimum microenvironment for wound healing to take place.

Before offering any treatment, the nurse should carefully assess the wound and the patient (see Wound Classification, p. 142). Once the nurse has decided upon the wound type, its condition and which dressing to use, a decision must be made about which cleansing solution to use before the dressing is applied.

Commonly Used Wound Cleansing Agents

Normal Saline
Normal saline (sodium chloride 0.9 per cent w/v) is a non-irritant wound cleansing solution, which is isotonic to body fluids. It has no adverse effects on tissue healing (Brennan and Leaper, 1985), but has no antiseptic qualities. It can be used for physically cleansing many types of wounds, but is ineffective against infection.

Cetrimide
Cetrimide has emulsifying and detergent properties, and is effective against gram-positive organisms but less effective against gram-negative ones (The Pharmaceutical Society of Great Britain, 1986). It can be used alone or in combination with chlorhexidine. However, it is inactivated by soaps and organic matter (Ayliffe, Coates and Hoffman, 1984), and has a marked toxic effect on fibroblast cells in culture, even in low concentrations (Deans, Bilings, Brennan *et al.*, 1986). Therefore, its value in routine use for regular wound cleansing is questioned.

Chlorhexidine
Chlorhexidine is available in several forms. It has a wide range of antibacterial activity, being effective against both gram-positive and gram-negative organisms (Gardener and Peel, 1986). It is relatively nontoxic to living tissue (Brennan, Foster and Leaper, 1986), except when used in combination with cetrimide. However, it is rapidly inactivated by blood, pus and bile (Leaper, 1986), and skin sensations may occur with some patients (British National Formulary, 1986). It is best used as a single sachet of sterile solution.

Iodine Compounds
Iodine compounds are effective against both gram-positive and gram-negative organisms. Their action has rapid onset and they do not encourage the emergence of resistant organisms. However, their action is affected by the presence of pus and exudate (Gardener and Peel, 1986). Some patients are sensitive to iodine, and allergic responses can occur, so the patient's skin should be tested before use; severe reactions are rare.

Hydrogen Peroxide
Hydrogen peroxide acts as a mechanical debriding agent. Its action is rapid but brief. When used for moderately sloughy wounds, it is believed that the bubbles which are released assist small particles of debris to dislodge from the wound (*The Dressing Times*, 1988). However, the oxygen bubbles may also lift newly formed epithelium from the dermis (Sleigh and Lister, 1985). Hydrogen peroxide is inactivated when it comes into contact with organic matter (Lawrence and Black, 1968), and it is caustic to surrounding skin in concentrations above 6 per cent (British National Formulary, 1986). It should not be used to irrigate closed cavity wounds as there is a risk that oxygen may pass into the bloodstream and cause a life-threatening embolus (Bassan *et al.*, 1982; Sleigh and Lister, 1985).

Hypochlorites
Hypochlorites are chemical debriding agents traditionally used on dirty, sloughy and necrotic wounds. They are also often used for packing sloughy wound cavities because of their supposed debriding properties. However, they may succeed in removing slough and necrotic material because the wet soak rehydrates the sloughy and dry necrotic tissue, which is then removed by autolysis, rather than by any direct chemical action of the hypochlorites on the slough itself (Thomas, 1986, 1988).

Hypochlorites are toxic to fibroblasts in culture (Deans, Bilings, Brennan, *et al.*, 1986). They delay wound healing and collagen production, interfere with epithelial migration and prolong the acute inflammatory response in wounds healing by secondary intention (Brennan and Leaper, 1985). They are inactivated rapidly when they come into contact with blood, pus and slough (Gardener and Peel, 1986; Russell, Hugo and Ayliffe, 1982), are caustic to surrounding skin (Bale and Harding, 1990; Morgan, 1986) and decay on storage (Ayliffe, Coates and Hoffman, 1984).

Clinical studies have also demonstrated that they can lead to the release of endotoxins and other toxic materials from bacteria present in pressure sores, which can lead to acute oliguric renal failure (Barton and Barton, 1981). It is thus difficult to justify their continued use in wound management.

Wound Dressing Technique

There is no single dressing technique which is suitable for all types of wounds. Before dressing a patient's wound, the nurse should consider what the aims of the aseptic dressing technique are. Thomlinson (1987) suggests that these aims are: (1) to minimize the risk of patients developing secondary wound infection; (2) to prevent any micro-organisms present from being transferred to other patients; and (3) to encourage early detection and prompt treatment of any infection. These aims are achieved partly by the use of a nontouch technique.

Because of the different techniques practised, nurses are advised to follow local policy. It should be remembered, however, that when blood and other body fluid contamination is expected, the wearing of gloves is always advised as an infection control measure to protect staff.

Wound Complications

Haematoma (Haemorrhage)

The nurse should know the location of the patient's incision so that the dressings may be inspected for haemorrhage at intervals during the first 24 hours after operation. Any undue amount of bleeding is reported. If a drain is *in situ*, the amount and type of drainage should be noted, and excessive blood loss reported. Sometimes concealed bleeding occurs in the wound, beneath the skin. This bleeding usually stops spontaneously but results in clot formation within the wound. If the clot is small, it will be absorbed and need not be treated. When the clot is large, the wound usually bulges somewhat, and healing will be delayed unless it is removed. After several stitches are removed, the clot can be evacuated, and the wound may then be dressed using an appropriate dressing that will encourage granulation tissue to grow, without traumatizing the healing tissue. Alternatively, a secondary closure may be performed.

Infection (Wound Sepsis)

A study to determine the prevalence of infection among hospital patients in England and Wales in 1980 demonstrated that the overall rate of infection of wounds was about 5 per cent, with four fifths of these infections being judged to have developed in hospital (*Journal of Hospital Infection*, 1981). The risk of developing wound infection can be reduced by a number of pre-, intra- and postoperative measures.

Preoperative Measures
The shorter the time a patient is in hospital preoperatively, the less will be the exposure to nosocomial infections. Coexisting infections must be treated because other infections, such as respiratory infection, can initiate pulmonary complications.

If the operation site is to be shaved, the nurse should use clippers or depilatories rather than a razor (Petterson, 1986; Winfield, 1986), and shaving should be carried out as near to the time of operation as possible. The fewer cuts and abrasions there are on the skin, the less opportunity there is for infection; and the shorter the time between shaving and the operation, the lower the incidence of infection.

Thorough skin cleansing will reduce the number of resident skin bacteria and skin contaminants to a minimum. Special preparation may be required for specific types of surgery, for example, bowel preparation for patients having elective colonic surgery (surgeons may follow their own programme of care before bowel surgery). In some types of surgery, for example, hip replacement and large bowel surgery, the use of prophylactic antibiotics can be justified to minimize wound infections. However, caution is necessary as misuse of antibiotics contributes to the development and spread of antibiotic-resistant strains of bacteria.

Intraoperative Measures
Thorough cleansing of the operation site in order to remove superficial flora, soil and debris will reduce the risk of contaminating the wound with the patient's own skin flora. A flawless aseptic technique in theatre will reduce the risk of introducing any contaminants into the wound.

Powder and talcum should be washed off sterile gloves as they can adversely affect the healing process.

Postoperative Measures
Hands and clothes should be clinically clean when in contact with the patient and the wound in order to reduce the risk of cross-infection. It may be advisable for the nurse to wear a disposable apron while attending to the patient and

Table 2.36 *Risk factors contributing to wound sepsis*

Local
Wound contamination
Foreign body
Faulty suturing technique
Devitalized tissue
Haematoma
'Dead' space

General
Debilitation
Dehydration
Malnutrition
Anaemia
Advanced age
Extreme obesity
Shock
Length of preoperative hospitalization
Length of operation
Associated disorders (e.g., diabetes mellitus)

the wound as this may also reduce the risk of cross-infection.

The nurse should use an aseptic technique when treating the wound, and also an appropriate wound cleansing agent and wound dressing. The dressing should be removed and replaced only when necessary. The patient's natural resistance to infection, for example, good nutritional state, should be improved. The patient should not be kept in hospital any longer than is necessary.

Good psychological care throughout the patient's stay may also reduce the incidence of postoperative wound infection (Boore, 1978). Risk factors contributing to wound sepsis are listed in Table 2.36.

When the inflammatory process occurs, it usually causes symptoms in 36 to 48 hours. The patient's pulse rate and temperature increase, the white blood cell count elevates and the wound usually becomes somewhat tender with incisional pain, and becomes swollen and warm. At times, when the infection is deep, there may be no local signs.

When a diagnosis of wound infection is made in a postoperative wound, the surgeon may remove one or two sutures and, under aseptic precautions, separate the wound edges with a pair of blunt scissors or a haemostat. Once the wound is opened, a drain is inserted. Alternatively, all the sutures may be removed to allow the wound to heal by second intention.

Cellulitis is a bacterial infection that spreads into tissue planes producing all the features of inflammation. Streptococcus is frequently the responsible organism and systemic antibiotics are usually effective. If an extremity is the focus of the infection, elevation will reduce dependent oedema and the application of heat will promote local blood supply. Rest will decrease muscular contractions, which otherwise would force offending organisms into the circulatory system.

An abscess is a localized bacterial infection characterized by a collection of pus (bacteria, necrotic tissue and white blood cells). Usually a tender 'point' develops. Because the area is under pressure, there is a tendency for the infection to seed bacteria, which may invade adjacent tissues (cellulitis) or vascular spaces (bacteraemia, sepsis). Treatment is surgical drainage or excision. Rest, elevation of the part and heat are helpful. Antibiotics are not given unless there is evidence of regional or systemic spread.

Lymphangitis is a spread of infection from a cellulitis or abscess to the lymphatic system. It is treated by rest and antibiotic therapy.

Disruption, Evisceration and Dehiscence

The complications of disruption, evisceration and dehiscence are especially serious when they involve abdominal wounds. These complications result from sutures giving way, from infection and, more frequently, after marked distension or cough. They may also occur because of advanced age and the presence of pulmonary or cardiovascular disease in abdominal surgical patients.

The earliest sign is usually a gush of serosanguineous peritoneal fluid from the wound. The rupture of the wound may occur suddenly. When a lower abdominal wound is disrupted, coils of intestine may push out of the abdomen. Such a catastrophe causes considerable pain and is often associated with vomiting. Frequently the patient says that 'something gave way'. When the wound edges part slowly, the intestines may protrude gradually or not at all, and the presenting symptom may be the sudden drainage of a large amount of peritoneal fluid into the dressings.

- When disruption of a wound occurs, the surgeon is notified at once. The protruding coils of intestine should be covered with sterile dressings moistened with sterile saline.

An abdominal binder, properly applied, is an excellent prophylactic measure against an evisceration of this kind, and it is often used along with the primary dressing, especially for operations on patients with weak or pendulous abdominal walls, or when rupture of a wound has occurred. Vitamin deficiency or lowered serum protein or chloride may require correction.

Keloid

Not infrequently in an otherwise normal wound, the scar develops a tendency to excessive growth. Sometimes the entire scar is affected; at other times the condition is segmented. This keloid tendency is unexplained, unpredictable and unavoidable in some people.

Much investigation has been done into prevention and cure. Careful closure of the wound, complete haemostasis and pressure support without undue tension on the suture lines have all been reputed to combat this distressing wound complication.

DRUGS

Administration of drugs is a practical skill carried out regularly by the nurse throughout the day. It is a skill that requires adherence to a set procedure (local policies may differ slightly), and knowledge to enable the nurse to assess the effects of the drug and the presence of any side-effects (RCN Department of Nursing Policy and Practice, 1987).

Drugs are prescribed by the doctor, but the nurse is responsible for their correct administration. All staff involved in drug prescription, supply and distribution have their responsibilities to carry out the procedure effectively and within the law (UKCC, 1986). The nurse also has responsibility for drug storage and for recording the drugs as they are administered, ensuring that they are given to the correct patient at the correct time. All drugs administered should be in the correct, prescribed dose. All errors relating to drugs should be reported immediately to the doctor and to the senior nurse.

Nurses should be aware of the routes of drug administration, and of drug interactions. This will enable prompt action to be taken if side-effects occur (Gould, 1988; Hunter, 1989; Pritchard and David, 1988).

Drug Administration

Drug administration is governed by three Acts of Parliament:

1. The Misuse of Drugs Act, 1971: this covers controlled drugs, such as diamorphine and pethidine (schedule 1 and 2 drugs). The control of these drugs is strict, as dependency and misuse can occur. Therefore, they are ordered on special forms by the senior nurse on duty and checked by two other nurses, one of whom must be registered. Records of all entries must be kept for two years. These drugs are stored separately in a locked cupboard, which is itself within another locked cupboard.
2. The Poisons Act, 1972: this deals with nonmedicinal poisons (a poisonous substance having medicinal properties is controlled under the Medicines Act).
3. The Medicines Act, 1968: this covers all aspects of medicine supplies for both humans and animals. Medicines can be purchased by a pharmacist or a doctor (which is more likely to occur within general practice).

All medicines must be stored in an appropriate cupboard within their own containers. Only trained health care professionals (e.g., first level nurses) may control and administer drugs (Stillwell, 1988). Drug prescriptions must be legible and written in ink. If the prescription is not signed and dated, or if the correct frequency and route of drug administration are not stated, then the nurse should contact the doctor before administering the drug so that the prescription can be corrected. Trade (proprietary) names for drugs should not be written on the prescription sheet. All appropriate information regarding the patient should be recorded on the prescription sheet, such as name, age, hospital number and known allergies (Gould, 1988).

The nurse is responsible for ensuring that the prescription sheet is correctly written out, and for recording on the appropriate sheet that the drug has been given. All drug side-effects should be recorded and reported to the doctor (Heenan, 1989).

Drug Storage

Drug storage and ordering are the responsibility of the nurse in charge. The keys for the drug cupboards are held by the senior nurse, with the controlled drug cupboard key being kept separately. There should be separate storage cupboards for tablets, lotions and creams, and injectable drugs. The medicine trolley should be locked and attached securely to the wall of a designated area when not in use.

Nonadherence to the correct storage of medicines, particularly those that need to be stored in a refrigerator (such as insulin and antibiotic liquids), will alter their effectiveness. If drugs are stored appropriately, there is less risk of errors occurring and of reduction in drug effectiveness (Fogarty, Hills and Sloan, 1986).

Side-Effects

Drug side-effects can be due to overdosage of a prescribed drug or to patient sensitivity. Some drugs are known to have systemic effects on certain patients: for example, phenothiazines can cause parkinsonism in some patients, and cytotoxic drugs can cause nausea and vomiting. Some side-effects can be reduced by lowering the drug dosage, such as with the antipsychotic drug haloperidol. Certain patients will be more likely to develop drug side-effects, such as immunosuppressed patients, those taking cytotoxic drugs and the elderly.

Drugs and the Elderly Person

Those administering medications to elderly patients must be aware of the commonly used drugs which are removed from the body primarily by renal excretion. Drugs excreted by the kidneys remain in the elderly person for a longer time and therefore drug dosages must often be reduced as overdosage and drug toxicity at usual therapeutic dosages may occur.

At the same time, it is important to realize that a decline in cardiac output may decrease the delivery rate to the target organ or storage tissue.

Changes in the gastrointestinal system may also affect drug therapy. In some elderly patients, a reduced number of mucosal cells and a slowing of gastric motility can prevent the drug from reaching therapeutic plasma and tissue concentrations, and delayed gastric emptying has undesirable effects on drugs which are acid labile or metabolized by the stomach mucosa. Alterations in intestinal motility and activity thus change the drug's contact time with the absorptive surface of the mucosa.

As a result of a slowing metabolism, the drug levels may increase in the tissues and plasma, leading to a prolongation of drug action.

Because some or all of the organ systems may be marginally operational, older patients may show paradoxical or unusual responses to drugs and may develop toxic reactions and complications. In addition, an elderly patient may have multiple medical problems requiring drug treatment.

Nutritional Considerations

In any drug regime for an elderly patient, it must be borne in mind that drugs are capable of altering the patient's nutritional state, which may already be compromised by a marginal diet and chronic disease and its treatment. Drugs can depress the appetite, cause nausea, irritate the stomach and decrease absorption of nutrients, in addition to altering the electrolyte balance and the carbohydrate and fat metabolism. A few examples of drugs that are capable of altering the nutritional state are the antacids (produce thiamine deficiency), laxatives (diminish absorption), corticosteroids (lower serum calcium by reducing its absorption), aspirin (associated with folate deficiency) and phenothiazines and tricyclic depressants (increase food intake and weight gain).

Possible Drug Side-Effects

The drugs commonly used by elderly people are capable of producing potentially serious problems.

- Because sedatives and hypnotics can lead to confusion, delusion, hallucinations, falls, dependency, agitation and altered behaviour, such drugs should be given in smaller doses, if at all. Caution should also be taken when opiates are administered because they act as respiratory depressants.
- Before a prescribed opiate is given, the respiratory rate should be counted; if the rate drops below 14 per minute, the drug should be withheld and the doctor informed.
- The side-effects of commonly used analgesics must be taken into account when older patients are concerned. Although salicylates are well tolerated, they can produce salicylism, electrolyte depletion and possibly serious bleeding from prolonged prothrombin time.
- If tranquillizers are used for older patients, it is important to note that some (the phenothiazines) can cause hypotension, cerebral depression and worsening of the agitated state. The minor tranquillizers, meprobamate and chlordiazepoxide, are useful in alleviating symptoms of anxiety in the ambulatory patient and in calming agitation. However, these drugs have a narrow therapeutic range, so that they may worsen the agitation and produce uninhibited, aggressive states and dependency in some patients.
- The tricyclic antidepressants may cause cardiac tachyarrhythmias and conduction disturbances.
- Because the heart conduction system, in general, is less effective in older patients, even small doses of digitalis can cause arrhythmias and gastrointestinal and mental symptoms. Digitalis is also not as well tolerated because of less effective kidney function, a decrease in myocardial potassium and a reduction in body weight. As a result, supplementary potassium and careful dosage maintenance of digitalis are

required. Digitalis toxicity and cardiac arrhythmias are enhanced by the depletion of intracellular potassium. Patients taking digitalis preparations in combination with non-potassium-sparing diuretics are at high risk of hypokalaemia and digitalis toxicity. Digitalis blood levels must be monitored regularly; correction of potassium loss with diet and supplements is necessary. The most common signs of digitalis toxicity are fatigue, visual disturbances, muscle weakness, nausea and anorexia.

With self-administered medication, it is important to consider possible sensory and memory losses as well as decreased manual dexterity. To help the patient manage medications and improve patient co-operation, the nurse can:

- Explain the action, side-effects and dosage of each medication.
- Write out the times that drugs should be taken.
- Encourage use of standard containers rather than safety lids.
- Destroy old, unused medications.
- Periodically review the medication regime.
- Discourage the patient's use of over-the-counter drugs without consulting a health professional.

Throughout the teaching process, the nurse should ask questions to ensure that the patient has learnt and understood what is required.

CARE OF THE PATIENT WITH CANCER

Cancer nursing is an area of practice that covers all age-groups and nursing specialties and is carried out in a variety of health care settings, including the home, community, acute care institutions, hospices, and rehabilitation and day centres. The field or specialty of cancer nursing, or oncology nursing, has paralleled the development of medical oncology and the major therapeutic advances that have occurred in the care of the person with cancer.

The scope, responsibilities and expected outcomes of cancer nursing are as diverse and complex as those of any nursing specialty. There is a special challenge inherent in caring for people with cancer because the word cancer is often equated with pain and death in our society. In order to meet this challenge, nurses must first identify their own reactions to cancer and realistically set goals that can be attained.

The nurse must be equipped to support the patient and loved ones through a wide range of physical, emotional, social, cultural and spiritual upheavals. In order to accomplish the desired outcomes, nurses provide realistic support to those in their care, using standards of practice and the nursing process as the basis of care. The major areas of responsibility for the nurse caring for the patient with cancer are listed in Table 2.37.

Epidemiology of Cancer

Incidence
Cancers affect every age-group; however, most cancers occur in people over 65 years of age. Overall, men experience a higher incidence of cancer than do women. Cancer incidence is higher in the industrialized nations of the world and in the industrial sectors of more developed countries.

Mortality Rates
Cancers are second only to cardiovascular disease as a leading cause of death in the United Kingdom. In the United Kingdom, in order of frequency, the leading causes of cancer deaths include cancers of the lung,

Table 2.37 *Responsibilities of the nurse caring for the patient with cancer and the family/home-carers*

- Support the idea that cancer is a chronic illness that has acute exacerbations rather than one that is solely synonymous with death and suffering
- Assess own level of knowledge relative to the pathophysiology of the disease process
- Make use of current research findings and practices in the care of the patient with cancer and the family/home-carers
- Identify people at high risk for the development of cancer
- Participate in primary and secondary prevention efforts
- Assess the nursing care needs of the person with cancer
- Assess the learning needs, desires and capabilities of the person with cancer
- Identify the nursing problems of the person and family/home-carers
- Assess the social support networks available to the person
- Plan appropriate care with the person and family/home-carers
- Assist the person to identify strengths and limitations
- Assist the person to design short-term and long-term goals for care
- Implement a nursing plan that interfaces with the medical care regime and that is consistent with established goals
- Collaborate with members of a multidisciplinary team to foster continuity of care
- Evaluate the goals and resultant outcomes of care with the patient, family and/or home-carers and the members of the multidisciplinary team
- Reassess and redesign the direction of the care as determined by the evaluation

colorectal area and prostate in men, and cancers of the lung, breast and colorectal area in women. Figure 2.28 gives the statistics for cancer incidence and cancer deaths by site and sex, for 1988.

Altered Physiology of the Malignant Process

Cancer is a disease process that begins when abnormal cells arise from normal body cells as a result of some poorly understood mechanism of change. As the disease progresses, these abnormal cells proliferate, still within a local area. However, a stage is then reached in which the cells acquire invasive characteristics, and changes occur in surrounding tissues. The cells infiltrate these tissues and gain access to lymph and blood vessels through which they are transported to form metastases (cancer spread) in other parts of the body.

Although the disease process can be described in the general terms used above, cancer is not a single disease with a single cause; rather it is a group of distinct diseases with different causes, features, treatments and prognoses.

Benign vs. Malignant Proliferative Patterns

During the life span, various body tissues normally experience periods of rapid or proliferative growth which must be distinguished from malignant growth activity. The patterns of cell growth, designated by the terms hyperplasia, metaplasia, dysplasia, anaplasia and neoplasia, may be described as follows:

Hyperplasia
Hyperplasia, an increase in the number of cells of a tissue, is a common proliferative process during periods of rapid body growth (e.g., fetal and adolescent growth and development) and during epithelial and bone marrow regeneration. It is a normal cellular response when a physiological demand exists, and an abnormal response when growth exceeds the physiological demand.

Metaplasia
Metaplasia occurs when one type of mature cell is converted to another type by means of an outside stimulus which affects the parent stem cell. Chronic irritation or inflammation, vitamin deficiency and chemical exposure may be factors leading to metaplasia. Metaplastic changes may be reversible or may progress to dysplasia.

Dysplasia
Dysplasia is bizarre cell growth resulting in cells that differ in size, shape or arrangement from other cells of the same type of tissue. Dysplasia can be caused by

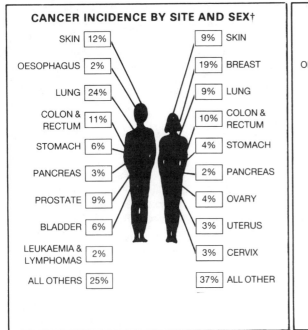

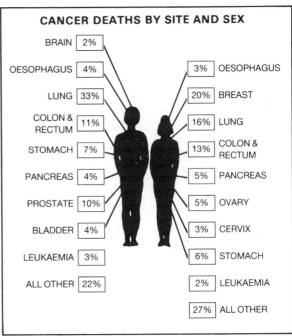

† Excluding non-melanoma skin cancer and carcinoma *in situ.*

Figure 2.28 Cancer statistics for 1990. The estimates of the incidence of cancer are based on data from the Cancer Research Campaign (Cancer Research Campaign (1990) *Facts on Cancer*, Cancer Research Campaign, London: by kind permission).

chemicals, radiation or chronic inflammation or irritation. It can be reversible or can precede irreversible neoplastic change.

Anaplasia

Anaplasia is a lower degree of differentiation of dysplastic cells. (Differentiation refers to the extent to which the cells differ from their cells of origin and to their degree of maturity.) Anaplastic cells are poorly differentiated, irregularly shaped or disorganized with respect to growth and arrangement. Anaplastic cells lack normal cellular characteristics and are nearly always malignant.

Neoplasia

Neoplasia, described as uncontrolled cell growth which follows no physiological demand, can be either benign or malignant. Benign and malignant neoplastic growths are classified and named by the tissue of origin (Table 2.38).

Benign and malignant cells differ in many cellular growth characteristics, as summarized in Table 2.39. The degree of anaplasia (lack of differentiation of cells) ultimately determines the malignant potential.

Malignant Cell Characteristics

Despite their individual differences, all cancer cells share some common cellular characteristics. Nuclei of cancer cells are often large and irregularly shaped (pleomorphism). Nucleoli, structures within the nucleus that house ribonucleic acid (RNA), are larger and more numerous in malignant cells, perhaps due to increased RNA synthesis. Chromosomal abnormalities and fragility of chromosomes are commonly found on analysis of cancer cells. Mitosis (cell division) occurs more frequently in malignant cells than in normal cells. Additionally, cancer cells have altered amounts of cyclic adenosine monophosphate (AMP) and cyclic guanosine monophosphate (GMP). These substances, which are the building blocks of nucleic acids, facilitate the utilization of nutrients and the synthesis of RNA. As a result, cell growth and division are promoted.

Invasion and Metastasis

Malignancies have the ability to spread or transfer cancerous cells from one organ or body part to another by invasion and metastasis. Invasion involves the growth of the primary tumour into the surrounding host tissues. The process of invasion occurs in several ways. Mechanical pressure exerted by rapidly proliferating neoplasms may force fingerlike projections of tumour cells into surrounding tissue. Malignant cells may break off from the primary tumour and invade adjacent structures. Malignant cells are thought to possess specific destructive enzymes (lysosomal hydrolases or collagenases) that

Table 2.38 *Names of selected benign and malignant tumours according to tissue types*

Tissue type	Benign	Malignant
Epithelial tumours		
Surface	Papilloma	Squamous cell carcinoma
Glandular	Adenoma	Adenocarcinoma
Connective tissue tumours		
Fibrous	Fibroma	Fibrosarcoma
Adipose	Lipoma	Liposarcoma
Cartilage	Chondroma	Chondrosarcoma
Bone	Osteoma	Osteosarcoma
Blood vessels	Haemangioma	Haemangiosarcoma
Lymph vessels	Lymphangioma	Lymphangiosarcoma
Muscle tumours		
Smooth	Leiomyoma	Leiomyosarcoma
Striated	Rhabdomyoma	Rhabdomyosarcoma
Nerve cell tumours		
Nerve cell	Neuroma	
Glial tissue		Glioma
Nerve sheaths	Neurilemmoma	Neurilemmic sarcoma
Haematological tumours		
Granulocytic		Myelocytic leukaemia
Erythrocytic		Erythroleukaemia
Plasma cells		Multiple myeloma
Lymphoid		Lymphocytic leukaemia

(Porth, C. M. (1986) Pathophysiology: Concepts of Altered Health States *(2nd edition), J. B. Lippincott, Philadelphia.)*

destroy surrounding tissue and facilitate invasion by malignant cells. The mechanical pressure of a rapidly growing tumour may enhance this process.

Metastasis is the dissemination of malignant cells from the primary tumour to distant sites by direct spread of tumour cells to body cavities or through lymphatic and haematogenous circulation. Tumours growing in or penetrating body cavities may shed cells or emboli that travel within the body cavity and 'seed' the surfaces of other organs. This can occur in ovarian cancer when malignant cells enter the peritoneal cavity and seed peritoneal surfaces of abdominal organs such as the liver or pancreas.

The most common mechanism of metastasis is transport of tumour cells through the lymphatic circulation. Tumour emboli enter the lymph channels by way of the interstitial fluid that communicates with lymphatic fluid. In addition, malignant cells may penetrate lymphatic vessels by invasion. After entering the lymphatic circulation, malignant cells either become lodged in the lymph nodes or pass between lymphatic and venous circulation. Tumours arising in areas of the body with rapid and extensive lymphatic circulation have a high risk of metastasis through lymphatic channels. Breast tumours frequently metastasize in this manner through axillary, clavicular and thoracic lymph channels.

Haematogenous spread, or dissemination through the bloodstream, of malignant cells is less common than spread by other means. Few malignant cells are able to survive the turbulent nature of arterial circulation. In addition, the structure of most arteries and arterioles is far too secure to permit malignant invasion. Malignant cells do have the ability to induce the growth of new capillaries from the host tissue in order to meet their needs for nutrients and oxygen. This process is referred to as angiogenesis. It is through this vascular network that tumour emboli may enter the systemic circulation and travel to distant sites. Large tumour emboli which become trapped in the microcirculation of distant sites serve as the origin of growth for metastasis.

Metastasis from the primary tumour to other sites is not a random process. Since the late 1800s, investigators have recognized the tendency for malignancies of specific cell classifications to spread, or metastasize, to specific organs. Several theories have been generated to explain how and why metastasis occurs. Investigators are focusing their attention on the following factors in metastasis: organ vascularity, immune defences at the tissue level,

Table 2.39 *Characteristics of benign and malignant neoplasms*

Characteristics	Benign	Malignant
Cell characteristics	Cells resemble normal cells of the tissue from which the tumour originated	Cells often bear little resemblance to the normal cells of the tissue from which they arose; there is both anaplasia and pleomorphism
Mode of growth	Tumour grows by expansion and does not infiltrate the surrounding tissues; encapsulated	Grows at the periphery and sends out processes that infiltrate and destroy the surrounding tissues
Rate of growth	Rate of growth is usually slow	Rate of growth is usually relatively rapid and is dependent on level of differentiation; the more anaplastic the tumour, the more rapid the rate of growth
Metastasis	Does not spread by metastasis	Gains access to the blood and lymph channels and metastasizes to other areas of the body
Recurrence	Does not recur when removed	Tends to recur when removed
General effects	Is usually a localized phenomenon that does not cause generalized effects unless by location it interferes with vital functions	Often causes generalized effects such as anaemia, weakness and weight loss
Destruction of tissue	Does not usually cause tissue damage unless location interferes with blood flow	Often causes extensive tissue damage as the tumour outgrows its blood supply or encroaches on blood flow to the area; may also produce substances that cause cell damage
Ability to cause death	Does not usually cause death unless its location interferes with vital functions	Will usually cause death unless growth can be controlled

(Porth, C. M. (1986) Pathophysiology: Concepts of Altered Health States *(2nd edition), J. B. Lippincott, Philadelphia.)*

surface recognition factors on tumour cells and differing behavioural characteristics among cells within one tumour.

Carcinogenesis

Malignant transformation is thought to be at least a two-step cellular process. In the first or initiation step, initiators such as chemicals, physical factors and biological agents escape normal enzymatic mechanisms and cause alterations in the genetic structure of the cellular deoxyribonucleic acid (DNA). These alterations are irreversible but usually are not of significance to cells until the second step of carcinogenesis occurs—promotion. During this step, repeated exposure to promoting agents causes the expression of abnormal or mutant genetic information. Once this genetic expression occurs in cells, they begin to produce mutant cell populations that are different from their original cellular ancestors. Those agents which initiate or promote cellular transformation are referred to as carcinogens.

Aetiologies

Certain categories of agents or factors have been implicated in the carcinogenic process. These include viruses, physical agents, chemical agents, genetic or familial factors, dietary factors and hormonal agents.

Viruses

Viral causation in human cancers is very difficult to ascertain because isolation of viruses is very difficult. Infectious aetiologies are considered when clusters of specific cancers are noted. Viruses are thought to incorporate themselves in the genetic structure of cells, thus altering future generations of that cell population—perhaps leading to a cancer. For example, the Epstein-Barr virus is highly suspect as a causative agent in Burkitt's lymphoma and nasopharyngeal cancers. Herpes simplex type II virus, cytomegalovirus and papillomavirus have all been associated with dysplasia and malignancy of the uterine cervix; the hepatitis B virus has been implicated in hepatocellular carcinoma.

Physical Agents

Physical factors associated with carcinogenesis include exposure to sunlight or to radiation and chronic irritation or inflammation.

Excessive exposure to the ultraviolet radiation of the sun, especially in fair-skinned, blue- or green-eyed people, increases the risk of skin cancers. Exposure to ionizing radiation can occur with repeated diagnostic radiographic procedures or radiotherapy, and from exposure to radioactive materials at atomic bomb test sites or nuclear power plants. Those exposed to extensive radiation have a higher incidence of leukaemia and cancers of the lung, bone, thyroid and other tissues.

Chronic irritation or inflammation is thought to damage cells, leading to abnormal cell differentiation. Cell mutations secondary to chronic irritation or inflammation are associated with lip cancers among pipe-smokers. Oral cancers are associated with prolonged tobacco use or ill-fitting dentures. Melanomas are associated with chronically irritated moles, colorectal cancers with ulcerative colitis, and liver cancers with cirrhosis.

Chemical Agents

Many chemical substances found in the workplace have proven to be carcinogens or co-carcinogens in the cancer process. The extensive list of suspected chemical substances continues to grow. Currently, approximately 80 per cent of all cancers are thought to be environmentally related. Most hazardous chemicals produce their toxic effects by altering DNA structure in body sites distant from chemical exposure. The liver and kidneys are the organ systems most often affected, presumably owing to their roles in detoxification of chemicals.

Genetic and Familial Factors

Genetic factors also play a role in cancer cell development. If DNA damage occurs in cell populations where chromosomal patterns are abnormal, mutant cell populations may develop. Abnormal chromosomal patterns and cancer have been associated with extra chromosomes, too few chromosomes or translocated chromosomes. Specific cancers with underlying genetic abnormalities include Burkitt's lymphoma, chronic myelogenous leukaemia, meningiomas, acute leukaemias, retinoblastomas and skin cancers.

Some adult and childhood cancers display familial predisposition. These cancers tend to occur at an early age and at multiple sites in one organ or pair of organs. Cancers associated with familial inheritance include retinoblastomas, nephroblastomas, pheochromocytomas, malignant neurofibromatosis, leukaemias and breast, endometrial, colorectal, stomach, prostate and lung cancers.

Dietary Factors

Dietary factors are thought to be related to 40 to 60 per cent of all environmental cancers. Dietary substances can be either proactive (protective) or carcinogenic/co-carcinogenic. The risk of cancer increases over long-term ingestion of carcinogens/co-carcinogens or chronic absence of proactive substances in the diet.

Hormonal Agents

Tumour growth may be promoted by disturbances in hormonal balance, by either the body's own (endogenous) hormone production or administration of exogenous hormones. Cancers of the breast, prostate and uterus are considered to be dependent on endogenous hormonal levels for growth. Administration of oral contraceptives and diethylstilboestrol has been associated with hepatocellular carcinomas and vaginal carcinomas, respectively.

The Role of the Immune System

The development of cancer is linked closely to failure of the normal immune system. The increased incidence of malignancies in organ transplant recipients who receive immunosuppressive therapy to prevent rejection of the transplanted organ supports this belief. In addition, patients receiving long-term chemotherapy to treat a malignancy are also at increased risk for the development of a second malignancy.

Malignant cells undergo many changes in structure and function. As a result, new surface antigens are formed on cell membranes. These antigens are capable of stimulating the cellular and humoral immune responses. The T lymphocyte, the soldier of the cellular immune response, is responsible for the recognition of tumour cell antigens. When tumour antigens are recognized by T lymphocytes, other T lymphocytes toxic to the tumour cells are stimulated, proliferate and are released into the circulation. In addition to possessing these cytotoxic properties, T lymphocytes are capable of stimulating other components of the immune system to rid the body of malignant cells. Certain lymphokines, which are substances produced by lymphocytes, are capable of killing or damaging various types of malignant cells. Other lymphokines are able to mobilize other cells such as macrophages that disrupt cancer cells. Interferon, a substance produced by the body in response to viral infection, also possesses some antitumour characteristics. Antibodies, produced by B lymphocytes of the humoral immune response, also defend against malignant cells.

How is it, then, that malignant cells are able to survive and proliferate despite the immune system defence mechanisms? There are several suggestions as to how tumour cells can overcome an apparently intact immune system. If the body fails to recognize the malignant cell as different from 'self', the immune response may fail to be stimulated. The failure of the immune system to respond promptly to the malignant cells allows the tumour to grow to a size that is too large to be managed by normal immune mechanisms.

The tumour cells may actually suppress the patient's immune defences. Tumour antigens may combine with the antibodies produced by the person and hide or mask themselves from normal immune defence mechanisms. Tumours are also capable of producing substances that impair usual immune defences. These substances not only promote growth of the tumour but also increase the patient's susceptibility to infection by a variety of pathogenic organisms. As a result of prolonged contact with a tumour antigen, the patient's body may be depleted of the specific lymphocytes and no longer be able to mount an appropriate immune response.

Abnormal concentrations of host suppressor T lymphocytes may play a role in the development of malignancies. Suppressor T lymphocytes normally assist in the regulation of antibody production and diminish immune responses when they are no longer required. Studies have demonstrated that low levels of serum antibodies and high levels of suppressor cells have been found in patients with multiple myeloma, a malignancy associated with hypogammaglobulinaemia (low amounts of serum antibodies). Carcinogens such as viruses or certain chemicals, including chemotherapeutic agents, may weaken the immune system and ultimately enhance tumour growth. Finally, altered immune mechanisms associated with the ageing process may allow malignant cells to overcome normal immune defences.

Detection and Prevention of Cancer

Nurses as well as doctors have traditionally been involved with tertiary prevention, the care and rehabilitation of the patient after cancer has been diagnosed and treated. However, in the past 20 years clinicians and researchers have placed greater emphasis on primary and secondary prevention of cancer. Primary prevention is concerned with reducing the risk or preventing the development of cancer in healthy people. Secondary prevention involves detection and screening efforts in order to achieve early diagnosis and prompt intervention to halt the cancerous process.

Nurses in all settings have an important role in cancer prevention. To participate in prevention of cancer, nurses must acquire the knowledge and skills necessary to provide the community with cancer prevention education

about health-related behaviours, risk factors associated with the development of cancer, and screening and detection methods. Epidemiological and laboratory studies have shown that cigarette smoking, dietary habits, sun exposure and alcohol consumption can greatly influence the risk of developing cancer. Nurses also need teaching and counselling skills to foster patient participation in cancer prevention programmes and to promote healthy lifestyles.

Public awareness about health promotion can be increased in a variety of ways. Health education and health maintenance programmes are sponsored by community organizations such as churches, senior citizen groups and parent–teacher associations. Primary prevention programmes may focus on the hazards of tobacco or the importance of nutrition. Secondary prevention programmes may include cervical smears, mammography, and breast and testicular self-examination. The Imperial Cancer Research Fund has produced guidelines for the public on how to reduce their risk of developing cancer. These are shown in Table 2.40. Nurses in acute care settings can identify risks for patients and caregivers, and incorporate teaching and counselling in discharge planning.

Diagnosis of Cancer

Patients with suspected cancer undergo extensive diagnostic testing to determine the presence of tumour and the extent of disease, to identify possible spread (metastasis) or invasion of other body tissues, to evaluate the function of involved as well as uninvolved body systems and organs, and to obtain tissue and cells for analysis of the cancer, including its stage and grade. A patient undergoing extensive testing is usually fearful of the procedures themselves and anxious about the possible results of the testing. The patient and loved ones require information about the tests to be performed and the patient's role in the testing procedures. The nurse provides opportunities for them to express their fears about the test results. The patient and loved ones are supported throughout the period of diagnostic testing and the nurse reinforces and clarifies information conveyed to them by the doctor. The nurse also encourages them to communicate and share their concerns and to discuss their questions with each other.

Staging and Grading

A complete diagnosis includes identifying the stage and grade of malignancy. This must be accomplished before the initiation of treatment to provide for and maintain a systematic and consistent approach to diagnosis, treatment and evaluation of care. Treatment options and prognosis are determined on the basis of staging and grading. This approach facilitates the exchange of information about similar types of cancer and their associated survival and response rates. Ultimately, these classifications can assist in ongoing cancer research.

Table 2.40 *Steps towards cancer prevention*

Action	Rationale
Stop smoking	This is the single most important thing anyone can do for their health; every year, cigarette smoking causes 40,000 deaths from cancer in the UK; another 70,000 die from other smoking-related diseases; this is equivalent to a jumbo crashing every day of the year, killing all the passengers
Avoid getting burnt by the sun	Use a sunscreen for protection or stay in the shade; most skin cancers are easily curable, but one type – malignant melanoma – is dangerous unless treated early; ask a pharmacist for advice on suitable sunscreens
Take care with sexual relationships	A virus is involved in cervical and anal cancer; if a woman or her partner has many sexual relationships, her risk of developing cervical cancer is increased; every woman, from the time she becomes sexually active until she is 65, should have cervical screening every three to five years, so that easily treatable, precancerous changes can be detected; over 2,000 women die from cervical cancer every year – the vast majority have never had a test
Follow safety rules at work	They are designed to protect workers; exposure to some industrial materials, such as asbestos dust and certain chemicals, is a real risk
Eat a healthy diet	A diet low in fats and high in fibre and fresh fruit and vegetables may reduce cancer risk and is certainly beneficial to general health; being grossly overweight adds to the risk of developing some forms of cancer
Treat alcohol with caution	Cancers of the mouth, throat and oesophagus are rare, but excess alcohol – particularly neat spirits – increases the risk; combining drinking and smoking is even more risky
Get to know your body	A monthly check for changes in the way your body looks and feels can help early detection of cancer of the skin, breast and testis; and this can have a dramatic effect on the chances of complete cure
Use screening services	Screening is designed to help early detection, and regular services are being set up for women at risk of cervical and breast cancer; research may lead to other screening programmes in the future – e.g., methods are being investigated for the early detection of bowel cancer

Warning signals for early diagnosis of cancer:

1. A change in bowel or bladder habits
2. A persistent sore throat, nagging cough or hoarseness
3. Unusual bleeding or discharge
4. Thickening or a lump in the breast, testis or elsewhere
5. Persistent indigestion
6. Difficulty in swallowing
7. Obvious change in size or bleeding of a mole

These symptoms may be due to minor illnesses, but patients should check with their family doctor if they have any of them, or if they have any change in their general health lasting more than two weeks

(By kind permission of Imperial Cancer Research Fund leaflet, Cancer – Cutting Your Risk, *PO Box 123, Lincoln's Inn Fields, London WC2A 3PX.)*

Staging determines the size of the tumour and the existence of metastasis. Several systems exist for classifying the anatomical extent of disease. The TNM system, developed from the work of the International Union Against Cancer (IUCC) and is most frequently used in describing malignancies such as breast, lung or ovarian cancer. In this system the T refers to the extent of the primary tumour, N refers to lymph node involvement and M refers to the extent of metastasis. Alternatively, tumours may be classified as stages 0 to IV, for example in cervical cancer: stage 0 represents carcinoma *in situ*; stage I early invasion but no metastases; stage II limited local invasion or minimal regional lymph node involvement; stage III extensive local tumour or extensive regional lymph node involvement; and stage IV usually inoperable extension of tumour or lymph nodes, or where there is any evidence of distant metastases.

Grading refers to the classification of the tumour cells. Grading systems seek to define the origin of tissue of the tumour and the degree to which the tumour cells retain the functional and histological characteristics of the tissue of origin. Tumours that closely resemble the tissue of origin in structure and function are said to be well differentiated. Tumours that do not clearly resemble the tissue of origin in structure or function are graded as poorly differentiated. These tumours tend to be more virulent and less responsive to treatment than well-differentiated tumours.

Management of Cancer

Treatment options offered to cancer patients should be based on realistic and achievable goals for each specific type of cancer. The range of possible treatment outcomes may include complete eradication of malignant disease (cure), prolonged survival with the presence of malignancy (control) or relief of symptoms associated with the cancerous disease process (palliation). It is imperative that the health care team, the patient and the patient's loved ones have a clear understanding of the treatment options and outcomes. Open communication and support are vital as the patient and loved ones periodically reassess treatment plans and outcomes when complications of therapy develop or disease progression occurs.

Multiple modalities are often employed in cancer treatment. A variety of therapies, including surgery, radiotherapy, chemotherapy and immunotherapy may be employed at various times during the course of treatment. An understanding of the principles of each and how they interrelate is important in understanding the rationale and expected outcomes of treatment.

Surgery

Surgical removal of the entire cancer remains the best and most frequently used treatment. However, the surgical approach may be selected for a variety of reasons. Surgery may be selected as the primary method of treatment, or it may be diagnostic, prophylactic, palliative or reconstructive.

Surgery as Primary Treatment

When surgery is used as the primary approach in the treatment of cancer, the goal is to remove the entire tumour (or as much as is feasible, a procedure often called debulking) and any involved surrounding tissue, including regional lymph nodes. Contrary to the design of surgical therapy in the past, the expected outcome is not to excise all possible tumour cells. It is now recognized that the growth and dissemination of cancer cells have often produced distant micrometastases by the time the patient seeks treatment. Therefore, attempting to remove wide margins of tissue in the hopes of 'getting all the cancer cells' is often not realistic. This reality substantiates the need for a co-ordinated multidisciplinary approach to cancer therapy. Once the surgery has been completed, one or more additional forms of treatment may be chosen to increase the likelihood of cancer cell destruction. There are, however, cancers which when treated surgically in the very early stages are considered to be curable (e.g., skin cancers, testicular cancers).

Diagnostic Surgery

Diagnostic surgery is usually performed to obtain a biopsy (excision of a piece of tissue from a suspicious growth) in order to analyse the tissues and cells of the suspected malignancy. The three most common biopsy methods are the excisional, incisional and needle methods. The excisional method is most frequently used for biopsies of the skin, the upper respiratory tract, and the upper and lower portions of the gastrointestinal tract, in which removal of the entire tumour is often possible. This approach not only provides the pathologist with the entire specimen but also decreases the chance of cellular seeding of the tumour. The incisional method is used if the tumour mass is too large to be removed. It is imperative that the biopsy be representative of the tumour mass so that the pathologist can provide an accurate diagnosis. Both of these approaches are often endoscopic procedures. Surgical incision is often required to determine the anatomic extent or stage of the tumour.

Needle biopsy is used to sample suspicious masses that are easily accessible, such as some growths in the breasts, lung, liver and kidney. The procedure is fast, relatively inexpensive and easy to perform. In general, the patient experiences minimal and temporary physical discomfort. In addition, the degree to which the surrounding tissue is disturbed is kept to a minimum, thus decreasing the likelihood of disseminating cancer cells (seeding). However, there is a chance that even the most skilled doctor will obtain a biopsy from such a small area that a full description of the cellular types is not possible.

The choice of biopsy to be performed takes into account many factors. Of greatest importance is the type of treatment anticipated if a diagnosis of cancer is confirmed. The surgical area includes the site of biopsy so that any cells that might have been dislodged during the procedure are excised at the time of surgery. In addition, the condition of the patient is considered. Assessment of nutrition and of respiratory, renal and hepatic systems is essential in determining the most appropriate method of treatment. If the biopsy requires general anaesthesia, and subsequent surgery is likely, the effects of total anaesthesia on the patient are considered. The patient and loved ones are given an opportunity to discuss the available options before definitive plans are made. The nurse, as the patient's advocate, serves as a liaison between the patient and the doctor in order to facilitate this process. Time should be set aside to minimize interruptions. Time for questions and for 'thinking through' all that has been discussed should be provided.

Prophylactic Surgery

Prophylactic surgery involves the removal of lesions that are apt to develop into cancer, such as small tumours (polyps) that often grow in the colon.

Palliative Surgery

When cure of the cancer is impossible, the expected outcome of treatment is to provide the patient with as much comfort as possible and a satisfying and productive life for as long as is possible. Whether the period of time is extremely short or lengthy, the major expected outcome is a high quality of life—with 'quality' defined by the patient and loved ones.

Palliative surgery is performed in an attempt to relieve complications of cancer, such as ulcerations, obstructions, haemorrhage, pain or infection. This type of surgery includes nerve blocks and cordotomies designed to relieve intractable pain; tumour resection, to relieve obstruction that may occur if a segment of bowel is obstructed (this may result in ostomies, depending on the extent of invasion); and simple mastectomies for ulcerative breast disease. The nurse provides appropriate counselling and referrals for patients and their families. Surgical removal of hormone-producing glands that might enhance tumour growth is often performed. These glands include the pituitary, adrenals, ovaries and testes.

Reconstructive Surgery

Reconstructive surgery may follow curative or radical surgery and is carried out in an attempt to produce a better return of function or a better cosmetic effect. It may be done in one operation or in stages. Presurgery counselling and evaluation are recommended. The surgeon who is to perform the reconstructive surgery is often called in preoperatively. For example, the woman who is to have breast reconstruction done may see the surgeon before hospitalization for a mastectomy. This approach provides the woman with something positive to focus on, at a time when thoughts of mutilation and death may be paramount. The surgeon performing the reconstructive surgery also benefits from seeing the way the woman's breasts appear normally and from establishing rapport with her. The nurse must recognize the woman's sexual needs and the impact that an altered body image may have on her sexuality. Providing the woman and her loved ones with opportunities to discuss these issues is imperative. The needs of the individual must be assessed accurately and validated in each situation for any type of reconstructive surgery.

Nursing Considerations

The patient undergoing surgery for the diagnosis or treatment of cancer is often anxious about the surgical procedure, possible findings, postoperative limitations, changes in normal body functions and prognosis. The patient and loved ones require time and assistance to deal with the possible changes and outcomes. At the same time, the patient requires expert medical and nursing care in the preoperative and postoperative phases of surgery and illness. Nurses who are asked about the results of diagnostic testing and surgical procedures are guided in their response by the information conveyed to the patient and loved ones by the doctor. Nurses may be asked by the patient and loved ones to explain and clarify information which was provided by the doctor at a time when their level of anxiety kept them from understanding the information and its implications. It is important for the nurse to communicate frequently with the doctor and other health care team members to be certain that a consistent approach is used. Plans for discharge and follow-up care and treatment are initiated as early as possible in order to ensure continuity of care from hospital to home or from a cancer referral centre to the patient's local hospital and health care provider.

Radiotherapy

Radiotherapy is the use of ionizing radiation to interrupt cellular growth. Approximately 50 per cent of patients with cancer receive a form of irradiation at some point in their course of treatment. This form of treatment may be chosen when the expected outcome of treatment is that of a cure, such as in Hodgkin's disease, testicular seminomas, localized cancers of the head and neck, and cancers of the uterine cervix. Radiotherapy may also be used to control malignant disease when a tumour cannot be removed surgically or when local nodal metastasis is present, or prophylactically to prevent leukaemic infiltration to the brain or spinal cord. Palliative irradiation is frequently used to relieve the symptoms of metastatic disease especially when it has spread to brain, bone or soft tissue.

Two types of ionizing radiation exist: electromagnetic rays (X-rays and gamma rays) and heavier particulate radiation (electrons, protons, neutrons, alpha particles and beta particles). Either type can lead to tissue disruption by ionization. The most harmful tissue disruption is the alteration of the DNA molecule within the cells of the tissue. Ionizing radiation causes breakage among the strands of the DNA helix, leading to cell death. Cell regulatory mechanisms are disturbed by radiation, shortening the life span of the cell.

Cells are most vulnerable to the disruptive effects of radiation during DNA synthesis and mitosis (S and M phases of the cell cycle, respectively). Therefore, those body tissues that undergo frequent cell division are most sensitive to radiotherapy. These tissues include bone marrow, lymphatic tissue, epithelium of the gastrointestinal tract and gonads. Those tissues that are slower growing or at rest are relatively radioresistant; they include muscle, cartilage and connective tissues. A radiosensitive tumour is one that can be destroyed by a dose of radiation that still allows for normal cell regeneration in the tissue. Tumours that are well oxygenated also seem to be more sensitive to radiation; therefore, radiotherapy might be enhanced if oxygen concentrations to tumours could be increased. In addition, if the radiation could be delivered at a time when most tumour cells were in either the S or M phases, the number of cancer cells destroyed ('cell kill') would be increased.

Radiation is delivered to tumour sites by either external or internal mechanisms. If external radiotherapy is used, one of several methods of delivery may be chosen, depending on the depth of the tumour to be radiated. Orthovoltage machines deliver the maximum radiation dose to superficial lesions such as lesions of the skin and breast, while megavoltage machines (cobalt-60 units) deliver radiation dose to deeper body structures and spare the skin from possible adverse effects. Other radiotherapy machines, linear accelerators (Figure 2.29), deliver their dosage to deeper structures without harming the skin and also create less scattering of radiation within the body tissues.

Internal radiation implants are used to deliver a high dose of radiation to a localized area. The specific radioisotope for implantation is selected on the basis of its half-life, which is the time it takes for half of its radioactivity to decay. This internal radiation can be implanted by way of needles, seeds, beads or catheters. With internal radiotherapy, as the distance from the radiation source increases, the dosage delivered to the patient decreases. This allows for sparing of tissue away from the local area. Patients receiving internal radiation emit radiation while the implant is in place. Principles of time, distance and shielding must be used in planning care for these patients to minimize exposure of staff to radiation.

Radiation Dosage

The radiation dosage is dependent on the sensitivity of the target tissues to radiation and the tumour size. The lethal tumour dose is defined as that dose that will eradicate 95 per cent of the tumour. The total radiation dose is delivered over several weeks to allow repair of healthy tissue and to achieve a greater cell kill by increasing the availability of a greater number of cells in the S or M phases of the cell cycle. Repeated radiation treatments over a period of time (fractionated doses) also allow time for the periphery of the tumour to be repeatedly reoxygenated, because tumours shrink from the outside inwards. This increases the radiosensitivity of the tumour, thus increasing tumour cell death.

Toxicity

Toxicity of radiotherapy is usually localized to the region being irradiated. Local reactions occur when normal cells in the treatment area are also destroyed and cellular regeneration falls behind cellular death. Body tissues most frequently affected are those that normally proliferate rapidly; they include the skin, the epithelial lining of the gastrointestinal system and the bone marrow. Alteration in skin integrity is a common effect and can include alopecia, erythema and desquamation (shedding of skin). Once treatments have been completed, re-epithelialization occurs. Alterations in oral mucosal membranes secondary to radiotherapy include stomatitis, dryness of the mouth (xerostomia) and decreased salivation. The entire gastrointestinal mucosal membranes may be involved, and oesophageal irritation with chest pain and dysphagia may result. Anorexia, nausea, vomiting and diarrhoea may occur if the stomach or colon is in the

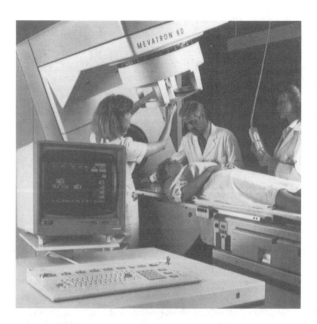

Figure 2.29 Mevatron, a linear electron accelerator used for radiotherapy. (By kind permission of Siemens Medical Engineering, Siemens plc.)

irradiated field. Symptoms subside and gastrointestinal re-epithelialization occurs once treatments are complete. Bone marrow cells proliferate rapidly, and if bone-marrow-producing sites are included in the field of irradiation, anaemia, leucopenia and thrombocytopenia may result. Patients are then at increased risk of infection and bleeding until blood cell counts return to normal.

Certain systemic side-effects are also commonly experienced by patients receiving radiotherapy. These manifestations, which are generalized, include fatigue, malaise, headache, nausea and vomiting. This syndrome may be secondary to substances released on the breakdown of tumour cells. The effects are temporary and subside with the cessation of treatments.

Late effects of radiotherapy may also occur in various body tissues. These effects are chronic, usually display fibrotic changes secondary to a decreased vascular supply and are irreversible.

Nursing Considerations

The patient who is receiving radiotherapy and the loved ones often have questions and concerns about its safety. The nurse is often in a position to answer questions and allay fears about its effects on others, on the tumour and on the patient's normal tissues and organs. The actual procedure for delivering the radiation is explained, along with a description of the equipment to be used, the duration of the procedure (often minutes only), the possible need for immobilization of the patient during the procedure and the absence of new sensations during the procedure. If the patient receives radiotherapy by means of a radioactive implant, explanations will be required about limitation of visitors and health care staff and other radiation precautions. Patients also need to understand their role before, during and after the procedure.

Attention is given by the nurse to the patient's skin, nutritional status and general feeling of wellbeing. The patient's skin and oral mucosa are assessed frequently for changes (particularly if radiotherapy is directed to these areas). The skin is protected from irritation, and the patient is advised to avoid using ointments, lotions or powders on the area. Gentle oral hygiene is essential to remove debris and prevent irritation. If the patient experiences systemic changes such as weakness and fatigue, assistance may be needed with activities of daily living and personal hygiene. Additionally, the nurse's explanation that these symptoms are a result of the treatment, and do not represent deterioration or disease progression, is often reassuring to the patient.

When a patient has a radioactive implant in place, nurses also take precautions to protect themselves and other personnel as well as the patient from the effects of radiation. Generally, the patient is either on bedrest or restricted to the room while the radioactive implant is in place. Specific instructions are frequently provided by the radiation safety officer from the radiology department, and usually include the maximum amount of time to be spent in the patient's room by any individual, shielding equipment to be used and special precautions and actions to be taken if the implant is dislodged. Patients are informed about the rationale for these precautions so that they do not feel unduly isolated.

Chemotherapy

Chemotherapy is the use of antineoplastic drugs to promote tumour cell death by interfering with cellular functions and reproduction. It is used primarily to treat systemic disease rather than lesions that are localized and amenable to surgery or irradiation. Chemotherapy may be combined with surgery or radiotherapy, or both, to reduce tumour size preoperatively, to destroy remaining tumour cells postoperatively or to treat some forms of leukaemia. The expected outcomes of chemotherapy (cure, control, palliation) must be realistic because they will define the drugs to be used and the aggressiveness of the treatment chosen.

Each time a tumour is exposed to a chemotherapeutic agent, a percentage of tumour cells (20 to 99 per cent, depending on dosage) is destroyed. Repeated doses of drugs are necessary over a prolonged period in order to achieve regression of the tumour. Eradication of 100 per cent of the tumour is nearly impossible, but an expected outcome of chemotherapy is to eradicate enough of the tumour so that the remaining tumour cells can be destroyed by the body's immune system.

Actively proliferating cells within a tumour (growth fraction) are the most sensitive to chemotherapeutic agents. Nondividing cells capable of future proliferation are the least sensitive to antineoplastic drugs and consequently are potentially dangerous. However, they must be destroyed in order to eradicate a malignancy completely. Repeated cycles of chemotherapy are used to enhance tumour cell kill by destroying these nondividing cells as they are signalled into active proliferation. These effects are related to the phases of the reproductive cycle of the cell—the cell cycle. Reproduction of both healthy and malignant cells follows the cell cycle pattern (Figure 2.30). The cell cycle time is the time required for one tissue cell to divide and reproduce into two identical daughter cells. The cell cycle of any cell has four distinct phases, each with a vital underlying function: (1) G_1 phase—RNA and protein synthesis occurs; (2) S phase—DNA synthesis occurs; (3) G_2 phase—premitotic phase, DNA synthesis complete; and (4) mitosis—cell division occurs. The G_0 phase, the resting or dormant phase of cells, can occur after mitosis and during the G_1 phase. In the G_0 phase are those dangerous cells which are not actively dividing but have the future potential for replication. The administration of certain chemotherapeutic agents (as well as of some other forms of therapy) is coordinated with the cell cycle.

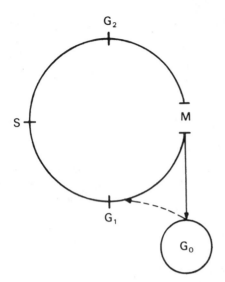

Figure 2.30 Phases of the cell cycle. The cycle represents the interval between the midpoint of mitosis to the subsequent end point in mitosis in one daughter cell or both. G_1 is the postmitotic phase during which RNA and protein synthesis is increased and cell growth occurs. G_0 is the resting or dormant phase of the cell cycle. The S phase represents synthesis of nucleic acids with chromosome replication in preparation for cell mitosis. During G_2, RNA and protein synthesis occurs as in G_1. (Porth, C. M. (1986) *Pathophysiology: Concepts of Altered Health States* (2nd edition), J. B. Lippincott, Philadelphia.)

Classification of Chemotherapeutic Agents

Certain chemotherapeutic agents (cell-cycle-specific drugs) destroy cells in specific phases of the cell cycle. Most cell-cycle-specific drugs affect cells in the S phase by interfering with DNA and RNA synthesis. Others, such as the Vinca or plant alkaloids, are specific to the M phase where they halt mitotic spindle formation.

Those chemotherapeutic agents which act independently of the cell cycle phases are termed cell-cycle-nonspecific drugs. These agents usually have a prolonged effect on cells, leading to cellular damage or death. Many treatment plans combine cell-cycle-specific and cell-cycle-nonspecific drugs in order to increase the number of vulnerable tumour cells killed during a treatment period.

Chemotherapeutic agents are also classified according to various chemical groups, each with a different mechanism of action. These include the alkylating agents, nitrosoureas, antimetabolites, anti-tumour antibiotics, plant alkaloids, hormonal agents and miscellaneous agents. The classification, mechanism of action, common drugs, cell cycle specificity and common side-effects of antineoplastic agents are listed in Table 2.41. Chemotherapeutic

agents from each category may be used in order to enhance the tumour cell kill during therapy.

Investigational Drugs and Clinical Trials

Investigational antineoplastic drugs undergo thorough trials to test their toxicities and effectiveness. Before new chemotherapeutic agents are approved for clinical use in the treatment of cancer, they are subjected to rigorous and often lengthy evaluation to identify beneficial effects, side-effects and safety.

Administration of Chemotherapeutic Agents

Routes of Administration

Chemotherapeutic drugs may be administered by topical, oral, intravenous, intramuscular, subcutaneous, arterial, intracavitary and intrathecal routes. The route of administration is usually dependent on the type of drug, the required dose and the type and extent of tumour being treated.

Dosage

Dosage of antineoplastic agents is based primarily on the patient's total body surface area, previous response to chemotherapy or radiotherapy and physical status.

Extravasation

Special care must be taken whenever intravenous vesicant agents are administered. Vesicant drugs are those agents that, if deposited into the subcutaneous tissue (extravasated), cause tissue necrosis and damage to underlying tendons, nerves and blood vessels. Although the complete mechanism of tissue destruction is unclear, it is known that the pH of many antineoplastic drugs is responsible for the severe inflammatory reaction. Sloughing and ulceration of tissue may be so severe that skin grafting may be necessary. The full extent of tissue damage may take several weeks to become apparent. Drugs classified as vesicant agents include dactinomycin, daunorubicin, doxorubicin, nitrogen mustard, mithramycin, mitomycin, vinblastine, vincristine and vindesine.

Only specially trained doctors and nurses should be involved in the administration of vesicants to prevent extravasation. Careful selection of peripheral veins, skilled venepuncture and careful drug administration are essential. Indications of extravasation during drug administration include loss of blood return from the intravenous device, resistance to intravenous fluid flow and swelling, pain or redness at the site. If extravasation is suspected, the drug administration should be stopped immediately and ice applied to the site (except for Vinca alkaloid extravasation). The doctor may aspirate any infiltrated drug from the tissues and inject a neutralizing solution into the area to reduce damage. Recommendations

Table 2.41 *Classification of antineoplastic agents*

Category	Mechanism of action	Common drugs	Cell-cycle specificity	Common side-effects
Alkylating agents	Alter DNA structure by • Misreading of DNA code • Breaks in DNA molecule • Cross-linking of DNA strands	Nitrogen mustard Cyclophosphamide Melphalan Chlorambucil Thiotepa Cisplatin Busulphan	Cell-cycle nonspecific	Bone marrow suppression, nausea, vomiting, cystitis (cyclophosphamide), stomatitis, alopecia, gonadal suppression
Nitrosoureas	Similar to alkylating agents; cross blood–brain barrier	Carmustine (BiCNU) Lomustine (CCNU) Semustine (methyl CCNU) Streptozocin	Cell-cycle nonspecific	Delayed and cumulative myelosuppression, especially thrombocytopenia; nausea, vomiting
Antimetabolites	Interfere with the biosynthesis of metabolites/ nucleic acids necessary for RNA and DNA synthesis	Cytarabine 5-fluorouracil Methotrexate (MTX) Hydroxyurea 6-Mercaptopurine 6-Thioguanine 5-Azacytadine	Cell-cycle specific (S phase)	Nausea, vomiting, diarrhoea, myelosuppression, proctitis, stomatitis, renal toxicity (MTX), hepatotoxicity
Anti-tumour antibiotics	Interfere with DNA synthesis by binding DNA; prevent RNA synthesis	Dactinomycin Bleomycin Daunorubicin Mithramycin Mitomycin Doxorubicin	Cell-cycle nonspecific	Bone marrow suppression, nausea, vomiting, alopecia, anorexia, cardiac toxicity (daunorubicin, doxorubicin)
Plant alkaloids	Cause metaphase arrest by inhibiting mitotic tubular formation (spindle); inhibit DNA and protein synthesis	Vincristine (VCR) Vinblastine Vindesine VP-16 VM-26	Cell-cycle specific (M phase)	Bone marrow suppression (mild with VCR), neuropathies (VCR), stomatitis
Hormonal agents	Bind to hormone receptor sites that alter cellular growth; block binding of oestrogens to receptor sites (anti-oestrogens); inhibit RNA synthesis	Androgens Oestrogens Anti-oestrogens Progesterone Steroids	Cell-cycle nonspecific	Hypercalcaemia, jaundice, increased appetite, masculinization, feminization, sodium and fluid retention, nausea, vomiting, hot flushes
Miscellaneous agents	Unknown; too complex to categorize	Asparaginase Procarbazine M-AMSA Hexamethylmelamine Dacarbazine (DTIC) Mitozantrone Methyl-GAG	?	Anorexia, nausea, vomiting, myelosuppression, hepatotoxicity, anaphylaxis, hypotension, altered glucose metabolism

and guidelines for management of vesicant extravasation have been issued by individual drug manufacturers, pharmacies and the Royal Marsden Hospital Society, and differ from one drug to the next.

When frequent, prolonged administration of vesicant antineoplastic agents is anticipated, right atrial catheters or venous access devices may be inserted. These devices promote safety during drug administration and reduce problems with access to the circulatory system.

Toxicity

Toxicity associated with chemotherapy can be acute or chronic. Cells with rapid growth rates (e.g., epithelium, bone marrow, hair follicles) are more susceptible to damage from these agents. Various body systems may be affected by these drugs and are discussed in the following paragraphs.

Gastrointestinal System

Nausea and vomiting are the most common side-effects of chemotherapy and may persist for up to 24 hours following drug administration. Stimulation of nausea and vomiting occurs by: (1) irritation of the gastrointestinal tract; (2) stimulation of the chemoreceptor trigger zone of the medulla; (3) stimulation of the true vomiting centre of the brain; (4) anticipatory stimulation; and (5) a combination of factors. Use of phenothiazines, sedatives and steroids, alone or in combination, is often effective in minimizing nausea and vomiting. Relaxation techniques and imagery can also help to decrease stimuli contributing to symptoms. Alterations in the patient's diet may reduce the frequency or severity of these symptoms.

Although the epithelium which lines the oral cavity quickly renews itself, its rapid rate of proliferation makes it susceptible to the effects of chemotherapy. As a result, stomatitis and anorexia are common. The entire gastrointestinal tract is susceptible to mucositis (inflammation of the mucosal lining), and diarrhoea is a common result. Antimetabolites and anti-tumour antibiotics are the major culprits in mucositis and other gastrointestinal symptoms.

Haematopoietic System

Most chemotherapeutic agents depress bone marrow function (myelosuppression), resulting in decreased production of blood cells. Myelosuppression decreases the number of white blood cells or leucocytes (leucopenia), red blood cells (anaemia), and platelets or thrombocytes (thrombocytopenia) and increases the risk of infection and bleeding. Depression of these cells is the usual reason for limiting the dose of the chemotherapeutic drugs. Frequent monitoring of blood cell counts is essential, and the patient must be protected from infection and injury, particularly while the blood cell counts are depressed.

Renal System

Chemotherapeutic agents can be harmful to the kidneys owing to direct effects of the drugs during their excretion and to the accumulation of end-products following cell lysis. Cisplatin, methotrexate and mitomycin are particularly toxic to the kidneys. Rapid cell lysis following chemotherapy results in increased urinary excretion of uric acid, which can lead to renal damage. Monitoring of blood urea nitrogen, serum creatinine and creatinine clearance is essential. Adequate fluid hydration, alkalinization of the urine to prevent formation of uric acid crystals and the use of allopurinol are frequently indicated to prevent these side-effects.

Cardiopulmonary System

Anti-tumour antibiotics (daunorubicin and doxorubicin) are known to cause irreversible cumulative cardiac toxicities, especially when total dosage reaches 550 mg/m^2. Cardiac ejection fraction, electrocardiographic (ECG) tracings and signs of congestive heart failure must be monitored closely. Bleomycin and busulfan are known for their cumulative toxic effects on lung function. Pulmonary fibrosis can be a long-term effect of prolonged dosage with these drugs. Therefore, the patient is monitored closely for changes in pulmonary function.

Reproductive System

Testicular and ovarian function can be affected by chemotherapeutic agents, resulting in possible sterility. Reproductive ability may return following chemotherapy; however, reproductive cells may have been damaged during treatment and result in chromosomal abnormalities in offspring. Therefore, banking of sperm is recommended for men before the initiation of treatments. Patients and significant others are informed about potential changes in reproduction resulting from chemotherapy.

Neurological System

The plant alkaloids, especially vincristine, can cause neurological damage with repeated doses. Peripheral neuropathies, loss of deep tendon reflexes and paralytic ileus may occur. These side-effects are usually reversible and disappear after completion of chemotherapy.

Nursing Considerations

The nurse has an important role in assessing and managing many of the problems experienced by the patient undergoing chemotherapy. Because of their systemic effects on normal as well as malignant cells, these problems are often widespread, affecting many body systems. Anorexia, nausea, vomiting, altered taste and diarrhoea put the patient at risk for nutritional and fluid and electrolyte disturbances. Changes in the mucosa of the gastrointestinal tract may lead to irritation of the oral cavity and intestinal tract, further threatening the patient's nutritional status. Therefore, it is important for the nurse to assess the patient's nutritional and fluid and electrolyte status frequently and to use creative ways to encourage an adequate fluid and dietary intake. Suppression of the bone marrow and immune system are expected consequences of chemotherapy, and frequently serve as a guide in determining appropriate chemotherapy dosage. However, this effect also increases the risk of anaemia, infection and bleeding disorders. Therefore, nursing assessment and care focus on identifying and modifying factors which further increase the risk to the patient. Asepsis and gentle handling are indicated to prevent infection and trauma. Laboratory test results, particularly blood cell counts, are monitored closely. Untoward changes in blood test results and the occurrence of signs of infection and bleeding are reported promptly to the patient's doctor. The patient and home carers are instructed about measures to prevent these problems at home.

Local effects of the chemotherapeutic agent are also of concern. The patient is observed closely during its administration because of the risk and consequences of extravasation (particularly of vesicant agents or those that may produce tissue necrosis if deposited in the subcutaneous tissues). Local difficulties or problems with administration of chemotherapeutic agents are promptly brought to the attention of the doctor so that corrective measures can be taken immediately.

Nurses involved in handling chemotherapeutic agents may be exposed to low doses of the drugs by direct contact, inhalation and ingestion. Personnel repeatedly exposed to cytotoxic drugs have demonstrated mutagenic activity in their urine. Although not all mutagens are carcinogenic, they do have the ability to produce permanent inheritable changes in the genetic material of cells. Although long-term studies of nurses handling chemotherapeutic agents have not been conducted, it is known that chemotherapeutic agents are associated with secondary formation of cancers and chromosome abnormalities. Nausea, vomiting, dizziness, alopecia and nasal mucosal ulcerations have been reported in health care staff who have handled chemotherapeutic agents. Because of known and potential hazards associated with handling chemotherapy, specific precautions for those involved in preparation and administration of chemotherapy have been developed. When followed, these precautions greatly minimize the risk of exposure (Pritchard and David, 1988).

Biological Response Modifiers

Biological response modifiers are agents or methods of treatment that have the ability to alter the immunological relationship between the tumour and the cancer patient (host) to provide a therapeutic benefit. Although the mechanisms of action vary with each type of biological response modifier, the expected outcome is destruction or cessation of the malignant growth. Over the years, the role of the body's natural immune defences against cancer has become better understood. The basis of biological response modifier treatment lies in the restoration, stimulation or augmentation of those natural immune defences.

Some of the early investigations of the stimulation of the immune system involved nonspecific agents such as bacille Calmette-Guérin (BCG) and *Corynebacterium parvum* (*C. parvum*). These agents serve as antigens which stimulate an immune response when injected into the patient. It is hoped that the stimulated immune system will then be able to eradicate malignant growths. Extensive animal and human investigations with BCG have yielded some promising results, especially in the treatment of malignant melanoma, bladder cancer and colorectal cancer. However, the exact role of these agents requires further investigation.

Interferons are another example of biological response modifiers with both antiviral and anti-tumour properties. When stimulated, all nucleated cells are capable of producing these glycoproteins, which are classified according to their biological and chemical properties: α-interferons are produced by leucocytes, α-interferons are produced by fibroblasts and γ-interferons are produced by lymphocytes.

Although the exact anti-tumour effects of interferons have not been thoroughly established, it is thought that they either stimulate the immune system or assist in prevention of tumour growth. Interferons enhance both lymphocyte and antibody production. They also facilitate the cytolytic role of macrophages and natural killer cells. Additionally, interferons are able to inhibit cell multiplication by increasing the duration of various phases of the cell cycle. The effects of interferons have been demonstrated in hairy cell leukaemia, non-Hodgkin's lymphoma, renal cell carcinoma, melanoma and Kaposi's sarcoma. Further efforts are underway to investigate the role of interferons in cancer treatment.

Monoclonal antibodies are another type of biological response modifier; they became available through recent technological advances that enabled investigators to grow and produce specific antibodies for specific malignant cells. The production of monoclonal antibodies involves injecting tumour cells into mice and harvesting the antibodies produced by the immune systems of the mice. The antibodies are then infused into the cancer patient. Preliminary investigations of monoclonal antibody therapy for leukaemia and lymphoma have been disappointing; however, initial reports of its use in treatment of solid tumours have been more promising. The feasibility of combining monoclonal antibodies and chemotherapeutic agents in hopes of improving the effectiveness of these agents is under investigation.

Lymphokines and cytokines, cell products of lymphocytes with known biological roles in the normal immune response, are also the focus of current research efforts. The most widely publicized agent is interleukin-2 (IL-2), which is known to stimulate the production and activation of T lymphocytes. Its role in the treatment of acquired immunodeficiency syndrome (AIDS) is under investigation.

Nursing Considerations

Patients receiving biological response modifier therapy have many of the same needs as other cancer patients undergoing more conventional therapies. However, for many patients who have failed to respond to standard treatment modalities, biological response modifier therapy may be viewed as a 'last chance' effort. Consequently, it is essential that the nurse assesses the need for education, support and guidance for both the patient and loved ones, and assists in planning and evaluating patient care. Nurses need to be familiar with each agent given and its potential adverse effects. Because of the investigational nature of these agents, the nurse will be administering them in a research setting. Accurate observations and careful documentation are essential components of the data collection process.

Nursing Care of the Patient With Cancer

The outlook for patients with cancer has greatly improved because of scientific and technological advances. However, as a result of the underlying malignancy or various treatments, the patient with cancer may confront or experience a variety of secondary problems. Regardless of the type of cancer, treatment used or prognosis, many patients with cancer are susceptible to these problems and complications. An important role of the nurse on the oncology team is to assess the patient for these problems and complications.

▶ NURSING PROCESS
▶ THE PATIENT WITH CANCER

▶ *Assessment*

At all stages of cancer, the patient is assessed for those factors which predispose to infection and bleeding problems. These factors include suppression of bone marrow and blood cell production by chemotherapy, radiotherapy or the malignancy itself. The nurse monitors laboratory studies, particularly the complete blood cell count and blood coagulation studies, to detect early changes in white blood cells, red blood cells and platelets. Common sites of infection and bleeding, such as the patient's pharynx, skin, perianal area, urinary tract and respiratory tract, are assessed frequently. However, it is important to keep in

mind that the typical signs of infection (fever, swelling, redness, drainage and pain) may be absent in the immunosuppressed patient. The patient is monitored for sepsis, particularly if invasive catheters or infusion lines are in place.

The functions of the white blood cells are often impaired in cancer patients. A decrease in circulating white blood cells is referred to as leucopenia or granulocytopenia. There are three types of white blood cells: neutrophils, basophils and eosinophils. The neutrophils, totalling 60 to 70 per cent of all the body's white blood cells, play a major role in combating infection through phagocytosis. Both the total white blood cell count and concentration of neutrophils are important in determining the patient's ability to fight infection. A differential count supplies the relative numbers of the various types of white blood cells and permits tabulation of polymorphonuclear neutrophils and immature forms of neutrophils. These numbers are compiled and reported as the absolute neutrophil count. The risk of infection rises as the absolute neutrophil count decreases.

The cancer patient is also closely monitored for signs of bleeding; the most common sites include the skin and mucous membranes, the intestinal, urinary and respiratory tracts, and the brain. Gross bleeding as well as oozing at injection sites, bruising (ecchymosis) and changes in mental status that may indicate intracranial bleeding are monitored and reported.

Skin and tissue integrity is at risk in cancer patients because of the effects of chemotherapy, radiotherapy, surgery and invasive procedures for diagnosis and therapy. As part of the assessment, the nurse identifies which of these predisposing factors are present and assesses the patient for other risk factors including nutritional deficits, bowel and bladder incontinence, immobility, immunosuppression and changes related to ageing. Skin lesions or ulceration secondary to the tumour are noted. Alterations in tissue integrity throughout the gastrointestinal tract are particularly bothersome to the patient. The oral mucous membranes and the appearance of lesions are noted, as is their effect on the patient's nutritional status and level of comfort. Hair loss (alopecia) is another form of tissue disruption common to cancer patients who receive radiotherapy or chemotherapy. In addition to noting its loss, the nurse also assesses the meaning of hair and hair loss to the patient and home carers.

Assessment of the patient's nutritional status is an important part of the nurse's role. Alterations in nutritional status and weight loss may be secondary to the effects of a local tumour, systemic disease, treatment-related side-effects or the emotional status of the patient. The patient's weight and calorie intake are monitored daily. Other information obtained through assessment includes diet history, frequency and duration of episodes of anorexia, changes in appetite, situations and foods that aggravate or relieve the anorexia, and medication history. Difficulty in chewing or swallowing is determined and the occurrence of nausea, vomiting or diarrhoea is noted. Clinical and laboratory data useful in assessing the patient's nutritional status include anthropometric measurements (triceps skin fold and mid upper arm circumference) serum protein levels (albumin and transferrin), lymphocyte count, haemoglobin levels, haematocrit, urinary creatinine levels and serum iron levels.

Pain and discomfort in cancer may be related to the tumour or malignancy itself, to pressure exerted by the tumour, to diagnostic testing procedures or to many of the cancer treatments that may be used. As in any other situation involving pain, the experience of cancer pain is affected by both physical and psychosocial influences. In addition to assessing the source and site of pain, the nurse also assesses those factors which increase the patient's perception of pain, such as fear and apprehension, fatigue, anger and social isolation. Assessment scales for pain are useful in assessing the patient's pain level before use of pain-relieving treatments and in evaluating the patient's response to them.

Assessment of the cancer patient is not limited to the physiological changes that may occur in the course of the disease but also focuses on the patient's psychological and mental status as both the patient and loved ones face this life-threatening experience, unpleasant diagnostic tests and treatment modalities, and progression of disease. The patient's mood and emotional reaction to the results of diagnostic testing and prognosis are assessed. Progression through the stages of grief is assessed, as is the patient's communication about the diagnosis and prognosis with loved ones.

Cancer patients are forced to cope with many assaults to body image throughout the course of disease and treatment. Entry into the health care system is often accompanied by depersonalization. Threats to self-concept are enormous as patients face the realization of illness, possible disability and death. Many cancer patients are forced to alter their lifestyles to accommodate treatments or as a direct result of disease pathology. Priorities and value systems are often forced to change when body image is threatened and physical characteristics become less important. Disfiguring surgery, hair loss, cachexia, skin changes, altered communication patterns and sexual dysfunction are some of the devastating results of cancer and its treatment that may threaten the patient's self-esteem and body image. During assessment, these potential threats are identified, as is the patient's ability to cope with these changes.

► *Patient's Problems*

Based on the assessment, the problems experienced by the patient with cancer may include the following:

- Potential for infection related to altered immunological response.

- Potential for injury related to bleeding disorder.
- Alterations in tissue integrity related to the effects of treatment and disease.
- Alterations in nutrition: less than body requirements related to anorexia and gastrointestinal changes.
- Alterations in comfort: pain related to disease and treatment effects.
- Grieving related to anticipated loss and altered role function.
- Disturbance in self-concept: altered body image related to changes in appearance and role functions.

► *Planning and Implementation*
► Expected Outcomes

The main expected outcomes for the patient may include prevention of infection, prevention of injury related to bleeding disorder, maintenance of tissue integrity, maintenance of nutrition, relief of pain or other symptoms, psychological adjustment to the cancer and its progression and changes in body image.

Nursing Care

Prevention of Infection

Despite advances in the care of patients with cancer, infection remains the leading cause of death. Defence against infection is compromised in many different ways. Skin and mucous membrane integrity, the body's first line of defence, is challenged by multiple invasive diagnostic and therapeutic procedures, adverse effects of irradiation and chemotherapy, and the detrimental effects of immobility. Impaired nutrition resulting from anorexia, nausea, vomiting and diarrhoea, and the underlying malignant process can alter the body's ability to combat invading organisms. Medications such as antibiotics disturb the balance of normal flora, allowing the overgrowth of pathogenic organisms. Other medications can also alter the immune response (see Chapter 26). Cancer itself may be immunosuppressive. Malignancies such as leukaemia and lymphoma are often associated with defects in cellular and humoral immunity. Advanced cancer can lead to tumour obstruction of hollow viscera, blood and lymphatic vessels, creating a favourable environment for proliferation of pathogenic organisms. In some patients, tumour cells infiltrate bone marrow and prevent normal production of white blood cells. Most often, however, a decrease in white blood cells is a result of bone marrow suppression following chemotherapy or irradiation.

Infections in the myelosuppressed or immunosuppressed patient are most often nosocomial, a result of organisms that have become part of the patient's resident flora after being acquired from the hospital environment. The most threatening pathogens are the gram-negative bacilli such as *Pseudomonas aeruginosa* and *Escherichia coli*. Gram-positive bacilli such as *Staphylococcus aureus* and fungal organisms such as *Candida albicans* can also contribute to serious infection.

Fever is probably the most important sign of infection in the immunocompromised patient. Although fever may be related to a variety of noninfectious conditions including the underlying malignancy, any temperature elevation of 38.3°C or above is reported and dealt with promptly. Antibiotic agents may be prescribed to treat infections after results of cultures and sensitivities of wound drainage, exudate, sputum, urine, stool or blood specimens are obtained. An important component of the nurse's role is to administer these medications promptly according to the drug chart to achieve adequate blood levels of the medication. Strict asepsis is essential when handling intravenous lines, catheters and other invasive equipment. The patient is protected from exposure to others with active infections and is strongly advised to avoid crowds. Handwashing and appropriate hygiene are necessary to reduce exposure to potentially harmful bacteria and to eliminate environmental sources of contamination. The patient is also encouraged to cough and take deep breaths frequently to prevent atelectasis and other potential respiratory problems.

Assessment of the patient for infection and inflammation is frequent and continues throughout the course of disease. Septicaemia and septic shock are life-threatening complications that must be prevented or detected early in their course. The patient and home carers are instructed about signs of septicaemia, preventive actions and actions to take if infection or septicaemia occurs.

Prevention of Injury Related to Bleeding Disorder

A decrease in the number of circulating platelets (thrombocytopenia) is the most common cause of bleeding in the patient with cancer. Thrombocytopenia is often a result of bone marrow depression following certain types of chemotherapy and radiotherapy. Tumour infiltration of bone marrow can also impair the normal production of platelets. In some cases, platelet destruction is associated with an enlarged spleen (hypersplenism) and abnormal antibody function that occur with leukaemia and lymphoma.

Platelets are essential for normal blood clotting and coagulation (haemostasis). Thrombocytopenia is defined as a platelet count less than $0.1 \times 10^{12}/l$. When the count falls to 0.02 to $0.05 \times 10^{12}/l$, the risk for bleeding increases. Counts less than $0.02 \times 10^{12}/l$ are associated with an increased risk for spontaneous bleeding. In addition to monitoring laboratory values, the nurse continues to assess the patient for evidence of bleeding. The nurse also takes steps to prevent trauma and minimize the risk of bleeding by replacing the patient's hard-bristled toothbrush with a soft-bristled one, by encouraging the patient to use an electric razor rather than a safety or straight-edge razor and by avoiding unnecessary invasive procedures (e.g., rectal temperatures, catheterization). The patient

and home carers are assisted in identifying and removing environmental hazards that may lead to falls or other trauma. Soft foods, increased fluid intake and stool softeners, if prescribed, may be indicated to reduce trauma to the gastrointestinal tract. The joints and extremities are handled and moved gently to minimize the risk of spontaneous bleeding.

Maintenance of Tissue Integrity

The person with cancer is at risk for the development of a variety of skin and mucous membrane impairments. The nurse in all health settings is in an ideal position to assess and assist the patient and home carers in the management of these problems. Some of the most frequently encountered disturbances include skin and tissue reactions to radiotherapy, stomatitis, alopecia and metastatic skin lesions.

The patient who is experiencing skin and tissue reactions to radiotherapy requires careful skin care to prevent further skin irritation, drying and damage. The skin over the affected area is handled gently; rubbing and use of hot or cold water, soaps, powders, lotions and cosmetics are avoided. Trauma to the area is prevented by use of loosely fitting clothes that do not constrict, irritate or rub the affected area. If blistering occurs, care is taken not to disrupt the blisters to reduce the risk of introducing bacteria. Aseptic wound care is indicated to minimize the risk of infection and sepsis.

Stomatitis. Stomatitis is a common problem in cancer patients as a result of chemotherapy or radiotherapy. It is an inflammatory response of the oral tissues that may progress from mild erythema and oedema to painful ulcerations, bleeding and secondary infection. This condition most often develops within 5 to 14 days of the administration of certain chemotherapeutic agents such as doxorubicin and 5-fluorouracil. It may also occur with irradiation to the head and neck area. In very severe cases of stomatitis, chemotherapy may be temporarily halted until resolution of inflammation.

As a result of normal everyday wear and tear, the epithelial cells that line the oral cavity have a very rapid turnover or routinely slough off. Chemotherapy and irradiation interfere with the body's ability to replace those cells. An inflammatory response develops as denuded areas appear in the oral cavity. Myelosuppression as a result of the underlying malignancy or treatment predisposes the patient to oral bleeding and infection. Pain associated with ulcerated oral tissues can significantly interfere with nutritional intake and willingness to maintain oral hygiene. Soft-bristled toothbrushes and nonabrasive toothpaste prevent or reduce the trauma to the oral mucosa. Restriction of foods which are difficult to chew, too hot or spicy may further reduce trauma and promote comfort. The patient's lips are lubricated to keep them soft. Topical antifungal agents and anaesthetics may be prescribed to promote healing and minimize patient discomfort. The patient who experiences severe pain and discomfort with stomatitis will require encouragement and assistance to use these prescribed agents and to maintain an adequate fluid and food intake.

Alopecia. The temporary or permanent thinning or complete loss of hair, referred to as alopecia, is a potential adverse effect of certain forms of radiotherapy and several chemotherapeutic agents. The extent of alopecia depends on the dose and duration of therapy. These treatments cause alopecia by damaging stem cells and hair follicles. As a result, the hair is brittle and may fall out or break off at the surface of the scalp. Loss of other body hair is less frequent.

Many health professionals view hair loss as a minor problem when compared with the potential life-threatening consequences of the underlying malignancy. However, for many patients, hair loss poses a major threat to body image, arousing feelings of anxiety, sadness, anger, rejection, ridicule and isolation. To patients and loved ones, hair loss can serve as a constant reminder of cancer, interfering with coping abilities, interpersonal relationships and sexuality. The nurse's role is to provide information about alopecia and to assist the patient and loved ones in coping with hair loss and changes in body image. While hair loss may be reduced by techniques such as scalp cooling, the patient is encouraged to acquire a wig or hairpiece before hair loss so that the replacement matches the patient's own hair. Use of attractive scarves and hats may make the patient feel more attractive. It is frequently of some comfort to patients that the hair usually begins to grow again after completion of the chemotherapy; however, the colour and texture of the new hair may be different.

Malignant Skin Lesions. Skin lesions may occur with local extension or tumour embolization into the epithelium and its surrounding lymph and blood vessels. Secondary growth of cancer cells into the skin may be characterized as erythematous areas progressing to wounds involving tissue necrosis and infection. The most extensive lesions are friable, purulent and malodorous. In addition, these lesions are a source of considerable pain and discomfort. Although this type of wound is most often associated with breast cancer, it can also accompany lymphoma, leukaemia, melanoma and cancers of the head and neck, lung, uterus, kidney, colon and bladder. The development of severe skin lesions is usually considered to be a very poor prognostic sign for expected length of survival.

Ulcerating skin lesions usually indicate the presence of widely disseminated disease. Therefore, eradication of the problem is usually not feasible. The management of these lesions becomes a nursing priority. Nursing care includes careful assessment, cleansing, reduction of superficial bacterial flora, control of bleeding, reduction of odour and protection against pain and further trauma to the skin. The patient and loved ones will require assistance and guidance to care for these skin lesions at home. Referral to a community nurse is indicated to provide assistance and evaluation of wound care at home.

Maintenance of Nutritional Status

Most cancer patients experience some degree of weight loss during their illness. Anorexia, malabsorption and cachexia are examples of nutritional problems commonly seen in cancer patients.

Anorexia. There are many theories about the aetiology of anorexia in the cancer patient. Alterations in taste manifested by increased salty, sour and metallic tastes and altered responses to sweet and bitter tastes lead to decreased appetite, decreased intake and protein–calorie malnutrition in the cancer patient. Taste alterations may be due to deficiencies of minerals such as zinc, increases in circulating amino acids and the administration of chemotherapeutic agents. Individuals undergoing radiotherapy to the head and neck may experience 'mouth blindness', which is a severe impairment of taste. Alterations in the sense of smell also alter taste, which is a common experience of patients with head and neck cancers. Anorexia may be related to early satiety and a sense of fullness secondary to decreased digestive enzymes, abnormalities of glucose and triglyceride metabolism and prolonged stimulation of gastric volume receptors. Psychological distress such as fear, pain, depression and isolation throughout illness may have a negative impact on appetite. Conditioned food aversions due to past experiences with nausea, and vomiting associated with treatment may also contribute to anorexia.

Malabsorption. Many cancer patients are unable to absorb nutrients from the gastrointestinal system secondary to tumour activity and cancer treatment. Tumours may impair enzyme production; create fistulae; secrete hormones and enzymes such as gastrin, which leads to increased gastrointestinal irritation, peptic ulcer disease and decreased fat digestion; and interfere with protein digestion. Chemotherapy and irradiation can irritate and damage mucosal cells of the bowel, inhibiting absorption. Radiotherapy can cause sclerosis of the blood vessels in the bowel and fibrotic changes in the gastrointestinal tissue. Surgical intervention may change peristaltic patterns, alter gastrointestinal secretions and reduce the absorptive surfaces of the gastrointestinal mucosa, all leading to malabsorption.

Cachexia. Cachexia (wasting syndrome) is common in the cancer patient, especially in advanced disease states. Cancer cachexia is related to inadequate nutritional intake along with increasing metabolic demand, increased energy expenditure due to anaerobic metabolism of the tumour, impaired glucose metabolism, competition of the tumour cells for nutrients, altered lipid metabolism and failure of appetite.

Creative dietary modification to overcome the factors contributing to anorexia must be planned for each patient.

Home carers are included in the dietary plan of care to maintain consistency and aid compliance. Factors contributing to the patient's anorexia (unpleasant sights and odours) are eliminated. The patient's preferences as well as physiological and metabolic requirements are considered in selecting foods. Small, frequent meals are provided with additional supplements between meals. Oral hygiene and pain relief measures are offered before mealtime to make meals more pleasant.

Care to relieve malabsorptive states may include enzyme and vitamin replacement, changes in feeding timetable, use of elemental diets and measures to relieve diarrhoea. If malabsorption is severe, parenteral nutrition may be necessary via a right atrial catheter, such as a Hickman catheter (see Figure 13.6). These catheters are surgically placed and are maintained for long-term venous access. In order to prevent infection, they are tunnelled under the skin through the subcutaneous tissue before entering the superior vena cava and the right atrium. A Dacron cuff located just under the skin at the exit site anchors the catheter and prevents entry of bacteria. Maintenance of the catheter requires heparinization to prevent clotting and dressing changes at the exit site to prevent infection. Specific procedures for catheter care will vary among health care institutions. General nursing care includes flushing the line with small doses of heparin in normal saline, infused over 24 to 48 hours or after each use of the catheter. The dressings are changed three times a week, and the exit site is assessed for redness, swelling, discharge, pain, or protrusion of the Dacron cuff. The site should be cleansed aseptically with alcohol followed by povidone-iodine. An anti-infective topical agent is applied to the site, and an occlusive gauze or transparent dressing is applied. The infusion cap at the end of the catheter is changed weekly to prevent infection. Patient education is essential for prevention and management of potential complications including catheter breakage, air emboli and infection.

Measures to reduce cachexia usually do not prolong survival but improve the quality of life. Creative dietary therapies, enteral (tube) feedings or total parenteral nutrition may be chosen to deliver nourishment. Nursing care is also directed towards prevention of trauma, infection and other complications that increase metabolic demands.

Relief of Pain

It is estimated that 60 to 96 per cent of all individuals with progressive malignant disease experience pain. Although patients with cancer may have acute pain, their pain is more frequently characterized as chronic. (For a complete discussion of pain, see following section.) As in other situations involving pain, the experience of cancer pain is influenced by both physical and psychosocial factors.

Malignancies can cause pain in a variety of ways. Bone destruction as a result of tumour invasion is one of the most devastating sources of pain. Bone involvement is seen commonly in multiple myeloma and cancers of the breast and prostate. Infiltration or compression of nerves can cause pain that is described as sharp and burning. Vertebral metastasis involving spinal nerves may occur with breast and lung cancer. Tumours causing lymphatic or venous obstruction may lead to a dull, throbbing type of pain. This is often associated with lymphoma or Kaposi's sarcoma. Ischaemic pain results from any tumour that occludes arterial circulation. Obstruction of hollow viscera is often associated with colon cancer. Patients with abdominal obstruction often complain of pain that is dull and poorly localized. Finally, tumours invading skin or mucous membranes may cause pain associated with inflammation, ulceration, infection and tissue necrosis; this is common in patients with progressive head and neck malignancies and Kaposi's sarcoma.

Pain is also associated with various cancer treatments. Acute pain is linked with trauma that results from surgical procedures. Tissue necrosis, peripheral neuropathies and stomatitis are potential sources of pain which may occur with certain chemotherapeutic agents. Radiotherapy can cause inflammation of the skin or irradiated organs.

In today's society, most people expect pain to pass quickly, and in fact it usually does. However, although it is controllable, cancer pain is often irreversible and not quickly resolved. For many patients, pain is a signal of continued tumour progression and impending death. As anticipation and anxiety about the pain increase, the patient's perception of the pain is heightened, producing fear and additional pain. Chronic cancer pain, then, can be best described as a cycle progressing from pain to anxiety to fear and back to pain again.

Pain tolerance, the point past which pain can no longer be tolerated, varies among patients. Pain tolerance is decreased by fatigue, anxiety, fear of death, anger, powerlessness, social isolation, changes in role identity, loss of independence and past experiences. Tolerance to pain is enhanced by adequate rest and sleep, diversion, mood elevation, empathy, antidepressants, anti-anxiety agents and analgesics.

Successful management of cancer pain is based on a thorough and precise pain assessment that examines physical, psychosocial, environmental and spiritual factors. A multidisciplinary team effort is essential to determine the optimal approach for pain management. Prevention and reduction of pain serve to lessen anxiety and break the previously described pain cycle. This can be best accomplished by administering analgesics on a regularly scheduled basis as prescribed and not as needed (prn). A variety of pharmacological and nonpharmacological approaches offer the best methods of providing effective cancer pain management. No reasonable approaches, even those that may be somewhat invasive, should be overlooked because of a poor or terminal prognosis. Improving the quality of life is as valuable as preventing a painful death.

Progression through the Grieving Process

Because there are so many kinds of cancer (over 100), the diagnosis of cancer need not indicate a fatal outcome. Many forms of cancer are curable; many others achieve 'cure' status if they are treated early. Despite these facts, many patients and their loved ones view cancer as a fatal disease that is inevitably accompanied by pain, suffering, debility and emaciation. Grieving is a normal response to these fears and to the losses anticipated or experienced by the patient with cancer. These may include loss of health, normal sensations, body image, social interaction, sexuality and intimacy. The patient, family and friends may grieve the loss of quality time to spend with others, the loss of a future and unfulfilled plans and the loss of control over one's own body and emotional reactions.

The patient and loved ones who have just been informed by their doctor about the diagnosis of cancer frequently respond with shock, numbness and disbelief. It is often during this stage that the patient and loved ones are called on to make important initial decisions about treatment, and they require the support of the doctor, nurse and other health care team members to make these decisions. An important role of the nurse is to answer questions and to clarify information provided by the doctor. In addition to assessing the response of the patient and significant others to the diagnosis and planned treatment, the nurse assists them in framing their questions and concerns, identifying resources and support people (e.g., spiritual adviser, counsellor) and communicating and sharing their concerns with each other.

As the patient and loved ones progress through the grieving process, they may express feelings of anger, frustration and depression. During this time, the nurse encourages them to verbalize their feelings in an atmosphere of trust and support. The nurse continues to assess their reactions and provides assistance and support as they confront and learn to deal with new problems.

If the patient enters the terminal phase of disease, it may become obvious that the patient and loved ones are at different stages of the grieving process. Therefore, the nurse assists them at these different stages to come to grips with their reactions and feelings. Physical support, including holding the patient's hand or just being present at the bedside, frequently contributes to feelings of trust and peace of mind. Maintaining contact with the surviving family members after death of the cancer patient may help them to progress through the process of grieving and to work through their feelings of loss.

Improved Body Image and Self-Esteem

A positive approach is essential when caring for the patient with an altered body image. Independence and continued participation in self-care and decision making are encouraged to help the patient retain control and a sense of self-worth. The patient is encouraged to express feelings about threats to body image. Assistance is provided to enable the patient to assume those tasks and participate in those activities of most importance and interest to the patient. The nurse serves as a good listener and counsellor to the patient as well as to loved ones. Referral to a support group for cancer patients, their families or both often provides additional assistance in coping with the changes resulting from cancer or its treatment.

The patient who is experiencing alterations in sexuality and sexual function is encouraged to share and discuss any concerns openly with the partner. Alternative forms of sexual expression are explored with the patient and partner to promote positive self-worth and acceptance. The nurse who identifies serious physiological, psychological or communication difficulties related to sexuality or sexual function is in a key position to assist the patient and partner to seek further counselling if necessary.

► *Evaluation*
► Expected Outcomes

1. Patient experiences no infection or inflammation.
2. Exhibits no bleeding.
3. Maintains adequate tissue (skin and mucous membrane) integrity.
4. Maintains adequate nutritional status.
5. Achieves relief of pain and discomfort.
6. Progresses through grieving process.
7. Exhibits improved body image and self-esteem.

Rehabilitation

The diagnosis of cancer may be accompanied by emotional turmoil and changes in lifestyle or daily habits. However, with advances in diagnosis and treatment, survival rates are improving. Many patients, including those who receive primary surgical treatment and adjuvant chemotherapy or irradiation, are returning to work and their usual activities of daily living. These patients may encounter a variety of problems, including coping with changes in functional abilities and attitudes of employers, co-workers, families and friends.

Nurses play an important role in the rehabilitation of the cancer patient. Assessment of body image changes as a result of disfiguring treatments is necessary in order to facilitate the patient's adjustment to changes in appearance or functional abilities. The nurse can refer the patient and loved ones to a variety of support groups such as BACUP (British Association of Cancer United Patients) and CancerLink, or, for example, to groups specifically for people who have had a mastectomy or laryngectomy. (BACUP and CancerLink provide information about sources of help and support for patients with cancer.) Nurses also collaborate with physiotherapists and occupational therapists in improving the patient's abilities and use of prosthetic devices.

Some patients return to work and continue to receive either chemotherapy or radiotherapy for extended periods of time. These people may experience transient problems such as lethargy, fatigue, anorexia, nausea or vomiting. Nurses assess for the existence of these problems and assist the patient in identifying strategies for coping with them. For patients with gastrointestinal disturbances following chemotherapy, altering work hours or receiving treatments in the evenings may prove to be helpful. Nurses collaborate with dieticians to help patients plan meals that will be tolerable and meet nutritional requirements.

Discrimination against recovering cancer patients has been demonstrated in several forms. Often employers lack the understanding of the variability that exists in the diagnosis of cancer in terms of functional capacity and prognosis. As a result, employers may be hesitant to hire or continue employment of people with cancer, especially if continued treatment regimes might require adjustments in work schedules. Attitudes of co-workers can become a problem when related to communication impairments such as those experienced by some head and neck cancer patients. Finally, employers, co-workers, friends and families may continue to view the person as being 'sick' despite ongoing recovery or completion of treatment.

Nurses can participate in efforts to educate employers and the public in general to ensure that the rights of patients with cancer are maintained. Whenever possible, nurses assist patients and families to resume pre-existing roles. Nurses can encourage patients to regain the highest level of independence possible. The diagnosis of cancer need not be a 'death sentence'. Many people can resume active roles in life.

Considerations for the Elderly

Cancer nurses are working with increasing numbers of elderly patients. Approximately 55 per cent of all cancers occur after 65 years of age. Common malignancies in the elderly include multiple myeloma, non-Hodgkin's lymphoma, oropharyngeal cancers and cancers of the bladder, breast, colon, lung and prostate.

It is important for nurses working with this population to understand the normal physiological changes that occur with ageing. These changes include decreased skin elasticity; decreased skeletal mass, structure and strength; decreased organ function and structure; impaired immune system mechanisms; alterations in neurological function; and altered drug absorption, distribution, metabolism and elimination. These changes ultimately influence the elderly patient's ability to tolerate treatment for cancer. In addition, many elderly patients have other chronic diseases that may also limit tolerance of treatment.

Potential toxicities associated with chemotherapeutic agents such as cisplatin may be enhanced by a decline in renal blood flow and creatinine clearance normally associated with the ageing process. Cardiac toxicities associated with chemotherapy with doxorubicin may be more pronounced in the elderly patient who already has a decreased cardiac output as a result of normal physiological ageing.

The elderly person receiving radiotherapy may have a delayed recovery of normal tissues as a result of the changes in tissue repair associated with ageing. The potential adverse effects involving the bone marrow, gastrointestinal tract and skin may be enhanced, leading to an increased incidence and severity of myelosuppression, skin impairments, anorexia, nausea, vomiting and diarrhoea.

The older patient is often slower to recover from surgical interventions. Decreased tissue healing capacity and pulmonary and cardiovascular functioning may increase the risk of the patient developing postoperative complications such as atelectasis, pneumonia and wound infections.

The nurse must be aware of the increased risk of complications following cancer treatment in the elderly and carefully assess for signs and symptoms of adverse effects. In addition, the elderly patient is instructed to report all symptoms to the doctor. It is not uncommon for the elderly patient to delay reporting symptoms, attributing them to 'old age'. Many elderly people do not want to report illness for fear of loss of independence, role functions and financial security. The nurse acts as a patient advocate, encouraging independence and providing support when indicated.

Care of the Patient With Advanced Cancer

The patient with advanced cancer is likely to experience many of the problems previously described, but all to a greater degree. Symptoms of gastrointestinal disturbances, nutritional problems, weight loss and cachexia predispose to skin breakdown, fluid and electrolyte problems and infection. Although not all cancer patients experience pain, those who do often fear that it will be treated inadequately. Although treatment at this stage of illness is likely to be palliative rather than curative, prevention and appropriate management of problems can improve the quality of the patient's life considerably. For example, use of analgesia on a regular basis at set intervals rather than on an 'as needed' basis frequently breaks the cycle of tension and anxiety associated with waiting until pain becomes severe and pain relief is inadequate once the analgesic is given. Working with the patient and loved ones as well as other health care providers on a pain management programme based on the patient's individual requirements frequently increases patient comfort and sense of control. In addition, the dose of opioid analgesic required is often reduced as pain becomes more manageable and other medications (e.g., sedatives, tranquillizers, muscle relaxants) are added to assist in relieving pain.

The patient may be a candidate for radiotherapy or surgical intervention to relieve severe pain. The consequences of these procedures (e.g., percutaneous nerve block, cordotomy) are explained to the patient and loved ones, and measures are taken to prevent complications resulting from altered sensation, immobility and changes in bowel and bladder function.

With the appearance of each new symptom, the patient often experiences dread and fear that the disease is progressing. However, one cannot assume that all symptoms are related to the cancer. The new symptoms and problems are evaluated and treated aggressively if possible to increase the patient's comfort and improve the quality of life.

Weakness, immobility, fatigue and inactivity often occur in the advanced stages of cancer as a result of the tumour itself, treatment, inadequate nutritional intake or dyspnoea. The nurse works with the patient to set realistic goals and to provide rest balanced with planned activities and exercise. The nurse assists the patient in identifying less energy-consuming methods of accomplishing tasks and activities which are most valued.

Efforts are made throughout the course of the disease to provide the patient with as much control and independence as is wanted, but with assurance that support and assistance will be provided. Additionally, the health care team works with the patient and loved ones to ascertain and adhere to the patient's wishes about treatment methods and care as the terminal phase of illness and death are approached.

Hospice

For many years society was unable to cope appropriately with patients in the most advanced stages of cancer, and patients were left in acute care settings to die rather than at home or in facilities specifically designed to manage the needs of patients with terminal disease. The needs of these people do not require advanced technology or sophisticated equipment, but are best managed by a comprehensive multidisciplinary programme that focuses on symptom relief and psychosocial and spiritual support for the patient and loved ones when cure and remission are no longer possible. The concept of hospice, which originated in Great Britain, best addresses these needs.

Because of high costs associated with maintaining free-standing hospices, care is often provided by co-ordinating hospital-based and community services. Although doctors, social workers, spiritual advisers, dieticians, physiotherapists and volunteers are involved in patient care, nurses are most often the co-ordinators of all

hospice activities. It is essential that community-based nurses possess great skill in the assessment and management of pain, nutrition, bowel dysfunction and skin impairments.

Specialist community nurses (such as MacMillan nurses) are also actively involved in bereavement counselling. Through collaboration with other support disciplines, nurses often assist patients and their loved ones to cope with changes in role identity, home structure, grief and loss. In many instances, family support for survivors continues for a period of approximately one year.

Oncological Emergencies

In addition to assessment and management of the previously described problems experienced by the patient with cancer, the nurse also has an important role in the prompt detection of complications of cancer and its treatment which are considered to be oncological emergencies.

As a result of the underlying malignancy, its metastasis or the effects of treatment, the oncology patient is at risk for the development of a unique group of acute conditions requiring immediate medical or surgical intervention. Common oncological emergencies include superior vena cava syndrome, spinal cord compression, hypercalcaemia, pericardial effusion, disseminated intravascular coagulation and the syndrome of inappropriate secretion of antidiuretic hormone.

Superior Vena Cava Syndrome

The superior vena cava is the major site of venous drainage from the head, neck, arms and upper thorax. Positioned within the rigid compartment of the mediastinum, it is closely surrounded by major structures, including the heart, lungs, vertebral bodies and oesophagus. Consequently, compression of the superior vena cava by tumour or enlarged lymph nodes can result in markedly impaired venous drainage of the head, neck, arms and thorax. In the vast majority of patients, the superior vena cava syndrome occurs with lung cancer, but it can also occur with lymphoma and metastasis from other sites.

The clinical features of impaired venous drainage usually develop gradually over a period of three to four weeks, but they may also appear suddenly. Progressive shortness of breath, dyspnoea, cough and facial swelling are common. Oedema of the neck, arms, hands and thorax may develop with associated sensations of skin tightness and difficulty swallowing. The jugular, temporal and arm veins may be engorged and distended. Dilated thoracic vessels often cause prominent venous patterns visible on the chest wall. Continued venous obstruction may lead to increased intracranial pressure, associated visual disturbances, headache and altered mental status. If untreated, the superior vena cava syndrome may lead to cerebral anoxia, laryngeal oedema bronchial obstruction and death.

Management

Prompt diagnosis and treatment are essential in managing this syndrome. Radiotherapy is the treatment of choice to decrease the tumour size and alleviate symptoms. Chemotherapy is used when the tumour is known to be responsive (lymphoma or small cell lung cancer). Other supportive measures such as oxygen therapy and diuretics may be used.

Nursing Care

Nursing care includes identifying patients at risk for developing superior vena cava syndrome. Clinical features detected by the nursing assessment are reported to the doctor and are investigated promptly. Continued assessment of the patient's cardiopulmonary and neurological status is essential. As a result of increasing difficulty in breathing and progressive oedema, many patients become anxious and fearful of suffocating. Nursing care is directed toward facilitating breathing by positioning, promoting comfort and reducing anxiety. Minimizing the patient's energy expenditure by energy conservation techniques may minimize shortness of breath. In addition, the patient's fluid volume status is monitored and fluids are administered cautiously to minimize oedema.

Spinal Cord Compression

Malignancies such as breast, lung, kidney and prostate cancers, myeloma and lymphoma that metastasize to the spine may cause spinal cord compression. Most lesions develop in the space between the periosteum of the vertebrae and the dura of the spinal cord (extradural), leading to destruction of the vertebral bodies and epidural tissue. Less commonly, tumours develop in the spinal cord itself.

Spinal cord compression is characterized by pain that may be constant and exacerbated by movement, coughing or sneezing. The location and characteristics of the pain depend on the area of involvement of the spinal cord. Neurological dysfunction develops when cord compression is prolonged or severe, and may include motor and sensory deficit. Sensory deficits generally begin as loss of pinprick sensation, progressing to decreased vibratory sense and finally to loss of position sense. The sense of touch usually remains intact even when motor dysfunction is advanced. Motor loss (weakness and ataxia) is often present at the time of diagnosis. Progression of compression ultimately leads to flaccid paralysis. The occurrence of other dysfunctions such as urinary and faecal incontinence is dependent on the level of the lesion compressing the cord. Compression of upper motor neurons above S2 can lead to bladder-overflow incontinence. Cord compression at levels S3, S4 and S5 can result in flaccid sphincter tone and bowel incontinence.

Prompt neurological assessment is essential if sensory and motor function is to be maintained or restored. Although a variety of diagnostic procedures may assist in identifying the compressing lesion, the myelogram is considered the most accurate means of localizing the site of compression. Once the diagnosis is established, medical intervention is quickly initiated because symptoms can progress within a relatively short period of time.

Management

Radiotherapy is most commonly used to reduce tumour size and halt disease progression. In most cases, surgical decompression is not used unless the symptoms progress despite irradiation or the patient has previously received a maximum amount of radiation to the area of the cord involved. Surgery may be indicated when the tumour involved in known to be insensitive or nonresponsive to radiotherapy. Steroids are often given in addition to radiotherapy to decrease the oedema and inflammation at the site of compression. Recovery of neurological function is influenced by promptness of diagnosis and treatment. Despite treatment, patients who develop complete paralysis usually do not regain neurological function.

Nursing Care

Nursing care includes ongoing assessment of neurological function in order to identify existing and progressing dysfunction. Most patients will require both pharmacological and nonpharmacological measures to control pain. Because of pain and decreased functional abilities associated with spinal cord compression, patients are often at risk for the hazards of immobility such as skin breakdown, urinary stasis, thrombophlebitis and decreased clearance of pulmonary secretions. Nursing measures are directed towards prevention of these problems and maintenance of muscle tone through range-of-motion exercises. For patients with bladder or bowel incontinence, intermittent urinary catheterization and bowel training programmes are essential. Additionally, the patient and loved ones will require assistance in coping with pain and alterations in body functioning, lifestyles, roles and level of independence.

Hypercalcaemia

Hypercalcaemia is a potentially life-threatening complication that is characterized by abnormal calcium metabolism resulting in serum calcium levels in excess of 2.74 mmol/l of blood. The skeletal system serves as the storage site for approximately 99 per cent of all the calcium in the body. Hypercalcaemia associated with cancer occurs when the release of calcium from the bones is more than the kidneys can excrete or the bones can reabsorb. (See section on fluid and electrolyte balance, above, for a discussion of normal calcium metabolism.) Hypercalcaemia is commonly seen in patients with multiple myeloma, and breast, squamous cell lung and prostatic cancer. Less commonly, it develops in patients with leukaemia, lymphoma or renal cancer.

The underlying cause of hypercalcaemia in the cancer patient varies. Approximately 70 per cent of all cancer patients with hypercalcaemia have metastatic bone disease. In this situation, direct invasion of the bone by tumour cells causes bone destruction and subsequent release of calcium. Hypercalcaemia may also be caused by the production of osteoclast-activating factor and prostaglandins. These substances, produced by cancer cells, stimulate the breakdown of bone and the release of calcium. Hypercalcaemia may also be caused by tumours that produce parathyroid-like substances and promote release of calcium from bones.

Nursing Care

Nursing care begins with identification of patients at risk for hypercalcaemia. Careful nursing assessment will assist in identifying the signs and symptoms of hypercalcaemia. Patients at risk are encouraged to maintain adequate fluid intake of 2 to 3 litres of fluid per day unless contraindicated by existing renal or cardiac disease. The importance of mobility must be emphasized in order to prevent demineralization and breakdown of bones. Patients with alterations in mental status and mobility as a result of hypercalcaemia will require additional nursing measures to prevent the hazards of immobility and promote safety.

Pericardial Effusion/Cardiac Tamponade

Cardiac tamponade is a cardiovascular disorder that occurs when fluid accumulates in the pericardial space and compresses the heart, impairing cardiac filling during diastole. Neoplastic disease or its treatment is the most common cause of cardiac tamponade. Pericardial disease secondary to neoplastic growth usually occurs by direct invasion from adjacent thoracic tumours (lung and breast cancers) or metastasis to the pericardium (lymphomas, leukaemias and melanomas). Fluid produced by the invasive tumour, metastatic lesion or pericardial tissue in response to the malignant processes accumulates in the pericardial space, increases pressure on the myocardium and impedes expansion of the ventricles. As ventricular volume and cardiac output fall, the cardiac pump fails and circulatory collapse develops. Radiotherapy to the mediastinal area has also been implicated in pericardial fibrosis, pericarditis and resultant cardiac tamponade, which may occur months or even years after the cessation of radiotherapy.

Pericardial disease and cardiac tamponade may occur gradually or very rapidly. Gradual fluid accumulation allows the parietal (outer) layer of the pericardial space to stretch and compensate for the increased pressure. Therefore, large fluid volumes may accumulate before symptoms appear. However, when fluid accumulates rapidly, the pericardial pressures rise quickly and compensatory stretching cannot occur. Increased central venous pressures and jugular distension develop. Distension of neck veins during inspiration (Kussmaul's sign) is suggestive of pericardial disease. Pulsus paradoxus (a decrease in systolic blood pressure of more than 10 mmHg during inspiration with strengthening of the pulse on expiration) may be detected in moderate cardiac tamponade. Heart sounds diminish, and increased areas of cardiac dullness may be percussed. As cardiac output decreases, compensatory tachycardia and systemic vascular resistance occur. As tamponade progresses, the systolic blood pressure continues to fall and the diastolic pressure rises in compensatory effort, creating a narrow pulse pressure. Shortness of breath and tachypnoea may also develop. Weakness, diaphoresis, lethargy and altered consciousness due to decreased cerebral perfusion may result. Circulatory collapse with cardiac arrest is imminent if untreated.

ECG tracings during pericardial effusion usually reveal nonspecific T-wave changes with reduced QRS voltage. Electrical alternans (QRS complexes that alternate in size) is common with tamponade. The chest X-ray film is not usually diagnostic with small-volume pericardial effusions. However, with larger effusions, a 'water-bottle' heart appearance (obliteration of vessel contour and cardiac chambers) becomes apparent on X-ray. Echocardiography and computed tomography are valuable in the diagnosis of cardiac tamponade and evaluation of the effectiveness of treatment.

Management

The usual treatment of cardiac tamponade is pericardiocentesis (the aspiration of the pericardial fluid by a large-bore needle inserted into the pericardial space). Unfortunately, the benefits of pericardiocentesis in malignant effusions are only temporary, and fluid accumulation frequently recurs. Pericardial windows are often created surgically as a palliative measure to drain pericardial effusions into the pleural space. Catheters may also be placed in the pericardial space, and sclerosing agents (such as tetracycline) may be injected to prevent effusive reaccumulation. In mild effusions, prednisone and diuretics may be prescribed with careful monitoring of patient status.

Nursing Care

Nursing assessment includes frequent monitoring of vital signs; assessment for pulsus paradoxus; monitoring of ECG tracings; assessment of heart and lung sounds, neck vein filling, level of consciousness, respiratory status, and skin colour and temperature; accurate monitoring of intake and output; and laboratory studies such as arterial blood gases and electrolytes.

Appropriate nursing actions may include elevation of the head of the patient's bed; minimization of physical activity to reduce oxygen requirements; supplemental oxygen as prescribed; frequent oral hygiene; turning and encouraging the patient to cough and take deep breaths every two hours; reorientation, if needed; supportive measures; maintenance of patent intravenous access; and appropriate patient education.

Disseminated Intravascular Coagulation

Disseminated intravascular coagulation (consumption coagulation) is the abnormal activation of both the coagulation and fibrinolytic mechanisms, resulting in the consumption of coagulation factors and platelets. Disseminated intravascular coagulation can occur with any malignant process; however, it is most commonly associated with cancers of the lung, gastrointestinal system and prostate, and melanoma and the leukaemias. Certain chemotherapeutic agents are also thought to precipitate disseminated intravascular coagulation. These drugs include vincristine, methotrexate, 6-mercaptopurine, prednisone and L-asparaginase. Certain disease processes commonly seen in the cancer patient may also initiate this condition, including sepsis, hepatic failure, and anaphylaxis.

Clot formation is initiated by triggering of the intrinsic or extrinsic mechanisms of normal coagulation. Malignant tumours stimulate the intrinsic coagulation pathway during metastasis when endothelial injury occurs. The extrinsic coagulation pathway is also activated by the release of thromboplastin (or thromboplastin-like substances) from tumour cells. Once activated, the clotting cascade continues to consume clotting factors and platelets and forms fibrin clots in the microvasculature. These clots place the patient at high risk for thrombus formation, infarction and bleeding. The last stage of the clotting cascade, fibrinolysis, also continues to occur at an abnormally high rate in disseminated intravascular coagulation. Fibrinolysis, or clot dissolution, breaks down clots that have formed and places the patient at an even higher danger of haemorrhage.

Laboratory results indicative of disseminated intravascular coagulation include prolonged prothrombin time and partial thromboplastin time, decreased platelet counts and fibrinogen levels and increased fibrin split products. Bleeding from multiple body sites is commonly found in patients with disseminated intravascular coagulation. Clinical symptoms of this syndrome are varied and depend on the organ system involved in thrombus/infarct or bleeding episodes.

Management

Treatment of disseminated intravascular coagulation centres on control of the underlying disease process. Supportive measures with antithrombinolytic agents such as heparin or antithrombin III are often employed to decrease stimulation of the coagulation pathways. Transfusion with fresh frozen plasma or cryoprecipitates (which contain clotting factors and fibrinogen) may be used in conjunction with heparin therapy, but is rarely effective when used alone. Antifibrinolytic agents such as E-aminocaproic acid are controversial forms of therapy and are associated with high incidence of thrombus formation.

Nursing Care

Indicated nursing assessments for the patient experiencing disseminated intravascular coagulation include monitoring of vital signs; accurate fluid intake and output measurement; assessment of skin colour and temperature; assessment of lung, heart and bowel sounds; assessment of level of consciousness; assessment of headache, visual disturbances, chest pain, decreased urinary output and abdominal tenderness; assessments of all body orifices, tube insertion sites, incisions and bodily excretions for bleeding; and monitoring of indicated laboratory test results.

Appropriate nursing care involves the minimization of physical activity to decrease risk of injury and oxygen requirements; increasing pressure to all venipuncture sites; minimization of invasive procedures; maintenance of adequate oral hygiene; assisting the patient to turn, cough and take deep breaths every two hours; reorientation, if needed; maintenance of a safe environment; and appropriate patient education and supportive measures.

Syndrome of Inappropriate Secretion of Antidiuretic Hormone

The syndrome of inappropriate secretion of antidiuretic hormone is characterized by continuous, uncontrolled release of antidiuretic hormone. This leads to increased extracellular fluid volume with decreased osmolality, water intoxication, hyponatraemia, increased urine osmolality and increased excretion of urinary sodium. The most common cause of the syndrome is malignancy; it occurs most often in patients with cancers of the lung, pancreas, duodenum, brain, oesophagus, colon, ovary, larynx, prostate and nasopharynx, and Hodgkin's disease, thymomas and lymphosarcomas. Two antineoplastic drugs, vincristine and cyclophosphamide, also stimulate antidiuretic hormone secretion. Certain processes commonly seen in the cancer patient, such as pain, stress, trauma and haemorrhage, are also associated with inappropriate secretion of antidiuretic hormone.

The antidiuretic hormone produced, stored and released by tumour cells is identical to antidiuretic hormone normally produced by the posterior pituitary gland. When antidiuretic hormone is produced, the distal renal tubules and collecting ducts of the kidney conserve and reabsorb water. In the syndrome of inappropriate secretion of antidiuretic hormone, the posterior pituitary becomes unresponsive to the normal feedback mechanisms, and water conservation continues despite decreasing serum osmolality and increasing urine osmolality. With continued absorption of fluid, circulatory volume increases and sodium is actively excreted by the kidneys in compensation. If the serum sodium levels fall below 120 mmol/l, patients usually display symptoms of hyponatraemia, which include personality changes, irritability, nausea, anorexia, vomiting, weight gain, lethargy and confusion. If serum sodium levels continue to fall below 110 mmol/l, then seizure, coma and death may result. Oedema is rarely seen.

Laboratory findings indicative of the syndrome of inappropriate secretion of antidiuretic hormone include: (1) serum hyponatraemia; (2) increased urine osmolality; and (3) increased urinary sodium. Decreased blood urea, creatinine and serum albumin levels secondary to dilution may also occur. Abnormal results of water load tests would also indicate the presence of the syndrome.

Management

Treatment of the syndrome of inappropriate secretion of antidiuretic hormone depends on the severity of symptoms. With mild symptoms, fluids are limited to 500 to 1,000 ml/day to increase the serum sodium level and decrease fluid overload. When neurological symptoms are severe, parenteral sodium replacement and diuretic therapy are indicated. Electrolytes are monitored carefully during treatment since secondary magnesium, potassium and calcium imbalances may occur.

Following control of the symptoms, the underlying malignancy is treated. If water excess continues despite oncological treatment, pharmacological intervention may be indicated to control symptoms.

Nursing Care

Nursing assessment of the patient with the syndrome of inappropriate secretion of antidiuretic hormone includes accurate measurement of intake and output and assessment of level of consciousness, lung and heart sounds, vital signs, daily weight and urine specific gravity. The patient is also assessed for nausea, vomiting, anorexia, oedema, fatigue and lethargy. The nurse monitors laboratory test results, including serum electrolytes, osmolality, urea, creatinine and urinary sodium and osmolality.

Indicated nursing care involves minimization of activity; appropriate oral hygiene measures; maintenance of environmental safety measures; reorientation, if necessary; fluid restriction, if necessary; and appropriate patient education and supportive measures.

THE PERSON EXPERIENCING PAIN

Pain disables and distresses more people than any single disease entity. It is probably the most common and compelling reason why a person seeks health care. Most medical–surgical problems are associated with pain, resulting either from the disease process, diagnostic tests or treatment modalities.

Ironically, little is known about pain. Algology—the study of pain—is a new science. Most experts consider pain a mysterious phenomenon that defies precise definition. At the very least, it appears to have three components: (1) a stimulus, physical or mental; (2) a bodily sensation of hurting; and (3) the reaction of the person experiencing it.

Despite the prevalence of pain, there is substantial evidence for the failure of health carers to relieve patients' pain. Marks and Sacher (1973) report that the majority of medical patients who took part in a survey reported severe distress from their pain, yet their doctors prescribed low doses of analgesics, and nurses under-administered the drugs prescribed. Seers (1987) reports evidence of poor pain control among postoperative patients, and Hunt, Stollar, Littlejohns *et al.* (1977) found that nurses accept too readily the presence of unrelieved pain, that they enquire about patients' pain only during drug rounds and that they do not appreciate their own potential as agents of pain relief.

The nurse spends more time with the patient with pain than any other member of the health care team and therefore has the opportunity to make a significant contribution towards increasing the patient's comfort and relieving pain. The doctor must seek to verify the patient's complaint of pain by establishing the cause and treating it. The nurse, in addition to collaborating with the doctor towards this goal, also makes a major contribution to palliative pain relief—relief of pain that does not necessarily involve curing the cause of the pain.

In clinical practice, when direct care is given to a patient with pain, it is essential that the nurse adopts the patient's point of view about pain. A cardinal rule in the care of patients with pain is that all pain is real, regardless of its cause—even when the cause remains unknown. Therefore, the nurse's verification of pain is based simply on the patient's indication that it exists.

Within this context, the nursing definition of pain may be stated as whatever bodily hurt patients say they have, existing whenever they say it does. This definition encompasses two important points that are ultimately relevant to assessment, care and evaluation.

First, the nurse believes patients when they indicate that they have pain. It is important to avoid making the erroneous judgement that patients do not have pain because no physical origin can be identified. Although some painful sensations are initiated by or sustained by patients' mental or psychological state, they actually feel a sensation of pain; they do not merely think or imagine that they have pain. Furthermore, painful states initiated by psychological states, such as anxiety, are usually accompanied by physical changes, such as decreased blood flow or muscle tension. Most painful sensations are the result of two sets of stimuli: physical and mental or emotional. Therefore, the assessment of pain involves obtaining information about the physical and mental or emotional causes of pain. Nursing care involves attempting to reduce or relieve both sources of pain.

The second point to keep in mind is that what the patient 'says' about pain need not be limited to verbal statements. Some patients cannot or will not express their pain verbally. Therefore, the nurse is also responsible for observing the many nonverbal behaviours that indicate the presence of the pain sensation and all that the patient experiences in relation to the pain.

Some patients deny pain, and they pose a different assessment problem. Although it is important to believe the patient who admits to pain, it is equally important to be alert to patients who deny pain when they do in fact 'hurt'. A very common reason is fear of becoming addicted to their drugs. A nurse who suspects pain in a patient who denies it should explore with the patient the reason for suspecting pain, such as the fact that the disorder or procedure is usually painful, or that the patient grimaces when moving, or avoids any movement. The nurse should also explore with the patient any reason that may cause the denial of pain, such as fear of addiction or further treatment.

Nursing Assessment

Assessment of the patient experiencing pain involves the following:

- Recognizing whether the pain is acute or chronic.
- Identifying the phases of the experience.
- Observing the patient's behavioural responses.
- Identifying the factors that influence the pain and the patient's response to it.

A thorough assessment is of the utmost importance. To help the patient with pain, the nurse must know that pain is occurring and how it is affecting the patient. This is not always obvious. The patient may try to hide the pain, or there may be a language barrier. Or, the patient may exhibit minimal responses to pain and, therefore, may appear not to experience pain.

Differences Between Acute and Chronic Pain

Pain specialists agree that there are two types of pain— acute and chronic. The differences between acute and chronic pain have implications for both assessment and care.

The terms acute and chronic are classifications of pain, based on the duration of pain. Quite simply, acute pain is of brief duration and chronic pain is prolonged. Acute does not necessarily mean severe; acute pain may range in intensity from mild to severe.

Acute Pain

Acute pain, which is a very common daily occurrence, is usually defined as an episode of pain that lasts from a split second to about six months. Generally, it serves the purpose of warning the patient that some degree of damage has occurred within the body that requires some form of treatment or care. Usually, organic disease or injury is present, although healing may also be accompanied by acute pain. As the healing process progresses, the pain subsides and gradually disappears.

Injuries or diseases that cause acute pain may require treatment or may heal spontaneously. For example, a prick of the finger may heal rapidly, the pain subsiding quickly, perhaps within a few minutes. In the case of a more drastic condition, such as appendicitis, surgery may be necessary. In these cases, the pain decreases with healing of the injury or surgical trauma.

Chronic Pain

Chronic pain is sometimes defined as pain that lasts for six months or longer, although six months is a rather arbitrary period of time for differentiating between acute and chronic pain. An episode of pain may assume the characteristics of chronic pain long before six months have elapsed, or some types of pain may remain primarily acute in nature for longer than six months. Nevertheless, after six months, the majority of pain experiences are accompanied by problems associated with chronic pain. Chronic pain serves no useful purpose, and if it persists, the pain itself may become the major disorder.

The following are four common types of chronic pain, that is, prolonged pain experiences: (1) recurrent acute pain; (2) pain with obvious ongoing peripheral pathology; (3) chronic benign pain that may have peripheral or central pathology; and (4) chronic intractable benign pain syndrome.

Recurrent acute pain is intermittent pain. The patient has fairly well-defined episodes of pain interspersed with pain-free intervals. Because these episodes may recur over a period of years, recurrent acute pain is sometimes considered a type of chronic pain. Examples of recurrent acute pain are migraine headaches, sickle cell crises and exacerbations of rheumatoid arthritis.

Chronic benign pain may be due to peripheral or central (brain and spinal cord) pathology. The pathology is often unclear, but it is not life threatening, as in cancer. (Benign means nonmalignant.) An example of chronic benign pain with central pathology is post-stroke syndrome following a brain infarct. Low back pain, a very common example of chronic benign pain, may be due to peripheral pathology, such as ischaemic muscles, or central pathology, such as emotions causing muscle tension. As long as patients function well in daily life in spite of the pain, they usually remain classified in this category of chronic benign pain.

Chronic intractable benign pain syndrome has the

same characteristics as chronic benign pain, but the patient copes poorly. For example, the patient with low back pain may begin to use the pain to avoid dealing with marital or employment problems. Eventually, the patient may cope poorly with job or marriage.

Pain with ongoing peripheral pathology may be of limited or unlimited duration. An example of time-limited pain with obvious ongoing peripheral pathology is the pain related to cancer. The pain may be of limited duration because the patient is eventually relieved after months of painful treatments, or the patient lives only a few months. In either case, the pain does not last for an extended period. An example of pain with ongoing peripheral pathology and unlimited duration is pain associated with degenerative arthritis.

Phases of the Pain Experience

The patient may experience any or all of the three phases of a pain experience:

1. The anticipation of pain.
2. The sensation of pain.
3. The aftermath of pain.

Each of these phases must be assessed because each requires nursing care, not just the phase during which pain is sensed. Even the patient who has relatively persistent and chronic pain may experience modified forms of these phases as the pain waxes and wanes in intensity.

The anticipation or fear of pain is sometimes more difficult for the patient to bear than the actual sensation of pain. The anticipation phase affects the patient's response to the sensation of pain.

Of the three phases, the most frequently overlooked is probably the aftermath. However, close observation may reveal any number of behavioural responses indicating such feelings as fear, embarrassment or guilt. These feelings may last from hours to months following the cessation of the pain sensation.

Behavioural Responses

The patient's responses during any of the three phases of pain experience may be any one or a combination of possible reactions. These may include physiological manifestations, verbal statements, vocal behaviours, facial expressions, body movements, physical contact with others or alterations in response to the surrounding environment. These behaviours vary greatly from one person to another and may differ within the same person from one time to the next.

The nurse observes the patient's behavioural response to identify the following:

● The phase of pain the patient is experiencing (i.e., anticipation, sensation or aftermath).
● The intensity of the patient's pain. Whenever possible, it is helpful to ask the patient to rate the pain on a verbal or numerical scale (e.g., none, slight, moderate, severe or very severe; or 0 to 10: 0 = no pain, 10 = worst possible pain).
● The patient's tolerance for this particular painful sensation. Pain tolerance may be defined as the maximum intensity or duration of pain the person is willing to endure.
● Characteristics of the painful sensation. These include

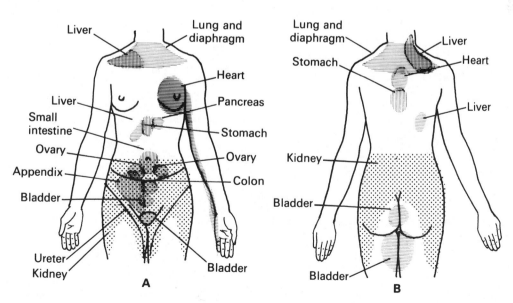

Figure 2.31 Referred pain. (A) Anterior view. (B) Posterior view. (Chaffee, E. E. and Lytle, I. M. (1980) *Basic Physiology and Anatomy* (4th edition), J. B. Lippincott, Philadelphia.)

location (see Figure 2.31 for areas to which pain in various organs may be referred), duration, rhythmicity (periods of waxing and waning of the intensity or existence of pain) and quality (e.g., pricking, burning, aching).

- Effects of pain on activities of daily living (e.g., sleep, appetite, concentration, interactions with others and physical movement). Acute pain is usually associated with anxiety, chronic pain with depression.
- What the patient believes will help relieve pain. Many patients have definite ideas about what will increase or decrease the intensity of their pain or what will make it more tolerable.
- The patient's concern about the pain. This may include a wide variety of items, such as financial burdens, prognosis, interference with role performance and body image changes.

Adaptation of Responses to Pain

Assessment of physiological and behavioural indications of pain is sometimes difficult, if not impossible, during periods of adaptation. During this time, observable clues to the existence and nature of pain may be absent or minimal. An understanding of adaptation, in contrast to the acute pain model, will help one avoid the mistaken conclusion that patients have no pain simply because they do not act as though they have pain (Figure 2.32).

Without realizing it, most members of the health care team are only familiar with the acute pain model. It is not unusual for the nurse or doctor to doubt the statement of a calm patient who says, ''I have severe pain in my right leg''. One mistakenly tends to expect all patients with pain to exhibit some behavioural or physiological responses associated with acute pain, including increased pulse and respiratory rates and the occurrence of pallor and perspiration. The patient in acute pain may also cry, moan, frown, immobilize a body part, clench the fist or withdraw.

The responses a particular patient makes to the sudden onset of acute pain may not be the ones made when pain lasts more than a few minutes or when it becomes chronic.

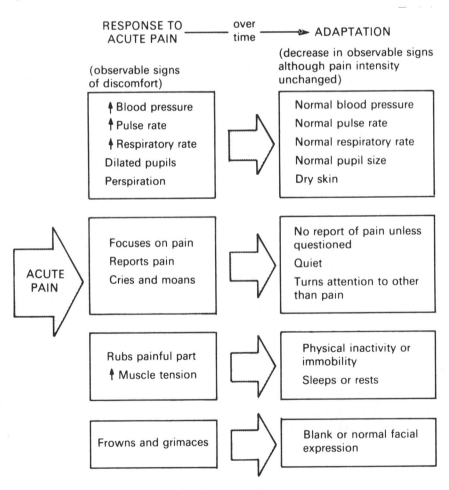

Figure 2.32 Adaptation to acute pain.

NAME ———————————————————————— DATE ———————————
LOCATION: Describe or point to area of pain. ———————————————————
——

QUALITY: What words best describe your pain?
——

INTENSITY: Rate your pain on a scale of 0 (no pain) to 10 (worst pain possible)
    At present ————————————————— 1 hour after medication ———————————
    Worst it gets ——————————————— Best it gets ———————————

ONSET: When did pain begin? ——————————— What time of day does it occur? ——————
    How often does it occur? ——————— How long does it last? ———————

EFFECT OF PAIN: What relieves the pain? ———————————————————————
    What makes the pain worse? ————————————————————————
    What other problems/symptoms occur with the pain? ——————————————
    How does the pain affect your life and your activities? ——————————————

PLAN:

Figure 2.33 Pain assessment tool.

Because the body is unable to sustain an intense physiological reaction to pain for weeks or years, or even several hours, a patient usually responds differently to acute and chronic pain.

Other behavioural features of pain may also change drastically. The fatigue of being in pain may leave the patient too exhausted to moan or cry. The patient may sleep even with severe pain. Or, patients may appear relaxed and involved in activities because they have become experts in the art of distracting themselves from pain. It is unfortunate when patients who have succeeded in minimizing the effect of chronic pain on their lives are then doubted by others.

Regardless of the type of adjustment made by the patient with chronic pain, pain over an extended period of time often produces behaviours typical of a disability. To some extent, the patient may be unable to continue the activities and interpersonal relationships engaged in before pain began. This may range from merely having to curtail participation in some vigorous sport to being unable to take care of personal needs, such as undressing.

Assessing the Harmful Effects of Pain

Special emphasis should be placed on assessing the harmful effects of pain. Frequently, the initial effect of a painful sensation is that of a helpful warning signal. Pain warns us that injury has occurred and that efforts must be taken to treat the injury or prevent further injury. After this initial warning signal, the existence of pain becomes a distressing and often harmful experience. Prolonged or chronic pain may prevent rehabilitation from an illness, or the pain itself may become a disability. Prolonged pain may result eventually in depression, persistent fatigue due to the inability to sleep well, weight gain or loss, problems with concentration, job loss and divorce or other interpersonal problems.

Acute pain may result in problems that delay recovery from the acute illness associated with the pain. Acute pain may disturb the amount and quality of sleep, decrease appetite, reduce fluid intake, and cause nausea and vomiting. For years, rest and nutrition have been recognized as important factors in recovery from illness. When pain interferes with sleep and nutritional intake, the patient is deprived of natural resources for getting well. In addition, nausea, vomiting or decreased fluid intake are potential threats to fluid and electrolyte balance.

Assessing the existence of pain, its nature and its distressing and harmful effects requires that the nurse ask specific questions and make careful observations. Global, nonspecific questions are insufficient because patients tend to give incomplete and inaccurate reports of their pain experience unless the nurse asks for details.

Assessment Tools

The initial assessment of pain may be accomplished using the assessment tool in Figure 2.33. If the location of pain is difficult to identify, the drawings in Figure 2.34 may also be used. Once completed, these forms may become a part of the health record. As the nurse gains experience in the assessment of pain, it may be necessary to expand the assessment tool.

To the extent possible, the information on the assessment tool should come from the patient. The health record and the patient's family or close friends may supplement the information obtained from the patient. However, it is important to remember that only the patient can feel the sensation of pain. Therefore, the patient is the only one who can rate it. Any verbal or numerical scale can be used as long the same scale is used with that patient each time.

The scale suggested on the assessment tool is 0 to 10 (0 = no pain, 10 = worst possible pain).

Pre-existing Factors Influencing the Pain Experience

All aspects of the patient's pain experience are subject to the influence of a large number of factors. These factors may increase or decrease the perceived intensity of pain, increase or decrease the patient's tolerance for pain and elicit one particular set of behavioural responses rather than other possible reactions.

Some are situational, arising from the immediate circumstances. Others, discussed here, were already a part of the patient's physical and emotional make-up before the onset of pain. This section focuses on only a few of

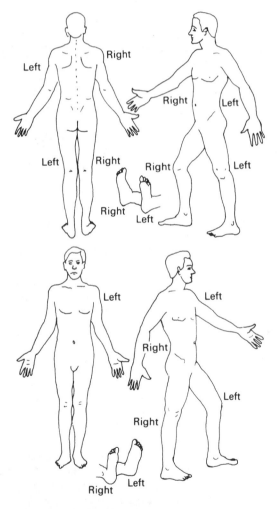

Figure 2.34 Pain assessment. The location of pain is noted and recorded on the figures as appropriate. (Melzack, R. (ed.) (1983) *Pain Measurement and Assessment*, Raven Press, New York, p. 216.)

these pre-existing factors that both influence the patient's pain experience and interfere with the nurse's understanding of it.

Neurophysiological Mechanisms of Pain

Specific neuroanatomical structures are involved in the transformation of a stimulus into a sensation perceived as painful by the patient. Unfortunately, this fact leads to the erroneous impression that there is a direct and predictable relationship between a stimulus and the occurrence of pain. As a result, the nurse may expect all patients exposed to the same stimulus (e.g., appendectomy) to experience the same intensity of pain. This is not true. Comparable lesions in different patients do not produce the same sensations of pain. A nurse who does not realize this may believe that the patient has pain when none exists, or that there is no pain or only slight pain when the patient is actually experiencing severe pain.

There is lack of agreement about the neurological mechanisms that underlie a sensation of pain. Currently, the three theories most frequently considered are (1) the specificity theory, (2) the pattern theory and (3) the gate control theory. These theories are not mutually exclusive, and none is considered entirely accurate or comprehensive. However, each makes a contribution to an understanding of what causes a person to perceive pain following a specific stimulus.

The gate control theory provides a particularly helpful basis for beginning to appreciate the individuality of the pain experience. It suggests that the existence and intensity of pain are dependent on various neurological activities that include the transmission of signals from the cortex and thalamus. These structures send signals that involve the individual's memories and feelings as well as cultural influences.

Endorphins and Encephalins

The term endorphin is a combination of two words: endogenous and morphine. It means 'morphine within'. Recently, it has been discovered that the human body manufactures its own supply of endorphins and encephalins, another morphine-like substance. (The terms endorphin and encephalin are sometimes used interchangeably.) When the body releases these substances, one effect is pain relief.

Endorphins and encephalins are peptides that are found in heavy concentrations in the central nervous system. These substances relieve pain by the same mechanism as morphine and other opioids. They are thought to inhibit impulses that would be felt as painful by blocking their transmission in the brain and spinal cord.

The fact that these substances exist in the body has several possible implications in clinical practice. First, it helps explain why different people feel different amounts of pain from comparable stimuli. There are individual differences in endorphin levels as well as certain factors, such as anxiety, that influence endorphin levels. Obviously, people with more endorphin feel less pain, and those with less endorphin feel more pain.

Second, certain techniques may relieve pain at least in part because they cause the release of endorphins. Studies have suggested that placebos, acupuncture and transcutaneous electric nerve stimulation may cause the release of endorphins.

Third, other methods of pain relief, such as mental imagery, may help patients to release their own endorphins.

Cultural Influences

Early in childhood people begin to learn what those around them expect and accept with respect to painful experiences. For example, someone may learn that an injury sustained during a sports activity is not expected to hurt as much as a comparable injury caused by an unexpected accident. Or, a person may learn that the latter warrants a greater expression of pain than the former. From all of the experiences with stimuli, the person begins to learn from others what stimuli are supposed to be painful and what kind of behavioural responses should be made. The people in a person's culture teach this by their behaviour towards that person. They may ignore, punish or praise, depending on the person's behaviour and their beliefs. Since these beliefs vary from one culture to another, it is apparent that patients reporting the same intensity of pain will not necessarily respond to it in the same ways.

Everyone learns their own culture's expectations about pain throughout life. Once these expectations are internalized, they are rarely altered by exposure to the differing values of other cultures. Consequently, people tend to grow up believing that their own perceptions of and reactions to pain are the only correct and normal ones.

Consider what may happen when a nurse from one culture cares for a patient with pain who comes from another culture. The expectations of the nurse's culture may include avoiding expressions of pain, such as crying and moaning; seeking immediate relief from pain; giving complete descriptions of the pain; and having confidence in the health professions. This nurse may tend to ignore or be sceptical of the patient whose cultural experiences have taught them to moan and complain about pain, to refuse pain relief measures that do not cure the cause of the pain, to use adjectives like 'unbearable' in describing the pain and to be somewhat distrustful of the doctor's ability. A patient with still another cultural background may behave differently, or may behave similarly but for different reasons.

Many other attitudes and behaviours—a patient's preference for having visitors or being alone or the attitude towards diagnosis—may vary from one culture to another. Recognizing the values of one's own culture and learning how these values differ from those of other cultures helps nurses overcome the tendency to evaluate behaviour on the basis of their own cultural expectations. A nurse who appreciates cultural differences will have greater understanding of what the patient is experiencing. Assessment is far more accurate when it takes into account the wide range of possible attitudes and behavioural responses, and measures for pain relief are more effective when the nurse is able to respond to the patient's particular beliefs and values.

It is important to avoid stereotyping patients and their pain experiences and reactions according to their cultural group. Each patient's personal experiences vary. It is more productive to use information about the patient's cultural background to identify those questions that the nurse must ask about every patient. For example, determining whether patients want to be alone with their pain, and why, is far more helpful in planning individualized care than assuming that their preferences will always correspond to those of their sociocultural group.

Past Experience With Pain

It is tempting to expect that a person who has had multiple or prolonged experiences with pain will be less anxious and more tolerant of pain than a person who has not experienced much pain. Occasionally, this may be observed, but the reverse is true for the majority of patients.

Probably the more experience patients have with pain, the more frightened they will be about subsequent painful events. They may also tend to be less willing to tolerate pain, that is, to want relief from the pain sooner and at lower levels of intensity. This is understandable if we realize that most patients with pain receive unsatisfactory or inadequate pain relief from time to time. Thus, patients with repeated pain experiences may learn to fear the escalation of pain and the possibility that they will not receive relief. Furthermore, once patients experience severe pain, they know just how bad pain can become. On the other hand, patients who have never experienced severe pain actually do not know what to be afraid of.

Sometimes the effect of past experience with pain is a result of an accumulation of many separate painful events throughout the patient's life. For other patients, past painful experiences may have been more or less constant, as in prolonged or chronic and persistent pain. The patient who feels pain for months or years may suffer additional effects from this type of past experience and the personality may undergo a change. The patient may become quite irritable, withdrawn and depressed, and others may find the person unpleasant to be around.

The undesirable effects that may result from past experiences point to the need for the nurse to be aware of all of the patient's experiences with pain. If patients' pain is relieved promptly and adequately, they may be less fearful of future pain and more able to tolerate it.

Considerations For the Elderly

Assessment of pain in the elderly may be difficult because of physiological, psychological and social characteristics found in the aged. Older people may experience reduced sensory perception and increased pain threshold because of degeneration of neurons in the dorsal column of the spinal cord. As a result, they may incur injury without being aware of it or may experience a painful condition in an atypical way. Acute pain may not be as sharply perceived in the elderly, although chronic pain may be more intense. The pain response and pattern may be different from those usually seen in younger patients, or the pain may be referred far from the site of injury or disease.

Although pain is one of the major reasons that many of the elderly seek health care, others are reluctant to seek help even if they are in severe pain because they think of pain as a problem expected in old age. Others fail to seek care because they fear that the pain may indicate a serious illness or they fear loss of control. The elderly person deals with pain according to lifestyle, personality and cultural background. Many elderly people are very fearful of addiction and as a result will not admit that they are in pain or ask for pain medication.

Contrary to the views of the elderly as well as many health care providers, pain in the elderly is often more significant than in younger people. For example, the onset of persistent headache in the elderly may be a symptom of serious intracranial bleeding.

Nursing Care

Basic Care Plan

Once information about the patient is organized, it provides a basis for designing individualized nursing care. First, the nurse plans to alter factors that influence the nature of the pain sensation and factors that increase the intensity of the patient's behavioural responses to the pain experience. Of course, some influencing factors cannot or should not be altered. For example, if a painful sensation is being caused by pressure from an inoperable malignancy, it is not possible to alter this factor because the tumour cannot be removed. However, in some cases, positioning, drug therapy or radiotherapy may decrease the pressure. The influence of the patient's cultural expectations usually cannot be altered, and no attempt should be made to do so.

Since it may not be possible or desirable to alter some of the patient's responses to the pain experience, the second part of the nurse's plan of care includes determining appropriate responses to the patient's behaviours and attitudes about pain. For example, patients' cultural and personal experiences may have taught them that the preferred and natural response to pain experiences is not to share their feelings and sensations with anyone. Other patients may feel quite the opposite, wanting to describe their feelings and pain in detail. Appropriate and helpful nursing approaches to these two types of patient will differ markedly.

After examining what can be done to assist a particular patient with the pain experience, the third phase of the nurse's plan is to select appropriate expected outcomes for nursing care. Whenever possible, these outcomes are shared with the patient. For some patients, they may include total elimination of the painful sensation. For most patients, however, this is rarely realistic. Other expected outcomes may include a decrease in intensity, duration or frequency of pain and a decrease in the detrimental effects of pain on the patient. For example, pain may decrease appetite or interfere with sleep and thereby retard recovery from an acute illness. Thus, the expected outcomes may be a good night's sleep and increased intake of nourishing food. Prolonged pain may decrease the quality of life by interfering with work or interpersonal relationships. Thus, an outcome may be to decrease time off from work or increase the quality of interpersonal relationships.

These goals may be accomplished by pharmacological or nonpharmacological, noninvasive means. In the acute stages of illness, the patient may be a less active participant in pain relief measures, but when both mental and physical energy are present, the patient may learn self-management techniques for pain relief, such as relaxation or imagery. Hence, as the patient progresses through the stages of recovery, one expected outcome may be to decrease reliance on medication for pain relief and increase the patient's use of self-management and noninvasive pain relief measures.

Managing Anxiety Related to Pain

It is well known that anxiety may have a profound influence on the sensation and response to pain. Therefore, anxiety related to the three phases of the pain experience—anticipation, sensation of pain and aftermath—will be discussed in some detail.

Anticipation Phase
During the anticipation phase of the pain experience, it may be desirable for patients to have a moderate amount of anxiety about the impending pain so that they will be motivated to find methods of coping with it. It is not unusual for such patients to worry about their anticipated pain some of the time but not all of the time. Usually, this useful level of anxiety results from informing patients

about when the pain will occur, its locations and the inten sity and duration of pain that are expected. The nurse then channels this anxiety into helping the patient to learn a variety of pain relief measures (see Noninvasive Pain Relief Measures, below).

During the anticipatory phase of pain, teaching the patient about the nature of the impending painful experience and what can be done to obtain relief usually minimizes the anxiety experienced when the pain sensation is actually felt. With this approach, the patient knows that something can be done about the pain when it occurs. Hence, anticipation of pain is less likely to increase anxiety as much as it would if the patient had no knowledge of what to do about the pain. Learning about pain relief measures may give the patient a sense of control over sensations of pain, since the pain is viewed as being less threatening.

One of two extremes of reaction sometimes occurs when a patient is taught about a future painful event: intense anxiety or no anxiety. Anxiety-reducing techniques that may be effective with patients who appear to be highly anxious include focusing the patient's attention on a specific problem or eliminating a source of anxiety; for instance, by helping an anxious relative to become less anxious. Administering tranquillizing drugs, if prescribed, or using desensitization, a form of behaviour therapy, may be necessary in cases of extreme anxiety.

Desensitization presents information to the patient in a sequence progressing from least to most frightening information. Working with the patient, family/close friends and other members of the health care team, the nurse first constructs a hierarchy of stimuli that are frightening to the patient. Then the nurse provides a relaxing and pleasurable environment for the patient, begins talking about the least frightening stimulus, and progresses up the hierarchy until the patient shows signs of anxiety. At this point, the nurse reverts to a less frightening stimulus. This process is repeated at intervals until the patient's anxiety about the most frightening stimulus decreases to a moderate level. Occasionally, it may be necessary to postpone a painful event if these measures are not effective in reducing the patient's anxiety to a moderate level.

People who show little or no anxiety about impending pain may know from past experiences that they have a high tolerance for pain. But some patients who show low anxiety or no anxiety are denying the fact that they may have pain. When pain actually occurs, these patients tend to be quite anxious and to have considerable difficulty in coping with pain. What can be done to assist these patients before the painful event is largely unknown. It is not yet known with certainty whether it is better to continue to give them information or to give them no information. When giving the patient specific information about pain does not result in moderate anxiety, further information

probably should be brief, essential and general. Emphasis should be placed on pain relief measures.

When the nurse suspects that the patient's lack of anxiety reflects an effort to deny the information received about pain, the nurse should explore whether the patient wants more information about either pain or its relief. It appears that this decision should be respected. However, the patient should be closely observed for a marked increase in anxiety as the time approaches for the painful event to occur. The previous suggestions regarding interactions with patients with moderate and severe anxiety can then be employed, depending on the level of anxiety noted.

At times, the nurse may be tempted not to tell a patient that pain may be experienced, or that the pain may be much greater than the patient seems to think. The nurse may reason that such knowledge will make the patient anxious. Indeed, this may be correct. The prospect of pain usually arouses some anxiety in the patient. However, if ways of coping with pain are to be learnt, the patient must first know that pain may occur. Failure to forewarn the patient of pain is probably a mistake unless one of the following conditions exists: (1) previous experience shows that forewarning this patient produces such a high level of uncontrollable anxiety that the patient is unable to take positive steps toward learning to handle the pain; (2) the patient specifically requests not to be forewarned, and this request has been thoroughly explored with the patient; or (3) previous experience shows that teaching this patient about pain and its relief impedes the coping mechanism of denial, and that no other effective mechanism for coping with stress exists.

What the nurse tells the patient about the available pain relief measures and their effectiveness may also be relevant to the anxiety component of the patient's pain experience. The nurse may prevent an increase in anxiety by explaining briefly to the patient the general type of pain relief to be expected from each pain relief measure. For example, if the patient expects distraction or medication to eliminate the pain totally, then anxiety may increase when this does not happen. These pain relief measures along with many others frequently do not eliminate the pain completely or even reduce its intensity. Instead they tend to increase the patient's tolerance for pain or render pain much less bothersome to the patient.

The Sensation of Pain
During the time when pain sensations are felt by the patient, it is desirable to reduce the patient's anxiety to as low a level as possible. When the patient is anxious about the pain, there is a tendency to perceive a greater intensity of pain or to be less tolerant of the pain. This in turn produces greater anxiety. Thus, a spiralling process is initiated in which the patient becomes more anxious and experiences greater pain or becomes progressively less tolerant of pain.

Table 2.42 _Nursing activities to assist the patient with the pain experience_

Category of nursing activity	Explanation	Example of nursing activity
1. Establishing a relationship with the patient with pain	Interacting with patient as a total person, believing what patient says is experienced, and respecting reactions and attitudes regarding pain (see text)	Telling the patient you believe what is said about the pain experience
2. Teaching the patient about pain and its relief	Using a variety of the patient's sensory mechanisms for the purpose of conveying information about the pain experience (see text)	Explaining the quality and location of impending pain by applying pressure and pulling the skin in the area where the patient will have an incision
3. Using the patient–group situation	Using the principles of small group functioning to teach the patient and family or friends about the patient's pain experience	The nurse, two female patients with arthritis, and their husbands discussing modifications in homemaking activities following discharge from the hospital
4. Managing other people who come in contact with the patient	Assisting other people to reach their maximum potential for helping the patient with the pain experience	Talking alone with a patient's partner who shows marked anxiety in the presence of partner when patient complains of undiagnosed abdominal pain
5. Using cutaneous stimulation	Using various qualities, locations, durations and intensities of stimuli in contact with the skin (see text)	Use of massage to back or head to relieve headache
6. Providing distraction from pain	Obtaining the patient's response to and participation in stimuli through the major sensory modalities (see text)	Helping the patient to use chant with breathing during a painful dressing change
7. Promoting relaxation	Using a variety of techniques to assist the patient to avoid fatigue and to achieve skeletal muscle relaxation	Helping the patient learn to use slow, rhythmic breathing
8. Using guided imagery	Assisting the patient to imagine a pleasant event as a substitute for the pain experience or to imagine a means of ridding the body of the pain (see text)	Helping the patient imagine that pain is being eliminated as patient exhales slowly
9. Administering pharmacological agents	Giving medications with the pain-relieving potential to the patient and explaining the effects; assisting the doctor in determining the patient's need for analgesics (see text)	Administering analgesics on a preventive basis
10. Decreasing noxious stimuli	Using a variety of techniques to reduce the transmission of pain signals to the cortex of the brain	Splinting an abdominal incision during coughing and deep breathing

Table 2.42 *Continued*

Category of nursing activity	Explanation	Example of nursing activity
11. Using the assistance of professionals	Assisting the patient, family, friends and doctor to identify the need for additional help in dealing with pain; assisting the patient and loved ones to obtain this help and to use it to their best advantage	Suggesting to the patient that a spiritual counsellor may be able to alleviate concern (reduce anxiety) that the pain is punishment for a supposed sin
12. Being with the patient	Identifying and responding to the patient who would benefit from the mere presence of the nurse or someone else	Getting a hospital volunteer to sit at the bedside of the patient who does not want to be alone with the pain experience
13. Conveying that the source of noxious stimuli has been removed or decreased	Conveying to the patient, when appropriate, that something has been done to diminish or eliminate a cause of pain (see text)	Telling the patient that the needle for the lumbar puncture has just been removed and that all that remains is to cleanse the back
14. Assisting with the assimilation of the painful experience	Identifying the patient's need for and assisting with the intellectual and emotional incorporation of a painful experience (see text)	Discussing with the patient what sensations were felt and what patient was thinking while experiencing the myocardial infarction on the previous day

(Adapted from McCaffery, M. (1983) Nursing Management of the Patient with Pain *(3rd edition) J. B. Lippincott, Philadelphia.)*

Obviously, it is important to interrupt this process as soon as possible. Low levels of anxiety or pain are easier to reduce or control than are higher levels. Consequently, pain relief measures should be utilized before pain becomes severe. Many patients believe that they should not request pain relief measures until pain approaches or exceeds the maximum level they are able to tolerate. Therefore, it is important to explain to all patients that pain relief or control is more successful if pain relief measures are used before pain becomes unbearable.

Anxiety during the anticipatory and sensation phases of the pain experience may be managed effectively by establishing a relationship with the patient with pain and by patient teaching (see Nurse–Patient Relationship and Teaching, below). Almost all nursing care for pain relief contributes in some way toward utilizing anxiety or decreasing anxiety.

Aftermath

During the aftermath phase of pain, when the pain sensation subsides, it is hoped that the patient's anxiety also will subside. When this does not happen, certain techniques may help the patient to integrate the pain experience (see Table 2.42).

For many patients, the experience of pain continues after the sensation of pain ceases or subsides. Some patients continue to fear pain simply because they do not know that there is no longer any danger that pain will occur. Conveying to patients that the noxious stimuli have been removed or decreased helps prevent them from anxiously expecting pain to continue or to occur again shortly.

Most patients do not simply forget about a painful experience as soon as pain is no longer felt or anticipated. Patients may be disturbed about their behaviour during the pain experience or they may be concerned about how others view their responses. They may have unclear and somewhat frightening ideas about the cause of their pain or the treatment for it. Their general sense of personal safety and control may be shaken by their having felt more intense pain than they had ever imagined was possible. Patients who are relieved of chronic pain actually may experience an identity crisis, fearing what they will be like without pain. In the aftermath phase, patients may also suddenly begin trembling or perspiring. They may have nausea, vomiting or chills. Some patients have nightmares about a painful experience for weeks and months after it is over. Obviously, the care of patients with pain, especially the management of anxiety, extends beyond the anticipation and sensation phases of pain into this aftermath phase to help them cope with these reactions.

Noninvasive Pain Relief Measures

Because of the lack of knowledge or time, many patients and health team members tend to regard analgesics as the major method of pain relief. However, there are many nursing activities that can be used to assist the patient with the pain experience. Various categories of such nursing activities are outlined in Table 2.42.

The purpose of the table is to introduce the nurse to the variety of nursing activities that may be used to help patients with their pain experiences. This brief synopsis is intended to introduce these measures. For help in acquiring additional knowledge, the nurse is referred to more complete sources of information (see Further Reading). Through reading and practice, the nurse may easily learn to use these activities with patients.

Some of the noninvasive nursing activities listed in Table 2.42 will be discussed here in more detail. 'Noninvasive' simply means that no physical or bodily intrusion is involved. Noninvasive methods of pain relief entail very low risks, compared with analgesics. Although noninvasive pain relief measures are not necessarily a substitute for analgesics, a noninvasive technique may be all that is necessary or appropriate for brief episodes of pain lasting only seconds or minutes. In other instances, especially when there is severe pain that lasts for hours or days, the use of some noninvasive techniques along with medications may be the most effective way to relieve pain.

Nurse–Patient Relationship and Teaching

The two pain relief measures basic to all others are the nurse–patient relationship and patient teaching about pain and its relief. These activities may reduce pain in the absence of any other pain relief measures. Certainly, each may enhance the effectiveness of all other pain relief measures used with the patient. Certain aspects of the relationship and teaching serve to reduce the patient's anxiety about pain, and, as was indicated earlier, reducing anxiety commonly results in pain relief, either by decreasing the intensity of pain or by rendering the pain more tolerable to the patient.

Trust is an important aspect of the nurse–patient relationship. Conveying to the patient that the complaints about pain are believed can help reduce any anxiety. Some patients spend considerable time and energy trying to convince others that they have pain. The presence of pain may be doubted by others because no cause can be found for it or because the person's behaviour is not 'typical' of what the health care team expects. To say to a patient, "I know you have pain (or discomfort); I only want to understand it better," often will set the patient's mind at rest. Occasionally, patients who have feared that no one will believe them will become tearful with gratitude and relief when they know that they can trust the nurse and that the nurse believes them.

Whenever nurses encounter patients with pain, they must convey to the patients that they care about helping them obtain pain relief. The patient may not know where to turn for help in relieving the pain; it is seldom that anyone on the health care team is explicitly responsible for providing pain relief. However, when the nurse says very simply, "Let me know when you begin to hurt so I can help you do something about it," the message is conveyed to the patient that the nurse cares and assumes responsibility for helping with the pain.

The nurse also provides information, through patient teaching, about how pain can be controlled. The patient needs to know, for example, that pain should be reported in the early stages. When the patient waits too long before reporting it, the pain may be intense and anxiety may be very high. It is much easier to prevent severe pain and panic than to relieve them once they occur.

Cutaneous Stimulation

According to the gate control theory, stimulation of large-diameter nerve fibres in the skin may reduce the intensity of pain. Skin stimulation may also cause the release of endorphins. Such skin stimulation can be accomplished in a variety of ways. In devising methods of cutaneous stimulation for pain relief, the nurse considers which quality of stimulation is to be used and the location, duration and intensity of stimulation. The approach is one of trial and error, but common sense often is an effective guide.

Various qualities of cutaneous stimulation are easily available at low cost. Although some form of cutaneous stimulation is usually acceptable, consultation with the patient's doctor may be necessary for some, and other forms may be contraindicated because of the patient's condition. Different types of skin sensations may be elicited when the following measures are applied: pressure, vibration, heat, cold, bathing, lotion, menthol cream and transcutaneous electric nerve stimulation (TENS). Although transcutaneous electric nerve stimulation is not as readily available as the other measures, it has proved to be very helpful in both acute and chronic pain relief, and its use is becoming more widespread. It consists of a battery-operated unit with electrodes that are applied to the skin to produce a tingling, vibrating or buzzing sensation in the area of pain (Figure 2.35).

Local application of cold to a painful part is an underused but often highly effective method of relieving pain. Compared with local applications of heat, cold relieves pain faster and has a longer carryover effect. Contrary to popular belief, cold does not necessarily cause muscle contraction but slows the conduction of impulses that maintain muscle tone and may cause muscle relaxation. Therefore, cold is not only indicated to decrease bleeding and swelling of a new injury but also may be continued for pain relief.

When cutaneous stimulation is employed, it is applied to different areas of the body. Usually, stimulating the skin on or near the pain site is effective. In other instances, direct stimulation over the pain site must be avoided because it elicits more pain. If stimulation of the skin near

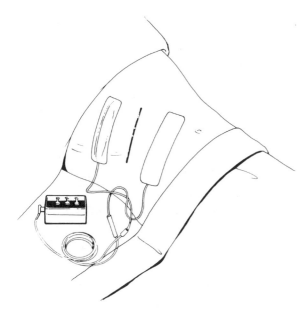

Figure 2.35 Transcutaneous electric nerve stimulation (TENS) being used for relief of incisional pain postoperatively. (Courtesy of 3M Electrotherapy Products, St Paul, Minnesota.)

the pain site is ineffective or painful, the side of the body opposite the painful area may be stimulated for pain relief. This is called contralateral stimulation. This is especially helpful to remember when the site of pain is difficult to stimulate directly, such as when a thick cast has been applied over a painful area or when the entire extremity is injured or burned.

The appropriate intensity of stimulation to be applied is generally moderate. Mild stimulation tends to be ticklish or annoying, whereas intense stimulation may cause pain.

In general, the duration of cutaneous stimulation indicated and the intervals between its applications vary considerably. Some patients experience pain relief for hours or days following cutaneous stimulation. Others obtain relief only while stimulation is being applied. For these patients, use of a menthol cream or a transcutaneous electric nerve stimulation unit is an efficient means of providing continuous stimulation without hampering activity. It takes only a few minutes to apply, but the stimulation lasts for hours. The unit may be worn 24 hours a day.

Distraction

Distraction, or focusing the patient's attention away from the painful sensations, may be an effective method of pain relief. It may decrease the perceived intensity of pain, but usually it increases tolerance for pain, making pain less bothersome. Pain tends to draw attention to itself; but if people are less aware of pain or pay less attention to it, they will be less bothered by pain and more tolerant of it.

There are many degrees and types of distraction, ranging from simply preventing monotony to the use of highly complicated physical and mental activity. When environmental stimuli are deficient in amount, patterning or variation, the person's centrally regulated thresholds for sensation tend to be lowered. This allows someone to use more of the available input, and the person becomes more sensitive to input such as pain and other sensations.

If the patient with pain is experiencing some form of sensory restriction, pain relief may result when the nurse provides environmental stimuli. This is a mild form of distraction that focuses the patient's attention away from the painful sensations. The distraction may involve minimizing strange noises, making brief but frequent visits to the patient, bringing snacks or teaching physical exercises appropriate to the patient's condition. The latter is a particularly effective method of reducing the effects of sensory restriction.

More deliberate and intense forms of sensory stimulation may be necessary to distract the patient from brief episodes of increased pain, such as pain from bone marrow aspiration or wound debridement, or longer periods of moderate to severe intensities of pain. Some patients are able to use distraction for hours.

The value of distraction techniques for pain relief is frequently misunderstood by the health care team. A common misconception is that patients who can be distracted from the pain do not have as much pain as they want others to believe. For example, nurses may erroneously assume that patients cannot have pain if they are laughing and talking with visitors. However, distraction is a powerful method of pain relief. Doubting the patient's pain because distraction is used effectively may result in the patient's discarding this effective way of coping with pain.

The effectiveness of distraction depends on the degree to which the patient is able to receive and create sensory input other than pain. As a rule, pain relief is increased in direct relation to the patient's active participation, the number of sensory modalities used and the patient's interest in the stimuli. Therefore, seeing, hearing and keeping score of a football game will distract the patient from the pain more than would only one or two of these activities. If the patient prefers rugby to football, stimuli related to rugby will distract the patient from pain more than stimuli associated with football.

Increasing the complexity of the distractor as pain increases will be effective in pain relief, however, only up to a certain level of pain intensity. With severe pain, the patient may be unable to concentrate well enough to engage in highly complicated mental or physical activities.

Many patients devise their own distraction strategies.

The patient may hum, mentally calculate mathematical problems or choose an absorbing television programme. The nurse may support these efforts and assist the patient to elaborate on them.

Under conditions of brief, severe pain, it may be effective to teach the patient a distraction strategy. A technique that may be taught quickly, even to patients who are debilitated, fatigued, sedated or in severe pain, is to combine rhythmic rubbing with visual concentration. The patient is asked to open the eyes, stare at a specific spot on the wall or ceiling and rub a part of the body. The rubbing may be done initially by the nurse. Then the nurse may take the patient's hand and guide the patient in doing the rubbing. Rubbing with a firm, circular motion on bare skin seems to be effective. The rubbing and staring involve a steady source of sensory input through visual and tactile-kinaesthetic modalities along with a focus of rhythm. If this is not distracting enough, the patient can be instructed to add another activity, such as breathing in and out slowly. The patient may chant silently, "Breathe in slowly, breathe out slowly". Sensory input through several modalities combined with rhythm and a focus on breathing are common characteristics of successful distraction techniques.

Another distraction technique that is very useful with patients who are fatigued or sedated, or when pain lasts longer than several minutes, is 'active listening'. The patient may use a tape recorder with an earphone or headset, select a cassette of fast music and listen to the music, while keeping time by tapping the finger or nodding the head. For visual input, the patient can focus on an object or close the eyes and imagine something about the music, such as dancing to the music. When the pain increases, the patient can increase the volume; when pain decreases, the volume can be decreased. For example, a burned patient undergoing a painful dressing change might use this method of distraction to make the painful experience more tolerable.

Relaxation

Skeletal muscle relaxation may reduce the intensity of pain or increase pain tolerance. It can also be combined with other pain relief measures, such as analgesics or a heating pad, to enhance their effectiveness. Many people learn relaxation techniques for the purpose of dealing with life stresses. Classes in transcendental meditation, yoga, hypnosis, music therapy and a variety of other potentially relaxing activities are available. If a patient already knows a technique for relaxing, the nurse may need only suggest that it is used in order to reduce or to prevent increased pain.

Almost all patients with chronic pain need to learn some method of relaxing and to employ it on a regular basis several times a day. Regular periods of relaxation are needed to combat the fatigue and muscle tension that

occur with chronic pain and decrease pain tolerance or increase the intensity of the pain.

A simple relaxation technique for patients with acute or chronic pain consists of abdominal breathing at a slow, rhythmic rate. The patient may close the eyes and breathe slowly and comfortably (not too deeply) at about six to nine breaths per minute. Patients can maintain a constant rhythm by counting silently and slowly to themselves as they inhale ("in, 2, 3") and exhale ("out, 2, 3"). Patients conclude this relaxation technique by taking another deep breath. When the nurse is teaching this technique, it is helpful to count out loud for patients at first. Initially, patients may benefit from keeping their eyes open as the nurse breathes in co-ordination with them.

Slow, rhythmic breathing may also be used as a distraction technique. However, it may require practice before the patient becomes skilful in using it.

A quick and easy method of helping the tense patient with severe pain to relax is to give the following instructions: "Clench your fists; breathe in deeply and hold it a moment. As you breathe out, feel yourself go limp. Now start yawning."

Guided Imagery

Therapeutic guided imagery may be defined as the use of one's imagination in an especially designed manner to achieve a specific positive effect. In this instance, the desired effects are relaxation and pain relief. Imagery of various types is capable of altering body functions over which we seem to have no direct or conscious control. Most people have experienced this in the form of increased cardiac rate (pounding heart) or perspiration when a distressing mental image comes to mind just before falling asleep. Although images of this sort seem to provoke a stress response, certain other images seem to evoke relaxation responses or pain relief. A considerable amount of the nurse's time is usually required to teach and explain the technique of guided imagery. The patient, too, must invest time and energy in practising it. For these reasons, guided imagery most often is taught to patients with chronic pain, although it is effective with acute pain as well. To learn to use guided imagery, patients must be able to concentrate, use their imagination and follow directions. It is not advisable to try to teach it when the patient is fatigued, sedated or in severe pain. One simple form of therapeutic guided imagery for relaxation and pain relief consists of combining the slow rhythmic breathing described as a relaxation technique with a mental image of relaxation and comfort. With eyes closed, patients imagine that each time they exhale slowly they are breathing out muscle tension and discomfort, leaving behind a relaxed and comfortable body. Each time they inhale, they can imagine that the air sends healing energy to the area of discomfort. Each time they exhale, they can imagine that the air floats away from their body, carrying with it the pain and tension. It enters the body again immediately, in a purified state, and can be circulated to the area of discomfort again.

Usually, the patient is asked to practise guided imagery for about five minutes, three times a day. Several days of practice may elapse before the patient finds that the intensity of pain can be reduced using this technique. Pain relief can continue for hours after the imagery is used. Most patients begin to experience the relaxing effects of guided imagery the first time they try it.

Medications for Pain Relief

Whether pain is acute or chronic, certain guidelines are useful when analgesics are indicated for the relief of pain. Usually, analgesics are most effective when a preventive approach is used and when the dose and interval between doses is individualized to meet the patient's needs. The only safe and effective way to administer narcotics is to observe the patient's response.

Preventive Approach

Using a preventive approach to pain relief means that prescribed drugs (analgesics in particular) are given before the pain occurs, if it can be predicted, or at least before it reaches a severe intensity. If the patient's pain is expected to occur daily for a great portion of the 24-hour period, a regular schedule around the clock may be indicated. Even if the analgesic is prescribed 'as needed' or 'prn', the nurse can administer the analgesic on a preventive basis before it is needed as long as the prescribed interval between doses is observed. This is preferable to the usual approach to a prn request, which may require that the patient have intense pain before requesting and receiving medication.

A preventive approach has many advantages. It usually takes a smaller dose to alleviate mild pain or prevent the occurrence of pain than it does to relieve severe pain. Thus, a preventive approach may result in a lower total 24-hour dose. This helps to prevent tolerance to analgesics and decreases the severity of side-effects such as sedation and constipation. Furthermore, pain relief can be more complete with a preventive approach. For example, there need not be any peaks of severe pain and the patient spends less time in pain. With a 'prn' approach to pain relief, the patient usually experiences pain, obtains the analgesic and waits for it to take effect. Within a 24-hour period, this may result in the patient spending a total of several hours in pain.

Better pain control achieved with a preventive approach may reduce the likelihood of the patient's craving the drug. Some health care team members seem to feel that the frugal use of opioids will help prevent addiction in the patient with acute pain. However, there is no basis for this belief. Certainly, a patient who is in pain and has an analgesic withheld is more likely to crave the drug than the patient whose pain is relieved before it becomes distressing.

Considerations For the Elderly

Physiological changes in the elderly make it important to administer analgesics with caution. Drug interactions are more of a possibility in the elderly because of the higher incidence of chronic illness and increased use of prescription and over-the-counter drugs. Before administering opioid and non-opioid analgesics to the elderly, it is important to obtain a careful drug history to identify potential harmful drug interactions.

Absorption and metabolism of drugs are altered in the elderly patient because of decreased liver, renal and gastrointestinal function. In addition, changes in body weight, protein stores and distribution of body fluid alter the distribution of drugs in the body. As a result, drugs are not metabolized as quickly and blood levels of the drug remain higher for a longer period of time. The patient is more sensitive to drugs and is at increased risk of drug toxicity.

Opioid and non-opioid analgesics can be given effectively to the elderly but must be used cautiously because of increased susceptibility to depression of the nervous system and respiratory system. Because the elderly are generally more sensitive to analgesics, it is advisable to begin with a smaller dose of a non-opioid analgesic first, increasing the dose slowly, and adding additional drugs carefully. Frequent monitoring is necessary for safe, effective pain relief.

Routes of Administration for Moderate to Severe Pain

The route of administration of analgesics selected is based on the patient's condition and desired effect of the drug. For moderate to severe pain, the most common routes of administration of an opioid analgesic are the intramuscular or subcutaneous routes. Parenteral administration of the medication produces more rapid analgesic effects than oral administration, but these effects are of shorter duration. Intravenous or rectal routes of administration may also be indicated if the patient is not permitted any oral intake or is vomiting. The rectal route may be indicated for patients with bleeding problems, such as haemophilia.

Intravenous opioides may be administered by bolus injection or by continuous intravenous drip using an infusion pump. The latter provides a more steady level of analgesia and is indicated when pain is to be controlled over a 24-hour period, such as postoperatively for the first day or so, or in a patient with prolonged cancer pain who cannot take medication by mouth.

If the patient can take medication by mouth, this route

is preferred to all others since it is easy, noninvasive and painless, unlike injections. Severe pain can be relieved with oral opioids if the doses are high enough. Certainly, patients with prolonged pain should receive analgesics orally rather than by injection if at all possible. Many opioids can be given effectively by mouth for severe pain. However, to be effective, dosage must be altered because of differences in absorption of drugs given by different routes. For example, 10 mg of diamorphine administered intramuscularly would be equivalent to 20 mg given orally or 30 mg of morphine. In terminally ill patients with prolonged pain, doses may gradually become much higher owing to increased pain or tolerance to analgesia. In the majority of these patients, the higher doses provide additional pain relief (i.e., there is no ceiling to the dose of opioids such as morphine providing the dose is titrated against pain) and the higher doses are not lethal (the patient is tolerant to respiratory depression and sedation as well as analgesia). If the patient's medication is changed from a parenteral dose to an oral opioid at a dose that is not equivalent in strength (equianalgesic), the lesser dose of oral opioid may result in a withdrawal reaction and the reappearance of pain and anxiety.

New Routes and Approaches to Pain Management

Recent attention to the problem of acute and chronic pain has led to the development of new methods of pain relief. Newer methods of delivering analgesics include intraspinal infusion and patient-controlled analgesia.

Intraspinal Infusion of Analgesics

Intraspinal infusion of opioids or local anaesthetic agents has been effective in pain control in postoperative patients as well as those with chronic pain unrelieved by usual methods of pain relief. A catheter is inserted by the doctor into the subarachnoid or epidural space in the thoracic or lumbar region for administration of opioids or local anaesthetics. Repeated infusion of these agents through the catheter results in pain relief without many of the side-effects of systemic analgesia, including sedation.

If analgesics are needed for a longer period of time or if the patient has chronic, terminal disease, the catheter may be tunnelled through the subcutaneous tissue and the inlet or port is placed under the skin in the abdominal region. The opioid analgesic is injected through the skin into the outlet or port and catheter, which delivers the medication directly into the subarachnoid or epidural space. This method may require injection of the opioid several times a day to maintain an adequate level of pain relief.

In those patients who are likely to require more frequent doses or continuous infusions of opioids to keep them pain free, an implantable infusion device may be used to administer the drug continuously. The dose is administered at a small, constant dose at a preset rate into the epidural or subarachnoid space. The infusion device has a reservoir that stores the medication for slow release and needs to be refilled once every one or two months, depending on the patient's needs. This eliminates the need for repeated injections through the skin and reduces the number of journeys to the hospital for frequent injections.

Very small doses of opioid analgesics can be administered by these methods to block pain pathways with little effect on pulse, respiration or blood pressure. The shortcomings of intramuscular administration of opioid analgesia, such as delay in pain relief and need for frequent injections, are eliminated. Adverse side-effects such as respiratory depression and sedation are reduced because of the small doses given by these methods. However, the patient must be monitored very closely when the loading dose of the medication is given, to detect respiratory depression. Delayed onset of respiratory depression has been reported with use of intraspinal analgesia; therefore, the patient must be monitored and antagonists such as naloxone should be available for administration to reverse respiratory depression if it occurs.

Patient-Controlled Analgesia

Patient-controlled analgesia has been used effectively with postoperative patients. This method of pain management allows patients to control their own intravenous medication within a predetermined time and dose using an automated and preloaded pump system. This results in a more consistent level of analgesia with few side-effects. Although the drug is under the patient's control within safety limits to prevent inadvertently administering an overdose, the amount of medication administered by the patient has not been greater than in traditional methods of pain relief. Pulmonary complications have been less frequent and patients have been more alert with this system.

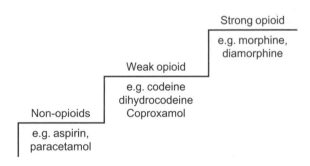

Figure 2.36 The 'analgesic staircase' (adapted from Regnard, C. F. B. and Davies, A. (1986) *A Guide to Symptom Relief in Advanced Cancer*, Haigh & Hochland, Manchester).

Choice of Analgesic

Nurses are in a strong position to influence prescriptions of analgesic for patients and so an understanding of the potency and action of different analgesics is useful. The concept of the 'analgesic staircase' can be helpful (Figure 2.36). As can be seen, if pain fails to be relieved by a non-opioid analgesic, then a weak opioid should be used. If a patient is still in pain while regularly taking a weak opioid (such as dihydrocodeine), there is little point in changing to another weak opioid (such as coproxamol), since the potency of the two drugs is the same. Instead, it is logical to move onto a strong opioid (such as morphine or diamorphine).

Combinations of non-opioids (nonsteroidal anti-inflammatory drugs) and opioids can be beneficial since they produce analgesia by acting at the peripheral nervous system level; opioids act primarily at the central nervous system level. Adjuvant drugs, such as tricyclic antidepressants, tranquillizers, anticonvulsants and steroids, may also be effective when used in conjunction with analgesics.

Patient Education

Acute Pain

Patients who have experienced acute pain as a result of injury, illness, investigations or surgery often fear its recurrence once they are discharged from hospital. Fear and anticipation of pain are further increased because nurses, doctors and pain relief are less available to the patient for control of pain in the home. The patient may leave the hospital with the expectation that the pain will not recur and is very frightened if it returns unexpectedly or persists longer than expected. In preparation for hospital discharge, the patient and caregivers receive instruction and guidance about what type of pain or discomfort to expect, how long that discomfort is expected to last and when the pain or discomfort signals a problem that should be reported. Additionally, they are prepared for home care by guidance about medication to be used in case of pain as well as its side-effects. The patient is reminded that those pain relief strategies that were effective in the hospital can be used at home. The nurse gives support and reassurance to the patient and carers that pain can be managed successfully at home.

Chronic Pain

Inadequate control of pain in the outpatient is a common cause of readmission to the hospital. If chronic pain was the primary reason for the patient's initial hospitalization, the anxiety and fear of the patient and carers are multiplied when the patient is about to return home. The patient and home carers are taught the techniques of pain assessment and administration of analgesics. This advice is given orally and in writing, and opportunities are provided for the patient and carer(s) to practise administration of the medication until they are comfortable and confident with the procedure. They are advised about how to monitor respiratory status and to recognize central nervous system depression and other side-effects of opioid and non-opioid analgesics. If the medications cause other predictable effects such as constipation, the patient and carers are advised about their treatment and prevention so that pain relief is not interrupted to resolve the problem.

If the patient is to receive analgesics at home by intramuscular or subcutaneous injection or intravenous or intraspinal infusions, a referral to a district nurse is indicated. The district nurse visits the patient in the home after discharge to assess the patient, to determine if the patient and carers are carrying out the pain management programme effectively and, if indicated, to evaluate the injection or infusion technique used by the patient and carers for accuracy and safety. If the patient has an implanted infusion pump in place, the nurse examines the condition of the pump or injection site and may refill the reservoir with medication as prescribed by the doctor, or supervise home carers in the procedure. The district nurse assesses the patient for changes in the need for analgesics, and assists the patient and carers in altering the prescribed dose in collaboration with the patient's doctor. The district nurse supports and encourages the patient and home carers to use noninvasive pain management techniques to supplement analgesic therapy. These efforts enable the patient to obtain adequate pain relief while remaining at home and with loved ones.

Evaluating the Effectiveness of Pain Relief Measures

To determine objectively the effectiveness of nursing activities designed to help the patient with the pain experience, the patient's behavioural responses before care are compared with those that follow care. After providing care, the nurse once again assesses the patient's behavioural responses, much as occurred in the initial assessment. This assessment is repeated at appropriate intervals following care.

The comparison of these assessments reveals the effectiveness of the pain relief measures. This provides a basis for continuing or modifying nursing care.

The expected outcome of nursing care for pain relief is usually one or more of the following possibilities, each having many possible manifestations:

1. Achieves pain relief or decreased intensity of pain.
   a. Rates pain at a lower intensity (on a scale of 0 to 10) following care.
   b. Rates pain at a lower intensity for longer periods of time.
2. Uses coping strategies effectively.

a. Is alert and pain free enough to engage in activities important to recovery (e.g., drinking fluids, coughing, ambulating).
b. Sleeps all night.
c. Increases the amount of time spent out of bed.
d. Increases the amount of time spent at work.
e. Says the pain is not as bothersome as before care was initiated.
f. Patient says less attention is paid to the pain.
g. Spends less time talking about pain.

CARE OF THE DYING PATIENT

Caring for the dying and for those facing the aftermath of the death of someone they love demands great skills of nurses, both in caring for patients' physical needs, and in the great sensitivity required to facilitate adjustment to impending death or the expression of grief in the bereaved. Increasingly, it is being recognized that such skills are derived through experience and training, and that caring for the dying and bereaved is a common element to all nursing roles.

Caring for the dying and their families is also an area where many nurses feel inadequately prepared and find undertaking such care stressful and distressing. Studies have demonstrated that nurses' first encounter with death during training can shape their feelings about this difficult area for the whole of their nursing careers (Quint, 1967). There is also evidence to suggest that the care dying patients receive is not always of a high quality. Symptoms such as pain may not be relieved adequately, and evidence of a reluctance to communicate with patients about their prognosis and condition have been noted frequently in research literature (Field, 1989; Hockley, Dunlop and Davies, 1988; Twycross and Lack, 1983).

The inadequacies of such care led to the development of the hospice movement in the 1960s, when centres were set up to provide an environment in which people could die with dignity, while receiving expert pain and symptom control. Since the 1960s, services for the dying have proliferated rapidly, and a body of knowledge has evolved contributing to skilled practice as well as resolving some of the many difficulties facing dying patients and their families. Nurses need to equip themselves with such skills so that high quality care can be made available to all dying patients regardless of where they are cared for or the disease causing their fatal illness.

Mortality Statistics and Definitions

Mortality statistics alone provide little information about the nature of caring for the dying, but if one examines places of death, causes of death and at what point an individual is identified as dying, a picture of this difficult area of nursing care begins to emerge.

Today, at least 60 per cent of deaths occur in hospital or in specialist units such as hospices rather than at home; in urban areas this figure is much higher at around 75 per cent (Taylor, 1983). This means that two thirds of people die in institutional settings, and a relatively small number of the dying receive specialist terminal care in hospices or under the care of support teams. This contrasts with research evidence that suggests that, if asked, patients who are dying would prefer to die at home with their family, in familiar and more personal surroundings (Bowling, 1983). As a result of this evidence, much of the recent work of the hospice and palliative care movement has focused on enabling patients to remain at home by providing support services in the community for them.

The task of nurses working in institutional settings is to facilitate patients to achieve their expressed wishes regarding their preference of place of death, and to liaise with support and community services in order to make this possible. However, the statistics would suggest that the majority of patients are unable to achieve this aim; therefore, the role of nurses working on general hospital wards is central in providing quality care for the dying. Many nurses working in such wards feel they have had no specialist training for the task.

Mortality statistics indicate that particular diseases are common causes of death. In Western societies, chronic degenerative diseases such as cardiovascular disease, cancer and respiratory disease are responsible for a much greater proportion of the total number of deaths than infectious diseases. This is represented in Kind's analysis of hospital inpatient enquiry data (1988), and is shown in Table 2.43.

It is clear from Table 2.43 that heart and circulatory disease and malignant neoplasms are responsible for over half of all inpatient deaths. This is important, since while the majority of patients die from these two diseases, the nature of the physical symptoms experienced by each group are quite different and will therefore present different challenges to the nurses caring for them. Nurses need to become expert in the care of potential problems facing their particular client group, and be aware that most of the literature regarding care of the dying refers to the person dying from cancer.

Identifying Terminal Illness and Prognosis

Identifying a patient as dying, and making some assessment of the length of time an individual might have left before they actually die (prognosis), is fraught with many problems. There is no doubt that terminal illness is the period of time from when the downward physical progression towards death caused by disease is irreversible

Table 2.43 *Death by diagnostic group*

Diagnostic group	Rate/100 hospital admissions
Infectious disease	2.48
Malignant neoplasm	15.74
Benign neoplasm	0.93
Endocrine and metabolic disease	4.34
Diseases of the blood	3.04
Mental disorders	7.74
Nervous system	2.31
Heart disease	17.98
Other circulatory disease	18.04
Respiratory disease	8.70
Digestive system	2.45
Nephritis and other urinary disease	5.28
Male genital	0.29
Female genital	0.06
Skin	1.21
Musculoskeletal system	1.01
Congenital anomalies	1.61
Perinatal conditions	2.73
Ill-defined	2.51
Other injuries	1.00
Poisoning	0.40
Other	2.52

Kind, P. (1988) Hospital Deaths – The Missing Link: Measuring Outcome in Hospital Activity Data. *Discussion Paper 44, Centre for Health Economics, York*

and no longer responsive to active curative therapy. The precise point in time at which this occurs is much more difficult to identify, however. Health carers involved in the treatment and care of such patients, and researchers studying the dying, have used different approaches. Terminal illness has been defined as the end of curative treatment and the beginning of palliative care; the final illness has been noted to span from days or weeks, from six weeks before death, to six months or several years. There is clearly confusion and differences of opinion as to when a patient should be identified as 'dying'. This is very important since crucial decisions need to be made at the time of identification of terminal illness by the health carers, the patient and the family. Many hospice units will only accept patients whose prognosis has been estimated as three months or less, so many patients who may need supportive care or who have particular symptom difficulties may fall outside of the remit of specialist services for the dying.

Further difficulties are encountered when attempting to estimate prognosis. There is evidence from several research studies to indicate that doctors tend to be inaccurate in their estimations of how long an individual might have before death, with a tendency to be over-optimistic (Murray-Parkes, 1972). The importance of this is that inaccurate assessment of what is likely to happen to dying patients makes planning for their care very difficult, and

much uncertainty is involved for both the dying individual and their carers.

How does one know a patient is dying, and how long does a dying patient have to live? These are very difficult questions to answer. But nurses and doctors act upon such decisions every day of their working lives.

Factors to be taken into account when deciding a patient is dying include the following:

● Treatment of the patient's disease no longer offers hope of cure or maintenance of their condition in *status quo*, or remission.
● The individual's physical condition is deteriorating month by month, week by week, day by day or hour by hour.
● This deterioration is considered to be irreversible.

These factors are more important than the precise diagnosis, since disease or condition alone is not always an accurate guide to a patient's hope of recovery, although there are particular diseases or conditions that, at diagnosis, are considered incurable. For example, a diagnosis of cancer is not a definition of terminal illness; however, a diagnosis of lung cancer is very likely to entail extremely grave consequences for the individual, given its low five-year survival rate (Cancer Research Campaign, 1988).

Decisions regarding how best to care for a patient, although reflecting prognosis, also need to be taken based upon the rate of physical deterioration, for example, Bale and Regnard (1989) have discussed management of pressure sores in the dying in relation to this. According to Regnard, active wound care aimed at healing pressure sores is realistic only in patients whose decline is relatively slow (month by month or week by week), whereas wound management aimed at comfort and pain relief is a more appropriate goal for the patient whose physical decline is obvious day by day. This approach can be applied to many aspects of nursing care for the dying.

There is now research evidence to suggest that doctors are unable to be any more precise about patients' prognosis than this. It is very difficult to predict accurately how long a patient has left to live. There are many reported instances where a doctor has told a patient that they have three or six months to live, only for the patient to live two years or more. Such inaccuracy in prediction is likely to cause great distress in patients and their relatives. Likewise is the situation when a patient's prognosis is predicted to be much longer, and the patient declines rapidly and dies sooner than predicted. This is a common occurrence and prevents individuals preparing for their own death or for comprehensive support services to be established for the patient and family. For this reason it is generally considered to be more appropriate to give patients less precise predictions for the time they have left. For example, it is more likely for patients to be told they have only months rather than years left to live.

This is not to suggest that being open with patients regarding their diagnosis and prognosis is not a good thing. There is now a body of evidence that suggests that patients want and need to know if they are dying (McIntosh, 1974). The majority of patients know at some level the seriousness of their condition whether or not the doctors or nurses tell them. Most patients adjust to the knowledge of their own impending death, and value the opportunity to complete unfinished business, say goodbyes to family and friends and prepare for death. Nurses have a great deal to learn from the courage of such individuals. The role of nurses in caring for dying patients is to facilitate their psychological and spiritual adjustment to the knowledge of their impending death, and help in the control of physical symptoms resulting from their disease process.

Adjustment to Terminal Illness

There is little doubt that the majority of patients want and need to know that they are dying. However, the extent to which this is made possible by those who are caring for them is very variable.

Glaser and Strauss (1965) have examined the way institutional environments greatly affect patients' adjustment to their disease. They identified two important factors: first, the dying trajectory the patient is following (that is, the speed of the downward progression towards death) and, second, that of 'awareness contexts'.

A patient's dying trajectory will be greatly influenced by the nature of the disease. Rapid dying trajectories are most commonly seen in emergencies or intensive care situations. Here, patients may have little or no time for awareness of and adaptation to inevitable death to occur. This is in contrast to chronic conditions where the downward progression is much slower. However, there is likely to be great uncertainty in either situation, making care of such patients very difficult.

Different ward settings are also likely to affect the extent to which an individual is likely to be aware of dying. Glaser and Strauss (1965) observed the behaviour of hospital staff as they cared for dying patients, and documented different levels of awareness which were exhibited by ward staff. Closed awareness occurred where the patient was kept totally unaware of the prognosis by staff and relatives. This was possible only where patients were unable to recognize their own physical deterioration, and where relatives and staff prevented patients from 'finding out'. More common behaviours were suspicion awareness, where patients were suspicious of their condition, and mutual pretence awareness, where both patient and staff were aware that the patient was dying but did not show this to each other. This could be extremely difficult to maintain, and caused considerable strain to patients, relatives and staff. Open awareness occurred where patient and staff were aware

of the situation, and were able to communicate openly about it with each other. This level of awareness, while preferable, was not without its problems; dying patients were expected by staff to act with dignity and decorum at all times. Thus institutions did, and still do, conspire to prevent individuals from finding out the seriousness of their condition. While the aim of this is to somehow prevent patients from suffering from the pain of such knowledge, it is felt to be detrimental and unethical to withhold information. Frequently, a great fear of talking to or telling patients is expressed by health carers, and relatives may put pressure on staff not to be open with patients.

The real issues are this: does one tell patients they are dying, and how does one offer support and assistance to such individuals? An understanding of the coping process is useful here.

The Coping Process

Lazarus, Averill and Opton (in Coelho, Hamburg and Adams, 1974) define coping as: 'problem-solving efforts made by an individual when the demands he faces are highly relevant to his welfare and when these demands tax his adaptive resources' (p. 251).

Therefore, coping is a process undertaken in response to stress (positive or negative) and involves the individual appraising the threat (whether internal or external), adopting strategies in order to deal with the threat and reappraising their effectiveness. The way an individual copes with the threat will be an important determinant of their ability to contain the stress and anxiety associated with it, and of their adjustment and adaptation to this change in life situation. Benner and Wrubel (1988) emphasize the individuality of this process, that is, that a person's individual make-up and history will determine what is perceived to be stressful and what their possibilities for coping are.

Several writers have examined coping in relation to patients who know they are dying. The most well known of these coping theories have identified sequences or stages through which an individual passes in adapting to the threat of imminent death. One of the best known authors to write on this subject is Kübler-Ross (1970), who interviewed over 200 dying patients and identified five stages in the process of adjusting to the knowledge of dying. These are: denial (or 'not me'), anger (or 'why me?'), bargaining (or 'yes me, but?'), depression and acceptance. While these were never presented as sequential stages through which individuals pass as they move closer to death, the ultimate goal identified for patients was that of acceptance of the inevitability of death within an environment of open communication and support provided by staff and family or home carers.

Kübler-Ross's work has been highly influential, although it is now regarded as problematic. These so-called stages of adaptation are actually not clearly visible in dying patients, and individuals rarely proceed through these in an ordered or forward progression. Denial is a common reaction to the news of terminal illness. Patients are simply unable psychologically to take in the news, and cope by being unable to believe it can be true; in fact, they may talk and act as if they had not been told.

The concept of acceptance in Kübler-Ross's (1970) stage theory of dying is also problematic, particularly as it presents the idea that passive acceptance of the inevitable is a pre-requisite of a 'good death'. This is not helpful since patients do not always reach this stage: some may fight or deny the reality of death to the very end and, depending on the individual, this may well be very normal and appropriate for them, however difficult it is for those caring for them. While there are individuals who do reach acceptance of their fate and are extremely rewarding to care for, patients frequently fluctuate in their ability to accept their own death, and more common is resignation, physical and mental, to the inevitability of death.

The reality is that individuals coping with dying tend to exhibit numerous and fluctuating responses, ranging from outright denial to despair or stoic acceptance. These reactions may be manifested all at once within a single conversation, or one response such as anger or bitterness may predominate.

Wiseman (1979) has identified strategies which appear to be associated with individuals who cope well with cancer and dying. These are as follows:

1. Avoid avoidance (do not deny).
2. Confront realities, and take appropriate action.
3. Focus on solutions, or redefine a problem into solvable form.
4. Always consider alternatives.
5. Maintain open, mutual communication with significant others.
6. Seek and use constructive help.
7. Accept support when offered.
8. Maintain hope.

While these do not represent a blueprint for good coping, they do suggest a list of strategies that nurses can help patients to use constructively. Reactions to knowledge of dying, coping and adjustment are also related to the individual's developmental stage. Children have a very different concept of death from that of adults, depending on their age and developmental stage. Young adults, the middle-aged and elderly are likely to face dying very differently, and previous experiences of illness and death are also likely to influence the way in which they cope.

Facilitating Coping In Dying Patients

The nurse's role in helping patients and families cope with dying is a vital one, and yet it is something most nurses find very difficult. It takes great bravery to talk about an event such as death, when most people have never confronted it for themselves, let alone considered helping someone else go through it. In order to be able to act as a facilitator, nurses must have faced, and feel comfortable with, the possibility of their own death. (Time spent thinking over personal experiences of death and how one might cope, and how one would plan life if there was only a short time left is invaluable, and is probably best shared with a friend or colleague.)

There are two levels of approach to the facilitation of coping in patients who are dying, as follows:

1. Facilitation of emotional expression.
2. Intervention.

Facilitation of Emotional Expression

All patients and relatives need to express their feelings in relation to the illness and the impact it is having on their life and relationships, regardless of how much they are aware of the fact that the person is dying or what coping strategies (such as denial) are being used. The nurse plays a vital role in the facilitation of such expression, which in itself is therapeutic. This might take the form of a one-off interview with the patient, or form part of an ongoing relationship a nurse develops with a patient during the time they are caring for them.

Helping the dying person to express their feelings and fears is difficult, but using certain skills can encourage the expression of feelings and convey to the patient that the nurse cares and wants to listen. Such skills might include: the use of open-ended statements like "You seem sad today" or "This must be very difficult for you right now" to initiate a meaningful conversation; reflecting statements the patient makes ("So you are saying that you feel you aren't getting any better"); prompting ("Can you tell me more about that?"); and the use of nonverbal communication (showing an interested expression, eye contact, sitting close to the patient and touch). Often, strategies as simple as these can open the emotional floodgates and the person will pour out their feelings. Many nurses feel worried about doing this in case they unleash something they cannot handle. This is unlikely; most patients welcome the chance simply to express their feelings and tell their story, and feel relieved afterwards. Buckman (1988) provides useful advice on using these techniques to support someone who is dying.

In conversation with dying patients for the first time, particularly when one is not sure quite how the person is coping in relation to knowledge of terminal illness, a useful strategy is simply to sit close to the person and ask them to tell their story: how they became ill; what doctors have said to them; what treatment they have had; where they are now; what they feel is happening now; and whether they have thought about the possibility that they may not get better. The nurse should keep to the point and not let the conversation deviate on to safer areas. A person who is not up to facing all of this is likely to turn the conversation onto other safer areas, and may well come back to it later in the conversation. Giving space and the careful use of silence help the dying person to set their own pace and agenda. Taking this approach also gives the nurse/facilitator the space to gear the level and depth of conversation to the person, and provides a way of dealing with difficult direct questions such as ''I'm going to die, aren't I?''. Such questions are dreaded by nurses because of fears of not knowing how to answer. One approach is, rather than immediately answering in the affirmative, wait until an understanding of why the question is being asked can be developed, by checking back with the patient whether that is really what they feel is happening to them. Questions like these also need to be backed up by an exploration of the person's feelings and fears in relation to dying and the dying process.

All nurses should be able to operate at this level at any stage in their career, particularly as it often does not involve imparting information about diagnosis and prognosis (an area that frequently worries junior nurses).

Intervention—As Facilitation of Adjustment

A second level of facilitation can be described broadly as intervention because it suggests a less passive role on the part of the facilitator or nurse. This might include giving information, breaking bad news, facilitation of decision making, identification of clinical symptoms such as anxiety and depression and the use of therapeutic counselling.

Breaking bad news, for example, telling an individual that there is no possibility of curing their condition, is often felt to be one of the most difficult tasks for health carers. Nurses frequently feel that the responsibility for giving such information lies solely with doctors, and that nurses play no part in this. This is a mistaken view; decisions regarding when and how to tell, and from whom the news should come, are decisions best made by the multidisciplinary team. Nurses have much to offer because of their prolonged work contact with patients. Such news cannot be softened and wrapped up so that the impact is lessened. For this reason, bad news needs to be conveyed directly and in a frank and clear manner, but also with great care and sensitivity so that individuals can assimilate what is said and are given the opportunity to express their feelings and emotions regarding the news. This takes time and may need to be repeated. It is unnecessary to convey all the information at once—patients will be unable to assimilate it, and so information should begin

simply and perhaps in short bursts, assessing how much has been understood. During each discussion, the person responsible for telling does not necessarily need to be a doctor; it may be more appropriate for someone who knows the individual well, such as a nurse or a relative, to tell the patient.

Regardless of who actually conveys bad news to the patient, the nurse's role is an important one, and it can be very useful to be present during the 'telling' so that the nurse understands what has been said and how the patient received the news. The nurse's role should be to support the patient in their reaction to the news, to clarify and interpret what has been said to the patient and to allow the patient to express their feelings. This is an ongoing process and needs to involve family and friends.

Important decisions need to be made by dying people in relation perhaps to treatment of their disease, or financial and family matters. Again, the nurse can play an important role in identifying patients' wishes and help as appropriate. Patients and relatives may also display signs of severe anxiety or despair, and nurses need to become skilled at recognizing when these go beyond what might be described as a normal and understandable response, and call for help from other professionals such as clinical psychologists, social workers and psychiatrists.

In all situations involving caring for dying patients and their families, listening and communication skills can be used therapeutically. Therapeutic counselling involves the use of such skills over a period of time, establishing and building on ongoing relationships with the individual so that trust can be developed. Identified issues can be explored and built on over a period of time. Counselling aims to help individuals interpret their own situations and make their own decisions. It does not seek to direct individuals in their adjustment and decisions. These are skills that need be developed, and specialist courses in counselling are available to nurses.

Family and Friends

The family, friends and other carers should be central to the care of the dying patient and, if they and the patient wish, participate maximally with the patient's care. This aids anticipatory grieving and can help to ensure a less stormy bereavement. Many families feel they want to be doing something to feel 'useful', however small. Thus the role of the nurse should be that of facilitator between patient and family rather than the primary caregiver to the exclusion of others.

The process of adjustment that has been outlined for patients is also a process that family members and others will go through. It is unlikely, however, that they will move through the process at the same rate as the patient. This may be difficult; for example, in the case where the patient accepts impending death before those close to them are ready to do so, it may seem as if their loved one has turned their back on them and given up. It is also arguable that, as the patient drifts into final coma, problems over adjustment to dying diminish in the patient, while stress among caregivers and family increases.

Lewis (1986), in her review of research into the impact of cancer on the family, has identified different sources of stress on the family:

- Emotional strain.
- Physical demand of caring (e.g., loss of sleep, physical fatigue).
- Uncertainty over the patient's health (the fear and anxieties are as great as those of the partner).
- Fear of patient dying.
- Altered household roles and lifestyles.
- Financial difficulties.
- Existential concerns (in one study, 81 per cent of women who stated they had talked with their husband about his death felt shared expression of dying made it easier to cope with bereavement).
- Ways to comfort the patient.
- Perceived inadequacy of services.
- Nonconvergent needs among household members.

The nurse's role in supporting and facilitating expression of feelings between patients and their families is an essential one. But how can the nurse best help? Freihafer and Felton (1976) asked relatives to rank identified behaviour of carers as either 'helpful' or 'unhelpful'.

Helpful behaviour included:

- Answering questions honestly.
- Keeping the patient well groomed and comfortable.
- Calming the patient (talking to patient, reducing fear).
- Not abandoning patient.

Unhelpful behaviour included:

- Trying to get relatives' minds off the patient's condition.
- Crying with relatives.
- Encouraging relatives to cry.
- Reminding relatives that the patient's suffering will soon be over.

As Donovan and Girton (1984) say:

> *In the hospital all family members are outsiders. This fosters frustration—the frustration of helplessly watching a loved one die without being able to do a single thing, while strangers bustle efficiently about doing many things...Each person is unique and has unique capabilities. A man can often lift, turn and move a patient more easily than a woman. He can engage the patient in diversionary conversation or read to him. A child can help change a bed, draw a picture and give a big hug.*

The nurse needs to assess continuously the family's or significant others' needs and desires to be involved, and also to assess when it is time for them to have a break to care for their own needs.

Giaquinta (1977), in her work with 100 families living through the death from cancer of a family member, described 10 phases of family functioning within the following four stages:

1. Living with cancer.
2. The living–dying interval.
3. Bereavement.
4. Re-establishment.

During the 'living with cancer' stage, the individual receives an initial diagnosis of cancer and the whole family moves through phases of coping with the impact of diagnosis. These include functional disruption of usual family roles during illness, treatment and hospitalization; a search for meaning while the family attempts to gain intellectual mastery over the cancer process; the need to inform others outside the family, which can cause feelings of despair, vulnerability and isolation; and displaying emotions. Nurses should aim to foster hope, family cohesion and security, and encourage problem-solving during these phases.

During the living–dying interval, the individual ceases to perform familiar roles and is cared for either at home or in hospital. The family and/or significant others must reorganize their roles to cope and lessen the strain. They also need time to remember the individual's life history. While this is emotionally painful, it is an important phase to go through for both patient and loved ones. Through the use of pictures, scrapbooks and family albums, the nurse may facilitate this process.

Bereavement coincides with imminent death of the individual. Separation and mourning are the tasks of the family at this stage. Nursing care here should be aimed towards promoting intimacy between the patient's loved ones, and fostering relief through the expression of grief.

Re-establishment signals the end of mourning when loved ones may re-enter their social environment, which extends beyond their immediate one.

The Hospice Movement and Palliative Care

While the concept of the hospice can be traced back to medieval times, the modern hospice movement can be attributed to the work of Dame Cicely Saunders who, during her time as medical officer at St Joseph's Hospital in East London, developed techniques of giving to patients strong opiate analgesic drugs at regular intervals, and a concept of 'total pain', which acknowledged the strong emotional and psychological as well as the physical components of pain. Consequently, she revol-

Table 2.44 *Characteristics of hospice services*

- Knowledge and expertise in the control of symptoms in advanced cancer, and a recognition that symptoms such as pain can have physical, psychological, social and spiritual components
- Care is family centred
- Care is by a multidisciplinary team, including doctors, nurses, social workers, spiritual adviser, occupational and physiotherapist
- Home care, respite care and day care services are provided in collaboration with inpatient facilities
- Bereavement follow-up services are offered for relatives
- Hospices also have an educational and research role

utionized the effectiveness of pain relief in advanced cancer patients. In 1967, Dame Cicely Saunders opened St Christopher's Hospice, a specialized, purpose-built unit devoted to the care and support of dying patients. Since the 1960s, the hospice movement has proliferated rapidly so that in Britain there are currently around 125 inpatient units, 80 hospice-based home care teams, 150 free-standing community-based teams, 20 hospital support teams and 64 day care centres (Hill and Oliver, 1988).

Table 2.44 lists the characteristics of hospice services. The philosophy of hospice care is one of providing a supportive environment in which the needs of the dying (physical, psychological, social and spiritual) can be met, and where the quality of the relationship between patient, staff and family is central and highly valued. Open communication is promoted at all times, and individuals are allowed choice in the place of care during their final illness; the nature of support they wish to receive is central to the philosophy of care. The aim of all care is the facilitation of a peaceful and dignified death.

Palliative Care

Palliative care as an area of specialist practice has evolved from the hospice movement and the principles of care on which it is based. Palliative medical care has recently become recognized as a distinct medical specialty. The concept of 'palliative' care for the dying has broadened the focus of care for patients, so that inpatient units provide continuing care, symptom control and respite care for relatives, and from which patients return home once symptoms have been improved or controlled. Thus, care is home-centred, and the expected outcome is to maximize patient's functional potential and quality of life by offering rehabilitation, day care and respite care so that relatives have some relief from the demands of care. Thus

hospice units can no longer be named as simply 'places to die'. Palliative care is also felt to be an important approach to care that should be commenced as early as possible in the course of the disease and not begun only when the patient is imminently dying.

Palliative care remains focused on advanced cancer patients, and most of the experience and understanding of symptom control is derived from this disease. Unfortunately, services for other groups of patients are not always as well developed, for example, for those suffering from respiratory or cardiovascular diseases or for the elderly, and there is now talk of certain groups of dying patients being 'disadvantaged' because of this. However, many of the concepts of symptom control are being applied across other disease categories, and services for particular groups of patients, such as individuals dying from acquired immunodeficiency syndrome (AIDS), are now becoming well established.

Symptoms and Needs of the Dying

A number of studies have been undertaken to identify the problems and needs of dying patients. Hockley (1983) surveyed dying patients in a general hospital and found that of 26 patients dying from cancer and of non-malignant disease, the most common symptom among them was anorexia; 21 also had sore mouths—12 had visible thrush and only 2 of these were receiving treatment for it. Twenty-three of the 26 patients complained of sleeping poorly; ward noise and being turned in their beds too frequently by nurses were identified as being common causes. Twenty of the patients complained of cough or breathlessness, and 18 of pain. Other common problems included pressures sores (many of these had developed after admission), depression and anxiety (particularly among patients who did not know their diagnosis).

Ward (1985) found that, among patients referred to a home care service for terminally ill cancer patients, not only were symptoms such as pain, dyspnoea, nausea and vomiting, sleeplessness and constipation very common, but they were not being controlled adequately at their time of referral to the home care team. There were also other more practical needs, such as advice and help for relatives about care, emotional support and reassurance, relief for housebound carer(s), night sitting and help with laundry and housework. Mudditt (1987) found that relatives of the dying being discharged from hospital to be cared for at home, had many anxieties and concerns over how they were going to manage and how best to undertake the care. They were also dissatisfied with the advice they had received from hospital nurses. More information was felt to be needed on nutrition, elimination, how to care for hygiene needs, positioning and moving the dying person, and how to cope with their medications. It is clear from such studies that nurses need to develop skills in pain and symptom control for dying patients, and to place a high priority on providing social support and co-ordinating services for dying people and their families, particularly following discharge from hospital. Nurses also have an important educational role in providing information to families about how best to care for the dying person.

Symptom Management in the Dying

Considerable expertise has been developed by palliative care experts in the pharmacological and nursing manage-ment of symptoms in the dying; pain has been discussed in depth in this chapter (pp. 179–97). The principles of symptom management in the dying are extremely im-portant, and the points outlined in the section on the per-son experiencing pain apply to the approach taken with other common symptoms such as breathlessness, nausea and vomiting, and anorexia. Assessment of causative and contributory factors to the symptom, and the perceived impact it is having on the dying patient's life, is essen-tial. Symptoms in the dying person are not necessarily caused only by the disease process, and the care and treatment of such symptoms are likely to vary from patient to patient. Once a careful and systematic assess-ment has been undertaken, symptom relief can be approached by referral to the medical team for appropri-ate pain- and symptom-relieving drugs. Nursing care aimed at providing comfort and support for the dying patient experiencing a range of symptoms is vital in im-proving quality of life.

Common symptoms that should be anticipated in the dying are as follows:

- Pain.
- Dry mouth.
- Sore mouth.
- Anorexia.
- Dysphagia.
- Heartburn.
- Nausea and vomiting.
- Gastrointestinal obstruction.
- Constipation.
- Faecal obstruction.
- Rectal discharge.
- Sleeplessness.
- Confusion.
- Anxiety.
- Cough.
- Dyspnoea.
- 'Death rattle'.
- Pressure sores.

Each symptom requires careful assessment, intervention and evaluation; aspects of the care of such symptoms are discussed in the relevant sections of this text.

Good Practice in Hospital Care For the Dying

Criticisms of hospital care for the dying led Henley (1986) to outline a blueprint for good practice for health carers. Two key themes occur throughout the recommendations in this report: that of the great importance of good com-munication between staff, patients and loved ones; and, second, the need for more training and support for doc-tors, nurses and other staff to ensure that they are able to offer dying patients and their relatives and others the indi-vidual emotional and practical care they need. The report outlines recommendations in three areas: care for patients and their loved ones before death; care for patients and their loved ones at the time of death; and administrative and other procedures after death.

Care For Patients and Their Loved Ones Before Death

Henley (1986) highlights the following aspects:

- The great need for staff to give time to dying patients.
- The need to give patients opportunities for private con-versations with staff, and for communication to be open and honest.
- Patients from religious and cultural minorities need special attention.
- There should be access to pain and symptom control.
- Great attention should be paid to practical care not based on routines, and free from medical interventions such as routine temperature and blood pressure record-ings or blood tests.
- Access to spiritual counselling was also highlighted as being very important.
- Staff should make a great effort to get to know family and friends; one key member of staff should be ident-ified to have the responsibility to get to know loved ones and to keep them informed.
- Loved ones should also be given the opportunity to talk to staff in private, to be allowed 24-hour visiting if they wish, to have access to meals and refreshments and to be allowed to stay with patients during nursing and other procedures if they wish.

Care For Patients and Loved Ones At the Time of Death

- Staff should attempt in advance to find out loved ones' wishes with regard to being with the patient at the time of death. They should also communicate the news of the patient's death sensitively, and be trained in how to do this by telephone or other means.
- When death is imminent, patients should have some-one sitting with them at all times.
- Following the patient's death, loved ones should be given the opportunity to be left to sit with the person

who has just died, or to view the body if they were not present at the time of death.

- Bereaved relatives need to be given time to themselves and privacy. All staff should have training and support in how to look after bereaved relatives.
- Loved ones should be offered the opportunity to speak in private to a doctor or nurse about the death and the circumstances surrounding it.
- Practices of removing the body from the ward and handling the patient's property after death need to be undertaken with great care and sensitivity. Drawing curtains around all the beds on a ward while a body is being removed and careless placing of patient's property (soiled clothes, half-eaten boxes of chocolates and so on) in property bags are unacceptable.
- Support for loved ones following sudden death is equally important; nurses may need to ensure that they have support and help once they leave the hospital.

Administrative and Other Procedures After a Death
Nurses must know about the various administrative procedures that need to be carried out following a death, such as: the death certificate; returning property to a patient's loved ones; procedures for postmortem and arranging funerals. This is so that clear and accurate information can be given to loved ones, preferably backed up with written information.

BIBLIOGRAPHY

NUTRITION

Anonymous (1988) Hospital malnutrition still abounds, *Nutrition Reviews*, Vol. 46, pp. 315–17.

Bistrian, B. R., Blackburn, G. L., Hallowell, E. and Heddle, R. (1974) Protein status of general surgical patients, *Journal of the American Medical Association*, Vol. 230, pp. 858–60.

Bistrian, B. R., Blackburn, G. L., Vitale, J. and Cochran, M. (1976) Prevalence of malnutrition in general medical patients, *Journal of the American Medical Association*, Vol. 235, pp. 1567–70.

Bradley, A. and Theobald, A. (1988) The effect of dietary modification as defined by NACNE on the eating habits of 28 people, *Human Nutrition and Dietetics*, Vol. 1, pp. 105–14.

British Dietetic Association (1988) *Malnutrition in Hospitals, Report of A working Party*, British Dietetic Association, Birmingham.

Butterworth, C. E. (1974) The skeleton in the hospital closet, *Nutrition Today*, Vol. 9, pp. 4–7.

Butterworth, C. E. and Blackburn, G. L. (1975) Hospital malnutrition, *Nutrition Today*, Vol. 10, pp. 11–12.

Crapo, P. A., Reaven, G. and Olefsky, J. (1977) Post-prandial plasma glucose and insulin responses to different complex carbohydrates, *Diabetes*, Vol. 26, pp. 1178–83.

Department of Health (1991) *Dietary Reference Values for Food Energy and Nutrients for the United Kingdom.*

Report on Health and Social Subjects No. 41, HMSO, London.

Department of Health and Social Security (1980) *Guidelines On Pre-cooked Chilled Foods*, HMSO, London.

Department of Health and Social Security (1984) *Committee on Medical Aspects of Food Policy. Diet and Cardiovascular Disease. Report on Health and Social Subjects No. 28*, HMSO, London.

Gibson, R. S. (1990) *Principles of Nutritional Assessment*, Oxford University Press, Oxford.

Glew, G. (1973) *Cook-Freeze Catering: An Introduction to Its Technology*, Faber & Faber, London.

Goodinson, S. M. (1987a) Anthropometric assessment of nutritional status, *The Professional Nurse*, Vol. 2, pp. 388–93.

Goodinson, S. M. (1987b) Biochemical assessment of nutritional status, *The Professional Nurse*, Vol. 2, pp. 8–12.

Heymsfield, S. B. and Casper, K. (1987) Anthropometric assessment of the adult hospitalized patient, *Journal of Parenteral and Enteral Nutrition*, Vol. 11, pp. 36S–41S.

Hill, G. L., Blackett, R. L. Pickford, I. *et al.* (1977) Malnutrition in surgical patients: an unrecognised problem, *Lancet*, Vol. i, pp. 89–92.

Holmes, A. (1986a) Food additives, *Nursing* (3rd series), Vol. 8, pp. 293–5.

Holmes, S. (1986b) Fundamentals of nutrition, *Nursing* (3rd series), Vol. 3, pp. 235–7.

Holmes, S. (ed.) (1986c) Malnutrition, wellbeing and the quality of life, *Nutrition in Nursing Practice*, Conference Proceedings, Division of Nursing Studies, University of Surrey, Guildford, pp. 30–5.

Holmes, S. (1986d) Determinants of food intake, *Nursing* (3rd series), Vol. 7, pp. 260–4.

Interdepartmental Committee on Nutrition for National Defense, *Manual of Nutrition Surveys* (2nd edition).

Kaminski, M. V. and Winborn, A. L. (1978) *Nutritional Assessment Guide*, Midwest Nutrition, Education and Research Foundation, Inc.

Metropolitan Height and Weight Tables (1983) *Build Study*, Society of Actuaries and Association of Life Insurance Medical Directors of America.

National Advisory Committee on Nutrition Education (1983) *A Discussion Paper on Proposals for Nutrition Education in Britain*, Health Education Council, London.

Paul, A. A. and Southgate, D. A. T. (1978) *McCance and Widdowson's 'The Composition of Foods'* (4th edition), HMSO, London.

Roubenoff, R., Roubenoff, R.A., Preto, J. and Balke, C. W. (1977) Malnutrition amongst hospitalized patients. A problem of physician awareness, *Archives of Internal Medicine*, Vol. 147, pp. 1462–5.

Wright, R. A. and Heymsfield, S. (1985) *Nutritional Assessment*, Blackwell Scientific Publications, Oxford.

FURTHER READING

Books

Committee on Medical Aspects of Food Policy (Department of Health and Social Security) (1984) *Diet and Cardiovascular*

Disease, Report on Health and Social Subjects No. 28, HMSO, London.

Committee of Medical Aspects of Food Policy (Department of Health) (1989) *Dietary Sugars and Human Disease, Report on Health and Social Subjects No. 37*, HMSO, London.

Fieldhouse, P. (1986) *Food and Nutrition: Customs and Culture*, Croom Helm, London.

Gibson, R. S. (1990), *Principles of Nutritional Assessment*, Oxford University Press, Oxford.

Gifft, H. H., Washbon, M. and Harrison, C. G. (1972), *Nutrition, Behaviour and Change*, Prentice-Hall, New Jersey.

Health Education Council (1983) *Discussion Paper on Guidelines for Nutrition Education in Britain, Report of the National Advisory Committee on Nutrition Education*, Health Education Council, London.

Krause, M. V. and Mahan, L. K. (1984) *Food, Nutrition and Diet Therapy* (7th edition), W. B. Saunders, Philadelphia.

LeFanu, J. (1987) Eat Your Heart Out: The Fallacy of the 'Healthy Diet', MacMillan, London.

Passmore, R. and Eastwood, M. A. (1986), *Davidson and Passmore's Human Nutrition and Dietetics* (8th edition), Churchill Livingstone, Edinburgh.

Suitor, C. W. and Crowley, M. F. (1984) *Nutrition: Principles and Applications in Health Promotion* (2nd edition), J. B. Lippincott, Philadelphia.

Wright, R. A. and Heymsfield, S. (1985) *Nutritional Assessment*, Blackwell Scientific Publications, Oxford.

Articles

Baker, J. P. *et al.* (1982) Nutritional assessment: A comparison of clinical judgment and objective measurements, *New England Journal of Medicine*, 22 April, Vol. 306, No. 16, pp. 969–72.

Butterworth, C. E. Jr and Blackburn, G. L. (1975) Hospital malnutrition, *Nutrition Today*, March/April, Vol. 10, No. 2, pp. 8–18.

Cockran, D. and Kaminski, M. V. (1986) Current concepts in nutritional assessment, *Nutritional Support Services*, May, Vol. 6, No. 5, pp. 14–15.

Hall, C. A. (1982) Nutritional assessment, *New England Journal of Medicine*, 16 September, Vol. 307, No. 12, p. 754.

Hinson, L. R. (1985) Nutritional assessment and management of the hospitalized patient, *Critical Care Nurse*, February, Vol. 5, No. 2, pp. 53–7.

Laffrey, S. C. (1986) Normal and overweight adults: Perceived weight and health behavior characteristics, *Nursing Research*, May/June, Vol. 35, No. 6, pp. 173–7.

Lipschitz, D. A. (1982) Protein–calorie malnutrition in the hospitalized elderly, *Medical Clinics of North America*, September, Vol. 9, No. 3, pp. 531–43.

McLaren, D. S. and Meguid, M. M. (1983) Nutritional assessment at the crossroads, *Journal of Parenteral and Enteral Nutrition*, June, Vol. 7, No. 6, pp. 575–9.

Morgan, J. (1984) Nutritional assessment of critically ill patients, *Focus on Critical Care*, June, Vol. 11, No. 3, pp. 28–34.

Morowitz, H. J. (1985) Ecology and the great cold cereal rip-off, *Hospital Practice*, 15 March, Vol. 20, No. 3, pp. 30–1.

Orme, J. F. and Clemmer, T. P. (1983) Nutrition in the critical care unit, *Medical Clinics of North America*, November, Vol. 67, No. 6, pp. 1295–302.

Seltzer, M. H. *et al.* (1982) Instant nutritional assessment: Absolute weight loss and surgical mortality, *JPEN*, May/June, Vol. 6, No. 3, pp. 218–21.

Superko, H. R., Haskell, W. L. and Wood, P. D. (1985) Modification of plasma cholesterol through exercise, *Postgraduate Medicine*, October, Vol. 78, No. 5, pp. 64–75.

Vitale, J. J. (1985) Nutrition and the elderly, *Postgraduate Medicine*, October, Vol. 78, No. 5, pp. 93–102.

Vitamin supplements (1985) *Medical Letters*, 2 August, Vol. 27, No. 693, pp. 66–7.

Warnold, J. and Lundholm, K. (1984) Clinical significance of preoperative nutritional status in 215 non-cancer patients, *Annals of Surgery*, March, Vol. 199, No. 3, pp. 299–305.

SLEEP

BIBLIOGRAPHY

Bouton, J. (1986) Falling asleep, *Nursing Times*, 10 December, Vol. 82, pp. 36–7.

Closs, J. (1988a) Patients' sleep–wake rhythms in hospital (Part 1), *Nursing Times*, 6 January, Vol. 84, No. 1, pp. 48–50.

Closs, J. (1988b) Patients' sleep–wake rhythms in hospital (Part 2), *Nursing Times*, 13 January, Vol. 84, No. 2, pp. 54–5.

Gournay, K. (1988) Sleeping without drugs, *Nursing Times*, 16 March, Vol. 84, No. 11, pp. 46–9.

Lyall, J. (1989) The unknown addicts, *Nursing Times*, 22 February, Vol. 85, No. 8, pp. 16–17.

Morgan, K. (1987) *Sleep and Ageing*, Croom Helm, Beckenham.

Neal, M. J. (1987) *Medical Pharmacology at a Glance*, Blackwell Scientific, Oxford.

Roper, N., Logan, W. and Tierney, A. J. (1985) *The Elements of Nursing* (2nd edition), Churchill Livingstone, Edinburgh, Chapter 17.

Trevelyan, J. (1988) The forgotten addicts, *Nursing Times*, 20 April, Vol. 84, No. 16, pp. 16–17.

Willis, J. (1989) A good night's sleep, *Nursing Times*, 22 November, Vol. 84, No. 47, pp. 29–31.

Wilson-Barnett, J. and Batchup, L. (eds) (1988) Fordham in *Patients' Problems*, Scutari Press, London.

FURTHER READING

Articles

Bredsdorff Gray, K. (1988) A man's best friend, *Nursing Times*, 24 August, Vol. 84, No. 34, pp. 40–4.

Clinical feature (1987) The need for sleep, *Nursing Standard*, 23 September, Vol. 1, Issue 3, p. 25.

Hamlin, M. and Hammersley, D. (1989) Drug withdrawal, *Nursing Times*, 30 August, Vol. 84, No. 35, pp. 66–8.

Kearnes, S. (1989) Insomnia in the elderly, *Nursing Times*, Vol. 85, No. 47, pp. 32–3.

Trevelyan, J. (1989) Now I lay me down to sleep, *Nursing Times*, 22 November, Vol. 85, No. 47, pp. 34–5.

HYGIENE

BIBLIOGRAPHY

Alderman, C. (1988) Oral hygiene, *Nursing Standard*, 9 July, Vol. 40, No. 2, p. 24.

Crosby, C. (1989) Methods in mouth care, *Nursing Times*, 30 August, Vol. 85, No. 35, pp. 38–41.

Gooch, J. (1985) Mouth care, *The Professional Nurse*, Vol. 1, No. 3, pp. 72–8.

Gooch, J. (1987) Skin hygiene, *The Professional Nurse*, February, Vol. 2, No. 5, pp. 153–4.

Greaves, A. (1985) 'We'll just freshen you up, dear . . .' (survey into the use of wash bowls and face cloths), *Nursing Times*, 6 March, Vol. 81, (*Journal of Infection Control Nursing*, Supplement, Vol. 27, pp. 3–4, 7–8).

Harris, M. D. (1980) *Nursing Times*, 21 February, Vol. 76, No. 8, pp. 340–1.

Harrison, A. (1987) Denture care, *Nursing Times*, 13 May, Vol. 83, No. 19, pp. 28–9.

Meckstroth, R. (1989) Improving quality and efficiency in oral hygiene, *Journal of Gerontological Nursing*, July, Vol. 15, No. 6, pp. 38–42.

Roth, P. T. and Creason, N. S. (1986) Nurse-administered oral hygiene: is there a scientific basis? *Journal of Advanced Nursing*, 11 May, Vol. 3, pp. 323–31.

Shepherd, G., Page, G. and Sammon, P. (1987) The mouth trap, *Nursing Times*, 13 May, Vol. 83, No. 19, pp. 25–7.

Webster, R., Thompson, D., Bourmay, G. and Sutton, T. (1988) Patients' and nurses' opinions about bathing, *Nursing Times*, 14 September, Vol. 84, No. 37, pp. 54–7.

FURTHER READING

McMahon, R. (1989) Partners in care, *Nursing Times*, 22 February, Vol. 85, No. 8, pp. 34–6.

Richardson, A. (1987) A process standard for oral care, *Nursing Times*, 12 August, Vol. 83, No. 32, pp. 38–40.

FLUID AND ELECTROLYTE BALANCE

FURTHER READING

Books

Muirhead, N. and Catto, G. R. (1986) *Aids to Fluid and Electrolyte Imbalance*, Churchill Livingstone, Edinburgh.

Nursing (1978) *Monitoring Fluid and Electrolyte Precisely*, *Nursing '78*, Skillbook Series, Internal Communications, Horsham, Pennsylvania.

Zila, J. F. (1984) *Clinical Chemistry in Diagnosis and Treatment* (4th edition), Lloyd-Luke (Medical Books), London.

Articles

Barton, I. K. and Mansell, M. A. (1984) Fluid and electrolyte disorders: sodium, *British Journal of Hospital Medicine*, July, Vol. 32, No. 1, pp. 15–18.

Folk-Lightly, M. (1984) Solving the puzzle of patients' fluid imbalances, *Nursing 84*, February, Vol. 14, No. 2, pp. 34–41.

Foss, M. (1988) Acid–base balance, *The Professional Nurse*, September, Vol. 3, No. 12, pp. 509–13.

Howland, S. M. (1980) Potassium deficit and excess, *Nursing*, May, 1st series, No. 13, pp. 560–1.

Iveson-Iveson, J. (1982) Fluid balance, *Nursing Mirror*, 16 June, Vol. 154, No. 24, p. 38.

Miller, J. (1989) Intravenous therapy in fluid and electrolyte imbalance, *The Professional Nurse*, February, Vol. 4, No. 5, pp. 237–41.

Piper, M. E. (1976) Fluid and electrolyte balance, *Nursing Mirror*, 28 October, Vol. 143, No. 18, pp. 55–7.

Schwartz, M. W. (1987) Potassium imbalances, *American Journal of Nursing*, October, Vol. 87, No. 10, pp. 1292–9.

Turner, J. (1988) Helping the dehydrated patient, *Nursing Times*, 4 May, Vol. 84, No. 18, pp. 40–1.

Willatts, S. M. (1984) Fluid and electrolyte disorders: water, *British Journal of Hospital Medicine*, July, Vol. 32, No. 1, pp. 8–14.

TEMPERATURE CONTROL

BIBLIOGRAPHY

Edholm, O. G. (1978) *Man—Hot and Cold*, Edward Arnold, London.

IATROGENIC EFFECTS OF BEING IN HOSPITAL

BIBLIOGRAPHY

Bradshaw, S. (1987) Treating yourself, *Nursing Times*, 11 February, Vol. 83, No. 5, pp. 40–1.

Campbell, C. (1988) Could do better, *Nursing Times*, 1 June, Vol. 84, No. 22, pp. 66–71.

Darbyshire, P. (1987) Mealtimes—or refuelling stops? *Nursing Times*, August, Vol. 83, No. 33, P. 39.

Dopson, L. (1986) Back to the drawing board, *Nursing Times*, 29 October, Vol. 82, No. 43, pp. 16–18.

Gidley, C. (1987) Now wash your hands, *Nursing Times*, 22 July, Vol. 83, No. 29, pp. 40–2.

Grazier, S. (1988) The loneliness barrier, *Nursing Times*, 12 October, Vol. 84, No. 41, pp. 44–5.

Hartley, J. (1988) Banishing the bacteria, *Nursing Times* (*Journal of Infection Control Nursing*, Supplement), 1 June, Vol. 84, No. 22, pp. 71–2.

Kennedy, J. (1989) Ring cushions—an outdated mode of treatment, *Nursing Times*, 29 November, Vol. 85, No. 48, pp. 34–5.

Levin, D. (1985) Care about food: hospitals can make you thin, *Nursing Times*, 8 May, Vol. 81, pp. 36–8.

Overton, E. (1988) Bed-making and bacteria, *Nursing Times* (*Journal of Infection Control Nursing*, Supplement), 2 March, Vol. 84, No. 9, pp. 69–71.

Sadler, C. (1987) On the track of a killer, *Nursing Times*, 7 October, Vol. 83, No. 40, p. 19.

Symington, I. (1987) Hepatitis B—an avoidable hazard, *Nursing Times*, 14 January, Vol. 83, No. 2, pp. 50–1.

Taylor, M. (1988) Malnutrition in hospital, *Nursing Standard*, 19 November, Vol. 3, pp. 30–1.

Thomlinson, D. (1987) To clean or not to clean? *Nursing Times* (*Journal of Infection Control Nursing*, Supplement), 4 March, Vol. 83, No. 9, pp. 71–5.

Webster, O., Cowan, M. and Allen, J. (1986) Dirty linen, *Nursing Times*, 29 October, Vol. 82, No. 43, pp. 36–7.

Whipp, P. (1987) MRSA: methods of prevention and control, *The Professional Nurse*, Vol. 2, No. 10, pp. 324–5.

Williams, E. and Buckles, A. (1988) A lack of motivation, *Nursing Times* (*Journal of Infection Control Nursing*, Supplement), 1 June, Vol. 84, No. 22, pp. 60–4.

Wright, E. (1988) Catheter care: the risk of infection, *The Professional Nurse*, September, Vol. 3, No. 2, pp. pp. 487–90.

FURTHER READING

Books

Roitt, I. (1984) *Essential Immunology* (5th edition), Blackwell Scientific Publications, Oxford.

Articles

Blackmore, M. (1987) Hand-drying methods, *Nursing Times* (*Journal of Infection Control Nursing*, Supplement), 16 September, Vol. 83, No. 37, pp. 71–4.

Crummy, V. (1985) Hospital-acquired urinary tract infection (study of infection rates from indwelling urinary catheters, and development of policy for management and care), *Nursing Times* (*Journal of Infection Control Nursing*, Supplement), 5 June, Vol. 81, pp. 7, 9, 11, 12.

Denton, P. F. (1986) Psychological and physiological effects of isolation, *Nursing*, March, Vol. 3, No. 3, pp. 88–91.

Dickerson, J. W. T. (1986) Hospital-induced malnutrition: a cause for concern, *The Professional Nurse*, August, Vol. 1, No. 11, pp. 293–6.

Dickerson, J. W. T. (1986) Hospital-induced malnutrition: prevention and treatment, *The Professional Nurse*, September, Vol. 1, No. 12, pp. 314–16.

Goodlad, J. (1989) Understanding hepatitis B, *Nursing Times*, 14 June, Vol. 84, No. 24, pp. 69–71.

Goodinson, S. M. (1987) Assessment of nutritional status, *The Professional Nurse*, August, Vol. 2, No. 11, pp. 367–9.

Goodinson, S. M. (1987) Assessing nutritional status: subjective methods, *The Professonal Nurse*, November, Vol. 3, No. 2, pp. 48–51.

Holmes, S. (1987) Diabetics—artificial feeding, *Nursing Times*, 5 August, Vol. 83, No. 31, pp. 49–55.

Jacques, L., McKie, S. and Harnes, C. (1986) Effects of short-term catheterization, *Nursing Times* (Supplement), 18 June, Vol. 82, No. 25, pp. 59–62.

Milne, C. (1989) Lying in wait (adverse effects of bedrest), *Nursing Standard*, 11 February, Vol. 3, pp. 30–1.

Mohun, J. (1989) Design for health (effect of hospital environment on patients, including use of art), *Nursing Times & Nursing Mirror*, 24 May, Vol. 85, No. 25, pp. 16–17.

Reed, S. (1987) Point taken? *Nursing Times* (*Journal of Infection Control Nursing*, Supplement), 2 December, Vol. 83, No. 48, pp. 64–9.

Taylor, M. (1985) 'Nurse, I'm starving' (nurses' responsibilities for monitoring patient nutrition), *Nursing Times*, 5 June, Vol. 81, p. 31.

BEDREST

BIBLIOGRAPHY

Green, J. H. (1978) *Basic Clinical Physiology* (3rd edition), Oxford University Press, Oxford.

Milne, C. (1989) Lying in wait (adverse effects of bedrest), *Nursing Standard*, 11 February, Vol.3, pp. 30–1.

Rubin, M. (1988) The physiology of bedrest, *American Journal of Nursing*, January, Vol. 88, No. 1, pp. 50–6.

FURTHER READING

Boore, J. R. P., Champion, R. and Ferguson, M. C. (1987) *Nursing the Physically Ill Adult: A Textbook of Medical/Surgical Nursing*, Churchill Livingstone, Edinburgh, pp. 275–6.

Milne, C. (1989) Preventing the problem (problems of bedrest), *Nursing Standard*, 18 February, Vol. 3, pp. 34–5.

AMBULATION

BIBLIOGRAPHY

Kubler Ross, E. (1970) *On Death and Dying*, Tavistock, London.

Robertson, I. (1986) Learned helplessness, *Nursing Times/ Nursing Mirror*, 17 December, Vol.82, pp. 28–30.

Roper, W., Logan, W. W. and Tierney, A. J. (1983) *Using a Model for Nursing*, Churchill Livingstone, London.

Stockwell, F. (1972) *The Unpopular Patient*, Royal College of Nursing, London.

FURTHER READING

Books

Wilson-Barnett, J. and Batehup, L. (1988) *Patient Problems (A Research Base for Nursing Care)*, Scutari Press, London, Chapter 10.

Articles

Griffiths, B. L. (1987) Back pain: why bother? *The Professional Nurse*, December, Vol. 3, No. 3, pp. 97–101.

Lloyd, P. (1986) Handle with care, *Nursing Times*, 19 November, Vol. 82, No. 47, pp. 33–5.

Love, C. (1986) Do you roll or lift? *Nursing Times*, 16 July, Vol.82, No. 28, pp. 44–6.

Thompson, C. (1987) Learning to lift, *Nursing Times*, 15 April, Vol. 83, No. 14, pp. 34–5.

Walsh, R. (1988) On the move (human kinetics), *Nursing Times*, 31 August, Vol. 84, No. 35, pp. 26–30.

Walsh, R. (1988) Good movement habits (human kinetics), 14 September, *Nursing Times*, Vol. 84, No. 37, pp. 59–61.

PRESSURE AREA CARE

BIBLIOGRAPHY

Barrett, E. (1988) A review of risk assessment methods, *Care— Science and Practice*, Vol. 6, No. 2, pp. 49–52.

David, J., Chapman, C., Chapman, R. and Locket, M. (1983) *An Investigation of the Current Methods Used in Nursing For the Care of Patients With Established Pressure Sores*, Nursing Practice Research Unit, Northwick Park Hospital and Clinical Research Centre, Harrow, Middlesex.

Dickerson, J. W. T. (1986) Hospital-induced malnutrition: prevention and treatment, *The Professional Nurse*, Vol. 1, No. 12, pp. 314–16.

Exton-Smith, N. (1987) The patient's not for turning, *Nursing Times*, Vol. 83, No. 42, pp. 42–4.

Hill, G. L., Blackett, R. L. and Pickford, I. (1977) Malnutrition in surgical patients, *Lancet*, Vol. i, pp. 289–92.

Lowthian, P. T. (1979) Turning clocks system to prevent pressure sores, *Nursing Mirror*, Vol. 148, No. 21, pp. 30–1.

Lowthian, P. T. (1987) The practical assessment of pressure sore risk, *Care—Science and Practice*, Vol. 5, No. 4, pp. 3–7.

Norton, D., Exton-Smith, A. N. and McLaren, R. (1975) *An Investigation of Geriatric Nursing Problems in Hospital*, Churchill Livingstone, Edinburgh.

Preston, K. W. (1988) Positioning for comfort and relief: the 30 degree alternative, *Care—Science and Practice*, Vol.6, No. 4, pp. 116–19.

Pritchard, V. (1986) Calculating the risk, *Nursing Times*, Vol. 82, No. 8, pp. 59–61.

Torrance, C. (1983) *Pressure Sores: Aetiology, Treatment and Prevention*, Croom Helm, Beckenham.

Tweedle, D. (1978) How the metabolism reacts to injury, *Nursing Mirror*, Vol. 147, No. 21, pp. 34–6.

Waterlow, J. (1985) A risk assessment card, *Nursing Times*, Vol. 81, No. 48. pp. 49–55.

INFECTION CONTROL

BIBLIOGRAPHY

Anonymous (1984) Needlestick transmission of HTLV-III from a patient infected in Africa, *Lancet*, 15 December, Vol. 2, pp. 1376–7.

Ayliffe, G. A. J., Babb, J. R., Davies, J. G. and Lilly, H. A. (1988) Hand disinfection: a comparison of various agents in laboratory and ward studies, *Journal of Hospital Infection*, Vol. 11, pp. 226–43.

Ayliffe, G. A. J., Collins, B. J. and Taylor, L. J. (1990) *Hospital-acquired Infection: Principles and Prevention* (2nd edition), Wright, London.

Broughall, J. M., Marsham, C., Jackson, B. and Bird, P. (1984) An automatic monitoring system for measuring handwashing frequency in hospital wards, *Journal of Hospital Infection*, Vol. 5, pp. 447–53.

Caddow, P. (ed.) (1989) Nursing Intervention (Chapter 8), B. Bowell in *Applied Microbiology*, Scutari Press, London, pp. 159–88.

Caddow. P. (ed.) (1989) The Control and Prevention of Hospital-Acquired Infection (Chapter 5), *Applied Microbiology*, Scutari Press, London, pp. 75–102.

Casewell, M. and Phillips, I. (1978) Food as a source of *Klebsiella* species for colonisation and infection of intensive care patients, *Journal of Clinical Pathology*, Vol. 31, pp. 845–9.

Centers for Disease Control (1985) Recommendations for preventing transmission of infection with human T-lymphotropic virus type III/lymphadenopathy-associated virus in the workplace, *Morbidity and Mortality Weekly Report*, Vol. 34, pp. 681–95.

Centers for Disease Control (1987) Recommendations for prevention of HIV transmission in health-care settings, *Morbidity and Mortality Weekly Report*, Vol. 36 (Supplement No. 2S), pp. 3S–18S.

Centers for Disease Control (1991) Update: Transmission of HIV infection during an invasive dental procedure— Florida, *Morbidity and Mortality Weekly Report*, Vol. 40, pp. 21–33.

Collins, C. H. and Kennedy, D. A. (1987) Microbiological hazards of occupational needlestick and 'sharps' injuries, *Journal of Applied Bacteriology*, Vol. 62, pp. 385–402.

Department of Health (1982) *The Safe Disposal of Clinical Waste (HN(82)22)*, Department of Health, London.

Department of Health (1986a) *Public Enquiry into the Cause of the Outbreak of Legionnaires' Disease in Staffordshire*, HMSO, London.

Department of Health (1986b) *The Report of the Committee of the Enquiry into an Outbreak of Food Poisoning at Stanley Royd Hospital*, HMSO, London.

Department of Health (1987) *Hospital Laundry Arrangements For Used and Infected Linen (HC(87)30)*, Department of Health, London.

Department of Health (1988) *Hospital Infection Control: Guidance On the Control of Infection in Hospitals*, prepared by the DHSS/Public Health Laboratory Service Hospital Infection Working Group, Department of Health, London.

Expert Advisory Group on AIDS (1990) *Guidance for Clinical Health Care Workers: Protection Against Infection With HIV and Hepatitis Viruses*, HMSO, London.

Fujita, K., Lilly, H. A. and Ayliffe, G. A. J. (1981) Gentamicin-resistant *Pseudomonas aeruginosa* infection from mattresses in a burns unit, *British Medical Journal*, Vol. 283, p. 219.

Haley, R. W. (1986) *Managing Hospital Infection Control for Cost-effectiveness*, American Hospital Association.

Haley, R. W., Culver, D. H., White, J. W., *et al.* (1985) The efficacy of infection surveillance and control programmes in preventing nosocomial infections in US hospitals, *American Journal of Epidemiology*, Vol. 121, pp. 182–205.

Greaves, A. (1985) We'll just freshen you up, dear, *Nursing Times,* 6 March, Supplement, Vol. 81, No. 10, pp. 3–8.

Kelsey, J. C. (1972) The myth of surgical sterility, *Lancet*, Vol. 2, pp. 1301–1303.

Kiddy, K., Josse, E. and Griffin, N. (1987) An outbreak of serious klebsiella infections related to food blenders, *Journal of Hospital Infection*, Vol. 9, pp. 191–3.

Larson, E. (1988) A causal link between handwashing and risk of infection? Examination of the evidence, *Infection Control Hospital Epidemiology*, Vol. 9, pp. 28–36.

Leclair, J.M., Freeman, J., Sullivan, B.F., *et al. (1987)* Prevention of nosocomial respiratory syncytial virus infections through compliance with glove and gown isolation precautions, *New England Journal of Medicine*, Vol. 317, 329–34.

Lynch, P., Jackson, M. M., Cummings, M. J. *et al.* (1987) Rethinking the role of isolation practices in the prevention of nosocomial infections, *Annals of Internal Medicine*, Vol. 107, pp. 243–6.

Lynch, P., Cummings, M. J., Roberts, P. L., *et al.* (1990) Implementing and evaluating a system of generic infection precautions: body substance isolation, *American Journal of Infection Control*, Vol. 18, pp. 1–12.

Meers, P. D., Ayliffe, G. A. J., Emmerson, A. M., *et al.* (1981) Report on the national survey of infection in hospitals, 1980, *Journal of Hospital Infection*, Vol. 2 (supplement), pp. 1–51.

Newsom, S. W. B. (1972) Microbiology of hospital toilets, *Lancet*, Vol. 2, pp. 700–3.

Overton, E. (1988) Bed-making and bacteria, *Nursing Times*, 2 March, Vol. 84, No. 9, pp. 69–71.

Roberts, D. (1990) Sources of infection: food, *Lancet*, Vol. 336, pp. 859–61.

Scottish Home and Health Department (1988) *The Hospital Infection Manual, Including a Code of Practice for the Scottish Health Service,* SHHD, Edinburgh.

Sedgwick, J. (1984) Handwashing in hospital wards, *Nursing Times*, 16 May, Vol. 80, No. 10.

Speller, D. C. E., Shanson, D. C., Ayliffe, G. A. J. and Cooke, E. M. (1990) Acquired immune deficiency syndrome: recommendation of a working party of the Hospital Infection Society, *Journal of Hospital Infection*, Vol. 15, pp. 7–34.

Taylor, L. J. (1978) An evaluation of handwashing techniques, parts I and II, *Nursing Times*, 12 and 19 January, Vol. 74.

Taylor, L. J. (1988) Segregation, collection and disposal of hospital laundry and waste, *Journal of Hospital Infection*, Vol. 11 (supplement A), pp. 57–63.

Webster, J. and Faoagali, J. L. (1989) An in-use comparison of chlorhexidine gluconate 4% w/v, glycol-poly-siloxane plus methylcellulose and a liquid soap in a special care baby unit, *Journal of Hospital Infection*, Vol. 14, pp. 141–51.

Wilson, J. and Breedon, P. (1990) Universal precautions, *Nursing Times*, 12 September, Vol. 86, No. 37, pp. 67–70.

World Health Organisation (1990) Report of the international survey of the prevalence of hospital-acquired infections, *Hospital Infection Control*, November, Vol. 17, No. 11, p.148.

FURTHER READING

Books

Ayliffe, G. A. J., Coates, D. and Hoffman, P. N. (1984) *Chemical Disinfection in Hospitals*, Public Health Laboratory Service, London.

Boore, J. (1978) *Prescription For Recovery*, Royal College of Nursing, London.

British Medical Association (1989) *A Code of Practice For Sterilisation of Instruments and Control of Cross-Infection*, BMA, London.

British Medical Association (1990) *A Code of Practice For the Safe Use and Disposal of Sharps*, BMA, London.

British Standards Institute (1990) *Specification for Sharps Containers (BS 7320)*, BSI, London.

Castle, M. and Ajemian, E. (1987) *Hospital Infection Control: Principles and Practice* (2nd edition), John Wiley & Sons, Chichester.

Cooke, E. M. (1991) *Hare's Bacteriology and Immunity For Nurses* (7th edition), Churchill Livingstone, Edinburgh.

Department of Health (1986) *Health Service Catering Hygiene*, HMSO, London.

Department of Health (1987) *Decontamination of Health Care Equipment Prior to Inspection, Service or Repair (HN(87) 22)*, Department of Health, London.

Hobbs, B. C. and Roberts, D. (1987) *Food Poisoning and Food Hygiene* (5th edition), Edward Arnold, London.

Kreier, J. P. and Mortensen, R. J. (1990) *Infection, Resistance and Immunity*, Harper & Row, London.

Larson, E. (1984) *Clinical Microbiology and Infection Control*, Blackwell Scientific Publications, Oxford.

Lowbury, E. J. L., Ayliffe, G. A. J., Geddes, A. M. *et al.* (eds) (1981) *Control of Infection: A Practical Handbook* (2nd edition), Chapman & Hall, London.

Maurer, I. (1985) *Hospital Hygiene* (3rd edition), Edward Arnold, London.

Smith, P. W. (ed.) (1984) *Infection Control in Long-Term Care Facilities*, John Wiley & Sons, Chichester.

Walsh, M. and Ford, P. (1989) *Rituals in Nursing*, Heinemann, London.

Worsley, M. A. (ed.) (1990) *Infection Control: Guidelines for Nursing Care*, Infection Control Nurses' Association, Great Britain.

Articles

Ashworth, P. (1984) Infection control and the nursing process—making the best use of resources, *Journal of Hospital Infection*, Vol. 5 (supplement A), pp. 35–44.

Austin, L. (1988) The salt bath myth, *Nursing Times*, 2 March, Vol. 84, No. 9, pp. 79–83.

Ayliffe, G. A. J., Babb, J. R. and Quoraishi, A. H. (1978) A test for 'hygienic' hand disinfection, *Journal of Clinical Pathology*, Vol. 31, pp. 923–8.

Ayliffe, G. A. J., Babb, J. R., Taylor, L. and Wise, R. (1979) A unit for source and protective isolation in a general hospital, *British Medical Journal*, Vol. 2, pp. 461–5.

Ayliffe, G. A. J., Collins, B. J. and Lowbury, E. J. L. (1967) Ward floors and other surfaces as reservoirs of infection, *Journal of Hygiene*, Vol. 65, pp. 515–36.

Babb, J. R., Davies, J. G. and Ayliffe, G. A. J. (1983) Contamination of protective clothing and nurses' uniforms in an isolation ward, *Journal of Hospital Infection*, Vol. 4, pp. 149–57.

Bartrop, R. W., Luckhurst, E., Lazarus, L., Kilon, L. G. and Penny, R. (1977) Depressed lymphocyte function after bereavement, *Lancet*, Vol. 1, pp. 834–6.

Burnie, J. P., Odds, F. C., Lee, W., *et al.* (1985) Outbreak of systemic *Candida albicans* in intensive care unit caused by cross-infection, *British Medical Journal*, Vol. 290, pp. 746–8.

Carter, R. (1990) Ritual and risk, *Nursing Times*, 28 March, Vol. 86, No. 13, pp. 63–4.

Claesson, B. E. B. and Claesson, U. L. E. (1985) An outbreak of endometritis in a maternity unit caused by spread of group A streptococci from a showerhead, *Journal of Hospital Infection*, Vol. 6, pp. 304–11.

Cousins, M. (1976) Anatomy of an illness (as perceived by the patient), *New England Journal of Medicine*, Vol. 295, pp. 1458–63.

Cruse, P. E. and Foord, R. (1980) The epidemiology of wound infection, *Surgical Clinics of North America*, Vol. 60, pp. 27–40.

Garibaldi, R., Burke, J. P. and Britt, M. R. (1980) Meatal colonisation and catheter-associated bacteriuria, *New England Journal of Medicine*, Vol. 303, pp. 316–18.

Gibbs, H. (1986) Catheter toilet and urinary tract infections, *Nursing Times*, 4 June, Vol. ?, No. ?, pp. 75–6.

Greer, S., Morris, T. and Pettingale, K. W. (1979) Psychological response to breast cancer: effect on outcome, *Lancet*, Vol. 2, pp. 785–7.

Haley, R. W., Gardner, J. S. and Simmons, B. P. (1985) A new approach to the isolation of hospitalised patients with infectious diseases: alternative systems, *Journal of Hospital Infection*, Vol. 6, pp. 128–39.

Hobbs, P. (1989) Enteral feeds, *Nursing Times*, 1 March, Vol. 85, No. 9, pp. 71–3.

Hoffman, P. N., Cooke, E. M., McCarville, M. R. *et al.* (1985) Micro-organisms isolated from skin under wedding rings worn by hospital staff, *British Medical Journal*, Vol. 290, pp. 206–7.

Hospital Infection Society (1990) Revised guidelines for the control of epidemic methicillin-resistant *Staphylococcus aureus*, *Journal of Hospital Infection*, Vol. 16, pp. 351-77.

Houang, E. T., Buckley, R., Smith, M. *et al.* (1981) Survival of *Pseudomonas aeruginosa* in plaster of Paris, *Journal of Hospital Infection*, Vol. 2, pp. 231–5.

Jackson, M. M. and Lynch, P. (1985) Isolation practices: a historical perspective, *American Journal of Infection Control*, Vol. 13, pp. 21–31.

Joseph, C. A. and Palmer, S. R. (1989) Outbreaks of salmonella infection in hospitals in England and Wales 1978–87, *British Medical Journal*, Vol. 298, pp. 1161–4.

Joynson, D. H. M. (1978) Bowls and bacteria, *Journal of Hygiene*, Vol. 80, pp. 423–5.

Kelso, H. (1989) Alternative technique, *Nursing Times*, 7 June, Vol. 85, No. 23, pp. 70–2.

Kerr, S., Kerr, G. E., Mackintosh, C. A. *et al.* (1990) A survey of methicillin-resistant *Staphylococcus aureus* affecting patients in England and Wales, *Journal of Hospital Infection*, Vol. 16, pp. 35–48.

Loomes, S. (1988) Is it safe to lie down in hospital? *Nursing Times*, 7 December, Vol. 84, No. 49, pp. 63–5.

Maki, D. G., Alvarados, C. A., Hassemer, C. A. *et al.* (1982) Relation of the inanimate hospital environment to endemic nosocomial infection, *New England Journal of Medicine*, Vol. 307, pp. 1562–6.

Nystrom, B. (1980) The disinfection of thermometers in hospitals, *Journal of Hospital Infection*, Vol. 1, pp. 345–8.

Nystrom, B. (1981) The disinfection of baths and shower trolleys in hospitals, *Journal of Hospital Infection*, Vol. 2, pp. 93–5.

Oldman, P. (1987) An unkind cut, *Nursing Times*, 2 December, Vol. 83, No. 48, pp. 71–4.

Riddle, H. (1984) Hospital cleaning contracts, *Nursing Times*, 8 August, Vol. 80, No. 32, pp. 57–9.

Roberts, J. (1987) Penny wise, pound foolish? *Nursing Times*, 16 September, Vol. 83, No. 37, pp. 68–70.

Ryder, C. J. (1990) UK Food legislation, *Lancet*, Vol. 336, pp. 1559–62.

Seropian, B. and Reynolds, B. M. (1971) Wound infections after pre-operative depilation versus razor preparation, *American Journal of Surgery*, Vol. 121, pp. 251–4.

Taylor, L. J. (1988) Hospital-acquired infection: the silent epidemic, *Medical Horizons*, October, Vol. 2, No. 3, p. 25.

Wilson, J. L. (1990) The price of protection, *Nursing Times*, 27 June, Vol. 86, No. 26, pp. 67–8.

Winfield, U. (1986) Too close a shave? *Nursing Times*, 5 March, Vol. 82, No. 10, pp. 64–8.

PERIOPERATIVE CARE/SHOCK

BIBLIOGRAPHY

Autton, N. (1968) *Pastoral Care in Hospitals*, SPCK, London.

Bateman, D. N. and Whittingham, T. A. (1982) Measurement of gastric emptying by real time ultrasound, *Gut*, Vol. 23, p. 524.

Boore, J. (1978) *Prescription For Recovery*, Royal College of Nursing, London.

Carbatt, P. and Van Crevel, H. (1981) Lumbar puncture headache: controlled study on the preventative effect of 24 hours' bedrest, *Lancet*, Vol. II, pp. 133–5.

Cochran, R. M. (1984) Psychological preparation of patients for surgical procedures, *Patient Education and Counselling*, Vol. 5, pp. 153–8.

Franklin, B. J. (1974) *Patient Anxiety On Admission to Hospital*, Royal College of Nurses, London.

Gidley, C. (1983) Now wash your hands, *Nursing Times*, 22 July, Vol. 83, p. 29.

Gray, C. (1989) Patients' perceptions of anxiety, *Surgical Nurse*, June, Vol. 2, No. 3, pp. 12–17.

Groen, J. J. (1971) Social change and psychosomatic disease, *Society, Stress and Disease: The Psychological Environment and Psychosomatic Diseases, Volume 1*, Oxford University Press.

Hayward, J. (1973) *Information—A Prescription Against Pain*, Royal College of Nursing, London.

Hildgard, E. R. and Atkinson, R. L. (1979) *Introduction to Psychology* (7th edition), Harcourt, New York.

McCaffery, M. (1983) *Nursing the Patient in Pain*, Harper & Row, London.

Nimmo, W. S. *et al.* (1983) Gastric contents at induction of anaesthesia: is a 4-hour fast necessary? *British Journal of Anaesthesiology*, Vol. 55, pp. 1185–7.

Pharo, C. (1989) The nurse's role in anaesthesia, *Surgical Nurse*, April, pp. 18–23.

Pugh, J. and Millar, B. (1989a) Nursing management for mobility, *Surgical Nurse*, June, Vol. 2, No. 3, pp. 24–7.

Pugh, J. and Millar, B. (1989b) Mobility in the perioperative phase, *Surgical Nurse*, August, Vol. 2, No. 4, pp. 11–15.

Pugh, J. and Millar, B. (1989c) Mobility in the postoperative phase of care, *Surgical Nurse*, October, Vol. 2, No. 5, pp. 15–19.

Summers, R. (1984) Should patients be told more? *Nursing Mirror*, Vol. 159, No. 16, p. 20.

Summerskill, H. (1976) Measurements of gastric function during digestion of ordinary solid meals in man, *Gastroenterology*, Vol. 70, p. 203.

Swindale, J. E. (1989) The nurse's role in giving preoperative information to reduce anxiety in patients admitted to hospital for elective minor surgery, *Journal of Advanced Nursing*, Vol. 14, pp. 899–905.

Thomas, E. A. (1987) Pre-op fasting—a question of routine, *Nursing Times*, Vol. 83, pp. 46–7.

Walsh, M. and Ford, P. (1989a) Rituals in nursing—'We always do it this way', *Nursing Times*, 11 October, Vol. 85, No. 41, pp. 26–35.

Walsh, M. and Ford, P. (1989b) Rituals in nursing—'It can't hurt that much', *Nursing Times*, 18 October, Vol. 85, No. 42, pp. 35–8.

Wilson-Barnett, J. (1981) Anxiety in hospitalised patients, *The Royal Society of Health Journal*, Vol. 101, pp. 118–22.

Winfield, U. (1986) Too close a shave, *Nursing Times*, Vol. 82, pp. 64–8.

FURTHER READING

Books

Game, C., Anderson, R. E. and Kidd, J. R. (eds) (1989) *Medical-Surgical Nursing: A Core Text*, Churchill Livingstone, Edinburgh.

Wachstein, J. (1976) *Anaesthetics and Recovery Room Techniques (Nursing Aids Series)* (2nd edition), Baillière Tindall, Eastbourne.

Watson, J. E. (1979) *Medical-Surgical Nursing and Related Physiology* (2nd edition), W. B. Saunders, Eastbourne.

WOUND CARE AND WOUND HEALING

BIBLIOGRAPHY

Ayliffe, G. A. J., Coates, D. and Hoffman, P. N. (1984) *Chemical Disinfection in Hospitals*, Public Health Laboratory Services, London.

Bale, S. and Harding, K. G. (1990) Using modern dressings to effect debridement, *The Professional Nurse*, Vol. 5, No. 5, pp. 244–8.

Barnett, S. E. and Varley, S. J. (1986) Wound healing and the effects of dressings, *Care Science and Practice*, December, Vol. 4, No. 3, pp. 10–12.

Barton, A. and Barton, M. (1981) *The Management and Prevention of Pressure Sores*, Faber & Faber, London.

Basson, M. M. *et al.* (1982) Near-fatal systemic oxygen embolism due to wound irrigation with hydrogen peroxide, *Postgraduate Medical Journal*, Vol. 58, pp. 448–51.

Boore, J. R. P. (1978) *Prescription For Recovery*, Royal College of Nursing, London.

Brennan, S. S. and Leaper, D. J. (1985) The effect of antiseptics on the healing wound: a study using the rabbit ear chamber, *British Journal of Surgery*, Vol. 72, pp. 780–2.

Brennan, S. S., Foster, M. E. and Leaper, D. J. (1986) Antiseptic toxicity on wounds healing by secondary infection, *Journal of Hospital Infection*, Vol. 8, pp. 263–7.

British National Formulary (1986) *Number 12*, British Medical Association and the Pharmaceutical Society of Great Britain, London.

Colebrook, L. and Hood, A. L. (1948) Infection through soaked dressings, *Lancet*, Vol. 2, p. 682.

Cutting, K. and Harding, K. (1990) Dressing cavities, *Nursing Times*, 12 December, Vol. 86, No. 50, pp. 62–4.

Deans, J., Bilings, P., Brennan, S. S. *et al.* (1986) The toxicity of commonly used antiseptics on fibroblasts in tissue culture, *Phlebology*, Vol. 1, pp. 205–9.

Draper, J. (1985) Making the dressing fit the wound, *Nursing Times*, 9 October, Vol. 81, No. 41, pp. 32–5.

Gardener, J. F. and Peel, M. M. (1986) *Introduction to Sterilisation and Disunfection*, Churchill Livingstone, Edinburgh.

Hellgren, L. (1983) Cleansing properties of stabilized trypsin and streptokinase-streptodornase in necrotic leg ulcers, *European Journal of Clinical Pharmacology*, Vol. 24, pp. 623–8.

Kenedi, R. M. and Cowden, J. M. (eds) (1976) The problem of clinical trials with new systems for preventing or healing decufiti, G. R. Fernie and J. Dornan in *Bedsore Biomechanics*, MacMillan, London.

Johnson, A. (1988a) Criteria for ideal wound dressings, *The Professional Nurse*, March, Vol. 3, No. 6, pp. 191–3.

Johnson, A. (1988b) Modern wound care products, *The Professional Nurse*, July, Vol. 3, No. 10, pp. 392–8.

Johnson, A. (1988c) Standard protocols for treating open wounds, *The Professional Nurse*, Vol. 3, No. 12, pp. 498–501.

Journal of Hospital Infection (1981) Vol. 2, Supplement.

Lawrence, C. A. and Black, C. M. (1968) *Disinfection, Sterilization and Preservation*, Lea & Febinger, Philadelphia.

Leaper, D. J. (1986) Antiseptics and their effect on healing tissue, *Nursing Times*, 28 May, Vol. 82, No. 22, pp. 45–7.

Morgan, D. A. (1986) *Formulary of Wound Management Products—A Guide for Health Care Staff* (produced as part of the 1984 UK CPA Boots Award), Whitchurch Hospital, Cardiff.

Petterson, E. (1986) A cut above the rest? *Journal of Infection Control Nursing/Nursing Times*, 5 March, Vol. 82, No. 10, pp. 68–70.

Russell, A. D., Hugo, W. B. and Ayliffe, G. A. (1982) *Principles and Practice of Disinfection, Preservation and Sterilization*, Blackwell Scientific Publications, Oxford.

Samson, I. G. and Spielberger, C. D. (eds) (1976) Stress reduction through sensation information, J. E. Johnson in *Stress and Anxiety 2*, Halstad Press, London.

Schmitt, F. E. and Wooldridge, J. (1973) Psychological preparation of surgical patients, *Nursing Research*, Vol. 22, pp. 108–16.

Sleigh, J. W. and Lister, S. P. K. (1985) Hazards of hydrogen peroxide, *British Medical Journal*, Vol. 291, p. 1706.

The Dressing Times (1988) Vol. 1, No. 3, December.

The Dressing Times (1989) Vol. 2, No. 1, March.

The Pharmaceutical Society of Great Britain (1986) *The Pharmaceutical Codex* (11th edition), The Pharmaceutical Press, London, p. 156.

Thomas, S. (1986) Milton and the treatment of burns (Letter), *Pharmaceutical Journal*, Vol. 236, pp. 128–9.

Thomas, S. (1988) Pressure points, *Community Outlook Supplement/Nursing Times*, Vol. 84, pp. 20–2.

Thomlinson, D. (1987) To clean or not to clean? *Journal of Infection Control Nursing/Nursing Times*, 4 March, Vol. 83, No. 9, pp. 71–5.

Turner, T. D. (1982) Which dressing and why—1. Wound care No. 11, *Nursing Times*, 21 July, Vol. 78, No. 29, pp. 41–4.

Turner, T. D. (1983) Absorbent dressings, *Nursing*, Vol. 12, pp. 1–7.

Turner, T. D. (1987) Product development, *Senior Nurse*, April, Vol. 6, No. 4, pp. 25—9.

Westaby, S. (1981) Wound care No. 4, *Nursing Times*, 16 December, Vol. 77, No. 51, pp. 13–16.

Wilson, P., Burroughs, D. and Dunn, L. (1988) Methicillin-resistant *Staphylococcus aureus* and hydrocolloid dressings, *Pharmaceutical Journal*, Vol. 241, pp. 787–8.

Winfield, U. (1986) Too close a shave? *Nursing Times*, 5 March, Vol. 82, No. 10, pp. 64–8.

Winter, G. D. (1978) Wound healing, Supplement, *Nursing Mirror*, Vol. 146, No. 10, p. 10.

Wood, R. A. B. (1976) Disintegration of cellulose dressings in open granulating wounds, *British Medical Journal*, Vol. 785, pp. 1444–5.

FURTHER READING

Bale, S. (1991) A holistic approach and the ideal dressing: cavity wound management in the 1990s, *The Professional Nurse*, March, Vol. 6, No. 6, pp. 316–23.

Senter, H. and Pringle, A. (1985) *How Wounds Heal: A Practical Guide For Nurses*, Calmic Medical Division, The Wellcome Foundation Ltd, Cheshire.

DRUGS

BIBLIOGRAPHY

Fogarty, A., Hills, S. and Sloan, C. (1986) Finding the facts on glyceryl trinitrate tablets, *Nursing Times*, 27 August, Vol. 82, pp. 37–8.

Gould, D. (1988) Called to account, *Nursing Times*, 23 March, Vol. 84, No. 12, pp. 28–31.

Heenan, A. (1989) Monitoring adverse reactions, *Nursing Times*, 27 September, Vol. 85, No. 39, pp. 25–9.

Hunter, R. (1989) Neuroleptic malignant syndrome, *Nursing Times*, 2 August, Vol. 85, No. 39, pp. 43–4.

RCN Department of Nursing Policy and Practice (1987) *Drug Administration: A Nursing Responsibility*, Royal College of Nursing, London.

Stillwell, B. (1988) Should nurses prescribe? *Nursing Times*, 23 March, Vol. 84, No. 12, pp. 31–4.

Pritchard, A. P. and David, J. A. (1988) *Manual of Clinical Nursing Procedures* (2nd edition), Harper & Row, London, Chapter 11.

UKCC (1986) *Administration of Medicines, UKCC Advisory Pages*, April, UKCC, London.

FURTHER READING

Books

Hector, W. (1982) *Modern Nursing: Theory and Practice* (7th edition), William Heinemann Medical Books, London.

Neal, M. J. (1987) *Medical Pharmacology At a Glance*, Blackwell Scientific Publications, Oxford.

Articles

Burton, S. M. (1988) Drug update: antibacterial agents, *The Professional Nurse*, February, Vol. 3, No. 5, pp. 171–3.

Durie, B. (1987) Drugs and sexual function, *Nursing Times*, 12 August, Vol. 83, No. 32, pp. 34–5.

Hill, J. (1987) Bottled up, *Nursing Times*, 19 August, Vol. 83, No. 33, pp. 36–7.

McGuire, J., Preston, J. and Pinches, D. (1987) Two pink and one blue, *Nursing Times*, 14 January, Vol. 83, No. 1, pp. 32–3.

Oldnall, A. S. (1988) The unit-dose system of drug distribution, *The Professional Nurse*, January, Vol. 3, No. 4, pp. 132–3.

Smith, S. (1987) Drugs and the heart, *Nursing Times*, 27 May, Vol. 83, No. 21, pp. 24–6.

Smith, S. (1987) Drugs in angina and myocardial infarction, *Nursing Times*, 3 June, Vol. 83, No. 22, pp. 52–4.

Smith, S. (1987) Diuretic agents, *Nursing Times*, 10 June, Vol. 83, No. 23, pp. 53–5.

Smith, S. (1987) Drugs and parasympathetic nervous system, *Nursing Times*, 17 June, Vol. 83, No. 24, pp. 36–8.

Smith, S. (1987) Drugs and gastrointestinal tract, *Nursing Times*, 1 July, Vol. 83, No. 26, pp. 50–2.

Stevenson, S. (1989) Administering pentamidine, *Nursing Times*, 27 September, Vol. 85, No. 39, pp. 30–2.

Walters, J. (1988) How antibiotics work, *The Professional Nurse*, April, Vol. 3, No. 7, pp. 251–4.

Walters, J. (1988) How antibiotics work—the cell membrane, *The Professional Nurse*, July, Vol. 4, No. 10, pp. 508–10.

CANCER

BIBLIOGRAPHY

Pritchard, A. P. and David, J. (1988) *Royal Marsden Hospital Manual of Clinical Nursing Procedures* (2nd edition), Harper & Row, London.

FURTHER READING

Books

American Cancer Society (1984) *American Cancer Society Special Report: Nutrition and Cancer: Cause and Prevention*, American Cancer Society, New York.

American Cancer Society (1982) *Unproven Methods of Cancer Management*, American Cancer Society, New York.

Baird, S.R. (ed.) (1987) *Decision-Making in Oncology Nursing*, B. C. Decker, Toronto.

Beyers, M., Durburg, S. and Werner, J. (1984) *Complete Guide to Cancer Nursing*, Edward Arnold, London.

Billings, J. A. (1985) *Outpatient Management of Advanced Cancer: Symptom Control, Support, and Hospice-in-the-Home*, J. B. Lippincott, Philadelphia.

Brager, B. L. and Yasko, J. M. (1984) *Care of the Client Receiving Chemotherapy*, Reston Publishing, Reston, Virginia.

Burns, N. (1982) *Nursing and Cancer*, W. B. Saunders, Philadelphia.

Carrieri, V. K., Lindsey, A. M. and West, C. M. (eds) (1986) *Pathophysiological Phenomena in Nursing*, W. B. Saunders, Philadelphia.

Cassileth, B. R. and Cassileth, P. A. (eds) (1982) *Clinical Care of the Terminal Cancer Patient*, Lea & Febiger, Philadelphia.

Chernecky, C. C. and Ramsey, P. W. (1984) *Critical Care Nursing of the Client With Cancer*, Appleton-Century-Crofts, Norwalk, Connecticut.

Corr, C. A. and Corr, D. M. (eds) (1983) *Hospice Care: Principles and Practice*, Springer, New York.

del Regato, J. A. and Spjut, H. J. (1984) *Cancer: Diagnosis, Treatment and Prognosis*, C. V. Mosby, St Louis.

Devita, V., Hellman, S. and Rosenberg, S. (eds) (1985) *Cancer: Principles and Practice of Oncology* (2nd edition), J. B. Lippincott, Philadelphia.

Donovan, M. and Girton, S. (1984) *Cancer Care Nursing* (2nd edition), Prentice Hall, Englewood Cliffs, New Jersey.

Griffiths, M. J., Murray, K. H. and Russo, P. C. (1984) *Oncology Nursing: Pathophysiology, Assessment and Intervention*, Macmillan, New York.

Groenwald, S. L. (1991) *Cancer Care Nursing* (3rd edition), Prentice Hall, New Jersey.

Hafen, B. Q. and Frandsen, K. J. (1983) *Faces of Death*, Morton, Englewood, Colorado.

Johnson, B.L. and Grose, J. (1985) *Handbook of Oncology Nursing*, John Wiley & Sons, New York.

Knobf, M. K. T., Fischer, D. S. and Welch-McCaffrey, D. (eds) (1984) *Cancer Chemotherapy, Treatment and Care*, G. K. Hall, Boston.

McCaffery, M. (1983) *Nursing Management of the Patient With Pain* (3rd edition), J. B. Lippincott, Philadelphia.

McCorkle, R. and Hongladarom, G. (1986) *Issues and Topics in Cancer Nursing*, Appleton-Century-Crofts, Norwalk, Connecticut.

McIntire, S. N. and Cioppa, A. L. (eds) (1984) *Cancer Nursing: A Developmental Approach*, John Wiley & Sons, New York.

McNally, J. C., Stair, J.C. and Somerville, E. T. (eds) (1985) *Guidelines for Cancer Nursing Practice*, Grune & Stratton, Orlando, Florida.

Meinhart, N. J. and McCaffery, M. (1983) *Pain: A Nursing Approach to Assessment and Analysis*, Appleton-Century-Crofts, Norwalk, Connecticut.

Oncology Nursing Society (1984) *Cancer Chemotherapy: Guidelines and Recommendations for Nursing Education and Practice*, Oncology Nursing Society, Pittsburgh.

Page, H. S. and Asire, A. J. (1985) *Cancer Rates and Risks*, U. S. Department of Health and Human Services, National Institutes of Health, Bethesda, Maryland.

Piper, B. F. (1986) *Pathophysiological Phenomena in Nursing*, W. B. Saunders, Philadelphia.

Porth, C. (1986) *Pathophysiology: Concepts of Altered Health States* (2nd edition), J. B. Lippincott, Philadelphia.

Tiffany, R. (ed.) (1988) *Oncology for Nurses and Health Care Professionals* (2nd edition), Vols 1–3, Harper & Row, London.

Tschudin, V. (ed.) (1989) *Nursing the Patient with Cancer*, Prentice Hall, Englewood Cliffs, New Jersey.

U. S. Department of Health and Human Services (1985) *Cancer Rates and Risks* (3rd edition), Public Health Services, National Institutes of Health.

Vredevo, D. L. *et al.* (eds) (1981) *Concepts of Oncology Nursing*, Prentice-Hall, Englewood Cliffs, New Jersey.

Wall, P. D. and Melzack, R. (1984) *Textbook of Pain*, Churchill Livingstone, New York.

Yasko, J. M. (1983) *Guidelines for Cancer Care: Symptom Management*, Prentice-Hall, Reston, Virginia.

PAIN

BIBLIOGRAPHY

Hunt, J. M., Stollar, T. D., Littlejohns, D. W. *et al.* (1977) Patients with protracted pain: A survey conducted at The London Hospital, *Journal of Medical Ethics*, Vol. 3, pp. 61–73.

Marks, R. M. and Sacher, E. J. (1973) Undertreatment of medical inpatients with narcotic analgesics, *Annals of Internal Medicine*,Vol. 78, pp. 173–81.

Seers, C. J. (1987) *Pain, Anxiety and Recovery in Patients Undergoing Surgery*, unpublished PhD Thesis, King's College, University of London.

FURTHER READING

Aronoff, G. M. (1985) *Evaluation and Treatment of Chronic Pain*, Urban & Schwarzenberg, Baltimore.

Bellissimo, A. and Tunks, E. (1984) *Chronic Pain: The Psychotherapeutic Spectrum*, Praeger, New York.

Benedetti, C, Chapman, C. R. and Moricca, G. (1984) *Recent Advances in the Management of Pain: Advances in Pain Research and Therapy*, Vol. 7, Raven Press, New York.

Bromm, B. (1984) *Pain Measurement in Man: Neurophysiological Correlates of Pain*, Elsevier, New York.

Fields, H. L., Dubner, R. and Cervero, F. (1985) *Proceedings of the Fourth World Congress on Pain: Advances in Pain Research and Therapy*, Vol. 9, Raven Press, New York.

Gildenberg, P. L. and DeVaul, R. A. (1985) *The Chronic Pain Patient: Evaluation and Management: Pain and Headache*, Vol. 7, S. Karger, New York.

Goldberg, I. K., Kurscher, A. H. and Malitz, S. (1986) *Pain, Anxiety, and Grief*, Columbia University Press, New York.

Holzman, A. D. and Turk, D. C. (1986) *Pain Management: A Handbook of Psychological Treatment Approaches*, Pergamon Press, New York.

Kotarba, J. A. (1983) *Chronic Pain—Its Social Dimensions*, Sage, Beverly Hills, California.

McCaffery, M. (1979) *Nursing Management of the Patient in Pain*, J. B. Lippincott, New York.

McCaffery, M. and Beebe, A. (1989) *Pain: Clinical Manual for Nursing Practice*, C. V. Mosby, St Louis.

Meinhart, N. T. and McCaffery, M. (1983) *Pain: A Nursing Approach to Assessment and Analysis*, Appleton-Century-Crofts, New York.

Melzack, R. (1983) *Pain Measurement and Assessment*, Raven Press, New York.

Smith, G. and Covino, B. G. (1985) *Acute Pain*, Butterworth & Co, Bosotn.

Stimmel, B. (1983) *Pain, Analgesia, and Addiction: The Pharmacologic Treatment of Pain*, Raven Press, New York.

Swerdlow, H. (1983) *Relief of Intractable Pain: Monographs in Anaesthesiology*, Vol. 13, Elsevier, New York.

Turk, D. C., Meichenbaum, D. and Genest, M. (1983) *Pain and Behavioural Medicine: A Cognitive-Behavioural Perspective*, Guilford Press, New York.

Twycross, R. G. and Lack, S. A. (1983) *Symptom Control in Far-Advanced Cancer: Pain Relief*, Pitman, London.

Vestal, R. E. (1984) *Drug Treatment in the Elderly*, ADIS Health Science Press, Boston.

Wall, P. D. and Melzack, R. (1984) *Textbook of Pain*, Churchill Livingstone, New York.

Wilson-Barnett, J. and Batehup, L. (eds) (1988) Pain, M. Fordham in *Patient Problems*, Scutari, London.

Wilson-Barnett, J. and Raiman, J. (eds) (1988) Pain and Its Management, J. Raiman in *Nursing Issues and Research in Terminal Care*, John Wiley, Chichester.

CARE OF THE DYING PATIENT

BIBLIOGRAPHY

Bale, S. and Regnard, C. (1989) Pressure sores in advanced disease; a flow diagram, *Palliative Medicine*, Vol. 3, No. 4, pp. 263–5.

Benner, P. and Wrubel, J. (1988) *The Primacy of Caring: Stress and Coping in Health and Illness*, Addison Wesley, California.

Bowling, A. (1983) The hospitalisation of death; should more people die at home? *Journal of Medical Ethics*, Vol. 9, pp. 158–61.

Buckman, R. (1988) *I Don't Know What To Say: How to Help and Support Someone Who Is Dying*, Papermac, London.

Cancer Research Campaign Statistics (1988) Cancer Research Campaign, London.

Coelho, G. V., Hamburg, D. A. and Adams, J. E. (eds) (1974) The psychology of coping: issues of research and assessment, R. S. Lazarus, J. R. Averill and E. M. Opton, in *Coping and Adaptation*, Basic Books, New York.

Donovan, N. I. and Girton, S. E. (1984) *Cancer Care Nursing*, Appleton Century Crofts, Norwalk, Connecticut.

Field, D. (1989) *Nursing the Dying*, Tavistock/Routledge, London.

Freihafer, P. and Felton, G. (1976) Nursing behaviours in bereavement; an explanatory study, *Nursing Research*, Vol. 25, pp. 332–7.

Giaquinta, B. (1977) Helping families face the crisis of cancer, *American Journal of Nursing*, Vol. 9, pp. 1585–9.

Glaser, B. G. and Strauss, A. L. (1965) *Awareness of Dying*, Aldine, Chicago.

Henley, A. (1986) Good practice in hospital care for the dying, *King's Fund, Project Paper 61*, King's Fund, London.

Hill, F. and Oliver, C. (1988) Hospice—an update on the cost of patient care, *Health Trends*, Vol. 3, August, pp. 83–6.

Hockley, J. (1983) An investigation to identify symptoms of distress in the terminally ill patient and his/her family in the general ward, *City and Hackney Health District, Nursing Research Papers, No. 2*.

Hockley, J., Dunlop, R. and Davies, R. J. (1988) Survey of distressing symptoms in dying patients and their families in hospital and the response to a pain and symptom control team, *British Medical Journal*, Vol. 277, pp. 1715–17.

Kind, P. (1988) *Hospital Deaths—The Missing Link: Measuring Outcome in Hospital Activity Data, Discussion Paper 44*, Centre for Health Economics, York.

Kübler-Ross, E. (1970) *On Death and Dying*, Tavistock, London.

Lewis, F. M. (1986) The impact of cancer on the family; a critical analysis of the research literature, in *Patient Education and Counselling*, Elsevier Scientific Publications Ireland Ltd, Belfast, pp. 269–89.

McIntosh, J. (1974) Processes of communication, information seeking and control associated with cancer: a selective review of the literature, *Social Science and Medicine*, Vol. 8, pp. 167–87.

Mudditt, H. (1987) Home truths, *Nursing Times*, Vol. 83, No. 35, pp. 31–3.

Murray-Parkes, C. M. (1972) Accuracy of predictions of survival in later stages of cancer, *British Medical Journal*, Vol. 2, pp. 29–31.

Quint, J. C. (1967) *The Nurse and the Dying Patient*, Macmillan, New York.

Taylor, H. (1983) The hospice movement in Britain: its role and its future, *Centre for Policy on Ageing*, Dorset Press, Dorchester.

Twycross, R. and Lack, S. A. (1983) *Symptom Control in Far Advanced Cancer: Pain Relief*, Pitman Books, London.

Ward, A. (1985) *Home Care Services for the Terminally Ill: A Report for the Nuffield Foundation*, Medical Care Research Unit, University of Sheffield.

Wiseman, A. D. (1979) *Coping with Cancer*, McGraw-Hill, New York.

Unit **2**

PROBLEMS AFFECTING INTERNAL AND EXTERNAL RESPIRATION

chapter 3

ASSESSMENT OF RESPIRATORY FUNCTION

OVERVIEW OF ANATOMY AND PHYSIOLOGY

The cells of the body derive the energy they need from the oxidation of carbohydrates, fats and proteins. For this process, as for any type of combustion, oxygen is required. Certain vital tissues, such as those of the brain and the heart, cannot survive for long without a continuing supply of oxygen. As a result of oxidation in the body tissues, carbon dioxide is produced and must be removed from the cells to prevent build-up of acid waste products.

Oxygen is supplied to cells and carbon dioxide is removed from cells by way of the circulating blood. Cells are in close contact with capillaries, whose thin walls permit easy passage or exchange of oxygen and carbon dioxide. Oxygen diffuses from the capillary, through the capillary wall to the interstitial fluid, and then through the membrane of tissue cells, where it can be used by mitochondria for cellular respiration. The movement of carbon dioxide also occurs by diffusion and proceeds in the opposite direction, from cell to blood.

After these tissue capillary exchanges, blood enters the systemic veins (where it is called venous blood) and travels to the lung circulation. The oxygen concentration in blood within the lung capillaries is lower than it is in the lung gas spaces, which are called alveoli. As a result, oxygen diffuses from the alveoli to the blood. Carbon dioxide, whose concentration in the blood is higher than in the alveoli, diffuses from the blood into the alveoli. Movement of fresh air in and out of the airways (called ventilation) continually replenishes the oxygen and removes the carbon dioxide from the air spaces in the lung. This whole process of gas exchange between the atmospheric air and the blood and between the blood and the cells of the body is called respiration.

Anatomy of the Lung

The lungs are elastic structures enclosed in the thorax, which is an airtight chamber with distensible walls.

Ventilation involves movements of the walls of the thorax and of its floor, the diaphragm. The effect of these movements is alternately to increase and decrease the capacity of the chest. When the capacity of the chest is increased, air enters through the trachea, because of the lowered pressure within, and inflates the lungs. When the chest wall and diaphragm return to their previous positions, the elastic lungs recoil and force the air out through the bronchi and trachea.

The outer surfaces of the lungs are enclosed by a smooth, slippery membrane, the pleura, which also extends to cover the interior wall of the thorax and the superior surface of the diaphragm. The pleura is termed 'parietal pleura' where it lines the thorax, and 'visceral pleura' where it covers the lungs. Between the two pleural surfaces is a small amount of fluid that lubricates the surfaces and allows them to slide freely during ventilation.

The mediastinum is the wall that divides the thoracic cavity into two halves. It is composed of two layers of pleura between which lie all of the thoracic structures except the lungs.

Each lung is divided into lobes. The left lung consists of upper and lower lobes, whereas the right lung has upper, middle and lower lobes. Each lobe is further sub-divided into two to five segments separated by fissures, which are extensions of the pleura. A schematic diagram of the airways and the lobes of the lungs is shown in Figure 3.1.

There are several divisions of the bronchi within each lobe of the lung. First are the lobar bronchi (three in the right lung and two in the left lung). Lobar bronchi divide into segmental bronchi (10 on the right and 8 on the left), which are the structures identified when choosing the most effective postural drainage position for a given patient. Segmental bronchi then divide into subsegmental bronchi. These bronchi are surrounded by connective tissue that contains arteries, lymphatics and nerves. The subsegmental bronchi then branch into bronchioles, which have no cartilage in their walls. Their patency depends entirely on the elastic recoil of the smooth muscle that surrounds it and on the alveolar pressure. The bronchioles contain submucosal glands, which produce mucus that forms an uninterrupted covering for the inside lining of the airway. The bronchi and bronchioles are also lined with cells whose surfaces are covered with short 'hairs' called cilia. These cilia create a constant whipping motion

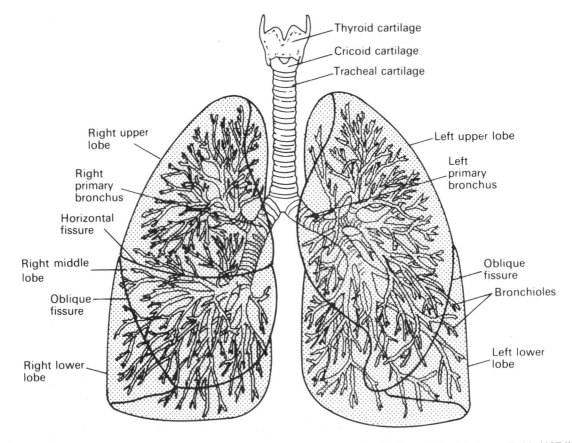

Figure 3.1 Larynx, trachea and bronchial tree (anterior view). (Chaffee, E. E. and Greisheimer, E. M. (1974) *Basic Physiology and Anatomy* (3rd edition), J. B. Lippincott, Philadelphia.)

that serves to propel mucus and foreign substances away from the lung toward the larynx.

The bronchioles then branch into terminal bronchioles, which do not have mucus glands or cilia. Terminal bronchioles then become respiratory bronchioles, which are considered to be the transition passageways between the conducting airways and the gas exchange airways. Up to this point the conducting airways contain about 150 ml of air caught in the tracheobronchial tree that does not participate in gas exchange. The respiratory bronchioles then lead into alveolar ducts and alveolar sacs and then alveoli. Oxygen and carbon dioxide exchange takes place in the alveoli.

The lung is made up of about 300 million alveoli, which are arranged in clusters of 15 to 20. So numerous are these alveoli that if their surfaces were united to form one sheet it would cover an area the size of a tennis court (or 70 square metres).

There are three types of alveolar cells. Type I alveolar cells are epithelial cells that form the alveolar walls. Type II alveolar cells, metabolically active cells, secrete surfactant, which is a phospholipid that lines the inner surface of the alveoli. Type III, alveoli cell macrophages, are large phagocytic cells that ingest foreign matter (e.g., mucus, bacteria) and act as an important defence mechanism.

Mechanics of Ventilation

During inspiration, air flows from the environment into the trachea, bronchi, bronchioles and alveoli. During expiration, alveolar gas travels the same route in reverse.

The physical factors that govern air flow in and out of the lungs are collectively referred to as the mechanics of ventilation. Air flows from a region of higher pressure to a region of lower pressure. During inspiration, contraction of the diaphragm and other muscles of respiration enlarges the thoracic cavity and thereby lowers the pressure inside the thorax to a level below that of atmospheric pressure. Therefore, air is drawn through the trachea and bronchi into the alveoli.

During normal expiration, the muscles of respiration relax and the thoracic cavity decreases in size. The alveolar pressure now exceeds atmospheric pressure, and air flows from the lungs into the atmosphere.

Resistance is determined chiefly by the radius of the airway through which the air is flowing. Any process that changes bronchial diameter will therefore affect airway resistance and alter the rate of air flow for a given pressure gradient during respiration. Common factors that may alter bronchial diameter include contraction of bronchial smooth muscle, as in asthma; thickening of bronchial mucosa, as in chronic bronchitis; or obstruction of the airway due to mucus, a tumour or a foreign body. Loss of lung elasticity, such as is seen in emphysema, may also alter bronchial diameter since the lung connective tissue encircles the airways and helps to keep them open during both inspiration and expiration. With increased resistance, greater than normal respiratory effort is required by the patient to achieve normal levels of ventilation.

The pressure gradient between the thoracic cavity and the atmosphere causes air flow in and out of the lungs and also stretches the lung tissue itself. The pressure required to stretch the lung is determined by the properties of its elastic tissue. A measure of how easily lungs can be stretched is called lung compliance.

A compliant lung (high compliance) distends easily when pressure is applied, whereas a noncompliant lung (low compliance) requires greater than normal pressure to distend it. The major factors that determine lung compliance are connective tissue (collagen and elastin) and the surface tension in the alveoli. The surface tension at the surface of the alveoli is normally maintained at a low level by the presence of the alveolar lining material (lung surfactant). Increased connective tissue or increased alveolar surface tension results in low compliance. In adult respiratory distress syndrome there is a surfactant deficiency and the lungs are stiff (low compliance). In pulmonary fibrosis, connective tissue proliferates and compliance is decreased. Lungs with low compliance require a greater than normal energy expenditure to achieve normal levels of ventilation.

The mechanics of ventilation can be measured to evaluate lung function (Figure 3.2). Included in these measurements are:

- Inspiratory reserve volume (IRV)—the maximum volume of air that can be inhaled after a normal inhalation.
- Tidal volume (V_T)—the volume of air normally inhaled or exhaled.
- Expiratory reserve volume (ERV)—the maximum volume of air that can be exhaled after a normal exhalation.
- Residual volume (RV)—the volume of air remaining in the lungs after a maximum exhalation.
- Total lung capacity (TLC)—the volume of air in the lungs after a maximum inhalation.
- Functional residual capacity—the volume of air in the lungs at resting and exhalation.

Several additional useful measurements include:

- Vital capacity (VC)—the maximum volume of air that is exhaled after a full inspiration (includes inspiratory reserve volume, tidal volume and expiratory reserve volume).
- Forced vital capacity (FVC)—same as vital capacity except that it is achieved by forceful expiration.
- Maximum voluntary ventilation (MVV)—the volume of air exhaled per minute while breathing fast and deep.

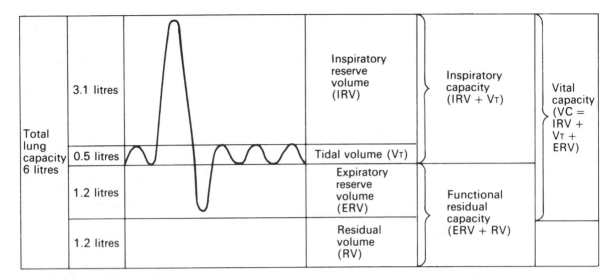

Figure 3.2 Respiratory volumes and capacities: normal spirogram of relative volumes in the lung. Inspiratory reserve volume (IRV)—maximum volume of air inhaled after a normal inhalation; tidal volume (VT)—volume of air normally inhaled or exhaled; expiratory reserve volume (ERV)—maximum volume of air exhaled after a normal exhalation; residual volume (RV)—volume of air remaining in the lungs after a maximum expiration; total lung capacity (TLC)—volume of air in the lungs after a maximum inhalation. These volumes change in disease states. They are useful in evaluating lung mechanics.

- Minute ventilation (È)—the volume of air exhaled in one minute.
- Flow volume curves—a single breath test that measures most of the above volumes and tends to be more accurate than the traditional volume–time curves of pulmonary function studies. (See Table 3.1.)

In healthy upright lungs, ventilation is greatest in the lower regions of the lung and decreases toward the apices. In addition to this regional inequality of ventilation, there is uneven ventilation among alveoli, permitting air to be distributed more evenly between them.

Certain changes occur in the respiratory system associated with ageing: chest wall compliance decreases and osteoporosis may cause chest wall rigidity. The elderly tend to rely on their abdominal and diaphragmatic contribution to breathing. The residual volume increases with age, while the vital capacity decreases.

Diffusion and Perfusion

Diffusion is the process by which oxygen and carbon dioxide are exchanged at the air–blood interface. The alveolar-capillary membrane is ideal for diffusion because of its large surface area and thin membrane. In healthy lungs oxygen and carbon dioxide travel across the alveolar-capillary membrane without difficulty.

Pulmonary perfusion is the actual blood flow through the pulmonary circulation. The blood is pumped into the lungs by the right ventricle through the pulmonary artery.

The pulmonary artery divides into the right and left branches to supply both lungs. These two branches divide further to supply all parts of each lung. The pulmonary circulation is considered a low pressure system since the systolic blood pressure in the pulmonary artery is 20 to 30 mmHg and the diastolic pressure is 5 to 15 mmHg. Because it is low, the pulmonary vasculature normally can vary its resistance to accommodate the blood flow it receives.

Perfusion is also influenced by alveolar pressure. The pulmonary capillaries are sandwiched between adjacent alveoli. If the alveolar pressure is sufficiently high, the capillaries will be squeezed. Depending on the pressure, some capillaries will be completely collapsed whereas others will be narrowed.

Pulmonary artery pressure, gravity and alveolar pressure determine the patterns of perfusion. In lung disease these factors vary and the perfusion of the lung may become very abnormal.

Shunting

Normally about 2 per cent of the blood pumped by the right ventricle does not perfuse the alveolar capillaries. This blood, which cannot participate in gas exchange with alveolar gas, is called shunted blood. It drains into the left side of the heart through the bronchial, pleural and thebesian veins. In some pathological states of the heart and great vessels (ventricular septal defect, patent ductus arteriosus) and lung diseases (pulmonary oedema, atelectasis)

Table 3.1 *Pulmonary function tests*

Description	Term used	Symbol	Remarks
Maximum volume of air exhaled from the point of maximum inspiration	Vital capacity	VC	Slow vital capacity may be normal or reduced in COAD patients
Vital capacity performed with a maximally forced expiratory effort	Forced vital capacity	FVC	Forced vital capacity is often reduced in COAD owing to air trapping
Volume of air exhaled in the specified time during the performance of forced vital capacity	Forced expiratory volume (qualified by $_{subscript}$ indicating the time interval in seconds)	FEV_t (usually FEV_1)	A valuable clue to the severity of the expiratory airway obstruction
FEV_t expressed as a percentage of the forced vital capacity	Ratio of timed forced expiratory volume to forced vital capacity	$FEV_t/FVC\%$ (usually $FEV_1/FVC\%$)	Another way of expressing the presence or absence of airway obstruction
Mean forced expiratory flow between 200–1,200 ml of the FVC	Forced expiratory flow	$FEF_{200-1200}$	Formerly called maximum expiratory flow rate (MEFR); an indicator of large airway obstruction
Mean forced expiratory flow during the middle half of the FVC	Forced mid-expiratory flow	$FEF_{25-75\%}$	Formerly called maximum and mid-expiratory flow rate; slowed in small airway obstruction
Mean forced expiratory flow during the terminal portion of the FVC	Forced end-expiratory flow	$FEF_{75-85\%}$	Slowed in obstruction of smallest airways
Volume of air expired in a specified period during repetitive maximal effort	Maximal voluntary ventilation	MVV	Formerly called maximum breathing capacity; an important factor in exercise tolerance

COAD: chronic obstructive airways disease

((1985) Chronic Obstructive Pulmonary Disease *(8th edition)*, American Lung Association, New York)

the amount of blood shunted exceeds the normal 2 per cent.

The shunted blood, which contains the same amount of oxygen as venous blood, mixes with the blood returning from the alveoli to produce arterial blood. The oxygen content of the arterial blood depends on both the oxygen content and the volume of each fraction. Severe hypoxia results when the amount of blood shunted exceeds 20 per cent. The hypoxia is not significantly improved by breathing even 100 per cent oxygen because the oxygen does not come in contact with the shunted blood.

Distribution of Ventilation and Perfusion

Ventilation is the flow of gas in and out of the lung, and perfusion is the filling of the pulmonary capillaries with blood. The pulmonary arterial pressure, gravity and alveolar pressure lead to uneven perfusion of the lung. The main factors leading to uneven distribution of ventilation of the lung include patency of the airways, local changes in compliance within the lung and gravity.

Any factor that reduces the airway calibre (mucosal oedema, inflammation, secretion, bronchospasm) will raise the resistance to air flow and decrease the ventilation of the corresponding alveoli. Similarly, any area in which the local compliance has decreased (i.e., that portion of the lung has become more stiff) will receive less ventilation than the surrounding more expandable portions of the lung.

The effect of gravity on ventilation is complex. In the early phase of inspiration, more of the tidal volume is distributed to the basal region of the lung. The basal region of the erect lung, therefore, receives more blood and air than the apex.

Matching of Ventilation and Perfusion

For optimum gas exchange the perfusion of each alveolus must be matched by optimum ventilation. In addition to the pressure–volume relationship of the lung, there are other mechanisms, such as changes in calibre of airways or capillaries, that ensure that ventilation and perfusion are properly matched in the normal lung.

Mismatching of ventilation and perfusion leads to hypoxia. It appears to be the main cause of hypoxia following thoracic or abdominal surgery and most types of respiratory failure. Its effects can be similar to those of shunts, or 100 per cent oxygen can eliminate hypoxia, depending on the type of ventilation–perfusion mismatch.

Partial Pressure

Partial pressure is the pressure exerted by each type of gas in a mixture of gases. The partial pressure of a gas is proportional to the concentration of that gas in the mixture. The total pressure exerted by the gaseous mixture is equal to the sum of the partial pressures.

The air we breathe is a gaseous mixture consisting mainly of nitrogen (78.62 per cent) and oxygen (20.84 per cent), with traces of carbon dioxide (0.04 per cent), water vapour (0.05 per cent), helium, argon and so on. The atmospheric pressure at sea level is about 760 torr (torr = mmHg). Based on these facts the partial pressure of nitrogen and oxygen can be calculated. Partial pressure of nitrogen is 79 per cent of 760 (0.79×760) = 600 torr, and that of oxygen is 21 per cent of 760 (0.21×760) = 160 torr.

The following is a reference list of expressions related to partial pressure:

P = pressure
P_{O_2}—partial pressure of oxygen
P_{CO_2}—partial pressure of carbon dioxide
P_{AO_2}—partial pressure of alveolar oxygen
P_{ACO_2}—partial pressure of alveolar carbon dioxide
P_{aO_2}—partial pressure of arterial oxygen
P_{aCO_2}—partial pressure of arterial carbon dioxide
P_{vO_2}—partial pressure of venous oxygen
P_{vCO_2}—partial pressure of venous carbon dioxide

P_{50}—partial pressure of oxygen when the haemoglobin is 50 per cent saturated

Once the air enters the trachea it becomes fully saturated with water vapour, which displaces some of the gases in order that the air pressure within the lung may remain equal with the air pressure outside (760 torr).

When a gas is exposed to a liquid, the gas will dissolve in the liquid until an equilibrium is reached. The dissolved gas also exerts a partial pressure. At equilibrium, the partial pressure of the gas in the liquid is the same as the partial pressure of the gas in the gaseous mixture. In the lung, venous blood and alveolar oxygen are separated by a very thin alveolar membrane. Oxygen diffuses across this membrane to dissolve in the blood until the partial pressure of oxygen in the blood is the same as that in the alveoli (104 torr). However, since carbon dioxide is manufactured in the cells, venous blood contains carbon dioxide at a higher partial pressure than that in the alveolar gas. In the lung, carbon dioxide diffuses out of venous blood into the alveolar gas. At equilibrium, the partial pressure of carbon dioxide in the blood and in alveolar gas is the same (40 torr).

The entire sequence of changes in partial pressure readings (in torr) may be summarized as shown below.

Oxygen Transport

Oxygen and carbon dioxide are carried simultaneously by virtue of their abilities to dissolve in blood or to combine with some of the elements of blood. Oxygen is carried in the blood in two forms: (1) as physically dissolved oxygen in the plasma and (2) in combination with the haemoglobin of the red blood cells. Each 100 ml of normal (P_{O_2} = 100) arterial blood carries 0.3 ml of oxygen physically dissolved in the plasma, and 19 ml of oxygen in combination with haemoglobin.

The volume of oxygen physically dissolved in the plasma varies directly with the P_{aO_2}. The higher the P_{aO_2}, the greater the oxygen dissolved. The amount of dissolved oxygen is directly proportional to the partial pressure, and this is true no matter how high the oxygen pressure rises.

The volume of oxygen that combines with haemoglobin also depends on P_{aO_2}, but only up to a P_{aO_2} of about 150 mmHg. Above this P_{aO_2}, haemoglobin is 100 per cent saturated, by which it is meant that haemoglobin will not combine with any additional oxygen. When

	Atmospheric air	Tracheal air	Alveolar air
P_{H_2O}	3.7	47.0	47.0
P_{N_2}	597.0	563.4	569.0
P_{O_2}	159.0	149.3	104.0
P_{CO_2}	0.3	0.3	40.0
Total	760.0	760.0	760.0

haemoglobin is 100 per cent saturated, 1 g of haemoglobin will combine with 1.34 ml of oxygen. Therefore, in a person with 14 g/dl of haemoglobin, each 100 ml of blood will contain about 19 ml of oxygen associated with haemoglobin. If the PaO_2 is less than 150 mmHg, the percentage of haemoglobin saturated with oxygen is lower. For example, at a PaO_2 of 100 mmHg (normal value) saturation is 97 per cent, and at a PaO_2 of 40 mmHg, the saturation is 70 per cent.

The oxygen dissociation curve of haemoglobin (Figure 3.3) shows the relationship between the partial pressure of oxygen and the percentage saturation of the haemoglobin more clearly (SaO_2). The unusual shape of the oxygen dissociation curve is a distinct advantage to the patient for two reasons:

1. If the arterial PO_2 decreases from 100 to 80 mmHg as a result of lung disease or heart disease, the haemoglobin of the arterial blood will still be almost maximally saturated (94 per cent) and the tissues will not suffer from anoxia.
2. When the arterial blood passes into tissue capillaries and is exposed to the tissue tension of oxygen (about 40 mmHg), haemoglobin gives up large quantities of oxygen for use by the tissues.

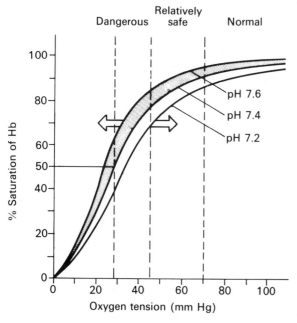

Figure 3.3 Oxygen–haemoglobin dissociation curve. The oxygen can attach to the haemoglobin more easily (higher SaO_2 per PO_2), but has more trouble coming off the haemoglobin at the tissues (less tissue oxygenation). Decreased oxygen affinity (shift to the right) means that it is more difficult for the oxygen to attach to the haemoglobin (lower SaO_2 per PO_2), but it can come off at the tissues more easily. P_{50} is normally 27 mmHg. A shift to the right gives a higher P_{50}, and a shift to the left gives a lower P_{50}.

Oxygen Dissociation Curve

The oxygen dissociation curve indicates the methods used by the body to release oxygen to the tissues so that the oxygen obtained from the lungs is stored and then released to the tissues in amounts sufficient for their needs. The oxygen dissociation curve in Figure 3.3 is marked to show three levels of sufficiency: (1) normal levels—PaO_2 above 70 mmHg; (2) relatively safe levels—PaO_2 45 to 70 mmHg; and (3) dangerous levels—PaO_2 below 40 mmHg.

Figure 3.3 shows that at a normal pH of 7.40, the steep part of the curve is between a PaO_2 of 40 mmHg (75 per cent haemoglobin saturation) and 20 mmHg (33 per cent haemoglobin saturation). P_{50} refers to the oxygen tension (27 mmHg) at 50 per cent haemoglobin saturation. When we talk about changes in PaO_2 and saturation, we talk about changes in P_{50}.

The oxygen–haemoglobin dissociation curve will shift to either the right or the left, depending on the presence of the following: CO_2, hydrogen ion concentration (acidity), temperature and 2,3-diphosphoglycerate.

A rise in these factors will shift the curve to the right, so that more oxygen is then released to the tissues at the same PaO_2. A reduction in these factors will cause the curve to shift to the left, making the bond between oxygen and haemoglobin stronger, so that less oxygen is given up to the tissues at the same PaO_2. In Figure 3.3, the normal (middle) curve shows that 75 per cent saturation occurs at a PaO_2 of 40 mmHg. If the curve shifts to the right, the same saturation (75 per cent) occurs at the higher PaO_2 of 57 mmHg. If the curve shifts to the left, 75 per cent saturation occurs at a PaO_2 of 25 mmHg.

Clinical Significance

With a normal haemoglobin of 15 g/dl (2.3 mmol/L) and a PaO_2 level of 40 mmHg (oxygen saturation 75 per cent), there is adequate oxygen available for the tissues but there is no reserve. With a catastrophe (e.g., bronchospasm, aspiration, hypotension or cardiac arrhythmias), which reduces the intake of oxygen from the lungs, tissue hypoxia would result. The normal value of PaO_2 is 80 to 100 mmHg (95–98 per cent saturation). With this level of oxygenation, there is a 15 per cent margin of excess oxygen available to the tissues.

An important consideration in the transport of oxygen is the cardiac output, which determines the amount of oxygen delivered to the body. If the cardiac output is normal (5 litres/minute), the amount of oxygen delivered to the body per minute will be normal. If cardiac output falls, the amount of oxygen delivered to the tissues will also fall. This is why cardiac output measurements are so important. Not all of the oxygen delivered to the body is used up. In fact, only 250 ml of oxygen is used up per minute. The rest of the oxygen returns to the right side of the heart, and the PO_2 of venous blood drops to about 40 mmHg.

Carbon Dioxide Transport

Simultaneously with the diffusion of oxygen from the blood into the tissues, carbon dioxide diffuses in the opposite direction (e.g., from tissue cells to blood) and is transported to the lung for excretion. The amount of carbon dioxide in transit is one of the major determinants of the acid–base balance of the body. Normally, only 6 per cent of the venous carbon dioxide is removed, and enough remains in the arterial side to exert a pressure of 40 mmHg. Most of the carbon dioxide (90 per cent) enters the red blood cells, and the small portion (5 per cent) that remains dissolved in the plasma (P_{CO_2}) is the critical factor that will determine carbon dioxide movement in or out of the blood.

In summarizing respiratory gas transport, it is important to emphasize that the many processes described do not take place in intermittent stages but occur rapidly, simultaneously and continuously.

Neurochemical Control of Ventilation

The rhythmicity of breathing is controlled by respiratory centres located in the brain. The inspiratory and expiratory centres located in the medulla oblongata control the rate and depth of ventilation to meet the body's metabolic demands.

There are several groups of receptor sites that assist in the brain's control of respiratory function. The central chemoreceptors are located in the medulla and respond to chemical changes in the cerebrospinal fluid, which are in turn due to chemical changes in the blood. They respond to an increase or decrease in the pH and convey a message to the lungs to change the depth and then the rate of ventilation to correct the imbalance. The peripheral chemoreceptors are located in the aortic arch and the carotid arteries and respond first to changes in Pa_{O_2}, then to $PaCO_2$ and pH. The Hering-Breuer reflex is brought about by stretch receptors located in the alveoli. This reflex is stimulated when the lungs are distended and inhibits inspiration so that the lungs do not become overdistended. There are also proprioceptors in muscles and joints that respond to body movements such as exercise, causing an increase in ventilation. Thus, range-of-motion exercises in an immobile patient will stimulate breathing. Baroreceptors, also located in the aortic and carotid bodies, respond to an increase or decrease in arterial blood pressure and cause a reflex hypoventilation or hyperventilation.

ASSESSMENT OF PATIENTS WITH PULMONARY DISEASE

The nursing assessment incorporates the physical findings and often indicates why the patient has certain signs and symptoms. The chief complaint usually relates to one of the following: dyspnoea, pain, shortness of breath, the accumulation of mucus, wheezing, haemoptysis, swelling of the ankles and feet, cough, general fatigue/weakness and altered sleep. In addition to identifying the chief reason why the patient is seeking health care, it is important to determine when the chief complaint started, how long it lasted, if it was relieved at any time and how relief was obtained. Information on precipitating factors, duration, severity and associated factors or symptoms is collected. In a respiratory history, factors that may contribute to the patient's lung condition are assessed:

- Smoking (the single most important factor that contributes to lung disease).
- Previous personal or family history of lung disease.
- Occupational history.
- Allergens and environmental pollutants.
- Hobbies.

Psychosocial factors that may affect the patient's life are evaluated and include anxiety, role changes, interpersonal relationships, financial problems and employment/unemployment. What are the patient's coping mechanisms? Is the patient reacting to problems in life with anxiety, anger, hostility, dependency, withdrawal, isolation, avoidance, nonco-operation, acceptance or denial? Finally, what are the support systems the patient uses to deal with the illness? Are supportive family members, friends or community resources available?

Inspection of the Thorax

Inspection of the thorax reveals much about musculoskeletal structure, nutrition and the status of the respiratory system. The skin over the thorax is observed for colour and turgor, and for evidence of loss of subcutaneous tissue. The musculature of the thorax may reflect recent weight loss. Asymmetry, if present, is noted.

Breathing Patterns

The manner in which the patient breathes is of particular importance. Normally, the ribs articulate with the spine at a 45-degree angle. The act of breathing elevates the ribs, thrusting the sternum forward and up. The intercostal spaces widen, and the angle that the ribs make with the spine more nearly approaches 60 degrees. Patients with emphysema have excessive residual volume; that is, they cannot expel the usual volume of air from the lungs during expiration. Because of the large residual volume, the ribs make a less acute angle with the spine, and the sternum is thrust forward excessively, even during expiration. This has the effect of increasing the anteroposterior diameter of the thorax.

Normally, the anteroposterior diameter, in proportion to the lateral diameter, is 1:2. In the patient with emphysema the ribs are more widely spaced and the intercostal spaces tend to bulge on expiration. As a result of over-inflation of the lungs, not only is the capacity of the thorax to expand limited, but the diaphragm is also depressed, limiting vertical filling. Consequently, the patient must bring into play accessory muscles of respiration, such as the sternocleidomastoids. The appearance of the patient with advanced emphysema is thus quite characteristic and allows the observer to diagnose the disease easily, even from a distance.

Observation of the rate and depth of respiration is also important. In the adult, the normal respiratory rate is 12 to 18 breaths per minute; it is regular in depth and rhythm. An increase in the rate of respiration is called tachypnoea; an increase in depth is called hyperpnoea. An increase in both rate and depth that results in a lowered arterial P_{CO_2} is referred to as hyperventilation. At the extreme of hyperventilation is the marked increase in rate and depth, associated with severe acidosis of diabetic or renal origin, that is called Kussmaul respiration. In the critically ill patient, alternating episodes of apnoea (cessation of breathing) and hyperpnoea may occur on a continuum. This cyclic phenomenon is referred to as Cheyne-Stokes breathing.

The inspiratory phase of respiration is the only one requiring energy in normal physiology. Expiration is passive. Inspiration occupies the first third of the respiratory cycle, expiration the latter two thirds. With rapid breathing, inspiration and expiration are nearly equal.

In thin people, it is quite normal to note a slight retraction of the intercostal spaces during quiet breathing. Bulging during expiration implies obstruction of expiratory air flow, as in emphysema. Marked retraction on inspiration, particularly if asymmetrical, implies blockage of a branch of the respiratory tree. Asymmetrical bulging of the intercostal spaces, on one side or the other, is created by an increase in pressure within the hemithorax. This may be a result of air trapped under pressure within the pleural cavity where it does not belong (pneumothorax) or the pressure of fluid within the pleural space (pleural effusion).

The severe pain associated with pleurisy causes intercostal muscle spasm and a 'lag' in respiration on the involved side.

Certain patterns of respiration are characteristic of specific disease states. Although nurses need not recognize the specific pattern or be acquainted with the association of a certain pattern with a disease state, they are expected to be able to describe abnormal patterns of rhythmicity.

Palpation of the Thorax

Following inspection, the thorax is palpated for tenderness, masses, lesions or inflammation. If the patient has reported an area of pain, or if lesions are apparent, direct palpation with the fingertips (for skin lesions and subcutaneous masses) or with the ball of the hand (for deeper masses or generalized flank or rib discomfort) is done.

Respiratory excursion is an estimation of thoracic expansion and may reveal significant information about the symmetry of breathing. Respiratory lag or impairment is often the result of pleurisy, fractured ribs or trauma to the chest wall.

Sound generated by the larynx travels distally along the bronchial tree to set the chest wall in resonant motion. This is especially true of consonant sounds. The capacity to feel sound on the chest well is called vocal or tactile fremitus.

Percussion of the Thorax

Percussion sets the chest wall and underlying structures in motion, producing audible and tactile vibrations. The examiner uses percussion to determine whether underlying tissues are filled with air, fluid or solid material. This technique is also used to estimate the size and location of certain structures within the thorax (diaphragm, heart, liver).

The examination is usually initiated with percussion of the posterior thorax. Ideally, the patient is in a sitting position with the head flexed forward and the arms crossed on the lap. This position separates the scapulae widely and exposes more lung area for assessment.

Auscultation of the Thorax

Auscultation is useful in assessing the flow of air through the bronchial tree and in evaluating the presence of fluid or solid obstruction in the lung structures. To determine the condition of the lungs, the examiner auscultates for normal breath sounds, adventitious sounds and voice sounds.

A thorough examination includes auscultation of the anterior, posterior and lateral thorax and is performed as follows. The diaphragm of the stethoscope is placed firmly against the chest wall as the patient breathes slowly and deeply through the mouth. Corresponding areas of the chest are auscultated in a systematic fashion from the apices to the bases and along the midaxillary lines. It is often necessary to listen to two full inspirations and expirations at each anatomical location to ensure valid interpretation of the sound heard. Deep breathing may result in symptoms of hyperventilation (e.g., lightheadedness) and can be avoided by getting the patient to rest and breathe normally once or twice during the examination.

Breath Sounds

Normal breath sounds are distinguished by their location over a specific area of the lung and are identified as vesicular and bronchial (tubular) breath sounds. Vesicular sounds are audible as quiet, low-pitched sounds that have a long inspiratory phase and a short expiratory phase. They are heard normally throughout the entire lung field, except over the upper sternum and between the scapulae, where they are replaced with bronchial breath sounds. Bronchial breath sounds are usually louder and higher pitched than vesicular sounds. In comparison, the expiratory phase is longer than the inspiratory phase. Bronchial sounds audible elsewhere in the lung are an indication of pathology and necessitate consultation with a doctor.

The quality and intensity of breath sounds are determined during auscultation. When air flow is decreased by bronchial obstruction (atelectasis) or when fluid (pleural effusion) or tissue (obesity) separates the air passages from the stethoscope, breath sounds are diminished or absent. For example, the breath sounds of the patient with emphysema are faint and often completely absent.

When heard, the expiratory phase is prolonged and may exhibit a high-pitched whistling tone called wheezing. This same sound is also heard in asthma and in any process associated with marked bronchoconstriction.

Adventitious Sounds

The presence of an abnormal condition that affects the bronchial tree and alveoli may produce additional or adventitious sounds. The terminology used to describe these abnormal sounds is changing. For this reason, verbal and written communication regarding the presence of adventitious sounds is sometimes confusing. The current view is as follows. Adventitious sounds are divided into two categories: discrete, noncontinuous sounds and continuous musical sounds. The duration of the sound is the important distinction to make in identifying the sound as noncontinuous or continuous. Crackles (râles) are discrete, noncontinuous sounds that result from delayed reopening of deflated airways. Fine crackles are usually audible at the end of inspiration and originate from the alveoli. Their sound can be re-created by rubbing several pieces of hair next to one's ear. Coarse crackles have a gross, moist sound. They are produced in the large bronchi and are audible in early to mid-inspiration. Crackles may or may not be cleared by coughing. Crackles are a reflection of underlying inflammation or congestion and are often present in such conditions as pneumonia, bronchitis, congestive heart failure, and pulmonary fibrosis.

Wheezes (rhonchi) are continuous musical sounds that are longer in duration than crackles. They may be audible during inspiration, expiration, or both. These sounds result from the passage of air through narrowed or partially obstructed passages. Obstruction is often due to the presence of secretions or swelling, and hence wheezes may clear with coughing. Wheezes originate in the smaller bronchi and bronchioles; they are high pitched and whistling. Rhonchi originate in the larger bronchi or trachea and are lower pitched and sonorous. They are heard in patients with increased secretions. Wheezes are commonly heard in patients with asthma and emphysema.

Inflammation of pleural surfaces induces a crackling, grating sound that is usually heard in both inspiration and expiration. The sound is called a friction rub. It seems to be quite 'close' to the ear and is enhanced by applying pressure with the head of the stethoscope. The sound is imitated by rubbing the thumb and index finger together near the ear. The grating sound of a friction rub is not altered by coughing. If audible only during inspiration, it may be difficult to distinguish from crackles, which may be multiple and so frequent that a continuous sound is perceived.

Voice Sounds

The sound heard through the stethoscope as the patient vocalizes is known as vocal resonance. The vibrations produced in the larynx are transmitted to the chest wall as they pass through the bronchi and alveolar tissue. During the process the sounds are diminished in intensity and altered so that syllables are not distinguishable. The spoken voice is usually assessed by having the patient repeat the phrase 'ninety-nine' while the examiner listens with the stethoscope in corresponding areas of the chest from the apices to the bases.

If the vocal resonance is increased in intensity and clarity, bronchophony is said to be present. Egophony is best appreciated by having the patient repeat the letter 'e'. The distortion produced by consolidation transforms the sound into a clearly heard 'a' rather than 'e'.

A routine assessment of the thorax and lungs includes the following: inspection of the thorax and respirations, percussion of the posterior thorax and auscultation of the thorax for breath sounds and the presence of adventitious sounds. Unless some facet of the history or a prior observation in the physical assessment leads the nurse to pursue additional information about respiratory status, palpation for fremitus and auscultation of voice sounds are omitted.

Assessment of Respiratory Signs and Symptoms

The major signs and symptoms of respiratory disease are dyspnoea, cough, sputum production, chest pain, wheezing, clubbing of the fingers, haemoptysis and cyanosis. These clinical manifestations are related to the duration and severity of the disease.

Dyspnoea

Dyspnoea (difficult or laboured breathing) is a symptom common to many pulmonary and heart conditions, particularly when there is increased lung rigidity and airway resistance. The right ventricle of the heart will ultimately be affected by lung disease since it must pump blood through the lungs. Sudden dyspnoea in a healthy person may indicate pneumothorax (air in the pleural cavity). Sudden shortness of breath in an ill patient or after surgery may denote pulmonary embolism. Orthopnoea (inability to breathe except in an upright position) is characteristic of cardiogenic pulmonary congestion. Shortness of breath with an expiratory wheeze is seen in chronic obstructive airways disease (asthma, bronchitis, emphysema). Noisy breathing may result from a narrowing of the airway or localized obstruction of a major bronchus by a tumour or foreign body. The presence of both inspiratory and expiratory wheezing usually signifies asthma, if the patient is not in congestive heart failure. Shortness of breath is quite commonly related to tension and anxiety. In general, the acute diseases of the lungs produce a more severe grade of dyspnoea than do the chronic diseases. The circumstances that produce the patient's dyspnoea must be determined. How much exertion triggers shortness of breath? Is there an associated cough? Is dyspnoea related to other symptoms? Patients tend to use words like 'suffocation' and 'tightness' to describe their dyspnoea, and they also complain of associated symptoms of fatigue, headache, nausea, numbness, tingling or pain (Jansen-Bjerklie, Carrier and Hudes, 1988). What was the mode of onset: sudden or gradual? At what time of day or night is it obvious? Is it worse when the patient is lying flat in bed? Does it occur at rest? With exercise? Walking? (How far?) Climbing stairs? Running?

The management of dyspnoea depends on the success with which its cause can be alleviated. Relief of the symptom is sometimes achieved by placing the patient at rest with the head elevated and, in severe cases, by administering oxygen.

Cough

Cough results from irritation of the mucous membranes anywhere in the respiratory tract. The stimulus producing a cough may arise from an infectious process or from an airborne irritant, such as smoke, smog, dust or a gas. 'The cough reflex is the watchdog of the lungs' and is the patient's chief protection against the accumulation of secretions in the bronchi and bronchioles.

On the other hand, the presence of cough may indicate serious pulmonary disease. Of equal importance is the type of cough. A dry, irritative cough is characteristic of upper respiratory tract infection of viral aetiology. Laryngotracheitis causes an irritative, high-pitched cough. Tracheal lesions produce a brassy cough. A severe or changing cough may indicate bronchogenic carcinoma. Pleuritic chest pain accompanying coughing may indicate pleural or chest wall (musculoskeletal) involvement.

The character of the cough is then evaluated. Is it dry? Hacking? Brassy? Wheezing? Loose? Severe? Note the time of coughing. Coughing at night may herald the onset of left-sided heart failure or bronchial asthma. A cough in the morning with sputum production is indicative of bronchitis. A cough that worsens when the patient is supine may indicate a postnasal drip (sinusitis). Coughing after food intake may indicate aspirated material in the tracheobronchial tree. A cough of recent onset is usually from an acute infectious process.

Sputum Production

A patient who coughs long enough will almost invariably produce sputum. Violent coughing causes bronchial spasm, obstruction and further irritation of the bronchi and may result in syncope. A severe, repeated or uncontrolled cough that is nonproductive is potentially harmful. Sputum production is the reaction of the lungs to any constantly recurring irritant. It may also be associated with a nasal discharge. If there is a profuse amount of purulent sputum (thick yellow or green) or a change in colour of the sputum, the patient probably has a bacterial infection. Rusty sputum indicates the presence of bacterial pneumonia, if the patient has not received antibiotics. A thin, mucoid sputum frequently results from viral bronchitis. A gradual increase of sputum over a period of time may reveal the presence of chronic bronchitis or bronchiectasis. Pink-tinged mucoid sputum is suggestive of a lung tumour, whereas profuse, frothy, pink material, often welling up into the throat, may indicate pulmonary oedema. Malodorous sputum and bad breath point to the presence of lung abscess, bronchiectasis or an infection caused by fusospirochaetal or other anaerobic organisms.

If the sputum is too thick to raise, it is necessary to decrease its viscosity by increasing its water content through adequate hydration (drinking water) and inhalation of aerosolized solutions. These may be delivered via any type of nebulizer.

Smoking is contraindicated since it interferes with ciliary action, increases bronchial secretions, causes inflammation and hyperplasia of the mucous membranes, and reduces production of surfactant. Thus, bronchial drainage is impaired. If smoking is stopped, sputum volume will decrease and resistance to bronchial infections will improve.

The patient's appetite may be depressed because of the odour of the sputum and the taste it leaves in the mouth. Adequate mouth hygiene, proper environment and wise selection of food will stimulate appetite. Serving citrus juices at the beginning of the meal will make the mouth feel better and will help to make the patient more receptive to the rest of the meal.

Chest Pain

Chest pain associated with pulmonary conditions may be sharp, stabbing and intermittent or dull, aching and persistent. The pain usually is felt on the side where the pathological process is located, but it may be referred elsewhere, for example, to the neck, the back or the abdomen. Chest pain is experienced by many patients with pneumonia, pulmonary embolism with lung infarction and pleurisy, and is a late symptom of bronchogenic carcinoma. In carcinoma the pain may be dull and persistent because of invasion into the chest wall, mediastinum or spine.

Lung disease does not always produce thoracic pain since the lungs and the visceral pleural covering lack sensory nerves and are insensitive to pain stimuli. But the parietal pleura has a rich supply of sensory nerves that are stimulated by inflammation and stretching of the membrane. Pleuritic pain due to irritation of the parietal pleura is sharp and seems to 'catch' on inspiration; patients say it is 'like the stabbing of a knife'. They are more comfortable when they lie on the affected side, a posture that tends to 'splint' the chest wall, restrict the expansions and contractions of the lung and reduce the friction between the injured or diseased pleurae on that side. Pain associated with cough may be lessened by manual splinting of the rib cage.

The quality, intensity and radiation of pain are assessed and factors that precipitate it are searched for. Whether there is a relationship between pain and the patient's posture should be determined. Also, the inspiratory and expiratory phase of respiration and its effect on pain are evaluated.

Analgesic medications are effective in relieving chest pain, but care must be taken not to depress the respiratory centre or a productive cough. For relief of extreme pain, a regional anaesthetic block is done by injecting local anaesthetic along the intercostal nerves that supply the painful area.

Wheezing

Wheezing is often the major finding in a patient with bronchoconstriction or airway narrowing. It is heard with or without a stethoscope, depending on its location. Wheezing is a high-pitched, musical sound heard mainly on expiration.

Clubbing of the Fingers

Clubbing of the fingers as a sign of lung disease is found in patients with chronic hypoxic conditions, chronic lung infections (bronchiectasis) and malignancies of the lung. This finding may be manifested initially as sponginess of the nailbed and loss of the nailbed angle.

Haemoptysis

Haemoptysis (expectoration of blood from the respiratory tract) is a symptom of pulmonary or cardiac disorders. It varies from blood-stained sputum to a large, sudden haemorrhage and always merits investigation. The most common causes are (1) pulmonary infection (bronchitis, bronchiectasis, tuberculosis), (2) carcinoma of the lung,

(3) abnormalities of the heart or blood vessels, (4) pulmonary artery–vein abnormalities, and (5) pulmonary emboli and infarction. The onset of haemoptysis is usually sudden and may be intermittent or continuous. Several investigations are usually done to determine the cause: blood examination, chest angiography, chest radiography and bronchoscopy. A careful history and physical examination are necessary to establish a diagnosis of the underlying disease, irrespective of whether the bleeding produced involved a fleck of blood in the sputum or a massive haemorrhage. The amount of blood produced is not always indicative of the seriousness of the cause.

First it is important to determine where the blood is coming from. Has it come from the gums, nasopharynx, lungs or stomach? The nurse may be the only witness to the episode. The following points should be borne in mind in making and recording observations. In patients whose bloody sputum originates from the nose or the nasopharynx, expectoration is usually preceded by considerable sniffing and blood may appear in the nares. Blood from the lung is usually bright red, frothy and mixed with sputum. Initial symptoms include a tickling sensation in the throat, a salty taste, a burning or bubbling sensation in the chest and perhaps chest pain, in which case the patient tends to splint the bleeding side. The term 'haemoptysis' is reserved for the coughing up of blood arising from a pulmonary haemorrhage. This blood has an alkaline pH (greater than 7.0).

In contrast, if the haemorrhage is in the stomach, the blood is vomited (haematemesis) rather than coughed up. Blood that has been in contact with gastric juice is sometimes so dark that it is referred to as 'coffeeground' material. This blood has an acid pH (less than 7.0).

Cyanosis

Cyanosis, a bluish colouring of the skin, is a very late indicator of hypoxia. In order for cyanosis to appear, there must be at least 5 g/dl (0.77 mmol/l) of unoxygenated haemoglobin. A patient whose haemoglobin is 15 g/dl (2.3 mmol/l) will not demonstrate cyanosis until 5 g/dl (0.77 mmol/l) of that haemoglobin becomes unoxygenated, resulting in an effective circulating haemoglobin of two thirds of the normal level. This determines cyanosis even if the haemoglobin level is low or high (the anaemic patient will rarely manifest cyanosis, and the polycythaemic patient will look cyanotic even if adequately oxygenated). Therefore the presence of cyanosis is not a reliable sign.

Assessment of cyanosis is affected by room lighting, skin colour and depth of the vessels from the surface of the skin. In the presence of a pulmonary condition, central cyanosis is looked for by observing the colour of the tongue and lips. This indicates a decrease in oxygen tension in the blood. Peripheral cyanosis results from decreased blood flow to a certain area of the body, as in vaso-constriction of the nailbeds or ear lobes from cold weather, and does not necessarily indicate a central systemic problem.

Assessment of Breathing Ability

Tests of the patient's breathing ability are easily assessed at the bedside by measuring the respiratory rate, tidal volume, minute ventilation, vital capacity, inspiratory force and compliance. These tests are particularly important for patients at risk of developing pulmonary complications, including those who have undergone chest or abdominal surgery, have experienced prolonged anaesthesia, have pre-existing pulmonary disease or are elderly.

Patients whose chest expansion is limited by external restrictions such as obesity or abdominal distension and who are unable to breathe deeply because of postoperative pain or sedation, produce low tidal volumes. Ventilation at low tidal volumes without sigh inflations can produce alveolar collapse or atelectasis. The functional residual capacity falls, lung compliance is reduced and the patient must breathe faster to maintain the same degree of tissue oxygenation. These events can be exaggerated in patients who have pre-existing pulmonary diseases and in elderly patients whose airways are less compliant owing to earlier closure of small airways during the expiratory cycle.

Respiratory Rate

The normal adult who is resting comfortably breathes at 12 to 18 breaths per minute. Except for occasional sighs, the breathing is reasonably regular.

- Bradypnoea, or slow breathing, is associated with raised intracranial pressure, brain injury and drug overdose.
- Tachypnoea, or rapid breathing, is commonly seen in

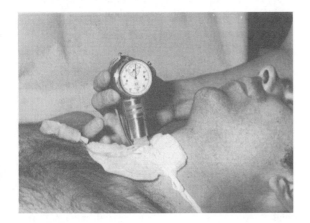

Figure 3.4 Wright respirometer connected to a tracheostomy tube with the cuff inflated. The small dial measures the tidal volume and vital capacity. The large dial measures the minute volume.

pneumonia, pulmonary oedema, metabolic acidosis, septicaemia and rib fracture.

Tidal Volume

The volume of each breath is referred to as the tidal volume. The simplest instrument commonly used to measure volumes at the bedside is known as the Wright respirometer (Figure 3.4).

If the patient is breathing via an endotracheal tube or tracheostomy, the respirometer is attached directly to it and the exhaled volume is obtained from the dial. In others, the respirometer is attached to a face mask, which is placed to cover the nose and mouth so that it is airtight, and the exhaled volume is measured as before. Hand-held electronic respirometers that provide digital readouts of lung volumes are also available.

The tidal volume may vary from breath to breath. To make the measurement reliable, the volumes of several breaths are measured, and the range of tidal volumes together with the average tidal volume are noted. The normal tidal volume is 5 to 8 ml per kilogram of body weight.

Minute Ventilation

Tidal volume and respiratory rates alone are unreliable indicators of the adequacy of ventilation because both can vary widely from breath to breath. Together, however, the tidal volume and respiratory rate are important because they determine the minute ventilation, which is useful in the detection of respiratory failure. Minute ventilation ($\dot{E}$) is the volume of air expired per minute. It is equal to the product of the tidal volume (V_T) and respiratory rate or frequency (f) according to the following equation:

$$\dot{E} = V_T \times f$$

In practice, the minute ventilation is not calculated but is measured directly using a respirometer. Minute ventilation may be decreased by a variety of conditions, including those that:

- Limit neurological impulses transmitted from the brain to the respiratory muscles, such as spinal cord trauma, cerebrovascular accidents, tumours, myasthenia gravis, Guillain-Barré syndrome, polio and drug overdose.
- Depress respiratory centres in the medulla, as with anaesthesia and narcotic sedative overdose.
- Affect the lungs by (1) limiting thoracic movement (kyphoscoliosis); (2) limiting lung movement (pleural effusion, pneumothorax); (3) reducing functional lung tissue (chronic pulmonary diseases, severe pulmonary oedema).

When the minute ventilation falls, the amount of alveolar ventilation reaching the lungs must also decrease, and the $PaCO_2$ increases.

Vital Capacity

Vital capacity is measured by getting the patient to inspire maximally and exhale fully through a respirometer. The normal value depends on age, sex, body build and weight.

● Most patients can generate a vital capacity twice their predicted tidal volume. If the vital capacity is less than 10 ml per kilogram of body weight, the patient will be too weak to sustain spontaneous ventilation and respiratory assistance will be required.

When the vital capacity is exhaled at a maximum flow rate, the forced vital capacity is measured. Most patients can exhale at least 75 per cent of their vital capacity in one second (forced expiratory volume in one second, or FEV_1) and almost all of it in three seconds (FEV_3). A reduction in the FEV_1 suggests abnormal pulmonary air flow. If a patient's FEV_1 and forced vital capacity are proportionately reduced, the maximum lung expansion is restricted in some way. If the reduction in FEV_1 greatly exceeds the reduction in forced vital capacity, the patient may have some degree of airway obstruction.

Inspiratory Force

Inspiratory force evaluates the effort a patient is making during inspiration. It does not require patient co-operation and hence is useful in the unconscious patient. The equipment needed for this measurement includes: (1) a manometre that measures negative pressure; and (2) adaptors for connection to an anaesthetic mask or a cuffed endotracheal tube. The manometer is attached and the airway is completely occluded (Figure 3.5). This is continued for 10 to 20 seconds while the inspiratory efforts of the patient are registered on the manometer. The normal inspiratory pressure is -100 cm H_2O. If the negative pressure registered after 15 seconds of occluding the airway is less than -25 cm H_2O, mechanical ventilation is usually required, because the patient lacks sufficient muscle strength for deep breathing or effective coughing.

Compliance

Compliance is the distensibility or stretchability of the lung. The healthy lung is usually said to be compliant. Compliance is calculated at the patient's bedside by measuring the tidal volume and airway pressure during inspiration. It can also be measured in the pulmonary laboratory using special instruments. When a patient is ventilated mechanically, ease of breathing is quickly and easily estimated by measuring the compliance.

If the pressure measurement is made while air is flowing into the lungs, it reflects changes in air flow resistance as well as lung and chest wall compliance (lung stiffness), and is termed 'dynamic compliance'. Low compliance is

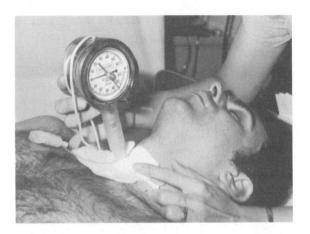

Figure 3.5 Measurement of inspiratory force. The inspiratory force manometer is connected to the tracheostomy tube. The tracheostomy cuff should be inflated. The hole in the connector between the tracheostomy and manometer is plugged so that the airway is obstructed on inspiration. Negative inspiratory force is reflected at -45 cm H_2O pressure. The patient is allowed to breathe between measurements by unplugging the hole.

a characteristic finding in pneumothorax, haemothorax, pleural effusion, pulmonary oedema, atelectasis and most acute illnesses of the lung. Compliance is useful in assessing the progress of the disease in adult respiratory distress syndrome.

● In general, a rapid reduction in static compliance suggests a pneumothorax. A gradual compliance reduction suggests progressive decreases in lung and chest wall compliance from conditions that restrict lung expansion, such as pleural effusion or atelectasis. A rapid reduction in dynamic compliance suggests air flow resistance, such as with accumulated secretions.

Atelectasis

Atelectasis refers to the collapse of an alveoli or a lobule or larger lung unit (Figure 3.6). It may be caused by obstruction of a bronchus, the effect of which is to impede the passage of air to and from the alveoli communicating with it. The alveolar air thus trapped soon becomes absorbed into the bloodstream, and, all external communication having been blocked, its replacement from the outside air is impossible. The net result is that the portion of lung so isolated becomes airless: it shrinks in size, causing the remainder of the lung to overexpand. Bronchial obstruction capable of causing atelectasis may follow inhalation of a foreign body. It may result from a plug of thick exudate that is not, or cannot be, expelled by coughing. Also, the supine position, splinting of respiratory function due to pain, respiratory depression from narcotics and relaxants, and abdominal distension increase the potential of airway closure. Atelectasis resulting from bronchial obstruction by secretions is the usual mechanism that produces the 'massive collapse' occasionally observed postoperatively and in debilitated, bedridden patients. In these patients there is likely to be long, continued respiratory depression, together with inadequate depth of respiratory excursion and perhaps unusually profuse or poorly expectorated bronchial secretions. Tumours of the bronchi often make their presence known first by an atelectasis resulting from their obstructive growth.

Atelectasis may result from pressure on the lung tissue, which restricts normal lung expansion on inspiration. Such pressure may be produced by a variety of causes: fluid accumulation within the thorax (pleural effusion), air in the pleural space (pneumothorax), an extremely large heart, a pericardium distended with fluid (pericardial effusion), tumour growth within the thorax or an elevated diaphragm that is displaced upward as the result of abdominal pressure. Under such circumstances there is crowding of the intrathoracic contents, and since the spongy lung tissue is most compressible, the lung collapses without resistance. Where it is compressed it becomes airless, or atelectatic, and the efficiency of pulmonary function is reduced accordingly. Atelectasis caused by pressure is encountered most often in patients with pleural effusion due to cardiac failure or pleural infection.

Clinical Features
If lung collapse occurs suddenly, and if sufficient lung tissue is involved, the following may be anticipated: marked dyspnoea, cyanosis, prostration and pleural pain, which usually is referred to the lower chest. Fever commonly occurs. Tachycardia and dyspnoea are unusually prominent. The patient characteristically sits bolt upright in bed, appears anxious and cyanotic, and has difficulty in breath-

ing. The chest wall on the affected side moves little, if at all, whereas on the opposite side the excursion appears excessive. Lungs that have collapsed because of the obstruction of a bronchus should be re-expanded as rapidly as possible to avoid the common complications of pneumonia or lung abscess.

Medical Management
The goal is to improve ventilation and remove secretions. If atelectasis has resulted from a pleural effusion or pressure pneumothorax, the fluid or air may be removed by needle aspiration. If bronchial obstruction is the cause, it must be removed in order to permit air to enter the lung again. If respiratory care measures fail to remove the obstruction, a bronchoscopy is done. It may be necessary to use endotracheal intubation and mechanical ventilation for a few days.

Nursing Care
Methods to relieve bronchial obstruction include aspirating secretions, encouraging the patient to cough, and using an aerosol nebulizer, followed by postural drainage and chest percussion. The patient should be turned frequently in an effort to stimulate coughing. If possible, the patient is assisted out of bed and walked to aid in mobilizing and in expelling secretions.

All stuporous, debilitated and sedated patients need frequent position changes in bed, a procedure that affords increased respiratory excursion on the uppermost side. Encouragement of coughing and deep breathing (at least every two hours) is important in preventing and treating atelectasis. The use of deep breathing enhances large-volume inhalation; this emphasis on inspiration is necessary to decrease the potential for airway closure. Judicious use of nasopharyngeal and nasotracheal suction is also helpful in stimulating patients to cough, thereby removing tenacious secretions.

Patients and their family and close friends are likely to be anxious and will benefit from support and information designed to help them cope.

DIAGNOSTIC ASSESSMENT OF RESPIRATORY FUNCTION

Radiographic Examinations of the Chest

Normal pulmonary tissue is radiolucent; therefore, densities produced by tumours, foreign bodies and other pathological conditions can be detected by means of radiographic examination. A chest X-ray film may reveal an extensive pathological process in the lungs in the absence of symptoms. The routine chest X-ray film consists of two views—the posteroanterior projection and the lateral projection. Chest films are usually taken after full inspiration (deep breath) since the lungs are best demon-

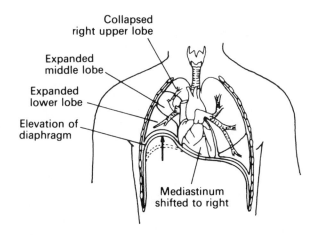

Collapsed
right upper lobe

Expanded
middle lobe

Expanded
lower lobe

Elevation of
diaphragm

Mediastinum
shifted to right

Figure 3.6 Atelectasis.

strated when they are well aerated. Also, the diaphragm is at its lowest level and the largest expanse of lung is visible.

Tomography

Tomography provides films of sections of the lungs at different planes within the thorax. It is valuable in demonstrating the presence of solid lesions, calcification or cavitation within a lesion, and the surrounding vascular patterns.

Computed Tomography

Computed tomography is an imaging method in which the lungs are scanned in successive layers by a narrow-beam X-ray. It has the capability to demonstrate the chest in cross sections and to distinguish small differences in tissue density, thus demonstrating lesions that cannot be detected by conventional radiology. It may be used to define pulmonary nodules and small tumours adjacent to pleural surfaces that are not visible on routine chest films.

Positron Emission Tomography

Positron emission tomography uses high-energy physics and sophisticated computer techniques. The patient inhales or is injected with a shortlived radioactive version of an element that occurs naturally in the body (oxygen, nitrogen, carbon, fluorine). The radioisotope emits subatomic particles called positrons (a positively charged electron). When a positron encounters an electron, which it does just after emission, both are destroyed and two gamma rays are released. These bursts of energy are recorded by the positron emission tomography scanner, and its computer determines where in the body the radioactive material is located. Positron emission tomography is particularly useful for quantitative measurements of regional pulmonary perfusion and for studying ventilation–perfusion relationships.

Fluoroscopy

Fluoroscopy is helpful in evaluating a lesion that has been previously identified on an X-ray film, to see if it is pulsatile. It is also useful in the study of pulmonary dynamics (the motion of pulmonary structures; diaphragmatic motion) and in detecting regional variations in ventilation.

Barium Swallow

A barium swallow outlines the oesophagus and reveals displacement of the oesophagus and encroachment on its lumen by cardiac, pulmonary and mediastinal abnormalities.

Bronchography

A bronchogram provides an outline of the bronchial tree or selected areas after a radio-opaque medium that coats the bronchial mucosa has been instilled directly into the trachea, bronchi and the entire bronchial tree. It reveals anomalies of the bronchial tree and is important in the diagnosis of bronchiectasis, since involved segments cannot always be outlined by other methods.

The procedure must be carried out while the patient is in a fasting state to reduce the possibility of aspiration of gastric contents. Preoperative medication may include atropine to decrease secretions and vagally mediated reflex bradycardia, and diazepam for sedation.

A topical anaesthetic is sprayed into the nose and then in the mouth and posterior pharynx to prevent gagging and coughing when the tube is passed. The contrast medium is instilled by dripping it over the glottis, by slowly injecting it through a tube in the trachea or by injecting it through a needle inserted percutaneously into the trachea below the glottis.
Nursing Care.
Bronchograms cause some discomfort to the patient, and the nurse should support the patient and provide relief where appropriate. After such a procedure, food and fluids are withheld until the patient demonstrates a cough reflex. Once the cough reflex has returned, the patient is encouraged to cough and clear the bronchial tree. Postural drainage may be required. A slight temperature elevation is common following this procedure.

Angiographic Studies of the Pulmonary Vessels

Angiographic studies include pulmonary angiography, angiocardiography, aortography, bronchial arteriography and superior vena cava angiography. Pulmonary angiography is most commonly used to investigate thromboembolic disease of the lungs and congenital abnormalities of the pulmonary vascular tree and to detect abnormal vasculature arising from tumours.

It is the rapid injection of a radio-opaque medium into the vasculature of the lungs for radiographic study of pulmonary vessels.

Endoscopic Procedures

Bronchoscopy

Bronchoscopy is the direct inspection and examination of the larynx, trachea and bronchi through either a flexible fibreoptic bronchoscope or a rigid bronchoscope. In current practice the fibreoptic scope is used more frequently (Figure 3.7).

The diagnostic purposes of bronchoscopy are: (1) to examine tissues or collected secretions; (2) to determine the location and extent of the pathological process and to obtain a tissue sample for diagnosis (by biting forceps, curettage or brush biopsy); (3) to determine whether a tumour can be resected surgically; and (4) to diagnose bleeding sites (source of haemoptysis).

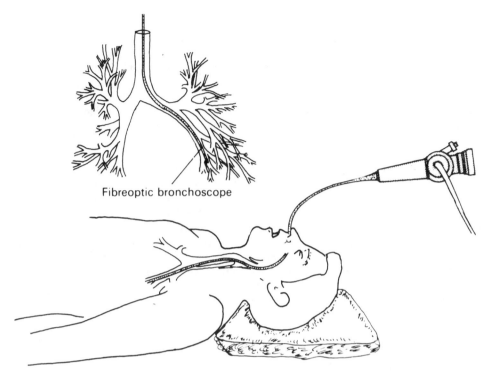

Fibreoptic bronchoscope

Figure 3.7 Fibreoptic bronchoscopy.

Therapeutically, bronchoscopy is used to: (1) remove foreign bodies from the tracheobronchial tree; (2) remove secretions obstructing the tracheobronchial tree when the patient is unable to clear them; (3) provide postoperative treatment in atelectasis; and (4) destroy and excise lesions.

Possible complications of bronchoscopy include reaction to the local anaesthetic, infection, aspiration, bronchospasm, hypoxaemia, pneumothorax, bleeding and perforation.

Nursing Care

Patients need to be made fully aware of the purpose and nature of the test, particularly the part they will be expected to play, in order to reduce fear and to correct misapprehensions. The explanation should include information about the actual procedure, staff and equipment involved, the sensations to be expected and the duration and likely outcome. Informed consent is then obtained.

Patients must be encouraged to practise breathing through the nose (if the bronchoscope is to be inserted through the mouth), and be prepared to expect blood-stained sputum, a sore throat and possibly an irritating cough for the first day or so after the procedure.

Food and fluids are withheld for six hours before the test to reduce the risk of aspiration when reflexes are blocked. Preoperative medications are given as prescribed to inhibit vagal stimulation (thereby guarding against bradycardia, arrhythmias, hypotension), suppress the cough reflex, sedate the patient and relieve anxiety.

Contact lenses, dentures and other prostheses are removed. The examination is usually done under local anaesthesia, but general anaesthesia may be given, especially if the rigid bronchoscope is used.

If local anaesthesia is used, the solution may be dropped on the epiglottis and vocal cords and into the trachea to reduce the cough reflex and pain. Diazepam may be administered as prescribed, intravenously for additional sedation and for amnesia.

Following the procedure, the patient is given nothing by mouth until the cough reflex returns, since the preoperative sedation and local anaesthesia impair the protective laryngeal reflex and swallowing for several hours. Once the patient demonstrates a cough, small pieces of ice and eventually fluids may be given. The patient is observed for evidence of cyanosis, hypotension, tachycardia, arrhythmias, haemoptysis and dyspnoea.

Sputum Studies

Sputum is obtained for study to identify pathogenic organisms and to determine whether malignant cells are present. It may also be used to assess for hypersensitivity states (in which there is an increase of eosinophils). Periodic sputum examinations may be necessary for patients receiving antibiotics, steroids and immunosuppressive drugs for prolonged periods, since these agents give rise to opportunistic infections. In general, sputum cultures are used in diagnosis, for drug sensitivity testing and as a guide in treatment. Sputum can be obtained by expectoration. If the patient cannot raise the sputum spontaneously, deep coughing can often be induced by the patient breathing an irritating aerosol. Other methods of collecting sputum specimens include endotracheal aspiration, bronchoscopic removal, bronchial brushing, transtracheal aspiration and gastric aspiration, usually for tuberculosis organisms. Generally, the deepest specimens are obtained in the early morning.

The patient is asked to clear the nose and throat, and to rinse the mouth in order to decrease contamination of the sputum. The patient then takes a few deep breaths; coughs (rather than spits), using the diaphragm; and expectorates into a sterile container.

The specimen is sent to the laboratory immediately; allowing it to stand for several hours in a warm room will result in the overgrowth of contaminant organisms and may make culture more difficult.

Transtracheal aspiration of sputum is accomplished by transtracheal puncture through the cricothyroid membrane and by the introduction of a fine catheter through the needle into the trachea (Figure 3.8).

This technique is also used to promote coughing and sputum production in thoracotomy patients and in those patients with an absent cough reflex. In this instance, the catheter is left in place for periodic instillation of saline to induce coughing.

Transtracheal aspiration bypasses the oropharynx and thus avoids specimen contamination by mouth flora, particularly anaerobes. It is of special value to the immunocompromised patient with pneumonia who does not produce sputum.

Possible complications include intratracheal bleeding, hypoxaemia, cardiac arrhythmias, pneumomediastinum, subcutaneous emphysema and infection.

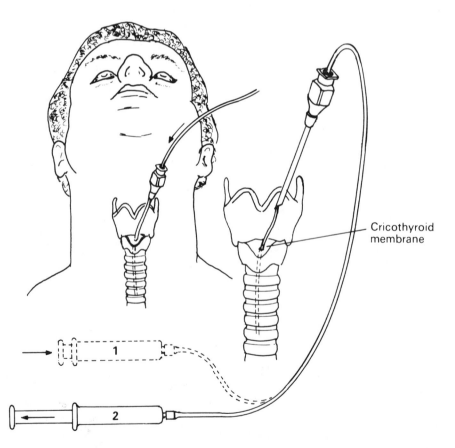

Figure 3.8 Transtracheal aspiration. After the catheter is positioned into the trachea, the needle is withdrawn, leaving the catheter in place. Sterile saline (2–5 ml) is injected into the catheter (1) to loosen secretions and induce coughing. Then the material is aspirated back through the catheter into a syringe (2).

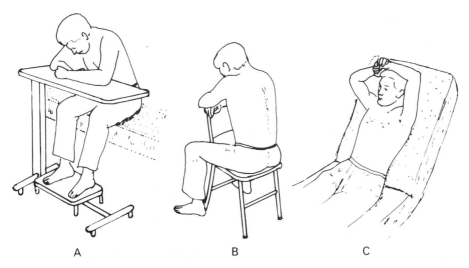

Figure 3.9 Positioning the patient for a thoracentesis. The nurse assists the patient to one of three positions, and offers comfort and support throughout the procedure. (A) Sitting on the edge of the bed with head and arms on and over the bed table. (B) Straddling a chair with arms and head resting on the back of the chair. (C) Lying on unaffected side with the bed elevated 30 to 45 degrees. (Brunner, L. S. and Suddarth, D. S. (1986) *The Lippincott Manual of Nursing Practice* (4th edition), J. B. Lippincott, Philadelphia.)

Thoracentesis

A thin layer of pleural fluid normally remains in the pleural space. A sample of this fluid can be obtained by thoracentesis or by tube thoracotomy. Thoracentesis is the aspiration of pleural fluid for diagnostic or therapeutic purposes (Figure 3.9).

Frequently, a needle biopsy of the pleura is taken at the same time. Studies of pleural fluid include Gram stain culture and sensitivity, acid-fast staining and culture, differential cell count, cytology, pH, specific gravity, total protein and lactic dehydrogenase.

Pleural Biopsy

Pleural biopsy is accomplished by needle biopsy of the pleura or by pleuroscopy, which is a visual exploration of the pleural space through a fibreoptic bronchoscope inserted into the pleural space. Pleural biopsy is done when there is pleural exudate of undetermined aetiology and when there is need for pathological tissue staining or tissue culture for tuberculosis and fungi.

Nursing Care

Patients need to be fully informed about the procedure, including its purpose and nature, especially the sensations of pressure they are likely to feel. They will need to be in a position where the area for needle insertion can be easily identified. Sitting upright will aid in the removal of fluid that localizes at the base of the chest. Patients must be advised to avoid coughing and other sudden movements that may result in trauma of the visceral pleura and the

lung. The procedure is performed under conditions of asepsis and local anaesthesia. Once the fluid has been withdrawn, the needle is removed and pressure is applied to the puncture site. Patients should be observed for alterations in breathing pattern, coughing, faintness and an increased pulse rate. Possible complications include pneumothorax, subcutaneous emphysema, infection, pulmonary oedema and cardiac distress.

Pulmonary Function Tests

Pulmonary function tests are done to detect abnormalities in respiratory function and to determine the extent of the abnormality. Such tests include measurements of lung volumes, ventilatory function, diffusing capacity, gas exchange, lung compliance, airway resistance and distribution of gases in the lung.

Pulmonary function tests are useful in following the course of a patient with established respiratory disease and assessing response to therapy. They are useful as screening tests in potentially hazardous industries, such as coal mining and those that involve exposure to asbestos and other noxious fumes, dusts or gases. Preoperatively, they are useful for patients scheduled for thoracic and upper abdominal surgery.

Pulmonary function tests require some type of spirometer that has a volume-collecting device attached to a recorder that demonstrates volume and time simultaneously.

A number of function tests are carried out since no single measurement can be done to evaluate pulmonary function. Usually, test results are interpreted on the basis of degree of deviation from normal, taking into consideration the patient's height, weight, age and sex.

The most frequently used pulmonary function tests are described in Table 3.1.

Arterial Blood Gas Studies

Measurements of blood pH and of arterial oxygen and carbon dioxide tensions are made when managing patients with respiratory problems and in adjusting oxygen therapy as needed. The arterial oxygen tension (PaO_2) indicates the degree of oxygenation of the blood, and the arterial carbon dioxide tension ($PaCO_2$) indicates adequacy of alveolar ventilation. Arterial blood gas studies aid in assessing the degree to which the lungs are able to provide adequate oxygen and remove carbon dioxide, and the degree to which the kidneys are able to reabsorb or excrete bicarbonate ions to maintain normal body pH. Serial blood gas analysis is also a sensitive indicator of whether the lung has been damaged following chest trauma. Arterial blood gases are obtained through an arterial puncture at the radial, brachial or femoral artery (Figure 3.10).

Radioisotope Diagnostic Procedures (Lung Scan)

A perfusion lung scan is done by injecting a radioactive isotope into a peripheral vein and then taking a scan of the chest and body to detect radiation. The isotope particles are distributed into the lungs in amounts proportional to the regional blood flow, making it possible to trace and measure the blood perfusion through the lung. This procedure is used clinically to measure the integrity of the pulmonary vessels relative to blood flow and to evaluate blood flow abnormalities as seen in pulmonary emboli. The nurse informs patients that the imaging time is 20 to 40 minutes, that they will lie under the camera and that a mask will be fitted over their nose and mouth during the test.

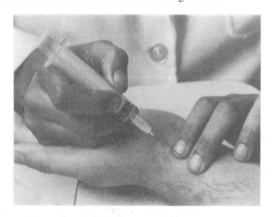

Figure 3.10 Technique of arterial puncture for blood gas analysis.

A ventilation scan is done after the perfusion scan. The patient takes a deep breath of a mixture of oxygen and radioactive gas, which diffuses throughout the lungs. A scan is done to detect ventilation abnormalities, especially in patients who have regional differences in ventilation (e.g., emphysema).

Lung Biopsy Procedures

When the chest X-ray film is inconclusive or reveals pulmonary density (indicating an infiltrate or lesion), it is desirable to examine lung tissue to establish the nature of the lesion. There are several nonoperative lung biopsy techniques that are being used because they yield accurate information with low morbidity: (1) transcatheter bronchial brushing; (2) percutaneous (through the skin) needle biopsy; or (3) transbronchial lung biopsy.

In transcatheter bronchial brushing, a fibreoptic bronchoscope is introduced into the bronchus under fluoroscopic monitoring. A small brush is attached to the end of a flexible wire, which is inserted through the fibrescope. Under direct vision, the area under suspicion is brushed back and forth, causing cells to slough off and adhere to the brush.

This procedure is useful for cytologic evaluations of lung lesions and for the identification of pathogenic organisms.

Nursing support for this procedure includes reinforcing the patient's understanding and seeing that the consent form has been signed. Following the procedure, the patient may have a mild sore throat and transient haemoptysis. Fluids and food are withheld for several hours following the procedure. Possible complications include anaesthetic reactions, laryngospasm, haemoptysis and, rarely, pneumothorax.

Percutaneous needle biopsy may be accomplished with a cutting needle or by aspiration with a spinal-type needle that provides a tissue specimen for histological study. A transbronchial lung biopsy uses cutting forceps introduced by fibreoptic bronchoscope.

A narcotic analgesic may be given before the procedure. The skin over the biopsy site is cleansed and anaesthetized, and a small incision is made. The biopsy needle is inserted through the skin into the pleura while the patient holds the breath in midexpiration. With fluoroscopic monitoring, the surgeon guides the needle into the periphery of the lesion and obtains a tissue sample from the mass. Possible complications include pneumothorax, pulmonary haemorrhage and empyema.

THE PATIENT REQUIRING SPECIFIC MANAGEMENT OF RESPIRATORY CONDITIONS

A wide variety of treatments are used when caring

for patients with different types of respiratory conditions. The most common are oxygen therapy, nebulizer therapy, hyperinflation manoeuvres and chest physiotherapy (postural drainage, percussion and vibration, breathing exercises and physical conditioning).

Oxygen Therapy

Oxygen therapy is the administration of oxygen at a concentration of pressure greater than that found in the environmental atmosphere. It is particularly useful in the treatment of hypoxaemic states that result in inadequate transport of oxygen by the blood. The goal in oxygen therapy is to treat the hypoxaemia while decreasing the work of breathing and the stress on the myocardium. Oxygen transport to the tissues depends on factors such as cardiac output, arterial oxygen content, adequate concentration of haemoglobin and metabolic requirements. All of these must be considered when oxygen therapy is considered.

Assessment
A change in the patient's respiration may be evidence of the need for oxygen therapy. The clinical signs of hypoxaemia (a decrease in the arterial oxygen tension in the blood) include changes in mental status (progressing through impaired judgment, agitation, disorientation, confusion, lethargy and coma), dyspnoea, increase in blood pressure, changes in heart rate, arrhythmias, cyanosis (late sign), diaphoresis and cool extremities. Hypoxaemia usually leads to hypoxia, which is a decrease in oxygen supply to the tissues. Hypoxia, if severe enough, can be life-threatening.

The signs and symptoms of the need for oxygen may depend on how suddenly this need develops. With rapidly developing hypoxia there are changes in the central nervous system since the higher centres are more sensitive to oxygen deprivation. The clinical picture may resemble that of drunkenness, with the patient exhibiting signs of inco-ordination and impaired judgment. Long-standing hypoxia (as seen in chronic obstructive airways disease and chronic heart failure) may produce fatigue, drowsiness, apathy, inattentiveness and delayed reaction time. The need for oxygen is assessed by arterial blood gas analysis as well as by clinical evaluation.

Types and Treatment of Hypoxia
There are four types of hypoxia: hypoxic hypoxia, anaemic hypoxia, stagnant hypoxia and histotoxic hypoxia.

Hypoxic hypoxia occurs when a decrease in the oxygen level in the blood results in decreased oxygen diffusion into the tissues. This is caused by hypoventilation, high altitude and diffusion defects, and it is corrected by increasing alveolar ventilation and providing supplemental oxygen.

Anaemic hypoxia is present when a decrease in the effective haemoglobin concentration causes a decrease in the oxygen carrying capacity of the blood to the tissues. It is caused by anaemia, and is corrected by giving whole blood or packed cells.

Stagnant hypoxia occurs when there is a decrease in cardiac function (cardiac output) and the blood is not adequately pumped to the tissues. This is caused by bradycardia, hypotension and cardiac arrest. Therapy includes hydration, cardiac stimulants, vasopressors and resuscitation.

Histotoxic hypoxia exists when a toxic substance blocks the release or use of oxygen at the tissue level resulting in rapid anoxia and death, as in cyanide poisoning.

Clinical Considerations
Oxygen is administered with care, and its effects on each patient are carefully assessed.

In general in patients with respiratory conditions, oxygen therapy is given only to raise the PaO_2 to 60 to 80 mmHg. At this level the blood is 80 to 90 per cent (0.80–0.90) saturated, and higher PaO_2 values will not add further significant amounts of oxygen to the red blood cells or plasma. Instead of helping, increased amounts of oxygen may possibly suppress ventilation in certain patients.

Excessive oxygen may produce toxic effects on the lungs and central nervous system or may result in depression of ventilation. For example, in patients with chronic obstructive airways disease, the stimulus for respiration is a decrease in blood oxygen rather than an elevation in carbon dioxide levels. Thus, sudden administration of a high concentration of oxygen will remove the respiratory drive that has been created largely by the patient's chronic low oxygen tension. This can cause a progressive increase in $PaCO_2$, ultimately leading to death from carbon dioxide narcosis and acidosis.

When oxygen is administered by any method, the patient is assessed frequently for signs of oxygen need: mental aberration, disturbed consciousness, abnormal colour, perspiration (diaphoresis), changes in blood pressure and increasing heart rate (tachycardia) and respiratory rate (tachypnoea).

Other precautions to be taken when administering oxygen involve the careful handling of the equipment. Since oxygen supports combustion there is always a danger of fire when oxygen is used. Smoking must be avoided. Oxygen therapy equipment is also a potential source of bacterial cross-infection and thus the tubing is changed frequently, depending on infection control policy and the type of oxygen delivery equipment.

Hazards of Oxygen Therapy

Oxygen is a drug and can cause serious side-effects, such as oxygen-induced hypoventilation (prevented by giving low-flow oxygen rates of 1 to 2 litres/minute) and atelectasis.

Perhaps the most serious and insidious hazard is oxygen toxicity, which is caused by too high a concentration of oxygen for an extended period of time. The altered physiology of oxygen toxicity is not fully understood, but is related to a destruction and decrease of surfactant, the formation of a hyaline membrane lining the lung and the development of pulmonary oedema that is not cardiac in origin. Signs and symptoms of oxygen toxicity include substernal distress, paraesthesias in the extremities, dyspnoea, anorexia, flaring of the nares, restlessness, fatigue, malaise and progressive respiratory difficulty.

Prevention of oxygen toxicity is achieved by using oxygen according to prescription. If high concentrations of oxygen are necessary, the duration of administration is kept to a minimum and reduced as soon as possible.

Methods of Oxygen Administration

Oxygen is dispensed from a cylinder or from a piped-in system. A reduction gauge is necessary to reduce the pressure to a working level, and a flowmeter regulates the control of oxygen in litres/minute. Oxygen is moistened by passing it through a humidification system to prevent the mucous membranes of the respiratory tree from becoming dry.

There are many different oxygen devices; all will deliver oxygen if used as prescribed and if proper installation is maintained (Table 3.2). The amount of oxygen delivered is expressed as a percentage concentration (as in 70 per cent). The appropriate form of oxygen therapy is best determined by arterial blood gas levels, which indicate the patient's oxygenation status.

The nasal cannula is used when the patient requires a low-to-medium concentration of oxygen for which precise accuracy is not essential. This method is relatively

Table 3.2 *Oxygen administration devices*

Device	Suggested flow rate (litres/min)	O₂ percentage setting	Advantages	Disadvantages
Cannula	1–2 3–5 6	23–30 30–40 42	Lightweight, comfortable, inexpensive, continuous use with meals and activity	Nasal mucosal drying, variable FIO_2
Catheter	1–6	23–42	Inexpensive	Variable FIO_2, needs frequent change, gastric distension
Mask, simple	6–8	40–60	Simple to use, inexpensive	Poor fitting, variable FIO_2, must remove to eat
Mask, partial rebreather	8–11	50–75	Moderate O₂ concentration	Warm, poor fitting, FIO_2 must remove to eat
Mask, non-rebreather	12	80–100	High O₂ concentration	Poor fitting
Mask, Venturi	4–6 6–8	24, 26, 28 30, 35, 40	Precise FIO_2, additional humidity available	Must remove to eat
Mask, aerosol	8–10	30–100	Good humidity, accurate FIO_2	Uncomfortable for some
Tracheostomy collar	8–10	30–100	Good humidity, comfortable, fairly accurate FIO_2	Uncomfortable for some
T-piece, Briggs	8–10	30–100	Same as tracheostomy collar	Heavy with tubing
Face tent	8–10	30–100	Good humidity, fairly accurate FIO_2	Bulky and cumbersome

FIO_2 = Fraction of inspired oxygen

simple and allows the patient to move about in bed, talk, cough and eat without interruption of oxygen flow. Flow rates in excess of 6 to 8 litres/minute may lead to air swallowing and cause irritation to the nasal and pharyngeal mucosa.

The oropharyngeal catheter is rarely used, but may be prescribed for short-term therapy to administer low-to-moderate concentrations of oxygen. This method can lead to irritation of the nasal mucosa. When oxygen is administered nasally (cannula or catheter), the percentage of oxygen reaching the lungs varies with the depth and rate of respirations.

Simple masks are used for low-to-moderate concentrations of oxygen whereas partial or nonrebreathing masks are used for moderate-to-high concentrations of oxygen. Although popular, these masks cannot be used for controlled oxygen concentrations and must be adjusted for proper fit. They should not press tightly against the skin and cut off circulation; adjustable elastic bands are provided to ensure comfort and security. Bags on partial and non-re-breather masks must remain inflated during both inspiration and expiration. This is accomplished by adjusting the litre flow so the bag does not collapse on inspiration.

The Venturi mask is the most reliable and accurate method for delivering precise oxygen concentration. The mask is constructed in such a way as to allow a constant flow of room air blended with a fixed flow of oxygen. It is used primarily for patients with chronic obstructive airways disease. The Venturi mask employs the principle of air entrainment (trapping in the air like a vacuum), which provides a high air flow with controlled oxygen enrichment. Excess gas leaves the mask through the perforated cuff, carrying with it the exhaled carbon dioxide. This method allows inhalation of a constant oxygen concentration regardless of the depth or rate of respiration.

The mask should fit snugly enough to prevent oxygen flow into the eyes, and the patient's skin is checked for irritation. The mask must be removed in order that the patient may eat, drink and take medications.

Aerosol masks, tracheostomy collars and face tents are used with aerosol devices (nebulizers) that can be adjusted for oxygen concentrations in ranges from 27 to 100 per cent (0.27–1.00). If the gas mixture flow falls below patient demand, room air will be pulled in, diluting the concentration. The aerosol mist must be constantly available for the patient during the entire inspiratory phase.

Home Health Care

At times oxygen must be administered to the patient at home. The patient and home carer should be instructed in the methods for administering oxygen and should be informed that oxygen is available in gas, liquid and concentrated forms. The gas and liquid forms come in portable devices so that the patient can leave the home while receiving oxygen therapy. Humidity must be provided while oxygen is used (except with portable devices) in order to counteract the dry, irritating effects of compressed oxygen on the airway.

Intermittent Positive Pressure Breathing

Intermittent positive pressure breathing is the breathing of air or oxygen (or a combination of both) at a pressure higher than atmospheric pressure to produce air flow into the lungs during inhalation. Intermittent positive pressure breathing is applied by a mechanical device that inflates the lungs through positive pressure, dispersing a prescribed medication. When the patient inhales, the machine delivers a positive pressure breath; after a preset pressure is reached on the machine, the machine cycles off and there is passive exhalation. The intermittent positive pressure breathing machine may be powered by electricity or gas and may be connected with a mouthpiece, mask or tracheostomy adaptor.

In recent years there has been controversy over the effectiveness of intermittent positive pressure breathing therapy. There is no clear evidence of its value in routine use.

Indications

Intermittent positive pressure breathing is typically used in chronic obstructive airways disease, acute pulmonary oedema, drug overdose and restrictive lung disorders, and to prevent postoperative atelectasis. It is intended to mobilize secretions, increase ventilation, bronchodilate mechanically, decrease the work of breathing and reduce cardiac output. Its primary indication is to deliver medications deep in the lower respiratory tract in patients who cannot take deep breaths on their own.

Hazards

Intermittent positive pressure breathing can cause pneumothorax, mucosal drying, increased intracranial pressure, haemoptysis, gastric distension, vomiting with possible aspiration, psychological dependency (especially with long-term use, as in chronic obstructive airways disease), hyperventilation, excessive oxygen (due to uncontrolled oxygen–air dilution) and cardiovascular problems.

Nebulizer Therapy

The nebulizer is a device that disperses a liquid (medication) into microscopic particles and delivers it to the lungs as the patient inhales. The nebulizer is usually air-driven by means of a compressor through connecting tubing. In some instances, the nebulizer is oxygen-driven rather than air-driven. To be effective, a visible mist must be available for the patient to inhale.

Inhaler Therapy

Fixed-dose inhalers in pressurized aerosol containers target medication directly to the bronchial mucosa with only minute amounts of drug escaping into the systemic circulation. Bronchodilators and corticosteroids are given via this method. Patients need to be advised to inhale slowly and to hold their breath for as long as possible while releasing the drug. Some patients find they are unable to co-ordinate their breathing with aerosol release and may find dry powder inhalers (Rotacaps) easier to use.

Incentive Spirometry (Sustained Maximum Inspiration)

The incentive spirometer gives visual feedback to guide the patient to inhale slowly and deeply to maximize lung inflation (Figure 3.11). The patient is placed in a sitting or semi-recumbent position, since the diaphragmatic excursion is greater with this posture. However, this treatment may be done with the patient in any position. The tidal volume of the spirometer is set according to the manufacturer's instructions. The purpose of the device is to measure a gradually increasing inhaled volume as the patient takes deeper and deeper breaths. The patient takes a deep breath from the mouthpiece, pauses at peak inflation, then

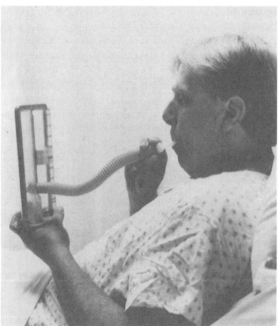

Figure 3.11 An incentive spirometer designed to encourage sustained maximum inspiration for patients who are predisposed to atelectasis. (Courtesy of Photography Department, Montefiore Hospital, Pittsburgh, Pennsylvania. Brunner, L. S. and Suddarth, D. S. (1986) *The Lippincott Manual of Nursing Practice* (4th edition), p. 208, J. B. Lippincott, Philadelphia.

relaxes and exhales. To avoid fatigue the patient should take several normal breaths before attempting another with the incentive spirometer. The volume is periodically increased as tolerated.

Indications

Incentive spirometry is used postoperatively to prevent or treat atelectasis, resulting in shunting. As prophylaxis, incentive spirometry may be more effective than intermittent positive pressure breathing since it encourages a maximal inspiratory effort.

Nursing Care

Nursing care of patients using incentive spirometry includes the following:

- Explaining the reason for therapy.
- Positioning patients in semi-recumbent or an upright position (although any position is acceptable).
- Teaching patients to use diaphragmatic breathing.
- Instructing patients to hold their breath at the end of inspiration (for three seconds), then to exhale slowly.
- Encouraging coughing during and after each session.
- Helping patients splint the incision while coughing postoperatively.
- Setting a reasonable volume goal (in order not to discourage patients).
- Placing the machine within patients' reach.
- Beginning therapy immediately postoperatively (atelectasis can start within one hour after hypoventilation begins).
- Encouraging approximately 10 breaths per hour while patients are awake.
- Recording effectiveness and number of breaths achieved every two hours.

Chest Physiotherapy

Chest physiotherapy includes postural drainage, chest percussion and vibration, breathing exercises/breathing retraining and effective coughing. The goals of chest physiotherapy are removal of bronchial secretions, improved ventilation and increased efficiency of the respiratory musculature.

Postural Drainage (Segmented Bronchial Drainage)

Postural drainage is the use of specific positions so the force of gravity can assist in the removal of bronchial secretions. The secretions drain from the affected bronchioles into the bronchi and trachea, and are removed by means of coughing or suctioning. It is used to prevent or relieve bronchial obstruction due to secretions.

Because the patient is usually in an upright position, secretions are likely to accumulate in the lower part of the

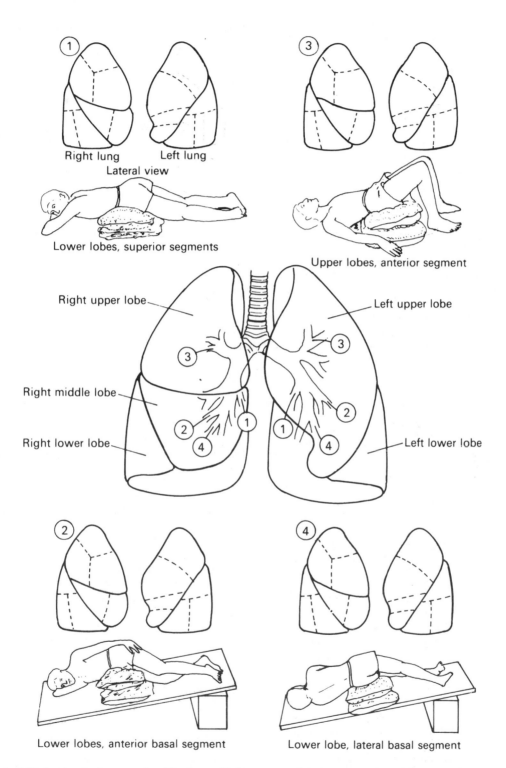

Figure 3.12 Anatomical segments of the lung with four postural drainage positions. The numbers relate the position to the corresponding anatomical segment of the lung.

lung. When postural drainage is used, the patient is positioned sequentially in different postures (Figure 3.12), so that the force of gravity helps to drain secretions from the smaller bronchial airways to the main bronchi and trachea. The secretions are then removed by coughing. Inhalation of prescribed bronchodilators before postural drainage assists in draining the bronchial tree.

Postural drainage exercises can be directed at any of the segments (bilateral) of the lung. The lower and middle lobe bronchi empty more effectively when the head is down; the upper lobe bronchi empty more effectively when the head is up. Frequently, the patient is placed in five positions, one for drainage of each lobe: head down, prone, right and left lateral and sitting upright.

Postural drainage is usually done two to four times a day, before meals (to prevent nausea, vomiting and aspiration) and at bedtime. If prescribed, bronchodilators, water or saline may be nebulized and inhaled before postural drainage to dilate the bronchial tubes, reduce bronchospasm, decrease thickness of mucus and sputum, and combat oedema of the bronchial walls. The patient is made as comfortable as possible in each position, and a sputum cup and paper tissues are provided. The patient is advised to remain in each position for 10 to 15 minutes and to breathe in slowly through the nose and then breathe out slowly through pursed lips to help keep airways open so that secretions can be drained while the various positions are assumed. If patients cannot tolerate the position, they are helped to assume a modified posture. When patients change position, they are asked to cough and remove secretions as follows:

1. Assume a sitting position and bend slightly forward because the upright position permits a stronger cough.
2. Keep the knees and hips flexed to promote relaxation and lessen the strain on the abdominal muscles while coughing.
3. Inhale slowly through the nose and exhale through pursed lips several times.
4. Cough twice during each exhalation while contracting (pulling in) the abdomen sharply with each cough.
5. Splint incision, using pillow support, if necessary.

The secretions may need to be suctioned mechanically if the patient is unable to cough. It may also be necessary to use chest percussion and vibration to loosen bronchial secretions and mucus plugs that adhere to the bronchioles and bronchi and to propel sputum in the direction of gravity drainage.

Following the procedure, the amount, colour, viscosity and character of the ejected sputum is noted; the patient's colour and pulse are evaluated the first few times the exercises are performed. It may be necessary to administer oxygen during postural drainage.

If the sputum is foul smelling, postural drainage is carried out in a room away from other patients and deodorizers are used.

Nursing Care

Patients need to be made fully aware of the purpose and nature of the intervention. They may find some positions intolerable, and compromises have to be made. Postural drainage is best carried out before meals to prevent nausea, vomiting and aspiration. Medications may be administered before the procedure to make expectoration easier. While in each position patients should be advised to inhale slowly through the nose and to exhale slowly through pursed lips to promote bronchodilation. Patients need to be advised to cough to remove secretions when they change position. A receptacle should be provided, and the nature of the sputum should be noted. After the procedure the patient may find it refreshing to brush the teeth and use a mouthwash before resting in bed.

Chest Percussion and Vibration

To aid in the loosening and removal of thicker secretions, the chest may be tapped (percussion) and vibrated. Percussion and vibration help to dislodge mucus adhering to the bronchioles and bronchi.

Percussion is carried out by cupping the hands and lightly striking the chest wall over the lung segment to be drained in a rhythmical fashion. A towel may be placed over the chest to prevent skin irritation and redness from direct contact. Percussion, alternating with vibration, is maintained for 3 to 5 minutes for each position. The patient uses diaphragmatic breathing during this procedure to promote relaxation. As a precaution, percussion over the sternum, spine, liver, kidneys, spleen or breasts (in females) is avoided. Percussion is done cautiously in the elderly because of their increased incidence of osteoporosis and risk of rib fracture.

Vibration is the technique of applying manual compression and tremor to the chest wall during the exhalation phase of respiration (Figure 3.13). This manoeuvre helps to increase the velocity of the expired tidal volume from the small airways, thus freeing the mucus. After three or four vibrations the patient is encouraged to cough, using the abdominal muscles. (Contracting the abdominal muscles increases the effectiveness of the cough.) A scheduled programme of coughing and clearing sputum, together with hydration, will reduce sputum in the majority of patients. The number of times the percussion and vibration cycle is repeated depends on the patient's tolerance and clinical response. Breath sounds are evaluated after the procedures.

Nursing Care

When performing chest physiotherapy it is important to make sure the patient is comfortable, is not wearing restrictive clothing and has not just eaten a meal. The uppermost areas of the lung are treated first. Medication is given for pain as prescribed before percussion and vibration,

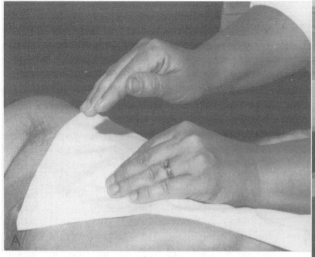

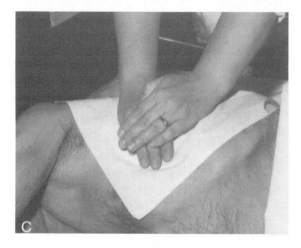

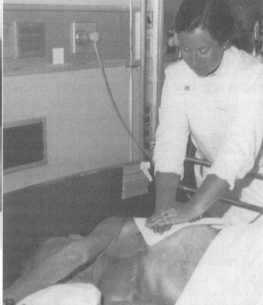

Figure 3.13 Percussion and vibration. (A) Proper hand positioning for percussion. (B) Proper technique for vibration. Note that the wrists and elbows are kept stiff and the vibrating motion is produced by the shoulder muscles. (C) Proper hand position for vibration.

any incision is splinted and pillows are used for support as needed. On completion of the treatment, the patient is returned to a comfortable position. The treatment is stopped if any of the following untoward symptoms develop: increased pain, increased shortness of breath, weakness, light-headedness or haemoptysis. Therapy ends when the patient has normal respirations, can mobilize secretions and has normal breath sounds, and when the chest film is normal.

Health Education

Chest physiotherapy is frequently indicated at home for patients with chronic obstructive airways disease, bronchiectasis and cystic fibrosis. The techniques are the same as described above, but gravity drainage is achieved by placing the hips over a stack of magazines, newspapers or pillows. The patient, family member or close friend are advised about the positions and the techniques of percussion and vibration, so that therapy can be continued throughout the day.

Breathing Retraining

Breathing retraining consists of exercises and breathing practices designed and carried out to achieve a more efficient and controlled ventilation, to decrease the work of breathing and to correct respiratory deficits. These exercises promote maximum alveolar inflation; promote muscle relaxation; relieve anxiety; eliminate useless, unco-ordinated patterns of respiratory muscle activity; slow the respiratory rate; and decrease the work of breathing. Slow, relaxed and rhythmic breathing also helps to control the anxiety that is present when the patient is dyspnoeic.

Breathing exercises may be practised in several positions, since air distribution and pulmonary circulation vary according to the position of the chest. Many patients will require additional oxygen, using a low-flow method, while doing breathing exercises.

Patients are told to breath slowly and rhythmically in a relaxed manner in order to permit more complete exhalation and emptying of the lungs. They are advised to always inhale through the nose since this filters, humidifies and warms the air. If patients become short of breath, they should concentrate on breathing slowly and rhythmically.

Diaphragmatic Breathing

The goal of diaphragmatic breathing is to use and strengthen the diaphragm during breathing. Diaphragmatic breathing can become automatic with sufficient practice and concentration. Such respiratory muscle training has been recommended for patients with chronic obstructive airways disease and to prevent respiratory failure (Kim, 1984).

The patient is advised to:

1. Place one hand on the stomach (just below the ribs) and the other hand on the middle of the chest. This increases awareness of the diaphragm and its function in breathing.
2. Breathe in slowly and deeply through the nose, letting the abdomen protrude as far as it will.
3. Breathe out through pursed lips while tightening (contracting) the abdominal muscles. Press firmly inward and upward on the abdomen while breathing out.
4. Repeat for one minute; follow by a rest period of 2 minutes. Work up to 5 minutes, several times a day (before meals and at bedtime).

Pursed Lip Breathing

Pursed lip breathing, which improves oxygen transport, helps to induce a slow, deep breathing pattern and assists the patient to control breathing, even during periods of physical stress. This type of breathing helps prevent alveolar collapse owing to loss of lung elasticity in emphysema.

The goal of pursed lip breathing is to train the muscles of expiration so as to prolong exhalation and increase airway pressure during expiration, thus lessening the amount of airway trapping and resistance.

The patient is advised as follows:

1. Inhale through the nose while counting to 3, and exhale slowly and evenly against pursed lips while tightening the abdominal muscles. (Pursing the lips increases intratracheal pressure; exhaling through the mouth offers less resistance to expired air.)
2. Count to 7 while prolonging expiration through pursed lips.
3. Sit in a chair and fold arms over the abdomen:
   a. Inhale through the nose (count to 3).
   b. Exhale slowly through pursed lips while bending forward.
   c. Count to 7.
4. While walking:
   a. Inhale while walking two steps.

b. Exhale through pursed lips while walking four or five steps.

The above steps may also be performed while practising diaphragmatic breathing.

THE PATIENT REQUIRING AIRWAY MANAGEMENT

Adequate ventilation is dependent on free movement of air through the upper and lower airways. In many conditions the airway becomes narrowed or blocked as a result of a disease process, bronchoconstriction (narrowing of airway by contraction of muscle fibres), a foreign body or secretions. Maintaining a patent airway is achieved through meticulous airway management, whether in an emergency situation, such as airway obstruction, or in long-term management, as in caring for a patient with an endotracheal or a tracheostomy tube.

Emergency Management of Upper Airway Obstruction

Upper airway obstruction is caused by food particles, vomitus, blood clots or any other particle that enters and obstructs the larynx or trachea. It may also occur from enlargement of tissue in the wall of the airway, as in epiglottitis, laryngeal oedema, laryngeal carcinoma or peritonsillar abscess, or from thick secretions. Collapse of the walls of the airway as occurs in retrosternal goitre, enlarged mediastinal lymph nodes, haematoma around the upper airway and thoracic aneurysm may also result in upper airway obstruction. Finally, the unconscious or comatose patient is at risk of obstructing the upper airway because such a patient loses the protective reflexes (cough and swallowing) and the tone of the pharyngeal muscles, causing the tongue to fall back and block the airway.

The patient is observed for the following signs of upper airway obstruction:

- Inspiration causing indrawing of parts of the upper chest, sternum and intercostal spaces.
- Exhalation that is characterized by a jerky protrusion and prolonged, somewhat sustained contraction of the abdominal muscles, followed by a brief relaxation before another contraction.
- Seesaw movement of the chest and abdomen (combination of the above). As the inspiratory muscles contract, an inward thoracic depression results while relaxed abdominal muscles are pushed up jerkily. Exhalation is produced by a laboured and prolonged abdominal muscle contraction, causing a jerky upward push of the thorax.

As soon as an upper airway obstruction is identified the following emergency measures are taken:

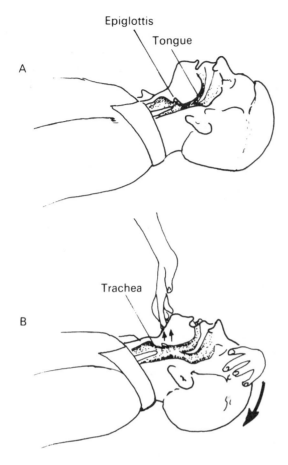

Epiglottis

Tongue

A

Trachea

B

Figure 3.14 Opening the airway. (A) Airway obstruction caused by the tongue and epiglottis. (B). Relieving the obstruction by using the head-tilt/chin-lift method. (Standards and guidelines for cardiopulmonary resuscitation and emergency cardiac care (1986) 6 June, Vol. 255, No. 21, p. 2916. Reprinted by permission of the *Journal of the American Medical Association*.)

- The mouth is opened to see if the tongue has fallen back or if there are secretions, blood clots or any particles obstructing the airway. Secretions are suctioned, and any particulate matter in the pharynx is removed immediately with forceps or by suctioning.
- Extension of the head is the simplest way of relieving upper airway obstruction caused by the tongue's falling back. The head is extended at the atlanto-occipital joint. This increases the distance between the chin and the cervical spine, which puts the muscles that support the tongue under tension and pulls the tongue forward.
- If simple extension of the head is not adequate to clear the airway, the mandible is forced forward. This manoeuvre is designed to put further tension on the musculature that supports the tongue. It is best achieved by the head-tilt/chin-lift method. The nurse

stands beside the patient and uses two fingers of one hand to lift up the jaw by pulling up on the chin. At the same time, the nurse's opposite hand pushes down on the forehead to tilt the head backward (Figure 3.14).

- If this manoeuvre is not adequate and partial airway obstruction still exists, then endotracheal intubation is done. Unconsciousness and loss of protective airway reflexes require endotracheal intubation to maintain a patent airway and prevent aspiration.
- If assisted ventilation is required, a resuscitator bag and mask are used initially before intubation and mechanical ventilation. The mask is sealed onto the patient's face by pressing the mask with the left thumb on the bridge of the nose while the index finger presses around the lips. At the same time the rest of the fingers of the left hand pull on the chin and the angle of the mandible to maintain the head in extension (Figure 3.15). The right hand inflates the lungs by periodically squeezing the bag to its full volume. A self-inflating or resuscitation bag is also used after the patient is intubated. The bag is squeezed in the same manner to its full volume, but head extension is not necessary because the upper airway is bypassed by the tube and thus always open. Ventilation through a self-inflating bag is accomplished by one person and is used not only for emergency ventilation but also during suctioning, ventilator maintenance and ambulation of the patient on a ventilator.

Endotracheal Intubation

Endotracheal intubation refers to the passing of a tube through the mouth or nose into the trachea. It is done to

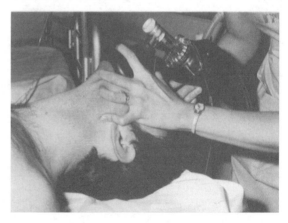

Figure 3.15 Bag and mask ventilation. The head is extended and the mask is sealed to the face by pressing the left thumb on the bridge of the nose and the index finger on the chin. The remaining three fingers pull the chin and mandible upward to maintain the head in extension. The right hand then squeezes the bag. Bag and mask ventilation should be performed only by specially trained staff.

provide an airway when the patient is having respiratory difficulty that cannot be treated by simpler methods. It is the method of choice in emergency care. Endotracheal intubation is used as a means of providing an airway for patients who cannot maintain an adequate airway on their own (comatose patients, those with upper airway obstruction), and it provides an excellent means for suctioning secretions from the pulmonary tree.

An endotracheal tube usually is passed with the aid of a laryngoscope by medical staff who are specifically trained in this technique. Once the tube is inserted, a cuff around the tube is inflated to prevent leakage around the outer part of the tube and to minimize the possibility of subsequent aspiration. Suctioning of the tracheobronchial secretions is done through the tube. Warm, humidified oxygen can be introduced through the tube, or the tube may be connected to ventilatory support. Endotracheal intubation may be used for up to two to three weeks. Then a tracheostomy is considered.

As in any other treatment, there are disadvantages associated with endotracheal or tracheostomy tubes. For one thing, the tube causes discomfort. In addition, the cough reflex is depressed because closure of the glottis is hindered, and this prevents the generation of the high intrathoracic airway pressure necessary to produce an expulsive cough. Secretions tend to become thicker because the warming and humidifying effect of the upper respiratory tract has been bypassed. The swallowing reflexes, composed of the glottic, pharyngeal and laryngeal reflexes, are depressed because of prolonged disuse and the mechanical trauma of the endotracheal or tracheostomy tube. Ulceration and stricture of the larynx or trachea may develop. Finally, the patient is not able to talk.

Tracheostomy

A tracheostomy is an operation in which an opening is made into the trachea. When an indwelling tube is inserted into the trachea, the term 'tracheostomy' is used. A tracheostomy may be either temporary or permanent.

A tracheostomy is done to bypass an upper airway obstruction, to remove tracheobronchial secretions, to permit the use of mechanical ventilation, to prevent aspiration of oral or gastric secretions in the unconscious or paralyzed patient (by closing off the trachea from the oesophagus) and to replace an endotracheal tube. There are many disease processes and emergency conditions that make a tracheostomy necessary.

An opening is made in the second and third tracheal rings. After the trachea is exposed, a cuffed tracheostomy tube of an appropriate size is inserted (Figure 3.16A). The cuff is an inflatable attachment to a tracheostomy or endotracheal tube that is designed to seal off the tracheal lumen for mechanical ventilation.

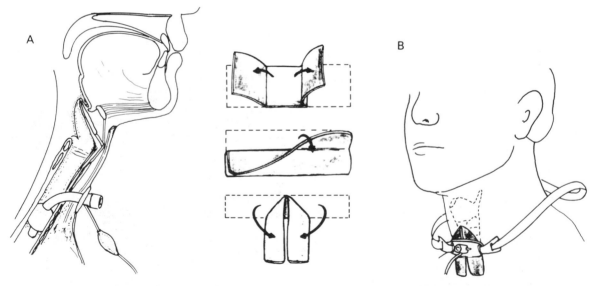

Figure 3.16 Tracheostomy tube dressing and tape changes. Drawing A shows how the cuff of the tracheostomy tube fits smoothly within the tracheal wall. Pressure should be great enough to ensure a snug fit but not so great as to produce a stenosis. Illustration B shows how to unfold a 3 × 3-inch gauze square and refold it so that it need not be cut (cut, frayed threads could be aspirated) and yet will provide a comfortable neck pad. Use tracheostomy gauze sponges with slits already made and oversewn if available. These are changed as often as necessary. Note the manner in which the neck twill tapes are fastened to the openings in the neck plate of the tracheostomy tube; this eliminates a knot, which may create pressure on the neck. Twill tape ends should be tied to the side of the neck rather than in back. (A knot at the back would be uncomfortable to lie on.)

The tracheostomy tube is held in place by tapes fastened around the patient's neck. Usually, a square of sterile gauze is placed between the tube and the skin to absorb drainage and prevent infection (Figure 3.16B).

Complications

Complications may occur early or late in the course of tracheostomy tube management. They may even occur years after the tube has been removed. Immediately after the tracheostomy is performed there may be bleeding, pneumothorax, air embolism, aspiration, subcutaneous or mediastinal emphysema, recurrent laryngeal nerve damage or posterior tracheal wall penetration. Long-term complications include airway obstruction due to accumulation of secretions or protrusion of the cuff over the opening of the tube, infection, rupture of the innominate artery, dysphagia, tracheo-oesophageal fistula, tracheal dilation or tracheal ischaemia and necrosis. Problems that may arise after the tube is removed include tracheal stenosis and vocal cord paralysis (secondary to laryngeal nerve damage).

Postoperative Nursing Care

The patient requires continuous monitoring and assessment. The newly made opening must be kept patent by proper suctioning of secretions. After the vital signs are stable, the patient is positioned to facilitate ventilation, promote drainage, minimize oedema and prevent strain on the suture lines. Analgesic and sedative drugs are given with caution since it is undesirable to depress the cough reflex.

Another objective of nursing care is to alleviate patients' apprehensions. They need reassurance, since they may have a real fear that they will asphyxiate while they are asleep. Since these patients cannot speak, paper and pencil are kept within reach so that they have a means of communication. A tap bell or other signalling device should be available.

Tracheal Suctioning (Tracheostomy or Endotracheal Tube)

When a tracheostomy or an endotracheal tube is present, it is necessary to suction patients' secretions, since their own cough mechanisms are not as effective. Tracheal suctioning is performed every one to two hours, or whenever secretions are present. Unnecessary suctioning can initiate bronchospasm and cause mechanical trauma to the tracheal mucosa.

Patients should be advised to spray normal saline directly into their tracheostomy tube every two hours to minimize the risk of dry or tenacious secretions that would inhibit suction. The nurse should explain precisely what is to be done. This should gain patients' co-operation and provide reassurance. Patients should be encouraged to perform their own suction if they are able to manage, in order to have control over their own care.

Hands need to be washed in an alcohol-based solution to minimize the risk of cross-infection. Wearing a plastic apron will protect the nurse's clothes, since suctioning tends to induce patients to cough.

The strength of suction will depend on the tenacity of the sputum—suctioning needs to be set at an appropriate level. The end of the catheter is attached to the suction tubing by a Y connector. The rest of the catheter is kept in its packaging to minimize the risk of contamination.

Disposable gloves need to be worn as the catheter is withdrawn from its packet. The catheter is then gently introduced, with the suction turned off, to about one third of its length into the tracheostomy tube, taking care not to damage the tracheal mucosa.

Suction is applied by placing the thumb over the open limb of the Y connector. Suction should not be applied for more than 15 seconds at a time—prolonged suctioning can result in infection and initiate a choking sensation for patients.

The catheter is gently withdrawn from the trachea, with the suction turned off, in a rotating motion so as to prevent trauma. Catheters are used only once in order to reduce the risk of introducing infection. The connection tubing is rinsed in a bowl of sodium bicarbonate with the suction turned on. This will loosen secretions adhered to the side of the tube.

Cuff Management

As a general rule, the cuff on a tracheostomy tube should be deflated. It is inflated in the following situations: continuous mechanical ventilation, during and after eating or during and one hour after a tube feeding, during intermittent positive pressure breathing treatments, when the patient is unable to handle oral secretions and when there is increased risk of aspiration (e.g., when the patient is unconscious or has continuous tube feedings).

Nursing Care

The tracheostomy tube and surrounding skin need to be kept clean with a solution such as saline. The dressing needs to be changed when soiled using a clean technique. Patients begin to adapt to breathing through their tracheostomy after the first 24 to 48 hours. Humidified oxygen may be required to prevent crust formation in the airway.

Spare tubes and tracheal dilators should always be available in case the tracheostomy tube becomes accidently dislodged. Tracheal bleeding and profuse secretions need to be controlled with suction. Patients with infected sputum need to be encouraged to cough up their secretions. Tracheostomy tubes should be changed every three to five days. Permanent stomas are protected with a bib or piece of gauze.

Complications include kinking of the tube; necrosis of

the trachea due to an overinflated cuff; malposition, which may lead to haemmorhage; tracheo-oesophageal fistula; damage during suctioning; and infection.

THE PATIENT REQUIRING MECHANICAL VENTILATION

A mechanical ventilator is a positive/negative pressure breathing device that can maintain respirations automatically for long periods of time.

If a patient is experiencing a continuous decrease in oxygenation (Pao_2) an increase in arterial carbon dioxide levels ($PaCo_2$), and a persistence of acidosis (a decreased pH), then mechanical ventilation may be necessary. Conditions such as postoperative thoracic or abdominal surgery, drug overdose, neuromuscular diseases, inhalation injury, chronic obstructive airways disease, multiple trauma, shock, multisystem failure and coma may all lead to respiratory failure and the need for mechanical ventilation. A patient with apnoea that is not reversible is also a candidate for mechanical ventilation.

Ventilators are classified according to the manner in which they support ventilation. The two general categories are negative pressure and positive pressure ventilators.

Negative pressure ventilators exert a negative pressure on the external chest and the underlying lung to expand it during inspiration. Air then flows into the lung, filling its volume. It is used mainly in respiratory failure associated with neuromuscular conditions such as poliomyelitis, muscular dystrophy, multiple sclerosis and myasthenia gravis.

Positive pressure ventilators inflate the lungs by exerting positive pressure on the airway, thus forcing the alveoli to expand during inspiration. Expiration occurs passively. For continuous use, endotracheal intubation or tracheostomy is necessary. There are three types of positive pressure ventilators.

The pressure-cycled ventilator is a positive pressure ventilator in which the inspiratory pressure to be reached with each inspiration is controlled. The ventilator cycles on, delivers a flow of air until a certain predetermined pressure is reached, and then cycles off.

Time-cycled ventilators terminate or control inspiration after a preset time. The volume of air the patient receives is regulated by the length of inspiration and the flow rate of the air.

Volume-cycled ventilators are the most commonly used positive pressure ventilators. With this type of ventilator, the volume of air to be delivered with each inspiration is controlled. Once this preset volume is delivered to the patient, the ventilator cycles off and exhalation occurs passively. From breath to breath, the volume of air delivered by the ventilator is constant, assuring consistent, adequate breaths.

Nursing Care of the Mechanically Ventilated Patient

► Assessment

The nurse has a vital role in assessing the patient's state and the functioning of the ventilator. In assessing the patient, the nurse evaluates the following:

- Vital signs.
- Evidence of hypoxia (restlessness, anxiety, tachycardia, increased respiratory rate, cyanosis).
- Respiratory rate and pattern.
- Breath sounds.
- Neurological state.
- Tidal volume, minute ventilation, forced vital capacity.
- Nutritional state.
- Suctioning needs.
- Psychological state.
- Patient's inspiratory effort and synchrony with the ventilator.

Alterations in cardiac output may occur as a result of positive pressure ventilation. The positive intrathoracic pressure during inspiration compresses the heart and great vessels, thereby reducing venous return and cardiac output. This is usually corrected during exhalation when the positive pressure is off.

The ventilator also needs to be assessed to make sure that it is functioning properly and that the settings are appropriate.

► Patient's Problems

Based on the assessment, the patient's main problems may include:

- Ineffective airway clearance related to increased mucus production associated with continuous positive pressure mechanical ventilation.
- Potential for injury/infection related to endotracheal intubation or tracheostomy.
- Impaired physical mobility related to ventilator dependency.
- Impaired verbal communication related to endotracheal tube attachment to ventilator.
- Ineffective individual coping and powerlessness related to ventilator dependency.

► Planning and Implementation
► Expected Outcomes

The main outcomes for the patient may include the following:

- Reduction of mucus accumulation.
- Absence of injury/infection.

- Attainment of optimum mobility.
- Adjustment to nonverbal methods of communication.
- Acquisition of successful coping measures.

► *Nursing Care*

Nursing care of the mechanically ventilated patient requires unique technical and interpersonal skills. Nursing interventions are similar whether the patient is in an intensive care unit, a medical-surgical unit or an extended care facility. The frequency of administering the care and the stability of the patient are the factors that vary from unit to unit.

Airway Management

Continuous positive pressure ventilation increases the production of secretions regardless of the patient's underlying condition. Measures to clear the airway of secretions include suctioning, chest physiotherapy, frequent position changes and ambulation as soon as it can be achieved.

Ventilators often have a sigh mechanism designed to give a greater than normal tidal volume. A hand resuscitator bag can also be used. Periodic sighing prevents atelectasis and the further retention of secretions. Humidification by way of the ventilator is maintained to help liquify secretions so they are more easily raised. Bronchodilators, either intravenous or inhaled, are administered as prescribed to dilate the bronchial tubes so that secretions are more easily mobilized.

Prevention of Injury and Infection

Airway management also involves maintenance of the endotracheal or tracheostomy tube. The ventilator tubing is positioned so there is minimal pulling or distortion of the tube in the trachea. Cuff pressure is monitored to keep the pressure under 25 cm H_2O. The presence of a cuff leak is evaluated at the same time. Tracheostomy care is performed to prevent the increased risk of infection. Oral hygiene is given because the oral cavity is a primary source of contamination of the lungs in the intubated and compromised patient.

Promotion of Optimal Level of Mobility

The patient's mobility is limited because of attachment to the ventilator. If the condition is stable, the patient should get out of bed and to a chair as soon as possible. Ambulation is also encouraged when indicated. A manual self-inflating bag with oxygen is used to ventilate the patient while walking. Mobility and muscle activity are beneficial because they stimulate respirations and improve morale.

If the patient is not able to get out of bed or walk, then active or passive range-of-motion exercises are performed to prevent muscle atrophy, contractures and venous stasis.

Promotion of Optimal Communication

Alternative methods of communication must be developed for the patient on a ventilator. The nurse assesses the patient's communication abilities:

- Is the patient's hand strong and available for writing? (If the patient is right-handed, the intravenous line is placed in the left hand.)
- Is the mouth unobstructed by tube for mouthing words?
- Is the patient conscious and able to communicate?

Once the patient's limitations are known, the nurse offers several appropriate communication approaches:

- Lip reading (use single key words).
- Pad and pencil or 'magic slate'.
- Communication board.
- Gesturing.
- Electric larynx.
- An electronic voice synthesizer.

Patients must be helped to find the communication method best suited for them. Some methods may be frustrating to the patient and they need to be identified and minimized. A speech therapist will assist in determining the most appropriate method for the patient.

Promotion of Coping Ability

Dependence on a ventilator is frightening to the patient, family and other informal carers, and can disrupt even the most stable relationships. They are helped to talk about their feelings about the ventilator, the patient's condition and the environment in general. Explaining procedures every time they are performed will help to reduce anxiety and familiarize the patient with hospital routines (Johnson and Sexton, 1990). To restore a sense of control, the patient is encouraged to participate in decisions about care, schedules and treatment when possible. There is a tendency to become withdrawn or depressed during mechanical ventilation, especially if it is prolonged. Consequently, the patient is encouraged about the progress being made when appropriate. Diversion is provided by watching television, playing music or taking a walk (if appropriate). Stress-reduction techniques (a back rub, relaxation measures) help release tension and enable the patient to deal with anxieties and fears about the condition and being dependent on the ventilator.

► *Evaluation*
► **Expected Outcome**

1. Patient manages ventilation with minimal mucus accumulation.
   a. Tolerates frequent suctioning.
   b. Assists with position changes.
   c. Attempts to ambulate within limitations of equipment and condition.

2. Is free of injury/infection.
   a. Assists with oral care if possible.
   b. Tolerates tracheostomy care.
3. Is mobile within limits of ability.
   a. Gets out of bed to chair as soon as possible.
   b. Walks around room as tolerated.
   c. Performs range-of-motion exercises every 6 to 8 hours.
4. Communicates effectively.
   a. Writes messages as necessary.
   b. Is able to use gestures to communicate.
5. Copes effectively.
   a. Expresses fears and concerns about the condition and the equipment.
   b. Participates in decision making when possible.
   c. Uses stress-reduction techniques when necessary.
   d. Seeks support groups when needed.

Problems with Mechanical Ventilation

Because of the seriousness of the patient's condition and the highly complex and technical nature of mechanical ventilation, a number of problems can arise. Such situations as inadequate alveolar ventilation, an air leak in the system, a cuff leak, obstruction or resistance to air flow, condensation in the ventilator tubing, secretions, bronchospasm and atelectasis all need to be identified and corrected. Patients may also 'fight' the ventilator when they are out of phase with the machine: the patient attempts to breathe in during the ventilator's mechanical expiratory phase.

Weaning the Patient From the Ventilator

Weaning the patient from dependence on the ventilator takes place in four stages. The patient is gradually weaned from the (1) ventilator, (2) cuff, (3) tube and (4) oxygen. Weaning from mechanical ventilation is done at the earliest possible time consistent with patient safety. It is essential that the decision be made from a physiological rather than from a mechanical viewpoint. A total understanding of the patient's clinical state is required in making this decision.

Weaning is started when the patient is recovering from the acute stage of the medical and surgical problems and when the cause of respiratory failure is sufficiently reversed.

Adequate psychological preparation is necessary before and during the weaning process. Patients need to know what is expected of them during the procedure. They are frightened by having responsibility for their own breathing again, and need reassurance that they are improving and are well enough to handle spontaneous breathing. The nurse explains what will happen during weaning and what the patients' role in the procedure will be. The nurse emphasizes that someone will be with them or near them at all times, and allows time to answer any questions simply and concisely.

Patients who have had short-term ventilatory assistance usually can be extubated within two or three hours of weaning and allowed spontaneous ventilation by means of a mask with humidified oxygen. Patients who have had prolonged ventilatory assistance usually require more gradual weaning, which may take several days. They are weaned primarily during the day and placed back on the ventilator at night to sleep.

THE PATIENT UNDERGOING THORACIC SURGERY

Assessment and management are particularly important in the patient undergoing thoracic surgery. Thoracic operations are done for a wide variety of reasons; in addition, the patient may have obstructive pulmonary disease with compromised breathing. Preoperative management is important because there may be a narrower margin of safety in chest operations.

Fortunately, the lungs have a large functional reserve. Newer techniques of anaesthesia, respiratory therapy, skilful surgery and intensive postoperative care have made possible more extensive thoracic surgery.

The objectives of preoperative care are to ascertain patients' functional reserve to determine if they can survive the operation, and to ensure the optimal condition of patients for surgery.

Diagnosis

A number of preoperative tests are done to determine the preoperative state of the patient and to assess his physical assets and liabilities. The initial investigation starts with the history and physical examination. The general appearance of the patient, the behaviour and mental alertness will indicate whether a significant surgical risk is involved.

Pulmonary function studies (especially lung volume and vital capacity) are done to determine whether the contemplated resection will leave sufficient functioning lung tissue. Arterial blood gas values are assessed to provide a more complete picture of the functional capacity of the lung. Exercise tolerance tests have predictive value. Such tests are especially important to determine whether the patient who is a candidate for pneumonectomy can tolerate whole lung removal.

Preoperative studies are done to provide a baseline for comparison during the postoperative period and to reveal any unsuspected abnormalities. These studies include chest radiography, electrocardiography, determination of blood urea nitrogen and serum creatinine, glucose tolerance or blood sugar (diabetes), assessment of blood electrolytes, serum protein studies, blood volume determinations and full blood cell count.

Operative Procedures

Lobectomy

When the pathology is limited to one area of a lung, a lobectomy (removal of a lobe of a lung) is performed. This operation, which is more common than pneumonectomy, may be carried out for bronchogenic carcinoma, giant emphysematous blebs or bullae, benign tumours, metastatic malignant tumours, bronchiectasis and fungus infections.

Pneumonectomy

The removal of an entire lung (pneumonectomy) is done chiefly for cancer when the lesion cannot be removed by a lesser procedure. It also may be performed for lung abscesses, bronchiectasis or extensive unilateral tuberculosis. The removal of the right lung is more dangerous than the removal of the left since the right lung has a larger vascular bed and its removal imposes a greater physiological burden.

Segmentectomy (Segmental Resection)

Some lesions are located in only one segment of the lung. Bronchopulmonary segments are subdivisions of the lung that function as individual units. They are held together by delicate connective tissue; disease processes may be limited to a single segment. Care is used to preserve as much healthy and functional lung tissue as possible, especially in patients who already have a limited cardiorespiratory reserve.

Wedge Resection

A wedge resection of a small, well-circumscribed lesion may be done without regard for the location of the intersegmental planes.

Bronchoplastic or Sleeve Resection

Bronchoplastic resection is a procedure in which only one lobar bronchus together with a part of the right or left bronchus is excised.

► NURSING PROCESS

► THE PATIENT UNDERGOING THORACIC SURGERY

Preoperative Nursing Care

► Assessment

The nursing assessment includes the following:

- What signs and symptoms are present—cough, expectoration (amount), haemoptysis, chest pain, dyspnoea?
- What is the smoking history? How long has the patient been smoking? How much is the patient currently smoking?

- What is the patient's cardiopulmonary tolerance while resting, eating, bathing, walking?
- What is the patient's breathing pattern? How much exertion is required to produce dyspnoea?
- What is the patient's general appearance, mental alertness, behaviour and nutritional state?
- What other medical conditions exist—allergies, etc?
- What are the patient's personal preferences and dislikes?
- What does the patient know about the disorder, impending surgery and recovery?
- How are the patient, family and close friends coping with the prospect of surgery? What resources are at their disposal?

► Patient's Problems

Based on the assessment data, the patient's major preoperative problems may include the following:

- Impaired breathing related to lung impairment.
- Ineffective airway clearance related to lung impairment.
- Lack of knowledge about the surgical procedure and self-care.
- Anxiety related to diagnosis and surgical procedure.

► Planning and Implementation
► Expected Outcomes

The main outcomes for the patient may include a perceived improvement in breathing, acquisition of knowledge about the surgical procedure and self-care, and relief of anxiety.

Nursing Care

Patients need to be given advice about the avoidance of bronchial irritants, especially cigarette smoking; drinking of more fluids and use of humidification to loosen secretions; administration of bronchodilators as prescribed to relieve bronchospasm; and instruction in diaghragmatic breathing for more effective ventilation.

Patients and their families need to be advised of what to expect in the postoperative period, that is, the possible presence of chest tube(s) and drainage bottles, the usual postoperative administration of oxygen to facilitate breathing and the possible use of a ventilator. The importance of frequent turning to promote drainage of lung secretions is explained. Diaphragmatic and pursed lip breathing are taught and should be practised at this time.

Since a coughing schedule will be necessary in the postoperative period to bring up secretions, the patient should be advised about the technique of coughing and warned that the coughing routine may prove to be uncomfortable. The patient is taught to splint the incision using the hands, a pillow or a folded towel.

The patient is taught coughing and huffing techniques as follows:

Coughing Technique

1. Sit upright with knees flexed and body bent slightly forward.
2. Splint the incisional area with firm hand pressure or support it with a pillow or rolled blanket while coughing. (The nurse can demonstrate this initially.)
3. Take three deep breaths followed by a deep inspiration (inhaling slowly and evenly through the nose).
4. Contract (pull in) the abdominal muscles and cough twice forcefully, with mouth open and tongue out.
5. If unable to sit, lie on one side with hips and knees flexed.

Huffing Technique

'Huffing' is the expulsion of air through an open glottis and may be helpful for the patient with diminished expiratory flow rates or for the patient in severe pain who refuses to cough. This type of forceful exhalation stimulates pulmonary expansion and assists in alveolar inflation.

1. Take a deep diaphragmatic breath and exhale forcefully against your hand. Exhale forcefully in a quick, distinct pant or 'huff'.
2. Practise doing small 'huffs' and progress to one strong 'huff' during exhalation.

Psychological Support

Patients are admitted only one or two days before surgery, which does not provide much time for the nurse to talk with them. To effectively use the time before surgery, the nurse listens to patients to evaluate how they feel about their illness and proposed treatment. She also determines their motivation to return to normal function. Patients may reveal significant reactions: the fear of haemorrhage because of bloody sputum, the discomfort of a chronic cough and chest pain, or the fear of death because of dyspnoea and tumour.

The nurse helps patients to overcome many of their fears and mobilize their intellectual functions to cope with the stress of surgery. This is done by correcting any false impressions, by offering reassurance and by dealing honestly with questions about pain and discomfort and their treatment. The management and control of pain begins before surgery when patients are informed that they can overcome many postoperative problems by following certain routines related to deep breathing, coughing, turning and moving.

► **Evaluation**
► **Expected Outcomes**

1. Breathing improves.
   a. Stops smoking.
   b. Avoids bronchial irritants.
   c. Demonstrates diaphragmatic breathing.
   d. Uses incentive spirometer correctly.
   e. Understands importance of measures to improve airway clearance (humidification, postural drainage, chest percussion, bronchodilators).
   f. Collects sputum so that it can be measured.
2. Attains knowledge of surgery and care.
   a. Understands what to expect in postoperative period.
   b. Demonstrates effective breathing, coughing and splinting techniques.
3. Improves ability to cope.
   a. Expresses confidence in the capability of the hospital staff.
   b. Demonstrates techniques to help control pain such as deep breathing, coughing, turning and moving.
   c. Has realistic expectations for recovery.

Postoperative Care

Potential Complications

Complications following thoracic surgery are always a possibility and are identified and managed early. Pulmonary oedema due to overinfusion of intravenous fluids is a real danger. The early symptoms are dyspnoea, crackles, bubbling sounds in the chest, cyanosis and pink, frothy sputum. In addition, the patient is monitored at regular intervals for signs of haemorrhage, mediastinal shift, bronchopulmonary fistula, infection, shock, atelectasis, pneumothorax, arrhythmias, pleural effusion and gastric distension.

Chest Drainage

Following thoracic surgery, chest tubes and a closed drainage system are used to reexpand the involved lung and to remove excess air and fluid (or blood).

Whenever the chest is opened, from any cause, there is a loss of negative pressure, which can result in the collapse of the lung. The collection of air, fluid or other substances in the chest can compromise cardiopulmonary function and even cause collapse of the lung. Pathological substances that collect in the pleural space include fibrin, or clotted blood; liquids (serous fluids, blood, pus, chyle); and gases (air from the lung, tracheobronchial tree or oesophagus).

Surgical incision of the chest wall almost always causes some degree of pneumothorax. Air and fluid collect in the intrapleural space, restricting lung expansion and reducing air exchange. It is necessary to keep the pleural space evacuated postoperatively and to maintain negative pressure within this potential space. Therefore, during or immediately after thoracic surgery, chest catheters are positioned strategically in the pleural space, sutured to the skin and connected to some type of drainage apparatus in order to remove the residual air and drainage fluid from the pleural or mediastinal space. This results in the re-expansion of remaining lung tissue.

A chest drainage system must be capable of removing whatever collects in the pleural space so that a normal pleural space and normal cardiopulmonary function may be restored and maintained. There are many types of commercial chest drainage systems in use, most of which use the water-seal principle. The chest catheter is attached to a bottle, using a one-way valve principle. Water acts as a seal and permits air and fluid to drain from the chest, but air cannot re-enter the submerged tip of the tube.

Drainage depends on gravity, the mechanics of respiration and, in some cases, suction provided by the addition of a controlled vacuum. Fluctuations in the water level in the tube show that there is effective communication between the pleural cavity and the drainage bottle, and is a valuable indication of the patency of the drainage system. 'Milking' the tube towards the drainage bottle prevents it from becoming clogged with clots or fibrin. Fluctuations in fluid level stop when the lung has re-expanded. Constant bubbling in the water seal chamber may indicate air trapped in the pleural space, and potential pneumothorax. The drainage bottle must be kept below the level of the patient's chest to prevent backflow of fluid into the pleural space. Pressure on the tubing should be avoided as this can also lead to backflow. Patients should be encouraged to breathe deeply and cough frequently to increase intrapleural pressure and promote emptying of secretions from the pleural space. Changing positions frequently helps to promote better drainage. The arm and shoulder of the affected side will benefit from frequent exercise, which minimizes stiffness. Patients must be observed for signs of respiratory disorder, including cyanosis, chest pain, shallow breathing and changes in blood pressure and pulse rate. The amount of drainage should be recorded accurately. In the event of accidental disconnection of the drainage tubing, artery clamps should be applied immediately to the intrapleural drain to prevent air entry into the pleural cavity.

The chest tube is removed when the lung is re-expanded (usually between 24 hours to several days). The tube is clamped during removal, and patients are asked to inhale deeply and hold their breath as the tube is pulled out gently; this minimizes the risk of occurrence of tension pneumothorax.

► *Assessment*

The character and depth of the respiration and the patient's colour serve as important criteria in evaluating whether the lungs are being expanded adequately. The heart rate and rhythm are monitored by auscultation and electrocardiography, since major arrhythmic episodes are common after thoracic and cardiac surgery. Arrhythmias can occur at any time but frequently are seen between the second and sixth postoperative days. The rate of occurrence of arrhythmias increases with patients over 50 years of age and with those undergoing pneumonectomy or oesophageal surgery.

An arterial line is maintained to facilitate frequent monitoring of blood gases, serum electrolytes, haemoglobin and hematocrit values, and arterial pressure. Central venous pressure is monitored for the early recognition of hypovolaemia.

► *Patient's Problems*

Based on the assessment, the patient's main problems may include:

● Altered breathing related to lung impairment and surgery.
● Alteration in comfort, pain, related to incision, drainage tubes and the surgical procedure.
● Impaired physical mobility of the upper extremities related to thoracic surgery.
● Dehydration related to the surgical procedure.
● Lack of knowledge about recovery and rehabilitation.

► *Planning and Implementation*
► **Expected Outcomes**
The main outcomes for the patient may include improvement of breathing, improvement of airway clearance, relief of pain and discomfort, mobility and shoulder exercises, maintenance of adequate fluid volume and understanding of self-care procedures.

Nursing Care

Improvement of Breathing
Gas exchange is determined by evaluating oxygenation and ventilation. In the immediate postoperative period, this is achieved by measuring the blood pressure, pulse and respirations every 15 minutes for the first 1 to 2 hours, then less frequently as the patient's condition stabilizes.

The diaphragmatic and pursed lip breathing taught preoperatively should be practised every 2 hours to expand alveoli and prevent atelectasis. Another technique to improve ventilation is sustained maximal inspiratory therapy. This technique optimizes lung inflation, improves the cough mechanism, and provides for early assessment of acute pulmonary changes.

When the patient is orientated and the blood pressure stabilized, the head of the bed is elevated 30 to 40 degrees during the immediate postoperative period. This facilitates ventilation and helps residual air to rise in the upper portion of pleural space, where it can be removed through the upper chest tube.

The patient with limited respiratory reserve may not be able to turn on the unoperated side, since this limits ventilation of the operated side. The position is varied from horizontal to semi-upright, since remaining in one position tends to promote the retention of secretions in the dependent portion of the lungs. Following a pneumonectomy, the operated side should be dependent so that fluid in the pleural space remains below the level of the bronchial stump.

Turning Procedure
1. Instruct patients to bend the knees and use the feet to push.
2. Ask patients to shift their hips and shoulders to the opposite side of the bed while pushing with the feet.
3. Ask patients to bring their arm over the chest, pointing it in the direction towards which they are being turned, and get them to grasp the side rail with their hand.
4. Turn patients in 'log roll' fashion to prevent twisting at the waist and possible pulling of the incision, which could be painful.

Trauma to the tracheobronchial tree during operation, diminished lung ventilation and diminished cough reflex all result in the accumulation of excessive secretions. If the secretions are not managed or removed, airway obstruction will occur, which causes air in the alveoli distal to the obstruction to become absorbed and the lung to collapse. Atelectasis, pneumonia and respiratory failure may result.

Secretions are suctioned from the tracheobronchial tree before the endotracheal tube is removed and continue to be removed by suctioning until the patient can cough up secretions effectively.

The patient is encouraged to cough effectively, since ineffective coughing will result in exhaustion and retention of secretions. To be effective, the cough is to be low pitched, deep and controlled. Since it is difficult to cough in a supine position, the patient is helped to a sitting

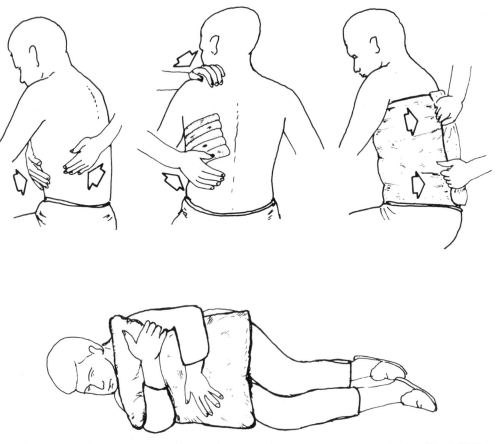

Figure 3.17 Techniques for support of incision while patient with thoracic surgery coughs. (Top left) The nurse's hands should support the chest incision anteriorly and posteriorly. The patient is asked to take several deep breaths, inhale and then cough forcibly. (Top middle) With one hand, the nurse exerts downward pressure on the shoulder of the affected side while firmly supporting beneath the wound with the other hand. The patient is asked to take several deep breaths, inhale and then cough forcibly. (Top right) The nurse can wrap a towel or sheet around the patient's chest and hold the ends together, pulling slightly as the patient coughs, releasing as the patient takes deep breaths. (Bottom) The patient can be taught to hold a pillow firmly against the incision while coughing. This can be done while lying down or sitting in an upright position.

position on the edge of the bed, with the feet resting on a chair. Coughing is carried out at least every hour during the first 24 hours and when necessary thereafter. If audible crackles are present, it may be necessary to use chest percussion with the cough routine until the lungs are clear. Aerosol therapy is helpful in humidifying and mobilizing secretions so that they can be readily coughed up. To lessen incisional pain during coughing, the nurse supports the incision firmly over the operated side and against the opposite chest (Figure 3.17).

If a patient is identified as being at high risk of developing postoperative pulmonary complications, then chest physiotherapy is started immediately (perhaps even preoperatively). The techniques of postural drainage, vibration and percussion help to loosen and mobilize the secretions so that they can be coughed up or suctioned.

Relief of Pain and Discomfort

Pain following a thoracotomy may be severe, depending on the type of incision and the patient's reaction to and ability to cope with pain. Deep inspiration is very painful following thoracotomy. Pain can lead to postoperative complications if it reduces the patient's ability to breathe deeply and cough and if it further limits chest excursions so that effective ventilation is decreased. Immediately after the surgical procedure and before the incision is closed, the surgeon may perform a nerve block with a long-acting local anaesthetic, which can reduce postoperative pain. Small, intravenous doses of a narcotic are given as prescribed and are titrated to relieve pain while still allowing the patient to co-operate in deep breathing, coughing and mobilization efforts. However, it is important to avoid depressing the respiratory system with too much narcotic, since the patient should not be so somnolent that coughing does not occur.

● The nurse should not confuse the restlessness of hypoxia with restlessness due to pain. Dyspnoea, restlessness, increasing respiratory rate, increasing blood pressure and tachycardia are warning signs of impending respiratory insufficiency.

Mobility and Shoulder Exercises

Thoracotomy involves the transection of large shoulder girdle muscles. Arm and shoulder exercises may be started on the evening of surgery (Figure 3.18) to restore movement, accelerate the recovery of muscle function and prevent painful stiffening of the affected arm and shoulder. Early mobilization limits long-term pain and prevents the complications of bedrest. Patients can often manage to sit out of bed several hours after surgery. Specific skeletal exercises designed to restore function following thoracic surgery need to be taught and encouraged. Patients may need assistance with daily activities

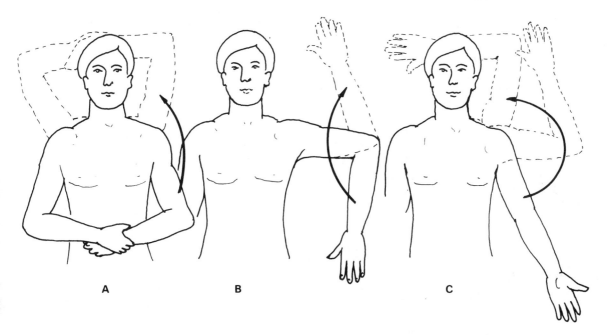

A **B** **C**

Figure 3.18 Arm and shoulder exercises are done following thoracic surgery to restore movement, prevent painful stiffening of the shoulder and improve muscle power. (A) Hold hand of the affected side with the other hand, palms facing in. Raise the arms forward, upward and then overhead, while taking a deep breath. Exhale while lowering the arms. Repeat five times. (B) Raise arm sideward, upward and downward in a waving motion. (C) Place arm at side. Raise arm sideward, upward and over the head. Repeat five times. Both exercises can also be done while lying in bed.

such as washing and dressing until they can comfortably move their arm and shoulder.

Fluid Volume and Nutritional Considerations

During the operation or immediately after, the patient may receive a blood transfusion, followed by an intravenous infusion to 'keep the vein open' until the blood volume can be reassessed. The rate of administration is slow (10 ml/hr), especially when there is evidence of limited cardiopulmonary reserve and when the pulmonary vascular bed has been greatly reduced, as in pneumonectomy.

A liquid diet is provided as soon as there is evidence of bowel sounds. The patient is progressed to a full diet as soon as possible. Well-balanced meals are crucial to the recovery and maintenance of lung function.

Health Education

Patients need to understand the importance of arm and shoulder exercises, and continue with the exercises taught in hospital once they have returned home. Some patients may have a tendency to lean sideways; an erect posture may be encouraged by standing in front of a full-length mirror.

Patients need to know how to effectively manage pain using local heat or oral analgesia. They should be aware that tiredness is common, and plan to space out their activities with frequent rest periods. They should be warned to stop exercising if they experience chest pain, shortness of breath or undue muscular pain. Walking is recommended and should be increased gradually in time and distance.

Chest muscles may be weaker than normal for 3 to 6 months following surgery, and patients need to be advised to limit lifting to weights of less than 20 lb during this time.

Breathing exercises taught in hospital should be continued for the first two to three weeks. Bronchial irritants must be avoided and patients helped to stop smoking. Colds and lung infections need to be prevented, and the rationale of having influenza vaccinations should be discussed. Patients must be advised of the importance of keeping follow-up appointments.

Psychological Support

Anxiety about the future, especially regarding a return to work, is likely to be alleviated if patients and their families, particularly the spouse, are given the opportunity to discuss issues and are provided with support and education.

► *Evaluation*
► **Expected Outcomes**

1. Improved breathing.
   a. Demonstrates diaphragmatic and pursed lip breathing.
   b. Demonstrates absence of dyspnoea.
   c. Is free of infection.
   d. Demonstrates deep, controlled coughing.
   e. Recognizes importance of humidity for keeping secretions moist.
2. Is relieved of pain and discomfort.
   a. Reports that pain is diminishing.
   b. Splints incision during coughing.
3. Improved mobility of shoulder and arm; demonstrates arm and shoulder exercises to relieve stiffening.
4. Maintains adequate fluid intake.
   a. Drinks 6 to 8 glasses of water a day (about 1,500 ml).
   b. Eats well-balanced meals.
5. Adheres to therapeutic programme.
   a. Demonstrates arm and shoulder exercises and the importance of practising them five times a day.
   b. Recognizes the importance of alternating walking and rest, practising breathing exercises, avoiding heavy lifting, relieving intercostal pain, avoiding bronchial irritants, preventing colds or lung infections, getting influenza and pneumonia vaccines, keeping follow-up appointments and stopping smoking.

BIBLIOGRAPHY

Jansen-Bjerklie, S., Carrier, V. K. and Hudes, M. (1988) The sensations of pulmonary dyspnea, *Nursing Research*, Vol. 35, pp. 154–9.

Johnson, M. M. and Sexton, D. L. (1990) Distress during mechanical ventilation: patients' perceptions, *Critical Care Nurse*, Vol. 10, No. 7, pp. 48–57.

Kim, M. J. (1984) Respiratory muscle training, *Heart and Lung*, Vol. 13, pp. 333–40.

FURTHER READING

Books

Burton, G. G. and Hodgkin, J. E. (eds) (1984) *Respiratory Care: A Guide to Clinical Practice* (2nd edition), J. B. Lippincott, Philadelphia.

Kacmarek, R. M., Mack, C. W. and Dimas, S. (1990) *The Essentials of Respiratory Care* (3rd edition), Mosby Year Books, St Louis.

Royal Marsden Hospital (1988) *Manual of Clinical Nursing Procedures* (2nd edition), Harper & Row, London.

Shapiro, B. A. *et al.* (1985) *Clinical Application of Respiratory Care* (3rd edition), Year Book Medical Publishers, Chicago.

Smith, S. A. (1989) Extended body image in the ventilated patient, *Intensive Care Nursing*, Vol. 5, pp. 31–8.

Wright, S. G. (ed.) (1988) Breathing, R. A. Webster and D. R. Thompson in *Nursing the Older Patient*, Harper & Row, London, pp. 93–119.

Articles

Allan, D. (1987) Making sense of tracheostomy, *Nursing Times*, Vol. 88, No. 45, pp. 36–8.

Altose, M. D. (1985) Assessment and management of breathlessness, *Chest*, August, Vol. 88 (supplement 2), pp. 77S–83S.

Assessing chest pain and cough (1984) *American Journal of Nursing* January, Vol. 84, No. 1, pp. 101, 150.

Carrieri, V. K. *et al.* (1984) The sensation of dyspnea: A review, *Heart Lung*, July, Vol. 13, No. 4, pp. 436–47.

Collins, B. J. (1986) Respiratory assistance—care of equipment, *Intensive Care Nursing*, Vol. 1, pp. 138–43.

Durie, M. (1984) Respiratory problems and nursing intervention, *Nursing*, Vol. 28, pp. 826–8.

Grosmaire, E. K. (1983) Use of patient positioning to improve Pao$_2$: A review, *Heart Lung*, November, Vol. 12, No. 6, pp. 650–3.

Mumford, S. P. (1986) Using jet nebulizers, *The Professional Nurse*, Vol. 1, pp. 95–7.

Nelsey, L. (1986) Mouthcare and the intubated patient—the aim of preventing infection, *Intensive Care Nursing*, Vol. 1, pp.187–93.

Quigley, R. L. (1988) Tracheostomy—an overview. Management and complications, *British Journal of Clinical Practice*, Vol. 42, pp. 430–34.

Smith, S. A. (1989) Extended body image in the ventilated patient, *Intensive Care Nursing*, Vol. 5, pp. 31–8.

Vasbinder-Dillon, D. (1988) Understanding mechanical ventilation, *Critical Care Nurse*, Vol. 8, No. 7, pp. 42–56.

Walsh, M. (1989) Making sense of chest drainage, *Nursing Times*, Vol. 85, No. 24, pp. 40–41.

Wilson, E. B. and Malley, N. (1990) Discharge planning for the patient with a new tracheostomy, *Critical Care Nurse*, Vol. 10, No. 7, pp. 73–9.

chapter 4

ASSESSMENT AND CARE OF PATIENTS WITH DISORDERS OF THE UPPER RESPIRATORY TRACT

ANATOMY AND PHYSIOLOGY OF THE UPPER RESPIRATORY AIRWAY

The upper respiratory tract consists of the nose, pharynx, larynx and the upper part of the trachea. It has three main functions: to allow the passage of air to the lower airway; to protect the lower airway from foreign matter; and to warm, filter and humidify inspired air.

The Nose

The nose filters, humidifies and warms the inspired air, and is also responsible for olfaction (smell), a function that diminishes with age.

The external, visible portion of the nose and the internal portion are separated into right and left nasal cavities by a narrow vertical divider, the septum. The anterior nares (nostrils) are the outside openings of the nasal cavities. The posterior nares open into the nasopharynx. The nasal cavities are lined with a highly vascular ciliated mucous membrane called the nasal mucosa. Mucus secreted continuously by goblet cells covers the surface of the nasal mucosa and is moved back to the nasopharynx by the action of the cilia.

The nasal cilia, hair and moisture collect small, airborne particles. Sensory receptors in the nasal mucosa respond to mechanical or chemical irritation initiating the deep inhalation and explosive exhalation known as sneezing.

The three turbinate bones that project from the lateral walls of the nasal cavities serve to increase the mucous membrane surface of the nasal passages.

The paranasal sinuses, cavities within the surrounding facial bones, drain into the interior nasal cavities. They include the frontal sinuses, located between and above the eyes; the ethmoidal sinuses, extending along the roof of the nostrils; and the sphenoidal sinuses, located on either side of the nose. A prominent function of the sinuses is to help give resonance and timbre to speech.

The current of air entering the nostrils is deflected upwards to the roof of the nose and follows a circuitous route before it reaches the nasopharynx. On its way, it comes into contact with a large surface of moist, warm mucous membrane that catches practically all of the dust and germs in the inhaled air. This air is moistened and warmed to body temperature and brought into contact with sensitive nerves. Some of these nerves detect odours, and others provoke sneezing to expel irritating dust.

Pharynx

The pharynx, or throat, is limited below by the larynx and the upper end of the oesophagus. Its upper extension is the nasopharynx, into which open the posterior nostrils and the auditory (eustachian) tubes from the middle ears. The nose and the nasopharynx are lined with the same type of ciliated epithelium as that which lines the trachea and bronchial tree; but the pharynx, which serves as both a respiratory and an alimentary passage, is lined with squamous (flat-celled) epithelium.

Tonsils and Adenoids

The tonsils are two almond-shaped bodies, one on each side of the oropharynx. The adenoids are located in the roof of the nasopharynx. The tonsils and the adenoids constitute only two of a ring of similar masses of lymphoid tissue that completely encircles the throat. These organs are important links in the chain of lymph nodes guarding the body from invasion by organisms entering the nose and the throat.

Larynx

The larynx is a cartilaginous epithelium-lined structure that is the transition between the upper airway and the lower airway (see Figure 4.1). The major function of the larynx is to permit speech and a variety of other sounds. It also protects the lower airway from foreign substances and facilitates coughing. It is frequently referred to as the voice box and consists of the following:

- Epiglottis—a valve flap of cartilage that covers the opening to the larynx during swallowing.
- Glottis—the opening between the vocal cords in the larynx.
- Thyroid cartilage—part of it forms the 'Adam's apple', the largest cartilage in the trachea.
- Cricoid cartilage—the only complete cartilaginous ring in the larynx (located below the thyroid cartilage).
- Arytenoid cartilages—used in vocal cord movement with the thyroid cartilage.

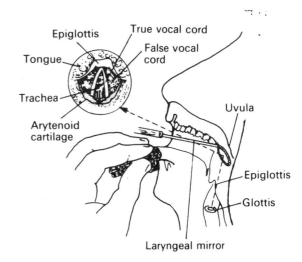

Figure 4.1 Normal laryngeal anatomy and indirect laryngoscopy. (Wolcott, M.W. (1988) *Ambulatory Surgery*, J. B. Lippincott, Philadelphia.)

- Vocal cords—ligaments controlled by muscular movements that produce vocal sounds; they are mounted in the lumen of the larynx.

ASSESSMENT OF THE UPPER RESPIRATORY TRACT

Assessment involves identifying problems and the effects of any disorder on a patient's lifestyle and wellbeing. Establishing the nature, extent and duration of any disorder, together with any relieving or aggravating factors, associated symptoms and coping strategies, will help to put any problems into perspective.

The Nose and Sinuses

Patients are asked to identify and describe any problems with breathing. For example, have they noticed any exudate, bleeding, swelling or tenderness around the nose; have they complained of headaches; do they identify any particular disorder with the nose?

The nose and sinuses are examined by inspection and palpation. For a routine examination, only a simple light source, such as a penlight, is necessary. A more thorough examination requires the use of a nasal speculum.

The external nose is inspected for lesions, asymmetry or inflammation. The mucosa is inspected for colour, swelling, exudate or bleeding. The nasal mucosa is normally more red than the oral mucosa but may appear swollen and hyperaemic in the presence of the common cold. Allergic rhinitis, on the other hand, is suspected when the mucosa appears pale and swollen.

The septum is inspected for deviation, perforation or bleeding. A slight degree of septal deviation is present in most people. Actual displacement of the cartilage into either vestibule may produce nasal obstruction, but such deviation is usually asymptomatic.

With the patient's head tilted back, the examiner attempts to view the inferior and middle turbinates. In chronic rhinitis, nasal polyps may develop between the inferior and middle turbinates and are distinguished by their grey appearance. Unlike the turbinates, they are gelatinous and freely movable.

The Pharynx

Patients are asked about any throat soreness, difficulty in swallowing and a sense of irritation or fullness in the throat. They are also asked if they have had any previous problems with the pharynx. They are asked to open the mouth wide and take a deep breath. Often this will flatten the posterior tongue and briefly expose a full view of the anterior and posterior pillars, tonsils, uvula and posterior pharynx.

These structures are inspected for colour, symmetry and evidence of exudate, ulceration or enlargement.

The Trachea

Patients are asked about any symptoms of chest pain or coughing that may be indicative of inflammation of the trachea.

The position and mobility of the trachea are usually noted by direct palpation. This is done by placing the thumb and index finger of one hand on either side of the trachea just above the sternal notch. The trachea is normally midline as it enters the thoracic inlet behind the sternum but may be deviated by masses in the neck or mediastinum. Pleural or pulmonary disorders, such as a significant pneumothorax, may result in displacement of the trachea.

UPPER RESPIRATORY TRACT INFECTIONS

Upper respiratory tract infections are by far the most common medical complaint in Great Britain, accounting for half the time lost from work through acute illness (Seaton, Seaton and Leitch, 1989). Such disorders tend to be self-limiting, varying in effect and seldom requiring admission to hospital.

However, they can be inconvenient and annoying for the individual and have important economic consequences for the community. Upper respiratory tract infections may be complicated by more serious lower respiratory tract infections, with exacerbations of other established disorders such as asthma and chronic bronchitis. It is important to recognize the signs and symptoms.

Common Cold

The phrase 'common cold' is usually used when referring to symptoms of an upper respiratory tract infection. Colds are highly contagious since patients shed virus for about two days before the symptoms appear and during the first part of their symptomatic phase. The incidence of colds is seasonal, increasing in the autumn and remaining high throughout the winter months before falling to a low level during the summer. Immunity after recovery is variable and depends on many factors, including natural host resistance and the specific causative virus.

Clinical Features

The signs and symptoms of a cold are nasal discharge and obstruction, sore throat, sneezing, malaise, fever, chills and often headache and muscle aching. As the cold progresses, coughing usually occurs. Most specifically, the term 'cold' refers to an afebrile, infectious, acute inflammation of the mucous membranes of the nasal cavity. More broadly, the word refers to an acute upper respiratory tract infection, whereas terms such as rhinitis, pharyngitis, laryngitis and chest cold distinguish the sites of the major symptoms.

The symptoms last five days to two weeks. If there is significant fever or more severe constitutional problems with the respiratory symptoms, it is no longer a common cold but one of the other acute upper respiratory tract infections. Many different viruses (over 100) are known to produce the signs and symptoms of the common cold, and about 10 per cent of colds seem to be associated simultaneously with more than one virus. Also, allergic conditions affecting the nose can mimic the symptoms of a cold.

Nursing Care

Nursing care of the patient with a common cold consists of adequate fluid intake, rest, prevention of chilling, aqueous nasal decongestants, vitamin C supplements, bronchodilators and expectorants as needed. Warm salt water gargles soothe the sore throat, and aspirin relieves the general constitutional symptoms. Antibiotics are not indicated in the uncomplicated common cold.

Using disposable tissues and discarding them hygienically, covering the mouth when coughing and avoiding crowds are important measures to prevent the spread of an upper respiratory airway infection.

Herpes Simplex Infection

The herpes simplex virus (HSV-1) most commonly produces the familiar herpes labialis (cold sore, fever blister or canker). Small vesicles, single or clustered, may erupt on the lips, the tongue, the cheeks and the pharynx. These soon rupture, forming sore, shallow ulcers that are covered with a grey membrane.

Herpes virus infections appear often in association

with other febrile infections, such as streptococcal pneumonia, meningococcal meningitis and malaria. The virus remains latent in cells of the lips or nose and is activated by febrile illnesses, extreme cold or sunburn. The painful stage lasts seven to ten days, with recovery and healing of the ulcers being complete within three weeks. As the sores are obvious, patients may feel embarrassed and shy.

Medical Management

The herpes virus does not respond well to many chemotherapeutic agents. Certain antiviral agents may be of use, either taken systemically or applied topically. Analgesics and codeine are helpful in relieving pain and discomfort. Topical anaesthetics, such as lignocaine give a measure of relief for oral pain. Applications of drying lotions or liquids may help to dry the lesions.

Sinusitis

The sinuses are involved in a high proportion of upper respiratory tract infections. If their openings into the nasal passages are clear, the infections resolve promptly. However, if their drainage is obstructed by a deflected septum or by hypertrophied turbinates, spurs, or polyps, sinusitis may persist as a smouldering secondary infection or flare up into an acute suppurative process.

Clinical Features

Acute sinusitis may be localized in one sinus or may involve several (Figure 4.2). The most prominent symptom of acute sinusitis is pain. The location of the pain is diagnostically important. In frontal sinusitis, patients complain of frontal headache; in ethmoidal sinusitis, the pain is usually in or about the eyes; in maxillary sinusitis, pain may be referred to the brow but usually is lateral to the nose and sometimes is accompanied by aching of the upper teeth of the corresponding side; in sphenoidal sinusitis, occipital headache may result. Pain also may be referred, for example, to the forehead. Nasal congestion and discharge are usually, but not necessarily, present. Patients feel generally miserable, quite apart from pain. Fever, if present at all, is usually mild.

The breath may smell foul and usually there is tenderness and swelling over the affected sinus. In chronic sinusitis, there is often persistent nasal obstruction due to discharge and oedema of the nasal mucous membrane.

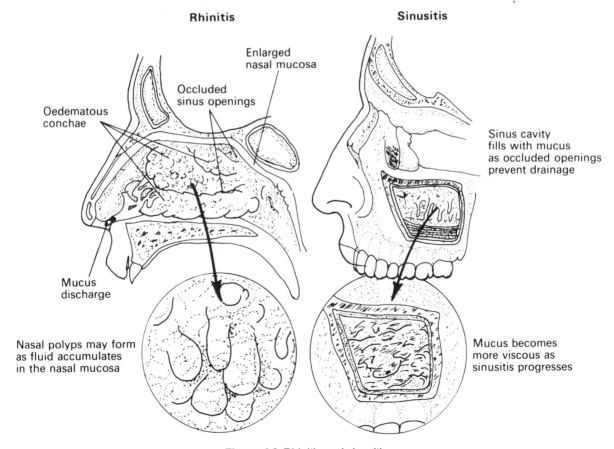

Rhinitis

Enlarged
nasal mucosa

Occluded
sinus openings

Oedematous
conchae

Mucus
discharge

Nasal polyps may form
as fluid accumulates
in the nasal mucosa

Sinusitis

Sinus cavity
fills with mucus
as occluded openings
prevent drainage

Mucus becomes
more viscous as
sinusitis progresses

Figure 4.2 Rhinitis and sinusitis.

Patients are likely to experience a cough, because of constant dripping of the discharge back into the nasopharynx, and headaches (often worse after lying flat), fatigue and nasal stuffiness.

A careful history and assessment is done to rule out other local or systemic disorders, such as tumour, fistula, allergy and viral infections.

Medical Management

The goals of treatment of sinusitis are relief of pain, shrinkage of the nasal mucosa and control of infection. Pain relief is achieved by administering prescribed analgesics. Bedrest is recommended for acute episodes. Antibiotics appropriate to the infecting organisms may be prescribed. With severe or chronic symptoms, the sinus contents may be aspirated by direct puncture, and the sinus explored. Increased humidity, steam inhalations, increased fluid intake and local heat applications will assist in promoting drainage. Local use of vasoconstricting agents in the form of nasal sprays and non-oily drops may be tried. Antihistamines may be prescribed if there is thought to be an underlying allergic inflammatory process. Structural deformities that obstruct the opening of the sinus may need surgical attention. Polyps may require excision or cauterization, and a deflected septum may have to be removed, or a narrow ostium widened. Some victims of severe chronic sinusitis obtain relief only on moving to a dry climate.

Nursing Care

Hot wet packs applied to the face over the involved sinus area will hasten resolution of the infection. Depending on the type of infecting organism and the extent of the infection, patients are advised to apply local therapy as prescribed until drainage is established. Patients need to be aware of the early signs of a sinus infection and the preventive measures:

- Avoid allergens if allergies are suspected.
- Maintain general health so that the body's resistance is not lowered (eat properly, get plenty of rest and exercise).
- Avoid others with upper respiratory tract infections.
- Notify doctor if pain in sinus areas persists or if nasal discharge is present and discoloured.
- Patients presenting with a headache may need reassurance and advice that their symptoms are not related to a disorder of the brain.

Rhinitis

Altered Physiology

Rhinitis is an inflammatory lesion involving the mucous membrane of the nose. It is sometimes a manifestation of allergy, in which instance the condition is referred to as 'allergic rhinitis'. Usually, however, rhinitis is due to a viral infection. The most common variety of infection

causing viral rhinitis is the common cold. Rhinitis is also encountered with regularity in the early stages of measles and other specific viral infections. Bacterial rhinitis is usually caused by a gram-positive bacterium and is characterized by a purulent nasal discharge. The infection is often secondary to a viral upper respiratory tract infection. If untreated, rhinitis can lead to sinusitis, otitis media, bronchitis and pneumonia.

In acute rhinitis, the nasal mucous membrane becomes congested, swollen, and oedematous for a short period of time and then quickly returns to normal. After repeated attacks, however, particularly in cases that originate as a result of chronic sinusitis, this swelling becomes obstinate and the patient has a chronic inflammation. Patients with this problem say that they are 'subject to colds'. The fact is that, excluding the recurring attacks of allergic rhinitis, their attacks are acute exacerbations of the same 'cold'. Patients may notice a decreased sense of smell.

If continued, chronic rhinitis leads to the deposition of abnormally large amounts of connective tissue in the nasal mucous membrane, which greatly thickens it and, in addition to hypertrophy, causes the formation of spurs and polyps on the nasal septum. Wasting or atrophy of the mucous membrane, the cartilage and the bones lining the nasal passages eventually may occur, and these passages become large, empty caverns. An abundant exudate builds up on the walls, giving off a disagreeable odour. This condition is called atrophic rhinitis.

Medical Management and Nursing Care

In acute viral rhinitis, symptomatic treatment includes topical or systemic vasoconstricting medications to relieve nasal obstruction, analgesics for headache and rest to alleviate general discomfort. Adults are advised to avoid crowds.

Patients need to be advised against blowing their noses too frequently or too hard. They should blow their noses by opening their mouths slightly and blowing through both nostrils to equalize the pressure. Physiotherapy, medications and surgery are used to treat rhinitis, but response to therapy is often disappointing and patients may become dispondent.

Pharyngitis

Pharyngitis is an inflammation of the pharynx. Acute pharyngitis is a febrile inflammation of the throat, caused predominantly by a virus. Chronic pharyngitis is common in adults who work in dusty surroundings, use the voice to excess and suffer from a chronic cough. It is also common in those who smoke.

The clinical manifestations of acute pharyngitis include a fiery red pharyngeal membrane, swollen lymphoid follicles of the throat and enlarged tonsils. The cervical lymph nodes may also become enlarged. Uncomplicated viral infections usually subside within 10 days of their onset. Complicated infections can lead to sinusitis, otitis media, mastoiditis, cervical adenitis, rheumatic fever and nephritis.

There are three types of chronic pharyngitis: (1) hypertrophic—characterized by general thickening and congestion of the pharyngeal mucous membrane; (2) atrophic—characterized by a thin, whitish, glistening mucous membrane; and (3) chronic granular—characterized by numerous swollen lymph follicles on the pharyngeal wall. Patients complain of a constant sense of irritation or fullness of the throat, mucus that collects in the throat and of difficulty in swallowing.

Medical Management

Treatment tends to be symptomatic in the case of uncomplicated pharyngitis. Antimicrobial agents may be prescribed if a bacterial cause is suspected. The treatment of chronic pharyngitis consists mainly of avoiding alcohol, tobacco or other irritants, resting the voice and correcting any upper respiratory, pulmonary or cardiac condition that might be responsible for a chronic cough. Nasal congestion may be relieved by nasal sprays. Antihistamines may be given if there is a history of allergy. The attendant malaise is controlled with an agent such as aspirin. Contact with other people should be avoided at least until any fever has subsided completely in order to prevent the infection from spreading. Throat cultures, nasal swabs and blood cultures may be taken for laboratory analysis to determine the nature of the causative organism (Figure 4.3).

Nursing Care

Patients should be advised to rest in bed during the febrile stage of an acute attack, and they are likely to need periods of rest once ambulatory. Any secretions should be disposed of carefully to limit the spread of infection. Warm saline gargles and throat irrigations may help to ease the discomfort and relieve soreness by reducing spasm in the pharyngeal muscles. The irrigating solution needs to be at a temperature tolerated by the patient.

A liquid or soft diet is offered during the acute stage of the disorder, depending on the patient's appetite and the degree of discomfort caused by swallowing. If sufficient fluids can not be taken by mouth, fluids are administered by the intravenous route. Patients need to be advised to try and drink at least 2,500 ml each day during the febrile stage: whenever possible drinks are prepared that suit personal tastes.

A linctus may be necessary if the disorder is complicated by a persistent and irritable cough. Mouth care may promote comfort and help prevent fissures of the lips and inflammation of the mouth associated with bacterial infection. Night sedation might prove to be beneficial to some patients who have difficulty in sleeping, although preference should be given to nonpharmacological approaches to promoting sleep.

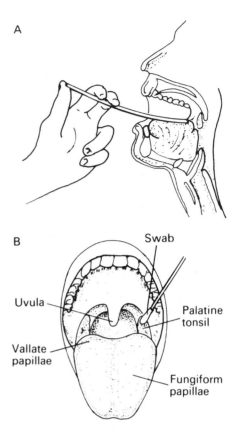

Figure 4.3 Taking a throat culture. When obtaining a throat culture from a patient who 'gags', it is helpful to get the patient to close the eyes. Since anticipation is lessened, the culture can be obtained with only a slight gag. (A) Grasp the tongue blade so that the thumb pushes the end upward (as a fulcrum) while the fingers push the middle section downward. (B) Vigorously rub a cotton wool swab over each tonsilar area and the posterior pharynx.

Convalescence from an acute attack needs to be gradual. Complications such as hepatitis or rheumatic fever may have their onset two or three weeks after the pharyngitis has subsided. Pharyngeal swelling may spread in the form of sinusitis, otitis media, mastoiditis or cervical adenitis. Patients and their families need to be advised about their illness, treatment and recovery, and be aware of the symptoms that may indicate possible complications.

Tonsillitis and Adenoiditis

The tonsils are composed of lymphatic tissue and are situated on each side of the oropharynx. They frequently serve as the site of acute infection. Chronic tonsillitis is less common and may be mistaken for other disorders such as allergy, asthma and sinusitis.

The adenoids consist of an abnormally large lymphoid tissue mass near the centre of the posterior wall of the nasopharynx. Infection of the adenoids frequently accompanies acute tonsillitis.

Clinical Features

The symptoms of tonsillitis include sore throat, fever, snoring and difficulty in swallowing. Adenoid hypertrophy may cause mouth-breathing, earache, draining ears, frequent head colds, bronchitis, fetid breath, voice impairment and noisy respiration. Tonsillitis usually resolves spontaneously after five to seven days and has a peaked incidence in the fifth and sixth years of life. Unusually enlarged adenoids may cause nasal obstruction. Extension of infection to the middle ears by way of the auditory (eustachian) tubes may result in acute otitis media, the potential complications of which include spontaneous rupture of the eardrums and further extension into the mastoid cells, causing acute mastoiditis. The infection may also reside in the middle ear as a chronic, low-grade, smouldering process that eventually may cause permanent deafness.

Diagnosis

A thorough physical examination is performed, and a careful history is obtained to rule out related or systemic conditions. A culture of the organisms at the tonsillar site is done to determine the presence of bacterial infection. In adenoiditis, if there are recurrent episodes of suppurative otitis media that are causing a hearing loss, it is important for patients to have a comprehensive audiometric examination.

Tonsillectomy and Adenoidectomy

Appropriate antibiotic therapy is initiated for both tonsillectomy and adenoidectomy. Tonsillectomy is usually not done unless medical treatment is unsuccessful and there is severe hypertrophy or peritonsillar abscess that occludes the pharynx, making swallowing difficult and endangering the airway.

Enlargement of the tonsils is rarely an indication for their removal; most children have normally large tonsils, which decrease in size with age.

Tonsillectomy or adenoidectomy is done only if the patient has had any of the following: repeated bouts of tonsillitis; hypertrophy of the tonsils and adenoids that could cause obstruction; repeated attacks of purulent otitis media; suspected hearing loss due to serous otitis media that has occurred in association with enlarged tonsils and adenoids; and some other conditions, such as an exacerbation of asthma or rheumatic fever.

Laser surgery has been tried, but it prolongs anaesthesia and causes other laser-related complications; therefore, in this situation laser surgery must be used judiciously.

Postoperative Nursing Care

Continuous nursing observation is required in the immediate postoperative and recovery period because of the significant risk of haemorrhage. After the operation, the most comfortable position is prone with the head turned to the side to allow for drainage from the mouth and pharynx. The oral airway is not removed until the patient demonstrates that the swallowing reflex has returned. An ice collar may be applied to the neck, and a basin and tissues are provided for the expectoration of blood and mucus.

Bleeding may be bright red if the patient expectorates blood at once. Often, however, the blood is swallowed and immediately becomes brown owing to the action of the acid gastric juice.

- If the patient vomits large amounts of altered blood or spits bright blood at frequent intervals, or if the pulse rate and temperature rise and the patient is restless, the surgeon is notified immediately.

Occasionally, it may be necessary to suture or ligate the bleeding vessel. In such cases the patient is returned to the operating theatre. After ligation under anaesthesia, continuous nursing observation and postoperative care are required, as in the initial postoperative period.

If there is no bleeding, water and cracked ice are given to the patient as soon as desired. Alkaline mouthwashes are useful in coping with the thick mucus that may be present after a tonsillectomy. A liquid or semiliquid diet is given for several days; acid juices (orange, apple, or lemon), which may cause burning when swallowed, are avoided.

On returning home, the patient needs to get plenty of rest, eat soft foods, drink fluids and resume activity gradually. Any bleeding is reported to the doctor; delayed haemorrhage may occur up to a week after surgery.

Peritonsillar Abscess

Peritonsillar abscess develops above the tonsil in the tissues of the anterior pillar and soft palate. As a rule, it is secondary to a tonsillar infection.

Clinical Features

The usual symptoms of an infection are present, together with such local symptoms as difficulty in swallowing (dysphagia), thickening of the voice, drooling and local pain. An examination shows marked swelling of the soft palate, often to the extent of half-occluding the orifice from the mouth into the pharynx.

Medical Management

Antibiotics (usually penicillin) are extremely effective in the control of the infection in peritonsillar abscess. If antibiotics are given early in the course of the disease, the abscess may be aborted and incision avoided. If antibiotics are not given until later, the abscess must be drained, but improvement in the inflammatory reaction is rapid.

The abscess is evacuated as soon as possible. The mucous membrane over the swelling is first sprayed with a topical anaesthetic and then injected with a local anaesthetic; after a small incision has been made, the points of artery forceps are forced into the abscess pocket and opened as they are withdrawn. This operation is performed best with the patient in the sitting position, since this will make it easier for him to expectorate the pus and blood that accumulate in the pharynx. Almost immediate relief is experienced.

Nursing Care
A considerable measure of relief may be obtained by throat irrigations or the frequent use of mouthwashes or gargles, using warm saline or alkaline solutions.

Laryngitis

Inflammation of the larynx often occurs as a result of voice abuse or as a part of an upper respiratory tract infection. It may also be caused by an isolated infection involving only the vocal cords.

The cause of this inflammation is almost always a virus. Bacterial invasion may be secondary. Laryngitis is usually associated with acute rhinitis or nasopharyngitis. The onset of infection may be associated with exposure to sudden temperature changes, dietary deficiencies, malnutrition and lack of immunity. Laryngitis is common in winter and is readily transmitted.

Clinical Features and Diagnosis
Acute laryngitis is manifested by hoarseness or complete loss of the voice (aphonia) and by severe cough, whereas chronic laryngitis, which is marked by persistent hoarseness, may follow repeated attacks of acute laryngitis. It is sometimes a complication of chronic sinusitis and chronic bronchitis. The condition also may be induced by the frequent inhalation of irritating gases, the excessive use of tobacco or alcohol or the habitual overuse of the voice, as in the case of public speakers. Laryngoscopic examination of the patient with chronic laryngitis is indicated in order to eliminate the possibility of tuberculosis or tumour of the larynx.

Nursing Care
For acute laryngitis, the treatment is abstinence from talking and smoking, bedrest and cool steam or aerosol therapy. If the laryngitis is part of a more extensive respiratory infection owing to a bacterial organism or if it is severe, appropriate antibacterial chemotherapy is instituted. The majority of patients recover with conservative treatment; however, the disease tends to be more severe in elderly patients and may be complicated by pneumonia.

For chronic laryngitis, the treatment of the condition is rest of the voice, elimination of any primary respiratory tract infection that may be present and restriction of smoking. Topical steroid preparations may be used to reduce local inflammatory reactions. A well-humidified environment is important, and expectorant drugs are helpful in thinning laryngeal secretions during acute episodes. An adequate fluid intake is also necessary to thin secretions. Patients may need help to communicate other than verbally.

NURSING PROCESS OVERVIEW FOR UPPER RESPIRATORY TRACT INFECTION

▶ *Assessment*

The nurse obtains a complete history of the patient's problem. Signs and symptoms may include headache, sore throat, pain around the eyes and on either side of the nose, difficulty in swallowing, cough, hoarseness, fever, stuffiness and generalized discomfort and fatigue. The nurse determines onset of the symptoms, what precipitated them, what relieves them, if anything, and what aggravates them. A history of allergy and the existence of a concomitant illness are identified.

On inspection, the nurse looks for swelling, lesions or asymmetry of the nose as well as for any bleeding or discharge. The nasal mucosa is inspected for abnormal findings such as a reddened colour, swelling or exudate, and nasal polyps, which may develop in chronic rhinitis, are searched for.

The frontal and maxillary sinuses are palpated for tenderness, which suggests inflammation. The throat is observed by asking the patient to open the mouth wide and take a deep breath. The tonsils and pharynx are inspected for the abnormal findings of reddened colour, asymmetry or evidence of drainage, ulceration or enlargement.

The trachea is palpated for midline position in the neck, and any lumps or deformities are identified. The neck lymph nodes are also palpated for associated enlargement.

▶ *Patient's Problems*

Based on the information gained from the assessment, the patient's problems may include the following:

● Alteration in normal breathing pattern as a result of excessive secretions secondary to an inflammatory process.
● Discomfort, soreness or pain related to upper respiratory tract irritation secondary to an infection.
● Risk of dehydration related to increased fluid loss secondary to sweating associated with fever.
● Lack of knowledge about the disorder and how to prevent recurrence.

▶ *Planning and Implementation*
▶ Expected Outcomes
The main outcomes for the patient may include

improvement in breathing, improvement in comfort, adequate hydration and knowledge of how to prevent upper respiratory tract infections.

Nursing Care

Airway Clearance

An accumulation of secretions can block the airway in many patients with an upper respiratory tract infection. Changes in the respiratory pattern result, and the work of breathing required to get beyond the blockage is increased. There are several measures that can be employed to loosen thick secretions or to keep the secretions moist so that they can be expectorated easily. Increasing fluid intake provides systemic hydration, which is an effective expectorant. Humidifying the environment by room vaporizers or steam inhalations also loosens secretions and reduces inflammation of the mucous membranes. Patients need to be advised on the best position to assume for facilitating drainage. This will depend on the location of the infection or inflammation. For example, drainage for sinusitis or rhinitis is achieved in the upright position. In some conditions, topical or systemic vasoconstricting medications are administered as prescribed to relieve nasal or throat congestion.

Comfort Measures

Upper respiratory tract infections usually produce localized discomfort. In sinusitis, pain may occur in the area of the sinuses or the patient may experience a headache. In pharyngitis, laryngitis or tonsillitis, a sore throat occurs. Nurses can help to relieve this discomfort by administering analgesics. Topical anaesthetics provide symptomatic relief for herpes simplex blisters and sore throats. Hot packs help relieve the congestion of sinusitis and promote drainage. Warm water gargles or irrigations relieve the pain of a sore throat. An ice collar may be applied in the immediate postoperative period following a tonsillectomy and adenoidectomy to reduce swelling and decrease bleeding. Encouraging the patient to rest will help relieve the generalized discomfort or fever that accompanies many upper airway conditions (especially rhinitis, pharyngitis and laryngitis). The patient needs information about general oral and nasal hygiene techniques to help relieve localized discomfort and to prevent the spread of infection.

Fluid Intake

In upper airway infections, the work of breathing and the respiratory rate increase as inflammation and secretions develop. This in turn increases insensible fluid loss. An associated fever increases the metabolic rate, which results in sweating and increased fluid loss. The patient is encouraged to drink two to three litres of water per day during the upper airway infection, unless contraindicated, to thin secretions and promote drainage.

Patient Education

The prevention of most upper airway infections is difficult because there are many potential causes. The responsible pathogen usually cannot be identified, and vaccines are unavailable except in rare instances. Allergies, pathological conditions of the septum and the turbinates, emotional problems and various systemic illnesses may be predisposing factors in isolated cases.

Patients need information about the following hygienic measures, which support the body's defences and reduce susceptibility to respiratory infections:

- Practise good health measures—nutritious diet, appropriate exercise, adequate rest and sleep.
- Avoid excesses in alcohol and smoking.
- Correct air dryness by proper home humidification, especially during cold weather.
- Avoid air contaminants (dust, chemicals) when possible.
- Avoid unnecessary chilling of the skin, especially the feet; chilling lowers resistance.
- Obtain influenza vaccination if advised by a general practitioner. This is usually recommended for the elderly and those with chronic illness.
- Avoid crowds during influenza epidemics.
- Maintain adequate dental hygiene.

▶ *Evaluation*
▶ **Expected Outcomes**

1. Patient reports an improved breathing pattern.
   a. Reports decreased congestion.
   b. Uses room humidifier or vaporizer.
   c. Assumes best position to facilitate drainage of secretions for the condition.
   d. Shows familiarity with use of vasoconstricting medications (oral or nasal spray) to relieve nasal congestion.
2. Patient is comfortable.
   a. States the use of analgesics helps relieve localized pain or headache.
   b. Demonstrates the application of hot packs for sinusitis, warm water gargles or irrigations for a sore throat, and an ice collar following a tonsillectomy and adenoidectomy.
   c. Shows an understanding of the need for rest.
   d. Demonstrates adequate oral hygiene.
3. Patient maintains an adequate fluid balance.
   a. States rationale for drinking plenty of fluids.
   b. Demonstrates no significant weight loss.
   c. Is not dehydrated.
4. Patient knows how to prevent upper respiratory tract infections.
   a. Eats a balanced diet daily.
   b. Does not smoke.
   c. Avoids enclosed areas polluted with smoke.

d. Stays away from crowded areas during influenza epidemics (shopping centres, crowded restaurants, cinemas).

e. Contacts general practitioner to receive an influenza vaccination.

f. Uses room humidifiers when necessary.

g. Wears protective clothing (hat, scarf, gloves, boots) to keep warm and avoid chilling.

OBSTRUCTION AND TRAUMA OF THE UPPER RESPIRATORY TRACT

Epistaxis (Nosebleed)

Altered Physiology

A haemorrhage from the nose, referred to as epistaxis, is caused by the rupture of tiny, distended vessels in the mucous membrane of any area of the nose. Most commonly, the site is the anterior septum, where three major blood vessels enter the nasal cavity.

Epistaxis results from injury or disease, although the usual cause of small nosebleeds is 'picking' of the nose. Other local causes are deviated septum, perforated septum, cancer and trauma. Epistaxis also occurs as a sign of acute rheumatic fever, acute sinusitis, arterial hypertension and haemorrhagic diseases.

Medical Management and Nursing Care

Patients are likely to be perturbed by the sight of blood and need reassurance that the amount lost probably looks worse than it is. Cessation of bleeding is aided by asking the patient to sit upright and compress the soft outer portion of the nose for five to ten minutes continuously. Patients should be advised not to talk or blow their noses, and to breathe through their mouths. An ice cold compress applied to the nose may arrest bleeding. Patients should be advised not to swallow any blood. Disposable tissues and receptacles for blood should be provided. The patient's heart rate, blood pressure and level of consciousness should be assessed, and the amount and colour of blood lost should be noted.

If bleeding persists, cauterization or packing may be carried out by the doctor. The packing is kept in place for up to five or six days if necessary. If the problem is recurrent, patients need advice appropriate to the likely cause. Some suggestions are avoidance of nose-picking and the possible benefits of air humidification if the cause is thought to be due to excessive dryness of the mucous membranes.

Nasal Obstruction

The passage of air through the nostrils is frequently obstructed by a deflection of the nasal septum, hypertrophy of the turbinate bones or the pressure of polyps, which are grapelike swellings that arise from the mucous membrane of the sinuses, especially the ethmoids. This obstruction also may lead to a condition of chronic infection of the nose and result in frequent attacks of nasopharyngitis. Very frequently, the infection extends to the sinuses of the nose and the drainage from these cavities is obstructed by deformity or swelling within the nose; pain is then experienced in the region of the affected sinus.

Medical Management

The treatment of nasal obstruction requires the removal of the obstruction, followed by measures to overcome whatever chronic infection exists. In many patients the underlying nasal allergy requires treatment. At times it is necessary to drain the nasal sinuses by a radical operation.

If a deflection of the septum is the cause of the obstruction, the surgeon makes an incision into the mucous membrane and, after raising it from the bone, removes the deflected bone and cartilage with bone forceps. The mucosa then is allowed to fall back in place and is held there by tight packing. This operation is called a submucous resection or septoplasty.

Nasal polyps are removed by clipping them at their base with a wire snare. Hypertrophied turbinates may be treated by astringent applications to shrink them close to the side of the nose.

After these procedures, the head of the bed is elevated to promote drainage and to help in alleviating discomfort owing to oedema. Frequent oral hygiene care is given because patients breathe through their mouths.

Fractures of the Nose

The location of the nose makes it susceptible to injury by a wide variety of causes. In fact, the nose sustains fractures more frequently than any other bone in the body. Fractures of the nose usually result from direct trauma. As a rule, no serious consequences result, but the deformity that may follow often gives rise to obstruction of the nasal air passages and to facial disfigurement.

Assessment

The nose should be examined internally to rule out the possibility that the injury may be complicated by a fracture of the nasal septum and submucosal septal haematoma. If a haematoma develops and is not drained, it may eventually become an abscess with a dissolution of the septal cartilage. The familiar saddle deformity of the nose results.

Clinical Features

Immediately after the injury there is usually considerable bleeding from the nose externally and internally into the pharynx. There is marked swelling of the soft tissues adjacent to the nose and, frequently, a definite deformity. Because of this swelling and bleeding, an accurate diagnosis can only be made after the swelling has subsided.

Medical Management and Nursing Care

As a rule, the bleeding is controlled with the use of cold compresses. With the application of local anaesthesia to the nose or with intravenous anaesthesia, it is usually possible to bring displaced fragments into alignment and then hold them by intranasal packing or external splints. In reducing the fracture it is important to re-form the nasal passages and to realign the bones so as to prevent a disfiguring deformity. After reduction the swelling that occurs may be decreased by the application of ice compresses with the patient in the sitting position.

Patients are likely to want to know how long the bruising and swelling will take to disappear, and how their nose will eventually look. They may need initial support to help them cope with a change in body image and altered self-perception.

Laryngeal Obstruction

Oedema of the larynx is a serious, often fatal, condition. The larynx is a stiff box that will not stretch, and the space within it between the vocal cords (glottis), through which the air must pass, is narrow. Swelling of the laryngeal mucous membrane, therefore, may close this orifice tightly, leading to suffocation. Oedema of the glottis occurs rarely in patients with acute laryngitis, occasionally in patients with urticaria and more frequently in severe inflammations of the throat. It is an occasional cause of death in severe anaphylaxis.

When caused by an allergic reaction, treatment includes the administration of adrenaline or an adrenal corticosteroid and the application of an ice pack to the neck.

Foreign bodies frequently are aspirated into the pharynx, the larynx or the trachea and cause a twofold problem. First they obstruct the air passages and cause difficulty in breathing, which may lead to asphyxia; later they may be drawn farther down, entering the bronchi or one of their branches and causing symptoms of irritation, such as a croupy cough, blood or mucous expectoration, and paroxysms of dyspnoea. The physical signs and X-ray films confirm the diagnosis.

In emergencies, when the signs of asphyxia are evident, immediate treatment is necessary. Frequently, if the foreign body has lodged in the pharynx and can be seen, it is dislodged by the finger. If the obstruction is in the larynx or the trachea, the abdominal thrust manoeuvre is tried. If all efforts are unsuccessful, an immediate tracheotomy is necessary.

● To perform the abdominal thrust manoeuvre, stand behind the person who is choking and place both arms around the waist, with one hand grasping the other fist. Then quickly and forcefully apply pressure against the victim's diaphragm, pressing slightly upward, just below the ribs. The pressure will compress the lungs and expel the aspirated object. Do this repeatedly until the object is expelled. Patients are likely to be anxious both because of the disorder and its treatment. Nurses need to spend time allowing patients to talk about their experience and to compose themselves after the incident.

CANCER OF THE LARYNX

Cancer of the larynx is potentially curable if detected early. It represents 3 to 5 per cent of all cancers, and occurs about eight times more frequently in men than in women, and most commonly in men aged 50 to 65 years.

Factors that contribute to laryngeal cancer are irritants such as cigarette smoke and alcohol (and their combined effects), vocal straining, chronic laryngitis, industrial exposure, nutritional deficiencies and family predisposition.

Clinical Features

A malignant growth may occur on the vocal cords (intrinsic) or on another part of the larynx (extrinsic). Hoarseness may be noted early in the patient since accurate approximation of the cords during phonation is interrupted by the presence of the tumour. Patients may complain of pain and burning in the throat when drinking hot liquids and citrus juices. Later a lump may be felt in the neck. Subsequently, too, dysphagia, dyspnoea, hoarseness and foul breath are noticed. Enlarged cervical nodes, weight loss, general debility and the discomfort of pain radiating to the ear may be suggestive of metastasis.

Diagnosis

Direct laryngoscopic examination may be necessary if the larynx cannot be seen completely; it is also used for biopsy of the tumour. The growth may involve any of the three areas (glottis, supraglottis or subglottis) and varies in appearance. The precise involvement is determined since this affects the treatment. Since many of these lesions are submucosal, biopsy may necessitate that an incision be performed with microlaryngeal techniques or laser to transect the mucosa and reach the tumour.

Mobility of the vocal cords is assessed; if normal movement is limited, the growth may affect muscle, other tissue and even the airway. The lymph nodes of the neck and the thyroid gland are palpated to determine spread of the malignancy.

Computed tomography and laryngography are effective in determining the extent of tumour growth.

Medical Management

Treatment varies with the extent of the malignancy. Precise determination of the exact location and involvement of the malignancy is done by indirect and direct laryngoscopy, biopsy and radiography before radiation therapy or surgery is prescribed.

If surgery is to be performed, thorough mouth hygiene before the procedure is imperative. Antibiotics may be prescribed to reduce the possibility of infection. In men, preoperative shaving includes the beard and the hair on the neck and the chest down to the nipple line.

Radiotherapy

Good results have been produced by radiotherapy in patients in whom only one cord was affected and which was normally mobile (i.e., moved with phonation). In addition, these patients retain a practically normal voice. A few may develop chondritis or stenosis; a small number may later require laryngectomy.

Partial Laryngectomy (Laryngofissure, Thyrotomy)

A partial laryngectomy is recommended in the early stages, especially in intrinsic cancer of the larynx (limited to the vocal cords), and has a cure rate of more than 80 per cent. In this operation, the thyroid cartilage of the larynx is split in the midline of the neck, and the portion of the vocal cord that is involved with tumour growth is removed. Sometimes a tracheostomy tube is left in the trachea when the wound is closed; it is usually removed after a few days.

Supraglottic (Horizontal) Laryngectomy

A supraglottic laryngectomy is used in the management of certain extrinsic tumours. After adequate resection, sufficient normal larynx is left so that the cords remain intact and their function is maintained. During surgery a radical neck dissection is also done on the involved side. Postoperatively, the patient may experience some difficulty in swallowing for the first two weeks. The chief advantage of this operation is that it preserves the voice. The major problem is that there may be local recurrence; therefore, patients have to be selected carefully.

Total Laryngectomy

For extrinsic cancer of the larynx (extension beyond the vocal cords), the entire larynx is removed; this includes the thyroid cartilage, the vocal cords and the epiglottis. A neck dissection may also be carried out on the affected side. With or without neck dissection, a total laryngectomy requires a permanent tracheal stoma (Figure 4.4). This is done to prevent aspiration of food and fluid into the lower respiratory tract, since the larynx that provides the protective sphincter is no longer present.

Total Laryngectomy With Laryngoplasty

In this delicate procedure, a dermal tube is fashioned from the upper end of the trachea into the hypopharynx. By closing the permanent tracheostomy opening with the finger, the patient can exhale air up through the dermal tube and into the pharyngeal cavity. The sound produced is transformed into speech that is almost normal and far superior to oesophageal speech.

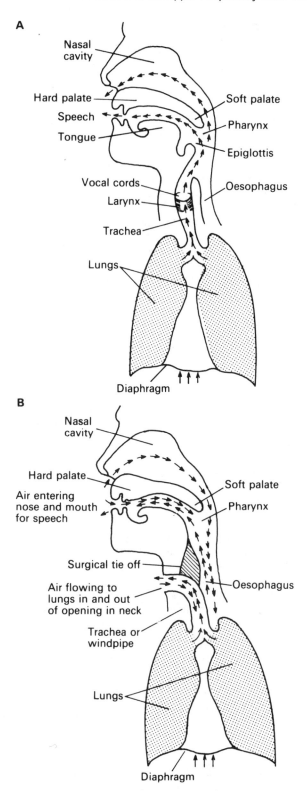

Figure 4.4 Direction of the air flow before (A) and after (B) total laryngectomy. (Courtesy of American Cancer Society.)

► **THE PATIENT UNDERGOING LARYNGECTOMY**

► *Assessment*

The nurse needs to assess the patient for the following symptoms: hoarseness, sore throat, dyspnoea, dysphagia or pain and burning in the throat. The patient's neck is palpated for swelling. Patients' feelings about their disorder must be ascertained and talked through. Establishing what patients think is their problem, and how they think it will affect their future lifestyle, may help in preparing for treatment and recovery. Family and friends are also likely to be anxious and need support.

If treatment includes surgery, it is important for the nurse to know the nature of the surgery in order to plan appropriate care. For example, some patients experience loss of speech.

A preoperative evaluation by a speech therapist will provide patients with an opportunity to ask questions.

In addition, the nurse needs to determine the psychological preparedness of the patient. The idea of cancer is terrifying to most people; this is compounded by the potential for permanent loss of speech. The nurse needs to evaluate the patient's coping methods in order to develop an effective approach to supporting them both preoperatively and postoperatively.

► *Patient's Problems*

Based on all the assessment data the patient's main problems may include the following:

● Lack of knowledge about the disorder, treatment, postoperative course and rehabilitation.
● Anxiety and depression related to the diagnosis of cancer.
● Altered breathing pattern as a result of surgery.
● Impaired communication as a result of impaired ability to speak words.
● Inadequate nutrition related to swallowing difficulties.
● Risk of non-co-operation with rehabilitation advice.

► *Planning and Implementation*
► **Expected Outcomes**
The main outcomes for the patient may include attainment of an adequate level of knowledge, reduction in anxiety and depression, attainment of a patent airway (patient is able to handle own secretions), improvement in communication by use of alternative methods, attainment of an optimal level of nutrition and co-operation with rehabilitation advice.

Preoperative Nursing Care

Patient Education
The diagnosis of cancer of the larynx is associated with preconceived notions and fears. Many categorize it with other 'cancers' and assume the worst. Others assume that loss of speech and disfigurement are inevitable with this condition. Once the doctor explains the diagnosis to the patient, the nurse clarifies any misconceptions by identifying where the larynx is, what it does, and what the particular procedure will be. The patient's role in the postoperative and rehabilitative period is explained (see below).

Measures to Reduce Anxiety and Depression
Since surgery of the larynx is done most commonly for a tumour that may be malignant, patients will have many questions: Will the surgeon be able to remove all of the tumour? Is it cancer? Will I die? Will I choke? Will I ever speak again? Therefore, the psychological preparation of patients is as important as the physical preparation. If patients are going to have a complete laryngectomy, they should know that they will lose their natural voice completely and that, with training, there are ways in which they can carry on a fairly normal conversation. (They will not be able to sing, laugh or whistle.) Until they receive this training, patients need to know how the nurse can be reached, and that they can communicate in the immediate postoperative phase by writing. The nurse answers questions about the nature of the surgery and tells patients that they will lose the normal use of their voice. Patients need to be given realistic expectations regarding recovery, and reassured that they will be able to perform most of their preoperative activities.

Patients are given the opportunity to vent their feelings and share their perceptions. Any misconceptions they might have about their condition are resolved. They are given complete but concise answers to their questions. During the postoperative period, someone who has had a laryngectomy should visit these patients. This visit should help them to realize that there are people willing to help them cope with the situation, and show that recovery is possible.

Postoperative Nursing Care

Airway Maintenance
Lying on the side will ensure a clear airway postoperatively. Patients should be observed for restlessness, laboured breathing, apprehension and increased pulse rate, since these suggest respiratory or circulatory problems. Medications that depress respirations should be avoided. Patients need to be reminded to cough and take deep breaths; suctioning may be necessary. Early ambulation, also, aids in preventing atelectasis and pneumonia. Some patients will have a tracheostomy tube in place for two or three days and this needs to be kept patent and clean.

If a total laryngectomy has been performed, a laryngectomy tube will most likely be in place. The laryngectomy tube (which is shorter than a tracheostomy tube but has a larger diameter) is the only airway the patient has. The care of this tube is the same as for a tracheostomy tube.

The stoma is kept clean by daily cleansing with saline solution or prescribed solution; antibiotic ointment (of a non-oil base), as prescribed, may then be applied around the stoma and suture line.

The laryngectomy tube may be removed when the stoma is well healed, usually within 3 to 6 weeks after the operation. Until that time, the patients will need to be taught how to clean and change the laryngectomy tube and how to clear their airway of secretions. Through the postoperative period, the nurse must be alert for the possible serious complication of rupture of the carotid artery, particularly if wound infection is present. Should this occur, the nurse would apply direct pressure over the artery, summon assistance and provide psychological support to the patient until the vessel can be ligated.

Nutrition

Nutrition is maintained for the first 2 or 3 days by means of a nasogastric catheter or a tube passed into the pharynx. Intravenous fluids will be administered concomitantly. The nurse can remove and pass the tube because there is no danger of getting it into the trachea since the trachea now bypasses the pharynx and upper airway. Tube feedings are given 2 to 3 days postoperatively depending on the patient's nutritional needs. After that, the tube is usually removed. The nurse explains to the patient that thick fluids such as custard, which are easy to swallow, will be given first. Solid foods are introduced as tolerated. Patients need to be advised to maintain good oral hygiene.

Communication and Speech Rehabilitation

Since a 'magic slate' is often used for communication, it is as well to remember which hand the patient uses for writing so that the opposite arm can be used for intravenous infusions. When notes are the means of communication, they should be destroyed to ensure the patient's privacy. If the patient is not able to write, flash cards can be used.

Another method of communication is oesophageal speech. This can be taught once the patient begins oral feedings or one week postoperatively. The patient first develops the ability to belch. An hour after the meal has been eaten, the nurse reminds the patient to belch. This is practised repeatedly. Later, this conscious action is transformed into simple explosions of air from the oesophagus for speech purposes. From here the speech therapist works with the patient in an attempt to make speech intelligible and as close to normal as possible.

If oesophageal speech is not successful, or until the technique is mastered, an electric larynx may be used for communication. This apparatus projects sound into the oral cavity. When words are formed by the mouth (articulated), the sound from the electric larynx becomes words that can be heard. The voice that is produced is obviously not the patient's normal voice, but the patient is able to communicate with relative ease.

Another form of communication that will help the patient be better understood is called tracheo-oesophageal puncture. In this method the voice is restored by diverting air, which travels from the lungs through a puncture in the posterior wall of the trachea, into the oesophagus and out of the mouth. Once the puncture is surgically created and has healed, a voice prosthesis is fitted over the puncture site. The prosthesis is removed and cleaned when there is mucus build-up in order to prevent airway obstruction. The patient is given lessons in voice production by the speech therapist, but the speech is produced just as before by moving the tongue and lips to form the sound into words.

Other alternatives or interim methods of communication include a call bell, sign language, lip reading and computer aids.

Patient Education

The following areas are addressed.

Tracheostomy and Stoma Care

Patients need information about what to expect from their tracheostomy. They will frequently cough up rather large amounts of mucus through this opening. Because air passes directly into the trachea without being warmed and moistened by the upper respiratory mucosa, the tracheobronchial tree compensates by secreting excessive amounts of mucus. Therefore, patients will have frequent coughing episodes and may be somewhat troubled by the brassy sounding, mucus-producing cough. However, they should be assured that these problems diminish in time as the tracheobronchial mucosa adapts to the patients' altered physiology.

When patients cough, the orifice should be wiped clean and cleared of mucus. In addition, the skin around the stoma should be washed twice daily. If crusting occurs, the skin around the stoma is lubricated with a non-oil base ointment and the crusts removed with sterile tweezers. It may be necessary that a bib be worn in front of the tracheostomy to keep the mucus from soiling the clothing.

One of the most important factors in decreasing cough and mucus production as well as crusting around the stoma is to provide adequate humidification of the environment. Mechanical humidifiers and aerosol generators (nebulizers) are excellent sources of humidification and help maintain comfort. Some system of humidification should be set up in the home before the patient is discharged from the hospital. An air-conditioned atmosphere may be distressing to the newly laryngectomized patient, since the air may be too cool or too dry and thus too irritating.

Changes in Taste and Smell

Patients can expect to have a diminished sense of taste and smell for a period after the operation. Because they are breathing directly into the trachea, air is not passing through the nose to the olfactory end organs. Because taste and smell are so closely connected, the patients' taste sensations are altered. However, in time patients usually accommodate to this problem and their olfactory sensation adapts to meet their needs.

Hygienic and Recreational Measures

Special precautions need to be taken in a shower to prevent water from entering the stoma. Wearing a loose-fitting plastic bib or simply holding a hand over the opening is effective. However, swimming is not recommended, because the patient with a laryngectomy can drown without getting the face wet. Hair sprays, loose hair and powder should be kept clear of the stoma, since they could cause blockage, irritation and possibly infection.

Recreation and exercise are important. Golf, bowling, bridge, spectator activities and walking can be enjoyed safely. Moderation in order to prevent fatigue is important because, when tired, the person who has had a laryngectomy has more difficulty speaking with the new voice. At such times the patient can easily become discouraged and depressed.

Follow-up and Emergency Care

Patients need to be advised to keep follow-up appointments for physical examinations and for advice concerning any problems relating to the convalescent programme. They should also carry proper identification, such as a card, to alert a first-aider to the special requirements of resuscitation should this need arise. On the back of the card can be included the name of a responsible person to notify in the event of emergency.

► *Evaluation*
► **Expected Outcomes**

1. The patient acquires an adequate level of knowledge.
   a. Shows an understanding of the specific surgical procedure.
   b. States the role to be played by patient in own care.
   c. Performs self-care adequately.
2. The patient experiences less anxiety and depression.
   a. Describes the reason for the surgery.
   b. Shows confidence that health care personnel will give the care patient needs.
   c. Develops a sense of hope about the condition.
   d. Patient expresses comfort with the support group.
   e. Meets with someone who has had a laryngectomy.
3. The patient maintains a clear airway and handles own secretions.
   a. Demonstrates practical and correct technique involved in cleaning and changing the laryngectomy tube.
   b. Demonstrates how to raise secretions from stoma or tube by coughing or by suctioning.
   c. Is afebrile and has a normal respiratory rate.
   d. Relates the significance of good hygienic measures in keeping mouth and stoma clean.
   e. Covers stoma opening securely when attending to

personal hygiene, taking a shower and so on.
4. The patient acquires effective communication techniques.
   a. Uses effective communication methods until able to whisper.
   b. Is comfortable with alternative communication techniques when voice is not audible: call bell, flash cards, sign language, lip reading, computer aids.
   c. Explains how the vocal problem can be improved by following the plan of care, eventually mastering own programme, whether it is 'belch' speech or artificial larynx.
   d. Communicates with family and friends using newly learned speech techniques.
   e. Practises the advice of the speech therapist.
5. The patient maintains balanced nutrition.
   a. Drinks fluids when experiencing swallowing difficulties.
   b. Avoids sweet foods as they depress appetite.
   c. Tolerates solid foods.
   d. Rinses mouth and brushes teeth frequently.
6. The patient follows rehabilitation and home care programme.
   a. No longer smokes.
   b. Practises recommended speech therapy in addition to keeping appointments with speech therapist.
   c. Demonstrates understanding of hygienic principles when caring for stoma and laryngectomy tube (if present).
   d. Involves partner/other carers with the care activities.
   e. Plans how to increase the humidity at home.
   f. Covers stomal opening securely when attending to personal hygiene.
   g. Shows understanding of symptoms that require medical attention.
   h. Makes follow-up appointments as appropriate.
   i. Carries a card indicating procedures to follow in the event of an emergency, including who to contact for assistance.

BIBLIOGRAPHY

Seaton, A., Seaton, D. and Leitch, A. G. (1989) *Crofton and Douglas's Respiratory Diseases* (4th edition), Blackwell Scientific, Oxford.

FURTHER READING

Books
Kacmarek, R. M., Mack, C. W. and Dimas, S. (1990) *The Essentials of Respiratory Care* (3rd edition), Mosby Year Books, St Louis.
Stokes, D. (1985) *Learning to Care on the ENT Ward*, Hodder & Stoughton, London.

chapter 5

ASSESSMENT AND CARE OF PATIENTS WITH THORACIC AND LOWER RESPIRATORY TRACT DISORDERS

RESPIRATORY INFECTIONS

Acute Tracheobronchitis

Acute tracheobronchitis is an acute inflammation of the mucous membranes of the trachea and the bronchial tree that often follows infections of the upper respiratory tract. A patient with a viral infection has a lessened resistance and can readily develop a secondary bacterial infection. Thus, the adequate treatment of upper respiratory tract infections is one of the major factors in the prevention of acute bronchitis. Aside from infection, inhalation of physical and chemical irritants, gases or other air contaminants can also cause acute bronchial irritations.

Clinical Features

The signs and symptoms of acute tracheobronchitis result from the mucopurulent sputum that is secreted by the inflamed mucosa of the bronchi. Initially, patients have a dry, irritating cough and expectorates a scanty amount of mucoid sputum. They complain of sternal soreness from coughing and have fever, headache and general malaise. As the infection progresses, the sputum is more profuse and purulent and the cough becomes looser.

Examination and culture of the sputum is essential to identify the specific causative organism.

Medical Management

The treatment is largely symptomatic. The patient is advised to rest. Moist heat to the chest will relieve the soreness and pain. Cool vapour therapy or steam inhalations are beneficial in relieving the laryngeal and tracheal irritation. Increasing the vapour pressure (moisture content) in the air will reduce irritation.

Cough depressants are not given or are prescribed only with caution when the cough is productive. Antihistamines may be excessively drying, making secretions more difficult to expectorate. An expectorant may be prescribed and the fluid intake increased to 'thin' the viscous and tenacious secretions. Antibiotic treatment is indicated when the sputum becomes purulent.

Nursing Care

The nurse's observations are important in determining the therapeutic plan because care of the patient is largely symptomatic.

A primary nursing function is to caution the patient against overexertion, which can induce a relapse or extension of the infection. The elderly patient can easily develop bronchopneumonia from acute tracheobronchitis if adequate care is not given. Patients are encouraged to change position frequently—sitting upright helps to facilitate effective coughing and prevent retention of mucopurulent sputum.

Pneumonia

Pneumonia is an inflammatory process of the lung substance that is commonly caused by infectious agents. Pneumonia is the most common infectious cause of death in the United Kingdom (Office of Population Censuses and Surveys, 1987), accounting for about 56 deaths per year per 100,000 of the population of England and Wales.

It is classified according to its causative agent, if known: for example, it may be a bacterial, viral, fungal, parasitic or lipid pneumonia. There is also a chemical pneumonia, such as that seen after ingestion of paraffin oil or inhalation of irritating gases. Radiation pneumonitis may follow radiotherapy for breast or lung cancer, and usually occurs six weeks or more after completion of radiotherapy.

If a substantial portion of one or more lobes is involved, the disease is referred to as lobar pneumonia. Bronchopneumonia implies that the pneumonic process is distributed in patchy fashion, having originated in one or more localized areas within the bronchi and extended to the adjacent surrounding lung parenchyma. Of these two types, bronchopneumonia is more common that lobar pneumonia.

In general, patients with bacterial pneumonia usually have acute or chronic underlying disease that impairs host defences. More often, pneumonia arises from endogenous flora of the patient whose resistance has been altered or from aspiration of mouth flora. Although most viral infections occur in previously healthy people, when bacterial pneumonia occurs in a healthy person there is usually a history of preceding viral illness. In recent years there has been an increase in the number of patients who have deficient defences against infections: those on corticosteroids or other immunosuppressive drugs, those on broad-spectrum antimicrobials, those with acquired immunodeficiency syndrome (AIDS), and those requiring the use of life-support technology. These patients who have suppressed immune systems often acquire pneumonia from organisms of low virulence. In addition, there are increasing numbers of patients with impaired defences who develop hospital-acquired pneumonia from gramnegative bacilli. Also, gram-positive cocci, anaerobes, mycobacteria, nocardial species, and viral, chlamydial, fungal and parasitic agents can cause pneumonia.

Altered Physiology

Most pneumonias are bacterial in origin, with the pneumonic process altering the normal process of ventilation. The pneumococci enter the alveoli, producing inflammation and exudate within the air spaces, which eventually become filled. Areas of the lung are inadequately ventilated because of secretions, mucosal oedema and bronchospasm, producing partial occlusion of the bronchi and alveoli. There is a fall in the alveolar oxygen tension and venous blood entering the lungs passes through the underventilated area without being oxygenated. In essence, the blood bypasses the lungs and is shunted from the right to the left side of the heart. This mixing of oxygenated and unoxygenated blood eventually results in arterial hypoxaemia.

Prevention and Risk Factors

The nurse should be acquainted with the factors and circumstances that commonly predispose the person to pneumonia in order to identify the patient at high risk and to engage in anticipatory and preventive nursing.

- Any condition producing mucus or bronchial obstruction and interfering with normal drainage of the lung (cancer, chronic obstructive airways disease) renders the patient susceptible to pneumonia.
- Immunosuppressed patients are at risk.
- People who smoke are at risk because cigarette smoke disrupts both mucociliary and macrophage activity.
- Any patient who lies passively in bed for prolonged periods, relatively immobile and breathing shallowly, is highly vulnerable to the risk of bronchopneumonia.
- Any person who has a depressed cough reflex (owing to drugs or weakness), has aspirated foreign material into the lungs during a period of unconsciousness (head injury, anaesthesia), or has an abnormal swallowing mechanism is very likely to develop bronchopneumonia.
- Any hospitalized patient on a nothing-by-mouth regime or who is receiving antibiotics has increased pharyngeal colonization or organisms and is at risk. In very ill people, the oropharynx is likely to be colonized by gram-negative bacteria.
- People who are intoxicated frequently are particularly susceptible to this infection, since alcohol suppresses the body's reflexes, white cell mobilization and tracheobronchial ciliary motion.
- Any person scheduled to receive a sedative is observed

for respiratory rate and depth before the drug is given; if respiratory depression is apparent, the drug should not be administered. Respiratory depression predisposes to the pooling of bronchial secretions and subsequent development of pneumonia.

- An important preventive measure is the frequent suctioning of secretions in patients who are unconscious or have poor cough and gag reflexes; this reduces the likelihood that secretions will be aspirated or accumulate in the lungs and induce bronchopneumonia.
- Elderly people are especially vulnerable to pneumonia. Postoperative pneumonia should be anticipated in the elderly and forestalled by frequent mobilization, effective coughing and breathing exercises.
- Anyone receiving treatment with respiratory therapy equipment can develop pneumonia if the equipment has not been cleaned properly.

Pneumonia has been known to be more prevalent with certain underlying disorders such as heart failure, diabetes, alcoholism and chronic obstructive airways disease. Certain diseases have also been associated with specific pathogens. For example, staphylococcal pneumonia has been noted after epidemics of influenza, and patients with chronic obstructive airways disease are at increased risk of developing pneumonia caused by pneumococci or *Haemophilus influenzae*.

Cystic fibrosis is associated with respiratory infection with *Pseudomonas* and *Staphylococcus*. *Pneumocystis carinii* pneumonia has been associated with acquired immunodeficiency syndrome (AIDS). Pneumonias occurring in hospitalized patients often involve organisms not usually found in the nonhospitalized population, including enteric gram-negative bacilli and *Staphylococcus aureus*.

Clinical Features

These are related to the underlying cause. Bacterial pneumonias include streptococcal, staphylococcal, klebsiella and pseudomonas pneumonia and Legionnaire's disease. Classic bacterial pneumonia usually starts with a sudden onset of shaking chills, rapidly rising fever (39.5–40.5C) and pleuritic chest pain that is aggravated by breathing and coughing. Patients will have an increased respiratory rate (25–45/min), often with nasal flushing, a respiratory grunt and the use of accessory muscles. Lying on the affected side may ease the symptoms by splinting the chest. Patients are likely to have a tachycardia, flushed cheeks, cyanosed extremities and prefer to sit upright to aid breathing and ease coughing. The cough is usually short, painful and incessant, producing purulent sputum, sometimes bloodtinged or rusty.

Patients with compromised pulmonary function, either as a result of ageing or chronic obstructive airways disease, may develop the symptoms of pneumonia insidiously, with purulent sputum possibly being the only indication of pneumonia.

Nonbacterial pneumonias include viral, *Pneumocystis carinii* and fungal pneumonia. Viral pneumonia tends to be associated with a cough, headache, anorexia, fever and myalgia. *Pneumocystis carinii* pneumonia tends to be of insidious onset and associated with increasing shortness of breath. Fungal pneumonia produces fever, chest pain, productive cough and haemoptysis.

Diagnosis

The diagnosis is made from the history (particularly of recent respiratory tract infection), physical examination, chest X-ray, blood cultures and sputum examination, microscopy and culture.

Medical Management

Management depends largely on the underlying cause. Bacterial pneumonia is managed by giving the appropriate antibiotic as determined by the results of the Gram stain of the sputum specimen. Effective drugs include the penicillins, cephalosporins and erythromycin.

Supportive measures include respiratory support, fluid and electrolyte replacement and total parenteral nutrition. Patients must be given sufficient inspired oxygen to correct hypoxia. Arterial blood gas analysis is performed to determine the need for oxygen and to evaluate therapy. Mechanical ventilation may be warranted for some patients.

► NURSING PROCESS
► THE PATIENT WITH PNEUMONIA

► Assessment

The presence of a fever in any hospitalized patient should alert the nurse to the possibility of the development of bacterial pneumonia. Use of assessment skills will further identify the clinical features of pain; tachypnoea; use of accessory muscles; rapid, bounding pulse; coughing; and purulent sputum. The nurse determines the severity, location and cause of the chest pain as well as what relieves it. Any changes in temperature, amount and colour of secretions, frequency and severity of the cough, and degree of tachypnoea or shortness of breath are also monitored.

The elderly patient is assessed for unusual behaviour, alterations in mental status and heart failure. A restless, excited delirium may be exhibited, especially in patients with alcoholism.

The potential complications of bacterial pneumonia are evaluated routinely so that intervention can begin early.

Complications

Lethal complications may develop during the first few days of antibiotic treatment. The patient is observed for continuing or recurring fever. Inadequate lung drainage or insufficient blood supply to the involved lung may reduce the amount of antibiotic agent reaching the invading organism. Resistant or recurring fever may be due to drug allergy (assess for rash), drug resistance or slow response of the susceptible organism, superinfection, infected pleural effusion or pneumonia caused by unusual organisms. Failure of the pneumonia to resolve raises the suspicion of underlying carcinoma of the bronchus.

Patients should respond to treatment within 24 to 48 hours after antibiotic therapy is initiated. Complications of pneumonia include sustained hypotension and shock (especially in gram-negative bacterial disease in the elderly). These complications are encountered chiefly in patients who have received no specific treatment, have been treated too little or too late, have received chemotherapy to which the infecting organism is resistant or are suffering from a pre-existing disease that complicates the pneumonia.

Atelectasis (from obstruction of bronchus by accumulated secretions) may occur at any stage of acute pneumonia. Pleural effusion also is fairly common and may signal the beginning of empyema. A chest tube may be required to control pleural infection by establishing proper drainage of the empyema.

Delirium is another possible complication and is considered a medical emergency when it occurs. It may be caused by hypoxia, meningitis or the delirium tremens of alcoholism. The patient with delirium is given oxygen, adequate hydration and mild sedation and is observed constantly. Congestive heart failure, cardiac arrhythmias, pericarditis and myocarditis are also complications of pneumonia.

Superinfection is an important complication that may occur with the administration of very large amounts of penicillin or with the use of combinations of antibiotics. If the patient improves and the fever diminishes after initial antibiotic therapy but subsequently there is a rise in temperature with increasing cough and evidence of spread of pneumonia, then a superinfection has occurred. Antibiotics are changed appropriately or, in some cases, discontinued entirely.

The influenza vaccine is recommended yearly to all patients at risk (the elderly, cardiac and pulmonary disease patients), since pneumonia is a complication of influenza.

► *Patient's Problems*

Based on the assessment, the patient's main problems may include:

- Altered breathing related to copious tracheobronchial secretions.
- Reduced activity tolerance related to altered respiratory function.
- Potential dehydration related to fever and dyspnoea.
- Lack of knowledge about the treatment regime and preventive health measures.

► *Planning and Implementation*
► Expected Outcomes

The major goals for the patient may include improvement of airway patency, obtaining enough rest to conserve energy, maintenance of proper fluid intake and an understanding of the treatment protocol and preventive measures.

Nursing Care

Improvement in Breathing

Retained secretions interfere with gas exchange and may cause slow resolution of the disease. A high level of fluid intake (2 to 3 litres/day) is encouraged, since adequate hydration thins and loosens pulmonary secretions and also replaces fluid losses owing to fever, diaphoresis, dehydration and dyspnoea. The air is humidified in order to loosen secretions and improve ventilation. A high-humidity face mask (using either compressed air or oxygen) delivers warm, humidified air to the tracheobronchial tree and liquefies secretions. The patient is encouraged to cough in the manner described for the postoperative patient.

Chest physiotherapy is extremely important in loosening and mobilizing secretions. Patients are asked to move into the proper position to drain the involved lung, and then the chest is vibrated and percussed. After the lung has drained for 10 to 20 minutes (depending on tolerance), patients are encouraged to breathe deeply and cough. If they are too weak to cough effectively, the mucus may have to be removed by nasotracheal suctioning or by bronchoscopic aspiration as determined by the doctor.

If oxygen is prescribed, the most appropriate means of delivery is selected. The effectiveness of the oxygen concentration must be monitored by assessing for the clinical features of hypoxia.

Rest and Energy Conservation.

Patients are encouraged to rest and remain in bed to avoid overexertion and possible exacerbation of symptoms. They need to choose a comfortable position for resting and breathing, and are encouraged to change position frequently.

If sedatives or tranquillizers are prescribed, the patient's sensorium is evaluated first. Restlessness, confusion and aggression may be due to cerebral hypoxaemia, in which case sedatives are contraindicated.

Patients are likely to need help with certain activities of living, the aim being to retain independence but to involve family members and close friends where appropriate.

Proper Fluid Intake.

The patient's respiratory rate increases because of dyspnoea and fever. With an increased rate there is an increase in insensible fluid loss during exhalation. The patient can quickly become dehydrated. Therefore, fluids are encouraged (at least 2 litres/day). Frequently, a patient who is dyspnoeic is anorexic and will only take fluids. Fluids, then, are beneficial for volume replacement as well as nutrition.

Patient Education

After the fever subsides, patients may gradually increase their activities. Fatigue, weakness and depression may be prolonged after pneumonia. Breathing exercises to clear the lungs and promote full lung expansion are encouraged.

The nurse explains to the patient that it is wise to stop cigarette smoking since it destroys tracheobronchial ciliary action, which is the first line of defence of the lungs. Smoking also irritates the mucous cells of the bronchi and inhibits the function of alveolar macrophage (scavenger) cells. The patient is advised to avoid fatigue, sudden changes in temperature and excessive alcohol intake, which lowers resistance to pneumonia. The nurse reviews with the patient the principles of adequate nutrition and rest, since one episode of pneumonia may make the patient susceptible to recurring respiratory tract infections. The patient is encouraged to obtain influenza vaccine at the prescribed times, because influenza increases susceptibility to secondary bacterial pneumonia.

► *Evaluation*
► Expected Outcomes

1. Patient has improved breathing.
   a. Subjective feeling of improved breathing.
   b. Has a normal temperature.
   c. Arterial blood gases are within normal limits.
   d. Demonstrates effective coughing technique.
   e. Adheres to humidification measures.
2. Attains proper amount of rest.
   a. Rests in bed/chair initially.
   b. Avoids the recumbent position.
   c. Shows no signs of restlessness, confusion or aggression.
3. Achieves an adequate fluid intake.
   a. Understands the importance of drinking at least two litres of fluid per day.
   b. Has sufficient skin turgor.
4. Understands the disorder, its treatment protocol and prevention.
   a. Is aware of factors that contribute to development of pneumonia.
   b. Talks of joining a support group to stop smoking.

LUNG ABSCESS

A lung abscess is a localized lesion in the lung containing pus and necrotic (dead) tissue that collapses and forms cavities, or pockets, in the lung. It may occur from aspiration of vomitus or infected material (nasotracheal secretions, blood) from the upper respiratory tract. After aspiration, pneumonitis develops and the area of pneumonia cavitates because the micro-organisms have necrotizing potential; hence a lung abscess may develop very rapidly. A lung abscess may also occur secondary to bronchial obstruction due to a tumour. Infection or necrosis within the tumour mass results in the accumulation of secretions. Or, it may be a sequela of necrotizing pneumonias, tuberculosis, pulmonary embolism, chest trauma or bronchial neoplasm.

In the initial stages the cavity in the lung may or may not communicate with a bronchus; eventually, however, it becomes surrounded, or 'encapsulated', by a wall of fibrous tissue, except at one or two points where the necrotic process extends until it reaches the lumen of some bronchus or the pleural space and thus establishes a communication with the respiratory tract, the pleural cavity, or both. In the first instance, its purulent contents are evacuated continuously in the form of sputum, whereas if a pleural exit is accessible, empyema (collection of pus in the pleural cavity) results; if both types of communication are furnished, the problem becomes one of bronchopleural fistula.

Clinical Features

The majority of patients have a cough that produces a small amount of sputum, a low-grade fever and malaise. In time the sputum becomes copious and often foul smelling and at time contains blood. This occurs frequently when the abscess extends into the bronchus and begins to drain. The patient may complain of a pleuritic type of chest pain. Sometimes the onset is acute, with chills, high fever, cough and malaise.

Diagnosis

Physical examination may reveal an area of consolidation and pleural thickening, dullness to percussion and suppressed breath sounds. Confirmation of the diagnosis is made by chest films, sputum culture and direct visualization with fibreoptic bronchoscopy, which is necessary to rule out the possibility of tumour or a foreign body in the lung.

Usually, sputum specimens are obtained by transtracheal aspiration since an expectorated sputum specimen will be contaminated by the indigenous flora of the mouth and gingivae. Several species of bacteria are often present in a lung abscess. The most common cause is the anaerobic bacteria that normally colonize the upper airway.

Medical Management

The goals of management of a lung abscess are prevention, eradication of the infection, and establishment of adequate drainage. The following measures will reduce the risk of suppurative lung disease:

1. Patients who must have teeth extracted while their gums and teeth are infected may be given appropriate antibiotic therapy before any dental treatment.
2. The patient is advised to maintain adequate dental and oral hygiene, since anaerobic bacteria play a role in the pathogenesis of lung abscess.
3. Appropriate antimicrobial therapy is given to patients with pneumonia.

Bronchoscopy is indicated if inhalation of foreign material is suspected. A patient with impaired cough reflexes and loss of glottis closure or one who has swallowing difficulties is apt to aspirate foreign material and hence develop lung abscess. Other patients at risk are those with an altered state of consciousness from anaesthesia, central nervous system disorders (seizures, stroke), drug addiction, alcoholism or oesophageal disease, as well as patients being fed by nasogastric tube.

Antimicrobial therapy depends on the results of sputum culture and sensitivity and is given for an extended period of time. High intravenous doses are generally required, because the antibiotic must penetrate necrotic tissue and abscess fluid.

Adequate drainage of the lung abscess is achieved through postural drainage aided by percussion, effective coughing and breathing exercises. Sometimes bronchoscopy is needed to drain the abscess.

A high-protein, high-calorie diet is necessary since chronic infection is associated with a catabolic state, which requires calories and protein to facilitate healing.

After the patient shows signs of improvement as demonstrated by normal temperature, lowering of white blood cell count and improvement in the chest film (resolution of surrounding infiltrate, reduction in the size of the cavity and absence of fluid), the antibiotic is administered orally rather than intravenously. If treatment is stopped too soon, a relapse may occur. The duration of antibiotic therapy may be from 6 to 16 weeks.

Surgical intervention is indicated only when medical therapy has been proved inadequate by failure of the cavity to resolve, by a continuing septic condition, or when major haemoptysis occurs. Pulmonary resection (lobectomy) is the procedure usually performed when there is a thick-walled abscess with purulent drainage. If the patient cannot tolerate thoracic surgery, tube thoracotomy is done.

Nursing Care

The nurse monitors the patient for any adverse effects. Chest physiotherapy is initiated as prescribed to drain the abscess. The patient is taught deep-breathing and coughing exercises to help expand the lungs. To ensure proper nutritional intake, a diet high in protein and calories is encouraged.

Emotional support is provided because the abscess may take a long time to resolve.

Patient Education

If surgery has been necessary, the patient will most likely return home before the wound closes entirely. It will be necessary to teach the patient or a caregiver how to change the dressings as needed to prevent skin excoriation and an offensive odour. Deep-breathing and coughing exercises are to be practised every two hours during the day. Postural drainage and percussion techniques are taught to a caregiver so that lung secretions can be removed. Counselling is provided for attaining and maintaining an optimal state of nutrition.

PLEURAL CONDITIONS

Pleurisy

Pleurisy (pleuritis) refers to inflammation of both the visceral and parietal pleurae. When these inflamed membranes rub together during respiration (particularly inspiration), the result is severe, sharp, 'knifelike' pain. The pain may become minimal or absent when the breath is held, or it may be localized or radiate to the shoulder or abdomen. Later, as pleural fluid develops, the pain lessens. In the early dry period, the pleural friction rub can be heard with the stethoscope, only to disappear later as fluid appears to separate the roughened pleural surfaces.

Pleurisy may develop with pneumonia or upper respiratory tract infection, tuberculosis, collagen disease, after trauma to the chest or pulmonary infarction or embolism, in primary and metastatic cancer, in the viral disease known as epidemic pleurodynia and after thoracotomy.

Careful radiographical and sputum examinations and thoracentesis with pleural fluid examination and possibly pleural biopsy are indicated in order to discover the underlying condition.

Medical Management

The objective of treatment is to discover the underlying condition causing the pleurisy. As the underlying disease is treated (pneumonia, infarction) the pleuritic inflammation usually resolves. At the same time it is necessary to watch for signs of pleural effusion, such as shortness of breath, pain and decreased local excursion of the chest wall.

Prescribed analgesics and applications of heat or cold will provide symptomatic relief. Indomethacin, an anti-inflammatory drug, may give pain relief while allowing the patient to cough effectively. If the pain is severe, a procaine intercostal block may be required.

Nursing Care

Since this patient has real pain on inspiration, the nurse can offer suggestions to enhance comfort, such as turning frequently on the affected side in order to splint the chest wall; this will lessen the stretch of the pleura. The nurse can also teach the patient to use the hands to splint the rib cage while coughing. Since pain on breathing produces anxiety, the patient will require support and understanding.

Pleural Effusion

Pleural effusion, a collection of fluid in the pleural space, is rarely a primary disease process but is usually secondary to other diseases. Normally, the pleural space may contain a small amount of fluid (5 to 15 ml) acting as a lubricant that allows the visceral and parietal surfaces to move without friction.

In certain intrathoracic and systemic diseases, fluid may accumulate in the pleural space to a point where it becomes clinically evident, and it is almost always of pathological significance. The effusion can be a relatively clear fluid, which may be a transudate or an exudate, or it can be blood, pus or chyle. A transudate (filtrates of plasma that move across intact capillary walls) occurs when factors influencing formation and reabsorption of pleural fluid are altered, usually by imbalances in hydrostatic or oncotic pressures. A transudate indicates that a condition such as ascites or a systemic disease such as heart failure or renal failure underlies the fluid accumulation. An exudate (extravasation of fluid into tissues/cavity) usually results from inflammation by bacterial products or tumours involving the pleural surfaces. In general, the differentiation is made on the basis of protein content and lactic dehydrogenase activity. Pleural effusion may be a complication of tuberculosis, pneumonia, heart failure, pulmonary viral infections and neoplastic tumours. In fact, 50 per cent of patients with cancer of the lung develop pleural effusion. In approximately one in four patients, pleural effusion is secondary to carcinoma.

Clinical Features

Usually, the clinical features are those caused by the underlying disease; pneumonia will cause fever, chills and pleuritic chest pain, whereas a malignant effusion may result in dyspnoea and coughing. A large quantity of pleural effusion will cause shortness of breath. Confirmation of the presence of fluid is obtained by chest film, ultrasound, physical examination and thoracentesis. Tests made of pleural fluid include bacterial cultures, Gram stain, acid-fast bacillus stain (for tuberculosis), red cell count, white cell count, chemistry studies (glucose, amylase, lactic dehydrogenase, protein) and pH.

Medical Management

The objectives of treatment are to discover the underlying cause to prevent fluid collection from recurring, and to relieve discomfort and dyspnoea. Specific treatment is directed to the underlying cause (e.g., heart failure, cirrhosis).

Thoracentesis is done to remove fluid, to collect a specimen for analysis and to relieve dyspnoea. However, if the underlying cause is a malignancy, the effusion may recur within a few days or weeks. Repeated thoracenteses result in pain, depletion of protein and electrolytes and sometimes pneumothorax. In this event the patient may be treated with chest tube drainage connected to a water-seal drainage system or suction to evacuate the pleural space and re-expand the lung. Sometimes drugs are instilled in the pleural space to obliterate the pleural space and prevent further accumulation of fluid. After drug instillation, the chest tube is clamped and the patient is assisted to assume various positions to ensure uniform drug distribution and to maximize drug contact with the pleural surfaces. The tube is unclamped as prescribed, and chest drainage is usually continued several days longer to prevent re-accumulation of fluid and to facilitate obliteration of the pleural space by formation of adhesions between the visceral and parietal pleurae. Other treatments for malignant pleural effusions include radiation of the chest wall, surgical pleurectomy and diuretic therapy.

If the pleural fluid is an exudate, more extensive diagnostic procedures are done in order to determine the cause. Therapy for pleural disease is then instituted.

Nursing Care

Patients will need information and support in relation to the disorder, diagnostic tests and treatment. Because the pleura is involved, there will be considerable pain; therefore, the patient is assisted to assume positions that are the least painful and pain medication is administered as prescribed and as needed. Patients may need help with certain activities of living, particularly if mobility is further restricted by a chest drain. Nursing care related to the underlying cause of the pleural effusion will be specific to that condition.

Empyema

Empyema is a collection of pus in the pleural cavity. At first the pleural fluid is thin, with a low leucocyte count, but frequently it progresses to a fibropurulent stage and finally to a stage where it encloses the lung within a thick exudative membrane.

In most instances an empyema is associated with an underlying pulmonary infection. Organisms may invade the pleural space by direct extension or as the result of the rupture of a lung abscess. An empyema may also follow thoracic surgery or penetrating wounds of the chest. The character of the exudate varies according to the infecting organism.

Clinical Features

The patient has fever, pleural pain, dyspnoea, anorexia and weight loss. If the patient has received antibiotic therapy, the clinical features may be altered. The diagnosis is established on the basis of chest films and thoracentesis.

Medical Management

The objectives of treatment are to drain the pleural cavity and to achieve full expansion of the lung. This is accomplished by adequate drainage and by appropriate antibiotics selected on the basis of the causative organism. Large doses of the drug are usually given.

Drainage of the pleural fluid or pus depends on the stage of the disease and is accomplished by:

- Needle aspiration (thoracentesis) if the fluid is not too thick.
- Closed-chest drainage using a large-diameter intercostal tube attached to water-seal drainage.
- Open drainage by means of rib resection to remove the thickened pleura, pus and debris and to resect the underlying diseased pulmonary tissue.

If the inflammation has been of long-standing, an exudate can form over the lung and interfere with its normal expansion. This will have to be removed surgically (decortication). The drainage tube is left in place until the pus-filled space is obliterated completely. The complete obliteration of the pleural space is checked radiographically, and the patient should be aware that this process may take a long time.

Nursing Care

Resolution of an empyema is a prolonged process. The nurse helps patients cope with the condition and advises them about breathing exercises (pursed lip and diaphragmatic breathing), which help to restore normal respiratory function. The nurse also provides care specific to the method of drainage of the pleural fluid.

CHRONIC OBSTRUCTIVE AIRWAYS DISEASE

Chronic obstructive airways disease is a common cause of death and disability in the United Kingdom, and is the largest single cause of absence from work (Office of Health Economics, 1977). The disorder produces long-term problems related to household management, ambulation, sleep and rest, recreation and work (Williams and Bury, 1989). Chronic obstructive airways disease is a broad classification that includes a group of conditions associated with chronic obstruction of air flow entering or leaving the lungs. Airway obstruction is diffuse airway narrowing, causing increased resistance to air flow. Included in the chronic obstructive airways disease category are chronic bronchitis, bronchiectasis, emphysema and asthma. Basically, the person with chronic obstructive airways disease has: (1) excessive secretion of mucus within the airways not due to specific causes (bronchitis or bronchiectasis); (2) an increase in the size of the air spaces distal to the terminal bronchioles with loss of alveolar walls and elastic recoil of the lungs (emphysema); and (3)

narrowing of the bronchial airways that varies in severity (asthma). As a result there is a subsequent derangement of airway dynamics—for example, loss of elasticity and obstruction of air flow. There is often an overlap of these conditions.

Chronic obstructive airways disease is likely to be a disease of genetic and environmental interaction; cigarette smoking and air pollution contribute to its development, which may occur over a 20- to 30-year span. It appears to begin fairly early in life and is a slowly progressive disorder that is present many years before the onset of clinical symptoms and impairment of pulmonary function.

► NURSING PROCESS
► THE PATIENT WITH CHRONIC OBSTRUCTIVE AIRWAYS DISEASE

► Assessment

The nurse's observations, history and recording should yield an understanding of the patient and the disorder. Data collection involves obtaining information about current symptoms as well as previous disease manifestations. The following is a list of questions that a nurse can use as a guide to obtain a clear history of the disorder:

- How long has the patient had respiratory difficulty?
- What are the pulse and the respiratory rates?
- Are the respirations even?
- Does the patient contract the abdominal muscles during inspiration?
- Does the patient have prolonged expiration?
- Are the accessory muscles of respiration used?
- Does exertion increase the dyspnoea? What type of exertion?
- What are the limits to the patient's exercise tolerance?
- Is cyanosis evident?
- Are the patient's neck veins engorged?
- Does the patient have peripheral oedema?
- Is the patient coughing?
- What is the colour, amount and consistency of the sputum?
- What is the patient's mental state?
- Is there increasing stupor or apprehension?
- At what times during the day does the patient complain most of fatigue and shortness of breath?
- Have the patient's habits of eating or sleeping been affected?
- What does the patient, the family and close friends know about the condition?
- How does the disorder affect the patient's ability to perform activities of living?
- Does the disorder limit the patient's ability to work, socialize and enjoy leisure pursuits?
- How much support is available?

► *Patient's Problems*

Based on the assessment, the patient's main problems may include the following:

- Difficulty in breathing related to ventilation-perfusion inequality, bronchoconstriction, increased mucus production, ineffective cough and bronchopulmonary infection.
- Chronic ineffective cough due to increased mucus production and bronchoconstriction, and exacerbated by bronchopulmonary infection.
- Inability to perform self-care activities due to fatigue as a consequence of the increased work of breathing and insufficient ventilation and oxygenation.
- Reduced activity tolerance related to altered respiratory function.
- Ineffective coping responses related to less socialization, denial, anxiety, depression and lower activity level.

- Dissatisfaction with life: inability to work and socialize.
- Lack of knowledge about the disorder and how to live with it.

► *Planning and Implementation*
► **Expected Outcomes**
The major goals for the patient may include a perceived improvement in breathing pattern, diminished cough, improvement in self-care activities, improvement in activity tolerance, improvement in coping ability, increase in life satisfaction and an improvement in knowledge of and ability to manage the disorder.

Nursing Care

See Nursing Care Plan 5.1, for the patient with chronic obstructive airways disease.

► NURSING CARE PLAN 5.1: CHRONIC OBSTRUCTIVE AIRWAYS DISEASE

Jack Morris is a 57-year-old bus driver who has chronic obstructive airways disease. He is married, is a nonpractising member of the Church of England and has three adult children, all of whom are also married.

Patient's problems	Expected outcomes	Nursing care	Rationale
1. Difficulty in breathing due to bronchoconstriction and ventilation–perfusion mismatch	Reports breathing is easier	1a. Encourage mobility and changes in posture 2–4 hourly	Encourages mobilization of secretions
		b. Teach and encourage deep-breathing exercises, pursed lip breathing and diaphragmatic breathing 2–4 hourly	It is reported that there is some evidence that these techniques help to relax breathing and improve the ratio of alveolar to dead space ventilation (Seaton, Seaton and Leitch, 1989)
		c. Teach about bronchodilator therapy, nebulizers, oxygen therapy. Ensure patient is able to use these appropriately	Many patients with chronic obstructive airways disease have a small but significant degree of reversible airflow obstruction
		d. Liaise with physiotherapist regarding chest physiotherapy and postural drainage	Physiotherapy has been reported to have shown a decrease in airways obstruction in patients with copious sputum (Seaton, Seaton and Leitch, 1989)
2. Chronic ineffective cough due to increased mucus production, bronchoconstriction and exacerbated by bronchopulmon- ary infection	Coughs effectively	2a. Instruct in correct coughing technique, assist to cough if necessary	Controlled coughing techniques have been reported to give subjective benefit to patients (Moser and Archibald, 1983)
		b. Instruct in diaphragmatic breathing	
		c. Encourage fluid intake of 2–2.5 litres/day unless contraindicated	Hydration helps keep secretions moist and easier to expectorate
		d. Provide sputum pot, tissues and washing facilities	
3. Risk of infection due to abnormal ciliary action and accumulation of secretions	Is free from the symptoms of infection	3a. Encourage fluid intake of 2–2.5 litres/day unless contraindicated	Hydration helps to keep secretions moist and easier to expectorate
		b. Teach early signs of infection:	Minor respiratory infections that are of no consequence to the

►

▶ NURSING CARE PLAN 5.1: CHRONIC OBSTRUCTIVE AIRWAYS DISEASE

Patient's problems	Expected outcomes	Nursing care	Rationale
		i. Increased sputum ii. Change in colour or thickness of sputum iii. Increased shortness of breath, chest tightness or fatigue iv. Increased coughing	person with normal lungs can prove fatal in those with chronic obstructive airways disease. Early detection is important so that treatment can be started
		c. Gives prophylactic antibiotic therapy as prescribed	It is reported (Seaton, Seaton and Leitch, 1989) that trials have shown a statistically significant reduction of acute exacerbations of the disorder if prophylactic antibiotics are given, especially in the winter
		d. Encourage adequate diet	There is reported to be a direct link between malnutrition and increased susceptibility to infection (Curgian and Pagano, 1985)
4. Inability to perform self-care activities due to fatigue as a consequence of the increased work of breathing and insufficient ventilation and oxygenation	Is able to perform self-care activities as desired	4a. Promote easier breathing and effective coughing (see problems 1 and 2) b. Advise to co-ordinate diaphragmatic breathing with activities c. Advise to space out activities to avoid activity directly after meals. Avoid excessive activity first thing in the morning d. Teach pursed-lip breathing e. Assist with activities until able to do them unassisted, encouraging maximum control and independence	Diaphragmatic breathing improves ventilation and removal of secretions without producing shortness of breath Bronchial secretions and oedema collect in the lungs when lying on the back overnight Pursed lip breathing slows expiration, prevents collapse of the lung and helps patient control the rate and depth of respiration, thus enabling a feeling of control and ability to carry out activity
5. Reduced activity tolerance related to altered respiratory function	Activity levels gradually improve	5a. Discuss reasoning behind reduced activity levels so patient understands why certain things can no longer be done b. Promote gradual increase in self-care activities (see problem 4) c. Promote easier breathing (see problem 1) d. Discuss and encourage long-term physical training programme	Muscles that are deconditioned consume more oxygen and place additional burden on the lungs Physical training has been shown to increase exercise capacity and diminish breathlessness (Cockcroft, Saunders and Berry, 1981; Unger, Moser and Hansen, 1980)
6. Risk of inappropriate levels of nutrition:	Is correct weight for height	6a. Encourage frequent, small, nutritious meals that patient will enjoy	

► NURSING CARE PLAN 5.1: CHRONIC OBSTRUCTIVE AIRWAYS DISEASE

Patient's problems	Expected outcomes	Nursing care	Rationale
a. Is obese as a result of inactivity, boredom, inability to shop for well-balanced meals b. Is malnourished as a result of unhealthy diet. Tissue hypoxia, increased energy expenditure on breathing, coughing and expectorating; anxiety and apathy contribute to malnutrition	Eats a healthy diet	b. Give advice about healthy eating c. Set realistic short-term goals about losing weight – advise why this is necessary d. Discuss practical ways of ensuring patient continues to have healthy diet at home	The obese have a heightened demand for ventilation, increased work of breathing and respiratory muscle inefficiency (Luce, 1980)
7. Risk of disturbed sleep pattern as a result of coughing, difficulty in breathing and the need for treatment. Inactivity, boredom and apathy may lead to an increase in daytime naps	To have satisfactory sleep pattern	7a. Assist patient to find a comfortable position b. Promote environment conducive to rest and sleep c. Promote daytime stimulation and activity d. Maintain near to normal bedtime routines e. Give medication as prescribed f. Monitor for difficulties in breathing overnight	Sjoberg (1983) considers sleep to be crucial when the lungs are damaged Hypnotics may be contraindicated in chronic obstructive airways disease The usual small changes in P_{CO_2} and P_{O_2} with deepening sleep are exaggerated in chronic lung disease (Fleetham and Kryger, 1981)
8. Ineffective coping responses related to less socialization, denial, anxiety, depression and lower activity level	Is able to cope with long-term nature of disorder	8a. Adopt a hopeful and encouraging attitude towards patient b. Ensure patient has adequate knowledge about the disorder (see problem 10) c. Teach relaxation techniques if thought to be appropriate d. Encourage patient to get involved in own care e. Carry out measures to improve activity levels (see problem 5)	There is a relationship between shortness of breath and anxiety and depression. Isolation and denial have been shown to be classic responses of patients with chronic obstructive airway diseases (Dudley, Glaser, Jorgenson and Logan, 1980) Relaxation techniques may help reduce shortness of breath and limit anxiety (Renfroe, 1988) Getting involved in own care is likely to build up self-esteen and prepares for management at home
9. Dissatisfaction with life; inability to work socialize, etc	Reports increased life satisfaction	9a. Discuss potential and actual problems – use of nursing assessment and history b. Involve family and social support systems	A consideration of the broader aspects of the quality of life has been reported to be important for delivering optimal care (Williams, 1989) Patients with chronic obstructive airways disease have been shown to experience problems

►

▶ NURSING CARE PLAN 5.1: CHRONIC OBSTRUCTIVE AIRWAYS DISEASE

Patient's problems	Expected outcomes	Nursing care	Rationale
			with household management, pastimes and work (Williams and Bury, 1989)
		c. Involve social worker as appropriate	Quality of life may influence the uptake of health care resources (Traver, 1988)
10. Lack of knowledge about the disorder and how to live with it	Demonstrates knowledge of condition Manages disorder effectively long term	10a. Give information and support regarding: i. Methods to improve breathing (see problem 1) ii. Methods to avoid infection (see problem 3)	Patients with chronic obstructive airways disease who participate in teaching sessions designed to help them manage their disorder have been shown to have fewer hospital admissions and shorter lengths of hospitalization (Howard, Davies and Roghmann, 1987)
		iii. Avoidance of potentially aggravating environment (dust, pets etc)	In some cases, the more severe the disorder, the more effective is the education (Boyer, Brough, Rasmussen and Schmidt, 1982)
		iv. Stopping smoking	The mortality for patients with chronic obstructive airways disease who smoke is higher than for those who do not (Doll and Peto, 1976)
		v. Having regular influenza vaccinations vi. Medications and treatment	
		b. Arrange for nurse to visit at home if this is thought to be appropriate	It has been shown that visits from a nurse have helped some patients with chest disorders (Heslop and Bagnall, 1988)

Improvement in Breathing Pattern

Bronchospasm, which is present in many forms of pulmonary disease, causes reduction in the calibre of the small bronchi, resulting in stasis of secretions and infection. Increased mucus production along with decreased mucociliary action contributes to further reduction in the calibre of the bronchi and results in decreased air flow and decreased gas exchange, which is aggravated by the loss of lung elasticity.

These changes in the airway demand that the nurse must frequently assess the level of dyspnoea and hypoxia in the patient. If bronchodilators are prescribed, the nurse must properly administer the medications and be alert for potential side-effects. The relief of bronchospasm is confirmed by measuring improvement in expiratory flow rates and assessing whether the patient has a reduction in dyspnoea.

Aerosol therapy helps to loosen secretions so that they can be removed. Inhaled bronchodilators are often added to the nebulizer to provide direct bronchodilator action on the airways, thereby improving gas exchange. Nebulizer treatments should be given before meals to improve lung ventilation and thus reduce the fatigue that accompanies eating. Following inhalation of nebulized bronchodilators, patients are advised to inhale moisture to further liquify secretions. Then expulsive coughing or postural drainage will aid patients in expectorating secretions. The patients are helped to do this in a manner that will not be exhausting to them.

Oxygen is given when hypoxaemia is present. The nurse must monitor the effectiveness of the oxygen therapy and ensure that patients are compliant in their use of the oxygen delivery device. The nurse advises them about the proper use of oxygen and cautions that smoking with or near oxygen is extremely dangerous. In some cases, patients may be discharged home with oxygen. Oxygen can be supplied to the home by compressed gas, liquid or concentrator systems. Portable oxygen systems are available that allow the patient to work and travel. Patient education includes reassuring the patient that oxygen is not 'addictive' and explaining the precautions involved in using oxygen (no smoking) and the necessity of having regular measurements of arterial blood gases.

Continuous oxygen therapy has been demonstrated to

prolong life for those with a PaO_2 of 55 mmHg (7.31 kPa[a]) or less on room air. Intermittent oxygen use has little value in the patient with chronic obstructive airways disease, except during an intensive exercise programme or in the form of nocturnal therapy.

Removal of Bronchial Secretions

A major goal in the treatment of chronic obstructive airways disease is to diminish the quantity and tenacity of sputum in order to improve pulmonary ventilation and gas exchange. All pulmonary irritants must be eliminated, particularly cigarette smoking, which is the most persistent source of pulmonary irritation. A high fluid intake (6 to 8 glasses) daily is encouraged to liquefy secretions. An added reason for encouraging fluid intake is the tendency for the patient to breathe through the mouth, which accelerates water loss.

Inhaling nebulized water is also helpful since it humidifies the bronchial tree, adding water to the sputum and decreasing its viscosity, so that evacuation of sputum is facilitated.

Postural drainage with percussion and vibration uses gravity to help raise secretions so that they can be coughed out or suctioned easily. When used in conjunction with bronchodilators and nebulizer therapy or an intermittent positive pressure breathing treatment, postural drainage should follow either of these therapies because drainage is facilitated after the tracheobronchial tree is dilated. The patient is advised about effective breathing and coughing to help raise the secretions. Postural drainage is usually carried out when the patient wakes up, to remove secretions that have accumulated overnight, and before the patient retires, to promote sleep. The frequency of these measures throughout the day will be dictated by the patient's needs.

Prevention of Bronchopulmonary Infection

Bronchopulmonary infections must be controlled to diminish inflammatory oedema and to permit recovery of normal ciliary action. Minor respiratory infections that are of no consequence to the person with normal lungs can produce fatal disturbances of pulmonary function in the person with chronic obstructive airways disease. The cough associated with bronchial infection introduces a vicious cycle with further trauma and damage to the lungs, further progression of symptoms, increased bronchospasm and further increase in susceptibility to bronchial infection. Infection compromises lung function and is a common cause of respiratory failure.

In chronic obstructive airways disease, infection does not manifest itself in the same way as it does elsewhere in the body. The patient is advised to report to the doctor immediately if the sputum becomes discoloured, since purulent expectoration or a change in the character, colour or amount of the sputum is evidence of infection. The patient should be taught that any worsening of the symptoms (increased tightness of the chest, increase in dyspnoea and fatigue) is also suggestive of infection and must be reported. Viral infections are hazardous to these patients because they are so often followed by infections.

Patients with chronic obstructive airways disease are prone to respiratory infections and should be immunized against influenza. During highly polluted or heavily pollinated days (in the spring) these people should avoid outdoor exposure since it may increase bronchospasm. Outdoor periods of high temperatures associated with high humidities should also be avoided.

Breathing Exercises and Retraining

Most people with chronic obstructive airways disease breathe shallowly from the upper chest in a rapid and inefficient manner. This type of upper chest breathing can be changed to diaphragmatic breathing with practice. Training in diaphragmatic breathing reduces the respiratory rate, increases alveolar ventilation and sometimes causes a reduction of functional residual capacity.

Pursed-lip breathing slows expiration, prevents collapse of lung units and helps patients to control the rate and depth of respiration and to relax, which enables them to gain control of the dyspnoea and feelings of panic.

Patients with chronic obstructive airways disease have definite periods of the day when exercise tolerance is decreased. This is especially true on arising in the morning, because bronchial secretions and oedema collect in the lungs during the night while patients are lying on their back. Male patients will often be unable to shave or wash. Activities requiring the arms to be supported above the level of the thorax may produce distress. These activities may be tolerated better after patients have been up and moving around for an hour or more. Because of these limitations, patients participate in planning their care with the nurse and in determining the best time for bathing and shaving. A hot beverage on arising, along with diaphragmatic breathing, will assist them to expectorate and will shorten the period of disability experienced on arising.

Another period of increased disability occurs immediately after meals, particularly the evening meal. Fatigue from the day's activities coupled with abdominal distension limits their exercise tolerance. The chief complaint by patients at this time is likely to be fatigue or dyspnoea.

Once patients have learned diaphragmatic breathing, an inspiratory muscle trainer may be employed to help strengthen the muscles used in breathing. This device requires that patients breathe against a resistance. The resistance is gradually increased and the muscles become better conditioned. Conditioning of the respiratory muscles takes a long time, and patients are asked to continue practising at home.

Self-Care Activities

As gas exchange, airway clearance and the breathing

pattern improve, patients are encouraged to assume some of their own care. They are taught to try to co-ordinate diaphragmatic breathing with activities such as walking, bathing, bending or climbing stairs. They should begin to bathe themselves, dress themselves and take short walks, resting as needed to avoid fatigue and excessive dyspnoea. Fluids should be readily available, and patients should be aware of the significance of maintaining fluid intake. If patients will be using postural drainage at home, they are advised and supervised by the nurse before discharge.

Physical Conditioning

Physical conditioning techniques include breathing and general physical conditioning exercises intended to conserve and increase pulmonary ventilation. There is a close relationship between physical fitness and respiratory fitness. Graded exercises and physical conditioning programmes employing treadmills, stationary bicycles and measured level walks have been shown to improve symptoms and to increase work capacity and exercise tolerance. It is useful for patients to have a physical activity that they can do on a regular, sustained basis. A lightweight portable oxygen system is available for the ambulatory patient who requires oxygen therapy during physical activity to improve hypoxia. This type of rehabilitation improves the quality of life.

Coping Measures

Any factor that interferes with normal breathing quite naturally induces anxiety, depression and changes in behaviour. Many patients find the slightest exertion exhausting. Constant shortness of breath and fatigue may render the patient irritable and apprehensive to the point of panic. Enforced inactivity (and possibly reversal of family/interpersonal roles owing to loss of employment), the frustration of having to work to breathe and the realization that they face a prolonged, unrelenting disease may cause patients to react with anger, depression and demanding behaviour. Sexual ability may be compromised, which also diminishes self-esteem.

It is important for the nurse and other health care staff to adopt a cautiously hopeful and encouraging attitude and keep patients active up to their level of symptom tolerance. Emphasis should be on controlling symptoms and increasing self-esteem and the sense of mastery and of well-being. Supportive medical and nursing care, ongoing patient teaching, exercise conditioning and possibly group therapy sessions help to relieve somewhat an almost overwhelming burden.

The patient should also be directed to support groups and to patients with a similar disorder. These will help to improve patients' knowledge of the condition, their ability to cope with the disease and their sense of self-worth.

Patient Education

Patients with chronic obstructive airways disease who participate in teaching sessions designed to enable them to manage their disorder have fewer hospital admissions and shorter stays (Howard, Davies and Roghmann, 1987). To help patients with chronic obstructive airways disease to live better, it is essential that they are educated about their disorder. One of the major teaching factors is helping patients accept realistic short-term and long-range goals. If they are severely disabled, the objective of treatment is to preserve their present pulmonary function and relieve their symptoms as much as possible. If their disease is mild, the objective is to increase their exercise tolerance and prevent further loss of pulmonary function. Patients have to be told what to expect. They and those caring for them need patience to achieve these goals.

Patients are advised to avoid extremes of heat and cold. Heat increases the body temperature, thereby raising the oxygen requirements of the body; cold tends to promote bronchospasm. High altitudes aggravate the hypoxia. Bronchospasm may also be initiated by air pollutants such as fumes, smoke, dust, and even talcum, lint and aerosol sprays.

Protection of the lung is basic for the preservation of lung function. Patients with chronic obstructive airways disease should be informed unequivocally that, for them, smoking is dangerous. Cigarette smoking depresses the activity of scavenger cells and affects the ciliary cleansing mechanism of the respiratory tract, the function of which is to keep the breathing passages free of inhaled irritants, bacteria and other foreign matter. Their is one of the major defence mechanisms of the body. When this cleansing mechanism is damaged by smoking, air flow is obstructed and air becomes trapped behind the obstructed airway. The air sacs greatly distend and the lung capacity is diminished. Cigarette smoking also irritates the goblet cells and mucous glands, causing an increased accumulation of mucus. The mucus accumulation produces more irritation, infection and damage to the lung capacity. Frequently, patients are unaware of what is happening until they notice that extra physical effort produces respiratory distress. At this point the damage may be irreversible. Therefore, patients with chronic obstructive airways disease should definitely refrain from smoking. There is a wide variety of smoking control strategies, including prevention, cessation and behaviour modification. (Unfortunately, not all patients are capable of stopping smoking completely.)

Patients with chronic obstructive airways disease should restrict themselves to a life of moderate activity, ideally in a climate with minimal shifts in temperature and humidity. Stress situations that might trigger a coughing episode or emotional disturbance should be avoided.

Patients should be directed to community resources such as pulmonary rehabilitation programmes, smoking cessation programmes and other programmes to help improve their ability to cope with their chronic condition and their therapeutic regime and to give them a sense of worth, hope and well-being.

▶ *Evaluation*
▶ **Expected Outcomes**

1. Patient demonstrates improved breathing.
   a. Recognizes need for bronchodilators and for taking them on time.
   b. Demonstrates ability to use and clean respiratory therapy equipment.
   c. Uses oxygen equipment appropriately.
   d. Shows stable arterial blood gas values (but not necessarily normal due to chronic changes in gas exchange capability of the lung).
   e. States that 6 to 8 glasses of fluids per day are needed.
   f. Understands that pollens, fumes, gases, dusts and extremes of temperature and humidity are respiratory irritants to be avoided.
   g. Stops smoking.
   h. Performs postural drainage correctly and reports that caregiver can do percussion/vibration.
   i. Coughs less.
   j. Knows signs of early infection and need to notify general practitioner at earliest sign of infection.
   k. Is free of infection on discharge.
   l. Recognizes need to stay away from crowds and people with colds during the influenza season.
   m. Plans to discuss influenza and pneumonia vaccines with their general practitioner to help prevent infection.
   n. Practises pursed-lip and diaphragmatic breathing and uses them during activity and when short of breath.
   o. Shows signs of decreased respiratory effort and reports feeling less short of breath.
2. Performs self-care activities.
   a. Paces activities of daily living with alternate rest periods to reduce fatigue and dyspnoea.
   b. Uses controlled breathing while bathing, bending to tie shoes and so on.
   c. Knows about personal energy conservation.
3. Achieves activity tolerance.
   a. Performs activities with less shortness of breath.
   b. Recognizes need to exercise daily and demonstrates an exercise plan to be carried out at home.
   c. Walks and gradually increases walking time and distance to improve physical conditioning.
4. Acquires effective coping mechanisms.
   a. Discusses activities or methods to ease shortness of breath.
   b. Has realistic expectations for the future.
5. Adheres to therapeutic programme.
   a. Is able to list those factors that improve their condition as well as those that make their condition worse.
   b. Recognizes the need to preserve existing lung function by adhering to treatment and rehabilitation programme.

Chronic Bronchitis

Clinical Features and Altered Physiology

The defining characteristic of chronic bronchitis is a productive cough that lasts for three months a year for two successive years. In chronic bronchitis, excessive mucus secretion and dyspnoea are associated with recurring infections of the lower respiratory tract and often with reduced ability to ventilate the lungs. The patient's major problem is the protracted and abundant production of inflammatory exudate that fills and obstructs the bronchioles and is responsible for a persistent, productive cough and shortness of breath. This constant irritation causes hypertrophy of mucus-secreting glands, goblet cell hyperplasia and increased mucus production, leading to bronchial plugging and bronchial narrowing. Alveoli adjacent to the bronchioles may become damaged and fibrosed. Further bronchial narrowing follows as a result of these fibrotic changes in the airways. In time, irreversible lung changes may occur, with resultant emphysema or bronchiectasis.

A wide range of viral, bacterial and mycoplasmal infections can produce acute episodes of bronchitis. Bronchitis is encountered in people who smoke heavily or are exposed to air pollutants that produce abnormal secretion of mucus and impair ciliary function. Hereditary factors and reaction to allergens also play a part in its development. Exacerbations of chronic bronchitis are most likely to occur during the winter. The inhalation of cold air produces bronchospasm in sensitive people. Progressive bronchitis will almost invariably result in chronic obstructive airways disease.

Preventive Measures

Because of the disabling nature of chronic bronchitis, every effort is directed toward its prevention. An important feature is the avoidance of respiratory irritants (particularly tobacco smoke). People who are prone to respiratory tract infections should be immunized against common viral agents. All patients with acute upper respiratory tract infections should receive proper treatment, including antibiotic therapy based on cultures and sensitivity studies at the first sign of purulent sputum.

Medical Management

The main objectives of treatment are to maintain the patency of the peripheral bronchial tree, to facilitate removal of bronchial exudates and to prevent disability. Changes in the sputum pattern (nature, colour, amount, thickness) and in the cough pattern are important signs to note. Recurrent bacterial infections are treated with antibiotic therapy after the completion of culture and sensitivity studies.

To facilitate the removal of bronchial exudates, bronchodilators are prescribed to relieve bronchospasm and reduce airway obstruction; thus, gas distribution and entilation are improved. Postural drainage and cussion following treatments are usually helpful. given orally or parenterally if bronchospasm is severe) is an important part of therapy, since proper hydration helps the patient cough up secretions. Steroid therapy may be used when the patient fails to respond to more conservative measures, but its use is still controversial. When there is an underlying bronchiectasis, postural drainage is most important. The patient should stop smoking because smoke inhalation causes bronchoconstriction, paralysis of ciliary activity and inactivation of surfactant. Smokers are also more susceptible to bronchial infection.

Bronchiectasis

Bronchiectasis is a chronic dilation of the bronchi and bronchioles. Bronchial dilation may be caused by a variety of conditions, including pulmonary infections and obstruction of the bronchus, aspiration of foreign bodies, vomit or material from the upper respiratory tract, and extrinsic pressure from tumours, dilated blood vessels and enlarged lymph nodes. A person may be predisposed to bronchiectasis as a result of respiratory infection in early childhood, measles, influenza, tuberculosis and immunoglobulin A (IgA) deficiency. Following surgery, bronchiectasis may develop when the patient's cough is ineffective, with the result that mucus obstructs the bronchus and leads to atelectasis.

Altered Physiology

The infection damages the bronchial wall, causing loss of its supporting structure and producing thick sputum that may ultimately obstruct the bronchi. The walls become permanently distended by severe coughing. The infection extends to the peribronchial tissues, so that in the case of saccular bronchiectasis, each dilated tube virtually amounts to a lung abscess, the exudate of which drains freely through the bronchus. The lower lobes are most frequently involved.

The retention of secretions and obstruction ultimately lead to collapse of the distally situated lung (atelectasis). Inflammatory scarring or fibrosis replaces functioning lung tissue. In time the patient develops respiratory insufficiency with reduced vital capacity, decreased ventilation and an increased ratio of residual volume to total lung capacity. There is impaired mixing of inspired gas (ventilation–perfusion imbalance) and hypoxaemia.

Clinical Features

Characteristic symptoms of bronchiectasis include chronic cough and the production of purulent sputum in copious amounts. A high percentage of patients with this disease experience haemoptysis. Clubbing of the fingers is also very common. Patients are likely to be subject to repeated episodes of pulmonary infection.

Medical Management

The objectives of treatment are to prevent and control infection and to promote bronchial drainage to rid the affected portion of the lung(s) of excessive secretions. Infection is controlled with antibiotic therapy. Patients may be put on a year-round regime of antibiotics, alternating types of drugs at intervals.

Postural drainage of the bronchial tubes underlies all treatment considerations because draining the bronchiectatic areas by gravity reduces the amount of secretions and the degree of infection. (Sometimes mucopurulent sputum must be removed by bronchoscopy.) The affected chest area may be percussed or 'cupped' to assist in raising secretions.

Patients are started out with short periods of postural drainage and the time is increased steadily. Bronchodilators may be given to persons who also have obstructive airway disease. Patients with bronchiectasis almost always have associated bronchitis. Beta-sympathomimetics may be used for bronchodilation and to increase the mucociliary transport of secretions.

To make sputum expectoration easier, the water content of the sputum is increased by aerosolized nebulizer treatments and by an increase in oral fluid intake.

Surgical intervention may be indicated for the patient who continues to expectorate fairly large amounts of sputum and experience repeated bouts of pneumonia and hemoptysis in spite of a successful treatment regime, provided the disease involves only one or two areas of the lung that can be removed without producing respiratory insufficiency.

Patient Education

Patients are taught diaphragmatic breathing and postural drainage exercises. They are encouraged to have regular dental care and to avoid all pulmonary irritants (cigarette smoke, noxious fumes). They should monitor their sputum and report any change in its character or quantity. A decrease in sputum production is as significant as is an increase. An important preventive aspect is immunization against influenza and pneumococcal pneumonia.

Pulmonary Emphysema

Pulmonary emphysema is a complex and destructive lung disease characterized by destruction of the alveoli, enlargement of air spaces and loss of airway support by the lung parenchyma. It appears to be the end stage of a process that has slowly progressed for many years. In fact, by the time the patient develops symptoms, pulmonary function is often irreversibly impaired.

Cigarette smoking is the major cause of emphysema. However, in a small percentage of patients there is a familial predisposition to emphysema associated with a plasma protein abnormality. The genetically susceptible person is sensitive to environmental influences (smoking, air pollution, infectious agents, allergens) and, in time, develops chronic obstructive symptoms. It is imperative that the carriers of this genetic defect be identified to permit genetic counselling, and that the environmental factors be modified to delay or prevent overt symptoms of disease.

Altered Physiology
In emphysema the major site of obstruction is the airways which become plugged with mucus and narrowed from inflammation. In later stages the obstruction is caused by loss of the supporting tissues of the airway (elasticity of the lung), which causes the bronchioles to collapse during expiration. The smaller air passages dilate and the alveoli fuse together, resulting in a loss of normal lung elasticity and an increase in dead space. Interference with alveolar ventilation may occur if there is bronchial obstruction or uneven expansion of the lungs with poor air distribution.

The person with emphysema has a chronic obstruction (marked increase in airway resistance) to the inflow and outflow of air from the lungs. The lungs are in a state of chronic hyperexpansion. In order to get air into and out of the lungs, negative pressure is required during inspiration and an adequate level of positive pressure must be attained and maintained during expiration. The rest position is one of inflation. Instead of being an involuntary passive act, expiration becomes a muscular active act. The patient becomes increasingly short of breath, the chest becomes rigid and the ribs are fixed at their joints. The 'barrel chest' of many of these patients is due to loss of lung elasticity in the presence of the continued tendency of the chest wall to expand (Figure 5.1). In some instances the barrel chest is due to kyphosis. Some patients bend forward to breathe, using the accessory muscles of respiration. There is also retraction of the supraclavicular fossae on inspiration (see Figure 5.1B). In advanced disease there is also contraction of the abdominal muscles on inspiration. There is a progressive reduction of the vital capacity. Full deflation becomes increasingly difficult and finally impossible. The total vital capacity may be normal, but the one-second vital capacity is low. The patient moves air more slowly and inefficiently and has to work hard to do it. Alveolar integrity begins to break down. As the walls of the alveoli are destroyed (a process accelerated by recurrent infections), the alveolar–capillary surface area continually decreases. In late stages of the disease there is interference with carbon dioxide elimination, and the increased carbon dioxide tension in arterial blood (called hypercapnia) causes respiratory acidosis. There is also impairment of oxygen diffusion resulting in hypoxaemia.

As the alveolar walls continue to rupture, the pulmonary capillary bed is reduced. The pulmonary blood flow is increased and the right ventricle is forced to maintain a higher blood pressure in the pulmonary artery. Thus, right-sided heart failure (cor pulmonale) is one of the complications of emphysema. The presence of leg oedema (dependent oedema), distended neck veins or pain in the region of the liver suggests the development of cardiac failure.

Secretions are increased and retained, since the person is unable to make a forceful cough to expel them. Chronic and acute infections thus take hold in the emphysematous lungs, adding to the air transfer problem.

Clinical Features
Dyspnoea is the presenting symptom in emphysema and has an insidious onset. Patients usually have a history of cigarette smoking and a long history of chronic cough, wheezing and increasing shortness of breath, especially with respiratory infection. In time even the slightest exertion, such as bending over to tie their shoelaces, produces dyspnoea and fatigue (exertional dyspnoea). The emphysematous lung is not contracted on expiration, and the bronchioles are not effectively emptied of their secretions.

Patients readily develop inflammatory reactions and infections owing to the pooling of these secretions. After these infections, patients experience a prolonged wheezing expiration. Anorexia, weight loss and weakness are common complaints.

Diagnosis
The patient's symptoms and the clinical findings on physical examination provide the initial clues to the

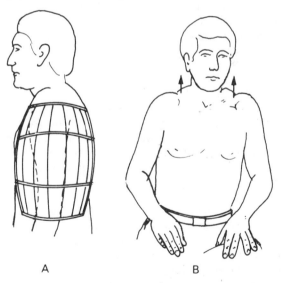

A   B

Figure 5.1 Comparison of typical findings in the patient with pulmonary emphysema. (A) The common 'barrel chest' condition of the patient with emphysema, showing characteristic increase of anteroposterior diameter. (B) Another posture of the patient with emphysema, showing elevation of shoulder girdle and retraction of the supraclavicular fossae on inspiration.

patient's problem. Other aids in diagnosis include chest films, pulmonary function tests (particularly spirometry) and blood gas studies (to assess ventilatory function and pulmonary gas exchange).

Medical Management

The major objectives of treatment are to improve the quality of life, to slow the progression of the disease process and to treat the obstructed airways to relieve hypoxia. The therapeutic approach includes: (1) treatment measures designed to improve ventilation and decrease the work of breathing; (2) prevention and prompt treatment of infection; (3) the use of physiotherapy techniques to conserve and increase pulmonary ventilation; (4) maintenance of proper environmental conditions to facilitate breathing; (5) supportive and psychological care; and (6) an ongoing programme of patient education and rehabilitation.

Bronchodilators

Bronchodilators are prescribed to dilate the airways, because they combat both bronchial mucosal oedema and muscular spasm and help in reducing airway obstruction and improving gas exchange. Bronchodilators may produce unwanted side-effects, which include tachycardia, cardiac arrhythmias and central nervous system excitation. The drug dosage is carefully adjusted for each patient in accordance with their tolerance and clinical response.

Aerosol Therapy

Aerosolization (the process of dispensing particles in a fine mist) of saline bronchodilators and mucolytics is frequently used to aid in bronchodilatation. The particle size in the aerosol mist must be small enough to allow the medication to be deposited deep within the tracheobronchial tree.

Nebulized aerosols relieve bronchospasm, decrease mucosal oedema, and liquefy bronchial secretions. This facilitates the process of bronchial clearance, helps to control the inflammatory process and improves ventilatory function. Nebulizer treatments driven with oxygen must be given with extreme caution in patients who have chronically elevated carbon dioxide tensions and are breathing on hypoxic stimuli.

Superimposed Infection

Patients with emphysema are susceptible to lung infections and must be treated at the earliest signs of infection. An antimicrobial regime is helpful in treating recurrent episodes of purulent bronchitis and appears to shorten the course of fever and cough. Steroids may be prescribed in selected patients with severe disease.

Removal of Secretions

Removal of secretions is achieved through chest physiotherapy to facilitate drainage of accumulated secretions and tracheal suctioning when patients are unable to cough up their secretions. Bronchoscopic removal of secretions may be necessary occasionally for the patient who is unable to cough and raise sputum. For the patient who

develops acute respiratory failure, endotracheal intubation or tracheostomy may be indicated to permit more effective suctioning of secretions, to prevent mucus plugging and to provide ventilatory assistance.

Oxygenation

Alterations in the level of oxygen in the arterial blood results in hypoxaemia in patients with severe emphysema. When present, low concentrations of oxygen are administered during acute episodes to correct the hypoxaemia. The amount and duration of oxygen is determined by the periodic measurement of arterial blood gas. For certain patients with advanced emphysema, continuous low-flow oxygen is used. This modality of treatment may alleviate patients' symptoms and improve their quality of life, and usually involves long-term home use of oxygen.

Asthma

Asthma is an intermittent, reversible, obstructive airway disease characterized by increased responsiveness of the trachea and bronchi to various stimuli. This results in narrowing of the airways, causing dyspnoea. This narrowing of the airway changes in degree, either spontaneously or because of therapy. Asthma differs from other obstructive lung diseases in that it is a reversible process, and patients may exhibit no symptoms for a prolonged period of time.

Asthma can begin at any age; about half of the cases develop in childhood and another third before the age of 40. General surveys of random samples of adult British populations indicate that the current prevalence of diagnosed asthma is about 2 to 6 per cent (Seaton, Seaton and Leitch, 1989). Although asthma is rarely fatal, it affects school attendance, occupational choices, physical activity and many other aspects of life.

Asthma is often characterized as extrinsic (allergic), intrinsic (idiopathic or nonallergic) or mixed (both factors):

Extrinsic asthma is caused by a known allergen or allergens (e.g., dust, pollens, animals, food). Patients with extrinsic asthma usually have a family history of allergies and a past medical history of eczema or allergic rhinitis. Exposure to the allergen triggers an asthmatic attack. Children with extrinsic asthma often outgrow the condition by adolescence.

Intrinsic asthma is not related to specific allergens. Factors such as a common cold, respiratory tract infections, exercise, emotions and environmental pollutants may trigger an attack. Aspirin or other nonsteroidal anti-inflammatory drugs may also be a factor. The attacks of intrinsic asthma become more severe and frequent with time and can progress to chronic bronchitis and emphysema. Some patients will develop mixed asthma.

Mixed asthma is the most common form of asthma. It has characteristics of both the extrinsic and the intrinsic forms.

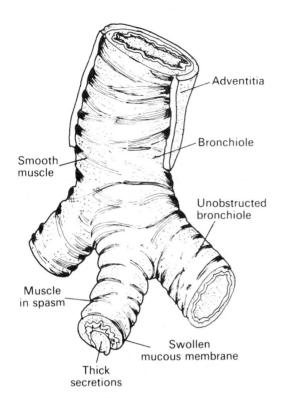

Figure 5.2 Obstruction of a bronchiole in asthma.

Altered Physiology

Asthma is a reversible diffuse airway obstruction. The obstruction is caused by one or more of three developments: (1) contraction of muscles surrounding the bronchi, which narrows the airway; (2) swelling of membranes that line the bronchi; and (3) filling of the bronchi with thick mucus (Figure 5.2). In addition, there is bronchial muscle enlargement, mucous gland enlargement, thick, tenacious sputum and hyperinflation or air trapping in the alveoli. The exact mechanism for these changes is not known, but most of what is known involves the immunological system and the autonomic nervous system.

Some people with asthma develop exaggerated immunoglobulin E (IgE) antibody responses to their environments. This means that abnormally large amounts of IgE are produced in response to certain antigens and allergens. The IgE antibodies then attach to mast cells, which are found in the lung. Re-exposure to the antigen results in the antigen's binding to the antibody. This causes the release of mast cell products (called mediators) such as histamine, bradykinin and prostaglandins and of the slow-reacting substance of anaphylaxis (SRS-A). The release of these mediators in the lung tissue affects the smooth muscle and glands of the airway, causing bronchospasm, mucous membrane swelling and excessive mucus production.

The autonomic nervous system innervates the lung.

Bronchial muscle tone is regulated by vagal nerve impulses via the parasympathetic system. In intrinsic asthma, when the nerve endings in the airway are stimulated by such factors as infection, exercise, cold, smoking, emotions and pollutants, an increased amount of acetylcholine is released. This can directly cause bronchoconstriction as well as stimulate the production of the chemical mediators discussed above. A proposed theory is that people with asthma have a low tolerance for parasympathetic responses.

In addition, - and ß-adrenergic receptors of the sympathetic nervous system are located in the bronchi. When the -adrenergic receptors are stimulated, bronchoconstriction occurs; bronchodilation occurs when the ß-adrenergic receptors are stimulated. The balance between - and ß-receptors is controlled primarily by cyclic adenosine monophosphate (cyclic AMP). Alpha-receptor stimulation results in a decrease in cyclic adenosine monophosphate, which leads to an increase in mast cell release of chemical mediators and bronchoconstriction. Beta-receptor stimulation results in increased levels of cyclic adenosine monophosphate, which inhibits release of chemical mediators and causes bronchodilation. A proposed theory is that ß-adrenergic blockade occurs in people with asthma. Consequently, asthmatics are prone to an increased release of chemical mediators and constriction of smooth muscle.

Clinical Features

It is interesting to note that cough may be the only symptom in some patients with asthma. In others, in addition to contraction of smooth muscles, there is oedema of the bronchial mucosa and production of excess mucus.

The asthmatic attack starts suddenly with coughing and a sensation of tightness in the chest. Then slow, laborious, wheezy breathing begins. Expiration is always much more strenuous and prolonged than inspiration, which forces the patient to sit upright and use every accessory muscle of respiration. Obstructed air flow creates the sensation of dyspnoea. The person becomes blue from hypoxia and breaks out into a profuse sweat; the pulse is weak; the extremities are cold; there may be fever, and, occasionally, pain, nausea, vomiting and diarrhoea. The cough at first is tight and dry, but it soon becomes more violent; a distinctive sputum of thin mucus containing small, round, gelatinous masses is coughed up with much difficulty. The attack may last from 30 minutes to several hours. Under certain circumstances, the attack may subside spontaneously. Such attacks are rarely fatal. However, occasionally 'status asthmaticus' occurs, in which therapeutic measures fail and the patient has repeated attacks or continuous asthma. This condition is life-threatening.

Related Reactions

Allergic reactions related to asthma include eczema (present at some time during life in 75 per cent of patients with asthma), urticaria and angioneurotic oedema (present in 50 per cent of patients). Emotional stress may bring on an attack in those who are susceptible, just as any other organ system in the body may be stimulated by psychic factors. However, rarely are emotions the sole cause of asthma.

Diagnosis

A clear history of hypersensitivity (at home or at work) to some known substance that may be inhaled or ingested, such as a pollen, a particular type of food, feathers, animal hair or face powder, or a history suggesting the probability of such a sensitivity is very important in determining the type and cause of asthma present in any given patient. The close association of the attacks with allergic rhinitis, together with the discovery, during the attack, of marked pallor and swelling of the nasal mucous membrane, aids in establishing the case as one of extrinsic allergic asthma (Table 5.1). The finding of an abnormally high count of eosinophilic cells in the blood or the sputum tends to confirm this diagnostic impression. Blood gas evaluation and simple spirometry are useful in evaluating gas exchange and providing baseline data that assist in identifying dangerous hypoxaemia and respiratory acidosis.

Physical exertion may induce acute bronchospasm in most patients with asthma. The key factor appears to be heat loss from the respiratory tract induced by hyperventilation. Inhalation of cold air during exercise rapidly increases bronchoconstriction, whereas warm, humid air does not.

With more industries releasing chemical irritants in the work place or into the environment, the asthmogenic result is increasingly apparent. Common air pollutants can depress pulmonary function. People exposed to grains and wood dusts often show symptoms of respiratory irritation and allergic reaction. Certain drugs, such as aspirin, indomethacin and related anti-inflammatory agents, may trigger asthmatic attacks.

In patients who do not have obvious clinical manifestations, testing in a pulmonary function laboratory can usually provide objective evidence of airway obstruction.

Often a diagnosis is confirmed by asking the patient to inhale a trial aerosol bronchodilator (during a coughing episode). If the wheezing is caused by bronchitis, the cough is not relieved; if the underlying cause is asthma, the cough is relieved. An even more effective diagnostic aid is the monitoring of peak expiratory flow rate. Since this is a simple test, patients can be asked to monitor their own flow rates.

Prevention

In every patient with recurrent asthma, evidence should be sought that might implicate a foreign protein to which patients are hypersensitive and which might precipitate the attacks. If attacks occur chiefly at night, when patients are in bed, skin tests are conducted with material from the mattress and pillows. If the test results are positive, then a mattress and pillow made from other materials are substituted. If attacks appear to be associated with the presence of a particular species of animal, such as a horse or a cat, similar skin tests are made with an antigen composed of hair or skin scrapings from the animal concerned. A seasonal incidence of attacks in a patient suggests an airborne allergen as the chief aetiological agent. In such cases, therapy may be attempted with pollen extracts. Air

Table 5.1 *Comparison of extrinsic and intrinsic asthma*

Extrinsic (allergic)	Intrinsic (infectious)
Age at onset 3 to 35	Under 3, over 35 or 40
Symptoms Season or perennial, frequently pollen or mould related	Worse in winter, exacerbated by cold air, air pollution and primarily by infection
Mucus Clear and foamy	Thick and white or discoloured
Family history of atopy Positive	No greater than in general population
Skin tests Positive and correlating	Negative or positive noncorrelating
Serum IgE High or normal	Normal
Response to therapy Good response to immunotherapy and bronchodilators	Poor response to bronchodilators; no response to immunotherapy

(Patterson, R. (ed.) (1985) Allergic Diseases (3rd edition), J. B. Lippincott, Philadelphia.)

conditioning offers possibilities in the prevention of attacks, depending on the extent to which patients can restrict their lives to air-conditioned rooms during the pollen season. A complete change of climatic environment to a locality with different flora during that period is the most satisfactory solution, when feasible.

Exercise-induced asthma can be prevented by inspiring air at 37C (body temperature) and 100 per cent relative humidity. Covering the nose and mouth with a mask necessitates rebreathing expired air that has been warmed and moistened by its passage through the respiratory tract. A simple face mask is an inexpensive, practical method for asthmatic ball players, runners and skiers.

Associated Psychological Aspects

People with asthma may perceive themselves as being chronically disabled. Inability to perform social, school or work commitments as they would wish may lead to depression and other inappropriate coping responses. Patients need to be given every opportunity to manage their own disorder and be given the information and support to enable them to have realistic expectations.

It is important to remember that asthmatic attacks, once started, may indicate that the patient will be susceptible to repeated attacks. In some patients, attacks may be induced by suggestion alone. Good general physical and mental health is most important.

Complications of Asthma

The acute asthmatic attack *per se* is seldom serious; however, death occasionally occurs as a result of respiratory exhaustion, which is particularly possible if sedatives are administered too freely.

Complications of asthma include pneumothorax; mediastinal or subcutaneous emphysema; chronic and recurrent acute bronchitis; bronchiectasis; pulmonary hypertension; and hypertrophy of the right side of the heart with right-sided heart failure (pulmonary heart disease). Chronic hypoxia due to these complications leads to symptoms and personality changes.

Medication to dilate the bronchioles is used in both prevention and treatment of asthma. Categories of bronchodilators usually prescribed include the xanthine derivatives; the sympathomimetics; and steroids, which moderate the inflammatory response.

In an acute attack, the sympathetic drugs and the theophyllines are used. Adrenaline is given initially. If this does not help, intravenous aminophylline is started. Status asthmaticus does not respond readily to the theophyllines and sympathomimetics. Administration of intravenous corticosteroids is necessary. In patients with chronic asthma or frequent attacks, continuous therapy is indicated. The same combination of medications is prescribed; sometimes oral steroids are added.

Sedatives or tranquillizers are administered to calm the anxious patient who is not in danger of developing respiratory failure. Antibiotics are prescribed if an infection occurs. Patients with extrinsic (allergic) asthma may undergo treatment to reduce their sensitivity to the allergens.

Airway obstruction, particularly during acute episodes, often results in hypoxaemia, requiring the administration of oxygen and the monitoring of arterial blood gases. The administration of fluids is also important because people with asthma are frequently dehydrated from diaphoresis and the insensible fluid loss of hyperventilation.

Breathing exercises along with postural drainage and aerosol therapy are prescribed in order to aid in removing retained secretions. Intermittent positive pressure breathing is not advocated for acute asthma attacks. If the patient's condition worsens to the point of acute respiratory failure, intubation and mechanical ventilation will be necessary.

Patients with acute asthma attacks are likely to be extremely anxious that their normal methods of managing the disorder appear to be failing. They may be experiencing a sense of loss of control and a fear of death. Relatives are likely to be distressed at seeing them in such difficulty, and feel unable to help. A calm, informative approach is needed by those involved in caring for such patients in order to minimize anxiety and help alleviate the symptoms. Once the attack has subsided, patients will need to understand the significance of what has happened so that they can continue to live with their disorder with an optimistic outlook.

Status Asthmaticus

Status asthmaticus is severe asthma that is unresponsive to conventional therapy and lasts longer than 24 hours. A vicious self-perpetuating cycle may occur as a result of infection, anxiety, overuse of tranquillizers, nebulizer abuse, dehydration, increased ß-adrenergic block and nonspecific irritants. An acute episode may sometimes be precipitated by hypersensitivity to aspirin.

Altered Physiology

A combination of factors, including constriction of the bronchiolar smooth muscle, swelling of bronchial mucosa and thickened (inspissated) secretions, contribute to one pathological problem—a decrease in the diameter of the bronchi. Another problem is the ventilation–perfusion abnormality that results from hypoxaemia and respiratory acidosis or alkalosis.

There is a reduced PaO_2, and an initial respiratory alkalosis with a decreased $PaCO_2$ and an increased pH. As the severity of status asthmaticus increases, the $PaCO_2$ increases and the pH falls, reflecting respiratory acidosis.

Clinical Features

Breathing is laboured, with a greater effort made on exhalation. The neck veins and even the face veins become engorged. Expelled air escapes with a wheeze; however, the amount of wheezing does not correlate with the severity of the attack. With greater obstruction, the wheeze may disappear.

Diagnosis

The rising P_{CO_2} suggests progressive pulmonary failure and requires aggressive drug intervention and other therapeutic measures to prevent death from respiratory failure. Therefore, blood gas determinations are an important guide to the severity of the condition and offer a reliable method of checking the patient's response to therapy.

Medical Management

Treatment is best given in an intensive care unit. Frequent serum electrolyte determinations are made to guide proper electrolyte therapy. Aminophylline is administered intravenously or at six-hourly intervals until adequate theophylline levels in the blood serum are reached.

To treat dyspnoea, cyanosis and hypoxaemia, oxygen therapy is initiated on low-flow humidified oxygen, either by Venturi mask or nasal catheter. The amount is determined following blood gas determinations. The P_{aO_2} is kept between 65 and 85 mmHg (8.64 to 11.30 kPaª).

Corticosteroids are also prescribed to restore bronchial reactivity. Mucolytic agents are effective after bronchodilation has occurred. Cough suppressants and sedatives are avoided. If symptoms suggest the presence of an infection, antibiotics are given.

Nursing Care

Signs of dehydration are assessed by checking skin turgor. Fluid intake is essential to combat dehydration, to loosen secretions and to facilitate expectoration. Intravenous fluids are administered as prescribed up to 3 to 4 litres a day.

Constant monitoring of patients is important for the first 12 to 24 hours, or until status asthmaticus is halted. When it is necessary to question them, the nurse should try to phrase the questions so that patients can answer in only one or two words. The room should be quiet and free of respiratory irritants, including flowers and cigarette smoke. Patients should have a nonallergenic pillow.

Mechanical assistance for breathing may be required when maximum medical therapy fails. Volume-cycled respirators are preferable to pressure-cycled ventilators, because large tidal volumes are necessary to overcome airway resistance. During mechanical ventilation, patients' cardiac function and blood gas values must be monitored carefully to avoid such complications as heart failure and pneumothorax.

Patient Education

Patient education is an important part of post-hospital care

if recurrences are to be kept to a minimum. Bronchodilators may be required on an 'around-the-clock' basis. Certain medications can be increased when asthmatic attacks occur. Adequate hydration must be maintained at home to keep secretions from thickening. Patients need to recognize that infection is to be avoided, since it can trigger an attack.

PULMONARY HYPERTENSION

Pulmonary hypertension is a condition that is not clinically evident until late in its disease progression. Pulmonary hypertension exists when the pulmonary arterial pressure exceeds 30 mmHg systolic, 10 mmHg diastolic and 15 mmHg mean pressure. These pressures, however, cannot be measured indirectly as can systemic blood pressure, but must be measured during right-sided heart catheterization. In the absence of these measurements, clinical recognition becomes the only indicator for the presence of pulmonary hypertension. There are two forms of pulmonary hypertension: primary (or idiopathic) and secondary. Primary pulmonary hypertension is of unknown cause and is rare. It occurs most often in women between 20 and 40 years of age and is usually fatal within seven years of diagnosis. Secondary pulmonary hypertension is more common and results from existing cardiac or pulmonary disease. Its prognosis depends on the severity of the underlying disorder and the changes in the pulmonary vascular bed. The most common cause of pulmonary hypertension is pulmonary artery vasoconstriction due to hypoxia from chronic obstructive airways disease.

Altered Physiology

Normally, the pulmonary vascular bed can handle whatever the right ventricle delivers. It has a low resistance to blood flow and compensates for increased blood volume by opening unused vessels in the pulmonary circulation. However, if the pulmonary vascular bed is destroyed or obstructed, as in pulmonary hypertension, the ability to handle whatever flow or volume of blood it receives is lost and the increased blood flow then increases the pulmonary arterial pressures. As the pulmonary arterial pressure increases, the pulmonary vascular resistance also increases. Both pulmonary artery vasoconstriction (as in hypoxia or hypercapnia) and a reduction of the pulmonary vascular bed (which occurs with pulmonary emboli) result in an increase in pulmonary vascular resistance and pressure. This increased workload affects right ventricular function. The myocardium ultimately is unable to meet the increasing demands imposed on it, leading to right ventricular hypertrophy (dilation) and failure (cor pulmonale).

Clinical Features

The signs and symptoms are usually associated with the

underlying cardiac or pulmonary disorder. Increasing dyspnoea on exertion is the most common symptom; chest pain occurs in 30 to 60 per cent of those affected. Other signs and symptoms include weakness; fatigability; syncope; signs of right-sided heart failure (peripheral oedema, ascites, distended neck veins, liver engorgement, crackles, heart murmur); electrocardiographic changes showing right ventricular hypertrophy, right axis deviation, tall peaked P waves in inferior leads and decreased PaO_2 (hypoxaemia).

Diagnosis

Cardiac catheterization of the right side of the heart will reveal elevated pulmonary arterial pressures. Pulmonary angiography will detect defects in pulmonary vasculature such as pulmonary emboli. Pulmonary function studies will reveal an increased residual volume and total lung capacity and a decreased forced expiratory volume in one second (FEV_1) in obstructive pulmonary diseases and a decreased vital capacity and total lung capacity in restrictive lung diseases.

Medical Management

The objective of treatment is to manage the underlying cardiac or pulmonary condition. Since hypoxia is the most common cause of pulmonary vasoconstriction leading to increased pulmonary vascular resistance and pulmonary hypertension, oxygen therapy is the major component of management. In acute conditions, appropriate oxygen therapy (see Table 3.2) will reverse the vasoconstriction and reduce the pulmonary hypertension in a relatively short time.

In more chronic, progressive conditions, continuous oxygen therapy may be necessary to slow down the progression of the disease. In the presence of cor pulmonale, treatment should include fluid restriction, digitalis to improve cardiac function, rest and diuretics to decrease fluid accumulation. In primary pulmonary hypertension, vasodilators have been administered with variable success.

PULMONARY HEART DISEASE (COR PULMONALE)

Pulmonary heart disease is a condition in which the right ventricle enlarges (with or without failure) as a result of diseases that affect the structure or function of the lung or its vasculature. Any disease that affects the lungs and has associated hypoxaemia may result in pulmonary heart disease. The most frequent cause is chronic obstructive airways disease in which changes in the airway and retained secretions reduce alveolar ventilation. Certain disorders of the nervous system, respiratory muscles, chest wall, and pulmonary arterial tree may be responsible for pulmonary heart disease.

Altered Physiology

Pulmonary disease can produce a chain of events that will in time produce hypertrophy and failure of the right ventricle. Any condition that deprives the lungs of oxygen can cause hypoxaemia (decreased arterial oxygen tension) and hypercapnia (increased carbon dioxide in the blood), resulting in ventilatory insufficiency. Airway hypoxia and hypercapnia cause pulmonary arterial vasoconstriction. There may be associated reduction of the pulmonary vascular bed, as in emphysema or pulmonary emboli. The result is increased resistance in the pulmonary circuit, with a subsequent rise in pulmonary blood pressure (pulmonary hypertension). Right ventricular hypertrophy may then result and be followed by right ventricular failure. In short, pulmonary heart disease results from pulmonary hypertension that causes the right side of the heart to enlarge because of the increased work required to pump blood against high resistance through the pulmonary vascular system.

Clinical Features

Usually, the symptoms of pulmonary heart disease are those of underlying lung disease. Chronic obstructive airways disease produces shortness of breath and cough. As the right ventricle fails, the patient develops oedema of the feet and legs, distended neck veins, an enlarged, palpable liver, pleural effusion, ascites and a heart murmur. Headache, confusion and somnolence may be manifested as a result of carbon dioxide narcosis.

Medical Management

The objectives of treatment are to improve the patient's ventilation and to treat both the underlying lung disease and the manifestations of heart disease. In chronic obstructive airways disease the airways have to be opened to improve gas exchange. With improved oxygen transport, the reactive pulmonary hypertension that leads to pulmonary heart disease is relieved. In short, the lung must be treated first. Oxygen is given to reduce pulmonary arterial pressure and pulmonary vascular resistance. Substantial patient improvement may require 4 to 6 weeks of oxygen therapy. This is usually carried out at home. Assessment of arterial blood gases is necessary to determine adequacy of alveolar ventilation and to monitor low-flow oxygen.

Additional measures include bronchial hygiene and the administration of bronchodilators and chest physiotherapy to improve ventilation.

Electrocardiographic monitoring is done when necessary, since there is a high incidence of arrhythmias in these patients. Respiratory infection must be treated, since it commonly precipitates pulmonary heart disease. The patient's prognosis depends on whether the hypertensive process is reversible.

Patient Education

Because management of pulmonary heart disease is

related to treating the underlying cause, it is often a long-term process. Consequently, most of the care and monitoring is done in the home. Patients are advised to avoid those things that irritate the airway if they have chronic obstructive airways disease. If continuous oxygen is administered, patients, their families and other informal carers are advised about its use. Most important, patients are urged to stop smoking. Nutrition counselling is necessary if they are on a sodium-restricted diet or are taking diuretics. The family and other carers are counselled that restlessness, depression and irritable or angry behaviour may be encountered with hypoxaemia or hypercapnia, and should decrease as the arterial blood gas values improve.

PULMONARY EMBOLISM

Pulmonary embolism refers to the obstruction of one or more pulmonary arteries by a thrombus (or thrombi) that originates somewhere in the venous system or in the right side of the heart, becomes dislodged and is carried to the lung. An infarction of lung tissue caused by interruption of the lung's blood supply results in 10 per cent of embolic episodes. Pulmonary embolism is a common disorder and is often associated with advanced age, postoperative states and prolonged immobility. It may occur in an apparently healthy person. People who are at risk of developing a pulmonary embolus include those with venous stasis as a result of varicose veins or prolonged periods of immobilization; hypercoagulability of the blood due to injury, tumour or increased platelet count; and venous endothelial disease such as thrombophlebitis, vascular disease or as a result of foreign bodies such as peripheral venous catheters.

The majority of thrombi originate in the deep veins or the legs. Other sources include the pelvic veins and the right atrium of the heart.

Altered Physiology

Following a massive embolic obstruction of the pulmonary arteries, there is an increase in alveolar dead space since the area, although continuing to be ventilated, receives little or no blood flow. In addition, a number of vasoactive and bronchoconstrictive substances are released from the clot. These substances compound the ventilation–perfusion imbalance, causing venous admixture and shunting.

The haemodynamic consequences are increased pulmonary vascular resistance due to reduction in the size of the pulmonary vascular bed, a consequent increase in pulmonary arterial pressure and, in turn, an increase in right ventricular work to maintain pulmonary blood flow. When the work requirements of the right ventricle exceed its capacity, right ventricular failure occurs. When this happens there is a decrease in cardiac output followed by a drop in systemic blood pressure and the development of shock.

Clinical Features

The symptoms of pulmonary embolism depend on the size of the thrombus and the area of the pulmonary artery occluded. Dyspnoea is the one symptom that is usually consistently present with pulmonary embolism. A massive embolism occluding the bifurcation of the pulmonary artery can produce pronounced dyspnoea, sudden substernal pain, rapid and weak pulse, shock, syncope and sudden death.

There may also be fever, cough and haemoptysis. The patient's respiratory rate is accelerated out of proportion to the degree of fever and tachycardia. The clinical picture may simulate that of bronchopneumonia or heart failure. In some instances, the disease presents in an atypical fashion with few signs and symptoms, while in other instances it mimics various cardiopulmonary disorders.

Diagnosis

The chest X-ray will reveal subtle or nonspecific changes. An electrocardiogram may show characteristic but nonspecific changes and needs to be compared with a previous electrocardiogram in order to correlate changes with the suspected embolism. Arterial blood gas analysis will show hypoxaemia, and pulmonary function studies will be abnormal but nonspecific to pulmonary embolism. A perfusion lung scan coupled with a ventilation lung scan will confirm the presence of emboli when the ventilation scan is normal in an area where there is a defect in the perfusion scan (indicating areas of diminished or absent blood flow). If lung scanning is not definitive, then pulmonary angiography will usually confirm the diagnosis of pulmonary emboli. A phlebogram may be done to detect 'silent' thrombi in the legs.

Emergency Interventions

Massive pulmonary embolism is a true medical emergency; the patient's condition tends to deteriorate rapidly. The immediate objective of treatment is to stabilize the cardiorespiratory system. The majority of patients who die of massive pulmonary embolism do so in the first two hours following the embolic event. Emergency management consists of the following:

- Nasal oxygen is administered immediately to relieve hypoxaemia, respiratory distress and cyanosis.
- An infusion is started to open an intravenous route for drugs/fluids that will be needed.
- Pulmonary angiography, haemodynamic measurements, arterial blood gas determinations and perfusion lung scans are carried out. A sudden rise in pulmonary resistance increases the work of the right ventricle, which can cause acute right-sided heart failure with cardiogenic shock.
- If the patient has suffered massive embolism and is hypotensive, an indwelling urethral catheter is inserted to monitor urinary volume.

- Hypotension needs to be treated.
- The electrocardiogram is monitored continuously for right ventricular failure, which may have a rapid onset.
- Sodium bicarbonate may be administered to correct metabolic acidosis. Intravenous diuretics and anti-arrhythmic agents are given when appropriate.
- Blood is drawn for serum electrolytes, blood urea, full blood count and haematocrit.
- If clinical assessment and arterial blood gases indicate the need, the patient is placed on a volume-controlled ventilator.
- Small doses of opiates are given to relieve patients' anxiety, to alleviate chest discomfort, to help them accept the discomfort of the endotracheal tube and to ease their adaptation to the mechanical ventilator.

Medical Management

The alteration in respiratory function is due to a reduction in the size of the pulmonary vascular bed caused by the pulmonary embolus. To correct or treat this alteration, drug therapy is administered initially to remove the thrombus/embolus and restore the pulmonary circulation to normal and then to prevent recurrence.

Anticoagulant therapy (heparin, warfarin) has traditionally been the primary method of management of acute deep vein thrombosis and pulmonary embolism, thrombolytic therapy (urokinase, streptokinase) is now used to dissolve thrombi in the deep veins and in the pulmonary circulation. This thrombolytic therapy results in a more rapid resolution of the thrombi/emboli. It restores more normal haemodynamic functioning of the pulmonary circulation, resulting in a reduction of pulmonary hypertension. On a long-term basis, thrombolytic therapy prevents permanent damage to the pulmonary vascular bed. Bleeding, however, is a significant side-effect. Consequently, thrombolytic agents are advocated only for patients with massive pulmonary emboli affecting a significant area of blood flow to the lung.

Before the thrombolytic infusion, prothrombin time, haematocrit values and platelet counts are obtained. During therapy all but absolutely essential invasive procedures are avoided, with the exception of careful venepuncture.

After completion of the thrombolytic infusion (which varies in duration according to the agent used and condition being treated) the patient is placed on anticoagulants. Anticoagulation slows or stops the underlying thrombotic process, thus preventing recurrence. Heparin is given and controlled according to standard procedures and is followed by warfarin sodium.

Other measures are initiated to support the patient's respiratory and vascular status. Oxygen therapy is administered to correct the hypoxia and to relieve the pulmonary vascular vasoconstriction and reduce the pulmonary

hypertension. Elastic stockings are used to compress the superficial venous system and increase the velocity of deep venous blood by redirecting the blood through the deep veins. Venous stasis is then reduced. However, simple leg elevation (above the level of the heart) with flexion at the knees also increases venous flow. Some authorities believe elastic stockings are unnecessary if the patient's legs are elevated.

Surgical Intervention

If the patient has persistent hypotension, shock and respiratory distress; if pulmonary artery pressure is greatly elevated; and if angiograms reveal obstruction of a large part of the pulmonary vasculature, embolectomy may be indicated. This requires a thoracotomy with cardiopulmonary bypass technique.

Another surgical technique used when pulmonary emboli recur, despite adequate medical therapy (or if the patient is intolerant of anticoagulant therapy), is an interruption of the inferior vena cava. This method prevents dislodged thrombi from being swept into the lungs while at the same time permitting adequate blood flow. This can be done by total ligation or the use of Teflon clips applied to the vena cava to divide the caval lumen into small channels without occluding caval blood flow.

Transvenous catheter embolectomy is a technique in which a vacuum-cupped catheter is introduced transvenously into the affected pulmonary artery. Suction is applied to the end of the embolus, and the embolus is aspirated into the cup. The surgeon maintains suction to hold the embolus within the cup, and the entire catheter is withdrawn through the right side of the heart and out the femoral venotomy. An inferior caval filter is often inserted at the same time to protect against a recurrence.

Nursing Assessment

The nurse examines each susceptible patient for a positive Homan's sign (pain on dorsiflexion of the foot), which may or may not indicate impending thrombosis of the leg veins.

A key role is to try to prevent the occurrence of pulmonary embolism in all patients and to identify those who are at high risk, particularly those with conditions predisposing to slowing of venous return. Such conditions include trauma to the pelvis (especially surgical) and lower extremities (especially hip fractures), obesity, history of thromboembolic disease, varicose veins, pregnancy, heart failure, myocardial infarction, oral contraceptive use and malignant disease; also, postoperative patients and the elderly often have a slower venous return.

Nursing Care

The nurse must be alert for the potential complication of

shock or right ventricular failure subsequent to the effect of the pulmonary embolus on the cardiovascular system.

Prevention of thrombus formation is a major nursing responsibility. Ambulation and active and passive leg exercises are encouraged to prevent venous stasis in patients on bedrest. When the legs are moved in a 'pumping' exercise, the leg muscles help to increase venous flow. Patients are advised to avoid prolonged sitting, immobility or constricting clothing. They are advised not to 'dangle' their legs and feet in a dependent position while sitting on the edge of the bed. The feet should be on the floor or on a chair and patients should avoid crossing their legs. Intravenous catheters (for parenteral therapy or measurements of central venous pressure) should not be left in the veins for prolonged periods of time.

Thrombolytic therapy (streptokinase) causes lysis of deep vein thrombi and pulmonary emboli, promoting resolution. During thrombolytic infusion, the patient remains on bedrest, pulse and blood pressure are assessed every three to four hours, and invasive procedures are limited. The infusion is discontinued immediately if uncontrolled bleeding occurs.

When chest pain is present, it is usually pleuritic. Narcotic analgesics are administered as prescribed for severe pain.

Careful attention is given to the proper use of oxygen. It is important to make sure that the patient understands the need for continuous oxygen therapy. Signs of hypoxia are a means of evaluating the effectiveness of the oxygen therapy. Nebulizer therapy, incentive spirometry, and/or postural drainage are administered if there is an accumulation of secretions complicating the pulmonary embolism.

Coping With Anxiety

After the patients' condition stabilizes, they are encouraged to express their feelings about this condition. Their questions are answered concisely and accurately. Their therapy is explained and they are told how they can help by early recognition of untoward effects. On discharge, patients are advised about how to prevent recurrence, and what signs and symptoms should alert them to seek medical attention.

Postoperative Nursing Care

If surgery was performed, the patient's pulmonary arterial pressure and urinary output are measured. The insertion site of the arterial catheter is checked for haematoma formation and infection. An adequate blood pressure must be maintained to ensure perfusion of the vital organs. To prevent peripheral venous stasis and lower extremity oedema, the foot of the bed is elevated. Isometric exercises, elastic stockings and walking are encouraged when the patient is out of bed. Sitting is discouraged, since hip flexion causes compression of the large veins in the legs.

Patient Education

The following patient advice is intended to help prevent recurrences:

● When taking anticoagulants, look for bruising and bleeding and try to protect yourself from bumping into objects that can cause bruising.
● Use a toothbrush with soft bristles.
● Do not take aspirin or antihistamine drugs while receiving warfarin. Always check with your general practitioner before taking any medication, including over-the-counter medications.
● Continue to wear anti-embolism stockings as long as directed.
● Avoid sitting with your legs crossed or sitting for prolonged periods.
● When travelling, change your position regularly, walk occasionally and do active exercises of the legs and ankles while sitting. Drink plenty of liquids while travelling to avoid haemoconcentration owing to fluid loss.
● Report dark, tarry stools to your general practitioner immediately.
● Carry a card stating that anticoagulants are being taken.

BREATHING DISORDERS DURING SLEEP

Respiratory abnormalities can occur during sleep. Some patients who have adequate blood oxygenation while awake develop hypoxaemia while sleeping. Apnoea is the cessation of air flow at the nose and mouth for more than 10 seconds. Sleep apnoea syndrome, which is evaluated in a sleep laboratory, is present when there are at least 30 apnoeic episodes during both rapid eye movement sleep and nonrapid eye movement sleep during seven hours of nocturnal sleep. Oxygen desaturation is usually evident in apnoeic episodes.

Sleep apnoea is classified into three types: (1) central—simultaneous cessation of both air flow and respiratory movements; (2) obstructive—lack of air flow due to pharyngeal occlusion; and (3) mixed—a combination of central and obstructive apnoea within one apnoeic episode.

The patient, usually male, snores loudly, stops breathing up to 10 seconds or more and then awakens abruptly with a loud snort as his blood oxygen level drops. He may have more than ten apnoeic episodes per hour to several hundred per night. This can seriously tax the heart and lungs. Increasing age and obesity correlate positively with alterations in breathing and nocturnal oxygen desaturation. Other symptoms include excessive daytime sleepiness, morning headache, sore throat and complaints by the bed partner that the patient snores loudly or is unusually restless during sleep.

Management is based on whether complications of life-threatening arrhythmias, chronic cardiovascular effects, memory loss and intellectual impairment are present. If obese, the patient is advised to lose weight. (Most patients with obstructive apnoea are obese.) Tricyclic antidepressants, respiratory stimulants and tracheostomy to bypass the obstruction may be modalities of treatment according to the problems of the individual patient. Nocturnal oxygen is beneficial for relieving hypoxaemia in some patients. Pacemaker stimulation of the phrenic nerves may be helpful in patients with central sleep apnoea.

OCCUPATIONAL LUNG DISEASES

Diseases of the lungs can occur in a variety of occupations as a result of exposure to organic or inorganic (mineral) dusts and noxious gases (fumes and aerosols). The effect of inhaling these materials depends on the composition of the inhaled substance, its antigenic (precipitating an immune response) or irritating properties, the dose inhaled, the length of time inhaled and the host's response (a person's susceptibility to the irritant). There are a growing number of occupational lung diseases owing to new and untested industrial substances and chemicals (presumed to be harmless). The problem may be compounded by smoking, which appears to have a synergistic effect on occupational lung disease and may increase the risk of lung cancers in people exposed to asbestos.

Preventive Measures and Health Maintenance

First, every effort is made to reduce the exposure of the worker to industrial products. The work environment must be ventilated properly to remove the noxious agent from the worker's breathing zone. Dust control can prevent many of the pneumoconioses and includes ventilation, spraying an area with water to control release of dust and effective and frequent floor cleaning. Air samples need to be monitored. Toxic substances should be enclosed to reduce their concentration in the air. Workers must wear protective devices (face masks, hoods, industrial respirators) to provide a safe air supply when in a toxic atmosphere. Every employee should be carefully screened and followed, especially the worker at high risk for developing occupational lung disease (hypersensitivity states, asthma). There is a risk of developing serious smoking-related illness (cancer) in industries in which there are unsafe levels of certain gases, dusts, fumes, fluids and other toxic substances. Ongoing educational programmes to teach workers to bear responsibility for their own health, including smoking cessation and influenza vaccination, have a major role in the prevention of occupational lung disease.

The Pneumoconioses

Pneumoconiosis refers to a non-neoplastic alteration of the lung resulting from exposure to inorganic dust (e.g., 'dusty lung'). The most common pneumoconioses are silicosis, asbestosis and coalworker's pneumoconiosis.

Silicosis

Silicosis is a chronic pulmonary disease caused by inhalation of silica dust (silicon dioxide particles). When the silica particles, which have fibrogenic properties, are inhaled, nodular lesions are produced throughout the lungs. With the passage of time and exposure, the nodules enlarge and coalesce. Dense masses form in the upper portion of the lungs, resulting in loss of pulmonary parenchymal volume. Restrictive lung disease (inability of the lungs to expand fully) and obstructive lung disease from secondary emphysema result. Exposure of 10 to 20 years is usually required before the disease develops and shortness of breath is manifested. Fibrotic destruction of pulmonary tissue can lead to emphysema, pulmonary hypertension and cor pulmonale.

There is no specific treatment, and therapy is directed at the complications of silicosis.

Asbestosis

Asbestosis is a disease characterized by diffuse pulmonary fibrosis due to the inhalation of asbestos dust.

The asbestos fibres are inhaled and enter the alveoli, which, in time, are eventually obliterated by fibrous tissue that surrounds the asbestos particles. There is fibrous pleural thickening and pleural plaque formation. The altered physiological pattern is that of restrictive lung disease with decrease in lung volume, diminished gas transfer and hypoxaemia. The patient has progressive dyspnoea, mild to moderate chest pain, anorexia and weight loss. Pulmonary heart disease and respiratory failure occur as the disease progresses. A significant proportion of workers exposed to asbestos dust die of lung cancer, especially those who smoke. In addition to lung cancer and asbestosis, exposure to asbestos can produce nonmalignant pleural disease, diffuse malignant mesothelioma and possibly neoplasms of other tissues. Avoidance, in general, is essential and asbestos workers should stop smoking.

There is no effective treatment for asbestosis. Management is directed at intercurrent infection and coexisting lung disease. In patients with severe gas transport abnormalities, continuous oxygen therapy may improve exercise tolerance.

Coal Worker's Pneumoconiosis

Coal worker's pneumoconiosis includes a variety of respiratory diseases found in coal workers in which there is an accumulation of coal dust in the lungs causing a tissue reaction to its presence.

The patient with complicated coal worker's pneumoconiosis has massive lesions of dense fibrotic tissue containing black material. These masses eventually destroy blood vessels and the bronchi of the affected lobe. Patients develop dyspnoea, cough and sputum production, with expectoration of varying amounts of black fluid (melanoptosis), particularly if they smoke. Eventually pulmonary heart disease and respiratory failure result. The treatment is symptomatic.

TUMOURS OF THE CHEST

A chest tumour may be primary, arising within the lung or the mediastinum, or it may represent a metastasis from a primary tumour site elsewhere. Metastatic tumours of the lungs occur frequently, since the bloodstream transports free cancer cells from primary cancers elsewhere in the body. Such tumours grow in and between the alveoli and the bronchi, which they push apart in their growth. This process may occur over a long period of time, causing few or no symptoms.

Primary tumours of the lung may be benign or malignant. Most arise from the bronchial epithelium. Bronchial adenomas are slow growing, usually benign tumours, but they very vascular and therefore produce symptoms of bleeding and bronchial obstruction. Bronchogenic carcinoma is a malignant tumour arising from the bronchus. Such a tumour is epidermoid, usually located in the larger bronchi, or is an adenocarcinoma, arising farther out in the lung. There are also several intermediate or undifferentiated types of lung cancer, identifiable by cell type.

Lung Cancer (Bronchogenic Carcinoma)

Lung cancer is responsible each year for 310 deaths per 100,000 of the male population of the UK (International Agency for Research on Cancer, 1986). The UK is top of the international standardized mortality league table.

The survival rate is low, for in approximately 70 per cent of patients, the disease has spread to regional lymphatics and other sites at the time of diagnosis.

It has been suggested that carcinoma tends to arise at sites of previous scarring (tuberculosis, fibrosis) in the lung.

Classification and Staging
The four major cell types of lung cancer (which differ significantly) are epidermoid (squamous cell) carcinoma, small cell (oat cell) carcinoma, adenocarcinoma and large cell (undifferentiated) carcinoma. Many tumours contain more than one cell type. The different cell types display different biological behaviour and have prognostic significance. Therefore, different approaches to treatment may be indicated by the cell type.

The stage of the tumour refers to the anatomical extent of the tumour, spread to the regional lymph nodes and metastatic spread. Staging is accomplished by tissue diagnosis, lymph node biopsy and mediastinoscopy. It is important in determining whether tumour resection should be attempted. Prognosis appears to be most favourable for epidermoid and adenocarcinoma, whereas undifferentiated small cell (oat cell) tumours have a poor prognosis.

Risk Factors
Lung cancer is ten times more common in cigarette smokers than in nonsmokers, with the prevalence being related to the length of time and the intensity of smoking. Epidermoid carcinoma, involving the larger bronchi, is thought to be almost entirely associated with heavy cigarette smoking. Few cases of this type of cancer have been reported in nonsmokers. For reasons unknown, the incidence of adenocarcinoma is rising faster than that of other types.

Adenocarcinoma of the peripheral bronchi is not associated with any known cause and occurs equally in smokers and nonsmokers. Another risk factor is occupational exposure to asbestos, radioactive dusts, arsenic and certain plastics alone or in combination with tobacco smoke. People at high risk who insist on continuing to smoke should have regular chest X-rays and sputum examinations in order to increase their chances that lung cancer will be detected while it is still treatable.

Clinical Features
Tumours of the bronchopulmonary system may affect the lining of the respiratory tract, lung parenchyma, pleura or chest wall. The disease begins insidiously (over several decades) and often is asymptomatic until late in its course. The signs and symptoms depend on the location and size of the tumour, the degree of obstruction and the existence of metastases to regional or distant sites.

The most frequent symptom is cough, probably from irritation by the tumour mass. It is frequently ignored as a 'cigarette cough'. Starting as a hacking, nonproductive cough, it later progresses to a point where it produces a thick, purulent sputum as secondary infection occurs.

● A cough that changes in character should arouse suspicion of lung cancer.

A wheeze in the chest (occurs when a bronchus becomes partially obstructed by the tumour) is noted in about 20 per cent of patients. The expectoration of blood-tinged sputum is common, particularly in the morning, and is due to sputum becoming streaked with blood as it passes over the ulcerated tumour surface. In some patients, recurring fever owing to a persisting infection in an area of pneumonitis distal from the tumour is the early symptom. In fact, cancer of the lung should be suspected in people with repeated unresolved upper respiratory tract infections. Pain is a late manifestation and is often found to be related to bone metastasis. If the tumour spreads to adjacent structures and regional lymph nodes, the patient may present with chest pain and tightness, hoarseness (involvement of recurrent laryngeal nerve), dysphagia, head and neck oedema, and symptoms of pleural or pericardial effusion. The most common sites of metastases are lymph nodes, bone, brain and adrenal glands. General symptoms of weakness, anorexia, weight loss and anaemia appear late.

Diagnosis

If the patient with pulmonary symptoms is a heavy smoker, cancer of the lung is suspected. Chest radiography is carried out to search for pulmonary density, a solitary peripheral nodule, atelectasis and infection. Cytological examination of fresh sputum obtained by cough or saline washings from a suspected bronchus is done to search for malignant cells. Bronchoscopy with a flexible fibreoptic instrument allows a detailed study of the bronchial segments, and identification of the source of malignant cells and the probable extent of anticipated surgery. Fluorescent bronchofibroscopy is used to detect small, early bronchogenic cancers.

Lung scans are part of the diagnostic process. Before surgery the patient is evaluated to determine whether the tumour is resectable and whether the patient can tolerate the physiological impairment resulting from such surgery. Pulmonary function tests combined with split-function perfusion scans are carried out to determine if the patient will have adequate pulmonary reserve following the procedure. The patient's ability to move air (vital capacity, FEV_1) is important since the ability to generate an effective cough is imperative in the postoperative period.

Medical Management

The objective of medical management is to provide the maximum likelihood of cure. The treatment depends on the cell type, the stage of the disease (anatomical event) and the physiological state (particularly cardiac and pulmonary state) of the patient. In general, treatment may involve surgery, radiotherapy, chemotherapy and immunotherapy, used separately or in combination.

Surgery

Surgical resection is the preferred method for patients with localized tumours with no evidence of metastatic spread and whose cardiopulmonary function is adequate. (Usually, surgery for small cell cancer of the lung is not advisable because this is a rapidly growing tumour that metastasizes early and widely.) Unfortunately, in a large number of patients with bronchogenic cancer the lesion is inoperable at the time of diagnosis. The usual operation for small, apparently curable tumour of the lung is lobectomy (removal of a lobe of the lung). An entire lung may be removed (pneumonectomy) in combination with other surgical procedures, such as resection of involved mediastinal lymph nodes. Before surgery, the cardiopulmonary reserve of the patient must be determined.

Radiotherapy

Radiotherapy may cure a small percentage of patients. It is useful in controlling radioresponsive neoplasms that cannot be resected. The small cell and epidermoid tumours are usually radiation sensitive. It may be used as palliative treatment to decrease tumour size and relieve pressure on vital structures. Respite may be obtained from cough, chest pain, dyspnoea, haemoptysis and bone and liver pain. Relief of symptoms may last from a few weeks to many months, and is important in improving the quality of the remaining period of life.

Attention is paid to the patient's nutrition and psychological outlook. The patient should be monitored for signs of anaemia and infection.

Chemotherapy

At present chemotherapy is used to manipulate tumour growth patterns, to treat patients with distant metastases, or with small cell cancer of the lung, and in combination with surgery or radiotherapy. Combinations of two or more drugs may be more beneficial than single-dose regimes. A large number of drugs are reported to have some activity against lung cancer. The choice depends upon the growth of the tumour cell and the specificity of the drug for cell cycle phase. These agents are toxic and have a narrow margin of safety. Chemotherapy may provide palliation, especially of pain, but does not cure and rarely prolongs life. It is valuable in reducing pressure symptoms of lung cancer and in treating brain, spinal cord and pericardial metastasis.

Nursing Care

Nursing care of the patient with lung cancer is similar to that of any cancer patient. Special attention is focused on the respiratory manifestations of the disease. Airway management is needed to maintain airway patency through the removal of secretions or exudate. As the tumour enlarges, there may be compression on a bronchus or involvement of a large area of lung tissue, resulting in an impaired breathing pattern and poor gas exchange. Deep breathing and coughing, aerosol therapy, oxygen therapy and mechanical ventilation may be necessary when there is respiratory impairment.

The psychological aspects of nursing the patient with lung cancer are extremely important.

CHEST TRAUMA

Injuries to the chest may cause minor or serious disturbances of cardiorespiratory function, depending on which part of the complex mechanism is involved. Thus, a fall against the side of a bath may fracture one or two ribs with painful but rather slight disturbance of respiratory function, whereas a car accident in which the driver of the car is thrown against the steering wheel may crush the chest, causing cardiac and lung injuries that may be rapidly fatal.

The most serious consequences of chest trauma are respiratory failure from damage to the chest wall, airways, diaphragm and lungs, and shock due to large vessel and extrathoracic injuries. Frequently, acute respiratory failure and shock are encountered in combination, a particularly lethal situation.

Chest injuries may be caused by nonpenetrating (blunt) trauma, which does not penetrate but injures by force, and by penetrating injuries. Both types of injuries can cause serious respiratory and haemodynamic dysfunction.

Immediate Assessment and Management

In the treatment of injuries to the chest, efforts are made to correct disturbances of cardiorespiratory function caused by the trauma. The first requirement is to evaluate the patency of the airway by assessing for signs of obstruction, sternal retraction, stridor, wheezing and cyanosis. Agitation, irrational behaviour and hostility are signs of decreased oxygen delivery to the cerebral cortex. To restore and maintain cardiopulmonary function, an adequate airway is created and ventilation is ensured. (This includes stabilizing and re-establishing chest wall integrity, correcting open pneumothorax, decompressing pneumothorax/haemothorax and eliminating cardiac tamponade.) Hypovolaemia and low cardiac output are corrected. Ongoing treatment is essential to see if the patient is responding to treatment or to detect early signs of a deteriorating condition.

Principles of management are essentially those pertaining to care of the postoperative thoracic patient.

Rib Fractures

Rib fractures are the most common chest injury and should be taken seriously, since they may result in underlying lung contusion. Such injuries are of special concern in middle-aged and elderly patients who may already have seriously reduced vital capacity. The fifth to the ninth ribs are those most commonly broken. If the rib fragments are driven inwards, the jagged edges of the rib(s) may lacerate the lungs, spleen or liver, as well as cause haemothorax, pneumothorax or haemopneumothorax.

If the patient is conscious, severe pain, tenderness and muscle spasm over the area of the fracture will be experienced, which is aggravated by coughing, deep breathing and motion. To reduce the pain the patient will breathe in a shallow manner, and will avoid sighs, deep breaths, coughing and moving. This results in diminished venti-

lation, collapse of unaerated alveoli (atelectasis), pneumonitis and hypoxaemia. Respiratory insufficiency and failure can be the outcome of such a cycle. Following blunt chest trauma, serial analysis of arterial blood gases is a sensitive indicator to determine whether the lung has been injured.

Medical Management

If there are no complications (pneumothorax, haemothorax), the objective is to relieve the pain so that the patient can breathe effectively. Sedation may be given to relieve pain and allow deep breathing and coughing. Using hands to support the injured area (or wrapping a towel around the chest), the patient is encouraged to breathe deeply and to cough. Usually the pain abates in five to seven days, and discomfort can be controlled with non-narcotic analgesia. Most rib fractures heal in three to six weeks.

Flail Chest

Flail chest is the loss of stability of the chest wall with subsequent respiratory impairment. It is usually the result of multiple rib or sternal fractures. When this happens one portion of the chest wall no longer has a bony connection with the rest of the rib cage. It is usually accompanied by a severe degree of respiratory distress.

Medical Management

If only a small segment of the chest wall is involved, the objectives are to clear the airway (coughing, deep breaths, gentle suctioning) in order to aid in the expansion of the lung, and to relieve pain by intercostal nerve blocks, high thoracic epidural blocks or careful use of intravenous narcotics.

For mild to moderate flail chest injuries, some doctors advocate treating the underlying pulmonary contusion with fluid restriction, diuretics, corticosteroids and albumin while relieving chest pain, and by chest physiotherapy, combined with close and continuing patient monitoring.

When a severe flail chest is encountered, endotracheal intubation and mechanical ventilation with a volume-cycled ventilator and sometimes positive end-expiratory pressure is used to splint the chest wall (internal pneumatic stabilization) and to correct abnormalities in gas exchange. This helps to treat the underlying pulmonary contusion, serves to stabilize the thoracic cage for healing of fractures and improves alveolar ventilation and intrathoracic volume by decreasing the work of breathing. However, this form of treatment requires long-term endotracheal intubation and ventilator support.

Haemothorax and Pneumothorax

Severe chest injuries usually are accompanied by the collection of blood in the chest cavity (haemothorax) because of torn intercostal vessels and lacerations of the lungs, or the escape of air from the injured lung into the pleural cavity (pneumothorax). Often, both blood and air are found in the chest cavity (haemopneumothorax). The lung on that side of the chest is compressed, which interferes with its normal function.

The seriousness of the problem depends on the amount and rate of thoracic bleeding. Needle aspiration (thoracentesis) or chest tube drainage of the blood or air allows decompression of the pleural cavity so that the lung is able to re-expand and again perform its function in respiration. Operative intervention is carried out if bleeding continues at a rate greater than 300 ml/hr for 3 to 4 hours, if the rate of bleeding increases or if it is impossible to evacuate the blood within the pleural space.

Medical Management

A large-diameter intercostal tube (catheter) is usually inserted in the second intercostal space or in the fifth space in the axilla. This usually brings about prompt and effective decompression of the pleural cavity (drainage of blood/air). If there is an excessive amount of bleeding from the chest tube in a relatively short period of time, autotransfusion may be employed. This technique takes the patient's own blood that is drained from the chest, filters it and then transfuses it back into the patient's vascular system.

Tension Pneumothorax

In some patients, air may be drawn into the pleural space from the lacerated lung or through a small hole in the chest wall. In either case, the air that enters the chest cavity with each inspiration is trapped there: it cannot be expelled through the air passage or small hole in the chest wall.

A tension (pressure) thus is built up within the pleural space, which produces a collapse of the lung and may even push the heart and the great vessels towards the unaffected side of the chest. This not only interferes with respiration but also disrupts circulatory function, because with increased intrathoracic pressure, venous return to the heart is compromised, causing decreased cardiac output and impairment of peripheral circulation. The clinical picture is one of air hunger, agitation, hypotension and cyanosis.

Medical Management

Immediate thoracentesis is carried out to relieve the positive pressure or 'tension' within the chest. If the lung expands and there is no continuing leakage from the lung, further drainage may be unnecessary. If the lung is still leaking, as evidenced by the reaccumulation of an inexhaustible volume of air during the thoracentesis, then constant egress of this air must be provided by a large-bore chest tube with water-seal drainage.

In an emergency situation a tension pneumothorax can be quickly converted to a simple pneumothorax by insertion of a large-bore needle into the pleural space, which relieves the pressure and vents the intrathoracic air to the outside. Then a chest tube can be inserted and connected to suction inorder to remove the remaining air and fluid and re-expand the lung.

Penetrating Wounds of the Chest

Open Pneumothorax

Open pneumothorax implies an opening in the chest wall large enough to allow air to pass freely in and out of the thoracic cavity with each attempted respiration. In such patients, not only is the lung collapsed, but the structures of the mediastinum (heart and great vessels) are also pushed towards the uninjured side with each inspiration, and in the opposite direction with expiration.

Medical Management

Open pneumothorax calls for emergency interventions. In such an emergency, anything may be used that is large enough to fill the hole—a towel, a handkerchief or the heel of the hand. A conscious patient needs to be told to inhale and strain against a closed glottis. This action assists in the re-expansion of the lung and the ejection of the air from the thorax. In the hospital, the opening is plugged by sealing it with gauze impregnated with petroleum. A pressure dressing is applied by circumferential strapping. Usually, a chest tube connected to water-seal drainage is inserted to permit egress of air and fluid. Antibiotics are usually prescribed to combat infection from contamination.

Stab Wounds

Stab wounds are a common cause of penetrating wounds of the chest, most of which are caused by knives and switchblades, and are frequently associated with alcohol or substance abuse. The appearance of the external wound may be very deceptive, since pneumothorax, haemothorax and cardiac tamponade, along with severe and continuing haemorrhage, can occur from any small wound, even one caused by an icepick.

Medical Management

The objective of immediate management is to restore and maintain cardiopulmonary function. After an adequate airway is ensured and ventilation is corrected, the patient is examined for shock and intrathoracic and intra-abdominal injuries.

After the status of the peripheral pulses is assessed, an intravenous line is secured. Blood is withdrawn for chemistries, typing and cross-matching. Simultaneously, a central venous pressure line is established. An indwelling catheter is inserted to monitor urinary volume and to collect a urine sample for laboratory study.

Shock is treated simultaneously with colloid solutions, crystalloids, blood or vasopressors, as indicated by the condition of the patient. Chest X-rays are taken, and other diagnostic procedures are carried out as indicated by the needs of the patient.

A chest tube is inserted in the pleural space in most patients with penetrating wounds of the chest in order to achieve rapid and continuing re-expansion of the lungs. The chest tube allows early recognition of continuing intrathoracic bleeding, which will make surgical exploration necessary.

If the patient has a penetrating wound of the heart and great vessels, the oesophagus and the tracheobronchial tree, surgical intervention is required. Associated intra-abdominal wounds also necessitate abdominal exploration.

THE CLINICAL PROBLEM OF ASPIRATION

Aspiration (inhalation) of stomach contents is a serious complication that may cause death. It can occur when there is loss of protective airway reflexes, such as is seen in patients who are unconscious from drugs, alcohol, stroke or cardiac arrest, or in instances when a non-functioning nasogastric tube allows the gastric contents to drain around the tube and cause silent aspiration.

Massive inhalation of gastric contents, if untreated, will, in a period of several hours, result in the clinical syndrome of tachycardia, dyspnoea, cyanosis and hypertension followed by hypotension, and finally death. The primary factors responsible for morbidity and mortality after aspiration of gastric contents are the volume of aspirated gastric contents and their character. A full stomach contains solid particles of food. If these are aspirated, the problem then becomes one of mechanical blockage of the airways and secondary infection. A fasting stomach contains acidic gastric juice, which, if aspirated, may prove destructive to the alveoli and the capillaries. The presence of faecal contamination (more likely seen in intestinal obstruction) will increase the likelihood of mortality because the endotoxins produced by intestinal organisms may be absorbed systemically, or the thick proteinaceous material found in the intestinal contents may obstruct the airway, leading to atelectasis and secondary bacterial invasion.

Chemical pneumonitis may develop from aspiration and result in destruction of alveolar-capillary endothelial cells, with a consequent outpouring of protein-rich fluids into the interstitial and intra-alveolar spaces. This results in loss of surfactant, which in turn causes early closure of the airway. Finally, the impaired exchange of oxygen and carbon dioxide causes respiratory failure.

Preventive Measures

When Reflexes Are Lacking
Aspiration is likely to occur if the patient cannot adequately co-ordinate the protective glottic, laryngeal and cough reflexes. This hazard is increased if the patient has a distended abdomen, is in a supine position and has the upper extremities immobilized by intravenous infusions or hand restraints. A normal person, when vomiting, can take care of the airway by sitting up or turning onto one side, and co-ordinating breathing, coughing, gag and glottic reflexes. If these reflexes are active, an oral airway should not be inserted. If an airway is in place, it should be pulled out the moment the patient gags on it so as not to stimulate the pharyngeal gag reflex and promote vomiting and aspiration. Catheter suction of oral secretions should be executed with minimal pharyngeal stimulation, yet at the same time should be effective.

During Tube Feeding
The patient who is receiving tube feedings should be positioned upright during the feeding and for 30 minutes thereafter to allow the stomach to partially empty. Small volumes given under low pressure will help to prevent aspiration.

With Delayed Emptying Time of Stomach
A full stomach may cause aspiration because of increased intragastric or extragastric pressure. The following clinical situations cause delayed emptying time of the stomach and may contribute to aspiration: intestinal obstruction; increased gastric secretions during anxiety, stress or pain; or abdominal distension because of ileus, ascites, peritonitis, drugs, severe illness or vaginal delivery.

Following Prolonged Endotracheal Intubation
Prolonged endotracheal intubation or tracheostomy can depress the laryngeal and glottic reflexes because of disuse. Patients with prolonged tracheostomies are encouraged to phonate and exercise their laryngeal muscles. The pharynx is suctioned before deflating the cuff to prevent aspiration of regurgitated material. It is important to remember that improperly administered intermittent positive pressure breathing (IPPB) treatments by mask can distend the stomach and promote aspiration.

ACUTE RESPIRATORY FAILURE

Adult Respiratory Distress Syndrome

Adult respiratory distress syndrome is pulmonary oedema that occurs as a result of increased permeability; i.e., it occurs in the presence of near-normal pulmonary vascular pressures. It is estimated that there are about 12,000 cases each year in the UK (Wardle, 1984), although difficulty in diagnosis makes any statistics questionable.

Clinical Features

The clinical features of the syndrome include initial severe illness with no pulmonary component, followed by a latent period in which pulmonary abnormalities are minimal. There is a subsequent period of progressive respiratory distress with dyspnoea and hypoxia. The X-ray will show bilateral involvement of the lungs leading to pulmonary oedema.

In spite of the different causes, the clinical picture, altered physiology and pathology are similar. Adult respiratory distress syndrome appears 6 to 48 hours after the onset of the illness. The patient develops respiratory distress; the rate of breathing increases (tachypnoea) and may reach 40 breaths per minute. Each breath is shallow and laboured (dyspnoea) and may be associated with grunting. Retraction of the intercostal and suprasternal areas is seen during inspiration. Contractions of the accessory muscles of respiration are other signs of respiratory distress.

Cyanosis appears and fails to respond to oxygen therapy. Evidence of cerebral hypoxia, such as anxiety, confusion, irritability, lack of co-operation and drowsiness may appear. Hypoxia of the heart will result in tachycardia, arrhythmias and hypotension.

Medical Management

The principles of management of acute respiratory failure are the following:

1. Treat the cause.
2. Maintain a patent airway.
3. Provide adequate ventilation.
4. Provide optimum oxygen.
5. Carry out chest physiotherapy.

Treatment of the cause may involve evacuating the pleural cavity, giving antibiotic treatment for infection, reversing effects of drugs or accelerating their excretion, and decreasing raised intracranial pressures. Diseases such as bronchial asthma and pulmonary oedema require specific therapy. In some illnesses, such as polyneuritis and poliomyelitis, one has to wait for the illness to resolve.

To maintain a patent airway it may be necessary to intubate the patient or to do a tracheostomy. Once the airway is clear, adequacy of ventilation is assessed by measuring the respiratory rate, tidal volume, vital capacity, inspiratory force, arterial carbon dioxide tension ($PaCO_2$) and oxygen tension (PaO_2). Depending on the results, the patient is allowed to breathe spontaneously or is helped by a ventilator and by being monitored in the intensive care unit.

The arterial oxygen tension (PaO_2) will show the degree of oxygenation.

Nursing Care

The patient in acute respiratory failure is seriously ill and requires close monitoring because the condition could quickly change to a life-threatening situation. Frequent assessment of the patient's status is necessary to evaluate the effectiveness of the management programme.

Patients are supported in whatever position they feel most comfortable, using pillows, blankets, or an overbed table. If fluids are not restricted, fluid intake is encouraged to correct fluid loss that occurs during rapid breathing and to loosen secretions. Patients will be extremely anxious because of the hypoxaemia and dyspnoea. The nurse should explain all procedures, and deliver care in a calm, patient manner. It is important to reduce patients' anxieties because its manifestations prevent rest and increase oxygen expenditure. Rest is essential to conserve oxygen use, thereby reducing the oxygen need.

BIBLIOGRAPHY

Howard, J. E., Davies, J. L. and Roghmann, K. J. (1987) Respiratory teaching of patients: how effective is it? *Journal of Advanced Nursing*, Vol. 12, pp. 207–14.

International Agency for Research on Cancer (1986) *Monograph on the Evaluation of the Carcinogenic Risk of Chemicals to Humans. Vol. 38. Tobacco Smoking*, World Health Organisation, Geneva.

Office of Health Economics (1977) *Preventing Bronchitis*, OHE, London.

Office of Population Censuses and Surveys (1987) *1985 Mortality Statistics. DH2. 12*, HMSO, London.

Seaton, A., Seaton, D. and Leitch, A. G. (1989) *Crofton and Douglas's Respiratory Diseases* (4th edition), Blackwell Scientific, Oxford.

Wardle, E. N. (1984) Shock lungs: the post-traumatic respiratory distress syndrome, *Quarterly Journal of Medicine*, Vol. 53, pp. 317–32.

Williams, S. J. and Bury, M. R. (1989) Impairment, disability and handicap in chronic respiratory illness, *Social Science and Medicine*, Vol. 29, pp. 609–16.

FURTHER READING

Books

Chalmers, H. (1988) *Choosing a Model: Caring for Patients With Cardiovascular and Respiratory Problems*, Edward Arnold, London.

Kacmarek, R. M., Mack, C. W. and Dimas, S. (1990) *The Essentials of Respiratory Care*, Mosby Year Books, St Louis.

Wright, S. G. (ed.) (1988) Breathing, R. A. Webster and D. R. Thompson in *Nursing the Older Patient*, Harper & Row, London, pp. 93–119.

Articles

Boyer, M., Brough, F. K., Rasmussen, T. and Schmidt, C. D. (1982) Comparison of two teaching methods for self-care training for patients with chronic obstructive airways disease, *Patient Counselling and Health Education*, Vol. 4, pp. 111–15.

Cockcroft, A. E., Saunders, M. J. and Berry, G. (1981) Randomized controlled trial of rehabilitation in chronic respiratory disability, *Thorax*, Vol. 36, pp. 200–3.

Curgian, L. M. and Pagano, K. (1985) Nutrition in chronic respiratory disease, *Rehabilitation Nursing*, Vol. 10, No. 6, pp. 22–3.

Doll, R. and Peto, R. (1976) Mortality in relation to smoking: 10 years' observation in British doctors, *British Medical Journal*, Vol. 2, pp. 1525–8.

Dudley, D. L., Glaser, E. M. G., Jorgenson, B. N. and Logan, D. L. (1980) Psychological concomitants to rehabilitation in chronic obstructive pulmonary disease, *Chest*, Vol. 77, pp. 413–19.

Fleetham, J. A. and Kryger, M. M. (1981) Sleep disorders in chronic airflow obstruction, *Medical Clinics of North America*, Vol. 65, pp. 549–61.

Grayden, J. E. (1988) Factors that predict patients' functioning following treatment for cancer, *International Journal of Nursing Studies*, Vol. 25, pp. 117–24.

Heslop, A. P. and Bagnall, P. (1988) A study to evaluate the intervention of a nurse visiting patients with disabling chest disease in the community, *Journal of Advanced Nursing*, Vol. 13, pp. 71–7.

Janson-Bjerklie, S., Carrier, V. K. and Hudes, M. (1988) The sensations of pulmonary dyspnea, *Nursing Research*, Vol. 35, pp. 154–9.

Kim, M. J. (1984) Respiratory muscle training, *Heart and Lung*, Vol. 13, pp. 333–40.

Ledger, S. D. (1986) Management of a patient in respiratory failure due to chronic bronchitis, *Intensive Care Nursing*, Vol. 2, pp. 30–43.

Luce, J. M. (1980) Respiratory complications of obesity, *Chest*, Vol. 78, pp. 626–31.

Moser, K. M. and Archibald, C. (1983) *Shortness of Breath: A Guide to Better Living and Breathing*, C. V. Mosby, St Louis.

Parkosewich, J. A. (1986) Sleep-disordered breathing: a common problem in chronic obstructive pulmonary disease, *Critical Care Nurse*, Vol. 6, No. 6, pp. 60–4.

Renfroe, K. L. (1988) Effects of progressive relaxation on dyspnea and state anxiety in patients with chronic obstructive pulmonary disease, *Heart and Lung*, Vol. 17, pp. 408–13.

Sjoberg, E. L. (1983) Nursing diagnosis and the COPD patient, *American Journal of Nursing*, Vol. 83, pp. 244–8.

Traver, G. A. (1988) Measures of symptoms and life quality to predict emergent use of institutional health care resources in chronic obstructive airways disease, *Heart and Lung*, Vol. 17, pp. 689–97.

Unger, K. M., Moser, K. M. and Hansen, P. (1980) Selection of an exercise program for patients with chronic obstructive pulmonary disease, *Heart and Lung*, Vol. 9, pp. 68–76.

Williams, S. J. (1989) Chronic respiratory illness and disability: a critical review of the psychosocial literature, *Social Science and Medicine*, Vol. 28, pp. 791–803.

Unit 3

CARDIOVASCULAR, CIRCULATORY AND HAEMATOLOGICAL PROBLEMS

chapter 6 ▬▬▬▬▬

ASSESSMENT OF CARDIOVASCULAR FUNCTION

Nursing assessment of a patient with heart disease includes taking a history, observing physical appearance and monitoring tests of cardiac functioning. A sound knowledge of cardiac anatomy, physiology and pathophysiology is necessary for developing assessment skills, defining patient problems, planning nursing care and understanding the purposes of diagnostic tests.

ANATOMY AND PHYSIOLOGY

The heart is a hollow, muscular organ located in the centre of the thorax where it occupies the space between the lungs and rests upon the diaphragm. It weighs approximately 300 g (10.6 oz), although heart weight and size are influenced by age, sex, body weight, frequency of physical exercise and heart disease. The function of the heart is to pump blood through the body thus supplying tissues with oxygen and other nutrients and at the same time removing carbon dioxide and other waste products of metabolism. There are actually two pumps within the heart, located on its right and left sides, respectively. The output of the right heart is distributed entirely to the lungs via the pulmonary artery, and the output of the left heart is distributed to the remainder of the body via the aorta. These two pumps eject blood simultaneously at approximately the same rate of output.

The pumping action of the heart is accomplished by the rhythmical contraction and relaxation of its muscular wall. During contraction of the muscle (systole), the chambers inside the heart become smaller as the blood is ejected. During relaxation of the muscles of the heart wall (diastole), the heart chambers fill with blood in preparation for the subsequent ejection. A normal adult heart beats approximately 60 to 80 times per minute, ejects approximately 70 ml of blood from each side per beat, and has a total output of approximately 5 l/min.

Cardiac Anatomy

The space in the middle of the chest between the two lungs is called the mediastinum. The bulk of the mediastinal space is occupied by the heart, which is encased in a thin, fibrous sac called the pericardium. The pericardium is not essential for the proper functioning of the heart, but serves as an envelope to protect its surface. The space between the surface of the heart and the pericardial lining is filled with a very small amount of fluid, which lubricates the surface and tends to reduce friction during cardiac muscle contraction.

Heart Chambers

The right and left sides of the heart are each composed of two chambers, an atrium (pl. atria) and a ventricle. The common wall between the right and left chambers is called the septum. The ventricles are the chambers that eject blood into the arteries. The functions of the atria are to receive incoming blood from the veins and to act as temporary storage reservoirs for subsequent emptying into the ventricles. The relationship of the four chambers of the heart is shown in Figure 6.1.

The atria and ventricles are easily distinguished by the greater thickness of the muscle that forms the ventricular wall. The left ventricle ejects blood against high systemic pressure, whereas the right ventricle ejects blood against the low-resistance pulmonary vasculature. Therefore, because of the increased work of the left heart, the left ventricular wall is about two and a half times as thick (approximately 1 cm) as the right ventricular wall.

Because of the rotation of the heart within the chest cavity, the right ventricle lies anteriorly (just beneath the sternum) and the left ventricle is situated posteriorly. The left ventricle is responsible for the apex beat or the point of maximum impulse, usually apparent on the left side of the chest wall.

Heart Valves

Heart valves permit blood to flow in only one direction through the heart. Valves, which are composed of thin leaflets of fibrous tissue, open and close passively in response to pressure changes and blood movement. There are two types of valves: atrioventricular and semilunar.

Atrioventricular Valves. Valves separating the atria from the ventricles are termed atrioventricular valves. The tricuspid valve, so named because it is composed of three cusps, or leaflets, separates the right atrium from the right ventricle. The mitral or bicuspid valve (two cusps) lies between the left atrium and left ventricle.

Semilunar Valves. Semilunar valves are situated between each ventricle and its corresponding artery. The valve between the right ventricle and the pulmonary artery is called the pulmonary valve; the valve between the left ventricle and the aorta is called the aortic valve. Both of the semilunar valves are normally composed of three cusps. There are no valves between the large veins and the atria.

Papillary Muscles and Chordae Tendineae

Normally, when the ventricles contract, ventricular pressure tends to push the atrioventricular valve leaflets upward into the atrial cavity. If enough pressure were to be exerted on the valves, blood would be ejected backward from the ventricles to the atria. Papillary muscles and chordae tendineae are responsible for maintaining unidirectional blood flow through the atrioventricular valves (from the ventricle to the respective artery). Papillary muscles are muscle bundles that are located on the sides of the ventricular walls. Chordae tendineae are fibrous bands extending from the papillary muscles to the edges of the valve leaflets, acting to tether the free edges of the valves to the ventricular wall. Contraction of the papillary muscles causes the chordae tendineae to become taut. This keeps the valve leaflets closed during systole, preventing backflow of blood. Papillary muscles and chordae tendineae are not necessary for proper functioning of the semilunar valves.

Coronary Arteries

The heart muscle is metabolically active in that its requirements for oxygen and nutrients are large and continuous. These required substances are supplied to the heart muscle by blood flowing in the coronary arteries (see Figure 6.2). The heart, with large metabolic requirements, uses approximately one half of the oxygen delivered through the coronary arteries; in contrast, other organs use, on the average, only one quarter of the oxygen

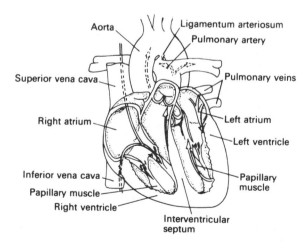

Figure 6.1 Interior of the heart. Arrows indicate the direction of blood flow. (Chaffee, E. E. and Greisheimer, E. M. (1974) *Basic Physiology and Anatomy* (3rd edition), J. B. Lippincott, Philadelphia.)

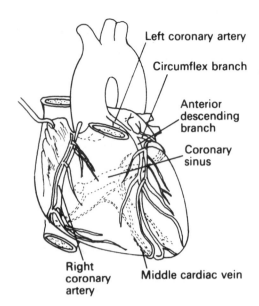

Left coronary artery

Circumflex branch

Anterior descending branch

Coronary sinus

Right coronary artery

Middle cardiac vein

Figure 6.2 Diagram of the coronary arteries arising from the aorta and encircling the heart. The coronary sinus and some of the coronary veins are also shown. (Chaffee, E. E. and Greisheimer, E. M. (1974) *Basic Physiology and Anatomy* (3rd edition), J. B. Lippincott, Philadelphia.)

delivered to them. The coronary arteries arise from the aorta near its origin at the left ventricle. The wall of the left side of the heart is supplied in large part through the left main coronary artery, which divides into several large branches that run down (left anterior descending coronary artery) and across the left side of the myocardium (circumflex artery). The right heart wall is supplied similarly from a separate right coronary artery. Unlike other arteries, the coronary arteries are perfused during diastole.

Cardiac Muscle

The specialized muscle tissue composing the wall of the heart is called cardiac muscle. Microscopically, cardiac muscle resembles striated (skeletal) muscle, which is under conscious control. However, heart muscle is not under conscious control and in that sense resembles smooth (involuntary) muscle. The cardiac muscle fibres are arranged in an interconnected manner (called a syncytium) so that they can contract and relax in co-ordination. The sequential pattern of contraction and relaxation of individual muscle fibres ensures the rhythmic behaviour of the heart muscle as a whole and enables it to function as a pump. The heart muscle itself is called the myocardium. The segment of cells on the inner surface of this muscle, which is in contact with the blood, is called the endocardium, and the portion of cells on the outer surface of the heart is called the epicardium.

Cardiac Physiology

Electromechanical Coupling

In the normal cardiac muscle cell, an electrical difference (voltage) exists between the inside and the outside of the cell across its membrane. The inside of the cell is negative relative to the outside of the cell. When the magnitude of this difference is reduced (the inside of the cell becomes less negative), depolarization has occurred and contraction of muscle cell results. A cardiac muscle cell is normally depolarized when a neighbouring cell is depolarized (although it can also be depolarized by external electrical stimulation). Sufficient depolarization of a single specialized conduction system cell will therefore result in depolarization and contraction of the entire myocardium. Repolarization occurs as the cell returns to its baseline state (becomes more negative), and corresponds to relaxation of myocardial muscle.

During depolarization the permeability of the cell membranes to certain ions (sodium, chloride, calcium, potassium) changes. One of those changes results in an increased permeability to calcium, allowing for uptake of calcium into the cell. This increase in intracellular calcium concentration leads to shortening of the muscle fibres and development of tension (contraction). After a short period, the membrane voltage returns to its original value, the calcium that has accumulated in its interior is removed and the cell relaxes. This interaction between changes in membrane voltage and muscle contraction is called electromechanical coupling.

Cardiac muscle, unlike skeletal or smooth muscle, has a prolonged refractory period during which it cannot be restimulated to contract. This protects the heart from sustained contraction (tetany), which would result in sudden cardiac death.

Normal electromechanical coupling and contraction of the heart are dependent on the composition of the interstitial fluid surrounding the heart muscle cells. The composition of this fluid is in turn influenced by the composition of the blood. A change in blood calcium concentration may therefore alter contraction of the heart muscle fibres. A change in blood potassium concentration is also important, because potassium affects the normal electrical voltage of the cell.

Conduction System of the Heart

Specialized cells of the conduction system generate and conduct electrical impulses to myocardial cells, resulting in myocardial contraction. Cardiac muscle cells have an inherent rhythmicity, which is illustrated by the fact that a segment of myocardium removed from the rest of the heart will continue to contract rhythmically if maintained under the proper conditions. The heart rate is determined by the group of myocardial cells with the fastest intrinsic

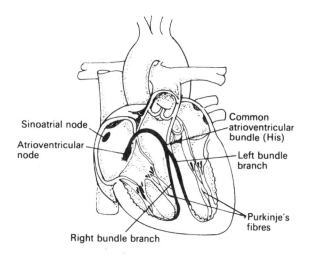

Figure 6.3 Conduction system, showing relationship between the sinoatrial node, the atrioventricular node and the common atrioventricular bundle and its branches. (Chaffee, E.E. and Greisheimer, E.M. (1974) *Basic Physiology and Anatomy* (3rd edition), J. B. Lippincott, Philadelphia.)

rate. These specialized cells, located at the junction of the superior vena cava and the right atrium, are known as the sinoatrial node and function as the pacemaker for the entire myocardium (see Figure 6.3). The sinoatrial node initiates approximately 60 to 100 impulses per minute in a resting normal heart but can change its rate in response to the needs of the body. The electrical signal initiated by the sinoatrial node is conducted along the myocardial cells of the atrium to the atrioventricular node. The atrioventricular node (located in the right atrial wall near the tricuspid valve) is another group of specialized muscle cells similar to the sinoatrial node, but with an intrinsic rate of about 40 to 60 impulses per minute. The atrioventricular node co-ordinates the incoming electrical impulses from the atria and relays an electrical impulse to the ventricles. This impulse is conducted away from the atrioventricular node through a bundle of specialized muscle fibres (the bundle of His) that travel in the septum separating the left and right ventricles. The His bundle divides into right and left bundle branches, which terminate in fibres called Purkinje fibres. The right bundle fans out into the right ventricular muscle. The left bundle divides again into the left anterior and left posterior bundle branches, which fan out into the left ventricular muscle. Further spread of depolarization through the rest of the myocardium takes place by conduction through the muscle fibres themselves.

If the sinoatrial node malfunctions, the atrioventricular node generally takes over the pacemaker function of the heart. Should both the sinoatrial and atrioventricular nodes fail in their pacemaker function, the myocardium will continue to beat at a rate of less than 40 beats per minute, the intrinsic pacemaker rate of the electrical impulse of the ventricular myocardial cells.

Cardiac Haemodynamics

Fluid flows from regions of high pressure to regions of low pressure. The pressures that are responsible for blood flow in the normal circulation are generated by contraction of the ventricular muscle. When the muscle contracts, blood is forced from the ventricle into the aorta during the period of time when left ventricular pressure exceeds aortic pressure. When these two pressures become equal, the aortic valve closes and output from the left ventricle ceases. The blood that has entered the aorta increases the pressure in that vessel. This provides a pressure gradient to force blood progressively through the arteries and capillaries and into the veins. The blood returns to the right atrium because pressure in this chamber is lower than pressure in the veins. Similarly, a gradient of pressure is responsible for blood flow from the pulmonary artery through the lung and back to the left atrium. The pressure gradients within the pulmonary circulation are considerably lower than those in the systemic circulation because the resistance to flow in the pulmonary vessels is lower.

Cardiac Cycle

Consider the pressure changes that occur in the chambers of the heart during the cardiac cycle, beginning with diastole when the ventricles are relaxed. During diastole the atrioventricular valves are open, and blood returning from the veins flows into the atrium and then into the ventricle. Towards the end of this diastolic period, the atrial muscle contracts in response to a signal initiated by the sinoatrial node. The contraction raises the pressure inside the atrium and forces an increment of blood into the ventricle. This blood augments the volume of the ventricles by an additional 10 per cent. At this point, the ventricles themselves begin to contract (systole) in response to propagation of the electrical impulse that began in the sinoatrial node some milliseconds previously. During systole, the pressure inside the ventricle rapidly rises, forcing the atrioventricular valves to close. The consequence of this action is that no further filling of the ventricle from the atrium can occur, and blood ejected from the ventricle cannot flow back to the atrium. The rapid rise of pressure inside the ventricles forces the pulmonary and aortic valves to open, and blood is ejected into the pulmonary artery and aorta, respectively. The exit of blood is at first rapid, and then, as the pressures in each ventricle and its corresponding artery approach equalization, the flow of blood gradually decreases. At the cessation of systole, the ventricular muscle relaxes and the pressure within the chamber rapidly decreases. This decrease in pressure creates a tendency for blood to come back from the artery into the ventricle, which forces the semilunar valves to close. Simultaneously, as the pressure within the ventricle drops to below atrial pressure, the atrioventricular valves open, the ventricles begin to fill, and the entire sequence is repeated. It is important to note that the mechanical events related to filling and ejection by the heart are closely coupled to the corresponding electrical events that cause cardiac contraction and relaxation.

The events just described lead to the repetitive rise and fall of pressures inside the ventricles. The maximum pressure reached is called systolic pressure and the minimum pressure diastolic pressure.

Cardiac Output

Cardiac output is the amount of blood pumped by either of the ventricles during a given period of time. The cardiac output of a typical adult is normally about 5 l/min but varies greatly, depending on the metabolic needs of the body. Cardiac output is equivalent to the stroke volume multiplied by the heart rate. Stroke volume is the amount of blood ejected per heartbeat. Cardiac output can be affected, therefore, by changes in either stroke volume or heart rate. The resting heart rate of an average adult is approximately 72 beats/min and the average stroke volume is about 70 ml/beat.

Control of Heart Rate

Since the function of the heart is to supply blood to all tissues of the body, its output varies as the metabolic needs of the tissues themselves change. For example, during exercise the total cardiac output may increase fourfold, to 20 l/min. This increase is normally accomplished by approximately doubling both the heart rate and the stroke volume. Changes in heart rate are accomplished by reflex controls mediated by the autonomic nervous system, including its sympathetic and parasympathetic divisions. The parasympathetic nerves, which travel to the heart through the vagus nerve, can slow the cardiac rate, whereas sympathetic nerves increase it. These nerves exert their effect on heart rate through their action on the sinoatrial node to either decrease or increase its rate of intrinsic depolarization. The balance between these two reflex control systems normally determines the heart rate. The heart rate is also stimulated by an increased level of circulating catecholamines (secreted by the adrenal gland) and by the presence of excess thyroid hormone, which produces a catecholamine-like effect.

Control of Stroke Volume

Stroke volume is determined primarily by three factors: (1) intrinsic contractility of the cardiac muscle, (2) the degree of stretch of the cardiac muscle before its contraction, and (3) the pressure against which the heart muscle has to eject blood during contraction.

Intrinsic contractility is a term used to denote the force that can be generated by the contracting myocardium

under any given condition. It is increased by circulating catecholamines, sympathetic neuronal activity and certain drugs (such as digitalis). It is depressed by hypoxaemia and acidosis. Increased contractility results in increased stroke volume.

The precontraction length of the ventricular muscle fibres is determined by the volume of blood within the ventricle at the end of diastole. This volume, the ventricular end-diastolic volume, is called preload. The larger the preload, the greater will be the stroke volume, until a point is reached when the muscle is so stretched it can no longer contract. The relationship between increased stroke volume and increased ventricular end-diastolic volume for a given intrinsic contractility is called Starling's Law of the Heart, which is based on the fact that a greater initial length leads to a greater degree of shortening of cardiac muscle. This results from increased interaction between thick and thin filaments of the sarcomeres (similar to that discussed more fully in Chapter 34 on skeletal muscle physiology).

The pressure against which the left ventricle ejects blood is the pressure in the aorta; right ventricular ejection works against the pressure in the pulmonary artery. The greater these pressures, the greater will be the tension in the ventricular wall during contraction. This tension is called afterload. Increased afterload leads to decreased stroke volume.

The heart can achieve a greatly increased stroke volume, as during exercise, by increasing preload (through increased venous return), by increasing contractility (through sympathetic nervous discharge) and by decreasing afterload (through peripheral vasodilation with decreased aortic pressure).

The fraction of the end-diastolic volume that is ejected with each stroke is called the ejection fraction. With each stroke, 56 to 78 per cent of the end-diastolic volume is ejected by the normal heart. The ejection fraction can be used as an index of myocardial contractility; it is decreased if contractility is depressed.

Considerations for the Elderly

Atherosclerosis of the coronary arteries and its resultant effects on the heart have long been associated with the ageing process. However, recent investigations show little evidence that age is the precipitating factor. Current evidence indicates that the cardiac changes once attributed to ageing can be minimized by modifying lifestyle and personal habits, that is, by following a low-sodium, low-fat diet, not smoking and exercising regularly.

Studies have shown that the normal ageing heart is able to provide an adequate cardiac output under ordinary circumstances, but may have limited functional ability to respond to situations that cause physical or emotional stress. In the elderly person who has decreased activity, the left ventricle may become smaller in response to the decreased workload demand. Ageing also results in decreased elasticity and widening of the aorta, thickening and rigidity of the cardiac valves and increased connective tissue in the sinoatrial and atrioventricular nodes and bundle branches. These changes lead to decreased myocardial contractility, increased left ventricular ejection time and delayed conduction. Thus, stressful physical and emotional conditions, especially those that occur suddenly, may have adverse effects on the aged person. The heart is unable to respond to such conditions with an adequate increase in rate, and more time is required for the heart rate to return to basal levels after even a minimal increase. In some patients heart failure may be precipitated.

NURSING HISTORY

Cardiac patients who are acutely ill require a different initial nursing history than do cardiac patients with stable or chronic problems. A patient experiencing an acute myocardial infarction requires immediate, and possibly lifesaving, medical and nursing care—for example, relief of chest discomfort or prevention of arrhythmias—rather than an extensive interview. For this patient, a few wellchosen questions about chest discomfort, associated symptoms (such as shortness of breath or palpitations),

drug allergies and smoking history should be asked at the same time one is assessing heart rate, rhythm and blood pressure. When the patient is more stable, a more extensive history should be obtained.

When caring for an acutely ill cardiac patient, one must first focus on assessment of the heart and cardiac output. Patients with atherosclerotic coronary artery disease commonly experience chest discomfort (angina pectoris or myocardial infarction); shortness of breath, fatigue and reduced urine output (left ventricular failure with decreased cardiac output); palpitations and dizziness (arrhythmias due to ischaemia, aneurysm, stress or electrolyte imbalance); oedema and weight gain (right ventricular failure); and postural hypotension with dizziness and light-headedness (saline depletion from diuretic therapy). Patients with valvular disease may have symptoms of heart failure, arrhythmias and chest discomfort.

Not all chest discomfort is related to myocardial ischaemia. Guidelines are useful in differentiating the chest discomfort of serious, life-threatening conditions from that of conditions less serious or that would be treated in a different manner. Table 6.1 summarizes characteristics of the pain associated with angina pectoris, myocardial infarction and pericarditis. Figure 6.4 illustrates the pain patterns both in these conditions and in noncardiac conditions. However, there are four important points to remember when evaluating chest discomfort:

Table 6.1 *Characteristics of pain associated with angina pectoris, myocardial infarction and pericarditis*

Location and radiation	Character and duration	Precipitating events
Angina pectoris		
Subternal or retrosternal pain spreading across chest	*Pressure*; squeezing, heavy discomfort	Usually related to exertion, emotion, eating
	Usually subsides within 1–10 min	
May radiate to *inside* of either arm or to both arms, neck or jaw		
Myocardial infarction		
Substernal or over precordium	Crushing, vice-like, gripping	Occurs spontaneously
May spread widely throughout chest; painful disability of shoulders and hands may be present	More severe and prolonged than angina May be associated with dizziness, perspiration and nausea 15–25% may be silent	Unrelated to emotion, exercise
Pericarditis		
Substernal or to left of sternum	Sharp, intermittent pain; made worse by swallowing, coughing, *rotation of trunk*	Often severe and sudden in onset; pain increases with inspiration and motion of trunk
May be felt in epigastrium		
May be referred to neck, arms, back		

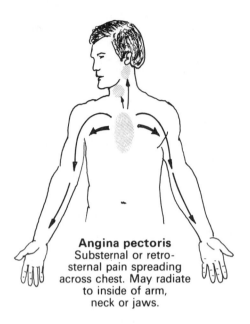

Angina pectoris
Substernal or retro-
sternal pain spreading
across chest. May radiate
to inside of arm,
neck or jaws.

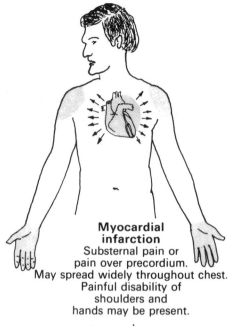

**Myocardial
infarction**
Substernal pain or
pain over precordium.
May spread widely throughout chest.
Painful disability of
shoulders and
hands may be present.

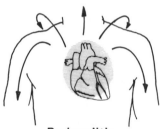

Pericarditis
Substernal pain or pain to
the left of sternum. May
be felt in epigastrium and
may be referred to neck,
arms and back.

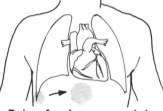

Pain of pulmonary origin
Pain arises from inferior
portion of pleura.
May be referred to costal
margins or upper abdomen.
Patient may be able to
localize the pain.

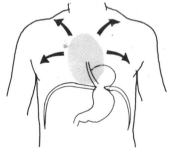

Oesophageal pain
(*Hiatus hernia, Reflux oesophagitis*)
Substernal pain. May be
projected around chest
to shoulders.

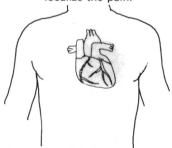

Anxiety
Pain over left chest.
May be variable.
Does not radiate. Assess
for hyperventilation, sighing
respiration, palpitations. Patient
may complain of numbness
and tingling of hands and mouth.

Figure 6.4 Assessment of chest pain.

- There is little correlation between the severity of the chest discomfort and the gravity of its cause.
- There is poor correlation between the location of chest discomfort and its source.
- The patient may have more than one clinical problem occurring simultaneously.
- In a patient with a history of atherosclerotic coronary artery disease, it is frequently assumed that the chest discomfort is secondary to ischaemia until proven otherwise.

To facilitate the gathering of information for a cardiovascular nursing history, the following areas should be assessed (adapted from Brunner and Suddarth (1989), Chapter 5, p. 213):

1. Breathing:
   a. Is the patient breathless?
   b. What precipitates or relieves the breathlessness?
   c. What position does the patient assume?
   d. What colour is the skin (e.g. pale, cyanosed)?
   e. What is the nature of the respiration (e.g. depth, frequency)?
   f. Is there any sputum? Is it, for example, frothy, pink, infected?
2. Pain:
   a. Is the patient in pain, and where is the pain located?
   b. What is the character of the pain (e.g. dull, sharp, crushing)?
   c. Are associated signs and symptoms present (e.g. sweating, nausea)?
   d. How is pain precipitated (e.g. exercise, cold, stress)?
   e. How is pain relieved (e.g. rest, glyceryl trinitrate)?
3. Colour:
   a. Is central cyanosis present?
   b. Is peripheral cyanosis present?
   c. Is pallor present?
4. Oedema:
   a. Is ankle oedema present?
   b. Is sacral oedema present?
   c. Is ascites present?
5. Arrhythmias:
   a. Is the pulse regular or irregular?
   b. Does the patient complain of palpitations?

All of these areas can be assessed by the nurse during the routine admission procedure, causing minimal stress and exertion for the patient, who will be given a more detailed examination by the medical staff. When the patient's condition permits, a more detailed nursing assessment can be made. However, it is important to phrase the questions according to the appropriateness of the situation and to pursue areas where further clarification is necessary.

Information obtained in the nursing history is needed in order to plan individualized care while the patient is hospitalized, to aid in discharge planning and to provide appropriate teaching. Knowing how the patient perceives the effects of the disease process on activities of daily living will help to identify specific aims for cardiac rehabilitation or to devise strategies for modifying certain activities.

Since dietary modification (reduction of sodium, saturated fat or caloric intake) will probably be prescribed, the history should include the following: food preferences (including cultural or ethnic); eating habits (canned or commercially prepared foods versus fresh foods, and restaurant cooking versus home cooking); who shops for groceries; and who prepares the meals. Knowing if any risk factors for coronary artery disease exist will enable the nurse to help the patient modify behaviours that may be contributing to the progression of heart disease.

RISK FACTORS IN CORONARY ARTERY DISEASE

The presence of coronary artery disease is associated with one or more characteristic findings known as risk factors. Risk factors have been determined on the basis of systematic observations of relationships between certain characteristics and the subsequent development of coronary artery disease. Current research is establishing physiological explanations for these relationships.

Effective patient teaching requires a knowledge base for recognizing the risk factors, for interpreting the data from studies that identify risk factors and for making effective explanations about the significance of the risk factors and how they can be modified. However, there is not complete agreement about the importance or the effectiveness of modifying risk factors in patients with known coronary artery disease.

Risk factors for atherosclerosis tend to make an individual more prone to developing coronary heart disease. These risk factors are classified according to whether or not they can be modified by changing an element of lifestyle or a personal habit. Nonmodifiable risk factors include the following:

- Positive family history.
- Increasing age.
- Sex (males greater than females).

Modifiable risk factors include the following:

- Hyperlipidaemia.
- Elevated blood pressure.
- Elevated blood sugar (diabetes mellitus).
- Obesity.
- Physical inactivity.
- Stress.
- Use of oral contraceptives.

PHYSICAL ASSESSMENT

Assessment of physical findings should confirm data obtained in the nursing history. Baseline information is obtained on admission. For the acutely ill cardiac patient, physical examination is performed with routine vital signs (every four hours, or more frequently if indicated). Because nurses spend 24 hours a day with the patient, they are in the best position to identify any changes that may occur.

It is to the patient's benefit to detect changes early, before serious complications develop. Any changes observed in the assessment are reported to the medical staff and noted in detail in the chart.

The cardiac physical assessment, which is carried out by the nurse, should include an evaluation of the following:

● Patient appearance.
● The heart as a pump.
● Filling volumes and pressures.
● Cardiac output.
● Compensatory mechanisms.

Factors that reflect decreased contractility and efficiency of the heart as a pump are reduced pulse pressure, cardiac enlargement and the presence of murmurs and gallop rhythms.

Filling volumes and pressures are estimated by the degree of jugular vein distension and the presence or absence of congestion in the lungs, peripheral oedema and postural changes in blood pressure.

Cardiac output is reflected by heart rate, pulse pressure, peripheral vascular resistance, urine output and central nervous system manifestations.

Examples of compensatory mechanisms that help maintain cardiac output are increased filling volumes and elevated heart rate.

The order of examination proceeds logically from head to toe, and with practice can be done in approximately 10 minutes: (1) general appearance, (2) blood pressure, (3) pulse, (4) hands, (5) head and neck, (6) heart, (7) lungs, (8) abdomen, and (9) feet and legs.

General Appearance

The nurse should observe the patient's level of distress. The level of consciousness should be noted and described. Appropriateness of thought content, reflecting the adequacy of cerebral perfusion, is particularly important to evaluate. Family members who are most familiar with the patient can be helpful in alerting the examiner to subtle behavioural changes.

The nurse should also take note of the patient's anxiety level and should know how anxiety affects the cardiovascular system. The nurse attempts to put the anxious patient at ease.

Examination of Blood Pressure

Blood pressure occurs as a cyclic phenomenon and is measured in millimetres of mercury (mmHg). The peak of the cycle is called the systolic pressure; the low point of the cycle is called the diastolic pressure. Blood pressure is usually expressed as the ratio of the systolic pressure over the diastolic pressure, with normal average values measuring 120/80 mmHg.

The difference between the systolic and the diastolic pressures is called the pulse pressure. Normally, this amounts to 40 mmHg. When the systolic pressure is elevated, a widening of the pulse pressure results. This happens in atherosclerosis (hardening of the arteries) and in thyrotoxicosis. Elevation of the diastolic pressure is always associated with elevation of the systolic pressure, and the circumstance represents true hypertension. An increase in the diastolic pressure to 95 mmHg gives rise to concern, particularly in younger patients; an increase in excess of 95 mmHg in the diastolic pressure constitutes true hypertension and requires investigation and control.

Postural Blood Pressure Changes

Postural (orthostatic) hypotension occurs when the blood pressure drops after an upright posture is assumed; it is usually accompanied by dizziness, light-headedness, or syncope. Although there are many causes of postural hypotension, the three most commonly seen in the cardiac patient are saline depletion, inadequate vasoconstrictor mechanisms, and autonomic insufficiency. Postural changes in blood pressure, along with appropriate history, can help the medical staff differentiate between these causes. Remember the following points when assessing postural blood pressure changes:

● Position the patient supine and as flat as symptoms permit for 10 minutes before the initial blood pressure and heart rate measurement.
● Always check supine measurements before checking upright measurements.
● Always record both heart rate and blood pressure at each postural change (lying down, sitting, standing).
● Do not remove the blood pressure cuff between position changes, but do check to see that it is still correctly placed.
● Assess postural blood pressure changes with the patient sitting on the edge of the bed with feet dangling and, if necessary, with the patient standing at the side of the bed.
● Wait one to three minutes after each postural change before recording blood pressure and heart rate.
● Be alert for any signs or symptoms of patient distress and, if necessary, return the patient to bed before the test is completed.
● Record any signs or symptoms that accompany the postural change.

Normal postural responses are increased heart rate (tooffset reduced stroke volume and maintain cardiac output), a slight to a 15 mmHg drop in systolic pressure, and a slight drop to an increase of 5 to 10 mmHg in diastolic pressure.

Saline depletion should be suspected (in the presence of a history of saline loss, e.g., diuretic therapy) when, in response to sitting or standing, the heart rate increases and either the systolic pressure decreases by 15 mmHg or the diastolic blood pressure drops by 10 mmHg. It is difficult to differentiate saline depletion from inadequate vasoconstrictor mechanisms by postural changes in vital signs alone.

With saline depletion, reflexes to maintain cardiac output (increased heart rate and peripheral vasoconstriction) function correctly but, because of lost extracellular fluid volume, the blood pressure falls. With inadequate vasoconstrictor mechanisms, the heart rate again responds appropriately but, because of diminished peripheral vasoconstriction, the blood pressure drops. The following is an example of a postural blood pressure recording showing either saline depletion or inadequate vasoconstrictor mechanisms:

	Blood pressure	Heart rate
Lying down	120/70	70
Sitting	100/55	90
Standing	98/52	94

In autonomic insufficiency, the heart rate is unable to increase to compensate for the gravitational effects of upright posture. Peripheral vasoconstriction may be absent or diminished. The presence of autonomic insufficiency does not rule out concurrent saline depletion. The following is an example of autonomic insufficiency as demonstrated by postural blood pressure changes:

	Blood pressure	Heart rate
Lying down	150/90	60
Sitting	100/60	60

Examination of the Pulse

The pulse should be examined bilaterally; peripheral pulses should be equal. The nurse should note the amplitude (fullness); this will depend on pulse pressure, i.e. the difference between systolic and diastolic pressures. It gives an estimate of stroke volume.

A small volume pulse may indicate low stroke volume and peripheral vasoconstriction caused by, for example, myocardial infarction or shock. Large pulse volume produced by large stroke volume may indicate, for example, aortic regurgitation or thyrotoxicosis (Brunner and Suddarth, 1989).

The rate of the pulse should also be examined; it may vary from 50 to 100 beats per minute, with the average adult pulse being 70 (Millar, 1975). Equally important is the assessment of pulse rhythm; if this is found to be irregular, the pulse should be counted apically and radially at the same time for a full minute, and any discrepancies noted. Pulse deficits are commonly found with atrial fibrillation/flutter, ventricular ectopics and heart block.

Hands

In the cardiac patient, the following are the most important findings to note:

● Peripheral cyanosis implies decreased flow rate of blood in the periphery, allowing more time for the haemoglobin molecule to become desaturated. This may occur normally with the peripheral vasoconstriction associated with a cold environment, or pathologically in conditions that reduce blood flow, for example, cardiogenic shock.
● Pallor can denote anaemia or an increased systemic vascular resistance.
● Capillary refill time provides the basis for an estimate of the rate of peripheral blood flow. Normally, reperfusion occurs almost instantaneously. More sluggish reperfusion indicates a slower peripheral flow rate, for example, as in heart failure.
● Hand temperature and moistness are controlled by the autonomic nervous system. Normally, hands are warm and dry. Under stress, they may be cool and moist. In cardiogenic shock, hands become cold and clammy due to stimulation of the sympathetic nervous system and resulting vasoconstriction.
● Oedema decreases skin mobility.
● Dehydration and ageing reduce skin turgor.
● Clubbing of the fingers and toes implies chronic haemoglobin desaturation, as in congenital heart disease.

Head and Neck

When examining the head of a cardiac patient, one needs to be concerned primarily with checking the lips and earlobes for cyanosis. In cyanosis, haemoglobin does not become fully saturated with oxygen and a bluish colour occurs.

A gross estimate of right heart function can be made by observing the pulsations of the jugular veins of the neck. This enables estimation of central venous pressure, which reflects right atrial or right ventricular end-diastolic pressure (the pressure immediately preceding right ventricular contraction).

Jugular vein distension is caused by increased filling volume and pressure on the right side of the heart.

Examination of this is normally carried out by the doctor, but observation of the pulsation of the external jugular veins may be made by the nurse. These are superficial and visible just above the clavicles adjacent to the sternomastoid muscles. They are frequently distended while the patient lies supine on the examining table or bed. As the patient's head is elevated, the distension of the veins will disappear. The veins are not normally apparent once the angle that the patient makes with the examining table exceeds 30 degrees.

Obvious distension of the veins with the patient's head elevated 45 to 90 degrees implies an abnormal increase in the volume of the venous system. This is associated with right-sided cardiac failure or, less commonly, with obstruction to flow in the superior vena cava.

Inspection, Palpation and Auscultation of the Heart

This will be carried out by the doctor and is necessary to establish abnormalities in heart size, position of the heart and abnormalities in heart sounds. Auscultation involves listening to each event of the cardiac cycle and allows diagnosis of, for example, stenotic valves. As stated with in connection with the pulse, nurses may be involved in recording apical/radial rates in order to assess for irregularities in heart rate or rhythm.

Lungs

Respiratory assessment is described in Chapter 3. Findings frequently exhibited by cardiac patients include the following:

- Tachypnoea. Rapid, shallow breathing may be noted in patients who have heart failure or pain, or who are extremely anxious.
- Cheyne-Stokes respirations. Patients in severe left ventricular failure may exhibit Cheyne-Stokes breathing. Of particular importance is the duration of the apnoeic period.
- Haemoptysis. Pink, frothy sputum is indicative of acute pulmonary oedema.
- Cough. A dry, hacking cough from irritation of small airways is common in patients with pulmonary congestion from heart failure.
- Crackles. Heart failure, or atelectasis associated with bed rest, splinting from ischaemic pain, or the effects of pain medication and sedatives, often results in the development of crackles. Typically, crackles are first noted at the bases (because of the effect of gravity on fluid accumulation and decreased ventilation of basilar tissue) but may progress to all portions of the lung fields. Examination for crackles is carried out by the doctor.
- Wheezes. Compression of the small airways by inter-

stitial pulmonary oedema may cause wheezing. Beta-blocking agents, such as propranolol, may precipitate airway narrowing, especially in patients with underlying pulmonary disease.

Abdomen

For the cardiac patient, two components of the abdominal examination are frequently performed.

- Determination of liver size. Liver engorgement occurs because of decreased venous return secondary to right ventricular failure. The liver will be enlarged, firm, nontender, and smooth. Hepatojugular reflux may be demonstrated by pressing firmly over the liver for 30 to 60 seconds and noting a 1 cm rise in jugular vein distension. Examination for this is carried out by the doctor.
- Assessment of bladder distension. Urine output is an important indicator of cardiac output. In a patient who has not voided or who is unable to void, always assess for bladder distension before initiating other measures.

Feet and Legs

Many patients with heart disease have associated peripheral vascular disease, or peripheral oedema secondary to right ventricular failure. Therefore, adequacy of peripheral arterial circulation and venous return should be assessed in all cardiac patients. In addition, thrombophlebitis is a complication associated with bedrest and requires careful monitoring.

Summary

Physical examination of the cardiovascular system is complex and much of it will be carried out by the medical staff. However, the physical observations carried out by the nurse are important and must be done accurately in order to assist with the patient's diagnosis.

DIAGNOSTIC TESTS AND PROCEDURES

Diagnostic tests and procedures are used to confirm data obtained by interview and examination. Some tests are easy to interpret, while others must be interpreted by expert medical staff. All require that basic explanations be given to patients. Some necessitate special procedures to be followed before the test and special monitoring by the nurse following the test.

Laboratory Tests

Laboratory tests may be requested for a variety of reasons:

to assist in the diagnosis of acute myocardial infarction (angina pectoris cannot be confirmed by either blood or urine studies); to measure abnormalities in blood chemistry that could affect the prognosis of a cardiac patient; to assess the degree of the inflammatory process; to screen for risk factors associated with the presence of atherosclerotic coronary artery disease; to determine baseline values before therapeutic intervention; to assess drug levels; and to screen generally for any abnormalities. Laboratory studies relating specifically to the cardiac patient are summarized. Because many different methods of measurement are used, individual hospitals should be referred to for their normal laboratory values.

Cardiac Enzymes and Isoenzymes

Acute myocardial infarction can be confirmed by the presence of abnormally high levels of enzymes or isoenzymes in the serum. Enzymes are released from cells when the cells are injured and their walls break down and die. Most of these enzymes are nonspecific in relation to the particular organ that has been damaged. Certain isoenzymes, however, come only from myocardial cells and are released when the cells are damaged by hypoxia resulting from ischaemia or infarction. The isoenzymes leak into the interstitial spaces of the myocardium and are carried into the general circulation by the lymph system and the coronary circulation. Because different enzymes are released into the blood at varying periods following myocardial infarction, it is crucial to time the drawing of blood in relation to the time of onset of chest discomfort. If blood is drawn too early, enzymes may not yet be elevated; if it is drawn too late, enzymes may already have returned to baseline. Enzymes used in the diagnosis of acute myocardial infarction are creatine phosphokinase (CPK) and its isoenzyme CPK-MB, and lactic dehydrogenase (LDH) and its isoenzymes.

The enzymes are evaluated as a part of the patient's total diagnostic profile, including history, symptoms and ECG.

Blood Chemistry

Serum Electrolytes

Serum electrolytes can affect the prognosis of a patient with acute myocardial infarction or any cardiac condition. Serum sodium reflects relative water balance. Calcium is necessary for blood coagulability and neuromuscular activity. Hypocalcaemia and hypercalcaemia can both cause ECG changes and arrhythmias.

Serum potassium is an indicator of renal function and may be decreased by diuretic agents that are often used to treat congestive heart failure. A decrease in potassium causes cardiac irritability and predisposes the patient receiving a digitalis preparation to digitalis toxicity and to the development of arrhythmias. Elevated serum potassium has a myocardial depressant effect and a ventricular irritability effect. Hypokalaemia and hyperkalaemia can each lead to ventricular fibrillation or cardiac arrest.

Blood Urea Nitrogen

Blood urea nitrogen is an end product of protein metabolism and is excreted by the kidneys. In the cardiac patient, elevated blood urea nitrogen could reflect reduced renal perfusion (due to decreased cardiac output) or saline depletion (due to diuretic therapy).

Glucose

Serum glucose is important to measure because many cardiac patients also have diabetes mellitus. Serum glucose may be mildly elevated in stressful situations when mobilization of endogenous noradrenaline results in conversion of liver glycogen to glucose.

Blood Lipids and Lipoproteins

Cholesterol and triglyceride levels may be measured to evaluate the risk of developing atherosclerotic disease. The patient should be fasting before the test. Stress may alter the results.

Measurement of lipoproteins is also useful in evaluating risk, especially if there is a positive family history of heart disease or to diagnose a specific lipoprotein abnormality. Decreased levels of high-density lipoprotein and elevated levels of low-density lipoprotein increase the risk of development of atherosclerotic coronary artery disease.

Chest X-Ray and Fluoroscopy

A chest X-ray is usually requested to determine the size, contour and position of the heart. It reveals cardiac and pericardial calcifications and demonstrates physiological alterations in the pulmonary circulation. It does not aid in the diagnosis of acute myocardial infarction, but can confirm the presence of some complications, e.g., congestive heart failure. Correct placement of heart catheters, such as pacemakers and pulmonary artery catheters, is also confirmed by chest X-ray.

Fluoroscopy provides visual observation of the heart on a luminescent X-ray screen. It shows heart and vascular pulsations and is useful in the assessment of unusual cardiac contours. Fluoroscopy is a useful tool for the placement and positioning of intravenous pacemaking electrodes and for guiding the catheter in cardiac catheterization.

Electrocardiography

The electrocardiogram (ECG) is a visual representation of the electrical activity of the heart as reflected by changes in electrical potential at the skin surface. The ECG is recorded as a tracing on a strip of paper or appears on the screen of an oscilloscope. In order to facilitate the interpretation of the ECG, data about the patient's age, sex, blood pressure, height, weight, symptoms and medications (especially digitalis and anti-arrhythmic drugs) should be noted on the ECG requisition. Electrocardiography is particularly useful in the evaluation of conditions that interfere with normal heart functions, such as disturbances of rate or rhythm, disorders of conduction, enlargement of heart chambers, presence of a myocardial infarction and electrolyte imbalances.

The standard ECG consists of 12 leads. Information regarding the electrical activity of the heart is obtained by placing electrodes on the skin surface at standardized anatomical positions. The various electrode positions that may be monitored are referred to as leads. For example, lead 1 measures the electrical activity between the left arm and the right arm. For a complete 12-lead ECG, the electroactivity of the heart is monitored from each of 12 different anatomical positions.

Procedure for Obtaining an Electrocardiogram

To obtain an ECG, electrodes are placed on the patient as shown in Figure 6.5. With the electrodes in these positions, the first six leads can be obtained. To ensure good contact between skin and electrode, the electrodes are placed on a flat surface just above the wrists and ankles, and electrode paste or an alcohol sponge is placed under each electrode. The extremity straps are adjusted firmly to hold the electrodes in place. These straps should not pinch the patient's skin or be so tight as to decrease circulation distal to the strap. The lead selected on the machine is then turned on to record each of the six leads. Next, the six V leads are obtained by moving the chest leads in the six precordial positions. A lead selector switch is turned to 'V' to record each of these leads. The arm and leg electrodes must be attached to the patient in order to obtain the V leads. There are some ECG machines that record three or six leads simultaneously.

Each ECG should include the following identifying information:

1. Patient name and identification number.
2. Location, date, and time of the recording.
3. Any unusual position of the patient during the record-

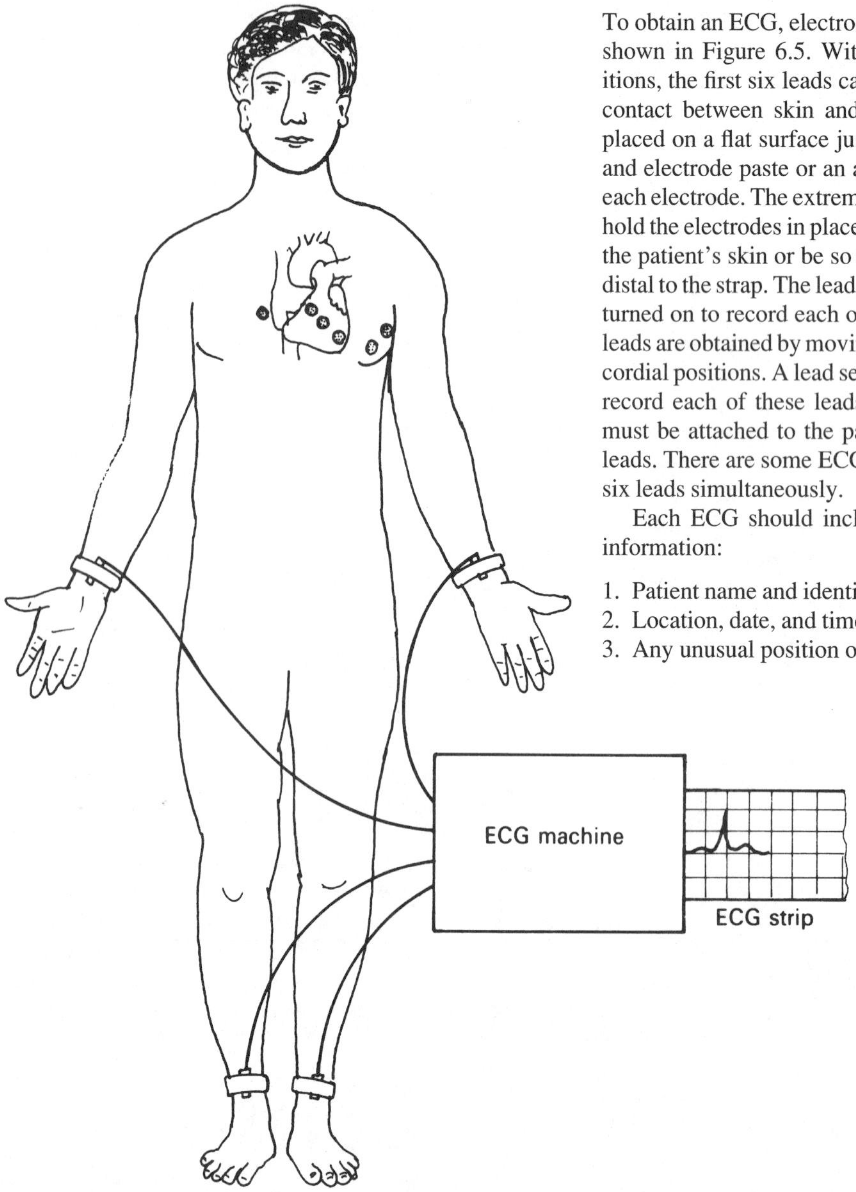

Figure 6.5 Twelve-lead ECG-electrode placement.

ing, or the presence of thoracic deformities, amputation, respiratory distress or muscle tremor.

Electrocardiographic Variations

In addition to the standard 12-lead ECG, the ECG can be used in other ways. One lead of the ECG can be monitored continuously on an oscilloscope (a fluorescent screen). The waveform from this lead can be written out to provide a permanent record. Continuous ECG monitoring is especially useful in the coronary care unit to detect arrhythmias.

One lead of the ECG can be monitored by a small tape recorder (Holter recorder) and recorded on a continuous (1 to 24 hours) magnetic tape recording. The patient can then be monitored day or night to detect arrhythmias or evidence of myocardial ischaemia during activities of daily living. The tape recorder weighs approximately 1 kg and can be carried over the shoulder. The patient keeps a diary of activity, noting the time of any symptoms, experiences or unusual activities performed. The tape recording is then examined (using a specialized instrument called a scanner), analysed and interpreted. Evidence obtained in this way is helpful in diagnosing arrhythmias and myocardial ischaemia and in evaluating therapy such as anti-arrhythmic and anti-anginal drugs or pacemaker function.

The ECG can also be transmitted by telemetry (telephone lines), thus freeing the patient from a cable connected to the oscilloscope. The ECG signal can then be monitored miles away.

Analysis of the ECG

When analysed accurately, the ECG offers important information about the electrical activity of the myocardium. ECG waveforms are printed on graph paper. Time or rate is measured on the horizontal axis of the graph, and amplitude or voltage is measured on the vertical axis. Because the conduction system of the heart is responsible for electrical activity, the ECG waveforms are representative of the conduction system's function.

Waves, Complexes and Intervals

The ECG is composed of several components or waves, including the P wave, the QRS complex, the T wave, the ST segment, the PR interval, and possibly a U wave (usually indicates an abnormality).

The P wave represents atrial muscle depolarization. It is normally 2.5 mm or less in height and is 0.11 seconds or less in duration. The first negative deflection after the P wave is the Q wave, which is less than 0.03 seconds in duration and less than 25 per cent of the R wave amplitude; the first positive deflection after the P wave is the R wave; and the S wave is the first negative deflection after the R wave (see Figure 6.6).

The QRS complex (beginning of Q wave to end of S wave) represents ventricular muscle depolarization. Not all QRS complexes have all three waveforms.

The T wave represents ventricular muscle repolarization. It follows the QRS complex and is usually of the same deflection as the QRS complex. If a U wave is seen, it will follow the T wave. The presence of a U wave may indicate an electrolyte abnormality.

The ST segment, which represents early ventricular repolarization, lasts from the end of the S wave to the beginning of the T wave.

The PR interval is measured from the beginning of the P wave to the beginning of the R wave and represents the time required for the impulse to travel through the atria and conduction system to the Purkinje fibres. In adults, the PR interval normally ranges from 0.12 to 0.20 seconds in duration.

The QRS complex is measured from the beginning of the Q wave, or the R wave if no Q wave is present, to the end of the S wave. The QRS complex is normally 0.04 to 0.10 seconds in duration.

The QT interval, which represents electrical systole, is measured from the beginning of the Q wave, or R wave if no Q wave is present, to the end of the T wave. The QT interval varies with heart rate, is usually less than half the RR interval (measured from the beginning of one R wave to the beginning of the next R wave), and is usually 0.32 to 0.40 seconds in duration if the heart rate is 65 to 95 beats/minute.

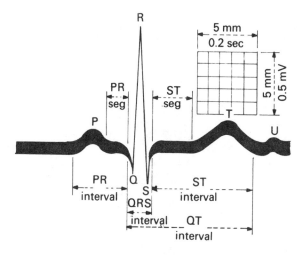

Figure 6.6 Commonly measured complex components. The PR interval is measured from the beginning of the P wave to the beginning of the QRS; the QRS is measured from the beginning of the Q wave to the end of the S wave; the QT interval is measured from the beginning of the Q wave to the end of the T wave.

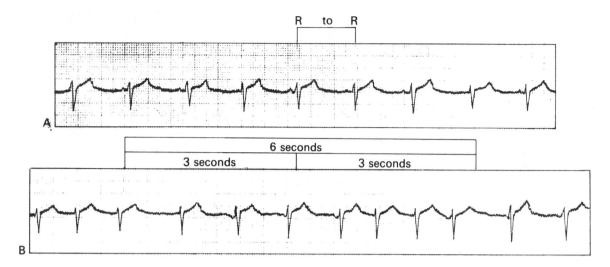

Figure 6.7 (A) Heart rate determination for a regular rhythm. There are approximately 25 little boxes between two R waves: 1,500 divided by this number equals 60. The heart rate is 60. There are five large boxes between R waves, thus the rate is approximately 60.(B) Heart rate determination if the rhythm is irregular. There are approximately seven RR intervals in six seconds. Seven multiplied by 10 equals 70, thus the heart rate is 70. (Underhill, S. L. *et al.* (1982) *Cardiac Nursing*, J. B. Lippincott, Philadelphia, p. 201.)

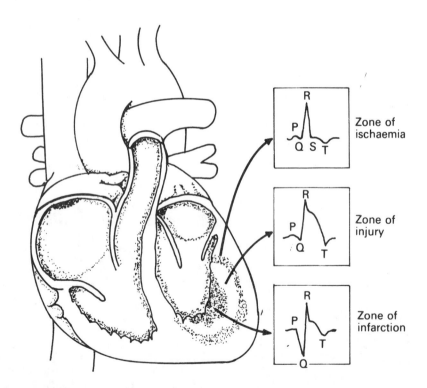

Figure 6.8 Effects of ischaemia, injury and infarction on ECG recording. Ischaemia causes inversion of T wave because of altered repolarization. Cardiac muscle injury causes elevation of the ST segment. Infarction causes Q or Q–S waves because of the absence of depolarization current from the dead tissue and opposing currents from other parts of the heart.

Determination of Heart Rate From ECG

Heart rate can be obtained from the ECG strip by several methods. The first, and most accurate, if the rhythm is regular, is to count the number of 0.04-second intervals (0.04 seconds equals one small box) between two R waves, and then divide 1,500 by that number. (There are 1,500 0.04-second interval boxes in a 1-minute strip.) See Figure 6.7A.

The second method for computing heart rate, especially used when the rhythm is irregular, is to count the number of R–R intervals in six seconds and multiply that number by 10. The ECG paper is usually marked at three-second intervals (15 large boxes, horizontally) by a vertical line at the top of the paper (see Figure 6.7B). The R–R intervals are counted rather than QRS complexes, because a computed heart rate based on the latter might be inaccurately high.

Abnormal Findings

Myocardial Ischaemia and Injury

Myocardial ischaemia causes the T wave to be larger and inverted owing to altered late repolarization. Possibly, the ischaemic region remains depolarized, whereas adjacent areas have returned to the resting state. The change is seen in the leads closest to the involved surface of the heart. Ischaemia also causes ST segment changes. If there is epicardial myocardial injury, the injured cells depolarize normally but repolarize more rapidly than do normal cells; thus, the ST segment is elevated. If the myocardial injury is on the endocardial surface, then the ST segment is depressed (1 mm or more) in the leads where the positive electrode faces the area of injury. With injury, the ST segment depression is horizontal or slopes downward and is 0.08 s in duration.

Myocardial Infarction

Myocardial infarction usually causes abnormal Q waves within one to three days, because of both the absence of depolarization current from necrotic tissue and opposing currents from other parts of the heart. An abnormal Q wave is 0.04 seconds or longer in duration and is, in depth, 25 per cent of the R wave (provided the R wave itself exceeds 5 mm). Old transmural myocardial infarction is usually indicated by significant Q waves without ST segment and T wave changes or by reduced voltage of the R wave. In some patients, Q waves disappear. With a transmural myocardial infarction (involving all three layers of the heart), injury and ischaemic changes are also present (see Figure 6.8). The ST segment elevation lasts from a few days to two weeks. The T wave becomes large and symmetric for 24 hours, and then inverts within one to three days for one to two weeks. During recovery from a myocardial infarction, the ST segment is often first to return to normal (one to six weeks), followed by the T wave (weeks to months). Q wave alterations are usually permanent.

Exercise Stress Testing

Exercise stress testing is a noninvasive means of assessing certain aspects of cardiac function. By evaluating cardiac action during physical stress, the heart's response to an increased demand for oxygen can be determined. The test is used for the following purposes: to assist in diagnosing the cause of chest pain, to screen for ischaemic heart disease, to determine the functional capacity of the heart after a myocardial infarction or after surgery, to assess the effectiveness of anti-anginal or anti-arrhythmic drug therapy, to identify arrhythmias that occur during physical exercise and to aid in the development of a physical fitness programme.

Exercise stress testing may be carried out by getting the patient to walk on a treadmill, pedal a stationary bicycle or climb a set of stairs. The patient is exercised by increasing walking speed and the incline of the treadmill or by increasing the load against which the bicycle is pedalled. ECG electrodes are applied to the patient, and tracings are made before, during and after exercise testing. Blood pressure, skin temperature, physical appearance and the occurrence or worsening of chest pain are monitored closely during and following the test.

The test is continued until the patient's predetermined target heart rate is reached, but it is terminated early if the patient experiences chest pain, extreme fatigue, a drop in blood pressure or pulse rate or other complications.

The patient is advised to avoid smoking, eating and drinking for four hours before the test and to wear comfortable shoes suitable for walking. Women should be told to wear a brassiere that provides adequate support. Following the test the patient should be advised to rest for a period of time and to avoid stimulants, eating or extreme temperature changes (i.e., hot or cold showers, going out into the cold). Blood pressure and ECG are monitored for 10 to 15 minutes after completion of the test, or until they return to baseline.

Vectorcardiography

Vectorcardiography, which is similar to electrocardiography, presents a three-dimensional view of the electrical forces of the heart: horizontal or transverse, frontal and left sagittal or lateral planes. This diagnostic modality amplifies understanding of the ECG and gives more accurate diagnostic information in certain areas of cardiac diagnosis, e.g., ventricular hypertrophy, conduction disturbances and myocardial infarction. The patient should be assured that the test is similar to an ECG and that it is safe and painless.

Cardiac Catheterization

Cardiac catheterization is an invasive diagnostic procedure in which one or more catheters are introduced into the heart and selected blood vessels in order to measure pressures in the various heart chambers and to determine oxygen saturation of the blood by sampling specimens. By far the most common use of cardiac catheterization is to assess the patient's need and readiness for coronary bypass surgery (see Chapter 8). During cardiac catheterization the patient is monitored electrocardiographically by means of an oscilloscope. Because the introduction of the catheter into the heart can induce potentially fatal arrhythmias, resuscitation equipment should be readily available when the procedure is being performed.

Angiography

Cardiac catheterization is usually done in conjunction with angiography, a technique of injecting a contrast medium into the vascular system to outline the heart and blood vessels. When a particular heart chamber or blood vessel is singled out for study, the procedure becomes selective angiography. Angiography makes use of cineangiograms, a series of rapid exposures on an intensified fluoroscopic screen that records the passage of the contrast medium through the vascular site(s). The recording of the information allows for comparison of information over time.

Four of the more common sites for selective angiography are the aorta, the coronary arteries and the right and left hearts.

Aortography

An aortogram is a form of angiography that outlines the lumen of the aorta and the major arteries arising from it. In thoracic aortography a contrast medium is used to study the aortic arch and its major branches. The translumbar or retrograde brachial or femoral approach may be used.

Coronary Arteriography

In coronary arteriography a radio-opaque catheter is introduced into the right brachial or femoral artery and is passed into the ascending aorta and manipulated into the appropriate coronary artery under fluoroscopic control. Coronary arteriography is used as an evaluation tool before coronary artery surgery. It is also used to study suspected congenital abnormalities of the coronary arteries.

Right-Heart Catheterization

Right-heart catheterization involves passing a radio-opaque catheter from an antecubital or femoral vein into the right atrium, right ventricle and pulmonary vasculature. This is carried out under direct visualization with a fluoroscope. Pressures within the right atrium are measured and recorded, and blood samples are removed for measurement of the haematocrit and oxygen saturation. The catheter is then passed through the tricuspid valve, and similar tests are performed on the blood within the right ventricle. Finally, the catheter is introduced into the

pulmonary artery (through the pulmonary valve) and as far as possible beyond that point, where 'capillary' samples are obtained and 'capillary' pressures (also known as wedge pressures) are recorded. Then the catheter is withdrawn.

Right-heart catheterization is considered a relatively safe procedure. Complications, when they do occur, include cardiac arrhythmias, venous spasm, infection of the cutdown site, cardiac perforation and, rarely, cardiac arrest.

Left-Heart Catheterization

Left-heart catheterization is usually done by retrograde catheterization of the left ventricle or by transseptal catheterization of the left atrium. In the retrograde technique, the catheter is inserted under direct vision into the right brachial artery (arteriotomy) and advanced under fluoroscopic control down into the ascending aorta and into the left ventricle; or the catheter may be introduced percutaneously by puncture of the femoral artery.

In the transseptal approach, the catheter is passed from the right femoral vein (percutaneously or by saphenous vein cutdown) into the right atrium. A long needle is passed up through the catheter and is used to puncture the septum separating the right and left atria. The needle is withdrawn and the catheter is advanced under fluoroscopic control into the left ventricle. In both of these techniques the patient is monitored by electrocardiogram.

Left-heart catheterization is most often performed to evaluate the function of the left ventricular muscle and the mitral and aortic valves or the patency of the coronary arteries. It is used to evaluate patients before and after cardiac surgery. Usually, the right side of the heart is catheterized before the left side is done. Complications include arrhythmias, myocardial infarction, perforation of the heart or great vessels and systemic embole.

Following catheterization, the catheter is slowly withdrawn, the artery is repaired and the cutdown site is closed and bandaged.

Nursing Care

Precatheterization nursing responsibilities include the following:

● Prepare the patient to fast prior to the procedure.
● Prepare the patient for the expected duration of the procedure; indicate that it will involve lying on a hard table for about two hours.
● Prepare the patient to experience certain sensations during the catheterization. Knowing what to expect can help the patient cope with the experience. An occasional thudding sensation (palpitation) may be felt in the chest because of extra systoles that almost always occur, particularly when the catheter tip touches the myocardium. When contrast medium is injected into

the right heart (during angiography), there may be a strong desire to cough. The injection of contrast medium into either side of the heart may produce a feeling of heat, particularly in the head, which disappears after a minute or less.

● Encourage the patient to express fears and anxieties. Provide teaching and reassurance to reduce apprehension.

Postcatheterization nursing interventions include the following:

● Watch the puncture (or cutdown) sites for haematoma formation, and check the peripheral pulses in the affected extremity (dorsalis pedis and posterior tibial pulses in the lower extremity, radial pulse in the upper extremity) every 15 minutes for one to two hours, and then every one to two hours until stable.

● Evaluate extremity temperature and colour and any patient complaints of pain, numbness or tingling sensations in the affected extremity to determine signs of arterial insufficiency. Report changes promptly.

● Watch for arrhythmias by observing the cardiac monitor or by listening to the apical heart rate and evaluating the pulse for rhythm changes.

● If protocol requires, see that the patient remains in bed with little movement of the involved extremity until the following morning.

● Report any complaint of chest discomfort immediately.

● Discomfort at the site is expected. Administer pain medication as prescribed.

Echocardiography

Echocardiography is a noninvasive ultrasound test used to examine the size, shape and motion of cardiac structures.

High-frequency sound waves are sent into the heart through the chest wall and are recorded as they return. The ultrasound is generated by a hand-held transducer (a device that converts one form of energy to another form of energy) applied to the front of the chest. The transducer picks up the echoes, converts them to electrical impulses and transmits them to the echocardiography machine for display on an oscilloscope and for recording on a videotape. This is the same sonar principle by which submarines detect ships. An ECG is recorded simultaneously to time events within the cardiac cycle. Echocardiography is a safe method that gives information similar in many respects to the data obtained with angiocardiography. It is especially useful in the diagnosis and differentiation of heart murmurs. An echocardiogram can show whether the heart is dilated, the walls or septum are thickened or pericardial effusion is present. It has also been used to study the motion of prosthetic heart valves.

Patients should be assured that the test is safe and painless. They should know that they will be expected to

change positions several times during the procedure, to breathe slowly and periodically to hold their breath.

Phonocardiography

Phonocardiography is the graphic recording of heart sounds and pulse waves and their relation to time. It helps the observer to identify, accurately time and differentiate among various sounds and murmurs. It is used to aid in the precise timing of cardiac events and in the diagnosis of valvular and other cardiac disorders.

Microphones containing miniature transducers are placed on the patient's chest at the apex and base of the heart. The transducers pick up heart sounds, amplify them, convert them to electrical impulses and transmit them to a recorder that produces a waveform graph of the sounds.

Patients should be assured that the procedure is safe and painless. They should know that they will be expected to remain still and quiet during the test except when asked to change positions, to breathe slowly or to hold their breath.

Radioisotope Studies

Radioisotope studies are useful for detecting myocardial infarction and decreased myocardial blood flow, and for evaluating left ventricular function. The radioisotopes are injected intravenously, and scans are done using a gamma scintillation camera.

Myocardial Infarction Imaging

Technitium pyrophosphate (^{99m}TC-PYP) is taken up in areas of the heart where there is damaged myocardial tissue, forming a 'hot spot' on a scan made with a scintillation camera. Hot spots appear within 12 hours of infarction, are most evident 48 to 72 hours after infarction, and usually disappear within one week unless there is continuing myocardial damage.

The patient is assured that the scan involves less radiation exposure than a chest X-ray and is told to remain motionless during the scan.

Myocardial Blood Flow Evaluation

Thallium-201 is used to evaluate blood flow through vessels that are too small to visualize with coronary arteriography. Thallium concentrates in normal myocardial tissue but not in ischaemic or necrotic tissues.

Often this test is paired with an exercise stress test to compare changes in myocardial perfusion during exercise and at rest. In this technique, 'cold spots' correlating with lack of myocardial perfusion correlate with infarcted areas. The patient should be assured that there is no known radiation danger from thallium.

Blood Pool Scanning

The technique of gated cardiac blood pool scanning

utilizes a computer to analyse left ventricular function. By determining the difference between the amount of the radioactive tracer technetium pyrophosphate (^{99m}Tc-PYP) in the end-diastolic volume and the amount in the end-systolic volume, the ejection fraction can be calculated. This test can also be used to assess the differences in left ventricular function during rest and exercise.

In multiple-gated acquisition scanning, the scintillation camera records 14 to 64 points of one single cardiac cycle. The sequential pictures are studied to evaluate ventricular wall motion and to determine the ejection fraction.

The patient is assured that there is no known radiation danger, and is told to remain motionless during the scan.

Haemodynamic Monitoring

Central Venous Pressure Monitoring

Central venous pressure is the pressure within the right atrium or in the great veins within the thorax. It represents the filling pressure of the right ventricle and indicates the ability of the right side of the heart to manage a fluid load. It serves as a guide to fluid replacement in seriously ill patients and is a measurement of effective circulating blood volume.

Abnormal central venous pressure reflects right ventricular failure. Most right ventricular failure is secondary to left ventricular failure. Therefore, an elevated central venous pressure can be a *late* sign of left ventricular failure.

Central venous pressure is a dynamic or changing measurement. The change in central venous pressure correlated with the patient's clinical status is a more useful indication of adequacy of venous blood volume and alterations of cardiovascular function than is a single measurement of central venous pressure. A lowered central venous pressure indicates that the patient is hypovolaemic, and this is verified when a rapid intravenous infusion causes the patient to improve. A rising central venous pressure may be due to either hypervolaemia or poor cardiac contractility.

The central venous pressure site should be prepared by shaving and cleansing with an antiseptic solution. A local anaesthetic may be used. The catheter is threaded through the external jugular, antecubital or femoral vein into the vena cava just above or within the right atrium. Once the central venous pressure catheter is inserted, povidine-iodine spray may be applied and the site is then covered with a clear adhesive dressing. This facilitates observation and reduces the frequency of changing the dressing. If the site is not visible, the dressing is usually changed daily or in accordance with the doctor's request (Wilson, 1983, p. 12).

Central venous pressure is measured by the height of a column of water in a manometer. The zero of the manometer is levelled with the right atrium. This is found at the mid-auxillary line if the patient is nursed in the upright position, or by using the sternal notch if the patient is lying flat (Pritchard and David, 1988, p. 87; Wilson, 1983, p. 13). Normal central venous pressure is 4 to 10 cm of water. The most common complications of central venous pressure monitoring are infection and air embolism.

Pulmonary Artery and Pulmonary Artery Wedge Pressure Monitoring

Pulmonary artery pressures reflect left-sided heart pressures and therefore are more useful in assessing left ventricular failure than is central venous pressure. Pulmonary artery pressures are monitored only in coronary care units or other intensive care units and not on general medical–surgical units.

A balloon-tipped, flow-directed catheter is inserted into a large vein that leads into the superior vena cava and right atrium. The balloon is inflated, and the catheter is carried rapidly by the flow of blood through the tricuspid valve, into the right ventricle, through the pulmonary valve and into a branch of the pulmonary artery. When the catheter reaches a small pulmonary artery, the balloon is deflated and the catheter is secured with sutures.

Pulmonary artery systolic and diastolic pressures are obtained via a transducer and blood pressure monitor. Normal pulmonary artery pressure is 25/9 mmHg, with a mean pressure of 15 mmHg. When the balloon is inflated, the catheter is 'wedged' in the pulmonary artery. Pressures transmitted to the catheter reflect left ventricular end-diastolic pressure. At end-diastole, when the mitral valve is open, pulmonary artery wedge pressure is the same as the pressure in the left atrium and the left ventricle, unless the patient has mitral valve disease or pulmonary hypertension. Pulmonary artery wedge pressure is a mean pressure and is normally 4.5 to 13 mmHg.

Catheter site care is the same as that for a central venous pressure catheter. The catheter flush solution is heparinized normal saline, delivered in small amounts using a pressure bag and flush device. As in measuring central venous pressure, it is essential to place the transducer at the phlebostatic axis to ensure accurate readings. Measurement of cardiac output can also be obtained by using a pulmonary artery catheter. Complications of pulmonary artery monitoring include infection, pulmonary artery rupture, pulmonary thromboembolism, pulmonary infarction, catheter kinking, arrhythmias and air embolism.

Systemic Intra-arterial Monitoring

Intra-arterial monitoring is used to obtain direct and continuous blood pressures in critically ill patients with severe high blood pressure or hypotension. Arterial catheters are also useful when obtaining arterial blood gases and serial blood samples. Intra-arterial monitoring is restricted to critical care units.

Once an arterial site is selected (radial, brachial, femoral or dorsalis pedis), collateral circulation to the area must be confirmed before catheter placement. This can be done by using the ultrasonic Doppler test. (If no collateral circulation existed, and the cannulated artery became occluded, ischaemia and infarction of the area distal to the cannulated site could occur.) Site preparation and care are the same as for central venous pressure catheters. The catheter flush solution is the same as for pulmonary artery catheters. A transducer is attached, and pressures are obtained in mmHg. Complications include local obstruction with distal ischaemia, external haemorrhage, massive ecchymosis, dissection, air embolism, blood loss, pain, arteriospasm and infection.

BIBLIOGRAPHY

Brunner, L. S. and Suddarth, D. S. (1989) *The Lippincott Manual of Medical-Surgical Nursing* (2nd edition), Chapter 5, Harper & Row, London.

Millar, A. (1975) *Systems of Life, Numbers 9-12; Cardiovascular System 1-4, Nursing Times,* Macmillan Journals, London.

Pritchard, A. P. and David, J. A. (1988) *The Royal Marsden Hospital Manual of Clinical Nursing Procedures* (2nd edition), Harper & Row, London.

Wilson, V. (1983) Cardiac Nursing, Blackwell Scientific, London, pp. 12–13.

FURTHER READING

Books

Anatomy and Physiology

Tortora, G. J. and Anagnostakas, N. P. (1984) *Principles of Anatomy and Physiology* (4th edition), Chapter 20, The Heart, Harper & Row, New York.

Cardiac Signs and Symptoms (general assessment)

Pritchard, A. P. and David, J. A. (1988) *The Royal Marsden Hospital Manual of Clinical Nursing Procedures* (2nd edition), Chapter 26, Observations, Harper & Row, London.

Swanton, R. H. (1984) *Cardiology*, Chapter 1, Blackwell Scientific, London.

Zoob, M. (1977) *Cardiology for Students*, Chapters 2 and 3, Churchill Livingstone, Edinburgh.

Investigatory Techniques

Swanton, R. H. (1984) *Cardiology*, Chapter 10, Blackwell Scientific, London.

Zoob, M. (1977) *Cardiology for Students*, Chapters 4, 5 and 6, Churchill Livingstone, Edinburgh.

Articles

Anatomy and Physiology

Millar, A. (1975) *Systems of Life, Numbers 9–12, Cardiovascular Systems 1–4, Nursing Times,* Macmillan Journals, London.

Roberts, A. (1980) *Systems of Life, Numbers 66–70, Systems and Signs, Cardiovascular Systems 1–5, Nursing Times,* Macmillan Journals, London.

Cardiac Signs and Symptoms (general assessment)

Willetts, K. (1989) Assessing cardiac pain, *Nursing Times,* 22 November, Vol. 8, No. 47, pp. 52–4.

Invasive Techniques

Allan, D. (1989) Arterial catheterization, *Nursing Times,* 4 October, Vol. 85, No. 4, pp. 45–7.

Miller, J. A. (1988) Recording central venous pressure, *The Professional Nurse,* March, Vol. 3, No. 6, pp. 188–9.

chapter 7

ASSESSMENT AND CARE OF PATIENTS WITH CARDIAC DISORDERS

CORONARY HEART DISEASE

Coronary Atherosclerosis

The United Kingdom has one of the highest rates of coronary heart disease in the world (Quested, 1989). The term 'coronary heart disease' refers to the symptoms of coronary occlusion caused by atherosclerosis (Goodinson, 1984). This pathological condition of the coronary arteries is characterized by an abnormal accumulation of lipid substances and fibrous tissue in the vessel wall that leads to changes in arterial structure and function and reduction of blood flow to the myocardium. Causes of atherosclerotic heart disease probably involve alterations in lipid metabolism, blood coagulation and the biophysical and biochemical properties of the arterial walls.

Altered Physiology

The functional lesion of atherosclerosis is called atheroma. Atherosclerosis begins when the waxy cholesterol atheroma, which looks like pearly grey mounds of tissue, becomes deposited on the intima of the major arteries. These deposits interfere with the absorption of nutrients by the endothelial cells that compose the vessel lining and obstruct blood flow by protruding into the lumen of the vessel (Figure 7.1). The vascular endothelium in involved areas becomes necrotic and then scarred, further compromising the lumen and impeding the flow of blood. At sites such as these, where the lumen is narrowed and the wall rough, there is a great tendency for clots to form, which explains the fact that intravascular coagulation, followed by thromboembolic disease, is among the most important complications of atherosclerosis.

Our knowledge of atherogenesis is limited. Several theories are propounded, but as yet none has been substantiated conclusively. Among suspected mechanisms are thrombus formation on the surface of the plaque followed by fibrous organization of the thrombus, haemorrhage into a plaque and continuing lipid accumulation. If the fibrous cap of the plaque ruptures, the lipid debris is

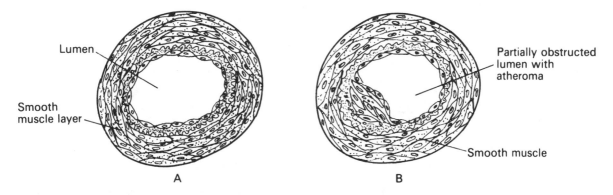

Figure 7.1 Cross-sections of a normal and an atherosclerotic artery. (A) Cross-section of normal artery showing patent lumen. (B) Cross-section of artery showing atheroma and diminished patency of artery lumen.

swept into the bloodstream and obstruction of the arteries and capillaries distal to the ruptured plaque results.

The coronary arteries are particularly susceptible to the effects of atherosclerosis. They twist and turn as they supply the heart, thereby creating angles and crevices ripe for atheroma development (Figure 7.2).

Clinical Features

Coronary atherosclerosis produces symptoms and complications as a result of the narrowing of the arterial lumen and obstruction of blood flow to the myocardium. This impediment to blood flow is progressive and the inadequate blood supply (ischaemia) that results deprives the muscle cells of the blood components they need for their survival. Varying degrees of cell damage are produced by ischaemia. The major manifestation of ischaemia of the myocardium is chest pain. Angina pectoris refers to recurrent chest pain that is not accompanied by irreversible damage to myocardial cells. More severe ischaemia with cell damage is termed myocardial infarction. Irreversibly damaged myocardium undergoes degeneration and is replaced by scar tissue. If the damage to the myocardium is extensive, the heart may eventually fail, that is, it may be unable to support the body's needs for blood by providing an adequate cardiac output.

Other clinical manifestations of coronary heart disease may be ECG changes, ventricular aneurysms, arrhythmias and sudden death.

Risk Factors and Prevention of Atherosclerotic Heart Disease

Epidemiological studies and observations reveal that there are risk factors for atherosclerosis that tend to make a person more prone to develop coronary heart disease. A risk factor may be modifiable or nonmodifiable. A modifiable risk factor is one over which an individual may exercise control by changing a lifestyle or personal habit; a nonmodifiable risk factor is a consequence of genetics over which an individual has no control (Table 7.1). A risk factor may operate independently or in tandem with other risk factors. The more risk factors a person has, the greater is the likelihood of developing coronary heart disease. People at risk should have periodic medical examinations, modify their lifestyles and alter their dietary habits.

Four modifiable risk factors—cigarette smoking, elevated blood pressure, hyperlipidaemia and behaviour patterns—have received major attention. The two risk factors cited as major causes of coronary heart disease and its consequent complications are cigarette smoking and hypertension.

Cigarette Smoking

Cigarette smoking contributes to the development and severity of coronary heart disease in two ways. First, the inhalation of smoke increases the blood carbon monoxide (CO) level. Haemoglobin, the oxygen-carrying compo-

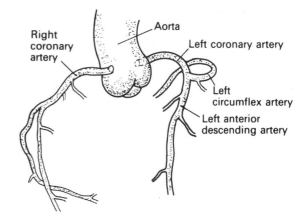

Figure 7.2 Angles of the coronary arteries. The many angles and curves of the coronary arteries contribute to the vessels' susceptibility to the development of atheromatous plaques.

Table 7.1 *Risk factors for atherosclerosis*

Nonmodifiable risk factors	Modifiable risk factors
Positive family history	Hyperlipidaemia
Increasing age	Elevated blood pressure
Sex – occurs three times more often in men than in women	Cigarette smoking
	Elevated blood sugar (diabetes mellitus)
Race – higher incidence in blacks than in whites	Obesity
	Physical inactivity
	Stress
	Use of oral contraceptives

nent of blood, combines more readily with CO than with O_2. Thus, the oxygen being supplied to the heart is severely limited, which makes the heart work harder to produce the same amount of energy. Second, nicotinic acid in tobacco products causes arteries to constrict, which compromises blood flow and subsequent oxygenation. A person with increased risk for coronary heart disease should therefore stop smoking.

Elevated Blood Pressure
Elevated blood pressure is the most insidious of all risk factors because it is asymptomatic until disease is well advanced. An elevated blood pressure creates a very high pressure gradient against which the left ventricle must pump. The continued high pressure forces the myocardial oxygen demands to exceed the supply. This initiates the vicious cycle of pain associated with coronary heart disease.

Early detection of high blood pressure and co-operation with a therapeutic regime can prevent the serious consequences associated with untreated elevated blood pressure.

Hyperlipidaemia
The association of elevated blood lipids (fats) with coronary heart disease has been established through epidemiologic studies. Lipids are a mixed group of biochemical substances that may be manufactured by the body or derived from metabolism of ingested substances. An endogenous lipid is one produced by the normal metabolic functions of the body; an example of an endogenous fat is sterol. An exogenous lipid is one derived from a source external to the body, for example, that derived from eating an egg.

Lipids have the common property of being more soluble in fat or organic solvents than in water. In the blood, the principal lipids are cholesterol, triglycerides and

phospholipids. To render them suitable for transport in the blood, the lipids are attached to a variety of proteins; the resulting product is called a lipoprotein.

There are five types of hyperlipidaemias. Determining the underlying lipid abnormality by blood studies is essential before suggesting dietary control.

Cholesterol and triglycerides are the lipids most frequently associated with coronary heart disease.

For clinical purposes, hyperlipidaemia may be suspected if the fasting blood cholesterol or triglyceride levels are elevated.

Hyperlipidaemia may be primary or secondary. Primary hyperlipidaemia is generally a hereditary disorder and is the rarest of the phenotypes. The secondary type occurs as a manifestation of numerous other diseases, including hypothyroidism, nephrotic syndrome, diabetes mellitus and alcoholism. Therapy consists in treating the basic disorder.

For some individuals, the control of fat consumption is an important factor in preventive nutrition. Dietary fat may be regulated by changing the total amount or the type of fat in the diet, or both. Assisting the patient to modify dietary fat intake through effective counselling requires an understanding of the differences between saturated and polyunsaturated fatty acids, cholesterol, medium-chain triglycerides and various other fractions as well as of their functions in the human body.

No single diet or drug will be effective in all conditions in lowering the particular elevated lipid abnormality, but in most people with such an abnormality the level can be brought within the upper average range.

For patients in whom diet alone cannot normalize the specific lipid, there are several medications that have a synergistic effect when taken with the prescribed diet. These agents are shown to be biochemically effective, in that elevated lipoprotein concentration tends to return toward normal and manifestations of the abnormalities, such as xanthomas (yellow papules in the skin caused by lipid deposits), may disappear. Drug treatment also varies with the type of hyperlipidaemia. The drugs used are usually grouped into two types: those that decrease lipoprotein synthesis, such as clofibrate, and those that increase lipoprotein breakdown (catabolism), such as cholestyramine.

The usefulness of diet and drugs in reversing coronary heart disease is still controversial. A major factor influencing the thoughts of researchers is that, because lipids are manufactured within the body, in certain cases dietary control may have no influence on serum lipid levels. Despite controversy due to such questions, however, it is now broadly accepted that preventive nutrition can have a significant impact on coronary heart disease.

Behaviour Patterns of Coronary-Prone People
It is believed that stress and certain behaviours contribute to the pathogenesis of coronary (atherosclerotic) heart

disease. Psychobiological and epidemiological studies have investigated behaviours that characterize people who are prone to coronary heart disease: competitive striving for achievement, exaggerated sense of time urgency, aggressiveness and hostility. A person who manifests these behaviours is classified as type A coronary-prone. It appears that, in addition to reducing other risk factors (smoking, dietary fats), such a person should make some effort to alter lifestyle and long-term habit patterns.

The type A behaviour pattern has been widely accepted as a risk factor for coronary heart disease, although contemporary research indicates that it may not be as significant as was once thought. As yet there is no conclusive evidence of its precise role.

Considerations for the Elderly

Atherosclerotic coronary heart disease is not a function of ageing. The longer a person survives without coronary heart disease, the less likely it is that the disease will develop. Ageing does, however, produce changes in the integrity of the lining of the walls of arteries (arteriosclerosis), thus impeding blood flow and tissue nutrition. These changes are often sufficient to diminish oxygenation and increase myocardial oxygen consumption (MVO_2). The result can be debilitating angina pectoris and eventually congestive heart failure.

Angina Pectoris

Definition, Aetiology and Altered Physiology

Angina pectoris is a clinical syndrome characterized by paroxysms of pain or a feeling of pressure in the anterior chest. The cause is considered to be insufficient coronary blood flow, resulting in inadequate oxygen supply of the myocardium.

Angina is usually caused by atherosclerotic heart disease and almost invariably is associated with a significant obstruction of a major coronary artery. (The characteristics of the various types of angina are listed in Table 7.2.)

Any number of factors can produce anginal pain. Physical exertion can precipitate an attack by increasing myocardial oxygen demands. Exposure to cold or even the drinking of iced beverages can cause vasoconstriction and an elevated blood pressure, with increased oxygen demand. Eating a heavy meal increases the blood flow to the mesenteric area and places a heavier demand on the heart. Stress and any emotion-provoking situation causing the release of adrenalin and increased blood pressure may accelerate the heart rate. If blood flow from the left ventricle is obstructed, as in aortic stenosis, the oxygen needs of the myocardium are drastically increased.

Clinical Features

Ischaemia of the heart muscle produces pain, varying in severity from upper substernal pressure to agonizing pain that is accompanied by severe apprehension and a feeling of impending death. The pain is usually felt deep in the chest behind the upper or middle third of the sternum (retrosternal). Although the pain frequently is localized, it may radiate to the neck, jaw, shoulders and inner aspects of the upper extremities. The patient often experiences a tightness, a choking or strangling sensation that has a vicelike, insistent quality. A feeling of weakness or numbness in the arms, wrists and hands may accompany the pain. Along with the physical pain, the patient also has a sense of impending death, an apprehension so characteristic of angina that if it occurs alone, as it sometimes does, it is sufficient for diagnosis.

Table 7.2 *Types of angina*

Unstable angina (pre-infarction angina; crescendo angina)	*Angina decubitis*
Progressive increase in frequency, intensity and duration of anginal attacks	Angina while lying down
Increasing danger of myocardial infarction within 3–18 months	*Intractable or refractory angina*
	Severe incapacitating angina
Chronic stable angina	*Prinzmetal's angina (variant: resting)*
Predictable, consistent, rarely occurs while at rest	Spontaneous type of anginal pain accompanied by ST-segment elevation in ECG
Nocturnal angina	Thought to be due to coronary artery spasm
Pain occurs at night usually during sleep; may be relieved by sitting upright	Associated with high risk of infarction
Commonly due to left ventricular failure	

Considerations for the Elderly

The elderly person who experiences angina may not exhibit the typical pain profile because of changes in neuroreceptors. Pain is often manifested in the elderly as weakness or fainting. When exposed to cold temperatures, elderly people may experience anginal symptoms more quickly because they have less subcutaneous fat to provide insulation. They should be encouraged to dress with extra clothing and advised to recognize feelings of weakness as an indication that they should rest or take prescribed medications.

Diagnosis

The diagnosis of angina is often made by an evaluation of the clinical manifestations of pain and the patient's history. In certain types of angina, ECG changes are helpful in making a differential diagnosis of the angina. The patient's response to exertion or stress may also be tested by means of electrocardiographic monitoring while the patient exercises on a bicycle or treadmill.

Medical Management

The objectives of medical management of angina are to decrease the oxygen demands of the myocardium and to increase the oxygen supply. Medically these objectives are met through pharmacological therapy and risk factor control. Surgically the objectives are met by revascularization of the blood supply to the myocardium, through coronary artery bypass surgery or percutaneous transluminal angioplasty (see Chapter 8). Frequently a combination of medical and surgical therapies is employed.

Pharmacological Therapy: Nitroglycerine

The nitrates are still the mainstay of treatment for angina pectoris. Nitroglycerine is given to reduce myocardial oxygen consumption, which decreases ischaemia and relieves anginal pain. Nitroglycerine is a vasoactive drug that acts to dilate both the veins and the arteries and thus has an effect on the peripheral circulation. Dilation of the veins causes venous pooling of blood throughout the body. As a result, less blood is returned to the heart and there is a reduction in filling pressure (preload). Nitrates also relax the systemic arteriolar bed and thus cause a fall in blood pressure (decrease afterload). These effects decrease myocardial oxygen requirements, bringing about a more favourable balance between supply and demand.

Nitroglycerine taken sublingually or in the buccal pouch alleviates the pain of ischaemia within three minutes.

● The patient should be advised to keep the tongue still and to avoid swallowing saliva until the nitroglycerine tablet is dissolved. If the pain is severe, the tablet can be crushed between the teeth to hasten sublingual absorption.

● As a precaution, the patient should carry the medication at all times in a securely capped dark glass bottle, not in a metal or plastic pillbox.

nitroglycerine is volatile and is inactivated by heat, moisture, air, light and time. If the nitroglycerine is fresh, the patient will feel a burning sensation under the tongue and often a feeling of fullness or throbbing in the head. The nitroglycerine supply should be renewed every six months.

Instead of using a fixed dosage, the patient regulates drug usage, taking the smallest dose that relieves pain. The drug should be taken in anticipation of any activity that may produce pain. Because nitroglycerine will increase the patient's tolerance for exercise and stress when taken prophylactically (e.g., before exercise, stair-climbing and sexual intercourse), it is best that it be taken before the pain develops.

● The patient should note how long it takes for the nitroglycerine to relieve the discomfort. If the pain lasts more than 20 or 30 minutes after the nitroglycerine has been taken, an impending myocardial infarction may be suspected.

Side-effects of nitroglycerine include flushing, throbbing headache, hypotension and tachycardia. The use of long-acting nitrate preparations is controversial. Isosorbide dinitrate appears to be effective for up to two to five hours and can be chewed or swallowed (Trounce, 1990).

Transdermal Nitrates. Nitroglycerine is also available in a lanolin-petrolatum base or skin patches. In this form it is applied to the skin to protect against anginal pain and promote its relief. It is especially useful when patients experience nocturnal angina or are involved in periods of extended activity (e.g., golfing) because it has a prolonged effect of up to 24 hours. The dose is usually increased until headache or an excessive effect on blood pressure or heart rate occurs and then is reduced to the largest dose that does not produce these side-effects. Instructions for application accompany the various products.

Beta-Adrenergic Blockers

If the patient continues to have chest pain despite treatment with nitroglycerine and modification of lifestyle, the beta-adrenergic blocking agent atenolol, which is cardioselective (Swanton, 1984), may be given. This drug appears to reduce myocardial oxygen consumption by blocking the sympathetic impulses to the heart. The result is a reduction in heart rate, blood pressure and myocardial contractility that establishes a more favourable balance between myocardial oxygen needs and the amount of oxygen available. This helps to control chest pain and allows the patient to work or exercise. Atenolol may be given with oral isosorbide dinitrate or isosorbide mononitrate for anti-anginal and anti-ischaemia prophylaxis. Atenolol is cleared by the kidney (Swanton, 1984). The usual dose is 100 mg once daily (Swanton, 1984). Side-effects include musculoskeletal weakness, hypotension and bradycardia.

When atenolol is started, blood pressure and heart rate should be monitored according to the doctor's request. If the blood pressure drops significantly, a vasopressor may be needed. If severe bradycardia occurs, atropine is the antidote of choice. It is also important to remember that atenolol can precipitate congestive heart failure and asthma.

● Caution the patient not to stop taking atenolol abruptly, because there is evidence that angina may worsen and myocardial infarction may develop if this drug is discontinued abruptly.

Calcium Ion Antagonists

The calcium blockers, or antagonists, possess properties that have profound effects on myocardial oxygen demands and supply, hence their value in the treatment of angina. Physiologically, the calcium ion performs at the cellular level to influence contraction of all types of muscle tissue and plays a role in the electrical stimulation of the heart.

Calcium ion antagonists increase myocardial oxygen supply by dilating the smooth muscle wall of the coronary arterioles and decrease myocardial oxygen demands by reducing systemic arterial pressure and thus the workload of the left ventricle.

The two calcium antagonists most commonly used are nifedipine and diltiazem. The vasodilating effects of these agents, particularly on the coronary circulation, have made them valuable in angina that results from coronary vasospasm (Prinzmetal's angina). Calcium blockers should be used with great caution in individuals with heart failure because they block the calcium that supports contractility. Hypotension may occur after IV administration. Other side-effects that may occur are constipation, gastric intolerance, dizziness or headache associated with dizziness.

Calcium ion antagonists are usually given every four to six hours. Therapeutic doses vary from one person to another.

Risk Factor Control

Several other measures may be necessary in order to decrease the oxygen demands of the myocardium. It is important that the patient stops smoking, because smoking produces tachycardia and raises the blood pressure, thus increasing the work of the heart. Obese people should lose weight to reduce cardiac work.

Physical conditioning should be encouraged because it increases exercise capacity and produces a lower heart rate and blood pressure in response to a given exercise.

► NURSING PROCESS
► THE PATIENT WITH ANGINA PECTORIS

► *Assessment*

In the hospital the nurse should observe and record all facets of the patient's activities, with particular regard for those that have been found to precede and precipitate attacks of anginal pain.

1. When do attacks tend to occur?
   a. Following a meal?
   b. After engaging in certain activities?
   c. After physical activities in general?
   d. After visits from members of the family, friends or others?
2. How does the patient describe the pain?
3. Is the onset of pain gradual or sudden?
4. How long does it last? Seconds? Minutes? Hours?
5. Is the pain steady and unwavering in quality?
6. Is the discomfort accompanied by other symptoms, such as excessive perspiration, light-headedness, nausea, palpitation, shortness of breath?
7. How many minutes after taking nitroglycerine does the pain last?
8. What is the mode of abatement?

The answers to these questions, ascertained from observation, can form a basis for designing a logical programme of prevention.

When sensing that an attack is imminent, a patient should cease all movement in order to reduce to a minimum the oxygen requirements of the ischaemic myocardium.

This is done with the hope that oxygen needs can be met by the limited supply available at the moment and the impending attack can thus be averted.

► *Patient's Problems*

Based on the assessment data, the patient's problems may include the following:

● Pain related to myocardial ischaemia.
● Anxiety related to fear of death.
● Lack of knowledge of underlying nature of disease and methods for avoiding complications.
● Potential nonadherence to therapeutic regime related to nonacceptance of necessary lifestyle changes.

► *Planning and Implementation*
► Expected Outcomes

The major goals of the patient include prevention of pain, reduction of anxiety, awareness of the underlying nature of the disorder and understanding of the prescribed care and adherence to the self-care programme.

Nursing Care

Prevention of Pain

The patient must understand the symptom complex and the need to avoid activities known to cause anginal pain, such as sudden exertion, walking against the wind, exposure to cold, emotional excitement and so on. The patient must learn to change, modify or adapt to these stresses.

There are patients whose attacks occur predominantly in the morning. This idiosyncrasy obviously calls for a change in the schedule of daily activities. As a first step, the patient should plan to rise earlier each morning in order to shave, wash and dress in a more leisurely fashion.

Ideally, this unhurried pace should be maintained throughout the entire day, so that scheduled tasks and commitments are handled without haste or a sense of pressure. Any patient with angina pectoris should be advised to initiate all movements with deliberation, avoid exposure to cold, avoid tobacco, eat regularly but lightly and maintain a proper weight. Use of over-the-counter drugs should be discouraged, especially diet pills, nasal decongestants or other drugs containing agents that will increase heart rate and blood pressure.

Reduction of Anxiety

This patient has a strong fear of death. It is important to

Table 7.3 *Patient education for the person with angina*

Goal: To improve the quality of life and promote health

Expected outcomes
1. Patient prevents an episode of anginal pain
   a. Uses moderation in all activities of life
      i. Participates in a normal daily programme of activities that do not produce chest discomfort, shortness of breath and undue fatigue
      ii. Exercises before work, after work or before meals
      iii. Avoids exercises requiring sudden bursts of activity; avoids all isometric exercise
      iv. Avoids activities that require heavy effort
      v. Alternates activities with periods of rest; some fatigue is normal and temporary
   b. Avoids situations that are emotionally stressful
   c. Avoids overeating
      i. Eats smaller portions
      ii. Avoids excessive caffeine intake (coffee, cola drinks), which can increase the heart rate and produce angina
      iii. Refrains from engaging in physical exercise for 2 hours after meals
      iv. Does not use 'diet pills', nasal decongestants or any over-the-counter medications that can increase heart rate
   d. Stops smoking, since smoking increases the heart rate, blood pressure and blood carbon monoxide levels
   e. Avoids cold weather if possible
      i. Wears scarf over nose, mouth during very cold weather to warm the air
      ii. Walks more slowly in cold weather
      iii. Dresses warmly in winter
   f. Follows general principles of good, hygienic living

2. Patient copes with an attack of anginal pain
   a. Carries nitroglycerin at all times
      i. Keeps nitroglycerin in a tightly capped, dark-coloured glass bottle
      ii. Discards the cotton wool pad/packing
      iii. Avoids opening the bottle unnecessarily
      iv. Tries to avoid carrying supply right next to body
      v. Discards tablets after 5 months
      vi. If tablets are fresh, they should cause a burning sensation when placed under the tongue
   b. Places nitroglycerin under the tongue at first sign of chest discomfort
      i. Does not swallow saliva until the tablet has dissolved
      ii. Stops and rests until all pain subsides
      iii. States the significance of using the upright position to potentiate the effects of nitroglycerin
      iv. Usually, another nitroglycerin tablet may be taken in 3–5 minutes if pain relief is not obtained. If pain persists, patient calls the doctor. If the anginal discomfort is unrelieved by the usual number of nitroglycerin tablets, or if it recurs after a short interval, the patient must go to the nearest emergency facility
   c. Takes nitroglycerin prophylactically to avoid pain known to occur with certain activities (stair-climbing, sexual intercourse)
   d. Is alert for the side-effects of nitroglycerin: headache, flushing and dizziness

---

stay with the patient in order to minimize this fear. Nursing care should be planned so that time away from the bedside is kept to a minimum, because this fear of death is often alleviated by the physical presence of another person. Essential information about the illness should be provided and an explanation given as to why it is important to follow prescribed directives.

Understanding of the Illness and Ways to Avoid Complications

The education of patients with angina is designed to acquaint them with the basic nature of their illness and to furnish them with the facts that they need if they are to reorganize their living habits in a way that will reduce the frequency and severity of anginal attacks; delay the progress of the underlying disease, if possible; and help protect them from other complications. The factors outlined in Table 7.3 are important in educating the patient with angina pectoris.

Adherence to the Self-Care Programme

The self-care programme is prepared in co-operation with the patient and any significant other (see Table 7.3). Activities should be planned so as to minimize the occurrence of episodes of angina. The patient should understand that any pain unrelieved by the usual methods employed should be treated at the nearest accident and emergency department.

▶ Evaluation
▶ Expected Outcomes

1. Is relieved of pain (see Table 7.3 on patient education.)
2. Reduces anxiety.
   a. Understands the illness and purpose of treatment.
   b. Adheres to medical regime.
   c. Knows to seek medical assistance if pain persists or changes in quality.
   d. Avoids being alone during painful episodes.
3. Understands ways to avoid complications and demonstrates freedom from complications.
   a. Describes the process of angina.
   b. Explains reasons for measures to prevent complications.
   c. Exhibits normal ECG and level of cardiac enzymes.
   d. Is free of signs and symptoms of acute myocardial infarction.
4. Adheres to self-care programme.
   a. Demonstrates an understanding of pharmacological therapy.
   b. Daily habits reflect modification of lifestyle.

Myocardial Infarction

Definition, Aetiology and Altered Physiology

Myocardial infarction refers to the process by which myocardial tissue is destroyed in regions of the heart that are deprived of an adequate blood supply because of a reduced coronary blood flow. The cause of the reduced blood flow is either a critical narrowing of a coronary artery owing to atherosclerosis or a complete occlusion of an artery owing to embolus or thrombus. Decreased coronary blood flow may also result from shock and haemorrhage. In this situation, there is a profound imbalance between myocardial oxygen supply and demand.

'Coronary occlusion', 'heart attack' and 'myocardial infarction' are all used synonymously, but the preferred term is myocardial infarction. In the United Kingdom, around 160,000 people die every year from myocardial infarction (Quested, 1989).

The pathophysiology of atherosclerotic heart disease and risk factors for it are discussed in the opening pages of this chapter.

Clinical Features

The patient with myocardial infarction is usually male, is over 40 years old and has atherosclerosis of the coronary vessels, often with arterial hypertension. Attacks also occur in women and in younger men in their early 30s or even 20s. Women who take oral contraceptives and also smoke are at very high risk. Overall, however, the rate of myocardial infarction is greater in men than in women at all ages.

In a typical patient, the pain starts suddenly, usually over the lower sternal region and the upper abdomen and is continuous, but it may increase steadily in severity until it becomes almost unbearable. It is a heavy, vicelike pain, which may radiate to the shoulders and down the arms, usually the left arm. Unlike the pain of true angina, it begins spontaneously (not following effort or emotional upset), persists for hours or days and is relieved neither by rest nor by nitroglycerine. The pulse may become very rapid, irregular and feeble, even imperceptible.

Considerations for the Elderly

The elderly patient may not experience the typical vicelike pain associated with myocardial infarction because of the diminished responses of neurotransmitters that occur in the ageing process. Often the pain is atypical, such as jaw pain, or fainting may be experienced.

The arteriosclerosis that accompanies ageing may compromise tissue perfusion because of increased peripheral vascular resistance. Because elderly patients may have a well-established collateral circulation of the myocardium, they are often spared the lethal complications associated with myocardial infarction.

Diagnosis

The person with a severe occlusion may be in shock, appearing ashen and becoming cold and clammy. Vomiting is common. In a few hours body temperature rises, blood pressure falls to an unusually low point and the leucocyte count rises to 15,000 or 20,000/mm^3. Changes may be seen in the electrocardiogram within 2 to 12 hours (but may take as long as 72 to 96 hours). These changes reveal not only the presence but also the location of the infarct. Serum enzymes and isoenzymes are elevated and can be correlated with the patient's clinical course. Even if the ECG is normal, elevation of serum enzymes reveals that caution is indicated in the management of this person.

Diagnosis is generally based on patient history, ECG and serial enzyme studies. Prognosis depends on the severity of coronary artery obstruction and hence the extent of myocardial damage.

Medical Management

Generally, medical management of myocardial infarction includes relief of pain, prevention of ventricular fibrillation and other lethal arrhythmias, prescription of rest and exercise, dietary modifications and the prevention and management of anxiety.

The most critical period for the patient with a myocardial infarction is the first 48 hours following the attack. The area of infarction can increase in size for several hours or days after the onset of the attack. Cardiogenic shock and ventricular fibrillation are common causes of sudden death during this time.

Thrombolytic Therapy

The goal of management is to minimize myocardial damage and thus reduce the probability of complications. Important in reducing the size of the infarction is the administration of thrombolytic agents. The purpose of these drugs is to dissolve any thrombus which may have formed in a coronary artery, minimizing the occlusion and hence the infarction size. Critical to the effectiveness of these agents is the early administration of the drug after the onset of chest pain.

It involves intracoronary or, more commonly, intravenous administration of a thrombolytic agent. The success rate is 70 to 80 per cent for reperfusion. The currently available agents are:

1. Streptokinase, which is most commonly used.
2. Urokinase.
3. Recombinant tissue-type plasminogen activator (rTPA).

4. Anisoylated plasminogen-streptokinase activator complex (APSAC).
5. Prourokinase.

There are several contraindications, and patients must be selected carefully. Complications include: (1) bleeding episodes, for example, from puncture sites; (2) reperfusion arrhythmias; (3) allergic reactions, for example, rash, fever, anaphylaxis. (Adapted from Brunner and Suddarth (1989), pp. 264–5.)

► NURSING PROCESS
► THE PATIENT WITH MYOCARDIAL INFARCTION

► *Assessment*

One of the most important aspects of care of the patient with a myocardial infarction is the nursing assessment. This serves to establish a baseline of information on the present status of the patient, so that any deviations may be noted immediately. The nursing assessment is orderly and inclusive and has as its objectives identification of the needs of the cardiac patient and determining their priority.

Systematic assessment of the patient includes a careful history, particularly as it relates to the description of symptoms: chest pain, dyspnoea, palpitations, faintness (syncope) or sweating. Each symptom must be evaluated with regard to time, duration and precipitating and relieving factors.

In addition, a precise and complete physical assessment is critical to the observations for complications. A systematic method is used and should include the following:

1. Level of consciousness. The patient's orientation to time, place and person is very important to determine. Often changes in sensorium are produced by drug therapies or impending cardiogenic shock. An altered sensorium can mean that the heart is not perfusing the cerebral circulation satisfactorily.
2. Cardiac rhythm. The incidence of arrhythmias after an acute myocardial infarction is approximately 90 per cent. Early detection allows for initiation of anti-arrhythmia drug therapy, which can prevent subsequent reduction in cardiac output, hypotension, reduction of perfusion to vital organs and progression to lethal arrhythmias. While the interpretation of complex arrhythmias is the responsibility of the coronary care nurse, every nurse should be able to recognize normal sinus rhythm and deviations from the normal. It is also important to be familiar with the most commonly occurring arrhythmias: premature ventricular contractions, ventricular tachycardia, ventricular fibrillation and bradyarrhythmias.

A cardiac monitor is used to continuously assess heart rate, rhythm and conduction. These are documented every four hours and before the administration of medications that have cardiovascular effects. A 12-lead ECG is taken when any marked change in rhythm occurs. This assists in the diagnosis of arrhythmias, conduction disturbances and any further myocardial damage.

3. Peripheral pulses. Rate, rhythm and volume of pulses are assessed. Cardiovascular disorders will be reflected here. For example, a rapid, regular, but weak pulse may indicate reduced cardiac output. A slow pulse may indicate heart block. An irregular pulse indicates cardiac arrhythmias. Diminished or absent pulses may indicate that the left ventricle has distributed a thrombus to the periphery. The femoral arteries are shown statistically to be a frequent site of peripheral arterial emboli.

4. Fluid volume status. Urinary output is important, especially in relation to intake. An early sign of cardiogenic shock is diminished or no urinary output. The nurse should observe for oedema. In addition, the sacrum should be observed for oedema in those patients who are on bedrest.

5. Pulse pressure. Careful attention is given to pulse pressure measurements. Pulse pressure is the numerical difference between the systolic and diastolic pressures. A narrowing pulse pressure is often seen after a myocardial infarction. Stroke volume may be inferred from the pulse pressure; that is, stroke volume is the amount of blood ejected with each ventricular contraction. Since effective ventricular contraction is a function of systole and diastole, the quantitative difference between these two haemodynamic parameters reflects the stroke volume.

▶ *Patient's Problems*

Based on the clinical manifestations, nursing history and the diagnostic assessment data, the patient's problems may include the following:

- Altered comfort, chest pain related to reduced coronary blood flow.
- Potential alteration in breathing patterns related to fluid overload.
- Potential alteration in tissue perfusion related to decreased cardiac output.
- Anxiety related to fear of death.
- Potential nonadherence to self-care programme related to denial of diagnosis of myocardial infarction.

▶ *Planning and Implementation*
▶ Expected Outcomes

The major goals of the patient include relief of chest pain, absence of respiratory difficulties, maintenance/attainment of adequate tissue perfusion, reduction of anxiety and adherence to the self-care programme.

Nursing Care

Relief of Chest Pain

The most expedient and appropriate method to relieve chest pain associated with myocardial infarction is the intravenous administration of an analgesic agent, as prescribed by the doctor. The drug of choice is morphine hydrochloride (or diamorphine hydrochloride). Two important criteria are met by the administration of this drug intravenously rather than intramuscularly: a more rapid absorption is assured and the serum enzyme levels are not falsely skewed as they would be by injection into a muscle. An additional benefit of morphine is the euphoric effect it produces, which is helpful in the management of anxiety. Morphine is also an effective preload and afterload reducer and thus serves to reduce myocardial workload. It accomplishes reduction in preload by causing vasodilation of the vascular smooth muscle, thus pooling the blood in the periphery. Arterial blood pressure is reduced concomitantly, which minimizes afterload. Because morphine is given intravenously and takes effect rapidly, the nurse monitors the patient closely for hypotension, respiratory depression and decreased mental acuity.

Administration of oxygen should occur in tandem with analgesia to assure maximal relief of pain. Inhalation of oxygen even in low doses raises the circulating level of oxygen and reduces pain associated with low levels of circulating oxygen.

Vigorous assessment of all vital signs should take place as long as the patient is experiencing pain. Physical rest, in bed with the backrest elevated or in a cardiac chair, will assist in decreasing chest discomfort and dyspnoea. The head-up position is beneficial for the following reasons: (1) tidal volume is improved because there is reduced pressure from abdominal contents on the diaphragm and thus oxygen exchange is improved; (2) drainage of the upper lobes of the lungs is improved; and (3) venous return to the heart is reduced, which reduces the work of the heart.

Absence of Respiratory Difficulties

Regular and vigorous assessment of respiratory function can help the nurse detect early signs of complications associated with the lungs. Scrupulous attention to fluid volume status will prevent overloading the heart and hence the lungs. Encouraging the patient to breathe deeply and change position frequently will prevent stagnation of fluid in the lung bases.

Maintenance/Attainment of Adequate Tissue Perfusion

Keeping the patient on bedrest or chair rest is particularly helpful in reducing myocardial oxygen consumption (MVO_2). Frequently checking skin temperature and peripheral pulses with frequency is important to the maintenance of adequate tissue perfusion. Oxygen can be administered to enrich the supply of circulating oxygen.

Reduction of Anxiety

Developing a trusting and caring relationship with such patients is critical in reducing their anxiety. Provide frequent and private opportunities for them to share their concerns and fears. Create an atmosphere of acceptance of their fears and help them to know that their feelings are both realistic and normal.

Adherence to a Self-Care Programme

The most effective way to increase the probability of adherence to a self-care regime is adequate education about the disease process. Working with patients in the developfurther enhances potential for adherence (see Table 7.4).

► *Evaluation*

► **Expected Outcomes**

1. Patient experiences relief of pain.
   2. Shows no signs of respiratory difficulties.
   3. Maintains adequate tissue perfusion.
   4. Anxiety is reduced.
   5. Adheres to self-care programme.

Care of the patient with an uncomplicated myocardial infarction is summarized in Nursing Care Plan 7.1, opposite.

Table 7.4 *Self-care for the patient with a myocardial infarction*

A patient who has had a myocardial infarction should learn to regulate activity according to personal responses to each situation

Goal: To improve the quality of life and promote health

Expected outcomes:

1. Patient modifies activities during convalescence so that complete recovery is realized
   a. Myocardial healing starts early but is not complete for varying periods, usually 6–8 weeks
   b. A myocardial infarction usually requires some modification of lifestyle; adaptation to a heart attack is an ongoing process
      i. Patient avoids any activity that produces chest pain, dyspnoea or undue fatigue
      ii. Avoids extremes of heat and cold, and walking against the wind
      iii. Loses weight as directed
      iv. Stops smoking
      v. Alternates activity with rest periods. Some fatigue is normal and expected during convalescence
      vi. Uses personal strengths to compensate for limitations
      vii Eats 3 or 4 meals daily, each containing the same amount of food
         (a) Avoids large meals and hurrying while eating
         (b) Restricts caffeine-containing beverages, because caffeine can affect heart rate, rhythm and blood pressure
         (c) Complies with prescribed diet, modifying calories, fat and sodium, as prescribed
      vii. Makes every effort to adhere to medical regime, especially in taking medications
      ix. Pursues a pleasurable hobby that affords release of tension
2. Patient undertakes an *orderly* programme of increasing activity and exercise for long-term rehabilitation
   a. Engages in a regime of physical conditioning with a gradual increase in activity levels
      i. Walks daily, increasing distance and time as prescribed
      ii. Monitors pulse during physical activity until the maximal level of activity is attained
      iii. Avoids activities that tense the muscles: isometric exercise, weight-lifting, any activity that requires sudden bursts of energy
      iv. Avoids physical exercise immediately after a meal
      v. Exercises before work, after work or before retiring
      vi. Shortens work hours when first returning to work
   b. Participates in a *daily* programme of exercise that develops into a programme of regular exercise for a lifetime
   c. Notifies doctor when the following symptoms occur
      i. Chest pressure or pain not relieved in 15 minutes by nitroglycerin (and reports to nearest emergency facility)
      ii. Shortness of breath
      iii. Fainting
      iv. Slow or rapid heartbeat
      v. Swelling of feet and ankles

► NURSING CARE PLAN 7.1: THE PATIENT WITH MYOCARDIAL INFARCTION

Mr Ellis lives with his wife, his 17-year-old son and his 14-year-old daughter. He is a partner in a large firm of solicitors, and enjoys golf and hill-walking in his leisure time. As well as these pursuits, he enjoys spending time with his family in outdoor activities such as camping, canoeing and skiing. The following care plan highlights problems that he may encounter during his stay in hospital.

Patient's problems	Expected outcomes	Nursing care	Rationale
1. Chest pain due to reduced coronary blood flow	The patient will be pain-free	1a. Give analgesia as prescribed by doctor and evaluate its effect with the patient	The state of being pain-free will reduce the workload of the heart by reducing sympathetic nervous activity, which is increased when pain is present (Watson and Royle, 1987, p. 131)
		b. Give psychological support and reassure the patient in order to reduce anxiety	See problem 3
		c. Administer oxygen therapy if prescribed	Oxygen is administered to increase arterial oxygen tension, which may help to relieve myocardial pain caused by hypoxia and prevent extension of the infarction (Watson and Royle, 1987, p. 335)
		d. Ensure that the patient is nursed in a quiet, stress-free area in order to promote psychological rest	
		e. Position patient carefully in a manner that minimizes discomfort	
		f. Limit unnecessary activity in order to promote physical rest	
2. Risk of haemodynamic instability due to reduced cardiac function	Haemodynamic stability will be maintained	2a. Continuous cardiac monitoring to observe for arrhythmias	Early detection of abnormalities will reduce the risk of developing the complications of myocardial infarction (Watson and Royle, 1987, pp. 338–9)
		b. Measure and record temperature, pulse, respirations and blood pressure 2–4 hourly or as prescribed by doctor	
		c. Measure and record fluid intake and urinary output	
		d. Observe the patient for the development of peripheral or pulmonary oedema	
3. Anxiety and fear	Anxiety and fear will be reduced	3a. Assess for the presence of anxiety, e.g. over-alertness, tachycardia, tremor, hyperventilation	Anxiety causes activation of the autonomic nervous system, which in turn increases the workload of the heart. A decrease in anxiety will lead to a reduction in the workload of the heart (Carpenito, 1983, pp. 78–87)
		b. Give full explanations of the environment to patient and family, and describe what he may expect during his stay	
		c. Explain all procedures to the patient	
		d. Encourage deep-breathing exercises and participation in his own care to attempt to reduce anxiety levels (Thompson, 1989, p. 35)	

►

► NURSING CARE PLAN 7.1: THE PATIENT WITH MYOCARDIAL INFARCTION

Patient's problems	Expected outcomes	Nursing care	Rationale
		e. If severe anxiety is present, administer medication as prescribed by doctor	
4. Risk of developing complications of bedrest	The development of complications will be minimized	4a. Explain the reason for bedrest b. Encourage patient to do deep-breathing and leg exercises in order to minimize the risk of deep venous thrombosis and pulmonary embolis c. Monitor condition of the skin and pressure areas for the development of redness or sores d. Encourage the patient to care for himself as far as his condition allows, e.g. feeding, shaving, washing, in order for the patient to maintain some independence and self-control, thus reducing anxiety or depression	Prevention of the development of complications will promote recovery and reduce anxiety-provoking situations for the patient (Thompson, 1989, pp. 35–6)
5. Risk of constipation due to inactivity and the administration of analgesia	Constipation will be prevented	5a. Ensure the patient drinks adequate fluids b. Encourage the patient to choose high-fibre foods from the menu c. Administer laxatives if prescribed	Prevention of constipation reduces the patient's activity in straining, which in turn may cause vagal stimulation leading to cardiac arrhythmias (Thompson, 1989, p. 36)
6. Worries and fears regarding his wife, children and lifestyle	Worries and fears will be minimized	6a. Discuss fully his condition with him and his family b. Facilitate open visiting for his family c. Provide health education counselling for the patient and his family on topics such as diet, smoking, exercise, work, stress, sex etc	Reduction of worries and fears for both the patient and family will reduce anxiety and fear (Thompson, 1988, p. 57; 1989, p. 59)
7. Concern about rehabilitation	The patient will be able to lead as normal a life as possible	7a. Encourage patient to mobilize gradually as per medical staff's instructions. Mobilization may begin after 24–48 hours and then a gradual increase in activity over the next 6–8 days b. Encourage patient to be independent for self-care providing he is pain-free c. Encourage patient to adhere to lifestyle modifications, e.g. change in diet, stopping smoking, reducing stress d. Design a plan of convalescence and exercise for the patient which includes leisure activities for when the patient is discharged	According to a WHO working group and experts of the International Society of Cardiology, 'The rehabilitation of cardiac patients can be defined as the sum of activities required to ensure them the best possible physical, mental and social conditions so that they may, by their own efforts, regain as normal as possible a place in the community and lead an active, productive life' (Deavin, 1984)

Cardiac Rehabilitation

Once an acute myocardial infarction has been diagnosed and the patients progress to symptom-free status, an active rehabilitation programme is provided.

The goals of rehabilitation for patients with myocardial infarction are to extend and improve the quality of life. The immediate objectives are to return patients as rapidly as possible to a normal or near-normal lifestyle. This includes training patients for physical activity, educating both patients and their families, and initiating psychosocial and vocational counselling when necessary.

Cardiac rehabilitation actually begins as soon as the acute episode occurs. During this stage the nurse can assist patients towards realizing their goals of independence, even when they are on strict bedrest. This is achieved by directing their thinking towards the time when they will be active again. The goal here is not to change their lifestyle but to make necessary modifications. It is best to avoid focusing on what patients should not do. Instead, they should be encouraged to develop short-term and long-range goals based on their needs. It is important to explain the nature of the disease, answer questions honestly and reassure patients that most people return to a useful economic life and resume their usual activities. These positive approaches help to keep patients from becoming cardiac invalids.

There is a divergence of opinion about the amount of activity in which patients may participate following a myocardial infarction. Complications commonly occur early during convalescence. Physiological resolution of the infarction continues to occur over time and varies among individuals. Scar formation over the infarcted area is seen at the beginning of the third week and the necrotic debris is resolved by the fourth week. Thus, there is an area of ischaemia in some patients for varying lengths of time, which affects their exercise prescriptions.

Physical Conditioning

Physical conditioning or exercise training is done to improve cardiac efficiency and enhance the patient's ability to perform work at reduced heart and blood pressure rates. This will reduce the oxygen requirements of the heart and enable the patient to perform more physical activity before developing symptoms of myocardial ischaemia (e.g., chest pain, ECG changes). Physical conditioning may be divided into the acute phase, convalescent phase (up to eight weeks) and maintenance phase (lifelong).

As soon as the patient's condition is stable, and the doctor allows it, the arms are put through range-of-motion exercises. Active motion of the muscles of the shoulder girdle helps to prevent anterior chest wall pain, which may be interpreted as being cardiac in origin. Once asymptomatic, the patient may be able to sit in a chair for 20 to 30 minutes several times a day. Encourage the patient to participate in self-care activities as soon as possible. Early mobilization under supervision is usually permitted after an uncomplicated myocardial infarction. Prolonged immobilization has a deconditioning effect and also contributes to anxiety and depression.

- Watch the patient closely and carefully during physical activity for chest pain, dyspnoea, weakness, fatigue and an increase in heart rate of more than 20 beats from baseline or more than 120 beats per minute.
- Watch also for a fall in systolic blood pressure, the development of an arrhythmia and ECG changes. If these occur, the activity is stopped immediately and the patient's clinical status is re-evaluated.

Isometric exercises are contraindicated because they may impose stress on the left ventricle by raising the blood pressure while at the same time decreasing coronary perfusion. The performance of the Valsalva manoeuvre (straining) is to be avoided.

A treadmill test with ECG monitoring is done to help in developing guidelines for the design of an appropriate exercise programme for the patient. This is usually carried out about four weeks after discharge (Swanton, 1984). The patient who demonstrates low functional capacity with ischaemic ST segment depression and premature ventricular beats will need a different activity programme than the patient who has good functional capacity with no significant ECG abnormalities. The level of the patient's physical activity before infarction is also considered.

In general, the activity is increased in distance and speed. The cardiovascular benefits of exercise depend on whether or not the patient can exercise long enough to reach and maintain the prescribed pulse rate for a period of 15 minutes.

Several months after myocardial infarction the maintenance phase begins. As a result of physical training, the patient may participate in activities that promote endurance—jogging, running, swimming, cycling. These appear to be useful for heart and lung conditioning. In general, the best type of exercise consists of rhythmic and repetitive movements (calisthenics, walking, running) that require maximal or submaximal effort. Short bursts of intensive effort are to be avoided because they produce a marked rise in blood pressure.

Sexual Activity

Many patients fear that sexual activity will be harmful to their heart condition and will precipitate chest pain.

If the patient can walk vigorously around the block or climb a flight of stairs without symptoms, sexual activity may usually be resumed. Some modifications may be necessary—that is, intercourse after a night's sleep and followed by a rest period, or the use of more passive positions to decrease cardiac workload. Sexual relations should be avoided after drinking alcohol or ingesting a large meal, if the situation produces anxiety, or if abnormal symptoms develop and persist.

INFECTIOUS DISEASES OF THE HEART

The endocardium is the endothelial layer of tissue that lines the heart's cavities and covers the flaps of its valves. Of the diseases that affect it, the majority represent various types and stages of inflammation (i.e., endocarditis or its aftermath). They include: (1) rheumatic endocarditis, one of the many complications of acute rheumatic fever; (2) infective endocarditis, produced by direct bacterial invasion of the endocardium, particularly that portion covering the valve leaflets; and (3) chronic valvular heart disease, based on structural deformities of the heart valves, whether of congenital origin or acquired as a result of either rheumatic or bacterial endocarditis in the past.

When an area of endocardium becomes inflamed, a fibrin clot, called a vegetation, may form. In time this clot becomes converted into a mass of scar tissue. The scarred endocardium becomes thickened, stiffened, contracted and deformed. A fringe of vegetations ranging along the free margins of the valve flaps, marking the site of earlier erosions, represents the basic lesion of endocarditis and is the forerunner of chronic valvular heart disease.

Two functional disorders of the valves may result from these pathological changes: stenosis or regurgitation. In stenosis the valvular opening becomes narrowed and does not permit the passage of normal amounts of blood. Regurgitation results from the valves' shrivelling and producing a wider opening. The valve leaflets can no longer perform their function of closing to prevent a backflow of blood.

Rheumatic Endocarditis

Altered Physiology
Rheumatic fever is a sequel to a Group A streptococcal infection. It is considered a preventable disease. The most prominent symptom of rheumatic fever is polyarthritis, but the most serious damage occurs in the heart, where every structural component is likely to be the site of an inflammatory reaction. The heart damage and the joint lesions are not infectious in origin, in the sense that these tissues are not invaded and directly damaged by destructive organisms; rather, they represent a sensitivity phenomenon occurring in response to the haemolytic streptococcus. Leucocytes accumulate in the affected tissues and form nodules, which eventually are replaced by scars. The myocardium is certain to be involved in this inflammatory process; that is, rheumatic myocarditis develops, which temporarily weakens the contractile power of the heart. The pericardium likewise is affected; that is, rheumatic pericarditis also occurs during the acute illness. These myocardial and pericardial complications usually are without serious sequelae; on the other hand,

the effects of rheumatic endocarditis are permanent and often crippling.

Infective Endocarditis

Infective endocarditis (bacterial endocarditis) is an infection of the valves and endothelial surface of the heart caused by direct invasion of bacteria or other organisms and leading to deformity of the valve leaflets. It may be acute, subacute, or chronic. Acute endocarditis usually occurs on normal valves. Causative micro-organisms include bacteria (streptococci, enterococci, pneumococci, staphylococci), fungi and rickettsiae. The subacute form is usually caused by *Streptococcus viridans*.

Aetiology
Infective subacute endocarditis usually develops in patients who have a history of valvular heart disease. At great risk are patients with rheumatic heart disease or mitral valve prolapse and individuals who have had prosthetic-valve surgery.

Hospital-acquired endocarditis occurs most often in patients with debilitating disease, those with indwelling catheters and those on prolonged intravenous or antibiotic therapy. Patients on immunosuppressive drugs or steroids may develop fungal endocarditis. Therefore, infective endocarditis often accompanies medical and surgical therapy. It is more common in older people, probably due to decreased immunological responses to infection, metabolic alterations arising from changes in the ageing body and increased instrumentation, especially in genitourinary disease. There is a high incidence of staphylococcal endocarditis among drug addicts, the disease occurring for the most part on normal valves.

Myocarditis

Acute myocarditis is an inflammatory process involving the myocardium. The heart is a muscle, hence its efficiency depends on the health of the individual muscle fibres. When the muscle fibres are healthy, the heart can function well in spite of severe valvular injuries; when the muscle fibres are poor, life is in jeopardy.

Altered Physiology
Myocarditis usually results from an infectious process, particularly of viral, bacterial, mycotic, parasitic, protozoal or spirochaetal origin, or it may be produced by hypersensitivity states such as rheumatic fever. Therefore, myocarditis may be seen in patients with acute systemic infections, those receiving immunosuppressive therapy, or those with infective endocarditis.

Myocarditis can cause heart dilation, mural thrombi, infiltration of circulating blood cells around the coronary vessels and between the muscle fibres and degeneration of the muscle fibres themselves.

PERICARDITIS

Definition and Aetiology

Pericarditis refers to an inflammation of the pericardium, the membranous sac enveloping the heart. It may be a primary illness or may develop in the course of a variety of medical and surgical diseases.

The following are some of the causes underlying or associated with pericarditis:

1. Idiopathic or nonspecific causes.
2. Infection.
   a. Bacterial (e.g., streptococcus, staphylococcus, meningococcus, gonococcus).
   b. Viral (e.g., coxsackie, influenza).
   c. Mycotic (fungal).
3. Disorders of connective tissue—systemic lupus erythematosus, rheumatic fever, rheumatoid arthritis, polyarteritis.
4. Hypersensitivity states—immune reactions, drug reactions, serum sickness.
5. Diseases of adjacent structures—myocardial infarction, dissecting aneurysm, pleural and pulmonary disease (pneumonia).
6. Neoplastic disease.
   a. Secondary to metastasis from lung cancer, breast cancer.
   b. Leukaemia.
   c. Following radiation.
   d. Primary (mesothelioma).
7. Trauma—chest injury, cardiac surgery, during cardiac catheterization, pacemaker implantation.
8. Association with renal disorders (uraemia).

Clinical Features

The characteristic symptom of pericarditis is pain and the characteristic sign is a friction rub. Pain is almost always present in acute pericarditis and is most common over the precordium. The pain may be felt beneath the clavicle and in the neck and left scapular region. Pericardial pain is aggravated by breathing, turning in bed and twisting the body; it is relieved by sitting up. In fact, the patient prefers to adopt a forward-leaning or a sitting posture. Dyspnoea may occur as the result of restriction of the heart contraction, which leads to a decreased cardiac output. The patient may appear extremely ill. Pericarditis *per se* often gives rise to no signs other than fever and the production of a friction rub.

Diagnosis

Diagnosis is most often made on the presentation of signs and symptoms. The ECG may be helpful in confirming the diagnosis.

Management

The objectives of management are to determine the cause, to administer therapy for the specific cause (when known) and to be on the alert for cardiac tamponade (compression of the heart from fluid in the pericardial sac). The patient is placed on bedrest when cardiac output is impaired until the fever, chest pain and friction rub have disappeared.

Nonsteroidal anti-inflammatory agents may be given for pain relief during the acute phase (Swanton, 1984, p. 279). Salicylates relieve pain and hasten reabsorption of fluid in the patient with rheumatic pericarditis. Corticosteroids are sometimes given to control symptoms, hasten resolution of the inflammatory process in the pericardium and prevent recurring pericardial effusion.

Patients with infections of the pericardium are treated with the antimicrobial agent of choice based on identification and sensitivity tests. The pericarditis of rheumatic fever may respond to penicillin. Isoniazid, ethambutol, rifampicin and streptomycin in various combinations are used in the treatment of tuberculosis that produces pericarditis. Amphotericin B is used in fungal pericarditis and adrenal steroids are used in disseminated lupus erythematosus.

As the patient's condition improves, activity may be increased gradually. However, if pain, fever or friction rub reappear, bedrest must be resumed.

► NURSING PROCESS
► THE PATIENT WITH PERICARDITIS

► Assessment

Pain is the primary distress of the patient with pericarditis. The pain of pericarditis is assessed by observation and by evaluation while getting the patient to vary positions in bed.

While observing the patient, try to discover whether or not the pain is influenced by respiratory movements, with or without the actual passage of air; by flexion, extension, or rotation of the spine, including the neck; by movements of the shoulders and arms; by coughing; or by swallowing. Recognizing these relationships may be very helpful in establishing a diagnosis.

A pericardial friction rub occurs when the pericardial surfaces lose their lubricating fluid because of inflammation. The rub is audible on auscultation and is synchronous with the heartbeat.

► Patient's Problems

Based on the assessment data, the patient's problems may include the following:

● Pain related to inflammation of the pericardium.
● Potential development of decreased cardiac output related to restriction of cardiac contraction.

► *Planning and Implementation*
► **Expected Outcomes**
The major goals of the patient may include relief of pain and maintenance/attainment of cardiac output.

Nursing Care

Relief of Pain
Relief of pain is achieved by ensuring that the patient remains resting in bed or a chair, whichever is more comfortable. Because the posture the patient assumes to relieve the pain is that of sitting upright and leaning forward, chair rest may be more comfortable. As the chest pain and friction rub abate, activities of daily living may be resumed gradually.

The responses of a patient who is receiving medications for the pericarditis, such as analgesics, antibiotics, or steroids, should be monitored and recorded.

If chest pain and the friction rub recur, the patient should be encouraged to resume bedrest.

Maintenance/Attainment of Adequate Cardiac Output
If the patient does not respond to medical management, fluid may develop or accumulate between the pericardial linings or in the sac. This condition is called pericardial effusion. Fluid in the pericardial sac can cause constriction of the myocardium and interrupt its ability to pump. Thus, the cardiac output will decline with each contraction. Failure to identify the onset of this problem can lead to cardiac tamponade and the possibility of sudden death.

Early signs and symptoms of this event to watch for are those that indicate a falling arterial pressure. Usually the systolic pressure falls while the diastolic remains stable; hence the pulse pressure narrows.

► *Evaluation*
► **Expected Outcomes**

1. Patient is free of pain.
   a. Performs activities of daily living comfortably.
   b. Temperature returns to patient's normal range.
2. Maintains/attains adequate cardiac output. Blood pressure remains in patient's normal range.

Chronic Constrictive Pericarditis

Chronic constrictive pericarditis is a condition in which chronic inflammatory thickening of the pericardium compresses the heart and prevents it from expanding to normal size. The major haemodynamic deficit results from a restriction of ventricular filling.

Often the adherent pericardium becomes calcified. The heart action is greatly restricted by this tough, unyielding enclosure and oedema, ascites and hepatic enlargement result. The fixation of the heart to the pericardium may produce a retraction of the chest wall with every beat.

Chronic restrictive pericarditis is caused by long-standing pyogenic infections, postviral infections, tuberculosis or haemopericardium.

The signs and symptoms are predominantly those of congestive heart failure, but dyspnoea on effort is the most prominent symptom. Chronic atrial fibrillation is commonly present.

Surgical removal of the tough encasing pericardium (pericardiectomy) is the only treatment of any benefit. The objective of the operation is to release both ventricles from the constrictive and restrictive inflammation. (See Chapter 8, p. 377.)

ACQUIRED VALVULAR DISEASES OF THE HEART

The function of normal heart valves is to maintain the forward flow of blood from the atria to the ventricles and from the ventricles to the great vessels. Valvular damage may interfere with valvular function by stenosis (narrowing) of the valve or by impaired closure that allows backward leakage of blood (valvular insufficiency, regurgitation or incompetence).

Acquired valvular heart disease often is a result of previous rheumatic carditis that has damaged one or more of the heart valves. The mitral valve is involved most frequently, followed by the aortic, tricuspid and pulmonary valves. If the heart muscle remains strong, the circulatory apparatus can adjust itself efficiently even though a valve is injured badly. The details of such adjustment, called compensatory changes, include modifications in the rate and character of the heartbeat, changes in the blood, hypertrophy of the myocardium, redistribution of the blood in the body and so on. All of these changes reduce the unfavourable impact of the valve defect.

Mitral Valve Prolapse Syndrome

The mitral valve prolapse syndrome is a dysfunction of the mitral valve leaflets that renders the mitral valve incompetent and results in valvular regurgitation. This syndrome may produce no symptoms or it may progress rapidly and result in sudden death. In recent years the syndrome has been diagnosed more frequently, ostensibly as a result of improved diagnostic methods. Many individuals have the syndrome but no symptoms. Often the symptoms are first identified during a physical examination of the heart, which reveals an extra heart sound referred to as a mitral click. The presence of a click indicates early valvular incompetence with disruption of normal blood flow. The mitral click may deteriorate into a murmur over a period of time as the valve leaflets become progressively dysfunctional. Concomitant with the progression of the murmur may be signs and symptoms of heart failure as mitral regurgitation ensues.

Mitral Stenosis

Mitral stenosis is the progressive thickening and contracture of the mitral valve cusps, which causes narrowing of the orifice and progressive obstruction to blood flow. It is by far the most common of the late cardiac lesions produced by rheumatic fever and is considered the typical lesion.

Mitral Insufficiency (Regurgitation)

Mitral insufficiency results when incompetence and distortion of the mitral valve prevent the free margins from coming into apposition during systole. The chordae tendineae may become shortened, preventing complete closure of the leaflets. Valvular movement is more restricted than in mitral stenosis. In about half of the patients, mitral regurgitation is caused by chronic rheumatic heart disease.

Aortic Valve Stenosis

Aortic valve stenosis is the narrowing of the orifice between the left ventricle and the aorta. In adults the stenosis may be congenital, or it may be a result of rheumatic fever or cusp calcification of unknown cause. There is progressive narrowing of the valve orifice over a period of several years to several decades.

Aortic Insufficiency (Incompetence; Regurgitation)

Aortic insufficiency is caused by inflammatory lesions that deform the flaps of the aortic valve, preventing them from completely sealing the aortic orifice during diastole and thus allowing a backflow of blood from the aorta into the left ventricle. This valvular defect may follow endocarditis of the rheumatic or bacterial type or may be due to congenital abnormalities or diseases that cause dilation or tearing of the ascending aorta (syphilitic disease, rheumatoid spondylitis, dissecting aneurysm).

Tricuspid Lesions

Tricuspid stenosis is the restriction of the tricuspid valve orifice as the result of commissural fusion and fibrosis usually following rheumatic fever. It is commonly associated with diseases of the mitral valve.

Tricuspid insufficiency allows the regurgitation of blood from the right ventricle into the right atrium during ventricular systole.

CARDIOMYOPATHIES

Definition, Aetiology and Altered Physiology

Myopathy is a disease of muscle. The cardiomyopathies are a group of diseases that affect the structure and function of the myocardium. They are considered to be primary or secondary according to their aetiology. The term primary cardiomyopathy is used if the condition is of unknown aetiology; secondary cardiomyopathy indicates that the myocardial involvement results from a systemic disorder such as excessive alcohol intake, infections, metabolic diseases, immune diseases, toxic response, pregnancy and hypertension.

When the cardiomyopathies are categorized by pathological, physiological and clinical signs, they are defined as (1) dilated cardiomyopathy, or sometimes congestive cardiomyopathy; (2) hypertrophic cardiomyopathy; and (3) restrictive cardiomyopathy.

Regardless of the category and the aetiology, these diseases lead to severe heart failure and often death.

Dilated or congestive cardiomyopathy is the most commonly occurring form of the cardiomyopathies. It is distinguished by a dilated and enlarged ventricular cavity along with decreasing muscle wall thickness, left atrial enlargement and stasis of blood in the ventricle. Microscopic examination of the muscle tissue reveals a diminishing of the contractile elements of the muscle fibres. Excessive alcohol intake is often implicated in this type of cardiomyopathy.

Hypertrophic cardiomyopathy occurs less frequently and is most often associated with idiopathic hypertrophic subaortic stenosis. In hypertrophic cardiomyopathies the heart muscle actually increases in mass weight, especially along the septum. The septal size increase may produce obstruction to the flow of blood from the atria to the ventricles; hence, this category is divided further into obstructive and nonobstructive types. Nonobstructive hypertrophic cardiomyopathy is usually associated with hypertension.

The last and least frequently occurring category is restrictive cardiomyopathy. This form is seen less frequently than all other forms and is characterized by an impairment of ventricular stretch and hence volume. Restrictive cardiomyopathy can be associated with amyloidosis and other such infiltrative diseases.

Regardless of the distinguishing features, the pathophysiology of cardiomyopathy is a series of progressive events that culminates in impaired pumping of the left ventricle. As the stroke volume becomes less and less, the sympathetic system is stimulated, resulting in increased systemic vascular resistance. As in the pathophysiology of heart failure from any cause, the left ventricle enlarges to accommodate the demands and eventually fails. Failure of the right ventricle usually accompanies this process.

Clinical Features

The cardiomyopathies may occur at any age and affect both men and women. Most people with cardiomyopathy present initially with signs and symptoms of heart failure. Dyspnoea on exertion, paroxysmal nocturnal dyspnoea, cough and easy fatigability are early symptoms. A physical examination usually indicates systemic venous congestion, jugular vein distension, pitting oedema of dependent body parts, hepatic engorgement and tachycardia.

Diagnosis

Diagnosis of cardiomyopathy is usually made from findings revealed by patient history and by ruling out other causes of the failure, such as myocardial infarction. There is no specific test that is best for diagnosing cardiomyopathy. The ECG will demonstrate changes consistent with left ventricular hypertrophy. The echocardiogram is probably one of the most helpful diagnostic tools in that the functioning of the left ventricle can be observed easily. Cardiac catheterization is sometimes used to rule out coronary heart disease as a causative factor.

Medical Management

Medical management is directed toward correcting the heart failure. When heart failure has progressed beyond being medically responsive, heart transplant is the patient's only hope for survival.

▶ **NURSING PROCESS**
▶ **THE PATIENT WITH CARDIOMYOPATHY**

▶ *Assessment*

The nursing assessment for the patient with cardiomyopathy begins with a detailed history of the presenting signs and symptoms. Because of the chronic nature of this problem, a careful psychosocial history is also important. The patient's family and friend support system should be identified very early and involved in the management of the patient.

The physical assessment should be directed toward signs and symptoms of congestive heart failure. A careful evaluation of fluid volume status and vital signs are important in a baseline assessment. The doctor may want to place the patient on a cardiac monitor; however, when the diagnosis is made and arrhythmia is not a significant problem, the patient may not need to be monitored. The acuteness of the heart failure will determine whether or not the patient needs to be in a critical care environment.

▶ *Patient's Problems*

Based on the assessment data, the patient's problems may include the following:

● Potential alteration in breathing pattern related to myocardial failure.
● Activity intolerance related to excessive fluid volume.
● Anxiety related to the disease process.
● Potential nonadherence to the self-care programme.

▶ *Planning and Implementation*
▶ **Expected Outcomes**
The major goals of the patient include absence of respiratory difficulties, increased activity tolerance, reduction of anxiety and adherence to a self-care programme.

Nursing Care

Absence of Respiratory Difficulties
Because many of the patient's signs and symptoms are corrected by pharmacological agents, attention to the timing of administration of prescribed medications is vitally important. Careful documentation of the patient's response is critical.

Supporting respiratory exchange with oxygen by way of a nasal cannula may be indicated.

The patient may be more comfortable if allowed to rest at the bedside in a chair. This position will be helpful in pooling venous blood in the periphery and reducing preload. Helping the patient to keep warm and to change position frequently will stimulate circulation and reduce the possibility of skin breakdown. Maintaining an environment free of dust, lint, flowers and such will also support easier respiratory exchange.

Increased Activity Tolerance
Planning nursing care so that the patient participates frequently in activities of short duration is important. Allowing the patient to accomplish a goal, no matter how small, will also enhance his sense of well-being. For example, working with the patient to determine what part of the bath can be completed without aid and then providing a period of rest before the nurse completes the bath, will help the patient conserve energy which is in short supply. Minimize or abolish activities that deplete the patient's energy.

Reduction of Anxiety
Provide patients with appropriate information about their signs and symptoms. Assist them to accomplish certain activities for themselves. Provide an atmosphere in which they feel free to express their fears and let them know that their concerns are legitimate. If patients are facing death or awaiting transplant surgery, allow them all the time they require to discuss their concerns. Spiritual support may be indicated for patients and their significant others.

Adherence to a Self-Care Programme

It is particularly important for the patient with cardiomyopathy to learn what self-care activities are necessary and how to perform them at home. Optimum health is crucial if the patient is a candidate for heart transplant. Satisfactory improvement can be obtained by meticulous attention to a medication programme, which usually consists of several different medications to maintain a state free of cardiac failure.

The nurse can be integral to the process as patients review lifestyle and work to incorporate the above therapeutic activities with minimal intrusion. Helping patients to accept their disease will facilitate their adherence to a self-care programme at home.

Establishing trust is vital to the relationship with these chronically ill and debilitated patients. Providing realistic hope helps to reduce their anxiety while awaiting a donor heart when transplant is an acceptable treatment modality.

When a patient can no longer be helped by any therapeutic technique, allowing the patient and significant others the freedom to begin the grieving process is vitally important.

► *Evaluation*
► **Expected Outcomes**

1. Patient demonstrates improved respiratory function.
   a. Respiratory rate is within normal limits.
   b. Blood gases are normal.
2. Increases activity tolerance.
   a. Carries out activities of daily living, e.g., brushes teeth, feeds self.
   b. Transfers self from chair to bed.
3. Experiences reduction of anxiety.
   a. Discusses prognosis freely.
4. Adheres to a programme of self-care.
   a. Takes medications according to prescribed schedule.
   b. Modifies lifestyle to accommodate activity limitations.
   c. Identifies signs and symptoms to be reported to the medical staff.

CARDIAC COMPLICATIONS: OVERVIEW

The complications of cardiac disease are responsible for many deaths from heart disease. The most common complications are arrhythmias, acute pulmonary oedema, cardiac failure, cardiogenic shock, thromboembolic episodes and myocardial rupture. The goals of medical and nursing management of patients with heart disease are the prevention of complications and the early identification of signs and symptoms that signal the onset of a complication.

Arrhythmias are the most common complication of cardiac disease. They may vary in severity from a benign premature beat to a malignant and fatal ventricular fibrillation. Mobile intensive care units, new drug therapies and increasingly sophisticated pacemakers have all contributed to improvement in the control of compromising arrhythmias.

Cardiac failure, which covers a spectrum of complications from acute pulmonary oedema to cardiogenic shock, remains a leading cause of cardiac morbidity and mortality. The factor of greatest importance in cardiac failure is the extent of myocardial fibre damage. The severity of failure will be directly proportional to the extent of damaged muscle mass.

Though not as common because of more aggressive activity programmes for patients with heart disease, thromboembolic episodes still occur. The cerebral, renal, femoral, mesenteric and pulmonary arteries are most often affected.

Myocardial rupture, too, is rare. It presents itself often enough, however, that observing for signs and symptoms in the high-risk patient population is critical.

All complications of cardiac diseases can result in cardiac arrest. Cardiopulmonary resuscitation is the treatment of choice and is a skill that is essential for all health-care workers.

The best resource in the prevention of complications is nursing care that involves early recognition and reporting of cardinal signs and symptoms of the various complications.

ARRHYTHMIAS

An arrhythmia is a disorder of the heartbeat that may include a disturbance of rate, rhythm or both. Arrhythmias are derangements of the heart's conduction system and not of heart structure. Arrhythmias are identified by analysing ECG waveforms. They are named according to the site of impulse origin and the mechanism of conduction involved. For example, an arrhythmia that originates in the sinus node (SA node) and is slow in rate is called sinus bradycardia. There are four possible sites of origin, as indicated in Table 7.5. Note also the possible altered conduction mechanisms that can occur.

Properties of Cardiac Muscle

The cardiac muscle possesses the following physiological properties: excitability, automaticity, conductivity and contractility.

Excitability is the ability of a myocardial cell to respond to a stimulus; automaticity allows a cell to reach a threshold potential and generate an impulse without being stimulated by another source. Conductivity refers to the ability of the muscle to move an impulse from cell to cell.

Table 7.5 *Identification of arrhythmias by site of origin*

Sites of origin	Mechanisms of conduction
Sinus node	Bradycardia
Atria	Tachycardia
Atrioventricular node or junction	Flutter
Ventricles	Fibrillation Premature beats Heart blocks

Contractility allows the muscle to shorten when stimulated.

When all of these properties are functioning without deviations, the heart muscle is stimulated by impulses originating in the sinus node; hence, the sinus node is referred to as the heart's pacemaker. If disequilibrium occurs in one of the heart's basic properties, an arrhythmia may result. The disequilibrium can be caused by normal activity such as exercise or by a pathological occurrence such as a myocardial infarction. In myocardial infarction, because reduced oxygenation to the myocardium can increase excitability, the myocardium has an increased response to stimuli. This is an example of one of the most common causes of an arrhythmia.

Autonomic Nervous System

The heart is under the control of the autonomic nervous system, which consists of sympathetic and parasympathetic fibres. The sympathetic system is also referred to as adrenergic, a word derived from the root word 'adrenalin'. Thus, stimulation of the sympathetic system accelerates heart rate, raises blood pressure and enhances the force of myocardial contraction. Parasympathetic stimulation, conversely, slows the heart rate, lowers blood pressure and reduces the force of contraction.

Manipulation of the autonomic nervous system forms the foundation for much of the drug therapy in arrhythmia control, e.g., ß-adrenergic blockers.

Arrhythmias Originating in the Sinus Node

Sinus Bradycardia

Sinus bradycardia may be due to vagal stimulation, digitalis intoxication, increased intracranial pressure or myocardial infarction. It is also seen in highly trained athletes, in people in severe pain, in those people under medication (propranolol, reserpine, methyldopa), in hypoendocrine states (myxoedema, Addison's disease, panhypopituitarism), in anorexia nervosa, in hypothermia and after surgical damage to the sinus node (Figure 7.3).

The characteristics of sinus bradycardia are the same as those of normal sinus rhythm, except for the rate. If slow heart rate is causing significant haemodynamic changes with resultant syncope, angina, or ectopic arrhythmias, then treatment is directed toward increasing the heart rate. If the decrease in heart rate is due to vagal stimulation such as bearing down at stool or vomiting, attempts are made to prevent further vagal stimulation. If the patient has digitalis intoxication, then digitalis is withheld. The drug of choice in treating sinus bradycardia is atropine. Atropine blocks vagal stimulation, thus allowing a normal rate to occur.

Sinus Tachycardia

Sinus tachycardia may be caused by fever, acute blood loss, anaemia, shock, exercise, congestive cardiac failure (CCF), pain, hypermetabolic states, anxiety or sympathomimetic or parasympatholytic drugs. The ECG pattern is as shown in Figure 7.4.

The characteristics of sinus tachycardia are the same as those of normal sinus rhythm, except for the rate.

Carotid sinus pressure may be effective in slowing the

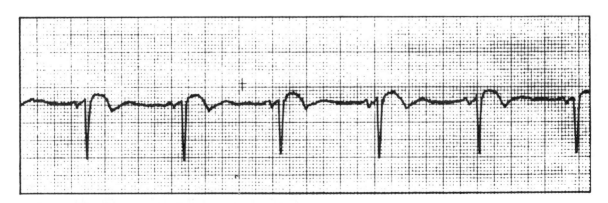

Figure 7.3 Sinus bradycardia.

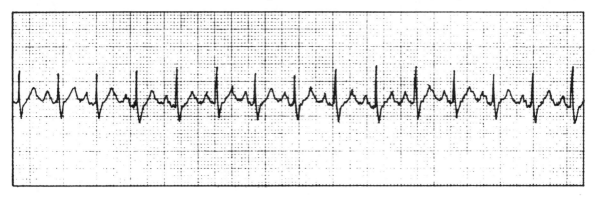

Figure 7.4 Sinus tachycardia.

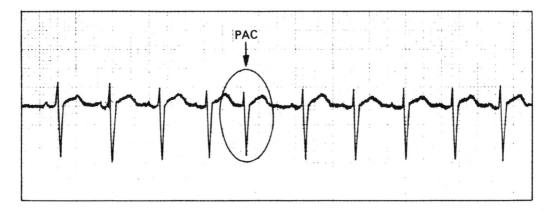

Figure 7.5 Premature atrial contraction (atrial ectopic).

rate temporarily, and thereby help to rule out other arrhythmias.

Arrhythmias Originating in the Atrial Muscle

Premature Atrial Contractions (Atrial Ectopics)

Premature atrial contractions may be due to atrial muscle irritability caused by caffeine; alcohol; nicotine; stretched atrial myocardium as in congestive cardiac failure; stress or anxiety; hypokalaemia; atrial ischaemia, injury or infarction; and hypermetabolic states.

Premature atrial contractions have the characteristics shown in Figure 7.5.

Paroxysmal Atrial Tachycardia

Paroxysmal atrial tachycardia is characterized by abrupt onset and abrupt cessation. Rhythm may be triggered by emotions, tobacco, caffeine, fatigue, sympathomimetic drugs or alcohol. Paroxysmal atrial tachycardia is not usually associated with organic heart disease. The rapid rate may produce angina due to decreased coronary artery filling. Cardiac output is reduced and heart failure may occur. The patient frequently does not tolerate this rhythm for long periods (Figure 7.6).

The patient may not be aware of paroxysmal atrial tachycardia. Treatment is directed toward eliminating the cause and decreasing the heart rate. Morphine sedation may slow the rate without further treatment. Carotid sinus pressure usually slows the rate or stops the attack and is usually more effective after digitalis or vasopressors. The use of vasopressors has a reflex effect on the carotid sinus by elevating the blood pressure and thus slowing the heart rate. Short-acting digitalis preparations may be used. Propranolol may be tried if digitalis is unsuccessful. The calcium channel blocker verapamil may be used. Cardioversion may be necessary if the patient does not tolerate the fast heart rate.

Atrial Fibrillation

Atrial fibrillation (disorganized and unco-ordinated twitching of atrial musculature) is usually associated with atherosclerotic heart disease, rheumatic heart disease,

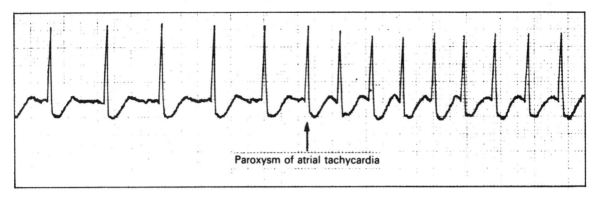

Figure 7.6 Paroxysmal atrial tachycardia.

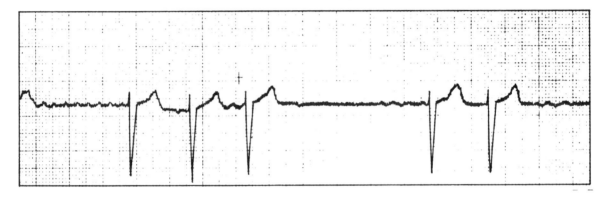

Figure 7.7 Atrial fibrillation.

congestive cardiac failure, thyrotoxicosis, cor pulmonale or congenital heart disease (Figure 7.7).

A rapid ventricular response reduces the time for ventricular filling and hence the stroke volume. The atrial kick, which is 25 to 30 per cent of the cardiac output, is also lost.

Congestive heart failure frequently follows. There is usually a pulse deficit, the numerical difference between apical and radial pulse rates.

Treatment is directed toward eliminating the cause, decreasing the atrial irritability and decreasing the rate of the ventricular response.

In patients with chronic atrial fibrillation, anticoagulant therapy may be used to prevent thromboemboli from forming in the atria.

At times a mixture of atrial flutter and atrial fibrillation is seen, sometimes called atrial flutter-fibrillation or coarse atrial fibrillation. Such an arrhythmia is best classified as atrial fibrillation when the criteria for atrial flutter are not satisfied.

Drugs of choice to treat atrial fibrillation are similar to those used in the treatment of paroxysmal atrial tachycardia. A digitalis preparation is used to slow the heart rate and an anti-arrhythmic such as quinidine is used to correct the arrhythmia.

Arrhythmias Originating in the Ventricular Muscle

Premature Ventricular Contractions (Ventricular Ectopics)

Premature ventricular contractions are the result of increased automaticity of the ventricular muscle cells. They can be due to digitalis intoxication, hypoxia, hypokalaemia, fever, acidosis, exercise or increased circulating catecholamines.

Infrequent premature ventricular contractions are not serious in themselves. Usually, the patient feels a palpitating sensation but has no other complaints. However, the concern lies in the fact that these premature contractions may lead to more serious ventricular arrhythmias.

In the patient with acute myocardial infarction, premature ventricular contractions are considered serious precursors of ventricular tachycardia and ventricular fibrillation when they (1) occur in increasing number, more than six per minute; (2) are multifocal or originate from several areas in the heart; (3) occur in pairs or triplets; and (4) occur in the vulnerable phase of conduction.

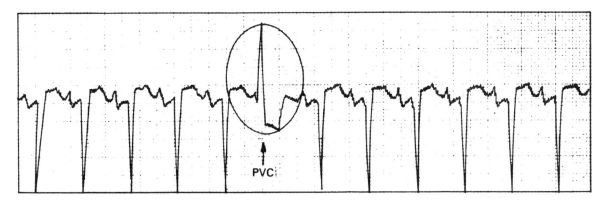

Figure 7.8 Premature ventricular contraction.

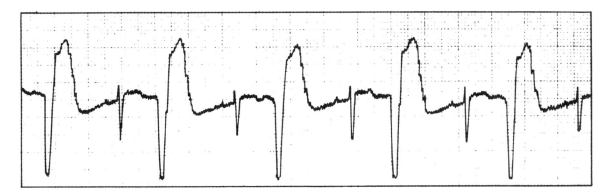

Figure 7.9 Ventricular bigeminy.

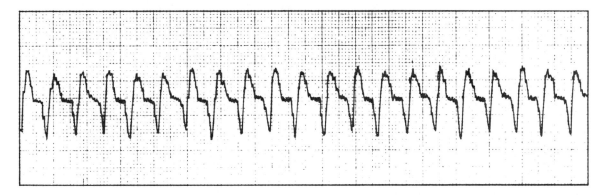

Figure 7.10 Ventricular tachycardia.

The T wave represents the period when the heart is most likely to respond to any stray beat and be excited in an arrhythmic manner. This phase of T wave conduction is said to be the vulnerable phase (Figure 7.8).

In order to decrease the myocardial irritability, the cause must be determined and, if possible, corrected. An anti-arrhythmic drug may be used for immediate and possibly long-term therapy. The drug most commonly used in acute care is lignocaine; disopyramide may be effective for long-term therapy.

Ventricular Bigeminy

Ventricular bigeminy is frequently associated with digitalis excess, coronary artery disease, acute myocardial infarction and congestive cardiac failure. The term

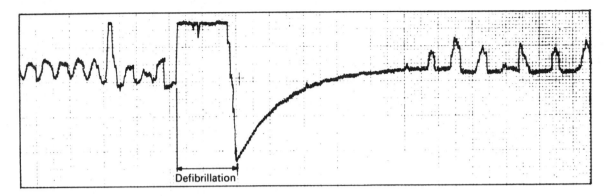

Figure 7.11 Ventricular fibrillation with defibrillation.

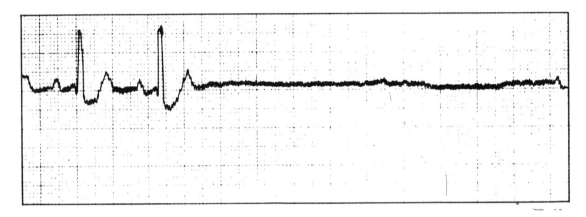

Figure 7.12 Ventricular asystole.

'bigeminy' refers to a condition in which every other beat is premature (Figure 7.9).

If the ectopic beats occur every third beat, this is termed trigeminy; every fourth beat, quadrigeminy.

The treatment for ventricular bigeminy is the same as for premature ventricular contractions. Since the underlying cause of ventricular bigeminy is frequently digitalis toxicity, this should be ruled out or treated if present.

Ventricular Tachycardia

This arrhythmia is caused by increased myocardial irritability, as are premature ventricular contractions. It is usually associated with coronary artery disease, atherosclerotic heart disease and rheumatic heart disease, and may precede ventricular fibrillation. Ventricular tachycardia is extremely dangerous and should be considered an emergency. The patient is generally aware of this rapid rhythm and is quite anxious (Figure 7.10).

The patient's tolerance or lack of tolerance for this rapid rhythm will dictate the therapy to be given. The cause of the myocardial irritability must be determined and corrected, if possible. Anti-arrhythmic drugs may be used. Cardioversion may be indicated if the reduction in cardiac output is marked.

Ventricular Fibrillation

Ventricular fibrillation is rapid, ineffective quivering of the ventricles. With this arrhythmia there is no audible heart beat, no palpable pulse and no respiration. This pattern is so grossly irregular it can hardly be mistaken for another type of arrhythmia (Figure 7.11). The immediate treatment is defibrillation.

Ventricular Asystole

In ventricular asystole there are no QRS complexes. There is no heartbeat, no palpable pulse and no respiration. Without immediate treatment ventricular asystole is fatal (Figure 7.12).

Cardiopulmonary resuscitation is necessary to keep the patient alive.

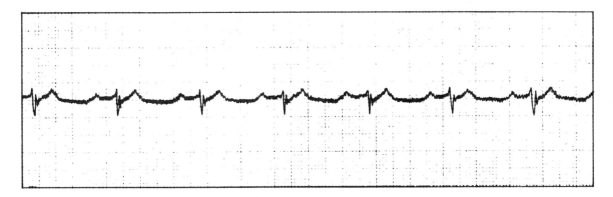

Figure 7.13 First-degree heart block.

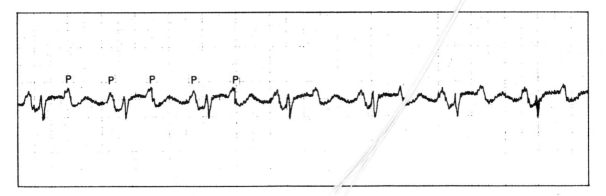

Figure 7.14 Second-degree heart block.

Conduction Abnormalities

First-Degree Atrioventricular Block

First-degree atrioventricular block is usually associated with organic heart disease or may be due to the effect of digitalis. It is seen frequently in patients with inferior myocardial infarctions (Figure 7.13).

This arrhythmia is important because it may lead to more serious forms of heart block. It is often a warning signal. The patient should be monitored closely for any advancing block.

Second-Degree Atrioventricular Block— Mobitz Type II

Second-degree atrioventricular block, Mobitz type II, is also caused by organic heart disease, by myocardial infarctions and by digitalis intoxication. This type of block results in a reduced heart rate and usually a reduced cardiac output (see Chapter 6, p. 312) (Figure 7.14.)

Treatment is directed toward increasing the heart rate to maintain a normal cardiac output. Digitalis intoxication should be ruled out and myocardial depressant drugs withheld.

Third-Degree atrioventricular Block

Third-degree atrioventricular block (complete heart block) is also associated with organic heart disease, digitalis intoxication and myocardial infarction. The heart rate may be markedly decreased, resulting in a decrease in perfusion to vital organs, such as the brain, heart, kidneys, lungs and skin (Figure 7.15).

Treatment is directed toward increasing perfusion to vital organs. The insertion of a temporary transvenous pacemaker is the usual treatment. A permanent pacemaker may be necessary if the block is persistent.

Medical Management

Arrhythmias are most commonly treated with drug therapy. In situations where drugs alone are not adequate, certain adjunctive mechanical therapies are available. The most common are elective cardioversion, defibrillation and pacemakers.

Cardioversion

Cardioversion is the use of electricity to terminate arrhythmias that have QRS complexes. It is usually an

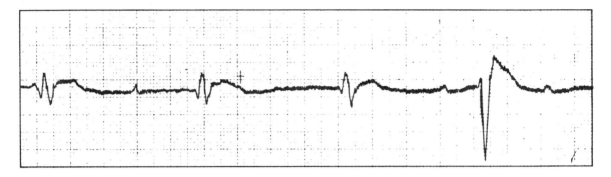

Figure 7.15 Third-degree atrioventricular block.

elective procedure, and informed consent is obtained. The patient is usually given some form of mild anaesthesia, and is usually intubated after being anaesthetized. The amount of voltage used varies from 25 to 400 watt-seconds. Digoxin is usually withheld for 48 hours before cardioversion to prevent post-cardioversion arrhythmias.

The synchronizer is turned on. The defibrillator is synchronized with a cardiac monitor so that an electrical impulse is discharged during ventricular depolarization (the QRS complex). If not synchronized, the defibrillator could discharge during the vulnerable period (T wave), resulting in ventricular tachycardia or fibrillation. The synchronizer switch is therefore turned on in advance so that the unit discharges immediately after the onset of the next QRS complex.

If ventricular fibrillation occurs after cardioversion, the defibrillator must be recharged immediately, the synchronizer turned off and defibrillation repeated. After use, the defibrillator should be turned off to prevent accidental discharge of the paddles. Oxygen flow should be stopped during cardioversion if possible, to avoid the hazard of fire.

Indications of a successful response are conversion to sinus rhythm, strong peripheral pulses and adequate blood pressure. Airway patency should be maintained, and the patient's state of consciousness assessed. Vital signs should be obtained at least every 15 minutes for one hour, every 30 minutes for two hours, and then every four hours. ECG monitoring is required during and after cardioversion; therefore, these patients are in a coronary care environment.

Defibrillation

Defibrillation is asynchronous cardioversion that is used in an emergency situation. Its use is usually confined to the treatment of ventricular fibrillation when there is no organized cardiac rhythm. Defibrillation completely depolarizes all the myocardial cells at once, allowing the sinus node to recapture its role as the pacemaker. The electrical voltage required to defibrillate the heart is much greater than that usually required for cardioversions. For defibrillation to be successful an electrical arc must be created, which is managed by maintaining good contact between the machine paddles and the skin. The following are some key points to remember in assisting with defibrillation or cardioversion:

● Use a good conducting agent between the skin and the paddles, such as saline pads or electrode paste.
● Position the paddles so as to create an effective arc (see Figure 7.16).

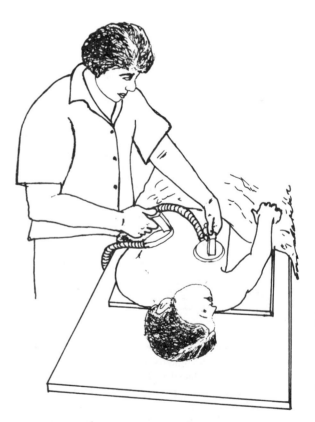

Figure 7.16 One method of paddle placement in cardioversion.

- Exert 20 to 25 lb of pressure on each paddle to ensure good skin contact.
- Practise safety by being certain no one is touching the bed or patient when the paddles are discharged.

If defibrillation has been unsuccessful, cardiopulmonary resuscitation is started immediately. Adrenaline may be used if the fibrillation is fine; it may make the fibrillation coarser and thus easier to convert with defibrillation. Sodium bicarbonate may be given to reverse the acidosis caused by lack of respiratory exchange. Adrenaline and sodium bicarbonate are incompatible when mixed together and must be given separately. Blood pressure is supported, using vasopressors. At no time during the resuscitation should the external cardiac massage and the assisted ventilation be stopped for longer than five seconds.

Pacemaker Therapy

Definition and Indications for Use

A pacemaker is an electronic device that provides repetitive electrical stimuli to the heart muscle for the control of heart rate. It initiates and maintains the heart rate when the natural pacemakers of the heart are unable to do so. Pacemakers are generally used when a patient has an arrhythmia, or the forerunner of an arrhythmia that causes failure of cardiac output. Pacemakers are most commonly used as part of the treatment in complete heart block following myocardial infarction. A pacemaker can also be used to control tachyarrhythmias that otherwise do not respond to drug therapy. Temporary pacing may also be done following open heart surgery.

Pacemaker Design

Pacemakers consist of two component parts: (1) the electronic pulse generator, which contains the circuitry and batteries that generate the electrical signal; and (2) the pacemaker electrodes (also called leads or wires), which transmit the pacemaker impulses to the heart. The stimuli from the pacemaker travel through a flexible catheter electrode that is threaded through a vein into the right ventricle or introduced by direct penetration of the chest wall. The pulse generator is usually implanted in a subcutaneous pocket in the pectoral or axillary region. Sometimes an abdominal site is selected.

Pacemaker generators are insulated to protect against body moisture and warmth. The pulse generator (or pacemaker) contains its own supply of power, which is provided by battery cells. The cells last for varying periods of time depending on their type.

Types of Pacemakers

The most commonly used pacemaker is the demand (synchronous; noncompetitive) pacemaker, which is set for a specific rate and stimulates the heart when normal ventricular depolarization does not occur. It functions only when the natural heart rate goes below a certain level. The fixed rate pacemaker (asynchronous; competitive) stimulates the ventricle at a preset constant rate that is independent of the patient's rhythm. It is used infrequently, usually in patients with complete and unvarying heart block.

Temporary Pacemaker Systems

Temporary pacing is usually an emergency procedure and permits the observation of the effects of pacing on heart function so that the optimum pacing rate for the patient can be selected before a permanent pacemaker is implanted. It is used in patients who have suffered myocardial infarction complicated by heart block, in patients with cardiac arrest with bradycardia and asystole, or in selected postoperative cardiac surgery patients. Temporary pacing may be done for hours, days or weeks and is continued until the patient improves or a permanent pacemaker is implanted.

Temporary pacing may be carried out either by an endocardial (transvenous) approach or by the transthoracic approach to the myocardium. The transvenous electrode is passed under fluoroscopic guidance through any peripheral vein (antecubital, brachial, jugular, subclavian, femoral) and the catheter tip is positioned in the apex of the right ventricle. The most common complication occurring during pacemaker insertion is ventricular arrhythmia. Cardiac perforation occurs rarely. A defibrillator should be immediately available.

Permanent Pacemaker Systems

For permanent pacing, the endocardial lead is passed transvenously into the right ventricle, and the pulse generator is implanted within the body underneath the skin below the right or left pectoral region or below the clavicle (Figure 7.17). This is termed an endocardial or transvenous implant. This procedure is usually done under local anaesthesia. Another method of permanent pacing is the implantation of the pulse generator in the abdominal wall. The electrode is passed transthoracically to the myocardium, where it is sutured in place. For this method, termed an epicardial or myocardial implant, a thoracotomy is required to provide access to the heart.

▶ NURSING PROCESS

▶ THE PATIENT WITH A PACEMAKER

▶ *Assessment*

Following the insertion of either a temporary or a permanent pacemaker, the patient is monitored by electrocardiogram. The pacemaker rate may vary as much as five beats above or below the preset pacemaker rate. An intravenous line is kept open to provide a readily accessible vein for drug administration, as prescribed, in the event of an arrhythmia and for fluids to combat dehydration.

The incision site where the pulse generator is implanted (or the entry site for the pacing electrode if the pacemaker is temporary) is watched for evidence of bleeding, haematoma formation or infection.

Infection is a major threat to the patient who has

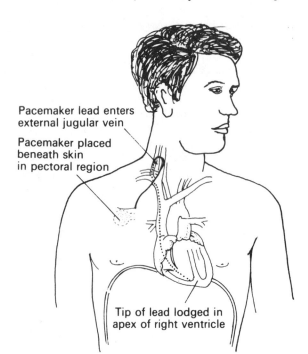

Pacemaker lead enters external jugular vein

Pacemaker placed beneath skin in pectoral region

Tip of lead lodged in apex of right ventricle

Figure 7.17 Implanted transvenous pacing electrode and pacemaker generator.

received a new pacemaker. The insertion site is observed primarily for swelling, unusual tenderness and increased heat. Any unusual drainage is reported to the doctor.

All electrical equipment used in the vicinity of the patient is grounded with three-pronged plugs inserted into a proper outlet. Improperly grounded equipment can generate leakage currents capable of producing ventricular fibrillation. A biomedical engineer, electrician or other qualified person should make certain that the patient is in an electrically safe environment.

The nurse observes for potential sources of electrical hazards. No metal parts of the output terminal or pacemaker wires should be exposed. All such bare metal should be scrupulously covered with nonconductive tape

to prevent accidental ventricular fibrillation from stray currents, which might reach the heart if exposed metal parts were to come in contact with a metal conductor, such as a bedrail. Aberrant current sources (from malfunctioning equipment) can travel over the surface of a damp skin and can also cause ventricular fibrillation. *The patient must be placed in an electrically safe environment.*

Complications

In the initial hours following the insertion of either a temporary or a permanent pacemaker, the most common complication is dislodgement of the pacing electrode. The identification of this complication is made by examination of the ECG pattern; the relationship between the pacing spike and the patient's QRS becomes asynchronous (Figure 7.18).

The nurse can help to avoid this complication by minimizing the patient's activities. If a temporary electrode is in place, the extremity used can be immobilized. The ECG is monitored very carefully for the presence of a pacing spike. Because of the importance of such monitoring, this patient is ideally in a coronary care unit.

Data about the model of pacemaker, date and time of its insertion, location of the pulse generator, stimulation threshold and pacer rate should be noted on the patient's record. This information is important for solving any unusual arrhythmia problem.

▶ *Patient's Problems*

Based on assessment data, the patient's problems may include the following:

● Potential for infection related to catheter or generator insertion.
● Lack of knowledge regarding self-care programme.

▶ *Planning and Implementation*
▶ Expected Outcomes

The major goals of the patient may include (1) absence of infection and (2) adherence to a self-care programme.

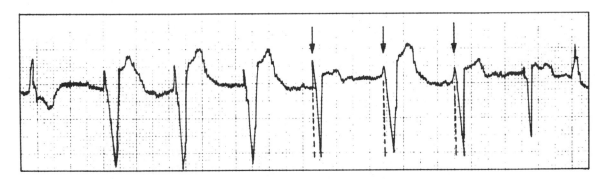

Figure 7.18 Synchronized pacemaker rhythm. Arrows indicate presence of sensed pacing spike.

Nursing Care

Prevention of Infection

The dressing should be changed each day and the wound inspected for redness, oedema, pain or any unusual bleeding. Changes are reported to the doctor.

Adherence to the Self-Care programme

Because of the nature of the need for a pacemaker, most patients are very compliant with the home health-care programme. Table 7.6 gives details of patient education.

▶ *Evaluation*
▶ Expected Outcomes

1. Patient is free of infection.
   a. Temperature normal.
   b. White blood cells within normal range (5,000–10,000/mm^3).
   c. Exhibits no redness or swelling of pacemaker insertion site.
2. Adheres to a self-care programme.
   a. Responds appropriately when queried about the signs and symptoms of infection.
   b. Knows when to seek medical attention (as demonstrated in responses to signs and symptoms).
   c. See Table 7.6.

ACUTE PULMONARY OEDEMA

Definition, Aetiology and Altered Physiology

Pulmonary oedema is the abnormal accumulation of fluid in the lungs, either in the interstitial spaces or in the alveoli.

Pulmonary oedema represents the ultimate stage of pulmonary congestion, in which fluid has leaked through the capillary walls and is permeating the airways, giving rise to dyspnoea of dramatic severity. Pulmonary congestion occurs when the pulmonary vascular bed has received more blood from the right ventricle than the left can accommodate and remove. The slightest imbalance between inflow on the right side and outflow on the left side of the heart may have drastic consequences. For example, if with each heartbeat the right ventricle pumps out just one more drop of blood than the left, within the space of only three hours the pulmonary blood volume may have expanded by as much as 500 ml!

Noncardiac pulmonary oedema has a wide variety of causes: toxic inhalants, drug overdose, neurogenic pulmonary oedema. Clinical management is directed toward reducing pulmonary blood flow and pulmonary arterial pressure.

The most common cause of pulmonary oedema is cardiac disease—atherosclerotic, hypertensive, valvular, myopathic. Most patients with pulmonary oedema have chronic heart disease of a type that imposes a strain on the left ventricle, such as arterial hypertension or aortic valve disease. The oedema is particularly likely to arise from the damage to the heart muscle caused by acute myocardial

Table 7.6 *Patient education: the patient with a pacemaker*

---

1. Report to doctor/pacemaker clinic periodically as prescribed, so that the rate of the pacemaker and its function can be checked. This is especially important during the first month after implantation
   a. Adhere to a weekly monitoring schedule during the first month after implantation
   b. Check pulse daily. Report *immediately* any sudden slowing or increasing of the pulse rate. This may indicate pacemaker malfunction
   c. Resume weekly monitoring when battery depletion is anticipated. (The time for reimplantation depends on the type used)
2. Wear loose-fitting clothing around the area of the pacemaker
   a. Understand the reason for the slight bulge over the pacemaker implant
   b. Notify doctor if the area becomes reddened or painful
   c. Avoid trauma to the area of the pacemaker generator
3. Study the manufacturer's instructions and become familiar with pacemaker
4. Physical activity does not usually have to be curtailed, with the exception of heavy contact sports
5. Carry an identification card/bracelet indicating doctor's name, type and model number of pacemaker, manufacturer's name, pacemaker rate and hospital where pacemaker was inserted
6. Avoid being close to microwave ovens, arc welders and large electrical generators, and electrical cautery and diathermy equipment (although at this time electrical interference is not a major problem)
7. Show identification card and request scanning by a hand scanner when going through weapon detector at airport
8. Remember that hospitalization is necessary periodically for battery changes/pacemaker unit replacement

---

infarction. The development of pulmonary oedema signifies that cardiac function has become grossly inadequate. There is an elevated left ventricular end-diastolic pressure and a rise in pulmonary venous pressure. This produces an increase in hydrostatic pressure, which results in transudation of fluid. Impaired lymphatic drainage contributes to the accumulation of fluid in the lung tissues.

The pulmonary capillaries, engorged with an excess of blood that the left ventricle is incapable of pumping, no longer are able to retain their contents. Fluid, first serous and later bloody, escapes into the adjacent alveoli through the communicating bronchioles and bronchi. It then mixes with air and, churned by respiratory agitation, is expelled from the mouth and nostrils, producing the ominous 'death rattle'. Because of the fluid build-up, the lungs become stiff and cannot expand, and air cannot enter. The result is severe hypoxia.

Death from pulmonary oedema is by no means inevitable. If appropriate measures are taken promptly, attacks can be aborted and patients can survive this complication to benefit from measures directed against its recurrence. Fortunately, pulmonary oedema usually does not develop precipitously but is preceded by the premonitory symptoms of pulmonary congestion.

Clinical Features

The typical attack of pulmonary oedema occurs at night after the patient has been lying down for a few hours. Recumbency increases the venous return to the heart and favours the resorption of oedema fluid from the legs. The circulating blood becomes diluted, and its volume expands. The venous pressure mounts and the right atrium fills with increasing rapidity. There is a corresponding increase in the right ventricular output, which eventually surpasses the output from the left ventricle. The pulmonary vessels become engorged with blood and proceed to leak. Meanwhile, the patient has become increasingly restless, anxious and unable to sleep.

There is a sudden onset of breathlessness and a sense of suffocation. The patient's hands become cold and moist, the nail beds become cyanotic and the skin colour turns grey. In addition, the pulse is weak and rapid and the neck veins are distended. There is incessant coughing, which produces increasing quantities of mucoid sputum. As the pulmonary oedema progresses, anxiety develops into near panic and the patient becomes confused, then stuporous. Breathing is noisy and moist, and the patient, nearly suffocated by the blood-tinged, frothy fluid now pouring into his bronchi and trachea, is literally drowning in his own secretions. The situation demands immediate action.

Diagnosis

The diagnosis is made upon evaluation of the clinical features resulting from pulmonary congestion. In complex cases, a pulmonary artery catheter may be inserted to facilitate the retrieval of haemodynamic data essential to the diagnosis and treatment.

Management

The goals of medical management for the patient with acute pulmonary oedema are to reduce total circulating volume and to improve respiratory exchange. These goals are accomplished through a combination of oxygen and drug therapies and nursing support.

Oxygenation

Oxygen is administered in concentrations adequate to relieve hypoxia and dyspnoea.

If signs of hypoxaemia persist, oxygen may be delivered by intermittent or continuous positive pressure. If respiratory failure occurs despite optimal management, endotracheal intubation and mechanical ventilation are required. The use of positive end-expiratory pressure is effective in reducing venous return, lowering pulmonary capillary pressure and improving oxygenation. Oxygenation is monitored by measurement of arterial blood gases.

Pharmacological Therapy: Morphine

Morphine is given intravenously in small doses to reduce anxiety and dyspnoea and to decrease peripheral resistance so that blood can be redistributed from the pulmonary circulation to the periphery. This action decreases pressure in the pulmonary capillaries and decreases transudation of fluid. The decrease in rate of respirations resulting from morphine is also beneficial.

- Morphine may not be given if pulmonary oedema is caused by cerebral vascular accident or if chronic pulmonary disease or cardiogenic shock are present.
- Watch for excessive respiratory depression and have a morphine antagonist (naloxone hydrochloride) available.

Diuretics

Usually frusemide will be given intravenously to produce a rapid diuretic effect. In addition, frusemide causes vasodilation and peripheral venous pooling, with a subsequent reduction in venous return that occurs even before the diuretic effect. Thus dyspnoea is rapidly relieved and pulmonary congestion is decreased. Because a large volume of urine will accumulate within minutes after administration of a potent diuretic, an indwelling catheter may be required.

- Watch for falling blood pressure, increasing heart rate and decreasing urinary output; these indicate that the total circulation is not tolerating diuresis.
- Patients with prostatic hypertrophy must be watched for signs of urinary retention.

Digitalis

To improve the contractile force of the heart, thus increasing the output of the left ventricle, the patient may be given a rapid-acting digitalis preparation. The improved cardiac contractility will increase cardiac output, enhance diuresis and reduce diastolic pressure. Thus pulmonary capillary pressure and the transudation of fluid into the alveoli will be reduced.

- Digitalis must be given with extreme caution to patients with acute myocardial infarction, because these patients are sensitive to digitalis and may develop toxic arrhythmias.
- The serum potassium level is measured at intervals because diuresis may have produced hypokalaemia. The effect of digitalis in the presence of hypokalaemia is enhanced, so digitalis toxicity may occur.
- If the patient has been on digitalis, the drug is usually withheld until the possibility of digitalis intoxication is ruled out.

Aminophylline

When the patient is wheezing and bronchospasm appears to play a significant role, aminophylline may be given to relax bronchospasm.

Phlebotomy

If the patient's condition is refractory to management, it is sometimes helpful to reduce the venous return to the heart by withdrawing 250 to 500 ml of blood from a peripheral vein (a phlebotomy or venesection). Phlebotomy is especially valuable when pulmonary oedema has followed overtransfusion or administration of excessive intravenous fluid.

The resulting decrease in venous return is accompanied by a corresponding decline in the right ventricular output. Accordingly, the pulmonary artery pressure drops, the pulmonary vessels become less congested, and the lung capillaries, no longer congested, reabsorb the fluid that has escaped. The oedema clears; the immediate danger has passed.

Positioning

Proper positioning can help reduce venous return to the heart.

- Place the patient upright, with legs and feet down, preferably with legs dangling over the side of the bed. This has the immediate effect of decreasing venous return, lowering the output of the right ventricle, and decongesting the lungs, e.g., reducing preload.

Psychological Support

Extreme fear and anxiety are cardinal features of pulmonary oedema. These emotions, which are self-perpetuating, make the condition more severe. Reassuring the patient and providing skilful anticipatory nursing are integral parts of the therapy. Because this patient experiences a sense of impending doom, it is essential that the nurse stays close. Touching the patient offers a sense of concrete reality. Nursing care should be organized to maximize the nurse's presence at the bedside. Offer the patient frequent information about what is being done to treat the condition and what the patient's responses to the treatment mean.

Prevention

Like most complications, pulmonary oedema is easier to prevent than to treat. It is important to recognize it in its early stages, when the presenting symptoms and signs are solely those of pulmonary congestion. A dry, hacking cough and the presence of a third heart sound (S_3) are often the earliest indications of pulmonary congestion. The S_3 is best heard at the apex with the patient lying in the left lateral decubitus position. The lung fields and heart sounds should be examined daily by the doctor.

In an early stage, the situation may be corrected by relatively simple measures. These include: (1) placing the patient in an upright position with the feet and legs dependent; (2) eliminating overexertion and emotional stress to reduce the left ventricular load; and (3) administering morphine to reduce anxiety, dyspnoea and preload.

The long-range approach to the prevention of pulmonary oedema must be directed at its precursor, pulmonary congestion.

It may be wise for the patient to sleep with the head of the bed elevated on 25-cm blocks. It is especially important to take extreme precautions when giving infusions and transfusions to cardiac patients and elderly people.

- In order to prevent circulatory overloading, which could precipitate acute pulmonary oedema, intravenous fluids are given at a slower rate, with the patient positioned upright in bed and kept under close nursing surveillance.
- Intravenous control devices are used to restrict the volume of fluid that can be delivered.

Surgical treatment may be necessary to eliminate or to minimize valvular defects that limit the flow of blood into or out of the left ventricle, because such defects impair the cardiac output and predispose the patient to the development of pulmonary congestion and oedema.

CARDIAC FAILURE

Definition, Aetiology and Altered Physiology

Cardiac failure, often referred to as congestive cardiac failure, is the inability of the heart to pump sufficient blood to meet the needs of the tissues for oxygen and nutrients. The term 'congestive cardiac failure' is most commonly used when reference is made specifically to left-sided and right-sided failure.

The underlying mechanism of cardiac failure involves impairment of the contractile properties of the heart, which leads to a lower than normal cardiac output (see Chapter 6, p. xxx).

Heart rate is controlled by the autonomic nervous system. When cardiac output falls, the sympathetic nervous system accelerates the heart rate to maintain adequate cardiac output. When this compensatory mechanism fails to maintain adequate tissue perfusion, the properties of stroke volume compensate.

In cardiac failure in which the primary problem is damaged and inhibited myocardial muscle fibres, stroke volume is impaired. Stroke volume is dependent upon three factors: preload, contractility and afterload (see Chapter 6, p. xxx).

Any one or more of these three factors may be altered in such a way that cardiac output is impaired. The relative ease of determining haemodynamic measurements via invasive monitoring procedures has greatly facilitated differential diagnosis and pharmacological manipulation of the problem.

Cardiac failure most commonly occurs with disorders of cardiac muscle that result in decreased contractile properties of the heart. Common underlying conditions that lead to disordered muscle function include coronary atherosclerosis, arterial hypertension and inflammatory or degenerative muscle disease.

Coronary atherosclerosis leads to myocardial dysfunction by interfering with the normal supply of blood to cardiac muscle. Hypoxia, acidosis (due to accumulation of lactic acid) and nutrient deprivation of heart muscle result. Myocardial infarction (death of myocardial cells) frequently precedes the development of overt cardiac failure.

Systemic or pulmonary hypertension (increased afterload) increases the work requirement of the heart, and this in turn leads to hypertrophy of myocardial muscle fibres. This effect (i.e., myocardial hypertrophy) can be considered a compensatory mechanism because it increases the contractility of the heart. However, for reasons that are not clear, the hypertrophied cardiac muscle does not function normally, and cardiac failure may eventually result.

Cardiac failure associated with inflammatory and degenerative diseases of the myocardium is due to direct damage to myocardial fibres, with a resultant decrease in contractility.

Cardiac failure may occur as a result of heart disease that only secondarily affects the myocardium. The mechanisms involved include impediment to flow of blood through the heart (e.g., stenosis of a semilunar valve), inability of the heart to fill with blood (e.g., pericardial tamponade, constrictive pericarditis or stenosis of

atrioventricular valves), or abnormal emptying of the heart (e.g., insufficiency of atrioventricular valves). Sudden increase in afterload due to elevated systemic blood pressure ('malignant' hypertension) may result in cardiac failure in the absence of myocardial hypertrophy.

A number of systemic factors can contribute to the development and severity of cardiac failure. Increased metabolic rate (e.g., fever, thyrotoxicosis), hypoxia and anaemia require an increased cardiac output to satisfy systemic oxygen demand. Hypoxia or anaemia also may decrease the supply of oxygen to the myocardium. Acidosis (respiratory or metabolic) and electrolyte abnormalities may decrease myocardial contractility. Cardiac arrhythmias, which may be present independently or secondary to cardiac failure, decrease the efficiency of overall myocardial function.

Clinical Features

The dominant feature in cardiac failure is increased intravascular volume. Congestion of tissues results from increased arterial and venous pressures due to decreased cardiac output in the failing heart. Increased pulmonary venous pressure can lead to pulmonary oedema, manifested by cough and shortness of breath. Increased systemic venous pressure can result in generalized peripheral oedema and weight gain.

The diminished cardiac output of cardiac failure has widespread manifestations because of diminished tissue and end-organ perfusion. Some commonly encountered effects related to low perfusion are dizziness, confusion, fatigue, exercise or heat intolerance, cool extremities and oliguria. Renal perfusion pressure falls, which results in the release of renin from the kidney, which in turn leads to aldosterone secretion, sodium and fluid retention and increased intravascular volume.

Left-Sided and Right-Sided Cardiac Failure

The left and right ventricles can fail separately. Left ventricular failure most often precedes right ventricular failure. Pure left ventricular failure is synonymous with acute pulmonary oedema. Because the outputs of the ventricles are coupled, failure of either ventricle may lead to decreased tissue perfusion. The congestive manifestations, however, may differ according to whether left or right ventricular failure exists.

Left-Sided Cardiac Failure

Pulmonary congestion predominates when the left ventricle fails, because the left ventricle is unable to adequately pump the blood coming to it from the lungs. The increased pressure in the pulmonary circulation causes fluid to be forced into the pulmonary tissues. The clinical manifestations that ensue include dyspnoea, cough, fatigability, tachycardia and anxiety and restlessness.

Dyspnoea results from the accumulation of fluid in the

alveoli, which impairs gas exchange. Dyspnoea may occur even at rest or may be precipitated by minimal to moderate exertion. Orthopnoea, difficulty in breathing when lying flat, may be present. Patients who experience orthopnoea will not lie flat, but instead will use pillows to prop themselves up in bed or will sit in a chair, even to sleep. Some patients experience orthopnoea only at night, a condition known as paroxysmal nocturnal dyspnoea. This occurs when the patient, who has been sitting for a long period with the feet and legs in a dependent position, returns to bed. After several hours the fluid that accumulated in the dependent extremities begins to be reabsorbed, and the impaired left ventricle is unable to adequately empty the increased volume. As a result, the pressure in the pulmonary circulation increases and causes further shifting of fluid into the alveoli.

The cough associated with left ventricular failure may be dry and nonproductive but is most often moist. Large quantities of frothy sputum, which is sometimes blood-tinged, may be produced.

Fatigability results from the low cardiac output that deprives tissues of normal circulation and decreases the removal of catabolic waste products. It is also a result of the increased energy expended for breathing and the insomnia that results from respiratory distress and coughing.

Restlessness and anxiety result from the impaired oxygenation of tissues, the stress associated with respiratory difficulty and the knowledge that the heart is not functioning properly. As anxiety increases, so does dyspnoea, which in turn further enhances the anxiety, creating a vicious cycle.

Right-Sided Cardiac Failure

When the right ventricle fails, congestion of the viscera and the peripheral tissues predominates. This is because the right side of the heart is unable to adequately empty its blood volume and thus cannot accommodate all of the blood that normally returns to it from the venous circulation. The clinical features that ensue include oedema of the lower extremities (dependent oedema), which is usually pitting oedema, weight gain, hepatomegaly, distended neck veins, fluid in the abdominal cavity, anorexia and nausea, nocturia and weakness.

The dependent oedema begins in the feet and ankles and can gradually progress up the legs and thighs and eventually into the external genitalia and lower trunk. Sacral oedema is not uncommon for patients who are on bed rest, since the sacral area is dependent. Pitting oedema, oedema in which pits remain after even slight compression with the fingertips, is obvious only after retention of at least 4.5 kg of fluid.

Venous engorgement of the liver leads to hepatomegaly and tenderness in the right upper abdominal quadrant. As this process progresses, pressure within the portal vessels can become great enough to cause fluid to be forced into the abdominal cavity, a condition known as ascites. This collection of fluid in the abdominal cavity can cause pressure on the diaphragm and thus precipitate respiratory distress. Anorexia and nausea result from the venous engorgement and venous stasis within the abdominal organs.

Nocturia occurs because renal perfusion is promoted by periods of recumbency. Diuresis results, and is most common at night because cardiac output is improved with physical rest. The weakness that accompanies right-sided failure is due to the reduced cardiac output, impaired circulation and inadequate removal of catabolic waste products from the tissues.

Diagnosis

The diagnosis is made by evaluation of the clinical manifestations of pulmonary and systemic congestion. Of extreme value in the determination of effective stroke volume is the use of the pulmonary artery catheter. This catheter may be inserted at the bedside. The catheter's technology has expanded to include a multi-lumen apparatus that allows one catheter to make more than one haemodynamic measurement. The catheter enters the right atrium via the superior vena cava. A balloon is then inflated, allowing the catheter to follow the blood flow through the tricuspid valve, through the right ventricle, through the pulmonary valve and into the main pulmonary artery. Waveform and pressure readings are noted during insertion to identify location of the catheter within the heart. The balloon is deflated once the catheter is in the pulmonary artery and properly secured (Figure 7.19).

Actual measurements of preload, afterload and cardiac output can be obtained. There are lumina at various intervals along the catheter. One lumen is attached to the proximal port of the catheter and lies at the level of the right atrium. Because preload is the amount of venous return to the heart and is therefore equal to the central venous pressure measurement, measuring the pressure at the proximal port yields an accurate preload and hence central venous pressure measurement. The tip of the catheter rests in the pulmonary artery where left ventricular pressure measurements are made. The balloon is inflated and flows into a small pulmonary capillary, occluding or wedging the capillary. A pressure measurement is made, which is the left ventricular end-diastolic pressure or afterload, the resistance against which the left ventricle must pump. Cardiac output is measured via a thermodilution lumen connected to a computer.

Measurements of the various pressures are made at intervals prescribed by the doctor, and drug therapy is adjusted based on the readings.

The nursing management of the patient who has a haemodynamic catheter is highly specialized and is ideally conducted in an intensive care environment.

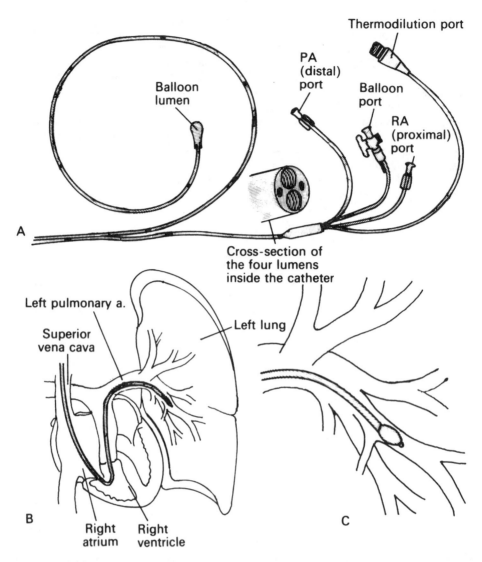

Figure 7.19 (A) The multilumen pulmonary artery catheter. (B) Location of the catheter within the heart. The catheter enters the right atrium via the superior vena cava. The balloon is then inflated, allowing the catheter to follow the blood flow through the tricuspid valve, through the right ventricle, through the pulmonary valve, and into the main pulmonary artery. Waveform and pressure readings are noted during insertion to identify location of the catheter within the heart. The balloon is deflated once the catheter is in the pulmonary artery and properly secured. (C) Pulmonary capillary wedge pressure. The catheter floats into a distal branch of the pulmonary artery when the balloon is inflated, and becomes 'wedged'. The wedged catheter occludes blood flow from behind, and the tip of the lumen records pressures in front of the catheter. The balloon is then deflated, allowing the catheter to float back into the main pulmonary artery. (Brunner, L. S. and Suddarth, D. S. (1986) *The Lippincott Manual of Nursing Practice* (4th edition), J. B. Lippincott, Philadelphia.)

Medical Management

The basic objectives in the treatment of patients with cardiac failure are the following:

1. To promote rest in order to reduce the workload on the heart.
2. To increase the force and efficiency of myocardial contraction through the action of pharmacological agents.
3. To eliminate the excessive accumulation of body water by means of diuretic therapy, diet and rest.

Pharmacological Therapy

Cardiac glycosides (digitalis), diuretics and vasodilators

form the basis of the pharmacological treatment of cardiac failure.

Digitalis

Digitalis increases the force of myocardial contraction and slows the heart rate. Several effects are produced: an increase in cardiac output; a decrease in heart size, venous pressure and blood volume; and diuresis, which relieves oedema. The effect of a given dose of digitalis depends on the state of the myocardium, electrolyte and fluid balance and renal and hepatic function.

A loading dose of digitalis may be given to induce the full therapeutic effect of the drug. This is usually done in the treatment of more severe forms of cardiac failure. Otherwise, the digitalis is started without a loading dose. A maintenance dose is given and continued daily. In either case, the patient is observed closely and given a daily dose just adequate to replace the amount of drug that is destroyed or excreted, in order to maintain the digitalis effect without producing toxicity. The optimal dosage is the amount that relieves the patient's signs and symptoms of cardiac failure or slows the ventricular response therapeutically *without causing toxicity*. The patient is observed closely for relief of signs and symptoms: lessening dyspnoea and orthopnoea, decrease in crackles and relief of peripheral oedema.

Digitalis Toxicity. Anorexia, nausea and vomiting are early effects of digitalis toxicity. There may be alterations in the heart rhythm, bradycardia, premature ventricular contractions, ventricular bigeminy (coupling of normal and premature beat) and paroxysmal atrial tachycardia.

● The apical heart rate is taken before digitalis is administered. If there is excessive slowing of the heart rate or change in rhythm, the drug is withheld and the doctor is notified. Frequently, the doctor will order that the digitalis preparation be withheld if the rate is 60 beats per minute or less.
● If prescribed, the serum digitalis level is checked by the doctor before administration of the drug.

Diuretic Therapy

Diuretics are given to promote the excretion of sodium and water through the kidneys. These drugs may not be necessary if the patient responds to restricted activity, digitalis and a low-sodium diet.

● When diuretics are given they should be administered in the morning so that the resultant diuresis will not interfere with the patient's night-time rest.
● An intake and output record is kept, because the patient may lose a large volume of fluid after a single dose of a given diuretic.
● As a basis for evaluating the effectiveness of therapy, a patient receiving diuretic drugs is weighed daily at the same time. In addition, skin turgor is examined for evidences of oedema or dehydration. The pulse rate is also monitored.

The dosage schedule is determined by the patient's daily weight, physical findings and symptoms. Although frusemide is a particularly useful diuretic in the treatment of heart failure because it dilates the venules, thereby increasing venous capacitance, which in turn reduces preload (venous return to the heart), it may be contraindicated in elderly patients when there is an increased risk of electrolyte imbalance.

Diuretic Side-Effects. Prolonged diuretic therapy may produce hyponatraemia (deficiency of sodium in the blood), which results in apprehension, weakness, fatigue, malaise, muscle cramps and twitching, and rapid, thready pulse.

Profuse and repeated diuresis can also lead to hypokalaemia (potassium depletion). Signs are weak pulse, faint heart sounds, hypotension, muscle flabbiness, diminished tendon reflexes and generalized weakness. Hypokalaemia poses new problems for the cardiac patient, because among the complications of hypokalaemia are marked weakening of cardiac contractions and the precipitation of digitalis toxicity in people receiving digitalis, both of which increase the likelihood of dangerous arrhythmias.

● Periodic assessment of the electrolytes will alert to hypokalaemia and hyponatraemia.
● To lessen the risk of hypokalaemia and its attendant complications, patients receiving diuretic drugs may be given a potassium supplement (potassium chloride). Bananas, orange juice, dried prunes, raisins, apricots, dates, figs, peaches and spinach are good dietary sources of potassium.

Other problems associated with diuretic administration are hyperuricaemia, volume depletion, hyperglycaemia and diabetes mellitus.

The elderly male patient requires ongoing nursing surveillance because the incidence of urethral obstruction due to prostatic hypertrophy is high in this age group. Signs of bladder distension should be sought regularly by palpation over the bladder.

Vasodilator Therapy

Of particular significance in the management of cardiac failure are the vasoactive drugs.

Vasodilator drugs have been used to reduce impedance (resistance) to left ventricular ejection of blood. The drug action allows more complete ventricular emptying and increases venous capacity, so left ventricular filling pressure is reduced and a dramatic decrease in pulmonary congestion may be achieved rapidly.

Sodium nitroprusside may be given intravenously by means of carefully monitored infusions. The dosage is titrated to keep the arterial systolic pressure at the prescribed level and the patient is monitored by measuring pulmonary artery pressures and cardiac output. Another commonly used vasodilator drug is isosorbide dinitrate, which can also be given intravenously in the acute stages of cardiac failure (Swanton, 1984).

Providing Dietary Support

The rationale in dietary support is to provide the type of diet that will cause the heart the least possible work effort and muscular strain and to maintain good nutritional status, taking into consideration the patient's likes, dislikes and cultural food habits.

Sodium Ion Manipulation

Restriction of the sodium ion is indicated for the prevention, control or elimination of oedema, as in hypertension or cardiac failure.

Sodium should be specified in describing the regime rather than 'low-salt' or 'salt-free', and the quantity should be indicated in milligrams. Very often mistakes are made in hospital units because of inconsistencies in the translation of salt to sodium. It is important to realize that salt is not 100 per cent sodium. There are 393 mg, or approximately 400 mg, of sodium in 1 g (1,000 mg) of salt.

Many types of natural foods contain varying amounts of sodium. Therefore, even if no salt is added in cooking and if salty foods are avoided, the daily diet may still contain approximately 1,000 to 2,000 mg of sodium.

Other sources of sodium can be found in some processed foods. Added food substances—such as sodium alginate, which improves texture; sodium benzoate, which acts as a preservative; or disodium phosphate, which improves cooking quality in certain foods—increase the sodium intake when included in the daily diet.

Therefore, patients on low-sodium diets should be advised not to buy processed foods and to check labels carefully for such words as 'salt' or 'sodium', especially on canned foods. For diets that call for less than 1,000 mg of sodium, low-sodium milk and bread and salt-free butter should be considered.

Patients on sodium-restricted diets should also be cautioned against using nonprescription medications, such as antacids, cough syrups, laxatives, sedatives or salt substitutes, because these products contain sodium or excessive amounts of potassium. Any over-the-counter medication of this type should not be purchased without first consulting the doctor.

When diets are very restrictive of both fat and sodium, the patient may find the food unpalatable and may refuse to eat. A variety of flavourings such as lemon juice and herb seasonings may be used to improve the taste of the food and encourage the patient to accept the diet. Every effort should be made to take into account the patient's likes and dislikes.

▶ **NURSING PROCESS**
▶ **THE PATIENT WITH CARDIAC FAILURE**

▶ *Assessment*

The focus of the nursing assessment for the patient with cardiac failure is directed toward observing for signs and symptoms of pulmonary and systemic fluid overload. All untoward signs are recorded and reported to the doctor.

Respiratory
The rate and depth of respirations are noted and evidence of wheeze is listened for. Observation is made for the presence of a cough.

Cardiac
The rate and rhythm are monitored. Rapid rates indicate that the ventricle has had less time to fill and there is therefore some stagnation of blood in the atria and eventually the pulmonary bed.

Sensorium/Level of Consciousness
As the intravascular volume increases, the circulating blood becomes dilute and its oxygen transport capacity is compromised. The brain tolerates inadequate oxygenation poorly, and the patient becomes confused.

Periphery
The dependent parts of the patient's body are assessed for oedema. If the patient is sitting upright, examine the feet and lower legs; if the patient is supine in bed, examine the sacrum and back for oedema. Fingers and hands may also become oedematous. In extreme cases of cardiac failure the patient may develop periorbital oedema, in which the eyelids may be swollen shut. Jugular vein distension may be visible.

Urinary Output
The patient may become oliguric or anuric. It is important to measure output frequently in order to develop a baseline to measure against in testing the efficacy of diuretic therapy. Intake and output records are rigorously maintained and the patient is weighed daily, at the same time and on the same scales.

▶ *Patient's Problems*

Based on the assessment data, major nursing diagnoses for the patient may include the following:

● Activity intolerance related to fatigue and dyspnoea secondary to decreased cardiac output.
● Anxiety related to breathlessness and restlessness secondary to inadequate oxygenation.
● Alteration in tissue perfusion—peripheral, related to venous stasis.

- Potential lack of knowledge of self-care programme related to nonacceptance of necessary lifestyle changes.

► *Planning and Implementation*
► **Expected Outcomes**

The major goals of the patient may include: (1) promotion of rest; (2) relief of anxiety; (3) attainment of normal tissue perfusion; and (4) knowledge of self-care programme.

Nursing Care

Promotion of Rest

It is essential that the patient has both physical and emotional rest. Rest reduces the work of the heart, increases heart reserve and reduces blood pressure. Periods of recumbency also promote diuresis by improving renal perfusion. Rest also decreases the work of the respiratory muscles and oxygen utilization. The heart rate is slowed, which prolongs the diastolic period of recovery and thus improves the efficiency of heart contraction. The patient will be impressed to hear that each day of complete rest spares the heart approximately 25,000 contractions.

Positioning

The head of the bed may be elevated on 20-cm to 30-cm blocks, or the patient may be placed in a comfortable armchair. In this position the venous return to the heart (preload) and the lungs is reduced, pulmonary congestion is alleviated and impingement of the liver on the diaphragm is minimized. The lower arms should be supported with pillows to eliminate the fatigue caused by the constant pull of their weight on the shoulder muscles. The orthopnoeic patient may sit on the side of the bed with feet supported on a chair, the head and arms resting on an over-the-bed table, and lumbosacral spine supported by a pillow. If pulmonary congestion is present, positioning the patient in an armchair is advantageous because this position favours the shift of fluid away from the lungs. oedema, which usually occurs in dependent parts of the body, shifts from the extremities to the sacral areas when the patient is confined to bed.

Relief of Anxiety

Because of their inability to maintain adequate oxygenation, patients in cardiac failure are apt to be restless and anxious. They feel overwhelmed by breathlessness. These symptoms tend to become exaggerated at night.

Raising the head of the bed and keeping a night light on are helpful. The presence of a member of the family or a close friend provides necessary reassurance to some people. The patient should be observed for possible respiratory irregularities such as Cheyne-Stokes respirations, a phenomenon that may occur in cardiac failure. If such a respiratory disturbance is present, it may be worthwhile to test the effect of oxygen inhalations administered (as prescribed) each night just before the hour of sleep. Oxygen may be given during the acute stage to diminish the work of breathing and to increase the comfort of the patient. Small doses of morphine may be prescribed for extreme dyspnoea.

- The patient with hepatic congestion is unable to detoxify drugs with normal rapidity and should be medicated with caution. As a result of cerebral hypoxia with superimposed nitrogen retention, the patient may react unfavourably to soporific drugs, becoming confused and increasingly anxious in response to medication. Such a patient should not be restrained; restraints are likely to be resisted, and resistance inevitably increases the cardiac load.

The patient who insists on getting out of bed at night should be seated comfortably in an armchair. As cerebral and systemic circulations improve, the quality of sleep will improve.

Avoiding Stress

Rest is not possible without relaxation. Emotional stress produces vasoconstriction, elevates arterial pressure and speeds the heart. Promoting physical comfort and avoiding situations that tend to promote anxiety and agitation may help the patient to relax. The period of rest is continued for a few days to a few weeks until the cardiac failure is controlled.

Attainment of Normal Tissue Perfusion

The decreased tissue perfusion occurring in cardiac failure results from inadequate levels of circulating oxygen and stagnation of blood in the peripheral tissues. Moderate daily exercise will enhance the blood flow to peripheral tissues. Adequate oxygenation and appropriate diuresis will also serve to provide good tissue perfusion. Effective diuresis reduces haemodilution, thus providing more oxygen-carrying capacity to the vascular system.

Adequate rest is essential to the promotion of adequate tissue perfusion.

- There are dangers inherent in bedrest, such as pressure sores (especially in oedematous patients), phlebothrombosis and pulmonary embolism. Changes of position, deep breathing, elastic stockings and leg exercises all help to improve muscle tone and at the same time aid venous return to the heart.

Knowledge About Self-Care

The self-care programme is prepared in co-operation with the patient or significant other. Activities of daily living should be planned to minimize breathlessness and fatigue. The patient should remember that intolerable breathlessness and fatigue associated with normal activities are reasons to seek medical attention.

Patient Education

After cardiac failure is under control, patients are encouraged to gradually resume the activities they were accustomed to before their illness, particularly their jobs. Patients' earlier lifestyles should be retained if possible. However, some modifications in their habits, work and interpersonal relationships usually have to be made. Any activity that produces symptoms must be curtailed or other adaptations made. Patients should be helped to identify their emotional stresses and to explore ways in which these may be ventilated and discharged.

All too frequently patients keep returning to the clinic and hospital for recurring episodes of cardiac failure. Not only does this create psychological, sociological and financial problems, but the physiological burden on the patient can be serious. Previously normal organs of the body may ultimately be damaged. Repeated attacks can lead to pulmonary fibrosis, liver cirrhosis, enlargement of the spleen and kidneys, and even brain damage due to insufficient oxygen during acute episodes.

To ensure that the patient will persevere in therapy requires patient education, involvement and co-operation. Many of the recurrences of cardiac failure appear to be preventable. These include failure to follow the drug therapy properly, dietary indiscretions, inadequate medical follow-up, excessive physical activity and failure to recognize recurring symptoms. A summary of what the patient should know is given in Table 7.7.

Table 7.7 *Patient education: cardiac failure*

Patients with heart disease should learn to regulate their activities according to their individual responses

Goal: To prevent progression of disease and the development of cardiac failure

Patients learn that to achieve these goals they will have to do the following:

1. Live within the limits of the cardiac reserve
   a. Obtain adequate rest
      i. Have a regular daily rest period
      ii. Shorten working hours if possible
      iii. Avoid emotional upsets
   b. Accept the fact that taking digitalis and restricting sodium intake may be a permanent way of life
      i. Take digitalis daily, exactly as prescribed
         (a) Check own pulse rate daily
         (b) Have a check-list to ensure that medicine(s) has been taken
      ii. Take diuretic as prescribed
         (a) Weigh at the same time daily to detect any tendency towards fluid accumulation
         (b) Report weight gain of more than 0.9–1.4 kg in a few days
         (c) Know the signs and symptoms of potassium depletion; if taking oral potassium, keep a check-list along with diuretic medication
      iii. Take vasodilator as prescribed
         (a) Know signs and symptoms of orthostatic hypotension and how to prevent it
   c. Restrict sodium as directed
      i. Consult the written diet plan and the list of permitted and restricted foods
      ii. Examine labels to ascertain sodium content (antacids, laxatives, cough remedies and so on)
      iii. Avoid using salt
      iv. Avoid excesses in eating and drinking
   d. Review activity programme
      i. Increase walking and other activities gradually, provided that they do not cause fatigue and dyspnoea
      ii. In general, continue at whatever activity level can be maintained without the appearance of symptoms
      iii. Avoid extremes of heat and cold, which increase the work of the heart. Air conditioning may be essential in a hot, humid climate
      iv. Keep regular appointments with doctor or clinic
2. Be alert for symptoms that may indicate recurring failure
   a. Recall the symptoms experienced when illness began. Reappearance of previous symptoms may indicate a recurrence
   b. Report immediately to the doctor or clinic any of the following
      i. Gain in weight
      ii. Loss of appetite
      iii. Shortness of breath on activity
      iv. Swelling of ankles, feet or abdomen
      v. Persistent cough
      vi. Frequent urination at night

It must be emphasized that many remedies such as cough medicines, antacids and pain pills contain fairly large amounts of sodium. The patient must be warned against using these products and advised to rinse the mouth with clear water when using toothpaste and mouthwashes. In some areas the drinking water has a high sodium content. To find out what this content is, the patient should contact the nearest department of environmental health.

As an added precaution for older patients whose eyesight is failing and whose fingers are less nimble as a result of arthritis, the printing on any drug bottle should be large and easily readable and the bottle should be equipped with an easy-open stopper.

Cardiac failure can be controlled. The patient must never become lax in following the prescribed therapeutic programme. Careful follow-up, maintenance of correct weight, sodium restriction, prevention of infection, avoidance of noxious agents such as coffee and tobacco, and avoidance of unregulated or excessive exercise all aid in preventing the onset of cardiac failure. In patients with valvular heart disease, surgical correction of the defect at the appropriate time may spare the heart and prevent failure.

► *Evaluation*
► **Expected Outcomes**

1. Patient reduces fatigue and dyspnoea.
   a. Obtains adequate physical and emotional rest.
   b. Assumes positions that reduce fatigue and dyspnoea.
   c. Adheres to medication regime.
2. Experiences less anxiety.
   a. Avoids situations that produce stress.
   b. Sleeps comfortably at night.
3. Attains normal tissue perfusion.
   a. Obtains adequate rest.
   b. Performs activities that promote venous return: moderate daily exercise; active range of motion of extremities if immobile or in bed for long periods of time; wearing support stockings.
   c. Skin warm and dry; colour is good.
   d. Exhibits no peripheral oedema.
4. Adheres to self-care regime.

CARDIOGENIC SHOCK

Cardiogenic shock is the end stage of left ventricular dysfunction, and occurs when the left ventricle is extensively damaged. The heart muscle loses its contractile power, and the result is a marked reduction in cardiac output with inadequate tissue perfusion to the vital organs (heart, brain, kidneys). The degree of shock is proportional to the level of left ventricular dysfunction. Although cardiogenic shock is seen most commonly as a complication of myocardial infarction, it can also occur with cardiac tamponade, pulmonary embolism and epidural or general anaesthesia.

Altered Physiology
The symptoms and signs of cardiogenic shock reflect the circular nature of the altered physiology of cardiac failure. The damage to the myocardium results in a decrease in cardiac output, which in turn reduces arterial blood pressure in the vital organs. Flow to the coronary arteries is reduced. This results in a decrease in the oxygen supply to the myocardium, which in turn increases ischaemia and further reduces the heart's ability to pump. Thus, a 'vicious cycle' is set in motion.

● The classic signs of cardiogenic shock are low blood pressure, rapid and weak pulse, cerebral hypoxia manifested by confusion and agitation, and decreased urinary output.

Arrhythmias are common and result from a decrease in oxygen to the myocardium. As in cardiac failure, the use of a pulmonary artery catheter to measure left ventricular pressure is important in assessing the severity of the problem and evaluating management. Continuing elevation of left ventricular end-diastolic pressure accompanied by a fall in arterial blood pressure indicates the failure of the heart to function as an effective pump.

Medical Management
There are many approaches to the treatment of cardiogenic shock. Any major arrhythmias are corrected because they may have caused or contributed to the shock. If low intravascular volume is suspected, or found through pressure readings (i.e., hypovolaemia), the patient is treated by infusion of volume expanders. If hypoxia is present, oxygen is given, often under positive pressure when regular flow is insufficient to meet tissue demands.

Drug therapy is selected and guided according to cardiac output and mean arterial blood pressure. One group of drugs used is the catecholamines, which raise blood pressure and increase cardiac output. However, they tend to increase the workload of the heart by increasing oxygen demand. Vasoactive drugs such as sodium nitroprusside and nitroglycerine are effective drugs that lower blood pressure and thus cardiac work. They cause arterial and venous dilatation, thereby shunting much of the intravascular volume to the periphery and causing a reduction in preload and afterload. These vasoactive drugs can be given in tandem with dobutamine, a vasopressor which assists in maintaining an adequate blood pressure.

Other therapies employed in treating cardiogenic shock involve the use of circulatory assist devices. The most frequently used mechanical support system is the intra-aortic balloon pump. The intra-aortic balloon pump uses internal counterpulsation to augment the pumping action of the heart by the regular inflation and deflation of a balloon located in the descending thoracic aorta. The device is connected to a control box that directs its activities by synchronization with the electrocardiogram. Haemodynamic monitoring is also essential to determine the patient's circulatory status during the use of the intra-aortic balloon pump. The balloon inflates during ventricular diastole and deflates during systole at a rate equal to the heart rate. The intra-aortic balloon pump augments diastole, which results in increased perfusion of the coronary arteries and myocardium and a decrease in left ventricular workload.

Nursing Implications

The patient with cardiogenic shock requires constant nursing care and observation. Careful patient assessment, measurement of haemodynamic parameters, and recording of fluid intake and urinary output are essential. The patient must be closely monitored for arrhythmias, which must be corrected immediately.

Because of the technology required for effective medical management in such cases, this patient is always treated in a critical care environment. Intensive care nurses with highly developed skills are responsible for the nursing management. Every nurse, however, needs to understand the rationale of the various treatments.

THROMBOEMBOLIC EPISODES

The decreased mobility of the patient and the impaired circulation that accompanies cardiac diseases contribute to the development of intracardiac and intravascular thrombosis. As the patient increases activities, a thrombus may become detached (the detached thrombus is called an embolus) and may be carried to the brain, kidneys, intestines or lungs.

The most common embolic episode is that of a pulmonary embolus. The symptoms of pulmonary embolism include chest pain, cyanosis, shortness of breath, rapid respirations and haemoptysis. The pulmonary embolus may block the circulation to a part of the lung, producing an area of pulmonary infarction. The pain experienced is usually pleuritic—that is, it increases with respiration and may disappear when the patient holds a breath. Cardiac pain is continuous, however, and usually does not vary with respirations.

Systemic embolism may occur from the left ventricle, and the resulting vascular occlusion may present as stroke or renal infarct; it may compromise the blood supply to an extremity.

The nurse must be aware of such possible complications and be prepared to identify and report signs and symptoms.

PERICARDIAL EFFUSION

Altered Physiology

Pericardial effusion refers to the escape of fluid into the pericardial sac. This may accompany pericarditis, advanced congestive heart failure or cardiac surgery.

The characteristic sign of pericardial effusion is an extension of flatness to percussion across the anterior aspect of the chest wall. The patient may complain of a feeling of fullness within the chest or have substernal or ill-defined pain.

Normally, the pericardial sac contains less than 50 ml of fluid. Pericardial fluid may accumulate slowly without causing noticeable symptoms. However, a rapidly developing effusion can stretch the pericardium to its maximum size and can cause decreased cardiac output and decreased venous return to the heart. The result is cardiac tamponade (compression of the heart).

Clinical Features

Symptoms include a feeling of precordial oppression due to the stretching of the pericardial sac; shortness of breath; and a drop and fluctuation in blood pressure. Blood pressure is lowest on inspiration (pulsus paradoxus), at which point the pulse may not be perceptible. The venous pressure tends to rise, as evidenced by the engorged neck veins.

The cardinal signs are falling arterial blood pressure, narrowing pulse pressure, rising venous pressure and distant heart sounds. *This is a life-threatening situation, demanding immediate intervention.*

Diagnosis

If the clinical features are not immediately life-threatening, the doctor may choose to confirm the diagnosis via echocardiogram. Bedside diagnosis based on clinical signs and symptoms is usually sufficient.

Management: Pericardial Aspiration (Pericardiocentesis)

If the cardiac function becomes seriously impaired, a pericardial aspiration (puncture of the pericardial sac) is performed to remove fluid from the pericardial sac. The major goal for it is to prevent cardiac tamponade, which restricts normal heart action.

During the procedure the patient is monitored by ECG, and central venous pressure measurements are made. Emergency resuscitative equipment is readily available.

The head of the bed is elevated to a 45° to 60° angle so that the needle can be inserted into the pericardial sac more easily. If not already in place, a peripheral intravenous device is inserted and a slow intravenous infusion of saline or glucose is started in case it becomes necessary to administer emergency drugs or blood.

The pericardial aspiration needle is attached to a 50-ml syringe by a three-way stopcock. The V lead (precordial lead wire) of the ECG may be attached to the hub of the aspirating needle with alligator clips, because the monitoring of ECG oscillation is useful in determining whether or not the needle has contacted the myocardium. Contact is evidenced by an elevation of the ST segment or stimulation of premature ventricular contractions.

There are several possible sites for pericardial aspiration. The needle may be inserted in the angle between the left costal margin and the xiphoid, near the cardiac apex, to the left of the fifth or sixth interspace at the sternal margin, or on the right side of the fourth intercostal space. The needle is advanced slowly until fluid is obtained.

A fall in central venous pressure associated with a rise in blood pressure indicates that relief of cardiac tamponade has occurred. The patient almost always feels immediate improvement. If there is a substantial amount of pericardial fluid, a small catheter may be left in place to drain recurrent bleeding or effusion.

During the procedure it is important to watch for the presence of bloody fluid. Pericardial blood does not clot readily, whereas blood obtained from inadvertent puncture of one of the heart chambers does clot.

Pericardial fluid is sent to the laboratory for examination for tumour cells, bacterial culture, chemical and serological analysis, and differential cell count. A haematocrit is done if the fluid is bloody.

● After pericardiocentesis, effective care involves careful monitoring of the blood pressure, venous pressure and heart sounds to evaluate for the possible recurrence of cardiac tamponade. If it recurs, repeated aspiration is necessary. Sometimes cardiac tamponade is treated by open pericardial drainage. The patient is ideally in an intensive care unit.

MYOCARDIAL RUPTURE

When a myocardial infarction, infectious process, pericardial disease or other myocardial dysfunction weakens the cardiac muscle, the heart may rupture, leading to immediate death in most cases. Cardiac rupture, although fairly rare, can occur.

Death is caused by cardiac tamponade (the heart is bleeding into its pericardial sac). Pericardiocentesis and repair of the myocardium can be life-saving measures.

CARDIAC ARREST

Cardiac arrest is defined as the sudden, unexpected cessation of the heartbeat and effective circulation. All heart action may stop, or asynchronized muscular twitchings (ventricular fibrillation) may occur.

There is an immediate loss of consciousness and an absence of pulses and audible heart sounds. Dilation of the pupils of the eyes begins within 45 seconds. Convulsions may or may not be present.

● There is an interval of approximately four minutes between the cessation of circulation and the appearance of irreversible brain damage. The interval varies with the age of the patient. During this period, the diagnosis of arrest must be made and the circulation must be restored.
● *The most reliable sign of arrest is the absence of a carotid pulsation.* Valuable time should not be wasted taking the blood pressure or listening for the heartbeat.

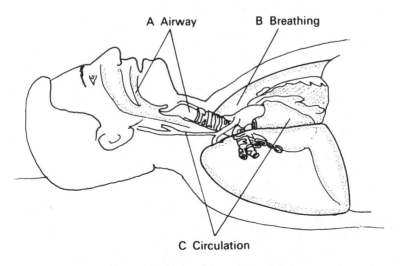

A Airway **B Breathing**

C Circulation

Figure 7.20 A, B, C of basic life support.

Cardiopulmonary Resuscitation

Basic cardiopulmonary resuscitation consists of the following sequence: airway, breathing and circulation (Figure 7.20). The resuscitation process consists of maintaining an open airway, providing artificial ventilation by means of rescue breathing and providing artificial circulation by external cardiac compression.

The first step in cardiopulmonary resuscitation is to secure an airway. Remove any material from the airway and lift the jaw forward. Insert an oropharyngeal airway if available. Ventilate the patient with 12 breaths per minute using direct mouth-to-mouth breathing or using the bag and mask technique.

The next step after ventilation is external cardiac compression. This must be done with the patient on a firm surface. The heel of one hand is placed on the lower half of the sternum, 3.8 cm from the tip of the xiphoid and toward the patient's head. Place the other hand on top of the first one. The fingers should not touch the chest wall. Using the body weight while keeping the elbows straight, apply quick, forceful compressions to the lower sternum, 3.8 to 5.0 cm toward the spine. Regular compression and release are made 60 times per minute.

When two people are available, the first person does the cardiac compressions and the second ventilates the patient after five compressions. If only one person is available, the rate is two ventilations to every 15 cardiac compressions.

The decision to terminate resuscitation is based on medical considerations and will take into account the cerebral and cardiac status of the patient.

Following successful resuscitation after cardiac arrest, the nurse should carefully monitor the situation because the patient is at great risk for another cardiac arrest. Continuation of ECG monitoring is essential, and any abnormalities of rhythm must be corrected. Electrolyte and acid–base balances must be established and maintained. Haemodynamic monitoring should be initiated if it was not previously instituted.

BIBLIOGRAPHY

Brunner, L. S. and Suddarth, D. S. (1989) *The Lippincott Manual of Medical-Surgical Nursing* (2nd edition), Harper & Row, London.

Carpenito, L. J. (1983) *Nursing Diagnosis, Application to Clinical Practice,* J. B. Lippincott, Philadelphia, pp. 78–87.

Deavin, J. E. (1984) Rehabilitation following myocardial infarction, *Nursing (2nd Series), The Add-On Journal of Clinical Nursing,* May, Vol. 2, No. 25, p. 13.

Goodinson, S. M. (1984) Coronary heart disease, *Nursing (2nd Series), The Add-On Journal of Clinical Nursing,* May, Vol. 2, No. 25, p. 5.

Quested, J. (1989) Preventing heartache, *Community Outlook,* February, p. 16.

Swanton, R. H. (1984) *Cardiology,* Blackwell Scientific, London, pp. 144, 148, 174, 279, 361.

Thompson, D. (1988) Supporting wives of coronary patients, *Nursing Times,* 24 August, Vol. 84, No. 34, p. 57.

Thompson, D. (1989) Management of the patient with acute myocardial infarction, *Nursing Standard,* 22 November, Vol. 4, No. 9, pp. 35–6.

Thompson, D. (1989) Counselling coronary patients and their partners, *Nursing Times,* 21 June, Vol. 85, No. 25, p.59.

Trounce, J. (1990) *Clinical Pharmacology for Nurses* (13th edition), Churchill Livingstone, Edinburgh, p. 34.

Watson, J. E. and Royle, J. R. (1987) *Watson's Medical-Surgical Nursing and Related Physiology* (3rd edition), Baillière Tindall, Eastbourne, pp. 131, 335, 338–9.

FURTHER READING

Books

Hampton, J. R. (1983) *Cardiovascular Disease,* William Heinemann Medical Books, London.

Hoechst UK *ECG Atlas,* Hoechst UK Ltd, Middlesex.

McCormick, E. W. (1984) *The Heart Attack Recovery Book,* Coventure Ltd, London.

McCulloch, J., Townsend, A. and Williams, D. (1985) *Focus on Coronary Care,* William Heinemann Medical Books, London.

Oliver, F. M., Julian, D. G. and Brown, M. G. (1974) *Intensive Coronary Care,* WHO, Geneva.

Scheidt, S. (1987) *Clinical Electrocardiography: Cardiovascular Problems in Everyday Practise,* Ciba-Geigy Ltd, Switzerland.

Speedling, E. J. (1982) *Heart Attack: The Family Response At Home and In Hospital,* Tavistock Publications, USA.

Swanton, R. H. (1984) *Cardiology,* Chapters 3–9, Blackwell Scientific, London.

Zoob, M. (1977) *Cardiology for Students,* Chapters 7–27, Churchill Livingstone, London.

Articles

Coronary Heart Disease

Bundy, C. (1988) Making sense of stress and coronary heart disease, *Nursing Times,* 2 November, Vol. 84, No. 44, pp. 35–7.

Holmes, S. (1988) Does a high-fat diet cause heart disease? *Nursing Times,* 30 March, Vol. 84, No. 13, pp. 34–5.

Holmes, S. (1989) Diet and Heart disease, *Nursing,* April, Vol. 3, No. 36, pp. 9–11.

Quested, J. (1989) Preventing heartache, *Community Outlook,* February, pp. 16–18.

Ritchie, M. (1988) Coronary heart disease: An *Occupational Health* survey, *Occupational Health,* February, Vol. 40, No. 2, pp. 459–60.

Scott, A. (1989) Diet combats coronaries, *Nursing Times,* 31 May, Vol. 85, No. 22, pp. 29–30.

Angina

Hayward, J. M. (1988) Living with angina, *The Professional Nurse,* October, pp.33–6.

Myocardial Infarction

Davison, V. L. (1989) Mending a broken heart, *Community Outlook*, February, pp. 19–20.

Jesson, A. (1986) Rehabilitation after a myocardial infarction, *Nursing Times*, 15 October, pp. 44–6.

Thompson, D. (1989) Management of the patient with acute myocardial infarction, *Nursing Standard*, 22 November, Vol. 4, No. 9, pp. 34–8.

Townsend, A. (1988) Analgesia in managing myocardial infarction, *Nursing Times*, 17 August, Vol. 84, No.33, p. 58.

Disorders of the Heart and the Elderly

Roberts, A. (1988) *Systems of Life 158. Senior Systems 23. Cardiovascular System 1, Nursing Times*, 23 March, Vol. 84, No. 12, pp. 59–62.

Roberts, A. (1988) *Systems of Life 159. Senior Systems 24. Cardivascular System 2, Nursing Times*, 6 April, Vol. 84, No. 14, pp. 43–6.

Drugs and Disorders of the Heart

Smith, S. (1987) How drugs act: Drugs and the heart, *Nursing Times*, 27 May, Vol. 83, No. 21, pp. 24–6.

Smith, S. (1987) How drugs act: Drugs in angina andmyocardial infarction, *Nursing Times*, 3 June, Vol. 83, No. 22, pp. 52–4.

Smith, S. (1987) How drugs act: Diuretic agents, *Nursing Times*, 10 June, Vol. 83, No. 23, pp. 53–5.

Cardiac Arrhythmias

Allen, D. (1988) Making sense of ECGs, *Nursing Times*, 21 September, Vol. 84, No. 38, pp. 39–41.

Roberts, A. (1988) *Systems of Life 162. Senior Systems 27. The Heart—Normal Conduction and Cardiac Arrhythmias, Nursing Times*, 13 July, Vol. 84, No. 28, pp. 43–6.

Pacemakers

Ambrose, C. (1988) Cardiac pacing: A new technique, *The Professional Nurse*, May, pp. 290–91.

Belshaw, M. (1989) Temporary transvenous pacing, *Nursing Times*, 4 January, Vol. 85, No. 1, pp. 39–41.

Toussaint, L. R. (1985) A pace apart, *Nursing Mirror*, 21 August, Vol. 161, No. 8, pp. 18–20.

Cardiopulmonary Resuscitation

Chan, E. S. (1989) Nursing assessment following cardiac resuscitation, *Nursing*, April, Vol. 3, No. 36, pp. 30–31.

Goodwin, R. (1988) Cardiopulmonary resuscitation, *Nursing Times*, 24 August, Vol. 84, No. 34, pp. 63–8.

Newbold, D. (1987) Critical care: External chest compression. The new skills, *Nursing Times*, 1 July, Vol. 83, No. 26, pp. 41–3.

Psychosocial Considerations

Pottle, A. (1988) Visiting in coronary care units, *Nursing Times*, 19 October, Vol. 84, No. 42, p. 59.

Rimmer, C. (1988) Who returns to coronary care? *Nursing Times*, 16 November, Vol. 84, No. 46, pp. 40–41.

Shaw, A. (1989) Visiting needs in coronary care units, *Nursing Times*, 10 May, Vol. 85, No. 19, p. 55.

Thompson, D. (1988) Supporting wives of coronary care patients, *Nursing Times*, 24 August, Vol. 84, No. 34, p. 57.

Thompson, D. (1989) Counselling coronary patients and their partners, *Nursing Times*, 21 June, Vol. 85, No. 25, p. 59.

chapter **8** ▬▬▬▬▬▬

ASSESSMENT AND CARE OF PATIENTS REQUIRING CARDIAC SURGERY

Since the introduction of valvular surgery in the 1940s, continued advances in technology associated with cardiac diagnosis and anaesthesia have made surgical intervention possible for many cardiac disorders. This chapter describes the main surgical procedures and care required by adults with a heart disorder.

CARDIAC CONDITIONS AND SURGICAL PROCEDURES

Cardiopulmonary Bypass

Many cardiac surgical procedures are performed while the patient is placed on partial or complete cardiopulmonary bypass (extracorporeal circulation) (Weiland and Walker, 1986). The bypass procedure provides a mechanical means of circulating and oxygenating the blood while diverting it from the heart and lungs. This affords the surgeon a quiet, bloodless field, and yet preserves tissue and organ perfusion and viability.

Extracorporeal circulation uses three main structure elements: a pump, an oxygenator and plastic circuitry. During cardiopulmonary bypass, the blood volume is circulated continuously between the patient and the apparatus, where it is filtered, temperature-regulated and oxygenated, as shown in Figure 8.1. Because of the mechanical limitations of the system, complications may result from alterations in cardiovascular dynamics unless measures are taken to provide for haemodilution, hypothermia and anticoagulation. Whole blood was originally used to prime the extracorporeal circuit but this was associated with various problems, including expense and transmission of disease. Current practice is to dilute autologous blood, usually with Ringer's lactate solution and 5 per cent dextrose (Weiland and Walker, 1986, p. 34).

Hypothermia (and rewarming at the completion of the procedure) is accomplished by the heat exchange element in the pump. During the operative procedure the patient is cooled to a temperature of 28° to 32°C, which decreases the tissue oxygen requirements by about 50 per cent, thereby providing major organs some protection against ischaemic injury, particularly if the pump apparatus fails. Although hypothermia increases blood viscosity, this effect is compensated for by haemodilution. Heparin is used to preclude the risk of massive extravascular coagulation in the mechanical parts of the bypass system. Anticoagulation is regulated carefully during the operation. Immediately after the bypass is discontinued, protamine sulphate is used to reverse the effects of the heparin.

During surgery the adequacy of tissue perfusion is determined by monitoring the electrocardiogram, arterial blood pressure, central venous pressure, urine output and arterial blood gases (Griffin and Treasure, 1989).

Cardiopulmonary bypass is not without risk; this risk increases when pump time exceeds two hours. Excessive pump time exacerbates blood trauma, produces abnormal capillary membrane permeability and predisposes the patient to tissue anoxia. All of these complications must be anticipated after surgery (Browett, 1989, p. 26).

Aortic Stenosis

Aortic stenosis is a narrowing of the valve orifice between the left ventricle and the aorta. It may be congenital or it can result from rheumatic heart disorders or calcification of unknown origin. Rheumatic changes include thickening and fibrosis of the cusps, fusion of the commissures and valve calcification.

Aortic stenosis results in left ventricular hypertrophy and decreased ventricular function. This causes a reduced cardiac output, which decreases cardiac and cerebral perfusion, which in turn may cause syncope, angina and arrhythmias. Severe aortic stenosis results in left ventricular failure, decreased cardiac output, pulmonary oedema and eventually right-sided heart failure. Some surgeons perform aortic valve replacement even on asymptomatic patients because of the risk of sudden death.

Aortic Incompetence

Aortic incompetence results from incomplete closure of the aortic valve cusps during ventricular diastole. This incomplete closure allows blood to flow backwards from the aorta into the left ventricle. With rheumatic heart problems and bacterial endocarditis, the valve leaflets become thickened and scarred, lose compliance and eventually become calcified. Other causes of aortic incompetence include congenital malformation and disorders that cause traumatic tearing of the ascending aorta.

The regurgitation of blood into the left ventricle results

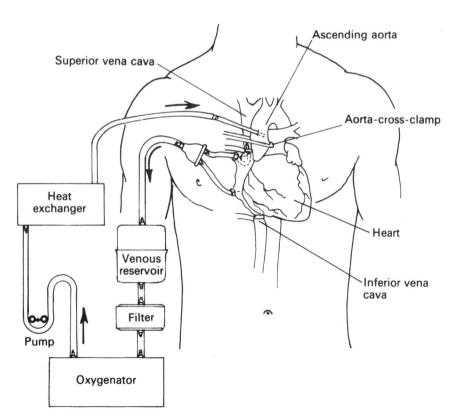

Figure 8.1 Schematic drawing of the cardiopulmonary bypass system.

in dilation and hypertrophy of the ventricle. Patients with aortic incompetence characteristically have an elevated systolic blood pressure, a low diastolic blood pressure and thus a wide pulse pressure. These patients also develop other symptoms including palpitations, dyspnoea on exertion, chest pain and dizziness due to sudden postural changes.

The treatment for patients who are symptomatic or who have documented left ventricular hypertrophy is aortic valve replacement.

Mitral Stenosis

Mitral stenosis is the progressive thickening and contracture of valve cusps, with narrowing of the orifice and progressive obstruction to blood flow. It is a late feature of rheumatic damage to the endocardium. Patients with mitral stenosis may experience dyspnoea, pulmonary congestion (haemoptysis, cough and orthopnoea) arrhythmias, angina pectoris and systemic embolism.

Patients with mitral stenosis can usually be managed initially with medical therapy. Patients with progressive symptoms are stabilized medically and then treated surgically.

Mitral Incompetence

Mitral incompetence is caused by rheumatic or bacterial endocarditis. These infectious processes cause fibrotic and calcific changes that thicken, shorten and deform the valve cusps so that they do not completely close. It may also be caused by congenital deformities or myocardial infarction. Patients with mitral incompetence have chronic pulmonary congestion, arrhythmias and symptoms of fatigue, orthopnoea, shortness of breath on exertion and palpitations. Surgical treatment is directed towards replacement with a prosthetic valve or a biological tissue valve. This procedure is done when there is extensive calcification and destruction of the chordae tendineae. Two of the most common valves used for mitral

valve replacement are the Starr-Edwards silastic ball and cage valve, and the Bjork-Shiley tilting disc valve. Patients who have a mechanical valve in place are usually maintained on anticoagulant therapy postoperatively to minimize the risk of embolisation. Figure 8.2 shows the mechanical and biological tissue valves in common use.

Tricuspid Stenosis

Tricuspid stenosis is characterized by the same fibrotic and calcific changes as stenosis of the other heart valves. These result in a narrowing of the valve orifice, which impedes the flow of blood from the right atrium to the right ventricle. The right atrium dilates and the right-sided heart failure leads to venous congestion with cyanosis, liver and hepatic malfunction, ascities, haemoptysis and dyspnoea.

Patients may have mitral and aortic disorders which must also be addressed. Surgical intervention may be carried out at the time of operation after correction of the mitral valve problem.

Tricuspid Incompetence

Tricuspid incompetence allows the regurgitation of blood from the right ventricle into the right atrium during ventricular systole. It is usually a functional disorder caused by failure and dilation of the heart due to severe mitral incompetence. The symptoms of tricuspid incompetence are the same as those of tricuspid stenosis. The patient will require surgical treatment of mitral valve disease, which may reverse tricuspid regurgitation, or a tricuspid valve replacement may be indicated.

Left Ventricular Aneurysm

Left ventricular aneurysm may affect some patients who suffer a myocardial infarction, and is secondary to the injury and scarring caused by the infarction. Surgical removal of the ballooned portion of the left ventricle may be indicated for a patient displaying symptoms otherwise

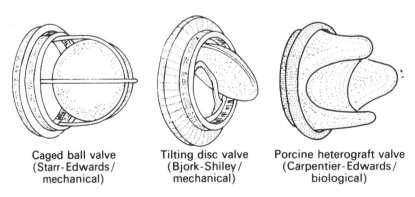

Caged ball valve (Starr-Edwards/ mechanical)

Tilting disc valve (Bjork-Shiley/ mechanical)

Porcine heterograft valve (Carpentier-Edwards/ biological)

Figure 8.2 Common mechanical and biological valve replacements.

it may cause the heart to become ineffective as a pump, leading to congestive heart failure, peripheral emboli and tachyarrhythmias.

Surgical Intervention for Coronary Artery Disease

Coronary artery disease is a narrowing and distortion of the coronary arteries resulting in decreased blood flow to the myocardium. It is caused by atherosclerosis, which causes proliferation of smooth muscle cells and accumulation of lipids in the intima of the artery wall. The actual cause of atherosclerosis is unknown, but according to Griffin and Treasure (1989, p.1771) certain risk factors have been identified, including high blood pressure, hyperlipidaemia, smoking and obesity. Some of the symptoms associated with coronary artery disease are angina pectoris, myocardial infarction and primary ventricular fibrillation.

Neutze and White (1987, p. 405) suggest that surgical intervention for coronary artery disease is aimed at improving the quality of life by reducing angina pectoris and allowing the patients to resume their previous activity levels. A criterion generally accepted for surgical treatment is disabling angina pectoris unrelieved by medical therapy (West and Wilson-Barnett, in Wilson-Barnett and Robinson (eds), 1989, p. 117).

Coronary artery disease is treated surgically by coronary artery bypass graft, heart transplantation and, less invasively, by percutaneous transluminal coronary angioplasty (dilation of diseased coronary arteries with a balloon-tipped catheter). Flynn and Frantz (1987, p. 59) suggest that because the decision as to when it is appropriate to use surgery remains controversial, it is imperative that the patient, family and close friends, where applicable, are fully aware of the benefits and risks associated with the proposed and alternative treatments. The patient is then able to make an informed decision as to the most appropriate treatment.

Coronary Artery Bypass Graft

Griffin and Treasure (1989, pl. 772) describe the operative technique utilized in coronary artery bypass graft surgery, which involves connecting a segment of a vein or artery between the aortic root and the affected coronary artery at a point distal to the obstruction. Usually a portion of the patient's saphenous vein is used for the graft or grafts as shown in Figure 8.3.

The operation is carried out through a median sternotomy. The patient is supported on cardiopulmonary bypass so that the heart can be arrested to allow for anastomosis of the saphenous vein to the coronary arteries. The vein is reversed from its normal direction so that the valves do not interfere with blood flow through the vein.

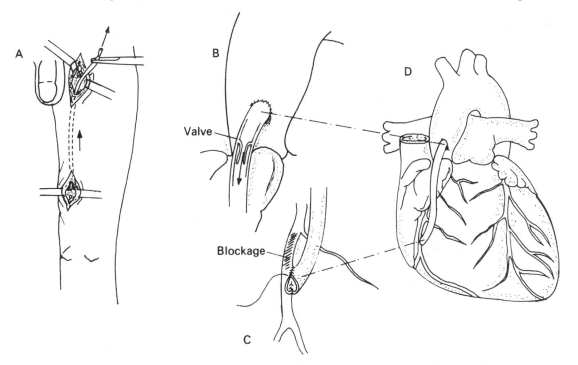

Figure 8.3 Saphenous vein revascularization procedure. (A) The saphenous vein is removed from the patient's leg. The vein is reversed so that the valves will not interfere with blood flow. (B) The distal end of the vein is sutured to the ascending aorta. (C) At a point distal to the blockage, the vein is sutured to the coronary artery by end-to-side anastomosis. (D) The completed bypass re-establishes the flow distal to the blockage.

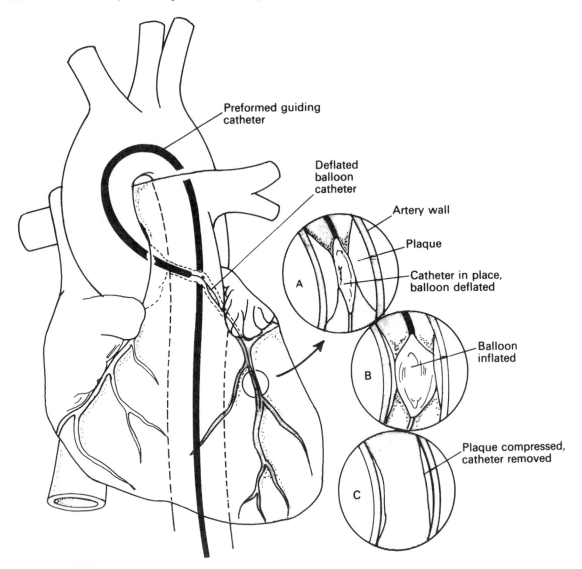

Figure 8.4 Percutaneous transluminal coronary angioplasty is a less invasive procedure than coronary artery bypass surgery in selected patients. (A) A balloon-tipped catheter is passed into the affected coronary artery and placed within the atherosclerotic lesion. (B) The balloon is then rapidly inflated and deflated with controlled pressure. (C) After the plaque is compressed, the catheter is removed, allowing improved blood flow of the vessel. (Redrawn from Purcell, J. A. and Giffen, P. A. (1981) Percutaneous transluminal coronary angioplasty, *American Journal of Nursing*, September, Vol. 81, No. 9, p. 1621.)

Percutaneous Transluminal Coronary Angioplasty

This procedure, which can be performed instead of coronary artery bypass graft surgery in some patients with single-vessel coronary artery disease, is described by Solomon (1988, p. 29). Potential candidates must also be eligible for coronary artery bypass graft surgery, as the complications of angioplasty may necessitate immediate bypass surgery: for example, coronary artery spasm, clot, rupture or myocardial infarction. The procedure is done by inserting a balloon-tipped catheter into the affected coronary artery and reducing the stenosis by inflating the balloon with controlled pressure (Figure 8.4).

Local anaesthesia is used and the procedure is performed in a cardiac catheterization department by a cardiologist. The procedure is carried out with the cardiac surgery team and an operating room on standby in case difficulties arise.

Patients who require percutaneous transluminal coronary angioplasty are hospitalized for two to four days and then may resume previous activity levels. While the long-term effects of this procedure are not fully evaluated, the advantage of its being less invasive makes it preferable to coronary artery bypass surgery for selected patients. Pre- and post-procedure care is similar to the care required by patients undergoing cardiac catheterization.

Heart Transplantation

Heart transplantation is performed for end-stage cardiac disorders that do not respond to surgical or medical therapy (Underhill *et al.*, 1983, p. 344).

Currently, it is performed only in selected centres because of the complex surgical and management techniques involved. The principal factor that restricts the number of transplants performed is the limited number of suitable donors. The primary focus of postoperative care is to prevent infection and rejection.

NURSING PROCESS: AN OVERVIEW

Patients who are to undergo heart surgery have many of the same needs as other surgical patients, and require the postoperative care described in Chapter 2. In addition, the patient, family and close friends, where applicable, are experiencing a major life crisis (Liddle, 1988, p. 147). Their psychological responses to the surgery are intense due to the association of the heart with life and death.

Preoperative care begins before admission and focuses on stabilizing any other disorders and optimizing cardiac function. Any sources of possible infection are investigated and treated.

Immediately after surgery, the patient is cared for in an intensive care unit where continuous assessment of cardiac function and prompt intervention are possible. Patients are taught to carry out self-assessment during the rehabilitation phase in order to regulate activity levels.

Assessment

Gortner *et al.* (1988, p. 649) indicate that the nursing assessment should focus primarily on obtaining baseline observations; assessing the patient's emotional and teaching needs, and those of any significant other. The history includes a social assessment of family roles and support systems and a description of the patient's usual activity levels.

Patients with nonacute heart disease are usually admitted one to two days before surgery. The preoperative history reviews past and present conditions, with emphasis on renal, respiratory, gastrointestinal and neurological function, as these systems can be affected due to alterations in cardiac output (Treasure, 1987, p. 9). An analysis of the patient's alcohol intake and smoking behaviour is made. Any disease that affects respiratory function may prolong postoperative respiratory support.

Many laboratory tests are carried out; a complete blood count, serum electrolytes, lipid profile, and nose, throat, sputum and urine cultures. Coagulation and antibody screens are obtained, as well as renal and hepatic function tests.

Patients who have some form of cardiac disorder are usually prescribed a combination of drugs, such as diuretics, digitalis, beta-adrenergic blockers and antihypertensives. Patients are assessed individually by the medical staff, who may advise some drugs to be stopped before admission, for example, digitalis and diuretics. Anticoagulant drugs are discontinued several days before operation to allow coagulation mechanisms to return to normal (Underhill, 1983, p. 338).

The psychological assessment and the assessment of teaching and learning needs of the patient, family and close friends are as important as the physical examination (Gortner *et al.*, 1988, p. 650). They may be anxious and fearful, and may have many unanswered questions. Anxiety levels usually increase as the day of admission to hospital approaches. Nurses are required to evaluate the patient's emotional state and allow feelings to be expressed. This facilitates a growing and supportive relationship to develop between nurse and patient. Patients need support whether they have high or low anxiety levels. Nurses provide this support by giving time, by listening and by showing an interest (West and Wilson-Barnett, in Wilson-Barnett and Robinson (eds), 1989, p. 118). Patients can be assured that they will be sedated before entering the operating room.

Questions should be asked to obtain the following information about the patient, family and close friends, where appropriate:

- The meaning to the patient and significant others of the surgery.
- Coping mechanisms that have and are being used to deal with stress.
- Anticipated changes in lifestyle.
- Support systems in effect.
- Fears regarding the present and the future.
- Knowledge and understanding of the operative procedure, postoperative course and long-term rehabilitation.

The fears most often expressed are fear of the unknown, fear of pain and fear of dying. The patient, family and close friends, where appropriate, are allowed repeated opportunities to express their feelings. If there is fear of the unknown, the nurse should describe what the patient may feel, for example, by comparing the similarities and differences between a cardiac catheterization and the impending surgery. Patients may want to discuss their fears regarding pain. The nurse can reassure them that the fear of pain is normal, and can confirm that while some pain may be experienced, the patient will be closely observed and the use of medication, positioning and relaxation will make the pain more tolerable (Dobson, 1982, p. 325).

The patient, family and friends are encouraged to talk about their fear of death; this is a normal emotion. Once this fear is expressed, the patient, family and friends can be helped.

During the assessment, the nurse determines how much the patient, family and close friends know about the surgery and the expected postoperative events. Teaching usually includes information about the hospital stay and the operation (preoperative care, length of surgery, visiting time) and rehabilitation. The patient, family or close friend may be taken on a tour of the intensive care unit. The patient should be less anxious having already seen and heard the environment, and having met personnel who will be on duty postoperatively (Turnock, 1990, p. 30). The patient and significant others should be informed about the presence of monitors, chest tubes, intravenous lines, endotracheal tube, pacing wires, arterial line and an indwelling catheter. Explaining the purpose and the approximate time that these will be in place should help to relieve the patient's anxiety. Most patients will be intubated and mechanically ventilated for 24 hours postoperatively; they need to be aware that this prevents them from talking and eating. They should be assured that nursing staff are skilled in other means of communication and that a liquid diet will be given.

All preoperative teaching is documented, including an evaluation of the patient's level of understanding.

McIvor and Thomson (1988, p. 142) suggest that by alleviating undue anxiety and fear, emotional preparation of the patient for surgery lessens the chance of preoperative problems, aids in smooth anaesthesia induction and enhances the patient's involvement postoperatively in care and recovery. Likewise, preparation of the family or close friends for the events to come helps them to cope, to be supportive to the patient and to participate in the postoperative and rehabilitative care (Gilliss, 1984, p. 103).

Assessing For Complications

Browett (1989, p. 27) suggests that the patient should be assessed continuously for indications of impending complications, as shown in Figure 8.5. The nurse and the medical staff work as a team to recognize early signs and symptoms of complications and to institute measures to reverse their progress.

Cardiac Tamponade. Cardiac tamponade results from bleeding into the pericardial sac or accumulation of fluids in the sac, which compresses the heart and prevents adequate filling of the ventricles (Solomon, 1988, p. 38). The nurse assesses for signs of tamponade: arterial hypotension accompanied by a rising central venous pressure; muffled heart sounds; weak, thready pulse; neck vein distension; and decreased urine output. A reduction in the amount of drainage in the chest-collection bottle may indicate that the fluid is accumulating elsewhere. The nurse should assist in preparing for a pericardiocentesis.

Myocardial Infarction. A myocardial infarction may occur during the postoperative period. When assessing the patient, the nurse is aware that symptoms may be masked by the usual postoperative chest discomfort. A careful assessment of the type of pain is made to differentiate it from incisional pain. The nurse watches for decreased cardiac output in the presence of normal circulating volume and central venous pressure. The doctor uses serial electrocardiograms and cardiac enzymes to make a definite diagnosis. Medical management is individualized; postoperative activity level may be reduced to allow the heart adequate time for healing.

Cardiac Failure. Cardiac failure causes deficient blood perfusion to different organs. The nurse observes for and reports the following signs and symptoms: a falling mean arterial pressure, a rising central venous pressure and an increasing tachycardia (Browett, 1989, p. 29). The patient may exhibit signs of restlessness and agitation, cold and blue exremeties, venous distension, laboured respirations, tissue oedema and ascites.

Persistent Bleeding. Griffin and Treasure (1989, p. 1775) suggest that persistent bleeding may be the result of tissue fragility, trauma to tissues or some unexplained clotting defect, usually transitory. However, a significant platelet deficiency may be present. The nurse watches for a steady and continuous drainage of blood and observes the central venous pressure. Medical management may include the administration of protamine sulphate, Vitamin K or blood components. Preparations are made to return the patient to surgery if bleeding persists (over 300 ml per hour) for four to six hours.

Hypovolaemia. The nurse observes for signs of hypovolaemia: arterial hypotension and low central venous pressure with an increasing pulse rate and low left atrial and pulmonary artery wedge pressures (Browett, 1989, p. 29). When indicated, the doctor will prescribe blood and intravenous solutions.

Renal Failure. Urine output depends on cardiac output, blood volume, the state of hydration and the condition of the kidneys. Renal injury may be caused by deficient perfusion, haemolysis and low cardiac output before and following open heart surgery (Weiland and Walker, 1986, p. 35). If urinary output falls below 20 ml per hour, it may indicate a reduced renal function. The nurse will assess the kidneys' ability to concentrate urine in the renal tubules by measuring specific gravity. Treatment is aimed at increasing cardiac output and renal blood flow. Urea, creatinine and electrolyte levels are also monitored. If this does not rectify the problem, the patient may be prepared for peritoneal dialysis or haemodialysis.

Hypotension. Hypotension may be caused by inadequate cardiac contractility and a reduction in blood volume or by mechanical ventilation, all of which can produce a reduction in cardiac output. Vital signs are monitored, including left atrial pressure, central venous pressure and arterial pressure. The nurse should note chest tube drainage, as hypotension may be caused by excessive

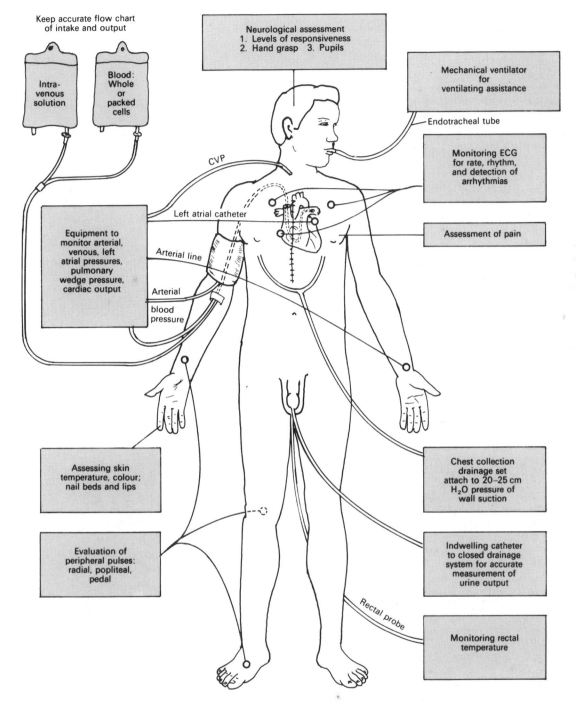

Figure 8.5 Postoperative care of the cardiac surgery patient.

bleeding. Medical management is geared to maintaining left atrial pressure at a level that will provide an adequate circulating volume for good tissue perfusion (Weiland and Walker, 1986, p. 37).

Embolization. Embolization may result from injury to the intima of the blood vessels, dislodgement of a clot from a damaged valve, venous stasis aggravated by certain arrhythmias, loosening of mural thrombi and coagulation problems (Browett, 1989, p. 29).

Common sites for emboli are the lungs, coronary arteries, mesentery, extremeties, kidneys, spleen and brain. The symptoms displayed will vary according to the site:

midabdominal or midback pain, painful cessation of pulses, numbness or coldness in an extremity; chest pain and respiratory distress with pulmonary embolus or myocardial infarction; and one-sided weakness and pupillary changes, such as occur in cerebral vascular accident. The nurse initiates preventive measures for the patient, such as the use of antiembolic stockings, the avoidance of pressure on the popliteal space (leg-crossing, leg-raising), and the commencement of passive and active exercises.

Postpericardiotomy Syndrome. This term refers to a group of abnormal behaviours that occur in varying intensity and duration. The cause is uncertain, but may be due to anticardiac antibodies or viral causes, for example. The features displayed include fever, malaise, arthralgias, dyspnoea, percardial effusion, pleural effusion and friction rub. The treatment is aimed at relieving symptoms (bedrest, aspirin) since the condition is self-limiting but may recur.

Evaluation

1. Reduction in anxiety: patient, family and close friends express a lessening of anxiety, patient participates and learns from preoperative teaching (states reasons for operation, events to occur before and after surgery, and the need for follow-up rehabilitation after surgery).
2. Alleviation of discomfort and an absence of incisional pain.
3. Maintains airway and tissue oxygenation, attains arterial blood gases within normal limits for patient. The patient will be extubated 24 hours post-surgery, and will breath spontaneously and unlaboured 14 to 18 breaths per minute.
4. Restoration of adequate cardiac output—blood pressure and heart rate within normal limits for patient; skin warm and dry; urine output greater than 50 ml per hour.
5. Attains fluid and electrolyte balance—normal serum electrolytes, lungs clear on auscultation and absence of oedema.
6. Adapts to the intensive care environment—orientated to time and place when asked, does not hallucinate and sleeps five hours without interruption.
7. Remains free from complications—an absence of life-threatening arrhythmias, presence of normal heart sounds and normal cardiac enzymes. The temperature is maintained within normal limits for the patient and there is an absence of bleeding.

Patient Education

Depending upon the type of surgery and postoperative progress, the patient may be discharged from the hospital between 7 to 10 days after surgery. Although the patient may be anxious to return home, usually the patient and family or close friends are apprehensive about this transition. Carers often express fears that they are incapable of caring for the patient at home. They are often concerned that complications will occur, which they are unprepared to handle.

The nurse helps the patient and home carers to set realistic and achievable outcomes (West and Wilson-Barnett, in Wilson-Barnett and Robinson (eds), 1989, p. 123). This plan is devised several days before discharge to allow ample time for its review and clarification. Specific written guidelines are provided regarding many aspects of the patient's rehabilitation. Some patients are placed on a minimum salt and cholesterol restriction, and will also be advised to weigh themselves and report a gain of more than 2.2 kg per week.

Patients are able to gradually increase activities, though avoiding strenuous activities until after the exercise tolerance test. It may be suggested that the patient should participate in activities that do not cause discomfort; increasing walking time and distance each day and attempting stairs once or twice a day in the first week, increasing as tolerated (West and Wilson-Barnett, in Wilson-Barnett and Robinson (eds), 1989, p. 124). The patient should plan to: take short rest periods; avoid lifting more than 9 kg; and avoid large crowds initially.

After the first post-operative check-up the patient is advised by the doctor about when to commence driving and work. Sexual relations can be resumed, and parallels the patient's ability to participate in other activities; this is usually about two weeks after surgery. Patients are advised to abstain if tired or after a heavy meal. The patient should consult a doctor if chest discomfort, breathing difficulties or palpitations occur and last longer than 15 minutes after intercourse.

Medications are labelled and the patient is made aware of their purpose and possible side-effects. Patients with prosthetic valves may continue on a warfarin regime indefinitely. Patients are advised to observe for bleeding and avoid the use of drugs that may interfere with the action of warfarin, for example, aspirin. Women with a prosthetic valve are discouraged from becoming pregnant. The patient is cautioned about the need for antibiotic cover following dental and surgical procedures. The patient is advised to carry an identification card stating the cardiac condition and current medication.

The nurse may find that some patients will have difficulty in learning and retaining information after cardiac surgery. West and Wilson-Barnett (in Wilson-Barnett and Robinson (eds), 1989, p. 117) have shown that many patients experience difficulties in cognitive function after cardiac surgery. The patient may experience recent memory loss, short attention span, difficulty with simple arithmetic, poor handwriting and visual disturbances. Patients may often become frustrated when they try to resume normal activities and learn how to care for themselves at

► NURSING CARE PLAN 8.1: THE PATIENT UNDERGOING CARDIAC SURGERY

Helen Murdoch is 45 years old and works part-time in a local government office. She is married and has a 17-year-old daughter.

Patient's problems	Expected outcomes	Nursing care	Rationale
1. Risk of mental and psychological disorientation due to sensory overload	Mental and psychological orientation	1a. Keep the patient orientated to time and place; explain all procedures and reiterate how much the patient's co-operation will aid treatment	Psychotic disturbances are more frequent after operations involving cardiopulmonary bypass (Treasure, 1987)
		b. Observe for manifestation of delirium (impairment of orientation, memory, intellectual functions, judgement) transient perceptual distortions and paranoid delusions	Symptoms may be related to sleep deprivation, increased sensory input, disorientation to night and day, prolonged inability to speak because of endotracheal intubation etc.
		c. Encourage visits by the family at regular times and allow them to touch each other	Helps patient to regain sense of reality
		d. Plan care to allow rest periods, day/night pattern and uninterrupted sleep	
		e. Reassure patient and family that psychiatric disorders following cardiac surgery are usually transient	
		f. Remove patient from intensive care unit as soon as possible; allow patient to express events of psychotic episode	Helps patient to deal with and assimilate experience
		g. Encourage mobility; keep environment as free as possible from excessive auditory and sensory input	
2. Risk of inability to maintain airway and therefore tissue oxygenation due to trauma and extensive chest surgery	Adequate airway maintenance	2a. Assisted or controlled ventilation	Respiratory support is used during the first 24 hours to provide an airway in the event of cardiac arrest, to decrease the work of the heart and to maintain effective ventilation (Browett, 1989)
		b. Monitor clinical status, arterial blood gases and tidal volume	Adequacy of ventilation is assessed by the patient's clinical status and by direct measurement of tidal volume and arterial blood gases (Brunner and Suddarth, 1989)
		c. Suction tracheobronchial secretions carefully using an aseptic technique	Retention of secretions leads to hypoxia and possible cardiac arrest (Pritchard and David, 1988)
		d. Sedate patient adequately	To help toleration of endotracheal tube and cope with ventilating sensations (Weiland and Walker, 1986)
		e. Chest physiotherapy– promoting coughing, deep breathing and alteration in position	To prevent retention of secretions and atelectasis (Brunner and Suddarth, 1989)

►

► NURSING CARE PLAN 8.1: THE PATIENT UNDERGOING CARDIAC SURGERY

Patient's problems	Expected outcomes	Nursing care	Rationale
		f. Restriction of fluid intake 1,000 ml/24 hr	Pulmonary congestion may develop from excessive fluid intake (Pritchard and David, 1988)
		g. Assess daily chest X-ray	To evaluate state of lung expansion and to detect atelectasis
3. Risk of inadequate cardiac output due to blood loss and compromised myocardial function	Adequate cardiac output	3a. Continuous assessment of cardiovascular status utilizing haemodynamic monitoring– recorded every 15 to 30 minutes; arterial blood pressure	Extreme vasoconstriction following cardiopulmonary bypass makes auscultatory blood pressure unobtainable (Weiland and Walker, 1986)
		b. Check peripheral pulses (pedal, tibial, radial) Palpate the carotid, brachial, popliteal and femoral pulses	As a further assessment of cardiac function Absence may be due to recent catheterization of the extremity; indicates blood volume, vascular tone and pumping effectiveness of the heart
		c. Central venous pressure	A high central venous pressure reading may be caused by hypervolaemia, heart failure, cardiac tamponade A low central venous pressure reading may be caused by a low blood volume (Pritchard and David, 1988)
		d. Monitor and record urine output hourly	Urine output is an indication of cardiac output and renal perfusion (Griffin and Treasure, 1989)
		e. Observe buccal mucosa, nail beds, lips, lobes and extremities for duskiness/ cynosis	Signs of low cardiac output
		f. Assess the skin, noting the temperature and colour	Cool, moist skin indicates vasoconstriction and decreased cardiac output
		g. Assess neurological status	The brain is dependent on a continuous supply of oxygenated blood and must rely on adequate and continuous perfusion by the heart. Hypoperfusion or air debris may produce central nervous system damage after heart surgery (Treasure, 1987)
		h. Observe for symptoms of hypoxia–restlessness, headache, confusion, dyspnoea, hypotension and cyanosis	
		i. Monitor the patient's neurological score utilizing the Glasgow Coma Scale; report any alterations to medical staff	

► NURSING CARE PLAN 8.1: THE PATIENT UNDERGOING CARDIAC SURGERY

Patient's problems	Expected outcomes	Nursing care	Rationale
4 Risk of fluid and electrolyte imbalance due to cardiopulmonary bypass	Fluid and electrolyte balance	4a. Keep intake and output flow	Adequate circulating blood volume is necessary for optimum cellular activity; metabolic acidosis and electrolyte imbalance can occur after bypass As a method of determining positive or negative fluid balance
		b. Measure postoperative chest drainage; should not exceed 200 ml/hr for first 4 to 6 hours; cessation of drainage may indicate linked or blocked chest tube	Excessive blood loss from chest cavity can cause hypovolaemia (Duncan *et al.*, 1987)
		c. Monitor serum electrolytes	A specific concentration of electrolytes is necessary in both extracellular and intracellular body fluids to sustain life
		i. Monitor ECG for specific changes (*hypokalaemia*)	Arrhythmias, asystole and cardiac arrest may be due to inadequate intake, diuretics, vomiting, excessive nasogastric drainage and stress from surgery (Pritchard and David, 1989)
		ii. Monitor for effects of low potassium levels: digitalis toxicity, metabolic alkalosis, weakened myocardium Monitor the rate of intravenous potassium replacement as directed	
		iii. *Hyperkalaemia* Effects: mental confusion, restlessness, nausea, weakness and paraesthesia of extremities	May be caused by increased fluid intake, red cell breakdown from the pump, acidosis, renal insufficiency, tissue necrosis
		Be prepared to administer an ion-exchange resin (sodium polystyrene sulphonate) or intravenous sodium bicarbonate or intravenous insulin and glucose	The resin binds potassium and promotes its intestinal excretion Drives potassium into the cells from extracellular fluid
		iv. *Hyponatraemia* Assess for weakness, fatigue, confusion, convulsions and coma (see problem 3)	May be due to reduction of total body sodium or an increased water intake, causing a dilution of body sodium (Browett, 1989)
		v. *Hypocalcaemia* Monitor for signs of reduced calcium levels – numbness and tingling in the fingertips, toes, ears and nose, carpopedal spasm, muscle cramps and tetany Be prepared to monitor replacement therapy as directed	May be due to alkalosis (which produces the amount of calcium in the extracellular fluid) and multiple blood transfusions

►

► NURSING CARE PLAN 8.1: THE PATIENT UNDERGOING CARDIAC SURGERY			
Patient's problems	**Expected outcomes**	**Nursing care**	**Rationale**
		vi. *Hypercalcaemia* Monitor for signs of ECG changes and digitalis toxicity	May be due to prolonged immobility Institute treatment as directed; this condition may lead to asystole and death (Brunner and Suddarth, 1989)
5. Risk of experiencing pain due to sternotomy incision and irritation of pleura	Alleviate pain	5a. Examine sternotomy incision and leg dressing; monitor temperature b. Assess and relieve the patient's pain; record the nature, type, location and duration of pain; monitor cardiovascular status – see problem 2 c. Differentiate between incisional and anginal pain d. Administer medication as prescribed, and evaluate effectiveness by asking the patient	Assess for signs of infection; pyrexia may indicate local or systemic infection Pain and anxiety increase pulse rate, oxygen consumption and cardiac work Allows the patient to comply with treatment and exercises

home. The patient and family or close friends are reassured that the problem is transient and will subside in six to eight weeks.

Patient education does not end at the time of discharge. The patient may be commenced on a rehabilitation and exercise programme after an exercise tolerance test. The patient is advised how and whom to contact in case of an emergency.

Nursing Care Plan 8.1 describes the care necessary for the patient undergoing cardiac surgery.

BIBLIOGRAPHY

Browett, A. (1989) Coronary artery bypass graft, *Nursing*, Vol. 3, No. 36, pp. 26–9.

Brunner, L. S. and Suddarth, D. S. (1989) *The Lippincott Manual of Medical-Surgical Nursing* (2nd edition), Harper & Row, London.

Dobson, M. E. (1982) A review of methods for relief of postoperative pain, *Annals of the Royal College of Surgeons, England*, Vol. 64, pp. 324–7.

Duncan, R. C. *et al.* (1987) Effect of chest tube management on drainage after cardiac surgery, *Heart and Lung*, Vol. 16, No. 1, pp. 1–8.

Flynn, M. K. and Frantz, R. (1987) Coronary artery bypass surgery, *Heart and Lung*, Vol. 16, No. 2, pp. 159–66.

Gillis, C. (1984) Reducing family stress during and after coronary bypass surgery, *Nursing Clinics of North America*, Vol. 19, No. 1, pp. 103–12.

Gortner, R. S. *et al.* (1988) Improving recovery following

cardiac surgery, *Journal of Advanced Nursing*, Vol. 13, No. 5, pp. 649–61.

Griffen, S. and Treasure, T. (1989) Coronary artery surgery, *Cardiothoracic Surgery*, Vol. 74, pp. 1771–6.

Liddle, K. (1988) Reaching out to meet the needs of relatives in intensive care units, *Intensive Care Nursing*, Vol. 4, No. 4, pp. 146–59.

McIvor, D. and Thomson, F. J. (1988) The self-perceived needs of family members with a relative in the intensive care unit, *Intensive Care Nursing*, Vol. 4, No. 4, pp. 139–45.

Neutze, M. J. and White D. H. (1987) What contribution has cardiac surgery made to the decline in mortality from coronary heart disease? *British Medical Journal*, Vol. 294, No. 6569, pp. 405–9.

Pritchard, A. P. and David A. J. (1988) *The Royal Marsden Manual of Clinical Nursing Procedures* (2nd edition), Harper & Row, London.

Soloman, J. (1988) *Introduction to Cardiovascular Nursing*, Williams & Wilkins, Baltimore.

Treasure, T. (1987) Heart and minds: how big is the risk of coronary surgery? *British Medical Journal*, Vol. 37, No. 1, pp. 9–11.

Turnock, C. (1990) Demystifying intensive care, *Nursing Standard*, Vol. 4, No. 4, pp. 30–1.

Underhill, S. L. (1983) *Cardiac Nursing*, J. B. Lippincott, Philadelphia.

Weiland, P. A. and Walker, E. W. (1986) Physiological principle and clinical sequelae of cardiopulmonary bypass, *Heart & Lung*, Vol. 15, No. 1, pp. 34–9.

Wilson-Barnett, J. and Robinson, S. (eds) (1989) Risk factors and recovery from coronary artery bypass surgery, S. West and J. Wilson-Barnett in *Directions in Nursing Research*, Scutari Press, London.

FURTHER READING

Books

Andreoli, K. *et al.* (1987) *Comprehensive Cardiac Care* (6th edition), C. V. Mosby, St Louis.

Darovic, G. O. (1987) *Hemodynamic Monitoring*, W. B. Saunders, Philadelphia.

Farrell, E. M. (ed.) (1990) *Advances in the Diagnosis and Treatment of Coronary Artery Disease*, Blackwell Scientific, Oxford.

Health Education Council (1984) *Coronary Heart Disease Prevention: Plans for Action*, Pitman, London.

Miller, G. (1989) *Invasive Investigations of the Heart*, Blackwell Scientific, Oxford.

Articles

Reyes, A. V. (1987) Monitoring and treating life-threatening ventricular dysrhythmias, *Nursing Clinics of North America*, Vol. 22, No. 1, pp. 61–76.

chapter 9

ASSESSMENT AND CARE OF PATIENTS WITH VASCULAR AND PERIPHERAL CIRCULATORY DISORDERS

PHYSIOLOGICAL OVERVIEW

Adequate perfusion, which results in oxygenation and nutrition of body tissues, is dependent in part upon a functionally intact cardiovascular system. Efficient pumping action of the heart, patent and responsive blood vessels and an adequate circulating blood volume are essential for adequate blood flow. Nervous activity, blood viscosity and the metabolic needs of tissues influence the rate of blood flow and hence the adequacy of blood flow.

The peripheral vascular system consists of the systemic circulation and the pulmonary circulation serially connected in a closed system with the right and left heart. The blood vessels provide distensible channels for the transport of blood from the heart to the tissues and back to the heart. Cardiac ventricular contraction supplies the driving force for movement of blood through the vascular system. Arteries distribute oxygenated blood from the left side of the heart to the tissues, while veins convey deoxygenated blood from the tissues to the right side of the heart.

Capillary vessels, located within the tissues, connect the arterial and venous systems and constitute the site of exchange of nutrients and metabolic wastes between the circulatory system and the tissues. Arterioles and venules immediately adjacent to the capillaries, together with the capillaries, comprise the microcirculation. A schematic representation of the circulation is shown in Figure 9.1.

The lymphatic system complements the function of the circulatory system. Lymphatic vessels transport lymph (a fluid similar to plasma) and tissue fluids (containing smaller proteins, cells and cellular debris) from the interstitial space to systemic veins.

Anatomy of the Vascular System

Arteries and Arterioles
Arteries are thick-walled structures that carry blood from the heart to the tissues. The aorta, which has a diameter of

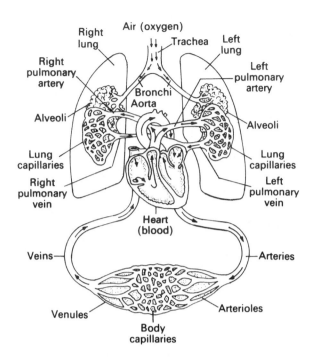

Figure 9.1 Schematic drawing of systemic circulation. (Start at bottom of diagram.) Loaded with carbon dioxide, blood from the body capillaries goes through venules and veins into the right chamber of the heart. It is pumped into the two lungs. Having dropped carbon dioxide and picked up oxygen, it goes back to the left chamber of the heart. From there it is pumped through the aorta into the body circulation (arteries and arterioles) until it reaches the body capillaries, where it gives up oxygen and picks up carbon dioxide. (National Tuberculosis and Respiratory Disease Association.)

approximately 25 mm, gives rise to numerous branches, which in turn divide into smaller vessels that approach 4 mm in diameter by the time they reach the tissues. Within the tissues, the vessels divide further, diminishing to approximately 30 microns in diameter; these vessels are called arterioles.

The walls of the arteries and arterioles are divided into three layers: an inner endothelial cell layer called the tunica intima, which is in contact with the blood; a middle layer called the tunica media; and an outer layer called the tunica adventitia. The intima provides a smooth surface for contact with the flowing blood. The adventitia is a layer of connective tissue that anchors the vessel to its surrounding structures. The media makes up the major portion of the vessel wall. In the aorta and other large arteries of the body, this layer is composed chiefly of elastic and connective tissue fibres that give the vessels considerable strength, allowing them to constrict and dilate for the purpose of accommodating stroke volume and maintaining an even, steady flow of blood. There is much

less elastic tissue in the smaller arteries and arterioles, and the media in these vessels is composed primarily of smooth muscle. Smooth muscle, by contraction and relaxation, controls vessel diameter. Chemical, hormonal and nervous system factors influence the activity of smooth muscle. Because arterioles can alter their diameter, thereby offering resistance to blood flow, they are often referred to as resistance vessels. Arterioles regulate the volume and pressure in the arterial system and the blood flow to the capillaries.

Because of the large amount of muscle, the wall of the arteries is relatively thick; it accounts for approximately 25 per cent of the total diameter of arterioles. The muscle and adventitia of the arterial wall have their own blood supplies to meet metabolic requirements. The blood vessels that supply the wall are the vasa vasorum. The intima is thin and is in such close contact with the blood within the vessel that it can receive its nourishment directly from that source.

Capillaries

Capillary wall lacks muscle and adventitia and are composed of a single layer of cells. This thin-walled structure permits rapid and efficient transport of nutrients to the cells and the removal of metabolic wastes. The diameter of capillaries ranges from 5 to 10 microns, so red blood cells must alter their shape to pass through these vessels.

The distribution of capillaries throughout the tissues varies with the type of tissue. For example, skeletal tissue, which is metabolically active, has a more dense capillary network than does less active tissue such as cartilage.

Veins and Venules

Capillaries join together to form larger vessels called venules, which in turn join to form the veins. The venous system is therefore structurally analogous to the arterial system. Venules correspond to arterioles, veins to arteries and the vena cava to the aorta. Analogous types of vessels in the arterial and venous systems have approximately the same diameter.

The walls of the veins, in contrast to those of the arteries are thinner and considerably less muscular. The wall of the average vein amounts to only 10 per cent of the vein diameter, in contrast to 25 per cent in the artery. The wall of a vein, like that of an artery is composed of three layers.

The thin, less muscular structure of the vein wall allows greater distensibility of these vessels. Greater distensibility permits the 'storage' of large volumes of blood in the veins under low pressure. For this reason, veins are referred to as capacitance vessels. Approximately 75 per cent of the total blood volume is contained in the veins. The sympathetic nervous system, which innervates the vein musculature, can stimulate venoconstriction, thereby reducing venous volume and increasing the general circulating blood volume.

Some veins, unlike arteries, are equipped with valves.

In general, veins that transport blood against the force of gravity, as in the lower extremities, have one-way valves that prevent the distal reflux of blood as it is propelled toward the heart. Valves are composed of endothelial leaflets, the competency of which depends on the integrity of the vein wall.

Lymphatic System

See page 386 for anatomy.

Circulatory Needs of Tissues

The amount of blood flow needed by body tissues is constantly changing. The percentage of the cardiac output received by individual organs or tissues is determined by the metabolic needs of the cells and the function of the tissues. An integrated and co-ordinated system of regulation is necessary so that blood flow to individual areas is maintained in proportion to the needs of that area. This regulatory mechanism is complex and consists of central nervous system influences, circulating hormones and chemicals and independent activity of the arterial wall itself.

Sympathetic nervous system activity, mediated by the hypothalamus, is the most important factor in regulating the calibre, and thus the blood flow, of peripheral blood vessels. Arteries are relatively abundantly innervated by the sympathetic nervous system. Stimulation of the sympathetic nerves causes vasoconstriction. The neurotransmitter responsible for sympathetic vasoconstriction is noradrenaline. Sympathetic activation occurs in response to a number of physiological and psychological stressors. Removal of sympathetic activity, as by drugs or sympathectomy, will result in vasodilation.

Other hormonal substances also affect peripheral vascular resistance. Adrenaline released from the adrenal medulla, acts like noradrenaline in constricting peripheral blood vessels. Angiotensin, a substance formed from the interaction of renin (synthesized in the kidney) and a circulating serum protein, stimulates arterial constriction. Although the blood concentration of angiotensin is usually small, its vasoconstrictor effects become important in certain pathophysiological states, such as congestive heart failure and hypovolaemia.

Alterations in local blood flow are influenced by a number of circulating substances that have vasoactive properties. Potent vasodilator substances include histamine, bradykinin and certain muscle metabolites. A reduction in available oxygen and nutrients and changes in local pH also affect local blood flow. Serotonin, a substance liberated from platelets that aggregate at the site of vessel wall damage, constricts arterioles.

When metabolic requirements increase, blood vessels dilate to increase the flow of oxygen and nutrients to the tissues. When the metabolic needs decrease, vessels constrict and blood flow to the tissues decreases. Metabolic demands of tissues increase with physical activity or exercise, local heat application, fever and infection. Reduced metabolic requirements of tissues accompany rest or decreased physical activity, local cold application and the cooling of the body. Failure of the blood vessels to dilate in response to the need for increased blood flow will result in tissue ischaemia (deficient blood supply).

Blood Flow

Blood flow through the cardiovascular system always proceeds in the same direction: left heart to aorta, arteries, arterioles, capillaries, venules, veins, vena cavae and finally to the right heart. The reason for this unidirectional flow is that a pressure difference exists between the arterial and venous systems. Because arterial pressure (approximately 100 mmHg) is greater than venous pressure (approximately 4 mmHg) and fluid always flows from an area of high pressure to an area of low pressure, blood flows from the arterial to the venous system.

Although the pressure difference or gradient in the vascular system provides the impetus for propulsion of blood forward, a force opposing blood flow provided by the blood vessels also exists. This is termed resistance. The most important factor in the vascular system determining the resistance is the vessel radius. Small changes in the vessel radius will lead to large changes in resistance. The predominant site for change in the calibre of blood vessels and therefore resistance, are the arterioles.

Blood viscosity and vessel length, under normal conditions, do not change significantly. Therefore, these factors do not usually play an important role in blood flow. However, a large increase in haematocrit may increase blood viscosity and reduce capillary blood flow. In the majority of blood vessels, flow is laminar or streamlined, with the blood in the centre of the vessel moving slightly faster than the blood near the vessel walls. Laminar flow is normally silent. In some instances, particularly at vessel bifurcations, laminar flow becomes turbulent. Turbulent blood flow creates sounds that can be heard superficially with a stethoscope. The sound created by turbulent blood flow is called bruit. Turbulent blood flow may also occur when its velocity is high, with decreased blood viscosity, with greater than normal vessel diameter or when vessels have narrowed or constricted segments.

Blood Pressure

See page 316 for physiology and measurement.

Capillary Filtration and Reabsorption

Fluid exchange across the capillary wall is continuous. This fluid, which has the same composition as plasma but without the proteins, forms the interstitial fluid. The equilibrium between hydrostatic and osmotic forces of the blood and interstitium, as well as capillary permeability, govern the amount and direction of fluid movement across the capillary. Normally, the blood pressure (hydrostatic pressure) at the arterial end of the capillary is relatively high, compared with that at the venous end. This high pressure at the arterial end of the capillaries tends to drive fluid out of the capillaries and into the tissue. The plasma proteins in the capillaries exert an osmotic force (oncotic pressure) that tends to pull fluid back into the capillary from the tissue space, but this osmotic force cannot overcome the high hydrostatic pressure at the arterial end of the capillary. At the venous end of the capillary, however, the osmotic force predominates over the low hydrostatic pressure and there is a net reabsorption of fluid from the tissue space back into the capillary. Virtually all of the fluid that is filtered at the arterial end of the capillary bed is reabsorbed at the venous end. The excess filtered fluid enters the lymphatic circulation. These processes of filtration, reabsorption and lymph formation aid in the maintenance of tissue fluid volume and in the removal of tissue wastes and debris. Capillary permeability, under normal conditions, remains constant.

Under certain abnormal conditions, the fluid filtered out of the capillaries may greatly exceed the amounts reabsorbed and carried away by the lymphatics. This can result from damage to the capillary walls and their resulting increased permeability, obstruction of lymphatic drainage, elevation of venous pressure or decrease in plasma protein oncotic force. The accumulation of fluid that results from these processes is known as oedema.

Considerations for the Elderly Patient
The ageing process produces changes in the walls of the blood vessels that affect the transportation of oxygen and nutrients to the tissues. The intima thickens as a result of cellular proliferation and fibrosis. Elastin fibres of the media become calcified, thinned and fragmented and collagen accumulates in both the intima and the media. These changes cause stiffening of the vessels, resulting in increased peripheral resistance, impairment of blood flow and increased left ventricular workload.

ALTERED PHYSIOLOGY OF THE VASCULAR SYSTEM

Reduced blood flow through peripheral blood vessels characterizes all peripheral vascular disorders. The physiological effects of altered blood flow depend on the extent to which tissue demands for oxygen and nutrients exceed the flow of blood delivered to the tissues. If the tissue needs are high, even modestly reduced blood flow may be inadequate to maintain tissue integrity, and tissues become ischaemic and malnourished and will ultimately die if adequate blood flow is not restored.

Heart Failure
Left-sided heart failure causes an accumulation of blood in the lungs and a reduction in cardiac output, resulting in inadequate arterial blood flow to tissues. Right-sided heart failure causes systemic venous congestion and a reduction in peripheral perfusion.

Alterations in Blood Vessels
Intact, patent and responsive blood vessels are necessary for the adequate delivery of oxygen to tissues and the removal of metabolic wastes. Arteries can become obstructed by atherosclerotic plaque, thrombus or embolus. Damage and subsequent obstruction of arteries follow chemical or mechanical trauma, infections and inflammatory processes. Complete arterial obstruction is associated with a greater incidence of tissue necrosis (death) than is a partial obstruction. Sudden arterial occlusion causes profound and frequently irreversible tissue ischaemia and necrosis. When arterial occlusions develop gradually, the opportunity for the growth of new vessels (collateral circulation) to replace the occluded ones is greater.

A reduction in venous blood flow can be caused by obstruction of the vein by thrombosis, incompetent valves or a reduction in the effectiveness of the pumping action of surrounding muscles. Decrease in venous blood flow results in the formation of oedema (see capillary filtration and reabsorption). Oedematous tissues cannot receive adequate nutrition from the blood and consequently are more prone to breakdown or injury and infection.

DISORDERS OF THE ARTERIES

Arteriosclerosis and Atherosclerosis

Arteriosclerosis is the most common disorder of the arteries; it literally means 'hardening of the arteries'. It is a diffuse process characterized by fibromuscular or endothelial thickening of the walls of small arteries and arterioles. Atherosclerosis refers to a generalized process characterized by focal changes in the intima of arteries. These changes consist of the accumulation of lipids, calcium, blood components and fibrous tissue (atheroma or plaque). Although the pathological processes of arteriosclerosis and atherosclerosis differ, one rarely occurs without the other and thus the terms are often used interchangeably. Because atherosclerosis is a generalized disorder of the arteries, when it is present in the extremities it is usually present elsewhere in the body.

Altered Physiology and Aetiology
The most common and direct results of atherosclerosis in arteries include narrowing (stenosis) of the lumen, obstruction by thrombosis, aneurysm development and rupture. Its indirect results are malnutrition and subsequent fibrosis of the organs which the sclerotic arteries

supply. If reduction in blood supply is severe and permanent, tissue cells undergo ischaemic necrosis and are replaced by fibrous tissue, which requires much less nutrition.

Atherosclerosis primarily affects the main arteries throughout the entire arterial tree in varying degrees, usually in a patchy manner. Branch arteries are usually affected only at their bifurcation.

There have been many theories to explain why and how atherosclerosis develops. No single theory has been proven and it may be that there is no single cause or mechanism for the development of atherosclerosis but rather that multiple processes are involved.

Morphologically, atherosclerotic lesions are of three types: fatty streaks, fibrous plaque and complicated lesions. Fatty streaks are yellow and smooth, protrude slightly into the arterial lumen and are composed primarily of cholesterol. They have been found in the arteries of all age groups, including infants. It is not clear whether fatty streaks predispose to the formation of fibrous plaques nor if they are reversible. They do not usually cause clinical symptoms.

The fibrous plaque characteristic of atherosclerosis is composed of smooth muscle cells, collagen fibres, plasma components and lipids. It is yellowish grey and protrudes in varying degrees into the arterial lumen, at times completely obstructing it. This plaque is believed to be irreversible.

The complicated atherosclerotic lesion is almost always associated with complete occlusion of the artery with subsequent ischaemia or infarction of the organ served by the involved vessel. In this lesion, fibrous plaque becomes calcified and ruptures with haemorrhage into the plaque or thrombosis development (Figure 9.2).

Gradual narrowing of the arterial lumen as the disorder progresses stimulates the formation of collateral circulation (Figure 9.3). While this natural vascular 'bypass' allows continued perfusion to the tissues beyond the arterial obstruction, it is often inadequate to meet imposed metabolic demands and ischaemia results.

Risk Factors

Many factors are associated with the development of atherosclerosis. While not completely clear whether modification of these risk factors will prevent the development of cardiovascular disease, there is evidence that it may slow the disease process. Genetically determined risk factors such as familial hyperlipidaemia are unavoidable; however, it is believed that they can be influenced by alteration of other risk factors and thereby be modified indirectly.

As indicated in Chapter 7, a diet high in fat has been strongly implicated in the causation of atherosclerosis. Approximately 42 per cent of the calories we ingest are derived from fats. Fats are classified according to their chemical structure. Saturated fats include fats of animal origin and solid vegetable fat. The intake of saturated fats is positively correlated with the elevation of serum

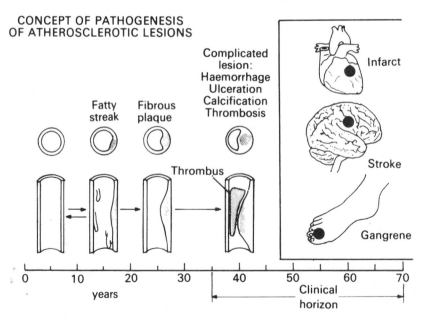

Figure 9.2 Schematic concept of the progression of atherosclerosis. Fatty streaks constitute one of the earliest lesions of atherosclerosis. Many fatty streaks regress, whereas others progress to fibrous plaques and eventually to atheromata. These may then become complicated by haemorrhage, ulceration, calcification or thrombosis and may produce myocardial infarction. (Adapted from Hurst, J. W. and Logue, R. B. *The Heart*, McGraw-Hill, New York.)

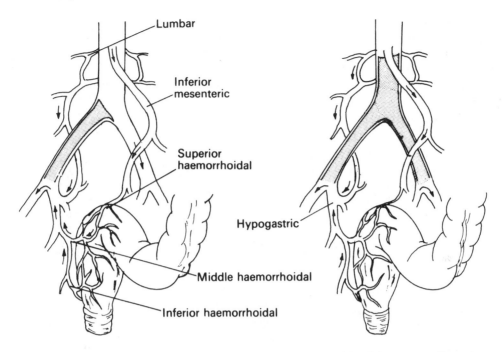

Figure 9.3 Development of collateral channels in response to occlusion of the right common iliac artery and the terminal aortic bifurcation.

cholesterol and triglycerides and with the development of atherosclerotic cardiovascular disease. Serum triglycerides are also elevated in diets high in refined carbohydrates (sugar). On the other hand, unsaturated fats such as corn oil, sunflower oil and the fats in fish, may be capable of reducing blood cholesterol and triglyceride levels. In 1983 the National Advisory Committee on Nutrition Education (NACNE) recommended that fat intake should comprise, on average, 30 per cent of our total energy intake and that saturated fat intake should comprise, on average, 10 per cent of our total energy intake (James, 1983). The committee made no recommendation about lowering cholesterol level.

Certain drugs are now being used to reduce blood lipid levels in conjunction with dietary modification. Among these are cholestyramine, nicotinic acid and clofibrate. Close observation of patients on long-term medication is required.

Smoking is another risk factor as it causes vasoconstriction by stimulating the sympathetic nervous system. It also causes a reduction in the carrying capacity of haemoglobin as the combustion of one or more of the toxic substances in tobacco has a much greater affinity for the haemoglobin than oxygen. This therefore diminishes the systemic availability of oxygen to the tissues. Lastly, smoking encourages platelet aggregation, which predisposes the smoker to thrombus formation.

Other risk factors include sedentary lifestyle, emotional stress and obesity. Lack of exercise does not promote circulation, stressful situations cause the release

large quantities of noradrenaline and adrenaline, which are thought to cause fatty acids to be mobilized from the fat stores.

The presence of hypertension or diabetes mellitus seems to accelerate the atherosclerotic process. Factors such as caffeine and alcohol may contribute in a minor way to the development of the disorder.

It is clear that the greater the number of risk factors, the greater the likelihood of developing the disorder. Therefore, the elimination of combined risk factors should be strongly encouraged.

Clinical Features

The clinical signs and symptoms of the atherosclerotic process depend on the organ or tissue affected. Coronary atherosclerosis, angina pectoris and acute myocardial infarction are discussed in Chapter 7. Cerebrovascular disease, including transient ischaemic attacks and stroke, is discussed in Chapter 32. Atherosclerosis of the aorta including aneurysm and atherosclerotic lesions of the extremities are discussed below.

Peripheral Arterial Occlusive Disease

Arterial insufficiency of the extremities is usually found in individuals over the age of 50 years, most often men and predominantly in the lower extremities. The age of onset and severity are influenced by the type and number of atherosclerotic risk factors present. Obstructive lesions are confined predominantly to segments of the arterial system extending from the aorta, below the renal arteries to the popliteal artery (Figure 9.4).

Clinical Features

The hallmark and only symptom of peripheral arterial insufficiency is intermittent claudication, that is, pain or discomfort in the lower extremities (buttock, hip, thigh, calf, arch of foot) occurring with exercise and terminating with rest. The site of arterial disease can be deduced from the location of claudication, for example, calf pain may accompany reduced blood flow through the superficial femoral artery, while pain in the thigh may result from obstruction in the pelvic arteries. The pain is insidious in onset and is produced by muscle hypoxia and the accumulation of metabolites. The pain may be described as aching, cramping, tiredness or weakness. One of the diagnostic features of intermittent claudication is that the amount of activity that produces claudication on one occasion will produce it again on repeated occasions.

The progression of vascular disease can be monitored by documenting the amount of exercise that can be tolerated or the distance a patient can walk before pain occurs. As the disorder progresses, this distance will become less and less until the pain is felt even at rest. Rest pain is indicative of a severe obstruction to blood flow. The pain is

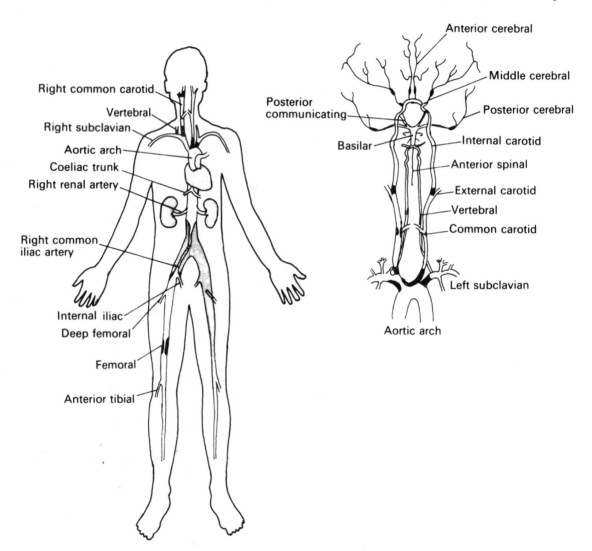

Figure 9.4 Common sites of atherosclerotic obstruction in major arterial systems of the body. (Lefthand figure redrawn from Crawford, E. S. and DeBakey, M. E., Surgical treatment of occlusive cerebrovascular disease, *Mod. Treat.*, Vol. 2, p. 36. Righthand figure from Beeson, P. B. and McDermott, W., *Textbook of Medicine*, W. B. Saunders, Philadelphia.)

persistent, aching or boring. Elevation or horizontal placement of the extremity will aggravate the pain, while dependency of the extremity will reduce the pain. Some patients sleep with the affected leg hanging over the side of the bed in an attempt to relieve the pain.

A feeling of coldness or numbness in the extremities may accompany intermittent claudication and is a result of the reduced arterial flow. Upon examination, the extremities may be cool and exhibit pallor on elevation or a ruddy cyanotic colour with dependency. The skin of the

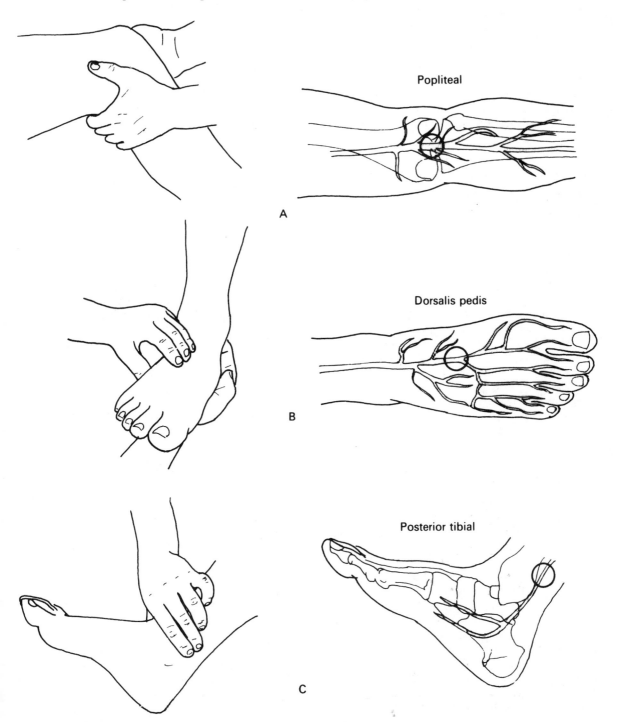

Popliteal

A

Dorsalis pedis

B

Posterior tibial

C

Figure 9.5 Assessing peripheral pulses. (A) Popliteal pulse. (B) Pedal pulse. (C) Posterior tibial pulse.

lower limbs becomes dry and scaly, there is muscle wasting, hair loss and thickened ridged nails, due to the decreased nutritional and oxygen supply to the tissues.

Ulcerations and gangrene may also be evident. Gangrene occurs when the blood supply to the limb is so poor that even the viability of the skin cannot be maintained. The skin indicates areas of impending death by changes in its colour and texture, i.e. dead white, to grey/blue, to mottled bluish purple.

Bruits may be auscultated with a stethoscope (a bruit is the sound produced by turbulent flow of blood through an irregular, stenotic lumen or through a dilated (aneurysm) segment of the vessel). Peripheral pulses may be diminished or absent (Figure 9.5).

Nursing Care of the Patient With Peripheral Vascular Insufficiency

From these clinical features, the following patient problems can be identified:

1. Alteration in peripheral tissue perfusion related to compromised circulation.
2. Pain related to impaired ability of peripheral vessels to supply tissues with oxygen.
3. Potential impairment of skin integrity related to compromised circulation.
4. Lack of knowledge regarding the disorder and how patients can actively help themselves. The care of the patient is aimed at increasing the arterial blood supply to the extremities, promoting vasodilation and preventing vasoconstriction, relief of pain, attainment or maintenance of tissue integrity and the education of patients regarding their disorder.

Increase in Arterial Blood Supply to the Extremities

Arterial blood supply to the lower extremities can be enhanced by elevating the head of the bed by 15 cm or allowing the patient to assume a sitting position with the feet resting on the floor. Walking or other moderate or graded exercises may be recommended to promote blood flow by muscular exercise and thus encourage the development of collateral circulation. To protect the feet, walking on uneven ground should be avoided. Pain can serve as a guide in determining the amount of exercise a person should engage in. Patients are advised to exercise within the limits of their claudication as the onset of pain indicates that tissues are not receiving adequate oxygen, so the patient should rest before continuing activity. Active postural exercises, such as the Buerger-Allen exercises, may be prescribed for some patients. The routine involves placing the extremities in three positions: elevation, dependency and then at the horizontal position. The

frequency of these exercises will vary between patients. Pain and dramatic colour changes indicate the need for termination of the exercise and rest. (See Figure 9.6 for more information.)

Not all patients with arterial insufficiency should exercise. Patients who have leg ulcers, rest pain, gangrene or acute thrombotic occlusions require bedrest as activity will worsen their disorder.

Promotion of Vasodilation and Prevention of Vasoconstriction

Arterial dilation increases blood flow to the extremities. However, in patients whose arteries are severely sclerosed, inelastic or damaged, dilation is impossible.

Warmth promotes arterial flow by preventing chilling and thus the vasoconstriction associated with exposure. Adequate clothing and warm environmental temperatures protect the patient from chilling. Direct heat should never be used on the extremities.

When heat is applied externally to an extremity, the demand for extra blood flow is increased. When heat is applied to an ischaemic limb, the demand for an increased blood supply cannot be met and damage to the tissue is increased in the form of burns or necrosis. The patient should be advised to avoid the extremes of hot and cold and be careful to bathe in warm water. Swimming in cold water and sunburn should be avoided.

Nicotine and other chemicals cause vasoconstriction, thereby reducing blood flow to the extremities. They also reduce the oxygen-carrying capacity of the haemoglobin and encourage platelet aggregation. Patients with arterial insufficiency who smoke must be fully informed of the circulatory conseqences of this habit (which could eventually lead to limb amputation), and be encouraged to stop smoking completely. Emotional upsets stimulate the sympathetic nervous system, which results in vasoconstriction. Although emotional stress is unavoidable, emotionally charged situations should be avoided. Advice in stress reduction techniques should be offered.

Constricting clothing such as girdles, garters and belts should be avoided as these will impede circulation to the extremities. Leg crossing should be discouraged because it compresses vessels in the legs.

Relief of Pain

Frequently, the pain associated with arterial insufficiency is chronic and continuous. It limits activities, affects work and responsibilities, disturbs sleep and alters one's sense of wellbeing and optimism. Because of this, patients are often depressed and irritable. As the patient's pain may be of a chronic, severe and unremitting type, the choice of analgesia is important. The use of addictive drugs should be restricted to the immediate pre- and postoperative periods.

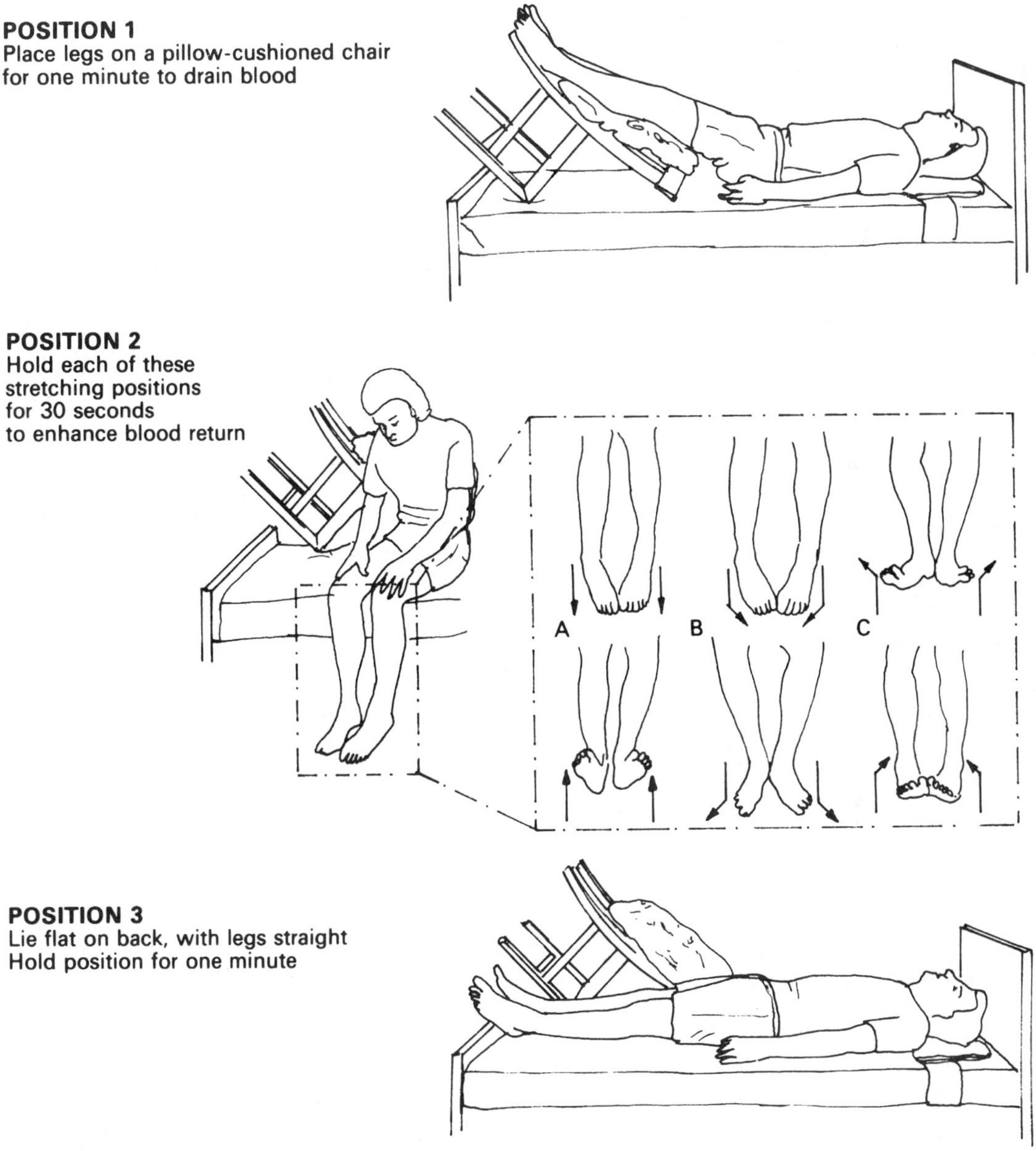

POSITION 1
Place legs on a pillow-cushioned chair
for one minute to drain blood

POSITION 2
Hold each of these
stretching positions
for 30 seconds
to enhance blood return

A   B   C

POSITION 3
Lie flat on back, with legs straight
Hold position for one minute

Figure 9.6 Buerger-Allen exercises. Do exercise series six times, four times a day. (Forshee, T. and Minckley, B. (1976) Lumbar sympathectomy, *RN*, July, Vol. 39, No. 2.)

Maintenance of Tissue Integrity

Poorly nourished tissues are more susceptible to damage and bacterial invasion. When lesions develop, healing may be delayed or inhibited due to the poor blood supply to the area. Infected, nonhealing ulcerations of the extremities can be extremely debilitating and can require prolonged hospitalization and treatments. Amputation of the extremity may eventually be necessary. Thus measures to prevent these complications should be of high priority and vigorously implemented. Trauma to the extremities should be avoided. Sturdy, well-fitting shoes or slippers will prevent foot injuries and blisters. Shoes should have adequate toe room, have a good arch support and feel comfortable. Seamed stockings should be avoided. The use of neutral soaps and body lotions such as lanolin or arachis oil prevents drying and cracking of the skin. Scratching and vigorous rubbing can abrade the skin and create a site for bacterial invasion. The use of talcum powder to the legs should be discouraged as this serves to dry the skin and mask the true colour of the extremity. Toenails should be cut by a chiropodist.

Protective padding over corns and callouses will prevent breakdown and alleviate pressure. All signs of blisters, ingrown toenails, infection or other problems should be reported to the doctor. People with diminished vision may require assistance in periodically examining the lower extremities for trauma. The elderly with problems of mobility may be helped by placing a mirror on the floor and examining their feet in this way.

Patients should be advised not to use any medication on the feet or legs unless it has been prescribed by the doctor. Good nutrition will promote healing and prevent tissue breakdown. Vitamins B and C and adequate protein are necessary.

Obesity strains the heart, increases venous congestion and reduces circulation. A diet low in lipids may be prescribed for patients with atherosclerosis.

Patient Education

It is important that the patient has an understanding of the disorder as, without it, compliance to changes in lifestyle will prove to be more difficult. The patient should be helped to accept the chronic nature of the disorder. Family and friends should be involved in these discussions as they can be of immense support to the patient.

The management of the disorder and the reasons why adherence to advice is so important, should be disclosed to the patient, the family and close friends. Care of the feet and legs is of prime importance in the prevention of trauma, ulceration and gangrene. (See Nursing Care Plan 9.1 for the patient with peripheral vascular disease.)

► NURSING CARE PLAN 9.1: THE PATIENT WITH PERIPHERAL VASCULAR DISEASE

Mr Patrick Riley is a 65-year-old retired policeman. Born in Northern Ireland, he has lived in England for the past 30 years. He lives with his wife in a bungalow, is a regular church attender (Church of England) and they have no children. Mr Riley smokes 20 cigarettes a day.

Patient's problems	Expected outcomes	Nursing care	Rationale
1. Alteration in peripheral tissue perfusion related to compromised circulation	Increase in arterial blood supply to extremities resulting in warmer extremities, improved colour and less muscle pain Able to perform exercises four times a day or as tolerated	1a. Elevate head of bed by 15 cm b. Encourage moderate amount of walking or graded leg exercises within limits of pain c. Encourage active postural exercises (Buerger-Allen exercises: see Figure 9.6)	Dependency of lower limbs enhances arterial blood supply Muscular exercise promotes blood flow and the development of collateral circulation With postural exercises, gravity alternatively fills and empties the blood vessels
2. Risk of vasoconstriction	Promotion of vasodilatation and prevention of vasoconstriction	2a. Maintain warm temperature and avoid chilling b. Discourage Mr Riley from smoking c. Assist Mr Riley in ways to avoid emotional stress d. Encourage Mr Riley to avoid wearing constrictive clothing e. Encourage Mr Riley to avoid crossing his legs	Warmth promotes arterial flow by preventing vasoconstriction effects of chilling Nicotine causes vasospasm, which impedes peripheral circulation Emotional stress causes peripheral vasoconstriction by stimulating sympathetic nervous system Constrictive clothing impedes circulation and promotes venous stasis Leg crossing causes compression of vessels with subsequuent impediment of circulation
3. Chronic continuous pain related to impaired ability of peripheral vessels to supply tissue with oxygen	Relief of pain	3a. Promote increased circulation	Enhancement of peripheral circulation increases the oxygen supplied to the muscle and decreases the accumulation of metabolites that cause muscle spasm

► NURSING CARE PLAN 9.1: THE PATIENT WITH PERIPHERAL VASCULAR DISEASE

Patient's problems	Expected outcomes	Nursing care	Rationale
		b. Administer analgesics as prescribed, with appropriate nursing considerations; evaluate its effectiveness	Analgesics help to reduce pain and allow Mr Riley to participate in activities and exercises that promote circulation
4. Potential impairment of skin integrity related to compromised circulation	Attainment or maintenance of tissue integrity	4a. Advise in ways to avoid trauma to extremities; use sheepskin bed cradle or heel protectors, as appropriate; avoid using tape of any kind on Mr Riley's skin	Poorly nourished tissues are susceptible to trauma and bacterial invasion; healing of wounds is delayed or inhibited due to poor tissue perfusion
		b. Inspect skin daily for evidence of traumatic injury; monitor temperature for signs of infection	
		c. Encourage Mr Riley to wear well-fitting shoes	Well-fitting shoes prevent foot injuries and blisters
		d. Encourage meticulous hygiene; bathing with neutral soaps, applying lotions	Neutral soaps and lotions prevent drying and cracking of skin
		e. Organize chiropodist to attend to Mr Riley's nails	Prevents injury to skin due to inexperience
		f. Avoid scratching or vigourously rubbing Mr Riley's skin	Scratching and rubbing can cause skin abrasions and bacterial invasion
		g. Promote good nutrition: adequate intake of vitamins B and C and protein; control obesity	Good nutrition promotes healing and prevents tissue breakdown; obesity strains the heart, increases venous congestion and reduces circulation
5. Lack of knowledge regarding his disorder	Increase Mr Riley's and his family's understanding of the disorder	5a. Explain his disorder in basic terms	Knowledge enhances compliance to necessary changes in lifestyle
		b. Explain the rationale for planned care at a level of their understanding	
		c. Provide written advice about foot and leg care	Assists the retention of information
		d. Give advice on how and why Mr Riley should stop smoking; give encouragement to do so	Helps Mr Riley to reduce/stop smoking; impress upon him the dangers of smoking to his health and circulation

Diagnosis of Arterial Occlusive Disease

The presence, location and extent of arterial occlusive disease are determined by a careful history of the patient's signs and symptoms and physical examination. Observation of the peripheral pulses is an important part of the examination and should include the femoral, popliteal, posterior tibial and pedal pulses (Figure 9.5). Inequality of pulses between extremities or the absence of a normally palpable pulse may be a sign of occlusion. The femoral pulse in the groin and the posterior tibial pulse behind the lateral malleolus are most easily found. The popliteal pulse is sometimes difficult to palpate behind the knee of an obese patient and the pedal artery varies in location on the dorsum of the foot. The colour and temperature of the extremity should be noted. The nails may be thickened and opaque, the skin shiny, atrophic, dry and has sparse hair growth. A comparative assessment is made of the two extremities.

To determine the qualitative and quantitative aspects of the problem, Doppler ultrasonic flow studies can be performed. The Doppler is an ultrasonic probe that detects blood flow, even at times when pulses are not palpable (Figure 9.7). Angiography may be used to confirm the diagnosis of arterial occlusive disease if surgery is contemplated. The procedure involves the injection of contrast medium directly into the vascular system and visualization of the vessels as the radio-opaque material flows through them. In this manner, the location of vascu-

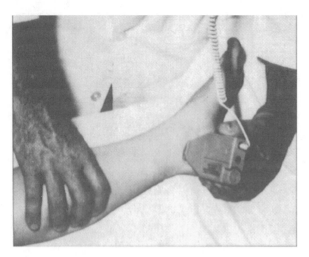

Figure 9.7 Doppler ultrasound transducer being used in screening for major deep-vein thrombosis. (Brunner, L. S. and Suddarth, D. S. (1986) *The Lippincott Manual of Nursing Practice* (4th edition), J. B. Lippincott, Philadelphia.)

lar obstructions or aneurysms and the presence of collateral circulation can be demonstrated. It is from the result of the angiogram that proposed surgery is planned. If there is inadequate 'run off' or collateral circulation, then bypass surgery or endarterectomy may not be suitable. It may be that amputation is the only option. Of all leg amputations performed, 84 per cent are as a result of arterial disease (Roberts, 1988b, p. 51). For the care of patients undergoing amputation see Chapter 36.

Usually, patients experience a temporary feeling of warmth as the contrast medium is injected. Infrequently, a patient may have an allergic response to the iodine contained in the contrast medium. This reaction may appear immediately after the injection or may be delayed. Symptoms may include dyspnoea, nausea and vomiting, sweating, tachycardia and numbness of the extremities. Any such reaction should be reported at once. Treatment may include the administration of adrenaline, antihistamines or steroids. Other complications include the risks of vessel injury, haemorrhage and/or formation of haematoma around the injection site and possibly stroke from thrombosis or distal occlusion of limb. Nursing care of a patient following Angiography involves planning and implementing care to allow prompt recognition of any of these potential complications.

Care of Patients With Peripheral Vascular Insufficiency

Patients are advised to exercise within the limits of their claudication, reduce weight where appropriate and to stop smoking. This regime can improve their activity limitations. In some instances, sympathectomy may be beneficial to improve collateral circulation in patients with intermittent claudication. Sympathectomy can also be useful in increasing the blood supply to the skin and therefore of benefit to patients with arterial skin ulceration. (See leg ulcers, page 415.)

Excision of the appropriate sympathetic ganglia will release arteriolar constriction and improve peripheral blood flow. Recently phenol has been used rather than subjecting the patient to an operation and a general anaesthetic. The phenol is injected, under radiological control, into the appropriate level of the lumbar sympathetic chain where it destroys the sympathetic ganglia. This too achieves vasodilation and has the added advantage of having less potential complications than those associated with general anaesthesia and abdominal surgery. It is also less costly; instead of spending five days in hospital following lumbar sympathectomy, patients who have had this phenol sympathectomy may go home the following day.

For patients who have a localized occlusion of less than 6 cm in length, a relatively new technique called percutaneous transluminal angioplasty of the arteries in the lower extremities is gaining acceptance as an alternative to vascular surgery, especially for those patients who are considered to be at high risk for surgical complications. Under local anaesthesia a balloon catheter is used to dilate mechanically the affected area of the artery and remodel the stenotic segment. As surgery and general anaesthesia are not required, the risks of morbidity are reduced, as are the length and cost of hospitalization. The patient is prescribed a low dose of aspirin and dipyridamole daily, which should be taken for a minimum of six months after the procedure. These drugs inhibit platelet aggregation. If re-occlusion occurs, subsequent percutaneous transluminal angioplasties can be performed, or if that is not feasible, vascular surgery can be used to alleviate the obstruction.

For other patients, when intermittent claudication has become gravely disabling, vascular grafting or endarterectomy may be helpful. In the grafting procedure, either the diseased segment of the artery is removed and a synthetic graft inserted in its place, or the obstructed segment is left intact and instead 'bypassed' by the use of a graft. Material used for arterial bypass grafts may be synthetic (Dacron, Teflon) or the patient's own saphenous vein is used. When the saphenous vein is used, the surgeon has to reverse the vein to ensure that the valves do not obstruct the blood flow. When an endarterectomy is performed, the atheromatous obstruction is 'shelled out' through an incision into the artery. The artery is then sutured to restore vascular integrity. Sometimes directly closing the artery will cause narrowing, in which case the surgeon will elect to use a vein patch to close the artery, thus ensuring the lumen of the artery is not narrowed.

Postoperative Nursing Care

The primary aim in postoperative management of patients who have had these vascular procedures is to maintain adequate circulation through the arterial repair. Circulation checks which include observations of pulses, colour, temperature and sensation in the extremities, should be performed and recorded frequently. Abnormalities should be reported promptly. Disappearance of a pulse may indicate thrombotic occlusion of the graft, so the surgeon should be notified immediately. An adequate circulating blood volume should be established and maintained. Continuous monitoring of urine output, central venous pressure or arterial pressure, mental status and pulse rate and volume will permit early recognition and treatment of fluid imbalances. Leg crossing and prolonged extremity dependency should be avoided in order to prevent thrombosis. Low-dose heparin may be given subcutaneously until the patient is fully mobile. Patients who have synthetic grafts may be discharged on dipyridamole and aspirin. All patients should be given discharge advice regarding looking after their skin, feet, adherence to any prescribed medication or diet and to stop smoking. Continuation of smoking increases the risk of occlusion of vascular grafts (Campbell, 1982, p. 478).

Thromboangiitis Obliterans (Buerger's Disease)

Buerger's disease is characterized by recurring inflammation of the arteries and veins of the lower and upper extremities, resulting in thrombus formation and occlusion of the vessels. The disease begins in the small arteries and progresses to the larger vessels.

Aetiology and Clinical Features

Buerger's disease is uncommon and its cause unknown. It occurs most often in men between the ages of 20 and 35 years and has been reported in all races in many areas of the world. There is considerable evidence that heavy smoking is either an aetiological or aggravating factor, since stopping smoking has a most beneficial effect on the disease. Generally, the lower limbs are affected first, but arteries in the arms or viscera are also commonly involved. Superficial thrombophlebitis may be present.

Arteriography will confirm arterial occlusive disease. Pain is the outstanding symptom of Buerger's disease. The patient complains of cramp-like pain in the feet or legs after exercise (intermittent claudication), which is relieved by rest; often there is a considerable burning pain, which is aggravated by emotional disturbances, smoking or chilling. Rest pain in the digits, a feeling of coldness or a sensitivity to cold may be early symptoms. Paraesthesia may develop, and pulses may be diminished or absent.

As the disease progresses, definite redness or cyanosis of the part appears when it is in the dependent position. Colour changes may affect only one extremity, only certain digits or certain parts of a digit.

Medical Management

The treatment of Buerger's disease is essentially the same as that for atherosclerotic peripheral vascular disease. The main objectives are to improve circulation to the extremities, prevent the spread of the disease and protect the extremities from trauma and infection. The continuation of smoking is highly detrimental and therefore patients are strongly advised to stop smoking. Symptoms are often relieved by cessation of smoking. Sympathectomy may be useful in patients whose disease has not progressed to gangrene. It will produce vasodilation and thereby increase blood flow. If gangrene of a toe does develop and bypass surgery is not feasible, amputation will be necessary. The indications for amputation are worsening gangrene, especially if moist, severe rest pain or sepsis secondary to gangrene.

Aortic Diseases

The aorta is the main trunk of the arterial system and is divided into the ascending aorta, the aortic arch and the descending aorta. The entire aorta is designated as thoracic above the diaphragm and abdominal below the diaphragm.

Aortic Aneurysms

Classification of Aneurysms

An aneurysm is a localized sac or dilation of an artery, formed at a weak point in the vessel wall (Figure 9.8). Very small aneurysms due to infection are designated mycotic aneurysms. An aneurysm that is somewhat larger but still limited in extent, projecting from one side of the vessel only, is called a saccular aneurysm. If an entire arterial segment becomes dilated, a fusiform aneurysm develops. Aneurysms are serious because rupture is always possible and can lead to haemorrhage and death.

Aneurysm of the Thoracic Aorta

As the most common cause of aneurysm of the thoracic aorta is atherosclerosis, they occur mostly in men over the age of 60. The thoracic area is the most common site for the development of a dissecting aneurysm (Harper, 1989, p. 1665). Dissecting aneurysms are often fatal, with death resulting from rupture (Horton, 1980, p. 74).

Clinical Features

Symptoms are variable and depend on how rapidly the aneurysm dilates and how the pulsating mass affects the surrounding intrathoracic structures. Most are asymptomatic. In most cases pain is the most prominent symptom. It is usually constant and boring in nature, and may be perceived only when the person is lying down. Other conspicuous symptoms are dyspnoea, the result of the pressure of the aneurysm sac against the trachea, a main bronchus or the lung itself; cough, frequently paroxysmal;

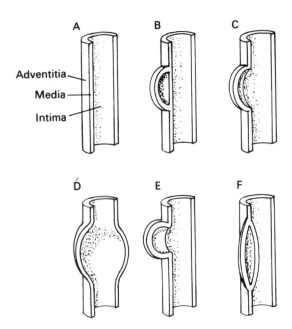

Figure 9.8 Characteristics of arterial aneurysm. (A) Normal artery. (B) False aneurysm—actually a pulsating haematoma. The clot and connective tissue are outside the arterial wall. (C) True aneurysm. One, two or all three layers may be involved. (D) Fusiform aneurysm—symmetrical, spindle-shaped expansion of entire circumference of involved vessel. (E) Saccular aneurysm—a bulbous protrusion of one side of the arterial wall. (F) Dissecting aneurysm—this usually is a haematoma that splits the layers of the arterial wall.

hoarseness, stridor or complete aphonia due to pressure against the laryngeal nerve; and dysphagia due to impingement on the oesophagus.

When large veins in the chest are compressed by the aneurysm, there is often evidence of dilated superficial veins on the chest, neck or arms; oedematous areas on the chest wall; and cyanosis. The process of dissection leads to shearing and occlusion of the arteries branching from the aorta in the area involved by the process. The tear occurs most commonly in the region of the aortic arch. The dissection of the aorta may progress backwards in the direction of the heart, obstructing the opening to the coronary arteries or producing a haemopericardium (effusion of blood into the pericardial sac), or aortic insufficiency, or it may extend in the opposite direction, causing occlusion of the arteries supplying the gastrointestinal tract, the kidneys, the spinal cord and even the legs.

The onset of symptoms is usually sudden. Severe and persistent pain, described as 'tearing' or 'ripping' may be reported in the anterior chest or below the scapulae. Patients may manifest pallor, sweating, tachycardia and hypotension.

Diagnosis

Diagnosis of a thoracic aneurysm is principally by chest radiography. Aortography allows the precise location of the aneurysm to be established.

Medical Management

Whether medical (conservative) or surgical management is selected depends on the type of aneurysm present. Medical management involves strict control of arterial blood pressure with an aim to prevent the extension of the aneurysm. Beta blockers and/or vasodilators are used to achieve a systolic blood pressure in the region of 100 to 120 mmHg. Surgery involves the removal of the aneurysm and restoring vascular continuity using a vascular graft. This operation often involves cardiopulmonary bypass, and therefore the patient is nursed in an intensive care area.

Abdominal Aortic Aneurysm

The most common cause of abdominal aortic aneurysm is atherosclerosis. Approximately 3 per cent of the population over the age of 50 have aortic aneurysms. Recently, an increase in the incidence of abdominal aortic aneurysm has been observed (Fowkes, MacIntyre and Ruckley, 1989, p. 33). Most of these aneurysms occur below the renal arteries. Left untreated, the eventual outcome may be rupture and death.

Altered Physiology

The factor common to all aneurysms is damaged media within the vessel. This may be caused by congenital weakness, trauma or disease process. Once an aneurysm develops, the tendency is towards an increase in size.

Clinical Features

About two fifths of patients with abdominal aortic aneurysm have symptoms; the remainder are asymptomatic. Some patients complain that they can feel their heart beating in their abdomen when lying down. The most common symptom is abdominal pain, which may be persistent or intermittent, and is often localized in the middle or lower abdomen. The next most common symptom is lower back pain. This is a serious symptom that usually signifies rapid expansion or impending rupture of the aneurysm. Patients may complain of feeling an abdominal mass or abdominal throbbing. More than 50 per cent will exhibit hypertension. There may be evidence of vascular insufficiency to the legs.

Clinical Features of Ruptured Abdominal Aortic Aneurysm

Signs of a rupturing abdominal aortic aneurysm include constant intense back pain, shock, tachycardia, hypotension, sweating, pallor and rigid abdomen. Bruising of the skin on the abdomen, loins and perineal area is a late sign. Rupture into the peritoneal cavity is rapidly fatal. Retroperitoneal rupture has a better prognosis. The overall

and determination of renin levels may also be performed to identify patients with renovascular disorders. The presence of additional risk factors is sought and evaluated.

Assessment of the patient also involves careful monitoring of the blood pressure at frequent intervals. Blood pressure readings are taken in both arms to reveal any differences between them and the readings are taken with the patient in the supine, sitting and erect positions to reveal any postural changes in pressure. Patients who can sense when their blood pressure is elevated should be asked what symptoms create the awareness of such changes and what events or factors seem to precipitate the symptoms. A thorough assessment can yield valuable information about the extent of the effects of the hypertension throughout the body and any psychological factors related to the problem.

Medical Management

The expected outcome of treatment for hypertension is to lower the blood pressure to as close to normal levels as possible without introducing adverse effects. The type of treatment regime selected for individual patients is determined by the degree of hypertension, the complications present, the number and extent of risk factors and the availability of personal and physical resources for compliance to the treatment regime. In cases of mild hypertension, conservative medical management is considered to be the most beneficial approach. Patients are counselled and taught ways to change poor health habits. Dietary control of salt and cholesterol, weight reduction, a regular exercise programme, abstinence from tobacco and alcohol and stress management are addressed, and modifications are realistically planned with the patient. Research by Collins, Peto, MacMahon, *et al.* (1990, p. 827) shows that reducing slightly elevated diastolic pressure by five to six points reduces the risk of coronary heart disease by up to 25 per cent, and can reduce the risk of stroke by up to 40 per cent.

When the conservative approach is ineffective, drug therapy is usually necessary. The selection of the appropriate drug or combination of drugs is highly individualized. In the 'stepped care' approach, drugs are used which have potential for the greatest effectiveness with the fewest side-effects and the best chance of acceptance by the patient (Table 9.1). In an attempt to promote compliance, complicated drug therapy should be avoided. Table 9.2 describes the various pharmacological agents used in the treatment of hypertension.

► **NURSING PROCESS**
► **THE PATIENT WITH HYPERTENSION**

► *Assessment*

Assessment of the patient with hypertension involves careful monitoring of the blood pressure at frequent inter-

vals. Blood pressure readings are taken in both arms to reveal any differences between them, and the readings are taken with the patient lying down, sitting and standing to reveal postural changes in pressure. Readings are also taken after activity and after anxiety-producing situations to indicate if such events have a significant effect on the pressure. When the patient is placed on an antihypertensive drug therapy regime, blood pressure readings are imperative to demonstrate the effectiveness of the drugs and to reveal drops in pressure that would necessitate a change in the dosage of the drugs.

Physical examination also includes assessment of apical and peripheral pulses, their rate, rhythm and character, to detect effects of the hypertension on the heart and the peripheral vessels. The patient is questioned about symptoms that would be indicative of multisystem sequelae of hypertension, such as nosebleeds, anginal pain, shortness of breath, alterations in vision, vertigo, headaches or nocturia. The patient who can sense when the blood pressure is elevated should be asked what symptoms create the awareness of such changes, and what events or factors seem to precipitate the symptoms. A thorough assessment can yield valuable information about the extent of the effects of the hypertension throughout the body and any psychological factors related to the problem.

► *Patient's Problems*

Based on the assessment, the main problems for the patient with hypertension may include the following:

● Lack of knowledge about the relationship between the treatment regime and control of the disease process.
● Potential nonadherence to the self-care programme related to negative side-effects of prescribed therapy and an inability to believe that treatment is needed when symptoms are absent.

Table 9.1 *Stepped care approach to drug therapy*

Step	Drug regime
1	Begin with either low-dose thiazide diuretic or beta-blocker
2	If blood pressure is not controlled, thiazide diuretic and beta-blocker are prescribed together
3	If control of blood pressure is still not achieved, a vasodilator is added to the thiazide diuretic and beta-blocker

Calcium antagonists or angiotensin-converting enzyme (ACE) inhibitors may be used as an alternative to steps 1 or 2.

Steps 1 or 2 control blood pressure in 75 to 80 per cent of patients (Reid et al., 1985, p. 84).

Table 9.2 *Drugs used in the management of hypertension*

Purpose: To maintain blood pressure within normal ranges by the simplest and safest means possible with the fewest side-effects for each individual patient

Medication	Major action	Advantages	Contraindications	Side effects and nursing considerations
Diuretics				
Thiazide diuretics				
Bendrofluazide Chlorthalidone Hydrochlorothiazide	Decrease the kidney's ability to reabsorb sodium and water from the distal tubules. An increased urine output results. Depletion of extracellular fluid occurs. Directly affects vascular smooth muscle tone thereby reducing vessel resistance, helping to lower the blood pressure	Effective orally. Effective during long-term administration. Mild side-effects. Enhance other antihypertensive drugs	Gout; severely impaired kidney function	Dry mouth, thirst, weakness, drowsiness, lethargy, muscle aches, muscle fatigue, tachycardia, Gastrointestinal disturbance. Postural hypotension may be potentiated by dehydration, alcohol, barbituates or narcotics. Postural hypotension may be more profound in the elderly. Hypokalaemia may result and potassium supplements may be necessary. Long-term use can cause glucose intolerance as they inhibit the release of insulin from the pancreas; therefore, diabetic patients receiving these drugs should be monitored closely. Joint pains from an increase in blood urate may occur
Loop diuretics				
Frusemide Ethacrynic acid Bumetamide	Inhibit sodium and water reabsorption in the loop of Henle. Volume depletion	Rapid action. Potent diuretics. To be used only when thiazides fail to have the desired effect	As for thiazides	Volume depletion is rapid – profound diuresis. Electrolyte depletion – replacement is required. Thirst, nausea, vomiting, skin rash, postural hypotension. Again, postural hypotension often more profound in the elderly
Potassium-sparing diuretics				
Spironolactone Triamterene Amiloride	Aldosterone antagonist Act on the distal tubule to inhibit sodium reabsorption	Spironolartone is effective in treating hypertension accompanying primary aldosteronism. All cause retention of potassium	Renal disease; uraemia; severe hepatic disease	Drowsiness, lethargy, confusion, ataxia – may indicate hyperkalaemia requiring a decrease in dosage. Diarrhoea and other gastrointestinal symptoms – give drug after meals. Skin

Table 9.2 *Continued*

Medication	Major action	Advantages	Contraindications	Side effects and nursing considerations
				eruptions, urticaria. Spironolactone can cause gynaecomastia
Beta-adrenoceptor blocking drugs				
Propranolol Oxyprenolol	These block both beta-1 receptors in the heart and beta-2 receptors in the lungs. Called non-selective	Non-selective beta-blockers block the effect of sympathetic stimulation of beta-1 and beta-2 receptors, producing a slower heart rate and lowered blood pressure, but also produce bronchospasm and vasoconstriction	Bronchial asthma; allergic rhinitis; heart failure; cardiogenic shock. They should be used with caution in diabetic patients	Depression, insomnia, nightmares, hallucinations, lassitude, weakness and fatigue. Bradycardia, heart failure, gastrointesinal disturbances which can be reduced if the drug is ingested before meals. Non-cardioselective drugs should not be given to patients with asthma or peripheral vascular disease because of their bronchospasm and vasoconstrictive effects
Atenolol Metoprolol	These are cardioselective drugs in that they have a relatively selective action on the beta-1 receptors	Cardioselective drugs tend to block beta-1 sites rather than the beta-2 sites and so do not produce the un- desirable effects of bronchospasm and vasoconstriction. Reduces pulse rate in patients with tachycardia and blood pressure elevation		
Vasodilators				
Hydralazine hydrochloride	Acts directly on the smooth muscle of blood vessels causing dilatation, thus lowering peripheral resistance and blood pressure	Used as a third drug of choice when patient does not respond to simpler regimes	Porphyria	Headache, tachycardia, flushing and dyspnoea may occur. Peripheral oedema may require diuretics. May produce lupus erythematosus-like syndrome which requires immediate withdrawal of the drug
Minoxidil	Has a direct vasodilating action on arteriolar vessels leading to decreased resistance and lowering of blood pressure	Has a more profound hypertensive effect than hydralazine hydrochloride and is reserved for the treatment of severe hypertension which is resistant to other drugs	Phaeochromocytoma, porphyria	Tachycardia, oedema. Take blood pressure and apical pulse before administration; monitor fluid balance and daily weight

▶

Table 9.2 *Continued*

Medication	Major action	Advantages	Contraindications	Side effects and nursing considerations
Calcium channel blockers				
Nifedipine	Interferes with the action of intracellular calcium in smooth muscle producing vasodilatation in coronary and peripheral arteries	Reduces peripheral resistance, thereby lowering blood pressure	Cardiogenic shock, porphyria	Headache, flushing, oedema of ankles and fingers, lethargy
Verapamil	Decreases conduction in the atrioventricular node and myocardial contractility. Reduces peripheral resistance		Bradycardia, heart block, heart failure, porphyria. Should not be given with a beta-blocker	Gastrointestinal disturbances, headache. Intravenous administration may cause hypotension, therefore the patient should be in the supine position. Bradycardia, heart block and asystole may occur following intravenous administration
Angiotensin-converting enzyme (ACE) inhibitors				
Captopril Enalapril	Block the effect of angiotensin-converting enzyme, thus preventing the formation of angiotensin II	Useful in the treatment of severe hypertension, particularly when other regimes have failed. Especially effective when plasma renin levels are raised, as in renovascular hypertension	Pregnancy; porphyria	May cause sudden drop in blood pressure. For this reason, patients are usually admitted for 24 hours while commencing this drug. Diuretics are discontinued if possible before commencement. Careful monitoring required for 24 hours. Persistent dry cough, hyperkalaemia, skin rash, altered taste, oral problems, gastric irritation, proteinuria, agranulocytosis and neutropenia

▶ *Planning and Implementation*
▶ Expected Outcomes

The main expected outcomes are to ensure that the patient understands the disease process, its treatment and the importance of adhering to the treatment and advice given.

Nursing Care

As the therapeutic regime becomes the responsibility of the patient, if able, or of a significant other, both the patient and the home carers should have the following explained at a level of their understanding.

Patient Education to Avoid Progression of Vascular Changes

Salt Reduction. Patients should be given the rationale for their treatment. They should reduce their intake of salt not merely by avoiding adding it to food, but also by avoiding salty foods such as hamburgers and sausages, and by checking the amount of salt contained in canned and frozen foods. Some controversy exists about the value of moderate restrictions in salt intake, but some studies have shown this to be beneficial (Beevers and Wilkins, in O'Brien, O'Malley, Beevers, *et al.* (1987), p. 23).

Weight Reduction. Patients should reduce weight if

they are considered to be obese, as this can reduce blood pressure. Every attempt should be made to motivate obese patients to reduce weight so that it lies within the normal range for their height. On average, a weight reduction of 1 kg results in a 2 mmHg fall in systolic pressure and a 1 mmHg fall in diastolic pressure. Moreover, a weight reduction of 10 kg produces a fall in blood pressure equivalent to that obtained using an antihypertensive drug (Curzio, 1987, p. 37). Patients should be given dietary advice and an opportunity to consult a dietician. Some local health education groups have developed dietary advice booklets that incorporate a food diary and a low-calorie cookbook catering for local tastes (Curzio, 1987, p. 38).

Stress Reduction. Since stress causes an elevation in blood pressure, patients should be advised to avoid stress-producing events as much as possible and be given advice regarding relaxation techniques. It has been noted by Beevers and Wilkins (1987) that the effects of behavioural therapy can have beneficial effects on blood pressure. It has been shown that an eight-week course of behavioural therapy can 'produce a sustained fall in blood pressure for as long as a year' (p. 24). Exercise helps to reduce the feeling of stress in patients, as well as lowering their blood pressure and reducing weight. If medical staff have recommended exercise as part of treatment, then patients should be warned to begin exercising gently and then gradually build up. Walking, swimming and cycling are all useful forms of exercise for these patients.

Stopping Smoking. Smoking increases liver enzymes and therefore can affect the metabolism of some drugs. There is evidence to suggest that smokers respond less well than nonsmokers to antihypertensive drugs, particularly beta-blockers. In addition, smoking is an independent risk factor for vascular disease and is therefore discouraged (Beevers and Wilkins, 1987, p. 24). Information should be given about how to stop smoking, and a referral to a stop-smoking clinic may be appropriate.

Limiting Alcohol Intake. A daily alcohol intake of 80 g (equivalent to four pints of beer) causes a rise in blood pressure, especially in hypertensive patients. Patients should be advised to abstain or limit their alcohol intake to a maximum of two drinks a day (Beevers and Wilkins, in O'Brien *et al.* (1987), p. 23).

A small study was undertaken by Rhodes (1989) to assess whether hypertensive patients attending a health centre were given health education by medical and nursing staff about the control of their hypertension. The findings suggested that little or no information was given regarding the disease process, prescribed drugs and their side-effects, smoking, diet, exercise or stress reduction. Patients commented that they would have liked more information about relaxation, their medication, dietary consumption and hereditary factors relating to hypertension. The study suggests that medical and nursing staff need to improve their communication with patients and help them to express their fears and anxieties (p. 55).

Nursing staff should emphasize that the patient's blood pressure can almost always be controlled, but only if the patient complies with the treatment and advice given. This is an important point as the hypertensive patient often does not feel unwell; without symptoms, the impetus for compliance is reduced. It should be explained that even though such patients feel well, their blood pressure could still rise dangerously, and that how they feel is not a reliable indicator of how well they are doing (Feury and Nash, 1990). The importance of keeping follow-up appointments should therefore be stressed.

Regular follow-up care is imperative so that the disease process can be assessed in terms of control or progression and treated accordingly. Symptoms of progression of the disorder with involvement of other body systems must be detected early so that appropriate changes in the treatment regime can be made.

Compliance to Treatment Regime

Noncompliance to the therapeutic regime is a significant problem in people with hypertension. McMillan (1984) quotes research by Cooper, Love and Raffoul (1982) who found that 41 per cent of hypertensive patients had poor compliance. Active participation of patients in their treatment regime, attempts to establish a therapeutic rapport and encouragement to attend for regular follow-up does help.

A great deal of commitment is required from patients with hypertension to adhere to lifestyle, diet and activity restrictions, and to take regularly prescribed medication. The effort needed does not always seem reasonable, particularly when patients are symptom- free without medication but experience side-effects with the medication. Much supervision, education and encouragement are often needed with hypertensive people to arrive at an acceptable plan for living with their hypertension and the treatment regime. Compromises may have to be made on some aspects of the therapy in order to achieve success in higher priority areas.

A thorough understanding of the disease process of hypertension as well as the impact of medication and health habits on this process is important. The concept of hypertension control rather than cure is important to explain. The temporary nature of medication side-effects should be emphasized. Consultation with a dietician may be useful in exploring the number of possible ways to modify salt and fat intake. Lists of low-salt foods and beverages should be provided. Beverages containing caffeine should be avoided. Alcohol may have synergistic effects with the medications so the patient should be fully informed of this and encouraged to abstain from the use of alcohol. As nicotine causes vasoconstriction, the use of tobacco should be discouraged. Support groups for control of weight, smoking and stress may be beneficial for some patients. Others may need more support from family and friends.

Written information about the expected effects and side-effects of medication is very useful in maintaining a safe self-administration programme. When side-effects do occur, patients need to know when and whom to contact. In addition, patients should be advised of the possibility of rebound hypertension with sudden discontinuation of antihypertensive medication, and the possibility of sexual dysfunction related to the drugs.

Considerations for Elderly Patients

Adherence to the therapeutic regime is even more difficult for the elderly person than for the general population. Drug therapy can be a significant problem because it must be continuous and it may require numerous daily doses. Special care must be taken to ensure that the patient understands the drug regime, is able to read the instructions and open the medicine bottle(s), and provision is made for having prescriptions refilled as required. The elderly patient's family and friends should always be included in the teaching programme so that they can understand the patient's needs, support adherence to the therapeutic regime and know when to seek guidance from the health professionals.

The patient and home carers should be especially cautioned that hypertensive drug therapy may cause problems of hypotension, which should be reported immediately. Because of their impaired cardiovascular reflexes, the elderly are often more sensitive than are younger people to the volume depletion caused by diuretic therapy and by the sympathetic inhibition effect of beta-adrenoceptor antagonists. In an attempt to prevent any postural hypotension that may ensue, the patient should be very careful to change positions slowly and to use supportive aids if necessary to prevent falls that could result from dizziness and syncope.

▶ *Evaluation*
▶ **Expected Outcomes**

1. Patient exhibits no progression of vascular changes.
   a. Maintains blood pressure within acceptable range with diet or medication therapy.
   b. Gives no evidence of angina.
   c. Reveals no ECG changes indicative of left ventricular hypertrophy.
   d. Has normal serum urea and creatinine levels.
   e. Exhibits no progression of retinal pathology.
   f. Gives no evidence of cerebral infarction.
2. Patient adheres to therapeutic regime.
   a. Explains rationale for all aspects of therapeutic regime.
   b. Includes family and friends in decisions regarding changes in lifestyle necessitated by therapeutic regime.
   c. Adheres to dietary regime as prescribed: sodium, cholesterol and calorie reduction.
   d. Loses weight as prescribed.
   e. Becomes involved in a regular programme of exercise.
   f. Takes medication as prescribed.
   g. Reports side-effects of medication to doctor before altering or discontinuing medication.
   h. Abstains from tobacco, caffeine and alcohol.
   i. Uses available community resources for stress management and reduction.
   j. Explains rationale for continuance of therapeutic regime, even though symptom-free.
   k. Keeps follow-up clinic or doctor appointments.

Hypertensive Emergencies

Occasionally, acute, life-threatening elevations in blood pressure occur that require prompt treatment. Hypertensive emergencies frequently occur in patients whose hypertension has been poorly controlled or in whom medication has been abruptly discontinued. The degree of organ failure present because of the hypertension will determine the rapidity with which the blood pressure must be lowered. The presence of acute left ventricular failure or cerebral dysfunction indicates the need for immediate reduction in blood pressure over the next 24 to 48 hours.

The drugs of choice in hypertensive emergencies are those that have immediate effect. However, the aim of treatment is to reduce the diastolic pressure gradually over a number of hours, since too rapid a reduction in blood pressure can cause cerebrovascular accidents, blindness and myocardial infarctions. Usually, a safe reduction in blood pressure can be achieved by confining the patient to bed and administering oral antihypertensive agents such as beta-blockers or nifedipine. Sodium nitroprusside is the drug of choice if the patient has heart failure and an associated diastolic blood pressure over 140 mmHg.

There are only a few indications for intravenous use of antihypertensive drugs. These include situations where the patient has 'gross ventricular failure due to hypertension, encephalography with fits or fluctuating neurological signs and eclampsia with fits' (Beevers and Wilkins, 1987, p. 34). Drugs used in these situations include labetolol, sodium nitroprusside, diazoxide and hydralazine. These drugs are potentiated by diuretics. Extremely close monitoring of the patient's blood pressure and cardiovascular status is required during treatment with these medications. A rapid drop in blood pressure can occur and action must be taken immediately to prevent shock.

VEIN DISORDERS

Venous Thrombosis, Thrombophlebitis, Phlebothrombosis and Deep Vein Thrombosis

Altered Physiology and Aetiology

Although the exact aetiology of venous thrombosis remains unclear, three antecedent factors are believed to play a significant role in its development: stasis of blood, injury to the vessel wall and altered blood coagulation. The presence of at least two factors appear to be necessary for thrombosis to occur.

Venous stasis occurs when blood flow is retarded, such as with heart failure or shock; when veins are dilated, such as following drug therapy; and when skeletal muscle contraction is reduced, such as with immobility, extremity paralysis or anaesthesia. Bedrest has been shown to reduce blood flow in the legs by at least 50 per cent.

Disruption of the lining of blood vessels creates a site for clot formation. Direct vessel trauma, such as after a fracture or dislocation; disorders of the veins and chemical irritation of the vein from intravenous drugs or solutions can all damage veins.

Increased coagulability of blood occurs most commonly in patients who have been withdrawn abruptly from anticoagulant medications. Oral contraceptives and a number of blood dyscrasias can also lead to hypercoagulability.

Thrombophlebitis is inflammation of the walls of the veins with formation of a clot. When a clot develops initially in the veins without inflammation, the process is referred to as phlebothrombosis. Venous thrombosis can occur in any vein but is most frequent in the veins of the lower extremities. Both superficial and deep veins of the legs may be affected. Of the superficial veins, the saphenous vein is most frequently affected. Of the deep leg veins, the iliofemoral, popliteal and small calf veins are most often affected.

Venous thrombi are composed of an aggregate of platelets attached to the vein wall and a tail-like appendage containing fibrin, white blood cells and many red blood cells. The 'tail' can grow larger or propagate in the direction of blood flow as successive layering of the clot constituents occurs. The danger associated with a propagating venous thrombosis is that parts of a clot can become detached and produce an embolic occlusion of the pulmonary blood vessels. Fragmentation of the thrombus can occur spontaneously as the clot undergoes natural dissolution, or it can occur in association with an elevation in venous pressure, such as occurs with standing or muscular activity after prolonged inactivity. Other complications are described in Figure 9.11.

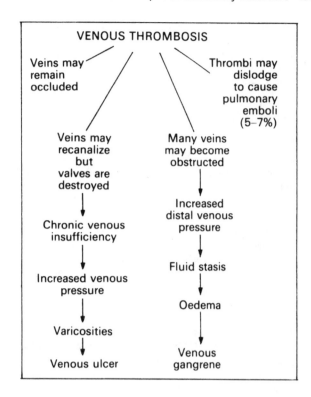

Figure 9.11 The seriousness of venous thrombosis is readily noted.

Clinical Features

At least one to two thirds of all patients with venous thrombosis of the lower extremities have no symptoms (Anonymous, 1989). In others, symptoms are variable and not usually specific for thrombophlebitis. However, despite this uncertainty, the presence of clinical signs should always be investigated further.

Obstruction of the deep veins of the legs produces oedema of the extremity because the outflow of venous blood is inhibited. The amount of swelling can be determined by measuring extremity circumference at various levels with a tape measure. One extremity is compared to the other at the same level for size differences. Bilateral swelling may be difficult to detect. The skin over the affected leg may become warmer and superficial veins may become more prominent. Tenderness, which usually occurs later, is produced by inflammation of the vein wall and can be detected by gentle palpitation of the extremity. Homan's sign, a pain in the calf following sharp dorsiflexion of the foot, is not specific for deep vein thrombosis because it can be elicited in any painful disorder of the calf. In some cases, signs of a pulmonary embolus are the first indication of a deep vein thrombosis.

Thrombosis of the superficial veins produces pain or tenderness, redness and warmth of the involved area. The risk of dislodgement and embolization of superficial venous thrombi is very low because the majority of them undergo spontaneous lysis; thus, this disorder can be treated at home with rest, extremity elevation, analgesics and possibly anti-inflammatory agents.

Prevention

Venous thrombosis, thrombophlebitis and deep vein thrombosis can often be prevented, especially if patients who are considered at high risk are identified and preventive measures are instituted without delay.

Elastic Compression Stockings

One approach to prophylaxis is the use of elastic compression stockings, which are usually prescribed for patients on a regime of restricted activity, particularly those who are confined to bed. These stockings, by exerting a sustained, evenly distributed pressure over the entire surface of the calves, reduce the calibre of the superficial veins of the lower extremities, resulting in increased flow in the deeper veins. It is important to note that any type of stocking, including the elastic type, can be converted into a tourniquet if applied incorrectly (i.e. rolled tightly at the top). In such instances, the stockings will produce stasis instead of preventing it. For correct application see Figure 9.12. Elastic compression stockings are removed for a brief interval at least twice daily. While they are off, the skin is inspected for signs of irritation and the calves are examined for possible tenderness. Any skin changes or signs of tenderness are reported.

Research studies have questioned the value of using elastic stockings on their own in the prevention of deep vein thrombosis. It is felt by some researchers that using elastic stockings in conjunction with subcutaneous injection of low-dose heparin provides the best results (Drinkwater, 1989, p. 25).

Considerations for Elderly Patients. Because of decreased strength and manual dexterity, elderly patients may be unable to apply elastic stockings properly. If such is the case, a family member or close friend should be taught how to assist the patient to apply the stockings so that they do not cause undue pressure on any part of the feet or legs.

Body Position and Exercise

When the patient is confined to bed, the feet and lower legs should be elevated periodically above heart level. The superficial and tibial veins empty rapidly in this position and remain collapsed. Active and passive leg exercises, particularly those involving calf muscles, should be performed to increase venous blood flow. Early ambulation is most effective in preventing venous stasis. Deep-breathing exercises are beneficial because they produce increased negative pressure in the thorax, which assists in emptying the large veins.

Nursing Assessment

Careful nursing assessment is invaluable in detecting early signs of venous disorders of the lower extremities. Patients who are at a high risk of developing thrombophlebitis are those whose treatment involves bedrest, for example, myocardial infarction, congestive cardiac failure, sepsis, traction; patients who have a history of varicose veins, hypercoagulation, recent major surgery, particularly if over 40 years old, major gynaecological surgery and those with leg trauma, especially fractures involving the wearing of casts; the elderly, the obese and women taking the oral contraceptive pill are also in the high risk group.

The patient should be asked about the presence of leg pain or tenderness, any functional impairment or oedema. The legs are inspected from the groin to the feet, noting asymmetry, and the calf circumference is measured and recorded. Any increase in temperature in the affected leg is reported. Any abnormalities should be reported promptly.

Diagnosis

Phlebography (venography) involves the injection of a radiographic contrast medium into the venous system through a dorsal foot vein. The diagnosis is based on the demonstration of an unfilled segment of vein in an otherwise completely filled vein with its connecting collaterals. The injection may cause a brief but painful vein inflammation.

Another method used to measure alterations in velocity of blood flow in leg veins is Doppler ultrasonography. When the Doppler probe is placed over veins that are obstructed, the Doppler flow recording will be diminished or absent in comparison to that for the opposite extremity. This method is relatively inexpensive, portable, rapid and noninvasive.

Impedance plethysmography is used to measure changes in venous volume. A blood pressure cuff is applied to the patient's thigh and is inflated enough to impede venous flow (about 50 to 60 mmHg) but not enough to impede arterial flow. Calf electrodes are used to measure electrical resistance that results from venous volume changes. In the presence of deep vein thrombosis, the increase in venous volume that normally results from blood trapped below the level of the cuff will be less than expected.

The use of both Doppler ultrasonography and impedance plethysmography can increase significantly the accuracy of diagnosis. I^{125}-labelled fibrinogen scanning has provided a sensitive method for the early detection of venous thrombosis. This test relies on the fact that radioactive fibrinogen, when injected intravenously, will concentrate in the forming clot. The level of radioactivity can then be measured serially, and the progression of

Put on supports early in the morning, before swelling occurs
Always begin with supports 'inside-out' . . . as they are when you receive them

1a

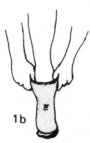

1b

1. Sit with feet in easy reach. Support must be 'inside-out' with its foot inverted back to heel. Seam faces down (a). Grasp each side firmly and pull onto foot (b).

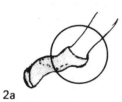

2a

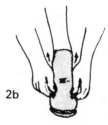

2b

2. Pull past midpoint of heel (a), so support will not slip back. Then, reach just beyond toes and grasp fabric between fingers and start pulling over foot. Pull from sides (b) never by seams.

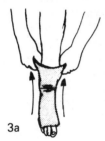

3a

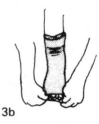

3b

3. Pull all the way past ankle (a). Seat heel in place. Pull foot portion of support out toward tips of toes (b) to set fabric evenly on foot. Allow to settle back normally.

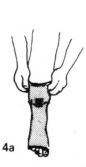

4a

4b

4. Using short (5 cm at a time), snappy pulls (a) pull support up to point it was measured to end (b). Smooth evenly down leg. **Never allow top to roll or turn down**.

Figure 9.12 Method of applying supporting hose. (Courtesy of Jobst.)

the clot can be monitored. However this test is costly and will not reveal thrombi in the groin or pelvic areas.

Medical Management

The aims of the medical treatment are to prevent propagation of the thrombus and the inherent risk of pulmonary embolism and to prevent recurrent thromboemboli. Therapeutic anticoagulation can accomplish these aims. Heparin can be administered by continuous or intermittent infusion but continuous pump infusion is the preferred method because evidence suggests a lower incidence of haemorrhagic complications. The dosage is regulated by the partial thromboplastin time. Heparin is usually continued for 10 to 12 days until organisation of the clot has taken place. The patient is then started on oral anticoagulants for long-term prevention. Oral anticoagulants, such as warfarin, are monitored by the prothrombin time. Because warfarin has a therapeutic lag period of three to five days, it is usually administered in conjunction with heparin until desired anticoagulation has been achieved (i.e., when the prothrombin time is kept at one-and-a-half times to twice the normal).

Anticoagulants cannot dissolve a thrombus that has already formed. Many centres use thrombolytic (fibrinolytic) therapy because lysis and dissolution of clots take place effectively. Streptokinase and urokinase are both from biological sources and are about equal in thrombolytic activity. Urokinase is much more expensive than streptokinase.

The patient's partial thromboplastin time, prothrombin time, haemoglobin and haematocrit are monitored frequently. If bleeding occurs and cannot be stopped, the drug is discontinued. Surgery for deep vein thrombosis is necessary when: (1) the patient cannot be given anticoagulants; (2) the danger of pulmonary embolism is extreme; and (3) the venous drainage is so severely compromised that permanent extremity damage will probably result. A thrombectomy is the treatment of choice when surgery is necessary.

Contraindications to anticoagulant therapy include the following: bleeding from the gastrointestinal, genitourinary or respiratory tract; haemorrhagic blood dyscrasias; aneurysms; severe hepatic or renal disease; recent cerebrovascular haemorrhage; severe trauma; alcohol or drug dependency; recent or impending surgery of the eye, brain or spinal cord; infections; or open ulcerative wounds.

Nursing Care

Bedrest, elevation of the affected extremity, elastic compression stockings and analgesics are adjuncts to anticoagulant therapy. Usually bedrest is required for five to seven days following a deep vein thrombosis. This is approximately the length of time necessary for inflammatory symptoms to subside and organization of the thrombus to occur. When the patient begins to ambulate, elastic stockings are used.

Walking is superior to standing or sitting for long periods. Bed exercises, such as dorsiflexion of the foot against a foot board, are also recommended.

When heparin is given via a continuous infusion pump, the nurse checks periodically for kinks or leaks in the tubing, and inspects the entire system frequently to ensure that the exact dose is being administered.

The principal complication of anticoagulant therapy is the occurrence of spontaneous bleeding anywhere in the body. Bleeding from the kidneys will be manifested by microscopic haematuria and is often the first sign of anticoagulant overdose. Bruises, nosebleeds and bleeding gums are also early signs. To promptly reverse the effects of heparin, the doctor may prescribe intravenous injections of protamine sulphate. The reversal of the effects of warfarin can be achieved by administration of vitamin K or concentrated factor replacement.

A further possible complication of heparin therapy is heparin-induced thrombocytopenia, which generally occurs 7 to 10 days after the treatment has started. The doctor will discontinue heparin when this occurs and use protamine sulphate to reverse the heparin effects.

Patient Education

The patient being discharged on warfarin should be informed about the medication, its purpose and the need to take the correct amount at the specific times prescribed. The patient should also be aware that the blood tests planned periodically are to determine how the blood is clotting and whether a change in medication dosage is required. If the patient is unable or unwilling to co-operate with the therapeutic regime, continuation of the drug should be questioned.

Specific teaching directives should include the following points:

1. Take the anticoagulant tablet at the same time each day.
2. Wear or carry identification indicating which anticoagulant is being taken.
3. Keep all appointments for blood tests.
4. Because other medications affect the way the anticoagulant normally acts, do not take any of the following medications without the doctor's consent: vitamins, cold medicines, antibiotics, aspirin, mineral oil and anti-inflammatory drugs.
5. The doctor should be contacted before taking any over-the- counter drugs.
6. Remember that alcohol may alter the body's response to an anticoagulant.
6. Avoid food fads, crash diets or marked changes in eating habits.
7. Do not take warfarin unless so directed by the doctor. Do not stop taking warfarin (when prescribed) unless

so directed by the doctor. When seeking treatment from another doctor, dentist or chiropodist, indicate that an anticoagulant is being taken. Contact the general practitioner before dental extraction or elective surgery. Be extra careful to avoid injury that can cause bleeding.

8. Women should notify their doctor if they suspect that they are pregnant.
9. If any of the following signs appear, report them immediately to the doctor:
    a. Faintness, dizziness or increased weakness.
    b. Severe headache or stomach pain.
    c. Red or brown urine.
    d. Any bleeding, such as cuts that do not stop bleeding.
    e. Bruises that increase in size, nose bleeds or unusual bleeding from any part of the body.
    f. Red or black bowel movements.
    g. Skin rash.

Chronic Venous Insufficiency

Altered Physiology and Clinical Features

Venous insufficiency is a disorder resulting from the incompetency of venous valves in the legs. Both superficial and deep veins can be involved. Valvular incompetence can occur whenever there has been a prolonged increase in venous pressure, such as occurs with deep vein thrombosis. Because the walls of veins are thinner and more elastic than the walls of arteries, they distend readily when venous pressure is consistently high. In this state, leaflets of the venous valves are stretched and prevented from closing completely, thereby allowing a backflow or reflux of blood in the veins. Venous stasis and oedema result.

When the deep veins in the legs have incompetent valves following a thrombus, postphlebotic syndrome may develop. This disorder is characterized by chronic venous stasis, resulting in oedema, altered pigmentation, pain, stasis dermatitis and stasis ulceration. Superficial veins may be dilated. The disorder is long-standing, difficult to treat and often disabling.

Stasis ulcers develop as a result of leakage of capillaries and subsequent ulcerations. The ulcerations usually occur in the lower part of the extremity in the area of the medial malleolus of the ankle. The skin becomes dry, cracks and itches, and develops a brown pigmentation. Subcutaneous tissues fibrose and atrophy. The risk of injury and infection of the extremities is increased.

Management and Patient Education

Management of the patient with venous insufficiency is directed at reducing venous stasis and preventing ulcerations. Measures which increase venous blood flow are antigravity activities and compression of superficial veins with elastic stockings.

Elastic compression of the legs reduces pooling of venous blood and enhances venous return to the heart. Thus elastic hose are recommended for patients with venous insufficiency. The fit of the stocking is important. It should provide for a greater pressure at the foot and ankle, gradually declining to a lesser pressure at the knee or groin. A tourniquet effect is created if the top of the stocking is too tight or if twisting has occurred, which worsens venous pooling. Stockings should be applied following a period of elevation, when the venous blood volume is at its lowest. The technique for putting on elastic hose is depicted in Figure 9.12.

Elevation of the legs above the heart should be performed frequently throughout the day (at least 30 minutes every two hours). At night, the patient should sleep with the foot of the bed elevated about 15 cm. Prolonged sitting or standing still is detrimental, but walking should be encouraged.

When sitting, the patient should avoid placing pressure on the popliteal spaces, such as occurs with leg crossing or sitting with the legs dangling over the side of the bed. Constricting garments such as girdles or garters should be avoided. Extremities with venous insufficiency are conscientiously protected from trauma. The skin is kept clean, dry and soft. Signs of ulceration are reported immediately to the health care professional for treatment and follow-up.

Leg Ulcers

Definition and Aetiology

A leg ulcer is an excavation of the skin surface that is produced by the sloughing of inflammatory necrotic tissue. The most frequent cause is vascular insufficiency, either venous or arteriolar. Venous leg ulcers constitute 95 per cent of all leg ulcers and it is estimated that 10 per 1,000 of the adult population have leg ulcers (Eagle, 1990, p. 32).

Altered Physiology

Inadequate exchange of oxygen and other nutrients in the tissue is the metabolic abnormality underlying the development of leg ulcers. When the cellular metabolism cannot maintain energy balance, cell death (necrosis) results. Alterations in blood vessels at the arterial, capillary and venous levels may affect cellular processes and lead to the formation of ulcers (see Figure 9.13).

Clinical Features

The patient with a leg ulcer usually complains of aching, fatigue, heaviness and swelling of the leg. The symptoms

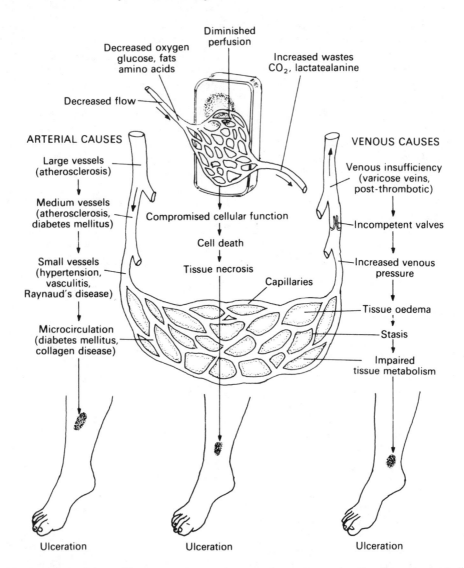

Figure 9.13 Altered physiology of leg ulcers. Some of the conditions that cause diminished blood flow to peripheral tissue are indicated on the left. Oxygen and energy sources are further aggravated by capillary changes brought about by diabetes mellitus and collagen disease. Cellular function is compromised when insufficient oxygen and energy substrates are supplied. Tissue necrosis takes place and results in ulceration. A somewhat similar situation occurs when there is venous insufficiency brought about by a different haemodynamic pattern. Increased venous pressure reduces capillary flow. Oedema and stasis result, impairing cellular metabolism and again leading to ulceration.

will vary depending upon whether the problem is one that is arterial or venous in origin (see Table 9.3). The severity of the symptoms depend on the extent and duration of the vascular insufficiency. The ulcer itself appears as an open sore that is inflamed. Exudate may be present or the area may be covered by a dark crust.

Diagnosis

There are many causes of ulcers and it is important that an accurate diagnosis is made so that appropriate therapy can be prescribed. The history of the condition is important in determining the presence of venous or arterial insufficiency. The extent and type of pain are assessed carefully, as are the appearance and temperature of the skin of both lower extremities. The quality of all pulses of the lower extremities (femoral, popliteal, posterior tibial and pedal) is carefully checked. The presence or absence of oedema is determined. If the extremity is oedematous, it is examined to see if pitting is present. Any limitation of mobility and activity that results from the vascular insufficiency is determined. In addition, the patient is questioned about

Table 9.3 *Characteristics of venous and arterial ulcers*

	Venous	**Arterial**
Site	Commonly above medial malleolus	Toes, heels, feet, anterior/lateral aspect of ankle
Progress	Gradual	Rapid
Pain	Intermittent, usually associated with severe oedema/ infection	Unremitting
Skin	Warm, oedematous, eczematous, atrophie blanche	Cold, shiny, bluish/pink
Size	Usually shallow, often extensive	Often small but deep
Pulse	Foot pulses present	Foot pulses absent or diminished

Thomas, L. (1988) Treating leg ulcers, Nursing Standard, 6 February, Vol.2, No.18, pp. 22–23.

nutritional status and about any chronic conditions that may exist, such as diabetes, collagen disease or varicose veins, that could be associated with the leg ulcer. More conclusive diagnostic aids are Doppler ultrasound studies, arteriography and venography.

Medical Management

All ulcers have the potential for becoming infected and antibiotic therapy is prescribed either when indicated by culture and sensitivity determinations or when there are clinical signs of infection. The route of administration prescribed is usually systemic because topical antibiotics have not proven to be effective for leg ulcers.

To promote healing, the wound is kept clean of exudate and necrotic tissue. This may be accomplished by flushing the area with normal saline; if that is unsuccessful, the doctor may decide that debridement is necessary. Debridement can be achieved by a variety of means; using instruments to cut away devitalized tissue, using enzymatic debridement agents such as streptokinase/streptodornase or using a dextranomer such as polymeric beads (the latter two methods are expensive). Some health authorities use less expensive 0.5 per cent silver nitrate as a debriding agent as this has the added advantage of being an antiseptic, which destroys pseudomonas. Once the devitalized tissue has been removed, the aim of treatment is to keep the ulcer clean and moist while healing takes place. There is a huge variety of dressings available which can be used to achieve this aim.

In patients where arterial insufficiency is the problem and the ulcer does not respond to antibiotics, cleansing and debridement, more aggressive therapy may be necessary. Phenol sympathectomy will increase blood supply to the skin but revascularization operations may often be necessary to correct arterial insufficiency.

► NURSING PROCESS
► THE PATIENT WITH LEG ULCERS

► *Assessment*

A careful nursing history and assessment of symptoms are important in determining venous or arterial insufficiency. The extent and type of pain are assessed carefully, as are the appearance and temperature of the skin of both lower extremities. The quality of all peripheral pulses is determined, and comparisons are made of the pulses bilaterally. The presence or absence of oedema is determined. If the extremity is oedematous, it is examined to see if pitting is present. Any limitation of mobility and activity that results from the vascular insufficiency is determined. In addition, the patient is questioned about any chronic conditions that may exist, such as diabetes, collagen disease or varicose veins that could be associated with the leg ulcer.

► *Patient's Problems*

Based on the assessment, the main problems facing the patient may include the following:

1. Impairment of skin integrity related to vascular insufficiency.
2. Impaired physical mobility related to the activity restrictions of the therapeutic regime and the presence of pain.
3. Potential nutritional deficit related to increased need for nutrients that promote wound healing.

► *Planning and Implementation*
► Expected Outcomes

The planning of nursing care for these patients will aim to restore skin integrity, improve physical mobility and attain adequate nutrition. The nursing challenge in caring for these patients is great, whether the patient is in hospital or at home. The physical problem is often a long-term one that causes a substantial drain on the patient's physical and emotional resources.

Nursing Care

Restoration of Skin Integrity

Measures are taken to keep the area clean to promote wound healing. Strict aseptic technique may be used in an attempt to prevent contamination. Ointments, lotions and dressings are applied as prescribed. Positioning of the legs depends on whether the cause of the ulcer is arterial or venous in origin. If there is arterial insufficiency, blood flow can be improved by elevating the head of the bed by 7.7 to 15 cm.

This improved flow of blood increases oxygenation of the tissue and promotes healing. If there is venous insufficiency, resolution of dependent oedema can be promoted by elevating the lower extremities. Decrease in the oedema will allow for improved exchange of cellular nutrients and waste products in the area of the ulcer. Thus healing is promoted. Compression bandages will be prescribed for venous insufficiency, but are contraindicated in arterial insufficiency.

Avoidance of trauma to the lower extremities is important in promoting skin integrity. When the patient is ambulant, all obstacles are moved from the path so that the patient's legs will not be bumped. When the patient is in bed, a bed cradle is used to relieve pressure from the bed clothes and to prevent anything from touching the legs. Heat in the form of heating pads, hot water bottles or hot baths is avoided. Heat increases the oxygen demands and thus blood flow demands of the tissues, which in this case are already compromised. Discontinuation of smoking will also help the healing process.

Improvement in Physical Mobility

Generally, physical activity is restricted at first in order to promote healing. When infection has improved and healing has begun, ambulation will be resumed gradually and progressively. Activity aids arterial flow and venous return and is encouraged after the acute phase of the ulcer process.

Until full activity can be resumed, the patient is encouraged to move about when in bed, to turn from side to side frequently and to exercise the upper extremities to maintain muscle tone and strength. Meanwhile, diversional activities that interest the patient are encouraged. Consultation with an occupational therapist may be helpful in the period of limited mobility and activity is prolonged.

If pain limits the patient's activity, analgesics are often prescribed by the doctor. The pain of peripheral vascular disease is often chronic in nature, so non-narcotic analgesics are more desirable than narcotics because of the problem of drug dependency is reduced. It is often desirable to administer the analgesic before planned activity periods in order to help the patient participate more comfortably in the activity.

Attainment of Adequate Nutrition

Nutritional deficiencies are determined from the patient's account of usual dietary intake. Alterations in the diet are made to remedy any deficiencies. In addition, a diet that is high in protein, vitamin C and iron is encouraged in an attempt to promote the healing process.

Many patients with peripheral vascular disease are elderly. Their calorie intake may need to be adjusted because of their decreased metabolic rate and decreased level of activity. Particular consideration should also be given to their iron intake because many elderly people are anaemic. Once a diet plan that meets the individual's nutritional needs has been developed, dietary advice is made available to the patient and home carer. The diet plan is designed to be compatible with the patient's and carer's lifestyle and preferences. Research has shown that patients who have an understanding of their disorder and the factors that inhibit the healing of their ulcer actually have a significantly quicker healing rate than those who do not have this knowledge. It is therefore important to include this type of knowledge in the education/discharge planning (Nudds, 1987).

► *Evaluation*
► **Expected Outcomes**

1. Skin integrity restored.
   a. Absence of inflammation.
   b. Absence of exudate.
   c. Patient uses measures to avoid trauma to the legs.
   d. Patient uses prescribed position of bed (head elevated or foot elevated) to promote circulation.
2. Patient increases physical mobility.
   a. Progresses gradually to optimum level of activity.
   b. Relates that pain does not impede activity.
3. Patient attains adequate nutrition.
   a. Selects foods high in protein, vitamins and iron.
   b. Discusses with family member or close friend dietary modifications that need to be made at home.
   c. Plans with carer a diet that is nutritionally sound.

Varicose Veins

Incidence

Varicose veins (varicosities) are abnormally dilated, tortuous superficial veins caused by incompetent venous valves. Most commonly, they occur in the lower extremities, the saphenous veins or the lower trunk; however, they can occur elsewhere in the body (e.g., oesophageal varices; see Chapter 16).

It is estimated that varicose veins occur in 20 per cent of the population in developed countries (Milne, 1988, p. 26). The condition is most common in women and in people in occupations requiring prolonged standing, such as salespeople, hairdressers, lift operators, nurses and doctors. An hereditary weakness of the vein wall may contribute to the development of varicosities, and it is not uncommon to see this disorder in several members of the same family.

Altered Physiology

There are three groups of veins in the lower extremities: superficial, deep and communicating veins (Figure 9.14).

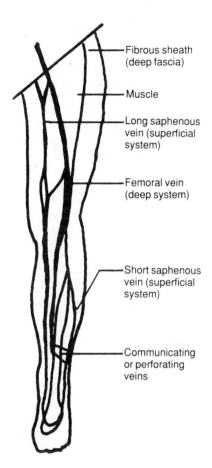

Figure 9.14 Normal deep and superficial veins of the leg (posterior view). (Green, S. and Wickenden, A. (1984) Varicose veins, *Nursing*, June, Vol. 2, No. 26, pp. 779–81.

An understanding of the normal blood flow through these will help the appreciation of altered physiology. The superficial veins are situated in the subcutaneous fat and are visible through the skin. Most superficial veins drain into the saphenous vein. They all have valves to prevent distal reflux of blood. The deep veins are situated close to the named arteries in the legs. Two or three deep veins accompany each artery. Deep veins are smaller than the superficial veins. They also have valves. Communicating veins, also known as perforating veins, have valves and join the superficial and deep veins. The main communicating veins are the ones that join the long saphenous vein to the femoral vein, and the short saphenous vein to the popliteal vein.

It is in these areas that the valves are most commonly involved. The veins become dilated so preventing the valves from closing and as a result they become incompetent (Figure 9.15). There is a back up of pressure, which is transferred to the next lower segment, resulting in pooling and stagnation of blood. This combi-nation of vein dilatation and incompetent valves produces the varicosity.

Incompetent valves in the communicating veins cause dilatation of the main saphenous trunks and their tributaries and the formation of incompetent valves and varicosities.

Clinical Features

If only the superficial veins are affected, the person may have no symptoms, but cosmetically the appearance of the dilated veins may be unappealing. If symptoms are present, they may take the form of dull aches, muscle cramps and increased fatigue of muscles in the legs. Ankle swelling and a feeling of heaviness of the legs may be present. Nocturnal cramps are a common symptom in patients with varicose veins.

When deep venous obstruction results in varicose veins, patients may demonstrate the signs and symptoms of chronic venous insufficiency (see page 415). Susceptibility to injury and infection is greater.

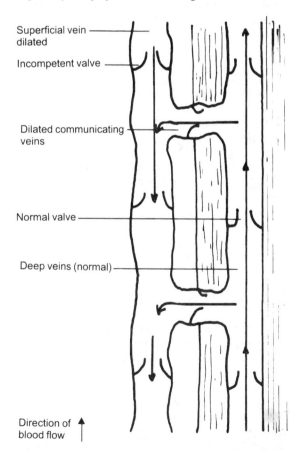

Figure 9.15 Incompetent valves and retrograde blood flow. (Green, S. and Wickenden, A. (1984) Varicose veins, *Nursing*, June, Vol. 2, No. 26, pp. 779–81.

Diagnosis

A common diagnostic test for varicose veins is the Brodie-Trendelenburg test, which will demonstrate backward flow of blood through incompetent valves of the superficial veins and of the branches that communicate with the deep veins of the leg. With the patient lying down, the affected leg is elevated to empty the veins. A soft rubber tourniquet is then applied around the upper thigh to occlude the veins and the patient is asked to stand. If the valves of the communicating veins are incompetent, blood flows into the superficial veins from the deep veins. If, upon release of the tourniquet, blood flows rapidly from above into the superficial veins, the inference is that the valves of the superficial veins are also incompetent. This test is used to determine the type of treatment to be recommended for the varicose veins.

Doppler ultrasonographic examination is often used to detect retrograde flow of blood in superficial veins with incompetent valves following compression of the leg proximally. Phlebography involves the injection of radiographical contrast medium into the leg veins so that the vein anatomy can be visualized during various leg movements.

Prevention and Patient Education

Activities that cause venous stasis should be avoided, such as wearing tight garters or a constricting girdle, crossing the legs at the thighs and sitting or standing for long periods of time. Changing position frequently, elevating the legs when they are tired and getting up to walk for several minutes of every hour, promote circulation. The patient should be encouraged to walk one to two miles a day if there are no contraindications. Walking up the stairs rather than using the lift is helpful in promoting circulation. Swimming is also a good exercise for the legs.

Support hose or elastic stockings are useful. The overweight patient should be assisted to lose weight.

Medical Management

Surgery for varicose veins requires demonstrated patency of deep veins. Once this has been established, ligation of the saphenous vein is accomplished under general anaesthesia. The vein is ligated high in the groin, where the saphenous vein meets the femoral vein. An incision is then made in the ankle and a metal or plastic wire is passed the full length of the vein, 'stripping' as it passes (Figure 9.16). The branches of the saphenous vein break off at their junctions. Pressure and elevation keep bleeding at a minimum during surgery.

Sclerotherapy

In sclerotherapy, an irritating chemical, such as 3 per cent sodium tetradecyl sulphate, is injected into the empty lumen of a varicose vein, which irritates the vein wall and produces localized phlebitis and fibrosis, thereby obliterating the vein lumen. Sclerosing is a palliative not a curative treatment, and is only used in varicosities below the knee as it is impossible to achieve the required compression above the knee.

Following injection, elastic compression bandages are applied to the leg. These may be worn for up to six weeks. Walking is important for maintenance of blood flow in the extremity and its importance should be emphasized.

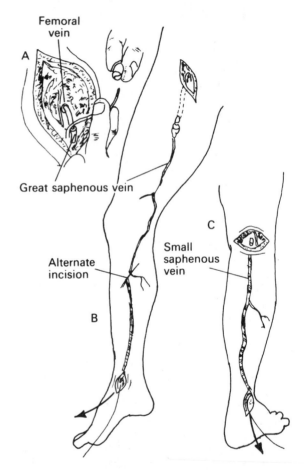

Figure 9.16 Ligation and stripping of the great and the small saphenous veins. (A) The tributaries of the saphenous vein have been ligated, and the saphenous vein has been ligated at the saphenofemoral junction. (B) Vein stripper has been inserted from the ankle superiorly to the groin. The vein is stripped from above downwards. A number of alternative incisions may be needed to remove separate varicose masses. (C) The small saphenous vein is stripped from its junction with the popliteal vein to a point posterior to the lateral malleolus. (Rhoads *et al.*, *Surgery*, J. B. Lippincott, Philadelphia.)

Postoperative Nursing Care

Elastic compression of the leg is maintained continuously for about one week after vein stripping. Exercise and movement of the legs and elevation of the foot of the bed are necessary. Walking may be started 24 to 48 hours after surgery. Standing still and sitting are contraindicated.

Analgesics may help patients to move affected extremities more easily. The bandages are inspected for bleeding, particularly at the groin because the greatest risk of bleeding occurs there. Sensations of 'pins and needles' or hypersensitivity to touch in the involved extremity may indicate a temporary or permanent nerve injury resulting from surgery. The saphenous vein and saphenous nerve are in close proximity to each other.

Patients will require long-term elastic support of the leg after discharge and plans are made to provide adequate supplies. Sutures are removed from around day 10 to day 14. Leg exercises will also be necessary, and the development of an individual plan will require consultation with the patient and doctor.

Post-sclerotherapy care: if the patient experiences a burning sensation in the injected leg for one or two nights, a mild sedative and walking will relieve the problem. Because bathing may be a problem during the six weeks, a plastic bag may be placed over the bandaged leg and secured above the bandage to allow the patient to shower.

THE LYMPHATIC SYSTEM

The lymphatic circulation begins in the tissues and is a one-way system that carries lymph from the tissues back to the venous circulation. The lymphatics are thin-walled capillaries similar to the blood capillaries, except that lymphatic vessels are more permeable to large molecules. Lymph is the fluid found in lymph vessels. Peripheral lymphatics join larger lymph vessels and pass through regional lymph nodes before entering the venous system. The lymphatics converge into two main trunks, the thoracic duct and the right lymphatic duct. These ducts empty into the junction of the subclavian and the internal jugular veins. The thoracic duct drains most of the lymph vessels in the body. The right lymphatic duct conveys lymph primarily from the right side of the head, neck, thorax and upper arms. Like veins, lymphatics contain one-way valves to prevent fluid reflux. Muscular contraction of the lymphatic walls and surrounding tissues aids in the propulsion of lymph toward venous drainage points.

Diagnosis By Lymphangiography

Radiological visualization of the lymphatic system is possible after the injection of contrast medium directly into lymphatic vessels in the hands and feet. This technique affords a means of detecting lymph node involvement by metastatic carcinoma, lymphoma or infection in sites that are otherwise inaccessible to the examiner except by direct surgical approach.

A lymphatic vessel is located in each foot (or hand) by injecting a patent blue violet dye into the subcutaneous tissues between the first and second digits. Approximately 15 minutes later, the skin proximal to the injection site is incised. A blue lymphatic segment is identified and isolated and a cannula inserted. The contrast medium is infused very slowly. Appropriate X-ray pictures are taken at the conclusion of the injection, 24 hours later and periodically thereafter, as indicated.

Lymphangitis and Lymphadenitis

Lymphangitis is an acute inflammation of the lymphatic channels. It arises most commonly from a focus of infection in an extremity. Usually, the infective organism is the haemolytic streptococcus. The characteristic red streaks that extend up the arm or leg from an infected wound outline the course of the lymphatics as they drain.

The lymph nodes located along the course of the lymphatic channels also become enlarged, red and tender (acute lymphadenitis) and can, although rarely, become necrotic and form an abscess (supporative lymphadenitis). The nodes involved most often are those in the groin, axilla or the cervical region. Recurrent episodes of lymphangitis are often associated with progressive lymphoedema.

After acute attacks, elastic support should be worn on the affected extremity for several months to prevent long-term oedema.

Lymphoedema and Elephantiasis

Lymphoedema is a swelling if tissues in the extremities due to an increased quantity of lymph that results from an obstruction of lymphatics. It is especially marked when the extremity is in a dependent position. Initially the oedema is soft, pitting and relieved by treatment. As the condition progresses, the oedema becomes firm, non-pitting and unresponsive to treatment. The most common type is congenital lymphoedema, which is caused by hypoplasia of the lymphatic system of the lower extremity. This disorder is usually seen in females, and appears first between the ages of 15 and 25 years. The obstruction may be in both the lymph nodes and the lymphatic vessels. At times, it is seen in the arm, after a mastectomy with lymph node clearance for carcinoma, and in the leg in association with varicose veins or chronic phlebitis. When chronic swelling is present, there may be frequent bouts of infection characterized by high fever and chills and increased residual oedema after the inflammation has resolved. These lead to chronic fibrosis, thickening of the subcutaneous tissues and hypertrophy of the skin. This disorder, in which chronic swelling of the extremity recedes only slightly with elevation, is given the name elephantiasis.

Medical Management

Lymphoedema is currently managed by physiotherapy and/or surgery. Lymphatic fluid can be compressed manually from the soft tissues by squeezing the extremity distally. Active and passive exercise assists in the movement of lymphatic fluid into the bloodstream. Mechanical pulsatile air pressure devices (e.g., Flowtron boots) are also available.

Surgical treatment of lymphoedema is performed in order to reduce the size of the extremity and improve its appearance, to reduce the incidence of inflammatory episodes and to limit secondary skin changes associated with chronic lymphoedema. Surgery involves the excision of affected subcutaneous tissue and fascia, with skin grafting to cover the defect or the transfer of superficial lymphatics into the deep lymphatics.

Postoperatively, the management of the skin grafts are the same as when they are used for other disorders. Prophylactic antibiotics may be prescribed for five to seven days. Constant elevation of the affected extremity and observations for complications are essential. Complications include necrosis of the skin graft, haematoma and abscess formation and cellulitis.

BIBLIOGRAPHY

Anonymous (1989) Diagnosis of deep vein thrombosis, *Lancet*, 1 July, Vol. II, No. 8653, pp. 23–4.

Beilin, L. (1989) Epidemiology of hypertension, *Medicine*, September, Vol. 69, pp. 2856–9.

Belch, J. J. F. (1990) Management of Raynaud's Phenomenon, *Hospital Update*, May, pp. 391–9.

Campbell, W. B. (1982) The ischaemic lower limb (1 and 2), *Hospital Update*, April/May, Vol. 8, No. 4, pp. 473–83, and Vol. 8, No. 5, pp. 549–61.

Campbell, W. B. (1990) Acute limb ischaemia, *Surgery*, June, Vol. 81, pp. 1937–41.

Collins, R., Peto, R., MacMahon, S., *et al.* (1990) Blood pressure, stroke and coronary heart disease, *Lancet*, 7 April, Vol. 335, No. 8693, pp. 827–38.

Cooke, E. D. and Nicolaides, A. N. (1990) Raynaud's syndrome, *British Medical Journal*, March, Vol. 300, pp. 553–5.

Cooper, J. K., Love, D. W. and Raffoul, P. R. (1982) Intentional prescription non-adherence (noncompliance) by the elderly, *Journal of the American Geriatric Society*, Vol. 30, pp. 329–33.

Curzio, J. (1987) Obesity in an outpatient hypertension clinic, *Nursing Times*, 29 July, Vol. 83, No. 30, pp. 37–9.

Drinkwater, K. (1989) Management of deep vein thrombosis, *Surgical Nurse*, February, pp. 24–6.

Eagle, M. (1990) The quiet epidemic below the knee, *Nursing Standard*, 3 January, Vol. 4, No. 15, pp. 32–6.

Feury, D. and Nash, D. T. (1990) Hypertension: the nurse's role, *RN*, November, Vol. 53, No. 11, pp. 54–60.

Fowkes, F. G. R., MacIntyre, C. C. A. and Ruckley, C. V. (1989) Increasing incidence of aortic aneurysms in England and Wales, *British Medical Journal*, 7 January, Vol. 298, pp. 33–5.

Harper, D. R. (1989) Aneurysms, *Surgery*, July, Vol. 70, pp. 1660–66.

Horton, R.E. (1980) *Vascular Surgery*, Hodder and Stoughton, London.

James, W. P. T. (1983) *A Discussion Paper on Proposals for Nutritional Guidelines for Health Education in Britain (NACNE Report)*, Health Education Council, London.

Macleod, J., Edwards, C. and Bouchier, I. (eds) (1987) Chapter 7, D. C. Julian in *Davidson's Principles and Practice of Medicine* (15th edition), Churchill Livingstone, Edinburgh.

McMillan, E. (1984) Patient compliance with anti-hypertensive drug therapy, *Nursing*, Vol. 26, pp. 761–4.

Milne, C. (1988) Varicose veins, *Nursing Standard*, 16 April, Vol. 2, No. 28, p. 26.

Nudds, L. (1987) Healing information, *Community Outlook*, September, pp. 12–13.

O'Brien, E., O'Malley, K., Beevers, D. G., *et al.* (1987) D. G. Beevers and M. R. Wilkins in *ABC of Hypertension* (2nd edition), BMJ Publicatons, London.

Rhodes, J. (1989) Patient education and hypertension, *Nursing Times*, 20 September, Vol. 85, No. 38, p. 55.

Roberts, A. (1988a) Peripheral vascular disease—1, *Nursing Times*, 4 May, Vol. 84, No. 18, pp. 49–52.

Roberts, A. (1988b) Peripheral vascular disease—2, *Nursing Times*, 8 June, Vol. 84, No. 23, pp. 51–4.

Thomas, L. (1988) Treating leg ulcers, *Nursing Standard*, 6 February, Vol. 2, No. 18, pp. 22–3.

Walsh, M. (1990) *Accident and Emergency Nursing—A New Approach* (2nd edition), Heinemann Nursing, Oxford.

FURTHER READING

Books

Beevers, D. G. and MacGregor, G. A. (1987) *Hypertension in Practice*, Martin Dunitz, London.

Booth, J. A. (ed.) (1983) *Handbook of Investigations*, Harper & Row, London.

Committee on Medical Aspects and Food Policy (COMA) (1984) *Panel on diet in relation to cardiovascular disease*, HMSO, London.

Fahey, V. A. (ed.) (1988) *Vascular Nursing*, W. B. Saunders, Philadelphia.

Gilbert, P. (1987) *You and Your Varicose Veins*, Sheldon Press, London.

Macleod, J., Edwards, C. and Bouchier, I. (eds) (1987) *Davidson's Principles and Practice of Medicine* (15th edition), Churchill Livingstone, Edinburgh.

Roath, S. (ed.) (1989) *Raynaud's—A Guide for Health Professionals*, Chapman & Hall, London.

Ryan, T. J. (1987) *The Management of Leg Ulcers* (2nd edition), Oxford University Press, Oxford.

Strasser, T. (ed.) (1987) *Cardiovascular Care of the Elderly*, World Health Organisation, Geneva.

Articles

General

Adams, C. W. M. (1990) Inflammation in atherosclerosis—the balance between necrosis and repair, *Surgery*, June, Vol. 81, pp. 1828–34.

Ball, M. J. (1987) The aetiology of atherosclerosis and coronary heart disease, *British Journal of Hospital Medicine*, November, Vol. 38, No. 5, pp. 404–10.

Beaver, B. M. (1986) Health education and the patient with peripheral vascular disease, *Nursing Clinics of North America*, June, Vol. 21, No. 2, pp. 265–72.

Collin, J. (1988) The epidemiology of abdominal aortic aneurysm, *British Journal of Hospital Medicine*, July, Vol. 40, No. 1, pp. 64–7.

Dalsing, M. C. *et al.* (1985) Surgery of the aorta, *Critical Care Quarterly*, Septemebr, Vol. 8, No. 2, pp. 25–38.

Ekins, M. A. (1986) Psychosocial considerations in peripheral vascular disease; Cause or effect?, *Nursing Clinics of North America*, June, Vol. 21, No. 2, pp. 255–63.

Loysen, E. and Silman, A. (1986) Dangerous smoke signals, *Nursing Times*, 15 January, Vol. 82, No. 3, pp. 42–3.

Marinelli-Miller, D. (1983) What your patient wants to know about angiography—but may not ask, *RN*, November, Vol. 64, No. 11, pp. 52–4.

McCarthy, W. J. and Williams, L. R. (1985) Femoral artery reconstruction, *Critical Care Quarterly*, September, Vol. 9, No. 2, pp. 39–50.

Ornish, D., Brown, S. E., Scherwitz, L. W. *et al.* (1990) Can lifestyle changes reverse coronary heart disease? *Lancet*, 21 July, Vol. 336, No. 8,708, pp. 129–133.

Pairitz, D. (1984) Peripheral vascular surgery: Postoperative assessment, *Journal of the Association of Operating Room Nurses*, November, Vol. 40, No. 5, pp. 23, 26–9.

Piper, S. (1988) Lessons in trauma, *Nursing Times*, 9 March, Vol. 84, No. 10, pp. 49–51.

Ronayne, R. (1989) Smoking: a decision-making dilemma for the vascular patient, *Journal of Advanced Nursing*, August, Vol. 14, No. 8, pp. 647.

Ronayne, R. (1990) Smoking and peripheral vascular disease, *Nursing Times*, 10 January, Vol. 86, No. 2, p. 48.

Stout, R. W. (1988) Cholesterol in the elderly: more questions than answers, *Geriatric Medicine*, January, Vol. 18, No. 1, pp. 23–32.

Turner, J. A. (1986) Nursing intervention in patients with peripherial vascular disease, *Nursing Clinics of North America*, June, Vol. 21, No. 2, pp. 233–40.

Wagner, M. M. (1986) Pathophysiology related to peripheral vascular disease, *Nursing Clinics of North America*, June, Vol. 21, No. 2, pp. 195–205.

Witteman, J. C. M. *et al.* (1989) Increased risk of atherosclerosis in women after the menopause, *British Medical Journal*, 11 March, Vol. 298, pp. 642–4.

Anticoagulant and Thrombolytic Therapy

Blakely, W. P. *et al.* (1983) Standard care plan for systemic administration of streptokinase, *Critical Care Nursing*, July/August, Vol. 3, No. 4, pp. 86–9.

Fennerty, A. (1988) Anticoagulants in venous thromboembolism, *British Medical Journal*, 19 November, Vol. 297, No. 6659, pp. 1285.

Gever, L. N. (1983) Streptokinase and urokinase: Minimizing the risks of these thrombolytics, *Nursing 83*, January, Vol. 13, No. 1, p. 76.

Gever, L. N. (1984) Anticoagulants ... and what to teach your patient about them, *Nursing 84*, November, Vol. 14, No. 11, p. 64.

John, R. M. and Swanton, R. H. (1990) Anticoagulants in cardiovascular disease, *British Journal of Hospital Medicine*, March, Vol. 43, No. 3, pp.207

McConnell, E. T. (1986) APTT and PT: Two common-but-important coagulation studies, *Nursing 86*, MØy, Vol. 16, No. 5, pp. 47–8.

Ryder, K. (1987) Anticoagulants and antiplatelet therapy, *Update*, 1 June, Vol. 34, No. 11, p. 1240.

Swithers, C. (1988) Tools for teaching about anticoagulants, *RN*, January, p. 57.

Arterial Conditions

Bryan, A. J. and Angelini, G. D.(1989) Traumatic rupture of the thoracic aorta, *British Journal of Hospital Medicine*, April, Vol. 41, pp. 320–6.

Charlesworth, D. (1986) Chronic ischaemia of the lower limbs, *Surgery*, Vol. I, No. 38, November, p. 905.

Cotton, L. T. (1986) One in four survives ruptured abdominal aortic aneurysm, *Geriatric Medicine*, December, Vol. 16, No. 12, pp. 7–9.

Czapinski, N. *et al.* (1983) Nursing plan for abdominal aortic aneurysms, *Journal of the Association of Operating Room Nurses*, February, Vol. 37, No. 2, pp. 205–8, 210.

Datta, P. K. (1982) A case for critical selection, *Nursing Mirror*, 3 March, Vol. 154, No. 9, pp. 34–7.

Datta, P. K. (1982) The pulsating mass, *Nursing Mirror*, 8 September, Vol. 155, No. 10, pp. 46–9.

Dormandy, J. (1989) Peripheral vascular disease, *Medicine International*, September, Vol. 69, p. 2872.

Eddison, M. and Reynolds, C. (1986) Minimising the risk of surgery for cerebral ischaemia, *Professional Nurse*, April, Vol. 1, No. 7, pp. 185–8.

Ellis, H. (1988) Arteriosclerosis disease of the lower limbs, *Update*, 1 April, Vol. 36, No. 7, p. 2031.

Ernst, E. (1989) Peripheral vascular disease, *British Medical Journal*, 7 October, Vol. 299, No. 6704, p. 873.

Horkin, L. (1985) Aortic aneurysm, *Nursing*, October, Vol. 42, p. 1244.

Hyland, F. (1985) Raynaud's disease, *Nursing Times*, 24 April, Vol. 81, No. 17, p. 36.

Jamieson, C. (1988) The management of intermittent claudication, *The Practitioner*, 23 May, Vol. 232, No. 1449, pp. 613–16.

Jenkins, A. M., Ruckley, C. V. and Nolan, B. (1986) Ruptured abdominal aortic aneurysm, *British Journal of Surgery*, May, Vol. 73, pp. 395–8.

McCallum, C. (1984) Femoro-popliteal bypass graft, *Nursing Times*, 3 October, Supplement, pp. 10–11.

Milne, C. (1988) Carotid endarterectomy, *Nursing Standard*, 27 February, Vol. 2, No. 21, pp. 28–9.

Quinless, F. (1984) Physiology, signs and symptoms, *Nursing 84*, March, Vol. 14, No. 3, pp. 52–3.

Raftery, A. T. (1991) Management of peripheral vascular disease, *Update*, 1 March, Vol. 42, No. 5, pp. 455–62.

Roberts, A. (1988) Peripheral vascular disease—1, *Nursing Times*, 4 May, Vol. 84, No. 18, p. 49.

Rowe, P. H. (1990) Vascular emergencies: the acute ischaemic limb, *Geriatric Medicine*, March, Vol. 20, No. 3, p. 71.

Russell, J. *et al.* (1983) Abominal aortic aneurysm: Standard postoperative care, *Critical Care Nurse*, May/June, Vol. 3, No. 3, pp. 124, 126.

Snooks, S. and Lumley, J. S. P.(1990) Management of infra-inguinal chronic arterial disease, *Surgery*, June, Vol. 81, pp. 1933–7.

Sutton, D. (1985) Aortofemoral bypass, *Nursing Mirror*, 17 July, Vol. 161, No. 3, pp. 42–3.

Thomas, L. (1989) Of mutual benefit, *Nursing Times*, Vol. 85, No. 19, pp. 38–41.

Varey, G. (1985) Resection of an aortic aneurysm, *Nursing Times*, 19 June, Vol. 81, No. 25, pp. 34–7.

Young, P. (1988) Anaesthesia for elective abdominal aortic surgery, *British Journal of Hospital Medicine*, August, Vol. 40, pp. 116–20.

Zimmerman, T. A. *et al.* (1983) Thoracoabdominal aortic aneurysms: Treatment and nursing interventions, *Critical Care Nurse*, November/December, Vol. 3, No. 6, pp. 54–63.

Assessment and Diagnosis

Bastarache, M. M., Giuca, J., Horowitz, L. M., *et al.* (1983) Assessing peripheral vascular disease: Noninvasive testing, *American Journal of Nursing*, November, Vol. 83, No. 11, pp. 1552–6.

Baum, P. L. (1985) Heed the early warning signs of PVD, *Nursing 85*, March, Vol. 15, No. 3, pp. 50–8.

Baum, P. L. (1986) Taking the PVD patient's history, *Nursing 86*, May, Vol. 16, No. 5, pp. 30–3.

Beli, A. M. (1990) Interventional radiology of the peripheral vasculature, *Hospital Update*, January, Vol. 16, No. 1, pp. 46–53.

Clark, C. R. and Gregor, F. M.(1988) Developing a sensation information message for femoral angiography, *Journal of Advanced Nursing*, Vol. 13, pp. 237–44.

Cudworth-Bergin, K. L. (1984) Detecting arterial problems with a Doppler stethoscope, *RN*, January, Vol. 47, No. 1, pp. 38–41.

Durbin, N. (1983) The application of Doppler techniques in critical care, *Focus on Critical Care*, June, Vol. 10, No. 3, pp. 44–6.

Halperin, J. L. (1988) Peripheral vascular disease: evaluation and treatment, *Geriatric Medicine*, June, Vol. 18, No. 6, pp. 83–9.

Herman, J. A. (1986) Nursing assessment and nursing diagnosis in patients with peripheral vascular disease, *Nursing Clinics of North America*, June, Vol. 21, No. 2, pp. 219–31.

Hudson, B. (1983) Sharpen your vascular assessment skills with Doppler ultrasound stethoscope, *Nursing 83*, May, Vol. 13, No. 5, pp. 54–7.

Kincaid-Smith, P. (1985) Investigation of hypertension, *Medicine*, July, Vol. 19, p. 792.

Massey, J. A. (1986) Diagnostic testing for peripheral vascular disease, *Nursing Clinics of North America*, Vol. 21, No. 2, pp. 207–18.

Mathewson, M. (1983) A Homan's sign is an effective method of diagnosing thrombophlebitis in bedridden patients, *Critical Care Nurse*, July/August, Vol. 3, No. 4, pp. 64–5.

McCreesh, M. (1985) The non-invasive vascular laboratory, *Nursing Times*, 26 June, Vol. 81, No. 26, pp. 32–4.

Peterson, F. Y. (1983) Assessing peripheral vascular disease at the bedside, *American Journal of Nursing*, November, Vol. 83, No. 11, pp. 1549–51.

Hypertension

Breckenridge, A. (1988) Drugs for hypertension, *Update*, 1 February, Vol. 36, No. 3, p. 1607.

Cerrato, P. L. (1990) Hypertension: the role of diet and lifestyle, *RN*, December, Vol. 53, No. 12, pp. 46–50.

Donavan, M. and Schrober, J. (1982) Hypertension, *Nursing*, January, Vol. 33 (1st series), pp. 1431–3.

Gwen, B. and Given, C. W. (1983) Adherence to hypertensive therapy, *Geriatric Nursing*, May/June, Vol. 4, No. 3, pp. 172–5.

Hinds, C. (1983) A hypertension survey: Respondants' knowledge of high blood pressure, *International Nursing Review*, January/February, Vol. 30, No. 1, pp. 12–14.

Jolly, A. (1991) Taking blood pressure, *Nursing Times*, 10 April, Vol. 87, No. 14, pp. 40–3.

Kerr, J. A. C. (1985) Adherence and self-care, *Heart Lung*, January, Vol. 14, No. 1, pp. 24–31.

Mathewson, M. A. (1983) Current vasodilator therapy, *Focus on Critical Care*, February, Vol. 10, No. 1, pp. 49–53.

Mitchell, J. R. A. (1989) Prognosis of hypertension, *Medicine International*, September, Vol. 69, p. 2864.

Morgan, M. and Watkins, C. J. (1988) Managing hypertension: beliefs and responses to medication among cultural groups, *Sociology of Health and Illness*, December, Vol. 10, No. 4, p. 561.

Raftery, E. (1985) Hypertension: who and when to treat, *Update*, July, Vol. 31, No. 2, p. 155.

Rhodes, J. (1989) Patient education and hypertension, *Nursing Times*, 20 September, Vol. 85, No. 38, p. 55.

Rodman, M. J. (1991) Hypertension: first line drug therapy, *RN*, January, Vol. 54, No. 1, pp. 32–40.

Rodman, M. J. (1991) Hypertension: step-care management, *RN*, February, Vol. 54, No. 2, pp. 24–30.

Simpson, F. O. (1985) Epidemiology of hypertension, *Medicine*, July, Vol. 19, pp. 781–5.

Smith, S. (1985) Drugs and hypertension, *Nursing Times*, 20 February, Vol. 81, No. 8, pp. 37–9.

Smith, W. C. S., Lee, A. H., Crombie, I. K. *et al.* (1990) Control of blood pressure in Scotland: the rule of halves, *British Medical Journal*, 14 April, Vol. 300, No. 6730, p. 981.

Stott, D. J. and Ball, S. G. (1986) Treatment of essential hypertension, *British Journal of Hospital Medicine*, October, Vol. 36, No. 4, pp. 261–8.

Truswell, A. S. (1985) Diet and hypertension, *British Medical Journal*, 13 July, Vol. 291, pp. 125–7.

Swales, J.D. (1985) Management of hypertension, *Medicine*, July, Vol. 19, pp. 792–7.

Wilkinson, P. (1987) Which hypotensive drug?, *Update*, October, Vol. 35, No. 7, p. 655.

Leg Ulcers

Bale, S. and Harding, K. (1989) Education for nurses and patients, *Nursing Standard*, 15 July, Vol. 3, No. 42, pp. 25–7.

Cornwall, J. V. (1983) Guidelines to leg ulcer care, *Nursing 83*, March, Vol. 2, No. 11, pp. 317–19.

Dale, J. and Gibson, B. (1986) Leg ulcers: The nursing assessment, *The Professional Nurse*, June, Vol. 1, No. 9, pp. 236–8.

Dale, J. and Gibson, B. (1986) Prevention of venous ulcers, *The Professional Nurse*, October, Vol. 2, No. 1, pp. 21–2.

Dale, J. and Gibson, B. (1990) Back-up for the venous pump, *The Professional Nurse*, June, Vol. 5, No. 9, pp. 481–6.

David, J. (1990) Recent venous ulcer treatments, *Nursing Standard*, 28 February, Vol. 4, No. 23, pp. 24–6.

Dent, P. and Weeden, L. (1985) Caring for leg ulcers, *Nursing Mirror*, 19 June, Vol. 160, No. 25, pp. 26–34.

Doyle, J. E. (1983) All leg ulcers are not alike: Managing and preventing arterial and venous ulcers, *Nursing 83*, January, Vol. 13, No. 1, pp. 58–63.

Evans, P. (1988) Venous disorders of the leg, *Nursing Times*, Vol. 84, No. 49, pp. 46–7.

Gee, C. F. (1990) Paste bandages for leg ulcers, *Nursing*, 26 April, Vol. 4, No. 9, pp. 25–9.

Hallows, L. (1987) Leg ulcers an underlying problem, *Community Outlook*, September, pp. 6-11.

Hopkins, S. (1987) Prophylactic treatment for venous ulcers, *Nursing Times*, 1 July, Vol. 83, No. 26, pp. 45–6.

Ivancin, L. A. (1983) Healing those fustrating stasis ulcers, *RN*, August, Vol. 46, No. 8, pp. 38–40, 68.

Nicholls, R. (1989) Leg ulcers: collecting the facts, *Nursing Standard*, 16 December, pp. 12–13.

Nicholls, R. (1990) Leg ulcers: a study in the community, *Nursing Standard*, Special Supplement 7, 3 April, pp. 4–6.

Pottle, B. (1987) Trial of a dressing for non-healing ulcers, *Nursing Times*, 25 March, pp. 54–8.

Shreeve, C. (1985) Chronic venous insufficiency, *Nursing Mirror*, 12 June, Vol. 160, No. 24, p. 28.

Solid, R. (1984) Give venous leg ulcers the boot … Unna's boot, *Nursing 84*, November, Vol. 14, No. 11, pp. 52–3.

Taylor, S. and Hoile, A. (1986) Treating chronic venous ulcers, *Nursing Times*, 28 May, Vol. 82, No. 22, pp. 33–7.

Thomas, L. (1988) Treating leg ulcers, *Nursing Standard*, 13 February, Vol. 2, No. 19, p. 28.

Venn, G. and Fox, A. (1987) Leg ulcers pointers to management, *Nursing Times*, Supplement, 25 March, Vol. 83, No. 12, pp. 49–52.

Lymphatics

Alderman, C. (1988) The lymphatic system, *Nursing Standard*, 19 November, Vol. 3, No. 8, pp. 26–7.

Badger, C. (1986) The swollen limb, *Nursing Times*, 30 July, p. 40.

Badger, C. (1987) Lymphoedema: management of patients with advanced cancer, *The Professional Nurse*, January, Vol. 2, No. 4, p. 100.

Badger, C. (1988) A problem for nurses: Lymphoedema, *Surgical Nurse*, October, p. 14.

Badger, C. (1990) The management of oedema, *Nursing Standard*, 20 June, Vol. 4, No. 39, pp. 28–30.

Baskerville, P. A. (1989) Primary lymphoedema, *Surgery*, February, Vol. 65, pp. 1550–5.

Getz, D. (1985) The primary, secondary and tertiary nursing interventions of lymphoedema, *Cancer Nursing*, June, Vol. 8, No. 3, p. 177.

Loefler, I. J. P. (1989) Elephantiasis, *Surgery*, August, Vol. 71, p. 1684.

Peripheral Vascular Disease

Black, C. A. (1990) Peripheral vascular disorders, *Nursing Clinics of North America*, December, p. 777.

Dormandy, J. (1989) Peripheral vascular disease, *Medicine International*, September, No. 69, p. 2872.

Raftery, A. (1991) Management of peripheral vascular disease, *Update*, 1 March, Vol. 42, No. 5, pp. 455–62.

Ronayne, R. (1989) Smoking: a decision-making dilemma for the vascular patient, *Journal of Advanced Nursing*, August, p. 647.

Varicose Veins

Fox, J. (1988) Management of varicose veins—surgery or injections?, *Update*, 15 July, Vol. 37, No. 2, p. 140.

Green, S. and Wickenden, A. (1984) Varicose veins, *Nursing*, June, Vol. 2, No. 26, pp. 779–81.

Jamieson, C. (1989) Management of varicose veins, *The Practitioner*, 22 April, Vol. 233, No. 1467, p. 578.

Mansfield, A. (1986) Varicose veins, *British Journal of Hospital Medicine*, August, Vol. 36, No. 2, pp. 124–7.

Murie, J. (1988) Recovery from surgery for varicose veins, *Update*, 1 December, Vol. 37, No. 11, p. 1042.

Venous Conditions

Fahey, V. A. and Bergan, J. J. (1985) Venous reconstruction: Surgery for severe venous stasis, *Journal of the Association of Operating Room Nurses*, February, Vol. 41, No. 2, pp. 423–9.

Hull, R. D. (1989) Pulmonary embolism and venous thrombosis, *Medicine*, September, Vol. 69, pp. 2877–83.

Kakkar, V. (1987) Venous thrombosis and pulmonary embolism, *Surgery*, January, Vol. 1, No. 40, p. 948.

Love, C. (1990) Deep vein thrombosis: threat to recovery, *Nursing Times*, 31 January, Vol. 86, No. 5, pp. 40–3.

Miller, J. (1989) Nursing patients with deep vein thrombosis, *Nursing*, 28 September–11 October, Vol. 3, No. 2, pp. 36–9.

Milne, C. (1988) Haemostasis, *Nursing Standard*, 22 October, Vol. 3, No. 4, pp. 26–7.

Mitchell, J. R. A. (1985) Thrombosis—pathophysiology and prevention, July, *Medicine*, Vol. 19, pp. 797–803.

Taylor, D. L. (1983) Thrombophlebitis: Physiology, signs and symptoms, *Nursing 83*, July, Vol. 13, No. 7, pp. 52–3.

chapter 10

ASSESSMENT AND CARE OF PATIENTS WITH HAEMATOLOGICAL DISORDERS

ANATOMY AND PHYSIOLOGY

The haematological system consists of the blood and the sites where blood is produced, including the bone marrow and lymph nodes. The blood is a specialized organ that differs from other organs in that it exists in a fluid state. The fluid consists of cellular components suspended in blood plasma. The blood cells are divided into erythrocytes (red blood cells, normally 5×10^{12}/l of blood) and leucocytes (white blood cells, normally $5–10 \times 10^9$/l of blood). There are approximately 500–1,000 erythrocytes for each leucocyte. Also suspended in the plasma are small, non-nucleated cell fragments called platelets (normally $150–300 \times 10^9$/l of blood). These cellular components of blood normally make up 40 to 45 per cent of the blood volume. The fraction of the blood occupied by erythrocytes is called the haematocrit. Blood appears as a thick, opaque, red fluid. Its colour is imparted by the haemoglobin contained within the red blood cells.

The volume of blood in humans is approximately 7 to 10 per cent of the normal body weight, which represents about five litres. The blood is recirculated through the vascular system and serves as a link between body organs, carrying oxygen absorbed from the lungs and nutrients absorbed from the gastrointestinal tract to the body cells for cellular metabolism.

The blood also carries waste products produced by cellular metabolism to the lungs, skin, liver and kidneys for subsequent transformation and elimination from the body. It also carries hormones, antibodies and other products of internal secretion to their sites of action or utilization.

In order to perform its functions, blood must remain in its normally fluid state. Because it is fluid, the danger always exists that trauma can lead to loss of blood from the vascular system. To prevent this, the blood has an intricate clotting mechanism that is activated when necessary to seal leaks in the blood vessels.

Excessive clotting is equally dangerous because it potentially obstructs blood flow to vital tissues. To prevent this complication, the body has a fibrinolytic mechanism that eventually dissolves the clots formed within blood vessels.

Bone Marrow

The bone marrow occupies the interior of spongy bones and the central cavity of the long bones of the skeleton. The marrow accounts for 4 to 5 per cent of the total body weight and therefore is one of the larger organs of the body. The marrow can be either red or yellow. Red marrow is the site of active blood cell production and constitutes the major haemopoietic (blood-producing) organ. Yellow marrow, on the other hand, is composed mainly of fat and is not active in the production of blood elements. During childhood, the major portion of the marrow is red. As a person ages, a large portion of the marrow in the long bones is converted into yellow marrow, but it retains the potential for reversion to haemopoietic tissue if necessary. Red marrow in the adult is confined chiefly to the ribs, vertebral column and other flat bones.

The marrow is a highly vascularized organ that consists of connective tissue containing free cells. The most primitive of this population of free cells are the stem cells, which are precursors of two different cell lines. The myeloid line includes erythrocytes, several types of leucocytes and platelets. The lymphoid line differentiates into lymphocytes.

Erythrocytes

The normal red blood cell is a biconcave disc, its configuration resembling that of a soft ball compressed between two fingers. It has a diameter of about 8×10^{-9} m but is a very flexible cell, so flexible that it is capable of passing easily through capillaries that may be as small as 4×10^{-9}m in diameter. The volume of a red blood cell is about 90 cubic microns. The red blood cell membrane is so thin that gases such as oxygen and carbon dioxide can easily diffuse across it. Mature red blood cells consist primarily of haemoglobin, which makes up 95 per cent of the cell mass. These cells have no nuclei and have many fewer metabolic enzymes than do most other cells. The presence of a large amount of haemoglobin enables the cell to perform its principal function, the transport of oxygen between lungs and tissues.

The oxygen-carrying pigment haemoglobin is a protein with a molecular weight of 64,000. The molecule is made up of four subunits, each containing a haem portion attached to a globin chain. Iron is present in the haem component of the molecule. An important property of the haem portion is its ability to bind to oxygen loosely and reversibly. When haemoglobin is combined with oxygen, it is called oxyhaemoglobin. Oxyhaemoglobin has a brighter red colour than haemoglobin that does not contain oxygen (reduced haemoglobin), so arterial blood is a brighter red than venous blood. Whole blood normally contains about 15 g of haemoglobin per 100 ml of blood (15 g/dl), or 30 µg of haemoglobin per million erythrocytes.

Production of Erythrocytes (Erythropoiesis)

Erythroblasts arise from the primitive stem cells in bone marrow. The erythroblast is a nucleated cell that in the process of maturing within the bone marrow accumulates haemoglobin and gradually loses its nucleus. At this stage, the cell is known as a reticulocyte. Further maturation into an erythrocyte entails the loss of dark staining material and a slight shrinkage in size. The mature erythrocyte is then released into the circulation. Under conditions of rapid erythropoiesis, reticulocytes and other immature cells may be released prematurely into the circulation.

Differentiation of the primitive multipotential stem cell of the marrow into an erythroblast is stimulated by erythropoietin, a substance produced mostly by the kidney. Under conditions of prolonged hypoxia, as in the case of people dwelling at high altitudes or after severe haemorrhage, erythropoietin levels are increased and red blood cell production is stimulated.

For normal erythrocyte production, the bone marrow requires iron, vitamin B_{12}, folic acid, pyridoxine (vitamin B_6) and other factors. If any of these factors is deficient during erythropoiesis, decreased red blood cell production and anaemia result.

Iron Stores and Metabolism

Total body iron content in the average adult is approximately 3 g, most of which is present in haemoglobin or one of its breakdown products. Normally, about 0.5 to 1 mg of iron is absorbed per day from the intestinal tract to replace losses of iron in the faeces. Additional amounts of iron, up to 2 mg per day, must be absorbed by the adult female to replace blood lost during menstruation. Iron deficiency in the adult (decreased total body iron content) generally indicates that blood has been lost from the body—for example, by haemorrhage or excessive menstruation.

The concentration of iron in blood is normally about 80–180 µg/dl (14–32 µmol/l) for men and 60–160 µg/dl (11–29 µmol/l) for women. With iron deficiency, bone marrow iron stores are rapidly depleted, haemoglobin synthesis is depressed and the red blood cells produced by the marrow are small and low in haemoglobin.

Vitamin B_{12} and Folic Acid Metabolism

Vitamin B_{12} and folic acid are required for DNA (deoxyribonucleic acid) synthesis in many tissues, but deficiencies of either of these vitamins has the greatest effect on erythropoiesis. Vitamin B_{12} or folic acid deficiency is characterized by the production of abnormally large red blood cells (called megaloblasts). Because these cells are abnormal, many are sequestered in the bone marrow and their rate of release is decreased. This condition results in megaloblastic anaemia.

Both vitamin B_{12} and folic acid are derived from the diet. Vitamin B_{12} combines with intrinsic factor produced in the stomach. The vitamin B_{12}-intrinsic factor complex is absorbed in the distal ileum. Folic acid is absorbed in the proximal small intestine.

Red Blood Cell Destruction

The average lifespan of a circulating red blood cell is 120 days. Aged red blood cells are removed from the blood by the reticuloendothelial system, particularly in the liver and the spleen. The reticuloendothelial cells produce a pigment called bilirubin from the haemoglobin that is released from the destroyed red blood cells. Bilirubin is a waste product that is excreted in the bile. The iron, freed from the haemoglobin during bilirubin formation, is carried in plasma bound to the protein called transferrin to the bone marrow, where it is reclaimed for production of new haemoglobin.

Function of Erythrocytes

The major function of the red blood cells is to transport oxygen from the lungs to the tissues. Erythrocytes are uniquely capable of performing this function because of their high concentration of haemoglobin. If haemoglobin were not present, the oxygen-carrying capacity of blood would be decreased by 99 per cent and would not be sufficient to meet the metabolic needs of the body. An important property of haemoglobin is that it binds oxygen loosely and reversibly. As a result, oxygen readily binds to haemoglobin in the lungs, is carried as oxyhaemoglobin in arterial blood, and readily dissociates from haemoglobin in the tissues. In venous blood, haemoglobin combines with hydrogen ions produced by cellular metabolism and thus buffers excess acid.

Leucocytes

Leucocytes are divided into two general categories, granulocytes and mononuclear cells (agranulocytes). In normal blood, the total leucocyte count is $5–10 \times 10^9/l$. Of these, approximately 60 per cent are granulocytes and 40 per cent are mononuclear cells. Leucocytes can be readily differentiated from erythrocytes by the presence of a nucleus, their larger size and different staining properties.

Granulocytes

Granulocytes are defined by the presence of granules in their cytoplasm. The diameter of a granulocyte is generally two to three times that of an erythrocyte. Granulocytes are divided into three subgroups, which are characterized by their staining properties as seen on microscopic examination. Eosinophils have bright red granules in their cytoplasm, whereas the granules in basophils stain deep blue. The third, and by far the most numerous, cell in this series is the neutrophil, with granules that show a dull violet hue. The nucleus of the mature granulocyte generally has multiple lobes (usually two to four) connected by thin filaments of nuclear material. Because of their nuclear characteristics, these cells are called polymorphonuclear leucocytes. The immature granulocyte has a single-lobed ovoid nucleus and is called a band cell. Ordinarily, band forms account for only a small percentage of circulating granulocytes, although their percentage can increase greatly under conditions in which the rate of production of polymorphonuclear leucocytes is increased. The number of circulating granulocytes found in the healthy person is maintained relatively constant, but in the presence of infection large numbers of these cells are rapidly released into the circulation. Granulocyte production from the stem cell pool is thought to be controlled in a manner similar to the regulation of erythrocyte production by erythropoietin.

Mononuclear Leucocytes (Agranulocytes)

Mononuclear leucocytes (lymphocytes and monocytes) are white blood cells with a single-lobed nucleus and a granule-free cytoplasm. In normal adult blood, lymphocytes account for approximately 30 per cent and monocytes approximately 5 per cent of the total leucocytes. Mature lymphocytes are small cells with scanty cytoplasm. They are produced primarily in the lymph nodes and in the lymphoid tissue of the intestine, spleen and thymus gland from precursor cells that originated as marrow stem cells. Monocytes are the largest of the blood leucocytes. They are produced by the bone marrow and give rise to tissue histiocytes, including Kupffer cells of the liver, peritoneal macrophages, alveolar macrophages and other components of the reticuloendothelial system.

Function of the Leucocytes

The function of the leucocytes is to protect the body from invasion by bacteria and other foreign entities. The major function of neutrophilic polymorphonuclear leucocytes is to ingest foreign material (phagocytosis). Neutrophils arrive at the site within an hour of the onset of an inflammatory reaction and initiate phagocytosis, but are relatively short-lived. The influx of monocytes is later, but these cells continue their phagocytic activities for long periods.

The function of lymphocytes is primarily to produce substances that aid in the attack of foreign material. One group of lymphocytes (T-lymphocytes) kills foreign cells directly or releases a variety of lymphokines, substances that enhance the activity of phagocytic cells. The other group of lymphocytes (B-lymphocytes) produces antibodies, protein molecules that destroy foreign material by several mechanisms.

Eosinophils and basophils function as reservoirs of potent biological materials such as histamine, serotonin and heparin.

Release of these compounds alters the blood supply to tissues, such as occurs during inflammation, and helps to mobilize body defence mechanisms. The increase in the number of eosinophils in allergic states indicates that these cells are involved in the hypersensitivity reaction.

Platelets

Platelets are small particles, $2–4 \times 10^{-9}$ m in diameter, that are present in the circulating blood plasma. Because they disintegrate quickly and easily, their number varies normally between $150–300 \times 10^9/l$ of blood, depending on the numbers that are produced, how they are used and how quickly they are destroyed. They are formed from the fragmentation (the pinching off of bits of membrane and cytoplasm) of giant cells of the bone marrow, called megakaryocytes. Platelet production is regulated by thrombopoietin.

Platelets play an essential role in the control of bleeding. When vascular injury occurs, platelets collect at the site. Substances released from platelet granules and other blood cells cause the platelets to adhere to each other and form a patch or plug, which temporarily stops bleeding. Additional substances released from platelets activate coagulation factors in the blood plasma.

Blood Coagulation

Blood coagulation is the process whereby the components of the liquid blood are transformed into a semi-solid material called a blood clot. The blood clot is composed mainly of blood cells entrapped in a meshwork of fibrin. Fibrin is formed from proteins in the plasma as the result of a complex series of reactions.

Many factors are involved in the reaction cascade that forms fibrin. The clotting factors are listed in Table 10.1, and the extrinsic and intrinsic pathways for fibrin generation are shown diagrammatically in Figure 10.1. When tissue is injured, the extrinsic pathway is activated by the release from the tissue of a substance called thromboplastin. As the result of a series of reactions, prothrombin is converted to thrombin, which in turn catalyzes the conversion of fibrinogen to fibrin in the presence of calcium (factor IV).

Clotting by the intrinsic pathway is activated when the collagen lining blood vessels is exposed. Clotting factors are then activated sequentially until, as with the extrinsic pathway, fibrin is ultimately formed. Although longer, this sequence is probably most often responsible for clotting *in vivo*. The intrinsic pathway is also responsible for initiating the clotting of blood that comes into contact with glass or other foreign surfaces, as when blood is withdrawn from the body into a test tube. It is for this reason that anticoagulants must often be used when drawing blood for chemical or other tests. The anticoagulants

Table 10.1 *Clotting factors*

Official number	Synonym	Contemporary version	
I	Fibrinogen	I	(fibrinogen)
II	Prothrombin	II	(prothrombin)
III	Tissue thromboplastin	III	(tissue factor)
IV	Calcium	IV	(calcium)
V	Labile factor	V	(labile factor)
		VI	PF$_3$ (platelet coagulation activities)
		VI	PF$_4$
VII	Stable factor	VII	(stable factor)
VIII	Anti-haemophilic factor	VIII	AHF (anti-haemophilic factor)
		VIII	VWF (von Willebrand factor)
		VIII	RAg (related antigen)
IX	Christmas factor	IX	(Christmas factor)
X	Stuart-Prower factor	X	(Stuart-Prower factor)
XI	Plasma thromboplastin (antecedent)	XI	(plasma thromboplastin antecedent)
XII	Hageman factor	XII	HF (Hageman factor)
		XII	PK (Prekallikrein, Fletcher)
		XII	HMWK (high molecular weight kininogen)
XIII	Fibrin stabilizing factor	XIII	Fibrin stabilizing factor

The Roman numerals and synonyms designating each clotting factor accepted by the International Committee on Blood Clotting Factors are located in the lefthand columns. Note the absence of factor VI. The version in the righthand column incorporates more recently recognized clotting factors, but is not officially recognized. (Green, D., General considerations of coagulation proteins, Ann. Clin. Lab. Sci., Vol. 8, No. 2, pp. 95–105.)

usually used are either citrate, which binds the plasma calcium, or heparin, which prevents the conversion of prothrombin to thrombin. Citrate cannot be used as an anticoagulant *in vivo* because binding of plasma calcium would cause death. Heparin can be used clinically as an anticoagulant. Warfarins are also used clinically for their anticoagulant action of interfering with the production of several of the plasma coagulating factors.

Clots that form in the body are eventually dissolved by the action of the fibrinolytic system, which consists of plasmin and other proteolytic enzymes. Through the action of this system, clots are dissolved as tissue is repaired and the vascular system is returned to its normal baseline state.

Blood Plasma

After cellular elements are removed from blood, the remaining liquid portion is called blood plasma. It contains ions, proteins and other substances. If plasma is allowed to clot, the remaining fluid is called serum. Serum has essentially the same composition as plasma except that its fibrinogen and several of the clotting factors have been removed.

Plasma Proteins

Plasma proteins consist primarily of albumin and globulins. The globulins in turn consist of alpha, beta and gamma fractions derived by a laboratory test called serum protein electrophoresis. Each of these groups is made up of distinct proteins. The gamma globulins, which consist mainly of antibodies, are called immunoglobulins. These proteins are produced by the lymphocytes and plasma cells. Important proteins in the alpha and beta fractions are the transport globulins and the clotting factors, which are made in the liver. The transport globulins carry various substances in bound form around the circulation. For example, thyroid-binding globulin carries thyroxin, and transferrin carries iron. The clotting factors, including fibrinogen, remain in an inactive form in the blood plasma until activated by the clotting cascade.

Albumin is particularly important for the maintenance of fluid volume within the vascular system. Capillary walls are impermeable to albumin, so its presence in the plasma creates an osmotic force that keeps fluid within the vascular space. Albumin, which is produced in the liver, has the capacity to bind to a number of substances that are often present in plasma. In this way, it functions as a transport protein for metals, fatty acids, bilirubin and drugs, among other substances.

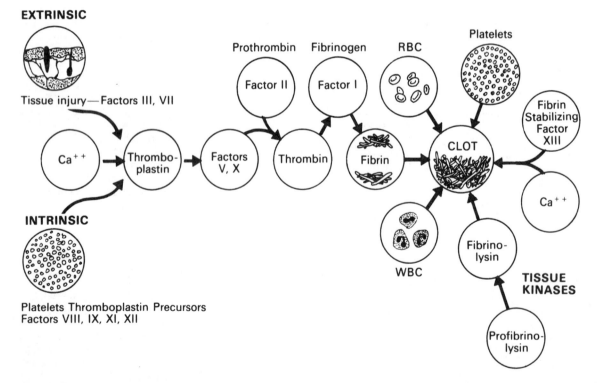

Figure 10.1 The blood-clotting mechanism. The schematic drawing represents the factors essential to change blood into a solid gel. The entire chain reaction in which fibrinogen (a plasma protein) is converted to fibrin (the clot) takes place at the site of vessel damage. (Adapted from Feller, I. and Archambeault, C., *Nursing the Burn Patient*, Institute for Burn Medicine, Ann Arbor, Michigan.)

Altered Physiology of the Haematological System

Anaemias

A frequent disorder of the haematological system is a decrease in the number of circulating red blood cells. This condition, called anaemia, can result from either under-production of red blood cells by the bone marrow or increased destruction of circulating red blood cells. Underproduction of red blood cells can be due to a deficiency in cofactors for erythropoiesis, including folic acid, vitamin B_{12} and iron. Red blood cell production may also be reduced if bone marrow is suppressed (by tumour or drugs) or is inadequately stimulated due to lack of erythropoietin, as occurs in chronic renal disease. Increased destruction of red blood cells may occur because of an overactive reticuloendothelial system (e.g., hypersplenism) or because the bone marrow produces abnormal red blood cells (e.g., sickle cell anaemia). Because the red blood cell and its contained haemoglobin are important for the delivery of oxygen to tissues, anaemias may result in tissue hypoxia.

Bleeding Disorders

Bleeding disorders can be attributed to deficiency in either platelets or clotting factors in the circulating blood. Platelet function in the blood plasma can be reduced as the result of bone marrow insufficiency, increased splenic destruction or abnormal circulating platelets. Deficiencies of clotting factors are usually due to underproduction of these factors by the liver. Haemophilia is a hereditary disorder that results from deficiency of clotting factors VIII and IX.

Clinical Features of Blood Disorders

Problems commonly seen in patients with blood disorders are outlined in Table 10.2.

HAEMATOLOGICAL INVESTIGATIONS

Methods of Obtaining Blood

Venepuncture

Most routine haematological tests are performed on venous blood.

Finger Puncture

The finger puncture method is used frequently for blood smears and counts. This method utilizes capillary blood, but for practical purposes the results are identical to those obtained with venous blood. A lancet makes a puncture of 1 to 2 mm. The most common haematological tests are described in Table 10.3.

Bone Marrow Aspiration

Bone marrow is usually aspirated from the sternum or iliac crest in adults. Most patients need no more preparation than a careful explanation of the procedure but, for some very anxious patients, pethidine and/or a sedative such as diazepam may be useful. It is always important for the doctor or nurse to describe and explain the procedure as it is being performed. First, the skin area is cleansed as for any minor operation. Then a small area is anaesthetized with lignocaine, through the skin and subcutaneous tissue to the periosteum of the bone. The bone marrow needle is introduced with a stylet in place. When the needle is felt to go through the outer cortex of bone and enter the marrow cavity, the stylet is removed, a syringe is attached, and a small volume (0.5 ml) of blood and marrow is aspirated. The actual aspiration always causes brief pain, and the patient should be warned of this. Taking deep breaths or using relaxation techniques often helps.

If a bone marrow biopsy is necessary, it is best performed after the aspiration and with a special needle. Several types of needles are available, the procedure varying according to the type of needle used. Because these needles are large, the skin should be punctured first with a surgical blade (No. 9 or 11) to make a 3-mm or 4-mm incision. Only the iliac bone is used for this procedure (Figure 10.2), because the sternum is too thin.

The major hazard of these procedures is a slight risk of haemorrhage. This risk is increased if the patient's platelet count is low. Following bone marrow aspiration, pressure should be applied to the site for several minutes. After a biopsy, pressure is applied to the posterior iliac crest for 60 minutes by the combination of a pressure dressing and ensuring the patient lies in a recumbent position in bed. Most patients have no discomfort after a bone

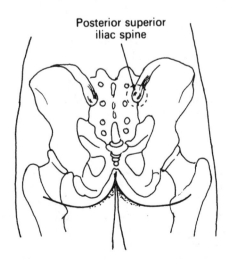

Figure 10.2 Site of bone marrow biopsy.

marrow aspiration, but the site of a biopsy may ache for a day or two.

ANAEMIA

Definition and Aetiology

Anaemia is a laboratory term that indicates a low red cell count and a below normal haemoglobin or haematocrit level. It is not a disease, but rather reflects a disease state or altered body function. Physiologically, anaemia exists when there is an insufficient amount of haemoglobin to deliver oxygen to the tissues.

There are many different kinds of anaemias. Some are due to inadequate production of red blood cells, while others are due to premature or excessive destruction of red blood cells. The most common cause is blood loss, but other aetiological factors include deficits in iron and other nutrients, hereditary factors and chronic diseases.

Altered Physiology

The appearance of anaemia reflects either marrow failure or excessive red cell loss, or both. Marrow failure (i.e., reduced erythropoiesis) may occur as a result of a nutritional deficiency, toxic exposure, malignancy or, as in many instances, from unknown causes. Red cells may be lost through haemorrhage or excessive haemolysis (increased destruction). In the latter case the problem may be rooted in some red cell defect that is incompatible with normal red cell survival or explainable on the basis of some factor extrinsic to the red cell that promotes red cell destruction.

Red cell lysis (dissolution) occurs mainly within the phagocytic cells of the reticuloendothelial system, notably in the liver and spleen. As a byproduct of this process, bilirubin, formed within the phagocyte, enters the bloodstream, and any increase in haemolysis is promptly reflected by an increase in plasma bilirubin. (This concentration is normally 1×10^{-2} g/l or less; levels above this produce visible jaundice of the sclerae.)

If, as happens in certain specific haemolytic disorders, red cells are destroyed within the circulating bloodstream, haemoglobin itself appears in the plasma (haemoglobinaemia). If its concentration there exceeds the capacity of the plasma haptoglobin to bind it all i.e., if the amount is more than about 1 g/l, then this pigment is free to diffuse through the renal glomeruli and into the urine (haemoglobinuria). Thus, the presence or absence of haemoglobinaemia and haemoglobinuria provides information about the location of abnormal blood destruction in a patient with haemolysis and can be a clue to the nature of the haemolytic process.

A conclusion as to whether the anaemia in a particular patient is caused by haemolysis or by inadequate erythropoiesis usually can be reached on the basis of: (1) the reticulocyte count in the circulating blood; (2) the degree to which young red cells are proliferating in the bone marrow and the manner in which they are maturing, as observed on biopsy; and (3) the presence or absence of hyperbilirubinaemia and haemoglobinaemia. Moreover, erythropoiesis can actually be quantitated by measuring the rate at which injected radioactive iron is incorporated into circulating erythrocytes. The life span of the patient's red cells (therefore, the rate of haemolysis) can be measured by tagging a portion of these with radioactive chromium, reinjecting them, and following their disappearance from the circulating blood over the course of the ensuing days or weeks. Methods by which one particular type of marrow failure can be distinguished from another type, and one haemolytic disease from another, are specified in relation to each of the conditions discussed.

Considerations in the Elderly Patient

Anaemia is common in older people and is the most common haematological condition that affects the elderly, but studies indicate that the ageing process does not cause changes in haemopoiesis. The cause is usually unexplained. Anaemia is generally considered to be part of a pathological process rather than a result of ageing. Because the elderly person may be unable to respond adequately to the anaemia with increased cardiac output or pulmonary ventilation, anaemia in this population can have serious effects on cardiopulmonary function if not properly treated. Thus, it is particularly important to identify the cause of the anaemia and not to attribute it to the ageing process.

Clinical Features

Aside from the severity of the anaemia, several factors affect the anaemic patient and tend to influence the severity and even the presence of symptoms: (1) the speed with which the anaemia has developed; (2) its duration (i.e., its chronicity); (3) the metabolic requirements of the particular patient; (4) any other disorders or disabilities with which the patient is currently afflicted; and (5) special complications or concomitant features of the condition that has produced this anaemia.

The more rapidly an anaemia develops, the more severe its symptoms. An otherwise normal person can tolerate as much as a 50 per cent gradual reduction in haemoglobin, red count or haematocrit without pronounced symptoms or significant incapacity, whereas the rapid loss of as little as 30 per cent may precipitate profound vascular collapse in the same individual. A person who has been anaemic for a very long period of time, with haemoglobin levels between 9 and 11 g/dl, experiences few or no symptoms other than slight tachycardia on exertion. Exertional dyspnoea is likely to occur below, but not

Table 10.2 *Common problems of patients with blood disorders*

Patient problem	Nursing care
Anxiety of patient and family/friends	Reinforce doctor's explanation of diagnosis, and its implications for patient Explain the nature, discomforts and limitations of activity associated with diagnostic procedures and treatments Offer patient the service of listening Provide an atmosphere of acceptance and understanding Promote patient's relaxation and comfort Remember patient's individual preferences Promote independence and self-care within patient's limitations Encourage family to participate in patient's care (as desired) Create a comfortable atmosphere for family visits with the patient
Fatigue and weakness	Plan nursing care to conserve the patient's strength and emotional energy Give frequent rest periods Encourage patient to walk as much as can be tolerated Avoid disturbance, noise and stress Promote optimal nutrition – high protein and high-calorie foods and drinks
Haemorrhagic tendencies	Keep the patient at rest during bleeding episodes Apply firm digital pressure to bleeding sites and call doctor Apply cold compresses to bleeding sites when indicated Do not disturb clots Avoid giving medications by injection Support patient during transfusion therapy Observe for symptoms of internal bleeding Summon the doctor immediately if patient begins to bleed from mouth or throat
Ulcers of the tongue, gums or mucous membranes	Avoid irritating foods or beverages Give frequent oral hygiene with mild, cool mouthwash solutions Use sponge applicators or soft-bristled toothbrush Keep the lips lubricated Give mouth care both before and after meals Encourage regular visits to the dentist Obtain advice from oral hygienist and hospital oral surgeon, as required
Dyspnoea	Elevate head of bed Use pillows to support patient in the orthopnoeic position Administer oxygen as prescribed by the doctor Prevent unnecessary exertion
Bone and joint pains	Relieve pressure of bedding by using a cradle Administer either hot or cold compresses as indicated Administer adequate analgesia as prescribed on a regular basis Provide for joint immobilization when prescribed; obtain advice from physiotherapist
Fever	Tepid sponge according to hospital procedure when indicated Give antipyretic (e.g. paracetamol) drugs as prescribed Encourage fluid intake unless contraindicated Maintain a cool environment, e.g. by fanning the room
Pruritis or skin eruptions	Keep patient's fingernails short (refer to chiropodist) Use soap sparingly Apply emollient lotions in skin care (obtain advice from dermatologist)

above, 7.5 g/dl; weakness, only below 6 g/dl; dyspnoea at rest, below 3 g/dl; and cardiac failure, only at the profoundly low level of 2 to 2.5 g/dl.

Patients who customarily are very active are more likely to experience symptoms, and symptoms that are more pronounced, than a more sedentary person. A hypothyroid patient, who requires less than the usual amount of oxygen, may be perfectly asymptomatic,

Table 10.3 *Common haematological laboratory tests*

Test	Definition
Full blood count	Includes enumeration of number of white cells, red cells and platelets per litre of venous blood, as well as differential count, percentage of each type of nucleated cell in the blood (i.e. percentage polymorphonuclears, lymphocytes, and so on)
Reticulocyte count	Percentage of young (1–2 days old), non-nucleated erythrocytes in peripheral blood; they are recognized in special stains of blood smears as cells with lacy inclusions, which consist of RNA
Haemoglobin electrophoresis	A drop of blood placed on a solid medium (paper, starch block, gel or cellulose acetate) is exposed to a current of electricity while being bathed by a buffer solution. The different haemoglobins (e.g. A, A-2, F, S) travel at varying speeds, depending on their charge. At the end of the procedure, the paper or gel is stained, and the haemoglobins in each sample can be identified
Sickling test	A drop of blood is mixed with a drop of a reducing agent (sodium metabisulphite). This substance deprives the red cells of oxygen and induces sickling if S haemoglobin is present. Sickling of red cells is observed under the microscope in 30 minutes if the blood was obtained from a person with either sickle trait or sickle cell anaemia. Normal blood does not undergo any change
Leucocyte alkaline phosphatase	Leucocyte alkaline phosphatase is an enzyme present in high concentrations in granules of neutrophils. A special stain of peripheral blood smears is used to estimate the amount of this enzyme present per cell. The normal score is 20 to 130. Untreated chronic myeloid leukaemia patients have scores of less than 20, and the test is useful to help diagnose chronic myeloid leukaemia. High scores are seen in infection and steroid-induced leucocytosis
Coombs' test	Determines the presence of immune globulin (hence, antibodies) on the surface of erythrocytes (direct Coombs' test), or in the plasma (indirect Coombs' test)
Bleeding time	A screening test for disorders of platelet function. It is the time taken for bleeding to cease after a standardized skin wound is produced, usually on the volar surface of the forearm. A prolonged time suggests an inherited or acquired platelet defect, e.g. von Willebrand's disease or aspirin ingestion
Platelet aggregation	A measure of the time and completeness of the formation of platelet aggregates in a sample of plasma, after the addition of an agent such as adrenaline or adenosine diphosphate (ADP)
Prothrombin time test	Measures the coagulant activity of the 'extrinsic' system, including fibrinogen, prothrombin and factors V, VII and X. It is used to monitor warfarin therapy as well as for a screening test for liver disease
Partial thromboplastin time test	A screening test for deficiencies of all plasma coagulation factors except VII and XIII. It is usually considered abnormally prolonged if levels of factors are less than 30 per cent of normal. It is often used to monitor heparin therapy

without tachycardia or increased cardiac output, at a haemoglobin level of 100 g/l. Contrary to this, at any given level of anaemia, patients with underlying heart disease are far more apt to experience angina or symptoms of congestive failure than someone without heart disease.

Finally, as will emerge in the discussions that follow, many anaemic disorders are complicated by various other abnormalities that do not depend on the anaemia but are inherently associated with these particular diseases. These abnormalities may give rise to symptoms that completely overshadow those of the anaemia, as is exemplified by the painful crises of sickle cell anaemia (see p. 441).

There are a number of haematological disorders in which anaemia is the presenting problem, or the problem of paramount concern, and that, as a group, exemplify all of the aetiological factors that have been discussed and all of the pathogenic mechanisms that have been formulated to date with respect to anaemia.

Diagnosis

A variety of haematological investigations are performed to determine the type and cause of the anaemia. These include measurements of haemoglobin and haematocrit, red cell indices, white blood cell studies, serum iron level, measurement of total iron binding capacity, folate level, vitamin B_{12} level, platelet count, bleeding time, prothrombin time and partial thromboplastin time. Bone marrow aspiration and biopsy may be included. In addition, diagnostic studies are done to determine the presence of acute or chronic illness and the source of any chronic blood loss.

Management

Management of anaemia is directed toward reversing the cause and replacing any blood that has been lost. The discussion below of each specific type of anaemia includes its management.

▶ NURSING PROCESS
▶ THE PATIENT WITH ANAEMIA

▶ *Assessment*

The nursing history and physical examination are important when caring for a patient with anaemia. They will reveal clues that may alert the nurse to problems and concerns that often can be alleviated. Weakness, fatigue and general malaise are common, as are pallor of the skin and mucous membranes. Jaundice may be present in patients with pernicious anaemia or anaemia that is of a haemolytic nature. Dryness of the skin and hair and spooning (concave surface) of the nails are often seen in iron deficiency anaemia.

Cardiac status is carefully assessed. When the haemoglobin is low, the heart will attempt to compensate by pumping faster and harder in an effort to deliver more blood to hypoxic tissue. This increased cardiac workload results in such symptoms as tachycardia, palpitations, dyspnoea, dizziness and orthopnoea. Congestive heart failure will eventually develop, as evidenced by cardiomegaly, hepatomegaly and peripheral oedema.

Neurological examination is also important because of the effects of pernicious anaemia on the central and peripheral nervous systems. The patient is assessed for peripheral numbness and paraesthesias, ataxia, poor co-ordination and confusion. Assessment of gastrointestinal function may reveal complaints of nausea, vomiting, diarrhoea, anorexia and glossitis (inflammation of the tongue).

The nursing history includes information about any drugs the patient may be taking that could depress bone marrow activity or interfere with folate metabolism. The patient is also questioned about any loss of blood, as evidenced by blood in the stools or, for women, excessive menstrual flow. Family history is important because certain anaemias are inherited. A nutritional history may reveal deficiencies in essential nutrients such as iron, vitamin B_{12} and folic acid.

▶ *Patient's Problems*

Based on the assessment data, the patient's main problems may include the following:

- Immobility secondary to weakness, fatigue and general malaise.
- Breathlessness or angina due to heart failure.
- Malnutrition due to loss of intake of essential nutrients.

▶ *Planning and Implementation*
▶ Expected Outcomes

The main outcomes for the patient may include tolerance of normal activity, attainment/maintenance of normal cardiac output and attainment/maintenance of adequate nutrition.

Nursing Care

Tolerance of Normal Activity

Nursing care is planned to conserve the patient's strength and physical and emotional energy. Frequent rest periods are encouraged, and support from the family or close friends is elicited to promote a restful environment. A regular schedule of rest and sleep is imperative for restoring strength and activity tolerance. Activities of daily living are encouraged as tolerated. As the anaemia is treated and blood studies return to normal, the patient is encouraged to resume normal activities gradually. Activities that are found to cause undue fatigue are postponed until greater endurance becomes evident. Safety precautions are taken to prevent falls resulting from poor co-ordination, paraesthesias and weakness.

Attainment/Maintenance of Normal Cardiac Output

With longstanding reduction of oxyhaemoglobin, the heart may begin to lose its ability to withstand the additional work of supplying blood to hypoxic tissue. It will begin to enlarge, and cardiac output will decrease. Nursing measures are directed toward decreasing activities and stimuli that cause an increase in heart rate and that necessitate increased cardiac output. The patient is encouraged to identify those situations that precipitate palpitations and dyspnoea and to avoid them until the anaemic condition improves. If dyspnoea is a problem, measures such as elevation of the head of the bed and the use of pillows for support are used. Unnecessary exertion is avoided. Oxygen is administered when necessary. Vital signs are monitored frequently and the patient is observed for indications of fluid retention, e.g., peripheral oedema, decreased urinary output and neck vein distension.

Attainment/Maintenance of Adequate Nutrition

Inadequate intake of essential nutrients, such as iron and folic acid, can cause some anaemias. The symptoms associated with anaemias, such as fatigue and anorexia, can also lead to malnutrition. A well-balanced diet high in protein and high-calorie foods, fruits and vegetables is encouraged. The patient's family and close friends are included in dietary teaching sessions because the diet plan should be acceptable to everyone involved in caring for the patient at home.

► *Evaluation*
► **Expected Outcomes**

1. Patient tolerates normal activity.
   a. Follows a progressive plan of rest, activities and exercises.
   b. Paces activities according to energy level.
2. Attains/maintains normal cardiac output.
   a. Avoids activities that cause tachycardia, palpitations, dizziness and dyspnoea.
   b. Rest is taken to relieve breathlessness.
   c. Has normal vital signs.
   d. Experiences no signs of fluid retention, e.g., peripheral oedema, decreased urinary output, neck vein distension.
3. Attains/maintains adequate nutrition.
   a. Eats foods high in protein, calories and vitamins.
   b. Avoids foods that cause gastric irritation.
   c. Develops a meal plan that promotes optimal nutrition.

Classification of Anaemias

There are several ways to classify the anaemias. The physiological approach is to determine whether the anaemia is due to a defect in production of red cells (hypoproliferative anaemia) or to destruction of the red cells (haemolytic anaemia).

In the hypoproliferative anaemias, red cells usually survive normally, but the marrow is unable to produce adequate numbers of cells; thus, the reticulocyte count is depressed. This situation may be a result of marrow damage by drugs or chemicals (e.g., chloramphenicol, benzene) or may be due to lack of erythropoietin (as in renal disease) or to lack of iron, vitamin B_{12} or folic acid.

When haemolysis is the major cause of anaemia, the abnormality is usually within the red cell itself (as in sickle cell anaemia or glucose-6-phosphate dehydrogenase deficiency), in the plasma (as in the immune hae-

molytic anaemias), or in the circulation (as in heart valve haemolysis). In all of these haemolytic anaemias, the reticulocyte count is elevated and the indirect bilirubin is high, often enough to cause clinical jaundice.

Hypoproliferative Anaemias

Aplastic Anaemia

Altered Physiology

Aplastic anaemia is caused by a decrease in precursor cells in the bone marrow and replacement of the marrow with fat. It may be idiopathic, auto-immune, result from certain infections or be caused by drugs, chemicals or radiation damage. Agents that regularly produce marrow aplasia in sufficient dosage include benzene and benzene derivatives; anti-cancer agents such as nitrogen mustard; the antimetabolites, including methotrexate and 6-mercaptopurine; and certain toxic materials, such as inorganic arsenic. Other agents occasionally responsible for aplasia or hypoplasia include certain antimicrobials, anticonvulsants, anti-thyroid drugs, antidiabetic agents, antihistamines, analgesics, sedatives, phenothiazines, insecticides and heavy metals. The most common offenders in this respect are the antimicrobials chloramphenicol and the organic arsenicals, the anticonvulsant phenytoin, the anti-inflammatory phenylbutazone, sulphonamides and gold compounds.

In many situations, aplastic anaemia occurs when a drug or chemical is ingested in toxic amounts. However, in a small minority of people it develops after a drug has been taken in the recommended dosage. These latter cases may be considered a type of idiosyncratic drug reaction in people who are hypersensitive for reasons as yet unknown. Provided that their exposure is arrested early, a prompt and complete recovery may be anticipated. (Unfortunately, one cannot be so optimistic in the case of chloramphenicol recipients. Reactions in people hypersensitive to this drug may be completely unrelated to dosage; they may develop long after the drug has been discontinued and can progress to a complete and fatal aplasia despite all available therapy.)

Whatever the offending drug, if exposure is allowed to continue after signs of hypoplasia have appeared, bone marrow depression almost certainly progresses to the point of complete and irreversible failure—hence, the importance of frequent full blood counts for every patient receiving a drug or exposed regularly to any chemical that has been implicated in the production of aplastic anaemia.

Diagnosis

Because the bone marrow is hypocellular, attempts at marrow aspiration frequently yield only a few drops of blood. A biopsy is usually necessary to demonstrate a severe decrease in normal marrow elements and replacement by fat. The abnormality is probably in the stem cell, the precursor for granulocytes, erythrocytes and platelets. As a result, pancytopenia (deficiency in all of the cellular elements of the blood) occurs.

Clinical Features

The onset of aplastic anaemia characteristically is a gradual one, marked by weakness, pallor, breathlessness on exertion and other features of anaemia. A presenting symptom in about a third of the patients is abnormal bleeding due to thrombocytopenia. When the granulocytic series is involved as well, the patient is likely to present with fever and sepsis, in addition to bleeding. Physical signs, except for pallor and skin haemorrhages, are unremarkable. The blood count is marked by pancytopenia. Red cells are normocytic and normochromic, that is, of normal size and colour.

Management

As might be expected from a condition that affects all haemopoietic cells, aplastic anaemia carries a very poor prognosis. Three methods of treatment are currently employed: (1) bone marrow transplantation; (2) administration of immunosuppressive therapy with antilymphocyte globulin (ALG); and (3) high-dose methylprednisolone therapy.

The goal of bone marrow transplantation is to provide the patient with an undamaged supply of functioning haemopoietic tissue. Successful transplantation requires the ability to match donor and recipient and to prevent complications during the recovery process. With the use of the immunosuppressant cyclosporin, the incidence of graft rejection is less than 10 per cent.

The goal of immunosuppressive therapy with antilymphocyte globulin is to remove the immunological functions that prolong the aplasia and thus allow the patient's bone marrow a chance to recover. Antilymphocyte globulin is given through a central venous catheter daily for seven to 10 days. Patients who respond to the therapy usually do so within six weeks to three months, but response may be as late as six months after treatment. Patients who have nonsevere aplastic anaemia and are treated early in the course of their disease have the best chance of responding to antilymphocyte globulin.

The response rate to high-dose methylprednisolone is similar to that achieved with antilymphocyte globulin. Currently, trials of moderately high doses of methylprednisolone with antilymphocyte globulin are in progress to see if the response rate can be improved further.

Supportive therapy plays a major role in the management of aplastic anaemia. Any offending drug is discontinued. The patient is supported with transfusions of red cells and platelets as necessary to prevent symptoms. Eventually, such patients may develop antibodies to minor red cell antigens and to platelet antigens, so that transfusions no longer raise the counts sufficiently. Death

is usually caused by haemorrhage or infection, although modern antibiotics, especially those active against gram-negative bacilli, have been a major advance for these patients. Patients with pronounced leucopenia are protected from contact with people who have infections. Antibiotics should not be used prophylactically in neutropenic patients, because this favours the emergence of resistant bacteria and fungi.

Prevention

An extremely important area is prevention of drug-induced aplastic anaemia. Because it is not possible to predict which patients will react adversely to a particular drug, potentially toxic drugs should be used only when alternative therapies are not available. Blood cell counts must be carefully monitored in patients receiving potentially marrow-toxic drugs, such as chloramphenicol. People taking toxic drugs on a long-term basis should understand the need for periodic blood studies and know what symptoms to report.

Nursing Care

Patients with diagnosed aplastic anaemia are vulnerable to the effects of leucocyte, erythrocyte and platelet deficiencies. They should be assessed carefully for signs of infection, tissue hypoxia and bleeding. Any wound, abrasion or ulcer of mucous membrane or skin is a potential site of infection and should be guarded against. Oral hygiene also is very important. Depending on the degree of weakness and fatigue, care should be planned to preserve the patient's energy. When thrombocytopenia is present, minor trauma, including subcutaneous and intramuscular injections, must be avoided. Regular atraumatic bowel movements are important, because haemorrhoids can develop and become infected or bleed.

Red Cell Aplasia

Red cell aplasia is an isolated anaemia caused by lack of red cell formation in the marrow. This is a rare disorder in which only the erythroid cells are affected. The marrow is cellular, but the erythroid element is almost absent. There is a severe anaemia without granulocytopenia or thrombocytopenia. The condition is sometimes associated with tumours of the thymus or certain drugs, such as phenytoin, or it may arise during the course of a haemolytic anaemia. Some patients can be shown to produce an antibody to immature red cells, and this may be the cause of the disease. Treatment measures include red cell replacement, thymectomy and administration of immunosuppressive drugs, such as corticosteroids and cyclosporin.

Myelophthisic Anaemias

Myelophthisic anaemias are a varied group of anaemias that differ as to cause but are similar in that all show partial replacement of normal marrow space by abnormal tissue. This tissue may be fibrous (in myelofibrosis) or it may consist of plasma cells (in multiple myeloma) or metastatic carcinoma cells. A marrow biopsy is often necessary for the diagnosis. Pancytopenia is present, although usually less severe than in aplastic anaemia, but there are also young marrow cells circulating, apparently because there is abnormal release from the damaged marrow. Myeloblasts and nucleated red cells are seen in small numbers. The treatment is that for the primary disease. Androgens occasionally improve the patient's condition.

Anaemias in Renal Disease

There is an association between anaemia and kidney disorders. The symptoms of anaemia often constitute the patient's major problems. The haematocrit usually falls to between 20 and 30 per cent and is lower for more severe uraemia, although it rarely falls below 15 per cent. The red cells appear normal on peripheral smear.

This anaemia is due to both a mild shortening of red cell survival and a deficiency of erythropoietin. Some erythropoietin is evidently produced outside the kidney, because some erythropoiesis does continue, even in anephric patients (those whose kidneys have been removed), and developing red cells can be seen in the bone marrow.

- Patients undergoing chronic haemodialysis lose blood into the artificial kidney and may thus become iron deficient. Folic acid deficiency develops because this vitamin passes into the dialysate.
- Dialysis patients should be treated with iron and folic acid and occasional transfusions.

Androgens have been shown to stimulate enough erythropoiesis to obviate the need for transfusions in some patients. Most patients with uraemia can tolerate moderate anaemia with few symptoms and should not be transfused unless symptoms are present.

Anaemias in Chronic Diseases

Many chronic inflammatory diseases are associated with anaemia of a normochromic, normocytic type (red cells are normal in colour and size). These include rheumatoid arthritis, lung abscesses, osteomyelitis, tuberculosis and many malignancies. The anaemia is usually mild and nonprogressive. It develops gradually over a period of six to eight weeks and then stabilizes at haematocrit levels that are seldom below 25 per cent. The haemoglobin rarely falls below 9 g/dl and the bone marrow has normal cellularity with increased stores of iron. Erythropoietin levels are low, perhaps because of decreased production, and there is a block in the utilization of iron by erythroid cells. There is also a moderate shortening of red cell survival.

Most of these patients are comfortable and do not require treatment for the anaemia. With amelioration of the underlying disorder, the marrow iron is used to make red cells, and the haemoglobin rises.

Iron Deficiency Anaemia

Iron deficiency anaemia is a condition in which the total body iron content is decreased below a normal level. (Iron is needed for the synthesis of haemoglobin.) It is the most common type of anaemia in all age groups.

Aetiology

The common cause of iron deficiency in men and postmenopausal women is bleeding (e.g., from ulcers, gastritis or gastrointestinal tumours) or malabsorption, especially after gastric resection. The most common cause in premenopausal women is menorrhagia (excessive menstrual bleeding). Rarely, iron can be lost in the urine during intravascular haemolysis, as in paroxysmal nocturnal haemoglobinuria or heart valve haemolysis.

Clinical and Laboratory Features

In people who are iron deficient, the haemoglobin and the red blood cell count are reduced. The haemoglobin is reduced more than the red cell count, and for this reason the red cells tend to be small and relatively devoid of pigment, that is, hypochromic. Hypochromia is the hallmark of iron deficiency. The cause of this deficiency is the failure of the patient to ingest, or absorb, sufficient dietary iron to compensate for the iron requirements associated with body growth or for the loss of iron that attends bleeding, whether the bleeding is physiological (e.g., menstrual) or pathological.

Patients with iron deficiency present primarily with the symptoms of anaemia. If the deficiency is severe, they may also have a smooth, sore tongue; thin, spoon-shaped fingernails; and pica (a craving to eat unusual substances, such as clay, laundry starch or ice). All of these symptoms subside after therapy.

The laboratory studies show a haemoglobin that is proportionately lower than the haematocrit and red count, because of the small, poorly haemoglobinized red cells (microcytosis and hypochromia). The serum iron concentration is low, the total iron-binding capacity is high and the serum ferritin (a measure of the iron stores) is low. The white count is usually normal, and the platelet count is variable.

Management

It is always important to search for a cause of iron deficiency. It may be a sign of a curable gastrointestinal malignancy or of uterine fibroids or cancer. Except in pregnancy, when the cause is obvious, stool specimens should be tested for occult blood.

Several oral iron preparations are available for treatment: ferrous sulphate, gluconate and fumarate. The cheapest and most effective preparation is ferrous sulphate. Tablets with enteric coating may be poorly absorbed and should be avoided. Usually, three or four doses a day are necessary. Although iron is absorbed best on an empty stomach, taking it with food is usually advised to minimize gastric distress. Patients may be better able to tolerate the therapy if the dose is started at one tablet daily and then raised. They should be warned that iron salts often change the stools to a darker colour. Generally, the iron is continued for a year after the source of bleeding has been controlled. This allows for replenishing of the iron stores.

Nursing Care

Preventive education is important because iron deficiency anaemia is so common in menstruating and pregnant women. Food sources high in iron include organ (for example, liver, kidney) and other meats, cooked white beans, leafy vegetables, raisins and molasses. Taking iron-rich foods with a source of vitamin C enhances absorption.

The selection of a well-balanced diet is encouraged. Nutritional counselling is provided for those whose normal diet is less than adequate. Patients who have a history of faddish diets are counselled that such diets often contain limited amounts of absorbable iron.

Iron therapy usually has to be continued for many months to replenish iron stores. In some cases, intramuscular administration of iron may be prescribed; that is, when oral iron is not absorbed or is poorly tolerated or when iron is needed in large amounts. The injection causes some local pain and can stain the skin. A method for parenteral administration of iron preparations follows:

1. Discard needle used to draw medication into syringe; use new needle for injection to avoid tracking medication through subcutaneous tissue.
2. Allow a small amount of air into syringe.
3. Use a needle 5 cm long—medication is injected deep into upper outer quadrant of buttock.
4. Retract skin over muscle laterally before inserting needle, to prevent leakage and staining of skin (that is, to 'Z' track the iron preparation in the muscle layer).
5. Inject solution slowly followed by air in syringe; wait a few seconds before withdrawing needle.

Occasional febrile or allergic reactions are seen. Total iron replacement with a single intravenous injection is possible, but it can cause a severe anaphylactic reaction.

Patients with iron deficiency anaemia are encouraged to continue their iron therapy as long as it is prescribed, even though they may no longer be fatigued. If the iron supplement causes gastric distress, the patient is told to take it with meals until the symptoms subside, and then to resume the between-meal schedule for maximum absorption. Because ferrous sulphate is apt to deposit on the teeth

and gums, patients are advised to brush their teeth frequently.

Megaloblastic Anaemias

The anaemias caused by deficiencies of the vitamins B_{12} and folic acid show identical bone marrow and peripheral blood changes. This is because both vitamins are essential for normal DNA synthesis. In each case, hyperplasia (abnormal increase in the number of normal cells) of the marrow occurs, and the precursor erythroid and myeloid cells are large and bizarre; some are multinucleated. But many of these cells die within the marrow, so the mature cells, which leave the marrow, are decreased in number. Thus, a pancytopenia develops. In a far advanced situation, the haemoglobin may be as low as 4 to 5 g/dl, the white blood count $2–3 \times 10^9/l$, and the platelet count less than $50 \times 10^9/l$. The red cells are large and the polymorphonuclears are hypersegmented.

Vitamin B_{12} Deficiency

Aetiology

A deficiency of vitamin B_{12} can occur in several ways. Inadequate dietary intake is very rare but can develop in strict vegetarians who consume no meat. Faulty absorption from the gastrointestinal tract is more common. An absence of intrinsic factor normally secreted by cells of the stomach is called pernicious anaemia. This is primarily a disorder of elderly people and has a familial tendency. The abnormality is in the gastric mucosa: the stomach wall becomes atrophic and fails to secrete intrinsic factor. This substance ordinarily binds with the dietary vitamin B_{12} and travels with it to the ileum, where the vitamin is absorbed. Without intrinsic factor, no orally administered B_{12} can enter the body. Even if adequate vitamin B_{12} and intrinsic factor are present, a deficiency can occur if disease involving the ileum or pancreas impairs absorption. Gastrectomy can also cause vitamin B_{12} deficiency.

Clinical Features

After the body stores of vitamin B_{12} are used up, patients begin to show signs of the anaemia. They gradually become weak, listless and pale. The haematological effects of deficiency are accompanied by effects on other organ systems, particularly the gastrointestinal tract and nervous system. Patients with pernicious anaemia develop a smooth, sore, red tongue and mild diarrhoea. They may become confused, but more often have paraesthesias in the extremities and difficulty keeping their balance because of damage to the spinal cord: they lose position sense. These symptoms are progressive, although the course may be marked by spontaneous partial remissions and exacerbations. Without treatment, patients die after several years, usually from congestive failure secondary to anaemia.

Diagnosis

One means of determining the cause of vitamin B_{12} deficiency is the Schilling test. After fasting for 12 hours, the patient is given a small dose of radioactive B_{12} in water to drink, followed by a large, nonradioactive intramuscular dose. When the oral vitamin is absorbed, it will be excreted in the urine; the intramuscular dose helps to flush it into the urine. A 24-hour urine specimen is collected and measured for radioactivity. If very little has been excreted, the test is repeated several days later (the 'second stage'), with a capsule of oral intrinsic factor added to the oral B_{12}. If the patient has pernicious anaemia, this time much more radioactivity will be found in the 24-hour urine. If the problem is due to an ileal or pancreatic defect, administration of digestive enzymes will increase absorption and subsequently increase urine radioactivity.

Management

Vitamin B_{12} deficiency is treated by replacement. Strict vegetarians can prevent or treat deficiency with oral supplementation with vitamins or fortified soy milk. When, as is much more common, the deficiency is due to defective absorption or absence of intrinsic factor, replacement is by intramuscular injections of vitamin B_{12}.

At first, B_{12} is given daily, but eventually most patients are managed with 100 µg intramuscularly monthly. This can produce dramatic recoveries in desperately ill patients. The reticulocyte count rises within a week, and in several weeks the blood counts are all normal. The tongue improves in several days. The neurological features require more time for recovery; if there is severe neuropathy, paralysis or incontinence, the patient may never recover fully.

● Vitamin B_{12} therapy must be continued for the life of the patient who has had pernicious anaemia or non-correctable malabsorption in order to prevent recurrence of the anaemia.

Nursing Care

These patients may need support during the diagnostic tests and nursing care for several aspects of their disease: anaemia, congestive failure, neuropathy. When they are incontinent or paralysed, care must be taken to prevent pressure sores and contracture deformities. The Schilling test can be useful only if the urine collections are complete; here, the nurse's assistance is essential. Patients must be taught about the chronicity of their disorder and the necessity for monthly injections even when they are asymptomatic. The gastric atrophy associated with pernicious anaemia increases the risk of gastric carcinoma, so these patients need to understand that ongoing medical follow-up is important.

Folic Acid Deficiency

Folic acid is another vitamin that is necessary for normal red blood cell production. It is stored as different compounds, referred to as folates. The folate stores in the body are much smaller than those of vitamin B_{12}, so it is much more common to see dietary folate deficiency. This occurs in patients who rarely eat uncooked vegetables or fruits (i.e., primarily elderly people living alone or people with alcoholism). Alcohol increases folic acid requirements, and at the same time people suffering from alcoholism usually have a diet that is deficient in the vitamin. Folic acid requirements are increased in chronic haemolytic anaemias and in pregnancy, so these patients may develop the anaemia while ingesting an adequate diet.

● Patients on prolonged intravenous feeding or hyperalimentation may become folate deficient after several months, unless the vitamin is given intramuscularly. Some patients with small bowel diseases may not absorb it normally.

Clinical Features and Laboratory Tests

All of these patients have the characteristic findings of megaloblastic anaemia along with a sore tongue. Symptoms of folic acid and vitamin B_{12} deficiencies are quite similar, and the two anaemias may coexist. However, the neurological features of vitamin B_{12} deficiency do not occur with folic acid deficiency, and persist if vitamin B_{12} is not replaced. Therefore, careful distinction between the two anaemias must be made. Serum levels of both vitamins can be measured.

Management

Treatment is administration of a good diet and 1 mg of folic acid a day. This should be given intramuscularly only in patients with malabsorption. With the exception of the vitamins given during pregnancy, most proprietary vitamin preparations do not contain folic acid, so it must be given as a separate tablet. When the haemoglobin returns to normal, the folic acid replacement can be stopped. However, people suffering from alcoholism should continue receiving folic acid as long as they continue drinking.

Haemolytic Anaemias

In haemolytic anaemias, the erythrocytes have a shortened life span. The bone marrow is usually able to compensate partially by producing new red cells at three or more times the normal rate. Consequently, all of these anaemias have certain laboratory features in common: the reticulocyte count is elevated, the fraction of indirect bilirubin is increased, and the haptoglobin (a binding protein for free haemoglobin) is often low. The bone marrow is hypercellular, with erythroid proliferation. The only truly diagnostic test for haemolysis is the red cell survival study. This is usually necessary only for difficult diagnostic problems. About 20–30 ml of the patient's blood is removed, incubated with radioactive chromium-51, and then reinjected. The chromium-51 labels the red cells exclusively. After these cells have equilibrated with the circulating blood, small samples are taken at intervals over the next days and weeks, and the radioactivity is measured. A normal chromium-51 survival time is 28 to 35 days. Red cells of patients with severe haemolysis (such as sickle cell anaemia) have survival times of 10 days or less.

Inherited Haemolytic Anaemias

Hereditary Spherocytosis

Hereditary spherocytosis is a haemolytic anaemia characterized by small, sphere-shaped red cells and splenomegaly (enlarged spleen). This is an uncommon disorder inherited in a dominant fashion.

Clinical Features and Diagnosis
An abnormality of the erythrocyte membrane causes cells to lose membrane as they pass through the spleen and to become spherical in shape. These spheres are relatively rigid and easily destroyed. The peripheral blood contains many of the characteristic small spherical cells, and the patient has an anaemia that may be exacerbated during infections, even minor viral illnesses. In addition, the spleen is enlarged. The disorder is usually diagnosed in childhood, but may be missed until adult life because there are few symptoms.

Management
Surgical removal of the spleen (splenectomy) is the treatment. It does not change the erythrocyte defect but removes the site of membrane loss and haemolysis. After splenectomy patients have normal haemoglobin levels, only slight shortening of red cell survival times and few spherical cells in the peripheral smear. Patients have a normal life expectancy. The major complications are all prevented by splenectomy: (1) aplastic crises after infection, often with severe anaemia; (2) nonhealing leg and ankle ulceration; and (3) gallstones.

Sickle Cell Anaemia

Definition and Aetiology
Sickle cell anaemia is a severe haemolytic anaemia resulting from a defective haemoglobin molecule and associated with attacks of pain. This disabling disease is found predominantly in black Afro-Caribbeans, but it also occurs in people from Mediterranean and Arab countries.

Altered Physiology
The defect is a single amino acid substitution in the ß chain of haemoglobin. Because normal haemoglobin A contains two and two ß chains, there are two genes for synthesis of each chain. People with sickle cell trait have inherited only one abnormal gene, so their red cells can synthesize both normal ß chains and ßˢ chains; thus, they have A and S haemoglobin. If two people with sickle trait marry, some of their children may inherit two abnormal genes and will then have only ßˢ chains and only S haemoglobin; these children have sickle cell anaemia.

Clinical Features
The sickle haemoglobin has the unfortunate property of acquiring a crystal-like formation when exposed to low oxygen tension. The oxygen in venous blood is low enough to cause this change; consequently, the cell containing S haemoglobin becomes deformed, rigid and sickle-shaped when in the venous circulation (see Figure 10.3). These long, rigid cells can become lodged in small vessels and, when they pile up against each other, blood flow to a region or an organ may be slowed. When ischaemia or infarction results, the patient may experience pain, swelling and fever. Such a chain of events is presumed to explain the painful crises of this disease, but what triggers the chain or how to prevent it is not understood.

Symptoms are secondary to haemolysis and thrombosis. Patients are always anaemic, with haemoglobin values in the 7–10 g/dl range. Jaundice is characteristic and is usually obvious in the sclerae. The bone marrow expands in childhood in a compensatory effort, sometimes leading to enlargement of the bones of the face and

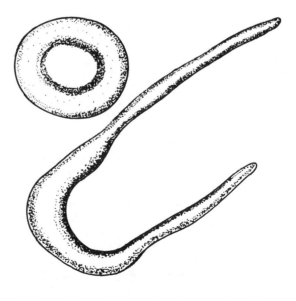

Figure 10.3 A sickled cell and a normal red blood cell.

skull. As a result, patients may have prominent foreheads and high cheekbones. The chronic anaemia is associated with tachycardia, flow murmurs and often cardiomegaly. Arrhythmias and heart failure may occur in older patients.

Like patients with spherocytosis, those with sickle cell anaemia may develop aplastic crises when infected and may have gallstones (due to increased haemolysis that leads to bilirubin stones) and leg ulcers. The latter may be chronic and painful and require skin grafting. These patients are unusually susceptible to infection, particularly pneumonias and osteomyelitis. Infection is one of the most common causes of death.

All of the patient's tissues and organs are constantly vulnerable to microcirculatory interruptions by the sickling process, and therefore are susceptible to hypoxic damage or true ischaemic necrosis at any time. Thrombotic episodes may result in minor pain in an extremity, in severe pain and swelling in a hand or knee, in chest pain due to pulmonary infarction, in pain simulating an acute abdominal crisis or in the sudden appearance of a 'stroke', with hemiplegia. These crises are completely unpredictable; they can occur monthly or very rarely and may last for hours, days or weeks. Events that seem to precipitate crisis include dehydration, fatigue, menstruation, intake of alcohol, emotional stress and acidosis. Certain effects of infarction are permanent, such as hemiplegia, aseptic necrosis of the femoral head and renal concentrating defects.

Diagnosis

The diagnosis can be made by haemoglobin electrophoresis or by 'sickle prep', in which a drop of blood is mixed with sodium metabisulphite and watched under the microscope for sickling. Sickling in this test occurs whether the patient has sickle trait or sickle cell anaemia; only the electrophoresis can show the distinction. The patient with sickle trait has normal haemoglobin and haematocrit levels as well as a normal blood smear. In contrast, the patient with sickle cell anaemia has a low haematocrit and sickled cells on smear.

Sickle Trait. Patients with sickle trait are protected from crises because the haemoglobin A in their cells prevents the cells from sickling under ordinary circumstances. Such people have no anaemia and look and feel well. About 10 per cent of the Black ethnic population in the UK have sickle cell trait.

Sickle Cell Anaemia. Patients with sickle cell anaemia are usually diagnosed in childhood, because they are anaemic in infancy and begin to have crises at one or two years of age. Many die in the first years of life, but antibiotics and patient and doctor education about this disease have probably improved the outlook in the last 10 to 20 years, and some patients live into the sixth decade. All siblings of a patient with sickle cell anaemia should be tested for the disease. In Britain, one in 400 people of Afro-Caribbean descent has sickle cell anaemia.

Management

There is no specific treatment for the haemoglobin abnormality. The disease could be prevented only by intensive genetic counselling of the population at risk, a difficult and controversial task. Crises cannot now be prevented. Researchers are evaluating several chemicals with antisickling properties, but these are still in the investigational stage. Because infection seems to predispose to crises in children, all infections should be treated promptly or prevented when possible. Since dehydration and hypoxia promote sickling, patients are advised to avoid high altitudes, anaesthesia or fluid loss. Because of the renal defect, these patients easily become dehydrated. Folic acid therapy is given continuously, because the marrow has an increased requirement.

When sickle crisis occurs, the mainstays of therapy are hydration and analgesia. Increased fluid intake helps to dilute the blood and reverse the agglutination of sickled cells within the small blood vessels. Patients and families can learn to handle minor crises at home but, if there is no relief after several hours, hospital admission may be necessary. The patients often have fever and leucocytosis with crisis, so infection or appendicitis or cholecystitis may be suspected and must be ruled out. Intravenous fluids (3–5 litres/day for adults) are essential. Narcotic analgesics are often necessary because of the severity of pain and should be given in adequate doses. They should never be used chronically, however, for some patients do become addicted. Relaxation techniques, breathing exercises, transcutaneous nerve stimulation and whirlpool baths are helpful for some patients.

Transfusions are reserved for particular situations: (1) aplastic crisis, when the patient's haemoglobin falls rapidly; (2) severe painful crisis not responding to any other therapy after several days; (3) as a preoperative measure, to dilute the amount of sickled blood; and (4) sometimes during the latter half of pregnancy in an attempt to prevent crises.

▶ NURSING PROCESS
▶ THE PATIENT WITH SICKLE CELL ANAEMIA

▶ *Assessment*

Because the sickling process can cause microcirculatory interruptions in any tissues and organs, with resultant hypoxia and ischaemia, a careful assessment of all body systems is necessary. Particular emphasis is placed on assessing for pain, swelling (e.g. of the joints and abdomen) and fever. Any sign of cerebral hypoxia should be reported.

The patient is also questioned about symptoms indicative of gallstones, such as food intolerances, abdominal pain or dyspepsia.

Because these patients are so susceptible to infections,

they are assessed for the presence of any infectious process, for example, expectoration of sputum, joint or limb pain, since pneumonia and osteomyelitis are especially common. Leg ulcers which may be infected are sometimes present. Chronic anaemia, another common problem associated with sickle cell anaemia, is also considered during the nursing assessment.

Patients in crisis are questioned about factors that could have precipitated the crisis. They are asked to recall whether they have recently had symptoms of infection or dehydration or have been experiencing situations that promote fatigue or emotional stress. History of alcohol intake is also discussed. In addition, patients are asked to recall factors that seemed to precipitate previous crises, and measures that they use to prevent crises. This information will provide guidelines for identifying and meeting their learning needs.

▶ *Patient's Problems*

Based on the assessment, the patient's major problems may include the following:

● Pain due to agglutination of sickled cells within blood vessels.
● Susceptibility to life-threatening infection.
● Health education needs regarding prevention of crisis—effects of this chronic disorder upon morale and occupation.

▶ *Planning and Implementation*

Nursing Care Plan 10.1 for the patient with sickle cell crisis is presented below.

The nurse can help the patient and family or close friends, as appropriate, to adjust to this chronic disease

▶ NURSING CARE PLAN 10.1: THE PATIENT IN SICKLE CELL CRISIS

Care plan for Carol Henry, a 23-year-old secretary who has sickle cell anaemia. Carol, whose parents both come from Guyana, was born in Birmingham, England.

Patient's problems	Expected outcomes	Nursing care	Rationale
1. Pain due agglutination of sickled cells within small blood vessels i.e. 'sickling'	Pain-free at rest, later, pain-free on movement when no longer immobilized or on bedrest	1a. Assess severity and location of pain. Common sites are joints, extremities, chest and abdomen, e.g. use a pain chart	Tissues and organs are prone to thrombosis, hypoxia and thus pain
		b. Give adequate analgesia according to doctor's prescription, e.g. intravenous opiate infusion pump	Using a tool to measure the patient's perception of the pain enhances morale and allows measurement of effectiveness of nursing actions (McCaffery
		c. Review effect soon and often	and Sofaer, 1983)
		d. Discuss with doctor as appropriate	Ives and Guerra (1987) suggest that a narcotic intravenous infusion is the only effective pain remedy in sickle cell crisis
		e. Nurse at rest in bed	
		f. Encourage to move joints gently and change position every 2–4 hours	To avoid muscle wasting and pressure sores
		g. Use other measures as preferred by patient, such as heat, cold, massage and relaxation	Joint pain can be minimized by careful positioning, and to some individuals these measures are helpful
		h. Encourage to drink at least 3 litres per 24 hours	Fluids promote haemodilution and reverse sickling within small vessels
		i. Give intravenous fluids as prescribed	
		j. Monitor intake and output	
		k. Report to doctor any sign of change in fluid balance	
2. Susceptibility to life-threatening infection	Restoration of temperature to within normal limits Breathing comfortably, free from pain and discomfort	2a. Check for signs of infection. Common sites are: lungs, long bones, joints, e.g. head of femur, leg ulcers	The physiological stress that results from infection precipates a crisis Resolution of an infection at its onset can often prevent or limit the severity of a crisis
		b. Encourage early ambulation within limits of pain	

▶

▶ **NURSING CARE PLAN 10.1: THE PATIENT IN SICKLE CELL CRISIS**

Patient's problems	Expected outcomes	Nursing care	Rationale
	No expectoration of sputum No pain in long bones or joints Absence of infective drainage from wounds	c. Refer to physiotherapist d. Teach deep-breathing exercises and encourage patient to perform them two-hourly e. Swab any wounds for microbiological culture; report same to doctor f. Use aseptic technique for all dressing changes g. Promote adequate nutrition h. Refer to dietician i. Promote adequate fluid balance (see problem 1)	Movement prevents stasis of pulmonary secretions and thus hypostatic pneumonia Asepsis deters the introduction of micro-organisms into wounds Optimal nutrition and fluid balance promote tissue integrity
3. Health education needs regarding prevention of crises	Patient identifies factors that precipitate crisis Describes acceptable changes in lifestyle to prevent crisis Elicits the support of family/friends in making these changes Drinks at least 2–3 litres per day every day Lists avoidable sources of infection Identifies the need to seek prompt medical attention when infection occurs	3a. Discuss factors that commonly precipitate crisis: namely, infection, dehydration, trauma, strenuous physical exertion, overtiredness, exposure to cold, hypoxia, e.g. at high altitude, emotional stress b. Discuss the chronic nature of the disease with patient and family/friends c. Stress the importance of adequate hydration and avoidance of infection	Avoidance of situations that precipate crises can often increase the intervals between crises Understanding the chronicity of the disorder and the ability to minimize crises gives the individual control over the illness and promotes adherence to a healthy lifestyle
4. Effect of this chronic disorder upon morale and occupation	Patient reconciles modest changes in lifestyle to stay well and lead a normal life Patient's employer is aware of the potential of occasional hospital stays and adopts a supportive role Financial commitments are managed to avoid emotional stress	4a. Make available contacts within local self-help groups, charities and national information bodies b. Refer to medical social worker for advice and guidance with financial problems c. If patient desires, ask doctor to write to employer explaining effects upon ability to continue in occupation	The reassurance of another sufferer experiencing the same emotions may be beneficial Organizations can provide information and literature for patients, their families and employers

and understand the importance of hydration and prevention of infection. When leg ulcers are present, they require careful dressing and protection from trauma and wound contamination. If they fail to heal, skin grafting may be necessary.

Cardiac disease is managed in the same way as for any patient who does not have sickle cell anaemia. During crisis, the patient is kept quiet and allowed to rest undisturbed. Swollen extremities should not be exercised and pain should be relieved. Male patients may develop sudden, painful episodes of priapism (persistent penile erection) and need to know that it is common and has no long-term deleterious effects.

Other Haemoglobinopathies

C Haemoglobin

C haemoglobin is less common among the United Kingdom black population than S haemoglobin. The C trait is asymptomatic, and homozygous C disease is a mild haemolytic anaemia with splenomegaly but no serious complications.

Thalassaemia

Thalassaemia is a group of hereditary disorders associated with defective haemoglobin-chain synthesis. These anaemias occur worldwide, but the highest prevalence is found in people of Mediterranean, African and Southeast Asian ancestry. In London, thalassaemia affects 3.5 per cent of the Maltese, 2.5 per cent of the Italian and 1.5 per cent of the West Indian populations. Of the Cypriot population, 17 per cent carry a thalassaemia gene. Thalassaemia is characterized by hypochromia (abnormal decrease in haemoglobin content of erythrocytes), microcytosis (smaller than normal erythrocytes), haemolysis and variable degrees of anaemia.

The thalassaemias are classified into two major groups according to the affected globin chain of haemoglobin: α-thalassaemias and ß-thalassaemias, which are associated with decreased or absent α-chain synthesis and ß-chain synthesis, respectively. The α-thalassaemias occur mainly in people from Southeast Asia and Africa, and the ß-thalassaemias are most prevalent in Mediterranean populations. The α-thalassaemias are milder than the ß-forms and are often without symptoms. Patients with severe ß-thalassaemia will die within the first few years of life if untreated; if treated with regular transfusion therapy they may survive into their 20s or 30s.

The ß-thalassaemias are classified according to their severity: minima, minor, intermedia and major. Patients with thalassaemia minima are asymptomatic; the majority of those with thalassaemia minor are also without symptoms, although significant anaemia that requires transfusion therapy may occur during pregnancy.

Thalassaemia intermedia is more severe, with life expectancy of only about three or four decades. These patients often suffer from chronic fatigue, debilitating bone pain, cardiac disease and hypersplenism. Because of an inadequate excretory pathway for iron, they often experience complications of iron overload (e.g., hepatic fibrosis and cirrhosis) which is worsened by transfusion therapy. However, iron-chelating agents (for example, desferrioxamine) administered nightly by subcutaneous pump can reverse this process. Although this treatment is inconvenient and distressing, it can lengthen the life of thalassaemia sufferers by many years.

Thalassaemia major (Cooley's anaemia) is characterized by severe anaemia, marked haemolysis and ineffective erythropoiesis. With early regular transfusion therapy, growth and development through childhood is facilitated. Organ dysfunction due to iron overload usually begins in adolescence, and death used to occur in the second or third decade of life. Recent advances with oral iron chelators and modest success with bone marrow transplantation in some experimental centres may yield greater hope for thalassaemia sufferers in the future.

Glucose-6-Phosphate Dehydrogenase Deficiency

The abnormality in this disorder is in glucose-6-phosphate dehydrogenase, an enzyme within the red cell that is essential for membrane stability. A few patients have in herited an enzyme so defective that they have a chronic haemolytic anaemia, but the most common type of defect results in haemolysis only when the red cells are stressed by certain situations, such as fever or the presence of certain drugs. The disorder came to the attention of researchers during World War II, when some soldiers developed haemolysis while taking primaquine, an antimalarial drug. Drugs that are haemolytic for glucose-6-phosphate-dehydrogenase-deficient people are antimalarial drugs, sulphonamides, nitrofurantoin, the common coal tar analgesics (including aspirin), the thiazide diuretics, the oral hypoglycaemic agents, chloramphenicol, para-aminosalicylic acid, vitamin K and, for certain individuals subject to 'favism', the fava bean. Blacks and people of Greek or Italian origin are those primarily affected. The type of deficiency found in the Mediterranean group is more severe than that in the black group, resulting in greater haemolysis and sometimes in life-threatening anaemias. All types are inherited as X-linked defects; thus, many more males are at risk than females. There are probably several million affected individuals in numerous racial groups worldwide. It is less common in indigenous northern Europeans.

Clinical Features

The patients are asymptomatic and have normal haemoglobin levels and reticulocyte counts most of the time. Several days after exposure to an offending drug, they may develop pallor, jaundice and haemoglobinuria, and the reticulocyte count will rise. Special strains of the peripheral blood may then show Heinz bodies (degraded haemoglobin). Haemolysis continues for a week, and then spontaneously the counts begin to improve because the new young red cells are resistant to lysis. In the Mediterranean type, this recovery does not occur.

Diagnosis and Management

The diagnosis is made by a screening test or a quantitative assay of glucose-6-phosphate dehydrogenase. The treatment is removal of the drug. Transfusion is only necessary in the Mediterranean variety. The patient should be educated about the disease and given a list of drugs to avoid.

Acquired Haemolytic Anaemias

There are a variety of acquired haemolytic anaemias, including paroxysmal nocturnal haemoglobinuria, immune haemolytic anaemia, microangiopathic haemolytic anaemia, heart valve haemolysis and spur cell anaemia, as well as those associated with infections and hypersplenism. Table 10.4 identifies the causes, manifestations and treatment of these anaemias. Immune haemolytic anaemia is addressed in the text discussion.

Table 10.4 *Acquired haemolytic anaemias*

Name	Cause	Symptoms and treatment
Paroxysmal nocturnal haemoglobinuria	Unknown–sometimes occurs after aplastic anaemia	Dark urine (haemoglobinuria) especially in morning Sometimes pancytopenia Multiple venous thrombosis No treatment known
Autoimmune haemolytic anaemia	Antibodies produced, sometimes secondary to drug (methyldopa, penicillin)	Jaundice, spherocytes Responds to steroids
Microangiopathic haemolytic anaemia	Red blood cells damaged during flow through abnormal, small blood vessels, as in malignant hypertension	Fragmented red blood cells seen on smears Treat primary disease
Heart valve haemolysis	Red blood cells damaged by regurgitant flow through incompetent valve prosthesis	Fragmented red blood cells Treatment: replace valve
Spur cell anaemia	Severe liver disease, usually hypertension Increased lipid in red blood cell membrane	Spur-shaped red blood cells No treatment
Infections	Malaria, *Clostridium welchii*, especially after septic abortion	Haemoglobinuria possible Treat the infection
Hypersplenism	Large spleen from any cause, e.g. cirrhosis, lymphomas	Sometimes pancytopenia Treatment: splenectomy

Immune Haemolytic Anaemia

When antibodies combine with red cells they can be either isoantibodies, reacting with foreign cells, as in transfusion reactions or erythroblastosis fetalis, or autoantibodies, which react with the cells of the host. The immune haemolysis that results may be very severe. Antibodies coat the red cells, producing a positive Coombs's test. These cells are then removed by the spleen and the rest of the reticuloendothelial system. Many cells are destroyed, and others return to the circulation as spherocytes with reduced membrane and a shortened survival rate.

In idiopathic autoimmune haemolytic states, what induces the immune system to produce the antibodies is not known. The disease usually begins suddenly, often in people over 40 years of age. In some cases, the haemolysis is associated with systemic disease (especially systemic lupus erythematosus, chronic lymphatic leukaemia or lymphoma). Other patients, with identical clinical pictures, can be shown to be producing antibodies to a drug (especially penicillin, cephalosporins or quinidine). The antibodies or the drug–antibody complexes then attach to red cells, resulting in haemolysis. Patients taking large doses of methyldopa may develop antibodies to their own red cells; only a few of these patients have a significant haemolytic anaemia.

Clinical Features
Presentation can be quite variable. A positive Coombs's test may be the only manifestation in mild cases. More often, signs of anaemia are present, such as fatigue, dyspnoea, palpitations and jaundice. Occasionally, the anaemia is so severe that the patient presents with overwhelming haemolysis and shock.

Management
Any possibly offending drug should be discontinued. The treatment consists of high doses of corticosteroids until haemolysis decreases. When, usually after several weeks, the haemoglobin has returned toward normal, the steroid dose can be lowered; in some patients it can be discontinued entirely. In severe cases blood transfusions may be required. Because the antibody may react with all possible donor cells, transfusion requires careful crossmatching and slow, cautious administration.

Splenectomy removes a major site of red cell destruction, so this operation is often performed if steroids do not produce a remission. If neither corticosteroids nor splenectomy is successful, immunosuppressive drugs may be administered, for example, azathioprine.

POLYCYTHAEMIA

Polycythaemia refers to an increased concentration of red cells; it is a term used when the red cell count is greater than $6 \times 10^{12}/l$, or the haemoglobin exceeds 18 g/dl. True polycythaemia is present when the total body red cell mass is increased. 'Relative' polycythaemia occurs when the red cell mass is normal but the plasma volume is reduced; this may be produced by diuretic therapy or by unknown factors. Red cell mass can be measured accurately by an isotopic technique.

Secondary Polycythaemia

Secondary polycythaemia is caused by excessive production of erythropoietin. This may occur in response to a hypoxic stimulus, as in chronic obstructive pulmonary disease or cyanotic heart disease, or in certain haemoglobinopathies in which the haemoglobin has an abnormally high affinity for oxygen (e.g., haemoglobin$_{Chesapeake}$). In some cases of secondary polycythaemia, the production of erythropoietin serves no purpose because there is no hypoxaemia; this is the situation in a few patients with renal carcinoma, renal cysts, cerebellar hemangioblastoma, hepatoma or uterine fibroids.

Management of secondary polycythaemia involves treatment of the primary problem. If the cause cannot be corrected, venesection can be used to treat the symptoms of hypervolaemia and hyperviscosity.

Polycythaemia Vera

Polycythaemia vera, or primary polycythaemia, is a proliferative disorder in which all the marrow cells seem to have escaped from the normal control mechanisms. The bone marrow is intensely cellular, and in the peripheral blood the red count, white count and platelets are often all elevated. Patients typically have a ruddy complexion and hepatosplenomegaly (enlarged liver and spleen). The symptoms are referable to the increased blood volume (headache, dizziness, fatigue and blurred vision) or to increased blood viscosity (angina, claudication, thrombophlebitis). Bleeding is also a complication, perhaps because of the engorged capillaries. Another common and unexplained problem is pruritus.

Management

The objective of management is to reduce the high blood viscosity. Venesection is an important part of therapy and can be done repeatedly to keep the haemoglobin within normal range. Radioactive phosphorus or chemotherapeutic agents can be used to suppress marrow function but may increase the risk of leukaemia. When the patient has an elevated uric acid level, allopurinol is used to prevent gout and uric acid nephropathy. Cyproheptadine may be administered to control pruritus.

LEUCOPENIA AND AGRANULOCYTOSIS

Leucopenia is a condition in which the white cells number fewer than normal. Agranulocytosis is a potentially fatal condition in which there is almost complete absence of polymorphonuclear cells. A leucocyte count of fewer than $5 \times 10^9/l$ or a granulocyte count of fewer than $2 \times 10^9/l$ is abnormal and may be a signal of a generalized bone marrow disorder, such as megaloblastic anaemia, aplasia, metastatic tumour, myelofibrosis or acute leukaemia. Viral infections and overwhelming bacterial sepsis can also cause leucopenia. Most commonly, the aetiology is drug toxicity: phenothiazines are implicated frequently, and anti-thyroid drugs, sulphonamides, phenylbutazone and chloramphenicol are also contributing factors. The patient is not symptomatic unless infection develops, which usually occurs when the granulocytes are fewer than $1 \times 10^9/l$. Fever and severe sore throat with ulcerations are common complaints. Bacteraemia may follow soon after.

Management

Any possibly offending drugs are withdrawn. If the granulocyte count is very low, the patient is protected from any obvious sources of infection. Cultures of all orifices and blood are essential, and when fever occurs it is treated with broad-spectrum antibiotics until the specific organism is known. Good oral hygiene is vital to avoid candida, candidal septicaemia and herpes infections.

Antiseptic/local anaesthetic irrigations of the throat are employed to keep it clear of necrotic exudate, with whatever analgesic, antipyretic or sedative drugs that may be indicated to promote comfort. The essence of treatment, apart from eradicating the infection, is to eliminate, if possible, the factor responsible for the bone marrow depression. Spontaneous restoration of marrow function, except in the case of neoplastic diseases, often occurs within two or three weeks or so, if death from infection can be averted.

HAEMOPOIETIC MALIGNANCIES

Normally, production of specialized blood cells from stem cell precursors is carefully regulated according to the body's needs. If homeostatic control of production is disrupted, neoplastic proliferation may result. A wide variety of haemopoietic malignancies can develop and are often classified according to the cell line involved. Leukaemia, literally white blood, is a neoplastic proliferation of white cells. The defect is believed to originate in the haemopoietic stem cell. The lymphomas are neoplasms of lymphoid tissue. Hodgkin's disease accounts for 40 per cent of all lymphomas and is believed to result from defective T-lymphocytes. Many other lymphomas are derived from B-lymphocytes. Both Waldenström's macroglobulinaemia and multiple myeloma are neoplasms affecting plasma cells produced by B-lymphocytes.

Leukaemia

The common feature of the leukaemias is an unregulated proliferation or accumulation of white cells in the bone marrow, replacing normal marrow elements. There is also proliferation in the liver, spleen and lymph nodes, and invasion of nonhaematological organs, such as the meninges, gastrointestinal tract, kidney and skin. The leukaemias are often classified according to the cell line involved, as either lymphocytic or myelocytic, and according to the maturity of the malignant cells, as either acute (immature cells) or chronic (differentiated cells). The aetiology is unknown, but there is some evidence that genetic influence and viral pathogenesis may be involved. Bone marrow damage with radiation (as in the atomic bomb survivors) or chemicals (benzene) can cause leukaemia.

Acute Myeloid Leukaemia

Acute myeloid leukaemia affects the haemopoietic stem cell that differentiates into all myeloid cells: monocytes, granulocytes (basophils, neutrophils, eosinophils), erythrocytes and platelets. All age groups are affected; incidence rises with age.

Clinical features

Most of the signs and symptoms evolve from insufficient production of normal blood cells. Vulnerability to infection results from granulocytopenia, weakness and fatigue occur due to anaemia, and bleeding tendencies arise as a result of thrombocytopenia. The proliferation of leukaemic cells within organs leads to a variety of additional symptoms: pain from enlarged liver or spleen; lymphadenopathy; headache or vomiting secondary to meningeal leukaemia (most common in lymphocytic leukaemia); and bone pain from expansion of marrow.

Onset is often insidious, with symptoms occurring over a period of one to six months. The peripheral blood will show a decrease in both erythrocyte and platelet counts. Although the total leucocyte count can be low, normal or high, the percentage of normal cells is usually vastly decreased. A bone marrow specimen is diagnostic.

Management

Chemotherapy is the major form of treatment and in most instances results in remissions lasting a year or longer. Drugs commonly used include daunorubicin or doxorubicin, cytarabine, thioguanine, etoposide, mitozantrone and amsacrine. Transfusions of red cells and platelets are administered to provide normal cells temporarily. When a tissue match with a close relative can be obtained, bone marrow transplantation is used to provide normal bone marrow after destruction of leukaemic marrow by chemotherapy and/or radiotherapy.

Prognosis

At present, survival of treated patients averages only 14 months, with death usually a result of infection. Untreated patients survive only about two months. However, for some patients bone marrow transplantation is curative.

Chronic Myeloid Leukaemia

Chronic myeloid leukaemia is also believed to be a malignancy of myeloid stem cells. However, more normal cells are present than in the acute form, and therefore the disease is milder. Uncommon before the age of 20 years, the incidence of chronic myeloid leukaemia rises with age.

Clinical Features

The clinical picture is similar to that of acute myeloid leukaemia, but signs and symptoms are less severe. Many patients are without symptoms for years. Onset is typically insidious. Leucocytosis is always present, sometimes at extraordinary levels.

Management and Prognosis

The drug of choice for chemotherapy is busulphan. Survival has been improved significantly with bone marrow transplantation. The final event in most patients is a transformation into an acute myeloid leukaemia that is usually resistant to all therapy. Overall, patients live for three to four years. Death usually results from infection or haemorrhage. The nursing care is similar to that for acute leukaemia (see p. 449).

Acute Lymphocytic Leukaemia

Acute lymphocytic leukaemia is believed to be a malignant proliferation of lymphoblasts. It is most common in young children, with a peak incidence at four years of age. After the age of 15, acute lymphocystic leukaemia is less common.

Clinical Features

Lymphocytes proliferate in marrow and peripheral tissue and crowd the development of normal cells. As a result of marrow proliferation of malignant cells, normal haemopoiesis is inhibited and leucopenia, anaemia and thrombocytopenia develop. Erythrocyte and platelet counts are low, and leucocyte counts may be either low or high but always include immature cells. Manifestations of leukaemic cell infiltration into other organs are more common with acute lymphocytic leukaemia than with other forms.

Management and Prognosis

Therapy for this childhood leukaemia has improved to the extent that approximately 50 per cent of children survive at least five years. The major form of treatment is chemotherapy with combinations of vincristine, prednisolone, daunorubicin and asparaginase used for initial therapy, and combinations of mercaptopurine, methotrexate, vincristine and prednisolone for maintenance. Irradiation of the craniospinal region and intrathecal injection of chemotherapeutic drugs help prevent central nervous system recurrence. For those children who fail to respond to chemotherapy, bone marrow transplantation, when already in remission, from a compatible donor is another treatment option.

Chronic Lymphocytic Leukaemia

A disease of elderly people, chronic lymphocytic leukaemia tends to be a mild disorder that primarily affects people over the age of 35.

Clinical Features

Many patients are asymptomatic and are diagnosed during physical examination or treatment for another disease. Possible manifestations are those of anaemia, infection or enlargement of lymph nodes and abdominal organs. The erythrocyte and platelet counts may be normal or decreased. Lymphocytosis is always present.

Management and Prognosis

If mild, chronic lymphocytic leukaemia may require no treatment. When symptoms are severe, chemotherapy with steroids and chlorambucil is often used. Highly variable in course, the average survival time is seven years.

Patients who no longer respond to therapy may be hospitalized for supportive care. They have often experienced remissions and exacerbations of the disease, and have known hope and despair. They are very tired and ill and require knowledgeable nursing assessment, support and expert physical care. (See also section on patients with advanced carcinoma, Chapter 2.)

► NURSING PROCESS
► THE PATIENT WITH LEUKAEMIA

► Assessment

Although the clinical picture will vary with the type of leukaemia involved, the nursing history may reveal weakness and fatigue, bleeding tendencies, petechiae and ecchymoses, pain, headache, vomiting, fever and infection. Blood studies may reveal alterations of the white blood cells, anaemia and thrombocytopenia. Specific features are identified under the discussion of each of the types of leukaemia.

► Patient's Problems

Based on the assessment data, the patient's problems may include the following:

- Anxiety and fear related to the diagnosis and prognosis.
- Risk of bleeding related to thrombocytopenia.
- Potential for infection related to neutropenia.
- Fatigue and breathlessness related to anaemia.
- Discomfort due to leukaemic infiltration of other body systems.
- Malnutrition related to gastrointestinal proliferative changes and toxic effects of chemotherapeutic agents.
- Disturbance in body image related to alopecia.

► Planning and Implementation
► Expected Outcomes

The main outcomes for the patient may include ability to cope with the diagnosis and prognosis, absence of bleeding, absence of infection, tolerance of activity, attainment/maintenance of comfort, attainment/maintenance of adequate nutrition and promotion of positive body image.

Nursing Care

Ability to Cope with the Diagnosis and Prognosis

Like other patients with malignant diseases, patients with leukaemia are often depressed, frightened and lonely. A well-informed and sympathetic nurse can contribute immeasurably to their comfort by explaining procedures, anticipating side-effects of drugs and encouraging patients to participate in the therapy regime. The treatment can become very complex, and too often patients feel that more is being done 'to' them than 'for' them. The nurse can be a sympathetic listener and help patients to cope with the emotional and physical stresses.

Prevention of Bleeding

These patients should be approached in the same manner as those with aplastic anaemia and should be assessed for thrombocytopenia, granulocytopenia and anaemia. The risk of bleeding correlates with the level of thrombocytopenia. In addition to having petechiae and ecchymoses, patients may develop major haemorrhages when their platelet counts drop below $20 \times 10^9/l$ of blood. For undetermined reasons, fever or infection also increases the likelihood of bleeding. Any increase in petechiae and any melaena, haematuria or nosebleeds should be reported. An oral contraceptive is often prescribed to be taken continuously to prevent anaemia due to profound menstrual loss. Undue trauma or intramuscular injections must be avoided, and paracetamol, rather than aspirin, should be used for analgesia. Haemorrhage is treated by bedrest and transfusions of red cells and platelets.

Prevention of Infection

Because of the lack of mature and normal granulocytes, these patients are always threatened by infection, the major cause of death in leukaemia. The likelihood of infection increases with the degree of neutropenia, so granulocyte counts under $1 \times 10^9/l$ of blood make the development of systemic infection highly probable. Immune dysfunction compounds the risk of infection. Patients must be systematically assessed for any evidence of infection.

The nurse should monitor the patient for temperature elevation, flushed appearance, chills, tachycardia, appearance of white patches in mouth; redness, swelling, heat or pain of eyes, ears, throat, skin, joints, abdomen, rectal and perineal areas; cough; changes in character and/or colour of sputum, stool; skin rash.

● Remember that the usual manifestations of infection are altered in patients with leukaemia. Steroids may blunt the normal febrile response to infection.

Some typical signs of infection, such as the appearance of exudates, are often not apparent and make the need for careful observation even greater. Frequent oral hygiene may decrease the likelihood of infection originating from the oral cavity. Because of the high risk of infection arising from intravenous cannulae, gloves should be worn to start infusions, daily site care should be provided and the cannula should be changed every 48 hours. Often, an indwelling skin-tunnelled central venous catheter is inserted for therapy, transfusions, hyperalimentation and blood sampling. This negates the need for repeated venepuncture; however, scrupulous asepsis in dealing with the line is vital to avoid the introduction of infection.

Rectal abscesses are not unusual, so it is important to ensure normal elimination and avoid rectal thermometers, enemas and rectal trauma. The urinary tract is another common site for infection. Avoidance of catheterization and, when catheterization is essential, scrupulous asepsis during catheter insertion and maintenance are important.

Tolerance of Activity

Anaemia results from defective erythropoiesis, accelerated red cell destruction and episodes of bleeding. If weak and easily fatigued, the patient may need assistance in choosing priorities and will need alternate rest and activity periods. Patients must also be assessed for dyspnoea, tachycardia and other evidence of inadequate oxygen supply to vital organs.

Attainment/Maintenance of Comfort

Infiltration of abnormal leucocytes into systemic tissues causes a variety of disabling symptoms. Pain is a common problem due to infiltration and enlargement of abdominal organs, lymph nodes, bones and joints. Signs of central nervous system infiltration include headache, confusion and other symptoms of meningeal irritation and raised intracranial pressure. Ongoing assessment of every body system will help to identify these widespread effects so that care can be planned to decrease symptoms as they occur.

Careful positioning is helpful in preventing undue pain in the abdomen, lymph node areas, bones and joints. Sudden movements are avoided and soft supports, such as pillows, are used to promote comfort. When necessary, analgesics are administered as prescribed to relieve pain. To avoid bleeding at puncture sites, indwelling intravenous devices are used when analgesics are given parenterally.

The massive cell destruction resulting from chemotherapy increases uric acid levels and makes patients vulnerable to uric acid nephropathy. Therefore, patients need a high fluid intake and allopurinol as prescribed to prevent crystallization of uric acid and subsequent acute renal failure.

Attainment/Maintenance of Adequate Nutrition

Gastrointestinal problems may result from the infiltration of abnormal leucocytes into the abdominal organs as well as from the toxicity of the chemotherapeutic agents. Anorexia, nausea, vomiting, diarrhoea and lesions in the mouth are common. Because good nutrition is so important for cancer patients, careful timing of chemotherapeutic drug administration, prophylactic use of prescribed antiemetics and the encouragement of foods and fluids that are the least irritating are essential. Frequent oral hygiene helps to prevent oral lesions and to promote appetite. Small, frequent meals of foods and fluids that are high in protein and calories and palatable to the patient are often helpful in maintaining nutrition. Early referral to the dietician and close monitoring of body weight are essential in the prevention of weight loss and the evaluation of the effectiveness of these measures.

Promotion of Positive Body Image

Because the hair is an important factor in a person's self-image, the development of alopecia is usually traumatic. Patients are prepared for the occurrence of this problem and helped to express and resolve their feelings about it. It is often helpful for them to obtain a wig that they find aesthetically appealing *before* the hair loss occurs. Family and friends are encouraged to assist in selecting the wig. Involvement and support of both family and friends are often invaluable in helping patients adjust to the problem.

► *Evaluation*
► Expected Outcomes

1. Patient copes with diagnosis and prognosis.
   a. Expresses feelings about prognosis to family, friends and support system.
   b. Utilizes coping mechanisms appropriately.
   c. Sets realistic outcomes.
   d. Participates in the treatment.
2. Is free of bleeding.
   a. Adheres to treatment plan.
   b. Avoids situations that predispose to physical trauma, e.g., razor and other sharp objects, forceful nose blowing, straining with stool, contact sports.
   c. Uses soft toothbrush for oral hygiene.
   d. Monitors urine, stools and vaginal secretions for evidence of bleeding.
   e. Alerts hospital staff at first sign of bleeding.
3. Is free of infection.
   a. Attempts to maintain adequate nutritional intake.
   b. Practises taught method and routine of oral hygiene.
   c. Describes signs and symptoms of infection and preventive measures.
   d. Avoids those with known infection.
   e. Alerts hospital staff to first signs of infection.
4. Experiences increased strength and endurance.
   a. Explains causes for weakness and fatigue.
   b. Spaces activities throughout the day.
   c. Rests at specified intervals.
   d. Makes appropriate alterations in lifestyle to accommodate decreased physical activity.
   e. Shows improvement from day to day.
5. Attains/maintains comfort.
   a. Identifies positions that promote comfort of abdomen and extremities.
   b. Positions self to relieve abdominal and extremity pain.
   c. Rests with head of bed elevated to decrease headache.
   d. Uses analgesics as prescribed.
   e. Drinks adequate fluids to prevent renal complications.
6. Attains/maintains adequate nutrition.
   a. Identifies factors that precipitate gastrointestinal discomfort.
   b. Uses antiemetics as prescribed to prevent nausea and vomiting.
   c. Chooses foods that do not cause gastric irritation.
   d. Attempts to increase intake of foods high in protein and calories.
   e. Performs regular and frequent oral hygiene.
   f. Maintains/gains weight.

7. Maintains positive body image.
   a. Discusses feelings about alopecia.
   b. Accepts help from nursing staff, wig specialist, family and close friends in preparing for and coping with alopecia.
   c. Obtains a wig that patient finds appealing.

MALIGNANT LYMPHOMAS

The lymphomas are neoplasms of the cells of the lymphoid system: the lymphocytes and histiocytes. They are often classified according to the degree of cell differentiation and the origin of the predominant malignant cell. These tumours usually start in lymph nodes, but can involve lymphoid tissue in the spleen, the gastrointestinal tract (for example, the tonsils or the wall of the stomach), the liver or the bone marrow. They often spread to all of these areas and to extralymphatic tissues (lungs, kidneys, skin) by the time of death. The aetiology of these tumours is unknown.

Hodgkin's Disease

Hodgkin's disease, like other lymphomas, is a malignant disease of unknown aetiology that originates in the lymphatic system and involves predominantly the lymph nodes. It is somewhat more common in males and has two peaks of incidence: one in the early 20s and the other after the age of 50. Because many features are similar to those occurring with infection, an infectious origin for the disease continues to be sought.

The malignant cell of Hodgkin's disease, its pathological hallmark and its essential diagnostic criterion, is the 'Reed-Sternberg cell', a gigantic atypical tumour cell, morphologically unique and of uncertain lineage, which many regard as an aberrant histiocyte.

Patients with Hodgkin's disease are customarily classified into subgroups based on pathological criteria that reflect the grade of malignancy and suggest the prognosis. Hodgkin's paragranuloma, for example, with fewest Reed-Sternberg cells and least disturbance of nodal architecture, carries a much more favourable prognosis than Hodgkin's sarcoma, in which the lymph nodes are virtually replaced by tumour cells of the most primitive type. The majority of patients with so-called Hodgkin's granuloma (which includes two conditions currently designated 'nodular sclerosis' and 'mixed cellularity') are in an intermediate position with respect to the density and destructiveness of tumour cells, therapeutic responsiveness and overall outlook.

Clinical Features

Hodgkin's disease usually begins as a painless enlargement of the lymph nodes on one side of the neck, which becomes increasingly conspicuous. However, for months generalized pruritus may be the first and only symptom and later is often a most distressing one. The individual nodes remain firm and discrete (that is, they do not soften and do not fuse) and are seldom tender and painful. Soon the lymph nodes of other regions, usually the other side of the neck, also enlarge in the same manner. The mediastinal and retroperitoneal lymph nodes may also enlarge, causing severe pressure symptoms: pressure against the trachea results in dyspnoea; pressure against the oesophagus causes dysphagia; pressure on the nerves causes laryngeal paralysis and brachial, lumbar or sacral neuralgias; pressure on the veins results in oedema of one or both extremities and effusions into the pleura or peritoneum; and pressure on the bile duct causes obstructive jaundice. Later the spleen may become palpable, and the liver may enlarge. In some patients the first nodes to enlarge are those of one axilla or of one groin. Occasionally, the disease starts in mediastinal or peritoneal nodes and may remain limited to them. In still other cases the enlargement of the spleen is the only conspicuous lesion.

Sooner or later a progressive anaemia develops. A leucocytosis is often seen, with an abnormally high polymorphonuclear count and an elevated eosinophil count. About half of the patients have a slight fever, the temperature seldom rising above 38.3°C. However, patients with mediastinal and abdominal involvement present a remarkable intermittent fever. The temperature goes as high as 40°C for periods of 3 to 14 days, returning to normal within a few weeks. Untreated, this disease is progressive in its course; the patient loses weight and becomes cachectic, the anaemia becomes marked, anasarca (severe generalized oedema) appears, the blood pressure falls and death is likely to ensue in one to three years.

Diagnosis

The diagnosis of Hodgkin's disease hinges on the identification of its characteristic histology in an excised lymph node. A diagnosis having been firmly established on the basis of the requisite criteria, it becomes necessary to assess as accurately as possible the total extent of tumour involvement and distribution. In other words, one attempts to pinpoint the location of every tumour lesion inside and outside the lymphatic system and to exclude the presence of a tumour in organs and tissues that are not yet involved. This is called staging and is a difficult, expensive and uncertain undertaking but an extremely important one because these are the very considerations on which treatment and prognosis are based.

Laboratory tests include a full blood count, erythrocyte sedimentation rate and liver and renal function tests. A bone marrow biopsy and liver and spleen scans are done to determine if there is involvement in these organs. Chest X-ray as well as bone scans of the pelvis, vertebrae and long bones are done to identify any involvement in these areas.

Rarely, if computerized tomography scanning fails to reveal the extent of disease, or an affected node is unavailable for biopsy, then a staging laparotomy is performed. The spleen is also removed in order to prevent tumour spread.

Management

Current concepts of treatment stem from the following observations and premises:

1. Hodgkin's disease spreads from its original location (usually a single node) by way of the lymphatic channels to contiguous lymph nodes, which in turn become the sites of tumour growth; it rarely skips lymph nodes en route to more distant sites of metastasis.
2. Rarely does Hodgkin's disease spread beyond the lymphatic system to involve other organs and tissues until late in the disease.
3. Hodgkin's disease can be completely and permanently eradicated 95 per cent of the time from any site that has received a radiation dose of 3,500 to 4,500 rads (3.5–4.5 Gray) within the space of about four weeks. Megavoltage radiation techniques permit the delivery of such a dose to one or more entire lymph node chains.
4. Areas of the body in which the lymph node chains are located can tolerate doses of this magnitude without serious damage (as can the area of the spleen and the oronasopharynx, both of which may become involved in Hodgkin's disease), provided that vital structures such as the lungs, liver, gastrointestinal tract, kidneys and bone marrow are protected by carefully shaped lead shields.

Hodgkin's disease is potentially curable by radiotherapy, provided it has not extended beyond the lymph node chains, spleen and oronasopharynx. Failing signs of such extension, patients with this disease should have the benefit of 'curative' radiotherapy in which doses large enough to destroy the tumours are delivered not only to obvious tumour nodes but to all adjacent nodes and lymph node chains as well. Conversely, any sign of spread beyond the treatable areas automatically disqualifies the Hodgkin's patient from such a course, in which case a combination of chemotherapy and palliative radiotherapy is indicated.

Staging of Hodgkin's Disease
For the sake of simplicity, uniformity and convenience in categorizing patients with Hodgkin's disease with respect to the extent and activity of their disease and hence their eligibility for curative radiotherapy, the disease generally is classified, or 'staged', as follows:

Stage I: Disease is limited to a single node and contiguous structures, or a single extralymphatic organ or site.

Stage II: Disease involves more than a single node or

group of contiguous nodes, but is confined to one side of the diaphragm only.

Stage III: Disease is present both above and below the diaphragm and may include solitary involvement of the spleen, one extralymphatic site, or both.

Stage IV: Disease has disseminated diffusely to one or more extralymphatic sites with or without associated lymph node involvement.

Stages are further subdivided on the basis of the presence or absence of constitutional symptoms, i.e., fever, night sweats and unexplained weight loss. Patients without these symptoms are designated A, and patients with them are designated B. Chemotherapy is often added for stage IIB and for stage IIIA. For stages IIIB and IV, combination chemotherapy is used, and radiation is generally reserved for the palliative treatment of local lesions that are especially damaging or painful. Currently, patients diagnosed at stage IA or IIA have a five-year survival rate of 90 per cent and essentially can be considered cured. Survival rates decrease progressively with more advanced stages.

Nursing Care

Radiation therapy often requires many weeks of daily trips to the hospital. The dose to the tumour and adjacent lymph node areas is generally 4,500 rads.

Patients often develop oesophagitis, anorexia, loss of taste, nausea and vomiting, diarrhoea, skin reactions and lethargy. Much ingenuity is needed to help patients cope with these unpleasant side-effects. They should be encouraged to make a concerted effort to eat. Bland soft foods that they normally like are usually most palatable and are tolerated best when served at mild temperatures. Antiseptic/anaesthetic sprays and anaesthetic throat lozenges may be helpful in relieving the mouth and throat discomfort that often interfere with eating. The antiemetic prescribed by the doctor should be given during the peak times of nausea.

Skin reactions that give the appearance of sunburned or tanned skin are common. Patients are alerted that these are expected and that rubbing of the area and application of heat, cold or lotions should be avoided unless prescribed by the doctor. If the reaction is severe and the skin is burned, the hospital staff should be notified.

The lethargy that accompanies radiation may cause patients to become discouraged about their progress. They are told that it is expected and that they must increase periods of rest and sleep in order to maintain a reasonable energy level. Family and friends are encouraged to help patients in their attempts to rest. Diversional activities that require minimal energy expenditure may help to prevent boredom.

A commonly used chemotherapy regime is MOPP-ChLVPP, a combination of nitrogen mustard, vincristine, prednisone, procarbazine, chlorambucil and vinblastine. As for any patient receiving chemotherapy (see Chapter 2), support is necessary to help these patients tolerate the toxic effects, which include bone marrow depression, gastrointestinal disturbances and alopecia. It often helps if patients are told that the therapy will end in a specific period of time. This, along with the knowledge that there is a high likelihood of cure, serves as an incentive for them to continue with the therapy. Referral to the hospital appliance officer and wig specialist is important to provide a wig that is aesthetically acceptable to the patients before the problem occurs. This often averts some of the distress commonly associated with the loss of hair.

Patients with Hodgkin's disease are extremely vulnerable to infection, both as a result of radiation and chemotherapy and as a consequence of defective immune responses caused by the tumour. They are urged to report fever or any other signs of infection (skin redness, tenderness, lesions, cough) immediately so that treatment can be instituted. They are also apprised of the importance of avoiding contact with people who are known to have infections.

Follow-up appointments with the doctor are important for determining the effectiveness of the treatment and to monitor its toxic effects. The patient and home carer(s) are encouraged to keep all appointments.

Non-Hodgkin's Lymphomas

Lymphocytic lymphomas are more indolent and have a better prognosis than histiocytic lymphomas. Non-Hodgkin's lymphomas are a group of disorders that can be defined as malignancies of the lymphoid tissue other than Hodgkin's disease. They are relatively uncommon in the United Kingdom. The aetiology is unknown. The prognosis is dependent upon the grade and stage of the malignancy.

The symptoms are similar to those of Hodgkin's disease, but patients with these disorders are more likely to have generalized lymph node disease or extranodal disease when the disorder is first discovered. If the disease is localized, irradiation is the treatment of choice. If there is generalized involvement, chemotherapy is used. As with Hodgkin's disease, infection is a major problem. Central nervous system involvement is also common.

Mycosis Fungoides (Cutaneous T-Cell Lymphoma)

Mycosis fungoides is a relatively rare lymphoma of the skin that is found equally among blacks and whites, and that is more common in men than women. It usually begins as a pruritic, red rash, and months or years later the skin becomes infiltrated with plaques and tumours of lymphoma. The specific lymphocyte involved is the T-cell lymphocyte. The body may be covered with mushroom-like growths varying in size from 1 to 5 cm. Eventually, the malignant process reaches nodes, liver, spleen and lungs. Patients are very uncomfortable with the itching and disfigurement of this disease. Treatment with nitrogen mustard (which may be used topically) or irradiation can achieve palliation.

The patient with painful ulcerative lesions will require skilled nursing. A bed cradle should be used to remove the weight of bedding from painful skin lesions. Bacteriostatic ointment may be prescribed as a preventive measure against secondary infection and to seal off air from open nerve endings. Other aspects of care are similar to those for the patient with Hodgkin's disease.

MULTIPLE MYELOMA

Multiple myeloma is a malignant disease of plasma cells that infiltrates bone, soft tissues, lymph nodes, liver, spleen and kidneys. It is not classified as a lymphoma. The malignant cell is the plasma cell, the neoplastic proliferation taking place mainly in the bone marrow.

Patients generally present with anaemia, back pain and sometimes leucopenia or thrombocytopenia due to marrow infiltration by malignant plasma cells. The diagnosis of myeloma can be made by aspiration or biopsy of the bone marrow. X-rays showing destructive lesions of many bones are common. The malignant plasma cells produce large quantities of abnormal globulins, which appear in 'the serum electrophoresis as a paraprotein 'spike'. Fragments of these globulins are excreted in urine as Bence Jones proteins. These also raise plasma viscosity, giving rise to renal dysfunction, heart failure and cerebral insufficiency.

Patients may be incapacitated by constant bone pain. Plasma cell tumours can appear in many sites in these patients, including skin, mouth and pleura; these are often painless. The osteolytic lesions are often associated with hypercalcaemia, and bone fractures are common, especially in the ribs and vertebrae, which may cause spinal cord compression.

Management

Melphalan, cyclophosphamide and steroids are the drugs most commonly used to decrease the tumour mass and relieve bone pain. They can prolong life from one year to two or three years. Radiation is very useful for palliation of bone pain and for reducing the size of extraskeletal plasma cell tumours. Good hydration is essential in order to prevent renal damage from precipitation of Bence Jones protein in the renal tubules, hypercalcaemia and hyperuricaemia. Thus, it is important to assess these patients for signs and symptoms of renal insufficiency. Allopurinol is used to prevent uric acid crystallization. When patients have severe pain they need narcotic anal-

gesics and local irradiation, and sometimes back braces to relieve pressure. Pathological fractures are also possible. It is important to keep the patients as active as possible, because bedrest only increases the likelihood of hypercalcaemia. Bacterial infections, especially pneumonia, are common in these patients, since they have impaired capacity for antibody production. Patients with multiple myeloma should not be made to fast for diagnostic tests because dehydrating procedures can precipitate acute renal failure.

The nurse should observe constantly for signs of spinal cord compression and report these so that emergency radiotherapy can be given to prevent ensuing, irreversible paralysis.

BLEEDING DISORDERS

Altered Physiology

The body is normally protected against excessive and lethal blood loss by numerous complicated and interrelated mechanisms. As indicated in Figure 10.1, haemostasis includes three phases. The first, the vascular phase, involves immediate vasoconstriction of injured vessels. This vessel spasm is sufficient to stop capillary bleeding. The second phase, or platelet phase, involves platelet aggregation at the site. These tiny cells are rapidly attracted to the damaged endothelium and form loose plugs. More platelets gather, and eventually these fuse together and contract, forming stable plugs. The platelet plug effectively stops bleeding in small vessels such as venules, and provides temporary protection in larger injuries. Complete and permanent sealing of vascular wounds is accomplished through the clotting of the blood, which results in the production of an adherent gel-like mass that effectively controls most types of haemorrhage.

Initiated through either the intrinsic or the extrinsic pathway, a chain reaction occurs in which blood proteins are sequentially activated until factor Xa is formed. At this point, factor Xa interacts with factor V, calcium and a platelet substance to convert prothrombin to thrombin. This is a very active enzyme that has several functions: one is to encourage further platelet aggregation; another is to convert fibrinogen to fibrin. Therefore, strands of fibrin begin to form in the vicinity of the platelet plug, reinforcing the plug and producing a larger clot. The fibrin clot is then further stabilized by the formation of bonds between the molecules, catalyzed by another plasma protein, factor XIII. The result is that the damaged vessel is sealed and blood flow in the area is slowed. Then, tissue repair of the vessel endothelium can proceed. Eventually, much of the fibrin clot will be lysed by another plasma protein system—the plasmin system, which produces fibrinolysis.

Several other homeostatic mechanisms contribute to

haemostasis. Haemorrhage from a large, lacerated vessel is retarded as a result of an abrupt lowering of the arterial blood pressure (i.e., 'shock'), which reduces the rate of blood flow throughout the body and therefore reduces the rate of its escape. Further protection also may be furnished by compression of the leaking vessel by the swelling mass of blood (haematoma) surrounding the vessel. A final factor of great importance in the prevention of bleeding is the normal resistance of blood vessels to mechanical rupture, either by the pressure of blood exerted from within the vessel or by traumatic pressures exerted from the outside.

Abnormalities that predispose to haemorrhagic diseases can affect vessels, platelets and any of the plasma coagulation factors, fibrin or plasmin. Some patients can have defects at several sites simultaneously. Bleeding may be a symptom of a primary coagulation defect (as in haemophilia), may occur secondary to another disease (as in cirrhosis, uraemia or leukaemia) or may even be due to drugs (overdose of warfarin).

Clinical Features

The symptoms and signs of bleeding disorders vary, depending on the type of defect. A careful history can often give clues to the diagnosis. Abnormalities of the vascular system give rise to local bleeding, usually into the skin. Because platelets are primarily responsible for the cessation of bleeding from small vessels, patients with thrombocytopenia will have petechiae—small red or purple spots, often in clusters, seen on the skin and mucous membranes. Trauma results in excessive bruising but not large, uncontrolled haematomas. After cuts or skin puncture, bleeding stops promptly with local pressure and does not recur when pressure is released. In contrast, in haemophilia and abnormalities of other coagulation factors, the platelets function normally so that there are no petechial or superficial haemorrhages. Instead, deep bleeding occurs after minor trauma, such as intramuscular haematomas and haemorrhage into joint spaces. External bleeding recurs several hours after pressure is removed—as, for example, severe bleeding starting several hours after a tooth extraction.

Patients who have bleeding disorders or who have the potential for developing such disorders as a result of disease processes or therapeutic agents are observed carefully and frequently for bleeding. All drainage and excreta such as faeces, urine, vomit and gastric drainage are observed for occult as well as frank blood. The skin is observed for petechiae and ecchymoses and the nose and gums are checked for bleeding. Abdominal, loin or joint pain are promptly reported because they may be indicative of internal bleeding. In addition, the patient is closely observed for evidence of hypovolaemia manifested by hypotension, tachycardia, pallor, cool clammy skin, altered responsiveness and oliguria.

Vascular Disorders

Spontaneous rupture of small vessels that are defective or injured results in leakage of blood into the skin, mucous membranes and serosal surfaces. The smallest haemorrhages, pinhead in size, are called petechiae. Haemorrhages up to 1 cm in diameter are referred to as purpura, and larger, blotchy lesions are ecchymoses.

Vascular dysfunction can be caused by a variety of mechanisms. Alterations in the connective tissue framework supporting blood vessels are believed to explain the bleeding associated with vitamin C deficiency and adrenocortical hormone excess. Vascular injury can also result from systemic diseases such as diabetes mellitus or the action of bacterial toxins. A particularly important cause of vascular injury is immunologically mediated. As a consequence of drug reactions, bacterial infections, allergic disorders, or collagen-vascular diseases, vascular damage occurs. Effects range from minor local injury to widespread thromboses or haemorrhage.

Platelet Defects

The sudden onset of petechiae, purpura or excessive bruising or bleeding from the nose or gums should stimulate a search for a platelet defect. Deficiencies of platelet number, or thrombocytopenias, are most common, but there are also some rare disorders of platelet function in which the platelet count is normal but the clinical picture is identical to that in thrombocytopenia. The platelet function disorders can be diagnosed by special tests for platelet factor 3 and platelet adhesiveness and aggregation. The most important functional disorder to remember is that induced by aspirin; even small amounts of aspirin prevent normal platelet aggregation, and the bleeding time test is prolonged for several days after aspirin ingestion. Although this defect does not cause bleeding in most normal people, patients with another coagulation disorder (such as thrombocytopenia or haemophilia) can experience life-threatening haemorrhage after taking aspirin.

Thrombocytopenia

Thrombocytopenia is the most common cause of generalized bleeding. It can result either from decreased production of platelets by the marrow or from increased peripheral destruction. Some of the causes are listed in Table 10.5. If the platelet deficiency is secondary to an underlying disease, this can usually be diagnosed from the examination of the patient or the bone marrow. When peripheral destruction is the cause of thrombocytopenia, the marrow shows increased megakaryocytes and normal platelet production. Bleeding and petechiae usually do not occur with platelet counts above 50×10^9/l, although excessive bleeding can follow surgery.

Table 10.5 *Thrombocytopenias*

Cause	Treatment
1. Failure of production	
a. Leukaemia	Treat the leukaemia
b. Tumour invasion of marrow	
c. Aplastic anaemia	Bone marrow transplant, androgens, antilymphocyte globulin
d. Megaloblastic anaemia	B_{12} or folic acid
e. Toxins	Discontinue toxin
f. Drugs: thiazides, heparin, chloramphenicol, cytotoxic drugs	Discontinue drug
g. Infection, especially septicaemia, viral infections, tuberculosis	Treat infection
h. Alcohol	Discontinue alcohol
2. Increased destruction	
a. Due to antibodies	
i. Diopathic thrombocytopenic purpura	Steroids, splenectomy
ii. Lupus erythematosus	Steroids, immunosuppressive drugs
iii. Malignant lymphoma	Steroids
iv. Drugs: quinine, digoxin, phenytoin, aspirin, sulphonamides, alcohol, gold	Discontinue drug
b. Due to entrapment in large spleen	
c. Due to infections	Splenectomy
i. Bacteraemia	
ii. Postviral infections	Treat infection
3. Increased utilization	
a. Disseminated intravascular coagulation	Fresh frozen plasma, cryoprecipitate and low-dose heparin

When the platelet count drops below $20 \times 10^9/l$, petechiae appear and there are nose bleeds, excessive menstrual bleeding and haemorrhage after surgery or dental extractions. When the platelet count is less than $5 \times 10^9/l$, spontaneous fatal central nervous system haemorrhage or gastrointestinal haemorrhage can occur.

Management

The management for secondary thrombocytopenia is usually that for the underlying disease. If platelet production is impaired, platelet transfusions may help to raise platelet counts and stop bleeding or prevent intracranial haemorrhage. If excessive destruction is the problem, transfused platelets will also be destroyed and will not raise the count.

Idiopathic Thrombocytopenic Purpura

Idiopathic thrombocytopenic purpura is a disease of all ages but commonly affects children and young women. Although the precise aetiology remains unknown, viral infections sometimes precede the disease in children. Antiplatelet antibodies are produced so platelet life span

is markedly shortened. Occasionally, the antibodies can be demonstrated *in vitro*, but usually the diagnosis is made from the decreased platelet count and survival time and increased bleeding time. Other overt causes of thrombocytopenia must be ruled out. Symptoms may begin suddenly, with petechiae and mucosal bleeding. The platelet count is generally below $20 \times 10^9/l$. Death may result from intracranial bleeding. There are no physical findings of note other than the haemorrhages.

Management

Corticosteroids are the treatment of choice; the bleeding ceases in one to two days, and platelet counts rise in a week or so. About three quarters of patients respond to steroids, but many have a relapse when the drug is withdrawn. These patients, as well as the nonresponders, are subjected to splenectomy. Splenectomy produces a lasting remission in 75 per cent of patients, although transient recurrences of thrombocytopenia sometimes occur months or years later. The rare patients who do not respond to splenectomy are sometimes treated with the immunosuppressive drugs azathioprine or cyclophosphamide.

Clotting Factor Defects

Haemophilia

Definition and Aetiology

There are two hereditary bleeding disorders that are indistinguishable clinically, but that can be separated by laboratory tests—haemophilia A and haemophilia B. Haemophilia A is due to a deficiency of factor VIII clotting activity, whereas haemophilia B stems from a deficiency of factor IX. Factor VIII deficiency is about five times more common. Both types of haemophilia are inherited as X-linked traits, so almost all affected people are males; their mothers and some of their sisters are carriers but are asymptomatic.

Clinical Features

The disease, which may be very severe, is manifested by large, spreading bruises and bleeding into muscles and joints after even minimal trauma. Patients often note pain in a joint before swelling and limitation of motion are apparent. Recurrent joint haemorrhages can result in damage so severe that chronic pain or ankylosis (fixation) of the joint occurs. Many of the patients are crippled by the joint damage before they become adults. Spontaneous haematuria and gastrointestinal bleeding can occur. The disease is recognized in early childhood, usually in the toddler age group.

Before the availability of factor VIII concentrates, many haemophiliacs died of the complications before reaching adulthood. Some people with haemophilia have a milder deficiency, having between 5 and 25 per cent of the normal level of factor VIII or IX. They do not experience the painful and disabling muscle and joint haemorrhages, but bleed only after dental extractions or surgery. Nevertheless, such haemorrhages can prove fatal if the cause is not recognized quickly.

Management

In the past, the only treatment was fresh frozen plasma, which had to be given in such large quantities that the patients became volume overloaded. Now factor VIII and IX concentrates are available to all blood banks. Patients are given concentrates when they are actively bleeding or as a prophylactic measure before dental extractions or surgery. Some families/carers are taught how to administer the concentrate at home, at the first sign of bleeding.

A few patients eventually develop antibodies to the concentrates, so their factor levels cannot be elevated. Treatment of this problem is extremely difficult and often unsuccessful. Aminocaproic acid is an inhibitor of fibrinolytic enzymes. This drug can slow the dissolution of blood clots that do form, and is sometimes used after oral surgery in patients with haemophilia.

In terms of general care, haemophiliacs should never be given aspirin or intramuscular injections. Dental because dental extractions are so hazardous. Splints and other orthopaedic devices may be very useful in those who have suffered joint or muscle haemorrhages.

In recent years several patients have contracted acquired immune deficiency syndrome (AIDS) through the administration of factor VIII manufactured in the United States from plasma inadvertently contaminated by the human immunodeficiency virus (HIV). These people will require reassurance that factor VIII is now made artificially by genetic engineering in the United Kingdom.

Those haemophiliacs who have AIDS face all the enormous problems it brings, together with the knowledge that they have contracted the disease through medical treatment. A great deal of psychological support is needed to help them overcome their feelings of fear, resentment and desperation. The nursing care of the person with AIDS is dealt with in greater detail in Chapter 26.

A high percentage of haemophiliacs are now HIV-positive, of whom an unknown percentage is thought to be at risk of developing overt AIDS; the prediction of this figure is controversial.

▶ NURSING PROCESS
▶ THE PERSON WITH HAEMOPHILIA

▶ *Assessment*

People with haemophilia are carefully assessed for evidence of internal bleeding (abdominal, chest or loin pain; haematuria; haematemesis; melaena), muscle haematomas and haemorrhage into joint spaces. Vital signs are checked for indications of hypovolaemia. All extremities and the torso are carefully examined for haematomas. All joints are assessed for swelling, limitation of mobility and pain. Range of motion of the joints is done slowly and carefully to avoid further damage. At the first indication of pain, joint motion is stopped. Haemophiliacs are questioned about any limitations of activities and movement experienced in the past and any need they have had for mobility aids such as splints, walking sticks or crutches.

If the person has had recent surgery, the surgical site is assessed for bleeding frequently and carefully. Continuous monitoring of vital signs may be necessary until it is certain that excessive postoperative bleeding is not present.

All haemophiliacs should be questioned about how they and their carers cope with their condition, measures that they use to prevent bleeding episodes and any limitations that the condition imposes on their lifestyle and daily activities. The person who has frequent hospitalizations for bleeding episodes due to traumatic injury is carefully questioned about the factors that have led to these episodes. Such data are particularly helpful in determining the extent of acceptance of the condition and the need for education regarding measures to prevent unnecessary trauma.

▶ Patient's Problems

Based on the assessment, the person's main problems may include the following:

- Pain related to joint haemorrhage and subsequent ankylosis.
- Risk of decreased tissue perfusion related to bleeding.
- Health education needs regarding prevention of bleeding.
- Ineffective coping related to the chronicity of the condition and its effects on lifestyle.

▶ Planning and Implementation
▶ Expected Outcomes

The main outcomes for the haemophiliac may include relief/minimization of pain, adequate tissue perfusion, utilization of measures to prevent bleeding and coping with chronicity and altered lifestyle.

Nursing Care

Relief/Minimization of Pain

Generally, analgesics are required to alleviate the pain associated with large muscle haematomas and joint haemorrhage. The doctor usually prescribes non-narcotic analgesics when possible, because pain may be of long duration and dependency on narcotics may become a problem with chronic pain. It is often helpful to administer the analgesic before activities that are known to precipitate pain. This not only helps the person to accomplish the activity, but also tends to decrease the amount of analgesia required.

All possible efforts are taken to prevent or minimize pain due to activity. The patient is encouraged to move slowly and to prevent undue stress on involved joints. Many patients report that warm baths promote relaxation, improve mobility and lessen pain. Heat is avoided during bleeding episodes, however, because it potentiates further bleeding.

Since joint pain restricts mobility, patients with excessive pain during activity may benefit from orthopaedic aids. Splints, walking sticks or crutches are helpful in some cases in shifting body weight off joints that are particularly painful. Splints must be properly applied and crutches must be properly fitted by the physiotherapist to prevent undue pressure on body surfaces that could cause tissue trauma and bleeding.

Attainment/Maintenance of Adequate Tissue Perfusion

The patient is assessed frequently for signs and symptoms of decreased tissue perfusion as evidenced by hypoxia to vital organs: restlessness, anxiety, confusion, pallor, cool clammy skin, chest pain and decreased urinary output. Hypotension and tachycardia will occur as a result of volume depletion. The blood pressure, pulse, respirations, central venous pressure and pulmonary artery pressure are monitored, as are the haemoglobin and haematocrit, coagulation and bleeding times and platelet counts.

The patient is observed frequently for bleeding from the skin, mucous membranes and wounds and for internal bleeding. During bleeding episodes the patient is kept at rest, and gentle pressure is applied to any external bleeding sites. Cold compresses are applied to bleeding sites when indicated. Parenteral medications are administered intravenously to decrease trauma and the risk of bleeding. All possible efforts are made to protect the patient from trauma. The environment is kept free of obstacles that could cause falls, and the patient is turned and moved with care. Side rails are padded when necessary. Blood and blood components are administered as prescribed, and precautions are taken to avoid complications (see p. 463).

Use of Measures to Prevent Bleeding

The haemophiliac and carers are informed of the risk of bleeding and the necessary safety precautions to be taken. They are encouraged to alter the home environment as necessary to prevent physical trauma. Obstacles that could cause falls are removed. An electric razor is used for shaving and a soft toothbrush is used for oral hygiene. Forceful nose blowing and coughing and straining at stool are avoided. A stool softener is used if necessary. Aspirin and aspirin-containing drugs are to be avoided.

Physical activity is encouraged, but with proper safety measures used. Noncontact sports such as swimming, hiking and golf are acceptable activities, whereas contact sports are always to be avoided.

The necessity for regular check-ups and laboratory studies is explained. With knowledge of the reasons for continued medical evaluation, the person will be more likely to keep appointments.

Coping with Chronicity and Altered Lifestyle

People with haemophilia often require assistance in coping with the condition because it is chronic, it places restrictions on their lives and it is an inherited disorder that can be passed to future generations. From childhood, haemophiliacs are helped to accept themselves and the disease and to identify the positive aspects of their lives. They are encouraged to be self-sufficient and to maintain independence by preventing unnecessary trauma that can cause acute bleeding episodes and temporarily interfere with normal activities. As they work through feelings about the condition and progress to acceptance of it, they will accept more and more responsibility for maintaining optimal health. They will co-operate with health care providers, keep regular medical and dental appointments and strive toward a healthy, productive life. Many people benefit from the services of haemophilia organizations and support groups. These provide co-ordinated, ongoing care and the opportunity to talk with others who are faced with the same situation.

► *Evaluation*
► **Expected Outcomes**

1. Experiences relief/minimization of pain.
   a. Pain-free at rest.
   b. Later, pain-free on movement.
   c. Later still, able to move joints through full range of motion without pain.
2. Maintains adequate tissue perfusion.
   a. Vital signs and haemodynamic pressure readings remain normal.
   b. Laboratory studies remain within normal ranges.
   c. Experiences no active bleeding.
3. Uses measures to prevent bleeding.
   a. Avoids physical trauma.
   b. Alters home environment to increase safety.
   c. Keeps outpatient appointments.
   d. Avoids contact sports.
   e. Avoids aspirin and aspirin-containing drugs.
   f. Wears Medic-Alert bracelet.
4. Copes with chronicity and altered lifestyle.
   a. Identifies the positive aspects of present life.
   b. Involves family members and other carers in decisions about the future and changes to be made in lifestyle.
   c. Strives toward independence.
   d. Makes specific plans for continuation of health care.

Von Willebrand's Disease

This is a common bleeding disorder, inherited as a dominant character and affecting males and females equally. It is due to a mild deficiency of factor VIII (15 to 50 per cent of normal) associated with an impairment of platelet function. The laboratory tests show normal platelet count, prolonged bleeding time and slightly prolonged partial thromboplastin time. Patients commonly have nose-bleeds, excessively heavy menses, bleeding from cuts and postoperative bleeding. They do not suffer from massive soft tissue or joint haemorrhages. Both of the defects can be corrected by the administration of cryoprecipitate, which contains factor VIII, fibrinogen and factor XIII.

Hypoprothrombinaemia

Prothrombin, as was previously noted, is essential for the clotting process. This protein is produced in the liver by a vitamin K-dependent chemical process. Vitamin K enters the body from food sources as well as from synthesis by bacteria that reside in the intestine. Normal prothrombin activity in the blood depends on adequate absorption of this vitamin from the gastrointestinal tract and on adequate liver function. Therefore, prothrombin deficiency may arise as a result of diarrhoea, from a lack of bile in the gastrointestinal tract (necessary for absorption of fat-soluble vitamin K) due to biliary tract obstruction, from surgical removal or mucosal damage of a large part of the small intestine, from prolonged antibiotic therapy or as the result of liver disease.

The principal symptom of prothrombin deficiency, as observed in patients with haemophilia, is prolonged haemorrhage from blood vessels that are damaged by trauma or disease, which explains the characteristic occurrence of ecchymoses, haematuria, gastrointestinal bleeding and postoperative haemorrhages.

Warfarin Toxicity

The coumarins (for example, warfarin) are drugs that are often employed for the express purpose of inducing a partial depression of prothrombin activity, because the drugs interfere with the action of vitamin K in the liver. Therapy is usually calculated to prolong the prothrombin time by two to two-and-a-half times the normal time. In this range, thrombosis is inhibited and thrombophlebitis is prevented. However, if taken in excessive dosages, whether intentionally or mistakenly, or if certain other drugs are administered simultaneously that interfere with metabolism, the complete picture of prothrombin deficiency, with a severe haemorrhagic disorder, may be produced. Among drugs that enhance coumarin-induced anticoagulation are phenylbutazone, indomethacin, chloral hydrate and salicylates. Other drugs, such as barbiturates, decrease coumarin effects.

Management

Hypoprothrombinaemia, if due to vitamin K deficiency, responds to treatment with any of several preparations that are available for oral or parenteral administration. However, when corrective measures are urgently required, particularly in patients with liver disease or coumarin toxicity, the effective treatment requires the direct replacement of prothrombin by means of transfusion because purified preparations of prothrombin are not yet available.

Liver Disease

The liver cell makes all the plasma protein coagulation factors except factor VIII. Therefore, in severe hepatic disease of any sort, deficiencies in these factors may occur. The prothrombin time and partial thromboplastin time will both be prolonged. If the spleen is enlarged as well (as in cirrhosis), the platelet count may also be depressed. These patients frequently bruise easily and may have life-threatening haemorrhage from peptic ulcers or oesophageal varices. Treatment includes fresh frozen plasma, fresh blood and factor IX complex. Vitamin K does not improve the disorder.

Disseminated Intravascular Coagulation

Occasionally, widespread clotting in small vessels of the body occurs, causing clotting factors and platelets to be used up. Thus, paradoxically, the patient presents with a bleeding disorder characterized by low fibrinogen, prolonged prothrombin time and partial thromboplastin time, low factor VIII and thrombocytopenia. Such patients may bleed from mucous membranes, venepuncture sites, and the gastrointestinal and urinary tracts. The bleeding can range from minimal occult internal bleeding to profuse haemorrhages from all orifices. Patients may also develop renal failure due to fibrin deposition in small vessels of the kidney. Many serious illnesses may predispose to disseminated intravascular coagulation, including septicaemia, premature separation of the placenta in a pregnant woman, metastatic malignancies, acute leukaemia, especially promyelocytic leukaemia, haemolytic transfusion reactions, massive tissue trauma and shock. Disseminated intravascular coagulation should be suspected in any patient with a predisposing cause who develops purpura, a bleeding tendency and signs of renal damage.

Serious haemorrhage requires replacement therapy: transfusions of red cells, platelet concentrates, fresh frozen plasma and, if indicated by very low fibrinogen level, cryoprecipitate. The best treatment is correction of the underlying disease, but in the meantime continuous intravenous, low-dose heparin may retard the coagulation process and permit normalization of clotting tests and a decrease in the haemorrhagic symptoms.

THERAPEUTIC MEASURES IN BLOOD DISORDERS

Splenectomy

The surgical removal of the spleen is sometimes necessary following trauma to the abdomen. Because the spleen is very vascular, severe haemorrhage can result after splenic rupture. Under such circumstances splenectomy becomes an emergency procedure.

Splenectomy is also often performed as a treatment for a number of haematological disorders. An enlarged spleen may be the site of excessive destruction of blood cells; when this destruction is life-threatening, the operation may prove palliative. This is the case in autoimmune haemolytic anaemia or idiopathic thrombocytopenic purpura when these disorders do not respond to corticosteroids. Some patients with severe anaemia due to inherited red cell defects (such as thalassaemia or pyruvate kinase deficiency) may benefit from splenectomy. Patients with

rheumatoid arthritis may develop splenomegaly with destruction of granulocytes and granulocytopenia; removal of the spleen may improve the blood count and reduce the tendency toward infection.

Very large, bulky and painful spleens (such as may occur in myelofibrosis or chronic myeloid leukaemia) usually do not need to be removed, but when the patient's symptoms and blood counts do not respond to drugs, splenectomy can be helpful. Most patients with hereditary spherocytosis (spheroid shape of erythrocytes) are essentially cured of their haemolytic process by splenectomy.

When the spleen is large, the operation can be difficult, but generally there is a very low mortality. Morbidity may result from postoperative atelectasis, pneumonia, abdominal distension and subphrenic abscess formation. Young patients are at increased risk of pneumococcal infections after splenectomy for the rest of their lives and should receive pneumococcal vaccine, and take penicillin continuously. All patients are advised to seek prompt medical attention when even relatively minor symptoms of infection occur. Patients with high platelet counts (such as those with myelofibrosis) often are found to have even higher counts after splenectomy—greater than a thousand—and this can predispose the patient to serious thrombotic or haemorrhagic problems.

Blood Transfusion

Blood Donation

Because blood and blood components are used so frequently, nearly all hospitals now have blood banks, and the regional transfusion services have facilities for removal of blood from donors. These donor clinics are often the responsibility of nurses, who must screen prospective donors, supervise the phlebotomies and care for the health and safety of the donors.

Donor Interviewing

All prospective donors are examined and interviewed before the donation for their own protection and that of the recipients. Donors should appear to be in good health and should be free of any of the following disqualifying factors:

- A history of viral hepatitis, recently or at any time in the past, or a history of close contact with a hepatitis or dialysis patient within six months. Donated blood is screened routinely for hepatitis B antigen.
- A history of syphilis or malaria, because these can be transmitted by transfusion even years later. A history of visiting a tropical country in the last six months. A person who has been free of symptoms and off therapy for three years after malaria may be a donor. Donor blood is screened routinely for syphilis.

- A history of evidence of drug abuse in which drugs were self-injected, because addicts have a high hepatitis carrier rate, and because of the risk of AIDS.
- A history of possible exposure to the AIDS virus. A test for the presence of antibodies to AIDS virus in donated blood is now mandatory. People who are members of high-risk groups, for example, homosexual and bisexual men, intravenous drug abusers, people with haemophilia, sexual partners of individuals at risk for AIDS, and people with signs and symptoms suggestive of the appearance of the disease are asked to self-defer from blood donation.
- A skin infection, because of the possibility of contamination of the phlebotomy needle.
- A history of recent asthma, urticaria or allergy to drugs, because hypersensitivity can be transferred transferred to the recipient.
- Pregnancy within six months, because of the nutritional demands of pregnancy on the mother.
- A history of tooth extraction or oral surgery within 72 hours, because such procedures are frequently associated with transient bacteraemia.
- A history of recent tattoo, because of the higher risk of hepatitis.
- A history of exposure to infectious disease within the past three weeks, because of the risk of transmission to the recipient.
- Recent immunizations, because of the risk of transmitting live organisms (two-week waiting period for live, attenuated organisms; two months for rubella; one year for rabies).
- Presence of cancer, because of the lack of knowledge about transmission.
- A history of whole blood donation within the past six months.
- Having omitted breakfast that morning, or lunch as the case may be.

Blood donors who pass this screen are then examined with regard to blood pressure, pulse, oral temperature, weight, and haemoglobin level. The last is often checked via a screening test that only estimates the haemoglobin. People under 18 and over 65 years of age are usually disqualified. Donors are expected to meet the following minimal requirements:

1. The body weight should exceed 50 kg for a standard 450-ml donation. Donors weighing less than 50 kg may be bled proportionately less.
2. The oral temperature should not exceed 37.5°C.
3. The pulse rate should be regular and between 50 and 100 beats per minute.
4. The systolic arterial pressure should be between 90 and 180 mmHg, and the diastolic pressure between 50 and 100 mmHg.
5. The haemoglobin level in the case of a woman should be at least 12.5 g/dl, and in the case of a man, 13.5 g/dl.

Phlebotomy

Phlebotomy consists of venepuncture and the withdrawal of blood. Donors lie in a recumbent position, the skin over the antecubital fossa is carefully cleaned with a spirit preparation, a tourniquet is applied and venepuncture is performed. Withdrawal of 450 ml of blood takes less than 15 minutes. Following removal of the needle, firm pressure is applied with sterile gauze for two or three minutes or until bleeding stops. A firm bandage is then applied. Donors are asked to remain recumbent until they feel able to sit up, usually after one or two minutes. If weakness or faintness is experienced, they should rest for a longer period. After getting up, they are given food and fluids in a reception area and asked to remain for another 15 minutes. Donors should be advised to leave the dressing on and avoid heavy lifting for several hours, to avoid smoking for one hour and alcoholic beverages for three hours, to increase fluid intake for two days and to be sure to eat well-balanced meals for two weeks. The labels on the blood bag and tubes are checked carefully before and after donation to avoid any error that could prove fatal to a recipient.

Complications

Excessive bleeding at the site of venepuncture is sometimes due to a bleeding disorder in the donor, but more often is the result of a technical error: laceration of the vein, excessive tourniquet pressure or failure to apply enough pressure following withdrawal of the needle.

Fainting is relatively common and may be related to emotional factors, vasovagal reaction or prolonged fasting before donation. Sometimes, because of the loss of blood volume, hypotension and syncope occur when the donor assumes an erect position.

- A donor who appears pale or complains of faintness should immediately lie down or sit with head lowered below the knees. The nurse should observe the donor for another 30 minutes.

Anginal chest pain may be precipitated in patients with unsuspected coronary artery disease.

Convulsions may occur in patients with epilepsy. Both angina and convulsions require further medical evaluation.

Blood and Blood Components

A unit of blood that has been drawn from a donor consists of approximately 450 ml of whole blood and 60 to 70 ml of preservative-anticoagulant. The latter serves as the anticoagulant and also provides the red cells with a sugar for metabolism. This blood can be maintained at 1 to 6°C in the blood bank for 21 to 35 days, depending on the type of preservative-anticoagulant used; after that it is discarded, because too many of the red cells are unable to survive *in vivo*. Whole blood stored for more than 24 hours does not contain functional platelets or practical amounts of coagulation factors V and VIII.

Samples of the unit are always taken immediately after donation so that the blood can be typed and tested for the presence of syphilis, hepatitis and antibodies. A test for the presence of AIDS antibodies in donated blood is now required. A label on the unit thereafter states the blood group, date drawn and expiry date.

Whole blood is a complex tissue with both cellular and many noncellular plasma components. Recently it has been recognized that whole blood is necessary only in certain clinical situations; often, component therapy can replace the particular deficiency without subjecting the patient to unnecessary risks, such as circulatory overload. In addition, the use of components is more economical because it makes it possible to meet the needs of more than one patient from a single blood donation. Transfusion laboratories are able to separate whole blood into these fractions, and all of the components are available from the National Transfusion Service.

Whole Blood

Whole blood may be used to treat acute, massive haemorrhage or hypovolaemic shock due to haemorrhage. It is not indicated for the correction of anaemia. Whenever possible, components should be used instead.

Packed Red Cells

Red cells are separated from whole blood by centrifugation or sedimentation; most of the plasma is removed, leaving a haematocrit of approximately 80 per cent. Packed red cells are indicated for transfusions in all anaemic patients, in surgical patients before and after operation and in many cases of acute blood loss. The use of packed cells instead of whole blood reduces the volume load. Thus, this method is safer for patients with incipient congestive failure and reduces the incidence of transfusion reactions due to plasma factors.

Frozen Red Cells

The method of freezing red cells allows storage for long periods of time—even years—but is expensive. Hence, frozen cells are used only under unusual circumstances, such as for patients with very rare blood types, or with antibodies to the common minor antigens or to store for autotransfusion to the donor later.

Platelets

Patients with thrombocytopenia and haemorrhage often require transfusions of large numbers of platelets. Platelets taken from four to eight units of blood are necessary to raise the count of a severely thrombocytopenic patient to a haemostatic level. Therefore, 'platelet-rich plasma' with a small volume is used rather than whole blood. Several

methods are available for harvesting fresh platelets: (1) Plasma can be removed after centrifugation of a unit of freshly collected whole blood; the plasma is then centrifuged again slowly to separate the platelets. Several such platelet 'units' can then be pooled and given to the recipient, who thus receives platelets from several different donors. (2) A single donor can undergo platelet aphoresis, in which blood is donated, the red cells are separated and returned to the donor immediately, and the plasma is spun down to obtain platelets in a volume of only 10 to 20 ml. In this way, multiple units can be donated.

Platelet concentrates are generally kept at room temperature with agitation and are administered within 48 hours of collection to ensure viability. Each unit of platelets will raise the recipient's platelet count by about $10 \times 10^9/l$. For an adult with severe thrombocytopenia, six or more units of platelets may be needed daily. Even larger doses are needed for patients with fever or infection because these conditions decrease platelet effectiveness.

Single donor platelet transfusions are especially valuable for patients who have received many transfusions and have developed antibodies to all except HLA- (transplantation antigen-) matched blood products.

Granulocytes

Severely granulocytopenic patients with infection can sometimes benefit from transfusions of normal white cells. Large numbers of granulocytes less than 24 hours old must be administered. The donor's white cells are removed continuously as blood is drawn from one vein and returned constantly to another vein. The process requires about four hours of donor time, and the donor must be anticoagulated during the procedure.

Plasma

Whole plasma was originally used in the treatment of hypovolaemic shock, but now, because plasma carries a risk of hepatitis equal to that of whole blood, other colloids (such as albumin) or electrolyte solutions (like Ringer's lactate) are usually preferred. Plasma can be used to replace deficient coagulation factors in acquired or inherited bleeding disorders. Only fresh frozen plasma (which can be stored for 12 months) contains all the coagulation factors, including V and VIII. However, fractions of plasma have now been prepared that can replace all the factors except V, in small volume concentrates. Fresh frozen plasma may be administered to replace clotting factors in patients who are bleeding and being massively transfused with whole blood or packed red cells. It is also used to treat patients with severe liver disease.

Albumin

Plasma albumin is a large protein molecule that usually stays within vessels and is a major contributor to plasma osmotic pressure. This material is used to expand the blood volume of patients in hypovolaemic shock and to elevate the level of circulating albumin in patients with hypoalbuminaemia. These preparations, in contrast to all other fractions of human blood, cellular or soluble, are subjected to heating at 60°C for 10 hours, and therefore can be certified unequivocally as free of all viral contaminants, including the hepatitis virus.

Cryoprecipitate
Cryoprecipitate is a plasma derivative that is rich in factor VIII, fibrinogen, factor XIII and fibronectin. It is prepared by thawing one unit of fresh frozen plasma and removing all but 10 to 15 ml of plasma and the cold-insoluble globulins. The product is then refrozen and can be used for up to one year for the treatment of haemophilia A, Von Willebrand's disease, disseminated intravascular coagulation and uraemic bleeding.

Factor IX Concentrate
A concentrated form of factor IX is prepared by pooling, fractionating and freeze-drying large volumes of plasma. It is used primarily for treatment of patients with factor IX deficiency (also called haemophilia B, or Christmas disease).

Prothrombin Complex
This fraction contains prothrombin and factors VII, IX and X, and some factor XI. It is useful for the treatment of bleeding in congenital or acquired deficiencies in these factors.

Transfusion Technique

Administration of blood and blood components demands knowledge of correct techniques for administration and possible complications. After checking the prescription and explaining the procedure to the patient, the nurse obtains the blood or blood component from the blood bank. Labels are carefully checked with another nurse. Vital signs should be recorded before initiating the transfusion.

Whole blood or packed red cells are generally administered through a large venous cannula via a special giving set that contains a blood filter to screen out fibrin clots and other particulate matter. For the first 15 minutes, the transfusion is run very slowly, at about 2 ml per minute, and the patient is observed carefully for adverse effects. If no ill effects occur during this time, the flow rate is then increased to the prescribed rate. The patient must continue to be observed frequently. A summary of major points to consider when administering blood components is listed in Table 10.6.

Assessment

Before initiating the transfusion, the blood product should

be checked by two nurses against the doctor's prescription, the patient's blood group (as stated in the case notes), the patient's cross-match form, the expiry date and the patient's identity band. It should also be checked for the presence of gas bubbles, which may indicate bacterial growth, and for any abnormal colour or cloudiness, which may be a sign of haemolysis. Temperature, pulse, respirations and blood pressure are taken in order to provide a baseline for comparing vital signs at a later time.

After the blood transfusion is started, the patient should be watched closely for 15 to 30 minutes to assure that no signs of reaction or circulatory overload occur. Monitoring vital signs is carried out at regular intervals as indicated.

Complications and Nursing Management

Every patient who receives a blood transfusion is subject to the possible development of complications of transfusion therapy. Nursing management is directed toward the prevention of these complications and prompt initiation of measures to control any complications that occur. Transfusion complications include the following:

Circulatory overload
Febrile reaction
Allergic reaction
Septic reaction
Haemolytic reaction
Delayed haemolytic reaction
Diseases transmitted by the transfusion (e.g., hepatitis, malaria, syphilis, AIDS)

Circulatory Overload
In patients with normal blood volume (as in chronic anaemia) or increased blood volume (as in renal failure or heart failure), the addition of whole blood or packed cells can precipitate pulmonary oedema. Packed red cells are safer to use and, if the rate of administration is sufficiently slow, circulatory overload may be prevented, particularly if concomitant diuretics are prescribed with the blood to avoid this.

● The signs to look for are dyspnoea, orthopnoea, cyanosis or sudden anxiety. If the transfusion is continued, severe dyspnoea and coughing of pink, frothy sputum can occur. Neck vein distension, crackles at the base of the lungs and rise in central venous pressure will occur.
● The patient is nursed in an upright position with the feet below waist height, the blood is discontinued and the doctor is called. The intravenous line is kept patent with a *very* slow infusion of normal saline to retain access to the vein in case intravenous medications are necessary. Phlebotomy or diuretics, oxygen, morphine and aminophylline may be necessary if improvement does not occur rapidly.

Table 10.6 *Administration of blood components*

Product	Administration technique	Major complications
Packed red cells	Use a blood giving set and prime blood filter so that cells cover entire surface Administer only with 0.9% NaCl (dextrose haemolyses red blood cells and Ringer's lactate causes coagulation) Administer 1 unit over 3–4 hours	Transfusion reactions less frequent than with whole blood
Platelets	Use special platelet giving set that has a nonwettable filter (do not use microaggregate filter) Administer only with 0.9% NaCl Administer as rapidily as can be tolerated, usually 6 units with the clamp fully open, to prevent platelets from clumping and sticking to side of bag	Febrile reactions common
Granulocytes	Use standard blood filter (do not use microaggregate filter) Administer only with 0.9% NaCl Administer over 2–4 hours to aid patient tolerance	Febrile and allergic reactions common Leucoagglutinin reactions possible, leading to hypotension, anaphylaxis and respiratory distress
Plasma	Use solution set (do not use microaggregate filter) Administer as rapidly as patient tolerates because coagulation factors become unstable after thawing	Risk of circulatory overload
Albumin	Undiluted 20% albumin should be administered at 1ml/minute if patient is normovolaemic	Risk of circulatory overload
Factor VIII	Administer by syringe or solution set	Allergic and febrile reactions common
Prothrombin	Administer by syringe or solution set	Allergic and febrile reactions possible

Febrile Reaction

Patients may develop a fever during transfusion because of the presence of bacterial pyrogens, sensitivity to leucocytes or platelets, haemolytic episodes or unknown factors. Due to the widespread use of disposable transfusion equipment, bacterial pyrogens are rarely a cause. Infrequently, blood can be grossly contaminated with large numbers of micro-organisms that survive in the 4°C storage. If such blood is infused, the patient develops fever and shaking chills within 30 minutes, and shock soon follows. Even when the cause of this reaction is recognized early (by gram stain of the donor blood), the mortality rate is high.

As soon as the reaction is recognized, the transfusion is discontinued and the intravenous line is kept open with normal saline. The doctor is summoned and the blood bag is returned to the laboratory for analysis. The temperature is checked 30 minutes after the chill and as indicated thereafter. Antipyretics are administered as prescribed.

Sensitivity to leucocyte or platelet antigens is much more common, especially in previously transfused patients or women who have borne children. The temperature rises during the administration of blood or shortly afterward and is rarely associated with chills, hypotension or nausea. This type of reaction has a good prognosis; the treatment is intravenous corticosteroids. Subsequent transfusions should utilize leucocyte-poor blood. Patients who receive multiple transfusions are often prescribed prophylactic intravenous corticosteroids and antihistamine, to be given concomitantly during a transfusion, to prevent manifestations of leucocyte reactions.

Allergic Reaction

Some patients may develop urticaria (hives) or generalized itching or, rarely, wheezing or anaphylaxis. The cause of these reactions is thought to be sensitivity to a plasma protein in the transfused blood, or passive transfer of antibodies from the donor that react with some antigen (for example, in a drug or food) to which the recipient is exposed. To avoid this, allergic individuals are disqualified as donors. The reactions are usually mild and respond to antihistamines. If urticaria is the only symptom, the transfusion can sometimes be continued at a slower rate. If the reaction is severe, intravenous adrenaline is used.

Septic Reaction

Septic reactions are severe reactions that result from transfusion of blood or components contaminated with bacteria. Preventive measures include administering blood as soon as it arrives on the ward before warm room temperatures promote bacterial growth, and inspecting blood or components for gas bubbles, clotting or abnormal colour before administration. If the transfusion is contaminated, the patient will respond with rapid onset of chills, high fever, vomiting, diarrhoea and marked hypotension. In such a case the transfusion is discontinued immediately and the intravenous line kept patent with normal saline. The doctor is summoned and the blood bag is returned to the laboratory. Blood cultures are taken, and the patient is treated for septicaemia with antibiotics, intravenous fluids, vasopressors and steroids.

Haemolytic Reaction

The most dangerous type of transfusion reaction occurs when the donor blood is incompatible with that of the recipient. Antibodies in the recipient's plasma rapidly combine with donor erythrocytes, and the cells are haemolyzed either in the circulation (for example, in the renal capillaries) or in the reticuloendothelial system.

● Symptoms consist of chills, low back pain, headache, nausea or chest tightness, followed by fever and hypotension and vascular collapse. Severe reactions usually start within 10 minutes after the transfusion is begun. Haemoglobinuria (red urine) appears at the next voiding.

● The reaction must be recognized promptly and the transfusion discontinued immediately; the chances of a fatal episode are much reduced if less than 100 ml of incompatible blood are transfused.

Treatment is directed toward correcting the hypotension and preventing the renal damage that can follow haemoglobinuria. The patient is supported with intravenous colloid and given mannitol as an osmotic diuretic to maintain a good urine flow, glomerular filtration and renal blood flow. An indwelling catheter may be necessary for accurate measurement of output. If, after 24 hours, urine flow cannot be maintained, mannitol is contraindicated because it can be assumed that acute tubular necrosis has occurred. The management henceforth will be that for the renal disorder and will include fluid restriction and possibly dialysis until spontaneous healing takes place.

Delayed Haemolytic Reaction

Delayed haemolytic reactions occur at about one to two weeks and are recognized by fever, mild jaundice, a gradual fall in haemoglobin level and a positive Coombs' test. There is no haemoglobinuria, and generally these reactions are not dangerous. However, recognition is important because subsequent transfusions may cause an acute haemolytic reaction.

Diseases Transmitted by Blood Transfusion

The following diseases are transmissible by blood transfusion.

Serum Hepatitis. Serum hepatitis is a risk of transfusion therapy, particularly abroad, both for whole blood and for most components (see above). Hepatitis is discussed further in Chapter 16.

Malaria. Malaria is sometimes transmitted in blood donated by asymptomatic people who have been exposed to the disease. Recipients develop high fever and headache several weeks after the transfusion.

Syphilis. Syphilis is rarely transmitted now because of the serological tests required on all units of blood and because the organism does not survive refrigeration.

Acquired Immunodeficiency Syndrome (AIDS). AIDS has been associated with transfusion of blood products. For this reason people in high-risk groups should not donate blood. All donated blood is now tested for the presence of antibodies to the AIDS virus.

Summary of Nursing Care in Transfusion Reaction

If it is suspected that a transfusion reaction is occurring because of any of the conditions mentioned above, the nurse should stop the transfusion and call the doctor immediately. The following steps are taken in order that a diagnosis may be made regarding the type and severity of the reaction:

● The transfusion set is disconnected, but the intravenous line is kept open with a saline solution in case intravenous medication should be needed rapidly.

- The blood bag and tubing are saved, not thrown away. They should be sent to the laboratory for repeat cross-matching and culture.
- A sample of the patient's blood is taken for plasma haemoglobin, culture and retyping.
- A urine sample is collected as soon as possible and sent to the laboratory for a haemoglobin determination. Subsequent voidings of urine should be ward tested, and fluid balance observed.
- The transfusion laboratory is notified that a suspected transfusion reaction has occurred.

Bone Marrow Transplantation

This is an exciting addition to the therapeutic possibilities for haematological disease. Bone marrow can be aspirated by needle from multiple sites of an anaesthetized normal donor and transfused easily intravenously into the recipient. The marrow cells immediately travel to the marrow spaces that have been emptied by disease (i.e., aplastic anaemia), by chemotherapy or by total body irradiation. The donor cells proliferate in the marrow, releasing functional cells into the peripheral circulation. Complete marrow recovery may take six to eight weeks.

The major barrier to the success of bone marrow transplantation is the antigenic difference between donor and recipient. Thus, transplants between identical twins are almost always successful, and sibling transplants are often successful. If the donor and the patient are not identical in HLA (transplantation antigen) types, preconditioning of the patient with immunosuppression is necessary. Many recipients succumb to graft vs. host disease or severe infections while awaiting the recovery of the transplanted marrow. However, methods of immunosuppression and supportive care have improved greatly over the last few years, and this is currently the best treatment for severe aplastic anaemia. Bone marrow transplantation is also used to treat some forms of leukaemia and thalassaemia.

BIBLIOGRAPHY

Ives, T. J. and Guerra, M. F. (1987) Constant morphine infusion for severe sickle cell crisis pain, *Drug Intelligence and Clinical Pharmacy*, July/August, Vol. 21, pp. 625–7.

McCaffery, M. and Sofaer, B. (1983) *Nursing the Patient in Pain*, Harper & Row, London.

FURTHER READING

Books

Bailey, R. D. (1985) *Coping with Stress in Caring*, Blackwell Scientific, Oxford.

Brunner, L. S. and Suddarth, D. S. (1989) *The Lippincott Manual of Medical-Surgical Nursing* (2nd edition), Harper & Row, London.

Capra, L. G. (1986) *Care of the Cancer Patient* (2nd edition), Macmillan, London.

Contreras, M. (1990) *ABC of Transfusion*, British Medical Journal Publications, London.

Darling, V. H. and Rogers, J. (1986) *Research for Practising Nurses*, Macmillan, London.

Guyton, A. C. (1987 *Human Physiology and the Mechanisms of Disease* (4th edition), Saunders, Philadelphia.

Health Education Council (1987) *Sickle Cell Disease: A Guide for GPs, Nurses and Other Health Professionals*, Health Education Council, London.

Hector, W. and Whitfield, S. (1982) *Nursing Care For the Dying Patient and the Family*, Heinemann, London.

Hewitt, P. E. (1985) *Blood Diseases: Pocket Picture Guides*, Gower Medical, London.

Hoffbrand, A. V. and Lewis, S. M. (1989) *Postgraduate Haematology* (3rd edition), Heinemann, London.

Hoffbrand, A. V. and Pettit, J. E. (1984) *Essential Haematology* (2nd edition), Blackwell Scientific, Oxford.

Hoffbrand, A. V. and Pettit, J. E. (1987) *Clinical Haematology Illustrated*, Gower Medical, London.

Hughes-Jones, N. C. (1984) *Lecture Notes on Haematology* (4th edition), Blackwell Scientific, Oxford.

Jones, P. (1986) *Proceedings the AIDS Conference 1986*, Intercept, Newcastle-upon-Tyne.

Kubler-Ross, E. (1969) *On Death and Dying*, Tavistock, London.

Malseed, R. T. and Harrigan, G. S. (1989) *Textbook of Pharmacology and Nursing Care*, Lippincott, Pennsylvania.

McGilloway, O. and Myco, F. (1985) *Nursing and Spiritual Care*, Harper & Row, London.

Neubeuger, J. (1987) *Caring for Dying People of Different Faiths*, Lisa Sainsbury Foundation and Austen Cornish, London.

New Nursing Skillbook (1984) *Dealing With Death and Dying*, Nursing 84 Books, Springhouse, Pennsylvania.

Nurses' Clinical Library (1985) *Immune Disorders*, Nursing 85 Books, Springhouse, Pennsylvania.

Nurses' Clinical Library (1985) *Neoplastic Disorders*, Nursing 85 Books, Springhouse, Pennsylvania.

Nursing Skillbook (1978) *Helping Cancer Patients Effectively*, Nursing 78 Books, Horsham, Pennsylvania.

Peplau, H. E. (1988) *Interpersonal Relations in Nursing*, Macmillan, London.

Porth, C. M. (1989) *Pathophysiology* (2nd edition), Harper & Row, London.

Prytchard, A. P. and David, J. A. (1988) *Royal Marsden Hospital Manual of Clinical Nursing Procedures* (2nd edition), Harper & Row, London.

Regnard, C. and Davies, A. (1986) *A Guide to Symptom Control in Advanced Cancer*, Haigh & Hochland, Manchester.

Richards, J. D. M., Lynch, D. C. and Goldstone, A. H. (1983) *A Synopsis of Haematology*, Wright, Bristol.

Robbins, J. (Ed.) (1989) *Caring for the Dying Patient and the Family*, Harper & Row, London.

Skeel, R. T. (1987) *Handbook of Cancer Chemotherapy*, Little, Brown & Co., Boston.

Tiffany, R. (Ed.) (1981) *Cancer Nursing Update*, Baillière Tindall, London.

Tiffany, R. (Ed.) (1987) *Oncology for Nurses and Health Care Professionals, Volumes 1 and 2* (2nd edition), Harper & Row, London.

Tiffany, R. (Ed.) (1988) *Oncology for Nurses and Health Care Professionals, Volume 3*, Harper & Row, London.

Tschudin, V. (1987) *Counselling Skills for Nurses* (2nd edition), Baillière Tindall, London.

Tschudin, V. (1986) *Ethics in Nursing: The Caring Relationship*, Heinemann, London.

Tschudin, V. (1988) *Nursing the Patient with Cancer*, Prentice Hall, London.

Williams, C. (1983) *All About Cancer*, John Wiley, Chichester.

Articles

General

Anderson, M. A., Aker, S. N. and Hickman, R. O. (1982) The double lumen Hickman catheter, *American Journal of Nursing*, February, Vol. 82, No. 2, pp. 272–3.

Bjetlich, J. and Hickman, R. O. (1980) The Hickman indwelling catheter, *American Journal of Nursing*, Vol. 80, No. 1, pp. 62–5.

Brandt, B. (1984) A nursing protocol for the client with neutropenia, *Oncology Nursing Forum*, March/April, Vol. 11, No. 2, pp. 24–8.

Cox, E. (1985) The Hickman catheter, *Nursing Mirror*, 25 September, Vol. 161, No. 13, pp. 34–6.

Ellerhorst-Ryan, J. M. (1985) Complications of the myeloproliferative system: Infection and sepsis, *Seminars in Oncology Nursing*, November, Vol. 1, No. 4, pp. 244–50.

O'Rourke, A. (1986) Bone marrow procedure guide, *Oncology Nursing Forum*, January/February, Vol. 3, No. 1, pp. 66–7.

Reheis, C. E. (1985) Neutropenia: Causes, complications, treatment and nursing care, *Nursing Clinics of North America*, March, Vol. 20, No. 1, pp. 219–25.

Richardson, A. (1987) A process standard for oral care, *Nursing Times*, 12 August, Vol. 83, No. 2, pp. 38–40.

Shepherd, G., Page, C. and Sammon, P. (1987) The mouth trap, *Nursing Times*, 13 May, Vol. 83, No. 19, pp. 24–7.

Waterworth, S. (1989) Blood investigations, *Nursing*, August, Vol. 3, No. 4, pp. 24–5.

Yeomans, A. C. (1987) Myelodisplastic syndromes: A preleukaemic disorder, *Cancer Nursing*, April, Vol. 10, No. 1, pp. 32–40.

Anaemia

Smith, E. C. G. (1985) Treatment of aplastic anaemias, *Hospital Practice*, 15 May, Vol. 20, No. 5, pp. 69–84.

Waterworth, S. (1989) Management of anaemia, *Nursing*, August, Vol. 3, No. 40, pp. 12–15.

Bleeding Disorders

Harris, A. (1983) Nursing care study—Idiopathic thrombocytopenic purpura, *Nursing Times*, 21 September, Vol. 79, No. 38, pp. 50–53.

Koch, P. M. (1984) Thrombocytopenia: Don't let it make a big problem out of nothing, *Nursing 84*, October, Vol. 14, No. 10, pp. 54–7.

Bone Marrow Transplantation

Bater, M. (1989) Preparing for bone marrow transplantation, *Nursing Times*, 15 February, Vol. 85, No. 7, pp. 46–7.

Cogliano-Shutta, N. A., Broda, E. J. and Gress, J. S. (1985) Bone marrow transplantation, *Nursing Clinics of North America*, March, Vol. 20, No. 1, pp. 49–66.

Gibson, L. (1987) Bone marrow transplant—the process, *Nursing Times*, 21 January, Vol. 83, No. 3, pp. 36–8.

Gibson, L. (1987) Bone marrow transplant—the recovery, *Nursing Times*, 28 January, Vol. 83, No. 4, p. 46.

Haberman, M. R. (1988) Psychosocial aspects of bone marrow transplantation, *Seminars in Oncology Nursing*, February, Vol. 4, No. 1, pp. 55–9. [This whole issue is devoted to bone marrow transplantation.]

King, L. (1981) Blood brothers, *Nursing Mirror*, 30 September, Vol. 153, No. 4, pp. 35–7.

Nuscher, R., Baltzer, L., Repinec, D. A. *et al.* (1984) Bone marrow transplantation, *American Journal of Nursing*, June, Vol. 84, No. 6, pp. 764–72.

Clotting Defects

Cartlidge, J. (1984) Haemophilia, *Nursing Mirror*, 15 February, Vol. 158, No. 7, Clinical Forum I–VIII.

Flavell, G. (1982) Disabilities and how to live with them. Haemophilia, *Lancet*, 10 April, Vol. 1, pp. 845–6.

Raw, A. Y. (1982) Home therapy for patients with haemophilia and Christmas disease, *Nursing Times*, 10 October, Vol. 78, No. 15, pp. 615–18.

Disseminated Intravascular Coagulation

Rooney, A. and Hawley, C. (1985) Nursing management of disseminated intravascular coagulation, *Oncology Nursing Forum*, January/February, Vol. 12, No. 1, pp. 15–22.

Siegrist, C. W. and Jones, J. A. (1985) Disseminated intravascular coagulopathy and nursing implications, *Seminars in Oncology Nursing*, November, Vol. 1, No. 4, pp. 237–43.

Thorne, T. (1984) Disseminated intravascular coagulation, *Nursing Times*, 10 October, Vol. 80, No. 41, pp. 46–7.

Leukaemias

Borley, D. (1984) Overcoming the fears, *Nursing Mirror*, 11 January, Vol. 158, No. 2, pp. 38–40.

Dobson, M. (1983) Caring for patients with leukaemia, *Nursing Times*, 11 May, Vol. 79, No. 19, pp. 56–7.

Gibson, L. (1983) Chronic myeloid leukaemia, *Nursing Times*, 8 June, Vol. 79, No. 23, pp. 66–7.

Lakhani, A. K. (1987) Current management of acute leukaemia, *Nursing*, Vol. 3, No. 20, pp. 755–8.

Morgan, G. (1989) Nursing the patient with leukaemia, *Nursing*, Vol. 3, No. 40, pp. 19–22.

Kelly, J. O. (1983) Standards of clinical nursing practice for leukaemia: Neutropenia and thrombocytopenia, *Cancer Nursing*, December, Vol. 6, No. 6, pp. 487–94.

Lymphomas

Brown, L. A. (1982) Priorities in a progressive illness, *Nursing Mirror*, 17 March, Vol. 154, No. 11, pp. 46–8.

Eddy, J. L., Selgas-Cordes, R. and Curran, M. (1984)

Cutaneous T-cell lymphoma, *American Journal of Nursing*, February, Vol. 84, No. 2, pp. 202–6.

Harwood, A. (1979) Hodgkin's disease, *Nursing Times*, 20 September, Vol. 75, No. 38, pp. 1617–23.

Hagan, S. J. (1983) Bring help and hope to the patient with Hodgkin's disease, *Nursing 83*, August, Vol. 13, No. 8, pp. 58–63.

Roques, P. (1983) A staging laparotomy, *Nursing Mirror*, 7 September, Vol. 157, No. 10, pp. 32–3.

Multiple Myeloma

Coward, D. D. (1986) Cancer-induced hypercalcaemia, *Cancer Nursing*, August, Vol. 9, No. 3, pp. 125–32.

Higginson, J. (1984) When interference can be good, *Nursing Mirror*, 11 January, Vol. 158, No. 2, pp. 36–8.

King, L. M. (1982) Myelomatosis, *Nursing Times*, 8 September, Vol. 78, No. 36, pp. 1518–20.

Yardley, J. (1989) Multiple myeloma, *Nursing*, August, Vol. 3, No. 40, pp. 4–7.

Sickle Cell Anaemia

Booram-Ogeer, S. B. and Alverez-Clarke, J. M. (1985) Sickle cell anaemia, *Nursing*, Vol. 2, No. 40, pp. 1196–7.

France-Dawson, M. (1985) Sickle cell disease: Implications for nursing care, *Journal of Advanced Nursing*, Vol. 11, pp. 729–37.

May, A. and Choiseul, M. (1986) Sickle cell anaemia and thalassaemia: Symptoms, treatment and effects on lifestyle, *Health Visitor*, July, Vol. 61, pp. 212–15.

Thalassaemia

May, A. and Choiseul, M. (1988) *ibid*.

Sawley, L. (1983) Thalassaemia: A shift to the north, *Nursing Mirror*, 14 December, Vol. 157, No. 24, pp. 38–9.

Transfusion Therapy

Cluroe, S. (1989) Blood transfusions, *Nursing*, August, Vol. 3, No. 4, pp. 11–15.

Laycock, L. (1983) Plasmaphoresis and exchange, *Nursing Times*, 24 August, Vol. 74, No. 34, pp. 50–2.

Nicholson, E. (1988) Autologous blood transfusion, *Nursing Times*, Vol. 84, No. 2, pp. 33–5.

Pauley, S. Y. (1984) Transfusion therapy for nurses. Part 1, *Journal of the National Intravenous Therapy Association (NITA)*, November/December, Vol. 7, No. 6, pp. 501–11.

Pauley, S. Y. (1985) Transfusion therapy for nurses. Part 2, *NITA*, January/February, Vol. 8, No. 1, pp. 51–60.

Querin, J. J. and Stahl, L. D. (1983) Twelve simple sensible steps for successful blood transfusions, *Nursing 83*, Vol. 13, No. 11, pp. 34–44.

Thomas, S. F. (1979) Transfusing granulocytes, *American Journal of Nursing*, May, Vol. 79, No. 5, pp. 942–4.

unit 4 ▬▬▬▬▬▬▬▬▬▬▬▬

DIGESTIVE AND GASTRO-INTESTINAL PROBLEMS

chapter 11

ASSESSMENT OF DIGESTIVE AND GASTROINTESTINAL FUNCTION

ANATOMY AND PHYSIOLOGY

Anatomy of the Gastrointestinal Tract

The gastrointestinal tract is a tube that is in contact with the external environment at either end. The pathway extends from the mouth through the oesophagus, stomach and intestines to the anus (Figure 11.1). The oesophagus is located in the thoracic cavity, anterior to the spine and posterior to the trachea and heart. It is a collapsible tube about 25 cm in length that becomes distended when food passes through it.

The stomach is situated in the upper portion of the abdomen to the left of the midline, just under the left diaphragm. It is a distensible pouch with a capacity of approximately 1,500 ml. The inlet to the stomach is called the gastro-oesophageal junction. It is surrounded by a ring of smooth muscle, which, on contraction, closes the stomach off from the oesophagus. The outlet from the stomach is called the pylorus. Circular smooth muscle in the wall of the pylorus forms the pyloric sphincter and controls the size of the opening between the stomach and small intestine.

The small intestine is the longest segment of the gastrointestinal tract and accounts for about two thirds of the total length. It is folded back and forth on itself and occupies a major portion of the abdominal cavity. It is divided into three parts: an upper part, called the duodenum; the middle part, called the jejunum; and the lower part, called the ileum. The common bile duct, the conduit for both bile and pancreatic secretions, empties into the duodenum.

The junction between the small and large intestines usually lies in the right lower portion of the abdomen. It is in this area that the appendix, a vermiform structure, is located. At the junction of the small and large intestines is the ileocaecal valve, which functions in a similar fashion to the pyloric sphincter and gastro-oesophageal junction. The large intestine consists of an ascending segment on the right side of the abdomen, a transverse segment that extends from right to left in the upper abdomen, and a

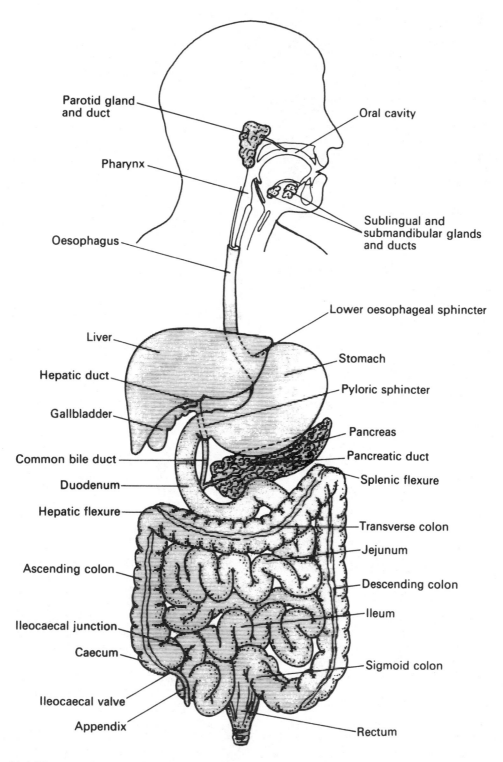

Figure 11.1 Diagram of the digestive system. (Chaffee, E. E. and Greisheimer, E. M. (1974) *Basic Physiology and Anatomy* (3rd edition), J. B. Lippincott, Philadelphia.)

descending segment on the left side of the abdomen. The terminal portion of the large intestine is the rectum, which is continuous with the anus. The anal outlet is surrounded by the external anal sphincter, which, unlike the other sphincters of the gastrointestinal tract, is composed of striated muscle and is under voluntary control.

Blood Supply to the Gastrointestinal Tract

Since the gastrointestinal tract is so long, its blood supply is from arteries that originate along the entire length of the thoracic and abdominal aorta. Of particular importance are the vessels to the large and small intestines: the superior and inferior mesenteric arteries. These two arteries form small loops, or arcades, which encircle the intestine, supplying its wall with oxygen and nutrients. Blood in the veins that drain the intestine is enriched by nutrients absorbed from the lumen of the gastrointestinal tract. These veins merge with others in the abdomen to form a large vessel called the portal vein, which carries the nutrient-rich blood to the liver. The blood flow to the entire gastrointestinal tract is about 20 per cent of the total cardiac output, and it is significantly increased after eating.

Nerve Supply

The gastrointestinal tract is supplied by both the sympathetic and parasympathetic components of the autonomic nervous system. The parasympathetic fibres travel in the vagus nerve and in nerves that arise from the sacral segment of the spinal cord. In addition, the upper oesophagus and the external anal sphincter are under voluntary control and are supplied by somatic nerves that arise from the cervical spinal cord and the sacral spinal cord, respectively.

The Process of Digestion

In order to perform their functions, all cells of the body require nutrients, which must be derived from the intake of food that contains protein, fat, carbohydrates, vitamins and minerals, as well as cellulose fibres and other vegetable matter without nutritional value. This diet provides the energy needs of the body and maintains body weight at approximately constant levels.

The intake of food is a voluntary act that is controlled by conscious sensations of hunger and satiety, modified by learned behaviour. These sensations originate in the higher centres of the brain, probably in the hypothalamus. The hypothalamus itself is influenced by visual and olfactory sensations, nervous and hormonal signals originating in the digestive tract and behavioural patterns.

The primary functions of the gastrointestinal tract are as follows:

- To break down food particles into their small constituent molecules for digestion.
- To absorb the small molecules produced by digestion into the bloodstream.

- To eliminate undigested and unabsorbed foodstuffs and other waste products from the body.

The pathway that foodstuffs take in the digestive tract begins at the mouth, where they are chewed and swallowed. The bolus of food is then conveyed down through the oesophagus into the stomach, where it remains for a variable length of time. It then enters the small intestine, where much of the digestion and absorption of nutrients takes place. The unabsorbed food passes from the small intestine into the colon (also called the large intestine) for further modification and storage before elimination (defaecation). The total length of the gastrointestinal tract, from mouth to anus, is approximately 7 to 8 metres.

Large volumes of fluid containing hormones and enzymes are secreted into the gastrointestinal tract in order to aid in the process of digestion, absorption and elimination. The total secretion into the lumen of the gastrointestinal tract is about eight litres per day, but less than 200 ml per day of liquid is excreted in the faeces. This illustrates the massive absorptive capacity of the gastrointestinal tract.

- Disturbances of the absorptive function of the digestive system can lead to serious disturbances of body fluid balance.

Gastrointestinal Motility and Secretions

Motility refers to the co-ordinated contractions of the muscles in the walls of the gastrointestinal tract that propel food and secretions from the mouth toward the anus. These sequential rhythmic contractions are referred to as peristalsis. At the same time that the food is being propelled through the gastrointestinal tract, it comes into contact with a wide variety of secretions that aid in breaking down and digesting the food particles.

Oral Digestion

The process of digestion begins with the act of chewing. Food is broken down into small particles that can be swallowed and mixed with digestive enzymes. The first secretion encountered is saliva, which is secreted in the mouth by the salivary glands at the rate of about 1.5 litres daily. Saliva contains an enzyme (salivary amylase or ptyalin) that helps in the digestion of starches. It also serves as a solvent for the molecules in the food that stimulate the taste buds. Eating or even the sight, smell or thought of food can cause reflex salivation. The major function of saliva is to lubricate the food as it is chewed, thereby facilitating swallowing.

Swallowing

Swallowing, the initial act in the propulsion of food, is under voluntary control. It is regulated by a swallowing centre in the medulla oblongata of the central nervous system. Voluntary efforts to initiate swallowing are ineffective unless there is something to swallow, such as air, saliva or food. As the food is swallowed, the epiglottis moves to cover the tracheal opening and thus prevents aspiration of food into the lungs. Swallowing results in the propulsion of the bolus of food into the upper oesophagus. The smooth muscle in the wall of the oesophagus undergoes rhythmic contractions that move sequentially from above to below and help to propel the bolus of food from the upper oesophagus toward the stomach. During this process of oesophageal peristalsis, smooth muscle around the gastro-oesophageal junction relaxes and permits the bolus of food to enter the stomach. Subsequently, the smooth muscle contracts to prevent reflux of stomach contents into the oesophagus.

● When there is reflux of the acid contents of the stomach into the oesophagus, an uncomfortable sensation occurs beneath the sternum. This sensation is commonly called heartburn.

Gastric Action

Within the stomach, food is exposed to gastric juice, which is very acidic. The acidity (pH as low as 1) is due to the secretion of hydrochloric acid by the glands of the stomach. The volume of gastric juice is 2.5 litres per day. The function of the highly acidic stomach secretion is to break down food into more absorbable components. The secretion of hydrochloric acid occurs in response to a meal. Between meals, the rate of secretion of acid into the stomach is low.

● People who chronically secrete excessive amounts of gastric acid are susceptible to development of gastric and duodenal ulcers.

The gastric secretions also contain the enzyme pepsin, which is an important enzyme for the digestion of proteins (Table 11.1).

Another component of gastric secretions is intrinsic factor. This compound is synthesized by cells of the stomach and combines with vitamin B_{12} in the diet, so that the vitamin can be absorbed in the ileum.

● In the absence of intrinsic factor, vitamin B_{12} cannot be absorbed, resulting in pernicious anaemia.

Peristaltic contractions in the stomach propel its contents toward the pylorus. Large food particles cannot pass through the pyloric sphincter and are churned back into the body of the stomach. In this way, food in the stomach is mechanically agitated and broken down into smaller particles. Therefore, different types of meals remain in the stomach for times varying from a half hour to several hours, depending on the size of food particles, composition of the meal and other factors.

Peristalsis in the stomach and contractions of the pyloric sphincter allow the partially digested food to enter the small intestine at a rate that permits efficient absorption of nutrients.

Intestinal Secretions

Secretions in the duodenum come from the pancreas, the liver and the glands in the wall of the intestine itself. The major characteristic of these secretions is their high content of digestive enzymes.

Pancreatic secretion has an alkaline pH, owing to a high bicarbonate concentration. This serves to neutralize the acid entering the duodenum from the stomach. The pancreas also secretes digestive enzymes, including trypsin, which aids in the digestion of protein; amylase, which aids in the digestion of starch; and lipase, which aids in the digestion of fats.

Bile (secreted by the liver and stored in the gallbladder) contains bile salts, cholesterol and lecithin (a phospholipid), which emulsify the ingested fats and make them more accessible to digestion and absorption. The bile salts themselves are reabsorbed into the portal blood when they reach the ileum.

Secretions from the intestinal glands consist of mucus, which coats the cells and protects the duodenum from attack by hydrochloric acid; hormones; electrolytes; and enzymes. The total amount of intestinal secretions is approximately 1 litre per day of pancreatic juice, 0.5 litre per day of bile and 3 litres per day from the glands of the small intestine.

Gastrointestinal Regulatory Substances and Bacteria

Hormones

Hormones and neuroregulators have been found to control the rate of secretion of the gastrointestinal fluids and gastrointestinal motility. Local regulators also play a role. Acetylcholine and histamine stimulate the gastric glands to increase the secretion of gastric acid. Noradrenaline and some prostaglandins inhibit gastric acid activity.

Gastrin is secreted by the cells of the stomach. It partially regulates the secretion of gastric acid and influences contraction at the gastro-oesophageal junction and pyloric sphincter. The stimulus to gastrin release is distension of the stomach.

Secretin, secreted by the mucosa in the upper portion of the small intestine, stimulates the secretion of bicarbonate in pancreatic juice and inhibits the secretion of gastric acid. The stimulus to the release of secretin is acid entering the small intestine from the stomach.

Cholecystokinin (CCK), also released from the cells in the upper small intestine, acts on both the gallbladder and the pancreas. It causes contraction of the gallbladder and release of digestive enzymes from the pancreas. The stimulus to the release of cholecystokinin is the presence of fatty acids and amino acids in the small intestine.

Bacteria

Bacteria are normal components of the contents of the gastrointestinal tract. Their presence is essential for normal gastrointestinal function. Few bacteria are present in the stomach or upper small intestine, probably because they are killed by the acid secretions in the stomach.

Table 11.1 *The major digestive enzymes*

Name of enzyme	Substrate	Products of reaction	Source of enzyme	Site of action
Action of enzymes that digest carbohydrate				
Salivary amylase (ptyalin)	Starch as in grains, potatoes, legumes	Dextrins, maltose, glucose	Secretions from parotid and submaxillary glands (saliva)	Mouth, if chewing is very thorough; some in fundus of stomach if mixing with acidic gastric juice is delayed
Pancreatic amylase	Starch	α-limit dextrins, maltose, glucose	Secretions from pancreas	Small intestine
	Dextrins	Maltose, glucose		
Disaccharidases	Disaccharides	Monosaccharides	Mucosal cells of small intestine (brush border)	Brush border of intestinal wall
Maltase	Maltose (in corn syrup, beer)	Glucose		
Sucrase	Sucrose (in table sugar, fruits)	Glucose and fructose		
Lactase	Lactose (in milk)	Glucose and galactose		
Action of enzymes that digest protein				
Pepsin	Protein	Polypeptides	Chief cells of gastric mucosa (secreted as enzyme precursor pepsinogen*)	Stomach
Trypsin Chymotrypsin Carboxypeptidase	Protein and polypeptides (polypeptides are primarily from the partial digestion of protein)	Peptides	Pancreas (secreted as the enzyme precursor trypsinogen, chymotrypsinogen, and procarboxy-peptidase*)	Lumen of the small intestine
Aminopeptidase	Polypeptides	Smaller peptides, amino acids	Mucosal cells of small intestine	Brush border of small intestine
Dipeptidase	Dipeptides	Amino acids		
Action of enzymes that digest fat (triglyceride)				
Pharyngeal lipase†	Triglycerides (in foods containing fat such as meat, butter, nuts, cheese)	Fatty acids, diglycerides, monoglycerides	Mucosa of pharynx	Fundus of stomach
Gastric lipase†	Short chain triglycerides (dairy fats)	Short chain fatty acids, diglycerides monoglycerides	Gastric mucosa	Stomach
Pancreatic lipase	Triglycerides, diglycerides	Diglycerides, monoglycerides, fatty acids (short, long and medium chain)	Pancreas	Lumen of small intestine

* Activation of enzyme precursor takes place in the lumen of the intestinal tract
† Not essential for adequate digestion of fat
(Suitor, C.W. and Hunter, M.F. (1984) Nutrition: Principles and Application in Health Promotion, *Philadelphia, J.B. Lippincott, p. 219.*)

However, the bacterial population increases in the ileum and becomes a major component of the contents of the large intestine. Bacteria function as an aid to digestion and also synthesize essential nutrients that otherwise might not be available for absorption. The bacterial mass comprises about 10 per cent of the dry weight of the stool.

Digestion and Absorption of Nutrients

Food, ingested in the form of fats, protein and carbohydrates, is broken down into its constituent nutrients by the process of digestion.

Carbohydrate digestion begins in the mouth with the breakdown of starches by the action of salivary amylase. It continues in the oesophagus but is inhibited in the stomach by gastric acid. Continuation of carbohydrate digestion occurs in the duodenum by the action of pancreatic amylase. The end result of this process is the liberation of small sugar molecules known as disaccharides (e.g., sucrose, maltose, galactose). Enzymes attached to the mucosal cells of the intestine convert the disaccharides into monosaccharides, such as glucose and fructose, which are then absorbed into the blood.

● Glucose is the major carbohydrate that the tissue cells use as fuel.

Proteins are long chains of amino acids linked together chemically. The hydrochloric acid in the stomach aids in breaking down proteins into smaller particles that are more easily attacked by the digestive enzymes. The process of protein digestion begins in the stomach by the action of pepsin and continues in the duodenum by the action of pancreatic enzymes, such as trypsin. When the proteins are broken down into their constituent amino acids, they are actively absorbed through the mucosal cells of the small intestine into the blood. The tissues use amino acids in synthesizing their constituent proteins.

Ingested fats must be dispersed into small droplets (emulsified) so that they can be attacked by digestive enzymes. Emulsification of fats takes place as the result of the churning action in the stomach and duodenum and contact with bile salts. Pancreatic lipase then breaks down the emulsified fats into monoglycerides and fatty acids. These are solubilized as micelles, which move to the mucosal surface of the intestine, where they are absorbed. Within the mucosal cells, the fatty acids are recombined into fats, which then enter the lacteals (part of the lymphatic system) and eventually enter the bloodstream. The tissues use fats as a fuel; excess fat is stored in the fat cells that are widely distributed throughout the body.

Vitamins in the diet are absorbed essentially unchanged from the gastrointestinal tract. The fat-soluble vitamins A, D, E and K are absorbed by a mechanism similar to that described above for fats. Vitamin B_{12} is absorbed after combination with intrinsic factor, as described previously.

Minerals in the diet, such as calcium and iron, are absorbed in the small intestine. Calcium absorption requires the presence of vitamin D and is modified by the action of parathyroid hormone.

● Iron in the diet is needed to replace small amounts of iron normally lost by the body, but only a limited fraction of the ingested iron can be absorbed. Therefore, repletion of iron stores of the body by oral therapy, in a patient with iron deficiency, is a long-term process.

Little of the water and electrolytes in the diet, and in the 8 litres per day of gastrointestinal secretions, is excreted in the stool.

Intestinal Peristalsis

Peristalsis propels the contents of the small intestine towards the colon. Intense peristaltic waves may be responsible for the gurgling sounds emanating from the gastrointestinal tract at various times. Segmental contractions of the intestinal smooth muscle occur in addition to its peristaltic contractions. These segmental contractions do not propel contents toward the colon, but rather churn it back and forth, to permit more efficient digestion and absorption. Food leaving the small intestine must pass through the ileocaecal valve to enter the colon. This valve is normally closed and helps prevent colonic contents from refluxing back into the small intestine. However, with each peristaltic wave of the small intestine, the valve opens briefly and permits some of the contents to pass through. The first part of a meal usually reaches the ileocaecal valve in about four hours, and all of the unabsorbed food has entered the colon by eight or nine hours after eating.

Motility of the colon consists of relatively weak peristaltic activity that moves the colonic contents slowly, and strong peristaltic rushes that propel the contents for considerable distances. When the contents reach and distend the rectum, an urge to defaecate is experienced. Eating stimulates the peristaltic rushes in the colon, resulting in a desire to defaecate shortly after a meal. This gastrocolic reflex is the reason that defaecation after meals is the rule in children. However, in adults, habit and cultural factors are more important in determining the time for elimination of faecal contents. The first part of a meal reaches the rectum about 12 hours after eating. From the rectum to the anus, transport is much slower, and as much as one fourth of the meal may still be in the rectum three days after ingestion. This slow transport of colonic contents allows efficient reabsorption of water and electrolytes.

Defaecation

Distension of the rectum reflexly initiates contractions of its musculature and relaxation of the internal anal sphincter, which is ordinarily closed. The internal sphincter is controlled by the autonomic nervous system; the external sphincter is under the conscious control of the cerebral cortex. When the desire to defaecate is felt, the external anal sphincter voluntarily relaxes, permitting expulsion of colonic contents. Normally, the external anal sphincter is maintained in a state of tonic contraction. Thus, defaecation is a spinal reflex that can be voluntarily inhibited by keeping the external anal sphincter closed. In this regard, it is similar to micturition. Contraction of abdominal muscles (straining) facilitates emptying of the colon.

- The presence of neurological lesions that disrupt the innervation of the rectum lessens the effectiveness of reflex evacuation and can lead to abnormal retention of faecal material (faecal impaction).

The average frequency of defaecation in humans is once daily, but the range is extremely variable. It is commonly observed that some people defaecate several times daily, while others may defaecate only a few times per week. More importantly, changes in bowel habits may signify colonic disease. An increase in frequency of defaecation is called diarrhoea, whereas decreased frequency is called constipation.

The elderly are prone to constipation because of limited mobility and a decreased intake of fibre and foods that are hard to chew. A detailed explanation of gastrointestinal problems in the elderly population is presented in Chapter 16.

Faeces and Flatus

Faeces consist of undigested foodstuffs, inorganic materials, water and bacteria. Their composition is relatively unaffected by alterations of diet, since a large fraction of the faecal mass is of nondietary origin, derived from the gastrointestinal tract. This is why appreciable amounts of faeces continue to be passed despite prolonged starvation. The brown colour of the faeces is due to breakdown of bile by the intestinal bacteria. With obstruction of the bile ducts, bile is absent from the intestine and the stools become white. Indole and skatole, arising from bacterial decomposition, are responsible in large part for the faecal odour.

The gastrointestinal tract normally contains approximately 150 ml of gas. Gas expelled from the upper gastrointestinal tract (belching) has its origin as swallowed air. Gas expelled from the lower gastrointestinal tract (flatulence) consists of swallowed air, as well as gas produced by bacteria in the colon. The gas in the colon contains methane, hydrogen sulphide, ammonia and other potentially harmful gases. These gases can be absorbed into the portal circulation and are detoxified by the liver.

- Patients with liver disease are frequently treated with antibiotics to reduce the number of colonic bacteria and thereby inhibit the production of toxic gases.

ALTERED PHYSIOLOGY

Abnormalities of the gastrointestinal tract are numerous and exemplify every type of major pathology that can affect other organ systems. A composite view of the various types of gastrointestinal disorders that may occur is presented in Figure 11.2. Congenital, inflammatory, infectious, traumatic and neoplastic lesions have been encountered in every portion, and at every site, along its length. In common with many other organ systems, it is subject to circulatory disturbances, faulty nervous control and senescence.

Psychosocial Considerations in Gastrointestinal Disorders

Apart from the many organic diseases to which the gastrointestinal tract is susceptible, there are many extrinsic factors—some related to disease, others not—that can interfere with its normal function and produce symptoms. An anxiety state, for example, often finds its chief expression in indigestion, anorexia or motor disturbances of the intestines, producing constipation or diarrhoea. Students facing examinations or stressed executives facing major decisions can readily be susceptible to gastrointestinal disorders. Also, some psychological problems are thought to have a role in physical dysfunction. For example, personality factors are thought to have an influence in peptic ulcer disease.

In addition to the state of mental health, physical factors such as fatigue and an unbalanced or abruptly changed dietary intake can markedly affect the gastrointestinal tract. In both the assessment of and advice to the patient, the nurse should realize that a combination of mental and physical factors affect the status of the gastrointestinal tract.

Diagnosis

Investigation of the gastrointestinal tract includes the use of X-rays and ultrasound and the passage of various oral and anal tubes. In general, the nurse has a supportive and educational role. Patients requiring such tests are frequently anxious, elderly or debilitated. The preparation for many of these studies includes fasting and the use of laxatives or enemas, measures that are poorly tolerated by weakened patients. In addition, many of these tests require seemingly endless waiting, either for the tests to begin or be completed or for the results to be known.

Radiography of the Upper Gastrointestinal Tract

The entire gastrointestinal tract can be delineated by X-rays, following the introduction of barium sulphate or a similar radio-opaque liquid as the contrast medium. This

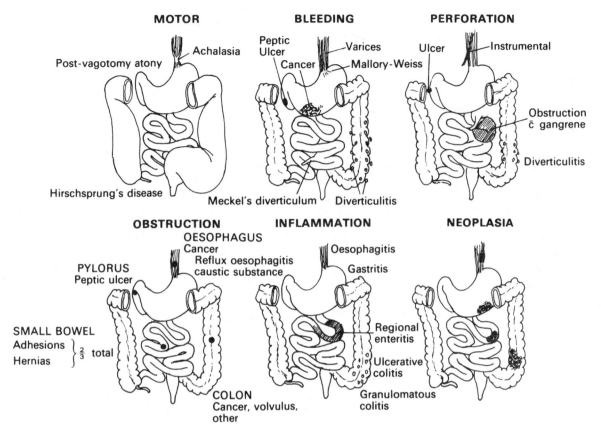

MOTOR

Post-vagotomy atony
Achalasia
Hirschsprung's disease

BLEEDING

Peptic Ulcer
Cancer
Varices
Mallory-Weiss
Meckel's diverticulum
Diverticulitis

PERFORATION

Ulcer
Instrumental
Obstruction c̄ gangrene
Diverticulitis

OBSTRUCTION

OESOPHAGUS
Cancer
Reflux oesophagitis caustic substance
PYLORUS
Peptic ulcer
SMALL BOWEL
Adhesions
Hernias } ⅔ total
COLON
Cancer, volvulus, other

INFLAMMATION

Oesophagitis
Gastritis
Regional enteritis
Ulcerative colitis
Granulomatous colitis

NEOPLASIA

Figure 11.2 Altered physiology of the gastrointestinal tract. (Hardy, J. D., *Rhoad's Textbook of Surgery* (5th edition), J. B. Lippincott, Philadelphia.)

material, an odourless and completely insoluble (hence, not absorbable) powder, is ingested in the form of a thick or thin aqueous suspension for purposes of upper gastrointestinal tract study (barium meal) and is instilled rectally for visualization of the colon (barium enema).

Patient Preparation

In preparation for a barium meal, the patient is to receive nothing by mouth six hours before the test. A laxative may be prescribed to clean out the intestinal tract. Since smoking can stimulate gastric motility, the patient is discouraged from smoking the morning before the examination.

Procedure

For the purposes of examining the upper gastrointestinal tract, the patient is required to swallow barium under direct fluoroscopic examination. Initially, the patient is asked to hold the barium drink in the mouth and swallow it at a precise moment in order for the oesophagus to be examined. The patient then drinks a further 200 to 300 ml, and its passage is followed down the oesophagus, into the stomach and duodenum. This usually takes 20 to 30 minutes, but will take much longer if a follow-through examination is needed. X-rays are taken at intervals and in different positions.

Possible findings of such studies include an obstruction due to a tumour or stricture, a hiatus hernia, gastric ulcer, pyloric stenosis, duodenal ulcer and Crohn's disease. There is no specific nursing care required following such investigations, although the patient may feel tired and slightly nauseated. The main problem to occur following a barium meal is constipation due to the barium (Booth, 1983).

Double Contrast Studies

The double contrast method of examining the upper gastrointestinal tract involves administering a thick barium suspension medium to outline the stomach and oesophageal wall. Next, tablets that release carbon dioxide in the presence of water are given. The primary advantage of this technique is the finer detail that can be shown within the oesophagus and stomach, permitting signs of early superficial neoplasms to be noted.

Barium Enema

The purpose of a barium enema is to reveal the presence of

polyps, tumours and other lesions of the large intestine and to demonstrate any abnormal anatomy or malfunction of the bowel.

Patient Preparation

The preparation of the patient includes those measures necessary to produce an empty and clear lower bowel. It will vary from one centre to another, but usually involves eating a low-residue diet for the two days before the investigation. The day before the barium enema, a laxative such as sodium picosulphate may be given in order to stimulate emptying of the bowel. Clear fluids only are allowed on the day of the investigation. It is important to ensure that bowel clearance has occurred, as the procedure is impossible otherwise.

In the X-ray department, the radio-opaque substance is instilled rectally; it is viewed in the fluoroscope and then filmed. If the patient has been prepared satisfactorily, the contour of the entire colon, including caecum and appendix (if patent), is clearly visible and the motility of each portion readily observed. The procedure takes about 15 minutes and is followed by an evacuating enema or laxative to facilitate barium removal.

Upper Gastrointestinal Endoscopy

Endoscopy of the upper gastrointestinal tract allows for direct visualization of the gastric mucosa and is especially valuable when gastric neoplasm is suspected. Endoscopes are flexible scopes equipped with fibreoptic lenses. Coloured photographs or motion pictures can be taken through them. However, precautions must be taken to protect the scope, since the fibreoptic bundles may be broken if the scope is bent acutely. Mouth guards are essential to prevent the patient from biting the scope.

An electronic video endoscope is available. The endoscope attaches directly to the video processor, which converts electronic signals to a television screen. A laser-compatible upper gastrointestinal endoscope also exists. Endoscopic laser therapy for gastrointestinal neoplasms is primarily palliative. It is used mainly to relieve obstruction, reduce tumour size, enlarge an obstructed lumen and treat bleeding sites.

Patient Preparation

The patient fasts for six to eight hours before the examination. A local anaesthetic spray, along with the intrave-

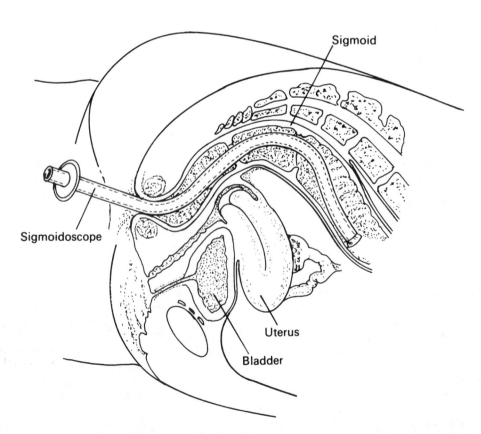

Figure 11.3 Sigmoidoscopy. Instrument is advanced past proximal sigmoid and then deflected into descending colon.

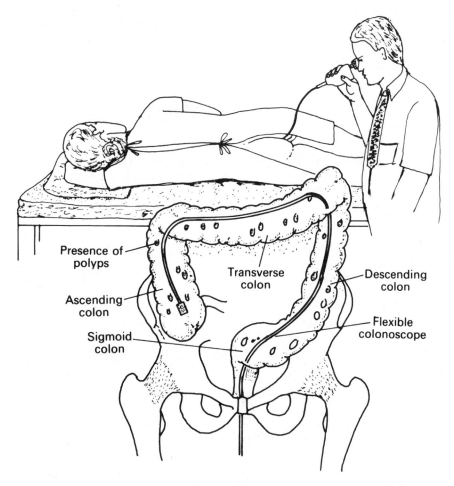

Figure 11.4 Colonoscopy. Flexible scope passes through rectum and sigmoid colon into the descending, transverse and ascending colon.

nous administration of diazepam just before the scope is introduced, helps to make the procedure more bearable. Sometimes atropine may be helpful in reducing secretions.

Follow-Up Care

Following endoscopy the patient is advised not to eat or drink until the gag reflex returns in three to four hours; this is done to prevent aspiration into the lungs. Postendoscopy assessment by the nurse includes observation for signs of perforation, such as pain, unusual discomfort and an elevated temperature. Pulse, respiratory rate, blood pressure and temperature are taken following the procedure to ensure that they are within normal limits. If any deviation from what is considered normal occurs, then the medical staff should be informed and the observations repeated until they return to within normal limits. Minor throat discomfort can be relieved with lozenges and oral analgesic medications.

Sigmoidoscopy and Colonoscopy

Procedures to view the lower bowel make use of a sigmoidoscope, a tubular instrument that incorporates a small electric light that allows the lumen of the lower bowel to be viewed directly.

The flexible sigmoidoscope permits an examination of up to 40 to 50 cm from the anus (Figure 11.3), more than the 25 cm that can be seen with the rigid sigmoidoscope. Although there is a more proximal distribution of lesions of the colon, polyps and cancer are found more commonly on the left side of the colon. Rectal bleeding and anaemia are indicators for a colonoscopy even if the patient has a negative barium enema. An enema may be given before the procedure to ensure that the lower bowel is clear.

Colonoscopy

Direct visual inspection of the colon is possible by means

of a flexible colonoscope. This procedure is used as a diagnostic aid, and the instrument may also be used to remove foreign bodies, polyps or tissue for biopsy (Figure 11.4).

Patient Preparation
To perform a colonoscopy, the lower bowel needs to be clear. The day before the examination the patient is asked to drink only clear fluids and is given an oral aperient such as socium picosulphate, which induces diarrhoea and clears the bowel. Care needs to be taken to ensure that the patient has an adequate fluid intake and does not become dehydrated.

It may be helpful to provide the patient with a leaflet concerning the procedure to read beforehand.

Procedure
Colonoscopy is performed with the patient lying on the left side with the legs drawn up. Discomfort may result from instilling air to open the colon or from tugging the colon so that the scope can be manoeuvred. Complications are rare following this procedure, although perforation or haemorrhage is possible.

Stool Examination

The basic examination of the stool includes an inspection of the specimen for its amount, consistency and colour. Special tests indicated in specific cases may include tests for occult blood, fat, parasites, food residues and other substances. The colour of stools varies from light to dark brown. (Milk-fed infants pass stools that are golden-yellow, owing to unchanged bilirubin.) Various foods and medications may affect stool colour.

- Blood in sufficient quantities, if shed into the upper gastrointestinal tract, produces a tarry black colour (melaena).
- Blood entering the lower portion of the gastrointestinal tract or passing rapidly through it will appear bright or dark red.
- Lower rectal or anal bleeding can be suspected if there is streaking of blood on the surface of the stool or if blood is noted on toilet tissue.

Stool Consistency and Appearance
In various disorders the stool assumes a typical appearance:

In steatorrhoea, the stools are generally bulky, greasy, foamy and foul in odour; stool colour is grey, with a silvery sheen.

With biliary obstruction, the stool becomes 'acholic' and is light grey or 'clay coloured', owing to the absence of urobilin.

In chronic ulcerative colitis, mucus or pus may be visible on gross inspection of the stool.

Constipation or faecal impaction may result in the passage of small, dry, rocky-hard masses called scybala. This type of stool may traumatize the rectal mucosa sufficiently to cause haemorrhage, in which case the faecal masses are streaked with bright red blood.

Ultrasound

Ultrasound is a noninvasive diagnostic technique in which sound waves are passed into internal body structures; varying deflections of these sound waves are bounced back, much like a reflection. Reflections, in turn, are displayed on an oscilloscope. Vertical deflections from a horizontal baseline represent the depth of the reflected tissues. When scans are taken from several angles, and a computer is added to the system, a two-dimensional image of the abdominal organs can be produced. Usually, for abdominal examination, a transducer is placed on the abdomen after a coating of lubricant jelly has been applied to the skin.

The chief advantage of ultrasound is the spatial reproduction of masses in transverse and longitudinal directions. There is no ionizing radiation or any noticeable biological side-effects in the energy range used for diagnostic purposes. It is relatively inexpensive. This type of diagnostic procedure is useful in studying the liver, pancreas, spleen, gallbladder and retroperitoneal tissues.

Disadvantages include the following:

- A high degree of skill is required of the operator.
- This technique cannot be used when a structure to be examined lies behind bony tissue, which prevents passage of sound waves to deeper structures.
- Gas in the abdomen or air in the lungs present a problem, since ultrasound is not well transmitted through gas or air.

Computed Tomography

Computed tomography (CT scanning) is a diagnostic method in which a very narrow X-ray beam is used to detect the density differences from very small cubes of tissue. These data are computerized and then reconstructed so that transverse cross-sections of the body can be shown on a television monitor.

The indications for computerized tomography scanning are diseases of the liver, spleen, kidney, pancreas and pelvic organs. However, good detail depends on the presence of fat, which means that this diagnostic tool is not useful for very thin, cachectic patients. Also, since a scanning time of five seconds is required, it is impossible to maintain complete stillness (e.g., heartbeat) during the procedure. Therefore, motion artifacts are produced and the results are a less than clear picture. Finally, radiation doses are appreciable.

ASSESSMENT

The patient will have a nursing assessment before any investigation is undertaken. This assessment will include the patient's ability to eat and drink, and to excrete waste products. Problems related to gastrointestinal function may include pain, indigestion, intestinal 'gas', vomiting, haematemesis, diarrhoea or constipation.

Pain

Pain can be a major symptom of gastrointestinal disease. The character, duration, frequency and time of the pain vary greatly, depending on the underlying cause, which also affects the location and distribution of referred pain. Other factors, such as meals, rest, defaecation and vascular disorders, may directly affect pain.

Indigestion

Indigestion can result from disturbed nervous control of the stomach or from a disorder in the stomach or elsewhere in the body. Fatty foods tend to cause the most discomfort because they remain in the stomach longer than proteins or carbohydrates. Coarse vegetables and highly seasoned foods can also cause considerable distress.

Upper abdominal pain associated with eating is the most common complaint of patients with gastrointestinal dysfunction. The basis for the abdominal distress may be the patient's own gastric peristaltic movements. Bowel movements may or may not relieve the pain.

Intestinal Bloating (Belching and Flatulence)

The accumulation of gas in the gastrointestinal tract may result in belching, the expulsion of gas from the stomach through the mouth, or flatulence, the expulsion of gas from the rectum.

Air that reaches the stomach is quickly expelled, but not necessarily by belching. Periodically, stomach gas moves into the lower oesophagus (simple reflux) and then returns to the stomach, owing to a peristaltic contraction of the distal oesophagus. Belching occurs when simple reflux is accompanied by contraction of the anterior abdominal muscles. At the first urge to belch, simply swallowing may interrupt the belch.

Usually, gases in the intestine pass into the colon and are released as flatus. Patients often complain of bloating or distension.

So-called heartburn and other associated problems are due to reverse peristalsis, probably gastro-oesophageal reflux.

Vomiting

The involuntary act of vomiting is preceded by closure of the glottis and pylorus, together with relaxation of the gastric wall and the smooth muscle surrounding the gastro-oesophageal junction. With retching, the gastro-oesoph- ageal junction remains closed so gastric contents are not expelled. Vomiting is usually preceded by nausea, an unpleasant sensation suggesting that vomiting is imminent.

Haematemesis

Haematemesis is the vomiting of blood. When this happens soon after haemorrhage, the vomitus is bright red. If blood has been retained in the stomach, digestive processes change the haemoglobin to a brown pigment, which gives the vomitus a coffee-ground appearance. Occasionally, the patient has difficulty in differentiating between haematemesis and haemoptysis (expectoration of blood-tinged sputum), particularly if a coughing paroxysm has preceded the bleeding.

Diarrhoea

Diarrhoea is an increase in the frequency, consistency (more fluid) and volume of stools, and is a major abnormality of gastrointestinal function. A common mechanism for diarrhoea is an increased rate of movement of the contents through the intestine and colon, so that inadequate time is available for absorption of the gastrointestinal secretions, resulting in an increased fluid content of the stool. Inflammation or other diseases of the colonic mucosa can also lead to diarrhoea, as can infection from pathogens or parasites or overuse of laxatives. When these occur, water and electrolytes are not sufficiently reabsorbed and increased amounts of fluids or liquid reach the rectum, resulting in increased stool volume. Steatorrhoea, defined as a large amount of fat in the stools, is commonly due to pancreatic disease. The decreased activity of pancreatic enzymes is responsible for decreased fat digestion. Disease of the biliary tract can also cause steatorrhoea, owing to the absence of bile salts. The consequences of diarrhoea are loss of potassium, causing electrolyte imbalance; loss of bicarbonate, leading to acidosis; and loss of nutrients, leading to malnutrition.

Constipation

Constipation is the retention of or a delay in expulsion of faecal content from the rectum. In this situation, water is absorbed from the faecal matter, producing stools that are hard and dry and of smaller volume than normal. For most patients, this means irregular, infrequent defaecation associated with the passage of hard faeces (Pritchard and David, 1988). Figure 11.5 illustrates some of the causes of constipation.

PLANNING AND IMPLEMENTATION

Nursing care for the individual requiring gastrointestinal investigation will include the following:

● Providing information about the test and the activities

required of the patient; oral and written instructions should be given.

● Alleviating anxiety: the patient will need time to express any fears or worries.

● Assuring the patient that there will be someone available to help them cope with any discomfort.

The need for nutritional assessment must not be ignored as, quite commonly, patients undergoing investigations of the gastrointestinal tract are already nutritionally compromised, and are likely to have to undergo periods of fasting while the investigations are carried out.

Specific preparation for gastrointestinal investigations will vary from one hospital to another.

BIBLIOGRAPHY

Booth, J. A. (ed.) (1983) *Handbook of Investigations*, Harper & Row, London.

Pritchard, A. P. and David, J. A. (1988) *The Royal Marsden Manual of Clinical Nursing Procedures* (2nd edition), Harper & Row, London.

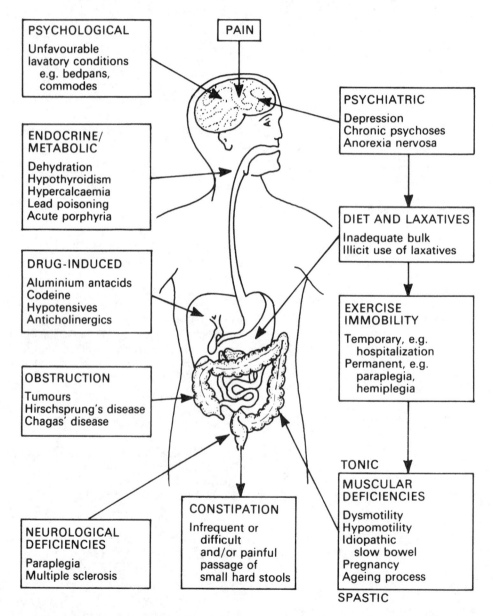

Figure 11.5 Classification of constipation. (Pritchard, A. and David, J. A. (1988) *The Royal Marsden Manual of Clinical Nursing Procedures* (2nd edition), Harper & Row, London.)

FURTHER READING

Books

Beattie, A. D. (1989) *Diagnostic Tests in Gastroenterology*, Chapman & Hall Medical, London.

Hinchliff, S. and Montague, S. (1988) *Physiology for Nursing Practice*, Baillière Tindall, Eastbourne.

Marieb, E. N. (1989) *Human Anatomy and Physiology*, Benjamin/Cummings Publishing, California.

Moshy, R. E. and Phillips, C. A. (1989) *From Ward to X-Ray: A Practical Guide*, Austen Cornish, London.

Suitor, C. W. and Hunter, M. F. (1984) *Nutrition: Principles and Application in Health Promotion*, J. B. Lippincott, Philadelphia.

Tortora, G. J. and Anagnostakos, N. P. (1990) *Principles of Anatomy and Physiology* (6th edition), Harper & Row, New York.

Articles

Clark, A. G. N. (1990) Constipation and faecal impaction in the aged: the management of a common problem, *Care of the Elderly*, Vol. 2, No. 2, pp. 66–8.

Holmes, S. (1990) Good food for long life: nutrition for elderly people, *The Professional Nurse*, Vol. 6, No. 1, pp. 43–6.

Newton, C. A. (1987) An overview of the large intestine: anatomy, physiology and normal function, *Nursing*, Vol. 3, No. 21, pp. 770–2.

chapter 12

ASSESSMENT AND CARE OF PATIENTS WITH UPPER GASTROINTESTINAL TRACT DISORDERS

The process of ingestion begins with the mastication of food in the mouth, and thus adequate nutrition is related both to good dental health and the general condition of the mouth. The presence and condition of the teeth directly affect nutritional wellbeing by influencing the type of food ingested and the degree to which food particles are properly mixed with salivary enzymes. Any discomfort in the mouth, due to lip lesions, inflammation of the buccal mucosa or other conditions, can have a deleterious effect on food intake. Oesophageal problems related to the apparently simple act of swallowing can also adversely affect food and fluid intake, thereby jeopardizing general health and wellbeing.

Given the close inter-relationship between adequate nutritional intake and all of the structures of the upper gastrointestinal tract (lips, mouth, teeth, oesophagus), health education should place heavy emphasis on helping people to avoid the discomfort caused by disorders associated with any of these structures.

NURSING PROCESS OVERVIEW: PATIENTS WITH CONDITIONS OF THE ORAL CAVITY

► Assessment

The nursing assessment includes questions about the patient's normal routine for brushing and flossing the teeth, the frequency of dental visits and awareness of any lesions or irritated areas in the mouth, tongue or back of the throat that interfere with eating. Are dentures or a partial plate worn? Are capped teeth or a dental bridge present? Has the patient recently experienced sore throats (note frequency, severity, duration and treatment used)?

Are there any difficulties with swallowing or chewing? Are gum problems present (pain or bleeding)? Is there a history of voice changes? Are foods that are hard to chew

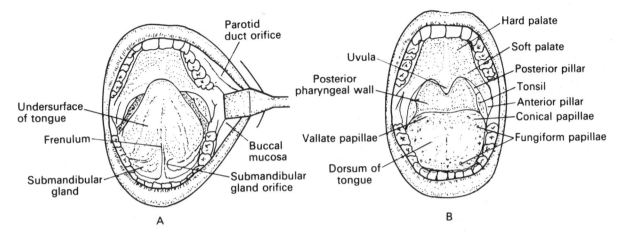

Figure 12.1 The mouth (A) and the pharynx (B). (Adapted from Bates, B. (1987) *A Guide to Physical Examination and History Taking* (4th edition), J. B. Lippincott, Philadelphia.)

avoided? Are spicy foods or very hot foods consumed regularly? What does the daily food intake consist of?

Physical assessment involves an inspection of the inside of the mouth with a pen torch and a spatula. Removal of dentures and partial plates is necessary to allow a thorough inspection of the gums. Observation begins with the lips, noting the colour, the presence or absence of moisture, hydration and the existence of any ulceration or fissures. The patient is requested to open the mouth wide; the spatula is inserted to expose the buccal mucosa for an assessment of colour and lesions (Figure 12.1).

The gums are inspected for inflammation, bleeding, retraction and discolouration. The odour of the breath is noted; the presence of any neoplasms that have ulcerated and become infected will be accompanied by a foul odour. The hard palate is examined for colour, shape and dried blood. The dorsum of the tongue is inspected for texture, colour and the presence of any lesions. Note any red (erythroplakia) or white (leucoplakia) patches. A thin white coat and large, vallate papillae in a V-shape on the back of the tongue are normal findings (see Figure 12.1B). By requesting the patient to move the tongue laterally, the size and range of movement can be observed, as well as the integrity of the hypoglossal nerve (12th cranial nerve). Requesting the patient to touch the palate with the tip of the tongue allows inspection of the ventral surface of the tongue and the floor of the mouth. Note should be taken of any abnormal tissue, red or white plaque, ulcers or warty growths.

The spatula can be used to depress the tongue to allow observation of the pharynx. Care is required to prevent the gagging response that will inhibit further examination. The spatula should be placed firmly behind the midline of the tongue after noting whether any painful areas are present. The patient is requested to tip the head back, open the mouth wide, take a deep breath and say 'ahh'. Often this will flatten the posterior tongue and briefly expose a clear full view of the anterior and posterior pillars, the tonsils, the uvula and the posterior pharynx. Any enlargement, ulceration or presence of exudate or blood should be noted. Normally, the uvula and soft palate rise with a deep inspiration, an indication of an intact vagus nerve (10th cranial nerve).

▶ Patient's Problems

Based on the assessment, the patient's main problems may include the following:

- Alteration in the oral mucous membranes related to a pathological condition, infection or chemical/mechanical trauma (drugs, ill-fitting dentures).
- Alteration in nutrition, related to inability to ingest adequate nutrients secondary to oral/dental disease conditions.
- Disturbance in self-concept/body image, related to a physical change in appearance subsequent to a disease condition or surgical/medical treatment.

▶ Planning and Implementation
▶ Expected Outcomes

The main outcomes for the patient may include improvement in the condition of the oral mucous membrane, improvement in nutritional intake and attainment of a positive self-image.

Nursing Care

Mouth Care

The cause of the oral mucous membrane disorder is identified so that it can be treated. The nurse monitors the intake of irritating substances (tobacco, alcohol, highly spiced foods) so that their influence as offensive agents can be evaluated. Dental treatment should be arranged if required, and the patient advised to make regular follow-up visits. The need for frequent brushing and flossing of the teeth is emphasized.

Nutritional Intake

The patient's weight, age and level of activity are recorded so that an adequate daily calorie intake can be estimated by the dietician if the patient has a nutritional deficit. A food diary may be maintained to determine the exact quantity of food and fluid ingested. The frequency and pattern of eating is recorded to determine whether there are psychosocial factors as well as physiological factors influencing ingestion. Dietary patterns may need to be altered in order to maintain an adequate nutritional intake. Changes will depend on the individual's particular needs. The goal is to help the patient attain a desirable body weight.

Positive Self-image

The patient is encouraged to verbalize any perceived change in body appearance and realistically discuss actual changes or losses. The nurse offers support while these patients verbalize their fears and negative feelings, and encourages them to identify their reactions (withdrawal, depression, anger) and to describe themselves and how they believe others see them so that they have a more realistic perception of themselves. The nurse listens attentively and determines whether their needs are primarily psychosocial or cognitive–perceptual. This determination will help individualize a plan of care. The patient's strengths and achievements are praised and positive attributes reinforced.

The nurse should determine the patient's major anxieties concerning interpersonal relations at home and at work. Recommendations should be made concerning specific ways for the patient to interact with others and cope with any anxieties and fears.

The patient's progress in developing a positive self-esteem is recorded. The nurse should be alert to signs of grieving and should keep a record of emotional changes. Repeated opportunities are provided for listening, and the nurse should accept the patient's expressions of hostility.

► *Evaluation*
► **Expected Outcomes**

1. Patient shows evidence of an intact oral mucous membrane.
   a. Is free of pain/discomfort in the oral cavity.
   b. Avoids spicy foods.
   c. Is able to identify foods that are irritating to the gums (nuts, crisp biscuits).
2. Attains a desirable body weight.
   a. Eats nutritionally balanced meals.
   b. Keeps a daily record of calories if indicated.
   c. Substitutes foods appropriately to maintain suggested caloric intake.
   d. Maintains a recommended body weight plus or minus 2 to 3 kg.
3. Attains a positive self-image.
   a. Freely discusses body change.
   b. Verbalizes anxieties.
   c. Talks about self as an important person.
   d. Is able to accept change and modify self-concept.
   e. Speaks positively about appearance.
   f. Focuses energies away from self towards new identified expected outcomes.

CONDITIONS OF THE ORAL CAVITY

Abnormalities of the Lips

Angular Cheilitis

Angular cheilitis is a condition of the junction of the lips. It can range from a simple erythema of the bilateral commissural fissures (junctions of upper and lower lips), to more serious complaints of pain accompanied by ulceration and/or fissuring. The contributing factors include age, the presence of dentures that often fit incorrectly, accompanying denture-induced stomatitis, usually the product of a candidial infection, and deficiencies of iron, folate or vitamin B_{12}. Treatment consists of demonstrating the correct cleansing of dentures; the dentures should be removed before sleeping and should be scrubbed with the appropriate cleanser and then stored overnight in chlorhexidine 0.2 per cent solution, to inhibit the growth of *Candida* species. A dental referral may be needed to ensure correct fitting of the dentures. Finally, any biochemical abnormalities should be corrected. All of these procedures should be accompanied by adequate explanation to prevent recurrence of the problem.

Herpes Simplex

A cold sore is produced by the *Herpes simplex* virus. Singular or clustered vesicles erupt on the lip. Vesicles rupture, forming ulcers that are covered with a grey membrane.

Chancre

A chancre is a reddened, circumscribed lesion that ulcerates and becomes crusted. A hard papule is the primary lesion of syphilis.

Contact Dermatitis

Lipsticks, cosmetics, ointments to prevent chapping and even toothpaste and chewing gum may be the source of allergens that cause erythema, vesiculation, burning and itching of the lips. These conditions are treated by eliminating the suspected contactant, applying topical corticosteroid ointment and using hypoallergenic cosmetics.

Nursing Care

An initial approach to the patient with lip lesions includes taking a nursing history concerning the length of time the lesions have existed, any known precipitating factors, methods of treatment used to date, known associates with similar problems and a statement of the problem in the patient's words.

The nurse inspects the lesions, noting their appearance, location, size and drainage, if any; and after identifying the abnormality, will recommend that the patient does the following:

- Avoids spicy/irritating foods.
- Uses warm rinses to clean the mouth without irritating the lips.
- Uses ice packs to soothe if necessary.
- Avoids emotional situations that increase stress and aggravate the condition.
- Eliminates causative factors (sun exposure, cosmetics).
- Refrains from direct contact with another through kissing.
- Seeks health care if necessary.

Abnormalities of the Gums

Enlargement of the gingival tissue can occur in response to normal body changes (puberty, pregnancy).

Gingivitis

Gingivitis (inflammation of the gums) is the most common disease of oral tissues. At first there is inflammation and slight swelling of the superficial gingivae and interdental papillae. Bleeding in response to light contact may occur and prompt the patient to refrain from adequately cleaning the teeth. Such neglect compounds the problem, because food debris, bacterial plaque and calculus (tartar) can result in chronic degenerative gingivitis and, later, in periodontal disease.

Necrotizing gingivitis is a pseudomembranous ulceration affecting the edges of the gums, the mucosa of the mouth, the tonsils and the pharynx. It is thought to be caused by a combination of two organisms, a spirochete and a fusiform bacillus. Smears made from the ulcerations are found to be teeming with the characteristic organisms and this establishes the diagnosis. However, the condition may also be due to poor oral hygiene, low tissue resistance and infection produced by a complex of micro-organisms.

The chief symptoms are painful, bleeding gums and acute halitosis. Swallowing and talking are also painful, especially when infection has spread to the tonsils and pharynx. There may be a mild fever and swelling of the lymph nodes in the neck.

Management. Conscientious mouth hygiene and periodic professional teeth cleaning can prevent plaque build-up and gum irritation. For necrotizing gingivitis, the plan of care includes washing and irrigating the mouth hourly with prescribed solutions rich in free oxygen, such as diluted hydrogen peroxide and/or metronidazole 200 mg three times daily to combat anaerobic organisms. Phenoxymethyl penicillin 250 mg given orally four times a day is effective. Definitive measures such as dental prophylaxis and gingival massage are postponed until the acute inflammation has subsided.

Herpetic Gingivostomatitis

Herpes simplex infection may take the form of an acute herpetic gingivostomatitis. The patient frequently experiences a burning sensation 24 to 48 hours before blisters appear. Small vesicles, single or clustered, may erupt and rupture, forming sore, shallow ulcers that are covered with a grey membrane. Herpes infections appear often in association with other febrile infections, such as streptococcal pneumonia, meningococcal meningitis and malaria.

Some patients may associate herpes simplex with hearsay stories relating this herpes virus to cancer. Although herpes virus type 2 has been associated with carcinoma of the cervix in women, there is no documented evidence to show the exact relationship between the two.

Management. Treatment is supportive. Nursing care aims to resolve problems as they arise, for example: (1) pain relief in adults is achieved by the topical application of lignocaine gel to ease local discomfort, or benzydamine hydrochloride 0.15 per cent mouthwash is prescribed; (2) secondary infection is prevented by rinsing the mouth with chlorhexidine gluconate 0.2 per cent; (3) regular antipyretics are given to reduce the patient's temperature; (4) a high fluid input is necessary, especially in children, to prevent dehydration; (5) acycloguanosine appears in trials to be effective against the causative virus.

Abnormalities of the Mouth

Leucoplakia

White patches that cannot be diagnosed as a specific disorder can be benign and hyperkeratotic (tissue overgrowth) or malignant. They occur most frequently between the ages of 50 and 70 years, and are commonly found in the buccal and mandibular mucosa. The majority have no evidence of abnormal tissue development; however, a small percentage develop into squamous cell carcinoma, so biopsy is recommended if the lesions persist for longer than two weeks.

Lichen Planus

Lichen planus is a mucocutaneous disease recognized as white papules at the intersection of a network of interlacing lesions. Often, the lesions are ulcerated and painful. If asymptomatic, reassurance is all that is needed. For lichen planus, the diet is limited to soft, bland foods. If there is pain, small amounts of benzydamine hydrochloride 0.15 per cent held in the mouth for two to three minutes may relieve soreness while eating. Direct application of triamcinolone acetonide in carmellose sodium after meals or at bedtime may promote healing. Corticosteroids given systemically or injected intralesionally have been effective. Periodical examinations of chronic lesions are necessary because of their potential for malignancy.

Candidiasis

Candidiasis (thrush) produces white, cheesy plaques that look like milk curds and can be rubbed off to leave an erythematous and, often, bleeding base. Diagnosis requires identifying the spores of *Candida albicans* from exfoliated cells (dead tissue cells scraped from the lesion). Predisposing factors may include diabetes mellitus, lymphoma or other debilitating conditions; corticosteroids; and antibiotics. Treating the basic cause may improve the condition. In addition, nystatin, taken orally or as an oral suspension, is effective. The suspension is a medicated fluid that should be swished about the mouth vigorously for at least one minute. If the condition becomes chronic, it is more difficult to treat and requires persistent attention to basic care.

Aphthous Stomatitis

Among the most common lesions of the mouth are recurrent aphthous ulcers. Aphthous ulcers are shallow ulcers found in the mucous membrane of the mouth, most often on the inner side of the lips and cheeks, and in the sulcus between the lips and gums. However, they may appear anywhere in the mouth, including on the tongue. The lesions begin with a burning, tingling sensation and slight swelling of the mucous membrane, which soon becomes a shallow ulcer with a whitish centre surrounded by a red border. These ulcers are especially painful when eating and are particularly aggravated by acid or spicy foods. Since these ulcers are tender to pressure, any abrasion or movement of the skin around the ulcer makes it painful to speak or move any of the facial muscles. The ulcers may be single or multiple, and they often tend to heal at one site and recur elsewhere. The sores may appear at any time in life; most often they begin in childhood or adolescence and may appear as frequently as once a month. In most cases, however, they do not occur more than once a year or so. These ulcers last only a short time (from 10 to 14 days) and eventually heal spontaneously, leaving no scar.

In spite of intense studies, no definite cause can be found for aphthous ulcers. An L-form of -haemolytic *Streptococcus* has been proposed as the microbial cause. There seem to be definite predisposing factors, such as stress, related to their occurrence. In women, they seem to appear at the time of menstrual periods, and they occur

much more frequently among women than men. Fatigue, change in a life situation and anxiety are other predisposing factors.

Because no cause is known there is no specific treatment for aphthous ulcers. When anxiety is an obvious aetiological factor, tranquillizing drugs may be beneficial. A soft, bland diet may reduce pain. Various antibiotic and steroid preparations applied locally, or injected systemically, offer some relief, specifically, hydrocortisone hemisuccinate pellets 2.5 mg (one pellet taken four times daily and allowed to dissolve over the ulcer). Fortunately, these ulcers eventually heal spontaneously in a relatively short time.

Leucoplakia Buccalis

Leucoplakia buccalis (also called 'smoker's patch') and the related keratosis labialis are seen in middle-aged adults, more than 80 per cent of whom are men. These conditions are characterized in the early stages by the appearance of one or two small, thin, often crinkled, pearly patches on the mucous membrane of the tongue, the mouth or both, owing to keratinization of the mucosa and sclerosis of its underlying tissue (Figure 12.2). In time, most of the tongue and the mouth may become covered by a creamy, white, thick, fissured or papillomatous mucous membrane that desquamates occasionally, leaving a beefy-red base. This condition results from chronic irritation by carious, infected or poorly repaired teeth; by tobacco; and by highly spiced foods. It will disappear in time after cessation of smoking. Occasionally, it is due to syphilis. Not infrequently, cancers start in the keratinized patches. Detection of these patches through a nursing assessment and examination is a prime nursing responsibility in this situation.

Erythroplakia

The lesions of erythroplakia are due to exudative or ulcerative processes that resemble a red patch on the oral mucous membrane. They are of short duration, are fairly

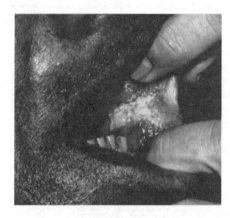

Figure 12.2 Leucoplakia. Note the white patches above and to the right of the teeth.

easy to remove and are nonspecific for an inflammatory disorder. Erythroplakia is more common than leucoplakia in the elderly and has a greater incidence of malignancy.

Kaposi's Sarcoma

Kaposi's sarcoma is a malignant mesenchymal skin tumour that occurs primarily on the legs of men between 50 and 70 years of age. Recently, it has been seen with increased frequency as a nonsquamous tutor of the oral cavity in patients with acquired immune deficiency syndrome (AIDS). The lesions are purplish and nonulcerated and are composed of spindle-shaped cells. Irradiation is the treatment of choice.

Abnormalities of the Salivary Glands

The salivary glands consist of: the parotid glands, one on each side of the face below the ear; the submaxillary and sublingual glands, both in the floor of the mouth; and the buccal gland, beneath the lips. About 1,200 ml of saliva is produced daily. The glands' primary functions are lubrication, antibacterial protection and digestion.

Parotitis

Parotitis (inflammation of the parotid gland) is the most common inflammatory condition of the salivary glands; however, infection can occur in the other glands as well. The essential lesion of mumps (epidemic parotitis) is an inflammation of the salivary gland (usually the parotid) and is primarily a paediatric communicable disease.

Elderly, acutely ill and debilitated people whose salivary glands fail to secret sufficiently because of general dehydration often develop parotitis. The infecting organisms travel from the mouth through the salivary duct. Because older people tend to have parched mouths and do not chew solid foods adequately, they offer poor defence against invasion of the parotid ducts by pathogenic organisms.

The offending organism is usually *Staphylococcus aureus* (except in mumps). The onset of this complication is sudden, with an exacerbation of the fever and of the symptoms of the primary condition. The gland swells and becomes tense and tender. Pain is felt in the ear, and there is interference with swallowing. The swelling increases rapidly, and the overlying skin soon becomes red and shiny.

Nursing Care. In order to prevent postoperative parotitis, patients are advised to have necessary dental work done before surgery. In addition, optimal patient preparation includes maintaining an adequate nutritional and fluid intake along with good mouth hygiene.

After surgery, encouraging the patient to suck boiled sweets may prevent obstruction of the salivary gland ducts. At the onset of the swelling, an icebag may be applied over the affected gland and chemotherapy may be instituted with penicillin or one of the sulphonamides. A suppurating gland may require incision and drainage.

Sialadenitis

Sialadenitis (infection of a salivary gland) is caused by dehydration, stress or improper oral hygiene and is associated with infection with *Staphylococcus aureus*, *Streptococcus viridans* or pneumococcus. Characteristics include pain, swelling and a purulent discharge.

Management. Antibiotics are used to relieve acute symptoms. Massage, hydration and steroids frequently cure the problem. Chronic sialadenitis, with uncontrolled pain, requires surgical excision of the gland and its duct.

Salivary Calculus (Sialolithiasis)

More than 80 per cent of all salivary stones are found in the submandibular gland. The cause may relate to a high concentration of saliva, infection or ductal stricture owing to trauma or inflammation. Sialograms (X-ray films taken with a radio-opaque substance injected into the duct) may be required to show obstruction of the duct by stenosis. Salivary stones are formed mainly from calcium phosphate. If located within the gland, they are irregularly lobulated and vary in diameter from 3 to 30 mm. Stones in the duct are small and oval.

Calculi within the salivary gland cause no symptoms unless infection arises; but a calculus that obstructs the gland's duct causes sudden, local and often colicky pain, which is suddenly relieved by a gush of saliva. This characteristic complaint can be elicited in a nursing assessment. Where this condition exists, the gland is swollen and quite tender, the stone itself often is palpable and its shadow may be seen on X-ray films.

The calculus can be extracted fairly easily from the duct in the mouth; sometimes enlarging the orifice permits the stone to pass spontaneously. It may be necessary to remove the gland if there are repeated recurrences of symptoms and calculi in the gland itself.

Neoplasms

Neoplasms of the salivary glands, although rare, can be of almost any type. The majority are benign but can turn malignant at a later time. In 80 per cent of these patients, tumours develop in one parotid gland. The tumours remain small and quiescent for years, then suddenly begin to increase in size. Diagnosis is based on the history and physical examination, frozen sections and fine-needle aspiration.

Minor salivary gland tumours are usually malignant and occur in patients aged about 70 years. Pleomorphic adenoma is the most common minor salivary gland tumour that is benign; adenoid cystic carcinoma is the most common malignant tumour. Biopsy determines tumour type, and surgical removal is recommended.

Management. Treatment of a parotid tumour will depend upon its nature. Benign lesions require a superficial parotidectomy. Superficial excision of the gland, along with all of the tumour, combined with careful dissection to preserve the vulnerable facial (seventh) nerve, is a common procedure. For malignant tumours, it may be necessary to sacrifice the nerve, and a radical parotidectomy is performed. If the tumour is malignant or mixed, radiotherapy follows surgery. Local recurrences are common; the recurrent growth usually is more malignant than the original one.

Nursing Care. Preoperatively, the patient is encouraged to ask questions about the procedure since there is the possibility that a radical neck dissection may be required. In the postoperative period, the nurse should be aware that the patient may have some facial paralysis (if the nerve was not excised) due to tissue trauma and oedema. This paralysis will gradually subside. Dressings are removed after 24 hours, and patients are allowed to shower and wash their hair.

CANCER OF THE ORAL CAVITY

Cancer of the oral cavity, which may occur in any part of the mouth, including the pharynx, is curable if discovered early. It accounts for around 1 per cent of the yearly cancer deaths in England and Wales. Of the 1,687 deaths from oral cancer in 1988, the distribution by site was as shown in Table 12.1.

Squamous cell carcinoma constitutes over 90 per cent of all mouth cancers. The next most common type, adenocarcinoma, arises mainly from the salivary glands. The third grouping includes malignancy of the jaw bone. The cure rate for these cancers is below 35 per cent.

In cancers of the lip, the most common types of tumours are the squamous and basal cell carcinomata. These tumours most frequently occur as chronic ulcers. Basal cell carcinoma usually occurs on the upper lip, and squamous cell carcinoma on the lower lip. Predisposing factors may be prolonged exposure to the sun, combined with age (these lesions are rare in people under the age of

Table 12.1 *Cancer of the mouth and pharynx, mortality statistics*

Site	Percentage	(Cases)
Lips	2	(36)
Tongue	21	(364)
Salivary glands	12	(179)
Gum, and floor of mouth	13	(224)
Pharynx	31	(522)
Unspecified sites within lips, oral cavity and pharynx, oropharynx, nasopharynx	21	(362)

(Source: Office of Population Census and Statistics (1990) Mortality Statistics: England and Wales, 1988, *HMSO, London.)*

40) and smoking. There is a significant tendency (about 10 per cent) for leucoplakic patches to develop into carcinoma. A typical lesion is a painless, indurated ulcer with raised edges. Any wart or ulcer of the lip that does not heal in three weeks should be referred for a medical opinion.

In cancer of the tongue, the constant expansion and contraction of the tongue can easily force small tumour cells into the lymphatic channels and eventually into the regional lymph nodes, where they become embedded. This cancer is most common in men in their later decades of life. Alcohol and tobacco are the two primary aetiological agents. Currently, the male to female ratio is 2:1. The disease is not common before the age of 30 (Toms, 1982).

Clinical Features

Most oral cancers cause no symptoms in the early stages. Often the patient feels a roughened area with the tongue. The first complaints may be difficulty in chewing, swallowing or speaking; swelling, numbness or loss of feeling in any part of the mouth may also occur. A lump in the neck may indicate metastatic spread. Any patient with a white, patchy area, sore spot or ulceration of lips, gums or mouth that fails to heal in three weeks should be urged to see a doctor (Scully, 1989).

Cancer of the lip is associated with discomfort and irritation due to the presence of a nonhealing sore that may be raised or ulcerated. Localized tenderness is characteristic; pain is usually absent.

With cancer of the tongue there is pain or soreness (when eating hot or highly seasoned foods). As the growth spreads to neighbouring structures, other symptoms develop, such as excessive salivation, slurred speech, blood-tinged sputum, trismus (spasm of the mastication muscles) and pain on swallowing liquids. If the cancer is untreated, the patient is unable to swallow, and earache, faceache and toothache become almost constant.

Malignancy at the base of the tongue (posterior) produces less obvious symptoms: dysphagia, sore throat, salivation and some blood-tinged sputum.

Diagnosis

An incisional biopsy is usually required to confirm a diagnosis, involving a local or general anaesthetic. Generally, large biopsies are required to include sufficient normal and potentially neoplastic tissue for the pathologist to make a diagnosis without further specimens. The biopsy wound may be up to 1.5 cm long, and require up to 10 days to heal (Shklar, 1984). The early stage of cancer of the anterior undersurface of the lateral aspects of the tongue is usually detected as a small ulcer that fails to heal within three weeks, or as an area of thickening. Confirmation of diagnosis is by biopsy.

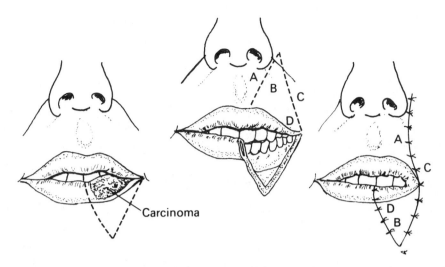

Figure 12.3 The Estlander procedure for repair of carcinoma of the lower lip. (1) A V-shaped excision is made wide enough to remove tumour and allow for a small margin of tissue on either side of the tumour. (2) A flap of the same shape (A–C) is excised from the opposite lip. (3) The new flap is rotated downwards to form a new buccal commissure. (Adapted with permission from del Regato, J. A., Spjut, H. J. and Cox J. D. (1985) *Ackerman and del Regato's Cancer: Diagnosis, Treatment, and Prognosis*, C. V. Mosby, St Louis.)

Management

Management varies with the nature of the lesion and the preference of the surgeon. Treatment consists of surgery, radiotherapy, chemotherapy or a combination of the three. In cancer of the lip, small lesions are usually excised liberally (Figure 12.3); larger lesions of the lip may require the services of two or more medical teams, including oral surgeons, radiologists and/or plastic surgeons. The choice depends on the extent of the lesion, the skill of the surgeon or radiologist and what is necessary to cure the patient while maintaining function and preserving appearance. There is a 70 per cent recurrence rate for tumours greater than 4 cm. Fortunately, only 10 to 15 per cent of lip cancers metastasise. The five-year survival rate is approximately 80 per cent if the lymph nodes are uninvolved, but only 30 per cent when there is lymph node involvement (Cocke, McShane and Silverton, 1979).

For cancer of the tongue the two major treatments of choice are radiation therapy and surgery (Figure 12.4). Laser excision is also used for certain types of surface lesions. Metastasis to the neck necessitates more extensive surgical neck dissection, combined with either external beam radiation or interstitial therapy involving implants of iridium or caesium. Irradiation and surgery are separated by a gap of four to six weeks. Enlargement of lymph nodes indicates metastasis, necessitating more extensive surgical neck dissection. When the tongue is involved, it is often necessary to perform a hemiglossectomy (removal of a lateral segment of the tongue). The tongue is a difficult site for effective irradiation, and because of the mutilating effects of total glossectomy, and

the likelihood of metastasis, the cure rate of posterior tongue cancer is low. There is a 50 per cent chance of a five-year survival period with early detection and no lymph node spread. However, only 20 per cent of cases are diagnosed early. With lymph node involvement, the five-year survival period is 20 per cent (Cocke, McShane and Silverton, 1979). For even the advanced lesions involving the tongue, mandible, larynx and neck, treatment may be palliative, involving combinations of surgery and radiotherapy.

▶ NURSING PROCESS
▶ THE PATIENT WITH CANCER OF THE ORAL CAVITY

▶ *Assessment*

The principal nursing activities in the assessment phase include a careful nursing history to detect symptoms requiring medical evaluation. Complaints of sores, lumps, pain in the mouth, stiffness in the neck and difficulty with swallowing, chewing or speaking require attention.

The nurse asks if the patient has an intolerance to hot, cold or highly seasoned foods. Is there a history of heavy alcohol and tobacco use? Is the mucosa inflamed? Are there signs of dehydration?

An oral examination is best carried out by the medical team in a dental chair with satisfactory lighting and equipment. The nurse may be asked to assist with the examination of the oral cavity, and provides a familiar face during a sometimes uncomfortable procedure.

► *Patient's Problems*

Based on the assessment, the patient's main problems may include the following:

- Alteration of the oral mucous membrane related to irritation, inflammation and dryness of the mouth secondary to the presence of a lesion.
- Alteration in nutrition, related to reduced intake of foods and fluids secondary to sensitive oral mucous membranes.
- Disturbance in self-concept/body image, related to disfiguring appearance of an oral lesion or reconstructive surgery.
- Fear of pain and social isolation and inability to cope related to the diagnosis and prognosis of the disease process.
- Potential for injury or infection related to altered immunological responses secondary to chemotherapy/radiotherapy.
- Anticipatory grieving related to the diagnosis of cancer.

► *Planning and Implementation*
► Expected Outcomes

The patient's expected outcomes may include maintenance of the integrity of the oral cavity, adequate intake of foods and fluids, attainment of a positive self-image and effective communication, acquisition of coping mechanisms, absence of infection and acceptance of the diagnosis.

Nursing Care

Mouth Care

The nurse teaches the patient how to keep the mouth clean. If use of a toothbrush and dental floss is impossible, an irrigating solution of thymol, or chlorhexidine gluconate 0.2 per cent, is refreshing. To be effective, antiseptic mouthwashes must be used frequently and held in the mouth for at least one minute. However, there is little evidence to suggest that any one solution is better than water for moisturising the mouth and washing away bacteria. Benzydamine hydrochloride 0.15 per cent mouthwash may be prescribed for discomfort. Commercial mouthwashes should be avoided owing to the irritation and pain caused by the alcohol content.

In the unconscious patient, the nurse is wholly responsible for maintaining optimal mouth hygiene. The use of a special mouth tray with all necessary applicator sticks, spatulae, mouthwashes and lubricants encourages regular care. Use of a lip moisturiser helps to prevent cracking of the lips.

Dryness of the mouth is a frequent sequel of oral cancer, and of chemotherapy and radiotherapy. To minimize this problem, the patient is advised to avoid dry, bulky and irritating foods and fluids as well as alcohol and tobacco. Encouragement is also given to increase the intake of fluids, if this is not contraindicated. The new artificial saliva sprays are of some benefit where salivary flow is reduced.

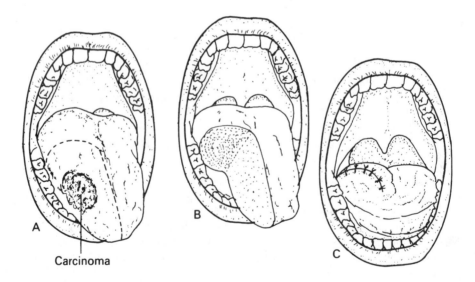

Carcinoma

Figure 12.4 Surgery for cancer of the tongue. (A) Small invasive cancer of the tongue. Tongue is extended and incision margins are outlined. (B) A deep resection provides for removal of a generous portion of nonmalignant tissue. (C) Sutured area results in a shallow margin which is less defined when the tongue is extended. (Adapted with permission from McQuarrie, D. G., Adams, G. L., Shons, A. R. *et al.* (1986) *Head and Neck Cancer*, Year Book Medical Publishers, Chicago.)

Adequate Food and Fluid Intake

Anorexia is a common problem in a patient with oral cancer because of the discomfort associated with eating. The nurse recommends the intake of soft, high-carbohydrate foods (pasta, potatoes) that are filling and have a protein-sparing action (i.e., protein catabolism for energy needs is saved, or 'spared', so that protein can be used for tissue regeneration). Creative approaches to food preparation are encouraged. The nurse suggests three moderate meals a day, rather than frequent small servings, to limit the frequency of coping with the oral discomfort associated with eating. Supplementary feeds help maintain an adequate protein and calorie intake. Fluid requirements can be met by suggesting sweetened juices that are nonacidic (gelatin desserts in liquid form, colas and milk shakes). Flexible straws or modified feeding utensils are helpful. Antiemetic agents are administered as prescribed.

The desires as well as the nutritional needs of the patient should be taken into consideration. If the patient is unable to take anything by mouth, it may be necessary to give feeds via a nasoenteric or nasogastric tube to maintain fluid and electrolyte balance and to prevent starvation and negative nitrogen balance.

Coping Measures

The patient with a mouth or facial problem requires patience and understanding. Quite naturally, the patient tends to withdraw from people, and is self-conscious about mouth odours and appearance. The nurse is challenged to communicate with the patient, encouraging expression of fears and concerns, and offering support and explanations as necessary. The immediate family and close friends need to be aware of their supporting role and, in turn, should be informed of the plan of therapy for the patient and urged to participate in the plan of care.

A particular area of concern that interferes with communication, feeding and swallowing is excessive salivation or drooling. The measures taken to control drooling depend on the cause, severity and relative permanence of the dysfunction. If the problem is moderate to severe but temporary, as may be the case following surgery, mechanical suction devices used with a soft catheter are effective. If drooling is mild, management may be obtained by training the patient to swallow more frequently, by providing emotional reassurance and, rarely, by the use of anticholinergic agents, which are of limited use owing to their side-effects (Wilkins, 1989). For more severe drooling, it may be necessary to resort to plastic reconstruction of the oral structures.

Mouth wipes, as well as a paper bag attached to the bed or the bedside stand to receive soiled tissues, should always be on hand. An effective way of holding dressings of the mouth or the lower jaw in place is by the use of a face mask. The strings can be tied at the top of the head.

Patients may express a strong desire for solitude and may be self-conscious about their appearance. (The need to remove, temporarily, any large mirrors in the room should be considered by the nurse.) The results of surgery or radiotherapy cause concern, especially the fear of disfigurement; if the resection is extensive, the possibility of prosthetics (fitting an artificial part) may be explained.

The patient may have problems with speech. Providing a pad of paper and a pencil or 'magic slate', so that the patient can express any needs and thoughts, may make a tremendous difference in the patient's depressed condition. Often these patients are reluctant to associate with other patients and prefer to be alone. If there are two or more patients with a similar condition, they can help each other. It is easier for them, and for others, if they have their meals apart from other patients.

Family and friends should be encouraged to visit so that patient are aware that others care. Patients can be helped to care for their appearance. With speech training and adjustment to a prosthesis, such patients will become increasingly aware that the future holds promise for them as people.

Alleviation of Fear

The nurse asks the patient to describe any fears related to pain, isolation, altered lifestyle and loss of control. The description may provide a clue for managing the problem and developing a plan of care. The nurse also assesses the patient's physical reactions to these fears. Common responses include muscle rigidity, fatigue, tachycardia, hypertension, dyspnoea and nausea.

The nurse can reduce fears in a number of ways. For example, the fear of pain can be managed by advising the patient that medication will be offered every three to four hours, and that if something more is needed the doctor will be called to adjust the dosage or frequency. A pain chart can be a useful tool. The nurse supports adaptive behaviours, encourages expressions of emotions, emphasizes the patient's abilities and fosters positive self-esteem.

Distorted perceptions are corrected by providing accurate information. Control is encouraged by encouraging the patient to participate in the treatment process. Support groups are recommended, and the nurse can offer to contact a representative from a support group to visit the patient.

The nurse should be receptive to the patient's expressions of potential loss. Behaviours associated with defence mechanisms such as projection, displacement and rationalization need to be recognized. Many patients withdraw, cry easily and experience a sense of hopelessness. Some of them progress through certain behaviours in anticipating death: denial, anger, depression, bargaining, resolution and acceptance. The nurse's role is one of offering support, and projecting an optimistic attitude, especially if the lesion has a high incidence of cure (80+ per cent for cancer of the lip) (Cocke, McShane and Silverton,

1979). Visits by an appropriate counsellor, social worker or religious adviser can be suggested.

Infection Control

Bone marrow suppression is a side-effect of both chemo- and radiotherapy, weakening defence mechanisms and making the patient more susceptible to infections. Anaemia, subsequent to malnutrition, is also common. Laboratory studies must be evaluated frequently, and the patient's temperature is checked every six to eight hours for an elevation that may indicate an infection. Visitors who may transmit micro-organisms are prohibited because the patient's immunological system is depressed. Trauma to sensitive skin tissues is avoided to maintain skin integrity and prevent infection. Strict aseptic technique is necessary when changing dressings. Desquamation (shedding of the epidermis) is a reaction to radiotherapy that causes dryness and itching, and can lead to a break in skin integrity and subsequent infection.

Benzydamine hydrochloride 0.15 per cent mouthwash and saline mouthwashes may be prescribed for the patient who develops mouth ulcers, stomatitis or xerostomia (dryness of the mouth caused by the arresting of salivary secretion) as a result of chemotherapy. The intake of a high-protein, high-carbohydrate diet with vitamin supplements is encouraged to promote tissue repair for the patient who is anorexic and anaemic.

Patient Education

The nurse has the responsibility to make sure that the patient receives accurate information about the disease process if the information is wanted. Some patients want to know everything about their diagnosis, while others only want to know what is necessary for them to manage their daily activities. The participation of family members or significant others is encouraged in any discussions.

The nurse must determine what the patient already knows and what extra information is required about the type of treatment recommended (chemotherapy, radiotherapy, surgery), the process involved and the implications for care. Information is presented at the patient's level of understanding and when the patient is relaxed, painfree and not distracted by visitors. A person must be physically and emotionally ready to learn for learning to occur. Pictures or diagrams can be used when appropriate, and family members or significant others are involved in the sessions whenever possible. Active participation is encouraged, but it is important to remember that the patient must have the energy to attend the session. Important facts are emphasized and repeated by the patient as necessary.

Home Health Care

The post-hospital objectives of patient care are similar to those in the hospital. The patient who is recovering from treatment of a mouth condition needs to breathe, to secure nourishment, to avoid infection and to be alert for adverse signs. The patient, family members, significant others, the nurse and whoever else may be involved, such as a speech therapist or dietician, need to prepare an individualized plan. If suctioning the mouth or a tracheostomy tube is required, it is important to determine what equipment is needed and how to use it, as well as where it can be obtained. Consideration is given to the humidification and aeration of the room, as well as measures to control odours. How to prepare foods that are nutritious, properly seasoned and of the right temperature can be explained. The use and care of prostheses must be understood. The importance of cleanliness with dressings and mouth care is reviewed. The person caring for the patient needs to know the signs of obstruction, haemorrhage, infection, depression and withdrawal, as well as what to do about these problems. Follow-up visits to the clinic or doctor are important to determine progression or regression and to make any modifications in medication or general care.

Over 90 per cent of recurrences will appear within the first 18 months; therefore, meticulous inspection by the doctor every four to six weeks is essential. Early detection of local recurrences or metastasis, followed by aggressive treatment, can cure as many as 50 per cent of these patients. Follow-up visits become less frequent after two years, but must be continued for life because of the frequency of other primary carcinomas. One important part of continuing care is the elimination of alcohol consumption and smoking. Because of further extension of a malignancy by metastasis and necrosis, it may be impossible medically to halt the spread of disease. All efforts are then directed toward the comfort measures—physical, psychological and spiritual. With help from the family or significant others, this may be continued in the hospital, a nursing home, a hospice setting or the patient's own home.

► *Evaluation*
► Expected Outcomes

1. Patient practises oral hygiene measures.
   a. Brushes teeth and flosses daily; performs mouth care after each meal.
   b. Inspects mouth routinely for the presence of lesions.
   c. Avoids foods and fluids that irritate the gums or mouth.
   d. Limits or avoids use of alcohol and tobacco (including smokeless tobacco).
   e. Uses lubricating agents for the mouth (lozenges, chewing gum).
2. Maintains adequate intake of foods and fluids.
   a. Eats soft, nonirritating foods several times a day.
   b. Uses a modified eating utensil if necessary.
   c. Maintains or gains weight.
   d. Is hydrated.
   e. Requests antiemetic agents as needed.

f. Adheres to parenteral feeding schedule.

3. Evidences a positive self-image.
   a. Interacts appropriately with family members or significant others.
   b. Is able to communicate effectively (verbally or by using a 'magic slate').
   c. Projects self-confidence.
   d. Participates in social gatherings.

4. Expresses personal feelings about diagnosis.
   a. Is aware of diagnosis and understands prognosis.
   b. Discusses feelings with family members and significant others.
   c. Verbally discusses emotional responses to the diagnosis.

5. Acquires information about disease process and course of treatment.
   a. Is motivated to learn about treatment and its implications, and participates in the teaching sessions.
   b. Involves family members and/or significant others in teaching sessions as a means of support.

6. Reduces fears related to pain, isolation and the inability to cope.
   a. Accepts that pain will be managed if not eliminated.
   b. Freely expresses fears and concerns.
   c. Agrees to talk with a support group.
   d. Communicates openly with family members and significant others.
   e. Writes down one positive thing about self each day.

7. Is infection free.
   a. Maintains normal laboratory values.
   b. Is afebrile.
   c. Maintains skin integrity.
   d. Practises oral hygiene after every meal and at bedtime.
   e. Avoids visitors with infectious conditions.
   f. Eats a high-protein, high-carbohydrate diet.

RADICAL NECK DISSECTION

Malignancies of the head and neck, including cancers of the lips, tongue, gums, palate, tonsils and of the mucosa of the mouth, pharynx and larynx, may be treated early by surgery, radiotherapy or chemotherapy, with good results. These cancers (stages I and II) are in an area that can be easily seen, making early prognosis and treatment possible. Most observers agree that such patients do not die of recurrence at the site of the primary growth, but rather of metastasis to the cervical lymph nodes in the neck, which often takes place by way of the lymphatics before the primary lesion has been treated. Only the nodes on one side of the neck are involved, unless the tumour is located at or near the midline, in which case the nodes of both sides of the neck may contain metastatic tumours.

Because radiotherapy does not by itself give good results in controlling the metastatic cancer in the lymph nodes in the neck, an operation called a radical neck dissection is performed. A radical neck dissection involves removal of all the tissue under the skin, from the ramus of the jaw down to the clavicle, and from the midline anteriorly back to the anterior border of the trapezius muscle posteriorly. This includes removing the sternomastoid muscle and other smaller muscles, as well as the jugular vein in the neck, because the lymphatic nodes are found widely distributed throughout these tissues (Figure 12.5).

A functional or modified neck dissection is similar to a radical neck dissection except that the sternomastoid muscle, internal jugular vein and the spinal accessory nerve are preserved. Obviously, this approach appears a reasonable alternative to radical radiation therapy, and is a preferred alternative to traditional neck dissection in the control of regional metastasis when neck disease is either occult or still confined to mobile lymph nodes.

Nursing Care

The nursing care for patients requiring radical neck dissection includes both physical and psychological preparation for major surgery. In addition to the impending physical rigors of this surgery, this patient is aware that the malignancy includes metastasis to the cervical nodes. This information is bound to cause concern and anxiety regarding the postsurgical outcome.

Before the operation, the patient should be informed about the impending surgery, what is to be done in the operating room (amplification of the surgeon's explanation) and what the postoperative period will be like. At the same time, the patient can be given an opportunity to express concerns about the forthcoming surgery. During this exchange, the nurse has an opportunity to assess the patient's coping abilities, encourage questions and develop a plan for offering assistance. A sense of mutual understanding and rapport will make the postoperative experience less troublesome for the patient. After the operation, any expressions of concern on the patient's part can guide the nurse in providing additional support. These caring activities deliberately include supportive family members and significant others.

The specific postoperative physical nursing care for this patient includes maintenance of a patent airway and continuous assessment of respiratory status; wound care and attention to dressings, including careful observation for haemorrhage; and management of oral hygiene and nutritional needs.

Airway Management
After the endotracheal tube or airway has been removed and the effects of the anaesthesia have worn off, the patient may be placed in a semi-recumbent position to facilitate breathing and promote comfort. This position also increases lymphatic and venous drainage, facilitates swallowing and decreases venous pressure on the skin flaps.

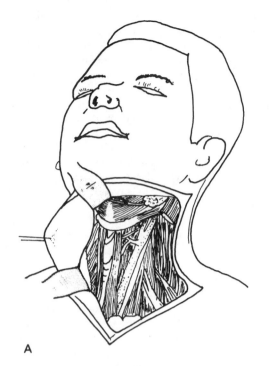

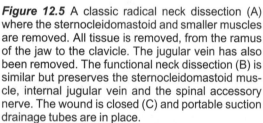

A   B

Figure 12.5 A classic radical neck dissection (A) where the sternocleidomastoid and smaller muscles are removed. All tissue is removed, from the ramus of the jaw to the clavicle. The jugular vein has also been removed. The functional neck dissection (B) is similar but preserves the sternocleidomastoid muscle, internal jugular vein and the spinal accessory nerve. The wound is closed (C) and portable suction drainage tubes are in place.

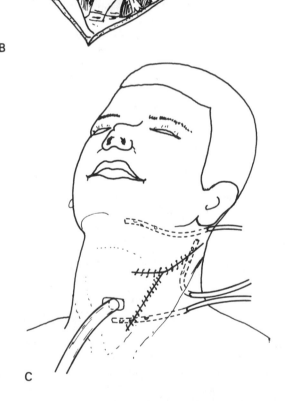

C

Signs of respiratory distress, such as dyspnoea, cyanosis and changes in vital signs, are watched for, since they may suggest oedema, throat irritation from the endotracheal tube, haemorrhage or inadequate drainage. Temperature is usually taken per axilla.

In the immediate postoperative period, the nurse may be able to detect the presence of stridor (coarse, high-pitched sound on inspiration) by listening frequently at the trachea with a stethoscope. In this situation, the doctor should be called.

Coughing is encouraged to aid in the removal of secretions. The patient should assume a sitting position, with the nurse supporting the patient's neck with the hands, so that bothersome secretions can be brought up. If this technique fails, the patient's respiratory tract may have to be suctioned. Care is exerted to protect the suture lines during suctioning. If a tracheostomy tube is in place, suctioning is done through this tube using sterile technique.

Wound Care

With portable wound suction drainage, there is no need for pressure dressings because the skin flaps are drawn down tightly. Dressings are observed for evidence of haemorrhage and constriction, which may affect respiration. Drains may be removed before the massive dressings are changed in about five days. Lighter dressings permit greater freedom of movement. Aeroplast or other antiseptic plastic sprays protect the wound. The patient is usually allowed out of bed the first postoperative day.

Possible Complications

Because of the extensiveness of the surgery, haemorrhage is a possible complication. Later, postoperative respiratory problems may cause pneumonia, unless the patient is turned and encouraged to breathe deeply. Wound infection has been reduced considerably, with the use of portable wound suction in place of pressure dressings. Neural complications can occur if the cervical plexus or spinal accessory nerves are severed.

Since lower facial paralysis may occur as a result of injury to the facial nerve during the dissection, this is watched for and reported if noted. Likewise, if the superior laryngeal nerve is damaged, the patient may have difficulty with swallowing liquids and food because of the partial lack of sensation of the glottis.

Prevention and Management of Haemorrhage. The following measures are indicated:

1. Assess vital signs. Tachycardia, tachypnoea and hypotension may indicate impending hypovolaemic shock subsequent to haemorrhage.
2. Observe dressings and wound drainage for excessive bleeding. The expected postoperative drainage should be serosanguineous and less than 200 ml in the first 24 hours. Blood loss is excessive if there is ligature separation or rupture of a vessel.
3. If haemorrhage occurs, apply pressure over dressings and over the carotid and internal jugular vessels. Direct pressure over the wound will slow blood loss. Pressure on surrounding major vessels will decrease blood flow to the area, thus decreasing blood loss.
4. Stay with the patient and summon assistance. Haemorrhage requires the continuous application of pressure to the bleeding site and/or major associated vessel. A controlled, calm manner will allay patient anxiety. A doctor is notified immediately because vessel or ligature tear will require surgical intervention.

Oral Hygiene and Nutrition

Mouth hygiene is necessary and welcomed by this patient. It is carried out frequently and helps to enhance the appetite. A nasogastric tube may be inserted for feeding purposes or to help decompress the stomach.

Coping Measures

The psychological postoperative nursing care is directed towards the support of a patient who has had a radical change in body image and who has major concerns regarding prognosis. Such a patient also has difficulty in communication and is concerned about the continuing ability to breathe and swallow normally. Adjustment to the results of this surgery will take time, and the nurse enlists the support of family members and significant others in encouraging and reassuring the patient.

The person who has had extensive neck surgery is often sensitive about appearance, either when the operative area is covered by bulky dressings or when an incision line is exposed, as with portable drainage. If the nurse conveys acceptance of both the patient and appearance, and expresses a positive, optimistic attitude, the patient is more likely to be encouraged. In spite of the wide removal of tissue, the cosmetic and functional defects are less than might be expected. The patient also needs an opportunity to voice any concerns regarding the success of the surgery and the prognosis. Most of these patients are able to maintain and gain weight and are soon restored to economic independence.

Rehabilitation Following Head and Neck Surgery

Many problems can be avoided with a conscientious exercise programme. The purpose of the exercises depicted in Figure 12.6 is to regain maximum shoulder function and neck motion following neck surgery. These exercises are recommended by the doctor when it is believed that the neck incision is sufficiently healed. Excision of muscle and nerves results in a weakness of the shoulder that can cause 'shoulder drop', with some forward curvature of the shoulder. Exercises will assist the patient in returning to normal activity.

Exercises are done in the morning and evening. At first each exercise is done once; thereafter, it is gradually increased by one, every day, until each is done ten times. Sweeping, smooth motions are used, in a relaxed manner. After each exercise the patient is directed to go limp and relax. Between exercises and when not using the arm or hand, the patient is encouraged to rest the arm and hand on a padded support to keep the shoulder lifted slightly.

FRACTURE OF THE MANDIBLE: JAW REPOSITIONING OR RECONSTRUCTION

Fractures of the mandible occur from two main causes: trauma and disease. Trauma may include violence, accidents and sports injuries, and involve not only fractures but also major tissue loss. Disease can include benign or malignant local tumours, metastasis, metabolic disorders and muscular contractions from an electrical shock.

Fractures of the mandible, as elsewhere, can be closed, where there is no break in the mucosa or skin, or open, where the bone has penetrated the surrounding tissue. Mandibular fractures are further classified as favourable or unfavourable. This depends upon the direction of the line of the fracture, and whether or not muscle action displaces the fracture alignment (unfavourable) or maintains it (favourable) (Figure 12.7).

Management

Treatment aims to realign the dental occlusion, and to sta-

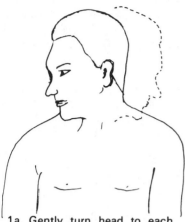

1a. Gently turn head to each side and look as far as possible.

1b. Gently tip right ear toward right shoulder as far as possible. Repeat on left side.

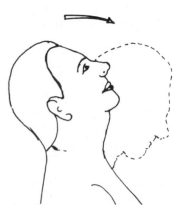

1c. Move chin to chest and then lift head up and back.

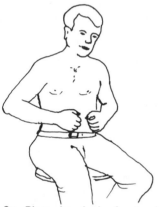

2a. Place hands in front with elbows at right angles away from body.

2b. Rotate shoulders back, bringing elbows to side.

2c. Relax whole body.

3a. Lean or hold onto low table or chair with hand on the unoperated side. Bend body slightly at waist and swing shoulder and arm from left to right.

3b. Swing shoulder and arm from front to back.

3c. Swing shoulder and arm in a wide circle, gradually bringing arm above head.

Figure 12.6 Three rehabilitation exercises following head and neck surgery. The objective is to regain maximum shoulder function and neck motion following neck surgery. (*Exercise for Radical Neck Surgery Patients*, Head and Neck Service, Department of Surgery, Memorial Hospital, New York, New York.)

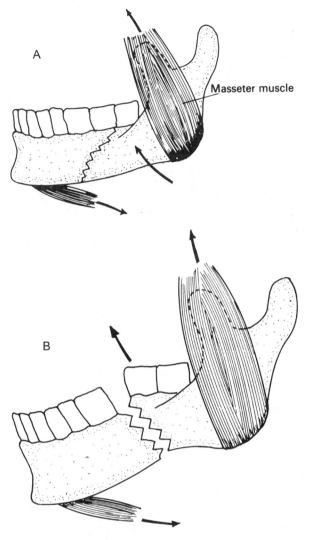

Figure 12.7 Fractures of the mandible. (A) Favourable fracture: muscle pull and direction of fracture maintain alignment. (B) Unfavourable fracture: muscle pull and direction of fracture cause displacement.

bilize the bone until healing has occurred. Either dental or interosseus fixation is used to achieve this. The choice depends on the type of fracture and the site.

Interosseus Fixation. This requires the surgical opening of the fracture, reduction and fixation either by means of a plate or by drilling small holes either side of the fracture and fixating with stainless steel wire threaded through the holes, and twisted tightly to maintain alignment. Both means remain in position permanently. This is the preferred method for complex fractures (Figure 12.8A).

Dental Fixation. Dental fixation is the preferred method for closed fractures. The means of fixation depends upon the existing dentition. Three main methods

are used: (1) eyelet wires, (2) dental arch bars and (3) Gunning splints.

1. Eyelet wires are used if the majority of teeth are present: eight stainless steel wires are twisted around the necks of teeth on both the mandible and maxilla. The jaws are then brought into occlusion and the opposing wires are joined together (Figure 12.8B).
2. Dental arch bars are usually used where only a few teeth remain: one bar is wired to the maxillary teeth and one to the mandibular teeth. Fixation and occlusion is maintained by the use of wires or rubber bands that attach to hooks on the arch bars (Figure 12.9).
3. Gunning splints are employed for the edentulous patient. The splints are made from casts of the gums, and are then wired to the maxilla and mandible. Gunning splints are premade with a hole in the region of the incisors, allowing easier consumption of a liquid diet.

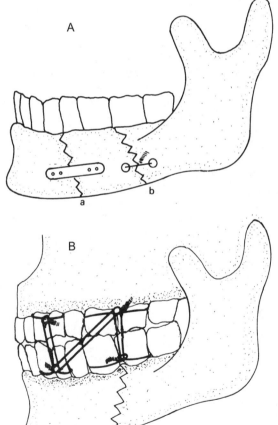

Figure 12.8 Fixation of fractures of the mandible. (A) Open reduction of fractured mandible using (a) a plate and (b) interosseus wire. (B) Closed reduction of fractured mandible using eyelet wires is indicated if the majority of teeth are present.

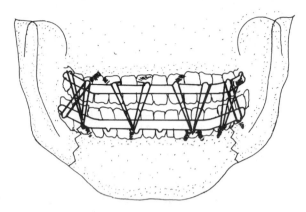

Figure 12.9 Mandibular fixation with arch bars. Arch bars and intermaxillary wiring are used if a significant number of teeth are missing.

Nursing Care

Preoperatively, explanation of the method of treatment of the fracture is given to the patient. Anxiety about appearance and effects of intermaxillary fixation must be explored, as well as the temporary change in body image. Reassurance can be given that the wires will be removed in six weeks' time when healing occurs, and that the patient's appearance will remain unaltered once the swelling has reduced. Emphasis is also given to explaining that breathing and swallowing are unimpaired. The patient is told that the diet will be in a liquid form, and that the dietician will make an assessment. To allay anxieties concerning vomiting with intermaxillary fixation in position, a practical demonstration by the nurse of the expectoration of liquid through clenched teeth can do much to relieve anxiety. A reassuring thought is that what goes down in a liquid form can come up in a liquid form.

In the recovery area, the patient is nursed on the side with the head elevated slightly.

- Vomit can be aspirated if consciousness is impaired. Until the patient is fully conscious in the ward environment, a competent nurse must remain with the patient, and know how to cut and remove wires. The nurse must know the exact position of any intermaxillary wires or bands, and must have wire cutters and artery forceps or scissors (if bands are used) at hand, at all times. The wires should be cut only if vomiting is likely to lead to aspiration, that is, before full consciousness is reached.

If an open reduction and interosseus fixation are employed, a fine-bore nasogastric tube will be inserted in theatre, and remain in place for up to five days to allow wound healing to occur. Antiemetic drugs will be prescribed to minimize the risk of vomiting.

On return to the ward, functioning suction equipment, wire cutters and artery forceps, if necessary, are placed at the head of the bed for emergency use. Suctioning of the nasopharyngeal area can be performed with a small catheter inserted through the nasal orifice, and that of the mouth by inserting a catheter between the gum and buccal membrane.

Particular attention must be paid to oral hygiene. When a closed reduction has been used, a small toothbrush accompanied by copious mouthwashing can be employed once the patient is fully conscious. A patient with an open reduction may wait for mucosal healing to occur before commencing toothbrushing, according to the doctor's wishes. Technique is the key to oral hygiene; the aim is the removal of food particles trapped behind arch bars and eyelet wires. A toothbrush is used in combination with mouthwashes. This should be demonstrated with the aid of a mirror. Sponge sticks and cotton buds must be avoided since they can become trapped in the ends of wires.

Nutritional input will be in a liquid form for the next six weeks; drinking is difficult because the mouth cannot be opened, but a drinking straw can be of assistance. Involvement of the dietician is important because adequate protein and carbohydrate input are required for healing.

Observation needs to made daily for loosening of any wires or trauma to buccal membranes, which can result in ulcers. Dental wax can be applied to proud wires to prevent such complications, or the wires can be repositioned by a doctor.

Patient Education and Preparation For Discharge

Patient education includes: (1) maintaining a high standard of oral hygiene; (2) monitoring for signs of complications, such as swelling, signs of infection or damage to the means of fixation; (3) maintaining a safe environment; (4) avoiding alcohol, which can impair consciousness; (5) warning that the antibiotic metronidazole, commonly prescribed prophylactically, can induce vomiting in conjunction with alcohol; (6) avoiding sports until advised otherwise; (7) such patients commonly request wire cutters to take home with them, but this is unnecessary; (8) maintaining calorie intake (the use of a food blender will greatly assist in the preparation of meals).

CONDITIONS OF THE OESOPHAGUS

The oesophagus is a mucous-lined, muscular tube that allows food to enter the stomach. It begins at the base of the pharynx and ends about 4 cm below the diaphragm. Its ability to transport food and fluid is facilitated by two sphincters: the pharyngo-oesophageal at the junction of the pharynx and the oesophagus, and the gastro-oesophageal at the junction of the oesophagus and the stomach.

An incompetent gastro-oesophageal sphincter allows reflux (backward flow) of gastric contents.

Difficulty in swallowing (dysphagia) is the most common symptom of oesophageal disease. This symptom may range from an uncomfortable feeling that a bolus of food is 'caught' in the upper oesophagus (before it eventually passes into the stomach), to acute pain on swallowing (odynophagia). Obstruction to the passage of food (solid and soft) and even liquids may be felt anywhere along the oesophagus. Often the patient can indicate whether the problem is located in the upper, middle or lower third of the oesophagus.

There are many pathological conditions of the oesophagus, with the order of frequency beginning with achalasia and progressing to diffuse spasm, diverticula, perforation, foreign bodies, chemical burns, hiatal hernias, benign tumours and carcinoma. A discussion of these conditions is preceded by an overview of nursing process for patients with oesophageal disorders.

NURSING PROCESS OVERVIEW: PATIENTS WITH CONDITIONS OF THE OESOPHAGUS

▶ Assessment

The nurse elicits a complete health history. If the patient is thought to have an oesophageal disorder, appropriate questions to ask will include those about changes in appetite. Has it remained the same, increased or decreased? Is there any discomfort with swallowing? If so, does it occur only with certain foods? Is it associated with pain? Does a change in position affect the discomfort? The patient is asked to describe the pain experience. Does anything aggravate it? Are there any other symptoms that occur regularly, such as regurgitation, nocturnal regurgitation, eructation (belching), heartburn, substernal pressure, a sensation that food is sticking in throat, a feeling of early satiety, nausea, vomiting or weight loss? Are the symptoms aggravated by emotional upset? If the patient reports any of these complaints, the nurse questions those factors that affect them, such as the time of their occurrence; their relationship to eating; factors that relieve or aggravate them, such as position change, belching, antacids or vomiting. The nursing assessment also includes questions about the existence of past or present causative factors, such as infections and chemical, mechanical or physical irritants. A history of alcohol and tobacco use is elicited. The nurse determines whether the patient looks emaciated.

▶ Patient's Problems

Based on the assessment, the patient's problems may include the following:

- Alteration in nutritional status, related to difficulty with swallowing.
- Pain related to ingestion of an abrasive agent, a tumour or frequent episodes of gastric reflux.
- Lack of knowledge about the oesophageal disorder, diagnostic studies, medical management, surgical intervention and rehabilitation.

▶ Planning and Implementation
▶ Expected Outcomes

The main outcomes for the patient may include attainment of an adequate nutritional intake, relief of pain and improvement in knowledge level.

Nursing Care

Adequate Nutritional Intake

The patient is encouraged to eat slowly and chew the food thoroughly to facilitate its passage to the stomach. Small, frequent feeds of bland food are recommended to promote digestion and prevent tissue irritation. Sometimes liquid swallowed with food will facilitate passage. An atmosphere for eating that will help stimulate the appetite should be provided. The patient should avoid using irritants such as tobacco and alcohol. A baseline weight is obtained and regular weights are recorded. A food chart may be used to calculate the patient's daily intake. Calories are counted to estimate daily food intake.

Relief of Pain

Small, frequent feeds are recommended because large quantities of food overload the stomach and promote gastric reflux. The nurse suggests that the patient avoid very hot and cold beverages and spicy foods because they stimulate oesophageal spasm and increase the secretion of hydrochloric acid. The patient is advised to avoid any activities that put strain on the thoracic area and increase pain. The patient should remain upright for one to four hours after each meal to prevent reflux by using gravity to decrease an elevated gastro-oesophageal pressure gradient. It may help to raise the head of the bed. Eating is discouraged before bedtime.

The patient is advised not to abuse over-the-counter antacids because excessive use can cause rebound acidity. Antacid use should be directed by a doctor who can recommend the daily, safe quantity needed to neutralize gastric juices and prevent oesophageal irritation. Histamine antagonists are administered as prescribed to decrease gastric acid irritation.

Patient Education

The patient is prepared physically and psychologically for diagnostic tests, treatments and possible surgical intervention. The main nursing care involves reassurance and discussion about the purposes and procedures involved. Some disorders of the oesophagus evolve over time, while others are the result of trauma (e.g., chemical burns or perforation). The emotional and physical preparation for the latter groups is more difficult owing to the shortened time period and the circumstances of the injury. Evaluation of treatment must be ongoing and directed to whether the patient has enough information to participate in care and diagnostic efforts. If surgery is involved, immediate and longterm evaluation is similar to that of a patient having chest surgery.

The expected outcomes of rehabilitation will reflect whether surgery or more conservative measures such as diet, positioning and use of antacids were used in the treatment phase. If the condition is corrected, short-term evaluative measures may be sufficient. If an ongoing condition exists, the nurse must help the patient plan for needed physical and psychological adjustment and for follow-up care. Many elderly patients may be found in the group with ongoing conditions. These patients need support for realistic meal planning, use of medications and participation in a full life. A multidisciplinary approach is helpful here, including the dietician, social worker, family members and significant others.

Home Health Care

Chronic conditions (diffuse spasm, diverticula) require an individualized approach to home management. There may be a need for special food preparation (liquidized foods; bland, soft diets) and increased frequency of eating (four to six small servings per day). The medication schedule is adjusted to the patient's daily activities as much as possible. Analgesics and antacids can be taken as needed every three to four hours.

Emergency conditions (perforation, chemical burns) usually happen in the home or away from medical help and require emergency management. The patient is treated for shock and respiratory distress and transported as quickly as possible to a medical facility. Specific emergency measures for chemical burns can be found on page 505.

Foreign bodies in the oesophagus do not pose an immediate threat to life unless pressure is exerted on the trachea resulting in dyspnoea or the cessation of respirations. Educating the public to prevent accidental swallowing of foreign bodies or corrosive agents is a major health issue. (See Chapter 39 for emergency resuscitation measures.)

Postoperative home health care focuses on nutritional support, management of pain and respiratory function. Some patients are discharged from the hospital with a gastrostomy tube or a fine-bore nasogastric feeding tube in place as a temporary measure. The patient, family and/or significant others need specific advice about the management of equipment and treatments. (See page 517 for caring for a patient receiving total parenteral nutrition, and page 516 for the care of the patient with a gastrostomy. Postoperative nursing care for thoracic and/or abdominal surgery patients can be found in Chapters 2 (Perioperative Care) and 4. Nursing care for a patient receiving radiotherapy or chemotherapy is discussed in Chapter 2, Care of the Patient With Cancer.)

► *Evaluation*
► Expected Outcomes

1. Patient achieves an adequate nutritional intake.
    a. Eats small, frequent meals.
    b. Drinks water with small servings of food.
    c. Stops using irritants (alcohol, tobacco).
    d. Maintains a desired weight.
2. Is free of pain or able to control pain within an acceptable level.
    a. Avoids large meals and irritating foods.
    b. Takes antacids as prescribed.
    c. Maintains the upright position after meals for one to four hours.
    d. Experiences less eructation and chest pain.
3. Increases knowledge about oesophageal condition, treatment and prognosis.
    a. Understands cause of condition.
    b. Expresses rationale for medical or surgical management and diet/medication regime.
    c. Describes treatment programme.
    d. Practises preventive measures so accidental injuries are avoided.

Achalasia

Achalasia is the term used to designate functional oesophageal obstruction caused by neuromuscular changes that prevent relaxation of the inferior oesophageal sphincter. Nerve degeneration, oesophageal dilation and hypertrophy are parts of the clinical picture. Achalasia is usually associated with a lack of peristaltic activity in the oesophagus itself and with a failure of the oesophageal sphincter to relax in response to swallowing. Narrowing of the oesophagus just above the stomach results in increasing dilation of the oesophagus in the upper chest.

Clinical Features

The primary symptom of achalasia is that of difficulty in swallowing both liquids and solids. The patient has a sensation of food sticking in the lower portion of the oesophagus. As the condition progresses, regurgitation of the food is common; this may occur spontaneously or may be brought about by the patient to relieve the discomfort that is produced by the prolonged distension of the oesophagus by food that will not pass into the stomach. There may be secondary pulmonary complications due to spillover of oesophageal contents (aspiration pneumonia).

Diagnosis

Radiological studies show oesophageal dilation above the narrowing at the cardio-oesophageal junction. The diagnosis is confirmed by manometry, which shows the absence of primary peristalsis. Balloon oesophagoscopy and barium swallow help to confirm the diagnosis.

Management

The conservative approach to treating early achalasia involves stretching the narrowed area of the oesophagus. This is done by passing a tube orally into the oesophagus. A distensible bag at the end of the tube is positioned and inflated (Figure 12.10). Vigorous dilation has a 75 per cent success rate and only a 3 per cent incidence of perforation. The procedure can be painful; therefore, an analgesic or sedative is administered before the treatment.

Oesophagoscopy is recommended every three to five years because oesophageal carcinoma is associated with achalasia.

Diverticulum

A diverticulum is an outpouching of mucosa and submucosa that protrudes through a weak portion of the musculature (pulsion type). If there is a pulling outward of the oesophageal wall from inflamed or scarred peribronchial lymph nodes, the term traction diverticulum is used (Figure 12.11).

Pharyngo-oesophageal Diverticulum

The most common type of diverticulum, which is found three times more frequently in men than in women, is pharyngo-oesophageal pulsion diverticulum (Zenker's diverticulum), which occurs posteriorly through the cricopharyngeal muscle in the midline of the neck. It is usually seen in people over 60 years of age. The patient first notices difficulty in swallowing and a fullness in the neck. There may be complaints of belching, regurgitation of undigested food and gurgling noises after eating. The diverticulum, or pouch, becomes filled with food or liquid. When the patient assumes a recumbent position, undigested food is regurgitated and may also cause coughing, owing to irritation of the trachea. Halitosis and a sour taste in the mouth are also common, because of the decomposition of food retained in the diverticulum.

Diagnosis and Management. To determine the exact nature and location of a diverticulum, barium is ingested and X-ray films are taken. Oesophagoscopy is usually

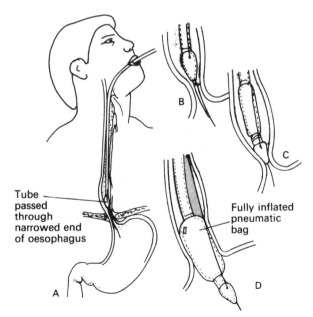

Figure 12.10 Treatment of achalasia: conservative approach. (A, B, C) The dilator is passed, guided by a previously swallowed thread, into the upper stomach. (D) When the balloon is in the proper position, it is distended by pressure sufficient to dilate the narrowed area of the oesophagus.

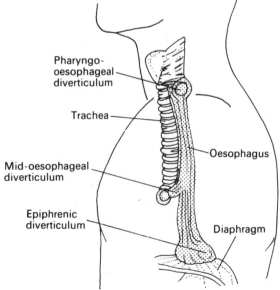

Figure 12.11 Possible sites for the occurrence of oesophageal diverticuli. The site will determine the location of the surgical incision to correct the problem.

contraindicated because of the danger of perforating the diverticulum, with resulting mediastinitis. The blind passing of a nasal tube should be avoided. The tube should be guided into the stomach under direct vision of a lighted endoscope. Because this patient is often a victim of unbalanced diet and fluid levels, an evaluation of the nutritional state is done to determine dietary needs.

Since the condition is progressive, the only means of cure is surgical removal of the diverticulum. Care is taken, surgically, to avoid undue trauma to the common carotid artery and internal jugular veins. The sac is dissected free and amputated flush with the oesophageal wall. In addition to a diverticulectomy, a myotomy of the cricopharyngeal muscle is often done, in order to relieve spasticity of the musculature, which otherwise seems to contribute to a continuation of the previous symptoms.

Nursing Care. When a patient has difficulty in swallowing, the diet is limited to foods that pass more easily. Liquidized meals supplemented with vitamins are usually prescribed. The nurse arranges for the dietician to see the patient and home carers to discuss plans for continuing this treatment at home.

Midoesophageal and Epiphrenic Diverticula

The occurrence of diverticula in the midtubular oesophagus is less common; symptoms are less acute, and usually the condition does not require surgery.

Traction diverticula are usually asymptomatic. They are found in the midoesophageal area and occur when inflamed lymph nodes near the tracheal bifurcation create a tension sac by adhering to the oesophagus as the tissue heals and contracts. No specific treatment is usually necessary.

Epiphrenic diverticula are usually larger pulsion diverticula occurring in the lower oesophagus just above the diaphragm, and occasionally higher. They are thought to be related to the improper functioning of the lower oesophageal sphincter.

Management. Surgery is indicated only if the symptoms are troublesome and growing progressively worse. A transthoracic (thoracotomy) approach is used, which means that preoperative and postoperative nursing management is similar to that for chest surgical patients (see Chapter 4).

Nursing Care. After surgery the patient is fed through a nasogastric tube that is usually inserted at the time of operation. The wound must also be observed for evidence of leakage from the oesophagus and a developing fistula.

If the operative risk is prohibitive, nursing care is similar to that advocated for the patient with a peptic ulcer: antacids, anticholinergics and abstinence from coffee, alcohol and smoking (see p. 527). In addition, reflux is avoided by: (1) keeping the head elevated; (2) remaining upright for two hours after meals; (3) avoiding abdominal compression from garments and posture; (4) eating small meals; and (5) losing weight, if necessary.

Perforation

The oesophagus is not an uncommon site of injury. Perforation may result from stab or bullet wounds of the neck or chest, as well as from accidental puncture by a surgical instrument during examination or dilation. Spontaneous perforation of the oesophagus has been known to occur during vomiting.

The patient experiences spontaneous pain followed by dysphagia. Infection, fever, leucocytosis and severe hypotension may be noted. Hyperpnoea and cervical tenderness are early signs of injury and crepitation. In some instances, signs of pneumothorax are observed. Radiographical examination and fluoroscopy can localize the injury.

Management
Because of the high risk of infection, broadspectrum antibiotic therapy is initiated. A nasogastric tube is passed, to provide suction and to reduce the amount of gastric juice that can reflux into the oesophagus and mediastinum. Nothing is given by mouth. Surgery is performed to close the wound, and postoperative nutritional support then becomes a primary concern. Total parenteral nutrition may be required. Depending on the incisional site and nature of surgery, the postoperative nursing care will be similar to that for patients who have had thoracic or abdominal surgery.

Foreign Bodies

Swallowed foreign bodies (dentures, fishbones, pins) may injure the oesophagus as well as obstruct its lumen. Pain and dysphagia may be present; dyspnoea may occur as a result of pressure. Radiographical findings are useful in identifying the foreign body.

Usually, foreign bodies can be removed with the aid of the oesophagoscope. When the foreign body is made of metal (pins, safety pins, needles, nails and tacks), it may not be safe to allow the object to make its way slowly through the stomach and intestinal tract. A bar magnet, fastened to a cable, may be manoeuvred into place with the aid of fluoroscopy and the object withdrawn. A Foley catheter can be manipulated past the object, the balloon inflated and the catheter and the foreign body removed. It is possible for a skilled oesophagoscopist to remove open safety pins through the oesophagoscope.

If an impacted bolus of meat is lodged in the oesophagus, it can usually be dissolved with proteolytic enzymes. The injuries to the oesophagus are the more serious part of the problem, because they may lead to deep cervical or mediastinal abscess or to stricture formation. Drainage of such abscesses requires thoracic surgery.

Chemical Burns

The patient who accidentally or intentionally swallows a strong acid or base is emotionally distraught as well as in acute physical pain. An acute chemical burn of the oesophagus is accompanied by severe burns of the lips, mouth and pharynx, with pain on swallowing and, sometimes, difficulty in respiration, due either to oedema of the throat or to a collection of mucus in the pharynx. The patient may be profoundly toxic, febrile and in shock. Emergency treatment consists of encouraging the patient to drink water to dilute the harmful substance. Dilution is not carried out if the patient has acute airway obstruction or swelling or if there is evidence of oesophageal, gastric or intestinal perforation. The patient is treated immediately for shock, pain and respiratory distress.

Management

Oesophagoscopy is performed as soon as possible to determine the extent and severity of damage. If the patient is able to swallow, fluids are given in small quantities. Secretions are aspirated from the pharynx if respiration is affected. The necessity for high fluid intake may require administration by parenteral means.

Corticosteroid therapy is also administered to suppress inflammation and to minimize subsequent scar and stricture formation. Antibiotics are given to combat infection and to prevent mediastinitis. A nasogastric tube is passed for feeding purposes and to ensure patency of the oesophageal lumen.

Occasionally, a patient is admitted after the acute phase has subsided but multiple stricture levels have formed in the oesophagus. These may be dilated by per oral use of bougies; if this is not successful, it may be necessary to try the retrograde bougienage method. A gastrostomy opening is made, and a braided silk string is swallowed. One end is brought out through the gastrostomy opening and the other end through the nose. The two ends are tied together and form a complete loop. Dilation is obtained by pulling larger and larger bougies upward through the oesophagus by means of the string. It is important that this string be left in place at all times. The gastrostomy is kept open by means of a gastrostomy tube, through which feeds may be given if necessary.

Hiatus Hernia

The oesophagus enters the abdomen through an opening in the diaphragm, to empty, at its lower end, into the upper part of the stomach. The opening in the diaphragm normally encircles the oesophagus tightly; therefore, the stomach lies completely within the abdomen. In a condition known as hiatus hernia, the opening in the diaphragm through which the oesophagus passes becomes enlarged, and part of the upper stomach tends to come up into the lower portion of the thorax. There are two types of hernias, sliding hernias and paraoesophageal hernias.

Sliding Hiatus Hernia

Sliding hiatus hernias occur when the upper stomach and the gastro-oesophageal junction are displaced upwards and slide in and out of the thorax. About 90 per cent of patients with oesophageal hiatus hernias have sliding hernias. Diagnosis is confirmed by radiographical studies and fluoroscopy (see Figure 12.12A).

Clinical Features and Management. The patient may experience heartburn, regurgitation and dysphagia. At least 50 per cent of the patients are asymptomatic. Medical management includes frequent, small feeds that can pass easily through the oesophagus. The patient is advised not to recline for one hour after eating to prevent reflux or movement of the hernia. The patient's bed should be elevated at the head on 10- to 20-cm blocks to prevent movement of the hernia by gravity. Surgery is indicated in about 15 per cent of patients.

Paraoesophageal Hernia

Paraoesophageal hernias occur when all or part of the stomach pushes through the diaphragm next to the gastro-oesophageal junction. Fewer than 10 per cent of patients experience paraoesophageal herniation, and many are asymptomatic. Reflux does not usually occur because the gastro-oesophageal sphincter is intact (Figure 12.12B).

Clinical Features and Management. The patient usually experiences a sense of fullness after eating. The complications of haemorrhage, obstruction and strangulation can occur, so an anterior gastropexy (fixation of prolapsed stomach in its normal position by suturing to the abdominal wall) is the treatment of choice.

Oesophageal Varices

Varices of the lower oesophagus are really a secondary feature of cirrhosis of the liver. This subject is discussed on page 593.

Benign Tumours

Benign tumours may arise anywhere along the oesophagus. The most common lesion is a leiomyoma, which can occlude the lumen of the oesophagus. Most benign tumours are asymptomatic and are distinguished from cancerous growths by a biopsy. Small lesions are excised during oesophagoscopy; thorocotomy may be necessary for intramural lesions.

Cancer of the Oesophagus

Carcinoma of the oesophagus occurs three times more frequently in men than in women in the United Kingdom,

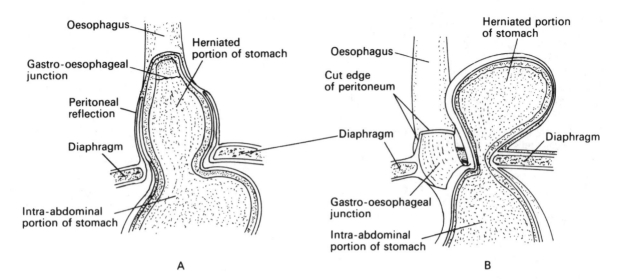

Figure 12.12 Sliding oesophageal and paraoesophageal herniae. (A) Sliding oesophageal hernia. Upper stomach and gastro-oesophageal junction are moved upwards and slide in and out of the thorax. (B) Paraoesophageal hernia. All or part of the stomach pushes through the diaphragm next to the gastro-oesophageal junction.

and usually occurs during the fifth decade of life. There is a 1 per cent incidence in the population (Office of Population Censuses and Surveys, 1988).

Altered Physiology and Clinical Features
Unfortunately, the patient may have an advanced ulcerated lesion of the oesophagus before symptoms present. Malignancy, usually of the squamous cell epidermoid type, may spread beneath the oesophageal mucosa, or it may spread directly into, through and beyond the muscle layers into the lymphatics. In the latter stages, obstruction of the oesophagus is noted, with possible perforation into the mediastinum and erosion into the great vessels.

Unfortunately, when symptoms exist that are related to oesophageal cancer, the disease is generally advanced. Symptoms include dysphagia, initially with solid foods and eventually with liquids; a feeling of a lump in the throat; painful swallowing; substernal pain or fullness; and, later, regurgitation of undigested food with foul breath and hiccoughs. The patient is first aware of intermittent and increasing difficulty in swallowing. At first only solid food gives trouble, but as the growth progresses and the obstruction becomes more complete, even liquids cannot pass into the stomach. Regurgitation of food and saliva occurs, haemorrhage may take place and there is a progressive loss of weight and strength owing to starvation. Later symptoms include substernal pain, hiccough, respiratory difficulty and foul breath. The delay between onset of early symptoms and the time when the patient seeks medical advice is often 12 to 18 months.

Diagnosis
Diagnosis is confirmed in 95 per cent of the cases by oeso-

phagoscopy with biopsy. Bronchoscopy is usually performed, especially in tumours of the middle and the upper third of the oesophagus, to determine whether the trachea has been involved by the tumour and to help in determining whether the lesion can be removed. Cancer of the lower end of the oesophagus may be due to adenocarcinoma of the stomach extending upwards into the oesophagus.

Management
Treatment includes surgery, radiotherapy, chemotherapy and, for some patients, laser endoscopy. The patient may be treated by surgical excision of the lesion, radiotherapy or a combination of both treatments. Usually, surgery is preferred for lower oesophageal tumours, whereas radiotherapy is favoured for upper oesophageal lesions. With radiotherapy, the lesion may shrink, thereby expanding the lumen and permitting the patient to swallow. Relatively few patients are cured; hence palliative therapy may be required, including combinations of treatment such as gastrostomy, jejunostomy, laser endoscopy, dilation of the stricture, insertion of the intraluminal prosthetic tube and chemotherapy.

The surgical approach may be through the thorax, or through the abdomen and thorax, depending on the location of the tumour. A common approach for lesions of the lower oesophagus is to remove the involved portion of the oesophagus and re-form the continuity of the gastrointestinal tract by bringing the stomach into the chest and implanting the proximal end of the oesophagus into it (oesophagogastrostomy). The chest is closed after a drain is inserted into the pleural cavity and connected to closed suction.

Lesions in the middle and upper thirds of the oesophagus, particularly, are often not suitable for surgical excision and, fortunately, occur less frequently.

Radiotherapy is used before surgery in some hospitals; in others, it is used after surgery. The ideal method of treating this problem has not yet been found; each patient is approached in a way that appears best for the individual. If the growth is found to be inoperable, either before or at operation, a gastrostomy is performed as a palliative procedure to permit the administration of food and fluids (see p. 516).

Prognosis

If the malignancy is detected early, removal is simplified and the continuity of the digestive system is easily maintained. However, the mortality rate among patients with cancer of the oesophagus is high, owing to three factors: (1) usually, the patient is an older person, in whom the incidence of pulmonary and cardiovascular disorders is high; (2) before significant symptoms occur, the tumour has already invaded surrounding structures, and it is impossible to excise a liberal area of tissue because of the proximity of vital structures; (3) the malignancy tends to spread to nearby lymph nodes, and the unique relation of the oesophagus to the heart and lungs makes these organs easily accessible to the extension of the tumour.

Nursing Care

Care is directed towards improving the patient's nutritional and physical condition in preparation for surgery, radiotherapy or laser therapy. A weight-gaining programme based on a high-calorie and high-protein diet, in liquid or soft form, is advocated, if it can be managed by mouth. If not, then feeding via a fine-bore nasogastric tube may be commenced.

The patient is educated about the nature of the postoperative equipment that will be used, including that required for closed chest drainage, nasogastric aspiration, intravenous fluid therapy and perhaps gastric intubation. Immediate postoperative care is similar to that provided for patients undergoing thoracic surgery (see Chapter 4). Following emergence from anaesthesia, the patient is placed in a semi-recumbent position, and later a recumbent position, to assist in preventing reflux of gastric secretions. The patient is observed carefully for regurgitation and dyspnoea. A common postoperative complication is aspiration pneumonia. Temperature is monitored to detect any elevation that may indicate seepage of fluid through the operative site into the mediastinum.

If a prosthetic tube has been inserted or an anastomosis has been done, the patient will have a functioning continuum between the throat and the stomach. Encouragement and patience will be needed as the patient begins to swallow small sips of water and, later, pureed small feeds. When the patient is able to increase food intake to a significant amount, intravenous fluids are discontinued. If a prosthetic tube (such as a pliable latex tube held open with fine wire coils) is used, it may easily become obstructed if food is not chewed sufficiently. After each meal, the patient is to remain upright for at least two hours to assist in the movement of food. The nurse is challenged to encourage this patient to eat, since the appetite is usually poor. Family involvement and home-cooked favourite foods may help the patient to eat. If gastric distress is a problem, antacids may help. When radiotherapy is part of the treatment, the patient's appetite is further depressed.

When the patient is ready to go home, the carer is advised about how to give nutritional care, what to observe, how to handle signs of complications, how to keep the patient comfortable and how to obtain needed physical and emotional support.

BIBLIOGRAPHY

Cocke, W. M., McShane, R. H. and Silverton, J. S. (1979) *Essentials of Plastic Surgery*, Little, Brown & Company, Boston.

Office of Population Censuses and Surveys (1988) *Mortality Statistics: England and Wales*, HMSO, London.

Scully, C. (1989) *Clinical Dentistry in Health and Disease: Volume 2—The Mouth and Perioral Tissues*, Heinemann Medical Books, Oxford.

Shklar, G. (ed.) (1984) *The Diagnosis, Therapy, Management and Rehabilitation of the Oral Cancer Patient*, W. B. Saunders, Philadelphia.

Toms, J. (1982) *Trends in Cancer Survival in Great Britain*, Cancer Research Campaign, London.

Wilkins, E. M. (1989) *Clinical Practice of the Dental Hygienist* (6th edition), Lea & Febiger, Philadephia.

FURTHER READING

Books

Conditions and Cancer of the Oral Cavity

Bates, B. (1987) *A Guide to Physical Examination and History Taking* (4th edition), J. B. Lippincott, Philadelphia.

Cawson, R. A. and Eveson, J. W. (1987) *Oral Pathology and Diagnosis*, Heinemann Medical Books, London.

del Regato, J. A., Spjut, H. J. and Cox, J. D. (1985) *Ackerman and del Regato's Cancer: Diagnosis, Treatment and Prognosis* (6th edition), C. V. Mosby, St Louis.

Forrest, J. (1985) *The Good Teeth Guide*, Granada, London.

McQuarrie, D. G., Adams, G. L. *et al.* (1986) *Head and Neck Cancer*, Year Book Medical, Chicago.

Moore-Gillon, V. and Stafford, N. (1987) *Aids to ENT*, Churchill Livingston, Edinburgh.

Pritchard, A. P. and David, J. A. (eds) (1988) *The Royal Marsden Hospital Manual of Clinical Nursing Procedures* (2nd edition), Harper & Row, London.

Salter, M. (1988) *Altered Body Image: The Nurse's Role*, John Wiley & Sons, London.

Radical Neck Dissection

Grabb, W. C. and Smith, J. W. (eds) (1978) *Plastic Surgery*, Little, Brown & Company, Boston.

Rowe, A. H. R., Alexander, A. G. and Johns, R. B. (eds) (1986) *Clinical Dentistry*, Blackwell Scientific, Oxford.

Articles

Conditions and Cancer of the Oral Cavity

Eilers, J. *et al.* (1988) Development, testing and application of the oral assessment guide, *Oncology Nursing Forum*, May/June, Vol. 15, No. 3, pp. 325–30.

Macleod Clark, J. (1982) *Nurse–Patient Verbal Interaction*, unpublished PhD thesis, University of London.

Parkinson, S. A. *et al.* (1987) Oral protein and energy supplements in cancer patients, *Human Nutrition: Applied Nutrition*, August, Vol. 41A, No. 4, pp. 233–43.

Roberts, A. (1986) Systems of Life, No. 141, Senior systems 6, *Nursing Times*, 17 September, Vol. 82, No. 38, pp. 51–4.

Vijayaram, S., Krishna Bhargava *et al.* (1989) Experience with oral morphine for cancer pain relief, *Journal of Pain and Symptom Management*, September, Vol. 4, No. 3, pp. 130–4.

Wilson Barnett, J. (1977) *Emotional Reactions to Hospitalization*, unpublished PhD thesis, University of London.

Fracture of the Mandible

Freedman, S. D. and Devine, B. A. (1987) A clean break: postoperative oral care, *American Journal of Nursing*, April, Vol. 87, No. 4, pp. 474–5.

Gotta, A. W. (1988) Airway management for maxillofacial trauma, *Nursing (USA)*, 14 April, Vol. 10, No. 5, pp. 34–40.

Mouthcare

Ferranti, G., Ash, R. C., Brown, A. T. *et al.* (1984) Chlorhexidine for prophylaxis against oral infections in patients receiving bone marrow transplant, *Journal of the American Dental Association*, Vol. 114, pp. 461–7.

McCord, F. and Stalker, A. (1988) Brushing up on oral care, *Nursing Times*, Vol. 84, No. 13, pp. 40–4.

Oliver, D. (1986) Oral thrush in hospice patients, *Nursing Times*, 5 November, Vol. 82, pp. 34–5.

Roberts, H. (1990) Mouthcare in oral cavity cancer, *Nursing Standard*, 31 January, Vol. 4, pp 26–9.

Torrance, C. (1990) Oral hygiene, *Surgical Nurse*, August, Vol. 3, No. 4, pp. 16–20.

Trenter Roth, P. T. and Creason, N. S. (1986) Nurse-administered oral hygiene: is there a scientific basis? *Journal of Advanced Nursing*, Vol. 11, No. 3, pp. 323–31.

chapter 13

GASTROINTESTINAL INTUBATION AND SPECIAL NUTRITIONAL SUPPORT

GASTROINTESTINAL INTUBATION

Gastrointestinal intubation is the insertion of a tube into the stomach or intestine by way of the mouth or nose to (1) decompress the stomach and remove gas and fluid, (2) diagnose gastrointestinal motility, (3) administer medications and feeds, (4) treat an obstruction or bleeding site and (5) obtain gastric contents for analysis. Any solution administered through a tube is either poured through a syringe or delivered from a drip reservoir by gravity or by an electric pump. Aspiration to remove gas and fluids is accomplished by using a syringe and/or a drainage bag. The tubes differ in composition (PVC, polyurethane, silicone), length (90 cm to 3 m), size (No. 6 Fr to No. 18 Fr), purpose and placement in the gastrointestinal tract (stomach, duodenum, jejunum).

Nasogastric Tubes

A nasogastric tube is introduced through the nose or the mouth into the stomach. Commonly used tubes include the Ryle's tube, Silk tube (Merck), Clinifeed tube (Roussel) and Flexiflo tube (Abbot).

Ryle's Tube
The Ryle's tube has a single lumen (No. 8 to 16 Fr) and is made of plastic with holes near its tip. The tube is used in adults to remove fluid and gas from the upper gastrointestinal tract, to obtain a specimen of gastric contents for laboratory studies and to administer medications or feed directly into the gastrointestinal tract. It must be noted that this particular tube is not ideally suited to longterm feeding due to the size of the tube and associated trauma.

Silk Tube
The Silk tube (Rees, Attrill *et al.*, 1986) is a polyurethane tube with a single lumen designed for longterm feeding purposes. Intubation is aided by a guide wire and it is possible to aspirate stomach contents due to the position

of holes on the side of the tube. Thus confirmation of feeding tube position is possible before removal of the guide wire. Polyurethane does not react with gastric juices like PVC, and the tube remains soft while *in situ*, promoting patient comfort. The Silk tube is 6 Fr and is available in a variety of lengths. It is vital that the tube is flushed with water at regular intervals to prevent blockage when used for feeding purposes.

Clinifeed Tube

The Clinifeed tube is a PVC tube appropriate for short-term feeding. It must be changed every 10 days as the tube reacts with the gastric juices and becomes hard. Position must be confirmed radiologically as it is not possible to aspirate stomach contents through such a tube. Intubation with a Clinifeed tube is achieved using a guide wire.

There are a variety of other feeding tubes available, such as Flexiflo tubes (Abbot Laboratories), which are made with PVC and polyurethane, and Prima tubes (Portex).

Nasoduodenal Tubes

A nasoduodenal tube is introduced through the nose and passed through the oesophagus and stomach into the intestinal tract. It may be used to aspirate intestinal contents to prevent gas and fluid from distending the coils of intestine or for feeding purposes. An example of a nasoduodenal tube is the Corsafe tube (Merck).

It usually takes 24 hours for the tube to pass through the stomach into the duodenum. Passage is facilitated by having the patient lie on the right side.

Because peristalsis either decreases or stops for 24 to 48 hours after an operation, owing to the effects of anaesthesia and of visceral manipulation, nasogastric or nasoduodenal aspiration are used for the following reasons:

● To evacuate fluids and flatus, so that vomiting is prevented and tension is reduced along the incision line.
● To reduce oedema, which can cause obstruction.

Usually, the tubes are allowed to remain in place after operation until peristalsis is resumed, as determined by the presence of bowel sounds.

Nursing Care of the Patient Undergoing Insertion of a Nasogastric Tube

Nursing care is organized into the following areas:

● Instructing the patient about the purposes of the tube and the procedures required for insertion.
● Inserting a nasogastric tube.
● Checking for placement of the nasogastric tube.
● Monitoring the patient.
● Providing oral and nasal hygiene.
● Removing the tube.

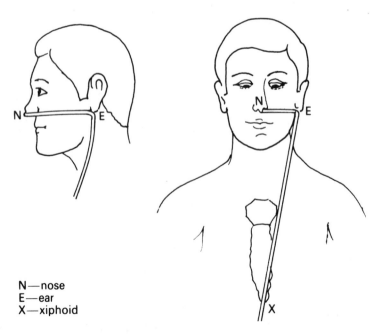

N—nose
E—ear
X—xiphoid

Figure 13.1 Determining the length of nasogastric tube to be inserted by measuring the distance from tip of nose, to ear lobe, to bottom of xiphisternum.(From: Hanson, R. L. (1979) Predictive criteria for length of nasogastric tube insertion for tube feeding, *Journal of Parenteral/Enteral Nutrition*, Vol. 3, No. 3, pp. 160–3.)

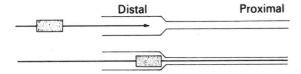

Figure 13.2 Diagram showing insertion of guide wire into tube before insertion into patient. A safety stopper prevents the guide wire from protruding through the proximal end of the tube. (From: Pritchard, P. A. and David, J. A. (1988) *The Royal Marsden Hospital Manual of Clinical Nursing Procedures* (2nd edition), Harper & Row, London.)

Instruction

Before the patient is intubated, the nurse explains the purpose of the tube. This information may make the patient more co-operative and tolerant of an initially unpleasant procedure. The general activities related to the passage of the tube are then reviewed, including the fact that the patient may have to breathe through the mouth and that passage of the tube may cause gagging until the tube has passed the gag reflex. It is sometimes appropriate to show the patient the tube to help allay anxiety. A signal by which the patient can communicate to the nurse that the procedure should be stopped must also be arranged.

Insertion of the Tube

During insertion, the patient sits upright, if possible, in order to allow easy passage of the tube. Having collected together all the necessary equipment, the nurse measures the distance on the tube from the patient's earlobe to the tip of the nose, to the bottom of the xiphisternum, and notes the mark on the tube (Figure 13.1). Tubes with guide wires will require insertion of the wire after lubrication with water, ensuring the wire does not protrude out of the proximal end of the tube (Figure 13.2).

Intubation with such tubes constitutes an extended role and must not be undertaken without adequate training and assessment. This is not the case for a tube without a guide wire. Instructions vary according to the type used and must always be read. The patient's nostrils need to be patent and clean. The tube is lubricated with water or lubricating jelly and inserted into the nostril. The tube slides backwards and inwards along the floor of the nose to the nasopharynx. The patient is asked to swallow and sip water as the tube passes over the nasopharynx, if possible, thus closing the glottis and enabling the passage of the tube into the oesophagus. The tube is advanced gently until the predetermined mark is reached (Figure 13.3). If a guidewire has been used, it is withdrawn gently and the tube is then secured using tape on an adhesive patch, if supplied (Figure 13.4).

Position of the Nasogastric Tube

Position is confirmed by aspirating gastric fluid through the tube and testing with litmus paper, introducing 5 ml of air into the stomach via the tube and checking for whooshing sounds using a stethoscope placed over the epigastrium (note: this should never be used as the only method of checking position), or by a chest X-ray on which the radio-opaque tube will show up.

Oral and Nasal Hygiene

Regular and conscientious oral and nasal hygiene are vital parts of patient care, since the tube may be in place for several days. Applicator sticks dipped in water can be used to clean the nose. This can be followed by cleansing with water-soluble oil. Frequent mouth attention is comforting. Throat lozenges, chewing gum (if permitted) and frequent movement assist in relieving discomfort. These activities will keep the mucous membranes moist and will help prevent mouth infection such as with *Candida*.

Assessment for Possible Complications

Patients undergoing intubation are susceptible to a variety of problems, including dehydration, pulmonary complications and mouth infections, which require careful ongoing assessment, as follows:

Dehydration

1. Symptoms indicating dehydration include:
   (a) Dryness of skin and mucous membranes.
   (b) Decreasing urinary output.
   (c) Lethargy and exhaustion.
   (d) Drop in body temperature.
2. Assessment of dehydration involves maintaining an accurate record of the following:
   (a) Drainage—amount, colour and type.
   (b) Amount and character of vomit, if any.
   (c) Effects produced by the treatment.

Pulmonary Complications

1. Nasogastric intubation produces a higher incidence of postoperative pulmonary complications by interfering with coughing and clearing of the pharynx.
2. The patient is encouraged to cough and to take deep breaths regularly. The nurse also carefully confirms the proper placement of the tube before instilling any fluids.

Mouth Infections

1. When administering oral hygiene, the nurse carefully inspects the mucous membranes for signs of irritation or excessive dryness.
2. The nostrils, oral mucosa, oesophagus and trachea are susceptible to irritation and necrosis. Visible areas are inspected frequently and the adequacy of hydration is assessed. In addition, the patient is assessed for the

presence of oesophagitis and tracheitis. Symptoms include sore throat and hoarseness.

Psychological Care

Patients with nasogastric tubes often feel uncomfortable and unattractive. It is vital that they are supported throughout the time the tube is in place and that they are given the time to talk about their frustrations and feelings. Many hospitals now have clinical nutrition nurses who may be available to provide psychological support to such patients.

ENTERAL FEEDING

Tube feeds are given to meet nutritional requirements when oral intake is inadequate or impossible. Tube feeds are delivered to the stomach (nasogastric) or the distal duodenum or proximal jejunum when it is necessary to

bypass the oesophagus and stomach. Some of the disorders that may result in an individual requiring enteral feeding are listed in Table 13.1.

Liquid formulas are designed to improve nutritional intake by either oral or tube administration. Tube feeds have several advantages:

- Intraluminal delivery of nutrients preserves gastrointestinal integrity.
- Tube feeds preserve the normal sequence of intestinal and hepatic metabolism before nutrient delivery to the arterial circulation.
- The intestinal mucosa and liver are important in fat metabolism and are the only sites of lipoprotein synthesis.
- Normal insulin–glucagon ratios are maintained with the intestinal administration of carbohydrates.

Commercial formulas frequently present problems because the composition is 'fixed'. Some patients may not

Figure 13.3 The enteral feeding tube (6 Fr) is passed readily into the stomach.

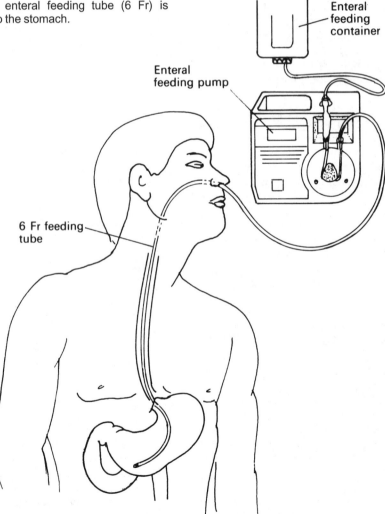

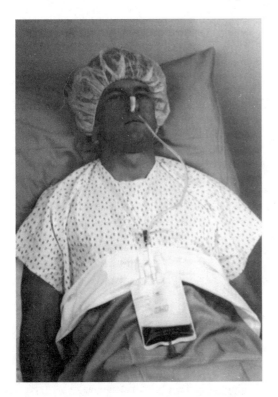

Figure 13.4 Nasogastric tube attachment and drainage bag. The tube is secured to the nose to prevent displacement. (Photograph courtesy of Towic Medical, Inc., Park Ridge, Illinois.)

Table 13.1 *Disorders and problems necessitating enteral feeding*

1. Gastrointestinal disorders such as Crohn's disease, short bowel syndrome, bowel fistulae and problems with absorption
2. Nutritional deficits occurring during radiotherapy and chemotherapy for malignant disease
3. Nutritional deficits following surgery
4. Coma, semiconsciousness following, for example, a cerebrovascular accident or head injury
5. Hypermetabolic states due to burns, major trauma or sepsis
6. Inability to maintain nutritional intake following maxillofacial or oral surgery
7. Oesophageal stenosis or obstruction
8. A loss of gag reflex
9. Renal failure

be able to tolerate certain ingredients, such as sodium, protein or potassium. In such cases, the dietician may be able to prepare an appropriate feed. Attention is given to including all essential minerals and vitamins. Total intake of calories and nutrients is assessed when there is a reduction in total intake, or excessive dilution, of feeds.

Many patients are highly resistant to tube feeds,

particularly those feeds administered via nasogastric tubes. Often a fine-bore polyurethane tube is tolerated better than a plastic one. The finer-bore tube, however, requires a finely dispersed formula and frequent flushing to prevent the tube from clogging.

A wide variety of containers, feeding tubes, delivery systems and pumps are available for use in tube or enteral feeds. It is suggested that reservoirs that can contain up to 1.5 litres of feed are preferable as this enables commercially prepared, sterile feeds to be dispensed with minimal handling. This reduces the risk of bacterial contamination. Larger reservoirs also improve the ratio of administered feed/prescribed feed (Payne-James, Rees, *et al.*, 1988). Some commonly used commercial tube feeds include Ensure, Clinifeed and Fortison. Pulmocare is a specialized formula for patients with pulmonary disorders that is high in fat and low in carbohydrates. Its high density (1.5 calories/ml) is ideal for patients who require fluid restriction, and it is also designed to reduce carbon dioxide production.

Some feeds are given as supplements, and others are provided to meet the patient's total nutritional needs. Dieticians work closely with doctors and nurses in determining the best formula for the individual patient.

Osmosis and Osmolality

Solutions that are highly concentrated upset the normal water balance within the body. Fluid balance is maintained by the process of osmosis. It is accomplished within the body by moving water through membranes from a dilute solution of lower osmolality to a more concentrated one of higher osmolality until the solutions are nearly of equal osmolality. The osmolality of normal body fluids is approximately 300 mOsm/kg. The body attempts to keep the osmolality of the contents of the stomach and intestines at approximately this level.

The proteins are extremely large particles and therefore have little or no osmotic effect. However, individual amino acids and carbohydrates are smaller particles and therefore have greater osmotic effect. Fats are not water soluble and do not form a solution in water; thus, they have no osmotic effect. Since electrolytes such as sodium and potassium are comparatively small particles, they have a great effect on osmolality, and consequently on tolerance.

Osmolality is an important consideration for patients being fed past the pylorus. When a concentrated solution of high osmolality is taken in large amounts, water will move to the stomach and intestines from fluid surrounding the organs and the vascular compartment. The patient experiences a feeling of fullness, nausea and diarrhoea, which can bring about dehydration, resulting, in some cases, in hypotension and tachycardia. Collectively, these symptoms have been termed 'dumping syndrome'. This problem can be avoided by starting with a low volume of feed administered at a slow rate, and increasing the rate over a few days (Jones, 1986).

There is a wide range of tolerance among patients as to the effects of osmolality. Usually, debilitated patients are more sensitive to such disorders. Therefore, the nurse should be knowledgeable about the osmolality of formulas and should observe the patient in order to detect or prevent such disorders.

► NURSING PROCESS
► THE PATIENT RECEIVING A TUBE FEED

► Overview

When caring for a patient receiving tube feeds, the nurse aims to establish an adequate nutritional intake while maintaining the patient's physical comfort, meeting psychological needs and avoiding complications.

► Assessment

The nurse participates in the nutritional assessment of patients. A preliminary assessment may include information from the patient's family or other informal carers, and should answer the following questions:

● What is the patient's nutritional status as judged by current physical appearance; dietary history, including a history of food allergies, likes and dislikes; and recent weight loss or gain?
● Are there any existing chronic illnesses or situations that will increase metabolic demands on the body?
● Is the patient's fluid and electrolyte balance in order?
● Is the patient's digestive tract functioning? Does it have good absorptive capacity?
● Does the patient have any renal impairment?
● What medications is the patient taking, and what other therapy is the patient receiving that may affect the digestive intake and digestive system?
● Does the patient's present dietary intake meet nutritional needs?

In addition, a more elaborate assessment is done for those patients who may require intensive nutritional therapy. This is done by a nutrition team that includes the nurse, doctor, dietician and pharmacist. In addition to the history and physical examination, nutritional assessment consists of recording any weight change, determining biochemical indications of malnutrition such as low plasma albumin levels.

► Patient's Problems

Based on the assessment, the patient's main problems may include the following:

● Inadequate nutritional intake resulting in weight loss.
● Dehydration due to an alteration in bowel habit, e.g., diarrhoea and an inadequate fluid intake.

● An inability to eat enough to meet the metabolic demands of the body.
● An inability to eat enough due to swallowing difficulties.
● Anxiety and possibly depression due to the necessity of having a tube in place.
● The potential problem of aspirating feed due to ineffective airway clearance.

► Planning and Implementation
► Expected Outcomes

The main outcomes for the patient may include achievement and maintenance of nutritional balance, maintenance of a normal bowel pattern, maintenance of a patent airway and improvement in individual coping mechanisms.

Nursing Care

Nutritional Balance

When preparing and administering a tube feed, it is essential that all measures of cleanliness be observed. Volume of the feed, flow rate and adequate fluid intake are all-important.

The prescribed quantity and frequency of tube feeds needs to be maintained. The nurse must therefore carefully monitor the rate of intravenous infusion and avoid too rapid administration of fluids. Several pumps have been designed specifically for enteral tube feeds and are lightweight, easy to handle and are readily available in most hospitals.

The newer polyurethane feeding tubes have small diameters (No. 6 to 8 Fr) and some have a water-activated lubricant that makes it easier to place the tube and insert and remove the guide wire. The various tubes come with instructions for ease of passage. Since they are softer, more pliable and much thinner than the conventional nasogastric tube, they provide greater patient comfort. However, kinking of tubing may present a problem.

Before and after the administration of tube feeds, water is administered to ensure tube patency and to decrease the chance of bacterial growth, tube crusting or occlusion. Feeds are administered either by gravity (intravenous infusion) or by continuous controlled pump.

Feeds are lactose free, with an osmolality of only 300 mOsm/kg; a feed may be given undiluted and provides 1 calorie/ml. Feeding rates of about 100 to 150 ml/hr (2,400 to 3,600 calories/day) are effective in inducing positive nitrogen balance and progressive weight gain, without producing abdominal cramps and diarrhoea. If the feed is intermittent, 200 to 350 ml is given in 10 to 15 minutes. Additional water after feeding is important to prevent hypertonic dehydration.

Continuous monitoring of the tube-feeding regime is necessary to determine its effectiveness.

- Assess placement of tube, position of patient and flow rate.
- Observe patient's ability to tolerate the formula (assess for feeling of fullness, bloating, nausea, vomiting, diarrhoea and constipation).
- Assess the patient's general condition by noting the appearance of the skin (turgor, dryness, colour) and mucous membranes; urinary output; state of hydration; and weight gain or loss.
- Observe for signs of dehydration (dry mucous membranes, thirst, decreased urine output).
- Record the actual formula intake by the patient, including incidents of vomiting and diarrhoea or distension.
- Note any signs of inability of the patient to communicate.
- Assess for possible complications (Table 13.2).

Bowel Pattern

Patients having nasogastric or nasoduodenal tube feeds frequently experience diarrhoea (watery stools occurring three or more times in 24 hours). Pasty, unformed stools are expected with enteral feeding because most formulas have little or no residue. The dumping syndrome also leads to diarrhoea. To confirm that the dumping syndrome is causing the diarrhoea, other possible causes must be ruled out: zinc deficiency, contaminated formula, malnutrition (a decrease in the intestinal absorptive area resulting from malnutrition can cause diarrhoea) and drug therapy. Antibiotics such as clindamycin, anti-arrhythmic drugs (quinidine, propranolol), aminophylline and digitalis are known to increase the frequency of the dumping syndrome in certain patients.

The dumping syndrome results from the rapid distension of the jejunum when hypertonic solutions are administered quickly (over 10 to 20 minutes). Foods high in carbohydrates and electrolytes draw extracellular fluid from the blood into the jejunum so that dilution and absorption can occur. The gastrointestinal symptoms (diarrhoea, nausea) associated with the dumping syndrome can be managed by the following:

- Decreasing the instillation rate to provide time for carbohydrates and electrolytes to be diluted.
- Giving the feeds at room temperature, because temperature extremes stimulate peristalsis.
- Administering the feed by continuous intravenous infusion rather than bolus (if permitted) to prevent sudden distension of the intestine.

Airway Management

Airway obstruction occurs when stomach contents or enteral feeds are regurgitated and aspirated or when a nasogastric tube is improperly placed and feeds are instilled into the pharynx or the trachea.

To maintain a patent airway, the nurse should always check tube placement before giving a feed. Aspiration is less likely to occur if the patient sits upright.

If aspiration is suspected, the feed is stopped, the nasogastric tube is removed and the pharynx and trachea are suctioned if necessary. The nurse should notify a doctor, remain calm and be supportive to such patients, who may feel that they are going to suffocate and die.

Promoting Coping Ability

The psychosocial goal of nursing care is to provide support, encouragement and a warm acceptance of the patient, while conveying hope that daily progressive improvement is possible. Nursing interventions may include the following:

- Praising patients when they adhere to the proposed plan of care.
- Encouraging self-care within the parameters of the patient's ability (making the bed, recording daily weight and intake and output).
- Reinforcing an optimistic approach by mentioning signs and symptoms that indicate progress (daily weight gain, electrolyte balance, absence of nausea and diarrhoea).

Patient Education

Preparation for home care management of enteral feeds begins when the patient is hospitalized. The nurse teaches while administering the feeds so that the mechanics of the procedure are observed and reinforced. Before discharge, information is provided about the equipment, supply of feeds and storage, and administration of the feeds (frequency, quantity, rate of instillation). Family members who will participate in the patient's care are invited to participate. Available printed information about the delivery equipment and formula is given to the patient. The patient is encouraged to handle the equipment under the supervision of a nurse.

Table 13.2 *Complications of enteral feeding*

Complication	Cause
Tube displacement	Excessive coughing Tension on the tube Tracheal suctioning Airway intubation
Nasopharyngeal irritation	Tube position
Diarrhoea	Hyperosmolar feeds Rapid infusion Feeding administered at a temperature that is either too hot or too cold
Dehydration	Hyperosmolar feeds with insufficient fluid intake
Atelectasis and possible pneumonia	Aspirated tube feeding

Nutrition teams are now more commonly taking responsibility for patients who are to be discharged home with nasogastric feeds. The nutrition nurse is able to help the patient, family and others learn the necessary procedures, and also provides a link between hospital and community.

▶ Evaluation

When evaluating the nursing care of a patient who is receiving tube feeds, it is important that the goals are realistic. For example, it may not be possible for a patient with an oesophageal tumour to achieve a positive nitrogen balance. However, such a patient may be able to maintain body weight and avoid the problems of dehydration.

Alterations in bowel habits are a common problem for patients receiving enteral feeds. Evaluation will assess whether the patient is able to avoid suffering from abdominal cramps and diarrhoea.

Psychological evaluation will include looking for signs of a willingness to participate in care, cues of an optimistic approach and perhaps a willingness to provide support to other individuals who require tube feeds.

GASTROSTOMY

A gastrostomy tube is inserted to create an opening into the stomach for the purpose of administering food and fluids. In some instances, a gastrostomy tube is used for prolonged feeds. Gastrostomy is preferred to nasogastric feeds in the comatose patient because regurgitation is less likely to occur. Gastrostomy tubes are placed either surgically or by using percutaneous endoscopic technique (Payne-James, Rees *et al.*, 1988).

▶ NURSING PROCESS
▶ THE PATIENT UNDERGOING A GASTROSTOMY

▶ Assessment

Preoperative Assessment
The focus of the preoperative assessment is on determining the patient's ability to understand the surgical experience and the manner in which the impending surgery is being dealt with. The ability to adjust to a change in body image and to participate in self-care is evaluated, along with the patient's, the family's and significant others' psychological states. Is the patient depressed, angry, withdrawn or optimistic? Will family and friends be supportive?

The purpose of the operative procedure is explained to the patient so that there is a better understanding of the postoperative course. The patient needs to know that the purpose of this surgery is to bypass the oesophagus, and that liquid feeds will be administered directly into the stomach by means of a tube. When the procedure is being done to relieve discomfort, prolonged vomiting, debilitation and the inability to eat, it is often viewed positively by the patient.

Postoperative Assessment
In the postoperative period the patient's fluid and nutritional needs are assessed to ensure proper food and fluid intake. The nurse checks the status of the tube and the wound for proper maintenance and any signs of infection. At the same time, the patient's reaction to the change in body image and understanding of the methods for carrying out the feeding procedure are evaluated to determine the care needed to help the patient cope with the presence of the tube and to learn self-care measures.

▶ Patient's Problems

Based on the assessment, the patient's main problems in the postoperative period may include the following:

● Inadequate nutritional intake to meet body requirements, related to enteral feeding problems.
● Potential infection related to the presence of wound and tube.
● Potential impairment of skin integrity related to enteral feeds.
● Ineffective coping related to the inability to eat normally.
● Disturbance in self-concept/body image related to the presence of the tube.
● Lack of knowledge about the feeding procedure.

▶ Planning and Implementation
▶ Expected Outcomes
The main outcomes for the patient may include attainment of the desired level of nutrition, maintenance of skin integrity, absence of infection, improvement in coping methods, adjustment to changes in body image and acquisition of sufficient knowledge about the tube feeding regime.

Nursing Care

Nutritional Needs
Water is administered in small volumes to the patient via the gastrostomy, as requested by the surgeon. The volume is increased gradually and, if tolerated, will be followed by an enteral feed recommended by the dietician. Reservoirs and pumps may be used as for the instillation of a nasogastric feed. In the long term, the patient may find bolus feeds more convenient.

Tube Care and Infection Precautions
The tube can be held in place by a thin strip of adhesive that is first twisted about the tube and then firmly attached

to the abdomen. A spigot may be used to close the tube following a feed to prevent leakage. A small dressing can be applied over the tube outlet. This protects the skin surrounding the incision from the seepage of gastric acid contents and the spillage of feeds.

Skin Care

The skin surrounding a gastrostomy opening requires special care. It may become irritated owing to the enzymatic action of gastric juices that leak around the tube. If untreated, the skin becomes macerated, red, raw and painful. Daily washing with soap and water around the tube, and the application of a bland ointment such as zinc oxide or petrolatum are protective measures.

Skin status is evaluated daily for signs of breakdown, irritation or excoriation. The patient and family members or significant others should be encouraged to participate in this inspection and in hygiene activities.

Body Image Adjustment

The patient with a gastrostomy has experienced a major assault on body image. A normal body function, eating, can no longer be taken for granted. The patient is also aware that gastrostomy as a therapeutic intervention is only done in the presence of a major, chronic or perhaps terminal illness. Calm discussion of the purposes and routines of gastrostomy feeding can help keep gastrostomy from becoming an overwhelming situation. Talking with a person who has had a gastrostomy can also help the patient to accept the expected changes. Adjusting to a change in body image takes time and requires support and acceptance from family and close friends. An evaluation of the existing personal support system is necessary. One family member or significant other may emerge as the primary support person. If so that person will become the major communicator between the patient and health care team.

Patient Education

The nurse assesses the patient's level of knowledge, interest in learning about the procedure and ability to understand and apply the information. Detailed instructions about management of the tube feeds are provided. To facilitate self-care, the patient is advised in post-hospital care and encouraged to establish as normal a routine as possible. These expected outcomes are achieved through teaching about tube feeds and tube and skin care and through ongoing evaluation by questioning and practice by the patient. Patients (or caregivers in the home setting) must view themselves as capable and responsible for care; know the method and frequency of administration of self-care activities; and have adequate supplies, including the physical, financial and social resources to maintain care. In addition to individual teaching, the use of printed instructions is necessary as a reinforcement. Adequate provision of supervision and support must be arranged.

Demonstration of feeding begins by showing the patient how to check for residual gastric content before the feeding. The patient then learns how to determine the patency of the tube by administering water at room temperature before the feeding and after to clear the tube of food particles, which could decompose if allowed to remain in the tube. All feeds are given at room temperature or near body temperature.

For a bolus feed, the patient is shown how to introduce the liquid into the catheter by using the barrel of a syringe. As the syringe fills with liquid, the feed is allowed to flow into the stomach by gravity by holding the syringe perpendicular to the abdomen (Figure 13.5). The rate of flow is regulated by raising or lowering the receptacle above the abdominal wall.

With a bolus feed, usually 300 to 500 ml is given for each meal and requires 10 or 15 minutes to complete. The amount is often determined by the patient's reaction. If the patient feels 'full' it may be desirable to give smaller amounts more frequently. Keeping the head of the bed elevated for at least half an hour after feeding facilitates digestion. Any obstruction requires that the feeding be stopped and the doctor notified.

Some patients smell, taste and chew small amounts of food before taking their tube feeds. This procedure stimulates the flow of salivary and gastric secretions and may give some sensation of normal eating.

A tube feed may also be given by intermittent or continuous infusion via a feeding pump. Instruction in the use of the particular pump is provided. Most enteral feeding systems have built-in alarms that signal when the bag is empty, when the battery is low, or if an occlusion is present.

TOTAL PARENTERAL NUTRITION

Total parenteral nutrition is the administration of nutrients directly into the venous circulation, and is reserved for those patients whose gastrointestinal tract is nonfunctional. It is an expensive form of nutritional support and, unless experienced care is available, carries with it a number of potential risks. Total parenteral nutrition consists of water, amino acids, glucose, fat, vitamins, electrolytes and trace elements, and is infused into a central vein or occasionally a peripheral vein. It is prepared in a sterile production unit by experienced pharmacists and usually comes in a single 'big bag' for infusion into the patient. This helps to reduce the risk of infection by cutting the number of times the system is manipulated once the feed is being administered to the patient.

Regimes will differ from one hospital to another according to the manufacturer used and the advice given by either the nutrition team or the medical staff managing nutritional care. Many hospitals have now decided to have a number of standard regimes available to simplify prescribing and to minimize mistakes.

Patients who need total parenteral nutrition include:

- Those who have a nonfunctioning gut, e.g., post-gastrointestinal surgery, paralytic ileus.
- Those who are hypercatabolic and unable to achieve an adequate intake enterally, e.g., patients with severe burns or major trauma.
- Those suffering an acute exacerbation of inflammatory bowel disease or pancreatitis.
- Those with high enterocutaneous bowel fistulae.
- Those who are unable to tolerate enteral feeding during and following chemotherapy and bone marrow transplantation.

Method of Administration

Once the decision to feed an individual parenterally has been made, the nutrition team or medical staff caring for the patient will decide on an appropriate regime according to the individual's nutritional requirements. The specific contents of regimes will vary according to the manufacturer and hospital policy.

Total parenteral nutrition is a potentially hazardous therapy and care needs to be taken at every stage to avoid complications. The solutions used are hypertonic and consequently are very irritant to veins. For this reason, solutions are normally infused into a large vein such as the subclavian vein or superior vena cava. A large vein with rapid blood flow ensures rapid dilution of the solutions. A catheter inserted to infuse total parenteral nutrition is used only for that purpose, except in unusual circumstances, e.g., following bone marrow transplantation a patient will have a multi-lumen catheter inserted (Figure 13.6). Medications, with the exception of insulin, are infused into different lines due to possible incompatibilities, and blood samples are taken from other available veins to avoid contamination of the system. Infection is one of the major complications that may occur during the infusion of total parenteral nutrition.

Preparation of Patient Before Insertion of Central Venous Line

Central venous lines to be used for feeding purposes are usually inserted in an operating theatre or in a room put

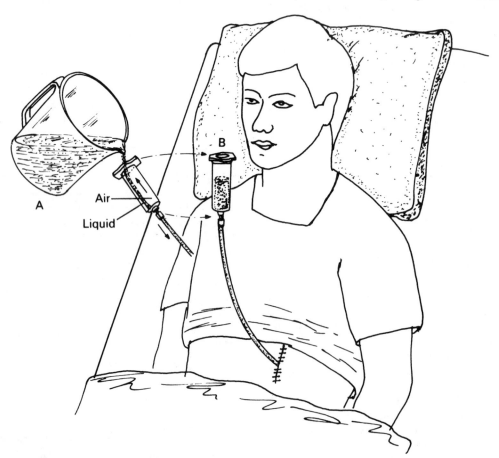

Figure 13.5 Gastrostomy feeding by gravity. (A) Feed is instilled at an angle so that air does not enter the stomach. (B) Syringe is raised perpendicular to stomach so that feed can enter by gravity.

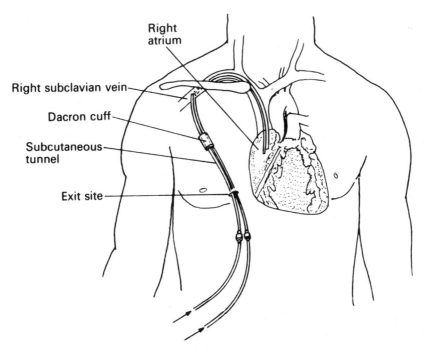

Right
atrium

Right subclavian vein

Dacron cuff

Subcutaneous
tunnel

Exit site

Figure 13.6 Double-lumen Hickman catheter used for total parenteral nutrition in those patients requiring other intravenous therapy in addition to total parenteral nutrition, e.g., drug therapy following bone marrow transplantation.

aside specifically for line insertion. The aim is to reduce the risk of infection. The patient needs to be prepared for this procedure as for any operation. In addition, time is needed to describe the concepts of total parenteral nutrition in terms that can be understood by the patient.

Individuals who have hairy chests may require assistance either to shave or use a depilatory cream.

If the procedure is to be carried out under local anaesthetic then a description of what to expect is also needed. This will include details of what the patient should expect to feel, the position that the patient will be asked to adopt and the length of time the procedure will take.

The most common site of insertion is the subclavian vein, although the jugular, cephalic or basilic veins are also used sometimes. The patient is positioned supine and the head is tilted downwards in order to dilate the blood vessels of the neck and shoulder. Sometimes a rolled sheet is placed vertically down the vertebral column in order to hyperextend the shoulders.

Following disinfection of the area, insertion of the catheter takes place. Commonly used catheters for feeding are the Hickman and Broviac catheters or the Nutricaths (Vygon). These are tunnelled through the subcutaneous tissue so that the exit site of the catheter is some distance from the entry point into the vein (Keohane, Jones *et al.*, 1983).

An image intensifier or X-ray is used to confirm the position of the catheter tip either in the superior vena cava or the right atrium, where rapid dilution of the nutrient solutions can take place. Following this, dressings are applied to the exit and insertion sites, and these are normally left in place for up to 10 days initially, unless excessive oozing occurs. Potential complications of insertion include pneumothorax and air embolism, and therefore careful observation of the individual after insertion is necessary.

▶ NURSING PROCESS
▶ THE PATIENT RECEIVING TOTAL PARENTERAL NUTRITION

▶ *Assessment*

It is possible that the nursing staff will be involved with the identification of those individuals who require total parenteral nutrition. The incidence of malnutrition in hospitals is high, and an awareness of nutritional needs is essential (see Chapter 2). Once an individual is receiving total parenteral nutrition, constant assessment is essential. This will include weighing the patient regularly; monitoring fluid input and output, and blood glucose levels; and observation of signs of any other potential problems such as infection, a mechanical problem associated with the system or other metabolic problems. An assessment of the individual's ability to cope psychologically with the method of feeding will also need to be made.

► *Planning and Implementation*

In the light of the information gathered when assessing the patient, a number of nursing needs will be identified, as follows:

● Potential infection due to contamination of the exit site of the catheter and/or feeding system (bag of feed, administration set, extension tube).
● Potential metabolic complications due to the administration of total parenteral nutrition, such as hyperglycaemia, fluid overload or hypophosphataemia.
● Potential mechanical problems with the feeding system.
● Potential difficulties in adapting psychologically to total parenteral nutrition.

Nursing Care

Infection Prevention

Any catheter used for total parenteral nutrition must be dedicated to that purpose to minimalize manipulation of the system and therefore the risk of contamination. It has been demonstrated that rigorous aseptic nursing care is the most significant factor in reducing catheter-related sepsis (Clarke, Tunbridge *et al.*, 1988; Keohane, Jones *et al.*, 1983).

In order to simplify the system, the feed for 24 hours is prepared under sterile conditions in a 'big bag', which can then be primed and set up by the bedside once a day. There is then no need to change bags and bottles of feed throughout the day. A sterile, non-touch technique is used to prime the administration set with the total parenteral nutrition and to attach it to the patient's catheter. Policy will vary from one hospital to another, but the principle of strict asepsis applies at all times.

Dressings over the exit site are changed aseptically according to the agreed hospital policy, which again may vary widely from one hospital to another. Changing both the total parenteral nutrition and the dressing constitute an 'extended role' and are carried out only by trained staff. Regular monitoring of temperature and pulse helps in the early detection of any signs of complications, as does observation of the exit site.

Metabolic Complications

It is important that the patient receives nutritional support at the correct rate. This is achieved by using an infusion pump, which ensures a constant and accurate flow of total parenteral nutrition. Some patients may be fed continuously, while others will be fed cyclically, allowing for a break during the day when the patient can be more mobile and free from restrictions. Fluid input and output is recorded. Hyperglycaemia is another potential problem, and blood sugar levels are therefore recorded regularly, particularly during the early stages of treatment. When the

individual proves to be tolerating total parenteral nutrition, with few fluctuations in blood sugar levels, then urinalysis can be used to detect any signs of glucose intolerance. However, when total parenteral nutrition is stopped, it should be done gradually as sometimes rebound hypoglycaemia may occur.

During the administration of total parenteral nutrition, the medical staff may request the collection of urine over a 24-hour period in order to determine the individual's nitrogen balance. Blood samples will also be taken regularly in order to monitor blood biochemistry as problems may occur and the composition of the feed may have to change accordingly. It is always important to check the contents of the feed against the prescription.

Mechanical Problems

Occasionally, catheters used for feeding purposes may fracture or block. This is unlikely if the correct infusion rate is maintained and atraumatic clamps are used to occlude the catheter when disconnection from the administration system is necessary. A short extension tube may be used between the catheter and the administration set for clamping purposes if the catheter is susceptible to a fracture. Flushing with saline, using an aseptic technique, will be necessary to avoid blockage if cyclical feeding is taking place.

Air embolism is another potential problem, which can be avoided by using luer-lock connections. These are most unlikely to disconnect. Correct clamping of the line will also help to avoid such a complication.

Psychological Care

The distress caused by preventing an individual from eating normally should not be underestimated, and it is important that support and time are given to the patient. It may be tactful to give an individual a bed away from where meals are served, and to offer some form of distraction during mealtimes. Eating is normally a pleasurable social activity: patients receiving total parenteral nutrition may go through a grief reaction as they cope with an inability to eat and an altered perception of body image related to the catheter system (Atkins, 1989).

Patient Education

It is now possible for patients to administer their own total parenteral nutrition at home, although careful planning and a well-established support system are essential (Field, 1988). Careful teaching by a nurse specialist will be necessary before the individual is discharged. The supply and storage of equipment will also need to be discussed. Involvement of family or close friends will be an important aspect of care, and the provision of a 'help line' is essential. Literature for patients receiving total parenteral nutrition at home is now available and will be an important reference source. A national support group set up by patients (PINNT) is available for individuals receiving total parenteral nutrition at home.

► *Evaluation*

Evaluation of the care given to a patient receiving total parenteral nutrition will focus on a number of factors, including whether the patient has achieved the nutritional goals set. It may not be realistic to expect a weight gain, but a maintenance of body weight may be achieved.

The avoidance of complications such as infection, metabolic problems or mechanical difficulties will be important. This can be achieved by observing the individual's catheter exit site, vital signs, fluid balance, blood glucose levels and the function of the feeding system.

Acceptance of the need for total parenteral nutrition and a determination to maintain normal activity for some individuals will provide a measure of coping. Evaluation needs to be realistic and ongoing in this area.

BIBLIOGRAPHY

Atkins, S. (1989) Parenteral nutrition—the nurse's role, *Surgical Nurse*, February, pp. 13–17.

Clarke, P. J., Tunbridge, A. *et al.* (1988) The total parenteral nutrition service: an update, *Annals of the Royal College of Surgeons of England*, Vol. 70, pp.296–9.

Field, J. (1988) Food down the line, *Journal of District Nursing*, May, pp. 4–5.

Jones, B. M. J. (1986) Enteral feeding: techniques of administration, *Gut*, Vol. 27, No. S1, pp. 47–50.

Keohane, P. P., Jones, B. J. M., *et al.* (1983) Effect of catheter tunnelling and a nutrition nurse on catheter sepsis during parenteral nutrition, *Lancet*, 17 December, pp. 1388–90.

Payne-James, J. J., Rees, R. G. P. *et al.* (1988) Enteral nutrition: clinical application, *Intensive Therapy and Clinical Monitoring*, November, pp. 239–46.

Rees, R. G., Attrill, D. *et al.* (1986) Improved design of nasogastric feeding tubes, *Clinical Nutrition*, Vol. 5, pp. 203–7.

FURTHER READING

Baughen, R. (1988) Nasogastric feeding—is your patient getting enough? *Nursing Standard*, October, Special Suppl., pp. 3–4.

Dickerson, J. W. T. and Booth, E. M. (1985) *Clinical Nutrition for Nurses, Dietitians and Other Health Care Professionals*, Faber & Faber, London.

Finnegan, S. (1989) Mechanical complications of parenteral nutrition, *The Professional Nurse*, Vol. 4, No. 7, pp. 325–7.

Finnegan, S. and Oldfield, K. (1989) When eating is impossible: TPN in maintaining nutritional status, *The Professional Nurse*, Vol. 4, No. 6, pp. 271–5.

Silk, D. B. A. (1983) *Nutritional Support in Hospital Practice*, Blackwell Scientific, Oxford.

chapter 14

ASSESSMENT AND CARE OF PATIENTS WITH GASTRIC AND DUODENAL DISORDERS

UPPER GASTROINTESTINAL TRACT BLEEDING

Gastritis and haemorrhage from peptic ulcer are the two most common causes of upper gastrointestinal tract bleeding. Haematemesis refers to the vomiting of blood. The vomited blood can be bright red or have a 'coffee-ground' appearance (haemoglobin changes to methaemoglobin in the stomach). The passage of dark, tarry stools (melaena) indicates upper gastrointestinal tract bleeding. Management depends on the amount of blood lost and the rate of bleeding.

Management
Management of upper gastrointestinal tract bleeding consists of (1) quickly determining the amount of blood lost and the rate of bleeding, (2) rapidly correcting the blood loss, (3) stabilizing the patient, and (4) diagnosing the cause. Specific medical and nursing care for upper gastrointestinal tract bleeding are discussed on pages 529–30 in the section entitled Complications of Peptic Ulcers.

Once the patient has been stabilized, endoscopy is performed in order to determine the cause. If the diagnosis is inconclusive, then upper gastrointestinal X-ray films can provide more information.

Rebleeding occurs in a number of patients depending on the cause of bleeding and whether risk factors (e.g. a visible vessel) were found. The patient is carefully monitored so that signs of bleeding can be quickly detected. These include decreased central venous pressure, tachycardia, tachypnoea, hypotension, mental confusion, thirst and oliguria.

GASTRITIS

Acute gastritis (inflammation of the stomach) is most commonly due to a dietary indiscretion. Other causes include alcohol, aspirin, uraemia or radiotherapy. Chronic

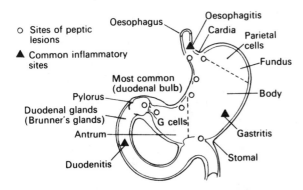

Figure 14.1 'Peptic' lesions may occur in the oesophagus (oesophagitis), stomach (gastritis) or duodenum (duodenitis). Note peptic ulcer sites and common inflammatory sites. Hydrochloric acid is formed by parietal cells in the fundus; gastrin is secreted by G cells in the antrum. The duodenal glands secrete an alkaline mucus solution.

gastritis may also occur. A diagnosis is usually made endoscopically and frequently the histology reveals the presence of *Helicobacter pylorri* (*Campylobacter pyloridis*), the relevance of which is unproven. Care of a patient with this condition is directed towards dietary modification and lifestyle changes in order to minimize symptoms.

PEPTIC ULCER

A peptic ulcer is a defect in the mucosal wall of the gastrointestinal tract anywhere in the presence of acid and pepsin. It most commonly occurs in the oesophagus, stomach and duodenum (Figure 14.1). Peptic ulcers more frequently occur in the duodenum than in the stomach, and tend to be single, but multiple ulcers may be present. Chronic gastric ulcers tend to occur in the lesser curvature of the stomach, near the pylorus. See Table 14.1 for a comparison of the features of gastric and duodenal ulcers.

Aetiology and Incidence

The aetiology of peptic ulcer is poorly understood. It is known that peptic ulcers occur only in the areas of the gastrointestinal tract that are exposed to hydrochloric acid and pepsin. The disease occurs with the greatest frequency between the ages of 40 and 60 but is relatively uncommon in women of childbearing age, although it has been observed in childhood and even in infancy. More men than women are affected, although there is some evidence that the incidence in women is increasing. After the menopause, the incidence of peptic ulcer in women is almost equal to that in men. Peptic ulcers in the body of the stomach can occur without excessive acid secretion; therefore, an attempt should be made to differentiate gastric from duodenal ulcers. Peptic ulcer remains a common disorder, but the incidence has declined over recent years.

Peptic ulcer seems to develop in people who are emotionally tense, but whether this is the cause or the effect of the condition is uncertain. Familial tendency also appears to be a significant predisposing factor, revealing that three times as many ulcer patients have relatives with the same diagnosis. A further hereditary link is noted in the finding that people in blood group O are 35 per cent more susceptible than people with type A, B or AB. Other predisposing factors associated with peptic ulcer include emotional stress, eating hurriedly and irregularly, and smoking excessively. Rarely, ulcers are due to excessive amounts of the hormone gastrin,

Table 14.1 *Comparison of duodenal and gastric ulcer*

Chronic duodenal ulcer	Chronic gastric ulcer
Age	
Usually 50	Usually 45 and over
Sex	
Male–female: 4:1	Male–female: 2:1
Blood group	
Most frequently–0	No differentiation
Social class	
More frequently in those groups subjected to stress and responsibility: executives, leaders in competitive fields	More common among labouring people
General nourishment	
Usually well nourished	Often malnourished
Acid production: stomach	
Hypersecretion	Normal–hyposecretion
Pain	
2 to 3 hours after a meal; night-time: often awakened between 1 and 2 a.m.	Occurs 30 minutes to 1 hour after a meal; night-time, rarely; relieved by vomiting
Ingestion of food relieves pain	Ingestion of food does not help; sometimes pain is increased
Vomiting	
Uncommon	Common
Haemorrhage	
Melaena more common than haematemesis	Haematemesis more common than melaena
Malignancy possibility	
Rarely	Perhaps in less than 10 per cent

produced by tumours (gastrinomas—Zollinger-Ellison syndrome).

Altered Physiology

Peptic ulcer occurs mainly in the gastroduodenal mucosa because this tissue is unable to withstand the digestive action of gastric acid and pepsin. The erosion is due to an increase in concentration or activity of acid-pepsin or to a decrease in the normal resistance of the mucosa. A damaged mucosa is unable to secrete enough mucus to act as a barrier against hydrochloric acid.

Gastric secretion occurs in three phases: (1) cephalic, (2) gastric and (3) intestinal. Since these phases are interactive and not independent of one another, a disturbance in any one phase may be ulcerogenic.

Cephalic (Psychic) Phase

The first phase is initiated by stimuli such as the sight, smell or taste of food, acting on cerebral cortical receptors that, in turn, stimulate the vagal nerves. Essentially, an unappetizing meal has little effect on gastric secretion, whereas a more tasty, appealing meal evokes a high secretion. This accounts for the traditional emphasis on serving a bland meal to the peptic ulcer patient. Today many gastroenterologists agree that the bland diet has no significant effect on gastric acidity or ulcer healing. However, excessive vagal activity during the night, when the stomach is empty, is a significant irritant.

Gastric Phase

The gastric phase of gastric secretion is mediated by the hormone gastrin. Gastrin enters the bloodstream from the antrum and is carried to glands in the fundus and body of the stomach; here it stimulates the production of gastric juice. Gastrin activity may be greater in patients with pyloric stenosis. The antrum of the patient with gastric ulcer contains less gastrin than that of the patient with a duodenal ulcer. Following partial gastrectomy or gastrojejunostomy, if part of the antrum is left in place but is no longer in contact with the acid-secreting portion of the stomach, the antrum continues to release gastrin, because acid no longer bathes the mucosa to inhibit gastrin release. Excess gastrin in the blood can lead to stomal ulcers. Excessive gastrin is also present in Zollinger-Ellison syndrome.

Intestinal Phase

During the intestinal phase a hormone, secretin, is secreted when hydrochloric acid enters the duodenum. Secretin, in turn, stimulates bicarbonate secretion from the pancreas, which neutralizes the acid. Secretin also inhibits the gastric phase of gastric secretion.

Gastric Mucosal Barrier

In humans, gastric secretion is a mixture of mucopoly-

saccharides and mucoproteins secreted continuously by the mucosal glands. This mucus adsorbs pepsin and protects it against acid. Hydrochloric acid is secreted continuously, but secretions increase owing to neurogenic and hormonal mechanisms that are initiated by gastric and intestinal stimuli. If hydrochloric acid were not buffered and neutralized, and if the outer layer of mucosa did not offer protection, hydrochloric acid, along with pepsin, would destroy the stomach. Hydrochloric acid comes into contact with only a small portion of the gastric mucosal surface: it diffuses into it very slowly. This impenetrability of the mucosa is called the gastric mucosal barrier. It is the main defence of the stomach against being digested by its secretions. Other factors that influence mucosal resistance are blood supply, acid–base balance, integrity of the mucosal cells and epithelial regeneration.

Note, then, that a person is likely to develop a peptic ulcer from one of two causes: (1) hypersecretion of acid-pepsin, and (2) a weakened gastric mucosal barrier. Anything that decreases the production of gastric mucus or damages gastric mucosa is ulcerogenic: salicylates, alcohol and indomethacin fall into this category.

Clinical Features

Symptoms of duodenal ulcer (the most common form of peptic ulcer) may last for varying amounts of time. Exacerbations seem to occur in the spring or autumn, but even this pattern is inconsistent. Many people have symptomless ulcers, and in 20 to 30 per cent perforation or haemorrhage may occur without any preceding features.

Pain

As a rule, the patient with duodenal ulcer complains of pain or a burning, sharply localized sensation in the midepigastrium or in the back. It is believed that the pain occurs when the increased acid content of the stomach and duodenum erodes the lesion and stimulates the exposed nerve endings. Another theory suggests that contact of the lesion with acid stimulates a local reflex mechanism that initiates contraction of the adjacent smooth muscle.

Pain precedes meals from one to three hours and becomes progressively more severe towards the end of the day. It may also waken the person between midnight and 3 a.m. However, there is no pain when the patient awakens in the morning because the flow of gastric acid is at its lowest at this time.

Typically, pain is relieved quite promptly by food or alkalies, either of which neutralizes the free acid in contact with the ulcer. If the patient takes neither food nor alkali, the pain gradually wears off as the secretion of acid stops and empties into the intestine. The character of the pain may be described as a dull, burning sensation, a feeling of emptiness or a gnawing so severe that the patient is in agony. When the ulcer has begun to affect the pancreas, pain in the back may become noticeable.

Pyrosis (Heartburn)

Some patients experience a burning sensation in the oesophagus and stomach, which moves up to the mouth, occasionally with sour eructation (burping). Eructation is common when the patient's stomach is empty.

Vomiting

Although rare in uncomplicated duodenal ulcer, vomiting may be a symptom of peptic ulcer. It is due to gastric outlet obstruction caused by either muscular spasm of the pylorus or mechanical obstruction. The latter may be due to scarring or to acute swelling of the inflamed mucous membrane adjacent to the acute ulcer. Vomiting may or may not be preceded by nausea; usually it follows a bout of severe pain, which is relieved by ejection of the acid gastric contents. The vomitus may contain food particles from the previous day.

Constipation and Bleeding

Constipation may be apparent in the patient with duodenal ulcer, probably as a result of diet and medications.

- About 20 per cent of patients who bleed from an acute duodenal ulcer have had no previous digestive complaints; however, they develop symptoms thereafter.

Diagnosis

Barium studies and upper gastrointestinal endoscopy are used to identify peptic ulcers. Gastric secretory studies are of value in diagnosing achlorhydria (the absence of hydrochloric acid in gastric juices) and Zollinger-Ellison syndrome. Pain that is relieved by ingesting food or antacids and the absence of pain on rising are also highly suggestive of duodenal ulcer.

A breath test has been developed that detects *Helicobacter pylori* (*Campylobacter pyloridis*), a bacterium linked to a variety of gastrointestinal disorders. This organism is present in patients with peptic ulcer disease and gastritis; however, no causative relationship has yet been established.

Care of the Patient With Peptic Ulcer

The patient may expect both remissions and recurrences but is able to control the symptoms to some extent.

Control of Gastric Secretions

Gastric acidity can be managed with neutralization of the gastric juice at frequent and regular intervals with drugs, nonirritating foods and antacids. Drugs that block the acid-secreting action of histamine (H_2 blockers), such as cimetidine and ranitidine, or that produce an acid-resistant barrier over the ulcer, such as sucralfate, have been shown to be effective in healing duodenal ulcers. Occasionally, anticholinergic agents are prescribed to inhibit gastric secretion, and antispasmodics given to reduce pylorospasm and intestinal motility.

Rest and Stress Reduction

Reducing environmental stress is a difficult task requiring physical and mental interventions on the patient's part and help from family members and significant others. The patient may need help in identifying situations that are stressful or exhausting. A rushed lifestyle and an irregular schedule may aggravate symptoms and interfere with regular meals taken in relaxed settings and with regular administration of medications.

Smoking

Studies have been shown that smoking decreases the secretion of bicarbonate from the pancreas into the duodenum. Therefore the acidity to the duodenum is higher when one smokes.

Diet

The objective of the diet for peptic ulcers is to avoid oversecretion and hypermotility in the gastrointestinal tract. These can be minimized by avoiding extremes of temperature and overstimulation by meat extracts, alcohol, seasonings (especially pepper and mustard) and coffee (including decaffeinated coffee, which also stimulates acid secretion). In addition, an effort is made to neutralize acid by eating three regular meals a day. Small, frequent feedings are not necessary as long as antacids or a histamine blocker is taken.

If the patient tolerates a particular food, it may be eaten. If it produces pain, it should be avoided. Milk and cream are no longer considered central to therapy. In fact, diets rich in milk and cream are potentially harmful over a long period because they increase serum lipids, a contributing factor in producing atherosclerosis. Skimmed milk stimulates acid secretion to some extent: the more effective the change in pH to neutral, the more enhanced is the stimulus to new acid secretion. As alkalinity increases, gastrin release is stimulated and acid secretion is increased.

Antacids

Antacids continue to be the mainstay of peptic ulcer treatment even though they are not capable of maintaining a pH of 3.5 or above (necessary for pepsinogen inactivity) for longer than 45 minutes. The objective is to select the antacid that provides the safest and longest period of acid neutralization. Usually, antacids leave the stomach rapidly, so that frequent doses are required. Recommended dosages should not be exceeded because systemic alkalosis or rebound hyperacidity can occur.

Antacids can be divided into those that contain magnesium or magnesium and aluminum and those that contain aluminum alone. Those that contain magnesium tend to cause diarrhoea, and those that contain aluminum cause constipation. Antacids that contain calcium are not recommended because calcium produces an increase in serum gastrin and in acid secretion. All antacids have been found to be more effective if given in the liquid form.

Antacid intake is scheduled to correspond to the delay in gastric emptying. A recommended schedule is one to three hours after each meal and at bedtime. For convenience, most people use the tablet forms. The effectiveness of antacid therapy can be prolonged if antacids are taken after a meal because gastric emptying is delayed by the presence of food. If the patient is awakened at night with epigastric pain, the time should be noted and thereafter the alarm clock should be set for an hour earlier to take the antacid.

H_2 Receptor Antagonists

Histamine has two receptors for its action. H_1 receptor is located on bronchial and nasal mucosa, cardiac tissue and blood vessels; H_2 receptor is found primarily in the parietal cells in the stomach, in uterine and bronchial muscle and in T lymphocytes. Even though H_2 receptors are distributed in body tissue, only gastric receptors appear to be affected by this drug. Common antihistamines block the action of H_1 receptors but have no effect on H_2 receptors in the stomach. Cimetidine and ranitidine, H_2 receptor antagonists, have a dramatic effect by lowering acid secretion in the stomach.

Cimetidine relieves ulcer pain and thus decreases the need for antacids. Short-term treatment with cimetidine has resulted in complete ulcer healing, but low-dose maintenance therapy may be needed to prevent recurrence. Side-effects may include leucopenia, bone marrow depression, diarrhoea, constipation, gynaecomastia and confusion in older patients. Cimetidine's effect on renal function is under investigation.

Ranitidine is as effective as cimetidine, and causes fewer side-effects. Side-effects that have been noted include dizziness, constipation, gynaecomastia and depression. Depression usually begins in six to eight weeks. It takes several weeks for the depression to lift after the drug has been stopped.

Famotidine is another H_2 antagonist. Trial clinical studies have shown rapid ulcer healing in four to eight weeks for about 85 per cent of those treated. Thereafter a reduced dosage is recommended for maintenance therapy. Famotidine's absorption rate is not affected significantly by antacids, which can be given at the same time. Studies on elderly patients have shown no significant changes in pharmacodynamics.

Anticholinergics

Anticholinergics block acetylcholine, which is a major stimulant of acid secretion. Their effectiveness is limited because undesirable side-effects may occur at therapeutic doses. Therefore, they are only prescribed for those patients who suffer from severe, persistent nocturnal pain and are rarely recommended for long-term use. Anticholinergics decrease gastric motor activity and thus allow an antacid to remain in the stomach longer. They are occasionally used at night-time with a double dose of antacid for persistent night pain.

Side-effects of anticholinergic drugs include dryness of the mouth and throat; excessive thirst; difficulty in swallowing; flushed, dry skin; rapid pulse and respiration; dilated pupils; and emotional excitement.

● Anticholinergic medications should not be used by patients with glaucoma, urinary retention or pyloric obstruction because of drug side-effects (increased central nervous system stimulation, increased intraocular pressure and urinary hesitation).

Other Drugs

Sucralfate is a locally acting drug that has also been shown to have anti-ulcer properties. Sucralfate forms complexes with proteinaceous exudates, such as albumin and fibrinogen, in the ulcer crater, producing an adherent barrier over the ulcer. This barrier is acid resistant, as opposed to acid reducing. The result is that acid is prevented from passing through to the ulcer, but the acid is not neutralized appreciably. Sucralfate is only minimally absorbed from the gastrointestinal tract and does not depend on systemic activity for its anti-ulcer effects.

Duration of Treatment

The patient should take the drugs as prescribed to ensure complete healing of the ulcer. Since most patients become free of symptoms in a week, it becomes a nursing goal to stress the importance of following the prescription so that the breakdown of the healing process and the return of chronic ulcer symptoms are averted.

After the first week, the purpose of using antacids switches from that of relieving symptoms to preventing symptoms. The best plan appears to be to encourage the patient to eat regular meals.

From the sixth or seventh week to six months, antacid is taken about an hour after meals and at bedtime. Thereafter, antacid therapy is usually dropped. If the person experiences a stressful situation or has been indiscreet with the diet and symptoms recur, antacid therapy may be resumed until the patient is free of symptoms.

Recurrence of an ulcer is possible and may happen within two years in about one third of all patients, although this incidence may be affected with prophylactic use of such drugs as cimetidine, ranitidine and famotidine. The likelihood of recurrence is lessened if the person avoids tea, coffee and cola (including decaffeinated), alcohol, highly seasoned and fried foods and ulcerogenic drugs, such as salicylates, corticosteroids and phenylbutazone.

► NURSING PROCESS
► THE PATIENT WITH A PEPTIC ULCER

► Assessment

The patient's history serves as an important base for assessment. The patient is asked to describe the pain and methods used to relieve it (food, certain antacids). Peptic ulcer pain is usually described as 'burning' or 'gnawing' and occurs about two hours after a meal. It frequently awakens the patient between midnight and 3 a.m. The patient will usually state that the pain is relieved by taking antacids or foods or by vomiting. During the assessment the nurse asks the patient to list the usual food intake for a 24-hour period and to include food habits (speed of eating, regularity of meals, preference for spicy foods, use of seasonings, use of caffeinated beverages).

The patient's level of tension or nervousness is assessed. Does the patient smoke cigarettes? How are the stressors of everyday life managed? How is anger expressed? How does the patient describe work and personal life? Are there occupational stresses? Are there problems within the patient's family or personal life? Is there a past family history of ulcer disease?

Vital signs are assessed for indicators of anaemia (tachycardia, hypotension), and the stool is examined for occult blood.

► Patient's Problems

Based on the assessment, the patient's main problems may include the following:

● Discomfort and/or pain, related to the effect of gastric acid secretion on damaged tissue.
● Anxiety related to coping with an acute disease.
● Nutritional deficiency related to dietary intake, effect of acid on gastric mucosa, work habits and methods of dealing with stress.
● Activity intolerance related to lack of sleep.
● Lack of knowledge about prevention of symptoms and management of the condition.

► Planning and Implementation
► Expected Outcomes

The main outcomes for the patient may include relief of pain, reduction of anxiety, promotion of a good nutritional intake, attainment of adequate rest and acquisition of knowledge about prevention and management.

Nursing Care

See Nursing Care Plan 14.1, for the patient with peptic ulcer.

► Evaluation
► Expected Outcomes

1. Patient experiences less pain.
   a. Is free of pain between meals.
   b. Uses antacids to prevent pain.
   c. Avoids foods and fluids that cause pain.
   d. Eats meals at regular times.
   e. Experiences no side-effects of antacids (diarrhoea, constipation, fluid retention).
2. Experiences less anxiety.
   a. Identifies situations that produce stress.
   b. Identifies lifestyle adjustments necessary to reduce stress.
   c. Alters lifestyle as appropriate.
   d. Involves family and close friends in decisions regarding lifestyle adjustments.
3. Maintains tissue integrity.
   a. Avoids irritating foods and beverages.
   b. Eats regular meals.
   c. Eats slowly and in a relaxed atmosphere.
   d. Takes medications as prescribed.
   e. Uses coping mechanisms to deal with stress.
4. Attains adequate rest.
   a. Alternates activity with rest periods.
   b. Uses energy-saving techniques for activities of daily living.
   c. Recognizes signs of overactivity.

Patient Education

Patient education for the individual with peptic ulcer aims at achieving the expected outcomes when planning care in the patient's own setting. It is necessary for such patients to have an understanding of their situation and of the factors that will influence it. Areas that need consideration are the following:

1. Medication. Does the patient know what medications are to be taken at home, including name, dosage, frequency and possible side-effects? Does the patient know which drugs to avoid?
2. Diet. What foods tend to upset the individual? Does the patient have a knowledge of foods that have acid-producing potential? What eating patterns and medication help to alleviate symptoms?
3. Rest and stress reduction. Has the patient had an opportunity to examine lifestyle and identify sources of stress? What strategies has the individual developed in order to avoid stress and being over-tired?
4. Awareness of complications. Is the patient aware of signs and symptoms of complications that should be reported?
5. Follow-up care. Follow-up in outpatients will be necessary. Does the patient understand that recurrence of an ulcer is possible? What does the patient do if symptoms recur?

► NURSING CARE PLAN 14.1: THE PATIENT WITH PEPTIC ULCER

Karen Jones is a 35-year-old shop assistant with three teenage children living at home with her. Karen has a peptic ulcer. Although she is still married, Karen and her husband separated two years ago.

Patient's problems	Expected outcomes	Nursing care	Rationale
1. Pain and discomfort in epigastrum due to increased hydrochloric acid secretion and thus irritated mucosa and muscle spasm	Karen will experience relief of discomfort and report this to the nursing staff	1a. Administer drug therapy, e.g. antacids. H$_2$ antagonists and anticholinergics as prescribed b. Explain the action of each medication given c. Assess level of pain and discomfort using a pain assessment tool such as a pain thermometer d. Establish whether eating particular foods helps to relieve pain	Antacids neutralize the hydrochloric acid and thus relieve pain. Histamine antagonists inhibit gastric acid secretion. Anticholinergic drugs suppress gastric acid secretion Providing information to patient will improve compliance Nurses tend to underestimate levels of pain (Hunt *et al.*, 1977). Use of a tool improves communication Pain is often worse when the stomach is empty
2. Irregular and hurried eating pattern causing pain and discomfort	To establish an eating pattern that minimizes pain and discomfort	2a. Refer to dietician and reinforce the importance of not eating food that causes pain b. Encourage patient to eat meals at frequent regular times and ensure that patient is given choices about menu and time of eating c. Avoid caffeine, spicy foods and fried foods, which are known to stimulate gastric secretion, in addition to very hot or cold food and drink d. Discuss ways of enabling patient to eat in a more relaxed, unhurried fashion	For patient's own comfort. To give patient access to expert nutritional advice In order to neutralize gastric secretions and to dilute stomach contents. Patient is best able to determine the frequency of intake required to avoid pain Known to stimulate gastric secretion Acid secretion is decreased when an individual is relaxed and unhurried
3. Tired most of the time due to work and home commitments. Also unable to sleep, thus worsening symptoms of peptic ulcer	To establish a routine that incorporates time to relax and rest	3a. Allow an opportunity to discuss strategies for coping with a busy lifestyle such as a rest during the day, establishing and investing time in a supportive friendship	Emotional and physical stress predispose to peptic ulcers and worsen symptoms
4. Anxiety related to knowledge of condition and apparent inpracticality of changing lifestyle	For Karen to feel confident about the possibility of gaining support and help	4a. Involve children in discussions concerning wellbeing of their mother b. Provide an opportunity to express fears and anxieties c. Explain rationale for treatment advised	Family support will make expected ooutcomes feasible Open communication and an opportunity to be heard help to allay anxiety Understanding will aid co-operation
5. Potential complications such as haemorrhage, perforation and pyloric obstruction	Will recognize signs of being unwell should they arise, and seek medical help quickly	5a. Reinforce the importance of taking advice given concerning management of peptic ulcers b. Describe symptoms that may occur should the complications arise	To avoid recurrence Knowledge improves patient's awareness and will enable action to be taken at an early stage

Complications of Peptic Ulcers

There are four major complications of peptic ulcer: haemorrhage, perforation, pyloric obstruction and intractable ulcer.

Haemorrhage

Manifested by haematemesis, melaena or both, haemorrhage is the most common complication of peptic ulcer. The most frequent site is the distal portion of the duodenum. When the haemorrhage is of large proportions (2,000 to 3,000 ml), most of the blood is vomited. The patient may become almost exsanguinated, and rapid correction of blood loss will be required to save his life. When the haemorrhage is small, much or all of the blood may be passed in the stools, which will appear tarry black owing to the digested haemoglobin.

Assessment. The nurse assesses the patient for early symptoms of faintness or giddiness; nausea may precede or accompany bleeding. Dyspepsia may not be present. Vital signs are evaluated for tachycardia, hypotension and tachypnoea.

Management. Because bleeding can be fatal, the doctor will identify the cause and severity of the haemorrhage and correct the blood loss to prevent hypovolaemic shock.

● Preparations are made for a peripheral intravenous line for infusion of saline and blood and possibly a central line for infusion and measurement of central venous pressure. Whole blood or plasma transfusions are given to keep the circulating blood volume at a safe level. The doctor does not wait for a drop in blood pressure before starting transfusion therapy if there are signs of tachycardia, sweating and coldness of the extremities.
● The haemoglobin and hematocrit are monitored to detect bleeding.
● An indwelling urinary catheter is inserted to monitor urinary output.
● Nasogastric intubation is used to distinguish fresh blood from 'coffee-ground' material.
● Oxygen therapy may be instituted.
● The patient is placed in the recumbent position to prevent hypovolaemic shock.
● Vital signs are monitored every 15 to 30 minutes.
● Hypovolaemic shock is treated as outlined in the section entitled Perioperative Care, Chapter 2.

If bleeding cannot be managed by the measures just described, then the following may be done:

● Endoscopic injection with adrenalin (if a stigmata of recent haemorrhage is seen).
● In some centres coagulation of the bleeding site is accomplished by a laser beam.

Surgical Treatment. If bleeding recurs in 48 hours after medical therapy has begun, or if more than five units of blood is required in 24 hours to maintain blood volume, the patient is likely to be operated upon. Some doctors recommend that if a patient with peptic ulcer haemorrhages three times, surgery is indicated.

Other determining factors for surgery are the patient's age (if over 60, massive haemorrhaging is three times more likely to be fatal), a history of chronic duodenal ulcer and a coincidental gastric ulcer.

The ulcer-bearing area is removed, or the bleeding vessels are ligated. In many patients a procedure is included that is aimed at controlling the underlying causes of the ulcer (e.g., vagotomy and pyloroplasty or gastrectomy).

Perforation

Perforation of a peptic ulcer may occur unexpectedly, without much evidence of preceding indigestion. Perforation into the free peritoneal cavity is an abdominal catastrophe and an indication that surgery is required.

Signs and symptoms to note during a nursing assessment include the following:

● Sudden, severe upper abdominal pain (persisting and increasing in intensity).
● Pain, which may be referred to the shoulders, especially the right shoulder, because of irritation of the phrenic nerve in the diaphragm.
● Vomiting and collapse (fainting).
● Extremely tender and rigid (boardlike) abdomen.
● Shock.

Immediate surgical intervention is indicated, because chemical peritonitis develops within a few hours following perforation and is followed by a bacterial peritonitis. Therefore, the perforation must be closed as quickly as possible. In a few patients, it may be deemed safe and advisable that surgery be performed for the ulcer disease, in addition to the perforation being sutured.

Postoperatively, the stomach contents are drained by means of a nasogastric tube. The nurse monitors fluid and electrolyte balance and assesses the patient for peritonitis or localized infection (increased temperature, abdominal pain, paralytic ileus, increased or absent bowel sounds, abdominal distension). Antibiotic therapy is given intravenously as prescribed.

Pyloric Obstruction

Pyloric obstruction occurs when the area distal to the pyloric sphincter becomes scarred and stenosed from spasm or oedema or from scar tissue that is formed when the ulcer alternately heals and breaks down. The patient has symptoms of nausea and vomiting, constipation, epigastric fullness, anorexia and (later) weight loss.

In treating the patient, the first consideration is the relief of the obstruction by gastric decompression. At the same time, attempts are made to confirm that obstruction is the cause of discomfort. This is done by checking the amount of fluid aspirated from the nasogastric tube. A residual volume of over 200 ml is strongly suggestive of obstruction.

Before surgery is undertaken, decompression continues and extracellular fluid volume and electrolyte and metabolic derangements are corrected. Conscientious monitoring of fluid balance is continued. With supportive measures, the patient's condition may improve. Surgery, in the form of a vagotomy and antrectomy, may be required. If the patient is severely malnourished during this time, total parenteral nutrition may be used.

Intractability

An intractable ulcer is one that continues to give problems and is resistant to all forms of treatment. It is the most common, persistent problem seen in patients with peptic ulcers and the most common reason given by patients for choosing surgery.

A careful patient history includes a thorough review of dietary and drug habits, which could reveal long-term use of caffeine-containing drinks or aspirin-containing medications. The entire gastrointestinal tract is assessed carefully to determine other possible problems, such as hiatus hernia, gallbladder disease or diverticulitis.

The patient, family and close friends are informed of the fact that surgery is no guarantee that an ulcer is cured. Possible postoperative sequelae, such as intolerance to dairy products and sweet foods, are also discussed.

Surgical Approaches

Surgery for ulcer disease is done when medical therapy has not been successful or when complications arise, such as haemorrhage, perforation or pyloric obstruction. Patients requiring ulcer surgery may have had a long illness, be discouraged, have interruptions in their work role and experience pressures in their personal or family life. Various types of surgical procedures may be used in treating peptic ulcer disease.

Peptic ulcer surgery aims to reduce acid secretion either by abolishing the vagal stimulus (vagotomy) or by removing the acid-secreting part of the stomach (partial gastrectomy). After a gastric resection, the stomach remnant may be joined to the duodenum (Billroth I), or to a loop of jejunum (Billroth II or polya) (Figure 14.2).

- Partial gastrectomy is the removal of two thirds to three fourths of the stomach.
- Antrectomy involves removing the antral (lower) portion of the stomach (which contains the G cells that secrete gastrin) as well as a small portion of the duodenum and pylorus. An antrectomy may also be performed in conjunction with a truncal vagotomy.
- Truncal vagotomy is the severing of the anterior and posterior vagal trunks as they enter the abdomen with

the oesophagus. This procedure reduces acid secretion from the stomach, but also denervates the pylorus and the small bowel. Failure of the stomach to empty necessitates a drainage procedure such as a pyloroplasty (Figure 14.2) or a gastroenterostomy (joining a loop of jejunum to the stomach).

- Parietal cell vagotomy (proximal gastric vagotomy or highly selective vagotomy) involves severing only those vagus nerves that innervate the parietal cell mass in the upper portion of the stomach. Antral innervation remains intact, avoiding the need for a pyloroplasty.

Sequelae

After gastrectomy or vagotomy with a drainage procedure, patients may experience symptoms of postprandial fullness, diarrhoea and dizziness (symptoms of the 'dumping syndrome'). Specific gastric problems are stomal ulceration and a relative increase in late gastric malignancy (occurring more than 20 years after such an operation).

The rate of recurrent ulcer is lowest after truncal vagotomy with antrectomy, and highest with proximal gastric vagotomy.

Nursing Care

Preoperative nursing care for the patient undergoing surgery for peptic ulcer disease includes the following:

- Preparing the patient for diagnostic tests. The patient undergoes blood tests, X-ray series and a general physical examination before surgery. The nurse prepares the patient for each of these diagnostic measures by explaining their nature and significance.
- Attending to the patient's fluid and nutritional needs. The nutritional and fluid needs of the patient are of major importance. In those patients with pyloric obstruction, there usually is prolonged vomiting, with resultant weight and fluid loss. Every effort is made to restore an adequate nutritional intake and to maintain an optimal fluid and electrolyte balance.
- Clearing and emptying the gastrointestinal tract. Nasogastric suction often is required to empty the stomach, especially in patients with pyloric obstruction. The tube is inserted before the operation and left in place for perioperative and postoperative use.
- Limiting fluid intake. The patient is usually limited to fluids during the 24-hour period preceding surgery.
- Shaving and preparing the skin. The abdomen should be prepared, from the nipple line to the symphysis, although the incision is usually made in the upper right quadrant or the midline.

Postoperative care is the same as that for gastric surgery. (See pages 535 to 537, Nursing Care of Patients Undergoing Gastric Surgery.)

ZOLLINGER-ELLISON SYNDROME (GASTRINOMA)

Zollinger-Ellison syndrome is considered as a possible diagnosis when a patient presents with several peptic ulcers. It is identified by the following findings: hypersecretion of gastric juice, multiple duodenal ulcers (second and third portions), an increase in parietal cell mass, hypertrophied duodenal glands and gastrinomas (islet cell tumours) in the pancreas. The gastrinomas may also be found in the duodenum and stomach. The incidence of malignancy is approximately 65 per cent. The huge amounts of secreted hydrochloric acid almost have the effect of the stomach's trying to digest itself. The serum gastrin level is increased. In Zollinger-Ellison syndrome, secretin stimulates gastrin secretion rather than inhibits it. Steatorrhoea (unabsorbed fat in the stool) may be evident, because excessive gastric acid inactivates lipase in the intestine, thereby precipitating bile salts and decreasing fat digestion. The result is steatorrhoea and diarrhoea. Gastrin also decreases water and salt absorption, which in turn leads to diarrhoea.

Management

Hypersecretion of acid can be controlled with cimetidine in doses up to 1,200 mg, four to six times a day. However, there is a high failure rate with prolonged drug therapy. The recommended surgical procedure is antrectomy with a truncal or parietal cell vagotomy (see p. 530). Total gastrectomy is the most successful treatment for those who cannot be managed with H_2 receptor blockers. In the postoperative period, dietary advice is necessary. Lifelong parenteral vitamin B_{12} therapy will be necessary if a total gastrectomy is done because intrinsic factor, secreted by

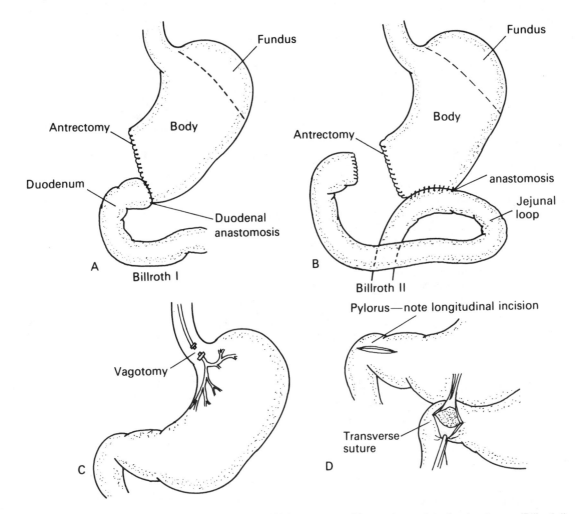

Figure 14.2 Surgical procedures for ulcer disease. (A) Antrectomy with anastomosis to the duodenum (Billroth I). (B) Antrectomy with anastomosis to the jejunum (Billroth II). (C) Severing of the vagus nerve (vagotomy). (D) A longitudinal incision into the pylorus followed by a transverse suture to enlarge the opening (pyloroplasty).

the gastric mucosal cells and necessary for vitamin B_{12} absorption, can no longer be produced. Careful follow-up monitoring is done to detect possible metastasis.

Nursing Assessment

Diarrhoea and hypercalcaemia are common problems. A nursing assessment frequently reveals that the patient's symptoms are often refractory (unyielding) to large amounts of antacids. The patient may disclose taking several pints of milk a day with no apparent relief from pain.

STRESS ULCER

Stress ulcer is the term given to a group of duodenal or gastric ulcers that occur following physiologically disturbing conditions.

Altered Physiology

Stressful conditions such as burns, shock, severe sepsis and multiple organ trauma can initiate the development of such ulcers. Fibreoptic endoscopy within 24 hours of injury reveals shallow erosions of the stomach wall; by 72 hours, multiple gastric erosions are observed. As the stressful condition continues, the ulcers spread. When the patient recovers, the lesions are reversed. This is typical of stress ulceration.

Differences of opinion exist as to the actual causation of mucosal ulceration. Usually, it is preceded by shock; this leads to a decrease in gastric mucosal blood flow and a reflux of duodenal content into the stomach. In addition, large quantities of pepsin are released. The combination of ischaemia, acid and pepsin creates an ideal climate to produce ulceration. When acute stress ulceration is combined with central nervous system trauma, stress ulcers (Cushing's ulcers) are often deeper and more penetrating. Gastric erosions are frequently observed about 72 hours after extensive burns (Curling's ulcers).

Management

Antacids are the basis of treatment. If the patient is acutely ill, antacids may be given through the nasogastric tube. Frequent gastric aspiration is done to check pH, in an attempt to get it to, or above, 3.5. Antacid therapy can also inhibit the activity of the proteolytic enzyme, pepsin. Stress ulcers are treated aggressively with antacid therapy and cimetidine therapy. Other methods of management of upper gastrointestinal tract haemorrhage are discussed on page 529.

MORBID OBESITY

Morbid obesity is a term applied to people with an excess of body fat. Body mass index, a ratio of weight (kg) to

height (m^2), is often used by doctors and dieticians. The normal range in adults is 19 to 25. Surgical management is reserved for those individuals for whom conservative measures have failed consistently. Options such as jaw wiring, intragastric balloons, jejunoileal bypass and gastric bypass have been used, but with only limited success. Another option is a vertical banded gastroplasty.

In vertical banded gastroplasty, a double row of staples is applied vertically along the lesser curvature of the stomach beginning at the angle of His. A small stoma is created at the end of the staples by adding a circle of staples or a band of polypropylene mesh or silicone tubing (Figure 14.3).

Nursing Care

General postoperative nursing care is similar to that for any patient experiencing gastric resection. Patients are usually discharged in one week with detailed dietary advice. Usually a daily 600- to 800-calorie diet is recommended, and fluid intake is encouraged to prevent dehydration. Patients are asked to report any excessive thirst or concentrated urine to their doctor. Outpatient visits are scheduled monthly.

Psychosocial considerations are essential for these patients. All efforts are directed towards helping them modify their eating behaviours and cope with their body image change. Nonco-operation usually results in patients eating too much or too fast. If this happens, vomiting and painful oesophageal distension may occur.

Postoperative complications usually occur in the immediate postoperative period and include peritonitis, stomal obstruction, stomal ulcers, atelectasis and pneumonia, thromboembolism and metabolic sequelae resulting from prolonged vomiting and diarrhoea.

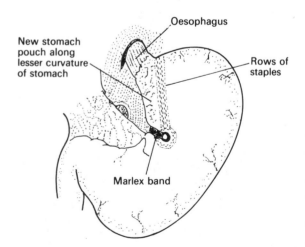

Figure 14.3 Vertical banded gastroplasty. A vertical row of staples along the lesser curvature of the stomach creates a new, smaller stomach pouch.

GASTRIC CANCER

Cancer of the stomach is still a serious problem, mostly in people over the age of 40, and occasionally in younger people. More than 90 per cent of cases arise from the mucosa but less than 5 per cent appear as gastric ulcers. The incidence of gastric cancer is four times greater in Japan, which has led to mass surveys for earlier diagnosis in that country. Hereditary factors appear to be significant, as do chronic inflammation of the stomach, pernicious anaemia and achlorhydria (25 per cent). The prognosis is poor. About 60 per cent of patients have clinical findings at the time of diagnosis, resulting in a low cure rate.

Clinical Features

The early symptoms of gastric cancer are often indefinite, since most of these tumours start on the lesser curvature, where they cause little disturbance to gastric functions. Later, after they have spread to the cardiac orifice, or especially to the pylorus, the suffering may be distressing; this is due not as much to the cancer as to the disturbance in gastric motility. Weight loss, weakness, anaemia and sometimes icterus appear late in the disease. Pain, in gastric cancer, as in cancer in almost all other parts of the body, is a late symptom. Whereas pain is a sensitive indicator of disturbed physiology or disease, it is ironic that pain rarely warns the person who has cancer while there is still an opportunity of curing it. The most important early symptoms of gastric cancer are as follows:

- A progressive loss of appetite and weight.
- The appearance of, or change in, gastrointestinal symptoms that have been increasingly apparent for only a matter of weeks or months.
- The appearance of blood in the stools.
- Vomiting. (If the tumour causes obstruction at the cardiac orifice, vomiting or a feeling of fullness will immediately follow a meal. If the tumour is near the pylorus, it eventually obstructs this channel, and vomiting becomes a prominent sign.)
- Occasional vomiting of 'coffee-ground' vomitus or signs of blood in the stool.

The blood that leaks slowly from the cancer (large haemorrhages are rare in patients with gastric cancer) is altered chemically and forms small clots or precipitates. The patient may not vomit, but traces of blood may be found in the stools when examined in the laboratory.

Diagnosis

Biopsies through the gastroscope are helpful in diagnosing gastric cancer. Cytological studies verify the diagnosis. Occasionally, the tumour is palpable, especially if it is located near the pylorus. Since metastasis frequently occurs before warning signs are experienced, X-ray films, fluoroscopy and gastroscopy are most valuable in determining the extent of the problem. Occult blood may be found in stools. Serum protein levels would be low. Dyspepsia of more than four weeks' duration in any person over the age of 40 calls for complete X-ray examination of the gastrointestinal tract.

Care of the Patient With Gastric Cancer

There is no successful treatment of gastric carcinoma except removal of the tumour. If the tumour can be removed while it is still localized to the stomach, the patient can be cured. If the tumour has spread beyond the area that can be excised surgically, cure cannot be effected. However, in many of these patients, effective palliation may be obtained by resection of the tumour (see pp. 535–7, Nursing Care of Patients Undergoing Gastric Surgery). If a radical subtotal gastrectomy has been performed, the stump of the stomach is anastomosed to the jejunum, as in gastrectomy for an ulcer. When total gastrectomy is performed, gastrointestinal continuity is restored by an anastomosis between the ends of the oesophagus and jejunum. Palliative, rather than radical, surgery is done if there is metastasis to other vital organs, such as the liver.

► NURSING PROCESS
► THE PATIENT WITH GASTRIC CANCER

► *Assessment*

When assessing the patient with gastric cancer, it is helpful to establish details concerning support from the family or significant others. Information about lifestyle, including occupation, are also useful. Does the patient smoke? A nutritional assessment (see Chapter 2) is also necessary.

Within the context of a relaxed, nonthreatening atmosphere, the nurse needs to discuss with these patients how they feel about their illness and the impending surgery. Specific worries need to be identified and then explored. Realistic information is vital, and it may be helpful to have some written literature for the patient to read at a later stage. The patient needs to be encouraged, and positive statements reinforced (Wilson-Barnett and Batehup, 1988).

► *Patient's Problems*

Based on the assessment, the patient's main problems may include the following:

- Anxiety related to anticipating the surgical procedure.
- Nutritional deficiency related to anorexia.

- Pain, related to the presence of abnormal epithelial cells.
- Anticipatory grieving related to the diagnosis of cancer.
- Lack of knowledge about self-care activities.

▶ *Planning and Implementation*

▶ **Expected Outcomes**

The main outcomes for the patient may include reduction of anxiety, attainment of optimum nutrition, relief of pain and adjustment to the diagnosis and to anticipated lifestyle changes.

Nursing Care

Promoting Optimum Nutrition

Small frequent feeds of nonirritating foods are encouraged to decrease gastric irritation. Food supplements should be high in vitamins A and C and iron so that tissue repair is facilitated. If a total gastrectomy is to be done, then parenteral vitamin B_{12} will need to be given indefinitely. The nurse monitors the rate and frequency of intravenous therapy; and records intake, output and daily weights to make sure the patient is maintaining or gaining weight. Signs of dehydration (thirst, dry mucous membranes, poor skin turgor, tachycardia) are assessed. Antiemetics are administered as prescribed.

Relief of Pain

Analgesics are administered as prescribed. A continuous intravenous infusion may be necessary for severe pain. The frequency, intensity and duration of the pain is assessed to determine the effectiveness of the analgesic being administered. The nurse works with the patient to help manage the pain (e.g., position changes, decreased environmental stimuli, restricted visiting). Nonpharmacological methods for pain relief such as imagery, distraction, relaxation tapes and massage are suggested, and periods of rest and relaxation are encouraged. A pain chart may be helpful (Pritchard and David, 1988).

Psychosocial Support

The nurse helps the patient express any fears and concerns about the diagnosis. The patient is allowed to grieve freely. Any questions are answered honestly, and the patient is encouraged to participate in treatment decisions. Some patients mourn the loss of a body part and perceive their surgery as a type of mutilation. Some express disbelief and need reality reinforcement. Privacy should be provided during periods of crying if the patient wants to be alone.

The nurse offers emotional support and involves family members and significant others whenever possible. Mood swings and defence mechanisms (denial, rationalization, displacement, regression) must be recognized by the nurse, and the patient, family members and significant others must be reassured that emotional responses are normal and expected. Professional services are provided if necessary, including those of religious adviser, social workers, cancer counsellors and others as appropriate. The nurse projects an empathetic approach and spends time with the patient. Most patients will begin to participate in self-care activities when they have acknowledged their loss.

Patient Education

The patient is advised that it may take six months before regular meals can be eaten after a partial resection. Small, frequent feeds are given initially, or tube feeding will be used. Total parenteral nutrition may be necessary. With any enteral feeding the possibility of the dumping syndrome exists, so it must be explained and ways to manage it reviewed.

The patient is told that it may take three months before normal activities can be resumed. Daily periods of rest are necessary, and the patient will have to visit the general practitioner frequently after discharge. Changes in lifestyle will be affected by irradiation or chemotherapy. The patient needs to know what to expect: length of treatments, expected reactions (nausea, vomiting, anorexia, fatigue), need for transportation to and from the treatments and need for a support person for the first 24 hours after the treatment because of generalized weakness. Counselling may be necessary for some.

Nutritional counselling is started in the hospital and reinforced at home. Any tube feeding procedure is supervised by a community nurse who teaches the patient, family members and/or significant others how to use the equipment and formulae and how to detect complications. (See p. 512 to review management of tube feeds.) The patient learns to record daily intake, output and weight and is taught how to cope with pain, nausea, vomiting and bloating. The patient is made aware of those complications that require medical attention, such as bleeding (overt or covert haematemesis, melaena), obstruction, perforation or any symptoms that become consistently worse.

The nurse teaches the patient how to care for the incision and how to examine the wound for signs of infection (malodorous drainage, pain, heat, inflammation, swelling). Any irradiation or chemotherapy regime is explained. The patient as well as the family and close friends need to know what kind of care will be needed during and after treatments. Patients who live alone or who are responsible for the care of children need to make arrangements for help for about 24 hours after a treatment.

▶ *Evaluation*

▶ **Expected Outcomes**

1. Patient experiences less anxiety.
   a. Understands the surgical procedure.
   b. Expresses fears and concerns about surgery.

c. Seeks emotional support.

d. Discusses feelings about surgery with family and significant others.

e. Discusses the surgical procedure and postoperative course.

2. Attains optimum nutrition.
   a. Eats small, frequent meals.
   b. Eats foods high in iron and vitamins A and C.
   c. Maintains a reasonable weight.
3. Experiences less pain.
   a. Takes prescribed medications as prescribed.
   b. Rests periodically during the day.
   c. Uses relaxation techniques.
4. Adjusts to diagnosis.
   a. Freely expresses fears and concerns.
   b. Seeks emotional support from family members and significant others.
   c. Discusses prognosis.
5. Performs self-care activities and adjusts to lifestyle changes.
   a. Resumes normal activities within three months.
   b. Alternates periods of rest and activity.
   c. Tolerates three regular meals daily within six months after surgery.
   d. Manages tube feeds.
   e. Adjusts to total parenteral nutrition.
   f. Adheres to radiotherapy/chemotherapy regime.
   g. Keeps follow-up appointments.

NURSING CARE OF PATIENTS UNDERGOING GASTRIC SURGERY

The major considerations in the nursing care of patients undergoing gastric surgery include providing physical and psychological support in the preoperative period, assessing and monitoring for complications in the postoperative period, and preparing the patient to deal with life following discharge and required self-care activities.

Preoperative Nursing Care

An important part of preoperative nursing care involves allaying the patient's fears and anxieties about the impending surgery and its implications. The nurse encourages the patient to express feelings and answers any questions. It is also necessary to explain the surgical procedure, thus preparing the patient for what to expect after the operation, such as nasogastric intubation and intravenous fluid therapy. However, if the operation is an emergency, because of haemorrhage, perforation or acute obstruction, adequate psychological preparation may not be possible. In this event, the nurse caring for the patient in the postoperative period should anticipate the concerns, fears and questions, and be available for support and explanation.

Gastric Resection (Partial Gastrectomy)

Postoperative nursing care following gastric resection include the following:

1. Positioning the patient. When recovery from anaesthesia is complete, the patient is nursed in a semi-recumbent position, for comfort and for easy drainage of the stomach.
2. Avoiding pulmonary complications. Analgesics are administered as prescribed, so that deep breathing and productive coughing may be effective in preventing pulmonary complications. This will overcome the patient's tendency to take shallow breaths for fear of incisional pain. The patient will be asked to take deep breaths and to cough hourly in the immediate postoperative period.
3. Checking nasogastric tube drainage. Drainage from the nasogastric tube may contain some blood for the first 12 hours, but excessive bleeding should be reported. Since a nasogastric tube is in place and peristalsis has not yet returned, fluids by mouth are withheld. It is important to observe for signs of distension (increased girth).
4. Giving nose and mouth care. The nostrils can be cleaned with an applicator stick moistened with water. To relieve dryness of the mouth, mouthwashes may be given frequently. Cool water sponges to the lips and ice help to keep the mouth moist.
5. Attending to fluid needs. Intravenous fluids are given to meet fluid and nutritional needs, as well as to compensate for fluid lost in drainage and vomitus. Fluid intake as well as output is recorded. Following the return of peristalsis and the removal of the nasogastric tube, fluids by mouth may be restricted for several hours, then begun sparingly. Small amounts of water are used at first, after which the amount is gradually increased as tolerated.
6. Providing dietary intake. Bland foods are gradually added until the patient is able to eat small meals and drink fluid between meals. The key to increasing the dietary content is to offer increments gradually as tolerated and to recognize that each person is different. If regurgitation occurs, the patient may be eating too fast or too much. It also may indicate that oedema along the suture line is preventing fluids and food from moving into the intestinal tract. If gastric retention does occur, it may be necessary to reinstitute nasogastric aspiration.
7. Encouraging mobility. Usually on the first postoperative day, the patient is encouraged to get out of bed. Mobility is then increased daily.
8. Providing wound care. Wound dressings may have serosanguineous drainage on them because of drainage tubes left in the wound. Dressings are reinforced or changed if necessary; however, excessive oozing is reported.

Nutritional Care After Gastric Surgery

Often a patient who has had gastric surgery has been under-nourished before the operation because of food intolerance or preoperative diagnostic testing. There may be significant protein deficiency, which may require parenteral nutritional support (see p. 517) for the first five or six post-operative days. Normal eating is resumed as soon as the patient feels hungry and bowel sounds are elicited.

Dysphagia may be noticed in those patients who have had truncal vagotomy, which causes trauma to the lower oesophagus. This patient may be more comfortable taking a soft diet for the first 10 days to 2 weeks. To encourage the patient to eat, attractive and appetizing food should be served in a pleasant atmosphere. With regard to long-term management of this patient, weight loss is a common problem because the patient experiences early fullness that curbs the appetite. Anorexia may also be due to the dumping syndrome, which occurs in about one fifth of patients following partial gastrectomy (see below).

Appropriate nursing care is to suggest the following patient teaching points:

- Fluids should be taken before or between meals, rather than with meals.
- Smaller but more frequent meals should be eaten.
- Meal composition should be more dry than fluid-filled.
- Diets with small-molecule carbohydrates, such as sucrose and glucose, should be avoided, but fat may be consumed to tolerable levels.
- It may be advisable to supplement the diet with vitamins and medium-chain triglycerides.

Other dietary deficiencies of which the nurse should be aware include: (1) malabsorption of organic iron, which may require supplementation with oral or parenteral iron; and (2) low serum level of vitamin B_{12}, which may require supplementation by the intramuscular route.

Postoperative Complications

Shock

Shock has been mentioned as a complication, especially in very ill patients. The restoration of normal temperature and the administration of fluids are the prophylactic measures necessary. For symptoms and treatment of shock, see appropriate section in Chapter 2.

Haemorrhage

Haemorrhage is occasionally a complication after gastric operations. The patient exhibits the usual signs (see Perioperative Care, Chapter 2) and may vomit bright red blood in considerable amounts. This experience can prove upsetting to the patient, and diazepam is effective in lessening the patient's apprehension. Nasogastric drainage or lavage may be doctor-initiated. Adrenaline may be given to produce vasoconstriction.

- When haemorrhage occurs, it is important to initiate action rapidly and to notify the doctor. Blood, blood substitutes and intravenous equipment are made available.
- Nursing support of the patient is given concurrently with emergency treatment.

Pulmonary Complications

Pulmonary complications frequently follow upper abdominal incisions because of the tendency for shallow respirations. Therefore, the nurse uses foresight and initiates appropriate breathing and leg exercises, and mobilization to promote optimum oxygen–carbon dioxide exchange and adequate circulation.

Steatorrhoea

Steatorrhoea (unabsorbed fat in the stool) is partially the result of rapid gastric emptying, which prevents adequate mixing with pancreatic and biliary secretions. In mild cases, steatorrhoea can be controlled by reducing the intake of fat and taking an antimotility drug.

Dumping Syndrome

The term 'dumping syndrome' designates an unpleasant set of vasomotor and gastrointestinal symptoms that occur after meals in 10 to 50 per cent of patients who have had gastrointestinal surgery or a form of vagotomy.

Clinical Features. Early symptoms may include a sensation of fullness, weakness, faintness, dizziness, palpitations, sweating, cramping pains and diarrhoea. Later, there is a rapid elevation of blood glucose followed by a compensatory reaction of insulin secretion. This results in a reactive hypoglycaemia, which is also unpleasant for the patient. Symptoms that may occur 10 to 90 minutes after eating are vasomotor and are manifested by pallor, perspiration, palpitations, headache and feelings of warmth, dizziness and even drowsiness.

Altered Physiology. The altered physiology underlying this syndrome is not completely understood, but there may be several causes for its occurrence. One is the mechanical result of surgery in which a small gastric remnant connects into the jejunum through a large opening. Foods that are high in carbohydrates and electrolytes have to be diluted in the jejunum before absorption can take place; yet the passage of food from the stomach remnant into the jejunum is too rapid. The ingestion of fluid at mealtimes is another factor that causes the stomach contents to empty rapidly into the jejunum. The symptoms that occur are probably brought about by rapid distension of the jejunal loop anastomosed to the stomach. The hypertonic intestinal contents draw extracellular fluid from the circulating blood volume into the jejunum to dilute the high concentration of electrolytes and sugars.

Nursing Care. In anticipation of the possibility of the patient's experiencing the dumping syndrome, nursing care is directed toward proper dietary advice.

- The patient should be positioned in a semi-recumbent position during mealtimes. Following the meal, the patient should lie down for 20 to 30 minutes to delay stomach emptying.
- Fluids are discouraged with meals but may be given up to an hour before mealtime or one hour following mealtime.
- Fat may be given to tolerance, but carbohydrate intake should be kept low (sucrose and glucose are avoided).
- Antispasmodics, as prescribed, also may aid in delaying the emptying of the stomach.

Surgery is resorted to only if absolutely necessary (less than 1 per cent of patients).

Gastritis and Oesophagitis

With the removal of the pylorus, which acts as a barrier to the reflux of duodenal contents, a bile reflux gastritis and oesophagitis may occur. This is manifested by burning epigastric pain and the vomiting of bilious material. Eating or vomiting does not relieve the situation. Binding agents such as cholestyramine, aluminum hydroxide gel or metoclopramide hydrochloride have been used with some success.

Vitamin B$_{12}$ Deficiency

Total gastrectomy brings to an abrupt, complete and final halt the production of 'intrinsic factor', the gastric secretion that is required for the absorption of vitamin B$_{12}$ from the gastrointestinal tract (see p. 473). Therefore, unless this vitamin is supplied by parenteral injection throughout life, the patient inevitably suffers from vitamin B$_{12}$ deficiency, which leads in time to a condition identical to that of a patient with pernicious anaemia in relapse. All of the manifestations of pernicious anaemia, including macrocytic anaemia and combined system disease, may be expected to develop within a period of five years or less, to progress in severity thereafter and, in the absence of therapy, to prove fatal. This complication is avoided by the regular monthly intramuscular injection of 100 to 200 g of vitamin B$_{12}$, a regime that should be started without delay after gastrectomy.

Evaluation

Nursing evaluation of the patient who has had gastric surgery involves confirming that the patient is free of physical complications and is coping effectively with the surgical experience and the postoperative concerns. Points to be noted include the following:

- Stable respiratory status. Respiratory rate between 14 and 20 per minute; clear breath sounds.
- Lack of infection or excessive drainage or haemorrhage. Vital signs stable; minimal blood in gastric drainage after 12 hours.
- Stable hydration and nutrition. Adequate intake and output; adequate urinary drainage; gradually tolerating fluids and bland foods; maintaining or possibly gaining weight; absence of dumping syndrome.
- Daily increases in activity and mobilization.
- Effective coping behaviour. Patient understands the purposes of the surgical procedure and the postoperative course; verbalizes any concerns about the surgical outcome; uses support of family or significant others appropriately.

Patient Education

Patient teaching is based on an assessment of the patient's physical and psychological readiness to return home and into the community. (If the patient has gastric cancer, the expected outcomes are for maintenance and palliation.) The patient and family/significant others will benefit from a team approach to discharge care. The team members include the community nurse, physician, dietician and perhaps the social worker. Written advice about meals, activities, medications and follow-up care are helpful. The post-discharge plan has to be individualized, and the patient's physical status, resources and prognosis taken into account. The plan should include the following:

- Nutrition and hydration. The patient may have small, frequent feeds or may have progressed to regular meals. Resumption of regular meals may require a period of six months. If a major portion of the stomach was removed, the patient may require enteral tube feeds or perhaps parenteral nutrition (see Chapter 13).
- Activity and rest. Gradual resumption of activities is encouraged according to the patient's abilities. This could require a period of at least three months but is dependent on the patient's previous activity schedule. Daily rest periods are encouraged.
- Analgesics. If the patient requires medication for pain, advice regarding usage and administration are given.
- Follow-up supervision. The patient should understand that follow-up care is necessary. Travel arrangements for clinic visits may be necessary.
- Long-term coping. The need for assistance for the patient, family and/or significant others in coping with the situation should be anticipated. Appropriate community agencies (e.g., church, hospice, community nurse) are identified and referrals made as needed.

THE PANCREAS

The pancreas has both endocrine and exocrine functions, and these functions are interrelated. The major exocrine function is to facilitate digestion through secretion of enzymes into the proximal duodenum. Secretin and cholecystokinin-pancreozymin (CCK-PZ) are hormones from the gastrointestinal tract that aid in digestion of food substances by control of secretions of the pancreas. Additionally, neural factors also influence pancreatic enzyme secretion. Considerable dysfunction of the pancreas must occur before enzyme secretion decreases and protein and fat digestion become impaired. Pancreatic enzyme secretion is normally 1,000 to 4,000 ml per day, with the amount depending on the quantity and type of food intake.

Pancreatitis

Pancreatitis (inflammation of the pancreas) is a serious disorder of the pancreas that can assume several forms. Acute pancreatitis, in which the structure and function of the pancreas usually return to normal after the acute attack, occurs most frequently as a result of gallstones. Chronic pancreatitis is characterized by permanent abnormalities of pancreatic function and is usually a result of long-term alcohol use. Patients with long-standing, undiagnosed chronic pancreatitis may develop acute episodes of pancreatitis, making the clinical picture less clear.

Several classification systems have been used to categorize the various stages and forms of pancreatitis. One classification system describes acute pancreatitis on the basis of findings on laparotomy or autopsy. These include interstitial (oedematous) and haemorrhagic (acute necrotizing) pancreatitis. The 1984 International Symposium on Classification of Pancreatitis categorizes the disease as acute or chronic pancreatitis, with obstructive chronic pancreatitis added as a type of chronic pancreatitis.

Several theories exist about the cause and mechanism of pancreatitis, which is generally described as the auto-digestion of the pancreas. Generally, these theories state that obstruction of the pancreatic duct is present and is accompanied by hypersecretion of the exocrine enzymes of the pancreas. These enzymes enter the bile duct where they are activated and, together with bile, back up (reflux) into the pancreatic duct, causing pancreatitis.

Acute Pancreatitis

Pathophysiology and Aetiology

Acute pancreatitis or inflammation of the pancreas is brought about by the digestion of this organ by the very enzymes it produces, principally trypsin. Biliary tract disease occurs in up to 80 per cent of patients with acute pancreatitis; however, only 5 per cent of patients with gallstones develop pancreatitis. Gallstones enter the common bile duct and lodge at the ampulla of Vater, obstructing the flow of pancreatic juice or causing a reflux of bile from the common bile duct into the pancreatic duct, thus activating the powerful pancreatic enzymes within the gland. Normally, these remain in an inactive form until the pancreatic juice reaches the lumen of the duodenum.

Spasm and oedema of the ampulla of Vater, resulting from duodenitis, can probably produce pancreatitis.

Long-term alcohol use is a common cause of acute episodes of pancreatitis, but the patient usually has had undiagnosed chronic pancreatitis before the first episode of acute pancreatitis occurs. Other less common causes of pancreatitis include bacterial or viral infection, with pancreatitis a complication of mumps virus. Blunt abdominal trauma, ischaemic vascular disease, hyperlipidaemia, hyperparathyroidism and the use of corticosteroids, thiazide diuretics and oral contraceptives have been associated with an increased incidence of pancreatitis. In addition, there is a small incidence of hereditary pancreatitis.

Mortality of acute pancreatitis remains high (10 per cent) owing to toxaemia, shock, anoxia, hypotension or fluid and electrolyte imbalances. Attacks of acute pancreatitis may result in complete recovery, may recur without permanent damage or may progress to chronic pancreatitis. The patient admitted to the hospital with a diagnosis of pancreatitis is acutely ill and requires skilled nursing and medical care.

Classification

Pancreatitis ranges in severity from a relatively mild, self-limiting disorder to a rapidly fatal disease that does not respond to any treatment. Oedema and inflammation usually confined to the pancreas itself are the major events in the more mild form of pancreatitis, which is termed interstitial or oedematous pancreatitis. Although this is considered the more mild form of pancreatitis, the patient is acutely ill and at risk of developing shock, fluid and electrolyte disturbances and sepsis.

Acute haemorrhagic pancreatitis represents a more advanced form of acute interstitial pancreatitis. Enzymatic digestion of the gland is more widespread and complete. The tissue becomes necrotic, and the damage extends to its vascular radicles, so that blood escapes into the substance of the pancreas and beyond into the retroperitoneal tissues. Late complications consist of pancreatic cysts or abscesses. The mortality rate of acute haemorrhagic pancreatitis is 30 per cent.

Clinical Features

Severe abdominal pain is the major symptom of pancreatitis that brings the patient to medical care. Abdominal pain and tenderness, along with back pain, result from irritation and oedema of the inflamed pancreas that stimulate the nerve endings. An increase in tension on the pancreatic capsule and obstruction of the pancreatic ducts also contribute to the pain. Typically, the pain occurs in the midepigastrium but can be supraumbilical. It is frequently acute in onset, occurring 24 to 48 hours after a very heavy meal or alcohol ingestion, and it may be diffuse and difficult to locate. It is generally more severe after meals and is unrelieved by antacids. Pain may be accompanied by abdominal distension and a poorly defined palpable abdominal mass.

The patient appears acutely ill. Abdominal guarding is present. A rigid or boardlike abdomen may occur and is generally a grave sign. Ecchymosis (bruising) in the flank or around the umbilicus may indicate severe, haemorrhagic pancreatitis.

Nausea and vomiting are common in acute pancreatitis. The vomitus is usually gastric in origin but may also be bile-stained. Fever, jaundice, mental confusion and agitation may also occur.

Although hypertension is not rare in acute pancreatitis, hypotension is more typical and may reflect hypovolaemia and shock in acute hemorrhagic pancreatitis. Hypovolaemia is due to loss of large amounts of protein-rich fluid into the tissues and peritoneal cavity. The patient may develop tachycardia, cyanosis and cold, clammy skin in addition to hypotension.

Respiratory distress is common, and the patient may develop diffuse pulmonary infiltrates, dyspnoea, tachypnoea and arterial hypoxaemia.

The diagnosis of acute pancreatitis is based on a history of abdominal pain, the presence of known risk factors, physical examination findings and selected diagnostic findings.

Diagnosis
Blood Studies. Serum amylase and lipase are the most important aids in diagnosing acute pancreatitis. Peak levels are reached in 24 hours, with a rapid fall to normal levels within 48 to 72 hours. Serum lipase and amylase levels in the urine also become elevated and remain elevated longer than serum amylase. The white blood cell count is usually elevated; hypocalcaemia is present in many patients and appears to be correlated with the severity of pancreatitis.

Transient hyperglycaemia and glucosuria and elevated serum bilirubin levels occur in some patients with acute pancreatitis.

X-Ray Studies. X-ray films of the abdomen and chest are obtained to differentiate pancreatitis from other disorders that may cause similar symptoms and to detect the development of pleural effusions.

Ultrasonography and Computed Tomography. Sonograms and tomograms are used to identify an increase in the diameter of the pancreas and to detect pancreatic cysts or pseudocysts.

Stools. Usually the stools of patients suffering with pancreatic disease are bulky, pale and foul smelling. Fat content varies between 50 and 90 per cent in pancreatic disease; normally, the fat content is 20 per cent.

Management
Management of the patient with acute pancreatitis is symptomatic and is directed towards preventing or treating complications. All oral intake is withheld to inhibit pancreatic stimulation and secretion of pancreatic enzymes. Although there is some controversy about the use of parenteral hyperalimentation in acute pancreatitis because of the possibility that it may stimulate pancreatic secretion, it is usually an important part of therapy, particularly in debilitated patients. Nasogastric suction is frequently used to decrease painful abdominal distension and paralytic ileus and to remove hydrochloric acid so that it does not enter the duodenum and stimulate the pancreas. Cimetidine is also used to decrease hydrochloric acid secretion.

Systemic treatment is necessary if vascular collapse and shock occur. Adequate correction of fluid and blood loss is necessary to maintain fluid volume and prevent renal failure. The patient is usually acutely ill and is monitored in the intensive care unit. Antibiotics are frequently administered to control infection; insulin may be required if hyperglycaemia occurs. Peritoneal lavage has been effective in severe pancreatitis or if ascites is significant.

Intense respiratory care is indicated because of the increased likelihood of elevation of the diaphragm, pulmonary infiltrates and effusion, and atelectasis. Hypoxaemia occurs in a significant number of patients with acute pancreatitis even without abnormalities present on X-ray films. Respiratory care may range from close monitoring of arterial blood gases to use of humidified oxygen to intubation and use of a ventilator. Adequate pain relief is essential during the course of acute pancreatitis.

Antacids may be used when the acute episode of pancreatitis begins to resolve. Oral feeds that are low in fat and protein content are initiated very gradually. Caffeine and alcohol are eliminated from the diet. If the episode of pancreatitis occurred during treatment with thiazide diuretics, glucocorticoids or oral contraceptives, these medications are discontinued. Follow-up of the patient may include ultrasound, X-ray studies, or endoscopic retrograde cholangiopancreatography to determine if the pancreatitis is resolving and to assess for abscesses and pseudocysts. Endoscopic retrograde cholangiopancreatography may also be used to identify the cause of acute pancreatitis if it is in question.

► NURSING PROCESS
► THE PATIENT WITH ACUTE PANCREATITIS

► *Assessment*

The nursing history focuses on the presence and character of the patient's abdominal pain and discomfort. The presence of pain, its location, its relationship to eating and to alcohol consumption, and the effect of the patient's efforts to bring about relief of pain are noted. The patient's nutritional status and history of gallbladder attacks and alcohol use are assessed. A history of gastrointestinal problems including nausea, vomiting, diarrhoea and passage of stools containing fat is elicited. Respiratory status, respiratory rate and pattern, as well as the breath sounds are assessed. Normal and adventitous breath sounds and abnormal findings on chest percussion, including dullness at the bases of the lungs and abnormal fremitus, are documented.

▶ Patient's Problems

Based on the assessment, the main problems for the patient with acute pancreatitis may include the following:

- Severe pain and discomfort related to inflammation, oedema, distension of the pancreas and peritoneal irritation.
- Altered fluid and nutritional status related to vomiting, inadequate fluid intake, fever, sweating and oedema.
- Alterations in respiratory function related to severe pain, pulmonary infiltrates, pleural effusion and atelectasis.

▶ Planning and Implementation
▶ Expected Outcomes

The main outcomes for the patient may include relief of pain and discomfort, improved fluid and nutritional status and improved respiratory function.

Nursing Care

Relief of Pain and Discomfort

Since the pathological process responsible for pain is autodigestion of the pancreas, the objectives of therapy are to relieve pain and to decrease secretion of the enzymes of the pancreas. The pain of acute pancreatitis is often very severe, necessitating the liberal use of analgesics. Pethidine may be used; morphine sulphate is to be avoided because it causes spasm of the sphincter of Oddi. Oral feeds are withheld to decrease the formation and secretion of secretin. The patient is maintained on parenteral fluids and electrolytes to restore fluid balance. Nasogastric suction is used to remove gastric secretions and to relieve abdominal distension. The patient will require frequent explanations by the nurse about the necessity of withholding fluid intake and maintaining gastric suction. Additionally, the nurse provides frequent oral hygiene and care to decrease discomfort from the nasogastric tube and relieve dryness of the mouth, which will be even more of a problem for the patient if he is receiving anticholinergic drugs to decrease pancreatic secretions.

The acutely ill patient will be nursed on bedrest to decrease the metabolic rate and reduce the secretion of pancreatic and gastric enzymes. If the patient experiences increasing severity of pain, this is reported to the doctor because the patient may be experiencing haemorrhage of the pancreas or the dose of analgesic may be inadequate.

Fluid Balance and Nutritional Status

Nausea, vomiting, gastric suction, movement of fluid from the vascular compartment to the peritoneal cavity and sweating and fever increase the patient's need for fluid and electrolyte replacement. Intravenous fluids will be administered and may be accompanied by transfusion of blood and albumin to maintain the patient's blood volume. The nurse assesses the patient's fluid and electrolyte status by noting skin turgor and moistness of mucous membranes. The patient is weighed daily, and fluid intake and output are carefully measured, including urine output, nasogastric secretions and diarrhoea. The nurse observes the patient for the presence of ascites and measures abdominal girth if ascites is suspected.

During the attack of acute pancreatitis, the patient will not be permitted food and oral fluid intake; however, it is important for the nurse to assess the patient's nutritional status and to note any events that alter the patient's fluid and nutritional needs. These signs include increased body temperature, restlessness and increased physical activity, and fluid and nutrient loss through diarrhoea. Circulatory collapse and shock are possible complications; therefore, frequent assessment of the patient is indicated and emergency medications are kept readily available.

As the patient's acute symptoms subside, oral feeds are reintroduced gradually. Between acute attacks, the patient receives a diet high in carbohydrates and low in fat and proteins. Heavy meals are to be avoided, as are alcoholic beverages.

Improvement of Respiratory Function

The patient is nursed in a semi-recumbent position to decrease pressure on the diaphragm by a distended abdomen and to increase respiratory expansion. Frequent changes of position are necessary to prevent atelectasis and pooling of respiratory secretions. Anticholinergic medications, if given to decrease gastric and pancreatic secretions, also dry the secretions of the respiratory tract, predisposing the patient to obstruction and infection. Assessment is essential to observe for any changes in respiratory status. The patient is advised in techniques of coughing and deep breathing to improve respiratory function.

Patient Education

The patient who has experienced and survived an episode of acute pancreatitis has usually been acutely ill, and will require a prolonged period of time to regain strength and return to previous levels of activity. Because of the severity of the acute illness, the patient may not recall many of the facts and explanations that have been given during hospitalization. As a result, this patient often requires repetition and reinforcement of information and advice. If acute pancreatitis is a result of biliary tract disease such as gallstones and gallbladder disease, the patient requires reinforcement about the need for a low-fat diet and avoidance of heavy meals. If the pancreatitis is a result of alcohol abuse, the patient needs to be reminded of the importance of eliminating *all* alcohol. When the acute attack has subsided and such patients return to their previous environments, they may be inclined to return to their previous habits. They need to be given specific information about resources and support groups that may be of assistance in avoiding alcohol in the future. Referral to Alcoholics Anonymous or other support groups is essential.

A referral to the community nurse is often indicated to permit the nurse to assess the patient's home situation, reinforce advice about fluid and nutrition intake and avoidance of alcohol, and permit the patient and home carers to discuss their questions and concerns.

▶ **Evaluation**
▶ **Expected Outcomes**

1. Patient experiences relief of pain and discomfort.
   a. Reports relief of pain and discomfort.
   b. Explains rationale for nasogastric tube and suction.
   c. Uses analgesics as prescribed, without overuse.
   d. Participates in oral hygiene measures.
   e. Maintains bedrest as prescribed.
   f. Uses anticholinergics appropriately if prescribed.
   g. Avoids alcohol to decrease abdominal pain.
2. Achieves improved fluid and nutritional balance.
   a. Demonstrates normal skin turgor and moist mucous membranes.
   b. Reports stabilization of weight.
   c. Demonstrates no increase in abdominal girth.
   d. Reports decrease in number of episodes of diarrhoea.
   e. Identifies and consumes high-carbohydrate, low-protein foods.
   f. Explains rationale for eliminating alcohol intake.
   g. Maintains adequate fluid intake within prescribed guidelines.
3. Experiences improved respiratory function.
   a. Maintains semi-recumbent position when in bed.
   b. Changes position in bed frequently.
   c. Coughs and takes deep breaths at least every hour.
   d. Demonstrates normal respiratory rate and pattern and full lung expansion.
   e. Demonstrates normal breath sounds and absence of adventitious breath sounds.
   f. Drinks at least eight glasses of nonalcoholic fluids per day (if within fluid allowance) to liquefy pulmonary secretions.
   g. Demonstrates normal body temperature and absence of indications of respiratory infection.

Chronic Pancreatitis

Chronic pancreatitis is an inflammatory disease characterized by progressive anatomical and functional destruction of the pancreas. As cells are replaced by fibrous tissue with repeated attacks of pancreatitis, pressure within the pancreas increases. The end result is mechanical obstruction of the pancreatic and common bile ducts and the duodenum. Additionally, there is atrophy of the epithelium of the ducts, inflammation and destruction of the secreting cells of the pancreas.

Alcohol consumption in Western societies and malnutrition worldwide are the major causes of chronic pancreatitis. In alcoholism, the incidence of pancreatitis is 50 times the rate in the nondrinking population. Chronic consumption of alcohol produces a hypersecretion of protein in pancreatic secretions. The result is protein plugs and calculi within the pancreatic ducts. There is also evidence that alcohol has a direct toxic effect on the cells of the pancreas. Damage to these cells is more likely to occur and to be more severe in patients whose diets are poor in protein content and either very high or very low in fat. The incidence of chronic pancreatitis is increased in adult men and is characterized by recurring attacks of severe upper abdominal and back pain, accompanied by vomiting. Attacks often are so painful that narcotics, even in large doses, do not provide relief. As the disease progresses, recurring attacks of pain will be more severe, more frequent and of longer duration. Some patients complain of continuous severe pain; others have a dull, nagging, constant pain. The risk of addiction to opiates is increased in pancreatitis because of the nature of the pain.

Weight loss is a major problem in chronic pancreatitis; over 75 per cent of patients experience significant weight loss usually due to decreased dietary intake secondary to anorexia or fear that eating will precipitate another attack. Malabsorption occurs late in the disease when as little as 10 per cent of function remains. As a result, the digestion of foodstuffs, especially proteins and fats, is disrupted. The stools become frequent, frothy and foul-smelling, owing to the impairment of fat digestion, which results in a stool with a high fat content. This condition is referred to as steatorrhoea. As the disease progresses, calcification of the gland may occur and calcium stones may form within the ducts.

Diagnosis
Endoscopic retrograde cholangiopancreatography is the most helpful study in the diagnosis of chronic pancreatitis. It provides detail about the anatomy of the pancreas and of the pancreatic and biliary ducts. It is also helpful in obtaining tissue for analysis and in differentiating pancreatitis from other conditions such as carcinoma. A computed tomography scan or ultrasonography is helpful to detect the presence of pancreatic cyst formation. A glucose tolerance test evaluates pancreatic islet cell function, information necessary for making decisions about surgical resection of the pancreas. An abnormal glucose tolerance test indicative of diabetes may be present. In

contrast to the patient with acute pancreatitis, serum amylase levels and the white blood cell count are unremarkable.

Management

The management of chronic pancreatitis depends on its probable cause in each patient. Nonsurgical approaches may be indicated for the patient who refuses surgery, is a poor candidate for surgery, or whose disease and symptoms do not warrant surgical intervention. Treatment includes prevention and management of acute attacks, the relief of pain and discomfort, and management of exocrine and endocrine insufficiency of pancreatitis. Treatment and prevention of abdominal pain and discomfort are similar to those used in acute pancreatitis; however, the focus is usually on use of nonopiate methods to prevent or treat pain. The doctor, nurse and dietician emphasize to the patient, family and other informal carers the importance of avoiding alcohol and other foods that the patient has found tend to produce abdominal pain and discomfort. The fact that no other treatment will be successful in relieving pain if the patient continues to consume alcohol is stressed.

Diabetes mellitus resulting from dysfunction of the pancreas islet cells is treated with diet, insulin, or oral hypoglycaemic agents. The hazard of severe hypoglycaemia if alcohol use continues is stressed to the patient and home carers. Pancreatic enzyme replacement is indicated in the patient with malabsorption and steatorrhoea.

Surgery is generally carried out to relieve abdominal pain and discomfort, to restore drainage of pancreatic secretions and to reduce the frequency of acute attacks of pancreatitis. The surgical procedure to be performed depends on the anatomical and functional abnormalities of the pancreas, including the location of disease within the pancreas, the presence of diabetes, exocrine insufficiency, biliary stenosis and pseudocysts of the pancreas. Other factors taken into consideration in determining if surgery is to be performed and what procedure is to be carried out include the presence of alcoholism and the ability of the patient to manage the endocrine or exocrine changes that are expected from surgical alterations.

Pancreaticojejunostomy with a side-to-side anastomosis or joining of the pancreatic duct to the jejunum allows drainage of the pancreatic secretions into the jejunum. Pain relief occurs by six months in over 80 per cent of the patients who undergo this procedure, but pain returns in a substantial number of these patients as the disease itself progresses. A variety of other surgical procedures are performed for different degrees and types of disease, ranging from revision of the sphincter of the ampulla of Vater, internal drainage of a pancreatic cyst into the stomach, to wide resection or removal of the pancreas. Attempts have been made to preserve the endocrine function of the pancreas by autotransplantation or implantation of the patient's pancreas islet cells. Testing and refinement of

this procedure continue in an effort to improve the results. Morbidity and mortality following these surgical procedures are high because of the poor physical condition of the patient before surgery and the concomitant occurrence of cirrhosis.

Despite the operative procedures, the patient is likely to continue having pain and digestive difficulties from the pancreatitis without complete abstinence from the use of alcohol. This point should be emphasized by the nurse in the course of advising the patient and carers.

Pancreatic Cysts

As a result of the local necrosis that occurs at the time of acute pancreatitis, collections of fluid may form in the vicinity of the pancreas. These become walled off by fibrous tissue and are called pancreatic cysts. They are the most common type of pancreatic cyst; other types develop as a result of congenital anomalies or secondary to chronic pancreatitis or trauma to the pancreas.

Diagnosis of pancreatic cysts is made by ultrasound, computed tomography scan and endoscopic retrograde cholangiopancreatography. Endoscopic retrograde cholangiopancreatography may be used to define the anatomy of the pancreas and to evaluate the patency of pancreatic drainage. Pancreatic cysts may attain considerable size. Because of their location behind the posterior peritoneum, when they enlarge, they impinge on and displace the stomach or the colon, which are adjacent. Eventually, through pressure or secondary infection, they produce symptoms, requiring that they be drained.

Management

Drainage into the gastrointestinal tract or through the skin surface of the abdominal wall may be established. In the latter instance, the drainage is likely to be profuse and destructive to tissue because of the enzyme contents. Hence, steps must be taken to protect the skin in areas adjacent to the drainage site to prevent excoriation. Ointments protect the skin, provided that they are applied before excoriation takes place. Another method involves the constant aspiration of digestive juice from the drainage tract by means of a suction apparatus, so that contact with the digestive enzymes is avoided. This method demands expert nursing attention to be sure that the suction tube does not become dislodged from the drainage tract and that the entire apparatus functions properly without interruption.

When chronic pancreatitis develops in association with gallbladder disease, efforts are made to relieve the difficulty by surgically exploring the common duct and removing the stones; usually, the gallbladder is removed at the same time. In addition, an attempt is made to improve the drainage of the common bile duct and the pancreatic duct by dividing the sphincter of Oddi, a muscle that is located at the ampulla of Vater (this operation is known as a sphincterotomy). Nursing care after such an operation is the same as that indicated for all patients undergoing biliary tract surgery. A T tube is usually placed in the common bile duct, requiring a drainage system to collect the bile after the operation.

Pancreatic Tumours

Carcinoma of the Pancreas

The incidence of pancreatic cancer has been steadily increasing for the past 20 to 30 years, especially in non-white males, and occurs most frequently in the sixth and seventh decades of life. Exposure to chemicals, a high-fat diet and cigarette smoking are associated with an increased incidence of pancreatic cancer, although their role in the aetiology is unclear.

Cancer may arise in any portion of the pancreas (in the head, the body or the tail), producing clinical features that vary, depending on the location of the lesion and whether or not functioning, insulin-secreting pancreatic islet cells are involved. Tumours that originate in the head of the pancreas, the most common location, give rise to a distinctive clinical picture (see below). Functioning islet cell tumours, whether benign (adenoma) or malignant (carcinoma) are responsible for the syndrome of hyperinsulinism (see p. 545). With these exceptions, the symptoms are nonspecific and patients usually do not seek medical attention until late in the course of their illness; 80 to 85 per cent of patients have advanced, unresectable disease when the tumour is first detected.

Clinical Features

Anorexia, weight loss, abdominal pain or jaundice may be the initial symptoms and may develop only when the disease is far advanced. Other signs include rapid, profound and progressive weight loss, as well as vague, upper or midabdominal pain or discomfort that is unrelated to any gastrointestinal function and difficult to describe. Such discomfort radiates as a boring pain in the midback and is unrelated to posture or activity. Patients with pancreatic carcinoma often find that they get some relief from pain by sitting hunched forward; pain is often accentuated by lying supine. A full-length foam-rubber pad placed under the patient has proven to be beneficial and protects the bony prominence from pressure. Pain is often progressive and severe, requiring the use of narcotic analgesics. The formation of ascites is common.

A very important sign, when present, is the onset of symptoms of insulin deficiency: glucosuria, hyperglycaemia and abnormal glucose tolerance. Diabetes may be an early sign of carcinoma of the pancreas. Meals often aggravate epigastric pain, which usually occurs weeks before the appearance of jaundice and pruritus. A gastrointestinal X-ray series may demonstrate deformities in adjacent viscera caused by the impinging pancreatic mass. Ultrasonography, computed tomography scanning and endoscopic retrograde cholangiopancreatography are useful in establishing the diagnosis.

Percutaneous fine-needle aspiration biopsy of the pancreas is used to diagnose pancreatic tumours and to confirm the diagnosis in patients whose tumours are not resectable, eliminating the stress and postoperative pain of ineffective surgery. In candidates for surgery, a preoperative diagnosis of the tumour is helpful in planning the surgical procedure. In this procedure, a needle is inserted through the anterior abdominal wall into the pancreatic mass under the guidance of computed tomography scan, ultrasound, endoscopic retrograde cholangiopancreatography or other imaging techniques. The aspirated material is examined for malignant cells.

Management

Therapy usually is limited to palliative measures. Definitive surgical treatment (i.e., total excision of the lesion) is often not feasible because of the extensive growth when the lesion is finally diagnosed and the probable widespread metastases–especially to the liver, lungs and bones.

The surgical procedure is usually extensive if carried out to remove resectable localized tumours. Pain management and attention to nutritional requirements are important measures to improve the patient's level of comfort.

Tumours of the Head of the Pancreas

Assessment

Tumours in this region of the pancreas cause obstruction of the common bile duct where it passes through the head of the pancreas to join the pancreatic duct and empty at the ampulla of Vater into the duodenum. Obstruction to the flow of bile produces jaundice, clay-coloured stools and dark urine.

Malabsorption of nutrients and fat-soluble vitamins may result from the obstruction and from the absence of bile from the gastrointestinal tract. Some degree of abdominal discomfort or pain and of pruritus may be noted. Nonspecific symptoms such as anorexia, weight loss and malaise may be present.

This disease must be differentiated from the jaundice due to a biliary obstruction caused by a gallstone in the common duct, which is usually intermittent and appears typically in obese patients, most often women, who have had previous symptoms of gallbladder disease. The tumours producing the obstruction may arise from the pancreas, from the common bile duct or from the ampulla of Vater.

Management

When these patients come into hospital, they are in such a poor nutritional and physical state that a fairly long period of preparation is necessary before operation can be attempted. Various liver and pancreatic function studies are carried out, vitamin K is given to restore the blood prothrombin activity and diets high in protein are often given with pancreatic enzymes. Blood transfusions are frequently used as well.

Following conventional blood and X-ray studies, more sophisticated diagnostic aids may be used, including duodenography, angiography by hepatic or coeliac artery catheterization, pancreatic scanning percutaneous transhepatic cholangiography, endoscopic retrograde cholangiopancreatography and percutaneous needle biopsy of the pancreas. Laparotomy with biopsy of the pancreas is a valuable diagnostic aid.

Surgical Management

A biliary–enteric shunt may be performed to relieve the jaundice and, perhaps, provide time for a suspicious lesion to be proven nonmalignant. Pancreatoduodenectomy (Whipple's procedure), which involves the removal of the gallbladder, distal portion of the stomach, duodenum and head of the pancreas and anastomosis of the remaining pancreas, stomach and common duct to the jejunum, is the operation of choice for potentially curable cancer of the head of the pancreas (Figure 14.4A, B). The result is removal of the tumour, allowing flow of bile into the jejunum. When excision of the tumour cannot be performed, the jaundice may be relieved by diverting the bile flow into the jejunum by anastomosing the jejunum to the gallbladder, a procedure known as cholecystojejunostomy (Figure 14.4C).

Nursing Care

Extensive preoperative preparation is indicated and includes adequate hydration and nutrition, correction of prothrombin deficiency with vitamin K and treatment of anaemia to minimize postoperative complications.

The postoperative care of patients who have undergone a pancreatuduodenectomy or Whipple's procedure is similar to the care of patients following extensive gastrointestinal and biliary surgery. The psychosocial considerations, however, are more specific and must be properly approached by the nurse. In view of the fact that the patient has undergone major and risky surgery and is severely ill, it is most likely that anxiety and depression will be experienced that will affect the response to treatment.

The mortality rate following this procedure had decreased recently because of advances in methods of nutritional support and improved techniques of surgical anastomosis. Preoperatively and postoperatively, the challenge for the nurse is to promote patient comfort, prevent complications and assist the patient in returning to and maintaining as normal and comfortable a life as possible.

Haemorrhage, vascular collapse and hepatorenal fail-

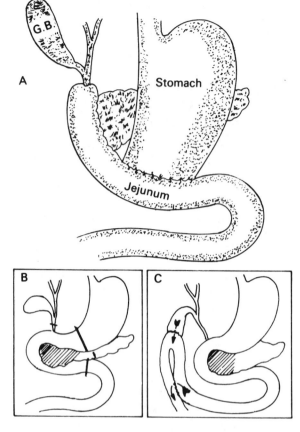

Figure 14.4 Pancreatoduodenectomy (after Whipple). (A) End result of resection of the carcinoma of the head of the pancreas or the ampulla of Vater. The common duct is sutured to the end of the jejunum, and the remaining portion of the pancreas and the end of the stomach are sutured to the side of the jejunum. (B) Lines indicate removal of head of pancreas, duodenum, adjacent stomach and distal segment of common bile duct. (C) Cholecystojejunostomy is an alternative operation if tumour of the head of the pancreas is inoperable. Bile flows into the intestine through the anastomosis of the jejunum and gallbladder.

ure remain the major complications of this extensive surgical procedure. The patient will be monitored closely in the intensive care unit following surgery, have multiple intravenous and arterial lines in place for fluid and blood replacement as well as monitoring arterial pressures, and be on a mechanical ventilator in the immediate postoperative period. Careful attention is given to changes in the patient's vital signs, arterial blood gases and pressures, blood test results and urine output. Although the patient's physiological status is the focus of the doctor and nurse, the psychological and emotional state must be considered, along with that of the patient's family and friends. The immediate and long-term outcome of this extensive surgical resection is uncertain, and the patient, family and friends require emotional support and understanding in the critical and stressful preoperative and postoperative periods.

Pancreatic Islet Tumours

The pancreas contains the islet (islands) of Langerhans—small nests of cells that secrete directly into the bloodstream and, therefore, are part of the endocrine system. The secretion, insulin, is essential for metabolism of glucose. Diabetes mellitus (Chapter 17) is the result of deficient secretion of insulin.

At least two types of tumours of the pancreatic islet cells are known: those that secrete insulin and those in which insulin secretion is not increased, known as 'nonfunctioning' islet cell cancer.

Tumours of the islet cells frequently produce hypersecretion of insulin and an excessive rate of metabolism of glucose. Hypoglycaemia, the resulting fall in serum glucose level, produces symptoms of weakness, mental confusion and even convulsions. These may be relieved almost immediately by taking sugar by mouth or by intravenous administration of glucose. The five-hour glucose tolerance test is helpful in diagnosing insulinoma, the tumour of the pancreatic islet cells that produces excessive insulin, and in distinguishing it from the more common functional hypoglycaemia.

Once the diagnosis of a tumour of the islet cells has been made, surgical treatment with removal of the tumour is usually recommended. The tumours may be benign adenomas or they may be malignant. Complete removal usually results in a dramatic cure. In some patients, such symptoms may not be produced by an actual tumour of the islet cells but by a simple hypertrophy of this tissue. In such cases a partial pancreatectomy–removal of the tail and part of the body of the pancreas–is performed.

Nursing Care

In preparing these patients for operation, the nurse must be alert for symptoms of hypoglycaemia and be ready to give sugar, usually with orange juice, should they appear. After operation, the nursing care is the same as that following any upper abdominal operation, with special emphasis on observation of serum glucose levels.

Hyperinsulinism

Hyperinsulinism results from the overproduction of insulin by the pancreatic islets. Symptoms resemble those of excessive doses of insulin and are attributable to the same mechanism—an abnormal reduction in the concentration of blood sugar. Clinically, it is characterized by episodes during which the patient experiences unusual hunger, nervousness, sweating, headache and faintness; in severe cases, convulsive seizures and episodes of unconsciousness may occur. The findings at operation or postmortem examination may indicate hyperplasia (overgrowth) of the islets of Langerhans or a benign or malignant tumour involving the islets and capable of producing large amounts of insulin (see preceding discussion). Occasionally, tumours of nonpancreatic origin produce an insulin-like material that can cause hypoglycaemia. This condition occasionally is responsible for convulsions coinciding with decreases in the blood glucose to levels that are inadequate to sustain normal brain function (i.e., below 1.6 mmol/l).

All of the symptoms that accompany spontaneous hypoglycaemia are relieved by the oral or parenteral administration of glucose. Surgical removal of the hyperplastic or neoplastic tissue from the pancreas offers the only successful method of treatment. About 15 per cent of patients with spontaneous or functional hypoglycaemia eventually develop diabetes mellitus.

BIBLIOGRAPHY

Hunt, J. M. *et al.* (1977) Patients with protracted pain: a survey conducted at the London Hospital, *Journal of Medical Ethics*, Vol. 3, No. 2, pp. 61–73.

Pritchard, P. A. and David, J. A. (1988) *The Royal Marsden Manual of Clinical Nursing Procedures* (2nd edition), Harper & Row, London.

Wilson-Barnett, J. and Batehup, L. (1988) *Patient Problems: A Research Base for Nursing Care*, Scutari Press, London.

FURTHER READING

Books

Brunner, L. S. and Suddarth, D. S. (1989) *The Lippincott Manual of Medical-Surgical Nursing* (2nd edition), Harper & Row, London.

David, J. A. (1986) *Wound Management: A Comprehensive Guide to Dressing and Healing*, Martin Dunitz, London.

Dickerson, J. W. T. and Booth, E. M. (1985) *Clinical Nutrition for Nurses, Dietitians and Other Health Care Professionals*, Faber & Faber, London.

Articles

Goodinson, S. (1986) Assessment of nutritional status, *Nursing*, Vol. 7, pp. 252–8.

Spencer, K. E. (1989) Postoperative pain: the alternatives to analgesia, *The Professional Nurse*, Vol. 4, No. 10, pp. 479–80.

ASSESSMENT AND CARE OF PATIENTS WITH INTESTINAL DISORDERS

Two of the major intestinal problems afflicting many people, especially the elderly, are constipation and diarrhoea. In all age groups, a fast-paced lifestyle, high levels of stress, irregular eating habits, insufficient intake of fibre and water and lack of daily exercise contribute to these problems. Laxatives are among the most popular over-the-counter medications purchased in the United Kingdom today, and laxative abuse is becoming a serious problem in the aged population. Nurses can have an impact on the chronicity of these problems by identifying behaviour patterns that put patients at risk, by educating the public about prevention and management and by helping those afflicted improve their condition and prevent complications.

CONSTIPATION

Constipation refers to an abnormal infrequency of defaecation, and also to abnormal hardening of stools that makes their passage difficult and sometimes painful.

Chronic Constipation

Most individuals have one bowel movement a day. However, the range of normal extends from three movements per day to three or fewer per week. In people who are constipated, defaecation is irregular and is complicated by hardened stools. Some constipated people occasionally have a diarrhoea of liquid stools as a result of the irritation caused by the presence in the colon of hard, dry faecal masses. Such stools contain a good deal of mucus, secreted by glands in the colon in response to these irritating masses. In severe constipation, the rectum may become impacted, that is, filled with masses of hard faeces that must be removed by the fingers or first softened by instillations of oil before they can be washed out by an enema.

Constipation can be caused by certain medications (tranquillizers, anticholinergics, narcotics, antacids with aluminum), rectal/anal disorders (haemorrhoids, fissures), obstruction (cancer of the bowel), metabolic and neurological conditions (diabetes mellitus, multiple sclerosis), lead poisoning and connective tissue disorders (scleroderma, lupus erythematosus). Other aetiological factors include weakness, debility, fatigue and inability to increase intra-abdominal pressure to facilitate the passage of stools, such as occurs with emphysema.

Altered Physiology

The altered physiology of constipation is poorly understood. However, it is believed to be related to interference with one of three major functions of the colon: mucosa transport (mucosal secretions facilitate movement of colon contents), myoelectric activity (mixing of the rectal mass and propulsive actions) or the processes involved in defaecation. The urge to defaecate is normally stimulated by rectal distension, which initiates a series of four actions: stimulation of the inhibitory rectoanal reflex, relaxation of the internal sphincter muscle, relaxation of the external sphincter muscle and muscles in the pelvic region and increased intra-abdominal pressure. Interference in any of these four processes can thus lead to nonorganic or idiopathic constipation.

When the urge to deaecate is ignored, the rectal mucous membrane and musculature become insensitive to the presence of faecal masses, and consequently a stronger stimulus is required to produce the necessary peristaltic rush for defaecation. The initial effect of this faecal retention, or hoarding, is to produce irritability of the colon, which, at this stage, frequently goes into spasm, especially after meals, giving rise to colicky midabdominal or low abdominal pains.

Clinical Features

Clinical features include abdominal distension, borborygmus (intestinal rumbling), pain and pressure, decreased appetite, headache, fatigue, indigestion, a sensation of incomplete emptying, straining at stool and the elimination of small-volume, hard, dry stool.

Diagnosis

Diagnosis is based on a complete physical examination, a sigmoidoscopy, a radiographic examination and stool testing for occult blood. Idiopathic constipation is diagnosed after an organic cause is eliminated.

Considerations for the Elderly

Elderly people report problems with constipation five times more frequently than younger people. A number of factors contribute to this increased frequency. People who have loose-fitting dentures or have lost their teeth have difficulty chewing and frequently choose soft, processed foods that are low in fibre. Convenience foods, also low in fibre, are popular for those who have lost interest in eating. Some older people reduce their fluid intake if they are not eating regular meals; decreased fluid intake decreases bulk and makes passage of stool more difficult. Lack of exercise and prolonged bedrest also contribute to constipation by decreasing abdominal muscle tone.

Sometimes older people imagine that they are constipated because they do not have a daily bowel movement and have misconceptions about what is and is not normal. This self-diagnosis frequently leads to laxative abuse or the habitual use of enemas.

Management

Management includes discontinuing abusive laxative use, recommending the inclusion of fibre in the diet, prescribing an exercise routine to strengthen abdominal muscles and patterning behaviours related to establishing a normal bowel movement (responding to reflexes, 'heeding the call', setting a daily defaecation time, drinking warm water with a meal).

If laxative use is necessary, one of the following may be prescribed: bulk-forming agents, saline/osmotic agents, lubricants, stimulants or faecal softeners. The physiological action and patient teaching related to these laxatives is described in Table 15.1. Enemas and rectal suppositories are not recommended for constipation and should be reserved for the treatment of impaction or for bowel preparation for surgery or diagnostic procedures. If long-term laxative use is absolutely necessary, the doctor will prescribe a bulk-forming agent in combination with an osmotic laxative.

▶ **NURSING PROCESS**
▶ **THE PATIENT WITH CONSTIPATION**

▶ *Assessment*

When talking with patients about their bowel habits, it is helpful to keep in mind that some may be embarrassed to discuss such a personal body function. Tact and respect for the reserved patient are generally appreciated. Questions of ' more personal matter may be placed later in the history after rapport has been established.

A complete nursing history includes onset and duration of constipation, lifestyle (exercise, nutrition, stress), occupation, past elimination pattern, current elimination pattern, laxative/enema use, current drug therapy and past medical-surgical history. The patient is asked to describe the colour, odour and consistency of the stool as well as any associated intestinal symptoms (rectal pressure/fullness, abdominal pain, pain and straining at defaecation, watery diarrhoea, flatulence). Does the patient have bleeding when trying to defaecate?

Table 15.1 *Laxatives: classification, agent, action and patient education*

Classification	Sample agents	Action	Patient education
Bulk-forming	Methyl cellulose	Increases faecal mass, which stimulates peristalsis	Do not take dry; report abdominal distension or unusual amount of flatulence
Osmotic	Magnesium hydroxide	Attracts fluid into bowel by osmosis	Only short-term use recommended because of toxicity (CNS or neuromuscular depression, electrolyte imbalance); magnesium laxatives should not be taken by patients with renal insufficiency
Stimulant	Bisacodyl	Irritates colon epithelium by stimulating sensory nerve endings and increasing mucosal secretions; action occurs within 6 to 8 hours	Catharsis may cause fluid and electrolyte imbalance, especially in the elderly; tablets should be swallowed, not crushed or chewed; avoid milk or antacids within 1 hour of taking the drug because the enteric coating may dissolve prematurely
Faecal softener	Liquid paraffin Docusate sodium	Hydrates stool by surfactant action on colonic epithelium (increases wetting efficiency of intestinal water); aqueous and fatty substances are mixed; drug does not exert laxative action	Can be used safely by patient who should avoid straining (cardiac patients, those with anorectal disorders)

(Adapted from Malseed, R.T. (1985) Pharmacology: Drug Therapy and Nursing Considerations, *J.B. Lippincott, Philadelphia.)*

► *Patient's Problems*

Based on the assessment data, the patient's main problems may include the following:

- Constipation or faecal impaction.
- Discomfort related to abdominal pressure.
- Fluid volume deficit related to inadequate fluid intake.
- Anxiety related to concern about irregular elimination pattern.
- Lack of knowledge about health maintenance practices to prevent constipation.

► *Planning and Implementation*
► Expected Outcomes

The main outcomes for the patient may include restoration or maintenance of a normal bowel function, relief of pain, adequate intake of fluids and fibre, relief of anxiety and understanding of methods for avoiding constipation.

Nursing Care

Patient Education

Most of the patient's expected outcomes can be achieved through a thorough teaching programme that presents information about the causes of constipation and the dietary practices and exercise activity that can promote healthy bowel habits.

In constipation, the role of the nurse is to assist with the re-education of the patient. The physiology of defaecation should be explained carefully, with particular emphasis on the importance of heeding promptly the urge to defaecate.

The patient must know what constitutes a normal diet and should be aware of the similarities and differences between prescribed diet and the normal diet. In general, a high-residue, high-fibre diet is prescribed for constipation.

The nurse recommends frequent mobilization in order to promote defaecation.

Patients who worry about having a daily bowel movement need reassurance. Carefully explain that some healthy people have a bowel movement three times daily, while others do so only two or three times a week. Knowing that some of the food eaten may normally remain in the intestinal tract 48 hours after ingestion will help the patient to understand and accept the fact that a daily bowel evacuation is not always necessary. The use of laxatives should be discouraged.

If a laxative regime has been prescribed, the nurse should explain the consequences of laxative dependency and possible faecal impaction.

Preventive measures include the gradual tapering off of laxative use; sufficient fluid and fibre intake; an adequate exercise programme; and modification of contributory lifestyle factors (for example, ignoring the urge to defaecate, stress).

► *Evaluation*
► **Expected Outcomes**

1. Patient establishes a regular pattern of bowel function.
   a. Participates in a regular exercise programme.
   b. Avoids laxative abuse.
   c. Drinks 2 to 3 litres of water daily.
   d. Includes foods high in bulk in the diet (fresh fruits, bran, nuts, whole grain breads and cereals, cooked fruits and vegetables).
   e. Reports soft, formed stool every day or every two to three days.
2. Experiences less abdominal discomfort.
   a. Is as physically active as possible.

Complications of Constipation

The maintenance of elimination is basic to the care of every patient. The effort entailed in defaecation is considerable. With the use of a bedpan the muscular strain is inevitably greater; when constipation is imposed in addition, the performance of this function can be extremely fatiguing if not altogether exhausting. This is a serious consideration in the management of patients with congestive heart failure, those who have suffered a recent myocardial infarction and are susceptible to cardiac rupture and those with arterial hypertension.

To facilitate elimination, the patient should assume the normal position for defaecation. The semi-squatting position maximizes the use of the abdominal muscles and the force of gravity.

Hospitalized patients who cannot use the bathroom experience less strain if assisted to a bedside commode, or seated on a bedpan at the side of the bed with feet supported on a chair. If the patient cannot sit up, a small support should be placed under the lumbosacral curve to minimize strain and increase comfort while using the bedpan.

Faecal Impaction

Faecal impaction refers to an accumulated mass of dry faeces that cannot be expelled. The mass may be palpable on digital examination, may cause pressure on the colon mucosa that results in ulcer formation and may cause the frequent seepage of liquid stools. Treatment consists of mineral oil and saline enemas and the digital extraction of the stool.

Megacolon

Megacolon refers to a dilated and atonic colon caused by a faecal mass that obstructs the passage of colon contents. Symptoms include constipation, liquid faecal incontinence and abdominal distension. The obstruction, which is diagnosed on radiographic examination, can lead to perforation and an emergency colectomy.

Cathartic Colon

Cathartic colon refers to mucosal atrophy of the colon with muscle thickening and fibrosis subsequent to the chronic use of laxatives. Symptoms include hypokalaemia, metabolic alkalosis, malabsorption and liquid faecal seepage. Treatment is directed at relieving the symptoms.

DIARRHOEA

Diarrhoea is a condition in which there is an unusual frequency of bowel movements, as well as changes in the amount, the character and the consistency of the stools. It is best described, quantitatively, as more than 200 grams of stool per day. Three factors determine its severity: intestinal secretions, altered mucosal absorption and increased motility.

Acute diarrhoea is caused by an increased secretion of water and electrolytes by the intestinal mucosa. This occurs because water is pulled into the intestines by the osmotic pressure of nonabsorbed particles or because intestinal secretions are increased. Diarrhoea may also be caused by increased peristaltic action of the intestines and is usually due to inflammatory bowel disease (ulcerative colitis, Crohn's disease). Infectious diarrhoea, which is caused by an infectious agent, results in an acute increase in the water content of faeces due to increased mucosal cell secretion of water. Peristaltic action is also increased. Common infectious agents are *Shigella*, *Escherichia coli* and *Campylobacter jejuni*.

Altered Physiology

The most common intestinal irritants are the products of certain bacteria grown either in the intestine or in the food before it was eaten. In the case of the enteric pathogens, the organisms causing bacillary dysentery, bacterial growth with release of the irritating toxins takes place in the intestine. On the other hand, many cases of food poisoning are due to the ingestion of food that is contaminated and already contains the toxin. *Staphylococcus aureus*, for example, if given an opportunity to grow in food, produces an exotoxin that is extremely irritating to the intestinal tract.

The inflammatory response to mild irritants is slight; little or no mucous membrane lining is destroyed on exposure to them unless their concentration in the intestinal fluid is excessive. Their chief effect is to produce hyperaemia (vascular dilation, with local increase in blood flow) of the intestinal mucosa and an increase in mucous secretion. A motor response of hyperperistalsis also occurs, persisting until the irritant is excreted, which explains the symptoms of crampy diarrhoea.

Clinical Features

In acute cases the stools are greyish brown, foul smelling and filled with undigested particles of food and mucus. The patient complains of abdominal cramps, distension, intestinal rumbling, anorexia and thirst. Painful straining of the anus may attend each defaecation.

The diarrhoea in food poisoning is explosive in onset, develops within a very few hours following the toxic meal and, except in severe cases, subsides within one or two days—as soon as the toxin is excreted and the inflammatory response lessens. There is little or no fever, and usually the only associated symptoms are those directly attributable to the diarrhoea, namely, dehydration and weakness.

Dysentery resulting from the growth of gastrointestinal pathogens within the gastrointestinal tract, on the other hand, develops with a more gradual onset and persists for several days or weeks, with striking constitutional symptoms in addition to the diarrhoea.

Considerations For the Elderly

The elderly can quickly become dehydrated and hypokalaemic from episodes of diarrhoea. Exact intake and output records are kept to determine fluid loss. All output is measured, including liquid stools. Urinary output of less then 30 ml/hour for two to three consecutive hours is reported to the doctor. Hypokalaemia is manifested by muscle weakness, paraesthesia, hypotension, anorexia and drowsiness.

The elderly need to have ready access to a bathroom because they may not be able to control elimination fully. They may need help with ambulation if a mobility problem exists.

The older person's skin is very sensitive because of decreased turgor and reduced subcutaneous fat layers. Enzymes from diarrhoeal stool are irritating and can cause excoriation.

The nurse should teach the patient to keep the anal area dry and clean. Washing with a mild soap is recommended. The area is patted dry, and zinc and caster oil cream can be applied after stool passage to serve as a protective barrier.

Preventive Health Measures

Precautions include ensuring that proper storage and refrigeration facilities are available and are used for the handling of all fresh fruits and meats. Meat products should be cooked thoroughly and either consumed promptly or refrigerated immediately. Milk and milk products should be refrigerated and protected against exposure.

Proper housekeeping, especially in the kitchen, is obviously very important in the prevention of epidemic diarrhoea. All materials used in the preparation and the serving of food must be cleaned rigorously and kept in immaculate condition. All food handlers should receive detailed instructions in hygienic principles and practices and, upon the development of any illness that is potentially infectious, should be relieved of their duties immediately.

Diagnosis

The diagnosis of an acute diarrhoea is based on the course of the disease: the type of onset and progression, the presence or absence of fever and a study of the stools, which are examined for bacteria as well as for blood and pus. The majority of cases (60 per cent) are diagnosed by microbiological, serological or tissue culture techniques; undiagnosed cases are usually of an infectious nature.

Management

Oral fluids are immediately increased and an oral glucose and electrolyte solution may be prescribed to rehydrate the patient. Nonspecific drugs such as diphenoxylate and loperamide are prescribed to decrease motility for diarrhoea of a noninfectious source. Antimicrobial agents are prescribed when an infectious agent has been identified. Intravenous therapy may be necessary for rapid hydration, especially for the very young or the elderly.

▶ NURSING PROCESS
▶ THE PATIENT WITH DIARRHOEA

▶ *Assessment*

Diarrhoea and its associated symptoms occur in a variety of disorders. The nurse will facilitate the diagnosis in each case by recording careful observations, including the patient's symptoms, behaviour and remarks. The patient is asked to describe the onset and pattern of the diarrhoea. Is it associated with abdominal pain, cramping or urgency? Does it occur at any specific time of the day? Assessment of stool frequency, consistency, colour and odour is carried out. Watery stools are characteristic of small-bowel disease, whereas loose, semisolid stools are associated more often with disorders of the colon. Voluminous, greasy stools suggest intestinal malabsorption, and the presence of mucus and pus in the stools denotes inflammatory enteritis or colitis. Oil droplets in the lavatory water are almost always diagnostic of pancreatic insufficiency. Nocturnal diarrhoea may be a manifestation of diabetic neuropathy.

The patient's usual daily dietary intake and drug therapy should be reviewed to identify any possible causative agents. Patients are asked if they are suffering from any chronic diseases, have any known allergies or have recently been exposed to an acute illness or an infected person. Note is made of whether the patient has travelled recently and, if so, to what geographical area.

Assessment for dehydration is done by checking for postural hypotension, tachycardia, a weak, thready pulse, decreased skin turgor, dry mucous membranes and inadequate urinary output. Because dehydration exists when weight loss exceeds 6 per cent of body weight, the patient is weighed daily and an accurate intake and output record is kept.

► *Patient's Problems*

Based on the assessment, the patient's main problems may include the following:

● Diarrhoea, related to the infection and ingestion of irritating foods.
● Potential for fluid volume deficit related to frequent passage of stools and insufficient fluid intake.
● Anxiety related to frequent, uncontrolled elimination.
● Potential impairment of skin integrity related to the passage of frequent, loose stools.
● Potential for transmission of infection related to faecal contamination.

► *Planning and Implementation*
► Expected Outcomes

The main outcomes for the patient may include cessation of diarrhoea, avoidance of fluid volume deficit, reduction of anxiety, maintenance of skin integrity and prevention of spread of infection.

Nursing Care

Measures to Control Diarrhoea

During an episode of acute diarrhoea, the patient is encouraged to rest in bed and take liquids and foods that are low in bulk until the acute period subsides. When food intake is tolerated, the nurse recommends a bland diet. Caffeine intake is limited because caffeine stimulates intestinal motility. Milk may be restricted for several days because transient lactase deficiency may be seen in some forms of acute diarrhoea. Antidiarrhoeal drugs such as diphenoxylate are administered as prescribed.

Maintaining Fluid Balance

Fluid balance is difficult to maintain during an acute episode of diarrhoea because the rapid propulsion of faeces through the intestines decreases water absorption; output exceeds intake. The nurse assesses for dehydration (decreased skin turgor, tachycardia, decreased pulse volume, decreased serum sodium) and keeps an accurate record of intake and output. The patient is weighed daily. The nurse encourages oral fluid replacement in the form of water, juices and commercial preparations such as Dyorolyte. Intravenous fluids may be required.

Reducing Anxiety

An opportunity should be provided for the patient to express fears/worry about being embarrassed by lack of control over bowel elimination. This fear of embarrassment is a major concern.

The nurse may suggest that the patient identifies irritating foods and stressors that precipitate an attack of diarrhoea. Elimination or reduction of these factors helps control defaecation. The patient is encouraged to be sensitive to body clues that warn of impending urgency (abdominal cramping, hyperactive bowel sounds). Special absorbent underwear and pads may be recommended to protect clothes if there is accidental faecal discharge.

The nurse should project an understanding, tolerant and relaxed demeanour. Support the patient's efforts to use coping mechanisms.

Skin Care

The perianal area becomes excoriated because diarrhoeal stool contains digestive enzymes that cause local irritation. The nurse advises the patient to follow a perianal care routine such as the following: wipe or pat the area dry after defaecation, cleanse with a mild soap and warm water, pat dry immediately and apply lotion/ointment as a skin barrier.

Precautionary Infection Measures

All patients with diarrhoea should be treated as potentially infectious until they are proven otherwise. If the diarrhoea is of an infectious origin, the nurse should determine whether there is any diarrhoea among the family, significant others and neighbours. Proper precautions following hospital isolation policies must be taken to prevent the spread of the disease through contamination of hands, clothing, bed linen and other objects with faeces or vomitus.

The nurse tries to determine if there is a causal relationship between episodes of diarrhoea and food intake. If a food contaminant is suspected, food is tested by bacteriological cultures. Food that is not contaminated can still act as an irritant to the patient's gastrointestinal tract.

▶ *Evaluation*
▶ **Expected Outcomes**

1. Patient avoids irritating foods.
   a. Identifies foods that act as an irritant.
   b. Eliminates irritating foods from diet.
   c. Reports a decrease in number and frequency of daily stools.
   d. Reports formed stools.
2. Maintains fluid and electrolyte balance.
   a. Takes sufficient fluids orally.
   b. Tolerates intravenous fluid/electrolyte replacement.
   c. States absence of fatigue and muscle weakness.
   d. Is alert and oriented.
   e. Displays moist mucous membranes and normal tissue turgor.
   f. Has a balanced intake and output.
   g. Has normal urine specific gravity.
3. Experiences less anxiety.
   a. Verbalizes concerns and fears.
   b. Recognizes symptoms that signal an impending attack.
   c. Uses coping mechanisms effectively.
   d. Wears special absorbent underwear and pads that protect clothing from soiling if needed.
4. Maintains skin integrity.
   a. Keeps area clean after defaecation.
   b. Uses lotion/ointment as a skin barrier.

DISEASES OF MALABSORPTION

Digestion is the process whereby nutrients are reduced to appropriate form for intestinal absorption. Intestinal absorption transports nutrients across the mucosa to the portal blood system.

Along with nutrients, the intestinal tract is the recipient of a large volume of fluid and electrolytes. Of about 1,500 ml of ingested liquid, plus about 7,000 ml from the gastrointestinal tract (salivary, biliary, pancreatic and intestinal sources), all but 500 ml are absorbed proximal to the ileocaecal valve. Thus, the intestine continually shifts the volume and composition of its contents to fulfil its major function of absorption.

Interruptions in the complex digestive process may occur anywhere to cause malabsorption, the inability of the digestive system to absorb one or more of the major nutrients—carbohydrates, fats and proteins. Malabsorption occurs when the digestive process has been altered by:

● The inability of nutrients to be readily catabolized and transported (gastric resection, Zollinger-Ellison syndrome, pancreatic insufficiency).
● The decreased absorption of nutrients by the intestinal mucosa (jejunal diverticula, ileal dysfunction).

● A combination of causes (parasitic diseases, Whipple's disease, coeliac disease).

In addition to these causes, certain inflammatory bowel disorders, such as ulcerative colitis and regional enteritis (Crohn's disease), cause increased protein breakdown (catabolism) in the small intestine, with resulting loss of protein into the lumen of the intestine (protein-losing enteropathy).

Altered Physiology and Clinical Features

Three primary malabsorption diseases are: (1) tropical sprue; (2) adult coeliac disease (nontropical sprue, gluten-induced coeliac disease); and (3) lactose intolerance. Tropical sprue and adult coeliac disease are similar in clinical features and pathological changes, but differ in their geographical incidence and causes, and also respond to different treatments. In adult coeliac disease, protein malabsorption is frequently seen as allergic reaction to gluten, which is found in wheat, rye, oats and barley. Gluten causes the mucosal villi to atrophy, thus restricting their absorptive abilities. Lactose intolerance occurs when there is a deficiency of lactase, a digestive enzyme that breaks down milk sugar (the disaccharide lactose). The resulting high concentration of lactose in the intestines causes an osmotic retention of water, which results in abdominal cramping, nausea and possibly diarrhoea.

The hallmarks of the malabsorption syndrome, of whatever cause, are diarrhoea or frequent loose, bulky, foul stools that have increased fat content and are often greyish in colour; associated weakness, weight loss and lack of wellbeing are often present. The chief result of malabsorption is malnutrition, manifested by weight loss.

Patients with the malabsorption syndrome, if untreated, become weak and emaciated due to starvation. Failure to absorb the fat-soluble vitamins A, D and K causes these patients to develop a corresponding vitamin deficiency. Manifestations of abnormal bleeding are likely to appear as a result of vitamin K deficiency and hypoprothrombinaemia (see p. 459). Anaemia develops, which is of the macrocytic type characteristic of folic acid deficiency (see p. 440). Impaired absorption of calcium may be responsible for gradual demineralization of the skeleton. Moreover, calcium deficiency may lead to extreme neuromuscular hyperirritability, including attacks of hypocalcaemic tetany.

Management

Investigations may include upper gastrointestinal endoscopy and faecal fat collections. Dietary considerations are pre-eminent in the treatment of adult coeliac disease and lactose intolerance. In coeliac disease, the elimination of gluten from the patient's diet is followed by striking clinical improvement. The diarrhoea ceases and nutritional status is restored to normal. This gratifying remission may be expected to last as long as the patient remains on a gluten-free diet, and no longer.

The treatment for lactose intolerance consists of removing lactose-containing foods from the diet e.g., milk, ice cream. Soy milk products can be substituted. Most adults can digest fermented milk products such as cheese and yogurt. These products supply a vital need for calcium, and their use is encouraged.

The factors primarily responsible for the onset and the progression of tropical sprue have not as yet been clarified. Of greatest benefit in this condition is the administration of folic acid, which usually is prescribed for a period of four to six months after remission has occurred. Broadspectrum antibiotics are equally important. The beneficial effects of folic acid in patients with tropical sprue appear with such regularity and on occasion are so striking as to suggest that this particular malabsorption syndrome may be attributable to, as well as productive of, folic acid deficiency.

ACUTE INFLAMMATORY INTESTINAL DISORDERS: APPENDICITIS AND PERITONITIS

Acute inflammatory intestinal disorders such as appendicitis and peritonitis may at first have similar clinical features: abdominal pain and tenderness, nausea and vomiting, anorexia, a low-grade temperature, tachycardia and leucocytosis. Diagnosis is based on a complete history and physical examination. Surgery is the treatment of choice. Common nursing outcomes are relief of pain, prevention of fluid volume deficit, reduction in anxiety, elimination of infection due to the potential/actual disruption of the gastrointestinal tract, maintenance of skin integrity and attainment of optimum nutrition.

Appendicitis

The appendix is a small, fingerlike appendage about 10 cm long, attached to the caecum just below the ileocaecal valve. No definite function can be assigned to it in humans. The appendix fills with food and empties as regularly as does the caecum, of which it is a part. It empties inefficiently, however, and its lumen is very small, so that it is prone to become obstructed and is particularly vulnerable to infection (appendicitis).

Appendicitis is the most common cause of acute inflammation in the right lower quadrant of the abdominal cavity. About 7 per cent of the population will have appendicitis at some time in their lives; males are affected more than females, and teenagers more than adults. It occurs most frequently between the ages of 10 and 30.

The disease is more prevalent in countries in which

people consume a diet low in fibre and high in refined carbohydrates.

Altered Physiology and Clinical Features

The appendix becomes inflamed and oedematous due to either kinking or an occlusion, possibly caused by a faecalith (hardened mass of stool), tumour or foreign body. The inflammatory process increases intraluminal pressure, initiating a progressively severe generalized or upper abdominal pain which, within a few hours, becomes localized in the right lower quadrant of the abdomen with rebound tenderness (production or intensification of pain when pressure is released). This pain is usually accompanied by a low-grade fever, nausea and often vomiting. A moderate leucocytosis is often present. Loss of appetite is common.

Eventually, the inflamed appendix fills with pus and then is apt to perforate. Once it has ruptured, the pain becomes more diffuse; abdominal distension develops as a result of paralytic ileus, and the patient's condition worsens.

Complications

The major complications of acute appendicitis are perforation, peritonitis, appendiceal abscess formation and pyelophlebitis. With perforation, the pain is severe and the temperature is elevated. The doctor is notified immediately. Patients over 50 years of age are considered to be at high risk because they have the highest mortality rate. Perforation can lead to an appendiceal abscess (a mass that is walled off from the peritoneal cavity by the omentum, or small bowel) or peritonitis. An abscess is managed with intravenous antibiotics that help localize the infection until surgical drainage can be performed; an appendectomy is done in about six weeks. The management of peritonitis is described on pages 554 to 555.

Care of the Patient With Appendicitis

Surgery is always indicated if acute appendicitis is suspected, unless there is good evidence that perforation has occurred recently and that a generalized peritonitis has developed.

When an operation is necessary, the patient is carefully prepared. An intravenous infusion is used to establish adequate urinary output and replace existing fluid loss. Antibiotic therapy is often instituted as a preventive measure against infection. If there is evidence or likelihood of paralytic ileus, a nasogastric tube may be passed. The patient is asked to void, the abdomen is prepared and the prescribed preoperative medications are given.

The patient who has been suffering from acute abdominal pain may view the operation as a means of relief. This acceptance of surgery makes the anaesthetic and

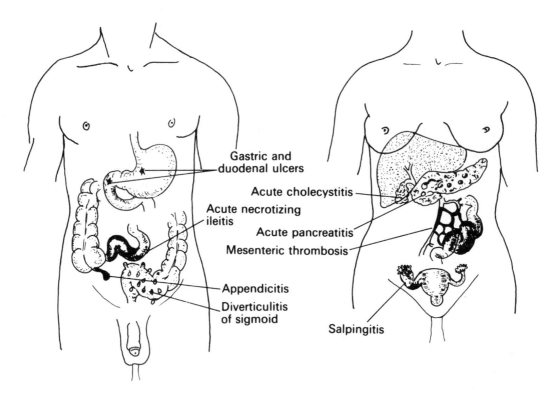

Figure 15.1 Common primary causes of peritonitis. (Dunphy, J. E. and Way, L. W. (1985) *Current Surgical Diagnosis and Treatment*, Lange Medical Publishers, Los Altos, California.)

postanaesthetic course a relatively easy one. The operation is usually performed under general anaesthetic.

Peritonitis

Peritonitis is inflammation of a part or all of the parietal and visceral surfaces of the abdominal cavity. Usually it is a result of bacterial infection, the organisms coming from disease of the gastrointestinal tract or, in women, the internal reproductive organs (Figure 15.1). Secondary peritonitis comes from external sources by injury or by extension of inflammation from an extraperitoneal organ, such as the kidney. The most common bacteria found are *Escherichia coli*, *Klebsiella*, *Proteus* and *Pseudomonas*. Inflammation and ileus are the direct effects of the infection.

Altered Physiology

Peritonitis is caused by leakage of contents from abdominal organs into the abdominal cavity, usually as a result of inflammation, infection, ischaemia, trauma or tumour perforation or, in the case of peritoneal dialysis, through the inadvertent introduction of contaminated material. Initially, the material that spills into the abdominal cavity is sterile (except in the case of peritoneal dialysis), but within 6 to 12 hours bacterial contamination occurs. Oedema of tissues results, and in a short while exudation develops.

Fluid in the peritoneal cavity becomes turbid with increasing amounts of protein, white cells, cellular debris and blood. The immediate response of the intestinal tract is hypermotility, but this is soon followed by paralytic ileus, with an accumulation of air and fluid in the bowel.

Clinical Features

Symptoms depend on the location and extent of the inflammation, which are determined by the infection causing the peritonitis. At first a diffuse type of pain is felt. This tends to become constant, localized and more intense near the site of the process. It is usually aggravated by movement. The affected area of the abdomen becomes extremely tender, and the muscles become rigid. Rebound tenderness and ileus may be present. Usually, nausea and vomiting occur and peristalsis is diminished. The temperature and pulse rate increase, and there is almost always an elevation of the leucocyte count. Shock may result from hypovolaemia or septicaemia. These early clinical features of peritonitis are frequently the symptoms of the disorder causing the condition.

Care of the Patient With Peritonitis

Fluid, colloid and electrolyte replacements are the major foci of medical management. Hypovolaemia occurs because massive amounts of fluids and electrolytes move from the intestinal lumen into the peritoneal cavity and deplete the vascular space. This in turn decreases renal perfusion. In addition, the fluid in the abdominal cavity can impair ventilation by causing pressure on the diaphragm.

Intestinal intubation and aspiration assist in relieving abdominal distension and in promoting intestinal function. Oxygen therapy by nasal cannulae or mask will promote ventilatory function.

If the cause of the peritonitis is removed at an early stage, the inflammation subsides and the patient recovers. Frequently, however, the inflammation is not localized and the whole abdominal cavity becomes involved, in which case the patient is acutely ill and has severe pain.

Because sepsis is the major cause of death from peritonitis, massive antibiotic therapy is usually initiated early in the treatment. Cultures of peritoneal fluid are taken but, until the laboratory reports are available, large doses of a broad-spectrum antibiotic are given intravenously.

Eventually, unless the cause of peritonitis is eliminated, the patient may succumb to intestinal obstruction. This is brought about by small bowel adhesions and even local abscess formation. If these can be localized, surgical drainage is effective.

Surgical objectives include removing the infected material and correcting the cause. Surgical treatment is directed toward excision (appendix), resection with or without anastomosis (intestine), repair (perforation) and drainage (abscess). With extensive sepsis, the creation of an ostomy is preferred to intestinal anastomosis because the colon could be damaged as a result of ischaemia.

Nursing Care

Accurate assessment of pain is important. A description of the nature of the pain, its location in the abdomen and any shifts in location may help ascertain the source of difficulty.

Accurate recording of input and output, including vomit, assists in calculating fluid replacement. In addition, determination of central venous pressure (see Chapter 6) may be helpful.

Drains are frequently inserted during the operation, and it is essential that the nurse observes and records the character of the drainage. Care must be taken in moving and turning the patient to prevent the drains from being dislodged accidentally.

Signs that the peritonitis is subsiding include a fall in temperature and pulse rate, softening of the abdomen, return of peristaltic sounds, passing of flatus and bowel movements. Foods and fluids (taken by mouth) will be gradually increased and intravenous fluids reduced.

Two of the most common complications that must be watched for are wound infection and abscess formation. Any suggestion from the patient that an area of the abdomen is tender or painful or 'feels as if something just gave way' should be reported. The sudden occurrence of serosanguineous wound drainage strongly suggests wound dehiscence (see Wound Care and Wound Healing, Chapter 2).

DIVERTICULAR DISORDERS

A diverticulum is an outpouching or herniation of the mucous membrane lining of the bowel through a defect in the muscle layer. Diverticula, in fact, may occur anywhere along the course of the gastrointestinal tract, from the oesophagus to the rectum.

Diverticulosis exists when multiple diverticula are present without inflammation or symptoms. Diverticulitis results when food and bacteria retained in a diverticulum produce infection and inflammation that can impede drainage and lead to perforation or abscess formation. A congenital predisposition is likely when the disorder is present in those under 40 years of age. A low intake of dietary fibre is considered a major cause of the disease.

It has been estimated that approximately 20 per cent of patients with diverticulosis experience diverticulitis at some point. Diverticulitis is most common in the sigmoid colon (95 per cent). It may occur in acute attacks or may persist as a long-continued, smouldering infection.

Altered Physiology

A diverticulum forms when the mucosa and submucosal layers of the colon herniate through the muscular wall because of high intraluminal pressure (thickened muscle layers occlude the lumen), low volume in the colon (fibre-deficient contents) and decreased muscle strength in the colon wall (muscular hypertrophy from hardened faecal masses). A diverticulum can become obstructed and then inflamed if the obstruction continues. The inflammation tends to spread to the surrounding bowel wall, giving rise to irritability and spasticity of the colon. An abscess may develop, leading to peritonitis, and erosion of the blood vessels (arterial) may produce bleeding.

Clinical Features

Constipation from spastic colon syndrome often precedes the development of diverticulosis by many years. Other signs of diverticulosis are bowel irregularity and diarrhoea. A moderately severe acute diverticulitis has as its most common symptom crampy pain in the left lower quadrant of the abdomen, and a low-grade fever. Following local inflammation of the diverticula, there may be a narrowing of the large bowel with fibrotic stricture, leading to cramps, narrow stools and increased constipation. With the development of granulation tissue, occult bleeding may occur, producing iron-deficiency anaemia.

In addition, weakness and fatigue are evident. If an abscess develops, there is tenderness, a palpable mass, fever and leucocytosis. If an inflamed diverticulum perforates, abdominal pain results that is localized over the involved segment—usually the sigmoid; local abscess or peritonitis results. With the development of peritonitis, the symptoms of rigidity, abdominal pain, loss of bowel sounds and shock develop. Uninflamed or slightly inflamed diverticula may erode areas adjacent to arterial branches, thus causing massive rectal bleeding.

The incidence of diverticular disease increases with age. There are structural changes in the circular muscle layers of the colon as well as cellular hypertrophy. The elderly may not notice abdominal pain until infection occurs. They may delay reporting symptoms because they fear surgery or may be afraid that they may have cancer.

Although blood in the stool is a common sign of diverticular disease in the elderly, it is frequently overlooked because a person fails to examine the stool or cannot see slight changes because of diminished vision.

Diagnosis

Diverticulosis may be diagnosed from X-ray studies that show narrowing of the colon and thickened muscle layers.

A history generally elicits the two main presenting symptoms of diverticulitis: pain in the lower left quadrant, along with a marked change in bowel habits (diarrhoea or constipation). Diagnosis is made on the basis of sigmoidoscopy (direct visualization), colonoscopy and X-ray findings with a barium enema (after inflammation has subsided). An obstruction may show with localized inflammation. A computerized tomography scan can reveal abscesses.

Care of the Patient With Diverticular Disorder

In diverticulosis, a high-fibre diet is prescribed to prevent constipation. In diverticulitis, the bowel is rested by withholding oral fluids, administering intravenous fluids and instituting nasogastric aspiration. Broad-spectrum antibiotics and analgesics are prescribed. Oral intake is increased as symptoms subside. A low-fibre diet may be necessary until signs of infection decrease.

For spastic pain, antispasmodics such as propantheline bromide are taken before meals and at bedtime. Bowel antimicrobials may also be required. Stool normalization can be achieved by the use of one or more of the following: bulk preparations, such as methyl cellulose; stool softeners, such as sodium docusate; instillation of warm oil into the rectum; and an evacuant suppository, such as bisacodyl. Such a prophylactic plan will reduce the bacterial flora of the bowel, diminish the bulk of the stool, and soften the faecal mass, so that it traverses more easily the area of inflammatory obstruction.

Surgery for diverticulosis is usually necessary only if severe haemorrhage occurs, and even then is controversial because studies show that in 50 per cent of cases, surgery is followed by a recurrence of diverticula. If surgery is decided upon, a total colectomy with an ileorectal/ileoanal anastomosis is recommended. In this surgery, the entire colon is removed and the end of the small intestine is joined to the rectum or the anus.

Although acute diverticulitis usually subsides with medical management, about 25 per cent of the cases require surgical intervention for perforation, peritonitis, abscess formation, haemorrhage and obstruction. There are two types of surgery: (1) one-stage resection of the involved sigmoid section, for recurrent attacks, and (2) multiple-staged procedures for complications, such as obstruction, perforation and fistulae (Figure 15.2). Surgery is preceded by barium studies. In preparing the patient for surgery, it is important to avoid irritating the colon, which is already sensitive and susceptible to perforation. A mild laxative and carefully administered cleansing enemas may be sufficient.

The surgery performed varies with the operative findings. When possible, the area of diverticulitis is resected and the remaining bowel joined end to end (primary resection and end-to-end anastomosis). A two-stage resection is sometimes done, in which the diseased colon is resected, as in a one-stage operation, but no anastomosis is performed and both ends of the bowel are brought out onto the abdomen as stomas. The 'double-barrel' colostomy is then anastomosed in a later procedure. In some

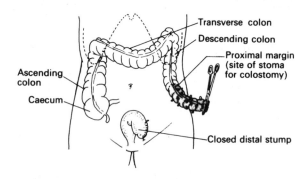

Figure 15.2 The Hartmann procedure for diverticulitis. Primary resection for diverticulitis of the colon. The affected segment (shaded) has been divided at its distal end. If primary anastomosis is to be done, the proximal margin (dotted line) is transected, and the bowel is anastomosed end-to-end. If a two-stage procedure is to be used, a colostomy is formed at the proximal margin and the distal stump is oversewn (Hartmann procedure, as shown), or brought to the surface as a mucous fistula. The second stage consists of reversal of colostomy takedown and anastomosis. (Way, L. W. (ed.) (1985) *Current Surgical Diagnosis and Treatment*, Lange Medical Publishers, Los Altos, California.)

patients such an operation may appear impossible or inadvisable, in which case a colostomy is performed in the right transverse colon. Diverting the faecal flow from the area of diverticulitis allows the inflammatory process to subside, and a later operation removing the colon containing the diverticulitis is done, followed by an anastomosis. When this method of treatment is chosen, the colostomy is only temporary; after the area of diverticulitis has been removed and the intestinal continuity established by the anastomosis, the colostomy is closed. This is thus a three-stage procedure, requiring care for a colostomy during only a part of the treatment (see p. 574). A colostomy on the right side of the transverse colon drains liquid or mushy faeces and requires that a bag be worn constantly. Irrigations are rarely of value in this type of colostomy, but ordinary cleanliness is obtained by baths or showers, using soap and water to cleanse the skin around the colostomy stoma.

▶ NURSING PROCESS
▶ THE PATIENT WITH DIVERTICULITIS

▶ *Assessment*

The main problems an individual with diverticulitis may suffer are pain in the left lower quadrant and more general abdominal tenderness due to inflammation and infection. Altered bowel habits may also worry the patient, including rectal bleeding, episodes of diarrhoea and constipation related to the narrowing of the colon. A dietary history may reveal a low fibre intake. Temperature and pulse may be elevated due to infection secondary to abscess formation, perforation and peritonitis.

▶ *Planning and Implementation*

Nursing Care

Elimination
If the patient is able to maintain an oral intake, the nurse should recommend a fluid intake of two to three litres a day (within limits of the patient's cardiac reserve), and suggest foods that are soft but have increased fibre, such as peas and prunes, to promote defaecation. For uncomplicated diverticular disease, suggest the addition of unprocessed bran to soups, salads and cereals. The nurse should help the patient identify undesirable habits that may have been used to suppress the urge to defaecate. The daily intake of bulk laxatives such as methyl cellulose should be recommended, which helps to propel faeces through the colon. Stool softeners should be administered as prescribed to decrease straining at stool which, in turn, decreases intestinal pressure.

Pain Relief
Analgesics and antispasmodic drugs are administered as prescribed. A low-fibre diet is recommended until the inflammation subsides. The intensity, duration and location of pain are recorded to determine severity and progression/remission of the inflammatory process. Pain is felt in the left lower quadrant and can be referred to the back. The nurse should immediately report any abdominal rigidity, which may indicate perforation and peritonitis.

Preventing Complications
The major nursing focus is prevention through identification of people at risk and management of those suffering from diverticular disease. The nurse encourages fluid intake to promote hydration in order to maintain normal stool consistency and prevent straining. During acute inflammation, however, oral foods and fluids may be restricted, in which case intravenous fluids are prescribed to prevent dehydration.

If food is tolerated while infection is present, a low-fibre diet is prescribed and the nurse advises the patient about dietary management. The nurse observes for indications of perforation: a tender, rigid abdomen; the presence or absence of pain; increased temperature; tachycardia; and hypotension. Perforation constitutes a surgical emergency.

The patient should understand the nature of the problem and recognize that the objective is to rest the intestinal tract.

▶ *Evaluation*
▶ Expected Outcomes

1. Patient attains a normal pattern of elimination.
   a. Reports less abdominal cramping and pain.
   b. Reports the passage, without pain, of soft, formed stool.
   c. Adds unprocessed bran to foods.
   d. Drinks at least 10 glasses of fluid a day (if fluid intake is tolerated).
   e. Exercises daily.
2. Experiences less pain.
   a. Requests analgesics as needed.
   b. Adheres to a low-fibre diet.
3. Achieves normal gastrointestinal tissue perfusion.
   a. Complies with food restrictions.
   b. Remains on bedrest.
   c. Is afebrile.
   d. Has a soft, nontender abdomen with normal bowel sounds.

Meckel's Diverticulum

Meckel's diverticulum is a congenital abnormality consisting of a blind tube, comparable to the appendix, that usually opens into the distal ileum near the ileocaecal valve. A portion of this duct persists as a diverticulum in approximately 2 per cent of the population. It is more common in men than in women.

The importance of Meckel's diverticulum lies in the fact that its mucosal lining not infrequently may become inflamed and may lead to intestinal obstruction, or it may perforate, causing peritonitis.

The most common symptoms of a diseased Meckel's diverticulum are abdominal pain, typically umbilical in location, or the passage of stools containing blood. The blood is a dark crimson colour. (A slowly bleeding gastric or upper intestinal lesion is tarry black; a colonic haemorrhage usually produces bright red bleeding.) The treatment is surgical excision of the diverticulum.

CHRONIC INFLAMMATORY BOWEL DISEASE: CROHN'S DISEASE AND ULCERATIVE COLITIS

The term 'inflammatory bowel disease' is used to designate two chronic inflammatory gastrointestinal disorders: Crohn's disease (granulomatous colitis) and ulcerative colitis. The disease is seen more frequently in whites and most frequently in the Jewish population. A familial history is found in 20 to 40 per cent of patients.

The current belief is that Crohn's disease and ulcerative colitis are separate entities with similar aetiologies. Both are characterized by exacerbations and remissions. Both diseases are associated with ankylosing spondylitis and the HLA antigen B27. A specific chromosomal abnormality has not been identified. Each disease may be triggered by environmental agents such as pesticides, food additives, tobacco and radiation. An immunological influence has been suggested because of studies that show abnormalities in humoral and cell-mediated immunity in people with these disorders. Lymphocytotoxic antibodies have been found in patients with inflammatory bowel disease, but more definitive research is needed to link immunological and environmental factors.

A psychological factor has also been suggested. Many individuals with ulcerative colitis are found to be dependent, passive, immature, perfectionist and anxious to please. Coping behaviours are often inappropriate and can include withdrawal, denial and repression. Some people have a decreased level of tolerance for the pain and discomfort associated with intestinal cramping and diarrhoea. They may react by being depressed or violent. Some clinicians suggest that the personality traits are the cause —not the result—of the disease symptoms, but more clinical research is needed to establish a causal relationship.

Altered Physiology

Although both diseases share certain similarities, they differ in many ways. Crohn's disease is an inflammatory disorder that erodes the wall of the intestine. It may involve any part of the intestine, although the ileum is most commonly affected. Ulcerative colitis is a recurrent ulcerative and inflammatory disease of the colon and rectum, with rare involvement of the distal ileum. It is a serious disease, accompanied by systemic complications and a high mortality rate. Eventually 10 to 15 per cent of the patients develop carcinoma of the colon. See Table 15.2 for a comparison of Crohn's disease and ulcerative colitis.

Crohn's Disease Crohn's disease is a subacute and chronic inflammation that extends through the intestinal mucosa. This transmural involvement accounts for the formation of fistulae, fissures and abscesses. The lesions are characteristically discontinuous or separated by normal tissue. Granulomas occur in 50 per cent of the cases. Advanced cases present with a 'cobblestone' appearance. As the disease advances, the intestinal lumen narrows, causing obstruction.

Ulcerative Colitis. Ulcerative colitis affects the superficial mucosa of the colon and is characterized by multiple ulcerations, diffuse inflammations and desquamation of the colonic epithelium, with alternating periods of exacerbation and remission. The lesions are continuous and ultimately spread throughout the large intestine. Eventually the bowel narrows, shortens and thickens due to muscular hypertrophy and the deposition of fat.

Clinical Features

Crohn's Disease. With Crohn's disease, the onset of symptoms is usually insidious, but abdominal pain, diarrhoea and weight loss are prominent, and are unrelieved by defaecation. Diarrhoea is present in 90 per cent of patients. Scar tissue and formation of granulomas interfere with the ability of the intestine to transport products of the upper intestinal digestion through the constricted lumen, resulting in crampy abdominal pains. Because intestinal peristalsis is stimulated by the eating of food, the crampy pains occur after meals. To avoid these bouts of crampy pain, the patient avoids food or takes it only in amounts and types inadequate for normal nutritional requirements, so that weight loss, malnutrition and secondary or macrocytic anaemia occur. In addition, ulcers form in the lining membrane of the intestine and other inflammatory changes take place, resulting in a constant irritating discharge that is emptied into the colon from the weeping, swollen intestine. This causes a chronic diarrhoea. The end result is a very uncomfortable person who is thin and emaciated from inadequate food intake and constant fluid loss. In some patients, the inflamed intestine may perforate and form intra-abdominal and anal abscesses. Melaena may occur, along with malabsorption syndrome. Fever and leucocytosis occur. Abscesses, fistulas and fissures are common.

Ulcerative Colitis. The predominant symptoms of ulcerative colitis are diarrhoea, abdominal pain, intermit-

Table 15.2 *Comparison of Crohn's disease and ulcerative colitis*

	Crohn's disease	Ulcerative colitis (mucosal)
History	Crippling	Exacerbations, remissions may be lethal Toxic megacolon
Pathology Early Late	 Transmural thickening Deep, penetrating granulomas	 Mucosal ulceration Mucosal minute ulceration
Clinical features Location Bleeding Perianal involvement Fistulae Rectal involvement Diarrhoea	 Illeum, right colon(usually) Usually not, but may occur Common Common About 20 per cent Less severe	 Rectum, left colon Common–severe Rare–mild Rare Almost 100 per cent Severe
Diagnostic studies X-ray films	Skip areas Shortening of colon Mucosal oedema Stenosis, fistulae	Diffuse involvement No shortening of colon No mucosal oedema Stenosis, rare; no fistulae
Therapeutic care	Steroids, sulphonamides (sulphasalazine) Total parenteral nutrition Partial or complete colectomy, with ileostomy or anastomosis Rectum can be preserved in some patients	Steriods, sulphonamides Proctocolectomy, with ileostomy Rectum can be preserved in only a few patients 'cured' by colectomy
Complications	Right-sided hydronephrosis Nephrolithiasis Cholelithiasis Retinitis, iritis Finger clubbing Erythema nodosum	Pyelonephritis Cholangiocarcinoma Pericholangitis Same Same Same

tent tenesmus and rectal bleeding. In addition, anorexia, weight loss, fever, vomiting and dehydration may be evident, as well as cramping and the feeling of an urgent need to defaecate. The patient may report passing 10 to 20 liquid stools daily. Hypocalcaemia and anaemia frequently develop. Rebound tenderness may occur in the right lower quadrant.

Diagnosis

Crohn's Disease. For Crohn's disease, the most conclusive diagnostic aid is a barium study of the upper gastrointestinal tract that reveals the classic 'string sign' on X-ray of the terminal ileum, indicating the constriction of a segment of intestine.

A proctosigmoidoscopic examination is usually done initially to establish whether there is an inflammatory process in the rectosigmoid area. If this area is normal, the diagnosis of ulcerative colitis is ruled out.

A stool examination may be positive for occult blood and fat. Leucocytosis and an elevated sedimentation rate may be present. Bowel sounds are exaggerated over the right lower quadrant.

Ulcerative Colitis. In the diagnosis of chronic ulcerative colitis, careful stool examination is done to rule out dysentery caused by the common intestinal organisms, especially *Entamoeba histolytica* infection. The stool tests positive for blood. Leucocytosis, anaemia and bone marrow depression are common. Other indicators include a loss of plasma proteins due to liver dysfunction, electrolyte imbalance, thrombocytosis due to the inflammatory process and decreased serum iron levels secondary to blood loss. Sigmoidoscopy and barium enema X-ray examination are of value in distinguishing this condition from other diseases of the colon with similar symptoms.

● In acute ulcerative colitis, aperients are contraindicated when the patient is being prepared for barium enema because they may cause severe exacerbation of the condition, which may lead to megacolon (excessive dilatation of the colon), perforation and death. If the patient is required to have this diagnostic test, a liquid diet for a few days before the X-ray and a gentle tap water enema on the day of examination may be sufficient preparation.

Care of the Patient With Inflammatory Bowel Disease

Medical treatment for both Crohn's disease and ulcerative colitis is aimed at reducing inflammation, suppressing inappropriate immune responses and providing rest for a diseased bowel, so that healing may take place.

Well-balanced, low-residue, high-protein diets with supplemental vitamin therapy and iron replacement are effective in meeting nutritional needs. Fluid and electrolyte imbalance due to dehydration caused by diarrhoea is corrected by intravenous therapy. Any foods that exacerbate diarrhoea should be avoided. Milk may contribute to diarrhoea if lactose intolerance is present. In addition, cold foods are to be avoided, along with smoking, because both increase intestinal motility.

Antidiarrhoeal/antiperistaltic medications are given to reduce to a minimum the colonic peristalsis, in order to rest the inflamed bowel. They are continued until the patient's stools approach normal frequency and consistency. Sulphonamides such as sulphasalazine are often effective for mild or moderate inflammation. Antibiotics are used for secondary infections, particularly for purulent complications such as abscesses, perforation and peritonitis. Sulphasalazine is helpful in preventing recurrences.

Adrenocorticotrophic hormone and corticosteroids are most effective early in the course of the acute inflammatory phase rather than in the chronic phase. When steroids are reduced or stopped, the symptoms of disease are likely to return. If steriods are continued, adverse sequelae such as hypertension, fluid retention, subcapsular cataracts and hirsutism may develop.

Psychotherapy is aimed at determining what factors distress the patient, dealing with these factors and attempting to resolve conflicts so that they no longer disturb the patient.

Surgical Intervention for Inflammatory Bowel Disorders

When conservative measures fail to relieve the severe symptoms of inflammatory bowel disease, surgery may be recommended.

Crohn's disease. If a lesion can be delineated in Crohn's disease (obstruction, abscess, fistula, stricture), it is removed and the remaining portions of the bowel are anastomosed. Loss of 50 per cent of the small bowel can usually be tolerated. The surgical procedures of choice are the following:

- Total colectomy (excision of the entire colon) with ileostomy (surgical creation of an opening into the ileum, usually by means of an ileal stoma on the abdominal wall).
- Segmental colectomy (removal of a segment of the colon) with colocolonic anastomosis (joining of the remaining portions of the colon).
- Subtotal colectomy (removal of nearly all of the colon) with ileorectal anastomosis (joining of the ileum and rectum).

The rate of recurrence following surgery is 20 to 40 per cent for the first five years. Patients under 25 years of age have the highest recurrence rate.

Ulcerative Colitis. Approximately 15 to 20 per cent of patients with ulcerative colitis require surgical intervention. Indications for surgery include lack of improvement or continued deterioration, profuse bleeding, perforation, stricture formation and indications that carcinoma has developed. The operation of choice is a total colectomy and ileostomy; any procedure more limited will prove to be of only temporary benefit in most patients. A proctocolectomy (complete excision of colon, rectum and anus) is recommended when the rectum is severely involved.

In the 1970s a surgical procedure was introduced that combined protocolectomy with a continent ileal reservoir (Kock's pouch). This procedure eliminates the need for an external faecal collection bag. Approximately 30 cm of the distal ileum is reconstructed to form a reservoir with a nipple valve that is created by intussusception of a portion of the terminal ileal loop (see Figure 15.3). Gastrointestinal effluent can be stored in the pouch for several hours and is then removed by means of a catheter inserted through the nipple valve. The major problem with the Kock pouch is malfunction of the nipple valve, which is seen in 20 to 40 per cent of patients.

A new surgical procedure, called a restorative proctocolectomy, is being performed for chronic ulcerative colitis and familial polyposis that eliminates the permanent ileostomy, establishes an ileal pouch and retains anal sphincter control of elimination. The procedure involves an ileoanal anastomosis done in conjunction with a total abdominal colectomy and a mucosal proctectomy. A temporary diverting-loop ileostomy is constructed at the time of surgery and closed about three months later. With ileoanal anastomosis, the diseased colon and rectum are removed, voluntary defaecation is maintained and anal continence is preserved. The ileal pouch decreases the number of bowel movements by 50 per cent, from approximately 14 to 20 per day, to 7 to 10 per day. Night-time elimination is gradually reduced to one bowel movement. Complications of the ileoanal anastomosis include

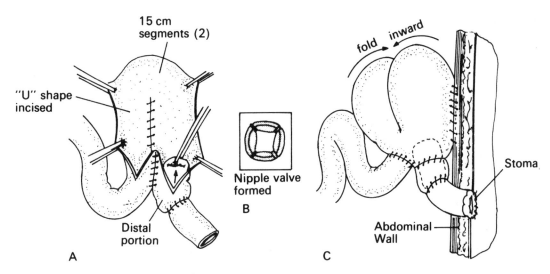

Figure 15.3 An ileal reservoir for the Kock pouch and for an ileoanal anastomosis. For the Kock pouch: (A) A 30-cm portion of the ileum is sutured together to form a 'U' shape. It is then excised open and the distal portion is pulled back into the ileum (similar to an intussusception). (B) A nipple valve is formed by suturing the pulled-back portion of the intestine to itself. (C) The top of the ileum is folded onto itself and a stoma is formed from the distal portion.

perianal skin excoriation from leakage of faecal contents, stricture formation at the anastomosis site and small bowel obstruction. See Table 15.3 for an description of common intestinal ostomies.

Preoperative Nursing Care

A period of preparation, with intensive fluid, blood and protein replacement, is necessary before surgery is attempted. Antibiotics may be prescribed. If the patient has been taking steroids for a long period of time, these will probably be continued during the surgical phase, and then gradually tapered off. Meanwhile, the patient should be assessed for adrenal insufficiency by observing and recording pulse, blood pressure, urinary output, general appearance and reactions.

Usually, the patient is given a low-residue diet offered frequently in small feeds. All other preoperative measures are similar to those for general abdominal surgery. The abdomen is marked for the proper placement of the stoma by the surgeon or the stoma nurse. Care is taken to see that the ostomy or stoma is conveniently placed. Information about an ileostomy is presented to the patient by means of literature, models and discussion. The patient should have a reasonably good idea of what the surgery entails and what to expect postoperatively, and may even be encouraged to wear an ileostomy appliance for a day or two before surgery to facilitate adjustment to it after the operation.

Preoperative preparation for a continent ileostomy is similar to that for the patient having a traditional ileostomy. Teaching before surgery will relate to managing the drains from the outlet, the nature of drainage and the need for nasogastric intubation, parenteral fluids and perineal packing and care.

Postoperative Nursing Care

General abdominal surgery wound care is required. As soon as the operation is completed, a temporary plastic bag with an adhesive facing is placed over the ileostomy and firmly pressed onto surrounding skin. The opening of the small intestine onto the abdomen continuously discharges the liquid contents of the small intestine, because the stoma does not have a controlling sphincter. The contents draining from the ileostomy drain into the plastic bag and are thus kept from coming into contact with skin. They are collected and measured as the bag becomes full. After the ileostomy has had a chance to heal, a permanent appliance is chosen with help from a stoma nurse. The stomal size should be rechecked after three weeks, when the oedema has subsided. The final size and type of bag may be selected after three months, after the patient's weight has stabilized and the stoma shrinks to a stable shape.

Because these patients lose much fluid and food in the early postoperative period, an accurate record of fluid intake, urinary output and faecal discharge is necessary to help gauge the fluid needs of the patient. Fluids and a low-residue, high-calorie diet are given until the patient becomes accustomed to the new digestive arrangement.

Nasogastric aspiration is also a part of immediate postoperative care, with the tube requiring frequent aspiration. The purpose of this is to facilitate healing and to

Table 15.3 *Common intestinal ostomies*

Ileostomy	Ileal loop (urinary conduit)	Transverse colostomy	Descending or sigmoid colostomy
Intestinal segment involved			
End of ileum	Loop of ileum is made into pouch into which transplanted ureters drain urine	Transverse colon	Descending or sigmoid colon
Effluent			
Liquid, semi-liquid, soft	Urine only	Soft and occasionally fairly firm; softer towards ileum	Descending–fairly firm stool; sigmoid–even more solid
Odour			
Slightly odorous	Nonodorous	Very malodorous	Usually malodorous
Skin effect			
Enzymes highly irritating	Urine is irritating to unprotected skin	Irritating, with continuous discharge	Fairly irritating
Types of appliances			
Open-ended bag worn at all times; if Koch pouch, no appliance is worn	Open-ended bag worn at all times	Bag worn at all times (either a large stoma with two openings or two separate stomas; faecal discharge from one and mucus from the other)	Depends on patient's level of control: some wear no appliance and irrigate regularly; others wear closed bag if effluent is firm (open-ended if discharge is more liquid continuously)
Indications			
Use meticulous skin care	Use meticulous skin care	Avoid irritating and gas-producing foods	Avoid irritating foods
Avoid irritating foods	Protect clothes from seepage		Protect skin
Wear nonconstricting garments	Drink sufficient fluids to maintain recommended daily output	Modify clothing to protect bag Protect skin	

relieve pressure on the suture line by preventing a build up of gastric contents. The patient receives intravenous fluids for four to five days until bowel sounds return. Thereafter, sips of clear liquids are offered, and the diet progresses gradually. Nausea and abdominal distension are observed as signs of an obstruction. Should they occur, the doctor is notified.

As with other patients undergoing abdominal surgery, early mobilization is encouraged. Prescribed analgesics are given if required. Changing the perineal dressings is painful and may be facilitated by moistening the dressings before they are removed. After the dressing is removed, the perineum is irrigated two to three times daily until full healing takes place.

Psychosocial Considerations

The patient, understandably, may think that everyone is aware of the ileostomy, and may view the stoma as mutilative in comparison with other abdominal incisions that heal and are hidden. Because there is loss of a body part and a major change in anatomy, the ileostomy patient often goes through the various phases of grieving. The nurse can expect the patient to experience shock, disbelief, denial, rejection, anger and restitution. Nursing support through these phases is important, and understanding of the patient's emotional outlook in each instance should determine the nurse's approach. For example, any form of teaching is of no avail until the patient has reached the stage of restitution.

Concern over body image may lead to questions related to personal relationships, sexual function and the ability to become pregnant and to deliver normally.

Finally, such patients need to know that someone understands and cares about them. Sincere friendliness and a nonjudgmental attitude exhibited by the nurse will aid in gaining the patient's confidence, so important to therapy and preoperative preparation. It is important to recognize the dependency needs of these patients.

Such patients probably are the most challenging of all to the nurse. Their prolonged illness can make them irritable, anxious and depressed.

On the other hand, an operation establishing an ileostomy can produce dramatic changes in patients who have suffered from colitis for several years. Once the misery of the disease has lifted and patients learn how to take care of an ileostomy, they can become normal, affable people. But until they progress to this phase, an empathetic and tolerant approach by the nurse will play an important part in recovery.

The support of other people with stomas is also a help. A charity called the Ileostomy Association exists and is able to offer extensive advice and information on all aspects of living with an ileostomy (see Useful Addresses, at end). Local hospitals may have a stoma therapist on the staff; this is a valuable resource person for the ileostomy patient.

Rehabilitation and Patient Education Following an Ileostomy

There are certain rehabilitation problems unique to the ileostomy patient, one of which is irregularity of bowel evacuation. The patient with an ileostomy cannot establish regular bowel habits because the contents of the ileum are fluid and are discharging continuously. Therefore, the patient must wear an appliance day and night. The appliance is regarded, then, as an intestinal prosthesis.

Several days after the operation, the ileostomy diameter is carefully measured with a stoma-measuring card (various apertures indicate different sizes) so that a suitable opening in the flange will be available in the permanent appliance. The flange is sealed to the skin with an adhesive disc that permits the patient to carry on normal activities without fear of leakage or odour.

The location and length of the stoma are significant in the management of the ileostomy by the patient. The surgeon places the stoma as close to the midline as possible and in a position where even an obese patient with a protruding abdomen can care for it readily. Usually, the ileostomy stoma is about 2.5 cm long, which makes it convenient for the attachment of an appliance.

The ileostomy may be noisy at first, due to oedema caused by slight obstruction of tissues. Eventually it will become quieter. A low-fibre diet is followed at first, with strained fruits and vegetables. These foods are important for vitamins A and C. Later there are few dietary restrictions, except for avoiding foods that are high in fibre or hard-to-digest kernels, such as celery, popcorn, corn-on-the-cob, poppy seeds or caraway seeds and coconut. Fluids may be a problem during the summer, when they are lost during perspiration as well as through the ileostomy. If the effluent (faecal discharge) is too watery, fibrous foods (such as whole grain cereals, fresh fruit skins, beans, corn and nuts) are restricted. If the effluent is excessively dry, salt intake is increased. An increased intake of water or fluid will not increase the effluent because excess water is excreted in the urine.

Another possible problem is skin excoriation around the stoma. Not only does the ileostomy drainage contain enzymes that rapidly excoriate the skin but, if cement is used in putting the appliance on, the skin may be irritated when the appliance is removed. To prevent irritation and yeast growth, nystatin powder is dusted lightly on the peristomal skin.

A regular schedule for changing the appliance before leakage occurs is established. In teaching the patient to use and care for the appliance, the nurse should stress the following essential points:

To Remove the Appliance

1. Sit or stand in a comfortable position.
2. Peel the adhesive off the skin with one hand while exerting gentle pressure on the skin with the other (Pritchard and David, 1988).

To Cleanse the Skin

1. Remove excess faeces or mucus with a dry tissue.
2. Wash the skin and stoma thoroughly with tepid water and mild soap. Dry thoroughly. During the time the skin is being cleansed, a gauze dressing may cover the stoma to absorb excess drainage.

To Put On the Appliance

1. If there is no irritation, a new flange and bag can be applied. A gel or spray may be used to prevent irritation and to give skin protection.
2. If there is skin irritation, a protective wafer is used to cover and protect the skin.
3. A new flange and bag can then be applied. Paste available from manufacturers of stoma products can be used to fill any dips or crevices.

The amount of time that a person can keep the appliance sealed to the body depends on the location of the stoma and on body structure. Usually, the normal wearing time is two to four days. The appliance is emptied every four to six hours, or at the same time the patient empties the bladder. An emptying spout at the bottom of the appliance is closed with a special clip made for this purpose.

The appliance is cleaned and aired according to the manufacturer's directions. Usually, thorough washing with soap and water using a soft nylon brush is effective. There are many deodorizers and cleaning aids available that the patient can use. Commercial liquid deodorizers are also available, and are preferred by some patients. Other inexpensive deodorants are pieces of charcoal, or two aspirin tablets crushed and dropped into the bag. Foods such as spinach and parsley act as deodorizers in the intestinal tract; foods that cause odours are cabbage, onions and fish. Some doctors prescribe a stool thickener, such as diphenoxylate (by mouth), to assist in odour control.

Patient Education

The partner or informal carer should be familiar with the adjustment that will be necessary when the patient returns home. They need to know why it is necessary for the patient to occupy the bathroom for 10 minutes at certain times of the day, and why certain equipment is needed. Their understanding is necessary to reduce tension—a relaxed patient tends to have fewer problems.

Complications

Minor complications occur in about 40 per cent of patients who have an ileostomy; less than 20 per cent of the complications require surgical intervention. Peristomal skin irritation, the most common complication of an ileostomy, is due to leakage of effluent. An ill-fitting bag is frequently the cause. The bag is adjusted by the nurse or a stoma therapist and skin barriers are applied. Diarrhoea, manifested by very irritating effluent that rapidly fills the bag (every hour or sooner), can quickly lead to dehydration and electrolyte losses. Supplemental water, salt and potassium are given to prevent hypovolaemia and hypokalaemia. Antidiarrhoeal agents are administered. Stenosis is caused by circular scar tissue formation at the stoma site. The scar tissue is surgically released. Urinary calculi occur in about 10 per cent of ileostomy patients because of dehydration secondary to decreased fluid intake. Intense lower abdominal pain that radiates to the legs, haematuria and signs of dehydration alert the nurse to strain all urine. Sometimes small stones are passed during urination; otherwise an invasive procedure is necessary to crush or remove the calculi. Cholelithiasis (formation of gallstones) due to cholesterol is seen three times more frequently than in the general population because of changes in the absorption of bile acids that occurs preoperatively. Spasm of the gallbladder causes severe upper right abdominal pain that can radiate to the back and right shoulder. Ileitis is usually seen with a recurrence of inflammatory bowel disease.

► NURSING PROCESS
► THE PATIENT WITH CHRONIC ULCERATIVE COLITIS

► *Assessment*

The nurse, when assessing the patient, will ask about symptoms such as diarrhoea, abdominal cramping, tenesmus, nausea, anorexia and weight loss. Exacerbations related to stress or dietary indiscretions and remissions are reported. Job-related stress factors are identified. A family history of inflammatory bowel disease is explored, because 15 per cent of those diagnosed have a family member with the disease. Any known allergies are recorded, especially an allergy to milk, because lactose

intolerance is common with Crohn's disease. The amounts of alcohol, caffeine and nicotine used daily/weekly are noted, because these agents stimulate the bowel and can initiate diarrhoea and abdominal cramping.

Nutritional status needs to be assessed. Malabsorption is not uncommon, and some patients can lose 10 to 20 pounds in two months. Because patients with inflammatory bowel disease may have 20 diarrhoeal stools per day, they isolate themselves from family and friends and become anxious, dependent and depressed. Sleep disturbances are common. Assessment includes psychosocial evaluation of the individual's coping mechanisms and emotional status.

Crohn's Disease

With Crohn's disease, pain is usually localized in the right lower quadrant where hyperactive bowel sounds can be heard due to increased peristalsis. The most prominent problem is intermittent pain associated with diarrhoea that does not decrease with defaecation. Pain in the periumbilical region usually indicates involvement of the terminal ileum.

Ulcerative Colitis. With ulcerative colitis, the abdomen may be distended and rebound tenderness may be present. Rectal bleeding is a dominant sign.

► *Patient's Problems*

Based on the assessment, the patient's main problems may include the following:

● Diarrhoea, related to the inflammatory process.
● Abdominal pain and cramping, related to increased peristalsis.
● Fluid volume and electrolyte deficits related to anorexia, nausea and diarrhoea.
● Nutritional deficit related to anorexia secondary to diarrhoea.
● Activity intolerance related to fatigue.
● Anxiety related to impending surgery.
● Ineffective individual coping related to repeated episodes of diarrhoea.
● Lack of knowledge concerning the process and management of the disease.

► *Planning and Implementation*
► Expected Outcomes

The main outcomes for the patient may include an improvement in the nature and frequency of elimination, reduction in abdominal pain and cramping, prevention of fluid volume deficit, improvement and maintenance of nutritional status, avoidance of fatigue, reduction of anxiety, attainment of emotional balance and acquisition of knowledge and understanding of the disease process.

Nursing Care

Bowel Elimination

The nurse ascertains if there is a relationship between diarrhoea and certain foods, activity or emotional stress. Any precipitating factors are reported, as well as stool frequency, consistency and amount. Ready access to a bathroom or bedpan is provided, and the environment is kept clean and odour-free. Anti-diarrhoeal agents are administered as prescribed, and the frequency and consistency of stools are recorded after therapy has started. Bedrest is encouraged to decrease peristalsis.

Pain Relief

The character of the pain is documented as dull, burning or cramp-like. Its onset is relevant: does it occur before or after meals, during the night or before elimination? Is the pattern constant or intermittent? Is it relieved with medications?

Anticholinergic medications are given as prescribed, 30 minutes before a meal to decrease intestinal motility, and analgesics are given as needed for pain. Pain can also be reduced by position changes, the local application of heat (as prescribed), diversional activities and the prevention of fatigue.

Fluid Intake

To detect fluid volume deficit, an accurate record of oral and intravenous fluids is kept as well as a record of output (urine, liquid stool, vomitus, wound or fistula drainage). Daily weights are taken because they indicate rapid fluid gains or losses. The nurse assesses for signs of fluid volume deficit: dry skin and mucous membranes, decreased skin turgor, oliguria, exhaustion, temperature decrease, increased haematocrit, elevated urine specific gravity and hypotension. Oral intake of fluids is encouraged, and intravenous flow rate is monitored. Measures to decrease diarrhoea are initiated: dietary restrictions, stress reduction and administration of anti-diarrhoeal agents.

Nutritional Measures

Total parenteral nutrition (see Chapter 13) is used when the symptoms of inflammatory bowel disease are severe. With this type of nutrition, the nurse maintains an accurate record of fluid intake and output, as well as the patient's daily weight. The urine is tested for sugar and ketones daily when total parenteral nutrition is being used. Elemental feeds that are high in protein and low in fat and residue may be instituted after total parenteral nutrition therapy because they are digested primarily in the jejunum, do not stimulate intestinal secretions and allow the bowel to rest. Intolerance is noted if the patient exhibits nausea, vomiting, diarrhoea or abdominal distension.

If oral foods are tolerated, small, frequent feeds are given to avoid overdistending the stomach and stimulating peristalsis. Activities are restricted to conserve energy, reduce peristalsis and limit calorie depletion.

Rest

Intermittent rest periods during the day are recommended, and activities are restricted in order to conserve energy and reduce the metabolic rate. Activity within the limit of such patients' capacities is desirable, so that they do not regard themselves as invalids. Bedrest is suggested for a patient who is febrile, has frequent diarrhoeal stools or is bleeding. Active and passive exercises are encouraged for anyone on bedrest in order to maintain muscle tone and prevent thromboembolic complications. Activity restrictions are evaluated and modified an a day-to-day basis.

Reducing Anxiety

Establish rapport by being attentive and displaying a calm, confident manner. Time should be provided for the patient to ask questions and express feelings. The nurse should listen carefully and be sensitive to nonverbal indicators of anxiety (restlessness, tense facial expressions). The patient may be emotionally labile because of the conditions of the disease, so information about impending surgery should be tailored to the patient's level of understanding and desire for details. Some people need to know everything to lessen their anxiety, while others want to know very little. If necessary, pictures and illustrations should be used to explain the surgical procedure and help the patient visualize what a stoma looks like.

Coping Measures

Because the patient feels isolated, helpless and out of control, the nurse should offer understanding and emotional support. The patient may be demanding and angry, and may exhibit inappropriate responses to stress: infantile behaviour, perfectionism, denial and social self-isolation.

The nurse needs to recognize that the patient's behaviour may be affected by innumerable factors. Any patient who is suffering from the discomforts of frequent bowel movements and rectal soreness is anxious, discouraged, and depressed. Thus, it is important to develop a relationship with patients that gives them a feeling that they are receiving support in their attempts to deal with the stresses that have plagued them. The nurse should communicate that the patient's complaints are understood, encourage talking and ventilation of feelings, and listen to matters that are disturbing to the patient, even if they seem trivial. An attempt should be made to direct attention away from the patient's intestinal tract. Stress reduction measures such as relaxation techniques, breathing exercises and biofeedback should be recommended.

Patient Education and Home Health Care

The patient's understanding of the disease process and need for additional information about medical management (medications, diet) and surgical interventions should be assessed. The nurse should mention that control is possible when the cause of exacerbations is determined.

Information about nutritional management should be provided. A bland, low-residue, high-protein, high-calorie, and high-vitamin diet relieves symptoms and decreases diarrhoea. The nurse should explain the rationale for the use of steroids, anti-inflammatory agents, antibacterial and antidiarrhoeal drugs, and antispasmodics. Emphasize that medications are to be taken as prescribed and not abruptly discontinued (especially the steroid agents, which can cause serious medical problems if suddenly stopped).

If surgery is required the nurse explains the procedure and the pre- and postoperative care. Ileostomy care is reviewed if necessary.

Patients who are being medically managed at home need to understand that their disease can be controlled and they can lead a healthy life between exacerbations. Control implies management based on an understanding of inflammatory bowel disease and its treatment.

During a flare-up, patients are encouraged to rest as needed and modify activities according to energy levels. If possible, they should limit activities to one floor in the house. Patients are advised to limit their housecleaning tasks and to avoid using a vacuum cleaner because this activity imposes strain on the lower abdominal muscles. Patients should sleep in a bedroom with an adjacent or nearby bathroom because of frequent diarrhoeal stools (10 to 20/day). Quick access to a toilet helps alleviate the worry of embarrassment if an accident occurs. Room deodorizers help control odours.

Patients in the home setting need information about their medications (drug name, dosage, side-effects, frequency of administration) and need to take them on time. Memory aids such as daily check lists may be helpful.

Dietary modifications can control but not cure the disease. A low-residue, high-protein, high-calorie diet is recommended, especially during an acute phase. Patients are encouraged to keep a record of those foods that irritate the bowel and eliminate them from the diet.

The prolonged nature of the disease causes a strain on family and personal life and financial resources. Support from the carer is vital; however, some carers experience resentment, guilt, fatigue and an inability to continue coping with the emotional demands of the illness as well as with the physical demands of caring for another.

Some people will not socialize for fear of being embarrassed. Many prefer to eat alone. Because they have lost control over elimination they feel that they have lost control over other aspects of their life. They need time to ventilate their fears and frustrations.

► *Evaluation*
► Expected Outcomes

1. Patient reports a decrease in the frequency of diarrhoeal stools.
   a. Recognizes a causal relationship between certain foods, activity or stress, and elimination.
   b. Restricts activities; maintains bedrest.
   c. Takes medications as prescribed.
2. Experiences less pain.
   a. Uses diversional activities to decrease anxiety and pain.
   b. Takes anticholinergics before meals, as prescribed.
   c. Takes analgesics as needed and prescribed.
3. Maintains fluid volume balance.
   a. Takes 2 to 3 litres of oral fluids daily.
   b. Has a normal body temperature.
   c. Displays adequate skin turgor and moist mucous membranes.
4. Attains optimum nutrition.
   a. Tolerates small, frequent feeds without diarrhoea.
   b. Complies with total parenteral nutrition therapy.
   c. Accepts elemental feeds if necessary.
5. Avoids episodes of fatigue.
   a. Rests periodically during the day.
   b. Adheres to bedrest restrictions.
   c. Performs exercises as needed.
6. Feels less anxious.
   a. Discusses fears and worries.
   b. Describes the surgical procedure in own words.
   c. Handles equipment with ease.
   d. Asks to speak with a stoma nurse specialist.
7. Copes successfully with diagnosis.
   a. Expresses feelings freely.
   b. Socializes with family members and friends.
   c. Uses appropriate stress reduction behaviours.
8. Acquires an understanding of the disease process.
   a. Modifies diet appropriately to decrease diarrhoea.
   b. Adheres to medication regime.
   c. Describes possible surgical interventions.

See Nursing Care Plan 15.1 for the patient with ulcerative colitis.

INTESTINAL OBSTRUCTION

The normal flow of the intestinal contents through the intestinal tract can be impeded by two types of intestinal obstruction:

1. Mechanical, in which there is an intraluminal obstruction or a mural obstruction from pressure on the intestinal walls, and
2. Paralytic, in which the intestinal musculature is unable to propel the contents along the bowel. (Stimuli that may inhibit intestinal peristalsis are laparotomy,

► NURSING CARE PLAN 15.1: THE PATIENT WITH ULCERATIVE COLITIS

Ken Macdonald, aged 44, a self-employed insurance broker with three teenage children (one from a previous marriage), suffering with ulcerative colitis.

Patient's problems	Expected outcomes	Nursing care	Rationale
1. Diarrhoea and rectal bleeding up to 12 times a day due to inflammatory process	Patient returns to a 'normal' bowel pattern of less than five bowel motions a day	1a. Monitor bowel motions on a stool chart	To ascertain frequency consistency and volume of bowel motion
		b. Investigate whether certain foods, activities or stressors exacerbate diarrhoea	To facilitate the elimination or reduction of such factors
		c. Ensure easy access to bathroom and toilet facilities	To help Ken feel secure and safe and able to avoid accidents
		d. Administer antidiarrhoeal agents as prescribed	To reduce number of bowel motions
		e. Encourage Ken to rest during exacerbation of disease process	To reduce peristalsis and therefore frequency of bowel motion
2. Abdominal pain, cramps and discomfort due to the disease process	Patient identifies what exacerbates pain and develops strategies for avoiding it	2a. Use a pain chart to assess nature and extent of pain (Pritchard and David, 1988)	To establish when pain occurs, what causes it and how it is relieved
		b. Investigate strategies such as analgesics, position, the use of a heat pad and avoiding tiredness and their role in reducing pain	In order to facilitate Ken's ability to minimalize pain
3. Anorexia, nausea and diarrhoea resulting in fluid and electrolyte deficits	Maintains fluid and electrolyte balance	3a. Keep an accurate fluid balance chart	To identify fluid deficits
		b. Administer intravenous fluids as prescribed	To maintain fluid intake when patient is unable to drink sufficient volumes
		c. Take measures to reduce frequency of bowel motions (see problem 1)	To reduce fluid output
4. Weight loss and nutritional deficits due to anorexia, secondary to diarrhoea	Patient maintains weight at 65 kg and nutritional input of at least 1,500 kcal	4a. If Ken's condition is very severe then total parenteral nutrition may be indicated (see Chapter 13)	To maintain nutritional intake
		b. Patient may require feeding via a nasogastric feeding tube using an elemental feed	To introduce easily absorbed food into the gastrointestinal tract
		c. If able to eat, Ken requires small, frequent meals high in protein and calories	To avoid over-distending the stomach, and to optimize nutritional intake
		d. When appetite is poor, encourage rest	To conserve energy
5. Patient is over-tired due to trying to continue to work while unwell	Ken will set realistic goals of what he can achieve	5a. Explore ways of Ken reducing activity within the constraints of what is compulsory	To ensure that periods of rest are part of patient's day
		b. Involve Ken's wife and children in discussions concerning this issue	To negotiate help for Ken if possible
6. Ken is extremely anxious about his work and feels depressed due to having constant diarrhoea	Patient establishes coping strategies	6a. Ensure patient is allowed time to express anxieties, and offer advice and information as appropriate	To help Ken feel supported
		b. Discuss ways in which Ken can find support and facilitate them	To ensure that patient knows something is being done
		c. Help family to understand Ken's anxiety and depression	To enable family to act as a support and a help

►

▶ **NURSING CARE PLAN 15.1: THE PATIENT WITH ULCERATIVE COLITIS**

Patient's problems	Expected outcomes	Nursing care	Rationale
		d. Use relaxation techniques if appropriate	To help patient feel more able to cope with his illness
7. Patient has only a limited knowledge of his condition due to a tendency to try and ignore it	Patient to comprehend the disease process involved and how it can be controlled	7a. Assess patient's understanding and provide additional information as required	To improve patient's knowledge base
		b. Refer to dietician	To provide a resource of nutrition information
		c. Discuss medication that Ken is taking	To ensure that patient understands the rationale for their use to improve compliance
		d. Investigate who Ken talks to about his illness	To facilitate support mechanisms

trauma, infection, mesenteric ischaemia and metabolic disorders.)

An obstruction is partial or complete. Its seriousness depends on the region of bowel that is affected, the degree to which the lumen is occluded and, especially, the degree to which the blood circulation in the bowel wall is disturbed.

Small Bowel Obstruction

Adhesions are the most common cause of small bowel obstruction (60 per cent incidence), followed by hernias and neoplasms. Other causes include intussusception, volvulus, paralytic ileus, inflammatory bowel disease, strictures and foreign bodies.

Altered Physiology

Proximal to the intestinal obstruction there is an accumulation of intestinal contents, fluid and gas. In the small intestine, distension reduces the absorption of fluids and stimulates gastric secretion. As a result, fluids and electrolytes are lost. With increasing distension, pressure within the intestinal lumen causes a decrease in venous and arteriolar capillary pressure. This, in turn, causes oedema, congestion, necrosis and eventual rupture or perforation of the intestinal wall.

With vomiting, there is a loss of hydrogen ions and potassium from the stomach, producing hypochloraemia, hypokalaemia and metabolic alkalosis. Then dehydration and acidosis develop because of water loss and sodium loss. When there are acute fluid losses, hypovolaemic shock may occur.

Clinical Features and Diagnosis

The initial symptom is usually pain that is wavelike in character. The patient may pass blood and mucus rectally, but no faecal matter and no flatus. Vomiting occurs. This pattern is often characteristic. If the obstruction is complete, the peristaltic waves become extremely vigorous and assume a reverse direction, the intestinal contents being propelled towards the mouth instead of towards the rectum. If the obstruction is in the ileum, faecal vomiting takes place. First, the patient vomits the stomach contents, then the bile-stained contents of the duodenum and the jejunum, and finally, with each paroxysm of pain, the darker, faecal-like contents of the ileum. Soon, due to the loss of water, sodium and chlorides in the vomit, the unmistakable signs of dehydration become evident. The patient complains of intense thirst, drowsiness, generalized malaise and aching. The tongue and the mucous membranes become parched; the face acquires a pinched appearance. The abdomen becomes distended; the lower the obstruction in the gastrointestinal tract, the more marked is the distension. If the situation is allowed to continue uncorrected, shock appears, due to dehydration and loss of plasma volume. The patient is prostrated; the pulse becomes increasingly weak and rapid; the temperature and the blood pressure are lowered; the skin is pale, cold and clammy. At this point, death may supervene rapidly.

X-ray studies indicate dilated bowel loops. With strangulation, the patient experiences severe abdominal pain and tenderness, high fever with leucocytosis and symptoms of shock.

Management

Decompression of the bowel via a nasoenteral tube is successful in the majority of cases. When the bowel is completely obstructed, the possibility of strangulation warrants surgical intervention.

The surgical treatment of intestinal obstruction depends largely on the cause of the obstruction. In the most common causes of obstruction, such as strangulated hernia and obstruction by adhesions, the operation consists of repair of the hernia or division of the adhesion to which the intestine is attached. In some hernias, the strangulated portion of bowel may be removed and an anastomosis performed. Operation for intestinal obstruction may be simple or complicated, depending on the duration of the obstruction and the condition of the intestine found at operation.

Preoperatively, the patient's vital signs are stabilized, intravenous fluids are administered for hydration and a nasogastric tube is inserted to prevent vomiting.

Postoperative Adhesions

After abdominal operations, there are many areas within the abdomen that may not be completely healed, and loops of intestine may become adherent to these areas. Such inflammatory adhesions are usually only temporary and of no particular importance. However, occasionally these adhesions may produce a kinking of an intestinal loop, which causes obstruction of the intestinal flow. This obstruction usually appears on the third or fourth day after operation, when peristalsis is normally resumed and when food and fluids are being given to the patient for the first time. The symptoms are typical of any intestinal obstruction—crampy abdominal pain, distension, vomiting and so on.

The difficulty is usually relieved by nasogastric aspiration. Decompressing the bowel above the site of the obstruction allows the inflammation to subside and relieves the obstruction. When the obstruction cannot be relieved by this conservative means, an operation may be necessary to free the adherent intestine and to permit the intestinal flow to be resumed.

Intussusception

Intussusception is a condition in which one part of the intestine slips into another part located below it, much as a telescope is shortened by pushing one section into the next. This occurs through peristalsis. The point at which intussusception develops most commonly is at or near the ileocaecal valve. The telescoping, or invagination, also may start at the point of attachment of a tumour in the colon—particularly a pedunculated tumour—as a result of its becoming engaged by a peristaltic wave and propelled along the colon, dragging into the lumen that portion of the wall to which its pedicle is attached. (See Figure 15.4A.)

Volvulus

A volvulus (Figure 15.4B) is a life-threatening obstruction in which the bowel is twisted upon itself and the intestinal lumen is obstructed both proximally and distally.

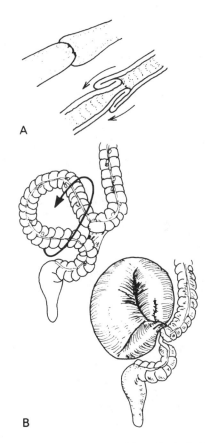

Figure 15.4 Two causes of intestinal obstruction. (A) Intussusception. Note invagination or shortening of colon by the movement of one segment of bowel into another. (B) Volvulus of the sigmoid colon. The twist is counterclockwise in most cases of sigmoid volvulus. Note the oedematous bowel. (B: Way, L. W. (ed.) (1985) *Current Surgical Diagnosis and Treatment*, Lange Medical Publishers, Los Altos, California.)

The accumulation of gas and fluid in the trapped bowel leads to necrosis, perforation and peritonitis.

Paralytic Ileus

A paralytic ileus is a paralysis of peristaltic movement due to the effect of trauma or toxins on the nerves that regulate intestinal movement. Functional paralytic ileus following abdominal surgery may last 12 to 36 hours. Because of this, food and fluids are withheld until normal peristalsis returns, as indicated by bowel sounds (heard with the stethoscope) or the passing of flatus. Paralytic ileus may also happen after back injuries, after operation on the kidney and frequently with peritonitis.

The lack of peristalsis results in a distension of the intestine with gas produced by decomposition of the intestinal contents or by swallowing of air. Few or no peristaltic sounds can be heard, and the patient may be extremely uncomfortable, if not in marked pain. Relief of the distension associated with paralytic ileus is often obtained by nasogastric intubation (see p. 509).

Abdominal Hernias

A hernia is a protrusion of an organ, tissue or structure through the wall of the cavity in which it is naturally contained. This definition may apply to any part of the body; for instance, the protrusion of the brain after a subtemporal decompression is called cerebral hernia. However, in general the term is applied to the protrusion of an abdominal viscus through an opening in the abdominal wall.

Inguinal hernia is a major reason for surgery, especially among men, in whom it occurs three times more frequently than in women. Most hernias result from congenital or acquired weakness of the abdominal wall, coupled with sustained increased intra-abdominal pressure from coughing or straining, or from an enlarging lesion within the abdomen. Once the hernia occurs, it has a tendency to increase in size.

The hernial sac is formed by an outpouching of the peritoneum and may contain the large or small intestine, the omentum and occasionally the bladder. When the hernia is initially formed, the sac is filled only when the patient is standing up; the contents return to the abdominal cavity as soon as the patient lies down.

Indirect inguinal hernia is the most common type of hernia. It is due to a weakness of the abdominal wall at the point through which the spermatic cord emerges in the male, and the round ligament in the female. Through this opening the hernia extends down the inguinal canal and often into the scrotum or the labia (Figure 15.5). It is common in the male, and it may appear at any age.

Direct inguinal hernia passes through the posterior inguinal wall. It also is more common in males. It is more difficult to repair than indirect inguinal hernia, and often recurs after surgery. It is believed to be hereditary or related to a defect in the synthesis of collagen.

Umbilical hernia results from failure of the umbilical orifice to close. It is most common in obese women and in children, as a protrusion at the umbilicus. This hernia is also seen with increased intra-abdominal pressure in cirrhosis and ascites.

Ventral or incisional hernias occur because of a weakness in the abdominal wall. They are due most frequently to previous operations in which drainage was necessary, complete closure of the tissues being impossible. Weakened by infection, only a slight bulge results at first, but this increases gradually in size until a definite hernial sac is produced.

Femoral hernia appears below the inguinal (Poupart's) ligament (i.e., below the groin) as a round bulge. It is more frequent in women because of changes during pregnancy.

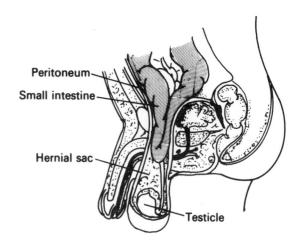

Figure 15.5 Inguinal hernia. Note that the sac of the hernia is a continuation of the peritoneum of the abdomen and that the hernial contents are intestine, omentum or other abdominal contents that pass through the hernial opening into the hernial sac.

A hernia is referred to as reducible when the protruding mass can be placed back into the abdominal cavity. This can occur naturally when the patient lies down, or it may require manual reduction (the mass is pushed back into the cavity). As time goes on, adhesions form between the sac and its contents, so that the hernia becomes irreducible or incarcerated. Such a hernia is one that cannot be reduced and in which the intestinal flow may be obstructed completely.

In a strangulated hernia, not only are the contents irreducible, but the blood and intestinal flow through the intestine in the hernia is stopped completely. This condition develops when the loop of intestine in the sac becomes twisted or swollen and a constriction is produced at the neck of the sac. The result then is an acute intestinal obstruction, with the added danger of gangrene of the bowel. The symptoms are pain at the site of strangulation, followed by colicky abdominal pain, vomiting, and swelling of the hernial sac.

Mechanical Reduction

Very often patients can reduce their own hernias. In order to keep the mass from protruding when a standing position is assumed, a corset (a pad made of firm material that is placed externally over the hernia and held in place with a belt) may be worn. Most authorities agree that a corset creates more problems than it can solve. Skin irritation and lesions may result from constant rubbing. When improperly fitted, it may cause strangulation of the hernia. However, a corset may be recommended (1) for infants, when there is need to wait for a weight gain before surgery or for remission of another problem, such as bronchitis or nappy rash; (2) for adults who have an underlying problem that needs to be resolved first; or (3) when a patient has worn a corset for years, is terrified of the hospital and will not part with the corset. In this last instance, the proper fitting of the corset must be done by a qualified person. Daily bathing can lessen the possibility of skin irritation. Usually the corset is worn directly over the hernia and not over clothing, which could cause slipping. It must be emphasized that a corset *does not cure a hernia*; it simply prevents the abdominal contents from entering the hernial sac.

The hernia should always be repaired by surgery; otherwise, it is in continual danger of strangulation. When strangulation occurs, an operation becomes imperative and is attended invariably by considerable risk.

The operation involves removal of the hernial sac after it has been dissected free from surrounding structures, the contents have been replaced in the abdominal cavity and the neck has been ligated. The muscle and the fascial layers then are sewn together firmly over the hernial orifice to prevent a recurrence. The incidence of recurrence is 5 to 25 per cent. When the tissues are not sufficiently strong, reinforcement can be obtained by overlaying the suture line with synthetic sutures or mesh, which is also sutured in place (hernioplasty). The presence of the mesh stimulates more than the usual amount of fibroblastic activity and thereby enhances the strength of the repair. When strangulation has occurred, the operation is complicated by intestinal obstruction and injury to the bowel.

Preoperative Nursing Care

Most patients undergoing a herniorrhaphy (surgical repair of a hernia) are in good physical condition and have elected to have the surgery. They may be prompted by the knowledge that an unrepaired hernia can become a serious emergency, or that the condition can cause difficulty in securing employment. In emergency conditions of strangulated or incarcerated hernia, the nurse prepares the patient as in any other acute surgical problem.

It is important to determine whether the patient has an upper respiratory infection, chronic cough from excessive smoking or sneezing due to an allergy. It may be necessary to postpone the operation, because coughing or sneezing could weaken the postoperative wound, thereby negating the purpose of surgery.

Postoperative Nursing Care

The patient is allowed out of bed several hours after surgery. Young, healthy patients without other problems are often discharged on the day of surgery. Following local or spinal anaesthesia, diet is determined by the desires of the patient. When general anaesthesia is used, fluid and food are restricted until peristalsis returns.

Urinary retention is common in the postoperative period. However, if the patient gets out of bed to void within several hours after surgery, there usually is no difficulty. In any case, it is necessary to prevent bladder distension; this may require catheterization if other nursing measures fail.

The patient who coughs or sneezes after the operation is requested to support the incision site with one hand, both to lessen the pain and to protect the incision site from the increased intra-abdominal pressure caused by the coughing and sneezing.

Following repair of an inguinal hernia, swelling of the scrotum may occur. Because this is extremely painful, the patient is reluctant to move. A narcotic may be prescribed for pain, and antibiotics to prevent epididymitis. A scrotal support may be applied for support and comfort.

Infection that interferes with healing occurs occasionally. Soreness in the operative region and temperature elevation may suggest such a problem. Systemic antibiotics or wound drainage may be required.

For more extensive hernia repair, such as may be required following umbilical or large incisional hernia, nasogastric aspiration may be used to prevent distension, vomiting and straining. Stool softeners are prescribed to prevent straining during defaecation.

Patient Education

Hospitalized patients may go home the day following herniorrhaphy or may stay three to five days or longer, depending on their age and medical condition. Many patients have same-day surgery with local anaesthesia. The patient at home needs to know that pain and scrotal swelling will be present after surgery for 24 to 48 hours. Use of a scrotal support and pain medication should relieve the pain. The patient is requested to report severe pain to the doctor.

Some surgeons permit patients to do whatever they wish if they agree not to engage in painful activity, thereby preventing injury to the incision. Most, however, recommend limited activities for five to seven days, and restriction of heavy lifting for four to six weeks. The use of correct body mechanics at all times is encouraged.

The patient is advised to report any drainage from the incision to the doctor. Straining during defaecation is avoided by diet modification, bulk aperients or stool softeners, and a daily fluid intake of 2,000 ml. Pain or difficulty with urination is reported to the doctor.

Evaluation

Short-term evaluation of nursing care can be carried out through an assessment of the return of peristalsis, adequate urinary output, decrease in scrotal swelling, absence of infection, relief of pain and avoidance of straining at stool. Long-term evaluation can be carried out through an assessment of the patient's understanding of the restrictions established.

Large Bowel Obstruction

About 15 per cent of intestinal obstructions occur in the

large bowel, and most are found in the sigmoid. The most common causes are carcinoma, diverticulitis, inflammatory bowel disorders and benign tumours.

Altered Physiology

Obstruction at the ileocaecal valve produces changes similar to those in small bowel obstruction. Obstruction in the colon can lead to severe distension and perforation unless some gas and fluid can flow back through the ileum (incompetent valve). Large bowel obstruction, even if complete, is also comparatively undramatic if the blood supply to the colon is not disturbed. However, if the blood supply is cut off, intestinal strangulation and necrosis (tissue death) occur, and the patient's life is in jeopardy. In the large intestine, dehydration occurs more slowly than in the small intestine because the colon is able to absorb its fluid contents and can distend to a size considerably beyond its normal full capacity.

Clinical Features and Diagnosis

Large bowel obstruction differs clinically from the small bowel type in that the symptoms develop and progress relatively slowly. In patients with obstruction in the sigmoid or the rectum, constipation may be the only symptom for days. Eventually, the abdomen becomes markedly distended, loops of large bowel become visibly outlined through the abdominal wall and the patient suffers from crampy lower abdominal pain. Finally, faecal vomiting develops. The terminal features are essentially those of ileum obstruction.

X-ray studies show a distended colon. Barium studies are contraindicated.

Management

The usual treatment is surgical resection, with the formation of a colostomy or ileostomy in right colon obstruction and perforation. Sometimes an ileoanal anastomosis is performed. A caecostomy (insertion of a tube into the lumen of the caecum) may be done for those patients who are poor surgical risks and need relief from the obstruction. The procedure provides a vent for releasing gas and a small amount of drainage.

CANCER OF THE LARGE INTESTINE: COLON AND RECTUM

Tumours of the small intestine are rare; on the other hand, tumours of the colon are relatively common, In fact, second only to lung cancer, cancer of the colon and rectum is now the most common type of internal cancer in men. In women, colorectal cancer ranks third as a cause of death, following cancer of the lung and cancer of the breast. More than 95 per cent of the cancer tumours are adenocarcinomas. The incidence increases with age (most patients are over the age of 50), and is higher in people with a family history of colon cancer and those with ulcerative colitis. The distribution of cancer sites throughout the colon can be seen in Figure 15.6. Changes in the percentage distribution have been recorded recently. The incidence of cancer in the sigmoid and rectal areas has decreased, whereas the incidence in the ascending and descending colon has increased.

The low five-year survival rate of 40 to 50 per cent is due primarily to late diagnosis. Most people are asymptomatic for long periods of time and only seek medical help when they notice a change in bowel habits or rectal bleeding.

Altered Physiology and Clinical Features

Cancer of the colon and rectum always arises from the epithelium lining the intestine. The effects produced depend largely on the location of the cancer.

The chief symptoms are changes in bowel habits (the most common presenting symptom), the passage of blood in the stools (second most common symptom), mucus, rectal/abdominal pain, anaemia, weight loss, obstruction and perforation. A suddenly developing obstruction may be the first symptom of cancer involving the colon anywhere between the caecum and the sigmoid, for in this region, where the bowel contents are liquid, a slowly developing obstruction will not become evident until the lumen is practically closed. Cancer of the sigmoid and the

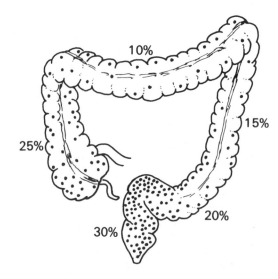

Figure 15.6 Distribution of cancer of the colon and rectum. (After Way, L. W. (ed.) (1985) *Current Surgical Diagnosis and Treatment*, Lange Medical Publishers, Los Altos, California.)

rectum causes earlier symptoms of partial obstruction, with constipation alternating with diarrhoea, lower abdominal crampy pains and distension.

● Any patient with a history of unexplained change in bowel habit, with changes in the shape of the stool or with passage of blood in the stools should be studied carefully to rule out cancer of the large bowel.

The possibility that a rectal carcinoma exists—detectable, but still asymptomatic and still operable—is one important reason for the inclusion of a rectal examination as part of every routine physical examination (see p. 580). A digital examination can reveal about 20 per cent of colorectal cancers. Additional symptoms, often present, are those of progressive weakness, anorexia, weight loss, anaemia and lower abdominal pain.

The incidence of carcinoma of the colon and rectum increases with age. These cancers are considered the most common malignancies in old age except for prostatic cancer in males. The presentation of symptoms is often insidious. Fatigue is almost always present, due primarily to iron deficiency anaemia. The symptoms most commonly reported by the elderly are abdominal pain, obstruction, tenesmus and rectal bleeding.

Colonic carcinoma in the elderly has been closely associated with dietary carcinogens. Lack of fibre is a major causative agent because faecal transit time is prolonged, which in turn prolongs exposure to possible carcinogens. Excess fat is believed to alter bacterial flora and convert steroids into compounds that have carcinogenic properties.

Diagnosis

Along with the abdominal and rectal examination, the most important diagnostic procedures for cancer of the colon are faecal occult blood testing, barium enema, proctosigmoidoscopy and colonoscopy. As many as 60 per cent of colorectal cancers can be identified by sigmoidoscopy.

Surgical Management

The operative treatment will depend on the location and the extent of the cancer. When the tumour can be removed, the involved colon is excised for some distance on each side of the growth to remove the tumour and the area of its lymphatic spread (Figure 15.7). If distant (liver) metastasis has occurred, the tumour may be excised for palliation (relief of symptoms without cure). The intestine is reunited by an end-to-end anastomosis of the colon. When the growth is situated low in the sigmoid or the rectum, the colon is cut above the growth and brought out through the abdominal wall, forming an abdominal anus called a colostomy. The growth then is removed from below by a perineal incision (abdominoperineal resection, Figure 15.8).

In the event that the tumour has spread and involves surrounding vital structures, it is considered to be inoperable. When the growth in the rectum or the sigmoid is inoperable, and especially when symptoms of partial or complete obstruction are present, a colostomy is performed.

A loop of the colon, near the junction of the descending colon and the sigmoid, is brought out of the abdomen through a lower left rectus incision and maintained in place by a plastic rod or rubber tube inserted underneath the loop. If the obstruction is complete, the loop may be drained by the insertion of a rubber tube or by the use of a right-angled tube, held in the intestine by a purse-string suture. When the obstruction is incomplete, the colostomy loop is allowed to remain unopened for several days to permit the peritoneal cavity to become thoroughly sealed off. During this time, the patient is given a liquid diet. The intestine is opened by electrocautery, because haemorrhage is slight after its use.

In some instances, when a tumour cannot be resected, a bypass procedure is performed; colocolostomy is the preferred method. In this procedure the ends of the remaining colon are joined, eliminating the need for a stoma. When the rectum is involved, a major concern is to save the sphincter, which controls defaecation. A low anterior resection of the rectum is done through an abdominal incision. However, the lesion must be located in the upper two thirds of the rectum, and there must be sufficient normal bowel tissue (2.5 cm) below the lesion to be resected and 10 cm of normal bowel proximal to the lesion to be removed. The sigmoid is anastomosed to the rectum, and no colostomy is needed.

Medical Management

Radiation is recommended for lesions that may not be resectable. Little benefit is obtained when chemotherapy and immunotherapy are used alone. However, radiation plus chemotherapy has been shown to result in longer survival rates.

Complications

The incidence of complications for colostomies is about half that seen with ileostomies. Some common complications are prolapse of the stoma (usually due to obesity), perforation (due to improper stoma irrigation), stoma retraction, faecal impaction and skin irritation. Leakage from an anastomotic site can occur if remaining bowel segments are diseased or weakened. Leakage from an intestinal anastomosis causes abdominal distension and rigidity, temperature elevation and signs of shock. Surgical repair is necessary.

Pulmonary complications are also always a concern with abdominal surgery. Patients over 50 years of age are

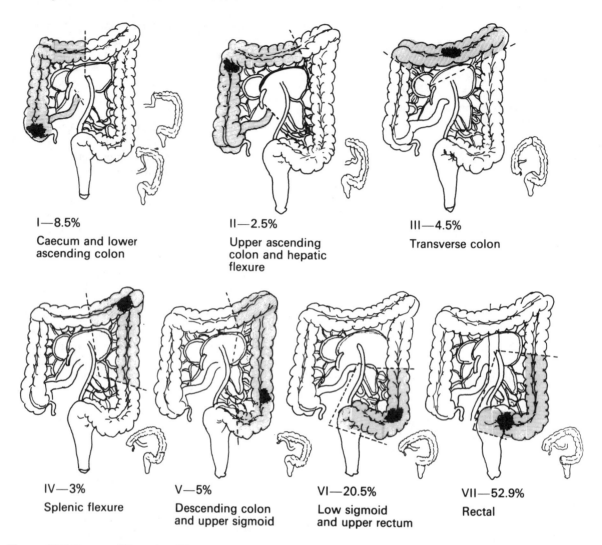

I—8.5%
Caecum and lower ascending colon

II—2.5%
Upper ascending colon and hepatic flexure

III—4.5%
Transverse colon

IV—3%
Splenic flexure

V—5%
Descending colon and upper sigmoid

VI—20.5%
Low sigmoid and upper rectum

VII—52.9%
Rectal

Figure 15.7 Cancer of the colon. Diagrams show areas where cancer can occur, what area is removed and (in the very small diagrams) how the anastomosis is done. For rectal cancer, an abdominoperineal resection is done with colostomy. (Adapted from American Cancer Society.)

considered to be at high risk, especially if they are hospitalized, are (or have been) receiving antibiotics or sedatives or are being maintained on bedrest for a prolonged period of time. Two primary pulmonary complications are pneumonia and atelectasis. Pneumonia can be prevented by frequent movement (turning the patient from side to side every two hours), deep abdominal breathing, coughing and early mobilization. For treatment, the nurse administers prescribed antipyretics and antibiotics such as penicillin G or erythromycin. Bedrest is maintained when the symptoms are severe. Atelectasis, a collapse of a lobule or lung unit, is manifested by dyspnea, cyanosis and tachycardia.

Preventive measures are similar to those used for pneumonia. Treatment consists of aspiration or bronchoscopy.

Care of the Patient With a Colostomy

When the possibility of a colostomy exists, the patient is informed by the surgeon. This is a lifesaving procedure that is compatible with active participation in social and work life. The nurse is in a position to help the patient accept a colostomy; with courage, optimism and determination, the patient can adjust to a new lifestyle, improving daily until an individual pattern of management has been established. Members of the health team, the stoma therapist, the family, close friends and other patients are available for assistance and support.

To give adequate support, care and advice to these patients, the nurse must know not only basic information about their physical condition, nutritional status and proposed surgery, but also the patients themselves. What do

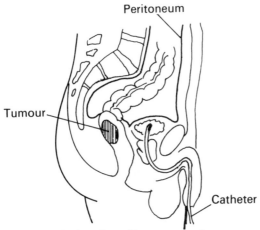

1. Presurgical patient. Note tumour in rectum.

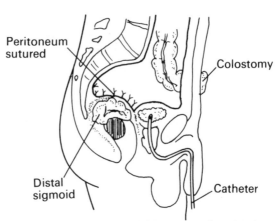

2. At operation, sigmoid is removed and colostomy established. The distal bowel has been dissected free to a point below pelvic peritoneum, which is sutured over the closed end of the distal sigmoid and rectum.

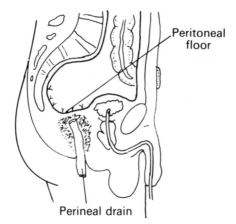

3. Perineal resection includes removal of the rectum and free portion of the sigmoid from below. A drain is inserted in this void.

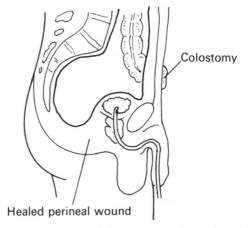

4. The final result after healing. Note healed perineal wound and the permanent colostomy.

Figure 15.8 Abdominoperineal resection for carcinoma of rectum.

they think, feel, express, suppress, desire, fear and so on? In daily contacts with patients who have a colostomy, valuable rapport can be established to facilitate their adjustment. The nurse must understand and practise psychology and the principles of learning as they apply to each particular individual. In addition to the shock of the colostomy, these patients are perhaps also dealing with a diagnosis of cancer. These two issues together can tax their coping ability and that of their families.

Elderly patients usually have some degree of decreased vision and impaired hearing, as well as difficulty with skills that require fine motor co-ordination. The nurse should encourage the patient to handle the stoma equipment preoperatively and simulate cleaning the peris-

tomal skin and irrigating the stoma, noting those skills that require assistance.

Accidents resulting from falls occur frequently among the elderly. The nurse should determine whether the patient can walk unassisted to the bathroom. Is the bathroom nearby?

Skin care is a major concern for the elderly patient because of skin changes that occur with ageing. The epithelial and subcutaneous fatty layers thin out; the skin is less hydrated and easily irritated. To prevent breakdown, special attention is paid to skin cleansing and the proper fit of an appliance. Arteriosclerosis causes decreased blood flow to the wound and stoma site. As a result, transport of nutrients is delayed, and healing takes longer.

Preoperative Nursing Care

Psychosocial Support

A patient diagnosed with cancer of the colon/rectum may require a permanent colostomy and may grieve about the diagnosis and the impending surgery. The nurse should assess emotional reactions and evaluate the ability of family and/or close friends to offer support and encourage coping behaviours. Those undergoing surgery for a temporary colostomy may express fears and concerns similar to those of a person with a permanent stoma. A temporary colostomy can become permanent for a patient whose condition deteriorates and who cannot tolerate additional surgery. The nurse should encourage emotional expressions and observe for adaptive behaviours.

The level of anxiety (mild, moderate, severe) should be identified as well as any measures the patient uses to cope with the diagnosis and impending surgery. The following questions should be considered: (1) Does the patient know what the stoma will look like, where it will be located and how it will function? (2) Is the patient aware of the type and frequency of drainage that is expected? (3) Have the available drainage bags been seen by the patient? (4) Has the patient spoken to a stoma therapist? (5) Does the patient know anyone who has a stoma, or spoken to another patient in a similar position?

Speaking with a person who is successfully managing a colostomy is often helpful. The Colostomy Welfare Group is a useful organization to be in touch with.

Anticipated changes in body image and lifestyle are profoundly disturbing, and patients will need empathetic support in trying to adjust to them. Because the excretory orifice is located on the abdomen, the patient may think that everyone will be aware of the stoma. The nurse can help to reduce this apprehension by presenting factual information about the surgical procedure and the creation and management of the stoma. If the patient is receptive, diagrams, photographs and appliances may be used to explain and clarify. Because the patient is experiencing emotional stress, the nurse may need to repeat some of the information. Time should be provided for the patient to ask questions. The nurse's acceptance and understanding of the patient's concerns and feelings convey a caring, competent attitude that promotes confidence and co-operation.

Preparation for Operation

Usually, a high-calorie, low-residue diet is given for several days before operation, if time and the patient's condition permit. In addition, mechanical cleansing of the bowel may be done by laxatives, enemas or colonic irrigations.

Careful attention is given to complaints of pain, which are assessed and described as to their nature, location and duration. The nurse records fluid losses such as occur with vomiting and diarrhoea. This will aid in regulating the fluid intake and maintaining adequate balance. If the haemoglobin is below 12 g/dl, a blood transfusion may be prescribed because anaemia is common. Preoperative nasogastric intubation facilitates the performance of intestinal surgery and minimizes postoperative distension.

Postoperative Nursing Care

Postoperative nursing care for patients undergoing a colectomy is similar to nursing care for any abdominal surgery patient. The patient is monitored for signs of the complications discussed earlier in this section (page 573). These include leakage from an anastomotic site, prolapse of the stoma, perforation, stoma retraction, faecal impaction and skin irritation, as well as pulmonary complications associated with abdominal surgery. Patients having a colostomy are helped out of bed on the first postoperative day and encouraged to care for the colostomy from the very first bag change, if appropriate. The return to normal diet is rapid, and every effort is made to encourage them to live as they did before the operation. Psychologically, this appears to de-emphasize the abnormality of the situation.

Once the stoma has healed and any initial oedema has disappeared, the patient will be able to discuss with the stoma care nurse the various appliances available. Equipment suited to the patient will be chosen and tried, and arrangements for a supply to be ordered will be made. Some patients may wish to learn to irrigate their stoma, thereby regulating when it works. This procedure would be taught by the nurse specialist and would be appropriate for those patients who are perhaps working or whose lifestyle would be hindered by the unpredictable working of their stoma.

Skin Care

The effluent discharge will vary with the type of ostomy. The stool is soft and mushy but irritating with a transverse colostomy, and fairly solid and slightly irritating with a descending or sigmoid colostomy. The patient is advised to protect the peristomal skin by frequently washing the area with a mild soap, applying a protective skin barrier around the stoma and securely attaching the drainage pouch. Nystatin powder can be dusted lightly on the peristomal skin to prevent irritation and yeast growth.

The skin is cleansed gently with a moist, soft cloth and a mild soap or solvent. Any excess flange is gently removed. Soap acts as a mild abrasive agent to remove enzyme residue from faecal spillage. During the time the skin is being cleansed, a gauze dressing may be used to cover the stoma to absorb excess drainage. The patient may bathe or shower before putting on the clean appliance. Tape applied to the sides of the flange will keep it secure during bathing. The skin is patted completely dry with a gauze pad, taking care to avoid rubbing the area.

Patting the skin prevents irritation because solvents can be damaging. A skin barrier (wafer, paste, powder) is used around the stoma to protect the skin from faecal drainage.

Application of the Drainage Bag

The stoma is measured to determine the correct size for the bag. The pouch opening should be about 0.6 cm larger than the stoma. The skin is cleansed according to the above procedure, and a peristomal skin barrier is applied. The backing is removed from the adherent surface of the bag and the drainage bag is pressed down over the stoma for 30 seconds.

Management of the Drainage Bag

Another aspect of care is the control of odours arising from the body excreta as they collect in the appliance. Inserting readily soluble deodorizing tablets in the appliance or putting a few drops of chlorophyll solution into the bag will help in the control of odours. Powdered charcoal, two crushed aspirin tablets or a teaspoon of baking soda may be sprinkled into the bag to absorb odours. Also effective are commercially available colostomy deodorants.

Removal of the Appliance

The drainage appliance is changed when it is one quarter to one third full so that the weight of its contents does not cause the bag to separate from the adhesive flange and spill the contents. The patient is asked to assume a comfortable sitting or standing position and gently push the skin down from the adhesive flange while pulling the bag up and away from the stoma. Gentle pressure prevents traumatizing the skin as well as preventing the spillage of any liquid faecal contents.

Care of Perineal Wound

If the malignancy has been removed by the perineal route, the wound is observed carefully for signs of haemorrhage. This wound usually contains a drain or packing that is removed gradually, so that at about the seventh day all drains are out. There are usually sloughing fragments of tissue that will come away during the following week or 10 days. This process is hastened by the mechanical irrigation of the wound.

It is appreciated by the patient if the prescribed medication for pain is administered before the procedure is begun. An irrigating container with normal saline is effective. The nurse should observe and record the condition of the perineal wound; note any bleeding, infection or necrosis. During the procedure it is important to protect the bed with an extra waterproof sheet and absorbent pads.

Changing the patient's position from one side to the other every two to four hours is desirable, because not only is it uncomfortable to lie in a dorsal recumbent position, but such a position may also interfere with healing by causing wound separation.

An indwelling catheter remains in place for several days to prevent urinary retention and pressure on the perineal area. Continuing assessment of the patient's urinary status is maintained to control infection and maintain hydration.

Patient Education

The patient's partner and family should be familiar with the adjustment that will be necessary when the patient returns home. They need to be encouraged to verbalize their concerns. Their understanding is necessary to reduce tension; a relaxed patient tends to have fewer problems.

Before discharge from the hospital, an individualized routine for stoma care and irrigation is reviewed with the patient and carer. Supplemental literature is helpful, because those involved may have questions when the patient is back in the home setting. Someone close to the patient should assume responsibility for purchasing the equipment and supplies that will be needed at home.

Nutritional Status

In general, the patient needs to be reminded that good health practices will materially aid feelings of wellbeing and positive adjustment to the colostomy. Diet is individualized as long as it is well balanced and does not cause diarrhoea or constipation.

The nurse should carry out a complete nutritional assessment and recommend the avoidance of certain foods that cause excessive odour and gas: foods in the cabbage family, eggs, fish, beans and cellulose products such as peanuts. If the elimination of food is causing any nutritional deficiencies, the dietician should be consulted about nonirritating foods to substitute for those that are restricted so that deficiencies are corrected. The patient should be advised to experiment with an irritating food several times before restricting it, because the reaction may be an initial sensitivity that will decrease with use.

The nurse should assess hydration status and report any signs of dehydration. If the patient has problems with diarrhoea, the frequency of diarrhoeal stools plus the occurrence of abdominal cramping, urgency and hyperactive bowel sounds should be noted. For constipation, prune or apple juice or a mild laxative is effective. The patient is helped to identify any specific foods that may precipitate elimination, for example, milk, fruits, sodas, coffee, tea, carbonated beverages and high-fibre foods.

Sexual Activity

The patient is encouraged to discuss plans to return to usual sexual activity. Some patients may initiate questions about sexual activity directly or give indirect clues about their fears. Some may view the surgery as mutilative and a threat to their sexuality; some fear impotence. Others may express worry about odour/leakage from the bag during sexual activity. Alternative sexual positions are recommended as well as alternative methods of stimulation to satisfy sexual drives. The nurse assesses the patient's needs and attempts to identify specific concerns. If the nurse is uncomfortable with this, or if the patient's concerns seem complex, the nurse should seek assistance from an appropriate source, such as the stoma nurse.

► NURSING PROCESS
► THE PATIENT WITH CANCER OF THE COLON OR RECTUM

► *Assessment*

The physical care of a patient with cancer of the colon or rectum will be the same as for a patient having any form of intestinal surgery, as previously described. A colostomy is usually necessary and therefore nursing care must meet the needs of such a patient. However, in addition, the patient has to adapt to the knowledge that cancer has been diagnosed. Anxiety will be heightened, and extra psychological support will be necessary. It may be that the patient will request the presence of a spiritual adviser; some hospitals have counsellors available to talk with patients who have been newly diagnosed as having cancer. It is important that the patient and significant others have time to talk and to express their fears and anxieties.

The nurse should interview the patient and ask for a description of the symptoms that resulted in medical care being sought. If there is any abdominal pain, a description is obtained (where it occurs and how often, how long it lasts, and whether it is associated with food intake or activities). Has there been a change in bowel habits? If so, what were the exact changes? Have blood or mucus been noticed in the stools? Has the patient lost weight? How many pounds and over what period of time? How much does the patient eat every day (amount and variety of foods)? Has there been unusual fatigue? Is a nap required during the day? Is the patient able to sleep well during the night?

A history of habits is taken (smoking, alcohol intake, exercise) and dietary preferences. The nurse should ask whether fruits and vegetables are eaten daily. How often does the patient eat fatty meats, dairy products (butter, ice cream, cheese) and 'junk foods' (potato crisps, chocolate, sweets)? How does the patient cope with stress? Has the patient ever had ulcerative colitis?

► *Patient's Problems*

Based on the assessment, the patient's main problems may include the following:

Preoperative

● Anxiety related to impending surgery and the diagnosis of cancer.
● Pain, related to tissue compression secondary to obstruction.
● Nutritional deficiency related to nausea and anorexia.
● Potential for dehydration related to vomiting and dehydration.

Postoperative

● Potential for infection related to possible contamination of the abdominal cavity during the surgical procedure.
● Lack of knowledge about the diagnosis, the surgical procedure and self-care after discharge.
● Actual impairment of skin integrity related to the surgical incisions (abdominal and perianal) and the formation of a stoma.

► *Planning and Implementation*
► Expected Outcomes

The main outcomes for the patient may include reduction in anxiety, reduction/alleviation of pain, attainment of an optimal level of nutrition, maintenance of fluid and electrolyte balance, prevention of infection, acquisition of information about the diagnosis, surgical procedure and self-care after discharge, and maintenance of optimal tissue healing.

Nursing Care

Reducing Anxiety
The patient's level of anxiety (mild, moderate, severe) should be established, and whether any coping mechanisms are being used to deal with stress. The nurse should arrange for periods of privacy if desired for meditation, relaxation exercises, biofeedback; time should be set aside to sit with the patient who wishes to talk, cry, or ask questions. The nurse should offer to contact the patient's religious adviser if desired; a time for the family and/or significant others to meet with the doctors and nurses, if wished, should be arranged to discuss the treatment/prognosis with them; the nurse should arrange a meeting with a stoma therapist if that seems useful; and suggest that a patient with a stoma be asked to visit.

The nurse should project a relaxed and empathetic attitude, and always be honest when answering questions. All tests and treatment procedures should be explained at the level of the patient's understanding. Any information the doctor has provided should be clarified, if necessary. Sometimes anxiety is relieved if the patient knows what physical preparation is necessary preoperatively and what to expect postoperatively.

Some patients appreciate seeing pictures or drawings, while others would prefer not to know details. The nurse should assess what the patient needs and wants to know.

Pain Reduction/Alleviation

Analgesics are administered as prescribed. The environment is made conducive to relaxation by dimming the lights, turning off the television or radio, and restricting visitors and telephone calls. Additional comfort measures are offered, such as: position changes, distraction and relaxation techniques.

Nutritional Measures

If the patient's condition permits, a diet high in calories, protein and carbohydrates and low in residue is given pre-operatively for several days to provide adequate nutrition and decrease excessive peristalsis, in order to minimize cramping. A liquid diet may be prescribed 24 hours before surgery to decrease bulk. Total parenteral nutrition is required for some patients to supply depleted nutrients (see Chapter 13). The nurse should record daily weights and notify the doctor if the patient continues to lose weight while receiving parenteral nutrition.

Anaemia is common. If the haemoglobin falls below 12 g (1.86 mmol/l), a blood transfusion may be prescribed by the doctor. When administering a blood transfusion, normal safety guidelines and agreed policy regarding safety are followed. The nurse should be alert for signs of an allergic reaction (rash, flushing, hives, chills, dyspnoea, vomiting, tachycardia) and stop the transfusion if a reaction appears.

Maintenance of Fluid and Electrolyte Balance

Intake and output, including vomitus, are measured in order to have an accurate record of fluid balance. The patient's intake of oral food and fluids is restricted to prevent vomiting. If vomiting is expected, antiemetics are administered as prescribed. Full or clear liquids may be tolerated, or the patient may be allowed nothing by mouth. A nasogastric tube will be inserted preoperatively to drain accumulated fluids and prevent abdominal distension. An indwelling catheter may be inserted to allow monitoring of hourly output. An output of less than 30 ml/hr is reported to the doctor.

The nurse should monitor intravenous administration of fluids and electrolytes. Vital signs are also monitored to detect hypovolaemia: tachycardia, hypotension and decreased pulse volume. Hydration status should be assessed and the nurse should report decreased skin turgor, dry mucous membranes, concentrated urine and increased urine specific gravity.

Prevention of Infection

The bowel may be cleansed by laxatives, enemas or colonic irrigations, as indicated by medical staff.

Preoperative Patient Education

The nurse determines the patient's present knowledge about the diagnosis, prognosis, surgical procedure and expected level of functioning postoperatively. Learning ability and interest are assessed in order to decide what information is needed, how it should be presented, when the patient would be most receptive and who should be present during the instruction. The patient is encouraged to participate in the learning process. A time and location conducive to learning are chosen and repetition and praise are used to reinforce learning.

The nurse should review information the patient needs about the physical preparation for surgery, the expected appearance and care of the wound postoperatively, the technique of ostomy care, dietary restrictions, pain control and medication management.

Wound Care

The abdominal wound is examined frequently during the first 24 hours to make sure that it is healing without complications (infection, dehiscence, haemorrhage, excessive oedema). Dressings are changed as needed to prevent infection. The patient is shown how to support the abdominal incision during coughing and deep breathing to lessen tension on the edges of the incision. The nurse monitors temperature, pulse rate and respirations for elevations that may indicate an infectious process.

The stoma is examined for swelling (slight oedema due to surgical manipulation is normal), colour (a healthy stoma should be pink), discharge (a small amount of oozing is normal) and bleeding (an abnormal sign). The peristomal skin is cleansed gently and patted dry to prevent irritation. Perineal wound care is carried out as described on page 577.

Patient Education

Discharge planning requires the combined efforts of the doctor, nurse, stoma therapist, social worker and dietician. Patients being discharged are given specific information, individualized to their needs, about ostomy care and complications to observe for: obstruction, infection, stoma stenosis, retraction or prolapse, and peristomal skin irritation. Dietary advice is essential to help patients identify and eliminate irritating foods that can cause diarrhoea or constipation. Patients are given a list of the medications prescribed for them, with information on the action, purpose, and possible side-effects of each. A system for remembering when to take the medication is developed with the patient.

Treatments (irrigations, wound cleansing) and dressing changes are reviewed, and the carers are encouraged to participate. Patients need very specific directions about when to call the doctor. They need to know exactly what complications require prompt attention (bleeding, abdominal distension and rigidity, diarrhoea and the 'dumping syndrome'—see p. 536). Patients are asked to weigh themselves weekly and notify a doctor if they experience continued or abrupt weight loss of one to two pounds per week. If radiotherapy is necessary, the possible side-effects of anorexia, vomiting, diarrhoea and exhaustion are reviewed.

▶ *Evaluation*
▶ **Expected Outcomes**

1. Patient experiences less anxiety.
   a. Expresses concerns and fears freely.
   b. Uses coping measures to deal with stress.
   c. Shares feelings/concerns with family members and significant others.
   d. Meets with support people (religious adviser, social worker, other patients).
2. Experiences less pain.
   a. Requests analgesics as needed.
   b. Uses diversional activities successfully.
   c. Reports a decrease in pain.
3. Achieves an optimal level of nutrition.
   a. Eats a low-residue, high-protein, high-calorie diet.
   b. Reports less abdominal cramping.
   c. Tolerates parenteral nutrition therapy, if needed.
4. Achieves fluid balance.
   a. Restricts oral intake of foods and fluids when nauseated.
   b. Urinates about 1.5 l/24 hrs.
   c. Does not have paraesthesia, dizziness, unusual fatigue (signs of hypokalaemia), excessive thirst.
   d. Does not have dry, itchy or scaly skin.
   e. Maintains desired weight.
5. Avoids infection.
   a. Is afebrile.
6. Acquires information about the diagnosis, surgical procedure and self-care after discharge.
   a. Discusses the diagnosis, surgical procedure, and postoperative self-care after discharge.
   b. Asks specific questions.
   c. Discusses concerns and fears.
   d. Participates actively in the learning process (listens attentively, clarifies procedures, restates important concepts, answers questions correctly).
   e. Communicates individual needs for self-care after discharge.
   f. Understands technique of ostomy care.
7. Maintains clean incision, stoma and perineal wound.
   a. Describes the appearance of incision site accurately.
   b. States that there is some pain in the incisional area, but that it is relieved by analgesics.
   c. Discusses the appearance of the stoma as raised and pink, with minimal oedema.
   d. Describes peristomal skin as pink in colour and without irritation.
   e. Assists the nurse with dressing changes.
   f. Begins to clean the stoma and peristomal skin whenever necessary.
   g. Co-operates with perineal wound irrigations.
   h. Supports incisional area with hand when coughing and taking deep breaths.
   i. Is afebrile.

POLYPS OF THE COLON AND RECTUM

Benign polyps are much more common in the large intestine than in the small intestine. If there are numerous growths, the condition is referred to as polyposis, often a congenital abnormality. Polyps occur in 10 to 60 per cent of the population; occurrence is most frequent in the fifth decade of life, with the majority of polyps found in the sigmoid and rectum.

Clinical features depend on the size of the polyp and the amount of pressure it exerts on intestinal tissue. The most common symptom is rectal bleeding. Diagnosis can be made by digital rectal examination, barium enema studies, proctosigmoidoscopy and colonoscopy, depending on the lesion's location and size. Once they are identified, polyps are excised because of the possibility that malignancy is already present or may develop.

Familial polyposis coli refers to a conditon in which there are hundreds of polyps in the large intestines. Surgery is always recommended because untreated cases invariably turn malignant, usually by the age of 40. A total colectomy with ileoanal anastomosis is the preferred surgical procedure.

DISEASES OF THE ANORECTUM

Patients with anorectal disorders seek medical care primarily because of pain and rectal bleeding. Other frequent complaints are protrusion of haemorrhoids, anal discharge, itching, swelling, anal tenderness, stenosis and ulceration. Constipation occurs because defaecation is delayed due to pain.

Rectal Examination and Patient Preparation

Visual inspection and digital examination of the anus and the rectum are indispensable for detecting and identifying lesions involving these structures. Moreover, rectal examination is extremely useful in diagnosing or excluding many intra-abdominal and pelvic conditions, including: appendicitis; diverticulitis; salpingitis; tumours of the ovary, uterus and colon; and prostatic lesions of various types.

Rectal examinations may be done with the patient in the knee–chest, lateral or inverted position or on a special proctoscopic table. Whatever position is used, the patient is informed of the procedure and how it is to be done, and is covered so that only the rectal area is exposed.

Anorectal Abscess

Anorectal abscess is located in the pararectal spaces. Usually, it is caused by infection of pathogenic micro-organisms. Incidence is higher in men than women.

Clinical Features and Management

An abscess may occur in a variety of spaces in and around the rectum. Often it contains a quantity of foul-smelling pus and is painful. If the abscess is superficial, swelling, redness and tenderness are observed. A deeper abscess may result in toxic symptoms and even lower abdominal pain, as well as fever. More than half of rectal abscesses will result in fistulae.

Surgical treatment consists of incision and drainage; this may be all that is necessary. When deeper infection exists, with the possibility of a fistula, it is necessary to remove the fistulous tract. This may be done initially, or it may require a second operation. Often no packing is used; if it is used, usually the wound is lined with saline-soaked gauze. Later, when it is necessary to remove the packing, soaking in a bath is helpful.

These wounds are allowed to heal by granulation. Bowel movements should be formed, rather than liquid or soft. A bulking agent such as methyl cellulose may be used.

Fistula in Ano

Fistula in ano is a tiny tubular tract that extends into the anal canal from an opening located beside the anus (Figure 15.9A). Fistulae usually result from an infection. Pus or faeces leak constantly from the cutaneous opening, making it necessary for the patient to wear a protective pad. This condition may be an early sign of Crohn's disease.

Management

A fistulectomy (excision of the fistulous tract) is the recommended surgical procedure. It is preferable for the patient to have had a bowel motion before surgery.

The patient is usually placed in the lithotomy position, and the sinus tract is identified by inserting a probe into it or by injecting the tract with methylene blue solution. The fistula is dissected out or laid open by an incision from its rectal opening to its outlet. The wound is packed with gauze.

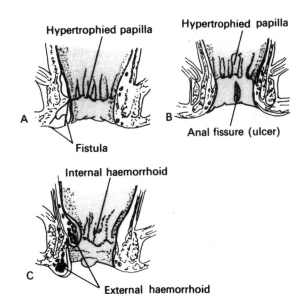

Figure 15.9 Various types of anal lesions. (A) Fistula. (B) Fissure. (C) External and internal haemorrhoids.

Fissure in Ano

Fissure in ano is a longitudinal ulcer in the anal canal (see Figure 15.9B). Fissures are usually caused by diarrhoeal stools and persistent tightening of the anal canal secondary to stress and anxiety (leading to constipation). Other causes include childbirth, trauma and laxative abuse. The most pronounced symptom is extreme pain during defaecation.

Clinical Features and Management

Fissures are characterized by painful defaecation and bleeding. The pain may be excruciating. More than half of these fissures will heal if treated by conservative measures, and the remainder will require minor surgery. Stool softeners and an increase in water intake are helpful; a bland laxative will prevent constipation. Anal dilation under anaesthesia may be required.

In surgical management, the same preoperative preparation as for fistula in ano is indicated. Several types of operations may be performed: in some cases, the anal sphincter is dilated and the fissure is excised; in others, a part of the external sphincter is divided. This establishes a paralysis of the external sphincter, with consequent relief of spasm, and permits the ulcer to heal. When there is a large, overhanging sentinel haemorrhoid, excision of the ulcer and of the haemorrhoid is performed.

Haemorrhoids

Haemorrhoids are simply varicose veins in the anal canal. They may come and go, and almost everyone has them at some time. They are very common in pregnancy. When they fade away, they may leave a telltale skin tag. They occur in two locations. Those occurring above the internal sphincter are called internal haemorrhoids, and those appearing outside the external sphincter are called external haemorrhoids (see Figure 15.9C). They cause itching, bleeding during bowel movements and pain. Internal haemorrhoids prolapse frequently through the sphincter and cause considerable discomfort. If the blood within them clots and becomes infected, they grow painful and are said to be thrombosed.

Clinical Features and Management

External haemorrhoids are associated with severe pain due to inflammation and oedema caused by thrombosis. Internal haemorrhoids are not usually painful until they bleed or prolapse with enlargement. Haemorrhoid symptoms and discomfort can be relieved by good personal hygiene and by avoiding excessive straining during defaecation. A diet that contains fruit and bran may be all the treatment that is necessary; failing this, perhaps a bulk laxative will help. Surgery is required when prolapsed haemorrhoids can no longer be reduced spontaneously or manually.

Many doctors have one or another preferred medications that, when injected above the sensitive squamous mucosa through an anoscope, has no direct effect on thrombosed veins, *per se*, but induces a fibrous reaction. This reaction in submucosal tissues of the upper anal canal and lower rectum tends to draw tissue upwards towards its normal site. This method has little effect on advanced haemorrhoids.

Cryosurgical haemorrhoidectomy involves freezing the tissues of the haemorrhoid for a sufficient time to cause necrosis. Although it is painless, it is not popular because the discharge is very foul-smelling and wound healing is prolonged.

Excision of an external haemorrhoidal tag can be done with laser therapy. The treatment is usually performed as an outpatient procedure, and is quick and relatively painless.

The methods of treating haemorrhoids just described are not effective for advanced thrombosed veins, which are usually treated by surgical haemorrhoidectomy.

The operation usually involves digital dilation of the rectal sphincter and removal of the haemorrhoids by the use of a clamp and cautery or by ligation and excision. Instead of a tube, some surgeons place pieces of soaked paraffin gauze over the anal wounds. Dressings, in such cases, are held in place by a T-bandage.

Patient Education

Stool softeners are usually prescribed for several days to prevent pain and discomfort during elimination. Ice packs help to reduce discomfort. Normal bowel elimination without pain should occur within a week. (See Nursing

Process: The Patient With an Anorectal Condition, p. 583.)

Pilonidal Sinus (Cyst)

A pilonidal sinus or cyst is found in the intergluteal cleft on the posterior surface of the lower sacrum (Figure 15.10). It is thought by some to be formed by an infolding of epithelial tissue beneath the skin, which may communicate with the skin surface through one or several small sinus openings. Hair frequently is seen protruding from these openings, and this gives the cyst its name—pilonidal—a nest of hair. The cysts rarely give symptoms until adolescence or early adult life, when infection produces an irritating drainage or an abscess. This area is easily irritated by perspiration and friction.

Management

In the early stages of the inflammation, the infection may be controlled by antibiotic therapy. Once an abscess has formed, as in cases of a hair-containing sinus, surgery is indicated. When an abscess is present, incision and drainage are performed. In patients with hair-containing

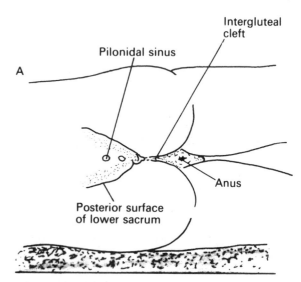

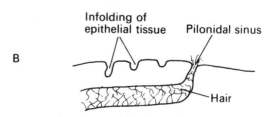

Figure 15.10 (A) Pilonidal sinus on lower sacrum about 5 cm above the anus in the intergluteal cleft. (B) Note hair particles emerging from sinus tract. Localized indentations of the skin (pits) can occur near the sinus openings.

sinuses without marked inflammatory reaction, surgery is also necessary to remove hair and debris, a potential source of irritation and infection. The entire cyst and the secondary sinus tracts are excised. In many patients the resulting defect may be sutured, but in some the defect may be so large that it cannot be closed entirely, and it is allowed to heal by granulation. Extensive excisions are no longer considered necessary.

Nursing Care
The nursing care of these patients is relatively simple. After excision of the cyst, the care is that of any superficial wound. For the first few days, the patient often is more comfortable lying on the abdomen or side with a pillow between the legs. Most patients are allowed out of bed soon after surgery, and their postoperative care is managed at home.

▶ NURSING PROCESS
▶ THE PATIENT WITH AN ANORECTAL CONDITION

▶ *Assessment*

Bleeding is frequently seen in anorectal disease. (The most common cause of rectal bleeding is haemorrhoids.) The patient is asked to describe the bleeding. It may be bright red, but occasionally it is a darker colour, due to its remaining in the rectal ampulla before expulsion and also its admixture with faeces. Bleeding from the anal canal usually has a bright red appearance. The stool is examined to see if blood is mixed with the faeces or just coating the stool.

The patient is asked to describe the pain. Does it occur during evacuation? Is there associated abdominal pain? How long does the pain last after evacuation? Is there a discharge? Can it be described as mucoid, purulent or bloody?

A dietary history is taken to establish whether there is an absence of fibre intake. Is there a history of constipation? How has it been handled before? Does the patient abuse laxatives? Is there straining at stool? Has any protrusion from the anus after defaecation ever been noticed? If so, did it resolve spontaneously?

The assessment should also cover whether the patient has a job that requires prolonged standing or sitting, whether there is a pregnancy history and whether any childbirth experience was normal.

▶ *Patient's Problems*

Based on the assessment, the patient's main problems may include the following:

- Constipation, related to ignoring the urge to defaecate because of pain during elimination.
- Anxiety related to impending surgery and embarrassment.

- Pain, related to irritation, pressure and sensitivity in the rectal/anal area secondary to anorectal disease and sphincter spasms postoperatively.
- Alteration in urinary elimination pattern related to postoperative fear of pain.
- Haemorrhage, related to the surgical incision.
- Potential nonadherence to the therapeutic regime.

▶ *Planning and Implementation*
▶ Expected Outcomes
The main outcomes for the patient may include attainment of adequate elimination, reduction in anxiety, relief of pain, promotion of urinary elimination, prevention of haemorrhage and adherence to the therapeutic regime.

Nursing Care

Measures for Relief of Constipation
The nurse encourages the intake of at least 2,000 ml of water daily to provide adequate hydration. High-fibre foods are recommended to promote bulk in the stool and facilitate easy passage through the rectum, as well as bulk laxatives such as methyl cellulose. Stool softeners are administered as prescribed. The nurse advises the patient to set aside a time for defaecation and to heed the urge. It is explained that relaxation exercises might be helpful before defaecation to relax the abdominal perineal muscles that may be constricted or in spasm due to anticipated pain with elimination.

Reducing Anxiety
Patients facing rectal surgery are usually upset and irritable because of discomfort, pain and embarrassment. The nurse should identify specific psychosocial needs and individualize a plan of care. Privacy is promoted by limiting visitors, if agreeable to patient, and the patient's privacy is always maintained when giving care. Soiled dressings are removed from the room to prevent unpleasant odours. Room deodorizers may be needed if dressings are foul-smelling.

Relieving Pain
During the first 24 hours after rectal surgery, there may be painful spasms of the sphincter and perineal muscles. Therefore, control of pain is a prime consideration. The nurse encourages the patient to assume positions of comfort (bedrest with prolapsed internal haemorrhoids, avoidance of walking with an abscess). Ice and analgesic ointments may be applied to decrease pain. After 24 hours have elapsed, topical anaesthetic agents may be beneficial for relief of local irritation and soreness.

The patient is asked to assume a prone position at intervals, since this position promotes dependent drainage of oedema fluid.

Medications may include suppositories that contain

anaesthetics, antibiotics, tranquillizers, antiemetics, analgesics and even bronchodilators. Patients will be more co-operative, and less apprehensive and uncomfortable, if the suppository is inserted properly. The most effective position for the patient to assume while the suppository is being inserted is side-lying, with the uppermost leg flexed. The suppository is unwrapped; the buttocks are spread apart with one hand and the suppository is inserted with the other. If the suppository was stored in the refrigerator (to prevent melting), it may be warmed to room temperature to lessen irritation of rectal mucosa. Water-soluble suppositories may be lubricated with water or lubricating jelly.

Promoting Urinary Elimination

Voiding may be a problem, due to a reflex spasm of the sphincter at the outlet of the bladder and a certain amount of muscle-guarding from apprehension and pain. All methods to encourage voluntary micturition (increasing fluid intake, listening to running water, dripping water over the urinary meatus) should be tried before resorting to catheterization. After rectal operations, patients are usually allowed out of bed to void.

Preventing Haemorrhage

The nurse examines the operative site for rectal bleeding and assesses for systemic indicators of excessive bleeding (tachycardia, hypotension, restlessness, thirst). Any unusual signs are reported to the doctor. After haemorrhoidectomy, haemorrhage may occur from the veins that were cut. If bleeding is obvious, direct pressure is applied to the area, the patient remains in bed and the buttocks are elevated on a pillow. Medical help is sought.

Patient Education

The patient should keep the perianal area as clean as possible. This is accomplished by gentle cleansing with warm water and drying with absorbent cotton wipes. The patient is asked not to rub the area with toilet tissue. Frequent warm baths may be helpful.

The patient prevents constipation by responding quickly to the urge to defaecate. Over-the-counter laxatives should be avoided. Diet is modified to increase fluids and fibre. The patient is encouraged to mobilize as soon as possible.

The patient is informed about the prescribed diet, made aware of the significance of proper eating habits and told what laxatives can be taken safely and why exercise is important.

▶ *Evaluation*

Evaluation of the care given to a patient following rectal surgery will include establishing a normal pattern of elimination. This will be dictated by the patient and aided by following advice concerning fluid and nutritional intake.

Anxiety is a common problem, and evaluation of care will examine whether the individual is coping with the situation and whether or not any problems have been discussed with a health care professional.

Care will also be aimed at reducing pain and discomfort; evaluation will take the form of observing and talking with the patient in order to ascertain the degree of pain.

Avoidance of complications such as retention of urine and bleeding from the surgical wound will also be indicators of the patient's progress.

BIBLIOGRAPHY

Pritchard, P. A. and David, J. A. (1988) *The Royal Marsden Hospital Manual of Clinical Nursing Procedures* (2nd edition), Harper & Row, London.

FURTHER READING

Books

Brunner, L. S. and Suddarth, D. S. (1989) *The Lippincott Manual of Medical-Surgical Nursing* (2nd edition), Harper & Row, London.
Hinchcliff, S. M., Norman, S. E. and Schober, J. E. (1989) *Nursing Practice and Health Care*, Edward Arnold, London.
Wilson-Barnett, J. and Batehup, L. (1988) *Patient Problems: A Research Base for Nursing Care*, Scutari Press, London.

Articles

Airey, S., Down, G. *et al.* (1988) An innovation in stoma care, *Nursing Times*, Vol. 84, No. 6, pp. 56–9.
Charlwood, J. (1987) Problems of the lower bowel causing constipation, *Nursing* (Third Series), Vol. 21, pp. 775–7.
Dalzell, T. (1989) Acute intestinal obstruction, *Nursing Times*, Vol. 85, No. 2, pp. 59–61.
Dyer, S., Clark, P. *et al.* (1988) Ileostomy and fistula appliances, *The Professional Nurse*, Vol. 3, No. 11, pp. 462–3.
Foston, L. R. (1989) A patient's view of ileostomy, *The Professional Nurse*, Vol. 5, No. 1, pp. 20–2.
Hanham, S. (1990) Management of constipation, *Nursing*, Vol. 14, No. 17, pp. 28–31.
Heading, C. (1987) Nursing assessment and management of constipation, *Nursing* (Third Series), Vol. 21, pp. 778–80.
Heading, C. (1987) Nursing factors—diarrhoea, *Nursing* (Third Series), Vol. 21, pp. 781–3.
Molitor, P. (1985) Constipation, *Nursing Mirror*, Vol. 160, No. 19, pp. 18–20.
Newton, C. A. (1987) An overview of the large intestine: anatomy, physiology and normal function, *Nursing* (Third Series), Vol. 21, pp. 770–2.
Swan, E. (1986) Emergency surgery for ulcerative colitis, *Nursing Times*, 22 January, pp. 49–53.

Unit 5

METABOLIC AND ENDOCRINE PROBLEMS

chapter 16

ASSESSMENT AND CARE OF PATIENTS WITH HEPATIC AND BILIARY DISORDERS

ANATOMY AND PHYSIOLOGY

The liver, the largest gland of the body, can be considered a chemical factory whose job is to manufacture, accumulate, alter and excrete a large number of substances involved in metabolism. The location of the liver is essential in this function, since it receives nutrient-rich blood directly from the gastrointestinal tract and then either stores or transforms these nutrients into chemicals that are used elsewhere in the body for metabolic needs. The liver's role is especially important in the regulation of glucose and protein metabolism. The liver manufactures and secretes bile, which has a major role in the digestion and absorption of fats in the gastrointestinal tract. It functions as an organ of excretion by removing waste products from the bloodstream and secreting them into the bile. The bile produced by the liver is stored temporarily in the gallbladder until it is needed for the process of digestion, at which time the gallbladder empties and bile enters the intestine.

The liver is located behind the ribs in the upper right portion of the abdominal cavity. It weighs about 1,500 g and is divided into four lobes. Each lobe is surrounded by a thin layer of connective tissue, which extends into the lobe itself and divides the liver mass into small units, called lobules. A schematic diagram of the liver and its anatomical relationships is shown in Figure 16.1.

The circulation of the blood into and out of the liver is of major importance in its function. The blood that perfuses the liver is derived from two sources. Approximately 75 per cent of the blood supply comes from the portal vein, which drains the gastrointestinal tract and is rich in nutrients. The remainder of the blood supply enters by way of the hepatic artery and is rich in oxygen. Terminal branches of these two blood supplies join to form common capillary beds, which constitute the sinusoids of the liver. Liver cells (hepatocytes) are thus bathed by a mixture of venous and arterial blood. The sinusoids empty into a venule that occupies the centre of each liver lobule and is called the central vein. The central veins join to form the hepatic vein, which constitutes the venous drainage from the liver and empties

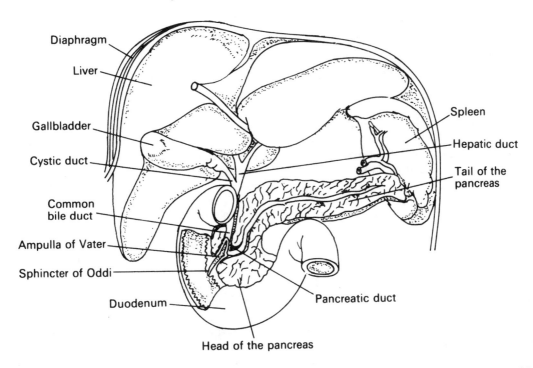

Figure 16.1 Liver and biliary system. (Chaffee, E. E. and Greisheimer, E. M. (1974) *Basic Physiology and Anatomy* (3rd edition), J. B. Lippincott, Philadelphia.)

into the inferior vena cava, close to the diaphragm. Thus, there are two sources of blood flowing into the liver but there is only one exit pathway.

In addition to hepatocytes, phagocytic cells belonging to the reticuloendothelial system are present in the liver. In the liver, these cells are called Kupffer cells. Their main function is to engulf particulate matter such as bacteria that enters the liver through the portal blood.

The smallest bile ducts, called canaliculi, are located between the lobules of the liver. These canaliculi receive secretions from the hepatocytes and carry them to larger bile ducts, which eventually form the hepatic duct. The hepatic duct from the liver and the cystic duct from the gallbladder join to form the common bile duct, which empties into the small intestine. The flow of bile into the intestine is controlled by the sphincter of Oddi, located at the junction where the common bile duct enters the duodenum.

The gallbladder, a pear-shaped, hollow, saclike organ, 7.5 to 10 cm long, lies in a shallow depression on the inferior surface of the liver, to which it is attached by loose connective tissue. The capacity of the gallbladder is 30 to 50 ml of bile. Its wall is composed largely of smooth muscle. The gallbladder is connected to the common bile duct by the cystic duct.

Metabolic Functions of the Liver

The liver plays a major role in the regulation of blood glucose concentration. After a meal, glucose is taken up from the portal venous blood by the liver and converted into glycogen, which is stored within the hepatocytes. Subsequently, the glycogen is converted back to glucose and released as needed into the bloodstream, in order to maintain normal levels of blood sugar. Additional glucose can be synthesized by the liver through a process called gluconeogenesis. For this process, the liver can use amino acids from protein breakdown or lactate produced by exercising muscles.

Use of amino acids for gluconeogenesis results in the formation of ammonia as a by-product. The liver converts this metabolically generated ammonia into urea. Ammonia produced by bacteria in the intestines is also removed from portal blood for urea synthesis. In this way, the liver converts ammonia, a potential toxin, into urea, a harmless compound that can be excreted in the urine.

The liver also plays an important role in protein metabolism. It synthesizes almost all of the plasma proteins (except γ-globulin), including albumin, α- and ß-globulins, blood-clotting factors, specific transport proteins and most of the plasma lipoproteins. Vitamin K is required by the liver for synthesis of prothrombin and some of the other clotting factors. Amino acids serve as the building blocks for protein synthesis.

The liver is also active in fat metabolism. Fatty acids can be broken down for the production of energy and production of ketone bodies (acetoacetic acid, ß-hydroxybutyric acid and acetone). Ketone bodies are small compounds that can enter the bloodstream and provide a source of energy for muscles and other tissues. Breakdown of fatty acids into ketone bodies occurs predominantly when the availability of glucose for metabolism is limited, as during starvation or in diabetic patients. Fatty acids and their metabolic products are also used for the synthesis of cholesterol, lecithin, lipoproteins and other complex lipids. Under some conditions, lipids may accumulate in the hepatocytes and result in the abnormal condition called fatty liver.

Vitamins A, B_{12}, D and several of the B complex vitamins are stored in large amounts in the liver. Certain metals, such as iron and copper, are also stored within the liver. Because the liver is rich in these substances, liver extracts have been used for therapy of a wide range of nutritional disorders.

Drug Metabolism

Many drugs, such as barbiturates and amphetamines, are metabolized by the liver. Metabolism generally results in loss of activity of the drug, although in some cases activation may occur. One of the important pathways for drug metabolism involves alteration of the drug by the cytochrome P-450 system. Another pathway of importance involves conjugation (binding) of the drug with a variety of compounds, such as glucuronic or acetic acid, to form more soluble substances. The conjugated products may be excreted in the faeces or urine, similar to bilirubin excretion.

Bile

Bile is continuously formed by the hepatocytes and collected in the canaliculi and bile ducts. It is composed mainly of water and electrolytes, such as sodium, potassium, calcium, chloride and bicarbonate, and also contains significant amounts of lecithin, fatty acids, cholesterol, bilirubin and bile salts. Bile is collected and stored in the gallbladder and is emptied into the intestine when needed for digestion. The functions of bile are excretory, as in the excretion of bilirubin, and as an aid to digestion through the emulsification of fats by bile salts.

Bile Salts

Bile salts are made by the hepatocytes from cholesterol. After conjugation with amino acids (taurine and glycine), they are excreted into the bile. The bile salts, together with cholesterol and lecithin, are required for emulsification of fats in the intestine. This process is necessary for efficient digestion and absorption. Bile salts are then reabsorbed, primarily in the distal ileum, into portal blood for return to the liver and are again excreted into the bile. This pathway from hepatocytes to bile to intestine and back to the hepatocytes is called the enterohepatic circulation. Because of the enterohepatic circulation, only a small fraction of the bile salts that enter the intestine is excreted in the faeces.

This decreases the demand for active synthesis of bile salts by the liver cells.

Bilirubin Excretion

Bilirubin is a pigment derived from the breakdown of haemoglobin by cells of the reticuloendothelial system, including the Kupffer cells of the liver. Hepatocytes remove bilirubin from the blood and chemically modify it through conjugation to glucuronic acid, which makes the bilirubin more soluble in aqueous solutions. The conjugated bilirubin is secreted by the hepatocytes into the adjacent bile canaliculi and is eventually carried in the bile into the duodenum. In the small intestine, bilirubin is converted into urobilinogen, which is in part excreted in the faeces and in part absorbed back into the portal blood. Much of this reabsorbed urobilinogen is removed by the hepatocytes and is secreted into the bile once again (enterohepatic circulation). Some of the urobilinogen enters the systemic circulation and is excreted by the kidneys in the urine. Elimination of bilirubin in the bile represents the major route of excretion for this compound. The bilirubin concentration in the blood may be increased either in the presence of liver disease or when the flow of bile is impeded (e.g., with gallstones in the bile ducts). With bile duct obstruction, bilirubin does not enter the intestine and, as a consequence, urobilinogen will be absent from the urine.

Gallbladder

The gallbladder functions as a storage depot for bile. Between meals, when the sphincter of Oddi is closed, bile produced by the hepatocytes enters the gallbladder. During storage, a large portion of the water in bile is absorbed through the walls of the gallbladder, so that gallbladder bile is five to ten times more concentrated than that originally secreted by the liver. When food enters the duodenum, the gallbladder contracts, and the sphincter of Oddi relaxes, allowing the bile to enter the intestine. This response is mediated by secretion of the hormone cholecystokinin (CCK) from the intestinal wall.

Altered Physiology

Liver dysfunction results from damage to the liver parenchymal cells, either directly, from primary liver diseases, or indirectly, due to obstruction to bile flow or to derangements of hepatic circulation.

Disorders that lead to hepatocellular dysfunction may be caused by infectious agents, such as bacteria and viruses, and by anoxia, metabolic disorders, toxins and drugs, nutritional deficiencies and states of hypersensitivity. Probably the most common cause of parenchymal damage is malnutrition, especially in alcoholism. The response of the parenchymal cells is much the same for most noxious agents: replacement of glycogen by lipids, producing fatty

Table 16.1 *Liver function studies*

Test	Normal	Clinical functions
Pigment studies		
Serum bilirubin, direct	0–5.1 μmol/l	These studies measure the ability of liver to conjugate and excrete bilirubin. Results are abnormal in liver and biliary tract disease and are associated with jaundice clinically
Serum bilirubin, total	1.7–20.5 μmol/l	
Urine bilirubin	0	
Urine urobilinogen	0.09–4.23 μmol/24 hr	
Faecal urobilinogen (infrequently used)	0.068–0.34 mmol/24 hr	
Dye clearances		
Indocyanine green	500–800 ml/m²/min	Dye is extracted from blood and excreted by liver; its clearance depends on hepatic blood flow, functioning liver cells and lack of obstruction. It is replacing the BSP test because of its fewer side-effects
Bromsulphthalein excretion (BSP test)	<5% retention 45 minutes after dye injection	BSP binds to albumin in blood. Liver cells unbind BSP, conjugate it and excrete it in bile. Normal clearance depends on hepatic blood flow, functioning liver cell mass and lack of obstruction. Retention is increased in liver cell damage or decreased liver blood flow.
Protein studies		
Total serum protein	70–75 g/l	Proteins are manufactured by the liver. Their levels may be affected in a variety of liver impairments
Serum albumin	35–55 g/l	Albumin (cirrhosis, chronic hepatitis, oedema, ascites)
Serum globulin	15–30 g/l	
Serum protein electrophoresis	32–56 g/l	Globulin (cirrhosis, liver disease, chronic obstructive jaundice, viral hepatitis)
Albumin/globulin (A/G) ratio	A > G or 1.5:1–2.5:1	A/G ratio is reversed in chronic liver disease (decreased albumin and increased globulin)
Prothrombin time	11 to 15 seconds	Prothrombin time may be prolonged in liver disease. It will not return to normal with vitamin K in severe liver cell damage
Serum alkaline phosphatase	Varies with method 20–90 IU/litre at 30°	Serum alkaline phosphatase is manufactured in bones, liver, kidneys and intestine and excreted through biliary tract. In absence of bone disease, it is a sensitive measure of biliary tract obstruction
Serum transaminase studies		
Aspartate aminotransferase (serum glutamic oxalacetic transaminase)	10 to 40 IU/l	The studies are based on release of enzymes from damaged liver cells. These enzymes are elevated in liver cell damage
Alanine aminotransferase (serum glutamic pyruvic transaminase)	5 to 35 IU/l	
LDH	165 to 400 IU/l	

▶

Table 16.1 *continued*

Test	Normal	Clinical functions
Blood ammonia	11.1–67.0 µmol/l	Liver converts ammonia to urea; ammonia level rises in liver failure
Cholesterol	3.9 to 6.5 mmol/l	Cholesterol levels are elevated in biliary
Ester	60 per cent of total cholesterol	obstruction and decreased in parenchymal liver disease

Additional studies	*Clinical functions*
Radiological studies	
Barium swallow	For oesophageal varices, which indicate increased portal pressure
Plain X-ray of abdomen	To determine gross liver size
Liver scan with radioisotope	To show size and shape of liver, to show replacement of liver tissue with scars, cysts or tumour
Cholecystogram and cholangiogram	For gallbladder and bile duct visualization
Coeliac axis arteriography	For liver and pancreas visualization
Laparoscopy	Direct visualization of anterior surface of liver, gallbladder and mesentery through a trocar
Liver biopsy	To determine anatomical changes in liver tissue
Oesophagoscopy/endoscopy	To search for oesophageal varices and abnormalities
Electroencephalogram	Abnormal in hepatic coma and impending hepatic coma
Ultrasound	To show size of abdominal organs and presence of masses
Computerized tomography (CT scan)	To detect hepatic neoplasms; diagnose cysts, abscesses and haematomas; and distinguish between obstructive and nonobstructive jaundice
Angiography	Visualizes hepatic circulation and detects presence and nature of hepatic masses

infiltration, with or without cell death or necrosis. This is commonly associated with inflammatory cell infiltration and growth of fibrous tissue. Cell regeneration can occur if the disease process is not too toxic to the cells.

Hepatocellular dysfunction is manifested by alteration of the metabolic and excretory functions of the liver. Serum bilirubin concentration rises, leading to jaundice or yellowing of the skin; this results from intrahepatic obstruction of bile channels. Abnormalities of carbohydrate, fat and protein metabolism occur with liver dysfunction. Abnormal protein metabolism results in decreased serum albumin concentration and oedema. Ammonia, a by-product of metabolism, is absorbed from the gastrointestinal tract but is not converted to urea by the damaged liver cells. An increased serum ammonia level may produce signs of central nervous system impairment.

The vascular architecture of the liver may be disturbed, causing increased portal vein blood pressure, which results in leakage of fluid into the peritoneal cavity, or ascites, and oesophageal varices. The lack of normal production of various blood-clotting factors can lead to bleeding from any site, but the patient is particularly prone to gastrointestinal bleeding.

Many endocrine abnormalities also occur with liver dysfunction as a result of the inability of the liver to metabolize hormones normally, including androgens or sex hormones. Although the exact mechanisms for their appearance are not well established, gynaecomastia, amenorrhoea, testicular atrophy and other disturbances of sexual function and sex characteristics are thought to result from failure of the damaged liver to normally inactivate oestrogens.

Acute liver damage may cause acute liver failure, may be completely reversible, or may progress to chronic disease. The end result of chronic liver damage is cirrhosis, characterized by replacement of parenchymal cells with fibrotic tissue. Liver failure is present when the ability of the liver to carry out its excretory and metabolic functions falls below the needs of the body. Hepatic coma results when liver dysfunction is so severe that the liver is unable to remove end products of metabolism from the bloodstream.

Considerations for the Elderly

The most frequently observed change in the liver in the elderly is a decrease in the size and weight of the liver accompanied by a decrease in total hepatic blood flow. In general, however, these decreases are in proportion to the decreases in body size and weight seen in normal ageing. Results of liver function tests do not normally change in the elderly; abnormal results in an elderly patient indicate abnormal liver function and are not the result of the ageing process itself.

The immune system is altered in the aged, and a less responsive immune system may be responsible for the increased incidence and severity of hepatitis B in the elderly and the increased incidence of liver abscesses secondary to decreased phagocytosis by the Kupffer cells.

Drug metabolism by the liver appears to be decreased in the elderly, but such changes are usually also accompanied by changes in intestinal absorption, renal excretion and altered body distribution of some drugs secondary to changes in fat deposition. These alterations necessitate careful administration of all medications with reduction of dosage to prevent drug toxicity.

ASSESSMENT OF HEPATIC FUNCTION

Liver Function Tests

The liver is a complex functioning organ and thus liver function tests are numerous (see Table 16.1). The patient needs to know why these tests are being done, why they are important and how co-operation can be achieved.

Over 70 per cent of the parenchyma of the liver may be damaged before liver function tests become abnormal (Beland and Passos, 1975). Function is generally measured in terms of serum enzyme activity (e.g., alkaline phosphatase, transaminases, lactic dehydrogenase), clearance of dyes such as indocyanine green or sulphobromophthalein (bromsulphthalein), and serum concentrations of proteins, bilirubin, ammonia, clotting factors and lipids. Several of these tests may be helpful for assessment of patients with liver disease; however, the nature and extent of hepatic dysfunction cannot be determined by these tests alone. Many other disorders can influence their results; therefore, the tests are not sensitive indicators of liver dysfunction.

Examination of the Liver

The liver may be palpable in the right upper quadrant. A palpable liver presents as a firm, sharp ridge with a smooth surface (Figure 16.2).If the liver is enlarged, the degree to which it descends below the right costal margin is recorded. The liver of a patient with cirrhosis is small and hard, while the liver of a patient with acute hepatitis is quite soft and the edge is easily moved by the hand. Tenderness of the liver implies recent acute enlargement with consequent stretching of the liver capsule. The absence of tenderness may imply that the enlargement is of long standing. Enlargement of the liver is an abnormal finding requiring further evaluation.

Liver biopsy (i.e., the sampling of liver tissue by needle aspiration for the purpose of histological study), ultrasonic scan and computerized tomography are all used in the diagnosis of structural changes in the liver.

CLINICAL FEATURES OF HEPATIC DISORDERS

The complications of liver disease are numerous and

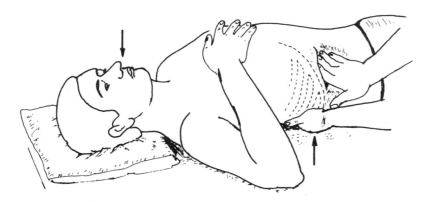

Figure 16.2 Technique for palpation of the liver. As the patient inhales, a palpable liver edge will descend to meet the index finger of the right hand. At the height of inspiration, the examiner releases the pressure of the right hand slightly and tries to feel the liver edge 'slip' under the fingertips.

varied. In many instances their ultimate effects are incapacitating or lethal; their presence is ominous, and their treatment is notoriously difficult.

Among the most frequent and important of these complications are the following:

● Jaundice, resulting from increased bilirubin concentration in the blood.
● Portal hypertension, ascites and oesophageal varices, resulting from circulatory changes within the diseased liver and producing excessive sodium and water retention, and a high risk of severe gastrointestinal haemorrhage.
● Nutritional deficiencies, attributable to the inability of the malfunctioning liver cells to metabolize certain vitamins, and responsible for impaired central and peripheral nervous systems and abnormal bleeding tendencies.
● Hepatic coma, reflecting the incomplete metabolism of protein by the diseased liver.

Jaundice

When, for any reason, the bilirubin concentration in the blood becomes abnormally increased, all the body tissue, including the sclerae and the skin, becomes tinged yellow or greenish yellow. This condition is called jaundice. There are several types of jaundice: (1) haemolytic; (2) hepatocellular; (3) obstructive; and (4) jaundice due to hereditary hyperbilirubinaemia. Hepatocellular and obstructive jaundice are the two types commonly associated with liver disease.

Haemolytic Jaundice
Haemolytic jaundice is the result of an increased destruction of the red blood cells, the effect of which is to flood the plasma with bilirubin so rapidly that the liver, although functioning normally, cannot excrete the bilirubin as quickly as it is formed. This type of jaundice is encountered in patients with haemolytic transfusion reactions and other haemolytic disorders. The bilirubin in the blood of these patients is predominantly of the unconjugated, or 'free', type. Faecal and urine urobilinogen are increased, although the urine is free of bilirubin. Patients with this type of jaundice, unless their hyperbilirubinaemia is extreme, do not experience symptoms or complications as a result of the jaundice *per se*. However, very prolonged jaundice, even if mild, predisposes to the formation of 'pigment stones' in the gallbladder, and extremely severe jaundice is attended by a definite risk of possible brain stem damage.

Hepatocellular Jaundice
Hepatocellular jaundice is caused by the inability of diseased liver cells to clear normal amounts of bilirubin from the blood. The cellular damage may be from infection,

such as in hepatitis or yellow fever virus, or from drug or chemical toxicity (e.g., carbon tetrachloride, chloroform, arsenic or certain psychotherapeutic drugs).

Cirrhosis of the liver is a form of hepatocellular disease that may produce jaundice; it is usually associated with excessive alcoholic intake. In prolonged obstructive jaundice, cell damage eventually develops, so that both types appear together.

Clinical Features. Patients with hepatocellular jaundice may be mildly or severely ill, with lack of appetite, nausea, loss of vigour and strength and possible weight loss. In some instances of hepatocellular disease there may be no jaundice clinically. However, the serum bilirubin concentration and urine urobilinogen level may be elevated. In addition, levels of serum aspartate aminotransferase and serum alanine aminotransferase may be increased, indicating cellular necrosis. At onset there may be complaints of headache, chills and fever, if the cause is infectious. Depending on the cause and extent of the liver cell damage, hepatocellular jaundice may or may not be completely reversible.

Obstructive Jaundice
Obstructive jaundice of the extrahepatic type may be caused by the bile duct's being plugged by a gallstone, by an inflammatory process, by a tumour or by pressure from an enlarged gland. The obstruction may also involve the small bile ducts within the liver substance (i.e., intrahepatic obstruction), caused, for example, by pressure on these channels from inflammatory swelling of the liver substance or by an inflammatory exudate within the ducts themselves. Occasionally, intrahepatic obstruction is due to stasis of the bile, following the ingestion of certain drugs, which accordingly are referred to as 'cholestatic' agents. These include phenothiazines, antithyroid medications and tricyclic antidepressants.

Hereditary Hyperbilirubinaemia
Increased serum bilirubin levels (hyperbilirubinaemia) due to several inherited disorders can also produce jaundice. Gilbert's syndrome is a familial disorder that is due to a diminution of glucuronyl transferase and an increased unconjugated bilirubin level. Others include Dubin-Johnson syndrome (chronic idiopathic jaundice, with pigment in the liver) and Rotor's syndrome (chronic familial conjugated hyperbilirubinaemia without pigment in the liver); 'benign' cholestatic jaundice of pregnancy, with retention of conjugated bilirubin, probably secondary to unusual sensitivity to the hormones of pregnancy; and probably also benign recurrent intrahepatic cholestasis.

Clinical Features of Jaundice
Whether the obstruction is intrahepatic or extrahepatic, and whatever its cause may be, if bile cannot flow normally into the intestine, but is dammed back in the liver

substance, it is reabsorbed into the blood and carried throughout the entire body, staining the skin, the mucous membranes and the sclerae. It is excreted in the urine, which becomes deep orange and foamy. The presence of bile salts in the blood causes histamine release, which produces pruritis, an intense itching, and the raised serum bilirubin interferes with haemoglobin metabolism, releasing peroxide that irritates the sclerae and causes photophobia (Taylor, 1983).

A number of problems may arise because of the decreased amount of bile in the intestinal tract: the stools become light or clay-coloured, and steatorrhoea (fatty, foul-smelling stools) will occur if there is total obstruction to bile; dyspepsia, and an intolerance to fatty foods may develop, owing to impaired fat digestion; a deficiency of fat-soluble vitamins, K, A, D and E, may occur; and a lack of alkaline bile may promote ulceration in the duodenum.

Drug Therapy

- Antihistamines such as piriton reduce the itching by lowering histamine levels.
- Sedatives, e.g. chlorpromazine or chlordiazepoxide, promote rest and raise the threshold of perception of itching.
- Resins such as cholestyramine bind bile salts in the gastrointestinal tract and aid excretion (Gillies, Rogers, Spector and Trounce, 1986). Unfortunately, it often produces nausea, and patients are reluctant to take it (Hinchcliff and Montague, 1988).

Nursing Care

The patient with jaundice may suffer from an altered body image, photophobia, pruritis and an increased tendency to bleed. The principles of nursing care of patients with jaundice include the following:

- The patient wears dark glasses to conceal yellow sclera and reduce photophobia.
- Soft lighting to tone down the yellowness of the skin.
- Preparation of visitors, to allay anxiety.
- Allow patient to be isolated, as a coping strategy.
- Apply calamine lotion to reduce itching.
- Keep skin cool by tepid sponging to reduce itching.
- Use soft, unstarched bed linen to reduce irritation.
- Keep patient's fingernails short and smooth to prevent skin damage and infection from damage.
- Give intramuscular vitamin K (or fresh blood if severe liver dysfunction) to increase prothrombin.
- Keep injections and blood-letting to a minimum to reduce risk of haemorrhage.
- Protect patient from trauma and ensure care is taken when shaving, blowing nose or brushing teeth to minimize risk of bleeding.
- Observe urine and stools for blood, which is a sign of possible internal bleeding.

Portal Hypertension

One set of problems associated with hepatic cirrhosis arises as a result of obstruction to the flow of portal venous blood through the liver, the effect of which is to elevate the blood pressure throughout the entire portal venous system. Although portal hypertension is commonly associated with hepatic cirrhosis, it can also occur with non-cirrhotic liver disease.

There are two major sequelae of portal hypertension:

1. The formation of oesophageal, gastric and haemorrhoidal varicosities occurs because of the elevated pressures transmitted to all of the veins that drain into the portal system. These varicosities are prone to rupture and often are the source of massive haemorrhages. The likelihood of bleeding is increased by the blood clotting abnormalities frequently present in patients with cirrhosis.
2. Accumulation of fluid (ascites) in the abdominal cavity. As ascites develops, intravascular volume tends to fall and renin is released by the kidneys. This results in secretion of increased quantities of the hormone aldosterone by the adrenal glands, which, in turn, causes the kidneys to retain sodium and water in an attempt to return intravascular volume to normal. Unfortunately, if portal hypertension continues, fluid retention will contribute to the formation of even more ascites.

Oesophageal Varices

Altered Physiology and Clinical Features

Oesophageal varices are dilated tortuous veins usually found in the submucosa of the lower oesophagus; however, they may develop higher in the oesophagus or extend into the stomach. Haemorrhage from ruptured oesophageal varices is the most common single cause of death in patients with cirrhosis. The collateral circulation develops due to the obstructed portal vein circulation. These collateral vessels are not very elastic but rather are tortuous and fragile and bleed easily. Other less common causes of varices are abnormalities of the circulation in the splenic vein or superior vena cava and hepatic venothrombosis.

Bleeding oesophageal varices are life threatening and can result in haemorrhagic shock, producing decreased cerebral, hepatic and renal perfusion. In turn, there will be an increased nitrogen load from bleeding into the gastrointestinal tract and an increased serum ammonia level which increase the risk of encephalopathy. Bleeding oesophageal varices should be suspected in the presence of haematemesis and melaena, especially in the patient who has been addicted to alcohol. Usually, the dilated veins cause no symptoms unless the mucosa over them becomes ulcerated. Then massive haemorrhage takes place. Factors that contribute to rupture are muscular strain from lifting heavy objects, straining at stool, sneezing, coughing or vomiting or irritation of vessels by rough foods or irritating fluids. Salicylates and any drug that erodes oesophageal mucosa or interferes with cell replication may also cause bleeding.

Assessment

Oesophagoscopy or endoscopy most clearly confirms the diagnosis because even the site of haemorrhage may be seen. The site of bleeding must be identified, since one third or more patients bleed from other sources. Gastritis and duodenal ulcer frequently coexist with cirrhosis. Nursing support before and during examination by oesophagoscopy or endoscopy can be effective in relieving a stressful experience. Careful monitoring can detect early signs of cardiac arrhythmias, perforation and haemorrhage. After the examination, fluids are not given until the gag reflex returns. Lozenges and gargles may be used to relieve throat discomfort if the patient's condition permits and the patient is able to participate in self-care.

Management

The patient with bleeding varices is critically ill, requiring aggressive medical care and expert nursing care. The extent of bleeding should be evaluated and vital signs monitored continuously when haematemesis and melaena are present. Signs of potential hypovolaemia are to be noted, such as cold, clammy skin, tachycardia, a drop in blood pressure, decreased urine output, restlessness and increased or shallow peripheral pulse. Blood volume is monitored by means of central venous pressure. Oxygen is required to prevent hypoxia and to maintain adequate blood oxygenation. Blood transfusion also may be needed.

Since patients with bleeding oesophageal varices are subject to electrolyte imbalance, intravenous fluids are provided to restore fluid volume and replace deficient electrolytes. Urinary output is carefully monitored; an indwelling catheter may be indicated.

Nonsurgical Management

Nonoperative treatment is the treatment of choice because of the high mortality of emergency surgery for control of bleeding oesophageal varices and because of the poor physical condition of the patient with severe liver disorder.

Drug Therapy. Vasopressin may be the initial mode of therapy because of its constriction of the splanchnic arterial bed and resulting decrease in portal pressure. It may be given intravenously or by intra-arterial infusion. Either method requires monitoring by the nurse. Gastric aspiration and vital signs offer indices of the effectiveness of vasopressin.

● Coronary artery disease in this patient would be a contraindication to the use of vasopressin, since coronary vasoconstriction is a side-effect that may precipitate myocardial infarction.

Electrolyte evaluation and monitoring of fluid intake and output are necessary, since hyponatraemia may occur and vasopressin may have an antidiuretic effect. The patient may also experience crampy abdominal pain.

Balloon Tamponade. To control the haemorrhage in certain patients, pressure is exerted on the cardia (upper orifice of the stomach) and against the bleeding varices by a double-balloon tamponade (Sengstaken-Blakemore tube) (Figure 16.3). The three openings in the tube are for specific purposes: gastric aspiration, inflation of the gastric balloon and inflation of the oesophageal balloon.

The balloon in the stomach is inflated, and the tube is pulled gently to exert a force against the cardia. Irrigation of the tubing is performed to detect bleeding; if returns are clear, the oesophageal balloon is not inflated. If bleeding continues, the oesophageal balloon is inflated. The desired pressure in both balloons is 25 to 30 mm Hg, i.e. greater than portal venous pressure. After the balloon is inflated, there is a possibility of injury or rupture of the oesophagus. Constant nursing surveillance is necessary at this time. Traction is placed on the tube at the site of insertion. A suction catheter may be inserted to aspirate oesophagopharyngeal secretions if a three-lumen tube is used. This is not necessary with the four-lumen tube (Figure 16.3C), because a fourth lumen provides a direct route for oesophageal aspiration.

Usually, a laxative such as magnesium sulphate is introduced through the tube to eliminate blood in the gastrointestinal tract; otherwise, ammonia absorption could occur, which may lead to hepatic coma.

Gastric suction is provided by connecting the catheter outlet to suction. The tubing is irrigated hourly, and drainage will indicate whether bleeding has been controlled. Iced saline lavage or irrigation may be used in the stomach balloon in order to constrict the gastric vessels. In such instances, the nurse will protect the patient from possible chilling.

Although this method has been fairly successful, it is important to note some inherent dangers. If the tube is left in place or inflated too long or at too high a pressure, ulceration and necrosis can develop in the stomach or oesophagus. Asphyxiation is another problem, caused by the counterweight pulling the tube into the oropharynx. These potential dangers suggest the need for intensive and expert care. The balloon must be deflated for five minutes at eight- to 12-hour intervals if prescribed, to prevent erosion and necrosis of the stomach and oesophagus.

Compression is not usually continued for longer than 48 hours. It is then cautiously released, and removed after 24 hours if no bleeding recurs. Nursing measures include monitoring to prevent accidental removal or displacement of the tube, and frequent mouth and nose care. For secretions that accumulate in the mouth, tissues should be within easy reach of the patient. The patient who has experienced oesophageal haemorrhage is usually anxious and frightened. The patient is less anxious if the procedure has been explained and the patient knows that the nurse is nearby and will respond immediately to a call.

Injection Sclerotherapy. In injection sclerotherapy (Figure 16.4) a sclerosing agent is injected through a fibreoptic endoscope into the bleeding oesophageal varices to promote thrombosis and eventual sclerosis. Although controlled studies have not yet demonstrated that injection sclerotherapy is superior to other treatments or improves long-term survival, the procedure has been used successfully to treat gastrointestinal haemorrhage. In addition, it has been used as a prophylactic measure to treat oesophageal varices before bleeding has occurred. Following treatment, the patient must be observed for bleeding, perforation of the oesophagus, aspiration pneumonia and oesophageal stricture. Antacids may be given following the procedure to counteract the effects of peptic reflux.

Repeated courses of sclerotherapy may be needed to obliterate all the varices. The patient, family and significant others need to be aware of the importance of these additional treatments even though the patient may not be actively bleeding.

Other Measures. Bleeding can also be treated by complete rest of the oesophagus (parenteral feedings). Straining and vomiting must be prevented. Gastric suction usually is employed to keep the stomach as empty as possible. The patient complains of severe thirst, which may be relieved by frequent oral hygiene and moist

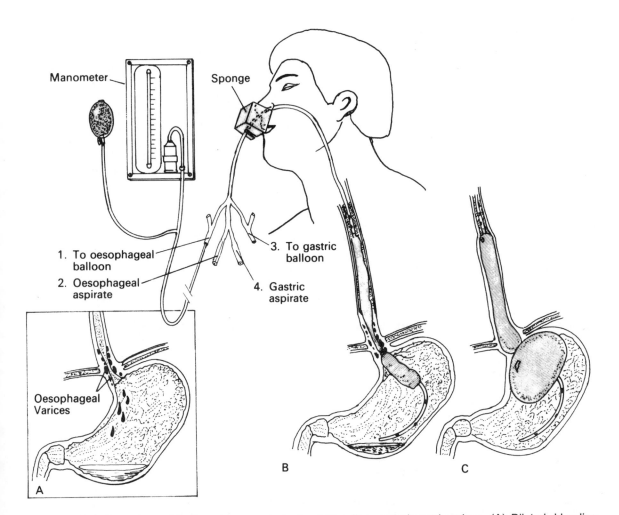

Figure 16.3 Oesophageal balloon tamponade to treat bleeding oesophageal varices. (A) Dilated, bleeding oesophageal veins (varices) of the lower oesophagus. (B) A four-lumen oesophageal tamponade tube with balloons (uninflated) in place. (C) Compression of bleeding oesophageal varices by inflated oesophageal and gastric balloons. The gastric and oesophageal outlets permit aspiration of secretions.

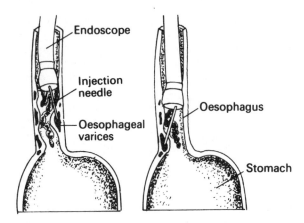

Figure 16.4 Injection sclerotherapy. Injection of sclerosing agent into oesophageal varices through an endoscope.

sponges to the lips. The nurse keeps close surveillance on the patient's blood pressure. Vitamin K therapy and multiple blood transfusions often are indicated. A quiet environment and calm reassurance will help to relieve the patient's anxiety.

Surgical Management

If none of the measures described above are effective, surgical procedures may be employed, such as direct surgical ligation of varices or portacaval and splenorenal venous shunt operations.

Surgical Bypass Procedures. The most common procedure is to create an anastomosis between the portal vein and the inferior vena cava, which is spoken of as a portacaval anastomosis (Figure 16.5). When portal blood is shunted into the vena cava, the pressure in the portal system is decreased, and consequently the danger of haemorrhage from oesophageal and gastric varices is reduced. When the portal vein cannot be used because of thrombosis, or for other reasons, a shunt may be made between the splenic vein and the left renal vein (splenorenal shunt) following splenectomy. Some surgeons prefer this shunt to the portacaval shunt, even when the portal vein can be used.

A mesocaval shunt is a third type of bypass procedure, to which the inferior vena cava is severed and the proximal end of the vena cava is anastomosed to the side of the superior mesenteric vein.

These operations are extensive procedures and are not always successful, because of secondary clotting in the veins used for the shunt. Trials have shown that the five-year survival rate after a shunt operation is similar to that found in patients treated conservatively. Nevertheless, a shunt is the only method by which a lowering of pressure in the portal system may be brought about, and since haemorrhages from the oesophageal varices are often fatal, it may be the only alternative.

Postoperative Nursing Care

Bleeding anywhere in the body is anxiety provoking, resulting in a crisis situation for the patient, family and friends. If the patient is an alcoholic, behavioural problems secondary to alcohol withdrawal can further complicate the situation. The nurse provides support and pertinent explanations regarding medical and nursing care. Monitoring the patient closely will help in detecting and managing complications.

Postoperative care is similar to that for any abdominal operation, but complications may arise, including haemodynamic shock, hepatic encephalopathy, electrolyte imbalance, metabolic and respiratory alkalosis, delirium tremens and seizures. These procedures do not alter the course of the progressive liver disease, and bleeding may recur as new collateral vessels develop.

Ascites

The presence and extent of ascites can be determined by percussing the abdomen. When fluid has accumulated in the peritoneal cavity, the flanks will bulge when the patient is supine. The presence of fluid accumulation can be confirmed either by percussing for shifting dullness (Figure 16.6A, B) or by detecting a fluid wave (Figure 16.6C). A fluid wave is likely to be found only when there is a large amount of fluid present. Daily measurement and recording of abdominal girth and body weight are indicated to assess the progression of ascites and its response to treatment. The role of dietary modification, drug therapy, paracentesis and shunting in controlling ascites are discussed below.

Controlling Fluid Retention and Ascites

Nutritional Control

The goal of treatment for the patient with ascites is a negative sodium balance to reduce fluid retention. Table salt, salty foods, salted butter and margarine and all the ordinary canned and frozen foods should be avoided. The taste of unsalted foods can be improved by using salt substitutes, such as lemon juice, oregano and thyme. Commercial substitutes need to be cleared with the doctor; for example, those containing ammonia could precipitate hepatic coma. Liberal use should be made of powdered, low-sodium milk and milk products. If fluid accumulation is not controlled on this regime, the salt restriction must be more stringent, with the daily sodium allowance reduced to 200 mg, and diuretics administered.

Diuretics

Another method of reducing oedema and ascites is to induce diuresis. This involves the reduction of sodium intake to 200 to 500 mg daily; restriction of fluids, if the serum sodium is low; and administration of an oral diuretic drug such as spironolactone, an aldosterone-

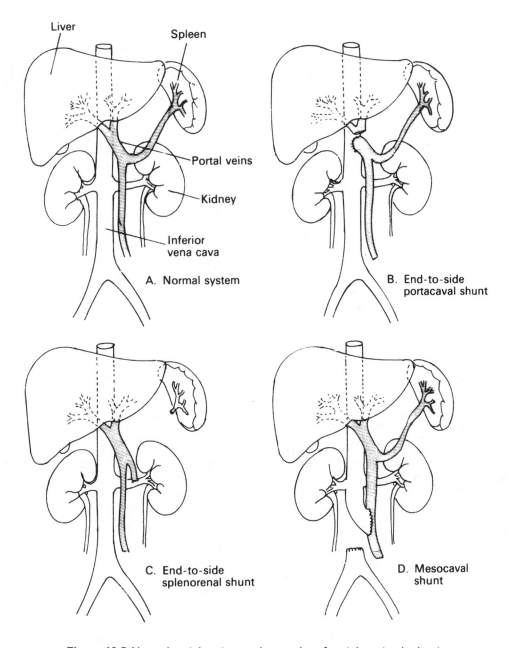

Figure 16.5 Normal portal system and examples of portal–systemic shunts.

blocking agent. This is a weak, potassium-sparing diuretic. If this fails it may be necessary to use a more potent diuretic, such as frusemide. These should be used cautiously, since long-term use may induce severe sodium depletion (hyponatraemia). Thiazide diuretics are contraindicated in liver disorders. Daily weight loss should not exceed 0.227 kg daily.

Diuretic therapy is carefully monitored by the nurse to detect possible complications: fluid and electrolyte disturbances such as hypovolaemia, hypokalaemia, hyponatraemia and hypochloraemic alkalosis, or encephalo-pathy precipitated by dehydration and hypovolaemia. Additionally, when potassium stores are depleted, the amount of ammonia in the systemic circulation increases, which may cause impaired cerebral functioning and encephalopathy.

Nursing Care
Skin integrity will be affected if meticulous care is not taken. Pressure over bony prominences and oedematous tissue must be relieved by frequently changing body position, or by using either a silicone or an alternating press-

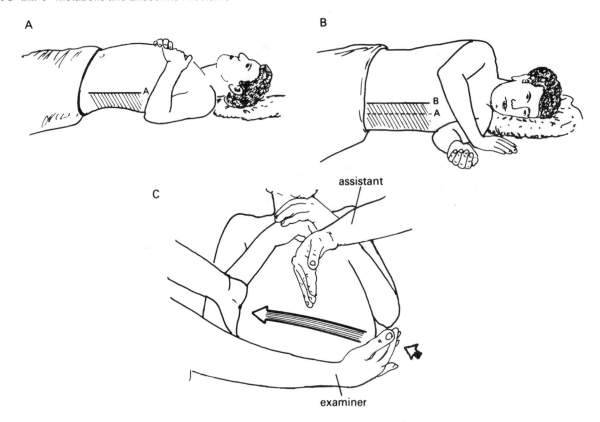

Figure 16.6 Assessing for ascites. (A) To percuss for shifting dullness, each flank is percussed with the patient in a supine position. If fluid is present, dullness will be noted at each flank. The most medial limits of the dullness should be marked as indicated in A. The patient should then be shifted to the side. (B) Note what happens to the area of dullness if fluid is present. (C) To detect the presence of a fluid wave, the examiner places one hand alongside each flank. A second person then places a hand, ulnar side down, along the patient's midline, and applies light pressure. The examiner then strikes one flank sharply with one hand, while the other hand remains in place to detect any signs of a fluid impulse. The assistant's hand dampens any wave impulses travelling through the abdominal wall. (Copyright © 1974, American Journal of Nursing Company. Reproduced with permission from *American Journal of Nursing*, Vol. 74, No. 9, September 1974.)

ure mattress (Crow, 1988). Lower extremities may have to be elevated and support hose applied. Salt-poor albumin may be given intravenously to temporarily elevate the serum albumin level, which increases serum osmotic pressure. This helps reduce oedema by causing the ascitic fluid to be drawn back into the bloodstream and ultimately eliminated by the kidneys.

Dyspnoea may also be experienced due to an enlarged abdomen; the patient may require oxygen, and attention must be given to positioning to facilitate adequate chest expansion.

Paracentesis

Paracentesis is the removal of fluid (ascites) from the peritoneal cavity through a small surgical incision or puncture made through the abdominal wall. Once considered an acceptable form of treatment for ascites, paracentesis is now primarily for diagnostic examination of ascitic fluid, for treatment of massive ascites resistant to other therapy and causing severe problems to the patient and as prelude to other procedures, including radiography, peritoneal dialysis, ascites reinfusion or surgery.

If paracentesis is warranted, the aspiration is limited to the slow removal of two to three litres, to relieve acute symptoms. Removing large amounts of fluid may cause hypotension, oliguria and hyponatraemia. If fluid in excess of this amount is removed, ascitic fluid tends to form again, drawing fluid from extracellular tissue throughout the body.

Nursing Care
The nurse prepares the patient for paracentesis by providing the necessary information, advice and reassurance.

● Ask the patient to void as completely as possible just before paracentesis, to lessen the danger of inadvertently piercing the bladder.

The patient is placed in the upright position on the edge of the bed or in a chair, fully supported, with the feet resting on a stool and one arm fitted with a sphygmomanometer cuff. The trocar is introduced with aseptic technique through a stab wound in the midline below the umbilicus, and the fluid is drained through an effluent tube into a container.

During the procedure the nurse helps the patient to maintain the proper posture.

● Observe the patient closely for evidence of vascular collapse, such as the appearance of pallor, increase in pulse rate or fall in blood pressure.

When the procedure is concluded, the patient is placed in a comfortable position. The amount of fluid collected is measured, described and recorded; and samples of the fluid, properly labelled, are sent to appropriate laboratories for examination of the cellular sediment, its specific gravity, protein concentration and bacterial content.

Shunts

Although surgical bypass procedures or shunts performed to treat oesophageal varices may also decrease ascites formation, the high operative mortality in patients with severe liver dysfunction limits surgical shunting as an effective treatment for ascites.

Attempts have been made to treat ascites through reinfusion of ascitic fluid into the general circulation; however, there is risk of infection from such treatment. In addition, this treatment is temporary, and reaccumulation of ascites occurs within two months in more than 70 per cent of patients.

The insertion of a LeVeen or peritoneovenous shunt has been successful in reducing ascites and maintaining intravascular protein and fluid volume by 'shunting' or redirecting the ascitic fluid from the peritoneal cavity into the systemic circulation, and avoids the need for major surgery (Figure 16.7). In this method, a perforated silicon tube is inserted into the peritoneal cavity and connected by a one-way valve to a tube in the superior vena cava. The valve is normally closed but opens when the pressure in the peritoneal cavity rises 3 cm H_2O above the pressure of the intrathoracic vena cava, which is located in the thorax. When the valve opens, the ascitic fluid flows into the superior vena cava. When pressure falls, the valve closes.

In the postoperative period, the patient is observed closely and the hematocrit is measured every four hours to monitor vascular volume expansion and haemodilution which may result from the inflow of ascitic fluid. Excessive haemodilution may be interrupted by placing the patient in a sitting position, which reduces the difference between the pressures of the peritoneal cavity and intrathoracic pressure, closing the valve and temporarily stop-

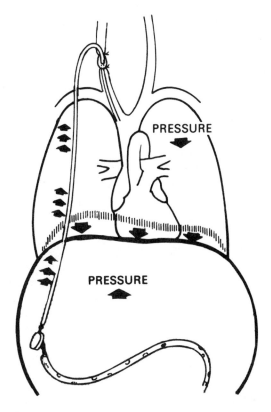

Figure 16.7 Peritoneovenous shunt for reducing ascites. The valve lies in the lower right side extraperitoneally, and a perforated collecting tube extends into the peritoneal cavity. (Schiff, L. (ed) (1987) *Diseases of the Liver* (6th edition) J. B. Lippincott, Philadelphia.)

ping the drainage of ascitic fluid to the vena cava. A diuretic such as frusemide may be prescribed to avoid the possibility of pulmonary oedema. Body weight, abdominal girth and urinary output are recorded every two hours. Ordinarily, the haematocrit falls, abdominal girth decreases, weight drops and urinary output rises. Reversal of these changes may indicate that the shunt is no longer patent and that the ascitic fluid is reaccumulating.

Following the relief of ascites, fluid and sodium intake will depend on the cardiac status and presence of peripheral oedema. These patients require continued care and monitoring, for even though the ascites may be cleared, the liver problem is not improved by the insertion of a peritoneovenous shunt.

Nutritional Deficiencies

Another group of complications that is common to patients with severe chronic liver disease of all types is caused by inadequate intake of vitamins. Among the specific deficiency states that occur on this basis are:

(1) vitamin A deficiency, beriberi, polyneuritis and Wernicke-Korsakoff psychosis, all attributable to a deficiency of thiamine; (2) skin and mucous membrane lesions characteristic of riboflavin deficiency; (3) pyridoxine deficiency; (4) hypoprothrombinaemia, characterized by spontaneous bleeding and ecchymoses, due to vitamin K deficiency; (5) the haemorrhagic lesions of scurvy (i.e., vitamin C deficiency); and (6) the macrocytic anaemia of folic acid deficiency.

- The threat of these vitamin deficiencies provides the rationale for supplementing the diet of every patient with chronic liver disease (especially when alcoholism is involved) with ample quantities of vitamins A, B complex, C, K and folic acid.

Hepatic Coma

Hepatic coma, one of the dreaded complications of liver disease, occurs with profound liver failure and results from the accumulation of ammonia and other identified toxic metabolites in the blood. Ammonia accumulates because damaged liver cells fail to detoxify and convert to urea the ammonia that is constantly entering the bloodstream as a result of its absorption from the gastrointestinal tract and its liberation from kidney and muscle cells. The increased ammonia concentration in the blood causes brain dysfunction and damage, resulting in hepatic encephalopathy and hepatic coma.

Assessment and Clinical Features

The earliest symptoms of hepatic coma include minor mental aberrations and motor disturbances. The patient appears to be slightly confused and experiences alterations in mood. The patient becomes untidy and experiences altered sleep patterns, tending to sleep during the day and to experience restlessness and insomnia at night. Asterixis or flapping tremor of the hands may be exhibited. Simple tasks, such as handwriting, become difficult. A sample of handwriting, taken daily, may provide graphic evidence of progression of hepatic coma. In the early stages of hepatic coma, the patient's reflexes are hyperactive; with deepening of coma these reflexes disappear and the extremities may become flaccid.

The electroencephalogram (EEG) shows generalized slowing and an increase in amplitude of brain waves. Occasionally, foetor hepaticus, a characteristic breath odour like freshly mowed grass, acetone or old wine, may be noticed. In a more advanced stage there are gross disturbances of consciousness as the patient passes from complete disorientation into frank coma, and may have convulsions. Approximately 35 per cent of all patients with cirrhosis of the liver die in hepatic coma.

Aggravating and Precipitating Factors

Circumstances that increase blood ammonia content tend to aggravate or precipitate hepatic coma. The largest source of blood ammonia is the enzymatic and bacterial digestion of proteins in the gastrointestinal tract. Ammonia from these sources is increased as a result of gastrointestinal bleeding, a high-protein diet, bacterial growth in the small and large intestines and uraemia. In the presence of alkalosis or hypokalaemia, increased amounts of ammonia are absorbed from the gastrointestinal tract and from the renal tubular fluid.

Other factors unrelated to increased blood ammonia that may induce hepatic coma in susceptible patients include overdiuresis, dehydration, infections, surgery, pyrexia and consciousness-altering drugs, such as sedatives, tranquillizers and narcotics.

Nursing Care

Principles of management of hepatic coma include the following:

- Neurological status is assessed frequently. A daily record is kept of handwriting and performance in arithmetic.
- Fluid intake and output and body weight are recorded daily.
- Vital signs are measured and recorded every four hours.
- Evidence of infection is reported promptly if observed.
- Serum ammonia level is monitored daily.
- Protein intake is reduced sharply or eliminated altogether.
- To reduce ammonia absorption from the gastrointestinal tract, lactulose may be prescribed.
- In addition, an antibiotic such as neomycin is given to reduce the number of intestinal bacteria capable of converting urea into ammonia.
- Electrolyte status is carefully monitored and corrected if abnormal.
- Sedative and analgesic drugs, if prescribed at all, are administered to this patient in very conservative doses and under very close observation.

Lactulose is hydrolyzed to form acids that cause a fall in colon pH, which traps the ammonia in the colon. The laxative effect of the lactulose increases the ammonia lost from the colon.

Other Features of Liver Disorder

Many patients with liver disorder develop generalized oedema due to hypoalbuminaemia resulting from decreased hepatic production of serum albumin. The production of blood clotting factors by the liver is also reduced, leading to an increased incidence of bruising, nosebleeds, bleeding from wounds and, as described above, gastrointestinal bleeding. Decreased production of several clotting factors is due to deficient absorption of vitamin K from the gastrointestinal tract. Vitamin K is essential in their synthesis. Absorption of the other fat-soluble vitamins (A, D and E) as well as dietary fats may also be impaired, owing to decreased secretion of bile salts into the intestine.

Abnormalities of glucose metabolism also occur; the blood sugar may be abnormally high shortly after a meal (i.e., a diabetic-type glucose tolerance test), but hypoglycaemia may occur during fasting because of decreased hepatic glycogen reserves and decreased gluconeogenesis.

● Because of decreased ability to metabolize drugs, usual drug dosages must be reduced for the patient with liver failure.

Decreased metabolism of oestrogens by the damaged liver can lead to gynaecomastia, testicular atrophy, loss of pubic hair in the male and menstrual irregularities in the female, as well as spider angiomata and reddened palms ('liver palms'). Splenomegaly (enlarged spleen) with possible hypersplenism occurs commonly as a feature of portal hypertension.

HEPATIC DISORDERS

Viral Hepatitis

The increasing incidence of viral hepatitis is a growing public health concern. Although the mortality rate is low, the disease is important because of its ease of transmission, morbidity and the prolonged loss of time from school or employment that it can cause.

Nursing Implications

The nurse is especially concerned with four major problem areas of viral hepatitis: (1) the care of the patient with hepatitis; (2) the increased risks in haemodialysis units and in users of illicit injectable drugs; (3) the fact that many people who have the disease are asymptomatic, which may present serious epidemiological problems; and (4) the apparent health needs of the community required for its elimination.

For a comparison of the many aspects of the major forms of viral hepatitis, see Table 16.2.

Table 16.2 *Hepatitis*

	Hepatitis A virus (HAV)	Hepatitis B virus (HBV)	Non-A, Non-B hepatitis virus (NANBH)
Other names	Type A hepatitis, infectious or epidemic hepatitis; IH virus	Type B hepatitis, serum hepatitis, SH virus, Dane particle	Hepatitis 'C', 'D'; Type C
Epidemiology			
Cause	Hepatitis A virus	Hepatitis B virus	Another virus
Method of transmission	Faecal–oral route; poor sanitation Person to person Waterborne, foodborne–shellfish Rarely, if at all, by blood transfusion	Parenterally, or by intimate contact with carriers or those with acute disease; male homosexuals Vertical transmission from mothers to infants Contaminated instruments, syringes, needles; renal dialysis*	Transfusion of blood and blood products Personnel in renal transplant and dialysis units Parenteral drug abusers Institutions with long-term residents*
Source of virus/antigen	Blood, faeces, saliva	Blood, saliva, semen, vaginal secretions	Appears to be blood-borne
Distribution by age	Young adults (aged 15 to 29) and middle-aged who have escaped childhood infection	Affects all ages, but mostly young adults	Same as HBV
Incubation period	3 to 5 weeks; average: 30 days	2 to 5 months; average: 90 days	Variable: 14 to 115 days; average: 50 days

*Recent intensive research suggests probably the same for HBV and NANBH.

Table 16.2 *Continued*

	Hepatitis A virus (HAV)	Hepatitis B virus (HBV)	Non-A, Non-B hepatitis virus (NANBH)
Occurrence	Worldwide	Worldwide	Worldwide Accounts for 20 per cent of sporadic cases
Antibody	Anti-hepatitis A virus Present in convalescent sera and immune serum globulin	Anti-HB$_c$ (core antigen) Anti-HB$_s$ (surface antigen)	
Immunity	Homologous	Homologous	
Severity	Most anicteric and asymptomatic	More severe than hepatitis A virus	Wide spectrum of severity, resembling HAV or HBV; often prolonged illness – months May progress to chronic hepatitis
Nature of illness			
Signs or symptoms	May occur with or without symptoms: 'flu-like illness Pre-jaundice phase: headache, malaise, fatigue, anorexia, lassitude, fever Jaundice phase: dark urine, yellow sclerae, jaundice, liver tenderness and perhaps enlargement	May occur without symptoms 1,000 IU/litre-serum transaminase level May develop antibodies to virus Similar to HAV, but more severe Fever and respiratory symptoms rare, but may have arthralgias, rash	Similar to hepatitis B virus Less severe and no jaudince
Diagnosis and method	Elevated serum transaminase Complement fixation rate Radioimmunoassay	Check serum for HB$_s$Ag, HB$_e$Ag, anti-HB$_c$ in absence of anti-HB$_s$ (obtainable as a panel) Elevated serum transaminase Radioimmunoassay – haemagglutination	
Severity	Usually mild Fatality rate 0 to 1 per cent	Variable, may be severe Fatality rate varies: 1 to 10 per cent	
Specific treatment	Adequate fluids, rest, nutrition	Same as hepatitis A virus In research: vaccine antiviral chemotherapy to eliminate chronic hepatitis B virus carrier state (being tested)	

Table 16.2 *Continued*

	Hepatitis A virus (HAV)	Hepatitis B virus (HBV)	Non-A, Non-B hepatitis virus (NANBH)
Prevention	Good sanitation Proper personal hygiene Effective sterilization procedures Careful screening of food handlers Immune globulin given within a few days of exposure	Specific hepatitis B immune globulin probably useful after exposure by ingestion, inoculation or splash involving hepatitis B surface antigen (HB$_s$Ag) Hepatitis B vaccine recommended for pre-exposure immunization of those at high risk	Mandatory screening of blood donors: For HB$_s$Ag, 20 per cent For non-A, non-B, 80 per cent

Hepatitis A Virus

Hepatitis A, formerly designated infectious hepatitis, is probably an RNA virus of the enterovirus family. The mode of transmission of this disease is the faecal–oral route, primarily through the ingestion of food or liquids infected by the virus. The virus has been found in the stool of infected patients before the onset of symptoms and during the first few days of illness. Typically, a young adult acquires the infection at school and brings it home, where haphazard sanitary habits spread it through the family. It is more prevalent in underdeveloped countries or in instances of overcrowding and poor sanitation. An infected food handler can spread the disease, and people can contract it by consuming water or shellfish from sewage-contaminated waters. Animal handlers can contract hepatitis A from infected primates. It is rarely, if ever, transmitted by blood transfusions.

The incubation period is estimated to be from one to seven weeks, with an average of 30 days. The course of the illness may be prolonged, lasting from four to eight weeks. It generally lasts longer and is more severe in those over the age of 40.

Assessment and Clinical Features

Most patients are anicteric (without jaundice) and symptomless. When symptoms appear, they are influenza-like with low-grade fever. Anorexia is an early symptom and is often severe. It is thought to result from release of a toxin by the damaged liver or by failure of the damaged liver cells to detoxify an abnormal product. Later, jaundice and dark urine may become apparent. Indigestion is present, in varying degrees, marked by vague epigastric distress, nausea, heartburn and flatulence. The patient may also develop a strong aversion to the taste of cigarettes or the presence of cigarette smoke and other strong odours. These symptoms tend to clear as soon as the jaundice reaches its peak—perhaps 10 days after its initial appearance. The liver and the spleen are often moderately enlarged for a few days after onset; otherwise, apart from jaundice, there are few physical signs to be elicited.

Nursing Care

Bedrest during the acute stage and the provision of a nutritious diet is important. During the period of anorexia, the patient should receive frequent small meals, supplemented, if necessary, by intravenous infusions of glucose. This often requires gentle persistence and ingenuity. Optimal food and fluid levels need to be maintained to counteract probable weight loss and prolonged recovery. Even before the jaundiced phase, however, many patients recover their appetites and thereafter maintain a good diet.

The patient's sense of wellbeing as well as laboratory test results are generally appropriate guides to bedrest and restriction of physical activity. Gradual but progressive ambulation seems to hasten recovery, provided the patient rests after activity and does not exercise to the point of fatigue.

Patient Education

The patient is usually managed at home unless symptoms are particularly severe. Therefore, the patient, family and other informal carers need support to cope with the incapacitation and fatigue, and specific guidelines about diet, rest, follow-up blood tests and hygiene, particularly handwashing, to prevent spread of the disease.

Prognosis

Recovery from hepatitis type A is the rule: the mortality rate of hepatitis A is approximately 0.5 per cent. No carrier state exists, and no chronic hepatitis is associated with hepatitis A. Hepatitis A confers immunity against itself; however, the person may contract other forms of hepatitis.

Control and Prevention

Ways to reduce the risk of contracting hepatitis A include:

● Good personal hygiene, stressing careful handwashing (after bowel movement and before eating).

- Environmental sanitation—safe food and water supply, as well as effective sewage disposal.
- Administration of immune globulin: Type A hepatitis can be prevented by the administration of globulin intramuscularly during the period of incubation, if this treatment is instituted within two to seven days following exposure. This bolsters the person's own antibody production and provides six to eight weeks of passive immunity. Immune globulin may suppress overt symptoms of the disease; the resulting subclinical case of hepatitis A would produce active immunity to subsequent attacks of the virus. Although rare, systemic reactions to immune globulin may occur.

Caution is required when anyone who has previously had angio-oedema, hives or other allergic reactions is treated with any human immune globulin. Adrenaline should be available for use during systemic or anaphylactic reactions.

Hepatitis B Virus

Hepatitis B virus is a double-shelled particle containing DNA. This particle is composed of a number of distinct antigens. Unlike hepatitis A, which is transmitted primarily by the faecal–oral route, hepatitis B is transmitted primarily through blood. The virus has been found in blood, saliva, semen and vaginal secretions and can be transmitted through mucous membranes and breaks in the skin. Therefore, those at risk of developing hepatitis B include all health care workers, especially staff and patients in haemodialysis and oncology units, homosexually active males and users of illicit injectable drugs. Mandatory screening of blood donors for HB_sAg has greatly reduced the occurrence of hepatitis B following blood transfusion.

Assessment and Clinical Features

Clinically, the disease closely resembles hepatitis A. However, the incubation period is relatively much longer (between two and five months). The mortality is appreciable, ranging from 1 to 10 per cent, depending on the infective dose and the condition of the patient. Symptoms and signs of hepatitis B may be insidious and variable. Pyrexia and respiratory symptoms are rare: some patients have arthralgias and rashes. The patient may lose his appetite and experience dyspepsia, abdominal pain, generalized aching, malaise, and weakness. Jaundice may or may not be evident. The patient's liver may be tender and enlarged, and the spleen is enlarged and palpable in a small number of patients.

Considerations for the Elderly

The elderly patient who contracts hepatitis B has a serious risk of severe liver cell necrosis or fulminant hepatic failure, particularly if other illnesses are present. The patient is seriously ill and the prognosis is poor.

Nursing Care

It is important that bedrest be continued until the hepatitis has definitely subsided. Subsequently, the patient's activities should be restricted until the hepatic enlargement and the elevation of the level of serum bilirubin have disappeared. Adequate nutrition should be maintained; proteins are restricted when the liver has a decreased ability to metabolize protein byproducts, as demonstrated by symptoms. Dyspepsia can be controlled with the use of antacids. If vomiting is a persistent problem, the patient may be hospitalized and given intravenous fluids.

Convalescence may be prolonged, with complete symptomatic recovery sometimes requiring three to four months or longer. During this stage, gradual restoration of physical activity is encouraged, following complete clearing of the jaundice.

The psychosocial effects of isolation and separation from family and friends during the acute and infective stages need to be considered. Special planning is required to minimize alterations in sensory perception. The family and significant others should be included in planning to decrease their fears and anxieties about the spread of the disease.

Patient Education

Because of the prolonged period of convalescence, the patient and carers must be prepared for home care. Adequate rest and nutrition is essential. Family and friends who have had intimate contact with the patient should be informed about the risks of contracting hepatitis B, and offered hepatitis B vaccine or hepatitis B immune globulin. Those at risk must be aware of early signs of hepatitis B and of ways to reduce risk to themselves. Follow-up home visits by a community nurse are indicated to assess the patient's progress and answer questions about transmission of the disease. A home visit also permits evaluation of the understanding of the patient and carers about the importance of adequate rest and nutrition. The patient who has had hepatitis B is advised against being a blood donor.

Prognosis

Mortality of hepatitis B has been reported to be as high as 10 per cent. Another 10 per cent of patients who have hepatitis B progress to a carrier state or develop chronic hepatitis.

Control and Prevention

The goals are (1) to interrupt the chain of transmission, (2) to protect those people at high risk through the use of hepatitis B vaccine, and (3) to use passive immunization for unprotected people exposed to hepatitis B virus.

Continued screening of potential blood donors for the presence of HB_sAg will further decrease the risk of transmission by blood transfusion. Washed red blood cells appear to reduce the risk of hepatitis transmission. The use of disposable syringes, needles and lancets reduce the risk of spreading this infection from one patient to another. Good personal hygiene practices are fundamental to infection control. In the laboratory, work areas should be disinfected daily. Gloves are to be worn when handling HB_sAg-positive specimens. Eating is prohibited in the laboratory.

Administering medication by individual-dose ampoules is essential. Where users of illicit injectable drugs share the same needle, serious outbreaks of hepatitis have occurred.

Hepatitis B Vaccine. Hepatitis B vaccine is available for prevention of hepatitis B. Its use is recommended for those at high risk of developing hepatitis B. Studies have shown that hepatitis B vaccine produces active immunity to hepatitis B virus in 90 per cent of healthy people. It provides no protection against other types of hepatitis and does not provide protection to those already exposed to the virus. Side-effects are infrequent. The most common postinjection complaint is soreness and redness at the injection site.

Hepatitis B Immune Globulin. Hepatitis B immune globulin is recommended for unprotected people exposed to hepatitis B virus through accidental contamination of mucous membranes or breaks in the skin, such as needle stick injuries. Hepatitis B immune globulin is prepared from pooled venous plasma of donors with a high titre of anti-HB_s antibodies and provides passive immunity. It is given intramuscularly as soon as possible, but no later than seven days after exposure. A second dose is given 25 to 30 days after the first.

Non-A, Non-B Hepatitis

Those varieties of hepatitis that are not identified as hepatitis A or B are classified as non-A, non-B hepatitis. Repeated episodes of non-A, non-B hepatitis and variations in incubation periods of this form of hepatitis suggest the existence of multiple causative agents. Non-A, non-B hepatitis is blood borne, and the possibility of a carrier state is likely. This form of hepatitis is now the major cause of transfusion-related viral hepatitis and is often observed in parenteral drug abusers.

Non-A, non-B hepatitis occurs not only in patients (following blood transfusion) and among drug users but also in personnel associated with renal transplantation units and in residents in homes for the mentally retarded. Another community health-related implication is that whereas only 10 to 20 per cent of post-transfusion hepatitis is type B, 80 to 90 per cent is non-A, non-B hepatitis.

Incubation time is variable, and severity covers a wide spectrum that most resembles hepatitis B. Most manifestations are without jaundice. Illness may be prolonged, lasting several months and resulting in chronic hepatitis. It is possible that immune globulin may offer limited protection against non-A, non-B hepatitis.

Toxic Hepatitis and Drug-Induced Hepatitis

Certain chemicals have poisonous effects on the liver and when taken orally or by injection produce acute liver cell necrosis, or toxic hepatitis. The chemicals most commonly implicated are carbon tetrachloride, phosphorus, chloroform and gold compounds. These are true hepatotoxins.

Many drugs may induce hepatitis but are sensitizing rather than toxic. The result, drug-induced hepatitis, is similar to acute viral hepatitis; however, parenchymal destruction tends to be more extensive. Some examples of drugs are monoamine oxidase inhibitors of the hydrazine type, isoniazid, methyldopa, halothane, phenothiazines and erythromycin.

Clinical Features and Management

Toxic hepatitis resembles viral hepatitis in onset. Anorexia, nausea and vomiting are the usual symptoms; jaundice and hepatomegaly are noted on physical assessment. Symptoms are more intense for the more severely poisoned patient.

Recovery from acute toxic hepatitis is rapid if the hepatotoxin is identified early and removed or if exposure to the agent has been limited. Recovery, however, is unlikely if there is a prolonged period between exposure and onset of symptoms. There are no effective antidotes. The pyrexia rises; the patient becomes deeply toxic and prostrated. Vomiting may be persistent, with the vomitus containing blood. Clotting abnormalities may be severe, and severe gastrointestinal symptoms may lead to vascular collapse. Delirium, coma and convulsions develop, and within a few days the patient usually dies.

There is little to be done by way of treatment, except to provide comfort measures, blood, fluids and electrolytes. A few patients recover from an acute toxic hepatitis only to develop chronic liver disease.

Drug-induced hepatitis may progress to hepatic failure. In the event that the liver heals, there may be scarring, followed by postnecrotic cirrhosis. Manifestations of sensitivity to a drug may occur on the first day of its use or not until several months later, depending on the drug. Usually, the onset is abrupt, with rigor, rash, pruritus, arthralgia, anorexia and nausea. Later, there may be jaundice and an enlarged and tender liver. When the offending drug is withdrawn, symptoms may gradually subside. However, once provoked, reactions may be severe and even fatal, even though the drug is stopped. If pyrexia, rash or pruritus occur from any medication, its use should be stopped immediately.

Halothane may cause serious, and sometimes fatal, liver damage. Precautions should preclude its use in: (1) patients with known liver disease; (2) repeated instances, particularly in patients who have had a pyrexia of unknown origin after the first administration of halothane; and (3) patients with evidence of prior sensitization.

Hepatic Cirrhosis

Cirrhosis of the liver refers to scarring of the liver. Three kinds are generally considered:

1. Laennec's portal cirrhosis (alcoholic, nutritional), in which the scar tissue characteristically surrounds the portal areas. This is most frequently due to chronic alcoholism and is the most common type of cirrhosis.
2. Postnecrotic cirrhosis, in which there are broad bands of scar tissue, as a late result of a previous acute viral hepatitis.
3. Biliary cirrhosis, in which there is pericholangitic, perilobular scarring. This type is usually the result of chronic biliary obstruction and infection (cholangitis) and is much more rare than Laennec's and postnecrotic cirrhosis.

The portions of the liver chiefly involved are the portal and the periportal spaces, where the bile canaliculi of each lobule communicate to form the liver bile ducts. These areas become inflamed, and the bile ducts become occluded with concentrated bile and pus. An attempt is made by the liver to form new bile channels; hence, there is an overgrowth of tissue made up largely of disconnected, newly formed bile ducts and surrounded by scar tissue, giving the cirrhotic liver its characteristic hobnail appearance.

Clinical features include intermittent jaundice and pyrexia and an enlarged, hard, irregular liver, which eventually becomes atrophic. The treatment is the same as that described for portal cirrhosis, that is, the treatment of any form of chronic liver insufficiency and, when indicated, surgical drainage to eradicate the biliary tract infection.

Altered Physiology

Although several factors have been implicated in the aetiology of cirrhosis, alcohol consumption is considered the major causative factor. Cirrhosis occurs with greatest frequency among alcoholics. However, many explain cirrhosis on the basis of nutritional deficiency with reduced protein intake, rather than on alcohol toxicity, and certainly some cases of cirrhosis are observed among people who do not drink alcohol. Nonetheless, several investigators have shown that although nutritional factors are undoubtedly involved, alcohol itself has to be incriminated in the pathogenesis of the alcoholic fatty liver and the associated effects, because cirrhosis has been observed in those with a high alcohol intake despite a normal diet.

Some people appear to be more susceptible than others to this disease, whether they are alcoholics or malnourished or not. Other factors may play a role, such as exposure to certain chemicals (carbon tetrachloride, chlorinated naphthalene, arsenic or phosphorus) or infectious schistosomiasis. Twice as many men as women are affected, and the majority of patients are between 40 and 60 years of age.

Clinical Features

Early in the course of cirrhosis, the liver tends to be large and its cells loaded with fat (Figure 16.8). The liver is firm and has a sharp edge noticeable on palpation. Abdominal pain may be present due to recent, rapid enlargement of the liver, producing tension on Glisson's capsule (the fibrous covering of the liver). Later in the course of the disease, the liver decreases in size as scar tissue contracts the liver tissue. The liver edge, if palpable, is nodular.

The late features are due partly to chronic failure of liver function and partly to obstruction of the portal circulation. Since a cirrhotic liver does not allow portal blood free passage, it is dammed back into the spleen and the gastrointestinal tract, with the result that these organs become the seat of chronic passive congestion, and thus cannot function properly. Such patients are apt to have chronic dyspepsia and changes in bowel habit, with constipation or diarrhoea. There is gradual weight loss. Fluid may accumulate in the peritoneal cavity, producing ascites, and splenomegaly may also be present. Spider telangiectases, or dilated superficial arterioles resembling bluish red spiders, are frequently observed on the face and trunk.

The obstructed portal circulation causes collateral blood vessels to develop, not only in the gastrointestinal tract (forming varices or haemorrhoids) but also in the

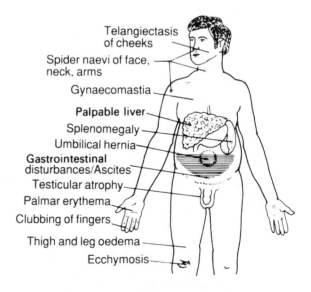

Figure 16.8 Common clinical findings in assessment of the patient with cirrhosis.

skin. As a result, the cirrhotic patient will often have prominent, distended abdominal blood vessels, which are visible on abdominal inspection (caput medusae).

Other late symptoms of cirrhosis are attributable to chronic failure of liver function. The concentration of plasma albumin is lowered, predisposing to the formation of oedema. Overproduction of aldosterone occurs in cirrhosis, causing sodium and water retention and potassium excretion. Vitamin deficiency is frequently encountered and mental function may deteriorate due to raised serum ammonia. Chronic gastritis and poor gastrointestinal function, together with poor diet and impaired liver function, account for anaemia, which together with a poor state of health result in severe fatigue, which interferes with the ability to carry out routine daily activities.

In addition to noting the occurrence of clinical manifestations, the nurse should obtain accurate information about the patient's dietary and alcohol intake. It is also important to note exposure to toxic agents encountered during work or recreation. Any medications or drugs, including anaesthetics, taken by the patient are recorded and checked for hepatotoxicity.

Diagnosis

The extent of liver disease and the kind of treatment are determined after studying the laboratory findings (see Table 16.1). In severe parenchymal liver dysfunction, the serum albumin level tends to decrease, and the serum globulin level rises. Enzyme tests indicate liver cell damage: serum alkaline phosphatase, aspartate aminotransferase and alanine aminotransferase levels increase, and the serum cholinesterase level may decrease. Excretory function is tested by the liver's ability to eliminate sulphobromophthalein (Bromsulphthalein) and indocyanine green dye. In cirrhosis, these dyes are retained. Bilirubin tests are done to measure bile excretion or bile retention. Photolaparoscopy, in conjunction with biopsy, permits direct visualization of the liver.

Ultrasound scanning will measure the difference in density of parenchymal cells and scar tissue. Computed tomography (CT scan) and radioisotopic liver scans give information about liver size and hepatic blood flow and obstruction.

Management

The management of the patient with cirrhosis is usually based on the patient's presenting symptoms. For example, antacids are prescribed to decrease gastric distress, vitamins and nutritional supplements to promote healing of damaged liver cells and improve the patient's general nutritional status, potassium-sparing diuretics (e.g., spironolactone) to decrease ascites, if present, and minimize fluid and electrolyte changes. The patient should be strongly encouraged to avoid further alcohol use. This should be reinforced in a nonjudgemental way by the nurse. The fibrosis of the cirrhotic liver cannot be cured, but its progression may be halted or slowed by such measures.

► NURSING PROCESS
► THE PATIENT WITH HEPATIC CIRRHOSIS

► *Assessment*

Nursing assessment focuses on history of precipitating factors, particularly long-term alcohol abuse, as well as changes in the patient's physical and mental status. The amount and duration of the patient's alcohol use are obtained and noted. Mental status is assessed through interview and other interaction with the patient; orientation to person, place and time is noted. The patient's ability to carry on a job or household activities provides some information about physical and mental status. Additionally, the patient's relationship with family, friends and co-workers may give some indication about incapacitation secondary to alcohol abuse and cirrhosis. Abdominal distension and bloating, bruising, gastrointestinal bleeding and weight changes are noted.

► *Patient's Problems*

Based on the assessment, the patient's major problems may include the following:

- Activity intolerance related to fatigue, general debility, muscle wasting, discomfort and dyspnoea.
- Alterations in nutrition related to chronic gastritis, decreased gastrointestinal motility and anorexia.
- Impairment of skin integrity related to oedema, jaundice and compromised immunological state.
- Potential for injury related to altered clotting mechanisms and portal hypertension.
- Alteration in thought processes related to deterioration of liver function and increased serum ammonia level.

► *Planning and Implementation*
► Expected Outcomes:
The outcomes for the patient may include independence in activities, improvement of nutritional state, improvement of skin integrity, decreased potential for injury and improvement of mental status.

Nursing Care

To achieve these expected outcomes, the major objectives of care are: (1) to promote rest to reduce the demands on the disordered liver; (2) to meet the patient's nutritional needs; (3) to prevent further threats to skin integrity; (4) to minimize risk of bleeding; and (5) to minimize metabolic derangements and limit those factors causing further deterioration of mental function.

Rest

The patient with active liver disease requires rest and other supportive measures to permit the liver to re-establish its functional ability. The patient's weight and fluid intake and output are measured and recorded daily. The patient's position in bed is adjusted for maximal respiratory efficiency, which is especially important if ascites is marked. Oxygen therapy may be required.

Rest permits the liver to restore itself by limiting the demands of the body and increasing the liver's blood supply. Since the patient is more susceptible to infection, efforts to prevent respiratory and vascular disturbances may help prevent pneumonia, thrombophlebitis and pressure sores. When the patient's nutritional state improves and the patient gains strength, the nurse should encourage a gradual increase in activity. Activity and mild exercise, as well as rest, are planned.

Improved Nutritional State

The cirrhotic patient who has no ascites or oedema and exhibits no signs of impending coma should receive a nutritious, high-protein, low sodium diet supplemented by vitamins. Since proper nutrition is so important, every effort must be made to encourage the patient to eat. Often, small, frequent meals are tolerated better than three large meals because of the abdominal pressure exerted by ascites.

Patient preferences are considered. Patients with prolonged or severe anorexia, or those who are vomiting, can be fed enterally.

Patients with fatty stools (steatorrhoea) should receive water-soluble forms of fat-soluble vitamins—A, D and E. Folic acid and iron are prescribed to prevent anaemia. If the patient shows signs of impending or advancing coma, a very low-protein diet should be given short-term (too little protein may cause negative nitrogen balance and wasting). A high-calorie intake should be maintained, and supplementary minerals given (e.g., oral potassium, if the serum potassium is normal or low and if renal function is normal). As soon as the patient's condition permits, the protein intake should be restored to normal, or above. Diet therapy is determined on an individualized basis.

Skin Care

Skin care should be observed meticulously, because of oedema, immobility, jaundice and increased susceptibility to skin breakdown and infection. Frequent position changes or use of an alternating pressure mattress are necessary to prevent pressure sores. Irritating soaps and use of adhesive tape are avoided to prevent trauma to the skin. Lotion may be soothing to irritated skin; measures are taken to minimize the patient's scratching of the skin.

Prevention of Bleeding

Precautionary measures include protecting the patient from trauma, and maintaining a safe environment, applying pressure to an injection site, and avoiding injury from sharp objects. The nurse should check urine and stools for blood as signs of possible internal bleeding and record vital signs regularly.

Improved Mental Function

The nurse should make every effort to prevent serum ammonia from rising, as this will cause a deterioration of mental function. Neurological status is assessed frequently and the patient is oriented to reality. Sedatives and analgesics should be avoided.

Patient Education and Home Health Care

The success of treatment depends on convincing the patient of the need to adhere completely to the care plan. This includes rest; probably a change in lifestyle; an adequate, well-balanced diet; and the elimination of alcohol. The patient and home carers should be taught about the symptoms of impending encephalopathy and the possibility of bleeding tendencies and easy susceptibility to infection. Recovery is neither rapid nor easy; there are frequent setbacks and apparent lack of improvement. Many patients find it difficult to refrain from using alcohol for comfort or escape. The understanding nurse can play a significant role in offering support and encouragement to this patient, the family and significant others. Referral of the patient to a community nurse may help with the transition from hospital to home, where use of alcohol may have been an important part of the patient's normal home life. The community nurse is able to observe the patient's progress at home and the manner in which the patient and home carers cope with the elimination of alcohol and restrictions on diet. Additionally, the nurse is able to reinforce previous teaching and answer questions that may not have occurred to the patient or carers until the patient was home and trying to re-establish new patterns of eating, drinking and lifestyle. The patient may need referral to Alcoholics Anonymous, psychiatric care or support from a religious adviser.

► *Evaluation*
► **Expected Outcomes**

1. Demonstrates ability to participate in activities.
   a. Plans activities and exercises to allow alternating periods of rest and activity.
   b. Reports increased strength and wellbeing.
   c. Displays increased weight gain without increased oedema and ascites formation.
   d. Participates in activities of daily living.
2. Increases nutritional intake.
   a. Demonstrates intake of appropriate nutrients and avoidance of alcohol.
   b. Gains weight without increased oedema and ascites formation.

c. Reports decrease in gastrointestinal disturbances and anorexia.

d. Identifies foods and fluids that are nutritious and allowed on diet.

e. Identifies foods restricted from diet.

f. Adheres to vitamin therapy regime.

g. Describes the rationale for small, frequent meals.

3. Demonstrates improved skin integrity.

   a. Shows intact skin without evidence of breakdown or infection.

   b. Achieves decreased oedema.

   c. Demonstrates normal skin tone.

   d. Changes position frequently.

   e. Inspects bony prominences daily.

   f. Avoids trauma to skin.

   g. Reports decreased or absent pruritus.

4. Experiences decreased risk of bleeding.

   a. Is free of bruises or haematoma formation.

   b. Reports absence of frank bleeding from gastrointestinal tract (e.g., absence of melaena and haematemesis).

   c. Uses measures to prevent trauma (e.g., uses soft toothbrush, blows nose gently, arranges furniture to prevent bumps and falls, avoids straining during defaecation).

5. Demonstrates improved mental function.

   a. Has serum ammonia level within normal limits.

   b. Is oriented to time, place and person.

   c. Demonstrates normal attention span (e.g., is able to complete reading of desired articles, books; able to watch television with interest).

   d. Converses with family, friends and health care team members appropriately.

   e. Reports urinary and faecal continence.

   f. Identifies early, reportable signs of impaired thought processes.

Cancer of the Liver

Hepatic tumours generally are cancerous. It has only been in recent years that benign liver tumours have gained any significance, since their incidence has increased with the use of oral contraceptives.

As for cancerous tumours, few cancers originate in the liver. Those that are primary tumours ordinarily occur in patients with cirrhosis, especially of the postnecrotic type. Such a hepatoma is generally inoperable because of rapid extension and metastasis elsewhere. Cholangiocarcinoma is a primary malignant tumour, usually arising in normal liver. If found early, there may be cure; however, the likelihood of early detection is small.

Metastases are found in the liver in about one half of all late cancer cases. The primary growth may be almost anywhere, and since the bloodstream and the lymphatics from the body cavities nearly all reach the liver, malignant tumours anywhere in the trunk are likely to reach this

organ eventually. Moreover, the liver apparently is an ideal place for these malignant cells to thrive. Often the first evidence of a cancer in an abdominal organ is the appearance of liver metastases, and, unless an exploratory operation or autopsy is performed, the primary growth may never be discovered.

Diagnosis of malignant disease of the liver is made, regardless of the location of the primary tumour, when there is a recent loss of weight, loss of strength and anaemia, which are the most common early features of any cancer that interferes with nutrition. Abdominal pain may be present and accompanied by rapid enlargement of the liver, which on palpation presents an irregular surface. Jaundice is present only if the larger bile ducts are occluded by the pressure of malignant nodules in the hilum of the liver. Ascites occurs if such nodules obstruct the portal veins or if tumour tissue is seeded in the peritoneal cavity.

Nonsurgical Management

Radiotherapy and Chemotherapy

Radiotherapy and chemotherapy have been used in the treatment of malignant disease of the liver with varying degrees of success. Although these therapies may prolong survival of some patients, the major effect is palliative.

An implantable pump has been used to deliver a high concentration of chemotherapy to the liver through the hepatic artery. This method provides a reliable, controlled and continuous infusion of drug that can be done in the patient's home, and may improve significantly the patient's quality of life (Reed *et al.*, 1981).

Biliary Drainage.

Percutaneous biliary drainage or biliary stent can be used to bypass biliary ducts obstructed by liver, pancreatic or bile duct tumours in patients with inoperable tumours or in those considered poor surgical risks, and thus reestablish biliary drainage, relieve pressure and pain from buildup of bile behind the obstruction, and decrease pruritus and jaundice. As a result, the patient's survival is increased and comfort is attained (Stoker, 1985).

Complications of percutaneous biliary drainage and biliary stent include sepsis, leakage of bile, haemorrhage and reobstruction of the biliary system by debris in the catheter or from encroaching tumour. Therefore, the patient is observed for rigor, bile leakage around the catheter, changes in vital signs and evidence of biliary obstruction, including increased pain or pressure, pruritus and recurrence of jaundice.

Surgical Management

Successful hepatic lobectomy for cancer can be done when the primary hepatic tumour is localized or when, in the case of metastasis, the primary site can be excised completely and the metastasis is limited. Metastases to the liver, however, are rarely limited or solitary. Capitalizing on the regenerative capacity of the liver cells, some surgeons have successfully removed 90 per cent of the liver (Groer and Shekleton, 1983).

Preoperative Assessment and Preparation

As the patient is being prepared for surgery, the nutritional, fluid, emotional and physical needs are assessed and met. Meanwhile, the patient may be undergoing extensive and exhausting diagnostic studies. The support, explanation and encouragement by the nurse will help the patient to achieve the most desirable level for surgery. It may be necessary to prepare the intestinal tract by way of laxatives, colonic irrigation and intestinal antibiotics to minimize the possibility of ammonium accumulation and to anticipate the possibility of incision into the intestines at surgery.

Surgical Intervention

If it is necessary to restrict blood flow from the hepatic artery and portal vein beyond 15 minutes (under normothermic conditions, 15-minute occlusion is permissible), it is likely that hypothermia will be used. The nurse needs to be aware of the extent of surgical resection carried out in order to anticipate the patient's care.

For a right-liver lobectomy, a thoracoabdominal incision is used. An extensive abdominal incision is made for a left lobectomy.

Postoperative Nursing Care

There are potential problems related to cardiopulmonary involvement, portal and general circulation, and respiratory and liver disorder. Metabolic abnormalities require careful attention. A constant infusion of 10 per cent glucose may be required in the first 48 hours to prevent a precipitous fall in blood sugar, resulting from decreased gluconeogenesis. Protein synthesis and lipid metabolism are also altered, necessitating infusions of albumin. Extensive blood loss may occur, and, as a result, the patient will receive infusions of blood and intravenous fluids. The patient requires constant attention for the first two or three days, as described for abdominal and thoracic postoperative nursing care (see Chapters 2 and 4, respectively). Early ambulation is encouraged. Liver regeneration is rapid; in one patient who had a 90 per cent resection of the liver, a normal liver mass was restored in six months.

Liver Abscesses

Whenever an infection develops anywhere along the gastrointestinal tract, there is danger that the infecting organisms may reach the liver. Most bacteria are promptly destroyed, but occasionally some gain a foothold. The bacterial toxins destroy the neighbouring liver cells, and the necrotic tissue produced serves as a protective wall for the organisms. Meanwhile, leucocytes migrate into the infected area. The result is an abscess cavity full of a liquid containing living and dead leucocytes, liquefied liver cells and bacteria. Pyogenic abscesses of this type may be either single or multiple and small. The result is a life-threatening disease. In the past the mortality rate was 100 per cent due to vague clinical symptoms, inadequate diagnostic tools, and inadequate surgical drainage of the abscess.

The clinical picture is one of sepsis with few or no localizing signs. The temperature is increased and may be accompanied by chills. The patient may complain of dull abdominal pain and tenderness in the right upper quadrant of the abdomen. Hepatomegaly, jaundice and anaemia may develop. With the aid of a computerized tomography scan and a liver scan for early diagnosis, and surgical drainage of the abscess, mortality has been greatly reduced.

Treatment includes intravenous antibiotic therapy; *Entamoeba histolytica* is the most common cause of liver abscess, but gram-negative bacilli may be implicated. Continuous supportive care is indicated because of the serious condition of the patient.

Liver Transplantation

Human liver transplantation has in most instances been done for life-threatening liver disease for which no other form of treatment was available. This includes biliary atresia, liver cirrhosis, chronic aggressive hepatitis and primary liver malignancies. Orthotopic liver transplantation is the preferred surgical procedure because it is technically the easiest to perform and has been successful. This procedure involves total replacement of the liver, with anatomical reconstruction of the vasculature, or replacement of the liver with a transplant in the same area of the right upper quadrant.

The main difficulties in hepatic transplantation are technical problems causing obstruction, drug toxicity, immunochemical rejection, hepatic arterial thrombosis or hepatic abscess. Because hepatic transplantation is performed only for severe liver disease, the patient is a poor surgical risk and frequently has many systemic problems that influence preoperative and postoperative care.

Cyclosporin, an immunosuppressive agent, used in combination with corticosteroids has considerably improved the success rate of liver transplantation. However, the patient must be monitored closely because of the regime's toxic effects on the liver and kidneys.

Postoperative Nursing Care

The patient is maintained in as sterile an environment as possible, because immunosuppressive drugs reduce the body's natural defence. The patient is artificially ventilated and monitored constantly. Suctioning is performed as required, and sterile humidification is provided. Rejection signs are monitored through liver function tests, and coagulation studies indicate the functioning of the transplanted liver. Infection is monitored closely.

Hourly progress determines when the patient is ready to be weaned from the ventilator, when oral fluids may be taken and when physical activity may gradually be resumed.

Constant emotional support is provided to assist the patient, family and close friends through the difficult and uncertain postoperative period. Family and/or close friends must be informed about the patient's condition at frequent intervals, since extensive care required in the immediate postoperative period minimizes their contact with the patient.

The patient and significant others will require teaching about immunosuppressive drugs, signs and symptoms of rejection, and the importance of follow-up care. Support will be needed to help them with the adjustments necessary for the patient to regain quality of life, for long-term survival after liver transplantation is uncertain. However, advances in donor organ transplantation techniques and immunosuppressive therapy are expected to improve survival rates.

BILIARY CONDITIONS

Several disorders affect the biliary system and interfere with normal drainage of bile into the duodenum. These disorders include carcinoma that obstructs the biliary tree and infection of the biliary system. However, gallbladder disease with gallstones is the most common disorder of the biliary system. Although not all occurrences of gallbladder infection (cholecystitis) are related to gallstones (cholelithiasis), 95 per cent of patients with acute cholecystitis have gallstones. However, a majority of people with gallstones have no pain and are unaware of the presence of stones.

Cholecystitis

At times the gallbladder may be the site of an acute infection that causes acute pain, tenderness and rigidity of the upper right abdomen, associated with nausea and vomiting and the usual signs of an acute inflammation. This condition is referred to as acute cholecystitis. If the gallbladder is found to be filled with pus, there is an empyema of the gallbladder.

Nursing Care Plan 16.1 is for the patient with cholecystitis, who has a history of intermittent, colicky abdominal pain, nausea and indigestion. This patient appears slightly jaundiced, with yellowish sclera, but does not complain of pruritis or photophobia. The patient's stools are clay-coloured and the urine is darker than normal. Preoperatively, it is important to give the patient a full explanation of any tests performed, such as ultrasound, and how the removal of the gallbladder will affect the patient. Preoperative teaching has been shown to reduce patient anxiety and enhance postoperative recovery (Hayward, 1975). Deep-breathing and coughing exercises must also be taught preoperatively in order to ensure co-operation postoperatively and to aid relaxation, thus promoting recovery (Boore, Champion and Ferguson, 1987). Reassurance about pain relief and the effects of the anaesthetic should also be given to help reduce the fear of surgery.

► NURSING CARE PLAN 16.1: THE PATIENT WITH CHOLECYSTITIS

Nasreen Khan is a 38-year-old Muslim woman, who is married with two teenage children. She has a history of intermittent, colicky abdominal pain (exacerbated by eating fatty foods), nausea and indigestion. She is very anxious about having an operation, and has a poor understanding of English.

Patient's problems	Expected outcomes	Nursing care	Rationale
1. Pain and discomfort due to high surgical incision, and presence of drains	Relief of pain	1a. Assess pain hourly and give analgesia as required	Regular assessment of pain leads to more effective treatment (McCaffery, 1983)
		b. Teach patient to support wound with pillow or hands when moving or coughing	Moving and coughing is less painful if wound is supported
		c. Position patient comfortably	
		d. Ensure drains not under tension by attaching to patient or bedside	Dislodged drain may lead to peritonitis (Allan, 1977)
2. Risk of haemorrhage following surgery, exacerbated by low vitamin K	No haemorrhage	2a. Monitor pulse and blood pressure	A raised pulse and fall in blood pressure may indicate haemorrhage
		b. Check wound for bleeding	

►

► NURSING CARE PLAN 16.1: THE PATIENT WITH CHOLECYSTITIS

Patient's problems	Expected outcomes	Nursing care	Rationale
		c. Monitor output from suction drain	Suction drain removes blood from operation site, internally. A large increase in output would indicate haemorrhage
		d. Observe for signs of shock	
		e. Withhold heparin	Heparin often given to prevent deep vein thrombosis, but if prothrombin level low, may lead to haemorrhage
3. Respiratory impairment related to high incision	Absence of chest infection	3a. Encourage deep breathing and coughing exercises every hour	Regular expansion of peripheral lung space will prevent consolidation of secretions. A high abdominal incision increases difficulty of respiration (Boore, Champion and Ferguson, 1987)
		b. Ensure good fluid intake (minimum 2 litres daily)	Reduces tenacity of sputum, and allows easier expectoration
		c. Mobilize from first day postoperatively	Encourages lung expansion
		d. Refer to physiotherapist	
4. Nausea, related to impaired bile secretion and anaesthetic	No nausea	4a. Aspirate nasogastric tube as required	Removes fluid and gas from stomach, thus relieving distension (Armstrong and MacKay, 1980)
		b. Give antiemetic (e.g. prochlorperazine, 12.5 mg) as required	
		c. Four-hourly mouth care	To keep mouth fresh
5. Dry mouth and risk of dehydration due to fasting	Moist mouth and minimum daily fluid intake of 2 litres	5a. Monitor fluid intake/output	
		b. Give intravenous fluids as prescribed	Intravenous fluids should be carefully monitored and recorded as they are a form of drug therapy
		c. Four-hourly mouth care using soft toothbrush and saline	Soft toothbrush is more effective than foamsticks in removing debris and plaque (Howarth, 1977)
		d. Offer chewing gum	Stimulates salivation
6. Abdominal discomfort and flatulence due to lack of bowel activity	No discomfort	6a. Aspirate nasogastric tube regularly	
		b. Keep nil by mouth for 24 hours and then gradually reintroduce fluids until bowel sounds return	Bowel inactive following handling during surgery. This leads to fluid build-up and distension. Bowel sounds are a sign of bowel activity recommencing
		c. Teach exercises to reduce flatulence	Planned external compression of large bowel can help reduce flatulence (Nichols, 1986)
		d. Mobilize as able	Exercise and use of skeletal muscle can induce tone in smooth muscle
		e. Give two suppositories, if no bowel action after diet recommenced	Stimulates bowel contraction
7. Poor understanding of English and ability to communicate	No barrier to communication	7a. Use daughter as interpreter	Enhanced communication reduces anxiety (Hayward, 1975), enables patient participation in care and allows optimum care to be given
		b. Use drawings, gestures to communicate directly	
		c. Speak slowly and simply	

► NURSING CARE PLAN 16.1: THE PATIENT WITH CHOLECYSTITIS

Patient's problems	Expected outcomes	Nursing care	Rationale
8. Risk of wound infection/peritonitis due to breach of skin integrity and presence of T-tube in common bile duct	Healing with no infection or leakage of bile	8a. Maintain strict asepsis when caring for drains or wound b. Ensure drains remain patent c. Change suction bottle daily d. Empty bile bag attached to T-tube as necessary; record output e. Check dressings for leakage, and change if necessary f. Remove suction drain once drainage is minimal (usually one to two days) g. Leave T-tube in place for one week, clamping once drainage is minimal, then remove after a clear T-tube cholangiogram h. Monitor temperature and pulse four-hourly i. Observe for signs of jaundice	Blocked tubing may lead to leakage of bile Suction bottles gradually lose their vacuum Considerable quantities of bile will drain at first due to oedema in common bile duct, but flow will diminish as inflammation subsides, and bile resumes normal outlet into duodenum A track will form around T-tube within five days due to latex-tissue reaction, allowing easy removal and reducing risk of bile leakage into peritoneum. Clamping will indicate any blockage to bile flow (Allan, 1977) Sign of infection Sign of obstruction of bile drainage
9. Risk of deep vein thrombosis	No deep vein thrombosis	9a. Mobilize, increasing activity daily b. Apply antiembolism stockings c. Teach patient the danger of crossed legs or pressure on calves	Calf pump aids venous return and reduces venous stasis (Tsapogas, 1971) Reduces incidence of deep vein thrombosis (Allan, Williams *et al.*, 1983) Increases venous stasis, and therefore increases risk of deep vein thrombosis
10. Anxiety about discharge home	Free of anxiety, and aware of aftercare	10a. Involve daughter as interpreter b. Advise patient to maintain nutritious diet and avoid excess fat; fat restriction may be lifted after six weeks if no nausea or flatulence occurs c. Advise patient to avoid vigorous exercise or lifting heavy objects (i.e., heavier than a saucepan or pot of tea) for six weeks d. Ask patient to report any increase in nausea or pain, or recurrence of jaundice	Bile now flows continuously into duodenum: reduces capacity to cope with fatty meal, but fats can be tolerated in small quantities. After two to three months, biliary ducts dilate to accommodate pool of bile and normal diet may be resumed. Many patients, however, never regain tolerance of fats (Bell, 1979) Abdominal muscles take 6 to 12 weeks to heal completely Indicates further bile obstruction

Cholelithiasis

Cholelithiasis (calculi, or gallstones) usually form in the gallbladder from the solid constituents of bile and vary greatly in size, shape and composition (Figure 16.9).

Gallstones are uncommon in children and young adults but become increasingly prevalent after the age of 40. One postmortem study on unselected patients found that 55 per cent of women and 25 per cent of men had gallstones (Roberts, 1976).

Altered Physiology

There are two major types of gallstones: those composed predominantly of pigment and those composed primarily of cholesterol. Pigment stones probably form when unconjugated pigments in the bile precipitate to form stones. The risk of developing such stones is increased in patients with cirrhosis, haemolysis and infections of the biliary tree. These stones cannot be dissolved and must be removed surgically.

Cholesterol stones account for most gallbladder disease in the United Kingdom. Cholesterol, a normal constituent of bile, is insoluble in water. Its solubility depends on bile acids and lecithin (phospholipids) in bile. In gallstone-prone patients, there is decreased bile acid synthesis and increased cholesterol synthesis in the liver. This results in a bile supersaturated with cholesterol, which precipitates out of the bile to form stones, and acts as an irritant, producing inflammatory changes in the gallbladder.

Four times more women than men develop cholesterol stones and gallbladder disease; they are usually over 40 years of age, multiparous and obese. There is increased incidence of stone formation in users of oral contraceptives, oestrogens and clofibrate, which are known to increase biliary cholesterol saturation. The incidence of stone formation increases with age as a result of increased hepatic secretion of cholesterol and decreased bile acid synthesis. In addition, there is increased risk because of malabsorption of bile salts in patients with gastrointestinal disease or T-tube fistula or in those who have had ileal resection or bypass.

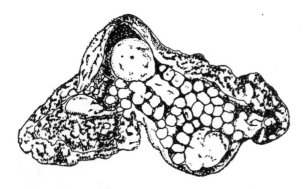

Figure 16.9 Multiple gallstones in a gallbladder.

Clinical Features

Gallstones may be silent, producing no pain and only mild gastrointestinal symptoms. Such stones may be detected incidentally during surgery or evaluation for unrelated problems.

The patient with gallstones may develop two types of symptoms: those due to disease of the gallbladder itself and those due to obstruction of the bile passages by a gallstone. The symptoms may be acute or chronic. Epigastric distress, such as fullness, abdominal distention and vague pain in the right upper quadrant of the abdomen, may occur following a meal high in fried or fatty foods.

If a gallstone obstructs the cystic duct, the gallbladder becomes infected and distended. The patient develops a pyrexia and may have a palpable abdominal mass. The patient experiences biliary colic with excruciating upper right abdominal pain that radiates to the back or right shoulder, is usually associated with nausea and vomiting, and is noticeable several hours after a heavy meal. The patient moves about restlessly, unable to find a comfortable position.

Such a bout of biliary colic is caused by contraction of the gallbladder, which has been stimulated by fat and cannot release bile because of obstruction by the stone. The distended gallbladder produces marked tenderness in the right upper quadrant on deep inspiration and prevents full inspiratory excursion. The pain of acute cholecystitis may be so severe that analgesics such as pethidine are required; antispasmodics have also been used effectively. Morphine is thought to increase spasm of the sphincter of Oddi and is therefore avoided.

If the gallstone is dislodged and no longer obstructs the cystic duct, the gallbladder drains and the inflammatory process subsides after a relatively short time. If the gallstone continues to obstruct the duct, abscess, necrosis and perforation with generalized peritonitis may result.

Jaundice usually only occurs with obstruction of the common bile duct, and results in: yellow skin and sclerae; pruritis; dark urine; and clay-coloured faeces (see p. 593).

Obstruction of bile flow also interferes with absorption of the fat-soluble vitamins A, D, E and K. Therefore, the patient may exhibit deficiencies of these vitamins if biliary obstruction has been prolonged. Vitamin K deficiency will interfere with normal blood clotting.

Diagnosis

Abdominal X-ray Films
An abdominal X-ray film may be obtained if gallbladder disease is suspected and to exclude other causes of symptoms. However only 15 to 20 per cent of gallstones are sufficiently calcified to be visible on such films.

Ultrasound
Ultrasound has replaced oral cholecystography as the

diagnostic procedure of choice because it is rapid and accurate and can be used in patients with liver disorders and jaundice. Additionally, it does not expose patients to ionizing radiation. The procedure is most accurate if the patient fasts overnight so that the gallbladder is distended. The use of ultrasound is based on reflected sound waves, and can detect calculi in the gallbladder or a dilated common bile duct. It is reported to detect gallstones with 95 per cent accuracy.

Cholecystogram

Although it has been replaced by ultrasonography as the test of choice, cholecystogram is still used if ultrasound equipment is not available or if the ultrasound results are questionable in a patient with chronic symptoms. Oral or occasionally intravenous cholangiography may be performed to detect gallstones and to assess the ability of the gallbladder to fill, concentrate its contents, contract and empty. An iodide-containing contrast medium that is excreted by the liver and concentrated in the gallbladder is administered to the patient. The normal gallbladder fills with this radio-opaque substance. If gallstones are present, they appear as negative shadows on the X-ray film.

During the interval between the administration of the iodide and the X-ray study, the patient is permitted nothing by mouth to prevent contraction and emptying of the gallbladder.

Nursing Care. Before administering the contrast medium to the patient, it is important to check for allergies to iodine or seafood. The use of iodine in such patients may produce a severe allergic reaction.

Note: Oral or intravenous cholecystogram in the obviously jaundiced patient is not useful since the liver cannot excrete the radio-opaque dye into the gallbladder in a jaundiced patient.

Endoscopic Retrograde Cholangiopancreatography

Endoscopic retrograde cholangiopancreatography permits direct visualization of structures once available only during laparotomy (Cotton, 1976). It involves insertion of a flexible fibreoptic endoscope into the oesophagus to the descending duodenum (Figure 16.10). The common bile duct and pancreatic duct are cannulated, and contrast material is injected into the ducts, permitting visualization of the biliary tree and access to the distal common bile duct to retrieve a retained gallstone.

Nursing Care. The procedure requires a co-operative patient to permit insertion of the endoscope without damage to the gastrointestinal tract. Before the procedure, adequate explanation of the procedure and the patient's role in it must be given by the nurse. The patient receives sedation immediately before the procedure. Following the procedure, the nurse monitors the patient's condition, observing vital signs and checking for signs of perforation or infection.

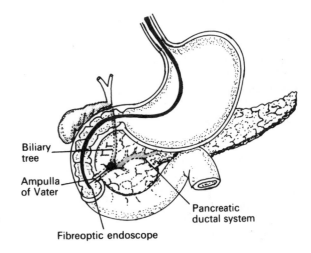

Biliary tree

Ampulla of Vater

Pancreatic ductal system

Fibreoptic endoscope

Figure 16.10 Endoscopic retrograde cholangiopancreatography. By means of a side-viewing fibreoptic duodenoscope, the ampulla of Vater is catheterized and the biliary tree injected with contrast material. The pancreatic ductal system is also assessed, if indicated. This procedure is of special value in ampullary or periampullary neoplasms, which may be simultaneously visualized and biopsied. Acute pancreatitis is a contraindication. (Redrawn from Misra, P. S. and Bank, S. (1982) Gallbladder disease: Guide to diagnosis, *Hospital Medicine*, February, p. 136.)

Percutaneous Transhepatic Cholangiography

Percutaneous transhepatic cholangiography involves the injection of dye directly into the biliary tree. Because of the relatively large concentration of dye that is introduced into the biliary system, all components of the system, including the hepatic ducts within the liver, the entire length of the common bile duct, the cystic duct and the gallbladder, are clearly outlined.

This procedure can be carried out even in the presence of liver disorder and jaundice. It is useful in distinguishing jaundice caused by liver disease (hepatocellular jaundice) from that due to biliary obstruction; for investigating the gastrointestinal symptoms of patients whose gallbladders have been removed; for locating stones within the bile ducts; and in diagnosing cancer involving the biliary system.

Although the complication rate following this procedure is low, the patient must be observed closely for symptoms of bleeding, peritonitis and septicaemia. Antibiotics should be administered as prescribed to minimize the risk of sepsis and septic shock.

Nonsurgical Management

The expected outcomes of medical therapy are to reduce the incidence of acute attacks of gallbladder pain and cholecystitis by supportive and dietary management, and, if possible, to remove the cause of cholecystitis by drug therapy, endoscopic procedures or surgical intervention.

Supportive and Dietary Management

Approximately 80 per cent of the patients with acute gallbladder inflammation achieve a remission with rest, intravenous fluids, nasogastric suction, analgesia and antibiotics. Unless the patient's condition deteriorates, surgical intervention is delayed until the patient's acute symptoms subside and complete evaluation can be carried out.

The diet, immediately after an attack, is usually limited to low-fat liquids, graduating to a light, low-fat diet. Eggs, cream, pork, fried foods, cheese and rich dressings, gas-forming vegetables and alcohol are avoided. The patient needs to be reminded that fatty foods may bring on an attack.

Dietary management may be the major mode of therapy in those patients who have experienced only dietary intolerance to fatty foods and vague gastrointestinal symptoms.

Drug Therapy

Chenodeoxycholic acid (chendol) has been effective in dissolving about 60 per cent of radiolucent gallstones composed primarily of cholesterol (Soloway, Balisteri and Trotman, 1980). It inhibits liver synthesis and secretion of cholesterol, thereby desaturating bile. Existing stones can be decreased in size, small ones dissolved and new stones prevented from forming. The therapy is most effective if the stones are small. The effective dose of chendol depends on body weight, and is generally indicated for those patients who refuse surgery or for whom it is considered too risky.

Certain other medications, such as oestrogens, oral contraceptives, clofibrate and dietary cholesterol, may adversely affect the results of treatment with chenodeoxycholic acid. This therapy does not cure the underlying abnormality and thus cholesterol stones may recur. Therefore, a prophylactic dose is probably necessary. Patients' adherence to this mode of therapy requires further study and follow-up.

If acute symptoms of cholecystitis continue or recur, drug therapy is inappropriate as a substitute for surgery, and surgical intervention is indicated.

Long-term follow-up and monitoring of the patient's liver enzymes are indicated. The patient is requested to report adverse side-effects and the recurrence of symptoms of gallstones.

Nonsurgical Removal of Gallstones

Methods of treating gallstones by infusion of solvents into the gallbladder are under investigation. One method involves infusion of a solvent through a catheter inserted

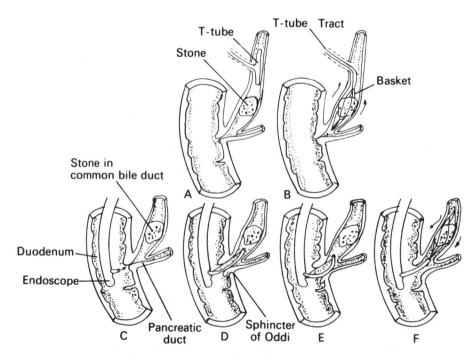

Figure 16.11 Removal of gallstone. (A) Use of T-tube tract for removal of retained stone. (B) Removal of stone with basket attached to catheter threaded through T-tube tract. (C) Endoscopic retrograde cholangiopancreatography endoscope inserted into duodenum. (D) Papillotome inserted into common bile duct. (E) Enlarging opening of sphincter of Oddi. (F) Retrieval and removal of stone with basket inserted through endoscope.

percutaneously directly into the gallbladder. Other procedures may involve infusion of the solvent via tube or drain inserted through a T-tube tract to dissolve stones not removed at the time of surgery or through an endoscopic retrograde cholangiopancreatography endoscope.

Other nonsurgical methods are available (Figure 16.11). A catheter and instrument with a basket attached can be threaded through the T-tube tract or fistula formed at the time of T-tube insertion; the basket is used to retrieve the stone lodged in the common bile duct. A second procedure is the use of the endoscopic retrograde cholangiopancreatography endoscope, where a cutting instrument is passed through the endoscope into the ampulla of Vater to enlarge the sphincter of Oddi, and allowing the lodged stone to pass spontaneously into the duodenum. Another instrument with a small basket or balloon at its tip may be inserted through the endoscope to retrieve the stone. Although complications following this procedure are rare, the patient must be observed closely for bleeding, perforation and the development of pancreatitis. This procedure is particularly useful in the treatment of patients presenting with symptoms after biliary tract surgery and for patients in whom surgery is particularly hazardous.

Extracorporeal shock wave therapy (lithotripsy) has also been successfully used for nonsurgical fragmentation of gallstones in selected patients (Rowland, Marks and Torres, 1989). This method (see Chapter 20) uses repeated shock waves directed at the gallstone located in the gallbladder or common bile duct to break up the stones. The fragments then pass the gallbladder or common bile duct spontaneously, are removed by endoscopy, or are dissolved with previously described solvents. It is expected that this mode of treatment will continue to be used only for select patients whose gallstones are not amenable to other forms of treatment.

These nonsurgical methods of removing stones are expected to decrease the need for surgery, reduce the length of hospital stay and enable patients to return to their normal activities more quickly than they could if they had undergone surgical removal of the stones.

Surgical Management

Surgical treatment of gallbladder disorders and gallstones is necessary for the relief of long-term symptoms, for the removal of the cause of biliary colic and for treatment of acute cholecystitis. Surgery may be elective when the patient's symptoms have subsided or may be performed as an emergency procedure if the patient's condition necessitates it.

Preoperative Management

Preparation for a gallbladder operation is similar to that for any upper abdominal laparotomy. Instruction and explanation are given before surgery with regard to turn-

ing and deep breathing. Because the abdominal incision is high on the abdomen (subcostal), the patient is often reluctant to move and turn; pneumonia and atelectasis are possible postoperative complications that are to be avoided by breathing deeply and by turning. Since drainage tubes are usually required after operation, the patient should be warned of this. The patient should also be informed about the likelihood of the need for nasogastric suction during the immediate postoperative period.

Surgical Intervention and Drainage Systems

Patients are usually placed on the operating table with the upper abdomen raised somewhat by an air pillow or sandbag to make the biliary area more accessible.

Cholecystectomy. In this operation, the gallbladder is removed after ligation of the cystic duct and artery. The operation is performed in most cases of acute and chronic cholecystitis. A low-suction drain (Redivac or similar) is placed in the gallbladder space and brought out through a stab wound for drainage of blood, serosanguinous fluids and bile into a vacuumed bottle.

Choledochostomy. In choledochostomy, an incision is made into the common bile duct for removal of stones. After the stones have been evacuated, a 'T' tube usually is inserted into the duct for drainage of bile until oedema subsides. This tube is connected to a drainage bag. The gallbladder also contains stones and, as a rule, a cholecystectomy is performed at the same time.

Cholecystostomy. Cholecystostomy is performed when the patient's condition prevents more extensive surgery or when an acute inflammatory reaction obscures the biliary system. The gallbladder is opened, the stones and the bile or the pus are removed and a drainage tube is secured with a pursestring suture. Following recovery from the acute episode, the patient may return for cholecystectomy.

Laparoscopic Cholecystectomy

Removal of the gallbladder and stones by a laparoscope is a less invasive alternative. The patient generally makes a faster recovery, has a reduced length of hospital stay and complications are less frequent.

Considerations for Elderly People.

Surgical intervention for biliary disorders are the most common operative procedures performed on elderly people. Although the incidence of gallstones increases with age, the symptoms experienced by the elderly patient may not be the typical pyrexia, pain and jaundice. Biliary tract disorders may be accompanied or preceded by symptoms of septic shock: oliguria, hypotension, mental changes, tachycardia and tachypnoea.

The risk of mortality and morbidity is increased in the elderly patient who undergoes emergency surgery for life-threatening disorders of the biliary tract. Despite associated or preoperative medical illness in older people, elective cholecystectomy is usually well tolerated and can be carried out with low risk if expert assessment and care are provided before, during and after the surgical procedure.

BIBLIOGRAPHY

Allan, A., Williams, J. T., Bolton, J. P. *et al.* (1983) Use of graduated compression stockings in prevention of postoperative deep vein thrombosis, *British Journal of Surgery*, Vol. 70, pp. 172–4.

Allan, D. (1977) Complications of T-tube drainage of the common bile duct, *Nursing Times*, 18 August, Vol. 73, No. 33, pp. 1270–1.

Armstrong, J. and Mackay, M. (1980) Patients with gastrointestinal problems, *Nursing*, Vol. 1, No. 13, pp. 567–8.

Beland, I. and Passos, J. (1975) *Clinical Nursing— Pathophysiological and Psychosocial Approaches*, Macmillan, New York.

Bell, J. (1979) Just another patient with gallstones, *Nursing* (USA), Vol. 9, No. 10, pp. 26–33.

Boore, J. R. P., Champion, R. and Ferguson, M. (eds) (1987) *Nursing the Physically Ill Adult*, Churchill Livingstone, Edinburgh.

Cotton, P. B. (1976) Endoscopic cannulation of the papilla of Vater, in Bouchier (ed.) *Recent Advances in Gastroenterology 3*, Churchill Livingstone, Edinburgh.

Crow, R. (1988) The challenge of pressure sores, *Nursing Times*, Vol. 84, No. 38, pp. 68–73.

Gillies, H. C., Rogers, H. J., Spector, R. G. and Trounce, J. R. (1986) *Textbook of Clinical Pharmacology* (2nd edition), Hodder & Stoughton, London.

Groer, M. E. and Shekleton, M. E. (1983) *Basic Pathophysiology: A Conceptual Approach* (2nd edition), Mosby, St Louis.

Hayward (1975) *Information—A Prescription Against Pain*, Royal College of Nursing, London.

Hinchcliff, S. and Montague, S. (1988) *Physiology for Nursing Practice*, Baillière Tindall, Eastbourne.

Howarth, H. (1977) Mouthcare procedures for the very ill, *Nursing Times*, 10 March, Vol. 73, No. 10, pp. 354–5.

McCaffery, M. (1983) *Nursing the Patient in Pain*, Harper & Row, London.

Nichols, R. (1986) Simple remedies for postoperative gas pains, *RN*, Vol. 49, No. 2, pp. 37–9.

Oakley, K. (1988) *Nurses' Guide to Radiological Procedures*, Edward Arnold, London.

Reed, M. L., Vaickevicius, V. K., Al-Safraf, M. *et al.* (1981) The practicality of hepatic artery infusion therapy of primary and metastatic hepatic artery malignancies, *Cancer*, Vol. 47, pp. 402–9.

Roberts, A. (1976) Systems of Life 19: Liver, *Nursing Times*, Vol. 72, No. 26, Occasional Paper.

Rowland, G. A., Marks, D. A. and Torres, W. E. (1989) The new gallstone destroyers and dissolvers, *American Journal of Nursing*, Vol. 89, No. 11, pp. 1473–6.

Soloway, R. D., Balisteri, W. F. and Trotman, B. W. (1980) Gallbladder and biliary tract in Bouchier (ed.) *Recent Advances in Gastroenterology 4*, Churchill Livingstone, Edinburgh.

Stoker, F. (1985) Improving biliary drainage management, *Nursing Times*, 3 July, Vol. 81, No. 27, pp. 32–5.

Taylor, D. (1983) Jaundice: physiology, signs and symptoms, *Nursing* (USA), August, Vol. 13, No. 8, pp. 52–4.

Tsapogas, M. J., Goussous, H. and Peabody, R. A. (1971) Postoperative venous thrombosis and the effectiveness of prophylactic measures, *Archives of Surgery*, Vol. 103, pp. 561–7.

FURTHER READING

Books

Sherlock, S. (1985) *Diseases of the Liver and Biliary System* (7th edition), Blackwell Scientific, Oxford.

Watson, J. E. and Royle, J. R. (1987) *Watson's Medical-Surgical Nursing and Related Physiology* (3rd edition), Baillière Tindall, Eastbourne.

Articles

Adinaro, D. (1987) Liver failure: Fluid and electrolyte concerns, *Nursing Clinics of North America*, Vol. 22, No. 4, pp. 843–52.

Berger, M., Mattioli, C. A., Dobbs, S. M. and Jackson, D. (1983) Bleeding oesophageal varices in the adolescent, *Heart Lung*, Vol. 12, No. 6, pp. 661–5.

Brookbanks, M. and Hampstead, N. (1987) Controlling an epidemic, *Nursing Times*, Vol. 83, No. 38, pp. 38–9.

Dodd, R. P. (1984) When the liver can't cope, *RN*, Vol. 47, No. 10, pp. 26–30.

Fredette, S. L. F. (1984) When the liver fails, *American Journal of Nursing*, Vol. 84, No. 1, pp. 64–7.

Gannon, R. B. and Pickett, K. (1983) Jaundice, *American Journal of Nursing*, Vol. 83, No. 3, pp. 404–7.

Gruber, M. (1985) Endoscopic injection scleropathy: Nursing responsibilities, *Crit. Care Q.*, Vol. 7, No. 4, pp. 73–80.

Guenter, P. and Slocum, B. (1983) Hepatic disease, *Nursing Clinics of North America*, Vol. 18, No. 1, pp. 71–80.

Gurevich, I. (1983) Viral hepatitis, *American Journal of Nursing*, Vol. 83, No. 4, pp. 571–86.

Janes, O. F. W. (1983) Gastrointestinal and liver function in old age, *Clinical Gastroenterology*, Vol. 12, No. 3, pp. 671–91.

Keith, J. S. (1985) Hepatic failure, *Critical Care Nurse*, Vol. 5, No. 1, pp. 60–86.

Klopp, A. (1984) Shunting malignant ascites, *American Journal of Nursing*, Vol. 84, No. 2, pp. 212–3.

McCormack, A., Itkin, J. and Cloud, C. (1984) The patient with liver failure, *RN*, Vol. 47, No. 10, pp. 32–3.

Miller, B. and Gavant, M. L. (1985) Biliary catheter care, *American Journal of Nursing*, Vol. 85, No.10, pp. 1115–7.

Mogadan, M., Alberelli, J., Ahmed, S. W. *et al.* (1984) Gallbladder dynamics in response to various meals: Is dietary fat restriction necessary in the management of gallstones? *American Journal of Gastroenterology*, Vol. 79, No. 10, pp. 745–7.

Schumann, K. (1982) Correction of ascites with peritoneovenous shunting, *Heart Lung*, Vol. 12, No. 3, pp. 248–55.

Sheets, L. (1989) Liver transplantation, *Nursing Clinics of North America*, Vol. 24, No. 4, pp. 881–90.

Smith, S. L. (1985) Liver transplantation: Implications for critical care nursing, *Heart Lung*, Vol. 14, No. 6, pp. 617–27.

Taylor, D. L. (1983) Gallstones, *Nursing* (USA), Vol. 13, No. 6, pp. 44–5.

Thistle, J. L., Cleary. P. A., Lachin, J. M. *et al.* (1984) The natural history of cholelithiasis: The national co-operative gallstone study, *Annals of Internal Medicine*, Vol. 101, No.2, pp. 171–5.

Thorpe, C. J. and Caprini, J. C. (1980) Gallbladder disease, *American Journal of Nursing*, Vol. 80, No. 12, pp. 2181–5.

Traiger, G. L. and Bohachick, P. (1983) Liver transplantation, *Critical Care Nurse*, Vol. 3, No. 5, pp. 96–103.

Tweed, S. H. (1989) Identifying the alcoholic client, *Nursing Clinics of North America*, Vol. 24, No. 1, pp. 13–32.

van Rensburg, L. C. J. (1984) The management of acute cholecystitis in the elderly, *British Journal of Surgery*, Vol. 71, No. 9, pp. 692–3.

Wimpsett, J. (1984) Trace your patient's liver dysfunction, *Nursing* (USA), Vol. 14, No. 8, pp. 56–7.

chapter 17

ASSESSMENT AND CARE OF PATIENTS WITH DIABETES MELLITUS

DEFINITION

Diabetes mellitus is a syndrome as opposed to a single disease. It is characterized by a chronic state of hyperglycaemia (raised blood glucose levels). This is due either to insufficient insulin or inadequate action of insulin. The syndrome results in the disorder of the metabolism of carbohydrate, protein and fat. The overall long-term effect is degenerative changes in all blood vessels.

TYPES OF DIABETES

There are several types of diabetes mellitus. The terminology used to describe these types has changed as more details have been discovered about the syndrome. The now internationally agreed titles are:

- Type I—insulin-dependent diabetes mellitus.
- Type II—non-insulin-dependent diabetes mellitus.
- Type III—diabetes mellitus associated with other syndromes.
- IGT—impaired glucose tolerance.
- GDM—gestational diabetes mellitus.

Table 17.1 shows the classification of diabetes mellitus.

AETIOLOGY

The aetiology of the disease is not completely understood. There are probably several causative factors within each type, varying from patient to patient. It remains to be proven whether the aetiology is related to an inherited defect, an environmental factor (e.g., viruses, obesity) or the interaction of both inheritance and environmental factors. In type I (insulin-dependent) diabetes, it is felt that genetics or viruses or an autoimmune response, alone or in combination, are involved. In type

Table 17.1 *Classification of diabetes mellitus*

Current classification	Previous classifications	Clinical characteristics	Nursing implications
Type: I: Insulin-dependent diabetes mellitus (5–10 per cent of all diabetes)	Juvenile diabetes Juvenile-onset diabetes Ketosis-prone diabetes Brittle diabetes	Any age, but usually young Mostly thin at diagnosis Causes may be genetic or viral but probably involve abnormal immune responses Often have islet cell antibodies	Critical to maintain normal range of blood glucose Potential future vaccine for immunization of susceptible people
		Little or no endogenous insulin	Essential to monitor status of blood glucose for good control
		Need insulin to preserve life	Knowledge emphasis on • Relationship between food, exercise and insulin in controlling blood glucose • Adjusting insulin • Interpreting glucose test results Skills emphasis on • Insulin administration • Testing for glucose and ketones • Pump care • Foot care
		Ketosis-prone	• Life-threatening situation, crucial for patient to detect and treat or prevent Peer pressure during adolescence and adulthood regarding compliance with diet, insulin and testing
Type II: Noninsulin-dependent diabetes mellitus (90–95 per cent of all diabetes: nonobese—20 per cent of type II; obese—80 per cent of type II)	Adult-onset diabetes Maturity-onset diabetes Ketosis-resistant diabetes Stable diabetes Maturity-onset diabetes of youth	Any age, usually over 40 but occasionally under 21 Causes may be related to genetic, obesity or environmental factors Mostly obese at diagnosis No islet cell antibodies Varying amounts of endogenous insulin present, often higher than normal levels	Very important to maintain near normal range of blood sugars Weight reduction crucial, but problems with motivation and compliance
		May need insulin to avoid hyperglycaemia	Insulin often overused as treatment; inappropriate use increases obesity
		Rare ketosis, except in stress or infection	Less life-threatening than type I, but majority of diabetics in this class
		Nonketotic hyperosmolar coma	Life threatening and often fatal

►

Table 17.1 *Continued*

Current classification	Previous classifications	Clinical characteristics	Nursing implications
Type III: diabetes associated with other conditions or syndromes	Secondary diabetes	Accompanied by conditions known to cause (or suspected of causing) diabetes: pancreatic or hormonal conditions, drug or chemical toxicity, certain genetic syndromes	As for types I and II (see above)
Impaired glucose tolerance (IGT)	Asymptomatic diabetes Chemical diabetes Subclinical diabetes Borderline diabetes Latent diabetes	Blood glucose levels between normal and that of diabetes Above-normal susceptibility to atherosclerotic disease Renal and retinal complications usually not significant	Both obese and nonobese should be screened periodically for diabetes, but obese should reduce weight
Gestational diabetes	Gestational diabetes	Begins or is recognized during or after pregnancy Above-normal risk of perinatal complications	Usually highly motivated to maintain normal blood glucose because of baby
		Glucose intolerance transitory, but frequently recurs: • 50 per cent go on to develop overt diabetes within 15 years • 80 per cent go on to develop overt diabetes after 20 years, particularly postmenopausally	Nursing challenge— maintain or reduce weight to ideal; may delay onset

II (noninsulin-dependent) diabetes, genetics and obesity play a more significant role.

Genetic Factors
Diabetes has always been thought of as a genetic or inherited disease. To date, no single mode of inheritance can explain all the types of diabetes adequately. In fact, many modes of inheritance have been proposed. Different types of diabetes may be inherited in different ways in different families—'genetic heterogeneity'.

The search for a genetic marker for diabetes has important implications for the understanding of the inheritance of diabetes. Research with the human leucocyte antigen (HLA) system that is used in tissue typing has demonstrated a relationship with some HLA antigens and diabetes.

Certain of these antigens are consistently found in insulin-dependent diabetes. There is often a family history in non-insulin-dependent diabetes mellitus, but this does not seem to be linked to human leucocyte antigen markers (Hassan, 1985).

Viral Factors
Viral infections have been shown to precede the onset of insulin-dependent diabetes mellitus. This is particularly true for patients who are genetically predisposed to diabetes mellitus.

Combined Factors
Viruses, heredity (including an immunological defect) and an autoimmune response may contribute to the development of insulin-dependent diabetes. Heredity by itself appears to be the least important contributor. Heredity and obesity significantly contribute to the development of non-insulin-dependent diabetes.

Although the exact mechanism of inheritance has not

yet been explained, blood relatives of known patients with diabetes should maintain life-long vigilance for this condition. Obese people and mothers who have delivered large babies are also susceptible.

ALTERED PHYSIOLOGY

Diabetes results from the inability of the body to produce and use insulin.

In the nondiabetic person, insulin is released from the pancreas in proportion to the amount of glucose in the blood. Normally, the beta cells in the pancreas stimulate or inhibit insulin secretion minute by minute, according to changing blood glucose levels. In diabetes, insulin is not secreted in proportion to blood glucose levels because of several possible factors: deficiency in the production of insulin by the beta cells; insensitivity of the insulin secretory mechanism of the beta cells; delayed or insufficient release of insulin; or excessive inactivation by chemical inhibitors or 'binders' in the circulation.

However, in some non-insulin-dependent people with diabetes, insulin secretion is increased, resulting in higher circulating insulin levels. Although excess insulin is present, it is not utilized because of an inadequate number of insulin receptors present on cells. This mechanism has been observed in obese non-insulin-dependent patients. With weight loss, the number of insulin receptors on the cells increases, thereby allowing glucose to enter the cell. This may result in return of a normal glucose tolerance.

An elevated fasting blood glucose level in diabetes reflects decreased uptake of glucose by the tissues or increased gluconeogenesis. If the concentration of glucose in the blood is sufficiently high, the kidney may not reabsorb all of the filtered glucose; the glucose then appears in the urine (glycosuria).

With increased gluconeogenesis (which is in part under the control of the adrenocortical hormones), protein and fats are mobilized, rather than stored or deposited in the cells. When there is deficiency of insulin, muscles cannot utilize glucose. Free fatty acids are then mobilized from adipose tissue cells and broken down by the liver into ketone bodies for energy. Ketoacidosis is characterized by excessive amounts of ketone bodies in the blood. Patients with ketoacidosis exhibit hyperventilation and loss of sodium, potassium, chloride and water from the body. The net metabolic result of acute, uncontrolled diabetes mellitus is loss of fat stores, liver glycogen, cellular protein, electrolytes and water. Over a period of years, blood glucose levels that are consistently above normal appear to hasten the complications that affect the large vessels in the brain, heart, kidneys and extremities, and the small vessels in the eyes, kidneys and nerves. The mechanisms have not yet been determined precisely, but several hypotheses have been proposed and will be discussed below with long-term complications. Table 17.2 presents an overview of the complications of diabetes.

Table 17.2 *Complications of diabetes*

Retinopathy

- Diabetes is a leading cause of new cases of blindness in adults between 20 and 74 years of age
- People with diabetes experience higher rates of cataracts and glaucoma
- The rupture of small aneurysms in the retinal vessels is the major cause of blindness in diabetic patients

Nephropathy

- 25 per cent of all new cases of end-stage renal disease are related to diabetes
- Renal disease causes 50 per cent of all deaths among adults with insulin-dependent diabetes
- Thickening of the glomerular capillary is the main specific renal problem related to diabetes; this is known as intercapillary glomerulosclerosis (Kimmelstiel-Wilson syndrome)
- Glomerular changes due to diabetes can result in hypertension, which accelerates other possible complications

Vascular complications

- Macrovascular degeneration (macroangiopathy): the presence of diabetes accelerates the development of atherosclerosis (deposition of fatty substances on the artery wall), resulting in a narrowing of the lumen. This can lead to angina, myocardial infarction, cerebrovascular accident, intermittent claudication and gangrene
- Microvascular degeneration (microangiopathy): microvascular changes affect the skin, kidneys and peripheral nerves. Microangiopathy is directly proportional to the rate, duration and poor control of diabetes

Neuropathy

- This affects mainly peripheral and autonomic nerves. Peripheral neuropathy results in paraesthesia of the limbs. Some loss of tendon reflexes may be apparent. Muscle atrophy may also be present. The combination of vascular changes and peripheral neuropathy puts the patient's feet at particular risk from damage. This can lead to gangrene, requiring amputation. Autonomic complications generally affect the gastrointestinal system. They also cause some sexual problems (e.g. impotence in males)

Ketoacidosis

- Ketoacidosis is a severe metabolic disorder that results in an acute hyperglycaemia

CLINICAL FEATURES

Type I Diabetes

Insulin-dependent diabetes mellitus usually begins in childhood, but may occur at any age and is not uncommon in adults. Measurable circulating insulin may still be present early in the course of the disease, but it soon disappears. In most instances the onset is abrupt, with weight loss, weakness, polyuria (excessive excretion of urine), polydipsia (excessive thirst) and polyphagia (excessive ingestion of food). As insulin production decreases, hyperglycaemia develops as a result of the body's inability to use glucose. Hyperglycaemia exceeds the renal threshold of glucose due to inability of the kidneys to absorb the extra glucose. Fluid loss through the kidneys results as the kidneys work to excrete the increased load of glucose, producing losses of water, sodium, magnesium, calcium, potassium chloride and phosphate. Because the body is not able to utilize ingested calories, body tissues are broken down to supply carbohydrate. An increased appetite is seen at first, but the hearty appetite may soon disappear as the metabolism becomes more unbalanced. Breakdown of protein and lipid (catabolism) produces loss of weight and muscular wasting. The patient is prone to develop ketosis (elevated level of ketone bodies in body tissues and fluids). Often the diagnosis is first made when the patient is brought to the hospital in a coma due to ketoacidosis. Insulin is always required.

Type II Diabetes

Non-insulin-dependent diabetes mellitus usually occurs after the age of 40. It can also occur in younger people who do not require insulin and who are not prone to developing ketosis. This type of diabetes is referred to as maturity onset diabetes of the young. In general, these patients may never require insulin and are usually managed adequately by diet alone.

The majority (about 80 per cent) of non-insulin-dependent diabetes mellitus patients are overweight when the condition is first diagnosed. The symptoms may be so minor that the diabetes is undetected for many years, and the diagnosis may be suspected as the result of a routine urinalysis. Diabetes is often detected when the patient seeks medical advice for some other complaint. Often, blood glucose tests are normal, with hyperglycaemia being detected only following a meal or as a result of a glucose tolerance test.

The onset is insidious and may take years to develop. Fatigue, tendency to drowse after a meal, irritability, nocturia, itching of the skin (especially of the vulva in the female), skin wounds that heal poorly, blurring of vision and cramps in the muscles are all warning symptoms of non-insulin-dependent diabetes.

DIAGNOSIS

Blood Glucose Tests

The presence of abnormally high blood glucose levels is the criterion on which the diagnosis of diabetes should be based. Blood glucose levels elevated above 6.7 mmol/l on more than one occasion suggest a diagnosis of diabetes. If fasting glucose levels are normal or nearly normal, the diagnosis must be based on a glucose tolerance test.

Glucose Tolerance Test

A glucose tolerance test should be carried out on the morning after the patient has fasted overnight. During the previous three days the patient should have a normal diet and should not be 'dieting', i.e., reduced carbohydrate intake. Venous blood samples are taken for fasting glucose levels. The patient then drinks a solution of 75 g of glucose in 250 to 300 ml of water. Venous blood samples are then taken every 30 minutes for the next two hours for blood glucose estimates. Pure lemon juice can be added to the drink to make it more palatable. Urine testing should be carried out before taking the glucose drink, at then at one and two hours following it.

A diagnosis of diabetes mellitus can be made if:

- Fasting blood glucose level $\geq$ 6.7 mmol/l.
- Two hours after the glucose drink $\geq$ 10 mmol/l.

A diagnosis of impaired glucose tolerance can be made if:

- Fasting blood glucose level < 6.6 mmol/l.
- Two hours after the glucose drink 6.7 to 9.9 mmol/l.

Urine Tests

Urine tests should not be used for diagnosis because both false-negative and false-positive results occur. Renal glycosuria occurs when the renal threshold for glucose is decreased. In this instance, glucose appears in the urine despite normal blood glucose values. In the elderly, renal threshold levels are higher than normal, so no glucose is found in the urine despite elevated blood glucose values.

MANAGEMENT

The basic problem of diabetes is impaired insulin secretion with a resulting abnormal carbohydrate metabolism. Over a period of years, this carbohydrate abnormality often leads to the vascular complications associated with diabetes. The main goal of treatment is to try to normalize insulin activity and blood glucose levels in an attempt to reduce the development of the vascular complications. The therapeutic goal within each type of diabetes is to lower blood glucose levels as much as possible without seriously disrupting the patient's usual activity patterns.

The management of diabetes depends on the type of diabetes the patient has. However, diet is the main factor that must be addressed in all types of diabetes.

Dietary Management

The basic principle used in diet management is the removal of glucose from the diet and the use of artificial sweeteners if required. Carbohydrate and fat intake should also be reduced. Increased fibre intake is thought to increase glucose tolerance. The aim of dietary adjustments is to provide a diet that contains adequate levels of all essential foods, while maintaining an ideal body weight, with glucose levels within the normal range. The balance between the dietary constituents is the main aim. The motto of the British Diabetic Association is 'Balance is life'.

Obesity

Obesity is known to be a contributory factor in diabetes. Therefore, obesity must be corrected as soon as possible. In patients who have developed non-insulin-dependent diabetes, normal glucose levels may be achieved by attaining and maintaining an ideal body weight.

Calorie Intake

Calorie Requirements
The first step in preparing the meal plan is to determine the patient's basic calorie requirements, taking into consideration age, sex, body weight and degree of activity. The calorific intake for an adult should be around 30 calories per kilogram of ideal weight. This should be increased to around 35 to 45 calories/kg for children and adults who are active (have heavy jobs or are involved in sports on a regular basis). Obese patients should reduce their calorie intake to 15 to 25 calories/kg. Of the total calorie intake, 15 to 20 per cent should come from protein intake, and 50 to 60 per cent from carbohydrates. The remainder of the calorie intake should come from fats.

Carbohydrates. The carbohydrate intake should be derived from complex sugars (polysaccharides). Carbohydrates should be distributed over the course of the day in order to prevent any extreme fluctuations in blood glucose levels. If a normal diet cannot be taken, the carbohydrate intake must be made up through carbohydrate exchanges. The diabetic patient must be made aware of how much carbohydrate is in each exchange, and adjust their intake accordingly.

Fat. Fat intake ranges from 0.5 to 1.5 g/kg of ideal body weight. The types of fat should be polyunsaturated fats rather than saturated fats.

Protein. The protein level of 15 to 20 per cent of calories is considered appropriate.

Fibre

Fibre intake in the diet has received much attention over recent years. This is also true of the diabetic diet. Fibre is thought to reduce glucose intolerance. This, in turn, can reduce the risk of long-term complications of diabetes mellitus, as well as the need for exogenous insulin. The benefits of a high-fibre diet that can be seen in a normal diet are also seen in a diabetic diet, i.e., reduced constipation and reduction of cholesterol levels. There are also some complications of which the diabetic patient must be aware; for example, increased bowel movement may lead to mineral deficiency.

Dietary Adaptation

Each individual diabetic patient must adapt their diet to reflect their individual circumstances. This must take into account their weight, occupation, sports activities, race and age. The British Diabetic Association has produced guidelines for dietary exchanges and adaptations, as well as a comprehensive recipe book specifically for diabetic patients.

Health Teaching About Diet

Each diabetic patient must have an intensive education programme about their diet. Their dietary control is the greatest single factor in controlling diabetes. There are now many food producers who publish the contents of their products, as well as manufacture specific products suitable for diabetic patients. The dietician's help is invaluable in this area of patient care. They will formulate a specific diet plan, and will follow-up the patient on an outpatient basis in order to monitor the patient's ability to maintain good dietary control.

Exercise

The amount of exercise the patient carries out will affect the control of diabetes. The patient must be aware of the adaptations that have to made to the diet and insulin intake (if required) when they are about to undergo increased exercise. The individual will soon learn how to make such adaptations to prevent hypoglycaemic attacks. They can either increase their calorie intake or reduce the insulin intake.

Management of Type I Diabetes Mellitus

Type I diabetes mellitus can present as an emergency situation. Therefore the first aim of management in such a situation is to preserve life. The treatment will depend on the patient's condition on presentation. Insulin will be required if blood glucose levels are elevated. Initially, this can be given intravenously, and then subcutaneously as the emergency is resolved. Correction of fluid and electrolyte imbalance is also essential. Future control is maintained by diet and exogenous insulin therapy.

Insulin Therapy

Exogenous insulin is required when an individual has insufficient or no endogenous insulin production from the beta cells of the islets of Langerhans. There are three main sources of exogenous insulin. These are traditionally pork and bovine pancreases and, more recently, semi-synthetic insulin. The latter is biosynthetic human insulin that has been produced using genetically altered bacteria. Insulins are either long- or short-acting. There are also some combination insulins available.

Routes of Insulin Administration
Insulin can be given intravenously if blood glucose levels need to be reduced over a relatively short period of time. Subcutaneous injections can be given in one of two ways: (1) intermittent injections can be given daily, twice daily or before each meal, according to the patient's blood glucose levels; or (2) a continuous subcutaneous infusion of insulin can be given, which delivers a constant stream of insulin that can be altered before meals to deliver extra insulin.

Regulation of Insulin Doses
The amount of insulin required initially will depend on the patient's blood glucose levels. The ultimate is to provide regular doses of insulin to maintain a stable blood glucose

level. This varies from one patient to another. It may be achieved in one patient by one injection in the morning of a mixed insulin; in another patient, it may involve an injection before both breakfast and the evening meal of a short-acting and a long-acting insulin. The 'honeymoon period' can last for several months; it occurs when the administration of exogenous insulin stimulates the production of endogenous insulin, and makes the control of blood glucose levels very difficult. It can be an extremely frustrating time for the patient.

Table 17.3 shows the types of insulin available and their duration of action.

Patient Education: Self-Administration of Insulin

As soon as the need for insulin has been established, and the initial period of control has been implemented, a patient education programme is essential. The patient will require support and information about every area of diabetes. The self-injection of insulin is the factor that worries most newly diagnosed diabetics.

Objectives of Patient Education
On completion of an education programme for insulin-dependent diabetic patients, the patient must be able to:

● Identify the type of insulin to be used.
● Show an awareness of the mode of action.
● Show an awareness of the time scales involved for the onset of action and the period of effectiveness.
● Appreciate the differences between U-100 syringes and normal syringes.
● Demonstrate an ability to charge the syringe with the appropriate insulin and in the prescribed dose.

Table 17.3 *Types of insulins and their actions*

Name	Source	Onset of action	Duration of action
Short-acting			
Actrapid	Porcine	30 mins	8 to 10 hours
Velosulin	Porcine	30 mins	8 to 10 hours
Long-acting			
Monotard	Human	2 hours	16 to 24 hours
Insulutard	Porcine	1 hour	16 to 24 hours
Ultratard	Bovine	4 hours	36 hours
Combination/mixed			
Mixtard	Porcine/human	30 mins	16 to 24 hours
Initard	Human	30 mins	16 to 24 hours

- Select an appropriate site for the injection of insulin.
- Appreciate the need to rotate injection sites.
- Demonstrate the ability to monitor accurately blood glucose levels.
- Adjust insulin doses as a result of lowered or elevated blood glucose levels.

Teaching Self-Injection

The expected outcome is for the patient to safely self-administer the correct dose of insulin into an appropriate site.

The following method is taught:

- Collect together the necessary equipment (insulin, U-100 syringe, alcohol wipe).
- Clean the rubber bung over the top of the vial of insulin with the alcohol wipe.
- Insert the needle of the U-100 syringe (needle is already attached to these particular syringes) and charge the syringe with the prescribed dose of insulin.
- Choose the appropriate site for injection.
- Inject the needle into the subcutaneous tissue. If the patient is thin, then advise pinching the skin between two fingers and injecting the insulin into the skin fold.
- Wipe the injection site with some cotton wool to aid the absorption of the insulin.

Recommended sites for insulin injection are shown in Figure 17.1.

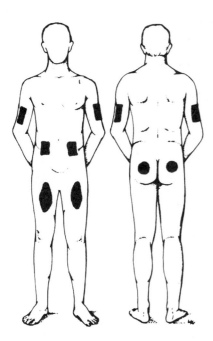

Figure 17.1 Recommended sites for insulin injection. (From *Keeping Well With Diabetes*, Novo Nordisk Pharmaceuticals Ltd.)

Rotation of Injection Sites

It is essential that the sites of injection are rotated on a daily basis. This aids absorption of insulin and helps to maintain skin integrity. Some patients may prefer to use the same site as it becomes less painful over time.

Some sites may also become less effective in the absorption of insulin and therefore control may become a problem. The main danger of not rotating the site is that lipohypertrophy will develop around the site. This will affect the absorption of the insulin, and episodes of hyperglycaemia may ensue.

Problems With Insulin Injection

Local Allergic Reactions

A local allergic reaction in the form of redness, swelling, tenderness and induration, or a wheal may appear at the site of injection. These reactions usually occur during the beginning stages of therapy and disappear with continued use of insulin. These allergic reactions are becoming less frequent because of the increased purity of insulins. The doctor may prescribe an antihistamine to be taken one hour before the injection if such a local reaction occurs.

Systemic Allergic Reactions

These reactions are very rare. If a systemic reaction occurs then desensitization is required. This may simply mean a change from porcine to human insulins.

Insulin Lipodystrophy

Lipodystrophy refers to a localized disturbance of fat metabolism, in the form of either lipoatrophy or lipohypertrophy. These reactions occur at the site of injection and may appear separately, in combination or in succession, in the same patient. Insulin-induced atrophy is loss of subcutaneous fat and appears as slight dimpling or more serious pitting of subcutaneous fat. It occurs most commonly in women and children. The use of U-100 insulin, which is 99 per cent pure, has almost eliminated this disfiguring complication. Lipoatrophy is treated by injection of purified insulin into the periphery of the lipoatrophic area.

Lipohypertrophy is the development of fibrofatty masses at the injection site; it occurs more often in children and adult men and is caused by the repeated use of an injection site. If insulin is injected into scarred areas, the absorption is irregular and the action of the insulin unpredictable. This is one reason why the rotation of injection sites is so important. The patient should avoid injecting insulin into these areas until the hypertrophy disappears.

Insulin Oedema

A generalized retention of fluid is sometimes seen after near-normal blood glucose levels are suddenly established in a patient who has had prolonged hyperglycaemia.

Monitoring for Glucose and Ketones

In order to maintain an effective control of diabetes, the patient must learn how to monitor glucose levels. This can be achieved in two ways:

1. Monitoring blood glucose levels.
2. Monitoring the presence of glucose and ketones in urine.

Monitoring blood glucose provides a more accurate picture of diabetic control.

Monitoring Blood Glucose Levels

1. Wash hands with soap and warm water, and dry thoroughly. Remove blood glucose test stick from tube and place on a clean, dry surface. Replace cap on tube immediately.
2. Prick the side of a fingertip with a lancet. Squeeze finger to obtain a large, suspended drop of blood.
3. Apply drop of blood to cover test pads on test stick. Do not spread or smear blood. Do not allow skin to touch test pads. Start timing.
4. *Time is important.* Leave blood on test pads for 60 seconds (use the second hand of a watch).
5. Hold test stick against a flat surface. The wipe away blood with clean cotton wool. Wipe twice more, each time using a clean area of cotton wool.
6. Wait for a further 60 seconds before comparing the test stick with the colour blocks on the tube. The colours remain stable, giving ample time to read or re-check results.
7. If the *upper* pad remains a buff colour, the blood glucose level is below 9 mmol/l. Compare only the *lower* (blue) pad on the test stick with the *lower* (blue) colour block on the tube to read the blood glucose level.
8. If the *upper* pad on the test stick changes to green, the blood glucose level is above 9 mmol/l. Compare only the *upper* (green) pad on the test stick with the *upper* (green) colour block on the tube to read the blood glucose level.
9. If the result after two minutes is above 17 mmol/l, the reaction is not complete. Wait for a further 60 seconds and then read again, using only the *upper* (green) colour block on the tube.
10. Record result immediately, in order to keep an accurate record for future reference (from *The BM-Test®* *1–44 Pocket Guide*, Boehringer Mannheim UK (Diagnostics and Biochemicals) Ltd, Bell Lane, Lewes, Sussex).

Haemoglobin A₁ (Glycosylated Haemoglobin A₁c)

At the present time, the haemoglobin A₁ test is carried out only in a laboratory and not at home. This test allows assessment of blood glucose levels over the four-week period before the date of the sample. When blood glucose levels are elevated, a glucose molecule attaches itself to haemoglobin in a red blood cell. The longer the glucose in the blood remains above normal, the more glycosylated haemoglobins form. This complex (the haemoglobin attached to the glucose) is permanent and lasts for the life of the red blood cell, approximately 120 days. If near-normal blood glucose levels are maintained, with only occasional rises in blood glucose, the overall value will not be greatly elevated. However, if the pattern of blood glucose values is consistently high, then the test result will also be elevated. The normal values vary from one laboratory to another, but a value of 6 to 8 mmol/l is considered within the 'normal' range. Values within the normal range indicate consistently near-normal blood glucose levels, a goal easier to attain for insulin-dependent patients who monitor blood glucose levels themselves, particularly if they use multiple insulin injections or insulin pump (continuous subcutaneous insulin injection) therapy.

Urine Testing for Glucose

Urine testing for glucose may be adequate for non-insulin-dependent diabetics, because their diabetes is fairly stable. However, many clinicians now feel that blood glucose monitoring in these patients is indicated. It has been found to be especially useful in the obese type II patient because of increased motivation to lose weight after seeing the daily blood glucose levels drop in response to diet therapy. Urine tests do not provide enough accuracy for the insulin-dependent patient, who must adjust insulin doses based on accurate test results in order to maintain near-normal blood glucose levels. Urine testing for glucose should be performed by insulin-dependent patients who cannot, for some reason, use blood glucose testing, because it can approximate levels of blood glucose.

The procedure for monitoring glucose in urine is as follows (from Day, 1986):

1. Collect the urine in a clean receptacle.
2. Draw the urine into a dropper and place five drops into the test tube.
3. Rinse the dropper.
4. Draw water into the dropper and add 10 drops to the test tube.
5. Drop one 'Clinitest' tablet into the test tube. Observe as the chemical reaction takes place. *Do not shake the test tube.*
6. *After the reaction is complete, wait 15 seconds and then compare the colour of the solution with the colour code chart.*

Urine Testing for Ketones

The procedure is as follows:

1. Place 'Acetest' tablet on a piece of blotting paper.
2. Place one drop of urine on top of the tablet.
3. Allow colour change to take place.
4. Compare result on colour chart.

Insulin Delivery Systems

The delivery of insulin is principally by subcutaneous injection. In an emergency it may be given intravenously. Other systems include pumps and several devices that will deliver small quantities of insulin as required.

Pump Systems

These devices can be attached to the patient's waist belt. A subcutaneous cannula is inserted into the patient and the pump delivers a regulated dose of insulin over a 24-hour period. It also has the ability to deliver a bolus dose before a meal.

Insulin Pen System

An insulin pen is similar in size to an ordinary pen, and can deliver a set amount of insulin by depressing a plunger. This allows the patient to carry around the insulin in a pocket, thus making the use of a syringe obsolete. This system is less cumbersome than the pump delivery system.

Management of Type II Diabetes Mellitus

Generally, type II diabetes mellitus is managed by using the diet or a combination of diet and oral hypoglycaemic agents. In cases where the control of type II diabetes is difficult, insulin may have to be given to regain the control previously maintained. There are two main types of oral hypoglycaemic agents: (1) sulphonureas and (2) biguanides. Sulphonureas work by stimulating the beta cells of the islets of Langerhans, whereas the mode of action of biguanides is to reduce the absorption of carbohydrates from the gastrointestinal tract. They are also thought to increase the glucose uptake in peripheral tissues. Table 17.4 lists oral hypoglycaemic agents.

Table 17.4 *Oral hypoglycaemic agents*

Name	Doses
Sulphonureas	
Tolbutamide	0.5 to 2 g
Chlorpropamide	100 to 375 mg
Glipizide	2.5 to 40 mg
Glibenclamide	2.5 to 15 mg
Biguanides	
Metformin	1 to 2 g

ACUTE COMPLICATIONS OF DIABETES

The main acute complications associated with diabetes are hypoglycaemia and severe hyperglycaemia. The hyperglycaemic states can lead to ketoacidosis or hyperglycaemic, hyperosmolar, nonketotic coma.

Hypoglycaemia ('Insulin Reactions')

Hypoglycaemia occurs when the blood glucose levels fall below 2.75 mmol/l. It can be caused by too much insulin, too little food or an excess of physical activity. It commonly occurs before meals or in the early morning.

When the blood glucose falls rapidly, the sympathetic nervous system is stimulated to produce adrenalin, causing sweating, tremor, tachycardia, palpitation and nervousness. When the blood glucose falls slowly, there is depression of the central nervous system, resulting in headache, lightheadedness, confusion, emotional changes, memory lapses, numbness of the lips and tongue, slurred speech, inco-ordination, staggering gait, double vision, drowsiness, convulsions and eventually coma. Because the brain depends on glucose for its energy supply, as hypoglycaemia progresses, brain function deteriorates. Permanent central nervous system damage may result from prolonged hypoglycaemia.

The combination of symptoms varies considerably in different patients and in the same patient at different times.

- Every patient taking insulin should be familiar with the warning symptoms so that sugar can be taken promptly.
- Hypoglycaemia must be treated promptly, because sustained hypoglycemia can lead to convulsions or coma and death. When the first warning symptoms appear, the patient should take some form of simple, fast-acting sugar orally: orange juice, sugar, glucose tablets or a soft drink containing sugar. If the symptoms persist for 10 to 15 minutes, the snack should be repeated. If it is more than an hour until the next meal, the patient should also eat a complex carbohydrate and protein.
- Every patient taking insulin should carry glucose tablets so that they can correct any hypoglycaemia as quickly as possible.

Prevention and Patient Education

Hypoglycaemia is prevented by following a regular pattern and timetable for eating, administering insulin and engaging in daily exercise. Between-meal and bedtime snacks are often needed to counteract the maximum insulin effect. In general, the patient should cover the time of peak activity of insulin by eating a snack and by taking additional food when engaging in an increased level of physical activity. Routine glucose tests are performed so that changing insulin requirements may be anticipated and adjusted.

Because unexpected hypoglycemia may occur, all patients treated with insulin should wear an identification bracelet or some form of documentation indicating that they have diabetes.

If the patient is conscious then hypoglycaemia can be rectified by getting the patient to take some oral glucose. If the patient is unconscious then intravenous glucose must be administered. This is in the form of a solution of 50 per cent glucose; 50 ml is delivered in the first instance. Severe hypoglycaemic states that are not treated successfully must be managed by the intravenous injection of glucagon, which stimulates glyconeogenesis in the liver.

Diabetic Ketoacidosis and Coma

Diabetic ketoacidosis is caused by an absence or inadequate amount of insulin, which results in hyperglycaemia and leads to a series of biochemical disorders. The altered physiology is the result of insulin deficiency affecting many aspects of the metabolism óf carbohydrate, protein and fat. As a result, the amount of glucose entering the cells is reduced, and fat is metabolized instead of carbohydrate. Free fatty acids are mobilized from adipose tissue. Liver oxidases act upon these fatty acids to produce ketone bodies. The ketone bodies escape into the blood, and metabolic acidosis results, with lowering of serum bicarbonate, PCO_2 and pH. The overall clinical picture is one of hyperglycaemia, water and electrolyte loss, acidaemia and coma.

Causes

Ketoacidosis may be precipitated by failure to take insulin, by insufficient insulin intake or by resistance to insulin. It may be caused by infection, by physiological stresses such as acute illness, surgery, trauma, pregnancy and/or by emotional stresses that reduce the effectiveness of the available insulin.

Anti-insulin factors (growth hormone, glucagon, cortisol) are released during stress and may play a part in the development of ketoacidosis. Ketoacidosis occurs more commonly in insulin-dependent diabetes. It is a serious complication, with a mortality rate ranging from 5 to 10 per cent.

Clinical Features

The clinical features occur as a result of changes in body fluid, electrolytes and acid–base status. Early features are polyuria (excessive urination), polyphagia (excessive appetite) and polydipsia (excessive thirst). Osmotic diuresis causes water loss (dehydration) and electrolyte depletion.

As the patient becomes more dehydrated, oliguria (diminished urination) develops. Malaise and visual changes may be noted by the patient. Headache, muscle aches and abdominal pain are frequent complaints, as are nausea and vomiting. If infection has precipitated the ketoacidosis, fever may be present. The patient's respiratory rate increases to compensate for acidosis. Coma and severe acidosis are ushered in with Kussmaul breathing (very deep, but not laboured, respirations) and a sweetish odour of the breath.

The patient is drowsy and soon becomes comatose. The blood glucose is elevated, the serum bicarbonate and the blood pH are decreased, the blood urea is increased and the plasma ketone is strongly positive. The urine is strongly positive for acetone. The patient's condition is serious at this stage, but recovery can be anticipated after prompt and vigorous treatment with insulin and intravenous fluids.

Management

The immediate goals in the management of ketoacidosis are:

1. To restore carbohydrate, protein and fat metabolism.
2. To reverse hypovolaemia.
3. To correct electrolyte imbalance.

These can be achieved by:

● Administration of intravenous insulin. This must be monitored closely using a volumetric pump to ensure accurate dosage.
● Administration of intravenous fluids—isotonic saline with added electrolytes (e.g. potassium) as required.

The patient who presents with diabetic ketoacidosis requires a high level of nursing intervention and monitoring. The routine care for an unconscious patient should be delivered, paying particular attention to the following areas:

1. The patient's blood glucose levels should be monitored one- to two-hourly.
2. The administration of intravenous insulin according to the prescription should be monitored.
3. Intravenous fluids should be administered according to prescription.
4. Fluid intake and output should be recorded accurately.
5. The patient should be assessed for evidence of fluid overload.
6. Vital signs should be monitored one- to two-hourly (temperature, pulse, respiration and blood pressure).
7. The patient's level of consciousness should be monitored using the Glasgow Coma Scale every one or two hours.

Consciousness should be restored and metabolic disturbances corrected within 12 to 24 hours. After the acute problem is corrected, the patient is regulated as described earlier. The precipitating cause of the coma should be determined to prevent a recurrence.

Hyperglycaemic, Hyperosmolar Nonketotic Diabetic Coma

This metabolic condition is characterized by hyperglycaemia with no significant level of ketoacidosis. The condition is seen most often in elderly, non-insulin-dependent diabetic patients, who are treated with oral hypoglycaemic agents. Polydipsia and polyuria are characteristic symptoms, with fluid and electrolyte imbalances. The patient's persistent hyperglycaemia causes an osmotic diuresis, resulting in loss of water and electrolytes. To maintain osmotic equilibrium, water shifts from the intracellular fluid space to the extracellular fluid space. Hypernatraemia and increasing hyperosmolality occur with glycosuria and dehydration.

Management

The objective of management is to correct the volume depletion and hyperosmolar state. Specific care of the patient is the same as that of the patient with diabetic ketoacidosis. A search is then made for the precipitating cause.

LONG-TERM COMPLICATIONS OF DIABETES

Patients who have longstanding diabetes may develop long-term complications. These are described as the diabetic-opathies, and include: diabetic retinopathy, nephropathy, neuropathy and angiopathy (see Table 17.2).

Foot and Leg Problems in Diabetes

Diabetic neuropathy most commonly manifests itself in the lower extremities. Pain and paraesthesia are the outstanding features. The pain has been described as dull or aching, cramping, burning or crushing.

The paraesthesias have been described as sensations of tingling or burning, or of coldness and numbness. Because of these varied discomforts, it is quite common for the patient to be depressed and irritable and to suffer from anorexia.

Loss of sensation can lead to infection, gangrene and amputation. The patient may be unaware of a blister, a protruding nail in a shoe, a burn from an electric blanket or other injury. Instruction and reinforcement of previous learning about foot care are vital.

Management. It is essential that diabetic patients seek the services of a chiropodist. They must be given expert advice on foot care and foot wear. Any lesions that appear on the foot must be treated quickly and effectively in order to prevent further problems, which may lead to amputation.

SPECIAL PROBLEMS IN DIABETES

Stress

The control of diabetes can be affected dramatically by stress. Stressors are many and diverse. The affect of stressors varies between each individual patient. Stress not only increases glyconeogenesis, but reduces the effectiveness of insulin. The overall result is an increase in blood glucose levels.

The psychological features of stress also affect diabetic control. Emotional stress may alter normal eating habits and exercise regimes. A loss of incentive to maintain control may also result from emotional disturbances.

The Diabetic Patient Undergoing Surgery

Because of the possibility of generalized vascular disease, decreased resistance to infection and changing insulin requirements due to stress, the patient must be followed very closely at the time of surgery. Surgical stress aggravates hyperglycaemia because of an increased secretion of adrenaline and glucocorticoids. The metabolic stress of anaesthesia also accentuates problems of hyperglycaemia and ketosis. In addition, the patient's normal schedule of food intake, which is the foundation of diabetic treatment, is interrupted.

Preoperative Care

All preoperative care should be carried out as described in Chapter 2. In the preoperative period, the aim is to have the diabetes well controlled and to correct any problems of hydration and electrolyte imbalance. The greatest danger is hypoglycaemia. During the fasting period the patient is given an intravenous infusion of 5 per cent dextrose to provide the necessary carbohydrate. A percentage of the insulin is given to control blood glucose levels.

Postoperative Care

All postoperative care must be given as described in Chapter 2. Nutrition is maintained by intravenous dextrose. Following surgery, the diabetes may intensify and become difficult to control. Healing may be delayed due to vascular disease, poor circulation and altered metabolism. A higher incidence of vascular complications (myocardial infarction, stroke) may occur due to increased incidence of atherosclerosis.

Infections

There appears to be a correlation between diabetes and susceptibility to infection, perhaps because of depleted host defences and higher than normal glucose concentration in the tissues. High blood glucose may impair the ability of granulocytes to carry out a number of vital functions. Hyperglycaemia also depresses leucocyte phagocytosis.

Infections are more serious in diabetes because resistance to infection is decreased by hyperglycaemia, and because diabetes becomes temporarily more severe in the presence of infection. Infections in diabetes are exacerbated by dehydration, insulin antagonism, impaired phagocytosis and neuropathy. Infection is a common precipitating cause of acute complications, such as ketoacidosis.

The extremities may be vulnerable to infection because of diminished arterial circulation, which lowers resistance to bacterial invasion and local injury. Cellulitis may spread rapidly. Fungal infections between the toes may produce fissures that provide further portals of entry for bacteria. Infections of the foot can lead to gangrene, with loss of toes or foot and lower leg.

Dental Disease

Dental disorders are exacerbated in the diabetic patient. Any dental disease can be either the cause or the result of poor diabetic control. Continued infection can interfere with blood glucose maintenance. Poor dentition may lead to chewing problems, which may interfere with proper nutrition, the cornerstone of diabetic control.

Premenstrual Syndrome

The changing levels of oestrogen and progesterone can cause premenstrual syndrome. In women with diabetes, blood glucose levels begin to rise approximately five days before menstruation. Symptoms include bloating, headache, food cravings, anxiety, mood swings, irritability and depression. The frequency of blood glucose monitoring should be increased during this period.

▶ NURSING CARE PLAN 17.1: THE PATIENT WITH NON-INSULIN-DEPENDENT DIABETES MELLITUS

Sydney Cohen, aged 54, is overweight and is married with two adult children. He is a Jewish Orthodox shop manager. Mr Cohen has presented with type II diabetes mellitus.

Patient's problems	Expected outcomes	Nursing care	Rationale
1. Due to alteration in metabolism, the patient's nutritional intake is altered	To achieve metabolic control by altering dietary intake and medication	1a. To balance carbohydrate, protein, fat, mineral and vitamin intake b. To adjust calorific intake to attain and maintain ideal body weight c. Food taken at regular intervals throughout a 24-hour period d. Maintain as 'normal' a diet as possible–taking into account the needs of the family as well as the patient's ethnic background e. Increase fibre intake	A balanced diet is essential in the treatment of diabetes mellitus (British Diabetic Association, 1988) Non-insulin-dependent diabetes mellitus can be caused and exacerbated by overweight. Therefore by maintaining ideal body weight a greater control of diabetes may be achieved (Day, 1986) Reducing the number of changes in the patient's diet to a minimum will help to ensure compliance, with minimal upset to the family (British Diabetic Association, 1988)
2. Due to deficiency in endogenous insulin replacement, hypoglycaemic agent is required	To provide a method to reduce blood glucose level	2a. Initially, the patient may require exogenous insulin to reduce blood glucose level b. Thereafter, an oral hypoglycaemic may be more appropriate than insulin	Patient should be given human insulin (i.e. *not pork*) due to ethnic background After the initial hyperglycaemia is brought under control it may be apparent that blood glucose levels may be maintained within normal limits by oral hypoglycaemic agents
3. Due to lack of knowledge of type and action of oral hypoglycaemic agents, the patient must be educated in their use	To provide patient and family with a full explanation of oral hypoglycaemic agents	3a. Discuss the various types of oral hypoglycaemic agents b. Discuss the type that has been prescribed c. Discuss their mode of action d. Discuss the dosages to be taken e. Discuss the timing of the doses f. Discuss the need to take these tablets at all times	By providing the patient with a full explanation of these tablets, the patient will have a fuller understanding of the control of the condition. This, in turn, will increase compliance with treatment and thus reduce the risk of long-term complications

► NURSING CARE PLAN 17.1: THE PATIENT WITH NON-INSULIN-DEPENDENT DIABETES MELLITUS

Patient's problems	Expected outcomes	Nursing care	Rationale
4. Due to lack of knowledge of diabetes mellitus, the patient will be unable to monitor its control	Give a full explanation of diabetes mellitus	4a. Discuss normal physiology b. Discuss normal action of insulin c. Discuss the changes that have taken place that have resulted in diabetes mellitus	Full explanation of normal and altered pathology will enhance patient's understanding of and compliance with treatment
	Monitor control	d. Monitor blood glucose levels e. Teach patient to monitor blood glucose levels	Monitoring of blood glucose gives a direct assessment of the control of diabetes mellitus. Blood glucose levels are a more accurate assessment of control than urine testing
5. Due to microvascular changes, skin integrity is compromised	To maintain skin integrity	5a. Stringent personal hygiene is essential	As the microvascular changes occur, blood flow is impeded. This, in turn, slows down any healing process
6. Due to microvascular changes, the patient's extremeties (in particular the feet) are at risk	To maintain skin integrity of feet	6a. Daily check of feet to assess for any lesions and for infection b. Daily bathing of feet c. Ensure that socks and shoes are well fitting	If great care is not taken to maintain the integrity of skin, then infection may lead to gangrene, which may require amputation. Chiropody care should be sought (Scottish Home and Health Department, 1987)
7. Insufficient knowledge about diabetes mellitus	Become self-regulating; prevent any major metabolic upset; alter lifestyle to take account of the condition	See problems 1 to 6	

► NURSING PROCESS
► THE PATIENT WITH DIABETES

► Nursing Care

The expected outcome of any diabetic control is to achieve metabolic control. The nursing care required will depend on the individual patient's presenting problems and the type of diabetes the patient has. The care of the patient with diabetic ketoacidosis is described earlier. Nursing Care Plan 17.1 is for the patient with non-insulin-dependent diabetes mellitus.

► Assessment

A full assessment must be carried out. Particular attention must be paid to the following areas when assessing a diabetic patient:

● Skin: check groin and axillae areas—moisture supports growth of candida. Check feet for the presence of athlete's foot and other lesions.

● Mouth: check for gum disease, and general state of dentition.
● Eyes: check for infection, e.g., 'weeping' eyes; check general eyesight—need for glasses?
● Cardiovascular assessment: check pulse, blood pressure; assess for signs of cardiac problems.
● Peripheral vascular assessment: check periphery for cool, thin, shiny skin; thick-ridged nails; pulse strength; ulcerations.

BIBLIOGRAPHY

British Diabetic Association (1988) *Dietary Recommendations—A Basic Guide*, BDA, London.

Day, J. L. (1986) *The Diabetes Handbook: Non-Insulin-Dependent Diabetes*, Thorsons, Wellingborough.

Hassan, T. (1985) *A Guide to Medical Endocrinology*, MacMillan, London.

Scottish Home and Health Department (1987) *Report of the Working Group on the Management of Diabetes*, HMSO, London.

FURTHER READING

Books

Ames Educational Services (1982) *An Introduction to Diabetes* (2nd edition), Miles Laboratories (Ames Division), Slough.

British Diabetic Association (1983) *The Diabetic's Handbook*, BDA, London.

Daly, H. (1988) *Diabetes Care: A Problem-Solving Approach*, Heinemann, London.

Day, J. L. (1986) *The Diabetes Handbook: Non-Insulin-Dependent Diabetes*, Thorsons, Wellingborough.

Hillson, R. (1987) *Diabetes: A Beyond-Basics Guide*, Macdonald Optima, London.

Kelleher, D. (1988) *Diabetes*, Routledge & Kegan Paul, London.

Kilo, C. (1987) *Diabetes: The Facts That Let You Regain Control of Your Life*, Wiley, New York.

Shillitoe, R. W. (1988) *Psychology and Diabetes: Psychosocial Factors in Management and Control*, Chapman & Hall, London.

Articles

General

Benn, J. (1989) Conversion, control and complications (even with tightening control), *Practical Diabetes*, Jan/Feb, Vol. 6, No. 1, p. 29.

Bodansky, H. (1989) The natural history of type I (insulin-dependent) diabetes, *Practical Diabetes*, Jan/Feb, Vol. 6, No. 1, p. 7.

Caiger, P. (1985) Monitoring diabetic control in the 1980s, *Midwife, Health Visitor and Community Nurse*, February, Vol. 21, No. 2, p. 56.

Conaglen, J. V. (1989) Diabetic ketoacidosis, *Medicine International*, May, Vol. 65, p. 2713.

Editorial (1986) Hyperkalaemia in diabetic ketoacidosis, *Lancet*, 11 October, Vol. 2, p. 845.

Editorial (1989) Insulin pen: mightier than the syringe? *Lancet*, 11 February, Vol. 1, p. 307.

Editorial (1989) Type 2 diabetes or NIIDM: looking for a better name, *Lancet*, 18 March, Vol. 1, p. 589.

Gatling, W. (1989) Home monitoring of diabetes, *Practical Diabetes*, May/June, Vol. 16, No. 3, p. 100.

Graham, M. (1986) Starting a diabetic clinic, *Practical Diabetes*, May/June, Vol. 3, No. 3, p. 135.

Grenfell, A. (1986) Complications in diabetes, *Maternal and Child Health*, May, Vol. 11, No. 5, p. 167.

Hoghton, M. (1987) Understanding of diabetes mellitus in non-diabetic adults, *Practical Diabetes*, March/April, Vol. 4, No. 2, p. 60.

Huzar, J. G. (1989) The role of diet and drugs, *Registered Nurse*, April, Vol. 52, p. 46.

Jennings, P. (1988) Diabetes: is self-help the answer? *The Professional Nurse*, May, Vol. 3, No. 3, p. 284.

Jones, K. (1989) Factors affecting weight loss in obese type II diabetes: role of the dietician, *Practical Diabetes*, Jan/Feb, Vol. 6, No. 1, p. 18.

Keen, H. (1989) The nature of the diabetic state, *Medicine International*, May, Vol. 65, p. 2672.

McAdams, R. (1986) When diabetes races out of control, *Registered Nurse*, May, Vol. 49, p. 46.

McAughey, D. (1989) All change (human insulin and problems of changeover), *Nursing Standard*, 1 April, Vol. 3, No. 27, p. 30.

Paton, R. (1989) The natural history of type II diabetes, *Practical Diabetes*, Jan/Feb, Vol. 6, No. 1, p. 10.

Reading, S. (1989) Blood glucose monitoring in diabetic control, *The Professional Nurse*, April, Vol. 4, No. 7, p. 354.

Samanta, A. (1986) Management of the acutely ill diabetic patient, *Intensive Care Nursing*, Vol. 1, No. 4, p. 194.

Wales, J. (1989) The natural history of diabetes mellitus, *Practical Diabetes*, Jan/Feb, Vol. 6, No. 1, p. 4.

Watkins, P. (1985) Pros and cons of continuous subcutaneous insulin infusion, *British Medical Journal*, 2 March, Vol. 290, No. 6469, p. 655.

Diabetes and the Adolescent

Alderman, C. (1989) A question of balance (compliance among diabetics), *Nursing Standard*, 1 April, Vol. 3, No. 27, p. 34.

Jenkins, H. (1989) Metabolic control and patient acceptibility in adolescent diabetics using Novopen, *Practical Diabetes*, Jan/Feb, Vol. 6, No. 1, p. 14.

Cardiovascular System

Salonen, J. T. (1989) Non-insulin-dependent diabetes and ischaemic heart disease, *British Medical Journal*, 22 April, Vol. 298, p. 1050.

Stout, R. W. (1989) Macroangiopathy, *Medicine International*, May, Vol. 65, p. 2706.

Diabetes and the Elderly

Thomas, L. (1989) Dealing with diabetes, *Geriatric Nursing and Home Care*, Dec/Jan, p. 14.

Diabetes and Exercise

Macleod, A. (1985) Exercise for diabetics, *Update*, 1 March, Vol. 30, No. 5, p. 468.

Diabetes and the Feet

Masson, E. (1989) Diabetic foot ulcers: do patients know how to protect themselves? *Practical Diabetes*, Jan/Feb, Vol. 6, No. 1, p. 22.

Reddy, P. (1989) Diabetes and incorrectly fitting shoes, *Practical Diabetes*, Jan/Feb, Vol. 6, No. 1, p. 16.

Samanta, A. (1989) Comparison between 'LSB' shoes and 'space' shoes in diabetic foot ulceration, *Practical Diabetes*, Jan/Feb, Vol. 6, No. 1, p. 26.

Drug Therapy

Chan, A. (1988) Pharmacology of oral agents used to treat diabetes mellitus, *Practical Diabetes*, March/April, Vol. 5, No. 2, p. 59.

Drury, M. (1989) Drugs for diabetes, *Practice Nurse*, April, Vol. 1, No. 10, p. 445.

Editorial (1986) Sources of insulin, *Journal of District Nursing*, October, Vol. 5, No. 4, p. 27.

Neuropathy

Macleod, A. F. (1989) Diabetic neuropathy, *Medicine International*, May, Vol. 65, p. 2700.

Obesity

Dunmore, S. (1989) Fat is a hormonal issue, *New Scientist*, 4 March, No. 1654, p. 52.

Jackson, R. (1986) Obesity: its pathogenesis and the doctor–patient relationship, *Practical Diabetes*, May/June, Vol. 3, No. 3, p. 126.

Ophthalmology

Hamilton, A. M. (1989) Diabetic retinopathy, *Medicine International*, May, Vol. 65, p. 2695.

Paediatrics

Schulte, J. (1989) Diabetes mellitus in childhood, *Midwife, Health Visitor and Community Nurse*, April, Vol. 25, No. 4, p. 153.

Transplantation

Editorial (1987) Pancreatic transplantation in diabetes, *Lancet*, 2 May, Vol. 1, p. 1015.

chapter 18

ASSESSMENT AND CARE OF PATIENTS WITH ENDOCRINE DISORDERS

PHYSIOLOGICAL OVERVIEW

The endocrine system consists of organs or groups of cells that release regulatory substances into the bloodstream. It is this property that distinguishes these organs from exocrine glands, which secrete into ducts. The regulatory substances secreted by endocrine glands are called hormones. Hormones regulate metabolic activity by controlling intracellular chemical reactions and transport across the cell membrane. Hormones are secreted by endocrine glands and act on target organs. Figure 18.1 shows the general location of the endocrine glands. Table 18.1 lists the principal hormones, their site of action and their functions.

The concentration of hormones in the bloodstream remains relatively constant. This is achieved by a feedback control system. Figure 18.2 depicts a feedback control mechanism.

The Hypothalamus

The hypothalamus is positioned just above the pituitary gland, which is situated in the hypophyseal fossa (sella turcica) of the sphenoid bone at the base of the brain. The hormones secreted by the hypothalamus stimulate or inhibit the secretion of pituitary hormones.

The Pituitary Gland

The pituitary gland, or the hypophysis, has been referred to as the 'master gland' of the endocrine system. It secretes hormones that, in turn, control the secretion of hormones by other endocrine glands. The pituitary itself is controlled in large part by the hypothalamus, an adjacent area of the brain. The pituitary gland is a round structure about 1.27 cm in diameter located on the inferior aspect of the brain and connected to the hypothalamus by the pituitary stalk. The pituitary gland is divided into anterior, intermediate and posterior lobes.

The hormones secreted by the posterior lobe of the

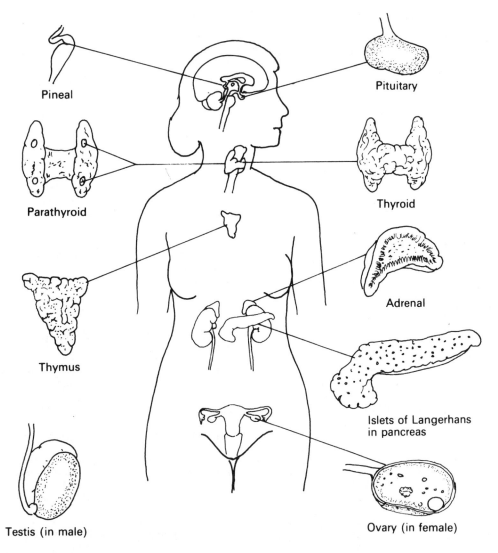

Pineal

Pituitary

Parathyroid

Thyroid

Thymus

Adrenal

Testis (in male)

Islets of Langerhans
in pancreas

Ovary (in female)

Figure 18.1 General location of the major endocrine glands. (Chaffee, E. E. and Greisheimer, E. M. (1980) *Basic Physiology and Anatomy* (4th edition), J. B. Lippincott, Philadelphia.)

pituitary gland are vasopressin (antidiuretic hormone) and oxytocin. These hormones are synthesized in the hypothalamus and travel down the nerve cells that connect the hypothalamus to the posterior pituitary gland, where they are stored. Vasopressin secretion is stimulated by an increase in the osmolality of the blood or by a decrease in blood pressure. The primary function of vasopressin is to control the excretion of water by the kidney. Oxytocin secretion is stimulated during pregnancy and at the time of childbirth. The primary functions of oxytocin are to facilitate milk ejection during lactation and to increase the force of uterine contractions during labour and delivery. Exogenous oxytocin can be used therapeutically to initiate labour.

The hormones of the anterior pituitary gland are follicle-stimulating hormone, luteinizing hormone, prolactin, adrenocorticotropic hormone, thyroid-stimulating hormone and growth hormone. The secretion of each of these major hormones is controlled by releasing factors that are secreted by the hypothalamus. These releasing factors reach the anterior pituitary by way of the bloodstream in a special circulation called the pituitary portal blood system.

The hormones released by the anterior pituitary enter the general circulation and are transported to their target organs. Thyroid-stimulating hormone, adrenocorticotropic hormone, follicle-stimulating hormone and luteinizing hormone have as their main function the release of hormones from other endocrine glands. Prolactin acts on the breast to stimulate milk production. Growth hormone has widespread effects on many target tissues and is discussed below. The other trophic hormones will be discussed in conjunction with their target organs.

Table 18.1 *Principal hormones of the body*

Endocrine organ	Hormonal secretion	Site of action	Function
Hypothalamus	Releasing factors	Anterior pituitary	Release of most pituitary hormones
	Inhibiting factor	Anterior pituitary	Prevention of prolactin, and growth hormone secretion
Anterior pituitary	Growth hormone (GH)	All tissues	Stimulates body growth and certain metabolic processes
	Adrenocorticotrophic hormone (ACTH)	Adrenal cortex	Stimulates corticosteroid production
	Thyrotrophic hormone (TSH)	Thyroid	Stimulates thyroid hormone production
	Gonadotrophins:		
	Follicle-stimulating hormone (FSH)	Ovary follicle	Ripening of follicle
		Testis	Formation of sperms
	Luteinizing hormone (LH)	Ovary follicle	Ovulation and the formation of the corpus luteum
		Testis (Leydig cells)	Testosterone production
	Prolactin	Pregnancy developed breast	Milk formation
Posterior pituitary	Vasopressin or antidiuretic hormone (ADH)	Renal tubules	Tubular absorption of water
	Oxytocin	Uterus	Contraction of pregnant uterus
		Breast after pregnancy	Expulsion of milk
Thyroid	Thyroxine and tri-iodothyronine	All tissues	Speeds metabolic rate
	Calcitonin	Bone	Maintenance of serum calcium
Parathyroid	Parathyroid (PTH) hormone	Bone, renal tubules	Maintenance of serum calcium
Adrenal cortex	Hydrocortisone	All tissues	Carbohydrate, fat and protein metabolism
	Aldosterone	Renal tubules	Sodium, potassium and water balance
Adrenal medulla	Adrenaline and noradrenaline	Adrenergic receptors	Controls circulatory, smooth muscle and metabolic activities
Pancreas			
Beta cells	Insulin	Most tissues	Carbohydrate, fat and protein metabolism
Alpha cells	Glucagon	Liver	Carbohydrate metabolism

(Source: Lewis, J.G., The Endocrine System, Churchill Livingstone, Edinburgh.)

Growth Hormone

Growth hormone, also referred to as somatotropin, is a protein hormone that increases protein synthesis in many tissues, increases the breakdown of fatty acids in adipose tissue and increases the glucose levels in the blood. These actions of somatotropin are essential for normal growth, although other hormones, such as thyroid hormone and insulin, are required as well. The secretion of growth

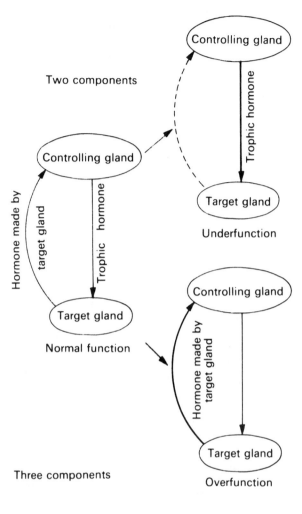

Two components

Controlling gland

Controlling gland

Trophic hormone

Target gland

Underfunction

Hormone made by target gland

Trophic hormone

Target gland

Normal function

Controlling gland

Hormone made by target gland

Target gland

Overfunction

Three components

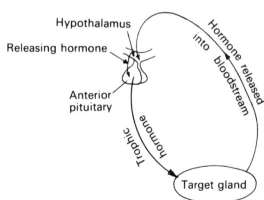

Hypothalamus

Releasing hormone

Anterior pituitary

Hormone released into bloodstream

Trophic hormone

Target gland

Figure 18.2 A feedback control mechanism.

hormone is increased by stress, exercise and low blood sugar. The half-time of growth hormone activity in the blood is 20 to 30 minutes. It is largely inactivated in the liver. If secretion of growth hormone is insufficient during childhood, generalized limited growth and dwarfism result. Conversely, oversecretion during childhood results in gigantism, with a person reaching seven or even eight feet in height. Excess growth hormone in adults results in deformities of bone and soft tissue and enlargement of viscera (acromegaly) but no increase in height.

Abnormal Pituitary Function

Abnormalities of pituitary function are caused by oversecretion or undersecretion of any of the hormones produced or released by the gland. Abnormalities of the posterior and anterior portions of the gland may occur independently. Oversecretion (hypersecretion) most commonly involves adrenocorticotropic hormone or growth hormone, resulting in the conditions known as Cushing's disease or acromegaly, respectively. Undersecretion (hyposecretion) commonly involves all of the anterior pituitary hormones and is termed panhypopituitarism. In this condition, the thyroid gland, the adrenal cortex and the gonads atrophy owing to loss of the trophic hormones. The most common disorder related to posterior lobe dysfunction is diabetes insipidus, a condition in which abnormally large volumes of dilute urine are excreted as a result of deficient production of vasopressin.

The Thyroid Gland

The thyroid gland is a butterfly-shaped organ located in the lower neck anterior to the trachea. It consists of two lateral lobes connected by an isthmus. The gland is approximately 5 cm long and 3 cm wide and weighs about 30 g. The blood flow to the thyroid, per gram of gland tissue, is very high (about 5 ml/min/g of thyroid), approximately five times the blood flow to the liver. This reflects the high metabolic activity of the thyroid gland. The thyroid gland produces three different hormones: thyroxine (T_4) and tri-iodothyronine (T_3), which are referred to collectively as thyroid hormone, and calcitonin.

Thyroid Hormone

Thyroid hormone is composed of two separate hormones made in the thyroid gland, thyroxine (T_4) and tri-iodothyronine (T_3). These hormones are amino acids that have the unique property of containing iodine molecules bound to the amino acid structure. Thyroxine (T_4) contains four iodine atoms in each molecule, while tri-iodothyronine (T_3) contains only three. These hormones are synthesized and stored bound to a glycoprotein called thyroglobulin in the cells of the thyroid gland until needed for release into the bloodstream.

Iodine Uptake and Metabolism

Iodine is essential to the thyroid gland for synthesis of its hormones. In fact, the major use of iodine in the body is by the thyroid and the major derangement in iodine deficiency is alteration of thyroid function. Iodide is ingested in the diet and absorbed into the blood in the gastrointestinal tract. The thyroid gland is extremely efficient in taking up iodide from the blood and concentrating it within the cells. There, iodide ions are converted to iodine molecules, which react with tyrosine (one of the common amino acids) to form the thyroid hormones.

Regulation of Thyroid Function

The secretion of thyrotropin, or thyroid-stimulating hormone, by the pituitary gland controls the rate of thyroid hormone release. In turn, the release of thyroid-stimulating hormone is determined by the level of thyroid hormones in the blood. If thyroid hormone concentration in the blood decreases, release of thyroid-stimulating hormone increases, which causes increased output of triiodothyronine (T_3) and thyroxine (T_4). This is an example of feedback control. Thyrotropin-releasing hormone, secreted by the hypothalamus, exerts a modulating influence on the release of thyroid-stimulating hormone from the pituitary. Environmental factors, such as a fall in temperature, may lead to increased secretion of thyrotropin-releasing hormone and, thereby, result in elevated secretion of thyroid hormones.

Function of Thyroid Hormones

The primary function of the thyroid hormones triiodothyronine and thyroxine is to control the cellular metabolic activity. These hormones serve as a general pacemaker by accelerating metabolic processes. The effects on the metabolic rate are frequently produced by increasing the level of specific enzymes that contribute to oxygen consumption and altering the responsiveness of tissues to other hormones. The thyroid hormones influence cell replication and are important in brain development. The presence of adequate thyroid hormone is also necessary for normal growth. The thyroid hormones, through their widespread effects on cellular metabolism, influence every major organ system.

Calcitonin

Calcitonin, or thyrocalcitonin, is another important hormone secreted by the thyroid gland. Its secretion is not controlled by thyroid-stimulating hormone. It is secreted by the thyroid gland in response to high plasma levels of calcium, and it reduces the plasma level by increasing calcium deposition in bone.

Abnormalities of Thyroid Function

Inadequate secretion of thyroid hormone during fetal and neonatal development will result in stunted physical and mental growth (cretinism), owing to general depression of body metabolic activity. In the adult, hypothyroidism (myxoedema) is manifested by lethargy, mental lassitude and generalized slowing of body functions. Oversecretion of thyroid hormones (hyperthyroidism) is manifested by

greatly increased metabolic rate. Many of the other characteristics of hyperthyroid patients result from the increased response to circulating catecholamines (adrenaline and noradrenaline). Hypothyroidism and hyperthyroidism are discussed in detail in a later section of this chapter. Oversecretion of thyroid hormones is usually associated with an enlarged thyroid gland (goitre). Goitre also commonly occurs in the presence of iodide deficiency. In this latter condition, lack of iodide results in low levels of circulating thyroid hormones, which causes increased release of thyroid-stimulating hormone; the elevated thyroid-stimulating hormone causes overproduction of thyroglobulin and hypertrophy of the thyroid gland. Euthyroid refers to thyroid hormone production that is within normal limits.

The Parathyroid Gland

The parathyroid glands, normally four in number, are situated in the neck, embedded in the posterior aspect of the thyroid gland. These small glands are easily overlooked and can be removed accidentally at the time of thyroid surgery. Inadvertent surgical removal is the most common cause of hypoparathyroidism.

Parathormone, the protein hormone from the parathyroid glands, regulates calcium and phosphorus metabolism. Increased secretion of parathormone results in increased calcium absorption from the kidney, the intestine and bones, thereby raising the blood calcium level. Some actions of this hormone are increased by the presence of vitamin D. Parathormone also tends to lower the blood phosphorus level. Excess parathormone can result in markedly elevated levels of serum calcium, a potentially life-threatening situation. When the product of serum calcium and serum phosphorus becomes high, calcium phosphate may precipitate in various organs of the body and cause tissue calcification.

The output of parathormone is regulated by the serum level of ionized calcium. Increased serum calcium results in decreased parathormone secretion, forming a feedback system.

The Adrenal Glands

There are two adrenal glands in the human, each attached to the upper portion of a kidney. Each adrenal gland is, in reality, two endocrine glands. The adrenal medulla at the centre of the gland secretes catecholamines, while the outer portion of the gland, the adrenal cortex, secretes corticosteroids.

Adrenal Medulla

The adrenal medulla functions as part of the autonomic nervous system. Stimulation of preganglionic sympathetic nerve fibres, which travel directly to the cells of the medulla, causes release of the catecholamine hormones adrenaline and noradrenaline. About 90 per cent of the secretion of the human adrenal medulla is adrenalin. Catecholamines regulate metabolic pathways to promote catabolism of stored fuels to meet calorie needs from endogenous sources. The major effects of adrenaline release are involved in preparation to meet a challenge (fight-or-flight response). Secretion of adrenaline causes decreased blood flow to tissues that are not needed in emergency situations, such as the gastrointestinal tract, and causes increased blood flow to those tissues that are important for effective fight or flight, such as cardiac and skeletal muscle. Catecholamines also induce release of free fatty acids, increase the basal metabolic rate and elevate the level of blood sugar.

Adrenal Cortex

The three kinds of steroid hormones produced by the adrenal cortex are glucocorticoids, the prototype of which is hydrocortisone; mineralocorticoids, mainly aldosterone; and sex hormones, mainly androgens (male sex hormones).

Glucocorticoids. The glucocorticoids are given their name because they have an important influence on glucose metabolism; increased hydrocortisone secretion results in elevated blood sugar levels. However, the glucocorticoids have major effects on the metabolism of almost all organs of the body. Glucocorticoids are secreted from the adrenal cortex in response to the release of adrenocorticotropic hormone from the anterior lobe of the pituitary gland. This system represents an example of negative feedback. The presence of glucocorticoids in the blood inhibits the release of corticotropin-releasing factor from the hypothalamus and also inhibits adrenocorticotropic hormone secretion from the pituitary. The resultant decrease in adrenocorticotropic hormone secretion causes diminished release of glucocorticoids from the adrenal cortex. A functioning adrenal cortex is necessary for life, although survival is possible by appropriate replacement with exogenous adrenocortical hormones.

The glucocorticoids are frequently administered to inhibit the inflammatory response to tissue injury and suppress allergic manifestations. Toxic effects of glucocorticoids include possible development of diabetes, osteoporosis, peptic ulcer, increased protein breakdown resulting in muscle wasting and poor wound healing, and redistribution of body fat. The presence of large amounts of exogenously administered glucocorticoids in the blood inhibits release of adrenocorticotropic hormone and endogenous glucocorticoids. Because of this, the adrenal cortex can atrophy. If exogenous glucocorticoid administration is suddenly discontinued, adrenal insufficiency results, owing to the inability of the atrophied cortex to respond adequately.

Mineralocorticoids. Mineralocorticoids exert their major effects on electrolyte metabolism. They act principally on renal tubular and gastrointestinal epithelium to cause increased sodium ion absorption in exchange for excretion of potassium or hydrogen ions. Aldosterone secretion is only minimally influenced by adrenocorticotropic hormone. It is primarily secreted in response to the presence of angiotensin II in the bloodstream. Angiotensin II is a substance that elevates the blood pressure by constricting arterioles. Its concentration is increased when renin is released from the kidney in response to decreased perfusion pressure. The resultant increased aldosterone levels promote sodium reabsorption by the kidney and the gastrointestinal tract, which tends to restore blood pressure to normal. The release of aldosterone is also increased by hyperkalaemia. Aldosterone is the primary hormone for the long-term regulation of salt balance.

Adrenal Sex Hormones (Androgens). Androgens, the third major type of steroid hormones produced by the adrenal cortex, exert effects similar to male sex hormones. The adrenal gland may also secrete small amounts of some oestrogens, or female sex hormones. Secretion of adrenal androgens is controlled by adrenocorticotropic hormone. When secreted in normal amounts, the adrenal androgens probably have little effect, but when secreted excessively, in certain inborn enzyme deficiencies, masculinization may result. This is termed the adrenogenital syndrome.

The Pancreas

The pancreas has an endocrine and an exocrine function. The exocrine function deals with digestive enzymes and is dealt with in Chapter 14.

Endocrine Pancreas

The islets of Langerhans, the endocrine part of the pancreas, are collections of cells embedded in the pancreatic tissue. They are composed of alpha, beta and delta cells. The hormone produced by the beta cells is called insulin; the alpha cells secrete glucagon, and the delta cells secrete somatostatin. A major action of insulin is to lower blood sugar by permitting entry of the sugar (glucose) into the cells of the liver, muscle and other tissues where the glucose can be either stored as glycogen or burned for energy. Insulin also promotes the storage of fat in adipose tissue and the synthesis of proteins in various body tissues. In the absence of insulin, glucose is not able to enter the cells and is excreted in the urine. This condition, called diabetes mellitus, can be diagnosed by high levels of glucose in the blood and urine (see Chapter 17). In diabetes mellitus, stored fats and protein are used for energy instead of glucose, with consequent loss of body mass. The rate of insulin secretion from the pancreas is normally regulated by the level of sugar in the blood. The effects of glucagon are chiefly to raise the blood sugar (opposite to those of insulin) by converting glycogen to glucose in the liver. Glucagon is secreted by the pancreas in response to a fall in the level of blood glucose. Somatostatin exerts a hypoglycaemic effect by interfering with release of growth hormone from the pituitary and glucagon from the pancreas, both of which tend to raise blood sugar levels.

THE THYROID GLAND

Assessment: Tests of Thyroid Function

Serum Thyroxine (T$_4$)
This is the total amount of circulating thyroid hormone in the bloodstream.

Serum Tri-iodothyronine (T$_3$)
This is the total amount of circulating T$_3$ in the bloodstream.

Thyroid-Stimulating Hormone.
A radioimmunoassay is carried out to determine the levels of thyroid stimulating hormone. The results of this investigation will prove that the problem lies with the thyroid gland or the pituitary gland.

Radioactive Iodine Uptake
This is a direct measurement of the rate of removal of iodine from the bloodstream by the thyroid gland. A small dose of radioactive iodine is given orally. Then at set intervals the radiation being omitted is measured. A hyperactive thyroid will have a high uptake of radioiodine; a hypoactive thyroid will have a low uptake of radioiodine.

Tri-iodothyronine (T$_3$) Suppression Test
The patient is given a seven-day course of T$_3$. A radioactive iodine uptake test is then carried out. The administration of T$_3$ should suppress the normal activity of the thyroid gland as the blood levels have increased. A hyperactive thyroid will not be suppressed by the administration of T$_3$.

T3 Resin Uptake Test
A sample of the patient's blood is taken and mixed with some T$_3$ that has been 'tagged' with radioiodine. The amount of binding between the T$_3$ and the patient's red blood cells is then measured. A hyperactive thyroid has a high degree of binding; conversely, a hypoactive thyroid has a low degree of binding.

Thyrotrophin-Releasing Hormone Test
An injection of thyrotrophin-releasing hormone is given to the patient. The levels of thyroid-stimulating hormone are then measured; they are suppressed in thyrotoxicosis.

Thyroid Scan
Some radioactive iodine is administered to the patient. Iodine uptake in the thyroid can then be measured. This investigation is often used to identify a localized area of hyperactivity in the thyroid gland.

Thyroid Stimulation Test
An injection of thyroid-stimulating hormone is administered to the patient. Radioiodine is then given, and the uptake by the thyroid is measured. The results will illustrate whether the problem lies with the thyroid gland itself or whether there is a secondary problem with the secretion of thyroid-stimulating hormone by the anterior pituitary.

Hypothyroidism and Myxoedema

Hypothyroidism is a condition in which there is a slow progression of thyroid hypofunction, followed by symptoms indicating thyroid failure. More than 95 per cent of patients with hypothyroidism have primary dysfunction of the thyroid gland itself. When the thyroid dysfunction is due to failure of the pituitary gland, it is known as secondary hypothyroidism; when failure of the hypothalamus is the underlying cause, the term tertiary hypothyroidism is used. When thyroid deficiency is present at birth, the condition is known as cretinism. In such instances, the mother may also suffer from thyroid deficiency.

The most common cause of hypothyroidism in adults is autoimmune thyroiditis (Hashimoto's thyroiditis), in which the immune system attacks the thyroid gland. Symptoms of hyperthyroidism may later be followed by those of hypothyroidism and myxoedema. Hypothyroidism also commonly occurs in patients with previous hyperthyroidism who have been treated with radioiodine, surgery or anti-thyroid drugs. It occurs most frequently in older women.

Clinical Features

Early symptoms of hypothyroidism are nonspecific, but extreme fatigue makes it difficult for the person to complete a full day's work or activities. Complaints of hair loss, brittle nails and dry skin are common, and numbness and tingling of the fingers may occur. On occasion, the voice may become husky, and the patient may complain of hoarseness. Menstrual disturbances such as menorrhagia or amenorrhoea occur, in addition to loss of libido.

With more severe hypothyroidism, the temperature and pulse rate become subnormal. The patient usually begins to gain weight even without an increase in food intake. (Severely hypothyroid patients, however, may be cachectic.) The skin becomes thickened because of an accumulation of mucopolysaccharides in the subcutaneous tissues (the origin of the term myxoedema). The hair thins and falls out; the face becomes expressionless and masklike.

At first the patient may be irritable and may complain of fatigue, but as the condition progresses, the emotional responses are subdued. The mental process becomes dulled, and the patient appears apathetic. Speech is slow, the tongue enlarges, and hands and feet increase in size. The patient frequently complains of constipation and intolerance to cold. Deafness also may occur. The advanced myxoedematous state may produce personality changes.

Myxoedema affects women five times more frequently than men and occurs most often between 30 and 60 years of age. It is not without its complications, because there is an associated tendency to the rapid development of atherosclerosis, with all the undesirable features of that disease. The patient with advanced myxoedema is hypothermic and abnormally sensitive to sedatives, opiates and anaesthetic agents. Therefore, these drugs are given with extreme caution.

Management

Hypothyroidism is treated by replacing the deficient hormone; in this case by a daily dose of thyroxine. If the patient presents with severe hypothyroidism and myxoedema coma, then tri-iodothyronine (T_3) may be given intravenously as it has a more immediate effect. Once the life-threatening period has ended, oral thyroxine is administered. The symptoms of hypothyroidism will disappear, and normal metabolic activity resumes, if the replacement therapy is adequate.

Precautionary Concerns

Myocardial ischaemia or infarction may occur in response to therapy in patients with myxoedema. Any patient who has been myxoedematous for a long period of time is almost certain to have elevated serum cholesterol levels, atherosclerosis and coronary artery disease. As long as metabolism is subnormal and the tissues, including the myocardium, require relatively little oxygen, a reduction in blood supply is tolerated very well. However, when thyroid hormone is given, the oxygen demand increases but oxygen delivery cannot be increased unless, or until, the atherosclerosis improves. This will occur very slowly, if at all. The signal that the oxygen needs of the myocardium exceed its blood supply is angina pectoris. Angina or arrhythmias may also occur when thyroid replacement is initiated, because thyroid hormones enhance the cardiovascular effects of catecholamines.

The nurse must be alert for signs of angina, especially during the early phase of treatment, and if detected, it must be heeded at once in order to avoid a fatal myocardial infarction. Obviously, the administration of thyroid hormone must be discontinued immediately, and later, when it can be resumed safely, substitution therapy should be given cautiously at a lower level of dosage and under the close observation of the doctor and the nurse.

Elderly arteriosclerotic patients may also become confused and agitated if their metabolic rates are raised too quickly in myxoedema.

Marked clinical improvement follows the administration of hormone replacement; such medication must be continued for life, even though signs of myxoedema disappear over a 3- to 12-week period.

Precautions must be taken during the course of therapy because of interaction of thyroid hormones with other drugs. Thyroid hormones may increase blood glucose levels, which may necessitate adjustment in doses of insulin or oral hypoglycaemic agents. The effects of thyroid hormone may be increased by phenytoin and tricyclic antidepressants. Thyroid hormones may also increase the pharmacological effects of digitalis, glycosides, anticoagulants and indomethacin, requiring careful observation and assessment by the nurse for side-effects of these drugs.

Severe untreated hypothyroidism is attended by an increased susceptibility to all hypnotic and sedative drugs. These agents, even in small doses, may induce profound somnolence, lasting far longer than anticipated. Moreover, they are prone to cause respiratory depression, which could easily prove fatal.

With this in mind, the dosage of any such drug is most conservative (e.g., no more than a half or one third the dosage ordinarily employed in patients of similar age and weight who are not myxoedematous). Sedative and hypnotic agents are not used unless the indications are very specific, and if they are given, the nurse must be unusually alert for signs of impending narcosis or respiratory failure.

Nursing Care

The patient with hypothyroidism experiences decreased energy and moderate to severe lethargy. As a result, such a patient is at risk of the complications of immobility. The ability to exercise and participate in activities is further limited by the changes in cardiovascular and pulmonary status resulting from the myxoedematous state. A major role of the nurse is to support the patient by assisting with care and hygiene, while giving encouragement to participate in activities within the patient's tolerance to prevent complications of immobility. The patient's vital signs and cognitive level are monitored closely during diagnostic investigations and initiation of treatment to detect: (1) deterioration of physical and mental status; (2) symptoms indicating that an increased metabolic rate resulting from treatment is outstripping the cardiovascular and pulmonary status; and (3) continued limitations or complications of myxoedema.

● Medications are administered to the patient with hypothyroidism very cautiously because of the altered metabolism and excretion and the patient's already depressed metabolic rate and respiratory status.

The patient often experiences chilling and extreme intolerance to cold even if the room temperature feels comfortable or hot to others. Extra clothing and blankets are provided, and the patient is protected from drafts. Although a heating pad or electric blanket may be asked for to decrease chilling and discomfort, these measures are avoided because of the risk of causing peripheral vasodilation, further loss of body heat and vascular collapse. Additionally, the patient could be burned by using these items without being aware of it because of delayed responses and decreased mental status.

The patient, family and significant others are often very concerned about the changes they have observed as a result of the hypothyroid state. It is often reassuring to be informed that many of the symptoms will disappear as treatment becomes effective. The patient is requested to continue to use medications as prescribed even after symptomatic improvement is experienced. Dietary advice is provided to promote weight loss once medication has been initiated and to promote return of normal bowel patterns. Because of the decreased mentation that occurs with hypothyroidism, it is important that a family member or significant other also be informed and advised about the expected outcomes of treatment, medication and side-effects that are to be reported to the doctor. Additionally, these instructions and guidelines are provided in writing for the patient, carers and community nurse to refer to once the patient returns home.

The patient with moderate to severe hypothyroidism may experience severe emotional reactions to the altered physical state. Changes in appearance and body image and the frequent delay in diagnosis of the disorder because of the nonspecific, early symptoms often produce negative reactions from family members and friends. The patient may have been labelled by family and friends as being mentally unstable, unco-operative or unwilling to carry out proper self-care. As hypothyroidism is treated successfully and symptoms subside, the patient may experience depression and guilt as a result of the progression and severity of symptoms that occurred. The patient, family and close friends are informed that the symptoms and inability to recognize them are common occurrences and part of the disorder itself. The patient and home carers may require assistance and counselling to deal with the emotional concerns and reactions that occurred.

Hyperthyroidism (Graves' Disease)

Hyperthyroidism constitutes a well-defined disease entity, commonly designated as Graves' disease or exophthalmic goitre. Its aetiology is unknown, but the excessive output of thyroid hormones is thought to be due to abnormal stimulation of the thyroid gland by circulating immunoglobulins. Long-acting thyroid stimulator is found in significant concentration in the serum of many of these patients, and may be related to a defect in the patient's immune surveillance system.

Clinical Features

Patients with well-developed hyperthyroidism exhibit a characteristic group of symptoms and signs. Their presenting symptom is often nervousness. They are often emotionally hyperexcitable, irritable and apprehensive (this disorder can be misdiagnosed as hypomania in some cases); they cannot sit quietly; they suffer from palpitations; and their pulse is abnormally rapid at rest as well as on exertion. They tolerate heat poorly and perspire unusually freely; the skin is flushed continuously, with a characteristic salmon colour, and is likely to be warm, soft and moist. A fine tremor of the hands may be observed. Many patients exhibit bulging eyes (exophthalmos), which produce a startled facial expression.

Other important symptoms include an increased appetite and dietary intake (unless gastrointestinal symptoms develop), progressive loss of weight, abnormal muscular fatigability and weakness, amenorrhoea and changes in bowel function, with constipation or diarrhoea. The pulse rate of these patients ranges constantly between 90 and 160 beats/min; the systolic, but characteristically not diastolic, blood pressure is elevated; atrial fibrillation may occur, and cardiac decompensation in the form of congestive heart failure is common, especially in elderly patients.

The thyroid gland invariably is enlarged to some extent. It is soft and may pulsate; a thrill often can be felt and a bruit heard over the thyroid arteries, which are signs of greatly increased blood flow through the organ.

In the more advanced cases, the diagnosis is made on the basis of the symptoms and the tests described previously: an increase in serum thyroxine (T_4) and an increased ^{131}I uptake by the thyroid, in excess of 50 per cent.

The course of the disease may be mild, characterized by remissions and exacerbations, and terminating with spontaneous recovery in the course of a few months or years. On the other hand, it may progress relentlessly, with the untreated person becoming emaciated, intensely nervous, delirious, even disoriented, and the heart eventually fails.

Symptoms of hyperthyroidism may occur with release of excessive amounts of thyroid hormone as a result of inflammation following irradiation of the thyroid or destruction of thyroid tissue by tumour. Such symptoms may also occur with excessive administration of thyroid hormone for treatment of hypothyroidism (see Table 18.2).

Table 18.2 *A comparison of systemic symptoms of hypo- and hyperthyroidism*

System	Hypoactive	Hyperactive
Central venous system	↓ Pulse ↓ Blood pressure Cardiomegaly	↑ Pulse ↑ Systolic blood pressure ↓ Diastolic blood pressure
Central nervous system	Intolerant of cold Depression Lethargy Monotone voice	Intolerant of heat Hyperexcitable Restless/irritable/anxious Tremor
Gastrointestinal system	Anorexia ↑ Weight Constipation	Appetite ↓ Weight Diarrhoea
Genitourinary system	Amenorrhoea Infertile ↓ Sex drive	Oligomenorrhoea Impotent ↓ Sex drive
Respiratory system	Dyspnoea ↑ Risk of pleural effusion	Hyperventilation Short of breath on exertion
Integumentary	Dry, thick skin Coarse hair Eyelids oedematous	↑ Sweating Loss of hair Eyelids retracted

Management

As yet, no treatment for hyperthyroidism has been discovered that combats its basic cause. However, reduction of thyroid hyperactivity provides effective symptomatic relief and removes the principal source of its most important complications.

Three forms of treatment are available for treating hyperthyroidism and controlling excessive thyroid activity: (1) pharmacotherapy, employing anti-thyroid drugs that interfere with the synthesis of thyroid hormones and other agents that control manifestations of hyperthyroidism; (2) irradiation, involving the administration of the radioisotope I^{131} or I^{125} for destructive effects on the thyroid gland; and (3) surgery, whereby most of the thyroid gland is removed.

Drug Therapy

The three possible methods of treating hyperthyroidism with drug therapies are to:

1. Inhibit thyroxine synthesis.
2. Treat hyperthyroid symptoms.
3. Limit the action of the thyroid gland.

Inhibition of Thyroxine Synthesis. This is achieved by using carbimazole. The drug should not be used during pregnancy as it can induce fetal goitre. Over-treatment can cause hypothyroidism, and therefore regular checks of thyroxine (T_4) are essential.

Treatment of Hyperthyroidism. Propranolol, a ß-adrenoreceptor blocking agent, can be used to treat the symptoms of hyperthyroidism. It reduces tachycardia, tremor, excess sweating and nervousness.

Limiting the Thyroid Gland. By damaging or destroying thyroid tissue, one can reduce the action of the thyroid gland. This can be achieved by giving radioactive iodine (I^{131}). The main considerations to take into account before initiating this treatment are the patient's age and hypersensitivity to iodine.

Surgical Intervention

The surgical removal of about seven-eighths of the thyroid tissue (subtotal thyroidectomy) practically assures a prolonged remission in most patients with exophthalmic goitre. Before surgery, the patient is given carbimazole until signs of hyperthyroidism have disappeared. Iodine is prescribed to reduce the size and the vascularity of the goitre. It may be given in the form of Lugol's solution, potassium iodide or hydriodic acid.

● Patients receiving iodine medication must be observed for evidence of iodine toxicity (iodism), the appearance of which is the signal for immediate withdrawal of the drug. Symptoms of iodism include swelling of the buccal mucosa, excessive salivation, coryza and skin eruptions.

Thyroidectomy for treatment of hyperthyroidism is usually scheduled within a few days after the patient's basal metabolic rate has been reduced to normal.

In appraising the value of surgery, it is considered a less than ideal form of treatment, because there is a possibility of permanent postoperative hypothyroidism, of hypoparathyroidism and of damage to the recurrent laryngeal nerve.

► NURSING PROCESS
► THE PATIENT WITH HYPERTHYROIDISM

► *Assessment*

The nursing history and examination focus on the occurrence of symptoms related to accelerated or exaggerated metabolism. These include the patient's and family's/friend's report of irritability and increased emotional reaction. It is also important to determine the impact that these changes have had on the patient's interaction with family, friends and colleagues. The history includes other stressful situations encountered and the patient's ability to cope with these stresses. Nutritional status and the presence of symptoms are assessed. The occurrence of symptoms related to excessive output of the nervous system and changes in vision and the appearance of the eyes are noted.

► *Patient's Problems*

Based on the assessment, the main problems for the patient with hyperthyroidism may include the following:

● Ineffective coping related to irritability, hyperexcitability, apprehension and emotional instability.
● Disturbance in self-esteem related to changes in appearance, excessive appetite, weight loss.
● Discomfort related to heat intolerance.
● Alteration in nutrition related to exaggerated metabolic rate, excessive appetite and increased gastrointestinal activity.

► *Planning and Implementation*
► Expected Outcomes

The patient's expected outcomes may include improved coping ability, improved self-esteem, relief of discomfort and improved nutritional status.

Nursing Care

Coping Measures

The patient with hyperthyroidism needs assurance that the emotional reactions experienced are a result of the disorder, and that with effective treatment those symptoms will be controlled. Because of the negative effect that these symptoms have on the interaction and communication of the patient with family and friends, they too need reassurance that these symptoms are expected to disappear with treatment. It is important to use a calm, unhurried approach with the patient. Additionally, the patient

needs to be isolated from stressful experiences; therefore, the patient is not placed in a hospital ward with very ill or talkative patients. The environment is kept quiet and uncluttered. Noises, such as loud music, conversation and equipment alarms, are minimized. Relaxing activities are encouraged if they do not overstimulate the patient.

If thyroidectomy is planned, the patient is likely to be apprehensive and anxious about the surgery. The patient is informed that while surgery is planned, a period of nonsurgical treatment is necessary to prepare the patient and the thyroid gland for surgical treatment. The patient is assisted by the nurse to take the medications as prescribed by the doctor and to develop a plan to encourage adherence to the therapeutic regime. The patient's hyperexcitability and shortened attention span may necessitate repetition of this information and advice.

Improved Self-Esteem

Hyperthyroid patients are likely to experience changes in appearance, appetite and weight that are beyond their control. These factors, along with the patients' recognition that they are not coping well with loved ones, environment and illness, may result in loss of self-esteem. The nurse conveys to the patient an understanding of the concern about these problems, and expresses willingness to help the patient to deal with them. Patients need to know that these changes are a result of the dysfunction of the thyroid gland and are in fact out of their control. If changes in appearance are very disturbing to the patient, the nurse may suggest that mirrors be removed from the room so that the patient is not constantly reminded of the changed appearance. In addition, home carers and health care staff are reminded to avoid bringing these changes to the patient's attention. The nurse explains to the patient that most of these changes are expected to disappear after effective treatment. If the patient experiences eye changes secondary to hyperthyroidism, eye care and protection may become necessary. The patient may need advice on how to instil eyedrops or ointment prescribed to soothe the eyes and protect the exposed cornea.

The patient may be embarrassed by the very large meals consumed as a result of the greatly increased metabolic rate. Therefore, the nurse arranges the setting so that the patient eats alone if desired and avoids commenting on the large dietary intake of the patient, while at the same time making sure that the patient does receive sufficient food.

Relief of Discomfort

The patient with hyperthyroidism frequently finds a normal room temperature too warm or often unbearably uncomfortable because of the exaggerated metabolic rate and heat production. The nurse provides a cool, comfortable environment for the patient and provides fresh bedding and gown as needed. Giving cool baths, providing cool or cold fluids and monitoring body temperature are important in providing relief. The reason for the patient's discomfort and the importance of providing a cool environment are explained to the family, friends and staff.

Improvement of Nutritional Status

Hyperthyroidism affects the gastrointestinal system. The patient's appetite is increased but may be satisfied by several well-balanced meals of small size, even up to six meals a day. Foods and fluids are selected to replace fluid lost through diarrhoea and diaphoresis and to control diarrhoea that results from increased peristalsis. Rapid movement of food through the gastrointestinal tract may result in nutritional imbalance and further weight loss. In order to reduce diarrhoea, highly seasoned foods and stimulants such as coffee, tea, cola and alcohol are discouraged. High-calorie, high-protein foods are encouraged. A quiet atmosphere during mealtimes may aid digestion. The patient's weight and dietary intake may be recorded to monitor nutritional status.

Patient Education

The patient with hyperthyroidism is advised about how and when to take prescribed medication. Additionally, the patient needs to know how the medication regime fits in with the broader therapeutic plan. Because of the patient's hyperexcitability and decreased attention span, the nurse provides the patient with a written plan to use at home. The type and amount of information given to the patient are individualized because of the resulting stress and possible emotional reactions by the patient. The patient, family and/or significant others receive verbal and written information about the desired effects as well as possible side-effects of the medications. The patient is advised by the nurse about which adverse effects should be reported to the doctor. The importance of long-term follow-up is stressed because of the possibility of hypothyroidism following thyroidectomy or treatment with anti-thyroid drugs or I^{131}.

If the patient is expected to have a total or subtotal thyroidectomy, then information is given about what to expect. This information, however, will be repeated to the patient as the time of surgery approaches. The patient is also requested to avoid those situations that have the potential to stimulate the life-threatening occurrence of thyroid storm.

▶ **Evaluation**
▶ **Expected Outcomes**

1. Patient demonstrates effective coping methods in dealing with family, friends and colleagues.
   a. Reports more effective conversation and interaction with family, friends and colleagues.
   b. Explains reasons for irritability and emotional instability.
   c. Identifies situations, events and people that are stress producing.
   d. Avoids stressful situations, events and people.
   e. Participates in relaxing, nonstressful activities.
   f. Explains to family and friends reasons for irritability and expectation that behaviour will change when treatment takes effect.
   g. Identifies expected outcomes of surgery or other treatment.
   h. Explains reason for delay in surgery and identifies own role during waiting period.
   i. Takes medications as prescribed in preparation for surgery or other treatment.
2. Achieves increased self-esteem.
   a. Expresses feelings about self and illness.
   b. Describes feelings of frustration and loss of control to others.
   c. Describes reasons for increased appetite.
   d. Discusses events in environment rather than concentrating on changes in own appearance.
   e. Dresses in attractive clothes that do not emphasize changes in physical appearance.
3. Experiences relief of discomfort.
   a. Reports relief of discomfort and a more comfortable environment.
   b. Uses clothing or bedding that is cool and comfortable.
   c. Notifies staff when fresh clothing or bedding is needed.
   d. Reports normal body temperature.
   e. Drinks cool fluids within fluid allowance.
   f. Uses air conditioner or fan if indicated.
   g. Avoids hot, uncomfortable environments.
4. Improves nutritional status.
   a. Reports adequate dietary intake and decreased feelings of hunger.
   b. Reports stabilization of weight.
   c. Identifies high-calorie, high-protein foods.
   d. Explains reasons for increased appetite.
   e. Identifies foods to be avoided on diet.
   f. Avoids use of alcohol and other stimulants.
   g. Reports decreased episodes of diarrhea.
   h. Demonstrates normal skin turgor and normal fluid balance.

Care of the patient with hyperthyroidism is described in Nursing Care Plan 18.1.

Thyroid Storm (Thyrotoxic Crisis)

Thyroid storm (thyrotoxicosis, thyrotoxic crisis) is a form of severe hyperthyroidism, usually of abrupt onset and characterized by high fever (hyperpyrexia), extreme tachycardia and altered mental state, which frequently appears as delirium. Thyroid storm is a life-threatening condition and is usually precipitated by stress such as

► **NURSING CARE PLAN 18.1: THE PATIENT WITH HYPERTHYROIDISM**

Gill King is a 31-year-old occupational therapist suffering from hyperthroidism. She is a lesbian and lives with her partner in a stable relationship; they are buying a house together.

Patient's problems	Expected outcomes	Nursing care	Rationale
1. Due to high levels of thyroxine, the patient becomes very anxious	To reduce anxiety	1a. A quiet environment is essential to reduce anxiety and therefore must be maintained b. Full explanation of tests, procedures and disease c. Avoid stress from outside the ward environment d. Restrict visitors to the immediate family and partner e. Gill's partner should be included in all the discussions and information-giving	A quiet, restful environment is essential to reduce the patient's anxiety levels By giving a full explanation the patient becomes less anxious about her condition and the procedures she may undergo Only visitors who are unlikely to cause the patient any distress will reduce the patient's stress levels (Watson and Royle, 1988)
2. Due to an increase in metabolic rate, Gill's nutritional intake must be increased	To maintain body weight	2a. Increase calorie intake over each 24 hours (i.e. 4,000 to 5,000 cals) b. Increase fluid intake i.e. 2,000 to 3,000 ml/24 hours c. Reduce any stimulant intake	Increasing Gill's nutritional intake will prevent any tissue breakdown due to increased metabolic demand Increased fluid intake will compensate for fluid loss due to increased metabolic rate and increased perspiration Reduce intake of tea, coffee etc to prevent stimulation from caffeine (Hinchliff and Montague, 1988)
3. Due to increased energy expenditure, Gill will be hyperactive	To decrease activity	3a. To reduce activity by encouraging Gill to rest b. Employ some diversional therapy, which expounds little energy c. Dispense prescribed sedatives	Activity increases metabolic rate; therefore, reducing activity will help to reduce metabolic rate Sedation may be required to aid rest; may also be required to promote sleep (Hinchliff and Montague, 1988)
4. Due to increase in metabolic rate, Gill is intolerant of hot environments	To keep the patient cool	4a. Try to keep environment cool b. Advise wearing light clothing c. Light bed linen should be used	As the patient is producing an abnormally high amount of body heat, any measures taken must be exogenous
5. Due to increased perspiration, skin is now compromised	To maintain skin integrity	5a. Daily cool bath or shower	Close attention to personal hygiene is essential in the maintenance of skin integrity
6. Due to exophthalmos, patient's eyesight may be compromised	To maintain eyesight	6a. Perform eye toilet with 0.9 per cent sodium chloride b. Regularly check eyesight c. Wear sunglasses as required	0.9 per cent sodium chloride is an isotonic solution similar to patient's own tears Exophthalmos can compress the optic nerve and artery, leading to visual impairment (Watson and Royle, 1988)
7. Due to exophthalmos, patient may be concerned about altered body image	The patient should express her feelings about body image	7a. Give full explanation of exophthalmos b. Encourage patient to take interest in grooming and general appearance	The exophthalmos may reduce as the thyroxine levels become reduced Promoting an interest in general appearance will increase the feeling of wellbeing

injury, infection, nonthyroid surgery, thyroidectomy, tooth extraction, insulin reaction, diabetic acidosis, pregnancy, digitalis intoxication, abrupt withdrawal of anti-thyroid drugs or vigorous palpation of the thyroid. These factors will precipitate thyroid storm in the partially controlled or completely untreated hyperthyroid patient. Patients who are maintained in a euthyroid state through the proper adjustment of an anti-thyroid drug may go through many of these episodes without a crisis being precipitated.

Untreated thyroid storm is almost always fatal, but with proper treatment, the mortality rate can be reduced substantially (see Figure 18.3).

Management
The immediate objective is to reduce body temperature and heart rate. Measures to reduce the temperature include tepid sponging, ice packs, a cool environment and hydrocortisone. Salicylates are not used since they displace thyroid hormone from binding proteins and worsen the hypermetabolism. Humidified oxygen is administered to improve tissue oxygenation and meet the high metabolic demand. Dextrose-containing intravenous fluids are administered to replace liver glycogen stores that have been decreased in the hyperthyroid patient. Carbimazole is given to impede formation of thyroid hormone and block conversion of thyroxine (T_4) to tri-iodothyronine (T_3), the more active form of thyroid hormone. Hydrocortisone is prescribed to treat shock or adrenal insufficiency. Iodine is administered to decrease output of T_4 from the thyroid gland. For cardiac problems such as atrial fibrillation, arrhythmias and congestive heart failure, sympatho-

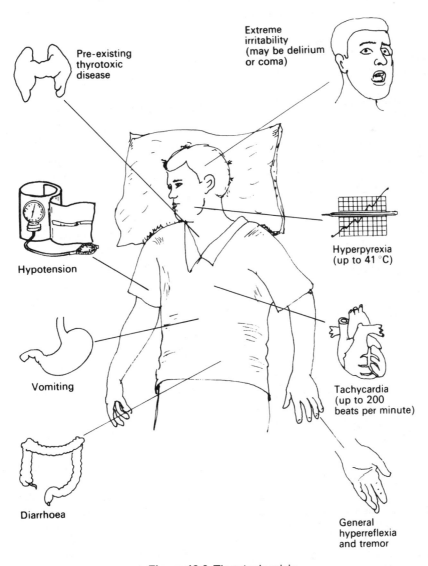

Pre-existing thyrotoxic disease

Extreme irritability (may be delirium or coma)

Hypotension

Hyperpyrexia (up to 41 °C)

Vomiting

Tachycardia (up to 200 beats per minute)

Diarrhoea

General hyperreflexia and tremor

Figure 18.3 Thyrotoxic crisis.

lytic agents may be given. Propranolol in combination with digitalis has been effective in reducing severe cardiac symptoms.

● The patient with thyroid storm or crisis is critically ill and requires astute observation and aggressive and supportive nursing care during and after the acute stage of illness. Care of the patient with hyperthyroidism is the basis of nursing care of the critically ill patient with thyroid storm or crisis.

Thyroiditis

Subacute or granulomatous thyroiditis (deQuervain's thyroiditis), an inflammatory disorder of the thyroid gland that predominantly affects women in their 50s, presents as a painful swelling in the anterior neck that lasts for one or two months and then disappears without residual effect. Evidence indicates that this disorder may be due to a viral infection. The thyroid enlarges symmetrically and occasionally is painful. The overlying skin is often reddened and warm. Swallowing may be difficult and uncomfortable. Irritability, nervousness, insomnia and weight loss–features of hyperthyroidism–are common, and many patients experience chills and fever as well.

Another form of thyroiditis occurs in the postpartum period and is thought to be an autoimmune reaction.

The purpose of treatment is to control the inflammation. In general, acetylsalicylic acid (aspirin) controls the symptoms of inflammation in mild cases but should be avoided if symptoms of hyperthyroidism occur, because it displaces thyroid hormone from its binding sites and increases the amount of circulating thyroid hormone. In more severe cases, glucocorticoids are effective but do not usually affect the underlying cause.

Chronic Thyroiditis (Hashimoto's Thyroiditis)

Chronic thyroiditis, which occurs most frequently in women aged 30 to 50 years, has been termed Hashimoto's disease, depending on the histological appearance of the inflamed gland. In contrast to acute thyroiditis, the chronic varieties are usually not accompanied by pain, pressure symptoms or fever, and thyroid activity is apt to be normal or low, rather than increased.

There is evidence that cell-mediated immunity plays a significant role in the pathogenesis of thyroiditis. A genetic predisposition also seems to be significant in aetiology. If untreated, the disease runs a slow, progressive course, leading eventually to myxoedema.

The objective of treatment is to reduce the size of the thyroid gland and prevent myxoedema. Thyroid hormone therapy is prescribed to reduce thyroid activity and the production of thyroglobulin. If hypothyroid symptoms are present, thyroid hormone is given. Anti-thyroid drugs may be given if an associated thyrotoxicosis exists. Surgery may be required if pressure symptoms persist.

Thyroid Tumours

Tumours of the thyroid gland are classified on the basis of being benign or malignant, as well as on the presence or absence of associated thyrotoxicosis, and the diffuse or irregular quality of the glandular enlargement. If the enlargement is sufficient to cause a visible swelling in the neck, the tumour is referred to as a 'goitre'.

All grades of goitre are encountered, from those that are barely visible to those producing an unsightly disfigurement. Some are symmetrical and diffuse, others nodular. Some are accompanied by hyperthyroidism, in which case they are described as 'toxic'; others are associated with a euthyroid state and are called 'nontoxic' goitres.

Thyroid Cancer

Cancer of the thyroid gland is a relatively rare disease. When it does occur, it is usually an adenocarcinoma. It tends to occur in younger females. Treatment is removal by surgery, and full thyroxine replacement is required afterwards.

Thyroidectomy

Partial or complete thyroidectomy may be carried out as primary treatment of thyroid carcinoma, hyperthyroidism or hyperparathyroidism. The type and extent of the surgery depends on the diagnosis, expected outcome of surgery and prognosis.

Preoperative Care

General preoperative care is discussed in Chapter 2. Before undergoing surgery for treatment of hyperthyroidism, the patient will be treated with appropriate drug therapy to return the thyroid hormone levels and metabolic rate to normal and to reduce the risk of thyroid storm and haemorrhage during the postoperative period.

Nutritional intake is regulated to include adequate carbohydrate and protein foods. A high daily calorie intake is necessary because of the increased metabolic activity and rapid depletion of glycogen reserves. Supplementary vitamins, particularly thiamine and ascorbic acid, are to be provided. Tea, coffee, cola and other stimulants are to be avoided.

If the patient is to undergo diagnostic testing before surgery, information is given about the purpose of the test and the preoperative preparations in order to reduce anxiety. In addition, a special effort is made to ensure a good night's rest preceding surgery.

Preoperative teaching includes demonstrating to the patient how to support the neck with the hands to prevent stress on the incision; that is, raising the elbows and placing the hands behind the neck will provide support and put much less strain and tension on the neck muscles and the surgical incision.

Postoperative Care

The patient is moved and turned carefully so as to support the head and avoid tension on the sutures. Narcotics are given as prescribed for pain. Occasionally, the patient is given humidified oxygen to facilitate breathing. The nurse should anticipate apprehension in such patients and inform them that oxygen will assist breathing and help them to feel less tired. Intravenous fluids will be administered during the immediate postoperative period, but water may be given by mouth as soon as nausea ceases. Usually, there is a little difficulty in swallowing; initially, cold fluids and ice may be taken better than other fluids.

The surgical dressings should be checked periodically and reinforced when necessary. It is important to remember that when the patient is in the dorsal position, evidence of bleeding should be looked for at the sides and the back of the neck as well as anteriorly. In addition to checking the pulse, temperature, respirations and the blood pressure for any indication of internal bleeding, it is also important to be on the alert for complaints from the patient of sensation of pressure or fullness at the incision site. Such signs may indicate haemorrhage subcutaneously and should be reported.

Occasionally, difficulty in respiration occurs, with the development of cyanosis and noisy breathing, as a result of oedema of the glottis or an injury to the recurrent laryngeal nerve.

The patient is advised to talk as little as possible, but when speaking does occur, the nurse should note any voice changes that might indicate injury to the recurrent laryngeal nerve that lies just behind the thyroid next to the trachea.

Complications

Haemorrhage, oedema of the glottis and injury to the recurrent laryngeal nerve are complications that have been reviewed previously. Occasionally, in thyroid operations, the parathyroid glands may be injured or removed, producing a disturbance of the calcium metabolism of the body. As the blood calcium level falls, hyperirritability of the nerves, with spasms of the hands and feet and muscular twitchings occurs. This group of symptoms is termed tetany, and its appearance should be reported at once since laryngospasm, although rare, may occur, blocking off the patient's airway. Tetany of this type is usually treated by the administration of calcium gluconate. This calcium abnormality may be temporary following thyroidectomy.

THE PARATHYROID GLANDS

Hyperparathyroidism

Hyperparathyroidism, which is due to overproduction of parathyroid hormone by the parathyroid glands, is characterized by bone calcification and the development of renal stones containing calcium in the kidneys. Primary hyperparathyroidism occurs two to four times more often in women than in men, and is most frequently seen in patients over 70 years of age. Secondary hyperparathyroidism with similar manifestations occurs in patients with chronic renal failure and so-called renal rickets, as a result of phosphorus retention, increased stimulation of the parathyroid glands and increased parathyroid hormone secretion.

Clinical Features and Diagnosis

The patient may have no symptoms or may experience signs and symptoms resulting from involvement of several body systems. There may be signs and symptoms of apathy, fatigue, muscular weakness, nausea, vomiting, constipation and cardiac arrhythmias, all attributable to an increased concentration of calcium in the blood. Psychological features may vary from emotional irritability and neurosis, to psychoses due to the direct effect of calcium on the brain and nervous system. An increase in calcium produces an increase in the excitation potential of nerve and muscle tissue.

The formation of stones in one or both kidneys, related to the increased urinary excretion of calcium and phosphorus, is one of the important complications of hyperparathyroidism. Renal damage results from the precipitation of calcium phosphate in the renal pelvis and parenchyma, resulting in nephrocalcinosis, obstruction, pyelonephritis and uraemia.

Musculoskeletal symptoms accompanying hyperparathyroidism may result from demineralization of the bones or bone tumours, composed of benign giant cells resulting from overgrowth of osteoclasts. The patient may develop: skeletal pain and tenderness, especially of the back and joints; pain on weight-bearing; pathological fractures; deformities; and shortening of body structure.

The incidence of peptic ulcer and pancreatitis is increased with hyperparathyroidism and may be responsible for many of the gastrointestinal symptoms that occur.

The diagnosis of primary hyperparathyroidism is established on the basis of increased serum calcium levels and an elevated level of parathormone. Radioimmunoassays for parathormone are very sensitive and differentiate primary hyperparathyroidism from other causes of hypercalcaemia. An elevated serum calcium level is a nonspecific finding since serum levels may be altered by diet, medications and renal and bone changes. Bone changes may be detected on X-ray films in advanced cases of the disease.

Management

The treatment of primary hyperparathyroidism is the surgical removal of abnormal parathyroid tissue. In the preoperative period it must be recognized that kidney involvement is possible, since these patients are subject to renal calculi. A fluid intake of 2,000 ml or more is encouraged to help prevent calculi formation. Because of the possibility of stone formation, urine is strained and any evidence of calculi is saved for laboratory analysis. The patient is observed for other features of renal calculi, such as abdominal pain and haematuria. Thiazide diuretics should not be used in the patient with hyperparathyroidism since they decrease the renal excretion of calcium, thereby causing further elevations in serum calcium levels.

Oral phosphate lowers the serum calcium level in some patients. Long-term use is not recommended because of ectopic calcium-phosphate deposits in soft tissues.

Nutritional needs are met, but foods high in calcium and phosphorus, such as milk and milk products, are limited. If the patient has a coexisting peptic ulcer, specifically prescribed antacids and protein feeds will be necessary. Since anorexia is common, efforts are made to encourage the patient's appetite. Prune juice, stool softeners and physical activity, along with increased fluid intake, should offset constipation, which is a common postoperative problem for this patient.

The nursing management of the patient undergoing parathyroidectomy is essentially the same as that for a thyroidectomy patient. Although not all parathyroid tissue will be removed during surgery in an effort to maintain control of calcium-phosphorus balance, the patient must be observed closely to detect symptoms of tetany, which may be an early postoperative complication. Most patients quickly regain function of the remaining parathyroid tissue and experience only mild, transient postoperative hypocalcaemia. In patients with significant bone disease or bone changes, a more prolonged period of hypocalcaemia should be anticipated.

Although it is rare, acute hypercalcaemic crisis can occur in hyperparathyroidism. This occurs with extreme elevation of serum calcium levels. Serum calcium levels higher than 3.7 mmol/l result in neurological, cardiovascular and renal symptoms that can be life threatening. Treatment includes rehydration with large volumes of intravenous fluids, diuretic agents to promote renal excretion of excess calcium and phosphate therapy to correct hypophosphataemia and decrease serum calcium levels by promoting calcium deposit in bone and decreasing gastrointestinal absorption of calcium. Calcitonin and dialysis may be used in emergency situations to decrease serum calcium levels quickly. The patient in acute hypercalcaemic crisis requires close monitoring for complications, deterioration of condition or reversal of serum calcium levels.

A combination of calcitonin and glucocorticoids has been administered in emergencies to reduce the serum calcium level by increasing calcium deposition in bone.

The patient requires expert assessment and care to minimize complications and reverse the life-threatening hypercalcaemia. Medications are administered with care and attention is given to fluid balance to promote return of normal fluid and electrolyte balance in this patient. Supportive measures are necessary for the patient, family and close friends.

Hypoparathyroidism

The most common cause of hypoparathyroidism is inadequate secretion of parathyroid hormone following interruption of the blood supply or surgical removal of parathyroid gland tissue during thyroidectomy, parathyroidectomy or radical neck dissection. Atrophy of the parathyroid glands of unknown aetiology is a less common cause of hypoparathyroidism.

Altered Physiology
Symptoms of hypoparathyroidism are due to a deficiency of parathormone that results in an elevation of blood phosphate, hyperphosphataemia and a decrease in the concentration of blood calcium–hypocalcaemia. Hypocalcaemia results because in the absence of parathormone there is decreased intestinal absorption of dietary calcium and decreased resorption of calcium from bone and through the renal tubules. Decreased renal excretion of phosphate causes hypophosphaturia, and low serum calcium levels result in hypocalciuria.

Clinical Features
Hypocalcaemia causes irritability of the neuromuscular system and contributes to the chief symptom of hypoparathyroidism, tetany–a general muscular hypertonia, with tremor and spasmodic or unco-ordinated contractions occurring with or without efforts to make voluntary movements. In latent tetany there is numbness, tingling and cramps in the extremities, with the patient complaining of stiffness in the hands and feet. In overt tetany the signs include bronchospasm, laryngeal spasm, carpopedal spasm (flexion of the elbows and wrists and extension of the carpophalangeal joints—Figure 18.4), dysphagia, photophobia, cardiac arrhythmias and convulsions. Other symptoms include anxiety, irritability, depression and even delirium.

Management
The object of therapy is to raise the serum calcium level to 2.2 to 2.5 mmol/l and to eliminate the symptoms of hypoparathyroidism and hypocalcaemia. When hypocalcaemia and tetany occur following a thyroidectomy, the immediate treatment is to administer calcium gluconate intravenously. If this does not control convulsive tendencies immediately, it may be necessary to administer sedatives such as chloral hydrate or pentobarbital.

Parenteral parathormone can be administered to treat acute hypoparathyroidism with tetany. The high incidence of allergic reactions to injections of parathormone

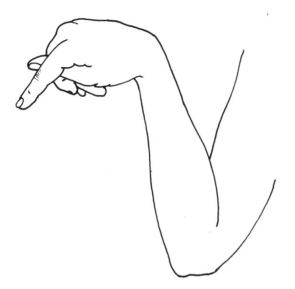

Figure 18.4 Carpopedal spasm.

limits its use to acute episodes of hypocalcaemia. The patient receiving parathormone is monitored closely for changes in serum calcium levels and allergic reactions.

Because of neuromuscular irritability, the patient with hypocalcaemia and tetany requires an environment that is free of noise, sudden drafts, bright lights or sudden movement.

Tracheostomy or mechanical ventilation may become necessary, along with bronchodilating medications, if the patient develops respiratory distress.

Nursing care of the patient with possible acute hypoparathyroidism includes the following actions:

- The attention of the nurse in the care of postoperative patients having thyroidectomy, parathyroidectomy and radical neck dissection is directed toward anticipating signs of tetany, convulsions and respiratory difficulties.
- Calcium gluconate is kept at the bedside with equipment necessary for intravenous administration. If the patient has cardiac problems, is subject to arrhythmias or is receiving digitalis, then calcium gluconate is administered by slow infusion.
- Calcium and digitalis increase systolic contraction and, furthermore, they potentiate each other. This may produce potentially fatal arrhythmias. Consequently, the cardiac patient requires constant vigilance and undoubtedly should be on continuous cardiac monitoring.

Therapy for the patient with chronic hypoparathyroidism is determined after serum calcium levels are obtained. The prescribed diet is high in calcium and low in phosphorus. Although milk, milk products and egg yolk are high in calcium, they are restricted because they also contain high

levels of phosphorus. Spinach is also avoided because it contains oxalate, which would form insoluble calcium substances. Oral tablets of calcium salts, such as calcium gluconate, may supplement the diet. Aluminum hydroxide gel or aluminum carbonate is also given after meals to bind phosphate and promote its excretion through the gastrointestinal tract.

Variable dosages of a vitamin D preparation–dihydrotachysterol or ergocalciferol (vitamin D_2) or cholecalciferol (vitamin D_3)–are usually required and enhance calcium absorption from the gastrointestinal tract.

The convalescent phase of patient care is the time to advise the patient in drug and diet therapy. The patient needs to know the reason for a high calcium and low phosphate intake, and the symptoms of hypocalcaemia and hypercalcaemia so that the general practitioner is contacted immediately should these symptoms occur.

THE ADRENAL GLAND

Phaeochromocytoma

A phaeochromocytoma is a tumour that is usually benign and originates from the chromaffin cells of the adrenal medulla. In 80 to 90 per cent of patients, the tumour arises in the medulla, and in the remaining patients it occurs in the extra-adrenal chromaffin tissue located in or near the aorta, ovaries, spleen or other organs. Phaeochromocytoma occurs at any age, but the peak incidence is between the ages of 25 and 50. It affects men and women equally. The patient's family should also be screened for this tumour because of the high incidence of phaeochromocytoma in family members. Fewer than 10 per cent of phaeochromocytomas are malignant.

Although uncommon, phaeochromocytoma is the cause of high blood pressure in 0.1 to 0.5 per cent of patients with hypertension. It is one form of hypertension that is usually treated successfully by surgery.

Clinical Features

Functioning tumours of the adrenal medulla cause arterial hypertension and other cardiovascular disturbances. The nature and severity depend on the relative proportions of adrenaline and noradrenaline secretion.

The hypertension may be intermittent or persistent. However, only 50 per cent of patients with phaeochromocytoma have sustained or persistent hypertension. If the hypertension is of the sustained type, it may be difficult to distinguish from so-called essential hypertension. In addition to hypertension, the symptoms are essentially the same as those encountered after the administration of adrenaline in large doses, namely tachycardia or palpitations, excessive perspiration, tremor, headache, flushing and nervousness. Hyperglycaemia may result from conversion of liver and muscle glycogen to glucose by adrenaline secretion, occasionally requiring insulin to maintain normal blood glucose levels.

The clinical picture in the paroxysmal form of phaeochromocytoma is usually characterized by acute, unpredictable attacks, lasting seconds or several hours, during which the patient feels excessively anxious, tremulous and weak and suffers from headache, vertigo, blurring of vision, tinnitus, air hunger and dyspnoea. Other symptoms include polyuria, nausea, vomiting, diarrhoea, abdominal pain and fear. Palpitations and tachycardia are common. Postural hypotension occurs in 70 per cent of untreated cases of phaeochromocytoma.

Blood pressures as high as 350/200 mm Hg have been recorded. Such blood pressure elevations are dangerous and may precipitate life-threatening complications, including cardiac arrhythmias, dissecting aneurysm, stroke and acute renal failure.

Diagnosis

The diagnosis of phaeochromocytoma is suspected if signs of sympathetic nervous system overactivity occur in association with marked elevation of blood pressure. However, determination of the catecholamines in urine and blood offers the most direct and conclusive test for overactivity of the adrenal medulla. Determination of levels of vanillylmandelic acid, an end-product of catecholamine catabolism, is particularly useful. These levels can be estimated by carrying out a 24-hour urine collection.

Diagnostic tests may also be carried out to localize the phaeochromocytoma and to determine if more than one tumour is present. Computed tomography, ultrasound scanning, intravenous pyelography and aortography or arteriography may be performed. However, these procedures are carried out only after the patient is prepared with blocking agents to prevent hypertensive attacks.

Management

The treatment of phaeochromocytoma is surgical removal of the tumour, usually with adrenalectomy, which occasionally is bilateral. Preliminary patient preparation includes effective control of blood pressure and blood volumes. Usually, this is carried out over 10 days to two weeks. Phentolamine or phenoxybenzamine may be used safely without causing undue hypotension. These agents inhibit the effects of catecholamines but do not alter their synthesis or degradation. Beta-adrenergic blocking agents may be used in patients with cardiac arrhythmias or in those unresponsive to alpha-adrenergic blocking drugs. Alpha-adrenergic and beta-adrenergic blocking agents must be used with caution, because patients with phaeochromocytoma may have increased sensitivity to them. Still another group of drugs that may be used preoperatively are catecholamine synthesis inhibitors such as alpha-methyl-p-tyrosine (metyrosine). These are occasionally used when the effects of catecholamines are not reduced by adrenergic blocking agents.

Manipulation of the tumour during surgical excision causes release of stored adrenaline and noradrenaline with marked increases in blood pressure and changes in heart rate. Therefore, use of sodium nitroprusside and alpha-adrenergic blocking agents may be required during and after surgery. Exploration of other possible sites of tumour is frequently undertaken to ensure removal of all tumour. As a result, the patient is subject to the stress and effects of a long surgical procedure, which may increase the risk of hypertension postoperatively.

Corticosteroid replacement is required if bilateral adrenalectomy has been necessary. Intravenous administration of corticosteroids (methylprednisolone sodium succinate) may begin the evening before surgery and continue during the early postoperative period to prevent adrenal insufficiency. Oral preparations of corticosteroids (prednisolone) will be prescribed after the acute stress of surgery diminishes.

The patient will be monitored for several days in the intensive care unit with special attention given to electrocardiographic changes, arterial pressures, fluid and electrolyte balance and blood glucose levels. Several intravenous lines will be inserted for administration of fluids and medications. Hypotension and hypoglycaemia may occur in the postoperative period owing to the sudden withdrawal of excessive amounts of catecholamines. Therefore, careful attention is directed to monitoring these changes.

Hypertension usually disappears with treatment. However, it can persist or recur if the blood vessels have been damaged by severe and prolonged hypertension or if all phaeochromocytoma tissue has not been removed.

Several days after surgery, 24-hour urine excretion of catecholamines and their metabolites is measured to determine whether surgery has been successful. When levels have returned to normal, the patient may be discharged. Thereafter, periodic checkups are required, especially in young patients or in patients whose families have a history of phaeochromocytoma.

Disorders of the Adrenal Cortex

The adrenal cortex is necessary for life. Adrenocortical secretions make it possible for the body to adapt to stress of all kinds. How well one adapts to stress varies from person to person. Without the adrenal cortex, severe stress will cause peripheral circulatory failure, shock and prostration. Life would be maintained only with nutritional and electrolyte replacement and replacement of adrenocortical hormones.

Adrenocortical hormones are classified into three groups: (1) mineralocorticoids, (2) glucocorticoids and (3) sex hormones. Mineralocorticoids are concerned with sodium and water retention and potassium excretion. Examples are aldosterone and desoxycorticosterone, a natural precursor of aldosterone. Glucocorticoids are concerned with metabolic effects, including carbohydrate metabolism. Examples are cortisol and corticosterone. Glucocorticoids enhance the metabolic breakdown of body proteins and fat to provide fuel during periods of fasting. They antagonize the action of insulin, enhance protein catabolism and inhibit protein synthesis. They affect defence mechanisms of the body and influence emotional functioning either directly or indirectly. In high concentrations, they suppress inflammation and inhibit scar tissue formation. In adrenal insufficiency, patients may be depressed and upset, whereas with excessive replacement they tend to become euphoric. The sex hormones secreted by the adrenal cortex are androgens and oestrogens.

Disorders of the adrenal cortex develop as a result of hyposecretion or hypersecretion of the adrenocortical hormones. Adrenal insufficiency may result from disease, atrophy, haemorrhage or surgical removal of the adrenal gland or glands.

Chronic Primary Adrenocortical Insufficiency (Addison's Disease)

Altered Physiology
Addison's disease, caused by a deficiency of cortical hormones, results when the adrenal cortex is surgically removed with bilateral adrenalectomy or is destroyed, often as a result of idiopathic atrophy or infections such as tuberculosis or histoplasmosis. Inadequate secretion of adrenocorticotrophic hormone from the pituitary gland results in adrenal insufficiency because of decreased stimulation of the adrenal cortex.

The symptoms of adrenocortical insufficiency may also result from sudden cessation of exogenous adrenocortical hormonal therapy, which suppresses the body's normal response to stress and interferes with normal feedback mechanisms.

Clinical Features
Addison's disease has a characteristic clinical picture. The chief clinical features include muscular weakness, anorexia, gastrointestinal symptoms, fatigue, emaciation, generalized dark pigmentation of the skin, hypotension, low blood sugar, low serum sodium and high serum potassium.

In severe cases of Addison's disease, the disturbance of sodium and potassium metabolism may be marked, with depletion of the sodium and water and severe chronic dehydration.

As the disease progresses, with acute hypotension developing due to hypocorticism, the patient moves into Addisonian crisis, which is a medical emergency marked by cyanosis, fever and the classic signs of shock: pallor, apprehension, rapid and weak pulse, rapid respirations and low blood pressure. In addition, the patient may complain of headache, nausea, abdominal pain, and diarrhoea and show signs of confusion and restlessness. Even slight overexertion, exposure to cold, acute infections or a decrease in salt intake may lead to circulatory collapse. The stress of surgery or dehydration resulting from preparation for diagnostic tests or surgery may precipitate an Addisonian or hypotensive crisis.

Diagnosis
Although the clinical features presented appear specific, the onset of Addison's disease usually occurs with non-specific symptoms. The diagnosis of Addison's disease is confirmed by laboratory test results. Suggestive laboratory findings include a decrease in the concentrations of blood sugar and sodium (hypoglycaemia and hyponatraemia), an increased concentration of serum potassium (hyperkalaemia) and an increased white blood cell count (leucocytosis).

The definitive diagnosis is confirmed by low levels of adrenocorticol hormones in the blood or urine. Serum cortisol levels are decreased in adrenal insufficiency. If the adrenal cortex is destroyed, baseline values are low and adrenocorticotrophic hormone injection fails to cause the normal rise in plasma cortisol and urinary 17-hydroxycorticosteroids.

If the adrenal gland is normal but not stimulated properly by the pituitary, a normal response to repeated dosages of exogenous adrenocorticotrophic hormone is seen but no response follows the administration of metyrapone, which stimulates endogenous adrenocorticotrophic hormone.

Nursing Care
Immediate treatment is directed toward combating shock: restoring blood circulation, administering fluids, monitoring vital signs and positioning the patient in a recumbent position with legs elevated. Hydrocortisone is given intravenously and followed with 5 per cent dextrose in normal saline. Vasopressor amines may be required if hypotension persists.

Antibiotics may be prescribed if infection has precipitated adrenal crisis in a patient with chronic adrenal insufficiency. Additionally, the patient will be examined closely to determine other factors or illnesses that led to the acute episode.

If the adrenal gland does not regain function, the patient will require life-long replacement of corticosteroids and mineralocorticoids to prevent recurrence of adrenal insufficiency and to prevent Addisonian crisis in times of stress and illness. Additionally, the patient will probably be required to supplement dietary intake with added salt during times of gastrointestinal losses of fluids through vomiting and diarrhoea.

► **NURSING PROCESS**
► **THE PATIENT WITH ADRENAL INSUFFICIENCY**

► *Assessment*

The nursing history and examination focus on the presence of symptoms of fluid imbalance and on the patient's level of stress. The blood pressure and pulse rate are observed as the patient moves from a lying to a standing position to detect inadequate fluid volume. Additionally, the patient's skin colour and turgor are assessed for changes related to chronic adrenal insufficiency and decreased blood volume. A history of weight changes, presence of muscle weakness and level of fatigue are obtained.

The patient, family and/or close friends are asked about the onset of illness or increased stress that may have precipitated the acute crisis.

► *Patient's Problems*

Based on the assessment, the main problems for the patient with adrenal insufficiency may include the following:

● Fluid volume deficit related to inadequate fluid intake and to fluid loss secondary to inadequate adrenal hormone secretion.
● Inadequate response to stress related to inadequate production of adrenal hormones.
● Lack of knowledge related to the need for hormone replacement and dietary modification.

► *Planning and Implementation*
► **Expected Outcomes**

The patient's outcomes may include improved fluid balance, improved response to stress and decreased stress in life, and increased knowledge about the need for hormone replacement and dietary modifications.

Nursing Care

Fluid Balance Measures
Weight changes are recorded daily since they provide very useful information about the adequacy of the patient's fluid and hormone replacement. Additionally, the patient's skin turgor and mucous membranes are assessed to provide information about fluid balance. The patient is requested to report increased thirst, which may indicate impending fluid imbalance.

The patient is encouraged to consume foods and fluids that will assist in restoring and maintaining fluid and electrolyte balance.

Stress Reduction
When the patient's condition is stabilized, precautions are taken to avoid stressful conditions, since stress could precipitate another hypotensive episode. Attempts are made to detect signs of infection or other stress that may have triggered the crisis in the first place. The nurse assists the patient to assess the level of stress and to determine if alternative approaches to dealing with stress are indicated.

During the acute crisis, a quiet, nonstressful environment is maintained. All procedures are explained to the patient in order to reduce fear and anxiety. The nurse explains to loved ones the rationale for minimizing stress during the acute crisis and the measures for helping the patient reduce or avoid stress.

► *Evaluation*
► **Expected Outcomes**

1. Patient achieves improved fluid balance.
   a. Exhibits normal skin turgor and moist mucous membranes.
   b. Reports stable weight and no excessive thirst.
   c. Reports absence of symptoms of postural hypotension (lightheadedness, dizziness, fainting on rising).
   d. Explains rationale for increasing salt and fluid intake in times of illness, increased stress and very hot weather.
   e. Identifies foods high in sodium.
   f. Consumes high-sodium foods during illness, in very hot weather and in times of increased stress.
   g. Seeks health care when illness or stress level exceeds the ability of patient to manage.
2. Improved response to stress and decreased stress level.
   a. Reports normal daily stresses without development of symptoms and adrenal crisis.
   b. Identifies sources of excessive stress and ways to avoid them.
3. Increases knowledge about the need for hormone replacement and dietary modifications.
   a. Explains rationale for hormone replacement.
   b. Identifies consequences of inadequate hormone replacement.
   c. Demonstrates proper technique of administering injectable hormone for use in emergencies.
   d. Explains how to modify hormone dosage and diet to meet changing needs during illness, stress and hot weather.
   e. Wears Medic Alert bracelet and carries medical information at all times.
   f. Designs schedule to ensure adherence to required medication therapy.
   g. Takes medication as prescribed.
   h. Identifies signs and symptoms of overdosage and underdosage of hormone.
   i. Exhibits absence of signs and symptoms of overdosage and underdosage of hormone.

Cushing's Syndrome

Cushing's syndrome is the opposite of Addison's disease, with its clinical characteristics reflecting excessive, rather than deficient, adrenocortical activity. The syndrome may result from excessive administration of cortisone or adrenocorticotrophic hormone or from hyperplasia of the adrenal cortex.

Altered Physiology

The basic lesion responsible for Cushing's syndrome may be a tumour arising in the cortex of one of the adrenal glands or a basophilic adenoma of the pituitary glands involving an overgrowth of pituitary cells, producing adrenocorticotrophic hormone, which stimulates the adrenal cortex despite adequate amounts of circulating adrenocortical hormones. The normal feedback mechanisms that control the function of the adrenal cortex become ineffective, and the usual diurnal pattern of cortisol is lost. The signs and symptoms of Cushing's syndrome are primarily a result of unregulated secretion of glucocorticoids and androgens or sex hormones, although there may also be altered mineralocorticoid secretion.

Clinical Features

When overproduction of the adrenal cortical hormone occurs, growth arrest, obesity and musculoskeletal changes occur.

The classic picture of Cushing's syndrome in the adult shows a characteristic central type obesity, with a fatty 'buffalo hump' in the neck and supraclavicular areas, a heavy trunk and relatively thin extremities (Figure 18.5). The skin is thinned, fragile and easily traumatized; ecchymoses and striae develop. The patient complains of weakness and lassitude. Sleep is disturbed because of altered diurnal secretion of cortisol. Excessive protein catabolism occurs, producing muscle wasting and osteoporosis. Kyphosis, backache and compression fractures of the vertebrae may result. Retention of sodium and water occurs as a result of increased mineralocorticoid activity, contributing to the hypertension and congestive heart failure commonly seen in Cushing's syndrome.

The patient takes on a 'moon-faced' appearance and may experience increased oiliness of the skin and acne. There is increased susceptibility to infection. Hyperglycaemia or overt diabetes may develop.

In females of all ages, virilization may occur as a result of excess androgens. Virilization is characterized by the appearance of masculine traits and the recession of feminine traits. There is an excessive growth of hair on the face (hirsutism), the breasts atrophy, menses cease, the clitoris enlarges and the patient's voice deepens. Libido is lost in males and females.

Changes occur in mood and mental activity; a psychosis may develop on occasion. Distress and depression are common and are increased by the magnitude of the physical changes that occur with this syndrome. If the Cushing's syndrome is a consequence of pituitary tumour, visual disturbances may occur.

The patient may also report weight changes, and slow healing of minor cuts and bruises.

Diagnosis

Diagnosis of this syndrome includes an increase in serum sodium and blood glucose levels and a decreased serum concentration of potassium, a reduction in the number of blood eosinophils and a disappearance of lymphoid tissue. Measurements of plasma and urinary cortisol levels are obtained. Several blood samples may be collected to determine if the normal diurnal variation in plasma levels is present. This variation is frequently abolished in adrenal dysfunction. If several blood samples are required, it is essential that they be collected at the times specified and the time of collection be noted on the requisition slip. Diagnostic studies frequently also include 24-hour urine collection for levels of 17-hydroxycorticosteroids and 17-ketosteroids, the urinary metabolites of cortisol and androgens. In Cushing's syndrome, these levels and plasma cortisol levels are elevated.

A low-dose dexamethasone suppression test may be conducted in which a low dose of dexamethasone, a potent synthetic glucocorticoid, is administered and plasma cortisol and urine 17-hydroxycorticosteroid levels are obtained. In patients with normal adrenal function, even low doses of the glucocorticoid will produce decreased cortisol and 17-hydroxycorticosteroid levels. In patients with bilateral adrenal hyperplasia or adrenal tumours, there will be no decrease in these levels.

A computerized tomography scan may be performed to localize adrenal tissue and detect tumours of the adrenal gland.

Management

If possible, the cause of Cushing's syndrome is removed. For pituitary disorders, hypophysectomy or pituitary irradiation may be required. Adrenalectomy (see p. 660) remains the treatment of choice in cases of adrenal hyperplasia. Rare hyperplasia cases may benefit from a primary therapy directed against the pituitary, for example, patients with large pituitary adenomas or those with mild adrenal hyperfunction. In the latter, slow but successful responses to radiation therapy may be anticipated.

Postoperatively, symptoms of adrenal insufficiency may begin to appear 12 to 48 hours after surgery because of removal of the source of high levels of adrenal hormones. Temporary replacement therapy with hydrocortisone may be necessary for several months until the remaining adrenal gland regains its ability to respond normally to the body's needs. If both adrenal glands have been removed (bilateral adrenalectomy), life-time

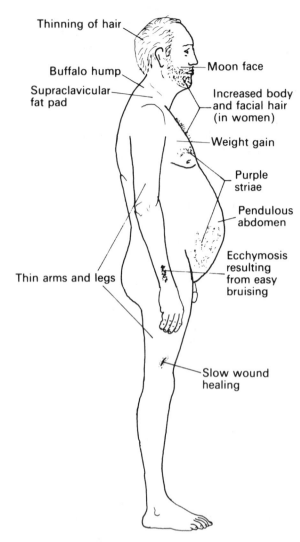

Figure 18.5 Features of Cushing's syndrome invariably include truncal obesity, thin extremities, moon face, buffalo hump and supraclavicular fullness. Broad purple striae appear at stretch points, such as the adbomen, hips and shoulders. Body and facial hair is increased, and thinning of scalp hair may be noted only if androgens are increased.

replacement of adrenal cortex hormones will be necessary.

If the Cushing's syndrome is a result of externally administered (exogenous) corticosteroids, an attempt will be made to reduce or taper the drug dose to the minimum level adequate to treat the underlying disease process (e.g., autoimmune and allergic diseases and rejection of transplanted organs). Frequently, alternate-day therapy decreases the symptoms of Cushing's syndrome and allows recovery of the adrenal glands' responsiveness to adrenocorticotrophic hormone.

► *Assessment*

The nursing history and examination focus on the effects on the body of high concentrations of adrenal cortex hormones and on the inability of the adrenal cortex to respond to changes in cortisol and aldosterone levels. The history includes information about the patient's level of activity and ability to carry out routine and self-care activities. The patient's skin is observed and assessed for trauma, infection, breakdown, bruising and oedema. Changes in physical appearance are noted, and the patient's responses to these changes are elicited. Throughout the interview and examination, the nurse assesses the patient's mental function, including mood, responses to questions, awareness of environment and level of depression.

► *Patient's Problems*

Based on the assessment, the main problems for the patient with Cushing's syndrome may include the following:

● Impaired ability to carry out self-care activities related to weakness, fatigue, muscle wasting and altered sleep patterns.
● Impaired skin integrity related to oedema, impaired healing and thin and fragile skin.
● Increased susceptibility to injury and infection related to altered protein metabolism and inflammatory response.
● Altered body image related to altered physical appearance, impaired sexual functioning and decrease in activity level.
● Altered mental function related to mood swings, irritability and depression.

► *Planning and Implementation*
► Expected Outcomes

The patient's main outcomes may include increased ability to carry out self-care activities, improved skin integrity, decreased risk of injury and infection, improved body image and improved mental function.

Nursing Care

Rest and Activity

Weakness, fatigue and muscle wasting make it difficult for the patient with Cushing's syndrome to carry out normal activities. Yet moderate activity should be encouraged to prevent complications of immobility and promote increased self-esteem. Insomnia often contributes to the patient's fatigue. Rest periods are planned and spaced throughout the day. Efforts are made to promote a relaxing, quiet environment for rest and sleep.

Skin Care

Meticulous skin care is necessary to avoid traumatizing the patient's fragile skin. Use of adhesive tape is avoided because it can irritate the skin, bony prominences are assessed frequently and the patient is encouraged to change position frequently to prevent skin breakdown.

Decreased Risk of Injury and Infection

A protective environment must be established to prevent falls, fractures and other injuries to bones and soft tissues. The patient who is very weak may require assistance in ambulating to prevent falls or bumping into sharp corners of furniture. Unnecessary exposure to visitors, staff or patients with infections is avoided. The patient is assessed frequently for subtle signs of infection since the anti-inflammatory effects of glucocorticoids may mask the common signs of inflammation and infection. Foods high in protein, calcium and vitamin D are recommended to minimize muscle wasting and osteoporosis.

Improved Body Image

If removal of the cause of Cushing's syndrome is possible and is carried out, the major physical changes will disappear in time. However, the patient may benefit from discussion of the impact the changes have had on self-concept and relationships with others. The weight gain and oedema seen with Cushing's syndrome may be modified by a low-carbohydrate, low sodium diet. A high-protein intake may reduce some of the other bothersome symptoms.

Improved Mental Function

Explanations to the patient, family and close friends about the cause of emotional instability are important in helping them cope with the mood swings, irritability and depression that may occur. Psychotic behaviour may occur in a few patients and should be reported. The patient and significant others are encouraged to verbalize their feelings.

Additionally, the patient is prepared for adrenalectomy, if indicated, and postoperative care (see below). Peptic ulcer and diabetes mellitus are common in the patient with Cushing's syndrome; therefore, management includes assessment of stools for blood and urine for glucosuria and appropriate intervention if indicated.

▶ Evaluation
▶ Expected Outcomes

1. Patient increases participation in self-care activities.
   a. Plans activities and exercises to allow alternating periods of rest and activity.
   b. Participates in hygienic care.
   c. Reports improved wellbeing.
   d. Sleeps soundly at night and during planned rest periods.
   e. Is free of complications of immobility.
2. Attains/maintains skin integrity.
   a. Has intact skin, without evidence of breakdown or infection.
   b. Shows evidence of decreased oedema in extremities and trunk.
   c. Avoids trauma to skin.
   d. Changes position frequently.
   e. Inspects bony prominences daily.
3. Decreases risk of injury and infection.
   a. Is free of fractures or soft tissue injuries.
   b. Is free of ecchymotic areas.
   c. Uses measures to prevent trauma (e.g., seeks assistance when necessary, arranges rugs and furniture to prevent falls and bumps).
   d. Avoids people with cold or influenza symptoms.
   e. Experiences no temperature elevation, redness, pain and other signs of infection and inflammation.
   f. Explains rationale for foods high in protein, calcium and vitamin D.
   g. Selects and eats foods high in protein, calcium and vitamin D.
4. Achieves improved body image.
   a. Uses make-up appropriately and selects clothes that enhance appearance.
   b. Socializes with others.
   c. Uses good grooming (e.g., skin care, hair care).
   d. Is not gaining weight.
   e. Adheres to diet (e.g., consumes high-protein, low-carbohydrate, low-sodium diet).
   f. Verbalizes feelings about changes in appearance, sexual function and activity level.
   g. States that physical changes are a result of excessive corticosteroids.
5. Exhibits improved mental functioning.
   a. Identifies reason for mood changes as excessive corticosteroid level.
   b. Expresses feelings to nurse and loved ones.
   c. Participates in social activities.
   d. Notifies nurse, doctor and family or close friends if feelings become overwhelming.

Primary Aldosteronism

The principal action of aldosterone is to conserve body sodium. Under the influence of this hormone, the kidneys excrete less sodium and more potassium and hydrogen.

Excessive production of aldosterone, which occurs in some patients with functioning tumours of the adrenal gland, causes a distinctive pattern of biochemical changes and a corresponding set of clinical features that are diagnostic of this condition. Such patients exhibit a profound decline in the blood levels of potassium (hypokalaemia) and hydrogen ions (alkalosis), as demonstrated by an increase in pH and carbon-dioxide combining power. The serum sodium level is normal or elevated depending on the amount of water reabsorbed with the sodium. Hypertension is usually present, although aldosteronism is the primary cause of only 3 per cent of cases of hypertension.

Hypokalaemia is responsible for the variable muscle weakness in patients with aldosteronism, as well as an inability on the part of the kidneys to acidify or concentrate the urine. Accordingly, the urine volume is excessive, leading to complaints of polyuria. Serum, by contrast, becomes abnormally concentrated, contributing to excessive thirst (polydipsia) and arterial hypertension. A secondary increase in blood volume and possible direct effects of aldosterone on nerve receptors such as the carotid sinus are other factors producing the hypertension. Hypokalaemic alkalosis may decrease the plasma-ionized calcium level and predispose the patient to tetany and paraesthesias.

Diagnostic studies reveal, in addition to a high or normal serum sodium level and low serum potassium level, high serum aldosterone levels and low serum renin levels.

Treatment of primary aldosteronism usually involves surgical removal of the adrenal tumour through adrenalectomy.

Adrenalectomy

Adrenalectomy is the treatment of choice in primary Cushing's syndrome and aldosteronism. In addition, it is also used in the treatment of adrenal tumours and for malignancy of the breast and prostate gland.

For Adrenal Tumours

All of the endocrine disturbances associated with a functioning tumour of the adrenal cortex or medulla can be relieved completely, and the patient improved dramatically, by surgical removal of the involved gland. Adrenalectomy is performed through an incision in the loin or the abdomen. In general, the postoperative care resembles that given for any abdominal operation. Following surgery for adrenal cortical tumours, the patient is susceptible to fluctuations in adrenocortical hormones and may require administration of corticosteroids, fluids and other agents to maintain blood pressure and prevent acute complication. Attention is also directed towards maintenance of a normal serum glucose level with insulin and appropriate intravenous fluids and dietary modifications.

Nursing care in the postoperative period includes frequent assessment of vital signs so that early indications of haemorrhage and possible adrenal crisis may be detected and treated. Stressful situations can be avoided by explaining the treatment, promoting comfort measures, establishing priorities of care and providing rest periods for the patient.

For Malignancy of Breasts or Prostate

Certain malignancies, notably those of the breast and the prostate are affected by the hormones produced by endocrine glands. Thus, ovarian hormones are known to have an effect on carcinoma of the breast, and hormones of the testes on carcinoma of the prostate. In some patients, even after suppression of endocrine stimulation, the hormones are still present, and they have been found to arise from adrenal glands. For this reason, bilateral adrenalectomy may be performed in an effort to control recurrent carcinoma of the breast or the prostate. The adrenals are approached either transabdominally or through the posterior bed of the twelfth rib.

Postoperatively, adrenocortical hormone must be administered in appropriate dosage to overcome the sudden deprivation of those hormones by the operation. The dosage of adrenocortical hormone may be reduced gradually as the body adjusts itself to its new level of hormone production.

Corticosteroid Therapy

Corticosteroids are used extensively for adrenal insufficiency and are also widely used in suppressing inflammation, controlling allergic reactions and reducing the rejection process in transplantation. Their anti-inflammatory and anti-allergy actions make corticosteroids effective in treating rheumatic or connective tissue diseases such as rheumatoid arthritis and systemic lupus erythematosus. High doses seem to permit patients to tolerate high degrees of stress. Such anti-stress action may be due to the ability of corticosteroids to aid circulating vasopressor substances in keeping the blood pressure elevated, or it may be due to other effects, such as the maintenance of the plasma glucose level.

Although the synthetic steroids are safer for some patients because of relative freedom from mineralocorticoid activity, most natural and synthetic corticosteroids produce similar kinds of chronic toxicity. The size of the dose required to bring about desired anti-inflammatory and anti-allergy effects also causes metabolic effects, pituitary gland suppression and changes in the function of the central nervous system. Such changes may be disabling and even dangerous.

In view of these possible effects, it is obvious that while adrenocorticosteroids are highly effective therapeutically, they may also be very dangerous. Dosages of these medications are frequently altered to allow high concentrations when absolutely necessary and then tapered in an attempt to avoid undesirable effects. This requires that patients be closely observed for side-effects and the dose reduced when high doses are no longer required. Suppression of the adrenal cortex may persist up to a year after a course of corticosteroids of only two weeks' duration.

Major Side-Effects of Corticosteroid Therapy

Adverse effects are more likely to occur when steroid therapy is used for long periods of time. In general, such effects are classified as follows:

Metabolic Effects

Changes in the metabolism may occur following large doses of glucocorticoids or mineralocorticoids. Excessive glucocorticoid activity (hypercorticism) causes clinical features of Cushing's syndrome, including the characteristic rounding of the face and an abnormal distribution of body fat.

Because of changes in the metabolism of carbohydrate, protein and fat, certain other complications may occur. For example, some patients may develop peptic ulcer, diabetes mellitus or osteoporosis. This does not mean that steroid therapy is to be avoided. It does mean that supportive therapy is required to minimize the threat of these other conditions. For example, it is necessary for the patient with a history of peptic ulcer to continue with antacids and perhaps antispasmodic medications, at the same time recognizing that peptic ulcer pain may not be present as a warning sign during the administration of corticosteroids. For the patient with diabetes, oral hypoglycaemic agents should be continued or insulin dosages adjusted as needed. For the patient with osteoporosis, it is helpful to adhere to a high-protein diet and to take calcium salt and vitamin D supplement, looking out for possible hypercalciuria. Special efforts are made to prevent an injury that may result in a fracture.

Infection may spread with minimal symptoms, because the patient's defence against invading organisms is lowered by the metabolic effects of the steroid. Viral and fungal infections create further problems because of the difficulty in treating these conditions.

Endocrine Effects

Prolonged steroid therapy has a tendency to suppress certain functions of the anterior portion of the pituitary gland. Hence, growth in children may be halted following long-term treatment with steroids owing to adrenal atrophy and suppression of the pituitary's capacity to release adrenocorticotrophic hormone. Although this effect may not be apparent under ordinary circumstances, it is obvious during times of unusual stress. During these periods of acute adrenal insufficiency, massive doses of corticosteroids are required to prevent adrenal collapse.

Central Nervous System Effects

Euphoria results from the action of corticosteroids on the central nervous system. Since such a reaction often creates psychological dependency on steroids, the patient may resist being removed from these drugs. With prolonged use of corticosteroids, the patient may experience mood swings that include excitement, restlessness, depression and sleeplessness. Nursing support and understanding are required as the patient moves through these experiences. Any tendency to emotional, psychological or psychotic difficulties needs to be brought to the attention of the doctor before steroids are prescribed.

Table 18.3 provides an overview of the management of the patient on steroid therapy.

Dosage Schedule

Attempts have been made to determine the best time to administer pharmacological doses of steroids. Once the patient's symptoms have been controlled on a six-hour or eight-hour programme, a switch is made to a once-daily or every-other-day schedule. In keeping with the natural secretion of cortisol, the best time of the day for the total steroid dose is in the early morning, from 7 to 8 a.m. Large-dose therapy at 8 a.m., when the gland is most active, produces maximal suppression of the gland. A large 8 a.m. dosage is more physiological, since it allows the body to escape effects of the steroids from 4 p.m. to 6 a.m., when serum levels are normally low, hence minimizing cushingoid effects. If symptoms of the disease being treated are suppressed successfully, alternative-day therapy is helpful in reducing pituitary-adrenal suppression in patients requiring chronic therapy. Taking the total steroid dose every other day presents some problems in that patients complain of discomfort on the second day. It may be necessary for the nurse to explain to the patient that this regime may be necessary to prevent toxic reactions.

Tapering of Steroids

Corticosteroid dosages are reduced gradually to allow normal adrenal function to return and to prevent steroid-induced adrenal insufficiency. Up to one year or more after use of corticosteroids, the patient is at risk of adrenal insufficiency in times of stress. For example, if surgery for any reason is necessary, the patient is likely to receive intravenous steroids during and after surgery to prevent the occurrence of acute adrenal crisis.

THE PITUITARY GLAND

Hypopituitarism

Hypopituitarism is pituitary insufficiency resulting from destruction of the anterior lobe of the pituitary gland. Panhypopituitarism (Simmonds' disease) is total absence of all pituitary secretions and is rare.

The total destruction of the pituitary gland by trauma, tumour or vascular lesion removes every stimulus that is normally received by the thyroid, the gonads and the adrenal glands. The resulting endocrinopathy is characterized by extreme weight loss, emaciation, atrophy of all endo-

Table 18.3 *The patient on steroid therapy*

Side effects	Nursing care	Possible medical management
Cardiovascular system effects: Hypertension Thromboembolic complications Arteritis	Report to doctor Continue assessment of patient	Reduce dosage of steroids
Infection	Assess for atypical indicators of infection Report to doctor Limit visitors and prevent exposure to infection if possible Promote cleanliness	Prescribe antimicrobial agents
Eye complications: Glaucoma Corneal lesions	Report to doctor	Refer to ophthalmologist
Adrenal insufficiency as manifested by peripheral circulatory collapse (orthostatic hypotension)	Report to doctor Remain with patient Decrease sources of stress Assist with administration of fluids and steroids	Prescribe hydrocortisone and intravenous normal saline; prescribe oral corticosteroid when patient's condition is stable
Musculoskeletal effects	Encourage diet high in calcium and vitamin D Use caution in moving and ambulating patient Avoid trauma and falls	Prescribe synthetic oestrogens or androgens Prescribe calcium supplement and oral preparations of vitamin D
Moon face (Cushing's syndrome) Weight gain and oedema Potassium loss	Suggest calorie restriction Suggest sodium restriction Report symptoms to doctor Suggest foods high in potassium	Consider switching steroid medication Prescribe diuretics Prescribe potassium supplement
Acne Increased urinary frequency and nocturia	Suggest frequent washing Assess for urinary tract infection and glycosuria	Prescribe topical medications Evaluate for diabetes mellitus and order urinalysis

Counselling of patients on long-term steroids

1. Recognize that steroids are valuable and useful medications but if taken for longer than two weeks, certain side-effects may be noticed
2. Side-effects that are to be reported to the doctor include dizziness when rising from chair or bed (postural hypotension indicative of adrenal insufficiency), nausea, vomiting, thirst, abdominal pain, pain of any type, feelings of depression or nervousness and development of an infection
3. Other side-effects may include weight gain (perhaps due to water retention), acne, headaches, fatigue and increased urinary frequency
4. If the patient has a fall or is in an accident, the condition may precipitate adrenal failure. Patient requires an immediate injection of hydrocortisone phosphate. (Patients on long-term steroid therapy should wear a Medic Alert tag and have a kit with hydrocortisone)

crine glands and organs, hair loss, impotence, amenorrhoea, hypometabolism and hypoglycaemia. Coma and death will ensue without replacement of the missing hormones.

Hypophysectomy

Hypophysectomy, or removal of the pituitary gland, may be done for several reasons, including treatment of primary tumours of the pituitary gland. In diabetic retinopathy, it is used to half the progress of haemorrhagic retinopathy and avoid blindness. Hypophysectomy is carried out as a palliative measure to relieve bone pain secondary to metastasis of malignant lesions of the breast and prostate. Pituitary hormones influence the growth of the normal breast and stimulate the function of the ovaries and the adrenal glands. Hypophysectomy removes the hormonal influences of these glands and reduces stimuli to the continued growth of the neoplasm.

There are several methods of pituitary ablation (removal). It can be done surgically through the transfrontal, subcranial or oronasal–transsphenoidal approaches. The pituitary can also be destroyed by irradiation or cryosurgery. (See Chapters 31 to 33 for care of the patient undergoing cranial surgery.)

The absence of the pituitary gland alters the function of many parts of the body. Menstruation ceases and infertility occurs after total or nearly total ablation of the pituitary gland. Substitution therapy with adrenal steroids (hydrocortisone) and thyroid hormone may be necessary.

Diabetes Insipidus

Diabetes insipidus is a disorder of the posterior lobe of the pituitary gland due to a deficiency of vasopressin, the antidiuretic hormone. It is characterized by great thirst (polydipsia) and large volumes of dilute urine. The cause is unknown, although it may be secondary to head trauma, brain tumour or surgical ablation or irradiation of the pituitary gland. Without the action of vasopressin on the distal nephron of the kidney, an enormous daily output of very dilute, waterlike urine with a specific gravity of 1.001 to 1.005 occurs. The urine contains no abnormal substances, such as sugar and albumin. Because of the intense thirst, the patient tends to drink 4 to 40 litres of fluid daily, with a special craving for cold water.

In the hereditary form of diabetes insipidus, the primary symptoms may begin at birth. When it occurs in adults, the polyuria may have an insidious onset, although sometimes it occurs suddenly and may be related to an injury.

The disease cannot be controlled by limiting the intake of fluids, since urine loss of high volumes of urine continues even without fluid replacement. Attempts to do this cause the patient to suffer extremely from an insatiable craving for fluid and to develop severe dehydration and hypernatraemia.

Diagnosis

The fluid deprivation test is carried out, in which fluids are withheld for 8 to 12 hours or until 3 per cent of the body weight is lost. The patient is weighed frequently during the time fluid is withheld. Plasma and urine osmolality studies are done at the beginning and end of the test. Inability to increase specific gravity and osmolality of the

urine are characteristic of diabetes insipidus. The patient with diabetes insipidus will continue to excrete large volumes of urine with low specific gravity and will experience weight loss, rising serum osmolality and elevated serum sodium levels. The patient's condition needs to be assessed frequently during the test, and the test is terminated if the patient develops problems such as tachycardia, excessive weight loss or hypotension.

Management

The objectives of therapy are: (1) to assure adequate fluid replacement; (2) to replace vasopressin (which is usually a life-long therapeutic programme); and (3) to search for and correct the underlying intracranial pathology.

Desmopressin (DDAVP), synthetic vasopression without the vascular effects of natural antidiuretic hormone, is particularly valuable because its action lasts longer and it has fewer adverse effects than other preparations previously used to treat the disease. It is administered intranasally with the patient sniffing the solution into the nose through a flexible plastic tube. Two administrations daily appear to control the symptoms.

Another form of therapy is the intramuscular administration of antidiuretic hormone, vasopressin tannate in oil, which is given at intervals of 36 to 48 hours or longer. The effect is a reduction in urinary volume for 24 to 48 hours. The vial of medication should be warmed or shaken vigorously before administration. The injection is given in the evening so that maximum results are obtained during sleep. Abdominal cramps are a side-effect of this drug.

The drug lypressin is absorbed through the nasal mucosa into the blood and is another method of administering vasopressin. Its duration may be too short for patients with severe disease. The patient should be observed for chronic rhinopharyngitis if this modality of treatment is used.

Clofibrate, a hypolipidaemic agent, has been found to have an antidiuretic effect on patients with diabetes insipidus who have some residual hypothalmic vasopressin. Chlorpropamide and thiazide diuretics are also used in mild forms of the disease, since they potentiate the action of vasopressin. The patient receiving chlorpropamide should be warned of the possibility of hypoglycaemic reactions.

The patient will require encouragement and support if studies are being undertaken for a possible cranial lesion. The patient and carers are advised about follow-up care and emergency measures. The patient is also advised to wear a Medic Alert bracelet and to carry information about this disorder and the medications at all times.

Syndrome of Inappropriate Antidiuretic Hormone Secretion

The syndrome of inappropriate antidiuretic hormone secretion (SIADH) refers to excessive antidiuretic hormone secretion from the pituitary gland even in the face of subnormal serum osmolarity. Patients with this disorder cannot excrete a dilute urine. They retain fluids and develop a sodium deficiency (dilutional hyponatraemia). The syndrome of inappropriate antidiuretic hormone secretion is often of nonendocrine origin. That is, the syndrome may occur in patients with bronchogenic carcinoma in which malignant lung cells synthesize and release antidiuretic hormone. This syndrome has also occurred with severe pneumonia, pneumothorax and other disorders of the lungs, in addition to malignant tumours that affect other organs.

Disorders of the central nervous system, such as head injury, brain surgery or tumour, or meningitis are thought to produce syndrome of inappropriate antidiuretic hormone secretion by direct stimulation of the pituitary gland. Some drugs (vincristine, phenothiazines, tricyclic antidepressants and others) have been implicated in syndrome of inappropriate antidiuretic hormone secretion; they either directly stimulate the pituitary gland or increase the sensitivity of renal tubules to circulating antidiuretic hormone.

This syndrome is generally managed by eliminating the underlying cause if possible and restricting the patient's fluid intake. Since retained water is slowly excreted through the kidneys, the extracellular fluid volume contracts and the serum sodium concentration gradually increases toward normal. Diuretics may be used along with fluid restriction if severe hyponatraemia is present.

BIBLIOGRAPHY

Hinchliff, S. and Montague, S. (1988) *Physiology for Nursing Practice*, Baillière Tindall, Eastbourne.

Watson, J. and Royle, J. (1988) *Watson's Medical/Surgical Nursing and Related Physiology*, Baillière Tindall, Eastbourne.

FURTHER READING

Books

Goldberg, K. (ed.) (1987) *Baillière's Clinical Endocrinology and Metabolism: International Practice and Research, Volume 1, Number 1*, Baillière Tindall, Eastbourne.

Burger, H. G. (1988) *Endocrine Problems*, Springhouse Corporation, Springhouse.

Edwards, C. (ed.) (1986) *Endocrinology*, Heinemann Medical, London.

Fletcher, R. F. (1987) *Lecture Notes on Endocrinology* (4th edition), Blackwell Scientific, Oxford.

Hall, R. (1989) *Fundamentals of Clinical Endocrinology* (4th edition), Churchill Livingstone, Edinburgh.

Hart, I. R. and Newton, R. W. (eds) (1983) *Endocrinology*, MTP, Lancaster.

Marsden, P. (1985) *Endocrinology*, MTP, Lancaster.

Muthe, N. C. (1981) *Endocrinology: A Nursing Approach*, Little, Brown & Co., Boston.

Plowman, P. N. (1987) *Endocrinology and Metabolic Diseases*, John Wiley, Chichester.

White, D. (1984) *Hormones and Metabolic Control*, Edward Arnold, London.

Wise, P. H. (1986) *Endocrinology*, Churchill Livingstone, Edinburgh.

Articles

General

Alderman, C. (1988) The adrenals, *Nursing Standard*, 1 October, p. 26.

Alderman, C. (1988) The thyroid and the parathyroid, *Nursing Standard*, 8 October, Vol. 52, No. 2, p. 26.

Arendt, J. (1985) The pineal: a gland that measures time? *New Scientist*, 25 July, No. 1466, p. 36.

Avioli, L. (1987) Hyperparathyroidism and prevention of osteoporosis, *Geriatric Medicine*, March, Vol. 17, No. 3, p. 47.

Baylis, P. (1989) Vasopressin: physiology and diabetes insipidus, *Medicine*, March, Vol. 63, p. 2616.

Behi, R. (1989) Treatment and care of thyroid problems, *Nursing*, September, Vol. 3, No. 41, p. 4.

Boyle, I. T. (1989) Parathyroid disorders and hypercalcaemia, *Medicine*, April, Vol. 64, p. 2624.

Caldwell, G. (1985) A new strategy for thyroid function testing (RIE), *Lancet*, 18 May, Vol. 1, p. 1117.

Cassar, J. (1989) Hyperparathyroidism, *Update*, 1 April, Vol. 38, No. 7, p. 756.

Collins, R. (1988) Parathyroid disease, *Surgery*, November, Vol. 62, p. 1486.

Connacher, A. (1987) Cushing's syndrome—overproduction of glucocorticoids, *Update*, 1 January, Vol. 34, No. 1, p. 66.

De Bruin, T. (1988) Graves' disease: immunological and immunogenetic, *British Medical Journal*, 7 May, Vol. 296, p. 1292.

De-Kretser, D. M. (1989) Male hypogonadism, *Medicine*, April, Vol. 64, p. 2643.

Edwards, C. (1989) Pituitary tumours, *Medicine*, March, Vol. 63, p. 2588.

Frost, G. (1985) Management of patients with congenital hypothyroidism, *British Medical Journal*, 18 May, Vol. 290, p. 1485.

Fry, J. (1986) Thyroid disease, *Update*, 15 May, Vol. 32, No. 10, p. 901.

Hardcastle, W. (1989) Management of Addison's disease, *Nursing*, September, Vol. 3, No. 41, p. 7.

Harris, G. (1983) The endocrine system; thyroid gland; adrenal glands, *Nursing*, May, Vol. 13, p. 359.

Howlett, T. (1989) Cushing's syndrome, *Medicine*, March, Vol. 63, p. 2605.

Howlett, T. (1989) Addison's disease, *Medicne*, March, Vol. 63, p. 2611.

Jeffcoate, W. (1986) Investigation of endocrine disorders in general, *The Practitioner*, September, Vol. 230, No. 1419, p. 765.

Klein, R. (1986) Screening for congenital hypothyroidism, *Lancet*, 16 August, Vol. 2, p. 403.

Laurance, B. (1985) The Prader Willi syndrome, *Maternal and Child Health*, April, Vol. 10, No. 4, p. 106.

McAvoy, B. (1986) Thyroid function tests, *Update*, 15 April, Vol. 32, No. 8, p. 719.

Milne, C. (1988) Endocrine system: the pituitary gland, *Nursing Standard*, 17 September, Vol. 2, No. 50, p. 26.

Ramsay, I. D. (1989) Thyroid disease, *Maternal and Child Health*, April, Vol. 14, No. 4, p. 112.

Reibsane, J. (1987) Thyroid crisis, *Nursing*, November, Vol. 87, p. 33.

Rodin, A. (1989) Thyroid disease in pregnancy, *British Journal of Hospital Medicine*, March, Vol. 41, No. 3, p. 234.

Sarsany, S. (1988) Thyroid storm, *Registered Nurse*, July, Vol. 51, p. 46.

Toft, A. (1989) Hypothyroidism, *Medicine*, March, Vol. 63, p. 2596.

Wheeler, M. (1988) Treatment of thyrotoxicosis, *Surgery*, November, Vol. 62, p. 1480.

Wheeler, M. (1988) Malignant goitre, *Surgery*, December, Vol. 63, p. 1505.

Young, A. (1989) Thyroiditis, *Surgery*, January, Vol. 64, p. 1519.

Pharmacology

Bloom, S. (1987) Somatostatin, *British Medical Journal*, 1 August, Vol. 295, p. 288.

Hague, W. (1987) Treatment of endocrine diseases, *British Medical Journal*, 31 January, Vol. 294, p. 297.

Howlett, T. (1986) Corticosteroid therapy, *The Practitioner*, September, Vol. 230, No. 1419, p. 813.

Surgery

Hughes, S. (1989) Surgical treatment of adrenal disease, *British Journal of Hospital Medicine*, April, Vol. 41, No. 4, p. 350.

Russell, R. (1986) Thyroidectomy, *British Journal of Hospital Medicine*, May, Vol. 35, No. 5, p. 327.

Young, E. (1988) Goitre, *Surgery*, December, Vol. 63, p. 1499.

Unit 6

RENAL AND URINARY PROBLEMS

chapter 19

ASSESSMENT OF RENAL AND URINARY FUNCTION

OVERVIEW OF PHYSIOLOGY

The kidneys, ureters, bladder and urethra compose the urinary system. The kidneys' main function is to remove unwanted substances, including water from the blood. These materials form the urine, which is transported through the ureters for temporary storage in the urinary bladder. During the act of micturition (urination), the bladder contracts and the urine is excreted from the body through the urethra. Urine formation regulates the water content and electrolyte composition of the body fluids. Although fluid and electrolytes can be lost by other routes, such as in perspiration or faeces, it is the kidneys that precisely regulate the internal environment of the body. The renal excretory function is necessary for maintenance of life. However, unlike the cardiovascular and respiratory systems, complete malfunction of the kidneys may not cause death for several days. Use of the artificial kidney or renal replacement therapy make it possible to substitute for certain functions of the kidneys.

An important feature of the urinary system is its ability to adapt to wide variations in fluid load based on individual habits and patterns. Basically, the kidneys must be able to excrete that which is ingested in the diet and not eliminated by other organs. This usually amounts to one to two litres of water per day, 6–8 g of salt (sodium chloride) per day, 6–8 g potassium chloride per day and 70 mg of acid equivalents per day. In addition, protein is ingested and metabolized by the body into urea and other waste products that must also be excreted in the urine.

Anatomy of the Urinary System

The kidneys are paired organs, each weighing approximately 125 g, located in a position lateral to the bodies of the lower thoracic vertebrae, a few centimetres to the right and left of the midline. They are surrounded by a thin, fibrous tissue known as the capsule. Anteriorly, the kidneys are separated from the abdominal cavity and its contents by layers of peritoneum. Posteriorly, they are shielded by the lower thoracic wall. Blood is supplied to each kidney through the renal artery and is drained through the renal vein. The renal arteries arise from the abdominal aorta, and the renal veins carry blood back into the inferior vena cava. The kidneys can efficiently clear the blood of waste materials, in part because their total blood flow is great and represents 25 per cent of cardiac output.

Urine is formed within the functional units of the kidneys, known as nephrons. The urine formed within these nephrons passes into collecting ducts that join to form the pelvis of each kidney. Each kidney pelvis gives rise to a ureter. The ureter is a long tube (25 cm) with a wall composed largely of smooth muscle. It connects each kidney to the bladder and functions as a conduit for urine.

The urinary bladder is a hollow organ that is situated anteriorly just behind the pubic bone. It acts as a temporary storage reservoir for the urine. The walls of the bladder consist largely of smooth muscle called the detrusor muscle. Contraction of this muscle is responsible mainly for emptying the bladder during urination. The urethra arises from the bladder; it runs through the penis in the male, and opens just anterior to the vagina in the female. A short distance from its origin, the urethra is encircled by a small bundle of muscle fibres that is called the external urinary sphincter. This sphincter is the major site for control of the initiation of urination.

The Nephron

The kidney is divided into an outer portion called the cortex and an inner portion known as the medulla (Figure 19.1). In the human, each kidney is composed of approximately one million nephrons, the functional units of the kidney. Each nephron consists of a glomerulus and a tubule (Figure 19.2); the glomerulus is about 0.2 mm in diameter, and the tubule is about 25 to 45 mm in length. The glomerulus, the beginning of the nephron, is composed of tufts of capillaries that are supplied with blood by an afferent arteriole and drained by an efferent arteriole. The latter is a thick-walled muscular vessel that helps to maintain a high pressure in the glomerular capillaries.

Like capillaries in general, the walls of the glomerular capillaries are composed of a layer of endothelial cells and a basement membrane. On the other side of the basement membrane are the epithelial cells that form the beginning of the tubule. The tubule itself is divided into three parts: a proximal tubule, the loop of Henle and a distal tubule. The distal tubules coalesce to form connecting ducts that are about 20 mm long. The ducts pass through the renal cortex and the medulla to empty into the pelvis of the kidney. The total length of a typical nephron, including the collecting duct, ranges from between 45 to 65 mm.

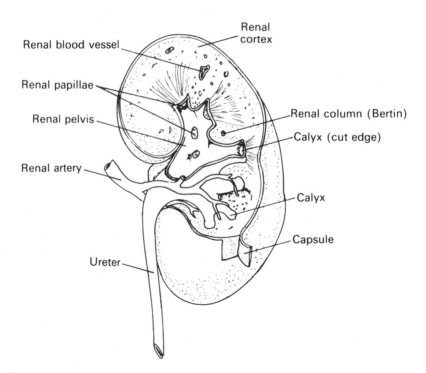

Figure 19.1 Diagram of internal structure of kidney, showing relationship of renal pelvis and calyces to pyramids in medullary region. (Chaffee, E. E. and Greisheimer, E. M. (1980) *Basic Physiology and Anatomy* (4th edition), J. B. Lippincott, Philadelphia.)

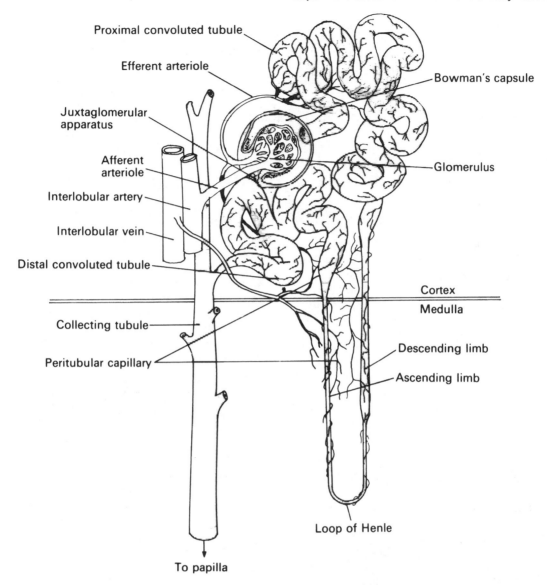

Proximal convoluted tubule

Efferent arteriole

Bowman's capsule

Juxtaglomerular apparatus

Afferent arteriole

Glomerulus

Interlobular artery

Interlobular vein

Distal convoluted tubule

Cortex

Medulla

Collecting tubule

Peritubular capillary

Descending limb

Ascending limb

Loop of Henle

To papilla

Figure 19.2 A nephron and its blood supply. The collecting tubule receives urine from neighbouring nephron units. Note that the loop of Henle dips into the medullary layer of the kidney. (Chaffee, E. E. and Greisheimer, E. M. (1980) *Basic Physiology and Anatomy* (4th edition), J. B. Lippincott, Philadelphia.)

Function of the Nephron

The process of urine formation begins as blood flows through the glomerulus. Fluid is filtered through the walls of the glomerular capillary tufts into the proximal tubule. Under normal conditions, approximately 20 per cent of the plasma passing through the glomerulus is filtered into the nephron, amounting to about 180 litres of filtrate per day. The filtrate, very similar to blood plasma without its proteins, consists essentially of water, electrolytes and other small molecules. Within the tubule and collecting ducts, some of these substances are reabsorbed selectively into the blood. Other substances are secreted into the filtrate as it travels down the tubule. The urine is the remaining fluid

(along with its contents) that reaches the pelvis of the kidney. Some substances, such as glucose, are usually completely reabsorbed in the tubule and do not appear in the urine. The processes of reabsorption and secretion in the tubule frequently involve active transport and require the utilization of metabolic energy. The amount of various substances normally filtered by the glomerulus, reabsorbed by the tubules and excreted in the urine is shown in Table 19.1.

Urine Composition

The kidney functions as the main excretory organ of the body. It disposes of unwanted materials that are ingested

Table 19.1 *Filtration, reabsorption and excretion of certain normal constituents of plasma*

	Filtered (g/24 hr)	Reabsorbed (g/24 hr)	Excreted (g/24 hr)*
Sodium	540	537	3.3
Chloride	630	625	5.3
Bicarbonate	300	300	0.3
Potassium	28	24	3.9
Glucose	140	140	0.0
Urea	53	28	25.0
Creatinine	1.4	0	1.4
Uric acid	8.5	7.7	0.8

* These are typical normal values. Wide variation is found, depending on diet.

as well as the byproducts of the body's metabolism. In the normal person, the amounts of these materials excreted per day are exactly equal to the amounts ingested and formed, so that over a period of time there is no net change in the total body composition.

Urine is composed primarily of water. A normal person ingests approximately one to two litres of water per day, and normally all but 400 to 500 ml of this fluid intake is excreted in the urine. The remainder is lost from the skin, from the lungs during breathing and in the faeces. The second major class of substances excreted in the urine is the electrolytes, including sodium, potassium, chloride, bicarbonate and other less abundant ions. The average diet contains about 6 to 8 g each of sodium chloride (salt) and potassium chloride per day, and nearly all of this is excreted in the urine. The third group of substances appearing in the urine is made up of the breakdown products of protein metabolism. The major breakdown product is urea, of which about 25 g are produced and excreted per day. Other products of protein metabolism that must be excreted are creatinine, phosphates and sulphates. Uric acid, formed as a breakdown product of nucleic acid metabolism, is also eliminated in the urine.

It is important to recognize that some substances that are present in high concentrations in the blood are ordinarily completely reabsorbed by active transport in the renal tubule. Amino acids and glucose, for example, are usually filtered at the glomerulus and reabsorbed so that none of either is excreted in the urine. Glucose, however, will appear in the urine if its blood level is so high that its concentration in the glomerular filtrate exceeds the capacity of the tubules to reabsorb it. Normally, the glucose is completely reabsorbed when its concentration in the blood is less than 11 mmol/l. In diabetes, in which the blood glucose levels exceed the kidney's reabsorption capacity, glucose will appear in the urine. Protein is also not normally found in the urine. These molecules are not filtered at the glomerulus because of their large size. The appearance of protein in the urine usually signifies damage to the glomeruli that causes them to become 'leaky'.

Regulation of Acid Excretion

The breakdown of proteins involves the generation of acid compounds, in particular phosphoric and sulphuric acids. In addition, a certain amount of acid material is ingested daily. Unlike CO_2, these are nonvolatile acids and cannot be eliminated by the lung. Because accumulation of these acids in the blood would lower its pH (more acidic), and inhibit cell function, they must be excreted in the urine. A normal person excretes approximately 70 mEq of acid each day. The kidney is able to excrete some of this acid directly into the urine to the extent of lowering its pH to 4.5, 1,000 times more acidic than blood.

More acid usually needs to be eliminated from the body than can be excreted directly as free acid in the urine. This is accomplished by the renal excretion of acid that is bound to chemical buffers. The acid (H^+) is secreted by the renal tubular cells into the filtrate, where it is buffered chiefly by phosphate ions and ammonia (NH_3). Phosphate is present in the glomerular filtrate, and ammonia is produced by the kidney cells and secreted into the tubular fluid. Through the buffering process, the kidney is able to excrete large quantities of acid in a bound form without furthering lowering the pH of the urine.

Regulation of Electrolyte Excretion

The amount of electrolytes and water that must be excreted by the kidney each day varies greatly, depending on the amounts ingested. The 180 litres of filtrate formed by the glomeruli each day contain about 1,100 g of sodium chloride. Approximately two litres of water and 6 to 8 g of sodium chloride are normally excreted per day in the urine. The small amounts excreted relative to the amount filtered reflect reabsorption of sodium from the filtrate into the blood as it travels down the tubules. Water from the filtrate follows the reabsorbed sodium in order to maintain osmotic balance. Thus, more than 99 per cent of the water and sodium filtered at the glomerulus is reabsorbed into the blood by the time the urine leaves the body. By regulating the amount of sodium (and therefore water) reabsorbed, the kidney can regulate the volume of body fluids.

● If sodium is excreted in excess of the amount ingested, the patient will become dehydrated. If less sodium is excreted than is ingested, the patient will retain fluid.

The regulation of the amount of sodium excreted depends on aldosterone, a hormone synthesized by and released from the adrenal gland. In the presence of increased aldosterone in the blood, less sodium is excreted in the urine.

Release of aldosterone from the adrenal gland is largely under the control of angiotensin, a peptide hormone manufactured in the liver and activated in the lung. Angiotensin levels are in turn controlled by the hormone renin, which is released from cells in the kidneys. This complex system is activated when pressure in the renal arterioles falls below normal levels, as occurs with shock and dehydration. The effect of activation of this system is to increase the retention of water and expansion of intravascular fluid volume.

Another electrolyte whose concentration in the body fluids is regulated by the kidney is potassium, the most abundant intracellular ion. The excretion of potassium by the kidneys is increased by elevated aldosterone levels, in contrast to the effects of aldosterone on sodium excretion.

● Retention of potassium is the most life-threatening effect of renal failure.

Regulation of Water Excretion

Regulation of the amount of water excreted is also an important function of the kidney. With a large water intake, a large volume of dilute urine must be excreted. Conversely, with a low water intake, the urine that is excreted must be concentrated. The relative degree of dilution or concentration of the urine can be measured in terms of its osmolality. This terms refers to the amount of solid material (electrolytes and other molecules) dissolved in the urine. The filtrate in the glomerular capillary normally has the same osmolality as the blood. As the filtrate passes through the tubules and collecting ducts, the osmolality may vary, reflecting the maximal diluting and concentrating abilities of the kidney.

The osmolality of the urine specimen can be measured. Osmolality reflects the number of particles of solute in a unit of solution, unlike specific gravity, which is less precise and reflects both the quantity and the nature of particles. Normal urine osmolality is 500 to 800 mOsm/l. Normal specific gravity is 1.003 to 1.030.

Regulation of water excretion and urine concentration is carried out in the tubule by varying the amount of water that is reabsorbed in relation to electrolyte reabsorption. The glomerular filtrate has essentially the same electrolyte composition as the blood plasma without the proteins. The amount of water that is reabsorbed is under the control of antidiuretic hormone (ADH). Antidiuretic hormone is secreted by the posterior part of the pituitary gland in response to changes in osmolality of the blood. With decreased water intake, blood osmolality tends to rise and stimulate antidiuretic hormone release. Antidiuretic hormone then acts on the kidney in order to cause increased reabsorption of water, thereby returning the osmolality of the blood towards normal. With excess water intake, the secretion of antidiuretic hormone by the pituitary is suppressed and, therefore, less water is reabsorbed by the kidney tubule. This latter situation leads to increased urine volume (diuresis).

● Loss of the ability to concentrate and dilute the urine is the most common early manifestation of kidney disease.

Renal Clearance

The test most commonly used to evaluate how well the kidney performs its excretory function is termed 'clearance'. Clearance of a substance A is shown by the following equation: clearance equals (the urine concentration of A) times (the urine volume in a given time) divided by the plasma concentration of A.

Clearance = (urine concentration of A) × (urine volume in a given time) ÷ plasma concentration of A

It is possible to measure the renal clearance of any substance, but the one that has proven to be particularly useful is the creatinine clearance. Creatinine is an endogenous waste product of skeletal muscle that is excreted by glomerular filtration and is not appreciably reabsorbed or secreted by the renal tubules. Therefore, creatinine clearance is a good measure of the glomerular filtration rate. The normal adult glomerular filtration rate is about 100 to 120 ml/min (1.67 to 2 ml/sec).

Storage of Urine and Micturition

Urine formed by the kidney is transported from the renal pelvis through the ureters and into the bladder. This movement is facilitated by peristaltic waves occurring about one to five times per minute and generated by the smooth muscle in the ureter wall. Urine flows into the bladder sporadically, propelled by peristaltic contractions. There are no sphincters between the bladder and the ureters, although reflux of urine from the bladder in normal people is prevented by the unidirectional nature of the peristaltic waves and because each ureter enters the bladder at an oblique angle.

● With overdistension of the bladder due to disease, the elevated pressure in the bladder can be transmitted back through the ureters, leading to ureteral distension and possible reflux or back-up of urine. This can lead to kidney infection (pyelonephritis) and damage from the elevated pressure (hydronephrosis).

The pressure in the bladder is normally very low, even as the urine accumulates, because the bladder's smooth muscle adapts to the increased stretch as the bladder is slowly filled. The first sensations of bladder filling ordinarily occur when about 100 to 150 ml of urine are present in the bladder. In most cases, there is a desire to void when the bladder contains approximately 200 to 300 ml. With 400 ml a marked feeling of fullness is usually present.

Voiding of urine is controlled by contraction of the external urethral sphincter. This muscle is under voluntary control and is innervated by nerves from the sacral area of the spinal cord. Voluntary control is a learned behaviour that is not present at birth. When there is a desire to urinate, the external urethral sphincter is relaxed, and the detrusor muscle (bladder smooth muscle) contracts and expels the urine from the bladder through the urethra.

Residual urine in the urethra drains by gravity in the female and is expelled by voluntary muscle contractions in the male.

The contraction of the detrusor muscle is regulated by a reflex involving the parasympathetic nervous system. The reflex is integrated in the sacral portion of the spinal tract. The sympathetic nervous system plays no essential part in micturition, but does prevent semen from entering the bladder during ejaculation.

● If the pelvic nerves to the bladder and sphincter are destroyed, voluntary control and reflex urination are abolished and the bladder becomes overdistended with urine. If the spinal pathways from the brain to the urinary system are destroyed (for example, after a spinal cord transection), reflex contraction of the bladder is maintained but voluntary control over the process is lost. In both of these types of loss of innervation, the muscle of the bladder can contract and expel urine, but the contractions are generally insufficient to empty the bladder completely, and residual urine is left behind.

Catheterization—passage of a catheter through the urethra into the bladder—can be used to assess bladder function by permitting measurement of the amount of urine left in the bladder after voiding (residual volume). Normally, this is no more than 50 ml. However, catheterization is avoided whenever possible, because it increases the risk of infection.

ALTERED RENAL PHYSIOLOGY

Diseases of the kidney can be classified according to the segment of the nephron that is primarily affected. Glomerulonephritis and the various forms of the nephrotic syndrome affect primarily the renal glomerulus. Vascular diseases, infections and toxins affect primarily the renal tubule, although some degree of glomerular dysfunction may coexist. Obstruction to the outflow of urine due to calculi (stones), protein or other material in the collecting ducts or ureters may eventually lead to damage throughout the nephron. When the degree of kidney damage is severe, renal failure occurs and may result in the condition called uraemia.

Glomerular Diseases

Nephritic Syndrome
The nephritic syndrome occurs in response to a group of diseases in which inflammation of the glomerulus (glomerulonephritis) is predominant. The major features are haematuria, proteinuria, sodium and fluid retention, hypertension and occasionally oliguria. These abnormalities are due to damage to the glomerular capillaries that permits leakage of red blood cells into the tubular lumen. Glomerulonephritis most commonly results from immune reactions. Common causes are the reaction to some streptococcal infections, predominantly in children, and the autoimmune diseases such as Goodpasture's syndrome and lupus erythematosus. Glomerulonephritis may resolve completely, although in some patients renal failure may result.

Nephrotic Syndrome
The nephrotic syndrome results from a group of glomerular diseases associated with increased permeability to proteins of the glomerulus. Frequently, there are no alterations of kidney structure observable by light microscopy. The primary manifestation of the disease is the loss of plasma proteins, particularly albumin, in the urine. Although the liver is capable of increasing its production of albumin, it is unable to keep up with the daily loss of albumin through the kidney; thus, hypoalbuminaemia results. The resultant decreased oncotic pressure leads to generalized oedema as fluid moves from the vascular system into the extracellular fluid spaces. A decreased circulating blood volume activates the renin–angiotensin system, leading to retention of sodium and further oedema. Patients with nephrotic syndrome also exhibit an elevated lipid concentration in their blood, the cause of which is not known. The nephrotic syndrome can occur with almost any intrinsic renal disease or systemic disease that affects the glomerulus. See Chapter 21, p. 718 for further discussion.

Renal Failure

Renal failure is present when the excretion of water, electrolytes and metabolic waste products is insufficient because of kidney damage that prevents the kidneys from maintaining the normal internal environment of the body. Acute renal failure has a sudden onset and is frequently reversible. Chronic renal failure usually develops gradually, but can also occur as a consequence of an acute episode. One normal kidney is generally sufficient for normal urinary function, so renal failure requires bilateral kidney damage. The signs and symptoms of renal failure are in large part a result of altered fluid and electrolyte balance of the body. The diagnosis is generally made by finding an elevation of nitrogenous waste products in the blood. Uraemia, characterized by the signs and symptoms resulting from accumulation of these waste products, occurs when the condition is severe.

Pathogenesis of Renal Failure
Decreased excretion of metabolic waste products can occur as a result of decreased blood flow to the kidney (pre-renal), acute obstruction to the flow of urine from the kidney (post-renal) or damage to the kidney itself (intra-renal).

- Decreased renal blood flow can occur with hypotension, congestive heart failure, dehydration or thrombosis of renal arteries. Acute decrease in renal blood flow may lead to secondary renal damage and renal failure. Decreased excretion of waste products due to decreased renal blood flow in the absence of kidney damage is called uraemia.
- Decreased urine output due to complete urinary obstruction can occur in patients who have an enlarged prostate, stones (calculi) in the ureters or urethra, or infiltrating tumours. Secondary damage to the kidneys and renal failure will result if the obstruction is not relieved promptly. This is termed obstructive or post-renal failure.
- Acute renal failure due to direct injury to the kidney results from acute vasculitis, acute glomerulonephritis, severe ('malignant') hypertension or, more commonly, acute damage to the renal tubules (acute tubular necrosis). The clinical conditions that may result in acute tubular necrosis include hypotension (shock), exposure to nephrotoxic chemicals, disintegration of blood components (intravascular haemolysis) leading to a build-up of haemoglobin in the urine (due to transfusion reactions, extensive burns or infusion of water intravenously), or crush injury of an extremity that damages muscle tissue. These injuries cause a release of myoglobin, which is carried to the kidneys and excreted in the urine (myoglobinuria).

Uraemia/Uraemic Syndrome

Uraemia is a term used to designate the features of chronic renal dysfunction that lead to an accumulation in the blood of substances normally excreted in the urine. Uraemia is a generalized condition that affects all organ systems of the body.

Fluids and Electrolytes
The fluid and electrolyte abnormalities that occur in renal failure are the result of a decreased number of functional nephrons. The basic altered physiology in kidney function is a decreased glomerular filtration rate due to a reduced number of filtering glomeruli, leading to decreased clearance of substances that depend on filtration for their excretion. Decreased glomerular filtration rate can be diagnosed by a decreased creatinine clearance. As creatinine clearance decreases, serum creatinine increases. Because of creatinine's constant production, it is the most specific and sensitive indicator of kidney disease. The blood urea also rises with kidney damage, but its level is also affected by protein intake and tissue breakdown. Uric acid also rises.

Calcium Metabolism and Bone Changes
Disorders of calcium metabolism with secondary bone changes are among the major features of uraemia. The primary finding is usually a decreased serum calcium concentration. One mechanism for hypocalcaemia is decreased conversion of vitamin D to its active form by the damaged kidneys, leading to diminished absorption of calcium from the gastrointestinal tract.

Decreased serum calcium secondarily stimulates the parathyroid glands to produce increased parathormone, resulting in the condition called secondary hyperparathyroidism. This condition is characterized by demineralization of bone and formation of bone cysts. The demineralization of bone leads to frequent fractures and bone pain. The term renal osteodystrophy is frequently used to designate the complex bone changes that occur with uraemia.

Anaemia
Anaemia, another common manifestation of uraemia, is generally caused by a decreased rate of production of red blood cells by the bone marrow and increased rates of red blood cell destruction. Decreased erythropoiesis (the formation of erythrocytes or red blood cells) is related to a decreased rate of production of erythropoietin by the kidneys.

Cardiovascular Features
Hypertension, frequently associated with chronic renal failure, may be either the cause or the result of renal damage. Primary hypertension leads to kidney damage as a result of atherosclerosis of the renal vasculature manifested by nephrosclerosis. Secondary hypertension occurs due to increased renin production by the diseased kidney, leading to generalized vasoconstriction as well as salt retention, which leads to fluid retention and an expansion of the vascular volume.

Other Features of Uraemia
Among the many diverse features of uraemia are gastrointestinal symptoms, including anorexia, nausea, vomiting and hiccoughs; neuromuscular symptoms, including mental clouding, inability to concentrate, drowsiness, lethargy, twitching, convulsions; and tetany, which is related to the low serum calcium. Dermatological symptoms, including severe itching (pruritis) are common. Patients with uraemia also have altered cellular immunity, with decreased delayed hypersensitivity and increased susceptibility to infection, probably related to a decreased ability of leucocytes to kill bacteria.

Course of Renal Failure

The basic mechanisms underlying the altered physiology of acute and chronic renal failure are similar. However, their clinical presentations are markedly different. (See Chapter 21, pp. 705–11.)

ASSESSMENT OF URINARY FUNCTION

Clinical Features of Urinary Dysfunction

The following symptoms and signs are suggestive of urinary tract disease: pain, changes in micturition and gastrointestinal symptoms.

Pain

Genitourinary pain is not always present in renal disease, but is generally seen in the more acute conditions. Pain of renal disease is caused by sudden distension of the renal capsule. Its severity is related to how quickly the distension develops.

Kidney pain may be felt as a dull ache in the costovertebral angle (the area formed by the rib cage and vertebral column) and may spread to the umbilicus. Ureteral pain produces pain in the back that radiates to the abdomen, upper thigh, testis or labium. Pain in the loin, radiating to the lower abdomen or epigastrium and often associated with nausea, vomiting and paralytic ileus, may indicate renal colic. Bladder pain (low abdominal pain over the suprapubic area) can be due to an overdistended bladder or bladder infection. Urgency, tenesmus (painful straining) and terminal dysuria (pain at the end of voiding) are usually present. Pain at the urethral meatus occurs with irritation of the bladder neck or urethra due to infection (urethritis), trauma or a foreign body in the lower urinary tract.

Severe pain in the scrotal region results from inflammation and oedema of the epididymis or testicle, or from torsion of the testicle, while perineal and rectal fullness and pain signal acute prostatitis or prostatic abscess. Back and leg pain may be due to metastasis of cancer of the prostate to the pelvic bones. Pain in the penile shaft may originate from urethral problems, while pain in the glans penis is usually due to prostatitis.

Changes in Micturition (Voiding)

Normal micturition is a painless function occurring five to six times daily and occasionally once at night. The average person voids 1,200 to 1,500 ml of urine in 24 hours. This amount, of course, is modified by fluid intake, sweating, outside temperature, vomiting or diarrhoea.

Urinary frequency is voiding that occurs more often than usual when compared with the patient's usual pattern or the generally accepted norm of once every three to six hours. It may result from a variety of conditions: infection, diseases of the urinary tract, metabolic disease, hypertension and certain medications (diuretics).

Urgency (strong desire to void) may be due to inflam-

matory lesions in the bladder, prostate or urethra; acute bacterial infections or chronic prostatitis in men; and chronic posterior urethrotrigonitis (inflammation of the urethra and trigone of the bladder) in women.

Burning on urination is experienced by patients with urethral irritation or bladder infection. Urethritis frequently causes burning during the act of voiding, whereas cystitis may produce burning both during and after urination.

Dysuria (painful or difficult voiding) stems from a wide variety of pathological conditions.

Hesitancy (undue delay and difficulty in initiating voiding) may indicate compression of the urethra or neurogenic bladder or outlet obstruction.

Nocturia (excessive urination at night) suggests decreased renal concentrating ability, heart failure, diabetes mellitus or poor bladder emptyings.

Urinary incontinence (involuntary loss of urine) may result from injury of the external urinary sphincter, acquired neurogenic disease or severe urgency from infection.

Stress incontinence (intermittent leakage of urine due to sudden strain) results from weakness of the sphincteric mechanism.

Enuresis (involuntary voiding during sleep) is physiological to the age of three years. After this it may be functional or symptomatic of obstructive disease of the lower urinary tract.

Polyuria (a large volume of urine voided in a given time) may be due to diabetes mellitus, diabetes insipidus, chronic renal disease, diuretics or excessive fluid intake.

Oliguria (a small volume of urine; output between 100 to 500 ml/24 hours) and anuria (absence of urine in the bladder); output less than 50 ml/24 hours indicates a serious renal dysfunction requiring immediate medical intervention. These conditions may result from such causes as shock, trauma, incompatible blood transfusion and drug toxicity. Complete absence of urine (absolute anuria) is usually indicative of complete obstruction of the urinary tract.

Haematuria (red blood cells in the urine) is considered to be a serious sign because it may indicate cancer of the genitourinary tract, acute glomerulonephritis or renal tuberculosis. The colour of bloody urine is dependent upon the pH of the urine and the amount of blood present; acid urine is a dark, smoky colour, while alkaline urine is red. Haematuria may also be due to systemic causes such as blood dyscrasias (abnormalities of clotting), anticoagulant therapy, neoplasms, trauma and extreme exercise.

Proteinuria (albuminuria) (abnormal amounts of protein in the urine) is characteristically seen in all forms of acute and chronic renal disease. Normal urine does not contain persistent protein in significant quantities.

Gastrointestinal Symptoms

Gastrointestinal symptoms may occur with urological conditions because the gastrointestinal and urinary tracts have common autonomic and sensory innervation and are closely related anatomically.

Health History and Nursing Assessment

When obtaining a health history, it is essential that the nurse uses language and terms understandable to the patient, and is aware of the patient's embarrassment or discomfort in discussing genitourinary functions and symptoms. The patient may 'forget' or deny symptoms because of anxiety or embarrassment. The following information related to urinary function is sought:

- What is the patient's chief concern or reason for seeking help?
- What is the patient's present or past occupation(s)? (Look for occupational hazards relevant to the urinary tract, including contact with chemicals, plastics, pitch, tar or rubber.)
- Has the patient been exposed to any environmental toxins?
- What is the patient's smoking history?
- What is the past history in relation to urinary problems?
- Is there a family history of renal disease?
- What childhood diseases did the patient have?
- Is there a history of urinary infections?
- Did enuresis extend beyond the usual age (past three years old)?
- Is nocturia present or absent?
- Are there any disorders of voiding? Dysuria? When does it occur? Where is it felt? Initial or terminal dysuria? Hesitancy? Straining? Pain during or after urination? Changes in colour of urine? Diminished urine output? Incontinence? Stress incontinence? Urgency incontinence? Any history of haematuria?
- Is pain present? Location? Character? Radiation? Duration? Related to voiding? What brings it on? What relieves it?
- Has the patient had fever? Chills? Passage of stones?
- Any history of genital lesions or sexually transmitted diseases?
- For the female patient: Number of children? Their ages? Forceps deliveries? Catheterized? When? Why? Any signs of vaginal discharge? Vaginal/vulvar itch or irritation?
- Does the patient have diabetes mellitus? Hypertension? Allergies?
- Has the patient ever been hospitalized with urinary tract infection? Before the age of 12? Cystoscopy? Indwelling catheter? Kidney X-ray procedures?
- Is the patient receiving any prescription or over-the-counter drugs that may affect urinary or renal function? Have any drugs been prescribed for treatment of renal or urinary problems?
- Is the patient at risk for urinary tract infection?

The nurse not only elicits information about the patient's physical complaints, but also assesses psychosocial status and educational needs. The nurse evaluates the patient's anxiety, perceived threats to body image, support systems and sociocultural patterns.

By putting together the information gathered during the initial and subsequent nursing assessments, the nurse can find valuable clues regarding misunderstandings, lack of knowledge and requirements for patient teaching.

DIAGNOSIS

Urinalysis

Although its value is often underestimated, urinalysis provides a wealth of important clinical information and is regarded as an indispensable part of every patient assessment. Urine examination of every patient includes evaluation of the following:

1. Urine colour and clarity.
2. Urine odour.
3. Measurement of urine acidity and specific gravity.
4. Tests for the presence of protein, glucose and ketone bodies in the urine (proteinuria, glucosuria and ketonuria, respectively).

Collection of Urine Samples

All urine tests are performed ideally on fresh specimens, preferably of the first voiding of the day because this specimen is most concentrated and more likely to reveal abnormalities. Random specimens are satisfactory for most analyses, provided that they have been collected in clean containers and have been protected adequately against bacterial contamination and chemical deterioration. All specimens should be refrigerated as soon as possible after they are obtained. If left standing at room temperature, the urine becomes alkaline due to contamination by urea-splitting bacteria from the environment. Microscopic examination should be carried out within 30 minutes after collection; delay allows dissolution of cellular elements and bacterial overgrowth in nonsterile specimens. Urine cultures should be processed immediately. If this is not possible, they should be stored at a temperature of 4°C.

Urine specimens should be collected from the patient by means of the midstream technique, using a wide-mouthed container (see Figure 19.3).

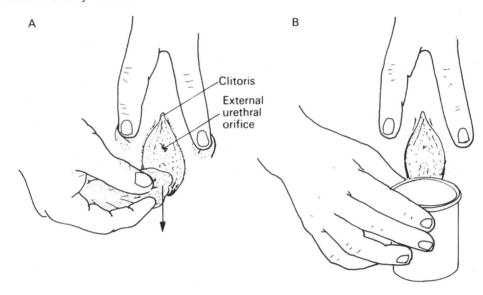

Figure 19.3 A midstream urine specimen from a female. (A) The patient is requested to hold the labia apart and wash right from the front towards the back with soap and water, and rinse. (B) The collection cup is held so that it does not touch the body, and the sample is obtained only while the patient is voiding with the labia held apart.

24-Hour Urine Collection

Many quantitative analytic tests are carried out on specimens of urine collected over a 24-hour period. The procedure is as follows:

The patient is requested to empty the bladder at a specified time (such as 8 a.m.). This urine is discarded. All urine voided during the next 24 hours is collected. The last specimen is collected and saved 24 hours after the collection began (i.e., 8 a.m.).

The patient's bladder should be empty when the tests starts and empty when it ends. The urine is collected in a clean container. Depending on the test to be performed, a preservative may be added or the urine may need to be refrigerated.

Discarding even one specimen voided during the test period invalidates the test. A successful collection requires the complete understanding and co-operation on the part of the patient and of all unit personnel concerned with the patient's care.

Midstream Urine Specimens

Urine specimens voided in the usual manner are practically useless for bacteriological study because of their inevitable contamination by organisms residing in the vicinity of the urethral meatus. Such contamination can be avoided by catheterizing the urinary bladder. However, catheterization is no longer recommended except for specific indications because of the risk of infection. Reliable bacteriological studies are possible without catheterization, provided that the midstream technique is utilized.

Instructions to the Male Patient

- Expose the glans and cleanse the area around the meatus with soap and water.
- Do not collect the first portion of the voiding; discard it.
- Collect the next portion by voiding into a sterile wide-mouthed bottle or tube that is protected by a sterile closure.
- Do not collect the last few drops of urine because prostatic secretions may be introduced into the urine at the end of the urinary stream.

Instructions to Female Patient

- Separate the labia to expose the urethral orifice (see Figure 19.3).
- Cleanse around the urinary meatus with soap and water.
- Wipe the perineum from the front to the back.
- Keep the labia separated and void forcibly, but do not collect the first portion of the voiding. (The distal portion of the urethral orifice is colonized by bacteria; the initial voiding washes away the urethral contaminants.)
- Collect the midstream portion of the urinary flow, making sure that the container does not come in contact with the genitalia.

Renal Function Tests

Renal function tests are used to evaluate the severity of kidney disease and to follow the patient's clinical progress. These tests also give information concerning the

Table 19.2 *Tests of renal function*

Test	Purpose/rationale	Test protocol
Renal concentration test 1. Specific gravity 2. Osmolality of urine	Tests the ability to concentrate solutes in the urine. Concentration ability is lost early in kidney disease; hence, this test shows early defects in renal function	Fluids may be withheld for 12–24 hr to assess the concentrating ability of the tubules under controlled conditions. Specific gravity measurements of urine are taken at specific times to determine urine concentration
Creatinine clearance* test	Provides an approximation of rate of glomerular filtration Measures volume of blood cleared of creatinine in 1 minute Most sensitive indication of early renal disease Useful to follow progress of patient's renal status	Collect all urine over 24-hr period Draw one sample of blood within the period
Serum creatinine test	A test of renal function reflecting the balance between production and filtration by renal glomerulus Most sensitive measure of renal function	Do test on blood serum
Serum urea test	Serves as an index of renal excretory capacity Serum urea is dependent on the body's urea production and on urine flow. (Urea is the nitrogenous end product of protein metabolism.) Affected by protein intake and tissue breakdown	Do test on blood serum

* Clearance is the amount of blood cleansed of a constituent per unit of time.

kidneys' effectiveness in carrying out their excretory function. Best results are obtained by combining a number of clinical tests. Table 19.2 lists the more common tests of renal function. Because of the important role of the kidneys in maintaining fluid and electrolyte balance, serum electrolyte levels also are assessed.

X-Ray Films

The examination usually begins with a plain film of the abdomen to delineate the size, shape and position of the kidneys, and to reveal any deviations, such as calcifications (stones) in the kidneys or urinary tract, hydronephrosis, cysts, tumours or kidney displacement by abnormalities in the surrounding tissues.

Computed Tomography

Computed tomography (CT or CAT scan) is a noninvasive technique that provides an excellent cross-sectional view of the kidney and urinary tract. It provides information on the extension of invasive lesions of the kidney. No special patient preparation is needed.

Intravenous Urogram or Intravenous Pyelogram

An excretory urogram or intravenous pyelogram permits visualization of the kidneys, ureter and bladder. A radio-opaque contrast medium is administered intravenously, and is cleared from the bloodstream and concentrated by the kidneys. A nephrotomogram may be carried out as part of the study to visualize different layers of the kidney and the diffuse structures within each layer, and to differentiate solid masses or lesions from cysts in the kidneys or urinary tract.

Intravenous pyelogram is conducted as part of the initial assessment of any suspected urological problem, especially in the diagnosis of lesions of the kidneys and ureters. It also provides a rough estimate of renal function. After the contrast material (sodium diatrizoate or meglumine diatrizoate) is given intravenously, multiple films are taken serially to visualize drainage structures.

Patient Preparation. The patient may be prepared for the procedure as follows:

1. The patient's history should be checked for any indications of allergies that might cause an adverse re-

action to the contrast material. The suspected allergy is noted prominently on the patient's record.

2. A laxative may be given the night before the scheduled examination to eliminate faeces and gas in the intestinal tract.

3. Liquids may be restricted 8 to 10 hours before the test to promote a concentrated urine. However, patients with marginal renal reserve or function, patients with multiple myeloma and those with uncontrolled diabetes mellitus may not tolerate dehydration. With the approval of the doctor, the nurse may give such patients water to drink during the hours before the test. The patient should not be overhydrated, as this may dilute the contrast material and thus cause inadequate visualization.

4. The procedure itself and the sensations produced by injection of the contrast medium and during the procedure (e.g., a temporary feeling of warmth and flushing of the face) are described to the patient.

Retrograde Pyelography

In retrograde pyelography, ureteral catheters are passed up through the ureters into the renal pelvis by means of cystoscopic manipulation. A contrast material is then introduced into the catheters by gravity or syringe. It is being used less frequently because of improved techniques in intravenous pyelography.

Cystogram

A catheter is inserted into the bladder and contrast material is instilled to outline the bladder wall and to aid in evaluation of vesicoureteral reflux (backflow or urine from the bladder into one or both ureters).

Cystourethrogram

A cystourethrogram provides visualization of the urethra and bladder either by retrograde injection of the contrast material into the urethra and bladder or by X-ray films taken while the patient excretes the contrast material.

Renal Angiography

The purpose of this procedure is to visualize the renal arterial supply. A special needle is used to pierce the femoral (or axillary) artery, and a catheter is threaded up through the femoral and iliac arteries into the aorta or renal artery. Contrast material is injected to opacify the renal arterial supply. Angiography enables evaluation of blood flow dynamics, demonstrates abnormal vasculature and helps to differentiate renal cysts from renal tumours.

Nursing Care. Before the procedure, an aperient may be prescribed to eliminate faecal material and gas from the colon so that unobstructed X-rays will be visualized. The patient is informed that a transient feeling of heat may be sensed along the course of the vessel when the contrast material is injected.

Following the procedure, the vital signs are taken until stable. The puncture site is examined for swelling and haematoma development. The peripheral pulses are palpated. The colour and temperature of the involved extremity are noted and compared with those of the uninvolved extremity.

Ultrasound

Ultrasound (ultrasonic scan) uses sound waves that are passed into the body. Organs in the urinary system create characteristic ultrasonic images. Abnormalities such as masses, malformations or obstructions can be identified. Ultrasound is a noninvasive technique, and so no special patient preparation is required.

Urological Procedures

The Cystoscopic Examination

Cytoscopy is a method of direct visualization of the urethra and bladder. The cystoscope, which is inserted through the urethra into the bladder, has a self-contained optical lens system that provides a magnified, illuminated view of the bladder (Figure 19.4). The cystoscope can be manipulated to allow complete visualization of the urethra and bladder as well as the ureteral orifices and prostatic urethra. Small ureteral catheters can be passed through the cystoscope, allowing assessment of the ureter and the pelvis of the kidney. The cystoscope also permits the urologist to obtain a urine specimen from each kidney to evaluate renal function. Cup forceps can be inserted through the cystoscope for biopsy. Calculi may be

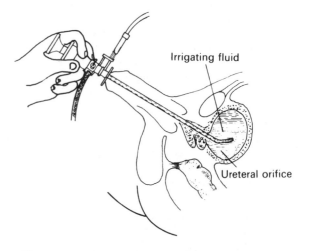

Figure 19.4 Cytoscopic examination. A cytoscope is introduced into the bladder of the male. The upper cord is an electric wire for the light at the distal end of the cytoscope. The lower tubing leads from a reservoir of sterile irrigating fluid that is used to inflate the bladder.

removed from the urethra, bladder and ureter via cystoscopy.

Before the procedure, a sedative may be given. A local topical anaesthetic is instilled into the urethra by the urologist before the cystoscope is inserted. Intravenous diazepam in combination with topical urethral anaesthesia may be administered.

Nursing Care

As with any diagnostic procedure, the nurse describes the examination and procedure in order to inform the patient and allay fears. Additional pre-procedure preparation may include encouraging the patient to drink one or two glasses of water before going to the radiology department.

Post-procedure management is directed at relieving any possible discomfort resulting from the examination. Some burning upon voiding, blood-tinged urine and urinary frequency from trauma to the mucous membrane may be expected after cystoscopic examination. Moist heat to the lower abdomen or warm baths are helpful in relieving pain and promoting muscle relaxation. Occasionally following cystoscopy, the patient with obstructive pathology may experience urinary retention as a result of oedema caused by the instrumentation.

Renal and Ureteral Brush Biopsy

Brush biopsy techniques provide specific information when abnormal X-ray findings for the ureter or renal pelvis raise uncertainty as to whether the defect is a tumour, a stone, a blood clot or an artifact. First, a cystoscopic examination is conducted. Then a ureteral catheter is introduced, followed by a biopsy brush that is passed through the catheter. The suspected lesion is brushed back and forth in order to obtain cells and surface tissue fragments for histological analysis.

Following the procedure, the patient may be given an intravenous infusion to help clear the kidneys and prevent clot formation. Urine may show blood (usually clearing in 24 to 48 hours) from oozing at the brushing site. Postoperative renal colic occurs occasionally, and responds to analgesics.

Needle Biopsy of the Kidney

Needle biopsy of the kidney is performed by percutaneous needle biopsy through renal tissue or by open through a small loin incision. It is useful in evaluating the course of renal disease and in securing specimens for electron and immunofluorescent microscopy, particularly for glomerular disease. Before the biopsy is carried out, coagulation studies are conducted to identify any patient at risk for postbiopsy bleeding.

The patient may be asked to fast for six to eight hours before the test. The patient is informed that it will be necessary to hold the breath in (to stop movement the kidney) during insertion of the renal biopsy needle.

Postbiopsy Nursing Care

The patient may be kept in a prone position immediately following biopsy and on bedrest for 24 hours to minimize the risk of bleeding.

The nurse observes for haematuria, which may appear soon after biopsy. The kidney is a highly vascular organ, and approximately 25 per cent of the entire cardiac output passes through it in about one minute. The passage of the biopsy needle punctures the kidney capsule, and bleeding can occur in the perirenal space. Usually, the bleeding subsides on its own, but a large amount of blood can accumulate in this space in a short period of time without noticeable signs until cardiovascular collapse is evident.

- To detect early signs of bleeding, it is important that the vital signs are taken about every 5 to 15 minutes for the first hour, and then with decreasing frequency as indicated.
- Signs suggestive of bleeding include a rise or fall in blood pressure, anorexia, vomiting and the development of a dull, aching discomfort in the abdomen.
- Any signs of backache, shoulder pain or dysuria should be reported to the doctor.

All urine voided by the patient is scrutinized for evidence of bleeding.

Patient Education

The nurse should keep in mind that a delayed haemorrhage can occur a number of days after biopsy. The patient is cautioned to avoid strenuous activity, strenuous sports and heavy lifting for at least two weeks. The doctor or clinic is to be notified if any of the following occurs: loin pain, haematuria, lightheadedness and fainting, rapid pulse or any other signs and symptoms of excessive bleeding.

Radioisotope Studies

Radioisotope studies are noninvasive procedures that do not interfere with normal physiological processes and require no specific patient preparation. Radiopharmaceuticals are injected intravenously. The resultant image (called a scan) indicates the distribution of the radiopharmaceutical within the kidney.

The Tc scan provides information about kidney perfusion and is useful when renal function is poor.

Urodynamic Measurements

Urodynamic measurements provide physiological and structural tests to evaluate bladder and urethral function by measuring: (1) the rate of urine flow; (2) bladder pressures during voiding and at rest; (3) internal urethral resistance; and (4) bladder contraction and relaxation. Abdominal, bladder and detrusor pressures, sphincter activity, bladder innervation, muscle tone and sacral reflex are assessed.

The following are the urodynamic measurements most frequently performed.

Uroflowmetry (flow rate) is the record of the volume of urine passing through the urethra per time unit (ml/second).

A cystometrogram is a graphic recording of the pressures in the bladder (intravesical) at various phases of filling and emptying of the urinary bladder to assess its function.

A cystourethrogram is visualization of the urethra and bladder either by retrograde injection or by voiding of contrast material.

In a micturating cystourethrogram, the bladder is filled with contrast medium, and the patient voids while rapid spot films are taken. The presence or absence of vesicoureteral reflux or congenital abnormalities in the lower urinary tract can be demonstrated. The voiding cystourethrogram is also used to investigate difficulty in bladder emptying and incontinence.

NURSING CARE OF PATIENTS UNDERGOING ASSESSMENT OF THE RENAL/URINARY SYSTEM

All patients, regardless of the extent or type of urinary tract dysfunction, undergo tests to assess the function of the urinary tract. Even those who have had these tests repeatedly in the past experience fear and apprehension about the procedures and the results. Additionally, they frequently feel discomfort and embarrassment about a previously private and personal function: voiding. Although this is a function that health care providers deal with frequently in the course of providing care, it is important to remember that it is not so routine to patients.

Patient's Problems

Potential problems for these patients may include the following:

- Lack of knowledge about the procedures and their meaning.
- Alteration in comfort; pain and discomfort related to renal dysfunction.
- Fear related to possible diagnoses of serious illness.
- Anxiety and embarrassment related to invasive techniques associated with private parts of the anatomy.

chapter 20

ASSESSMENT AND CARE OF PATIENTS WITH RENAL AND URINARY DYSFUNCTION

PSYCHOSOCIAL CONSIDERATIONS

Conditions of the genitourinary tract may generate emotional stresses and feelings of guilt and embarrassment when the external genitalia are examined and treated or urinary function is discussed. Problems of incontinence may cause disgust and feelings of helplessness. Some patients are constantly uneasy over the possibility of an 'accident', although others appear indifferent.

Surgical procedures affecting the male reproductive organs can pose a threat to the masculinity of the patient, no matter what his age. Although many men may hide their fears of impotency by blaming 'prostate trouble', many sexual problems of males (such as difficulty in achieving erection and premature ejaculation) are psychological in origin and related to a variety of causes—fear, guilt, aversion to partner and fatigue. Because of such fears and feelings, a male patient may react with anger and hostility to those caring for him, or he may turn his anger inward, resulting in more than the usual amount of pain. Patients with urinary infections may become depressed when they undergo prolonged periods of treatment. Anxiety in any stressful situation can produce urinary frequency and urgency.

Urological patients, like any other patients, need to be respected as individuals and understood. They want their questions answered, fears allayed and discomfort relieved. Additionally, their modesty and privacy need to be maintained. These patients may require reassurance, support and acceptance from the nurse.

FLUID AND ELECTROLYTE IMBALANCE

A major problem for patients with renal disorders is fluid and electrolyte imbalance. The nurse must be skilled in observing and documenting the clinical condition of the patient. Every patient with a urological disorder has a fluid intake–output chart on which is recorded all fluid intake, whether by ingestion or by parenteral administration. The volume of urine excreted and of other output is recorded.

In addition, other sources of fluid loss and the patient's weight are monitored and recorded. These records are essential in determining the patient's fluid allowance.

The following signs and symptoms may occur in patients with renal disease:

1. Acute weight loss (in excess of 5 per cent), a drop in body temperature, dryness of skin and mucous membranes, longitudinal wrinkles or furrows of tongue and oliguria or anuria could indicate fluid volume deficit.
2. Acute weight gain (in excess of 5 per cent), oedema, moist crackles in lungs, puffy eyelids and shortness of breath could indicate fluid volume excess.
3. Abdominal cramps, apprehension, convulsions, fingerprinting on sternum and oliguria or anuria could indicate sodium deficit.
4. Dry, sticky mucous membranes, flushed skin, oliguria or anuria, thirst and a rough and dry tongue could indicate sodium excess.
5. Anorexia, gaseous distension of intestines, silent intestinal ileus, weakness and soft, flabby muscles could indicate potassium deficit.
6. Diarrhoea, intestinal colic, irritability and nausea could indicate potassium excess.
7. Abdominal cramps, carpopedal spasm, muscle cramps, tetany and tingling of ends of fingers could indicate calcium deficit.
8. Deep bone pain, loin pain and muscle hypotonicity could indicate calcium excess.
9. Deep, rapid breathing (Kussmaul), shortness of breath on exertion, stupor and weakness could indicate primary base bicarbonate deficit.
10. Depressed respiration, muscle hypertonicity and tetany could indicate primary base bicarbonate excess.
11. Chronic weight loss, emotional depression, pallor, fatigue and soft, flabby muscles could indicate protein deficit.
12. Convulsions, disorientation, hyperactive deep reflexes and tremor could indicate magnesium deficit.

The nurse needs a thorough understanding of the patient's gains and losses of body fluids, and shares this information with other members of the health care team.

Repeated blood samples are obtained for surveillance of electrolyte balance; the nurse explains the purpose of the studies.

MAINTAINING ADEQUATE URINARY DRAINAGE

For the patient with urological disease, as for any other person, urinary excretion of waste materials is necessary for life. The composition of the body fluids is determined not so much by what the patient ingests as by what the kidneys retain. In health, the kidneys are very efficient, excreting the substances that are not needed and retaining those that are. But in the patient with damaged kidneys, therapeutic efforts are necessary to ensure that the limited function of the kidneys is not exceeded.

When artificial drainage of the urinary system becomes necessary, catheters may be inserted directly into the bladder, the ureters or the kidney pelves. Catheters are available in various sizes, shapes and lengths, and may have one or more openings placed in various positions near the tip.

Catheterization

Principles of Management

There are times when the catheter is a lifesaving instrument, as is the case when the patient is unable to void. At other times, catheterization may be necessary in determining the amount of residual urine in the bladder after the patient has voided, to bypass an obstruction that blocks the flow of urine, to provide postoperative drainage following bladder, vaginal or prostate surgery, or in monitoring of hourly urinary output in critically ill patients.

- A patient should be catheterized only if absolutely necessary because catheterization commonly leads to urinary tract infection.

When catheters are used, micro-organisms may gain access to the urinary tract by three main pathways: (1) by introduction from the urethra into the bladder at the time of catheterization; (2) from the thin film of urethral fluid outside of the catheter at the catheter–mucosa interface; and (3) by migration to the bladder along the internal lumen of the catheter after contamination (most common).

To safeguard the patient, the following points of care are essential in urethral catheter management:

- Strict surgical asepsis is employed.
- The urethra is adequately cleansed.
- The catheter should be smaller than the external urinary meatus to minimize trauma and allow secretions to drain out alongside the catheter.
- The catheter is well lubricated with an appropriate antimicrobial lubricant.
- The catheter is passed gently and skilfully.
- The catheter is removed as soon as possible.

Nursing Care of the Patient With an Indwelling Catheter and a Closed Urinary Drainage System

When an indwelling catheter is necessary, a closed drainage system—one designed to minimize or prevent disconnection and risk of contamination—is essential. Such a system may consist of an indwelling catheter, a connecting tube and a collecting bag emptied by a drainage valve.

> ► **NURSING PROCESS**

► THE PATIENT WITH AN INDWELLING CATHETER AND A CLOSED URINARY DRAINAGE SYSTEM

► *Assessment*

The patient with an indwelling catheter is observed for signs and symptoms of urinary tract infection: cloudy urine, haematuria, fever, chills, anorexia and malaise. The area around the urethral orifice is observed for drainage and excoriation. Urine cultures provide the most accurate means for assessment of infection. The colour, odour and volume of urine are also monitored.

Nursing assessment includes observation of the drainage system to ensure that the system provides adequate drainage of urine. The catheter itself is observed to make sure that it is properly anchored, to prevent pressure on the urethra at the penoscrotal junction in the male patient, and tension and traction of the bladder in both male and female patients. An accurate record of the patient's fluid intake and urine output provides additional information about the adequacy of urine elimination.

Additionally, patients at risk for urinary tract infection from catheterization are identified; these include persons who are elderly, debilitated, chronically ill, immunosuppressed, or diabetic. The patient's understanding of the purpose of catheterization is also assessed. Because of the increased risk of infection and subsequent septicaemia, assessment for signs and symptoms of bacteriuria, infection and sepsis is essential.

► *Patient's Problems*

Based on the assessment, the patient's major problems may include the following:

- Potential for infection of the urinary tract related to contamination of the urinary tract.
- Potential impairment of the tissue integrity (urethra and bladder) related to catheterization.

► Expected Outcomes
The main outcomes for the patient may include absence of urinary tract infection and absence of trauma to the urethra and bladder.

Nursing Care

Infection Control
Certain principles of care are essential when managing a closed urinary drainage system.

- Gloves must be worn whenever a urinary drainage system is handled.
- Strict asepsis is necessary during insertion of the catheter.
- A preassembled and sterile closed urinary drainage system is necessary and should not be disconnected before, during or after insertion of the catheter.
- To prevent contamination of a closed system, the tubing is never disconnected. No part of the collection bag or drainage tube should ever be contaminated.
- The bag is never raised above the level of the patient's bladder because this will cause flow of contaminated urine into the patient's bladder from the bag.
- Urine should not be allowed to collect in the tubing because a free flow of urine must be maintained to prevent infection.
- The drainage bag is not allowed to touch the floor. The bag and collecting tubing are changed if contamination occurs.
- The bag is emptied at least every eight hours through the drainage valve, and more frequently if there is a large volume of urine, to lessen the risk of bacterial proliferation.
- Care is taken to see that the drainage tube (valve/spout) is not contaminated.
- Irrigation of the catheter is *not* carried out routinely.
- The catheter is not disconnected from the tubing to obtain urine samples, irrigate the catheter or ambulate or transport the patient.
- Inadvertent handling or manipulation of the catheter by the patient or staff is avoided.
- Handwashing is necessary before and after handling of the catheter, tubing and drainage bag, and gloves must be worn.

The catheter is a foreign body in the urethra, and produces a reaction in the urethral mucosa with some urethral discharge. However, meatal care during catheterization is discouraged, as catheter manipulation during cleansing may result in increased rates of infection. Gentle washing with soap during the daily bath is warranted to cleanse and to remove obvious encrustations from the external catheter surface. The catheter is anchored as securely as possible to prevent to-and-fro movement in the urethra. Drainage and encrustation occur at the exit of any tube.

A liberal fluid intake and an increased urine output must be assured to mechanically flush the catheter and to dilute urinary elements that might form encrustations.

Urine cultures are obtained as prescribed or indicated in monitoring for infection. Many catheters have an aspiration (puncture) port from which a specimen can be obtained.

- There must be renewed emphasis on hand washing and glove changing between patients, and before and after handling any part of the catheter or drainage system.
- Catheterized patients with bacteria in the urine should not be in the same room with noninfected catheterized patients. It is best to assign only one patient with an indwelling catheter to a room to minimize risk of cross-contamination.

Minimizing Trauma

The catheter selected is of an appropriate size to minimize trauma to the urethra during its insertion. The catheter is lubricated adequately so that it can be inserted easily and gently. It is inserted far enough into the bladder to prevent trauma to the urethral tissues when the retention balloon of the catheter is inflated. The catheter is secured properly to prevent it from moving, causing traction on the urethra or being accidentally removed. Care is taken to ensure that any patient who is confused does not accidentally remove the catheter with the retention balloon still inflated, because such an action would cause considerable trauma to the urethra and bleeding.

In the male patient, the catheter is taped laterally to the thigh or to the abdomen (Figure 20.1) to prevent pressure on the urethra at the penoscrotal junction.

In the female patient, the drainage tubing attached to the catheter is taped to the thigh to prevent tension and traction on the bladder.

▶ *Evaluation*
▶ **Expected Outcomes**

1. Patient is free of urinary tract infection.

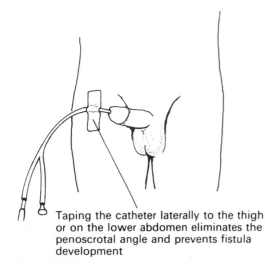

Taping the catheter laterally to the thigh or on the lower abdomen eliminates the penoscrotal angle and prevents fistula development

Figure 20.1 For the male patient, the catheter is taped to the thigh or to the abdomen.

   a. Excretes urine that is clear and yellow or amber, with a specific gravity of 1.005 to 1.025.
   b. Has a urine culture negative for micro-organisms.
   c. Has a normal temperature.
   d. Demonstrates adequate fluid intake and urine output.
   e. Does not have excessive drainage or excoriation around the urethral orifice.
   f. Avoids kinking or twisting of the catheter or drainage tubing.
   g. Maintains position of the drainage bag below the level of the bladder when in bed, sitting or moving about.
   h. Maintains proper anchoring of the catheter to prevent movement and accidental removal of the catheter.
2. Is free of trauma to urethra and bladder.
   a. Reports absence of pain or discomfort in urethra or bladder.
   b. Demonstrates no blood in urine or irritation of urethra.
   c. Is free of pain or discomfort on voiding following catheter removal.
   d. Eliminates 200 to 400 ml of urine with each voiding following catheter removal.
   e. Shows no signs of urinary incontinence.

Intermittent Self-Catheterization

Intermittent self-catheterization provides periodic drainage of urine from the bladder. It is the treatment of choice following spinal cord injury and other neurological disorders in which bladder emptying is impaired. Aseptic techniques are required during the in-hospital training period because of the risk of cross-contamination. The patient may use a 'clean' (nonsterile) technique at home, where the risk is reduced. Self-catheterization promotes independence, results in fewer complications and permits more normal sexual relations. The objectives are to decrease the morbidity associated with the longterm use of an indwelling catheter and to achieve catheter-free status if possible.

If the patient is unable to perform intermittent self-catheterization, then a family member or close friend is taught to carry out the procedure at regular intervals during the day.

Suprapubic Bladder Drainage

Suprapubic bladder aspiration is a method of establishing drainage from the bladder by inserting a catheter or tube into the bladder through a suprapubic ('above the pubis') incision or puncture. It is used as a temporary measure to divert the flow of urine from the urethra when the urethral route is impassable (due to injuries, strictures, prostatic obstruction), after gynaecological operations when bladder

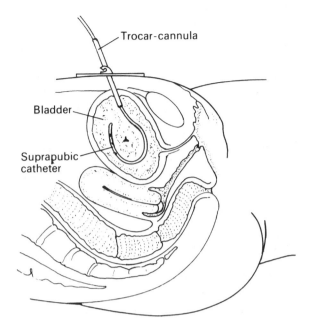

Figure 20.2 Suprapubic bladder drainage. A trocar-cannula is used to puncture the abdominal and bladder walls. The catheter is threaded through the trocar-cannula, which is then removed, leaving the catheter in place. The catheter is secured by tape or sutures to prevent accidental removal.

dysfunction is likely to occur (vaginal hysterectomy, vaginal repair surgery), and after pelvic fractures (Figure 20.2).

To facilitate insertion of the suprapubic catheter, the patient is placed in a supine position and the bladder is distended by administration of oral or intravenous fluids or by instillation of sterile saline into the bladder via a urethral catheter. These measures make it easier to locate the bladder.

Suprapubic bladder drainage may be maintained continuously for several weeks. If the patient's ability to void is to be tested, the catheter is clamped for four hours, during which time the patient attempts to void. After the patient voids, the catheter is unclamped and the residual urine measured.

ALTERATIONS IN VOIDING PATTERNS

Urinary Retention

Urinary retention (both acute and chronic) refers to the inability to urinate despite the patient's urge or desire to do so. Chronic retention will often lead to overflow incontinence (due to pressure of retained urine in the bladder) or residual urine. Residual urine refers to urine that remains in the bladder after voiding.

Retention may occur in any postoperative patient, particularly in those who have undergone surgery on the perineal or anal regions that resulted in reflex spasm of the sphincters. It may also occur in the acutely ill, the elderly or the bedridden. Urinary retention may be due to anxiety, prostatic enlargement, urethral pathology (infection, tumour, calculus), trauma, neurogenic bladder dysfunction and other conditions.

Urinary retention may lead to infection, which may develop as a result of overdistension of the bladder, compromised blood supply to the bladder wall and proliferation of bacteria. Impaired renal function may also occur, particularly if obstruction of the urinary tract is present.

Management

Measures are instituted to prevent overdistension of the bladder and to treat infection or obstruction. Many problems, however, can be prevented by careful nursing assessment and appropriate nursing interventions.

▶ NURSING PROCESS
▶ THE PATIENT WITH URINARY RETENTION

▶ *Assessment*

The signs and symptoms of urinary retention may easily be overlooked unless the nurse consciously assesses for them.

● Determine the time and volume of the last voiding.
● Is the patient passing small amounts of urine frequently?
● Is the patient dribbling?
● Is the patient complaining of pain or discomfort in the lower abdomen? (Note, however, that discomfort may be relatively mild if the bladder distends slowly.)
● Check for signs of a rounded swelling arising out of the pelvis, which could indicate retention.
● Palpate the suprapubic area for an oval-shaped mass, and percuss for dullness of a full bladder.
● Assess the patient for other indicators of urinary retention, such as restlessness and agitation.

▶ *Patient's Problems*

Based on the assessment, the patient's major problems may include the following:

● Urinary retention related to pain, tension, lack of privacy, or unfamiliar surroundings and position for voiding.
● Discomfort related to bladder distension.

▶ Expected Outcomes

The main outcomes for the patient may be return of normal voiding patterns and relief of discomfort.

Nursing Care

Promoting Urinary Elimination

Nursing measures to encourage voiding include providing privacy, helping the patient to the bathroom or commode in order to provide a more natural setting for voiding, or allowing the male patient to stand beside the bed while using the urinal (because most men find this position more comfortable and natural for urination).

Additional measures include providing warmth to relax the sphincters, giving the patient hot tea to drink and offering psychological reassurance and support whenever it is required.

Relief of Discomfort

Relief of urinary retention generally brings relief of abdominal distension and discomfort. Treatment of the cause (i.e., obstruction) usually relieves the patient's fear that the problem will recur.

▶ *Evaluation*
▶ Expected Outcomes

1. Patient demonstrates normal voiding patterns.
   a. Voids 300 to 400 ml of urine every three hours.
   b. Exhibits no abdominal distension.
   c. Is free of sensation of bladder fullness.
2. Experiences relief of discomfort.
   a. Reports no abdominal or bladder pain and discomfort.
   b. Uses appropriate measures to prevent recurrence of urinary retention and bladder discomfort.

Urinary Incontinence

Urinary incontinence is the involuntary or uncontrolled loss of urine from the bladder. If urinary incontinence results from an inflammatory condition (cystitis), it will probably be temporary in nature. However, if it results from a serious neurological condition (paraplegia), it could easily be a permanent problem.

Stress incontinence is the involuntary loss of urine through an intact urethra as a result of a sudden increase in intra-abdominal pressure.

It is seen mostly in women, and is due to congenital conditions (exstrophy of the bladder, ectopic ureter) or to obstetrical injury, lesions of the bladder neck, extrinsic pelvic disease, fistulae, detrusor dysfunction and a variety of other conditions.

Nursing Care

Most patients with urinary incontinence can be conditioned to gain urinary control through systematic habit training or the establishment of an automatic bladder. Such a programme helps a patient lose the fear of embarrassment as progress is made in rehabilitation.

Neurogenic Bladder

Neurogenic bladder refers to a bladder disturbance that results from a lesion of the nervous system. It may be caused by spinal cord injury or tumour, certain neurological diseases (multiple sclerosis), congenital anomalies (spina bifida, myelomeningocele) and infection. There are two types of neurogenic bladders: (1) spastic or hypertonic bladder, characterized by automatic, reflex or uncontrolled expulsion of urine from the bladder with incomplete emptying; and (2) flaccid bladder, with loss of sensation of bladder fullness and thus overfilling and distension of the bladder.

The major complication of neurogenic bladder is infection that results from stasis of urine and subsequent catheterization. Hypertrophy of the bladder walls also results, ultimately leading to vesicoureteral reflux (backing up of urine from the bladder to the ureters) and hydronephrosis (dilation of the internal structures of the kidney by increased pressure of the backed-up urine). Urolithiasis (stones in the urinary tract) may develop from urinary stasis and infection and from demineralization of bone due to the patient's prolonged bedrest. Renal failure is the major cause of death of patients with neurological impairment of the bladder.

Nursing Care

The care of the patient with neurogenic bladder is a major challenge to the health care team. There are several long-term objectives appropriate for all types of neurogenic bladders: (1) to prevent overdistension of the bladder; (2) to empty the bladder regularly and completely; (3) to maintain urine sterility with no stone formation; and (4) to maintain adequate bladder capacity without vesicoureteral reflux.

The immediate management of the patient with a neurogenic bladder consists of catheterizing the patient intermittently or inserting a three-way catheter with closed drainage to avoid overdistension.

With the use of either intermittent or continuous catherization, a liberal fluid intake is encouraged to reduce the urinary bacterial count, reduce stasis, decrease the concentration of calcium in the urine and minimize the precipitation of urinary crystals and subsequent stone formation. The patient is kept as mobile as possible, through early ambulation if feasible, or through the use of a wheelchair or tilt table.

Spastic Bladder

The spastic (reflex, automatic or hypertonic) bladder disorder is caused by any lesion of the cord above the voiding reflex arc (upper motor neuron lesion). The result is a loss of conscious sensation and cerebral motor control. There is reduced bladder capacity and marked hypertrophy of the bladder wall. As a result, the bladder empties on reflex, with minimal or no controlling influence to regulate its activity.

Flaccid Bladder

The flaccid (atonic, nonreflex or autonomous) neurogenic bladder is caused by a lower motor neuron lesion, most commonly due to trauma. The bladder continues to fill and becomes greatly distended. The bladder muscle does not contract forcefully at any time. Sensory loss may accompany a flaccid bladder, so the patient feels no discomfort. Overdistension causes damage to the bladder musculature, infection due to stagnant urine and damage to the kidneys as a result of pressure from the urine.

Patients can also be taught to perform self-catheterization at intervals until spontaneous complete emptying of the bladder is achieved.

Sometimes it is not possible for the patient to achieve reflex bladder control or self-catheterization. The male patient then may use an external (condom catheter) collecting device if the bladder empties well and no residual urine remains. The female patient may need to wear pads or waterproof pants. Surgical intervention may be carried out to correct bladder neck contractures or vesicoureteral reflux or to perform some type of urinary diversion procedure (see Urinary Diversion, below).

THE PATIENT UNDERGOING KIDNEY SURGERY

Preoperative Considerations

All operations on the kidney should be attempted only after a period of study and preparation. Every effort is made to ensure that renal function is as good as possible. This is the major preoperative goal. Fluids are encouraged to promote increased excretion of waste products before surgery, unless contraindicated because of pre-existing renal dysfunction. If kidney infection is present preoperatively, a wide-spectrum antimicrobial agent may be given to avoid the hazards of bacteraemia. Coagulation studies may be done if the patient has a history of bruising and bleeding. The general preoperative preparation is similar to that described in the section entitled Perioperative Care, Chapter 2.

Patients facing kidney surgery are apprehensive. They may enter the hospital with pain, fever and haematuria. Thus, the nurse encourages the patient to recognize and express any feelings of anxiety. Confidence is reinforced by establishing a relationship of trust and by providing expert and considerate care. Patients faced with the prospect of losing a kidney may think that they will be dependent on dialysis for the rest of their lives. However, normal function may be maintained by a single kidney.

Surgery on the kidney may be performed:

1. To remove obstructions (tumours, calculi).
2. To insert a tube for drainage of the kidney.
3. To remove the kidney itself (may be removed to treat unilateral kidney disease, in preparation for transplantation or to treat renal carcinoma).

Perioperative Concerns

The operative incisions for renal surgery include loin, intercostal, lumbodorsal and transverse abdominal or thoracoabdominal incisions (Figure 20.3). The difficulties in renal surgery are related to difficulty in access to the kidney. Additionally, plans are made for managing altered urinary drainage and drainage systems.

Postoperative Management

Because the kidney is such a vascular organ, haemorrhage and shock are the chief complications following renal surgery. Fluid and blood replacement are frequently indicated in the immediate postoperative period to prevent or treat intraoperative blood loss.

Abdominal distension and paralytic ileus are fairly common following operations on the kidney and ureter, and are thought to be due to a reflex paralysis of intestinal peristalsis and to manipulation of the colon or duodenum in gaining access to the kidney during surgery. Oral fluids are avoided until active bowel sounds return or until the passage of flatus is noted. Abdominal distension is relieved by decompression via a nasogastric tube. (See section entitled Perioperative Care, Chapter 2, for treatment of paralytic ileus.)

Antibiotics are given as necessary on the basis of culture identification of the causative organism. The toxic features of these agents must be kept in mind when assessing the patient. Therapy with low doses of heparin subcutaneously has been shown to prevent thromboembolism in urologic patients.

Management may also include insertion of a nephrostomy or other drainage tube, and the use of ureteral stents. See pages 688–9 for a description of these devices and nursing implications.

Management of Drainage Tubes

Almost all postoperative kidney and urological patients, and many other patients with kidney and urological disturbances, have drains, tubes or catheters in place. Following operations such as nephrostomy, pyelotomy and ureterotomy, drainage tubes may be placed directly in the kidney, pelvis or ureter in order to divert the urine and keep the wound dry. All catheters and tubes must remain functioning (e.g., draining) to prevent obstruction by blood clots, which can cause infection. Pain similar to

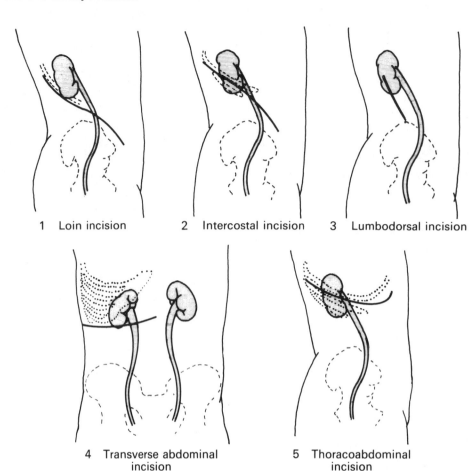

Figure 20.3 Standard incisions for urological surgical procedures.

renal colic is caused by the passage of clotted blood down the ureter.

Nephrostomy Drainage

A nephrostomy tube is inserted directly into the kidney for temporary or permanent urinary diversion either by open operation or percutaneously. This may be accomplished by a single tube or by a self-retaining U-loop or circular nephrostomy tube. The purposes of nephrostomy drainage are to provide drainage from the kidney after surgery, conserve and permit physiological restoration of renal tissue traumatized by obstruction, and provide drainage when the ureter is no longer draining. The nephrostomy tube is attached to closed gravity drainage or to a urostomy appliance.

Percutaneous nephrostomy is the insertion of a tube through the skin into the renal collecting system. It is done to provide external drainage of urine from an obstructed ureter, to provide a route for insertion of an ureteral stent (see following discussion), to dissolve renal calculi, to dilate strictures, to close fistulas, to administer drugs, to allow insertion of a brush biopsy instrument and nephro-

scope, and to perform selected surgical procedures.

The patient and tubing are observed for signs of bleeding (immediate or delayed), urinary debris and stones, fistulae formation and infection.

- Assess for bleeding at the nephrostomy site (main complication).
- Assure unobstructed drainage of the nephrostomy tube/catheter. Obstruction of the tube produces pain, trauma, pressure and stress on the suture lines, and infection. If the tube is dislodged inadvertently, it must be replaced immediately by the surgeon because the nephrostomy opening will contract, making it difficult to reinsert the tube.
- A nephrostomy tube is never clamped, as such an action will precipitate acute pyelonephritis.
- The nephrostomy tube is rarely irrigated. If necessary, irrigation may be carried out by the surgeon.

Ureteral Stents

A ureteral stent is a tubular device designed for placement

within the ureter to maintain ureteral flow in patients with ureteral obstruction (from oedema, stricture, fibrosis, advanced malignancy), to restore kidney function, to divert urine, to promote healing and to maintain the patency of the ureter after surgery (Figure 20.4).

The stent, usually of soft, flexible silicone, may be temporary or permanent. It may be inserted through a cystoscope or nephrostomy tube or by open operation. Complications include infection from a foreign body in the genitourinary tract, tube encrustation, bleeding or clot obstruction within the stent and dislodgement of the stent.

The nursing care includes: monitoring for bleeding; observing and measuring output; looking for purulent drainage at the insertion site or in the drainage bag; and monitoring for stent dislodgement, which is denoted by colicky pain and a decrease in urine output.

An indwelling stent usually induces local ureteral reaction, including mucosal oedema, which can cause temporary obstruction of the ureter.

▶ NURSING PROCESS

▶ THE PATIENT UNDERGOING KIDNEY SURGERY

▶ *Assessment*

Immediate concerns of the nurse caring for the postoperative patient who has undergone surgery of the kidney include assessment of respiratory and circulatory status,

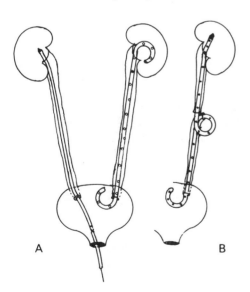

Figure 20.4 Ureteral stents. (A) Retrograde passage of ureteral stent. The double-J ureteral stent is shaped to resist migration. The proximal J hooks into the lower calix or renal pelvis, and the distal J curves into the bladder. (B) Open surgical placement of double-J stent before an ureteral anastomosis. (Courtesy of Surgitek, Racine, Wisconsin.)

pain level, and patency and adequacy of urinary drainage.

The patient's respiratory status is assessed by monitoring the rate, depth, and pattern of respirations. The location of the surgical incision frequently causes pain on inspiration and coughing.

The vital signs and arterial or central venous pressure are monitored. Skin colour, temperature and urine output will also provide information about the adequacy of circulatory status. The surgical incision and drainage tubes are observed frequently to aid in detection of unexpected blood loss and haemorrhage.

Pain is a major problem for the patient postoperatively because of the site of the surgical incision and the position assumed on the operating table to permit adequate access to the kidney. The location and severity of pain are assessed before and after administration of analgesics. Abdominal distension, which increases the patient's level of discomfort, is also monitored.

The patient's urinary output and drainage from tubes inserted during surgery are monitored for amount, colour and type of output and drainage. Decreased or absent drainage is reported promptly to the doctor, as it may indicate obstruction that may cause pain, infection and disruption of the suture lines.

▶ *Patient's Problems*

Based on the history and assessment and the type of surgical procedure carried out, the major problems for the patient may include the following:

● Potential impaired gas exchange related to the location of the surgical incision.
● Potential decreased cardiac output related to blood loss.
● Pain and discomfort related to the location of the surgical incision, the position assumed on the operating table during surgery and abdominal distension.
● Alteration in urinary elimination.

▶ *Planning and Implementation*
▶ Expected Outcomes

The main outcomes for the patient may include adequate gas exchange, maintenance of cardiac output, relief of pain and discomfort and maintenance of urinary elimination.

Nursing Care

Assuring Gas Exchange

The surgical approaches to the kidney predispose the patient to respiratory complications and paralytic ileus. Also, with a subcostal or posterior incision, the patient may have severe pain on breathing and coughing. If the pleura has been opened, pneumothorax may be a problem. The incision is generally close to the diaphragm and, with a substernal incision, the nerves may be stretched and bruised.

Adequate use of analgesic medications is necessary to relieve pain so that the patient is able to take deep breaths and cough. If the analgesic is given at proper intervals, the patient will be able to perform deep-breathing and coughing exercises more effectively. The patient is encouraged to cough after each deep breath to loosen secretions.

Assessing for Complications

Bleeding, haemorrhage, hypovolaemia and shock are the major complications of kidney surgery. The nurse's role is to observe for these complications, to report their signs and symptoms and to administer prescribed parenteral fluids and blood if complications occur. Continuing to monitor the patient's vital signs, skin condition, urinary drainage system and surgical incision is necessary to detect evidence of decreased circulating blood and fluid volume and cardiac output.

Relieving Pain

In addition to the incisional pain, the patient may experience discomfort from distension of the renal capsule (tumour, blood clot), ischaemia (from occlusion of blood vessels) and stretching of the intrarenal blood vessels. Adequate pain relief is necessary to permit the patient to take deep breaths, cough, turn and move about. This type of patient also frequently experiences muscular aches and pains resulting from the position assumed on the operating table, which places anatomical and physiological stresses on the body. Massage, moist heat and analgesic medications provide relief.

Promoting Urinary Elimination

Attention to the patient's urinary output and drainage is essential to preserve and protect the patient's remaining kidney function. Therefore, adequate drainage is critical to prevent obstruction and infection. The output from each urinary drainage tube is recorded separately; very accurate output measurements are essential in monitoring renal function and the patency of the urinary drainage system. Strict asepsis is used during manipulation of the drainage catheter and tube. Handwashing and the wearing of sterile gloves is indicated before and after touching any parts of the system. Use of closed drainage systems is essential to reduce contamination of the system and infection. The patient's urinary drainage is monitored closely for changes in volume, colour, odour and constituents. Urinalysis and urine cultures are important in following the patient's progress. Care is taken to ensure that the collection bag is suspended below the patient's bladder to prevent reflux of urine back into the urinary tract. (However, the bag is kept off the floor to prevent contamination.) Most urinary drainage systems do not require routine irrigation. If irrigation is necessary and prescribed, however, it should be performed carefully, using sterile solution, with minimal pressure, consistent with the doctor's instructions and with strict asepsis without interruption of the closed drainage system.

Patient Education and Home Care

If the patient is to be discharged from the hospital with the drainage system in place, measures are taken to be sure that both the patient and carer understand the importance of maintaining the system correctly and preventing infection. Written advice and guidelines are given to the patient before discharge.

A nursing care plan for a patient with renal colic is shown in Nursing Care Plan 20.1.

► NURSING CARE PLAN 20.1: THE PATIENT WITH RENAL COLIC

Care plan for Ali Bin Hussan, who is suffering from renal calculi and colic. He is 37 years old and is a practising Muslim. He is married and has two children. He works in a factory.

Patient's problems	Expected outcomes	Nursing care	Rationale
1. Severe pain due to the presence of renal stones causing inflammation and abrasion of the urinary tract	Path will be reduced to a tolerable level and episodes of severe pain will not occur	1a. Administer analgesics every 2–3 hours or as prescribed, and record effects	Promotes pain relief
		b. Assess Ali's pain level and the location of the pain at frequent intervals. Give analgesia before pain becomes severe	Pain is unique to each individual (McCaffery, 1983)
		c. Allow Ali to express his pain in his own way	Different cultures express pain in different ways
2. Anxiety due to: a. Pain and lack of knowledge b. Ali's concern for his wife and	Anxiety will be reduced to a level that is acceptable and tolerable for Ali	2a. Give explanation of what is wrong and what is being done to help him. Explain possible further diagnostic investigations and treatment	Helps to reduce anxiety and stress

► NURSING CARE PLAN 20.1: THE PATIENT WITH RENAL COLIC

Patient's problems	Expected outcomes	Nursing care	Rationale
children while he is in hospital c. Possible difficulty in communication due to language problems		that may be required, e.g. surgery/lithotripsy b. Make sure Ali's wife is informed of his diagnosis and allow visiting c. Locate an interpreter if necessary	
3. Risk of clinical shock due to intense pain	Shock will be avoided	3a. Monitor vital signs hourly or two hourly, i.e. blood pressure, respirations and pulse b. Elevate foot of the bed c. Prepare for and assist in setting up an intravenous infusion if required d. Administer analgesia; see problem 1	Early detection of relevant clinical changes Increases blood flow to the brain Replaces fluid loss and corrects electrolyte balance Reduces pain and neurogenic shock
4. Risk of: a. Obstruction of the urinary tract b. Urinary tract infection c. Urinary retention due to movement of renal stones	The urinary tract will remain patent and free from infection	4a. Observe for frequent urination of small amounts, oliguria or anuria b. Observe urine for presence of blood and strain urine for presence of stones or gravel c. Give plenty of fluids to drink unless vomiting; see problem 5 d. Monitor temperature four-hourly e. Give antibiotics as prescribed f. Measure fluid intake and output and chart it g. Observe for patient discomfort and a distended bladder	Obstruction of the urinary tract can cause acute renal failure The presence of stones can cause distension of the renal pelvis and proximal ureter Infection of the urinary tract can lead to pyelonephritis, which can permanently damage the renal parenchyma Early detection of urinary retention
5. Risk of nausea, vomiting and gastrointestinal disturbances due to pain and proximity of the kidneys to the gut	Minimal unpleasant aspects of vomiting	5a. Stay with Ali to give support and reassurance b. Provide vomit bowl and frequent mouthwashes c. Give antiemetic drugs if prescribed d. Ensure comfortable position in the bed e. Monitor fluid loss; see problem 4 f. Monitor intravenous infusion if required; see problem 5 g. Insert nasogastric tube if requested by doctor and aspirate stomach contents; chart volume	Relieves further anxiety Reduces nausea and vomiting Relieves abdominal muscle spasm Prevents dehydration High fluid intake required to increase hydrostatic pressure behind the stone to flush it out Reduces vomiting and monitors fluid loss
6. Lack of information about further treatment for renal stones	Ali will be aware of the implications and complications of renal stones	6a. Involve medical staff in explanations to Ali and his wife about further treatment options b. Give information with regard to fluids and diet which will assist Ali in self-care following discharge	Explicit information-giving will help Ali to make an informed choice about further treatment Patient education prepares the patient for better self-care

▶ *Evaluation*
▶ **Expected Outcomes**

1. Patient achieves adequate gas exchange.
   a. Exhibits clear and normal breath sounds.
   b. Demonstrates normal respiratory rate and unrestricted thoracic excursion.
   c. Performs deep-breathing exercises and coughs every two hours.
   d. Demonstrates normal temperature and vital signs.
2. Maintains cardiac output.
   a. Demonstrates normal vital signs and arterial and central venous pressures.
   b. Exhibits normal skin turgor, temperature and colour.
   c. Demonstrates no additional losses of blood or fluid.
   d. Exhibits no signs or symptoms of shock and hypovolaemia (e.g., decreased urine output, restlessness, rapid pulse).
3. Experiences reduced pain and discomfort.
   a. Reports progressive decrease in pain.
   b. Requires analgesics at less frequent intervals.
   c. Turns, coughs and takes deep breaths as suggested.
   d. Ambulates progressively.
   e. Uses moist heat and massage to reduce muscular aches.
4. Maintains urinary elimination.
   a. Demonstrates unobstructed urine flow from drainage tubes.
   b. Exhibits normal fluid and electrolyte balance (normal skin turgor, serum electrolytes within normal, absence of symptoms of imbalances).
   c. Reports no increase in pain, tenderness or pressure at drainage site.
   d. Exhibits cautious handling of own drainage system.
   e. Washes hands before and after handling drainage system and handles it only when necessary.
   f. States rationale for use and maintenance of a closed drainage system.
   g. Identifies signs and symptoms that should be reported to the health care provider.
   h. Exhibits no signs of infection (such as fever and pain).

UROLITHIASIS

Urolithiasis refers to the presence of stones (calculi) in the urinary system. Stones are found in the urinary tract by the deposit of crystalline substances (calcium oxalate, calcium phosphate, uric acid) excreted in the urine. They may be found anywhere from the kidney to the bladder, and vary in size from minute granular deposits, called sand or gravel, to bladder stones the size of an orange. The different sites of calculus formation in the urinary tract are shown in Figure 20.5.

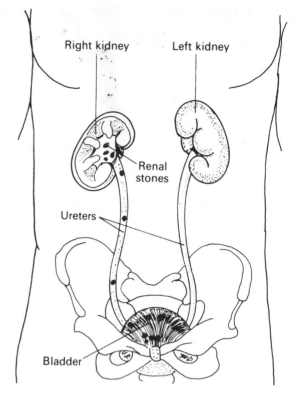

Figure 20.5 Various sites of calculous disease of the urinary tract (urolithiasis).

Certain factors favour the formation of stones, including infection, urinary stasis and periods of immobility (produces slowing of renal drainage and altered calcium metabolism). Hypercalcaemia (abnormally high concentration of blood calcium compounds) and hypercalciuria (abnormally large amounts of calcium in the urine) may be caused by hyperparathyroidism, renal tubular acidosis, excessive intake of vitamin D, excessive intake of milk and alkali and certain myeloproliferative diseases (leukaemia, polycythaemia vera, multiple myeloma), which produce an unusual proliferation of blood cells derived from bone marrow. These factors promote increased calcium concentrations in blood and urine, causing precipitation of calcium and formation of stones. Some stones are caused by an excessive excretion of uric acid, the end product of purine metabolism. Urinary stone formation may also occur with inflammatory bowel disease and in those with an ileostomy or bowel resection, particularly of the small bowel since these people absorb more oxalate. Vitamin A deficiency may be another cause. In many patients, however, no cause may be found.

The problem occurs predominantly in the third to fifth decades, and affects men more than women. People who have had two stones tend to have recurrences. The majority of stones contain calcium or magnesium in combination with phosphorus or oxalate. Most stones are radio-opaque and can be detected on X-ray.

Clinical Features

The clinical features of stones in the urinary tract depend on the presence of obstruction, infection and oedema. When the stones block the flow of urine, obstruction develops, and the constant irritation of the stone may be followed by a secondary infection that causes pyelonephritis and cystitis with chills, fever and dysuria. Some stones cause few if any symptoms while slowly destroying the functional units of the kidney (nephrons); others cause excruciating pain and discomfort. Stones in the renal pelvis may be associated with intense, deep ache in the loin (part of the back between the thorax and pelvis) and with voiding of increased amounts of urine containing blood and white blood cells (pus). The stone produces an increase in hydrostatic pressure and distends the renal pelvis and proximal ureter. Thus, painful afferent sensations are initiated. Pain originating in the renal area radiates anteriorly and downward toward the bladder in the female and toward the testis in the male. If the pain suddenly becomes acute, the loin exquisitely tender, and nausea and vomiting appear, the patient is having an attack of renal colic. Diarrhoea and abdominal discomfort may accompany the attack.

When stones lodge in the ureter, acute, excruciating, colicky pain is experienced, radiating down the thigh and to the genitalia. The pain usually occurs in waves. There is usually a frequent desire to void, but very little urine is passed, and it usually contains blood because of the abrasive action of the stone. This group of symptoms is called ureteral colic. In general, the patient will spontaneously pass stones 0.5 to 1 cm in diameter. Those over 1 cm in diameter usually must be removed or broken up so that they can be removed or passed spontaneously. When stones lodge in the bladder, they usually produce symptoms of irritation and may be associated with urinary tract infection and haematuria. If the stone obstructs the bladder neck, there will be urinary retention.

Diagnosis

The diagnosis is confirmed by intravenous urography or retrograde pyelography. Blood chemistries and a 24-hour urine test for measurement of calcium, uric acid, creatinine, sodium, pH and total volume are part of the diagnostic assessment. A dietary and drug history and family history of renal stones are obtained to identify factors predisposing the patient to the formation of stones.

Medical Management

The basic goals underlying the management of the patient's disease are to eradicate the stone, to determine the stone type, to prevent nephron destruction, to control infection and to relieve any obstruction that may be present. Infection and back-pressure of obstructed urine can destroy the renal parenchyma.

The immediate objective of treatment for renal or ureteral colic is to relieve the pain until its cause can be eliminated; strong analgesia is administered to prevent shock and syncope that may result from the excruciating pain. Hot baths are also useful. Unless the patient is vomiting, fluids are encouraged, since this treatment tends to increase the hydrostatic pressure behind the stone and thus assists it in its downward passage. A high round-the-clock fluid intake reduces the concentration of urinary crystalloids and ensures a high urinary output. Encouraging fluid intake also lowers the specific gravity of the urine.

When stones are recovered, chemical analysis is carried out to determine their composition.

If the stone cannot be passed spontaneously or complications occur, the stone must be removed surgically or through a percutaneous nephrostomy. It may also be fragmented through extracorporeal shock wave lithotripsy (ESWL) or dissolved.

Surgical Removal

Surgical intervention is indicated if the stone is causing obstruction, unremitting pain, infection that does not respond to treatment or progressive renal damage. Surgery is also done to correct any anatomical abnormalities within the kidney to improve urinary drainage.

If the stone is in the kidney, the operation performed may be a nephrolithotomy (incision into the kidney with removal of the stone) or a nephrectomy, if the kidney is nonfunctional secondary to infection or hydronephrosis. Stones in the kidney pelvis are removed by a pyelolithotomy, those in the ureter by ureterolithotomy and those in the bladder by cystotomy. Sometimes an instrument is inserted through the urethra into the bladder, and the stone is crushed in the jaws of this instrument. Such an operation is called a cystolithopaxy.

Methods of Stone Removal

The field of endourology integrates the skills of the radiologist and urologist to extract renal calculi without major surgery. A percutaneous nephrostomy is performed (see p. 688), and a nephroscope is introduced through the dilated percutaneous tract into the renal parenchyma. Depending on its size, the stone may be extracted with forceps or by a stone basket, or an ultrasound probe is introduced through the nephrostomy tube and ultrasonic waves are used to pulverize the stone. Small stone fragments and stone dust are irrigated and suctioned out of the collecting system. Larger stones may be further reduced by ultrasonic disintegration and then removed with forceps or stone basket. Using a similar method, an electrical discharge is used to create a hydraulic shock wave to crack the stone, or a laser can be used. A probe is passed through the cystoscope, and the tip of the lithotriptor is placed near the stone. The strength of the discharge and pulse frequency can be varied. This procedure is performed under local or general anaesthesia.

After stone extraction, the percutaneous nephrostomy tube is left in place for a time to ensure that the ureter is not obstructed from oedema or blood clots. The most common complications are haemorrhage, infection and urinary extravasation. Only a very small skin incision is required to remove the stone, a shorter hospital stay is required and postoperative morbidity is minimal. After removal of the tube, the nephrostomy tract closes spontaneously.

Extracorporeal Shock Wave Lithotripsy

Extracorporeal shock wave lithotripsy (ESWL; Figure 20.6) is a new, nonsurgical procedure used to break up stones in the calyx of the kidney. After the stones are reduced to small fragments the size of grains of sand, the remnants of the stones are passed in the urine through the lower urinary tract and voided.

Shock waves are generated by the lithotriptor, transmitted through the water bath, and directed precisely at the stone identified in the renal pelvis by fluoroscopy. The shock waves are timed with the patient's electro-cardiogram to prevent cardiac arrhythmias. Multiple shocks are necessary, with their number depending on the size of the kidney stone to be fragmented. Although the shock waves usually do not damage other tissue, discomfort from the multiple shocks may occur. Sometimes the urine is strained following the procedure; voided gravel or sand is sent to the laboratory for chemical analysis. The patient is encouraged to increase fluid intake to assist in the passage of stone fragments, which may occur for six weeks to several months after the procedure.

Although lithotripsy is a costly treatment, it is expected to decrease hospital stay and expenses by reducing for most patients the amount of time required to recover, since an invasive surgical procedure to remove the kidney stone is avoided.

► **NURSING PROCESS**
► **THE PATIENT WITH RENAL STONES**

► *Assessment*

The patient with suspected renal stones is assessed for pain and discomfort. The severity and location of pain are assessed along with the area of radiation of the pain. The

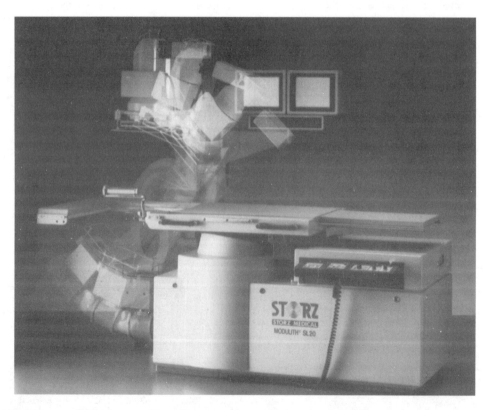

Figure 20.6 Extracorporeal shock wave lithotripsy (ESWL). 'Third generation lithotripter' featuring combination in-line ultrasound, X-ray localization and water cushion coupling. It is a powerful therapy source requiring no anaesthesia and has low running costs. (Courtesy of Storz Medical.)

patient is also assessed for the presence of associated symptoms such as nausea, vomiting, diarrhoea and abdominal distension. Additionally, the nursing assessment includes observations for signs of urinary tract infection (chills, fever, dysuria, frequency and hesitancy) and obstruction (frequent urination of small amounts, oliguria, or anuria). The urine is observed for the presence of blood, and strained for stones or gravel.

► Patient's Problems

Based on the assessment data, the problems of the patient with renal stones may include the following:

- Alterations in pain and discomfort related to inflammation, obstruction and abrasion of the urinary tract.
- Potential for infection and obstruction related to blockage of the urinary tract by a stone or oedema.
- Lack of knowledge about prevention of recurrence of renal stones.

► Planning and Implementation
► Expected Outcomes

The main outcomes for the patient may include relief of pain and discomfort, prevention of infection and obstruction and prevention of recurrence of renal stones.

Nursing Care

Relieving Pain

Immediate relief of severe pain from renal or ureteral colic is promoted through the use of analgesics as prescribed. The patient is encouraged and assisted to assume a position of comfort. If the patient obtains some pain relief by ambulating, then help is given to do so. The patient's pain is monitored closely, and increases in severity are reported promptly to the doctor so that relief can be provided and additional treatment initiated. The patient is prepared for other treatment (e.g., surgery, lithotripsy) if severe pain is unrelieved and the stone is not passed spontaneously.

Preventing Infection and Obstruction

The patient with suspected renal stones is at risk of infection and obstruction of the urinary tract. A decreased urine volume and bloody or cloudy urine must be reported by the patient. The total urine output as well as patterns of voiding are monitored. Increased fluid intake will be encouraged to prevent dehydration and increase hydrostatic pressure within the urinary tract to promote passage of the stone. If the patient is unable to take adequate fluids orally, intravenous fluids will be prescribed. The patient is assisted with walking since ambulation may help to move the stone through the urinary tract.

The nursing care of patients with calculi requires constant observation to detect the spontaneous passage of a stone. All urine should be strained through gauze, since uric acid stones may crumble. Any blood clots passed in the urine should be crushed and the sides of the urinal and bedpan inspected for clinging stones.

Patient Education

Because it is known that urinary calculi may recur after the first stone is found, the patient is encouraged to follow a regime to avoid further stone formation. One facet of prevention is to maintain a high fluid intake since stones form more readily in a concentrated urine. A patient who has shown a tendency to form stones should drink enough to excrete 3,000 to 4,000 ml of urine every 24 hours, should adhere to the prescribed diet and should avoid sudden increases in environmental temperatures, which may cause a fall in urinary volume. Occupations and sports that produce excessive sweating can lead to severe temporary dehydration; therefore, fluid intake should be increased. Sufficient fluids should be taken in the evening to prevent urine from becoming too concentrated at night. Urine cultures are done every one to two months in the first year and periodically thereafter. Recurrent urinary infection must be treated vigorously.

Because of the high risk of recurrence, the patient with renal stones is taught the signs and symptoms of stone formation, obstruction and infection, and is directed to report these promptly to the doctor.

► Evaluation
► Expected Outcomes

1. Patient experiences relief of pain.
   a. Reports decreased pain and discomfort.
   b. Assumes a position of comfort.
   c. Ambulates progressively with assistance.
   d. Requests analgesia as prescribed.
   e. Exhibits no signs of pain-induced shock or syncope.
2. Exhibits no indications of urinary tract infection or obstruction.
   a. Voids clear urine without red blood cells.
   b. Voids 200 to 400 ml of urine at each voiding.
   c. Reports absence of dysuria, frequency, hesitancy.
   d. Exhibits normal body temperature.
   e. Reports no chills.
3. Exhibits increased knowledge of health behaviours to prevent recurrence.
   a. Consumes high fluid intake (10 to 12 glasses of fluid/day).
   b. Voids dilute urine that is clear in colour and free of blood.
   c. Identifies actions to take to avoid dehydration.
   d. Avoids prolonged periods of immobilization and activity if possible.
   e. Identifies symptoms to be reported to health care provider (fever, chills, loin pain, haematuria).

f. Monitors urinary pH as directed.
g. Takes prescribed medication as directed to reduce stone formation.

RENAL TUMOURS

Renal tumours may arise from the renal capsule, parenchyma (renal cell carcinomas), connective tissue (sarcomas) or fatty tissue, or they may be neurogenic or vascular. Almost 90 per cent of all tumours are adenocarcinomas. These tumours occur more frequently in males, and may metastasize early to the lungs, bone, liver, brain and contralateral kidney. Twenty-five to 50 per cent of patients will have metastatic disease at the time of diagnosis.

Clinical Features

Many renal tumours produce no symptoms and are discovered on a routine physical examination as a palpable abdominal mass. The classic triad, occurring late in the course of the disease, is blood in the urine (haematuria), pain and a mass in the flank. *The usual sign that first calls attention to the tumour is painless haematuria*, which may be either intermittent and microscopic or gross. There may be a dull pain in the back from back-pressure produced by compression of the ureter, extension of the tumour into the perirenal area or haemorrhage into the substance of the kidney. Colicky pains occur if a clot or mass of tumour cells passes down the ureter. Symptoms from metastasis may be the first manifestation of renal tumour and include unexplained weight loss, increasing weakness, and anaemia.

Medical Management

The goal of management is to eradicate the tumour before metastasis occurs. A radical nephrectomy is the preferred treatment if the tumour can be removed. (See pp. 689–92 for nursing care following renal surgery.) Radiotherapy may be used adjunctively with surgery. Chemotherapy or hormonal therapy may be tried. Immunotherapy may be helpful.

Renal Artery Embolization

In patients with metastatic renal carcinoma, embolization of the renal artery is performed to cut off the blood supply to the tumour and thus cause the death of tumour cells. In other words, an infarct (area of dead cells) is created. This is based on the concept that infarction of the renal cell carcinoma will release tumour-associated antigens that will enhance the patient's response to metastatic lesions. The procedure may also reduce the number of tumour cells entering the venous circulation during surgical manipulation of the patient.

Nursing Care

The patient with a renal tumour may undergo extensive diagnostic and therapeutic procedures, including surgery, radiation therapy and chemotherapy. Following surgery, the patient usually has catheters and drains in place to ensure a patent urinary tract, to remove drainage and to permit very accurate measurement of urine output. Because of the location of the surgical incision and the position of the patient during the surgical procedure, pain and muscle soreness are common. The patient requires frequent analgesia during the postoperative period and assistance with turning. The patient also needs to be encouraged to turn, cough and take deep breaths to prevent atelectasis and other pulmonary complications. The patient and family or significant others require assistance and support to cope with the diagnosis and uncertainties about outcome.

Follow-up care is essential to detect signs of metastases as well as to reassure the patient and family or friends about the patient's continued wellbeing. The patient who has had surgery for renal carcinoma should undergo a yearly physical chest examination and chest X-ray throughout life, since late metastases are not uncommon. All subsequent symptoms should be evaluated with possible metastases in mind.

Renal Cysts

Cysts of the kidney may be multiple (polycystic) or single. Polycystic disease of the adult is inherited as an autosomal dominant trait and usually involves both kidneys. The patient presents with abdominal or lumbar pain, haematuria, hypertension, palpable renal masses and recurrent urinary tract infections. Renal insufficiency and failure usually develop in the terminal stages. Polycystic renal disease is also associated with cystic diseases of other organs (liver, pancreas, spleen) and aneurysms of the cerebral arteries. It is characteristically seen in midlife.

Medical Management

Since there is no specific treatment for polycystic renal disease, care of the patient is directed towards relief of pain, symptoms and complications. Hypertension and urinary tract infections are treated aggressively. Dialysis is indicated when signs of renal insufficiency and failure occur.

Genetic counselling is part of patient education, since polycystic kidney disease is a hereditary disease. The patient is advised to avoid sports and occupations that present a risk of trauma to the kidney.

Simple cysts of the kidney usually occur unilaterally and differ clinically and pathophysiologically from polycystic kidney disease. The cyst may be drained percutaneously.

CONGENITAL ANOMALIES

Congenital anomalies of the kidney are common. Occasionally, there is fusion of the two kidneys, forming what is called a horseshoe kidney. One kidney may be small and deformed and often is nonfunctioning. Frequently, there may be a double ureter or congenital stricture of the ureter. The treatment of these anomalies is necessary only if they cause symptoms, but it is important to determine that the other kidney is present and functioning before surgery is undertaken.

RENAL TRAUMA

Various types of injuries of the loin, back or upper abdomen may result in bruising, lacerations or rupture of the kidney or pedicle injury. The kidneys are protected by the musculature of the back posteriorly and by a cushion of abdominal wall and viscera anteriorly. They are highly mobile and are 'fixed' only at the renal pedicle. With traumatic injury, the kidney can be thrust against the lower ribs, resulting in contusion and rupture. Rib fractures occurring with renal displacement or a fracture of the transverse process of the upper lumbar vertebrae may be associated with renal contusion or laceration. Injuries may be blunt (car and motorcycle accidents, falls, athletic injuries) or penetrating (gunshot wounds, stabbings). Renal trauma is frequently associated with other injuries.

The most common renal injuries are contusions, laceration, rupture and renal pedicle injuries, or small internal laceration of the kidney. The kidneys receive half of the blood flow from the abdominal aorta; therefore, a fairly small renal laceration can produce massive bleeding.

Clinical Features
The clinical features include pain, renal colic (due to clots/fragments obstructing the collecting system), haematuria, flank mass, ecchymoses and lacerations or wounds of the lateral abdomen and flank.

Medical Management
The goals of management are to control haemorrhage, pain and infection; to preserve and restore renal function; and to maintain urinary drainage.

Haematuria is the most common feature of renal trauma; therefore, the appearance of blood in the urine following an injury to the loin indicates the possibility of renal injury. There is no correlation between the degree of haematuria and the degree of injury. Haematuria may be absent or detectable only on microscopic examination. Therefore, all urine is saved and sent to the laboratory for analysis to detect the presence of red cells and to follow the course of bleeding. The time the urine is voided and the volume should be recorded. Decreased haematocrit and haemoglobin levels indicate haemorrhage.

The patient is monitored for oliguria and signs of haemorrhagic shock since a pedicle injury or shattered kidney can lead to rapid exsanguination (lethal blood loss). An expanding haematoma may cause rupture of the kidney capsule. Skin abrasions, lacerations and entry and exit wounds in the muscles of the upper abdomen, flank and lower thoracic regions are important signs to check. It is important to remember that renal trauma is often associated with other injuries to the abdominal organs (liver, colon, small intestines).

In minor injuries to the kidney, healing may take place with conservative measures. The patient is kept on bedrest until haematuria clears.

The patient should be evaluated frequently during the first few days following injury in order to detect loin and abdominal pain, muscle spasm and swelling over the loin.

- Any sudden change in the patient's condition may indicate haemorrhage and require surgical intervention. The vital signs are monitored to detect evidence of bleeding. Analgesia is avoided since this may mask accompanying abdominal symptoms.
- The patient is prepared for surgical exploration if increasing pulse rate, hypotension and impending shock occur.

Most penetrating injuries require surgical exploration because of the high incidence of involvement of other organ systems and serious complications if untreated. The damaged kidney may have to be removed (nephrectomy), although on occasion it is possible to repair it.

The postoperative management is discussed on pages 689–92. Early complications (within six months) include rebleeding, abscess, sepsis, urine extravasation and fistula formation.

Patient Education
Follow-up care includes monitoring the blood pressure to detect hypertension that may occur on a renovascular basis. Activity is usually restricted for one month following trauma to minimize the incidence of delayed or secondary bleeding. The patient is advised about what changes should be reported to the doctor. Guidelines for increasing activity gradually are also provided.

BLADDER INJURIES

Injury to the bladder may occur with pelvic fractures and multiple trauma or from a blow to the lower abdomen when the bladder is full. Blunt trauma may result in contusion or in rupture of the bladder, extraperitoneally, intraperitoneally or a combination of both. Complications from these injuries (haemorrhage, shock, sepsis and extravasation of blood into the tissues) must be treated promptly.

A retrograde urethrogram is done first to evaluate for urethral injury. The patient is catheterized after the urethrogram is done.

Medical Management

Treatment for traumatic rupture of the bladder involves immediate surgical exploration and repair of the laceration, with suprapubic drainage of the bladder and the perivesical space (around the bladder) along with insertion of an urethral indwelling catheter.

In addition to the usual postoperative care following urological surgery, the drainage systems (suprapubic, indwelling urethral catheter and perivesical drains) are observed to ensure adequate drainage until healing takes place. The patient with a ruptured bladder may have gross bleeding for several days after repair. Complications of urethral injuries include stricture, incontinence and impotence.

CANCER OF THE BLADDER

Cancer of the urinary bladder is seen more frequently in people from the age of 50 onwards, and affects men more than women (3:1). Statistics indicate that these tumours make up approximately 2 per cent of all cancers in the body and are on the increase. The most common type is transitional cell cancer.

Risk factors for cancer of the bladder include cigarette smoking and carcinogens in the work environment, such as dyes, rubber, leather, ink or paint. There may be a relationship between coffee drinking and bladder cancer. Cancers arising from the prostate, colon and rectum in males and from the lower gynaecological tract in females may metastasize to the bladder.

Clinical Features

These tumours usually arise at the base of the bladder and involve the ureteral orifices and bladder neck. Gross, painless haematuria is the most common symptom of cancer of the bladder. Infection of the urinary tract is a common complication, producing frequency, urgency and dysuria. However, any disturbance of micturition or change in the urine may indicate cancer of the bladder. Pelvic or back pain may be due to metastasis.

Medical Management

Treatment of bladder cancer depends on the grade of the tumour (based on the degree of cellular differentiation), the stage of growth (the degree of local invasion and the presence or absence of metastasis) and the multicentricity (having many centres) of the tumour. The patient's age and physical, mental and emotional status are considered in determining treatment modalities.

Transurethral resection may be done for simple papillomas (benign epithelial tumours), although aggressive malignancies may develop from these tumours. One of the greatest challenges is the management of superficial bladder cancers, as it is now known that there are widespread abnormalities in the bladder mucosa of these patients. People with benign papillomas should be followed with cytology and cystoscopy periodically for the rest of their lives.

Topical chemotherapy is considered when there is high risk of recurrence, when cancer *in situ* is present, or when tumour resection has been incomplete.

The tumour may be irradiated preoperatively to reduce microextension of the neoplasm and viability of tumour cells, thus reducing the chances that the cancer may recur in the immediate area or spread by way of the circulatory or lymphatic systems. Radiation therapy is also used in combination with surgery or to control the disease in the inoperable patient.

A simple cystectomy (removal of the bladder), a partial cystectomy or a radical cystectomy is done for invasive or multifocal bladder cancer. Radical cystectomy in the male involves removal of the bladder, prostate and seminal vesicles and immediate adjacent perivesical tissues. In the female, radical cystectomy involves removal of the bladder, lower ureter, uterus, tubes, ovaries, anterior vagina and urethra. It may or may not include a pelvic lymphadenectomy (removal of lymph nodes). Removal of the bladder requires a urinary diversion procedure (see below).

URINARY DIVERSION

Urinary diversion refers to a means of diverting the urinary stream from the bladder so that it exits via a new route and opening in the skin (stoma). This is done primarily when a large or invasive bladder tumour requires that the entire bladder be removed. Other conditions requiring urinary diversion include pelvic malignancy, birth defects, strictures and trauma to ureters and urethra, neurogenic bladder and chronic infection causing severe ureteral and renal damage.

The most common methods of urinary diversion are listed below:

1. Ileal conduit: transplanting the ureters to an isolated section of the terminal ileum and bringing one end to the abdominal wall (Figure 20.7A). The ureter may also be transplanted into the transverse colon (colon conduit) or proximal jejunum (jejunal conduit).
2. Ureterosigmoidostomy: introducing the ureters into the sigmoid, thereby allowing urine to flow through the colon and out of the rectum (Figure 20.7B).
3. Cutaneous ureterostomy: bringing the detached ureter through the abdominal wall and attaching it to an opening in the skin (Figure 20.7C).

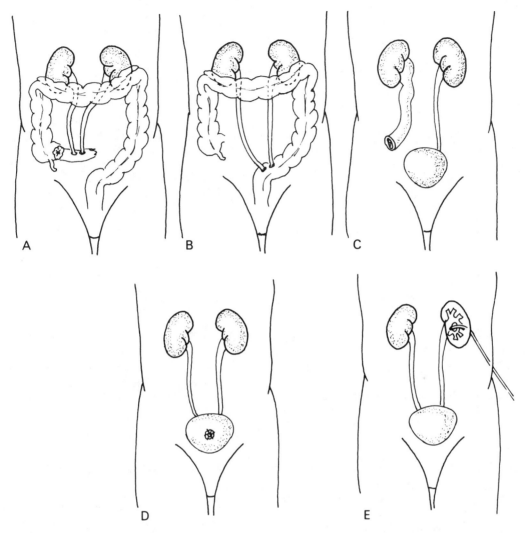

Figure 20.7 Methods of urinary diversion. (A) Ileal conduit. (B) Ureterosigmoidostomy. (C) cutaneous ureteros-tomy. (D) Vesicostomy. (E) Nephrostomy.

4. Vesicostomy: suturing the bladder to the abdominal wall and creating an opening (stoma) through the abdominal and bladder walls for urinary drainage (Figure 20.7D).
5. Nephrostomy: inserting a catheter into the renal pelvis via an incision into the flank or by percutaneous catheter placement into the kidney (Figure 20.7E).
6. Continent ileal urinary reservoir (Kock pouch): transplanting the ureters to an isolated segment of ileum (pouch) with a nipple-like one-way valve; urine is drained by catheter (Figure 20.8).

Ileal Conduit Urinary Diversion (Ileal Loop)

In an ileal conduit, the urine is diverted by implanting the ureter into a loop of ileum that is led out through the ab-dominal wall. This loop of ileum is a simple conduit (passageway) for urine from the ureters to the surface. A loop of the sigmoid colon may also be used. An ileostomy bag is used to collect the urine. The resected (cut) ends of the remaining intestine are anastomosed (connected) to provide an intact bowel.

Nursing Care

Urine volumes are checked hourly, since an output below 30 ml/hr may indicate an obstruction in the ileal conduit with possible backflow or leakage from the ureteroileal anastomosis. A catheter may be inserted through the urinary conduit to check for possible stasis or residual urine from a tight stoma.

The stoma is inspected frequently for bleeding. Minimal bleeding may be seen and implies good blood supply. A change in colour of the stoma from a normal pink to red

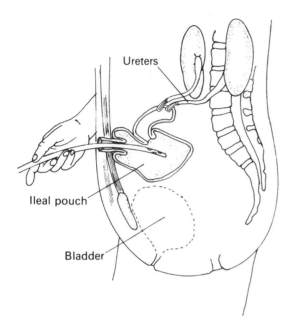

Figure 20.8 Continent ileal urinary reservoir (Kock pouch). Insertion of a catheter through the valve to drain stored urine.

colour to a dark purplish colour suggests that the vascular supply may be compromised. If cyanosis and compromised blood supply persist, surgical intervention may be required.

The stoma is insensitive to touch, but the skin around the stoma is exquisitely sensitive if it becomes irritated by urine or the appliance. The skin is inspected for: (1) signs of irritation and bleeding of the stomal mucosa; (2) alkaline encrustation with skin irritation around the stoma (from alkaline urine coming in contact with exposed skin); and (3) wound infections.

The odour of urine around the patient should alert the nursing personnel to the possibility of leakage from the appliance, the presence of an infection, or a problem in hygienic management. Since severe alkaline encrustation can accumulate rapidly around the stoma, the urine pH is kept below 6.5. Urine pH can be determined by testing the urine draining from the stoma, not from the collecting appliance. A properly fitted appliance is essential to prevent the peristomal skin (skin around the stoma) from being exposed to urine. If the urine is foul smelling, the stoma may be catheterized if prescribed in order to obtain a specimen for culture and sensitivity or to determine if the stoma is patent and draining properly and to detect the presence of residual urine. Scarring of the stoma can interfere with urine drainage.

A high-fluid diet is encouraged, in order to flush the ileal conduit and prevent mucus from congealing. The patient may excrete a fairly large amount of mucus with the urine as a result of the urine's irritating the intestine.

To relieve anxiety, the patient is reassured that this is a normal occurrence following an ileal conduit.

Patient Education

Appliance Selection
The urinary appliance may consist of one or two pieces and is usually disposable. The choice of appliance is determined by the location of the stoma and the patient's normal activity and body build.

Changing the Appliance: Skin Care
The appliance is changed at a time that will be most convenient to the patient. Early in the morning, before drinking fluids, when urinary output is lower, is the most preferred time.

● Clean all adhesive cement from the skin with warm water or adhesive solvent, using a soft cloth. Wash the skin with a noncream-based soap and water. Rinse well, since a soap film will prevent the appliance from adhering to the skin. Pat dry. The skin must be dry or the appliance will not adhere.

1. Insert a tampon or gauze or tissue wick at the stoma opening to absorb the urine and keep the skin dry while the appliance is being changed.
2. Inspect the skin for signs of irritation. Keep the skin free from direct contact with urine.
3. Apply a skin protector or barrier if required (Figure 20.8). Centre the appliance directly over the stoma and apply it carefully. Apply gentle pressure around the appliance to remove air bubbles and creases so that it will adhere securely.

● Apply hypoallergenic tape in a picture-frame effect around the pouch. The skin under the appliance may be dusted with pure talcum powder. An appliance cover may be used to absorb perspiration and eliminate warmth from the appliance.

Since the degree to which the stoma protrudes is not the same in all patients, there are various accessories and custom-made appliances to solve individual problems.

Odour Control
The patient should be advised to avoid foods and medications that give the urine a strong odour. A few drops of liquid deodorizer or diluted white vinegar may be introduced through the drain spout into the bottom of the pouch with a syringe or eyedropper. Taking ascorbic acid by mouth helps acidify the urine and suppresses urine odour problems.

Managing the Ostomy Appliance
The pouch is emptied by a drain valve when it is one third to one half full, since the weight of the urine may cause it

to separate from the skin. Some patients prefer wearing a leg bag attached with an adaptor to the drainage apparatus.

The patient is encouraged to contact the local ostomy association for visits, reassurance and practical information and help.

Ureterosigmoidostomy

Ureterosigmoidostomy is an implantation of the ureters into the sigmoid colon. It is usually done for the patient who has had extensive pelvic irradiation, previous small bowel resection or coexisting small bowel disease. In addition to the usual preoperative regime, the patient may be placed on a liquid diet for several days preoperatively to reduce residue in the colon. Antimicrobial agents are administered for bowel disinfection. Ureterosigmoidostomy requires a competent anal sphincter, adequate renal function and active renal peristalsis. The degree of anal sphincter control may be determined by assessing the patient's ability to retain enemas.

The patient will be informed that, following surgery, voiding will occur from the rectum for the rest of the patient's life, and that an adjustment in lifestyle will be necessary because of urinary frequency (as often as every two hours), which will have a consistency equivalent to a watery diarrhoea. There will be some degree of nocturia. Activities will have to be planned around the frequent need to urinate, which in turn may restrict the patient's social life. However, the patient has the advantage of urinary control without having to wear an external appliance.

Cutaneous Ureterostomy

A cutaneous ureterostomy is accomplished by bringing the detached ureters through the abdominal wall and attaching them to an opening in the skin. This procedure is used in selected patients with ureteral obstruction (advanced pelvic cancer); for poor-risk patients, since it requires less extensive surgery than other urinary diversion procedures; and for patients who have had previous abdominal irradiation.

A urinary appliance is fitted immediately following surgery. The management of the patient with a cutaneous ureterostomy is very similar to the care of the patient with an ileal conduit (see p. 699).

Continent Ileal Urinary Reservoir (Kock Pouch)

The continent ileal urinary reservoir is another type of urinary diversion created for patients whose bladder is removed or can no longer function (neurogenic bladder). In this procedure, a segment of the small intestine is surgically isolated from the intestine and serves for storage of urine (Figure 20.8). The ureters are implanted in the isolated segment and an opening is created connecting the new 'bladder' to the abdominal wall. A nipple-like valve is created by intussuscepting (telescoping) the intestine to prevent leakage of urine. To drain the stored urine, a catheter is inserted through the nipple valve and urine is drained. The advantage of this urinary diversion is that the valve prevents leakage of urine and the drainage of urine is under the control of the patient. The pouch must be drained at regular intervals to prevent absorption of metabolic waste products from the urine and reflux of urine to the ureters.

General Management of Patients Undergoing Urinary Diversion Procedures

Preoperative Management

A careful preoperative assessment of cardiopulmonary function is done since patients undergoing cystectomy (excision of the urinary bladder) are usually older people who may not fare well in a lengthy, complex procedure. As part of preoperative management, the bowel is cleansed (to minimize faecal stasis, to decompress the bowel and to minimize postoperative ileus), a low-residue diet is prescribed and antimicrobial drugs are administered for bowel disinfection to reduce pathogenic flora and to lessen potential complications of wound infection and sepsis. Adequate preoperative hydration is imperative to ensure urine flow during surgery and to prevent hypovolaemia during the prolonged operative procedure. The patient with urogenital tract cancer may have severe problems with malnutrition because of increased tumour mass and decreased food intake. Enteral or parenteral hyperalimentation can be used to support the patient, minimize toxicity, promote healing and improve response to treatment.

Postoperative Management

Postoperative management focuses on maintaining urinary function, preventing postoperative complications (respiratory complications, fluid and electrolyte imbalances) and promoting patient comfort. Catheters or drainage systems are observed and urine output monitored carefully. A nasogastric tube is inserted during surgery to allow for decompression and to relieve pressure on the intestinal anastomosis. It is usually kept in place for several days following surgery. As soon as bowel function resumes, as manifested by bowel sounds, the passage of flatus and a soft abdomen, the patient is given fluids by mouth. Until that time, fluids and electrolytes are given intravenously. The patient is ambulated as soon as possible.

Nursing Care

The role of the nurse in the immediate postoperative phase is to assess the patient for complications and prevent their occurrence. The catheters and urinary collection receptacle inserted during surgery are monitored closely. Urine volume, patency of the drainage system and colour of drainage are noted. A sudden decrease in urine volume or increase in drainage is reported promptly to the doctor since this may indicate obstruction of the urinary tract, inadequate blood volume or bleeding. Analgesia is administered as prescribed to promote patient comfort and permit the patient to turn, cough and take deep breaths without excessive pain and discomfort. The nursing care indicated for this patient includes measures for the patient undergoing intestinal surgery (see Chapter 15) and surgery of the urinary tract (pp. 687 and 689–92). The remainder of the postoperative management and the nursing care related to the physical needs of the patient are covered under the previous discussions of the specific urinary diversion procedures.

▶ NURSING PROCESS

▶ THE PATIENT UNDERGOING A URINARY DIVERSION SURGICAL PROCEDURE

▶ *Assessment*

The patient admitted to the hospital for a urinary diversion surgical procedure is assessed thoroughly. The nursing history focuses on the patient's and the family's/friend's understanding of the procedure and the changes in physical structure and function that will result from the surgery. The patient's self-concept and self-esteem are also assessed in addition to the patient's usual way of coping with stress and loss. The patient's mental status, dexterity and preferred method of learning are noted since these will influence the ability to participate in self-care postoperatively.

▶ *Patient's Problems*

Based on the assessment, the problems for the patient undergoing urinary diversion surgery may include the following:

Preoperative Problems

- Anxiety related to anticipated losses associated with the diagnosis and surgical procedure.
- Lack of knowledge about outcomes of the surgical procedure.

Postoperative Problems

- Lack of knowledge about management of urinary function.

- Potential alterations in self-concept related to altered body image.
- Difficulty in coping with fear of the diagnosis and the impact of surgery.
- Lack of self-care ability related to maintenance of ostomy.
- Altered sexuality patterns related to after-effects of surgery and self-consciousness about stoma.

▶ *Planning and Implementation*
▶ Expected Outcomes Preoperatively

The main outcomes preoperatively for the patient may include relief of anxiety and increased knowledge about expected outcomes of the surgery.

▶ Expected Outcomes Postoperatively

The patient's main postoperative outcomes may include increased knowledge about management of urinary function, improved self-concept and appropriate coping mechanisms to accept and deal with altered urinary function.

Preoperative Nursing Care

Relieving Anxiety

The threat of bladder removal and cancer creates fear related to losses—loss of love, body image and security. In addition to problems in adapting to an external appliance, a stoma and a scar, the patient must also adapt to alterations in toileting habits, and the male patient must also adapt to sexual impotency. (A penile implant is considered if the patient is a candidate for the procedure.) Women face the fear of loss of appearance because of changed body image. A supportive approach is needed that includes physical, psychological and psychosocial support. It involves taking a personal interest in the patient, assessing the patient's concept and perception of self and the manner in which the patient responds to stress and loss and helping to maintain the usual lifestyle and independence, with as few modifications as possible. The patient is encouraged to express any fears and anxiety. A visit from the stoma therapist can give support and make adaptation easier, both before and after surgery.

Patient Education

A stoma therapist is invaluable for preoperative teaching. Explanations of the surgical procedure and the reasons for wearing a collection device postoperatively are given to the patient and the carer. The stoma site is planned preoperatively with the patient standing, sitting and lying in order to locate the stoma away from bony prominences, skin creases and fat folds. *The patient should be able to see the site for ease of self-care.* The optimum site is marked with indelible ink for intraoperative location. It is best to encourage the patient to practise wearing the appliance partially filled with water before surgery.

Postoperative Nursing Care

Patient Education
A major postoperative objective is to assist the patient to achieve the highest level of independence and self-care possible. The nurse, or stoma therapist, if available, works closely with the patient and family/friends to advise and assist them in all phases of management of the ostomy. The patient is encouraged to participate in decisions regarding type of collecting appliance and time of day to change the appliance. The patient is assisted and encouraged to look at and touch the stoma early so that any fears are overcome.

The patient and home carers are advised about the signs and symptoms to be reported to the doctor and about problems that they can handle themselves. Information and increased responsibility for self-care are provided according to the patient's physical recovery from surgery and the ability to accept and acquire knowledge and skill needed for independence. Oral and written advice is provided, and the patient is given the opportunity to practise and demonstrate skills in the management of urinary drainage.

Improving Self-Concept
In addition to alterations in urinary drainage, the patient with a urinary diversion also experiences loss or fear of loss of relationships with others, altered sexuality and sexual function, dependence and changes in lifestyle. The patient's ability to cope with these potential changes depends to some degree on body image and self-esteem before the surgery and the support and reaction of others around the patient.

► **Evaluation**
► **Expected Outcomes**

Preoperative
1. Patient experiences reduced anxiety.
   a. Verbalizes fears and anxieties about the diagnosis, the surgery and its outcomes.
   b. Grieves openly about alterations, as appropriate.
   c. Shares fears, anxieties and concerns with partner.
   d. Accepts visit from stoma therapist.
   e. Reports reduction in level of anxiety.
2. Increases knowledge about expected outcomes of surgery.
   a. States purpose and expected outcomes of surgical procedure.
   b. Describes anticipated alterations in urinary drainage in own words.

c. Asks relevant questions related to postoperative course.
   d. Exhibits co-operation in identifying stoma site.

Postoperative
1. Increases knowledge about management of urinary function.
   a. Participates in management of urinary drainage system.
   b. Verbalizes own preferences and opinions in making decisions about care and management.
   c. Describes anatomical alteration due to surgery.
   d. Describes and uses recommended skin care measures.
   e. Revises daily routine to accommodate urostomy (urinary drainage) management.
   f. Identifies potential problems and measures to handle them.
   g. Identifies reportable signs and symptoms.
   h. Asks questions relevant to care at home.
2. Exhibits improved self-concept.
   a. Verbalizes acceptance of urinary diversion, stoma and appliance.
   b. Demonstrates increasing independence in self-care.
   c. Verbalizes plans to resume normal activities of daily living and return to usual lifestyle.
   d. Verbalizes acceptance of support and assistance from family and friends and health care providers.
   e. Exhibits proper hygiene and grooming.
   f. Volunteers to visit other patients about to undergo urinary diversion.

URETHRAL CONDITIONS

Caruncle

A caruncle is a small, red, extremely vascular polyp-like growth situated just within, and protruding from, the external urethral meatus of women. On rare occasions, it causes no subjective symptoms. However, it may be acutely sensitive, causing a local burning pain exaggerated by exertion and frequency of urination, which is exquisitely painful. Local excision of the caruncle will relieve the symptoms.

Urethritis

Urethritis, inflammation of the urethra, is usually an ascending infection and may be classified as gonorrhoeal (see Chapter 38) or nongonorrhoeal. However, both conditions may be present in the same patient.

Gonorrhoeal Urethritis
Gonorrhoeal urethritis is caused by *Neisseria gonor-*

rhoeae and is transmitted by sexual contact. In the male, inflammation of the meatal orifice occurs with burning on urination. A purulent urethral discharge appears 3 to 14 days (or longer) after sexual exposure. However, the disease may be asymptomatic. In the female, a urethral discharge is not always present and the disease also is often essentially asymptomatic. Therefore, gonorrhoea in the female is frequently not reported and diagnosed. In the male, the infection involves the tissues around the urethra, causing periurethritis, prostatitis, epididymitis and urethral stricture. Sterility may occur as a result of vasoepididymal obstruction. Treatment of gonorrhoea is discussed and patient education information is provided in Chapter 38.

Nongonorrhoeal Urethritis

Urethritis not associated with *Neisseria gonorrhoeae* is usually caused by *Chlamydia trachomatis* or *Ureaplasma urealyticum*. If the male patient is symptomatic, he will complain of mild to severe dysuria and a scanty to moderate urethral discharge. Nongonorrhoeal urethritis requires prompt antimicrobial treatment. Follow-up care is necessary to make certain that a cure is achieved. All people who are sexual partners of patients with nongonorrhoeal urethritis must be examined for sexually transmitted disease and treated.

Urethral Strictures

A urethral stricture is a narrowing of the lumen of the urethra due to scar tissue and contraction. Strictures result from urethral injury (caused by insertion of surgical instruments during transurethral surgery, indwelling catheters or cystoscopic procedures), straddle injuries and car accidents, untreated gonorrhoeal urethritis and congenital abnormalities.

The force and size of the urinary stream is diminished and symptoms of urinary infection and retention occur. Stricture causes urine to back up, resulting in cystitis, prostatitis and pyelonephritis. An important element of prevention is to treat all urethral infections promptly. Prolonged urethral catheter drainage is to be avoided and utmost care taken in any type of instrumentation involving the urethra, including catheterization.

Medical Management

The treatment may be palliative (gradual dilation of the narrowed area with metal sounds or bougies) or operation under direct vision (internal urethrotomy). If the stricture has become so small as to prevent the passage of a catheter, the urologist uses several small filiform bougies in search of the opening. When one bougie passes beyond the stricture into the bladder, it is fixed in place, and urine will drain from the bladder. The stricture then can be dilated to larger size by the passage of a larger sound (a dilating instrument) following behind the filiform bougie as a guide. Following dilation, hot baths and non-narcotic analgesics are given to control the pain. Antimicrobials are given for several days after dilation to minimize the infectious reaction, thus lessening discomfort.

BIBLIOGRAPHY

McCaffery, M. (1983) *Nursing the Patient in Pain*, Harper & Row, London.

chapter 21

ASSESSMENT AND CARE OF PATIENTS WITH RENAL AND URINARY DISORDERS

RENAL FAILURE

Renal failure results when the kidneys are unable to remove the body's metabolic wastes or perform their regulatory functions. The substances normally eliminated in the urine accumulate in the body fluids as a result of impaired renal excretion and lead to a disruption in endocrine and metabolic functions as well as fluid, electrolyte and acid–base disturbances. Renal failure is a systemic disease and is a final common pathway of many different kidney and urinary tract diseases.

Acute Renal Failure

Altered Physiology

Acute renal failure is a sudden and almost complete loss of kidney function caused by failure of the renal circulation or by glomerular or tubular dysfunction. It is manifested by sudden oliguria (less than 500 ml of urine per day), high urinary output or anuria (less than 50 ml of urine per day). Regardless of the volume of urine excreted, the patient with acute renal failure experiences rising serum creatinine and urea levels, and retention of other metabolic waste products normally excreted by the kidneys. Any condition that causes reduction in renal blood flow, such as volume depletion, hypotension or shock, leads to a reduction in glomerular filtration, renal ischaemia and tubular damage. Renal failure may also result from the adverse effects of burns, crushing injuries and infection, as well as from nephrotoxic agents that cause acute tubular necrosis and temporary cessation of renal function. With burns and crush injuries, myoglobin (a protein released from muscle when injury occurs) and haemoglobin are liberated, causing renal toxicity, ischaemia or both. Severe transfusion reactions may also cause renal failure as the haemoglobin, released through haemolysis, filters through the kidney glomeruli and becomes concentrated in the kidney tubules to such a degree that precipitation occurs, halting the excretion of urine.

Table 21.1 *Causes of acute renal failure*

1. Ischaemia (severe haemorrhagic shock, open heart surgery, cross-clamping of the aorta, surgery of the aorta or renal vessels or of the biliary tree, and extensive surgery in the elderly)

2. Septic shock

3. Pigment:
   a. Haemoglobin (transfusion reaction, haemolytic anaemia)
   b. Myoglobin (crush injury, exercise, electrical shock, seizures, diabetes)

4. Nephrotoxins:
   a. Aminoglycoside antibiotics (e.g., streptomycin, gentamicin)
   b. Other antibiotics
   c. Arsenic
   d. Mercury and other heavy metals
   e. Nonsteroidal anti-inflammatory drugs

Following these events, the kidneys become swollen and oedematous, and the epithelial cells in the tubules may undergo necrosis (Table 21.1).

Although the exact pathogenesis of acute renal failure and oliguria is not always known, various possible mechanisms have been suggested. In many instances, there is a clear-cut underlying disease, mechanical obstruction of the urinary tract by calculi or tumour or renal artery obstruction. A new causative factor in acute renal failure is the use of nonsteroidal anti-inflammatory agents, especially in the elderly. These agents interfere with prostaglandins that normally protect renal blood flow, and their use impairs this protective mechanism, leading to hypoperfusion of the kidneys.

It is important to know that some of the factors that lead to acute renal failure may be reversible if identified and treated promptly, before kidney function is impaired. This is true of the following conditions that reduce blood flow to the kidney and impair kidney function: (1) hypovolaemia; (2) hypotension; (3) reduced cardiac output and congestive heart failure; (4) obstruction of the kidney or lower urinary tract by tumour, blood clot or kidney stone; and (5) bilateral obstruction of the renal arteries or veins. If treated and corrected before the kidneys are permanently damaged, the increased serum urea, oliguria and other signs associated with these conditions may be reversed.

There are three clinical phases of acute renal failure: the period of oliguria, a period of diuresis and a period of recovery. The period of oliguria (urinary volume less than 400 to 600 ml/24 hr) is accompanied by a rise in the serum concentration of the elements usually excreted by the kidneys (urea, creatinine, uric acid, organic acids and the intracellular cations—potassium and magnesium). The oliguric phase lasts approximately 10 days.

In some patients, there can be a decrease in renal function with increasing nitrogen retention, yet the patient is actually excreting two or more litres of urine daily. This is the so-called high-output failure or nonoliguric form of renal failure and occurs predominantly after nephrotoxic antibiotics are administered to the patient; it may occur with burns, traumatic injury and halogenated anaesthesia.

In the second phase, the period of diuresis, the patient experiences a gradually increasing urinary output, which signals that glomerular filtration has started to recover. Although the volume of urinary output may reach normal or elevated levels, renal function may be markedly abnormal in the diuretic phase. Therefore, expert medical and nursing management is still required.

The period of recovery signals the improvement of renal function and may take from 3 to 12 months. Usually, there is a permanent partial reduction in the glomerular filtration rate and the ability to concentrate urine.

Clinical Features

Almost every system of the body is affected when there is failure of the normal renal regulatory mechanisms. The patient appears to be critically ill and is lethargic with persistent nausea, vomiting and diarrhoea. The skin and mucous membranes are dry from dehydration, and the breath may have the odour of urine. Central nervous system features include drowsiness, headache, muscle twitching and convulsions. The urinary output is scanty, may be bloody and has a low specific gravity. There is a steady daily rise in the serum creatinine value with the rate of rise dependent on the degree of catabolism (breakdown of protein).

A patient with renal disease in which the glomerular filtration rate is reduced has a decreased ability to excrete potassium. Protein catabolism results in the release of cellular potassium into the body fluids, causing serious potassium intoxication. High serum potassium levels are dangerous and lead to cardiac arrhythmias and arrest. Sources of potassium are tissue breakdown; dietary intake; blood anywhere outside the vascular system, such as in the gastrointestinal tract; or blood transfusion and other sources (intravenous infusions, potassium penicillin and extracellular shift in response to metabolic acidosis).

Additionally, there may be large losses of sodium from the gastrointestinal tract from diarrhoea and vomiting. Patients with acute oliguria cannot eliminate the daily metabolic load produced by the normal metabolic processes. This is reflected by a fall in the blood carbon dioxide combining power and blood pH. Thus, progressive acidosis accompanies renal failure. There may be an increase in serum phosphate concentrations, and serum calcium levels may be low in response to decreased absorption of calcium from the intestine and in association with an elevation of serum phosphate levels.

Anaemia inevitably accompanies acute renal failure from blood loss due to uraemic gastrointestinal lesions, reduced red cell life span and reduced erythropoietin production.

Prevention and Health Maintenance

A careful history is indicated to determine if the patient has been taking potentially nephrotoxic antimicrobial agents. The kidneys are especially susceptible to the adverse effects of drugs because they receive such a large blood flow (25 per cent of the cardiac output at rest) and are a major excretory pathway for antimicrobial drugs. The nephrons are exposed to high concentrations of antimicrobials as a result of glomerular filtration and tubular secretion and reabsorption, and thus are more likely to suffer toxic effects of drugs. Therefore, in patients taking potentially nephrotoxic drugs, renal function should be monitored by evaluating serum urea and creatinine levels within 24 hours of initiation of drug therapy, and at least twice a week while the patient is receiving therapy. Any agent that reduces renal blood flow (i.e., chronic analgesic abuse) may cause renal deterioration. Chronic analgesic abuse causes interstitial nephritis and papillary necrosis as the result of a complicated metabolic insult.

Medical Management

The kidney has a remarkable ability to recover from insult. Therefore, the objective of treatment of acute renal failure is to restore normal chemical balance and prevent complications so that repair of renal tissue and restoration of renal function can take place. A search for any possible cause is made in order to treat and eliminate it.

Early dialysis is indicated to prevent serious complications of uraemia, such as hyperkalaemia (potassium intoxication), pericarditis and seizures. Dialysis produces a more sustained correction of biochemical abnormalities; allows for liberalization of fluid, protein and sodium intake; diminishes bleeding tendencies; and may help wound healing. Haemodialysis, haemofiltration or peritoneal dialysis may be carried out.

Fluid and electrolyte imbalances are a major problem in acute renal failure; hyperkalaemia is the most life-threatening of these disturbances.

- A patient with a high and rising level of serum potassium requires immediate peritoneal dialysis, haemodialysis or haemofiltration. Details of dialysis treatment can be found on pages 711–15.
- Intravenous glucose and insulin or calcium gluconate is sometimes used as an emergency and temporary measure for potassium intoxication.
- All external sources of potassium are eliminated or reduced.

Guides to establishing fluid balance include daily body weight, serial measurements of central venous pressure, serum and urine concentrations, fluid losses, blood pressure and the clinical status of the patient. This information should be kept on a flow chart to indicate the degree to which the patient's condition is improving or deteriorating.

Adequate blood flow to the kidneys in some patients may be restored by intravenous fluids and medications. Shock, if present, is controlled, and any infection is treated.

The oliguric phase of acute renal failure may last from 10 to 20 days and is followed by the diuretic phase, at which time urinary output begins to increase, signalling that glomerular filtration is taking place. Blood chemistry evaluations are made to determine the amounts of sodium, potassium and water needed for replacement along with assessment for overhydration or underhydration.

After the diuretic phase, the patient is prescribed a high-protein, high-caloric diet and is encouraged to resume activities gradually since muscle weakness will be present from excessive catabolism.

Nursing Care

The nurse has an important role in caring for the patient with acute renal failure. In addition to directing attention to the patient's primary disorder, which may be a factor in the development of acute renal failure, the nurse monitors the patient for complications, participates in emergency treatment of fluid and electrolyte imbalances, assesses the patient's progress and response to treatment, and provides physical and emotional support. Additionally, the nurse keeps the patient's family and close friends informed about the patient's condition, assists them in understanding the treatments and provides psychological support. Although the development of acute renal failure may be the most life-threatening problem, the nurse must continue to include in the plan of care those nursing measures indicated for the patient's primary disorder (e.g., burns, shock, trauma, obstruction of the urinary tract).

The patient with acute renal failure will require treatment with haemodialysis, peritoneal dialysis or haemofiltration to prevent serious complications; the length of time that these treatments will be necessary varies with the cause and extent of damage to the kidneys. The patient and loved ones will need assistance, explanation and support during this time. The purpose and rationale of the treatments will be explained to the patient and carers by the doctor. However, their high levels of anxiety and fear may necessitate repeated explanation and clarification by the nurse. Continued assessment of the patient for complications of acute renal failure and of its precipitating cause is essential. (See Nursing Care Plan 21.1 for a patient with acute renal failure.)

► NURSING CARE PLAN 21.1:   THE PATIENT WITH ACUTE RENAL FAILURE

Care plan for Miriam Sachs, a 52-year-old Orthodox Jewish woman, who has acute renal failure. Mrs Sachs lives with her husband, and cares at home for her 79-year-old mother who has Alzheimer's disease. She has a son and daughter who are both married.
Note: This care plan covers the care needed in relation to her acute renal failure. The underlying cause of the acute renal failure must be treated, and will give rise to specific additional problems for which further care planning will be needed.

Patient's problems	Expected outcomes	Nursing care	Rationale

1. Anxiety due to:
  a. Sudden onset of illness
  b. Lack of knowledge, loss of control
  c. Miriam's responsibility towards her mother
  d. Possible complications affecting recovery
	Reduced anxiety	1a. Give explanation of what is wrong and what is being done for Miriam
		b. Keep Miriam's son and daughter informed of Miriam's progress and encourage visiting
		c. Refer to social worker with regard to Miriam's mother
			To reduce the problem of anxiety and stress
			
			Develops relationships and Miriam will feel supported by keeping in contact with her family unit
			Miriam's mother may need temporary placement elsewhere until Miriam's recovery

2. Alteration in fluid balance due to inability of the kidneys to excrete water, resulting in:
  a. Oliguria or anuria
  b. Risk of pulmonary oedema due to fluid retention
  c. Risk of dehydration (later)
  See problem 6
	To achieve fluid balance and prevent over-hydration until diuresis occurs and kidney function is restored
	Miriam will be able to breathe easily and comfortably
		2a. Restrict fluid intake to 500 ml + volume of previous day's urine output in 24 hours
		b. Strictly record fluid intake and output on a fluid balance chart
		c. Explain reason for fluid restriction to Miriam
		d. Observe for signs of generalized oedema
		e. Observe for breathlessness. Monitor respirations and blood pressure four hourly
		
		f. Weigh Miriam daily at the same time each day
			The 500 ml replaces insensible loss through skin and lungs
			
			Monitors fluid balance and enables calculation of daily fluid intake
			Enables Miriam to cope and comply more readily
			Retention of fluid causes increase in tissue fluid, especially if Miriam is anuric. Blood pressure and respirations will rise in pulmonary oedema
			Reflects retention of fluid (1 litre water = 1 kg in weight)

3. Alteration in electrolyte balance and accumulation of urea in the bloodstream due to the inability of the kidneys to clear and excrete superfluous electrolytes and urea from the bloodstream	To achieve and maintain the desired nutritional status and electrolyte balance	3a. Sodium and potassium restriction in diet b. Low-protein diet as prescribed by dietician (30–40 g/24 hr) c. High carbohydrate diet d. Refer to dietician Miriam's desire to keep within a Kosher diet e. Monitor total parenteral nutrition if necessary f. Explain rationale of diet to Miriam and her relatives g. Monitor levels of serum urea, electrolytes and creatinine daily, and report to medical staff	Kidneys are unable to secrete sodium and potassium; retention of which can cause pulmonary oedema and cardiac arrest. Urea is the end product of protein metabolism; retention of which causes uraemia Helps maintain Miriam's energy needs. Minimizes utilization of her own body protein, causing catabolism and raised serum creatinine. Promotes adequate nutrition to help prevent infection Miriam needs reassurance that her strict Kosher diet will not be compromised Ensures Miriam's co-operation and aids her acceptance of the regime Minimize further uraemia, hyperkalaemia and raised creatinine levels Approximate normal levels in an adult:

► NURSING CARE PLAN 21.1: THE PATIENT WITH ACUTE RENAL FAILURE

Patient's problems	Expected outcomes	Nursing care	Rationale
			Urea 2.5–6.6 mmol/l Potassium 3.5–5.0 mmol/l Creatinine 40–110 µmol/l
4. Fear of being maintained on intensive treatment procedures, i.e. replacement therapy in the form of haemodialysis or peritoneal dialysis	Miriam will be able to understand the need for the present treatment procedures	4a. Establish a good nurse/patient relationship b. Keep Miriam informed of her progress c. Encourage self-care of independent functions when Miriam can tolerate them d. Involve other disciplines in Miriam's care, e.g. social worker, rabbi, counsellor etc.	Miriam is not able to control her own care and wellbeing, and is dependent on the delivery of nursing care and psychological support
5. Risk of infection due to uraemic state	Miriam will be kept free of infection	5a. Aseptic care of wounds, intravenous infusion sites, dialysis access sites b. If a catheter is at first *in situ*, see problem 2 – give catheter care until it is removed c. Monitor temperature four-hourly d. Encourage deep breathing, coughing e. Assist with and maintain Miriam's oral and skin hygiene f. Maintain optimum nutrition; see problem 3	Minimize entry of pathogenic organisms Catheter is usually removed after 24 hours due to oliguria or anuria To prevent chest infection
6. Later problem of the passage of large amounts of dilute urine due to the diuretic phase, causing: a. Potential dehydration b. Potential excessive loss of sodium and potassium due to the kidneys' inability to concentrate the urine by selective reabsorption	Adequate hydration over the diuretic phase until the kidneys return to normal function	6a. Monitor fluid balance and maintain intake at 500 ml + previous day's urine output in 24 hours b. Urine specimens sent to laboratory for chemical tests such as creatinine clearance c. Reintroduce sodium and potassium into the diet, but continue to monitor serum sodium, potassium, urea and creatinine levels	Monitors recovery of the kidneys It takes several days for the kidneys to restore selective reabsorption Replacement therapy may still be necessary, urea and creatinine levels are sometimes slow to fall. Dialysis will be less frequent until no longer required

Chronic Renal Failure

Chronic renal failure or end-stage renal disease is a progressive, irreversible deterioration in renal function in which the body's ability to maintain metabolic and fluid and electrolyte balance fails, resulting fatally in uraemia (an excess of urea and other nitrogenous wastes in the blood). It may be caused by chronic glomerulonephritis; pyelonephritis; uncontrolled hypertension; hereditary lesions, such as in polycystic kidney disease; vascular disorders; obstruction of the urinary tract; renal disease secondary to systemic disease; drugs; toxic agents; or infections. Dialysis or kidney transplantation eventually becomes necessary to maintain life.

Altered Physiology

As renal function declines, the end products of protein metabolism, which are normally excreted in urine, accumulate in the blood. There are imbalances in the body chemistry and in the cardiovascular, haematological, gastrointestinal, neurological and skeletal systems. Skin and reproductive changes are also seen.

The patient tends to retain sodium and water. This is one factor that leads to oedema formation, congestive heart failure and hypertension. Hypertension may also result from activation of the renin–angiotensin axis and concomitant increased aldosterone secretion.

Other patients have a tendency to lose salt and run the risk of hypotension and hypovolaemia. Episodes of vomiting and diarrhoea may produce sodium and water depletion, which worsens the uraemic state. Metabolic acidosis occurs as a result of the reduced ability of the kidney to excrete hydrogen ions, produce ammonia and conserve bicarbonate.

The body's serum calcium and phosphate levels are reciprocal: as one rises, the other decreases. Secretion of parathormone increases in response to this decreased calcium level. However, in renal failure the body does not respond normally to the increased secretion of parathormone and, as a result, calcium leaves the bone often producing bone changes and bone disease. Uraemic bone disease (renal osteodystrophy) develops from changes in calcium, phosphate and parathormone balance. Also, the active metabolite of vitamin D (1,25-dihydroxycholecalciferol) normally manufactured by the kidney decreases with the progression of renal disease.

Anaemia develops owing to inadequate erythropoietin production, the shortened life span of red cells and the uraemic patient's tendency to bleed, particularly from the gastrointestinal tract. Erythropoietin, a substance normally produced by the kidney, stimulates bone marrow to produce red blood cells. In renal failure, erthyropoietin production decreases and anaemia results.

Neurological complications of renal failure may occur from renal failure itself, severe hypertension, electrolyte imbalance, water intoxication and drug effects. Such manifestations include altered mental function, changes in personality and behaviour, convulsions and coma.

A decrease in libido, impotence and amenorrhoea are sexual and menstrual changes that occur. Skin changes include pruritus (in part from calcium/phosphate imbalance), which adds to the patient's distress.

Clinical Features

Although at times the onset of chronic renal failure is sudden, in the majority of patients it begins with one or more symptoms—fatigue and lethargy, headache, general weakness, gastrointestinal symptoms (anorexia, nausea, vomiting, diarrhoea), bleeding tendencies and mental confusion. There is decreased salivary flow, thirst, a metallic taste in the mouth, loss of smell and taste, and parotitis or stomatitis. If active treatment is begun early, the symptoms may disappear. Otherwise, these symptoms become more marked, and others appear as the metabolic abnormalities of uraemia affect virtually every body system.

The patient gradually becomes more and more drowsy; the respiration becomes Kussmaul in character; and a deep coma develops, often with convulsions, which may occur as muscle twitchings or severe spasms (myoclonic jerks) quite similar to those of epilepsy. A white, powdery substance, 'uraemic frost', composed chiefly of urates, appears on the skin. Unless treatment is initiated, death soon follows.

Medical Management

The aim of management is to help the diseased kidneys to maintain homeostasis for as long as possible. All factors that contribute to the problem and those that are reversible (e.g., obstruction) are identified and treated.

With the deterioration of renal function, dietary intervention is necessary with careful regulation of protein intake, fluid intake to balance fluid losses, sodium intake to balance sodium losses and some restriction of potassium. At the same time, adequate calorie intake and vitamin supplementation must be ensured. Usually, the fluid allowance is 500 to 600 ml of fluid more than the 24-hour urine output.

Hypertension is managed by intravascular volume control and a variety of antihypertensive medications. The metabolic acidosis of chronic renal failure usually produces no symptoms and requires no treatment; however, sodium bicarbonate supplements or dialysis may be needed to correct the acidosis.

The patient is observed for early evidence of cerebral abnormalities. These may vary from slight twitching, headache or delirium. Heart failure, infection and volume depletion may also require treatment.

The patient is referred to a dialysis and transplantation centre early in the course of progressive renal disease. Dialysis is usually begun when the patient cannot maintain a reasonable lifestyle with conservative treatment.

Nursing Care

The patient with chronic renal failure requires astute nursing care to avoid the complications of reduced renal function and the stresses and anxieties of dealing with a life-threatening illness.

Potential problems for these patients may include the following:

- Alterations in fluid and electrolyte balance related to decreased urine output and dietary and fluid restrictions.
- Alteration in nutrition, less than body requirements, related to anorexia, gastrointestinal discomfort and dietary restrictions.
- Lack of knowledge about the condition and the treatment regime.
- Activity intolerance related to fatigue.
- Altered self-concept related to dependency and role changes.

Nursing care is directed at assessing fluid and electrolyte

status and identifying potential sources of imbalance, encouraging a dietary programme to ensure proper nutritional intake within the limits of the treatment regime, providing explanations and information to the patient and carers concerning the ramifications of reduced renal function and the need to follow the protocols prescribed by the doctor, and promoting positive feelings by encouraging increased self-care and greater independence.

DIALYSIS

Dialysis is a process used to remove unwanted fluid and waste products from the body when the kidneys are unable to do so because of impaired function or when toxins or poisons must be removed immediately to prevent permanent or life-threatening damage. In dialysis, solute molecules diffuse through a semipermeable membrane, passing from the side of higher concentration to that of lower concentration. Fluids pass through the semipermeable membrane by means of osmosis or ultrafiltration (application of external pressure to the membrane).

The purposes of dialysis are to maintain the life and wellbeing of the patient until kidney function is restored and to remove unwanted substances from the blood. Methods of therapy include haemodialysis, haemofiltration and peritoneal dialysis.

Dialysis is used in renal failure to remove toxic substances and body wastes normally excreted by healthy kidneys. The main indications for acute dialysis are a high and rising level of serum potassium, fluid overload (or impending pulmonary oedema), pronounced acidosis, pericarditis and severe mental confusion. It may also be used to remove certain drugs or other toxins taken in accidental or intentional poisonings or drug overdose.

The reasons for initiating chronic dialysis in renal failure are nausea and vomiting with anorexia, mental confusion, chronic high potassium, fluid overload (in the presence of diuretics and fluid restriction) and a general lack of wellbeing.

Haemodialysis

Haemodialysis is a process used for patients who are acutely ill and require short-term dialysis (days to weeks) or for patients with end-stage renal disease who require longterm therapy. A synthetic, semipermeable membrane replaces the renal glomeruli and tubules and acts as the filter for the impaired kidneys.

For patients with chronic renal failure, haemodialysis provides reasonable rehabilitation and life expectancy. However, haemodialysis does not cure renal disease and is not able to compensate for losses of the kidneys' endocrine or metabolic activities. These patients must undergo regular dialysis treatment for the rest of their lives or until they receive a successful kidney transplant. Patients have

chronic dialysis when they require dialysis therapy for survival.

The requirements for haemodialysis for a patient with end-stage renal failure are (1) access to the patient's circulation, (2) a dialyzer with a semipermeable membrane (the artificial kidney), and (3) an appropriate dialysis machine.

Access to the Patient's Circulation

Access to the patient's circulation is achieved through an arteriovenus (A–V) shunt (external silastic tubing placed in an adjacent artery and vein), a fistula (internal access using the patient's own vessels) (Figure 21.1) or a double- or single-lumen catheter into a main vein, e.g., subclavian or jugular.

Underlying Principles of Haemodialysis

The objectives of haemodialysis are to extract toxic nitrogenous substances from the blood and to remove excess

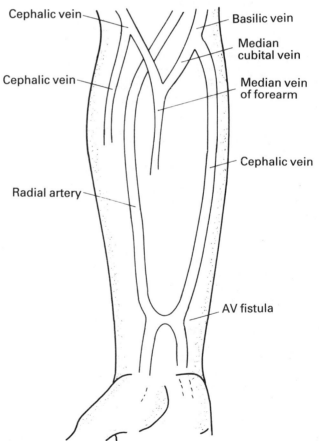

Figure 21.1 An arteriovenous (AV) fistula (vascular access) used in the forearm for haemodialysis (Galpin, C., St Thomas' Hospital, London.)

water. Heparin is added to the blood to prevent clotting. The blood passes, by means of a pump, through the artificial kidney machine to the semipermeable membrane or artificial kidney, and the dialysate fluid flows on the other side of the membrane. The toxins and wastes in the blood are removed by diffusion, moving from an area of greater concentration in the blood to an area of lesser concentration in the dialysate. The blood and dialysate do not mix. The dialysate is composed of all the important electrolytes in their ideal extracellular concentrations. (Small pores in the semipermeable membrane do not allow the loss of red blood cells and proteins.)

Excess water is removed from the blood by osmosis. The removal of water can be controlled by creating a desired pressure gradient (ultrafiltration). Purified blood is returned to the body through the patient's vein.

During dialysis, constant monitoring is required to detect the numerous complications that can arise. The nurse in the dialysis unit has an important role in monitoring and supporting the patient and in carrying out a continuing programme of patient assessment and education.

Complications

Although haemodialysis can prolong life indefinitely, it does not halt the natural course of the underlying kidney disease, nor does it completely control uraemia. The patient is subjected to a number of problems and complications. The leading cause of death among patients undergoing chronic haemodialysis is arteriosclerotic cardiovascular disease. Congestive heart failure, coronary heart disease and anginal pain, stroke and peripheral vascular insufficiency may incapacitate the patient. Anaemia and fatigue contribute to diminished physical and emotional wellbeing, lack of energy and drive, and loss of interest. Gastric ulcers and other gastrointestinal problems occur from the physiologic stress of chronic illness, medication and related problems. Disturbed calcium metabolism leads to renal osteodystrophy that produces bone pain and fractures. Other problems include fluid overload associated with congestive heart failure, malnutrition and disequilibrium syndrome following rapid fluid and electrolyte changes. Patients with virtually no renal function have been maintained for a number of years by intermittent haemodialysis. For some, a successful kidney transplant would eliminate the need for chronic, longterm haemodialysis treatment.

Long-term therapy presents a problem for the patient and for society of cost. With improved techniques and a greater number of patients on treatment, the cost of chronic dialysis is of great concern.

Psychosocial Considerations

People undergoing longterm haemodialysis are concerned with very real problems. Generally, their medical status is unpredictable and their lives are disrupted; they often have financial problems, difficulty in holding a job, waning sexual desires and impotence, depression from living the life of a chronically ill person and fear of dying. Younger people worry about marriage, having children and the burden that they bring to their families. A regimented lifestyle necessitated by the need for frequent dialysis treatments and restrictions in food and fluid intake is often demoralizing to the patient and loved ones.

Dialysis Settings

For selected patients, haemodialysis is carried out in the home. However, not all people are candidates because this procedure requires a highly motivated patient who is willing to take responsibility for the dialysis procedure and able to adjust each treatment to meet the body's changing needs.

Haemofiltration

Haemofiltration or continuous arteriovenous haemofiltration is another system for temporarily replacing kidney function. It is used for patients with fluid overload secondary to oliguric (low urinary output) renal failure or those patients whose kidneys are unable to handle their acute high metabolic or nutritional needs.

Although haemofiltration shares many of the limitations and problems of haemodialysis, its advantage is that it does not require dialysis machines or dialysis personnel, and it can be initiated quickly in hospitals without dialysis facilities.

Peritoneal Dialysis

In peritoneal dialysis, the surface of the peritoneum, which amounts to approximately 22,000 cm^2, acts as the diffusing surface. An appropriate sterile dialyzing fluid (dialysate) is introduced into the peritoneal cavity at intervals. Urea and creatinine, both metabolic end-products normally excreted by the kidneys, are removed (cleared) from the blood during peritoneal dialysis. Urea is cleared at a rate of 15 to 20 ml/min, while creatinine is removed more slowly.

It usually takes 36 to 48 hours to achieve with peritoneal dialysis what haemodialysis accomplishes in six to eight hours. Peritoneal dialysis can be intermittent (several times per week, each 6 to 48 hours) or continuous.

Although there are variations in the scheduling of dialysis treatments with the different forms of peritoneal dialysis, the underlying principles are the same.

Principles of Peritoneal Dialysis

Approximately two litres of sterile dialyzing solution (dialysate) are infused through an abdominal catheter into the peritoneal cavity. The solution flows into the cavity by gravity. The fluid comes in close contact with the blood vessels of the peritoneal cavity, which serves as the dialyzing membrane. Toxic wastes and excess fluid move from the patient's circulation by diffusion and osmosis into the peritoneal cavity during the dwell time, the period in which the fluid remains in the abdominal cavity before it is drained. At the end of the dwell time, the solution is allowed to drain from the abdominal cavity and is discarded. A new container of fluid is added and infused.

Expected Outcomes and Indications for Peritoneal Dialysis

The expected outcomes for this method of treatment are to assist in the removal of toxic substances and metabolic wastes, to re-establish normal fluid balance by removing excessive fluid and to restore electrolyte balance. Peritoneal dialysis may be the treatment of choice for patients with renal failure who are unable or unwilling to undergo haemodialysis or renal transplantation. It may be more effective than haemodialysis in patients who are susceptible to the rapid fluid, electrolyte and metabolic changes that occur during haemodialysis. Therefore, patients with diabetes or cardiovascular disease and those who may be at risk of side-effects of systemic use of heparin would be likely candidates for peritoneal dialysis to treat their renal failure. Additionally, severe hypertension, congestive heart failure and pulmonary oedema not responsive to usual treatment regimes have been successfully treated with peritoneal dialysis.

Preparation of the Patient for Peritoneal Dialysis

The patient about to undergo peritoneal dialysis may be acutely ill, thus requiring the treatment to correct extreme changes in fluid and electrolyte status, or may be undergoing one of many peritoneal dialysis treatments.

The procedure is explained to the patient and a signed consent is obtained. Baseline vital signs, weight, and serum electrolyte levels are obtained and recorded. Emptying of the bladder and bowel may be indicated to minimize the risk of puncture of internal organs and structures. The nurse also has an opportunity to assess the patient's anxiety about the procedure and to provide support and advice.

Continuous Ambulatory Peritoneal Dialysis (CAPD)

Continuous ambulatory peritoneal dialysis is a form of dialysis for patients with end-stage renal disease who want to take an active part in their treatment. However, it is not appropriate for all patients requiring chronic dialysis. It is performed at home by the patient. Sometimes a family member or close friend is trained to perform the exchanges for the patient. The technique is adjusted to the patient's physiological requirements for dialysis and ability to learn the procedure.

The dialysate is delivered from flexible plastic containers through a permanent peritoneal catheter (Figure 21.2). After the dialysate is infused into the peritoneal cavity, the bag is folded and tucked underneath the clothing during the dwell or equilibration time. This provides the patient with some freedom and reduces the number of connections and disconnections necessary at the catheter end of the tubing, thereby reducing the accompanying risk of contamination and peritonitis.

Patients who want control over their lives and are willing to co-operate in their care do well on continuous ambulatory peritoneal dialysis. Almost half of all new end-stage renal disease patients are choosing continuous ambulatory peritoneal dialysis for their form of therapy. The number of patients receiving continuous ambulatory peritoneal dialysis is expected to continue to increase.

Principles

Continuous ambulatory peritoneal dialysis works on the same principles as do other forms of peritoneal dialysis: diffusion and osmosis. However, because continuous ambulatory peritoneal dialysis is a continuous treatment, a steady state of blood values of the nitrogenous waste products results. The precise blood levels depend on the residual kidney function, on the daily dialysate volume and, of course, on the rate of production of the waste products. There are less extreme fluctuations in the serum chemistries on continuous ambulatory peritoneal dialysis, as the dialysis is constantly in progress. The serum electrolytes usually stay in the normal range.

An exchange is performed usually four times a day and the fluid is changed four times a day. This technique is continuous, 24 hours a day, seven days a week. The patient performs the exchanges at intervals spread throughout the day and sleeps during the night.

Indications

Continuous ambulatory peritoneal dialysis is the treatment of choice for most patients who want to perform their own dialysis at home. Continuous ambulatory peritoneal dialysis is indicated for those patients on maintenance or chronic haemodialysis who have problems with their present treatment.

Patients awaiting a kidney transplant can be safely maintained on continuous ambulatory peritoneal dialysis. Diabetic people with end-stage renal disease may be a group for whom continuous ambulatory peritoneal dialysis is an absolute indication. The excellent control of hypertension, the control of uraemia, and the satisfactory control of glycaemia by intraperitoneal administration of insulin may arrest the diabetic complications.

Older patients generally do well on continuous ambulatory peritoneal dialysis if personal or community supports are adequate. Patients who want to take an active part in their treatment, want more freedom and are motivated and willing to carry out the required treatment also

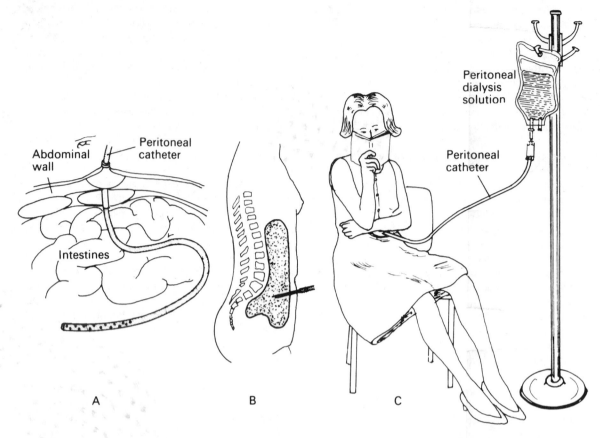

Figure 21.2 Continuous ambulatory peritoneal dialysis. (A) The peritoneal catheter is implanted through the abdominal wall. (B) Fluid infusing into the peritoneal cavity. (C) The patient allows for the prescribed dwell time (four to five hours) and drains the peritoneal cavity by gravity. (Brunner, L. S. and Suddarth, D. S. (1986) *The Lippincott Manual of Nursing Practice* (4th edition), J. B. Lippincott, Philadelphia.)

do well on continuous ambulatory peritoneal dialysis. When deciding on the treatment, it is important to consider the patient's personal support system, as well as ability to perform self-dialysis.

Complications

Continuous ambulatory peritoneal dialysis is not without complications. Most complications are minor in nature, but several, if left unattended, can have serious consequences for the patient.

Peritonitis

Peritonitis is the most common complication and also the most serious. Most peritonitis episodes are due to accidental contamination caused by *Staphylococcus epidermidis*. Fortunately, these episodes result in mild symptoms and have a good prognosis. Peritonitis due to *Staphylococcus aureus* produces a higher morbidity rate, has a more serious prognosis and runs a longer course.

Peritonitis is treated in the hospital if patients are not

well enough to do their own exchanges. Antibiotics are usually added to the dialysate and are also taken orally for 10 days. The infection usually clears in two to four days. Careful culture techniques are important for the treatment of the organism by the correct antibiotic.

Leakage

Leakage of dialysate through the incision/insertion site may be noted immediately after catheter insertion. Usually, the leak stops spontaneously if dialysis is withheld for several days to give the incision and exit site enough time to heal.

Altered Body Image and Sexuality

Although continuous ambulatory peritoneal dialysis has given end-stage renal disease patients more freedom and control over their treatment, it is not without its problems. The patients often experience an altered body image due to the abdominal catheter and the presence of the bag and tubing. The presence of fluid in the abdomen affects patients' clothing selection as well as their feeling of 'being fat'. Body image may be so altered that the patient does not want to look at or care for the catheter for days or weeks. Some patients seem to have no psychological problems with the catheter; they think of it as their lifeline and are quite glad to have it as a life-sustaining device.

Sexuality and sexual activity can be altered; the patient and partner may be reluctant to engage in sexual activities, partly due to the presence of the catheter being psychologically 'in the way' of natural performance. The presence of the two litres of dialysate, peritoneal catheter and empty bag may interfere with the sexual function and body image of these patients.

Considerations for the Elderly

Changes in kidney function with normal ageing increase the susceptibility of elderly people to kidney dysfunction and renal failure. Alterations in renal blood flow, glomerular filtration and renal clearance increase the risk of drug-associated changes in renal function. Precautions are indicated with administration of all medications because of the frequent use of multiple prescription and over-the-counter drugs and the risk of side-effects. The incidence of systemic diseases such as atherosclerosis, hypertension, cardiac failure, diabetes and malignancy increases with advancing age, predisposing the elderly to renal disease associated with these disorders. Fluid and electrolyte balance in the elderly is usually maintained in normal circumstances. However, with age, the kidney is less able to respond to acute fluid and electrolyte changes. Therefore, acute problems need to be prevented if possible or recognized and treated quickly. Precautions are warranted when the elderly patient must undergo extensive diagnostic tests or when new medications (e.g., diuretics) are added, to prevent dehydration which can compromise marginal renal function and lead to acute renal failure. An elderly patient may develop nonspecific and atypical signs of disturbed renal function and fluid and electrolyte imbalances. Recognition of these problems is further hampered by their association with previously existing disorders and the mistaken belief that they are normal changes of the ageing.

KIDNEY TRANSPLANTATION

Kidney transplantation involves transplanting a kidney from a living donor or human cadaver to a recipient who has endstage renal disease. Most patients have been on dialysis for months or years before transplantation. Transplantation provides the patient with a more normal lifestyle and is less expensive than dialysis. Selected patients with irreversible end-stage renal disease are considered for kidney transplantation. Kidney transplants from well-matched living donors who are related to the patient (those with compatible ABO and HLA antigens) are more successful than those from cadaver donors.

The patient's kidneys, which are nonfunctioning, may or may not be removed, and dialysis is instituted until a kidney from a suitable donor is obtained. The transplanted kidney is placed in the patient's iliac fossa anterior to the crest of the ilium. The ureter of the newly transplanted kidney is transplanted into the bladder or anastomosed to the ureter of the recipient (Figure 21.3).

Preoperative Management

The expected outcome of preoperative management is to bring the patient's metabolic state to a level as close to normal as possible. Tissue typing is done to determine compatibility of the tissues and cells of the donor and recipient. Antibody screening is also carried out. Immunosuppressive drugs are given to suppress the body's immunological defence mechanism and prevent later rejection of the transplanted kidney. Haemodialysis is usually performed the day before the scheduled transplant. The patient must be free of infection at the time of renal transplantation because of immunosuppression and the risk of spread of infection. The mouth must be treated for gingival disease and dental caries. The lower urinary tract is studied to assess bladder neck function and to detect ureteral reflux.

Nursing Care

The nursing aspects of preoperative management are essentially the same as those for patients undergoing renal and vascular surgery. The patient may have experienced considerable discouragement, depression and anxiety while on dialysis awaiting a cadaver kidney. Dealing with these concerns is part of the nurse's role in preoperative care.

Postoperative Management

The expected outcome of care is to maintain homeostasis until the transplanted kidney is functioning well. The major limiting factor of this procedure is the body's immunological response, which may lead to rejection and destruction of the transplanted kidney. The survival of a transplanted kidney depends on the success of techniques that suppress this immunological reaction. In order to overcome or minimize the body's defence mechanism, immunosuppressive drugs are given. This therapy is continued indefinitely.

Renal graft rejection and failure may occur early (24 to 72 hours), within a few days (3 to 14 days) or later (after three weeks). Ultrasound may be used to detect enlargement of the kidney, while renal biopsy and radiographic techniques are used to evaluate a failing renal transplant. When severe rejection occurs or when excessive immunosuppression is required to maintain the kid-

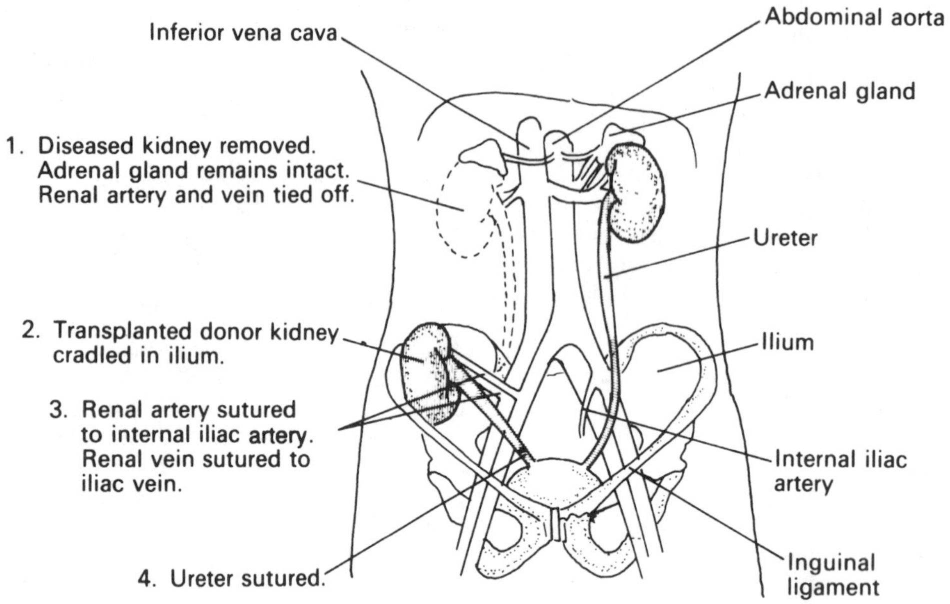

Figure 21.3 Renal transplantations. (1) The diseased kidney may be removed and the renal artery and vein are tied off. (2) The transplanted kidney is placed in the iliac fossa. (3) The renal artery of the donated kidney is sutured to the internal iliac artery, and the vein is sutured to the iliac vein. (4) The ureter of the donated kidney is sutured to the bladder, or sometimes to the patient's own ureter.

ney, the transplanted kidney is removed (graft nephrectomy) and the patient is returned to dialysis.

ACUTE GLOMERULONEPHRITIS

Acute glomerulonephritis refers to a group of kidney diseases in which there is an inflammatory reaction in the glomeruli. It is not an infection of the kidney *per se* but rather the result of untoward side-effects of the defence mechanism of the body. In most types of glomerulonephritis, IgG, the major immunoglobulin (antibody) found in the serum of humans, can be detected in the glomerular capillary walls. As a result of an antigen–antibody reaction, aggregates of molecules (complexes) are formed and circulate throughout the body. Some of these complexes lodge in the glomeruli, the filtering bed of the kidney, and induce an inflammatory response.

In most cases, the stimulus of the reaction is group A streptococcal infection of the throat, which ordinarily precedes the onset of glomerulonephritis by an interval of two to three weeks. The streptococcal product, acting as an antigen, generates circulating antibodies and results in deposit of the complexes in the glomeruli and injury to the kidney. Glomerulonephritis may also follow scarlet fever and impetigo (infection of the skin). The many forms of glomerulonephritis include proliferative, membranous, membranoproliferative, focal proliferative and rapidly

progressive. The pathology of these various types of glomerulonephritis has yet to be defined satisfactorily.

Altered Physiology
Cellular proliferation (increased production of endothelial cells lining the glomerulus), infiltration of the glomerulus by leucocytes and thickening of the glomerular filtration membrane or basement membrane result in scarring and loss of filtering surface. In acute glomerulonephritis, the kidneys become large, swollen and congested. All the renal tissues—glomeruli, tubules and blood vessels—are affected in all forms of glomerulonephritis, but in each form, the tissues are involved in varying degrees. With electron-microscopy and immunofluorescent identification of the immune mechanism, the nature of the lesion can be studied.

Clinical Features
The disease may be so mild that it is discovered accidentally through a routine urinalysis, or the history may reveal a preceding episode of pharyngitis or tonsillitis with fever. In the more severe form of the disease, the patient presents with headache, malaise, facial oedema and loin pain. Mild to severe hypertension is seen, and tenderness over the costovertebral angle is common.

Acute glomerulonephritis is predominantly a disease of youth. Some cases that develop later are acute exacerbations of a glomerulonephritis that is already present but undetected.

Diagnosis

The urine is scanty and bloody; there may even be no urine (anuria) for one or more days, although this is rare. The urine contains large amounts of protein. Usually, there are rising values of urea and serum creatinine. The patient may be anaemic because of loss of the red blood cells in the urine and changes in the haematopoietic mechanism of the body.

As the patient improves, the amount of urine increases, while the urinary protein and urinary sediment diminish. Usually, more than 90 per cent of children recover. The percentage of recovery for adults is not well established but is probably about 70 per cent. Some patients become severely uraemic within weeks and require dialysis for survival. Others, after a period of apparent recovery, insidiously develop chronic glomerulonephritis.

Medical Management

The expected outcomes of management are to protect the patient's poorly functioning kidneys and to treat complications promptly. If residual streptococcal infection is suspected, penicillin is given. Bedrest is encouraged during the acute phase until the urine clears and the serum urea, creatinine and blood pressure return to normal. Rest also facilitates diuresis. The urine of the patient may serve as a guide to the duration of bedrest, since excessive activity may increase proteinuria and haematuria.

Dietary protein is restricted when renal insufficiency and nitrogen retention develop. Sodium is restricted when hypertension, oedema and congestive heart failure are present. Carbohydrates are given liberally to provide energy and reduce the catabolism of protein.

Fluids are given according to the patient's fluid losses and daily body weight. Insensible fluid loss through respiration and faeces is estimated at 500 to 1,000 ml. The intake and output are measured and recorded. Usually, diuresis starts one to two weeks after the onset of symptoms. Oedema decreases and hypertension lessens. In some patients, the disease may progress to chronic glomerulonephritis.

Patient Education

Instructions to the patient include explanations and scheduling for follow-up evaluations of (1) blood pressure, (2) urinalysis for protein, and (3) blood for serum urea and creatinine studies to determine if there is exacerbation of disease activity.

CHRONIC GLOMERULONEPHRITIS

Altered Physiology

Chronic glomerulonephritis may have its onset as acute glomerulonephritis or may represent a milder type of antigen–antibody reaction, one so mild that it is overlooked. After repeated occurrences of these reactions, the kidneys are reduced to as little as one fifth their normal size, consisting largely of fibrous tissue. The cortex shrinks to a layer of 1 to 2 mm in thickness or less. Many glomeruli and their tubules become scarred and the branches of the renal artery are thickened. The result is severe glomerular damage which results in chronic glomerulonephritis, a common cause of chronic renal failure.

Clinical Features

The symptoms of chronic glomerulonephritis are variable. Some patients with severe disease have no symptoms at all for a long time. They may discover their condition as the result of a blood test or when their blood pressure is found to be elevated. Many patients merely notice that their feet are slightly swollen at night. The majority of all patients also have such general symptoms as loss of weight and strength, increasing irritability and nocturia. Headaches, dizziness and digestive disturbances are common.

Physical examination may reveal a poorly nourished patient with a yellow-grey pigmentation of the skin and periorbital and peripheral (dependent) oedema. Blood pressure may be normal or severely elevated.

A number of laboratory abnormalities occur. Urinalysis reveals a fixed specific gravity of 1.010, variable proteinuria and urine sediment changes. As glomerular filtration becomes depressed, hyperkalaemia and decreased serum bicarbonate (metabolic acidosis) develop.

Medical Management

The treatment of the ambulatory patient is guided by the patient's symptoms. Therefore, if hypertension is present, treatment is directed toward readjusting the diet and fluid intake in an effort to maintain as normal a metabolic state as possible. Protein intake (of high biological value) is adjusted according to the response of the patient, with adequate calories to prevent body protein from being used for energy. If there is a urinary tract infection, a possible factor in producing further renal damage, steps are taken to diagnose it and to treat it.

If severe oedema develops, the patient is nursed on bedrest and the head of the bed is elevated to promote comfort and diuresis. Weight is monitored daily, and diuretics are used to reduce fluid overload. Sodium and fluid intake is adjusted according to the ability of the patient's kidneys to excrete water and sodium.

Initiation of dialysis, which was previously used only in extreme cases of chronic glomerulonephritis, is considered early in the course of the disease to keep the patient in optimal physical condition, prevent fluid and electrolyte imbalances, and minimize the risk of complications of renal failure. The course of dialysis is smoother if treatment is initiated before the patient develops significant complications.

Nursing Care

The nurse has a major role in explaining to the patient and loved ones what is occurring. Additionally, the nurse provides emotional support throughout the course of the disease and treatment by providing opportunities for the patient and family or friends to verbalize their concerns and have their questions answered and their options discussed.

The nurse observes the patient for changes in fluid and electrolyte status and for signs of deterioration of renal function. Changes in fluid and electrolyte status and in cardiac and neurological status are reported promptly to the doctor. If dialysis is initiated, the patient and loved ones will require considerable assistance and support in dealing with the need for this therapy and its longterm implications.

NEPHROTIC SYNDROME

The nephrotic syndrome is a clinical disorder characterized by: (1) marked increase in protein in the urine (proteinuria); (2) decrease in albumin in the blood (hypoalbuminaemia); (3) oedema; and (4) excess cholesterol in the blood (hypercholesterolaemia). It is seen in any condition that seriously damages the glomerular capillary membrane. Causes include chronic glomerulonephritis, diabetes mellitus with intercapillary glomerulosclerosis, amyloidosis of the kidney, systemic lupus erythematosus and renal vein thrombosis. The altered physiology of nephrotic syndrome is discussed on page 672.

Clinical Features

There is slow onset of fluid retention that progresses to pitting oedema. The patient loses protein in the urine, leading to depletion of body proteins. In addition, the blood cholesterol level is high. The diagnosis is made on assessment of the patient's signs and symptoms, physical examination, renal function tests, measurements of 24-hour urine protein and serum electrolyte evaluations. Urinalysis shows microscopic haematuria, urinary casts and other abnormalities. Needle biopsy of the kidney is done for histological examination of renal tissue to confirm the diagnosis.

Medical Management

The objective of management is to preserve renal function. It may be necessary to keep the patient on bedrest a few days to promote diuresis to reduce the oedema. A high-protein diet is given to replenish wasted tissues and restore body proteins. If the oedema is severe, the patient is given a low-sodium diet. Diuretics are given in severe oedema, and adrenocorticosteroids (prednisone) may be used to reduce proteinuria.

Nursing Care

In the early stages, the nursing care is similar to that of the patient with acute glomerulonephritis, but as the disease worsens, care is similar to the care of the patient with chronic renal failure (see pp. 709–11).

NEPHROSCLEROSIS

Nephrosclerosis is hardening, or sclerosis, of the arteries of the kidney and is usually seen in association with hypertension. It is the renal manifestation of generalized arteriosclerosis. There are two forms: malignant and benign. Malignant nephrosclerosis is thought to be a generalized vascular disease that starts in the kidney and finally involves the entire vascular tree. Patients with the malignant type progress rapidly through the stages of proteinuria, increasing hypertension, failing renal function and retinal vessel changes. They usually die within several months. The factor responsible for death may be uraemia, congestive heart failure due to hypertensive heart disease or a cerebrovascular accident. It occurs most commonly from the third to the fifth decade of life.

Patients who develop benign nephrosclerosis are found in older age groups. These patients rarely complain of renal symptoms, although for years the urine has a low and fixed specific gravity and contains a small amount of protein and an occasional hyaline or granular cast. Only late in the disease does renal insufficiency appear.

HYDRONEPHROSIS

Hydronephrosis due to obstruction of urinary flow is dilation of the pelvis and calyces of one or both kidneys with resulting thinning of the renal parenchyma. Obstruction to the normal flow of urine causes the urine to back up, resulting in increased pressure in the kidney. If the obstruction is in the urethra or the bladder, the back-pressure affects both kidneys, but if the obstruction is in one of the ureters due to a stone or kink, only one kidney is damaged.

Partial or intermittent obstruction may be caused by a renal stone that has formed in the renal pelvis but has dropped into the ureter and blocked it. Or the obstruction may be due to a tumour of some other abdominal or pelvic organ pressing on the ureter or to bands of scar tissue resulting from an abscess or inflammation near the ureter that pinches it. The disorder may be due to an odd angle of the ureter as it leaves the renal pelvis or to an unusual position of the kidney, favouring a ureteral twist or kink. In elderly males, the most common cause is urethral obstruction at the bladder outlet by an enlarged prostate.

Whatever the cause, as the fluid accumulates in the renal pelvis it distends the pelvis and its calyces. In time, atrophy of the kidney results. As one kidney undergoes gradual destruction, the contralateral kidney gradually enlarges (compensatory hypertrophy). Ultimately, there is impairment of renal function.

Clinical Features

The patient may be asymptomatic if the onset is gradual. Acute obstruction may produce aching in the loin and back. If infection is present, there are symptoms of bladder irritability (dysuria) and chills, fever, tenderness and pyuria. The hydronephritic kidney may bleed from congestion, causing haematuria. Signs and symptoms of chronic renal failure develop as the condition progresses.

Medical Management

The expected outcomes of management are to identify and correct the cause of the obstruction, to treat infection and to restore and conserve renal function.

To relieve the obstruction, the urine may have to be diverted by nephrostomy (see p. 688) or other types of diversion. The infection is treated with antimicrobials since residual urine in the calyces produces infection and pyelonephritis. The patient is prepared for surgical removal of obstructive lesions (calculus, tumour, obstruction of the ureter). If one kidney is severely damaged and its function is destroyed, nephrectomy (removal of the kidney) is performed. (See The Patient Undergoing Kidney Surgery, pp. 687 and 689–92.)

INFECTIONS OF THE URINARY TRACT

Urinary tract infections are caused by the presence of pathogenic micro-organisms in the urinary tract, with or without signs and symptoms. Infection may occur at any site within the urinary tract and may affect the bladder (cystitis), urethra (urethritis), prostate (prostatitis) or kidney (pyelonephritis). The normal urinary tract is sterile except near the urethral orifice.

Bacteriuria refers to the presence of bacteria in the urine. A colony count of at least 100,000 colonies per millilitre of urine on a midstream or catheterized specimen usually indicates infection. However, urinary tract infection and subsequent sepsis have been reported with lower bacterial colony counts. Infections in any part of the urinary tract may persist for months or even years without symptoms.

The bacteria most commonly responsible for urinary tract infections are *Escherichia coli* (80 to 90 per cent); *Proteus mirabilis*; one or more species of *Klebsiella*, *Enterobacter*, *Proteus* and *Pseudomonas*; and the various enterococci. All these are normally found in the faecal flora.

Factors Contributing to Urinary Tract Infections

The majority of urinary tract infections result from bowel organisms that ascend from the perineum to the urethra and the bladder, adhering to the mucosal surfaces. Defence mechanisms of the bladder, including an 'anti-adherence' defence or fluid on the surface of the bladder wall and a 'washout factor' (flushing bacteria away with voiding), normally protect the urinary tract from infection. Interference with these mechanisms by inflammation, abrasion of the urethral mucosa or incomplete emptying of the bladder increases susceptibility to urinary tract infection.

Women are more prone to develop bladder infections because of the short female urethra and its anatomical proximity to the vagina, periurethral glands and rectum. In the male, the length of the urethra and the antibacterial properties of the prostatic secretions tend to ward off ascending urethral infections. Adult males who develop urinary tract infections should be examined for urinary obstruction, prostatic infection, renal stones or systemic disease.

Urethrovesical reflux refers to the reflux (flowing back) of urine from the bladder into the urethra. It is caused by an increase in intrabladder pressure (coughing, sneezing), which may squeeze the urine out of the bladder into the urethra. When the pressure returns to normal, the urine flows back from the urethra, bringing back into the bladder the bacteria from the anterior portions of the urethra. Urethrovesical reflux is also caused by dysfunction of the bladder neck or urethra.

Ureterovesical or vesicoureteral reflux refers to the flowing back of urine from the bladder into one or both ureters. In the normal person, the ureterovesical junction prevents urine from travelling back into the ureter, particularly at the time of voiding. When the ureterovesical valve is incompetent (congenital causes, ureteral abnormalities), the bacteria may reach the kidneys and there may be subsequent dilation of the ureter, renal pelvis and calyces with ultimate kidney destruction.

Faecal contamination of the urethral meatus is a common way in which bacteria are introduced into the urinary tract. Sexual intercourse plays a role in the ascent of organisms from the perineum into the bladder in women. Instrumentation (from catheterization, cytoscopic examinations) is also implicated in producing infections. Stasis of urine in the bladder may lead to infection, which may ultimately spread through the entire urinary system. Any obstruction to urinary flow renders the kidney more susceptible to infection. Common causes of urinary tract obstruction are congenital anomalies, urethral strictures, contracture of the bladder neck, bladder tumours, ureteral stones, compression of the ureters and neurological abnormalities. Infections may spread to the urinary tract by way of the blood or the lymphatic system. Diabetes mellitus also predisposes to urinary tract infections. Common causes of urinary tract infection are summarized in Figure 21.4.

Clinical Features

Signs and symptoms of urinary tract infections cover a broad range. Frequently, the patient is asymptomatic and

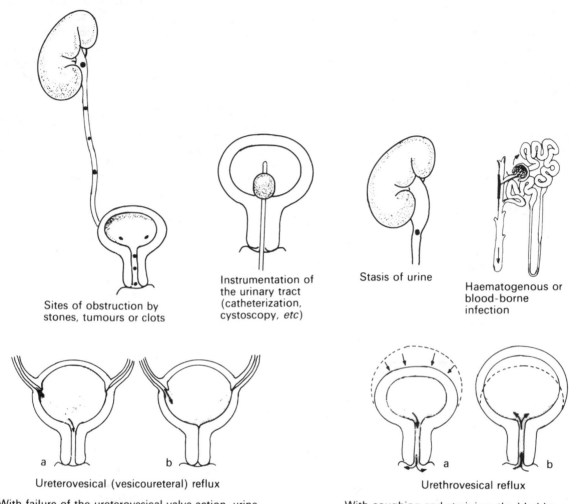

Sites of obstruction by
stones, tumours or clots

Instrumentation of
the urinary tract
(catheterization,
cystoscopy, *etc*)

Stasis of urine

Haematogenous or
blood-borne
infection

Ureterovesical (vesicoureteral) reflux

With failure of the ureterovesical valve action, urine
moves up the ureters during voiding (*a*) and flows into
the bladder when voiding has stopped (*b*). This prevents
complete emptying of the bladder, stasis and
contamination of the ureters with bacteria-laden urine

Urethrovesical reflux

With coughing and straining, the bladder
pressure rises, which may force urine from
the bladder into the urethera (*a*). When
bladder pressure returns to normal, the
urine flows back to the bladder (*b*), which
introduces bacteria from the urethra to the
bladder

Figure 21.4 Causes of urinary tract and kidney infections.

is found to have bacteria in the urine (bacteriuria) while
undergoing a routine health check. Signs and symptoms
of lower urinary tract infection (cystitis) include frequent
painful and burning urination, sometimes accompanied
by bearing-down sensations and spasms in the region of
the bladder and suprapubic area. Haematuria and back
pain may also be present. Signs and symptoms of upper
urinary tract infection (pyelonephritis) include fever,
chills, loin pain and painful urination.

Diagnosis

Urinary tract infection is diagnosed by bacteria in the

urine specimen collected by a midstream clean-catch
technique. A bacterial count of 100,000 organisms (colonies) per millilitre of urine indicates a urinary infection.

Cystitis (Lower Urinary Tract Infection)

Cystitis is an inflammation of the urinary bladder that is
most often caused by an ascending infection from the
urethra. It may be caused by urine flowing back from the
urethra into the bladder (urethrovesical reflux), faecal
contamination or the use of various instruments such as a
catheter or cystoscope.

Cystitis is seen more commonly in women. The distal portion of the urethra is frequently colonized with bacterial flora following colonization of the vaginal vestibule. A defect of the mucosa of the urethra, vagina or external genitalia of these patients may allow enteric organisms to adhere and colonize at periurethral sites and to invade the bladder. Acute cystitis in women is usually caused by *Escherichia coli* and often follows sexual intercourse.

About half of the women who present with symptoms of acute cystitis (frequency, dysuria) without bacteriuria have acute urethral syndrome (symptoms suggesting urinary tract infection but occurring in the presence of urine with fewer than 100,000 organisms). Cystitis in men is secondary to some other factor, such as infected prostate; epididymitis by reflux of urine along the vas or perivesical lymphatics, as from an infected prostate; or bladder stones. Therefore, men undergo diagnostic testing usually after the first episode of cystitis to identify and treat the cause.

The patient with cystitis complains of urgency, frequency, burning and pain on urination, nocturia and a bearing-down sensation in the region of the bladder and suprapubic area. There is pus, bacteria and often red cells in the urine.

Medical Management

The expected outcomes of medical management are to eradicate the causative pathogens, to decrease morbidity and to prevent recurrences. The specific treatment depends on the cause and location of the infection. A urine specimen is usually obtained for smears and culture so that the appropriate drug may be selected.

For an uncomplicated, nonobstructed lower urinary tract infection, the female patient may be treated with single-dose or short-term therapy with an antimicrobial agent to which the organisms are susceptible. These infections usually respond favourably to antimicrobials that result in high urinary drug levels. A potentially effective drug should rapidly eradicate the organism and relieve the patient's symptoms. The urine is re-examined 24 hours to three days after initiation of treatment to determine if the urine is free of bacteria. In the male patient, prostatitis may require prolonged antimicrobial therapy.

There is a tendency for these infections to recur. Recurrences are of two types: (1) reinfection, the occurrence of sequential infections caused by different organisms, and (2) persistent infection, the occurrence of repeated infections caused by the same organism. Repeated or persistent infection due to the same organism usually results from a persistent source of infection in the urinary tract, such as infected urinary tract stones or structural anomalies of the urinary tract. Although the incidence of such infections is relatively small, the potential for irreversible kidney damage and its prevention, if the source of persistent infection is treated, make differentiation of the type of recurrent infection important.

Since there is a marked tendency for infection to recur, follow-up urine studies are recommended for at least two years to determine whether asymptomatic infection is present. It is especially important to have follow-up studies if urinary tract infections occur during pregnancy.

▶ NURSING PROCESS
▶ THE PATIENT WITH LOWER URINARY TRACT INFECTION

▶ *Assessment*

A history of urinary signs and symptoms is obtained from the patient with a possible urinary tract infection. The presence of pain, frequency, urgency and hesitancy, and changes in urine are assessed, documented and reported. The patient's usual pattern of voiding is assessed to detect factors that may predispose the patient to urinary tract infection. Infrequent emptying of the bladder, the association of symptoms of urinary tract infection with sexual intercourse and personal hygiene are assessed. The patient's knowledge about prescribed antimicrobial medications and preventive health care measures is also assessed. Additionally, the patient's urine is checked for volume, colour, concentration, cloudiness and odour, all of which are altered by bacteria in the urinary tract.

▶ *Patient's Problems*

Based on the assessment, the patient's problems may include the following:

- Discomfort related to inflammation and infection of the urethra, bladder and other urinary tract structures.
- Lack of knowledge about factors predisposing to recurrence, detection and prevention of recurrence, and drug therapy.

▶ *Planning and Implementation*
▶ Expected Outcomes

The main outcomes for the patient may include relief of pain and discomfort and increased knowledge of preventive measures and treatments.

Nursing Care

Relieving Pain and Discomfort

Dysuria, frequency, hesitancy, urgency and other types of discomfort associated with urinary tract infection are frequently relieved quickly once antimicrobial therapy is initiated. Antispasmodic drugs may be useful in relieving bladder irritability and pain. Aspirin, heat to the perineum and hot baths help relieve urgency, discomfort and spasm. The patient is encouraged to drink liberal amounts of fluids to promote renal blood flow and to flush the bacteria from the urinary tract. However, fluids that may be irritating to the bladder (e.g., coffee, tea, colas) are avoided. Frequent voiding (every two to three hours) is encouraged to empty the bladder completely since this can significantly lower urine bacterial counts, reduce urinary stasis, and prevent reinfection.

Patient Education

Women who have repeated urinary tract infections should receive detailed advice on the following points:

1. Reduce concentrations of pathogens at the vaginal introitus by hygienic measures:
   a. Shower rather than bath, since bacteria in the bath water may enter the urethra.
   b. Cleanse around the perineum and urethral meatus (cleansing from the front to the back) after each bowel movement.
2. Drink liberal amounts of fluid during the day to flush out bacteria.
3. Void every two to three hours during the day and completely empty the bladder. This prevents overdistension of the bladder and compromised blood supply to the bladder wall, which predisposes the patient to urinary tract infection.
4. If sexual intercourse is the initiating event for development of bacteriuria:
   a. Void immediately after sexual intercourse.
   b. Take the prescribed single dose of an oral antimicrobial agent following sexual intercourse.
5. If bacteria continue to appear in the urine, longterm antimicrobial therapy may be required to prevent colonization of the periurethral area and recurrence of infection. The drug should be taken after emptying the bladder just before going to bed to ensure adequate concentration of the drug during the overnight period.
6. See doctor regularly for follow-up, recurrence of symptoms, infections nonresponsive to treatment or further involvement of the urinary tract.

► *Evaluation*
► **Expected Outcomes**

1. Patient experiences relief of pain, urgency, dysuria and fever.
   a. Reports absence of pain, urgency, dysuria, hesitancy on voiding.
   b. Takes antimicrobial agent as prescribed.
   c. Takes analgesics and hot baths for discomfort.
   d. Drinks 8 to 10 glasses of fluids daily.
   e. Voids every two to three hours.
   f. Voids urine that is clear and free from odour.
2. Increases knowledge of preventive measures and prescribed treatment modalities.

   a. States rationale for using shower rather than bath for daily hygiene.
   b. Uses appropriate cleansing action (front to back) following each bowel movement.
   c. States rationale for appropriate cleansing method following each bowel movement.
   d. Consumes seven to eight glasses of fluid per day.
   e. Voids frequently during day and at bedtime to prevent overdistension of bladder.
   f. Voids immediately after sexual intercourse.
   g. Takes oral antimicrobial agents as prescribed following sexual intercourse.
   h. Takes entire course of antimicrobial agent as prescribed.
   i. Reports recurrence of symptoms to doctor.
   j. Adheres to follow-up schedule as recommended by doctor.
   k. Reports symptoms of further involvement of the urinary tract.

Considerations for the Elderly

Urinary tract infection is the most common cause of sepsis in the elderly. Gram-negative sepsis resulting from urinary tract infection in the elderly is associated with a mortality rate exceeding 50 per cent. Obstruction from an enlarged prostate is the most frequent cause of urinary tract infection in elderly men; elderly women often have incomplete emptying of the bladder and urinary stasis. Postmenopausal women also are susceptible to colonization and increased adherence of bacteria to the vagina and urethra in the absence of oestrogen. The recognition of urinary tract infection and sepsis in the elderly is made more difficult by the frequent lack of typical symptoms. Although frequency, urgency and dysuria may occur, nonspecific symptoms such as lethargy, anorexia, hyperventilation and a low-grade fever may be the only clues to the presence of a urinary tract infection. The probability of frequent reinfection appears with advancing age.

Pyelonephritis (Upper Urinary Tract Infection)

Pyelonephritis is a bacterial infection of the renal pelvis, tubules and interstitial tissue of one or both kidneys. Bacteria may gain access to the bladder via the urethra and ascend to the kidney, or may reach the kidney through the bloodstream. Pyelonephritis is frequently secondary to ureterovesical reflux in which an incompetent ureterovesical valve allows the urine to back up (reflux) into the ureters, usually at the time of voiding (see Figure 21.4). Urinary tract obstruction (which renders the kidneys more susceptible to infection) and renal diseases are among other causes. Pyelonephritis may be acute or chronic.

Acute pyelonephritis is an active infection that presents with chills and fever, loin pain, costovertebral angle tenderness, leucocytosis, bacteria and pus in the urine, and frequently symptoms of lower urinary tract involvement, such as dysuria and frequency.

Low-grade interstitial inflammation may result in atrophy and destruction of tubules and the glomeruli. Eventually, when pyelonephritis becomes chronic, the kidneys become scarred, contracted and nonfunctioning.

Diagnosis and Medical Management

An intravenous urogram and other diagnostic tests are carried out to locate any obstruction in the urinary tract. The relief of obstruction is essential to save the kidney from destruction. The treatment is essentially the same as that of cystitis. Culture and sensitivity tests are done on the urine since the choice of antimicrobial is determined by the causative organism. Medication should produce sustained antibacterial concentration of the drugs within the renal parenchyma. The antimicrobial drug must be given for a long enough period to prevent reseeding of residual foci of infection.

A possible problem in treatment is a chronic or recurring infection persisting for months or years without symptoms. After the initial antimicrobial regime, the patient is kept on continuous antimicrobial treatment until there is no evidence of infection, all causative factors have been treated or controlled and kidney function is stabilized. The patient is monitored with serum creatinine determinations and blood counts for the duration of the longterm therapy.

Chronic Pyelonephritis

Repeated bouts of acute pyelonephritis may lead to chronic pyelonephritis (chronic interstitial nephritis).

The patient with chronic pyelonephritis usually has no symptoms of infection unless an acute exacerbation occurs. Noticeable signs may include fatigue, headache, poor appetite, polyuria, excessive thirst and weight loss. Persistent and recurring infection may produce progressive scarring of the kidney with ultimate kidney failure.

Complications of chronic pyelonephritis include uraemia (from progressive loss of nephrons secondary to chronic inflammation and scarring), hypertension and formation of kidney stones (from chronic infection with urea-splitting organisms, resulting in stone formation).

Diagnosis and Medical Management

The extent of the disease is assessed by intravenous urogram and measurements of serum urea, creatinine levels and creatinine clearance. Eradication of bacteria from the urine is undertaken if present. The choice of an antimicrobial is based on culture identification of the pathogen. Hypertension and chronic renal failure are the major complications of chronic pyelonephritis.

Perinephric Abscess

Perinephric abscess is an abscess in the fatty tissue of the kidney that may arise secondary to an infection of the kidney or as a haematogenous (spread through the bloodstream) infection originating elsewhere in the body. It may be secondary to a staphylococcal infection of the kidney or to the spread of infection from adjacent areas, such as from diverticulitis or appendicitis. The symptoms often are acute in onset, with chills, fever, leucocytosis and other signs of suppuration. Locally, there is loin or abdominal tenderness or pain. The patient usually appears to be seriously ill.

Medical Management

The treatment consists of administration of the appropriate antimicrobial agent and incision and drainage of the abscess. Drains are usually inserted and left in the perinephric space until all significant drainage has ceased. Because the drainage often is profuse, frequent changes of the outer dressings may be necessary. As in the treatment of an abscess in any site, the patient is monitored for sepsis, fluid intake and output, and general response to treatment.

Carbuncle of the Kidney

Carbuncle of the kidney is an infection of blood-borne origin usually caused by *Staphylococcus*. It usually follows a cutaneous boil or carbuncle and is characterized by fever, malaise and dull pain in the region of the kidney. This type of infection, if recognized, usually subsides with chemotherapy. Recently, carbuncles of the kidney from gram-negative bacteria have increased in incidence.

Tuberculosis of the Kidney and Genitourinary Tract

Altered Physiology and Clinical Features

Tuberculosis of the kidney and urinary tract is caused by the organism *Mycobacterium tuberculosis* and usually spreads from the lungs by way of the bloodstream to the kidneys and to other organs of the genitourinary tract. At first the symptoms are mild; there is usually a slight afternoon fever and a loss of weight and appetite. The process of tuberculosis generally starts in one of the renal pyramids; ulceration into the kidney pelvis follows. The organisms are carried down with the urine into the bladder so that the bladder is likely to become infected.

Tuberculosis of the urinary bladder is an extension of tuberculosis of a kidney. This disease gives rise to several small ulcers, the majority of them near the trigone of the bladder. The symptoms of bladder tuberculosis are those of cystitis in general but with an unusual degree of bladder irritability because of the location of the lesions.

Medical Management

A search for tuberculosis elsewhere in the body is conducted when tuberculosis of the kidney or urinary tract is found. Inquiry is made to determine if the patient has had known exposure to tuberculosis. Three or more clean-voided first morning urine specimens are obtained for culture for *M. tuberculosis*.

The objective of treatment is to eradicate the offending organism. Combinations of drugs are used to delay the emergence of resistant organisms. Shorter-course chemotherapy (four months) has been proven effective in eradicating the organism and in penetrating renal tissue. Since renal tuberculosis is a manifestation of a systemic disease, all measures to promote the general health of the patient are used. Surgical intervention may be necessary to prevent obstructive problems and to remove an extensively diseased kidney. The patient is advised about the need for follow-up examinations (urine cultures, excretory urograms) usually for a period of a year.

FURTHER READING

Books

Dialysis and Transplantation

Areopoulos, D. G. (ed.) (1982) *Peritoneal Dialysis in the Treatment of Renal Failure*, MTP Press, Lancaster.

Atkins, R. C., Thomson, N. M. and Farrell, P. C. (1981) *Peritoneal Dialysis*, Churchill Livingstone, Edinburgh.

Cogan, M. G. and Garovoy, M. R. (1985) *Introduction to Dialysis* (1st edition), Churchill Livingstone, Edinburgh.

Coles, G. A. (1988) *Manual of Peritoneal Dialysis*, Kluwer Academic Publications, London.

Gabriel, R. (1982) *A Patient's Guide to Dialysis and Transplantation* (2nd edition), MTP Press, Lancaster.

Renal Disorders

Black, D. and Jones, N. F. (eds) (1979) *Renal Diseases* (4th edition) Blackwell Scientific, Oxford.

Brooks, D. and Mallick, N. (1982) *Renal Medicine and Urology*, Churchill Livingstone, Edinburgh.

Brundage, D. (1980) *Nursing Management of Renal Problems*, C. V. Mosby, St Louis.

Cameron, S. (1981) *Kidney Disease—The Facts*, Oxford University Press, Oxford.

Cameron, S. (1985) *Manual of Renal Disease*, Churchill Livingstone, Edinburgh.

Castro, J. E. (ed.) (1982) *The Treatment of Renal Failure*, MTP Press, Lancaster.

Davison, A. M. (1981) *A Synopsis of Renal Diseases*, Billing & Sons, London.

Evan, D. B. and Henderson, R. G. (1985) *Lecture Notes on Nephrology*, Blackwell Scientific, Oxford.

Gabriel, R. (1981) *Renal Medicine* (2nd edition), Baillière Tindall, London.

Gower, P. E. (1983) *Nephrology (Pocket Consultant Series)*, Grant McIntyre, London.

Lancaster, L. E. (1984) *The Patient With End Stage Renal Failure* (2nd edition), John Wiley, New York.

Levine, D. Z. (1983) *Care of the Renal Patient*, W. B. Saunders, Philadelphia.

Parson, F. M. and Ogg, C. (1983) *Renal Failure—Who Cares?* MTP Press, Lancaster.

Rasmussen, J. M. (1980) *Renal Problems: A Critical Care Nursing Focus*, Prentice-Hall International, London

Schoengrund, L. and Balzar, P. (eds) (1985) *Renal Problems in Critical Care*, John Wiley, Chichester.

Vennegoor, M. (ed.) (1985) *Nutrition for Patients With Renal Failure*, EDTNA-ERCA Publications, Portsmouth. (Obtainable only from Caroline Galpin, St Thomas's Hospital, London.)

de Wardener, H. E. (1985) *The Kidney: An Outline of Normal and Abnormal Function* (5th edition), Churchill Livingstone, Edinburgh.

Winder, E. and Faber, S. (1982) *Renal Nursing*, Macmillan, London.

Urology and Urinary Tract Disorders

Asscher, A. N. and Moffat, D. B. (1983) *Nephro-Urology*, Heinemann, London.

Blandy, J. P. and Moors, J. (1989) *Urology for Nurses*, Blackwell Scientific, Oxford.

Feneley, R. C. L. and Blannin, J. P. (1984) *Incontinence*, Churchill Livingstone, Edinburgh.

James, J. (1984) *Handbook of Urology*, Harper & Row, London.

Kilmartin, A. (1980) *Understanding Cystitis*, Pan, London.

King's Fund (1983) *Action on Incontinence*, Report of a Working Group, Project Paper No. 43, King's Fund, London.

Mandelstrom, D. (1986) *Incontinence and Its Management* (2nd edition), Croom Helm, London.

Mitchell, J. P. (1981) *Endoscopic Operative Urology*, John Wright, Bristol.

Norton, C. (1986) *Nursing for Incontinence*, Beaconsfield Publishers, England.

Scott, R., Deane, R. F. and Callender, R. (1982) *Urology Illustrated* (2nd edition), Churchill Livingstone, Edinburgh.

Slade, N. and Gillespie, W. A. (1985) *The Urinary Tract and the Catheter: Infection and Other Problems*, John Wiley, Chichester.

Whitfield, H. N. (1985) *Urology (Pocket Consultant Series)*, Blackwell Scientific, Oxford.

Articles

Dialysis and Transplantation

Chambers, J. K. (1981) Assessing the dialysis patient at home, *American Journal of Nursing*, Vol. 81, No. 4, pp. 750–4.

Dryden, M. S., Ludlam, H. A., Wing, A. J. *et al.* (In press) Active intervention dramatically reduces CAPD-associated infection, *Peritoneal Dialysis International*.

Lancaster, L. E. (1982) Kidney transplant rejection: pathophysiology, recognition and treatment, *Critical Care Nursing*, Vol. 2, No. 5, pp. 50–3.

Lancaster, L. E. (1983) Renal failure: pathophysiology, assessment and intervention, *Nephrology Nurse*, Vol.5, No. 2, pp. 38–41, 51.

Lane, T., Stroshal, V. and Woldorf, P. (1982) Standards of care for the CAPD patient, *Nephrology Nurse*, Vol. 4, No. 5, pp. 34–45.

Ludlam, H. A., Young, A. E., Berry, A. J. *et al.* (1989) The prevention of infection with *Staphylococcus aureus* in continuous ambulatory peritoneal dialysis, *Journal of Hospital Infection*, November, Vol. 14, pp. 293–301.

Powers, A. M. (1981) Renal transplantation: the patient's choice, *Nursing Clinics of North America*, Vol. 16, No. 3, pp. 551–64.

Ward, E. (1986) Dialysis or death? Doctors should stop covering up for an inadequate health service, *Journal of Medical Ethics*, Vol. 12, June, pp. 61–3.

Renal Disorders

Cameron, J. S. (1986) Acute renal failure in the intensive care unit today, *Intensive Care Medicine*, Vol. 12, No. 2, pp. 64–70.

Coccarelli, C. M. (1981) Haemolytic therapy for the patient with chronic renal failure, *Nursing Clinics of North America*, Vol. 16, No. 3, pp. 531–550.

Lewis, S. M. (1981) Pathophysiology of chronic renal failure, *Nursing Clinics of North America*, Vol. 16, No. 3, pp. 501–13.

McConnell, E. A. (1982) Urinalysis: A common test but never routine, *Nursing 82*, Vol. 12, No. 2, pp. 108–11.

Murphy, L. M. and Cole, M. J. (1983) Renal disease: Nutritional implications, *Nursing Clinics of North America*, Vol. 18, No. 1, pp. 57–70.

Pickering, L. and Robbins, D. (1980) Fluid, electrolyte and acid–base balance in the renal patient, *Nursing Clinics of North America*, Vol. 15, No. 3, pp. 577–92.

Stark, J. L. (1982) How to succeed against acute renal failure, *Nursing 82*, Vol. 12, No. 7, pp. 26–33.

Urology and Urinary Tract Disorders

Barrett, N. (1981) Cancer of the bladder, *American Journal of Nursing*, Vol. 81, No. 12, pp. 2192–5.

Blannin, J. P. (1984) Assessment of an incontinent patient, *Nursing*, Vol. 2, September, pp. 863–5.

Clark, N. and O'Connell, P. (1984) Prostatectomy: a guide to answering your patient's unspoken questions, *Nursing*, Vol. 84, No. 14, pp. 48–51.

Cole, R. S. and Shuttleworth, K. E. D. (1988) Is extracorporeal shockwave lithotripsy suitable treatment for lower ureteric stones? *British Journal of Urology*, Vol. 62, pp. 525–30.

Gooch, J. (1986) Catheter care, *The Professional Nurse*, Vol. 1, May, pp. 207–8.

Gooch, J. (1986) Care of the urinary incontinent patient, *The Professional Nurse*, Vol. 1, August, pp. 298–300.

Granise, C. A. (1984) Indwelling catheter care: a run-through, *Nursing*, Vol. 84, pp. 26–7.

Gould, D. (1985) Management of indwelling urethral catheters: a report on research, *Nursing Mirror*, Vol. 161, 4 September, pp. 17–18, 20.

Johnson, A. (1986) Urinary tract infection, *Nursing*, Vol. 3, March, pp. 102–5.

Killion, A. (1982) Reducing risk of infection from indwelling urethral catheters, *Nursing 82*, Vol. 15, No. 5, pp. 26–30.

Latham, E. and Marden, W. (1986) Percutaneous Nephrolithotripsy, *Nursing Times*, Vol. 82, 18 June, pp. 65–6.

Mitchell, J. P. (1984) Management of chronic urinary retention, *British Medical Journal*, Vol. 289, September, pp. 515–6.

Norton, C. (1984) The promotion of continence, *Nursing Times*, *Incontinence Supplement*, Vol. 80, 4 April, pp. 4, 6, 8, 10.

Tattersall, A. (1985) Continence: getting the whole picture. A holistic approach to continence promotion, *Nursing Times*, Vol. 81, 3 April, pp. 55, 57–8.

Webb, C. (1984) Promoting continence: how would you feel? The effects of incontinence on sexuality, *Community Outlook*, February, pp. 45–6.

Winder, A. (1986) Intermittent self-catheterization, *The Professional Nurse*, Vol. 2, No. 2, p. 58.

chapter *22*

ASSESSMENT AND CARE OF FEMALE PATIENTS DURING THE REPRODUCTIVE CYCLE

ANATOMY AND PHYSIOLOGY

The female reproductive system consists of two ovaries, two uterine tubes, uterus and vagina. The vulva is the region of the external genitalia; it includes two thick folds of tissue called the labia majora and two smaller lips of delicate tissue called the labia minora, which lie within the labia majora. The upper portions of the labia minora unite to form a partial covering for the clitoris, a highly sensitive organ made of erectile tissue. Between the labia minora, below and posterior to the clitoris, is the urinary meatus, the external opening of the female urethra, measuring approximately 3 cm. Below this is the vagina (Figure 22.1). Either side of the vagina is a vestibular (Bartholin's) gland, a bean-sized structure. The opening of the duct is found within the labia minora, external to the hymen. The tissue between the external genitalia and the anus is called the perineum.

The vagina is a canal approximately 7.5 to 10 cm long, extending downwards and forwards from the uterus to the vulva. The bladder lies anteriorly to the vagina; the rectum is posterior. The walls of the vagina normally lie in contact with one another. The upper part of the vagina, the fornix, surrounds the cervix (the neck of the uterus).

The uterus is a pear-shaped muscular organ approximately 7.5 cm long and about 5 cm wide. Its walls are about 1.25 cm thick. The uterus is divided into a narrow cervix, projecting into the vagina, and the fundus or body, covered posteriorly and partly anteriorly by peritoneum. The uterus lies posterior to the bladder and is held in position in the pelvic cavity by ligaments. The round ligaments extend anteriorly and laterally to the internal inguinal ring and down the inguinal canal, where they blend with the tissues of the labia majora. The broad ligaments are folds of peritoneum extending from the lateral pelvic walls and enveloping the uterine tubes. The uterosacral ligaments extend posteriorly to the sacrum, and the uterovesical ligaments pass anteriorly.

The ovaries, lying behind the broad ligament, are oval

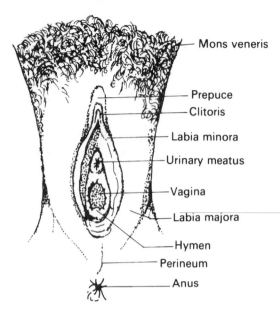

Figure 22.1 External female genitalia. (Chaffee, E. E. and Greisheimer, E. M. (1974) *Basic Physiology and Anatomy*, J. B. Lippincott, Philadelphia.)

in shape, and 2.5 to 5 cm long. Collectively, the ovaries and uterine tubes are called the adnexa (Figure 22.2).

Each ovary contains approximately 40,000 ova, which begin to mature when the girl reaches puberty (12 to 14 years). Each cyst enlarges until it reaches the surface of the ovary, where rupture occurs, and the ovum is discharged into the peritoneal cavity. This periodic discharge of matured ova is referred to as ovulation. The ovum usually finds its way into the uterine tube, where it is carried to the uterus. If it meets a spermatozoon, a union occurs and conception takes place. Following the discharge of the ovum, the cells of the graafian follicle undergo a rapid change. Gradually they become yellow (corpus luteum) and produce progesterone that prepares the uterus for the reception of the fertilized ovum.

If conception does not occur, the ovum dies and the endometrial lining of the uterus, which has become thickened and highly vascular, is shed as menstrual loss. Menstruation occurs approximately every 28 days throughout the fertile years. Each menstrual period lasts four to five days, and about 75 ml of blood are lost. Ovulation usually occurs 13 to 14 days before the first day of menstruation.

The menopause is the last menstrual period, usually experienced between the ages of 45 and 55 years. Ultimately, the breasts and reproductive organs atrophy, although this may take several years. During the climacteric, the time before the menopause, emotional distress may occur and women may complain of vasomotor disturbances ('hot flushes').

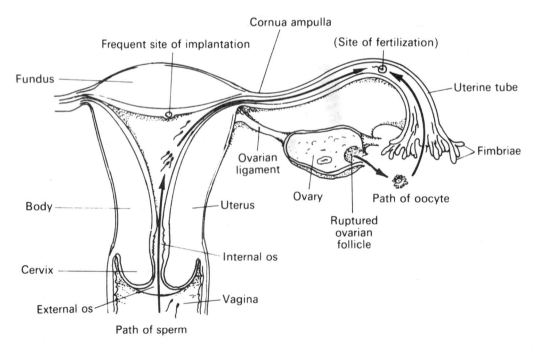

Figure 22.2 The female reproductive organs, showing path of oocyte from ovary into uterine tube, path of spermatozoa and the usual site of fertilization. (Chaffee, E. E. and Greisheimer, E. M. (1974) *Basic Physiology and Anatomy*, J. B. Lippincott, Philadelphia.)

HEALTH MAINTENANCE

Women are becoming increasingly conscious of health education and the value of a healthy lifestyle. Nurses are in a key position to provide information about diet, contraception, damaging health practices (for example, smoking and alcohol abuse), physical exercise and interventions designed to relieve stress. They can also point out the importance of good personal hygiene, taking into consideration the individual views and cultural and religious persuasions of women. Instruction about sexually transmitted disease may also be provided by nurses.

ASSESSMENT

Nursing History

Women with gynaecological conditions require sensitive nursing care because emotional considerations are as important as physical outcome. Women may feel embarrassed about physical examination of the genitourinary system and discussion of sexual practices. Explanations of anatomy and of the outcome of procedures such as sterilization may be required. The decision to undergo a particular treatment must rest with the individual woman, recognizing that this may be influenced by religious or cultural factors. Gynaecological conditions are often of a very personal and private nature, and this must be accepted by the nurse, who must treat any information given about or by the patient as highly confidential.

Pelvic Examination

In the United Kingdom, pelvic examination is usually performed by a doctor. The nurse prepares the woman for examination and is present to provide support throughout, as well as to assist the doctor. After the examination, the nurse may provide explanations and clarify information given by the doctor.

Although several positions may be used for performing the pelvic examination, the supine lithotomy position is used most frequently. A newer technique employs the lithotomy position in which the woman assumes a semi-sitting stance. This position offers several advantages: (1) it is more comfortable; (2) it allows better eye contact between patient and examiner; (3) it provides an easier means for the examiner to carry out the bimanual examination; and (4) it enables the woman to use a mirror to see her anatomy, note the presence of any lesions and learn methods for certain types of contraceptive techniques (Swartz, 1984).

In the Sims' position, the patient lies on her left side, with her left arm behind her and her right leg bent at a 90-degree angle. The right labia may be retracted for adequate access to the vagina.

The patient is asked to void before the pelvic examination. The urine is retained if a urine specimen is part of the total assessment procedure. The patient is then placed on the examination couch, with her feet together and knees flexed and separated; she is encouraged to relax so that her buttocks are presented at the edge of the examination table and her thighs are spread as widely apart as possible. The patient is appropriately draped to avoid embarrassment. The following equipment is necessary: good light source, vaginal speculum, unsterile gloves, lubricant, spatula, cotton-tipped applicators, glass slides and fixative solution.

When the patient is prepared, the labia majora and minora are examined. The epidermal tissue of the labia majora, with its hair follicles characteristic of skin, fades to the pink mucous membrane of the vaginal introitus. In the nulliparous woman the labia minora should come together at the opening of the vagina. In women who have borne children, the labia minora may gape, and vaginal tissue may protrude. The patient is asked to 'bear down'. Obstetric damage to the anterior vaginal wall may have resulted in muscular weakness, so that a bulge representing bladder intrusion into the submucosa of the anterior vaginal wall may be seen. This is called a cystocele. Birth trauma may also have affected the posterior vaginal wall, so that a bulge representing the cavity of the rectum may protrude, presenting as a rectocele. The cervix or the uterus itself may descend under pressure through the vaginal canal and present itself at the introitus. This is termed prolapse of the uterus.

The introitus should be free of hair follicles and of superficial mucosal lesions. The labia minora may be separated by the fingers of the gloved hand and the lower part of the vagina palpated. In virginal women, a hymen of variable thickness may be felt circumferentially within 1 or 2 cm of the vaginal opening. The hymenal ring will usually permit the admission of two fingers but occasionally is sufficiently restricting so that only one finger may enter the vagina. Rarely, the hymen totally occludes the vaginal entrance. In nonvirginal women, a rim of scar tissue representing the remnants of the hymenal ring may be felt circumferentially around the vagina near its opening. The greater vestibular glands (Bartholin's glands) lie between the labia minora and the remnants of the hymenal ring. These glands frequently become infected in gonococcal disease. Patients may occasionally present with an abscess of one of these glands.

Speculum Examination

Assorted sizes of the bivalved speculum are available in metal or plastic. A metal speculum is warmed with running tap water to make it less uncomfortable when it is inserted. The speculum is not lubricated, since lubrication with commercial jellies may interfere with cervical

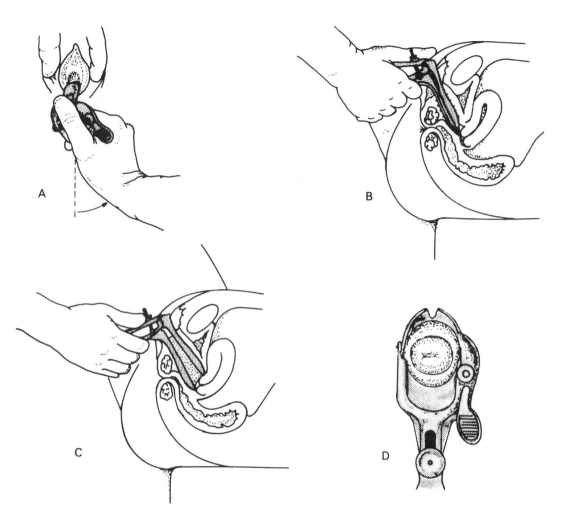

Figure 22.3 Speculum examination of the vagina and cervix. (A) The labia are spread apart with a gloved left hand, while the speculum is grasped in the right hand and turned anticlockwise before being inserted into the vagina. (B) The closed speculum is inserted into the vagina. (C) The blades of the speculum are then spread apart to reveal the cervical os, as shown in D.

cytology. The technique for speculum examination of the vagina and cervix is shown in Figure 22.3.

The cervix is inspected. In nulliparous women, the cervical os is 2 to 3 mm in diameter and smooth. Women who have borne children may have a laceration, usually transverse, frequently giving the cervical os a 'fishmouth' appearance. Moreover, epithelium from the endocervical canal may have grown out onto the surface of the cervix, appearing as beefy red surface epithelium circumferentially arranged around the os. This is commonly called a cervical erosion. Although not always differentiable from a cervical carcinoma, the cervical erosion is, in general, less sharply outlined than malignant tissue. Indeed, malignant change may not be obviously differentiated from the remainder of the cervical mucosa. The presence of endo-

cervical epithelium around the cervical os can lead to chronic infection and discharge from the orifice. Swabs should be taken if necessary, placed in culture medium and sent to the laboratory. Small cysts may appear on the surface of the cervix under these circumstances. These are usually bluish and are termed nabothian cysts. A polyp of endocervical mucosa may protrude through the os and appears dark red. A carcinoma may appear as a cauliflower-like growth. It is friable and will bleed easily when traumatized. A bluish colour of the cervix is a sign of early pregnancy (Chadwick's sign).

The vagina is examined as the speculum is withdrawn. It is smooth in young girls and becomes more thickened after puberty, with many rugae and much folding of the epithelium. Vaginal discharge may be present.

Bimanual Examination

The forefinger and middle finger of the gloved, lubricated hand are advanced vertically along the vaginal canal, and the vaginal wall is palpated. Firmness of any part of the vaginal wall may represent old scar tissue from obstetric trauma. Such tissue may be tender. Anterior tenderness or burning may represent urethritis associated with a urinary tract infection.

The cervix is palpated and noted for its consistency, mobility, size and position. The normal cervix is uniformly firm but not hard. Softening of the cervix and elongation of the cervical canal are seen in early pregnancy. Hardness may reflect invasion by neoplasia. The cervix and uterus are normally freely movable. Fixation in the pelvis may reflect extension of malignancy. The body of the uterus is normally twice the diameter and twice the length of the cervix. The body may be felt on either side of the cervix, curving anteriorly toward the abdominal wall. One in five women will, however, have a retroflexed uterus, which curves posteriorly toward the sacrum.

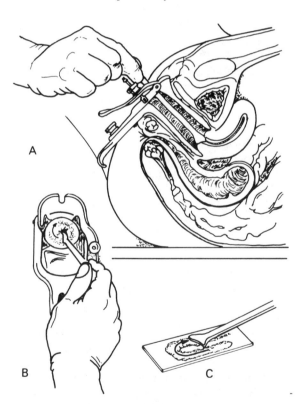

Figure 22.4 Method for obtaining a cervical smear. (A) Speculum in place and the Ayre spatula in position at the cervical os. (B) The tip of the spatula is placed in the cervical os and the spatula rotated 360 degrees, firmly but nontraumatically. (C) Cellular material clinging to the spatula is then smeared smoothly on a glass slide, which is promptly placed in a fixative solution.

The opposite hand is now placed halfway between the umbilicus and the pubis and pressed firmly toward the opening of the pelvis. If the uterus is in an appropriate position, movement of the abdominal wall will cause the body of the uterus to descend and the pear-shaped organ will be freely movable between the abdominal hand and the examining fingers of the pelvic hand. A reasonably accurate impression can be gained of the size, mobility and regularity of the contour of the uterus.

The right and left parametria are now palpated. The tube and ovary are contained within these structures. The fingers of the pelvic hand are moved first to one side, then to the other, while the abdominal hand is moved correspondingly to either side of the abdomen. The adnexa are trapped between the two examining hands and are palpated for an obvious mass, tenderness of adnexal tissue and mobility of the parametrial contents.

It is common for the ovaries to be slightly tender. Bimanual palpation of the vagina and rectovaginal pouch is accomplished by placing the index finger in the vagina and the middle finger in the rectum. A gentle movement of these fingers towards each other compresses the posterior vaginal wall and the anterior rectal wall and assists the examiner in identifying the integrity of these structures. This procedure may give the patient the sensation of having a bowel movement. The examiner reassures the patient that although she has the urge to defaecate, she is not in fact doing so.

To prevent cross-contamination between the vaginal and rectal orifices, the examiner changes gloves between these examinations.

Diagnosis

Tests Performed During the Gynaecological Examination

Cervical Cytology

The purpose of this test is to detect premalignant and malignant lesions. Some cells shed from the cervical os are gently scraped away with an Ayre spatula (see Figure 22.4), transferred to a glass slide and placed in fixative. A technician examines the slide and the cells are classified as shown in Table 22.1. If a finding is abnormal, colposcopy is indicated.

Endometrial Aspiration (Vabra Curettage)

Endometrial aspiration is performed to obtain endometrial cells and secretions for histological examination. The way the endometrium is responding to cyclical hormone stimulation may be determined. Some gynaecologists do not consider that it is adequate to detect endometrial malignancy, and dilatation and curettage (D&C) is performed if cancer is suspected.

Endometrial biopsy is done as an outpatient procedure.

Table 22.1 *The cervical intraepithelial (CIN) staging system (premalignant) and the clinical staging system for cervical carcinoma (malignant)*

Stage	Histological change	Treatment	
CIN I	Mild dysplasia (reversible)	Laser	
CIN II	Moderate dysplasia	Laser	Completely curable
CIN III	Severe dysplasia grading into overt early malignancy, not yet invasive	Laser/cone biopsy	

Stage	Clinical staging	Treatment	Five-year survival rate
0	Malignancy not yet invasive	Cone biopsy	Curable
1	Limited to cervix		81%
2	Spread to upper third of vagina/ lower part of uterus	Wertheim's hysterectomy	60%
3	Involvement of parametrium	Radiotherapy	30%
4	Infiltration of bladder/rectum/ distant metastases	Sometimes with palliative surgery	8%

Note: CIN III and Stage 0 of malignant disease overlap.
Reprinted by kind permission, Prentice Hall International. Taken from Gould, D. (1990) Nursing Care of Women.

It can usually be done without anaesthesia; however, a paracervical block is effective if required. A sound is inserted into the uterus followed by a thin, hollow curette. Suction is performed to obtain the specimen.

Schiller Test

With the patient in the lithotomy position (cervix exposed by speculum), a long cotton-tipped applicator is used to paint the cervix with aqueous iodine solution. The appearance of a mahogany-brown colour covering the entire surface indicates a reaction between the iodine and the glycogen of normal cells. Such a reaction is considered negative. If the cervix is abnormal, immature cells are present and tissues are not stained brown, indicating that the test is positive. The absence of staining directs attention to the sites requiring additional study (i.e., biopsy), such as those related to cancer, scars, erosion and zones of non-malignant leucoplakia.

Cervical Biopsy

The type and extent of biopsy of the cervix vary according to the abnormality or to the results of an abnormal cervical smear. When a lesion is clearly visible or can be seen with a magnifying instrument called a colposcope, one or more punch biopsies may be done without anaesthesia because the cervix is less sensitive to cutting procedures than the vagina. For more extensive lesions, biopsy of an inverted cone of tissue (cone biopsy) is performed (see Chapter 23).

Dilatation and Curettage

Dilatation and curettage (D&C) involves widening of the cervical canal with a dilator to obtain endometrial scrapings for cytological examination. It is also performed as a therapeutic measure for incomplete abortion.

The procedure is usually performed under general anaesthesia. The nurse's role is to ensure that the woman understands the doctor's explanations and to provide psychological support.

Perineal shaving is not necessarily performed today; damage to the adjacent bladder and bowel are avoided by asking the woman to empty her bladder immediately before being taken to theatre. The bowel is emptied using suppositories.

Postoperatively, the patient must be observed carefully for shock and excessive bleeding. Pulse and blood pressure are monitored every 30 minutes until stable, and the sanitary pad is inspected for vaginal loss. Mild analgesia may be required, and the remainder of the day is spent resting in bed. Postoperatively, there are no dietary restrictions once the effects of the anaesthetic have worn off.

Endoscopic Examinations

Laparoscopy

A laparoscope is a fibreoptic instrument approximately 10 mm in diameter and is inserted into the peritoneal cavity via a 2 cm subumbilical incision while the woman is anaesthetized in theatre (Figure 22.5). It allows direct visualization of the pelvic structures, lower abdomen and intestines. This is facilitated by the injection of a small amount of carbon dioxide into the peritoneum (insufflation) to separate the intestines from the pelvic organs. Minor surgical procedures such as tube ligation (sterilization), ovarian biopsy and separation of peritubal adhesions, may be performed via the laparoscope. Dilatation and curettage is usually performed at the same time as laparoscopy to provide an endometrial biopsy, and

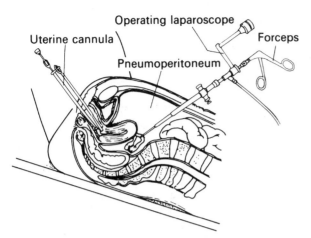

Figure 22.5 Laparoscopy. The laparoscope (on the right) is inserted through a small incision in the abdomen. A forceps is inserted through the scope to grasp the uterine tube. To improve the view, a uterine cannula (on the left) is inserted into the vagina to push the uterus upward. Insufflation of gas creates an air pocket (pneumoperitoneum), and the pelvis is elevated (note the angle), which forces the intestines higher in the abdomen.

because the presence of an intrauterine sound permits manipulation of the uterus, improving visualization. At the end of the procedure, the laparoscope is withdrawn, the carbon dioxide is allowed to escape through the cannula and the incision is closed with clips or sutures. A dressing is applied.

On return to the ward, the patient's pulse, blood pressure and vaginal loss are monitored half-hourly until her condition is stable.

Culdoscopy

Culdoscopy is not often performed in the United Kingdom. It is a diagnostic procedure in which an incision is made into the rectovaginal pouch, so that the culdoscope can be inserted to visualize the uterus, tubes, broad ligaments, uterosacral ligaments, rectal wall, sigmoid and small intestines.

● The woman is prepared as for any vaginal operation.
● Anaesthesia may be local, general or regional.
● The woman is placed in the knee–chest position.
● After the examination, when the culdoscope is withdrawn and the sutures have been inserted, the woman returns to the ward.

Hysteroscopy

Hysteroscopy permits direct endoscopic visualization of the uterine cavity. Fibreoptic lighting and distension of the uterine cavity with dextrose solution optimize visualization.

This procedure is used mainly to complement other

diagnostic procedures when diagnosis is difficult, as follows:

● Infertility.
● Uterine bleeding of unknown aetiology.
● To detect the presence of foreign bodies, e.g., fibroids or intrauterine device, which may be removed during the procedure.
● To diagnose and separate intrauterine adhesions.

Contraindications for hysteroscopy include:

1. Pelvic infection.
2. Uterine perforation.
3. Pregnancy, because it may be disturbed. In this case there is also the risk of infection.

Colposcopy

Colposcopy is the stereoscopic examination of the cervix using a binocular instrument of low magnification (10 to 25 times) with strong illumination.

The purposes of colposcopy are:

1. To identify distribution of abnormal squamous epithelium.
2. To identify areas from which tissue biopsy may be obtained.

Colposcopy is indicated in the following cases:

● After atypical vaginal or cervical cytology.
● When possibly malignant or premalignant cervical lesions are present.
● When there has been previous treatment of malignant or premalignant cervical lesions.

Before colposcopy became available, women had to undergo cone biopsy or dilatation and curettage.

Preparation for colposcopy is the same as for a woman undergoing pelvic examination, but with a careful explanation by the nurse of the longer length of the procedure. Women should be told that biopsy may be performed, as this is sometimes painful and will be followed by bleeding.

During the procedure, the gynaecologist may perform the following actions:

● Dry the cervix using a long cotton application stick, to clear away mucus and other secretions.
● Swab the cervix with saline. Moistening the cervical epithelium reveals the presence of blood vessels and the junction between the squamous and columnar epithelium.
● Examine the cervix via the colposcope.
● Paint the cervix with 3 per cent acetic acid, which digests mucus, thus enhancing visualization.
● Inspect colposcopic patterns, especially the transformation zone where squamous and columnar epithelia meet. Acetic acid draws moisture from tissues of high nuclear density; thus, cells undergoing rapid mitosis,

which are likely to be undergoing malignant change, are more readily detected.

- Perform punch biopsy of suspicious lesions (the nurse should warn the woman when biopsy is about to take place). The cervix contains few nerve endings and, in theory, biopsy should be associated with minimal discomfort, but in practice this is not always so.
- If bleeding occurs, direct pressure will usually control it. Suturing may be required for persistent bleeding.

The woman is provided with a sterile sanitary towel, and follow-up is organized. As for any pelvic examination, the woman should be told to contact the clinic or her doctor should bleeding continue for more than two or three days. She should know when to expect the results of biopsy and the date of her next appointment.

X-Ray Studies

Hysterosalpingogram
This is an X-ray examination of the uterus and uterine tubes following the injection of contrast medium through the cervical os. Its purpose is to identify possible causes of infertility, e.g., tubal occlusion, bicornuate uterus.

The procedure involves the following steps:

- The woman is placed on the X-ray table in the lithotomy position.
- The cervix is exposed with a bivalve speculum.
- Contrast medium is injected via a cannula into the uterine cavity.
- X-rays are taken.
- The presence of uterine lesions will be shown on the X-ray screen. If the tubes are patent, the contrast medium is seen to escape via the fimbriae.

After the procedure the woman should be advised to rest before going home. She may require analgesia, because hysterosalpingography is a painful procedure. A sanitary pad should be worn as the contrast medium will stain clothing.

THE MENSTRUAL CYCLE

Physiology

Ovarian Hormones
The ovaries are the female gonads, responsible for producing ova (reproductive function) and oestrogens and progesterone, which are steroid hormones (endocrine function).

The most important oestrogen is oestradiol, released by the ovarian follicle. It is responsible for the development and maintenance of the female reproductive organs, breasts and the secondary sexual characteristics typical of

the adult female, as well as helping to control the menstrual cycle.

Progesterone, secreted by the corpus luteum left after the escape of the ovum following ovulation, prepares the endometrium to receive a fertilized egg during the second half of the menstrual cycle. If pregnancy occurs, progesterone secretion becomes a function of the placenta. It is vital in the maintenance of pregnancy and prepares the breasts for lactation.

Androgens are also secreted in small amounts by the ovaries, but little is known about their function.

Control of Ovarian Secretion
Secretion of the sex steroids is controlled by two hormones released from the anterior pituitary—follicle-stimulating hormone (FSH) and luteinizing hormone (LH). The control of these hormones is in turn regulated by feedback mechanisms. Increased plasma levels of oestrogen inhibit follicle-stimulating hormone secretion by promoting luteinizing hormone secretion.

Menstrual Cycle
Secretion of ovarian hormones follows a cyclic pattern that results in changes of the endometrium and in menstruation (Figure 22.6). At the beginning of the cycle (just after menstruation), follicle-stimulating hormone output is increased and oestrogen secretion is stimulated. This causes the endometrium to thicken and become more vascular. Near the middle portion of the cycle, luteinizing hormone output increases and progesterone secretion is stimulated. It is at this time that ovulation occurs. Under the combined stimulus of oestrogen and progesterone, the endometrium reaches its peak of thickening and vascularization. If the ovum has been fertilized, oestrogen and progesterone levels remain high and the complex hormonal changes of pregnancy follow. If fertilization has not occurred, the output of follicle-stimulating hormone and luteinizing hormone diminishes; secretion of oestrogen and progesterone falls rapidly; and the vascularized, thickened endometrium is sloughed, with resultant vaginal bleeding (menstruation). The cycle then recommences.

Psychosocial Considerations

Young girls approaching the menarche (onset of menstruation) should know what to expect and be taught to regard menstruation as a normal physiological process. Although most women probably experience some pelvic pain (dysmenorrhoea) associated with their periods at some time or another, pelvic discomfort and backache are likely to be diminished by adequate nutrition, good posture and a balance between rest and exercise. Slight deviations from the usual pattern of daily living are considered normal during menstruation. Mild analgesia may be required, and mood swings are sometimes apparent.

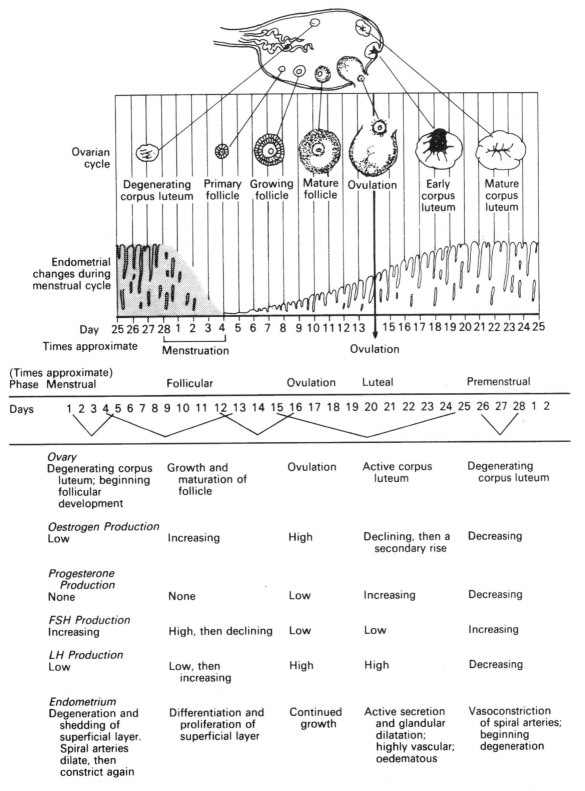

Figure 22.6 The menstrual cycle. Correlation of hormonal activities with ovarian and uterine changes. (Adapted from Chaffee, E. E. and Greisheimer, E. M. (1974) *Basic Physiology and Anatomy* (3rd edition), J. B. Lippincott, Philadelphia.)

Severe pain and incapacitation merit investigation, as this is not normal. Girls should be aware that menstruation does not increase vulnerability to illness, and need not interfere with sports or swimming. However, nurses must be aware that menstruation may be regarded differently in different cultures, and that it is surrounded by numerous myths and taboos.

Premenstrual Syndrome

Premenstrual syndrome (PMS) is a combination of symptoms experienced by some women before the onset of menstruation. The aetiology is unknown, but several theories suggest oestrogen–progesterone imbalance, vitamin deficiencies, excessive prostaglandins and/or abnormal magnesium metabolism. Major symptoms include headache, fatigue, low back pain, engorged or painful breasts and a feeling of abdominal fullness. General irritability may even include mood swings, fear of losing control, binge eating and crying spells. Symptoms vary widely from one woman to another and from one cycle to the next in the same person. A generally stressful life appears related to the intensity of physical symptoms. Women report moderate to severe life disruption, affecting interpersonal exchanges among family members. Premenstrual syndrome is regarded by some people as a factor in reduced productivity, work-related accidents and absenteeism.

The timing of the above symptoms is what helps in determining diagnosis. Symptoms recur regularly at the same phase of each menstrual cycle and, in the same cycle, are followed by a symptom-free phase.

Management

No single effective treatment for premenstrual syndrome so far exists. Symptoms are treated as they occur. Gynaecologists prescribe analgesia as required, diuretics to help reduce fluid retention, natural progesterone or vitamin supplements. Women may be encouraged to record their own symptoms so that they participate in their own care and recognize that they are not to 'blame' for premenstrual syndrome (Figure 22.7).

► NURSING PROCESS
► THE PATIENT WITH PREMENSTRUAL SYNDROME

► Treatment and Nursing Care

The nurse should establish rapport with the women when taking a nursing history to establish the particular symptoms experienced, onset in relation to the menses and severity. The nurse may ask the woman whether premenstrual syndrome was first experienced or became exacerbated following pregnancy, tubal ligation or after discontinuing oral contraceptives. Symptoms may be

	Jan	Feb	Mar	Apr
1				
2				
3				
4				
5				
6		h		
7				
8				
9				
10				
11				
12				
13			Hd	
14			HD	
15			HD	
16		D	HD	
17		Hd	Md	
18	d	HD	M	
19	Hd	HD	M	
20	D	M	M	
21	HD	M	M	
22	HD	M		
23	Mh	M		
24	M			
25	M			
26	M			
27	M			
28				
29				
30				
31				

Figure 22.7 Chart for recording timing and pattern of premenstrual symptoms as an aid to diagnosis of premenstrual syndrome. Capital letters signify intense symptoms; lowercase letters, mild symptoms. M, menstruation; H, h, headache; D, d, depressive symptoms. (Lindemann, J. C. (1984) *Premenstrual syndrome—a practical approach*, Wisc. Med. J., Vol. 83, No. 11, p. 32.)

exacerbated by vitamin deficiency (especially B$_6$) or excessive intake of salt, alcohol or caffeine, which are diuretics.

Keeping a chart to record the timing of premenstrual symptoms may help (Figure 22.7). The chart should be maintained for at least three cycles. Some measures that have been reported as being beneficial include:

● Whenever possible, avoiding stressful activities at times when premenstrual syndrome is likely to occur. The woman's partner and children may be encouraged to provide support and help with this.

- Maintaining the 'premenstrual diary'. (However, diary-keeping may cause a woman to focus more attention on her symptoms and therefore be counterproductive.)
- Eating small, nutritious meals, restricting fluid and salt intake and avoiding caffeine and alcohol. A hypoglycaemic diet has been reported as being helpful.
- Taking vitamin B$_6$ supplements. These may be prescribed or can be purchased from health food shops, for example, as evening primrose oil. Calcium and magnesium supplements may also be prescribed.
- Encouraging exercise and relaxation.
- Providing the address of a self-help group (see Useful Addresses).

Dysmenorrhoea

Dysmenorrhoea is painful menstruation. There are two types, primary and secondary dysmenorrhoea.

Primary Dysmenorrhoea
This condition is very common among young women, but can occur in women in their late 20s and 30s, especially those who have not had children. It appears to be related to the establishment of ovulatory cycles. The pain is due to uterine spasm and is usually colicky or a dull ache experienced in the lower abdomen, sometimes radiating down the back of the legs. It may severe enough for the woman to require bedrest for a few days. Very severe pain is associated with headache, diarrhoea, vomiting and fainting.

Aetiology. The cause of primary dysmenorrhoea is unknown, but excess production of prostaglandins from the endometrium is likely to be a causative or contributory factor. Prostaglandins have been isolated in large quantities from the menstrual loss of women with primary dysmenorrhoea. The systemic effects of prostaglandins include vomiting and diarrhoea. It is also widely believed that a small, poorly developed uterus and general ill health are associated with dysmenorrhoea, but this has never been proven. Healthy attitudes towards menstruation promoted among young women are said to be associated with low incidence of pain.

Treatment and Nursing Care. Since there is no single treatment for dysmenorrhoea, a three-pronged approach seems best to relieve symptoms: combine therapies as they relate to constitutional, hormonal and psychological factors.

1. Be selective, according to the needs of the individual and the severity of the problem.
   a. Proper psychological preparation of girls for menarche.
   b. Good posture; use special exercises to improve posture and correct weak musculature and imbalance.
2. Complete physical examination to rule out other physical abnormalities.

3. Instructions to patient:
   a. Usual activity is possible—and should be encouraged.
   b. Mild analgesics for discomfort are permissible, e.g., aspirin, paracetamol.
   c. Avoid the use of habit-forming drugs such as narcotics and alcohol.
4. Dysmenorrhoea can usually be eliminated by low-dose oral contraceptives that block ovulation.
5. Regular exercises (as well as physical activity) are recommended.
6. Administration of a prostaglandin inhibitor such as ibuprofen, mefenamic acid or naproxen sodium are recommended in relieving primary dysmenorrhoea.
   a. Medications are to be taken with water; milk may be used if the medication causes an upset stomach.
   b. If medication causes drowsiness or sleepiness, the woman should not drive a car or operate machinery.
7. Psychological counselling may also benefit some individuals.

Secondary Dysmenorrhoea
The distribution of this pain is often somewhat different from that associated with primary dysmenorrhoea, with headaches and backache featuring more prominently. It is always due to some secondary factor such as endometriosis, uterine fibroids or an intrauterine device. The underlying condition should be treated.

Amenorrhoea

Amenorrhoea is the absence of menstrual flow.

Primary Amenorrhoea
Primary amenorrhoea is said to occur when a girl is 16 or 17 years old and has not menstruated. This may be due to embryonic maldevelopment; treatment is according to aetiology.

Secondary Dysmenorrhoea
Secondary dysmenorrhoea is said to occur when menstruation has begun (initial menarche) but then stops.

1. Criteria:
   a. No bleeding for 6 months after having regular cyclic bleeding.
   b. No bleeding for 12 months after a history of irregular bleeding.
2. Causes:
   a. Normal pregnancy and lactation.
   b. Psychogenic (minor emotional upsets). Hypothalamic disturbances (autonomic nervous system) may also be the cause (e.g., anorexia nervosa).
   c. Constitutional (any disturbance of metabolism and nutrition, for example, diabetes, tuberculosis, obesity).

d. Exercise-related—rigorous involvement.
3. Assessment:
   a. Progesterone challenge test:
      i. Positive—if bleeding (or even 'spotting'); anovulation is most likely;
      ii. Negative—no bleeding occurs; indication of end organ failure. Other tests are indicated.
4. Treatment—directed at cause: constitutional therapy, psychotherapy, hormone therapy or surgery.

Abnormal Uterine Bleeding

Menorrhagia

Menorrhagia is excessive bleeding during menstruation at the time when monthly bleeding is expected.

The causes of menorrhagia may include the following:

- An endocrine disturbance, probably an imbalance between plasma oestrogen and progesterone levels. This is often described as 'dysfunctional uterine bleeding'.
- Benign or malignant pelvic tumours. Fibroids are the most common cause.
- Endometriosis.

Treatment is of the underlying cause; any haematological deficiency must be corrected.

Metrorrhagia

Metrorrhagia is the appearance of blood from the uterus between the regular menstrual periods or after menopause. It is always the symptom of some disease, often cancer or benign tumours of the uterus; therefore, it merits early diagnosis and treatment. Metrorrhagia is probably the most significant form of menstrual dysfunction; the fact that it occurs warrants further investigation.

The Menopause

The menopause is the time of the last menstrual period. It is caused by ovarian failure, and the symptoms that many women experience around this time are due to oestrogen withdrawal.

The climacteric is the transitional or perimenopausal period during which the woman's reproductive function gradually diminishes. It usually occurs between the ages of 45 and 55 years (average 51 to 52 years).

Clinical Features

- Menstrual flow in most women gradually decreases with each successive month, and then ceases altogether.
- Hot flushes and other vasomotor disturbances are reported by many women. These are a consequence of oestrogen withdrawal and are an early sign of the menopause.

- Later in the postmenopausal period, longer-term effects of oestrogen withdrawal gradually become apparent; sagging breasts and reproductive structures, loss of skin elasticity, occasionally stress incontinence and calcium deficiency, leading to osteoporosis, atrophic vaginitis and dyspareunia.
- Symptoms are more rapid in onset and more severe if the ovaries are removed or destroyed by irradiation.

Management

Most women respond positively when time is taken by the nurse to explain that the menopause is a normal physiological event that is not inevitably accompanied by ill health and nervous symptoms. Measures to promote general health are usually beneficial, although initially troublesome hot flushes may require hormone replacement therapy.

Medication usually consists of oestrogen and progesterone given for 25 days each month. Long-term administration of hormone replacement therapy to prevent other degenerative changes such as osteoporosis remains controversial because of the association between prolonged oestrogen therapy and neoplastic changes oestrogen-responsive tissues.

Patient Education

- Menopausal symptoms such as hot flushes resolve spontaneously even when hormone replacement therapy is not prescribed.
- Weight gain is not inevitable, especially if a sensible diet is adhered to and physical exercise is taken.
- Outside interests help to absorb anxiety and reduce tension.
- Social relationships can be expected to change for everyone in this age group; it is normal and desirable for children to become independent and leave home. This can be viewed in a positive light, as it allows time to be spent on new pursuits.
- The menopause does not indicate the end of the woman's sex life.

A number of physical discomforts may accompany the menopause, but self-help measures are efficacious:

1. A water-soluble lubricant helps to prevent dyspareunia.
2. Perineal muscle tone may be improved by daily pelvic floor exercises.
3. Bland lotions may be used to prevent dry, sore skin. Strongly scented preparations may be best avoided as they tend to exacerbate this problem.
4. A sensible diet combined with physical exercise prevents weight gain. Attention must be paid to calcium intake as a woman's requirement increases after the menopause (see Chapter 37).

CONTRACEPTION

Fertility control has been practised since ancient times. Many methods exist and their acceptance has fluctuated. An ideal method has not been developed; all have advantages and disadvantages. Most methods apply to women.

In the United Kingdom, contraceptives are provided free of charge under the NHS, although provision of the service is not uniform in all areas. Advice and supplies may be obtained at a family planning clinic organized by the local health authority, from a general practitioner who has received special training or from one of the private or charitable organizations such as the Marie Stopes Clinics, the British Pregnancy Advisory Service (BPAS) or the Brook Clinics, established to cater particularly for younger women.

Patient Education

The method of choice is likely to vary not only between one couple and another, but at different stages in the life cycle of the same couple. Factors such as religion and culture are likely to affect choice as well as age, parity and general health. Clients are more likely to use a method if they have chosen it themselves, understand how it works and have received clear explanations.

Natural Methods

The advantages of natural methods of contraception include the following: (1) they are not hazardous to health; (2) they are inexpensive; and (3) they are preferred by some religions. The disadvantages are that they require discipline by the couple and periods of abstinence. Also, they may be less effective than other methods. Abstinence or celibacy is the only completely effective means of preventing pregnancy. Coitus interruptus is the withdrawal of the penis from the vagina before ejaculation, which requires strong willpower. The uncertainty in this method is due to the presence of sperm in the pre-ejaculatory fluid.

Rhythm Method

The rhythm method of contraception can be difficult to use because it is based on the woman's ability to determine her time of ovulation and on the avoidance of intercourse during the fertile period. The fertile phase (when intercourse must be avoided) is estimated to occur about 14 days before menstruation, although it may occur between the tenth and seventeenth days. It is assumed that spermatozoa can fertilize an ovum three to five days after intercourse and that the ovum can be fertilized for about 24 hours after it leaves the ovary. Studies reveal that of 100 women practising the rhythm method, up to 40 will conceive during a year.

According to some researchers, if a woman carefully determines her 'safe period', based on precise recording of her menstrual dates for at least one year, and follows a carefully worked out formula, she may achieve 80 per cent protection. However, it requires a long period of abstinence during each cycle. New biochemical methods of detecting ovulation have improved statistics.

For ensuring success, the woman is encouraged to:

- Keep a daily chart recording the nature of cervical mucus; this changes as the menstrual cycle progresses.
- Check her temperature at waking (temperature rises for a few days after ovulation).
- Estimate when ovulation will occur based on past experience.

It is now possible to predict the time of ovulation by sampling cervical mucus using a colour-coded test kit. An enzyme, guaiacol peroxidase, in cervical mucus signals ovulation six days before it occurs.

Oral Contraception—'The Pill'

There are two types of oral contraceptive: the combined pill, containing oestrogen and a synthetic progestogen, and the progesterone-only pill (POP), which is less popular and slightly less effective. The combined pill operates by preventing ovulation, as the oestrogen it contains inhibits follicle-stimulating hormone, preventing ripening of the graafian follicle. Progestogen suppresses luteinizing hormone, inhibiting the luteinizing hormone surge and release of the egg. This form of contraception is taken for 21 days of the month. The woman is instructed to take the first pill on the first day of bleeding and to take one pill each day until the pack of 21 pills is completed.

The progesterone-only pill interferes with cervical mucus production and prevents the endometrium from developing sufficiently to receive a fertilized egg. Tablets are taken continuously, one every day.

Side-Effects

In a small percentage of women, side-effects may be noted, such as nausea, pelvic discomfort, backache, irritability, depression, headache, weight gain, leg cramps, breast soreness, hirsutism and acne. Usually, these disappear after three or four months. Because such symptoms are related to sodium and water retention caused by oestrogen, a smaller dose of the hormone and salt reduction in the diet may alleviate the problem.

Other problems encountered are the occurrence of thromboembolic disorders, more rapid growth of uterine fibroids and jaundice. Therefore, these drugs should not be used by women who have had thromboembolic disorders, uterine fibroids, diabetes or liver or gallbladder disease. Noted also is an increased incidence of heart attacks in smokers over the age of 35 who are on the pill. Occasionally, neuro-ocular complications arise, but a cause-and-effect relationship is unknown at present. Should visual disturbances occur, use of the pill should be terminated. An increased incidence of candidal vulvovaginitis has also been reported.

Fertility is delayed two to three months in approximately 20 per cent of users after stopping the pill. For some women it is longer; since ovulation may be delayed for varying periods, it is probably helpful (for calculating expected delivery date) for the woman desiring to become pregnant to use a mechanical contraceptive barrier for the first menstrual cycle.

The contraindications for the use of oral contraceptives are listed in Table 22.2.

Table 22.2 *Contraindications for the use of oral contraceptives*

Absolute contraindications
1. Known or suspected oestrogen-dependent neoplasia
2. Known or suspected cancer of the breast
3. Thrombophlebitis or thromboembolic disease
4. A history of thrombophlebitis, thromboembolism or thrombotic disease
5. Cerebrovascular and coronary artery disease
6. Abnormal uterine bleeding from an unknown cause
7. Known or suspected pregnancy

Other contraindications

Hypertension, hyperlipidaemia, diabetes mellitus, liver disease, cholestatic jaundice, amenorrhoea, migraine headache, leiomyoma of the uterus, cigarette smoking

Oral contraceptives are recommended mainly for young women; side-effects increase with age

Mechanical Barriers

Diaphragm
The diaphragm is an effective contraceptive device. It is a round flexible spring (50 to 90 mm in diameter) that is covered with a domelike latex rubber cup. A spermicidal jelly or cream is used to coat the concavity of the diaphragm before it is inserted deep into the vagina, covering the cervix. The combination of a diaphragm and spermicide prevents spermatozoa from entering the cervical canal. The diaphragm presents no discomfort, since it is lodged against the back wall of the vagina and anteriorly against the edge of the pubic bone. Since women vary in size, diaphragms are designed to fit the individual; therefore, it is necessary for the woman to be fitted for the proper size by a doctor or a nurse practitioner. At this time the woman is instructed in its use and care. The woman should reinsert the diaphragm herself and the nurse should check that it is correctly placed.

Each time the diaphragm is used, it must be examined carefully by holding it up to a bright light and making sure it has no pinpoint holes, cracks or tears. Contraceptive jelly or cream is applied in a prescribed manner to the dome of the diaphragm. If it is applied more than two hours before intercourse, it must be reapplied. The diaphragm is then positioned to cover the cervix completely. The diaphragm is left in place for at least six hours after coitus. Upon removal, it is cleansed thoroughly with mild soap and water, rinsed and dried before it is stored in its original container.

Cervical Cap
The cervical cap is much smaller (22 to 35 mm) than the diaphragm and covers only the cervix; it is used with a spermicide. If the woman knows how to insert a diaphragm, it is easy to apply a cervical cap. The main advantage is that the cap may be left in place for several days.

Sponge and Spermicide
A more recent contraceptive is a sponge made of urethane and a spermicide (nonoxynol-9) that is marketed under the trade name of Today. It is inserted into the vaginal tract, fits loosely over the cervix and may be left in place up to 24 hours. A polyester loop attached to the sponge permits its retrieval. It is available without prescription and appears according to some tests to be as effective as the diaphragm.

Condom
The condom is an impermeable snug-fitting rubber or plastic cover applied to the erect penis before it enters the vaginal canal. The penis with condom in place is to be removed from the vagina while still erect to prevent leakage of ejaculate.

Intrauterine Device

An intrauterine device (IUD) is a plastic or metal piece (frequently copper) of varying shapes, usually 2.5 × 2 cm, that is inserted by a gynaecologist through the cervix into the endometrial cavity to prevent pregnancy. The method by which an intrauterine device prevents contraception is thought to be due to a local inflammatory reaction caused by the presence of a foreign body in the uterus. The inflammatory reaction appears to be toxic to spermatozoa and blastocytes. One type of intrauterine device, the Progestasert-T, releases progestin and is replaced each year. Other types are replaced every two to three years unless there is a problem.

The advantages of this method are that it is effective over a long period of time, appears to have no systemic effects and reduces the factor of patient error. The disadvantages are that such a device may cause excessive bleeding, become displaced, perforate the cervix and uterus and may cause infection. There is also the risk of pregnancy-related complications, such as congenital anomalies, spontaneous or septic abortion and ectopic pregnancy.

Because several commonly used intrauterine devices have caused problems, many have been taken off the market. The popularity of this method has consequently decreased.

Postcoital Contraception

Pregnancy will be prevented if 50 mg of oestrogen are given within 24 hours of unprotected intercourse, followed by 50 mg 12 hours later. Such a 'morning after' pill is not applicable for use in long-term contraception, but is of real value in emergency situations such as rape, defective or torn condom or diaphragm, or other 'accidental' intercourse. Such medication given immediately after fertilization and before the occurrence of implantation is effective. Nausea can be minimized by taking the medication with meals and with an antiemetic drug. Other side-effects may be experienced, such as breast soreness and irregular menses, but these are transient. An intrauterine device inserted within five days will also prevent pregnancy, but oestrogen is the preferred method.

Sterilization

Sterilization is becoming increasingly popular for couples who no longer desire to have children. Sterilization may be achieved by hysterectomy, oophorectomy or tubal ligation in the female and by vasectomy in the male. With increasing research, ligations may be reversible; however, they are still considered a permanent means of sterilization.

Tubal Sterilization

Tubal sterilization (ligation or electrocoagulation of uterine tubes) terminates a woman's ability to have children without affecting her ovulatory or menstrual function. Various surgical techniques have been developed using the abdominal or vaginal approach.

Laparoscopy is the most common method of tubal ligation in the United Kingdom. The small incision is either subumbilical or at the pubic hairline.

The surgeon inserts a laparoscope through the incision, locates the uterine tubes and occludes them with clips or sutures. Another possible technique is to resect a segment of the tube. This operation may be done during other abdominal surgery or a Caesarean section, provided an informed consent has been obtained.

Patient Education. Usually before a sterilization is performed, any intrauterine device, if present, is removed. If the patient is taking oral contraceptives, these are usually stopped for a month before the procedure. Postoperatively, there is some abdominal soreness for a few days. The woman is advised to report any of the following: bleeding, pain that continues or increases, and elevated temperature. She should avoid intercourse, strenuous exercise and lifting for one week.

Vasectomy

A vasectomy is the ligation and transection of a section of the vas deferens in the male, with or without removal of a segment of the vas. The severed ends are occluded with ligatures or clips, or the lumen of each vas is coagulated. Bilateral vasectomy interrupts the transportation of the sperm.

Seminal fluid is manufactured in the seminal vesicles and prostate gland, which are unaffected by vasectomy. Thus, there will be no noticeable decrease in the amount of ejaculated fluid, except that it contains no spermatozoa. Because the sperm cells have no exit, they are reabsorbed into the body. The procedure has no effect on sexual potency, erection, ejaculation or production of male hormones.

Two behavioural responses seem to be common after vasectomy. People previously anxious about intercourse because of fear of pregnancy due to contraceptive failure often report a decrease in anxiety and an increase in spontaneous sexual arousal. Some men adopt stereotyped masculine behaviour, supposedly to allay concerns that the surgery has decreased their masculinity. Concise and factual preoperative discussion may minimize or prevent the latter behaviour. Some studies report that vasectomy can lead to autoimmune disorders, in that antibodies that agglutinate the patient's own spermatozoa may form and persist for many years after the procedure. However, an increased incidence of autoimmune disorders following vasectomy has not yet been clinically proven, and the implications are not clear.

The patient is advised that he should not have unprotected intercourse until at least three specimens of ejaculate are found to be free of sperm. Potency will not be altered following a bilateral vasectomy. The procedure does not prevent sexually transmitted disease. On rare occasions, a spontaneous re-anastomosis of the vas deferens occurs, which may result in pregnancy of the partner.

Complications of vasectomy include scrotal bruising and swelling, superficial wound infection, vasitis (inflammation of the vas deferens), epididymitis or epididymoorchitis, haematomas and sperm granuloma. A sperm granuloma is an inflammatory response to the collection of sperm in the scrotum due to leakage from the severed end of the proximal vas. This can initiate recanalization of the vas, possibly resulting in pregnancy of the partner.

Patient Education. After vasectomy, which is usually performed as an outpatient procedure, the man is advised:

1. To spend the remainder of the day resting, in bed if he prefers.
2. That he will feel most comfortable wearing loosely fitting clothes for a day or so.

3. To report persistent pain or oozing from the wound that cannot be controlled, signs of infection and a raised temperature.
4. That contraceptive precautions must continue until the ejaculate is free of sperm.

Reversal of Sterilization (Vasovasostomy)

Microsurgical techniques are being used for vasectomy reversal (vasovasostomy), which restores patency to the vas deferens. However, the success rate of this procedure is still under investigation.

Sperm Banking

Storage of fertile semen in a sperm bank before a vasectomy is a possibility should unforeseen life events cause a desire in the patient to father a child. The success rate in achieving pregnancy with frozen sperm is uncertain.

ABORTION

Abortion is the interruption of pregnancy up to the twenty-eighth week of gestation, whether it occurs accidently or is therapeutically induced. The layperson's term for nontherapeutic abortion is 'miscarriage'. After the twenty-eighth week of gestation, the fetus is considered to be viable, and stillbirth is said to have occurred. However, fetuses of less than 28 weeks' gestation are known to be capable of independent existence, and in the United Kingdom there are moves to reduce the time limit for legal therapeutically induced abortions.

The Human Fertilization and Embryology Bill was passed on 18 October 1990 by the House of Lords and received Royal Assent in November 1990. The upper time limit for abortion should not now exceed 24 weeks' gestation in cases where there would be physical or mental risks to the woman or any existing children. There are no time limits where the grounds for abortion involve the risk of grave permanent injury or death, or a substantial risk of serious handicap to the unborn child (Hall, 1990).

Estimates of spontaneous abortion vary, but it is believed that a high proportion of conceptions (perhaps one in five or ten) results in spontaneous abortion. Most occur because of faulty implantation or because the uterus has some mechanism of rejecting a defective conceptus. Systemic disease, hormone imbalance or anatomic abnormalities may also result in spontaneous abortion.

Spontaneous Abortion

Spontaneous abortion occurs most commonly at about 12 weeks' gestation, probably owing to a defective ovum and subsequent developmental defects of the fetus and placenta.

There are various kinds of spontaneous abortion, depending on the nature of the process (threatened, inevit-

able, incomplete and complete). Uterine bleeding and pain (uterine contractions) are suggestive of an abortion in a woman of childbearing age. In such a threatened abortion, the cervix does not dilate; with bedrest and conservative treatment, abortion may be prevented. If it cannot be prevented, an inevitable abortion is imminent. If some of the tissue, but not all, is passed, the abortion is referred to as incomplete; however, if the fetus and all related tissue are lost, the abortion is complete.

Habitual Abortion

Habitual abortion is successive (three), repeated abortions of unknown cause; immunological rejection is suspected. Fetal tissue may be sent for chromosomal analysis in an attempt to determine the cause.

In the condition known as 'incompetent cervix', the cervix dilates painlessly in the second trimester of pregnancy, resulting in spontaneous abortion. A surgical procedure called the Shirodkar operation is designed to prevent the cervix from dilating prematurely. A pursestring of non-absorbable suture is tied snugly around the cervix at the level of the internal os. It is most important that the patient and the nurses attending her, including those in community health agencies and industry, be informed that such a suture is in place. As soon as labour begins, the suture is removed to allow delivery.

The 1967 Abortion Act

The British abortion laws currently permit termination of pregnancy on the following grounds:

- If allowed to continue, the pregnancy would involve greater risks to the woman's health than if terminated.
- The pregnancy, if allowed to continue, would risk greater physical or mental damage to the woman than if terminated.
- If allowed to continue, the pregnancy would be likely to risk the mental or physical welfare of any existing children.
- If the baby was born, there would be substantial risk of physical or mental handicap.
- To save the life of the pregnant woman.
- To prevent serious permanent physical or mental health problems to the pregnant woman.

Before an abortion can be performed legally, two doctors must provide signed agreement. One may be the woman's general practitioner or doctor at a family planning clinic; the other is the surgeon who will actually perform the operation. Abortions may be performed in an NHS hospital or in a registered nursing home. Most institutions of this kind are private or funded charitably.

Therapeutic abortions may be carried out in the following ways in the operating room, usually under general anaesthesia.

Dilatation and Evacuation (Suction Curettage). The cervix is dilated, and a uterine aspirator is introduced. Suction from a pump is applied, and fetal tissue is removed from the uterus. This method is not used if the pregnancy has advanced beyond 12 weeks, since the fetus at this stage is too large and too firmly implanted.

Intra-Amniotic Injection of Oxytocic Agent. This procedure is used beyond the fourteenth week of pregnancy. Under local anaesthesia, a needle is inserted in the mid-abdomen, and an amniocentesis is performed. Over 200 ml of fluid is withdrawn and replaced by hypertonic saline. In some clinics, after six hours, oxytocin is administered intravenously, with lactated Ringer's solution, to initiate labour. If no oxytocics are administered, labour will usually begin spontaneously within 8 to 20 hours, but may be delayed for several days. Subsequent curettage is necessary to completely remove any remaining placental and residual tissue. The dangers of this procedure, such as accidental intravenous injection of saline, cerebral convulsion and acute renal failure, need to be realized.

Prostaglandins. Intra-amniotic instillation of natural or synthetic prostaglandins produces strong uterine contractions, causing cervical dilatation and expulsion of the fetus and placenta within 24 hours. This method appears safer than using hypertonic saline, because it avoids the complication of disseminated intravascular coagulation and hypernatraemia.

Prostaglandins may result in side-effects such as nausea, vomiting, diarrhoea, tachycardia, substernal 'pressure' and paralytic ileus, although the incidence and frequency of such problems vary according to the medication, dosage and technique of administration. Transvaginal extra-amniotic administration is used to initiate uterine contractions, as are vaginal suppositories. The latter methods are noninvasive with decreased morbidity and ease of administration.

Hysterotomy. A hysterotomy is a 'miniature' caesarean section; usually, this method is reserved for pregnant women who also want to be sterilized at the same time. The patient remains in the hospital for three to six days; care is essentially the same as for a patient having an abdominal operation. Hysterotomy is seldom performed in the United Kingdom.

The 'abortion pill' RU484 is awaiting a product licence, and some trials have been performed.

Septic Abortion

Septic abortion is associated with unskilled, criminal operations, but can occur when the operation is performed legally if some of the products of conception are retained. This is most likely when pregnancy is further advanced than anticipated. However, septic shock is fortunately a rare complication of abortion in the United Kingdom today. It requires treatment with broad-spectrum antibiotics, fluid and blood replacement.

Treatment and Nursing Care

Signs of a threatening abortion are vaginal discharge or bleeding and abdominal cramps. The woman should consult a doctor, who will probably recommend bedrest, a light diet and no straining on defaecation. According to some estimates, when first seen, fewer than 30 per cent of patients who are actually threatening to abort have viable fetuses, and 80 per cent or more will proceed to abortion regardless of management.

All tissue passed vaginally is saved for examination by the doctor. If there is much bleeding, the patient may require transfusions and fluid replacement. An estimate of the amount of bleeding can be determined by recording the number of sanitary pads and the nature of saturation per 24 hours. For an incomplete abortion, oxytocin may be prescribed to contract the fundus before the woman has a dilatation and evacuation of retained products of conception. The woman will require the same care as for dilatation and curettage (see p. 732). Information given to women before they return home is listed in Table 22.3.

Since this person often experiences a severe emotional reaction, the component of 'caring' for her is an important aspect of nursing. The cause of the abortion colours the problem and the patient's reaction. The response of the woman who desperately wants the baby is quite different from that of the woman who does not want to be pregnant but may be frightened of the possible consequences of an abortion. The nurse must not overlook the fact that in

Table 22.3 *Information for women who have undergone therapeutic abortion*

1. Bleeding similar to menstruation will continue for seven days or less. Report:
   a. If bleeding is heavier than usual menstrual flow
   b. If bleeding is followed by severe cramps, backache, nausea, or if you have a raised temperature
2. During bleeding:
   a. Do not use tampons – use sanitary pads (tampons may be used during your next period)
   b. Do not have intercourse; preferably, wait until you have one normal period
   c. Avoid strenuous exercise for at least one week, since it may cause further bleeding
3. Normal expected signs due to hormonal changes (these will pass):
   a. Tearfulness
   b. Breasts may be sore and perhaps leak. To combat this, wear a supportive brassiere and restrict fluids

(Adapted from Easterbrook, B. and Rust, B. (1977) Abortion counseling, Canadian Nurse, January, Vol. 73, p. 30.)

many instances, particularly for the woman having a spontaneous abortion, there is a grieving period that must be handled. Such grieving may be delayed or unresolved, resulting in other problems until the grief reaction has been worked out. There are many reasons for delayed grief reaction: friends may not have known the woman was pregnant; the woman may not have seen the lost fetus and can only imagine the sex, size and so on of the person who never developed; there is no funeral; those who know about the abortion (family, friends, caregivers) encourage denial, rarely crying and talking about the loss.

Providing opportunities for the woman to talk and express her emotions will not only help her but will also provide clues for the nurse in planning more specific care. Those closest to the woman are encouraged to hug her and allow her to talk and cry. If grief is unresolved, it may manifest itself by persistent vivid memories of the events surrounding the time of loss, persistent sadness or anger and frequent flooding of emotion when recalling the loss. Signs of pathological grief may require the assistance of a therapist skilled in bereavement counselling.

INFERTILITY

Infertility usually refers to a couple's failure to achieve a pregnancy in one or two years of unprotected intercourse. Primary infertility refers to a couple who have never had a child. Secondary infertility means that at least one conception has occurred but currently the couple is unable to achieve a pregnancy. In the United Kingdom, research suggests that approximately one couple in every six is unable to conceive (Hull, 1985).

Aetiology
Possible causes of infertility include uterine tumours, congenital anomalies, inflammation and possibly uterine displacement. It is also known that pH influences the survival and capacity of sperm to fertilize. Semen is alkaline, as is cervical mucous, but vaginal secretions are acid. Several factors may contribute to infertility. In the United Kingdom, investigations may be performed by a general practitioner, but often couples are referred to a gynaecologist and may receive treatment in an infertility clinic.

Investigations

Careful investigation includes the following:

- Full physical examination, including possible contributory psychosocial factors.
- Diagnostic tests to rule out damage from previous sexually transmitted disease, congenital abnormalities, injury or other infection that could damage the reproductive structures, such as abortion (endometritis) or mumps (oophoritis, orchitis).

Research has shown that the major causes of infertility are: ovarian (20 per cent), tubal damage (30 per cent), cervical (18 per cent) and seminal (30 per cent).

Ovarian Factors. Investigations are designed to determine:

1. Regular ovulation.
2. Adequate stimulation of the endometrium by progesterone following the luteinizing hormone surge midway through the cycle.

Women may be required to record basal body temperature to detect ovulation for at least four cycles. Alternatively, urinary or plasma hormone assays may be performed with endometrial biopsy.

Tubal Factors. To determine tubal patency, carbon dioxide is introduced through a sterile cannula into the uterus, tubes and peritoneal cavity. By listening with a stethoscope on the abdomen, the gynaecologist may hear gas swishing into the abdomen, indicating that the tubes are open. Another positive indication of tubal patency is the feeling by the patient of referred pain under the scapula or shoulder on the side of the patent tube. This suggests that the gas is under the diaphragm, exerting pressure on the phrenic nerve. If normal patency is present, there is a rise in pressure of 80 to 120 mm, with a sudden drop to 50 to 70 mm as gas passes into the peritoneal cavity. If the gas pressure gauge reaches 200 mm, the test is considered negative, indicating an occlusion.

Hysterosalpinogography (see p. 734) is an X-ray study that is useful when tubal occlusion is apparent since other abnormalities may be found, such as bicornuate uterus.

Laparoscopy (see p. 732) permits direct visualization of tubes and adnexa. Follicles may be seen on the ovarian surface if ovulation is occurring.

Cervical Factors. Cervical mucus can be examined to determine whether changes occur at ovulation that are favourable to sperm penetration and survival.

A postcoital cervical mucus test is done between 6 and 12 hours after intercourse. The gynaecologist aspirates cervical secretions via a cannula. The woman has been instructed not to pass urine or bathe between coitus and the examination; a perineal pad is worn until she is placed in a lithotomy position in the examination room. Aspirated material is placed on a slide and examined under the microscope for presence and viability of sperm.

Uterine Factors. Fibroids, polyps and congenital malformations may be determined by pelvic examination or by hysterosalpingography.

Seminal Factors. After four or five days of sexual abstinence, the sperm specimen is collected in a clean, dry glass container, kept at or below room temperature, and examined within two to four hours for volume, sperm motility, morphology and cell count. Normally, 3 to 5 ml of viscid alkaline semen is obtained; a normal count is 60 to 100 million sperm per millilitre.

Miscellaneous Factors. Miscellaneous factors,

▶ NURSING CARE PLAN 22.1: FOR THE INFERTILE COUPLE

Nursing care plan for Cath and Michael Donovan, who are undergoing investigations for infertility. They are both 34 years old, and have been married for 10 years. Cath is a primary school teacher and Michael is a sales executive. They have been trying to have a baby for seven years.

Patient's problems	Expected outcomes	Nursing care	Rationale
1. Anxiety concerning nature and invasiveness of investigations	Anxiety will be allayed	1a. Provide information about the physical examination of both partners and investigations ordered by doctor	Information allays anxiety; it is usual for less complex, less expensive tests to be performed first when subfertility is investigated
		b. Explain that noninvasive procedures are performed before complicated ones, e.g., involving hospital admission	
		c. Explain that each partner will see the doctor separately for physical examination	Provides privacy; some infertility problems may result from previous sexually transmitted disease, septic abortion. Even in close relationships, couple may not share everything
2. Embarrassment about investigations	Embarrassment will be alleviated	2a. Provide privacy during all tests	Co-operation is essential for the success of infertility investigations
		b. Explain all procedures in 'matter of fact' terms	Clients should not have to ask for information or instructions as they may be afraid of seeming foolish. False modesty may prevent co-operation or clients asking for clarification of instructions
3. Fear that cause of infertility will not be found	Fear will be allayed	3a. Provide explanations about the causes and possible treatments for infertility	Some causes are more easily treated than others, e.g., ovulation failure is much more amenable to treatment than pelvic adhesions
		b. Dispel myths by providing accurate information	With modern techniques, diagnosis and treatment are both more reliable than formerly, *but* the notion that once a couple has started treatment they relax and often conceive easily is not true

including immunological factors, are currently being investigated.

Management

Infertility may be difficult to treat, since it is often due to a combination of factors. Some couples undergo all tests, but the cause of the problem may remain undiscovered. However, with new techniques, these are declining in number. Many problems, simple as well as complex, can be discovered and corrected. Between 25 and 50 per cent of all infertile couples can conceive.

Therapy may require correction of faulty coital tech-nique, surgery to correct a malfunction or anomaly, hor-monal supplements and attention to proper timing of intercourse (see Nursing Care Plan 22.1 for the infertile couple).

Reproductive Technologies

Numerous technologies have been developed to help couples who cannot conceive.

Artificial Insemination

Artificial insemination is the introduction of semen into the female genital tract by artificial means. If the sperm

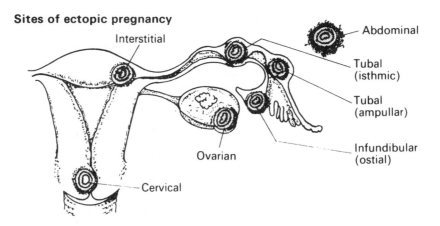

Sites of ectopic pregnancy

Figure 22.8 The various possible sites for ectopic pregnancy.

cannot penetrate the cervical canal normally, consideration may be given to artificial insemination, using the husband's semen (AIH). In the event of azospermia (lack of sperm in the semen), semen from carefully selected donors may be used (AID).

Indications for using artificial insemination are: (1) inability of the male to deposit semen in the vagina, which may be due to premature ejaculation, pronounced hypospadias or dyspareunia (painful intercourse experienced by the female); and (2) inability of semen to be transported from the vagina to the uterine cavity (this is usually due to faulty chemical conditions, such as may be produced with an abnormal cervical discharge, which may be corrected with chemotherapeutic agents). Another indication for artificial insemination is the desire of a single woman to have a child.

Partner's Semen. Certain conditions need to be established before semen is transferred to the vagina. The woman must have no abnormalities of the genital system, the tubes must be patent and ova must be available. In the male, sperm need to be normal in shape, amount, motility and endurance. The time of ovulation in the woman should be determined as accurately as possible, so that the two or three days during which fertilization is possible each month can be utilized. Fertilization seldom occurs from a single insemination. Usually, insemination is attempted between the tenth and seventeenth days of the cycle; three different attempts are made. Semen is collected in a wide-mouth jar following masturbation.

Donor's Semen. A donor may be used when the husband's sperm is defective or absent, or when, for hereditary reasons, it is feared that an undesirable disease may be transmitted. Safeguards need to be set up to prevent legal, ethical, emotional and religious problems.

Donors should have no family history of epilepsy, diabetes or known genetic defects, and a negative test result for syphilis should be obtained. In the United Kingdom, donor and woman are unknown to one another.

Insemination Procedure. The woman is placed in the lithotomy position on the examining table, a speculum is inserted and the vagina and cervix are swabbed clean with a cotton-tipped applicator. Semen is drawn into a sterile syringe, and a cannula is attached. The semen is then directed to the external os. If this is contraindicated, the semen may be inserted directly into the cervical canal. Following withdrawal of the syringe, the woman lies flat on the examining table for 30 minutes. Thereafter, there are no restrictions on the woman's activities.

The success rate for artificial insemination is about 50 per cent. About three to six inseminations are required over a two- to four-month period. Since this procedure is opposed by the Roman Catholic Church, this method should not be suggested to members of this faith.

In Vitro Fertilization

In vitro fertilization (IVF) is accomplished by first stimulating the ovary to produce multiple eggs because pregnancy success rates are greater with more than one embryo. At the appropriate time, the egg is recovered by laparoscopy and follicle aspiration. Sperm and eggs are incubated for 12 to 18 hours so that fertilization can occur. Following an additional 48 to 72 hours, the resulting embryo is transferred to the uterine cavity via a catheter positioned transcervically. Within two or three days, implantation takes place. Success rates vary.

The most common indications for *in vitro* fertilization are tubal damage or destruction, endometriosis that has not responded to therapy and anomalies of the uterus and reproductive tract. *In vitro* fertization may also be considered if the male has oligospermia (very low sperm concentration).

Many reservations have been expressed about *in vitro* fertilization: procreation is separated from sexual union, there are ethical dilemmas such as the fate of spare embryos and much in the way of expertise and resources are being used. However, on the whole, *in vitro* fertilization is considered an acceptable method for treating intractable infertility.

ECTOPIC PREGNANCY

Ectopic pregnancy occurs when the fertilized ovum does not reach the uterine cavity but becomes implanted on the uterine tube or, occasionally, in the ovary or the abdomen, or even the cervix (Figure 22.8). As the fertilized ovum increases in size, the tube becomes increasingly distended, until finally, four to six weeks after conception, rupture takes place, and the ovum is discharged into the abdominal cavity.

Aetiology and Incidence

The highest incidence of ectopic pregnancy occurs in women aged 35 to 44. Precipitating causes may be salpingitis, endometriosis, pelvic inflammatory disease, congenital anomalies of the tubes or spasm of the tubes with muscular insufficiency. Factors inherent in the embryo (embryonic abnormalities) may also predispose to ectopic gestation. Epidemiological studies suggest that increasing use of tubal ligation, abortion and the intrauterine device have been directly associated with ectopic pregnancy. Studies have shown the incidence to vary from 0.5 to 2.5 per cent (1 in 50 to 1 in 250 pregnancies).

Clinical Features

Delay in menstruation from one to two weeks followed by slight bleeding (spotting) may suggest the problem of an ectopic pregnancy, or amenorrhoea may continue several weeks. Symptoms may start with vague soreness on the affected side, probably due to uterine contractions and distension of the tube; frequently the patient experiences sharp, colicky pain.

When tubal rupture occurs, there is agonizing pain, dizziness, faintness, nausea and vomiting. These symptoms are related to peritoneal reaction to blood escaping from the tube. Symptoms of shock indicate that the patient is desperately ill; all the signs of haemorrhage—rapid, thready pulse; low temperature; restlessness; pallor; sweating—are in evidence. Later the pain becomes generalized in the abdomen and radiates to the shoulder and neck because of intraperitoneal accumulation of blood causing irritation to the diaphragm. By vaginal examination, the surgeon is able to feel a large mass of clotted blood that has collected in the pelvis behind the uterus.

Diagnosis

Laparoscopy is helpful because the doctor can visually note an unruptured ectopic pregnancy, thereby circumventing the risks of tubal rupture. Ultrasonography may be effective in differentiating an intrauterine pregnancy from an unruptured tubal gestation.

Management

The goal of treatment is the surgical removal of the ectopic pregnancy, since it is a life-threatening problem; the woman is then relieved of pain and discomfort.

When the operation is performed early, practically all patients recover with remarkable rapidity, but without operation the mortality is 60 to 70 per cent. The type of surgery is determined by the size and extent of local tubal damage; surgery ranges from conservative to more extensive. Very conservative surgery would include 'milking' an ectopic pregnancy from the tube. Perhaps a resection of the involved tube with end-to-end anastomosis may be effective. Some surgeons today perform a salpingostomy, which involves opening and evacuating the tube, controlling bleeding and resuturing the tube to preserve it. More radical surgery includes salpingectomy or salpingo-oophorectomy. Depending on the amount of blood lost, blood transfusions and treatment for shock may be necessary preoperatively and operatively.

Prognosis

The expectancy of another ectopic pregnancy or miscarriage is five to six times greater than for a woman who has not had an ectopic gestation.

► NURSING PROCESS
► THE PATIENT WITH ECTOPIC PREGNANCY

► Assessment

The meaning of a tubal pregnancy to the couple should be assessed, if possible, noting its psychological impact, how they are coping with the problem and evidence of grief. Vital signs, level of consciousness and nature and amount of vaginal bleeding are monitored.

► Patient's Problems

Based on the assessment, the patient's major problems may include the following:

● Pain, related to the progression of the tubal pregnancy.
● Grieving related to the loss of pregnancy and effect on future pregnancies.
● Lack of knowledge about treatment and impact on future pregnancies.

A potential complication of ectopic pregnancy is haemorrhage and shock. Careful assessment is essential to detect the development of this serious problem.

► Planning and Implementation
► Expected Outcomes

The major outcomes for the patient may include relief of pain, correction of fluid volume deficit, acceptance and resolution of grief and pregnancy loss and achievement of understanding of the unnatural pregnancy, its treatment and outcome.

Nursing Care

Potential Haemorrhage

Continuous monitoring of vital signs, level of conscious-ness, amount of bleeding and fluid balance will provide information regarding the possibility of haemorrhage and the need for intravenous therapy. Bedrest is indicated. Laboratory results for haemoglobin and blood gases are noted. Significant deviations in these laboratory values are reported to the doctor, and the patient is prepared for the possibility of surgery.

Relief of Pain

Analgesia is given as prescribed to relieve pain.

Grief Support

Reactions to the loss of early pregnancy may or may not be expressed verbally. The impact may not be fully re-alized or even accepted until much later. The nurse should be available to listen and provide support. The patient's partner should share in this loss.

Patient Education

With rapid changes, confusion may occur in the early hos-pital experience of the patient. Life-threatening symptoms resulting from possible haemorrhage and shock must be addressed and treated first. At this time the patient's atten-tion is focused on a crisis and not on learning. Therefore, it may be later that the patient is in a position to learn and ask questions about what has happened and why certain diag-nostic measures and interventions were carried out. Treat-ments are explained as they are presented and understood by the patient. The patient's partner is included when pos-sible. On recovering from the postoperative discomforts, the time may be more appropriate to address any questions and deep-seated problems, such as the effect of this lost pregnancy on future pregnancies.

▶ *Evaluation*
▶ **Expected Outcomes**

1. Patient experiences a lessening of pain and discomfort.
2. Shows no signs of haemorrhage and shock.
   a. Has reduced amounts of vaginal loss (sanitary pad).
   b. Has normal skin colour and turgor.
   c. Has stable vital signs.
3. Begins to accept pregnancy loss/expresses grief.
   a. Expresses sorrow over loss.
   b. Expresses the future hope for another child.
4. Acquires knowledge about tubal pregnancy and its resolution.
   a. Demonstrates an understanding of the causes of tubal pregnancy.
   b. Describes the need for careful health assessment during any future pregnancy.

BIBLIOGRAPHY

Hall, W. H. (1990) 'Changes in the Law on Abortion', *British Medical Journal*, Vol. 301, pp. 1109.–10.

Hull, M. G. R. (1985) Population study of causes, treatment and outcome of infertility, *British Medical Journal*, Vol. 284, pp. 803–5.

Swartz, W. H. (1984) The semi-sitting position for pelvic examination, *Journal of the American Medical Association*, 2 March, Vol. 251, No. 9, p. 1163.

FURTHER READING

Books

Abortion
Frankle, L. B. (1980) *The Ambivalence of Abortion*, Penguin, Harmondsworth.

Contraception
Grant, E. (1975) *The Bitter Pill*, Corgi, London.
Guillebaud, J. (1984) *The Pill*, Oxford University Press.
Guillebaud, J. (1986) *Contraception: Your Questions Answered*, Churchill Livingstone, Edinburgh.
Pauncefoot, Z. (1984) *Choices in Contraception*, Pan, London.
Potts, M. and Diggory, P. (1983) *Textbook of Contraceptive Practice*, Cambridge University Press.

Infertility
Decker, A. and Loebl, S (1980) *We Want To Have A Baby*, Penguin, London.
Kovacs, G. and Wood, C. (1984) *Infertility. Patient Handbook No. 22*, Churchill Livingstone, Edinburgh.
Winston, R. M. L. (1986) *Infertility: A Sympathetic Approach*, Martin Dunitz, London.

Miscarriage and Ectopic Pregnancy
Berezin, N. (1982) *After a Loss in Pregnancy*, Simon & Schuster, New York.
Oakley, A. McPherson, A. and Roberts, H. (1984) *Miscarriage*, Fontana, Glasgow.
Webb, C. (1986) *Using Nursing Models: Women's Health*, Hodder & Stoughton, Sevenoaks.

Articles

General
Abrums, M. (1986) Health care for women, *JOGNN*, May/June, Vol. 15, No. 3, pp. 250–5.
Bernhard, L. A. and Dan, A. J. (1986) Redefining sexuality from women's own experiences, *Nursing Clinics of North America*, March, Vol. 21, No. 1, pp. 125–36.
Leslie, L. A. and Swider, S. M. (1986) Changing factors and changing needs in women's health care, *Nursing Clinics of North America*, March, Vol. 21, No. 1, pp. 111–23.

Nolan, J. W. (1986) Developmental concerns and the health of midlife women, *Nursing Clinics of North America*, March, Vol. 21, No. 1, pp. 151–9.

Abortion

Kemp, J. (1984) Attitudes to abortion, *Nursing Mirror*, Vol. 158, No. 17, pp. 34–5.

Llewelyn, S. P. and Pytches, R. (1988) An investigation of anxiety following termination of pregnancy, *Journal of Advanced Nursing*, Vol. 13, pp. 468–71.

Neidhardt, A. (1986) Why me? Second trimester abortion, *American Journal of Nursing*, October, Vol. 86, No. 10, pp. 1133–5.

Webb, C. (1985) Barriers to sympathy, *Nursing Mirror, Research Forum*, Vol. 160, No. 1, pp. v–vii.

Well-Haas, C. L. (1985) Women's perceptions of first trimester spontaneous abortion, *JOGNN*, January/February, Vol. 14, No. 1, pp. 50–53.

Hysterectomy

Gould, D. J. (1986) Hidden problems after a hysterectomy, *Nursing Times*, Vol. 82, No. 23, pp. 43–6.

Webb, C. (1983) Hysterectomy—dispelling the myths, *Nursing Times*, Vol. 79, No. 47, pp. 52–4, Vol. 79, No. 48, pp. 44–6.

Infertility

Lovell, B. (1986) *In vitro* fertilization: a way of hope, *Nursing Times*, Vol. 82, No. 44, pp. 26–9.

Menopause

Aloia, J. F. *et al.* (1985) Risk factors for postmenopausal osteoporosis, *American Journal of Medicine*, January, Vol. 78, No. 1, pp. 95–100.

Bowles, C. (1986) Measure of attitude toward menopause using the semantic differential model, *Nursing Research*, March/April, Vol. 35, No. 2, pp. 81–5.

Bungay, G. T. (19??) Study of symptoms in middle life, *British Medical Journal*, Vol. 2, pp. 181–3.

Nolan, J. W. (1986) Developmental concerns and the health of midlife women, *Nursing Clinics of North America*, March, Vol. 21, No. 1, pp. 151–9.

Menstruation

O'Rourke, M. (1983) Self-reports of menstrual and nonmenstrual symptomatology in university-employed women, *JOGNN*, September/October, Vol. 12, No. 5, pp. 317–24.

Patterson, E. T. and Hale, E. S. (1985) Making sure: Integrating menstrual care practices into activities of daily living, *Advances in Nursing Science*, April, Vol. 7, No. 3, pp. 18–31.

Woods, N. F. (1985) Relationship of socialization and stress to perimenstrual symptoms, disability, and menstrual attitudes, *Nurs. Res.*, May/June, Vol. 34, No. 3, pp. 145–9.

Miscarriage and Ectopic Pregnancy

Nash, T. G. (1984) Extrauterine pregnancy, *Nursing Times*, Vol. 70, No. 42, pp. 1623–4.

Westrom, L. (1981) Incidence, trends and risks of ectopic pregnancy, *British Medical Journal*, Vol. 1, pp. 15–18.

Premenstrual Syndrome

Brush, M. G. (1985) The premenstrual syndrome before and after pregnancy, *Maternal and Child Health*, Vol. 10, No. 1, pp. 19–20.

Frank, E. P. (1986) What are nurses doing to help PMS patients? *American Journal of Nursing*, February, Vol. 86, No. 2, pp. 137–40.

Lancet (1981) Premenstrual syndrome: a disease of the mind? *Lancet*, Vol. 2, pp. 1238–40.

Laws, S., Hey, V. and Egan, A. (1985) *See Red. The Politics of Premenstrual Tension*, Hutchinson, London.

Walton, J. and Youngkin, E. (1987) The effect of a support group on self-esteem of women with premenstrual syndrome, *JOGNN*, May/June, Vol. 16, No. 3, pp. 174–8.

chapter 23

ASSESSMENT AND CARE OF PATIENTS WITH GYNAECOLOGICAL DISORDERS

INFECTIONS OF THE FEMALE REPRODUCTIVE SYSTEM

Vulvovaginal Infections

Overview and Prevention

The vagina is protected against infection by its pH (3.5 to 4.5), which is maintained by the actions of Dôderlein's bacilli (a part of the normal vaginal flora) and the hormone oestrogen. The risk of infection is greater if the woman's resistance is lowered, pH is altered, the number of invading organisms is increased and if oestrogen levels are low, as after the menopause.

Vulvovaginal disorders are common. The nurse has a key role in providing information that will assist in preventing and treating many of these conditions. Women need to understand female anatomy, personal hygiene and suitable choice of clothing.

The epithelium of the vagina is highly responsive to oestrogen, which induces the formation of glycogen. The break down of glycogen into lactic acid produces a low vaginal pH. When oestrogen decreases postmenopausally, there is a decrease in glycogen. In adolescents or young women who take oral contraceptives, the normal vaginal flora and glycogen formation are reduced. Compounding the problem, many in this age-group develop acne for which tetracycline is prescribed; this drug further destroys the normal vaginal flora, needed to maintain the lower pH that inhibits the growth of most organisms. With reduction in glycogen formation, infections are common and require careful diagnosis for treatment to be prescribed.

As the vaginal epithelium matures during the reproductive years, other causative factors initiate infections, such as sexual intercourse with an infected partner, poor feminine hygiene and the wearing of tight, nonabsorbent and heat-retaining clothing.

During the perimenopausal period when oestrogen

production ceases, the vaginal mucosa becomes atrophied and fragile, making the area more susceptible to injury and infection.

Vulvitis, Leucorrhoea and Nonspecific Vaginitis

Vulvitis (inflammation of the vulva) usually occurs in conjunction with other local or systemic disorders, such as a dermatological problem, poor local hygiene or sexually transmitted disease, or it may be secondary to a specific vaginitis.

Vaginitis (inflammation of the vagina) occurs when organisms such as *Escherichia coli*, staphylococci and streptococci invade the vagina. The normal whitish vaginal discharge (known as leucorrhoea), which occurs during ovulation, before menarche or the onset of menstruation, becomes more profuse and yellowish when vaginitis occurs. Often vaginitis is accompanied by urethritis because of the proximity of the urethra to the vagina. The discharge may cause itching, redness, burning and oedema, which may be aggravated by voiding and defaecation.

Treatment for vaginitis involves destruction of the offending micro-organism by antibiotics, usually applied locally as pessaries or cream. The woman may need advice about insertion and personal hygiene.

Considerations For Elderly Patients

Postmenopausal women are prone to infection by pyogenic bacteria as a result of atrophy of the vaginal mucosa (atrophic vaginitis). An annoying leucorrhoea causes itching and burning. Management is similar to that for nonspecific vaginitis. In addition, oestrogen taken orally or applied locally as an ointment is effective.

Specific Vaginal Infections

Specific vaginal infections include candidiasis, *Gardnerella*-associated vaginitis, trichomoniasis and chlamydial infections.

Candidiasis

Candidiasis is a fungal infection caused by *Candida albicans*. This organism is frequently a normal inhabitant of the mouth, throat, large intestine and vagina; it propagates where it is moist and warm, in mucous membranes and folds of tissue. *C. albicans* is also found in patients who have been on penicillin, cephalosporin or tetracycline therapy, since these medications reduce the natural protective organisms usually present in the vagina. Clinical infection may occur during pregnancy, when there is a systemic condition such as diabetes mellitus, or when the patient is taking steroids or oral contraceptives.

Clinical features are a vaginal discharge that causes intense pruritus;) is irritating, watery and tenacious; and may contain white, cheesy particles. A burning sensation may follow micturition especially if there is excoriation from scratching. Symptoms are often more severe just before menstruation and more difficult to treat during pregnancy. Diagnosis is made by identifying spores on a microscope slide after Gram staining. In most cases, this organism can also be cultured from the intestinal tract.

Management. The goal is to eliminate infection. Assessment of the patient includes identifying underlying factors that may contribute to the overgrowth of candidal organisms, such as pregnancy, diabetes or oestrogenic or oral contraceptive medications.

Preferred medications are antifungal agents such as clotrimazole. Clotrimazole cream is applied topically by vaginal applicator, usually at bedtime for seven nights. The cream may be applied to the vulva for pruritus. Treatment is continued through a menstrual cycle.

Gardnerella-Associated Vaginitis

Gardnerella vaginalis, acting with a vaginal anaerobic micro-organism, causes a nonspecific vaginitis characterized by excessive discharge and odour (fishy odour, especially after intercourse). This condition occurs throughout the menstrual cycle and does not produce local discomfort. The discharge is creamy greyish white to yellowish white. The odour can be readily detected ('whiff test') by using a dropper to deposit 10 per cent potassium hydroxide solution onto a sample of the discharge that clings to the removed vaginal speculum.

Management. Metronidazole given twice or three times a day for a week is effective. If this medication is contraindicated, ampicillin is administered. If the infection recurs, the male partner is also treated.

Trichomoniasis

Trichomonas vaginalis is a flagellated protozoan that causes a common sexually transmitted disease (see also Chapter 38). If trichomoniasis is transferred sexually, the male may be an asymptomatic carrier who harbours the organisms in his urogenital tract.

Clinical features are a vaginal discharge that is thin, frothy, yellow to yellow-brown, malodorous and very irritating. An accompanying vulvitis may result, with intense vulvovaginal burning and itching. In some women, the problem tends to be become chronic. It is diagnosed by microscopic detection of the pear-shaped, mobile, flagellate organisms. On inspection with a speculum, tissue may reveal generalized vaginal erythema with multiple small petechiae ('strawberry spots').

Management. The most effective treatment is metronidazole, orally one or two times a day with meals for seven days. Both partners should be treated because of inaccessible trichomonads in the urinary system. Some clinics suggest treating the patient and her sexual partner in one day by giving them one or two concentrated doses of metronidazole. Some patients complain of an unpleasant but temporary metallic taste when taking metronidazole. Some also note nausea and vomiting, as well as a hot and flushed feeling when this medication is taken in combination with an alcoholic beverage. In view of these possible side-effects, the patient should be advised not to take alcohol while on the drug.

In addition, intercourse is avoided unless a condom is used. For those who have uncomfortable side-effects from metronidazole, antitrichomonal suppositories are available. Relief may be experienced but not a complete cure. Metronidazole therapy is contraindicated in patients with some blood dyscrasias or central nervous system diseases or those who are pregnant or breast-feeding.

Chlamydial Infections

Sexually transmitted infection with *Chlamydia trachomatis* has increased in recent years. Clinical features in women resemble those of gonorrhoea (cervicitis and mucopurulent discharge). In males, urethritis and epididymitis are noted. Chlamydia attack the genitourinary tract and can cause dysuria. The condition also may be asymptomatic. Diagnosis can be confirmed by cytological and serological studies. Direct smear packets are commercially available but are expensive.

Treatment is with tetracycline, doxycycline or erythromycin usually for one week at prescribed doses. Pregnant women are cautioned not to take tetracycline because of adverse effects on the fetus.

Results of treatment are usually good if it is begun early enough. Possible complications from delayed treatment are tubal disease, pelvic inflammatory disease and infertility.

Management

For more painful vulvovaginal infections such as an abscess, the patient may require an incision to drain the affected area. This procedure is performed by the doctor. Relief is almost immediate, but soreness may continue for one or two days.

▶ NURSING PROCESS

▶ THE PATIENT WITH A VULVOVAGINAL INFECTION

▶ *Assessment*

The woman with a vulvovaginal problem should be examined soon after the onset of symptoms. A nursing history and physical examination include inspection of vaginal mucosa and vulva. The area is observed for erythema, oedema, excoriation and discharge. Each of the organisms producing infections appears to have its own characteristic discharge and effect. The patient is asked if there has been an increase in the amount of secretions and how she would describe any sensations, such at itching or burning. Dysuria often occurs as a result of local irritation of the urinary meatus. Abdominal cramps and fullness may indicate spread of infection in the pelvic area.

Factors that may be involved should be assessed: (1) physical and chemical factors, such as increased perspiration plus decreased evaporation (from tight or synthetic clothing), antiperspirants, perfumes and powders, soaps, bubble bath, a soiled perineal area, contraceptive jellies, feminine hygiene products and vaginal discharges; (2) psychogenic factors; and (3) medical conditions or endocrine factors such as a predisposition for vulva involvement in the diabetic, postmenopausal or chronically ill patient. The medications the patient has been taking are noted, since hormones and antibiotics, for example, may have altered the vaginal flora, resulting in an overgrowth of *C. albicans*.

Nurses who work in special clinics help diagnose these conditions by preparing and examining vaginal smears. *Trichomonas* is visible in a wet preparation, but Gram staining is necessary to identify *Candida*.

▶ *Patient's Problems*

Based on the nursing assessment and other data, the patient's main problems may include the following:

- Pain and discomfort related to burning or itching from the infectious process.
- Potential for reinfection or spread of infection.
- Lack of knowledge about proper hygiene and preventive measures.

▶ *Planning and Implementation*
▶ Expected Outcomes

The main goals of the patient may include relief of pain and discomfort; prevention of reinfection, complications and infection of sexual partner; and acquisition of knowledge about methods for preventing vulvovaginal infections and managing self-care.

Nursing Care

Relief of Discomfort and Pain

Vulvovaginal conditions are usually treated on an outpatient basis, unless the patient has other medical problems. Tact and gentleness in all contacts is important in providing comfort. Psychosocial comfort is significant since many women express embarrassment and even guilt that the infection may have been acquired from a sexual partner. Treatment plans may include the partner.

The nurse's role is to reinforce instructions for hygiene after each voiding and defaecation. A bidet may be used. If chafing of the upper thighs is present, a dusting of talcum powder may alleviate the discomfort.

Sexual intercourse is discouraged until a cure is achieved. Use of a condom is suggested to prevent reinfection and irritation of sensitive tissues. If dyspareunia is experienced, the woman may wish to discuss other ways of showing affection.

Prevention of Reinfection or Spread of Infection

One of the basic goals of preventing reinfection is to reduce tissue irritation. Good hygiene is essential.

In postmenopausal patients, the level of naturally secreted oestrogen decreases. Vaginal mucosal cells and vulva skin lose glycogen. Vaginal acidity declines, and the atrophic tissues become more fragile and susceptible to trauma and infection. This may be overcome by applying a bland lubricant or vaseline.

In teaching the patient how to use medications such as pessaries and applicators to dispense cream, the nurse may demonstrate by using a model of the pelvis. The importance of handwashing is stressed before and after administration. To prevent loss of medication from the vagina, the patient should lie down for 30 minutes following insertion. If there is seepage, a sanitary pad is worn to prevent soilage of clothing. When drugs are prescribed, the nurse can instruct the patient about precautions. For example, tetracycline, if prescribed for infection with *Gardnerella*, is taken one to two hours after meals and not with dairy products, iron or other mineral-containing substances. Sunlight exposure should be avoided. Long-term use of antibiotics should be avoided to prevent candidiasis, which can result when normal flora is destroyed by antibiotics.

The patient is advised that her sexual partner should be treated if infection recurs.

Patient Education and Self-Care

In addition to reviewing way of preventing reinfection, the nurse assesses the individual learning needs of the patient. The patient needs to know the characteristics of a normal and abnormal discharge. Douching has a tendency to eliminate normal flora that nature provides; this tends to reduce the woman's ability to ward off infection. Repeated douching may result in vaginal epithelial breakdown and chemical irritation and is never recommended.

The woman should keep the perineum dry: a hair dryer turned on low is an effective aid. She is advised to wear loose-fitting cotton underwear, not tight-fitting synthetic, nonabsorbent, heat-retaining garments (tights, tight trousers and jeans). It is suggested that the woman also avoid wearing damp bathing costumes for long periods of time.

Sexual intercourse should be avoided until cure is achieved. If pain during intercourse (dyspareunia) is no longer a problem, a condom may be used and efforts made not to injure the vaginal tissue. The use of water-soluble lubricant will decrease excoriation. If infection recurs, it may be necessary to repeat the treatment regime and include the partner.

► *Evaluation*
► **Expected Outcomes**

1. Patient experiences reduced pain and discomfort.
   a. Attends to personal hygiene as instructed.
   b. Reports that itching is relieved.
2. Is free from infection.
   a. Has no signs of inflammation, pruritus or dysuria.
   b. Notes vaginal discharge appears normal (thin, clear, nonfrothy).
   c. Reports that her partner is free from infection.
3. Acquires helpful information related to self-care.

Herpesvirus Type 2 Infection (Herpes Genitalis, Herpes Simplex Virus)

Herpes genitalis is a viral infection that causes herpetic (blisters) lesions on the cervix, vagina and external genitalia: it is a sexually transmitted disease.

This form of herpes is of major concern to health care providers and consumers because of the increasing prevalence of the disease. Not only is the infection painful, but it also can recur and affect future wellbeing. There is no cure at present. The condition requires accurate diagnosis, effective care and specific measures to prevent possible complications.

Aetiology and Pathophysiology

Of the known herpesviruses, six affect humans: (1) herpes simplex type 1 (HSV-1), usually causing 'cold sores' of lips; (2) herpes simplex type 2 (HSV-2); (3) varicella zoster; (4) Epstein-Barr virus; (5) cytomegalovirus; and (6) HBLV (human B-lymphotropic virus). Herpes simplex type 2 appears to be the causative virus in over 80 per cent of genital and perineal lesions; about 20 per cent are HSV-1.

There is considerable overlap between the two forms, which are clinically indistinguishable. Close human contact via mouth, oropharynx, mucosal surface, vagina and cervix seems necessary to acquire infection. Other susceptible sites are skin lacerations and conjunctivae. Usually the virus is killed at room temperature by drying. When virus replication diminishes, the virus ascends the peripheral sensory nerves and remains inactive in the nerve ganglia. Another outbreak occurs when the host is subjected to stressors, such as fatigue or illness.

It is significant to note that the incidence of cervical cancer is higher in women who have had cervical herpes. In pregnant women with cervical herpes, babies delivered vaginally may become infected with the virus; there is significant fetal morbidity and mortality.

Clinical Features

Itching and pain accompany the process as the area becomes red and oedematous. The vesicles may appear as pimples, which later coalesce, ulcerate and encrust. In the female, the cervix is the usual primary site, and then possibly the labia, vulva, vagina and perianal skin. The male is affected on the glans penis, foreskin and penile shaft. Influenza-like symptoms occur three to four days after the appearance of lesions. Inguinal lymphadenopathy, pyrexia, malaise, headache, myalgia and dysuria are noted. In the female, a purulent discharge may develop from a secondary bacterial infection. Pain is evident during the first week and then lessens. The lesions disappear in about three weeks unless they become secondarily infected.

Complications arise from extragenital spread, to the buttocks, upper thighs and to the eyes as a result of touching them with unwashed hands. Other potential problems are hepatitis, aseptic meningitis, autonomic nervous system dysfunction and psychological stress.

Management

There is no cure for herpesvirus type 2 infection, but treatment is aimed at relieving the symptoms. The goals are to prevent the spread of infection, to make the patient comfortable, to decrease potential health risks, and to be supportive and initiate a counselling and education programme. Acyclovir, an antiviral agent that can alter the course of the infection, is available for topical, oral and intravenous use. In general, acyclovir may reduce the duration of the infection but is only marginally effective in preventing recurrences. Of concern is the potential for drug resistance and longterm side-effects. The most effective management at present remains the care of local lesions and supportive care of systemic illness. Antibacterial agents help prevent secondary infections.

▶ NURSING PROCESS

▶ THE PATIENT WITH A GENITAL HERPESVIRUS INFECTION

▶ Assessment

The patient's history, physical and pelvic examination and the results of laboratory investigations establish diagnosis.

▶ Patient's Problems

Based on the assessment, the patient's main problems may include the following:

- Pain related to the presence of genital lesions.
- Potential for reinfection or spread of infection.

- Anxiety and distress related to embarrassment over the presence of the disease.
- Lack of knowledge about the disease process and methods for avoiding spread or reinfection.

▶ Planning and Implementation
▶ Expected Outcomes

The main outcomes for the patient may include relief of pain and discomfort, control of infection and its spread, relief of anxiety, and knowledge of and adherence to treatment regime and self-care.

Nursing Care

Relief of Pain

The local lesions are to be kept clean, and good hygiene is advocated. Small ice packs may be applied intermittently to painful areas to bring relief. Clothing should be clean, loose, soft and absorbent. Tepid baths are comforting. Aspirin and other analgesics are effective to control pain. A topical anaesthetic such as lignocaine gel is effective. Occlusive ointments and powders are to be avoided since they will prevent the lesions from drying, which in turn helps to kill the virus.

If there is considerable pain and malaise, bedrest may be required. It is necessary to assess the fluid intake of the patient, the presence of bladder distension and the frequency of voiding. Adequate fluid intake is encouraged; voiding is assisted by pouring warm water over the vulva. Such measures will help in preventing urinary retention and infection. Acyclovir is taken as prescribed, and side-effects such as rash, headache, insomnia, acne, sore throat, muscle cramps and lymphadenopathy are monitored. Rest and an appropriate diet are recommended. An indwelling urinary catheter may be necessary in severe cases of urethritis.

Control of Infection

Since herpesvirus can spread from the discharge of lesions, efforts are made to keep these areas dry. Using a hair dryer turned on low and cool is comforting and drying. Acyclovir as prescribed may be applied locally to the lesions four to five times daily to control the spread of infection. Other forms of administration may be recommended by the doctor. For general methods of preventing the spread of the infection, see the recommendations mentioned in the next section on self-care instruction.

Patient Education

The problems of genital herpes are both physical and psychological. Usually, the patient experiences a great deal of stress on learning the diagnosis, and this aggravates the problem. Therefore, when counselling the patient, the nurse should review the causes of the condition and the manner in which it progresses. The patient's questions are encouraged since such questions indicate receptive time to learn. The highly individual nature of the disease, its widespread incidence, the prevention of complications and promising research are discussed. The nurse can reassure the patient that in time she will be able to enjoy a normal social and sex life.

► *Evaluation*
► **Expected Outcomes**

1. Patient experiences minimal pain and discomfort.
   a. Takes aspirin/analgesic/acyclovir as prescribed.
   b. Rests and conserves energy.
   c. Uses warm baths.
   d. Wears clean, loose, cotton clothing.
   e. Abstains from sexual activity while infected.
   f. Develops a plan of relaxation/stress reduction.
2. Keeps infection under control.
   a. Practises good hygiene.
   b. Washes hands after going to the bathroom/cleansing perineum.
   c. Avoids use of occlusive ointments.
3. Acquires knowledge and keeps updated.
   a. Defines the limitations of social and sexual practices as the condition permits.
   b. Understands the nature and implications of sexually transmitted infection.
   c. Indicates a willingness to arrange for follow-up care.

Toxic Shock Syndrome

Toxic shock syndrome, a condition first identified in the late 1970s, is caused by the bacterium *Staphylococcus aureus* and usually occurs in women under the age of 30 who are menstruating and using tampons (particularly highly absorbent tampons). Research studies suggest that magnesium-absorbing fibres in the tampons may lead to lower levels of magnesium in the body. Such low levels contribute to providing an ideal condition for toxins to be produced by the bacteria. Toxic shock syndrome has also occurred in nonmenstruating women and in men and has been associated with such conditions as cellulitis, surgical wound infections and subcutaneous abscesses.

Clinical Features
In an otherwise healthy person the onset of toxic shock syndrome occurs with a sudden fever (up to 38.9C), vomiting, diarrhoea, myalgia, hypotension and signs suggesting the onset of septic shock. At times sore throat and headache are noted. A red, macular rash often develops. In some patients, this rash makes its first appearance on the torso, and in others, it first appears on the hands (palms

and fingers) and feet (soles and toes); it may then desquamate in 7 to 10 days.

Urinary output is decreased and the blood urea nitrogen becomes elevated; such urinary dysfunction may initiate disorientation due to fluid deficit and toxins. Respiratory distress or signs of 'shock lung' have been reported as a result of pulmonary oedema. Inflammation of mucous membranes may also occur. Blood studies indicate leucocytosis and elevated bilirubin, urea, nitrogen and creatine phosphokinase values.

Diagnosis
Blood and urine cultures are taken, along with throat cultures when appropriate. Vaginal and possibly cervical specimens are also examined.

Management
The patient is nursed on bedrest, and the treatment plan is directed primarily at controlling the infection with chemotherapeutic agents. General assessment may reveal shock and fluid imbalance, which is corrected. If there is respiratory distress, oxygen therapy is instituted; if signs of acidosis appear, sodium bicarbonate is given. Calcium is prescribed for hypocalcaemia.

Treatment is according to the individual patient's condition, which may vary from mild to very acute. The patient's emotional and psychological concerns are of importance.

► **NURSING PROCESS**
► **THE PATIENT WITH TOXIC SHOCK SYNDROME**

► *Assessment*

The nursing history is directed towards determining if the patient has used tampons recently, what kind she used, how long she retained a single tampon before changing it and whether she noted any problems when inserting the tampon, which may have injured the vaginal tissue. Sometimes, rough edges on the cardboard applicator can scratch or injure the mucosa when the tampon is inserted. Broken tissue allows organisms to invade the bloodstream.

► *Patient's Problems*

Based on the nursing assessment, the patient's main problems may include the following:

● Anxiety related to the severity and suddenness of the symptoms.
● Fluid volume deficit related to vomiting and diarrhoea.
● Nausea due to systemic toxicity.
● Lack of knowledge about use of tampons and personal hygiene.

► *Planning and Implementation*
► **Expected Outcomes**

The main outcomes for the patient may include reduction of anxiety and emotional stress, absence of vomiting and diarrhoea, absence of discomfort, absence of complications and acquisition of relevant knowledge.

Nursing Care

The patient will be reassured to relieve anxiety and apprehension. Close monitoring of vital signs and blood gases will be necessary. The nurse notes skin changes as well as fluid intake and loss to monitor level of hydration and renal function.

Nasal, throat, vaginal and cervical swabs are sent for culture, so that appropriate antibiotics can be prescribed.

Since disseminated intravascular coagulation has been observed in patients with toxic shock syndrome, it is essential for the nurse to be observant for haematomas, petechiae, oozing from needle puncture sites, cyanosis and coolness of the extremities.

Patient Education

Since the use of tampons during menstruation has been linked with toxic shock syndrome, it is recommended that superabsorbent tampons not be used. If tampons are preferred, women should be advised to alternate their use with pads. Tampons be changed every four hours and not left in place longer than eight hours. Tampons should be inserted carefully to avoid abrasions (applicators with rough edges should not be used). If a diaphragm is used, it should not be left in place for longer than six hours. Use of tampons is discouraged if the patient has had toxic shock syndrome.

► *Evaluation*
► **Expected Outcomes**

1. Patient exhibits reduced anxiety and emotional stress.
2. Does not have signs and symptoms of fluid and electrolyte imbalance.
   a. Notes absence of vomiting and diarrhoea.
   b. Takes fluids and food well.
3. Is comfortable and oriented.
   a. Reports absence of pain and nausea.
   b. Has vital signs within normal limits.
   c. Is free of purulent discharge.
   d. Has normal laboratory values.
   e. Is free of infection.
4. Demonstrates awareness of self-care measures.

Endocervicitis

Endocervicitis is an inflammation of the cervical mucosa and its glands. It is not a common problem but may occur when organisms gain access to the cervical glands after abortion, intrauterine manipulation or delivery. It is an infection that, if untreated, may extend into the uterus, uterine tubes and pelvic cavity. In the majority of patients, the inflammation is caused by ordinary pyogenic organisms, but gonococcal infection can occur.

Inflammation can cause erosion of the cervical tissue, resulting in spotting or bleeding. The main symptom is leucorrhoea, associated with sacral backache, low abdominal pain and urinary and menstrual disturbances.

Management

Treatment should be preventive as well as curative. Prevention of gonorrhoea will reduce the incidence of endocervicitis. Good obstetric care can also prevent occurrence. Delivery ought not to be attempted until the cervix completely dilates spontaneously; cervical lacerations should be repaired immediately.

Palliative treatment consists of antibiotics, but often a cure is effected only after the cervical glands are destroyed with cautery or after the diseased tissue is excised. Anaesthesia may or may not be required, since cauterization in the cervical area is painless.

For more severe chronic cervicitis, conization may be performed, possibly under anaesthesia. In the operating theatre, the tip of an electric instrument is inserted into the external os of the cervix and rotated to cut and coagulate a cone of tissue. A vaginal pack may be inserted, but aftercare is otherwise the same as for cautery.

Patient Education

Following cauterization, the patient should rest for a few days. The nature of vaginal discharge is explained to the patient so that she can expect a greyish green, malodorous discharge for up to three weeks, because of sloughing cervical tissue. A follow-up visit is recommended by the gynecologist after two or three weeks, when the cervix is checked for possible stenosis, which may require dilation. Usually, six to eight weeks are required for healing. Sexual relations are resumed on recommendation of the doctor. The patient should note any excess bleeding and report it to her doctor.

Pelvic Inflammatory Disease

Pelvic infection may involve the uterine tubes (salpingitis), ovaries (oophoritis), pelvic peritoneum or pelvic vascular system. Infection may be acute, subacute, recurrent or chronic and may be localized or widespread. It is usually bacterial but may also be caused by a virus, fungus or parasite.

Aetiology

Pathogenic organisms usually enter the body through the vagina, pass through the cervical canal and into the uterus, and may proceed to one or both uterine tubes and ovaries and into the pelvis. In bacterial infections occurring after childbirth or abortion, and in some IUD-related infections, pathogens are disseminated directly through the parametrium via the lymphatics and blood vessels. The increased blood supply required by the placenta provides more pathways for infection. Postpartum and postabortion infections tend to be unilateral. In sexually transmitted infections, the micro-organisms pass through the cervical canal and into the uterus, where the environment, especially during menstruation, allows them to multiply rapidly and spread to the uterine tubes and into the pelvis. The infection is usually bilateral. In rare instances some diseases (e.g. tuberculosis) gain access to the reproductive organs by way of the bloodstream from the lungs.

Clinical Features

The onset of pelvic infection is usually manifested by vaginal discharge and lower abdominal and pelvic pain and tenderness. The type of discharge varies with the infecting organism. It is usually heavy and purulent for gonorrhoea or staphylococcal infection; the discharge tends to be more mucoid and thinner. Systemic symptoms include fever, general malaise, anorexia, nausea, headache and possibly vomiting. On pelvic examination, intense tenderness may be noted.

Management

The aim of treatment is to control and eradicate infection by preventing spread. Even before the specific organism is determined, the patient is placed on broad-spectrum antibiotic therapy. Women with mild to moderately severe infections are usually treated as outpatients. However, patients who are acutely ill may be hospitalized.

In hospital, intensive therapy includes bedrest and intravenous fluids to correct dehydration and acidosis. If abdominal distension or ileus is present, nasogastric intubation and suction will be initiated. Careful monitoring of vital signs and symptoms will indicate whether infection has spread.

Complications

Pelvic or generalized peritonitis may develop, as may abscess formation, strictures and obstruction in the uterine tubes. Obstruction may result in an ectopic pregnancy at some future time if a fertilized egg is unable to pass the stricture. Scar tissue may close the uterine tubes, resulting in sterility. Adhesions are a common development that eventually may require removal of the uterus, tubes and ovaries. Other complications include bacteraemia with septic shock and thrombophlebitis with possible formation of septic emboli.

Nursing Care

'Care' for the patient with pelvic infection is as important as 'cure'. This infection may be very distressing, both physically and emotionally. The patient may feel well one day and develop vague symptoms and discomfort the next. She often suffers from constipation and menstrual difficulties.

The hospitalized patient is maintained on bedrest. For comfort, local warmth can be applied to the abdomen externally. In addition, the patient is supported nutritionally and with selective antibiotic therapy as prescribed. Catheterization and the use of tampons are avoided to prevent the spread of the infection.

The recording of vital signs and the nature and amount of vaginal discharge are necessary.

Infection control precautions include:

● Sanitary pads are handled carefully with gloves, and the soiled pad is deposited in a paper bag for incineration.
● Hands are washed carefully.

Patient Education

Patient teaching consists of explaining how pelvic infections occur and how they can be controlled.

● Be aware that organisms can gain entrance to the reproductive area during sexual intercourse or following pelvic surgery, abortion and childbirth.
● Realize that users of intrauterine devices are more susceptible to infections.
● Follow proper perineal care, especially wiping from front to back.
● Do not douche since this practice will reduce natural flora that can combat infecting organisms.
● Wear clean, cotton, loose-fitting undergarments.
● Avoid strongly scented soaps, bubble bath, sprays, powders and deodorants in the perineal area.
● Consult with a general practitioner or attend STD clinic if unusual vaginal discharge or odour is noted.
● Avoid tampons if they have caused problems.
● Do not wear pads or tampons for longer than six hours; preferably change them every four hours.
● Remember to remove a diaphragm after using it for six hours.
● Maintain optimum health by eating sensibly, exercising and relaxing.
● Remember that barrier methods of contraception afford some protection against sexually transmitted disease.

STRUCTURAL DISORDERS

Vaginal Fistulae

A fistula is an abnormal opening between two internal hollow organs or between an internal hollow organ and the exterior of the body. A ureterovaginal fistula is an opening between the ureter and vagina; a vesicovaginal fistula, an opening between the bladder and the vagina;

and a rectovaginal fistula, an opening between the rectum and the vagina (Figure 23.1).

Aetiology

Fistulae may occur congenitally, but in the adult, the usual cause is tissue damage resulting from injury sustained during surgery, delivery, radiotherapy or malignant disease.

Clinical Features

The immediate problem is infection and resulting excoriation. For example, the patient who has a vesicovaginal fistula has a continuous trickling of urine into the vagina. With a rectovaginal fistula, there is faecal incontinence, and flatus is discharged through the vagina. A malodorous condition develops that is difficult to control.

Methylene blue dye can be used to delineate the course of the fistula. In vesicovaginal fistula, the dye is instilled into the bladder and appears in the vagina. Following a negative methylene blue test, indigo carmine is injected intravenously; if the dye appears in the vagina, a ureterovaginal fistula is indicated.

Management

The goal is to heal the fistula, thereby also controlling infection and excoriation. Healing may occur without surgical intervention, but otherwise surgery is essential. Usually the vaginal approach is used for vesicovaginal and urethrovaginal fistulae. The abdominal approach is used for fistulae higher in the abdomen. Fistulae that are difficult to repair or very large may require urinary or faecal diversion.

Nursing Care

Nursing measures are planned to relieve discomfort, prevent infection, and improve the patient's self-esteem and self-care abilities.

Healing is promoted by optimal nutrition with an increase in intake of vitamin C and protein, by local cleanliness, keeping the bowel empty, by rest and by taking prescribed intestinal antibiotics. A rectovaginal fistula will heal faster if the patient is on a low-residue diet and if proper drainage of affected tissues is initiated.

More rest is required than in most postoperative patients because of a higher incidence of debilitation and the delicate as well as sensitive nature of the tissues. Warm perineal irrigations and controlled heat-lamp treatments are effective in stimulating the healing process.

For the patient who has had repair of a vesicovaginal fistula, an indwelling catheter is usually inserted. Drainage from the catheter is observed carefully, and care is taken to ensure that the catheter is functioning properly. If the catheter becomes clogged, urine may collect in the bladder, causing pressure that may damage the repaired tissue. Bladder and vaginal irrigations are done gently, with minimal pressure.

Effective measures to assist the woman whose fistula cannot be repaired must be planned on an individual basis. Cleanliness, frequent baths and deodorizing douches are required, as well as the use of perineal pads and protective undergarments. Particular attention to skin care is necessary to prevent excoriation. Bland creams or a light dusting of talcum powder may be soothing. Morale boosters and attention to the social and psychological needs of this patient are essential components of effective care.

Cystocele, Rectocele, Enterocele and Lacerations of the Perineum

Cystocele is a downward displacement of the bladder towards the vaginal opening (Figure 23.2). It is usually the result of obstetric injury to the pelvic floor occurring during labour, although the effects may not become apparent until after the menopause when oestrogen withdrawal causes the pelvic structures to become lax. The cause of rectocele is similar, but damage is to the muscles below the vagina, causing upward pouching of the rectum,

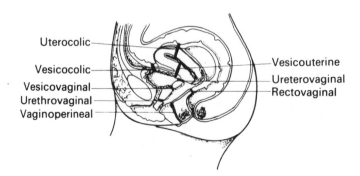

Figure 23.1 Sites of possible fistula formation: uterocolic—uterus and colon; vesicocolic—bladder and colon; vesicovaginal—bladder and vagina; urethrovaginal—urethra and vagina; vaginoperineal—vagina and perineal area; vesicouterine—bladder and uterus; ureterovaginal—ureter and vagina; rectovaginal—rectum and vagina.

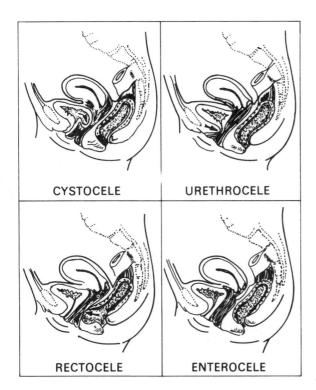

Figure 23.2 Pelvic floor relaxation: cystocele, ureth-rocele, rectocele and enterocele. Arrows depict sites of maximum protrusion. (Kistner, R. W. (1986) *Gynecology: Principles and Practice* (4th edition), Year Book Medical Publishers, Chicago.)

pushing the posterior wall of the vagina in front of it. Lacerations of the anal sphincter may cause an enterocele, in which there is protrusion of the intestinal wall into the vagina.

Clinical Features

1. Cystocele causes a sense of pelvic pressure and fatigue, frequently accompanied by urinary symptoms such as incontinence, frequency and urgency. Backache is common.
2. Rectocele and anterocele result in symptoms similar to those experienced with cystocele, but instead of urinary symptoms there will be constipation and flatulence.

Cystocele and rectocele often coexist.

Treatment

1. Surgery is the treatment of choice. Repair of the anterior vaginal wall is termed anterior colporrhaphy. Posterior colporrhaphy is the repair of the posterior vaginal wall. Repair of perineal lacerations and an enterocele is called a perineorrhaphy.
2. Conservative treatment may be attempted when the

patient is too frail to undergo anaesthesia and surgery, or does not wish to do so.

Perineal exercises may help to strengthen weak pelvic floor muscles, and a pessary may be inserted into the upper vagina to keep the uterus in position (Hodge or ring pessary). The gynaecologist fits the pessary and the nurse is responsible for instructing the patient in the need for scrupulous hygiene if irritation of the vaginal walls and infection are to be avoided. Regular gynaecological follow-up is necessary.

Uterine Displacements

Under normal circumstances, the uterus is anteverted (cervix at right angles to the vaginal vault). The body of the uterus is free to move, allowing for expansion during pregnancy, but the cervix is held in position by ligaments. When these are weakened or if pelvic adhesions form, backward displacement of the uterus occurs, a condition known as retroversion (Figure 23.3). Retroversion sometimes causes backache and in the past was sometimes thought to be the cause of pelvic pain, but is now known to be asymptomatic in most women. If retroversion is troublesome, a pessary may be used to hold the uterus forward or surgery may be performed to shorten the uterine ligaments, thereby achieving anteversion.

Prolapse and Procidentia

Because of weakening of the supports of the uterus, most

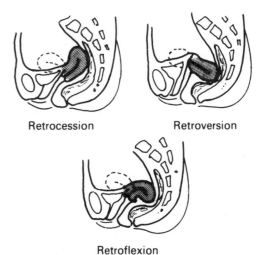

Figure 23.3 Displacements of the uterus. The dotted line indicates the normal position of the uterus. In retrocession, the uterus tilts posteriorly. In retroversion, the uterus turns posteriorly as a whole unit. In retroflexion, the fundus bends posteriorly above the cervical end. (Hardy, J. D. (1988) *Hardy's Textbook of Surgery* (2nd edition), J. B. Lippincott, Philadelphia.)

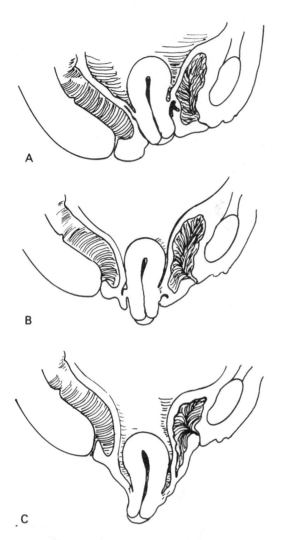

Figure 23.4 Prolapse of the uterus and vagina. (A) First-degree prolapse—cervix comes down to introitus. (B) Second-degree prolapse—cervix protrudes through introitus. (C) Third-degree prolapse—total procidentia: uterus protrudes through introitus. (Adapted from Gray, L. A. *Postgraduate Medicine*, Vol. 30, p. 209.)

often brought about by childbirth, the uterus may work its way down the vagina (prolapse) and even appear outside the vaginal orifice (procidentia) (Figure 23.4).

In its descent, the uterus pulls with it the vaginal walls, the bladder and the rectum. The symptoms caused are similar to those mentioned for backward displacements, plus urinary symptoms (incontinence and retention) from displacement of the bladder. These symptoms are aggravated when the woman coughs, lifts a heavy object or stands for a long while. Normal activities are troublesome tasks; even walking up steps may aggravate the problem. The nurse can encourage women who have such difficul-

ties to seek medical attention, because time is not likely to correct the problem.

Surgery is the treatment of choice. The uterus is sutured back into place, and repair work is done to strengthen and tighten muscles. In postmenopausal women, the uterus may be removed (hysterectomy). For elderly women or those who are too ill to stand the strain of surgery, pessaries may be the treatment of choice.

Treatment and Nursing Care

Today, damage to the pelvic muscles can be prevented to a large extent by good antenatal and obstetric care. Perineal exercises taught by the midwife during pregnancy enable the woman to tighten and control muscles of the pelvic floor, as does learning to start and stop the urinary flow during micturition. These exercises should be continued postnatally.

The nurse can correct any misconceptions older women may have. It is incorrect to assume that muscle damage is the natural consequence of childbirth or ageing and that nothing can be done, as failure to seek professional advice may result in further complications such as infection, cervical ulceration, urinary symptoms and haemorrhoids.

Preoperative Nursing Care

1. The patient must be told what surgery will entail, what it is expected to achieve and its effects on sexual activity.
2. In many hospitals, a midstream specimen or urine is sent to the laboratory to detect the presence of infection.
3. An enema may be given.
4. The perineal area may be shaved.
5. For other preoperative details see page 765.

Postoperative Nursing Care and Rehabilitation

1. Scrupulous hygiene of the perineal area is necessary to prevent infection and consequent pressure on the suture line. A bidet may be used.
2. Some patients return to the ward with an indwelling urinary catheter that remains in place for two to four days, although many surgeons now prefer to keep the bladder empty with a suprapubic catheter, as this reduces the risk of urinary tract infection. Other aspects of bladder management are discussed in Chapter 20.
3. A heat lamp may be used to dry the perineum after micturition and defaecation.
4. Anaesthetic sprays may provide local relief.
5. An ice pack may be applied to relieve congestion and discomfort.
6. A normal diet may be taken after the first postoperative day. Fluids are encouraged.

Patient Education

1. Women must be given information about the need for rest and the amount of exercise they can be allowed to safely undertake.
2. Lifting heavy objects and standing for long periods should be avoided.
3. Information concerning the resumption of sexual relations should be given.
4. Women must be reminded of the date and time of the next outpatient appointment.
5. Patients are instructed to report any pelvic pain, discharge or vaginal bleeding at once.
6. Exercises are recommended to help strengthen the pelvic floor muscles. Patients are instructed to tense the perineal muscles, hold the position and then relax. This exercise, which should be carried out 10 to 20 times every hour, can be performed standing or lying down.

BENIGN CONDITIONS

Vulvar Cysts

Bartholin's glands are positioned bilaterally in the posterior third of the vulva, near the vestibule. Cysts commonly result through obstruction of the duct and may remain asymptomatic, although infection by *Escherichia coli, Staphylococcus aureus* or gonococci are frequent complications. Abscesses may then develop, with or without inguinal lymphadenopathy. Treatment involves incision and drainage, with antibiotic cover.

Lichen Sclerosus

Lichen sclerosus et atrophicus, often mistaken for leucoplakia, presents as slightly raised whitish papules or macules of the vulval dermis. Symptoms are usually mild or absent, in contrast to the intense pruritus of leucoplakia. It is believed that at least 10 per cent of patients with cancer of the vulva have an associated lichen sclerosus, with or without leucoplakia. Biopsy and a careful follow-up programme are definitely recommended. If cancer cells are detected on biopsy, a simple vulvectomy is performed, with continued follow-up.

Ovarian Cysts

Altered Physiology

The ovary is a frequent site for the development of cysts. These may be simply pathological enlargements of normal ovarian constituents, the graafian follicle or corpus luteum, or they may arise from abnormal growth of the ovarian epithelium. Most arise as benign tumours, but may be subject to malignant change.

Dermoid cysts are tumours that are believed to arise from parts of the ovum that disappear normally as ripening (maturation) takes place. They consist of undifferentiated embryonic cells. They grow slowly and at operation are found to contain a thick, yellow, sebaceous material arising from a skin lining. Hair, teeth, bone, brain, eyes and many other tissues often are found in a rudimentary state within these cysts.

Clinically, cysts are manifested by their obvious presence as an ovarian mass. There may be lower abdominal pain that may be acute or chronic. Rupture may occur and simulate an acute abdominal emergency, such as appendicitis or ectopic pregnancy. Larger cysts may produce abdominal swelling and pressure on adjacent abdominal organs.

Management

The treatment of ovarian cysts is surgical removal. However, if malignant degeneration has taken place, with invasion of the abdomen and general emaciation (general carcinomatosis), operation is of little benefit. The patient may be given radiotherapy or chemotherapy (this treatment is used widely in the United Kingdom). The abdomen may be tapped to relieve distension from ascites. The postoperative nursing care after cystectomy is similar to that for abdominal surgery.

Benign Tumours of the Uterus: Leiomyomas ('Fibroids', Myomas or Fibromyomas)

Myomatous or fibroid tumours of the uterus are benign tumours arising from the muscle tissue of the uterus. They are common, occurring in about 20 per cent of white women and 40 to 50 per cent of black women. They develop slowly between the ages of 25 and 40, and often become large. There are instances in which such a tumour causes no symptoms. The most common symptom is abnormal endometrial bleeding. Other symptoms are due to pressure on the surrounding organs—pain, backache, constipation and urinary symptoms. In addition, such tumours often cause menorrhagia and infertility.

Management

Treatment depends on the size of the fibroid, its location and the woman's preference.

- Usually, surgery involves total abdominal hysterectomy, preserving the ovaries (see page 765 for nursing care).
- Individual fibroids may be removed surgically (myomectomy) if the woman wishes to preserve fertility.
- Small, asymptomatic fibroids require no intervention.

Endometriosis

Endometriosis is a benign lesion in which cells similar to

those lining the uterus are found growing aberrantly in the pelvic cavity outside the uterus. Symptoms vary and may be misleading. Extensive endometriosis may cause few symptoms, whereas an isolated lesion may produce considerable symptomatology.

Altered Physiology

In order of frequency, pelvic endometriosis attacks the ovary, ureterosacral ligaments, rectovaginal pouch, uterovesical peritoneum, cervix, umbilicus, laparotomy scars, hernial sacs and appendix. The misplaced endometrium responds to ovarian hormonal stimulation. When the uterus goes through the process of menstruation, this ectopic tissue bleeds—mostly into areas having no outlet—which then causes pain and adhesions. At surgery, these lesions are typically small, puckered and brown or blue-black, indicating concealed bleeding. If the endometrial tissue is within an ovarian cyst, there is no outlet for the bleeding and the formation is referred to as a pseudocyst (chocolate cyst).

Incidence

Endometriosis has increased in recent years. There is a high incidence among patients who marry later, bear children later, and have fewer children. In countries such as India, where tradition favours early marriage and early childbearing, endometriosis is rare.

It is characteristically found in the young, nulliparous female, aged 25 to 35. A similar condition affecting the endometrium in older, multiparous patients is referred to as adenomyosis. At present, these two conditions, which at one time were thought to be related, are now considered separate entities. There appears to be a predisposition to endometriosis; it is about seven times more common in women whose close female relatives have this condition.

Aetiology

The more popular theories regarding the origin of endometrial lesions are the transplantation theory and the metaplasia theory. The transplantation theory suggests that a backflow of menses (retrograde menstruation) causes endometrial tissue to be transported to ectopic sites through the uterine tubes. Transplantation can also occur during surgery if endometrial tissue is transferred inadvertently on instruments. Endometrial tissue can also be spread by lymphatic or venous channels. The metaplasia theory relates to retained remnants of embryonic epithelial tissue, which during development process may be transformed into endometrial tissue by means of environmental stimuli. The real cause of endometriosis may be a combination of factors.

Clinical Features and Diagnosis

Symptoms vary with the location of endometrial tissue. Usually the chief symptom is a type of dysmenorrhoea, unlike typical uterine cramps. The patient complains of a deep-seated aching in the lower abdomen, vagina, posterior pelvis and back that occurs one or two days before the menstrual cycle and lasts two or three days. Some patients, however, have no pain. Abnormal uterine bleeding and dyspareunia (painful intercourse) may also be evident in sexually active women. Infertility is another possible effect.

A health history including the menstrual pattern is necessary to elicit specific symptoms. On bimanual pelvic examination, fixed tender nodules may be detected and the uterus may be restricted in motility, indicating the presence of adhesions. Laparoscopy confirms the diagnosis.

Management

Treatment depends on the nature of the symptoms, desire for pregnancy and the extent of the disease. If the woman is asymptomatic, observation every six months may be all that is required. Other therapy for varying degrees of symptoms may be palliation, hormone administration or surgery. Palliative efforts include analgesics, prostaglandin inhibitors and pregnancy; the latter will alleviate symptoms because of the residual reaction in the various endometrial sites.

Hormonal therapy, in which oestrogen and progesterone is given for six to nine months, will suppress menstruation and relieve menstrual pain (dysmenorrhoea). However, there may be side-effects such as fluid retention (diuretics may be recommended), nausea, weight gain, some vaginal discharge and possibly thromboembolism. If these side-effects are troublesome, treatment is stopped. Another type of hormonal therapy involves the use of a synthetic androgen, danazol, which causes atrophy of the endometrium and subsequent amenorrhoea. The drug inhibits the release of gonadotropin with minimal overt sex hormone stimulation. This medication is expensive and may cause troublesome side-effects such as fatigue, depression, weight gain, oily skin, mild acne, hot flushes and atrophy of the vagina and breasts.

If conservative measures are not helpful, surgery may be necessary. The procedure will depend on the individual patient's needs. Laparoscopy may be performed when it may be feasible to fulgurate (cut with high-frequency current) endometrial lesions and to lyse (cut) adhesions. Lasers can be used to vaporize the endometrial lesions or to coagulate them.

Depending on circumstances, other surgical procedures may be used, including laparotomy, abdominal hysterectomy, bilateral salpingo-oophorectomy and appendectomy.

Prognosis

In mild to moderate endometriosis, the use of hormonal or surgical treatment relieves pain and enhances the chance of pregnancy. For women over age 35 or those willing to sacrifice reproductive capability, total hysterectomy provides good results.

Nursing Care

The nursing history and physical examination concentrate on detecting specific symptoms and determining when and how they occur. The woman's desire to have (more) children must be explored as this will guide the approach taken to treatment.

Relief of dysmenorrhoea involves pain assessment and evaluation of treatments, including prescribed medications that are designed to provide relief. Relief of dyspareunia and infertility are important patient goals.

Emotional support is important, especially if the chance of a wanted pregnancy seems slender. Unusual menstrual bleeding should always be reported and investigated.

Adenomyosis

In this condition, endometriosis involves the uterine wall; the incidence is highest in women from 40 to 50 years of age. Symptoms are menorrhagia, dysmenorrhoea, polymenorrhoea (abnormally frequent bleeding) and premenstrual staining. On physical examination, the uterus is felt to be enlarged, firm and tender. Treatment depends on the severity of bleeding and pain; hysterectomy offers greater relief than more conservative forms of therapy.

MALIGNANT CONDITIONS

Malignant tumours of the reproductive tract are the second highest cause of death in the United Kingdom. Recent statistics are presented in Table 23.1.

Cancer of the Cervix

Cervical cancer is the eighth most common malignancy of the female reproductive tract. Its incidence has increased significantly in recent years, and premalignant lesions are now frequently detected in young women in their early twenties, although diagnosis of malignancy still occurs most often between the ages of 30 and 50. Epidemiological studies strongly suggest a link between cervical cancer and number of sexual partners, since women who have sexual intercourse at an early age and have many partners seem to be most at risk.

Diagnosis

Premalignant lesions can be detected by a cervical smear. A staging system has also been developed, which allows the doctor to estimate the extent of the disease (premalignant and malignant lesions) so that treatment can be planned and prognosis estimated (see Table 22.1, p. 732).

Clinical diagnosis involved evaluation of signs and symptoms, X-ray and laboratory studies, colposcopy and biopsy. If the disease is advanced, then dilatation and curettage, computed tomography, lymphangiography and magnetic resonance imaging may also be of value.

Clinical Features

Early cancer of the cervix is asymptomatic. The two early symptoms are vaginal discharge and irregular vaginal bleeding. The discharge increases gradually in amount and becomes watery and, finally, dark and foul smelling because of necrosis and infection of the tumour. Bleeding occurs at irregular intervals, between periods (metrorrhagia) or after menopause. It may be very slight, just enough to spot the undergarments, and it is noted usually after some form of trauma (intercourse or defaecation). As the disease continues, the bleeding may become constant and may increase in amount.

As the cancer advances, the tissues outside the cervix become invaded, including lymph glands anterior to the sacrum. In one third of patients with invasive cervical cancer, the disease involves the fundus. The nerves in this region become involved, producing excruciating pain in the back and the legs that is relieved only by narcotics. The final picture, when untreated, is one of extreme

Table 23.1 *Cancer statistics in the United Kingdom for women*

	Incidence (1983)	%	Rank (incidence in female population)	Mortality (1984)	%	Rank (mortality in female population)	Rate per (million in UK)	5-year survival rate (%)
Breast	24,410	20	1	15,070	20	1	844	64
Ovary	5,130	4	6	4,290	6	5	177	27
Cervix	4,400	4	8	2,200	3	8	152	57
Uterus	3,720	3	9	1,143	No figures provided	15	128	72

Total incidence of malignancy in the female population in the UK (1983) = 124,170
Total mortality from malignant disease in the female population in the UK (1985) = 75,970
Note: Information on this table is obtained from Cancer Registries set up by the DHSS in 1962, which report annually. However, there is no statutory requirement to report details of cancer registrations so the incidence of malignancy seen here may be underestimated. Mortality statistics may also be unreliable because it is often difficult to determine the exact cause of death, especially in older people who are likely to suffer from several degenerative conditions simultaneously, of which cancer may be only one.
(Sources: (1) HMSO (1985) Mortality Statistics: Cause. England and Wales, 1984; (2) Cancer Research Campaign (1987) Facts on Cancer. By kind permission. [Collates figures from England and Wales with those from Scotland and Northern Ireland, citing sources of all figures.])

emaciation and anaemia, often with pyrexia due to secondary infection and abscesses in the ulcerating mass.

Management

Premalignant lesions detected on colposcopy may be destroyed by laser. Larger lesions may be removed by cone biopsy (removal of a cone-shaped section of the cervix). Pregnancy is still possible, but there is some risk of spontaneous abortion, especially if the cone is large. Follow-up is always necessary to detect recurrence. For invasive cervical carcinoma, treatment of choice is radiotherapy, but this may be combined with radical pelvic surgery for advanced malignancy. This involves removal of the uterus, tubes, ovaries, parametrium and the upper two thirds of the vagina (Wertheim's hysterectomy). Pelvic lymph nodes are removed to prevent metastasis. Local infiltration backwards to the rectum and forwards to the bladder may require pelvic exenteration (removal of the pelvic organs).

Cancer of the Endometrium

Cancer of the endometrium (fundus or corpus) of the uterus has increased in incidence partly because people are living longer and there is more accurate reporting. As part of their role in health education, nurses should alert all women of the need to report irregular or unusual vaginal bleeding, especially after the menopause.

Women who take oestrogens have an increased risk of acquiring endometrial cancer. Low doses are prescribed wherever possible.

For older women, the increased risk of endometrial cancer from oestrogen use is proportional to the length of time during which they are taken (particularly five years or longer). Oestrogens are effective for the vasomotor symptoms of menopause if doses are kept low and treatment is limited to less than a year.

Clinical Features

About 50 per cent of all patients with postmenopausal bleeding have cancer of the fundus. Its progress is slow, metastasis occurs later and irregular vaginal bleeding often appears early enough in the disease to allow cure by removal of the uterus. In late metastasis, radium and radiotherapy are the usual therapeutic measures.

Diagnosis

Diagnosis may be made from the clinical history, followed by dilatation and curettage to obtain endometrial curettings. All women taking hormone replacement therapy must be kept under medical surveillance.

Hysterectomy

A total hysterectomy involves the removal of the uterus, including the cervix. This procedure is done for dysfunctional uterine bleeding; endometriosis; malignant and nonmalignant growths on the uterus, cervix and adnexa; problems of pelvic relaxation and prolapse; and irreparable injury to the uterus.

▶ NURSING PROCESS
▶ THE PATIENT UNDERGOING A HYSTERECTOMY

▶ *Assessment*

The nursing history and physical and pelvic examination with the laboratory studies give a picture of the patient's problems. Additional questions will include psychosocial implications since hysterectomy affects personal and deep-seated experiences and relationships.

▶ *Patient's Problems*

Based on the assessment, the patient's major problems may include the following:

● Anxiety related to the diagnosis of cancer, fear of pain, loss of femininity and disfigurement.
● Disturbance in self-concept related to altered body image, sexuality, fertility and relationships with family and partner.
● Pain related to surgery and other adjuvant therapy.
● Grieving related to loss of reproductive organs.
● Lack of knowledge about the perioperative aspects of hysterectomy as well as adjustment to postoperative recovery and convalescence.

▶ *Planning and Implementation*
▶ Expected Outcomes

The major outcomes for the patient may include relief of anxiety, acceptance of self as altered, absence of pain/discomfort, reduction of grief and acquisition of knowledge and understanding of what a hysterectomy means.

Nursing Care

Relief of Anxiety

Anxiety in the woman undergoing a hysterectomy stems from: unfamiliar environment, effects of surgery on body image and reproductive ability, fear of pain and other discomforts and sensitivity and possibly feelings of embarrassment. She may fear that a sexually transmitted disease may be discovered or that she may no longer fulfil her role as a woman. Conflicts between medical treatment and religious beliefs may trouble her. It is necessary for the nurse to determine the meaning of this experience to the patient, and it is also necessary for the patient to verbalize her feelings to someone who understands and can help.

The nurse identifies the patient's strengths that will produce a positive effect. Through the preoperative period, explanations are given concerning physical preparation.

Preoperative Preparation

The pubic and perineal regions usually are carefully shaved and cleansed with soap and water (some hospitals do not require shaving). The intestinal tract and the bladder must be empty before the patient is sent to the operating room. This is most important to prevent contamination and accidental injury to the bladder or intestinal tract. Preoperative medications the morning of surgery will help the patient relax.

Self-Concept

The nursing history will reveal how the woman feels about having a hysterectomy. Concerns may surface such as the inability to have children, loss of femininity and questions about the impact on sexual relationships. The patient needs to be reassured that she will still have a vagina and that sexual intercourse can be experienced following a temporary period of abstinence postoperatively while the tissues heal.

When hormonal balances are upset, as often occurs in disturbances of the reproductive system, the patient may exhibit depression and heightened emotional sensitivity to people and situations. Understanding must be shared by the family as well as the health care providers. The nurse who exhibits interest, concern and willingness to listen to the patient's fears will add immeasurably to the patient's progress throughout the surgical experience. Since the decision to have a hysterectomy rests with the patient, this must be respected and supported.

Postoperative Care

The principles of general postoperative care for abdominal surgery apply. Particular attention is given to peripheral circulation, such as noting the presence of varicosities and promoting circulation with leg exercises and anti-embolic stockings.

Problems of voiding may be expected because of the proximity of the surgical intervention to the bladder; oedema or nerve trauma may cause temporary loss of bladder tone, but catheterization is avoided if possible because of the risk of urinary tract infection. Constipation is often a problem.

Patient Education

Information is provided to the patient according to her needs. It is important for her to know what kind of operation she has had and what limitations may be expected. Menstruation will no longer occur; symptoms of menopause will not result if ovaries are intact, but if they have been removed, hormonal replacement may be considered. A hysterectomy causes some reduced strength and lassi-

tude for a few weeks. This is to be expected and should gradually improve.

The patient should resume activities gradually; however, this does not mean sitting for long periods of time since this may cause pooling of the blood in the pelvis and the potential for thromboembolism. Showers are preferable to bathing to reduce vaginal infection. The patient is advised to avoid straining, lifting, sexual intercourse, or driving until she has been seen again by the gynaecologist. Vaginal discharge, excessive bleeding and elevated temperature must be reported to a health care professional.

► *Evaluation*
► **Expected Outcomes**

1. Patient is free of anxiety.
   a. Asks specific questions regarding the effects of surgery on menstruation, fertility, sexual relations and cancer.
   b. Discusses the surgical procedure and postoperative course.
2. Accepts herself as she now is.
   a. Includes her partner in planning convalescence.
   b. Verbalizes understanding of her problem and projected solution.
   c. Takes time and care with her appearance.
   d. Shares her plans with the nurse regarding her first two weeks at home.
   e. Displays no depression or regret.
3. Experiences minimal pain and discomfort.
   a. Is apyrexial for 24 hours before discharge.
   b. Has stable vital signs.
   c. Ambulates early.
   d. Notes absence of calf pain, redness, tenderness or swelling in extremities.
   e. Reports no urinary problems or abdominal distension.
4. Understands the need for, and practises:
   a. Deep breathing, turning and leg exercises as taught.
   b. Increasing activity and ambulation daily.
   c. Adequate fluid intake and adequate urinary output.
   d. Alternating periods of rest with activity.
   e. Reporting appropriate symptoms.
   f. Relating what hormonal replacement she is prescribed and its purpose.
   g. Keeping follow-up clinic appointments.

(See Nursing Care Plan 23.1 for the patient undergoing hysterectomy.)

Cancer of the Vulva

Primary cancer of the vulva represents 3 to 4 per cent of all gynaecological malignancies and is seen mostly in postmenopausal women. More Caucasians than non-

► NURSING CARE PLAN 23.1: THE PATIENT UNDERGOING HYSTERECTOMY

Nursing care plan for Bindoo Chopra, a 47-year-old Hindu woman who works full-time in a factory. She is married and has three teenaged children.

Patient's problems	Expected outcomes	Nursing care	Rationale
1. Risk of shock and haemorrhage	No shock or haemorrhage	1a. Monitor vital signs until stable and within normal limits (pulse, blood pressure, temperature, vaginal loss); report any abnormality to doctor	Detect early signs of shock and haemorrhage
2. Risk of deep vein thrombosis	No venous thrombosis, pulmonary embolus	2a. Encourage early ambulation (first day postoperatively) b. Encourage leg exercises as taught by physiotherapist	Calf muscles act as pumps, enhancing venous return; bedrest encourages venous pooling in deep leg veins, haemostasis and increases risk of thrombus formation
		c. Observe calves for swelling; ask about tenderness; report abnormalities to doctor	Early detection of signs and symptoms of deep venous thrombosis, allowing prompt investigation and effective treatment
		d. Observe colour and consistency of sputum; breathlessness	Bloodstained sputum is a sign of pulmonary embolism
		e. Give anticoagulants as prescribed	Prophylactic, given patient's age, nature of surgery and prolonged inactivity in bed
3. Risk of postoperative chest infection	No chest infection	3a. Encourage deep breathing as taught by physiotherapist	Ventilates airways fully; anaesthesia depresses cough reflex and ciliary action
		b. Encourage change of position	Helps pulmonary secretions drain
		c. Provide analgesia before physiotherapy as prescribed	Allows full participation
		d. Teach to support incision when coughing or expectorating	Prevents undue discomfort/pain at incision site
		e. Monitor temperature and report pyrexia (above 37°C) to doctor	Detect signs and symptoms of infection early
		f. Monitor condition of sputum: amount, consistency, colour, odour	As above
4. Risk of postoperative pain (especially during first 48 hours)	Pain controlled; will get out of bed and start physiotherapy within 24 hours	4a. Provide analgesia as prescribed; evaluate effectiveness 30 to 60 minutes later	Pain serves no useful purpose here and its effects are counterproductive as they prevent active participation in
		b. Provide comfort measures, e.g., most comfortable position in bed, heat pad to abdomen	Additional comfort measures demonstration of concern help, especially when patient is anxious
5. Risk of urinary tract infection	No urinary tract infection	5a. Encourage patient to drink at least 2 litres clear fluid daily	Catheterized in theatre; flushing action of urine will avoid bacteriuria
		b. Monitor fluid input and output	Ensure correct fluid balance

► NURSING CARE PLAN 23.1: THE PATIENT UNDERGOING HYSTERECTOMY

Patient's problems	Expected outcomes	Nursing care	Rationale
		c. Observe urine for colour, odour, cloudy deposits; check that patient does not complain of dysuria or frequency (report abnormalities to doctor)	Detect signs and symptoms of urinary tract infection promptly, so that treatment can begin
		d. Monitor temperature; report pyrexia (above 37°C) to doctor	Early detection of infection so that effective treatment can begin
6. Risk of infection to abdominal incision	No infection	6a. Keep intact dressing applied in theatre until third postoperative day	Wounds should be re-epithelialized by this time
		b. Encourage showering and not bathing	Prevents secondary infection
		c. Reapply nonadherent dressing after showering	Prevents trauma and contamination of new, delicate granulation tissue by clothing or environment
		d. See problem 5d	
		e. Observe wound condition at each dressing change: erythema, discharge, odour	As for problem 5d
7. Risk of infection to internal wound (vaginal stump)	No infection	7a. Encourage showering and not bathing	Prevents cross-infection
		b. Provide sterile sanitary pads, changed regularly	Prevents ascending infection
		c. Monitor vaginal loss; instruct patient to report bright or heavy blood loss, discharge with odour — report to doctor	Detect signs and symptoms of infection and secondary haemorrhage due to infection
		d. See Problem 5d	
8. Nausea and vomiting	No nausea or vomiting	8a. Provide antiemetic intramuscularly as prescribed, as prophylaxis	Anaesthetics and opiates induce vomiting, which serve no useful purpose
		b. Provide clear fluids when bowel sounds return, progressing to light then normal diet	Lack of food may exacerbate feelings of nausea
9. Risk of constipation	No constipation; normal bowel habit re-established within 5 days	9a. Encourage diet rich in fibre, fluids	Fibre attracts fluid thus easing passage of stool
		b. Give aperient as prescribed if bowels are not opened by third postoperative day	Lack of mobility in hospital and effect of opiates may slow bowel action despite attention to diet
10. Anxiety because of strange surroundings, not knowing what to expect during hospital stay, effects of operation	Anxiety within normal limits	10a. Provide explanations of each procedure, and why treatment is necessary, e.g., early ambulation	Anxiety delays recovery and suppresses the inflammatory response, depressing healing and resistance to infection; explanation allays anxiety
		b. Provide leaflets or written information about hysterectomy	Written information is a useful adjunct to verbal information

►

► NURSING CARE PLAN 23.1: THE PATIENT UNDERGOING HYSTERECTOMY

Patient's problems	Expected outcomes	Nursing care	Rationale
		c. Arrange for visit from interpreter of same sex	Communication problems may exist undetected
		d. Involve partner and family to discussions where appropriate	Family will wish to share patient's fears
11. Lack of knowledge about beneficial behaviour during longer term recovery at home	Will be able to describe expected course of recovery and how to optimize progress	11a. Provide written and verbal information to include partner, family and interpreter, as necessary	See problem 10
		b. Ensure patient knows date and time of follow-up appointment in outpatient department	

Caucasians are affected. The most common form is squamous cell carcinoma, although adenomas and melanomas have been reported. Aetiology is poorly understood.

Clinical Features and Diagnosis

Long-standing pruritus is the most common symptom of vulvular cancer. Bleeding, foul-smelling discharge and pain may also be present. Early lesions appear as a chronic dermatitis; later a lump may be noted that continues to grow and becomes a hard ulcerated, cauliflower-like growth. Diagnosis is confirmed by biopsy. Any vulval lesion that is persistent, ulcerated or does not heal with proper therapy should undergo biopsy.

The nurse is in a unique position to encourage a woman with this disease to seek help, since this is one of the most curable of all malignant conditions: it is visible and accessible and grows relatively slowly. Unfortunately, women so affected seem reluctant to seek medical attention. Procrastination causes more extensive involvement, jeopardizing cure.

Management

Vulvectomy is the treatment of choice. Small, uncomplicated lesions may simply be excised (simple vulvectomy), but radical vulvectomy is necessary once carcinoma has become invasive, with dissection of pelvic and inguinal lymph nodes. Occasionally, part of the urethra, vagina and rectum may be removed. For women too elderly or frail to withstand surgery and anaesthesia, radiotherapy is the treatment of choice, but results are less encouraging.

► NURSING PROCESS
► THE PATIENT UNDERGOING A VULVECTOMY

► Assessment

Physical and pelvic examination are important in estab-

lishing the extent of the disease, and may be used as an opportunity to establish rapport, as delay in seeking medical help is common through modesty, denial or neglect. Psychosexual factors can be assessed, and preoperative teaching and psychological encouragement are then possible.

► Patient's Problems

Based on the assessment and other data, the patient's major problems may include the following:

● Anxiety related to the diagnosis and aftermath of surgery.
● Alteration in skin integrity related to wound drainage.
● Potential for infection related to proximity of excretory function.
● Alteration in comfort related to surgical incision and subsequent wound care.
● Sexual dysfunction related to change in body image.
● Lack of self-care related to lack of understanding of perineal care and general health status.

► Planning and Implementation
► Expected Outcomes:

The major outcomes for the patient may include acceptance of and preparation for surgical intervention, avoidance of infection and postsurgical complications, recovery of the best possible sexual function and ability to perform adequate and appropriate self-care.

Preoperative Nursing Care

Relieving Anxiety

The patient must be allowed time to talk and ask questions. Fear of mutilation and loss of function is lessened when a woman of childbearing age learns that the possibility of having sexual relations is good and that pregnancy is possible following simple vulvectomy. The nurse must know what the surgeon has told the patient.

Preoperative Preparation

Preoperative preparation is described in Chapter 2. Additionally, some surgeons may require skin preparation. Antibiotic prophylaxis and heparin may be commenced and continued postoperatively.

Postoperative Nursing Care

Wound Care

When the patient returns from theatre, perineal dressings are more likely to remain in place and be comfortable if a T-binder is used. Groin wounds may be covered with simple dressings. Pressure dressings may be placed over the wounds to prevent accumulation of lymph and serum. Many surgeons insert plastic tubes through stab wounds in each inguinal area with attachment to portable suction. This arrangement facilitates apposition of tissue flaps and prevents accumulation of serum.

The wound is cleansed daily with warm normal saline irrigations or other antiseptic solutions as prescribed. After a gentle cleansing, irrigation is pleasant and non-traumatizing and enhances circulation.

Comfort Measures

Since sutures may be taut because of the surgeon's attempt to approximate tissues, comfortable positioning is required. Perhaps a pillow placed under the knees will relieve tension on the incision. When placed on her side, it is more comfortable for the patient and reduces tension on the wound to have a pillow placed between her legs and against the lumbar region.

Pressure-relieving devices, e.g., low air loss bed or mattress, will help distribute weight and relieve pressure. Moving from one position to another requires time and patience on the part of both patient and nurse. Ambulation may be attempted on the second day.

Analgesics are given as required for comfort. Since primary healing rarely occurs, debridement is usually performed to provide satisfactory conditions for healing by secondary intention. Because the healing process is slow and the nature of the surgery is often disquieting, the patient is apt to be discouraged. The nurse must be aware of the patient's uneasiness about being 'caught' unduly exposed when visitors arrive or someone enters the room. She will be sensitive about odours. Thus, cleanliness, deodorant sprays, immediate removal of soiled dressings, and adequate ventilation contribute to a more pleasant environment.

Prevention of Infection

A low-residue diet will prevent straining on defaecation and wound contamination. An indwelling urinary catheter may be necessary. The incidence of infection is high, and every attempt must be made to prevent it. Showers are safer than bathing.

Patient Education

The patient is encouraged to share her concerns as she convalesces and begins to assume increasing responsibility for her care. As she participates in changing her dressings and cleansing herself, she can use a mirror to see the perineal area. By commenting on how well the tissues are healing, and that they are looking more normal, the nurse will be able to lift the patient's spirits.

The nurse explains the need for the patient to share her concerns with her partner. Activities are gradually increased and words of encouragement mean a great deal.

Post-hospital care requires giving complete instructions to a family member who will assist in caring for this patient at home or to the community nurse who will be visiting her. Gradual resumption of physical and social activities is encouraged. The cure rate of properly treated vulvar carcinoma is 50 to 60 per cent. In the absence of lymph node metastasis, the cure rate is around 85 to 90 per cent.

A radical vulvectomy is often extensive and may require a second admission and operation for skin grafting. This is determined on an individual basis.

► *Evaluation*
► **Expected Outcomes**

1. Patient adjusts to the effects of surgery.
   a. Uses available resources in coping with and alleviating emotional stress.
   b. Asks questions relating to postoperative expectations.
   c. Demonstrates willingness to discuss alternate methods for expressing love.
2. Avoids infection and postoperative complications.
   a. Is free of any signs and symptoms of infection: vital signs within normal limits.
   b. Begins to move with a minimum of discomfort.
   c. Maintains cleanliness of the site following micturition or defaecation.
3. Assumes appropriate self-care.
   a. Participates more each day in her dressing changes.
   b. Uses the mirror to observe progress in wound healing.
   c. Irrigates the wound for comfort and to stimulate healing.

Cancer of the Vagina

Cancer of the vagina usually occurs as a result of metastasis from choriocarcinoma or from cancer of the cervix or adjacent organs, such as from the uterus, vulva, bladder or rectum. Primary cancer of the vagina is rare. Before 1970, it occurred predominantly postmenopausal women. In the 1970s it was revealed that maternal ingestion of diethyl-stilboestrol (DES) affected female offspring who were exposed *in utero*. Benign genital tract abnormalities have occurred in a majority of these young women. Adenosis of the vagina is a common finding.

Nursing Care

Encouraging close co-operation with health care staff is the prime target of nursing intervention with daughters who have been exposed to diethylstilboestrol *in utero*. They are at an age when sexuality in all its ramifications, including pregnancy, is of significance. Emotional support for mothers and daughters undoubtedly needs constant bolstering. For young women who have had vaginal reconstructive surgery, specific vaginal dilating procedures may be initiated. Water-soluble lubricants are helpful in reducing dyspareunia. If a possible malignancy develops, requiring treatment, all aspects and effects of radiation therapy, chemotherapy or surgery need to be explored on an individual basis.

Cancer of the Ovary

Ovarian cancer is difficult to diagnose and is unique in that primary cancers may occur and the ovary may be the recipient of metastases from other cancers. It carries an annual mortality rate of over 5,000, and is the sixth most prevalent cancer in women. The peak incidence is in the sixth to eighth decades of life, and it is slightly more common in non-Caucasians.

Of the many studies attempting to relate some causative factor to ovarian cancer, the most significant study by the Centers for Disease Control, Atlanta, United States, indicated that a protective effect was identified in those women who used oral contraceptives. Hereditary factors are being studied for additional clues.

Clinical Features

Because early signs and symptoms are similar to those of ovarian cysts or endometriosis, other means of differentiating benign from potentially malignant growths must be used. Features include irregular menses, increasing premenstrual tension, menorrhagia with breast tenderness and an early menopause. Before puberty and after menopause there may be precocious breast development and uterine bleeding. Virilization may be noted. Ovarian malignancy may be observed more frequently in women who are infertile, nulliparous, anovulatory or habitual aborters. In addition to a long history of ovarian dysfunction or malfunction, persistent gastrointestinal symptoms in a woman aged 40 or over that cannot be definitely diagnosed should raise a suspicion of ovarian malignancy. Early and insidious symptoms include vague abdominal discomfort, dyspepsia, flatulence, eructations and a feeling of fullness after a light meal.

Diagnosis

Because these tumours are located deep in the abdomen and are often painless, it is difficult to obtain an early diagnosis. Pelvic examination is unlikely to detect early ovarian cancer. Pelvic imaging techniques are unhelpful in screening patients who are asymptomatic. Tumour antigens are being studied for their potential as tumour markers.

Management

For ovarian cancer, surgical removal is the goal. Because of high morbidity and mortality, every effort is made to stage the tumour as accurately as possible and to direct treatment accordingly. A total abdominal hysterectomy with bilateral salpingo-oophorectomy may be done. Chemotherapy using cisplatin in combination with other agents such as doxorubicin may be used. It is not uncommon to do an exploratory laparotomy ('second look') following adjunct therapies in order to determine whether malignancy persists. Further chemotherapy may be required.

Nursing Care

The combination of two major clues—(1) a long history of ovarian dysfunction and (2) vague, undiagnosed, persistent gastrointestinal symptoms in the woman over 40—should alert the nurse to the possibility of early malignancy. Usually, ovarian malignancy is extensive at the time of diagnosis. Following assessment and evaluation, nursing measures will include those related to the various treatment modalities of surgery, chemotherapy and palliation. Emotional support and comfort measures plus attentiveness and caring are of major importance to this patient and her family.

Radiotherapy

Radiotherapy plays a central role in the treatment of many gynaecological malignancies (see also Chapter 2, Care of the Patient With Cancer).

External Beam Therapy

Betatrons, linear accelerators and cobalt 60 units are capable of delivering high doses of well-collimated irradiation deep within the pelvis to the site of the tumour. Side-effects are cumulative and express themselves as the total dose exceeds the body's natural capacity to repair the radiation effect. Radiation enteritis, expressed by diarrhoea and abdominal cramping, and radiation cystitis, manifested by frequency, urgency and dysuria, may ensue. This does not indicate an overdosage. It is a natural manifestation of the normal tissues' response to the radiotherapy programme. The radiologist and nurse inform the

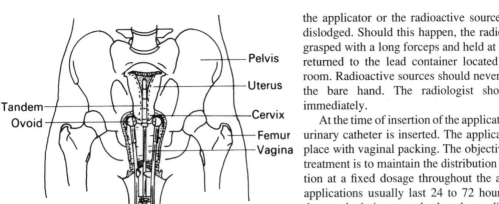

Figure 23.5 Placement of tandem and ovoids for internal radiotherapy. (© 1987 J. Wolfe.)

patient in advance of these possible side-effects and employ a variety of measures to modify their impact when they occur, such as dietary control (by restricting the amount of fibre), the maintenance of fluid intake and the use of antispasmodic drugs. On occasion, severe reactions will require that treatment be suspended briefly until the normal tissues repair themselves.

Internal (Intracavitary) Irradiation

In the operating room, an examination is performed under anaesthesia, after which specially prepared applicators are inserted into the endometrial cavity and vagina. These devices are not loaded with radioactive material until the patient has returned to her room. X-ray films are obtained to determine the precise relationship of the applicator to the normal pelvic anatomy and tumour. When preparations are complete, the radiologist loads the applicators with predetermined amounts of radioactive material. This is called after-loading and allows for precise control of the radiation exposure received by the patient, with minimal exposure of the health care team. A patient undergoing internal radiation treatment is nursed in a single room.

Various applicators have been developed for intracavitary treatment. Some are inserted into the endometrial cavity and endocervical canal as multiple small irradiators (e.g., Heyman's capsules). Others consist of a central tube (tandem or intrauterine 'stem') placed through the dilated endocervical canal into the uterine cavity, which remains in fixed relationship with irradiators placed in the upper vagina on each side of the cervix (vaginal ovoids) (Figure 23.5).

Finally, the radiologist takes steps to secure the internal applicator in place. Nursing personnel need not fear that the applicator will be prematurely extruded. However, one should check from time to time to see that the applicator or the radioactive sources have not been dislodged. Should this happen, the radioactive source is grasped with a long forceps and held at arm's length and returned to the lead container located in the patient's room. Radioactive sources should never be grasped with the bare hand. The radiologist should be notified immediately.

At the time of insertion of the applicator, an indwelling urinary catheter is inserted. The applicator is secured in place with vaginal packing. The objective of the internal treatment is to maintain the distribution of internal radiation at a fixed dosage throughout the application. Such applications usually last 24 to 72 hours, depending on dose calculations made by the radiologist and the radiation physicist.

Nursing Care During Caesium Treatment

The patient is carefully observed and attended, although the nursing staff must try to reduce as much as possible radiation exposure to themselves. Nurses should stay in the immediate vicinity of the patient no longer than is necessary to deliver essential nursing care, and no nurse should attend the patient more than a half hour per day. Of course, a pregnant nurse should not be involved in the immediate care of such patients. Nurse–patient contacts provide a good opportunity for the patient to talk about her anxiety and fear. To minimize radiation exposure, the nurse may stay at the foot of the bed or at the entrance to the room.

During the application, the patient will be on absolute bedrest. She may move from side to side with her back supported by a pillow, and the head of the bed may be raised to 45 degrees. The patient should be encouraged to practise deep-breathing and cough exercises, and to flex and extend the feet to stretch the calf muscles in order to promote venous return. Pressure area care is much appreciated, but adequate care is given within the minimum amount of time at the bedside.

Usually, the patient is on a low-residue diet to prevent frequent bowel movements, otherwise the applicators may become dislodged. The nurse should inspect the catheter frequently to make sure that it is draining properly. The chief hazard of improper drainage is that the bladder may become distended. Discharge should be reported immediately to the doctor.

The patient is observed for evidence of pyrexia, nausea and vomiting. These symptoms should be reported, since they may indicate infection or perforation.

Caesium Removal

At the end of the prescribed period, the nurse may help to remove the applicator. Since the sources are 'afterloaded', they can be removed by the doctor in the same manner as they were inserted. A mild sedative may be required before the applicator is removed.

Postinsertion Care

Progressive ambulation is recommended after the period of enforced bedrest. The patient may shower as soon as she wishes. Diet may be offered as tolerated.

FURTHER READING

Books

General

Cavanagh, D., Ruffolo, E. H. and Marsden, D. E. (1985) *Gynecologic Cancer*, Appleton-Century-Crofts, Norwalk, Connecticut.

DiSara, P. J. and Creasman, W. T. (1984) *Clinical Gynecologic Oncology* (2nd edition), C. V. Mosby, St Louis.

Griffith, N. W., McEvers, J. and Becker, R. (1984) *Instructions for Obstetric and Gynecologic Patients*, W. B. Saunders, Philadelphia.

Hacker, N. (1986) *Essentials of Obstetrics and Gynecology*, W. B. Saunders, Philadelphia.

Kistner, R. W. (1986) *Gynecology* (4th edition), Year Book Medical Publishers, Chicago.

Sexually Transmitted Diseases

Adler, M. (1986) *ABC of Sexually Transmitted Diseases*, BMA, London.

DHSS (1988) *New Cases Seen At NHS Genitourinary Medicine Clinics in England 1976–86: Statistical Bulletin, 2 July*, HMSO, London.

Holmes, K. K. *et al.*

(1984) *Sexually Transmitted Diseases*, McGraw-Hill, New York.

Articles

General

Hill, E. C. (1985) Obstetrics and gynecology, *Journal of the American Medical Association*, October, Vol. 254, No. 16, pp. 2308–9.

Huppert, L. C. (1987) Hormonal replacement therapy: Benefits, risks, doses, *Medical Clinics of North America*, January, Vol. 71, No. 1, pp. 23–39.

King, L. A. (1987) Pelvic inflammatory disease, *Postgraduate Medicine*, March, Vol. 81, No. 4, pp. 105–14.

Cervical Cancer

Broadley, K. (1986) Cervical cancer, *Nursing Times*, Vol. 82, No. 24, pp. 29–32.

Yule, R. (1984) Cervical cancer: screening and prevention, *Nursing Mirror*, Vol. 159, No. 13, pp. 37–9.

Considerations For the Elderly

Parker, R. T. and Piscitelli, J. (1986) Gynecologic surgery in the elderly patient, *Clinical Obstetrics and Gynecology*, June, Vol. 29, No. 2, pp. 453–61.

Soper, J. T. and Creasman, W. T. (1986) Vulvar dystrophies, *Clinical Obstetrics and Gynecology*, June, Vol. 29, No. 2, pp. 431–9.

Steinke, E. E. and Berge, M. B. (1986) Sexuality and aging, *Journal of Gerontological Nursing*, June, Vol. 12, No. 6, pp. 6–10.

Endometriosis

Davis, G. D. (1986) Management of endometriosis and its associated adhesions with the CO_2 laser laparoscope, *Obstetrics and Gynecology*, September, Vol. 68, No. 3, pp. 422–5.

Parmley, T. H. (1983) Diagnosis: Endometriosis, *Hospital Medicine*, October, Vol. 19, No. 10, pp. 152–67.

Herpes Genitalis

Bryson, Y. G. *et al.* (1983) Treatment of first episodes of genital herpes simplex virus infection with oral acyclovir, *New England Journal of Medicine*, 21 April, Vol. 308, No. 16, pp. 916–21.

Corey, L. *et al.* (1983) Intravenous acyclovir for the treatment of primary genital herpes, *Annals of Internal Medicine*, January, Vol. 98, No. 6, pp. 914–21.

Fife, K. H., Raab, B. and Strauss, S. E. (1986) New options for genital herpes: Diagnosis/treatment, *Patient Care*, 15 April, Vol. 20, No. 7, pp. 20–46.

Reichman, R. C. *et al.* (1984) Treatment of recurrent genital herpes simplex infections with oral acyclovir, *Journal of the American Medical Association*, 27 April, Vol. 251, No. 16, pp. 2103–7.

Warmbrodt, L. (1983) Herpes: The shock, the stigma, the ways you can ease the emotional pain, *Registered Nurse*, May, Vol. 46, No. 5, pp. 47–9.

Hysterectomy

O'Laughlin, K. M. (1986) Changes in bladder function in the woman undergoing radical hysterectomy for cervical cancer, *JOGNN*, September/October, Vol. 15, No. 5, pp. 380–5.

Webb, C. and Wilson-Barnett, J. (1983) Self-concept, social support and hysterectomy, *International Journal of Nursing Studies*, Vol. 20, No. 2, pp. 97–107.

Wells, M. P. and Villano, K. (1985) Total abdominal hysterectomy, *AORNJ*, September, Vol. 42, No. 3, pp. 368–73.

Ovarian Cancer

Barber, H. R. K. (1986) Ovarian cancer, *CA*, May/June, Vol. 36, No. 3, pp. 149–83.

Copeland, L. J. (1985) Second-look laparotomy for ovarian carcinoma, *Clinical Obstetrics and Gynecology*, December, Vol. 28, No. 4, pp. 816–23.

Freedman, R. S. (1985) Recent immunologic advances affecting the management of ovarian cancer, *Clinical Obstetrics and Gynecology*, December, Vol. 28, No. 4, pp. 853–71.

Jenkins, J. F., Hubbard, S. M. and Howser, D. M. (1982) Managing intraperitoneal chemotherapy: A new assault on ovarian cancer, *Nursing*, May, Vol. 12, No. 5, pp. 76–83.

Jolles, C. J. (1985) Ovarian cancer: Histogenetic classification, histologic grading, diagnosis, staging, and epidemiology, *Clinical Obstetrics and Gynecology*, December, Vol. 28, No. 4, pp. 787–99.

Kavanagh, J. J. (1985) Investigational therapies for epithelial ovarian cancer, *Clinical Obstetrics and Gynecology*, December, Vol. 28, No. 4, pp. 846–52.

Malfetano, J. H. (1985) Current approaches to treatment of advanced ovarian cancer, *Current Concepts in Oncology*, Fall, Vol. 7, No. 3, pp. 3–9.

Weiss, G. R. (1986) Second-line chemotherapy for ovarian cancer, *Clinical Obstetrics and Gynecology*, September, Vol. 29, No. 3, pp. 665–77.

Radiotherapy

Vigliotti, A. P. G. *et al.* (1986) Radiotherapy research in gynecologic cancer, *Clinical Obstetrics and Gynecology*, September, Vol. 28, No. 3, pp. 647–64.

Reproductive Malignancy

Benedict, J. L. and Murphy, K. J. (1985) Cervical cancer screening, *Postgraduate Medicine*, December, Vol. 78, No. 8, pp. 69–79.

Hartz, A. *et al.* (1985) Obesity and endometrial cancer, *Internal Medicine*, September, Vol. 6, No. 9, pp. 61–6.

Kaplan, A. (1984) Carcinoma of the uterine corpus, *Hospital Medicine*, September, Vol. 20, No. 8, pp. 93–122.

Mansey, F. M. (1986) Vulvovaginal reconstruction following radical resections, *Clinical Obstetrics and Gynecology*, September, Vol. 29, No. 3, pp. 617–27.

Robertson, B. J. (1985) Tuboplasty: Use, resources, and nursing implications, *Perioperative Nursing Quarterly*, June, Vol. 1, No. 2, pp. 49–56.

Rubin, D. (1987) Gynecologic cancer: Cervical, vulvar, and vaginal malignancies, *Registered Nurse*, May, pp. 56–63.

Wabrek, A. J. and Gunn, J. L. (1984) Sexual and psychological implications of gynecologic malignancy, *JOGNN*, November/December, Vol. 13, No. 6, pp. 371–6.

Toxic Shock Syndrome

Cibulka, N. J. (1983) Toxic shock syndrome and other tampon-related risks, *JOGNN*, March/April, Vol. 12, No. 2, pp. 94–9.

MacDonald, K. L. *et al.* (1987) Toxic shock syndrome, *Journal of the American Medical Association*, 27 February, Vol. 257, No. 8, pp. 1053–9.

Morrison, V. A. and Olafield, E. C. (1983) Postoperative toxic shock syndrome, *Archives of Surgery*, July, Vol. 118, No. 7, pp. 791–4.

Smirniotopoulos, T. T. (1983) Update on toxic shock syndrome, *Postgraduate Medicine*, October, Vol. 74, No. 4, pp. 369–72.

Tofte, R. W. and Williams, D. N. (1983) Toxic shock syndrome, *Postgraduate Medicine*, January, Vol. 73, No. 1, pp. 275–88.

Toxic shock syndrome (1985) *Nursing*, October, Vol. 15, No. 10, p. 74.

Wheltam, J. (1984) Update on toxic shock: How to spot it and treat it, *Registered Nurse*, February, Vol. 47, No. 2, pp. 55–60.

Vaginal and Vulvar Cancer

DiSaia, P. (1985) Management of superficially invasive vulvar carcinoma, *Clinical Obstetrics and Gynecology*, March, Vol. 28, No. 1, pp. 196–203.

Hurley, M., Meyer-Ruppel, A. and Evans, E. (1983) Emma needed more than standard teaching (radical vulvectomy), *Nursing*, March, Vol. 13, No. 3, pp. 63–4.

Iverson, T. (1985) New approaches to treatment of squamous cell carcinoma of the vulva, *Clinical Obstetrics and Gynecology*, March, Vol. 28, No. 1, pp. 204–10.

Kaplan, A. L. (1985) Vulvar reconstruction, *Clinical Obstetrics and Gynecology*, March, Vol. 28, No. 1, pp. 211–19.

Peters, W. A., Kumar, N. B. and Morley, G. W. (1985) Carcinoma of the vagina: Factors influencing treatment outcomes, *Cancer*, 15 February, Vol. 55, No. 4, pp. 892–7.

Piver, M. S. (1984) Early diagnosis and treatment of vulvar cancer, *Hospital Medicine*, February, Vol. 20, No. 2, pp. 163–77.

Smerz, L. R *et al.* (1985) Second-look laparotomy after chemotherapy in the management of ovarian malignancy, *American Obstetrics and Gynecology*, 15 July, Vol. 152, No. 6, pp. 661–8.

Wilkinson, E. J. (1985) Superficial invasive carcinoma of the vulva, *Clinical Obstetrics and Gynecology*, March, Vol. 28, No. 1, pp. 188–95.

Vulvovaginal Infections

Bourcier, K. M. and Seidler, A. J. (1987) Chlamydia and condylomata acuminata: An update for the nurse practitioner, *JOGNN*, January, Vol. 16, No. 1, pp. 17–22.

Burnhill, M. S. (1986) Taking a serious approach to vulvovaginitis, *Contemporary Obstetrics and Gynecology*, September, Vol. 28, No. 3, pp. 69–79.

Chlamydia: The silent epidemic (1985) *Time*, 4 February, Vol. 125, No. 5, p. 67.

Gilly, P. A. (1986) Vaginal discharge, *Postgraduate Medicine*, December, Vol. 80, No. 8, pp. 231–7.

Kaufman, C. A. and Jones, P. G. (1986) Candidiasis, *Postgraduate Medicine*, July, Vol. 80, No. 1, pp. 129–34.

Kaufman, R. H. (1986) Common causes of vaginitis, *Hospital Medicine*, November, Vol. 22, No. 11, pp. 23–44.

King, J. (1984) Vaginitis, *JOGNN*, March/April, Vol. 13, No. 2, pp. 41s–8s.

King, L. A. (1987) Pelvic inflammatory disease, *Postgraduate Medicine*, March, Vol. 81, No. 4, pp. 105–14.

Ladogana, L. (1985) Pelvic inflammatory disease: Diagnosis and management, *Medical Times*, November, Vol. 113, No. 11, pp. 25–31.

Salvio, K. and Aprezzio, J. J. (1984) New antibiotics in the treatment of pelvic infections, *JOGNN*, September/October, Vol. 13, No. 5, pp. 308–11.

Smith, L. S. and Lauver, D. (1984) Assessment and management of vaginitis and cervicitis, *Nurse Practitioner*, June, Vol. 9, No. 6, pp. 34, 39–47, 67.

Washington, D. (1984) Helping the patient with vaginitis, *Registered Nurse*, September, Vol. 47, No. 9, pp. 63–71.

chapter 24 ▬▬▬▬▬▬▬▬▬▬

ASSESSMENT AND CARE OF PATIENTS WITH BREAST DISORDERS

BREAST DEVELOPMENT AND PHYSIOLOGY

The breasts of males and females begin to differ at puberty. In females, marked enlargement begins between the ages of 10 and 14 years through hormone stimulation, and the nipple develops its adult, protruding shape. Anatomically, the adult breast is glandular. It consists of a series of lobules connected to the main ducts in the nipples by a series of smaller ducts. Many women notice cyclical changes and breast tenderness before menstruation. During pregnancy the breasts enlarge greatly and the nipples become more sensitive and prominent from about the eighth week of gestation. These changes reverse when lactation ceases.

Psychosocial Implications

In Western cultures, where emphasis is placed on youth and sexual attractiveness, women are likely to react strongly to any actual or suspected disease or injury affecting the breasts. Fear of disfigurement may prevent a woman from seeking immediate medical attention after she has detected suspicious breast changes.

All health professionals, including nurses, should be aware of the need to teach women to be alert to early signs of breast disease, to report suspicious changes as soon as they are detected and to promote breast self-examination.

INCIDENCE OF BREAST DISEASE

The breast is the most common primary site for malignancy to develop in women in the United Kingdom. Although the area is fairly accessible to medical examination, detection and diagnosis of breast disease can be difficult because of the normal physiological changes in breast tissue that accompany menstruation, pregnancy, lactation and the menopause.

Approximately 25 per cent of all women have irregular

areas in their breasts at some time, usually as a result of hyperplasia and involution just before menstruation. These irregularities, mainly apparent in the upper, outer quadrant, feel granular or nodular, but do not grow or consolidate. They are usually bilateral. Abnormal areas of breast tissue do not fluctuate throughout the menstrual cycle, and are usually unilateral.

In women and men, benign lesions of the breast occur more frequently than malignant lesions (70 per cent benign vs. 30 per cent malignant); 99 per cent of malignant tumours occur in females. Benign lesions occur frequently in premenopausal women.

Benign lesions, according to order of frequency and the age of presentation, include: fibrocystic disease (20 to 45 years), fibroadenoma (20 to 39 years) and intraductal papilloma (35 to 45 years). By contrast, cancer of the breast is manifested chiefly in the menopausal and postmenopausal years, with incidence increasing progressively as the woman gets older. Approximately 75 per cent of breast cancers occur in patients over the age of 40; less than 2 per cent occur before the age of 30.

Every year approximately 24,000 new cases of breast malignancy are diagnosed, and over 15,000 women die of the disease.

ASSESSMENT

Breast Examination

Breast examination forms part of every general medical or gynaecological examination. It involves inspection and palpation to detect abnormalities.

Inspection

The woman is asked to strip to the waist and is seated in a comfortable position facing the examiner, with her hands in her lap. Size and symmetry are noted. Slight differences in size is normal. The skin is inspected for inflammation, thickening, oedema and vascular pattern. Erythema may indicate local inflammation or presence of a neoplasm. Increased vascularity may signal increased blood supply to a growing malignancy. Lymphatic obstruction by tumour cells may cause oedema, producing characteristic pitting of the skin (orange peel appearance). Nipples vary between one woman and another, but in the same woman they are usually similar in size and shape. Signs that require further investigation include ulceration, rashes, assymetry of the nipples, recent retraction and dimpling. The latter may most easily be detected if the woman is asked to lift her arms above her head. Finally, the clavicular and axillary regions are inspected for swelling.

Palpation

Palpation of the axillae and clavicular areas is easily performed with the patient in a sitting position. To examine axillary lymph nodes, the patient's arm is gently abducted from the thorax by the examiner's hand. The patient's left forearm is grasped and supported with the examiner's left hand (Figure 24.1). The right hand is then free to palpate the axilla, noting the presence or absence of nodes that may be lying against the thoracic wall. The fingertips are used to gently palpate the areas of the central, lateral, subscapular and pectoral nodes. Normally these lymph nodes are not palpable. If enlarged, their size, location, mobility, consistency and tenderness are noted. The arm is put through a full range of motion in order to uncover any swellings that may be hidden under the pectoralis muscle or under subcutaneous fat. The procedure is reversed to examine the right axilla. In a similar fashion, the supraclavicular and infraclavicular areas are palpated.

The patient is now asked to lie flat on the examining table. Before palpation of the breast, the shoulder is elevated on a small pillow in order to balance the breast on the chest wall (Figure 24.1B). Otherwise, a mass may be missed in the thick tissue if the breast is allowed to fall to the side.

Light palpation in an orderly fashion includes the entire surface of the breast, including the breast tail. The examiner may choose to proceed in a clockwise direction following imaginary concentric circles from the outer limits of the breast toward the nipple. Another acceptable method is to palpate from each 'number' on the face of the clock toward the nipple in a clockwise fashion (Figure 24.1C).

When the medial half of the breast is palpated, the arm is actively or passively moved above the head in order to tense the pectoralis muscles and provide a flatter surface. When the lateral half of the breast is palpated, the arm is brought back to the patient's side (Figure 24.1D). The examiner may do this by simple manipulation of a relaxed elbow. A prolongation or 'tail' of breast tissue may extend toward the axilla along the pectoralis tendon toward its insertion. This breast tissue also requires palpation and should not to be mistaken for disease.

During palpation, the consistency of the tissue and the presence of tenderness or swellings are noted. If a swelling is felt, it is described by its location (e.g., left breast, 2 cm from nipple at 2 o'clock), size, shape, consistency, delimitation, mobility and presence of tenderness.

Lastly, the areola around the nipple is gently compressed to determine any secretion.

The breast tissue of the adolescent is firm and lobular, while the postmenopausal women often has breast tissue that feels stringy and granular. During pregnancy and lactation, the breasts are larger and firmer, and the lobules are more distinct. Cysts are common in menstruating women and are usually well defined and freely mobile. Premenstrually, they may be larger and more tender. Malignancies, on the other hand, tend to be hard, poorly defined, fixed to the skin or underlying tissues and painless. Any abnormalities detected during inspection and palpation require further investigation.

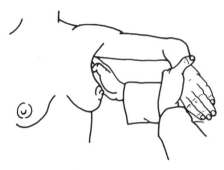

A. Palpation of axillae. Positioning of patient.

B. Palpation of breast. The patient's shoulder is elevated on a small pillow.

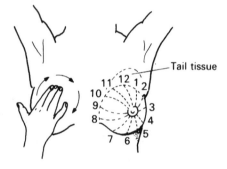

C. The entire surface of the breast, including the tail, is palpated in a clockwise fashion.

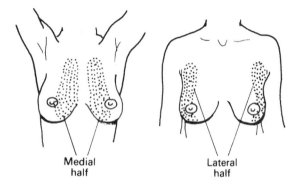

D. The medial half of the breast is examined with the patient's arm overhead, the lateral half with the arm at the side.

Figure 24.1 Breast examination.

Self-Examination of the Breast

Priority must be given to teaching women how to examine their breasts since 95 per cent of breast cancers and 65 per cent of early minimal breast cancers are detected by women themselves. It is estimated that only a minority (25 to 30 per cent) perform breast self-examination on a monthly basis. Even among women who perform breast self-examination, there often are delays in seeking medical attention. The reasons for this include: lack of education, reluctance to do anything if there is no pain, psychological factors, fear (a predominant deterrent), modesty and depression. The nurse is in a unique position in all contacts with women to inform and educate. The method of breast self-examination, which should be performed monthly, is shown in Figure 24.2.

The importance of this examination should be stressed, especially in the light of recent findings related to the occurrence of 'interval cancers' (cancer that may develop after a negative screening visit and before the subsequent medical examination). Breast self-examination is essential to detect these 'interval cancers'.

The rate at which breast cancer develops is very variable, as is known survival after diagnosis.

Mammography (X-Ray)

Mammography is a painless, non-invasive diagnostic procedure that can detect nonpalpable lesions. It is performed on an outpatient basis and takes about 20 minutes.

With mammography, breast cancer may be diagnosed before the appearance of any clinical features, permitting recognition of abnormal breast lesions smaller than 1 cm, the minimal size detectable by breast self-examination. However, a skilled radiologist is required to interpret the findings. At the same time, it should be noted that this form of diagnostic examination has limitations, since some carcinomas noted on clinical examination are not detectable by mammography. In addition, mammography

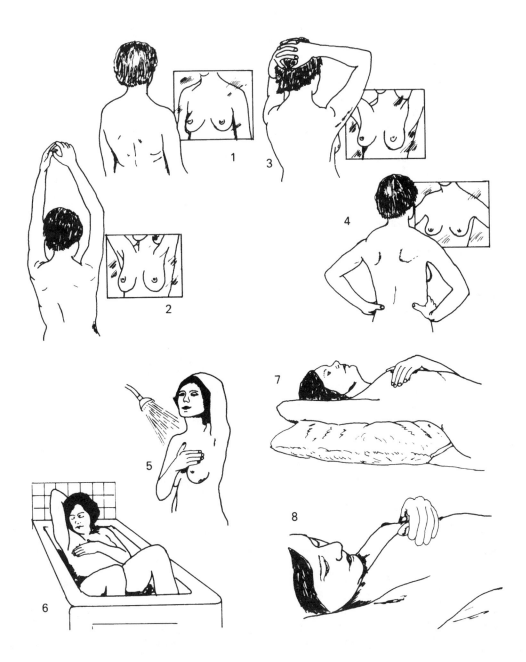

Figure 24.2 (1) Breast self-examination begins with visual inspection in the mirror, giving attention to breast contours and skin. (2) Arms are held high above the head to look for abnormal motion or skin retraction. (3) Pressure is placed on the back of the head to tense the pectoralis major muscles that underlie mammary tissues. (4) Inward pressure on hips serves to tense pectoralis major muscles. Retraction of skin is a sign of abnormality. (5) Wet, soapy skin makes detection of lumps easier. (6) Bathing is a good time to detect lumps. Wet skin allows the fingers to glide easily over the skin, and a reclining position flattens breast tissues against the chest wall. (7) Women find it easier to feel their breasts lying flat with the side to be examined supported on a pillow. Lumps are most evident when the breast is flattened and evenly distributed on the chest wall. As a woman gains familiarity with the appearance and feel of her breast through repeated examinations, she becomes more capable of appreciating changes. (8) Self-examination is completed with a squeeze of the nipple to detect abnormal discharge. (Danforth, D. N. and Scott, J. R. (eds) (1986) *Obstetrics and Gynecology* (5th edition) J. B. Lippincott, Philadelphia.)

is not as effective in studying very small breasts as it is for large, well-developed breasts. More recently, certain architectural patterns of the breast have been distinguished, making it possible to identify patients who are at high risk of developing breast cancer.

Concern about the possibility of inducing breast cancer by exposure to low-dose radiation of mammography is invalid. Experience suggests that today's radiographic techniques are much safer and better at detecting early cancers in women of all ages. In the United Kingdom, mammography is available routinely for every woman over the age of 50 years (DHSS, 1987).

Indications for immediate mammography include the following:

- A lump or some other abnormality has been detected by the woman herself or during routine examination.
- The woman falls into the high-risk group (see Incidence of Breast Cancer, p. 774).
- Physical examination is difficult because of scarring, implants, large breasts.
- Cancer is present in the other breast.

As health educators, nurses should teach women about the advantages of routine mammography and reassure them of its safety.

Thermography and Xeroradiography

The technique of diagnostic thermography provides a picture of the surface temperature of the skin covering the breast. Abnormal vascular signs are detected by infrared photography, and signals are displayed on an oscilloscope. The patient is prepared and given the same information as for mammography, then asked to sit naked from the waist up for 20 to 30 minutes in a room cooled to 21C. By means of a sophisticated heat-sensing apparatus, it is possible to detect minute amounts of heat generated in and around areas of increased vascularity, indicating the existence of disease. The method requires a well-trained radiologist to interpret abnormal patterns. Thermography is recommended only as an adjunct to, and not instead of, physical examination and mammography.

Xeroradiography provides an X-ray film of the soft tissue of the breast using a very limited amount of radiation. In this procedure, a selenium-coated plate is subjected to an electrical charge, the X-ray exposure is made and the plate is then developed by a special process under careful monitoring. The result is a xeroradiograph in which all tissues of the breast, including the skin, are portrayed in a bas-relief effect.

Other Diagnostic Methods

Ultrasonography is the use of a transducer to focus a beam of high-frequency sound waves through the skin and into the breast. These sound waves reflect back to the transducer like an echo that varies with the density of the underlying tissues. The waves are then processed by computer for display on a screen to be interpreted.

Diaphanography uses a fibreoptic light (transillumination of the breast) and synchronizes mapping of the breast to show areas through which the light does not pass.

Mammography is used much more frequently than any other method, although this may change in the future. It is likely that magnetic resonance imaging (MRI), presently used in the diagnosis of malignancy in other body systems, will eventually replace all other diagnostic for breast conditions.

Needle Biopsy: Aspiration Cytology

Breast biopsy can be performed in the outpatient department. Local anaesthesia is injected, then a fine needle is directed into the site to be sampled. The plunger is withdrawn to create a vacuum allowing tissue to be aspirated into the syringe. This is spread on a microscope slide and a fixative is added before the specimen is sent for histological examination. Accurate diagnosis is achieved in over 90 per cent of cases.

Open Biopsy

A specimen of tissue is obtained in theatre after the patient has been anaesthetized. It is sent to the laboratory for frozen section. This is then stained and subjected to histological examination to provide rapid diagnosis. It is preferable to delay mastectomy so that the type of operation can be discussed with the patient.

Excisional biopsy involves sending the entire lesion for histological examination. Incisional biopsy is performed when only part of the lesion is examined. If cancer is diagnosed, oestrogen-receptor and progesterone-receptor assays must be performed. If the tumour cells have receptor sites for these hormones, the patient is more likely to respond to hormone manipulation. Fewer than 10 per cent respond in the absence of receptor sites.

CONDITIONS AFFECTING THE NIPPLE

Fissure of the Nipple

A fissure is a longitudinal ulcer that develops occasionally in women who are breastfeeding. Prophylaxis is achieved by washing and drying the nipple after every feed, and by preparing for breastfeeding during pregnancy (careful hygiene and lubricating the nipples). If a fissure develops it is irritated by the baby's sucking, and is very painful. The nipple may bleed. Treatment involves frequent washes with sterile solutions and the use of an artificial nipple. If these measures do not initiate healing, a breast pump must be used.

Bleeding or Bloodstained Discharge From the Nipple (Intraductal Papilloma)

Although a bloody nipple discharge may be caused by malignancy, it is most commonly due to a benign epithelial tumour (papilloma) growing in one of the larger collecting ducts at the edge of the areola, or in an area of cystic disease. This bleeds on trauma, and the blood collects until it is expressed at the nipple. The duct can be identified and the papilloma excised.

Paget's Disease of the Breast

Paget's disease of the breast is seen most frequently in women over the age of 45; usually, it is unilateral. Most often, it begins as a mild eczematous condition of the nipple that may spread over the areola and even part of the breast; later, it may become ulcerated or eroded. In the more advanced stages, retraction of the nipple may occur. This is carcinoma of the ducts of the breast that converge at the nipple.

When any lesion of the nipple has not healed after a few weeks of treatment by simple cleansing and protective measures, a suspicion of Paget's disease should be confirmed by biopsy examination. This disease demands early and total removal of the breast.

BENIGN CYSTS AND TUMOURS OF THE BREAST

All breast lesions merit thorough investigation and should be excised surgically, even if benign.

Cystic Disease of the Breast

In cystic disease, many small cysts are produced owing to an overgrowth of fibrous tissue around the ducts. The disease occurs most commonly between the ages of 30 and 50. These cysts are labile, that is, they may develop quickly to a considerable size in a few days and decrease just as rapidly. They may be noted as lumps, which may be either painless or tender when palpated, particularly before menstruation. Occasionally, shooting pains may be felt. For tenderness, a supporting brassiere worn day and night may be helpful. The cyst itself rarely has any malignant potential, although breasts containing cysts may be more prone to developing cancer than normal breasts. Most cysts can be treated by simple aspiration of the fluid under local anaesthesia. Usually, the fluid will not recur. If the fluid is atypical on aspiration, biopsy may be recommended.

When pain is severe, danazol may be prescribed. By inhibiting secretion of follicle-stimulating hormone and luteinizing hormone, ovarian production of oestrogen is suppressed. This hypo-oestrogenic effect may be the reason for a decrease in breast pain and nodularity. Possible side-effects are fluid retention and hepatic disturbance.

Fibroadenoma (Adenofibroma)

Fibroadenomas are firm, round, mobile, benign tumours of the breast, usually appearing in girls in their late teens and early 20s. They are not tender. They can be removed through a small incision and have no malignant potential.

Patient Education

The physical and psychological needs of the woman with benign breast disease demand individual nursing care and patient education. The nurse can emphasize the need for monthly breast self-examination, explaining its importance, and suggest the following comfort measures:

● Wear a well supporting brassiere 24 hours a day.
● Decide whether warm or cool appliances are effective (warm compresses, heating pad, cool compresses, ice bag).
● Reduce or eliminate use of caffeine (coffee, tea, cola, chocolate) since this appears to reduce fibrocystic masses.
● Adhere to a low-salt diet, especially the two weeks before menstruation (diuretics may be helpful).

The nurse can reduce the patient's fear and anxiety through education, reassurance and follow-up support.

BREAST CANCER

Breast cancer is now recognized as a systemic rather than a local disease, as micro-metastases have usually disseminated by the time the primary tumour is detected. Early detection by mammography is therefore essential to halt spread, but at present over 90 per cent of breast cancers are detected by women themselves. Under these circumstances, the average tumour size is 2.5 cm. About 50 per cent already have lymph node spread, and the majority will die of their disease.

Incidence and Aetiology

Breast cancer is the commonest malignancy affecting women in the United Kingdom; currently, 1 woman in every 13 is affected. In 1983, total incidence in the United Kingdom was 24,410, and 15,070 women died (DHSS, 1987). The risk of developing breast cancer increases with age. Other women who stand a high chance of being affected include:

● Those in whom one malignant breast lesion has already been detected.
● Those who are nulliparous or who had their first baby after the age of 30 years.
● Those who experienced an early menarche and late

menopause; risk seems to increase with the years of hormonal fluctuations associated with the menstrual cycle.

- Those who have a familial incidence of breast cancer, especially if their mothers were affected.
- Those whose diets include a high proportion of fat.
- There is now some evidence that taking oestrogen as the combined oral contraceptive pill may increase risk, as does hormone replacement therapy.

There is little doubt that susceptibility to breast cancer is associated with western lifestyle, especially repeated menstrual cycles due to delay in childbearing and suppressed lactation, but cause and effective means of prevention remain obscure.

Altered Physiology

Breast cancer is a local disease capable of rapid systemic involvement. In its early stages it is non-invasive, affecting mainly the ducts, but once a local lesion has attained a size of 5 mm, there is an increasing risk that it will invade the lymph nodes and gain access to the systemic circulation. Because the same factors affect both breasts, the opposite breast must be watched carefully for the development of a second carcinoma.

The tumour is located most frequently in the upper outer quadrant of the breast. As it grows, it becomes attached to the chest wall or the overlying skin. If no treatment is given, the tumour invades the surrounding tissues and extends to the lymph glands of the adjacent axilla. When the tumour arises in the medial half of the breast, its extension may involve the lymph nodes within the chest along the internal mammary artery. Metastases occur most commonly in the lungs, bone, mediastinal lymph nodes or liver. In untreated cases, death usually results in two or three years.

Clinical Features

Symptoms are insidious. A painless, mobile lump appears in the breast, usually in the upper outer quadrant. Pain is usually absent, except in the very late stages. Some women are first made aware of a problem by a well-localized discomfort that may be described as burning, stinging or aching. Eventually, dimpling or 'orange peel' appearance of the skin may be observed. On examination in the mirror, the patient may note asymmetry and an elevation of the affected breast. Nipple retraction may be evident. Later, the breast becomes more or less fixed on the chest wall, and nodules appear in the axilla. Finally, ulceration occurs and malnutrition and general ill health become prominent.

Prognosis

Breast cancer is more unpredictable than most other cancers because of hormone dependence, immune response, host resistance and other variable factors. If the lymph nodes have not been involved, prognosis is better than in those instances when cancer cells are found in the nodes. In clinical assessment, the absence of palpable nodes does not necessarily mean absence of malignancy (the growth may be microscopic). However, the presence of a palpable node, even a large node, may reflect inflammation rather than a tumour. Tumour spread at the time of treatment appears to be more significant in prognosis than the type of treatment.

Diagnosis

The key to better cure rates is to diagnose the disease as early as possible before the stage of microscopic metastasis has been reached. When the tumour is less than 1 cm in size (stage 0), the likelihood of recovery (for at least 10 years) is 85 per cent.

Staging is done to assess the local extent of the disease, regional lymph node involvement, status of opposite breast and possibility of systemic metastasis (Table 24.1).

Management

The approach to treating breast cancer has altered during the past few decades, reflecting the basic premise that this disease is not local but systemic. Because of this assumption, not only is the local cancer treated, but the micrometastatic cancer, which may have disseminated throughout the body or may be present within the surrounding breast tissue, is also treated. Surgery combined with adjuvant chemotherapy is more effective than surgery alone for certain patients. Postoperative radiotherapy (following simple or modified radical mastectomy) decreases local recurrence but does not improve survival. Studies are being conducted to determine the best strategy, the correct combination of chemotherapeutic agents and the optimum timing in the multidisciplinary approach.

Surgical Management

The usual treatment of carcinoma of the breast is removal or destruction of the whole tumour. Complete removal of the tumour is only possible when the cancer is still confined to the breast. This is borne out by clinical experience, which shows a rate of cure better than 80 per cent if the tumour is confined to the breast. When cancer cells have spread to the nodes of the axilla, the cure rate falls to 40 per cent.

Types of surgical intervention include the following:

1. Simple excision (lumpectomy or tumourectomy) followed by irradiation of remaining breast tissue and axillary nodes.
2. Quadrantectomy: resection of the involved breast quadrant (usually upper outer quadrant), dissection of axillary lymph nodes, and irradiation to the residual breast tissue.
3. Simple (total) mastectomy: resection extends from the

Table 24.1 *TNM staging for breast cancer*

Stage	Appearance
T0	Tumour not palpable
T1	Tumour 2 cm or less; no fixation to other tissues
T1a	Not attached to underlying muscles
T1b	Tumour attached to underlying muscle
T2	Tumour more than 2 cm but less than 5 cm, not fixed to underlying tissues
T2a	Size as above, not attached to underlying muscles
T2b	Fixed tumour, size as above, now attached to underlying muscles
T3	Tumour more than 5 cm in diameter
T3a	Tumour more than 5 cm, not attached to underlying muscles
T3b	Tumour more than 5 cm, attached to underlying muscles
T4	Tumour of any size with skin ulceration **or** fixed to chest wall
	Nodes
N0	Axillary nodes not palpable
N1	Axillary nodes palpable, but not fixed to skin
N1a	Axillary nodes palpable, but do not appear to contain tumour
N1b	Axillary nodes palpable and appear to contain tumour
N2	Nodes greater than 2 cm fixed to one another and to underlying tissues
N3	Involvement of supraclavicular lymph nodes
	Metastases
M0	No distant metastases apparent
M1	Distant metastases apparent

clavicle to the costal margin and from the midline to the latissimus dorsi. The entire axillary tail and the pectoral fascia are removed. Usually this is followed by irradiation of remaining axillary nodes plus radiotherapy.

4. Modified radical mastectomy: entire breast and axillary lymph nodes are removed along with the pectoralis major but not pectoralis minor.
5. Radical mastectomy: removal of entire breast, axillary lymph nodes, and both pectoral muscles.

Following the removal of the tumour, bleeding points are ligated and the skin is closed over the chest wall. Skin grafting is done if the skin flaps are not large enough to close the wound. Haematoma formation is prevented by suction drainage, with the drainage tubes inserted in the axilla and beneath the superior skin flap. Pressure dressings are sometimes necessary.

Functional Considerations
The objective is to restore normal function to the hand, arm, and shoulder girdle on the affected side. Before surgery is performed, the surgeon plans an incision that will excise the tumour and affected nodes. The patient's lifestyle should be considered, and efforts made to avoid a scar that will be visible and restrictive. Skin flaps and tissue are handled gently to ensure proper viability, haemostasis and drainage.

Variations in Approach
There has been a gradual but marked departure from the radical mastectomy to more conservative surgery for primary breast tumours. After a biopsy performed in theatre, treatment options are discussed with the woman. Previously, it was usual to proceed to mastectomy following biopsy if the result was positive; thus the woman went to theatre not knowing whether she would awaken to find her breast removed. Approaches vary with the stages of the malignancy. In most instances, therapy includes combinations of chemotherapy, anti-oestrogens or oophorectomy and adrenalectomy for oestrogen receptor–positive patients. Another trend followed in some clinics is to do a breast reconstruction immediately following mastectomy or subsequently (e.g., six months later).

Hormonal Therapy
Hormonal therapy for breast cancer is greatly influenced by the index of oestrogen receptor protein, an assay performed on biopsied tissue. Normal breast tissue contains receptor sites for oestrogen. However, only about one third of breast malignant tumours are oestrogen dependent, or oestrogen receptor protein positive. An oestrogen receptor protein-positive assay indicates that tumour growth depends on oestrogen supply and that surgical measures to cut down on hormone production (oophorectomy, adrenalectomy or hypophysectomy) would be appropriate. These procedures are effective for palliative treatment. If oestrogen receptor protein is negative, surgery of this type is ineffective. Hormones may also be manipulated by anti-oestrogen drugs (tamoxifen and nafoxadine).

Adjuvant Chemotherapy of Breast Cancer
Cytotoxic drugs may be given as adjuvant chemotherapy (combined with or to supplement some other treatment—in this case, surgery) following primary excision; the purpose is to eliminate micrometastases. Drugs must be started almost immediately following definitive treatment of the primary neoplasm, because they are most effective when only a few malignant cells are present.

Combined chemotherapy (combining two or three chemotherapeutic agents) is usual today. When assessing the value of any form of therapy, it is important to weigh its efficacy against its toxic effects.

Common chemotherapeutic regimes include:

- Cyclophosphamide, methotrexate, 5-fluorouracil.
- Cyclophosphamide, methotrexate, 5-fluorouracil, plus vincristine and prednisone.
- Cyclophosphamide, doxorubicin, fluorouracil.
- Melphalan or phenylalanine mustard.

Radiotherapy

Radiotherapy is usually instituted following excision of the tumour. An external beam irradiates the area including adjacent lymph nodes and is repeated at specified intervals for several weeks. Alternatively, hollow needles may be inserted into the area to undergo treatment, then radioactive inserts are placed inside for a prescribed period. The purpose of both methods is to destroy migrant or remaining cancer cells after surgical removal of the tumour.

► NURSING PROCESS
► THE PATIENT WITH BREAST CANCER

► *Assessment*

The nursing history can be significant in revealing the reaction of the patient to diagnosis and ability to cope. Some pertinent questions are:

- How has the patient reacted to her diagnosis?
- How will she cope? What inner resources or strengths can she draw upon?
- Who will provide psychological and social support?
- Does she have a partner who can help her in making decisions about the treatment choices?
- Can problem areas such as misinformation about the therapeutic plan or unwarranted self-incrimination related to the subsequent development of cancer be identified?
- Is she experiencing any discomfort?

Her partner, family and close friends may help develop a nursing care plan.

A breast examination is performed as described on pp. 776–777. Results of other investigations such as mammography, breast biopsy, thermography and transillumination are reviewed.

► *Patient's Problems*

Based on the nursing and assessment, the patient's major problems may include the following:

- Fear and ineffective coping related to the diagnosis of cancer, its treatment and prognosis.

- Disturbance in self-concept related to extent of surgery and side-effects of radiation and/or chemotherapy.
- Pain from tissue trauma from incision(s).
- Lack of self-care because of partial immobility of upper extremity on side of breast surgery.
- Possible sexual dysfunction related to loss of body part and fear of partner's reaction to this loss.

Potential complications include: infection, injury, oedema formation and neurovascular deficits in upper extremity on affected side.

► *Planning and Implementation*
► Expected Outcomes:

The outcomes for the patient may include reduction of emotional stress, fear and anxiety, and evidence of ability to cope; realistic adaptation to changes that will occur relative to treatment; absence of pain/discomfort; avoidance of impaired mobility and achievement of self-care to the fullest possible level; and identification of alternative satisfying/acceptable sexual experiences.

Preoperative Nursing Care

Psychosocial Preparation

Psychosocial preparation should begin as soon as the woman learns that further investigation or treatment are necessary. She should never be blamed for delaying to seek medical advice, as it is recognized that fear prevents many women seeking help when a breast lump is detected (see p. 774). She and her partner should be given the opportunity to discuss their concerns, receive information about the treatment options available and any misunderstandings should be corrected. The cosmetic effect of surgery and skin grafting are important considerations, especially for women who participate in sports and swimming, and information about the Mastectomy Association may be appreciated (see Useful Addresses).

Preoperative Preparation

Once a plan of treatment has been decided, it is fully discussed with the patient, who should be in the best physical, psychological and nutritional condition before it is initiated. She will need to know the location and extent of surgical incisions, the extent and side-effects of radiotherapy, and the nature, frequency and method of administration of chemotherapy. Information about prostheses, plastic surgery and any necessary adjustments to clothing must be discussed *before* treatment begins.

Postoperative Nursing Care

- Vital signs are monitored to detect early signs of shock and haemorrhage. The arm on the unaffected side is used to obtain blood pressure readings.

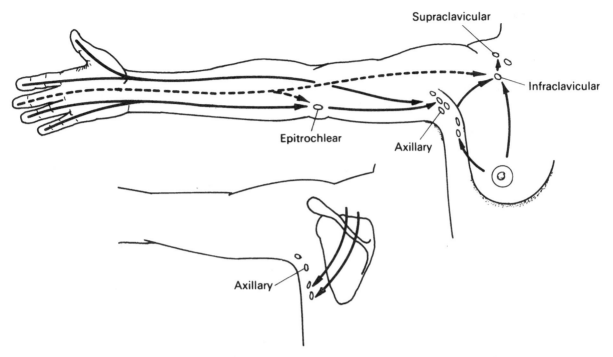

Figure 24.3 Lymphatic drainage of the breast and associated structures. The lymphatic vessels draining the fingers and the hand converge on the dorsum of the hand. From here the lymphatic drainage pursues three courses. The lymph vessels draining the ulnar aspect (little finger and ring finger) accompany the basilic vein and drain into the epitrochlear nodes and thence into the axillary nodes. The lymph vessels draining the thumb and the index fingers bypass the epitrochlear nodes and go directly to the axillary nodes. The lymph vessels draining the middle fingers may drain into the epitrochlear or the axillary, or they may bypass both of these groups of nodes to drain directly into the intraclavicular, and thence into the supraclavicular, and finally into the bloodstream. The axillary nodes also receive lymph from the posterior scapular region (insert).

- Dressings are inspected for bleeding, and drainage from the incisions is noted. Care of the suction apparatus is vital to prevent haematoma formation—it must be inspected regularly to ensure that the vacuum action is intact.
- Turning and deep breathing are encouraged to prevent respiratory complications.
- Grafts (skin, muscle, fatty tissue) are assessed for unusual redness, pain, swelling or drainage to detect early signs of infection.
- Some surgeons request elevation of the arm on the affected side so that venous and lymphatic return are aided by gravity. This helps prevent lymphoedema, especially after radical mastectomy when there is considerable disruption of circulatory and lymphatic systems (Figure 24.3).
- Analgesia is required for pain relief.
- Dressing changes must be performed gently to avoid local injury and discomfort.
- Exercises are introduced gradually to avoid undue stress on the healing tissues.
- The aetiology of lymphoedema is obscure, although removal of lymphatic ducts is known to contribute. It

may affect only the upper arm or be more extensive, first appearing soon after surgery or not until years later. Exercises help to reduce the problem by establishing collateral drainage channels.

Patient Education

Since lymphoedema may occur much later, one of the most important teaching points to emphasize with the patient is that she must always take extra precautions to avoid cuts, bruises and infection of the hand and arm on the side of her operation. She should also avoid undue stress on the suture line during shoulder range-of-motion exercises and gravity-dependent positions for prolonged periods of time. Carrying for extended periods should also be avoided.

Care of Incision Site

When dressings are changed, the nature of the incision, the way it looks and feels, and how it will gradually change are explained. The patient needs to know that sensation in the newly healed area may have decreased because nerves have been severed; however, the area should be bathed gently and blotted dry to avoid injury.

Signs of irritation and possible infection are described, so that if they occur, the patient will recognize and report them. When talking about the incision, the nurse should use the term *incision* rather than *scar*, since scarring connotes defect and deformity to many people. The arm on the affected side may be supported in a sling for a time to prevent tension on the wound. Gentle massage of the healed incision helps to increase the elasticity of the skin and encourages circulation.

Psychosocial Considerations

Problems may arise if the woman is reluctant to look at the incision, but she should not be forced to do so, as denial may be an important, sometimes effective, coping mechanism in the immediate postoperative period. Drawing diagrams and gentle encouragement to look when the dressing is changed may be the best strategy.

Ambulation and Exercise

Ambulation is encouraged the day after surgery when the effects of the anaesthetic have worn off and the patient is free of nausea and has been able to take fluids and nutrients. The nurse supports the patient from the unoperated side. After the surgeon's assessment postoperatively and the removal of drainage tubes, passive range of motion of the affected arm is initiated to increase circulation and muscle strength and to prevent stiffness of the shoulder. Hand exercises are also begun. These activities can be increased as the patient is encouraged to do more for herself by brushing her teeth, washing her face and combing her hair with the hand on the affected side. Failure to encourage exercises may prolong the disuse of the arm and promote the development of a contracture. Exercise should not be accompanied by pain; if the patient has had a skin graft or if the incision was closed with considerable tension, exercises are greatly limited and must be done very gradually. In all exercises, it is important to emphasize bilateral activity. The value of proper posture must be emphasized; the purpose of the exercise will be defeated if the patient hunches towards the affected side.

Difficulty with arm movement is much greater in the patient who has undergone radical mastectomy. Limitation of motion after simple and modified radical mastectomy is unusual, and the patient is encouraged to use the arm to the point of complete mobility almost immediately.

The exercises done in the hospital and illustrated in Figure 24.4 can be related to household activities. Putting dishes on a shelf, dusting, typing and piano playing are activities that promote and maintain muscle tone. Other suggestions are to swing the arm while walking; wear loose clothing; keep the mastectomy site, underarm and arm scrupulously clean; and avoid injury to the hand and arm.

Follow-up visits are very important to check healing, mental outlook, general physical condition and any evidence of recurrence.

► *Evaluation*
► Expected Outcomes

1. Patient demonstrates willingness to deal with the anxiety of the diagnosis and the impact of surgery on sexual functioning and self-image.
   a. Talks about her concerns related to possible future course of disease.
   b. Expresses understanding that mastectomy need not have a negative effect on sexuality.
2. Experiences little or no discomfort.
   a. Is apyrexial 48 hours before discharge.
   b. Experiences minimal pain in the incision.
   c. Demonstrates a drainage-free incision site.
   d. Has satisfactory wound healing; knows to report signs of redness, heat and pain.
3. Participates actively in self-care activities.
   a. Carries out exercises as prescribed.
   b. Performs additional activities that will enhance the exercises taught.
4. Uses means that will help in preventing complications.
   a. Knows possible complications and that they should be reported.
   b. Describes side-effects of chemotherapeutic agents; understands what measures to take in minimizing these effects.
   c. Avoids cuts, bruises, infection and excessive stress on hand and arm on operative side.
   d. Knows when to attend for her follow-up appointment.
   e. Notes the telephone number of health care staff to call should untoward signs arise.

Care of the patient with a breast lump is described in Nursing Care Plan 24.1.

Care of the Patient With Advanced Breast Cancer

Following mastectomy, the woman must attend regular follow-up visits. Frequency depends on the centre where treatment was performed. Recurrence is unfortunately common, and attempts are made to detect metastases as early as possible by X-ray, bone scans, mammography, blood chemistry and imaging procedures.

Of those women who have recurrence, lymph node involvement occurs in almost half; over a quarter have metastases in other organs and a quarter have bony metastases in the spine, hips or pelvis.

A. *Wall handclimbing.* Stand facing the wall, with the toes as close to the wall as possible—feet apart. With elbows somewhat bent, place the palms on the wall at shoulder level. By flexing the fingers, work hands up the wall until arms are fully extended. Work hands down to starting point.

B. *Rope turning.* Stand facing the door. Take free end of light rope in hand of the operated side. Place other hand on hip. With arm extended and held away from the body—nearly parallel with the floor—turn rope, making as wide swings as possible. Slow at first—speed up later.

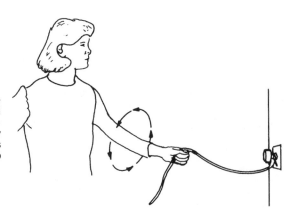

C. *Rod or Broom.* Grasp rod with both hands, held about 2 feet apart. With arms straight, raise rod over the head. Bend elbows lowering rod behind the head. Reverse maneuver, raising rod above the head, then to starting position.

D. *Pulley.* Toss rope over shower curtain rod or doorway curtain rod. Stand as nearly under rope as possible. Grasp an end in each hand. Extend arms straight and away from body. Pull left arm up by tugging down with right arm, then right arm up and left down—like a seesaw.

Figure 24.4 Exercises after mastectomy. The purpose of the exercise programme is to secure a complete range of motion of the affected shoulder joint. (Adapted from Radler, A. *A Handbook for Your Recovery*, The Society of Memorial Center, New York.)

► NURSING CARE PLAN 24.1: THE PATIENT WITH A BREAST LUMP

Nursing care plan for Carol Thompson, who is to have a breast lump removed. She is a 41-year-old practising Roman Catholic who is divorced, and who works as a legal secretary.

Patient's problems	Expected outcomes	Nursing care	Rationale
1. Anxiety concerning diagnosis, prognosis and possible nature and extent of surgery	Anxiety will be allayed to within realistic limits	1a. Explain that the purpose of this exploratory operation, emphasizing that only tissue for biopsy will be removed b. No other procedure may be necessary but if it is, Carol will be able to discuss her hopes and feelings with the surgeon and her nurse	Initially only a biopsy will be performed: the nature of the lump will be determined by histological examination. A high proportion of lumps prove to be benign. If malignancy is present, women benefit from the opportunity to discuss treatment options
2. Nervous about unfamiliar hospital environment and what to expect before and after operation	Will not be nervous: will know what to expect before and after operation	2. Show patient around ward: introduce to other patients; explain typical day; pre- and postoperatively	Providing information allays anxiety and enhances recovery from general surgical procedures
3. Anxiety about leaving teenage children alone while in hospital (Carol is divorced and a single parent)	Anxiety will be allayed within reasonable limits	3. Discuss alternatives to leaving children alone. Offer a referral to social worker. Ensure visiting times and telephone number of hospital are known to children	Worry about events at home may impede recovery
4. Anxiety about loss of time from work as a legal secretary if loss of function in left arm. Has heard 'horror' stories about arm swelling after mastectomy	Will not be anxious	4a. Explain that providing she needs no further treatment Carol can return to work in one or two weeks, when she feels well b. Swelling/oedema does not always follow mastectomy, and is *not* a problem after removal of lump, but movement may be restricted temporarily by drainage apparatus for 24–48 hours postoperatively	Lymphoedema is a complication of surgery involving lymph drainage. Haematoma formation is prevented by insertion of a suction drain, e.g. Redivac type, for 24–48 hours postoperatively
5. Fear of pain and nausea post-operatively (had an unfortunate experience of anaesthesia as a child)	Will not fear pain and nausea because she will understand these can be controlled	5. Explain use of analgesia and antiemetics postoperatively; will be offered drugs routinely and can ask if necessary	Knowing about prevention of pain and nausea gives patient 'control' of situation and allays fears

Nursing Care

The expected outcome is regression of symptoms for as long as possible, with emphasis on improving quality of life. When recurrence occurs, all the nurse's skills of assessing physical and psychosocial condition are challenged to the utmost. Information about behavioural change can be provided by the woman's family. The nurse may help the doctor to determine palliative approaches most likely to benefit the individual, so that she remains as comfortable as possible, even though the disease may not be arrested. Treatment options are outlined in Chapter 2, Care of the Patient With Cancer.

RECONSTRUCTIVE AND PLASTIC SURGERY OF THE BREAST

Hypertrophy of the Breast

The breasts are such an important part of the female figure that abnormalities often lead to requests for surgical management. The variations most often encountered are in size: breasts are too large or too small. Those that are too large are said to be hypertrophied; when the condition occurs in early life, it is called virginal breast hypertrophy. The condition is usually bilateral but may occur on only one side. The hypertrophied breasts that occur in later life are always bilateral.

Symptoms of Breast Hypertrophy

- Tenderness, diffuse pain and fatigue, especially towards the end of menstruation.
- Dragging sensation on the shoulders. Foundation garments provide inadequate support and straps may cut into the skin.
- Psychological problems, especially in younger women. Social life may be restricted, and sports are avoided.
- Insecurity and fear of losing partner's affection may lead to interpersonal relationship problems.

Mammoplasty

The operation performed to reduce the size of the breasts is termed a reduction mammoplasty. In this operation, the surgeon makes one incision beneath the breast and a similar curved incision in the skin of the anterior breast. The nipple is transplanted to a new location after the redundant tissue is cut away. The remaining skin edges are approximated with sutures, and the nipple is sutured to its new location. Drains are placed in the incision and remain for only one or two days. Simple dressings are used without pressure.

Postoperative Nursing Care. Nursing care is minimal. These patients sit up in bed the same day or day after operation and may be out of bed and eating a normal diet thereafter. The results of these plastic operations are good for both relief of symptoms and appearance. There is no recurrence of the hypertrophy, and the operation is not a serious one. The new transplanted nipple may turn black and be covered by a dry scab. This is to be expected, but the scab will come away after a week or two as the nipple regains a blood supply in its new location. It must be accepted that the breast cannot function for lactation after such an operation.

Usually, these patients are euphoric about the results, but it is not uncommon for some patients to experience negative psychological reactions related to the loss of a part of the body. The patient may feel anxious about this reaction, but it helps to let her know that these feelings occur frequently.

Operations to Enlarge or Uplift the Breasts

Operations to enlarge or uplift the breasts are requested fairly frequently. The operations are performed through an incision along the undermargin of the breast (circumareolar). The breast is elevated, and a pocket is formed between the breast and the chest wall, into which are inserted plastic or other inert synthetic materials intended to enlarge and uplift the breast. This procedure is called an augmentation mammoplasty and may be done on an outpatient basis with local anaesthesia by an experienced plastic surgeon. These operations are not serious, but complications do occur occasionally, in some instances requiring the removal of the inserted substance.

Breast Reconstruction Following Mastectomy

Restoration of the breast following mastectomy in patients who have an early stage cancer and favourable prognosis is becoming increasingly popular. The skin and subcutaneous tissue have been found to be far looser and more supple than was previously thought, and the blood supply to the area has been shown to be sufficient.

Opinions differ about whether postmastectomy breast reconstruction should be done immediately after surgery or delayed. Concern about immediate reconstruction stems from the fear that any recurrence of a local tumour will not be recognized early enough because of the musculocutaneous flap used in reconstruction or the presence of the implanted prosthesis. Proponents for immediate reconstruction argue that delay in diagnosis would be minimal, especially in view of the psychological benefits to be gained from the procedure. Meanwhile, the criteria used for selecting patients for breast reconstruction following mastectomy are being developed to reduce the risk of potential recurrence of malignancy. Varying opinions for delay suggest waiting two to five years after completion of chemotherapy or radiation therapy or six months after mastectomy.

Procedures. The choice of the method used for reconstruction is based on the condition of the overlying skin and the status of the underlying muscle. The latissimus dorsi and the abdominis myocutaneous flap are two of the more popular sources of tissue. The surgical procedures are described in Figures 24.5 and 24.6.

Postoperative Nursing Care. Suction tubes attached to closed drainage are placed in the breast and the donor area. Measures are used to reduce tension on the incisions. Elevating the head of the bed 30 degrees and flexing the knees will relieve tension on the abdominal incision. Antiemetics may be prescribed to control nausea and vomiting. Analgesics may help to relieve discomfort. The colour and temperature of the newly reconstructed breast area should be observed frequently to assess circulation. Mottling or an obvious temperature drop should be reported immediately as possible signs that circulation is impaired. Drainage of more than 50 ml/hr must also be reported. Dietary and other measures are taken to prevent flatus and abdominal distension.

When the patient commences ambulation, she is encouraged to adopt an upright posture. A brassiere is not worn for several weeks, and the breast is not massaged

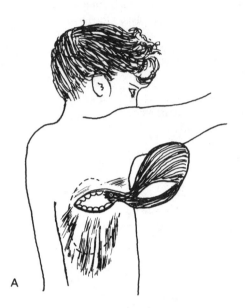

A

An elliptical incision identifies the skin tissue (island) that will be attached to dissected latissirnus dorsi muscle (dissected underneath skin in area of dotted line). When freed but with one end attached, this muscle and skin flap (note arrow) is then threaded through a tunnel under the skin (subaxillary) and brought out at the breast site.

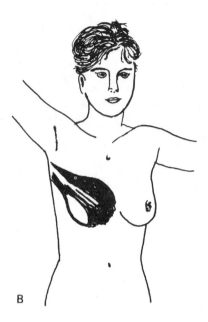

B

Flap in place after being tunnelled from back to front of the chest.

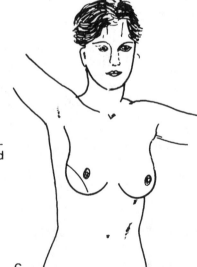

Flap is in place re-creating breast contour with reconstructed nipple and areola.

C

Figure 24.5 Breast reconstruction: myocutaneous flap procedure using latissimus dorsi muscle. (Adapted from *The Breast Cancer Digest* (2nd edition), US Department of Health and Human Services, Public Health Service, Bethesda, Maryland.)

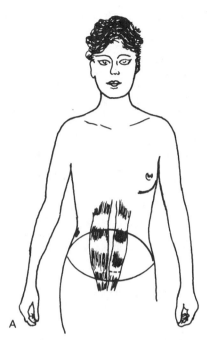

A

An elliptical lower abdominal incision is made, and one of two vertical abdominal muscles is cut.

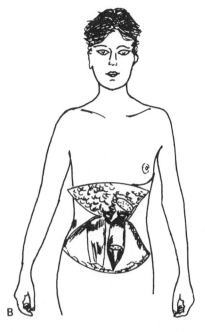

B

The skin flap including muscle and fat is then tunnelled under the skin of upper abdominal and lower chest to the breast site.

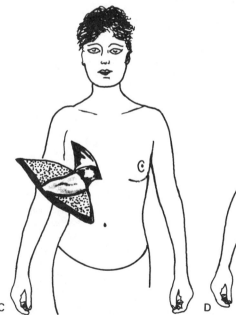

C

The flap will be positioned and moulded to the contour of the breast. Blood supply continues with flap.

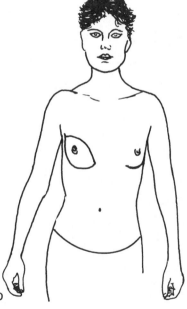

D

Flap in place re-creating breast contour with reconstructed nipple and areola.

Figure 24.6 Breast reconstruction: myocutaneous flap procedure using abdominis rectus muscle. (Adapted from *The Breast Cancer Digest* (2nd edition), US Department of Health and Human Services, Public Health Service, Bethesda, Maryland.)

until the surgeon indicates that no injury will result. The woman should not elevate her arms above the shoulder level or lift more than 2.5 kg for at least a month.

DISEASES OF THE MALE BREAST

In the male, gynaecomastia (overdeveloped breast tissue) is the most frequently encountered breast condition. It affects about 40 per cent of adolescent males, probably in relation to hormones being secreted by the testes, and disappears within one or two years. It may occur in prepubertal boys as well as adult males. Gynaecomastia is usually unilateral and presents as a firm, circular, tender mass beneath the areola. In the adult male, diffuse gynaecomastia may be related to certain drugs the patient is taking, such as stilboestrol. Pain and tenderness are initial symptoms. One per cent of malignant breast lesions occur in the male. Usually, the man discovers the malignancy as a painless lump beneath the areola. Other symptoms are nipple discharge (occasionally bloody), possible nipple retraction and skin ulceration. Diagnosis and treatment are similar to those used for women. Since the average age of the male breast cancer patient is five years older than women, the mortality appears higher. When the age difference is taken into account, the mortality rate is about the same.

BIBLIOGRAPHY

DHSS (1987) *Breast Cancer Screening (The Forrest Report)*, HMSO, London.

FURTHER READING

Books

Ariel, I. M. and Cleary, J. B. (1987) *Breast Cancer*, McGraw-Hill, New York.

Harris, J. R. *et al.* (1987) *Breast Diseases*, J.B. Lippincott, Philadelphia.

Pfeiffer, C. H. and Mulliken, J. B. (eds) (1984) *Caring for the Patient with Breast Cancer*, Reston Publishing Co., Reston, Virginia.

Articles

General

Holleb, A.I. (1984) Interview: Progress against breast cancer, *Cancer Nursing*, Spring/Summer, Vol. 38, No. 2, pp. 7–9.

LaCroix, A. Z. and Hukla, B. S. (1984) Are OCS (oral contraceptives) dangerous for women with benign breast disease or a family history of breast cancer? *Your Patient and Cancer*, May, Vol. 9, No. 6, pp. 27–32.

Rutledge, D. N. (1987) Factors related to women's practice of breast self-examination, *Nursing Research*, March/April, Vol. 36, No. 2, pp. 117–21.

Advanced Breast Cancer

Cristina, A. G. *et al.* (1983) Intraosseous metastatic breast cancer treatment with internal fixation and study of survival, *Annals of Surgery*, February, Vol. 197, No. 2, pp. 128–34.

Aetiology

Larson, E. (1983) Epidemiological correlates of breast, endometrial, and ovarian cancers, *Cancer Nursing*, August, Vol. 6, No. 4, pp. 295–301.

Rosenberg, L. *et al.* (1984) Breast cancer and cigarette smoking, *New England Journal of Medicine*, 12 January, Vol. 310, No. 2, pp. 92–4.

Senie, R. T., Rosen, P. P. and Kinne, D. W. (1983) Epidemiologic factors associated with breast cancer, *Cancer Nursing*, October, Vol. 6, No. 5, pp. 367–71.

Assessment and Detection

Baines, C. J. Breast self-examination: The doctor's role, *Hospital Practice*, March, Vol. 19, No. 3, pp. 120–7.

Bennett, S. E. *et al.* (1983) Profile of women practicing breast self-examination, *Journal of the American Medical Association*, 28 January, Vol. 249, No. 4, pp. 488–91.

Bolsen, B. (1982) Ultrasound breast scanning: (only) a complement to mammography? *Journal of the American Medical Association*, 3 September, Vol. 248, No. 9, pp. 1025–7.

Brailey, L. J. (1986) Effects of health teaching in the workplace on women's knowledge, beliefs, and practices regarding breast self-examination, *Res. Nurs. Health*, September, Vol. 9, No. 3, pp. 223–31.

Champion, V. L. (1985) Use of the health belief model in determining frequency of breast self-examination, *Res. Nurs. Health*, December, Vol. 8, No. 4, pp. 373–9.

Cohen, M. I. *et al.* (1985) Mammography in women less than 40 years of age, *Surgery, Gynecology and Obstetrics*, March, Vol. 160, No. 3, pp. 220–2.

Edgar, L., Shamian, J. and Patterson, D. (1984) Factors affecting the nurse as a teacher and practicer of breast self-examination, *International Journal of Nursing Studies*, Vol. 2, No. 4, pp. 255–65.

Hallal, J. C. (1983) The relationship of health beliefs, health locus of control, and self-concept to the practice of breast self-exam in adult women, *Nursing Research*, May/June, Vol. 31, No. 3, pp. 137–42.

Harper, A. P. (1985) Mammography, *Hospital Medicine*, April, Vol. 21, No. 4, pp. 189–208.

Holmes, P. (1987) Examining the evidence (for and against breast self-examination), *Nursing Times*, Vol. 83, No. 31, pp. 28–30.

King, R. C. (1982) Detailed guidelines for a thorough examination of the breast, *Registered Nurse*, July, Vol. 45, No. 7, pp. 57–63.

Lashley, M. E. (1987) Predictors of breast self-examination, *Advanced Nursing Science*, July, Vol. 9, No. 4, pp. 16–24.

Lauver, D. (1987) Theoretical perspectives relevant to breast self-examination, *Advanced Nursing Science*, July, Vol. 9, No. 4, pp. 16–24.

Marty, P. J., McDermott, R. J. and Gold, R. S. (1983) An assessment of three alternative formats for promoting breast self-examination, *Cancer Nursing*, June, Vol. 6, No. 3, pp. 207–11.

Moskowitz, M. (1985) Benefit/risk ratio for mammography screening, *Medical Times*, October, Vol. 113, No. 10, pp. 48–52.

Oberst, M. T. (1981) Testing approaches to teaching breast self-examination, *Cancer Nursing*, June, Vol. 4, No. 3, pp. 246.

Rudolph, A. and McDermott, R. J. (1987) The breast physical examination, *Cancer Nursing*, April, Vol. 10, No. 2, pp. 100–6.

Wertheimer, M. D. *et al.* (1986) Increasing the effort toward breast cancer detection, *Journal of the American Medical Association*, 14 March, Vol. 255, No. 10, pp. 1311–15.

Breast Augmentation/Reconstruction

Dinner, M. I. (1984) Postmastectomy reconstruction, *Surgical Clinics of North America*, December, Vol. 64, No. 6, pp. 1193–207.

Frazier, T. G. and Noone, R. B. (1985) An objective analysis of immediate simultaneous reconstruction in the treatment of primary carcinoma of the breast, *Cancer*, 15 March, Vol. 55, No. 6, pp. 1202–5.

Hutcheson, H. A. (1986) TAIF: New option for breast reconstruction, *Nursing*, February, Vol. 16, No. 2, pp. 52–3.

Solomon, J. (1986) The good news about breast reconstruction, *Registered Nurse*, November, pp. 47–54.

Breast Cancer

Ashikari, R. H. (1984) Modified radical mastectomy, *Surgical Clinics of North America*, December, Vol. 64, No. 6, pp. 1095–102.

Baker, R. R. (1984) Preoperative assessment of the patient with breast cancer, *Surgical Clinics of North America*, December, Vol. 64, No. 6, pp. 1039–50.

Bullough, B. (1981) Nurses as teachers and support persons for breast cancer patients, *Cancer Nursing*, June, Vol. 4, No. 3, pp. 221–5.

Charlson, M. E. (1985) Delay in the treatment of carcinoma of the breast, *Surgery, Gynecology and Obstetrics*, May, Vol. 160, No. 5, pp. 393–8.

Cohen, R. J. (1984) Diagnosis: Breast cancer, *Hospital Medicine*, July, Vol. 20, No. 7, pp. 81–102.

Cooperman, A. M. and Hermann, R. E. (1984) Breast cancer: An overview, *Surgical Clinics of North America*, December, Vol. 64, No. 6, pp. 1031–8.

Foster, R. S. (1984) Breast cancer: Detection, diagnosis, staging, and adjuvant systemic therapy, *Current Concepts in Oncology*, Summer, Vol. 6, No. 2, pp. 2–9.

Greifzu, S. (1986) Breast cancer: The risks and the options, *Registered Nurse*, October, pp. 26–31.

Greiner, L. and Weiler, C. (1983) Early-stage breast cancer. What do women know about treatment choices? *American Journal of Nursing*, November, Vol. 83, No. 11, p. 1570.

Gump, F. E. (1984) Premalignant diseases of the breast, *Surgical Clinics of North America*, December, Vol. 64, No. 6, pp. 1051–9.

Harris, J. R. (1986) Management of localized breast cancer, *Hospital Practice*, 15 October, Vol. 21, No. 10, pp. 61–72.

Hermann, R. E. *et al.* (1984) Partial mastectomy without radiation therapy, *Surgical Clinics of North America*, December, Vol. 64, No. 6, pp. 1103–13.

Holmes, P. (1986) 'Why me?' *Nursing Times*, 8 January, Vol. 82, No. 2, pp. 16–17.

Lierman, L. M. (1984) Support for mastectomy: A clinical nursing research study, *AORNJ*, June, Vol. 39, No. 7, pp. 1150–7.

Lipnick, R. J. *et al.* (1986) Oral contraceptives and breast cancer, *Journal of the American Medical Association*, 3 January, Vol. 255, No. 1, pp. 58–61.

Lippman, M. E. (1986) Management of breast cancer with hormones and drugs, *Hospital Practice*, 15 May, Vol. 21, No. 5, pp. 119–31.

Massey, V. (1986) Perceived susceptibility to breast cancer and practice of breast self-examination, *Nursing Research*, May/June, Vol. 35, No. 3, pp. 183–5.

Ray, C. *et al.* (1984) Nurses' perceptions of early breast cancer and mastectomy, and their psychological implications, and of the role of health professionals in providing support, *International Journal of Nursing Studies*, Vol. 21, No. 2, pp. 101–11.

Wertheimer, M. D. *et al.* (1986) Increasing the effort toward breast cancer detection, *Journal of the American Medical Association*, 14 March, Vol. 255, No. 10, pp. 1311–15.

Fibrocystic Breast Disease

Love, S. M., Gelman, R. S. and Silen, W. (1982) Fibrocystic 'disease' of the breast a non-disease? *New England Journal of Medicine*, 14 October, Vol. 16, No. 307, pp. 1010–14.

Male Breast Cancer

Roses, D. F. and Harris, M. N. (1985) Male Breast Cancer, *Hospital Medicine*, October, Vol. 21, No. 10, pp. 23–40.

Management

Surgery

Aitken, D. R. and Minto, J. P. (1983) Complications associated with mastectomy, *Surgical Clinics of North America*, December, Vol. 63, No. 6, pp. 1331–52.

Gilliland, M. D *et al.* (1983) The implications of local recurrence of breast cancer as the first site of therapeutic failure, *Annals of Surgery*, March, Vol. 197, No. 3, pp. 284–7.

O'Brien, R. L. (1983) Breast cancer treatment—current status, *Postgraduate Medicine*, September, Vol. 74, No. 3, pp. 124–5.

Radiation

Carrier, R. and Martel, G. (1985) Working with radiation: Reducing the risks, *Canadian Nurse*, October, Vol. 81, No. 9, pp. 18–20.

Gilman, C. J. (1982) Primary radiotherapy in early breast cancer, *American Family Physician*, April, Vol. 25, No. 4, pp. 113–7.

Hassey, K. M., Bloom, L. S. and Burgess, S. L. (1983) Radiation—alternative to mastectomy, *American Journal of Nursing*, November, Vol. 83, No. 11, pp. 1567–9.

Rosenal, L. (1985) Radiotherapy nurse: Developing a new role, *Canadian Nurse*, October, Vol. 81, No. 9, pp. 21–3.

Wilson, J. F. (1983) Breast cancer treatment: III. Simple excision with irradiation, *Postgraduate Medicine*, September, Vol. 74, No. 3, pp. 151–8.

Chemotherapy

Derby, C. E. (1985) Alternate methods of chemotherapy administration, *Canadian Nurse*, October, Vol. 81, No. 9, pp. 44–5.

Hopkins, M. B. (1986) Information-seeking and adaptational outcomes in women receiving chemotherapy for breast cancer, *Cancer Nursing*, October, Vol. 9, No. 5, pp. 256–62.

Kiang, D. T. *et al.* (1985) A randomized trial of chemotherapy and hormonal therapy in advanced breast cancer, *New England Journal of Medicine*, 14 November, Vol. 313, No. 20, pp. 1283–4.

Psychosocial Implications

Meyerowtiz, B. E., Watkins, I. K. and Sparks, F. C. (1983) Quality of life for breast cancer patients receiving adjuvant chemotherapy, *American Journal of Nursing*, February, Vol. 83, No. 2, pp. 232–5.

Scott, D. W. (1983) Quality of life following the diagnosis of breast cancer, *Topics in Clinical Nursing*, January, Vol. 4, No. 4, pp. 20–37.

Scott, D. W. (1983) Anxiety, critical thinking and information processing during and after breast biopsy, *Nursing Research*, January/February, Vol. 32, No. 1, pp. 24–8.

Risks

Webster, L. A. *et al.* (1983) Alcohol consumption and risk of breast cancer, *Lancet*, 24 September, Vol. 2, No. 8352, pp. 724–6.

Wynder, E. L. and Rose, D. P. (1984) Diet and breast cancer, *Hospital Practice*, April, Vol. 19, No. 4, pp. 73–88.

ASSESSMENT AND CARE OF MALE PATIENTS WITH DISORDERS RELATING TO THE REPRODUCTIVE SYSTEM

In the male, several organs serve as parts of both the urinary tract and the reproductive system. Disease of these organs may produce functional abnormalities of either or both systems. For this reason, diseases of the entire reproductive system in the male usually are treated by the urologist.

ANATOMY AND PHYSIOLOGY

The structures included in the male reproductive system are the testes, the vas deferens and the seminal vesicles, the penis and certain accessory glands, such as the prostate gland and Cowper's gland (Figure 25.1). The testes are formed in embryonal life within the abdominal cavity near the kidney. During the last month of fetal life, they descend posterior to the peritoneum, to pierce the abdominal wall in the groin. Later they progress along the inguinal canal into the scrotum. In this descent they are accompanied by blood vessels, lymphatics, nerves and ducts, which, along with supporting tissue, make up the spermatic cord. This cord extends from the internal inguinal ring through the abdominal wall and the inguinal canal to the scrotum. As the testes descend into the scrotum, a tubular process of peritoneum accompanies them. This normally is obliterated, the only remaining portion being that which covers the testes, the tunica vaginalis. (When this peritoneal process is not obliterated but remains open into the abdominal cavity, a potential sac remains, into which abdominal contents may enter to form an indirect inguinal hernia.)

The testes consist of numerous seminiferous tubules in which the spermatozoa are formed. These are transmitted by a system of collecting tubules into the epididymis, which is a hoodlike structure lying on the testes and containing tortuous ducts that lead into the vas deferens. This firm tubular structure passes upward through the inguinal canal to enter the abdominal cavity behind the peritoneum and then extends downward toward the base of the bladder. An outpouching from this structure is the seminal vesicle, which acts as a reservoir for the secretion of the

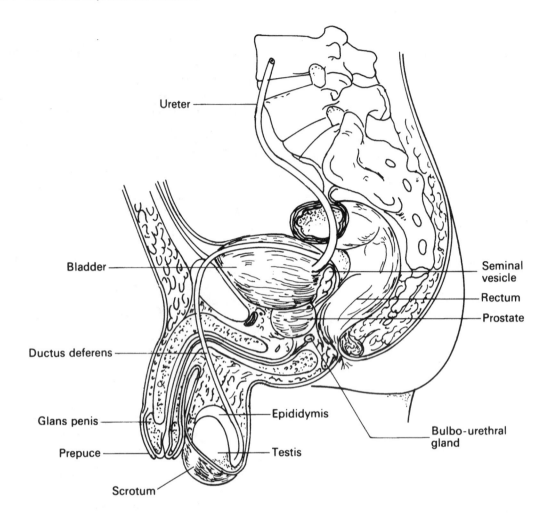

Figure 25.1 Organs of the male reproductive system. (Chaffee, E. E. and Greisheimer, E. M. (1974) *Basic Physiology and Anatomy* (3rd edition), J. B. Lippincott, Philadelphia.)

testes. The tract is continued as the ejaculatory duct, which then passes through the prostate gland to enter the urethra. The testicular secretions are carried by this pathway to the end of the penis in the reproductive act.

The testes have a dual function. The primary function is reproduction—the formation of spermatozoa from the germinal cells of the seminiferous tubules. However, the testes are also important glands of internal secretion. This secretion, called testosterone, is produced by the Leydig or interstitial cells, and induces and preserves the male sex qualities.

The prostate gland lies just below the neck of the bladder. It surrounds the urethra posteriorly and laterally and is traversed by the ejaculatory duct, the continuation of the vas deferens. This gland produces a secretion that is chemically and physiologically suitable to the needs of the spermatozoa in their passage from the genital glands.

The penis is both the organ of copulation and of urination. Anatomically, it consists of a glans penis, a body

and a root. The glans penis is the soft, rounded portion at the end that retains its soft structure even when erect. The urethra opens at the extremity of the glans. The glans normally is covered or protected by an elongation of the skin of the penis—the foreskin—which may be retracted to expose the glans. The body of the penis is composed of erectile tissues that contain numerous blood vessels that may become distended during sexual excitement. Through it passes the urethra, which extends from the bladder through the prostate to the end of the penis.

Congenital Malformations

Of the many disturbances of normal growth that may occur, the most common is a failure of the testes to descend into the scrotum. This condition is called cryptorchidism.

Failure of the urethra to form normally in the penis can result in hypospadias or epispadias. Hypospadias occurs when the urethral opening is a groove on the underside of the penis; when the urethral opening is on the dorsum of the penis the condition is called epispadias. These anatomical abnormalities may be repaired by various types of plastic surgery.

Considerations in the Elderly Patient

As the male ages, the prostate gland hypertrophies (enlarges), prostate secretion decreases, the scrotum hangs lower, the testes become smaller and more firm and pubic hair becomes sparser and stiffer.

Changes in gonadal functioning cause a decline in the concentration of plasma testosterone and a reduction in the amount of progesterone produced.

Male reproductive capability is maintained with advancing age. Although degenerative changes occur in the seminiferous tubules, spermatogenesis (production of sperm) remains. However, sexual function, involving libido (desire) and potency, lessens. This decline is more evident in men over age 70 but is also noted in males in their 60s. The lessening of sexual function is affected by a number of factors such as psychological problems, illnesses and medications. In general, the sexual act takes longer. Sexual activity is closely correlated with the man's sexual activity of his earlier years; if he was more active than the average male as a young man, he will most likely continue to be more active than average in his later years.

Impotence is usually due to either organic or psychogenic factors. Organic causes include vascular insufficiency, diabetes mellitus and neuropathy that cause erectile dysfunction. Drugs and alcohol may also affect sexual performance.

CONDITIONS OF THE PROSTATE

Prostatitis

Prostatitis is an inflammation of the prostate gland caused by infectious agents (bacteria, fungi, mycoplasma) or by a variety of other problems (e.g., urethral stricture, prostatic hyperplasia). Micro-organisms usually are carried to the prostate from the urethra.

The symptoms of prostatitis are many and include perineal discomfort, burning, urgency and frequency. Prostatodynia (pain in the prostate) is manifested by pain on voiding or perineal pain symptoms, but there may be no evidence of inflammation or bacterial growth in the prostatic fluid.

Acute bacterial prostatitis may produce a sudden onset of fever and chills and perineal, rectal or low back pain. Urinary symptoms of burning, frequency, urgency, nocturia and dysuria may be evident. Some patients, however, are asymptomatic.

Diagnosis requires a careful history, culture of prostatic fluid or tissue and, occasionally, a histologic examination of tissue. The doctor may perform prostatic massage and any prostatic fluid that is expressed is collected in a container. If it is not possible to collect prostatic fluid, the patient is requested to void a small quantity of urine. This specimen may contain the bacteria present in the prostatic fluid.

Medical Management

The goal of management is to avoid the complications of abscess formation and septicaemia. A broad-spectrum antimicrobial (to which the organism causing the infection is susceptible) is given for a period of 10 to 14 days. Intravenous administration of the drug may be necessary to achieve high serum and tissue levels. The patient is encouraged to remain on bedrest since this will alleviate symptoms rapidly. Comfort is promoted with analgesics (pain relief), antispasmodics and bladder sedatives (relieves bladder irritability), baths (relieves pain and spasm) and stool softeners (prevent straining at stool, which increases pain).

Swelling of the gland may produce urinary retention. Other complications include epididymitis, bacteraemia or septicaemia and pyelonephritis.

Chronic bacterial prostatitis is a major source of relapsing urinary tract infection in men. The treatment of chronic prostatitis is difficult, because of poor diffusion of most antimicrobials from the plasma into the prostatic fluid. Antimicrobials (trimethoprim-sulphamethoxazole, tetracycline, minocycline, doxycycline) may be given. Continuous suppressive treatment with low-dose antimicrobial drugs may be indicated. The patient is advised of the possibility of relapsing infection. Comfort is promoted with antispasmodics (to relieve bladder irritability), bathing and stool softeners.

The treatment of nonbacterial prostatitis is directed toward symptomatic relief: bathing, analgesics, etc. The sexual partner should be investigated because of the possibility of cross-infection.

Patient Education

The patient is instructed to take the prescribed antibiotic for the full time period. Hot baths (10 to 20 minutes) may be taken several times daily. Fluids are encouraged to satisfy thirst, but fluids are not 'forced' because an effective drug level must be maintained in the urine. Foods and drink that have diuretic action or increase prostatic secretions should be avoided: alcohol, coffee, tea, chocolate, cola and spices. During periods of acute inflammation, sexual arousal and intercourse should be avoided. However, sexual intercourse may be beneficial in the treatment of chronic prostatitis. The patient should avoid sitting for long periods of time. Medical follow-up is necessary for at least six months to one year since recurrence of prostatitis due to the same or different organisms can occur.

Benign Prostatic Hypertrophy

In many patients over 50 years of age, the prostate gland enlarges, extending upward into the bladder and obstructing the outflow of urine by encroaching on the bladder opening. This condition is known as benign prostatic hypertrophy (enlargement of the prostate). The aetiology is uncertain, but evidence suggests a hormonal cause as initiating hypertrophy of the supporting stromal tissue and of glandular elements in the prostate.

Since enlargement of the prostate gland produces an obstruction to flow of urine, a gradual dilation of the ureters (hydroureter) and kidneys (hydronephrosis) results. The hypertrophied lobes may obstruct the bladder neck or prostatic urethra and thus cause incomplete emptying and urinary retention. Urinary tract infection may result from urinary stasis.

The symptoms (referred to as prostatism) include increasing frequency of urination, nocturia, hesitancy in starting urination, a decrease in size and force of urinary stream; interruption of urinary stream; terminal dribbling, in which urine dribbles out after urination; a sensation of incomplete emptying of the bladder; incontinence; and acute urinary retention. Other generalized symptoms may be noted, including fatigue secondary to nocturia, anorexia, nausea and vomiting due to impaired renal function, and perhaps epigastric discomfort from a distended bladder.

A number of diagnostic tests may be performed to determine the degree of prostatic enlargement, the pre-sence of bladder wall changes, the efficiency or renal function and to assess the patient's general condition. These will include: intravenous urography, renal function tests, midstream specimen of urine, full blood count, serum acid phosphatase, chest X-rays and electrocardiography.

Medical Management

Treatment depends on the severity of the obstruction and the general condition of the patient. If the patient is unable to void he is catheterized immediately, usually with a urethral indwelling catheter. This can be a difficult procedure due to the resistance encountered due to the enlarged prostate, and a stylet (a thin metal wire) may be inserted into the catheter to prevent it collapsing within the urethra on insertion.

In extreme circumstances, when the urethra is totally obstructed, insertion of a suprapubic catheter may be necessary to provide adequate drainage. Surgery to remove the hypertrophied prostatic tissue, called a prostatectomy, is usually necessary to provide permanent relief. This may not be performed immediately and the patient may be discharged with an indwelling catheter and readmitted later for surgery. It is estimated that two out of every 1,000 patients catheterized die from acquired urinary tract infection; therefore, careful and appropriate handling of drainage equipment and patient education may help in reducing the risk to the patient (Bard, 1984; Pritchard and David, 1988). See Nursing Care Plan 25.1.

► NURSING CARE PLAN 25.1: THE PATIENT UNDERGOING PROSTATECTOMY

Nursing care plan for Mr Herbert Dixon, a 73-year-old West Indian man admitted to hospital for transurethral prostatectomy. Mr Dixon lives alone in a one-bedroomed council flat and has become housebound. His symptoms of frequent urination and dribbling have been increasing in severity and have been affecting his sleep.

Patient's problems	Expected outcomes	Nursing care	Rationale
1. Maintaining adequate bladder drainage and kidney function	Adequate bladder drainage occurs	1a. Monitor intake and output	Fluid balance disturbance is common following urinary catheterization for chronic retention (Burkitt and Randall, 1987a)
		b. Encourage an oral intake of 2 to 3 litres daily	Individuals are often dehydrated before catheterization as a consequence of limiting intake to reduce urinary symptoms (Brunner and Suddarth, 1983, p. 660)
		c. Take blood pressure four-hourly and monitor patient for signs of altered renal function: reduced urine output, drowsiness, lethargy	Renal function often declines and blood pressure fluctuates initially, in chronic retention, on catheterization (Brunner and Suddarth, 1989, p. 660)
		d. Tape drainage tube *not* catheter to thigh	Prevents urethral trauma and traction occurring to the bladder neck

► NURSING CARE PLAN 25.1: THE PATIENT UNDERGOING PROSTATECTOMY

Patient's problems	Expected outcomes	Nursing care	Rationale
2. Risk of hospital-acquired urinary tract infection	No infection occurs	2a. Ensure gravity drainage can occur within a closed system and that drainage points do not come in contact with contaminants (e.g., floor)	Prevents pooling and avoids risk of contamination
		b. Employ a clean technique when emptying drainage bag: wash hands, apply disposable gloves, drain urine into sterile or heat-disinfected receptacle	Avoids introduction of contaminants (Crow *et al.*, 1986; Pritchard and David, 1988, p. 400)
		c. Observe urine for cloudiness, debris, 'fishy' odour and report. Test for blood and protein. Collect catheter specimen of urine as directed	Evidence of urinary infection. To obtain confirmation of infection, organism and drug sensitivity
		d. Clean around the catheter and urethral meatus twice daily or more often if necessary (or teach patient if appropriate)	Removes crusts that encourage bacterial growth
		e. Ensure foreskin is *not* retracted	Prevents paraphimosis (Burkitt and Randall, 1986b; Pritchard and David, 1988, p. 402)
3. Risk of patient distress, discomfort and immobility due to urethral catheter	No distress or discomfort occurs and able to move freely	3a. Explain the purpose and mechanism of indwelling catheter	Education reduces anxiety
		b. Ask the patient to report any discomfort, bladder spasms, burning, desire to pass urine, pain in the penis	Bladder irritability and urethral irritation can occur (Burkitt and Randall, 1987b; Pritchard and David, 1988)
		c. Provide a leg bag for daytime use, ensuring it fits snugly around the leg but does not put traction on the catheter. Connect or teach patient to attach, large drainage bag to leg bag at night	Encourages mobility and allows dignity to be maintained. Appliance can be obscured by clothing
4. Lack of knowledge regarding planned surgery and outcome	Operation, potential postoperative care and outcomes understood	4a. Explain the operation and that he will have continuous bladder irrigation for 24 to 48 hours, and will remain catheterized for four or five days	Information reduces anxiety and enhances recovery (Hayward, 1975)
		b. Explain that a degree of incontinence may be experienced after catheter removal, and teach pelvic floor exercises	Urinary incontinence is common following this type of operation, and pelvic floor exercises may improve bladder neck control (James, 1984; Brunner and Suddarth, 1989, p. 661)
		c. Explain that retrograde ejaculation will occur postoperatively and implications for fertility, and that sexual activity can be resumed six to eight weeks postoperatively	Erectile function is usually undamaged by the operation, but retrograde ejaculation occurs (Brunner and Suddarth, 1989, p. 662). It cannot be assumed that age or marital status alter the significance this may have to an individual

►

▶ NURSING CARE PLAN 25.1: THE PATIENT UNDERGOING PROSTATECTOMY

Patient's problems	Expected outcomes	Nursing care	Rationale
5. Risk of fluid and electrolyte disturbance, and physiological shock	No fluid and electrolyte disturbance occurs. Vital signs remain within normal range. Shock does not occur	5a. Monitor blood pressure and pulse (initially half-hourly, decreasing to four-hourly) b. Maintain accurate intake and output assessment, including irrigation, intravenous and oral fluid intake c. Observe patient for evidence of electrolyte disturbance: drowsiness, thirst, confusion d. Monitor temperature four-hourly, and observe for rigor. Report any abnormalities	Blood pressure and pulse are indicators of cardiovascular status Overhydration and electrolyte disturbance can occur rapidly particularly when patient has impaired renal or cardiac function (Brunner and Suddarth, 1989, p. 661; Pritchard and David, 1988, p. 49). Bladder-irrigating fluid can be absorbed Contamination by pathogens can occur from any invasive technique, and direct access to the cardiovascular system occurs during transurethral resection of prostrate. Bacteraemia and septicaemia can cause physiological shock
6. Risk of haemorrhage and/or clot retention	Haemostasis occurs without clot formation	6a. Monitor colour and quality of haematuria, and report any abnormalities b. Ensure irrigation fluid flows freely and is adjusted in relation to the degree of haematuria. Ensure tubing drains freely c. 'Milk' tubing to assist drainage as directed d. Observe patient for bladder distension and discomfort e. Perform bladder lavage as directed if clots form or if patient complains of bladder pain or spasms	Bright red urine indicates arterial bleeding; dark red, venous bleeding. Excessive haematuria may require surgical intervention to resolve Continuous irrigation cleanses the bladder of residual debris and blood. Clot formation in the urethral catheter causes acute retention of urine and can result in severe pain for the patient (James, 1984; Brunner and Suddarth, 1988, p. 661; Pritchard and David, 1988, p. 49) Ensures tubing remains patent Pain or bladder distension would indicate catheter obstruction Evacuation of clots will relieve obstruction and pain (Brunner and Suddarth, 1988, p. 661)
7. Risk of urethral irritation	No urethral irritation occurs	7a. Cleanse area around urethral meatus with water, disposable wipes (wear disposable gloves), twice daily or more frequently if necessary b. Ensure foreskin is freely mobile and not retracted over the glans c. Tape drainage tubing to shaved area on the thigh	Blood clots and crusts can form around the urethral meatus, which provide a rich medium for bacterial growth and a source of ascending urinary tract infection. Gloves should be worn to prevent cross-infection and as protection against blood-borne pathogens (Pritchard and David, 1988, p. 9) Prevents paraphimosis developing Prevents traction being applied to the prostatic bed, which could induce bleeding (Brunner and Suddarth, 1988, p. 661)

▶ NURSING CARE PLAN 25.1: THE PATIENT UNDERGOING PROSTATECTOMY

Patient's problems	Expected outcomes	Nursing care	Rationale
		d. Request patient to refrain from pulling on catheter, and ensure catheter tubing is free of clothing and bedding	Prevents unnecessary bleeding
		e. Request patient to report any burning or irritation felt in the urethra	Urethral irritation can be caused by local tissue reaction to the catheter itself. Some relief may be obtained, should this occur, by application of sterile local anaesthetic lubricating jelly. Removal of the catheter should relieve irritation (Burkitt and Randall, 1987a; Pritchard and David, 1988, p. 401)
8. Risk of urinary retention or incontinence following catheter removal	Able to pass urine freely with volumes more than 150 ml	8a. Monitor fluid intake and output including frequency and volume of micturition	Micturition patterns can be disturbed following catheter removal. Frequency with small volumes can indicate the bladder is not comletely emptying
		b. Ask patient to report any abdominal discomfort or distension	May indicate urinary retention
		c. Ensure patient has a urinal (steam-disinfected or disposable) at all times	Delaying voiding can affect the establishment of normal micturition patterns or cause unnecessary episodes of incontinence
		d. Ask patient to report any burning or discomfort when passing urine. If present: report, obtain midstream specimen, encourage oral intake of more than two litres daily, administer antibiotics as prescribed	Urethral and bladder discomfort can indicate presence of urinary tract infection, which should be treated (Pritchard and David, 1988, p. 403)
		e. Reinforce preoperative teaching of pelvic floor exercises and encourage patient to perform them regularly (10 times per hour)	To increase bladder neck tone and aid bladder emptying
		f. If patient is incontinent: assess nature of problem, provide appropriate equipment to contain it, reassure patient of the temporary nature of the problem, and refer to continence advisor (if available)	Important to establish nature and pattern of problem. Incontinence often brings associated feelings of disgust and patient dignity should be maintained. Appropriate use of equipment reduces patient distress (James, 1984, p. 152)
9. Lack of knowledge concerning diagnosis or further treatment	Understands diagnosis and planned future management	9a. Establish patient's understanding of his condition and results of surgery	Enlargement of the prostate treated by transurethural resection of prostate can be benign or malignant. If cancer is diagnosed, further treatment will be necessary
		b. Encourage patient to discuss his diagnosis and treatment with urologist doctor	Feelings of loss of control, helplessness and depression are common responses to the diagnosis of cancer (Jones, 1989, p. 11)
		c. Reinforce information given to patient and encourage him to express his feelings and concerns regarding this	

► NURSING CARE PLAN 25.1: THE PATIENT UNDERGOING PROSTATECTOMY

Patient's problems	Expected outcomes	Nursing care	Rationale
		d. Explain treatment plan using patient information material to increase understanding e. Educate patient about symptoms that should be reported f. Provide contact addresses of support organizations (i.e. BACUP, Cancerlink, etc) if appropriate	Provision of information increases sense of control, positively influences physical and psychological wellbeing (Jones, 1989, p. 14)
10. Preparation for discharge	Successful discharge achieved	10a. Encourage patient to resume self-care in preparation for discharge b. Encourage patient to express worries and concerns about impending discharge c. Establish support (formal and informal) available on discharge d. Obtain information about patient's home and ability to perform self-care within home environment e. Ensure medication, outpatient's appointments, that incontinence aids are provided, and that patient understands them f. Explain to patient how to obtain further supplies of equipment or medication g. Establish if patient wishes to be referred to support agencies—Social Services (Medical Social Work), district nurses continence advisor h. Ensure transport arrangements are organized for discharge	Baseline information is important to establish individual's needs and appropriate use of limited resources. Early identification of problems and appropriate referral will ensure smooth transition from hospital to community, and reduce risk of readmission resulting from an inability to cope (Pritchard and David, 1988, p. 18)

The Patient Undergoing Prostatectomy

Ideally, prostactectomy should be performed before acute urinary retention develops, and certainly before the upper urinary tract and collecting system are damaged.

Four different approaches are possible in removing the hypertrophied fibroadenomatous portion of the prostate gland (these are compared in Table 25.1). In all four techniques, all hyperplastic tissue is removed, leaving behind the surgical capsule of the prostate. The transurethral approach is a closed procedure, while the other three are open surgical procedures.

A transurethral resection of the prostate is the most usual procedure and can be carried out by means of an endoscopic instrument that has ocular and operating systems. The instrument is introduced through the urethra to the prostate, which can be viewed directly. The gland is then removed in small chips with an electrical cutting loop (Figure 25.2A). Suprapubic prostatectomy is one method of removing the gland through an abdominal wound. An opening is made into the bladder, and the gland is removed from above (Figure 25.2B). Such an approach can be used for a gland of any size, and few complications occur.

Perineal prostatectomy involves the removal of the gland through an incision in the perineum (Figure 25.2C).

Retropubic prostatectomy involves a low abdominal incision, and the prostate gland is approached between the pubic arch and the bladder (without entering the bladder) (Figure 25.2D).

Table 25.1 *Comparison of surgical approaches for prostatectomy*

The operation of choice depends on (1) the size of the gland, (2) the severity of the obstruction, (3) the age of the patient, (4) the condition of patient and (5) the presence of associated diseases

Surgical approach	Advantages	Disadvantages	Nursing care
Transurethal resection (removal of prostatic tissue by instrument introduced through urethra)	Avoids abdominal incision Safer for surgical-risk patient Shorter period of hospitalization and convalescence Lower morbidity rate Causes less pain	Requires highly skilled operator Recurrent obstruction, urethral trauma and stricture may develop Delayed bleeding may occur Infection risks due to instrumentation	Observe evidence of haemorrhage (drainage in bag) and clot retention Observe for symptoms of urethral stricture (dysuria, straining, small urinary stream) Observe for evidence of infection (elevated temperature, raised pulse, rigors)
Open surgical removal			
Suprapubic	Technically simple Offers wider area of exploration Permits exploration for cancerous lymph nodes Allows more complete removal of obstructing gland Permits treatment of associated lesions in bladder	Requires surgical approach through the bladder Control of haemorrhage difficult Urinary leakage around suprapubic tube Recovery more prolonged and uncomfortable	Observe for indications of haemorrhage and shock Give meticulous aseptic attention to area around suprapubic tube
Perineal	Offers direct anatomical approach Permits gravity drainage Particularly efficacious for radical cancer therapy Allows haemostasis under direct vision Low mortality rate Less incidence of shock Ideal for very old, feeble and poor-risk patient with large prostate	Higher postoperative incidence of impotency and urinary incontinency Problem of damage to rectum and external sphincter Restricted operative field Greater potential for infection	Avoid use of rectal tubes, rectal thermometers and enemas after perineal surgery Use drainage pads to absorb excess urinary drainage Provide aids to alleviate, discomfort on sitting Urinary leakage may occur around wound for several days after catheter removal
Retropubic	Avoids incision into the bladder Permits easier visualization and control of bleeding Shorter period of convalescence Less bladder sphincter damage	Cannot treat associated bladder disease Increased incidence of haemorrhage from prostatic venous plexus; osteitis pubis	Watch for evidence of haemorrhage Posturinary leakage may occur for several days after catheter is removed

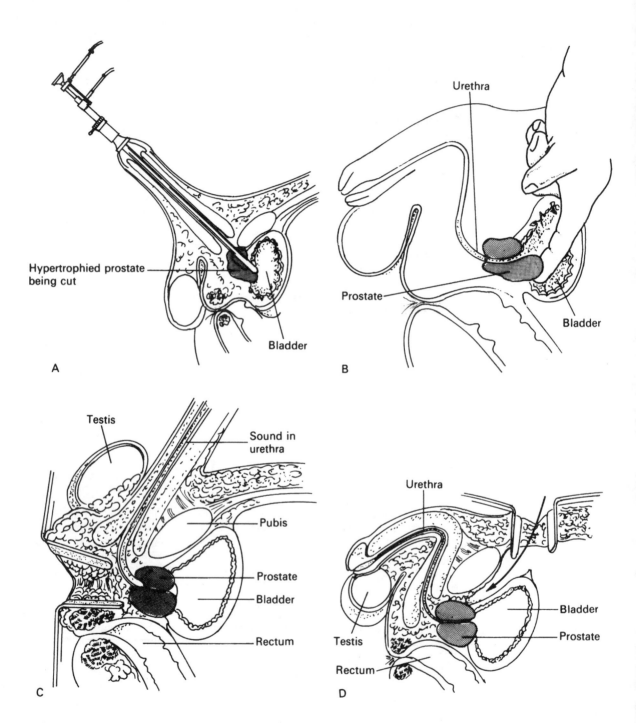

Figure 25.2 Prostatectomy procedures. (A) Transurethral resection. A loop of wire connected with a cutting current is rotated in the cystoscope to remove shavings of prostate at the bladder orifice. (B) Suprapubic prostatectomy. Using an abdominal approach, the prostate is shelled out of its bed by the surgeon's fingers. (C) Perineal prostatectomy. Two retractors on the left spread the perineal incision in providing a view of the prostate. (D) Retropubic prostatectomy is done through a low abdominal incision. Note two abdominal retractors and arrow approaching the prostate gland.

▶ THE PATIENT UNDERGOING PROSTATECTOMY

▶ *Assessment*

During the assessment, the following specific areas should be explored with the patient: his understanding of the condition, his urinary problems and how they affect his ability to care for himself and manage his lifestyle, how he currently manages his problems, including use of appliances, aids and services, any associated or underlying conditions that limit his activities and any pain or discomfort experienced. This assessment will usually include collection of baseline information regarding vital signs (blood pressure, pulse and respiratory rate and temperature), urinalysis, weight, appetite, mobility and condition of skin.

▶ *Patient's Problems*

Based on the nursing history and all other assessment data, the patient's major problems may include the following:

Preoperative
● Anxiety related to difficulties with voiding.
● Lack of knowledge related to his problems and planned treatment.

Postoperative

● Fluid and electrolyte disturbance due to changes in renal functioning, fluid loss and possible bleeding.
● Pain related to the surgical incision, catheter placement and bladder spasms.
● Potential risk of infection related to bacterial contamination of the incision and/or urinary tract.
● Lack of knowledge about postoperative care and preparations for discharge.

▶ *Planning and Implementation*
▶ Expected Outcomes

The patient's major preoperative outcomes may include reduction of anxiety and learning about the prostate problem and the perioperative experience. His major postoperative outcomes may include correction of fluid volume disturbances, relief of pain and discomfort, prevention of infection and ability to perform self-care activities.

Preoperative Nursing Care

Reduction of Anxiety

The nurse familiarizes the patient with the hospital environment and initiates measures to reduce anxiety. Communication is established regarding the patient's understanding of his problem and what the surgeon has already told him. He may be sensitive and embarrassed to discuss problems related to the genital area. Privacy is provided, and a trusting and professional relationship is developed with the patient since he often has related sexual concerns that may need to be discussed. Guilt feelings often surface as he falsely assumes a cause-and-effect relation between early sexual practices and his current problems. In short, his verbalization of concerns should be encouraged.

Patient Education

A convenient time is established for the patient (ensuring his privacy) to review the anatomy of the affected parts and how they function in relation to the urinary and reproductive systems. The use of diagrams may be effective in the teaching process. The nurse reinforces what will take place as the patient is prepared for diagnostic tests and then for surgery. The nurse describes the nature of the planned operation, the type of anaesthesia and the recovery room procedure. The amount of information is limited to the point of meeting the patient's needs and relieving his concerns. All procedures in the immediate perioperative period are explained, questions are answered and support is provided. Booklets and other written information may be useful aids to reinforce teaching and promote discussion.

Comfort Measures

If the patient presents with signs and symptoms of discomfort, he is nursed on bedrest and comfort measures such as reducing his anxiety and administering the prescribed sedation are initiated. The nurse monitors the patient's voiding patterns, observes for bladder distention and assists with catheterization for retention. An indwelling catheter is introduced if the patient has continuing urinary retention or if there is evidence of azotaemia (accumulation of nitrogenous waste products in the blood). If the patient is elderly or hypertensive or has diminished renal function or an excessive amount of urinary retention that has existed for many weeks, it may be advantageous for the patient's condition to be stabilized before surgery. *The blood pressure may fluctuate and renal function declines the first few days after bladder drainage is instituted.* If the patient cannot tolerate a urethral catheter, he is prepared for insertion of a suprapubic catheter.

Preoperative Preparation

When the patient is scheduled for a prostatectomy, the preparation described in Chapter 2 is followed. Antiembolism stockings are applied before the operation and are particularly important if the patient is placed in a lithotomy position during surgery. An enema may be given preoperatively to prevent postoperative straining and to improve access to the prostate.

Postoperative Nursing Care

Assessing for Potential Complications

Following prostatectomy, it is important to be on the alert for major complications such as haemorrhage, infection, thrombosis and catheter obstruction.

Haemorrhage

Since a hypertrophied prostate gland is very vascular, the immediate dangers following a prostatectomy are bleeding and shock. Bleeding may occur from the bed of the prostate. Bleeding may also result in the formation of clots, which then obstruct the flow of urine. The drainage begins as almost frank haematuria and then becomes light pink within 24 hours after operation.

● Bright red bleeding with increased viscosity and numerous clots usually indicates arterial bleeding. Venous bleeding appears darker and less viscous.
● Arterial haemorrhage usually requires surgical intervention (e.g., suturing or transurethral coagulation of bleeding points), while venous bleeding may be controlled by applying traction to the catheter so that the balloon applies pressure to the prostatic fossa.

Infection and Thrombosis

Following perineal prostatectomy, careful aseptic technique is practised, since the possibility of infection is great. Dressings can be held in place by a double-tailed T bandage or a padded scrotal support.

Rectal temperatures, rectal tubes and enemas are to be avoided because of the danger of causing trauma and bleeding in the prostatic fossa. After the perineal sutures are removed, the perineum is cleansed as necessary. Bathing is also used to encourage healing and the patient may gain relief from the use of a cool air hairdryer directed on the perineal area to aid drying.

In addition to haemorrhage, urinary tract infections and epididymitis are possible complications following prostatectomy. A vasectomy may be performed during surgery to prevent retrograde spread of infection from the prostatic urethra through the vas and into the epididymis. If epididymitis occurs, it is managed as discussed on page 807.

Patients undergoing prostatectomy (with the exception of transurethral resection) have a high incidence of deep-vein thrombosis and pulmonary embolism. Low-dose heparin therapy may be prescribed prophylactically.

Catheter Obstruction

Following a transurethral prostatic resection, the catheter must drain well; an obstructed catheter will produce distension of the prostatic capsule with resultant haemorrhage. Frusemide is prescribed to initiate postoperative diuresis, thereby helping to keep the catheter patent.

● Watch and palpate the lower abdomen to see that no blockage of the catheter is occurring. An over-distended bladder presents a distinct rounded swelling above the pubis.
● Check the drainage bag, dressings and incision site for evidence of bleeding. Note colour of urine; change in colour from pink to amber indicates lessened bleeding.
● Monitor the blood pressure, pulse and respirations and compare with the preoperative vital signs to assess for hypotension. Observe the patient for restlessness; cold, sweating skin; pallor; fall in blood pressure; and an increasing pulse rate.

Drainage of the bladder is usually accomplished through a closed sterile system of drainage. A three-way system is usually used following transurethral resection of the prostate. Irrigation fluid can, via an input channel, cleanse the bladder, thus preventing clot formation. Urine drains out into a drainage bag by gravity, and a third channel can provide access to perform bladder lavage without breaking the closed system should catheter obstruction occur (Pritchard and David, 1988, pp. 48–50).

● If the patient complains of pain, check the tubing and irrigate the system, thereby correcting any obstruction, before administering an analgesic. Usually, the catheter is irrigated with 50 ml of irrigating fluid at a time, making sure that the same amount is recovered in the drainage bag.
● Avoid overdistending the bladder, which can produce secondary haemorrhage by stretching the coagulated vessels in the prostatic capsule.
● Maintain an input and output record, including the amount of fluid used for irrigation.

The drainage tube (not the catheter) is taped to the shaved inner thigh to prevent traction on the bladder. If a suprapubic catheter is in place, it is taped to the abdomen. The nurse re-explains to the patient the purpose of the catheter and assures him that the urge to void is from the presence of the catheter and bladder spasms. The patient should be cautioned not to pull on the catheter, since this causes bleeding, subsequent plugging of the tubing and urinary retention.

Catheter Removal. After the catheter is removed (usually when the urine clears), urinary leakage may occur around the wound for several days in patients who have undergone perineal, suprapubic and retropubic surgery. Some urinary incontinence may occur after the catheter is removed. The patient is told that this will probably disappear in time, and aids or appliances should be provided to contain the problem and reduce distress.

Pain Relief

Usually following a prostatectomy, the patient is kept on bedrest for the first 24 hours. If pain occurs, the cause and location must be determined. It may be related to the incision; to excoriation of the skin at the catheter site; in the loin area, indicating a kidney problem; or it may be due to bladder spasms. Bladder irritability can initiate bleeding and result in clot retention.

Before administering the prescribed medication for pain relief, the patient's vital signs, including blood pressure, are checked; then the drainage tubing is checked and the system is irrigated as prescribed, thus correcting any obstruction that may cause discomfort.

Discomfort may be caused by dressings that are too snug or have become saturated with drainage or are not properly placed.

Patient Education

When the patient is able to mobilize, he is encouraged to walk but not to sit for prolonged periods, since this increases intra-abdominal pressure and increases the possibility of discomfort and bleeding. The bowel movements are kept soft (using fruit juice, fibre, stool softeners) to prevent excessive straining. If an enema is prescribed, it is administered with caution to avoid possible rectal perforation.

As the days pass and drainage tubes are removed, the patient may show signs of discouragement and depression because he is unable to regain bladder control immediately. Urinary frequency and burning may occur after the catheter is removed. The following exercises are helpful for regaining urinary control:

● Tense the perineal muscles by pressing the buttocks together; hold this position; relax. This exercise, done 10 to 20 times each hour, can be performed while sitting or standing.
● Try to shut off the urinary stream after starting to void; wait a few seconds and then continue to void.

Perineal exercises are continued until full urinary control is gained. The patient should be instructed to urinate as soon as the first desire to do so is felt. It is important for the patient to know that regaining urinary control is a gradual process, and that even though he may continue to 'dribble' after being discharged from the hospital, the dribbling should gradually diminish (up to one year). The urine may be cloudy for several weeks but should clear as the prostate area heals.

While the prostatic fossa is healing (six to eight weeks), the patient should not engage in any Valsalva efforts (straining at stool, heavy lifting), since this increases venous pressure and may produce haematuria. He should avoid long car journeys and strenuous exercise, which increase the tendency to bleed. He may also benefit from knowing that certain foods (spicy), alcohol and coffee can cause discomfort. The patient is cautioned to drink enough fluids to avoid dehydration, which increases the tendency for a clot to form and obstruct the flow of urine. Any bleeding, or dysuria or decrease in the size of the urinary stream should be reported to his doctor.

Sexual Function

A prostatectomy does not usually cause impotence. (Perineal prostatectomy may cause impotence due to unavoidable damage of the pudendal nerves.) In most instances, sexual activity may be resumed in six to eight weeks, the time required for the prostatic fossa to heal. Following ejaculation, the seminal fluid will go into the bladder and is excreted with the urine. (The anatomical changes in the posterior urethra lead to retrograde ejaculation).

After total prostatectomy (usually for cancer), impotence is almost always expected. For the patient who does not desire to give up sexual activity, a plastic insert (penile implant) may be used to make the penis rigid for sexual intercourse (see Impotence, p. 810).

▶ *Evaluation*
▶ **Expected Outcomes**

Preoperative

1. Patient is free of anxiety.
   a. Expresses his concerns and accepts solutions offered.
   b. Expresses relief that the bladder problem can be treated and that the condition is not a malignant tumour.
2. Relates his understanding of the surgical procedure and postoperative course.
   a. Discusses the surgical procedure and expected postoperative course.
   b. Practises perineal muscle exercises and other techniques useful in facilitating control of bladder function.
   c. Participates in all preoperative preparations for surgery.

Postoperative

1. Maintains acceptable level of urinary elimination.
   a. Maintains optimum drainage of catheter/drainage tubes.
   b. Verbalizes his understanding that urinary incontinence will gradually disappear.
2. Is free of pain.
   a. Relates relief of discomfort.
   b. Relates signs/symptoms of problems that are to be reported.
3. Is free of infection and hemorrhage.
   a. Maintains vital signs within normal limits.
   b. Exhibits good wound healing; no signs of inflammation.
   c. Relates what signs are to be reported if an infection is developing.
4. Responds positively to self-care measures.
   a. Increases activity and mobilizes daily.
   b. Keeps urinary output within normal ranges and consistent with intake.

c. Uses perineal exercises and interruption of urinary stream to promote bladder control.

d. Drinks adequate amounts of fluids daily.

e. Avoids straining and lifting heavy objects.

f. Says he is looking forward to resuming sexual activity when permitted.

Cancer of the Prostate

Cancer of the prostate is the third most common cause of cancer and the second most common cause of cancer deaths in United Kingdom males. With increasing numbers of men in the older age-group, greater attention will be focused on this condition.

Clinical Features

Early cancer of the prostate does not usually produce symptoms. The obstructive symptoms occur late in the disease. This cancer tends to be variable in its course. If the neoplasm is large enough to encroach on the bladder neck and cause obstruction of urine, there are symptoms and signs of obstruction, namely, difficulty and frequency of urination, urinary retention and decreased size and force of the urinary stream. Prostatic cancer commonly metastasizes to bone, lymph nodes, brain and lungs. Symptoms due to metastases are backache, hip pain, perineal and rectal discomfort, anaemia, weight loss, weakness, nausea and oliguria. Haematuria may be present from urethral or bladder invasion, or both.

Early Detection

Every male over the age of 40 should have a digital rectal examination as part of his health check. Earlier detection is the clue to a higher cure rate. Routine repeated rectal palpation of the gland is important because early cancer may be felt as a nodule within the substance of the gland or as a diffuse induration in the posterior lobe. A digital rectal examination in addition to being more accurate, readily available and less costly than other screening tests for prostatic cancer provides useful clinical information regarding the rectum, anal sphincter and quality of stool.

Diagnosis

On rectal examination, an area of increased firmness within the prostate is noted. The more advanced lesion is 'stony hard' and fixed. The diagnosis is made on histological examination of tissue removed surgically by transurethral resection, open prostatectomy or needle biopsy (perineal or transrectal). Fine needle aspiration is a quick painless method of obtaining prostate cells for cytological examination. It is a helpful method for determining staging of the tumour if cancer is present.

Investigations may include: haemoglobin to exclude anaemia, acid phosphatase (and/or) prostatic specific antigen raised in prostatic cancer, urea and electrolyte estimation to assess renal function, intravenous urogram to detect ureteric obstruction, lymphangiography, computerized tomography and nuclear magnetic resonance scans to demonstrate pelvic lymph node involvement, and bone scans and skeletal X-rays to detect metastatic bone disease.

Medical Management

Treatment selection is based on the stage of the disease and on the patient's general condition and symptoms. A transurethral prostatectomy is the standard operative approach that may be followed by bilateral orchidectomy (removal of the testes). Curative radiotherapy using external beam or interstitial irradiation may be used when patients have underlying conditions that make surgery hazardous. Side-effects include proctitis (inflammation of the rectum) and cystitis (inflammation of the bladder), due to proximity to the prostate. Radiotherapy is also used for palliation in advanced disease.

The prostate gland is dependent on testosterone for its development and is inhibited by oestrogens; similarly, prostatic cancer is usually hormone sensitive. Hormone manipulation is therefore used to control, but not cure, advanced local and metastatic disease.

Bilateral orchidectomy lowers plasma testosterone levels, since 93 per cent of circulating testosterone is of testicular origin, thereby inducing prostatic atrophy. However, orchidectomy does carry a significant emotional and physical impact, and impotence may be a lasting side-effect.

An alternative approach is the administration of oestrogens, usually diethylstilboestrol, which inhibits pituitary gonadotrophin release, which reduces testicular testosterone production. Diethylstilboestrol provides symptomatic control by reducing tumour size, lessening metastatic pain and imparting a sense of wellbeing. Evidence suggests that diethylstilboestrol, in high doses, does carry a significant risk of death from cardiovascular conditions.

Gynaecomastia (enlargement of the breasts), nausea and vomiting, and fluid retention can be side-effects of oestrogen therapy. Also, the patient may experience embarrassing feminizing effects, such as loss of facial and pubic hair and alteration in voice pitch. Impotence almost always occurs with oestrogen therapy.

In patients whose condition progresses, androgen blockade may be employed. Anti-androgens block the binding of androgens to their receptors within the tumour cell. Side-effects include gynaecomastia and gastrointestinal disturbance, but sexual functioning does not appear to be affected. Drugs that affect adrenal androgen production (aminogluthethimide, spironolactone, ketoconozole and corticosteroids) are used in advanced prostatic cancer (Pritchard, 1988a).

Regular transurethral resection may be necessary to maintain patency of the urethral passage. Urethral or suprapubic catheterization may be used when repeated surgery is impractical. Patients with disseminated disease are treated symptomatically: radiotherapy, narcotic analgesia and anti-inflammatory agents to relieve bone pain, blood transfusions when haemoglobin levels fall from tumour infiltration of the bone marrow, corticosteroids to increase appetite and improve mood. Patients with metastatic spread to the spinal column can develop neurological symptoms due to the collapse of vertebrae onto the spinal column (see also Nursing Management of the Patient With Pain, Chapter 2, Care of the Patient With Advanced Cancer, Chapter 2, Care of the Patient With Spinal Injury, Unit 11).

CONDITIONS AFFECTING THE TESTES AND ADJACENT STRUCTURES

Undescended Testis (Cryptorchidism)

Cryptorchidism is the absence of one or both testes from the scrotum. The testes may be located in the abdominal cavity or inguinal canal. If the testis does not descend, hormone therapy or surgery (orchidopexy) is employed to secure proper positioning.

In orchidopexy, an incision is made over the inguinal canal, and the testis is brought down and placed in the scrotum. If fixation cannot be achieved by surgery, or if the testis is missing or abnormal, a silastic implant resembling a normal testicle can be inserted.

Orchiditis

Orchiditis is an inflammation of the testes (testicular congestion). The aetiology is usually pyogenic, viral, spirochaetal, parasitic, traumatic, chemical or idiopathic.

When mumps is contracted in the postpubertal male, four to seven days after swelling of the jaw and neck, approximately one in five men will develop some form of orchiditis. The testis may show some atrophy. In past years, sterility and impotence often resulted. Current practice is for the man who has not previously had mumps and is now exposed to the disease to receive γ-globulin immediately. The disease is likely to be less severe, with reduced or no complications.

Management

If the causes are bacterial, viral or fungal, therapy is specific. Rest, elevation with a scrotal support, ice packs, antibiotics, analgesics and anti-inflammatory medications are recommended.

Epididymitis

Epididymitis is an infection of the epididymis that usually descends from an infected prostate or urinary tract. It may also develop as a complication of gonorrhoea. In men under 35 years of age, the major cause of epididymitis is *Chlamydia trachomatis*. The infection passes upward through the urethra and the ejaculatory duct, and thence along the vas deferens to the epididymis.

The patient complains of pain and soreness in the inguinal canal along the course of the vas deferens, and then develops pain and swelling in the scrotum and the groin. The epididymis becomes swollen and extremely painful; the temperature is elevated. The urine may contain pus (pyuria) and bacteria (bacteriuria), and the patient may experience resulting chills and fever.

Medical Management

If the epididymitis is chlamydial in origin, the patient and the patient's sexual partners must also be treated with antibiotics. The patient is observed for abscess formation. If no improvement occurs within two weeks, an underlying testicular tumour should be considered. An epididymectomy (excision of the epididymis from the testis) may be performed for patients with recurrent, incapacitating episodes or for those with chronic, painful conditions.

Nursing Care

The patient is nursed on bedrest with the scrotum elevated with a scrotal bridge or folded towel to prevent traction on the spermatic cord and to improve venous drainage and relieve pain. Antimicrobials are given as prescribed until all evidence of the acute inflammatory reaction has subsided.

Intermittent cold compresses to the scrotum may help ease the pain. Local heat or bathing later in the infection may hasten resolution of the inflammatory process. Analgesics are given for pain relief as prescribed. Once mobile, the patient should be encouraged to wear a scrotal support for two to three weeks.

Patient Education

The patient should avoid straining (lifting) and sexual excitement until the infection is under control. He should be instructed to continue with analgesics for pain and antibiotics as prescribed and to use ice packs if necessary for discomfort. It may take four weeks or longer for the epididymis to return to normal.

Tumours of the Testes

Testicular cancer accounts for only 1 per cent of all malignant tumors, but it ranks first in cancer incidence among males in the 20- to 35-year age-group. Such cancers are classified as germinal or nongerminal. There are two systems of classification of germinal tumours—the United Kingdom system and the WHO/United States system (shown in brackets):

1. Seminoma—classical or spermatocyte.
2. Teratoma differentiated (teratoma).

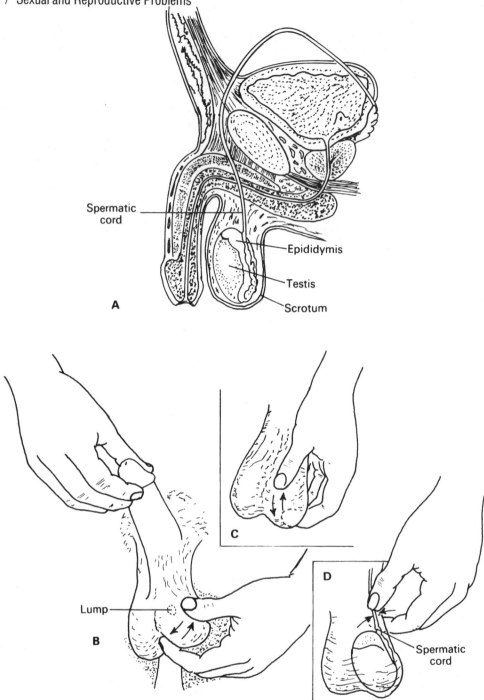

Figure 25.3 Testicular self-examination is to be performed once a month; it is neither difficult nor time-consuming. A convenient time is often after a warm bath or shower when the scrotum is more relaxed. Both hands are used to palpate the testis; the normal testicle is smooth and uniform in consistency. (A) Normal anatomy. (B) With the index and middle finger under the testis and the thumb on top, roll the testis gently in a horizontal plane between the thumb and fingers, feeling for any evidence of a small lump or abnormality. (C) Follow the same procedure for palpation in the 'vertical' plane. (D) Locate the epididymis (cordlike structure on the top and back of the testicle that stores and transports sperm). Repeat the examination for the other testis; it is normal to find one testis larger than the other. Any evidence of a small, pea-size lump should be checked by a doctor. It may be due to an infection or a tumour growth.

3. Malignant teratoma intermediate (teratocarcinoma).
4. Malignant teratoma undifferentiated (embryonal carcinoma).
5. Malignant teratoma trophoblastic (choriocarcinoma).

Clinical Features

The symptoms appear very gradually with a mass in the scrotum and generally painless enlargement of the testis. The patient may complain of heaviness in the scrotum. Backache (from retroperitoneal node extension), gynaecomastia (due to raised ß-human chorionic gonadotrophin levels), pain in the abdomen, loss of weight and general weakness may be from metastatic disease. The metastatic growth may be more marked than the local testicular one. *The enlargement of the testis without pain is a significant diagnostic finding.*

One method of early detection of testicular cancer is self-examination. Part of health promotion practices for men should include testicular self-examination. Teaching men to perform self-examination as depicted in Figure 25.3 is an important intervention for early detection of this disease.

Diagnosis

Alpha-fetoprotein and ß-human chorionic gonadotrophin are tumour markers that may be elevated in patients with testicular cancer. (Tumour markers are substances synthesized by the tumour cells and released into the circulation in abnormal amounts. Other diagnostic tests include an intravenous urogram to detect ureteral deviation secondary to tumour mass, lymphangiography to assess extent of lymphatic spread of the tumour, computed tomography to identify lesions in the retroperitoneum and mediastinum, abdominal ultrasound and chest X-ray.

Medical Management

The expected outcomes of management are to eradicate disease and achieve a cure. Disseminated testicular cancer is regarded as a treatable and probably curable disease. Treatment selection is based on cell type and anatomical extent of the disease (stage). Initial treatment involves removal of the testis (unilateral orchidectomy) through an inguinal incision. Occasionally, when metastatic spread is life-threatening, chemotherapy is commenced immediately, followed by orchidectomy (Borley, 1989; Hubbard and Jenkins, 1983).

Testicular tumours are highly responsive to drug therapy. Chemotherapy regimes vary, but a commonly used combination in the United Kingdom is: bleomycin, etoposide, vincristine sulphate and cisplatin. Chemotherapy employed in the management of these cancers is extremely toxic and expert intensive therapeutic support is a very important aspect of care in order that side-effects are minimizes (Borley, 1989; Tschudin, 1988).

Radiotherapy is used in the treatment of early stage seminomas. External beam therapy is delivered to pelvic lymph nodes on the affected side and the para-aortic nodes.

Surgery is sometimes performed following chemotherapy on those patients with teratomas to remove residual tissue and obtain histological specimens for examination. The operation employed is a para-aortic node dissection (Pritchard, 1988b). This is a major thoraco-abdominal operation and, as the patient is often debilitated following chemotherapy, careful preoperative preparation and skilled postoperative care is essential (Tschudin, 1988).

Fertility, Paternity and Sexuality

Before commencing chemotherapy, patients should be given the opportunity to bank sperm if their sperm count is suitable for cryopreservation (minimum sperm count >10 million/ml semen; minimum sperm motility >40 per cent). Men who recover spermatogenesis following treatment may wish to discuss the potential risk of congenital defects when considering paternity. Current evidence suggests that there is no greater risk for these individuals than for men who have not received chemotherapy or radiotherapy (Borley, 1989). Some patients may wish to have a testicular prosthesis for cosmetic reasons. Some centres routinely insert these at the time or orchidectomy. Para-aortic node dissection does the carry the potential risk of ejaculatory difficulties, and this should be discussed with the patient before surgery.

Patient Education

The patient may have difficulty in accepting his condition. He needs encouragement to maintain a positive attitude during what may be a long course of therapy.

A patient with a history of one tumour of the testes has a greater chance of developing another. Follow-up evaluation includes chest X-rays, intravenous urography, computerized tomography and levels of ß-human chorionic gonadotrophin and -fetoprotein.

Hydrocele

A hydrocele is a collection of fluid generally in the tunica vaginalis of the testis, although it may also occur within the spermatic cord. The tunica vaginalis becomes widely distended with fluid. Hydrocele may be acute or chronic and is differentiated from a hernia by the fact that a hydrocele transmits light when transilluminated.

Acute hydrocele occurs in association with acute infectious diseases of the epididymis or as a result of local trauma or systemic infectious diseases, such as mumps. The cause of chronic hydrocele is unknown.

Treatment is only necessary if the hydrocele becomes tense and compromises testicular circulation or if the scrotal mass becomes large, uncomfortable or embarrassing.

In the surgical treatment of hydrocele, an incision is made through the wall of the scrotum down to the distended tunica vaginalis. The sac is resected or, after being opened, is sutured together to collapse the wall. Postoperatively, a scrotal support is worn for comfort and support. The major complication is the formation of a haematoma in the loose tissues of the scrotum. The nursing care is the same as for a varicocele.

Varicocele

A varicocele is an abnormal dilation of the veins in the scrotum, and often involves the spermatic cord. Varicoceles are associated with subfertility. The main symptom is a dragging sensation in the scrotum. Surgical correction is achieved by ligating and excising the congested veins (varicocelectomy). Postoperatively, an ice pack may be applied to the scrotum to reduce oedema and bruising. The patient should wear a scrotal support for comfort (Brunner and Suddarth, 1989, p. 663).

IMPOTENCE

Impotence is the alteration of a man's sexual capability to either achieve or maintain an erection sufficient to accomplish intercourse. Impotence can be either erectile or ejaculatory. Erectile impotence has both psychogenic and organic causes. Causes of psychogenic impotence include anxiety, fatigue, depression and cultural pressure to perform sexually. Research suggests, however, that organic impotence may account for a larger percentage of cases of impotence than previously realized. Organic causes include occlusive vascular disease, endocrine disease (diabetes, pituitary tumours, hypogonadism), genitourinary conditions (radical pelvic cancer surgery), haematological conditions (Hodgkin's disease, leukaemia), neurological disorders (neuropathies, parkinsonism), trauma to the pelvic or genital area and drugs (alcohol, psychoactive drugs, anticholinergics) and drug abuse.

Diagnosis of impotence involves taking a sexual and medical history, an analysis of presenting symptoms, physical examination and various laboratory studies. The advent of sleep laboratories has made the nocturnal penile tumescence test possible. Research revealed that normal males have nocturnal penile erections closely paralleling rapid eye movement (REM) sleep in their occurrence and duration. Organically impotent men show inadequate sleep-related erections that correspond to their waking performance. Changes in penile circumference are monitored (using a mercury strain gauge placed around the penis) and recorded. The nocturnal penile tumescence test is a means of determining whether erectile impotence has organic or psychogenic aetiology (Gingell and Desai, 1987).

Arterial blood flow to the penis is measured with the Doppler probe. Psychological evaluation of the patient may be part of the diagnostic process.

Management

Treatment, which depends to some extent on the cause, can be medical, surgical or a combination of both. A patient's response to nonsurgical therapy, such as treatment of alcoholism and readjustment of hypertensive agents or other medications, is examined. Impotence secondary to hypothalamic-pituitary-gonadal dysfunction may be reversible with endocrine therapy. Insufficient penile blood flow may be treated with recently developed vascular surgery. Patients with impotence from psychogenic causes are directed to a professional specializing in psychosexual therapy. Patients with impotence secondary to organic causes may be candidates for surgical implantation of penile prostheses or taught the technique of autoinjection of papaverine (Brindley, 1986; Gingell and Desai, 1988). Noninvasive devices that use suction to produce penile engorgement and constriction bands to maintain the erection have been found successful in some cases (Wiles, 1988).

Two basic types of penile implants are available: the semirigid rod and the inflatable prosthesis. Complications following implant procedures include infection, erosion of the prosthesis through the skin and persistent pain, which may require removal of the implant (Gingell and Desai, 1988).

Impotence, regardless of its cause, has vast psychological and psychosocial implications for most men. Therefore, sound interpersonal skills are necessary in order that sensitivity and support are given.

CONDITIONS AFFECTING THE PENIS

Phimosis

Phimosis is a condition in which the foreskin is constricted so that it cannot be retracted over the glans. There has been a trend away from routine circumcision of newborns. Therefore, the child and adult will require early instruction in cleansing of the prepuce. In the adult, when the cleansing of the preputial area is neglected or no longer possible, the accumulation of normal secretions and subsequent inflammation (balanitis) occur. This causes adhesions and scarring. The thickened secretions become encrusted with urinary salts and calcify. In the aged, penile carcinoma may develop. Phimosis is corrected by circumcision (see below). The patient may require education concerning hygiene.

Paraphimosis is a condition in which the foreskin is retracted behind the glans and, because of narrowness and subsequent oedema, cannot be reduced back to its usual position (covering the glans). This can occur in the catheterized patient and results in severe discomfort. It is treated by manual reduction (compressing the glans firmly, to reduce its size, and then pushing the glans back as the prepuce is moved forward). Circumcision may be necessary once the inflammation and oedema subside.

Circumcision

Circumcision is the excision of the foreskin (prepuce) of the glans penis. It is sometimes performed in infancy for hygienic or religious reasons. In adults, it is indicated for phimosis, paraphimosis, recurrent infections of the glans and foreskin and personal desire of the patient.

Postoperatively, the patient is observed for bleeding. The wound is usually covered with petroleum jelly gauze dressing and should be changed as necessary. Since the adult male may experience a considerable amount of pain following circumcision, analgesics are given when needed.

Cancer of the Penis

Cancer of the penis is a rare disorder and accounts for less than 1 per cent of cancer deaths in the United Kingdom. The commonest type of penile cancer is squamous cell in origin and appears as a painless, wartlike growth or ulcer on the glans or coronal sulcus under the prepuce. It is associated with poor hygiene in uncircumcised, elderly men. In some countries, the cancer incidence is as high as 10 per cent. Often, diagnosis is delayed, probably because of guilt, embarrassment or ignorance.

Smaller lesions involving only the skin may be controlled by excisional biopsy. Topical chemotherapy with 5-fluorouracil cream may be one option in selected patients. Radiotherapy or radioactive needle implant produces varying results. Partial penectomy (removal of the penis) is preferred to total penectomy if possible; approximately 40 per cent of patients are then able to participate in sexual intercourse and to stand for voiding. Total penectomy is indicated when the tumour is not amenable to conservative treatment. Radiotherapy may be used as treatment for small squamous cell carcinomas of the penis or for palliation in advanced tumours or lymph node metastasis.

Sarcoma of the penis is a rare and unpredictable type of cancer. It occurs in a younger age group of patient and is less amenable to treatment. This tumour is not associated with poor hygiene.

Patient Education

Circumcision in infancy almost eliminates the possibility of penile cancer, since chronic irritation and inflammation of the glans penis predisposes to penile tumours. Personal hygiene is an important preventive measure in uncircumcised males.

Priapism

Priapism is an uncontrolled, persistent erection of the penis that causes the penis to become very large, hard and often painful. It occurs from either neural or vascular causes, including sickle cell thrombosis, spinal cord tumours and tumour invasion of the penis or its vessels. This condition may result in gangrene and often results in impotence, whether treated or not.

Priapism is considered a urological emergency. The expected outcome of therapy is to improve venous drainage of the corpora cavernosa to prevent ischaemia, fibrosis and impotence. Initially, treatment is directed at relieving the erection and includes bedrest and sedation. The corpora may be irrigated with an anticoagulant, which allows aspiration of stagnant blood. Shunting procedures to divert the blood from the turgid corpora cavernosa to the venous system (corpora cavernosa–saphenous vein shunt) or into the corpus spongiosum–glans penis compartment may be tried.

BIBLIOGRAPHY

Bard (1984) *Guidelines for the Management of the Catheterized Patient*, Bard Ltd, Marketing Services Department, Pennywell Industrial Estate, Sunderland SR4 9EW.

Borley, D. (ed.) (1989) Nursing patients with testicular tumours (Chapter 11), C. Blackmore in *Oncology For Nurses and Health Care Professionals, Volume 3* (2nd edition), Harper & Row, London, pp. 366–88.

Borley, D. (ed.) (1989) Nursing patients having cancer surgery (Chapter 1), E. A. Jones in *Oncology For Nurses and Health Care Professionals, Volume 3* (2nd edition), Harper & Row, London.

Brindley, G. S. (1986) Maintenance treatment of erectile impotence by cavernosal unstriated muscle relaxant injection, *British Journal of Psychiatry*, Vol. 149, pp. 210–15.

Brunner, L. S. and Suddarth, D. S. (1989) Care of the patient with a renal or genitourinary disorder (Chapter 9), *The Lippincott Manual of Medical-Surgical Nursing* (2nd edition), Harper & Row, London, p. 663.

Burkitt, D. and Randall, J. (1987a) Catheterization: Urethral trauma, *Nursing Times*, Vol. 83, No. 43, pp. 59–63.

Burkitt, D. and Randall, J. (1987b) Safe procedures, *Nursing Times*, Vol. 83, No. 43, pp. 65–6.

Crow, R. A., Chapman, R. C., Roe, B. H. and Wilson, J. A. (1986) *A Study of Patients With Indwelling Urethral Catheters and Related Nursing Practice*, Nursing Practice Research Unit, University of Surrey, Guildford.

Gingell, J. C. and Desai, K. M. (1987) Investigation of impotence with particular reference to the diabetic, *Practical Diabetes*, Vol. 4, No. 6, pp. 257–9.

Gingell, J. C. and Desai, K. M. (1988) Treatment of erectile failure, *Practical Diabetes*, Vol. 5, No. 1, pp. 7–9.

Hayward, J. (1975) *Information—A Prescription Against Pain*, Royal College of Nursing, London.

Hubbard, S. M. and Jenkins, J. (1983) An overview of current concepts in the management of patients with testicular tumors of germ cell origin—Part I: Pathophysiology, diagnosis and staging, *Cancer Nursing*, Vol. 6, No. 1, pp. 39–47.

James, J. (1984) *Handbook of Urology*, Harper & Row, London.

Pritchard, A. P. (ed.) (1988a) Endocrine therapy (Chapter 14), I. Judson and T. Powles in *Oncology for Nurses and Health Care Professionals, Volume 1*, Harper & Row, London, pp. 313–16.

Pritchard, A. P. (ed.) (1988b) Surgical oncology (Chapter 9), G. Westbury in *Oncology for Nurses and Health Care Professionals, Volume 1, Pathology, Diagnosis and Treatment* (2nd edition), Harper & Row, London, pp. 202–22.

Pritchard, A. P. and David, J. A. (1988) Bladder lavage and irrigation (Chapter 4), *The Royal Marsden Manual of Clinical Nursing Procedures* (2nd edition), Harper & Row, London, pp. 44–51.

Tschudin, V. (ed.) (1988) Male reproductive system cancers (Chapter 18), K. Wright in *Nursing the Patient With Cancer*, Prentice Hall, Hemel Hempstead, pp. 299–307.

Wiles, P. G. (1988) Successful noninvasive management of erectile impotence in diabetic men, *British Medical Journal*, Vol. 296, No. 16, pp. 161–2.

FURTHER READING

Books

General

Blandy, J. P. (1982) *Lecture Notes on Urology* (3rd edition), Blackwell Scientific, Oxford.

Borley, D. (ed.) (1989) Nursing patients with urinary tract cancer (Chapter 12), K. Havard in *Oncology for Nurses and Health Care Professionals, Volume 3*, Harper & Row, London, pp. 389–421.

Brunner, L. S. and Suddarth, D. S. (1989) Care of the patient with a renal or genitourinary disorder (Chapter 9), *The Lippincott Manual of Medical-Surgical Nursing* (2nd edition), Harper & Row, London, pp. 586–669.

Hinchcliff, S. and Montague, S. (eds) (1988) Reproduction (Chapter 6.3), R. Herbert in *Physiology for Nursing Practice*, Baillière Tindall, Eastbourne, pp. 605–12.

James, J. (1984) *Handbook of Urology*, Harper & Row, London.

Continence

Bard (1987) *You, Your Patients and Urinary Catheterization*, Bard Ltd, Sunderland.

Mandelstrom, D. (1986) *Incontinence and Its Management* (2nd edition), Croom Helm, London.

Norton, C. (1986) *Nursing For Continence*, Beaconsfield Publishers, Beaconsfield.

Impotence

Cole, M. and Dryden, W. (eds) (1988) Assessing the basis of sexual dysfunction: Diagnostic procedures (Chapter 6), D.

Friedman in *Sex Therapy in Britain*, Open University Press, Milton Keynes, pp. 103–24.

Patient Education

Royal Marsden Hospital *Patient Information Series*, distributed by Haigh & Holland, International University Booksellers, The Precinct Centre, Oxford Road, Manchester M13 9QA.

Testicular Cancer

Peckham, M. J. (1981) *The Management of Testicular Tumours*, Edward Arnold, London.

Articles

Continence

Alderman, C. (1989) Catheter care, *Nursing Standard*, Special Supplement, Vol. 4, No. 3, pp. 1–15.

Blannin, J. P. (1984) Assessment of the incontinent patient, *Nursing*, Vol. 2, September, pp. 863–5.

Gooch, J. (1986) Catheter care, *The Professional Nurse*, Vol. 1, May, pp. 207-8.

Gooch, J. (1986) Care of the urinary incontinent patient, *The Professional Nurse*, Vol. 1, August, pp. 298–300.

Mulhall, A. (1991) Biofilms and urethral catheter infections, *Nursing Standard*, Vol. 5, No. 18, pp. 26–8.

Roe, B. H. and Brocklehurst, J. C. (1987) Study of patients with indwelling catheters, *Journal of Advanced Nursing*, Vol. 12, pp. 713–18.

Roe, B. H. (1989) Study of the information given by nurses for catheter care to patients, *Journal of Advanced Nursing*, Vol. 14, pp. 203–11.

Roe, B. H. (1990) Syudy of the effects of education on patients' knowledge and acceptance of their indwelling urethral catheters, *Journal of Advanced Nursing*, Vol. 15, No. 2, pp. 223–31.

Impotence

Gingell, J. C. (1987) Pathophysiology of erection, *Practical Diabetes*, Vol. 4, NO. 5, pp. 211–12.

Robinette, M. A. and Moffat, M. J. (1986) Intracorporal injection of papaverine and phentolamine in the management of impotence, *British Journal of Urology*, Vol. 58, pp. 692–5.

Williams, G., Mulcahy, M. J. and Keily, E. A. (1987) Impotence: Treatment by autoinjection of vasoactive drugs, *British Medical Journal*, Vol. 295, pp. 595–6.

Testicular Cancer

Blackmore, C. (1988) The impact of orchidectomy upon the male with testicular cancer, *Cancer Nursing*, Vol. 11, No. 1, pp. 33–9.

Stanford, J. R. (1988) Testicular cancer, *Nursing (3rd series)*, Vol. 3, No. 26, pp. 957–60.

Stanford, J. (1987) Testicular self-examination: teaching, learning and practice for nurses, *Journal of Advanced Nursing*, Vol. 12, pp. 13–19.

Unit 8

PROBLEMS RELATED TO IMMUNOLOGY

chapter 26

THE IMMUNE SYSTEM, IMMUNOPATHOLOGY AND IMMUNODEFICIENCY

The term immunity refers to the body's specific protective response to an invading foreign agent or organism. However, pathological developments within the immune system lead to certain disease manifestations. Therefore, the term immunopathology is used to describe the study of diseases caused by the immune reaction–the protective response that the body initiates but which paradoxically turns against the body and causes tissue damage and disease. Immunodeficiencies, on the other hand, are disorders characterized by a defect in the immune system that leads to suppression of the immune response. To understand immunopathology and immunodeficiency, one must first understand how the body's immune system functions normally.

TYPES OF IMMUNITY: NATURAL AND ACQUIRED

There are two general types of immunity: natural immunity and acquired immunity. Natural immunity, which is a nonspecific immunity, is present at birth, while acquired or specific immunity develops after birth. Although each type of immunity plays a distinct role in the defence against harmful invaders, it is important to remember that the various components often act in an interdependent manner.

Natural Immunity

Natural immunity provides a nonspecific response to any foreign invader, regardless of the composition of the invader. The basis of natural defence mechanisms is merely the ability to distinguish between 'self' and 'nonself'. Such natural mechanisms include physical and chemical barriers, the action of white blood cells and inflammatory responses.

Physical barriers consist of intact skin and mucous membranes, which prevent pathogens from gaining access to the body, and the cilia of the respiratory tract along with coughing and sneezing responses, which act to clear pathogens from the upper respiratory tract before they can invade the body further. Chemical barriers such as acid gastric juices, enzymes in tears and saliva and substances in sebaceous and sweat secretions, act in a nonspecific way to destroy invading bacteria and fungi. Viruses are countered by other means, such as interferon, which is a nonspecific viricidal substance naturally produced by the body and capable of stimulating the activity of other components of the immune system.

White blood cells, or leucocytes, participate in both the natural and the acquired immune responses. Granular leucocytes, or granulocytes (so-called because of granules in their cytoplasm), include neutrophils, eosinophils and basophils. Neutrophils are the first cells to arrive at the site of inflammation. Eosinophils and basophils, other type of granulocytes, increase in number during allergic reactions and stress responses. Granulocytes assist in fighting invasion by foreign bodies or toxins by releasing cell mediators, such as histamine, bradykinin and prostaglandins, and engulfing the foreign bodies or toxins (phagocytosis). Nongranular leucocytes include monocytes or macrophages (referred to as histiocytes when they enter tissue spaces) and lymphocytes. Monocytes also function as phagocytic cells and are able to engulf greater numbers and quantities for foreign bodies or toxins than neutrophils. Lymphocytes, consisting of B and T cells or lymphocytes, play major roles in humoral and cell-mediated immunity, as will be discussed later.

The inflammatory response is a major component of the nonspecific or natural immune system elicited in response to tissue injury or invading organisms. Chemical mediators assist in the inflammatory response to minimize blood loss, wall off the invading organism, activate phagocytes and promote fibrous scar formation and regeneration of injured tissue. (The inflammatory response is discussed in detail in Chapter 2, Inflammation, p. 140.)

Acquired Immunity

Acquired immunity consists of immunological responses that are not present at birth but acquired during life. Most acquired immunity develops as a result of contracting a disease or generating a protective immune response through immunization. Weeks or months after exposure to the disease or immunization, an immune response develops sufficiently to prevent contraction of the disease on re-exposure to it. This type of acquired immunity is referred to as active acquired immunity because the immunological defences are developed by the body of the person being defended. Active acquired immunity generally lasts many years or even the person's lifetime.

Passive acquired immunity is temporary immunity transmitted from another source that has developed immunity through previous disease or immunization. Gamma globulin and antiserum, obtained from blood plasma of people with acquired immunity, are used in emergencies to provide passive immunity to diseases when risk of contracting a specific disease is great and there is not time for a person to develop adequate active immunity. Antibodies transferred from the mother to the developing child (i.e. maternal antibodies) is another form of passive immunity.

Both types of acquired immunity involve humoral and cell-mediated (cellular) immunological responses, described below.

THE IMMUNE SYSTEM

General Immune Responses

When the body is invaded or attacked by bacteria or viruses, it has three means of defending itself—the phagocytic immune response, the humoral or antibody immune response and the cellular immune response.

The first line of defence, the phagocytic immune response, involves the neutrophils, monocytes and macrophages, which have the ability to ingest foreign particles. These cells can move to the point of attack to engulf and destroy the foreign agents.

The second protective response, the humoral or antibody response, begins with the lymphocyte cells, which can transform themselves into plasma cells that manufacture antibodies. It is the antibodies, which are highly specific proteins, which are transported in the bloodstream and have the ability to disable the invaders.

A third mechanism of defence, the cellular immune response, also involves the lymphocytes which change into various activated subsets, e.g. killer T cells that can attack the microbes themselves.

Antigens and Antibodies

The part of the invading or attacking organism that is responsible for stimulating the production of an antibody is called an antigen or an immunogen. An antigen is a small patch of proteins on the outer surface of the microorganism. A single bacterium, even a single large molecule such as a toxin (diphtheria or tetanus toxin), may have several such antigens or 'markers' on its surface and can therefore induce the body to produce a number of different antibodies. Once an antibody is produced, it is released into the bloodstream and carried to the attacking organism, where it combines with the antigen on its surface, binding with it like a complementary piece of a jigsaw puzzle.

Stages of the Immune System Response

There are four well-defined stages in an immune

response: recognition, proliferation, response and the effector stage. An overview of these stages is presented here, followed by descriptions of humoral immunity, cell-mediated or cellular immunity and the complement system.

Recognition

The basis of any immune reaction is, first and foremost, recognition. It is the immune system's ability to recognize antigens on materials as 'foreign', or 'nonself', that is the initiating event in any immune reaction. The body must first recognize invaders as 'foreign' before it can react to them.

Surveillance by Lymph Nodes and Lymphocytes
The body accomplishes its surveillance in two ways. First, because the immune system is widely dispersed and distributed close to all of the body's surfaces, internal as well as external, in the form of tiny organs called lymph nodes. Second, small lymphocytes are continuously being discharged from each lymph node into the bloodstream, where they patrol the tissues and vessels that drain the areas served by that node. Basically, it is the lymph nodes and lymphocytes that make up the immune system.

Circulating Lymphocytes
There are lymphocytes in the lymph nodes themselves and those that circulate. Taken in aggregate, the total number of lymphocytes in the body is impressive. Radioactive labelling of circulating lymphocytes has shown that these cells circulate from the blood to lymph nodes and from the lymph nodes back into the bloodstream again, in a never-ending series of patrols. Some circulating lymphocytes can survive for decades. Some of them may maintain their solitary circuits for the lifetime of the person.

The exact way in which circulating lymphocytes recognize antigens on foreign surfaces is not known. At present, the accepted theory is that recognition depends on specific receptor sites on the surface of the lymphocytes. It appears that macrophages, a type of nongranular phagocytic cell found in the tissues of the body, play an important role in helping these circulating lymphocytes to process the antigens. Foreign materials enter the body and a circulating lymphocyte comes into physical contact with the surfaces of these materials. Upon contact, the lymphocyte, with the help of macrophages, either removes the antigen from the surface or in some way picks up an imprint of its structure. For example, during a streptococcal throat infection, the streptococcal organism gains access to the mucous membranes of the throat and a circulating lymphocyte moving through the tissues of the neck comes in contact with the organism. The lymphocyte, familiar with the surface markers on the cells of its own body, recognizes the antigens on the microbe as being different

(nonself) and the streptococcus as being antigenic (foreign). This triggers the second phase of the immune response—proliferation.

Proliferation

The circulating lymphocytes containing the antigenic message return to the nearest lymph node. Once in the node, these 'sensitized' lymphocytes stimulate some of the dormant lymphocytes residing there to enlarge, divide, proliferate and differentiate into either T lymphocytes or B lymphocytes. Enlargement of the lymph nodes in the neck, in conjunction with a sore throat, is one example of the immune response.

The Response Stage

In the response stage, the changed lymphocytes will function in either a humoral or a cellular fashion.

Humoral. The production of antibodies to a specific antigen is called a humoral response, humoral referring to the fact that the antibodies are released into the bloodstream and so reside in the plasma or fluid fraction of the blood, one of the classical four 'humors' of the body.

Cellular. The returning sensitized lymphocytes migrate to areas of the lymph node (other than those areas containing lymphocytes programmed to become plasma cells), where they stimulate the residing lymphocytes to becomes cells that will attack microbes directly rather than through the action of antibodies. These transformed lymphocytes have been given the descriptive name killer T cells. The T stands for the fact that during the embryological development of the immune system, these lymphocytes spent some time in the thymus of the developing fetus, at which time they were genetically programmed to become T cells rather than the antibody-producing B lymphocytes. Viral rather than bacterial antigens induce a cellular response. This response is manifested by the increasing number of lymphocytes seen in the blood smears of people with viral illnesses—for instance, in the lymphocytosis occurring in infectious mononucleosis.

Most immune reactions to antigens involve both humoral and cellular responses, though usually one predominates. During transplantation rejections the cellular reaction predominates, whereas in the bacterial pneumonias and sepsis it is the humoral response that plays the dominant protective role.

The Effector Stage

In the effector stage, the antibody of the humoral response or the killer T cell of the cellular response reaches and couples with the antigen on the surface of the foreign object. The coupling initiates a series of events that in the majority of instances results in the total destruction of the invading microbes or the complete neutralization of the

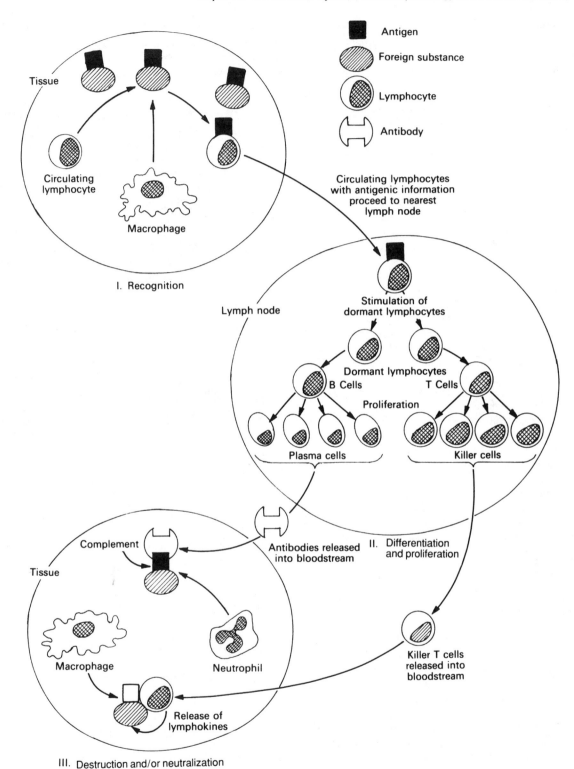

Figure 26.1 The phases of the immune response. I. Recognition of the antigen by circulating lymphocytes and macrophages. II. Stimulation of dormant lymphocytes, and differentiation and proliferation of T cells and B cells with formation and release of antibodies. III. Destruction or neutralization of antigens through the action of antibodies, complement, macrophages and killer T cells.

toxin. The events involve an interplay of antibodies (humoral immunity), complement and action by the killer T cells (cellular immunity). Figure 26.1 summarizes the phases of the immune response.

Humoral Immune Response

The humoral response is characterized by production of antibodies by the B-cell lymphocytes in response to a specific antigen. Although the B lymphocyte is ultimately responsible for the production of antibodies, both the macrophages of natural immunity and the special T-cell lymphocytes of cellular immunity are involved in recognition of the foreign substance and in antibody production.

Antigen Recognition

Several theories exist about the mechanisms by which the B cells recognize the invading antigen and produce appropriate antibodies in response. The existence of several theories probably results from the fact that there are several different methods of recognition of antigens by the B lymphocyte. These different means of antigen recognition may also be responsible for different types of antibody response. Some antigens seem to have the ability to trigger antibody formation by the B lymphocytes directly, while others require the assistance of T cells.

T cells, or T lymphocytes, are part of a surveillance system dispersed throughout the body. The lymphocytes recycle through the general circulation, tissues and lymphatic system. It is suggested that, with the assistance of macrophages, the T lymphocyte recognizes the antigen of a foreign invader. The T lymphocyte picks up the antigenic message or 'blueprint' of the antigen and returns to the nearest lymph node with that message.

Antibody Production

B lymphocytes, which are stored in the lymph nodes, are subdivided into thousands of clones, each responsive to a single group of antigens having almost identical characteristics. The T lymphocyte carries the antigenic message back to the lymph node and stimulates specific clones of the B lymphocyte to enlarge, divide, proliferate and differentiate into plasma cells capable of producing specific antibodies to the antigen. Other B lymphocytes differentiate into B-cell clones with a memory for the antigen. These 'memory cells' are responsible for the more exaggerated and rapid immune response in a person who is repeatedly exposed to the same antigen.

Antibody Structure

Antibodies are large proteins that are referred to as immunoglobulins because they are found in the globulin fraction of the plasma proteins. Each antibody molecule consists of two subunits, each of which contains a light and a heavy peptide chain. The subunits are held together by a chemical link composed of disulphide bonds. Each subunit has a portion that serves as a binding site for a specific antigen. This site, referred to as the Fab fragment, provides the 'lock' portion that is highly specific for an antigen. An additional portion, known as the Fc fragment, allows the antibody molecule to take part in the complement system (to be discussed later).

The body is able to produce five different types of antibodies or immunoglobulins. Immunoglobulins in general are designated by the symbol Ig, and each of the five types, or classes, is identified by a specific letter of the alphabet (IgA, IgD, IgE, IgG and IgM). Classification is based on the chemical structure and biological role of the individual immunoglobulin. Some of the outstanding characteristics of the immunoglobulins may be summarized as follows:

1. IgG (75 per cent of total).
   a. Present in serum and tissues (interstitial fluid).
   b. Major role in bloodborne and tissue infections.
   c. Activates complement system.
   d. Enhances phagocytosis.
   e. Crosses placenta.
2. IgA (15 per cent of total).
   a. Present in body fluids (blood, saliva, tears, breast milk, and pulmonary, gastrointestinal, prostatic and vaginal secretions).
   b. Protects against respiratory, gastrointestinal and genitourinary infections.
   c. Prevents absorption of antigens from food.
   d. Passed in breast milk to protect neonate.
3. IgM (10 per cent of total).
   a. Mostly limited to intravascular serum.
   b. First immunoglobulin produced in response to bacterial and viral infections.
   c. Activates complement system.
4. IgD (0.2 per cent of total).
   a. Present in small amounts in serum.
   b. Role unclear; may influence B-lymphocyte differentiation.
5. IgE (0.004 per cent of total).
   a. Present in serum.
   b. Involved in allergic and hypersensitivity reactions.
   c. May help in defence against parasites.

Antibody Function

Antibodies defend against foreign invaders in several ways. The type of defence employed depends on the structure and composition of both the antigen and the immunoglobulin. An antibody can act as a cross-link between two antigens, causing them to bind or clump together. This clumping effect, referred to as agglutination, helps in clearing the body of the invading organism by facilitating phagocytosis. Some antibodies have the ability to assist in the removal of offending organisms through the process of opsonization. In this process, the antigen–antibody molecule is coated with a sticky substance that also facilitates phagocytosis.

Antibodies also promote the release of vasoactive substances, such as histamine and slow-reacting-substance, two of the chemical mediators of the inflammatory response. In addition, antibodies are involved in the activation of the complement system.

Antigen-Antibody Binding

The portion of the antigen involved in binding with the antibody is referred to as the antigenic determinant. The binding of the antibody to the antigenic determinant can be likened to a 'lock and key' situation. The most efficient immunological responses occur when the antibody and antigen fit exactly. Poor fit can occur with an antibody that was produced in response to a different antigen. This phenomenon is known as cross-reactivity. For example, in acute rheumatic fever, the antibody produced against *Streptococcus pyogenes* in the upper respiratory tract may cross-react with the patient's heart tissue, leading to damage to valves of the heart.

Cell-Mediated (Cellular) Immune Response

While the B lymphocytes are the soldiers of humoral immunity, the T lymphocytes, also referred to as T cells, are primarily responsible for cellular immunity. These lymphocytes spend time in the thymus, where they are programmed to become T cells rather than antibody-producing B lymphocytes. There are several types of T cells, each with designated roles in the defence against bacteria, viruses, fungi, parasites and malignant cells. T cells attack foreign invaders directly rather than through the production of antibodies.

Cell-mediated reactions are initiated by the binding of an antigen with an antigen receptor located on the surface of a T cell. This may occur with or without the assistance of macrophages. The T cells then carry the antigenic message or blueprint to the lymph nodes, where the production of other T cells is stimulated. Some T cells remain in the lymph nodes and retain a memory for the antigen. Other T cells, known as killer T cells, migrate from the lymph nodes into the general circulatory system and ultimately to the tissues, where they remain until they either come in contact with their respective antigens or die.

Upon contact with foreign cells (or antigens), some killer T cells release chemical mediators known as lymphokines. These lymphokines are low-molecular-weight proteins with the ability to influence the inflammatory and immune responses to facilitate destruction and removal of

the foreign cells or toxins. Lymphokines can recruit, hold and activate other lymphocytes and macrophages to assist in removing the invading antigen. The actions of specific lymphokines are described in Table 26.1. One killer lymphocyte can, by releasing lymphokines, quickly recruit a large number of other cells into the area of antigenically foreign cells, amassing in a short time a large number of effector cells to protect the body. Unfortunately, such cellular activation can cause tissue injury and disease if the supposedly 'foreign' cell under attack is in reality part of the person.

Other types of T-cell lymphocytes also contribute to the destruction and removal of antigens. They include cytotoxic T cells, K cells and helper and suppressor T cells. Cytotoxic T cells attack the antigen directly by altering its cell membrane and ultimately causing cell lysis

Table 26.1 *Lymphokines and their biological effects*

Lymphokine	Effect
Permeability factor	Increases vascular permeability, allowing white cells into area
Interferon	Interferes with viral growth, stopping the spread of viral infection
Migration inhibitory factor	Suppresses movement of macrophages, keeping macrophage in area of foreign cells
Skin reactive factor	Induces inflammatory response
Cytotoxic factor (lymphotoxin)	Kills certain antigenic cells
Macrophage chemotatic factor	Attracts macrophages into the area
Lymphocyte blastogenic factor	Stimulates more lymphocytes, recruiting additional lymphocytes into the area
Macrophage aggregation factor	Causes clumping of macrophages and lymphocytes
Macrophage activation factor	Causes macrophages to adhere to surfaces more readily
Proliferation inhibitor factor	Inhibits growth of certain antigenic cells
Cytophilic antibody	A factor that binds to a receptor on macrophages that permits them to bind to antigens

(destruction). K cells, a subpopulation of lymphocytes that lack the usual characteristics of T cells, defend against antigens already coated with antibody.

The discovery of T-lymphocytes known as helper and suppressor cells has contributed to the understanding that humoral and cellular immune responses are not separate, unrelated processes, but branches of the immune response that can and do affect each other. Upon contact with the antigen, helper T cells (T_4 cells) release substances that enhance B-lymphocyte function and the production of antibodies. In addition, helper T cells contribute to differentiation of K cells and killer T cells. Suppressor T cells (T_8 cells) have the ability to decrease B-cell production, thereby keeping the immune response at a level that is compatible with health, (e.g., sufficient to fight infection adequately without attacking the body's healthy tissues).

Complement

The term complement refers to circulating plasma proteins made in the liver that can be activated when an antibody couples with its antigen. Once activated, these proteins interact sequentially with one another in a cascade or 'falling domino' effect. This causes alterations of the cell membranes on which antigen and antibody complex form, permitting fluid to enter the cell and leading eventually to cell lysis and death. In addition, activated complement molecules attract macrophages and granulocytes to areas of antigen–antibody reactions. These cells continue the body's defence by devouring the antibody-coated microbes.

Complement plays a very important role in the immune response. Destruction of an invading or attacking organism or toxin is not achieved merely by the binding of the antibody and antigens, but also requires activation of complement, the arrival of killer T cells or the attraction of macrophages.

Classical Complement Activation

There are two ways to activate the complement system. One, termed the classical pathway because it was the first method discovered, involves the reaction of the first of the circulating complement proteins (C_1), with the receptor site of the Fc portion of an antibody molecule following formation of an antigen–antibody complex. The activation of the first complement component then activates all the other components in the sequence in which the other components were discovered, namely C_1, C_4, C_2, C_3, C_5, C_6, C_7, C_8 and C_9.

Alternate Pathway of Complement Activation

The alternative method of complement activation occurs without the formation of antigen–antibody complexes. This alternate pathway can be initiated by the release of bacterial products such as endotoxins. When complement is activated through this pathway, the process bypasses the first three components (C_1, C_4 and C_2) and begins with C_3. Whatever the method of activation, however, once activated, the complement can and does destroy cells by altering or damaging the cell membrane of the antigen, by chemically attracting phagocytes to the antigen (chemotaxis) and by rending the antigen more vulnerable to phagocytosis (opsonization). The complement system enhances the inflammatory response by the release of vasoactive substances.

This response is usually therapeutic and can be lifesaving if the cell attacked by the complement system is a true foreign invader, such as a streptococcus or staphylococcus. However, if that cell is in reality part of the person, e.g. a cell of the brain or liver, the tissue lining the blood vessels or the cells of a transplanted organ or skin graft, the result can be devastating disease and even death. The result of the immune response, i.e. the vigorous attack on any material read as foreign, and the deadliness of the struggle is obvious in the pus (the remains of microbes, granulocytes and macrophages, T-cell lymphocytes, plasma proteins, complement and antibodies) that accumulates in wound infections and abscesses.

Interferons

Biological response modifiers are currently under investigation to determine their roles in the immune system and their potential therapeutic effects in disorders characterized by disturbed immune responses. Interferons, one example of the compounds known as biologic response modifiers, have antiviral and anti-tumour properties. In addition to responding to viral infection, they are produced by T cells, B cells and macrophages in response to antigens. They are thought to have a role in modifying the immune response by suppressing antibody production and cellular immunity. They also facilitate the cytolytic role of macrophages and natural killer cells. Interferons are undergoing extensive study to determine their effectiveness in treatment of tumours and acquired immunodeficiency syndrome (AIDS).

FACTORS AFFECTING IMMUNE SYSTEM FUNCTIONING

Age

People at the extremes of the life span are more likely to develop problems related to immune system functioning than those in their middle years. There is an increased frequency and severity of infections in the elderly, which may be a result of a decreased ability to respond adequately to invading organisms. The production and the function of both T- and B-cell lymphocytes may be impaired. The incidence of autoimmune diseases also also increases with age; this may be related to a decreased ability of antibodies to differentiate between 'self' and 'nonself'. Failure of the surveillance system to recognize mutant, or abnormal cells may be responsible for the high incidence of cancer associated with increasing age.

Declining function of various organ systems associated with increasing age also contributes to impaired immunity. Decreased gastric secretions and motility allow normal intestinal flora to proliferate and produce infection, causing gastroenteritis and diarrhoea. Decreased renal circulation, filtration, absorption and excretion contribute to urinary tract infections. Prostatic enlargement and neurogenic bladder can hinder the passage of urine and subsequently bacterial clearance through the urinary system. Urinary stasis, common in the elderly, permits the growth of micro-organisms.

Exposure to tobacco and environment toxins will impair pulmonary function. Prolonged exposure to these agents causes decreased elasticity of lung tissue, decreased effectiveness of cilia and a decreased ability to cough effectively. These impairments hinder the removal of infectious organisms and toxins, increasing the elderly person's susceptibility to pulmonary infections and malignancies.

Finally, with age the skin becomes thinner and less elastic. Peripheral neuropathy and the accompanying decreased sensation and circulation may facilitate stasis ulcers, pressure sores, abrasions and burns. Impaired skin integrity predisposes the ageing person to infection from organisms that are part of normal skin flora.

Nutrition

Adequate nutrition is essential for function of the immune system. Depletion of protein reserves results in atrophy of lymphoid tissues, depression of antibody response, reduction in the number of circulating T cells and impairment of phagocytic function. As a result, susceptibility to infection is greatly increased. During periods of infection and serious illness, nutritional requirements may be exaggerated further, potentially contributing to protein depletion and an even greater risk of impaired immune response and sepsis.

Existence of Other Organ Diseases

Conditions such as burns or other forms of trauma, infection and cancer may contribute to altered immune system function. Major burns or other factors cause impaired skin integrity and compromise the body's first line of defence. Loss of large amounts of serum with burn injuries depletes the body of essential proteins, including immunoglobulins. The physiological and psychological stressors induced during surgical disruption of tissue integrity stimulate cortisol release from the adrenal cortex; increased serum cortisol also contributes to suppression of normal immune responses.

Cancer

Immunosuppression contributes to the development of malignancies. However, cancer itself is immunosuppressive. Large tumours are able to release antigens into the blood that combine with circulating antibodies and prevent them from attacking the tumour cells. Furthermore, tumour cells may possess special blocking factors that coat tumour cells and prevent destruction by killer T lymphocytes. During the early development of tumours, the body may fail to recognize the tumour antigens as foreign and subsequently fail to initiate destruction of malignant cells.

Medications

Certain drug therapies are capable of causing both desirable and undesirable alterations in immune system functioning. Four major types of medications have the potential for causing immunosuppression: corticosteroids, nonsteroidal anti-inflammatory drugs (NSAIDS), cytotoxic drugs and specific immunosuppressants. Therapeutic use of these agents requires striking a delicate balance between therapeutic benefit and dangerous suppression of host defence mechanisms.

Radiotherapy

Radiotherapy may be used in the treatment of cancer or in the prevention of allograft rejection. It destroys lymphocytes and decreases the population of cells required to replace them. The size of extent of the irradiated area determines the extent of immunosuppression. Whole-body radiotherapy renders the individual totally immuno-incompetent.

DISORDERS OF THE IMMUNE SYSTEM

Disorders of the immune system can be divided into two general categories, one related to immunopathology and the other to immunodeficiencies. Disorders related to immunopathology are those diseases in which the normally protective immune response paradoxically turns against or attacks the body, leading to tissue damage. Disorders related to immunodeficiencies are those diseases in which there is either an unexplained (primary) or explained (secondary) defect in one or more components of the immune response.

Immunopathology

When the body fails to differentiate between self and nonself, immunopathology may develop. This is a determining factor that allows the disease-producing potential of the immune response to take precedence over its protective nature. If the antigen is truly foreign, the body is protected; if not, autoimmune disease and associated tissue damage result. The underlying problems of immunopathology may involve any component of the immune system in a variety of adverse interactions referred to as hypersensitivity reactions.

Allergic/Anaphylactoid Reaction (Hypersensitivity Type I)

An allergic reaction is a result of antigen-antibody reactions (specially IgE) that attract and destroy mast cells. Mast cells are found in most tissues of the body but are particularly abundant in connective tissue found in the lungs, intestinal mucosa, skin and blood vessels. These cells serve as storage sites for histamine. As a result of mast cell destruction, histamine is released, causing sneezing, rhinitis and watery eyes. Anaphylaxis, the most extreme reaction, involves laryngobronchospasm, shock, hypotension and potentially death.

Cytotoxicity Reaction (Hypersensitivity Type II)

A cytotoxicity reaction occurs when the immune system mistakenly identifies a normal constituent of the body as foreign. Such reactions may be a result of a cross-reacting antibody and eventually lead to cell and tissue damage. An example of this is seen in myasthenia gravis, in which the body mistakenly generates antibodies against normal receptors of nerve endings. Another example is seen in Goodpasture's syndrome, in which antibodies against lung and renal tissue are generated, producing lung damage and renal failure.

Immune-Complex-Mediated Reaction (Hypersensitivity Type III)

Immune complexes (antigen-antibody molecules) normally circulate in the bloodstream during the course of infectious diseases. Usually, these complexes cause no symptoms and eventually disappear from the circulation. However, in some people these large complexes are deposited in the lining of blood vessels or on tissue surfaces. As a result, the complement system is activated and vasculitis (inflammation of blood vessels) and other tissue damage may occur. The vessels of the joints and kidneys are particularly susceptible to this type of injury. Examples of this process include glomerulonephritis and systemic lupus erythematosus. Antigen–antibody complexes involving streptococcus are often responsible for glomerulonephritis. In systemic lupus erythematosus, abnormal suppressor T-cell function may contribute to the development of antibodies generated against the body's own DNA. DNA/antiDNA complexes may lead to arthritis and a form of glomerulonephritis associated with systemic lupus erythematosus.

Delayed Hypersensitivity (Hypersensitivity Type IV)

A delayed hypersensitivity reaction may occur as a result of exposure to microbial infections or skin irritants, such as chemicals found in cosmetics or poison ivy. This type of hypersensitivity is dependent on lymphokines released from T-cell lymphocytes. As a result of the release of the lymphokines, inflammatory reactions can occur, leading to such problems as contact dermatitis, graft rejection and the formation of granulomas.

In an attempt to isolate, contain and block an invading microbe, the body may recruit a large mass of cells. This mass of cells surrounds and 'walls off' the microorganism from the rest of the body in order to prevent dissemination and further infection. As a result, a granuloma is formed. An example of this type of response is the body's response to the tubercle bacillus. Unfortunately, as in tuberculosis, large caseating lung abscesses may be formed, compromising organ function.

Management

Treatment of immunopathology falls into two categories: (1) removal of the offending antigens, and (2) suppression of the immune response through immunosuppression. Unfortunately, the vast majority of antigens that cause immune disease have not yet been identified or, if known, cannot be removed from the body because they constitute normal cellular elements. Use of immunosuppression has become the most common method for dealing with immune reactions.

Immunosuppressive drugs may be classified according to their chemical structure and/or mechanism of action. Regardless of classification, must immunosuppressive drugs work by interfering with normal cell growth and metabolism. Some of these drugs were first used by cancer specialists in the treatment of malignancies because of their detrimental effects on cancer cells. It is now known that immunosuppressive drugs also impede the growth and metabolism of T- and B-cell lymphocytes. For this reason, they are used in the treatment of immunopathology.

Immunosuppressive therapy, however, is not without potential adverse effects. The use of antimetabolites, for example, may increase the risk of infections and malignancies such as leukaemia and non-Hodgkin's lymphoma. Steroid therapy may increase the risk of infections or mask the signs and symptoms of infection. In addition, steroids may contribute to the development of hypertension, diabetes, gastrointestinal bleeding, cataracts, changes in appearance and psychosis.

In view of the potential adverse effects of immunosuppressive therapy, the nurse has a key role in patient education and continuing assessment for potential complications. This role has special importance for nurses involved in the care of the older adult, who is already at risk for immune dysfunction.

Immunodeficiency

The second type of disorder of the immune system is immunodeficiency. Regardless of the underlying cause of immunodeficiency, the cardinal symptoms include recurrent, severe infections often involving unusual organisms. Immunodeficiencies may be classified as either primary or secondary, and also according to which components of the immune system are affected.

Primary Immunodeficiencies

Immunodeficiencies for which there are no known causes or underlying medical conditions are referred to as primary immunodeficiencies. They may involve one or a combination of components of the immune system (Table 26.2).

Secondary Immunodeficiencies

Secondary immunodeficiencies, which are more common than primary deficiencies, often occur in the course of underlying disease or health care problems as a result of the treatment or of the conditions themselves. People with secondary immunodeficiencies are immunosuppressed and are often referred to as immunocompromised hosts. A variety of factors contribute to the development of sec-

ondary immunodeficiency (Table 26.3). The goals of treatment include elimination of the contributing factors and use of sound principles of infection control. Acquired immunodeficiency syndrome (AIDS) is an example of a devastating secondary immunodeficiency that results in increased susceptibility of the patient of a variety of infections and rare malignancies.

ACQUIRED IMMUNODEFICIENCY SYNDROME (AIDS)

Acquired immunodeficiency syndrome (AIDS) is defined as the most severe form of a continuum of illness associated with human immunodeficiency virus (HIV) infection. Human immunodeficiency virus has previously been referred to as human T-cell lymphotropic virus type III (HTLVIII) and lymphadenopathy-associated virus (LAV). Manifestations of human immunodeficiency virus infection range from mild abnormalities in the immune response without overt signs and symptoms, to profound immunosuppression associated with a variety of life-threatening infections and rare malignancies.

Pathology

Human immunodeficiency virus belongs to a group of viruses known as retroviruses. The designation of retro-

Table 26.2 *Primary immunodeficiences*

Immune component	Underlying abnormality
Nonspecific immunity	Phagocytic dysfunction: chemotaxis, opsonization, ingestion and digestion
Humoral immunity	Immunoglobulin production: decrease in or absence of one or all of the immunoglobulins (hypogammaglobulinaemia)
Cellular immunity	Abnormal or absent T-lymphocyte production
Combined deficiencies	Abnormalities of more than one component of the immune system

Table 26.3 *Factors contributing to secondary immunodeficiencies*

Immune deficit	Examples
Alteration in skin integrity	Venipunctures, burns, trauma
Alteration in nutrition (deficit)	Anorexia, malabsorption and impaired ingestion, digestion and assimilation; severe protein losses in urine
Alteration in urinary elimination	Urinary stasis, bladder catheterizatrion
Immunosuppressive therapy	Chemotherapy, steroids
Malignancy	Leukaemia, lymphoma
Infectious processes	Septicaemia, human immunodeficiency virus (HIV)

virus indicates that these viruses carry their genetic material in ribonucleic acid (RNA) rather than deoxyribonucleic acid (DNA). Human immunodeficiency virus is known to selectively infect helper T-cell lymphocytes. Through the use of an enzyme known as reverse transcriptase, human immunodeficiency virus is able to reprogramme the genetic materials of the infected T_4 cell. As a result, human immunodeficiency virus can use the T_4 cell to reproduce the virus instead of itself. Consequently, whenever the infected T_4 cell is stimulated to reproduce by invading organisms, human immunodeficiency virus is reproduced instead of the T_4-lymphocyte. The newly produced virus can then infect other T_4-lymphocytes.

As was discussed earlier in this chapter, the T_4-lymphocyte plays several important roles in the immune response, including recognition of foreign antigens, activation of antibody-producing B-cell lymphocytes, stimulation of cytotoxic T lymphocytes, production of lymphokines and defence against parasitic infections. When T_4-lymphocyte function is impaired, organisms that do not usually cause disease are given the opportunity to invade and cause serious illness. Infections and malignancies that develop as a result of immune system impairment are referred to as opportunistic diseases.

Incidence

By April 1991, the Communicable Diseases Surveillance Centre (CDSC) and the Communicable Diseases (Scotland) Unit had reported over 5,000 cases of AIDS in the United Kingdom. By the end of 1991, it is likely that over 7,000 cases will have been reported.

Currently, 80 per cent of individuals who today have AIDS are male homosexuals, but as the incubation period is 10 or more years, this is only a reflection of what was happening many years ago. Increasing numbers of injecting substance misusers, heterosexuals and infants are today becoming infected.

AIDS is largely a disease of young people, the majority of cases affecting men between the ages of 20 and 49. This is expected to change, however, as heterosexual transmission and the number of individuals with AIDS increase in the next few years. AIDS has reached epidemic proportions in other parts of the world.

Transmission

The routes of transmission of human immunodeficiency virus are very similar to those of hepatitis type B. In male homosexuals, anal intercourse or manipulation increases chances of trauma to the rectal mucosa and subsequently increases chances of exposure to the virus through body secretions. Increased frequency of this practice and multiple sexual partners have contributed to the spread of this disease. Heterosexual intercourse with individuals who

are infected with human immunodeficiency virus is also a means of transmission.

Transmission among injecting substance misusers occurs through direct blood exposure to contaminated needles and syringes. Blood products, including those used by haemophiliacs, are capable of transmitting human immunodeficiency virus to the recipients. The virus may also be transmitted *in utero* from mother to child. Transmission through breast milk has occurred but is infrequent.

In an attempt to screen blood products for evidence of human immunodeficiency virus, the Blood Transfusion Service licensed an human immunodeficiency virus antibody assay for all blood and plasma donations. The ELISA (enzyme-linked-immunosorbent assay) test determines the presence of antibodies directed specifically against human immunodeficiency virus. The ELISA test does not establish a diagnosis of AIDS, but rather indicates that the individual has been infected with human immunodeficiency virus. People whose blood contains antibodies for human immunodeficiency virus are said to be seropositive. The Western blot assay is another test that can identify the presence of human immunodeficiency virus antibodies, and is used to confirm seropositivity as identified by the ELISA procedure. These tests are also used by doctors to assist in identifying patients who are infected with human immunodeficiency virus. It is expected that, in the future, human immunodeficiency virus infections related to blood products will be largely eliminated as a result of screening efforts.

Diagnosis

The features of human immunodeficiency virus infections vary. Diagnosis is based on clinical history, identification of risk factors, physical examination, laboratory evidence of immune dysfunction, presence of opportunistic disease based on biopsy or culture and identification of human immunodeficiency virus antibodies.

Clinical Features

The clinical features of AIDS are widespread and may involve the pulmonary, gastrointestinal and neurological systems as well as several types of malignancy and chronic illness due to opportunistic pathogens.

Pulmonary

Shortness of breath, dyspnoea, cough, chest pain and fever are associated with a variety of opportunistic infections such as those caused by *Mycobacterium avium intracellulare*, cytomegaloviruses and *Legionella*. However, the most common infection in people with AIDS is *Pneumocystis carinii* pneumonia (PCP), which has a high mortality rate. *Pneumocystis carinii*, thought to be a protozoan although it has recently been suggested that it is, in fact, a fungus, causes disease only in immunocompromised hosts. It invades and proliferates within the pulmonary alveoli, resulting in consolidation of the pulmonary parenchyma.

The clinical presentation of *Pneumocystis carinii* pneumonia in the AIDS patient is generally less acute than in people who are immunosuppressed as a result of other conditions. The period of time between the onset of symptoms and the actual documentation of disease may be weeks to months. Patients with AIDS initially develop nonspecific signs and symptoms such as fevers, chills, nonproductive cough, shortness of breath, dyspnoea and occasionally chest pain. *Pneumocystis carinii* pneumonia may be present despite the absence of crackles or rhonchi. Room air arterial oxygen concentrations may be mildly decreased, indicating minimal hypoxaemia. Untreated, *Pneumocystis carinii* pneumonia will eventually progress to cause significant pulmonary impairment and ultimately respiratory failure. A small number of patients have a dramatic onset and fulminant course, involving severe hypoxaemia, cyanosis, tachypnoea and altered mental status. Respiratory failure can develop within two to three days of initial onset of symptoms.

Pneumocystis carinii pneumonia can be diagnosed definitively by identification of the *Pneumocystis carinii* pneumonia protozoa in bronchial secretions, lung tissue or by induced sputum specimens.

Gastrointestinal

The gastrointestinal features of AIDS include loss of appetite, nausea, vomiting, oral and oesophageal candidiasis and chronic diarrhoea. Diarrhoea is a problem for 50 to 90 per cent of all AIDS patients. Some of the enteric pathogens that occur most frequently, which are identified by stool cultures or intestinal biopsy, include *Cryptosporidium muris, Salmonella*, cytomegalovirus (CMV), *Clostridium difficile* and *Mycobacterium avium intracellulare*. For patients with AIDS, the effects of diarrhoea can be devasting in terms of profound weight loss (more than 10 per cent of body weight), fluid and electrolyte imbalances, perianal skin excoriation, weakness and inability to carry out usual activities of daily living. Although many forms of infectious diarrhoea respond to treatment, it is not unusual for the infections to recur and become a chronic problem.

Oral candidiasis, a fungal infection, is nearly universal in all patients with AIDS and AIDS-related conditions. The development of oral candidiasis often precedes other life-threatening infections. It is characterized by the presence of creamy white patches in the oral cavity. When untreated, oral candidiasis will progress to involve the oesophagus. Associated signs and symptoms include difficult and painful swallowing and retrosternal pain. Some patients also develop ulcerating oral lesions, and are particularly susceptible to dissemination of candidiasis to other body systems.

Neurological

Most patients with AIDS will experience some form of neurological involvement during the course of human immunodeficiency virus infection. Neurological complications may involve both the central and the peripheral nervous systems. Signs and symptoms may be subtle and difficult to distinguish from fatigue, depression or the adverse effects of treatment for infections and malignancies.

Subacute encephalopathy is a common neurological dysfunction in individuals with AIDS. This syndrome is characterized by a progressive dementia, followed by death. Extensive neurological evaluation, including radiological procedures, lumbar puncture and brain biopsy, may fail to identify the underlying aetiology.

Progressive multifocal leukoencephalopathy is a central nervous system demyelinating disorder that is associated with AIDS. This disorder, which is caused by a virus, may begin with mental confusion and rapidly progress to include blindness, aphasias, paresis and ultimately death. Other common infections involving the nervous system include *Toxoplasma gondii* and *Cryptococcus neoformans*. Computed tomography and brain biopsy are often useful in identifying the source of neurological impairments.

Malignancy

Kaposi's sarcoma, some forms of non-Hodgkin's lymphoma and primary brain lymphoma are associated with AIDS. Kaposi's sarcoma, the complication that occurs most commonly, is a disease involving the endothelial layer of blood and lymphatic vessels. When first noted in 1872, Kaposi's sarcoma characteristically presented as lower extremity skin lesions in elderly men of Eastern European ancestry. In that population, the disease was slow to progress and easily treated. However, in the AIDS population, Kaposi's sarcoma is far more aggressive and often widely disseminated at the time of diagnosis. Kaposi's sarcoma can effect any organ system, including skin, lymphatic, pulmonary, gastrointestinal and central nervous systems. Skin involvement may range from purple lesions found on the trunk, face, oral mucosa or extremities, to fungating wounds that increase the patient's susceptibility to infection (Figure 26.2). Involvement of internal organs may eventually lead to organ failure, haemorrhage and death. Diagnosis of Kaposi's sarcoma is confirmed through biopsy of suspected lesions.

Chronic Illness

All AIDS patients develop at least one opportunistic infection during the course of their disease. Although many infections are treated successfully, some people never fully recover and are at increased risk for developing a second infection or malignancy. Treatment is often complicated by the debilitating signs and symptoms of

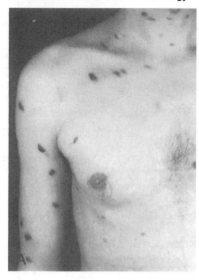
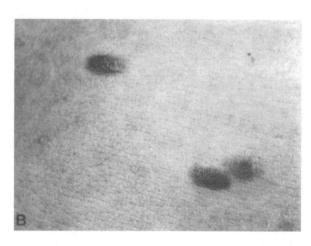

Figure 26.2 Epidemic Kaposi's sarcoma. (A) With time, an increasing number of patch, plaque and eventually nodular lesions may appear throughout the course of the disease. The symmetrical distribution of lesions along the lines of skin cleavage (Langer's lines) is typical of AIDS-associated Kaposi's sarcoma. (B) The ovoid shape of the lesions is a common feature of AIDS-associated Kaposi's sarcoma. (DeVita, V. T. Jr, Hellman, S. and Rosenberg, S. A. (1985) *AIDS: Etiology, Diagnosis, Treatment and Prevention*, J. B. Lippincott, Philadelphia.)

human immunodeficiency virus infection that include unexplained fatigue, headache, profuse night sweats, unexplained weight loss, dry cough, shortness of breath, extreme weakness, diarrhoea and persistent lymphadenopathy. Chronic illness develops when opportunistic diseases and the symptoms of human immunodeficiency virus do not resolve.

The effects of chronic illness, repeated and prolonged hospitalizations, can be devastating. People who progress to the terminal phases of human immunodeficiency virus infection are usually severely immunocompromised. Multiple local and disseminated infections involving several organ systems are common. Many people become profoundly malnourished as a result of impaired oral intake, gastrointestinal malabsorption and the effects of opportunistic diseases. Pulmonary, renal and hepatic failure may develop as a result of infection or malignancy. Skin breakdown related to immobility, profuse diarrhoea and progression of Kaposi's sarcoma is common. Neurological impairments may progress to dementia, coma and eventually death.

Patients in the advanced stages of AIDS are often no longer able to work, maintain current roles or relationships or care for themselves independently. Although the length of survival varies from months to years, approximately half of all the cases that have occurred since 1981 have resulted in death. Death occurs because either there is no known effective treatment for the opportunistic diseases or the patient no longer responds to standard therapy.

Management

At this time, no curative treatment exists for the underlying viral infection and subsequent immunodeficiency seen in AIDS. Medical management is aimed at treating and preventing opportunistic infections and malignancies, and includes supportive care for the debilitating effects of chronic illness such as malnutrition, skin breakdown, weakness, immobility and altered mental status.

Trimethoprim-sulphamethoxazole is an antibacterial drug that is used to treat a variety of organisms causing infection. It has long been the treatment of choice for *Pneumocystis* pneumonia (*Pneumocystis carinii* pneumonia) in non-AIDS patients. Unfortunately, AIDS patients with *Pneumocystis carinii* pneumonia who are treated with trimethoprim-sulphamethoxazole have experienced an increased incidence of adverse effects such as rashes, decreased white blood cell counts and drug-related fevers. These adverse effects have been reported in as many as 65 per cent of all AIDS patients treated with trimethoprim-sulphamethoxazole. Pentamidine, an antiprotozoal drug, is a second option for combating *Pneumocystis carinii* pneumonia. Many doctors initiate treatment with trimethoprim-sulphamethoxazole and change to pentamidine if adverse effects develop or patients do not show evidence of clinical improvement when treated with trimethoprim-sulphamethoxazole. The adverse effects of pentamidine include impaired glucose metabolism, renal damage and bone marrow suppression. Both trimethoprim-sulphamethoxazole and pentamidine are usually given intravenously, although trimethoprim-sulphamethoxazole can be given orally and pentamidine can also be given in a nebulized form.

The treatment of Kaposi's sarcoma remains experimental and has had limited success. Radiotherapy has been used to eradicate localized lesions that are disfiguring and anatomically inconvenient. Unfortunately, recurrence of irradiated lesions is not uncommon. Various single-agent and combination chemotherapy regimes have been tried with limited effectiveness. Chemotherapeutic drugs attempt to stop the growth of malignant tumours by interfering with cell metabolism and reproduction. Some of the chemotherapeutic agents that have been used in treating Kaposi's sarcoma are vinblastine, etoposide, adriamycin and bleomycin. Unfortunately, chemotherapy may induce bone marrow suppression and opportunistic infections in an already immunocompromised patient.

People who become weak and debilitated as a result of chronic illness associated with human immunodeficiency virus infection often require many forms of supportive care. Nutritional support may be as simple as providing assistance for obtaining or preparing meals. For people with more advanced nutritional impairment that results from decreased intake or gastrointestinal malabsorption associated with diarrhoea, total parenteral nutrition may be required. Fluid and electrolyte imbalances that result from nausea, vomiting and profuse diarrhoea often necessitate intravenous replacement. Skin breakdown associated with Kaposi's sarcoma, perianal skin excoriation and immobility is managed with thorough and meticulous skin care involving turning schedules, cleansing and application of ointments and dressings as prescribed by the doctor. Pulmonary symptoms such as dyspnoea and shortness of breath may be related to infection, Kaposi's sarcoma or fatigue. For these patients oxygen therapy, relaxation training and energy conservation techniques may be helpful. Patients with severe respiratory dysfunction may require mechanical ventilation in order to sustain life. Pain associated with skin breakdown, abdominal cramping or Kaposi's sarcoma is managed by analgesics given at regular intervals around the clock. Relaxation and guided imagery can be helpful in reducing pain and anxiety.

Future Treatment Options

The advent of zidovudine (Retrovir, formerly known as AZT) has led to a dramatic change in the concept of treatment. Zidovudine acts by interfering with human immunodeficiency virus replication, and evidence is now available that not only can it greatly prolong both the quantity and quality of life for individuals with symptomatic human immunodeficiency virus disease, but it may be useful in preventing symptomatic disease in those individuals who are currently asymptomatically infected with human immunodeficiency virus.

Zidovudine is given orally and is associated with significant side-effects, especially in those individuals who are symptomatically unwell as a result of human immunodeficiency virus infection. The most common side-effects are serious haemolytic anaemia and bone marrow suppression.

Many other drugs are now under investigation, and it is likely that, in the 1990s, several therapeutic agents will be available to treat individuals infected with human immunodeficiency virus.

In addition to identifying ways to halt human immunodeficiency virus replication, investigators are also studying a variety of approaches that will reconstitute and enhance immune system functions. Interferons and interleukin-2 (IL2) are examples of substances occurring naturally in the body that enhance immune system functions. Their success in clinical trials has been mixed. Although interferon has shown positive results in the treatment of Kaposi's sarcoma, its effectiveness in the treatment of patients with opportunistic infections has been disappointing. Patient improvement and survival depend not only on eliminating the human immunodeficiency virus but also on restoring the damaged immune system.

► NURSING PROCESS
► THE PATIENT WITH ACQUIRED IMMUNODEFICIENCY SYNDROME (AIDS)

The nursing care of people with AIDS is quite challenging because of the potential for any organ system to be the target of infections or malignancies. In addition, this disease is complicated by several controversial emotional and ethical issues. The plan of care for the patient with AIDS is individualized to meet the needs of the patient.

► *Assessment*

Nursing assessment includes identification of potential risk factors, including sexual history and history of intravenous drug use. The patient's physical status and psychological status are assessed. All factors reflecting immune system functioning are thoroughly explored.

Nutritional status is assessed by obtaining a dietary history and identifying factors that may interfere with oral intake, such as anorexia, nausea, vomiting, oral pain or difficulty swallowing. In addition, the patient's ability to purchase and prepare food is investigated. Weight, triceps skin fold measurements and blood urea nitrogen, serum protein, albumin and transferrin levels provide objective measurements of nutritional status.

The skin and mucous membranes are inspected daily for evidence of breakdown, ulceration and infection. The oral cavity is monitored for redness, ulcerations and the presence of white creamy patches indicative of candidiasis. It is especially important to assess the perianal area for excoriation and infection in those patients with profuse diarrhoea. Wound cultures are obtained in order to identify infectious organisms.

Respiratory status is assessed by monitoring the patient for cough, sputum production, shortness of breath, orthopnoea, tachypnoea and chest pain. The presence and quality of breath sounds are also assessed. Other objective parameters of pulmonary function include chest X-rays, arterial blood gas concentrations and pulmonary function tests.

Neurological status is determined by assessing the patient's level of consciousness and orientation to person, place and time, and the occurrence of memory lapses. The patient is also observed for sensory impairments such as visual changes, headaches or numbness and tingling in the extremities. Motor impairments, such as altered gait and paresis, may also occur. Finally, the patient is observed for evidence of seizure activity.

Fluid and electrolyte status is assessed by examining the skin and mucous membranes for turgor and dryness. Increased thirst, decreased urine output, low blood pressure or a decline in systolic blood pressure of 15 mm Hg with concurrent rise in pulse when the patient sits up, weak rapid pulse and urine specific gravity of 1.025 or more may indicate dehydration. Electrolyte imbalances such as decreased serum sodium, potassium, calcium, magnesium and chloride often result from profuse diarrhoea. The patient is assessed for signs and symptoms of electrolyte depletion. These may include decreased mental status, muscle twitching, muscle cramps, irregular pulse, nausea and vomiting and shallow respirations.

The patient's level of knowledge about the disease and means of transmission is evaluated. In addition, the level of knowledge of family and friends is investigated. The patient's psychological reaction to the diagnosis of AIDS is important to explore. Reactions vary among individuals and may include denial, anger, fear, shame, withdrawal from any social interactions and depression. It is often helpful to gain an understanding of how the patient has dealt with illness and major life stressors in the past. The patient's resources for support are also important to identify.

▶ *Patient's Problems*

The list of potential problems for the patient is quite extensive because of the complex nature of this disease. However, based on the assessment, the patient's main problems may include the following:

- Alteration in perianal skin integrity related to excoriation and diarrhoea.
- Alteration in bowel elimination: diarrhoea related to enteric pathogens and/or human immunodeficiency virus infection.
- Potential for infection related to immunodeficiency.

- Activity intolerance related to weakness, fatigue, malnutrition, impaired fluid and electrolyte balance and hypoxia associated with pulmonary infections.
- Alteration in thought processes related to shortened attention span, impaired memory, confusion and disorientation associated with AIDS encephalitis.
- Alteration in fluids and electrolyte balance related to losses associated with persistent diarrhoea.
- Ineffective airway clearance related to pulmonary infection, increased bronchial secretions and decreased ability to cough related to weakness and fatigue.
- Alteration in comfort: pain related to diarrhoea and impaired perianal skin integrity.
- Inadequate nutritional status related to decreased oral intake, decreased intestinal absorption and/or diarrhoea.
- Lack of knowledge concerning means of preventing transmission of human immunodeficiency virus.
- Social isolation related to stigma of the disease, withdrawal of support systems, isolation procedures and fear of infecting others.
- Grieving related to changes in lifestyle and roles and to unfavourable prognosis.

▶ *Planning and Implementation*
▶ Expected Outcomes

The patient's expected outcomes may include achievement and maintenance of perianal skin integrity, resumption of usual bowel habits, absence of infection, improved activity tolerance, improved thought processes, maintenance of fluid and electrolyte status, improved airway clearance, increased comfort, improvement of nutritional status, increased knowledge concerning means of preventing disease transmission, decreased sense of social isolation and expression of grief.

Nursing Care

Perianal Skin Care

The patient's perianal region is assessed frequently for impairment of skin integrity and infection. The patient is requested to keep the area as clean as possible. The perianal area is cleaned after each bowel movement with nonabrasive soap and water to prevent further excoriation and breakdown of the skin and infection. If the area is very painful, soft cloths or cotton sponges may prove to be less irritating than washcloths. In addition, baths or gentle irrigation may facilitate cleansing and promote comfort. The area is dried thoroughly after cleansing. The doctor is consulted concerning topical lotions or ointments to promote healing. Wounds are cultured if infection is suspected so that the appropriate antimicrobial treatment can be initiated. Debilitated patients may require assistance in maintaining hygienic practices.

Resumption of Usual Bowel Habits

The patient's bowel patterns are assessed for signs and symptoms of diarrhoea, including frequency and consistency of stools and the presence of abdominal pain or cramping associated with bowel movements. Factors that exacerbate the frequency of diarrhoea are also assessed. The quantity and volume of liquid stools are measured in order to document fluid volume losses. Stool cultures are obtained in order to identify pathogenic organisms.

The patient is advised about ways to decrease diarrhoea. Restriction of oral intake may be indicated and recommended by the doctor in order to rest the bowel during periods of acute bowel inflammation associated with severe enteric infections. As the patient's dietary intake is advanced, the patient is advised to avoid foods that act as bowel irritants such as raw fruits and vegetables, carbonated beverages, spicy foods and foods of extreme temperatures. Small, frequent meals will also help to prevent abdominal distension. The doctor may prescribe medications such as anticholinergic antispasmodics or opiates, which decrease diarrhoea by decreasing intestinal spasms and motility. Antibiotics and antifungal agents may also be prescribed in order to combat offending pathogens that are identified by stool cultures.

Preventing Infection

The patient and caregivers are requested to monitor for signs and symptoms of infection: fever, chills, night sweats, cough with or without sputum production, shortness of breath, difficult breathing, oral pain or difficulty swallowing, creamy white patches in the oral cavity, unexplained weight loss, swollen lymph nodes, nausea, vomiting, persistent diarrhoea or frequency, urgency or pain of urination; headache, visual changes or memory lapses; redness, swelling or drainage from skin wounds, and vesicular lesions on the face, lips or perianal area. The nurse also monitors laboratory values that indicate the presence of infection such as the white blood cell count and differential blood cell count. The doctor may request culture specimens of wound drainage, skin lesions, urine, stool, sputum, mouth and blood in order to identify pathogenic organisms and the most appropriate antimicrobial therapy.

The patient will require education about ways of preventing infection. The importance of personal hygiene is emphasized. Kitchen and bathroom surfaces should be cleansed regularly with disinfectants in order to prevent fungal and bacterial growth. Patients with pets are requested to use gloves when cleaning areas soiled by animals such as bird cages and litter boxes. Patients are advised to avoid exposure to others who are sick or who have been recently vaccinated. Patients with AIDS and their sexual partners are strongly urged to avoid exposure to body fluids during sexual activities and to use condoms for any form of sexual intercourse, as are any individuals engaging in penetrative sexual activity outside of a long-established, monogamous relationship. Intravenous drug use is discouraged because of risk to the patient of other infections and transmission of human immunodeficiency virus infection to others. Needle and syringe facilities and safe injecting techniques should be discussed as many patients are unable to discontinue drug use. 'Safer' sexual behaviour is also discussed.

The importance of avoiding smoking and maintaining a balance between diet, rest and exercise is also addressed. All health professionals must remember to maintain strict aseptic technique when performing invasive procedures such as venipunctures and bladder catheterizations.

Improving Activity Tolerance

Activity tolerance is assessed by monitoring the patient's ability to ambulate and perform activities of daily living. Patients may be unable to maintain usual levels of activity because of weakness, fatigue, shortness of breath, dizziness and neurological involvement. Assistance in planning daily routines that maintain a balance between activity and rest may be necessary. In addition, patients benefit from advice about the use of energy-conservation techniques, such as sitting while washing or while preparing meals. Personal items that are frequently used should be kept within the patient's reach so that they can be obtained without walking any distance. Measures such as relaxation and guided imagery may be beneficial in decreasing anxiety that contributes to weakness and fatigue.

Promoting Improvement of Thought Process

Thought processes are assessed by monitoring the patient for decreased attention span, memory lapses, confusion, disorientation, agitation and decreased levels of consciousness, which may range from somnolence to coma. The nurse consults with the family, friends and the doctor in order to identify factors that might contribute to altered thought process, such as use of illegal drugs, prescribed medications, hypoxia, fluid and electrolyte disturbances and severe depression.

The patient, family and friends are helped to understand and cope with changes in thought processes. The patient is reoriented to person, place and time whenever necessary. It is often helpful to have a clock and calendar within the patient's view to facilitate sustained orientation. The patient's family and friends are encouraged to bring favourite objects from home in order to provide a familiar and less threatening environment while the patient is hospitalized. All advice given to the patient are delivered in a slow, simple and clear manner. Measures to protect the patient from injury are instituted. These may include placing the call bell with easy reach, keeping side rails up and the bed in a low position, requesting the patient to wear shoes and slippers with nonskid soles and monitoring the patient who is smoking or shaving.

Maintaining Fluid and Electrolyte Balance

Fluid and electrolyte status is monitored on an ongoing basis. The skin is assessed for dryness and turgor. Fluid intake and output and specific gravity of urine are measured daily. The patient is also monitored for decreases in systolic blood pressure or increases in pulse associated with sitting or standing. Signs and symptoms of electrolyte disturbances such as muscle cramping, weakness, irregular pulse, decreased mental status, nausea and vomiting are documented and reported to the physician. Serum electrolyte values are monitored and abnormalities reported to the doctor when indicated. The nurse assists the patient in selecting foods that will replenish electrolytes, such as oranges and bananas (potassium) and cheese and soups (sodium). A fluid intake of 2,500 ml or more, unless contraindicated, is encouraged in order to regain fluid lost from diarrhoea. In addition, measures to control diarrhoea are initiated. If fluid and electrolyte imbalances persist, the nurse may administer intravenous fluid and electrolytes as prescribed by the doctor. It then becomes important for the nurse to monitor the therapeutic or potentially adverse effects of such therapy.

Improving Nutritional Status

Nutritional status is assessed by monitoring weight, dietary intake, anthropometric measurements and serum albumin, blood urea nitrogen, protein and transferrin levels. The patient is also assessed for factors that interfere with oral intake, such as anorexia, nausea, pain, weakness and fatigue. Based on the results of assessment, the nurse can implement specific measures to facilitate oral intake.

When fatigue and weakness interfere with intake, the patient is encouraged to rest before meals. In addition, meals should be planned so that they do not occur immediately after painful or unpleasant procedures. The patient with diarrhoea and abdominal cramping is encouraged to avoid foods that stimulate intestinal motility and distension, such as foods high in fibre or of extreme temperatures. The dietician is consulted to determine the patient's nutritional requirements. The patient is advised about ways in which to supplement nutritional value of meals. The addition of eggs, butter, margarine and fortified milk to gravies, soups or drinks can provide additional calories and protein. Use of commercial supplements such as puddings and powders may be advised. Patients who are unable to maintain nutritional status through oral intake often require enteral or parenteral feeds. Instruction is provided to patients and families about how to administer such feeds when patients are able to return home. Community nurses provide additional teaching and support for these patients after discharge from the hospital. The nurse often consults with social workers in order to identify sources of financial support for patients who are unable to purchase or prepare meals. Referral to voluntary agencies or other community re-

sources may be indicated if the patient is unable to shop for or prepare meals. These resources are often able to provide volunteers who can assist patients after discharge from hospital.

Patient Education

Patients, families and friends are advised about the routes of transmission of human immunodeficiency virus. All fears and misconceptions are thoroughly discussed. In addition, the nurse discusses precautions necessary to prevent transmission of human immunodeficiency virus, including use of condoms during vaginal or anal intercourse, avoiding oral contact with the penis, vagina or rectum, avoiding sexual practices that might cause cuts or tears in the lining of the rectum, vagina or penis, and avoiding sexual contact with multiple partners. The dangers of sharing needles and syringes are also discussed. Patients with AIDS, or who may be infected with human immunodeficiency virus, are instructed not to donate blood or other body organs.

Improving Airway Clearance

Respiratory status including rate, rhythm, use of accessory muscles, breath sounds, mental status and skin colour must be assessed at least daily. The presence of cough and the quantity and characteristics of sputum are documented. Sputum specimens are tested for the possible presence of infectious organisms. Pulmonary measures (coughing, deep breathing, postural drainage, percussion and vibration) are provided as often as every two hours to prevent stasis of secretions and promote clearance of airways. Because of weakness and fatigue, many patients may require assistance in attaining a position that will facilitate breathing and airway clearance. The provision of adequate rest periods is essential to maximize the patient's energy expenditure and prevent excessive fatigue. The patient's fluid volume status is evaluated so that adequate hydration can be maintained. Unless contraindicated by renal or cardiac disease, an intake of two to three litres of fluid daily is encouraged. Humidified oxygen may be prescribed and nasopharyngeal or tracheal suctioning may be indicated to maintain adequate ventilation. Mechanical ventilation may be necessary for patients who are unable to maintain adequate ventilation as a result of pulmonary infection, fluid and electrolyte imbalance or respiratory muscle paresis.

Increasing Comfort

The patient is assessed for the quality and quantity of pain associated with diarrhoea and peripheral neuropathy. In addition, the effects of pain on elimination, nutrition, sleep, affect and communication are explored, along with exacerbating and relieving factors. Cleansing the perianal area as previously described can promote comfort. Topical anaesthetics or ointments may be prescribed. Soft cushions or foam pads may be used to increase comfort while sitting. The patient is advised to avoid foods that act as bowel irritants, such as milk products, caffeine, prunes, cabbage, spicy foods, carbonated beverages and extremely hot or cold foods. Antispasmodics and antidiarrhoeal preparations may be prescribed to reduce discomfort and frequency of bowel movements. If necessary, systemic analgesics may also be prescribed.

Decreasing Sense of Social Isolation
AIDS patients are at risk for 'double stigmatization'. They have what society often refers to as 'a dread disease', and they may have a lifestyle (homosexuality or drug use) that differs from what is considered acceptable. The majority of people with AIDS are young adults at a developmental stage in which they should be establishing intimate relationships and personal and career goals. Their focus changes as they are faced with a disease that has no cure and a limited life expectancy. In addition, they may be forced to reveal hidden lifestyles to family, friends, colleagues and health care providers. As a result, AIDS patients are often flooded with emotions such as anxiety, guilt, shame and fear. Patients may be faced with multiple losses, such as rejection by family and friends and loss of financial security, normal roles and functions, self-esteem, privacy, ability to control bodily functions, ability to interact meaningfully with the environment and sexual functioning. Some patients may harbour feelings of guilt because of chosen lifestyle or because of the possibility of having infected others in current or previous relationships. Other patients may feel anger towards sexual partners who may have been responsible for transmission of the virus. Infection control measures used in the hospital or at home may further contribute to the patient's emotional isolation. Any or all of these stressors may cause the AIDS patient to withdraw both physically and emotionally from social contact.

Nurses are in a key position to provide an atmosphere of acceptance and understanding for AIDS patients and their families and partners. A patient's usual level of social interaction is assessed as early as possible, to provide a baseline for monitoring changes in behaviour indicative of social isolation (e.g., decreased interaction with staff, family or friends, hostility, nonco-operation). Patients are encouraged to express feelings of isolation and loneliness, and assured that these feelings are not unique or abnormal.

Providing information about how to protect themselves and others can help to prevent patients from avoiding social contact. Patients, family and friends must be assured that AIDS is not spread through casual contact. Educating ancillary personnel, nurses and doctors will help to reduce factors that might contribute to feelings of isolation. Patient care conferences concerning the psychosocial considerations regarding AIDS patients may help to sensitize nurses to patients' needs.

The nurse can help patients explore and identify resources for support and mechanisms of coping. Patients are encouraged to telephone family and friends as well as local or national AIDS support groups and 'hotlines'. If at all possible, barriers to social contact are identified and eliminated. For patients who are able to participate, social interaction with family, friends or colleagues is encouraged. Patients are also encouraged to engage in their usual diversional activities whenever possible.

Home Health Care Considerations
Many people with AIDS are able to return to the community and resume their usual daily activities. Others who return home are unable to continue employment or maintain their pre-existing level of independence. Families or caregivers need assistance in providing supportive care. They must receive advice about how to prevent disease transmission, including hand washing and methods of safely handling items soiled with body fluids. Caregivers in the home are taught how to administer medications, including intravenous preparations. Guidelines about infection, follow-up care, diet, rest and activities are also necessary. Both the patient and caregivers will require support and guidance in coping with this debilitating and usually fatal disease.

Community nurses and hospice nurses are in an excellent position to help provide the support and guidance so often needed in the home setting. Community nurses must be able to assist in administration of parenteral antibiotics, chemotherapy and nutrition. In addition, complicated wound care or respiratory care is often required in the home. Both patients and families are often unable to meet these skilled care needs without the assistance of nurses. Hospice nurses are increasingly called upon to provide emotional support to patients and families as AIDS patients enter the terminal stages of disease. This support takes on special meaning when AIDS patients lose the support of friends and families who have turned away from them because of fear of the disease or anger concerning lifestyles adopted by patients, or who have themselves died as a result of human immunodeficiency virus disease.

Prevention of Human Immunodeficiency Virus Transmission
As discussed earlier in this chapter, AIDS is not transmitted by casual contact. Epidemiological evidence has indicated that human immunodeficiency virus is transmitted only through intimate sexual contact, parenteral exposure to infected blood or blood products and perinatal transmission from mother to neonate. Studies of nonsexual household contacts of AIDS patients as well as nonsexual person-to-person contact that generally occurs in the work place have not demonstrated any increased risk for transmission of AIDS through such contact.

Human immunodeficiency virus has been isolated from blood, semen, saliva, tears, breast milk, urine and other body fluids, secretions and excretions. Health professionals therefore need to take special precautions when dealing with blood and body fluids in order to safeguard themselves and other patients. Many health authorities, and the Royal College of Nursing, have developed guidelines for the care of patients infected with human immunodeficiency virus. Although nurses will need to consult local policies closely, many of the precautions are based on the concept of 'Universal Precautions', i.e. *all* blood and body fluids from *all* patients should be treated with caution. This ensures that there is no need to single out so-called 'high risk' patients (with the possible risk of further stigma being attached), and also protects the health professional against other similarly transmitted diseases, especially hepatitis B.

A full description of Universal Precautions can be found in Chapter 2, Infection Control.

▶ *Evaluation*
▶ **Expected Outcomes**

The outcomes expected for the patient with AIDS are as follows:

1. Patient resumes usual bowel habits.
2. Experiences no infections.
3. Maintains usual level of thought processes.
4. Maintains fluid and electrolyte balance.
5. Maintains effective airway clearance.
6. Experiences increased sense of comfort.
7. Maintains perianal skin integrity.
8. Maintains adequate nutritional status.
9. Understands means of preventing disease transmission.
10. Experiences decreased sense of social isolation.
11. Maintains adequate level of activity tolerance.
12. Progresses through grieving process.

FURTHER READING

Books

Amos, W. M. G. (1981) *Basic Immunology*, Pergamon Press, London.

Brostoff, R. J., Roitt, I. M. and Male, D. K. (1985) *Immunology*, Gower Medical, London.

Flaskerud, J. H. (1989) *AIDS/HIV Infection: A Reference Guide For Nursing Professionals*, W. B. Saunders, Eastbourne.

Green, J. and McCreaner, A. (1989) *Counselling in HIV Infection and AIDS*, Blackwell Scientific, Oxford.

Miller, D. (1987) *Living With AIDS and HIV*, MacMillan Education, London.

Miller, R. and Bor, R. (1988) *AIDS—A Guide To Clinical Counselling*, Science Press, London.

Pratt, R. J. (1991) *AIDS: A Strategy For Nursing Care* (3rd edition), Edward Arnold, London.

Sande, M. A. and Volberding, P. A. (1990) *The Medical Management of Aids* (2nd edition), W. B. Saunders, London.

Sims, R. and Moss, V. (1991) *Terminal Care For People With AIDS*, Edward Arnold, London.

UK Health Departments (1990) *Guidance For Clinical Health Care Workers: Protection Against Infection With HIV and Hepatitis Viruses, Recommendations of the Expert Advisory Group on AIDS*, HMSO, London.

Articles

Centers for Disease Control (1987) Recommendations for prevention of HIV transmission in health care settings, *MMWR*, 21 August, Vol. 36, No. 2s, p. 3-S-18S.

Centers for Disease Control (1988) Update: Universal Precautions for prevention of transmission of human immunodeficiency virus, hepatitis B virus and other blood-borne pathogens in health care settings, *MMWR*, 24 June, Vol. 37, pp. 377–88.

chapter 27

ASSESSMENT AND CARE OF PATIENTS WITH RHEUMATIC DISORDERS

The Arthritis and Rheumatism Council of the United Kingdom identifies over 200 different conditions that are included under the term 'arthritis and rheumatism' (1986) and report the following:

> *As many as 20 million people experience some form of rheumatic complaint during the course of a year, and more than 8 million consult their family doctor about these problems. Arthritis and rheumatism are one of the leading causes of sickness incapacity, causing 65 million days to be lost from work despite a shrinking work force. These conditions form the biggest single class of physically disabling disorder in this country. The economic costs are very considerable, as is the impact on other members of the family or close friends of those affected.*
>
> *Some forms of arthritis attack children, even under the age of one year; other types single out people in the prime of life; and most forms of arthritis get more common in the elderly. Women are generally affected more often, but some conditions afflict men preferentially. Socioeconomic status, occupation and inheritance all exert an influence. The burden of rheumatic suffering has increased dramatically since the last war and different regions of the country appear to vary in how frequently people are affected; in general, the north suffers more than the south. The total cost of statutory services and benefits for arthritis and rheumatism approach £1.5 billion. Expenditure on research to conquer the problems amounts to about 0.5 per cent of this sum.*

The spectrum of diseases can be described in the following way:

1. The arthropathies (i.e., 'arthritis', inflammation of joints).
   a. The two major problems are rheumatoid arthritis and osteoarthritis.

b. Other forms of arthritis under this heading include gout, chondrocalcinosis and juvenile arthritis.

c. Arthritis associated with infection include septic, postinfective or reactive arthritis.

d. The spondylarthropathies—associated with psoriasis, inflammatory bowel disease, Reiter's disease, Behçet's disease and after dysentery.

Arthritis with disease of other major systems—endocrine, haematological, neurological, gastrointestinal, dermatological, neoplastic disorder, renal transplantation, bone disease, respiratory disorder and hypersensitivity.

2. The connective tissue diseases:
   a. Systemic lupus erythematosus.
   b. Systemic sclerosis (scleroderma).
   c. Polyarteritis nodosa.
   d. Polymyositis.
   e. Dermatomyositis.

3. Dorsopathies (i.e., 'back problems'):
   a. Ankylosing spondylitis and sacrolitis.
   b. Spondylosis—cervical, thoracic, lumbo, sacral (i.e. osteoarthritis of spine).
   c. Intervertebral disc disorders—displacement or degeneration, cervicalgia, lumbago, sciatica and 'neuritis', 'radiculitis', ankylosing vertebral hyperostosis (Forestier's disease).
   d. Other disorders—spinal stenosis, Baastrup's syndrome, torticollis, backache.

4. Soft-tissue disorders (i.e., 'rheumatism', non-articular pains):
   a. Polymyalgia rheumatica; tenosynovitis; sinovitis.
   b. Bursitis (including those of occupational origin, e.g., housemaid's knee).
   c. Shoulder—adhesive capsulitis ('frozen shoulder') and rotator cuff syndrome (scapulohumeral fibrositis, periarthritis of shoulder).
   d. Enthesopathies—epicondylitis (tennis elbow), periarthritis of the wrist, gluteal tendinitis, iliac crest spur, psoas and trocanteric tendinitis, Pellegrini-Stieda syndrome, Achilles bursitis, calcaneal spur.
   e. Fibromatoses—Dupuytren's contracture, Garrod's pads, plantar fasciitis, rheumatism, myalgia, 'neuralgia', panniculitis and other pains in the limbs. Strains and sprains of joints and adjacent muscles (including sports injuries).
   f. Other disorders—hypermobility syndrome, metatarsalgia, myositis ossificans.

5. Other rheumatic disorders:
   a. Rheumatic fever.
   b. Bone disease—Paget's disease (osteitis deformans), osteoporosis, osteomalacia, hallux valgus and other related problems, acquired deformities of the musculoskeletal system.
   c. Other conditions: Teitze's disease, algoneurodystrophy and osteitis condensans.

RHEUMATOID ARTHRITIS

Rheumatoid arthritis is the most common and serious type of inflammatory polyarthritis that comes under the heading of arthropathies. It is a chronic inflammatory disease of unknown aetiology. Although there is a marked systemic aspect to the disease that can affect many organs other than the joints throughout the body, it more commonly affects the joints, which are involved in a symmetrical fashion, with the small peripheral joints being most affected.

Epidemiology

Rheumatoid arthritis affects about 3 per cent of females and 1 per cent of males worldwide (Huskisson and Dudley Hart, 1987, p. 128). Although it may affect all ages from 16 to 70 years, the commonest incidence is between 20 to 55 years.

Altered Physiology

Immune complexes are formed within the joint space, and these help to activate complement and attract neutrophils. The phagocytosis of immune complexes by neutrophils produces inflammation in the joint, thus stimulating the synovium to produce granulation tissue (pannus), which then erodes the underlying cartilage and bone (Figure 27.1). Blood serum contains rheumatoid factors, which are auto-antibodies directed against immunoglobulin G (IgG). Progression to an advanced and chronic phase of rheumatoid synovitis is accompanied by accumulations of normal cells and new alterations of cellular composition. Increasing numbers of fibroblast cells appear and many of the synovium lining cells are swollen and contain cellular debris, cartilage fragments, complement components and immunoglobulin. Monocytoid cells become increasingly activated and fuse, leading to the formation of multinucleated giant cells. These blast-like cells are often located in clumps with T-cell blasts. They somewhat resemble lymphoid follicles, resulting in the synovial thickening becoming more prominent within an increased villous hypertrophy. As the synovium becomes more inflamed, fusions develop within the joint space, which clearly result from the increased capillary permeability and a reduction in the return of synovial fluid via the lymphatics within the subsynovial inflammatory layers.

Destructive Stage

As inflammation continues, adgrowths of vascular granulation tissue or pannus spread from the synovial margin across the cartilage to invade through the cartilage and into the bone ends, producing erosions. Tendon sheaths which are also lined with synovial lining undergo similar inflammatory changes.

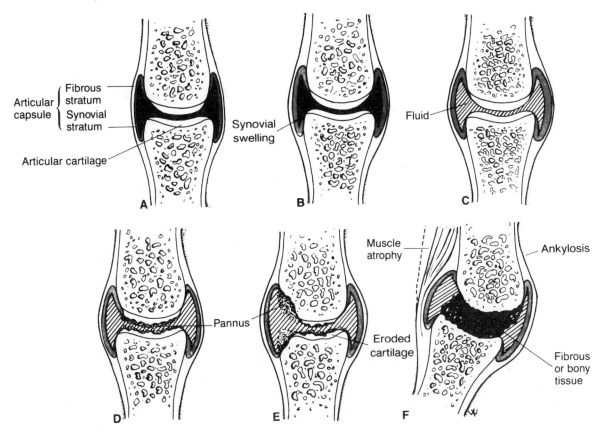

Figure 27.1 Altered physiology of rheumatoid arthritis. (A) Normal. (B) Synovial swelling. (C) Fluid collects in joint. (D) Pannus. (E) Eroded articular cartilage. (F) Ankylosis and muscle atrophy.

Clinical Features

The patient often describes an insidious onset of joint pain and stiffness, with generalized morning stiffness usually lasting up to six hours. Inflammation of many joints, a high temperature, sweating and weight loss also form important milestones for the onset of this disease. On examination, affected joints are usually swollen and tender with limitation of movement. Swelling is normally due to a fusion or synovial thickening and in later cases to bony overgrowth. It is important to identify muscle wasting around affected joints and to locate pain.

Joints Affected

Wright and Hazlock (1977) describe the hand as the 'arthritic patient's calling card'. The joints involved in rheumatoid arthritis are the proximal interphalangeal joints and the metacarpophalangeal joints, especially those of the index and middle fingers. Three types of deformity are noted in the hand, as follows:

1. Ulnar deviation—this results when the fingers drift towards the ulnar border of the hand from the metacarpophalangeal joints.

2. Swan neck deformity—this results when the proximal interphalangeal joint and the distal interphalangeal joint are flexed.

3. Boutonnière deformity—this results when the proximal interphalangeal joint is fixed in flexion and the distal interphalangeal hyperextended. Another major deformity within the hand results when the metacarpophalangeal joints become subluxed. The wrist is also often involved in rheumatoid arthritis, with the ulnar styloid often developing an overlying swelling and tenderness that later leads to it becoming prominent because the radio-ulnar joint subluxes. Movement of the hand and wrist joint together must be considered as the extensor tendons of the fingers cross the wrist, and interruption of movement may take place due to inflammation there (see Figure 27.2).

All other synovial joints in the body may become involved by rheumatoid arthritis with resulting disability, especially if weight-bearing joints are involved. In severe cases the tempero-mandibular joints (jaws) may also be involved, which will cause great problems with eating and swallowing.

A

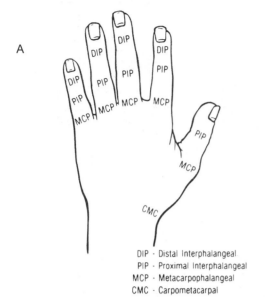

DIP · Distal Interphalangeal
PIP · Proximal Interphalangeal
MCP · Metacarpophalangeal
CMC · Carpometacarpal

B

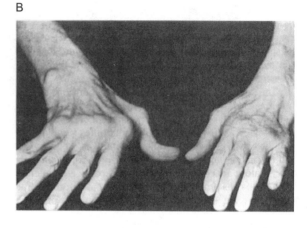

C

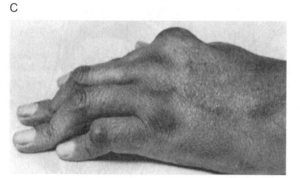

D

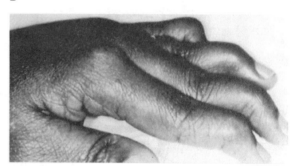

Figure 27.2 Rheumatoid arthritis of the hand. (A) Common reference points. (B) Boutonnière deformity, characterized by flexion of the proximal interphalangeal joint, hyperextension of the distal interphalangeal joint, and inability to straighten the joint. (C) Swelling and atrophy of the metacarpophalangeal joints in both hands. Ulnar deviation and subluxation of the metacarpophalangeal joints occur (as seen in right hand). (D) Swan neck deformity, in which the proximal interphalangeal (middle) joint is hyperextended and the distal interphalangeal joint is in flexion. (Reprinted from the Arthritis Teaching Slide Collection, © 1980. Used by permission of the Arthritis Foundation.)

Extra-Articular Features

In addition to joint problems, patients may experience many other symptoms (Hart, 1969, 1970):

1. 20 per cent of patients with rheumatoid arthritis develop nodules below bony prominences almost anywhere on the body.
2. Tenosynovitis around the hands or wrists causes pain, local swelling, tenderness, trigger fingers and flexion deformities.
3. Bursitis, especially in the hand and wrist.
4. Baker's cyst, which may need to be distinguished from deep vein thrombosis.
5. Ligamentous laxicity.

6. Skin—vasculitic ulcers and skin lesions around fingernails.
7. Eyes:
   a. Scleritis, episcleritis and sclera malacia perforans.
   b. Sjögren's syndrome (Bloch *et al.*, 1965).
8. Heart:
   a. Granulomatous lesions in myocardium.
   b. Pericarditis vasculitis.
9. Neuropathy:
   a. Compression, carpal tunnel syndrome, lymphadenopathy and splenomegaly (rare).
10. Lung involvement (Scadding, 1969):
    a. Fibrosing alveolitis.
    b. Pleurural fusion, nodules in lungs or pleura.

11. Anaemia—common and proportional to disease activity.
12. Felty's syndrome—splenomegaly and leucopenia, with infections also commonly occurring.
13. Osteoporosis—aggravated by steroid therapy.
14. Amylodosis—presents as proteinuria and can progress to renal failure. Diagnosis by rectal fat or renal biopsy.

Nursing History

The patient's history is the most valuable diagnostic aid to the physical assessment. The public's concept about 'rheumatism' can distort patients' descriptions of pain, which they believe is due to joint disease. Pain is the symptom that most commonly causes a person to seek medical attention. Other common symptoms include joint swelling, limited movement, stiffness, weakness and fatigue.

The patient's general appearance should be noted during initial contact. Gait, posture and general musculoskeletal size and structure are observed. Gross deformities and abnormalities in movement are noted. Deviations away from the body midline are called varus deformities (for example, bow legs); deviations towards the midline are called valgus deformities (for example, knock knees). The symmetry, size and contour of other tissues such as the skin and adipose tissue are also noted and recorded. A complete physical assessment is performed, with special attention given to the examination of each joint and its adjacent structures.

Joint stiffness is often difficult to separate from pain as both may arise from common factors such as capsular tension. However, certain types of stiffness are highly characteristic. Early morning stiffness occurs in rheumatoid arthritis, with the patient waking with distressing painful stiffness of all affected joints. The time it takes for this stiffness to wear off provides a reliable measure of inflammatory activity.

Swelling is another important indicator which should be noted during the history-taking, with particular reference as to whether the swelling is beside or over a joint.

Loss of Function
Function can be graded in the following way:

Grade 1—completely independent without any adaptations.
Grade 2—independent with some adaptations (e.g., aids and appliances).
Grade 3—partially dependent (e.g., needing help with bathing or dressing).
Grade 4—confined to bed/wheelchair.

Joint noises or crepitus occurs in rheumatoid arthritis on hyperextension of a finger or full knee flexion under load; this is as a result of the sudden formation of a gas bubble in the synovial fluid and therefore is of no pathological significance.

Family History
It is important to note if there has been any familial clustering as although the disease is not known to be hereditary it appears likely that the incidence of the disease is higher in those families with a known sufferer.

Psychological Impact of the Disease
It is helpful for the nurse to identify how the disease has been accepted by the patient, family and significant others, as this will have a great bearing on how they cope and adjust to the disease.

► NURSING PROCESS
► THE PATIENT WITH RHEUMATOID ARTHRITIS

► *Assessment*

The nurse must assess the patients' mobility as they enter the room, looking for impeding factors such as poor posture, gait, physique and deformity (Smith Pigg, Webb-Driscoll and Caniff, 1985). The nurse should examine paired joints together, for example, hands and wrists, alternating between the two to aid comparison. All joints need to be palpated for swelling, tenderness and movement of the joint through its full range of movement. Note should be made as to whether any swelling is due to bony outgrowths such as osteophytes, soft tissue swellings such as synovial swelling or due to synovial effusion, which is a collection of fluid within the joint's base. It is unusual for joints in rheumatoid arthritis to have an appearance of redness in the overlying skin. However, it is more usual when a joint is inflamed to have a rise in skin temperature, so the overlying skin of paired joints needs to be noted for warmth. The nurse can test the skin temperature by feeling the skin with the back of the fingers of one hand, moving backwards and forwards between the same skin area as the joint on either side of the body. When palpating joints, the nurse needs to test for tenderness of joints, which will give valuable information on such things as disease activity and whether the patient is in an acute phase of the disease or not.

Range of Movement
The nurse will need to put most joints through a passive range of movement with the patient lying on a bed or couch. All movements are measured with a protractor or goniometer. Measurements are graded from 0 when the patient's leg is flat on the couch, to flexion of 90 degrees and is recorded as degrees of flexion, extension, supination, pronation and so on. It is also extremely important to examine the lower limb joints while the patient is weight-bearing during walking as deformities will only

really become apparent once weight is put through the joint.

Pain

During the physical examination the nurse must record those joints which are inflamed and painful. The nurse must also note those joints which click or crunch during examination (crepitus), and time must be spent reassuring patients that this indicates only a roughening of the weight-bearing surfaces, or a gas bubble in the synovial fluid.

During physical examination of the joints, the nurse needs to assess how stable the joints are, and an assessment of muscle weakness is also made. Some of this information will be obtained during the history-taking when nurses may describe, for example, how knees suddenly give way or the problems patients may have in getting out of chairs due to muscle weakness.

► *Medical Diagnosis*

In addition to the nursing history and physical assessment, the nurse needs to understand how a medical diagnosis is reached. It is therefore useful in this instance to use the American Rheumatism Association's criteria for the diagnosis of rheumatoid arthritis, as follows:

1. Morning stiffness.
2. Pain on motion or tenderness in at least one joint.
3. Swelling (soft tissue thickening of fluid) in at least one joint.
4. Swelling (observed by a doctor) of at least one other joint within three months.
5. Symmetrical joint swelling (not terminal interphalangeal joints).
6. Subcutaneous nodules.
7. X-ray changes typical of rheumatoid arthritis, which must include at least bony decalcification around the involved joints.
8. Positive agglutination test—demonstration of immunoglobulin G 'rheumatoid factor'.

Patients are classified according to the number of criteria satisfied into 'classical'—7, 'definite'—5 and 'probable'—3. There are 21 exclusion criteria used to avoid confusion with other causes of arthritis.

X-rays are important in evaluating patients' rheumatoid arthritis, and it is normal procedure to take yearly X-rays of the hands and feet of these patients, as it is easier to determine factors such as bony erosion, bone density and texture and loss of joint space. There are no routine diagnostic tests for rheumatoid arthritis, except that of joint aspiration. This is performed to withdraw synovial fluid from a painful joint with a large effusion; the most common joints for this procedure are the knees and shoulders. A large-bore needle is inserted into the joint space to aspirate the fluid. Since this procedure has the potential

for introducing bacteria into the joint, aseptic technique is followed. Following aspiration, a sample of the fluid can be sent to the laboratory for culture.

Normally, synovial fluid is clear, viscous, straw-coloured and scanty in volume, with few cells. The fluid is examined for volume, viscosity, glucose value, white blood cells and its ability to form a mucin clot. It is examined microscopically for cell count, cell identification, Gram stain and formed elements. In inflammatory joint disease, the fluid often becomes cloudy, milky or dark yellow and contains numerous inflammatory cells such as leucocytes and complement, a plasma-protein associated with immunological reactions. The viscosity is reduced in inflammatory disease, and copious amounts of fluid may be present. Blood in the fluid specimen suggests trauma or tendency to bleed.

► *Patient's Problems*

Based on the nursing assessment, the patient's main problems may include the following:

1. Pain, related to movement of inflamed joints.
2. Impaired physical mobility related to restricted joint movement.
3. Self-care deficits (feeding, bathing, dressing, toileting) related to fatigue and joint stiffness.
4. Disturbances in self-concept related to the physical and psychological tendency seen with this chronic illness and a loss of independence.
5. Alteration in nutrition related to inadequate food intake.
6. Alteration in body weight— underweight due to anorexia or overweight due to the inability to cook a balanced diet and a reliance on 'convenience' foods.

► *Planning and Implementation*
► Expected Outcomes

The main outcomes for the patient may include the relief of pain and discomfort, increased mobility, activity and exercise tolerance, achievement of an optimal, individual level of independence in activities of living, attainment/maintenance of a positive self-concept, an attainment/maintenance of optimal nutrition and correct body weight for age and height.

Nursing Care

Relieving Pain and Discomfort

Nursing measures to relieve pain include warm and cold applications, promotion of rest, proper positioning of body and limbs and the use of supportive devices.

Warm and Cold Applications. Heat applications are often helpful in relieving pain, stiffness, inflammation and muscle spasm. Superficial heat may be supplied in the form of warm baths and warm, moist compresses. Physiotherapy exercises can sometimes be carried out more comfortably and effectively after heat has been applied. However, in some cases, heat may actually increase pain, muscle spasm and synovial fluid volume. If the inflammatory process is acute, cold applications may be applied in the form of moist packs or ice-bags. At home, the patient may use a packet of frozen peas from the freezer in this way. Both heat and cold are analgesic to nerve pain receptors and relax muscle spasms.

Rest. Rest can also help to allay pain. Since rheumatoid arthritis is a systemic disease, the whole patient and not merely the joints must be treated. The amount of rest required is indicated by the amount of inflammatory involvement and by the patient's needs. When in bed the patient should lie flat on a firm mattress with two or three pillows layered under the shoulders, cervical spine and head to prevent the risk of dorsal kyphosis. Pillows can be used as a support for some joints in bed but should never be placed under the knee, as this promotes flexion deformities of these joints.

The patient should be encouraged to pace the day by having frequent periods of rest either in a bed or chair to take the weight off the joints and relieve fatigue. If joint inflammation is severe, the patient may undergo modified bedrest for brief periods. If this is the case, the physiotherapist should be involved as soon as possible to help the patient with a range of passive exercises to maintain muscle tone; the nurse will then carry on with these out-of-hours but should always ensure that joints are supported in a position of optimum function.

Positioning and Posture. Proper body posture is essential for the patient in pain in order to minimize stress on inflamed joints. It includes walking as erect as possible and sitting in chairs that have straight backs so that the feet can rest flat on the floor and the shoulders and hips can rest against the back of the chair. When in bed, the patient should avoid extreme joint flexion, and the patient's knees should not be flexed on pillows. Passive exercises are encouraged because they help to prevent joint stiffness.

Assistive and Supportive Devices. Cervical collars may be prescribed to support the cervical spine for periods during the day or night if patients are experiencing pain, stiffness and limitation in movement of the cervical spine. However, it is important that the physiotherapist and the nurse ensure that the patient does not become too dependent on this device. Metatarsal pads may be put into standard shoes if pain or deformity is present. Splints can be used to support and immobilize joints such as wrist joints; they provide rest, support the joints in an optimal position to relieve pain and spasm and help to prevent deformity. Above all, the joints should not be permitted to be immobilized in positions of flexion, which is their natural tendency because of the predominant strength of flexor muscles. The knee is splinted at full extension, and the wrist at slight dorsoflexion. Splints may need to be modified when changes occur in joint structure.

Medication

Drug therapy is used to relieve inflammation and pain, to suppress the disease and to alter its progression. Nursing responsibilities include assessing the patient's need for medication and identifying the cause of the pain. For example, if the patient is in an acute phase of the disease, the nurse will have to consider the pain management holistically, supplementing medication with alternative forms of pain control such as relaxation in the treatment plan (Maycock, 1985). However, if the patient is in the chronic stage of rheumatoid arthritis, pain may well be due to mechanical damage within the joint space, in which case medication will probably not be of any value. When teaching the patient about medication, the nurse needs to help the patient understand how it affects the disease process and also how to observe for side-effects.

Increasing Mobility, Activity and Exercise Tolerance

Inflammation or structural damage to joints results in pain and disability. In an effort to avoid pain, the patient tends to immobilize the affected joints, and muscular spasm further limits their motion. Muscle, ligament and tendon atrophy and deformity may occur. All exercise regimes need to be prescribed by a trained physiotherapist as patients with rheumatoid arthritis have vulnerable joints, especially during a flare of the disease. Although it is imperative that muscle strength is maintained and in some cases increased, this should be done with great care.

Promoting Independence

In order to become independent the patient should be referred to the occupational therapist by the nurse for advice on aids for daily living, for example, a bath board to enable the patient to get into the bath on their own. After this assessment, it is important that the nurse works with the patient to achieve the expected outcomes of self-care and independence. The patient with rheumatoid arthritis will often take longer to do things, but nurses must be patient and allow extra time for patients to perform simple tasks on their own, such as the delicate movements needed for fastening items of clothing and opening small packages. The nurse should work with the occupational therapist and physiotherapist to teach the patient how to perform difficult tasks. There are many self-help devices available to assist with dressing, bathing and eating (Figure 27.3). When there is difficulty in mobilization, sticks or frames can be prescribed as assistive devices to reduce the amount of weight-bearing on the joints of the lower extremities. Well-fitted supportive shoes should be worn when walking to protect ankle joints and feet and prevent falls. Custom-made corrective shoes are used to prevent further foot deformity and provide support. When mobility is severely impaired and relief of pain by conventional

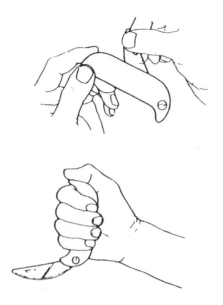

Figure 27.3 Special knife handle fits comfortably into the hand, and a simple rocking action can be used for cutting. (From *Joint Protection and Rehabilitation in Chronic Rheumatic Disorders*, Wolfe Medical, p. 156.)

drug therapy fails, reconstructive joint surgery may restore some function and reduce pain. Many patients receive total joint replacement to achieve pain control and increase mobility.

Promoting a Positive Self-Concept

Patients with arthritis show the same fundamental psychological responses to their disease as people with other chronic disease: fear, anxiety, depression, anger and loss. However, the unpredictability and uncertainty of the course of the disease will disadvantage this patient still further.

All aspects of the patient's life, including work role, social life, sexual functioning and financial status may be altered. Body image changes may cause social isolation and depression (Maycock, 1988, p. 129). The resulting strain on the patient, family and close friends contributes in many instances to the patient's low morale. The nurse should encourage patients to express their feelings of hostility or depression rather than to suppress them. Failure of communication also leads to deterioration of interpersonal relationships. The nurse and the patient's friends and/or relatives should try to understand the patient's personality and emotional reactions to the disease. Presenting a realistic but optimistic view by pointing out that only a small percentage of patients become totally disabled can help reassure the patient and loved ones. It is also important that the multidisciplinary team have frequent meetings and liaise closely to formulate a common treatment strategy to eliminate confusion of information given to the

patient by individual professionals. This will then serve as a valuable resource for reassurance and promotion of a patient's positive self-concept.

Promoting Optimal Nutrition

Patients with rheumatoid arthritis frequently experience anorexia, weight loss and anaemia. A dietary history should be taken by a dietician for each patient to determine usual eating habits and food preferences. The dietician and nurse can then teach the patient how to select foods to include the daily requirements from the basic four food groups (proteins, fats, carbohydrates and minerals), with emphasis on foods high in vitamins, protein and iron for tissue building and repair. For the extremely anorexic patient, small, frequent meals with increased protein supplement may be prescribed. Care must be taken to prevent obesity. Excess weight causes increased stress on weight-bearing joints, creating further joint damage. If obesity is already present, a reduction diet is prescribed.

Patient Education

Patient are usually unfamiliar with their disease process and treatment regime and need to feel confident to talk about their concerns and ask questions. The nurse begins by assessing the patient's knowledge-base (Maycock, 1991), interest level, ability to learn and degree of physical comfort. Information is provided in a quiet and private area at a time when the patient is comfortable and well rested. Teaching sessions should not exceed 30 minutes at one sitting. A family member or support person should be present when the patient is discharged from hospital, when advice is given for treatments such as ice-packs, baths, positioning, exercises and the use of assistive devices. The patient should be allowed sufficient time to ask questions, handle equipment and practise as necessary. Reinforcement and encouragement should be provided as needed.

When the patient has returned home, a district nurse will be asked to make an assessment in the patient's home to identify whether the patient is functioning independently without any mobility problems, and is able to safely manage treatments and drug therapy. Referral to voluntary group such as Arthritis Care, a support group for sufferers of arthritis, can be an extremely valuable source of support in the community.

Before the nurse can plan nursing care for this patient, clear criteria must be formed to enable information to be collected and an assessment of the patient's problems to be made.

The Arthritis Impact Measurement Scale (AIMS) forms such a framework and targets the nurse's questioning on particular patient problem areas such as: (1) mobility (activities of daily living); (2) dexterity; (3) social role (depression); and (4) social activity (see Table 27.1).

Table 27.1 *Arthritis Impact Measurement Scales (AIMS)**

Mobility

4* Are you in a bed or in a chair for most of the day because of your health?

3 Are you able to use public transportation?

2 When you travel around your community, does someone have to assist you because of your health?

1 Do you have to stay indoors most or all of the day because of your health?

Physical activity

4 Are you unable to walk unless you are assisted by another person or by a stick, crutches, artificial limbs or braces?

3 Do you have any trouble either walking several streets or climbing a few flights of stairs because of your health?

2 Do you have any trouble bending, lifting, or stooping because of your health?

1 Does your health limit the kinds of vigorous activities you can do, such as running, lifting heavy objects or participating in strenuous sports?

Dexterity

5 Can you easily write with a pen or pencil?

4 Can you easily turn a key in a lock?

3 Can you easily button articles of clothing?

2 Can you easily tie up a pair of shoe-laces?

1 Can you easily open a tin of food?

Social role

7 If you had to take medicine, could you take all your own medicine?

6 If you had a telephone, would you be able to use it?

5 Do you handle your own money?

4 If you had a kitchen, could you prepare your own meals?

3 If you had laundry facilities (washer, dryer) could you do your own laundry?

2 If you had the necessary transport, could you go shopping for groceries or clothes?

1 If you had household tools and appliances (e.g. vaccuum cleaner, mops) could you do your own housework?

Social activity

5 About how often have you been on the telephone with close friends or relatives during the past month?

4 Has there been a change in the frequency or quality of your sexual relationships during the past month?

3 During the past month how often have you had friends or relatives to your home?

2 During the past month how often have you got together socially with friends or relatives? '

1 During the past month, how often have you visited friends or relatives at their homes?

Activities of daily living

4 How much help do you need to use the toilet?

3 How well are you able to move around?

2 How much help do you need in getting dressed?

1 When you wash by strip wash, bath or shower, how much help do you need?

Pain

4 During the past month, how often have you had severe pain from your arthritis?

3 During the past month, how would you describe the arthritis pain you usually have?

2 During the past month, how long has your morning stiffness usually lasted from the time you wake up?

1 During the past month, how often have you had pain in two or more joints at the same time?

▶

* High scores reflect more limitation. (From: Meenan, R. F., Gertman, P. M. and Mason, J. H. (1980) Measuring health status in arthritis: The Arthritis Impact Scales, Arthritis and Rheumatism, Vol. 23, No. 2, pp. 146–52. Used by permission of the American Rheumatism Association.)

Table 27.1 *Continued*

Depression

6 During the past month, how often have you felt that others would be better off if you were dead?

5 How often during the past month have you felt so down in the dumps that nothing could cheer you up?

4 How much of the time during the past month have you felt downhearted and blue?

3 How often during the past month have you felt that nothing has turned out for you the way you wanted it to?

2 During the past month, how much of the time have you been in low or very low spirits?

1 During the past month, how much of the time have you enjoyed the things you do?

Anxiety

6 During the past month, how much of the time have you felt tense or 'highly strung'?

5 How much have you been bothered by nervousness and your 'nerves' during the past month?

4 How often during the past month have you found yourself having difficulty trying to calm down?

3 How much of the time during the past month have you been able to relax without difficulty?

2 How much of the time during the past month have you felt calm and peaceful?

1 How much of the time during the past month have you felt relaxed and free of tension?

► NURSING CARE PLAN 27.1: THE PATIENT WITH RHEUMATOID ARTHRITIS

Mary Hughes is 77 years old and lives alone, her husband having died two years previously. She has no children, but her elderly brother and sister (both married) live nearby. Mrs Hughes is a practising Christian (Church of England).

Patient's problems	Expected outcomes	Nursing care	Rationale
1. Complaining of an acute episode of the disease process resulting in hot, swollen and painful shoulders, wrists and knee joints	Reduction of inflammation and pain	1a. Regular administration of anti-inflammatory and analgesic drugs b. Ensure correct position in bed, with good support of cervical spine, shoulders c. Check mattress for bumps and ridges d. Encourage the use of cervical collar and resting splints for wrists e. Frequent position changes f. Apply cold packs to wrists and shoulders g. Use of a bed cradle h. Use of adjustable height table at meal times i. Adjust height of bed to facilitate ease of getting in and out on own	Anti-inflammatory analgesic drugs will help to reduce inflammation and pain but it is equally important to identify problems that increase pain (Maycock, 1985)
2. Change in skin integrity	Improve condition of skin	2a. Ensure rheumatoid nodules on elbows are protected by use of sheepskin pads b. Ensure elbow crutches are padded to ensure elbows are protected from hard edges c. Frequent change of position to relieve pressure on thin, fragile skin d. Avoid trauma to skin when moving patient – educate all staff, i.e. porters and radiologist	Changes in the skin integrity in rheumatoid arthritis are known to be related to the disease process, the drugs used for treatment and difficulty in maintaining skin integrity (Maycock, 1983)

► NURSING CARE PLAN 27.1: THE PATIENT WITH RHEUMATOID ARTHRITIS

Patient's problems	Expected outcomes	Nursing care	Rationale
		e. Ensure skin is kept clean and dry, particularly around deformities of joints, i.e. toes f. Observe for fasculitic lesions on skin, especially around nail folds and legs g. Observe for skin rash due to gold treatment h. Observe for skin fragility and bruising i. If skin is dry and thin encourage patient to use a hydrating cream in the washing water and apply to skin after washing (Aqueous Cream BP)	
3. Decreased mobility	Improve mobility	3a. Ensure analgesic and anti-inflammatory drugs are given before activity b. Refer to physiotherapist for muscle strengthening exercises once the 'flare' of symphonis has reduced c. Reinforce therapist's instructions on how to use walking aids d. Refer patient for hydrotherapy and passive range of movements to be carried out e. Flexion deformity of knees require implementation of the physiotherapist's exercise plan f. Encourage patient to understand the cause of the impaired mobility, i.e. muscle wasting, unstable or painful joints g. Help patient to understand that joint noises may be experienced (crepitus) when weight bearing, but that this is not harmful	The occurrence of flexion deformities and inflammation of ligaments and tendons will hinder mobilization. In addition pain, stiffness and/or decreased strength or endurance can be influencing factors
4. Disturbed sleep pattern	Improve sleep pattern	4a. Ensure patient is given anti-inflammatory drugs and analgesics at night b. Help patient into a comfortable position for sleep, ensuring cervical spine is not flexed and no pillows are under knees c. Assist patient to apply resting splints for night use d. Help patient to change position at regular intervals to reduce stiffness in joints e. Offer patient warm packs for painful joints before going to sleep	Rest is an important part of treatment as it provides freedom from physical and emotional activity and serves to decrease the inflammatory process, thus restoring affected tissues

►

► **NURSING CARE PLAN 27.1: THE PATIENT WITH RHEUMATOID ARTHRITIS**

Patient's problems	Expected outcomes	Nursing care	Rationale
		f. Reduce anxiety about treatment by explaining treatment programme and allow frequent opportunities to answer questions as they arise g. Explain to patient that the requirement for sleep diminishes as one gets older	
5. Stiffness in all joints	Reduction of stiffness lasting approximately 4 hours	5a. Administer anti-inflammatory and analgesic drugs at least one hour before expected mobility b. Warm bath before mobilizing c. Encourage to soak hands and wrists in warm water at regular intervals to reduce stiffness d. Help to understand relationship between activity and stiffness e. Careful use of hot packs to stiff joints f. Help to put joints through a gentle range of movement after bath or hot packs	Stiffness usually occurs after a period of inactivity such as night-time rest. Application of warmth and the scheduling of strenuous activity such as weight bearing after the peak of stiffness is of great benefit (Rodnan, Schumacher and Zaifler, 1983)
6. Low self-esteem	Build up self-confidence, promote independence and achieve goals	6a. Set achievable goals with patient b. Encourage and demonstrate improvement, i.e. measured walks and group strength recording c. Obtain aids for daily living from occupational therapist to encourage independence d. Help patient to feel 'in control' of what is happening to her by offering choices e. Help patient to understand disease process and relevant medication f. Help brother and sister to learn how to be supportive listeners but not to be over-protective	If realistic goals are achieved so as to give the patient as much control as possible over her treatment and a good understanding of the disease, reconciliation between self-concept, physical and psychological changes may be achieved (Miller, 1963)
7. Anorexia and weight loss	Reduce anorexia and maintain or increase body weight	7a. Identify those foods which will tempt patient to eat b. Refer to dietician for a dietary assessment c. Provide dietary supplements high in calories but low in volume d. Provide assistive eating devices, e.g. large-handled cutlery e. Provide small, regular meals f. Offer fluids at meal times to relieve dry mouth due to Sjögren's syndrome g. Ensure patient is in an upright position during meal times to aid swallowing	Inadequate nutrition may be related to lack of knowledge about a good diet, disability or the disease process. Therefore, the nurse needs to identify the reason for anorexia and weight loss (Smith Pigg, Webb-Driscoll and Caniff, 1985)

Patient's problems	Expected outcomes	Nursing care	Rationale
		h. Provide unhurried atmosphere at meal times i. Encourage brother or sister to bring in small, home-cooked snacks or meals j. Ensure that referral for a home help and Meals on Wheels is made when the patient is discharged if she is unable to shop and prepare food	

Nursing Care Plan 27.1 is an example of how the nurse identifies the patient's problems and the expected out comes of nursing care, and formulates a plan of care based on a sound rationale.

OSTEOARTHRITIS (OSTEOARTHROSIS)

Osteoarthritis is often known as degenerative joint disease and is a common disorder caused by the degeneration of the articular cartilage in synovial joints. It is linked closely to the process of ageing, and its prevalence increases sharply with advancing age. Osteoarthritis is the most frequently encountered of all the rheumatic diseases; it is interesting to note that it occurs in about 20 per cent of the population and is more common in women. The most common age of onset is around 50 years, although it can start between 40 and 65 years of age. Although about 50 per cent of the population will have X-ray changes after the age of 55 (Huskisson and Dudley Hart, 1987, pp. 102–3), only about 50 per cent of these patients will have actual symptoms.

Altered Physiology

The histological changes include irregularity and flaking of the surface of the articular cartilage, known as fibrillation. This irregularity increases in depth and width, and eventually the appearance of vertical fissures may be seen. In parallel to this, the underlying bone becomes more dense with the development of chondrocytes which form around the fissures, and as the bone becomes more dense or sclerotic, projections called osteophytes (formed from ossified cartilage) grow out from the edges of the joint margin (Figure 27.4). All these processes within the articular cartilage may continue until the underlying bone is exposed, after which the bone ends may become smooth and polished, a process known as eburnation. Fibrosis of the capsule and mild inflammatory changes in the synovium then take place.

As the joint undergoes repeated chemical stress, the elasticity of the joint capsule, articular cartilage and ligaments is reduced. The articular plate is thinned, and its function as a shock-absorber is decreased. The joint cartilage degenerates and atrophies. The bone hardens and hypertrophies at articular surfaces and the ligaments calcify. As a result, sterile joint effusions and secondary synovitis may be present, particularly in the knee.

It is important to realize that certain other medical conditions can lead to osteoarthritis or determine its develop-

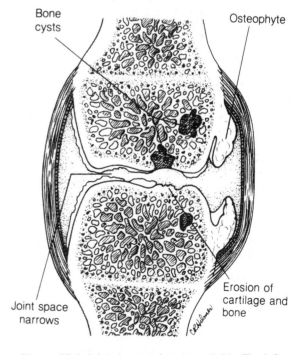

Figure 27.4 Joint changes in osteoarthritis. The left side denotes early changes, joint space narrowing with cartilage breakdown. The right side shows more severe disease progression with lost cartilage and osteophyte formation. (Porth, C. M. (1986) *Pathophysiology: Concepts of Altered Health States* (2nd edition), J. B. Lippincott, Philadelphia.)

ment at a particular site. This is known as secondary osteoarthritis:

1. Hypermobility of joints, which results in abnormality in the position of joint surfaces.
2. Traumatized joints, for example dislocation, fractures involving the joint surface, obesity.
3. Gout due to crystal deposition in the joint.
4. Avascular necrosis.

Clinical Features

The primary clinical features are pain, stiffness and functional impairment. Pain gets worse towards the evening and is aggravated by weight-bearing. Morning stiffness occurs in 80 per cent of patients; it lasts between 10 and 30 minutes and is often localized to one or two joints. Stiffness after inactivity is also noted and can last from 5 to 30 minutes. Functional impairment is due to a reduced range-of-joint movement that occurs when structural changes develop in the joint. Joint crepitus is the sensation of roughness that is transmitted from a moving joint on weight-bearing or palpation, which gives an audible crunch.

Although osteoarthritis occurs most often in weight-bearing joints (hips and knees), finger joints are frequently involved. Osteoarthritis is seen in the uppermost and middle joints of the fingers (distal interphalangeal joints and the proximal interphalangeals). Characteristic bony nodules, called Heberden's nodes may be present, which may be painful and inflamed on inspection. After months or years, the inflammatory features pass, leaving bony swelling and sometimes flexion, valgus or varus deformities. Nodes that appear on the proximal interphalangeal joints are called Bouchard's nodes. Both are bony enlargements that appear in a bilateral and symmetrical pattern (Figure 27.5).

Because osteoarthritis is a chronic disease, it progresses slowly with exacerbations and remissions. During the course of the disease, joints may develop painful restrictions of movement with resulting deformities, particularly of weight-bearing joints.

Diagnosis

As osteoarthritis is not a systemic disease, the sedimentation rate and haemoglobin are not altered in any way by the progression of the disease, and so laboratory testing is not indicated. It must be remembered that local synovitis may cause a slight elevation in sedimentation rate. The use of X-rays is important, however, both in establishing the diagnosis of osteoarthritis, grading its severity, and in differentiating inflammatory from degenerative arthritis. In osteoarthritis, the X-rays will build up a picture of what the bone density looks like and, if it is sclerotic, the joint space will be noted as to any reduction and cysts, and osteophytes will be identified easily.

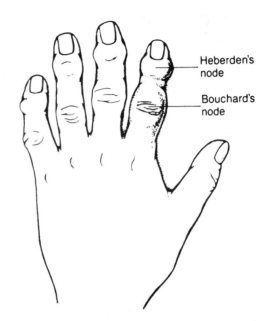

Heberden's node

Bouchard's node

Figure 27.5 Hand deformities commonly seen in osteoarthritis.

Management

Medical management focuses on treating the symptoms because there is no treatment available at present that slows down the degenerative joint disease process (Panayi, 1980). The use of medication for this form of arthritis is limited. The first line of treatment should be to use simple analgesics, and to progress to the nonsteroidal anti-inflammatory agents only when the patient gives a history of stiffness and pain. Intra-articular injections of cortisone are rarely used in osteoarthritis as there is rarely any synovitis in the joint and its use carries the risk of degradation of the articular cartilage.

Physiotherapy has an important role in the treatment of osteoarthritis. This treatment can be extremely helpful in aiding the build-up of wasting and weak muscles, as joint stability depends on the pull of these muscles. Conservative measures include the use of heat, weight reduction and encouraging the patient to keep the joints mobile. Surgery is recommended when conservative measures are ineffective and joint pain and immobility is spoiling the patient's quality of life. Therefore, in severe cases surgery such as total hip replacement, total knee replacement or osteotomy to relieve pain or correct deformity may be offered.

▶ **NURSING PROCESS**
▶ **THE PATIENT WITH OSTEOARTHRITIS**

▶ *Assessment*

The nursing history is structured to obtain information about mobility, social activities and the emotional response to the disorder. The patient's ability to perform activities of living adequately is assessed. Because osteoarthritis is specific to the musculoskeletal system, the nurse uses techniques of inspection, palpation and joint movement to assess function or impairment. The patient's gait and mobility and any difficulties with ambulation are observed, and muscle spasm and crepitus are noted, if present. Joints are palpated for swelling, effusion, enlargement and the presence of bony nodules. Palpation may elicit tenderness in early degeneration or severe pain in the advanced stages of the disease. Pain which tends to worsen with activity and improve with rest is the most common symptom of osteoarthritis.

Once joints are inspected and palpated, they are evaluated for range of movement. In severe disease, joint movement is markedly compromised. The vertebral column is assessed because the spine is frequently involved in patients with degenerative disease. Limitations in movement of the cervical and lumbar areas, with the accompanying increase in pain, are indicative of spinal involvement. A detailed discussion of the technique for joint assessment is found in the appropriate section for Rheumatoid Arthritis, above.

▶ Patients' Problems

Based on the nursing history, the patient's major problems may include the following:

1. Pain, related to joint degeneration and muscle spasm.
2. Impaired physical mobility related to limited joint movement.
3. Self-care deficit related to limited joint movement.

▶ Planning and Implementation
▶ Expected Outcomes

The main outcomes for the patient may include some relief of pain and discomfort, an increase in physical mobility and endurance, and attainment of an optimal level of independence in activities of living.

Nursing Care

Relief of Pain and Discomfort

Measures for relief of pain, stiffness and muscle spasm are generally the same as those used for rheumatoid arthritis. They include rest with alternating periods of activity, an exercise programme, heat application and joint protection. A weight reduction diet may be required to reduce stress on weight-bearing joints. The nurse should help the patient to understand the purpose of the prescribed regime and work with the patient in planning the implementation of rest, exercise, diet and heat treatment. The purpose, action, side-effects and schedule for taking the prescribed drugs are also part of the nurse's role in helping patients to understand their treatment.

Independence

Nursing care for promoting mobility and independence is the same as that employed for patients with rheumatoid arthritis. Joint pain and muscle spasm decrease joint movements and the ability of patients to care for themselves. Nurses need to work closely with patients and families to help them understand the disease process, as all too often these patients have experienced being told by health professionals and the public that they have arthritis and that they must learn to live with it. Because of the chronic nature of the pain, patients often feel that they cannot unburden themselves too often upon those closely around them, so it is important that the nurse offers time in private to the patient to discuss these feelings.

SYSTEMIC LUPUS ERYTHEMATOSUS

Systemic lupus erythematosus is a chronic inflammatory disease of unknown origin that can affect virtually any part of the body. It is an autoimmune disease, producing circulating immune complexes, and is characterized by the presence of anti-nuclear factor and other auto-antibodies. These proteins may accumulate in the skin, for example, causing a variety of skin rashes, or stick to the walls of blood vessels or deposit in the kidney, brain, lungs and joints. The onset of the disease is most common between the ages of 20 and 40, more specifically in women, is rare before the start of menstrual periods and very rare after the menopause. There is a high incidence in non-Caucasians.

The aetiology of systemic lupus erythematosus is unknown. Although a genetic link has not been found, there is a familial association, which suggests that a genetic predisposition may be related to environmental factors or susceptibility to certain viruses. Certain drugs such as hydralazine hydrochloride, and some anticonvulsant drugs have been thought to trigger the onset of symptoms or aggravate an existing disease.

Clinical Features

The onset of systemic lupus erythematosus may be insidious or acute. If insidious, the symptoms may be mild and vague, and for this reason the patient with systemic lupus erythematosus may have a delayed diagnosis. Alternatively, the disorder may strike as an acute and severe illness. Early diagnosis and effective early treatment has meant that a normal life span and lifestyle can be expected for the majority of patients (Hughes, 1982, p. 229). Initially, the patient may experience extreme fatigue, generalized weakness and anorexia. Fatigue has been reported to be the most frustrating symptom. Weight loss, fever, rash and signs of joint inflammation alert the doctor to suspect the diagnosis of systemic lupus erythematosus.

About 50 per cent of patients have no tangible signs of the disease, although slight soft tissue swelling can be identified on examination. This is often disproportionate to the symptoms. Fever will be experienced by 90 per cent of patients. Huskisson and Dudley Hart (1987, pp. 153–4) suggest that 80 per cent of patients will have skin involvement, 65 per cent will have renal involvement, 40 per cent will present with pleural effusion, 30 per cent with pericarditis and 30 per cent with disorders of mental function. Another presenting problem is photosensitivity in 30 per cent of cases. Life-threatening vasculitis (vessel wall inflammation) decreases the blood supply to major organs, causing necrosis and dysfunction. Hepatomegaly but not jaundice is experienced by 25 per cent of patients, and 10 per cent of patients experience splenomegaly. Gastrointestinal problems such as nausea and vomiting, oesophagitis and abdominal pain are common. Recurrent pneumonitis and unexplained dyspnoea may be due to airway obstruction, reduced vital capacity or reduced lung compliance. Hypertension and peripheral vascular disease result from peripheral vasculitis.

Raynaud's phenomenon is common in systemic lupus erythematosus and results from vasospasm from smaller vessels in the hands and feet. On exposure to cold, the vessels constrict, resulting in the characteristic white to blue to red colour changes. These attacks of vasoconstriction and may lead to necrosis with eventual distal digital amputation. This condition appears in 30 per cent of patients with systemic lupus erythematosus. Seventy per cent of patients survive five years, and 50 per cent ten years. However, prognosis is much worse with renal involvement.

Diagnosis

Diagnosis is based on a complete history and an analysis of the results of blood investigations. The doctor is looking for the classic symptoms of fever, fatigue and weight loss, and assessing for arthritis, pleurisy and pericarditis. There is no single definitive laboratory test in the diagnosis of systemic lupus erythematosus. Serum testing reveals moderate to severe anaemia, thrombocytopenia and leucocytosis or leucopenia. Other diagnostic immunological tests support but often do not confirm the diagnosis.

Management

Management is directed towards quick treatment of the clinical symptoms. Corticosteroids are usually the first line of management, being the only drugs that will suppress systemic lupus erythematosus inflammation. They are usually started in quite high doses of between 30 to 600 mg of prednisolone daily, but in severe disease may be up to 120 mg daily. The dose is then gradually reduced to a maintenance of 15 mg daily, as the condition im-

proves. It is common practice to introduce another drug, known as a steroid sparer, to suppress the disease; in many cases, the antimalarial drugs (e.g., chloroquine) are of great use (Hughes, 1982, p. 303). Antimalarial drugs take a few weeks to work. However, once they are effective the steroid dose will be reduced. Other classes of drugs used in the treatment of systemic lupus erythematosus are the nonsteroidal anti-inflammatory drugs and immunosuppressive and cytotoxic agents. Antibiotics and certain other drugs are used with caution because of the possibility of hypersensitivity reactions.

► NURSING PROCESS
► THE PATIENT WITH SYSTEMIC LUPUS ERYTHEMATOSUS

► *Assessment*

The nurse performs a thorough, systematic physical assessment of the patient, beginning with the major body organs. The skin is inspected for any skin rashes, which are examined for appearance, size and sensitivity to sunlight. The typical butterfly rash over the bridge of the nose is characteristic of systemic lupus erythematosus (Figure 27.6). If alopecia is present, the patient is advised that the hair loss is usually temporary. Any behavioural changes, neurosis or psychosis are noted. The nurse will record the heart rate and rhythm because valvular damage can occur when scar tissue forms as a result of tissue inflammation. Pericarditis and myocarditis may be present, along with friction rubs, tamponade and heart murmurs. Peripheral pulses are palpated for rate and volume. The patient's respiratory rate will also be assessed for signs of respiratory insufficiency or wheeziness.

Renal involvement is seen in 65 per cent of patients, but only 5 per cent of these will demonstrate symptoms. The nurse therefore assesses the patient for oedema of the ankles, haematuria and proteinuria. A 24-hour urinary collection is sent to the laboratory for serum creatinine levels to be quantified. Any behavioural changes indicating confusion or extreme lethargy are reported to the doctor.

The patient usually complains of pain and stiffness in some of the joints. A complete joint assessment similar to that described under 'Rheumatoid Arthritis' should be conducted. Patients with systemic lupus erythematosus usually have a low grade fever, fatigue and a diminished sense of self-worth related not only to the symptoms of the disease but also to the impact of being told that they have a multi-faceted, serious illness.

► *Patient's Problems*

The patient's main problems should have been identified based on the information collected in the nursing assessment, and may include the following:

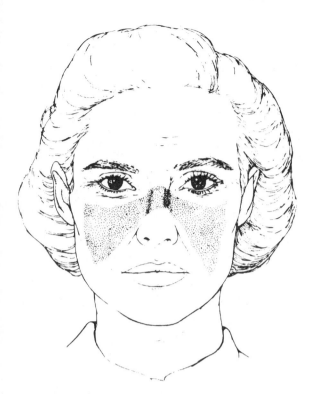

Figure 27.6 Butterfly rash of systemic lupus erythematosus.

1. Impairment of skin integrity related to photosensitivity and vasculitis.
2. Activity intolerance related to fatigue.
3. Disturbance in self-concept related to body image changes.
4. Pain, related to restricted joint movement.
5. Anticipatory grieving related to the unpredictability of a chronic, potentially fatal disease.
6. Self-care deficits related to musculoskeletal impairment.
7. Alteration in nutrition related to inadequate food intake.

► *Planning and Implementation*
► **Expected Outcomes**

The main outcomes for the patient may include maintenance of skin integrity, decreased fatigue and weakness, attainment of a positive self-concept, relief of pain and discomfort, appropriate use of the grieving process, attainment of independence in activities of daily living and attainment of optimal nutrition.

Nursing Care

Maintenance of Skin Integrity

The skin rash of systemic lupus erythematosus is often scaly, itchy and red. Cool baths may decrease discomfort and scaliness. The skin should be kept clean, and the patient should be helped to understand that cosmetics with perfumes should not be used because they could dry the skin. Topical corticosteroid creams or ointments may be applied, as prescribed, to decrease inflammation.

The nurse reinforces the doctor's explanation concerning the need to avoid sunlight and ultraviolet lights. Long-sleeved clothing, wide-brimmed hats and trousers are worn to protect the skin. Sunscreen with a maximum protection factor rating should be applied to uncovered skin areas, and sunglasses should be worn to decrease photosensitivity.

The nurse should observe for the presence or spread of superficial vasculitic lesions. Appropriate skin hygiene measures, such as keeping the skin clean and dry but moisturized, help to prevent skin breakdown.

Fatigue and Weakness

Patients with systemic lupus erythematosus often experience severe fatigue and generalized weakness. One of the first priorities in looking after these patients is helping them to understand how to conserve energy. Frequent rest periods combined with a 10 to 12 hour sleep each night is usually helpful in decreasing fatigue. The principles of energy conservation must be followed to avoid severe fatigue. The patient is helped to participate in a moderate exercise programme under the direction of a physiotherapist, which can increase endurance, strengthen muscle groups and improve activity tolerance.

Promoting a Positive Self-Concept

One of the major changes in body image is the presence of the erythematous rash on the face and other parts of the body. Even when the disease is in remission, the rash may not disappear. Patients with systemic lupus erythematosus, particularly young women, are usually very concerned about disfigurement caused by the rash (Maycock, 1988, pp. 130–1). The patient can be advised by the nurse how to use non-allergic cosmetics to camouflage the rash. However, some people may need specialized help, and the British Red Cross Society provides cosmetic counsellors.

In addition to the skin abnormalities, joint swelling, severe fatigue and weakness and the unpredictability of the disease contribute to poor self-concept. The nurse, family and close friends should try to understand this reaction and approach the subject in a realistic but optimistic manner. Further discussion on this expected outcome is found in the section on rheumatoid arthritis.

Relief of Pain

In addition to administering anti-inflammatory drugs or other prescribed drugs for the relief of joint and muscle pain, the nurse helps the patient to achieve maximum comfort by establishing ways of coping with the disease during a flare-up. Because fatigue, a major symptom of systemic lupus erythematosus, increases vulnerability to pain, the nurse reinforces the importance for adequate sleep and daily rest periods balanced with moderate exercise. Because stress also exacerbates pain, the patient is encouraged to express feelings about the problems associated with systemic lupus erythematosus. The patient and caregiver are involved with planning daily activities to prevent the build-up of pressure, and in promoting a supportive environment that helps reduce emotional stress. The nurse can direct both the sufferer and caregiver to self-help groups where they can meet similar people with similar problems.

The patient with systemic lupus erythematosus may be overwhelmed by the effects and implications of the condition. Grief is a common reaction to the discomforts and restrictions imposed by the disease and to the possibility of life-threatening complications. Helping patients to come to terms with this is an important part of the nursing role. The nurse accepts and validates these feelings and encourages the expression of fear and concern. The patient and caregiver are helped to identify their individual and collective strengths to support one another to enable the patient to resume some activities that were enjoyed previously. The nurse and other members of the health care team should be supportive throughout the grieving process.

Independence

Joint involvement combined with fatigue, weakness and muscle inflammation may alter a patient's ability to perform normal everyday tasks independently. The nurse assesses the coping ability of patients and helps them to identify coping mechanisms that have worked in the past. They are encouraged to resume activity gradually and to increase efforts as they gain skill in managing their lives. Activity is alternated with rest periods, to avoid over-fatigue and stress.

Nutrition

Anorexia may be compounded by dysphagia from oesophagitis. Food selection for the dysphagic patient includes foods of soft, bolus type consistency such as mashed potato and minced meat. Liquids and hard, brittle foods are the most difficult for the dysphagic patient to swallow. Foods high in protein, vitamins and iron are encouraged, with supplementary feeding added as necessary to maintain weight.

SYSTEMIC SCLEROSIS (SCLERODERMA)

Systemic sclerosis is a progressive disease characterized by inflammation of subcutaneous connective tissue, followed by progressive fibrosis and degenerative changes and a fibrotic process in other organs, particularly the oesophagus. Progressive fibrosis leads to secondary atrophy of the skin, subcutaneous fat, sweat glands and hair follicles, plus arteritis of the skin vessels. Scleroderma is thought to be an autoimmune disease that affects females three times more commonly than males, the peak age being between 20 and 50 years of onset. The fingers are the most common joints affected but any other joint may also be affected. The worst prognosis is seen when onset starts over the age of 40.

The disease has a variable course with remissions and exacerbations. It often begins with skin involvement (Currie, 1983). Mononuclear cells cluster on the skin and stimulate lymphokines to stimulate procollagen. Insoluble collagen is formed and accumulates successively in the tissues. Initially, the inflammatory response causes oedema formation, with the resulting taut, smooth and shiny skin appearance. The skin then undergoes fibrotic changes leading to loss of elasticity and movement. Eventually, the tissue degenerates and becomes non-functional. The chain of events from inflammation to degeneration also occurs in blood vessels, major organs and body systems and often results in death.

Clinical Features

The disease starts insidiously on the face and hands where the skin acquires a tense, wrinkle-free, bound-down appearance. The skin and subcutaneous tissues become increasingly hard and rigid and cannot be pinched up from the underlying structures. Wrinkles and lines are obliterated. The skin is dry because sweat secretion over the involved region is suppressed.

The face appears mask-like, immobile and expressionless, and the mouth becomes rigid. The buccal mucosa may likewise be affected. For years these changes may remain localized in the hands and feet. The condition spreads slowly. The extremities become stiff and immobile, the fingers semi-flexed, immobile and useless, and the hands become claw-like.

There may also be changes within the body, which, while not directly visible, may nevertheless be severe. The heart muscle becomes fibrotic, causing dyspnoea; the oesophagus is hardened, interfering with swallowing; the lungs are scarred, impeding respiration; digestive disturbances occur due to hardening of the intestine; progressive renal failure may occur.

The patient may manifest a variety of symptoms: calcinosis (calcium deposits in the tissues), Raynaud's phenomenon, oesophageal hardening and dysfunctioning, sclerodactyly (scleroderma of the digits) and telangiectasia (capillary dilatation that forms a vascular lesion).

Diagnosis

There is no one conclusive test to diagnosis scleroderma. A complete history and physical examination are performed to note any fibrotic changes in the skin, lungs, heart or oesophagus. The skin is biopsied to identify cellular changes specific to scleroderma. Lung tests will show ventilation and perfusion abnormalities. Pericardial effusion, valve lesions and cardiomyopathy are rare.

Management

X-rays are useful to identify the following categories of involvement (Huskisson and Dudley Hart, 1987, p. 137):

1. Resorption of tufts of distal phalanges.
2. Subcutaneous calcification.
3. Joint narrowing.
4. Peri-articular osteoporosis.

Barium swallow is useful in showing oesophageal changes. Huskisson and Dudley Hart also identify the importance of laboratory screening and report the following findings:

Erythrocyte sedimentation rate raised (50 per cent).
Positive latex test (30 per cent).
Positive antinuclear antibody (80 per cent) not DNA.
Anti-centromere antibody absent particularly in CREST syndrome.

Treatment is dependent on the clinical features associated with the disease. Patients need help to understand that there is no drug regime at present that has proved to be effective, although the use of analgesics and anti-inflammatory drugs are very useful in these cases. The physiotherapist can prescribe physiotherapy exercise to promote joint involvement. Patients are advised to avoid extremes in temperature and to use lotions to minimize excessively dry skin.

► NURSING PROCESS
► THE PATIENT WITH SYSTEMIC SCLEROSIS

► Assessment

Because of the inflammatory processes seen with scleroderma, the nurse assesses the patient for joint pain, stiffness, tenderness and localized oedema; polyarthritis may also be present. The fingers and hands are inspected for any colour changes or skin disruption indicative of Raynaud's disease. The patient is asked if stiffness or blanching occurs in the fingers after exposure to cold or stress, because either can trigger vasospasm. A complete musculoskeletal examination is performed as described in the assessment section of rheumatoid arthritis. Because scleroderma is a systemic disorder, the nurse also inspects and palpates the skin, evaluates gastrointestinal functioning, for instance dysphagia, constipation or diarrhoea, assesses the pulmonary and renal systems and ensures that the impact body changes have had on the patient's self-image are identified and assessed.

► Patient's Problems

Based on the information gained from the nursing history, the patient's main problems may include:

1. Impairment of skin integrity related to disruption of the skin surface and tissue layers.
2. Activity intolerance related to fatigue.
3. Self-care deficits related to musculoskeletal impairment.
4. Disturbance in self-concept related to changes in body image.
5. Alteration in nutrition related to inadequate food intake due to poor swallowing.
6. Pain, related to restricted joint movement.

► Planning and Implementation
► Expected Outcomes

The main expected outcomes for the patient may include attainment of maintenance of optimum skin integrity, activity tolerance without fatigue, attainment of optimal independence in activities of daily living, attainment of a positive self-concept, attainment or maintenance of optimal nutrition and management of pain and discomfort.

Nursing Care

The nursing care for a patient with scleroderma includes maintaining joint mobility by encouraging and reinforcing the physiotherapist's exercise regime and helping the patient to understand that keeping the hands and fingers warm is important, if Raynaud's disease is present.

For patients with gastrointestinal involvement, the nurse may help them to understand the usefulness of medications such as antacids, and to cope with the discomforts of constipation or diarrhoea by giving them dietary advice.

The patient who is having problems with swallowing needs frequent, small meals and encouragement to chew food thoroughly. It is also useful to note that advising patients to have frequent drinks between mouthfuls using a greasy fluid such as milk will aid swallowing.

The patient needs encouragement to take periodic deep breaths if there is pulmonary involvement, and the nurse needs to record respiration rate at rest throughout the day.

For those patients who show evidence of renal failure, the nurse should assess their weight on a weekly basis, and keep a regular record of urinary output and observe constantly for ankle oedema. Patients should also be given time to discuss the disease with the nurse, with particular reference as to how it is affecting their lives and that of their carers.

GOUT

Primary gout is a disease manifested by joint inflammation caused by the deposit of uric acid crystals in the joints and connective tissues, as the result of a disorder of purine metabolism. Hyperuricaemia occurs in conditions in which there is an increase in cell turnover and an increase in cell breakdown, or it may occur because renal excretion of uric acid is somehow blocked. Other causes of hyperuricaemia and gout include prolonged ingestion of certain diuretic agents, and attacks can be precipitated by surgery, trauma, dietary or alcoholic excess and starvation.

Altered Physiology

Because uric acid is relatively insoluble it tends to precipitate and form deposits at various sites where blood flow is least active, including cartilaginous tissue. The clumps of sodium urate crystals, called tophi, are deposited in the vicinity of joints, particularly the great toe, on the knuckles (Figure 27.7) and on the ear lobes. Around 20 per cent of patients have these signs. In the latter stage of the disease, there is deposition of urate crystals in the soft tissues and the kidneys.

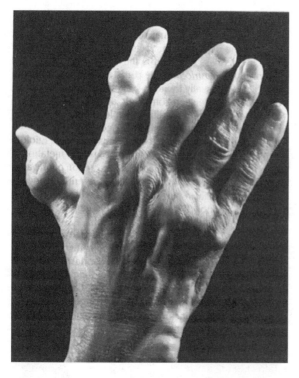

Figure 27.7 Accumulation of uric acid crystals on the knuckles of a patient with gout. (Photograph courtesy of National Institute of Arthritis, Metabolism, and Digestive Diseases.)

Clinical Features

An acute attack of gout usually begins with sudden onset of severe pain in one of the peripheral joints, which may be accompanied by intense inflammation, swelling and tenderness. Attacks most commonly happen between 3 and 6 o'clock in the morning. The most common joint to be involved is the big toe joint. Untreated acute attacks last for a few days or weeks but recur at regular intervals, sometimes many years apart. Gout may become chronic, leaving certain joints permanently disabled, deformed and painful.

Diagnosis

Diagnosis is based on the presence of uric acid crystals in fluid aspirated from the joint cavity. The appearance of tophi is considered to be a positive sign of gout. Blood taken for uric acid usually proves to be greater than 6 mg in 100 ml. A raised erythrocyte sedimentation rate and leucocytosis is found in an acute attack. The use of X-rays is not helpful in the early stages of the disease. In the latter stages when tophi are developing, X-rays show 'punched-out' radiolucent areas around the affected joints.

Management

The treatment of an acute attack is directed towards relieving pain and inflammation (Bergman, 1987; Scott, 1989). An acute attack requires quick action with a drug such as indomethacin, 50 mg to 100 mg given immediately. Subsequent does would be given in quantities of 25 to 50 mg three times a day. Treatment is designed to reduce the inflammation by using anti-inflammatory therapy as soon as possible.

Allopurinol may be given to patients in whom there is an over-production of uric acid or in whom there is renal impairment. Allopurinol is an oxidase inhibitor that interferes with the conversion of the products of purine metabolism to uric acid and thus inhibits uric acid synthesis. The administration of allopurinol generally produces a prompt fall in both serum and urinary uric acid.

Long-term treatment involves re-education on such issues as a low purine diet, less alcohol, weight reduction if obese, adequate fluid intake and the withdrawal of any diuretic therapy.

► **NURSING PROCESS**
► **THE PATIENT WITH GOUT**

► *Assessment*

A patient going through an acute attack of gout will be unable to tolerate the involved joint being touched, any alteration in temperature or even disturbances in air-flow.

► Patient's Problems

Based on the assessment, the patient's main problems may include the following:

1. Pain, related to restricted joint movement.
2. Impairment of skin integrity relating to changes in joint structure due to presence of tophi.
3. Potential alteration in nutrition relating to intakes of food high in purins.

► Planning and Implementation
► Expected Outcomes

The main outcomes for the patient may include relief of joint pain, maintenance of skin integrity and attainment of optimum nutrition.

Nursing Care

Pain Control

The patient will be encouraged to rest in bed or in a chair, whichever is most comfortable, with the affected joint protected by a well-padded bed cradle, and the limb should be elevated. Weight-bearing is avoided until the attack subsides, because early ambulation may precipitate a recurrence. If hand, wrist or elbow joints are involved, a splint may be custom made to immobilize the hot and tender joint, but it should be remembered that this may not be a comfortable option for the patient.

Care of the Skin

Tophi may become ulcerated and infected due to irritation by clothing and subsequent draining. Care is taken to provide gentle skin hygiene; draining tophi are covered with a dry, padded dressing.

Nutrition

Foods high in purine may sometimes need to be avoided. The patient may need help to understand the importance of modifying their lifestyle with reference to such things as reducing alcohol consumption, the taking of a balanced diet and ensuring that clear fluids in quantities of three litres a day are taken.

OTHER CONNECTIVE TISSUE DISORDERS

Seronegative Spondarthritis

Seronegative spondarthritis is an umbrella term for inflammatory disorders of the skeleton, including ankylosing spondylitis, Reiter's syndrome and psoriatric arthritis.

Ankylosing Spondylitis

Ankylosing spondylitis is a systemic inflammatory disease of unknown aetiology that affects the cartilaginous joints of the spine and surrounding tissues, and affects mainly young adult men. The age of onset is between 15 and 30 years, and there is a 6 per cent incidence of a familial history.

Its most characteristic clinical feature is back pain localizing in the spinal sacroiliac joints, in which early inflammatory changes cause back pain and stiffness. As the disease progresses the entire spine may become ankylosed, and thus the patient loses spinal movement. Diagnosis is based on a comprehensive history, physical examination and radiological studies. Sacroiliac joint changes are considered to be an early sign. An elevated erythrocyte sedimentation rate and a negative rheumatoid factor are relevant laboratory clues. Other features such as aritis (inflammation of the iris) affect 25 per cent of patients, and cardiac conduction defects affect 8 per cent of patients.

Medical management focuses on treating the pain and maintaining mobility by referring the patient for education and treatment from the physiotherapist. The drugs of choice are usually nonsteroid anti-inflammatory drugs.

Reiter's Syndrome

Reiter's syndrome affects young adult males and is characterized primarily by urethritis, arthritis and conjunctivitis, and is often known in the UK as 'the triad of arthritis'. It is 20 times more common in men than in women, and the usual age of onset is between 20 and 40 years. Conjunctivitis occurs in 30 per cent of cases. Management involves treatment of the symptoms because no cure is available. Bedrest is advised during the acute stage, and analgesic and anti-inflammatory drugs are used to reduce inflammation and pain. Joints inflamed with fluid effusions can be aspirated and local steroid injected.

BIBLIOGRAPHY

Arthritis and Rheumatism Council (1986) *Arthritis and Rheumatism in the 80s—A Report on an Investigation into the Burden of Suffering and the Availability of Facilities for Treatment and Relief*, Arthritis and Rheumatism Council, 41 Eagle Street, London, WC1R 4AR.

Bergman, H. D. (1987) Gout—medical management, *Journal of Practical Nursing*, Vol. 37, No. 3, pp. 48–53.

Bloch, K. J. *et al.* (1965) Non-articular manifestations of rheumatoid arthritis, *Medicine*, Vol. 44, p. 187.

Currie, H. L. F. (1983) *Essentials of Rheumatology*, Pitman Books, London, pp. 39–42.

Hart, F. D. (1969) Rheumatoid arthritis: extra-articular manifestations, Part 1, *British Medical Journal*, Vol. 3, p. 131.

Hart. F. D. (1970) Rheumatoid arthritis: extra-articular manifestations, Part 2, *British Medical Journal*, Vol. 2, p. 747.

Hughes, G. R. V. (1982) *The Treatment of SLE: The Case For Conservative Management: Clinics in Rheumatic Diseases, Volume 8, No. 1*, W. B. Saunders, Eastbourne.

Huskisson, E. C. and Dudley Hart, S. (1987) *Joint Disease: All the Arthropathies*, John Wright, Bristol.

Maycock, J. A. (1983) *Care of the Skin in Rheumatology Arthritis*, Graves Medical Audiovisual Library, Holly House, 220 New London Road, Chelmsford, Essex CM2 9BJ (tel: 0245 283351).

Maycock, J. A. (1985) Towards pain relief: special reference to rheumatic disease, *Nursing Mirror*, Vol. 160, pp. 40–1.

Maycock, J. A. (1988) *Altered Body Image: The Nurse's Role*, John Wiley, Chichester.

Maycock, J. A. (1991) Role of health professionals in patient education, June, *Annals of the Rheumatic Diseases, Heberden Papers, Health Education in Rheumatology, British Medical Journal*.

Miller, J. F. (1983) *Coping With Chronic Illness: Overcoming Powerlessness*, F. A. Davies, Philadelphia, p. 278.

Panayi, G. S. (1980) *Essential Rheumatology for Nurses and Therapists*, Ballière Tindall, pp. 20–1.

Rodnan, G. P., Schumacher, H. R. and Zaifler, N. J. (eds) (1983) *Primer on the Rheumatic Diseases* (8th edition), Arthritis Foundation, Atlanta, p. 137.

Scadding, J. G. (1969) Rheumatoid arthritis: lung involvement, *Proceedings of the Royal Society of Medicine*, Vol.62, p. 227.

Scott, J. T. (1989) Gout and its treatment, *Arthritis Research Today*, No. 75, pp. 8, 13.

Smith Pigg, J., Webb-Driscoll, P. and Caniff, R. (1985) *Rheumatology Nursing—A Problem-Orientated Approach, Volume 2*, John Wiley, New York, pp. 15–22, 237–67.

Unsworth, H. (1986) *Coping with Rheumatoid Arthritis*, Chambers, Edinburgh, pp. 10–12.

Wright, V. and Haslock, I. (1977) *Rheumatism for Nurses and Remedial Therapists*, William Heinemann Medical Books, London, p.25.

FURTHER READING

Books

Berry, H. and Jawad A. S. M. (1985) *Rheumatology—Management of Common Diseases in Family Practice*, MTP Press, Lancaster, England.

Clarke, A. K. (1987) *Rehabilitation in Rheumatology—The Team Approach*, Martin Dunitz, London.

Currie, H. L. F. (1983) *Essentials of Rheumatology*, Pitman, London.

Dudley Hart (1984) *Practical Problems in Rheumatology*, Methuen, Australia.

Fleet Croft, J.P. (1983) *The Musculo-Skeletal System, Orthopaedics, Rheumatology and Fractures*, Churchill Livingstone, Edinburgh.

Hollingsworth, E. (1988) *Rheumatology*, William Heinemann Medical Books, London.

Moll, J. N. H. (1987) *Manual of Rheumatology*, Churchill Livingstone, Edinburgh.

Moll, J. N. H. (1988) *Essentials of Rheumatology*, Churchill Livingstone, Edinburgh.

Moskowitz, R. W. and Haug, M. R. (1986) *Arthritis and the Elderly*, Springer Publishing, New York.

Panayi, G. S. (1980) *Essential Rheumatology for Nurses and Therapists*, Ballière Tindall, Eastbourne.

Salter, M. (1988) *Altered Body Image*, John Wiley, Chichester.

Scott, J. T. (1986) *Copeman's Textbook of Rheumatic Diseases, Volumes 1 and 2*, Churchill Livingstone, Edinburgh.

Shipley, M. (1984) *Pocket Picture Guide to Rheumatic Diseases*, Gower Medical Publishing, London.

Smith Pigg, J., Webb-Driscoll, P. and Caniff, F. R. (1980) *Rheumatology Nursing—A Problem-Orientated Approach*, John Wiley, Chichester.

Unsworth, H. (1986) *Coping with Rheumatoid Arthritis*, Chambers, Edinburgh.

Wright, V. and Haslock, I. (1977) *Rheumatism for Nurses and Remedial Therapists*, William Heinemann Medical Books, London.

Articles

Bergman, H. D. (1987) Gout—medical management, *Journal of Practical Nursing*, Vol. 37, No. 3, pp. 48–53.

Bergman, H. D. (1989) The treatment of systemic lupus erythematosus, *Journal of Practical Nursing*, Vol. 39, No. 1, pp. 50–5.

Brain, E. (1989) All about lupus (systemic lupus erythematosus), *Nursing Standard*, Vol. 3, p. 41.

Burchhardt, C. S. (1985) The impact of arthritis on quality of life, *Nursing Research*, Vol. 34, No. 1, pp. 11–16.

Burton, S. (1989) Drugs to treat rheumatic disorders, *Nursing*, Vol. 3, No. 34, pp. 27–9.

Byers, P. H. (1985) Effective exercise on morning stiffness and mobility in patients with rheumatoid arthritis, *Research in Nursing Health*, Vol. 8, No. 3, pp. 275–81.

Clegg, D. O. and Ward, J. R. (1987) Slow-acting anti-rheumatic therapy for rheumatoid arthritis, *Nurse Practitioner*, Vol. 12, No. 3, pp. 44, 49–50, 52.

Chesson, S., Hosking, S. and Stevenson, V. (1984) Nursing care of the patient with a rheumatic disease, *Rheumatic Diseases* (published by the Arthritis and Rheumatism Council, Report No. 90, July).

Davies, G. C. (1989) The clinical assessment of chronic pain in rheumatic disease: evaluating the use of two instruments (using the Mcgill and Mcgill comprehensive pain questionnaires), *Journal of Advanced Nursing*, Vol. 14, No. 5, pp. 397–402.

Dieppe, P. (1988) Arthritis in the 80s: osteoarthritis—a case of joint failure, *Arthritis and Rheumatism Council/Arthritis Today*, No. 71, pp. 3–5.

Holt, F. D. (1989) Overcoming arthritis exercise, *Arthritis Research Today*, No. 73, pp. 3–4.

Lorig, K. (1987) Arthritis— patient education: a review of a review of the literature, *Patient Education and Counselling*, Vol. 10, No. 3, pp. 207–52.

Maycock, J. A. (1988) Joint action (care of rheumatoid arthritis patients in general wards, using Mazlo's hierarchy of needs), *Nursing Standard*, Vol. 2, September, pp. 28–9.

Melville, J. (1988) Troubleshooter in the clinic (nurse practitioner in an OA clinic), *New Society*, Vol. 84, p. 42.

Miller, B. (1987) Osteoarthritis in the primary health care setting, *Orthopaedic Nursing*, Vol. 6, No. 5, pp. 42–6.

Mooney, N. E. (1983) Coping with chronic pain in rheumatoid arthritis: patient behaviours and nursing interventions, *Rehabilitation Nursing*, Vol. 8, No. 2, March/April.

Panayi, G. S. and Welsh, I. K. (1988) The immunogenetics of rheumatoid arthritis, *Arthritis and Rheumatism Council Topical Reviews*, No. 9, pp. 1–3.

Phillips, K. S. (1983) The use of gold therapy with rheumatoid arthritis, *Orthopaedic Nursing*, Vol. 2, No. 4, July/August.

Rice, T. (1988) Into the light (the disease lupus), *Nursing Standard*, Vol. 3, pp. 36–7.

Roberts, A. (1989) Systems of Life, No. 167: Senior Systems, No. 32: Locomotor Systems, No. 3, Joints (osteoarthritis and rheumatoid arthritis), *Nursing Times*, Vol. 85, 11 January, pp. 45–8.

Ross, E. R. (1988) Too high a price (septic arthritis), *Community View*, No. 478, pp. 3–5.

Venables, P. E. (1989) Systemic lupus erythematosus, *Arthritis Research Today*, Spring, No. 73, pp. 7–8.

Wathen, G. (1985) Arthritis—self-management American style, *British Journal of Occupational Therapy*, Vol. 48, No. 5, pp. 129–30.

Whitwam, L. (1989) Arthritis, social problems and practical solutions, *Nursing Times*, Vol. 85, No. 5, pp. 36–7, 39.

Unit 9

INTEGUMENTARY PROBLEMS

chapter 28

ASSESSMENT AND CARE OF PATIENTS WITH SKIN DISORDERS

Skin problems are encountered frequently in nursing practice. Skin-related complaints account for approximately 10 per cent of all general practitioner visits in this country. Because the skin mirrors the general condition of the patient, many systemic conditions may be accompanied by dermatological features. Any patient hospitalized with a medical or a surgical problem may suddenly develop itching and a rash. In certain systemic conditions, such as hepatitis and cancer, dermatological features may be the first sign that these disorders are present.

PHYSIOLOGY OF THE SKIN

The skin is a structure that is indispensable for human life. It forms a barrier between the internal organs and the external environment and participates in many vital functions of the body. The skin is continuous with the mucous membrane at the external openings of the organs of the digestive, respiratory and urogenital systems. Because disorders of the skin are readily visible, skin complaints are frequently the primary reason for patient visits.

Anatomy of the Skin

The skin is composed of two layers of tissue, the epidermis, an outer layer in contact with the environment, and a deeper layer called the dermis. The epidermis consists of live, continuously dividing epithelial cells covered on the surface by dead cells that were originally deeper in the dermis but were pushed upward by newly developing cells underneath. The dead cells are constantly flaking off from the skin, frequently in irregular patches. These dead cells contain large amounts of keratin, an insoluble, fibrous protein that forms the outer barrier of the skin. The epidermis is devoid of blood vessels and has few nerve endings. The superficial layers of the epidermis can be shaved from the body without pain or blood loss. The epidermis is modified in different areas of the body. Over the palms of the hands and the soles of the feet it is thickened and contains increased amounts of keratin, in contrast to the thin epidermis over most of the rest of the body. The thickness of the epidermis can increase with use, as is the case, for example, with the hands of a labourer.

The dermis is a thicker layer of connective tissue that underlies the epidermal layer. It is composed of collagen and elastic fibres and contains blood and lymph vessels, nerves, sweat and sebaceous glands and hair roots. Interlocking between dermis and epidermis produces ripples on the surface of the skin. On the fingertips, these ripples are called fingerprints. They are perhaps a person's most individual characteristic, and they almost never change. With ageing, the number of elastic fibres in the dermis progressively decreases, and the skin becomes wrinkled.

The colour of the skin is determined by the pigment called melanin, which is produced by the cells in the epidermis called melanocytes. The skin of black people and the darker areas of the skin on white people (for example, the nipple) contain large amounts of this pigment. Production of melanin by melanocytes is largely under the control of a hormone secreted from the hypothalamus, called melanocyte-stimulating hormone. Increased production of melanin occurs on exposure to ultraviolet light, such as occurs with a suntan.

The skin is anchored to the muscles and bones underneath by subcutaneous tissue composed of connective tissue interlaced with fat. Fat is deposited and distributed according to the person's gender, and in part accounts for the difference in body shape between men and women. Overeating results in increased deposition of fat beneath the skin.

Hair

Hair is present over the entire body except for the palms of the hands and soles of the feet. The hair consists of a root formed in the dermis and a hair shaft that projects beyond the skin. It grows in a cavity called a hair follicle. The proliferation of cells in the bulb of the hair causes the hair to form. Hairs in different parts of the body serve different functions. The hairs of the eyes (eyebrows and lashes), nose and ears screen dust, insects and airborne debris. Hair of the skin serves as thermal insulation in lower animals. This function in enhanced during cold or fright by the piloerection (hairs 'standing on end'), caused by contraction of the tiny arrector muscles attached to the hair follicle. The piloerector response that occurs in humans is probably vestigial. The colour of hair is due to the presence of varying amounts of melanin within the hair shaft. Grey or white hair is the result of loss of pigment. Growth of hair in certain locations on the body is under the control of sex hormones. The best examples are the hair on the face (beard and moustache) and on the body trunk that are controlled by the presence of the male hormones (androgens).

Nails

On the dorsal surface of the fingers and toes, a hard, transparent plate of keratin, called the nail, overlies the skin, The nail grows from its root, which lies under a thin fold of skin called the cuticle. The nail helps to protect the fingers and toes, in order to preserve their highly developed sensory function, and aids in the performance of certain fine functions of the fingers, such as picking up small objects.

Glands of the Skin

Sebaceous glands are associated with hair follicles. The ducts of the sebaceous glands empty an oily secretion onto the space between the hair follicle and the hair shaft. For each hair there is a sebaceous gland, whose secretions oil the hair and render the skin soft and pliable.

Sweat glands are found in the skin over most of the body surface. They are heavily concentrated on the palms of the hands and soles of the feet. Only the glans penis, the margins of the lips, the external ear and the nail bed are devoid of sweat glands. Sweat glands are subclassified into two categories: eccrine and apocrine. The eccrine sweat glands are found in all areas of the skin. Their ducts open directly onto the skin surface. The apocrine sweat glands are larger and, in contrast to that of the eccrine glands, their secretion contains parts of the secretory cells. They are located in the axillae, anal region, scrotum and labia majora. Their ducts generally open onto hair follicles. The apocrine glands become active at the time of puberty. In the female, they enlarge and recede with each menstrual cycle.

Apocrine glands produce a milky sweat that is broken down by bacteria to produce the characteristic underarm odour. Specialized apocrine glands called cerumenous glands are found in the external ear, where they produce wax (cerumen).

The thin, watery secretion called sweat is produced in the basal coiled portion of the eccrine gland and is released into its narrow duct. Sweat is composed predominantly of water and contains about half of the salt content of the blood plasma. Sweat is released from eccrine glands in response to a raised ambient temperature. The rate of sweat secretion is under the control of the sympathetic nervous system. Excessive sweating of the palms and soles, axillae, forehead and other areas may occur in response to pain and stress.

Functions of the Skin

Protective Function

The skin protects the body against invasion by bacteria and foreign matter. The thickened skin of the palms and soles provides the tough covering necessary for the constant trauma occurring in these areas.

The epidermis is relatively impermeable to most chemical substances. It is this property of skin that allows it to be an effective barrier for protection. Some substances go through the skin more readily than others. A variety of different lipids (fatty substances) may be absorbed through the skin. Fat-soluble vitamins (A and D) and steroid hormones are examples. Substances may enter the skin through the epidermis—the transepidermal route—or via the follicle openings.

Sensory Function

Stimulation of the receptor endings of nerves in the skin allows constant monitoring of the conditions of the immediate environment. The primary functions of the receptors in the skin are to sense temperature, pain, light touch and pressure (or heavy touch). Different nerve endings are responsible for responding to each of the different stimuli. Although the nerve endings are distributed over the entire body, they are more concentrated in some areas than in others. For example, the fingertips are much more densely supplied with nerve endings than the skin of the back.

Water Balance

Skin forms a barrier that prevents loss of water and electrolytes from the internal environment and also prevents the subcutaneous tissues from drying out. When skin is damaged, as occurs with a severe burn, for example, large quantities of fluids and electrolytes can be lost rapidly, possibly leading to circulatory collapse, shock and death. On the other hand, the skin is not completely impermeable to water. Small amounts of water continuously evaporate from the skin surface. This evaporation, called insensible perspiration, amounts to approximately 500 ml per day for a normal adult. Insensible water loss may vary with the body temperature, and in the presence of fever these losses can increase. During immersion in water, the skin can accumulate water up to approximately three or four times its normal weight. A common example of this is the swelling of the skin after prolonged bathing.

Temperature Regulation

The body continuously produces heat as a result of the metabolism of foodstuffs to produce energy. This heat is dissipated primarily through the skin. Three major physical processes are involved in loss of heat from the body to the environment. The first process, radiation, is the ability of a body to give off its heat to another object of lower temperature situated at a distance. The second process, conduction, is the transfer of heat from the body to a cooler object in contact with it. Heat transferred by conduction to the air surrounding the body is removed by the third process, convection, where warm air molecules move away from the body. Evaporation from the skin aids the process of heat loss by conduction. Heat is conducted through the skin into water molecules on its surface, causing the water to evaporate. The source of the water on the skin surface may be insensible perspiration, sweat or water from the environment. Normally, all of these mechanisms for heat loss are utilized. However, when the ambient temperature is very high, radiation and convection are not effective, and evaporation from the skin constitutes the only means for heat loss.

Under normal conditions, metabolic heat production is exactly balanced by heat loss, and the internal temperature of the body is maintained constant at approximately 37°C. The rate of heat loss depends primarily on the surface temperature of the skin, which is in turn a function of the skin blood flow. Skin is richly supplied with blood vessels that carry heat to the skin from the core of the body. Blood flow through these vessels is controlled primarily by the sympathetic nervous system. Increased blood flow to the skin results in delivery of more heat to the skin and a greater rate of heat loss from the body. On the other hand, decreased skin blood flow decreases the skin temperature and helps conserve heat for the body. When the temperature of the body begins to fall, as occurs on a cold day, the blood vessels of the skin constrict and reduce heat loss from the body.

Sweating is another process by which the body can regulate the rate of heat loss. Sweating is increased when body temperature starts to rise. In extremely hot environments, the rate of sweat production may be as high as one litre per hour. Under some circumstances, for example, with emotional stress, sweating may occur on a reflex basis unrelated to the necessity to lose heat from the body.

ASSESSMENT

Physical Assessment

Assessment of the skin includes all body surfaces, mucous membranes and the nails. The skin is a reflection of a person's overall health, and alterations often correspond to disease in other organ systems. Inspection and palpation constitute the chief techniques of the skin assessment.

A thorough examination of the skin includes an assessment of colour, lesions, vascularity, temperature, texture, mobility and the presence of oedema. Skin colour varies from person to person and ranges from ivory to deep brown. The skin of exposed portions of the body, especially in sunny, warm climates, tends to be more pigmented than that of the rest of the body. Fever, sunburn and inflammation produce a pink or reddish hue in the skin, caused by vasodilation. Pallor is an absence of or decrease in normal skin tones and vascularity, and is best observed in the conjunctivae. The bluish hue of cyanosis indicates cellular hypoxia and is easily observed in the nail beds, lips and mucous membranes. Jaundice is directly related to a raised serum bilirubin and is often noted in the sclerae and mucous membranes.

Assessing colour changes in the dark-skinned or black person may be difficult. Additional lighting may be helpful during inspection. The overall surface of dark skin normally has a reddish base or undertone; the buccal mucosa, tongue, lips and nails have a pink colour. Erythema is often visible as a purplish grey cast to the skin. Dark-skinned people normally have yellow conjunctivae; thus, it may be necessary to inspect the hard palate for the yellowing hue of jaundice. Rashes are more easily identified by palpation. Differences in skin texture are detected and borders of the rash defined.

The presence of any eruptions or lesions on the skin is noted. Careful observation of the eruption or lesion helps to identify the type of dermatosis (abnormal skin condition) and indicates whether the lesion is primary or secondary. At the same time, the anatomical distribution of the eruption is noted, because certain diseases affect certain sites of the body and are distributed in characteristic patterns and shapes. To determine the extent of the distribution, the left and right sides of the body are compared while the colour and shape of the lesion are noted. Following observation, the lesions are palpated to determine their texture and to see if they are hard or soft or filled with fluid. A metric ruler is used to measure the size of the lesions so that any further extension can be compared with this initial baseline measurement. The dermatosis is then documented clearly and in detail.

It is essential for the examiner to use precise and accurate terminology in any verbal or written communication about the state of the skin. This facilitates the ultimate identification and diagnosis of local and systemic diseases, and requires memorization and the reinforcement of clinical experience.

Once the colour of the skin has been inspected and lesions have been noted, an assessment of vascular changes in the skin is carried out. A description of vascular changes includes location, distribution, colour, size and the presence of pulsations. Common vascular changes include petechiae, ecchymosis, telangiectasia, angiomas and venous stars.

Skin moisture, temperature and texture are assessed primarily by palpation. The elasticity of the skin, which lessens in normal ageing, may be a factor in assessing the hydration status of a patient.

A brief inspection of the nails includes observation of configuration, colour and consistency. Many of the alterations seen in the nail or nail bed reflect local or systemic abnormalities in progress, or are the result of past events. Transverse depressions (Beau's lines) in the nails may reflect retarded growth of the nail matrix secondary to severe illness or, more commonly, are the result of local trauma. Ridging, hypertrophy and other changes may also be visible with local trauma. Inflammation of the skin around the nail (paronychia) is usually accompanied by tenderness and erythema. The angle between the normal nail and its base is 160 degrees. When palpated, the base of the nail is usually firm. Clubbing is manifested by a straightening of the normal angle (180 degrees or greater) and a softening of the nail base. This softening is perceived as spongelike when palpated.

Considerations for the Elderly

The major changes in the skin of older people include dryness, wrinkling, laxity, uneven pigmentation and a variety of proliferative lesions. The histological features of skin associated with ageing include a thinning at the junction of the dermis and epidermis, loss of dermal and subcutaneous tissue, reduction of the vascular bed (especially of the capillary loops), marked reduction of the vascular network surrounding hair bulbs and the eccrine, apocrine and sebaceous glands, and reduced numbers of melanocytes, specialized epidermal cells and mast cells (Figure 28.1).

Loss of dermal thickness approaches 20 per cent in elderly people, accounting for the thin, sometimes nearly transparent quality of their skin. The ageing skin, like all other ageing organ systems, has a loss of functional capacity. Functions affected include cell replacement, the barrier function, sensory perception, thermoregulation and sweat and sebum production. The result is an increasing vulnerability to injury and to certain disease. Skin problems are common among older people.

Diagnosis

Dermatology is a visually oriented specialty. In addition to listening to the patient's history, the examiner inspects the appearance of the primary and secondary lesions and their configuration and distribution. Certain diagnostic procedures may also be used to help in identifying skin conditions.

Skin Biopsy

A skin biopsy is performed to obtain tissue for micro-

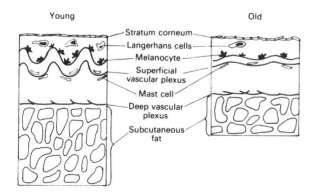

Figure 28.1 Histological changes in ageing normal skin. Schematic drawings emphasize the age-associated flattening of the dermo-epithelial junction; loss of dermal and subcutaneous mass; shortened capillary loops; and reduced numbers of melanocytes, Langerhans' cells and mast cells. (Reprinted with permission from the American Geriatrics Society: Gilchrest, B. A. (1982) Age-associated changes in the skin, *Journal of the American Geriatrics Society*, Vol. 30, No. 2, p. 140.)

scopic examination. It may be obtained by excision or by a punch biopsy that removes a small core of tissue. Biopsies are performed on skin nodules of uncertain aetiology to rule out malignancy and to obtain an exact diagnosis.

Immunofluorescence Testing

Immunofluorescence testing is a technique in which antigen or antibody is combined with a dye and used to localize the site of an immune reaction. (Antibodies can be made fluorescent by attaching them to a dye). Immunofluorescence tests on skin (direct immunofluorescence test) are techniques to detect autoantibodies directed against portions of the skin. The indirect immunofluorescence test detects specific antibodies in the patient's serum.

Patch Testing

Patch testing is done to identify substances to which the patient has developed an allergy. The suspected allergens are applied to normal skin under occlusive patches. After about 48 hours, the patches are removed and the underlying skin is inspected for any eczematous reaction, which may indicate a positive response to the allergen (Treadgold, 1983). During testing the patient is advised to leave the patch in place and not to bathe or scratch under the patch site.

Skin Scrapings

Skin scrapings are taken of suspected fungal lesions. This is done with a scalpel blade and the scraped material is transferred to a glass slide, covered with a cover slip and examined under the microscope.

Tzanck Smear

A Tzanck smear is used to examine cells from blistering skin conditions. The suspected lesion is opened and its contents are applied to a glass slide and examined after staining.

Wood's Light Examination

The Wood's light examination uses a special lamp for producing long-wave ultraviolet rays that cause the skin to produce a characteristic fluorescence in the presence of some microbial agents. This is seen best in a darkened room. The patient is reassured that the light is not harmful to skin or eyes.

Clinical Photographs

Clinical photographs are taken to show the nature and extent of the skin condition and to reveal progress or improvement resulting from treatment.

Skin Lesions

Skin lesions represent the most prominent characteristic of dermatological conditions. They vary in size, shape and cause, and are classified according to their appearance and origin.

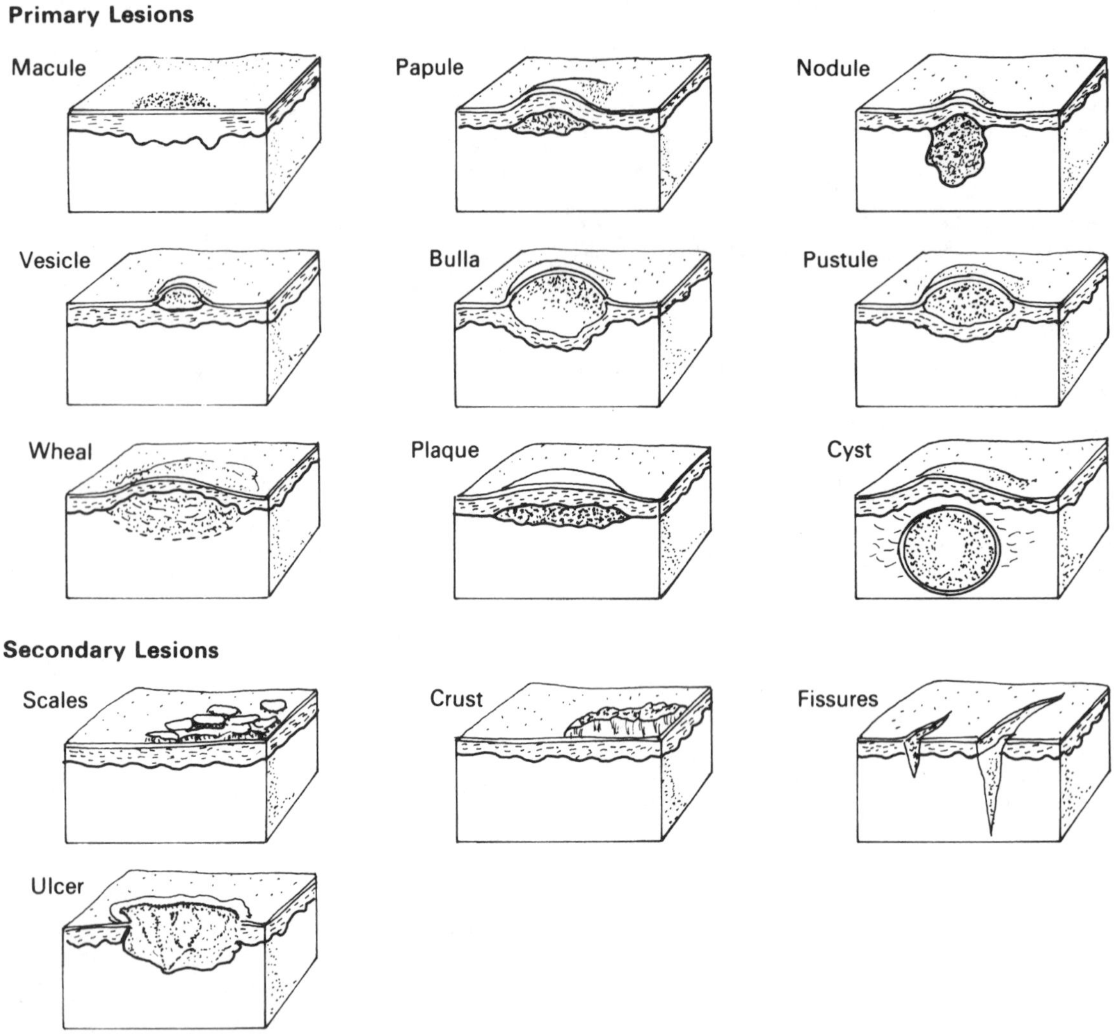

Primary Lesions

Secondary Lesions

Figure 28.2 Types of skin lesions.

Skin lesions can be described as primary or secondary. Primary lesions are the initial lesions and are characteristic of the disease itself. Secondary lesions result from external causes, such as scratching, trauma, infections or changes caused by wound healing. Depending on the stage of development, skin lesions are further divided according to type and appearance, as indicated in the following definitions and illustrated in Figure 28.2.

Primary Lesions (Initial Lesions)

Macule—a flat discolouration of the skin of various sizes, shapes and colours.

Papule—a solid, raised, palpable lesion; lesions may vary in colour

Nodule—a raised, solid lesion that is larger and deeper than a papule.

Vesicle—a small collection of fluid in or under the epidermis.

Bulla—a large vesicle or blister.

Pustule—a lesion that contains pus; may form as a result of purulent changes in a vesicle.

Wheal—transient elevation of the skin caused by oedema of the dermis and surrounding capillary dilation.

Plaque—a solid, elevated lesion on the skin or mucous membrane.

Cyst—a tumour that contains semi-solid or liquid material.

Secondary Lesions

As the term implies, secondary lesions are the changes that take place in primary lesions and possibly modify them. Secondary lesions include the following:

Scales—heaped-up, horny layers of dead epidermis; may develop as a result of inflammatory changes.

Crusts—a covering formed from serum, blood or pus drying on the skin.

Excoriations—linear scratch marks or traumatized area of skin.

Fissures—cracks in the skin, usually from marked drying and longstanding inflammation.

Ulcers—lesions formed by local destruction of the epidermis and part or all of the underlying dermis.

Lichenification—thickening of skin accompanied by exaggeration of skin markings.

Scar—a fibrotic change in the skin following a destructive process.

Atrophy—loss of one or more of the skin components.

Shape and Configuration

Once the type of lesion is identified, the shape of the lesion and the configuration (arrangement) of the lesions relative to each other are noted. 'Shape' may refer to a single lesion or to the appearance of multiple lesions. The following are descriptions frequently employed:

Annular—ring-shaped.

Circinate—circular.

Confluent—lesions run together or join.

Discoid—disc-shaped.

Discrete—lesions remain separate.

Generalized—widespread eruption.

Grouped—clustering of lesions.

Guttate—droplike.

Herpetiform—grouped vesicles.

Iris—a ring or a series of concentric rings.

Keratosis—horny thickening.

Linear—in lines.

Nummular—coin-shaped.

Polymorphis—more than one kind of skin lesion.

Reticulated—lacelike network.

Serpiginous—snakelike or creeping eruption.

Telangiectasia—tiny, superficial, dilated cutaneous vessel; can be seen as a red thread or line.

Zosteriform—bandlike distribution limited to one or more dermatomes of skin.

MANAGEMENT OF SKIN DISORDERS

Therapeutic regimes used in the treatment of patients with dermatological problems include topical and systemic medications, wet dressings, other special dressings and therapeutic baths.

The major expected outcomes of therapy are: (1) prevent damage to the healthy skin; (2) prevent secondary infection; (3) reverse the inflammatory process; and (4) relieve the symptoms.

Preventing Damage to Healthy Skin

Some skin problems are markedly aggravated by soap and water. Therefore, bathing routines are modified according to the condition being treated.

Damaged skin, whether the area of desquamation is large or small, is further affected by chemicals and trauma. The friction of a towel, if applied vigorously, is sufficient to excite a brisk inflammatory response that may result in any existing lesion flaring up and increasing in size. Thus, the essence of skin care and protection in bathing a patient with abnormal skin is to use a mild, superfatted soap or soap substitute and to ensure the complete removal of the soap when rinsing, before blotting the area dry with a soft cloth. Perfumed or deodorant soaps should be avoided with these patients.

Cotton wool balls saturated with oil will aid in loosening crusts and removing exudates. Adherent dry dressings may be saturated with sterile normal saline or another prescribed solution, which softens them and permits them to be pulled away gently.

Preventing Secondary Infection

Potentially infectious skin lesions should be regarded strictly as such, and proper precautions should be observed until the diagnosis is established. Some lesions with pus contain infectious material. Although some genital lesions are suspect, most are minor irritations.

Reversing the Inflammatory Process

The type of skin lesion (oozing, infected or dry) usually suggests the local medication or treatment that is prescribed. As a rule, if the skin is acutely inflamed (hot, red and swollen) and is oozing, it is best to apply wet dressings and creams. In chronic conditions in which the skin surface is dry and scaly, water-soluble emulsions, creams, ointments and pastes are used. The therapy must be changed according to patient preference and as the response indicates. Explain that the patient must contact the doctor or clinic if the medication or dressings seem to irritate the skin. Success or failure of skin therapy rests upon adequate advice to and motivation of the patient and the interest and support of the dermatology team.

Open, Wet Dressings

Open, wet dressings (wet compresses applied to areas of the skin) are usually used for acute, weeping inflammatory lesions. They may be either sterile or unsterile, depending on the condition being treated. The purposes of wet dressings are: (1) to reduce inflammation by producing constriction of blood vessels (thus decreasing vasodilation and the local blood flow in inflammation); (2) to cleanse the skin of exudate, crusts and scales; and (3) to maintain drainage of infected areas.

Wet dressings are used for vesicular, bullous, pustular and ulcerative disorders, as well as for acute inflammatory

Table 28.1 *Open wet dressings*

Solution and material	Desired effect	Nursing action
Solution Cool tapwater Normal saline Burrow's solution (aluminium acetate solution) Magnesium sulphate Potassium permanganate	Effective in treating oozing dermatosis or swollen, infected dermatitis (furunculitis, cellulitis)	Keep dressing cool or at room temperature Moisten compress to the point of slight dripping Compresses may be remoistened with *asepto* syringe
Material Soft towelling Napkins Soft cotton sheeting	Relieves inflammation, burning and itching Has cooling effect Useful for removing crusts Cleansing and soothing	Add ice cubes to solution if coolness is desired Apply for 15 minutes every two to three hours, unless otherwise indicated Keep patient warm if extensive areas are to be compressed Do not treat more than a third of the body at one time Discard dressing material daily *Caution:* Avoid burns

Table 28.2 *Types of bath*

Bath solution and medication	Desired effect	Nursing action
Water	Same effects as wet dressings	Fill the bath half full – 120 litres
Saline	Used for widely disseminated lesions	
Colloidal-Oatmeal or Aveeno	Antipruritic and drying	Keep the water at a comfortable temperature (approximately 36°C)
Sodium bicarbonate	Cooling	Do not allow the water to cool excessively
Starch		Use a bath mat – *medications may cause bath to be slippery*
Medicated tars (follow package directions Polytar emollient, psoriderm bath emulsion, liquor picis carbonis	Tar baths are used for psoriasis and chronic eczematous conditions	Apply a lubricating agent to wet skin after bath if emollient action is desired – increases hydration Dry by blotting with a towel
Bath oils Oilatum emollient, emulsifying ointment	Bath oils are used for antipruritic and emollient actions Used for acute and subacute eczematous eruptions	Keep room warm to minimize temperature fluctuations Encourage patient to wear light, loose clothing after the bath
Antiseptics Potassium permanganate, hexachlorophane Antifungal Sterzac	Used for infected lesions and when mild antiseptic action is required	

disorders, erosions and exudative, crusted surfaces (see Table 28.1).

Therapeutic Baths

Baths or soaks are useful when large areas are involved, to remove crusts, scales and old medications, and to relieve the inflammation and itching that accompany acute dermatoses. The temperature of the water should be comfortable, and the bath should not exceed 20 to 30 minutes because of the tendency of baths/soaks to produce maceration. For the different types of therapeutic baths and their uses, see Table 28.2.

Topical Medications

Medications in the form of lotions, creams, ointments and powders are frequently used to treat skin lesions.

Lotions exert a cooling action through water evaporation; they also have a protective effect, relieve itching and promote drying. Lotions are applied easily with a soft paintbrush or cotton gauze, or by hand, and are not usually washed off between applications.

Powders usually have a talc, zinc oxide, bentonite or cornstarch base and are dusted on the skin with a shaker or with cotton sponges. Although their medical action is brief, powders act as hygroscopic agents, absorbing moisture and reducing friction between skin surfaces and between the skin and bedding.

Creams are suspensions of oil and water, are easily applied, and usually are the most cosmetically acceptable to the patient. Creams are generally smoothed onto the skin by hand. They are used for their moisturizing and emollient effects.

Gels are semisolid emulsions that become liquid when applied to the skin. They are cosmetically acceptable to the patient, as they vanish after application, and are greaseless and nonstaining.

Pastes are mixtures of powders and ointments and are used in inflammatory conditions. They adhere best to the skin and may need to be removed with mineral or vegetable oil.

Ointments retard water loss, lubricate and protect the skin, and are preferred in the more chronic or localized skin conditions. Both pastes and ointments are applied with a wooden tongue depressor or by hand.

In all types of topical medication, the patient should be taught to apply the medication gently but thoroughly and, when necessary, to cover these medications with a dressing.

Corticosteroids are being widely used in the treatment of many dermatological conditions. Topical steroids frequently are used to suppress inflammation, thus relieving pain and itching. The patient is taught to apply this medication sparingly on hydrated skin. Topical corticosteroids may be covered with occlusive dressings to enhance skin penetration. (See below.) However, this can cause obstruction of sweat glands and overgrowth of skin bacteria.

Wet dressings may be used with topical steroids to enhance steroid absorption by softening and hydrating the skin.

When steroids are applied around the eyes, a great deal of caution is required, as long-term use around the eyes may cause glaucoma, cataracts and viral and fungal infections. Also, when strong (fluorinated) steroids are put on the face, precautions must be taken because they may produce an acne-like dermatitis, steroid-induced rosacea (characterized by lesions around the nose and cheeks) and hypertrichosis (excessive hair growth).

Intralesional therapy consists of the injection of a sterile suspension of medication (usually a corticosteroid) into or just below a lesion. Although this treatment may have an anti-inflammatory effect, local atrophy may result if the injection is made into subcutaneous fat. Skin lesions treated with intralesional therapy include psoriasis, keloids and cystic acne.

Systemic medications are also given for skin conditions. These include the corticosteroids, antibiotics, antifungals, antihistamines, sedatives and tranquillizers, analgesics and cytotoxic drugs.

Dressings for Skin Conditions

Skin dressings are used to keep topical medication in place and to allay itching and pain. One very effective type of dressing is the occlusive dressing, which increases the local skin temperature and hydration and enhances the absorption of topically applied medications. Occlusive dressings also promote the retention of moisture, and keep the medication from evaporating. An airtight plastic film, such as self-adherent food wrap, is applied to cover the treated skin. Plastic film is advantageous because it is thin and adapts itself readily to anatomical structures of all sizes and shapes. The patient is given the following advice:

1. Wash the area, then pat dry.
2. Smooth the medication into the lesion while the skin is moist.
3. Cover with plastic wrap (e.g., food wrap, plastic gloves, plastic bags).
4. Cover with a cotton bandage.

Plastic surgical tape containing corticosteroid in the adhesive layer can be cut to size and applied to individual lesions.

It is important to remember that prolonged use of occlusive dressings may cause local skin atrophy, striae, telangiectasia, inflammation of hair follicles, nonhealing ulceration or erythema and systemic absorption of corticosteroids. Dressings should be removed for 12 out of 24 hours to prevent some of these complications.

Other Dressings

1. Fingers and toes—tubular gauze or, when required, bigger gauze or cotton dressings held in place with tubular gauze.
2. Hands—disposable polyethylene gloves, sealed at wrists; cotton gloves.
3. Feet—cotton socks or disposable plastic bags; tubular gauze socks.
4. Extremities (arms and legs)—cotton cloth covered with tubular material.
5. Groin, perineum—disposable nappies; cotton cloth folded in nappy fashion; napkin, tubular gauze pants.
6. Axillae—cotton cloth taped in place or held by cotton bandage or tubular gauze.
7. Trunk—cotton or light flannel pyjamas or tubular gauze suit.
8. Scalp—turban or plastic shower cap or tubular gauze cap.
9. Whole body—a suit is made of the various sizes of tubular gauze.
10. Face—mask made from gauze with holes cut out for eyes, nose and mouth.

If the patient is troubled with itching at night-time, the nurse can advise that wearing cotton clothes next to the skin may be helpful. Excessive warmth is avoided, and the room is kept cool and humidified. The fingernails should be trimmed to prevent injury from scratching while asleep, and cotton gloves should be worn.

▶ NURSING PROCESS
▶ THE PATIENT WITH AN ABNORMAL SKIN DISORDER

▶ *Assessment*

Nursing History

The information that constitutes the basis of the nursing history may be obtained by asking the following questions:

- When did you first notice this skin problem (onset, duration, intensity)?
- Has it occurred previously?
- Are there any other symptoms?
- What site was first affected?
- What did the rash/lesion look like when it first appeared?
- Where and how fast did it spread?
- Are there itching, burning or tingling sensations? Loss of sensation?
- Is it worse at a particular time? Or season?
- Do you have any idea how it started?
- Do you have a history of hay fever, asthma, hives, eczema, allergies?

- Does anyone in your family have skin problems or rashes?
- Did the eruptions appear after certain foods were eaten?
- Had there been recent intake of alcohol?
- Was there a relationship between a specific event and the outbreak of the rash/lesion?
- What medications are you taking?
- What medication (ointment, cream) have you put on the lesion? (Include over-the-counter medications.)
- What skin products do you use?
- What is your occupation?
- What in your immediate environment (plants, animals, chemicals, infections) might be precipitating this problem? Anything new or any changes in the environment?
- Does anything touching your skin cause a rash?
- Is there anything else you wish to talk about in regard to this problem?

Physical Assessment

Assessment of the skin involves the entire skin area, including the mucous membranes, scalp and nails. Inspection and palpation constitute the chief procedures used in examining the skin, and require that the room be well-lit and warm.

The general appearance of the skin should be examined, observing colour, temperature, moisture, dryness, skin texture (rough or smooth) and the condition of the hair and nails. Skin elasticity is also determined by palpation.

A preliminary look at the eruption or lesion should help to identify the type of dermatosis and indicate whether the lesion is primary or secondary. At the same time, the anatomical distribution of the eruption should be noted because certain diseases tend to affect certain sites of the body and are distributed in characteristic patterns and shapes. To determine the extent of the regional distribution, the left and right sides of the body should be compared while the colour and shape of the lesion(s) are noted. Following observation, the lesions are palpated to determine their texture, shape and border and to see if they are soft or filled with fluid, or hard and fixed to the surrounding tissue.

The dermatosis is documented on the patient's record; it should be described clearly and in detail, using precise terminology.

After the characteristic distribution of the lesions has been determined, the following information should be obtained and described clearly and in detail:

- What is (are) the colour(s) of the lesion(s)?
- Is there redness, heat, pain, or swelling?
- How large an area is involved? Where is it?
- Is the eruption macular, papular, scaling, oozing, discrete, confluent?

- What is the distribution of the lesion(s)—symmetrical, linear, circular?

Assessing Patients With Dark or Black Skin

The gradations of colour that occur in dark-skinned people are determined largely by genetic transmission; they may be described as light, medium or dark. In dark-skinned people, melanin is produced at a faster rate and in larger quantities than in lighter-skinned people. Healthy, dark skin has a reddish base or undertone. The buccal mucosa, tongue, lips and nails normally appear pink.

In examining the dark-skinned or black patient, it is important to have good lighting and to look at the skin and the nail beds as well as in the mouth. All suspect areas should be palpated.

The degree of pigmentation of the black patient's skin may affect the appearance of the lesion. Lesions may be black, purple or grey instead of the tan or red colour seen in white patients.

Erythema. Because there is a tendency for black skin to assume a purplish greyish cast when an inflammatory process is present, it may be difficult to detect erythema (redness of skin due to congestion of the capillaries). To determine possible inflammation, the skin should be palpated for increased warmth or for signs of smoothness (oedema) or hardness. The adjacent lymph nodes are also palpated.

Rash. In instances of itching, the patient should be asked to indicate what areas of the body are involved. Usually the borders of the rash can be felt by running the tips of the fingers lightly over the skin. The patient's mouth and ears should also be examined. (Sometimes rubella will cause a red cast to appear on the tips of the ears.) Finally, the patient's temperature is checked.

Cyanosis. When a person with black skin goes into shock, the skin usually assumes a greyish cast. To determine signs of cyanosis, the areas around the mouth and lips and over the cheekbones and earlobes should be checked. When the conjunctivae of the eyelid are checked for petechiae (small red spots due to escape of blood), it is important to realize that deposits of melanin may normally appear in this area and should not be misinterpreted as petechiae.

Changes in Skin Colour. Changes in skin colour that occur in black people are noticeable and often cause distress to the patient. For example, hypopigmentation (loss of or decrease in skin colour), which may be due to vitiligo (a condition characterized by destruction of melanocytes in limited or extensive skin areas), may cause more concern in the dark-skinned person because it is so readily visible.

Hyperpigmentation (increase in colour) may occur after disease or injury to the skin. A pigmented nasal crease below the eye may be an external sign of allergy. However, pigmented streaks in the nails are considered to be normal.

Black and other dark-skinned people have a greater propensity for keloid or scar formation and for disorders resulting from occlusion or blockage of hair follicles.

Psychosocial Assessment

Because patients with skin conditions (1 in 20 people) can see and feel their problems, they are more apt to be disturbed by their ailments than are patients with other conditions. Skin conditions can lead to cosmetic disfigurement, social isolation and economic hardship. Some conditions are often erroneously associated with contagion.

Some conditions can cost the patient a job, with devastating effects on the person's life. Others may subject the patient to a protracted course of illness, leading to feelings of depression, frustration, self-consciousness and rejection. Itching and skin irritation may also be a constant annoyance and are common features of most skin diseases.

The result of these discomforts may be loss of sleep, anxiety and depression, all of which reinforce the general distress and fatigue that so frequently accompany skin disorders. The meanings attached to skin diseases may concerns self-image and interpersonal relationships.

Patients suffering from such physical and psychological discomforts require understanding, explanations of the problem and its treatment, nursing support, unending patience and continual encouragement. It takes time to help patients gain insight into their problems and work through their difficulties. Since very few conditions are contagious, there is no need to fear touching the patient. In fact, touching reduces the patient's sense of isolation, and conveys human warmth and compassion.

▶ Patient's Problems

The problems patients with dermatoses may have include the following:

- Potential alteration in skin integrity related to change in barrier function of the skin.
- Disturbance in self-image related to unsightly appearance of the skin.
- Discomfort related to skin lesions.
- Degree of awareness of skin care and methods of treating the skin ailment, and knowledge about sleep pattern disturbance related to pruritis.
- Degree of awareness of treatment regime related to length of treatment or the lifestyle adjustment required.
- Potential fluid and serum loss from damaged skin.
- Individual coping mechanisms related to emotional stress of dealing with an unsightly and often uncomfortable skin disorder may be affected.

► NURSING CARE PLAN 28.1: FOR PEOPLE WITH DRY SKIN CHANGES RELATED TO TRAUMA AND INFECTION

Patient's problems	Expected outcomes	Nursing care	Rationale
1. Potential alteration in skin integrity related to changes in barrier function of skin	Maintenance of skin integrity • Patient maintains skin integrity • Absence of maceration • No signs of thermal injury • Absence of infection • Patient applies prescribed topical medication • Takes prescribed medication on schedule	1a. Protect healthy skin from maceration (excessive hydration of stratum corneum) when applying wet dressings b. Remove moisture from skin by blotting gently and avoiding friction c. Guard carefully against risks of thermal injuries from excessively hot, wet dressings and from subtle heat injuries (heating pads, radiators) d. Advise patient to use sun-screening agents	Friction and maceration play a major role in some skin diseases Many cosmetic problems can be attributed to chronic skin damage
2 Changes from infection (related to entry of organisms through break in skin)		2a. Infection in patients with compromised immune systems b. Teach the patient clearly and in detail about treatment c. Apply intermittent wet dressings to reduce inflammation d. Provide baths and soaks e. Administer prescribed antimicrobial f. Use topical medications containing corticosteroids as prescribed and as indicated i. Observe lesion periodically for changes in response to therapy ii. Teach the patient about possible ill effects of long-term use of potent topical steroids g. Advise patient to stop using any skin agent that makes the problem worse	Any condition that compromises the immune status increases the risk of cutaneous infection Effective patient education is dependent on the interpersonal skills of the health professionals and in giving clear instructions reinforced by written advice A wet dressing cools the skin by evaporation, causing constriction of superficial cutaneous vessels and thereby decreasing erythema and serum production. Wet dressings help in debridement of crusts and control inflammatory processes Loosens exudates and scales Corticosteroids have an anti-inflammatory action, resulting in part from their ability to induce vasoconstriction of the small vessels in the upper dermis Extensive prolonged use of corticosteroids can lead to adrenal suppression and other side-effects A contact allergic reaction may develop from any ingredient in the medication
3. Self-consciousness related to unsightly skin appearance	Development of increasing self-acceptance • Patient develops increasing acceptance of own body • Follows through and participates in self-care measures	3a. Assess patient for disturbance of self-image (avoidance of eye contact, self-deprecating remarks and negative feelings about skin condition) b. Identify psychosocial stage of development	Disturbance of self-perception may accompany any disease or condition that is apparent to the patient. An impression of one's own body has an effect on self-concept There is an interaction among the patient's reaction and interpretation of skin condition

► NURSING CARE PLAN 28.1: FOR PEOPLE WITH DRY SKIN CHANGES RELATED TO TRAUMA AND INFECTION

Patient's problems	Expected outcomes	Nursing care	Rationale
	• Reports feeling in control of situation • Gives self positive reinforcement • Displays a more healthy self-regard • Appears less self-conscious; is not afraid to socialize and be seen by others • Uses cosmetics to enhance appearance as appropriate	c. Provide opportunity for expression. Listen, in an open, nondefensive way to expressions of grief/anxiety about changes in self-image d. Find out what the patient worries about and fears. Assist anxious patient to improve insight and identify and cope with problems e. Support patient's efforts to improve self-image (participation in skin treatments; grooming) f. Help patient towards self-acceptance g. Encourage socialization with others h. Advise patient of available cosmetic measures to conceal disfiguring conditions	The patient needs the experience of being heard and understood This gives the nurse an opportunity to allay undue anxiety and restore reality to the situation

4. Discomfort (itching) related to skin lesions	Relief of discomfort
	• Patient achieves relief of discomfort
	• Says that itching has been relieved
	• Demonstrates absence of scratch marks
	• Complies with prescribed treatment
	• Keeps skin hydrated and lubricated
	• Demonstrates intact skin; skin regaining healthy appearance
		4a. Examine area of involvement:
		  i. Attempt to discover cause of discomfort
		  ii. Record observations in detail using descriptive terminology
		  iii. Be aware that *sudden* onset of generalized rash may indicate drug allergy
		
		b. Control environmental and physical factors:
		  i. Provide humid environment
		  ii. Maintain a cool environment
		  iii. Use mild soap made for sensitive skin or a soap substitute
		  iv. Remove excess clothing or bedding
		  v. Wash bed linen and clothing with mild soap
		  vi. Stop repeated exposures to detergents, cleansers and solvents
		
		c. Use skin-care measures to maintain skin integrity
		
		  i. Provide tepid cooling baths or cool dressings for itching
		  ii. Treat dryness (xerosis) as prescribed
		  iii. Apply skin lotion/cream immediately after bathing
			An accurate description of a cutaneous eruption is necessary for diagnosis and treatment. Many skin conditions appear similar but have different aetiologies. Cutaneous inflammatory response may be muted in the elderly
			Itching is aggravated by heat, chemicals, physical irritants
			At low humidity, the skin loses water
			
			These contain no detergents, dyes or hardening agents
			
			Anything that removes water, lipids or protein from the epidermis alters the barrier function of the skin
			The skin is an important barrier that must be maintained intact in order to function properly
			Gradual evaporation of water from dressings cools the skin and relieves pruritus
			Dry skin can produce areas of dermatitis
			Effective hydration of the stratum corneum prevents compromise of the barrier layer of the skin

►

► NURSING CARE PLAN 28.1: FOR PEOPLE WITH DRY SKIN CHANGES RELATED TO TRAUMA AND INFECTION

Patient's problems	Expected outcomes	Nursing care	Rationale
		iv. Keep nails trimmed and smooth v. Apply prescribed topical therapy vi. Help the patient accept the prolonged treatment that some conditions require vii. Advise the patient to refrain from using medications that are commercially available	Trimming reduces skin damage from scratching The patient's problem may be caused by irritation or sensitization from self-medication
5. Sleep pattern disturbance related to pruritus	Achievement of restful sleep ● Patient achieves restful sleep ● Reports relief of itching ● Maintains appropriate environmental conditions ● Avoids caffeine in late afternoon/evening ● Identifies measures to promote sleep ● Experiences satisfactory rest/sleep pattern	5a. Prevent and treat dry skin i. Advise patient to keep bedroom well ventilated and humidified ii. Keep skin moisturized iii. Bathe/shower only as absolutely necessary if skin is excessively dry. Use emollient as a soap substitute. Apply skin lotion/cream immediately after bathing while skin is damp	Nocturnal pruritus interferes with normal sleep Dry air will make skin feel itchy. A comfortable environment promotes relaxation This prevents water loss. Dry, itchy skin can usually be controlled but not cured This will trap some of the water absorbed into the skin surface during bathing
		b. Advise patient of the following measures that may be helpful in promoting sleep: i. Maintain a regular sleep pattern ii. Avoid caffeinated drinks late in the evening iii. Exercise regularly iv. Use a bedtime routine or ritual	Regularity of sleep is important in maintaining sleep hygiene Caffeine has peak effect 2–4 hours after being consumed Exercise appears to have beneficial sleep effect if done in late afternoon This eases transition from wakefulness to sleep
6. Educational needs about skin care and methods of treating skin ailment	Understanding of skin care ● Patient acquires understanding of skin care ● Follows treatment as prescribed and can state rationale for measures taken ● Carries out prescribed baths, soaks, wet dressings ● Uses topical medication appropriately ● Understands importance of nutrition to skin health	6a. Determine what the patient knows about the condition b. Keep the patient informed; correct misconceptions/ misinformation c. Demonstrate application of prescribed therapy (wet compresses; topical medication) d. Advise the patient to keep skin moist and flexible with hydration and application of skin cream/lotion e. Encourage the patient to attain a healthy nutritional state	Assessment of what patients know and how they perceive the present problem is part of nursing assessment Patients need to have a sense that there is something they can do. Most patients benefit from explanations and reassurance The stratum corneum needs water to stay flexible. Application of skin cream/lotion to damp skin prevents dry, rough, cracked and scaly skin The appearance of the skin reflects a person's general health. Skin changes may be a feature of abnormal nutrition

► *Planning and Implementation*
► **Expected Outcomes**
The main outcomes for the patient may include mainten-ance of skin integrity, relief of discomfort, achieving rest-ful sleep, development of self-acceptance and acquiring knowledge of skin care.

Nursing Care

Maintaining Skin Integrity
Many people have dry and sensitive skin that is easily irri-tated. This is especially true of the elderly. Too much washing and scrubbing can increase the problem. Soaps are also irritating. People with sensitive skin should be bathed in tepid water with minimal soaping, taking care to rinse well and dry by gently patting the skin with a towel. An emollient can be applied to moist skin to trap moisture. Dry air is irritating because it reduces skin moisture, so keeping the environment humidified is also helpful.

Skin problems of the hands are a common complaint. The skin of the back of the hand is thin, accounting for its sensitivity and dryness and its poor resistance to soaps and detergents. People with this problem should protect the hands from contact with soaps, solvents, detergents and other chemicals by wearing cotton-lined heavy-duty vinyl gloves when handling these agents. People with hand irri-tations can be advised to wear cotton gloves for dry house-work. The hands should be kept out of water.

In patients with diagnosed skin conditions, the skin should be protected from maceration (excessive hydration of stratum corneum) when applying wet dressings. Ther-mal injuries should be carefully guarded against.

The patient with a compromised immune system is at increased risk for cutaneous infection. Nursing Care Plan 28.1 summarizes the nursing care for people with dry skin changes related to trauma and infection.

Relieving Discomfort
A rash that seems trivial to the observer may be causing extreme discomfort to the patient. Cystic lesions may be tender and painful. Many skin disorders produce itching. Itching is a significant symptom which scratching does not relieve. The patient is advised to keep cool, especially at night, and to avoid taking hot baths and wearing wool-len clothing. If itching persists, the sufferer is advised to see their doctor, who may prescribe a topical and/or sys-temic agent.

In providing care for a patient with itching skin lesions, the nurse attempts to discover the cause of discomfort. A sudden onset of generalized rash may indicate a drug al-lergy. Other causes are discussed under 'Pruritus' (below).

Nursing care appropriate for the relief of itching include humidifying the environment, maintaining a cool temperature, removing excess bedding and clothing and limiting the use of soap and using soap substitutes. The nails are trimmed to decrease skin damage from scratch-ing. Every effort should be made to keep the skin hydrated and moisturized to reduce the risk of skin breakdown. The patient is advised to refrain from using over-the-counter preparations to relieve itching because the skin problem may be caused by irritation or sensitization from self-medication.

Gradual evaporation of water from dressings cools the skin and relieves pruritus. The nurse reinforces this teach-ing, making sure that the patient understands that normal skin should be protected during the application of wet dressings. In removing an adherent dressing, the patient is taught to moisten it before removal to relieve discomfort. When taking therapeutic baths, the patient is advised to limit bathing time to no longer than 20 minutes to prevent skin maceration.

Achieving Restful Sleep
Irritation and itching interfere with normal sleep. The nurse may advise the patient of the following measures to promote sleep:

● Keep a regular sleep pattern.
● Avoid caffeinated drinks late in the evening.
● Use a bedtime routine or ritual to ease the transition from wakefulness to sleep.
● Exercise regularly.

In addition, the bedroom should be well-ventilated and humidified. Other measures to promote skin comfort so that the patient may feel more relaxed are found in Nurs-ing Care Plan 28.1.

Increasing Self-Acceptance
Physical appearance exerts a profound influence in the social world and in the way people are treated. Preferen-tial treatment is often bestowed on someone who is per-ceived as being attractive. A clean and healthy skin is intimately correlated with self-esteem.

Skin diseases can be unattractive, causing emotional suffering and affecting social relationships and business and recreational opportunities. People with eczema often have difficulty convincing others that their disease is not contagious. Those with flaking and scaling conditions are usually wary of meeting new people. Comments from strangers may be difficult to deal with. A lowering of self-confidence, excessive fixation on skin defects and worry about scarring are frequently found in people with acne. All of these factors can generate negative emotions in the patient.

The nurse understands that body image is a complex psychological concept that is related to the mental concept of self and self-esteem. Allowing patients to express their feelings freely gives them a sense of support and accept-ance from which strength can be gained. Mutual trust and respect between patient and nurse are necessary to clear the lines of communication. It is helpful to explore with the patient the strategies that may be used to cope with body image changes.

Informed patients may be less anxious and more co-operative. Thus, teaching them about their condition and its treatment may make them more hopeful, which may reinforce their ability to use their resources effectively.

Self-care, particularly hair and skin care, can make a difference in the perceptions of others. Appropriate cosmetics can bring substantial benefits to a person with a chronic skin condition or disfigurement. A referral to an expert on how to camouflage birthmarks, mottled skin, scars and chronic dermatitis can work wonders. People who remain despondent over their condition may benefit from psychological counselling.

Patient Education

A healthy skin reflects general health. Principles of good nutrition, exercise, rest and sleep are emphasized in any teaching programme dealing with skin care. Each person can learn that sunlight permanently damages the skin, leading to roughening, freckling and wrinkling.

A patient who is under treatment for a skin condition is usually told by the doctor what the skin condition is, its aetiology and what to expect from treatment. The nurse reinforces this teaching. It may be advisable to have a relative or friend of the patient nearby for emotional support and also to listen to the advice. Some patients do not listen, do not hear or hear only part of what is being said.

The patient is taught how to apply topical medication, particularly the amount to be used, the size of area to be treated and the frequency of application. The topical medication is smoothed gently onto the affected areas, never rubbed vigorously. In general, the treatment is not used on normal skin. Effects and potential side-effects of the treatment are discussed. Printed information sheets serve to reinforce what has been told.

► **Evaluation**
► **Expected Outcomes**

1. Patient maintains skin integrity.
   a. Indicates absence of skin cracking.
   b. Protects skin from contact with irritating substances.
   c. Applies emollient to skin as prescribed.
2. Achieves relief of discomfort.
   a. Uses topical medication and treatments as taught.
   b. Reports relief of itching.
3. Achieves more restful sleep.
   a. States that better sleeping is taking place.
   b. Reports an increased feeling of well-being.
4. Demonstrates increasing self-acceptance.
   a. Makes fewer self-depreciating remarks.
   b. Pays attention to appearance.
5. Acquires understanding of skin care.

a. Discusses rationale of prescribed treatment.
b. Demonstrates ability to perform treatments.

PRURITUS

Pruritus (itching) is one of the most common complaints in dermatology, causing alteration in comfort and changes in the integrity of the skin. Although pruritus is most frequently due to primary skin disease, it may also reflect systemic disease. Thus, it may be the first indication of an internal disease such as diabetes mellitus, blood disorders or cancer. Itching may also accompany renal, hepatic and thyroid diseases. Pruritus may be caused by certain oral medications; by the external application of certain drugs, soaps and chemicals; by prickly heat (miliaria); and by contact with woollen garments. Patients may also experience pruritus as a side-effect of radiotherapy or reaction to chemotherapy, analgesics or antibiotic therapy or as a symptom of infection. Pruritis may occur in the elderly as a result of dry skin. Itching may also be caused by psychological factors.

Because pruritus usually leads to scratching, the secondary effects include excoriations, redness, raised areas on the skin (wheals), infections of the skin and changes in pigmentation. Severe itching is debilitating.

Management

The cause of pruritus, if known, should be removed. The presence of signs of infection and environmental clues such as warm, dry air or irritating bed linen should be checked. In general, washing with soap and hot water is avoided. The application of a cold agent to the skin to help constrict the blood vessels may be helpful. Emollients (e.g., emulsifying ointment) mixed with water in the bath may be sufficient for cleansing. Soothing baths containing starch or water-soluble tar derivatives may be prescribed.

Topical steroids may prove useful for their anti-inflammatory effect, which may decrease itching.

Nursing Care: Patient Education

The nurse reinforces the reasons for the prescribed treatment and guides the patient on specific points of care. If baths have been prescribed, the patient is reminded to use tepid, not hot, water, and to shake off the excess water and blot between intertriginous areas with a towel. Rubbing vigorously with the towel is avoided because this over-stimulates the skin, causing more itching. Immediately after bathing, the skin should be lubricated with an emollient that traps moisture.

Perianal Itching

Pruritus of the anal and genital regions may be caused by small particles of faecal material lodged in the perianal crevices or attached to anal hairs, or by perianal damage caused by scratching, moisture and decreased skin resistance due to steroids or antibiotics. Other possible causes of perianal itching include local irritants such as scabies and lice, local lesions such as haemorrhoids, fungal or yeast infections, and pinworm infestation. Conditions such as diabetes mellitus, the anaemias, hyperthyroidism and pregnancy may also result in perianal pruritus.

Patient Education

The patient is requested to follow proper hygienic measures and to discontinue home and over-the-counter remedies. The perianal area should be rinsed with lukewarm water and the area blotted dry. If cleansing after defaecation is not possible, premoistened tissues may be used.

As part of health teaching, the patient is advised to avoid bathing in water that is too hot and to avoid using bubble baths, sodium bicarbonate or detergent soaps, all of which aggravate dryness. To keep the perianal skin as dry as possible, patients should avoid wearing underwear made of synthetic fabrics. Local anaesthetic agents should not be used because of possible allergic reactions. The patient should avoid vasodilating agents or stimulants that increase emotional tension (alcohol, coffee), and mechanical irritants such as rough or woollen clothing.

SECRETORY DISORDERS

The main secretory function of the skin is performed by the sweat glands, which help to regulate body temperature. These glands excrete a fluid, perspiration, which evaporates and thus cools the body. The sweat glands are located in various parts of the body and respond to different stimuli; those on the trunk generally respond to thermal stimulation; those on the palms and soles respond to nervous stimulation; and those in the axillae and forehead respond to both kinds of stimulation.

As a rule, moist skin is warm, and dry skin is apt to be cool. However, this is not a hard and fast rule. It is not unusual to observe cold sweats; warm, dry skin in a dehydrated patient; and very hot, dry skin peculiar to some febrile states.

Seborrhoeic Dermatoses

Seborrhoea is excessive production of sebum (secretion of sebaceous glands) in those areas where glands are normally found in large numbers (face, scalp, eyebrows, eyelids, at the sides of the nose and upper lip, malar or cheek regions, ears, axillae, under the breasts, groin, gluteal crease of the buttocks).

Seborrhoeic dermatitis is a chronic inflammatory disease of the skin with a predilection for areas that are well supplied with sebaceous glands or lie between folds of the skin, where the bacterial count is high.

The characteristic lesions are remarkably variable, but this is a dermatitis of the seborrhoeic areas. It may start in childhood with fine scaling of the scalp or other areas, and may continue throughout life. The scales may be dry, moist or greasy. There may be patches of sallow, greasy-appearing skin, with or without scaling, and slight erythema, predominantly on the forehead, nasolabial fold and scalp, and between adjacent skin surfaces in the regions of the axillae, groin and breasts.

The dry, flaky desquamation of the scalp with a profuse amount of fine, powdery scales is commonly called dandruff. The mild forms of the disease are asymptomatic. When scaling is present, it is often accompanied by pruritus, which may lead to scratching and result in secondary complications, such as infections and excoriations.

Seborrhoeic dermatitis has a genetic predisposition; hormones, nutritional status, infection and emotional stress influence its course. There are remissions and exacerbations of this condition, which should be explained to the patient.

Management

Because there is no known cure for seborrhoea, the objective of therapy is to control the disorder and allow the skin to repair itself. Seborrhoeic dermatitis of the body and face may respond to a topically applied corticosteroid cream, which allays the secondary inflammatory response. However, this medication should be used with caution on the eyelids, because it can induce glaucoma in predisposed people. Patients with seborrhoeic dermatitis may develop a secondary *Candida* yeast infection in body creases or folds. To reduce this, patients should be advised to wear loose clothing and to clean and dry intertriginous areas carefully. Patients with persistent candidiasis should be evaluated for diabetes.

The mainstay of dandruff treatment is with medicated shampoos. Two or three different types of shampoo should be used in rotation to prevent the seborrhoea from becoming resistant to a particular shampoo. The shampoo should be left on for at least 5 to 10 minutes. As the problem gets better, the treatment can be less intense. Antiseborrhoeic shampoos include those containing selenium sulphide suspension, zinc pyrithione shampoos, salicylic acid sulphur shampoos and tar shampoos that contain sulphur and salicylic acid.

Nursing Care: Patient Education

A person with seborrhoeic dermatitis is advised to remove external irritants and to avoid excess heat and perspiration, because rubbing and scratching will prolong the disorder. To avoid secondary infections, the patient should air the skin and keep skin folds clean and dry.

Instructions on the use of medicated shampoo are reinforced for those with dandruff that requires treatment.

The patient is advised that seborrhoeic dermatitis is a chronic problem that tends to wax and wane. The expected outcome is to keep it under control. Patients need to be encouraged to adhere to the treatment programme. Those who become discouraged and disheartened by the effect on body image should be treated with sensitivity and an awareness of their need to express their feelings.

Eczema

Eczema is one of the most common abnormal skin disorders (the terms eczema and dermatitis are often used synonymously). In eczema, the epidermis becomes erythematous and thickened, and this is followed by a vesicular eruption. When the vesicles rupture, the serous exudate dries and forms a crust. The skin becomes scaly and may be thickened in patches of varying shapes and sizes. Itching can be severe, causing the patient to scratch, and lichenification can develop in the affected areas.

Atopic Eczema

This is a chronic, fluctuating disease that may occur at any age. It is a genetically determined disorder in which there may be a family history of eczema, asthma or hay fever. The distribution of the lesions may vary considerably. The common symptom is itching. Atopic eczema may also be classified as infantile eczema, atopic eczema of childhood, or adolescent or adult atopic eczema. In the adolescent or adult it may follow childhood eczema, or may occur at the first manifestation of atopic eczema. The limbs, flexures and face are the sites commonly affected, and it may spread to the neck and the trunk. In severe cases, the total skin surface may be affected.

Nummular Eczema

Nummular eczema appears as a well-defined, round or oval coin-like patch of eczema. The common sites are the calves, shins, forearms, backs of fingers and hands. Itching is usually severe, as in atopic eczema.

Pompholyx

Pompholyx is eczema of the thick skin, e.g., of the hands and feet. It occurs on the sides of the fingers and hands, and the sides and soles of toes and feet. The thick horny layer of skin at these sites inhibits rupture of vesicles; thus vesicles may remain for days, looking like whitish grains in the skin.

An eczematous reaction is also seen in seborrhoeic dermatitis and contact dermatitis. Skin care for the patient with eczema is similar to that of the patient with seborrhoeic dermatitis (see p. 873). Patients are advised to remove any known irritants, and patch testing is carried out on any patient suspected of having contact dermatitis

to confirm its presence. Topical therapy must be used regularly. Moisturizing creams (e.g., aqueous cream) should be used regularly. They should be applied liberally and frequently during the day and after washing, to dry or inflamed areas. The patient should be encouraged to have regular emollient baths (see p. 864), and soap substitutes should be used (e.g., emulsifying ointment). Moisturizers and emulsifying ointments should be used even after the eczema has cleared as this helps to prevent the skin from becoming dry and a recurrence of the eczema.

Steroid Therapy
Topical corticosteroids (e.g., hydrocortisone, betamethasone, clobetasol) should be used only when prescribed, and only on the affected areas. Nurses treating patients with these steroids must wear gloves. More potent preparations (e.g., betamethasone, clobetasol) should never be used on the face. Systemic corticosteroid therapy (prednisolone) may be used in acute exacerbations.

Antibiotic Therapy
Antibiotics are given for secondary infection. Systemic antibiotics are given as choice. Topical antibiotics may be prescribed. These should be used with care as they often cause sensitivity to develop.

Baths (see p. 864)
Antiseptic baths may be used for eczema, and bath oils are used for emollient and antipruritic effects.

Open, Wet Dressings
These may be used as described on page 864.

Systemic Therapy
Antihistamines may be prescribed to relieve itching, and sedatives may be given to help the patient sleep and to prevent scratching.

Diet
The patient's history should be reviewed for any indication of allergies. The patient should be advised to avoid substances that have a high potential for sensitization, such as milk, eggs, wheat cereal, chocolate, orange juice and products containing artificial colouring. If an elimination diet is prescribed, the patient's reactions must be monitored closely. A trial diet is started and a new food added every three to five days, during which time response to that food is observed. If no response is apparent, the food is added to the diet. This continues until food allergen is discovered.

Patient Education
The patient is advised on the importance of continuing moisturizing therapy. The patient should avoid any aggravating factors and well-known allergens (e.g., woollen clothing, blankets, rubber). The nurse provides reassur-

ance and support to the patient and loved ones who are coping with long-term problems. This may be achieved by helping the patient to plan skin self-care and management, particularly if the condition is chronic. Involvement of loved ones in planning patient care and in carrying out the treatment can help to reduce stresses between them. The patient should be advised about the National Eczema Society (see 'Useful Addresses').

Evaluation

Expected Outcomes

1. Patient maintains skin integrity.
   a. Indicates absence of skin cracking.
   b. Protects skin from contact with irritating substances.
   c. Applies emollient to skin as prescribed.
2. Achieves relief of discomfort.
   a. Uses topical medication, as taught.
   b. Reports relief of itching.
3. Achieves more restful sleep.
   a. States that better sleep is achieved.
   b. Reports an increased feeling of wellbeing.
4. Demonstrates increasing self-acceptance.
   a. Voices fewer self-deprecating remarks.
   b. Pays attention to appearance.
5. Acquires understanding of necessary skin care.
   a. Demonstrates understanding of rationale of prescribed treatment.
   b. Demonstrates ability to perform treatment.

The nursing care is discussed further in Nursing Care Plan 28.1.

Acne Vulgaris

Acne vulgaris is a common disorder of the sebaceous (oil) glands and their hair follicles (pilosebaceous follicles). It is characterized by the presence of closed comedones (whiteheads), open comedones (blackheads), papules, pustules, nodules and cysts. The outbreaks occur most readily on the face and back, where the sebaceous follicles are more numerous.

Acne is the most commonly encountered skin condition affecting an estimated 85 per cent of the population between 12 and 35 years of age. It becomes more marked at puberty and during adolescence, perhaps because at this age certain endocrine glands of the body that influence the secretions of the sebaceous glands are functioning at peak activity. It may persist well into adulthood. The aetiology of acne appears to be multiple, reflecting an interplay of genetic, hormonal and bacterial factors.

Pathogenesis

During childhood, the sebaceous glands are small and vir-

tually nonfunctioning. These glands are under endocrine control, especially the androgens. During puberty, the presence of androgen stimulates the sebaceous glands, causing them to enlarge and to secrete a natural oil, sebum, which rises to the top of the hair follicle and flows out onto the skin surface. In adolescents who develop acne, androgenic stimulation produces a heightened responce in the sebaceous glands. Acne occurs when the pilosebaceous ducts through which the sebum flows become plugged, resulting in an accumulation of the sebaceous material that plugs the duct. This accumulation of material forms comedones.

Clinical Features

The initial lesions of acne are comedones. Closed comedones ('whiteheads') are obstructive lesions formed from impacted lipids or oils and keratin that plug the dilated follicle. Whiteheads are small, whitish papules with minute follicular openings that generally cannot be seen. These closed comedones may evolve into open comedones, in which the contents of the ducts are in open communication with the external environment. Open comedones ('blackheads') are due to an accumulation of lipid, bacterial and epithelial debris that obstructs the flow of sebum.

Although the exact cause is not known, some closed comedones may rupture and result in an inflammatory reaction due to the leakage of follicle contents (sebum, keratin, bacteria) into the dermis. This inflammatory response may result from the action of certain skin bacteria, such as *Propionibacterium acnes*, that live in the hair follicles and break down the triglycerides of the sebum into free fatty acids and glycerin. The resulting inflammation is seen clinically as papules, pustules, nodules, cysts or abscesses.

Management

The expected outcomes of management are to reduce colonization by the bacteria, decrease sebaceous gland activity, prevent the follicles from becoming plugged, reduce inflammation, combat secondary infection, minimize scarring and eliminate factors that may predispose to acne. The therapeutic regime depends on the type of lesion (comedonal, papular, pustular, cystic). A combination of therapies may be tried.

Topical Therapy

Benzoyl Peroxide

Benzoyl peroxide preparations are widely used because they produce a rapid and sustained reduction of inflammatory lesions. They also have an antibacterial effect by suppressing *Propionibacterium acnes*. They depress sebum production and lead to the breakdown of the comedone plugs. Initially, benzoyl peroxide causes redness and scaling, but generally the skin adjusts quickly to its use.

Usually the patient applies a gel preparation of benzoyl peroxide once daily. In many instances this will be the only treatment needed. Benzoyl peroxide is available over the counter and by prescription.

Vitamin A Acid

Topically applied vitamin A acid is used to clear the keratin plugs from the pilosebaceous ducts. Vitamin A acid speeds up the cellular turnover, forces out the comedones and prevents occurrence of new comedones. Thus it is effective in the treatment of comedonal acne. However, the patient should be informed that symptoms may worsen during early weeks of therapy because inflammation may occur during the process. Erythema and peeling are also a frequent result. Improvement may take up to 8 to 12 weeks. Some patients cannot tolerate this therapy. The patient is advised against sun exposure while using this topical medication because it may cause an exaggerated sunburn. Package insert directions are to be followed implicitly.

Topical Antibiotics

The use of topically applied antibiotics for the treatment of acne has become widespread. Topical antibiotics suppress the growth of *P. acnes*; reduce skin-surface free fatty acid levels; decrease comedones, papules and pustules; and do not have systemic side-effects. Topical preparations containing clindamycin are frequently used (Stoughton, 1979).

Systemic Therapy

Systemic Antibiotics

Oral antibiotics given in small doses over a long period are very effective in the treatment of patients with moderate and severe acne, especially when the acne is inflammatory and results in pustules, abscesses and scarring. Therapy may be continued for months to years. The patient is advised to take tetracycline at least one hour before or two hours after meals with clear fluids, because the drug is poorly absorbed with food. Side-effects of tetracyclines include photosensitivity, nausea, diarrhoea, vaginitis in women and cutaneous infection in either sex. (In some women, broad-spectrum antibiotics may predispose the patient to candidiasis.)

Oral Retinoids

Synthetic vitamin A compounds (retinoids) are being used with dramatic results in patients with nodular cystic acne that is unresponsive to conventional therapy. One compound is isotretinoin, which is also used for active inflammatory papular pustular acne that has a tendency to scar. Isotretinoin causes a reduction in sebaceous gland size and inhibits sebum production. It also causes the epidermis to shed (epidermal desquamation), thereby unseating and expelling existing comedones. The most common side-effect, experienced by almost all patients, is cheilitis (inflammation of the lips). Drying and chapping of the skin and mucous membranes are also frequently encountered. These changes are reversible with the withdrawal of the medication. Most importantly, isotretinoin is teratogenic in humans, meaning that it can have an adverse effect on a fetus. Therefore, contraceptive measures for females of childbearing age are obligatory during treatment and for as long as advised by the doctor. Patients are also cautioned not to take vitamin A supplements while on this drug, to avoid additive toxic effects.

Hormone Therapy

Oestrogen therapy (progesterone–oestrogen preparations) has been found to suppress sebum production and reduce skin oiliness. It is usually reserved for young women when the acne begins somewhat later than usual and tends to flare at certain times in the menstrual cycle, which is often irregular. Oestrogen in the form of oestrogen-dominant oral contraceptive compounds may be given on a prescribed cyclic regime. Oestrogen is not given to males because of undesirable side-effects.

Surgical Treatment

Surgical treatment of acne consists of comedone extraction, injections of steroids into the inflamed lesions and incision, and drainage of large, fluctuant, nodular cystic lesions. Cryosurgery (freezing with liquid nitrogen) may be used for nodular and cystic forms of acne. Patients with deep scars may be treated with deep abrasive therapy (dermabrasion, p. 906), in which the epidermis and some superficial dermis are removed down to the level of the scars.

Comedone Extraction

Comedones may be removed with a comedone extractor. The site is first wiped with an alcohol swab. The comedone is nicked with an 18-gauge needle or scalpel blade to widen the follicular opening and facilitate the removal of the comedone. The opening of the extractor is then placed over the lesion, and direct pressure is applied to cause extrusion of the plug through the expressor.

Removal of comedones will leave areas of erythema, which may take several weeks to subside. Recurrence of comedones after extraction is common because part of the comedone frequently remains in the pilosebaceous canal. However, the procedure is mainly of cosmetic benefit and may encourage the patient with its immediate result.

▶ NURSING PROCESS
▶ THE PATIENT WITH ACNE

▶ *Assessment*

Virtually all people will develop an occasional blemish or lesion during adolescence. The nurse, through observation and listening, finds out how patients perceive their skin condition. One young person will view a small blemish as intolerable, while another teenager will regard more extensive involvement as 'normal'. Adolescents, who are in their formative years of development, are vulnerable and need to be approached with empathy and compassion as they attempt to deal with acne. The nurse keeps this in mind during the assessment and other contacts with them.

When assessing the patient, stretch the skin gently and inspect the lesions. Closed comedones (which are precursors of larger inflammatory lesions) appear as slightly elevated small papules. Open comedones appear flat or slightly raised with a central follicular impaction. Look for and document the presence of inflammatory lesions: papules, pustules, nodules or cysts.

► *Patient's Problems*

Based on the nursing assessment, the patient's main problems may include the following:

- Lack of knowledge about cause and treatment of acne.
- Lack of self-esteem related to embarrassment and frustration over appearance

► *Planning and Implementation*
► Expected Outcomes

The main outcomes for the patient may include development of knowledge and understanding of the condition, and development of self-acceptance.

Nursing Care

Patient Education

Before treatment is initiated, patients are counselled and assured that the problem is not related to uncleanliness, dietary indiscretions, masturbation, sexual activity or any of the other popular misconceptions. The concept that acne arises because of a combination of factors, including heredity, large sebaceous glands and large numbers of *P. acnes* bacteria, all of which are beyond the control of the patient, needs to be reinforced.

When treatment is instituted, it may take four to six weeks or longer for results to be seen. Patients are taught to wash the face with mild soap and water twice a day to remove the surface oils and prevent obstruction of the oil glands. Patients need to be cautioned against scrubbing the face constantly, since acne is not caused by dirt and cannot be washed away. Mild abrasive soaps and drying agents may be prescribed to eliminate the oily feeling that troubles many patients. However, excessive abrasion is to be avoided because it only makes acne worse. It is also important to realize that soap itself can be irritating to the skin. The use of a polyester sponge pad provides the mechanical removal of superficial skin cells (epidermabrasion) and may be helpful to some patients. Hair should be kept off the face and shampooed daily if necessary.

All forms of friction and trauma are to be avoided: propping the hands against the face, rubbing the face and wearing tight collars and helmets. Patients are requested to keep hands away from the face and not to squeeze pimples or blackheads. Squeezing merely worsens the problem, because a portion of the blackhead is pushed down into the skin which may cause the follicle to rupture. There is no evidence that a particular food can cause or worsen acne.

Patients are counselled that acne is not something that can be cleared up in a short time, and that they must be consistent with treatment every day. The patient should be encouraged to use the cleansing product prescribed by the doctor. Reassurance is necessary that most acne medications cause some degree of drying and peeling, although the sudden appearance of diffuse redness and vesicles suggests contact allergy.

Development of Self-Acceptance

The patient is enrolled as a partner in therapy. It is of great importance that the problems be taken seriously and that the patient be given understanding, reassurance and support. All facets of the emotional factors involved must be taken into account. Stressful situations (e.g., examinations) cause exacerbations. Learning stress reduction techniques may be helpful.

► *Evaluation*
► Expected Outcomes

1. Patient develops increasing understanding of the skin problem.
   a. Reviews drawings of obstructive and inflammatory lesions of acne.
   b. Reads patient education brochures.
   c. Understands that picking and squeezing blemishes/ lesions will worsen the condition and may cause scarring.
   d. Reads the product information brochure of the prescribed medication.
2. Adheres to the prescribed therapy.
   a. States that a major commitment to required treatment, that may take months or years, will be made.
   b. Understands that the treatment must be continued when the skin clears.
   c. Follows cleansing programme.
   d. Avoids overcleansing.
3. Develops self-acceptance.
   a. Avoids mirror-gazing.
   b. Identifies someone with whom the problems can be talked over.
   c. Expresses optimism about outcome of treatment.

INFECTIONS AND INFESTATIONS OF THE SKIN

Bacterial Infections

Bacterial infections of the skin may be primary or secondary. Primary skin infections originate in previously normal-appearing skin and are usually caused by a single organism. Secondary skin infections arise from a pre-existing skin disorder in which several micro-organisms may be implicated.

The most common primary bacterial skin infections are impetigo and folliculitis. Folliculitis may lead to furuncles or carbuncles.

Impetigo

Impetigo is a superficial infection of the skin caused by streptococci, staphylococci or multiple bacteria. The lesions begin as small, red macules, which quickly become discrete, thin-walled vesicles that soon rupture and become covered with a loosely adherent honey-yellow crust. These crusts are easily removed and reveal smooth, red, moist surfaces on which new crusts soon develop. The exposed areas of the body, face, hands, neck and extremities are most frequently involved. Impetigo is contagious and may spread to other parts of the patient's skin or to other members of the family or significant others who touch the patient or use towels that are soiled with the exudate of the lesions.

Although impetigo is seen at all ages, it is particularly common among children living in poor hygienic conditions. Often it appears secondary to pediculosis capitis, scabies, herpes simplex, insect bites, poison ivy or eczema. In adults, ill health, poor hygiene and malnutrition may predispose to impetigo.

Bullous impetigo, a superficial infection of the skin caused by *Staphylococcus aureus*, is characterized by the formation of bullae from original vesicles. The bullae rupture, leaving a raw, red area.

Management

Systemic antibiotic therapy is the usual treatment. It is used to reduce contagious spread, treat deep infection and prevent acute glomerulonephritis, which has been known to occur as an aftermath of streptococcal skin diseases. In nonbullous impetigo, benzathine penicillin or oral penicillin may be given. Bullous impetigo is treated with a penicillinase-resistant penicillin (cloxacillin, dicloxacillin).

An antiseptic preparation (povidone-iodine; chlorhexidine) may be used to cleanse the skin in the vicinity of the infection to prevent spread.

The lesions are soaked or washed with soap solution to remove the central site of bacterial growth and to give the topical antibiotic an opportunity to reach the infected site. After the crusts are removed, a prescribed topical medication (e.g., neomycin, bacitracin) is applied. Topical treatment must be done several times a day. Gloves should be worn when care is given to these patients.

Patient Education

The patient and family/significant others should be advised to bathe daily with bactericidal soap. Cleanliness and good hygienic practices help prevent the spread of the lesions from one skin area to another and from one person to another. Each person should have a separate towel and washcloth. Since impetigo is a contagious disorder, an infected child should be kept away from other children.

Folliculitis, Furuncles and Carbuncles

Folliculitis refers to a staphylococcal infection that arises within the hair follicles. Lesions may be superficial or deep. Single or multiple papules or pustules appear close to the hair follicles.

Sycosis barbae ('shaving bumps') is an inflammatory reaction on the face of curly-haired males caused by ingrowing hairs that pierce the skin and cause an irritative reaction. Curly hair has a curved root that grows at a more acute angle. This is a common problem in black males but may also occur in others. The initial treatment is to avoid shaving and grow a beard. If this is not possible, a hand-brush may be used over the facial area to dislodge the hairs mechanically. If the patient must shave, a depilatory cream may be useful.

A furuncle (boil) is an acute inflammation arising deep in one or more hair follicles and spreading into the surrounding dermis. It is a deeper form of folliculitis. (Furunculosis refers to multiple or recurrent lesions.) Furuncles may occur anywhere on the body but are more prevalent in areas subjected to irritation, pressure, friction and excessive perspiration, such as the back of the neck, the axillae or the buttocks.

A furuncle may start as a small, red, raised, painful 'pimple'. Frequently, the infection progresses and involves the skin and subcutaneous fatty tissue, causing tenderness, pain and surrounding cellulitis. The area or redness and induration represents an effort of the body to keep the infection localized. The bacteria (usually staphylococcus) produce necrosis of the invaded tissues, followed in a few days by the characteristic pointing of a boil. When this occurs, the centre becomes yellow or black, and the boil is said popularly to have 'come to a head'.

A carbuncle is an abscess of the skin and subcutaneous tissue representing an extension of a furuncle that has invaded several follicles and is larger and more deep-seated. It is usually caused by a staphylococcal infection. Carbuncles appear most commonly in areas in which the skin is thick and inelastic. The back of the neck and the buttocks are common sites. In carbuncles, the extensive inflammation frequently is not associated with a complete walling off of the infection, so that absorption occurs, resulting in high fever, pain, leucocytosis and even extension of the infection to the bloodstream.

Furuncles and carbuncles are more apt to occur in patients with underlying systemic diseases, such as diabetes or haematological malignancies, and those receiving immunosuppressive therapy for other diseases.

Management

In the treatment of staphylococcal infections, it is important not to rupture or destroy the protective wall of induration that has localized the infection. Therefore, the boil or pimple should never be squeezed.

The follicular disorders (folliculitis, furuncles, carbuncles) are usually caused by staphylococci. If the immune system is impaired, the causative organisms may be gram-negative bacilli.

Systemic antibiotic therapy, selected by sensitivity study, is generally indicated. Intravenous infusions, tepid sponging and other supportive treatments are indicated for the very ill and toxic patient. Warm, moist compresses increase vascularization and hasten resolution of the furuncle or carbuncle. The surrounding skin is cleansed gently with antibacterial soap, and an antibacterial ointment is applied to prevent spillage and seeding of the bacteria in the event that the lesion ruptures or is incised.

When the pus has localized and is fluctuant (moving in palpable waves), a small incision with a scalpel will speed resolution by relieving the tension and ensuring a direct evacuation of the pus and slough. The patient is requested to keep the draining lesion covered with a dressing. Soiled dressings should be wrapped in paper and burned. Nurses should carefully follow isolation precautions in order to avoid becoming staphylococcus carriers. Disposable gloves should be worn when caring for these patients.

Special precautions must be taken with boils on the face, for the skin area drains directly into the cranial venous sinuses. Sinus thrombosis, with fatal pyaemia, has been known to develop after manipulation of a boil in this location.

Bedrest is advised for patients who have boils on the perineum or in the anal region, and a course of systemic antibiotic therapy is indicated to control the spread of the infection.

Patient Education

To prevent and control staphylococcal skin infections (boils, carbuncles), the staphylococcus must be eliminated from the skin and environment. Efforts must be made to increase the patient's resistance and provide a hygienic environment. If lesions are actively draining, the mattress and pillow should be covered with plastic material and wiped off with disinfectant daily; the bed linen, towels and clothing should be laundered after each use; the patient should shower and shampoo with an anti-bacterial soap and shampoo for an indefinite period. The prescribed antibiotic should be taken for the full length of time as directed.

Viral Infections

Herpes Zoster (Shingles)

Herpes zoster (shingles) is an inflammatory viral condition in which the virus produces a painful vesicular eruption along the distribution of the nerves from one or more posterior ganglia. It is caused by the varicella virus, which is a member of a group of DNA viruses. It is assumed that herpes zoster represents a reactivation of latent varicella (chicken pox) virus and reflects a lowered immunity. After a case of chicken pox runs its course, it is believed that the varicella virus responsible for the outbreak lies dormant inside nerve cells near the brain and spinal cord. Later, when these sleeping viruses are reactivated, they travel by way of the peripheral nerves to the skin. There, the viruses multiply, creating a red rash of small fluid-filled blisters. About 10 per cent of adults get shingles during their lifetime, usually after the age of 50. There is an increased frequency of herpes zoster in patients with weakened immune systems and malignancies, especially the leukaemias and the lymphomas.

Clinical Features

The eruption is generally accompanied or preceded by pain, which may radiate over the entire region supplied by the nerves. The pain may be burning, stabbing or aching. In some patients the pain is absent. Some itching and tenderness may occur over the area. At times malaise and gastrointestinal disturbances precede the eruption.

The patches of grouped vesicles appear on the red and swollen skin. The early vesicles contain serum and later become purulent, rupture and form crusts. The inflammation is usually unilateral, involving the thoracic, cervical or cranial nerves in a bandlike configuration. The blisters are usually confined to a narrow region of the face or trunk. The clinical course varies from one to three weeks. If an ophthalmic nerve is involved, the patient may have a painful eye. Inflammation and a rash on the trunk may cause pain at the slightest touch. The healing time varies between 7 and 26 days.

Herpes zoster in healthy adults is usually localized and benign. However, in immunosuppressed patients, the disease may be severe and the clinical course acutely disabling.

Management

The expected outcomes of management are to relieve the pain and to reduce or avoid complications. These include infection, scarring and postherpetic neuralgia and eye complications.

The pain is controlled with analgesics, because adequate pain control during the acute phase will help prevent persistent pain patterns.

Systemic corticosteroids are given to patients over the age of 50 to reduce the incidence and duration of postherpetic neuralgia (persistent pain of affected nerve following healing). Healing is usually more rapid in those who have been treated with steroids. There is some evidence that infection is arrested if oral acyclovir is given within 24 hours of the appearance of the eruption. Intravenous acyclovir, if started early, is effective in significantly reducing the pain and halting the progression of the disease.

If the eye is involved, the patient is referred to an ophthalmologist, because keratitis, uveitis, ulceration and blindness may occur.

A susceptible person can acquire chicken pox through contact with the infective vesicular fluid of a zoster patient. A person with previous history of chicken pox is immune and thus not at risk of infection after exposure to zoster patients. In older people, the pain from herpes zoster may persist as postherpetic neuralgia for months after the skin lesions disappear.

Patient Education

The nurse assesses the patient's discomfort and response to medication. The patient is taught how to apply wet dressings or medication to the lesions and to follow proper hand washing techniques to avoid spreading the herpes zoster virus.

Diversionary activities, such as television or crafts, and relaxation techniques are encouraged to assure restful sleep—all of which help to alleviate discomfort.

Because so many of these patients are elderly, a caregiver may be required to assist with dressings. Relatives, neighbours or a community nurse may need to help with dressing changes and general care, as necessary.

Fungal Infections (Mycoses)

The fungi, tiny representatives of the plant kingdom that feed on organic matter, are responsible for a variety of common skin infections. In some cases, they affect only the skin and its appendages (i.e., hair and nails), but in others, the internal organs are involved. In the latter instance, fungal disease may be so serious as to constitute a threat to life. Superficial infections, on the other hand, rarely cause temporary disability and respond readily to treatment. Secondary infection with bacteria or *Candida*, or both, may occur.

To obtain material for diagnosis, a scalpel is used to scrape scales from the margin of the lesion. The scales are dropped onto a slide to which potassium hydroxide has been added. The diagnosis is made by examining the infected scales microscopically and by isolating the organism in culture.

Wood's light induces fluorescence of a specimen of infected hair and may be helpful in diagnosing some cases of tinea capitis.

Tinea Pedis (Ringworm of the Feet; Athlete's Foot)

Tinea pedis, the most common fungal infection, is a superficial infection that affects the soles of the feet or the space between the toes. It may be acute or chronic in nature. As an acute infection, it is characterized by the appearance of inflamed vesicles. As a chronic condition, it is manifested as a scaly, dusky or reddened rash. The toenails may or may not be affected; if involved, they are apt to be discoloured, brittle and heaped-up. As a rule, there is moderate to severe itching. Lymphangitis and cellulitis may be seen occasionally when bacterial superinfection occurs. Sometimes a mixed fungal, bacterial and yeast infection occurs.

Preventive Measures and Patient Education

Because footwear provides a hospitable environment for fungi, the causative fungi may be in the shoes and socks. Because moisture encourages the growth of fungi, the patient is advised to keep the feet as dry as possible, including the areas between the toes. Small pieces of cotton can be placed between the toes at night to absorb moisture. Socks should be made of absorbent cotton, and hosiery should have cotton feet, since synthetic material does not absorb perspiration as well as cotton. For people whose feet perspire excessively, open-toed shoes or sandals should be worn whenever possible. Plastic or rubber-soled footwear should be avoided. Talcum powder or antifungal powder applied twice daily helps to keep the feet dry. Shoes should be alternated so that they may dry completely before they are worn again.

Management

During the acute (vesicular) phase, soaks of Burow's solution, saline or potassium permanganate are used to remove the crusts, scales and debris and to reduce the inflammation. Topical antifungals (miconazole; clotrimazole) are applied to the infected areas. Topical therapy is continued for several weeks, as there is a high rate of recurrence. Clinical and laboratory examinations are done to confirm the causative agent and indicate the treatment. An antifungal agent, griseofulvin, is given orally if there is an extension of the infection or resistance to topical therapy.

Tinea Capitis (Ringworm of the Scalp)

Ringworm of the scalp is a contagious fungal infection of the hair shafts and a common cause of hair loss in children. *Microsporum* and *Trichophyton* species are the dermatophytes (cutaneous fungi) that infect hair. Clinically, one or several round patches of redness and scaling are present. Small pustules or papules may be seen at the edges of such patches. As the hairs in the affected areas are invaded by the fungi, they become brittle and often break off at or near the surface of the scalp, resulting in areas of baldness. Most cases of tinea capitis heal without scarring, so the hair loss is only temporary. Sometimes a boggy swelling resembling a furuncle occurs in an area of involvement; this lesion is known as a kerion.

A second form of ringworm caused by *Trichophyton tonsurans* has become prominent in the inner city. It presents as a scaling dermatitis, similar to seborrhoea. The skin may be slightly red and scaly, and there are broken-off hairs.

Diagnosis
When fungi invade and interact with the superficial layers of the hair shaft, the infected hairs produce a yellow green fluorescence when irradiated by Wood's light. However, infection by the *Trichophyton* species is nonfluorescent.

Management
Griseofulvin, an antifungal agent, is given to patients with tinea capitis. Side-effects of griseofulvin include photosensitivity, headache, skin eruptions and gastrointestinal disturbances. Infected hairs break off, leaving noninfected ones in place. The hair should be shampooed two to three times weekly, and a topical antifungal preparation should be applied to reduce dissemination of the organisms.

Patient Education
Because the disease is contagious, the patient and family/significant others should be advised to set up a hygienic regime for home use. Each person should have a separate comb and brush and should avoid exchanging headgear. All infected members of the patient's household, including pets, must be examined because familial infections are relatively common.

Tinea Corporis (Ringworm of the Body)

Tinea corporis or tinea circinata is ringworm of the body. It begins as an erythematous (red) macule advancing to rings of vesicles with central clearing. The lesions appear in clusters, usually on the exposed areas of the body. These may extend to the scalp, hair or nails. As a rule, there is an elevated border consisting of small papules or vesicles. Coalescence of individual rings may result in large patches with bizarre scalloped borders. Ringworm of the body may cause intense itching. A frequent cause is the presence of an infected pet in the home.

Management
Topical antifungal medication may be applied to small areas. Griseofulvin is used in extensive cases.

Patient Education
The patient is advised to use a clean towel and washcloth daily. All areas and skin folds that retain moisture must be dried thoroughly, because fungal infections are fostered by heat and moisture. Clean cotton clothing should be worn next to the skin.

Tinea Cruris (Ringworm of the Groin)

Tinea cruris is ringworm infection of the groin, which may extend to the inner thighs and buttock area. It is commonly associated with tinea pedis. It occurs most frequently in joggers, obese people and those who wear tight underclothing. The infection starts with small, red, scaly patches and extends to form circinate (circular) plaques with elevated scaly or vesicular borders. Itching is usually present.

Mild infections may be treated with topical medication (clotrimazole, miconazole) for at least three to four weeks to ensure complete eradication of the infection. Oral griseofulvin may be required for more severe infections.

Patient Education
Heat, friction and maceration (from sweating) predispose to the infection. The patient is advised to avoid as far as possible excessive heat and humidity, nylon underwear, tight-fitting clothing and the prolonged wearing of a wet bathing suit. Concomitant tinea pedis must be treated to minimize reinfection. The groin area should be cleansed, dried thoroughly and dusted with a topical antifungal agent (tolnaftate) as a preventive measure, since the infection is apt to recur.

Tinea Unguium (Onychomycosis)

Tinea unguium (ringworm of the nails) is a chronic fungal infection of the toenails or, less commonly, the fingernails, and is usually caused by *Trichophyton* species (*T. rubrum*, *T. mentagrophytes*) or *Candida albicans*. It is usually associated with longstanding fungal infection of the feet. The nails become thickened, friable (easily crumbled) and lustreless. In time, debris accumulates under the free edge of the nail, and ultimately the nail plate becomes separated. The nail may be destroyed.

Management
Griseofulvin is usually given orally for six months to a year when the fingernails are involved. Of course, griseofulvin is not of value in treating candidal infections; these must be treated topically with amphotericin-B lotion, miconazole, clotrimazole, nystatin or other preparations. These products penetrate poorly, and the infections are difficult to treat. Response to griseofulvin in fungal infections of the toenails is poor at best. Toenails are slow-growing, with growth from the matrix of the nail to its free edge taking 130 to 160 days (4 to 5 months). Therefore, medications have to be used for a year or more, with only a limited chance of cure. Frequently, when the treatment is stopped the infection returns.

PARASITIC SKIN DISEASES

Pediculosis (Infestation by Lice)

Lice infestation affects people of all ages. Three varieties of lice infest humans: *Pediculus humanus capitis* (head louse); *Pediculus humanus corporis* (body louse); and *Phthirus pubis* (pubic, or 'crab', louse). They depend on the host for their nourishment, feeding on human blood approximately five times a day. They inject their digestive juices and excrement into the skin, which causes severe itching.

Pediculosis Capitis

Pediculosis capitis is an infestation of the scalp by the head louse, *Pediculus humanus capitis*. The female head louse lays her eggs (nits) close to the scalp. The nits become firmly attached to the hair shafts with a tenacious substance. The young lice hatch in about 10 days and reach maturity in two weeks. Head lice are found most commonly along the back of the head and behind the ears. The eggs are visible to the naked eye as silvery, glistening oval bodies that are difficult to remove from the hair. The bite of the insect causes intense itching, and the resultant scratching often leads to secondary bacterial infection with pustules, crusts, matted hair, impetigo and furunculosis. The infestation is more common in children and people with long hair. Head lice may be transmitted by direct physical contact or indirectly by the use of infested combs, brushes, wigs, hats and bedding.

Management
Treatment involves washing the hair with a shampoo containing gamma-benzene hexachloride or malathion. The patient is taught to shampoo the scalp and hair according to the product directives. After the hair is rinsed thoroughly, it is combed with a fine-toothed comb that is dipped in vinegar to remove any remaining nits or nit shells freed from the hair shafts. These are extremely difficult to remove and may have to be picked off by the fingernails, one by one (thus, the term 'nit picking'). All articles, clothing, towels and bedding that might have lice or nits should be washed in hot water (at least 54°C) or dry-cleaned to prevent reinfestation. Upholstered furniture, rugs and floors should be vacuumed frequently. Combs and brushes are also disinfected with the shampoo. All family members and close contacts are treated at the same time.

Complications such as severe pruritus, pyoderma (pus-forming infection of the skin) and dermatitis are treated with antipruritics, systemic antibiotics and topical corticosteroids.

Patient Education
The patient is reassured that head lice infestation may happen to anyone and is not a sign of uncleanliness. This condition spreads rapidly, so treatment must be started immediately. Control of school epidemics may be helped by having all of the pupils shampoo their hair on the same night. Students should be warned not to share combs, brushes or hats. Each household member should be inspected for head lice daily for at least two weeks.

Pediculosis Corporis and Pediculosis Pubis

Pediculosis corporis is an infestation of the body by the body louse, *Pediculus humanus corporis*. The body louse lives chiefly in the seams of underwear and clothing, to which it clings as it pierces the skin with its proboscis. Its bites cause characteristic minute haemorrhagic points. Widespread excoriation may appear as a result of intense itching and scratching, especially on the trunk and neck. Among the secondary lesions produced are parallel linear scratches and a slight degree of eczema. In longstanding cases, the skin may become thickened, dry and scaly, with dark pigmented areas. The areas of the skin chiefly involved are those that come in closest contact with the underclothing (i.e., the neck, trunk and thighs). The lice may be seen even in the seams of the clothing, so the clothing and bedding must be laundered or dry-cleaned to destroy the parasite and its eggs. A shower should be taken and precautionary methods followed to prevent reinfestation.

Complications, such as severe pruritus, pyoderma (pus-forming infection of the skin) and dermatitis are treated with antipruritics, systemic antibiotics and topical corticosteroids. It is important to remember that body lice are capable of transmitting epidemic disease in humans, namely rickettsial disease (epidemic typhus, relapsing fever and trench fever). The causative organism may be in the gastrointestinal tract of the insect and may be excreted on the skin surface of the infested person.

Pediculosis pubis, infestation by *Phthirus pubis* ('crab louse'), is an extremely common problem that is generally localized in the genital region and transmitted chiefly by sexual contact.

Reddish brown 'dust' from the excretions of the insects may be found in underclothing. Lice may also infest the hairs of the chest, axillary hair, beard and eyelashes. Grey-blue macules may sometimes be seen on the trunk, thighs and axillae as a result of either the reaction of the insects' saliva with bilirubin (converting it to biliverdin) or an excretion produced by the salivary glands of the louse. The pubic crease should be examined with a magnifying glass to detect the presence of *Phthirus pubis* crawling down a hair shaft, or nits cemented to the hair or at the junction with the skin. Itching is the most common symptom, particularly at night.

Management and Patient Education
The patient is requested to bathe with soap and water.

Then either gamma-benzene hexachloride or malathion in isopropyl alcohol is applied to affected areas of the skin and to hairy areas, according to the product information. If the eyelashes are involved, petrolatum may be thickly applied twice daily for eight days, followed by mechanical removal of any remaining nits.

All sexual contacts and household members must be treated. The patient and partner(s) may need to be investigated for coexisting sexually transmitted diseases.

Scabies

Scabies is an infestation of the skin by the mite, *Sarcoptes scabiei*. Infestations are not dependent on sexual activity, because the mites frequently involve the fingers, and hand contact may produce infection. In children, overnight stays with friends or the exchange of clothes may be a source of infection. Health care staff who have prolonged 'hands on' physical contact with an infected patient may likewise become infected.

The adult female burrows into the superficial layer of the skin and remains there for the rest of her life. With her jaws and the sharp edges of the joints of her forelegs, the mite extends the burrow, laying two to three eggs daily for up to two months. She then dies. The larvae (eggs) hatch in three to four days, and progress through larval and nymphal states to form adult mites in about 10 days.

Clinical Features

It takes approximately four weeks from the time of contact for the patient's symptoms to appear. The patient complains of severe itching caused by a delayed type of immunological reaction to the mite or its faecal pellets. During examination, the patient is asked where the itch is most severe. A magnifying glass and a light are held at an oblique angle to the skin while a search is made for the small, raised burrows. The burrows may be multiple, straight or wavy, brown or black, threadlike lesions, most commonly observed between the fingers and on the wrists. Other sites are the extensor surfaces of the elbows, the knees, the outer borders of the feet, around the nipples, in the axillary folds, under pendulous breasts and in or near the groin or gluteal fold, penis or scrotum. Red pruritic eruptions usually appear between adjacent skin areas. The burrow, however, is not always seen. Any patient with a rash may have scabies.

One classic sign of scabies is the increased itching that occurs at night, perhaps because the increased warmth of the skin has a stimulating effect on the parasite. Also, hypersensitivity to the organism and its products of excretion may contribute to the itching. If the infection has spread, other members of the household and close friends will also complain of itching about a month later.

Although the older patient itches severely, the vivid inflammatory reaction seen in younger people is usually absent. Scabies may not be recognized in the elderly, and the itching may erroneously be attributed to the dry skin of old age or to anxiety.

Secondary lesions are quite common and include vesicles, papules, excoriations and crusts. Bacterial superinfection may result from constant excoriation of the burrows and papules.

The diagnosis is confirmed by recovering *Sarcoptes scabei* or the mites' by-products from the skin. A sample of superficial epidermis is scraped off the top of the burrows or papules with a small scalpel blade. The scrapings are placed on a microscope slide and examined through a low-powered microscope to demonstrate the presence of any stage of the mite (adult, eggs, egg casings, larva, nymph) and faecal pellets.

Patient Education

The patient is advised to take a warm, soapy bath or shower to remove the scaling debris from the crusts and then to dry thoroughly and allow the skin to cool. Then a scabicide, such as gamma-benzene hexachloride or crotamiton, is applied thinly to the entire skin from the neck down, sparing only the face and scalp (which are not affected in scabies). The medication is left on as prescribed, after which the patient is advised to wash thoroughly. One application is usually curative. The patient should wear clean clothing and sleep between freshly laundered bed linens. All bedding and clothing should be washed in very hot water.

All household members and close contacts should be treated simultaneously to eliminate the mites. If scabies is sexually transmitted, the patient may require treatment for coexisting sexually transmitted disease. Scabies may also coexist with pediculosis.

After the treatment is completed, a bland ointment may be applied because the solution may be irritating to the skin. The hypersensitivity state does not cease upon destruction of the mites. Itching may remain a troublesome problem for a few days or weeks because itching is a manifestation of hypersensitivity, particularly in atopic (allergic) people. However, this is not a sign that the treatment has failed. The patient is requested not to apply more scabicide (as this will cause more irritation and increased itching) and not to take frequent hot showers (as this dries the skin and produces itching).

For patients in extended care facilities, health care staff should wear gloves when providing hands-on care for a patient suspected of having scabies until the diagnosis is confirmed and treatment accomplished.

CONTACT DERMATITIS

Contact dermatitis is an inflammatory reaction of the skin to physical, chemical or biological agents. The epidermis is damaged by repeated physical and chemical irritations. Contact dermatitis may be of the primary irritant type, in which a nonallergic reaction results from exposure to an irritating substance, or it may be allergic in nature (allergic contact dermatitis), resulting from exposure of sensitized people to contact allergens. Common causes of irritant contact dermatitis are soaps, detergents, scouring compounds and industrial chemicals. Predisposing factors include extremes of heat and cold, frequent immersion in soap and water, and a pre-existing skin disease.

Clinical Features

The eruptions begin at the point at which the offending agent contacts the skin, and may appear as urticaria or eczema.

Management

The objectives of management are to rest the involved skin, carry out symptomatic treatment and protect it from further damage. The distribution pattern of the reaction is determined in order to differentiate between allergic contact dermatitis and the irritant type. A detailed history is obtained. Then the offending agent is identified by patch-testing. Local irritation should be avoided, and soap is not generally used until healing occurs.

Patient Education.

The patient is advised as follows:

● Study the pattern of your dermatitis (location on the skin) and think about things that have touched your skin and may have caused the problem.
● Try to avoid contact with these materials.
● Avoid heat, soap and rubbing, all of which are external irritants.
● Avoid topical medications except when specifically prescribed.
● Wash the skin thoroughly immediately after exposure to irritants or antigens.
● When gloves are used for washing dishes, use cotton-lined gloves but do not wear them for more than 15 to 20 minutes at a time.

The advice should be followed for at least four months after the skin appears to be completely healed, because the resistance of the skin is lowered.

NONINFECTIOUS INFLAMMATORY DERMATOSES

Psoriasis

Psoriasis is a chronic inflammatory disease of the skin in which the production of epidermal cells occurs at a rate that is approximately six to nine times faster than normal.

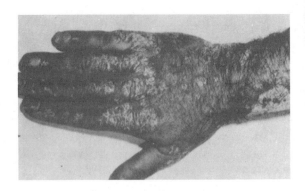

Figure 28.3 Psoriasis of the hand. (Sauer, G. C. (1973) *Manual of Skin Diseases* (3rd edition), J. B. Lippincott, Philadelphia.)

The cells in the basal layer of the skin divide too quickly, and the newly formed cells move so rapidly to the skin surface that they become evident as scaly plaques of epidermal tissue. The psoriatic epidermal cell may travel from the basal cell layer of the epidermis to the stratum corneum (skin surface) and be shed in three to four days, which is in sharp contrast to the normal 26 to 28 days. As a result of the increased number of basal cells and rapid cell passage, the normal events of cell maturation and growth cannot take place. This abnormal process does not allow formation of the normal protective layers of the skin.

Psoriasis, one of the most common skin diseases, affects approximately 2 per cent of the population. There appears to be a hereditary defect that causes overproduction of keratin. The cause is unknown. A combination of specific genetic make-up and environmental stimuli may trigger the onset of the disease. There is some evidence that the cell proliferation is mediated by the immune system. Periods of emotional stress and anxiety may aggravate the condition, and trauma, infections and seasonal and hormonal changes are trigger factors. The onset may occur at any age, but is most common between the ages of 10 and 35 years. Psoriasis has a tendency to improve and then recur throughout life.

Clinical Features

The lesions appear as red, raised, well-demarcated patches of skin covered with silvery scales (Figure 28.3). If the scales are scraped away, classical pinpoint bleeding is exposed in the base of the lesion. These patches are not moist and may or may not itch. The lesions may remain small, giving rise to the term 'guttate psoriasis'. Usually, the lesions enlarge slowly, but after many months they coalesce, forming extensive irregularly shaped patches. Psoriasis may range from a cosmetic source of annoyance to a physically disabling and disfiguring affliction. Psoriasis has a predilection for the scalp, the area over the elbows and knees, the lower part of the back and the genitalia.

Psoriasis also appears on the extensor surfaces of the arms and legs, on the scalp and ears and over the sacrum and the gluteal fold. Bilateral symmetry is often a feature of psoriasis. Where the nails are involved, pitting, discolouration, crumbling beneath the free edges and separation of the nail plate may occur. When psoriasis occurs on the palms and soles, it may present as pustular lesions. Psoriasis may be associated with arthritis of multiple joints, causing a crippling disability. The relationship between arthritis and psoriasis is not understood. Another complication is an exfoliative psoriatic state in which the disease progresses to involve the total body surface.

Psychological Considerations

Psoriasis may cause despair and frustration for the patient; observers may stare, comment, ask embarrassing questions or even avoid the person. The disease can eventually exhaust the patient's resources, interfere with job or schooling and make life miserable in general. The family and other informal carers may also be affected, since time-consuming treatments, messy ointments and constant shedding of scales may disrupt home life and cause resentment. Occasionally, the patient's frustrations are expressed through hostility directed at health care staff.

Management

The expected outcomes of management are to reduce the rapid turnover of epidermis and to promote resolution of the psoriatic lesions. Thus, the outcome is limited to control of the problem, because there is no known cure as yet.

The therapeutic approach should be one that the patient understands; it should be cosmetically acceptable and not too disruptive of lifestyle. It will involve the commitment of time and effort by the patient and possibly relatives and friends.

First, any precipitating or aggravating factors are removed. Then an assessment is made of lifestyle, since psoriasis may be affected significantly by stress. The patient must also be advised that treatment of a severe psoriasis can be time-consuming, expensive and aesthetically unappealing at times.

Therapy can be divided into two types: topical and systemic.

Topical Therapy

Topically applied agents are given to slow down the overactive epidermis without affecting other tissues. Medications include such agents as tar preparations, anthralin (dithranol), salicylic acid and corticosteroids. These therapies seem to act by suppressing the formation of epidermal cells.

Tar is formulated as lotions, ointments, pastes, creams and shampoos. Tar baths or tar preparations may retard and inhibit the rapid growth of psoriatic tissue. This aspect of therapy may be combined with carefully graded doses of ultraviolet-B light, which produces radiation in wavelengths between 280 and 320 nm (Goekerman's regime). Ultraviolet-B light seems to potentiate the action of tar. The tar is partially removed prior to ultraviolet light exposure to allow maximum transmission of light. During this phase of treatment, the patient is advised to wear goggles and to protect the eyes. Using a timer will prevent the danger of severe burns due to overexposure to the light rays. A daily tar shampoo may be used for scalp lesions. The patient is also taught to remove excess scales by rubbing with a soft brush while bathing.

Anthralin preparations (a distillate of crude coal tar) are useful for thick and resistant psoriatic plaques. The patient is taught to apply anthralin medication with a tongue depressor and gloved fingers, taking special care not to cover normal skin. The hands must be washed after the medication is handled, because a chemical conjunctivitis can be produced if the patient touches the eyes while medication is still on the hands. Anthralin stains badly and should be covered in some way (gauze dressings, stockinette, old pyjamas) when applied. The preparation is left on the skin for 8 to 12 hours. Anthralin is commonly combined with tar baths and ultraviolet-B therapy (Ingram's regime). Short-contact anthralin therapy is being used more frequently in treatment of psoriasis on a day-patient basis or in the home. With this therapy, the anthralin preparation may be left on the skin for as little as 20 minutes before being removed.

Topical Steroids. Topical steroids may be applied for their anti-inflammatory activity. However, once the steroid treatment is stopped, the psoriasis may quickly reappear (rebound phenomenon) and, in some instances, be more extensive than the original lesions.

Systemic Therapy

Systemic cytotoxic preparations, such as methotrexate, have been used in treating extensive psoriasis that fails to respond to other forms of therapy. Methotrexate appears to function by inhibiting DNA synthesis in epidermal cells, therefore reducing the turnover time of the psoriatic epidermis. However, the drug can be very toxic, especially to the liver, which can suffer irreversible damage. Thus, laboratory studies must be monitored to ensure that the hepatic, haematopoietic and renal systems are functioning adequately.

The patient should avoid drinking alcohol while taking methotrexate, because this increases the possibility of liver damage. The drug is teratogenic (producing physical defects in the fetus) in pregnant women.

Oral retinoids (synthetic derivatives of vitamin A and its metabolite, vitamin A acid, e.g., etretinate) modulate the growth and differentiation of epithelial tissue and thus show great promise in treating the patient with severe psoriasis.

Another drug that may be used is hydroxyurea, which

inhibits cell replication by affecting DNA synthesis. The patient is monitored for signs and symptoms of bone marrow depression.

Cyclosporin. Cyclosporin A is of fungal origin and used as an immunosuppressant. It has received increasing attention in clinical dermatology and, in particular, the treatment of psoriasis. However, it appears that its effect as an antipsoriatic drug is not fully understood. There are many theories postulated on its mode of action in relation to psoriasis, but observations indicate that even after a short period of three to seven days of high-dose cyclosporin A treatment, the epidermal mitotic activity in psoriatic skin is decreased significantly (Ellis, 1986). However, low-dose cyclosporin A might be of use in limited courses for the treatment of severe episodes of psoriasis—'crisis intervention' (van Joost, 1986). Apparently, the main side-effects are hypertension and elevated serum creatinine levels (van Joost, 1986). Therefore, low-dose cyclosporin A treatment could be important in maintaining clearance or improvement of severe psoriasis for long periods, if indeed there are no serious side-effects. As research is continued, the mode of action, the dosage required and further recognition of the side-effects will become apparent.

Photochemotherapy (Psoralen Ultraviolet-A Light Therapy; PUVA Therapy)

A treatment for severe psoriasis is PUVA (psoralen and ultraviolet-A) therapy, which involves the patient taking a photosensitizing drug (usually 8-methoxypsoralen) in a standard dose with subsequent exposure to long-wave ultraviolet light when peak drug plasma levels are obtained. Although the mechanism of action is not completely understood, it is assumed that there is an interaction between the psoralen molecule and light energy, resulting in decrease in cellular proliferation. PUVA is not without its hazards; it has been associated with long-term risks of skin cancer, cataracts and premature ageing of the skin.

PUVA therapy requires that psoralen be taken orally, followed in two hours by irradiation with high-intensity, long-wave ultraviolet light (UVA). UVA is the portion of the electromagnetic spectrum containing wave lengths from 320 nm to 400 nm. Psoralen may also be applied topically or in a bath in the form of 3-methoxypsoralen, 15 minutes before UVA exposure.

The PUVA unit consists of a light cabinet containing high-output blacklight lamps and an external reflectance system. The exposure time is calibrated according to the specific unit in use and the anticipated tolerance of the patient's skin. The patient is usually treated two to three times a week until the psoriasis clears. An interim period of 48 hours between treatments is necessary, because it takes this long for any PUVA burns to become evident. The patient is then provided with a maintenance programme. Once little or no disease is present, less potent therapies are used to keep minor flare-ups under control.

Patient Education During PUVA Therapy. PUVA treatment produces photosensitization, which means that the patient is sensitive to sunlight until oral methoxsalen has been excreted from the body (about six to eight hours). Therefore, exposure to the sun must be avoided at this time. If exposure is unavoidable, the skin must be protected with sunscreen and clothing. Protective spectacles (e.g., polarized sunglasses) should be worn to protect the eyes during and after treatment. Ophthalmic examinations are carried out on a regular basis. Nausea, which may be a problem in some patients, is lessened when methoxsalen is taken with food. Lubricants and bath oils may be used to help remove scales and prevent excess dryness. No other creams or oils should be used except on areas that have been shielded from ultraviolet light. Contraceptives should be used by sexually active women of reproductive age, as the teratogenic risk of PUVA has not been established. The patient must remain under constant and careful supervision and is encouraged to look for unusual changes in the skin.

► NURSING PROCESS
► THE PATIENT WITH PSORIASIS

► *Assessment*

The nursing assessment focuses on how the patient is coping with the skin condition, the appearance of the skin and the skin lesions. (See Clinical Features, above. Examine the areas especially favoured by psoriasis: elbows, knees, scalp, gluteal cleft, fingers and toenails (for small pits).

► *Patient's Problems*

Based on the nursing assessment, the patient's main problems may include the following:

- Lack of knowledge about the disease process and treatment.
- Impairment of skin integrity related to diminished protective function of the stratum corneum.
- Disturbance in self-image related to appearance and self-perception.
- Potential sexual dysfunction related to physical and psychological effects.

► *Planning and Implementation*
► Expected Outcomes

The main outcomes for the patient may include acquisition of knowledge about psoriasis and its treatment, a positive self-image and achievement of smoother skin with control of lesions.

Nursing Care

Patient Education

The patient is told with sensitivity that at the present time there is no permanent cure for psoriasis, that lifetime management is necessary, but that the condition can usually be cleared and controlled. It is necessary to review what psoriasis is and that the method by which the patient's skin replenishes itself is abnormal. The factors that provoke psoriasis are reviewed: any irritation or injury to the skin (cut, abrasion, sunburn), any current illness (e.g., sore throat) and emotional stress. It is emphasized that repeated trauma to the skin as well as an unfavourable environment (cold) and any drug (lithium, beta blockers, indomethacin) may exacerbate psoriasis. The patient should be advised not to pick or scratch the psoriasis areas to avoid injuring the skin. In addition, any topical irritant or allergy-producing substance is to be avoided. The patient should report to the doctor any infection, especially a streptococcal sore throat, that appears to aggravate the psoriasis. The patient is advised about taking any medication, as some drugs may worsen a mild psoriasis.

Too frequent washing may produce more soreness and scaling. Water should not be too hot, and the skin is dried by patting with a towel rather than vigorous rubbing. Emollients have a moisturizing effect by providing an occlusive body film on the skin surface so that normal water loss through the skin is halted, allowing the trapped water to hydrate the stratum corneum. A bath oil or emollient cleansing agent can give comfort to sore and scaling skin. Softening the skin can prevent fissuring. (See also Nursing Care Plan 28.1.)

Successful treatment of psoriasis takes persistence and patience because treatment is constant, interminable and can be expensive. Some patients spend two or more hours daily in applying medications. The patient is taught to use topical therapy appropriately. Care should be aimed at education and support, and should help the patient move towards self-acceptance. Mental health professionals can ease emotional strain and give recognition and support. Belonging to a support group helps patients to acknowledge that they are not alone in experiencing life adjustments in response to a visible, chronic disease. The National Psoriasis Association publishes periodic bull-

etins and reports updating new and relevant developments about this condition. (See 'Useful Addresses'.)

► *Evaluation*
► Expected Outcomes

1. Patient acquires knowledge and understanding of psoriasis.
   a. Describes psoriasis and the prescribed therapy.
   b. Identifies that trauma, infection and emotional stress may be trigger factors.
2. Achieves smoother skin and control of lesions.
   a. No new lesions appear.
   b. Keeps skin lubricated and soft.
3. Adheres to the therapeutic regime.
   a. Maintains control with appropriate therapy.
   b. Demonstrates proper application of topical therapy.

Nursing Care Plan 28.2 summarizes the nursing care of the patient with psoriasis.

Exfoliative Dermatitis

Exfoliative dermatitis is a serious condition characterized by a progressive inflammation in which erythema and scaling often occur in a more or less generalized distribution. It may be associated with chills, fever, prostration, severe toxicity and an itchy scaling of the skin. There is a profound loss of stratum corneum (outermost layer of the skin), which causes capillary leakage, hypoproteinaemia and negative nitrogen balance. The iron loss from the skin produces anaemia. Thus, exfoliative dermatitis has a marked effect on the entire body.

Exfoliative dermatitis has a variety of causes. It is considered to be a secondary or reactive process to an underlying skin or systemic disease. It may appear as a part of the lymphoma group of diseases, and may actually precede the appearance of lymphoma. It also appears as a severe reaction to a wide number of drugs, including penicillin and phenylbutazone.

This condition starts acutely as either a patchy or a

► NURSING CARE PLAN 28.2: THE PATIENT WITH PSORIASIS

Clement Momah is a 43-year-old Nigerian who suffers from psoriasis. He is married, has three adult children and is a practising Christian. He is a supervisor in a supermarket.

Patient's problems	Expected outcomes	Nursing care	Rationale
1. Discomfort from skin condition	Skin will be clear from psoriasis	1a. Bath with prescribed medication, followed by b. Prescribed regime of skin care c. Observe and document at least daily progress of any untoward effects of topical medication (irritation,	Skin needs to be lubricated to reduce water loss from the already dry skin Dithranol and tar may cause severe irritation to normal skin if not applied accurately Skin lesions should show

►

▶ NURSING CARE PLAN 28.2: THE PATIENT WITH PSORIASIS

Patient's problems	Expected outcomes	Nursing care	Rationale
		tenderness, warmth, erythema)	evidence of resolution of the psoriatic process by a reduction in turnover rate of skin cells. This should be demonstrated by absence of scaling, flattening of lesions and a reduction of erythema
		d. Advise patient to rest after therapy and not to do strenuous exercise or sunbathe while treatment is taking place	Rest allows the treatment to remain in place and encourages the patient to rest. Sunbathing should be avoided as it may cause further skin irritation and reduce the risk of treatment spreading (on to normal skin) with the added heat. Excess ultraviolet light from natural sunlight would occur in conjunction with the prescribed ultraviolet light B and create an overdose
2. Discomfort due to itching	Reduction and absence of pruritis	2a. Give oral antipruritic agents as needed and chart the effects. Observe for side effects, e.g. drowsiness	Systemic agents may be useful in the control of pruritis in addition to the topical therapy
		b. Observe for scratching and rubbing. Actively discourage scratching	Habitual scratching causes thickening of the skin, and an unacceptable cosmetic result
		c. Apply liberal and frequent amounts of emollients	Scratching may damage the skin and increase the risk of infection, particularly with *Staphylococcus aureus*
		d. Teach the relationship between itching and scratching	This should be explained to the patient, and alternative topical agents may help alleviate the itch, e.g. emollients
		e. Ensure nails are short and smooth – cotton gloves may be worn	
		f. Wear tubular gauze suits after treatment	Application of the tubular gauze suit not only feels comfortable and may reduce the risk of damage from finger nails, but it keeps the medication in place, preventing spreading. It also reduces the risk of staining clothing and furniture with which the patient may come into contact
3. Disturbed psychological effect due to the skin disorder and fear of rejection by others	Patient will discuss his feelings towards the condition and interact with fellow patients, family and friends	3a. Provide privacy as needed b. Spend time with the patient during treatment therapy – at least twice a day, then at intervals	Patient needs time to adjust. Use the treatment times, at least one hour each, to allow the patient to express his feelings and help to allay anxiety. This time can be used usefully and therapeutically to explore attitudes, evaluate skin condition and educate patient regarding care and management of his skin
		c. Touch the skin lesions during the course of treatment	Touching the skin in a subtle way not only helps in evaluation of progress but demonstrates there is no fear of contagion

► NURSING CARE PLAN 28.2: THE PATIENT WITH PSORIASIS

Patient's problems	Expected outcomes	Nursing care	Rationale
		d. Encourage interaction with patient, allowing him to share experiences	Sharing his thoughts about his condition with others who can show empathy may be helpful in acceptance of the condition
		e. Encourage wife and children to participate in treatments and to learn	Sharing treatment application with his family will enable them to see the condition and contribute positively in helping the patient towards recovery. Understanding of the condition and treatment will help them cope in a more informed way
4. Condition is liable to be chronic and unpredictable in its course	Patient demonstrates independence in caring for the skin. Patient's wife and children exhibit understanding of patient's progress and treatments by time of discharge	4a. Teach the patient about the disease process b. Evaluate understanding and reinforce areas of importance, particularly compliance c. Recommending available literature may supplement learning and understanding	A better-informed patient will aid coping mechanisms. Application of treatments forms a large part of therapy and it is important to understand the effects and expectations of the treatments to ensure the patient is committed to a regular treatment regime and has a positive attitude
		d. Document learning outcomes e. Teach and demonstrate treatments at each application, giving rationale	Documenting learning outcomes enables a progressive teaching and learning strategy, building up knowledge
		f. Encourage maximum independence, under supervision, and initiate in carrying out treatments	Independence is encouraged so the patient can continue treatment at home and be confident in the applications
		g. Discuss home environment and help to adapt if necessary	Full-length mirrors may be useful to examine the body and enable application of treatments
		h. Ensure the patient develops a routine preparation for discharge that he can adapt for his lifestyle	A plastic bath may stain with some medications – plastic liners may be an alternative. Discussing a routine and how this would fit into his lifestyle may aid better compliance. The family may need to participate in treatment regimes and adapt accordingly
		i. Work colleagues at the supermarket may need to be educated – verbally and in written form	Ensuring work colleagues are informed may help reduce anxieties about acceptance Contacting the Psoriasis Association may provide helpful information

generalized erythematous eruption accompanied by fever, malaise and, occasionally, gastrointestinal symptoms. The skin colour changes from pink to dark red; then, after a week, the characteristic exfoliation (scaling) begins, usually in the form of thin flakes that leave the underlying skin smooth and red, new scales forming as the older ones exfoliate (cast off). Hair loss may accompany this disorder. Relapses are the rule. The systemic effects include high-output congestive heart failure, intestinal disturbances, breast enlargement (gynaecomas-

tia), elevated levels of uric acid in the blood (hyperuraemia) and temperature disturbances.

Management

The objectives of management are to maintain fluid and electrolyte balance and to prevent intercurrent or cutaneous infection. The treatment is individualized and supportive, and depends on the cause. The patient is hospitalized and placed on bedrest. All drugs that may be implicated are stopped. A comfortable room temperature should be maintained, since the patient does not have normal thermoregulatory control because of fluctuations in temperature due to vasodilatation and evaporative water loss. The fluid and electrolyte balance must be maintained, since there is considerable water and protein loss from the skin surface. Plasma expanders may be indicated.

Continual nursing assessment is carried out to detect intercurrent and cutaneous infection. The erythematous, moist skin is receptive to infection and becomes colonized with pathogenic organisms, which produce more inflammation. Antibiotics are given if infection is present, and are selected on the basis of culture and sensitivity.

● Watch for signs and symptoms of congestive heart failure, because hyperaemia and increased cutaneous blood flow can produce a cardiac failure of high output origin.

Hypothermia may also occur as increased skin blood flow, coupled with increases in water loss through the skin, leads to heat loss by radiation, conduction, and evaporation.

As in any acute dermatitis, topical therapy is used to give symptomatic relief. Soothing baths, compresses and lubrication with emollients are used to treat the extensive dermatitis. The patient is likely to be extremely irritable because of the severe itching. Oral or parenteral steroids may be given when the disease is not controlled by more conservative therapy. When a specific cause is known, more specific therapy may be used.

Patient Education

The patient is advised to avoid all irritants in the future, particularly drugs.

Pemphigus Vulgaris

Pemphigus vulgaris is a serious disease of the skin characterized by the appearance of bullae (blisters) of various sizes (1 to 10 cm) on apparently normal skin (Figure 28.4) and mucous membranes (mouth, vagina).

Available evidence indicates that pemphigus is an autoimmune disease. (See Chapter 26.) Genetic factors may also play a role in its development. The disorder usually occurs in middle and late adult life.

Clinical Features

Most patients initially present with oral lesions appearing as irregularly shaped erosions that are painful, bleed easily and heal slowly. The skin bullae enlarge, rupture and leave large, painful eroded areas that are accompanied by crusting and oozing. A characteristic offensive odour emanates from the bullae and the exuding serum. There is blistering or sloughing of uninvolved skin when minimal pressure is applied (Nikolsky's sign). The eroded skin heals slowly, so that eventually huge areas of the body are involved. Bacterial superinfection is common.

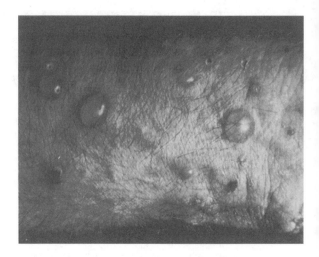

Figure 28.4 Pemphigus vulgaris bullae on the wrist. (Sauer, G. C. (1973) *Manual of Skin Diseases* (3rd edition), J. B. Lippincott, Philadelphia.)

Diagnosis

A biopsy specimen from the blister and surrounding skin will demonstrate acantholysis (separation of epidermal cells from each other because of damage to or an abnormality of the intracellular substance). Circulating antibodies (pemphigus antibodies) may be demonstrated by immunofluorescent studies of the patient's serum.

Management

The expected outcomes of therapy are to bring the disease under control as rapidly as possible, to prevent loss of serum and the development of secondary infection and to promote re-epithelialization of the skin.

Corticosteroids (prednisone) are administered in large doses to control the disease and keep the skin free of blisters. The high dosage level is maintained until remission is apparent. Prednisone is given with or immediately after a meal and may be accompanied by an antacid as prophylaxis against gastric complications. Essential to the patient's therapeutic management are daily evaluations of body weight, measurement of blood pressure, testing of blood for glucose and recording of fluid balance. (High-dosage corticosteroid therapy has its own serious toxic effects.)

Immunosuppressive agents (azathioprine; cyclophosphamide; gold) may be given to help control the disease and reduce the steroid dose.

▶ NURSING PROCESS
▶ THE PATIENT WITH PEMPHIGUS

▶ *Assessment*

Patients with pemphigus are invariably hospitalized at one time or another during exacerbations of the disease.

Disease activity is monitored clinically by examining

the skin for the appearance of new blisters, which are usually tense and not easily broken. The scalp, chest and adjacent skin areas need to be examined for blistering. Particular attention is given to assessing for signs and symptoms of infection.

▶ Patient's Problems

Based on nursing assessment, the patient's main problems may include the following:

- Alteration in oral mucous membranes related to blistering and erosions.
- Alteration in skin integrity related to ruptured bullae and denuded areas of the skin.
- Potential fluid and electrolyte imbalance related to loss of tissue fluids.
- Anxiety and ineffective coping related to appearance of the skin.

Possible complications that might develop include opportunistic infections, psychosis and hyperglycaemia.

▶ Planning and Implementation
▶ Expected Outcomes

The main outcomes for the patient may include relief of discomfort from oral lesions, achievement of skin healing, fluid and electrolyte balance, avoidance of infection, reduction in anxiety and an improvement in coping capacity.

Nursing Care

Relieving Oral Discomfort

The patient's entire oral cavity may be affected with erosions and denuded surfaces. A necrotic slough may develop over these areas, adding greatly to the patient's misery and interfering with food intake. Weight loss and hypoproteinaemia may thus result. Meticulous oral hygiene is important to keep the oral mucosa clean and allow for regeneration of epithelium. Prescribed mouth washes are used to rinse the mouth of debris. This is done frequently to soothe ulcerative areas. Commercial mouth washes are avoided. The lips are kept moist.

Cool, non-irritating fluids are encouraged to maintain hydration. Small, frequent meals of high-protein, high-calorie foods will help maintain nutritional status. Parenteral nutrition is considered if the patient is unable to eat.

Secondary infection may be associated with offensive odour from oral lesions. *Candida albicans* of the mouth is frequently seen in patients on high-dose steroid therapy. The oral cavity should be inspected daily and any changes noted and reported. Oral lesions are slow to heal.

Control of Infection

The patient is susceptible to infection because the barrier function of the skin is compromised. Bullae are also susceptible to infection, and septicaemia may follow.

Infection is the leading cause of death. Particular attention is given to assessing the patient for signs and symptoms of local and systemic infection. Steroids mask or alter typical signs and symptoms of infection. The vital signs are taken and temperature fluctuations recorded. The patient is observed for chills, and all secretions and excretions are monitored for suspicious changes. Results of culture and sensitivity tests are followed. Antimicrobials are administered as prescribed, and response to treatment is noted.

Skin Care

Cool, wet dressings or baths are protective and soothing. Patients with large areas of blistering have a characteristic odour that is lessened when secondary infection is controlled. Potassium permanganate baths help keep the areas from becoming infected and to some extent precipitate some of the protein that oozes through the open skin. They also have deodorant properties. Following the bath, the patient is dried carefully and the prescribed medication is applied. Nonadherent, foambacked dressings may be applied to the affected areas, or the patient may lie on a nonadherent, foam-backed sheet dressing when large areas are affected. Adhesive tape should never be used on the skin because it may produce small blisters.

The patient may benefit from the use of a special bed such as a temperature-controlled microsphere flotation bed, where the patient floats on a bed of fluidized beads. The advantages include:

- High prevention of pressure sores.
- Greater maintenance of body heat.
- Easing of discomfort, which may help to reduce the need for, or quantity of, medication for pain relief.
- Absorption of any excessive exudate.
- May help to increase the rate of healing of the skin.

Achieving Fluid and Electrolyte Balance

Extensive denudation of the skin leads also to fluid and electrolyte imbalance.

A large amount of protein and blood is lost from the denuded skin areas. Blood or component therapy may be prescribed to maintain the blood volume as well as the haemoglobin and plasma protein concentrations. The patient is encouraged to maintain adequate oral fluid intake. Serum albumin and protein levels are monitored.

Reducing Anxiety

Attention to the psychological needs of this patient require being available, giving expert nursing care and educating the patient and the family or close friends. This provides support from which the patient gains strength. Arranging for a family member/significant other to spend more prolonged periods of time with the patient can be supportive. When patients receive information about the disease and its treatment, uncertainty is reduced and the patients' capacity to act on their own behalf is enhanced.

If the patient continues to exhibit fear, anxiety and depression, a referral for psychological counselling may be helpful.

Patient Education

The disease can be characterized by recurrent relapses that require continuing therapy to maintain clinical control. Regular monitoring for the side-effects of corticosteroids is necessary. Long-term administration of immunosuppressive drugs is associated with increased risk of cancer. The patient is to report for follow-up regularly.

► *Evaluation*
► **Expected Outcomes**

1. Patient achieves relief from pain of oral lesions.
   a. Identifies therapies that reduce pain.
   b. Uses mouth washes and anaesthetic–antiseptic aerosol mouth spray.
   c. Drinks fluids at two-hourly intervals.
2. Achieves skin healing.
   a. States purpose of therapeutic regime.
   b. Co-operates with soaks/bath regime.
3. Maintains fluid and electrolyte balance.
   a. Keeps input record to assure adequate fluid intake.
   b. Understands the need to maintain fluid intake.
   c. Reports that urine output is within normal limit.
   d. Has serum chemistries within normal limits.
4. Is free of infection.
   a. Cultures from bullae, skin and orifices are negative for pathogenic organisms.
   b. Shows signs that skin is clearing.

Toxic Epidermal Necrolysis

Toxic epidermal necrolysis is a severe, potentially fatal skin disease. Its aetiology is unknown, but it is probably linked to the immune system as a reaction to drug ingestion or possibly secondary to a viral infection. Antibiotics, barbiturates and sulphonamides are the drugs most frequently implicated. Toxic epidermal necrolysis is characterized by initial signs of conjunctival burning or itching, cutaneous tenderness, fever, headache, extreme malaise and myalgias. These signs are followed by rapid onset of erythema, involving much of the skin surface. Large, flaccid bullae develop in some areas, while in other areas large sheets of epidermis are shed, exposing the underlying dermis. Fingernails, toenails, eyebrows and eyelashes may all be shed along with the surrounding epidermis. The skin is excruciatingly tender, and the loss of skin leaves a weeping surface similar to that of a second-degree burn. The patient with toxic epidermal necrolysis is severely ill. High fever, tachycardia and extreme weakness and fatigue are seen,

perhaps as a result of the process of epidermal necrosis, increased metabolic needs and possible gastrointestinal and respiratory mucosal sloughing. (The mucosa can have an injury similar to that of the skin.)

The major cause of death is infection, and the most common sites of infection are the skin and mucosal surfaces, lungs and blood. The organisms most frequently recovered are *Staphylococcus aureus*, *Pseudomonas*, *Klebsiella*, *Escherichia coli*, *Serratia* and *Candida*. The patient is monitored for ophthalmic complications to avoid keratoconjunctivitis. Hypertrophic scarring of the skin is not unusual.

Frozen histological studies of peeled skin from a fresh lesion of toxic epidermal necrolysis and cytodiagnosis of collections of cellular material from a freshly denuded area are diagnostic procedures used.

Management

The goals of treatment are control of fluid and electrolyte balance and prevention of death from infection. Supportive care is the mainstay of treatment.

All nonessential drugs are stopped immediately. It is desirable that the patient be treated in a regional burn centre because aggressive treatment similar to that of a severe burn is required. Skin loss may approximate 100 per cent of the total body surface area. Cultures are taken of the nasopharynx, eyes, ears, blood, urine, skin and unruptured blisters to determine the presence of pathogenic organisms. Intravenous infusions are started to maintain fluid and electrolyte balance. However, because an indwelling intravenous catheter may result in infection, fluid replacement is carried out by nasogastric tube and orally as soon as possible.

Protecting the skin with topical agents is paramount. A variety of topical antibacterial agents are used to prevent wound sepsis. Temporary biological dressings (pigskin; amniotic membrane) or plastic semipermeable dressings may be used to reduce pain, decrease evaporative losses and prevent secondary infection while awaiting re-epithelialization.

► **NURSING PROCESS**
► **THE PATIENT WITH TOXIC EPIDERMAL NECROLYSIS**

► *Assessment*

A careful inspection of the skin is made, with emphasis on its appearance and extent of involvement. The 'normal' skin is closely observed to determine if new areas of blistering are developing. Skin seepage is monitored for amount, colour and odour. An inspection of the oral cavity for blistering and erosive lesions is carried out daily. The patient's ability to drink fluids is determined.

The patient's vital signs are monitored, with special at

tention given to the presence and character of fever and the respiratory rate, depth, rhythm and cough. The character and amount of respiratory secretions are noted. Urine volume, specific gravity and colour are monitored. The intravenous insertion sites are inspected for local signs of infection. The patient's height is noted, and daily weight checks are made.

The patient is asked about fatigue and pain. An attempt is made to evaluate the patient's level of anxiety. The nurse asks what the patient usually does to deal with anxious feelings. The patient's basic coping mechanisms, which may be altered because of acute illness, are evaluated.

► *Patient's Problems*

Based on the assessment, the patient's main problems may include the following:

● Impaired tissue integrity (oral and skin) related to epidermal shedding.
● Fluid volume deficit and electrolyte losses related to loss of fluids from denuded skin.
● Potential alteration in body temperature related to heat loss secondary to skin loss.
● Pain related to raw, denuded skin, oral lesions and possible infection.
● Anxiety related to the appearance of skin and fear for survival.

► *Planning and Implementation*
► Expected Outcomes

The main expected outcomes for the patient may include achievement of skin and oral tissue healing, attainment of fluid balance, prevention of heat loss, relief of pain and lessening of anxiety.

Nursing Care

The nursing care of patients with toxic epidermal necrolysis is similar to that of patients with extensive burns (see Chapter 2).

It is well to remember that the lifestyle of toxic epidermal necrolysis patients has been abruptly changed to one of complete dependence. Assessment of their emotional state may reveal anxiety, fear of dying and depression. Patients can be reassured that these reactions are normal. They need nursing support, honesty, candour and some hope that things can get better. They are encouraged to express their feelings to someone with whom they have developed a trusting relationship. Listening to their concerns and being readily available with skilful and compassionate care are anxiety-relieving interventions.

Emotional support by a psychiatric nurse, chaplain, psychologist or psychiatrist may be invaluable for providing coping methods during the long period of recovery.

► *Evaluation*
► Expected Outcomes

1. Patient achieves increasing skin and oral tissue healing.
   a. Skin reveals larger areas of healing.
   b. Patient is able to swallow fluids.
2. Maintains fluid balance.
   a. Laboratory reports are within normal range.
   b. Urine volume and specific gravity are within acceptable range.
3. Maintains normal body temperature.
4. Reports lessening of intensity of pain.
5. Appears less anxious.
   a. Discusses concerns freely.
   b. Sleeps at longer intervals.

ULCERS AND TUMOURS OF THE SKIN

Ulcerations

The superficial loss of surface tissue due to death of the cells is called an ulceration. A simple ulcer, such as is found in a small, superficial, second-degree burn, tends to heal by granulation if kept clean and protected from injury. If it is exposed to the air, the serum that escapes will dry and form a scab, under which the epithelial cells will grow and cover the surface completely. Certain diseases cause characteristic ulcers—tuberculous ulcers and syphilitic ulcers are examples.

Ulcers Due to a Deficient Arterial Circulation

Ulcers related to problems with arterial circulation are seen in patients with peripheral vascular disease, arteriosclerosis, Raynaud's disease and frostbite. In these patients, the treatment of the ulceration must be carried out in conjunction with the treatment of the arterial disease. The danger is from secondary infection. Frequently, amputation of the part is the only effective therapy.

Pressure Sores

Pressure sores (decubitus ulcers) result from continuous pressure on a particular area of the skin (see Chapter 2).

Tumours of the Skin

Cysts

Cysts of the skin are epithelium-lined cavities containing fluid or solid material.

Epidermal cysts occur frequently and may be described as slow-growing, firm, elevated tumours found most frequently on the face, neck, upper chest and back. Removal of the cysts provides cure.

Sebaceous cysts are frequently found on the scalp. They apparently originate from the middle portion of the hair follicle and from the cells of the outer root sheath. The treatment is surgical removal.

Benign Tumours

Seborrhoeic Keratoses

These tumours are benign, wartlike lesions of varying size and colour, ranging from light tan to black. They are usually located on the face, shoulders, chest and back and are the most common skin tumours seen in middle-aged and elderly people. They may be cosmetically unacceptable to the patient, and a black keratosis may be erroneously diagnosed as malignant melanoma. The treatment is removal of the tumour tissue by excision, curettage and cautery, or the application of carbon dioxide or liquid nitrogen.

Actinic keratoses are premalignant skin lesions that develop in chronic sun-exposed areas of the body. They appear as rough, scaly patches with underlying erythema. An estimated 10 to 20 per cent of these lesions gradually transform into invasive squamous cell carcinoma.

Verrucae (Warts)

Warts are common benign skin tumours caused by infection with the human papilloma virus that belongs to the DNA virus group. All age groups may be affected, but the condition occurs most frequently between the ages of 12 and 16. Warts come in many varieties.

As a rule, warts are asymptomatic, except when they occur on weight-bearing areas, such as the soles of the feet. They may be treated with locally applied liquid nitrogen, salicylic acid plasters, electrodesiccation or the application of cantharidin.

Venereal Warts

Warts occurring on the genitalia and perianal areas are known as condyloma acuminata and have been shown to be sexually transmitted. These are treated with podophyllin in tincture of benzoin, which is applied to the wart and washed off later.

Angiomas (Birthmarks)

Birthmarks are benign vascular tumours involving the skin and the subcutaneous tissues. They may occur as flat, violet red patches (port-wine angiomas) or as raised, bright red nodular lesions (strawberry angiomas). The latter have a tendency to involute spontaneously. Port-wine angiomas, on the other hand, usually persist indefinitely. Patients may use masking cosmetics to camouflage the defect. The argon laser is being used on various angiomas with some success.

Pigmented Naevi (Moles)

Moles are common skin tumours of various sizes and shades, ranging from yellowish brown to black. They may be flat, macular lesions or elevated papules or nodules that occasionally contain hair. The great majority of pigmented naevi are harmless lesions. However, in rare cases, malignant changes supervene and a melanoma develops at the site of the naevus. Some authorities feel that all congenital moles should be removed, since these may have a higher incidence of malignant change. Naevi that show change in colour or size or become symptomatic (itch) or change shape should be removed to determine if malignant changes have occurred. Moles that occur in unusual places should be examined carefully for any irregularity of the border and variation in colour. (Early melanomas may frequently show some redness and irritation and areas of bluish pigmentation where the pigment-containing cells have become deeper in the skin.) Naevi larger than 1 cm should be examined carefully. Excised naevi should be examined histologically.

Keloids

Keloids are benign overgrowths of fibrous tissue at the site of a scar or trauma. They appear to be more common among black people. Keloids are asymptomatic but may cause disfigurement and cosmetic concern. The treatment, which is not always satisfactory, consists of surgical excision, intralesional corticosteroid therapy and radiation.

Dermatofibroma

A dermatofibroma is a common benign tumour of connective tissue that occurs predominantly on the extremities. It is a firm, dome-shaped papule or nodule that may be skin-coloured or a pinkish brown hue. Excisional biopsy is the recommended method of treatment.

Neurofibromatosis (von Recklinghausen's Disease)

Neurofibromatosis is a hereditary condition manifested by pigmented patches (café au lait macules), axillary freckling and cutaneous neurofibromas that vary in size. Developmental changes may occur also in the nervous system, muscles and bone. Malignant degeneration of the neurofibromas is found in 2 to 5 per cent of the patients.

CANCER OF THE SKIN

Skin cancer is the most common form of cancer. Because the skin is accessible to direct visualization, skin cancer is readily detected and is the most successfully treated type of cancer.

Causes and Prevention

The sun is the leading cause of skin cancer; incidence is related to the total amount of exposure to the sun. Sun damage is cumulative, and harmful effects may be severe by the age of 20. The increase in skin cancer is probably due to changing lifestyles and emphasis on sunbathing and related activities. Protective measures should be started in childhood and carried on throughout life. People who do not produce sufficient melanin pigment in the skin to give protection to underlying tissue are very susceptible to sun damage; those at greatest risk are fair, blue-eyed, red-haired people of Celtic ancestry or people with ruddy or light complexions, as well as those who suffer prolonged sunburn and do not tan. Others at risk are outdoor workers, such as farmers, sailors, fishermen and people who are exposed to the sun over a period of time. Elderly people with sun-damaged skin are also at risk, as are people who have had a history of X-ray treatment for acne or benign skin lesions. Workers exposed to certain chemical agents (arsenic, nitrates, coal, tar and pitch, oils and paraffins) are also included in the risk group. People who have scars due to severe burns may develop skin cancer 20 to 40 years later. Squamous cell cancer can develop in areas of chronic draining osteomyelitis. Neoplastic changes can develop in chronic fistulae. Chronic ulcers of the lower extremity may be the site of origin of skin cancer. In fact, any condition causing scarring or chronic irritation may lead to cancer. Immunosuppressed patients have an increased incidence of malignant skin tumours. Genetic factors are also involved.

Types of Skin Cancer

The most common types of skin cancer are basal cell carcinoma (rodent ulcer), squamous cell carcinoma and malignant melanoma.

Basal cell carcinomas arise from the basal cell layer of the epidermis or the hair follicles. This is the most common type of skin cancer. It generally appears on the sun-exposed areas of the body, and is more prevalent in regions where the population is subjected to intense and

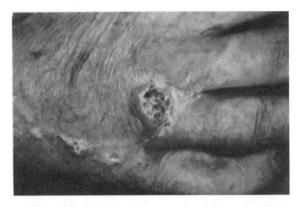

Figure 28.6 Squamous cell carcinoma. (Courtesy of Mervyn L. Elgart, MD.)

extensive exposure to the sun. The incidence is proportional to the age of the patient (average age of 60) and the total amount of sun exposure, and is inversely proportional to the amount of melanin pigment in the skin.

Basal cell carcinoma usually presents as a small, waxy nodule with rolled, translucent, pearly borders; telangiectatic vessels may be present. As it grows, it undergoes central ulceration and sometimes crusting (Figure 28.5). The tumours appear most frequently on the face between the hairline and the upper lip. Basal cell carcinoma is characterized by invasion and erosion of contiguous (adjoining) tissues, but it rarely metastasizes. However, a neglected basal cell carcinoma can account for the loss of a nose, an ear or a lip. Other lesions of this disease may appear as shiny, flat, grey or yellowish plaques.

Squamous cell carcinoma is a malignant proliferation arising from the epidermis. Although it usually appears on sun-damaged skin, it may arise from normal skin or from pre-existing skin lesions. It is of greater concern than basal cell carcinoma because it is a truly invasive carcinoma. The lesions may be primary, arising both on the skin and mucous membranes, or may develop from a precancerous condition, such as actinic keratosis (lesions occurring in sun-exposed areas), leucoplakia (premalignant lesion of the mucous membrane), or scarred or ulcerated lesions. It appears as a rough, thickened, scaly tumour that may be asymptomatic or may involve bleeding (Figure 28.6). The border of the lesion may be wider, more infiltrated and more inflammatory than that of basal cell carcinoma. Secondary infection can occur. Exposed areas, especially of the upper extremities and of the face, lower lip, ears, nose and forehead, are common sites.

Skin cancer is diagnosed by biopsy and histological evaluation.

The incidence of metastases is related to the histological type and the level or depth of invasion. Usually, tumours arising in sun-damaged areas are less invasive and rarely cause death, whereas squamous cell carcinoma arising without a history of sun or arsenic exposure or scar

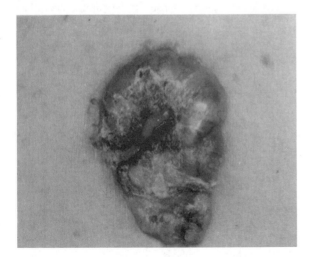

Figure 28.5 Basal cell carcinoma. (Courtesy of Mervyn L. Elgart, MD.)

formation appears to have a greater chance of metastatic spread. The patient should be evaluated subsequently for regional lymph node metastases.

Management of Basal Cell and Squamous Cell Carcinomas

The expected outcome of treatment is to eradicate or completely destroy all the tumour. The method of treatment depends on the tumour location, cell type (location and depth), cosmetic desires of the patient, history of previous treatment, whether or not the tumour is invasive and the presence or absence of metastatic nodes.

The usual methods of treatment of both basal cell carcinoma and squamous cell carcinoma are curettage and cautery, surgical excision, cryosurgery, radiotherapy and microscopically controlled chemosurgery.

Curettage Followed by Cautery
Curettage is carried out by excising the skin tumour by scraping its surface with a curette; cautery is then applied to achieve haemostasis and to destroy any viable malignant cells at the base of the wound or along its edges. It is useful for small lesions (smaller than 1 to 2 cm in diameter). This method takes advantage of the fact that the tumour in each instance is softer than surrounding skin and therefore can be outlined by a curette, which 'feels' the extent of the tumour. The tumour is removed and the base cauterized. The process is repeated three times. Usually, healing occurs within a month.

Surgical Excision
Wide surgical excision may be necessary. The adequacy of excision is verified by microscopic study of sections of the specimen. Such a histological study of excised tissue shows whether or not the margins are free of tumour. Skin grafting may be necessary if primary closure is not possible.

Radiotherapy
Radiotherapy is frequently carried out for cancer of the eyelid, the tip of the nose and areas in or near vital structures (e.g., facial nerve).

The patient should be informed that the skin may become red and blistered. A bland skin ointment (prescribed by the doctor) may be applied to relieve discomfort. The patient should also be advised against exposure to the sun.

Cryosurgery
Cryosurgery employs deep freezing to destroy the tumour tissue selectively. Liquid nitrogen is directed to the centre of the tumour until a temperature of −50°C is reached at the tumour base. The tumour tissue is frozen, allowed to thaw and then refrozen. The site thaws naturally and then becomes gelatinous and heals spontaneously. Swelling and oedema follow the freeze. The appearance of the lesion varies. Normal healing may take four to six weeks, occurring faster in areas with a good blood supply.

Microscopically Controlled Surgery (Chemosurgery)
Chemosurgery combines the use of topically applied chemicals and serial surgical excisions of tumours layer by layer. Immediate microscopic examination is made of frozen sections for evidence of cancer cells. This procedure may be repeated until the specimens are cancer-free and all peripheral extensions of the tumour are eradicated. Chemosurgery is useful for recurrent tumours or for infiltrating tumours whose margins cannot be determined.

Nursing Care

Because many skin cancers are removed by excision, patients are treated in outpatient surgical units. The role of the nurse is that of teaching the patient postoperative care.

The wound is usually (but not always) covered with a dressing to protect the site from physical trauma, external irritants and contaminants.

The patient is advised to watch for excessive bleeding and dressings so tight that circulation is compromised. If the lesion is in the perioral area, the patient is requested to drink liquids through a straw and limit excess talking and facial movement.

After the sutures are removed, an emollient cream may be used to help reduce dryness. Sunscreens over the wound to prevent postoperative hyperpigmentation are advised if the patient spends time outdoors.

Patient Education
The follow-up treatment should be regular, including palpation of the adjacent nodes. The following points of emphasis should be made part of patient education:

1. Avoid unnecessary exposure to the sun, especially during times when ultraviolet light radiation is most intense (10 am to 3 pm).
2. *Do not become sunburned.*
3. Apply a protective sunscreen if you must be in the sun; sunscreens block out harmful rays. Use a sunscreen with a solar protection factor of 15.
4. Oils applied before or during sunbathing do not protect against sunburn or sun damage.
5. Use a lip salve that contains a sunscreen with the highest solar protection factor number.
6. Wear appropriate protective clothing (e.g., broadbrimmed hat, long-sleeved clothing). However, clothing does not provide complete protection, as up to 50 per cent of the sun's damaging rays can go through clothes. Ultraviolet rays also penetrate clouds.
7. Do not use sun lamps for indoor tanning; avoid commercial tanning sunbeds.
8. Have moles treated that are accessible to repeated friction and irritation.

9. Watch for indications of potential malignancy in moles (e.g., increase in size, ulceration, bleeding or serous exudation).
10. Have a regular follow-up throughout lifetime. Watch for development of new lesions. (There is also an incidence of internal malignancy associated with squamous cell cancer.)
11. Caution your children and grandchildren, especially those with fair skin, to avoid excessive exposure to the sun and to use sunscreen so as to prevent later skin cancers.

Malignant Melanoma

A malignant melanoma is a malignant neoplasm in which atypical melanocytes (pigment cells) are present in both the epidermis and the dermis (and sometimes the subcutaneous cells). It can occur in one of several forms: superficial spreading melanoma, lentigo-maligna melanoma, nodular melanoma and acral-lentiginous melanoma. These types have certain clinical and histological features as well as different biological behaviours. Most melanomas derive from cutaneous epidermal melanocytes, but some appear in pre-existing naevi (moles) in the skin or develop in the uveal tract of the eye. Melanomas frequently appear simultaneously with cancer of other organs.

The incidence of melanoma has doubled during the past few decades, a rise that is probably related to increased recreational sun exposure. The incidence of melanoma is increasing faster than that of almost any other cancer, and the mortality rate is increasing faster than that of any other cancer except lung cancer.

Clinical Features

The superficial spreading melanoma occurs anywhere on the body and is the most common form of melanoma. It usually affects people of middle age, and occurs most frequently on the trunk and lower extremities. The lesion tends to be circular with irregular outer portions. The margins of the lesion may be flat or elevated and palpable. This type of melanoma may appear in a combination of colours, with hues of tan, brown and black mixed with grey, bluish black or white. Sometimes there is a dull pink rose colour in a small area within the lesion.

The lentigo-maligna melanomas are slowly evolving pigmented lesions that occur on exposed skin areas, especially of the head and neck, in elderly people. They first appear as tan, flat lesions, and in time undergo changes in size and colour.

The nodular melanoma is a spherical, blueberry-like nodule with a relatively smooth surface and relatively uniform blue black colour. It may be dome-shaped with a smooth surface. It may have other shadings of red, grey or purple. Sometimes nodular melanomas appear as irregularly shaped plaques. The patient may describe this as a 'blood blister' that fails to resolve. A nodular melanoma invades directly into subjacent dermis (vertical growth), and hence has a poorer prognosis.

Acral-lentiginous melanoma are a form of melanoma that occurs in areas not exposed excessively to sunlight and where hair follicles are absent. They are found on the palms of the hands, soles, nail beds and mucous membranes in black and other dark-skinned people. These melanomas appear as irregular pigmented macules, which develop nodules. They may become invasive early.

An excision biopsy specimen is taken to gain histological information on the type, level of invasion and thickness. In addition, the patient is thoroughly examined to determine the extent of the disease.

Prognosis

The prognosis is related to the depth of dermal invasion and the thickness of the lesion. The deeper and thicker the melanoma, the greater the likelihood of metastases. If the melanoma is growing radially (horizontally) and is characterized by peripheral growth with minimal or absent dermal invasion, the prognosis is favourable. When the melanoma progresses to the vertical growth phase (dermal invasion), the prognosis is poor. The presence of ulceration correlates with a poor prognosis. Malignant melanoma can spread through both the bloodstream and the lymphatic routes, and can metastasize to every organ of the body. Melanomas of the trunk appear to have a poorer prognosis than those of other sites, perhaps because the network of lymphatics in the trunk permits metastasis to regional nodes.

Causes and People at Risk

The aetiology is unknown, but ultraviolet rays are strongly suspected. In general, at greatest risk are patients with fair complexions, blue eyes, red or blonde hair and freckles. These people synthesize melanin more slowly. People of Celtic or Scandinavian origin are at greater risk. People who burn and do not tan are also at risk. In areas where sunlight is intense, there is a disproportionate increase in incidence. Others at risk have had a melanoma in the past, have a family history of melanoma, have giant congenital naevi or have a significant history of severe sunburn.

Up to 10 per cent of melanoma patients are members of melanoma-prone families who have multiple changing moles (dysplastic naevi) that are susceptible to malignant transformation. People with dysplastic naevus syndrome have been found to have unusual moles, larger and more numerous moles, lesions with irregular outlines and pigmentation located all over the skin. Microscopic examination of dysplastic moles shows disordered, faulty growth.

Management

The therapeutic approach to the treatment of malignant melanoma depends on the level of invasion and the measurement of thickness.

Surgery

Small superficial lesions are treated by local excision. Deeper lesions require wide local excision and coverage with a skin graft. This is the primary mode of treatment at this time. A regional node dissection may be done.

Immunotherapy

The term immunotherapy encompasses treatment methods that modify not only immune but other biological responses to cancer. There have been some encouraging results with several new forms of immunotherapy (interleukins; interferons; monoclonal antibodies directed against melanoma antigens). Research continues to define an effective systemic therapy.

► NURSING PROCESS
► THE PATIENT WITH MALIGNANT MELANOMA

► Assessment

An assessment of the patient with malignant melanoma is based on the history and symptomatology. Ask specifically about pruritus, tenderness and pain, which are not features of a benign naevus. Question the patient about changes in pre-existing moles or the development of a new pigmented lesion.

Use a magnifying lens in good lighting to look for irregularity and changes in the mole. Signs that suggest malignant changes include the following:

1. Variegated colour.
   a. White areas within a pigmented lesion are suspicious.
   b. Some malignant melanomas are not variegated but uniformly coloured (bluish-black; bluish-grey; bluish-red).
2. Irregular border.
   a. Look for angular indentation or notch in the border of the mole.
3. Irregular surface.
   a. Look for uneven elevations of the surface; irregular topography may be palpable or visible. The change in the surface may be from smooth to scaly.
   b. Some nodular melanomas have a smooth surface.

The common sites of melanomas are the skin of the back, the legs (especially in women), between toes and on the feet, face, scalp, fingernails and backs of hands. In black people, melanomas are most apt to occur in the less pigmented sites: palms, soles, subungual areas and mucous membranes.

The diameter of the mole is measured, because melanomas are often larger than 6 mm. Satellite lesions (those situated near the mole) are noted.

► Patient's Problems

Based on the nursing assessment, the patient's main problems may include the following:

● Pain related to surgical excision and grafting.
● Anxiety and depression related to possible life-threatening consequences of melanoma.
● Potential for recurrence.

► Planning and Implementation
► Expected Outcomes

The main outcomes for the patient may include relief of pain and discomfort, reduction of anxiety and absence of recurrence.

Nursing Care

Surgical removal of melanoma in different locations (head and neck, eye, trunk, abdomen, extremities, central nervous system) presents different challenges, taking into consideration the removal of the primary melanoma, the intervening lymphatics and the lymph nodes to which metastases may spread. Nursing care of the patient having surgery in these regions is discussed in the appropriate chapters.

Patient Education

The best hope of controlling the disease lies in the education of patients regarding the early signs of melanoma. Patients are taught to examine their skin monthly in an orderly manner, including scalp examination (Figure 28.7). The following are points to stress in patient education:

1. Use a full-length mirror and a small hand mirror to aid in examination.
2. Learn where moles and birthmarks are located.
3. Inspect all moles and other pigmented lesions; report to the doctor/clinic immediately moles that change colours, enlarge, become raised or thicker, itch or bleed.
4. Have a doctor examine your skin at least twice yearly. A person who has had a malignant melanoma should have lifelong follow-up. A person developing a malignant melanoma has a higher risk of developing a second one.

A key factor in development of malignant melanoma is exposure to sunlight. See page 896 for preventive measures.

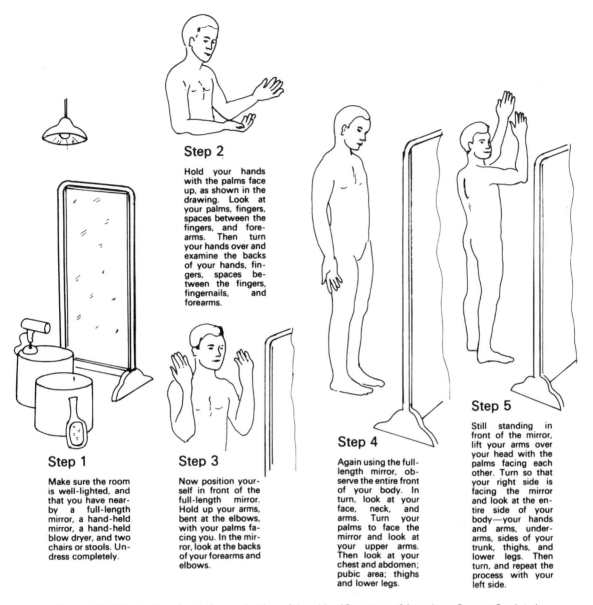

Step 1

Make sure the room is well-lighted, and that you have nearby a full-length mirror, a hand-held mirror, a hand-held blow dryer, and two chairs or stools. Undress completely.

Step 2

Hold your hands with the palms face up, as shown in the drawing. Look at your palms, fingers, spaces between the fingers, and forearms. Then turn your hands over and examine the backs of your hands, fingers, spaces between the fingers, fingernails, and forearms.

Step 3

Now position yourself in front of the full-length mirror. Hold up your arms, bent at the elbows, with your palms facing you. In the mirror, look at the backs of your forearms and elbows.

Step 4

Again using the full-length mirror, observe the entire front of your body. In turn, look at your face, neck, and arms. Turn your palms to face the mirror and look at your upper arms. Then look at your chest and abdomen; pubic area; thighs and lower legs.

Step 5

Still standing in front of the mirror, lift your arms over your head with the palms facing each other. Turn so that your right side is facing the mirror and look at the entire side of your body—your hands and arms, underarms, sides of your trunk, thighs, and lower legs. Then turn, and repeat the process with your left side.

Figure 28.7 Technique for self-examination of the skin. (Courtesy of American Cancer Society.)

► *Evaluation*
► **Expected Outcomes**

1. Patient experiences relief of pain and discomfort.
   a. States pain has lessened and is diminishing.
   b. Exhibits healing of surgical scar with no evidence of heat, redness or swelling.
2. Achieves reduction of anxiety.
   a. Expresses fears and fantasies.
   b. Asks questions about medical condition.
   c. Requests repetition of facts about melanoma.
   d. Identifies family member or significant other for positive reinforcement.

3. Demonstrates an understanding of the means for detecting melanoma.
   a. Demonstrates how to conduct self-examination of skin on a monthly basis.
   b. Expresses the following danger signals of melanoma: change in size of mole, colour of mole, mole surface, shape or outline of mole or skin around mole.
   c. Recalls measures to protect self from sun.

Metastatic Skin Tumours

The skin is an important, although not a common, site of metastatic cancer. All types of cancer may metastasize to the skin, but carcinoma of the breast is the primary source of cutaneous metastases in women. Cancer of the large intestine, ovaries and lungs are other sources. In men, the primary site is most commonly the lungs, large intestine, oral cavity, kidneys or stomach. Skin metastases from melanomas are found in both sexes. The clinical appearance of metastatic skin lesions is not distinctive, except perhaps in some cases of breast cancer in which diffuse, brawny hardening of the skin of the involved breast is seen ('cancer en cuirasse'). In most instances, metastatic lesions occur as multiple cutaneous or subcutaneous nodules of varying size that may be skin-coloured or show different shades of red.

DERMATOLOGICAL AND PLASTIC RECONSTRUCTIVE SURGERY

The word 'plastic' comes from a Greek word meaning 'to form'. Plastic or reconstructive surgery is done to reconstruct or alter congenital or acquired defects in order to restore or improve the body's form and function. (Often the terms plastic and reconstructive are used interchangeably). This type of surgery includes the closure of wounds, removal of skin tumours, repair of soft tissue injuries or burns,

correction of deformities of the breast and repair of cosmetic defects. Frequently, plastic surgery is done primarily for aesthetic and cosmetic improvement, but it is applicable to many parts of the body and to numerous structures, such as bone, cartilage, fat, fascia, mucous membrane, muscle, nerve and cutaneous structures. Bone inlays and transplants for deformities and nonunion can be done; muscle can be transferred; nerves can be reconstructed and spliced; and cartilage can be replaced. Last, but as important as any of these measures, is the reconstruction of the cutaneous tissues around the neck and the face; this is usually referred to as aesthetic or cosmetic surgery.

Wound Coverage: Grafts and Flaps

Skin Grafts

Skin grafting is a technique in which a section of skin is detached from its own blood supply and transferred as free tissue to a distant (recipient) site. Skin grafting can be used to repair almost any type of wound, and is the most common form of reconstructive surgery. In dermatology, skin grafts are commonly used to repair defects that result from excision of skin tumours, to cover areas denuded of skin and to cover wounds in which insufficient skin is available to permit wound closure. They are also used when primary

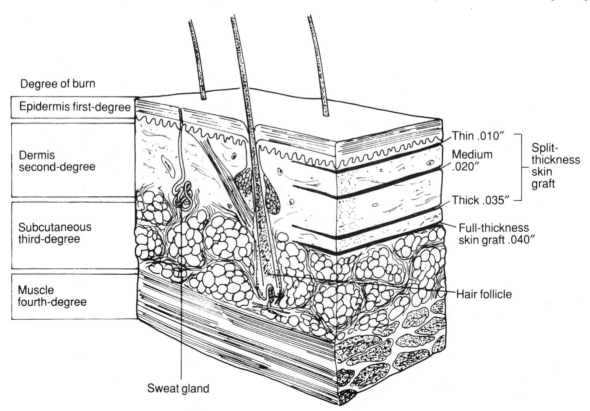

Figure 28.8 Layers of skin showing split-thickness graft.

closure of the wound increases risk of complications or when primary wound closure will interfere with function.

Skin grafts may be classified as autografts, allografts or xenografts. Autografts are grafts done with tissue transplanted from the patient's own skin. Allografts involve the transplant of tissue from one individual to another individual of the same species. These grafts are also called allogenic or homograft. A xenograft or heterograft involves the transfer of tissue from another species.

Grafts are also referred to by their thickness. A skin graft may be split-thickness (thin, intermediate or thick) or full-thickness, depending upon the amount of dermis included in the specimen. A split-thickness graft can be cut at varying thicknesses, and is commonly used to cover large wounds or defects for which a full-thickness graft or flap is impractical (Figure 28.8, p. 900). A full-thickness graft consists of epidermis and the entire dermis without the underlying fat. It is used to cover wounds that are too large to close directly.

Application of the Graft

A graft is obtained by a variety of instruments: razor blades, skin-grafting knives, electric- or air-powered dermatomes or drum dermatomes. The skin graft is taken from the 'donor' or 'host' site and applied to the wound/ulcer site, called the 'recipient' site or 'graft bed'.

For a graft to survive and be effective, certain conditions must be met: (1) the recipient bed must have an adequate blood supply so that normal physiological function can resume; (2) the graft must be in close contact with its bed (to avoid accumulation of blood or fluid); (3) the graft must be fixed firmly (immobilized) so that it remains in place on the recipient site; and (4) the area must be free of infection.

The graft, when applied to the recipient site, may or may not be sutured in place. It may be slit and spread apart to cover a greater area. The process of revascularization and reattachment of a skin graft to a recipient bed is referred to as a 'take'.

After a skin graft is put in place, the graft may be left exposed (in areas that are impossible to immobilize) or covered with a light dressing or a pressure dressing, depending on the area.

Patient Education

The patient is advised to keep the affected part immobilized as much as possible. For a facial graft, strenuous activity must be avoided. A graft on the hand or arm may be immobilized with a splint. When a graft is placed in a lower extremity, the part is kept elevated because the new capillary connections are fragile and excess venous pressure may cause rupture. When ambulation is permitted, the patient wears an elastic stocking to counteract venous pressure.

The patient or caregiver is requested to inspect the dressing daily. Unusual drainage or an inflammatory reaction around the wound margin suggests infection and should be reported to the doctor. Any fluid, purulent drainage, blood or serum that has collected will be gently evacuated by the surgeon, because this material would cause the graft to separate from its bed.

When the graft appears pink, it apparently is vascularized. After two to three weeks, mineral oil or a lanolin cream is massaged into the wound to moisten the graft and stimulate circulation. Because there may be loss of feeling or sensation in the grafted area for a prolonged period, the application of heating pads and exposure to sun are avoided.

Donor Site for Skin Grafting

Selection Criteria. The donor site is selected with several criteria in mind: (1) to obtain the closest possible colour match in keeping with the amount of skin graft required; (2) to match the texture and hair-bearing qualities; (3) to obtain the thickest possible skin graft without jeopardizing the healing process of the donor site (Figure 28.9); and (4) to consider the cosmetic effects of the donor site after healing, so that it is in an inconspicuous location.

Donor Site Care. Detailed attention to the donor site is just as important as the care of the recipient area. The donor site heals by re-epithelialization of the raw, exposed dermis. Usually a single layer of nonadherent fine-mesh gauze is placed directly over the donor site. Absorbent gauze dressings are then placed on top to take up blood or serum from the wound. A membrane dressing may be used, and provides certain advantages: it is transparent and allows the wound to be checked without disturbing the dressing, it permits the patient to shower without fear of saturating the dressing with water and it is virtually painless.

After healing, the patient is advised to keep the donor site soft and pliable with cream (e.g., lanolin). Extremes in temperature, external trauma and sunlight are to be avoided for both donor sites and grafted areas because these areas are sensitive, especially to thermal injuries.

Flaps

Another form of wound coverage may be provided by flaps. A flap is a segment of tissue that has been left attached at one end (called a base or pedicle) while the other end has been moved to a recipient area. It is dependent for its survival on functioning arterial and venous blood supplies and lymphatic drainage in its pedicle or base. A flap differs from a graft in that a portion of the tissue is attached to its original site and retains its blood supply. (An exception is the free flap, described below). Flaps may consist of skin, mucosa, muscle, adipose tissue, omentum and bone. They are used for wound coverage and provide bulk, especially when bone, tendon, blood vessels or nerve tissue is exposed. Flaps are used to repair defects

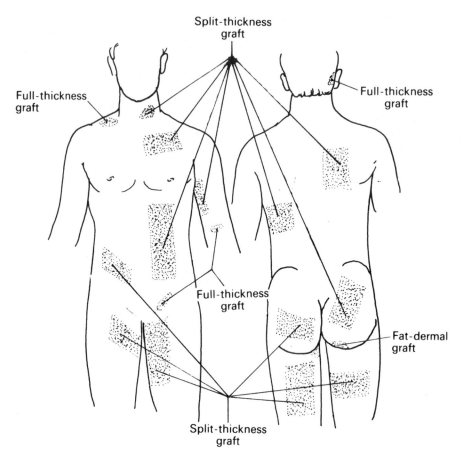

Figure 28.9 Commonly employed sites for donor areas of skin grafts. (Converse, J. M. and Brauer, R. A. (1977) *Reconstructive Plastic Surgery*, W. B. Saunders, Philadelphia.)

caused by congenital deformity, trauma or tumour ablation in an adjacent part of the body.

Flaps have the advantage of offering the best aesthetic solution because a flap retains the colour and texture of the donor area, is more apt to survive than a graft and can be used to cover nerves, tendons and blood vessels. However, a series of operations is usually required to move a flap. The major complication is necrosis of the pedicle or base due to failure of the blood supply.

Free Flaps

A striking advance in reconstructive surgery is the use of free flaps or free-tissue transfer, achieved by means of microvascular techniques. A free flap is completely severed from the body and transferred to another site, and receives early vascular supply from microvascular anastomosis with vessels at the recipient site. Thus the procedure is generally done in one step, eliminating a series of operations to move the flap. Microvascular surgery has opened an era that allows surgeons of differing specialties to use a variety of donor sites for tissue reconstruction.

Fascial, Cartilage and Bone Transplants

Transplants of fascial or muscle tissue have numerous uses. The tissue is usually obtained from the fascia lata of the thigh, and is adaptable for use as suture material, for repair of hernia defects and for replacement of tendon loss. Cartilage transplantation may be immediate and direct, taken from the costal cartilages and transferred to the nose. Bone grafts demand careful aseptic technique and rigid fixation in their new site. They may be taken from the crest of the tibia, the upper border of the iliac bone or a rib. All donor areas should receive the same careful treatment given any other surgical wound.

Management of the Patient With Facial Reconstructive Surgery

Reconstructive procedures on the face are designed to suit the individual patient and to repair deformities or restore normal function as much as possible. They may vary from closure of small defects to complicated procedures involving implantation of prosthetic devices to conceal a large defect or replace a lost part of the face (e.g., nose reconstruction, ear reconstruction; resection of the mandible). Each surgical solution is custom-tailored and involves a variety of incisions, flaps and grafts.

In correcting a primary defect, the surgeon may have to create a secondary defect. Although the operation may restore some function, such as eating or talking, the cosmetic or aesthetic results are sometimes limited. The original appearance of a patient with severe damage to soft tissue and bone structure can seldom be restored. Multiple surgical procedures may be required. The process of facial reconstruction is often slow and tedious.

► NURSING PROCESS
► THE PATIENT WITH FACIAL RECONSTRUCTIVE SURGERY

► Assessment

The face is a part of the body that every person desires to keep at its best or improve because most human interactions centre on the face. When the face loses its appearance and function (e.g., by accident or cancer), an emotional reaction occurs. Changes in appearance frequently cause anxiety and depression. Patients with facial changes frequently mourn for the lost part, suffer a loss of self-esteem due to reactions or rejection by others, and withdraw and isolate themselves. Health care staff can legitimize these emotions by acknowledging that anxiety and depression are appropriate for what the patient is experiencing.

In addition to assessing emotional responses, the nurse identifies strengths as well as usual coping mechanisms to determine how the patient will handle the surgical procedure. Any area in which the patient, family and other carers will need extra support is also highlighted.

Preoperative Nursing Care

The patient is prepared as thoroughly as possible for the extent of disfigurement and improvement that can be anticipated. The nurse is able to reinforce factual information and clarify misconceptions when the surgeon has fully informed the patient about the procedure, the functional defects that may result, the possible need for a tracheostomy and/or other prosthesis and the necessity for additional surgery.

Preoperative teaching also includes an explanation of intravenous feedings, the use of a nasogastric tube to allow gastric decompression and prevent vomiting and the frequent and lengthy dressing periods that may be necessary to care for wounds, flaps and skin grafts. Extra time is needed when presenting this information to anxious patients because they may not listen, may not comprehend or may distort what is being said.

► Patient's Problems

Based on the nursing assessment, the patient's main problems may include the following:

● Ineffective airway clearance related to tracheobronchial secretions.
● Discomfort and pain related to facial oedema and effects of procedure.
● Potential alteration in nutrition (less than body requirements) related to changed physiology of oral cavity, dribbling, impairment of chewing and swallowing, excision surgery affecting the tongue.
● Impaired verbal communication related to trauma/surgery producing anatomical and physiological abnormalities of speech.
● Alteration in self-image related to disfigurement.
● Alteration in family/home process related to grief reaction and disruption of personal life

► Planning and Implementation
► Expected Outcomes

The major outcomes for the patient may include maintenance of a patent airway and pulmonary function, achievement of increased comfort, attainment and maintenance of adequate nutritional status, development of some form of effective communication, reinforcement of positive self-concept and achievement of effective coping.

Nursing Care

Nursing care is similar to that of the patient undergoing mandibular and maxillary surgery (see Chapter 12).

Improving Self-Esteem
Success in rehabilitation of the patient undergoing reconstructive surgery is determined in no small measure by the relationship between the patient, nurse, surgeon and other staff.

Mutual trust, respect and clear lines of communication are essential for an effective relationship. Unhurried visits provide emotional reassurance and support. Giving attention to the details of care brings physical and emotional relief and release.

Often the kinds of dressings that have to be worn, the unusual positions that have to be maintained and the temporary incapacities that must be experienced can be upsetting to the most stable person. Honest praise for the patient's coping and fortitude reinforces self-respect. If prosthetic devices are to be used, the patient is taught how to use and care for them in order to gain a sense of greater independence. Once involved in self-care activities, the patient may feel new control over what was previously an overwhelming situation.

Patients with a severe disfigurement are encouraged to socialize in the hospital to experience the reactions of others in a more protected environment. Gradually they can widen this sphere of contact. Every effort is made to cover or mask defects. Patients may require support by members of the mental health team to accept their changed appearance.

Helping Family/Friends Coping

The family/friends are informed about the patient's appearance following surgery, the presence of supportive equipment and how the equipment aids in recovery. It is helpful to join the patient's loved ones for a few minutes during their first postoperative visit to help them cope with the changes they will see.

A major nursing task is to support the family or close friends in their decision to participate (or not to participate) in the patient's treatment. Nursing care also includes helping loved ones to communicate by suggesting techniques for reducing anxiety and stress, and promoting problem-solving and decision-making.

► *Evaluation*
► **Expected Outcomes**

1. Patient maintains patent airway.
   a. Demonstrates respiratory rate within normal limits.
   b. Has normal breath sounds.
   c. Has no signs of choking or aspiration.

2. Is free of complications.
   a. Demonstrates vital signs within normal limits.
   b. Undergoes normal wound healing.
   c. Is free of signs of infection.

3. Achieves increasing comfort.
   a. Reports decreasing pain.
   b. Demonstrates lessening facial oedema.
   c. Adheres to oral hygiene regime to prevent infection/subsequent pain.

4. Communicates effectively.
   a. Uses appropriate aids to enhance communication.
   b. Interacts with health team members and family/support people.

5. Develops positive self-image.
   a. Expresses positive feelings about surgical changes.
   b. Has appropriate eye contact and attention span.
   c. Demonstrates increasing independence in self-care activities.
   d. Uses prosthetic devices independently (when appropriate).
   e. Plans for resumption of pre-illness activities (e.g., work, recreation).

6. Family and other carers cope with situation.
   a. Demonstrate lessening anxiety and conflict among family and close friends.
   b. Shows awareness of what to expect.

Laser Treatment of Cutaneous Lesions

Lasers are devices that amplify or generate highly specialized rays of potent light. They are capable of mobilizing immense heat and power when focused at close range, and are a valuable tool in surgical procedures. Two main types of lasers, the argon laser and carbon-dioxide laser, have application in dermatological surgery.

Argon Laser

The argon laser produces a blue-green light that is absorbed by vascular tissue and hence is useful in treating vascular lesions: port-wine stains, telangiectasias, vascular tumours and pigmented lesions. The argon beam passes through the overlying skin and reaches the pigmented layer of the skin, causing protein coagulation in this area. An immediate effect is that tiny blood vessels under the skin are coagulated, causing the area to turn a much lighter colour. A crust forms within a few days, persisting about two weeks.

Patient Education

Cold compresses are usually applied over the treatment area for approximately six hours to minimize oedema, exudate and loss of capillary permeability. The patient is advised that there may be swelling of the treated area, and to avoid picking at the crust. Sun exposure over the treated area is avoided to prevent the development of hypopigmentation, and a sunscreen of at least solar protection factor 15 is to be used when exposure is unavoidable.

Carbon-Dioxide Laser

The carbon-dioxide laser emits light in the infrared spectrum that is absorbed at the skin surface because of the high water content of the skin and the long wavelength of the carbon dioxide light. As the laser beam strikes human tissue, it is absorbed by the intra- and extracellular water, which vaporizes, destroying the tissue. The carbon-dioxide laser is a precise surgical instrument for use in vaporizing and excising tissue with minimal tissue damage. Because of the ability of the beam to seal blood and lymphatic vessels, it creates a dry surgical field that makes many procedures easier and quicker. It is useful for removal of epidermal naevi, tattoos and certain warts. Incisions made with the laser heal in much the same way as those made by a scalpel.

Patient Education

The wound is covered with a nonstick dressing. The patient is requested to keep the wound dry. After re-epithelialization is complete, the dressing is removed. A steroid ointment may be prescribed at this stage to reduce chances of hypertrophic scarring.

Aesthetic Surgery

Rhytidectomy (face lift) is an operation on the face to remove soft-tissue folds and minimize cutaneous wrinkles. It is done to improve and create a more youthful appearance.

Psychological preparation requires that the person recognize the limitations of surgery and that miraculous rejuvenation will not occur. The patient is informed that the face may appear bruised and swollen after the dressings are removed, and that several weeks may pass before the oedema subsides.

The procedure is done under local or general anaesthesia, and the outpatient setting has become an increasingly popular site for the surgery. The incisions are placed in areas of concealment (natural skin folds and creases and areas hidden by hair). The loose skin, separated from underlying muscle, is pulled upwards and backwards. Excess skin that overlaps the incision line is removed. More recently, liposuction-assisted rhytidectomy is being done, in which fat is suctioned via a cannula through a small incision.

Patient Education

The patient is encouraged to rest quietly for the first two postoperative days until the dressings are removed. The head of the bed is elevated and neck flexion is discouraged to avoid compromising the circulation in the cervical (neck) flap. There is some degree of tightness of the face and neck due to pressure created by the newly tightened muscles, fascia and skin. Analgesics may be prescribed for discomfort. A liquid diet may be given by means of straws, and a soft diet is permitted if chewing is not too uncomfortable.

When the dressings are removed, the skin is gently cleansed of crusting and oozing and coated with the prescribed topical ointment. The matted hair may be combed with warm water and a wide-tooth comb.

The patient is advised not to lift or bend for 7 to 10 days because this activity may increase oedema and provoke bleeding. Activities are gradually increased. When all sutures are removed, the hair may be shampooed and blown dry with warm, not hot, air to avoid burning the ears, which may be numb for a period of time. Sudden pain indicates that blood is accumulating underneath the skin flaps, and should be reported to the surgeon immediately. Complications include sloughing of the skin, deformities of the face and neck and partial facial paralysis. Cigarette smoking has been implicated as a cause of skin slough in some patients.

The effects of a face lift will not stop the ageing process. With time, the tissues drift downwards. Some patients have two or more face lifts.

Rhinoplasty

Rhinoplasty is an operation designed to alter the shape of the nose. There are many variations of the procedure, and the operation is tailored to the specific nose. The patient may request that the nose be made narrower, that the tip be thinned or that a hump be removed. If the function of the nose is altered, the term nasal reconstruction is used. Nasal reconstruction is usually done for developmental and traumatic deformities.

Rhinoplasty is done through intranasal incisions under local or general anaesthesia. Following the operation, packing may or may not be placed inside the nose.

Patient Education

The patient is advised to rest sitting upright and reminded not to touch, pick or blow the nose in order to avoid bleeding. Chewing may be uncomfortable for a time, and liquids are advised. Some degree of bruising may be noted. Due to swelling inside the nose, the patient will have symptoms of a head cold. This is to be expected.

Complications include unexpected bleeding, haematoma and infection (rare).

Blepharoplasty

Blepharoplasty is an aesthetic operation designed to remove skin or fat from the upper or lower eyelids. The goal is restoration of the eyelids for a more youthful appearance. The procedure may be combined with a face lift. Although it is effective in tightening the eyelid skin and eliminating or reducing fat pads around the eye, blepharoplasty does not eliminate fine wrinkles, laugh lines, age lines or pigmentation around the eyes.

The procedure is done in an outpatient or hospital care facility under local or general anaesthesia. The incisions are made in the upper lid crease line and in the lower lid immediately below the eyelashes.

Patient Education

The following are teaching points applicable to most patients:

- Considerable eyelid swelling can be expected within 24 hours, and may last up to three weeks. Sleeping with the head elevated will help to diminish swelling.
- Ice compresses may be applied (with approval by the surgeon) to the eyelids for 20 minutes, three to four times daily, to reduce postoperative swelling and ecchymoses and to provide a soothing effect. (This self-care activity also serves to distract the patient from the discomfort.) Warm compresses are applied after 48 hours to hasten resolution of bruising.
- During the early postoperative period, the lashes are cleansed with cotton-tipped applicators moistened with clear water or prescribed solution.
- A sunscreen should be used after healing because sun-damaged skin wrinkles more easily. Usually there are no contraindications to the application of eye cosmetics after sutures are removed.

● Complications include spontaneous bleeding, which may result in a haematoma and require surgical drainage. The patient is advised to contact the surgeon immediately if bleeding occurs. Epiphora (excessive tearing) and ectropion (pulling-down of lower eyelid) may occur.

Dermabrasion

Dermabrasion (skin planing) is a form of skin abrasion used to correct acne scarring, ageing and sun-damaged skin. A special instrument (motor-driven wire brush, diamond-impregnated disk, serrated wheel) is used in the procedure. The epidermis and some superficial dermis is removed, while enough of the dermis is preserved to allow re-epithelialization of the dermabraded areas. Results are best in the face because it is rich in intradermal epithelial elements.

Patient Instruction and Preparation

The primary reason for undergoing dermabrasion is to improve appearance. The surgeon explains to the patient what can be expected from dermabrasion. The patient should also be informed about the nature of the postoperative dressing, what discomfort may be experienced and how long it will be before the tissues look normal. Dermabrasion may be carried out in the operating theatre or an outpatient setting. It is done under local or general anaesthesia. During and after planing, the area is irrigated with copious amounts of saline solution to remove debris and allow the surgeon to see the area. A dressing impregnated with ointment is usually applied to the abraded surface.

Patient Education

The nurse advises the patient about the after-effects of the surgery. Oedema occurs during the first 48 hours. Facial dermabrasion may cause the eyelids to close, and the patient should elevate the head of the bed to hasten fluid drainage. Erythema occurs, and can last for weeks or months. After 24 hours, the dressing may be removed (if the surgeon so wishes). When the serum oozing from the skin begins to gel, the patient applies the prescribed ointment several times a day to prevent hard crusting and to keep the abraded areas soft and flexible. Clear water cleansing/soaking is started with the surgeon's approval to remove crusts from the healing skin.

The patient is advised to avoid extreme cold and heat, and excessive straining or lifting, which may bruise delicate new capillaries. Direct or reflected sunlight is avoided for three to six months, and a sunscreen should be used.

Body Contouring Surgery

Suction lipectomy is the removal of localized deposits of fat by suction after small incisions are made through the skin. It is done to reduce the volume of localized fat deposits and improve the contour of the body. A cannula is inserted through the skin incision into the fatty tissue, and fat is aspirated through the suction tube as the cannula is removed. The procedure is done most often on the abdomen, hips, buttocks and thighs. Intraoperatively, blood is removed with fat and therefore blood loss is directly proportional to the size of the area being treated.

Suction lipectomy is more successful in younger people because they have greater skin elasticity and better potential for the aspirated areas to contract smoothly. Ageing and flabbiness impose limitations.

Patient Education

The nurse advises the patient that there is minimal postoperative pain and discomfort, although bruising may be seen in the aspirated areas, and that a rapid recovery can be anticipated. The dressings over the area are to be kept dry. A compression garment or bandages aid in the reduction of oedema. The patient is advised that full improvement may not be apparent for several months.

Potential complications include hypovolaemia, infection and failure of the skin to shrink adequately over the treated areas, which leaves irregular waves or depressions on the skin that can mar the aesthetic effect.

Tissue Expanders

A new trend in plastic and reconstructive surgery is the use of tissue expanders to produce tissue growth through

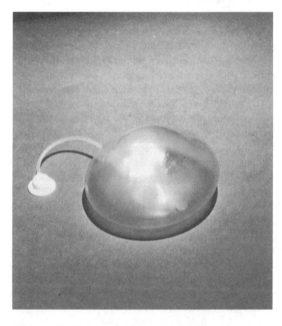

Figure 28.10 A round tissue expander, one of several types available. The expander is implanted to produce tissue growth in order to provide tissue of similar colour and texture for reconstructive surgery. (Courtesy of CUI Corporation.)

stretch and moulding techniques (Figure 28.10). Skin has the ability to increase in surface area (expand) when mechanically stimulated from beneath by an enlarging mass. (This occurs naturally during pregnancy.)

An inflatable expander is implanted beneath subcutaneous tissue and can be stretched by injections of fluid to produce an enlargement in the area of overlying skin and subcutaneous tissue. When the desired expansion is obtained, the expander is removed. Tissue expanders are used in breast reconstruction, for repair of tissue defects and to facilitate the development of soft-tissue flaps in areas in which such flaps are not readily available.

Potential problems include compression and functional compromise of structures such as nerves and arteries.

HAIR DISORDERS

Growth Cycle of Hair

Human scalp hair constantly renews itself and progresses through different phases of growth. Hair grows during the anagen (growth) phase, which may last three to five years (an average of four years). Approximately 90 per cent of the hairs on the scalp are in this anagen phase. Hair grows at the rate of approximately 1 cm per month.

The second phase, catagen phase, lasts one to two weeks. The blood supply to the hair root slowly diminishes, the hair root becomes smaller, and the cells in the papilla slowly stop dividing.

The final phase is the telogen (end of growth) phase, lasting four to six months. The hair, which has only a superficial root, pulls out easily when it is combed or brushed, or it is forced out of the scalp when a new hair, growing in the same follicle, enters the anagen phase. Thus, hair naturally falls out, with an average of 65 to 80 hairs being shed each day.

Alopecia

Alopecia is loss of hair or baldness. It may occur due to illness, drug therapy, hormonal imbalance or nutritional problems. In these events, it usually can be reversed when the underlying disorder is corrected. Other causes include excessive traction on the hair (from braiding too tightly), excessive use of dyes, straighteners and oils, fungus infection of the scalp and moles or cancer on the scalp.

The most common cause of alopecia is male pattern baldness, affecting more than half of the male population. This is believed to be caused by a combination of factors including heredity, increasing age and androgen (male hormone) levels. (The presence of androgen is necessary for male pattern baldness to develop.) The pattern of hair loss begins with receding of the hairline in the frontal-temporal area, and progresses to gradual thinning and complete loss of hair over the top of the scalp and crown.

Management

There are literally hundreds of over-the-counter products claiming to grow hair or prevent hair loss. Most, if not all, of these products are not effective. Search continues for a suitable anti-androgen to prevent hair loss.

Topical minoxidil is currently receiving a great deal of publicity as a method for treating baldness. The medication is applied to the scalp twice daily. It stimulates hair growth in some men with male pattern baldness, presumably by increasing the blood supply to the scalp. Hair growth is only maintained while treatment continues.

Some people may prefer to wear natural-appearing hair pieces.

Hair Transplantation Surgery

Hair transplantation surgery (hair replacement surgery) involves transplanting hair-bearing skin from the sides and posterior portions of the scalp to recipient spaces in the bald areas. This redistributes the patient's remaining hair as naturally and evenly as possible over the bald scalp area, and is accomplished by punch grafting, scalp reduction or the use of flaps of various kinds.

Punch grafting is the transplantation of small plugs of hair-bearing scalp from the uninvolved areas at the back and side of the head to the bald areas. It is done in four or more sessions, one to two months apart, and is an outpatient procedure.

Scalp reduction is a surgical procedure in which the bald portion of the scalp is reduced by staged surgical excisions. It is usually the procedure of choice for baldness of the vertex (top of head) and anterior vertex regions.

Hair-bearing flaps can be transposed from adjacent areas into bald areas. This procedure may be performed in several stages over a period of several months. With the use of flaps, 200 to 250 hairs per square centimetre, about normal density, can be transferred. Thus hair is obtained instantly as soon as the flap is rotated over the bald area. (Flaps are discussed on p. 901.)

Infection and bone necrosis can occur in scalp operations.

BIBLIOGRAPHY

Ellis, C. N., Gorsulowsky, D. C., Hamilton, T. A. *et al.* (1986) Cyclosporine improves psoriasis in a double-blind study, *Journal of the American Medical Association*, 12 December, Vol. 256, No. 22, pp. 3110–16.

Stoughton, R. D. (1979) Topical antibiotics for acne vulgaris, *Archives of Dermatology*, Vol. 115, pp. 486–9.

Treadgold, A. (1983) Patch testing for contact dermatitis, *Nursing*, Vol. 26, No. 9, pp. 255–8.

van Joost, T., Heule, F., Stolz, E. *et al.* (1986) Short-term use of cyclosporin A in severe psoriasis, *British Journal of Dermatology*, May, Vol. 114, No. 5, pp. 615–20.

FURTHER READING

Books

Buxton, P. K. (1988) *ABC of Dermatology*, British Medical Association, London.

Cronin, E. (1980) *Contact Dermatitis*, Churchill Livingstone, London.

David, J. A. (1986) *Wound Management*, Martin Dunitz, London.

Fregert, S. (1981) *Manual of Contact Dermatitis* (2nd edition), Munksgard, Copenhagen.

Fry, L., Wojnarowska, F. and Shahrad, P. (1981) *Illustrated Encyclopaedia of Dermatology*, MTP Press, London.

Hughes, G. V. R. (1985) *Lupus: A Guide for Patients*, Rheumatology Department, St Thomas's Hospital, London.

Levene, G. M. and Calnan, C. D. (1974) *A Colour Atlas of Dermatology*, Wolfe Medical Publications, London.

McKie, R. (1983) *Eczema and Dermatitis*, Martin Dunitz, London.

Malten, K. E., Nater, J. P. and Venketel, W. G. (1976) *Patch Testing Guidelines*, Dekker & van de Vegt, Nijmegen, Netherlands.

Marks, R. (1981) *Psoriasis*, Martin Duntiz, London.

Marks, R. (1984) *Acne*, Martin Dunitz, London.

Meneghini, C. and Bonifazi, E. (1986) *An Atlas of Paediatric Dermatology*, Martin Dunitz, London.

Murphy, G. (1987) *Answers to Acne*, Optima (MacDonald & Co.), London.

Murray, D. (1981) *The Anti-Acne Book*, Arlington Pocket Books, London.

Orton, C. (1981) *Learning to Live With Skin Disorders*, Souvenir Press, London.

Rook, A., Wilkinson, D. S. and Ebling, A. (1979) *A Textbok of Dermatology* (3rd edition), Blackwell Scientific, London.

Stone, L. A. (1989) *The Lippincott Manual of Medical-Surgical Nursing* (2nd edition), Chapter 11, Care of the patient with a skin disorder or burn, Harper & Row, London, p. 728.

Stone, L. A., Lindfield, E. M. and Robertson, S. (1989) *A Colour Atlas of Nursing Procedures in Skin Disorders*, Wolfe Medical, London.

Articles

Amann, L. P. (1981) The management of psoriasis, *Nursing*, Vol. 26, pp. 1123–5.

Armstrong-Esther, C. A. (1981) Skin and hypersensitivity, *Nursing*, Vol. 26, pp. 1152–6.

Bremer Schulte, M., Cormane, R. H., van Dijk, E. *et al.* (1985) Group therapy of psoriasis, *Journal of the American Academy of Dermatology*, Vol. 12, pp. 61–6.

Chaplain, S. (1981) Skin problems in the community, *Nursing*, Vol. 26, pp. 116–8.

Deener, D. (1980) Plastic surgery: result—a lip to be kissed with relish, *Nursing Mirror*, Vol. 151, pp. 30–33.

Editorial (1984) Management of toxic epidermal necrolysis, *Lancet*, 1 December, Vol. 2, No. 8414, pp. 1250–52.

Fincham-Gee, C. (1988) Safe use of topical steroids, *Nursing*, Vol. 29, No. 3, pp. 1043–5.

Fincham-Gee, C. (1990) Cosmetic camouflage, *Nursing*, Vol. 4, No. 6, pp. 20–2.

Fincham-Gee, C. (1990) Paste bandages for leg ulcers, *Nursing*, Vol. 4, No. 9, pp. 25–9.

Fincham-Gee, C. (1990) Cultured keratinocyte grafts, *Nursing*, Vol. 4, No. 11, pp. 17–22.

Fincham-Gee, C. (1990) A concept of caring, *Nursing*, Vol. 4, No. 16, p. 35.

Fincham-Gee, C. (1990) Nutrition and wound healing, *Nursing*, Vol. 4, No. 18, pp. 26–8.

Fincham-Gee, C. (1990) Nursing management—skin, *Midwife, Health Visitor and Community Nursing*, September, Supplement, pp. 8–10.

Fincham-Gee, C. and Stone, L. A. (eds) (1988) Skin, *Nursing*, Vol. 3, p. 29.

Greenhow, M. M. (1983) Topical treatments—a simple guide, *Nursing*, Vol. 2, No. 10, pp. 281–4.

Herrick, M. (1983) Surgery in dermatology, *Nursing*, Vol. 2, No. 10, pp. 272–3.

Jowett, S. and Ryan, T. (1985) Skin disease and handicap: An analysis of the impact of skin conditions, *Social Science Medicine*, Vol. 20, No. 4, pp. 425–9.

Logan, R. A. (1988) Self-help groups for patients with chronic diseases, *British Journal of Dermatology*, Vol. 118, No. 4, pp. 505–7.

Lovell, C. R. (1983) The skin and systemic disease, *Nursing*, Vol. 2, No. 10, pp. 277–9.

Marks, R. (1986) Psoriasis and its treatment with etretinate, *Retinoids Today and Tomorrow*, Vol. 2, pp. 4–6.

Martin, V. (1981) Preventing hypertrophic scarring: a burning issue, *Nursing Mirror*, Vol. 153, pp. 32–3.

Maunder, J. W. (1981) Clinical and laboratory trials employing carbaryl against the human head louse, *Pediculosis human capitis (de Gear)*, *Clinical and Experimental Dermatology*, Vol. 6, pp. 605–12.

Millard, L. D. (1983) Dermatology in pigmented skin, *Nursing*, Vol. 2, No. 10, pp. 274–6.

Mohlnycky, N. (1983) Parasitic skin infections, *Nursing*, Vol. 2, No. 9, pp. 246–8.

Muller, S. A. and Perry, H. O. (1984) The Goeckerman treatment in psoriasis: six decades of experience at the Mayo Clinic, *Cutis*, September, Vol. 34, No. 3, pp. 265–8.

Orfanos, C. E. *et al.* (1985) Current developments of oral retinoid therapy with three generations of drugs, *Current Problems in Dermatology*, Vol. 13, pp. 33–49.

Runne, V. and Kunze, J. (1982) Short duration ('minutes') therapy with dithranol for psoriasis: a new outpatient regime, *British Journal of Dermatology*, Vol. 106, pp. 135–9.

Ryan, T. J. (1981) The handicap of skin diseases, *Nursing*, Vol. 26, pp. 1144–5.

Sidhanee, A. C. (1983) Structure and function of the skin, *Nursing*, Vol. 2, No. 9, pp. 239–42.

Sidhanee, A. C. and Stone, L. A. (eds) (1983) Skin, *Nursing*, Vol. 2, pp. 9–10.

Stone, L. A. (1983) Contact dermatitis, *Nursing*, Vol. 2, No. 9, pp. 252–3.

Stone, L. A. (1983) Infections of the skin, *Nursing*, Vol. 2, No. 10, pp. 285–7.

Storer, J. S. *et al.* (1986) Review: Topical minoxidil for male pattern baldness, *American Journal of Medical Science*, May, Vol. 29, No. 5, pp. 328–33.

Tring, F. C. (1981) Warts and their treatment, *Nursing Times*, Vol. 77, pp. 1415–7.

Turner, T. D. (1985) Semiocclusive and occlusive dressings: An environment for healing—the role of occlusion, *The Royal Society of Medicine, International Congress and Symposium Series*, No. 88, pp. 5–14.

unit **10**

SENSORINEURAL
PROBLEMS

chapter *29*

ASSESSMENT AND CARE OF PATIENTS WITH VISUAL DISTURBANCES AND EYE DISORDERS

ANATOMY AND PHYSIOLOGY

The eyeball is a spherical organ situated in a bony cavity called the orbit. It is rotated easily in all the necessary directions by six muscles attached to its outer surface; these muscles act in a manner similar to the reins on a team of horses. Four of the muscles are located on each side of the eye and on the top and the bottom of the eye. Each of these four muscles, the rectus muscles, leads back to the apex of the orbit and turns the eye in or out, up or down. The other two muscles of the eye, the oblique muscles, run from the globe toward the medial wall of the orbit (Figure 29.1).

For the purpose of study, the eyeball may be divided into three coats or tunics (Figure 29.2). The dense, white, fibrous outer coat is called the sclera. Anteriorly, the sclera becomes continuous with the cornea, the translucent structure that bulges forward slightly from the general contour of the eye. Posteriorly, the sclera has an opening through which the optic nerve passes into the eyeball. The nerve spreads out over the posterior two thirds of the inner surface of the globe in a thin layer called the retina. In it are situated the tiny nerve endings, which, when properly stimulated, transmit visual impulses to the brain that are interpreted as sight.

Between the sclera and the retina is the pigmented middle coat known as the uveal tract. This tract is composed of three parts. The posterior part, the choroid, contains most of the blood vessels that nourish the eye. The anterior part is a pigmented muscular structure, the iris, which gives the characteristic colour to the eye (e.g., blue, brown). The circular opening at its centre, the pupil, dilates or contracts according to the intensity of light. These reactions are controlled by two sets of muscle fibres. Contraction of the circular fibres constricts the pupil; the radial fibres enlarge it. Between the iris and the choroid is the third portion of the uveal tract, a muscular body known as the ciliary body. It is composed of radial processes arising from a triangular-shaped muscle (ciliary muscle). Between these processes, and to them, are

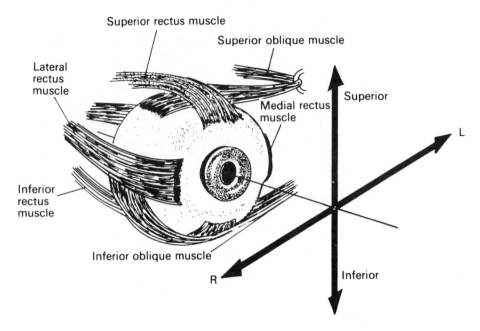

Figure 29.1 The extraocular muscles and their insertions onto the right eye. The arrows and the line to the pupil indicate the six cardinal positions of gaze. (Gittinger, J. W. Jr. (1984) *Ophthalmology*, Little, Brown & Co, Boston.)

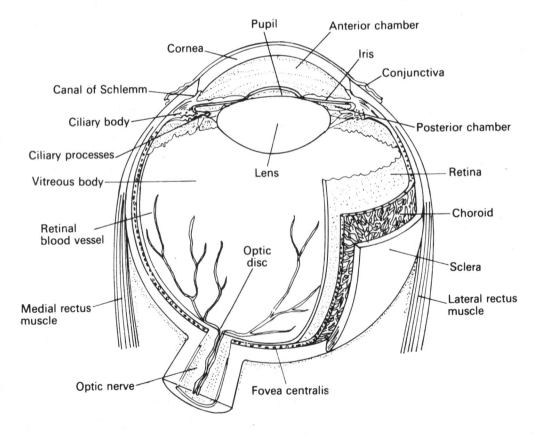

Figure 29.2 Transverse section of eye. (Chaffee, E. E. and Greisheimer, E. M. (1974) *Basic Physiology and Anatomy*, J. B. Lippincott, Philadelphia.)

attached delicate ligaments that pass centrally and become inserted in the capsule of the crystalline lens.

The lens is a semisolid body consisting of three anatomical components: the nucleus, the cortex, and the capsule. The nucleus is located in the central zone and is surrounded by a thick layer of softer cortical material, which in turn is enveloped by a thin transparent elastic capsule. The lens is capable of being modified to varying degrees of convexity by the contraction and the relaxation of the ciliary muscles, and zonules ('guy wires'). This adjustment in vision is referred to as accommodation.

The cavity within the eye is divided by the lens into two parts. The posterior part contains a jelly-like, translucent substance called the vitreous humour, which is the chief factor in maintaining the form of the eyeball. The anterior part contains a clear, watery fluid, the aqueous humour, which is secreted by the ciliary processes. It bathes the anterior surface of the lens, escapes at the pupil and enters the space between the iris and the cornea, known as the anterior chamber. Finally, it is drained from the eye through lymph channels (the canal of Schlemm) located at the junction of the iris and the sclera.

Appendages

The eyelids are the protective coverings of the eye. Lining the lids and entirely covering the anterior part of the eye except for the cornea, is a highly sensitive membrane, the conjunctiva, the surface of which is kept moist by a constant flow of lacrimal fluid tears. This fluid is excreted from the lacrimal gland, which is located in the upper and outer part of the orbit. It flows downwards and inwards across the eye and drains into tiny channels (lacrimal puncta). These channels conduct the fluid to the lacrimal sac and duct, which pass downwards and outwards, and open into the nasal cavity beneath the inferior turbinate bone.

Considerations for the Elderly

As a person ages, vision becomes less efficient. The pupil becomes less responsive to light owing to sclerosis of the pupillary sphincter, which results in a decrease in pupil size. The lens becomes more opaque, and the visual field decreases, making peripheral vision more difficult. Eyes adapt to darkness less rapidly; therefore, vision at night or in dimly lit areas is less clear than in younger people. With advancing years, there is a slowing in the process of accommodation as the lens gradually loses its elastic nature and becomes a relatively solid mass. When the lens becomes almost totally nonaccommodating, the condition is called presbyopia. Ciliary muscles with time also become less flexible and functional. Since near vision requires the greatest work by the ciliary muscles, near vision is compromised earliest, a condition that requires the wearing of reading glasses, bifocal lenses and even perhaps trifocal lenses.

The vitreous begins to have a clumping of collagen materials; such clumping is referred to as 'floaters', which may be apparent in the field of vision. The retina shows fewest changes with ageing, except for the macula. The macula is a minute area in the centre of the retina that is especially capable of detailed and acute vision. Very small sclerotic changes in the macula will result in impaired vision.

EYE CARE SPECIALISTS

The importance of adequate eye examinations cannot be emphasized too strongly. The care of the eye is undertaken by four groups of specialists:

1. The oculist, the ophthalmologist or the ophthalmic physician is a medical doctor who is skilled in the treatment of all conditions and diseases of the eye. Training and experience enable the oculist to make a more thorough and complete examination of the eye for refractive errors and other changes.
2. The ophthalmic optician examines the eyes and related structures to determine the presence of vision problems, eye diseases or other abnormalities, and to prescribe and adapt lenses or other optical aids.
3. The dispensing optician dispenses glasses or contact lenses, and adjusts spectacles to ensure a correct fit.
4. The ocular prosthetist is a technician who makes artificial eyes and other prostheses used in ophthalmology.

EXAMINATION OF THE EYE AND ASSESSMENT OF VISION

Examination of the eye is an essential component of the physical examination, not only because of the importance of the function of the eye to the wellbeing of the patient, but also because the eye reflects many facets of the general state of health. The retina, which may be viewed with the ophthalmoscope, is the only site in the human body where a vascular bed may be examined directly. Diseases such as hypertension and diabetes, both exceedingly common in the population, produce changes that are readily observable. The pupil may be said to be a window to the human microcirculation.

Visual Acuity

Formal testing of visual acuity is a part of the assessment of every patient. Testing of visual acuity is accomplished by means of an eye chart placed 6 metres from the patient. If space is lacking, an inverted eye chart may be placed directly behind the patient's head, and a mirror placed 3 metres from the patient. The patient is requested to cover one eye with a card, to keep both eyes open and to read each line of the chart until the details for a given size of print are no longer distinguishable. If the patient wears glasses, the acuity should be assessed with and without corrective lenses.

Illiteracy may be circumvented by the use of charts that display the letter 'E' in four different positions. This enables the vision of children as young as five years of age to be assessed. The Kay picture test can be used to enable the assessment of vision in children under school age.

Visual acuity is expressed in a ratio that relates what the patient *should* see at 6 metres to what the patient *can* see at 6 metres. Acuity of 6/24 means that patients can see at 6 metres what they should see at 24 metres; 6/60, the boundary of legal blindness, indicates that patients can see at 6 metres what they should be able to see at 60 metres. Such patients can only discern with accuracy the large letter at the top of the chart. Patients whose visual acuity is less than 6/6 when corrected by their own glasses should be referred to an ophthalmologist.

Near vision is not assessed routinely unless the patient is complaining of difficulty in reading at close range or is over the age of 40. After the age of 40, the lens may become rigid and less capable of accommodating its shape to close-range vision (presbyopia). Asking the patient to read newsprint at a distance of 30.5 cm provides a general screening for this disorder. Patients who experience difficulty with this examination are referred to an optician.

External Evaluation of the Eye

The external structures of the eye are assessed primarily by inspection. These structures include the eyebrow, eyelid, eyelashes, lacrimal apparatus, conjunctiva, cornea, anterior chamber, iris and pupil. The examination begins with an assessment of the position and alignment of the eyes. The eyebrows are observed for the quantity and distribution of the hair. The positioning of the lids in relationship to the eyeballs is noted. With the eyes open, no sclera should be visible above the corneas. Ptosis (drooping of the lid) may be due to lid oedema, muscle weakness, congenital defect or involvement of the third cranial nerve. The lids are also inspected for colour, swelling, lesions and the presence and direction of eyelash growth. Common abnormalities of the lids are discussed later in this chapter.

The region of the lacrimal gland in the upper lateral orbit is inspected. If enlargement is suspected, the upper lid can be everted to expose the lacrimal gland for further inspection. Next, the lacrimal apparatus is inspected for swelling. Obstruction or inflammation of the nasolacrimal duct can often be identified by pressing on the medial aspect of the lower lid just inside the orbital rim. The area is palpated for tenderness, and regurgitation of fluid from the puncta is watched for.

The sclera and bulbar conjunctiva are inspected concurrently. The lids are separated by placing the index finger on the patient's upper orbital rim and the thumb on the lower rim. As the lids are separated, the patient is requested to look up, down and to each side. Small capillaries are normally visible in the conjunctiva, and the white, fibrous sclera is normally clearly visible. In black people, however, the sclera is often yellowish. This is a normal finding, not to be confused with jaundice. The palpebral conjunctiva of the lower lid is readily inspected by asking the patient to look upwards while the lower lid is gently everted.

To inspect the cornea and anterior chamber for opacities, the examiner shines a light from a penlight held at an oblique angle. Normally, the cornea is smooth and transparent. Irregularities are often detected by defects in the light reflection through the cornea. Shadows cast on the iris may be indicative of a corneal lesion. The iris is inspected for continuity and unusual markings.

The pupils are normally round, regular and equal in diameter and in their reaction to light. Although a small percentage of the population may have unequal pupils that may be considered normal, the phenomenon is sufficiently unusual that it should lead to thorough examination in order to ascertain that the inequality is not due to central nervous system disease. When confronted with light, the normal pupil promptly constricts in a regular concentric fashion. The unstimulated opposite pupil constricts as well. This pupillary reaction is assessed by requesting the patient to focus on a distant object while the examiner shines a bright light on each pupil, in turn.

Constriction of the stimulated pupil is called the direct light reflex, whereas constriction of the opposite pupil is termed consensual light reflex. Exploration of this phenomenon allows one to separate damage to the optic nerve from blindness owing to more central disease. Direct light stimulation of the nerve-damaged eye results in neither a direct nor a consensual light reflex. Stimulation of the uninvolved eye, however, results in consensual constriction of the pupil of the damaged eye, since the consensual reflex is not dependent on transmission through the optic nerve.

Pupillary reaction to accommodation (adjustments that occur when vision is shifted from near to far objects or vice versa) is best observed by asking the patient to focus on an object in the distance and then at the examiner's finger, which is positioned 7.5 to 12.5 cm from the patient's nose. A normal response is for the pupils to constrict as the eyes converge and focus on the examiner's finger.

Autonomic disease due to central nervous system syphilis or to diabetes may result in a pupil that is incapable of responding to light but retains its capacity to respond to accommodation. Such a pupil is known as an Argyll Robertson pupil.

Ocular Tension

An increase in intraocular tension is the cardinal manifestation of glaucoma, a disease responsible for more than

12.5 per cent of all new patients registered as blind, and 11.5 per cent of all new patients registered as partially sighted in the United Kingdom. A general determination of intraocular pressure can be made by applying gentle finger pressure over the sclera of the closed eye. The tips of both forefingers are placed on the closed upper lid. One finger gently presses inward while the adjacent finger senses the amount of pressure exerted against it. Some examiners then compare the tension 'felt' or perceived in the patient's eye to their own. At best, this manoeuvre is a general estimation. When a more accurate measurement must be relied on, tonometry is indicated.

Assessment of Extraocular Muscles

The extraocular muscles (Figure 29.1) are six small muscles attached to each eye. They are innervated by three of the cranial nerves. Synergistic (correlated) action of the extraocular muscles of both eyes results in parallel gaze. Although the mechanism by which this takes place is highly complex, and analysis of abnormality requires medical consultation, this assessment can be done by the nurse.

Parallel alignment of the eyes may be easily detected by shining a light directly into the face while the patient is staring at the light source. The light should be reflected from the pupils of both eyes identically. Light reflexes that vary from one pupil to the other indicate disturbance in parallax vision. In spite of normal alignment of both eyes when they function together, the tendency of either eye to drift to the nasal or temporal side (and the necessity to involuntarily compensate for this with effort) may be assessed by the cover test. One eye is covered by a card or by the hand of the examiner, and the patient is asked to focus the free eye on a stationary object, while keeping the covered eye open. The card or hand is abruptly removed from the covered eye, which is then observed for any ab-

normal movement. If the eye, when covered, has drifted to the temporal side, it will snap back into alignment when the cover is removed. The tendency of an eye to drift, when covered, to the temporal side is called an exophoria; a tendency of an eye to drift to the nasal side is called an esophoria.

Integrity of the nervous control of the muscles of the eye may be assessed by directing the patient to move the eyes in the six cardinal positions of gaze (Figure 29.1) while following an object. The object is moved laterally to either side along the horizontal axis and then along two oblique axes, each of which makes a 60-degree angle with the horizontal. Each of the cardinal positions of gaze represents the function of one of the six extraocular muscles attached to each eye. If diplopia, or double vision, develops during the transition to any one of the cardinal positions of gaze, the examiner has an indication that one or more of the extraocular muscles are failing to function properly.

When extraocular movements are checked, the eye is observed for nystagmus, an irregular jerking movement of the eyes as gaze is shifted to a lateral position. Nystagmus has two components: a quick component in one or the other direction, and a slower subsequent component that brings the eye back to the intended position. However, nystagmus on extreme lateral gaze is a normal finding and can be avoided by not placing the object too far laterally beyond binocular gaze. A number of conditions cause nystagmus. Although many of these conditions are benign, others may reflect severe pathological processes.

Assessment of Field of Vision

Although the visual field (Figure 29.3) may be assessed with a high degree of precision by an ophthalmologist, a rough estimate may be made in the office or at the patient's bedside when the examiner is concerned with

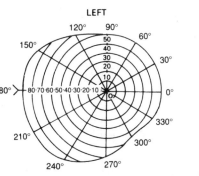
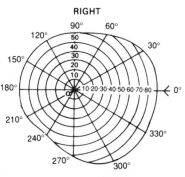

Figure 29.3 (A) Visual field charts showing peripheral vision of 180° with both eyes. (B) Photograph representing a street scene as viewed by a person with normal or 6/6 vision. (Photograph courtesy of The Lighthouse Inc., New York, New York.)

any general disturbance of the visual field. Such a circumstance may arise, for example, in assessing the patient who has suffered a stroke. Such patients commonly lose one fourth or one half of the visual fields of both eyes.

A simple and reliable method of testing the fullness of the visual field is direct confrontation. The examiner and patient sit directly facing each other at a distance of 60 cm. The patient is asked to cover one eye with a card while looking directly at the examiner's nose. The examiner in turn covers one eye as a method of comparison. If the patient has covered the left eye, for instance, the examiner covers the right eye (the examiner's own). The examiner then takes an object (pen, finger) in the right hand and moves it along a plane halfway between the examiner and the patient. The nasal, temporal upward and downward fields are assessed by bringing the object into view from various peripheral points. During each manoeuvre, the patient informs the examiner the moment the object can be seen. In order to test the nasal fields of gaze for the same eye, the examiner switches the object from the right hand to the left hand. The entire procedure is reversed for an assessment of the fields of the left eye. When confrontation testing reveals decreases in visual fields, or 'blind spots', the patient is referred immediately to an ophthalmologist for further evaluation.

Ophthalmoscopy

The internal eye is referred to as the fundus and comprises the retina, optic disc, macula and retinal vessels. It is visualized with the aid of an instrument called an ophthalmoscope. With practice and repetition, the nurse can become proficient in the use of the ophthalmoscope. The ophthalmoscope is an instrument that projects light through a prism and bends the light at 90 degrees, allowing the observer to view the retina through a lens in such a way that the line of vision is parallel to the bent ray of light. A number of lenses are available and are arranged on a wheel so that they may be chosen by rotating the

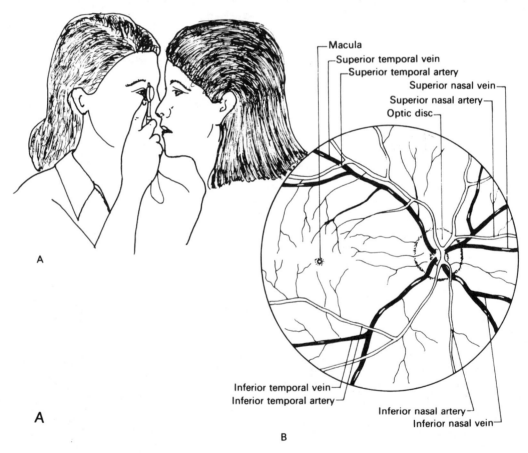

A

Figure 29.4 (A) Technique for the proper use of the ophthalmoscope. The right eye of the examiner looks into the patient's right eye. The index finger is used to adjust the lens for proper focus. (B) Display of the retina of the right eye as seen through the ophthalmoscope. The ophthalmoscope is capable of visualizing only a portion of the retina at any one time. It is best to identify the disc, ascertain the sharpness of disc margins and then follow each of the vessels that emerge from the disc at least three disc diameters along their course. The macular area should then be identified for any lesion that may be present.

wheel with the index finger without interrupting the inspection. The standard ophthalmoscope contains an array of gadgetry that includes grids, slits, filters and so on—none of which are particularly useful. The small, unfiltered aperture is appropriate and most useful for standard ophthalmoscopy.

In order to avoid a confrontation of noses, the right eye of the patient is examined with the right eye of the examiner, and the left eye of the patient with the left eye of the examiner (see Figure 29.4A). The room is darkened so that the pupil will be dilated. The patient is asked to hold the eyes still and focus on a real or imaginary distant object. The ophthalmoscope is gripped firmly in the hand, with the index finger resting on the lens wheel. The head of the ophthalmoscope is braced within the angle made by the brow and the nose. The lens chosen for initial inspection should be the one labelled zero unless the examiner is knowingly correcting his or her own defect in visual acuity. If the examiner wears glasses, it may be better to remove the glasses and become familiar with which lens is analogous to zero for the examiner with 6/6 vision; or, the examiner may prefer to keep the glasses on and use a zero lens setting. Provided that the patient has 6/6 vision, the zero lens should enable the examiner to obtain a precise focus on the retina. If the retina is out of focus, the lens wheel is rotated until it is brought into focus. The choice of a lens labelled with a red numeral implies that one is focusing farther away than normal; the choice of a lens labelled with a black numeral implies that one is focusing nearer to the examiner. The examiner will choose lenses among the red series for patients who are hypermetropic (farsighted) and lenses in the black series for patients who are myopic (nearsighted).

With the room in darkness, the patient appropriately gazing into the distance and the ophthalmoscope properly positioned within the cradle of the brow and nose, the examiner may now approach the patient. The examiner stands approximately 37.5 cm from the patient and about 15 degrees lateral to the patient's gaze. When the light is focused on the pupil, the retina will glow red through the dilated pupil opening. This is known as the red reflex. The examiner then approaches the patient until the examiner's forehead touches the left hand, which has been placed on the patient's forehead (Figure 29.4A). At this point, provided that the proper lens has been selected, the retina should be in focus, and the venules and arterioles that course through the retina are readily apparent (Figure 29.4B). In scanning the surface of the retina, it is important that the examiner holds the ophthalmoscope firmly and moves the head rather than the instrument.

The examiner should first focus on the optic disc. In the event that the disc is not in view when the retina is first visualized, the veins that are within the field of vision should be followed down their tributaries toward the disc from which the arterioles emerge and the venules enter. This is analogous to following the limbs of a tree until one

sees the trunk. The optic disc is examined for size, shape, colour and the sharpness of its margin. The disc is circular and yellowish pink. The margin is sharp and occasionally surrounded by a rim of dark pigment (choroidal crescent). One must become familiar with what is regarded as a normal-sized disc. In the centre of the disc there is frequently a small physiological cup into which the central vein of the retina recedes. To focus on the base of this cup accurately, one may have to choose another lens in the direction of the red sequence. A deep cup is seen in glaucoma. Oedema of the optic disc with concomitant blurring of the disc margin is seen with increases in cerebrospinal fluid pressure. The disc becomes pink, and accurate focus may require shifting to a lens in the direction of the black sequence. This is termed papilloedema. Optic atrophy is characterized by extreme pallor of the disc and reduction of its size.

The remainder of the retina is now examined. Abnormalities may be located precisely for other observers by using a standard nomenclature that makes reference to an imaginary clock face and by referring to the diameter of the disc to delineate distance. Thus, a haemorrhage may be noted to be one half of the disc diameter in size, located two disc diameters away from the disc margin at 2 o'clock. Another observer is then able to replicate this finding.

The examiner now follows each of the major vessels from the margin of the disc. The arterioles are lighter in colour and narrower than the venules. Under normal circumstances, arterioles are two thirds to four fifths the diameter of veins. The walls of the vessels are essentially transparent, and what is being observed is the blood column itself. The size and character of the arteriovenous crossings are noted, as well as any lesions in the retina. The retinal changes associated with diabetes are quite distinctive and are discussed in Chapter 17.

Lastly, the macular area of the retina is visualized by asking the patient to look directly at the light source. This causes the patient slight discomfort and tearing, and provides the examiner with only a brief second or two during which to inspect the small, circular, red area of the macula. The glistening reflection of its centre is called the fovea centralis retinae. Any oedema, haemorrhages or lesions are noted and brought to the attention of an ophthalmologist.

All of the techniques that have been discussed for the examination of the eye will not be performed on every patient. Routinely, one inspects the conjunctiva, the cornea and the pupil, and assesses extraocular motion. Ophthalmoscopic examination is a part of every reasonably complete physical examination. Although visual acuity is a part of the assessment, it need not be assessed more often than once every year or two, except in the elderly.

Letter Chart

The most widely accepted method of screening for visual problems is the Snellen letter chart. Although its accuracy is limited, it is the most widely used available test in the United Kingdom.

Echography

In echography (ultrasound, ultrasonography), high-frequency pulses of ultrasound are emitted from a small probe placed on the eye. After striking the ocular tissues, the sound energy is reflected to the probe, which, in turn, is displayed on an oscilloscope. Two primary types of ultrasound are used in ophthalmology:

A-scan—Oscilloscopic reflection is a vertical deflection from the baseline (one-dimensional).
B-scan—Oscilloscopic reflections are lines or dots (two-dimensional).

When used jointly, over 100 lesions or groups of lesions may be detected and differentiated in the orbital and periorbital region. Measurements for intraocular lenses can be done by ultrasound and analysed by computer. This is referred to as biometry and it enables the surgeon to determine lens power for an implant and postoperative refractive power.

This procedure is painless but requires the instillation of topical anaesthetic eyedrops. After the examination, the patient is cautioned not to rub the eyes, since corneal lesions may occur.

REFRACTIVE ERRORS

Vision is made possible by the passage of rays of light from an object through the cornea, the aqueous humour, the lens and the vitreous humour to the retina. In the normal eye, rays coming from an object at a distance of 6 metres or more are brought to a focus on the retina by the lens while perfectly at rest.

Types of Refractive Errors

Due to abnormalities in the eye structure or in the lens structure, defective vision may occur because objects are not focused correctly on the retina. If the rays of light are brought to a focus in front of the retina, the condition is referred to as myopia (nearsightedness); if the rays are focused behind the retina, the condition is called hypermetropia (farsightedness) (Figure 29.5). In such conditions, corrective lenses are prescribed. These, in association with the lenses of the eye, will correct the fault and restore a normal focus at the retina.

Rays from objects situated at shorter distances (less than 6 metres) require a 'stronger' lens to focus them on the retina. This is brought about by a contraction of the ciliary muscle that relaxes the lens capsule and causes the lens to become more convex. This function, as mentioned earlier, is called accommodation. By means of accommodation, objects at different distances from the eye may be seen distinctly. With increasing age, the elasticity of the lens decreases, so that accommodation for near vision is not complete, a condition called presbyopia. This explains why it is so common to see older people reading a paper while holding it at arm's length. 'Reading glasses' may be prescribed for these patients to enable them to focus rays from near objects to the retina.

In the case of presbyopia, two different types of lenses may be used (bifocals), one for far distance and one for near vision and reading. Trifocal lenses are also available; these add a third dimension that gives sharp focus in the 68- to 127-cm range. Lenses are prescribed for use in eyeglasses, or the lens may be applied directly to the surface of the eye (contact lens).

Astigmatism results from uneven curvature of the cornea—instead of curving equally in all directions the cornea is shaped somewhat like the bowl of a spoon. Two foci thus occur instead of one, and, as a consequence, the

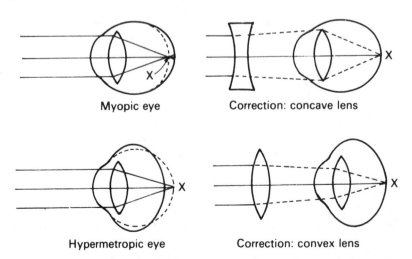

Myopic eye Correction: concave lens

Hypermetropic eye Correction: convex lens

Figure 29.5 Myopia and hypermetropia. (Brunner, L. S. and Suddarth, D. S. (1986) *The Lippincott Manual of Nursing Practice* (4th edition), J. B. Lippincott, Philadelphia.)

patient is unable to focus horizontal and vertical rays on the retina at the same time. These defects may be corrected with lenses called cylinder lenses. A patient may be myopic or hypermetropic and also have astigmatism. In such a situation a compound spherocylinder is prescribed by the optician.

Assessment of Refractive Errors

The strength and type of lens that will overcome refractive errors are determined by means of a retinoscope, which measures the refractive error. On the basis of this examin-

ation, an appropriate corrective lens is selected and then further refined by asking the patient to read letters on the Snellen chart through several different lenses.

CONTACT LENSES

More and more people are wearing contact lenses as a means of correcting refractive errors. Better techniques for measuring the eye and improved methods for supervising and advising those who wish to wear the lenses

Table 29.1 *Types of corrective lenses*

Durability	Advantages	Disadvantages
Eyeglasses (spectacles)		
Excellent	Excellent vision correction	Fogging in cool weather
New styles may suggest change	Easily cared for	Some cosmetic objections
		Unsuitable for certain activities: sports, some occupational drawbacks
		May need to be replaced more frequently than soft contact lenses
Hard contact lenses		
With care, may last for 15–20 years	Excellent vision correction	Uncomfortable for some
	Usually less costly than other types	Require period of adaptation
	Effective for people with astigmatism	Possibility of eventual intolerance
		May 'pop' out of position
Soft contact lenses		
May require more frequent replacement (usually replaced 1–3 years)	More comfortable than hard lenses	Require time daily for cleansing/ sterilizing
	Can be worn longer than hard lenses	Greater risk of eye irritation and infection
		Not as effective for astigmatism
		Possibility of eventual intolerance
Gas-permeable lenses		
Usually last longer than soft lenses but not as long as hard lenses	More comfortable than hard lenses	Eventual intolerance
	May claim more effective vision than with soft lenses	May be more costly
Extended-wear lenses		
Most fragile of all lenses	Provide corrected vision around the clock	Expensive
May have to be replaced every 6 months or more often	May be left in place for 2 weeks at a time	More frequent visits to ophthalmologist
		Risk of corneal injury
		May not correct vision as well
		Possibility of eventual intolerance

have increased the appeal of such lenses. They are particularly effective in certain occupations and are desirable for cosmetic reasons. However, not everyone can wear contact lenses; therefore, all potential candidates should be thoroughly screened by an ophthalmologist (see Table 29.1).

Medical conditions in which corneal lenses are recommended included absence of lens (aphakia), absence of iris (aniridia), congenital absence of pigment, myopia and hypermetropia, some types of astigmatism, cone-shaped deformity of the cornea (keratoconus) and turned-in eyelashes. Contraindications include allergic and inflammatory conditions (such as chronic blepharoconjunctivitis, corneal infection, iritis, uveitis), epiphora (abnormal overflow of tears), severe exophthalmus, pterygium or local neoplasm.

Contact lenses are usually not recommended for people who do not require full-time visual correction or lack sufficient manual dexterity to insert and remove lenses. Contact lenses are available in either hard or soft form. The hard lens was introduced in the early 1960s, the soft lens in the late 1960s.

When properly fitted, contact lenses 'float' on the fluid layer of the eyeball and are held loosely in place by the capillary attraction of the tears and the upper lid. The lens moves with the eye and is centred over the cornea.

Contact lenses have many advantages over framed lenses; they do not steam up when the wearer goes from the cold outside to a warm room; they are cleaned automatically with each blink of the eyelid; they can be worn safely during sports; they eliminate the need for less attractive lenses; they provide increased peripheral vision; and they do not break easily.

However, there are certain disadvantages and dangers in wearing contact lenses: contact lenses may be more expensive than framed lenses; solutions used to clean the lenses are costly; the adjustment period in learning to use them properly is longer; contact lenses can be lost easily, such as down the sink drain or in a swimming pool; and in the event of a chemical splash to the eye, the chemical agent may seep beneath the lens and cause extensive damage before the contact lens can be removed. Some types of contact lenses can result in injury to the cornea if the lenses are worn for an extended period of time.

Hard Lenses

Hard lenses are a form of plexiglass called polymethylmethacrylate (PMMA). They are nonporous, do not absorb water and cover only the central area of the cornea. Oxygen exchange to the cornea can develop and lead to discomfort if the lenses are worn too long (8 to 12 hours).

When fitting hard lenses, the ophthalmologist usually instils fluorescein into the eye in order to identify changes that occur in the formation of tear film as the lid blinks. However, fluorescein cannot be used with soft lenses because the dye stains the lenses permanently. To offset

microbial contamination, special procedures are used to disinfect soft lenses while they are stored during the night.

Soft Lenses

Soft contact lenses are made of polymer gel, although new formulations are being tested as soft lenses grow in popularity. They are porous, water-absorbent, hydrophilic, soft and flexible.

Soft lenses have certain advantages over hard lenses. They are comfortable from the start and can be worn up to 18 hours a day. They are effective for those who participate in sports, except for swimming. Since these lenses absorb pool chemicals and ocean salt, they should not be worn while swimming unless goggles and a mask are used. If they are worn only occasionally, rather than daily, the wearer will not lose his tolerance to them, as is the case with hard lenses. Finally, it is easier to switch from soft lenses to eyeglasses than from hard lenses to eyeglasses.

Soft lenses are inserted by placing the lens on the inferior conjunctiva while drawing the lower lid downwards. With the release of the lid, the wearer then rolls the eye around or massages the eye through the closed lid to position the lens on the cornea. To remove, the lens is grasped between the clean thumb and forefinger.

Gas-Permeable Lenses

Gas-permeable lenses are made of cellulose acetate butyrate (CAB). Cellulose acetate butyrate lenses are usually heat-tempered, which results in a harder, scratch-resistant surface and permits good optic use without affecting gas permeability. These lenses result in fewer problems from lens warpage and flattening.

Extended-Wear Lenses

Extended-wear lenses are highly permeable plastic lenses that are thinner and more pliable than ordinary soft or hard contact lenses, and can be worn continuously for weeks or months. They are more expensive than the usual soft contact lenses but are not completely trouble free. Extra fitting time is necessary, and the lenses may no longer be worn if certain conditions develop. Such conditions include microprotein accumulation on the anterior lens surface (soft lens spoilage) and corneal revascularization.

Spoilage or deterioration of soft contact lenses is due to extraneous deposits, physical and chemical changes in the lens material and microbial invasion. This includes soft lenses of acrylic origin, vinyl origin and silicone. Removal of encrusted deposits leaves surface irregularities and matrix defects; these lenses should be discarded. At present, no soft contact lenses are completely 'safe' for extended wear.

Flexible-Wear Lenses

Flexible-wear lenses are gaining in popularity over extended-wear lenses since fewer complications occur. These newer lenses need not be inserted and removed daily or cleaned on a daily basis. They are permeable enough to wear for extended periods. However, to avoid problems, it is advisable to remove the lenses at night and limit extended wear to special occasions.

For a comparison of the various types of corrective lenses, refer to Table 29.1.

Complications

The improper use of contact lenses (both hard and soft) can cause corneal abrasions, ulcerations and infection, which result from poorly fitted lenses, improper technique in applying or removing the lenses, poor technique in cleansing the lens and insufficient tear circulation under the lenses.

Patient Education

Although the advantages of contact lenses outweigh the disadvantages, precautions and safeguards must be understood by the nurse, the wearer and the employer. The contact lens must be regarded as a medical prosthesis, not a cosmetic device.

Care and precaution must be given to any medical prosthesis, and this certainly applies to contact lenses:

1. Wash hands thoroughly before touching the lenses, whether applying them or removing them.
2. Cleanse lenses only with the recommended sterile solution (noncaustic). (Some individuals are sensitive to thimerosal, a preservative in cleaning solutions that causes the eyes to sting when the lenses are inserted. Thus, it is recommended that lenses are soaked in distilled water.)
3. Keep the storage kit clean.
4. Do not wear lenses beyond the prescribed time.
5. Do not sleep with contact lenses in place; to do so may cause abrasion and erosion of the corneal epithelium. (Exception: extended wear lenses.)
6. Do not wet lenses with saliva before insertion; this can cause infection.
7. Restrict the wearing of contact lenses, in order to avoid potential corneal abrasions, if the following signs are present: photophobia, dryness, excessive burning, tearing.
8. Follow specialist's recommendations concerning eye makeup. Some ophthalmologists discourage patients from wearing eye makeup. Some advise applying mascara after lenses are in position.
9. Keep chemicals such as soaps, lotions and creams away from lenses, since they may adversely affect the lens; ask the wearer to keep eyes tightly closed when applying hair perfume and deodorant sprays. Stay away from areas where household sprays are used.
10. Have an ophthalmological examination every six months to ensure proper fit and to check corneal integrity.
11. With the expansion of available products, it is import-

ant to check with the ophthalmologist before changing types of lenses or disinfecting solutions.

Removal of Contact Lenses

Many types of contact lenses are designed to be worn only while the person is awake and fully conscious (exception: extended-wear lenses). They should be removed as a safety measure if the wearer is incapacitated due to accident, sickness or other cause. In emergency situations, the following directives should be followed:

1. Determine whether the patient is wearing contact lenses. Ask the patient directly if conscious or semiconscious. The patient may even be able to remove the lenses, perhaps with assistance, depending, of course, on the patient's condition. If the patient is unconscious, look for observable indications that contact lenses are being worn by gently separating the patient's eyelids. Shining a light (preferably a small penlight) on the eye from the side will help.
2. Remove the patient's contact lenses if patient cannot. With clean hands, position one thumb on the upper eyelid and one thumb on the lower eyelid, with thumbs near the margin of each eyelid. Separate the eyelids. A visible lens should slide easily with a gentle movement of the eyelids (Figure 29.6A–C). If the lens does not drop out easily, observe for possible lens position and follow instructions given in Figure 29.6D–F for removal of the lens. Remember that force should not be used. If the lens is seen but cannot be removed, gently slide it onto the sclera, where it can remain with relative safety until experienced help is available.

If the patient is wearing soft contact lenses, it is best to wait until someone experienced in removing these types of lenses is available to lend assistance. If flexible lenses are left in place for many hours, they will do little harm. However, if the emergency is such that they must be removed, then the steps described in Figure 29.6G–H should be followed.

EYE SAFETY: PRECAUTIONS, TREATMENT

Trauma to the Eye

The prevention of eye injuries is a phase of child and adult education that cannot be emphasized too strongly. Children need to be reminded frequently of the dangers of sticks, arrows, darts, 'sparklers', catapults, rubber bands and even harmless-looking toys. Precautions that should be taken when power tools are used need to be explained, along with the reasons protection is necessary from very bright lights, the sun shining on the snow, chemical fumes, sprays and flying chips of wood. The use of goggles gives protection against most foreign bodies, but

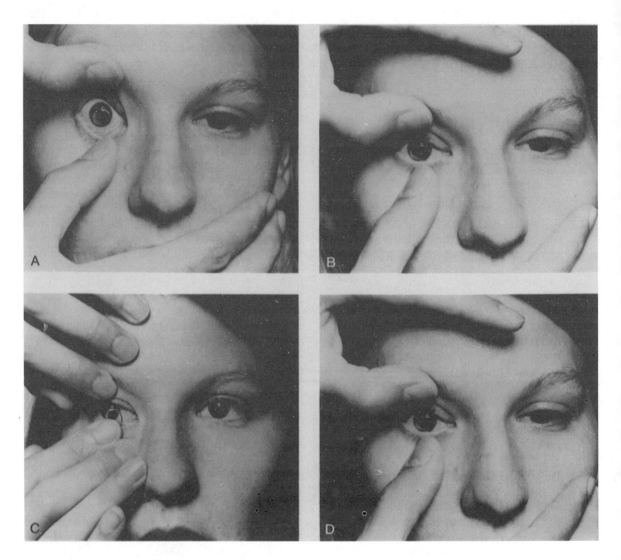

Figure 29.6 Removal of contact lenses.
Primary stages in hard lens removal: (A) After the eyelids have been separated and the hard contact lens has been correctly positioned over the cornea, widen the eyelid margins beyond the top and bottom edges of lens. (B) After the lower eyelid margin has been moved near the bottom lens edge and then the upper eyelid margin has been moved near the top lens edge, you are ready to move under the bottom edge of the lens by pressing slightly harder on the lower eyelid while moving it upward. (C) After the lens has tipped slightly, move the eyelids towards one another; this causes the lens to slide out between the eyelids.

Possible lens positions: (D) Directly over the cornea. This normal wearing position of a contact lens is also the correct position for removing it. If the lens cannot be removed, however, slide it onto the sclera. (E) On the sclera only. Here the lens can remain with relative safety until experienced help is available; other white areas of the eye to the side or above the cornea might also be used. If the lens is to be removed, however, slide it to a position directly over the cornea. (F) On both the cornea and the sclera. A lens in this position—or a similar one anywhere around the periphery of the cornea—should be moved as soon as possible. If the lens is to be removed, slide it to a position directly over the cornea; if the lens cannot be removed immediately, slide it onto the sclera.

Soft contact lens removal: (G) With clean hands, pull down the lower lid with the middle finger and place the index fingertip on the lower edge of the lens. Slide the lens down to the white part of the eye. (H) Compress the lens lightly between the thumb and index finger. Bring thumb and index finger together in a 'pinching' motion, causing the lens to double-up between fingers and allowing air underneath. Remove the lens from the eye. (Courtesy of The American Optometric Association.)

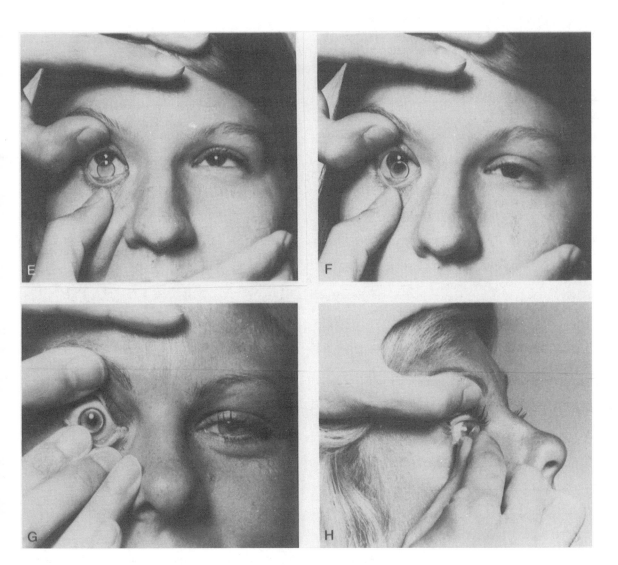

specially designed safety goggles or glasses with impact-resistant lenses are preferable if there is danger of flying metal or wood objects that may break the glass. Elderly people or those unsure of their footing need safeguards where there is a possibility of injury.

Any possible damage to the eye arising from trauma should be referred to an ophthalmologist immediately.

Foreign Bodies

Foreign bodies (e.g., dust, cinders) frequently cause considerable discomfort by irritating the sensitive conjunctiva. If the foreign body has been in the eye only a short time, it may be removed by a nurse. One way to detect foreign particles in the eye is to ask the patient to close the eyes, then darken the room and gently place a penlight on the lid. The foreign particle will show up as a black shadow. The lower lid is everted, the patient asked to look up and the lower half of the conjunctival sac examined. If the particle is not found, the upper eye is examined by everting the upper lid. The examiner stands in front of the patient and asks the patient to look down at the ground. The lashes are grasped between the thumb and fingers of one hand, and a matchstick, an applicator or the blunt end of a toothpick is placed across the upper part of the lid. The lashes are pulled downwards and forwards, away from the eye, as the applicator is pressed downwards, gently. The foreign body may be removed by touching it gently with a small applicator tipped with cotton and moistened in saline solution.

If this method is unsuccessful, or if the offending particle has been in the eye for a considerable time, no attempt should be made to remove it. It may have become embedded in the cornea, and there is considerable danger of serious injury if removal is attempted by unskilled hands. The ophthalmologist usually requires local anesthesia, a hand lens, fluorescein, an sterile needle, normal saline for irrigating the eye and, as a prophylaxis against infection, an antibiotic solution to instil after the offending particle is removed.

Acid and Alkali Burns

Careless use of hair sprays and other spray-on products has increased the incidence of chemical burns of the eye.

● Whenever acid or alkali gets on the lids or in the eye, an emergency exists, requiring that immediate action be taken. In such an instance, the lids, the conjunctiva and the cornea must be flushed copiously.

The easiest and quickest way to flush the eye is to hold the patient's head under a tap and allow the water to run over the eye and wash it out. However, it is more satisfactory to use a syringe, if available, taking care not to contaminate the other eye if it has not already been contaminated. Continuous flushing for at least 15 minutes is desirable. Plain tap water is adequate under such circumstances.

Actinic Trauma

Ultraviolet rays may damage the cornea as a result of excessive sunlight, snow blindness and the use of a welder's arc ('welder's flash') or a sun lamp. Treatment consists of instilling mydriatic drops and applying patches to both eyes.

Contusions and Haematoma ('Black Eye')

Trauma to the eye frequently results in haemorrhage. The bleeding that enters the loose tissues of the orbit spreads rapidly, discolouring the lids and surrounding skin. In itself, the injury is not too serious, but frequently it is frightening to patients because the discolouration and swelling is so prominent. The bleeding usually stops spontaneously, but it may be reduced and the swelling lessened by the application of cold compresses. Absorption of the blood may be hastened after the first 24 hours by the use of warm compresses applied 15 minutes at a time at intervals throughout the day.

Corneal Abrasions

Abrasions of the cornea can be detected after being stained with sodium fluorescein. A blue penlight more clearly identifies the abrasion than a white light.

Usually, a local anaesthetic and antibacterial drops are administered, and an eye pad is applied for 24 to 36 hours. Self-administration of a local anaesthetic is discouraged, since it may delay the diagnosis of complications and may even lead to further injury. The patient is asked to keep the eyes at rest to promote comfort and facilitate the healing process. The danger to be guarded against with an abra-

sion is the development of a corneal ulcer. Therefore, if there is no improvement after 24 hours, an ophthalmic consultation is desirable.

Lacerations

Lacerations of the eyelids are serious because the lids become scarred and are unable to close. Injuries to the lids are treated in the same way as any other wound, but an ophthalmologist is usually requested to care for them.

Lacerations of the eyeball are more serious because visual defects may result. Since more extensive injuries may endanger the entire eye, such injuries are invariably referred to the ophthalmologist for appropriate care. Injuries of this type may entail transplantation of conjunctival flaps to prevent leakage of ocular fluids, excision of the prolapsed iris and, in severe injuries, even removal of the eye.

NURSING CARE OF PATIENTS WITH EYE DISORDERS

Preventive Care

The eye is such an important organ that its care and protection are major considerations from the day of birth. The nurse, as an important member of the health team and as a teacher and a practitioner of sound health habits, can provide excellent health education in eye care and in the prevention of eye diseases.

Sound principles of safe care need to be stressed at an early age. Such problems as headache, dizziness, tiredness after close eye work ('the letters run together') and scratchy or itchy eyes should be checked by a health care practitioner. Also significant are inflamed or watery eyes; red-rimmed, encrusted or puffy lids; recurring styes; crossed eyes; and unequal pupils. Unusual behaviour should also be noted, such as holding a book too close, frowning, blinking, squinting, rubbing the eyes and failing in school or study work.

Faulty diet may account for the onset of many eye disorders. For instance, deficiencies of vitamins A and B may cause changes in the retina, the conjunctiva and the cornea.

The importance of eye care has been recognized by industries that require workers to wear protective devices in activities that pose a danger of injury from foreign objects. Safety glasses should be worn when the task at hand requires it. Eyes should be protected from bright sun, sun lamps, ultraviolet rays and hair spray. In the home, ammonia and alkali products present a particularly dangerous hazard for both children and adults, and should be stored in safe places out of reach and used with care.

Eyes need to rest after being used for close work for a period of time. Occasionally glancing out the window or around the room provides relaxation.

Table 29.2 *Medications used frequently in eye conditions*

Medication	Action
Local anaesthetics	
Amethocaine hydrochloride 0.5%, 1%	Rapid effect; anaesthesia produced in 1 minute
Cocaine hydrochloride 2% or 4%	Complete anaesthesia of conjunctiva and cornea produced in 5 minutes
Oxybuprocaine hydrochloride 0.2% to 0.4%	Anaesthesia produced in 5 minutes; lasts 1 hour
Anti-infective agents	
Acyclovir 1%	Anti-viral agent; effective against *Herpes simplex* keratitis
Chloramphenicol 0.5% and 1%	Most commonly used broad-spectrum antibiotic
Gentamicin 0.3%	Bactericidal against a wide range of gram-positive and gram-negative organisms, including *Pseudomonas aeruginosa*
Idoxuridine 0.1% and 0.5%	Anti-viral agent that heals dendritic ulcers in 3 to 5 days
Neomycin 0.5%	Common bactericidal agent used in conjunctivitis, blepharitis and other superficial infections
Penicillin 0.3%	Primarily used in conjunctivitis of the newborn
Dyes (for corneal staining to detect superficial abrasions)	
Fluorescein sodium 1% and 2%	*Note:* Because *Pseudomonas aeruginosa*, highly pathogenic for corneal tissues, grows well in fluorescein solutions, the sterile single-dose containers or fluorescent papers are recommended
Rose bengal 1%	Selective dye to stain devitalized conjunctivae and corneal cells; is very painful when instilled
Carbonic anhydrase inhibitor (carbonic anhydrase is an enzyme present in body tissues; in the ciliary body it is directly involved in the production of aqueous humour)	
Acetazolamide, 250 mg or 500 mg	Used to decrease production of aqueous humour by the ciliary body in the treatment of glaucoma
Dichlorphenamide, 50 mg	Used as an alternative to acetazolamide
	Note: Because of side-effects with both of these drugs (gastric upset, shortness of breath, acidosis, tingling of extremities, dermatitis, urethral stones), they are prescribed cautiously for selected patients
Sympathomimetic drugs (used primarily for mydriasis and occasionally as vasoconstrictors)	
Adrenaline 0.1%	Used as vasoconstrictor or in treatment of open-angle glaucoma
Phenylephrine hydrochloride 2.5% to 10%	Produces mydriasis within 20 minutes, lasting 3 hours
Parasympathomimetic drugs (used as miotics for controlling intraocular pressure in glaucoma)	
Group I: Act directly on myoneural junction	
Philocarpine nitrate 0.25% to 4%	Drug of choice in glaucoma; miosis within 30 minutes, lasting 4–8 hours

▶

Table 29.2 *Medications used frequently in eye conditions* (*continued*)

Group II: Cholinesterase inhibitors	
Physostigmine salicylate 0.25% to 1%	Produces miosis within 30 minutes; action persists for 6–8 hours
Ecothiopate iodide 0.3% to 0.25%	Potent miotic; action persists up to 12 hours
Group III: Sympatholytics	
Guanethidine monosulphate 1% to 5%	Often used in combination with adrenaline
Parasympatholytic drugs (used as mydriatics to facilitate ophthalmoscopic examination, and for mydriasis and cycloplegia in refraction and in treatment of uveitis)	
Mydriatics and cycloplegics	
Atropine sulphate 1%	Most powerful of this group; its action is not readily reversed by miotics; produces mydriasis in 30 minutes, lasting up to 14 days; contraindicated in narrow-angle glaucoma
Cyclopentolate hydrochloride 0.5% to 1%	Produces maximum mydriasis in 30 minutes and maximum cycloplegia in 45 minutes; action lasts less than 24 hours
Homatropine hydrobromide	Produces mydriasis within 30 minutes and maximum cycloplegia within 1 hour; action lasts 24 to 36 hours
Tropicamide 0.5% and 1%	Rapid acting; produces mydriasis and cycloplegia within 20 minutes; action lasts 6 hours
Adrenal corticosteroids (effective in treating inflammatory conditions of the eye; uveitis, apiscleritis, chemical burns; decreases vascularization and scarring following burns, trauma and severe inflammation)	
Hydrocortisone acetate 1%	Greater potency than cortisone, so it can be used in lower concentrations
Dexamethazone 0.1% Betamethazone sodium phosphate 0.1% Prednisolone acetate 0.5%	These three drugs are thought to be more potent than hydrocortisone; often used in combination with neomycin

Note: Corticosteroids are highly dangerous when used in the presence of Herpes simplex keratitis. The patient should definitely be under the care of an ophthalmologist when using these medications. All steroids are now known to produce glaucoma in certain predisposed patients. Use of steroids locally or systemically must be supervised carefully.

The importance of adequate and well-placed light in preventing eyestrain is essentially no longer a medical problem but one of general, industrial and social concern.

With many eye conditions, the medical management of patients has changed drastically in recent years and has resulted in less frequent need for hospitalization. For example, a patient with a cataract no longer needs to stay in the hospital for several days, and extended bedrest, which can result in sensory deprivation and a feeling of losing contact with the world, is no longer required. Cataract surgery and many other ophthalmic operations are performed in 'day surgery' units, thus allowing the patient to return home on the same day as the surgery. The result has been a reduced incidence of complications. On the other hand, such brief contact by the nurse with the patient, family or close friends allows only a short time for observation, assessment, goal determination, nursing care and patient evaluation. Therefore, any teaching sessions or demonstrations of self-care procedures must be done in such a way as to ensure that the patient and carers understand their responsibilities for self-care, and can recognize those signs and symptoms that may require professional consultation and intervention. Although outpatient surgery is common for some eye disorders, many eye problems do require more prolonged hospital care.

General Management

Eye Drops

Various drug solutions are inserted into the eyes in the treatment of nearly every kind of eye disorder (Table 29.2).

Before drops are instilled, it is important to check that the correct drug is being given. Some drugs (e.g., miotics and mydriatics) act in exactly opposite ways (Figure 29.7). Therefore, if one of these drugs is indicated in the treatment of a certain eye disease, the other is contraindi-

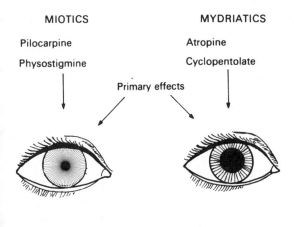

MIOTICS	MYDRIATICS
Pilocarpine	Atropine
Physostigmine	Cyclopentolate

Primary effects

Constriction of pupil (vasoconstriction)	Dilation of pupil (vasodilation)
Spasm of accommodation	Paralysis of accommodation
Decrease of intraocular pressure	Increase of intraocular pressure

Indications

To decrease intraocular pressure as in glaucoma	To facilitate examination of retina and optic disc and put ciliary body at rest, in inflammation. In uveitis, prevent synechiae

Figure 29.7 Effects and indications of miotics and mydriatics.

cated. It may seem needless to emphasize this warning, but experience has taught how easy it is to pick up the wrong bottle from a tray containing similar vials when the room is dimly lit.

In addition, the solution should be checked for colour changes or sedimentation, which indicate that the solution must be discarded. Patients especially are warned to avoid using medication of any kind if it has been in the medicine cabinet at home for months or years.

Instillation

Before the medication is instilled into the eyes (Figure 29.8A), the lids and the lashes are cleansed. Then the patient's head is tilted backwards and inclined slightly to the side, so that the solution will run away from the tear duct. This latter precaution is especially necessary when toxic solutions, such as atropine, are employed, because absorption of the excess drug by way of the nose and the pharynx may lead to toxic symptoms. In most patients, it is well to press the inner angle of the eye after instilling the drops to prevent the excess solution from entering the nose.

● The lower lid is depressed with the fingers of the left hand, the patient is told to look upward, and the solution is dropped on the everted lower lid.
● *Care must be taken that the nozzle does not touch any part of the eye or the lids, to guard against contamination of the bottle and injury to the eye.*
● After the drops (one or two at most) are placed in the eye, the lid is released and any excess fluid is sponged gently from the lids and the cheeks with sterile cotton wool.

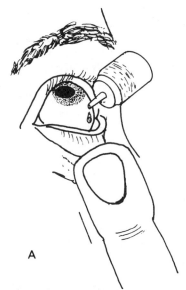

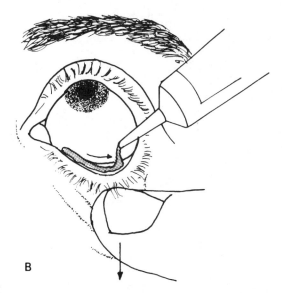

Figure 29.8 Instillation of eye drops. (A) When instilling eye drops, ask the patient to look upwards, then gently pull down the lower lid to form a receptacle for the dropped medication. (B) In applying ointment, ask the patient to look upwards, then depress the lower lid and gently squeeze ointment along the everted lid, beginning at the inner canthus (close to the nose) and then moving outward.

- After the medication is instilled, the patient is requested to close the eyes *gently* and keep them closed for three to five minutes. Patients often have a tendency to 'squeeze' their eyes closed, thereby expelling the medication. When the lids are kept closed as directed, the pumping action of the eyelids (to remove fluids from the eye) is stopped. This keeps the medication on the eye longer.
- If the solution has been contaminated, it must be replaced by a fresh bottle. Patients must have their own individual supply of drops and ointments.

Ointments

Ointments of various kinds are used frequently in the treatment of inflammatory diseases of the lids, the conjunctiva and the cornea. Those prescribed most commonly are sulphonamides, neomycin, chloramphenicol, steroids and various combinations.

Ointments are applied best by gently pulling down the lower lid and expressing a small amount of the ointment from the tube onto the conjunctiva of the lower lid. Care is taken not to touch the eye or the eyelid with the tube (Figure 29.8B).

Ocular Irrigations

Ocular irrigations are indicated following chemical splashes to the eye. Irrigation by water or normal saline is effective in removing most chemicals. The irrigating apparatus consists of a commercially prepared irrigating bottle containing sterile normal saline, an irrigating set and curved receiver for catching the fluid.

- The patient sits with the head tilted backwards and inclined slightly towards the side to be treated. A drop of 1 per cent amethocaine hydrochloride is instilled as a local anaesthetic. The receiver may be held by the patient so that it will catch the fluid as it runs from the eye. The patient's clothing is protected by a waterproof cape.
- The nurse stands in front of the patient and holds the lids open with the thumb and fingers of one hand. The solution is directed onto the eyeball away from the nose in order to avoid spillage of fluid into the other eye. The patient is requested to look in all directions of gaze in order to irrigate the whole anterior surface of the eye. The upper lid should be everted and irrigated so that no pooling of chemicals remains under the upper lid. Irrigation should be maintained for a minimum of 15 minutes in order to ensure complete removal of the chemical.
- When irrigation has been completed, the eye and the cheek are dried gently with cotton wool. The patient should then be seen by an ophthalmologist in order to determine whether any burns have affected the ocular structures.

Warm Wet Compresses

Heat relieves pain and increases the circulation, thereby promoting absorption and reducing tension in the eye. It is especially valuable for local inflammations of the eyelid, for example, styes and meibomian cysts. Heat is best applied in the form of compresses composed of two or three layers of gauze just large enough to cover the closed eye.

- A towel is used to cover the patient's clothing. The skin of the lids and the adjacent cheek are lightly coated with vaseline or yellow soft paraffin.
- The compresses then are moistened in a basin of water or any other prescribed solution that has been heated.
- The fluid, which should be kept at a temperature between 46°C to 49°C, is expressed or squeezed from the pad, and the compress, after being tested for temperature on the back of the hand, is placed gently over the closed lids.
- The pads are changed every 30 to 60 seconds for 10 to 15 minutes, and the application is repeated every two or three hours.
- At the completion of the period of application, the lids are dried gently with cotton wool.

► NURSING PROCESS
► OVERVIEW OF PATIENTS WITH EYE PROBLEMS

► Assessment

An initial nursing history is taken to determine the patient's primary problem, such as difficulty in reading, blurred vision, a burning sensation in the eyes, 'watering of the eyes', double vision, spots and isolated areas of lost vision (scotomas, itching, myopia or hypermetropia). The nurse should determine whether the problem is in one or both eyes and how long the patient has had this difficulty.

It is also important to ascertain the patient's general ocular condition or status. Does the patient wear glasses, contact lenses or use other vision assistive devices? When were they checked last? Is the patient under the regular care of an ophthalmologist? When was the last eye check-up? Was the patient's eye pressure checked? Does the patient have difficulty seeing (focusing) at close range or at a distance? Does the patient have problems reading or watching television? What about problems differentiating colours or problems with lateral or peripheral vision? Has the patient had any past eye trauma or eye infections? If so, when? What eye problems exist in the patient's family?

A pertinent past ocular history is essential. What past illnesses has the patient had?

Childhood: strabismus, amblyopia, injuries?
Adult: glaucoma, cataract, eye trauma, refractive errors—how corrected? Any previous eye surgery? Hypertension,

diabetes, thyroid disorders, sexually transmitted diseases, allergies, cardiovascular and collagen diseases? Family illnesses: Is there a history of eye disorders in parents or grandparents?

The patient's understanding of eye care and treatment is elicited in order to determine misconceptions or misinformation that can be corrected early.

▶ Patient's Problems

The patient's major problems may include the following:

- Alteration in comfort (pain) related to injury of or pressure in the eye.
- Fear and anxiety related to impaired vision and potential for further loss of sight.
- Alteration in visual sensory perception related to ocular trauma, inflammation, infection, tumour or degeneration.
- Lack of ability to care for self related to impaired vision and limited knowledge regarding eye care.
- Social isolation related to limited ability to participate in recreational and social activities secondary to impaired vision.

▶ Planning and Implementation
▶ Expected Outcomes

The patient's expected outcomes may include relief of pain, control of anxiety, prevention of further visual deterioration and acceptance of treatment, accomplishment of self-care activities including medication administration, and avoidance of social isolation and participation in diversional activities.

Nursing Care

Providing Eye Care

Regardless of the cause of a visual problem, measures can be initiated in an attempt to control as well as prevent further progression of deterioration. This can be accomplished by putting the eye at rest, restricting activities, wearing dark glasses or instilling a prescribed local anaesthetic. If the problem is related to an infection, an antibiotic or antimicrobial medication may be prescribed as eyedrops.

Relieving Pain and Anxiety

Pain may be due to trauma, such as a scratched cornea or increasing pressure within the eye. An eye pad will help to limit eye movement. However, it must be remembered that the uncovered eye should also rest because eyes move in synchrony.

Because light causes pain in many eye conditions, and because the eyes should be rested as much as possible before and after an operation to facilitate the healing process, it is best to maintain subdued lighting in the room. If those assisting the patient need light to carry out their activities, then dimmed artificial lights may be used.

Prescribed analgesics and antibiotics will help to control discomfort. Avoiding emotional disturbances and physical stresses promotes relaxation, which in turn helps to relieve pain.

Following a physical examination and investigations, a diagnosis is made; anxieties are frequently lessened when a specific treatment plan to correct the problem is finalized.

Dealing With Sensory Deprivation

When the eyes are bandaged, distortions in perception can occur, such as 'eye-patch delirium', inappropriate behaviour, loss of position sense and a sensation of floating. Often these problems are magnified and become frightening and upsetting. One way to assist the patient in overcoming these unsettling feelings is to reorient the patient constantly to reality and offer reassurance, explanations and understanding. Anyone entering the patient's room should speak and explain what is happening so as not to startle the patient. To minimize problems of sensory deprivation, it is usual to operate only on one eye at a time so that the other remains uncovered.

Preoperative Nursing Care

The preparation of the patient for an ophthalmic operation must be carried out with scrupulous care so that complications are minimized, comfort is achieved, and delay is minimized. The type of anaesthesia often determines how the patient is prepared. For example, if the patient is having a general anaesthetic, it will be necessary to ensure that a starving period of six hours before surgery is adhered to. However, if the patient is having a local anaesthetic, no starving period is necessary. Before the eyes are prepared for surgery, the patient's hair is covered with a cap and the forehead above the eye to be operated on is marked with an arrow in ink. If the eyelashes are to be cut, round-ended scissors are coated lightly with yellow soft paraffin so that the lashes adhere to the scissors and do not fall into the eye. An antibiotic is usually instilled as prescribed prior to surgery, while the patient is awake. The patient is encouraged to discuss any worries so that they may be addressed before surgery.

Postoperative Nursing Care

Following surgery, the operated eye is padded and covered with a protective eye shield, and unless specifically indicated otherwise, the patient is allowed to sit up in bed reclined against pillows. The patient's locker is placed on the unoperated side to facilitate easy reach of personal articles. The patient is provided with a call bell system and advised to ask for help if needed.

Following general anaesthesia, the patient is usually kept on bedrest until the next day. If a local anaesthetic is used, the patient may be able to get up within four hours of surgery or remain on bedrest until the next day, depending on the surgeon's wishes.

The ophthalmologist is notified immediately if the patient has excessive pain or if the dressings are disturbed.

● Morphine is never given to ophthalmic patients unless it is certain that vomiting will not injure the eye.

Diversional or recreational therapy is important but should be of such a nature that the eyes are not fatigued in any way. Even the patient's environment is an important consideration. Light is regulated so that it is not bright and does not produce a glare.

Enhancing Self-Care Activities

The patient is encouraged to carry out as much self-care as possible in order to promote a feeling of self-sufficiency. Nursing assistance is given as needed. Patients who cannot see are assisted with eating, but if they are accustomed to feeding themselves, they are encouraged to do so. Proper elimination is promoted by proper diet, stool softeners or enemas, as prescribed. Ophthalmic patients are not allowed to read, smoke or shave unless given permission to do so by the doctor. They must be cautioned against rubbing their eyes or wiping them with a soiled handkerchief. All patients receiving medications that dilate the pupils should wear dark glasses.

Medication bottles and instructions should be labelled in large letters and kept and used where there is plenty of light. Before patients use any medication they must wash their hands. When instilling eye drops, patients are supervised so that they develop a technique specific to their own needs. They may find it convenient to rest the base of the hand that is holding the medicine bottle against the forehead. With the other hand, they can lightly pull down the lower lid to form a V-trough to catch the eye drop.

Promoting Coping Mechanisms and Diversional Activities

The mental anxiety frequently experienced by the ophthalmic patient requires as much consideration as the physical condition. A person's dependence on sight is emphasized when one faces a temporary or possible permanent loss of this vital sense. Worry, fear and depression are common reactions in addition to tension, resentment, anger and rejection. By encouraging the patient to express any feelings, the nurse may discover the basic problems involved and can then take steps to alleviate them.

The patient should be encouraged to have visitors and to socialize. Depending on the patient's interests and preferences, suggestions can be made for diversional and interesting activities. When permissible, the radio and occupational therapy may be used to keep the patient's mind occupied. Although it is important not to be oversolicitous, showing interest, empathy and understanding

enhances the patient's sense of wellbeing. Because of differences of personality, the approaches in overcoming the anxiety of individual patients vary. When permanent blindness is apparent, re-education may be done by specially trained personnel or similarly afflicted people.

► *Evaluation*
► Expected Outcomes

1. Patient experiences less pain.
   a. Takes prescribed medication to counteract irritant, to rest the eyes, and to attack the cause of the infection.
   b. Applies prescribed warm compresses depending on the situation.
   c. Reduces eye activity by applying appropriate eye dressing and resting.
   d. Protects eye from additional injury by using a protective shield.
2. Shows evidence of calmness and absence of anxiety.
3. Accepts treatment regime and carries out recommendations.
   a. Washes hands before using eye drops and taking medications.
   b. Reports any untoward signs such as accumulation of granulations, watering of eyes and pain.
   c. Asks questions about progress and discusses any worries as they arise.
4. Practises self-care activities effectively.
   a. Demonstrates how treatments are managed; forms a V-trough in lower lid to receive eye drops.
   b. Cleans lenses effectively as taught.
   c. Lists safety measures to prevent falls such as being aware of loose carpeting and cluttered steps.
   d. Describes proper lighting for reading and hand crafts.
5. Participates in diversional and social activities.

CONDITIONS OF THE EYELIDS

Blepharitis

Blepharitis, or inflammation of the eyelids, is a common disorder that can be controlled through cleanliness and the prevention of excessive dryness. Since blepharitis is frequently associated with seborrhoea (excessive oiliness of the skin), attempts are made to keep the scalp clean. Daily cleaning of the eyelids by rubbing them gently with a clean, wet washcloth helps to remove scales. Usually, an antibiotic ointment is prescribed, such as chloramphenicol ointment, to be applied to the lid margin twice a day. Moist heat is helpful.

Stye (External Hordeolum)

A stye is an infection of the Zeis glands or Moll's glands

that empty at the free edge of the eyelid. When a stye develops, this area becomes swollen, red, tender and painful. Frequently, an eyelash will be found in the centre of the yellow point that appears. Warm compresses applied in the early stage hasten the pointing of the abscess. Removal of the central lash is often followed by drainage of pus, but incision is necessary if resolution does not begin within 48 hours. An antibiotic instilled into the conjunctival sac hastens control of the infection.

Chalazia

A chalazion is a cyst of the meibomian glands. It appears as a small, hard, painless lump in the lid and usually occurs secondary to infection of the gland, which results when the opening on the lid margin becomes plugged. Occasionally, such a cyst may become infected. When this occurs, warm compresses are used; incision and drainage may also be necessary. Incision and drainage (or excision of the cyst) are indicated if the mass distorts vision, causes astigmatism or becomes a cosmetic blemish.

Trachoma

Trachoma is a chronic, highly communicable disease of the conjunctival and corneal epithelium. It is one of the most common diseases of humans and affects about 15 per cent of the world's population. It is the greatest single cause for progressive loss of sight in the world. Trachoma is common in Asian countries and in countries around the Mediterranean Sea, particularly Egypt. It is rarely seen in the United Kingdom.

Management. Trachoma is spread by direct contact; therefore, personal cleanliness is a key factor in prevention. Isolating known cases and initiating antibiotic therapy early may help to control the disease. If untreated, it will last for months or years. Medical treatment consists of a three- to four-week course of tetracycline or erythromycin. The World Health Organisation is making great strides in eliminating this curable disease.

INFLAMMATIONS OF THE EYE

Conjunctivitis

Conjunctivitis, or inflammation of the conjunctiva, may result from bacterial, viral and rickettsial infections or from allergy, trauma or chemical injury.

No matter what the cause, the symptoms are similar: redness, pain, swelling and lacrimation. The amount and the nature of discharge depend on the offending organisms; for instance, the pneumococcus and the gonococcus cause an abundant purulent discharge.

Ointments such as sulphacetamide or gentamicin, or chloramphenicol drops or ointment may be instilled to clear the infection in one to three days. Untreated, the infection usually subsides in 7 to 10 days. Precautions must be taken to prevent dissemination of infection to the other eye, as well as to other people. Hands should be kept clean when treating the eye; individual clean washcloths and towels should be used.

Uveitis

Uveitis is a general term for inflammatory conditions of the uveal tract (iris, ciliary body, choroid). Anterior uveitis refers to iritis and cyclitis. Posterior uveitis refers to choroiditis and chorioretinitis; panuveitis involves the entire uveal tract. Uveitis (iritis) is usually unilateral and is characterized by pain, photophobia, blurring of vision, redness (circumcorneal flush) and a constricted pupil.

Some authorities prefer to classify the various forms of uveitis as granulomatous and nongranulomatous. In some aspects, the two forms are similar, but in others there occurs a significant difference (Table 29.3).

Complications and sequelae may result if uveitis is not treated. Adhesions may develop, impeding aqueous outflow at the anterior chamber angle and causing glaucoma. If adhesions hinder the flow of aqueous humour from the posterior to the anterior chamber, cataracts may develop. Even retinal detachment may occur as a result of traction exerted on the retina by vitreous strands.

Management. Treatment is directed to the specific type of involvement. For granulomatous uveitis, treatment is by systemic corticosteroids. Medications for comfort and relief of pain are also prescribed. Intraocular tension should be monitored regularly on all patients with uveitis.

Table 29.3 *Comparison between granulomatous and nongranulomatous uveitis*

Granulomatous	Nongranulomatous
Location Any portion of uveal tract, but predilection for posterior part	Anterior portion; iris, ciliary body
Onset Insidious	Acute
Pain None or minimal	Marked
Circumcorneal flash Slight	Present
Photophobia Slight	Marked
Course Chronic	Acute
Prognosis Fair to poor	Good
Recurrence Sometimes	Common

Nongranulomatous uveitis is treated with cyclopentolate to keep the pupil dilated. Local, and possibly systemic, steroids may be required. Initially, topical treatment may be required one- to two-hourly, with the frequency being reduced as the inflammation subsides.

Nongranulomatous uveitis subsides with treatment in a few weeks. Granulomatous uveitis may last months and even years in spite of treatment.

Sympathetic Ophthalmitis

Sympathetic ophthalmitis is a severe granulomatous bilateral uveitis that may occur from one week to several years after an eye injury. Fortunately, this is a rare condition, but it may be suspected when there is a history of a penetrating eye injury in one eye (exciting eye) and the patient complains of photophobia, blurring vision and infection in the other eye (sympathizing eye).

Medical management may take one of two forms: corticosteroids administered both locally and systemically, while cyclopentolate is given locally. This has been shown to be effective. The other, more radical procedure is preventive enucleation or removal of the severely injured eye before sympathetic ophthalmitis develops. This decision is a difficult one; often, a patient can think more clearly and reach a satisfactory decision if given the time and opportunity to express any thoughts and feelings about the operation. In such a case, it helps to understand the nature of the problem, the patient's ability and condition and the desired goals. Untreated, the disease progresses to bilateral blindness.

Pterygium

Pterygium is an abnormal triangular fold of membrane that extends onto the cornea from the white of the eye; it always occurs toward the nose. It is thought to be caused by chronic irritation, as from dust or wind. Surgical intervention prevents its growth and protects against loss of vision. In some eye clinics, surgery is followed by ß-radiation therapy, which helps to prevent recurrence of pterygium. Patients often erroneously refer to pterygium as a cataract.

CORNEAL DISORDERS

Corneal Ulcers

Inflammation of the cornea (keratitis) with loss of corneal

Table 29.4 *Assessment of acute eye conditions*

Acute conjunctivitis	Acute iritis (anterior uveitis)	Acute glaucoma (closed-angle)	Corneal ulcer or trauma
Incidence Very common	Common	Not common	Common
Vision Normal	Some blurring	Marked blurring	Blurred (usually)
Pain None	Moderate	Severe	May have pain
Intraocular pressure Normal	Normal or low	Elevated	Normal
Cornea Clear	Clear	Steamy	May have abrasion, foreign body or ulcer
Ocular discharge Moderate to copious	None	None	Watery and perhaps purulent
Pupillary response to light Normal	Weak	Weak	Normal
Pupil size Normal	Small	Dilated	Normal or small
Conjunctival vessels dilated Yes	Mostly circumcorneal	Yes	Yes
Prognosis Self-limited; 3 to 5 days	Good with treatment	Poor without proper treatment	Poor without proper treatment

tissue results in corneal ulcer. The inflammatory reaction often spreads deeper to the iris (iritis), resulting in the formation of pus, which collects as a white or yellow deposit behind the cornea (hypopyon). If the ulceration perforates, the iris may prolapse through the cornea or other serious complications may follow.

Because the cornea is so important to vision, any ulceration must be considered a most serious condition. The healing of all but the most superficial ulcers is attended with some degree of opacity of the cornea, and therefore with some diminution of vision.

The symptoms of corneal ulceration are pain, marked photophobia and increased lacrimation. The eye usually appears somewhat injected or 'bloodshot' (see Table 29.4).

Management

Prevention is much simpler and easier than cure. Prompt removal of foreign bodies and early treatment of scratches and infections may prevent the occurrence of a corneal ulcer.

Dark glasses are provided to relieve the photophobia. Mydriatics are given at frequent intervals. Fluorescein is generally used to outline the ulcers before the healing solutions are applied. Antibiotic solutions and chemotherapeutic agents are prescribed for the specific type of infection, since the micro-organism may be bacterial, viral or fungal.

*The United Kingdom Transplant Service was founded in Bristol in 1983. Eyes have been donated from people all over the country and distributed to qualified ophthalmologists throughout the United Kingdom.

Corneal Transplantation (Keratoplasty)

A keratoplasty in which the damaged cornea is replaced with a transplanted cornea may be done to repair a corneal opacity (scar), keratoconus or chemical burn of the eye. The circular segment of cornea removed from the patient must be matched exactly and replaced by a similar segment of cornea from a donor eye (Figure 29.9). For best results, the graft should be removed within 8 to 10 hours following the death of the donor (to prevent softening of the cornea) and transplanted within two days if a fresh cornea is used. Alternatively, it can be stored in organ culture medium at 34°C in an incubator for up to 30 days.*

The graft may be a penetrating graft (including all layers of the cornea) or a lamellar graft (involving only the outer layers of the cornea). The lamellar graft, popular in the past, is gradually being replaced by the penetrating graft.

Preoperative Nursing Care

Since keratoplasty is an elective operation, the patient should be aware of the nature of the operation and is no doubt optimistic about the likelihood of improved vision. The nurse, nevertheless, must allow time for the expression of concerns or questions that the patient may still have. Psychological and cultural concerns regarding the disability may have to be explored before the patient is in optimal condition for surgery. Physically, the patient should be free from respiratory or eye infections in order to promote postoperative healing.

Intraoperative Procedure

Usually, a transplant is done under general anaesthesia and takes one to two hours. The instrument used, a

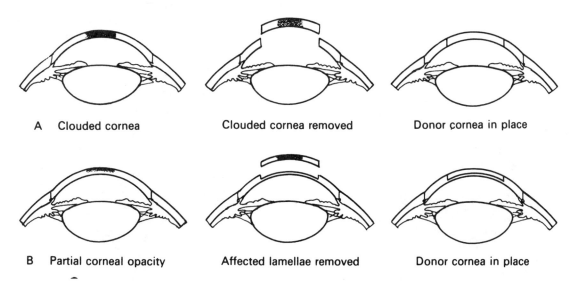

A Clouded cornea   Clouded cornea removed   Donor cornea in place

B Partial corneal opacity   Affected lamellae removed   Donor cornea in place

Figure 29.9 Corneal transplantation (keratoplasty). (A) Penetrating keratoplasty: a full-thickness (7- to 8-mm) disc is removed from the host and replaced with a matching full-thickness button from the donor. (B) Lamellar keratoplasty: a thin layer of corneal tissue is excised from the host eye. Stroma and entire endothelium are spared.

trephine, has an end that resembles a round pastry cutter in the size needed to remove the desired circular area of cornea. The donor material is prepared first with the trephine; the same instrument is used to remove the diseased cornea so that the graft is a perfect fit. Ultrafine sutures are placed evenly to create a tight seal; this is done with the use of an operating microscope.

Postoperative Nursing Care

The expected outcomes for postoperative patient care are: (1) to monitor for and avoid activities that will cause an elevation of intraocular pressure as well as pressure on the operated eye; (2) to rest the eye so that healing progresses smoothly; and (3) to institute measures that will prevent infection of the eye.

Elevated intraocular pressure constricts the vascular supply and can cause retinal atrophy or damage to the graft. To prevent pressure from increasing within the eye, the nurse must be aware of those activities that can elevate pressure (sneezing, coughing, straining during defaecation or lifting heavy objects). Loss of aqueous humour through the suture line by increased pressure could cause dislocation of the newly transplanted cornea, prolapse of the iris, adhesions of the iris to the cornea or malformation of the anterior chamber. To avoid these problems, when the patient is transferred from the operating table to the bed or stretcher, adequate staff are required to move the patient horizontally in one smooth lift, giving adequate support to the head. Intraocular pressure can be measured by sensitive electronic applanation tonometers. If the pressure is elevated, pharmacological control can be achieved with such drugs as acetazolamide, which inhibits the production of aqueous humour.

Healing is slow because the cornea is avascular, which also increases the possibility of infection. Thus, meticulous sterile technique is followed in dressing changes to protect the susceptible corneal epithelium from infection. Another means of reducing the chance for infection is to provide the patient with soft contact lenses which protect the suture line. This is particularly effective in patients who have chemical burns. To prevent herpes simplex infection, the administration of antiviral agents may be indicated.

RETINAL DISORDERS

Detached Retina

A retinal detachment occurs when the sensory retina separates from the pigment epithelium of the retina. The retina is that layer of the eye that perceives light and transmits impulses from its nerve cells to the optic nerve. When a tear or rip occurs in the retina, vitreous humour and transudate seep out between the rods and cones of the retina and the pigment epithelium. Tears or holes in the retina may occur suddenly or slowly, as a result of trauma or degeneration. They may also result from haemorrhage, exudation or tumour in front of or behind the retina. Studies have shown that approximately 8 per cent of the population have degenerations that can cause retinal holes or tearing to occur.

The most frequent type of retinal detachment is rhegmatogenous (induced by a rip or tear), which occurs in 1 in 10,000 of the population each year. Tractional retinal detachment may occur in patients with diabetes or other vasculopathies that cause an abnormal bonding of vitreous membrane to the internal surface of the retina. Exudative retinal detachment arises from choroidal tumours.

Clinical Features and Diagnosis

The usual symptoms include flashes of light and blurred or 'sooty' vision that is sudden in onset; the patient may

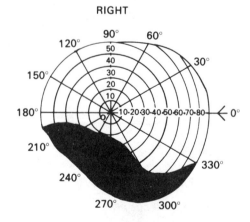

Figure 29.10 Retinal detachment, shown here in the active stage. There are many causes for detachment, but the hole or tear allows fluid to lift the retina from its normal position. This elevated retina causes a field or vision defect, seen as a dark shadow in the peripheral field. It may be above, or below as illustrated. (Photograph courtesy of The Lighthouse Inc., New York, New York.)

have the sensation of particles moving in his line of vision. These floating particles consist of retinal cells and blood that are released at the time of the tear and cast shadows on the retina as they drift by. Definite areas of vision may be blank (Figure 29.10), and in a few days the patient may have the sensation of a veil coming up or down in front of the eye, finally resulting in loss of vision. To diagnose the condition, the pupils are fully dilated and the eye is examined by slit lamp and ophthalmoscope. A determination of visual fields and ultrasonography may also be required.

Conservative Management

The suddenness of the incapacity creates confusion and apprehension in most patients, as well as a fear of blindness. Usually, it means that patients must abandon their business or activity, with little or no time to make plans. The patient is treated with rest immediately. The eye is padded and specific positioning, whether sitting or lying flat or on one side, will be requested by the ophthalmologist in the hope that the retina will fall back into place as much as possible before surgery, and thus facilitate the retina's adhering to the choroid.

Surgical Intervention

The objective in surgical treatment is to create a scar that seals the retina to the choroid as it heals. Such treatment may be accomplished in one of several ways: photocoagulation, cryosurgery or scleral buckling.

Photocoagulation makes use of a strong beam of light (from a carbon-arc source) that is directed through the dilated pupil to form a small burn, causing a choroid retinal inflammatory exudate. The LASER beam (light amplification by stimulated emission of radiation) can be used in photocoagulation. This method of treatment is used for limited retinal detachments and also may be used after operation to reattach small areas.

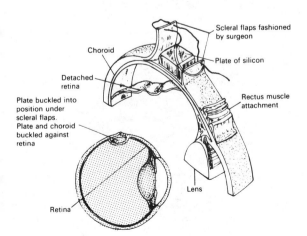

Figure 29.11 Scleral buckling for detached retina. (Ephicon, Inc.)

In cryosurgery, a supercooled probe is applied to the sclera, causing minimal damage; the choroid, pigment epithelium and retina adhere as a result of the scarring. The advantage of this method over diathermy is the reduced damage to the sclera.

A silicone explant (scleral plomb) may be sutured onto the sclera over the location of the tear or hole, which provides local indentation. This moves the choroid closer to the detached retina and may be done in conjunction with scleral buckling.

In scleral buckling, the idea is to shorten the sclera to enhance contact between the choroid and retina (Figure 29.11). After the subretinal fluid is withdrawn, the detachment is treated by one of the methods described above. The treated area is then indented to 'buckle' inward toward the vitreous humour.

Postoperative Nursing Care

The operated eye is padded and the patient may be kept in bed as directed, depending on the surgical procedure undertaken. During and following cryotherapy, the patient may experience periocular ache similar to the effect one gets sometimes from eating ice cream; usually this discomfort is controlled with an analgesic.

Precautions are taken to prevent the patient from bumping the head, which could dislodge the retina from the desired position. After a gradual resumption of function, the patient may resume usual activities in three to five weeks.

The psychological nursing care of this patient is of major importance. Diversion that is relaxing is desirable, such as conversation, listening to music, having someone read a favourite book and so forth.* These patients become depressed easily; therefore, every attempt should be made to prevent this reaction.

At the time of discharge, the nurse should be sure that the patient understands all advice for post-hospital care and follow-up visits.

Prognosis

If retinal detachment is not treated, further detachment and eventual blindness will occur. About 90 per cent of patients can be cured with treatment. Twenty per cent of all detachments are or will become bilateral.

Senile Macular Degeneration

Senile macular degeneration is a degeneration of the retina that increases in incidence with age. Normally the retina is closely adherent to the pigment epithelium, which is next to Bruch's membrane. Underneath Bruch's membrane are the minute capillaries. The complicated

---

*Recordings of books may be obtained from public libraries or the Royal National Institute for the Blind.

process of degeneration may reveal a defect in Bruch's membrane that permits fluid and a capillary to push through the defect and the pigment epithelium, resulting in a subretinal haemorrhage. Usually the haemorrhage and subsequent scar occur at the most vulnerable part of the retina, the macula. (The macula is an oval area of the retina that is devoid of blood vessels and appears darker than the surrounding retina on the posterior eye.)

Gradual progression of the deterioration occurs over months or years until the macula is destroyed. Central vision is affected so that reading becomes impossible. Peripheral vision permits a measure of orientation and allows ambulation in familiar areas.

Management

Light rays from an argon LASER are focused on the tiny involved area of the retina (away from the macula) to seal abnormal blood vessels, thereby preventing further fluid leakage (photocoagulation). The success rate is remarkable in patients who are treated early. Success depends on the location of the neovascular membranes. Argon LASER photocoagulation on vessels closer than 200µm to the centre of the fovea (the centre of the macula) is not successful. Clinical trials using other kinds of LASERS are being studied.

The nurse should recognize that this condition causes the patient to be anxious and depressed. Most often the patient is seen after considerable deterioration has taken place. Such patients need to be reassured that although their central vision is affected, they can still manage activities of daily living in an independent manner. When patients are unable to read or watch television, they can continue to be 'in contact' with the radio and friends.

CATARACTS

A cataract is an opaque (nontransparent) area of the crystalline lens or its capsule. Occasionally, it occurs at birth (congenital cataract) or in younger people as a result of trauma or disease, but most commonly it occurs in adults past middle age (senile cataract).

Altered Physiology

The normal lens is a clear, transparent, button-like structure lying behind the iris; it possesses strong refractive powers. The lens consists of three anatomical components. In the central zone is the nucleus, peripherally is the cortex and surrounding both is a capsule. With ageing, the nucleus takes on a yellowish brown hue. Surrounding opacities are spokelike, white densities occurring anteriorly and posteriorly to the nucleus. Opacity of the posterior capsule is the most significant form of cataract—it looks like frost on a window.

Physical and chemical changes may produce a loss of transparency of the lens. Changes in the multiple fine fibres (zonules) that extend from the ciliary body to the outer circumference of the lens, for example, may cause a distortion of the image. A chemical change in lens protein may cause coagulation, thereby producing cloudy vision by blocking the passage of light to the retina. Cataracts may be caused by ageing, trauma, radiation or as a result of certain diseases. One theory postulates that a breakdown in normal lens protein occurs with an influx of water into the lens. This process disrupts the tight lens fibres and interferes with the transmission of light. Another suggestion is that an enzyme plays a part in protecting the lens from degeneration. It decreases with ageing and is absent in many patients with cataracts.

Clinical Features

Because the rays of light entering the eye must pass through the pupil and the lens to reach the retina, any opacity in the lens behind the pupil will produce alterations in vision. Objects may seem distorted, blurred or hazy. The patient may describe it as a 'film' over the eye

Figure 29.12 Effects of cataract (left) and glaucoma (right) on vision. Photographs representing the eye diseases are done as if the camera were the right eye. (Photographs courtesy of The Lighthouse Inc., New York, New York.)

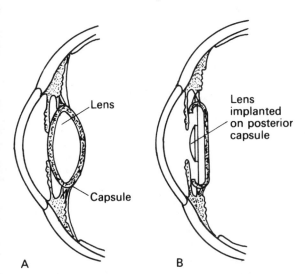

Figure 29.13 The most commonly used technique for cataract removal is the extracapsular method (B), with normal eye anatomy shown in (A). During extracapsular extraction, the contents of the lens are removed, but the posterior capsule is left intact, leaving a good site for attachment of an intraocular lens. (Reproduced with permission from *Patient Care*, 15 August, 1986. Copyright © 1986, Patient Care Communications, Inc., Darien, Connecticut. Artist: Paul J. Singh-Roy. All rights reserved.)

or 'looking through a fog' (Figure 29.12). In bright light, a cataract tends to scatter the light, causing an unpleasant glare. The patient experiences no pain, and visual loss is usually gradual.

In time, the degenerative processes cause more opacification of the lens until the opacity becomes complete. Ordinarily, the lens is not visible; however, when a cataract develops, it can be seen through the pupil as grey and, later, milky white. A cataract usually develops in one eye first. Later, one begins to develop in the other eye.

Medical Management

The affected lens may be removed by various surgical techniques. The most commonly used technique at present is extracapsular extraction (Figure 29.13).

Extracapsular Extraction

Extracapsular extraction is the removal of the nucleus, cortex and only the anterior capsule. The posterior capsule is left intact. Often extracapsular extraction is done by phacoemulsification. This is the removal of the lens by a mechanized instrument that is composed of three systems: irrigation, ultrasonic vibration and aspiration. As the titanium tip of the instrument vibrates 30,000 times per second, the lens is broken up into minute particles, which are then aspirated. The procedure can be done

under general or local anaesthesia with the use of a microscope.

When the lens is removed, the eye is referred to as aphakic (lacking the lens) and has no accommodative power. Refractive ability is almost totally gone. Aphakia is corrected by thick eyeglasses, contact lenses or an implanted intraocular lens. The thick eyeglasses have disadvantages, including an adjustment period that can be frustrating. Contact lenses are more effective, but they require manual dexterity to insert and remove. This kind of skill may be a problem for an older person. Far more popular and successful is the intraocular lens implant, which is incorporated at the time of lens extraction.

An intraocular lens implant, of which there are over 400 styles, is a prosthetic lens usually made of polymethylmethacrylate (PMMA) that is slipped into the vacated lens pocket and attached to surrounding tissues in an anatomically correct position. The chief advantage of this procedure is the minimal distortion in the size or shape of the image. The operation can be done under local anaesthesia and can be completed in less than an hour.

More recent intraocular lens implants have built-in protection against ultraviolet light damage (a controversial complication) and contain a coating to reduce risk of damage to the cornea. Some of the newer types of intraocular lens implants can be folded or compressed before insertion to reduce the size of the incision through which it is slipped into place. A type of rubber may be used in the future, since it more closely resembles a natural lens. Enzymes are also being studied as a means of emptying the capsular area, followed by the injection of a substance that could function as a lens when it gels or semi-hardens.

In summary, the most successful type of surgery currently for a senile cataract is an implant following extracapsular cataract extraction with an intact posterior capsule. This membranous capsule supported the patient's own lens, and it now supports the artificial lens implant.

► NURSING PROCESS
► THE PATIENT UNDERGOING SURGERY FOR CATARACT REMOVAL

► *Assessment*

The nursing history of the patient with a cataract will focus on how the cataract has affected lifestyle. Questions to be asked include the following: Describe how your vision has become impaired. How long have you noticed this change? What activities has your altered visual acuity affected (such as shopping, watching television, driving a car or close work such as hand crafts)? What has the doctor told you about treatment? Do you understand the nature of the proposed surgery?

The nurse should elicit misconceptions and the psychological/sociological impact.

► *Patient's Problems*

The problems for a patient undergoing surgery for cataract removal may include the following:

- Fear/depression related to sensory impairment and lack of understanding of the procedure.
- Potential for trauma (preoperative) related to increasing vulnerability to injury/attack.
- Potential for postoperative complications related to recent surgical intervention.
- Visual sensory perception alteration related to adjustment to new lens.

► *Planning and Implementation*
► Expected Outcomes

The patient's major expected outcomes may include reduction of emotional stress, fear and depression; prevention of ocular injury; avoidance of complications; and adjustment to altered visual status.

Preoperative Nursing Care

Reducing Preoperative Anxiety

Because this particular surgery can be performed safely on elderly people, even those in their 90s, the nurse is in a position to dispel the belief that the patient may be 'too old' for the procedure. Likewise, it is no longer necessary to lie immobile for days following surgery; one does not have to wait for treatment until the cataract is mature; thick eyeglasses are not the only means of assisting vision after cataract surgery. Patients may need to be in hospital only for two or three days following surgery, and some centres are now developing facilities for day-care surgery. Patients can be encouraged that significant progress has been made that permits improved vision with minimal discomfort.

The nurse should be sure that the patient understands the nature of surgery before signing the consent form. The patient should know that it will be several weeks before the best visual result is realized. Usually the lens selected is designed to leave the patient slightly myopic since this facilitates reading vision. For distance vision, a pair of glasses may be required.

The patient is informed that a local anaesthetic will be given in the operating room and that the injection may be uncomfortable at first but that this discomfort will abate quickly.

Further advice includes such details as what to expect in the operating room: quiet conversation among the members of the surgical team, sounds of equipment being used and frequent blood pressure checks. The surgeon may converse with the patient during the procedure. The patient needs to understand the importance of lying still during the procedure. After the operation, the patient should not bend forwards for extended periods of time. Lifting and strenuous activities are to be avoided. Any pain, eye discharge, increased redness or swelling around the eye must be reported by the patient.

Preventing Injury

Because of increasing impaired vision, the person with a cataract has a tendency to limit activities and reduce any venturing out in the community. When such patients do

Table 29.5 *Patient education for self-care following cataract surgery*

Activity limitations
Permissible

- Watch television; read if necessary – use moderation
- Do everything in moderation
- At first 'sponge baths'; later use bath or shower (with assistance)
- Wash hair in about 2 weeks; do not bend over sink or bath; tilt head backwards slightly
- Sleep with protective eyeshield (3 weeks); lie on back or side, not stomach
- Sedentary activities – 2 weeks
- Wear sunglasses if soothing

Avoid

- Rubbing the eyes; squeezing eyelids
- Straining at bowel movement
- Getting soap near eyes
- Lifting anything over 7–9 kg
- Sexual relations until . . . (date)
- Driving, if possible
- Bending head down below waist; bend knees only, and keep back straight to pick up something from the floor

Medications and eye care

- Wash hands before and after instilling eye medications
- Clean around eye with sterile cotton wool balls or gauze sponges moistened with sterile water; wipe lid gently from inner corner to outer corner
- To instil eye drops, be seated and tilt head back; gently pull down lower lid margin
- At follow-up visit, take all eye medications so that dosages can be checked and adjusted

Report unusual signs and symptoms

- Eye pain in and around eyes
- Changes in visual acuity, blurring diplopia, a film over visual field, light flashes, showers of spots before eyes
- Persistent headaches
- Inflammation, discharge from eyes

Note: To be reviewed with patient or caregiver. Directions should be printed in large letters using felt-tipped pen for strong contrast.

eventually go out, hesitating steps make them more vulnerable to being pushed, shoved or even attacked. To prevent bodily injury and additional ocular injury, it is important for patients and their families to seek medical attention.

When the patient is to have surgery and be hospitalized, the patient is oriented to the bed and ward so that they will be familiar to the patient after surgery. In this way, the patient will avoid bumping into furniture or doors before and after surgery when the eye is padded.

Preoperative teaching stresses those activities and restrictions that patients will experience after the operation, as well as the position they will be expected to maintain if they are kept in bed. Patients should know that their eye will be patched, and that they probably will require assistance when eating or going to the bathroom.

Eyelashes may be cut using scissors with blades coated with yellow soft paraffin to which the lashes will adhere and not enter the patient's eye.

Preoperative Preparation

Depending on the type of anaesthesia and on the time of day that the operation is to be performed, the patient will be either starved for six hours preoperatively or may be given a light breakfast. Preoperative sedation may be given one to two hours before surgery. Eye medications may include antibiotics, a topical mydriatic (which facilitates removal of the cataract when the pupil is dilated) and a cycloplegic (to paralyse the muscles of accommodation).

Postoperative Nursing Care

Avoiding Complications

The expected outcomes of postoperative care of the cataract patient (excluding phacoemulsification) are to prevent haemorrhage and stress on the sutures. The eye is kept padded for one day, and an eye shield is worn over the dressing to protect the eye from injury. Only the operated eye is covered.

Pain is usually slight after cataract extraction, but should it become severe, the surgeon should be notified since severe pain may be a symptom of a serious complication, such as haemorrhage.

A soft or regular diet is resumed when desired. The effects of sensory deprivation can be minimized if the patient is kept interested in diversional activities, such as listening to the radio, 'talking books' or visitors. Any signs of decreased vision may be due to haemorrhage, infection, corneal oedema or corneal scarring and must be reported.

Complications following an intraocular lens implant may occur at any time, even years later. Any visual changes must be reported, including loss of corneal clarity, bleeding, retinal detachment and signs of glaucoma.

Patient Education

Teaching points emphasized by the nurse are summarized in Table 29.5.

► *Evaluation*
► Expected Outcomes

1. Patient copes with psychosocial adjustment required to treat a cataract.

   Preoperatively:

   a. Accepts the progressive nature of cataract development and the need to have the treatment.
   b. Discusses the condition and the need for surgery.
   c. Asks direct questions relating to mobility during the postoperative phase.

   Postoperatively:

   a. Describes activities that can or cannot be done immediately following surgery.
   b. Participates in stress-relieving experiences.
   c. Relates a positive attitude that reveals optimistic thinking.

2. Prevents ocular injury
   a. Limits eye activity before and immediately after surgery.
   b. Adheres to proper head positioning until requested to elevate and move head.
   c. Avoids bending at the waist for prescribed number of days/weeks.
   d. Takes precautions to avoid colds (sneezing, coughing) and lifting in order keep ocular pressure from rising.

3. Takes precautions to avoid complications.
   a. Recites the precautions to be taken to ensure optimum vision.
   b. Keeps fingers and tissue wipes away from eye (it is expected eye will tear, blur or itch because of reaction to sutures).
   c. Asks for sunglasses when eye patch is removed (because of sensitivity to light).
   d. Washes hands before and after treating eye.
   e. Instils eye drops as prescribed and as taught.
   f. Demonstrates effective technique in keeping periorbital area clean, including eyelashes.

4. Adjusts to altered visual status.
   a. Adapts to the changes required, such as using eyeglasses or contact lenses.
   b. Indicates the range of vision possibilities with 'new lenses'.
   c. Describes the widened scope of activities that can now be pursued.
   d. Relates an understanding of the need for follow-up visits to the doctor and ophthalmologist.

Care of the patient with a cataract is outlined in Nursing Care Plan 29.1 on page 940.

► **NURSING CARE PLAN 29.1: THE PATIENT WITH CATARACT**

Nursing care plan for Natalie Goldberg, a 71-year old, non-practising Liberal Jewish patient. She is single, has no children and is a former dressmaker.

Patient's problems	Expected outcomes	Nursing care	Rationale
1. Anxiety due to sensory impairment and fear of the unknown	Patient will be aware of aspects of treatment and care and will report anxiety levels acceptable to her before surgery	1a. Determine patient's concerns and provide information to allay fears b. Orientate patient to her new surroundings c. Provide information on surgery and care d. Outline expected visual prognosis and restrictions required during the postoperative period e. During conversations, observe for reduction in anxiety levels	When the patient finds answers to her fears, she is more likely to accept treatment willingly Familiarity with surroundings will facilitate independence and help allay fears Knowledge of condition, treatment and visual prognosis will help in relaxing the patient and allowing her to feel in control of the situation. It will also facilitate postoperative recovery Determine whether nursing care has been effective
2. Risk of injury to self when mobilizing due to visual impairement	To be as independent as is safely possible during her stay in hospital	2a. Determine patient's normal mobility levels b. Ensure obstacles are not in the patient's way when she is mobilizing, and inform her of any changes in floor levels or of wet surfaces c. Observe the patient when mobilizing and offer assistance if necessary	Provides baseline for determining nursing care needed Allows independence during hospital stay Help keep the patient free from injury and provide reassurance that help is available if it is required
3. Risk of postoperative complications due to forthcoming surgical intervention	Avoidance of postoperative complications	3a. Ensure preoperative investigations such as chest X-ray, electrocardiograph, blood investigations, urinalysis and blood pressure measurements are carried out and results recorded b. Take conjunctival swabs for culture and sensitivity c. Cut eyelashes on the eye for surgery explaining to the patient that they will regrow fully in six weeks d. Instil prescribed antibiotic treatment and advise patient to avoid touching the eye with her fingers e. Advise the patient of postoperative restrictions: no bending or lifting; not to strain on defaecation; avoid coughing and sneezing; and ensure she understands the reasons for this	Ensure any underlying medical conditions such as diabetes, hypertension, heart or chest disease are ruled out or treated before surgery Identifies and allows for treatment of pathogenic micro-organisms within the eyes before surgery Reduces risk of infection, makes a clearer operating field and enables easier cleaning of the lids postoperatively, thus minimizing any discomfort to the patient Minimizes opportunities for infection and enhances healing process Prevents tension on the suture line, thus reducing the risk of postoperative complications such as haemorrhage and leaking wound
4. Risk of supplying inappropriate diet and religious support	Dietary and religious needs met to patient's satisfaction	4a. Determine patient's dietary needs and note foods to be avoided, e.g. pork b. Determine whether patient wishes to be visited by Rabbi, and arrange this if required	Provides patient with suitable diet and thus maintains nutritional state Meets patient's religious and cultural needs

► NURSING CARE PLAN 29.1: THE PATIENT WITH CATARACT

Patient's problems	Expected outcomes	Nursing care	Rationale
5. Risk of patient inhaling aspirate during surgery and being physically unprepared for surgery	Safely and efficiently prepared for surgery before transfer to theatre	5a. Ensure the patient remains nil orally for six hours preoperatively	Lessens likelihood of patient inhaling aspirate
		b. Prepare in gown and cap before giving premedication	Keeps patient's hair away from operating site
		c. Check consent form is signed	Legal requirement
		d. Administer premedication at prescribed time	Helps calm the patient before surgery
		e. Remove dentures, jewellery and any prosthesis before transferring to theatre	Prevents hazards to the patient during surgery
		f. Answer any queries the patient may have	Helps alleviate fears and worries, and calms the patient
		g. Provide toilet facilities before transfer to theatre	Ensures patient comfort
		h. Check correct eye is marked for surgery and ensure all relevant documents are transferred to theatre with the patient	Safeguards against wrong operation and provides for continuity of care
6. Risk of blocked airway due to loss of cough reflex	Patent airway and safe recovery from anaesthesia	6a. Nurse in semi-prone position on operated side	Permits jaw and tongue to fall forward thus facilitating drainage of secretions. Prevents damage through pressure on operated eye
		b. Monitor half-hourly pulse and blood pressure measurements until stable, then reduce to four-hourly for 24 hours. Report to nurse in charge if any deviations from baseline observations occur	Allows for swift medical intervention if any complications occur
7. Visual sensory alterations due to operated eye being occluded by a pad	Adjustment to altered visual status	7a. Place locker on patient's unaffected side and ensure all articles are within reach	Allows patient to be independent in reaching personal belongings without damaging the operated eye
		b. When attending to patient, approach from unoperated side	Avoids startling the patient
8. Risk of boredom due to inactivity	The patient will have an appropriate amount of activity and rest acceptable to her during her stay in hospital	8a. Take time to converse with the patient on topics that interest her	Provides diversionary activities and stimulation for the patient
		b. Encourage normal interests if visual handicap and surgical considerations allow	
		c. Encourage friends and relatives to visit	
		d. Provide radio, television, cassette tapes, large print books if patient wishes	
9. Unable to instil own eye medications due to lack of knowledge and practice	Patient should be confident of her ability to carry on treatment following discharge home	9a. Explain need for compliance with treatment, and ensure patient understands	Gives rationale to patient for treatment
		b. Explain the procedure for instilling drops, using appropriate terminology	Increases patient's knowledge
		c. Observe the patient instilling her own drops	Allows for assessment of competence
		d. Explain the effects of treatment, including visual effects and ensure patient understands	Will facilitate compliance with treatment

GLAUCOMA

Glaucoma is a condition characterized by increased tension or pressure within the eye causing progressive structural or functional damage to the eye. If unchecked, it may lead to blindness. Medication will not cure glaucoma but can keep it under control. Surgery is often curative.

Classification

The following is a simplified classification of glaucoma:

1. Adult primary glaucoma.
   a. Open angle (chronic simple, simple).
   b. Closed angle (narrow angle, angle-closure).
2. Congenital glaucoma—see paediatric or ophthalmology texts.
3. Secondary glaucoma—this is related to such conditions as trauma, aphakia, iritis, tumour and haemorrhage.

Adult Primary (Open Angle) Glaucoma

The cause of primary glaucoma is unknown. Glaucoma is the leading cause of preventable blindness, yet it is responsible wholly or in part for 13 per cent of those on the register for the blind in England and Wales. Glaucoma of some type is found in about 2 per cent of the population over the age of 40. It is estimated that about 500,000 people suffer from glaucoma in the United Kingdom alone; about half of these have the chronic form of the disease, and in this group two thirds remain undetected (International Glaucoma Association, 1987). Health care professionals have a responsibility to encourage annual eye check-ups, because early detection could reduce substantially the incidence of blindness from glaucoma.

Altered Physiology

The total volume and pressure of intraocular fluid is regulated by the balance between the formation and reabsorption of aqueous humour. Ordinarily, the pressure-regulating mechanism maintains an almost constant balance throughout life. The exact action of this mechanism is not known; however, pathological changes at the iridocorneal angle prevent the usual outflow of aqueous humour through the trabecular meshwork (connective tissue with perforations that permit fluid to pass through) to a tubular structure, the canal of Schlemm, and into the venous system. As a result, intraocular pressure is increased (Figure 29.14), however, increased ocular pressure (22 to 30 mmHg) does not necessarily mean that the patient will develop frank glaucoma.

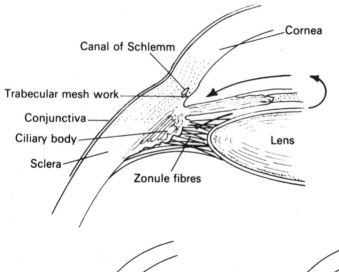

Canal of Schlemm

Cornea

Trabecular mesh work

Conjunctiva

Ciliary body

Sclera

Zonule fibres

Lens

Figure 29.14 Effects of ageing and of glaucoma on secretion of aqueous humour. Normal anatomy is identified in the upper illustration. (A) Arrows indicate the secretion of aqueous humour from the ciliary body to the posterior chamber, through the pupil into the anterior chamber, and out through the trabecular meshwork to the canal of Schlemm and then into the venous system. (B) The same pathway is followed in the ageing person, except that the amount of fluid is less. (C) In glaucoma, more fluid enters the anterior chamber than leaves it. This accounts for hardness of the eyeball due to the increase of pressure.

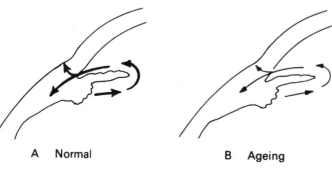

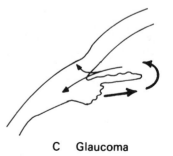

A   Normal

B   Ageing

C   Glaucoma

Apparently, both physical and emotional factors are involved in increasing pressure within the eye. The underlying mechanism is episcleral (overlying the sclera) venous pressure engorgement transmitted by the Valsalva phenomenon. That is, intraocular pressure increases when the patient exerts energy, as in climbing the stairs, bending over to pick up an object, sneezing or even turning the head suddenly. It also occurs in relation to emotional upsets (e.g., apprehension about the nature of prognosis of surgery may cause an increase in pressure).

Clinical Features

Symptoms are insidious and develop slowly. The patient may have mild discomfort, such as a tired feeling in the eye, trouble in focusing and headache. Impairment of peripheral vision occurs long before any effects on central vision are noted. The patient may become aware of peripheral visual impairment by bumping into things that were not seen at the side. Driving a car may be a hazard to others because of an inability to see pedestrians or vehicles approaching from the side. The patient may also note halos around lights.

Diagnosis and Measurement of Intraocular Pressure

An increase in intraocular pressure or hardening of the eyeball may be noted with the fingers, but more accurately it is measured by means of tonometry, tonography and peripheral vision testing. Tonometry (Figure 29.15) is a simple and painless test to measure the intraocular pressure. It is most reliably measured by applanation tonometry. The cornea is anaesthetized by a drop of 1 per cent amethocaine, and the circular area of contact of the tonometer prism is made visible by instilling 1 per cent fluorescein. The tonometer prism is brought into contact with the patient's eye, and measurements are taken either with patient seated at a slit lamp or with the patient lying down and then using a hand-held tonometer. A normal reading is 11 to 22 mmHg.

Gonioscopy is the direct visualization of the anterior chamber angle. Local anaesthesia is used. The examiner places a goniolens over the cornea. Sterile saline solution is injected between the cornea and the lens. The examiner uses a microscope and illuminating source to view the contents of the anterior chamber, particularly the anterior chamber angle.

Medical Management

Treatment depends on the stage of the condition, the degree of the reduced angle between the iris and the cornea, the response to medication and the reliability of the patient in adhering to the regime. In general, pharmacotherapy can keep the condition under control.

Pharmacotherapy

Primary (open-angle) glaucoma is often treated by one or a combination of the following medications:

- Miotics, such as pilocarpine, increase outflow of aqueous humour.
- Timolol maleate, a ß-adrenergic receptor blocking agent, is popular for the treatment of primary open-

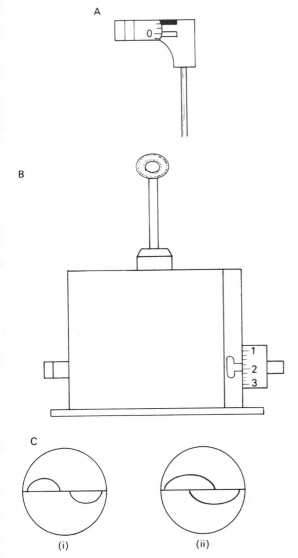

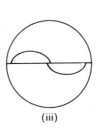

Figure 29.15 Applanation tonometry. (A) Applanation tonometer with prism attached. (B) Applanation tonometer viewed from the rear. (C) Semicircular rings seen by observer: (i) pressure too low; (ii) pressure too high; (iii) correct reading.

angle glaucoma, aphakic glaucoma and, in selected patients, secondary glaucoma. It appears to be better tolerated than previously used drugs. When applied topically, timolol decreases production of aqueous humour and reduces intraocular pressure for as long as 24 hours. Pupillary size is not changed, and the tone of the ciliary body is not altered; hence, this medication does not interfere with vision. In some patients, timolol may cause palpitations and tachycardia, and the nurse must be alert for these manifestations.

Drug dosage of timolol is usually one drop twice a day. Occasionally, mild eye irritation or brief blurring of vision occurs with timolol. This medication is prescribed with caution for patients who may have adverse effects from systemic use of ß-adrenergic receptor blocking agents (such as patients with asthma, heart block or heart failure).

- Carbonic anhydrase inhibitors, such as acetazolamide, can decrease the production of aqueous humour.
- Anticholinesterases, such as echothiophate iodide (phospholine iodide), can facilitate the outflow of aqueous humour.
- Epinephrine drops decrease production of aqueous humour and promote its outflow from the eye.

Surgical Management

Surgical treatment may consist of trabeculectomy or LASER or argon laser trabeculoplasty.

Trabeculectomy

In trabeculectomy, a small fistula or opening is made into the anterior chamber at the junction (limbus) of the cornea and sclera, allowing aqueous humour to flow into the subconjunctival space.

Nursing Considerations

One major risk in these surgical procedures is endophthalmitis, an inflammation of the internal structure of the eye due to infection. To prevent infection, meticulous care must be taken when administering eye medications or when touching the eyes.

Since the patient has undergone surgery in which general anaesthesia is usually required, the nurse must monitor vital signs and the intravenous infusions and provide comfort measures and pain control as the patient emerges from the anaesthesia. To prevent blood from entering the anterior chamber following a trabeculectomy, the patient's head is elevated or the patient is placed in a sitting position as soon as possible following recovery from anaesthesia. An eye shield is worn during the hospital stay. At the time of discharge, the patient is requested to wear the eye shield at night for three to four weeks.

LASER Trabeculoplasty or Argon LASER Trabeculoplasty

In these two procedures, referred to as LTP or ALT, a narrow LASER beam (usually blue-green argon) is focused on the trabecular meshwork of an open angle, resulting in a nonpenetrating burn that changes the meshwork pattern and facilitates drainage of the aqueous humour. Laser trabeculoplasty is a painless outpatient procedure that may have to be done several times to lower eye pressure. Meanwhile the patient continues to use the eye drops prescribed and possibly steroid eye drops to control inflammation. With primary open-angle glaucoma, the success

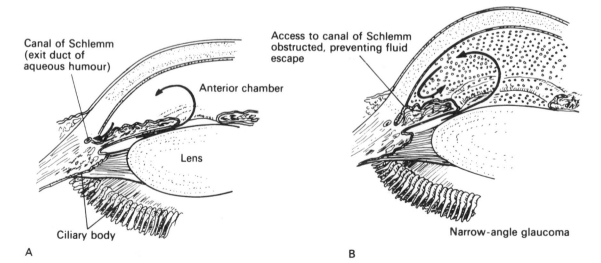

Canal of Schlemm (exit duct of aqueous humour)

Anterior chamber

Lens

Ciliary body

Access to canal of Schlemm obstructed, preventing fluid escape

Narrow-angle glaucoma

A   B

Figure 29.16 Obstruction of flow of aqueous fluid in glaucoma. (A) Normal flow of aqueous fluid through canal of Schlemm. (B) Obstruction to the flow of fluid, causing closed-angle glaucoma. (Lechliger, M. and Moya, F., *Introduction to the Practice of Anesthesia* (2nd edition), Harper & Row, New York.)

rate of this procedure is about 80 per cent; it is less effective with other types of glaucoma.

Acute Closed-Angle Glaucoma

Acute closed-angle glaucoma is the sudden building up of intraocular pressure (within 30 minutes to 1 hour) due to a complete blockage of the filtering angle caused by a bunching up of the iris (Figure 29.16B). This is an emergency situation, which, if left untreated, may lead to blindness.

● Acute closed-angle glaucoma may be precipitated in patients who have narrow anterior chamber angles by administering anticholinergic drugs such as atropine and scopolamine.

Clinical Features

When pressure increases rapidly, severe pain occurs in and around the eye (periocular). Artificial lights appear to have a rainbow around them, and vision becomes cloudy or blurred. The eye is red and the cornea is steamy; nausea and vomiting, as well as pupil dilation may be noted. The nausea and vomiting may be severe enough to distract attention from the eye and confuse the diagnosis. Intraocular pressure is elevated; as the pressure rises, the retinal artery is compressed, reducing nutrition to the eye. This can cause retinal and corneal atrophy.

Diagnosis

Intraocular pressure is measured, and the angle between the involved cornea and the iris is observed with a gonioscope. Pressure above 22 mmHg is suggestive of an early form of glaucoma. A tight or closed angle condition causes the pressure to increase in excess of 50 mmHg.

Medical Management

Treatment is principally surgical, however, before surgery, medications may be prescribed by the ophthalmologist. Miotic drugs will cause the pupil to contract and the iris to draw away from the cornea, thus allowing the aqueous humour to drain through the lymph spaces into the canal of Schlemm. Pilocarpine or timolol maleate may also be prescribed. Dosage and frequency of drops are regulated to meet individual requirements.

Carbonic anhydrase inhibitors restrict the action of the enzyme that is necessary to produce aqueous humour. Acetazolamide is an example of such an agent. Decreased production of aqueous humour aids in improving some patients' conditions before surgery, and may control intraocular tension in other patients to such an extent that surgery may not be necessary.

Ordinary glycerin given orally reduces intraocular pressure through the mechanism of osmotic balance exchange. Glycerol 50 per cent also administered orally has a high osmotic pressure; it withdraws fluid from the eye through the membrane and lowers pressure. Mannitol 20 per cent may be used intravenously.

Surgical Management

For surgical intervention, an incision is made through the cornea so that a portion of the iris may be drawn out and excised (peripheral iridectomy). An iridectomy prevents the iris from bulging forwards to crowd the chamber angle and permits drainage of aqueous humour from the anterior chamber, thereby reducing intraocular tension. With surgery there is a risk of haemorrhage and infection that must be monitored by the nurse.

Argon LASER beam surgery is an alternative treatment; it burns the iris and has the same effect as an iridectomy. This is often a preferred treatment because it avoids an incision, is relatively painless, and is done under topical anaesthesia on an outpatient basis.

About 30 minutes before LASER treatment, pilocarpine eye drops are administered to prevent further iris contraction. Amethocaine is applied topically to permit placement of a fundus contact lens (this keeps the lid open during the treatment). There is little discomfort during the delivery of LASER beams. The patient will be seated during the treatment, resting the chin in a chin rest as the ophthalmologist asks the patient to focus on a fixed point.

Following treatment there may be headache and blurring of the vision, which disappears after 24 hours. Discomfort is controlled with an analgesic. Topical steroids may be prescribed to reduce inflammation. Patients should be driven home by someone after the treatment. If necessary, these treatments are repeated in one or two weeks.

► NURSING PROCESS
► THE PATIENT WITH GLAUCOMA

► *Assessment*

The nursing history is important in evaluating the patient with glaucoma because there are several kinds of glaucoma with differing symptoms. Also many patients are aware that untreated glaucoma can lead to blindness. All patients need to be aware of the seriousness of the condition. Through a nursing history, the nurse is able to determine the patient's understanding about glaucoma and the awareness that this condition can be controlled with conscientious adherence to the treatment plan.

The nurse determines how long the patient has had glaucoma and what is understood by the patient about the problem. Does the patient have mild or extensive discomfort, difficulty focusing, problems with peripheral vision, cloudy or blurred vision or halos around lights? Does the patient have frequent headaches, nausea and vomiting? Are the eyes red? Is there a steamy cornea and signs of infection? Does the patient complain that the eyeball feels hard or is painful?

► *Patient's Problems*

The patient's major problems may include the following:

- Alteration in visual sensory perception related to progressive nature of glaucoma.
- Alteration in comfort; pain related to increasing pressure within the eye.
- Anxiety/fear related to possible or actual loss of vision.
- Lack of ability to care for self due to impaired vision.
- Potential social isolation related to fear of injury, which may further complicate the visual problem.

► *Planning and Implementation*
► Expected Outcomes

The major expected outcomes of the patient may include control of the condition of glaucoma by whatever means are necessary, relief of pain and discomfort, realistic adaptation to treatment measures and reduction of anxieties, resumption of responsibility for self-care to the best of patient's ability and participation in social activities within the constraints of any limitations.

Nursing Care

Relieving Pain

Except in the case of acute closed-angle glaucoma, there is often little discomfort experienced early on, but as the condition progresses, with degenerative changes of the trabecular meshwork, more fluid enters the anterior chamber than leaves. Fluid accumulation 'hardens' the eye and exerts pressure on the optic nerve, which causes discomfort. The patient is reminded that relief can be obtained by conscientiously using the prescribed eye drops. The technique in using these drops may need to be reviewed for effectiveness. Any habits that might cause an infection must be corrected.

Since emotional upsets, anger, fear or excitement can cause increased intraocular pressure, emotional stress needs to be minimized. Therefore, maintaining a calm atmosphere can help to keep eye discomfort under control. Excessive straining or lifting is also to be avoided.

The patient is cautioned to use only the medication prescribed; if the wrong eye drops are used accidentally, it could have adverse effects.

Promoting Self-Care Measures

Support systems are important for the patient with glaucoma. The patient and caregivers should be aware of the necessity of administering eye medications regularly. Although this will not cure the problem, it will keep it under control. The patient is told of the side-effects of the medication, and the ability to read labels, particularly those of the medications, is checked. The nurse discusses with the patient the nature of all treatments and the role played by the patient in keeping the condition under control. The nurse encourages questions and anticipates the patient's fears so that they can be addressed.

When vision is blurred, there is a tendency not to be as particular about one's appearance. All who contact this patient, therefore, can encourage the patient and give compliments when appropriate. The patient is encouraged to maintain proper eating habits and to participate in enjoyable activities.

The patient is assisted in modifying the environment so that it will be safe; light fixtures can be placed where they will do the most good. Advice to suit a patient's particular self-care needs can be individualized, and assistance should be provided if the patient is unable to manage self-care.

Patient Education and Home Health Care

Ineffective coping related to a lack of knowledge can be averted by teaching and repeating the basic fundamentals of care. The need to be consistent in administering eye medications must be re-emphasized even though the patient may feel all right and see no need to continue (nor even note any benefit). The nurse can discuss with the patient the need for periodic check-ups with the ophthalmologist, and can review the patient's lifestyle and assist in making adaptations if necessary.

Although glaucoma cannot be cured, it can be controlled to a great extent. Whether the patient has had surgery or not, certain limitations must be set.

Activities that may increase intraocular pressure and should be avoided are:

- Excessive fluid intake.
- Use of antihistamines or sympathomimetic medications without proper medical supervision.

Eye drops are an essential part of the treatment of a patient with glaucoma. It is imperative that fresh eye drops be used and that they be administered consistently.

Promoting Social Activities

The patient is encouraged to contact family, relatives or friends when company or assistance is needed. It can help significantly if someone can accompany the patient when shopping in order to read labels on the shelves and carry heavier packages. Whatever can be suggested to prevent isolation will help to keep the patient's condition under control; brooding, worry and isolation may aggravate the problem by increasing intraocular pressure.

► *Evaluation*
► Expected Outcomes

1. Patient reports that pain and discomfort are relieved/controlled.

a. Uses prescribed eyedrops regularly, with proper technique.

b. Avoids or manages stress.

c. Avoids straining or lifting.

2. Increases self-care skills.

a. Makes use of family/friends support systems.

b. Maintains personal grooming.

c. Takes part in modifying the environment for safety and efficiency.

3. Maintains social contacts with family and friends.

Considerations For the Elderly

Most patients with glaucoma are in the older age-group. Often dimming vision is accepted as part of the ageing process and medical assistance is not sought. Therefore, as part of the physical examination of anyone over the age of 65, tonometry should be recommended and eye pressure checked periodically thereafter. The major problem of patients with glaucoma is the tendency to stop taking eye drops and claiming that it does not help. However, it keeps glaucoma from worsening. To stop medication means that glaucoma will continue insidiously until the patient is blind. Other problems of ageing such as arthritis, loneliness and depression, constipation (straining on defaecation), and an increasing potential for falling/accidents have a direct affect on glaucoma.

BLINDNESS OR PARTIAL SIGHT

Telescopic eyeglasses and magnifying glasses are easily accessible aids that can be recommended by the nurse for those who have exhausted conventional prescribed lenses.

Mobility aids are probably the most basic need for the visually impaired. Such people need reassurance that they can move safely from one place to the next. Only about 3 per cent of the blind use guide dogs—probably the reason is that most sightless people are over the age of 65, and they are less trusting of dogs and may even have difficulty keeping up with them. The most useful aid is a long, lightweight cane that very subtly provides accurate information by simple manoeuvres and ensures that the next step is safe in a small, limited area. Overhead hazards are not detected, however.

For reading (work, study, leisure), a portable electronic magnifying system is available. In this system, one moves a small hand-held camera across the page and then views on a display screen a bright magnified image of the text (Viewscan by Wormald).

Additional aids are telescopic lenses, glasses combined with mirrors, nightscopes, closed-circuit television cameras and fibreoptic systems. By being aware of these possibilities, the nurse is able to recommend invaluable aids to the person with such a need.

ENUCLEATION

Removal of the eyeball, enucleation, is necessitated by a variety of factors, including trauma that forces the contents of the globe to escape, infections and other injuries that threaten to lead to sympathetic ophthalmitis (see p. 932). During the removal of the eye, muscles are cut as close to the globe as possible. These muscles are approximated with sutures over a plastic prosthesis, thereby providing the means for co-ordinated motion of the prosthesis with the patient's other eye. A plastic, gold or Teflon ball is placed in the area of the removed eyeball to form a stump on which the ocular prosthetist fixes the prosthesis (artificial eye). This prosthesis is coloured to match the patient's eye. In successful cases, it is difficult to distinguish the prosthesis from the normal eye.

In certain cases, the sclera can be retained and the rest of the contents of the eye 'scooped' out; this procedure is known as evisceration. The main advantage of evisceration is that it provides better motion to the artificial eye. The disadvantage is that sympathetic ophthalmitis may occur.

Exenteration is usually performed in advanced malignancy or severe war injuries. In this procedure, the eyelids, the eyeball and all contents of the orbit are removed, down to the bone. This operation is *very* disfiguring, and the ocular prosthetist is required to build a facial prosthesis that is usually attached to a pair of spectacles.

THE NEWLY BLIND

The number of blind people in the world is estimated at 28 million, only 6 per cent of whom live in the developed countries. There are 120,000 registered blind people and 56,000 partially sighted people in the United KIngdom. Of the newly blind cases, it is known that a significant number could have been prevented with present knowledge.

When a patient has marked visual impairment or is newly blind, a great deal of help is needed in making a healthy adjustment. For the most part, this help is entrusted to those skilled in such rehabilitation. However, a nurse can follow certain practices when caring for such a patient.

The nurse recognizes that there are stages through which this person moves:

1. Denial—this phase of the sightless person's experience must not be discredited, since it is a stage through which the person must go.

2. Value changes—adapting to aids that the patient thought would never have to be used.

3. Independence–dependence conflict—attempting to accept the situation without becoming completely dependent.

4. Coping with stigma—this person must adjust to unfortunate stigmata that are so prevalent among the sighted towards the sightless, such as that they are 'helpless', 'unemployable', 'completely dependent' or 'depressed'.
5. Learning to communicate in social settings without visual cues.

Expected Outcomes

The major expected outcomes for the patient are to accept the sightless or nearly sightless condition by:

1. Adaptation to the use of auxiliary aids.
2. Acceptance of the new visual role without becoming completely dependent.
3. Continuing with physical self-care.
4. Coping with the social climate and stigmata that are prevalent.
5. Learning to communicate without visual clues.
6. Adherence to the prescribed therapeutic regime.

Nursing Care

The nurse is able to assist the patient in several ways: (1) patient teaching, (2) patient support, (3) patient care, and (4) collaboration with the doctor.

Patient teaching is done to familiarize the patient with the anatomy of the eye and its function. By monitoring what the doctor has told the patient relative to diagnosis, anticipated treatment and prognosis, the nurse is able to reinforce this information, answer questions, provide support and relay back to the ophthalmologist the reaction of the patient, family and close friends, where appropriate. If information is withheld, such as little hope for recovery of vision, this will interfere with the patient's adjustment and rehabilitation. The nurse is often helpful in determining when the time is right for conveying such information. Fears are to be described because they can unearth misinformation. Frequently, self-imposed limitations are more restricting than physical disabilities, such as blindness. Even attitudes and beliefs of the nurse can have a direct or indirect effect on the patient. Such attitudes need to be confronted so that only genuine feelings are transmitted. A positive attitude by those who care for patients will affect the patient's self-esteem and body image in a beneficial way.

A blind person should always be treated with the dignity accorded any other person. Expressions of pity are to be avoided. The patient can be kept from becoming discouraged by ensuring that there is someone to talk to, or that there is some other form of diversion, such as the radio. The patient can be helped to overcome any feelings of awkwardness as simple activities are performed.

If the patient is allowed out of bed, the blind person should survey the room or area around the bed by walking around and touching the furniture. Thereafter, the nurse should be sure that the furniture remains in the same position. A door should never be left half open; it should be either open or shut. When walking together, the blind person should be allowed to follow the nurse by lightly touching the nurse's elbow. The blind person should not be pushed ahead of the nurse. When walking alone, the blind person should learn to use a lightweight walking stick to warn of obstacles.

Personal appearance is a significant part of the patient's care. Such patients should be allowed to dress by themselves; they can learn to brush and comb their hair, and even use cosmetics if they wish. Activities such as table etiquette and writing can be acquired with practice.

Familiarity with resources that are available to help the patient is a nursing responsibility. When patients are declared legally blind, they should be referred to the statutory and voluntary agencies. A directory of agencies serving the visually handicapped in the United KIngdom is available from the Royal National Institute for the Blind.

Interesting and effective aids are devices that 'talk', such as clocks, calculators, thermometers and scales. There also is an optical scanner that when passed over lines of text in a book send signals to a computer (programmed to recognize letters) that turns them into words and pronounces them. Another similar device scans words and records the shape of letters, which are then converted into vibrations felt by the fingertips of the user.

Technology continues to provide devices that are becoming available and useful in expanding the world of the sightless.

BIBLIOGRAPHY

International Glaucoma Association (1987) *Glaucoma '87—A Guide For Patients*, International Glaucoma Association, London.

FURTHER READING

Books

Department of Health and Social Security (1988) *Causes of Blindness and Partial Sight Among Adults in 1980/81 in England—New Registrations*, HMSO, London.

Dobree, J. H. and Boulter, E. (1982) *Blindness and Visual Handicap: The Facts*, Oxford University Press, Oxford.

Ford, M. and Heshel, T. (1988) *The In Touch 1988 Handbook* (5th edition), Broadcasting Support Services, London.

Leydbecker, W. and Crick, R. P. (1981) *All About Glaucoma*, Faber & Faber, London.

Rooke, F. C. E., Rothwell, P. J. and Woodhouse, D. F. (1980) *Ophthalmic Nursing, Its Practice and Management*, Churchill Livingstone, Edinburgh.

Stollery, R. (1987) *Ophthalmic Nursing*, Blackwell Scientific, Oxford.

Vale, J. and Cox, B. (1985) *Drugs and the Eye* (2nd edition), Butterworths, London.

Vaughan, D. and Asbury, T. (1989) *General Ophthalmology* (12th edition), Lange, California.

Wybar, K. and Muir, M. K. (1984) *Ophthalmology* (3rd edition), Baillière Tindall, London.

Articles

Donnelly, D. (1987) Focus on disability—Registered hopeless? *Nursing Times*, Vol. 83, No. 24, pp. 49–51.

Donnelly, D. (1987) Focus on disability—Information gap, *Nursing Times*, Vol. 83, No. 25, pp. 55–6.

Felinski, S. (1989) Not seeing eye to eye, *Nursing Times*, Vol. 85, No. 20, pp. 57–9.

Fox, J. (1989) Conjunctivitis, keratitis and iritis, *Nursing*, Vol. 3, No. 45, pp. 20–3.

French, S. (1988) Understanding partial sight, *Nursing Times*, Vol. 84, No. 3, pp. 32–3.

Jones, N. P., Hayward, J. M., Khaw, P. T. *et al.* (1986) Function of an ophthalmic 'accident and emergency' department: results of a six-month survey, *British Medical Journal*, Vol. 292, pp. 188–90.

Kershaw, J. E. M. (1980) The nursing care of ophthalmic patients in general wards, *Nursing Times*, 7 February, pp. 234–7.

Nelligan, B. (1989) Eye investigations, *Nursing*, Vol. 3, No. 45, pp. 10–12.

Smith, S. (1987) Drugs and the eye, *Nursing Times*, Vol. 83, No. 25, pp. 48–50.

Voke, J. (1980) Colour vision defects—their industrial and occupational significance, *Nursing Times*, 7 February, pp. 240–3.

Walker , C. (1987) Retinopathy of prematurity, *Nursing Times*, Vol. 83, No. 43, pp. 46–7.

Watkinson, S. (1989) Visual handicap in childhood, *Nursing*, Vol. 3, No. 45, pp. 13–16.

Watkinson, S. (1989) The blind child in hospital, *Nursing*, Vol. 3, No. 45, pp. 17–18.

Watkinson, S. (1989) Drugs and the eye, *Nursing*, Vol. 3, No. 45, pp. 24–6.

chapter 30

ASSESSMENT AND CARE OF PATIENTS WITH HEARING DISTURBANCES AND EAR DISORDERS

ANATOMY OF THE EAR

The ear can be divided into three parts: the external ear, the middle ear and the inner ear.

External Ear

The Pinna
Known as the auricle or pinna, this part of the external ear is composed of cartilage covered in perichondrium and then skin. It sits on the petrous part of the temporal bone of the skull.

External Auditory Meatus
This is a downwards sloping S-shaped canal, which is covered in epithelium continuous with the eardrum. At the entrance to the canal sit the hair-like projections that protect the ear from foreign bodies. The canal also contains cerumen secretory cells that have the same function.

Tympanic Membrane
The tympanic membrane is a 1 cm disc that lies across the end of the external auditory meatus at an angle of 45 degrees. It is covered on the outside with epithelium continuous with that of the external auditory meatus. It is pearly grey in colour and has three layers: outer, middle and inner.

In the middle fibrous layer is embedded the handle of the malleus, one of the three ossicles. The inner layer is flat epithelium continuous with the inner ear cavity.

Middle Ear

The middle ear consists of the inner layer of the eardrum, the ossicles (malleus, incus and stapes) embedded in the oval window of the cochlea, and the eustachian tube, which equalizes pressure on each side of the eardrum. The cavity of the middle ear is continuous posteriorly with a further cavity (the mastoid antrum) and beyond this with a variable interconnective arrangement of air-filled spaces in the mastoid bone.

Inner Ear

The inner ear contains the cochlea and semicircular canals with their respective branches of the auditory nerve (VIII). The cochlea is concerned with hearing and is served by the auditory branch of the VIII nerve. The semicircular canals are concerned with balance and are served by the vestibular branch of the VIII nerve.

How Do We Hear?

Sound waves transmitted by the eardrum to the ossicles of the middle ear are transferred to the cochlea, the organ of hearing, lodged in the labyrinth or inner ear. An important ossicle is the stapes, which rocks on its posterior portion, not unlike a piston, and sets up vibrations in fluids contained in the labyrinth. The fluid waves cause the basilar membrane in which the hair cells of the organ of Corti rest to move in a wavelike manner. The waves set up electrical currents that stimulate the various areas

of the cochlea. The hair cell sets up a neural impulse that is encoded and then transferred through the auditory cortex in the brain, where it is decoded into a sound message (Figure 30.1).

EXAMINATION OF THE EAR

The ear is examined primarily by inspection with a head mirror. The internal ear is looked at directly as far as the eardrum by using an auroscope. Assessment of hearing ability can be carried out using voice, tuning fork tests or audiometry.

Inspection of the External Ear
The pinna is examined for any abnormalities in shape or position; scarring indicating previous surgery or skin conditions are noted.

Inspection Using an Auroscope
Inspection of the ear canal and eardrum (tympanic membrane) requires the external auditory meatus to be free of cerumen or wax. Wax can be removed by a doctor using a wax hook. If the cerumen is firmly adherent and hard it

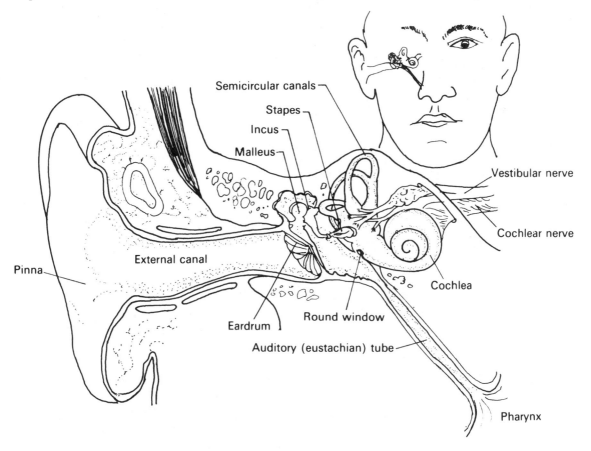

Figure 30.1 Anatomy of the ear.

may be removed by ear surgery. If the wax is not readily removed, softening drops may be prescribed for instillation and the patient requested to return in a week for a further attempt.

To examine the ear canal and tympanic membrane, the pinna is gently pulled upward and backward. This straightens the S-shaped external auditory meatus and allows better visualization. The auroscope is held like a pencil with the little finger resting on the patient's cheek. This prevents the speculum going right into the canal and causing trauma if the patient suddenly moves. The speculum of the auroscope rests just at the edge of the entrance to the canal.

Any discharge, inflammation or foreign body in the ear canal is noted. The examiner looks at the eardrum, its position and the colour of the membrane, as well as any unusual markings (Figure 30.2).

Testing For Auditory Acuity

Initially when testing a patient who has a suspected hearing deficiency, the otologist may assess the patient's ability to hear the spoken word. This is done by avoiding the patient's face and talking to the patient, or by the otologist momentarily turning away while talking to the patient. This rules out the possibility of the patient lip reading and is successful in diagnosing some patients who are profoundly deaf.

CLASSIFICATION OF HEARING LOSS

Conductive Deafness

Conductive hearing loss results from an impairment of the outer ear canal, tympanic membrane and ossicles. The inner ear is not involved in this type of loss and it can still analyse clearly the sounds that come to it (Figure 30.3).

Perceptive Deafness (Sensorineural) Loss

A disorder of the inner ear or nerve pathways produces a hearing loss in which sensitivity to and discrimination of sounds are impaired. Sounds may still be conducted through the external ear but cannot correctly be translated.

Hearing Tests

It is essential to understand two things when trying to appreciate tuning fork tests as a tool for diagnosing deafness: (1) to be clear about the two types of deafness described above; and (2) to understand the significance of air and bone conduction.

Air conduction, that is, sound travelling from the pinna through the external auditory meatus to the eardrum and hence to the ossicles and stapes in the oval window, will always be better than bone conduction. Bone conduction

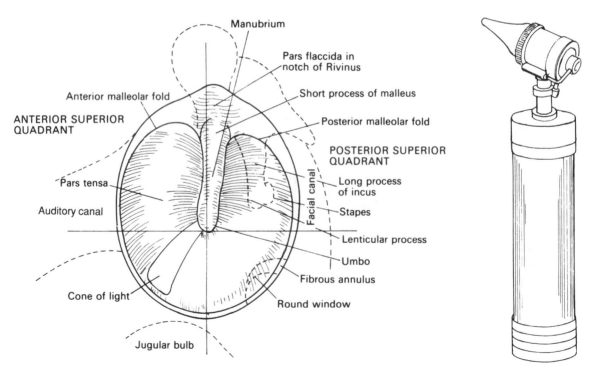

Figure 30.2 Inspection of external auditory meatus and tympanic membrane using an auroscope (J. Duncan).

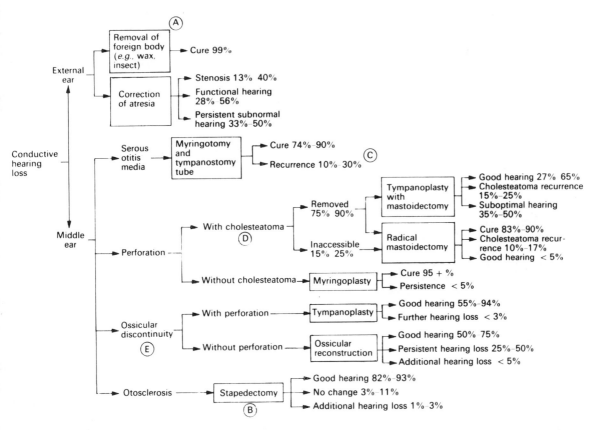

Figure 30.3 Conductive hearing loss. When a patient presents with this problem, the above flow chart indicates how the diagnosis determines the management of the patient and further predicts the outcome. (Eiseman, B. (ed.) (1980) Conductive hearing loss, B. W. Jafek and T. J. Balkany in *Prognosis of Surgical Disease*, W. B. Saunders, Philadelphia.)

is sound conducted from the mastoid bone to the cochlear in the inner ear, in the normal hearing person.

Rinne Test

The Rinne test compares hearing by bone conduction with hearing by air conduction. A tuning fork of 12 Hz is sounded and held in front of the ear in line with the external auditory meatus. The patient is asked to indicate when the sound is no longer heard. As soon as the patient ceases to hear the sound, the tuning fork is transferred to the mastoid process. If the sound is not heard there, the procedure is reversed. If the tuning fork is heard by air conduction after bone conduction, the Rinne test is said to be positive, i.e. air conduction of sound is greater than bone conduction.

If the tuning fork is heard on the mastoid process after it has ceased to be heard by air conduction, the Rinne test If the tuning fork is heard on the mastoid process after it has ceased to be heard by air conduction, the Rinne test is said to be negative (bone conduction is greater than air conduction) (Figure 30.4, p. 954).

A false negative Rinne test is when the patient has a 'dead' ear and thinks the tuning fork can be heard better by bone conduction than by air conduction. In fact, the sound is referred from the mastoid, through the bones of the skull to the other ear, where, with a functioning cochlea, it is heard. A masking device such as a Barony box can be used to exclude this phenomenon.

Weber Test

The tuning fork is sounded and placed upon the patient's forehead. The patient is then asked in which ear the sound is heard best. In conductive deafness of one ear, the patient can be expected to point to the ear in which there is conductive deafness as the ear in which the sound is heard clearest. If both ears are affected by conductive deafness, the tuning fork will be heard in the ear that is the more affected.

In sensorineural deafness, the position is reversed. The sound will be heard better by the ear with an intact and functioning cochlea and auditory nerve (see Figure 30.5, p. 954).

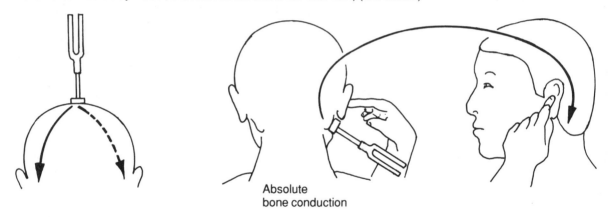

Figure 30.4 Rinne's test. (A) A tuning fork (512 Hz) is struck and held close to the patient's ear until it can no longer be heard by the patient, who signals to that effect. (B) The fork is then placed immediately on the patient's mastoid process. If the patient can hear it, then bone conduction of noise is greater than air conduction (negative Rinne's test). Thus the patient's perceptive hearing is satisfactory, and so there must be something affecting the conducting mechanism. (In a patient with severe unilateral perceptive deafness, bone conduction may appear better than air conduction because sound is carried by the skull to the better ear. If so, hearing of the 'good' ear should be masked by 'noise'; this restricts the test to the 'bad' ear.) (J. Duncan.)

Figure 30.5 (A) Weber's test. The tuning fork is set vibrating and its base put on the patient's vertex or forehead. Sound is conducted via the skull to both cochleas. The patient is then asked in which ear the sound is loudest. In perceptive deafness, it is louder in the 'good' ear, which has better cochlear function. However, in conductive deafness, it is heard better by the 'bad' ear because the 'good' ear is distracted by normal sounds from the environment while the deafer ear can concentrate on the sound arriving by bone conduction. (B) Absolute bone conduction. The ear to be tested is blocked by pressure on the tragus, a tuning fork is set vibrating, the base of which is applied to the patient's mastoid process on the side under test. The patient signals when the sound can no longer be heard. The fork is immediately applied to the examiner using the same method. If the examiner (who should not suffer from perceptive deafness) can hear the tone, it may be concluded that the patient has some degree of perceptive deafness. (J. Duncan.)

Audiometry

After tuning fork tests have made an initial diagnosis of the type of deafness, audiometric examination can indicate the level of the deafness or hearing acuity.

Pure Tone Audiometry
The sound stimulus consists of a pure or musical tone. The intensity is measured in decibels (dB) on a logarithmic scale, increasing by 10 dB each time (the louder the tone before the patient perceives it, the greater the hearing

loss). Normal hearing on the audiogram (Figure 30.6) lies in the 0 to 20 dB range.

Speech Audiometry
The spoken word is used to determine the ability to understand and discriminate sounds. For accuracy, audiometric tests are done in a soundproof room. The patient wears earphones and is asked to signal when the tone is heard, and again when it can no longer be heard. When the tone is applied directly over the external auditory opening, air conduction is measured. When the stimulus is applied to

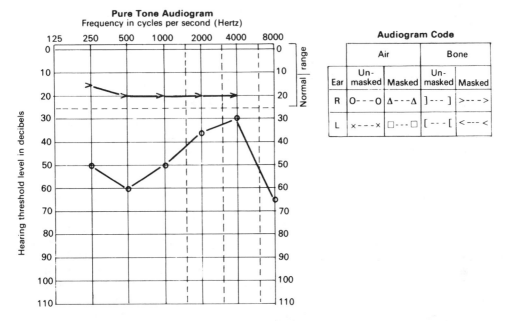

Figure 30.6 Pure tone audiogram. An audiogram presents a graphic outline of the person's hearing as measured by tones of different pitches ranging from 125 to 8,000 cycles per second (Hz). This audiogram of the right ear shows a conductive loss. Thresholds for these different tones as heard by air and bone conduction are plotted. The information is important for determining the type of hearing loss. Also, by testing through the critical speech range (approximately 300 to 3,000 Hz), one can predict how much difficulty there may be in hearing and understanding speech. The code box to the right indicates the signs used on the chart. (Dayal, V. S. (1981) *Clinical Otolaryngology*, J. B. Lippincott, Philadelphia.)

the mastoid bone, thereby bypassing the conductive mechanism, nerve conduction is tested.

Hearing Loss in the Elderly

With ageing, changes occur in the ear that eventually lead to hearing deficits. Not much change occurs in the external ear except that cerumen tends to become harder and there is a greater chance of impaction. In the middle ear, the tympanic membrane may atrophy or sclerose. The inner ear changes with a degeneration of cells at the base of the cochlea. This is manifested by a loss in the ability to hear high-frequency sounds, followed in time by the loss of middle and lower frequencies. The term 'presbycousis' is used to describe this progressive hearing loss.

Early signs of hearing loss may include tinnitus, increasing inability to hear at group meetings, a need to turn up the volume of the television, and so on. Presbycousis may progress rapidly over a few years, or slowly over a decade.

Other factors affect hearing in the elderly, such as lifelong exposure to loud noises such as that caused by jets, guns and heavy machinery in the workplace. Also, certain drugs, such as streptomycin, neomycin and even aspirin, may have an ototoxic effect because renal changes in the older person result in delayed drug excretion. Psycho-

genic factors and other diseases (e.g. diabetes) are also partially responsible for sensory changes.

Hearing impairment should not be assumed to be a normal consequence of ageing, and thus be ignored. When a problem occurs, an audiometric evaluation should be done. Hearing aids should not be invested in without a medical referral. Even with the best of medical care, the older person will have to learn to adjust to varying degrees of hearing deficit.

By understanding what type of hearing loss a patient has, the nurse will more successfully be able to relate to that patient. Trying to speak in a loud voice to a person who cannot adequately hear high-frequency sounds will only make matters worse. Talking into the least impaired ear using sign language, gestures and facial expressions may help.

NOISE AND ITS EFFECT ON HEARING

One of the waste products of the twentieth century is noise (unwanted and unavoidable sound). The sheer volume of noise that surrounds us daily has grown from a simple annoyance into a potentially dangerous source of physical and psychological damage.

Sound Intensity and Frequency

Scientists measure sound intensity (pressure exerted by sound) in decibels (dB). For example, the shuffling of papers in quiet surroundings represents about 15 dB, a low conversation, 40 dB, and a jet plane 100 feet away about 140 dB (Table 30.1). Sound above 80 dB begins to grate harshly on the human ear. (Frequency refers to the number of sound waves emanating from a source per second—cycles per second (Hz). Pitch is the term used to describe frequency.)

Hearing Loss

Psychosocial Considerations

Impairment of hearing may cause changes in personality and attitude, in the ability to communicate, in the awareness of surroundings and even in the ability to protect oneself.

In a classroom, a student with impaired hearing may show disinterest, inattention and failing grades. A pedestrian may attempt to cross the street at the wrong time because of failure to hear an approaching car. People with hearing loss may miss parts of a conversation and may believe that people are talking about them. Many people are not even aware that their hearing is gradually becoming impaired. In 1986, the total number of registered deaf people in England was 94,431 (Table 30.2).

Table 30.1 *Decibels produced by common sound sources*

dBs	Sound Source
0	Silence, threshold of audibility
10	Rustling paper
20	Whispering, ticking watch 2.5 cm from ear
30	Quiet home
40	Quiet conversation
50	Average home or office
60	Average conversation
70	Noisy office
80	Heavy traffic, factory workshop
90	Loud street noise
100	Thunder, artillery
110	Road drill
130	Jet engine
140	Shotgun blast – threshold of pain and perforation of ear drum

REHABILITATION

It is important to classify the kinds of hearing impairment so that rehabilitative efforts can be directed at meeting a particular need.

Hearing Aids

A hearing aid is an instrument through which sounds, both speech and environmental, are received by a microphone, converted into electrical signals, amplified and reconverted to acoustical signals. A hearing aid is not a new ear. It is, as its name implies, only an aid to hearing. Many aids available for nerve deafness depress the low tones and give better hearing for the high tones. Whether a person would benefit by having a hearing aid can best be determined by an otologist in conjunction with an audiologist. When the hearing loss is more than 30 dB in the range of 500 to 2,000 cycles per second (Hz) in the better ear, a patient may benefit (but not with certainty) from a hearing aid. A variety of aids are available; the problem is to select the best aid for the individual patient. Even this does not ensure optimal benefit from such an instrument. Psychological factors, such as vanity, may be involved, as well as other types of sensitivity.

The patient needs to know that the aid will not restore hearing to the level of the person with normal hearing, but will improve it in the range of 300 to 3,500 Hz (range of primary speech).

A hearing aid makes speech louder, but it does not always make it clear enough for the deaf person to understand what is said. The wearer must experiment and adjust the controls for optimal results. It must be recognized that the wearer will never hear what others hear, nor will hearing be as good as that of someone who has no hearing impairment. It may be necessary to receive auditory training and lessons in speech reading (lip reading) in order to make the new hearing aid effective. With such assistance, this person can learn to interpret sounds and use advantageously whatever hearing remains. Speech reading can help fill in the gaps of those words that might be missed. In auditory training, speech discrimination and listening skills are emphasized. The otologist, nurse clinician or the hearing centre can direct the patient to such classes.

A problem with most hearing aids is that background noise is also amplified, which may be distressing to the wearer (see Table 30.3).

Care of a Hearing Aid

A hearing aid must be cared for carefully. The ear mould, which is the only part of the instrument that may be washed, is washed in soap and water every day, and the cannula is cleansed with a small applicator or pipe cleaner. The mould must be dry before it is snapped into the receiver. The transmitter is usually worn off the

Table 30.2 *Number of people on the register of the deaf and hard of hearing, by age (England 1976 to 1986)*

As at 31 March	Numbers registered as:												Total
	Deaf with speech				Deaf without speech				Hard of hearing				
	<16	16–64	65+	Total	<16	16–64	65+	Total	<16	16–64	65+	Total	All persons
1976	1,799	7,312	3,990	13,101	1,593	9,899	2,879	14,371	1,182	5,823	18,526	25,531	53,003
1977R	1,784	7,352	4,325	13,461	1,721	9,687	2,887	14,295	1,250	6,114	19,641	27,005	54,761
1978	1,665	7,865	4,619	14,149	1,745	9,955	3,052	14,752	1,272	7,031	22,822	31,125	60,342*
1979	1,550	7,888	4,812	14,250	1,629	10,080	3,116	14,825	1,137	7,295	24,017	32,449	61,524
1980	1,566	8,215	5,089	14,870	1,545	9,995	3,255	14,795	1,086	7,841	26,196	35,123	64,788
1981–1982	..	..	..	..	..	..	..	..	..	..	..	..	..
1983	1,663	8,766	5,684	1,6113	1,663	10,620	3,439	15,722	1,648	9,982	35,549	47,179	79,014
1984–1985	..	..	..	..	..	..	..	..	..	..	..	..	..
1986	1,630	9,344	6,382	17,356	1,495	11,133	4,093	16,721	1,269	12,672	49,413	63,354	97,431

R Revised

* Includes 316 people for whom age breakdown not available

.. Data not available for these years

It is impossible to state to what extent increases in the numbers of people registered with a hearing impairment over the period 1976 to 1986 are due either to increased registration efforts by SSDs or to any 'natural' increase in numbers. Those registered as hard of hearing have shown the greatest increase, their numbers more than doubling over the period. Over three fifths of the total number of registered people in 1986 were aged 65 and over.

(*Source:* DHSS (1986) Registers of Deaf and Hard of Hearing at 31.3.86, DHSS, London. Reproduced by kind permission of the Controller of Her Majesty's Stationery Office.)

Table 30.3 *Hearing aid problems*

Whistling noises
1. Loose ear mould:
    Improperly made
    Improperly worn
    Worn out
2. Improper aid selection:
    Too much power required in aid, with inadequate
        separation between microphone and receiver
    Open mould used inappropriately

Pain from mould
1. Improperly fitted mould
2. Ear, skin or cartilage infection
3. Middle ear infection
4. Ear tumour
5. Unrelated causes:
    Temporomandibular joint
    Throat or larynx
    Other

Inadequate amplification
1. Dead batteries
2. Wax in ear
3. Wax or other material in mould
4. Wires or tubing disconnected from aid
5. Aid turned off or volume too low
6. Improper mould
7. Improper aid for degree of loss

(Source: Salatoff, R. T. (1981) Choosing the right hearing aid, Hospital Practice, *May, Vol. 16, No. 5, p. 32A.)*

body, behind the ear or in the frame of eyeglasses. A spare battery and cord should be carried by the wearer at all times. (This is suggested, but most patients do not do it.)

When a hearing aid is not functioning properly, the following steps should be taken: (1) note whether the on-off switch is on; (2) check the positioning of the batteries; (3) try a new battery; (4) examine the cord for breaks and check whether it is plugged in correctly; and (5) examine the ear mould for cleanliness. If the aid will not work, notify the hospital where the aid was acquired. If the aid requires repair, another may be lent while the other is being seen to.

Hearing Guide Dogs

Specially trained dogs are available to assist the person with hearing loss. At home, the dog reacts to the sound of a telephone, a doorbell, an alarm clock, a baby's cry, a knock at the door, a smoke alarm or an intruder. The dog alerts the person not by barking but by jumping on the person; the dog then runs to the source of the noise. In public, the dog positions itself between the person with a hearing problem and any potential hazard that the person cannot hear, such as an oncoming vehicle or a hostile person.

Communication With a Person Who Has a Hearing Impairment

Strategies for improving communication with a deaf person include the following:

1. When speaking, always face the person as directly as possible.
2. Make sure your face is as clearly visible as possible; locate yourself so that your face is well-lit; avoid being silhouetted against strong light; do not obscure the person's view of your mouth in any way; avoid talking with any object held in your mouth.
3. Be sure the patient knows the topic or subject of your verbal expression before going ahead with what you plan to say—this will enable contextual clues to be used in the lip-reading process.
4. Speak slowly and distinctly, pausing more frequently than you would normally.
5. If you are unsure whether or not the patient has understood some important direction or request, check to be certain that the full meaning of your message has got across.
6. If for any reason your mouth must be covered (as with a mask) and you must direct or advise the patient, there is no alternative but to write down the message (see Figure 30.7).

PROBLEMS OF THE EXTERNAL EAR

The auricle or external ear, which varies in size, shape and position on the head, aids in the collection of sound waves and their passage into the external auditory canal. The external auditory canal is an S-shaped skin-lined tube that ends at the tympanic membrane (eardrum), which is also lined with skin.

The skin of the canal contains highly specialized glands that secrete a brown, waxlike substance called cerumen (ear wax). The ear's self-cleaning mechanism moves skin debris and cerumen to the outer part of the ear. The cerumen seems to have antibacterial properties and serves as a protection for the skin.

Otitis Externa

Otitis externa involves inflammation of the skin lining the cartilaginous part of the ear canal. Deafness and discharge may be present with pain. Movement of the pinna is painful. Oedema in the walls of the external meatus may lead to physical blockage of the external canal. There is a collection of debris harbouring the organisms responsible.

The goals of management are relief of discomfort, reduction of swelling and eradication of infection.

**For all who meet the
hearing impaired**

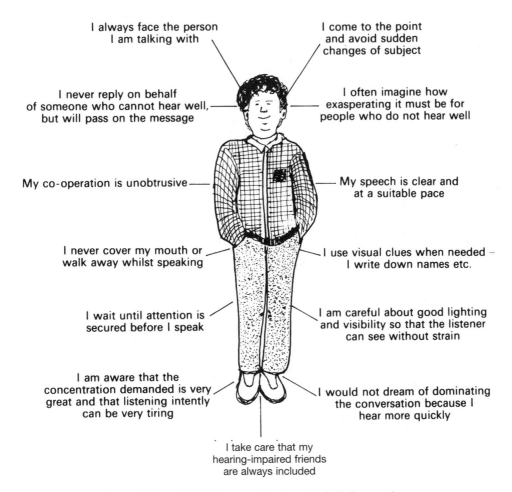

I always face the person
I am talking with

I come to the point
and avoid sudden
changes of subject

I never reply on behalf
of someone who cannot hear well,
but will pass on the message

I often imagine how
exasperating it must be for
people who do not hear well

My co-operation is unobtrusive

My speech is clear and
at a suitable pace

I never cover my mouth or
walk away whilst speaking

I use visual clues when needed –
I write down names etc.

I wait until attention is
secured before I speak

I am careful about good lighting
and visibility so that the listener
can see without strain

I am aware that the
concentration demanded is very
great and that listening intently
can be very tiring

I would not dream of dominating
the conversation because I
hear more quickly

I take care that my
hearing-impaired friends
are always included

Figure 30.7 Are you a hearing aide? (J. Duncan.)

Suction clearance under the microscope and insertion of a wick will be necessary. The wick will be soaked in antibiotic or steroid drops. Daily aural toilet at the outpatients department may be necessary. Systemic antibiotics and analgesics are prescribed.

Otitis externa can also be due to dermatosis eczema or allergic reactions to hair sprays.

Foreign Bodies in the External Canal

Foreign bodies may be removed by a wax hook or by irrigation. If vegetable matter is suspected, irrigation should be avoided as vegetable matter tends to swell.

Ear Surgery

Ear surgery may be performed for the following reasons:

1. Deafness—to try and correct or establish the cause.
   a. Stapedectomy for otosclerosis.
   b. Tympanoplasty and ossiculoplasty, in which the tympanic membrane and the middle ear structure are reconstructed.
   c. Myringoplasty—as above, but no middle ear restructuring takes place.
   d. Tympanotomy, in which the middle ear is opened and the middle ear cavity inspected (for cases of conductive deafness where there is an intact tympanic membrane, i.e. otosclerosis).
2. Infection.
   a. Removal of diseased material from the middle ear.
   b. To create a dry (safe) ear in cases of chronic suppurative otitis media.

Mastoidectomy

1. Cortical (or simple).

a. For localized infection in the mastoid antrum or surrounding air cells.

b. The aim is to remove the infected tissues in the mastoid bone without interfering with the sound-conducting mechanism further forward in the middle ear.

2. Radical mastoidectomy, in cases where there is a colesteatoma or where chronic infection involves the attic as well as the antrum. The disease will continue to cause damage in the attic region and the ossicles will be damaged irrevocably by disease. The ossicles and tympanic membrane are removed (except the stapes).

3. Modified radical mastoidectomy. In some cases the attic may be involved by disease, with parts of the ossicles and tympanic membrane remaining normal. These healthy remnants are left in place in order to maintain hearing after the operations.

PROBLEMS OF THE MIDDLE EAR

The middle ear contains the eardrum and ossicles and is vital to the function of hearing. The eustachian tube connects the postnasal space to the middle ear and allows equal air pressure to be maintained on either side of the eardrum. The tube, which is normally closed, opens by the action of the muscles of the palate on yawning or swallowing. At the base of the tube sits the adenoid pads. It is easy for the tube to become inflamed and it then offers an easy passage for infection into the middle ear.

Complications of Middle Ear Infection

Intracranial Infection
Infection can spread into the skull cavity occupied by the brain. If the membranous coverings of the brain (the meninges) are involved, the patient will develop meningitis. If the brain itself is involved then a brain abscess will occur either in the cerebellum or in the temporal lobe. Large veins pass through the cranial cavity and the lateral sinus. The largest lies very close to the mastoid bone and adjacent infection causes the vein to thrombose with consequent thrombonoplebitis.

Facial Paralysis
The facial nerve, encased in a covering of bone, passes through the middle ear. If the bony covering is eroded by a cholesteatoma then the nerve is damaged and the face becomes paralyzed on that side.

Extensions Into the Inner Ear
The nearest part of the inner ear to the attic is the lateral semicircular canal, and it is this structure that is most commonly affected by an eroding cholesteatoma, resulting in a condition known as labyrinthitis.

There are three approaches that can be taken when performing ear surgery (Figure 30.8):

1. Postauricular approach—from behind the pinna.
2. Endaural approach—in front of the pinna.
3. Transcanal approach—via the external auditory meatus.

Trauma to the Tympanic Membrane (Perforation)

Permanent perforation of the tympanic membrane occurs most frequently as a result of road traffic accidents resulting in skull fracture. The next most frequent cause is infection; perforations of the eardrum membrane that fail to heal are often the end result of acute or chronic suppurative otitis media. Traumatic damage may also result from the blast effects of high explosives or from intense compression caused by a severe blow on the ear, which can rupture the eardrum.

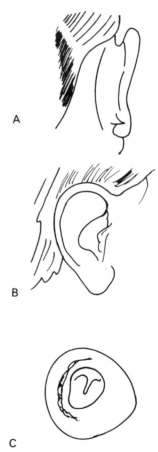

Figure 30.8 Surgical approaches for ear surgery. (A) Postauricular. (B) Endaural. (C) Transcanal. (J. Duncan.)

Less frequently, perforation is caused by foreign objects, water, burns of the face that include the external ear and the eardrum membrane, postmyringotomy defects, scuba diving and accidental or deliberate blows to the face. Perforations may also occur when cotton buds are used to clean ears. A bud may be inserted into the external ear, and the applicator pushed deeper into the ear, or the tip may be bumped and pushed into the canal. In either case, this may result in severe destruction of the eardrum, ossicles and even the inner ear. *Thus, all attempts to clean the ear with cotton buds should be discouraged.*

Most accidental perforations of the eardrum membrane heal spontaneously. Some persist because of the growth of scar tissue over the edges of the perforation, thus preventing extension of the epithelial areas across the margins and final healing.

Acute Otitis Media (Infection of the Middle Ear)

Acute otitis media is an acute infection (or abscess) of the middle ear (Table 30.4). The essential cause of acute otitis media is the entrance of pathogenic bacteria into the normally sterile middle ear when the patient's resistance is lowered or when the virulence of the organism is great enough to produce inflammation. Bacteria commonly found, in the order of importance, are *Streptococcus pneumoniae*, *Staphylococcus* and *Haemophilus influenzae*. The mode of entry of the bacteria in most patients is spread by way of the auditory canal or the eustachian tube.

Clinical Features
The symptoms of otitis media may vary with the severity of the infection; they may be either very mild and transient or very severe and fraught with serious complications. Pain in and about the ear is the first symptom. It may be intense and is relieved after spontaneous perforation of the eardrum or after myringotomy. The patient may be pyrexial. Deafness, ear noises, headache, loss of appetite, nausea and vomiting are other symptoms.

The end results of otitis media depend on the virulence of the bacteria, the efficiency of the therapy and the resistance of the patient. With early and appropriate widespectrum antibiotic therapy, otitis media may clear with healing, and with no serious sequelae. However, the condition may become subacute, with persistent purulent discharge from the ear. In this case, healing may take place but with permanent deafness.

Perforation as the result of rupture of the eardrum may persist and develop into a chronic form of otitis media. Secondary complications, with involvement of the mastoid and other serious intracranial complications, such as meningitis or brain abscess, may result.

Chronic Otitis Media

Chronic otitis media results from repeated attacks of otitis media causing persistent perforation of the eardrum. It is due to particular virulence of the infecting organisms or to bacterial resistance to antibiotic therapy. The chronically infected ear is characterized by persistent or recurrent purulent discharge, with or without pain, and varying degrees of deafness, usually conductive or mixed. Most chronic otitis media begins in childhood and may persist to adult life.

Classification
Chronic suppurative middle ear infection has been classified into five groupings, as indicated in Table 30.5.

Table 30.4 *Clinical features of acute diffuse external otitis and acute otitis media*

Feature	Otitis externa	Otitis media
Pain	Persistent	Subsides in 6 to 9 hours
	Aggravated by moving jaw	Relieved immediately if tympanic membrane ruptures
		Aggravated by swallowing, belching
Tenderness	Prominent	Absent
Systemic symptoms	Usually absent	Fever, rhinitis, sore throat
Hearing loss	Conductive type	Conductive type
Swelling of ear canal	Prominent	Absent
Discharge	Foul odour; blue pus, never profuse	No odour
Tympanic membrane	Inflamed but intact; no middle ear fluid	May be perforated; fluid in middle ear

(Reprinted from Farmer, H. S. (1980). A guide for the treatment of external otitis, American Family Physician, June, Vol. 21, No. 6, p. 98, published by the American Academy of Family Physicians.)

Table 30.5 *Classification of chronic otitis media*

Type	Specific condition	Involvement	Features
I	Chronic otitis media simplex	Central perforation of the tympanic membrane	Mucoid serous discharge
II	Chronic otitis media with cholesteatoma*	Usually, attic perforation (posterior superior part of eardrum) With or without perforation	Usually odorous discharge
III	Chronic adhesive otitis media	Marked retraction of tympanic membrane	No discharge; marked hearing loss
IV	Chronic otitis media with tympanosclerosis	Tympanosclerosis, a degenerative process in eardrum and middle ear Plaque of amorphous connective tissue	Severe hearing loss; no discharge
V	Chronic serous otitis media	If untreated or neglected, may result in severe deafness, chronic adhesive otitis media, cholesteatoma* or tympanosclerosis	Repeated bout of serous or fluid ear

*Cholesteatoma is due to the ingrowth of the skin of the external ear canal (squamous epithelium) into the middle ear. The skin from the external canal forms the outer sac, which fills with degenerated skin and sebaceous material. The sac is attached to the structures of the middle ear and mastoid, and produces changes by pressure necrosis. (Woodrow D. Schlesser, MD, personal communication.)

Clinical Features

The symptoms of chronic otitis media may be minimal, with varying degrees of deafness and the presence of a persistent or intermittent foul-smelling discharge of variable quantity. Pain may or may not be present. Symptoms such as sudden facial paralysis, unusually profound deafness or dizziness, onset of headache with dizziness and stiff neck may herald the beginning of meningitis or brain abscess, or erosion into the semicircular canals. The diagnosis is corroborated by the physical findings but, in addition, X-ray films of the mastoid usually show pathological changes.

Local treatment consists of: (1) careful cleansing of the ear; (2) instillation of antibiotic drops or application of antibiotic powder; and (3) X-ray study. Tympanoplastic procedures may be required early to prevent further damage to hearing and more serious complications.

Mastoiditis and Mastoidectomy

Mastoiditis is an inflammation of the mastoid resulting from an infection of the middle ear; if it is untreated, osteomyelitis may occur. Symptoms are pain and tenderness behind the ear, discharge from the middle ear and swelling of the mastoid. Usually this is treated successfully with antibiotics and occasionally myringotomy.

When there is recurrent or persistent tenderness, fever, headache and discharge from the ear, it may be necessary to remove the mastoid process (mastoidectomy).

Preoperative Care

Aside from general preoperative preparation of the patient, the postauricular or endaural (whichever is selected as the incision site) is cleansed thoroughly. To keep hair out of the operative field, water-soluble jelly may be applied to the hairline in the operating theatre, or a commercially available plastic cape with a small, central hole to expose the operative site may be used. (The edge of the hole adheres to the skin with adhesive.)

During the operation, the infection is removed completely from the mastoid process by removing the mastoid cells, and the middle ear is drained (myringotomy), thus preventing spread of infection to surrounding structures. The middle ear can be saved from further damage, and possible permanent hearing loss can be prevented.

Postoperative Care

The patient returns to the ward with a pressure bandage *in situ* over the ear and around the head (Figure 30.9). This is removed in 48 hours and a smaller dressing applied. The patient is nursed flat, lying on the unoperated side. Some centres recommend nursing patients after mastoid surgery with the affected ear down to allow drainage of the cavity. There is a pack in the ear canal.

Tympanoplasty

Tympanoplasty denotes a number of reconstructive operations on middle ear structures that have become diseased

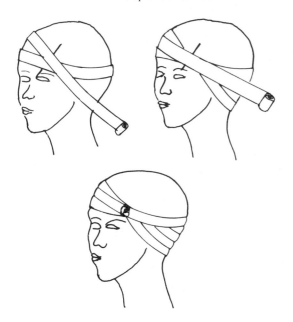

Figure 30.9 Application of a pressure bandage (from Serra, Bailey and Jackson, 1986).

or are congenitally deformed (Table 30.6). Using an operative microscope, the otologist is able to visualize and reconstruct defective conductive mechanisms to maintain or improve hearing. Chemotherapy or antibiotics maintain an infection-free area so that healing is promoted.

Tympanoplasty, Type I (Myringoplasty)

Myringoplasty is a plastic surgical procedure designed to close perforations of the tympanic membrane. The operation has dual goals: (1) to create a closed middle ear

cavity by graft over the perforation and (2) to improve hearing.

The most important advantage of the closed tympanic membrane is the avoidance of the risk of contamination of the middle ear during bathing, swimming or diving. Thus the reactivation of a chronic otitis media or mastoiditis may be prevented. Dramatic improvement in hearing may result from closure of a perforation if there is no involvement of the ossicles. Improvement can be tested by comparing pre- and postoperative audiometry.

During the surgical repair of a perforation, a careful inspection of middle ear contents, with particular attention to the continuity of the ossicles, is important.

Contraindications

Medical or surgical closure of perforations of the eardrum in the presence of an active infection is usually contraindicated. Surgery is also contraindicated in chronic disease of the middle ear with malfunction of the auditory canal (eustachian tube), and therefore inadequate drainage from the middle ear (the only avenue for egress of discharges). Involvement of the nasopharynx because of chronic infectious discharge from sinusitis or allergy, plus a history of acute exacerbations of otitis media, is an obvious contraindication.

Tympanoplasty, Types II to V and Modified Versions

Tympanoplasty may be done by various techniques. Either the postauricular or the endaural approach is used. Skin grafts have been replaced by fascial grafts. The operation may be done in one or two stages. When done in two stages, the first is performed to clear the infection or remove cholesteatoma, and the second stage is directed to mechanical correction of the deficient sound transmission system. Ossicular interruption is most frequent in otitis

Table 30.6 *Tympanoplastic procedures*

Type	Damage of middle ear	Methods of repair
I	Perforated tympanic membrane with normal ossicular chain	Closure of perforation; same as myringoplasty
II	Perforation of tympanic membrane with erosion of malleus	Closure with graft against incus or remains of malleus
III	Destruction of tympanic membrane and ossicular chain *but* with intact and mobile stapes	Graft contacts normal stapes; also gives sound protection to round window
IV	Similar to type III, but head, neck and crura of stapes missing; footplate mobile	Mobile footplate left exposed; air pocket between round window and graft provides sound protection for round window
V	Similar to type IV plus fixed footplate	Fenestra in horizontal semicircular canal; graft seals off middle ear to give sound protection for round window

Reproduced by kind permission of DeWeese, D.D. and Saunders, W.H. (1982) Textbook of Otolaryngology (6th edition), C.V. Mosby, St Louis.)

media, but problems of reconstruction occur with malformations of the middle ear and ossicular dislocations due to head injuries.

Polyethylene tubing, stainless steel, wire, bone and cartilage have been used as replacements, either to use the remaining parts of the ossicles or to create a columella (lttle column) effect for the transmission of impulses from the tympanic graft to the oval window.

Patients with a lengthy history of disease may regain as much hearing as those with less protracted infections. In the patient whose otitis media has been healed and whose ear has remained dry for a lengthy period, hearing improvement may be marked after tympanoplasty. Younger patients achieve better results than older patients. The simpler the surgery, the better the chance for hearing gain; this, of course, relates directly to the functional integrity of the ossicular chain and the efficiency of the newly created tympanic covering.

Continued research is being done to improve tympanoplasty procedures. In some instances, clinical failures have been due to infection, poor technique and tissue rejection of graft or prosthesis.

Otosclerosis

Otosclerosis is the term applied to a form of progressive deafness caused by the formation of new, abnormal, spongy bone in the labyrinth that eventually locks the stapes in a fixed position (clinical otosclerosis) and prevents sound transmission because the stapes is unable to vibrate and carry the stimulus of the vibrating malleus and incus to the inner ear fluids.

The cause of the condition is unknown, but it occurs most commonly in women, beginning after puberty, and it has an hereditary basis.

The condition, which involves both ears, but unequally, begins with insidious loss of hearing and a ringing or buzzing. The patient gives a history of slowly progressive hearing loss without middle ear infection. Sound transmission by air as tested with a tuning fork is markedly reduced, while intensification of sound is noted by placing the tuning-fork handle over the mastoid and recording the marked difference in hearing between air and bone. The bone conduction is far better than air conduction, which is the reverse of normal. Of all the tests, the diagnosis is evident from the findings of audiometry.

Stapedectomy

There is no known medical treatment for this form of deafness other than the help offered by amplification with an electric hearing aid or, preferably, a stapedectomy. A stapedectomy involves removing the otosclerotic lesion at the footplate of the stapes and creating a suitable implant with a prosthesis to replace this portion of the conductive mechanism.

▶ **THE PATIENT UNDERGOING EAR SURGERY**

▶ *Assessment*

A thorough nursing history should reveal a subjective description of the ear problem. This should include whether the patient has had pain, discharge and a noticeable hearing loss. The ear should be inspected for scarring, which might indicate previous surgery, and any abnormalities or discolouring or swelling of the auricle. Internal inspection with the otoscope looks for redness, swelling, lesions and discharge. The assessment of the patient should take into account the whole of the patient's medical history and not focus solely on the ear. It is useful to compare the good ear with the bad ear. A nursing care plan can be drawn up after assessing the patient (see Nursing Care Plan 30.1).

PROBLEMS OF THE INNER EAR

Body balance is maintained by the co-operation of muscles, joints, tendons, visceral senses, eyes and inner ear or vestibular apparatus. The last is the most important in this function. The inner apparatus of the ear provides feedback regarding the movements and the position of the head in space, co-ordinates all body muscles and positions the eyes during rapid motion or head movement.

The vestibular apparatus consists of the utricle, the saccule and the semicircular canals, of which there are three in each ear. Each canal lies in a plane at right angles to the others, with the entire apparatus grouped in working pairs for this complex function. The mechanism of action of the semicircular canals may be likened to the cochlea or organ of hearing. Here, also, fluids are set in motion by head or body movement, which in turn stimulate extremely delicate nerve fibres that transmit messages as electrical impulses along the nerve to centres in the brain, where they are interpreted.

Motion Sickness

Motion sickness is a disturbance of equilibrium caused by constant motion, such as occurs aboard a ship or boat, riding on a merry-go-round or swing, or even riding a distance in the back seat of a car. Symptoms are dizziness, nausea and, frequently, vomiting. These features may persist several hours after the stimulation stops.

Endolymphatic Hydrops (Menière's Disease)

Menière's disease is an inner ear problem stemming from

▶ NURSING CARE PLAN 30.1

This is a comprehensive care plan that can be applied to ear surgery in general, i.e. it is not specific.

Patient's problems	Expected outcomes	Nursing care	Rationale
1. Patient may feel anxious about hospital admission; communication may be difficult if patient is deaf	Patient will feel more relaxed in the hospital setting; deaf patients will not feel isolated	1a. Explanation – identify cause for anxiety at interview b. Provide information about ward routine, geography c. Establish communication with deaf patient – reassure patient that hearing aid may be worn up to theatre d. Provide information about pre- and postoperative events	Information hastens postoperative recovery
2. Busy surgical ward with many admissions; patient will not know correct procedure for preoperative preparation; some important aspect of preparation may be forgotten	Safe preparation for all patients preoperatively	2a. Explanation to patient of pre- and postoperative events b. Ensure patient notes/X-ray/ECG are on ward c. Ensure identity band *in situ* d. Ensure patient had preoperative audio in last 6 weeks e. Ensure patient has ECG and chest X-ray if aged over 50 and has had previous history of heart disease f. Ensure doctor sees and examines patient g. Ensure consent form is signed	Patient is at risk from misidentification
3. Patient may fail to disclose information, which may directly affect postoperative recovery	All relevant information is recorded by nurse on anaesthetic chart	3a. Establish if patient has any allergies to drugs, premedication, anaesthetic b. Ensure patient has no allergies to packing c. Ensure patient has no allergies to tape d. Establish if patient wears dentures or has loose, crowned or capped teeth e. Establish if patient wears contact lenses f. Ask patient to remove nail varnish if worn	Patient does not have any adverse reaction due to surgical intervention
4. Patient is at risk of postoperative infection	To detect signs of infection preoperatively	4a. Routine urinalysis b. Temperature recorded; if pyrexial with pain or discharge from ear, report c. If patient has previous history of heart conditions contact physiotherapist	Signs of infection will be anticipated and appropriate nursing action taken
5. Potential respiratory failure due to incomplete reversal of anaesthesia	Patient will not have breathing problems postoperatively	5a. Observation of respiration and adapt as condition dictates b. Observation for signs of cyanosis – finger beds, around nose	There is a high risk of airway obstruction due to general anaesthesia
6. Potential chest infection due to immobility as patient is nursed flat for 12 to 24 hours postoperatively	Patient will not get chest infection	6a. Record temperature four-hourly; report if elevated b. Give analgesia c. Encourage deep breathing d. Note rate and sound of respirations	Chest infection is anticipated and prevented or treated

▶

► NURSING CARE PLAN 30.1

Patient's problems	Expected outcomes	Nursing care	Rationale
7. Potential risk of disorientation in the immediate postoperative period especially, due to reduced hearing because of ear pack and patient bandage	To prevent disorientation that may endanger patient	7a. Orientate patient to ward and time, explain operation is over b. Keep patient informed as to postoperative events, i.e. explain observations, bandage	Information will orientate patient
8. Potential undetected haemorrhage will lead to circulatory collapse and cardiac arrest	To detect haemorrhage	8a. Constant observation of wound and pressure dressing if bleeding marked b. Observation of face; check facial nerve; ask patient to grimace; look for asymmetry c. Monitor pulse and blood pressure rate, particularly rise in pulse, fall in blood pressure; report	Pressure on facial nerve may indicate bleeding. Patient is at risk of bleeding after surgical intervention
9. Potential risk of shock due to haemorrhage or hypotensive anaesthesia	To detect signs of shock	9a. As for haemorrhage b. Be aware of low blood pressure after hypotensive anaesthesia; do not confuse it with haemorrhage	Patient having ear surgery has hypotensive anaesthesia to reduce bleeding to give clear surgical field
10. Potential risk of undetected facial palsy due to damage to VII nerve	Facial nerve will be intact and functioning	10a. Assess VII function one-hourly for 8 hours; ask patient to grimace; look for signs of asymmetry; report b. Ensure pressure bandage not too tight c. As for haemorrhage (see problem 8)	VII nerve runs through middle ear and is easily cut at surgery
11. Potential risk of dislodging prosthesis if surgery has been reconstructive in nature	Patient will not dislodge prosthesis	11a. Nurse patient flat or with affected ear uppermost b. Discourage violent movements or mobilizing until next day c. Give antiemetics to prevent retching and vomiting; monitor effectiveness d. Give analgesics	Prosthesis very fragile; needs approximately two weeks to settle in ear
12. Potential risk of deep vein thrombosis due to immobility (patient may be female on contraceptive pill)	To prevent deep vein thrombosis	12a. Bed stockings will be worn until mobile b. Four-hourly temperature recorded; inform doctor if patient is pyrexial and not due to infection and complaining of pain in calf, which feels hot c. Encourage passive and active leg movements while in bed	Patient on bedrest is prone to deep vein thrombosis in legs; contraceptive pill increases blood viscosity
13. Potential risk of nausea, vomiting and vertigo due to anaesthesia and proximity of surgery to inner ear	To prevent nausea and vomiting	13a. Give antiemetics postoperatively 6 to 8 hourly as prescribed b. Discourage from mobilizing for the first 12 to 24 hours	Inner ear surgery increases the risk of vomiting and vertigo

► NURSING CARE PLAN 30.1

Patient's problems	Expected outcomes	Nursing care	Rationale
		c. Position patient comfortably with operated ear uppermost d. Commence oral fluids and light diet as tolerated	
14. Potential risk of taste disturbance due to affected branch of facial nerve (chorda tympani) which supplies anterior two thirds of tongue	Inform patient of this phenomenon to allay anxiety	14a. Tell patient food may taste slightly metallic b. Encourage use of condiments on food c. Assure patient this is only temporary	Surgery of facial nerve can cause disturbances further along nerve
15. Potential risk of urinary retention due to anaesthesia; difficulty in passing urine due to position in bed	Patient will pass urine within 12 hours postoperatively	15a. Help patient on to bedpan or commode b. Provide privacy c. Stimulate elimination by providing sound of running water, i.e. taps d. Encourage oral fluids if not nauseous e. Record time of voiding	There is a risk of urinary retention after anaesthesia
16. Patient may feel weak and lethargic in the post-operative period; may feel nauseous and unable to perform adequate personal hygiene	Patient will be comfortable and have a clean mouth	16a. Hands and face wash; change patient into own night clothes on first postoperative night; may need to give assisted wash or blanket bath on first postoperative day	A dry, dirty mouth is uncomfortable and susceptible to infection
17. Patient has a wound that needs cleansing and dressing	Patient's wound will not become infected	17a. Pressure bandage is removed in 48 hours; ear is cleaned and dressed aseptically; ear dressing applied	Asepsis is maintained
18. Potential risk of skin damage due to pressure bandage	To prevent skin damage	18a. Ensure pressure bandage not too tight; should be able to get one finger under it easily b. Observe eye for puffiness or swelling c. Observe for signs of pressure on the facial nerve (see problem 10)	Haematoma will occur if pressure bandage too loose; pressure sore will occur if too tight; also eye swelling
19. Patient's ordinary routine and relationships are disrupted on admission to hospital; may be experiencing pain, which will further disrupt normal living activities; may be unable to sleep in hospital	To prevent pain and promote sleep	19a. Give analgesia when required as per regime or when patient says it is needed b. Position patient comfortably with head supported and affected ear uppermost c. Encourage visitors but initially discourage long visits d. Give night sedation if sleep is difficult e. Give advice on discharge and while in hospital about resuming normal activities and work	Patient makes good recovery and is prepared for discharge

a labyrinthine dysfunction, the cause of which has not been definitely established. Many theories have been advanced, such as abnormal hormonal and neurochemical influences on the blood flow to the labyrinth, electrolyte disturbance within labyrinthine fluids or an allergic reaction. Some attribute impairment of the microvasculature of the inner ear to abnormal metabolites (sugar, insulin, triglycerides and cholesterol) in the bloodstream.

Clinical Features

Menière's disease is most frequently characterized by the presence of a triad of symptoms: paroxysmal whirling vertigo (with nausea and vomiting), tinnitus and neurosensory hearing loss. Some add a fourth feature, that of a sense of pressure in the ear. At the onset of the condition, perhaps only one or two of these symptoms are manifested; however, the disease is not diagnosed as Menière's syndrome until all three signs are present (Figure 30.10).

Vertigo, the outstanding symptom of Menière's disease, occurs as a sudden attack, appearing at irregular intervals and possibly persisting for several hours. Early in this condition, weeks or months pass between attacks, but the time is gradually reduced so that they may be experienced every two to three days. Usually only one ear is involved. Nystagmus and ataxia may also be present. Tinnitus is characteristically a low, fluctuating, buzzing sound in the ears. It is often louder preceding and during an attack. Sensorineural loss applies to low tones and usually occurs in only one ear. It gets progressively worse and may cause severe cochlear damage if untreated.

Diagnosis

Because Menière's disease simulates the signs and symptoms of acoustic neuroma and other cerebellopontine angle tumours, careful diagnostic evaluation is required, including an audiogram, head scan and allergy evaluation. Early in the condition, patients are evaluated for glucose tolerance and for abnormal insulin levels. If results are abnormal, these patients are regarded as prediabetic and are managed by a controlled-carbohydrate weight reduction diet.

Electronystagmography is the preferred test; it measures the electropotential of the eye movements when nystagmus is produced and provides a graphic record of labyrinthine function.

Nursing Care and Medical Management

The goals of treatment are to eliminate vertigo and improve or stabilize the patient's hearing. This is accomplished by a combination of methods done early in the disease in order to avoid severe hearing loss. For an acute attack, the patient is permitted to assume whatever position is most comfortable. Usually, an intravenous line is started to permit the administration of medications and fluids. Vital signs and the patient's condition are monitored. Oral antivertiginous drugs may be prescribed.

Three quarters of the patients respond to the treatment of a salt-free diet and a diuretic. If there is an immediate favourable reaction to this regime, it is continued for two or three months before the amount of diuretic (urea) is

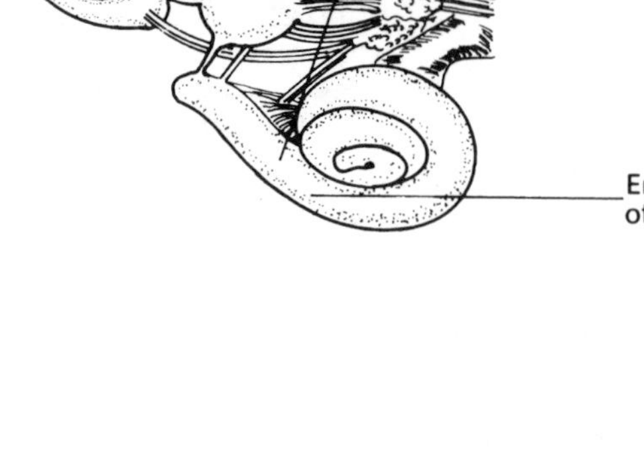

TYPE	SYMPTOMS AND SIGNS
Endolymphatic hydrops of the vestibular variety	• dizziness only episodic • reduced vestibular response or total lack of response in affected ear • no cochlear symptoms • no objective hearing loss • may eventually develop cochlear symptoms and signs
True endolymphatic hydrops	Clinical triad of typical Menière's disease present 1. Episodic vertigo 2. Fluctuating neurosensory hearing loss 3. Tinnitus
Endolymphatic hydrops of the cochlear variety	Symptoms and signs confined to cochlear portion of labyrinth • fluctuating hearing loss • sense of fullness in ear • tinnitus • neurosensory hearing loss demonstrated on testing • no dizziness • normal vestibular labyrinthine tests • may eventually develop vestibular symptoms and signs

Figure 30.10 A practical classification of Menière's disease.

gradually decreased. However, the patient never returns to the full use of salt. Food allergy is investigated and may require that certain elements be eliminated from the diet.

Surgical Management

A variety of medical and surgical treatments exist for Menière's disease, one of which may give a particular patient the needed relief. Research continues in an effort to find the cause of this syndrome, which will more clearly suggest definitive therapy.

An endolymphatic subarachnoid shunt is a procedure favoured by many otolaryngologists. The procedure is successful in two thirds of patients in providing relief without destroying function. It involves decompressing the endolymphatic sac and sectioning the vestibular nerve.

An endolymphatic system–mastoid shunt with valve implant is an alternative procedure carried out instead of a destructive labyrinthectomy. This type of surgery was first done in 1975 in Sweden, and in 1976 in the United States. Results appear more promising for those patients having early surgery before the endolymphatic sac is obliterated by the disease process.

Total labyrinthectomy (destruction of the membranous labyrinth—inner ear) is probably the most helpful technique when medical management fails (in 10 to 20 per cent of patients), and the patient has had progressive hearing loss and experiences severe vertigo attacks (increased loss of hearing, loss of nerve response and poor discrimination). This is done through the ear canal in the same manner as a stapedectomy. The stapes is removed and the endolabyrinth is aspirated with suction. The inner ear is packed with a pack impregnated in an ototoxic drug such as streptomycin to ensure the destruction of the labyrinth.

Cochlear Implant

A cochlear implant is an auditory prosthesis used for people who are profoundly deaf and designated as untreatable by other methods.

The process includes an otological history, physical examination and audiological assessment. A determination is made as to whether the patient would do better with properly fitted powerful hearing aids or the cochlear implant. Some patients do best when a hearing aid is used in the ear with the least impairment and with the implant in the other ear.

The surgical procedure involves a mastoidectomy and the opening of the facial recess to permit access for the placement of the electrode into the scala tympani of the cochlea. Surgery takes about one and a half hours; after

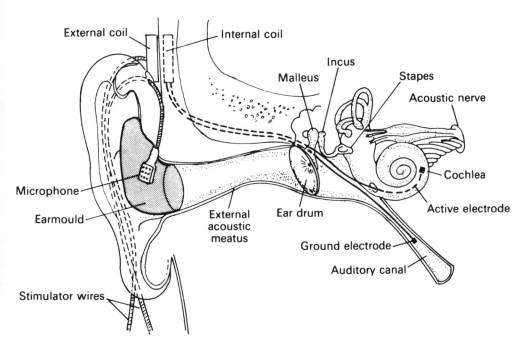

Figure 30.11 The cochlear implant. The internal coil has a stranded electrode lead. The electrode is inserted through the round window into the scala tympani of the cochlea. The external coil (the transmitter) is held in alignment with the internal coil (the receiver) by a magnet. The microphone receives the sound. The stimulator wire receives the signal after it has been filtered, adjusted and modified so that the sound is at a comfortable level for the patient. Sound is passed by the external transmitter to the inner coil receiver by magnetic conduction and is then carried by the electrode to the cochlea.

two months of recuperation, the patient is fitted with the external portion of the device. The patient carries the signal processor, approximately the size of a small cigarette package (9×5×2 cm), which uses mercury batteries that last about three weeks (Figure 30.11).

During rehabilitation, the patient learns about the use and care of the implant, determines the appropriate settings for the signal processor and attends an auditory training programme. These sessions are an important part of the whole process to ensure that the implant is used and that the person has made progress in differentiating sounds. Although clearly spoken word sounds will not be heard, the patient is able to differentiate between one kind of sound and another—such as the difference between the doorbell and the telephone.

Continued development of this device, the input of patients who are using it and the dedication of researchers will undoubtedly lead to greater advancements in this facet of care.

FURTHER READING

Books

Colman, M.B., Hall and Simpson, I. (1981) *Diseases of the Nose, Throat and Ear* (12th edition), Churchill Livingstone, Edinburgh.

Department of Health and Social Security (1988) *Say It Again* (report of an inspection of contemporary social work practice with people who are deaf or hard of hearing), DHSS, London.

McNaught and Callander (1976) *Illustrated Physiology* (3rd edition), Churchill Livingstone, Edinburgh.

Serra, A. M., Bailey, C. M. and Jackson, P. (1986) *Ear, Nose and Throat Nursing*, Blackwell Scientific Publications, Oxford.

chapter 31

ASSESSMENT OF NEUROLOGICAL FUNCTION

PHYSIOLOGICAL OVERVIEW

The nervous system consists of the brain, the spinal cord and the peripheral nerves. Its function is to control and to co-ordinate cellular activities throughout the body. It controls these activities through the transmission of electrical impulses. These impulses are routed by way of nerve fibres and nerve pathways that are direct and continuous. The responses elicited are practically instantaneous because changes in electrical potential transmit the signals.

The Brain

The brain is divided into the cerebrum, brain stem and cerebellum. It is enclosed in a rigid, bony box—the skull, or cranium. At the base of this box is the foramen magnum, an opening through which the spinal cord forms a continuous connection with the brain (Figure 31.1). The brain has three coverings: (1) the dura, the outer covering of dense fibrous tissue that closely hugs the inner wall of the skull; (2) the arachnoid, a very delicate membrane beneath the dura mater; and (3) the pia mater, a layer of delicate connective tissue that adheres closely to the brain and the spinal cord.

The brain stem from the top down consists of the midbrain, the pons and the medulla oblongata.

The cerebrum is divided into two hemispheres and consists of four lobes: frontal, parietal, temporal and occipital (Figure 31.2). The cerebrum is the largest part of the brain. On its surface, or cortex, are located the 'centres' from which motor impulses are carried to the muscles and to which sensory impulses come from the various sensory nerves.

The midbrain connects the pons and the cerebellum with the cerebral hemispheres. The cerebellum is located below and behind the cerebrum. Its function is the control or the co-ordination of muscles and equilibrium.

The pons is situated in front of the cerebellum between the midbrain and the medulla and is a bridge between the

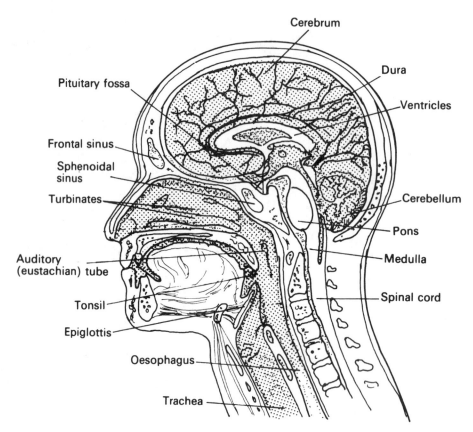

Figure 31.1 Cross-sectional view showing the anatomical position and the relation of structures of the head and the neck.

two halves of the cerebellum as well as between the medulla and the cerebrum.

The medulla oblongata transmits motor fibres from the brain to the spinal cord and sensory fibres from the spinal cord to the brain. The majority of these fibres cross, or decussate, at this level. The pons also contains important centres controlling heart, respiration and blood pressure and is the site of origin of the fifth, sixth, seventh and eighth cranial nerves.

There are two glands present in the brain: the pituitary and the pineal. The pituitary gland lies at the base of the brain in a bony fossa termed the sella turcica, just posterior to the optic chiasma, on which it may press when the gland is enlarged.

Cerebral Cortex

Although the cells in the cerebral cortex are quite similar in appearance, their functions vary widely, depending on their geographical location. The topography of the cortex in relation to certain of its specific functions is shown in Figure 31.2. The posterior portion of each hemisphere (i.e., the occipital lobe) is devoted to all aspects of visual perception. The lateral region, or temporal lobe, incorporates the auditory centre. The postcentral gyrus, pos-

terior to the central sulcus, is concerned with sensation; the precentral gyrus is concerned with voluntary muscle movements. The large, uncharted area beneath the forehead (i.e., the frontal lobes) contains the association pathways that determine emotional attitudes and responses and contribute to the formation of thought processes. Damage to the frontal lobes as a result of trauma or disease is by no means incapacitating from the standpoint of muscular control or co-ordination but has a decided effect on the person's personality, as reflected by basic attitudes, sense of humour and propriety, self-restraint and motivations.

Internal Capsule, Pons and Medulla

Nerve fibres from all portions of the cortex converge in each hemisphere and make their exit in the form of tight bundles known as the 'internal capsule'. Having entered the pons and the medulla, each bundle crosses the corresponding bundle from the opposite side. Some of these axons make connections with axons from the cerebellum, basal ganglia, thalamus and hypothalamus; some connect with the cranial nerve cells. Other fibres from the cortex and the subcortical centres are channelled through the pons and the medulla into the spinal cord.

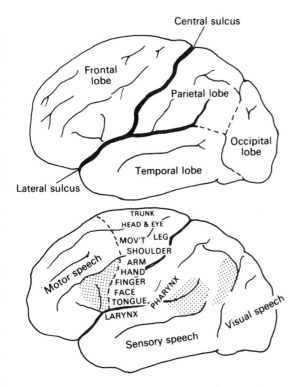

Figure 31.2 (Top) Diagrammatic representation of the cerebrum, showing relative locations of various lobes of the brain and the principal sulci. (Bottom) Diagrammatic representation of cerebral localization for motor movements of various portions of the body.

The Spinal Cord and Its Connections

The spinal cord, a direct continuation of the medulla oblongata, is that part of the nervous system contained within the vertebral column (Figure 31.3). It is a cord about 45 cm long and approximately the thickness of a finger, extending from the foramen magnum of the skull, where it is continuous with the medulla oblongata, to the first lumbar vertebra, where it tapers off into a fine thread of tissue. The spinal cord is an important centre of reflex action for the body and contains the conducting pathways to and from the higher centres in the cord and the brain. Like the brain, it consists of grey and white matter, but, although in the brain the grey matter is external and the white internal, in the cord the grey matter is in the centre and is surrounded on all sides by the white fibres, both those of sensory tracts running up to the brain and those of motor fibres coming down from the brain.

Grey Matter

The grey matter is shaped like two pairs of horns, the anterior horn and the posterior horn. The cord gives off 31 pairs of spinal nerves. Each is formed by the union of two roots, an anterior or motor root and a posterior or sensory

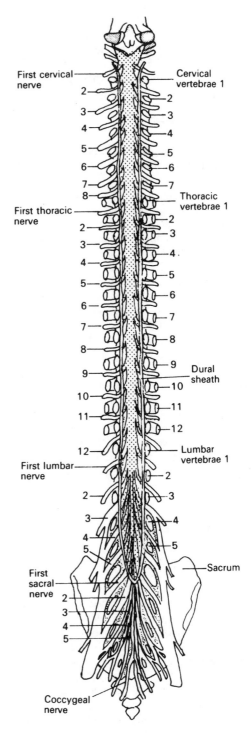

Figure 31.3 Spinal cord lying within the vertebral canal; spinous processes and laminae have been removed; dura and arachnoid have been opened. Spinal nerves are numbered on the left side; vertebrae are numbered on the right side. (Chaffee, E. E. and Greisheimer, E. M. (1980) *Basic Physiology and Anatomy* (4th edition), J. B. Lippincott, Philadelphia.)

root on which is the sensory ganglion. These two roots unite to form one spinal nerve. As a result, all the spinal nerves are mixed. Those leaving the right side of the cord supply the muscles, the skin and the organs on the right side of the body; those of the left side supply the corresponding muscles on that side of the body.

Cerebrospinal Fluid

Within each cerebral hemisphere is a central cavity, the lateral ventricle, which is filled with clear cerebrospinal fluid. This fluid is extracted from the blood as it circulates through the capillaries of the choroid plexus. It then passes through well-defined channels from the lateral ventricles through narrow, tubular openings to the third and the fourth ventricles. From this narrow cavity it escapes to the subarachnoid space to bathe the entire surface of the brain and the spinal cord. The cerebrospinal fluid normally is absorbed by the large venous channels of the skull and along the spinal and the cranial nerves.

Cerebrospinal fluid is clear and colourless and has a specific gravity of 1.007. The average patient's ventricular and subarachnoid systems contain about 150 ml of this fluid. The organic and inorganic contents of the cerebrospinal fluid are very similar to that of the plasma; however, their concentration is somewhat different.

Disease produces changes in the composition of the cerebrospinal fluid. Determinations of the protein content and the quantity of glucose and chloride present constitute the chief chemical examinations. In a state of health, there are a minimal number of white cells and no red cells in the spinal fluid. Cerebrospinal fluid is also tested for immunoglobulins.

ALTERED PHYSIOLOGY

Vision and Cortical Blindness

There is a definite area in the rear of each hemisphere where the fibres of the corresponding optic nerve end. It is by means of these receiving cells that vision is possible. The eyes may be normal and the optic nerve perfect, but if these cells in one hemisphere are diseased, the person is half-blind and has cortical blindness. This person cannot see to one side of the midline; only half of any object can be seen. This is known as hemianopia (half-blindness).

Cortical blindness of one optic area (i.e., of the posterior tip of one cerebral hemisphere) always affects both eyes equally. Total blindness in one may be due to disease of that eye itself or to disease of its optic nerve. Just behind the two eyes, however, the two optic nerves become confluent (the chiasma), then again become separate and continue to the brain as two optic tracts.

In each of these tracts is just half of each optic nerve, so that if one tract is injured, there is blindness of exactly one half of each retina. For example, if the right tract is injured, the patient is blind on the right half of each retina, so that with either eye the patient can see nothing to the left but will see perfectly to the right. If the cortical optical area of the hemisphere to which that tract runs is destroyed, this same form of hemianopia occurs.

The pituitary gland is located just beneath the chiasma; a tumour of this gland often disturbs the chiasma and produces blindness of both inner halves of the retinas, since it is only the fibres in the nasal halves of the optic nerves that cross. In many cases of blindness, it is thus possible to locate the disorder.

Motor Controls: Paralysis and Dyskinesia

A vertical band of cortex on each cerebral hemisphere governs the voluntary movements of the body. This region, known as the 'motor cortex', can be located accurately.

The exact location is known of the cells in which originate the voluntary movements of the muscles of the face, the thumb, the hand, the arm, the trunk or the leg. Before a person can move a muscle, these particular cells must send the stimulus down along their fibres. If these cells are stimulated with an electric current, the muscles they control will contract.

En route to the pons, the motor fibres converge into a tight bundle known as the capsule. A comparatively small injury to the capsule causes paralysis in more muscles than does a much larger injury to the cortex itself.

The brain is like a telephone exchange, in which one blow of an axe can sever all the wires at the point where they leave the building, but a similar blow on the switchboard would sever only a few.

The ordinary cause of a stroke, followed by paralysis of one half of the body (hemiplegia), is usually a small haemorrhage from a blood vessel in the capsule. A much larger haemorrhage nearer to or in the cortex might paralyze one extremity, but hardly half of the body. Hemiplegia may be due to the rupture of a microaneurysm of a tiny artery running to the internal capsule or to the plugging of this artery by a thrombus or an embolus, and the subsequent death of the fibres that it supplies with blood.

Immediately after a stroke, one half of the body, as a rule, is paralyzed. Then, gradually, the person recovers the use of certain muscles, usually those of the leg, often those of the upper arm, least often those of the hand. Although the haemorrhage actually destroys the fibres of only a few nerves, it temporarily injures all those in its surrounding area, perhaps by the pressure of the escaped blood or by the oedema. As the swelling from the haemorrhage diminishes, these latter fibres resume their function, but those actually destroyed never do.

Within the medulla, the motor axons from the cortex form two well-defined bands known as the corticospinal or pyramidal tracts. Here the majority of these fibres cross (or decussate) to the opposite side, continuing thereafter as the 'crossed pyramidal tract'. The remaining fibres then enter the spinal cord on the original side as the 'direct pyramidal tract', each fibre in this tract finally crossing to the opposite side of the cord near the point of termination and coming to an end within the grey matter comprising the anterior horn on that side, in close proximity to a motor nerve cell. Fibres of the crossed pyramidal tract terminate within the anterior horn and make connections with anterior horn cells on the same side. All of the motor fibres of the spinal nerves represent extensions of these anterior horn cells, with each of these fibres communicating with only one particular muscle fibre.

Thus, each muscle fibre is under voluntary control through a combination of two nerve cells. One is located in the motor cortex, its fibre in the direct or crossed pyramidal tract, and the other is located in the anterior horn of the spinal cord, its fibre running to the muscle. The former is referred to as the upper motor neurone; the latter, as the lower motor neurone. Every motor nerve serving a muscle is a bundle comprised of several thousand lower motor neurones.

Several motor nerve tracts, other than the corticospinal, are contained in the spinal cord. Some represent the pathways of the so-called extrapyramidal system, establishing connections between the anterior horn cells and the automatic control centres located in the basal ganglia and the cerebellum. Others are components of reflex arcs, forming synaptic connections between anterior horn cells and sensory fibres that have entered adjacent or neighbouring segments of the cord.

Motor Paralysis

Paralysis of a muscle may be due to pathological changes in either the upper or the lower motor neurone. If a motor nerve is cut somewhere between the muscle and the spinal cord, the muscle becomes paralyzed, and the person is not able to move it. Furthermore, it takes no part in reflex movements. Moreover, this muscle becomes limp and wastes away; that is, it atrophies due to disuse. The injury to the spinal nerve trunk may heal, and the patient may regain the use of the muscles that it supplies. However, if the anterior horn motor nerve cells are destroyed, the nerve cannot regenerate, and that muscle never will be useful again. This is what occurs in anterior poliomyelitis.

If the upper motor neurone is destroyed, a different condition exists in the muscle. It is paralyzed as far as voluntary movement is concerned but not necessarily for reflex (involuntary) movements, because these originate in the nerve cells in the cord or the medulla. The muscle does not atrophy, and it will not become limp; on the contrary, it remains permanently more tense than normal.

This paralysis seldom affects simply a part of one muscle, one single muscle or only a few muscles; it usually affects a whole extremity, both extremities or an entire half of the body.

A good illustration of this form of paralysis is the spastic (stiff) paralysis of those infants who during birth receive some mechanical injury that may have caused the rupture of a subdural blood vessel. The long-continued pressure of the escaped blood may injure large areas of cortex; hence, these children are frequently mentally retarded. Many have convulsions. When such a child begins to walk, the legs and the arms are stiff. During life, movements are awkward, stiff and weak. Since those muscles that draw the feet and the knees toward each other (the adductor muscles) are naturally stronger than those that spread those extremities apart (the abductor muscles), these patients walk by a cross-legged progression, called also the scissors gait; that is, in each step the leg is moved not only forward but is also swung round across the front of the other. When both legs are paralyzed, the condition is called paraplegia; and when the arm and the leg on the same side are paralyzed, the term hemiplegia is used. Paralysis of all four extremities is quadriplegia.

A common illustration of upper motor neurone paralysis is hemiplegia. If a haemorrhage, an embolus or a thrombus destroys the fibres from the motor area in the internal capsule, the arm and the leg of the opposite side promptly become stiff and more or less paralyzed, and the reflexes are exaggerated. Another illustration of upper neurone disease is seen in adults with spastic paraplegia, a chronic stiffness of both legs due to a gradual degeneration of the fibres in the pyramidal tract. The person so afflicted walks stiffly, as though wading through water, the knees always touching each other and the feet scarcely raised from the ground (the spastic gait).

Both an upper and a lower motor neurone paralysis may result from an injury that crushes the spinal cord, a type of injury that is all too common. A person diving into too-shallow water, for example, strikes the head and 'breaks' the neck. That is, at one point the vertebrae are no longer in line, and the cord is badly crushed at the point of the dislocation. Knuckling of the backbone due to tuberculosis may accomplish the same thing, only more slowly. The result of such crushing of the cord leads to a rigid paralysis on both sides of all muscles whose nerves leave the cord below the crushed spot. Flaccid paralysis also occurs in those muscles whose motor nerve fibres come from cells in the crushed area. There also will be insensibility of the skin below the crushed area, since the sensory fibres from below the injury no longer reach the brain. Tumours of the cord ultimately cause this same picture. At first, only that part of the cord directly involved is disturbed, but as the tumour grows, it may completely crush the cord.

Extrapyramidal Motor Controls

The smoothness, the accuracy and the strength that characterize the muscular movements of a normal person are attributable to the influence of the cerebellum and the basal ganglia.

The cerebellum (see Figure 31.1), nestled beneath the posterior lobe of the cerebrum, chief assistant to the higher motor centres in the cerebral cortex, is responsible for co-ordinating, balancing, timing and synergizing with precision all muscular movements that originate in those centres. Through the agency of the cerebellum, the contractions of opposing muscle groups are adjusted in relation to each other to maximal mechanical advantage; muscular contractions can be sustained evenly at the desired tension and without significant fluctuation, and reciprocal movements can be reproduced at high and constant speed, in stereotyped fashion and with relatively little effort.

The basal ganglia are masses of grey matter within the white matter of each cerebral hemisphere. These border or project into the lateral ventricles and lie in close apposition to the internal capsule. It is their function to control habitual or automatic acts and to maintain a 'postural background' against which voluntary movements are performed. These ganglia, aided by their connections with the organs of special sense, keep the contractile tone of every muscle in the trunk and the extremities in a constant state of adjustment, so that a person is able to maintain balance regardless of the posture of the body, in darkness as well as in light and irrespective of the status underfoot. Moreover, thanks to this control station, the person is equipped to react swiftly, appropriately and automatically to any smell, sight or sound that demands an immediate response.

Dyskinesias

Loss of cerebellar function, which may occur as a result of intracranial injury, haemorrhage, abscess or tumour, results in muscular flabbiness, weakness and fatigue. The patient exhibits a coarse involuntary tremor that increases in intensity in association with voluntary movements. Such a person is unable to control movements accurately or to co-ordinate the muscles efficiently or smoothly, every act being performed in disjointed fashion, according to stages, or 'by the numbers'. This patient is incapable of performing alternating movements with speed or uniformity, a characteristic of cerebellar disease called dysdiadochokinesis. When walking, the patient staggers, lurching from side to side as though intoxicated, with feet wide apart, but the steps are short and not stamping (i.e., with the vertiginous, reeling gait of cerebellar ataxia).

Destruction or dysfunction of the basal ganglia does not lead to paralysis but to muscular rigidity, with consequent disturbances of posture and movement. Such patients are afflicted by a tendency to display involuntary movements. These may take the form of coarse tremors, characterized by approximately six oscillations per second; athetosis, namely, movement of a slow, squirming, writhing, twisting type; or chorea, marked by spasmodic, purposeless and grotesque motions of the trunk and the extremities, and facial grimacing. Clinical syndromes based on lesions involving the basal ganglia include Parkinson's disease (see p. 1031).

Sensory Pathways and Disturbances

The Thalamus

The thalamus, a major receiving and communication centre for the afferent sensory nerves, is a large and complicated structure located in the midbrain. It lies in close relation to the third ventricle, forming its lateral wall, and to the lateral ventricle, forming its floor, and is in close proximity to the basal ganglia and adjacent to the internal capsule. To the thalamus may be attributed the vague awareness of sensations described as 'feelings' of pleasure, discomfort or pain. Moreover, it is responsible for the routing of all sensory stimuli to their many destinations, including the cerebral cortex, which receives them and translates them automatically into appropriate responses.

Sensory Pathways

The transmission of sensory impulses from their points of origin to their cerebral destinations involves three neurone relays; moreover, there are three major pathways by which they may be routed, depending on the type of sensation that is registered. Specific knowledge regarding these paths is of great importance from the standpoint of neurological diagnoses, being indispensable for the accurate localization of brain and cord lesions in many patients.

The axon of the nerve in which the sensory impulse originates enters the spinal cord by way of the posterior root. Axons conveying sensations of heat, cold and pain immediately enter the posterior grey column of the cord, where they make connections with the cells of secondary neurones. Pain and temperature fibres cross immediately to the opposite side of the cord and course upward to the thalamus. Fibres carrying sensations of touch, light pressure and localization do not connect immediately with the second neurone but ascend the cord for a variable distance before entering the grey matter and completing this connection. The axon of the secondary neurone crosses the cord and proceeds upward to the thalamus.

The third category of sensation, produced by stimuli arising from muscles, joints and bones, includes position sense and vibratory sense. These stimuli are conveyed, uncrossed, all the way to the brain stem by the axon of the primary neurone. In the medulla, synaptic connections are made with cells of the secondary neurones, whose axons then cross to the opposite side and proceed to the thalamus.

Sensory Losses. Severance of a sensory nerve results in total loss of sensation in its area of distribution. Transection of the spinal cord yields complete anaesthesia below the level of injury. Selective destruction or degeneration of the posterior columns of the spinal cord is responsible for a loss of position sense in segments distal to the lesion, unaccompanied by loss of touch, pain or temperature perception. Such people, unless they look, cannot tell where their feet are or in what direction they are pointing. Moreover, they cannot perceive vibrations in the affected area. A lesion, such as a cyst, in the centre of the cord causes dissociation of sensation, that is, loss of pain at the level of the lesion. This is explained by the fact that the fibres carrying pain and temperature cross the cord immediately on entering; thus, any lesion that divides the cord longitudinally divides these fibres likewise. Other sensory fibres ascend the cord for variable distances, some even to the medulla itself, before crossing, thereby bypassing the lesion and avoiding destruction.

Dysaesthesias. Irritative lesions affecting the posterior spinal nerve roots may cause intermittent severe pains that are referred to their areas of distribution. This phenomenon explains the pains of tabes dorsalis. The sensation of tingling of the fingers and the toes constitutes a prominent symptom of combined systems disease, presumably due to degenerative changes in the sensory fibres that extend to the thalamus (i.e., belonging to the spinothalamic tract).

Autonomic Nervous System

The contractions of muscles that are not under voluntary control, including the heart muscle, the secretions of all digestive and sweat glands, and the activity of certain endocrine organs as well, are controlled by a major component of the nervous system known as the autonomic nervous system. The term autonomic refers to the fact that the operations of this system are independent of the desires and the intentions of the person. It is not subject to someone's will; that is, it is in a sense autonomous.

To the extent that it is not subject to regulation by the cerebral cortex, the autonomic nervous system resembles the extrapyramidal systems that are centred in the cerebellum and the basal ganglia. However, in other respects it is unique. First, its regulatory effects are exerted not on individual cells but on large expanses of tissue and on entire organs. Second, the responses that it elicits do not appear instantaneously, but only after a lag period, and they are sustained far longer than other neurogenic responses, a type of response that is calculated to ensure maximal functional efficiency on the part of receptor organs, such as the blood vessels and the hollow viscera.

The quality of these responses is explained by the fact that the autonomic nervous system transmits its impulses only partly by way of nerve pathways, the remainder of the route being serviced by chemical mediators, resembling in this respect the endocrine system. Electrical impulses, conducted through nerve fibres, stimulate the formation of specific chemical agents at strategic locations within the muscle mass, the diffusion of these chemicals being responsible for the contraction.

The Hypothalamus

Overall supervision of the autonomic nervous system is considered to be a function of the hypothalamus. The hypothalamus is a portion of the diencephalon (interbrain) located immediately beneath and lateral to the lower portion of the wall of the third ventricle. It includes among its components the optic chiasma; the tuber cinereum; the pituitary stalk, which originates from the latter; and the pituitary gland itself. Large cell groups in adjacent portions of the hypothalamus have been assigned the role of the probable centres of autonomic regulation. These centres are richly endowed with connections linking the autonomic system with the thalamus, the cortex, the olfactory apparatus and the pituitary gland. Here reside the mechanisms for the control of visceral and somatic reactions that were designed originally for defence or attack, but in humans these are associated with emotional states (i.e., fears, anger, anxiety); for the control of metabolic processes, including fat, carbohydrate and water metabolism; for the regulation of body temperature, arterial pressure and all muscular and glandular activities of the gastrointestinal tract; for control of the genital functions; and for the sleep rhythm. The close proximity, histological similarity and multiple connections between the pituitary gland, master gland of the endocrines, and this portion of the brain suggest that here may be located the supreme headquarters of the endocrine and autonomic nervous systems, commanding all vital processes.

Sympathetic and Parasympathetic Nervous Systems

The autonomic nervous system comprises two divisions that are anatomically and functionally distinct, referred to as the sympathetic and the parasympathetic nervous systems. The majority of the tissues and the organs under autonomic control are innervated by both systems. Sympathetic stimuli are mediated by noradrenaline, and parasympathetic impulses are mediated by acetylcholine. These chemicals produce opposing and mutually antagonistic effects.

Sympathetic Nervous System

Sympathetic neurones are located in the thoracic and the lumbar segments of the spinal cord; their axons, called preganglionic fibres, emerge by way of all anterior nerve roots from the eighth cervical or first thoracic segment to the second or third lumbar segment, inclusive. A short distance from the cord these fibres diverge to join a chain composed of 22 linked ganglia that extends the entire length of the spinal column, flanking the vertebral bodies on both sides. Some form multiple synapses with nerve cells within the chain. Others traverse the chain without making connections or losing continuity to join large 'pre-vertebral' ganglia in the thorax, the abdomen or the pelvis, or one of the 'terminal' ganglia in the vicinity of an organ, such as the bladder or the rectum. Postganglionic nerve fibres originating in the sympathetic chain rejoin the spinal nerves that supply the extremities and are distributed to blood vessels, sweat glands and smooth muscle tissue in the skin. Postganglionic fibres from the prevertebral plexuses (i.e., the cardiac, pulmonary, splanchnic and pelvic plexuses) supply structures in the head and the neck, the thorax, the abdomen and the pelvis, respectively, having been joined in these plexuses by fibres from the parasympathetic division.

The adrenals, the kidneys, the liver, the spleen, the stomach and the duodenum are under the control of the giant coeliac plexus, familiarly known as the 'solar plexus'. This receives its sympathetic nerve components by way of the three splanchnic nerves, composed of preganglionic fibres from nine segments of the spinal cord (i.e., T4 to L1), and is joined by the vagus nerve, representing the parasympathetic division. From the coeliac plexus, fibres of both divisions travel along the course of blood vessels to their target organs.

Parasympathetic Nervous System

The preganglionic nerve cells of the sympathetic division, as described above, are consolidated in consecutive segments of the cord, from C7 to L1 or L2. Those of the parasympathetic system, on the other hand, are located in two sections, one in the brain stem and the other from spinal segments below L2. On this account, the parasympathetic system is referred to as the 'craniosacral' division, as distinct from the 'thoracolumbar' division of the autonomic nervous system.

The cranial parasympathetics arise from the midbrain and the medulla oblongata. Fibres from cells in the midbrain travel with the third oculomotor nerve to the ciliary ganglia, where postganglionic fibres of this division are joined by those of the sympathetic system. Forming the ciliary nerve, these innervate the ciliary muscles of the eye to control the calibre of the pupil. Parasympathetic fibres from the medulla travel with the seventh (facial), ninth (glossopharyngeal) and tenth (vagus) cranial nerves. Those from the facial nerve end in the splenopalatine ganglion, from which emanate the fibres that innervate the lacrimal glands, the ciliary muscle and the sphincter of the pupil. Those from the glossopharyngeal nerve innervate the parotid gland. The vagus nerve carries preganglionic parasympathetic fibres without interruption to the organs that it innervates, joining ganglion cells within the myocardium and within the walls of the oesophagus, the stomach and the intestine.

Preganglionic parasympathetic fibres from the anterior roots of the sacral nerves coalesce to become the pelvic nerves, consolidate and regroup in the pelvic plexus, and terminate around ganglion cells in the musculature of the pelvic organs. These innervate the colon, the rectum and the bladder, inhibiting the muscular tone of the anal and the bladder sphincters and dilating the blood vessels of the bladder, the rectum and the genitalia.

The vagus, splanchnic, pelvic and other autonomic nerves carry impulses generated in the viscera to the dorsal nucleus of the vagus, where connections are made with efferent parasympathetic neurones, forming a series of reflex arcs. These provide the basis for self-regulation, a cardinal feature of the autonomic nervous system, and are one reason for 'autonomy'.

Both sympathetic and parasympathetic divisions are in a constant state of activity, the activity of each relative to the other being one of controlled opposition, with a delicate balance maintained between the two at all times.

Sympathetic Syndromes. Certain syndromes are distinctive of diseases of the sympathetic nerve trunks. Among these are dilation of the pupil of the eye on the same side as a penetrating wound of the neck (evidence of disturbance of the cervical sympathetic cord); temporary paralysis of the bowel (indicated by the absence of peristaltic waves and the distension of the intestine by gas) following fracture of any one of the lower dorsal or upper lumbar vertebrae with haemorrhage into the base of the mesentery; and the marked variations in pulse rate and rhythm that often follow compression fractures of the upper six thoracic vertebrae.

THE NEUROLOGICAL EXAMINATION

The neurological examination is a sophisticated and subtle process, comprising a large number of tests of highly specialized function. Although neurological examinations are carried out by doctors, nurses will gain a better understanding of their patients' condition if they accompany them.

A neurological assessment is divided into five components: cerebral function, cranial nerves, motor system, sensory system and reflex status. As in other facets of the physical assessment, the neurological examination follows a logical sequence and is pursued from higher levels of cortical function through to a determination of the integrity of peripheral nerves.

Much of the patient's neurological function is assessed during the history and during the routine of the earlier parts of the physical examination. One can learn much about speech patterns, mental status, gait, stance, motor power and co-ordination. The simple act of shaking a patient's hand on entering the room conveys an enormous amount of information to the alert observer.

Cerebral Function

Cerebral abnormalities may cause disturbances in communication, in intellectual functioning and in patterns of emotional behaviour. Adequate cerebral functioning is determined by assessing the patient's mental status. The examiner observes the patient's appearance and behaviour, noting the patient's dress, grooming and personal hygiene. Observation of posture, gestures, movements, facial expressions and motor activity often provides important information about the patient's attitude. The manner of speech and the patient's level of consciousness are also observed: Is speech clear and coherent? Is the patient alert and responsive, or drowsy and difficult to rouse?

Intellectual function is tested when doubts exist about the patient's intellectual competence. Often, patients in a toxic state or those who have destruction of frontal cortex appear superficially normal until or unless one or more tests of integrative capacity are performed. First, the examiner determines whether patients are oriented to time, place and person. Does the patient know what day it is, what year it is or who is the present Prime Minister? Are patients aware of where they are? Is they aware of who you are and of their purpose for being in the room? Is the capacity for immediate memory intact? A person with an average IQ is able to repeat seven digits without faltering and is able to recite five digits backward. The examiner might ask the patient to count backward from 100, or to subtract 7 from 100, and then to continue subtracting 7 from each answer. The capacity to interpret well-known proverbs is a test of even higher intellectual function (abstract reasoning). For example, does the patient know what is meant by 'the early bird catches the worm'?

It is important to determine the patient's thought content as it emerges during the course of the interview. Are the patient's thoughts spontaneous, natural and clear? Are the patient's ideas relevant and coherent? Does the patient have any fixed ideas, illusions or preoccupations? What are the patient's insights into these thoughts? Preoccupation with death or morbid events, evidence of hallucinations and paranoia are all important and require further evaluation.

An assessment of cerebral functioning also includes the patient's emotional status. Is the patient's affect natural and even, or is the patient irritable and angry, anxious, apathetic or euphoric? Does the patient's mood fluctuate normally, or does the mood swing unpredictably from joy to sadness during the interview? Is the patient's affect appropriate to the patient's words and thought content? Are the patient's verbal communications consistent with the nonverbal communications?

The examiner may now look at more specific areas of higher cortical function. Agnosia is the inability to interpret or recognize objects seen through the special senses. The patient may see a pen but not know what it is called or what to do with it. The patient may even be able to describe it but not to interpret its function. The patient may experience auditory or tactile agnosia, as well as visual agnosia. Each of the dysfunctions implicates a different part of the cortex.

An assessment of cortical motor integration is carried out by asking the patient to perform a skilled act (throw a ball, move a chair). Successful performance hinges on the person's ability to understand the activity desired. There must also be normal motor strength. Failures signal cerebral dysfunction.

Lastly, language function is assessed. The normal person is able to understand and communicate in spoken and written language. Does the patient answer questions relevantly? Can the patient read a sentence from a newspaper and explain its meaning? Can such patients write down their own names or copy a simple figure that the examiner has drawn? A deficiency in language function is called dysphasia.

Interpretation of neurological abnormalities is a highly sophisticated and technical process. It is the obligation of the examiner to record and report what is found. Analysis and the conclusions that may be drawn from these findings will usually depend on the doctor's extensive knowledge of neuroanatomy, neurophysiology and neuropathology.

Examination of the Cranial Nerves

There are 12 pairs of cranial nerves that emerge from the undersurface of the brain. They are designated by the Roman numerals I to XII, according to the order of their placement. The cranial nerves are often assessed during a complete head and neck examination. These nerves, their functions and the tests for their measurement are outlined in Table 31.1.

Examination of the Motor System

The motor system is quite complex, and the end result of motor function is a synthesis of the integrity of the corticospinal tracts, the extrapyramidal system and cerebellar function. A motor impulse traverses two neurones. The upper motor neurone begins in the cortex of the opposite side of the brain, descends through the internal capsule, crosses to the opposite side in the brain stem, descends through the corticospinal tract and synapses with the lower motor neurone in the cord. The lower motor neurone receives the impulse in the posterior part of the cord and runs to the myoneural junction. The other two systems, the extrapyramidal system and the cerebellar system, act as modifiers.

A thorough examination of the motor system includes an assessment of muscle size, muscle tone, muscle strength, co-ordination and balance. The patient is requested to walk across the room while the examiner notes the patient's posture and gait. The muscles are inspected, and palpated if necessary, for their size and symmetry. Any evidence of atrophy or involuntary move-

Table 31.1 *Cranial nerves*

Cranial nerve	Function	Clinical examination
CN I (olfactory)	Sense of smell	With eyes closed, patient identifies familiar odours (coffee, tobacco); each nostril is tested separately
CN II (optic)	Visual acuity	Distance and near vision; examination of the fundi
CN III (oculomotor) CN IV (trochlear) CN VI (abducens)	Cranial nerves III, IV and VI function in the regulation of eye movements; CN III also innervates the levator muscle of the eyelid, the constrictor muscle of the pupil and the ciliary muscle, which controls accommodation	Test for ocular movements; test pupillary reactions; and inspect eyelids for ptosis
CN V (trigeminal)	Facial sensation	Get patient to close eyes; touch forehead, cheeks and jaw with cotton wool. Opposite sides of face are compared; sensitivity to superficial pain is tested by using a safety pin – alternate between sharp point and dull end. Patient reports 'sharp' or 'dull' with each movement; if responses are incorrect, test for temperature sensation – test-tubes of cold and hot water are used alternately
	Corneal reflex	While patient looks up, lightly touch a wisp of cotton wool against a temporal surface of each cornea; a blink and tears is a normal response
	Mastication	Get patient to clench jaw and move it from side to side; palpate masseter and temporal muscles, noting strength and equality
CN VII (facial)	Facial muscle movement	Assessment of motor function of facial muscles, while patient frowns, raises eyebrows, lightly closes eyes, whistles, blows out cheeks; note any asymmetry
	Taste; anterior two thirds of tongue	Patient extends tongue; ability to distinguish between sugar and salt is tested
CN VIII (vestibulocochlear)	Hearing and equilibrium	Whisper or watch-tick test; bone and air conduction of sound tested using a vibrating tuning fork; also used to test lateral hearing discrimination
CN IX (glossopharyngeal)	Taste; posterior third of tongue	Assess patient's ability to discriminate between sugar and salt on posterior third of tongue
CN X (vagus)	Pharyngeal contraction	Depress a tongue blade on posterior tongue, or stimulate posterior pharynx to elicit gag reflex

Table 31.1 *Continued*

Cranial nerve	Function	Clinical examination
	Symmetrical movement of vocal cords	Note any hoarseness in voice
	Symmetrical movement of soft palate	Ask patient to say 'ah'; observe symmetrical rise of uvula and soft palate
CN XI (spinal accessory)	Movement of sternocleidomastoid and trapezius muscles	Palpate and note strength of trapezius muscles while patient shrugs the shoulders against resistance
		Palpate and note the strength of each sternocleidomastoid muscle as patient turns head against opposing pressure of examiner's hand
CN XII (hypoglossal)	Movement of tongue	While patient protrudes tongue, any deviations or tremors are noted; the strength of the tongue is tested by getting patient to move the protruded tongue from side to side against a tongue depressor

ments (tremors, tics) is noted. Muscle tone is evaluated by palpating various muscle groups at rest and during passive movement. The resistance to these movements is noted. Abnormalities in tone include spasticity, rigidity or flaccidity.

Muscle strength is tested by ascertaining the patient's ability to flex or extend the extremity against resistance. The function of an individual muscle or group of muscles is evaluated by placing the muscle at a disadvantage. The quadriceps, for example, is a powerful muscle responsible for straightening the leg. Once the leg is straightened, it is exceedingly difficult for the examiner to flex the knee. On the other hand, if the knee is flexed, and the patient is asked to straighten the leg against resistance, a more subtle disability can be brought out. It is critically important to compare the two sides if one is looking for minor degrees of disability.

Some authorities advocate the use of a five-point scale for strength of motor power. Zero grade implies no contraction, increasing to grade five, indicating full contracting power.

Assessment of motor power can be as restricted or detailed as the examiner wishes. One may quickly test the strength of the proximal muscles of the upper and lower extremities, comparing the two. The motor capacity of the finer muscles that control the function of the hand and of the foot can then be assessed.

Cerebellar influence on the motor system is reflected in balance control and co-ordination. Co-ordination in the hands and upper extremities is tested by asking the patient to perform rapid, alternating movements and point-to-point testing. First, the patient is asked to pat the thigh as fast as possible with the hand. Each hand is tested separately. Then, the patient is asked to turn the hands from a supine to a prone position as rapidly as possible. Lastly, the patient is asked to touch each of the fingers with the thumb in a consecutive motion. Speed, symmetry and degree of difficulty are noted.

Point-to-point testing is accomplished by getting the patient to touch the examiner's extended finger and then the patient's own nose. This is repeated several times. This assessment is then carried out with the patient's eyes closed.

Co-ordination in the lower extremities is tested by getting the patient run the heel down the anterior surface of the tibia. Each leg is tested in turn. Inability to perform these manoeuvres is referred to as ataxia. The presence of ataxia or tremors (rhythmic, involuntary movements) during these movements suggests cerebellar disease.

It is not necessary to carry out each of these assessments for co-ordination. During a routine examination, it is advisable to perform a simple screening of the upper and lower extremities by getting the patient to perform either rapid, alternating movements or point-to-point testing. When abnormalities are observed, a more thorough examination is indicated.

The Romberg test is a screening measurement for balance. Patients stand with their feet together, arms extended in front and eyes closed. The examiner stands close to them and reassures them that they will be supported if they begin to lose their balance. Slight swaying is normal. Additional cerebellar tests for balance in the ambulatory patient include hopping in place, alternating knee bends and heel-to-toe walking.

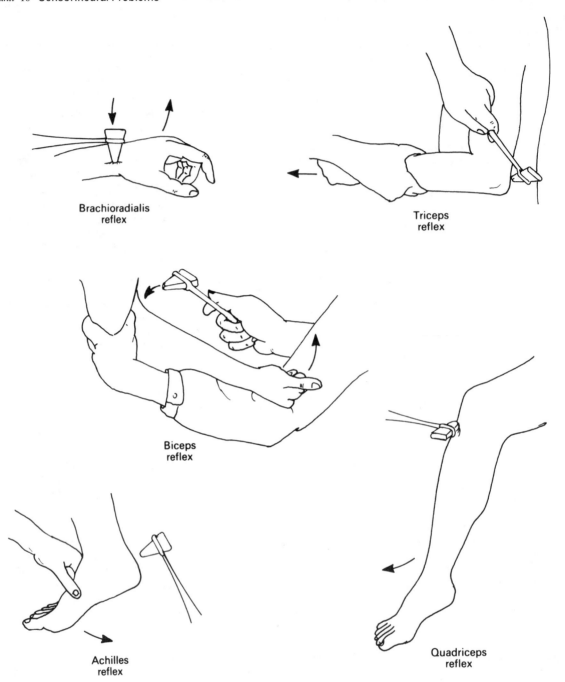

Brachioradialis
reflex

Triceps
reflex

Biceps
reflex

Achilles
reflex

Quadriceps
reflex

Figure 31.4 The proper technique for eliciting the major tendon reflexes. The tendon can be struck *directly* with the reflex hammer or *indirectly* by striking the examiner's thumb, which is placed on the tendon. Arrows indicate the normal movement expected.

Examination of the Reflexes

The motor reflexes are involuntary contractions of muscles or muscle groups in response to abrupt stretching near the site of the muscle's insertion. The tendon is struck directly with a reflex hammer, or indirectly by striking the examiner's thumb, which is placed firmly against the tendon. In testing the reflexes, one is examining involuntary reflex arcs that depend on the presence of afferent stretch receptors, spinal synapses, efferent motor fibres and a variety of modifying influences from higher levels. Common reflexes that may be tested include the biceps, the brachioradialis, the triceps, the patellar and the ankle (or Achilles) reflexes (Figure 31.4).

A reflex hammer is used to elicit a deep tendon reflex. The tendon is struck briskly and the response compared with the corresponding reflex on the opposite side of the body. Wide variation in reflex response may be considered normal. However, it is more important that the reflexes be symmetrically equivalent. When the comparison is made, both sides should be relaxed equivalently and each tendon struck with equal force.

The absence of reflexes is significant, although ankle jerks (Achilles reflex) may be absent in older people.

Reflex responses are often graded on a 0 to 4+ scale, but scale ratings are highly subjective and some examiners prefer to use the terms 'present', 'absent' and 'diminished' when describing reflexes.

A well-known reflex, indicative of central nervous system disease afflicting the corticospinal tracts, is the extensor plantar response. If the lateral aspect of the sole of the foot is stroked, in normal people the toes will contract and be drawn tightly together. In patients with central nervous system disease of the motor system, the toes will fan out and be drawn back. This is normal in newborn babies but represents serious pathology in the adult. There are a variety of described reflexes that convey similar information. Many of them are interesting but not particularly informative.

Sensory Examination

The sensory system is even more complex than the motor system because sensory modalities are carried in different tracts, located in different portions of the cord (Figure 31.5). It should be remembered that the sensory examination is largely subjective and requires the co-operation of the patient. Most sensory deficits result from peripheral neuropathy and will follow anatomical dermatomes. Exceptions to this include major destructive lesions of the brain; loss of sensation, which may affect an entire side of the body; and the neuropathies associated with alcoholism, which occur in a glove and stocking distribution.

Assessment of the sensory system involves tests for tactile sensation, superficial pain, vibration and proprioception. Throughout the sensory assessment, the patient's eyes are closed. The co-operation of the patient is encouraged by simple directions and reassurance that the examiner will not hurt the patient.

Tactile sensation is assessed by lightly touching a cotton wisp to corresponding areas on each side of the body. The sensitivity of proximal parts of the extremities are compared to distal parts.

Pain and temperature sensation are carried together in the lateral part of the cord. Thus, it is not necessary to test for temperature sense in most circumstances. Superficial pain is assessed by determining the patient's sensitivity to pinprick. The sharp and dull ends of a safety pin are alter-

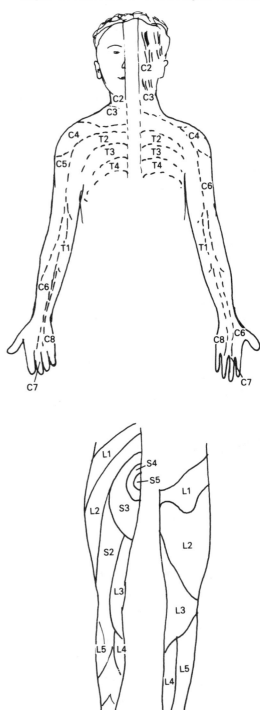

Figure 31.5 Sensory modalities in dermatome distribution. (From Hickey, J. (1981) *Neurological/Neurosurgical Nursing*, J. B. Lippincott, Philadelphia.)

nately applied to symmetrical areas of the body. The patient is asked to differentiate between a sharp and dull sensation.

The pin is applied with equal intensity at all times, and the two sides are tested symmetrically.

Vibration and proprioception (the subjective sense of joint position) are carried together in the posterior part of the cord. Vibration may be evaluated through the use of a tuning fork. The handle of the vibrating fork is placed against a bony prominence and the patient is asked whether a buzz is felt. The patient is asked to signal the examiner when the buzz ceases. If the patient does not perceive the vibrations at the distal bony prominences, the examiner progresses upwards with the tuning fork until the vibrations are felt. As with all measurement of sensitivity, side-to-side comparison is made.

Position sense may be determined by asking the patient to close the eyes and indicate, as the toes are moved, in which direction movement has taken place. Vibration and position sense are often lost together, frequently in circumstances where all others remain intact.

Having tested peripheral sensation, one now asks whether integration of sensation in the brain is being carried out properly. This may be done by testing two-point discrimination. That is, if the patient is touched with two sharp objects simultaneously, are they perceived as two or as one? If a patient is touched simultaneously on opposite sides of the body, then it should normally be recognized that the body has been touched in two places. If the patient recognizes only one place has been touched, the one not recognized is said to demonstrate extinction. A good test of higher cortical sensory ability is that of stereognosis. The patient is requested to close the eyes and identify a variety of objects (keys, coins, etc.) that are placed in the patient's hand by the examiner.

Neurological Assessment in the Elderly

The nervous system in older adults is vulnerable to general systemic illness and readily affected by disorders of other body systems. In addition, a number of neurological alterations occur with the ageing process: sluggishness of pupil response to light, diminished or absent Achilles reflexes, loss of strength and some muscle wasting. Loss of neurones occurs in selected layers and regions of the cerebral cortex. Another characteristic of the ageing nervous system is slowing of nerve conduction. Thus, a little more time is required to obtain a history of neurological disorder and its associated symptoms when an older person is being assessed.

Mental status is evaluated while the history is obtained, and areas of judgement, intelligence, memory, affect, mood, orientation, speech and grooming are assessed. Changes in mental status may be discerned by family members or close friends who bring the patient to the health care setting. Drug toxicity should always be suspected as an aetiological factor when the patient has a change in mental status. Mental confusion, usually with delusions and hallucinations, is seen in elderly patients who have underlying central nervous system damage or are experiencing an acute condition such as infection or dehydration. Dementia may be reversible and treatable (as in drug toxicity or thyroid disease) or chronic and irreversible. Depression may produce impairment of attention and memory.

Common neurological problems of the aged include headache, low back pain, dizziness, weakness and falling.

DIAGNOSTIC TESTS AND PROCEDURES

Imaging Procedures

Skull X-rays, usually lateral and anteroposterior views, can reveal fractures, calcification, erosion of bone and displacement of midline strictures.

Computed Tomography (CT) Scanning

Computed tomography makes use of a narrow beam of X-ray to scan the head in successive layers. The images that are produced provide cross-sectional views of the brain, with distinguishing differences in tissue densities of the skull, cortex, subcortical structures and ventricles. A computer printout is obtained of the absorption values of the tissues in the plane that is being scanned. The data are transformed into an image through a series of complex equations. Therefore, the brightness of each portion or 'slice' of brain in the final image is proportional to the degree to which it absorbs X-ray. The image is displayed on an oscilloscope or television monitor and is photographed.

Lesions within the brain are seen as variations in tissue density differing from the surrounding normal brain tissue. Abnormalities of tissue indicate possible tumour masses, brain infarction, displacement of the ventricles and cortical atrophy.

Computed tomography scanning is usually done first without contrast material and then with intravenous contrast enhancement. The patient lies on an adjustable table, with the head held in a fixed position, while the scanning system rotates around the head. (The patient is used as the axis, and the machine is rotated around this axis, resulting in a cross-cut image). The patient must lie with the head held perfectly still and with a careful effort not to talk or move the face, since head motion may cause considerable distortion of the image.

Computed tomography is the most revolutionary development in neurological diagnosis in this century. It is noninvasive, painless and has high degree of sensitivity for detecting lesions.

Positron Emission Tomography (PET)

Positron emission tomography is a computer-based nuclear imaging technique that can produce pictures of the metabolism of glucose within the brain and thus may allow a better understanding of brain function in disorders where blood flow is disrupted, in dementia and epilepsy.

Single Photon Emission Computed Tomography

Single photon emission computed tomography (SPECT) is a three-dimensional imaging technique using nuclear medicine procedures that employ radionuclides and instruments that emit and detect (respectively) single photons.

Magnetic Resonance Imaging (MRI)

Magnetic resonance imaging relies on magnets and computers to produce images of different areas of the body (Figure 31.6). A magnetic field surrounds the patient and causes hydrogen atoms in the body to line up in a certain fashion. When the atoms move back to their original places a signal is released that is processed by a computer. In central nervous system conditions, magnetic resonance imaging has the potential for identifying cerebral pathology earlier and more clearly than other diagnostic tests. It can provide information about the chemical changes within cells, thus allowing the doctor to monitor a tumour's response to treatment. It does not require ionizing radiation.

Before the test the patient must remove all metallic objects (jewellery, including wedding ring and watch), as well as credit cards which the magnetic field can erase. The patient will lie on a flat platform that will be moved into a tube containing the magnet. Nothing will be felt during the scanning process, but the patient will hear the thumping of the sound of the magnetic coils as the magnetic field is being pulsed. Throughout the scan the patient can talk to and hear the staff by means of a microphone placed in the scanner.

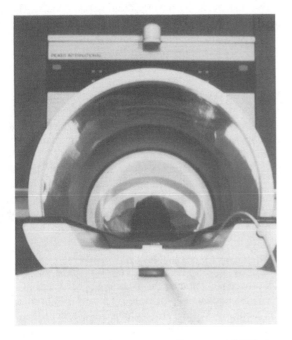

Figure 31.6 Magnetic resonance imaging (MRI). In central nervous system conditions, magnetic resonance imaging has the potential for identifying cerebral pathology earlier and more clearly. (Courtesy of National Institutes of Health.)

Cerebral Angiography

Cerebral angiography is an X-ray study of the cerebral circulation following injection of contrast material into a selected artery. Cerebral angiography is a valuable tool for investigating vascular disease, aneurysms (dilation of a segment of a blood vessel) and arteriovenous malformations. It is frequently done before craniotomy.

The majority of cerebral angiograms are carried out by threading a catheter through the femoral artery in the groin and up to the desired vessel. The procedure may also be accomplished by direct puncture of the carotid/vertebral artery or by retrograde injection of contrast medium into the brachial artery.

Patient Preparation

The patient should be well hydrated, and clear liquids are usually permitted up to the time of the study. Before going to the radiology department, the patient is asked to pass urine. The locations of the appropriate peripheral pulses are marked with a felt-tip pen. The patient is asked to remain immobile during the film sequence, and told that a brief feeling of warmth in the face, behind the eyes or in the jaw, teeth, tongue and lips, and a metallic taste are likely to be expected.

After the groin is shaved and prepared, a local anaesthetic is used for patient comfort and to reduce arterial spasm. A catheter is introduced into the femoral artery, flushed with heparinized saline, and filled with contrast medium. Under fluoroscopic guidance, the catheter is advanced to the appropriate vessel(s). During injection of the contrast medium, X-rays are made of the arterial and venous phases of circulation through the brain.

Postprocedure Nursing Care

In some instances, patients may experience major or minor arterial block due to embolism, thrombosis or haemorrhage, producing a neurological deficit. Signs of such an occurrence include alterations in the level of responsiveness and consciousness, weakness on one side of the body, motor or sensory deficits or speech disturbances. It is necessary to observe the patient repeatedly for these signs and to report them immediately if they occur.

The injection site is observed for haematoma formation (a localized collection of blood), and an ice cap may be applied intermittently to the puncture site to relieve swelling and discomfort. Since a haematoma at the puncture site or embolization to a distant artery will affect the peripheral pulses, these signs are monitored frequently. The colour and temperature of the involved extremity are also noted as a means of detecting possible embolism.

Myelography

A myelogram is an X-ray of the spinal subarachnoid space taken after an opaque medium or air is injected into the spinal subarachnoid space through a spinal puncture. It outlines the spinal subarachnoid space and shows any distortion of the spinal cord or spinal dural sac caused by tumours, cysts, herniated intervertebral discs or other lesions.

After the contrast medium is injected by varying the degree of table tilt, the course of the contrast medium is observed radioscopically. The contrast medium may be water soluble or oil based. Metrizamide is a water-soluble contrast agent that is absorbed by the body and excreted by the kidneys. It does not have to be removed via the needle route from the spinal canal because it is highly soluble and clears relatively quickly from the cerebrospinal fluid. Side-effects include headache, which is most probably due to central nervous system irritation by the metronidazole.

If iophendylate, an oil-based iodine compound, is used for myelography, the radiologist may remove it by syringe and needle aspiration. The patient may complain of sharp pain down the leg during aspiration if a nerve root is affected. This is remedied by rotating the needle point or adjusting the depth of the needle.

Nursing Care

Since most patients have some misconceptions about this procedure, the nurse can answer questions and clarify the explanation offered by the doctor. The patient should be aware that the X-ray table may be tilted in varying positions during the study. The meal that would normally be eaten before the procedure is omitted. The patient may be given a light sedative to help cope with a rather lengthy test.

Following myelography, when a water-soluble medium has been used, the patient sits upright in bed for at least six hours to reduce the rate of upward dispersion of the medium. The patient may be ambulant or remain in bed depending on the doctor's request.

Following a procedure in which an oil-based medium has been used, the patient should lie in a recumbent position for the amount of time specified by the doctor (usually 12 to 24 hours) to reduce cerebrospinal fluid leakage and decrease the frequency of headache. Usually, the patient is permitted to turn from side to side.

The patient is encouraged to drink liberal amounts of fluid for rehydration and replacement of cerebrospinal fluid and to decrease the incidence of post-lumbar puncture headache. The blood pressure, pulse, respiratory rate and temperature are monitored, as well as the ability to pass urine. Other untoward signs to watch for include fever, stiff neck, photophobia (sensitivity to light) or signs of chemical or bacterial meningitis.

Lumbar Epidural Venography

In lumbar epidural venography, a catheter is inserted percutaneously into the femoral vein and guided into the ascending lumbar vein or internal iliac veins. The contrast medium is injected to fill the epidural veins overlying the disc spaces and to opacify the epidural venous plexus. The procedure may be useful in the diagnosis of herniated lumbar discs that are not demonstrated by myelography. It reveals deviation or compression of the epidural veins due to a herniated disc or tumour. The procedure is relatively easy to perform, well tolerated, fairly painless and not associated with arachnoiditis. Lumbar epidural venography and myelography may be done as complementary diagnostic studies. Following the test, the site is observed for evidence of haematoma formation.

Radionuclide Imaging Studies (Brain Scan)

Radionuclide imaging is based on the principle that a radiopharmaceutical may diffuse through the blood–brain barrier at a point where it has been disrupted and collect in abnormal cerebral tissue. (Normal brain tissue is relatively impermeable.) There is increased uptake of radioactive material at the site of pathology.

In this procedure, the patient is given an intravenous injection of a radiopharmaceutical. The radioactivity subsequently transmitted through the skull is traced by a scanner that prints out a picture, or a gamma camera is used to monitor the passage of the radiopharmaceutical through the cerebral circulation to gain information about cerebral blood flow.

Brain scanning is particularly useful in evaluating vascular lesions of the brain and meninges and in locating vascular neoplasms and brain tumours. It is useful in the early detection and evaluation of stroke, abscess and follow-up of surgical or radiation therapy of the brain. Newer techniques permit the evaluation of cerebral circulation during the brain scan. However, computed tomography scanning is replacing traditional radioisotope scanning.

Echoencephalography

Echoencephalography is the recording of echoes from the deep structures within the skull by means of ultrasound. Ultrasonic transducers are positioned over specified areas of the head, while echoes are transcribed into images. Echoencephalography is a rapid and useful technique to determine the position of midline structures of the brain, and the distance from the midline to the lateral ventricular wall or the third ventricular wall. Therefore, it is done to detect a shift of the cerebral midline structures caused by subdural haematoma, intracerebral haemorrhage, massive cerebral infarction and neoplasms. It is useful in the evaluation of hydrocephalus, since it can detect dilation of the ventricles.

The nurse may explain that this is a noninvasive test, and that some type of water-soluble jelly is used to eliminate the air gap between the hand-held transducer and the patient's head.

Air Studies

The cerebrospinal fluid spaces in and around the brain may be seen in X-ray examination when the fluid is replaced with a gas. This is based on the principle that gas, replacing the fluid within the ventricular and subarachnoid systems, serves as a contrast medium, because air is less dense than fluid to X-rays. The cerebrospinal fluid may be partially replaced with air through pneumoencephalography and ventriculography.

Pneumoencephalography is a diagnostic procedure in which air or gas is instilled through a lumbar puncture as a means of demonstrating the ventricular system and subarachnoid space overlying the hemispheres and basal cisterns. A small amount of cerebrospinal fluid is removed and an equal amount of air injected. A special chair allows the patient to be rotated in all directions so that air may be placed selectively in the desired cavities. Films are then taken and studied.

A ventriculogram is an X-ray taken of the lateral ventricles following withdrawal of cerebrospinal fluid and injection of air or gas into the lateral ventricles through openings in the skull.

● These procedures are used infrequently since the advent of computed tomography.

Electrophysiological Tests

Electroencephalography (EEG)

An electroencephalogram represents a record of the electrical activity generated in the brain and obtained through electrodes applied on the scalp surface or through microelectrodes placed within the brain tissue. It provides physiological assessment of cerebral activity. Electroencephalography is a useful test for diagnosing seizure disorders such as the epilepsies and is a screening procedure for coma or organic brain syndrome. It also serves as an indicator of brain death. Tumours, abscesses, brain scars, blood clots and infection may cause electric changes to differ from normal patterns of rhythm and rate.

Electrodes are arranged on the scalp to record the electrical activity in various regions of the head. The amplified activity of the neurones is recorded on a continuously moving paper sheet; this record is the encephalogram (Figure 31.7). For a baseline recording, the patient lies quietly with the eyes closed. Then the patient may be asked to hyperventilate for three to four minutes and then to look at a bright, flashing light for photic stimulation. These are activation procedures done to evoke abnormal electrical discharges, especially seizure potentials. A sleep electroencephalogram may be recorded following sedation because some abnormal brain waves are seen only when the patient is asleep. If the epileptogenic area is

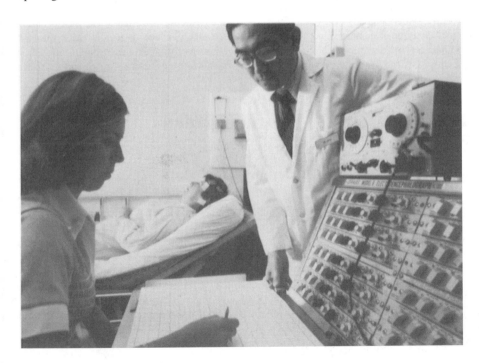

Figure 31.7 Neurologist and electroencephalography technician checking the electroencephalogram, which is a valuable diagnostic instrument in epilepsy and other neurological disorders. (Courtesy of National Institute of Neurological and Communicative Disorders and Stroke.)

inaccessible to the conventional scalp electrodes, nasopharyngeal or sphenoidal electrodes may be used.

Depth recording of electroencephalography is carried out by introducing electrodes stereotactically into a target area of the brain as dictated by the patient's seizure pattern and scalp electrencephalogram. It is used to select patients who may benefit from surgical excision of epileptogenic foci.

Patient Preparation

Tranquillizers and stimulants may be withheld 24 to 48 hours before an electroencephalogram, since these medications can alter the electroencephalography wave patterns or mask the abnormal wave patterns of seizure disorders. Coffee, tea or cola drinks are omitted in the meal before the test because of their stimulating effect. However, the meal is not omitted because an altered blood sugar level can also cause changes in the brain wave patterns.

The patient is informed that the electroencephalogram will take 45 to 60 minutes or longer if a sleep electroencephalography is performed. At the same time, the patient is assured that the procedure will not cause an electric shock and that the electrencephalogram is a test, not a form of treatment.

Evoked Potential Studies

Evoked potential studies evaluate the changes and responses in brain waves recorded from scalp electrodes that are evoked (elicited) by the introduction of an external stimulus. Evoked changes are detected with the aid of computerized devices that extract the signal, display it on an oscilloscope and store the data on magnetic tape or disc. These studies are based on the concept that any insult or dysfunction that can alter neuronal metabolism or disturb membrane function may change evoked responses in brain waves. In neurological diagnosis they reflect conduction times in the peripheral nervous system. In clinical practice, the visual, auditory and somatosensory systems are most often tested.

In visual evoked responses the patient looks at a visual stimulus (flashing light, checkerboard pattern on a screen). The average of several hundred stimuli is recorded by electroencephalography leads placed over the occiput. The transit time from the retina to the occipital area is measured using computer averaging methods.

To measure auditory evoked responses an auditory stimulus (repetitive auditory click) is given and the transit time up the brain stem into the cortex is measured. Specific lesions in the auditory pathway will modify or delay the response.

In somatosensory evoked responses the peripheral nerves are stimulated (electrical stimulation through skin electrodes) and the transit time up the spinal cord to the cortex is measured and recorded from scalp electrodes. This test is used to detect a deficit in spinal cord conduction and to monitor cord function during operative procedures.

There is no specific patient preparation other than reassurance and encouragement of relaxation. The patient is advised to remain perfectly still throughout the recording in order to prevent artifacts (potentials not generated by the brain) that interfere with the recording and interpretation of the test.

Electromyography (EMG)

An electromyogram is obtained by introducing needle electrodes into the skeletal muscles in order to study changes in the electrical potential of the muscles and the nerves leading to them. The electrical potentials are shown on an oscilloscope and amplified by a loudspeaker so that both the sound and appearance of the waves can be analysed and compared simultaneously. Electromyographies are useful in determining the presence of a neuromuscular disorder and myopathies. They help to distinguish weakness due to neuropathy (functional or pathological changes in the peripheral nervous system) from weakness due to other causes.

No special patient preparation is required. The patient is told that a sensation similar to that of an intramuscular injection will be experienced as the needle is inserted into the muscle. The muscles examined may ache for a short time following the procedure.

Nerve Conduction Studies

Nerve conduction studies are performed by stimulating a peripheral nerve at several points along its course and recording the muscle action potential or the sensory action potential that results. Surface or needle electrodes are placed on the skin over the nerve to stimulate the nerve fibres. This test is useful in the study of peripheral nerve neuropathies.

Special Procedures

Lumbar Puncture and Examination of Cerebrospinal Fluid

A lumbar puncture is carried out by inserting a needle into the lumbar subarachnoid space in order to withdraw cerebrospinal fluid for diagnostic and therapeutic purposes. The purposes are to obtain spinal fluid for examination, to measure and relieve spinal fluid pressure, to determine the presence or absence of blood in the spinal fluid, to detect spinal subarachnoid block and to administer antibiotics intrathecally in certain cases of infection.

The needle is usually inserted into the subarachnoid space between the third and fourth lumbar interspace. Since the spinal cord divides into a sheaf of nerves at the first lumbar vertebra, the needle is inserted below the level of the third lumbar vertebra (Figure 31.8) to prevent the spinal cord from being punctured.

A successful lumbar puncture requires that the patient be relaxed, since an anxious patient may become tense, thereby causing an increase in the pressure reading. The normal range of spinal fluid pressure with the patient in a lateral recumbent position is 70 to 170 mm H_2O. Pressures over 200 mm H_2O are considered to be abnormal. A lumbar puncture may be quite dangerous in the presence of an intracranial mass lesion, because when pressure is released the intracranial contents may herniate.

A lumbar manometric test (Queckenstedt test) may be performed by compressing the jugular veins on each side of the neck during the lumbar puncture. The increase in the pressure caused by the compression is noted. Then the pressure is released and pressure readings are made at 10-second intervals. In normal people, the cerebrospinal fluid pressure rises rapidly in response to compression of the jugular veins and returns quickly to normal when the compression is released. A slow rise and fall in pressure indicates a partial block due to a lesion compressing the spinal subarachnoid pathways. If there is no pressure change, a complete block is indicated. This test is not done if an intracranial lesion is suspected.

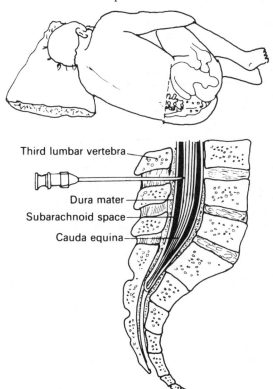

Figure 31.8 Technique of lumbar puncture. The interspaces between L3 and L5 are just below the line connecting the anterior–superior iliac spines.

Nursing Support

During the initial explanations, the patient should be assured that inserting a needle into the spine will not result in paralysis. Before the lumbar puncture, the bladder and bowel should be emptied. The patient is placed on the side with the back toward the doctor. The thighs and head are flexed as much as possible to increase the space between the spinous processes of the vertebrae and afford easier entry into the subarachnoid space. A pillow fixed between the legs will prevent the upper leg from rolling forward. A small pillow is placed under the patient's head so that the spine is maintained in a horizontal position. The nurse may assist the patient to maintain the position in order to avoid sudden movement, which can produce a traumatic (bloody) tap. During the procedure, the patient is requested to breathe normally since hyperventilation may lower an elevated pressure. Following the procedure, patients can adopt a comfortable position, although they may be advised to lie flat for 6 to 12 hours, or while any headache persists. A liberal fluid intake is encouraged.

Examination of the Cerebrospinal Fluid

Spinal fluid should be clear and colourless. Bloody spinal fluid may indicate cerebral contusion, laceration or subarachnoid haemorrhage. Usually, specimens are sent to the laboratory for cell count, culture and chemical analysis. The specimens should be sent immediately, since changes will take place and alter the result if the specimens are allowed to stand. (See Appendix for the normal values of cerebrospinal fluid.)

Post-Lumbar Puncture Headache

A post-lumbar puncture headache, ranging from mild to severe, may appear in a few hours to several days following the procedure. It is particularly severe when the patient sits or stands upright, but lessens or disappears when the patient lies down in a horizontal position.

The cause of this unpleasant complication is the leakage of spinal fluid at the puncture site. The fluid continues to escape into the tissues by way of the needle tract from the spinal canal.

The post puncture headache is usually managed by bedrest, analgesics and hydration.

Other complications of a spinal puncture include herniation of the intracranial contents, traumatic complications, spinal epidural abscess, spinal epidural haematoma and meningitis.

FURTHER READING

Lindsay, K. W., Bone, I. and Callender, Q. (1986) *Neurology and Neurosurgery Illustrated*, Churchill Livingstone, Edinburgh.

chapter 32

ASSESSMENT AND CARE OF PATIENTS WITH NEUROLOGICAL DYSFUNCTION

SPECIAL PROBLEMS OF PATIENTS WITH NEUROLOGICAL DISORDERS

The Patient With Increased Intracranial Pressure

Altered Physiology

Intracranial pressure is the result of the amount of brain substance, intracranial blood volume and cerebrospinal fluid within the skull at any one time. The normal intracranial pressure varies depending on the position of the patient and is considered to be less than or equal to 15 mmHg.

The rigid cranial vault contains brain (1,400 g), blood (75 ml) and cerebrospinal fluid (75 ml). The volume and pressure of these three components are usually in a state of equilibrium. Since there is limited space for expansion within the skull, an increase of any one of these components causes a change in the volume of the other, by either displacing or shifting cerebrospinal fluid, increasing the absorption of cerebrospinal fluid or decreasing cerebral blood volume. Under normal circumstances, minor changes in blood volume and cerebrospinal fluid volume occur constantly when there are changes in intrathoracic pressure (coughing, sneezing, straining), posture and blood pressure, and fluctuations in arterial blood gas levels.

Pathological conditions such as head injury, stroke, inflammatory lesions, brain tumour or intracranial surgery have a negative influence on the relationship between intracranial volume and pressure. Increased intracranial pressure may significantly reduce cerebral blood flow. The resultant ischaemia stimulates the vasomotor centres, and the systemic pressure rises to maintain cerebral blood flow. Usually this is accompanied by a slow bounding pulse and respiratory irregularities. These changes in blood pressure, pulse and respiration are of importance clinically because they are clues to the existence of increased intracranial pressure. The ultimate effect of raised intracranial pressure is cerebral ischaemia. The brain is very vulnerable to ischaemia and generally will not recover function if it is subjected to more than three to five minutes of complete ischaemia.

The concentration of carbon dioxide in the blood (PCO_2 and in brain tissues also has a role in the regulation of cerebral blood flow. A rise in PCO_2 causes the cerebral blood vessels to dilate, leading to increased cerebral blood flow and increased intracranial pressure, while a fall in PCO_2 has a vasoconstrictor effect. Decreased venous outflow may also increase cerebral blood volume, thus raising intracranial pressure.

Cerebral swelling or oedema occurs when there is an increase in the water content of the central nervous system. Certain brain tumours are associated with the development of large quantities of water. Even a small tumour may create a great increase in intracranial pressure.

Although an elevated intracranial pressure is most commonly associated with head injury, an elevated pressure may be seen as a secondary effect in a variety of other conditions: brain tumours, subarachnoid haemorrhage, and toxic and viral encephalopathies.

Thus, increased intracranial pressure is the summation of a number of physiological processes. Increased intracranial pressure from any cause affects cerebral perfusion and produces distortion and shifts of brain tissue.

Clinical Features

When intracranial pressure increases to the point where the brain's ability to adjust has reached its limits, neural function is impaired and may be expressed by changes in the level of consciousness and by abnormal respiratory and vasomotor responses.

The level of responsiveness/consciousness is the most important measure of the patient's condition.

● The earliest sign of increasing intracranial pressure is lethargy. Watch for slowing of speech and a delay in response to verbal suggestions.

Any sudden change in condition, such as shifting from quietness to restlessness (without apparent cause), shifting from orientation to confusion or increasing drowsiness, has neurological significance. These signs may result from compression of the brain due to either swelling from haemorrhage or oedema or an expanding intracranial lesion (haematoma or tumour) or a combination of both.

As pressure increases, the patient may react only to loud auditory or painful stimuli. At this stage, serious impairment of brain circulation is probably taking place and immediate surgical intervention may be required. If the unconsciousness deepens, the patient responds to painful stimuli by moaning but may not attempt to withdraw. As

the condition worsens, the extremities become flaccid and reflexes are absent. The jaw sags and the tongue becomes flaccid, producing inadequate respiratory exchange. When the coma is profound, with the pupils dilated and fixed and the respirations impaired, a fatal outcome is usually inevitable.

Medical Management

● Increased intracranial pressure constitutes a true emergency and must be treated promptly. As pressure rises, the brain substance is compressed. Secondary phenomena caused by circulatory impairment and oedema may lead to death.

The immediate management for relief of increased intracranial pressure is based on reducing the size of the brain by decreasing brain oedema, lowering the volume of cerebrospinal fluid or decreasing blood volume. These goals are accomplished by administering osmotic diuretics, restricting fluids, draining cerebrospinal fluid, hyperventilating the patient, controlling fever and reducing cellular metabolic demands.

Osmotic diuretics (mannitol, glycerol) may be given to dehydrate the brain and reduce cerebral oedema. They act by drawing water across intact membranes, thereby reducing the volume of brain and extracellular fluid. An indwelling catheter is usually inserted into the bladder for the management of the ensuing diuresis.

Steroids (such as dexamethasone) help reduce oedema surrounding brain tumours when a brain tumour is the cause of increased intracranial pressure.

Cerebrospinal fluid drainage is frequently employed since the removal of even a small amount of cerebrospinal fluid may dramatically reduce intracranial pressure and restore cerebral perfusion pressure.

Hyperventilation (with a volume ventilator) produces respiratory alkalosis, which in turn causes cerebral vasoconstriction. The result of this action is a reduction in cerebral blood volume and lowering of intracranial pressure. It is considered a short-term means of control.

Temperature control is aimed at preventing an elevation of temperature, since fever increases cerebral metabolism and the rate at which cerebral oedema forms. Cardiac output is monitored if measures are taken to reduce the patient's temperature.

Reducing cellular metabolic demands may also be accomplished through the administration of high doses of barbiturates when the patient is not responsive to conventional treatment. The mechanism by which barbiturates decrease intracranial pressure and protect the brain is uncertain, but the resultant comatose state is thought to reduce metabolic requirements of the brain, thus giving it some protection.

● The patient receiving high doses of barbiturates experiences loss of all neurological clinical parameters.

GEN 293

.... HOSPITAL

NAME

CONSULTANT

UNIT No

D. of B.

WARD

NEUROLOGICAL OBSERVATION CHART

DATE

TIME

C O M A S C A L E	Eyes open	Spontaneously	4					
		To speech	3					
		To pain	2					
		None	1					
	Best verbal response	Orientated	5					
		Confused	4					
		Inappropriate words	3					
		Incomprehensible Sounds	2					
		None	1					
	Best motor response	Obey commands	6					
		Localize pain	5					
		Normal flexion	4					
		Abnormal flexion	3					
		Extension to pain	2					
		None	1					

Eyes closed by swelling = C

Endotracheal tube or Tracheostomy = T

Usually records the best arm response

COMA SCALE TOTAL 3–15

INTRACRANIAL PRESSURE

Pupil scale
(m.m.)

1 •   240 230 220 210 200 190 180 170 160 150 140 130 120 110 100 90 80 70 60 50 40 Respiration 30 26 22 18 14 10 6

Temperature °C   40 39 38 37 36 35 34 33 32 31 30

PUPILS	right	Size						
		Reaction						
	left	Size						
		Reaction						

+ reacts
– no reaction
c. eye closed

L I M B M O V E M E N T	A R M S	Normal						
		Mild weakness						
		Severe weakness						
		Extension						
		No response						
	L E G S	Normal power						
		Mild weakness						
		Severe weakness						
		Extension						
		No response						

Record right (R) and left (L) separately if there is a difference between the two sides

Figure 32.1 Neurological observation chart (Glasgow Coma Scale).

Barbiturates are significant cardiorespiratory depressants. Thus, prolonged barbiturate anaesthesia requires a high level of nursing surveillance and support, since the patient is totally dependent and vulnerable to many complications. The patient is placed in the intensive care unit, and the following parameters are monitored: intracranial pressure, electroencephalogram, arterial pressures, and blood and serum barbiturate levels.

▶ NURSING PROCESS

▶ THE PATIENT WITH INCREASED INTRACRANIAL PRESSURE

▶ *Nursing Assessment*

Neurological Observations

Raised intracranial pressure may require emergency action. Although the nurse should be aware of the clinical features, i.e. the 'classical triad', widening pulse pressure, rising systolic blood pressure and bradycardia that often accompanies increased intracranial pressure, this does not always occur, or may happen too late for effective management. Since the responsibility for neurological observation is primarily a nursing one, a standardized method of assessing the patient's level of consciousness is useful. The Glasgow Coma Scale provides this and is based on three objective behaviours: eye opening, verbal responses and motor responses. Each is assessed independently and recorded Figure 32.1).

1. Eye opening.
    a. Spontaneous eye opening.
    b. Opens eye to speech.
    c. Opens eye to pain (eyes open to nailbed pressure).
    d. No eye opening.
2. Verbal responses. This assesses the patient's orientation. Any speech deficit, presence of tracheostomy or endotracheal tubing may influence the response but is taken into account.
    a. Orientated.
    b. Confused in conversation.
    c. Inappropriate words. Monosyllabic response.
    d. Incomprehensible sounds in response to pain.
    e. No verbal response.
3. Motor response. This assesses the arm response (not legs), and if a difference is noted between right and left, the best response is recorded.
    a. Obeys command.
    b. Localizes pain. Patient locates source of irritation.
    c. Flexion to pain. Nailbed pressure elicits withdrawal.
    d. Extension to pain. Nailbed pressure causes arm extension.
    e. No response. If the patient does not obey commands, the response can be tested by applying steady nailbed pressure.

Vital Signs

The vital sign recordings can also be useful in determining alterations in intracranial pressure. A rising systolic blood pressure with a widening pulse pressure and bradycardia may be indicative of a rise in intracranial pressure.

Pupil Reaction

Using the millimetre scale incorporated within the Glasgow Coma Scale, each pupil is assessed separately for size and equality, and their reaction is obtained by using a small pencil torch. For accuracy, the patient's environment should be dimmed.

The patient's gaze and the ability of the eyes to abduct and adduct can be assessed at this time. The doctor can also inspect the retina and optic nerve for signs of haemorrhage and papilloedema.

Limb Movements

In addition to assessing the best motor response (arms), the limbs are also assessed for motor power, comparing both sides. Any discrepancy is recorded separately. The response can be obtained by verbal command or by painful stimuli.

It is important that the nurse maintains serial observations, the frequency of which is dictated according to the patient's condition. Any changes should be reported as quickly as possible.

A paediatric version, the Adelaide Coma Scale, is at present undergoing trials. This modification of the Glasgow Coma Scale, affecting more the motor and verbal responses, is more applicable to a child under the age of five years.

Monitoring Intracranial Pressure

Clinical assessment is not always a reliable guide in recognizing increased intracranial pressure, especially in patients with altered consciousness. In certain situations, intracranial monitoring may be employed, which is the recording of the pressure exerted within the skull by the brain, cerebral blood and cerebrospinal fluid. The volume of any of these can expand as a result of tumour, trauma, oedema, haemorrhage and so on. Thus monitoring provides a continuous reflection of the intracranial state. Intracranial pressure is expressed by ventricular fluid pressures that normally fluctuate in the range of 0 to 10 mmHg (110 to 140 mmH$_2$O). Sustained elevations above 150 mmHg (200 mmH$_2$O) are generally considered to be abnormal.

The purposes of intracranial monitoring are therefore to:

1. Identify increased pressure early in its course.
2. Initiate appropriate treatment.
3. Act as a guide to the outcome.
4. Gain access to cerebrospinal fluid for sampling and drainage.
5. Evaluate the effectiveness of treatment.

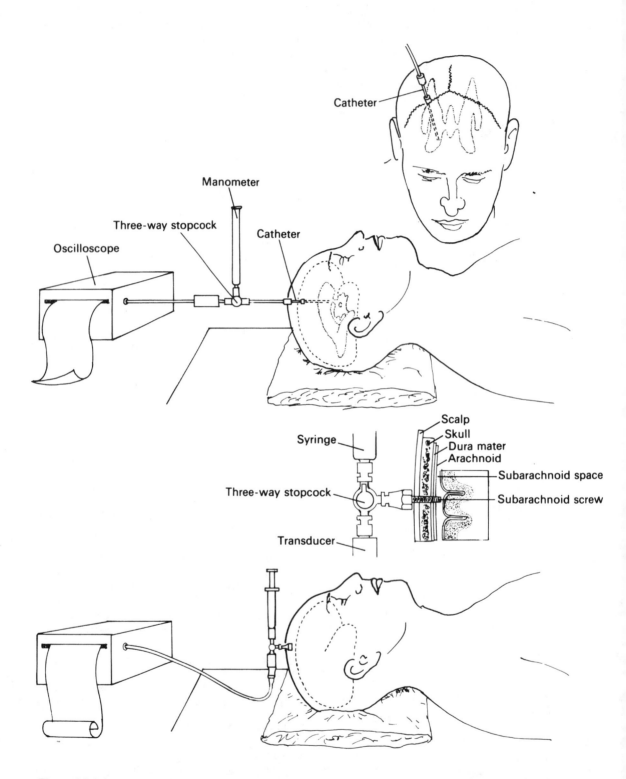

Figure 32.2 Intracranial pressure monitoring. (Top) Ventricular catheter. (Centre) Subarachnoid or hollow screw. (Bottom) Monitoring system connected to pressure transducer and display system.

The methods available are all invasive, incorporating a cannula/screw attached to a pressure transducer, and an oscilloscope with a chart recorder (Figure 32.2).

Planning and Implementation of Nursing Care

The nurse should maintain a strict aseptic technique when handling any part of the monitoring system. The insertion site is inspected for any signs of infection, and the patient's vital signs are monitored closely for systemic infection. All connections are checked for leaks since they can distort pressure recordings. When the monitoring system is set up, the transducer is zeroed at a particular reference point on the patient's head; therefore, for subsequent readings, the nurse should ensure the patient's head is in the same position relative to the transducer.

A number of factors are known to cause an increase in intracranial pressure that could be detrimental to the patient. With good nursing care, they can be avoided. For example, the nurse should be aware that venous outflow obstruction from the head results in increases in intracranial pressure. This may occur due to bad body positioning, or to prolonged suctioning, coughing, sneezing or straining at stool. Nursing care should be adapted accordingly and those actions likely to produce increases in intracranial pressure should be well spaced apart.

Whenever technology is associated with patient care, the nurse, while ensuring such technology remains functional, must always remember that a patient is attached to the machinery. Explanation and reassurance by the nurse may be helpful in reducing the patient's emotional stress.

Hyperthermia

Because of damage to the heat-regulating centre in the brain or severe intracranial infection, neurological and neurosurgical patients often develop very high temperatures. Such temperature elevations must be controlled, because the increased metabolic demands by the brain will overburden brain circulation and oxygenation, resulting in cerebral deterioration. Persistent hyperthermia is indicative of brain stem damage and has a poor prognosis. It has been shown that body temperatures well below normal decrease cerebral oedema, reduce the quantity of oxygen and metabolites required by the brain, and protect the brain from continued ischaemia. Also, the collateral circulation in the brain may be able to provide an adequate blood supply to the brain if the body metabolism can be lowered. Hyperthermia is also seen in the neurologically impaired patient with central nervous system, respiratory, urinary and wound infections. Drug reactions may also be the cause.

Nursing Considerations
The induction and maintenance of hypothermia is a major clinical procedure and requires knowledge and skilled nursing observation and care. It is desirable to begin treatment before the patient's temperature gets too high.

● All bedding over the patient should be removed (with the possible exception of a light sheet or loin cloth).
● Repeated doses of aspirin may be given as prescribed.
● Cool water sponging or an electric fan blowing over the patient to increase surface cooling are also helpful.
● The use of the hypothermia blanket and equipment is usually effective in controlling neurogenic hyperthermia.

The Unconscious Patient

Unconsciousness is a condition in which there is a depression of cerebral function. The causes of unconsciousness may be neurological (head injury, stroke), toxicological (drug overdose, alcohol intoxication) or metabolic (hepatic or renal failure).

Diagnosis

Laboratory tests that may be helpful in diagnosing the cause of unconsciousness include tests for blood sugar, electrolytes, blood urea nitrogen, osmolality, calcium, prothrombin time, serum ketones and arterial blood gases. Computerized tomography may support the diagnosis of a neurological disorder.

▶ NURSING PROCESS
▶ THE UNCONSCIOUS PATIENT

▶ *Nursing Assessment*

Clinical Features
The level of responsiveness is assessed by evaluating eye opening responses, verbal responses and motor responses to a command or painful stimulus using the Glasgow Coma Scale (Figure 32.1). The pupils are evaluated as to size, equality and reaction to light. In addition, the movement of the eyes is noted. Facial symmetry and swallowing reflexes are noted.

The vital signs are monitored, careful note being made of respiratory function. The nurse should also make note of any leakage from the nose and ears, neck stiffness and injection sites (diabetic/drug addict). The nurse should alert the medical staff about fluctuations from baseline recordings that may be indicative of a change in intracranial pressure.

▶ *Planning and Implementation*

Nursing Care
The quality of nursing care given to an unconscious patient may literally mean the difference between life and

death, since the patient's protective reflexes are impaired. The nurse must assume responsibility for the patient until the basic reflexes return (coughing, blinking and swallowing) and the patient becomes conscious and orientated. Thus, the major nursing objective is to assume these protective reflexes for such patients until they are aware of themselves and can function consciously.

Maintaining the Airway

The most important consideration in the care of the unconscious patient is the establishment of an adequate airway and ventilation. Circulation to the brain must be ensured. Obstruction of the airway is a risk facing the unconscious patient, since the epiglottis and tongue may relax, occluding the oropharynx, or the patient may inhale vomitus or nasopharyngeal secretions.

- The patient is positioned in a lateral or semiprone position, which permits the jaw and tongue to fall forward and thus facilitates drainage of secretions. *Unconscious patients must not be allowed to remain on their backs.* The airway can be maintained by the insertion of an oral airway. Occasionally a tracheostomy or endotracheal intubation may be necessary, especially if assisted ventilation is required. Oxygen may be administered until the cause of the unconsciousness or the arterial blood gas estimations are known.

The accumulation of secretions in the pharynx presents a serious problem that demands intelligent and conscientious management. Since the patient is unable to swallow and lacks pharyngeal reflexes, these secretions must be removed to eliminate the danger of aspiration.

- Under medical direction, elevating the head of the bed to a 30-degree angle helps to prevent aspiration of secretions.
- Suction is employed to remove secretions from the posterior pharynx and upper trachea. With the suction turned *off*, a suction catheter is attached to the suction equipment, and then manoeuvred to the desired level. The suction is turned on while the suction catheter is withdrawn with a twisting motion of the thumb and forefinger, which prevents the suctioning end of the catheter from irritating the tracheal or pharyngeal mucosa. Suction should not be prolonged. Such procedures should be limited to a few seconds, giving the patient adequate rest between episodes. Oxygenation should be continued between episodes of suction, if in use.
- The chest is auscultated periodically for crackles, rhonchi or absence of breath sounds.

Attaining Fluid and Nutritional Balance

An unconscious patient is unable to ingest oral fluids or meet nutritional requirements. These initial needs will be met, therefore, by intravenous infusion. Serial laboratory electrolyte evaluations will enable the doctor to achieve a proper balance.

Feeding via nasogastric tube enables better nutrition than by intravenous feeding. Initially, an adynamic ileus is common in the unconscious patient, and a nasogastric tube assists in gastric decompression. When gastric aspirate diminishes, gastric feeding can commence. When feeding a patient nasogastrically, it is important to aspirate the stomach before feeding. A residual exceeding 50 ml may result in gastric distension and vomiting. If possible, the patient's head should be elevated and the patient given 100 to 150 ml of preparatory feed, gradually increasing until 400 to 500 ml are given at each feeding. The elevated position reduces the likelihood of oesophageal reflux, regurgitation and aspiration. Sometimes it is necessary to replace the aspirated contents if a large aspirate is obtained to prevent fluid and electrolyte imbalance.

An unconscious patient requires high protein and adequate fluids in the order of 2,000 to 2,500 ml a day. Fever, excessive sweating or fluid loss elsewhere in the body increases fluid requirements. The tube should be rinsed with water after each feed and the preparatory feed is kept refrigerated until it is required. However, it is always allowed to return to room temperature before being administered.

Prolonged nasogastric intubation can cause oesophagitis and erosion of the nasal septum.

Maintaining Healthy Oral Mucous Membranes

The unconscious patient requires conscientious oral care because there is a risk of parotitis if the mouth is not kept scrupulously clean. The mouth is cleansed with mouth sponges or swabs to remove secretions and crusts and to keep the membranes moist. A thin coating of white paraffin on the lips prevents drying, cracking and the formation of encrustations.

Maintaining Skin Integrity

Preventing skin breakdown requires continuing nursing assessment and intervention. Special attention is given to unconscious patients because they are insensitive to external stimuli. The skin should be kept clean, dry and free from pressure. Pressure can cause skin necrosis, and a regular schedule of turning should be instituted. After turning, the patient is repositioned carefully to prevent ischaemic necrosis over pressure areas. Dragging the patient up in bed must be avoided since this creates a shearing force and friction on the skin surface. The patient's nails should be kept well clipped to prevent skin damage.

Maintaining correct body position is important; equally important is passive exercise of the extremities so that contractures are prevented. The use of a footboard aids in the prevention of footdrop and eliminates the pressure of bedding on the toes. Trochanter rolls supporting the hip joints keep the legs in a good position. The arm should be in abduction, the fingers lightly flexed and the hand in a position of slight supination.

Maintaining Corneal Integrity

Some unconscious patients lie with their eyes open and have inefficient or absent corneal reflexes. The cornea is likely to become irritated or scratched, leading to keratitis and corneal ulcers.

The eyes may be cleansed with cotton wool balls moistened with sterile normal saline to remove debris and discharge. It may be necessary to instil artificial tears every two hours. (This is an interdependent action requiring consultation with the doctor.) It is important to protect the cornea; therefore, the nurse must ensure that the patient's eye does not come into contact with bedding. The eyelids may be taped shut with hypoallergic tape and, if unconsciousness is prolonged, a tarsorrhaphy may be performed.

Attaining Thermoregulation

High fever in the unconscious patient may be caused by infection of the respiratory tract or urinary tract, drug reactions, or damage to the hypothalamic temperature-regulating centre. A slight elevation of temperature may be caused by dehydration. The temperature of the environment is determined by the patient's condition. An elevated body temperature would call for a minimum amount of bedding—a sheet or perhaps only a loin cloth.

● The body temperature of an unconscious patient is never taken by mouth. Rectal temperature is preferred to the less accurate axillary temperature.

Hyperpyrexia is treated by measures described on p. 995.

Preventing Urinary Retention

The unconscious patient is either incontinent or has urinary retention. The patient's bladder is palpated at intervals to determine whether urinary retention is present, since a full bladder may be an overlooked cause of incontinence. If there are signs of urinary retention, initially an indwelling catheter attached to a closed drainage system is inserted. Since the catheter is a major cause of urinary infection, the patient is observed for fever and cloudy urine. The area around the urethral orifice is inspected for suppurative drainage, and regular urethral toilet is given. To prevent traction of the urethra, the urinary catheter should be attached to the inner thigh of a female patient, and either to the abdomen or horizontally to the side of a male patient. The urinary catheter is usually removed when the patient has a stable cardiovascular system.

An external penile catheter (condom catheter) can be used for the unconscious male patient who can urinate spontaneously, although involuntarily. As soon as consciousness is regained, a bladder training programme is initiated.

Promoting Bowel Function

Abdominal distension is evaluated by listening for bowel sounds and measuring the girth of the abdomen with a tape measure. There is a risk of diarrhoea from infection, antibiotics and hyperosmolar fluids. Frequent loose stools are also an indication of faecal impaction.

Immobility and lack of dietary fibre may cause constipation. The nurse monitors the number and consistency of bowel movements and performs a rectal examination for signs of faecal impaction. The patient may require an enema every other day to empty the lower colon. However, enemas may be contraindicated if the Valsalva manoeuvre increases a compromised intracranial pressure. A glycerine suppository stimulates bowel emptying. Stools softeners may be prescribed and can be given with the tube feeds.

Safety

A certain degree of restlessness may be favourable as it may indicate that the patient is regaining consciousness. However, the nurse should be aware of the various phases of restlessness, as it is quite common in cerebral hypoxia, when there is a partially obstructed airway, a distended bladder, overlooked bleeding or a fracture. It may also be a sign of brain injury.

For the protection of the patient, padded siderails should be provided. Every measure that is available and appropriate for calming and quietening the disturbed patient should be carried out. Any form of restraint is likely to be countered by resistance, whether the patient is fully conscious or not, and fury so incited may lead to self-injury or to a dangerous increase in intracranial pressure.

Promoting Sensory Stimulation

Continuing sensory stimulation is provided to help overcome the profound sensory deprivation of the unconscious patient. Efforts are made to maintain the sense of daily rhythm by keeping the usual day and night patterns for activity and sleep. The nurse should direct conversation to the patient, encouraging loved ones to talk to the patient, and attempt to arouse the patient by touching and stimulating the senses. Introducing meaningful sounds, for example, from the home or work environment, may help to stimulate the patient's cortical levels.

The patient should be orientated periodically to the present situation. It is also important to avoid making any negative comments about the patient's status and prognosis in the patient's presence.

Attaining Self-Care

The unconscious patient is dependent on the nursing staff for all activities of daily living. As soon as consciousness returns, the nurse begins to teach, support, encourage and supervise these activities until the patient gains independence.

Supporting the Patient's Loved Ones

The unconscious patient's family and friends may be thrown into a sudden state of crisis and go through the process of high anxiety, denial, anger, remorse, grief and reconciliation. They will require constant information and reinforcement about the condition of their relative. Permitting loved ones to be involved in the patient's care, if they wish, may make them feel as if they are doing something to help.

► *Evaluation*
► **Expected Outcomes**

1. Patient has maintained a clear airway and has attained and sustained adequate fluid and nutritional status.
2. Patient regains consciousness without any long-term complications that could be attributed to the altered conscious state.

Dysphasia (Language Disorder)

A disturbance of language function may occur from injury or disease (head trauma, tumour, cerebrovascular accidents) to the 'speech centres' that are found in the dominant hemisphere of the brain. In right-handed people, the left hemisphere is dominant, and in most left-handed people, the left hemisphere is dominant, although 25 per cent of them have a dominant right hemisphere.

The cortical centres are:

1. Broca's area, located in a lateral convolution of the inferior part of the frontal lobe at the beginning of the lateral sulcus. Here the combinations of muscular movements necessary to speak each word are stored.
2. Receptive area (Wernicke's) lies at the posterior end of the lateral sulcus where the spoken word is understood and action initiated.

Language impairment, therefore, may involve the ability to read and write as well as to speak, listen and comprehend. Absence of speech is termed aphasia; dysphasia is a partial loss of production or comprehension of the spoken or written word, although both are used interchangeably. Dysphasia may be divided into:

1. Motor or expressive dysphasia, whereby the spoken word is understood but patients have difficulty in expressing themselves.
2. Sensory or receptive dysphasia, where patients are unable to understand the written or spoken word.
3. Central or global dysphasia, which is a combination of both motor and sensory dysphasia.

When weakness of the muscles involved in speaking occurs due to cranial nerve damage, the patient may have difficulty in articulating (dysarthria), and speech becomes slurred.

A speech assessment to determine the communication abilities of the patient is carried out by the speech therapist; thereafter the care is individualized for that patient.

Nursing Care

1. The patient should be given as much psychological security as possible.
2. The nurse should face the patient when communicating and establish eye contact.
3. The nurse should speak slowly, in short phrases, pausing in between.
4. It should be ensured that the patient understands what is being asked.
5. Conversation should be confined to practical matters and supplemented with gestures.
6. Consistency is important: the same word or gesture is repeated each time instructions are given and questions asked.
7. Extraneous noises and sounds must be kept to a minimum since the patient cannot sort out the various stimuli when the environment is noisy.
8. Sensory input should be provided.
   a. Auditory stimulation supplemented with visual stimulation.
   b. Communication cards and visual pictures should be provided.
   c. Reading and writing should be encouraged.
   d. Games, videos, television may be used to stimulate interest.
   e. The nurse should try to elicit responses from the patient, for example, a 'thumbs up' sign if a question is understood.
9. Patients should be assured that their intelligence is unaffected.
   a. The nurse should continue to provide a social contact by talking to patients while caring, giving.
   b. The nurse should never force patients to correct mistakes nor finish their sentences for them.
10. Patients should be encouraged to socialize with family and friends.
11. Periods of emotional lability will perhaps cause speech that is motivated by emotions to be expressed (for example, swearing). This should be ignored.
12. Speech may be unintelligent, filled with jargon.
    a. The nurse should observe any gestures that may offer a clue.
    b. The nurse should continue to listen to the patient.
    c. It is helpful if the nurse nods and makes neutral statements occasionally.

Family Education

The family (or significant others) will require as much support as the patient, and advice and supervision must be given on how to communicate with the patient. Loved ones should be encouraged to act naturally and to treat the patient in the same manner as before the illness. They should be aware that the patient's ability to communicate may alter daily, and that fatigue and distraction will have an adverse effect. They should also be aware that the patient may strike out verbally when emotional controls are low and the patient will become easily frustrated.

Relearning speech and language skills may take several years, but support groups and stroke clubs can often help to motivate and socialize the patient.

▶ *Evaluation*
▶ **Expected Outcomes**

1. Patient is able to socialize without embarrassment.
2. Communicates with others according to ability/disability.
3. Family members recognize the patient's limitations and give encouragement and support. They continue to pursue their own interests.

NEUROLOGICAL DEFICITS DUE TO CEREBROVASCULAR DISEASE

Cerebrovascular disease refers to any functional abnormality of the central nervous system caused by interference with the normal blood supply to the brain. The pathology may involve an artery, a vein or both, when the cerebral circulation becomes impaired as a result of partial or complete occlusion of a blood vessel or haemorrhage resulting from a tear in the vessel wall. The blood vessel most frequently associated with cerebrovascular disease is the internal carotid artery.

Vascular disease of the central nervous system may be caused by arteriosclerosis (most common), hypertensive changes, arteriovenous malformations, vasospasm, inflammation, arteritis or embolism. As a result of vascular disease, blood vessels lose their elasticity, become hardened and develop atheromatous deposits, or plaques, which may be the source of an embolus. The lumen of the vessel may gradually close, causing impairment of cerebral circulation and ischaemia of the brain. If cerebral ischaemia is transient, there is usually no lasting neurological deficit. However, occlusion of a large vessel produces cerebral infarction (Figure 32.3). The vessel may rupture and produce haemorrhage.

Stroke (Cerebrovascular Accident)

A stroke is a sudden loss of brain function resulting from a disruption of the blood supply to a part of the brain, which lasts for more than 24 hours. Frequently, it is the culmination of cerebrovascular disease of many years' standing, and is the commonest neurological disorder requiring hospital admission. Each year about 100,000 people in the United Kingdom have a first stroke, and 25,000 have a

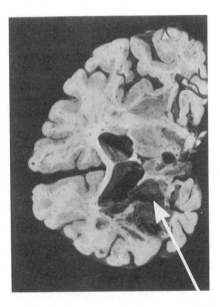

Figure 32.3 Impairment of cerebral circulation leading to a stroke. The arrow points to the area of cerebral infarction. (Armed Forces Institute of Pathology: Neg. No. 55-13956.)

first transient ischaemic attack. In affluent societies, stroke ranks behind heart disease and cancer as a cause of death.

Causes of Stroke

The causes of stroke can be classified as follows:

Cerebral Thrombosis
Cerebral arteriosclerosis and slowing of the cerebral circulation are major causes of cerebral thrombosis, which is the most common cause of stroke.

Headache is rather uncommon at the onset of cerebral thrombosis. Some patients may experience dizziness, mental disturbances or convulsions, and some may have an onset indistinguishable from that of intracerebral haemorrhage or cerebral embolism. In general, cerebral thrombosis does not develop abruptly, and a transient loss of speech, hemiplegia or paraesthesias in one half of the body may precede the onset of a severe paralysis by a few hours or days.

Cerebral Embolism
Pathological abnormalities of the left side of the heart, such as infective endocarditis, rheumatic heart disease and myocardial infarction, as well as pulmonary infections, are the sites where emboli originate. It is possible that the insertion of a prosthetic heart valve may precipitate a stroke since there seems to be an increased incidence of embolism following this procedure. The incidence of stroke following this procedure can probably

be reduced with postoperative anticoagulant therapy. Pacemaker failure, atrial fibrillation and cardioversion for atrial fibrillation are other possible causes of cerebral emboli and stroke.

The embolus usually lodges in the middle cerebral artery or its branches, where it disrupts the cerebral circulation.

● Sudden onset of hemiparesis or hemiplegia with or without dysphasia or loss of consciousness in a patient with cardiac or pulmonary disease is characteristic of cerebral embolism.

Cerebral Ischaemia

The most common manifestation is transient ischaemic attacks. A transient ischaemic attack is a transient or temporary episode of neurological dysfunction commonly manifested by a sudden loss of motor or sensory function, lasting a few seconds or minutes but no longer than 24 hours. Complete recovery usually occurs between attacks.

A transient ischaemic attack may serve as a warning of impending stroke, which has its greatest incidence in the first month after the first attack. The cause of this clinical entity is a temporary impairment of blood flow to a specific region of the brain due to a variety of reasons, including atherosclerosis of the vessels supplying the brain, obstruction of cerebral microcirculation by a small embolus, a fall in cerebral perfusion pressure, cardiac arrhythmias and so on.

The most common sites of atherosclerosis in the extracranial arteries are located at the bifurcation of the common carotid and at the origin of the vertebral arteries. Among the intracranial arteries, the middle cerebral artery is the most common location of atherosclerosis, where a 'bruit' may be heard on auscultation. Digital subtraction angiography is helpful in defining carotid artery obstruction and providing information on cerebral blood flow.

Medical Management. Patients who are not candidates for surgical intervention may be placed on anticoagulant therapy in order to prevent future attacks and a possible massive cerebral infarction. Platelet-inhibiting drugs (particularly aspirin) are useful in decreasing the occurrence of cerebral infarction in patients who have experienced multiple transient ischaemic attacks.

Surgical intervention procedures in common use are endarterectomy (surgical removal of an arteriosclerotic plaque or thrombus) and angioplasty in which a balloon on a catheter is inserted in the artery to break up the plaque and dilate the artery.

Cerebral Haemorrhage

Extradural Haemorrhage. Extradural haemorrhage (epidural haemorrhage) is a neurosurgical emergency that requires urgent care. It usually follows skull fracture with a tear of the middle artery or other meningeal artery. If the patient is not treated within hours following the accident, there is very little chance of survival (see p. 1049).

Subdural Haemorrhage. Subdural haemorrhage (excluding the acute subdural) is basically the same as an epidural haemorrhage, except that in subdural haematoma usually a bridging vein is torn. Thus, a longer period of time (longer lucid interval) is required for the haematoma to form and cause pressure on the brain. (This is discussed in the section on head injury on p. 1040.)

Subarachnoid Haemorrhage

Subarachnoid haemorrhage (haemorrhage occurring in the subarachnoid space) may occur as a result of trauma or hypertension, but the most common cause is a leaking aneurysm in the area of the circle of Willis and congenital arteriovenous malformations of the brain. Any artery within the brain can be the site of an aneurysm. (The treatment of intracranial aneurysms is discussed on p. 1027.)

Intracerebral Haemorrhage

Haemorrhage or bleeding into the brain substance is most common in patients with hypertension and cerebral atherosclerosis, since degenerative changes due to these diseases usually cause rupture of the vessel. It may also be due to certain types of arterial pathology, presence of brain tumour and the use of oral anticoagulants. The clinical picture and the prognosis depend mainly on the degree of haemorrhage and brain damage. Occasionally, the bleeding ruptures the wall of the lateral ventricle and causes intraventricular haemorrhage, which is frequently fatal.

Usually, the onset is abrupt, with severe headache. As the haematoma enlarges, a more pronounced neurological deficit occurs in the form of decreased alertness and abnormalities in the vital signs. If the bleeding is limited or develops gradually, there may be no significant pressure effects. On the other hand, the full deficit may evolve in a matter of hours. A marked reduction in consciousness in the early phase of the bleeding episode usually has an ominous prognosis.

The treatment of intracerebral haemorrhage is controversial. If the haemorrhage is small, the patient is treated conservatively and symptomatically.

● The blood pressure is carefully lowered with antihypertensive drugs. The patient's neurological deficit may worsen if the blood pressure is dropped too low or lowered too rapidly. The most effective form of treatment is the prevention of hypertensive vascular disease.

Risk Factors and Prevention of Stroke

Prevention of cerebrovascular disease is the best possible approach and as such depends on identification of the risk factors and thus their correction.

- Control of hypertension, the major risk factor, is the key to prevention of stroke.
- Patients with cardiovascular disease, rheumatic heart disease, rhythm abnormalities, congestive heart failure and left ventricular hypertrophy are at increased risk since cerebral embolism may originate in the heart.
- A high normal haematocrit level is related to an increased incidence of cerebral infarction.
- Diabetes is associated with accelerated atherogenesis.
- There appears to be an increased risk of stroke among women taking oral contraceptives, which is enhanced by coexisting hypertension, the patient being over 35 years, cigarette smoking and high oestrogen levels.
- An excessive or prolonged fall of blood pressure following shock.
- Drug abuse is a cause of stroke, particularly in adolescents and young adults.
- In younger people, attention should be directed at controlling blood lipids (particularly cholesterol), blood pressure, cigarette smoking and obesity.
- There appears to be a link between alcohol consumption and stroke.

Clinical Features

A stroke causes a wide variety of neurological deficits depending on the location of the lesion (which vessels are obstructed), the size of the area of inadequate perfusion and the amount of collateral (secondary or accessory) blood flow. The damaged brain cannot be fully restored.

Motor Loss

Stroke is a disease of the upper motor neurones and results in loss of voluntary control over motor movements. Since the upper motor neurones decussate (cross), a disturbance of voluntary motor control on one side of the body may reflect damage to the upper motor neurones on the opposite side of the brain. The most common motor dysfunction is hemiplegia (paralysis of one side of the body) due to a lesion of the opposite side of the brain. Hemiparesis, or weakness of one side of the body, is another sign.

In the early stage of stroke, the initial clinical feature may be flaccid paralysis and loss or decrease in the deep tendon reflexes. When these deep reflexes reappear (usually by 48 hours), increased tone is observed along with spasticity (abnormal increase in muscle tone) of the extremities on the affected side.

Communication Loss

Other brain functions affected by stroke are language and communication. Dysfunction in these areas may be manifested by:

- Dysarthria (difficulty in speaking), as demonstrated by poorly intelligible speech caused by paralysis of the muscles responsible for producing speech.

- Dysphasia or aphasia (defective speech or loss of speech), which is mainly expressive or receptive.
- Dyspraxia (inability to perform a previously learned action), as may be seen when a patient picks up a fork and attempts to comb the hair with it.

Perceptual Disturbances

Perception is the ability to interpret sensation, and disturbances may present as:

1. Visual disorders due to disturbances of sensory pathways between the eye and the visual cortex. This results in the loss of half of the patient's visual field, corresponding to the paralyzed side of the body, so that the patient neglects that side and the space on that side.
2. Visual/spatial disturbances, frequently seen in patients with a left hemiplegia. The patient fails to recognize familiar faces and objects, and becomes easily disorientated, even in familiar surroundings.
3. Sensory loss in the form of slight impairment of touch, to the more severe loss of proprioception.

Impairment of Mental Activity and Psychological Effects

If damage has occurred to the frontal lobe, then learning capacity, memory or other higher cortical intellectual functions may be impaired. Such dysfunction may be reflected in a limited attention span, difficulties in comprehension, forgetfulness and a lack of motivation, which cause these patients to encounter frustrating problems in their rehabilitation. Depression is a natural response to such a catastrophic illness. Other psychological problems are myriad and are manifested by emotional lability, hostility, frustration, resentment and nonco-operation.

Bladder Dysfunction

Following a stroke, the patient may have transient urinary incontinence due to confusion, inability to communicate need and inability to use the urinal/bedpan because of impaired motor and postural controls. Occasionally, following a stroke the bladder becomes atonic with impaired sensation in response to bladder filling. Sometimes control of the external urinary sphincter is lost or diminished.

Care of the Patient With Stroke (Acute Phase)

A patient who is deeply unconscious on admission to hospital is considered to have a poor prognosis; conversely, a fully conscious patient has a more favourable outcome. The acute phase usually lasts for 48 to 72 hours. The principles underlying the nursing care are as follows:

1. Care of the unconscious patient (see p. 995).
2. Neurological observations.
   a. A change in the level of responsiveness as evidenced by movement, resistance to position change

and response to stimulation: orientation to person/time/place.

b. Presence or absence of voluntary or involuntary movement of the extremities; the tone of muscles, body posture and position of the head.

c. Stiffness or flaccidity of the neck.

d. Eye opening—the comparative size of pupils, their reaction to light and ocular position.

e. The colour of the face and extremities, temperature and and skin moisture.

f. The quality and rates of pulse and respiration; the body temperature.

g. The volume of fluids ingested or administered, and volume of urine excreted each 24 hours.

3. Adequate cerebral blood flow and metabolism should be maintained.

a. Oxygen therapy, if necessary, should be given at the prescribed volume.

b. The blood pressure and cardiac output are maintained to sustain cerebral blood flow, and hydration must be ensured to reduce blood viscosity.

c. The patient should be monitored for evidence of pulmonary complications, which may be due to loss of airway reflexes, immobility or hypoventilation.

d. Endotracheal intubation and ventilation may be necessary in patients with respiratory embarrassment.

e. The patient should be observed for cardiac involvement, especially arrhythmias that may cause further embolic episodes.

4. The nurse should observe and report any deterioration in the patient's condition that may indicate surgical intervention, as required.

5. The nurse should communicate and reassure patients as consciousness is regained.

a. Patients should be stimulated by talking to them while giving care.

b. The nurse should attempt to reorientate patients (it should be remembered that they will fatigue easily).

c. Any dysphasia should be noted, and patients reassured that help with communication will be given.

d. The nurse should listen attentively as patients attempt to communicate.

6. Any increase in bladder tone should be recognized and the urinary catheter removed.

a. The patient should be toiletted frequently, with the nurse observing the voiding pattern.

Rehabilitation Phase

Although rehabilitation begins on the day the patient has the stroke, the care is intensified during the rehabilitative phase, requiring a multidisciplinary team approach; the nursing staff are in a good position to reinforce the care given by physiotherapists and the speech therapist.

Nursing Care

Planning and Implementation

A hemiplegic patient has unilateral paralysis. When control of the voluntary muscles is lost, the strong flexor muscles exert control over the extensors. The arm tends to adduct and rotate internally, with the elbow and wrist flexing. The affected leg tends to rotate externally at the hip joint and flex at the knees, while the foot and ankle joints supinate towards plantar flexion (Figure 32.4).

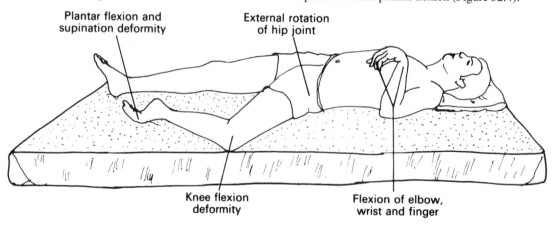

Plantar flexion and supination deformity

External rotation of hip joint

Knee flexion deformity

Flexion of elbow, wrist and finger

Figure 32.4 Hemiplegic deformities. The involved leg immediately falls into external rotation. The knee almost invariably flexes. As soon as knee flexion occurs, abduction of the upper leg follows. The foot falls into plantar flexion, so that there is always a footdrop and a shortening of the Achilles tendon. This position of the leg is assumed whether the leg is flaccid or spastic. The arm of the affected side is held against the body. Often, a flail arm is placed across the body for convenience in handling the patient, but if spastic, the elbow flexes to about 90 degrees. With the arm across the body, the wrist is dropped. If the arm is spastic, the fingers curl into a fist, with the thumb adducted and flexed under the fingers. (After Covalt, N. K., Preventive techniques of rehabilitation for hemiplegic patients, *GP*, Vol. 17, p. 131.)

1. Positioning—prevention of deformities. Correct positioning in bed is of prime importance (Figure 32.5) in preventing abnormal positioning, which could lead to increased spasticity contractures and pressure sores, and thus a reduction in the patient's opportunity to achieve maximum potential.
    a. Carefully place patient in positions to oppose the developing spasticity. As an alternative to the supine and lateral positions, the upright position may be used as the patient progresses.
    b. The patient's position should be changed every two hours, and can best be achieved by rolling the patient from side to side.
    c. The amount of time spent lying on the affected side may be limited by because of impaired sensation.
    d. A posterior splint may be applied to the affected limb at night to prevent flexion of the affected extremity during sleep.
    e. A palmar splint may be applied to a flaccid upper extremity to support the hand and wrist in a functional position.
    f. Ensure that the patient's affected shoulder is not

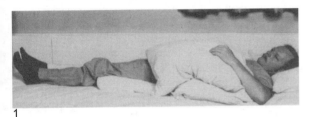

1

2

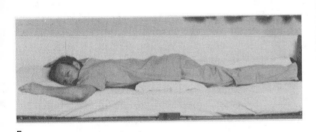

3

5   4

Figure 32.5 Positioning for a patient following a stroke. (Dark side of pyjamas represents affected or hemiplegic side.)
1. A pillow is placed in the axilla to prevent adduction of the affected shoulder. Pillows are placed under the arm, which is in a slightly flexed position with each joint positioned higher than the preceding one.
2. The trochanter roll should extend from the crest of the ilium to the midthigh, since the hip joint lies between these two points. The trochanter roll acts as a mechanical wedge under the projection of the greater trochanter and prevents the femur from rolling.
3. Lateral or side-lying position. The patient should be turned onto unaffected side. The upper thigh should not be acutely flexed
4. A volar resting splint may be used to support the wrist and hand if the upper extremity is flaccid.
5. Prone position. A pillow is placed under the pelvis to help promote hyperextension of the hip joint, which is essential for normal gait. Note position of arms.

pulled. A flaccid shoulder may be overstretched by excessive force; an incomplete dislocation can occur from overstretching the joint capsule and musculature, resulting in severe pain.

    g. The physiotherapist may advise a sling to be worn on the affected arm if the patient complains of pain or if the arm is very flaccid, but the nurse must ensure that:

      ii. the patient continues to exercise the affected arm;

      ii. the affected arm is supported on a pillow.

2. Retraining the affected extremities—exercise. The affected extremities are exercised passively and put through a full range of movement four or five times a day to maintain joint mobility, prevent contractures, gain motor control, prevent further deterioration of the neuromuscular system and to enhance circulation.

    a. Encourage the patient to exercise the affected limbs at intervals throughout the day to prevent them developing contractures.

    b. Supervise and support the patient to move and turn.

      i. Teach the patient to place the unaffected leg under the affected one to move it when turning and exercising.

      ii. Instruct the patient to lift the affected arm with the unaffected hand.

    c. Regularity is important, but frequent short periods of exercise are more beneficial than longer periods at infrequent intervals.

    d. Encourage relatives to become involved in the patient's care, demonstrating to them the special handling techniques.

3. Gaining independence in activities of daily living: loss of sensory/perceptual ability. This can be more of a disability to patients and a barrier to rehabilitation than loss of motor function. Patients may neglect the affected side or have a distorted body image. They may have spatial disorientation and neglect the environment on the affected side. Patients may fail to appreciate and recognize the size/shape/texture of familiar objects placed in their hands (astereognosis), as well as be unable to recognize objects by their sound or vision. Another form of sensory impairment is failure to perform a learned movement where the command is understood and no motor weakness exists (apraxia). Related to sensory/perceptual problems are visual field defects due to interruption of the visual pathway, producing a homonymous hemianopia, i.e. loss of vision in the nasal half of one eye and the temporal half of the other.

    a. Approach the patient from the unaffected side.

    b. Place bedside table, call bell on side of awareness.

    c. Place affected limbs within field of vision.

    d. Increase tactile sensation to affected side by touching, stroking.

    e. Avoid referring to right and left if spatial disorientation is a problem.

    f. Encourage the patient to turn head from side to side.

    g. Ensure the patient wears spectacles if required.

4. Language. Function may also be damaged (see p. xxx).

5. Swallowing. Initially and during the acute phase, the patient may have difficulty in swallowing (dysphagia).

    a. If indicated, continue with tube feeds according to the patient's requirements.

    b. Observe for any vomiting, regurgitation or diarrhoea.

    c. Institute oral feeding on the return of the cough and swallow reflexes. It is often easier for the patient to swallow semi-solids than fluids placed into the unaffected side of the mouth.

    d. Remind patient to chew on unaffected side, and inspect mouth for food collecting between cheek and gums.

    e. Give frequent oral hygiene.

    f. Encourage family and friends to assist the patient but explain the need for the patient to gain independence as the condition improves.

6. Elimination.

    a. Establish and maintain a bladder and bowel management programme.

    b. Attend to patients promptly when they need to eliminate.

    c. Reassure patient that regaining control of elimination will become established.

    d. Encourage independence in patients attending their own elimination needs.

7. Preparing for ambulation. As soon as possible, the patient is assisted out of bed. Usually when hemiplegia is the result of a thrombosis, active rehabilitation is started as soon as possible, whereas patients who have had a cerebral haemorrhage cannot participate actively until treatment is given to the underlying cause.

    a. Sitting balance. A hemiplegic patient tends to lose the sense of balance and thus needs first to learn sitting balance before learning to stand.

      i. Adjust the height of the bed.

      ii. Assist the patient into the sitting position by swinging legs over the side of the bed (Figure 32.6).

      iii. Ensure the feet are flat on the ground.

      iv. Stand in front of the patient and, if necessary, help to maintain this position.

      v. Observe any change in colour, shortness of breath, profuse perspiration and, if necessary, return patient to recumbent position.

      vi. Increase sitting time as rapidly as the patient's condition permits.

    b. Standing balance. Once sitting balance is achieved, standing balance is developed.

      i. Place chair parallel to the head of the bed on the patient's affected side (see Figure 32.6).

ii. Patient should wear strong, supportive walking shoes (slippers are not advised; bare feet are safer).

iii. Place patient into a sitting position.

iv. Help patient come to the standing position (see Figure 32.6).

v. The nurse's hands should be placed under the patient's shoulders, resting the arms on the patient's scapulae. The patient should be allowed to rest the arms on the nurse's shoulders. The patient's feet and knees are then wedged with the nurse's and, with the nurse's back being kept straight, the nurse leans back slightly to bring the patient into the standing position. The nurse pivots the patient round, and lowers the patient into the chair.

vi. The nurse stands behind and stabilizes the patient at waist level.

vii. The patient is observed for dizziness, pallor or tachycardia and, if necessary, is returned to bed.

viii. The standing time should be increased throughout the day.

c. Walking balance. Patients are usually ready to walk as soon as standing balance is achieved.

i. Patients should be assisted to walk as soon as they are able. Parallel bars are useful when patients first start to walk.

ii. A chair should be readily available in the event of sudden fatigue or dizziness.

iii. Patients should be encouraged to look occasionally at their feet, since proprioceptive loss may accompany hemiplegia. Better position sense may be achieved by the use of a posterior knee splint.

iv. A more stable support, in the early phases of rehabilitation, may be provided by a walking tripod.

8. Wheelchair. If the patient cannot manage ambulation, the physiotherapist can acquire a wheelchair to suit a particular patient. Wheelchair mobility provides greater independence in self-care activities and allows the patient to propel it with the unaffected foot and arm.

9. Achieving self-care. The patient is encouraged to assist in personal hygiene as soon as possible.

a. Realistic goals should be set and, if feasible, a new task should be set daily.

b. The patient should carry out all self-care activities on the unaffected side.

c. The nurse should encourage activities that can be carried out with one hand, such as combing the hair, shaving, brushing teeth and eating.

d. The patient's morale should be improved by encouraging dressing.

i. Clothing of a size larger than that normally worn, with Velcro fastenings, may be preferred.

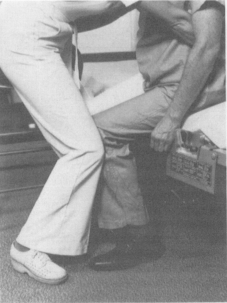

Figure 32.6 Getting the patient out of bed following a stroke. (Left) Place the bed in the low position so that the patient's feet are resting on the floor. Observe the patient's reaction and increase the sitting time as rapidly as the patient's condition permits. (Centre) Getting ready to rise to a standing position. Positioning the nurse's knees on the outside of the patient's knees will prevent the patient's knees from buckling. (Right) Stabilizing the patient as a standing postition is assumed. Note that the nurse is (1) stabilizing the patient's lower back and knees and (2) assessing the reaction to standing. (Courtesy of Washington Adventist Hospital; Glenn Dalby, photograher.)

ii. The sitting position achieves better balance while the patient is dressing.

10. Discharge.
    a. A home visit should be arranged with the occupational therapist and physiotherapist to assess the need to make home adaptations.
    b. There should be co-ordination with community services.

11. Education of relatives and friends. Members of the patient's family and circle of friends play an important role in the patient's recovery. They may have difficulty in accepting the patient's disability and may be unrealistic in their expectations. They should be prepared to expect occasional episodes of emotional lability—the patient may laugh or cry easily, be irritable, demanding, depressed or confused—but they should also know that this behaviour usually improves with time. Close relatives and friends should be given advice concerning the expected outcome and, although they should be sympathetic and supportive, they should also be firm, avoiding doing those things that patients can do for themselves, and focus on the abilities that remain. They need to be informed that rehabilitation may take many months, and that progress may be slow. Outpatient appointments should be kept and advantage taken of 'stroke clubs', or respite care may ease the burden for the caregivers. They also need to know that sexual function can be altered following stroke,

and that advice can be obtained by contacting a local branch of SPOD (The Association to Aid the Sexual and Personal Relationships of People With a Disability).

Evaluation

Expected Outcomes

1. Patient achieves optimum mobility.
   a. Avoids contractures by use of exercise and careful positioning.
   b. Achieves sitting, standing balance, transfer.
   c. Increases walking ability.
   d. Has no complaints of shoulder pain.
2. Demonstrates improved communication skills.
3. Patient is aware of sensory/perceptual difficulties.
   a. Will look at position of feet when walking.
   b. Is more aware of affected side of body and environment.
4. Achieves activities of daily living. Increases independence in ability to cope for self.
5. Bladder and bowel control attained and maintained.
6. Emotional lability becomes less.
7. Self-esteem improves. Patient again becomes valued member of the family and community.

See Nursing Care Plan 32.1 for the patient who has had a stroke.

► NURSING CARE PLAN 32.1: CARE OF A PATIENT WHO HAS HAD A STROKE

Mrs Alice Squibb is an overweight, 85-year old widow who lives in warden-controlled accommodation. She is a practising Methodist.

Patient's problems	Expected outcomes	Nursing care	Rationale
1. Impaired limb mobility with risk of spasticity	Full range of movements will be maintained on both sides. Joint contractures will be avoided. Spasticity in the affected limbs will be kept to the minimum	1a. Ensure all carers are aware of correct methods of handling the patient b. Range of movement and passive limb exercise performed four or five times daily c. Position limbs in anti-spasticity patterns d. Handle affected shoulder carefully. Avoid pulling on joint. Place in sling to avoid arm dangling e. Assist patient when turning from side to side f. Stimulate affected side with touch (see problem 2)	Muscle tone is lost. The weakened limb is flaccid, which over some weeks becomes spastic as tone increases. Bobath (1978) advocates that abnormal patterns of muscle tone can be lessened by correct positioning. Joint contractures will occur when no movement exists (Newman, 1985). Smith, Cruikshank, Dunbar *et al.* (1982) demonstrated that pulling on an affected shoulder joint capsule during the flaccid period can cause subluxation
2. Impaired sensory/ perceptual ability. Risk of injury to Mrs Squibb due to visual	Mrs Squibb and carers are aware of sensory/ perceptual difficulties	2a. Adapt approach to Mrs Squibb according to visual defect, e.g. approach from unaffected side	Neglect can be minimized if Mrs Squibb's affected arm/leg is kept within her field of vision. Descriptive terms, i.e. lift up

► NURSING CARE PLAN 32.1: CARE OF A PATIENT WHO HAS HAD A STROKE

Patient's problems	Expected outcomes	Nursing care	Rationale
field defect, motor deficit and/or perceptive deficits		b. Place call bell, bedside table on side of patient's awareness c. Avoid use of words 'right' and 'left' d. Provide tactile sensation to stimulate affected side e. Encourage Mrs Squibb to turn head from side to side f. Liaise with occupational therapist to establish a therapeutic programme g. Encourage patient to occasionally look at position of feet when mobilizing	your unaffected arm rather than 'left' will help the patient with spatial relationship difficulties
3. Impaired physical mobility	Patient will achieve the greatest potential in her mobility	3a. Plan a retraining programme in consultation with the physiotherapist b. Teach patient to move from side to side independently, initially with help c. Teach patient to sit up independently from lying position, initially with help (Figure 32.6) d. Transfer from bed to chair and return with one nurse, will be taught when sitting balance has been achieved (Figure 32.6) e. Transfer from bed to chair and return independently f. Assist the patient in the method of mobilizing according to physiotherapist's instructions g. Demonstrate to and support family/carers, assisting patient to gain independence	Patient loses the ability to maintain and restore balance in all movement and thus must relearn movement with a series of small progressive steps (Boyle, 1984; Johnstone, 1987).
4. Impaired verbal communication related to dysphasia and/or dysarthria	Strategies for improving communication will be developed	4a. Provide a relaxed atmosphere to allow free communication b. Try to understand Mrs Squibb's needs c. Listen carefully and attentively d. Reassure Mrs Squibb that, in consultation with the speech therapist, a suitable method of communication will be developed e. Avoid jargon, speak slowly, giving clear explanations f. Eye contact, gestures, writing, touch are all means of communication g. Provide help to relatives/friends h. Recognize that tiredness, poor concentration, agitation and depression may all affect communication	When communication is disrupted, the patient becomes isolated and alone, without the means to make needs known or to respond (Chalmers, 1985)

►

► NURSING CARE PLAN 32.1: CARE OF A PATIENT WHO HAS HAD A STROKE

Patient's problems	Expected outcomes	Nursing care	Rationale
5. Potential fluid volume and dietary deficit due to decreased gag and swallowing reflex. Risk of aspiration of food into upper respiratory tract	Adequate nutrition and hydration will be maintained safely according to the recommended requirements	5a. Provide the appropriate physical and social environment b. Evaluate gag and swallowing ability to determine when patient can swallow safely c. Liaise with dietician to provide food of a consistency (within patient's likes) that can be swallowed safely d. Arrange for the use of appropriate utensils to enable the patient to be more independent e. Provide protective clothing f. Ensure suction equipment is within easy reach g. Give assistance when required h. Encourage the placement of food on unaffected side i. Ensure fluids between mealtimes are within easy reach of patient j. Give advice to Mrs Squibb or her carers regarding the need to reduce weight	Food and fluid can be aspirated easily into the patient's lungs, leading to aspiration pneumonia if there are swallowing/gag deficits. Increased risk of cerebrosvascular accidents may be due to obesity (Warlow, 1987)
6. Impaired social interaction with risk of sensory deprivation and depression	The patient and carers will have gained insight into problems associated with impaired social interactions	6a. Support the patient and carers during periods of emotional lability b. Encourage Mrs Squibb to discuss her feelings c. Be aware of the possibility of depression occurring d. Make Mrs Squibb feel wanted e. Give positive reinforcement when relearning skills f. Reinforce that emotional lability/depression, like limb weakness, is a feature of the disorder and should improve	Emotional lability and low self-esteem are very common, and can be embarrassing both to patient and friends. Depression is common following stroke (Robinson and Price, 1982). Sensory deprivation as a result of inability to communicate/ immobility can occur (*see* problem 4) (Kratz, 1979)
7. Impairment of skin/ mucous membrane integrity	Patient's skin and mucous membranes will remain intact and free from infection	7a. Assess the skin integrity and establish a plan for regular skin inspection b. Change Mrs Squibb's position regularly to avoid sustained pressure (*see* problems 1, 2 and 3) c. Protect skin from heat and irritation d. Pay particular attention to areas with diminished sensation or lack of awareness e. Inspect the oral cavity after mealtimes for sores, pockets of food	Use of Norton Scale may be used to assess patient's risk of developing pressure sores (Norton, McLaren and Exon-Smith, 1978). Skin/mucous membrane damage increased due to immobility, motor and/or sensory impairment/neglect and incontinence
8. Impaired bladder and bowel function	Maintenance or the restoration of normal bladder and bowel function	8a. Observe urinary output for possible retention and/or incontinence b. Observe and document pattern of urinary elimination	Loss of bladder tone, sphincter control and inability to perceive full bladder may lead to urinary incontinence. Urinary catheterization should be used

► NURSING CARE PLAN 32.1: CARE OF A PATIENT WHO HAS HAD A STROKE

Patient's problems	Expected outcomes	Nursing care	Rationale
		c. Establish bladder training programme when indicated d. If possible, position Mrs Squibb's chair near toilet e. Adjust fluid requirements if necessary f. Provide suitable catheter toilet for patients with indwelling catheter g. Establish bowel programme h. Take measures to minimize constipation	only as a last resort (Alderman, 1989), and then using strict catheter care (Gooch, 1986; Wright, 1988). Immobility/inadequate fluid/fibre may result in altered bowel evacuation
9. Limited ability to perform daily living tasks	Achieves activities of living by increasing independence in the ability to cope for self	9a. Assist patient with daily living skills b. Initially choose activities that are within capabilities, e.g. grooming, brushing teeth c. Begin each activity from the upright position d. Allow patient to assume some responsibility for own needs e. Give assistance when necessary but recognize when to stand back	Setting and achieving realistic goals will improve self-esteem and confidence (see problem 6) The repetitious nature of many of the activities of living allows relearning/redevelopment of voluntary movement Too much assistance may result in dependence, whereas too little will cause frustration

NEUROSURGICAL TREATMENT OF PAIN

The management of long-term pain requires a multidisciplinary approach. (The reader is referred to Chapter 2 for a discussion of the basic theories of the psychophysiology of pain and its management.)

Intractable pain refers to pain that cannot be relieved satisfactorily by drugs without causing drug addiction or incapacitating sedation. Such pain usually is the result of malignancy (especially of the cervix, bladder, prostate and lower bowel), but it does occur in many other conditions, such as post-herpetic neuralgia, trigeminal neuralgia, spinal cord arachnoiditis and uncontrollable ischaemia and other forms of tissue destruction.

Neurosurgical methods available for pain relief include: (1) stimulation procedures (intermittent electric stimulation of a tract or centre to inhibit the transfer of pain information; (2) administration of intraspinal opiates; and (3) interruption of the tracts conducting the pain between the periphery and the cerebral integration centres. The latter are destructive or ablative procedures.

Stimulation Procedures

Electrical stimulation or neuromodulation is a method of suppressing pain by applying controlled low-voltage electrical pulses to the different parts of the nervous system. Electrical stimulation is thought to relieve pain by preventing messages from reaching the brain by blocking small afferent fibre input at the dorsal horn or by stimulating the release of endogenous opiates (natural pain-relieving peptides). This pain-modulating technique is administered by many modes. At present transcutaneous electrical nerve stimulation and dorsal column stimulation are the procedures most frequently done.

Transcutaneous Electric Nerve Stimulation

Transcutaneous electric nerve stimulation is the passage of small electrical currents through the skin for the purpose of controlling pain. The stimulating electrodes are placed over the site of pain or along the course of the major peripheral nerves innervating the area or over the peripheral plexus. The patient operates the amplitude control until stimulation, detected by a vibration, buzzing or tapping sensation, is felt within the deeper tissue. The amplitude is increased slowly until the sensation is perceived at the site or origin of pain and/or along radiating pathways. The patient controls the amplitude, frequency and duration of stimulation. It appears very useful to the well-instructed patient in the early management of acute pain as well as for the patient with chronic pain. It is best used as an adjunct to a comprehensive rehabilitation programme for relief and elimination of pain.

Patient Education for Transcutaneous Electric Nerve Stimulation

The patient is given the instruction booklet provided by the manufacturing company that explains care of the skin, electrodes and generator. The skin is cleansed and electrode gel is applied to the electrodes, which are then placed over the nerves that serve the painful area. The electrodes are secured with hypoallergenic tape. The major problem of transcutaneous electric nerve stimulation is skin irritation from the tape (from mechanical stresses created by shearing forces between tape and skin), gels or electrodes. The patient is advised to keep a record evaluating the effectiveness of transcutaneous electric nerve stimulation. If there is a progression of pathology (as in advanced cancer), changes in amplitude and so on may be adjusted.

Dorsal Column Stimulation

Dorsal column stimulation is a technique used for the relief of chronic intractable pain in which a surgically implanted device allows the patient to apply pulsed electrical stimulation to the dorsal aspect of the spinal cord to block pain impulses. (The largest accumulation of afferent fibres is found in the dorsal column of the spinal cord.)

The dorsal column stimulation unit consists of a radiofrequency stimulation transmitter, a transmitter antenna, a radiofrequency receiver and a stimulation electrode. The battery-powered transmitter and antenna are worn externally, while the receiver and electrode are implanted. A laminectomy is performed above the highest level of pain input, and the electrode is placed in the epidural space over the posterior column of the spinal cord. (The placement of the stimulating systems is varied.) The subcutaneous pocket is constructed over the clavicular area or some other site for placement of the receiver. The two are connected by a subcutaneous tunnel.

Postoperative Nursing Care

Preoperative assessment is carried out, which includes careful physical and psychological evaluation and pain assessment. The patient will possible also have benefit from transcutaneous nerve stimulation.

The postoperative nursing care is similar to that following a laminectomy (see p. 1059). The patient is assessed for evidence of paraplegia, tetraplegia and urinary incontinence. The extremities are evaluated for movement. Leakage of cerebrospinal fluid at the laminectomy site is also checked for, since the dura is opened during surgery. The implant site is checked for signs of infection. As soon as the patient is fully alert, the dorsal column stimulation system may be tested, although initial testing may not be accurate because a bandage may cover the receiver site. Complications include infection, cord trauma, cerebrospinal fluid leakage and pain around the implantation site.

Patient Education

The patient is given the manufacturer's booklet to become acquainted with the system. Proper skin care is taught as well as the method for attaching the antenna to the skin, connecting the transmitter and adjusting the settings. Different stimulation frequencies should be tried to determine which one gives the best pain relief. A record is kept of the stimulation used. The patient is also requested to keep several batteries in reserve. (Battery life depends on the extent of use.) The transmitter and antenna are cleaned according to the manufacturer's directions.

Intraspinal Opiates

Opiate receptors have been demonstrated not only in the brain but also in the spinal cord. These receptors can combine with locally administered opiates (morphine) injected epidurally or intrathecally to produce longlasting pain relief with little or no blunting of the patient's level of responsiveness and no losses of sensory, motor or sphincter function.

There are numerous techniques employed, but most include placing a catheter in the epidural or subarachnoid space via a spinal needle and inserting the catheter as near as possible to the spinal segment where the pain is projected. Small doses of preservative-free morphine diluted in saline are injected into the system at 6- to 24-hour intervals. If the patient requires long-term management, an implantable programmable pump is used.

Following the procedure the patient is evaluated for the degree of pain relief, which ranges from good to excellent. The puncture site is examined for evidence of infection.

With this method patients may be at home. The necessary dose of drug is small, the patients' mind is clear and they are usually able to function at a relatively high level. With long-term use there can be tolerance build-up and mechanical failure (catheter obstructed, dislodged, broken) of the application system. If the patient has rapid tumour growth, the dosage of morphine is increased, but the doses needed are low in comparison to that required for systemic administration for intractable pain.

Destructive or Ablative Procedures

Pain-conducting fibres can be interrupted at any point from their origin to the cerebral cortex. There is destruction of some part of the nervous system that can result in varying amounts of neurological deficit and incapacity (Figure 32.7). In time, pain usually returns as a result of either regeneration of axonal fibres or the development of alternative pain pathways.

Sympathectomy

Part of the sympathetic chain is resected. This procedure

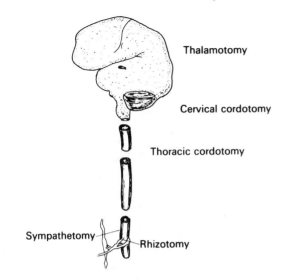

Figure 32.7 Pain-relieving procedures.

is often used to relieve spasm of peripheral vascular disorders and the intense, burning pain, causalgia, that occurs following trauma.

Rhizotomy

Rhizotomy is the surgical division selected posterior spinal nerve roots and is used in controlling severe chest pain of lung cancer and for pain relief in head and neck malignancies resulting in loss of sensation.

Since many patients with metastatic malignancies may not be able to tolerate an open rhizotomy, a percutaneous rhizotomy may be done, whereby a radiofrequency current is used to selectively coagulate the pain fibres, while the fibres concerned with touch and proprioception are preserved.

A chemical rhizotomy is one in which alcohol, phenol or a mixture of drugs is injected into the subarachnoid space. The medication is manoeuvred over the affected nerve roots by tilting the patient to the desired level. This renders the sensory nerve roots functionless. The patient's perception of pain is absent, but the motor nerve roots are usually not affected.

Patient Education

Patients should be taught the importance of the loss of sensation and pain, and to protect themselves from extremes of temperature. Patients should always test the temperature of water before bathing.

Cordotomy

Cordotomy is the division of sensory fibres in the lateral spinothalamic tract. It may be performed percutaneously, by the open method after laminectomy or by other techniques.

Percutaneous cordotomy uses radiofrequency currents to produce lesions in the anterolateral surface of the spinal cord. Under local anaesthesia, a needle is guided into the spinal cord under X-ray control, and then an electrode is inserted through it. By means of radiofrequency currents, a lesion is made at the desired spinal cord level.

Verification of electrode placement is determined by the patient's response to stimulation. The procedure is tolerated by wasted and debilitated patients.

An open cordotomy is the surgical division of the anterolateral columns of the sensory fibres. This procedure interrupts or destroys conduction of pain and temperature sense, while touch and position sense are preserved. The cord is exposed by laminectomy. Cordotomy is used most frequently in controlling the severe pain of terminal cancer, especially of the thorax, abdomen or lower extremities. Since a significant percentage of cordotomies lose their effectiveness in one to five years, the procedure is used for pain associated with conditions in which survival time is limited.

Postoperative Nursing Care

The principles of nursing care following a laminectomy are applicable in the postoperative and rehabilitation requirements of this patient.

Assessment for Complications

The patient is watched for respiratory complications, as well as for signs of fatigue and weakening of the voice. The patient may ventilate adequately while awake but may experience progressive hypercarbia and hypoxia while asleep. Therefore, arterial blood gases are monitored, and assisted mechanical ventilation is initiated when required.

Since haemorrhage may result in motor and sensory loss, the motion, strength and sensation of each extremity must be tested every few hours (or more frequently if necessary) during the first 48 hours postoperatively, and immediate surgical intervention is initiated. Because the patient has no sense of temperature, the skin should be felt at intervals to ascertain any changes in temperature. Since pressure sores may develop without the patient realizing it, the patient is taught to inspect the skin using a hand mirror to view the hard-to-see areas. Urinary retention may be encountered. There is usually a slow return to normal voiding, but this cannot be guaranteed. If there is permanent loss of urinary control from a high cervical procedure, a bladder training programme is started.

Psychosurgical Approaches

The purpose of psychosurgical procedures is to alter the patient's response to pain. A thalamotomy is the destruction (either unilateral or bilateral) of the specific cell groups within the thalamus. Burr holes are made in the skull, electrodes are placed in the target area by stereo-

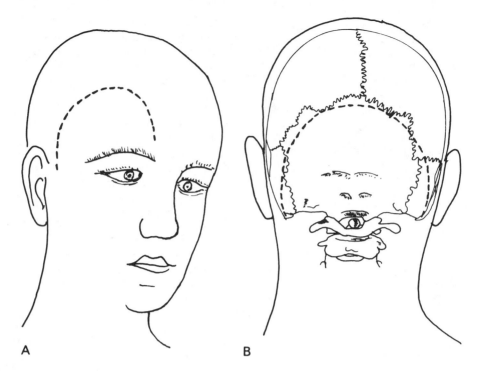

Figure 32.8 Surgical approaches for craniotomy (surgical opening of the cranial cavity). The dotted lines indicate scalp incisions. (A) Supratentorial approach. (B) Infratentorial approach. See text, below.

taxic techniques and a radiofrequency current is then directed through the electrodes to create the lesion. This procedure represents the highest level in the central nervous system in which pain pathways can be interrupted and is usually done for malignancy of the head and neck.

THE PATIENT UNDERGOING INTRACRANIAL SURGERY

In recent years, certain technological advances have helped to refine existing neurological procedures and develop newer ones. Superior neuroradiological techniques have made it possible to localize intracranial lesions. Improved illumination and magnification have made it possible to obtain a three-dimensional view of the field of operation. Lasers enable neurosurgeons to remove tumours precisely, and microsurgical instruments allow delicate tissue to be separated without trauma. Ultrasonic dissecting systems permit rapid and gentle removal of certain brain and spinal cord tumours with amazing precision.

Surgical Approaches

A craniotomy is the surgical opening of the skull to gain access to intracranial structures, allow removal of a tumour to relieve intracranial pressure, evacuate a blood clot and to control haemorrhage. The skull is opened by making a bony flap that is replaced following surgery and fixed in position by periosteal or wire sutures. In general, two approaches are used: (1) above the tentorium (supratentorial craniotomy) into the supratentorial compartment; and (2) below the tentorium into the infratentorial (posterior fossa) compartment (Figure 32.8).

The intracranial structures may be approached through burr holes (Figure 32.9), which are circular openings made in the skull by either a hand drill or an automatic craniotome (which has a self-controlled system to stop the drill when the bone is penetrated). Burr holes are made for exploration or diagnosis. They may be used to determine the level of brain tension and the size and position of the ventricles. They are also a means of evacuating an intracranial haematoma or abscess, making a bone flap in the skull and allowing access to the ventricles for decompression purposes, ventriculography or shunting procedures.

Other cranial procedures include craniectomy (an excision of a portion of the skull) and cranioplasty (repair of a cranial defect by means of a plastic or metal plate).

Diagnosis

Preoperative diagnostic procedures may include computed tomography and/or magnetic resonance imaging (see Chapter 31, p. 984) to demonstrate the lesion and reveal the degree of surrounding brain oedema, the

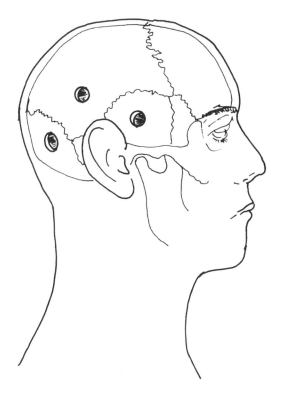

Figure 32.9 Burr holes may be used in neurosurgical procedures for making a bone flap in the skull, for aspiration of a brain abscess or to evacuate a haematoma.

ventricular size and any displacement. Cerebral angiography may be used to study the tumour blood supply or give information about vascular lesions.

Preoperative Care

The prospect of a neurosurgical operation, especially on the brain, is daunting to the patient and relatives, and the nurse should do everything possible to alleviate their anxiety by answering queries sympathetically. A full set of preoperative neurological observations should be made to allow postoperative comparative evaluation.

Observations of paralysis, visual disorders, personality changes, language disorder and bladder and bowel dysfunction are made and documented. Writing materials, picture or word cards can be supplied for those with language disorders, and support given to patients with sensory or motor deficits. Ambulation should be continued.

The patient and loved ones should be made aware of the nature and length of surgery and of postoperative expectations. Although some patients will not be aware of impending surgery, attention to their needs will usually reinforce confidence in the nurse.

The physical preoperative preparation may include:

1. Drug therapy, e.g. steroids are often introduced preoperatively to reduce cerebral oedema. Mannitol, a hyperosmotic solution, may be given intravenously before and during surgery.
2. A urethral catheter may be inserted before surgery to drain the bladder during the administration of dehydrating agents, to measure urinary output, to test for glucose and for specific gravity estimations.
3. The hair is usually washed the night before surgery; the head is shaved in the operating theatre. Many patients find this alteration in their appearance distressing. Reassuring patients that a dressing will normally cover the head and that it is possible to obtain a wig through the NHS helps to alleviate anxiety.

► NURSING PROCESS
► THE PATIENT UNDERGOING INTRACRANIAL SURGERY

Patients who have speech difficulties, failing vision and hearing loss are a challenge to the nurse's ingenuity. If the patient is dysphasic, writing materials or picture and word cards showing the bedpan, glass of water, blanket and so on may be supplied to help improve communication. If the patient is able to ambulate, encouragement is given in a quiet, unhurried way.

The emotional preparation of the patient is also important, including information about postoperative expectations. The large head dressing applied following surgery may impair hearing ability temporarily, and seeing may be difficult if the eyes are swollen. The patient will be unable to talk if an endotracheal tube or tracheostomy tube is *in situ*. Thus, an alternate method of communication should be developed before surgery.

Patients may not realize that they are about to undergo surgery. Even so, encouragement and attention to their needs usually will reinforce their confidence. Whatever the state of awareness of the patient, the family and close friends need reassurance and consideration, since they recognize the seriousness of a brain operation.

► *Postoperative Assessment*

Postoperative nursing monitoring of patients having intracranial surgery is done minute by minute and/or hour by hour depending on their clinical status. Assessment of respiratory status is essential because small degrees of hypoxia can aggravate cerebral ischaemia. The respiratory rate and patterns of respiration are monitored, and arterial blood gas values are reviewed. Fluctuations in the patient's vital signs are carefully watched for because they indicate increased intracranial pressure. The patient's rectal temperature is taken at intervals to evaluate for hyperthermia that may result from damage to the hypothalamus, which regulates body temperature.

Neurological checks are made frequently to detect increased intracranial pressure resulting from oedema or bleeding following intracranial surgery. A change in the level of responsiveness/consciousness may be the first sign of increasing intracranial pressure. Assessment of neurological status includes determining the level of responsiveness/consciousness, eye signs, motor response and vital signs. The nurse carefully observes for the insidious development of any neurological deficit, such as diminished response to stimuli, speech problems, difficulty in swallowing, weakness or paralysis of an extremity, visual changes (diplopia, blurred vision) and paraesthesias. The patient is observed for restlessness, which may reflect a return to consciousness or be due to pain, confusion, an obstructed urinary drainage system or other stimuli. Any evidence of seizure activity is reported immediately.

The patient's head dressing is inspected to determine the presence of bleeding and cerebrospinal fluid drainage. In patients undergoing transsphenoidal surgery, the nasal packing is checked for signs of bloody or cerebrospinal fluid drainage.

The intravenous infusion drip rate monitoring device is checked to see that it is working properly to prevent uncontrolled infusion. The infusion site is observed for redness, pain, swelling or purulent drainage.

Patient positioning depends on the surgical approach used. However, the patient's neck should be in a straight line because neck flexion may interfere with cerebral drainage.

The nurse is always alert to the development of complications, and all assessment is carried out with these problems in mind.

Nursing Care of the Patient Having Intracranial Surgery

Postoperative Care

Patient's Problem. Potential for ineffective breathing pattern related to postoperative cerebral oedema.

Expected Outcome. Achievement of adequate respiratory function.

1. Establish proper respiratory exchange and adequate brain oxygenation to eliminate systemic hypercarbia and hypoxia, which increase cerebral oedema.
   a. Place the patient in a lateral or semiprone position to facilitate respiratory exchange until consciousness returns, unless contraindicated.
   b. Employ tracheopharyngeal aspiration cautiously to remove secretions; suctioning can raise intracranial pressure.
   c. Elevate the head of the bed by 30 cm after patient is conscious to aid venous drainage of the brain, unless otherwise specified by the doctor.
   d. Ensure that the patient has nothing by mouth until

an active coughing and swallowing reflex is demonstrated; this prevents regurgitation.
   e. Ensure cardiovascular stability.

Potential Complication. Brain oedema secondary to intracranial surgery.

Expected Outcome. Prevention of brain oedema.

1. Assess and document patient's level of responsiveness/consciousness using the Glasgow Coma Scale (see p. 993); the diminution of the level of consciousness may be the first sign of increased intracranial pressure.
2. Evaluate for signs and symptoms of increasing intracranial pressure, which can lead to ischaemia and further impairment of brain function.
   a. Assess patient minute by minute, hour by hour, for:
      i. Diminished response to stimuli.
      ii. Fluctuations of vital signs.
      iii. Restlessness.
      iv. Weakness and paralysis of extremities.
      v. Increasing headache.
      vi. Changes or disturbances of vision; pupillary changes.
3. Control postoperative cerebral oedema as prescribed.
   a. Give steroids and osmotic dehydrating agents when prescribed in the postoperative period to reduce brain swelling.
   b. Monitor fluid intake; basic fluid requirements are usually precisely met; care is taken not to overload the patient.
   c. Maintain a normal temperature during the postoperative period. Temperature control may be lost in certain neurological states, and fever increases the metabolic demands of the brain.
      i. Take rectal temperature at specified intervals. Assess temperature of extremities, which may be cold and dry due to paralysis of heat-losing mechanisms (vasodilation and sweating).
      ii. Employ measures to reduce excessive fever when present. Use electrocardiogram monitoring to detect arrhythmias during hypothermia procedures.
         (a) Remove blankets.
         (b) Give tepid sponge.
         (c) Apply ice bag to axillae and groin.
         (d) Fan patient to increase surface cooling. Do not allow patient to shiver.
         (e) Drugs may be prescribed, e.g. aspirin suppositories, salicylates, chlorpromazine, to prevent excessive sweating.
         (f) Assist in monitoring intracranial pressure if required.
   d. Elevate head of bed to reduce intracranial pressure and facilitate respirations.
   e. Avoid excessive stimuli.

Patient's Problem. Potential alteration in fluid volume related to intracranial pressure or diuretics.

Expected Outcome. Attainment of fluid and electrolyte balance.

1. Monitor for polyuria, especially during first postoperative week; diabetes insipidus may develop in patients with lesions around the pituitary or hypothalamus.
   a. Take urinary specific gravity readings at intervals.
2. Evaluate patient's electrolyte status, since following certain major procedures patients have a tendency to retain water and sodium.
   a. Early postoperative weight gain indicates fluid retention; a greater than estimated weight loss indicates negative water balance. Weigh patient if indicated.
   b. Low potassium will cause confusion and decreased level of responsiveness.
3. Give prescribed intravenous fluids, including osmotic dehydrating solution, with care—rate and composition depend on fluid deficit, urine output and composition, and blood loss. Fluid intake and fluid losses should remain relatively equal.

Patient's Problem. Alteration in sensory perceptions (visual/auditory) related to periorbital oedema and head dressings.

Expected Outcome. Compensate for sensory deprivation.

1. Perform supportive measures until such patients can care for themselves.
   a. Change patient's position, as indicated; be aware that position changes can increase intracranial pressure.
   b. Give prescribed analgesics that do not mask the level of responsiveness (codeine).
2. Relieve signs of periocular oedema.
   a. Frequently bathe eyes with normal saline.
   b. Apply ointment or instil eye drops, as prescribed.
   c. Watch for signs of keratitis if cornea has no sensation.
3. Put extremities through range of motion exercises.
4. Evaluate and support patient during episodes of restlessness.
   a. Evaluate for airway obstruction, distended bladder, meningeal irritation from bloody cerebrospinal fluid.
   b. Pad patient's hands and bed rails to protect the patient from injury.
5. Reinforce blood-stained dressings with sterile dressing; blood-soaked dressings act as a culture medium for bacteria.
6. Orientate patient frequently to time, place and person.

Assessing the Patient For Complications

1. Intracranial haemorrhage.

   a. Postoperative bleeding may be intraventricular, intracerebellar, subdural or extradural.
   b. Watch for progressive impairment of state of responsiveness and other signs of increasing intracranial pressure.
   c. Prepare patient for diagnostic investigation, e.g. computerized tomography.
   d. Prepare deteriorating patient for reoperation and evacuation of haematoma.
2. Increased intracranial pressure; cerebral oedema.
3. Epilepsy (there is a greater risk with supratentorial operations).
   a. Administer prescribed anticonvulsants.
   b. Watch for status epilepticus, which may occur after any intracranial operation.
4. Infections.
   a. Urinary tract infections: strict aseptic techniques must be used in the management of indwelling urinary catheters.
   b. Pulmonary infections related to aspiration secondary to depressed level of responsiveness; may result in atelectasis and bronchopneumonia.
   c. Central nervous system infections (postoperative meningitis).
   d. Wound infections/septicaemia.
5. Venous thrombosis.
6. Leakage of cerebrospinal fluid, which may lead to meningitis.
   a. Differentiate between cerebrospinal fluid and mucus.
      i. Collect fluid on a glucose test strip; the indicator will have a positive reaction if cerebrospinal fluid is present, since cerebrospinal fluid contains sugar.
      ii. Assess for moderate elevation of temperature and mild neck rigidity.
   b. Caution patient against nose blowing or sniffing.
   c. Elevate head of bed as prescribed.
   d. Assist with insertion of lumbar subarachnoid drainage catheter that is placed to lower spinal fluid pressure.
      i. Ventricular catheters may be inserted in the patient undergoing surgery of the posterior fossa; the catheter(s) is connected to a closed reservoir system.
      ii. Give antibiotics as prescribed.
7. Gastrointestinal ulceration; monitor for signs and symptoms of haemorrhage, perforation or both.

Evaluation
Expected Outcomes.

1. Patient achieves neurological homeostasis/improved cerebral tissue perfusion.
   a. Opens eyes on request; utters recognizable words, progressing to normal speech.

b. Obeys commands with appropriate motor responses.

2. Attains thermoregulation.

3. Attains fluid and electrolyte balance.

　a. Demonstrates serum chemistries within acceptable limits for a patient undergoing intracranial surgery.

　b. Complies with fluid restriction, if necessary.

4. Copes with sensory deprivation.

5. Has no intracranial infection.

6. Has no pulmonary infection.

7. Demonstrates an improving self-concept.

　a. Pays attention to grooming.

　b. Visits and interacts with others.

Planning and Implementation

Achieving Neurological Homeostasis

Attention to the respiratory status is essential because even slight deficiencies in oxygen supply (hypoxia) can aggravate cerebral ischaemia. Nursing assessment and monitoring will affect the clinical course. The endotracheal tube is left in place until the patient shows signs of awakening and is breathing spontaneously as evaluated clinically and by arterial blood gas analysis. Secondary brain damage can result from impaired cerebral oxygenation.

Cerebral oedema is an increase in the water content of brain tissue leading to an increase in brain volume. Some degree of brain oedema occurs following brain surgery, which tends to be at its maximum 24 to 36 hours postoperatively. This is why there may be a slump in the patient's level of responsiveness on the second postoperative day. The control of cerebral oedema is discussed on page 991. The nursing strategies employed to eliminate factors contributing to the elevation of intracranial pressure are found on page 993. Intraventricular drainage is carefully monitored, using strict asepsis if any part of the system is handled.

Patient Education

The convalescence at home of a neurosurgical patient depends on the extent of the procedure and the success with which it was carried out. Those who will be caring for the patient at home are made aware of the patient's strengths as well as limitations and their part in promoting recovery. The patient may need to be accompanied while walking if sudden attacks of dizziness or seizures occur.

Usually the patient does not have any dietary restrictions unless there is another health problem requiring a special diet. The patient may take a shower or bath but should avoid getting the scalp wet until all the sutures have been removed. A clean scarf or cap may be worn until a wig or hairpiece is purchased. If skull bone has been removed, the neurosurgeon may advocate a protective helmet.

Following a craniotomy the patient is usually more sensitive to loud noises. Television noise can be very irritating to the convalescing person. If the patient is dysphasic, speech therapy may be necessary. This is likely to become a long-term and time-consuming project. It demands great patience and continuing encouragement on the part of all who are working with the patient.

When tumour, injury or disease is of such a nature that the prognosis is poor, care is directed toward making the patient as comfortable as possible. With return of the tumour or cerebral compression, the patient becomes less alert and aware. Other possible sequelae include paralysis, blindness and seizures. If the family or close friends are unable to give this type of care, the community nursing services and social worker plan together with them in making arrangements for additional home health care or in placing the patient in an extended-care or hospice facility.

Transsphenoidal Surgery

Pituitary tumours, representing about 5 per cent of all intracranial tumours, may be treated by surgery or irradiation. Surgical removal may be carried out through an open craniotomy (usually transfrontal) or by the transsphenoidal approach. The choice is determined by anatomical considerations and the extent and nature of the pathological process.

Tumours located within the sella turcica and small adenomas of the pituitary gland can be removed by way of the transsphenoidal approach (Figure 32.10). The incision is made beneath the upper lip, and entry is then gained successively into the nasal cavity, sphenoidal sinus and sella turcica.

This approach, using microsurgical techniques, is being used with greater frequency, and offers direct access to the sella with minimal risk of trauma and haemorrhage. It avoids many of the risks of craniotomy, and the postoperative discomfort is similar to that of other transnasal operations.

Preoperative Evaluation

The preoperative assessment includes a series of endocrine tests and neuroradiological studies. Funduscopic examination and visual field determinations are done, since the most serious effect of pituitary tumour is localized pressure on the optic nerve or chiasma. In addition, the nasopharyngeal secretions are cultured because a sinus infection is a contraindication to an intracranial procedure through this approach. Cortisone may be given preoperatively and postoperatively (since the source of adrenocorticotrophic hormone is removed). Antibiotics may or may not be administered prophylactically. Deep

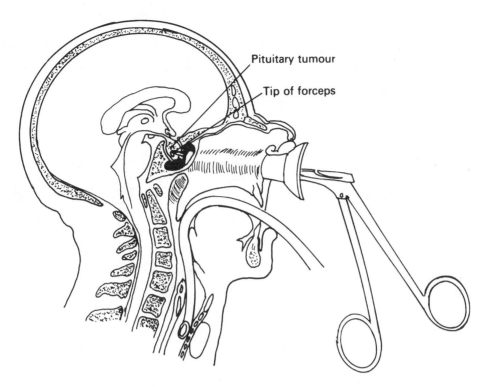

Figure 32.10 Transsphenoidal approach to the pituitary. A special nasal speculum is used to view the sinus cavity. After the dura is opened, the tumour is removed using microcurettes or other specially designed instruments.

breathing is taught preoperatively. The patient is advised that vigorous coughing and sneezing may cause a cerebrospinal fluid leak after surgery. Instructions are give to apply pressure on the inner aspect of both sides of the nose to control sneezing.

Postoperative Nursing Care

The vital signs are taken to monitor haemodynamic, cardiac and ventilatory status. Because of the anatomical proximity of the pituitary gland to the optic chiasma, visual acuity is checked at regular intervals. One method is to ask the patient to count the number of fingers held up by the nurse. Evidence of decreasing visual acuity suggests an expanding haematoma.

The major discomfort of the patient is related to the nasal packing and to mouth dryness and thirst from mouth-breathing. Oral care is provided every four hours or more frequently. Usually, the patient's teeth are not brushed until the incision above the teeth has healed.

The head of the bed is raised to decrease pressure on the sella turcica and to promote normal drainage. The patient is cautioned against blowing the nose or engaging in any activity that raises intracranial pressure, such as bending over or straining during urination or defaecation.

The intake and output are measured as a guide to fluid and electrolyte replacement. The urinary specific gravity is measured after each voiding to detect the development of diabetes insipidus. The patient's daily weight is monitored.

Fluids are generally given when nausea ceases, and the patient then progresses to a regular diet.

Medications given to the patient include antimicrobials, cortisone replacement therapy, analgesics for discomfort and agents for the control of diabetes insipidus, when necessary. The nasal packing is removed 24 to 48 hours postoperatively, and the area around the nares is cleansed to dissolve crusted blood. A sling dressing may be placed in position to obtain any discharge. The nurse must note any cerebrospinal fluid rhinorrhoea (see p. 1042).

Complications

Manipulation of the posterior pituitary gland during operation may produce transient diabetes insipidus of several days' duration that is treated with vasopressin. Occasionally, there is more persistent diabetes insipidus. Other complications include cerebrospinal fluid leakage, postoperative meningitis and inappropriate secretion of antidiuretic hormone.

BIBLIOGRAPHY

Alderman, C. (1989) When to catheterize, *Nursing Standard*, 11 October, Supplement, Vol. 4, No. 3, p. 10.

Boyle, A. (1984) The adult hemiplegic patient—a functional approach, *Nursing* (2nd series), Vol. 2, No. 32, pp. 952–4.

Bobath, B. (1978) *Adult Hemiplegia, Evaluation and Treatment* (2nd edition), Heinemann Medical Books, London.

Chalmers, C. (1985) Talking to stroke patients, *Nursing Times*, Vol. 81, No. 32, pp. 41–2.

Gooch, J. (1986) Catheter Care, *The Professional Nurse*, Vol, 1, Issue 8, pp. 207–8.

Johnstone, M. (1982) *The Stroke Patient: Principles of Rehabilitation*, Churchill Livingstone, Edinburgh.

Kratz, C. (1979) Sensory deprivation (3); In the elderly, *Nursing Times*, Vol. 75, No. 8, pp. 330–2.

Newman, D. (1985) Essential physical therapy for stroke patients, *Nursing Times*, Vol. 81, N0. 6, pp. 16–18.

Norton, D., McLaren, R. and Exon-Smith, A. N. (1978) *An Investigation of Geriatric Nursing Problems in Hospital*, Churchill Livingstone, Edinburgh.

Robinson, R. G. and Price, T. R. (1982) Post-stroke disorders: A follow-up study of 103 patients, *Stroke*, Vol. 13, pp. 635–40.

Smith, R. G., Cruikshank, J. G., Dunbar, S. *et al.* (1982) Malalignment of the shoulder after stroke, *British Medical Journal*, Vol. 284, pp. 1224–6.

Warlow, C. (1987) Cerebrovascular Disease, *Medicine International*, Vol. 2, pp. 1919–27.

Wright, E. (1988) Catheter care: The risks of infection, *The Professional Nurse*, Vol. 3, Issue 12, pp. 487–90.

chapter 33

ASSESSMENT AND CARE OF PATIENTS WITH NEUROLOGICAL DISORDERS

HEADACHE

Possibly the most common of all human afflictions is headache. Headache may arise from a variety of sources due to a variety of mechanisms, such as vascular spasms caused by muscle contraction or inflammation of pain-sensitive structures inside or outside the skull. Most headaches are not caused by structural diseases but are a symptom of the patient's problems in coping with or adapting to a life situation.

BRAIN TUMOURS

A brain tumour is a localized intracranial lesion that occupies space within the skull and tends to cause a rise in intracranial pressure. In adults, the majority of brain tumours originate from glial cells, that is, the support system of the brain and spinal cord. The highest incidence of brain tumours in adults occurs between 30 and 60 years of age, and the majority of these are supratentorial (above the covering of the cerebellum). Brain tumours rarely metastasize outside the central nervous system but cause death by impairing vital functions, either by direct involvement or by increasing intracranial pressure.

Classification

Brain tumours may be classified into several groups: (1) those arising from the coverings of the brain, such as the dural meningioma; (2) those developing in or on the cranial nerves, best exemplified by the acoustic neuroma and the optic nerve glioma; (3) those originating in the brain tissue, such as the various gliomas; and (4) metastatic lesions originating elsewhere in the body (Table 33.1). The major concerns are the location and the histological character of the tumour. Tumours may be benign or malignant. However, because a benign tumour may occur in a vital area, its effects may be as serious as those of a malignant tumour.

Table 33.1 *Classification of brain tumours*

Tumours originating in the brain tissue
Gliomas – infiltrating tumours that may invade any portion of the brain; most common type of brain tumour:

Astrocytomas
Ependymomas
Medulloblastomas   } Subclassified according to cell type
Oligodendrogliomas
Colloid cysts

Tumours arising from covering of brain
Meningioma – encapsulated, well-defined, growing outside the brain tissue; compresses rather than invades brain

Tumours developing in or on the cranial nerves
Acoustic neuroma – derived from sheath of acoustic nerve
    Optic nerve glioma

Metastatic lesions
Most commonly from lung and breast

Tumours of the ductless glands
Pituitary
Pineal

Blood vessel tumours
Haemangioblastoma
Angioma

Congenital tumours

Clinical Features

Brain tumours produce clinical features when they cause increased intracranial pressure or produce localizing signs and symptoms as a result of the tumour interfering with specific regions of the brain.

Symptoms of Increasing Intracranial Pressure
Symptoms of increased intracranial pressure are caused by a gradual compression of the brain due to the growth of the tumour. The effect is to disrupt the equilibrium that exists between the brain, the cerebrospinal fluid and the cerebral blood—all located within the skull. As the tumour grows, adjustments may occur through compensatory mechanisms: cerebrospinal fluid is reduced by increased absorption or decreased production, intracranial veins become compressed, cerebral blood flow decreases and the intracellular and extracellular brain tissue mass decreases. When these mechanisms fail, the patient develops features of increased intracranial pressure.

The most common general symptoms produced by pressure are headache, vomiting and papilloedema with associated blurred vision, diplopia and altered consciousness.

Headache, though not always present, is most common

in the early morning, made worse by coughing, straining or sudden movement. It is thought to be caused by the tumour invading, compressing or distorting the pain-sensitive structures (e.g. dural stretching), or by the oedema that accompanies the tumour.

Vomiting, seldom related to food intake,is usually due to irritation of the vagal centres in the medulla and, if forceful, is described as projectile.

Papilloedema, or oedema of the optic nerve, is present in a large percentage of patients and can lead to impaired vision.

Specific Features

Because the functions of different parts of the brain are known, the location of the tumour can be determined in part by identifying functions that are affected.

- Frontal lobe: headache, personality changes (antisocial behaviour, loss of initiative, intellectual impairment), focal seizures, disordered vision, hemiparesis (contralateral), dysphasia, (dominant hemisphere involved).
- Temporal lobe: dysphasia (dominant hemisphere), visual field defect, altered behaviour.
- Parietal: Jacksonian epilepsy (i.e. localized to one side), motor seizures, sensory impairment (sensory inattention, astereognosis), visual field defect.
- Occipital: visual field defect (one half of each eye).
- Cerebellar: dizziness, ataxia (tendency to fall to the side of the lesion), nystagmus (rhythmical vibration of eyeballs), inco-ordination.
- Brain stem: cranial nerve palsies.
- Hypothalamus/pituitary: endocrine imbalance, visual field defect.
- Ventricular area: obstruction to cerebrospinal fluid, increased intracranial pressure symptoms.

Further increases in intracranial pressure occur when the cerebrospinal flow is obstructed due to tumour enlargement, which leads to the development of hydrocephalus.

Specific Tumours

Gliomas

The malignant glioma is the brain neoplasm most frequently seen. Usually, these tumours cannot be totally removed because they spread by infiltrating into the surrounding neural tissue.

Pituitary Adenomas

The pituitary gland is a relatively small gland located in the sella turcica. It is attached to the hypothalamus by a short stalk and is divided into the anterior and the posterior lobes. The anterior lobe secretes growth hormone (GH), adrenocorticotrophic hormone (ACTH), thyroid-stimulating hormone (TSH), prolactin and the gonadotropic hormones,

follicle-stimulating hormone (FSH) and luteinizing hormone (LH). The posterior pituitary stores and releases antidiuretic hormone (vasopressin) and oxytocin.

Pituitary tumours may cause symptoms due to pressure on adjacent structures, such as compression of the optic nerves/chiasma producing a visual field defect, with expansion/erosion of the sella turcica, leading to headache.

Functioning pituitary tumours can produce one or more hormones normally produced by the anterior pituitary. These hormones may cause prolactin-secreting pituitary adenomas (prolactinomas), growth hormone-secreting pituitary adenomas that produce acromegaly in adults, and adrenocorticotrophic hormone-producing pituitary adenomas that give rise to Cushing's disease. Adenomas secreting thyroid-stimulating hormone or follicle-stimulating hormone-luteinizing hormone occur infrequently, while adenomas that produce both growth hormone and prolactin are relatively common.

The female patient whose pituitary gland is secreting excessive quantities of prolactin will present with amenorrhoea and/or galactorrhoea (excessive or spontaneous flow of milk). Male patients with prolactinomas may present with impotence and hypogonadism.

Acromegaly, caused by excess growth hormone, produces enlargement of the hands and feet, distortion of the facial features and peripheral nerve entrapment syndromes.

The clinical features of Cushing's disease, a condition associated with prolonged overproduction of cortisol, include a form of obesity with redistribution of fat to the facial, supraclavicular and abdominal areas, hypertension, purple striae and ecchymoses, osteoporosis, glucose intolerance and emotional disorders.

The majority of pituitary adenomas are treated by transsphenoidal microsurgical removal (see Chapter 32, p. 1016), while the remainder of tumours that cannot be removed completely are treated by radiation.

Angiomas

Brain angiomas (masses composed largely of abnormal blood vessels) are found either in or on the surface of the brain. Some persist throughout life without causing symptoms; others give rise to symptoms of brain tumour. Occasionally, the diagnosis is suggested by the presence of another angioma somewhere in the head or by a bruit (an abnormal sound) audible over the skull. Since the walls of the blood vessels in angiomas are thin, a cerebral vascular accident (stroke) frequently occurs. In fact, cerebral haemorrhage in people under 40 years of age should suggest the possibility of an angioma.

Acoustic Neuroma

An acoustic neuroma is a tumour of the eighth cranial nerve, the nerve of hearing and balance. It usually arises just within the internal auditory meatus, where it frequently expands before filling the cerebellopontine recess.

An acoustic neuroma may grow slowly and attain a considerable size before it is correctly diagnosed. The patient usually experiences loss of hearing, tinnitus and episodes of vertigo and staggering. As the tumour becomes larger, painful sensations of the face may occur on the same side as a result of the tumour's compressing the fifth cranial nerve.

With improved radiological techniques and the use of the operating microscope and microsurgical instrumentation, even large tumours can be removed through a relatively small craniotomy.

Diagnosis

The history of the illness and the manner in which the symptoms evolved are important. A neurological examination indicates the areas of the central nervous system involved. To assist in the precise localization of the lesion, a battery of tests is performed.

Skull X-Ray

A skull X-ray may demonstrate signs of increased pressure, thinning of bone, widening of sutures, calcification of the pineal gland and erosion of the sella turcica.

Computed Tomography

Computed tomography will give specific information concerning the number, size and density of the lesion(s) and the extent of secondary cerebral oedema. It also provides information about the ventricular system. Computer-assisted stereotactic (three-dimensional) biopsy can be used to diagnose deep-seated brain tumours and to provide a basis for treatment and prognostic information. Cerebral angiography provides visualization of cerebral blood vessels and can localize most cerebral tumours.

Brain Scan

A brain scan may be valuable, because an abnormal amount of radioactive material will accumulate in the area of the tumour and can be localized with a scintillation counter.

Electroencephalography

An electroencephalogram can detect abnormal brain waves in regions occupied by the tumour and can enable evaluation of temporal lobe seizures.

Echoencephalography

Echoencephalography can show whether certain structures have been displaced from the midline by a lesion in one hemisphere.

Pneumoencephalography

Pneumoencephalography may also be used in selected patients.

Cerebrospinal Fluid

Cytological studies of the cerebrospinal fluid may be done to detect malignant cells, because tumours of the central nervous system are capable of shedding cells into the cerebrospinal fluid.

Chest X-Ray

A chest X-ray may be useful in patients with metastatic disease since the primary tumour may be found in the lung.

Audiometric Studies

Audiometric studies may be performed if a lesion is suspected at or around the cerebellopontine angle.

Management

An untreated brain tumour ultimately causes death either from increasing intracranial pressure or from the brain damage it causes. Patients with possible brain tumour should be investigated and treated as soon as possible before irreversible damage occurs.

The objective of management is to remove all of the tumour or as much as possible without increasing the neurological deficit (paralysis, blindness) or to achieve relief by partial tumour removal and by decompression, radiation, chemotherapy or a combination of these. The majority of patients with brain tumours undergo a neurosurgical procedure, when possible, followed by radiation therapy and/or chemotherapy when indicated. Corticosteroids are highly effective in combating cerebral oedema, thus allowing for a thorough diagnostic assessment and a carefully planned surgical approach. (Also, appropriate dosages of corticosteroids treat postoperative swelling and facilitate a smoother, more rapid recovery.) In general, patients with meningiomas, acoustic neuromas, cystic astrocytomas of the cerebellum, colloid cyst of the third ventricle, congenital tumours such as dermoid cyst and some of the granulomas can be cured by surgical removal of the tumour. A complete removal of the infiltrating gliomas is not possible. In these patients, the treatment consists of biopsy to establish the diagnosis; partial removal; decompression; cerebrospinal fluid shunt diversion; and radiotherapy. (See Chapter 32, p. 1014 for nursing care of the patient following cranial surgery.) Certain chemotherapeutic agents combined with radiation therapy may also be used. More recently, deep-seated brain tumours have been removed using the carbon dioxide laser with computed tomography scanning and stereotactic techniques.

Radioisotopes (^{125}I) implanted directly into the brain tumour will permit high total doses of radiation to the localized tumour. With sophisticated guided systems, the radioisotope can be implanted precisely into the tumour, which helps to avoid radiation toxicity to the surrounding normal brain.

Newer drugs are being evaluated continually, and there is hope that these will eventually be more successful.

Cerebral Metastases

A significant number of patients suffer central nervous system complications as a result of systemic cancer and neurological deficits caused by cerebral metastases. Cancer of the lung commonly metastasizes to the brain, as do tumours of the breast, kidney, prostate gland, uterus, thyroid, skin (melanoma) and gastrointestinal tract.

Neurological symptoms and signs include headache, disturbances of gait, deterioration of vision, personality changes, intellectual impairment, focal weakness, paralysis, dysphasia and seizures. These problems can be devastating to both patient and loved ones.

Management

The treatment is palliative and involves eliminating or reducing serious symptomatology. Even distressing signs and symptoms can be resolved, thereby improving the quality of life that remains. Patients with intracerebral metastases who are not treated have a steady downhill course with a very limited survival time.

The therapeutic approach includes surgery (usually for a single intracranial metastasis), radiation and chemotherapy. Adrenocorticosteroid hormones may be helpful in relieving headache and alterations of consciousness, by reducing the inflammatory reaction around the metastatic deposits and decreasing the oedema surrounding them.

If the patient has severe pain, morphine can be infused into the epidural or subarachnoid space via a spinal needle and insertion of a catheter as near as possible to the spinal segment where the pain is projected. Small doses of morphine are injected into the system at prescribed intervals.

For the nursing care of a patient with cancer, see Chapter 2.

► NURSING PROCESS

► THE PATIENT WITH CEREBRAL METASTASES OR INCURABLE BRAIN TUMOUR

► Assessment

The nursing assessment focuses on how the patient is functioning, moving and walking, adapting to weakness/paralysis, visual loss and speech loss, and dealing with seizures.

A dietary history is taken to find out dietary intake and food intolerances and preferences. Biochemical measurements are reviewed to assess the degree of malnutrition, impaired cellular immunity and electrolyte imbalance.

Cachexia is seen in patients with metastases and is characterized by anorexia, pain, weight loss, altered metabolism, muscle weakness, malabsorption and diarrhoea. Mouth infections, dysphagia, weakness and depression may lead to lack of interest and enjoyment of food. Changes in smell and anosmia are a possibility among these patients.

Assessment is made for symptoms that cause distress to the patient, including pain, respiratory problems, problems with elimination and urination, disturbances in sleep, and impairment of skin integrity, fluid balance and temperature regulation. These problems may be caused by tumour invasion, compression or obstruction.

The nurse may discuss with the social worker the impact of the patient's illness on the family in terms of home care, interpersonal relationships and any financial problems. This information is important in helping family members strengthen their coping skills.

► Patient's Problems

Based on the assessment, the patient's main problems may include the following:

- Self-care deficits related to loss/impairment of motor and sensory function and decreased cognitive abilities.
- Insufficient nutritional intake related to cachexia due to treatment and tumour effects, decreased nutritional intake and malabsorption.
- Anxiety related to fear in anticipation of death, uncertainty, change in appearance, discontinuity in lifestyle.
- Potential alterations in family processes related to anticipatory grief and the burdens imposed by the care of the person with a terminal illness.

Other problems for the patient with cerebral metastases may include: pain related to tumour compression; impaired gas exchange related to dyspnoea; alteration in bowel elimination (constipation) related to decreased fluid and dietary intake and medications; alteration in urinary elimination patterns related to reduced fluid intake, vomiting and reactions to medications; sleep pattern disturbances related to discomfort and fear of dying; impairment of skin integrity related to cachexia, poor tissue perfusion and decreased mobility; potential or actual fluid volume deficit related to fever, vomiting and low fluid intake; impaired thermal regulation related to hypothalamic involvement, fever and chills. The reader is referred to the section on cancer in Chapter 2 for appropriate assessment and nursing care for these conditions.

► Planning and Implementation
► Expected Outcomes
The expected outcomes for the patient may include compensating for self-care deficits, attaining improved nutrition, relief of anxiety and enhancement of family coping skills.

Nursing Care

Compensating For Self-Care Deficits

The patient may have difficulty in participating in goal-setting as the tumour metastasizes and affects mental capabilities. The nurse should work with the family in keeping the patient mobile and at the highest level of functioning possible. Increasing assistance with self-care activities will be required. The patient with cerebral metastasis (and the family) lives with uncertainty. The nurse should encourage them to plan for each day and make that day count. The tasks and challenges for the nurse are to assist the patient to find useful coping mechanisms, adaptations and compensations in solving problems that arise. This helps patients to maintain some sense of control even though they may be in a marginal state. An individualized exercise programme will help to maintain strength, endurance and range of motion. Eventually, referral may have to be made to community services for assistance.

Improving Nutrition

Patients with nausea, vomiting, breathlessness and pain are disinterested in eating. These symptoms must be managed or controlled by assessment, planning and appropriate nursing and medical care. The nurse should consult the patient regarding food preferences.

The nurse teaches the family optimum positioning of the patient for comfort during meals. The timing of meals is important. Food is offered in small, attractive dishes when the patient is more rested and in less distress from pain or effects of treatment. The patient needs to be clean, comfortable and free of pain, with an environment that is as attractive as possible. This requires planning to minimize offensive sights, sounds and odours. Oral hygiene helps to improve oral intake. It may be necessary to record the quantity of food eaten to determine the daily calorie count. Nursing ingenuity is called for to make food more palatable and provide enough fluids. This involves communication and interaction with the dietician, doctor, patient and family.

Dietary supplementation, as preferred by the patient, can be encouraged to take care of increased caloric needs. If the patient refuses to eat the foods needed, it may be wise to offer whatever diet will be accepted.

When the patient shows marked deterioration as a result of tumour growth and effects, some other form of nutritional support (tube feeding, total parenteral nutrition) may be used. Nursing care includes assessment to ensure vein integrity, monitoring the insertion site for infection, checking the infusion rate, keeping intake and output records and changing intravenous tubing and feeding. These techniques can be taught to the caregivers at home.

The quality of life for the patient may serve to guide in the selection, institution and maintenance of nutritional support. The patient may become weary with all the urging to eat and the discussions about food, and may not desire aggressive nursing care. This is a real dilemma. The subsequent course of action should be ethical, and humane, taking into consideration the wishes of the patient and family.

Relieving Anxiety

Patients with cerebral metastases may be restless, with changing moods that may include intense depression, euphoria, paranoia, severe anxiety and a sense of impending doom. The response of patients to terminal illness reflects their pattern of reaction to other crisis situations. Serious illness imposes additional strains that often bring other unresolved problems to light. Learning to use patients' own coping strategies to help them deal with their feelings can be very beneficial. This requires experience and sensitivity to the patients' stated concerns.

Patients need the opportunity to exercise some control over their situation. An understanding of the disease and treatment will help the patient to participate in planning immediate and future care. The presence of family, friends, spiritual advisers and health professionals may be supportive. Support groups such as BACUP (British Association of Cancer United Patients), CancerLink and Tak Tent may provide a feeling of support and lessen the isolation that many families may experience.

Time spent with patients is helpful. The nurse should give them time to talk and to communicate their worries. Encouraging open communication and acknowledging fears is therapeutic. Touch is also a form of communication. These patients need assurance of the continuation of the relationship with the nurse and that they will not be abandoned. Life becomes more endurable when others share in the experience of dying.

If a patient's emotional reactions are very intense or prolonged, additional help from a spiritual adviser, social worker, occupational therapist, clinical psychologist or diversional therapy may be in order.

Enhancing Family Coping

The family needs to be reassured that their loved one is receiving optimal care and that attention will be paid to the patient's changing symptoms and to their problems. When the patient can no longer engage in self-care, the family is helped with the essentials of the patient's physical care and assisted in finding support systems (social worker, community services, hospice care). The expected outcome from the nursing point of view is to keep the patient's anxiety at a manageable level.

▶ *Evaluation*
▶ **Expected Outcomes**

1. Patient engages in self-care activities as long as possible.
   a. Uses supportive devices.
   b. Accepts assistance.

2. Demonstrates some improvement in nutritional status.
   a. Shows no additional weight loss.
   b. Has increased calorie intake.
3. Appears less anxious.
   a. Seems less restless and is sleeping better.
   b. Talking about concerns.
4. Family members seek help as needed.
   a. Demonstrate ability to bathe, feed and care for patient.
   b. Express feelings and concerns to appropriate health professionals.

INTRACRANIAL INFECTION: BRAIN ABSCESS

A brain abscess is a collection of pus within the substance of the brain itself. It may occur by direct invasion of the brain from intracranial trauma or surgery; by spread of infection from nearby sites such as the sinuses, ears and teeth; or by spread of infection from other organs (lung abscess, infective endocarditis). Brain abscess is a complication encountered increasingly in patients whose immune systems have been suppressed through either therapy or disease. To prevent brain abscesses, otitis media, mastoiditis, sinusitis, dental infections and systemic infections should be treated promptly.

Assessment

Clinical Features
The clinical features of a brain abscess result from alterations in intracranial dynamics (oedema, brain shift), infection or the location of the abscess. Headache, usually worse in the morning, is the patient's most continuing symptom. Vomiting is also common. Focal neurological signs (weakness of an extremity, decreasing vision, seizures) may occur, depending on the site of the abscess. The patient may display altered consciousness. Fever may or may not be present.

Diagnostic Evaluation
Repeated neurological examinations and continuing assessment of the patient are necessary to determine accurately the location of the abscess. Computed tomography is invaluable in showing the site of the abscess, following the evolution and resolution of suppurative lesions and determining the optimum time for surgical intervention.

Management

The aim of management is to eliminate the abscess, which is treated with antimicrobial therapy and/or surgery. Antimicrobials are given in large doses as they are able to cross the blood–brain barrier and gain access to the abscess cavity, allowing encapsulation to occur.

It is important that the nurse maintains close observation of the patient using the Glasgow Coma Scale (see p. 993), observing for the signs and symptoms of increased intracranial pressure that may result suddenly from cerebral oedema surrounding a rapidly growing abscess. This increased pressure may limit further blood flow to the brain, leading to brain damage.

Secondary compression of the midbrain and brain stem can lead quickly to coma and death. Corticosteroid may be given if the patient shows evidence of an increasing neurological deficit, to help reduce the inflammatory cerebral oedema. Anticonvulsant medication may be given as a prophylaxis against seizures, a common complication.

A definitive treatment of a brain abscess is usually surgical intervention, either to aspirate or to excise the abscess. Drainage may be done through burr holes, or the abscess excised via craniotomy (see p. 1014 for the nursing care of the patient undergoing cranial surgery).

Following surgery, drainage may be copious and dressings should be reinforced as necessary, maintaining strict asepsis. The patient may be advised to lie on the operative side to promote drainage.

Nursing Care

Compensating For Self-Care Deficits
The patient may have difficulty in participating in goal-setting as the tumour metastasizes and affects mental capabilities. The nurse should work with the family in keeping the patient mobile and at the highest level of functioning possible. Increasing assistance with self-care activities will be required. The patient with cerebral metastasis (and the family) lives with uncertainty. The nurse should encourage them to plan for each day and make that day count. The tasks and challenges for the nurse are to assist the patient to find useful coping mechanisms, adaptations and compensations in solving problems that arise. This helps patients to maintain some sense of control even though they may be in a marginal state. An individualized exercise programme will help to maintain strength, endurance and range of motion. Eventually, referral may have to be made to community services for assistance.

INTRACRANIAL ANEURYSMS (RUPTURE OF INTRACRANIAL ANEURYSM WITH SUBARACHNOID HAEMORRHAGE)

An intracranial (cerebral) aneurysm is a dilation of the walls of a cerebral artery (Figure 33.1). An aneurysm is the result of a defect and subsequent weakness of the

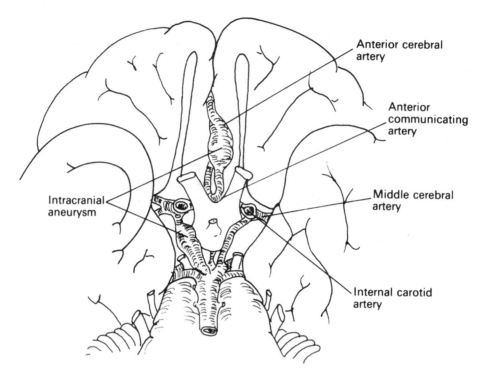

Figure 33.1 Intracranial aneurysm.

vessel wall. This may be either a congenital defect or due to atherosclerosis, hypertensive vascular disease, head trauma or advancing age. The cerebral arteries most commonly affected by an aneurysm are the internal carotid, anterior cerebral, anterior communicating and middle cerebral arteries. A small percentage develop in the vertebrobasilar territory. Multiple cerebral aneurysms are not uncommon.

Altered Physiology

Symptoms are produced when the aneurysm enlarges and presses on nearby cranial nerves or brain substance, or more drastically, when the aneurysm ruptures, causing subarachnoid haemorrhage (haemorrhage into the cranial subarachnoid space). Normal brain metabolism is disrupted by the brain being exposed to blood; by an increase in intracranial pressure resulting from the sudden entry of blood into the subarachnoid space, which compresses and injures brain tissue; or by ischaemia of the brain resulting from the reduced perfusion, pressure and vasospasm that frequently accompany subarachnoid haemorrhage.

In addition to aneurysms, other causes of subarachnoid haemorrhage include arteriovenous malformations, tumours, trauma, blood dyscrasias and unknown causes.

Clinical Features

Rupture of the aneurysm usually produces a sudden, un-usually severe headache and often loss of consciousness for a variable period of time. There may be pain and rigidity of the back of the neck and spine due to meningeal irritation. Visual disturbances (visual loss, diplopia, ptosis) occur when the aneurysm is adjacent to the oculomotor nerve. Tinnitus, dizziness and hemiparesis may also occur.

At times, an aneurysm will 'leak' blood, leading to the formation of a clot that seals the site of rupture. In this instance, the patient may show little neurological deficit, or there may be severe bleeding, resulting in cerebral damage followed rapidly by coma and death. The mortality rate corresponds to the level of consciousness and neurological deficit, but there is a high immediate mortality rate. Prognosis depends on the neurological condition of the patient, age, associated diseases and the extent and location of the aneurysm. Subarachnoid haemorrhage from an aneurysm is truly a catastrophic event.

Diagnosis

The diagnosis is confirmed by computed tomography scanning; lumbar puncture, which reveals blood in the cerebrospinal fluid; and cerebral angiography, which shows the location and size of the aneurysm and gives information about the affected vessel, adjoining vessels and vascular branches.

Analgesics (e.g., codeine; acetaminophen) may be prescribed for head and neck pain. The patient is fitted with graduated pressure elastic stockings to prevent deep vein thrombosis, a threat to any patient who is on bedrest.

Nursing Care

The aims of treatment are to allow the brain to recover from the initial haemorrhage, to prevent or minimize the risk of re-bleeding and to prevent or treat other complications.

The patient is prescribed immediate and absolute bedrest in a quiet, nonstressful setting, because activity, pain and anxiety elevate the blood pressure, thus increasing the risk of bleeding. Dim light may be helpful to relieve photophobia. Visitors are restricted, but appropriate reassurance will help to relieve anxiety. The head of the bed may be elevated for comfort, to provide drainage and to decrease intracranial pressure. However, some doctors may prefer the patient to remain flat to increase cerebral perfusion.

The patient's neurological status is monitored using the Glasgow Coma Scale, observing for deterioration which may be an indication of recurrent bleeding, increasing intracranial pressure or vasospasm. (The mechanism for this is not well known, but it correlates well with increasing amounts of blood in the basal cisterns. Vasospasm narrows the lumen of the involved cerebral blood vessels, thus impeding the cerebral blood flow, causing ischaemia and infarction. The symptoms exhibited reflect the areas of the brain involved. Recent research indicates that intravenous administration of the calcium blocker nimodipine, given during the critical time when vasospasm may develop (4 to 12 days post-bleed), may offer protection against delayed ischaemic deterioration.) Any activity that causes sudden increases in blood pressure or obstructs venous return should be avoided. This includes the Valsalva manoeuvre, straining, forceful sneezing and any activity requiring exertion.

Sudden systemic hypertension is guarded against. If blood pressure is elevated, antihypertensive therapy (nitroprusside) may be prescribed. Constant monitoring of the blood pressure by arterial line is carried out to avoid a precipitous drop in blood pressure, which can produce brain ischaemia. Because seizures cause blood pressure elevation, anticonvulsant agents are administered prophylactically. Stool softeners are prescribed to prevent straining, which can elevate the blood pressure, and some consultants will allow patients to use a commode at the bedside, which is less stressful. During this time, the patient is supported during investigations (see p. 993). If the blood pressure is elevated, antihypertensive therapy may be prescribed, but a precipitous drop should be avoided because cerebral ischaemia may ensue. Codeine-based analgesics should be administered regularly to reduce any headache.

If surgery is delayed or contraindicated, some centres give antifibrinolytic agents (e.g., aminocaproic acid, tranexamic acid) to delay or prevent clot dissolution at the site of aneurysmal rupture. Surgical intervention is indicated following positive diagnostic intervention and when the patient is in a fit condition. (Nursing Care, p. 1014.)

Surgical Management

The expected outcome of surgery is to prevent further bleeding. This is done by isolating the aneurysm from its circulation or by strengthening the arterial wall. An aneurysm may be treated intracranially by excluding it from the cerebral circulation by means of a ligature or a clip across its neck (Figure 33.2). If this is not anatomically possible, the aneurysm can be reinforced by wrapping it with plastic, muscle or some other substance. The

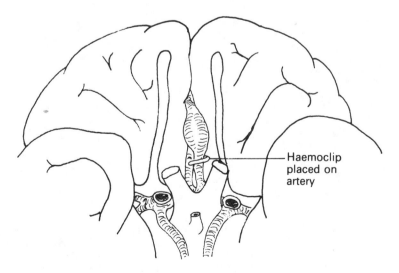

Figure 33.2 Cerebral aneurysm isolated by means of a haemoclip.

aneurysm may be both clipped and wrapped. Alternatively, an extracranial method may be used, whereby the carotid artery is occluded in the neck in order to reduce pressure within the blood vessel.

MULTIPLE SCLEROSIS

Multiple sclerosis (MS) is a chronic, frequently progressive disease of the central nervous system characterized by the occurrence of small patches of demyelination in the brain and spinal cord. (Demyelination refers to the destruction of myelin, the fatty and protein material that ensheathes certain nerve fibres in the brain and spinal cord.) Demyelination results in a disorder in the transmission of nerve impulses.

The aetiology of multiple sclerosis is unknown, but it is thought that it may be an autoimmune disease or is triggered by an infection or virus (Gay and Dick, 1986).

Epidemiological findings indicate that multiple sclerosis is more common in people living in the northern latitudes. It is one of the most disabling neurological diseases of young adults (20 to 40 years of age) in this country, affecting twice as many women as men. Its occurrence when patients are young increases the medi-

cal, psychological, social and economic problems encountered by the patient and loved ones.

Altered Physiology

In multiple sclerosis, the demyelination is scattered irregularly throughout the central nervous system (Figure 33.3). In time, myelin peels off the axis cylinders, and the axons themselves degenerate. The plaques or patches in the involved areas become sclerosed, interrupting the flow of nerve impulses and resulting in a variety of manifestations, depending on which nerves are affected. The areas most frequently affected are the optic nerves, chiasma and tracts, the cerebrum, the brain stem and cerebellum, and the spinal cord.

Clinical Features

The signs and symptoms of multiple sclerosis are varied and multiple, reflecting the location of the lesion (plaque) or combination of lesions. Fatigue is said to be the most disabling factor. Visual disturbances due to lesions in the optic nerve or tract are also common. Involvement of the pyramidal tracts gives rise to spastic weakness of the extremities, and disruption of the sen-

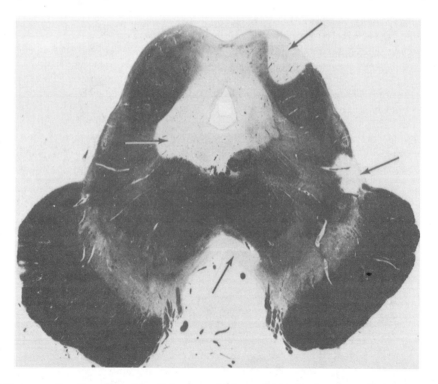

Figure 33.3 Cross-section from the midbrain (enlarged) of a patient with chronic multiple sclerosis. Specimen stained to show myelin (black). The four white areas indicated by the arrows are typical plaques in which the myelin has been destroyed. The nerve fibres in these plaques have lost their myelin sheaths and, as a consequence, conduction of stimuli in these areas would be impeded or lost. (Courtesy of Cedric S. Raine, M.D., Professor of Pathology [Neuropathology] and Neuroscience, Albert Einstein College of Medicine of Yeshiva University.)

sory axons may produce disturbances of feeling, numbness and paraesthesia. Lesions of the cerebellum and/or basal ganglia can produce ataxia, tremor dysarthria and inco-ordination.

Emotional lability (e.g. euphoria or depression) results from disruptions to the connections between the cortex and the basal ganglia. Bladder, bowel and sexual problems (e.g., impotence) can also occur.

Secondary features are related to complications: urinary tract infections, rectal distension, pressure sores, contracture deformities, dependent pedal oedema, pneumonia and reactive depressions. Tertiary problems (emotional, social, marital, economic, vocational) may result as a consequence of the disease.

Multiple sclerosis is characterized by exacerbations (the appearance of new symptoms and worsening of existing ones) and remissions (periods in which symptoms decrease or disappear). Relapses are often associated with periods of emotional and physical stress. Many patients are not seriously incapacitated but have long periods of remission between episodes. There is evidence that remyelination occurs in some patients.

Diagnosis

Electrophoresis of the cerebrospinal fluid usually reveals the presence of immunoglobulin abnormalities. Evoked potential studies are carried out to help to define the extent of the disease process and to monitor changes. Computed tomography scans may reveal cerebral atrophic changes. Magnetic resonance imaging has become a primary diagnostic tool for visualizing small plaques and for evaluating the course of the disease and the effect of the treatment. Underlying bladder dysfunction is diagnosed by urodynamic studies.

► **NURSING PROCESS**
► **THE PATIENT WITH MULTIPLE SCLEROSIS**

► *Assessment*

Nursing assessment is carried out with an awareness of actual and potential problems associated with the disease, including neurological problems, secondary complications and the consequences of the disease on the patient and family. The nurse should watch movements and walking to determine if the patient is in danger of falling. The patient should be observed functioning when well rested and when fatigued. The nurse should ask what the major problems are: for example, weakness, spasticity, visual impairment, incontinence. The nurse should find out how the condition has affected the patient's lifestyle, how well the patient is coping and what the patient would like to do better.

► *Patient's Problems*

Based on the assessment, the patient's potential problems may include the following:

● Impaired physical mobility related to weakness, muscle paresis, spasticity.
● Potential for injury related to sensory and visual impairment.
● Alteration in urinary and bowel elimination related to spinal cord dysfunction.
● Difficulties with speech and swallowing.
● Potential periods of exacerbation.
● Impaired patient and family education.

► *Planning and Implementation*
► **Expected Outcomes**

The patient's main expected outcomes may include promotion of physical mobility, avoidance of injury, achievement of bladder and bowel continence, improvement of cognitive dysfunction, adaptation to sexual dysfunction and development of coping strengths.

Nursing Care

At this time, there is no cure for multiple sclerosis. Of those who develop the disease, 20 per cent will run a benign course; 25 per cent have exacerbating attacks with some permanent residual symptoms; 40 per cent experience moderate or severe disability; and 15 per cent will have a chronic and progressive disease, often culminating in death from brain stem involvement. Therefore, patients will require intermittent hospital treatment, aimed at controlling the disease and adapting the patient to new symptoms. The major aim throughout is to assist the patient to maintain a positive attitude and an optimum quality of life within the constraints of the disease.

Impaired Physical Mobility
Impaired physical mobility relates to motor weakness and spasticity. The patient should be given exercises to strengthen non-affected muscles and to ensure maximum use of those weakened by disease. Vigorous exercise is to be avoided since extreme fatigue may exacerbate symptoms. Walking exercises may help to improve gait, especially when proprioception is diminished. Ambulation should be continued as long as possible and will be helped by the use of ambulatory aids. Muscle spasm is common and interferes with normal function; it is often painful and increases the probability of contractures and pressure sores. Swimming and stretching exercises may relieve spasticity, although muscle relaxants (diazepam) or antispasmodics (e.g., baclofen) may also have to be prescribed.

Motor dysfunction also causes problems with inco-ordination and clumsiness, and this can be overcome by encouraging the patient to walk with the feet wide apart in order to widen the base of support, and increase walking stability. Intention tremor of the upper limbs may be helped by the use of weighted wrist cuffs.

Sensory and Visual Impairments

Since sensory loss may occur in addition to motor loss, pressure sores are a continuing threat to skin integrity. Relief of pressure should be encouraged by careful positioning and frequent position change. The patient should avoid the use of hot water bottles and having the bath water too hot, and strict attention should be paid to sacral and perineal hygiene.

When diplopia is present, the use of an eyepatch or a frosted lens inserted into the spectacles frame may block out visual impulses to one eye. For those patients who cannot reach or hold books, arrangements should be made for access to tape cassettes, books that are recorded on tape and page-turning machines. Prism spectacles may be helpful for the bedridden.

Alteration to Bladder and Bowel Function

The patient may have urinary frequency. Urgency and/or incontinence require special support. The sensation of voiding should be heeded immediately. A voiding time regime can be initiated every one-and-a-half to two hours initially, gradually lengthening the time as progress is made.

- Instruct the patient to drink a measured amount every two hours.
- Voiding should be attempted 30 minutes after drinking.
- If bladder sensation is diminished, an alarm clock may be set to warn the patient to micturate.

In a female with permanent urinary incontinence, a urinary diversion may be considered. The male patient may wear a condom appliance for urinary collection.

Patients with a neurogenic bladder and urinary retention (page 686) may require indwelling urinary catheterization under aseptic technique, and they will be encouraged to maintain a fluid intake of around three to four litres a day.

Bowel problems include constipation, faecal impaction and incontinence. Adequate fluids and dietary fibre should be taken, and a bowel training programme instituted. The patient should be encouraged to defaecate at the same time each day, preferably after breakfast. Mechanical stimulation with a glycerine suppository may be required initially.

Difficulties With Speech and Swallowing

The cranial nerves controlling both articulation and swallowing may be affected. Dysarthrias, marked by slurred speech and dysphonia, are seen. The speech therapist can assist the patient to overcome communication problems and with the use of compensatory techniques. Inhalation of food particles due to the inability to swallow safely may occur, and the patient should be observed carefully while eating and drinking. Food of a semi-solid consistency may be easier for the patient to swallow. Occasionally, nasogastric supplementation is required overnight to maintain an adequate intake.

Periods of Exacerbation

In acute exacerbations, steroid therapy may bring about a more rapid improvement and improve nerve conduction. However, the residual effects of multiple sclerosis tend to increase with each exacerbation, and the patient may become dependent on steroid therapy, thus increasing the risk of complications such as urinary tract infection and sepsis. Immunosuppressant medication may also modulate the immune response and reduce the rate at which the disease progresses.

Over the past few years, there has been an increased interest in the use of hyperbaric oxygen therapy. Although a number of patients using this have gone into remission, the value of hyperbaric therapy is not conclusive.

Patient and Family Education

The patient's ability to understand the disease condition and its implications should be assessed. The amount of information given at any one time should not be too much for the patient to grasp; opportunities should be made for further reinforcement. The implication of multiple sclerosis will also affect those close to the patient, and they and the patient should always be considered as a unit. The patient's coping ability may be low and support can be offered. For example, the health visitor can discuss difficulties and give emotional support, the community nurse can assist with personal care and the social worker can arrange meals-on-wheels and make arrangements for house adaptations.

Financial help in the form of heating, mobility and attendance allowances is an entitlement in the United Kingdom. The patient and loved ones should be aware of groups such as the Multiple Sclerosis Society, ARMS (Action Research Multiple Sclerosis) and SPOD (Association to Aid the Sexual and Personal Relationships of People with a Disability). Through them, the positive attitude of those involved may motivate the recently diagnosed patient. The patient should continue to feel a valuable member within the home, and expression of sexuality should be encouraged.

The patient and loved ones should be made aware that the main problem is to learn to adapt to fatigue, which, since it is not a visible manifestation, is often misinterpreted by friends as disinterest. A daily routine, with short-term goals should be arranged, allowing for rest periods. Physical and emotional stresses, which may worsen symptoms and impair performance, should be avoided.

All the available resources of the multidisciplinary team can assist in maintaining a positive attitude and an optimum quality of life within the constraints of multiple sclerosis. Many people associate multiple sclerosis with a wheelchair, yet less than one person in ten will eventually be confined to one.

► *Evaluation*
► **Expected Outcomes**

1. Patient adapts to impaired mobility and spasticity.
2. Patient avoids injury, and demonstrates an intact skin.
3. When necessary, patient seeks assistance.
4. Bladder and bowel control is attained.
5. Independence in activities of daily living are achieved.
6. Patient maintains self-esteem.
7. The value of counselling services is recognized, e.g. SPOD (Association to Aid the Sexual and Personal Relationships of People with a Disability), and patient can adapt to sexual dysfunction.

PARKINSON'S DISEASE

Parkinson's disease is a progressive neurological disorder affecting the brain centres responsible for control and regulation of movement. It is characterized by bradykinesia (slowness of movement), tremor and muscle stiffness or rigidity.

Altered Physiology

The major lesion appears to be the result of a loss of melanin-pigmented neurones, particularly those in the substantia nigra of the brain (Figure 33.4). One of the major neurotransmitters in this area of the brain, and in other parts of the central nervous system, dopamine, which has an important inhibiting function in the central control of movement, is depleted.

In the majority of patients, the cause of the disease is unknown. Arteriosclerotic parkinsonism is seen more frequently in older age groups. It may follow encephalitis, poisoning or toxicity, or hypoxia, or may be drug-induced.

The disease most frequently attacks people in their 50s and 60s, and is the second most common neurological disorder of the elderly.

Clinical Features

The syndrome is associated with three main features:

1. Bradykinesia: slowness or poverty of movement whereby the patient has difficulty in initiating, maintaining and performing motor activities. There is loss of normal arm swing and, with absence of posture reflexes, the patient stands with the head bent forward and

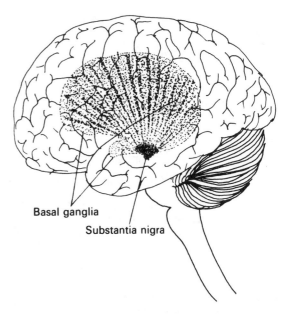

Basal ganglia

Substantia nigra

Figure 33.4 The loss of dopamine nerve cells from the brain's substantia nigra is thought to be responsible for the symptoms of parkinsonism. (Courtesy of National Institutes of Health.)

walks bent forward with a shuffling gait. Difficulty in pivoting and loss of balance may lead to frequent falls. little facial muscle movement gives expressionless, unblinking features.
2. Tremor: this frequently begins in one hand and arm, progressing later to the other, and later still to involve the head. The tremor is characteristic, as if the patient is rolling a pill between the fingers ('pill rolling'), and is present at rest, increasing when the patient is anxious or concentrating.
3. Stiffness or rigidity: the extremities become rigid because the muscles opposing an action cannot relax. When a limb is flexed passively, it is likened to bending a lead pipe, and cog wheel rigidity is encountered if this is superimposed by tremor (Figure 33.5).

Frequently, these patients show signs of depression and dementia.

Diagnosis

Early diagnosis of Parkinson's disease can be difficult, as the patient can rarely pinpoint when symptoms started. Often someone close to the patient notices a change such as stooped posture, a stiff arm, a slight limp or tremor. Handwriting changes may be an early diagnostic clue. A diagnosis of Parkinson's disease can usually be made with certainty when there is evidence of tremor, rigidity and bradykinesia (abnormally slow movements). The results of the patient's history and neurological examination are carefully evaluated.

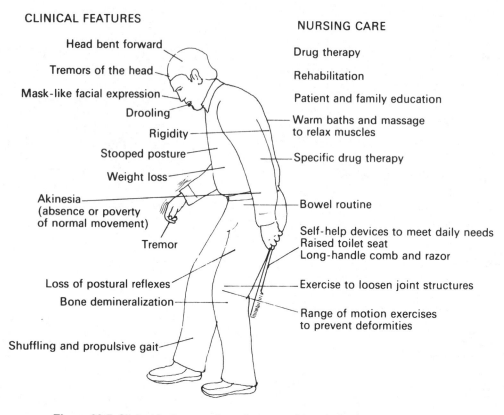

CLINICAL FEATURES

Head bent forward
Tremors of the head
Mask-like facial expression
Drooling
Rigidity
Stooped posture
Weight loss
Akinesia
(absence or poverty
of normal movement)
Tremor
Loss of postural reflexes
Bone demineralization
Shuffling and propulsive gait

NURSING CARE

Drug therapy
Rehabilitation
Patient and family education
Warm baths and massage
to relax muscles
Specific drug therapy
Bowel routine
Self-help devices to meet daily needs
Raised toilet seat
Long-handle comb and razor
Exercise to loosen joint structures
Range of motion exercises
to prevent deformities

Figure 33.5 Clinical features and nursing care of the patient with parkinsonism.

▶ NURSING PROCESS

▶ THE PATIENT WITH PARKINSON'S DISEASE

▶ Assessment

The nursing history and assessment focus on how the disease has affected the patient's activities and functioning abilities. The nurse should observe what the patient can do and what changes in function occur throughout the day. The nurse should observe responses following the administration of medications. Patients should be asked what they would like to do better. The following questions may be asked:

● Have you experienced any irregular jerking of your arms or legs?
● Have you ever been 'frozen' or rooted to the spot and been unable to move?
● Does your mouth water excessively?
● Have you (or others) noticed yourself grimacing or making faces or chewing movements?
● What specific activities do you have difficulty doing?

During this process, the nurse should observe the patient rolling over in bed, getting out of bed, getting out of a chair, walking, drinking and eating.

▶ Patient's Problems

Nearly every patient with a movement disorder has some functional alteration and may have some type of behavioural dysfunction. Based on the assessment, the patient's main problems may include the following:

● Impaired physical mobility related to muscle rigidity and weakness.
● Alteration in nutrition—less than body requirements related to tremor, slowness in eating, difficulty in chewing and swallowing.
● Alteration in bowel elimination related to medication and reduced activity.
● Self-care deficits related to tremor and motor disturbance.
● Impaired verbal communication related to decreased speech volume, slowness of speech, inability to move facial muscles.

▶ Planning and Implementation
▶ Expected Outcomes

The patient's expected outcomes may include: improvement of mobility; attainment of independence in activities of living; achievement of adequate bowel elimination; attainment and maintenance of satisfactory nutritional status; achievement of communication; and development of positive coping mechanisms.

Nursing Care

Improving Mobility
The aim of care is to promote maximum independence and this is achieved by keeping the patient as active as possible. Physiotherapy should be provided to increase muscle strength, improve co-ordination and dexterity, reduce muscular rigidity and prevent contractures in unused muscles. Walking, swimming and gardening are all exercises which maintain joint mobility, while stretching exercises help to loosen joint structures. Special walking techniques, for example, a conscious effort to swing the arms, lengthen stride and mentally humming a marching tune all help to maintain posture. Frequent rest periods aid in preventing fatigue and subsequent frustration. Warm baths and massage, in addition to passive and active exercises, help to relax muscles and relieve painful muscle spasms that accompany rigidity.

Ensuring Adequate Nutrition
Patients with Parkinson's disease have a problem in maintaining their weight. They become embarrassed by their slowness and untidiness in eating. Medications cause dry mouths, and patients experience difficulty in chewing and swallowing. These patients are 'silent aspirators' with decreased cough reflexes; unknowingly, they can aspirate and develop bronchopneumonia. Others may accumulate saliva due to a slow rate of swallowing. Such problems in eating eventually cause considerable weight loss.

Swallowing disorders are also due to tongue tremor, hesitancy in initiating swallowing, difficulty in shaping food into a bolus and disturbances in pharyngeal motility. To overcome these problems, the patient should sit in an upright position during mealtimes. Food should be of a soft consistency and cut into easily managed pieces. The patient should be encouraged to place food on the tongue, close the lips and teeth, lift the tongue up and then back, and swallow. The nurse should advise the patient to chew first on one side of the mouth and then the other. To control the build-up of saliva, the nurse should remind the patient to hold the head upright and make a conscious effort to swallow. Massaging the facial and neck muscles before meals may be beneficial. The use of nonslip mats and specially adapted crockery and cutlery may be of help.

Promoting Bowel Elimination
Patients with parkinsonism may have severe problems with elimination. Constipation is common and is often due to muscle weakness, lack of exercise, inadequate fluid intake, decreased autonomic nervous system activity and drug therapy. It can be relieved by increasing dietary fibre and fluids, and by establishing a regular bowel routine.

Enhancing Self-Care Activities
The nurse should teach, support and supervise the patient during activities of living. Environmental modifications may need to be made to compensate for functional disabilities. Poverty in movement and rigidity makes turning and getting out of bed difficult; bedside rails or a rope tied to the foot of the bed will provide assistance in moving without help from another.

Episodes of urinary incontinence, which are often embarrassing, are sometimes due to the patient's limited mobility and slowness in manual dexterity. A raised toilet seat and adaptations to clothing may avoid accidents.

Improving Communication
Communication by the patient can be frustrating. Speech is low-pitched, monotonous and requires a conscious effort to speak slowly, with deliberate attention to what is to be said. Patients should face the listener and exaggerate the pronunciation of words, speaking in short sentences. Taking a few deep breaths before speaking will help. Because patients will often withdraw from company due to embarrassment, they should be encouraged to be active participants in their own care, including social and recreational events.

Medical Management

Drug therapy is symptomatic and does not halt the disease process, but aims at restoring the dopamine/acetylcholine imbalance by either restoring dopamine levels or reducing acetylcholine.

Anticholinergic Agents
Anticholinergic agents inhibit the action of acetylcholine in an attempt to counteract the possible excess, and are often effective in controlling the tremor and rigidity. They may be used in conjunction with levodopa (see below). The main anticholinergic agents is use are: benhexol hydrochloride, benztropine, orphenadrine hydrochloride and procyclidine hydrochloride. The side-effects include blurred vision, rash, flushing, constipation, urinary retention and mental confusion.

Antihistamines
Antihistamines have mild anticholinergic action, which is again useful in controlling tremor.

Dopaminergic Agents
The precursor levodopa is converted to dopamine in the basal ganglia. It is not a cure but is effective in controlling the bradykinesia and rigidity. Levodopa should be given after meals to reduce gastric irritation, and the dose increased gradually until side-effects appear. These include nausea, vomiting, confusion, involuntary movement and postural hypotension. The beneficial effects of

levodopa are most pronounced in the first few years of treatment; the benefits, however, wane, and adverse side-effects become more severe with time. These include abnormal involuntary movements, e.g. facial grimacing, and choreoathetoid movements of the extremities. The patient may also experience 'on–off' reactions, with sudden periods of immobility.

Levodopa can be given in combination with a decarboxylase inhibitor (carbidopa), which allows a greater concentration of levodopa to reach the brain and decreases unwanted peripheral side-effects.

Dopamine Agonist (Bromocriptine)

Bromocriptine mimics the action of dopamine at the receptor site and has a similar central effect to that of levodopa. It may be useful when added to levodopa, especially if 'on–off' reactions occur, after which levodopa can be reduced gradually.

Antiviral Agents

Amantadine hydrochloride can be used early in the treatment of parkinsonism to reduce rigidity tremor and bradykinesia. Its mode of action is unknown. Adverse reactions include visual impairment, psychiatric disturbances and epigastric upsets.

Antidepressants

Antidepressants may be given to alleviate the depression that so commonly accompanies Parkinson's disease.

Drug therapy advances in recent years have superseded surgical therapy. However, stereotactic surgery may be beneficial for intractable tremor in young patients. This involves destruction of a small area of thalamus, where the tremor originates. More recent developments have shown that once ethical issues are resolved, it may be possible to transplant dopamine-producing fetal brain cells into the basal ganglia. The cells implanted are either adrenal medulla cells or those from the substantia nigra, that is, part of the basal ganglia which dies prematurely in patients with Parkinson's disease. Adult brain cells cannot repair or regrow, whereas immature fetal cells of basal ganglia can. The British Medical Association has drawn up guidelines for such operations in an attempt to deal with the moral and ethical issues which this procedure raises.

Patient Education

The patient and loved ones should be made aware of the problems associated with immobility, and the precautions necessary to maintain safety. Advice can be given on how to adapt the home environment. The patient should understand the role of drug therapy and the recognition of unwanted side-effects.

The disorder may affect the patient's ability to socialize and to continue employment. The medical social worker, occupational therapist and the disablement resettlement officer may give advice regarding future help available. Information can also be given about the disorder, and the help available through groups such as the Parkinson's Disease Society.

▶ *Evaluation*
▶ **Expected Outcomes**

1. The patient achieves maximal independence.
2. Daily exercise is taken.
3. Activities of daily living are achieved with minimal help.
4. An adequate nutritional status is maintained; the patient is able to swallow safely and eats slowly.
5. Communicates effectively, and practises speech exercises.
6. Patient is aware of contacts regarding future help.
7. Patient had a good knowledge of drug therapy, action and side-effects.

NEUROMUSCULAR DISEASES

Myasthenia Gravis

Myasthenia gravis is a disorder affecting the neuromuscular transmission of the voluntary muscles of the body; it is characterized by excessive weakness and fatigability of muscle function. It mainly affects younger women; men who develop the disease do so later in life.

Altered Physiology

The basic abnormality in myasthenia gravis is a defect in the transmission of impulses at the neuromuscular junction. Myasthenia gravis is considered to be an autoimmune disease in which antibodies directed against acetylcholine receptor impair neuromuscular transmission.

Clinical Features

The disease is characterized by extreme muscular weakness and easy fatigability, which generally is worse after effort and is relieved by rest. Patients with this disease tire on such slight exertion as combing the hair, chewing and talking, and must stop for rest. Symptoms vary according to the muscles affected. Those innervated by cranial nerves, e.g. the ocular muscles, produce diplopia (double vision) and ptosis (drooping of the eyelids). The patient has a sleepy, masklike expression because the facial muscles are affected. Laryngeal involvement produces a dysphonia (voice impairment), and weakness of the bulbar muscles causes problems with chewing and swallowing, presenting a danger of choking and aspiration. Some patients complain of weakness of arm and hand muscles and, less commonly, of leg muscle weakness, which makes the patient subject to falls.

● Progressive weakness of the diaphragm and intercostal muscles may produce respiratory distress or myasthenic crisis, which is an acute emergency.

Diagnosis

The signs and symptoms of myasthenia gravis are sometimes so striking that a presumptive diagnosis can be made on the basis of the patient's clinical history. An injection of edrophonium chloride, a drug that facilitates the transmission of nerve–muscle messages, is used to confirm the diagnosis. Within 30 seconds of an intravenous injection of edrophonium, most patients will improve substantially, but only temporarily. Demonstration of the anti-acetylcholine receptor antibodies in the serum is found in nearly 90 per cent of patients with myasthenia gravis.

Electromyography is used to measure the electrical potential of muscle cells.

Management

Management of myasthenia gravis is directed at improving remaining function through the administration of anticholinesterase medications, reducing antibodies and removing circulating antibodies. Therapy includes anticholinesterase drugs and immunosuppressive therapy, including plasmaphoresis, and thymectomy.

Anticholinesterase drugs act by prolonging the action of acetylcholine by inhibiting anticholinesterase release at the neuromuscular junction, and therefore increasing the response of the muscles to nerve impulses and improving strength. However, these provide only symptomatic relief.

Drugs in current use include pyridostigmine bromide, ambenonium chloride and neostigmine bromide. Most patients prefer pyridostigmine because it produces less marked side-effects, and its effect lasts longer than other anticholinesterase drugs. It can therefore be prescribed at night. The dosage is increased gradually until maximal benefits are obtained (additional strength, less fatigue), although normal muscle strength may not be achieved and the patient may have to adapt to some disability. Anticholinesterase medications are given with milk, biscuits or other buffering substances to relieve the associated gastric discomfort. Small doses of atropine, given once or twice daily, may ameliorate or prevent these side-effects. Other side-effects of anticholinesterase therapy include adverse effects on skeletal muscles, such as fasciculations (fine twitching), spasm and weakness. The effects on the central nervous system include irritability, anxiety, insomnia, headache, dysarthria, syncope, convulsions and coma. Increased salivation and lacrimation, increased bronchial secretions, and moist skin may also be noted.

● Priority is to give the drug prescribed according to an exact time schedule in order to control the patient's symptoms. *Any delay in drug administration may result in the patient's losing the ability to swallow.* The nurse should watch for an increase in muscle weakness within one hour after the patient takes the anticholinesterase drug, and be particularly alert for signs of respiratory distress.

After the initial doses have been adjusted, the patient learns to take the medication according to needs and time plan. Further adjustments may be necessary in the presence of physical or emotional stress and intercurrent infection.

Corticosteroid Therapy

Corticosteroid therapy may be of use in patients who do not respond well to anticholinesterase therapy. However, a deterioration in the patient's condition may occur initially before any improvement is seen, and so these drugs should be administered only under supervision.

Immunosuppressive therapy, e.g. azathioprine, may be used to stabilize the disorder if the optimum therapeutic dose of pyridostigmine is reached without maximal effect, or if patients resist corticosteroid therapy. A beneficial response should occur six to 12 months later. Removal of immunoglobulins by plasmaphoresis may produce short-term remissions.

Surgical Intervention

Thymectomy (removal of the thymus gland) causes substantial remission, especially in patients with a tumour or hyperplasia of the gland. It appears to have most benefit in the younger patient who has a history of myasthenia gravis of less than five years. Thymectomy may be carried out using a transcervical approach or a stenotomy. Careful postoperative evaluation, usually in an intensive care unit, is aimed at recognizing respiratory difficulties.

Myasthenic Crisis

Myasthenic crisis is the sudden onset of muscular weakness. Respiratory distress combined with varying signs (dysphagia, dysarthria, ptosis and diplopia) are symptoms of impending crisis. Weakness of respiratory, laryngeal, pharyngeal and bulbar musculature causes respiratory depression and airway obstruction as well as cerebral hypoxia with its attendant sequelae of central nervous system injury and death.

Myasthenic crisis may result from progression of the disease, emotional upset, systemic infections, certain drugs, surgery or trauma, or it may be brought about by adrenocorticotrophic hormone therapy.

Cholinergic crisis occurs from overmedication with anticholinesterase drugs, which release too much acetylcholine at the neuromuscular junction. Brittle crisis occurs when the receptors at the neuromuscular junction become insensitive to anticholinesterase medication. It is not controlled by increasing or decreasing anticholinesterase therapy.

Nursing Care During Myasthenic Crisis

The patient is admitted to an intensive care unit for constant monitoring, since this condition is marked by intense and sudden fluctuations, especially in respiratory function. Providing adequate ventilatory assistance takes precedence in the immediate management of the patient during crisis. Aspiration is a common problem; thus a clear airway must be maintained—endotracheal intubation and mechanical ventilation may be needed.

Intravenous edrophonium chloride is given to differentiate the type of crisis. It improves the condition of patients in myasthenic crisis, temporarily worsens that of patients undergoing cholinergic crisis and is unpredictable in brittle crisis.

If the patient is in true myasthenic crisis, neostigmine methylsulphate is administered parenterally. If the edrophonium test is uncertain, or there is increasing respiratory weakness, all anticholinesterase drugs are withdrawn, and atropine sulphate is given to reduce excessive secretions.

Other supportive measures include the following:

- If the patient is unable to swallow, nasogastric feeds are given until food can be taken orally.
- If the patient is to enjoy meals without being fatigued it is essential that drugs are timed carefully some 30 minutes before eating.
- The table should be at the correct height to prevent fatigue from having to lean forward to eat; the neck may also be supported in a cervical collar.

Constipation is not normally a problem due to the effects of anticholinesterase and enemas should in any case be avoided as they may precipitate a collapse. The patient with respiratory difficulty will experience anxiety, sometimes bordering on panic, and compounded by a tendency to choke and an inability to swallow. Acknowledgement by the nurse of these fears, and the development of effective communication, can reassure the patient.

To help the patient cope with visual impairment due to ptosis, it is possible for the nurse to tape open the patient's eyelids for short intervals, or to place an eyepatch over one eye when diplopia is problematic.

The use of sedatives and tranquillizers should be avoided since they may aggravate hypoxia and hypercarbia, causing respiratory and cardiac depression.

The nurse should reassure patients that they will not be left alone and that the crisis should pass.

Patient Education
The patient should learn the basic facts about anticholinergic drugs—their action, timing, dosage adjustment, symptoms of overdose and toxic effects.

There are a number of drugs that aggravate myasthenia gravis, and the patient is advised to consult with the doctor before taking any new medications. Lignocaine injections should be avoided, and so the patient's dentist should be informed.

Mealtimes should coincide with the peak effects of anticholinesterase if the patient has difficulty in swallowing. If choking occurs frequently, liquidized food may be easier to swallow. Standby suction should be available at home.

Certain factors may increase weakness and precipitate a myasthenic crisis: emotional upset, infections (particularly respiratory infections), vigorous physical activity and exposure to heat (hot baths, sunbathing) and cold. These situations should be avoided. To avoid the risk of fatigue, it is best to rest *before* becoming too tired. The patient is also advised to wear an identification bracelet.

Motor Neurone Disease

Motor neurone disease is a degenerative disorder characterized by selective neuronal loss in the motor system, affecting several levels. It is a progressive disease with no specific treatment.

Aetiology

The aetiology is unknown although several theories exist, including the ageing process triggered by genetic and environmental factors, viral infection, disordered carbohydrate metabolism and toxic poisoning.

Clinical Features

The clinical features depend on which part of the motor system is affected. If lower motor neurones are affected, progressive wasting of muscles occurs, whereas upper motor neurone damage results in exaggerated tendon reflexes. Progressive bulbar paralysis, leading to dysphagia and dysarthria ensues when cranial nerves are damaged. Attempts by the patient to eat and drink often result in aspiration pneumonia, the commonest cause of death in such patients. There is no sensory loss or intellectual impairment.

Treatment

There is no effective treatment. Support and symptomatic treatment are given when indicated.

CONVULSIVE DISORDERS

The Epilepsies

The epilepsies are paroxysmal disturbances of neurological function caused by uncontrolled discharge of neurones in the central nervous system, which may be manifestations of many disorders. No cause is found in 50 per cent of cases.

The basic problem is thought to be an electrical disturbance in the nerve cells in one section of the brain, causing them to give off abnormal, recurring, uncontrolled electrical discharges, during which parts of the body controlled by the errant cells may perform erratically. When these uncontrolled abnormal discharges happen repeatedly, the patient is said to have epilepsy. The erratic physical movements are called 'seizures' (the use of the terms 'fit' and 'convulsion' are synonymous with 'seizure').

Causes

The cause of epilepsy in unknown in the majority of cases, i.e. it is idiopathic; in other cases, epilepsy is usually a symptom of a disease that may be due to one of the following:

1. Metabolic and nutritional disorders.
   a. Hypoglycaemia.
   b. Hypoxia.
   c. Toxicity (poisoning with drugs, alcohol, lead).
   d. Congenital defects in metabolism.
2. Infections.
   a. Meningitis.
   b. Abscess.
   c. Encephalitis.
3. Structural damage.
   a. Tumour.
   b. Trauma.
   c. Vascular problems.
   d. Degenerative disease.

Clinical Features/Assessment

Depending on the location of the discharging neurones, seizures may range from a simple staring spell to prolonged convulsive movements with loss of consciousness. Based on the nature of the attack rather than the underlying pathology, an international classification has been formulated. Seizures are identified as being partial, generalized or unclassified (Table 33.2).

The initial pattern of the seizures (uncontrollable, inappropriate behaviour, sensations or mood) indicates the region of the brain in which the attack originates. Also, it is important to determine if the patient has had an aura (premonitory or warning sensation before an epileptic seizure), which may indicate the origin of the seizure (e.g., seeing a flashing light may indicate the seizure originated in the occipital lobe). The patient may not recall the episode when it is over.

In simple partial seizures, only a finger or hand may shake, or the mouth may jerk uncontrollably. The person may speak nonsense, may be dizzy and may experience unusual or unpleasant sights, sounds, odours or tastes, but

Table 33.2 *International classification of seizures*

Partial seizures (seizures beginning locally)
1. Simple partial seizures (with elementary symptomatology, generally without impairment of consciousness)
   a. With motor symptoms
   b. With special sensory or somatosensory symptoms
   c. With autonomic symptoms
2. Complex partial seizures (generally with impairment of consciousness). Psychomotor seizures or temporal lobe epilepsy
   a. With impairment of consciousness only
   b. With cognitive symptomatology
   c. With affective symptomatology
3. Partial seizures secondarily generalized

Generalized seizures (bilaterally symmetrical, without local onset)
1. Absences (petit mal)
2. Myoclonic (sudden, unilateral)
3. Clonic seizures
4. Tonic seizures
5. Tonic–clonic seizures
6. Atonic or akinetic seizures

Unclassified epileptic seizures
(Incomplete data)

without loss of consciousness. If the focal seizure spreads it is described as Jacksonian epilepsy.

In complex partial seizures, the person either remains motionless or moves automatically but inappropriately for time and place, or may experience excessive emotions of fear, anger, elation or irritability. Whatever the manifestations, the person does not remember the episode when it is over.

Generalized seizures, more commonly referred to as grand mal seizures, involve both hemispheres of the brain, causing both sides of the body to react. There may be intense rigidity of the entire body, followed by jerky alternations of muscle relaxation and contraction (generalized tonic–clonic contraction). The simultaneous contractions of the diaphragm and chest muscles may produce a characteristic 'epileptic cry'. Often the tongue is chewed, and stools and urine may be passed involuntarily. After one or two minutes, the convulsive movements begin to subside; the patient relaxes and lies in deep coma, breathing noisily. The respirations at this point are chiefly abdominal. In the post-ictal state (after the seizure), the patient is often confused and hard to arouse, and may sleep for hours. Many patients complain of headache or sore muscles.

Diagnosis

The diagnosis often depends on the patient's and witnesses's description of the attack(s). Since seizures are symptomatic, physical examination and neurological investigations, e.g. computerized tomography, may reveal underlying cerebral pathology.

The electroencephalogram furnishes diagnostic evidence in a substantial proportion of patients with epilepsy and aids in classifying the type of seizure. Abnormalities in the electroencephalogram usually continue to be apparent between attacks, or, if concealed, may be brought out by hyperventilation or during sleep. It should be noted, however, that some people with seizures may have normal electroencephalograms, whereas people who have never had seizures may have abnormal electroencephalograms.

► NURSING PROCESS
► THE PATIENT WITH EPILEPSY

► Assessment

The nurse serves as an historian and observer to elicit information about the patient's seizure history. The nurse should find out if the patient knows the factors or events that precipitate the seizures. The nurse should ask about alcohol intake, and find out how epilepsy has interfered with the patient's lifestyle. Does the patient lead as normal a life as possible? Does work or recreation suffer as a result? What are the limitations imposed by the seizure disorder?

Observation and neurological nursing assessment during and after a seizure are important for determining the type of seizure and its management. In particular, the following should be noted:

1. Description of the circumstances before the attack (visual stimuli, auditory stimuli, olfactory stimuli, tactile stimuli, emotional or psychic disturbances, sleep, hyperventilation).
2. The first thing the patient does in an attack—where the movements or the stiffness starts, position of the eyeballs and the head at the beginning of the attack. This information gives clues as to the location of the epileptogenic focus in the brain. (In recording, always state whether or not the beginning of the attack was observed.)
3. The type of movements of the part involved.
4. The parts involved. (Turn back bedding and expose patient.)
5. The size of both pupils. Are the eyes open? Did the eyes/head turn to one side?
6. Whether or not automatisms (involuntary motor activity such as lip smacking or repeated swallowing) were observed.
7. Incontinence of urine or faeces.
8. Duration of each phase of the attack.
9. Unconsciousness, if present, and its duration.
10. Any obvious paralysis or weakness of arms or legs after the attack.
11. Inability to speak after the attack.

12. Movements at the end of the seizure.
13. Whether or not the patient sleeps afterward.
14. Whether or not the patient was confused following the attack.

► Patient's Problems

Based on the assessment, the patient's main problems may include the following:

- Fear related to concern about the ever-present possibility of having seizures.
- Social isolation related to stresses and stigmas imposed by epilepsy.
- Lack of knowledge about epilepsy and its control.
- Potential for injury during seizures.

► Planning and Implementation
► Expected Outcomes

The main expected outcomes for the patient may include maintenance of control of seizures, achievement of a satisfactory psychological adjustment and acquisition of knowledge and understanding about the condition. The long-term goal is to achieve a satisfactory life adjustment.

Nursing Care During a Seizure

- Provide privacy and protect the patient from curious onlookers. (The patient who has an aura [warning of an impending seizure] may have time to seek a safe place.)
- Ease the patient to the floor, if there is enough time.
- Protect the head with a pad to prevent injury (from striking a hard surface).
- Loosen constrictive clothing.
- Push aside any furniture that may be struck by the patient during the attack.
- If the patient is in bed, remove the pillows.
- If possible, place the patient on one side with the head flexed forward, which permits the tongue to fall forward and facilitates drainage of saliva and mucus.
- *Do not attempt to pry open jaws that are clenched in a spasm to insert a mouth gag.* Broken teeth and injury to the lips and tongue may result from such an action.
- No attempt should be made to restrain the patient during the seizure, since muscular contractions are strong and restraint can produce a fracture.
- After the seizure, remain with the patient and turn on one side to prevent aspiration. Make sure the airway is adequate.
- Following the convulsion, the patient may experience a period of confusion, and should be reoriented to the environment when possible.
- If the patient experiences severe excitement following a seizure (post-ictal), try to handle the situation with calm persuasion and gentle restraint.

Medical Management

The long-term management of epilepsy includes determining the underlying cause and to control and prevent seizure recurrences. In approximately 70 per cent of newly diagnosed patients, complete control can be achieved using anticonvulsant therapy.

Drug Therapy

Many anti-epileptic drugs are available to control seizures, although the mechanisms of their actions are still unknown. The objective of drug therapy is to achieve seizure control with minimal side-effects. Drug therapy is a form of control, not cure. The drug is selected according to the type of seizure being treated and the effectiveness and safety of the drug.

Usually, treatment is started with a single drug. The starting dose and the rate at which the dosage is increased depend on patient co-operation and plasma serum levels. Changing to another drug may be necessary if seizure control is not achieved or when toxicity makes it impossible to increase the dosage. The drug may have to be adjusted because of intercurrent illness, weight gain or increases in stress. Sudden withdrawal of anti-epileptic medication can cause seizures to occur with greater frequency or can precipitate the development of status epilepticus (see p. 1040).

The side-effects of these medications may be divided into three groups: (1) idiosyncratic or allergic disorders, which present primarily as skin reactions; (2) acute toxicity, which may be manifested when the drug is initially prescribed; or (3) chronic toxicity, which occurs late in the course of drug therapy. Periodic physical examinations and laboratory tests are done on patients receiving drugs known to have toxic effects on the haematopoietic, genitourinary or hepatic systems. Table 33.3 summarizes the anti-epileptic drugs in current use.

Patient Education

The patient and loved ones need to know that epilepsy can be controlled, that it does not reflect insanity or a supernatural condition and that it should not be seen as a stigma. The complete co-operation of the patient and relatives will help to control the seizures.

Patients should be encouraged to examine their lifestyles and environment to determine whether certain factors precipitate the seizures, for example, emotional disturbances, new environmental stresses, onset of menstruation in female patients or fever.

The patient is encouraged to follow a regular and mod-

Table 33.3 *Major anti-epileptic drugs*

Generic name	Dose-related side-effects	Toxic effects	Indications

Carbamazepine	Dizziness; drowsiness
	Unsteadiness; nausea
	  and vomiting
	Diplopia; mild leucopenia
		Severe skin rash
		Blood dyscrasias
		Hepatitis
			All seizure types
			  (except absences)

Primidone	Lethargy; irritability Diplopia; ataxia Sexual impotence	Skin rash	All seizure types (except absences)
Phenytoin	Drowsiness; ataxia Visual problems Hirsutism Gingival hyperplasia	Severe skin reaction Peripheral neuropathy	All seizure types (except absences)
Phenobarbital	Sedation; irritability Diplopia Ataxia	Skin rash	All seizure types (except absences)
Ethosuximide	Nausea and vomiting Headache Gastric distress	Skin rash Blood dyscrasias Hepatitis Lupus	General absences
Valproate	Nausea and vomiting Weight gain Loss of hair	Skin rash Blood dyscrasias Nephritis Hepatotoxicity	All seizure types

erate routine in lifestyle, diet, exercise and rest, avoiding excessive stimulation. Tension, anxiety and frustration may induce seizures and should be avoided. If seizures follow alcohol intake, such beverages should be restricted.

The patient should not allow the supply of anticonvulsants to run out, and should never stop taking medication; sudden withdrawal is likely to precipitate seizures. If seizures become repetitive, a diary should be kept detailing the frequency and the time of day seizures take place and so on. The consultant may be able to use such a diary to help monitor drug therapy.

Anticonvulsants should not be discontinued when any other illness occurs, and they may require readjustment if the patient vomits. Anticonvulsant therapy may interact with the efficiency of the contraceptive pill, and seizures may increase premenstrually.

Patients should maintain good oral hygiene and have regular dental care to counteract the effects of long-term anticonvulsant therapy. A personal identification card, stating the patient's name and dose of drugs should be carried. Controlled epilepsy should not prevent the patient from driving or working; activity tends to inhibit seizures, not stimulate them.

Patients and their relatives should be encouraged to discuss their feelings and attitudes—and those of society—regarding epilepsy. Patients often fear humiliation in public, and ostracism and social rejection, which may extend to loved ones; for the observer, however, an epileptic fit is a frightening experience.

The patient should be informed about the services of the British Epilepsy Association. It may be possible to withdraw anticonvulsant therapy in those patients who have been seizure-free for two or three years.

People who have uncontrollable seizures and psychological and social maladaptation with other overwhelming problems can be referred to comprehensive epilepsy centres where continuous television and electroencephalogram monitoring, specialized treatment and rehabilitation services are available.

► *Evaluation*
► **Expected Outcomes**

1. Patient understands the nature of the disorder.
2. Patient maintains control of seizures by co-operating with the drug regime and avoiding factors recognized as initiating attacks.
3. Psychological adjustments are coped with.
4. Patient recognizes the need to alert others to the disorder, and wears or carries medical identification.
5. Discusses feelings and attitude, and those of loved ones, about epilepsy.

Surgery for Epilepsy
Surgery is indicated for patients whose epilepsy results from intracranial tumours, abscess, cysts or vascular anomalies.

Some patients with a single focal lesion who suffer from recurrent seizures that interfere with a normal lifestyle may be offered surgery. The commonest surgical procedure is the resectioning of either a cortical or temporal eleptogenic focus. Occasionally, a temporal lobectomy may be performed. Dividing the corpus callosum may be indicated in order to prevent the seizure spreading to the opposite hemisphere. Less frequently, stereotactic lesions may be made in the limbic system. The pre- and postoperative care is the same as that of other craniotomy patients.

Status Epilepticus

Status epilepticus (acute prolonged seizure activity) is a series of generalized convulsions that occur without full recovery of consciousness between attacks. It is considered to be a major medical emergency. Status epilepticus produces cumulative effects. Vigorous muscular contractions impose a heavy metabolic demand and can interfere with respirations. There is some respiratory arrest at the height of each seizure that produces venous congestion and hypoxia of the brain. Repeated episodes of cerebral anoxia and swelling may lead to irreversible and fatal brain damage.

Common factors that precipitate status epilepticus include withdrawal of anti-epileptic medication, fever and infection.

Medical and Nursing Care
The aims of treatment are to stop the seizures as quickly as possible, to ensure adequate cerebral oxygenation and to maintain the patient in a seizure-free state. An airway and adequate oxygenation are established. An intravenous infusion is set up. Intravenous diazepam (short-acting) is given slowly, directly into the bloodstream, in an attempt to halt the seizures immediately. However, repeated injections may cause respiratory depression. If the condition persists and cannot be controlled, then longer-acting anticonvulsants may be used, e.g. phenytoin, thiopentone, with assisted ventilation.

Electroencephalogram monitoring may be useful in determining the nature of the epileptogenic activity. Vital signs and neurological observations are monitored regularly.

HEAD INJURIES

Head injuries are the most frequent and serious neurological disorder in the United Kingdom. An estimated 300 per 100,000 population per year require hospitalization due to head injuries, and the mortality rate is 9 per 100,000. The morbidity rate is quite high; there are some

70,000 severely head-injured patients at present in the United Kingdom, many being under 30 years old.

Head injuries as a result of road traffic accidents and vehicle/pedestrian accidents are common causes of severe head injury, the majority of which are alcohol-related. Injuries to the head include trauma to the scalp, skull and brain, damage occurring both at the time of impact and as a result of the development of secondary complications. A large percentage of severely head-injured patients have significant injuries to other parts of the body.

Classification of Head Injuries

Although head injuries can be classified as blunt (nonpenetrating/closed) or penetrating, this does not indicate the cause. Therefore, it is now more useful to classify according to injury type. Most peacetime injuries are Type 1 and 2, whereas in conventional warfare, Type 3 and 4 injuries are common.

- Type 1—the head strikes a static surface, e.g. a fall from a height, thus causing a blunt or acceleration injury.

- Type 2—a moving object hits the stationary head, crushing or compressing the head.
- Type 3—Weaponry, e.g. an axe, knife or low-velocity bullet, penetrates the cranial cavity.
- Type 4—a high-velocity bullet causes massive brain destruction: small entry, large exit wound.

Scalp and Skull Injuries

Scalp Injury

Trauma may result in an abrasion, contusion, laceration or avulsion. The scalp can bleed profusely due to its many blood vessels, and it can also provide an entry for infection.

Skull Injury—Fractures of the Skull (Types 1 and 2)

A skull fracture is a break in the continuity of the skull caused by trauma (Figure 33.6). It may occur with or with-

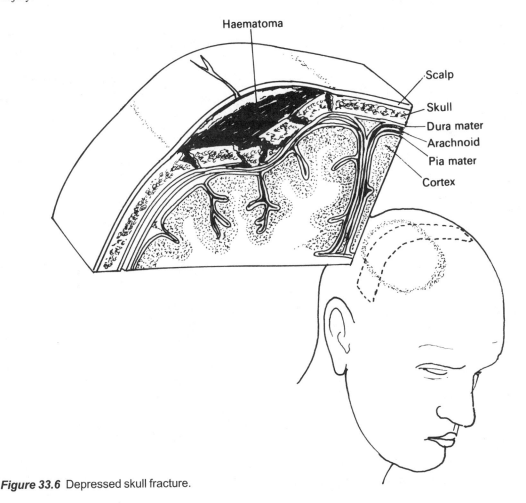

Figure 33.6 Depressed skull fracture.

out damage to the brain. The presence of a skull fracture usually means that there was considerable force upon impact. The majority of skull fractures are linear crossing points of weaknesses, e.g. sinuses, temporal, squamous areas, which may also tear underlying blood vessels, giving rise to haematoma formation.

Clinical Features

Fractures of the base of the skull frequently produce haemorrhage from the nose, the pharynx or the ears, and blood may appear under the conjunctivae. An area of ecchymosis, or bruising, may be seen over the mastoid. The escape of cerebrospinal fluid from the ears (cerebrospinal fluid otorrhoea) and the nose (cerebrospinal rhinorrhoea) suggests skull fracture. Bloody spinal fluid, if present, suggests brain laceration or contusion.

Brain Injury

The most important consideration in any head injury is whether or not the brain has been injured. Even 'minor' injury can cause permanent brain damage.

Serious brain injury may occur following blows or injuries to the head, with or without fracture of the skull, that produce contusions, laceration and haemorrhage of the brain.

Concussion

The degree of concussion should be estimated from those who witnessed the accident. Generally, concussion following head injury involves a temporary loss of consciousness lasting from a few seconds to several weeks, with associated post-traumatic amnesia, again perhaps lasting from hours to weeks. Both relate to the severity of diffuse brain damage.

Type 3 and 4 Injuries

Scalp wounds in these types of injuries tend to be small puncture wounds or lacerations.

- Skull—fractures are depressed.
- Brain—the clinical features of Type 3 injuries depend very much on the site and degree of damage, e.g. hemiparesis and speech disturbances may occur if damage occurs to the dominant hemisphere. The damage tends to be more localized. Type 4 damage is associated with massive tissue destruction from the explosive effects of a high-velocity bullet, and is usually fatal.

Assessment of Head Injuries

Clinical Features

Brain trauma may affect every system of the body. The clinical features of brain injury include disturbances of consciousness, confusion, pupillary abnormalities, sudden onset of neurological deficits and changes in vital signs. There may be visual impairment, hearing impairment, sensory dysfunction, spasticity, headache, vertigo, movement disorders, seizures and many other effects. The presence of hypovolaemic shock alerts to the possibility of multisystem injury, because central nervous system injury alone is not apt to produce shock.

Diagnosis

The initial physical and neurological examinations are the baseline upon which all future examination comparisons are made. Computed tomography is the primary neuroimaging diagnostic tool, and is useful in the evaluation of soft tissue injuries. Lateral and anteroposterior views of the skull are also obtained.

Planning and Implementation

Management in Accident and Emergency

A person with a head injury is presumed to have a cervical spine injury until proven otherwise, and should be transported with the head and neck maintained in alignment with the axis of the body.

The main priority is directed towards the preservation of brain homeostasis and prevention of secondary brain function. This includes stabilization of cardiovascular and respiratory function to maintain cerebral perfusion. This is achieved by maintaining a clear airway, giving suctioning and adequate oxygenation where necessary. Patients who are unconscious are intubated and may be placed on mechanical ventilation to control and protect the airway. Inadequate respiratory function leads to hypercarbia, in turn causing vasodilation, which increases cerebral blood flow and cerebral oedema with subsequent irreparable brain damage. Controlled ventilation has the opposite effect.

The level of responsiveness and consciousness is assessed constantly using the Glasgow Coma Scale (see Figure 32.1, p. 992) because an alteration in the level of consciousness will precede all other changes in vital and neurological signs. Although deterioration of the patient's level of consciousness is the most sensitive neurological indication of impending danger, the vital signs are also monitored at frequent intervals to assess the intracranial state. Bradycardia, widening pulse pressure and increasing systolic pressure are signs of increasing pressure (pp. 990–1).

If brain compression encroaches upon cerebral circulation, the vital signs tend to be reversed, the pulse and respirations become rapid and the blood pressure may fall. A rapid rise in temperature is also regarded unfavourably; hyperthermia increases the metabolic demands of the brain. Tachycardia and arterial hypotension may indicate bleeding occurring elsewhere in the body. Therefore, the haemorrhage must be located and the hypovolaemia corrected.

The strength and quality of limb movements are also assessed. It is important that the nurse recognizes that a unilaterally dilated and poorly reacting pupil may indicate developing pressure (haematoma, oedema) on the third cranial nerve due to a shifting of the brain. Overwhelming injury and intrinsic damage to the upper brain stem may result in both pupils becoming fixed and dilated.

It is also important to the management of the head-injured patient that an accurate history of the events leading up to and including the accident are obtained.

- What time did the accident occur?
- What caused the injury? (A high-velocity missile; object striking the head; a fall?)
- What was the direction and force of the blow?
- Was there loss of consciousness?
- What was the duration of unconsciousness?
- Any related amnesia? Fits?
- Any neurological deficit noted at the time?

Nursing Care

If the patient is unconscious, care is given according to page 995. As soon as the initial assessment and diagnostic tests are made, the nurse monitors and maintains the patient's consciousness using the Glasgow Coma Scale (see Figure 32.1, p. 992). The nurse also assesses the vital signs, pupillary changes and limb power. The factors associated with nursing care that may cause intracranial pressure to rise should be recognized (see Chapter 32, pp. 990–5).

Maintaining the Airway

One of the most important nursing goals in the management of the patient with a head injury is to establish and maintain an adequate airway. The brain is extremely sensitive to hypoxia, and a neurological deficit can be made worse if the patient is hypoxic. Therapy is directed toward maintenance of adequately oxygenated circulation. An obstructed airway causes CO_2 retention and hypoventilation, which produce cerebral engorgement and increases intracranial pressure.

Therapeutic and nursing activities to ensure an adequate exchange of air include the following:

- Keep the unconscious patient in a semiprone or prone position, with the head of the bed elevated about 30 degrees to decrease intracranial venous pressure, if directed by the doctor.
- Establish effective suctioning procedures. (Pulmonary secretions produce coughing and straining, which increase intracranial pressure.)
- Guard against aspiration and respiratory insufficiency.
- Assist medical staff in obtaining arterial blood gas levels to assess adequacy of ventilation. (Blood gases are kept within normal range to ensure adequate cerebral blood flow.)
- Keep the patient who is on mechanical ventilation under supervision.

Nursing Care Plan 33.1 describes the care required for a patient with head injury.

► NURSING CARE PLAN 33.1: NURSING CARE IN THE ACUTE PHASE FOR THE PATIENT WITH HEAD INJURY

Ravinder Singh is a 22-year-old unemployed Indian-Sikh who has suffered a head injury. He shares a rented flat with two male friends.

Patient's problems	Expected outcomes	Nursing care	Rationale
1. Difficulty in maintenance of airway due to altered consciousness	Adequate respiratory function. Respiratory complications will be avoided by early recognition of problems	1a. Maintain an open airway b. Position patient according to doctor's instructions (*see* problem 3) c. Use oral airway if indicated d. Assess respiratory rate, depth and breath sounds e. Suction patient as required (*see* problem 3) f. Provide oxygenation before suction (*see* problem 3) g. Assist with endotracheal intubation and possible mechanical ventilation	Depression of respiratory function may lead to cerebral hypoxia and vasodilatation, causing oedema with subsequent irreparable brain damage (Hume-Adams, 1975) Suction of secretions and vomitus, and positioning maintains airway patency, and prevents airway obstruction and aspiration pneumonia An adverse effect of airway suction is hypoxia (Young, 1984a and b)

►

► **NURSING CARE PLAN 33.1: NURSING CARE IN THE ACUTE PHASE FOR THE PATIENT WITH HEAD INJURY**

Patient's problems	Expected outcomes	Nursing care	Rationale
2. Alteration of consciousness and neurological function due to head injury	Further deterioration in patient's consciousness will be prevented. Changes in neurological function will be identified	2a. Establish accurate assessment of baseline neurological observations b. Continue monitoring consciousness and neurological function, as dictated by patient's condition c. Pay close attention to vital signs d. Report any deterioration immediately e. Assist and support patient during any emergency investigation f. Give adequate support and explanation to his friends and relatives g. Explain to relatives and friends in simple terms the equipment surrounding the patient h. Be aware of possible communication/language difficulties i. Arrange a translator if necessary	The ability to assess a patient's consciousness level is of clinical importance. The Glasgow Coma Scale provides a standardized, objective method for assessment (Allan, 1984)

3. Increased intracranial pressure with risk of brain herniation	Intracranial pressure will be maintained within normal limits. Factors known to increase intracranial pressure will be avoided	3a. Monitor for clinical features of increased intracranial pressure:
		  i. Depressed consciousness
		  ii. Changes in pupillary size and reaction
		  iii. Developing neurological dysfunction, e.g. limb weakness, abnormal posturing
		  iv. Alterations in vital signs
		  v. Changes in pressure waves/normal limits if intracranial pressure monitored
			Early detection enables measures to be initiated to prevent intracranial pressure rising (Alan, 1986)

		b. Take measures to avoid increasing intracranial pressure i. Plan and deliver nursing care at an optimum time based on vital signs and intracranial recordings	Dangerous increases in intracranial pressure may occur if nursing care that is known to increase intracranial pressure is not well planned
		ii. Elevate head of bed by 30 degrees or as directed by doctor	Elevation of head promotes venous drainage, thus lowering intracranial pressure
		iii. Position patient carefully, maintaining head and neck in neutral position	Maintaining head and neck in neutral position prevents cerebral venous drainage obstruction, which would increase intracranial pressure
		iv. If directed, provide oxygenation before suction	Hyperventilation decreases carbon dioxide levels, causing vasoconstriction and thus decreases intracranial pressure

► NURSING CARE PLAN 33.1: NURSING CARE IN THE ACUTE PHASE FOR THE PATIENT WITH HEAD INJURY

Patient's problems	Expected outcomes	Nursing care	Rationale
		v. Restrict suction to 15 seconds at any one time	Suctioning for more than 15 seconds at one time increases carbon dioxide levels, increasing intracranial pressure
		vi. Modify nursing care if necessary as indicated by changes in intracranial pressure	
		vii. Prevent patient from pushing/straining (valsalva manoeuvre)	Valsalva manoeuvre increases intrathoracic pressure/intracranial pressure
		viii. Maintain normal temperatures	Temperature elevation increases the need for oxygen due to increased metabolic requirements: the end-product of the increased cell metabolism rise causes an increase in intracranial pressure
		ix. Assist in restriction of fluid if requested	Fluid restriction may be employed to reduce cerebral oedema/intracranial pressure
		x. Care for patient with ventricular cerebrospinal fluid drainage, if employed: maintain strict asepsis; maintain level specified by doctor; observe patency, drainage and colour of cerebrospinal fluid	Removal of cerebrospinal fluid will reduce ventricular pressure and thus intracranial pressure
		xi. Administration of medication as directed by doctor to reduce intracranial pressure, e.g. mannitol	Volume of fluid is reduced by use of the hyperosmotic diuretic, mannitol
4. Potential for seizure activity	Seizure will be recognized, treated and controlled	4a. Be aware of possibility of post-traumatic seizures b. Observe onset, duration and seizure activity c. Protect patient from injury d. Guide movements e. Maintain airway f. Record and report any seizure to doctor g. Assist in the administration of anticonvulsants h. Assist in the monitoring of anticonvulsant blood level estimations	Seizures increase the metabolic rate, cause hypercarbia and increase intracranial pressure
5. Potential for fluid and electrolyte imbalance	Fluid and electrolyte balance will be maintained	5a. Maintain accurate intake and output chart b. Monitor urine specific gravity c. Test urine for presence of glucose d. Assist doctor in monitoring electrolytes, serum and urine osmolarities e. Recognize features of developing diabetes insipidus/hyperglycaemia	Early recognition of altered specific gravity/presence of glucose enables appropriate treatment Diabetes insipidus may develop due to hypothalamic/adjacent structural damage. Stress response in some patients can cause hyperglycaemia

►

► **NURSING CARE PLAN 33.1: NURSING CARE IN THE ACUTE PHASE FOR THE PATIENT WITH HEAD INJURY**

Patient's problems	Expected outcomes	Nursing care	Rationale
6. Potential for altered nutrition due to possible altered consciousness/other injuries	Adequate nutrition will be maintained	6a. Assess nutritional status, e.g. weight loss or gain b. Be aware that patient's religion prevents him from eating beef (*see* problem 9). Refer to dietician	Poor nutritional status may lead to decreased wound healing and lowered resistance to infection (Goodison, 1986)
7. Potential for injury due to altered consciousness, restlessness, confusion and aggression	Patient will not be injured	7a. Report any increased restlessness to doctor b. Avoid, if possible, the use of restraints c. Reorientate the patient to time, place and person d. Check for other injuries or retention of urine as possible causes of restlessness e. Keep cot sides in position	Sedation is contraindicated; may alter consciousness. Use of restraints will increase agitation
8. Potential for development of infection, due to head wound/invasive procedures	Infection will not develop/or will be identified as early as possible	8a. Maintain strict asepsis b. Monitor wounds for signs of infection c. Take routine specimens of urine, sputum, cerebrospinal fluid for culture and sensitivity d. Observe patient for any abnormal nasal or ear discharge e. Prevent patient from blowing nose or sneezing f. Note any neck rigidity	Early detection of sepsis will enable early treatment to commence Leakage of cerebrospinal fluid (ear/nasal) increases risk of meningitis
9. Potential difficulties in nursing care due to religious beliefs	An understanding of the beliefs and customs of the Sikh religion should avoid any nursing difficulties	9a. Accept patient's religious practices and rituals to prevent distress to him and friends b. Provide opportunity for the patient, friends or ethnic religious leader to maintain religious practices c. Be aware that Sikh's have three names: personal, title and family name d. Be aware that Sikh religion does not allow the eating of beef e. Be aware that removal of hair or other symbol may cause patient distress f. Recognize the problems associated with washing in bed g. Maintain patient's privacy, dignity and individuality during hygienic activities	According to Sikh religion, all those baptised adopt the family name of Singh (lion): 1. Patient's personal name is Ravinder; 2. Title, i.e. 'Singh' for all men 'Kaur' for all women; 3. Family name. Sikhs usually prefer to be called by their first name or by their first name and then honorific title Other meats will be accepted, although dishes such as 'hotpot', Scotch broth, Irish stew, will not be familiar and will require explanation Sikhs wear five symbols of brotherhood: 'the 5 Ks' – uncut hair, comb, steel bangle, short dagger and white shorts Sikhs prefer to wash in running water rather than by sitting in a bath (Henley, 1980; Shukla, 1979)

Fluid and Electrolyte Balance

Brain damage can produce metabolic and hormonal dysfunctions due to hypothalamic and pituitary damage. The monitoring of serum electrolyte concentrations is important, especially in patients receiving osmotic diuretics, e.g. mannitol, those with inappropriate antidiuretic hormone secretion and those with post-traumatic diabetes insipidus.

- Endocrine dysfunctions are evaluated by monitoring serum electrolytes, glucose values, and input and output records. The severely head-injured patient is prone to stress ulceration, and signs of gastrointestinal bleeding may be noted in the aspirate.
- Urine is tested regularly for sugar and acetone.
- The unconscious patient may require to be catheterized to monitor accurate output.
- Fluids and electrolytes are given as prescribed. In some cases, the patient may be underhydrated in an attempt to reduce extracellular volume and thus cerebral oedema.

Adequate Nutrition

A nasogastric or orogastric tube may be inserted since reduced gastric motility and reverse peristalsis are associated with head injury. As soon as the patient's condition has stabilized, nasogastric feedings are started. An orogastric tube may be passed in patients with a fractured base of the skull and/or cerebrospinal fluid rhinorrhoea. Small, frequent feeds lessen the possibility of vomiting and diarrhoea. Elevating the head of the bed and aspirating the tube before feeding (for evidence of residual feeding in the stomach) are measures used to prevent distension, regurgitation and aspiration. A continuous intravenous infusion or controlling pump may be used to regulate the feeding. The principles and technique of nasogastric feeds are discussed in Chapter 13. The feeding tube is usually retained until the swallowing reflex returns.

Cerebrospinal Fluid Leakage

The nurse should observe any cerebrospinal rhinorrhoea or otorrhoea, which may indicate a basal skull fracture. A sling dressing under the nose or a pad over the ear should be applied lightly to collect drainage. The conscious patient should be cautioned against sneezing or blowing the nose. The head of the bed may be elevated 30 degrees, as directed by medical staff, to reduce intracranial pressure and promote spontaneous closure of the leak. Persistent leakage usually requires surgical intervention.

Seizure Prevention

Seizures (see p. 1036) are common after head injury and can cause secondary brain damage from hypoxia. Anticonvulsants should be given as prescribed.

Preventing Injury

The patient emerging from a period of unconsciousness may become increasingly agitated. Restlessness may be due to hypoxia, fever or a full bladder, or it may indicate injury to the brain, or be due to annoyance from an undiagnosed injury. The nurse should ensure that the patient's airway is adequate and that the bladder is not distended. Likewise, bandages and casts should not be constrictive. Bedrails should be padded and the patient's hands wrapped to protect the patient from self-injury and dislodged tubes. Restraints should be avoided where possible because straining against them may increase intracranial pressure. A tranquillizer, e.g. chlorpromazine, can be prescribed if the patient is very agitated.

Environmental stimuli should be kept to a minimum by keeping the room quiet, limiting visitors, speaking calmly and reorientating frequently the patient to the surroundings. Adequate lighting may prevent visual hallucinations and every effort should be made to avoid disturbing the patient's sleep–wake cycle.

When the patient is able to mobilize, the use of a floor mat allows freedom of movement and promotes patient safety. An external urethral sheath may be used by the male patient if incontinence is a problem.

Detecting Complications

Deterioration in the patient's neurological or respiratory status should be reported immediately, and may be due to an expanding haematoma, progressive brain engorgement, oedema or a combination of these factors. (See section on Intracranial Haemorrhage, below.)

Improving Cognitive Functioning

Although many brain-damaged victims survive because of resuscitative and supportive technology, they frequently sustain significant mental sequelae that may not be noticed during the acute phase of injury. Cognitive impairment includes memory deficits, decrease in the ability to focus and sustain attention to a task (easily distracted), reduced ability to process information and slowness in thinking, perceiving, communicating, reading and writing. Psychiatric problems also occur in a percentage of patients. Such psychosocial, behavioural and emotional impairments are devastating to the loved ones as well as to the patient.

These problems require collaboration among many disciplines. A neuropsychologist plans a programme and initiates therapy or counselling that is designed to help the patient reach maximum potential. Training programmes include the use of computer training programmes, video games, sensory stimulation and reinforcement, behaviour modification and reality orientation. Assistance from many disciplines is necessary during this phase of recovery. Intellectual ability may not improve after a period of time, but social and behavioural aspects may improve.

Delayed Effects of Head Injury

- Infection (meningitis, abscess formation).
- Post-traumatic epilepsy.
- Post-concussional syndrome (headache, increased irritability, dizziness, lack of concentration, fatigue, depression).
- Diabetes insipidus.
- Hydrocephalus.

Patient and Family Education

The patient is encouraged to continue the rehabilitation programme after discharge, since improvement in status may continue up to three years or more following injury. The presence or absence or headache may be the most reliable guide to recovery. A second pillow or backrest at night may be helpful to alleviate some head discomfort.

Because post-traumatic seizures occur frequently, anticonvulsants may be prescribed for one to two years following injury. The patient is encouraged to return gradually to normal activities.

The patient's memory and orientation may fluctuate. The patient may be distracted easily. Such patients should increase gradually their physical and mental activity; pushing patients beyond their limits increases stress and fatigue. Stress is also common among the patient's loved ones. Relatives report difficulties in dealing with changes in the patient's temperament, behaviour and personality.

Self-help groups such as Headway may be useful to the patient and relatives (see Useful Addresses).

Evaluation

Expected Outcomes

1. Patient attains/maintains effective airway clearance, spontaneous ventilation and brain oxygenation.
   a. Blood gas levels are within normal limits.
   b. Has normal breath sounds on auscultation.
   c. Coughs up secretions.
2. Achieves satisfactory fluid and electrolyte balance.
3. Attains adequate nutritional status.
4. Patient continues with rehabilitation programme, and shows improved physical and emotional stability.

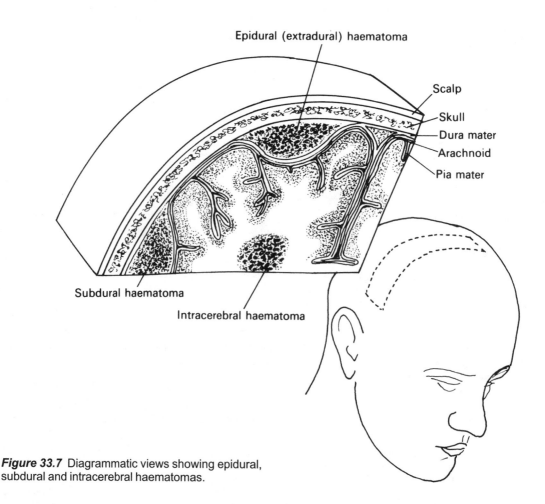

Figure 33.7 Diagrammatic views showing epidural, subdural and intracerebral haematomas.

Intracranial Haemorrhage

As a result of brain injuries, haematomas may develop within the cranial vault (Figure 33.7). The haematoma is referred to as epidural, subdural or intracerebral, depending on its location. The main effects are frequently delayed until the haematoma is large enough to cause distortion and herniation of the brain and increased intracranial pressure. The signs and symptoms of brain ischaemia resulting from compression caused by a haematoma are variable and depend on the speed with which vital areas are encroached upon and/or the changes that involve the underlying brain. In general, a small haematoma that develops rapidly may be fatal, while a more massive haematoma that develops slowly may allow the patient to adapt.

Epidural Haematoma (Extradural Haematoma or Haemorrhage)

Following a head injury, blood may collect in the epidural (extradural) space between the skull and the dura. This often results from fractures of the skull that cause rupture or laceration of the middle meningeal artery, which runs between the dura and the skull; haemorrhage from this artery causes pressure on the brain.

The symptoms are caused by the expanding haematoma. There is usually a momentary loss of consciousness at the time of injury, followed by an interval of apparent recovery. During the lucid interval, compensatory measures occur (p. 1020) to allow expansion of the haematoma. When these mechanisms can no longer compensate, even a small increase in the volume of the blood clot will produce a marked elevation of intracranial pressure. Then, often suddenly, signs of compression appear (usually deterioration of consciousness and signs of focal neurological deficits such as dilation and fixation of a pupil or paralysis of an extremity), and the patient deteriorates rapidly.

Medical Management

An epidural haematoma is considered to be an extreme emergency, since marked neurological deficit or even cessation of breathing may occur within minutes. The treatment consists of making openings through the skull (burr holes), removing the clot and controlling the bleeding point.

Subdural Haematoma

A subdural haematoma is a collection of blood between the dura and the underlying brain, a space normally occupied by a film of fluid. The most common cause is trauma, but it may also be caused by various bleeding disorders or aneurysms. A subdural haemorrhage is more frequently venous in origin and is attributed to the rupture of small vessels that bridge the subdural space.

A subdural haematoma may be acute, subacute or chronic, depending on the size of the involved vessel and the amount of bleeding present. The patient is usually unconscious, and the clinical signs are similar to those of epidural haematoma.

If the patient can be transported rapidly to the hospital, an immediate craniotomy is performed to open the dura, allowing for the solid subdural clot to be evacuated. Successful outcome also depends on the control of intracranial pressure and careful monitoring of respiratory function (see The Patient Undergoing Intracranial Surgery, p. 1012).

Chronic subdural haematoma imitates other conditions and may be mistaken for a stroke. Symptoms may appear weeks after what may have seemed to be a minor injury. The bleeding is less profuse and there is compression of the intracranial contents. The blood within the brain changes in character in two to four days, becoming thicker and darker, with a consistency similar to motor oil, eventually calcifying. The brain adapts to this foreign body invasion, and the patient's clinical signs and symptoms fluctuate. There may be severe headache, which tends to come and go; alternating focal neurological signs; personality changes; mental deterioration; and focal convulsions. Unfortunately, the patient may be labelled 'neurotic' or 'psychotic' if the cause of the symptoms is overlooked.

The treatment of chronic subdural haematoma consists of surgically evacuating the clot by suctioning or irrigating the area. The procedure may be carried out through multiple burr holes, or a craniotomy may be performed for a sizable subdural mass lesion that cannot be drained through burr holes.

Intracerebral Haemorrhage/Haematoma

Intracerebral haemorrhage is bleeding into the substance of the brain. It is commonly seen in Type 3 and 4 head injuries. These haemorrhages within the brain may also result from hypertension and other systemic disorders.

There may be an insidious development with the onset of neurological deficits followed by headache. Medical therapy involves careful administration of fluids and electrolytes, antihypertensive medications, control of intracranial pressure and supportive care. Surgical intervention via craniotomy or craniectomy permits removal of the blood clot and provides opportunity for control of the sites of haemorrhage. Physiotherapy is usually required for the rehabilitation of these patients.

SPINAL CORD INJURY

Damage to the spinal cord as a result of spinal vertebral injuries is a major problem affecting around 15 to 20 per million population every year. Vertebral injuries commonly result from indirect violence such as hyperextension or hyperflexion; 50 per cent result from road traffic accidents, with most of the others occurring from falls, sporting and industrial accidents, and gunshot wounds. Three quarters of the victims are under the age of 40 years; a quarter are younger than 20 years. Infections and pathological fractures from metastatic deposits may also cause cord damage. The vertebrae most frequently involved in spinal cord injuries are the fifth, sixth and seventh cervical (neck), the twelfth thoracic and the first lumbar vertebrae. These vertebrae are the most susceptible because there is a greater range of mobility in the vertebral column in these areas.

Pathogenesis

Damage to the spinal cord ranges from transient concussion to complete transection of the cord, rendering the patient paralyzed below the level of the injury. Following injury, swelling occurs at and around the damaged area, curtailing spinal cord vasculature and resulting in further damage from ischaemia, hypoxia and oedema. These secondary reactions are believed to be the principal cause of spinal cord degeneration at the level of the injury.

Emergency Management

The immediate management of the patient at the scene of the accident is critical, because improper handling can cause further damage and loss of neurological function. Any victim of a motor vehicle or diving accident, a contact sport injury, a fall or any direct trauma to the head and neck, however slight, should be suspected of having a spinal cord injury until such an injury is ruled out, especially if the victim complains of paraesthesia in the limbs, neck pain or limb weakness.

- At the scene of the accident, the victim should be immobilized on a spinal (back) board, with the head and neck in a neutral position, to prevent an incomplete injury from becoming complete.
- The board on which the patient is strapped is placed directly on the posterior frame.
- Unstrap the patient from the board, but do not remove the head strappings.
- Place a blanket roll between the legs.
- Place the anterior frame in position, and secure the frame straps.
- Turn the frame so that the patient is in the prone position.
- Remove the frame straps and the posterior frame. Remove the head strapping with care. Then remove the transfer board.

Clinical Features

If conscious, the patient will probably complain of acute pain in the back or neck, which may radiate along the involved nerve. Often the patient will speak of fear that the neck or back is broken. *The consequences of spinal cord injury depend on the level of injury of the cord* (Figure 33.8). Neurological level refers to that lowest level at which sensory and motor functions are normal. There is total sensory and motor paralysis, loss of bladder and bowel control (usually with urinary retention and bladder distension), loss of sweating and vasomotor tone below the neurological level, and marked reduction of blood pressure from loss of peripheral vascular resistance.

Respiratory problems are related to compromised respiratory function, the severity of which depends on the level of injury. The muscles contributing to respiration are the abdominals, intercostals (T1 to T11) and the diaphragm. In high cervical cord injury, acute respiratory failure is the leading cause of death.

Diagnosis

A detailed neurological examination is performed. Radiographical examination (lateral cervical spine X-rays and computed tomography scanning) is carried out. A search is made for other injuries because spinal trauma is associated with multiple injuries, commonly affecting the head and chest. Continuous ECG monitoring may be indicated, because bradycardia (slow heart rate) and asystole (cardiac standstill) are common in acute cervical injuries.

► NURSING PROCESS
► THE PATIENT WITH SPINAL CORD INJURY

► *Assessment*

The nurse should note any complaints of pain and tenderness in the back or neck. The patient should be monitored constantly for any changes in motor or sensory function, and for symptoms of progressive neurological damage. The breathing pattern in cervical cord damage should be observed since respiratory function may be compromised.

► *Patient's Problems*

Based on the assessment, the patient's main problems in the acute phase may include the following:

- Ineffective breathing patterns related to weakness/paralysis of abdominal and intercostal muscles and an inability to clear secretions.
- Impaired physical mobility related to motor and sensory impairment.
- Potential for further cord damage due to inexpert and incorrect transfer method.
- Alteration in comfort related to prolonged immobility.

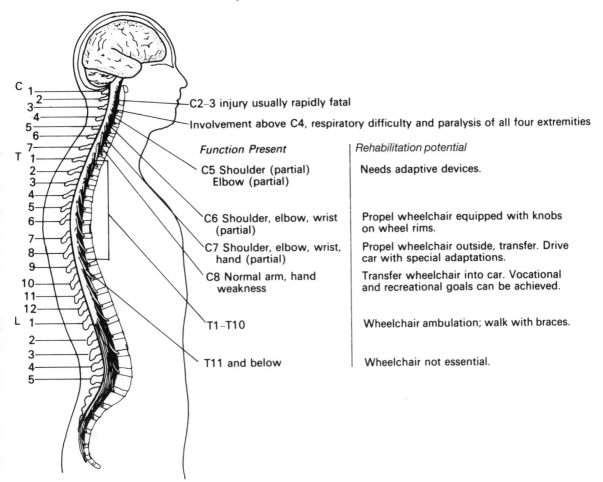

C2–3 injury usually rapidly fatal

Involvement above C4, respiratory difficulty and paralysis of all four extremities

Function Present	*Rehabilitation potential*
C5 Shoulder (partial) Elbow (partial)	Needs adaptive devices.
C6 Shoulder, elbow, wrist (partial)	Propel wheelchair equipped with knobs on wheel rims.
C7 Shoulder, elbow, wrist, hand (partial)	Propel wheelchair outside, transfer. Drive car with special adaptations.
C8 Normal arm, hand weakness	Transfer wheelchair into car. Vocational and recreational goals can be achieved.
T1–T10	Wheelchair ambulation; walk with braces.
T11 and below	Wheelchair not essential.

Figure 33.8 Sequelae of spinal cord injury and rehabilitation challenges. (The vertebrae are numbered on the left side of the drawing and the spinal nerves are numbered on the right.)

- Alteration in bladder and bowel function due to spinal shock.
- Potential impairment of skin integrity related to immobility and sensory loss.

► Planning and Implementation
► Expected Outcomes

The patient's expected outcomes may include the following: improvement of breathing pattern; improvement of mobility; achievement of skin integrity; relief of urinary retention; improvement of bowel function; and promotion of comfort.

Nursing Care of the Patient With Cervical Spinal Injuries (Acute Phase)

The aim of treatment is to preserve as much cord function as possible, observing for symptoms of progressive neurological deficit. The care involves immobilization, reduc-

tion of dislocations and stabilization of the vertebral column.

Airway Maintenance

Since there is the potential in cervical cord injuries of respiratory problems due to paralysis of the intercostal and abdominal muscles, the nurse's first priority is the maintenance of an airway, and the patient's respiratory pattern should be observed frequently.

The patient may be unable to cough up bronchial and pharyngeal secretions due to the paralysis, and tracheostomy and ventilatory support are necessary in some patients. Caution must be taken during suctioning since stimulation of the vagus nerve can precipitate bradycardia or cardiac arrest.

Motor and Sensory Function

The patient is monitored constantly for any changes in motor or sensory function and for symptoms of progressive neurological damage. It may be impossible

1052 unit 10 Sensorineural Problems

initially to determine whether the cord has been transected, since features of cord oedema are indistinguishable from those of cord transection. Motor and sensory function are determined by careful neurological examination; all observations are recorded so that any changes from the baseline status can be evaluated accurately.

Motor ability is tested by asking the patient to spread the fingers, squeeze the nurse's hand, move the toes and turn the feet. Sensation can be evaluated by pinprick, starting at the shoulder level and working down both sides to the extremities. The patient is asked where sensation is felt.

Transferring the Patient

The patient is kept on the transfer board during emergency treatment, and should always be maintained in an extended position. No part of the body should be twisted or turned, nor should the patient be allowed to assume a sitting position. Movement should be supervised by a doctor.

After the initial assessment, the patient can be placed on a Stryker frame if transfer to a bed is planned. Later, if it is proved that there is no cord injury, the patient can always be moved to a conventional bed without harm; the reverse, however, is not true. Transfer should occur in the following way under medical supervision:

● The board on which the patient is strapped is placed directly on the posterior frame. The patient is unwrapped from the frame, but the head strappings are not removed.
● A blanket roll is placed between the patient's legs.
● The anterior frame is placed into position and secured.
● The patient is turned into the prone position; the straps and the posterior frame are removed.
● The head strapping and transfer board are removed.

Reduction of Fracture/Dislocation

Some form of skeletal traction such as skull tongs/callipers or the halo-vest device is used to reduce the fracture or dislocation and to maintain alignment of the cervical spine (Figure 33.9). A variety of skeletal tongs are available, all of which involve fixation in the skull in some manner.

Traction is applied to the tongs by weights, the amount depending on the patient's size and the degree of fracture displacement. The traction is increased gradually by the addition of more weights, which widens the intervertebral disc spaces so that the vertebrae can slip back into position. Reduction usually takes place after correct alignment has been regained. Once reduction is achieved, as verified by cervical spine films and neurological examination, the weights are removed gradually until the amount needed to maintain alignment is obtained. The weights should hang free so as not to interfere with the traction.

Care of Traction

When skull tongs, callipers or skull pins from the halo frame are in place, the patient's skull is assessed for signs of infection, including drainage around them. Daily cleansing should take place. The back of the head is checked periodically for signs of pressure, with care taken not to move the neck. The hair may be shaved around the tong site to facilitate inspection. Probing under encrusted areas should be avoided. The patient may experience a slight discomfort/headache for a few days around the area of skull traction. The nurse should observe for any loosening of the callipers, pins or tongs, which may contribute to infection and cause instability. In cases of loosening, the nurse should stabilize the patient's head in a neutral position while another nurse notifies the neurosurgeon.

The skin under a halo vest is examined for excessive perspiration, redness and blistering, especially over bony prominences. The vest is opened at the side for washing purposes. The inside of the vest must not become wet because this will cause skin problems. Talcum powder must not be put inside the vest because it may contribute to skin excoriation.

Assessment of Spinal Shock

The patient is assessed for spinal shock in which there is complete loss of reflex, motor, sensory and autonomic activity below the level of the lesion. This causes bladder distension from paralysis of the bladder. The area over the bladder is palpated for signs of urinary retention and overdistension. An indwelling catheter or intermittent catheterization should be carried out to prevent overstretching of the bladder and detrusor muscle, which may delay the return of normal bladder function. A bladder training programme is established as soon as possible.

Further assessment is made for gastric dilation and ileus due to an atonic bowel as a result of autonomic disruption. The nurse should measure the patient's abdominal girth and listen for bowel sounds. Gastric intubation will relieve the gaseous distension and prevent vomiting and aspiration, which can further add to any respiratory embarrassment. The passage of a flatus tube may be of help in relieving the distension. Meanwhile, the circulation should be supported with intravenous fluids. Bowel activity usually returns within the first week. As soon as bowel sounds are heard via auscultation, the patient should begin a high-calorie, high-protein and high-fibre diet, with the amount of food increased gradually.

Temperature is also monitored because the patient may have hyperthermia as a result of alteration in temperature control, due to autonomic disruption. Hypotension and an inability to perspire in the paralyzed areas can also be problematic.

Pressure Area Care

As a result of spinal shock and recumbency due to inadequate peripheral circulation, pressure sores have been

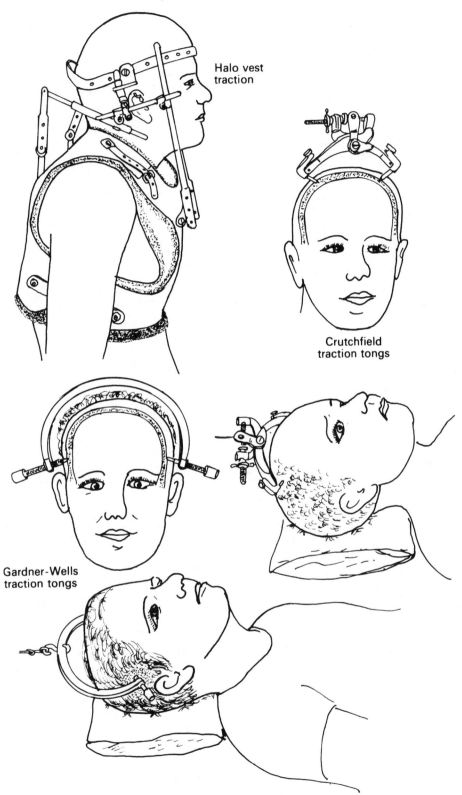

Halo vest traction

Crutchfield traction tongs

Gardner-Wells traction tongs

Figure 33.9 Methods of cervical traction. (Brunner, L. S. and Suddarth, D. S. (1986) *The Lippincott Manual of Nursing Practice* (4th edition), J. B. Lippincott, Philadelphia.)

known to develop within six hours. There is the ever-present danger of developing such sores because the patient with spinal cord injury is immobilized and has motor and sensory loss. However, not all patients can, or are able to, adapt to turning.

Turning patients with vasovagal instability may cause cardiorespiratory arrest. Others may have associated injuries that prevent positional change. If allowed, therefore, the Stryker frame or mechanical bed can reposition the patient every two hours. This should be supervised by a trained member of the medical or nursing staff.

Careful inspection of the skin is made each time the patient is moved, especially over pressure areas, for signs of redness and excoriation. Proper body alignment is maintained at all times. The feet should be placed against a padded footboard to prevent footdrop. There should be a space between the end of the mattress/frame and the footboard to allow free suspension of the heels. Tronchanter rolls can be applied from the iliac crest to the mid-thigh of both extremities to prevent external rotation.

Promoting Ambulation

For patients with a cervical fracture without neurological deficit, reduction in traction followed by rigid immobilization for approximately 16 weeks will restore skeletal function in most patients. These patients will be allowed to move gradually to an erect position. It should be anticipated that a four-poster neck brace or moulded collar will be applied when the patient is mobilized after traction is removed.

The rehabilitation of the patient with a permanent spinal cord injury is discussed in the section on the paraplegic patient (below).

Complications

Deep vein thrombosis with pulmonary embolism is a common complication of immobility; its clinical features include anxiety, shortness of breath and changes in blood gas values. Thigh and calf measurements are made daily. The patient is prepared for venography if there is a significant increase in the circumference of one extremity.

Autonomic dysreflexia (autonomic hyper-reflexia) is an acute emergency that occurs as a result of exaggerated autonomic responses to stimuli that are innocuous in normal individuals. This syndrome is characterized by severe, pounding headache with paroxysmal hypertension, profuse sweating (most often of the forehead), nasal congestion and bradycardia. It occurs among patients with cord lesions above the T6 level (the sympathetic visceral outflow level), generally after spinal shock has subsided. A number of stimuli may trigger this reflex: distended bladder (the most common cause), distended bowel or stimulation of the skin (tactile, pain, thermal stimuli). Since this is an emergency situation, the objective is to remove the triggering stimulus and to avoid the possibly serious complications.

The following measures are carried out:

- Place the patient in a sitting position to lower the blood pressure.
- Drain the bladder via the catheter. If the catheter is not patent, irrigate it with no more than 30 ml of irrigating solution or insert another catheter.
- After the symptoms subside, the rectum is examined for a faecal mass.
- Any other stimulus that can be the triggering event, such as an object on the skin or a draft of cold air, must be removed.
- If these measures do not relieve the patient's hypertension and excruciating headache, a ganglionic blocking agent (hydralazine hydrochloride) may be given intravenously by the doctor.
- Instruct the patient in prevention and management measures.

Any patient with a lesion above the T6 segment should be informed that such an episode is possible and may even occur many years after the initial injury.

▶ *Evaluation*
▶ **Expected Outcomes**

1. Patient demonstrates improvement in breathing.
   a. Has no evidence of respiratory infection.
   b. Is able to clear secretions.
2. Further damage and loss of neurological function is avoided by proper handling and early recognition of neurological deterioration.
3. Complications of spinal shock (e.g., pressure sores, urinary infections) are avoided.
4. The patient shows no discomfort around skull pin sites.
5. Appropriate adjustments to the immobilization have been made, and the patient now participates actively in the rehabilitation programme within the limits of any neurological deficits.

THE PARAPLEGIC PATIENT

Paraplegia refers to loss of movement and sensation in the lower extremities and all or part of the trunk as a result of damage to the thoracic or lumbar spinal cord or to the sacral root. It most frequently follows trauma due to accidents and gunshot wounds, but may be the result of spinal cord lesions (intervertebral disc, tumour, vascular lesions), multiple sclerosis, infections and abscesses of the spinal cord, and congenital defects.

Diagnosis

Evaluation includes the observations and studies performed for the patient with a spinal cord injury: full neurological examination, X-ray studies and ECG monitoring.

► NURSING PROCESS
► THE PATIENT WITH PARAPLEGIA

► *Assessment*

Patients with paraplegia have experienced varying degrees of loss of motor power, deep and superficial sensation, vasomotor control, bladder and bowel control, and sexual function. They are faced with threats of dysfunction related to paraplegia including mobility, skin breakdown and pressure sores, recurring urinary infection, contractures and psychosocial problems. Nurses in any health care setting must recognize these potential problems in the lifetime management of these people.

Psychosocial Assessment
It is usually some time before these patients comprehend the magnitude of their disability. They may go through stages of adjustment, including shock and disbelief, denial, depression, grief and acceptance. During the acute phase of the injury, denial can be a protective mechanism to shield patients from the overwhelming reality of what has happened. As they realize the finality of paraplegia, the grieving process may be prolonged. A period of depression follows as the patient experiences a loss of self-esteem in areas of self-identity, sexual functioning and social and emotional roles.

► *Patient's Problems*

Based on the assessment, the patient's main problems may include the following:

● Immobility related to an inability to walk.
● Impairment of skin integrity related to permanent sensory loss and immobility.
● Alteration in patterns of urinary elimination—retention related to level of spinal cord injury.
● Alteration in bowel elimination related to effects of spinal cord disruption.
● Sexual dysfunction related to neurological dysfunction.
● Complications related to cord damage.
● Ineffectual coping mechanisms related to the impact of dysfunction to patient's lifestyle.

► *Planning and Implementation*
► Expected Outcomes
The patient's expected outcomes may include attainment of some form of mobility, maintenance of healthy, intact skin, achievement of bladder management without infection, achievement of bowel control, achievement of sexual expression and strengthening of coping mechanisms.

Nursing Care

The patient requires extensive rehabilitation, which will be less difficult if appropriate nursing care has been carried out during the acute phase of the injury or illness. (See Nursing Care of the Patient With Cervical Spinal Injuries, p. 1051.). The nursing care is one of the determining factors in the success of the rehabilitation programme. The main objective is for the patient to live as independently as possible in the home community.

Achieving Mobility
A patient with complete severance of the cord can begin weight-bearing early, because no further damage can be incurred. The sooner muscles are strengthened, the less is the chance they will atrophy, and the less opportunity there will be for osteoporotic changes to take place in the long bones. Weight-bearing also reduces the possibility of urinary infections and formation of renal calculi, and enhances many other metabolic processes.

The unaffected parts of the body are built up to optimal strength to enable the patient to ambulate with braces and crutches. The muscles of the hands, arms, shoulders, chest, spine, abdomen and neck must be strengthened, since the patient must bear full weight on these muscles. The muscles of the abdomen and the back also are necessary for balance and the maintenance of the upright position.

Because vasomotor tone is lacking in the lower extremities, the patient may become hypotensive when placed in an upright position. Profound postural hypotension is seen in all patients with lesions above the midthoracic level. There is pooling of blood in the peripheral veins and splanchnic bed from lack of muscle tone and poor skin turgor. Reduced venous return to the heart, orthostatic hypotension, and decreased cerebral blood flow also occur.

To counteract this problem, a tilt table may be used to help the patient overcome vasomotor instability and tolerate the upright posture. Other possible measures include using elastic stockings to facilitate venous return in the legs and applying an abdominal binder to alleviate the pooling of blood in the abdominal area.

When a tilt table is used, the patient is gradually elevated to an upright position. At first the patient may be able to tolerate only an elevation of 45 degrees (or less), but gradually the angle of elevation is increased. Observe closely for signs of intolerance, including nausea, perspiration, pallor, dizziness and syncope. Blood pressure is taken before the patient is allowed up and when positioned on the tilt table, since periods of recumbency also favour the development of orthostatic hypotension.

If no tilt table is available, a high-backed reclining wheelchair with extension leg rests may be used. To overcome the effects of hypotension, the backrest is raised slowly and the leg rests are lowered gradually over a period of 7 to 10 days.

When the spine is stable enough to allow the patient to assume an upright posture, mobilization activities are initiated. A brace or vest may be used, depending on the level of the lesion. Braces and crutches enable some patients to ambulate for short distances and even to drive manually operated cars.

The nurse should teach and help when necessary, but should not take over activities that patients can do for themselves with a little effort. This type of nursing care more than repays itself in the satisfaction of seeing a completely demoralized and helpless patient begin to find meaning in a newly emerging lifestyle.

Achieving Healthy Skin
Because paraplegic patients spend a great portion of their lives in a wheelchair, pressure sores are ever-present threat, causing sickness and loss of time and money. Contributing factors are permanent sensory paralysis and loss of sensation over pressure areas, immobility that makes pressure relief a problem, trauma from bumps that cause unperceived abrasions and wounds, loss of protective function of the skin from excoriation and maceration due to excessive sweating and possible urine and faecal incontinence, and poor general health (anaemia, oedema, malnutrition) leading to poor tissue perfusion.

The prevention and management of pressure sores are discussed in detail in Chapter 2 and in the section about the care of the patient with a spinal cord injury (pp. 1050–54).

Patients with paraplegia must take responsibility for monitoring their own skin condition. This involves relieving pressure and avoiding holding any position for longer than two hours, in addition to seeing that the skin receives meticulous attention and cleanliness. Patients are taught that sores develop over bony prominences exposed to unrelieved pressure in the lying and sitting positions. The most vulnerable areas are pointed out, and patients are asked to use mirrors to inspect these areas morning and night, observing for redness, slight oedema or any abrasions. While in bed patients should turn at two-hourly intervals and then inspect the skin again for redness that does not fade on pressure. Sheets should be free from moisture and creases.

Patients are taught to relieve pressure in the wheelchair by doing push-ups, leaning from side to side to relieve ischial pressure and tilting forward while leaning on a table. Each person requires a wheelchair cushion prescribed to meet individual needs, which may change in time with changes in posture, weight and skin tolerance.

The diet for the patient with paraplegia should be high in protein, vitamins, and calories to ensure minimal wasting of muscle, well-functioning kidneys and the maintenance of healthy skin.

Achieving Bladder Management
The effect of the spinal lesion on the bladder depends on the level of the cord injury, degree of cord damage and length of time after injury. A patient with paraplegia usually has either a reflex or a nonreflex bladder, which are discussed under the section on the neurogenic bladder on page 686. Both problems increase the risk of urinary tract infection.

The nurse emphasizes the importance of maintaining an adequate flow of urine by encouraging the drinking of three to four litres of fluid a day, emptying the bladder frequently so there is minimal residual urine and giving attention to personal hygiene because infection of the bladder and kidneys almost always occurs by the ascending route. The perineum is to be kept clean and dry, and attention given to perianal skin after defaecation. Underwear should be cotton (more absorbent) and changed at least daily.

If an external catheter (condom catheter) is used, the sheath is removed nightly; the penis is cleansed to remove urine and dried carefully because warm urine on the periurethral skin promotes growth of bacteria. Attention is also given to the collection bag. The nurse emphasizes the importance of monitoring for indications of urinary tract infection: cloudy urine or haematuria (blood in the urine), fever, chills or loin pain.

The female patient who cannot achieve reflex bladder control or self-catheterization may need to wear pads or waterproof undergarments. Surgical intervention may be necessary in the form of some type of urinary diversion procedure.

Bowel Control: Bowel Training Programme.
The objective of a bowel training programme is to establish bowel evacuation through reflex conditioning. If a cord injury occurs above the sacral segments or nerve roots and there is reflex activity, regular digital examination and the use of suppositories may stimulate reflex emptying. The patient is also taught the symptoms of impaction (frequent loose stools; constipation) and cautioned to watch for the development of haemorrhoids. A diet with sufficient fluids and fibre is essential to a bowel training programme.

Finding Sexual Expression
Most patients with cord injury can have some form of meaningful sexual relationship, although some modifications will have to be made to cope with anxiety. The patient and partner will benefit from counselling on the range of sexual expression possible, special techniques, positions, exploration of body sensations offering sensual feelings and urinary and bowel hygiene as related to sexual activity. Penile prostheses are available for men with erectile failure. Sexual education and counselling services are being included in the rehabilitation services at spinal centres.

Complications
Autonomic dysreflexia is an acute emergency (see

p. 1054). Other long-term complications of paraplegia include bladder and kidney infections, pressure sores with complications of sepsis, osteomyelitis, fistulas and depression. Flexor muscle spasms may be particularly disabling. Overgrowth of bone occurs in 20 to 40 per cent of spinal cord injury patients in the hips, knees shoulders and elbows. This complication can produce a loss of range of motion.

Strengthening Coping Mechanisms

Adjustment to the disability leads to the development of realistic goals for the future, making the best of those abilities that are left intact and reinvesting in other activities and relationships. Caregivers usually require counselling, social services and other support systems to help them cope with the changes that will be made in their lifestyle and socioeconomic status.

Patient Education

Patients with a spinal injury are at special risk during the first few weeks after their return home. Urinary infections may appear and require rehospitalization. For the rest of their lives, patients are at risk of developing pressure sores which pose a serious threat to life. To avoid these complications, the patient and a family member or close friend are taught skin care, catheter care, range-of-motion exercises and other care techniques while the patient is still in the hospital. The teaching is reinforced during home visits by the district nurse and spinal nurse co-ordinator. Environmental modifications are made and specialized equipment is purchased before the patient comes home. Other complications during the extended care period may include lower extremity oedema, ankle and feet contractures, pain and alcohol abuse.

The community health nurse provides continuing follow-up evaluation to reinforce previous teaching and to determine if further physical help is needed. The patient's self-esteem and body-image perceptions may be very low at this time.

The patient requires continuing, lifelong follow-up by the doctor, physiotherapist and other rehabilitation team members, because the neurological deficit is permanent and new problems can erupt that require prompt attention before they take their toll in additional physical impairment, time, morale and money.

► *Evaluation*
► **Expected Outcomes**

1. Patient attains some form of mobility.
2. Maintains healthy, intact skin.
3. Achieves bladder control, absence of urinary tract infection.
4. Achieves bowel control.
5. Reports sexual satisfaction.
6. Shows improved adaptation to environment and others.

INTRASPINAL TUMOURS

Tumours within the spine are classified according to their anatomical relation to the spinal cord. They include intramedullary lesions (within the spinal cord); extramedullary–intradural lesions (within the subarachnoid space) and extradural lesions (outside the dural membrane).

Tumours that occur within the spinal cord or exert pressure on it cause symptoms ranging from weakness and loss of reflexes above the tumour level and localized or shooting pains, to progressive loss of motor function and paralysis.

Usually, sharp pain occurs in the area that is innervated by the spinal roots that arise from the cord in the region of the tumour. In addition, increasing paralysis develops below the level of the lesion.

The diagnosis is made by neurological examination and myelography in combination with computed tomography scanning.

Preoperative Care

The patient is assessed for weakness, muscle wasting, spasticity and sensory or sphincter disorders. A search is made for potential pulmonary problems, especially if a cervical tumour is present. The patient is also evaluated for coagulation deficiencies. Breathing exercises are taught and demonstrated preoperatively.

Surgical Management

Removal of the tumour is usually desirable but not always feasible. The goal is to remove as much tumour as possible while sparing intact portions of the spinal cord. The prognosis is related to the degree of neurological impairment at the time of surgery, the speed of occurrence of symptoms and the tumour's origin. Patients with large neurological deficits before surgery usually do not make significant functional recovery following successful tumour removal.

Other treatments include subtotal removal of the tumour, decompression of the spinal cord, chemotherapy and radiation therapy.

If the patient has epidural spinal cord compression resulting from metastatic cancer (from breast, prostate or lung), high-dose dexamethasone combined with radiotherapy may be effective in relieving pain.

Postoperative Nursing Care

The postoperative nursing care is similar to that following laminectomy (p. 1059). In addition, removal of a tumour within the cervical region may compromise respiratory function postoperatively and therefore close observations of the patient should be made.

Patient Education

Patients with residual sensory involvement are cautioned about the dangers of extremes in temperature and they should be alert to the dangers of heating devices (e.g., space heaters, fireplaces). The patient is taught to check skin integrity daily.

A patient who has impaired motor function related to motor weakness or paralysis may require training in activities of daily living and an ambulatory aid such as a walking stick or frame.

HERNIATION OR RUPTURE OF AN INTERVERTEBRAL DISC

The intervertebral disc is a cartilaginous plate that forms a cushion between the vertebral bodies. In herniation of the intervertebral disc (ruptured disc), the nucleus of the disc protrudes into the annulus (the fibrous ring around the disc), with subsequent nerve compression (Figure 33.10). Protrusion or rupture of the nucleus pulposus is usually preceded by degenerative changes that occur with ageing. Following trauma (falls, accidents and repeated minor stresses, such as lifting), the cartilage may be injured.

Clinical Features

A herniated disc with accompanying pain may occur in any portion of the spine: cervical, thoracic (rare) or lumbar. The clinical features depend on the location, the rate of development and the effect on the surrounding structures.

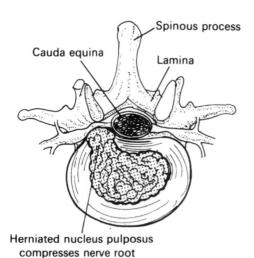

Cauda equina
Spinous process
Lamina
Herniated nucleus pulposus compresses nerve root

Figure 33.10 Ruptured vertebral disc. (Chaffee, E. E. and Greisheimer, E. M. (1974) *Basic Physiology and Anatomy* (3rd edition), J. B. Lippincott, Philadelphia.)

Cervical Disc

Cervical spondylosis involves degenerative changes in the disc and adjacent vertebral bodies. It usually occurs at the C5–6/C6–7 interspaces. Pain and stiffness may occur in the neck, at the top of the shoulders and across the scapulae. Pain may also occur in the upper extremities and head. Paraesthesia and numbness of the upper extremities can take place.

Lumbar Disc

The majority of lumbar disc herniations occur at the L4–5 or L5–S1 interspace, producing the following:

- Low back pain accompanied by varying degrees of sensory and motor impairment.
- Pain that is aggravated by actions that increase intraspinal fluid pressure, for example, bending, sneezing, lifting.
- Radiation of pain into one hip and down into the leg, i.e. sciatica.
- Posture deformity.
- Alteration in tendon reflexes.
- Sensory loss.

Diagnosis

1. History and clinical findings.
2. Positive straight leg raising test.
   a. Patient lies on back and attempts to raise a leg in the straight position.
   b. Pain will radiate into the leg because this manoeuvre stretches the sciatic nerve.
3. Positive Lasègue's test: while the leg is elevated, dorsiflexion of the foot aggravates the pain.
4. Spinal X-rays to exclude other pathology.
5. Myelogram/radiculogram usually demonstrates the area of pressure, localizing the herniation of the disc.

Nursing Care (Conservative)

Cervical Disc

Initially, treatment is conservative, the aim being to rest and immobilize the cervical spine to give the soft tissues time to heal, and to reduce inflammation in the supporting tissues and the affected nerve roots in the cervical spine. This can be achieved by bedrest, which eliminates the stress of gravity and frees the cervical spine from having to support the weight of the head. It also reduces inflammation and oedema in soft tissues around the disc, relieving pressure on the nerve roots.

The cervical spine may be rested and immobilized by a cervical collar or cervical traction. A collar allows maximal opening of the intervertebral foramina and holds the head in a neutral or slightly flexed position. The patient may have to wear the collar 24 hours a day during the acute phase. The skin site under the collar is inspected for irritation. When the patient is free of pain, cervical isometric exercises are started to strengthen the muscles in the neck.

Cervical traction is accomplished by means of a head halter attached to a pulley and weight. It increases vertebral separation and thus relieves pressure on the nerve roots. The head of the bed is elevated to provide countertraction. If the skin becomes irritated, the halter can be padded.

The use of local heat applied to the back of the neck several times daily will increase blood flow to the muscles and help to relax the spastic muscles, as well as the patient. Analgesics are given during the acute phase to relieve pain, and sedatives may be administered to control the anxiety often associated with cervical disc disease. Muscle relaxants are prescribed to relieve muscle spasm and to allow for patient comfort. Anti-inflammatory drugs or steroids may be given to treat the inflammatory response that usually occurs in the supporting tissues and affected nerve roots. Occasionally, an injection of a corticosteroid drug into the epidural space may be tried as a means of relieving radicular pain. Food and antacids are given with anti-inflammatory agents to prevent gastrointestinal irritation.

Lumbar Disc
The objectives of treatment are to relieve the pain and slow the progression of the disease and to increase the functional ability of the patient. Bedrest on a firm mattress (to limit spinal flexion) is encouraged to reduce the weight load and gravitational forces, thereby freeing the disc from stress. The patient is allowed to assume a comfortable position; usually, one with moderate hip and knee flexion to relax the back muscles is most satisfactory. While in the side-lying position, a pillow is placed between the legs. To get out of bed, the patient lies on one side while pushing up to a sitting position.

Since muscle spasm is prominent during the acute phase, muscle relaxants are used. Anti-inflammatory drugs and systemic steroids may be administered to counter the inflammation that usually occurs in the supporting tissues and the affected nerve roots. Heat and massage help to relax spastic muscles.

During conservative management, surgery may be indicated in cases of unrelieved pain or the development of a neurological deficit, for example, motor or sensory loss, muscle weakness or atrophy, or loss of sphincter control.

Surgical Management

The aim of surgical treatment is to relieve pressure on the nerve root in order to relieve pain. Several operative techniques are employed, as follows.

Laminectomy
Laminectomy is the removal of the lamina to expose the neural elements in the spinal canal, thus allowing inspection of the canal, and identification and removal of pathology and compression from the cord and nerve roots.

Microdiscectomy
Microdiscectomy incorporates the use of the operating microscope to visualize the offending disc and compressed nerve roots; it permits a smaller incision (2.5 cm) and minimal blood loss. Generally, it involves a shorter hospital stay, and the patient makes a more rapid recovery.

Anterior Cervical Approach (Discectomy and Fusion)
The disc space is opened and degenerate tissue is curetted. A bone graft (bovine, or from the patient's iliac crest) is used to fuse and thus stabilize the spine to reduce the chances of recurrence.

► NURSING PROCESS
► THE PATIENT UNDERGOING A CERVICAL DISCECTOMY

► *Assessment*

The patient is asked about past injuries to the neck (whiplash) because unresolved trauma may cause persistent discomfort, pain and tenderness, and the development of arthritis in the injured joint of the cervical spine. Assessment of the patient's problems includes determining the onset, location and radiation of the pain, paraesthesias, limited movement and diminished function of the neck, shoulders and upper extremities. The nurse should determine whether or not the symptoms are bilateral because, with large herniations, bilateral symptoms may be due to cord compression. Examination of the area around the cervical spine may cause tenderness.

Range of motion in the neck and shoulders is evaluated. The patient is asked about any health problems that may influence the postoperative course. The nurse determines the patient's need for information about the operative procedure, and reinforces what has been explained by the surgeon.

Most patients fear surgery on any part of the spine, and therefore need assurance and explanations throughout. Any complaint of pain, paraesthesia and muscle spasm are recorded in order to have a baseline for comparison after surgery. Preoperative assessment should also include an evaluation of movement in the extremities as well as bladder and bowel function. To facilitate the postoperative turning procedure, the patient is taught to turn as a unit (logrolling), as part of the preoperative preparation. Other facets of the postoperative regime that should be practised before the operation are deep-breathing and coughing exercises.

▶ *Patient's Problems*

Based on the assessment, the patient's main problems may include the following:

● Alteration in comfort, related to the surgical procedure.
● Alteration in mobility related to the postoperative surgical management.
● Lack of knowledge about the postoperative course and management following discharge.

▶ *Planning and Implementation*
▶ **Expected Outcomes**

The patient's expected outcomes may include achievement of comfort, attainment of improved mobility and participation in self-care.

Nursing Care

Postoperative Assessment

The patient may be kept flat for 12 hours postoperatively with the head immobilized in a neutral position. If a bone has been grafted, a check X-ray should be performed before the patient is mobilized. Vital signs and neurological assessment of limb power are assessed frequently. Haematoma and oedema may compress cord function. If the anterior approach is used, a haematoma at this site can rapidly obstruct the airway as well as dislodge any graft onto the spinal cord.

If the patient has had bone removed from the iliac crest, the donor site should also be observed for leakage and haematoma formation.

If the patient has had a bone fusion in which bone has been removed from the iliac crest, considerable pain may be experienced. Nursing care includes giving the prescribed postoperative analgesic according to the patient's needs, positioning for comfort and reassuring the patient that the pain can be controlled. If the patient experiences a sudden reappearance of radicular pain, extrusion of the graft may have occurred, a situation requiring reoperation and surgical repositioning of the graft.

A major complaint of the patient is usually sore throat, hoarseness or dysphagia, especially following an anterior approach. This can be relieved temporarily by throat lozenges. The nurse should observe for pulmonary secretions since the patient may be afraid to cough due to throat pain. Occasionally during an anterior approach, the recurrent laryngeal nerve may be damaged, resulting in hoarseness and an inability to cough effectively.

Improving Mobility

A cervical collar is usually worn postoperatively, which contributes to limitations in neck movements and altered mobility. Patients are taught to turn the body instead of the neck when looking from side to side. The neck should be kept in a neutral position, and the patient may require assistance during positional changes, making sure that the head, shoulders and thorax are aligned during turning. The nurse should provide support behind the neck and shoulders when helping the patient into the sitting position.

Patient Education

Following conservative or surgical treatment on the cervical spine, a cervical collar may be worn for six weeks postoperatively. Patients are cautioned against flexing, extending or rotating the neck in any extreme manner while stretching, exercising or working.

The prone position should be avoided while sleeping, and the head kept in a neutral position. The use of several pillows or cushions that produces unwanted neck flexion should be avoided. Standing or sitting for longer than 30 minutes can induce considerable neck strain. Vibration on the spine from long car journeys should also be discouraged.

Following treatment on the lumbar spine, the patient is advised that, since it takes up to six weeks for the ligaments of the muscles to heal, activity is to be increased gradually up to the point of tolerance. Excessive activity may result in spasm of the paraspinal muscles.

Activities that produce flexion strain on the spine (e.g., driving a car) should be avoided until healing has taken place. Heat may be applied to the back to soothe and relax muscle spasm and help absorb exudates in the tissues. Scheduled rest periods are important. Usually, the patient is advised to avoid heavy work for two to three months after surgery. Exercises are prescribed to strengthen the abdominal and erector spinal muscles. A back brace or corset may be necessary if back pain persists.

Following Lumbar Surgery

Following lumbar disc excision, the vital signs are checked frequently and the wound is inspected for evidence of haemorrhage, because vascular injury is a complication of disc surgery. Since postoperative neurological deficits may occur from nerve root injury, the sensation and motor power of the lower extremities are evaluated at specified intervals, along with the colour and temperature of the legs and sensation of the toes. Another important sign to check for is possible urinary retention.

The patient is positioned with a pillow is placed under the head, and the knee rest is elevated slightly, since slight knee flexion relaxes the muscles of the back. When the patient is lying on one side, however, extreme knee flexion must be avoided. The patient is encouraged to move from side to side to relieve pressure, but is first reassured that no injury will result from moving. When the patient is ready to turn, the bed is placed in a flat position and a pillow is placed between the legs. Turning is done with the body as a unit (logrolling), without twisting the back.

Most patients walk to the bathroom the following day, but if they cannot pass urine in the first 12 hours postoperatively, it may be necessary to allow them to use the commode.

To get out of bed, the patient lies on one side while pushing up to a sitting position. At the same time, a second person eases the patient's legs over the side of the bed. Coming to a sitting or standing posture is accomplished by one long, smooth motion. Sitting is discouraged except for toilet purposes.

Prescribed postoperative analgesia must be given according to the patient's needs. The patient should be aware that sciatic pain may not resolve for some time postoperatively due to oedema.

CRANIAL NERVE DISORDERS

There are 12 pairs of cranial nerves that emerge from the lower surface of the brain and pass through the foramina (openings) in the skull. They are classified as motor, sensory and mixed nerves. The cranial nerves are numbered in the order in which they arise from the brain. The names of the cranial nerves suggest their primary function or some anatomical characteristic. Most cranial nerves originate in the brain stem and innervate the head, neck and special organs.

The cranial nerves are examined separately and in sequence (see Chapter 31, Table 31.1). Some cranial nerve deficits can be detected by observing the patient's face, eye movements, speech and swallowing. Electromyography is used to investigate motor and sensory dysfunction. Magnetic resonance imaging produces excellent images of the cranial nerves and brain stem.

Since the brain stem and cranial nerves control vital motor, sensory or autonomic functions of the body, they may be involved in conditions arising primarily within these structures or in secondary extension from adjacent disease processes. The following discussions will centre on trigeminal neuralgia, a condition affecting the fifth cranial nerve, and on Bell's palsy, caused by involvement of the seventh cranial nerve. The cranial nerves are illustrated in Figure 33.11.

Trigeminal Neuralgia (Tic Douloureux)

Trigeminal neuralgia is a condition of the fifth cranial nerve characterized by an explosive onset of pain similar to an electric shock or a lancinating burning sensation in the area distributed by one or more branches of the trigeminal nerve. The pain ends as abruptly as it starts. The aetiology is uncertain, but chronic compression or irritation of the trigeminal nerve or degenerative changes in the Gasserian ganglion are suggested causes. The condition may be associated with pressure from a vascular anomaly encroaching upon the trigeminal nerve or its distribution.

Clinical Features

Assessment
Early attacks, appearing most often in the fifth decade of life, are usually mild and brief. Pain-free intervals may be measured in terms of minutes, hours, days or longer. With

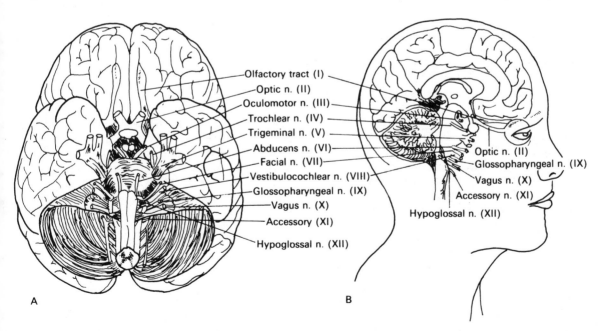

Figure 33.11 The cranial nerves. (A) Inferior view of the brain showing the cranial nerves. (B) Lateral view of the brain showing a schematized version of the cranial nerves.

advancing years, the painful episodes tend to become more and more frequent and agonizing. The patient lives in constant fear of attacks.

The pain of this neuralgia is felt in the skin, not in the deeper structures, but it is more severe at the peripheral areas of distribution of the affected nerve, notably over the lip, the chin, the nostrils and in the teeth. Paroxysms of sudden, severe pain are aroused by any stimulation of the terminals of the affected nerve branches, such as washing the face, shaving, brushing the teeth, eating and drinking. A draft of cold air and direct pressure against the nerve trunk may also cause pain. Certain areas are called trigger points, since the slightest touch immediately starts a paroxysm. To avoid stimulating these areas, patients with trigeminal neuralgia try not to touch or wash their faces, shave, chew or do anything else that might cause an attack. Behaviour of this type is a clue to diagnosis.

Medical and Nursing Care

Care of the patient with trigeminal neuralgia includes requesting the patient to recognize factors and trigger points that may precipitate and attack, and adapting care to avoid such attacks.

The anti-epileptic drugs carbamazepine and phenytoin, by reducing the transmission of impulses at certain nerve terminals, will relieve pain in most patients. Carbamazepine is taken with meals, in dosages gradually increased until relief is obtained. Side-effects include nausea, dizziness, drowsiness and hepatic dysfunction. The patient's blood is monitored for bone marrow depression.

When medication fails to provide pain relief, a number of surgical options are available.

Alcohol injection of the Gasserian ganglion and peripheral branches of the trigeminal nerve will give complete anaesthesia. However, the pain returns after the nerve regenerates.

Percutaneous Radiofrequency Trigeminal Gangliolysis

Percutaneous radiofrequency interruption of the Gasserian ganglion, whereby the small unmyelinated and thinly myelinated fibres that conduct the pain are thermally destroyed, is becoming the surgical procedure of choice for trigeminal neuralgia.

Under local anaesthesia, the needle is introduced through the cheek on the affected side. Under fluoroscopic control, the needle electrode is guided through the foramen ovale into the Gasserian ganglion, which is divided. The nerve is stimulated with a small current in a conscious patient, who then reports when a tingling sensation is felt. The patient is anaesthetized briefly and a radiofrequency current is passed to thermally injure the trigeminal ganglion and rootlets. The patient is then awakened from

the anaesthetic and examined for sensory deficits. Repeat lesions may be produced until the desired effect is achieved. The operative procedure takes less than one hour and gives permanent pain relief in most patients. Touch and proprioceptive functions are left intact.

Open Surgical Procedure

The trigeminal nerve root may be identified through either a subtemporal or posterior fossa approach and surgically divided, following which the patient will have loss of sensation in the distribution of the divided nerve fibres.

Microvascular Decompression of the Trigeminal Nerve

Since trigeminal neuralgia may be due to vascular compression by an arterial loop, and occasionally by a vein, an intracranial approach can be used. The arterial loop is lifted from the nerve and a small, nonabsorbable sponge is inserted to relieve the pressure. This is a major procedure; the postoperative management is the same as for any intracranial surgery (see p. 1012).

Complications

Troublesome dysaesthesia (abnormal sensations) affects some patients. Corneal anaesthesia may result in keratitis and corneal ulceration.

Bell's Palsy

Bell's palsy (facial paralysis) is due to peripheral involvement of the seventh cranial nerve on one side, which results in weakness or paralysis of the facial muscles. The aetiology is unknown, although possible causes may include vascular ischaemia, viral disease (herpes simplex, herpes zoster), autoimmune disease or a combination of all of these factors.

Altered Physiology

Bell's palsy is considered by some to represent a type of pressure paralysis. The inflamed, oedematous nerve becomes compressed to the point of damage, or its nutrient vessel is occluded to the point of producing ischaemia necrosis of the nerve within the facial foramina. There is distortion of the face from paralysis of the facial muscles; increased lacrimation (tearing); and painful sensations in the face, behind the ear, and in the eye. The patient may experience speech difficulties and may be unable to eat on the affected side because of relaxation of the facial muscle.

Clinical Features

The patient often experiences pain behind an ear, following which complete unilateral flaccid paralysis of the face develops. The patient is often unable to close the affected eyelid, raise the eyebrow, smile or show the teeth, resulting in grotesque appearance.

Nursing Care

While paralysis lasts, the affected eye is vulnerable to dust and foreign particles and must be protected. Corneal irritation and ulceration are a major threat to this patient. Sometimes there is an overflow of tears down the cheek (epiphora) from keratitis caused by drying of the cornea and absence of the blink reflex. The laxity of the lower lid alters the proper drainage of tears. To counter these problems, the eye should be covered with a protective shield at night. However, the eye patch may abrade the cornea, since there is some difficulty in keeping the partially paralyzed eyelids closed. The application of eye ointment at bedtime will cause the eyelids to adhere to one another and remain closed during sleep. The patient can be taught to close the paralyzed eyelid manually before going to sleep. Wrap-around sunglasses or goggles are worn to decrease normal evaporation from the eye.

If the nerve is not too sensitive, facial massage several times daily may help to maintain muscle tone. The technique is to massage the face with a gentle upward motion. Facial exercises, such as wrinkling the forehead, blowing out the cheeks and whistling, may be performed with the aid of a mirror and are intended to prevent muscle atrophy.

To help maintain the muscle tone and to prevent or minimize denervation, corticosteroids (prednisolone) may be given. This will reduce inflammation and oedema, which in turn reduces vascular compression and permits restoration of blood circulation to the nerve and relieves pain. Facial pain can also be controlled with analgesics. Local heat to the face also provides comfort and increases blood flow through the facial muscles.

Patient Education

The face should be kept warm. The patient should be reassured that the facial palsy is not the result of a stroke, and that spontaneous recovery occurs within three to five weeks in most patients. The patient should be taught to care for the affected eye, and continue to exercise the facial muscles to prevent atrophy.

DISORDERS OF THE PERIPHERAL NERVOUS SYSTEM

Peripheral Neuropathies

A peripheral neuropathy is a disorder affecting the peripheral motor, sensory or autonomic nerves. Peripheral nerves, by connecting the spinal cord and brain to all other body organs, transmit motor impulses outward and relay back sensory impulses to encode sensation in the brain. Involvement may be single or multiple. Polyneuropathies are characterized by bilaterally symmetrical disturbance of function, usually beginning in the feet and hands. (Most nutritional, metabolic and toxic neuropathies take this form.)

The most common causes of peripheral neuropathy are diabetes, alcoholism and occlusive vascular disease. Many bacterial and metabolic toxins and exogenous poisons also affect the structure and function of the peripheral nerves. Due to the growing use of chemicals in industry, agriculture and medicine, the number of substances known to cause peripheral neuropathies is increasing. In the developing countries, leprosy is a major cause of severe nerve disease.

The major symptoms of peripheral nerve disorders are loss of sensation, muscle atrophy, weakness, diminished reflexes, pain and paraesthesia (tingling, prickling) of the extremities. The patient frequently describes some part of the extremity as 'numb'. Autonomic features include decreased or reduced sweating, orthostatic hypotension, nocturnal diarrhoea, tachycardia, impotence and atrophic skin and nail changes.

Peripheral nerve disorders are diagnosed by electromyography and the recording of the nerve and muscle responses evoked when electrical stimulation is applied to a nerve.

Mononeuropathy

Management

The objective of treatment of mononeuropathy is to remove the cause if possible, such as by freeing the compressed nerve. Local steroid injections may lessen inflammation, resulting in less pressure on the nerve. Pain may be relieved by aspirin or codeine.

Guillain-Barré Syndrome (Acute Infective Polyneuritis)

Guillain-Barré syndrome is a clinical syndrome of unknown cause involving the peripheral and cranial nerves. In the majority of patients, the syndrome is preceded by an infection (respiratory or gastrointestinal), one to four weeks before the onset of neurological deficits. In some instances, it has occurred following vaccination or surgery. It may be due to a primary viral infection, an immune reaction, some other process or a combination of processes. One hypothesis is that a viral infection induces an autoimmune reaction that attacks the myelin of the peripheral nerves.

Proximal portions of the nerves tend to be affected most often, and the nerve roots within the subarachnoid space are commonly involved. Autopsy findings have revealed inflammatory oedema and demyelination with some lymphocytic infiltration that is especially prominent in the spinal nerve roots.

Clinical Features/Assessment

There is variation in the mode of onset. The initial neurological symptoms are paraesthesia (tingling and numbness) and muscle weakness of the legs, which may progress to the upper extremities, trunk and facial muscles. Muscle weakness may be followed quickly by complete paralysis. The cranial nerves are frequently affected, leading to paralysis of the ocular, facial and oropharyngeal muscles, causing marked difficulty in talking, chewing and swallowing. Autonomic dysfunction frequently occurs and takes the form of over- or underactivity of the sympathetic or parasympathetic nervous systems, manifested by cardiovascular and vasomotor disturbances. There may be severe and persistent pain in the back and calves of the legs. Frequently, the patient exhibits loss of position sense as well as diminished or absent tendon reflexes. Sensory changes are manifested by paraesthesias.

The majority of patients make a full recovery over several months to a year, but about 10 per cent are left with a residual disability.

Diagnosis

The spinal fluid shows an increased protein concentration with a normal cell count. Electrophysiological testing demonstrates marked slowing of nerve conduction velocity.

► NURSING PROCESS
► THE PATIENT WITH GUILLAIN-BARRÉ SYNDROME

► *Patient's Problems*

Based on the assessment, the patient's main problems may include the following:

- Ineffective breathing pattern related to rapidly progressive weakness and impending respiratory failure.
- Impaired physical mobility related to paralysis.
- Altered nutrition—less than body requirements, related to inability to swallow, which is secondary to cranial nerve dysfunction.
- Impaired verbal communication related to cranial nerve dysfunction.
- Fear related to loss of control and paralysis.

Nursing Care

Ensuring Respiratory Function
The patient with Guillain-Barré syndrome is absolutely

dependent on nursing surveillance and care for recovery. Artificial ventilation will probably be required if serial measurements of the patient's vital capacity show progressive deterioration indicating worsening of respiratory muscle power. A particularly dangerous situation occurs when the patient has difficulty in coughing and swallowing, which may cause aspiration of saliva and precipitate acute respiratory failure. The management of the patient requiring mechanical ventilation is a team effort and is discussed in Chapter 3. Chest physiotherapy is usually indicated if crepitations are heard on auscultation.

Promoting Mobility
The paralyzed extremities are supported in functional positions and given passive range-of-motion exercises at least twice daily. For severely paralyzed patients, the principles of nursing care of the unconscious patient (Chapter 32, p. 995) may be applied, although these patients are in full possession of their mental faculties. Patients may be distressed by paraesthesias and muscle pain and should be given mild analgesics.

When recovery begins to take place, these patients may experience orthostatic hypotension (from autonomic dysfunction) and will probably require the use of a tilt table to help them assume an upright posture.

Establishing Normal Nutrition
Attention is paid to adequate nutrition and prevention of muscle wasting. Paralytic ileus may result from insufficient parasympathetic activity. In this event, intravenous feedings are prescribed by the doctor and monitored by the nurse until bowel sounds are heard. If the patient is unable to swallow, nasogastric tube feeds may be prescribed. When the patient can swallow normally, oral feeding is gradually resumed. Constipation and retention of urine are common features due to autonomic involvement, and require bowel management and possibly urinary catheterization.

Improving Communication
Because of paralysis, tracheostomy and intubation, the patient is unable to communicate, and thus has no outlet for emotional expression. These problems are compounded by boredom, dependency, isolation and frustration. Some form of communication, for example, blinking the eyes to indicate 'yes' or 'no', must be established. Diversional therapy (television, cassette tapes, visits from the family or close friends) can alleviate some of the frustrations that are encountered.

Relieving Anxiety and Fear
Specific immunosuppressive therapy may be given, although this has not proved to be effective. More recently, plasma exchange has been tried, but again has not proved to be beneficial.

Naturally, patients will be afraid and so giving information about their disorder and its treatment may be re-assuring. Involving loved ones with selected patient care may help to reduce the sense of isolation felt by the patient.

Patient Education
It is important that the patient and relatives realize that recovery may take some months, but that usually improvements will begin once the maximum deficit occurs. Milder cases often have an excellent prognosis, but those patients with respiratory failure may face some disability.

After discharge from the hospital, patients are encouraged to continue with the exercise programme. A walking frame may be required for ambulation. Patients are cautioned about avoiding fatigue and overworking muscles. 'Take one day at a time' is good advice when the patient feels overwhelmed with problems of fatigue. The Guillain-Barré support group offers emotional support and information booklets.

► *Evaluation*
► **Expected Outcomes**

1. Patient attains spontaneous breathing and normal respiratory function.
   a. Vital capacity is within normal range.
   b. Has been weaned from mechanical ventilation.
2. Shows increasing mobility.
   a. Is able to move all extremities.
   b. Is working on ambulation techniques.
3. Demonstrates an ability to swallow.
   a. Expresses desire for food.
   b. Is taking adequate oral fluids and food.
4. Demonstrates recovery of speech.
   a. Is talking without undue breathlessness.
   b. Can make needs known.
5. Is less frightened.
   a. Patient is sleeping for longer intervals.
   b. Appears more relaxed and less anxious.

BIBLIOGRAPHY

Allan, D. (1984) Glasgow Coma Scale, *Nursing 2*, Vol. 2, No. 23, pp. 668–9.
Allan, D. (1986) Raised intracranial pressure, *The Professional Nurse*, Vol. 2, No. 3, pp. 78–80.
Gay, D. and Dick, G. (1986) Is multiple sclerosis caused by an oral spirochaete? *Lancet*, 12 July, Vol. 2, pp. 75–7.
Goodison, S. (1986) Assessment of nutritional status, *The Professional Nurse*, Vol. 3, No. 7, pp. 252–7.
Henley, A. (1980) Practical care of Asian patients, *Nursing*, Vol. 1, No. 16, pp. 683–6.
Hume-Adams, J. (1975) Brain damage caused by cerebral hypoxia, *Nursing Times*, Vol. 71, No. 17, pp. 654–6.
Shukla, K. (1979) Diet and culture, *Nursing*, Vol. 1, No. 12, pp. 523–5.

Young, C. (1984a) A review of the adverse effects of airway suction, *Physiotherapy*, Vol. 70, No. 3, pp. 104–6.
Young, C. (1984b) Recommended guidelines for suction physiotherapy, *Physiotherapy*, Vol. 70, No. 3, pp. 106–8.

FURTHER READING

Books

Anatomy and Physiology
Tortora, G. J. and Anagnostakos, N. P. (1990) *Principles of Anatomy and Physiology* (6th edition), Harper & Row, New York.

Multiple Sclerosis
Matthews, B. (1985) *MS: The Facts* (2nd edition), Oxford University Press, Oxford.
Simons, A. F. (1984) *MS: Psychological and Social Aspects*, William Heinemann Medical, London.

Neurology
Allan, D. (ed.) (1988) *Nursing and Neurosciences*, Churchill Livingstone, Edinburgh.
Hickey, J. V. (1986) *The Clinical Practice of Neurological and Neurosurgical Nursing* (2nd edition), J. B. Lippincott, Philadelphia.
Jennet, B. and Galbraith, S. (1983) *An Introduction to Neurosurgery* (4th edition), William Heinemann Medical, London.
Lindsay, K. W. *et al.* (1986) *Neurology and Neurosurgery Illustrated*, Churchill Livingstone, Edinburgh.
Pallet, P. J. and O'Brien, M. T. (1985) *Textbook of Neurological Nursing*, Little, Brown & Company, Boston.
Purchase, G. and Allen, D. (1984) *Neuromedical and Neurosurgical Nursing* (2nd edition), Baillière Tindall, Eastbourne.
Springhouse Corporation (1984) *Coping With Neurological Problems Proficiently (New Nursing Skillbook)* (2nd edition), Springhouse, Pennsylvania.
Warlow, C. and Garfield, J. (eds) (1987) *More Dilemmas in the Management of the Neurological Patient*, Churchill Livingstone, Edinburgh.

The Spine
Bedbrook, G. M. (1981) *The Care and Management of Spinal Cord Injury*, Springer-Verlag, New York.
Grungy, D., Swain, A. and Russell, J. (1986) *ABC of Spinal Cord Injury*, British Medical Journal Publications, London.
Spinal Injury Association (1980) *People With Spinal Injury: Treatment and Care*, Spinal Injury Association, London.

Articles

Anatomy and Physiology
Duthie, J. (1983) The nervous system: Structure and function, *Nursing*, Vol. 2, No. 15, pp. 431–4.

Roberts, A. (1977/1978) Systems of life, Nos. 31–9: Nervous system, *Nursing Times*, Vols. 73/74, Nos. 27, 31, 35, 39, 44, 48, 1, 5, 9.

Roberts, A. (1982) Systems of life, Nos. 86–9: Signs and symptoms, Vol. 78, Nos. 5, 9, 14, 18, 22, 27, 31, 35, 40.

Roberts, A. (1977) Signs and symptoms, *Nursing Times, Systems of Life, Nos 86–94*.

Voke, J. (1986) Transmitting the right signals, *Nursing Times*, Vol. 82, No. 39, pp. 47–9.

Voke, J. (1986) Reflex action, *Nursing Times*, Vol. 82, No. 40, pp. 52–3.

Voke, J. (1986) Parts of the brain, *Nursing Times*, Vol. 82, No. 41, pp. 44–7.

Assessing Consciousness

Boylam, A. and Brown, P. (1985) Neurological observations, *Nursing Times*, Vol. 81, No. 27, pp. 36–40.

Harrison, M. (1987) Coma, *Medicine International*, Vol. 2, No. 47, pp. 1908–17.

Simpson, D. and Reilly, P. (1982) Paediatric coma scale, *Lancet*, Vol. 2, No. 8295, p. 450.

Teasdale, G. (1975) Assessing 'conscious level', *Nursing Times*, Vol. 71, No. 24, pp. 914–7.

Teasdale, G. and Galbraith, S. (1975) Observation record chart, *Nursing Times*, Vol. 71, No. 25, pp. 972–3.

Brain Tumours

Copson, C. and Burridge, L. (1983) Cerebral tumours, *Nursing*, Vol. 2, No. 16, pp. 466–72.

Ford-Krauss, M. (1980) Management of patients with brain tumours, *Nursing*, Vol. 1, No. 9, pp. 383–88.

Ryan, P. (1989) Barts' pioneers brain tumour treatment, *BACUP News*, Issue 9, p. 3.

Teddy, P. (1987) Intracranial tumours, *Medicine International*, Vol. 2, No. 47, pp. 1932–9.

Cerebrovascular Disorders

Bartlett, J. (1983) Aneurysms and arteriovenous malformations, *Medicine International*, Vol. 1, No. 31, pp. 1448–55.

Connolly, D. (1982) Cerbral circulatory problems, *Nursing*, Vol. 1, No. 33, pp. 1460–4.

Galbraith, S. (1979) Management of the patient with subarachnoid haemorrhage, *Nursing Times*, Vol. 75, No. 43, pp. 1852–4.

Mitchell, S. K. and Yates, R. S. (1986) Cerebral vasospasm: Theoretical causes, medical management and nursing implications, *Journal of Neuroscience Nursing*, Vol. 18, No. 6, pp. 315–23.

Roberts, A. (1989) Cerebrovascular disease 1, *Nursing Times, Systems of Life, No. 173*.

Roberts, A. (1989) Cerebrovascular disease 2, *Nursing Times, Systems of Life, No. 174*.

Wright, ? (1985) Learning to walk again: How to help the elderly, *Nursing*, Vol. 2, No. 33, pp. 982–4.

Epilepsy

Lindsay, M. (1983) Epilepsy in adults, *Nursing*, Vol. 2, No. 15, pp. 453–6.

Markham, G. (1979) Epilepsy, *Nursing*, Vol. 1, No. 8, pp. 356–9.

Schneiderman, J. (1987) The first fit, *Medicine International*, Vol. 2, No. 46, pp. 1869–73.

Shorvon, S. (1987) Management of epilepsy in adults, *Medicine International*, Vol. 2, No. 46, pp. 1874–79.

Head Injury

Jennett, B. (1983) Medical aspect of head injury, *Medicine International*, Vol. 1, No. 30, pp. 1415–22.

Beetson, H. and Webber, E. (1983) Head injuries, *Nursing*, Vol. 2, No. 15, pp. 442–4.

Gurusinghe, N. (1985) Penetrating injuries of the head and spine, *Nursing Times*, Vol. 30, No. 81, pp. 28–34.

Mendelow, D. and Teasdale, G. (1986) Accident and emergency management of head injuries, *Nursing Times*, Vol. 82, No. 20, pp. 56–7.

Intracranial Pressure

Dearden, M. (1985) Intracranial pressure monitoring, *Care of the Critically Ill*, Vol. 1, No. 5, pp. 8–13.

Hugo, M. (1987) Alleviating the effects of care on the intracranial pressure of head-injured patients by manipulating nursing care activities, *Intensive Care Nursing*, Vol. 3, pp. 78–82.

Synder, M. (1983) Relation of nursing activities to increases in intracranial pressure, *Journal of Advanced Nursing*, Vol. 8, pp. 273–9.

Intracranial Surgery

Arsenault, L. (1985) Selected post-operative complications of cranial surgery, *Journal of Neurosurgical Nursing*, Vol. 17, No. 3, pp. 155–63.

McCash, A. M. (1985) Meeting the challenge of craniotomy care, *Registered Nurse*, June, pp. 26–35.

Investigations

Davit, M. (1979) Pictures in nursing: Taking an EEG, *Nursing*, Vol. 1, No. 8, pp. 376–9.

Dening, F. (1987) Nuclear magnetic resonance, *The Professional Nurse*, Vol. 3, No. 2, pp. 45–6.

Smaje, J. (1987) Clinical neurophysiology, *Medicine International*, Vol. 2, No. 46, pp. 1887–93.

Valentine, A. and Platts, A. (1987) Neuroradiolgy, *Medicine International*, Vol. 2, No. 46, pp. 1894–1900.

Motor Neurone Disease

Ross, F. (1980) Motor neurone disease, *Nursing Times*, Vol. 76, No. 41, pp. 1789–92.

Summers, D. H. (1981) Motor neurone disease, *Nursing Times*, Vol.77, No. 1, Occasional Paper.

Multiple Sclerosis

Anderson, L. (1985) Hyperbaric O_2 treatment for multiple sclerosis, *Nursing Times*, Vol. 81, No. 47, pp. 47–8.

Maggs, A. (1981) Multiple sclerosis 1, *Nursing Times*, Vol. 77, No. 10, pp. 414–8.

Matthews, B. (1983) Multiple sclerosis, *Medicine International*, Vol. 2, No. 48, pp. 1961–6.

Montegue, K. (1985) Take a deep breath, *Nursing Mirror*, Vol. 161, No. 15, pp. 37–41.

Wise, G. (1985) Learning to live with multiple sclerosis, *Nursing Times*, Vol. 81, No. 15, pp. 37–40.

Myasthenia Gravis

Lindsay, M. (1984) Myasthenia gravis, *Nursing Times*, Vol. 80, No. 4, pp. 38–40.

Newson-Davis, J. (1987) Myasthenia gravis, *Medicine International*, Vol. 2, No. 48, pp. 1988–91.

Pain

Crow, R. (1979) The nature of pain, *Nursing*, Vol. 1, No. 1, pp. 6–10.

Latham, J. (1986) Assessment, observation and measurement of pain, *The Professional Nurse*, Vol. 1, No. 4, pp. 107–10.

Latham, J. (1987) Transcutaneous nerve stimulation, *The Professional Nurse*, Vol. 2, No. 5, pp. 133–5.

Wright, B. (1983) Pain, *Nursing*, Vol. 2, No. 16, pp. 476–8.

Parkinson's Disease

Calne, D. and Pallis, C. (1987) Parkinsonism, *Medicine International*, Vol. 2, No. 47, pp. 1945–50.

Cole, K. (1988) Is Parkinson's disease preventable? *The Professional Nurse*, Vol. 4, No. 1, pp. 15-17.

Ferry, G. (1987) New light on Parkinson's disease, *New Scientist*, Vol. 113, No. 1546, pp. 56–9.

Lindsay, M. (1983) Developing understanding of Parkinson's disease, *Nursing Times*, Vol. 79, No. 10, pp. 24–66.

Roberts, A. (1989) Parkinsonism, *Nursing Times, Systems of Life, No. 175*, Vol. 85, No. 37.

Peripheral Nerve (Guillain-Barré)

Cooksley, P. (1981) Fading away, *Nursing Mirror*, Vol. 152, No. 1, pp. 38–9.

Lindsay, M. (1983) Trigeminal neuralgia, *Nursing*, Vol. 2, No. 15, pp. 451–2.

Matthews, D. (1987) Bell's palsy, *Medicine International*, Vol. 2, No. 48, pp. 1985–7.

Speech

Enderby, P. (1980) A nurse's guide to managing the patient with speech handicap following a stroke or head injury, *Nursing Times*, Vol. 76, No. 48, p. 2114.

Tomlinson, A. and Williams, A. (1985) Communication skills in nursing—a practical account, *Nursing*, Vol. 2, No. 38, pp. 1121–3.

The Spine

Allan, D. (1984) Care of patient on a wedge turning frame, *Nursing Times*, Vol. 80, No. 33, pp. 40–1.

Allen, G. (1985) Cervical spinal injuries, *Nursing*, Vol. 2, No. 44, pp. 1314–17.

Hamilton, A. (1979) Sexual problems of the disabled, *Nursing*, Vol. 1, NO. 5, pp. 220–5.

Horgen, M. (1985) Low back pain and its management, *Nursing*, Vol. 2, No. 44, pp. 1298–1300.

McCay, J. (1979) Patient's rehabilitation: The nurse's role, *Nursing*, Vol. 1, No. 5, pp. 217–19.

Rogers, E. (1979) Paralyzed patients and their nursing care, *Nursing*, Vol. 1, NO. 5, pp. 207–11.

Rogers, M. (1979) Paralysis, *Nursing*, Vol. 1, No. 5, pp. 203–6.

The Unconscious Patient

Allan, D. (1986) Nursing the unconscious patient, *The Professional Nurse*, Vol. 2, No. 1, pp. 15–17.

James, E. (1982) Nursing aspects of tube feeding, *Nursing*, Vol. 2, No. 4, pp. 101–4.

Pretty, J. (1979) Alternative methods of feeding, *Nursing*, Vol. 1, No. 12, pp. 538–40.

Wilmot, W. (1980) Pictures in nursing. Turning and positioning the unconscious patient, *Nursing*, Vol. 1, No. 9, Part 2, pp. 414–16.

chapter 34 ━━━━━━━━━━━━━━━━━━

ASSESSMENT OF MUSCULOSKELETAL FUNCTION

The musculoskeletal system includes the bones, joints, muscles, tendons, ligaments and bursae of the body. The occurrence of problems associated with these structures is very common and affects all age groups. Problems with the musculoskeletal system are generally not life-threatening, but they have a significant impact on one's productivity and financial situation. Problems associated with the musculoskeletal system will be encountered by the nurse practising in any field of nursing and in order to be able to assess abnormality, today's nurse must understand the expected 'norm'.

PHYSIOLOGICAL OVERVIEW

The musculoskeletal system is collectively the largest organ system in the body. Bony structures and connective tissue account for approximately 25 per cent of the body weight, and muscle accounts for approximately 50 per cent of the body weight. The health and functions of the musculoskeletal system are interdependent with the rest of the body systems.

The functions of the musculoskeletal system include protection, support, locomotion, mineral storage, haemopoiesis and heat production. The bony structure provides protection for vital organs, including the brain, heart and lungs. The bony skeleton supports body structures by providing a strong and sturdy framework. The muscles attached to the skeleton allow the body to move. Calcium, phosphorus and magnesium are among the minerals deposited and stored in the bone matrix. The red bone marrow located within the bone cavity is responsible for the production of red and white blood cells. Muscle contraction results in mechanical action for movement as well as heat production to maintain body temperature.

The Skeletal System

Anatomy of the Skeletal System
There are 206 bones in the human body, divided into four

categories: long bones (e.g., the femur), short bones (e.g., the tarsals), flat bones (e.g., the sternum) and irregular bones (e.g., the vertebrae). The shape and construction of a specific bone are determined by its function and the forces exerted on the bone.

Bones are constructed of cancellous (trabecular or spongy) or cortical (compact) bone tissue. Long bones are shaped like rods or shafts with rounded ends. The shaft, or diaphysis, is primarily cortical bone. The ends of the long bones are called epiphyses and are primarily cancellous bone. The epiphyseal plate separates the epiphysis from the diaphysis and is the centre for longitudinal growth in children. In the adult, it is calcified. The ends of long bones are covered by articular (hyaline) cartilage at the joints. Long bones are for weight-bearing and movement.

Short bones consist mainly of cancellous bone covered by a layer of compact bone.

Flat bones are important sites for haemopoiesis (formation of blood), and frequently provide vital organ pro-

tection. They are made of cancellous bone layered between compact bone.

Irregular bones have unique shapes related to their function. Generally, irregular bone make-up is similar to that of flat bones.

Bone is composed of cells, protein matrix and mineral deposits. The cells are of three basic types—osteoblasts, osteocytes and osteoclasts. Osteoblasts are involved in bone formation by secreting bone matrix. The matrix is 98 per cent collagen and 2 per cent ground substances (glucosamine glycans [acid polysaccharides] and proteoglycans). The matrix is a framework in which inorganic mineral salts are deposited. Osteocytes are mature bone cells involved in homeostatic bone functions and are located in osteons (bone matrix units). Osteoclasts are multinuclear cells involved in bone destruction, resorption and remodelling.

The osteon is the microscopic functioning unit of mature bone. The centre of the osteon contains a capillary.

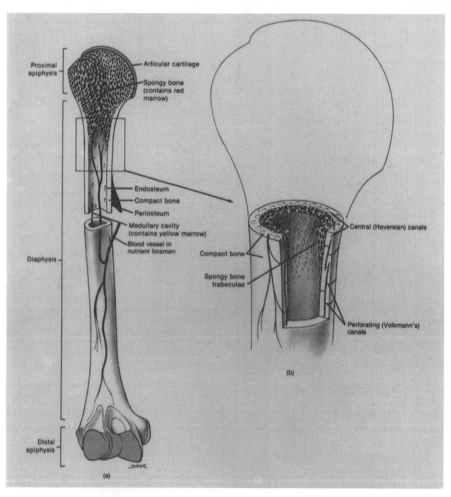

Figure 34.1 Osseous tissue. (A) Macroscopic appearance of a long bone that has been partially sectioned. (B) Histological structure of bone. (From Tortora, G. J. and Anagnostakos, N. P. (1990) *Principles of Anatomy and Physiology* (6th edition), Harper & Row, New York.)

Around the capillary are circles of bone matrix called lamellae. Within the lamellae are osteocytes (mature, living bone cells). They are nourished by processes extending into tiny canaliculi (canals that communicate with the blood vessel). The size of the osteon is limited by the nutritional supply. Bone cells and their nourishing blood vessels must be less than 0.1 mm apart (Figure 34.1).

Covering the bone is a dense, fibrous membrane known as the periosteum. The periosteum functions in the nutrition and growth of bone, and provides for the attachment of tendons and ligaments. The periosteum contains nerves, blood vessels and lymphatics. The layer closest to the bone contains osteoblasts, which are bone-forming cells.

Endosteum is a thin, vascular membrane covering the marrow cavity of long bones and the spaces in cancellous bone. Osteoclasts, which dissolve away bone to maintain the marrow cavity, are located near the endosteum and in Howship's lacunae (indentations on bone surfaces).

Bone marrow is a vascular tissue located in the medullary (diaphyseal) cavity of long bones and in flat bones. Red bone marrow is responsible for the production of red and white blood cells. In the adult, the red bone marrow in the long bone cavity is replaced mostly by fatty, yellow marrow. Red bone marrow in the adult is located mainly in the sternum, ilium, vertebrae and ribs.

Bone tissue is well vascularized. Periosteal vessels connect with bone tissue through minute Volkmann canals. In addition, nutrient arteries penetrate the periosteum and enter the medullary cavity through foramina (small openings). Nutrient arteries supply blood to the marrow and bone. The venous system may accompany arteries or may exit independently.

Bone Formation

Bone begins to form long before birth. The process by which intercellular material is formed and hardening minerals are deposited into the bone is known as ossification. There are two basic models of ossification: intramembranous and endochondral. Intramembranous ossification, in which bone develops within membrane, occurs in the bones of the face and skull. Therefore, when the skull heals, it is by fibrous union. The other kind of bone formation is known as endochondral ossification, in which a cartilage model exists and is resorbed and replaced by bone. Most bones in the body are formed and healed by endochondral ossification.

The exact mechanism by which ossification occurs is unknown. The cell mitochondria probably play a vital role in the formation of microcrystallites, which are deposited in the matrix as precursors of larger mineral deposits. The ground substances may be the stimulus for the deposition of crystals. In addition, a specific charge may occur on the collagen fibres that initiate the crystal formation and electrostatically hold the crystals, once formed, in place. Actively growing bone is electronegative. More than 99 per cent of the total body calcium is present in the bones.

Other minerals deposited within the bone matrix include sodium, magnesium, fluoride and carbonate.

Bone Maintenance

Bone is a dynamic tissue in a constant state of turnover (resorption and reforming). Calcium in bone in an adult is replaced at the rate of about 18 per cent a year. The important regulating factors that determine the balance between bone formation and bone resorption include local stress, vitamin D, parathyroid hormone, calcitonin and circulation.

Local stress (weight-bearing) acts to stimulate local bone resorption and formation and can result in extensive remodelling. In this way, deformed bones may tend to straighten out. This phenomenon also explains why important weight-bearing bones are thick and strong. When weight-bearing or stress is prevented, as in prolonged bedrest, calcium is lost from the bone. If the stress on the bone is excessive, bone necrosis will occur.

Vitamin D functions to increase the amount of calcium in the blood by promoting absorption of calcium from the gastrointestinal tract and accelerating mobilization of calcium from the bone.

Parathyroid hormone and calcitonin are the major hormonal regulators of calcium homeostasis. Parathyroid hormone regulates the concentration of calcium in the blood, in part by promoting movement of calcium from the bone. Excessive mobilization of calcium due to excess parathyroid hormone results in demineralization of the bone and formation of bone cysts. Calcitonin, from the thyroid gland, increases the production of bone.

Blood supply to the bone also affects bone formation. With diminished blood supply or hyperaemia (congestion), osteogenesis is reduced and the bone becomes osteoporotic. Bone necrosis occurs when the bone is deprived of blood.

The Articular System

The bones of the body are joined together at joints or articulations that allow for a variety of movements. Regardless of the amount of movement possible, the junction of two or more bones is called a joint. There are three basic kinds of joints: synarthrosis, amphiarthrosis and diarthrosis joints (also called synarthroses, amphiarthroses and diarthroses).

Synarthrosis joints are immovable, as exemplified by the skull sutures. Amphiarthroses, such as the vertebral joints and symphysis, allow some limited motion. The bones are separated by fibrous cartilage. Diarthroses, like the elbow, are freely movable joints. Synovial fluid lubricates the movement of diarthroses (or synovial) joints.

At a typical movable joint, the ends of the articulating bones are covered with a smooth hyaline cartilage. The articulating bones are surrounded by a tough, fibrous sheath, the joint capsule. The capsule is lined with a membrane, the synovium, which secretes the lubricating and shock-absorbing synovial fluid into the joint capsule.

Therefore, the bone surfaces do not come in direct contact. In some synovial joints, fibrocartilage discs are located between the articular cartilage surfaces. They provide shock absorption. In some joints, such as the knee, interosseous ligaments, which add strength to the joint, are found within the capsule.

Ligaments (fibrous connective tissue bands) bind the articulating bones together. Ligaments and muscle tendons, which pass over the joint, provide joint stability.

Movable joints are of several different kinds.

- Ball and socket joints, best exemplified by the hip or the shoulder, permit full freedom of movement.
- Hinge joints permit bending in one direction only, and is best exemplified by the elbow joint.
- A saddle joint allows movement in two planes at right angles to each other. The joint at the base of the thumb is a saddle, biaxial joint.
- The pivot joint is characterized by the articulation between the radius and the ulna. It permits rotation for such activities as turning a doorknob.
- Gliding joints allow for limited movement in all directions and are located at the joints of carpal bones in the wrist.

Bursae are additional structures associated with some joints. A bursa is a sac filled with synovial fluid that is located at a point of friction. Bursae are generally found cushioning the movement of tendons, ligaments and bones at the elbow, shoulder, knee and other joints.

The Skeletal Muscle System

Anatomy of Skeletal Muscles

Skeletal (striated) muscles are involved in body movement, posture and heat-production functions. Muscles are attached by tendons (cords of fibrous connective tissue) or aponeurosis (broad, flat sheets of connective tissue) to bones, connective tissue, other muscles, soft tissue or skin. Muscles contract to bring the two points of attachment closer together. Muscles vary in shape and size according to the activity for which they are responsible. Muscles develop and are maintained when actively used. Age and disuse cause loss of muscular function as fibrotic tissue replaces the contractile muscle tissue.

The muscles of the body are composed of parallel groups of muscle cells (fasciculi) encased in fibrous tissue called epimysium or fascia. The more fasciculi contained in a muscle, the more precise the movements.

The speed of the muscle contraction is variable. Myoglobulin, a haemoglobin-like protein pigment, is present in striated muscle cells and transports oxygen from the blood capillaries to the muscle cell mitochondria for cellular metabolic needs. Muscles containing large quantities of myoglobulin (red muscle) have been observed to contract slowly and powerfully (e.g., respiratory and postural muscles). Muscles containing little myoglobulin

(white muscles) contract quickly and for extended periods of time (e.g., extraocular eye muscles). Most body muscles contain both red and white muscle fibres.

Each muscle cell (also referred to as a muscle fibre) contains myofibrils, which in turn are composed of a series of sarcomeres, the actual contractile units of skeletal muscle. The components of the sarcomeres are known as thick and thin filaments. The thin filaments are composed mainly of a protein known as actin. The thick filaments are composed mainly of myosin, another protein material.

Skeletal Muscle Contraction

Contraction of a muscle is due to the contraction of each of its component sarcomeres. The contraction of a sarcomere is due to interactions between the myosin in the thick filaments and the actin in the thin filaments, brought about by a local increase in the calcium ion concentration. The thick and thin filaments slide across one another. When calcium concentration in the sarcomere subsequently falls, the myosin and actin filaments cease to interact and the sarcomere returns to its original resting length (relaxation). Interaction between actin and myosin does not occur in the absence of calcium.

Muscle fibres contract in response to electrical stimulation. When stimulated, muscle cells release calcium ions which allow actin and myosin to intereact. Shortly afterwards, the muscle cell is depolarized and calcium is removed rapidly (from the sarcomere) and the muscle relaxes. Depolarization of the muscle cells normally occurs in response to a stimulus from a nerve cell. Neurones that control the activity of skeletal muscle cells are called lower motor neurones; they originate in the anterior horn of the spinal cord.

Energy is consumed during muscle contraction and relaxation. The rate of energy used by skeletal muscle varies; it increases markedly during exercise. During isometric contraction, almost all energy is released in the form of heat; during isotonic contraction, some of the energy is expended in mechanical work. In some situations, such as shivering, the need for heat generation is the primary stimulus for muscle contraction.

Muscle Status

The contraction of muscle fibres can result in either isotonic or isometric contraction of the muscle. In isometric contraction, the length of the muscles remains constant, but the force generated by the muscles is increased. An example of this is when one pushes against an immovable wall. Isotonic contraction, on the other hand, is characterized by shortening of the muscle with no increase in tension within the muscle. An example of this is flexion of the forearm. In normal activities, many muscle movements are a combination of isometric and isotonic contraction. For example, during walking, isotonic contraction results in shortening of the leg and, during isometric contraction, the stiff leg pushes against the floor.

Relaxed muscles demonstrate a state of readiness to respond to contraction stimuli. This state of readiness is known as muscle tone (tonus), and is due to the maintenance of some of the muscle fibres in a contracted state. Sense organs in the muscles (muscle spindles) monitor muscle tone. Muscle tone is found to be minimal during sleep and increased when anxious. In lower motor neuron destruction (e.g., polio), the denervated muscle becomes atonic (soft and flabby) and atrophies. A muscle that has less than normal tonus is known as flaccid. The term 'spastic' describes the muscle with greater than normal tonus.

Muscle Actions

Muscles accomplish movement only by contraction. They cannot push. Through the co-ordination of muscle groups, the body is able to perform a wide variety of movement. The prime mover is the muscle that causes a particular motion. The muscles assisting the prime mover are known as synergists. The muscle causing movement opposite to that of the primary mover is known as the antagonist. The antagonist must relax to allow the prime mover to contract, producing motion. For example, when contraction of the biceps causes flexion of the elbow joint, the biceps is the prime mover and the triceps is the antagonist. With muscle paralysis, a person may be able to retrain functioning muscles within a synergistic group to co-ordinate in such a way as to effect the required movement. Secondary movers then become the primary mover.

The body movements that muscle contractions can produce are many. Flexion is characterized by bending at a joint (e.g., elbow). The opposite movement is extension or straightening at a joint. Abduction is the action of moving away from the midline of the body. To move toward the midline is adduction. Rotation describes turning around a specific axis (e.g., shoulder joint). Circumduction is the conelike movement of the thumb. Special body movements include supination (turning the palm up), pronation (turning the palm down), inversion (turning the sole of the foot inward), eversion (the opposite of inversion), protraction (the jaw is pulled forward), and retraction (the jaw is pulled backward).

Exercise, Disuse and Repair

Muscles need to be exercised to maintain function and strength. When a muscle is caused repeatedly to develop maximum or close to maximum tension over a long period of time, as in regular exercise with weights, the cross-sectional area of the muscle increases (hypertrophies). This is due to an increase in the size of individual muscle fibres without an increase in the number of muscle fibres. Hypertrophy will persist only if the exercise is continued.

The opposite phenomenon occurs with disuse of muscle over a long period of time. The decrease in the size of a muscle is called atrophy. Bedrest and immobility will cause loss of muscle mass and strength. When immobility is due to a treatment mode (e.g., casting or traction), the patient can decrease the effects of immobility by isometric exercise of the muscles of the immobilized part. Quadriceps exercises (tightening the muscles of the thigh) and gluteal setting exercises (tightening of the muscles of the buttocks) help maintain the larger muscle groups that are important in ambulation. Active and weight-resistant exercises of uninjured parts of the body prevent degeneration.

When muscles are injured, they need rest and immobilization until tissue repair occurs. The healed muscle then needs progressive exercise to resume its pre-injury functional state.

Considerations for Elderly People

Multiple changes in the musculoskeletal system occur with ageing. Bone mass peaks at about the age of 35, after which there is a universal gradual loss of bone. Numerous metabolic changes, including menopausal withdrawal of oestrogen and decreased activity, contribute to the loss of bone mass (osteoporosis). Women lose more bone mass than men. By the age of 75, the average women has lost 25 per cent of her cortical (compact) bone and 40 per cent of her trabecular (cancellous) bone. Additionally, bones change in shape and have reduced strength. If fractured, fibrous tissue develops more slowly in the aged.

In elderly people, the ability of the collagen structures to absorb energy is reduced. This contributes to the development of osteoarthritis. The articular cartilage degenerates in weight-bearing areas and has a reduced ability to heal.

Likewise, muscle strength is diminished. There is an actual loss in the number of muscle fibres due to myofibril atrophy, which begins in the fourth decade.

Many of the effects of ageing can be overcome if the body is kept healthy and active.

Remote musculoskeletal problems for which the patient has compensated may become new problems with age-related changes. For example, patients who have recovered from polio and who have been able to function normally by using synergistic muscle groups may discover increasing incapacity. They have a reduced compensatory ability.

PHYSICAL ASSESSMENT

An examination of the musculoskeletal system ranges from a basic assessment of functional capabilities to sophisticated physical examination manoeuvres that facilitate diagnosis of specific muscle and joint disorders. The nurse's assessment is primarily a functional evaluation. Additional techniques of inspection and palpation will be employed to evaluate the patient's posture and gait, joint function, bone stability, muscle integrity and strength, and ability to perform activities of daily living.

The musculoskeletal assessment is commonly integrated with that of the physical examination. This system relates closely to the neurological and cardiovascular systems, and thus all three assessments are often carried out together. The basis of the assessment is a comparison of symmetrical regions of the body. The extent of the assessment depends on the patient's physical complaints, health history and any physical clues detected by the examiner that warrant further exploration.

When specific symptoms or physical findings of musculoskeletal dysfunction are apparent, the examination is carried out and carefully documented, and the information is given to the doctor, who may decide that a more extensive examination and diagnostic work-up are necessary.

Gait Assessment

An assessment of gait is carried out by asking the patient to walk normally for a short distance away from the examiner. The examiner observes the gait for smoothness and rhythm. Any unsteadiness or irregular movements (frequently noted in elderly patients) are considered abnormal. When a limping motion is noted, it is most likely due to painful weight-bearing. In such instances, the patient can usually pinpoint the area of discomfort, thus guiding any further examination. When one extremity is shorter than another, a limp may also be observed as the patient's pelvis drops downward on the affected side with each step. Paralysis in the lower extremities results in a variety of gaits. These gaits are associated with such neurological disorders as Parkinson's disease and cerebrovascular accidents.

Joint Assessment

The joints are evaluated for their size and range of motion, and for the strength of the muscles that flex and extend the joints. The examiner is familiar with the normal range of motion of major joints, and focuses on specific joints if functional loss is apparent. Most people are able to hyperextend all joints. If the maximum extension of a joint still reveals some residual degree of flexion, the range of motion is said to be limited.

In the event that joint motion is compromised, or that the joint is painful, the joint is examined for the presence or absence of fluid within its capsule (effusion) and for an increase in temperature that might reflect active inflammation. An effusion is suspected when the joint is swollen in size and the normal bony landmarks are obscured. The most common site for joint effusion is in the knee.

Passive movement of the joint may produce an audible crunching sound, called crepitus. Crepitus may be palpable as well.

Joints and the tissues surrounding them are also observed for nodule formation. Rheumatoid arthritis, gout, osteoarthritis and rheumatic fever all produce characteristic nodules that are diagnostic of the disease. The subcutaneous nodules of rheumatoid arthritis are soft and occur within and along tendons that provide extensor function to the joints. The nodules of gout are hard and lie within and immediately adjacent to the joint capsule itself. The nodules of osteoarthritis are hard and painless and represent bony overgrowth that has resulted from destruction of the cartilaginous surface of bone within the joint capsule. These are frequently seen in older adults.

Atrophy of muscle results from disuse and from neurological damage. Thus, the muscles that provide function to a diseased joint will atrophy when the joint is kept passive to avoid the pain that may arise from moving it. This is dramatically seen in rheumatoid arthritis of the knees, in which the quadriceps muscle may atrophy in a very dramatic way. Often, the size of a diseased joint is exaggerated by the atrophy of muscles proximal and distal to that joint.

Examination of the Spine

Inspection of the spine is carried out with the patient's gown open to expose the entire back, buttocks and legs. The examiner will stand behind the patient, noting any differences in the height of the shoulders or iliac crests. The gluteal folds are normally symmetrical. Shoulder and hip symmetry, as well as the straight line of the vertebral column, are inspected with the patient erect and bending forward (flexion).

The normal curvature of the spine is convex through the thoracic portion and concave through the cervical and lumbar portions. The concavity of the lumbar spine is referred to as lumbar lordosis and is normal. Excessive curvature of the thoracic spine is called kyphosis. Deviation of the spine to the left or right is termed scoliosis. Kyphosis and scoliosis may result from damage to the paraspinal musculature in poliomyelitis or from disease of the vertebral column, as may be seen in tuberculosis.

DIAGNOSIS

Radiological Procedures

X-rays are important in evaluating patients with musculoskeletal disorders. Bone films determine bone density, texture, erosion and changes in bone relationships. Multiple X-ray views are needed for full assessment of the structure being examined. X-ray of the cortex of the bone reveals widening, narrowing and any signs of irregularity. Joint X-rays will reveal the presence of fluid, irregularity, spur formation, narrowing and changes in the joint structure.

Tomography shows in detail a specific plane of involved bone.

Computerized axial tomography can be useful in orthopaedic diagnosis by revealing tumours of the soft tissue or injuries to the ligaments or tendons. It is helpful in identifying the location and extent of fractures in areas difficult to define (e.g., the acetabulum).

Myelography, the injection of contrast medium into the subarachnoid space of the lumbar spine, is carried out to determine disc herniation, spinal stenosis (narrowing of the spinal canal) or the site of a tumour. This technique is discussed in Chapter 31.

Discography is a study of the intervertebral discs in which a contrast medium is injected into the disc and its distribution is noted.

Arteriography is a study of the arterial system. A radio-opaque contrast medium is injected into the selected artery, and serial films are taken of the supplied arterial system. It is useful for determining arterial perfusion and aids in determining the amount of extremity that needs to be amputated.

Arthrography is the injection of a radio-opaque substance or air into the joint cavity in order to outline soft tissue structures and the contour of the joint. The joint is put through its range of motion while a series of radiographs are taken. Arthrography is useful in identifying acute or chronic tears of the joint capsule or supporting ligaments of the knee, shoulder, ankle, hip or wrist. (If a tear is present, the contrast medium will leak out of the joint and show on X-ray.)

Other Studies

An arthrocentesis is carried out to obtain synovial fluid for purposes of examination. A needle is inserted into the joint, and fluid is then aspirated. Since this procedure has the potential for introducing bacteria into the joint, aseptic techniques must be followed. Following aspiration, no special precautions are necessary.

Normally, synovial fluid is clear, pale, straw-coloured and scanty in volume. The fluid is examined grossly for volume, colour, clarity, viscosity and formation of mucin clot. It is examined microscopically for cell count, cell identification, Gram's stain and formed elements. Examination of synovial fluid is helpful in the diagnosis of rheumatoid arthritis and other inflammatory arthropathies, and will reveal the presence of haemarthrosis (bleeding into the joint cavity), which suggests trauma or a tendency to bleed.

Arthroscopy is an endoscopic procedure that allows direct visualization of a joint. The procedure is carried out in the operating room, under sterile conditions and following the injection of a local anaesthetic into the joint or a general anaesthesia. A large-bore needle is inserted and the joint is distended with saline. The arthroscope is introduced and the knee joint visualized, including the synovium, articular surfaces and joint structures. If an arthrotomy is not indicated, the puncture wound is covered with a sterile sticking plaster and the extremity is wrapped from the midthigh to the midcalf with a compressive wrap that is worn for 24 to 48 hours for support. The joint is kept in extension and elevated to reduce swelling, and neurovascular function is evaluated periodically. The patient is advised to limit activity following the procedure. Complications are rare, but may include infection, haemarthrosis (blood in the joint cavity), thrombophlebitis, stiffness and delayed wound healing.

A bone scan reflects the degree to which the matrix of bone 'takes up' a bone-seeking radioactive isotope that is injected into the system. The degree of nuclide uptake is related to the metabolism of the bone. An increased uptake of isotope is seen in primary skeletal disease (osteosarcoma), metastatic bone disease, inflammatory skeletal disease (osteomyelitis) and certain types of fractures.

Thermography measures the degree of heat radiating from the skin surface. It is used to investigate the pathophysiology of inflamed joints (rheumatoid arthritis) and to assess the patient's response to anti-inflammatory drug therapy.

Electromyography provides information on the electric potential of the muscles and the nerves leading to them. The purpose of this procedure is to determine any abnormal physiology involving the motor unit. Needle electrodes are inserted into selected muscles, and responses to electrical stimuli are recorded on an oscilloscope.

Single and dual photon absorptiometry are noninvasive tests to determine bone mineral content in particular. Osteoporosis may be monitored with this type of densitometry.

Magnetic resonance imaging produces similar images to computerized axial tomography. Generally, it is a noninvasive technique used for the assessment of soft tissue lesions.

Bone biopsy may be done to determine the structure and composition of bone tissue, which may be helpful in diagnosing specific diseases.

Laboratory Studies

Examination of the patient's blood and urine can provide information concerning a primary musculoskeletal problem (e.g., Paget's disease), a developing complication (e.g., infection), baseline information for instituting therapy (e.g., anticoagulant therapy) or response to therapy. The complete blood count will provide information concerning the haemoglobin level (frequently lower after bleeding associated with trauma) and the white blood cell count. Before surgery, coagulation studies may be carried out to determine bleeding tendencies, because bone is a very vascular tissue. Blood chemistry studies provide data concerning a great variety of musculoskeletal conditions, including osteomalacia and muscle trauma. Alkaline phosphatase is elevated during fracture healing and in diseases with increased osteoblastic activity (e.g., osteomalacia, osteoblastic bone tumours). Urine calcium levels increase with bone destruction (e.g., metastatic bone tumours, multiple myeloma). Serum calcium levels increase with prolonged immobilization and diseases, including Paget's disease and metastatic cancers. Serum phosphorus levels are inversely related to calcium levels and are diminished in rickets associated with malabsorption syndrome. Serum enzyme levels of creatinine phosphokinase (CPK) and aspartate aminotransaminase (SGOT) become elevated with muscle damage.

NURSING PROCESS CONSIDERATIONS

The patient with a musculoskeletal problem will require support and nursing care during the period of examination and subsequent testing. There will be a need for physical and psychological preparation. Before any examinations, patient education (including what is to be done, why it is being done and what patient participation is expected) will help to reduce anxiety and enable the patient to be an active participant in care (Hayward, 1975).

The resulting diagnosis and prescribed treatment regime will affect the nursing management of the patient. The nursing plan of care will reflect nursing measures that will facilitate the resolution of the patient's problems.

The nursing assessment will enable the nurse to identify the health problems that can be improved by nursing interventions. Actual and potential nursing diagnoses common to patients with musculoskeletal disorders include the following:

- Impaired physical mobility.
- Alteration in comfort—pain.
- Impairment of skin integrity, actual or potential.
- Alteration in bowel elimination—constipation.
- Alteration in tissue perfusion—peripheral.
- Potential for infection.
- Lack of knowledge about the disease process and treatment regime.
- Inability to care for self.
- Disturbance in body image.
- Ineffective individual coping.
- Alteration in family/home process.
- Potential sexual dysfunction.
- Helplessness.
- Sleep pattern disturbance.
- Lack of diversional activities.
- Potential for alteration in nutrition—less than body requirements.

In collaboration with the patient, health goals and nursing strategies are formulated to achieve the expected outcomes and resolve the identified problems.

BIBLIOGRAPHY

Hayward, J. (1975) *Information—A Prescription Against Pain*, Royal College of Nursing, London.

FURTHER READING

Books

Adams, J. C. (1983) *Outline of Orthopaedics* (7th edition), Churchill Livingstone, London.
Arthroscopy of the Knee (Monograph) (1983) National Association of Orthopaedic Nurses, Pitman, New Jersey.
Bates, B. (1987) *A Guide to Physical Examination and History Taking* (4th edition) J. B. Lippincott, Philadelphia.
Birnbaum, J. S. (1982) *The Musculoskeletal Manual*, Academic Press, New York.
Dandy, D. J. (1989) *Essential Orthopaedics and Trauma*, Churchill Livingstone, Edinburgh.
Farrell, J. (1986) *Illustrated Guide to Orthopedic Nursing* (3rd edition), J. B. Lippincott, Philadelphia.
Malasanos, L. *et al.* (1981) *Health Assessment* (2nd edition), C. V. Mosby, St Louis.
McRae, R. (1983) *Clinical Orthopaedic Examination* (2nd edition), Churchill Livingstone, New York.
Pellino, T. *et al.* (eds) (1986) Anthony J. Jannetti in *National Association of Orthopedic Nurses: Core Curriculum for Orthopaedic Nursing*, Pitman, New Jersey.
Rockwood, C. A. and Green, D. P. (eds) (1984) *Fractures in Adults* (2nd edition), J. B. Lippincott, Philadelphia.
Sculco, T. P. (ed) (1985) *Orthopedic Care of the Geriatric Patient*, C. V. Mosby, St Louis.
Tortora, G. J. and Anagnostakos, N. P. (1987) *Principles of Anatomy and Physiology* (5th edition), Harper & Row, New York.
Turek, S. L. (1984) *Orthopedics: Principles and Their Application* (4th edition), J. B. Lippincott, Philadelphia.

Articles

Aggleton, P. and Chalmers, H. (1985) Models and theories 7: Henderson's model, *Nursing Times*, Vol. 81, No. 10, pp. 33–5
Burggraf, V. and Donlon, B. (1985) Assessing the elderly, Part 1: System by system, *American Journal of Nursing*, Vol. 85, No. 9, pp. 974–84.
Dunn, B. H. (1982) Musculoskeletal assessment: Components of the musculoskeletal examination, *Orthopedic Nursing*, Nov/Dec, Vol. 1, No. 6, pp. 33–7.
Dunn, B. H. (1983) Musculoskeletal assessment: Gait assessment. *Orthopedic Nursing*, May/June, Vol. 1, No. 3, pp. 33–6.
Farrell, J. (1984) Orthopedic pain: What does it mean? *American Journal of Nursing*, Vol. 84, No. 4, pp. 466–9.
Henderson, M. L. (1985) Assessing the elderly, Part 2: Altered presentations, *American Journal of Nursing*, Vol. 85, No. 10, pp. 1103–11.
Jones-Walton, P. (91984) Orthopedic health promotion: Injury and disability prevention, *Orthopedic Nursing*, Nov/Dec; Vol. 3, No. 6, pp. 35–42.
Kleinstuber, M. and Reed, D. (1985) Performing knee arthroscopy under local anesthesia, *Today's OR Nurs*, Nov, Vol. 7, No. 11, pp. 22–7.
Kostopoulos, M. R. (1985) Reducing patient falls, *Orthopedic Nursing*, Nov/Dec, Vol. 4, No. 6, pp. 14–15.
Ross, D. G. (1983) Musculoskeletal assessment: The knee, *Orthopedic Nursing*, Sept/Oct, Vol. 2, No. 5, pp. 23–8.
Unbanski, P. A. (1984) The orthopedic patient: Identifying neurovascular injury, *Journal of American Operating Room Nurses*, Nov, Vol. 40, No. 11, pp. 707–11.
Vanderbeck, K. A. (1984) Getting the facts: A guide to orthopaedic assessment, *Orthopedic Nursing*, Sept/Oct, Vol. 3, No. 5, pp. 31–4.
Woolf, A. D. and Dixon, A. StJ. (1984) Osteoporosis—an update on management, *Drugs*, Vol. 28, No. 5, pp. 565–76.

chapter 35

ASSESSMENT AND CARE OF PATIENTS WITH MUSCULOSKELETAL DYSFUNCTION

NURSING PROCESS OVERVIEW

► Assessment

The nursing assessment of the patient with musculoskeletal dysfunction includes an evaluation of the impact of the musculoskeletal problem on the patient. The nurse is concerned with assisting people with musculoskeletal problems to maintain their general health, accomplish their activities of daily living and manage their treatment. Systemic homeostasis is assured; optimum nutrition is encouraged; and problems related to immobility are prevented. The nurse helps the patient achieve a balance between periods of exercise and rest through an individualized plan of care, using an appropriate nursing model.

In the initial interview, the nurse obtains a general impression of the patient's status. A general inspection of the body will reveal the existence of any gross deformity, asymmetry of contours or size, swelling, oedema, bruising or breaks in the skin. Observing the patient's posture, movement and gait will provide information concerning alterations in ability to move, the existence of discomfort or the presence of involuntary movements (fasciculations or twitches). The nurse will gather information concerning existing concurrent health problems, the patient's perceptions and expectations related to the health problems and socioeconomic factors that may affect restoration of wellbeing.

History

The nurse needs to obtain subjective data from the patient concerning the onset of the problem and how it has been managed to this point. The existence of other health problems (e.g., diabetes, heart disease, a cold) needs to be noted for consideration when developing the plan of care. A history of medication use and response to analgesia will aid in designing future drug management regimes. Allergies are noted and should include the type of reaction the patient has experienced. The use of tobacco, alcohol and other drugs should be assessed in order to evaluate the effects of these habits on the patient's needs. Details of the patient's ability to learn, economic status and current occupation are needed for discharge planning and for rehabilitation. Additions to the initial interview data will be made as the nurse interacts with the patient. Such data allows for any adjustment of the patient's individualized plan of care.

Physical Assessment

Much information about the structure and functioning of the musculoskeletal system can be obtained by physical assessment. The nurse is interested in identifying the functional abilities of the patient and the effects that any disabilities and medical treatment have on the patient's ability to meet needs effectively. The patient's posture and gait, bone stability, joint function, muscle integrity and strength and ability to perform activities of daily living are assessed. Any deviations from normal are noted. Throughout the initial assessment, the nurse establishes a baseline for noting and evaluating changes in the person's abilities.

Assessment of Bony Skeleton

The bony skeleton is assessed for deformities and alignment. Abnormal bony growths due to bone tumours may be observed. Shortened extremities, amputations and body parts out of anatomical alignment are noted. Loss of height occurs with loss of vertebral cartilage in the aged.

Possible common deformities of the spine that may be noted include scoliosis (a lateral curving deviation of the spine), kyphosis (an increased roundness of the thoracic spine curve) and lordosis (swayback; exaggeration of the lumbar spine curve). Kyphosis is frequently seen in the elderly patient.

Abnormal angulation of long bone or motion at points other than joints is frequently indicative of fracture. Crepitus (grating sensation) at the point of abnormal motion may also be detected. Movement of bony fragments must be minimized to avoid additional injury.

Assessment of Articular System

The articular system is evaluated by noting joint swelling, nodule formation, deformity, stability and range of motion. Joint swelling might be noted with arthritis, inflammation or effusion (fluid accumulated in the joint capsule). Rheumatoid arthritis, gout and osteoarthritis produce characteristic nodules. Hard, painless, overgrowth nodules associated with osteoarthritis are frequently seen in older adults.

Joint deformity may indicate contracture (shortening of surrounding joint structures), dislocation (complete separation of joint surfaces), subluxation (partial separation of articular surfaces) or disruption of structures surrounding the joint. Weakness or disruption of joint-supporting structures may result in a joint that is too weak to function as designed and may therefore require external supporting appliances. Range of motion is evaluated both actively (joint is moved by the muscles surrounding the joint) and passively (joint is moved by the examiner).

Assessment of Muscular System

The muscular system is assessed by noting the patient's ability to change position, muscular strength and co-ordination, and individual muscle size. Muscular weakness of a group of muscles might indicate a variety of conditions, such as polyneuropathy, electrolyte disturbances (particularly potassium and calcium), myasthenia gravis, poliomyelitis and muscular dystrophy. By palpating the muscle while passively moving the relaxed extremity, the nurse can determine muscle tone. Muscle strength can be estimated by asking the patient to perform certain tasks with and without added resistance. For example, the biceps can be tested by requesting the patient to fully extend the arm and then flex it while the nurse applies resistance to prevent the arm from flexing. A simple handshake provides an indication of grasp strength.

Assessment of Skin and Peripheral Circulation

In addition to the musculoskeletal system, the nurse must inspect the skin and assess peripheral circulation. Cuts, bruises, skin colour and evidence of decreased circulation or infection can influence nursing care. Feeling the skin can reveal if any areas are warmer or cooler than others and if oedema is present. Peripheral circulation is evaluated by assessing peripheral pulses, colour, temperature and capillary refill time.

Subjective Assessment Data

During the interview and physical assessment, the patient may report the presence of pain, tenderness, tightness and abnormal sensations. This information needs to be noted and assessed.

Pain

Most patients with diseases and traumatic conditions of muscles, bones and joints experience pain. Bone pain is characteristically described as a dull, deep ache that is boring in nature, whereas muscular pain is considered sore and aching and is frequently referred to as 'muscle cramps'. Fracture pain is sharp and piercing and is relieved by immobilization. Sharp pain may also result from bone infection with muscle spasm or pressure on a sensory nerve.

Most musculoskeletal pain is relieved by rest. Pain that increases with activity may indicate joint sprain or muscle strain, while steadily increasing pain points to a progression of an infectious process (osteomyelitis), a malignant tumour or vascular complications. Radiating pain is seen in conditions in which pressure is exerted on a nerve root. Pain is variable, and its assessment and nursing management must be individualized by incorporating the use of pain assessment scales and charts (Davies, 1985).

Assessment of Pain

- What was the patient doing before the complaint of pain?
- Is the body in proper alignment?
- Is there pressure from traction, bed linen, a cast or other appliances?
- Is the position of a muscle mass causing tension on the skin at a pin site?
- Is the patient over-tired due to lack of sleep, exciting stimuli or too much activity?
- Can the pain be localized?
- How does the patient describe it?
- What was the manner of onset?
- Is there radiation of pain? If so, in what direction does it occur?
- Is there pain in any other part of the body?
- What is the character of the pain (sharp, dull, boring, shooting, throbbing, cramping)?
- Is it constant?
- What relieves it?
- What makes it worse?

Pain and discomfort are important to the patient and must be managed successfully. Not only is pain exhausting, but if prolonged it can force the patient to become increasingly preoccupied and dependent.

Altered Sensations

Sensory disturbances are frequently associated with musculoskeletal problems. The patient may describe the presence of paraesthesias (burning or tingling sensations) and numbness. These sensations may be due to pressure on nerves or circulatory impairment. Soft tissue swelling or direct trauma to these structures can impair their function. Assessment of the neurovascular status of the involved musculoskeletal area provides information for management. Loss of function can result from impaired nerves and circulatory structures located throughout the musculoskeletal system.

Assessment of Neurovascular Integrity

- Is the patient experiencing any abnormal sensations or numbness?
- When did this begin? Is it getting worse?
- Is the patient also experiencing pain?
- What is the colour of the part distal to the problem? Pale? Dusky? Cyanotic?
- Is there a pulse present distal to the problem?
- Is there rapid capillary refill? (Compress the patient's nail and release. When pressure is released, the colour of the nailbed should quickly assume a pink hue.)
- Is the motor component of the nerve intact? Is the patient able to move the innervated part?
- Is oedema present?
- Is any constrictive device or clothing causing nerve or vascular compression?
- Is it relieved by elevation of the affected part or modification of position?

► Planning and Implementation
► Expected Outcomes

The major outcomes for the patient with musculoskeletal dysfunction may include reduced anxiety, understanding of the therapeutic regime, relief of discomfort and improved physical mobility.

Nursing Care

Reducing Anxiety

Musculoskeletal problems may be due to an acute traumatic injury or may be of a persistent, recurrent, long-term nature. The psychological and social/economic impact of the problem causes a variety of reactions in these patients. The nurse needs to assist the patient in coping with the problems associated with musculoskeletal dysfunction and the associated therapies.

Most patients with acute musculoskeletal problems are anxious and have pain. People who have long-term disabilities often experience repeated reconstructive operations. They are familiar with the routines of the hospital and are concerned with the ultimate outcome of the procedure. Their patience and hope may be limited. People with musculoskeletal problems need an understanding, supportive nurse.

Patient Education. One way to aid these patients is to prepare them for the anticipated therapeutic approach. If patients are given information concerning preparatory measures and are involved in this preparation, they will be more inclined to accept the care given. Information about what to expect during and following the therapy will encourage active participation in treatment and care. When possible, specific information concerning anticipated equipment (e.g., casts, traction), mobilization aids (e.g., trapeze, crutches), exercises (e.g., quadriceps setting, deep breathing) and medications (e.g., analgesics, antibiotics) should be shared with the patient. Cognitive preparation decreases anxiety and alerts patients as to what is expected of them and what is usually involved in recovery. Patients can practise recuperative activities, such as using a urinal in a recumbent position, before they are immobilized and need to tend to basic bodily functions in unusual positions.

Relieving Pain and Discomfort

Patients who have bone and joint problems frequently experience severe pain. Often the person who has undergone surgery to correct a foot condition is much more uncomfortable than one who has had extensive abdominal surgery. Narcotics and other pain-relieving measures are given as prescribed, taking into consideration the type and the site of the musculoskeletal problem, the patient's age and the anticipated duration of treatment.

Pain may result from associated problems rather than from the primary musculoskeletal problem. When it occurs under restrictive bandages or casts, the blood supply may be diminished and excruciating pain may result. Swelling will occur distal to the constriction. Capillary refill will be diminished, as evidenced by gently squeezing a fingernail or toenail until it blanches, and then releasing pressure and noting the time it takes for the normal colour to return. (Colour normally returns quickly, within about three seconds.) The skin will feel cool to the touch and will appear dusky, pale or blue. Sensory or motor function may be altered or diminished.

Usually, swelling can be controlled and prevented by elevating the injured part slightly above the level of the heart and intermittently applying an ice pack to the injury for 20 to 30 minutes.

Prolonged pressure over bony prominences (e.g., heel, head of fibula, tibial tuberosity) may cause a burning type of pain. Relieving the pressure is necessary to relieve the pain and prevent further tissue damage.

Muscle spasm is another associated cause of pain. When a muscle is injured, the natural response of the muscle is to contract, thereby splinting and protecting the injured area. Prolonged muscle contraction is painful. Relaxation techniques, traction or medications may be used to reduce pain from muscle spasm.

Additional information and guidelines to nursing care of the patient with pain are presented in Chapter 2.

Improving Mobility and Patient Rehabilitation

Throughout the treatment period, the nurse is concerned with health maintenance and maximal restoration of function. The immobility necessitated by some treatments must not result in undue deterioration. Exercise of non-immobilized muscles and joints helps maintain their strength and function, minimizes cardiovascular deterioration and prevents disuse osteoporosis. Isometric exercises of immobilized extremities help to maintain muscle strength.

Involvement in activities of daily living (e.g., hygiene, dressing, eating) provides a sense of independence and accomplishment. Co-ordinating nursing interventions with special therapy approaches (e.g., physiotherapy, occupational therapy) makes it easier for the patient to learn and practise the therapeutic regimes. Emphasis is placed on what the patient is able to do within the limits of the treatment and care.

Before the time of discharge, patients should have explicit advice that they understand, indicating those activities they may and may not perform. It is not enough to bid them 'goodbye, and take things easy'. Patients must know any untoward signs and symptoms that should be reported to the doctor. They must be aware of the importance of follow-up visits. If they have any difficulties, they ought to know where and how to get help. The nurse has a major part of the responsibility for educating these patients before they leave the hospital.

► *Evaluation*
► **Expected Outcomes**

1. Patient exhibits minimal anxiety.
   a. Appears relaxed and confident in abilities.
   b. Uses effective coping strategies.
   c. Participates in care.
2. Relates plan for continued health management.
   a. Describes planned treatment regime.
   b. States signs and symptoms to report to doctor.
   c. Makes appointment for follow-up care.
3. Achieves comfort.
   a. Controls discomfort with occasional oral medications.
   b. Moves with minimal discomfort.
   c. Uses positioning to increase comfort.
4. Demonstrates improved physical mobility.
   a. Transfers self independently or with minimal assistance.
   b. Participates in activities of daily living.
   c. Uses mobility aids safely.

CARE OF THE PATIENT IN A CAST

A cast is a rigid external immobilizing device that is moulded to the contours of the body to which it is applied. The purpose of a cast is to immobilize a body part in a specific position and to apply uniform pressure on encased soft tissue. It may be used to immobilize a reduced fracture, correct a deformity, apply uniform pressure to underlying soft tissue or provide support and stability for weakened joints. Generally, casts permit mobilization of the patient while restricting movement of some body part.

Types of Casts

The condition being treated influences the type and thickness of the cast applied. Generally speaking, the joints proximal and distal to the area to be immobilized are included in the cast. However, with some fractures, cast construction and moulding may allow movement of a joint while immobilizing a fracture (e.g., three-point fixation in a patellar tendon weight-bearing cast).

Figure 35.1 illustrates some of the common types of cylindrical casts and areas in which pressure problems commonly occur.

Short arm cast—extends from below the elbow to the proximal palmar crease, secured around the base of the thumb. If the thumb is included, it is known as a thumb spica or gauntlet cast.

Long arm cast—extends from the upper level of the axillary fold to the proximal palmar crease; the elbow usually is immobilized at a right angle.

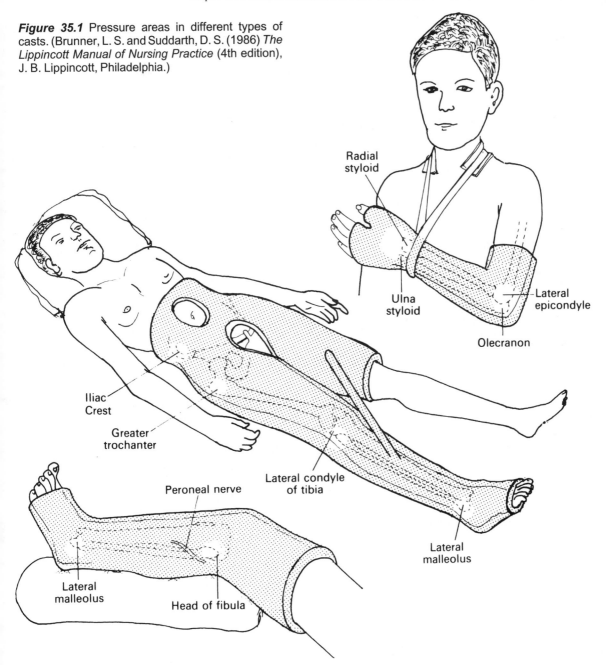

Figure 35.1 Pressure areas in different types of casts. (Brunner, L. S. and Suddarth, D. S. (1986) *The Lippincott Manual of Nursing Practice* (4th edition), J. B. Lippincott, Philadelphia.)

Short leg cast—extends from below the knee to the base of the toes. The foot is at a right angle in a neutral position.
Long leg cast—extends from the junction of the upper and middle third of the thigh to the base of the toes. The knee should be slightly flexed.
Walking cast—a short- or long-leg cast reinforced for strength. (May incorporate a walking heel.)
Plaster jacket—encircles the trunk.
Spica cast—incorporates a portion of the trunk and one or two extremities (single or double spica cast).

● Shoulder spica cast—a body jacket that encloses the trunk and the shoulder and elbow.
● Hip spica cast—encloses the trunk and a lower extremity; may be a single or double hip spica cast.

Casting Materials

Plaster

The traditional cast is made of plaster of Paris (POP). Plaster bandages mould very smoothly to the body contours. Rolls of crinoline are impregnated with powdered, anhydrous calcium sulphate (gypsum crystals). When wet, a crystallizing reaction occurs and heat is given off (an exothermic reaction).

● The heat given off during this reaction may be uncomfortable for the patient.

This crystallization produces a rigid dressing. The speed at which the reaction occurs varies from a few minutes to 15 to 20 minutes, dependent upon the temperature of the water used. The cooler the water, the longer the crystallization process.

After the plaster has set, the cast is still wet and somewhat soft. It does not have its full strength until dry. While damp, it can be dented if handled with the fingertips instead of the palms of the hand or if allowed to rest on hard surfaces or sharp edges. These dents may produce pressure sores on the skin under the cast. The cast requires 24 to 72 hours to dry, depending on the thickness of the cast and the environmental drying conditions. A freshly applied cast should be exposed to circulating air to dry. Covers restrict the escape of moisture. A dry cast is white and shiny, resonant and odourless as well as firm; a wet cast is grey and dull in appearance, is dull to percussion, feels damp and has a musty odour.

Nonplaster

Generally referred to as fibreglass casts, these water-activated polyurethane materials have the versatility of plaster and the additional advantages of being of lighter weight and increased strength, water-resistant and durable. They are made of an open-weave, nonabsorbent fabric impregnated with hardeners that reach full rigid strength in minutes.

Nonplaster casts are porous and therefore diminish skin problems. They do not soften when wet, which allows for hydrotherapy (use of water for treatment). When wet, some are dried with a hair drier on a cool setting. Thorough drying is important to prevent skin breakdown.

Splints and Braces

Contoured splints of plaster or pliable thermoplastic materials may be used for conditions that do not require rigid immobilization or for those in which swelling may be anticipated. The splints need to provide for adequate immobilization. They should be designed to support the body part in a functional position. The splints must be well padded to prevent pressure, skin abrasion and skin breakdown. To avoid burns from the exothermic reaction of the plaster, cool water is used to make the splint and the heat is allowed to dissipate before the splint is overwrapped with an elastic bandage. The bandage is applied in a spiral fashion, and the pressure is uniform so that the circulation is not restricted. The circulatory

status of the splinted extremity is assessed frequently by the nurse.

For long-term use, braces (orthoses) are designed to provide support, control movement and prevent additional injury. They are custom-fitted to various parts of the body, such as the back of leg. Braces may be constructed of plastic materials or of metal and leather. The orthotist adjusts the brace for fit, positioning and permitted mobility. The nurse helps the patient learn how to apply the brace and how to protect the skin from irritation and breakdown. The nurse assesses the patient's neurovascular integrity and comfort when wearing the brace. The patient needs to be encouraged to wear the brace as prescribed and to be assured that minor adjustments of the brace by the orthotist will increase comfort and minimize problems associated with the long-term use of the brace.

Cast Application

It is important to prepare the patient for the application of any cast. The patient needs to know what to expect during application, and that the casted body part will be immobilized following application. The patient is positioned to facilitate casting and is draped to prevent undue exposure and to prevent the plaster materials from coming in contact with other body parts. The anatomical part should be supported adequately when the cast is applied in order to increase the patient's comfort and maintain reduction and alignment.

The part to be casted should be clean and dry. Skin abrasions, if present, need to be cleaned and dressed before cast application. When the skin has been prepared, a knitted material (e.g., stockinette) is placed over the part to be casted. This material needs to be applied smoothly and in a nonconstrictive manner. Enough material is cut to allow the ends to be folded over the nearly finished cast to provide a smooth, padded edge. Soft, nonwoven, rolled padding is then wrapped smoothly and evenly around the part. Extra padding is placed around bony prominences and at nerve grooves (e.g., head of fibula, olecranon process). Nonabsorbent materials are used with nonplaster casts.

When padding is adequate, the casting material is applied. The plaster and nonplaster materials come in bandaging rolls of various widths to facilitate smooth, contoured application. The bandage is applied evenly on the extremity, turn upon turn, with each turn overlapping the preceding turn by one half the width of the roll. The motion is continuous, without pause, while the bandage is maintained in constant contact with the extremity. The turns or layers of the bandage are smoothed and rubbed to form a smooth, solid and well-contoured cast. Proper shaping of the cast to the body part is required for adequate support. At the joints and at points of anticipated cast stress, additional casting material is incorporated for additional strength.

During the application, care is taken to ensure that the anatomical part is immobilized in the desired position. Improper extremity position can result in contracture or malunion of fractures.

To enhance comfort and the patient's ability to participate in activities, the cast must be 'finished' properly. The edges need to be smooth and padded to prevent skin abrasion. Full range of motion of joints adjacent to the immobilized part needs to be assured. Before the patient's discharge, the cast can be trimmed and reshaped with a cast knife or manual cutters, if necessary, to allow for full motion and to eliminate any restriction due to the cast.

Plaster materials that have adhered to the skin during application are removed. If not cleaned off, these will loosen, crumble and slide underneath the cast, causing discomfort and possible skin breakdown.

▶ NURSING PROCESS
▶ THE PATIENT IN A CAST

▶ *Assessment*

The main concern following the application of a cast is to avoid complications. Experience has taught that any complaint of discomfort must not go unheeded. Two types of complications occur: constriction of circulation and pressure on tissues and bony parts.

Trauma or surgery affecting an extremity will produce swelling as a result of haemorrhage from bone and surrounding tissue and from tissue oedema. Vascular insufficiency and nerve compression due to unrelieved swelling can reduce or cut off blood supply to an extremity and result in peripheral nerve damage.

The nurse monitors for pain, swelling, discolouration (paleness or blueness), tingling or numbness, diminished or absent pulses, paralysis and coldness of the extremity. Signs of circulatory impairment are noted by assessing the toes or fingers of a leg or arm that has recently been placed in a cast. The toes and fingers should be pink in colour and warm to the touch. The capillary refill response is another means of assessing circulatory insufficiency. The nailbeds and the fleshy pulp of toes/fingers are pressed lightly and then released to check how quickly colour returns. The colour should return rapidly, indicating good perfusion. A blue tinge to the toes or fingers suggests venous obstruction, while white and cold fingers or toes suggest arterial obstruction. The temperature of the injured extremity is compared with that of the uninjured one, as are the pulses. Nerve status is assessed by asking the patient about sensations in the toes/fingers and ability to move (wiggle) toes/fingers. Inability to move the fingers or toes, pain on extension of the hand or foot and coldness of an extremity indicate ischaemia. If there is swelling, the cast will seem tight to the patient.

Prolonged pressure of the cast on neurovascular structures and bony structures causes necrosis, pressure sores

and nerve palsies or paralysis, such as may occur when a leg cast damages a peroneal nerve. A severe initial pain over bony prominences is a warning symptom of an impending pressure sore. Pain decreases when ulceration occurs. The nurse also monitors for an odour emanating from the cast and observes for discharge staining on the cast.

Sites most susceptible to pressure on the lower extremity are the heel, malleoli, dorsum of the foot, head of the fibula and anterior surface of the patella. On the upper extremity, the main pressure sites are located at the medial epicondyle of the humerus and the ulnar styloid (see Figure 35.1).

▶ *Patient's Problems*

Based on all the assessment data, the patient's identified problems may include the following:

● Alteration in comfort (pain; paraesthesias) related to cast pressure.
● Alteration in tissue perfusion (peripheral) related to cast pressure.
● Potential alteration in skin integrity related to cast pressure.
● Impaired physical mobility related to presence of cast.
● Lack of knowledge about cast management.

▶ *Planning and Implementation*
▶ Expected Outcomes

The outcomes for the patient may include achievement of comfort, attainment of tissue perfusion, attainment of skin integrity, achievement of mobility and acquiring knowledge of cast management.

Nursing Care

Promoting Comfort, Tissue Perfusion and Skin Integrity

Although it takes minutes for a cast to harden, it will take 24 to 72 hours for the plaster cast to dry and achieve maximum strength. A moist cast must be handled with the palms of the hands and should not rest on a hard surface or sharp edge, which may dent the cast and cause pressure areas.

The affected extremity is elevated above the level of the heart, if practical, on cloth-covered pillows to control swelling. The patient is encouraged to wiggle fingers/toes. If any symptom such as blueness/paleness of fingernails/toenails accompanied by pain and tightness, numbness, cold or tingling sensations occurs, the doctor should be notified. The capillary refill response is checked frequently for signs of circulatory impairment.

If the patient complains of pain, analgesics are not given until the cause of pain is determined. The first step in determining the cause is to ask the patient to indicate the exact site of pain.

● Do not ignore the complaints of pain of the patient in a cast: suspect circulatory complications or a pressure sore.

If the patient continues to have pain, the cast may be exerting pressure on a nerve, blood vessels or bony prominences.

● Unrelieved pain, excessive swelling, poor capillary refill response or inability to move toes/fingers must be reported to the doctor immediately to avoid possible paralysis and necrosis.
● If constriction of circulation is suspected, the cast may need to be bivalved (cut in half) to relieve pressure. Bivalving a cast does not disturb the alignment of the fracture.

The procedure for bivalving a cast is as follows:

1. Two longitudinal cuts are made in the cast, dividing it into two halves.
2. The underlying padding is also cut, since blood-soaked padding may shrink and constrict the circulation.
3. The cast is spread apart sufficiently to relieve constriction.
4. The anterior and posterior parts of the cast may be held together with a supportive bandage.
5. After the cast is bivalved, the extremity is elevated until the circulation is restored, swelling diminishes, and pain is relieved.

Another method of checking the cause for discomfort or for viewing a surgical wound is to cut an opening or 'a window' in the cast. This procedure is achieved by cutting a small oblong or square piece out of the cast, which can then be removed and replaced. Any padding below the plaster at this point must also be cut and removed. After the window is opened, a soft pad is inserted into the opening and the 'window' is replaced with tape to prevent the underlying tissue from swelling through the window and forming pressure areas around its margins.

The skin around the cast edges is inspected periodically for signs of irritation. Rough edges of the cast may be covered with tape to protect the skin.

Promoting Mobility

While in a cast, the patient should be taught to tense or contract muscles without moving the joints. The patient may actually forget how to 'will' a motion through the central nervous system pathways to the immobilized muscle. Therefore, isometric muscle contractions (contracting the muscle without moving the part) may be carried out to prevent atrophy and maintain muscle strength. Isometric contractions should be done at least hourly while the patient is awake.

● If the patient has a leg cast, ask the patient to 'push down' so that the knee touches the bed mattress or 'back' of the immobilizing cast.

● If the patient has an arm cast, encourage them to 'make a fist'.

Every joint that is not immobilized may be exercised. The patient is encouraged to exercise toes/fingers frequently and actively. Encourage the patient to participate in goal-setting and self-care activities. It is important that the patient remain actively involved so that any untoward psychological reaction (e.g., depression) associated with immobility, dependence and loss of control is avoided.

Patient Education

When the cast is dry, the patient should be advised as follows:

1. Maintain acts of living as normally as possible. Avoid excessive use of the injured extremity.
2. Continue any prescribed exercises regularly.
3. Elevate the casted extremity above heart level frequently to reduce the risk of swelling.
4. Keep the cast dry.
   a. Wetness diminishes the effectiveness of plaster casts.
      i. Do not cover the cast with plastic or rubber, as this causes condensation and wetting of the cast.
      ii. Avoid walking on wet floors or pavements.
   b. Fibreglass casts, after being wet, must be dried thoroughly with a hair drier on a cool setting to avoid skin problems.
5. Cushion rough edges of the cast with tape.
6. Report to your general practitioner if the cast breaks; do not attempt to fix it yourself.
7. Do not attempt to scratch the skin under the cast. This may cause a break in the skin and result in the formation of a cast sore. Cooler air may alleviate an itch.
8. Note odours about the cast, Stained cast areas, warm spots and pressure spots. Report them to the general practitioner.
9. Report to the general practitioner: persistent pain, swelling that does not respond to elevation, changes in sensation, decreased ability to move exposed fingers/ toes and changes in skin colour and temperature.

Note: Verbal advice to patients and their relatives or other carers should be reinforced by the provision of written instructions from the nurse before discharge.

Removing a Cast

Plaster of Paris casts may be removed with either a cast cutter—an electric saw with an oscillating circular blade—or cast shears. The usual method of cutting a cast is to bivalve it. If the saw is to be used (by an experienced or supervised nurse), the patient should have the procedure fully explained before it is started, and be assured that the saw blade will not cut the skin. Alternatively, when the shears are used, a full explanation of the procedure must be given, and any anticipated sensations by the patient of pressure on the affected limb must be highlighted. To conclude the procedure, any padding is cut with orthopaedic scissors.

Management of the Patient After the Cast is Removed. Remember when a cast is removed that the part or parts involved have probably been immobilized for a considerable period of time. When the support and protection of the cast have been removed, stresses and strains are placed on parts that have been at rest. The patient may complain of pain and stiffness, often very different from the original injury, and may be discouraged and depressed because the anticipated release from the cast has apparently only added problems to the situation.

To help the patient adjust to this new discomfort, the nurse may support the part so that it is maintained in the same position as when in the cast. A small pillow can be used to support the knee, the lumbar spine and similar body parts. The support is then gradually removed. When the extremity is moved, adequate support must be provided.

Exercises are prescribed to redevelop and to increase strength. The patient who has been doing isometric muscle contractions will not have to relearn to contract the muscles and will progress more rapidly with the rehabilitation programme.

Once the cast is removed, there will be a considerable amount of desquamated epithelium (dead skin) that may adhere to the skin surface. The skin is washed carefully and gently dried, and some type of emollient lotion may be applied. The patient should be cautioned against rubbing or scratching the skin, which could cause a break in the skin.

Atrophy of the part may be noted, but this diminishes gradually with the return of muscle function. Swelling after a cast is removed is common, and is treated by elevating and supporting the tissues with compression bandages or a support stocking.

If a new cast is to be applied, the patient's skin should be washed and dried carefully. The patient will need to be reminded again of the care of wet casts, continued neurovascular observations and general cast care advice.

Patient Education After Cast Removal
1. Cleanse the skin gently with soap and water. Dry gently.
2. Apply emollient lotion. Avoid scratching the skin.
3. Resume activities and exercise gradually.
4. Control swelling by elevating the extremity above heart level, and use compression bandages as directed.

► *Evaluation*
► **Expected Outcomes**

1. Patient maintains adequate circulation to extremity.
   a. Is free of pain.
   b. Has normal skin colour.
   c. Demonstrates skin temperature of injured extremity

that is similar to that of uninjured extremity.
   d. Achieves satisfactory capillary refill on testing.
2. Shows no signs of necrosis, pressure sores or nerve paralysis.
   a. Is free of pain over bony prominences.
   b. Demonstrates normal sensory and motor function of injured extremity.
   c. Shows no evidence of musty cast odours, cast staining or warm spots within cast.
   d. Exhibits intact skin at time of cast removal.
3. Has adequate knowledge about therapeutic regime.
   a. Elevates extremity that is in the cast.
   b. Exercises according to advice.
   c. Keeps cast dry.
   d. Reports any problems that develop.
   e. Keeps follow-up clinic or general practitioner appointments.

Arm Casts

The patient whose arm is immobilized in a cast must readjust to many activities of daily living. The unaffected arm must assume all the upper extremity activities. The patient may experience muscle fatigue due to the additional activities and the weight of the cast. Frequent rest periods are therefore encouraged.

To diminish and control swelling when the patient is lying down, the arm should be elevated, with each joint positioned higher than the preceding proximal joint (e.g., hand higher than the elbow). When the patient becomes ambulatory, a sling may be used to minimize venous congestion and oedema. The patient should be encouraged to remove the arm from the sling frequently and to extend it above the head.

Slings should distribute the supported weight over a large area and not on the back of the neck. Triangular slings, when used, need to be pinned at the sides and not tied with a knot behind the neck, to prevent pressure on cervical spinal nerves.

Circulatory disturbances in the hand may become apparent with signs of cyanosis, swelling and an inability to move the fingers.

Leg Casts

The application of a leg cast imposes a degree of immobility on the patient. The leg cast may be short, extending to the knee, or long, extending to the groin.

As with other cast applications, the leg must be assessed for swelling, adequate circulation and normal nerve function. The immobilized leg is supported initially on soft pillows to control swelling. Ice packs may be applied over the fracture site for the first 24 to 48 hours. Any reported numbness, tingling or burning sensations in the foot may be due to peroneal nerve injury from pressure at the head of the fibula.

● Injury to the peroneal nerve as a result of pressure is a common cause of footdrop.

When the cast is dry, the patient is taught how to transfer and ambulate safely with walking aids (e.g., crutches). The gait to be used depends on whether or not the patient's problem allows weight-bearing. If weight-bearing is allowed, the cast will be reinforced and a walking heel (a rubber pad) may be incorporated into the bottom of the cast, or the patient may be given a cast boot to wear over the casted foot (Figure 35.2). Cast boots are preferred to walking heels because they provide a broader support surface and do not disturb the patient's balance or posture by elevating the injured leg.

After ambulation begins, elevation of the cast should be encouraged when the patient is seated. Several times during the day, the patient should lie down, because a sitting position does not promote complete venous drainage.

Functional Bracing

A cast brace is a special type of cast in which hinges are incorporated to allow for joint motion while maintaining adequate alignment and immobilization (Figure 35.3). Some cast braces are constructed with hinges at the hip, knee, ankle, elbow or wrist. Most frequently, cast braces are used when femoral shaft fractures demonstrate some healing and little thigh swelling. Usually, the patient has been in skeletal traction for a few weeks before cast brace application.

Fracture healing is often enhanced with cast braces. Weight-bearing (stress) stimulates bone healing. In addition, the cast brace produces hydraulic pressure on the soft tissues, which facilitates fracture healing (Bastiani, Aldegheri and Brivio, 1984).

The patient managed with a cast brace is better able to

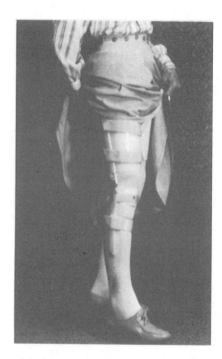

Figure 35.3 A type of cast brace. This moulded plastic knee–ankle–foot orthosis with total contact femoral section orthosis is useful when long-term (greater than six-month) immobilization is required. It is removable by the patient. (Courtesy of the University of Texas Southwestern Medical Center at Dallas.)

maintain physiological homeostasis. Rehabilitation is promoted by maintaining muscle strength and joint mobility. After the cast is dry (about 48 hours for plaster cast braces), the patient can ambulate with crutches, progressing from partial to full weight-bearing on the fractured extremity.

Problems that the patient may have after cast brace application include angulation deformity of the fracture site (malalignment of bone resulting in a bend in the bone), oedema at the knee, skin breakdown on the thigh as a result of pressure from the edge of the cast and soiling of the thigh cast. The patient is monitored for excessive swelling, neurovascular problems and skin breakdown. Since the cast may extend to the groin, measures should be taken to protect this area of the cast from becoming soiled with urine and faeces. To promote venous return, lower limbs in cast braces should be elevated when the patient is not walking.

Body or Spica Casts

Casts that encase the trunk (body cast) and portions of the trunk and one or two extremities (spica cast) require special nursing techniques. Body casts may be used in situations requiring spinal immobilization. Hip spicas are used for

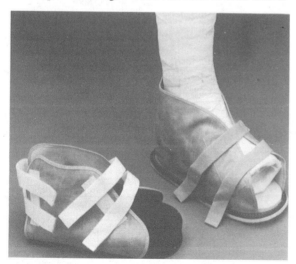

Figure 35.2 Two types of cast boots. (Courtesy Sroufe Manufacturing Inc., Ligonier, Indiana.)

patients following femoral fractures and some hip joint surgeries. Shoulder spica casts are used for some humeral neck fractures. Patient preparation, turning and skin and hygienic care are the nurse's primary concerns.

Preparing the patient for the casting by explaining the procedure will help reduce the patient's apprehension about being encased in a large cast, and will help the patient to relax, co-operate and feel involved throughout.

Following cast application, the patient needs to be supported by flexible, waterproof pillows until the cast is dry to prevent it from being dented. Inadequate cast support will cause a soft cast to crack or become dented, resulting in subsequent pressure points. It is important to see that a pillow is not placed under the head and shoulders (of a patient in a body cast) while the cast is drying, since this will cause pressure on the chest.

Patients should be assisted to change position every two hours to relieve pressure and to allow the cast to dry. Sufficient personnel (at least three people) are needed for this activity so that the fresh cast can be supported adequately with the palms of the hands. Vulnerable points in the cast are located at the body joints and need to be supported to prevent the cast from cracking. The patient is encouraged to assist in the repositioning by using the overhead trapeze or bedrail. Any abduction bars that are incorporated in spica casts to stabilize cast positioning must NOT to be used as turning devices. Pillows should be readjusted so that support is provided without pressure areas being present. The patient is repositioned with one smooth movement towards the uninjured side to prevent stress on the cast and twisting of the body within the cast.

The patient is repositioned to a prone position, twice daily if tolerated, in order to provide postural drainage of the bronchial tree and relieve pressure on the back. A small pillow under the abdomen will be an added comfort measure. Placing a pillow lengthwise under the dorsum of the feet will prevent footdrop (Table 35.1).

Cast Syndrome

Patients immobilized in large casts may develop psychological and physiological responses to the confinement. The psychological component of cast syndrome is similar to a claustrophobic reaction. The patient exhibits an acute anxiety reaction characterized by behavioural changes and autonomic responses (e.g., increased respiratory rate, diaphoresis, dilated pupils, increased heart rate, elevated blood pressure). The nurse needs to recognize the anxiety reaction and provide an environment in which the patient feels secure.

The physiological responses to large casts are associated with the imposed immobility. With decreased physical activity, gastrointestinal motility decreases. With accumulation of intestinal gases, pressure increases and actual ileus occurs. The patient complains of distension, abdominal discomfort, nausea and vomiting. As with

Table 35.1 *Repositioning the patient in a hip spica cast*

* The patient is moved with a steady, even, pulling motion to the side of the bed

* Pillows are placed along the other side of the bed for cast support

* The nurse should advise the patient to assist by using the arm on the involved side to pull the shoulder over when turning

* Two nurses are on the side to which the patient is being turned to provide support for the cast while rolling the patient towards them

* The third nurse assists in rolling the patient from behind, adjusts the patient's shoulder and adjusts the pillows

* The patient's body should be repositioned with one smooth movement and positioned comfortably in good alignment

paralytic ileus, the patient is usually treated conservatively with decompression (nasogastric intubation connected to suction) and intravenous fluid therapy until gastrointestinal motility is restored. If the cast restricts the abdomen, a window needs to be cut in the cast over the abdominal area. Occasionally, the condition will progress to complete obstruction or the bowel may become gangrenous. Then surgical intervention is required.

The nurse needs to be aware of the possible development of cast syndrome in patients with large casts and ensure its prevention or resolution.

CARE OF THE PATIENT IN TRACTION

Traction is the application of a pulling force to a part of the body. Traction is used to minimize muscle spasms; to reduce, align and immobilize fractures; to lessen deformity; to preserve limb length; and to increase space between opposing surfaces within a joint. In order for traction to be effective, a fixed point from which to work, for example, the Thomas splint or an equal countertraction, is required.

At times, traction needs to be applied in more than one direction to achieve the desired line of pull. When this is done, part of one of the lines of pull counteracts the other line of pull. These lines of pull are known as the vectors of force. The actual resultant pulling force is somewhere between the two lines of pull (Figure 35.4). The effects of applied traction are evaluated with an X-ray, and adjustments may be necessary. As the muscle and soft tissue relax, the amount of weight used may be changed to obtain the desired pulling force.

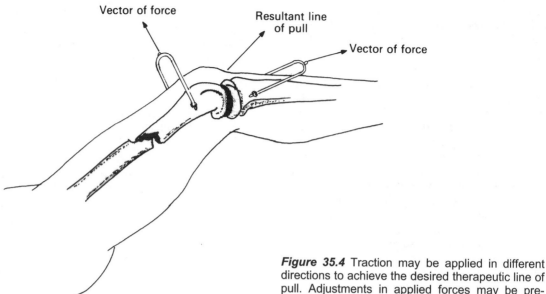

Figure 35.4 Traction may be applied in different directions to achieve the desired therapeutic line of pull. Adjustments in applied forces may be prescribed over the treatment period.

Types of Traction

Straight or running traction applies the pulling force in a straight line with the body part resting on the bed. Pugh's extension traction (Figure 35.5) and pelvic traction are examples of straight traction.

Balanced suspension traction (Figure 35.6) supports the extremity (being treated) off the bed and allows for some patient mobility without disruption of the line of pull.

Traction may be applied to the skin (skin traction) or directly to the bony skeleton (skeletal traction) via a Steinmann's or Denham pin.

Traction can also be applied with the hands (manual traction). However, this is a very temporary traction that may be used when applying a cast, facilitating skin care or adjusting traction apparatus.

Principles of Effective Traction

Whenever traction is applied, a countertraction must be considered. Countertraction is the force acting in the opposite direction. (Newton's third law of motion states that for every action there is an equal and opposite reaction.) Generally, the patient's body weight and bed position adjustments supply the needed countertraction.

- Countertraction must be maintained for effective traction.

For traction to be effective in reducing fractures and in providing immobilization, it must be continuous. Pelvic and cervical skin tractions are frequently used to reduce muscle spasm and are usually prescribed as an intermittent traction.

- Never interrupt skeletal traction.
- Do not remove weight unless the traction is prescribed intermittently.

Maintain the line of pull. Any factor that might reduce the pull or alter its resultant line of pull must be eliminated.

- The patient is centred in bed and in a good body alignment when traction is applied.
- Weights should hang free and not rest on the bed or floor.
- Ropes should be unobstructed in a straight alignment.
- Knots in the rope should not touch the pulley or the foot of the bed.
- The resultant line of pull should be in line with the long axis of the affected bone.
- The patient must be helped to maintain a therapeutic and comfortable position.

▶ **NURSING PROCESS**
▶ **THE PATIENT IN TRACTION**

▶ *Assessment*

The application of traction results in impaired physical mobility and can be a frightening experience. The equipment looks threatening. The patient's anxiety level needs to be assessed.

Additionally, the physiological impact on the patient of the immobilization, the traction device and the musculoskeletal problem must be considered.

The nurse needs to assess the skin integrity of the extremity to be placed in traction. Its neurovascular status (i.e., colour, temperature, capillary refill, oedema, pulses,

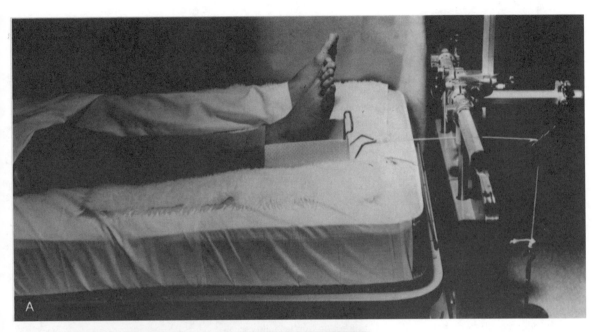

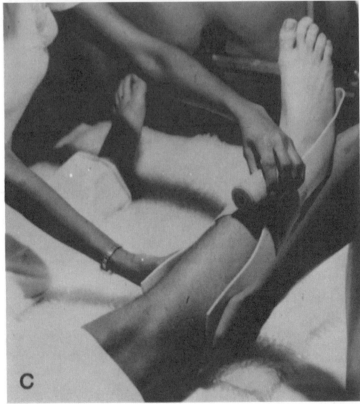

Figure 35.5 Pugh's extension. (A) Lower extremity in Pugh's extension traction. (B) Applying elastic bandage for Pugh's extension traction.

sensations and ability to move) is assessed, and compared with that of the unaffected extremity. The alignment of the body part in traction must be maintained as prescribed. Systemic assessment is appropriate. A patient may have problems with the skin, respiration, gastrointestinal tract or urinary tract when immobilized in traction. Development of deep vein thrombosis is assessed by checking for calf tenderness and a positive Homans's sign (discomfort in the calf when the foot is forcibly dorxiflexed). Disorientation and behavioural problems may also develop,

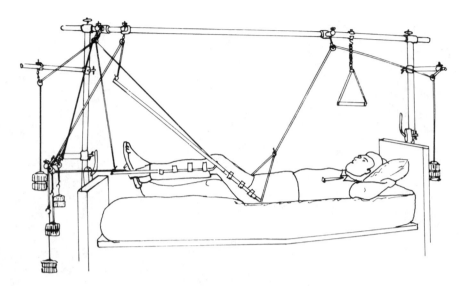

Figure 35.6 Principles of balanced suspension traction with Thomas leg splint. Vertical movement of the patient is permitted as long as resultant line of pull is maintained. In the nursing care of the patient in traction, it is necessary to understand the direction in which the force is operating. Study the line drawing carefully. Notice that the force produced by the weights is changed in direction by the pulleys.

related to confinement in a limited space for an extended period of time.

► *Patient's Problems*

Based on the nursing assessment, the patient's major identified problems related to traction may include the following:

- Anxiety related to health status.
- Alteration in comfort related to immobility.
- Impaired physical mobility related to mechanical devices restricting mobility and increasing the risk of complications of bedrest.
- Lack of knowledge about the treatment regime.
- Inability to care for self due to traction devices.

► *Planning and Implementation*
► Expected Outcomes

The major outcomes for the patient in traction may include reducing anxiety, increasing comfort, increasing mobility, understanding the rationale for traction interventions and increasing the ability to perform self-care.

Nursing Care

Reducing Anxiety

Before the application of any traction, the patient needs to be informed about the procedure, its purpose and its implications. Informing the patient about what is being done and why, helps to reduce apprehension. After being in

traction for a period of time, the patient may react to being confined to a limited space. Frequent visits by the nurse will reduce feelings of isolation and confinement. Family, friends and other informal carers should be encouraged to visit frequently for the same reason. Diversional activities that can be achieved within the limits of the traction are encouraged.

Increasing Comfort

Because the patient will be immobilized in bed, the mattress needs to be firm and supportive. Special mattress pads designed to minimize the development of pressure sores can be placed on the bed before application of the traction, if the patient has been assessed as being 'at risk'.

- The patient's skin should be examined frequently for evidence of pressure or friction over bony prominences.
- Pressure on dependent body parts should be relieved by regular changes of position, promoting patient comfort within the limits of the traction.
- Bed linen must be kept wrinkle-free and dry.

The problems associated with immobility that affect other body systems and cause the patient discomfort are minimized through active preventive nursing measures. Deep-breathing exercises that aid in full expansion of the lungs are taught; ankle and foot exercises possible within the limits of the traction decrease venous stasis and the development of deep vein thrombosis; adequate fluid intake ensures urine flow and aids in preventing constipation.

The nurse assesses the function of each body system in order to identify alterations in function. The patient is monitored closely for the development of complications associated with immobility.

● Every complaint of the patient in traction should be investigated immediately.

Improving Mobility Within the Limits of Traction
During traction therapy, the patient needs to exercise non-immobilized muscles and joints to diminish their deterioration due to immobilization. Active motion of all unaffected joints is encouraged. The physiotherapist can be consulted to design exercises that minimize loss of muscle strength. The nurse needs to encourage and support the patient in exercising. During exercising, the nurse must ensure that traction forces are maintained and that the patient is properly positioned to prevent complications resulting from poor alignment.

Patient Education
The patient must accurately perceive the rationale for the use of traction. The information needs to be repeated and reinforced frequently. With increased understanding of the therapy, patients become active participants in their own health care.

Improving Self-Care
Initially the patient may require much assistance with self-care activities. The nurse will help the patient learn how to provide for such needs as eating, bathing, dressing and toileting while immobilized in the traction device. Devices such as 'helping hands' and an overbed trapeze to facilitate self-care may be useful. The patient will feel less dependent and less frustrated and will experience improved self-esteem with resumption of self-care activities. Some assistance will be required throughout the period of immobility; however, the nurse and the patient can creatively develop routines that will maximize the patient's independence.

▶ *Evaluation*
▶ Expected Outcomes

1. Patient's anxiety is reduced.
   a. Patient appears relaxed.
   b. Uses effective coping mechanisms.
   c. Expresses concerns and feelings.
2. Feels increased comfort.
   a. Expresses feelings of comfort.
   b. Develops no pressure sores.
   c. Avoids problems related to immobility.
3. Demonstrates increased mobility.
   a. Performs prescribed exercises.
   b. Uses appropriate assistive devices.
4. Understands rationale for traction interventions.
   a. Describes traction regime.
   b. Participates in plan of care.

5. Shows increased ability to perform self-care.
   a. Feeds, bathes, dresses and toilets self with minimal assistance.

Specific Traction Applications

Skin Traction

Skin traction is accomplished by a weight pulling on 'tapes' attached to the skin. Traction on the skin transmits forces to other musculoskeletal structures. However, only limited traction can be applied in this way. The amount of weight applied must not exceed the tolerance of the skin, and is usually prescribed dependent on the weight of the patient. Therefore, when prolonged or heavy traction weight is necessary, skeletal traction is usually preferred to skin traction.

Two forms of skin traction used for adults are Hamilton-Russell's traction and Pugh's extension traction.

Hamilton-Russell's Traction. Hamilton-Russell's traction, which may be used for fractures of the neck of the femur, supports the flexed knee in a sling and applies the horizontal pulling force to the lower leg. If prescribed, the leg may be supported by a pillow to assure proper knee flexion and to prevent pressure on the heel (see Figure 35.7).

Pugh's Traction. Pugh's traction (unilateral or bilateral) is a form of skin traction in which the pull is exerted in one plane when partial or temporary immobilization is desired (see Figure 35.5A). It is used following injuries to the hip, e.g. dislocations, or as a treatment for low back pain.

Before the traction is applied, the skin is inspected for abrasions and circulatory disturbances, since the skin and circulation must be in healthy condition to tolerate the traction. The extremity should be clean and dry before the traction tapes are applied (Figure 35.5B).

To apply Pugh's traction, foam-rubber-padded straps are applied with the foam surface against the skin (Ventfoam), or self-adhesive extensions are applied on each side of the affected leg. A loop of the straps about 10 to 15 cm long is extended beyond the sole of the foot. The malleoli and proximal fibula are padded with cast padding to help prevent pressure sores and skin necrosis. While one person elevates and supports the extremity under the patient's heel and knee, another person wraps a supporting bandage circumferentially over the traction straps, beginning at the ankle and wrapping up to the tibial tubercle. This bandage helps the straps to adhere to the skin and prevents slipping. A spreader is applied to the distal end of the tape to prevent pressure along the side of the foot (only required if using Ventfoam straps). A rope is attached to the spreader and passed over a pulley fastened to the end of the bed. Then a weight is attached to the rope. A sheepskin pad may be placed under the leg to reduce friction of the heel against the bed.

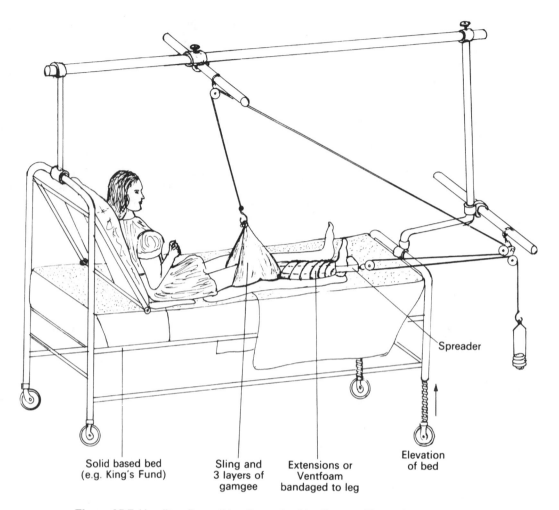

Solid based bed
(e.g. King's Fund)

Sling and
3 layers of
gamgee

Extensions or
Ventfoam
bandaged to leg

Spreader

Elevation
of bed

Figure 35.7 Hamilton-Russell traction using Ventfoam or Elastoplast extensions.

Skin and Nerve Pressure

Skin traction can irritate the skin and cause pressure on peripheral nerves. If skin straps are used, the circumferential wrappings should not impair circulation, but must be firm enough to ensure that the straps will remain in contact with the skin.

- To detect pressure points while the patient is in skin traction, the area over the Achilles tendon should be inspected several times daily because pressure in this region may occur when skin traction is applied to the leg. Care must be taken to avoid pressure on the peroneal nerve at the point at which it passes around the neck of the fibula just below the knee. Pressure at this point can cause footdrop (Figure 35.1). The patient needs to be asked about sensation and requested to move the toes and foot. Dorsiflexion of the foot—'point your toe at your nose'—demonstrates the function of the peroneal nerve.

Plantar flexion demonstrates the function of the tibial nerve.

An assessment must be made for altered sensation, weakness of dorsiflexion or foot movement, and inversion of the foot, which might indicate pressure on the common peroneal nerve. Any complaint of burning sensation under the traction bandage should be investigated immediately.

- When skin traction is applied to the arm, the area around the elbow where the ulnar nerve is located should not be bandaged tightly.
- Sensation and motion need to be assessed.
- Wrappings applied around the leg should be removed and the skin inspected regularly.
- A second nurse needs to support the extremity in position during skin inspection and care.
- Special care is given to the back at regular intervals, as the patient maintains a supine position.
- Prevent shearing forces on the skin.

Circulation

Following application of skin traction, the foot or hand is inspected for circulatory difficulties within a few minutes, and then every two hours.

- Check peripheral pulses and the colour, capillary refill and temperature of the fingers or toes.
- Check for calf tenderness and for a positive Homans's sign for indications of thrombophlebitis.
- Encourage active foot exercise hourly.

Ensuring Effective Traction

To ensure effective traction, observe for wrinkling and slipping of the traction bandage and maintain counteraction. Proper positioning must also be maintained to keep the leg or arm in a neutral position.

Skeletal Traction

Skeletal traction is applied directly to the bone. This method of traction is used most frequently in the treatment of fractures of the femur, the humerus, the tibia and the cervical spine. The traction is applied directly to the bone by use of a metal pin or wire (e.g. Kirschner wire, Steinmann's pin), which is inserted through the bone distal to the fracture. Crutchfield or Gardner-Wells head tongs are fixed in the skull to apply traction and immobilize cervical fractures.

Skeletal traction is applied under surgical asepsis.

Patient preparation contributes to the patient's comfort and co-operation during the pinning procedure. Frequently, the skeletal traction is inserted while the patient is in the ward and not in the theatre suite.

The insertion site is prepared with surgical scrub, such as povidone-iodine. A local anaesthetic is administered at the insertion site and periosteum. A small skin incision is made, and the sterile pin or wire is drilled through the bone. The patient feels pressure during this procedure and possibly some discomfort when the periosteum is penetrated.

Following insertion, the pin or wire is attached to a Bohler stirrup or loop. The ends of the wire are covered, e.g. with corks or tape, to prevent injury to the patient. The weights are attached to the stirrup by a rope-pulley system that exerts the appropriate amount and direction of pull for effective traction. Often the skeletal traction is balanced traction, which supports the affected extremity and facilitates patient independence and nursing care while maintaining effective traction.

The Thomas splint with the Pearson attachment is frequently used with skeletal traction in fractures of the femur (see Figure 35.6). It may be used with skin traction and other balanced suspension apparatus. Because upward traction is required, an overbed frame is utilized. Figure 35.8 shows suspension traction using slings.

The Pin Site

The wound at the insertion site requires attention. Gener-

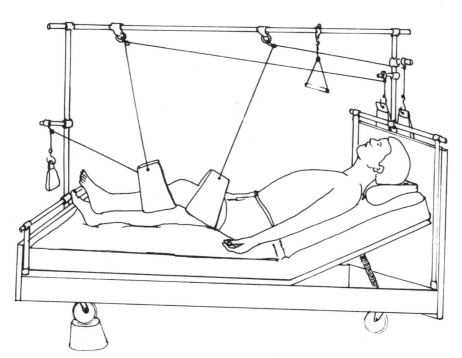

Figure 35.8 A type of balanced suspension traction for the lower extremity. Weights elevate the patient's injured leg, which is supported in slings. Skeletal traction is applied.

ally, the site is covered with a sterile dressing. Subsequent care of the pin is prescribed individually. The area must be kept clean. It is assessed for odour and other signs of infection. The goal is to avoid infection and the development of osteomyelitis. Slight serous oozing at the pin site is to be expected. This decreases the bacteria in the pin tract. Crusting is prevented, and the area is kept clean.

- Inspect the pin site daily for signs of inflammation and evidence of infection.

Neurovascular Status

The skin around the traction device is inspected for signs of circulatory impairment. Neurovascular assessment of the immobilized extremity is conducted at least every two hours initially and later several times a day.

Pressure

Specific pressure points need to be checked for redness and skin breakdown. Pressure areas caused by the traction apparatus may include the ischial tuberosity, popliteal space, Achilles tendon and heel. The unsupported muscle may cause discomfort due to the tension at the pin.

Often patients use the heel of the unaffected leg to act as a brace when they raise themselves. This digging of the heel into the mattress may cause injury to the tissues; hence, the heel must also be inspected to prevent pressure sores. If patients are unable to raise themselves, the nurse

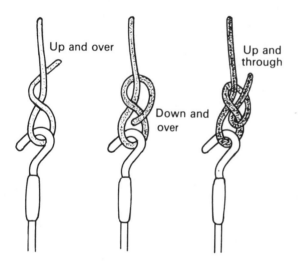

Figure 35.9 Guidelines for traction knot tying. Tying knots correctly is an orthopaedic nursing activity essential for the safety of the patient in traction. To save time, follow this simple phrase:
Up and over
Down and over
Up and through
Practise a few times with a traction cord. It is a good idea to secure all knots tightly with adhesive tape. (Courtesy of Zimmer Inc.)

should assess and initiate appropriate preventive measures.

Positioning

The foot should be positioned to avoid footdrop (plantar flexion), inward rotation (inversion) or outward rotation (eversion). The patient's foot may be supported in a neutral position by orthopaedic devices (e.g., foot supports). Frequent active flexion–extension ankle exercises are encouraged.

Maintaining Effective Traction

When traction is being used, the apparatus is checked to see that the ropes are in the wheel groove of the pulleys; that the ropes are not frayed; that the weights hang freely; and that the patient has not slipped down in bed, causing ineffective traction. The knots in the rope are tied securely. Figure 35.9 suggests a secure knot-tying method.

The weights that are applied initially are sufficient to overcome the shortening spasms of the affected muscles. As muscles relax, the traction weight is reduced to prevent fracture distraction and to promote fracture healing.

- Weights should never be removed from a patient with a fracture unless a life-threatening situation occurs. If the weights are removed, the whole purpose of their use has been defeated.

Skin Care

When traction frames are used, a trapeze may be suspended overhead within easy reach of the patient. This apparatus is of great help in assisting the patient to move about in bed and on and off bedpans. It is also a help to the nurse in caring for these patients.

The patient's elbows may become sore, and nerve injury may occur if most repositioning is done by pushing on the elbows. When a patient is not permitted to turn on one side or the other, the nurse must make a special effort to provide good pressure area care of the back and to keep the bed dry and free of crumbs and wrinkles. This can be accomplished by having the patient raise the hips from the bed by holding onto the overhead trapeze.

Exercise

Patient exercises are valuable in maintaining muscle strength and tone and in promoting circulation. Exercises need to be planned within the therapeutic limits of the traction. Active exercise frequently permitted includes pulling up on the trapeze, flexing and extending the feet, and range-of-motion and weight-resistance exercises for noninvolved joints. The immobilized extremity benefits from isometric exercises. Quadriceps- and gluteal-setting exercises promote the strength of these muscles, which are important in ambulatory stability. Without bed exercises, the patient will lose much muscle mass and strength, and rehabilitation time will be greatly extended.

Development of thrombophlebitis is a real concern for anyone immobilized for a period of time. Daily assessment for the development of deep vein thrombophlebitis is necessary. Antiembolic stockings, heparin and warfarin may be prescribed to help prevent thrombus formation. Prompt identification and treatment of thrombophlebitis is essential.

Pin Removal

When X-ray studies demonstrate the presence of sufficient callus, skeletal traction is discontinued. The extremity is gently supported while the weights are removed. The pin is removed by the doctor and a cast or brace is used to support the healing bone.

Summary of Nursing Care

When the patient is in traction, the nurse's responsibilities include the following:

1. Assess the neurovascular status of the extremity frequently.
2. Ensure that the ropes and pulleys are freely movable.
3. Maintain continuous traction for effectiveness.
4. Observe for skin irritation around the traction bandage.
5. Assess the patient for signs of infection.
6. Observe for pressure under the sling and equipment and at common pressure points (e.g., ischial tuberosity, popliteal space, heel).
7. Encourage active foot exercises, and use foot supporters as required.
8. Encourage exercises to minimize deconditioning of the immobilized patient.
9. Involve the patient in care to help reduce the depression and boredom that frequently accompany weeks of traction therapy.

CARE OF THE PATIENT UNDERGOING ORTHOPAEDIC SURGERY

Many patients who have musculoskeletal dysfunction need to undergo surgery to correct the problem. Problems that may be corrected by surgery include impaired function due to an unstabilized fracture, deformity or joint disease; necrotic or infected tissue; impaired circulation (e.g., compartment syndrome); and tumours or growths. Frequent surgical procedures include open reduction with internal fixation for fractures; arthroplasty, meniscectomy and joint replacement for joint problems, amputation for severe extremity problems (e.g., gangrene, massive trauma); bone graft for joint stabilization, defect-filling or stimulation of healing; and tendon transplants for improvement of motion. The goals of most orthopaedic surgery include improving function by restoring motion and stability and relieving pain and disability.

Types of Surgery

Orthopaedic surgery falls into the following categories:

Open reduction—the reduction and alignment of the fracture following surgical dissection and exposure of the fracture.

Internal fixation—the stabilization of the reduced fracture by the use of metal screws, plates, nails and pins.

Bone graft—the placement of bone tissue (autologous or homologous grafts) to promote healing, stabilization or replacement of diseased bone.

Amputation—the removal of a body part.

Arthroplasty—the repair of joint problems through the operating arthroscope (an instrument that allows the surgeon to operate within a joint without a large incision) or through open joint surgery.

Meniscectomy—the excision of damaged knee joint fibrocartilage.

Joint replacement—the substitution of joint surfaces with metal or plastic materials.

Total joint replacement—the replacement of both articular surfaces within a joint with metal or synthetic materials.

Tendon transfer—the movement of tendon insertion to improve function.

Fasciotomy—the cutting of the muscle fascia to relieve muscle constriction or to reduce fascia contracture.

► NURSING PROCESS
► PREOPERATIVE CARE OF THE PATIENT UNDERGOING ORTHOPAEDIC SURGERY

► *Assessment*

The nurse assesses the patient for adequate hydration, current medication history and possible infection.

Adequate hydration is an important goal for orthopaedic patients. Immobilization and bedrest contribute to urinary stasis and associated bladder infections and to stone formation. Adequate hydration assures adequate urine flow and helps to prevent the occurrence of urinary tract problems. In order to avoid preoperative dehydration, the nurse assesses the skin, vital signs, urinary output and laboratory values for evidence of dehydration.

It should be determined whether the patient has undergone previous therapy with corticosteroids. The person with rheumatoid arthritis or chronic pulmonary disease frequently has had steroid medications to control the disease. Steroid therapy, whether current or past, may adversely affect the body's ability to withstand the stress of surgery. Any steroids should be given preoperatively as prescribed to assure adequate corticosteroid levels, and to reduce the risk of steroid crisis.

The patient may be on other long-term medications, such as anticoagulants, cardiovascular drugs, insulin and so on. All of these need to be documented and discussed with the surgeon and anaesthetist.

The patient needs to be asked specifically about the existence of colds, dental problems, urinary tract infections and other possible loci of infection occurring in the two weeks before surgery. Osteomyelitis could develop from spread of infection through the bloodstream. In no instance are antibiotics relied on solely to prevent the spread of infection. Permanent disability can result if infection occurs within a bone or joint.

Other areas of preoperative assessment are similar to those for any patient undergoing surgery.

► *Patient's Problems*

Based on the nursing assessment data, the patient's major preoperative nursing diagnoses related to the orthopaedic status may include the following:

- Alteration in comfort—pain related to fracture, swelling, or inflammation.
- Actual or potential alteration in tissue perfusion (peripheral) related to swelling, constricting devices, impaired venous return.
- Alteration in health maintenance related to loss of independence.
- Impaired physical mobility related to pain, swelling and possibly an immobilizing device.
- Disturbance in self-concept (body image, self-esteem, role performance) related to impact of musculoskeletal problem.

► *Planning and Implementation*
► Expected Outcomes

The major outcomes for the patient before orthopaedic surgery may include relief of pain, adequate tissue perfusion, health maintenance, improved mobility and improved self-concept.

Nursing Care

Relieving Pain

Physical, pharmacological and psychological management techniques to control pain are useful in the preoperative period. Specific methods selected are tailored to the individual patient and prescribed by the doctor. Immobilization of a fractured bone or injured, inflamed joint will decrease discomfort. Elevation of a swollen extremity will promote venous return and reduce associated discomfort. Ice, if prescribed, will relieve swelling and directly reduce discomfort by diminishing nerve stimulation. Drugs are frequently prescribed to control the acute pain of musculoskeletal injury and associated muscle spasm. During the immediate preoperative period, the nurse needs to discuss and co-ordinate administration of analgesic medications with the anaesthetist and surgeon. Alternative methods of pain control (e.g., distraction, focusing, guided imagery, quiet environment) may be used to decrease pain perception.

Promoting Adequate Tissue Perfusion

Trauma, swelling or immobilization devices may interrupt tissue perfusion. Venous return is promoted by avoiding pressure in the popliteal area and by using antiembolic stockings unless contraindicated. The circulatory status (i.e., colour, temperature, capillary refill, pulse, pain, oedema, paraesthesia) of the extremity must be assessed frequently. If compromised circulation is noted, measures to restore adequate circulation are instituted. The doctor is notified promptly, the extremity is elevated, and constricting wraps and casts are released.

Health Maintenance

The nurse needs to assist the patient in activities that will promote health during the perioperative and rehabilitative periods. Nutritional needs and hydration are assessed. Generally, nutrition for orthopaedic patients is a reflection of their normal eating patterns. It may be appropriate to discuss ways of modifying the diet or to refer the patient to the dietician. The preoperative fasting regime is usually tolerated well. If the patient is diabetic, elderly and frail, or the victim of multiple trauma, special provisions may be necessary. Abnormal urinalysis findings and complaint of burning on micturition require further investigation before surgery. The nurse monitors fluid intake and urinary output. The use of an indwelling catheter should be limited to avoid urinary tract infection.

Smoking should be stopped during the preoperative period to facilitate optimum respiratory function. Coughing, deep breathing and use of the incentive spirometer are practised for improved respiratory function during the postoperative period.

Exercises are taught during the preoperative period. Gluteal-setting and quadriceps-setting isometric exercises are taught for maintenance of the muscles needed for ambulation. Unless contraindicated, isometric contraction of the calf muscles (calf pumping) is practised to minimize venous stasis and prevent thrombophlebitis. Active range-of-motion exercises of uninvolved joints are encouraged. The patient who will be using ambulatory aids may exercise to strengthen the upper extremities and shoulders. If possible, assistive devices (e.g., trapeze) are used and transfer techniques practised before surgery.

Improving Mobility

Preoperatively, the patient's mobility is impaired by pain, swelling and immobilizing devices (e.g., splints, casts, traction). The nurse must gently assist the patient in moving the injured part while providing adequate support. Swollen extremities are elevated and adequately supported with hands and pillows. Pain is controlled before an injured part is moved by splinting it and by administering medication in time to take effect before the injured part is moved. Skin care is provided, especially around pressure points. The use of pressure-reducing devices (e.g., convoluted foam mattress, alternating air mattress) needs to be instituted before surgery for those at risk of skin breakdown. Movement within the limits of therapeutic immobility is encouraged.

Improving Self-Concept

Preoperative orthopaedic patients may need assistance in accepting changes in body image, diminished self-esteem or inability to perform the responsibilities of their life roles. The degree of assistance required in this area varies greatly, depending on the events preceding hospitalization, the surgery and rehabilitation planned, the temporary or permanent nature of the altered body image and the extent of changes required in role performance. The nurse promotes a trusting relationship for patients to express concerns and anxieties, and helps them examine their feelings about changes in self-concept. The nurse can clarify any misconceptions patients may have, and help them work through modifications that may be necessary due to alterations in physical capacity and self-concept.

► *Evaluation*
► Expected Outcomes

1. Patient experiences less pain.
   a. States medication is effective in controlling discomfort.
   b. Uses multiple approaches to reduce pain.
   c. Requests assistance when moving to increase comfort.
2. Exhibits adequate tissue perfusion.
   a. Demonstrates reduced swelling.
   b. Experiences reduced inflammation.
   c. Exhibits normal capillary refill.
   d. Has palpable peripheral pulses.
   e. Has warm skin.
   f. Participates in exercise programme.
3. Promotes health.
   a. Eats balanced diet appropriate to meet nutritional needs.
   b. Maintains adequate hydration.
   c. Abstains from smoking.
   d. Practises respiratory exercises.
   e. Engages in strengthening and preventive exercises.
4. Functions within limits of therapeutic mobility or immobility.
   a. Moves with less discomfort.
   b. Elevates swollen extremity after transfer.

c. Uses immobilizing devices.
   d. Repositions self to relieve skin pressure.
5. Expresses positive self-concept.
   a. Acknowledges temporary or permanent changes in body image.
   b. Discusses role performance changes.
   c. Views self as valuable and capable of assuming responsibilities.

► NURSING PROCESS
► POSTOPERATIVE CARE OF THE PATIENT UNDERGOING ORTHOPAEDIC SURGERY

► *Assessment*

In major orthopaedic surgery, shock may be a problem, because orthopaedic wounds have a tendency to ooze and bleed more than do other surgical wounds. As a result, the nurse must be on the alert for symptoms of shock. A rising pulse rate or slowly falling blood pressure indicates persistent bleeding or the development of shock. Changes in the respiratory rate or in the patient's colour indicate obstruction of respiratory exchange and pulmonary or cardiac complications. Fat embolus (p. 1115) may occur. Thromboembolic disease (see Chapter 9) is one of the most common and most dangerous of all complications occurring in the postoperative orthopaedic patient.

Other complications that may occur are similar to those of patients undergoing general surgery, including abdominal distension and wound infection. In addition, elderly men may have some degree of prostatism and may have difficulty in voiding, so it is important to monitor urinary output.

The patient is assessed regularly for the presence of pain as skeletal trauma and surgery performed on bones, muscles and joints can produce significant pain.

► *Patient's Problems*

Based on all assessment data, the patient's major postoperative orthopaedic nursing diagnoses may include the following:

● Alteration in comfort—pain related to the surgical procedure and immobilization.
● Potential for infection related to the surgical procedure.
● Impaired physical mobility related to the surgical procedure and presence of immobilizing devices (splints, traction, cast, external fixator).
● Alteration in self-concept (body image, self-esteem, role performance) related to the impact of musculoskeletal problems. (Nursing care for this patient's problem has been discussed under the section on preoperative care on page 1095.)

► *Planning and Implementation*
► **Expected Outcomes**

The major outcomes for the patient after orthopaedic surgery may include relief of pain, absence of infection, improved mobility and restoration of function.

Nursing Care

Relieving Pain

Pain can be a limiting factor, and every effort is made to relieve its intensity. The preoperative teaching and exercise programmes help the patient understand what to expect following surgery. The patient is monitored closely, and the prescribed analgesic is administered before the pain occurs if its onset can be predicted, or at least before it reaches a severe intensity. The nurse can administer the analgesic on a preventive basis as long as the prescribed interval between doses is observed. Eventually, pain should diminish; increased pain suggests that a problem exists and needs to be checked.

Patients may be afraid to move after orthopaedic surgery and may therefore maintain a rigid extremity, which can cause painful muscle spasm and guarding. Reassuring patients that they cannot hurt themselves by moving and that some discomfort is normal and to be expected may help patients relax and go forward in their programme.

If the dressing becomes too tight and painful, the surgeon must be notified.

Setting realistic goals; motivating for self-care; using relaxation, distraction and guided imagery techniques; and establishing a relationship with the patient are nursing activities that can be used to help the patient cope with pain.

The nurse also monitors for any evidence of pressure sores, which are a constant threat to any patient who must spend a prolonged period in bed or who is elderly, malnourished or unable to move without assistance. Repositioning the patient, washing, blotting dry and massaging the skin are encouraged to avoid this complication as well as to promote comfort.

Monitoring for Potential Infection

Infection is a potential problem following any surgery. It is of particular concern for the postoperative orthopaedic patient because of the risk of osteomyelitis. The nurse monitors the patient's vital signs, assesses the appearance of the wound, and notes the character of the drainage. Prompt recognition of the development of an infective process is necessary. Prophylactic systemic antibiotics are frequently prescribed during the perioperative and immediate postoperative period. The nurse assesses the patient's response to these antibiotics. When changing dressings and emptying wound drainage devices, aseptic technique is essential. Patient education concerning reporting of the signs and symptoms of infection, hand washing and wound care reduces the development of infections.

Improving Mobility and Restoring Function

Some orthopaedic operations may require prolonged periods in bed. Bone does not mend as rapidly as soft tissues. Therefore, even when the skin incision is healed, bony structures underneath still need time to repair. This is especially important to remember in surgery of the lower extremities because, in addition to allowing normal movement, bone must be able to bear weight in ambulation. Metal pins, screws, rods and plates used in internal fixations are not strong enough to support the body's weight and will bend and break if stressed. The stability of the fracture, reduction and fixation, and bone healing are the important considerations in determining the amount of weight-bearing a reduced fracture can tolerate.

The exercise programme is tailored to the individual's clinical problem. The goal is to return the patient to the highest level of function in the shortest period of time consistent with the surgical procedure. In the postoperative period, rehabilitation is started by increasing the exercises that have been prescribed and increasing the patient's activities. Usually, some form of walking aid, for example, crutches, is used for postoperative mobility. Within the limits of the patient's weight-bearing tolerance (determined by the type of surgery), the nurse monitors the patient's gait, making sure that it is safe and does not have a potentially destructive pattern. (Crutch walking is discussed in Chapter 2, Ambulation).

Well-balanced diets with adequate protein and vitamins are needed for healthy tissue and wound healing. The patient is given a normal diet as soon as possible. However, large amounts of milk should not be given to orthopaedic patients who are on bedrest, because this only adds to the calcium pool in the body and requires that more calcium be excreted by the kidneys, which can lead to formation of urinary calculi.

► *Evaluation*
► **Expected Outcomes**

1. Patient achieves progressive pain relief.
   a. Utilizes relaxation techniques.
   b. Requires decreasing amounts of analgesic medication.
   c. Participates in own care.
2. Does not develop an infection.
   a. Shows no signs or symptoms of wound infection.
   b. Maintains vital signs within normal limits.
   c. Shows no purulent drainage.
   d. Wound heals without erythema, induration or swelling.
   e. Wound heals well.
3. Patient attains improved mobility.
   a. Increases independence in position changes.

b. Regains muscle strength and joint mobility.

c. Participates in exercise programme.

d. Keeps a progress chart.

4. Demonstrates some restoration of function.

a. Assumes increased responsibility for own care.

b. Walks with crutches using prescribed gait.

Reconstructive Joint Surgery

At times, the impact of joint disease or deformity will necessitate surgical intervention to relieve pain, improve stability and improve function. Surgical therapies used for joint disease include excision of damaged and diseased tissue, repair of damaged structures (e.g., ruptured tendon), removal of loose bodies (debridement), immobilizing fusion of a joint (arthrodesis) and replacement of all or part of the joint surfaces (e.g., arthroplasty, prosthesis).

The procedure is selected according to the patient's underlying problem(s), general physical health, impact of joint disability on life and age. Timing of these procedures

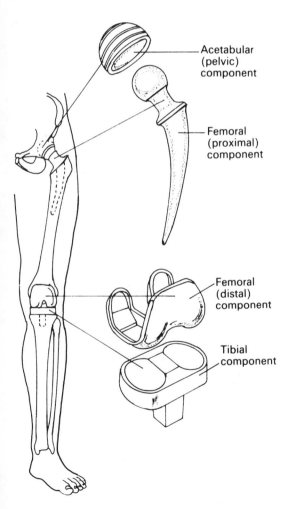

Figure 35.10 Hip and knee replacement.

is important for gaining maximum function. Surgery should be performed before surrounding muscles become contracted and atrophied and serious structural abnormalities occur. A holistic approach to patient care is encouraged to ensure the most appropriate treatment procedure is undertaken.

Total Joint Replacement

Patients with severe pain and disability associated with the joint may be selected for total joint replacement. Conditions contributing to joint degeneration include rheumatoid arthritis, osteoarthritis (degenerative joint disease), trauma and congenital deformity. At times, total joint replacement is a salvage procedure due to disruption of the blood supply and subsequent avascular necrosis. Joints frequently replaced include the hip, knee, shoulder and finger joints (Figure 35.10). Less frequently, more complex joints (elbow, wrist and ankle) are replaced.

Most joint replacements consist of metal and high-density polyethylene components. Finger prostheses are generally silastic. The joint implants may be cemented in the prepared bone with methyl methacrylate (a bone-bonding agent), which has properties similar to bone. Loosening of the bone in 5 to 15 years is the most common reason for prosthesis failure, as well as infection. Ingrowth prostheses (porous-coated, cementless, artificial joint components) that allow the patient's bone to grow into and securely fix the prosthesis are continually being evaluated. Accurate fitting and the presence of healthy bone stock with adequate blood supply are important in the use of cementless components.

With total joint replacement, excellent pain relief is obtained in 85 to 90 per cent of patients. Return of motion and function depends on the preoperative soft tissue condition, soft tissue reactions and general muscle strength. Early failure of total hip replacement is associated with higher levels of activity and prereplacement joint pathology.

Infection is a major concern because it is not always possible to achieve a functional extremity when the reconstruction procedure has to be repeated. Strict surgical asepsis and surgical environment controls are used to diminish surgical infection. Careful preoperative assessment of the patient for loci of infection is necessary. Prophylactic perioperative antibiotics are common. Infection occurs nearly twice as often in patients with rheumatoid arthritis as in those with osteoarthritis. (This may be associated with a deficit in polymorphonuclear leucocyte function observed in many rheumatoid arthritis patients.)

Total Hip Replacement

Total hip replacement is the replacement of a severely damaged hip with an artificial joint. Although a large number of implants are available, most consist of a metal femoral component topped by a spherical ball fitted into a plastic acetabular socket. Following a successful operation and rehabilitation, the hip is free or nearly free of pain, has good motion, is more stable and usually permits normal or near normal ambulation.

The operation is usually reserved for patients over 60 with unremitting pain or irreversibly damaged hip joints. The following conditions are amenable to this type of surgery: arthritis (degenerative joint disease, rheumatoid arthritis), femoral neck fractures, failure of previous reconstructive surgery (osteotomy, cup arthroplasty, femoral head replacement) and problems resulting from congenital hip disease.

The procedure is generally an elective one. Assessment of the patient's status and preoperative management are aimed at establishing the patient in an optimal condition for surgery. Any infection two to four weeks before planned surgery may result in postponement of surgery.

Assessment

A complete preoperative evaluation is carried out, with emphasis on cardiovascular, respiratory, renal and hepatic function. Every effort is made to prevent deep vein thrombosis and pulmonary embolism, the most common cause of postoperative mortality. Obesity, preoperative leg oedema, history of deep vein thrombosis and varicose veins increase the risk of postoperative pulmonary embolism.

Infection is the most feared complication, because it generally means that the implant unit must be removed. A search is made before the operation for any possible source of infection. Preoperative urine cultures may be taken, because urinary tract infection is a likely portal of entry for bacteria. Research suggests that the majority of deep infections are caused by bacteria that are implanted into the wound at the time of surgery, mostly from airborne sources. During operation, there is strict adherence to aseptic principles and the operating area is controlled and made as bacteria-free as possible. Preoperative skin preparation frequently begins a day or two before the surgery. Antibiotics may be administered in loading-dose fashion just before surgery or started intraoperatively.

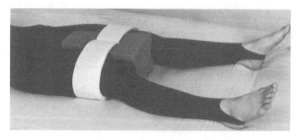

Figure 35.11 An abduction splint may be used after a total hip replacement to prevent dislocation of the prosthesis.

Preoperatively, the nurse needs to assess the patient's physiological parameters and the neurovascular status of the lower extremities. Postoperative assessment data are compared with preoperative data to identify deficits and changes. Nerve palsy can occur during surgery. Absence of peripheral pulses postoperatively may be of concern, unless the pulse was also absent preoperatively.

The home environment is evaluated early. Stair climbing and stooping are to be avoided during the first three months following surgery and kept to a minimum for the next three months. Modifications of the home environment may need to be made before the patient gets home.

Preoperative Patient Teaching

The nurse clarifies what the patient can reasonably expect from the surgery, during hospitalization and during rehabilitation. Establishing rapport early in this process helps patients to become active participants in their care.

Patient education is necessary in relation to coughing and deep breathing, muscle exercises, positioning, turning and transfer techniques. Coughing and deep-breathing regimes are reviewed and practised with the patient. The pulmonary complications of atelectasis and pneumonia are frequently seen and may be related to the patient's age, pre-existing pulmonary disease, deep anaesthesia, minimal activity and analgesic therapy. Learning how to use the incentive spirometer and intermittent positive pressure breathing equipment before surgery is helpful in maximizing the benefits from these devices and therapy. Isometric contraction of calf muscle and foot and ankle exercises are taught to prevent thrombophlebitis.

The patient is taught about positioning the leg in abduction to prevent dislocation of the prosthesis. The use of abduction splints (Figure 35.11), wedge pillows or two to three pillows between the legs is demonstrated. Review the patient's responsibility in maintaining abduction. Explain and demonstrate the limits for hip flexion.

The patient is taught upper extremity strengthening and isometric exercises of the quadriceps and gluteal muscles. When fitted with crutches or a Zimmer frame, the patient is taught a nonweight-bearing gait (no weight-bearing on the affected extremity) to facilitate postoperative ambulation. Practice is given in how to transfer from the bed to the wheelchair without flexing the hip joints beyond the prescribed limits. The use of the overhead frame and trapeze is practised. When using the fracture bed pan, the patient is requested not to bear down on the operated hip in flexion when getting on to it, but to flex the unoperated hip and knee and use the trapeze to lift the pelvis onto the pan.

The more familiar the patient is with what will be expected postoperatively, the better the chances of cooperation. Practising activities before surgery facilitates the ability to do them postoperatively, when the patient is less agile.

Postoperative Care

Before the patient's return from surgery, the bed should be equipped with a supportive mattress and an overbed trapeze. An adequate supply of pillows is needed to ensure proper positioning and comfort.

Positioning

Following surgery, the patient usually is positioned recumbent in bed with the affected extremity held in abduction by either an abduction splint or pillows to prevent dislocation of the prosthesis. At first the patient is repositioned only 45 degrees on the unoperated side, with the hip kept fully abducted and the entire length of the leg supported by pillows. As the repositioning routine becomes familiar, the patient is encouraged to assist by using the overbed trapeze but told not to adduct or flex the operated hip. The head of the bed should not be elevated more than 45 degrees to prevent acute flexion of the hip.

Exercise

On the day following surgery, specific exercises are begun and supervised by the physiotherapist. Exercises are carried out to increase range of motion and muscle strength in the operated hip and to work toward the goal of independence in ambulation.

Ambulation

When the patient is helped out of bed, usually on the first or second postoperative day, an abduction splint or pillows are kept between the legs. Once the patient is out of bed, the hip is kept at maximum extension. The procedure for helping patients out of bed consists of teaching them to get out of bed on the unaffected side and to return on the opposite, in order to maintain abduction of the operated hip. Active participation of the patient is always encouraged. Frequent short periods of time out of bed are preferred to occasional long periods of sitting.

At first the patient may merely be able to stand because of weakness or light-headedness from orthostatic hypotension. Specific weight-bearing limits are determined by the doctor based on the patient's condition, the procedure and the prosthesis used. If the patient has an in-growth prosthesis, weight-bearing may not be advocated in order to minimize motion of the prosthesis in the bone. This type of motion can disrupt the bone growth into the prosthesis, causing the prosthesis to loosen and fail.

When ready to ambulate, the patient is taught to use a walking frame by first advancing the frame and then advancing the involved extremity to the frame, bearing most of the weight on the hands. After mastering ambulation with the walking frame, the patient progresses to crutch walking and is taught the three-point gait. The patient moves the crutches and involved extremity while supporting the weight on the crutches, and then moves the unin-volved extremity. The choice of ambulatory aids depends on the patient's balance and comfort.

Patient Education

A programme of patient education involves teaching how important it is that the hip be maintained in abduction at all times and that stooping be avoided. Until otherwise advised, the patient should use a pillow between the knees when lying in a supine or side-lying position, and when turning. This prevents possible dislocation of the affected hip before the soft tissue has had a chance to heal and adequate muscle control has been restored. The patient is not to sleep on the operated side until directed to do so by the surgeon and, when seated, should keep the operated leg elevated. At no time should the legs be crossed.

Postoperative Complications

Dislocation of the Hip Prosthesis

Dislocation of the prosthesis needs to be recognized and reduced early so that circulatory and nerve damage to the leg does not occur. Dislocation may occur following movement several days postoperatively or through positioning that exceeds the limits of the prosthesis. The indicators of dislocation are shortening of the leg, inability to move it, malalignment, abnormal rotation and increased discomfort. If a prosthesis dislocates, the surgeon needs to be notified to reduce and stabilize the hip as soon as possible. As the muscles and joint capsule heal, the chance of dislocation diminishes. Stresses to the new hip joint should be minimal for the first three to six months.

Pain

Pain in the immediate postoperative period is controlled by intramuscular analgesia. Injection sites should be rotated, avoiding the operative hip and thigh. Muscle spasm may contribute to the pain experienced. At times the patient will indicate that the degree of postoperative pain is less than that experienced preoperatively, and only moderate amounts of analgesics are needed. By the second or third postoperative day, the pain has generally decreased to the point at which oral analgesics provide relief. Planned administration of an analgesic half an hour before exercise sessions may allow increased participation because comfort is increased. Haematomas and oedema are controlled, reducing the discomfort associated with pressure caused by the accumulation of fluid. An ice pack to the operative site may be prescribed to reduce oedema and bleeding. Portable suction of the wound will decrease fluid accumulation and haematoma formation, which could be a focus of infection. Drainage of 200 to 500 ml in the first 24 hours is expected; by 48 hours postoperatively, the total drainage in 24 hours has decreased to 50 ml or less, and the suction device is then removed.

Thromboembolism

Patients undergoing lower-extremity orthopaedic surgery are at high risk of developing deep venous thrombosis. Advancing age, conditions contributing to haemostasis and immobilization are additional risk factors. The nurse checks the legs daily for calf oedema, tenderness and a positive Homans's sign (see Chapter 9). The incidence of deep vein thrombosis in hip and knee reconstruction surgery is 45 to 70 per cent. Of these patients, 20 per cent develop pulmonary emboli, with 1 to 3 per cent being fatal. Therefore, the nurse must institute preventive measures and monitor the patient closely for the development of deep venous thrombosis and pulmonary emboli. Antiembolic stockings, elevation of the foot of the bed, ankle exercises and early ambulation facilitate circulation. Prophylactic warfarin or heparin may be prescribed, for seven days or as long as the patient is nonambulatory. Measures to promote circulation and decrease venous stasis are priorities for the hip and knee reconstruction patient.

Infection

Infection is the most serious complication following total hip replacement. Deep infection may require removal of the implant. Acute infections may occur within three months of surgery, and are associated with progressive superficial infections or draining haematomas. Delayed surgical infections may appear 4 to 26 months following surgery. Infections occurring more than two years after surgery are attributed to the spread of infection by the bloodstream from another place in the body.

Classic signs of infection may be present, or the patient may at some time months to years after surgery indicate return of discomfort in the hip, which could mean a late infection. The infection rate of patients having total hip surgery with rheumatoid arthritis is greater than those with osteoarthritis. This may be due to altered immunocompetency that results in an overall lower level of health and resistance. Patients who are diabetic, extremely elderly, obese or poorly nourished, or who have concurrent infections (e.g., urinary tract infections, dental abscesses) or develop large haematomas, are at higher risk of infection.

Because total joint infections are so disastrous, all efforts are undertaken to minimize their occurrence. Potential sources of infection are scrupulously avoided. A sterile operating room environment is essential, and surgery is conducted in such a way as to minimize trauma and promote wound healing. Prophylactic antibiotics are used. If an indwelling urinary catheter or portable wound suction is used, it is removed as soon as possible to avoid infections. Antibiotic therapy may be continued for 7 to 10 days. Prophylactic antibiotics may be advised if the patient needs any future surgical instrumentation, such as tooth extraction or cystoscopic examination.

If an infection occurs, antibiotics are used to treat the infection. Management of severe infections may require surgical debridement or removal of the prosthesis. Some patients may be candidates for implantation of a new prosthesis.

Temperature

Monitoring the patient's temperature can provide good clues to the source of the problem. Temperature elevations within the first 48 hours are frequently related to atelectasis or other respiratory problems. Temperature elevations during the next few days are associated with urinary tract infections. Superficial wound infections take about five to nine days to develop. Phlebitis-associated temperature elevations occur during the second and third week.

Other Complications

Other complications of total hip replacement include those associated with immobility, loosening of the prosthesis, heterotrophic ossification (formation of bone in the periprosthetic space) and avascular necrosis (bone death caused by loss of blood supply). Methods for improved cement fixation, ingrowth prosthesis and bone grafts are aimed at reducing the chance of prosthesis loosening.

Patient Education and Home Health Care

Before the patient prepares to leave the acute care setting, the nurse provides a thorough teaching programme to promote continuity of the therapeutic regime and work toward full rehabilitation. The patient should accept the responsibility for being the primary rehabilitative resource.

The patient is advised to keep to the daily exercise programme in order to maintain the functional motion of the hip joint and strengthen the abductor muscles of the hip. It will take time to strengthen and reeducate the muscles.

Ambulatory aids (crutches, Zimmer frame or walking stick) are used for a period of time. When sufficient muscle tone has developed to permit a normal gait without discomfort, the walking stick may be abandoned. Walking efficiency after total hip replacement is improved because of the acquired painless normal gait. In general, by three months the patient is able to resume all routine daily living activities. Frequent walks, swimming and use of a high rocking chair are excellent for hip exercises. Sexual activities should be carried out in the dependent position for three to six months to avoid adduction and flexion of the new hip.

At no time should the patient cross the legs or assume positions of acute flexion, more than 90 degrees. Assistance in putting on shoes and socks may be needed. Low chairs are avoided, as well as sitting for more than 30 minutes at a time, to minimize hip flexion and the risk of prosthetic dislocation and to prevent hip stiffness and flexion contracture. Travelling long distances is to be avoided unless frequent changes in position are possible. Other activities to avoid include overexertion, lifting heavy loads and excessive bending and twisting (lifting, shovelling snow, forceful turning).

Total Knee Replacement

Total knee replacement surgery is considered for patients who have severe pain and functional disabilities related to joint surfaces destroyed by arthritis (rheumatoid arthritis, osteoarthritis, post-traumatic arthritis) and haemophilia. There are a large variety of metal and acrylic prostheses that are designed to provide the patient with a functional, painless, stable joint. If the patient's ligaments have weakened, a fully constrained (hinged) or semiconstrained prosthesis may be used to provide joint stability.

Preoperative Care. Preoperative evaluation and patient education are important for postoperative nursing care. Measures are taken to prevent infection. Thigh-high antiembolic stockings are used to help prevent thrombophlebitis.

Postoperative Care. Postoperatively, the knee is dressed with a compression bandage. Ice may be applied to control oedema and bleeding. The neurovascular status of the leg is assessed (see p. 1079). Active flexion of the foot is encouraged.

A wound suction drain removes fluid accumulating in the joint. Drainage during the first eight hours following surgery is usually about 200 ml; it diminishes to less than 25 ml by 48 hours postoperatively, and then the drains can be removed.

Frequently, the patient's leg is placed on a continuous passive motion device (Figure 35.12) in the postoperative phase. This device promotes healing by increasing circulation and movement of the knee joint. The rate and amount of extension and flexion are prescribed. Usually 10 degrees of extension and 50 degrees of flexion are initiated, and progress to 90 degrees of flexion by discharge. If satisfactory flexion is not achieved, gentle manipulation of the knee joint under general anaesthesia may be undertaken about two weeks after surgery.

Efforts are directed at preventing complications (thromboembolism, peroneal nerve palsy, infection). The patient begins nonweight-bearing transfers out of bed on the first postoperative day. Support and elevation of the leg are needed when the patient is out of bed in a chair. The physiotherapist supervises exercises for strength and range of motion. Progressive ambulation, using ambulatory aids and within the prescribed weight-bearing limits, is begun within days of the surgery.

Following discharge from the hospital, the patient may continue with physiotherapy on an outpatient basis. Late complications that may occur include infection and loosening and wear of prosthetic components. Generally, the patient is able to achieve a pain-free, functional joint and participate more fully in life activities.

BIBLIOGRAPHY

Bastiani, G., Aldegheri, R. and Brivio, L. R. (1984) The treatment of fractures with a dynamic axial fixator, *JBJS*, Vol. 66B, No. 4, pp. 539–45.

Davies, P. (1985) *The Painful Process of Implementing Research* (unpublished), study undertaken at the Royal National Orthopaedic Hospital, Stanmore, Middlesex (copies held in the Nurse Education Library).

FURTHER READING

Books

Adams, J. C. (1987) *Outline of Fractures* (9th edition), Churchill Livingstone, Edinburgh.

Apley, G. A. and Solomon, L. (1988) *Concise System of Orthopaedics and Fractures*, Butterworths, Cambridge.

Benjamin, A. and Helal, B. (1980) *Surgical Repair and Reconstruction in Rheumatoid Disease*, John Wiley & Sons, New York.

Dandy, D. J. (1989) *Essential Orthopaedics and Trauma*, Churchill Livingstone, Edinburgh.

Duthie, R. B. and Bentley, G. (eds) (1983) *Mercer's Orthopaedic Surgery* (8th edition), University Park Press, Baltimore.

Epps, C. H. (1986) *Complications in Orthopaedic Surgery* (3rd edition), J. B. Lippincott, Philadelphia.

Farrell, J. (1986) *Illustrated Guide to Orthopaedic Nursing* (3rd edition), J. B. Lippincott, Philadelphia.

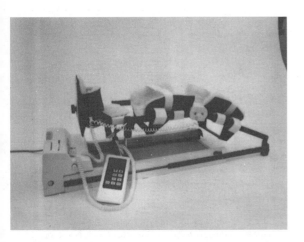

Figure 35.12 Continuous passive motion device used for postoperative total knee arthroplasty patients to facilitate joint range of motion. (Courtesy of Sutter Corporation.)

Gartland, J. (1979) *Fundamentals of Orthopedics* (3rd edition), W. B. Saunders, Philadelphia.

Heppenstall, R. (ed.) (1980) *Fracture Treatment and Healing*, W. B. Saunders, Philadelphia.

Hilt, N. and Cogburn, S. (1981) *Manual of Orthopedics*, C. V. Mosby, St Louis.

Intermediate Communications (1982) *Photobook: Working with Orthopedic Patients*, Springhouse, Pennsylvania.

MacKinnon, P. and Morris, J. (1986) *Oxford Textbook of Functional Anatomy—Volume 1: Musculoskeletal System*, Oxford University Press, Oxford.

Pearson, A. (1987) *Living in a Plaster Cast*, Royal College of Nursing London.

Pellino, T. *et al.* (eds) (1986) *National Association of Orthopaedic Nurses: Core Curriculum for Orthopaedic Nursing*, Pitman, New Jersey, Anthony J. Jannetti.

Powell, M. (ed.) (1986) *Orthopaedic Nursing and Rehabilitation* (9th edition), Churchill Livingstone, Edinburgh.

Roaf, R. and Hodkinson, L. (1980) *Textbook of Orthopaedic Nursing* (3rd edition), Blackwell Scientific, Oxford.

Rockwood, C. A. and Green, D. P. (eds) (1984) *Fractures in Adults* (2nd edition), J. B. Lippincott, Philadelphia.

Steward, J. D. M. and Hallett, J. P. (1983) *Traction and Orthopaedic Appliances* (2nd edition) Churchill Livingstone, Edinburgh.

Turek, S. L. (1984) *Orthopaedics: Principles and Their Application* (4th edition), J. B. Lippincott, Philadelphia.

Webb, J. T. (1985) *Notes on Orthopaedic Nursing* (2nd edition), Churchill Livingstone, Edinburgh.

Articles

General

Aaron, R. K. and Ciombor, D. (1983) Venous thrombosis in the orthopedic patient, *Surgical Clinics of North America*, June, Vol. 63, No. 3, pp. 529–38.

Celeste, S. M. *et al.* (1984) Identifying a standard for pin site care using the quality assurance approach, *Orthopedic Nursing*, July/Aug, Vol. 3, No. 4, pp. 17–24.

Collier, M. E. (1989) Pressure sore prevention and development: May the force be without you, *Educational Paper 3*, Wound Care Society, England.

Crutchley, C. (1984) Trends in orthopedic surgery, *Today's OR Nurs*, December, Vol. 6, No. 12, pp. 22–4.

Fahey, V. A. (1989) An in-depth look at depp vein thrombosis, *Nursing*, Vol. 19, No. 1, pp. 86–93.

Farrell, J. (1984) Positioning postoperative orthopedic patients. *Today's OR Nurs.* October, Vol. 6, No. 12, pp. 12–16.

Farrell, N. A. (9185) Cast syndrome, *Orthop. Nurs.*, July/August, Vol. 4, No. 4, pp. 61–4.

Gates, S. J. (1984) Helping your patient on bedrest cope with perceptual/sensory deprivation, *Orthop. Nurs.*, March/April, Vol. 3, No. 2, pp. 35–8.

Gill, K. P. *et al.* (1984) External fixation: The erector sets of orthopedic nursing, *Can. Nurs.*, May, Vol. 80, No. 5, pp. 29–31.

Goldstone, L. A. *et al.* (1982) A clinical trial of a bead bed system for the prevention of pressure sores in elderly orthopaedic patients, *Journal of Advanced Nursing*, November, Vol. 7, No. 6, pp. 545–8.

Hankin, F. *et al.* (1983) Bleeding beneath postoperative casts, *Orthop. Nurs.*, January/February, Vol. 2, No. 1, pp. 27–32.

Harris, W. H. *et al.* (1985) Prophylaxis of deep-vein thrombosis after total hip replacement, *Journal of Bone and Joint Surgey (America)*, January, Vol. 67, No. 1, pp. 57–62.

Johnson-Pawlson, J. and Koshes, R. (1985) Exercise is for everyone, *Geriatric Nursing*, November/December, Vol. 6, No. 6, pp. 322–7.

Kelly, D. J. (1983) The use of fiberglass as reinforcement with plaster casts, *Orthop. Nurs.*, November/December, Vol. 2, No. 6, pp. 33–6.

Lane, P. L. *et al.* (1982) New synthetic casts: What nurses need to know, *Orthop. Nurs.*, November/December, Vol. 1, No. 16, pp. 13–20.

McFarland, M. B. (1984) Encircling cast drainage: Is it valuable? *Orthop. Nurs.*, March/April, Vol. 3, No. 2, pp. 41–3.

Miller, M. C. (1983) Nursing care of the patient with external fixation therapy, *Orthop. Nurs.*, January/February, Vol. 2, No. 1, pp. 11–15.

Mindell, E. R. (1985) Orthopedic surgery, *Journal of the American Medical Association*, October 25, Vol. 254, No. 18, pp. 2213–15.

Moran-Higgins (1985) Perioperative concerns for the patient with osteoporosis, *Orthop. Nurs.*, May/June, Vol. 4, No. 3, p. 68.

Morse, J. *et al.* (1985) The patient who falls and falls again: Defining the aged at risk, *Journal of Gerontological Nursing*, November, Vol. 11, No. 11, pp. 15–21.

Scales, J. T. *et al.* (1982) Vaperm patient support system: A new general purpose hospital mattress, *The Lancet*, 25 November, pp. 1150–2.

Searls, K. *et al.* (1983) External fixation: General principles of patient management, *Crit. Care Q*, June, Vol. 6, No. 1, pp. 45–54.

Simchen, E. *et al.* (1984) Multivariate analysis of determinants of postoperative wound infection in orthopaedic patients, *Journal of Hospital Infections*, June, Vol. 5, No. 2, pp. 137–46.

Smith, C. (1984) Nursing the patient in traction, *Nursing Times*, 18–24 April, Vol. 80, No. 16, pp. 36–9.

Smith & Nephew (1976) *Gypsona Technique*, Broadwater Press, England.

Sproles, K. J. (1985) Nursing care of skeletal pins: A closer look, *Orthop. Nurs.*, January/February, Vol. 4, No. 1, pp. 11–12, 15–20.

Sullivan, D. (1985) Complications from intraoperative positioning, *Orthop. Nurs.*, July/August, Vol. 4, No. 4, pp. 56–7.

Trigueiro, M. (1983) Pin site care protocol, *Can. Nurs.*, September, Vol. 79, No. 8, pp. 24–6.

Voluz, J. M. (1983) Surgical implants; orthopedic devices, *Journal of American Operating Room Nurses*, June, Vol. 37, No. 7, pp. 1341–9.

Wittert, D. and Barden, R. (1985) Deep vein thrombosis, pulmonary embolism, and prophylaxis in the orthopedic patient, *Orthop. Nurs.*, July/August, Vol. 4, No. 4, pp. 27–32.

Total Joint Arthroplasty

Aaron, R. K. (1983) Total joint arthroplasty, *Surgical Clinics of North America*, June, Vol. 63, No. 3, pp. 697–714.

Barrington, R. (1987) Hip replacment on HP, *The Health Service Journal*, Vol. 97, No. 5037, p. 148.

Doheny, M. O. (1985) Porous coated femoral prosthesis: Concepts; and care considerations, *Orthop. Nurs.*, January/February, Vol. 4, No. 1, pp. 43–5.

Engh, C. A. (1983) Hip arthroplasty with a Moore prosthesis with porous coating: A five-year study, *Clin. Orthop.*, June, Vol. 176, pp. 52–66.

Harris, W. *et al.* (1985) Prophylaxis of deep vein thrombosis after total hip replacement: Dextran and external pneumatic compression compared with 1.2 or 0.3 gm of aspirin daily, *Journal of Bone and Joint Surgery (America)*, January, Vol. 67-A, No. 1, pp. 57–62.

Lotke, P. A. *et al.* (1984) Indications for the treatment of deep venous thrombosis following total knee replacement, *Journal of Bone and Joint Surgery (America)*, February, Vol. 66, No. 2, pp. 202–8.

Love, C. (1986) Do you roll or lift? *Nursing Times*, Vol. 82, No. 29, pp. 44–6.

McConnell, E. (1986) The short-term effects of the modular knee prosthesis, BSc Thesis, University of Ulster (unpublished).

Olivo, J. *et al.* (1985) Total knee arthroplasty: A team approach, *Today's OR Nurs.*, September, Vol. 7, No. 9, pp. 10–17.

Rand, J. A. *et al.* (1984) Management of the infected total joint arthroplasty, *Orthopedic Clinics of North America*, July, Vol. 15, No. 3, pp. 491–504.

Sachs, B. L. *et al.* (1985) An improvised passive motion apparatus, *Clin. Orthop.*, April, Vol. 194, pp. 205–6.

Strang, E. L. and Johns, J. L. (1984) Nursing care of the patient treated with continuous passive motion following total knee arthroplasty, *Orthop. Nurs.*, November/December, Vol. 3, No. 6, pp. 27–32.

Stulberg, B. N. *et al.* (1984) Deep-vein thrombosis following total knee replacement, *Journal of Bone and Joint Surgery (America)*, February, Vol. 66, No. 2, pp. 194–201.

Walsh, C. R. and Wirth, C. R. (1985) Total knee arthroplasty: Biomechanical and nursing considerations, *Orthop. Nurs.*, January/February, Vol. 4, No. 1, pp. 29–34, 70.

Wong, S. *et al.* (1984) Total hip replacements: Improving post-hospital adjustment, *Nurs. Manage.*, July, Vol. 15, No. 7, pp. 34C–D, 34F–G.

chapter 36

ASSESSMENT AND CARE OF PATIENTS WITH MUSCULOSKELETAL TRAUMA

Injury to one part of the musculoskeletal system usually produces injury or dysfunction of adjacent structures and of structures enclosed or supported by them. If the bones are broken, the muscles cannot function; if the nerves do not send impulses to the muscles, as in paralysis, the bones cannot move; if the joint surfaces do not articulate normally, neither the bones nor the muscles can function properly. Thus, although a fracture affects primarily the bone, it may also produce injury to the muscles surrounding the injured bone, and to the blood vessels and the nerves in the vicinity of the fracture.

In the treatment of injury of the musculoskeletal system, support is provided for the injured part until nature has time to heal it. Support may be accomplished by bandages, adhesive strapping, splints or casts, applied externally. Support may be applied directly to the bone in the form of pins or plates. At times, traction must be applied to correct deformity or shortening.

After the immediate and the painful effects of the injury have passed, consideration must be given to the prevention of fibrosis and the resulting stiffness in the injured muscles and the joint structures. Active function by the patient is the best form of treatment to guard against this disability. In some cases, the support applied may permit active function almost from the start. The healing process and recovery of function may be hastened by various forms of physiotherapy.

CONTUSIONS, STRAINS, SPRAINS AND DISLOCATIONS

Contusions

A contusion is an injury of the soft tissues, produced by blunt force (e.g., a blow, kick, fall). There is always some bleeding into the injured part (ecchymosis), due to the rupture of many small vessels. This produces the well-known discolouration of the skin (bruising), which gradually turns to brown and then to yellow, and finally disappears as absorption becomes complete. When the bleeding is sufficient to cause an appreciable collection of blood, it is called haematoma. The local symptoms (pain, swelling and discolouration) are present.

Care

Care consists of elevating the affected part and applying moist or dry cold for the first 24 hours to produce vaso-constriction, which results in decreased bleeding and oedema. Application of cold should be intermittent for 20 to 30 minutes. In the recovery phase, moist heat is applied for 20 minutes at a time to promote vasodilation, absorption and repair. Support bandages wrapped over the contused area controls bleeding and reduces associated swelling.

Strains

A strain is a 'muscle pull' due to over-use, overstretching or excessive stress. Strains are microscopic, incomplete muscle tears with some bleeding into the tissue. The patient experiences gradual soreness or sudden pain and then local tenderness. Pain is experienced with muscle use and isometric contraction.

Care

The injured muscle must be allowed to rest and repair itself. Intermittent ice compresses for the first day followed by intermittent heat provide both comfort and increased circulation to the injured muscle, promoting healing. Elevation and a pressure bandage control any associated oedema. Patient education needs to emphasize minimal exercise until healing has taken place, and then gradual progression of activity. Too much exercise too soon will cause restrain and delayed recovery.

Sprains

A sprain is an injury to the ligamentous structures surrounding a joint, caused by a wrench or a twist. The function of a ligament is to maintain stability while permitting mobility. A torn ligament loses its stabilizing ability. As is the case with contusions, blood vessels are ruptured, and ecchymosis and oedema occur. The joint is tender and movement of the joint becomes painful. The degree of disability and pain increases during the first two to three hours after the injury because of the associated swelling and bleeding. To be certain that there is no bone injury, these patients should have an X-ray examination. Avulsion fracture (a bone fragment is pulled away by a ligament or tendon) may be associated with sprains.

Care

Sprains are treated initially with cold, elevation and splinting or cast immobilization. The application of cold reduces the associated pain and causes vasoconstriction, which retards extravasation of blood and the development of oedema. Support bandages reduce swelling and oedema. The part should be elevated and rested.

After 24 hours, mild heat may be applied (15 to 30 minutes, four times a day) to promote healing. If the sprain is severe (torn muscle fibres and disrupted ligaments), surgical repair or cast immobilization is necessary so that the joint will not lose its stability. A severe sprain will take about a month to heal, and then active exercise can begin and build gradually.

Joint Dislocations

A dislocation of a joint is a condition in which the articular surfaces of the bones forming the joint are no longer in anatomical contact. The bones are literally 'out of joint'. A subluxation is a partial dislocation of the articulating surfaces. Traumatic dislocations are orthopaedic emergencies, because the associated joint structures, blood supply and nerves are distorted and severely stressed. Avascular necrosis (tissue death due to anoxia and diminished blood supply) and nerve palsy may occur.

Dislocations may be: (1) congenital (present at birth, due to some maldevelopment, most often noted at the hip); (2) spontaneous or pathological, due to disease of the articular or the periarticular structures; and (3) traumatic, due to injury, such as the application of force in such a manner as to produce disruption of the joint.

The signs and symptoms of a traumatic dislocation are: (1) pain; (2) change in contour of the joint; (3) change in the length of the extremity; (4) loss of normal mobility; and (5) change in the axis of the dislocated bones.

X-ray films confirm the diagnosis and should be taken in every case, because there is often an associated fracture.

Care

The part needs to be immobilized while the patient is transported. The dislocation is reduced (i.e., displaced parts brought into normal position), usually under anaesthesia. The head of the dislocated bone is manipulated back into the joint cavity. The joint is immobilized by bandages, splints, casts or traction. It is kept in a stable position. With a stable, reduced dislocation, gentle, active movement three or four times a day is begun several days to weeks after reduction. This is to preserve range of motion. The joint is supported between exercise sessions.

Nursing concerns are directed at providing comfort, evaluating the neurovascular status and protecting the joint during healing. The patient needs to learn how to manage the immobilizing devices and how to protect the joint from re-injury.

Sports Injuries

More and more people are participating in recreational

sports. These recreational athletes may push themselves beyond the level of their physical conditioning and incur sports injuries. Injuries to the musculoskeletal system may be of an acute nature (sprains, strains, dislocations or fractures) or may result from gradual overuse (chondromalacia patella, tendinitis, stress fractures). Professional athletes are also susceptible to injury, even though their training is supervised closely to minimize the occurrence of injury and to enhance the development of athletic performance.

Musculoskeletal contusions result from direct falls or blows from sporting equipment. The initial dull pain becomes greater, with oedema and stiffness occurring by the next day. Sprains occur commonly in fingers, ankles and knees. If the ligamentous damage is major, the joint becomes unstable and surgical repair may be required. An avulsion fracture may exist. Strains present with a sharp, stabbing pain from bleeding and immediate protective muscle contraction. Tennis players often suffer calf muscle strains; soccer players experience quadriceps strains; swimmers, weight lifters and tennis players suffer shoulder strains. Tendinitis (inflammation of a tendon) is due to overuse and is seen in tennis players (epicondylar tendinitis), runners and gymnasts (Achilles tendinitis), and runners and basketball players (infrapatellar tendinitis). Meniscal injuries of the knee occur with excessive rotational stress. Dislocations are seen with throwing and lifting sports. Fractures occur with falls. Skaters and bikers frequently suffer Colles's fractures of the wrist when they fall on outstretched arms; ballet dancers and field and track athletes experience metatarsal fractures. Stress fractures occur with repeated bone trauma from activities such as jogging, gymnastics, basketball and aerobics. The tibias, fibulas and metatarsals are most vulnerable.

Care

Generally, musculoskeletal injuries need to be recognized and managed early to facilitate healing and to minimize residual disabilities. The basic principle of management for most soft-tissue injuries is RICE (Rest, Ice, Compression, Elevation). Ice is applied for 20 to 30 minutes every three to four hours during the first 24 to 48 hours to control swelling and relieve pain. The area is wrapped with a compression bandage to minimize effusion, support the area and provide comfort. The wrap must not be constricting. Monitoring the neurovascular status of the extremity becomes an important nursing function. The injured extremity is elevated above the heart to control swelling and to promote rest. Depending on the site and the severity of the injury, the extremity may be immobilized and/or surgical intervention may be required. Arthroscopic surgery may be required for meniscus tears and other joint injuries that limit joint function and contribute to articular cartilage wear.

Patients who have experienced a sports-related injury are highly motivated to return to their previous level of activity. Compliance with restriction of activities and resumption of them on a gradual, progressive timetable may be a real problem for these patients. They need to be taught how to avoid further injury or new injury. With recurrence of symptoms, they need to learn to diminish the level and intensity of activity to a comfort level and to treat the symptoms (RICE). Activity should be resumed gradually and sensibly. Recovery from sports-related injury can take a few days to six or more weeks.

Prevention of sports-related injuries can be achieved by use of appropriate equipment (e.g., running shoes) and by training and conditioning the body. Changes in activities and stresses should occur gradually.

FRACTURES

A fracture is a break in the continuity of bone and is defined according to type and extent (Figure 36.1). Fractures occur when the bone is subjected to stress greater than it can absorb. Fractures can be caused by direct blow, crushing force, sudden twisting motion and even extreme muscle contraction.

While the bone is the part most directly affected, other structures also may be involved, resulting in soft-tissue oedema, haemorrhage into the muscles and joints, joint dislocations, ruptured tendons, severed nerves and damaged blood vessels. Body organs may be injured by the force that caused the fracture or by the resultant bony fragments.

Types of Fractures

A complete fracture involves a break across the entire cross-section of the bone and is frequently displaced (removed from normal position). In an incomplete fracture, the break occurs through only part of the cross-section of the bone.

A closed fracture does not produce a break in the skin. An open fracture is one that extends through the skin or mucous membrane. Open fractures can be graded, for example: grade I—a clean wound less than 1 cm long; grade II—a larger wound without extensive soft-tissue damage; and grade III—the most severe, with extensive soft-tissue damage.

Fractures may also be described according to anatomical placement of fragments—displaced/nondisplaced fracture.

The following are specific types of fractures (see Figure 36.1):

Greenstick—a fracture in which one side of a bone is broken and the other side is bent (usually seen in children). Transverse—a fracture that is straight across the bone.

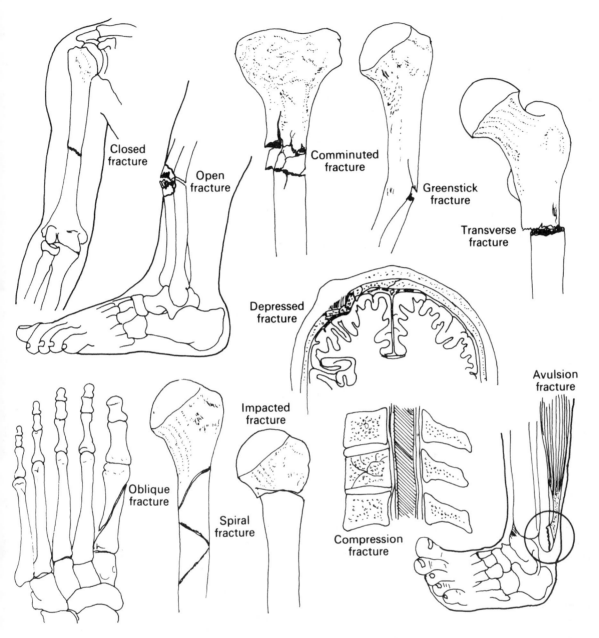

Figure 36.1 Types of fractures. (Brunner, L. S. and Suddarth, D. S. (1986) *The Lippincott Manual of Nursing Practice* (4th edition), J. B. Lippincott, Philadelphia.)

Oblique—a fracture occurring at an angle across the bone (less stable than transverse).

Spiral—a fracture twisting around the shaft of the bone.

Comminuted—a fracture in which bone has splintered into three or more fragments.

Depressed—a fracture in which fragment(s) is (are) indriven (seen frequently in fractures of skull and facial bones).

Compression—a fracture in which bone has been compressed (seen in vertebral fractures).

Pathological—a fracture that occurs through an area of diseased bone (bone cyst, Paget's disease, bony metastasis, tumour).

Avulsion—a pulling away of a fragment of bone by a ligament or tendon at its attachment.

Epiphyseal—a fracture through the epiphysis, only seen before skeletal maturity.

Clinical Features

The clinical features of a fracture are pain, loss of function, false motion, deformity, shortening, crepitation, local swelling and discolouration. In an open fracture, the bone penetrates through the skin.

1. The pain is of a continuous type and increases in severity until the bone fragments are immobilized.
2. Following the break, the part cannot be used and tends to move unnaturally instead of remaining rigid as it normally would. The displacement of the fragments in a fracture of the arm or leg causes a deformity (either visible or palpable) of the extremity, detectable when it is compared to the normal extremity. The extremity cannot function properly because normal function of the muscles depends upon the integrity of the bones to which they are attached.
3. In fractures of long bones, there is actually shortening of the extremity because of the contraction of the muscles that are attached above and below the site of the fracture. The fragments may often overlap as much as 2.5–5 cm. The muscle spasm that accompanies fracture is natural splinting to minimize further movement of the fracture fragments.
4. When the extremity is examined with the hands, a grating sensation, called crepitus, can be felt due to the rubbing of the fragments one upon the other. (Testing for crepitation can produce further tissue damage.)
5. Localized swelling and discolouration of the skin occur as a result of trauma and haemorrhage that follow a fracture. These signs may not develop for several hours or days following the injury.

All of these signs and symptoms are not necessarily present in every fracture. When there is a linear or fissure fracture, or in cases in which the fractured surfaces are driven together (impacted fractures), many of these symptoms do not occur.

The diagnosis of a fracture depends on the symptoms of the patient, the physical signs and X-ray examination. Usually, the patient reports having sustained an injury to the area.

Emergency Care of the Patient With a Fracture

The fractured extremity is rendered as immobile as possible *before the patient is moved.* If an injured patient must be removed from a vehicle before splints can be applied, the extremity is supported above and below the fracture site to prevent rotation as well as angular motion. Movement of fracture fragments will cause additional pain, soft-tissue damage and additional haemorrhage. Adequate splinting is essential to prevent damage to the soft tissue by the bony fragments. It must be remembered that the pain associated with a fractured bone is severe, and that the best way to decrease pain and haemorrhage and prevent possible shock is to prevent movement of the bone fragments and the joints adjacent to the fracture.

The peripheral pulses distal to the injury should be palpated to ensure that circulation has not been compromised and that tissue perfusion is sufficient.

In an open fracture, the wound is covered with a clean (sterile) dressing to prevent contamination of deeper tissues. No attempt is made to reduce the fracture, even if one of the bone fragments is protruding through the wound.

Immediately following injury, a patient who is in a state of confusion may not be aware of the fracture (i.e., a fractured extremity may be walked upon).

When a patient comes to a hospital suffering from a fracture, a narcotic sufficient to relieve the pain should be given, provided there is no head injury. The intravenous route allows for smaller dosage and prompt action.

Then, with care and gentleness, the clothes are removed, first from the uninjured side of the body and then from the injured side. Sometimes the patient's clothing must be cut away on the injured side. The fractured extremity is moved as little as possible.

PHYSIOLOGY OF BONE HEALING

When the bone is injured, the bone fragments are not merely patched together with scar tissue. The bone regenerates itself.

Stages of Bone Healing

There are several stages in fracture healing: (1) inflammation/haematoma formation; (2) cellular proliferation; (3) callus formation; (4) callus ossification; and (5) remodelling into mature bone.

Inflammation
With a fracture, the body response is similar to that of injury to other systems. There is bleeding, extravasation of blood and the formation of a fracture haematoma. The area exhibits oedema, swelling, inflammation and pain. The fracture fragment ends become devitalized because of the interrupted blood supply. The injured area is invaded by macrophages (large, white blood cells), which débride the area. The inflammatory stage lasts a couple of days, and resolution of the inflammatory response is characterized by a decrease in pain and swelling.

Cellular Proliferation
Fibrin strands form within the fracture haematoma and adjacent tissue, migrating into the clot. Revascularization begins. Fibroblasts and osteoblasts (developed from osteocytes, endosteal cells and periosteal cells) produce collagen and proteoglycans for a collagen matrix at the fracture. Cartilage and fibrous connective tissue develop. From the periosteum, a collar of growth is in evidence.

This is the beginning of an external cartilaginous callus. Minimal micromotion at the fracture site stimulates callus formation and healing.

Callus Formation

Tissue growth continues and the cartilage collar from each bone fragment grows toward the others until the fracture gap is 'bridged'. The fracture fragments are joined by fibrous tissue, cartilage and immature bone. An internal callus also develops and invades the remaining blood clot. The shape of the callus and the volume of tissue required to bridge the defect are directly proportional to the amount of bone damage and displacement. It takes three to four weeks for fracture fragments to be united by cartilage or fibrous tissue. Clinically, the fragments will no longer be easily moved.

Ossification

Ossification of the developed callus begins within two to three weeks postfracture, through the process of endochondral ossification (see Chapter 34, Bone Formation, p. 1071).

The mineral deposition continues, and produces a firmly reunited bone. With major adult long bone fractures, ossification takes three to four months.

Remodelling

The final stage of fracture repair consists of removal of any remaining devitalized tissue and reorganization of the new bone into its former structural arrangement. Bone architecture is related to its function. Compact bone and cancellous bone develop according to functional stresses. Depending on the extent of bone modification needed, remodelling may take months to years. Cancellous bone heals and remodels more rapidly than compact cortical bone, especially at points of direct contact.

The progress of bone healing is monitored by serial X-rays. Adequate immobilization is essential until there is radiological evidence of callus.

Bone Healing With Fragments Firmly Approximated

When fractures are treated with open rigid fixation techniques, the bony fragments can be placed in direct contact. Motion at the fracture is eliminated. In this situation, the stages of bone healing are modified. Haematoma formation is not essential and is not observed. Little or no external cartilaginous callus develops. Primary bone healing occurs.

Immature bone develops from the endosteum. There is an intensive regeneration of new osteons. The new osteons develop in the fracture line by a process similar to normal bone maintenance. Fracture strength is obtained when the new osteons have become established. With rigid internal fixation, the bone heals through cortical bone remodelling. This process is slower than bone healing by callus formation.

Table 36.1 *Approximate immobilization time necessary for union*

Fracture site	Number of weeks
Phalanx	3–5
Metacarpal	6
Carpal	6
Scaphoid	10
	(or until X-ray shows union)
Radius and ulna	10–12
Humerus:	
Superacondylar	8
Midshaft	8–12
Proximal (impacted)	3
Proximal (displaced)	6–8
Clavicle	6–10
Vertebra	16
Pelvis	6
Femur:	
Intracapsular	24
Intratrochanteric	10–12
Shaft	18
Supracondylar	12–15
Tibia:	
Proximal	8–10
Shaft	14–20
Malleolus	6
Calcaneus	12–16
Metatarsal	6
Toes	3

(Compare, E. L. et al. Pictorial Handbook of Fracture Treatment (5th edition), Year Book Medical Publishers, Chicago.)

Healing Time of Fractures

Many factors influence the speed with which healing occurs. The reduction of the displaced fracture fragments must be accurate and successfully maintained to ensure healing. The affected bone must have an adequate blood supply. The age of the patient and the type of fracture also affect healing time. In general, fractures of flat bones (pelvis, scapula) heal quite rapidly. Fractures at the ends of long bones where the bone is more vascular and cancellous heal more quickly than do fractures in areas where the bone is dense and less vascular (midshaft). Weight-bearing will stimulate healing of stabilized fractures of the long bones in the lower extremities. In addition, activity minimizes the development of immobility-related osteoporosis (a reduction of total bone mass producing porous and fragile bones due to imbalance in homeostatic bone turnover). Table 36.1 shows the approximate immobilization times necessary for union of the most common types of fractures.

If fracture healing is disrupted, the bone union time may be delayed or stopped completely. Factors that may interrupt fracture healing include loss of fracture haematoma by débridement, devitalization of adjacent tissue by inadequate blood supply, extensive space between bone fragments, interposition of soft tissue between bone ends, inadequate fracture immobilization, infection, complications from the treatment and metabolic disorders.

PRINCIPLES OF FRACTURE MANAGEMENT

The principles of fracture treatment (the 'four Rs') include recognition (e.g., X-ray), reduction, rest (e.g., immobilization in a plaster cast) and rehabilitation (restoration of 'normal' function).

Fracture Reduction and Immobilization

Reduction of a fracture ('setting' the bone) refers to restoration of the fracture fragments into anatomical alignment as soon as possible. This is accomplished by closed or open manipulation.

Before fracture reduction, the patient should be prepared for the procedure. Medications for pain relief are administered. The extremity that is to be manipulated should be handled gently to avoid additional damage, elevated to minimize swelling and gently cleaned if required before being dressed in a cast or splint.

After the fracture has been reduced, bone fragments must be immobilized or held in correct position and alignment until union has had time to take place. Immobilization may be accomplished by external or internal fixation. Methods of external fixation include bandages, casts, splints, continuous traction, pin and plaster technique or external fixators. Internal fixation devices (metal implants) include nails, plates, screws, wires and rods. These serve as internal splints to hold the fractured bone in alignment while healing takes place.

Methods of Fracture Reduction

Several methods are used to obtain reduction of a fracture; the method selected depends on the nature of the fracture. Variations of these methods are carried out, but the underlying principles are the same. Usually, fractures are reduced as soon as possible because tissues may lose their elasticity if infiltrated by oedema or haemorrhage. At times, the patient may need anaesthesia when a fracture is reduced and immobilized. In most cases, fracture reduction becomes more difficult as the injury begins healing.

Closed Reduction

In most instances, closed reduction is accomplished by bringing the bone fragments into apposition (ends in contact) by manipulation and manual traction.

Following the manipulation, X-ray films are taken to determine that the bone fragments are in correct align-

ment. A cast is usually applied to immobilize the extremity and maintain the reduction. A second person may hold the extremity in the desired position while it is being encased in plaster.

Traction

Traction may be used to effect fracture reduction and immobilization. Adjustments of the magnitude of traction are made as muscle spasm is overcome. X-rays are used to monitor the fracture reduction and approximation of the bony fragments. As the fracture heals, evidence of callus formation is noted radiologically. When the callus is well established, a cast is frequently used for the immobilization technique. Traction and the nursing care of a patient in traction are discussed more fully on page 1087.

Open Reduction or Open Operation

Some fractures require an operation or open reduction. The fracture fragments are reduced (put into alignment). Internal fixation devices in the form of metallic pins, wires, screws, plates, nails or rods may be used to hold the bone fragments in position until solid bone healing occurs. Internal fixation devices may be attached to the sides of bone or inserted through the bony fragments or directly into the medullary cavity of the bone (Figure 36.2). These devices assure firm approximation and fixation of the bony fragments.

Nursing Care Following Open Reduction. During the immediate postoperative period following open reduction, the nursing care is the same as for any other major surgical procedure (see Chapter 2). If the patient is to be immobilized in traction following surgery, the traction may be applied immediately following surgery in the operating room. Ice to control oedema may be prescribed. Neurovascular monitoring is carries out at frequent intervals. The affected part is elevated.

● Symptoms of pain, pallor, pulselessness, paraesthesia, paralysis (the 'five Ps'), or coolness, indicate abnormal circulatory changes or neurological disturbances.
● The medical staff should be notified immediately so that the dressings may be loosened or the cast bivalved in order to relieve pressure (see p. 1084). Haematoma drainage or fasciotomy may be needed. Dressings should be inspected at regular intervals.

The assessment and management of postoperative pain is an individualized problem. During the immediate postoperative period, narcotics may be prescribed. As soon as possible, oral non-narcotic analgesics should be given as prescribed, since patients who have undergone orthopaedic operations may have prolonged musculoskeletal complaints. Restlessness, anxiety and general discomfort may be relieved by appropriate nursing measures, including psychological support, position changes and pain modification techniques.

Orthopaedic wounds have a tendency to ooze more

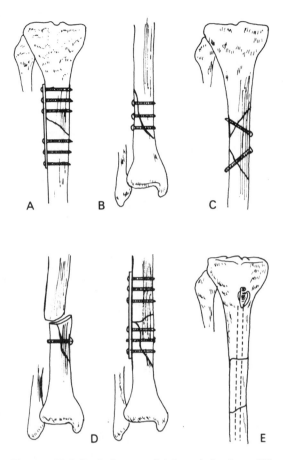

Figure 36.2 Techniques of internal fixation. (A) Plate and six screws for a transverse or short oblique fracture. (B) Screws for a long oblique or spiral fracture. (C) Screws for a long butterfly fragment. (D) Plate and six screws for a short butterfly fragment. (E) Medullary nail for a segmental fracture. (Smith, H. Fractures. In Speed, J. S. and Smith, H. (eds.) (1949), in *Campbell's Operative Orthopaedics, Volume 1*, (2nd edition), The C. V. Mosby Co., St Louis.)

than other surgical wounds. External muscle dissection frequently produces wounds in which haemostasis is poor. Wounds that are closed while under tourniquet control may bleed when the tourniquet is released in the postoperative period. Drains and portable wound suction are used to minimize blood accumulation and the possibility of infection.

Maintenance of good aseptic technique is essential when caring for patients having bone surgery. Osteomyelitis (bone infection) is difficult to treat, and prevention is the objective. Aseptic wound dressing technique is necessary. Prevention of wound infections will eliminate that source for subsequent osteomyelitis.

Usually, internal fixation will allow early mobilization of the patient. The actual stability of the fracture fixation determines the amount of movement and stress the

extremity can withstand. The surgeon can estimate the degree of stability obtained and will prescribe activity limits. An overbed trapeze is available to assist the patient moving in bed.

Removal of Internal Fixation Devices

Internal fixation devices may be removed after bony union has taken place, but for the majority of patients a device is not removed unless it produces symptoms. Pain and decreased function are the prime indicators that a problem has developed. Such problems may include mechanical failure (inadequate insertion and stabilization); material failure (faulty or damaged internal fixation devices); corrosion of the device, causing local inflammation; allergic response to the metallic alloy used; and osteoporotic remodelling adjacent to the fixation device (stress needed for bone strength is carried by the device, causing a disuse osteoporosis). If the device is removed, the bone needs to be protected from refracture related to osteoporosis, altered bone structure and accident. Bone remodelling re-establishes the bone's structural strength.

Nursing Care of the Patient With a Simple Fracture

An important objective in treating fractures is to help patients return to their usual activities as rapidly as possible. Weeks to months are required for most fractures to heal. Patients are taught how to control swelling and pain associated with the fracture and soft-tissue trauma. They are encouraged to be active within the limits of the fracture immobilization. Bedrest is kept at a minimum. Exercises are begun to maintain health of unaffected muscles and to increase strength of muscles needed for transferring and using ambulatory aids. Patients are taught how to use these devices safely. Planning is done to help patients modify their home environment as needed and secure personal assistance if necessary. Patient teaching includes self-care, medication information, monitoring for potential problems and the need for continuing health care supervision. The goal is to return to the prior level of activity, but it may take months for fracture healing and restoration of full strength and mobility.

Management of Open Fractures

In an open fracture (one associated with an open wound extending through the skin surface and above the area of bone injury) there is risk of infection—osteomyelitis, gas gangrene and tetanus. The objectives of management are to minimize the chance of infection of the wound, soft tissue and bone and to promote healing of soft tissue and bone.

The patient is taken to the operating theatre, where the wound is cleansed, débrided (foreign matter and devitalized tissue removed) and irrigated. The wound is swabbed for culture and sensitivity studies. Devitalized bone fragments are usually removed. Bone grafting may be done to bridge the defect, provided that the recipient tissue is healthy and able to facilitate union. The fracture is carefully reduced and stabilized by external fixation. Repair of damage to blood vessels, soft tissue, muscles, nerves and tendons is usually carried out.

Primary closure may not be accomplished because of oedema and potential ischaemia, restricted wound drainage and anaerobic infection. A heavily contaminated wound may be left open, dressed with sterile gauze and not closed until it is clear that infection has been aborted or overcome. Tetanus prophylaxis is given. Usually, intravenous antibiotics are started to prevent or treat serious infection. The wounds are closed by suture or by autogenous skin or flap grafts in five to seven days.

Nursing Care
On return from the operating theatre, the patient is observed for signs of shock because considerable loss of blood usually occurs during surgery. The extremity is ele-

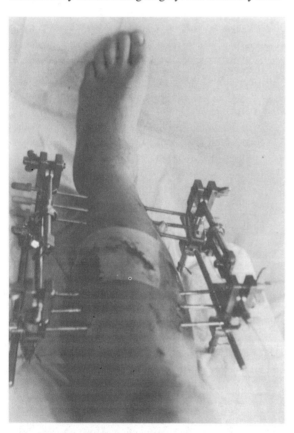

Figure 36.3 External fixation device. Pins are inserted into bone fragments. The fracture is reduced and aligned. The reduction is stabilized by attaching the pins to a rigid, portable frame. The device facilitates treatment of soft tissue damaged in complex fractures.

vated to minimize the development of oedema. The distal pulses are palpated and neurovascular status is assessed frequently. The temperature is taken at regular intervals, and the patient is observed for signs of infection.

External Fixators

External fixation devices are used to manage open fractures with soft-tissue damage and provide stable support for severe comminuted fractures while permitting active treatment of damaged soft tissue (Figure 36.3).

Complicated fractures of the humerus, forearm, femur, tibia and pelvis are managed with external skeletal fixators. The fracture is reduced, aligned and immobilized by a series of pins inserted in the bone fragments. The pins are maintained in position through attachment to a portable frame. The fixators facilitate patient comfort, early mobility, active exercise of adjacent uninvolved joints and shortened hospitalization. In addition, complications related to disuse and immobility are minimized.

The fixator is removed when the soft tissue has healed; the fracture may be stabilized by cast or moulded orthosis until the bone has healed by callus formation. (Continuous compression at the fracture site with an external fixator for primary bone healing is difficult to achieve.)

Nursing Care
Psychological preparation for application of the external fixator is important. The apparatus looks clumsy and foreign to the patient. Reassurance that the discomfort associated with the device is mild and that early mobility is anticipated aids in the acceptance of the device. Involvement of the patient in the care associated with the fixator after it is applied will also help.

Following application of the external fixator, the extremity is elevated to reduce swelling. The neurovascular status of the extremity is monitored frequently. The injured area and pin sites are checked for signs of infection. Some serous drainage from the pin sites is to be expected. Each pin site is assessed for redness, drainage, tenderness, pain and loosening of the pin.

● NEVER adjust the clamps on an external fixator frame when being used for primary fracture treatment.

Pin care to prevent pin tract infection is carried out according to the prescribed regime. Crusts should not form at the pin site, and the fixator must be kept clean.

Isometric and active exercises are encouraged within the limits of tissue damage. The nurse must be alert for potential problems due to pressure by the device on the skin, nerves or blood vessels, and prevent device-induced injury by covering any sharp points on the fixator or pins. When the swelling has subsided, the patient is mobilized within the limits of any other injuries. Weight-bearing limits need to be prescribed to minimize the chance of pins loosening when stress is applied at the bone-pin interface.

COMPLICATIONS OF FRACTURES

Immediate Complications

The immediate complications following fracture are: shock, which may be fatal within a few hours after injury; fat embolism, which may occur within 48 hours or later; compartment syndrome, which may result in permanent loss of extremity function; infection; thromboembolism (pulmonary embolism), which may cause death several weeks after injury; and disseminated intravascular coagulation.

Shock

Hypovolaemic or traumatic shock, resulting from haemorrhage (both external and internal) and loss of extracellular fluid into damaged tissues, may occur in fractures of the extremities, thorax, pelvis and spine. Because the bone is very vascular, large quantities of blood may be lost as a result of trauma, especially in femoral and pelvic fractures.

Treatment consists of replacing the depleted blood volume, relieving the patient's pain, providing adequate splinting and protecting the patient from further injury.

Fat Embolism Syndrome

Following fracture of long bones or pelvis, multiple fractures or crush injuries, fat emboli may develop, especially in the young, adult (20- to 30-year-old) male. At the time of fracture, innumerable fat globules may move into the blood because the marrow pressure is greater than the capillary pressure, or because catecholamines elevated by the patient's stress reaction cause mobilization of fatty acids and the development of fat globules in the bloodstream. The fat globules combine with platelets to form emboli, which then occlude the small blood vessels that supply the brain, lungs, kidneys and other organs. The onset of symptoms may occur a few hours after injury to a week after, but usually occurs within 48 hours. The onset of symptoms is rapid.

The presenting feature is usually cerebral disturbance manifested by bizarre mental symptoms varying from mild agitation and confusion to delirium and coma that occur in response to hypoxia, caused by the lodging of fat emboli in the brain. In addition, tachycardia is noted.

The respiratory response includes tachypnoea, dyspnoea, crackles, wheezes and large amounts of thick, white sputum. The chest X-ray exhibits a typical 'snow storm' infiltrate.

With systemic embolization the patient appears pale. Petechiae are noted in the buccal membranes and conjunctival sacs, on the hard palate, on the fundus of the eye and over the chest and anterior axillary folds. Free fat may be found in the urine when emboli reach the kidneys.

● Personality changes, restlessness, irritability or confusion in a patient who has sustained a fracture is an indication that immediate blood gas studies should be carried out.

Care

Immediate immobilization of fractures, minimal fracture manipulation and adequate support for fractured bones during turning and positioning are measures that may reduce the incidence of fat emboli. Frequently, fat emboli syndrome becomes apparent through subtle changes in the patient's mental status. Monitoring high-risk patients will aid in the early identification of this problem. Prompt institution of respiratory support is essential.

The objectives of management are to support the respiratory system and to correct homeostatic disturbances. Arterial blood gas analysis is done to determine the degree of respiratory impairment, as respiratory failure is the most common cause of death. Respiratory support is provided with oxygen given in high concentrations. Controlled volume ventilation with positive end-expiratory pressure (PEEP) may be employed to decrease and inhibit the formation of pulmonary oedema. Steroids may be given to treat the inflammatory lung reaction and to control cerebral oedema. Low-molecular-weight dextran may improve pulmonary and capillary flow because of its desludging effect. Heparin may be used for its lipolytic action (breakdown of fat globules), but its anticoagulant effect may cause haemorrhage at the fracture site.

Fat emboli are a major cause of death in patients with fractures. Respiratory support must be instituted early. Response to therapy frequently occurs within 48 hours.

Compartment Syndrome

Compartment syndrome is a problem that develops when tissue perfusion in the muscles is less than that required for tissue viability. This can be due to (1) reduction of the muscle compartment size because the enclosing muscle fascia is too tight or a cast or dressing is constrictive, or (2) an increase in muscle compartment contents because of oedema or haemorrhage associated with a variety of problems (e.g., ischaemia, crush injuries, injection of tissue-destroying (toxic) substances, fractures). The forearm and the leg muscle compartments are involved most frequently. Permanent function can be lost if the situation continues for more than six to eight hours and myoneural (muscle and nerve) ischaemia and necrosis occur. Volkmann's contracture (Figure 36.4) is an example of this complication.

The patient complains of deep, throbbing, unrelenting pain, which is not controlled by analgesics. Palpation of the muscle, if that is possible, will reveal it to be swollen

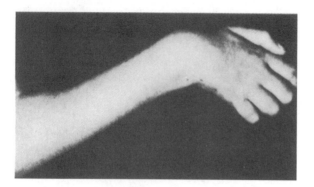

Figure 36.4 The forearm and hand of a patient with late Volkmann's ischaemic contracture. (Rockwood, C. A. and Green, D. P. (eds) (1984) *Fractures (Volume 1)*, J. B. Lippincott, Philadelphia.)

and hard. Passive stretching movement of the muscle will cause acute pain. If it does not, the patient's pain may be due to nerve ischaemia. Diminished capillary refill, cyanotic nailbeds, paralysis and paraesthesia may be present. The pulse may be obscured by swelling. Usually, major arteries are not occluded by compartment syndrome. Nerve and muscle tissues deteriorate as compartment pressures increase.

Prevention and Care

Compartment syndrome can be prevented by elevating the injured extremity and by applying ice after injury. If it occurs, restrictive dressings must be released, and fasciotomy may be needed if conservative measures have not restored tissue perfusion and relieved pain within an hour.

The extremity is splinted in a functional position, and passive range-of-motion exercises are usually prescribed every four to six hours. The wound is débrided and closed in three to five days when the oedema has resolved and tissue perfusion has been restored.

Other Immediate Complications

Thromboembolism, infection (all open fractures are considered to be contaminated—see p. 1113), and disseminated intravascular coagulation are other possible complications of fractures. The treatment of disseminated intravascular coagulation is discussed in Chapter 10.

Delayed Complications

Delayed Union and Nonunion

Delayed union occurs when healing does not advance at a normal rate for the location and type of fracture. Nonunion results from failure of the ends of a fractured bone to unite. The patient complains of persistent discomfort and movement at the fracture site. Factors contributing to union problems include infection at the fracture site; inter-

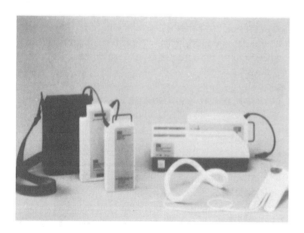

Figure 36.5 Electromagnetic bone-healing stimulator. Pulsed electromagnetic fields generated through coils included in the cast produce bone growth (osteogenesis) at the fracture site. The system is portable and battery powered. The therapy is used for 10 to 12 hours a day. (Courtesy of EBI Medical Systems Inc., Parsippany, New Jersey.)

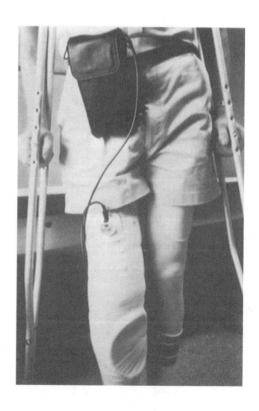

position of tissue between the bone ends; inadequate immobilization or manipulation, which disrupts callus formation; excessive space between bone fragments (bone gap); limited bone contact; and restricted blood supply that results in avascular necrosis.

In nonunion, fibrocartilage or fibrous tissue exists between the bone fragments; no bone salts have been deposited. A false joint (pseudoarthrosis) often develops at the site of the fracture. Fractures of the middle third of the humerus, of the neck of the femur in elderly people and of the lower third of the tibia most frequently result in nonunion.

Nonunion may be managed by bone grafting. Surgically, the fractured bone fragments are freshened, infection if present is removed, and a bone graft, frequently from the iliac crest, is placed in the bony defect. The bone graft provides a lattice work for invasion by bone cells. Following grafting, rigid immobilization is required.

Electrical Stimulation of Osteogenesis. Osteogenesis in nonunion may be stimulated by electricity, and is approximately as effective as bone grafting. It is not effective with large bone gaps or synovial pseudoarthrosis. The electrical stimulation modifies the tissue environment, enhancing mineral deposition and bone formation.

In some situations, pins that act as cathodes are inserted percutaneously directly into the fracture site, and direct current is passed over the fracture continuously. Direct current methods cannot be used when infection is present.

Another method is noninvasive inductive coupling. Pulsing electromagnetic fields are delivered to the fracture for 10 to 12 hours a day by an electromagnetic coil implanted in the dressing over the nonunion site (Figure 36.5). During the electrical stimulation treatment period, rigid fracture fixation with adequate support is needed.

Avascular Necrosis of Bone

Avascular necrosis occurs when the bone loses its blood supply and dies. It may follow a fracture (especially of the femoral neck), dislocations, prolonged high-dosage steroid therapy, chronic renal disease, sickle cell anaemia and other diseases. The devitalized bone may collapse or reabsorb and be replaced by new bone. The patient develops limitation of movement and pain. X-ray demonstrates calcium loss and structural collapse. Treatment generally consists of attempts to revitalize the bone with bone grafts, prosthetic replacement or arthrodesis (joint fusion).

FRACTURES OF SPECIFIC SITES

An injury to the skeletal structure may vary from a simple linear fracture to a severe crushing injury. The therapeutic programme is determined by the type and location of the fracture and the degree of involvement of surrounding structures. Maximum functional recovery is the goal of fracture management.

Fractures of the skull and cervical spine have been considered in Chapter 33 in the section on management of patients with neurological disorders. Fracture of the mandible is discussed in Chapter 12.

Clavicle (Collar Bone) Fractures

Fracture of the collar bone is a common fracture that results from a fall or a direct blow to the shoulder. Associated head or cervical spine injuries are seen with these fractures.

The clavicle helps to hold the shoulder upward, outward and backward from the thorax. Therefore, when the clavicle is fractured, the patient assumes a protective position—slumping the shoulders and immobilizing the arm to prevent shoulder movement. The objective of management is to hold the shoulder in its normal position by means of closed reduction and immobilization.

More than 80 per cent of these fractures occur in the

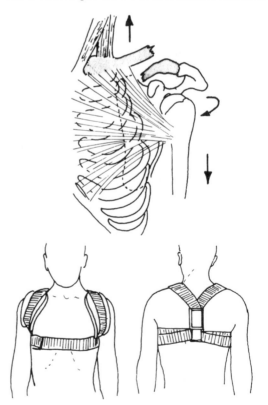

Figure 36.6 Fracture of the clavicle. (Top) Anteroposterior view, showing typical displacement of midclavicle fracture. (Bottom) Method of immobilization with a clavicular strap. (Hardy, J. D., *Rhoads' Textbook of Surgery*, J. B. Lippincott, Philadelphia.)

middle or inner two thirds of the clavicle. A modified shoulder spica (clavicular cast) or a figure-of-eight bandage or a commercially available clavicular strap (Figure 36.6) may be used to pull the shoulders back and hold them in that position. When a clavicular strap is used, the axillae are well padded to prevent a compression injury to the brachial plexus and axillary artery. There should be no restriction of circulatory or nerve function in either arm.

Fracture of the distal third of the clavicle without displacement and ligament disruption is treated with a sling and restricted use of the arm. When a fracture in the distal third is accompanied by a disrupted coracoclavicular ligament, there is displacement and it is more difficult to obtain healing. Open reduction and internal fixation with a Kirschner wire are recommended. Immobilization of the shoulder with a shoulder spica is considered to ensure that the bone fragments are reduced in proper anatomical alignment.

Complications of clavicular fractures include trauma to the nerves of the brachial plexus, injury to the subclavian vein or artery from a bony fragment and malunion. Malunion may be a cosmetic problem when low-neckline clothing is worn.

Patient Education
The patient is cautioned not to elevate the arm above shoulder level until the fracture has united, about six weeks, but is encouraged to exercise the elbow, wrist and fingers as soon as possible. When the patient is able, shoulder exercises (Figure 36.7) are prescribed to obtain full shoulder motion. Heavy activity is limited for three months.

Rib Fractures

Uncomplicated fractures of the ribs occur frequently in adults, and usually result in no impairment of function. However, because fractures of the ribs produce painful respirations, the patient tends to decrease respiratory excursions and refrains from coughing. As a result, tracheobronchial secretions are not coughed up, aeration of the lung is diminished and a predisposition to pneumonia and atelectasis is created. To help the patient cough and take deep breaths, the nurse may support the chest with the hands.

Chest strapping to immobilize the rib fracture is not usually used, because this may exacerbate decreased chest expansion, increasing the risk of respiratory complications of pneumonia and atelectasis. The pain associated with rib fracture diminishes significantly in three or four days, and the fracture is usually healed in six weeks.

Other serious problems may result: Multiple rib fractures may lead to a flail chest (see Chapter 5), while severe rib fractures may result in puncture of the

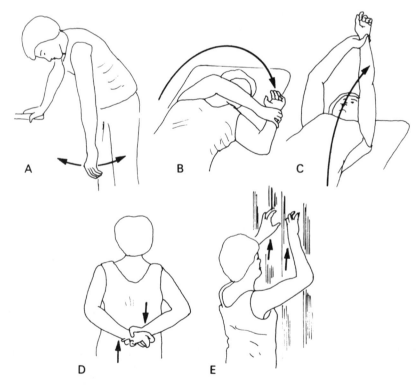

Figure 36.7 Exercises to develop range of motion of shoulder. (A) Pendulum exercise. (B) External rotation. (C) Elevation. (D) Internal rotation. In all of these exercises, the unaffected arm is used for power. (E) Wall climbing.

lung with the escape of air into the pleural space (pneumothorax) or of blood into the pleural space (haemothorax). The care of these patients is discussed in Chapter 5.

Upper Extremity Fractures

Fractures of the Humeral Neck

Fractures of the proximal humerus may occur through either the anatomical or the surgical neck of the humerus. The anatomical neck is located just below the humeral head. The surgical neck is the region below the tubercles. Impacted fractures of the surgical neck of the humerus are seen most frequently in older women following a fall on an outstretched arm. These are essentially nondisplaced fractures. Active middle-aged patients may suffer severely displaced humeral neck fractures with associated muscle (rotator cuff) damage.

The patient comes for aid with the affected arm hanging limp at the side and supported by the uninjured hand.

Neurovascular assessment of the involved extremity is essential to fully evaluate the extent of injury and possible involvement of the neurovascular bundle (nerves and blood vessels) of the arm.

Many of the impacted fractures of the surgical neck of the humerus do not require reduction. The arm is supported by a sling supplemented by a modified body bandage. When this sling arrangement is used, a soft pad is placed in the axilla to prevent skin maceration.

In any fracture of the arm, limitation of motion and stiffness of the shoulder occur from disuse. Therefore, pendulum exercises are begun as soon as tolerated by the patient. (In pendulum or circumduction exercises, the patient is requested to lean forward and to allow the affected arm to abduct and rotate [see Figure 36.7]). Early motion of the joint does not displace the fragments if motion is carried out within the limits imposed by pain.

These fractures require six to eight weeks to heal, and the patient should avoid vigorous activity, such as tennis, for an additional four weeks. Residual stiffness, aching and some limitation of range of motion may persist for six or more months.

When a humeral neck fracture is displaced, treatment consists of closed reduction under X-ray control, open reduction or replacement of the humeral head with a prosthesis. In this type of fracture, there must be a specified period of immobilization before exercises are started.

Fractures of the Shaft of the Humerus

Fractures of the shaft of the humerus are most frequently caused by (1) direct violence that results in a transverse, oblique or comminuted fracture, or (2) an indirect twisting force that results in a spiral fracture. The nerves and brachial blood vessels may be injured with these fractures. Wrist drop is indicative of radial nerve injury. Initial neurovascular assessment is essential to differentiate between trauma from the injury and complications from treatment.

Frequently, the weight of the arm helps to correct any displacement so that surgery is not required. With oblique, spiral or displaced fracture that has resulted in shortening of the humeral shaft, a hanging cast may be used. This cast is designed so that its weight provides traction to the arm when the patient is upright, thereby reducing and immobilizing the fracture. The hanging cast must be dependent (allowed to hang free without support), since the weight of the cast is the means by which continuous traction is applied to the long axis of the arm. The patient is advised to sleep in an upright position so that traction from the weight of the cast is maintained constantly.

Problems encountered with this mode of therapy are fracture distraction (pulling fracture fragments too far apart) due to the weight of the cast, and fracture angulation due to excessive fracture motion.

Finger exercises are started as soon as the cast is applied, while pendulum-shoulder exercises are done as directed to provide active movement of the shoulder, thereby preventing adhesions of the shoulder joint capsule. Isometric exercises may be prescribed to prevent muscle atrophy.

After the cast is removed, a sling is applied and exercises of the shoulder, elbow and wrist are begun. It requires about 10 weeks for humeral fractures to heal when treated with hanging casts.

Functional bracing is another form of treatment being used for these fractures. A hanging cast is applied for about one week, and then a contoured thermoplastic sleeve is secured in place with Velcro closures around the upper arm. As swelling decreases, the Velcro is tightened, applying uniform pressure and stability to the fracture. Functional bracing allows active use of muscles, shoulder and elbow motion and good approximation of fracture fragments. The callus that develops is substantial, and the sleeve can be discontinued in about nine weeks. Shoulder spica casts may be used during early treatment of unstable humerus fractures.

Skeletal traction may be appropriate for patients who must remain in bed due to other injuries (Figure 36.8). Active exercises of the hand and wrist are encouraged.

Open reduction of a humerus fracture is necessary with evidence of nerve palsy, pathological fractures or when other systemic or neurological disease (e.g., Parkinson's disease) would make management with a hanging cast inappropriate.

Fractures at the Elbow

Fractures of the distal humerus result from road traffic accidents, from falls on the elbow or the flexed elbow or by

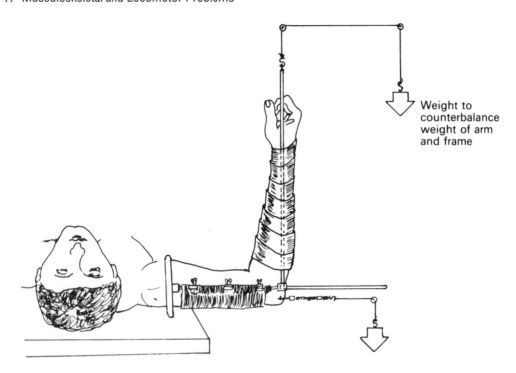

Weight to counterbalance weight of arm and frame

Figure 36.8 Dunlops traction. The arm is passed through the ring, which is then passed up so that it encompasses the shoulder. The upright attachment for the forearm may be moved in either direction to accommodate the length of the humerus. A cloth sling is placed on the horizontal segment to provide a surface on which the arm may rest. The olecranon extends just past the vertical extremity, so that the pin drilled through the olecranon will be clear and allow unimpeded traction. The forearm is placed between the two upright supports, and is usually held there with a circumferentially applied supportive bandage. A rope is attached to the vertical section and is passed through pulleys. A weight is attached to exactly counterbalance the weight of the arm and the frame. Skeletal traction is then applied in the desired amount through the pin in the olecranon. The entire extremity is counterbalanced so that a balanced traction system is created. (Lewis, R. C., *Handbook of Traction, Casting and Splinting Techniques*, J. B. Lippincott, Philadelphia.)

direct blow. These fractures may result in nerve damage from injury to the median, radial or ulnar nerves. The patient is evaluated for paraesthesias and also for signs of compromised circulation in the forearm and hand. The most serious complication of a supracondylar fracture of the humerus is Volkmann's ischaemic contracture, which results from antecubital swelling or damage to the brachial artery (see Figure 36.4).

- Observe the hand for swelling, skin colour (blueness and blanching of the nailbeds) and temperature, comparing it with the unaffected hand.
- Evaluate the strength of the radial pulse. If it weakens or disappears, the orthopaedic surgeon must be informed immediately because irreversible ischaemia may result. Fasciotomy may become necessary.
- Assess for paraesthesias (prickling and burning sensations) in the hand, since such signs may indicate nerve injury or impending ischaemia. Early treatment is indicated to restore circulation before irreparable damage occurs.
- Encourage the patient to move the fingers frequently.

Prompt reduction is desired. Haemarthrosis (blood in the joint) may be aspirated to relieve pain. The articular surfaces may be injured. The goal of therapy is reduction and stabilization of the fracture, followed by controlled active motion when swelling has subsided and healing has begun.

If the fracture is not displaced, the arm is immobilized in a cast or posterior splint with the elbow at 45 to 90 degrees of flexion, or the elbow may be supported with a pressure dressing and a sling.

A displaced fracture is usually treated by traction and/or open reduction and internal fixation. Sometimes the bone fragments are excised. Additional external support with a plaster splint is then applied.

Gentle range-of-motion exercise of the injured joint is begun about one week after internal fixation and after two weeks with nondisplaced closed reduction. Motion aids healing of injured joints by movement of synovial fluid into the articular cartilage. Active exercise of the elbow is carried out when prescribed, as limitation of motion is common unless an intensive rehabilitation programme is undertaken.

Radial and Ulnar Fractures

Fractures of the Radial Head

Radial head fractures are common, and are usually produced by a fall on the outstretched hand with the elbow in extension. If blood has collected in the elbow joint (haemarthrosis), it is aspirated to relieve pain and allow early range of motion. Immobilization for these undisplaced fractures is accomplished by a sling. Active joint motion may be prescribed as early as one to two days after injury.

If the fracture is displaced, an open operation is required, with excision of the radial head when necessary. Postoperatively, the arm is immobilized in a posterior plaster splint and sling. The patient is encouraged to carry out a programme of active motion of the elbow and forearm as prescribed.

Fractures of the Shafts of the Radius and Ulna

Fractures of the shaft of the bones of the forearm occur most frequently in children. Either the radius, the ulna or both bones may be broken at any level. Frequently, displacement occurs when both bones are broken.

The forearm has the unique functions of pronation and supination, and those motions must be preserved by good anatomical position and alignment.

If the fragments are not displaced, the fracture is commonly treated by closed reduction and application of a long arm cast.

The circulation, sensation and motion of the hand are assessed after the cast is applied. The arm is elevated to control oedema. Frequent finger flexion and extension are encouraged to reduce oedema. Active motion of the involved shoulder is essential. The reduction and alignment are monitored closely by X-ray to ensure adequate immobilization.

The fracture is immobilized for about 12 weeks; during the last six weeks the arm may be in a functional forearm brace that allows exercise of the wrist and elbow.

Displaced fractures are managed by open reduction with internal fixation, using a compression plate with screws, intramedullary nails or rods. The arm is usually immobilized in a plaster splint or cast. Open fractures may be managed with external fixation devices. The arm is elevated to control swelling. Neurovascular status is monitored. Elbow, wrist and hand exercises are begun as permitted by the immobilization device.

Fractures of the Wrist

A fracture of the distal radius (Colles's fracture) is a common fracture and is usually the result of a fall on an open dorsiflexed hand. It is frequently seen in elderly women with osteoporotic bones and weak soft tissues that do not dissipate the energy of the fall. The patient has a deformed wrist with radial deviation, pain, swelling, weakness, limited finger range of motion and numbness.

Treatment usually consists of closed reduction and immobilization with a cast. For more severe fractures, an external fixation device may be used to maintain reduction.

The wrist and forearm are elevated for 48 hours after reduction. The arm may be suspended from an overhead frame or intravenous stand.

It is essential to observe for swelling of the fingers (from decreased venous and lymphatic return) and to treat this actively. Constricting casts and bandages must be released promptly. The median nerve is assessed for function. Active motion of the fingers and shoulder is begun on recovery from anaesthesia.

The patient is encouraged to do the following finger exercises to reduce swelling and prevent stiffness:

1. Hold the hand above the level of the heart.
2. Move the fingers from full extension to flexion. Hold and release.
   (Repeat above at least 10 times every half hour when awake).
3. Use the hand in functional activities.
4. Actively exercise the shoulder and elbow.

Fracture of the Hand

Because trauma to the hand can be a complex problem, requiring extensive reconstructive surgery, the reader is referred to specialized books on the hand. The objective of treatment is always to regain maximum function of the hand.

For an undisplaced fracture of the distal phalanx (finger bone), the finger is splinted (for three to four weeks) to relieve pain and to protect the fingertip from further trauma. Displaced fractures and open fractures may require open reduction with internal fixation, using wires or pins.

Neurovascular status of the injured hand is evaluated. Swelling is controlled by elevation of the hand. Functional use of the uninvolved portions of the hand is encouraged.

Lower Extremity Fractures

The objectives of management of a fracture of the lower extremity are: (1) to obtain adequate bony union with full length and normal alignment and without rotational or angular deformity; (2) to restore muscle power and joint motion; and (3) to restore the pre-injury ambulatory status of the patient.

Special Rehabilitation Nursing Measures

● A fractured lower extremity should not be placed in a dependent position for prolonged periods, because oedema is a common problem following all injuries of the lower extremities.

- The patient is encouraged to exercise regularly all joints that do not move the bone fragments.
- The extremity is elevated intermittently when the patient becomes ambulatory to minimize recurrence of oedema. It is best for the patient to lie down when elevating the healing leg.
- After the immobilizing device is removed, elastic stockings can be worn to support venous circulation, thus reducing the problem of oedema.

Because practically all fractures of the lower extremity require the use of crutches, a walking frame or walking stick during convalescence, adjustable equipment should be acquired for the patient. The safe use of these ambulatory aids is discussed in Chapter 2.

Femur Fractures

Fractures of the femur can occur at several sites (Figure 36.9). When the head, neck or trochanteric region of the femur is involved, a hip fracture results.

Hip Fractures

There is a high incidence of hip fractures among elderly people because their bones are more likely to be brittle from osteoporosis and they are more at risk from falls. This occurs because of the increased likelihood of general frailty and conditions that produce a decrease in cerebral arterial perfusion (transient ischaemic attacks, anaemia, side-effects of other drug therapy). Their therapeutic and nursing management is further complicated by associated medical diseases (cardiovascular, pulmonary, renal and endocrine disorders). Hip fractures are the most frequent cause of traumatic death after the age of 75, occurring more frequently in women with osteoporosis, often after insignificant injuries. A hip fracture is viewed by the patient and loved ones as a catastrophic event in the patient's life.

Classification
There are two major types of hip fractures. Intracapsular

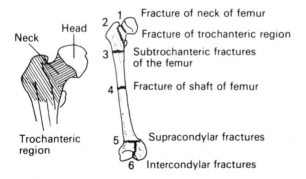

Figure 36.9 Sites of fracture of the femur.

fractures are fractures of the neck of the femur. Extracapsular fractures are fractures of the trochanteric region (between the base of the neck and the lesser trochanter of the femur) and the subtrochanteric region.

Fractures of the neck of the femur are more difficult to heal than those of the trochanteric region, because the vascular system supplying blood to the head and the neck of the femur may be damaged with the fracture. The nutrient supplying vessels within the bone may be interrupted, and bone cells may die. For this reason, nonunion or avascular necrosis is common in patients with these types of fractures.

Extracapsular intertrochanteric fractures have an excellent blood supply and heal more readily. However, there is a fairly high mortality rate following intertrochanteric hip fractures, mainly because the patients tend to be older (ages 70 to 85) and are poorer operative risks. Their conditions are further compromised by the degree of soft-tissue damage that occurs at the time of injury. Added difficulties can be anticipated when the fracture is comminuted and unstable, as is frequently the case.

Clinical Features
Because of the fracture, the leg is shortened, adducted and externally rotated. The patient may complain of slight pain in the groin or in the medial side of the knee. With most fractures of the femoral neck, the patient is in pain, is unable to move the leg without significant increase in pain and is able to achieve some comfort with the leg slightly flexed in external rotation. Impacted femoral neck fractures cause moderate discomfort even with movement, may allow the patient to bear weight and may not demonstrate obvious shortening or rotational changes. With extracapsular femoral fractures, the extremity is significantly shortened, presents external rotation to a greater degree, exhibits muscle spasm that resists positioning of the extremity in a neutral position, and has an associated large haematoma or area of ecchymosis.

The diagnosis of fractured hip is confirmed with X-ray films.

Considerations for Elderly People
Elderly people are more at risk from confusion, not only as a result of the stress of the trauma and unfamiliar surroundings, but also because of underlying systemic illness. Disorientation that develops in some elderly patients may be due to mild cerebral ischaemia. Examination of the legs may reveal oedema due to congestive heart failure and absent peripheral pulses due to arteriosclerotic vascular disease. Elderly people are more likely to be taking cardiac or anti-hypertensive medications that need to be continued and monitored. Likewise, chronic respiratory problems may be present and contribute to the possible development of inadequate pulmonary ventilation. Coughing and deep-breathing exercises are encouraged.

Dehydration and poor nutrition may be present. At

times elderly people who live alone are unable to summon help at the time of injury. A day or two may pass before assistance is provided, and as a result dehydration occurs. Dehydration contributes to haemoconcentration and predisposes to thromboembolism problems. Therefore the patient needs to be encouraged to consume adequate fluids and a balanced diet.

Muscle weakness and wasting may have contributed to the fall and fracture. Bedrest and immobility will cause an additional loss. The nurse needs to encourage movement of all joints except the involved hip and knee. Patients are encouraged to use their arms and the overhead trapeze to reposition themselves, thereby improving arm and shoulder strength, which are required for walking with ambulatory aids.

Care

Surgical intervention is carried out as soon as possible after the injury. The preoperative objective is to ensure that the patient is in as favourable a condition as possible. Displaced femoral neck fractures may be treated as elective emergencies, and reduction and internal fixation is undertaken as soon as possible after admission. This is to minimize the effects of diminished blood supply and the development of avascular necrosis.

Temporary skin traction may be applied to reduce muscle spasm, to immobilize the extremity and to relieve pain. Sand bags may be used to control the external rotation.

The goal of surgical treatment of hip fractures is to obtain a satisfactory fixation so that the patient can be mobilized quickly and thereby avoid secondary medical complications. Operative treatment consists of (1) reduction of the fracture and internal fixation, or (2) replacement of the femoral head with a prosthesis (hemiarthroplasty).

After general or spinal anaesthesia, the femoral neck fracture is reduced under radiographic control, using an image intensifier. A stable fracture is usually fixed with nails, a nail-and-plate combination, multiple pins or compression screw devices (Figures 36.10 and 36.11). The choice of fixation device is determined by the fracture site and the preference of the orthopaedic surgeon. A Zickel nail is particularly useful with subtrochanteric fractures, permitting earlier weight-bearing (Figure 36.11). Adequate reduction is important for fracture healing. (The better the reduction, the better the healing.)

Replacement of the head of the femur with a prosthesis is usually reserved for a fracture that cannot be reduced satisfactorily or nailed securely. Some orthopaedic surgeons prefer this method because nonunion and avascular necrosis of the head are common complications of internal fixation techniques. Salvage of the hip is usually preferred to prosthetic replacement. Total hip replacement may be used in selected patients with identified acetabular defects.

Postoperative Care

The immediate postoperative care of a patient with a hip

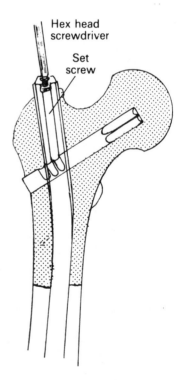

Figure 36.10 Examples of internal fixation for trochanteric fractures. In fractures of the femoral neck and trochanteric region, internal fixation is achieved through the use of nails and plates designed specifically for stability and fixation. (Courtesy of Zimmer Inc, Warsaw, Indiana.)

a   b

Smith-Petersen nail
with McLaughlin plate

Jewett nail
with overlay plate

Figure 36.11 Zickel nail for subtrochanteric fractures. The triflanged nail is locked in the Zickel rod by a set screw. The Zickel nail fixation controls rotation and maintains alignment, permitting early active hip movement and early progressive weight-bearing ambulation. (Courtesy of Howmedica, Inc.)

Hex head screwdriver

Set screw

fracture is similar in many ways to that for other major surgery patients. However, additional attention is given to preventing secondary medical problems and to early mobilization of the patient so that independent functioning can be restored.

During the first 24 to 48 hours, the priorities are the relief of pain and the prevention of respiratory complications. Hourly foot flexion exercises are encouraged. Intravenous antibiotics may be used prophylactically. Hydration, general nutrition and output are monitored. Movement in bed is encouraged. A pillow is used between the legs to maintain alignment and to provide needed support when turning the patient.

Turning. The patient may be helped to change position on the unaffected extremity by the following method:

● A pillow is placed between the legs to keep the affected leg in an abducted position. Then the patient is positioned on the unaffected side. After the initial soreness has gone and the incision has healed, the patient may usually be repositioned in the same manner on the affected hip.

Exercise. It is important that the patient exercise as much as possible by means of the overbed trapeze. This helps strengthen the triceps and shoulders in preparation for ambulatory activities.

On the second or third postoperative day, the patient is generally fairly comfortable and can transfer to a chair with assistance. On the third day, assisted ambulation can begin. The amount of weight-bearing that can be permitted depends on the stability of the fracture reduction and the location of the fracture. The doctor will prescribe the amount of weight bearing permitted and the rate at which the patient can progress to full weight-bearing. Physiotherapists will work with the patient on transfers, ambulation and the safe use of the walking frame and crutches.

Patients with hip fractures can anticipate discharge with the use of an ambulatory aid. Some modifications may be needed in the home to permit safe use of Zimmer frames and crutches and for the patient's continuing care.

Complications

Elderly people who suffer hip fractures are particularly prone to developing complications that may require more vigorous treatment than the fracture itself. In some instances, the shock of the injury may prove fatal. In less drastic responses, shock following this traumatic experience may cause bladder incontinence, although urinary control is usually gradually regained. In general, the routine use of an indwelling catheter is to be avoided. Yet urinary problems may occur. Therefore, the colour, odour and volume of urine are monitored to detect problems such as urinary retention, which is common following orthopaedic operations, especially on older people. To assure proper kidney function, a liberal fluid intake is encouraged.

As in many postoperative situations, thromboembolism is the most common complication. To prevent thromboembolism, prophylactic anticoagulation therapy is frequently used, along with support stockings and ankle exercises. The patient's legs are checked daily for evidence of thrombophlebitis.

Pulmonary complications are also a threat to elderly patients undergoing hip surgery. Deep-breathing exercises, a change of position at least every two hours and the use of an incentive spirometer help to prevent the development of respiratory complications.

Because patients with hip fractures generally have poor circulation and tend to remain in one position, pressure sores frequently develop. Giving proper skin care, especially to the back and heels and under the hips and shoulders, helps relieve the constant pressure. Pressure-relieving mattresses may provide protection by reducing pressure at the interface.

Delayed complications of hip fractures include protrusions of the fixation device through the bone, metal fatigue failure of the device, avascular necrosis of the femoral head (particularly with intracapsular fractures), nonunion and infection. Infection is suspected if the patient complains of moderate discomfort in the hip and has a mildly elevated temperature and a moderately elevated sedimentation rate.

The nursing management of the patient with a hip fracture is summarized in Nursing Care Plan 36.1.

Fractures of the Shaft of the Femur

Considerable force is required to break the shaft of the femur in adults. Most of these fractures are seen in the young male who has been involved in a vehicular accident or has fallen from a height. Frequently, these patients have problems associated with multiple trauma.

The patient presents with an enlarged, deformed, painful thigh. The patient cannot move the hip or the knee. The fracture may be transverse, oblique, spiral or comminuted. Frequently, the patient is in impending shock, since the loss of two to three units of blood into the tissues with this fracture is common. An expanding thigh may indicate continued bleeding.

Assessment includes checking neurovascular status of the extremity, especially circulatory perfusion of the foot. A Doppler ultrasound monitoring device may be needed to assess blood flow.

Dislocation of the hip and knee may accompany these fractures. Knee effusion suggests ligament damage and possible instability of the knee joint.

Care

Treatment is begun with skin traction for comfort and to immobilize the fracture so that additional soft-tissue dam-

► **NURSING CARE PLAN 36.1: TREATMENT OF THE PATIENT WITH A FRACTURED HIP**

Wan Da Lee is a 73-year-old Chinese woman who has sustained a fractured hip. She speaks no English and her son translates for her. She works every evening in a Chinese restaurant run by her son and his wife. There are three grandchildren, aged 3, 7 and 9. ('Wan' is her family name; 'Lee' is her personal name.)

Patient's problems	Expected outcomes	Nursing care	Rationale
1. Pain due to fracture or any additional discomfort as reported	Patient will be pain free at time of discharge and comfortable at all times	1a. Assess location and type of pain – utilize appropriate pain assessment charts (Davies, 1985)	*Pain is expected following fracture.* Pain is subjective and is evaluated through description of location and type. This information is important for determining cause of discomfort and for proposing care (Brunner and Suddarth, 1988)
		b. Handle affected extremity gently, supporting it with both hands when moving patient	Movement of bone fragments is painful; muscle spasms occur with movement; adequate support diminishes soft tissue tension
		c. Check skin traction if appropriate	Immobilization of fracture diminishes pain and additional tissue trauma by decreasing muscle spasm
		d. Facilitate pain relief: i. Administer analgesia as prescribed and indicated	Analgesia reduces pain; observing patient's nonverbal signs, i.e. facial grimaces, may indicate patient is experiencing pain (Martinelli, 1987)
		ii. Evaluate effectiveness of any analgesia given	Notation of effectiveness provides basis for future care; early identification of adverse reactions is necessary in order to initiate corrective measures and modify care plan information
		iii. Modify patient environment – utilize diversional therapy	Sensory overload or deprivation may modify pain experiences.
		iv. Call orthopaedic surgeon if necessary	A change of prescribed analgesia may be necessary
		e. Facilitate patient positioning for comfort and function	Facilitation of neutral body alignment aids patient comfort; functional positioning diminishes stress on musculoskeletal system
		f. Assist with frequent changes of position	Change of position relieves interface pressure and associated discomfort
2. Communication difficulties due to patient not speaking any English (see also Chapter 1)	Patient will feel secure within ward environment and demonstrate understanding of, and actively participate in, identified care	2a. Ensure patient's son or relevant translator is available at times of information exchange, e.g. initial assessment, care plan updating and explanation of all proposed care/treatment	Patient information given in an understanding manner helps to reduce pre- and postoperative anxiety and helps promotion of patient involvement in care (Boore, 1979; Hayward, 1975)
		b. Encourage patient to express any concerns to ward staff via son or translator	Verbalization and clarification of thoughts and feelings help the patient deal with perceived problems
		c. Agree method of communication with patient when son or translator not available, e.g., call bell, picture cue cards, pen and paper	Understanding of plan of care helps to diminish fears of the unknown

►

► NURSING CARE PLAN 36.1: TREATMENT OF THE PATIENT WITH A FRACTURED HIP

Patient's problems	Expected outcomes	Nursing care	Rationale
3. Risk of disorientation due to shock (see Chapter 2) as a result of the fracture sustained	Patient establishes effective communication (*see* problem 2). Verbally demonstrates orientation to time, place and person	3a. Assess orientation status on admission and prior to injury through discussions with family b. Ensure patient is in a safe environment at all times	Evaluation of patient orientation helps to determine changes due to unfamiliar surroundings, coexisting systemic disease or other factors Prevents patient from sustaining further injury
4. Impaired mobility related to fracture	Patient achieves pain-free, functional, stable hip and is able to participate actively in a progressive mobilization regime	4a. Maintain neutral positioning of hip b. Ensure affected hip abducted when turning, e.g. utilize pillows between legs c. Ensure positive skin care, especially to pressure points. Nurse patient on a pressure-relieving mattress, e.g. Vaperm (see Chapter 2) d. Advise and assist in position changes – encourage patient use of overhead trapeze e. In consultation with the physiotherapist, supervise a safe mobilization regime (within limitations of prescribed weight-bearing) f. Instruct in and supervise use of ambulatory aids, e.g. crutches, sticks, Zimmer frame	Prevents undue stress on fixation Supports leg, prevents adduction and therefore reduces risk of hip dislocation Immobility causes pressure, especially over bony prominences. Position changes relieve pressure (see also problem 1f), as does the use of specific mattresses (Scales, 1982) Promotes patient comfort and independence Amount of weight-bearing depends on the patient's condition, fracture stability and fixation device. Ambulatory aids are used to assist the patient with nonweight-bearing mobilization (Brunner and Suddarth, 1988) Prevents injury from unsafe use
5. Risk of alteration in urinary elimination pattern related to immobility	Patient maintains normal urinary elimination pattern	5a. Encourage patient intake of between 2,000 to 3,000 ml of fluid per day b. Accurately monitor all fluid intake and output c. Avoid use of indwelling catheter	Adequate fluid intake ensures hydration and helps to prevent renal calculi, infected mouth and chest infection (Beckwith, 1985) Adequate urinary output (1,500 ml daily) minimizes urinary stasis Reduces risk of urinary tract infection

6. Risk of complications such as diminished neurovascular status and thrombophlebitis	Patient experiences no complications	6a. *Haemorrhage*
		  i. Monitor and record vital signs – observing for hypovolaemic shock
		  ii. Note character and amount of drainage from any surgical incision and/or drainage system
		  iii. Inform surgeon of any 'excessive' bleeding and change in vital signs
		  vi. Be aware of any available haemoglobin results
			Changes in vital signs may indicate development of shock
			
			'Excessive' drainage (related to the individual patients anticipated drainage), may indicate active bleeding
			Corrective measures may need to be instituted
			
			Anaemia due to blood loss may develop and therefore blood replacement therapy may be needed

► **NURSING CARE PLAN 36.1: TREATMENT OF THE PATIENT WITH A FRACTURED HIP**

Patient's problems	Expected outcomes	Nursing care	Rationale
		b. *Diminished neurovascular status*	
		i. Assess affected extremity for colour and temperature	Skin becomes pale and feels cool with decreased tissue perfusion. Venous congestion may cause cyanosis
		ii. Assess toes for capillary refill response	Following compression of a nail bed, rapid return of pink colour indicates good capillary perfusion
		iii. Assess extremity for oedema and swelling	Surgery may cause swelling and oedema; excessive swelling and haematoma formation can compromise circulation and function of the affected limb
		iv. Assess ability to move foot and toes	Lack of the ability to move the foot may indicate nerve damage or compression
		v. Assess for sensations and numbness	Diminished pain and paraesthesia may indicate nerve damage
		vi. Assess pedal pulses	Pedal pulses indicate extremity circulation
		vii. Inform surgeon if diminished neurovascular status occurs (*Note:* Compare all assessments with unaffected extremity)	Intervention may be necessary to preserve function of extremity
		c. *Thrombophlebitis*	
		i. Utilize antiembolic compression stockings as prescribed – remove twice a day to facilitate skin care	Compression stockings aid venous blood return and reduce risk of stasis. Skin care is necessary to avoid breakdown
		ii. Administer prophylactic anticoagulant medications as prescribed	Anticoagulant therapy inhibits blood clotting factors and therefore reduces the risk of stasis
		iii. Avoid additional external pressure on popliteal blood vessels, e.g. from pillows	Compression of blood vessels diminishes blood flow
		iv. Encourage patient to change position and exercise ankles regularly; increase activity as prescribed	Activity and muscle exercise promote circulation and diminish venous stasis
		v. Assess lung status; promote coughing and deep breathing	Provides for optimal ventilation
		vi. Monitor body temperature; in particular assess skin	Body temperature elevates with inflammation; local inflammation will increase local skin temperature
		vii. Assess for Homans' sign	Pain in calf on dorsiflexion of ankle may indicate thrombophlebitis

►

► NURSING CARE PLAN 36.1: TREATMENT OF THE PATIENT WITH A FRACTURED HIP

Patient's problems	Expected outcomes	Nursing care	Rationale
7. Skin impairment related to surgical incision	The normal wound healing process will be achieved prior to patient discharge (see also Chapter 2)	7a. Assess wound appearance and character of drainage: (see also problem 6a (haemorrhage) ii.) b. Monitor vital signs	A wound that is oozing, swollen or with erythema noted around its edges is indicative of the presence of infection Temperature, pulse and respirations elevate in response to infection
		c. Ensure aseptic dressing changes	Reduces the risk of introducing wound infection
		d. Administer prophylactic antibiotics if prescribed and observe for any side-effects	Reduces the risk of pathogenic (bone) infection, e.g. osteomyelitis
8. Discharge planning should be commenced taking into account this patient's individual identified needs, her communicating difficulties (see also problem 2), and her home situation and other environmental/social/cultural factors (see also Chapter 1)			

age does not occur. Generally, skeletal traction (suspension traction with Thomas splint and Pearson attachment or with slings) is used for a while to achieve separation of the fracture fragments (which facilitates the operative procedure) for internal fixation or to achieve reduction and immobilization of the fracture site for subsequent cast bracing (Figure 36.12).

To preserve muscle strength, the patient should exercise the lower leg, foot and toes on a regular basis. A common complication following fracture of the femoral shaft

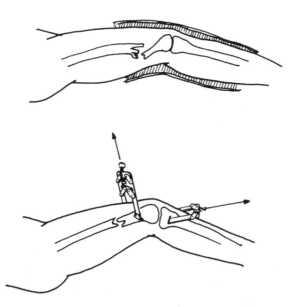

Figure 36.12 Two-wire skeletal traction for fracture of the femur in distal third. (Top) Deformity on admission to hospital. (Bottom) Adequate reduction when additional wire is inserted in lower femoral fragment and vertical lift is secured. (Hampton, O. P. Jr, *Wounds of the Extremities in Military Surgery*, C. V. Mosby, St Louis.)

is restriction of knee motion. Thus, quadriceps-setting exercises should be started early. Active and passive knee exercises are encouraged as soon as possible, depending on the stability of the fracture and knee ligaments. Progressive strengthening exercises for the upper extremities are needed to prepare for ambulation. Continued neurovascular monitoring is needed.

Internal fixation is generally carried out as soon after admission as the patient's overall condition allows. Intramedullary nailing using a Küntscher rod, Schneider rod or similar fixation rod obtains adequate internal fixation, which allows for early mobilization. The active muscle movement is important for increasing blood supply and increasing generated electrical potentials at the fracture site, which enhances healing. Compression plates may also be used, but need external support from a cast or brace for stability. Intramedullary implant and compression plates should be removed after 18 months. Following plate removal, the bone remodels and requires 'support' for several months.

A cast brace is commonly used for fractures of the mid- and distal shaft (supracondylar). Two to four weeks after the injury, when pain and swelling have subsided, the patient is removed from skeletal traction and placed in a cast brace (see p. 1086). The cast (fracture) brace is a total contact device that holds the reduced fracture. The muscle, through hydrodynamic compression, stabilizes the bone and stimulates healing. Minimal partial weight-bearing is begun and is progressed to full weight-bearing as tolerated. Functional ambulation stimulates fracture healing. The cast brace is worn for 12 to 14 weeks. In management of femoral shaft fractures, a major goal is rapid functional healing with sufficient strength to support the multiple stresses placed on the femur.

An external fixator may be used if the patient has experienced a grade III fracture, has extensive soft-tissue trauma, has lost bone, has an infection or has hip and tibial fractures also.

Fractures of the Tibia and Fibula

The most common fracture below the knee is a fracture of the tibia (and fibula) that results from a direct blow, falls with the foot in a flexed position or a violent twisting motion. Fractures of the tibia and fibula often occur in association with each other. The patient presents with pain, deformity, obvious haematoma and considerable oedema. Frequently, these fractures involve severe soft-tissue damage because there is little subcutaneous tissue in the area.

Peroneal nerve functioning needs to be assessed for baseline data. If the nerve is not functioning, the patient is unable to dorsiflex the great toe and has diminished sensation in this region. Tibial artery damage is assessed by testing the capillary refill response. Development of an anterior compartment syndrome could occur. Articular fracture may be complicated by haemarthroses and/or ligament damage.

Most closed tibial fractures are treated with closed reduction and initial immobilization in a long leg-walking or patellar-tendon-bearing cast. Reduction must be relatively accurate in relation to angulation and rotation. The patient attains partial weight-bearing status in 7 to 10 days. A cast (fracture) boot decreases pivoting and rotary stress. This activity decreases oedema, increases circulation and minimizes displacement because of the cast influence on the distribution of forces to the fracture site. The cast is changed to a short leg cast or brace in three to four weeks, which allows for knee motion. Fracture healing takes 16 to 24 weeks.

Open and comminuted fractures may be treated with traction or with an external fixator. The pins-in-plaster technique is used for those situations in which it is hard to maintain reduction. The patient is not allowed to bear weight for about six weeks. Intramedullary nails and compression plates may be selected for certain situations. External plaster support is needed with nailing. Compression plates allow for anatomical reduction, early foot and knee motion and early partial weight-bearing.

As with other lower extremity fractures, the leg should be elevated to control oedema. Continued neurovascular evaluation is needed. The development of compartment syndrome requires prompt recognition and resolution or there will be a permanent functional deficit.

Internal Derangement of the Knee

Injury to most joints consists of a tear of the supporting ligaments. In the knee joint, however, there may also be a displacement or tear of the semilunar cartilages, which are two crescent-shaped cartilages attached to the edge of the shallow articulating surface of the head of the tibia. They normally move slightly backward and forward to accommodate the change in the shape of the condyles of the femur when the leg is in flexion or extension. In sports and in certain accidents, the body is often twisted with the foot fixed. Since little torsion movement is normally permitted in the knee joint, either the cartilage is torn from its attachment to the head of the tibia or an actual tear of the cartilage itself occurs.

These injuries leave a loose cartilage in the knee joint that may slip between the femur and the tibia, preventing full extension of the leg. If this happens during walking or running, patients often describe the disability as their 'leg giving way' under them. Patients may hear or feel a click in the knee when they walk, especially when they extend the leg that is bearing weight, as in going upstairs. When the cartilage is attached front and back, but torn loose laterally (bucket-handle tear), it may slide between the bones to lie between the condyles and prevent full flexion or extension. As a result, the knee 'locks'.

These various types of injury are spoken of as internal derangements of the knee joint, and they produce a disturbing disability because the patient never knows when the knee will give trouble. The treatment of this disability is removal of the injured cartilage while preserving normal intra-articular structures. This can be done through an arthroscopic incision and procedure, frequently as an outpatient, allowing the patient to resume activities in one to two days and sports in a couple of weeks. Joint function can return to normal.

Postoperative Care

A pressure dressing is applied, and the leg should be elevated on pillows to minimize oedema. The most common complication is an effusion into the knee joint, which produces marked pain. If this occurs, the surgeon should be notified. Relief can be obtained by loosening the pressure dressing. The surgeon may need to aspirate the joint to relieve any further pressure.

To prevent atrophy of the thigh muscles, these patients are taught to contract their quadriceps muscles. Additional exercises are given to achieve full function, stability and strength.

Rupture of the Achilles Tendon

Traumatic rupture of the Achilles tendon is a common occurrence. Sudden contraction of the calf muscle with the foot fixed firmly to the floor may cause snapping of the tendon, generally within the tendon sheath. The patient is acutely aware of the problem because of the pain and inability to plantar flex the foot. Immediate surgical repair usually obtains satisfactory results. Conservative management with a plantar-flexed cast for six to eight weeks can be used.

Fractures of the Thoracolumbar Spine

Fractures of the thoracolumbar spine may involve (1) the vertebral body, (2) the lamina and articulating processes and (3) the spinous processes or transverse processes. Five per cent or fewer of spinal fractures are associated with neurological deficits. The fractures are generally due to indirect trauma caused by excessive loading, sudden muscle contraction or excessive motion beyond physiological limits. Osteoporosis contributes to vertebral body collapse. Lower regions of the spine are most vulnerable to fracture.

The patient with a spinal fracture presents with acute tenderness, swelling, paravertebral muscle spasm and possibly changes in normal spinal curvature. Pain is greater when moving, coughing or weight-bearing. The most important assessment carried out initially is to determine if there is injury to the spinal cord and if the fracture is stable or unstable. Immobilization is essential until these determinations are made. With a neurological deficit, immediate spinal cord decompression and fusion is usually performed.

With a stable spinal fracture, only the anterior structural column (vertebral bodies and discs) or the posterior structural column (neural arch, articular processes, ligaments) has been disrupted. Unstable fractures occur with fracture dislocations, and exhibit disruption of both anterior and posterior structural columns and the potential for neural damage exists.

Stable spinal fractures (due to flexion, extension, lateral bending, and vertical loading) are treated conservatively. The patient is placed on bedrest until the acute pain subsides (days to two to three weeks). Analgesics control pain. The patient is monitored for the development of a transient ileus due to associated retroperitoneal haemorrhage. Sitting is avoided until the pain subsides. A spinal brace or thoracolumbar orthosis may be used for support during progressive ambulation and resumption of activities.

With unstable spinal fractures, the patient may be placed on a turning frame. Within 24 hours, open reduction and fixation with spinal fusion and Harrington or Luque rod stabilization are usually accomplished. The patient is cared for on a turning frame postoperatively. Neurological status is monitored closely during the preoperative and postoperative periods. Progressive ambulation is begun about two weeks after surgery, with the patient in a body jacket cast or brace.

Patient education emphasizes good posture, good body mechanics and, when healing is sufficient, back-strengthening exercises.

Pelvic Fractures

The severity of pelvic fractures varies (Figure 36.13). Most fractures of the pelvis heal rapidly because the innominate bone (hip bone) is made up mostly of cancellous bone, which has a rich blood supply.

Type I pelvic fractures exhibit no break in the pelvic ring. They include fractures of the coccyx and single ramus of the pubis or ischium bone. Fractures of the coccyx can be disabling, causing pain on sitting and defaecation. Treatment includes bedrest, baths and medicines to soften faeces for easier bowel movements. Other type I pelvic fractures are treated with bedrest until the discomfort resolves. A bedboard under the mattress is desirable to give more stability. The patient is helped to change position in one smooth movement. Patients with a fractured sacrum should be monitored for bowel sounds and activity.

The most common type II pelvic fracture (single break in the pelvic ring) is the fracture of two ipsilateral rami. Bedrest is used, with the addition of a pelvic sling and/or bilateral Pugh's traction for slightly displaced fractures. Full activity can be resumed in 10 to 16 weeks.

A double break in the pelvic ring (type III fracture) occurs as a result of road traffic accidents, crush injuries and falls from buildings and scaffolds. General symptoms include deformity, local swelling, ecchymosis, tenderness over the symphysis pubis, anterior iliac spines, iliac crest, sacrum or coccyx, and inability to bear weight without discomfort. In addition, shock and haemorrhage may occur.

Pelvic fractures are serious because at least two thirds of these patients have significant and multiple injuries. (The care of the patient with multiple injuries is discussed in Chapter 39.) A high mortality rate accompanies these fractures. Death may ensue from local haemorrhage in view of the rich blood supply to the pelvis and the possibility of massive and hidden bleeding in the retroperitoneal region. Bleeding also arises from the cancellous surfaces of the fracture fragments and the laceration of veins and arteries by bone spicules. There is also the added danger of intra-abdominal haemorrhage from a torn iliac artery. In addition to haemorrhage, the bladder, the urethra or the intestines may be lacerated, resulting in conditions that can prove to be more serious than the fracture itself. To check for possible damage to the urinary tract, the patient's urine is examined for blood. A cystourethrogram and an intravenous urogram are often done if injury to the urinary tract is suspected. Since haemorrhage is possible in these injuries, the abdomen is examined for evidence of intra-abdominal haemorrhage with peritoneal lavage. The peripheral pulses of both lower extremities are palpated, because absence of peripheral pulses may indicate the possibility that an iliac artery or one of its branches is torn. The patient is moved carefully and gently to minimize further bleeding and shock. Management of haemorrhage and associated intra-abdominal, thoracic or cranial injuries has priority over treatment of fractures. Ongoing and continuing nursing assessments are done for injuries to the bladder, rectum, intestines and intra-abdominal organs.

For fractures that disrupt the pelvic ring or involve weight-bearing areas, skeletal traction to reduce the displacement, lateral recumbent positioning with spica cast,

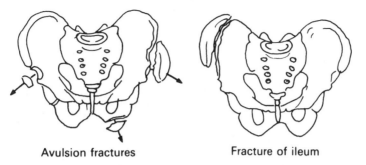

Avulsion fractures   Fracture of ileum

Type I

Fracture of sacrum   Separation of symphysis   Fracture of pubic ramus (unilateral)

Type II

Fracture of pubic rami (bilateral)   Fracture of hemipelvis   Fracture of acetabulum

Type III   Type IV

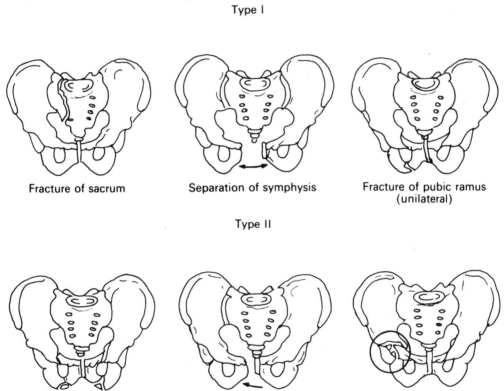

Figure 36.13 Fractures of the pelvis.

pelvic sling, open reduction with internal fixation or an external fixator may be considered.

When both sides of the pelvis are fractured, a pelvic sling is used to immobilize the pelvis into a single unit so that the patient can move the rest of the body with less pain. The pelvic sling lifts the weight of the pelvis very slightly from the mattress (Figure 36.14A). The sling may be folded back over the buttocks in order to permit the patient to use the bedpan. (Some orthopaedic surgeons may advise that the sling may be loosened for certain nursing care activities if the patient's condition permits.)

Since skin care is a problem, sheep skins may be used to line the sling to prevent excoriation. It is necessary to reach under the sling to give skin care.

If separation of the symphysis pubis has occurred, a compression force must be applied. This is obtained by crossing the ropes from the sling to the weights on the opposite side (Figure 36.14B). The pelvic sling is adjusted to exert a compression effect from side to side to correct the separation of bones. Because the sling exerts pressure over the trochanteric region, the patient may become quite uncomfortable.

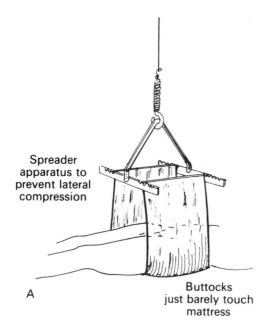

Spreader
apparatus to
prevent lateral
compression

A

Buttocks
just barely touch
mattress

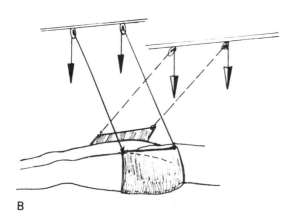

B

Figure 36.14 Pelvic sling suspension for fractures
of the pelvis. (A) A suspension of the pelvis without
an attempt at compression. The sling is suspended
by means of a large metal frame, and weight is
applied so that the pelvis is largely counterbalanced
and becomes, to a certain extent, 'weightless'.
Movement can then occur without moving the pelvis
fragments. (B) The method for applying compression when there has been separation of the anterior
pelvic ring, particularly at the symphysis pubis. This
suspension compresses the pelvis from side to side
correct any diastasis that may have occurred. Pain
developing at pressure points over the trochanters is
unavoidable; it will often limit the duration of time that
compression traction is useful. (Lewis, R. C., *Handbook of Traction, Casting and Splinting Techniques*,
J. B. Lippincott, Philadelphia.)

Pelvic slings are not used with fractures that have collapsed inward or when the acetabulum is fractured.

Undisplaced fractures of the acetabulum (type IV fractures) are seen following motor vehicle accidents in which
the femur is jammed into the dashboard. Open reduction
and fixation with multiple screws or direct lateral skeletal
traction is usually necessary. Traction is maintained for
six weeks, followed by non-weight-bearing for another
six weeks. Internal fixation permits earlier motion and
function.

During the period of immobility, exercises (leg, respiratory, range-of-motion and strengthening), support
stockings and elevation of the foot of the bed to aid venous
return are appropriate measures to help diminish the
effects of prolonged bedrest. Paralytic ileus may accompany pelvic fractures and immobility. When bony
healing has taken place in a pelvic fracture, the patient is
mobilized with a method of progressive weight-bearing,
usually with crutches.

AMPUTATION

Amputation of an extremity is often necessary as a result
of progressive peripheral vascular disease, trauma (crushing injuries, burns, frostbite), congenital deformities or
malignant tumour. Of all these causes, peripheral vascular
disease accounts for the majority of amputations of lower
extremities.

Amputation is really reconstructive surgery designed
to improve the patient's quality of life. It is used to relieve
symptoms and to facilitate improved function. If the
health care team is able to communicate a positive attitude, the patient will be more likely to adjust to the amputation and actively participate in the rehabilitative plan.

The loss of an extremity requires major adjustments.
The patient's perception of the amputation must be understood by the health care team. The patient must adjust to a
permanent change in body image, which must be incorporated in such a way that self-esteem is not lost. Physical
mobility and/or ability to perform activities of daily living
are altered, and the patient needs to learn how to modify
activities and environment to accommodate the use of
mobility aids and assistive devices. The rehabilitation
team is multidisciplinary, and helps the patient achieve
the highest possible level of function and participation in
normal activities.

Factors Affecting Amputation

Patients who require amputation are most likely to be
either young with severe extremity trauma or tumour, or
elderly with peripheral vascular disease. The young are
generally healthy, heal rapidly and participate in a vigorous rehabilitation programme. Since the amputation is
usually the result of an injury, much psychological sup-

port is needed in accepting the sudden change in body image and in dealing with the stresses of hospitalization, long-term rehabilitation and modification of lifestyle. These patients need time to work through their feelings about their permanent loss. Their reactions are unpredictable and can range from open, bitter hostility to euphoria.

On the other hand, elderly patients with peripheral vascular disease frequently have concurrent health problems. These cardiovascular, respiratory or neurological problems may limit their rehabilitation potential. Therapeutic amputations for longstanding problems may relieve a patient of pain, disability and dependency. These patients have had time to work through some feelings and come to terms with the amputation. Adjusting to the change in body image may be easier. Planning for psychological and physiological rehabilitation can be commenced before the amputation.

Levels of Amputation

Amputation is performed at the most distal point that will heal. The site of amputation is determined by two factors: circulation in the part and the requirements of the prosthesis.

The circulatory status of the extremity is evaluated through physical examination and specific studies. Muscle and skin perfusion are important for healing. Doppler flowmetry, segmental blood pressure determinations, and transcutaneous PO_2 are valuable studies. Angiography may be undertaken, especially if revascularization is considered to be an option.

For the most part, every attempt is made to preserve as much length as possible and to keep the knee and elbow joints intact. (Figure 36.15 shows the different levels at which an extremity may be amputated.) Almost any level of amputation can be fitted with a prosthesis.

Energy requirements and resultant cardiovascular demands for mobility increase as the patient progresses from using a wheelchair to a prosthesis or to crutch-walking without a prosthesis. Therefore, careful cardiovascular and nutritional monitoring is essential so that physiological limits and demands can be met.

The amputation of toes and portions of the foot causes minor changes in gait and balance. A Syme amputation (modified ankle disarticulation amputation) is done most frequently for extensive foot trauma, and produces a painless, durable extremity end that can withstand full weight-bearing. Below-knee amputations are preferred to above-knee amputations because of the importance of the knee joint and the energy requirements for walking. Preserving the knee joint of an elderly patient can mean the difference between walking with aids or being confined to a wheelchair. Knee disarticulations are most successful with young, active patients who are able to develop precise control of the prosthesis. When above-knee amputations

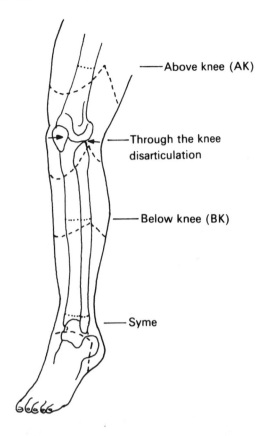

Figure 36.15 Levels of amputation are determined by circulatory adequacy, type of prosthesis, function of the part and muscle balance.

are done, all possible length is preserved, muscles are stabilized and shaped, and hip contractures are prevented for maximum ambulatory potential. If a hip disarticulation amputation is done, most elderly people must rely on a wheelchair for mobility.

Upper-extremity amputations are performed to preserve the maximum functional length. The prosthesis is fitted early for maximum function.

Management

The major surgical objective is to achieve uncomplicated healing of the amputation wound, resulting in a nontender residual limb (stump) with healthy skin for prosthesis use. Elderly people may be at risk of slower healing due to pre-existing poor nutrition and other health problems. Healing is enhanced by gentle handling of the residual limb, controlling residual limb oedema through rigid or soft compression dressings and using aseptic technique in wound care to avoid infection.

Rigid Cast Dressings

A closed rigid cast dressing is frequently used to provide

uniform compression, to support soft tissues and thereby control pain and to prevent contractures. Immediately following surgery, a rigid plaster dressing is applied and is equipped to attach a temporary prosthetic extension (pylon) and an artificial foot. A surgically clean limb sock is applied to the residual limb. Felt pads are placed over pressure-sensitive areas. Starting from the distal end, the limb is wrapped with plaster of Paris bandages while firm, even pressure is maintained. Care is taken not to constrict circulation. This rigid dressing technique is used as a means for creating a socket for postoperative prosthetic fitting. The length of the prosthesis is tailored to the individual patient.

The original cast may be left on for 10 to 14 days unless contraindicated by factors such as elevated body temperature, severe pain or loose-fitting cast. A second cast is then applied, and changed usually 10 to 14 days after the initial cast is changed.

Soft Dressings

When frequent inspection of the residual limb (stump) is desired, a soft dressing, with or without compression, may be used. Stump (wound) haematomas are avoided in order to minimize the risk of infection.

Staged Amputation

A staged amputation may be used when gangrene and infection exist. Initially, a guillotine amputation is done to remove the dead and septic tissue. The wound is then débrided and allowed to drain. Sepsis is treated with systemic antibiotics. In a few days, when the infection has been controlled and the patient's condition has stabilized, a definitive amputation with skin closure is done.

▶ NURSING PROCESS

▶ THE PATIENT UNDERGOING AN AMPUTATION

▶ *Assessment*

Before surgery, the neurovascular and functional status of the extremity must be evaluated through history and physical observation (e.g., colour, temperature, palpable pulses, hair distribution, condition of skin, responses to positioning, sensations, pain). Limitation of range of motion and presence of hip and knee flexion contractures may affect the function and fit of any prosthesis. The circulatory status and function of the sound extremity are also assessed.

If infection or gangrene exists, the patient may have associated enlarged lymph nodes, fever and purulent drainage. Swab cultures are required to determine appropriate antibiotic therapy. If the patient has experienced a traumatic amputation, the function and condition of the residual limb are assessed.

The patient's nutritional status is evaluated and a plan for nutritional care is made when necessary. For wound healing, a balanced diet with adequate vitamins and protein is essential.

Any concurrent health problems (e.g., dehydration, anaemia, cardiac insufficiency, chronic respiratory problems, diabetes mellitus) need to be identified and corrected so that the patient is in the best possible condition to withstand the trauma of surgery. Chemotherapy regimes may influence management and wound healing.

An assessment of the patient's psychological status is very important. Determination of the patient's emotional reaction to amputation is essential for nursing care. Grief response to a permanent alteration in body image is to be expected. Even if the amputation decreases pain and increases functioning, major adjustments are needed. Coping will be facilitated by the presence of an adequate support system and professional help.

▶ *Patient's Problems*

Based on the assessment, the patient's major problems may include the following:

● Alteration in comfort—pain, related to surgery and phantom limb sensation.
● Impairment of skin integrity, actual and potential, related to surgical amputation and skin irritation.
● Disturbance in self-concept—body image, related to amputation.
● Grieving—dysfunctional, related to loss of body part.
● Lack of self-care as regards feeding, bathing, dressing, grooming and toileting related to loss of body part.
● Impaired physical mobility related to loss of extremity.

▶ *Planning and Implementation*
▶ Expected Outcomes

The major outcomes for the patient may be relief of pain and absence of phantom sensations, restoration of intact skin, improvement of self-concept, resolution of grieving process, independence in self-care and restoration of physical mobility.

Nursing Care
Assessing for Complications

Following any surgery, efforts are made to prevent problems related to surgery, anaesthesia and immobility.

The most threatening problem is massive haemorrhage due to a loosened ligature. The patient is monitored carefully for any signs or symptoms of bleeding. The patient's vital signs are monitored, and suction drainage is observed frequently.

● Immediate postoperative bleeding may develop slowly or take the form of a massive haemorrhage resulting from a loosened ligature.
● Notify the surgeon promptly in the event of excessive bleeding.

Positioning

Postoperative positioning to prevent development of hip and/or knee contracture is important. According to the surgeon's preference, the residual limb may be placed in an extended position or elevated for a brief period following surgery. If the residual limb is to be elevated, the foot of the bed should be raised.

- The residual limb should not be placed on a pillow because a flexion contraction of the hip may result. A contracture of the next joint above the amputation is a frequent complication.

In a lower extremity amputation, after the first 24 to 48 hours, the patient should be encouraged to turn from side to side and to assume a prone position to stretch the flexor muscles and to prevent flexion contracture of the hip. A pillow may be placed under the abdomen and the residual limb, with the sound foot resting over the edge of the mattress. The legs should remain close together while the patient is in the prone position in order to prevent an abduction deformity. It is important that the patient recognizes the value of moving the residual limb. Sitting for prolonged periods should be discouraged.

Relieving Pain and Phantom Limb Sensation

Surgical Pain. Surgical pain is located at the incision and can be controlled readily with analgesics or evacuation of the haematoma or accumulated fluid.

Expressions of pain are individual. If the patient has experienced much discomfort before surgery, the postoperative pain may be interpreted as minimal and may be controlled effectively by minimal analgesics. On the other hand, the pain may be combined with the expression of grief and alteration of body image, and not modified adequately by analgesics. Severe pain may be due to excessive pressure on a bony prominence or haematoma. The surgeon must be notified and the cause of the discomfort determined. Any cast may be split to facilitate examination of the residual limb. Evaluation of the patient's pain and responses to chosen interventions is an integral part of the nurse's care of the patient in pain, and may be assisted by the use of pain assessment charts.

Patients who are managed with a cast dressing experience less pain than those with soft dressings. Within a few days, the surgical pain is generally controlled effectively with oral analgesics and pain-modifying techniques.

Phantom Sensations. Amputees also experience phantom pain, in which the patient describes pain or unusual sensation in the part that has been amputated. The sensation creates a feeling that the extremity is present and possibly crushed, cramped, or twisted in an abnormal position. These sensations are real and need to be accepted by the patient and the health care team.

Phantom sensation will eventually disappear, but while it lasts it can have a disquieting effect on the patient. The pathogenesis of phantom limb phenomena is unknown. However, keeping the patient active helps decrease the occurrence of phantom limb pain. Phantom limb pain may occur two to three months after amputation, and is seen more frequently in patients following above-knee amputations.

When the patients describe phantom pains/sensations, the nurse needs to acknowledge these disquieting feelings and help patients modify their perception of them. Distraction techniques and activity are helpful. Transcutaneous electrical nerve stimulation may provide relief for some patients.

Muscle Spasms. Muscle spasms may add to the patient's discomfort during convalescence. Changing the patient's position, application of heat or placing a light sandbag on the residual limb to counteract the muscle spasm may improve the patient's level of comfort.

Promoting Wound Healing

Skin integrity has been altered due to the surgical amputation. Potential healing problems may exist in relation to associated peripheral vascular, nutritional or other concurrent health problems such as diabetes mellitus. Immobilization and pressure from various aids may contribute to skin breakdown. The prosthesis may cause pressure areas to develop. The nurse assesses the patient to identify any potential problems.

To promote healing of the incision, oedema is controlled by means of the cast dressing or compression dressing. This helps to re-establish the circulation and lymph drainage.

- *A most important consideration is that the residual limb remains in the plaster cast socket during the patient's entire hospitalization.* If the cast inadvertently comes off, the residual limb must immediately be wrapped tightly with a compression bandage and the surgeon notified so that another cast can be applied. Excessive oedema will develop in a very short time and will result in a delay in rehabilitation.

The residual limb must be handled gently. Whenever the dressing is changed, aseptic technique is required to prevent wound infections and possible osteomyelitis. If a cast dressing is used, the nurse needs to observe for drainage, odour and increasing discomfort, which may indicate infection or necrosis. These problems should be reported to the surgeon promptly. Systemic indicators of infection need to be monitored.

Residual limb shaping is important for prosthesis fitting. When the incision is healed, the patient is taught to care for the residual limb.

Careful skin hygiene is essential to prevent skin irritation, infection and breakdown. The residual limb is washed and dried (gently) at least twice daily. The skin is inspected for pressure areas, eczema and blisters. If present, they must be treated before a major problem develops. Usually, a residual limb sock is worn to absorb perspiration and avoid direct contact between the skin and the prosthetic socket. The residual limb sock is changed daily and must fit smoothly to prevent the irritation caused by wrinkles. The socket of the prosthesis is washed with a mild detergent, rinsed and dried thoroughly with a clean cloth. The patient is advised that the socket must be thoroughly dry before the prosthesis is applied.

Enhancing Self-Concept

Although amputation is a reconstructive procedure, it alters the patient's body image. The patient will need to accept the irreversible changes. The nurse establishes a trusting relationship with the patient and communicates acceptance of the patient who has experienced an amputation. The patient and loved ones are encouraged to express and share their feelings concerning the loss of an extremity and to work through the grief process. The patient is encouraged to look at, feel and then care for the residual limb. Strengths of and resources available to the patient are identified to facilitate rehabilitation. Care is provided to assist the patient to regain the previous level of independent functioning. When patients perceive that others accept them as whole people and they are able to resume responsibility for self-care, their self-concept improves and changes in body image are accepted. This process may take months.

Resolution of Grieving. The realization that an extremity has been removed may come as a shock even though the patient had been prepared preoperatively. The patient's behaviour (e.g., crying, withdrawal, apathy, anger) and expressed feelings (e.g., depression, fear, helplessness) will demonstrate how the patient is beginning to cope with the loss and work through the grieving process. The nurse acknowledges the reality of the loss by listening and providing support.

Acceptance and support of the patient and loved ones through a trusting relationship during all phases of the process will assist them in dealing with the loss. The patient must feel free to express feelings. Support available from family and friends promotes acceptance of the loss. The nurse helps the patient deal with immediate needs and become oriented to realistic rehabilitation goals and future independent functioning.

Attaining Independent Self-Care

Amputation of an extremity affects the ability of patients to care for themselves. Patients should be encouraged to be active participants in self-care. They need time to accomplish these tasks, and must not be hurried. Practising an activity with consistent supportive supervision in a relaxed environment will enable them to learn self-care skills. Both patient and nurse need to maintain positive attitudes and minimize fatigue and frustration during the learning process.

Independence in dressing, toileting and bathing (bath or shower) depends on balance, transfer abilities and physiological tolerance of the activities. The nurse works with the physiotherapist and occupational therapist in teaching and supervising the patient in these self-care activities.

The upper-extremity amputee will have problems with self-care relating to feeding, bathing and dressing. Assistance is provided only as needed; the patient is encouraged to learn to do the task without help and to learn how to use feeding and dressing aids for eventual independent activities of daily living. The nurse and other members of the multidisciplinary team work with the patient to achieve maximum independence.

Promoting Physical Mobility

Exercises. If the amputation is not an emergency procedure, efforts should be made preoperatively to strengthen the upper extremities as well as the trunk and the abdominal muscles. The muscles in the arm and the shoulder especially need to be strengthened, since these muscle groups play an important part in crutch walking. The patient may flex and extend the arms while holding weights. Doing push-ups while in a prone position and sit-ups while seated will strengthen the triceps muscles.

In addition, the patient should be taught to crutch walk before the surgical procedure in order to prepare for postoperative mobility.

Postoperatively, range-of-motion exercises are started early because contracture deformities develop rapidly. Range of motion exercises are carried out to the hip and knee for below-the-knee amputations and to the hip for above-the-knee amputations.

An overhead trapeze can be used by the patient to change position and strengthen the biceps. The triceps, necessary in crutch walking, can be strengthened by pressing the palms against the bed while pushing the body upward (push-up exercises).

Assessment of body systems (e.g., respiratory, gastrointestinal, genitourinary) for problems associated with immobility (e.g., pneumonia, anorexia, constipation, urinary stasis) is needed, and corrective management is instituted. Avoiding problems associated with immobility and restoring physical activity are necessary for maintenance of health.

Strength and endurance are assessed, and activities are increased gradually in order to prevent fatigue. As the patient progresses to independent use of the wheelchair, ambulation with aids or ambulation with prosthesis, safety considerations are emphasized. Environmental barriers (e.g., steps, inclines, doors, wet surfaces) are identified, and methods of managing them are practised. Problems associated with the use of the mobility aids (e.g., pressure on the axilla from crutches, skin irritation of the hands from wheelchair use, residual limb irritation from prosthesis) are identified and dealt with.

Ambulation. Amputation changes the patient's centre of gravity, so the patient may need to practise position changes (e.g., standing from sitting and standing on one foot). A well-fitting shoe with a nonslip sole should be worn. During position changes, the patient should be guarded and possibly stabilized at the waist to prevent falling.

The patient is taught transfer techniques early. When the patient gets out of bed, good posture must be maintained.

● Excessive pressure on the residual limb is to be avoided because it may compromise wound healing.

Soon after surgery the patient is allowed to 'touch down' the artificial foot, depending on such factors as age and physical status and the condition of the other foot.

The patient usually stands between parallel bars twice daily. As endurance increases, ambulation is started within the parallel bars, but full weight-bearing is not permitted on the amputated side. Crutch walking is started when stable balance is achieved.

While crutch walking, the patient should learn to use a normal gait. The residual limb should move back and forth while the patient is walking with the crutches. To prevent a permanent flexion deformity from occurring, the residual limb should not be held up in a flexed position.

Prosthesis Preparation

Patients who are candidates for prosthesis will be seen by the prosthetist. Effective preprosthetic care is important to ensure proper fitting of the prosthesis. The major problems that can delay the prosthetic fitting during this period are: (1) flexion deformities; (2) nonshrinkage of the residual limb; and (3) abduction deformities of the hip.

The prosthesis socket is custom-moulded to the residual limb. Prostheses are designed for specific activity levels and patient abilities. Types of prostheses include hydraulic, pneumatic, biofeedback-controlled, myoelectrically controlled joints, synchronized joints and others.

Gait training is continued under the supervision of a physiotherapist until optimal gait is achieved. Adjustments of the prosthetic socket are made by the prosthetist to accommodate the residual limb changes that take place during the first six months to a year after surgery. A light plaster cast or a tensor bandage is used to limit oedema when the patient is not wearing the permanent prosthesis.

Residual Limb Shaping and Conditioning. The residual limb must be shrunk and shaped into a conical form to permit accurate measurement and maximum comfort and fit of the prosthetic device. This is done by applying bandages, a compression sock or an air splint. The patient, a member of the family or other informal carers can be taught the correct method of bandaging.

Bandaging supports the soft tissue and minimizes the formation of oedematous fluid while the residual limb is in a dependent position. The bandage is applied in such a manner that the remaining muscles required to operate the prosthesis are as firm as possible, while those muscles that are not longer useful will atrophy (Figure 36.16). An improperly applied bandage contributes to circulatory problems and a poorly shaped residual limb.

In order to 'toughen' the residual limb in preparation for a prosthesis, activities to condition the residual limb are usually prescribed. The patient begins by pushing the residual limb into a soft pillow, then into a firmer pillow, and finally against a hard surface. The patient is taught to massage the residual limb to mobilize the scar, decrease tenderness and improve vascularity. Massage is usually started when healing takes place, and is first done by the physiotherapist. Skin inspection and preventive care are encouraged.

Rehabilitation

The complete rehabilitation of an amputee requires the concerted efforts of the entire rehabilitation team. The orthopaedic surgeon, the nurse, the prosthetist (limb maker), the physiotherapist and the occupational therapist all unite their efforts to help the patient to make a satisfactory adjustment to the prosthesis. The establishment of prosthetic clinics has improved the outlook of amputees. With vocational counselling and job retraining where necessary, many of these patients can return to work.

Nonambulatory Amputees. Some patients may not be candidates for a prosthesis. Conditions that may limit a patient's ability to walk with a prosthesis include diabetes mellitus, heart disease, stroke, hypertension, circulatory insufficiency, obesity, infections, delayed healing of the residual limb (amputation stump) and peripheral vascular disease. If use of a prosthesis is not possible, the patient can be taught to participate in self-care activities in a wheelchair.

A special wheelchair designed for amputees is advocated for people who have lost one or both legs. Because of the decreased weight in the front, a regular wheelchair is in danger of tipping backwards when an amputee sits in it.

Home Health Care

After discharge from hospital, rehabilitation will continue either in a rehabilitation centre, if available, or at home. Continued support and supervision by the community nurse are essential.

Before discharge from the hospital, the home should be assessed in terms of the patient's continuing care, safety and mobility. Modifications are made according to the individual patient's needs. An overnight or week-end experience at home may be tried to identify problems that were not identified on the assessment visit. Physiotherapy and occupational therapy may continue in the home or on an outpatient basis. Transportation to appointments may need to be arranged. The social services department can provide help with adjustments to the home environment.

During follow-up health visits, the nurse evaluates the patient's physical and psychosocial adaptation. Periodic preventive health assessments are necessary. In many circumstances, partners or other informal carers at home have difficulty in giving the assistance required, and additional help is needed. Modifications in the care plan are made on the basis of such findings. Often, the patient and others find involvement in an amputee support group to be of value. Here they are able to share problems, solutions

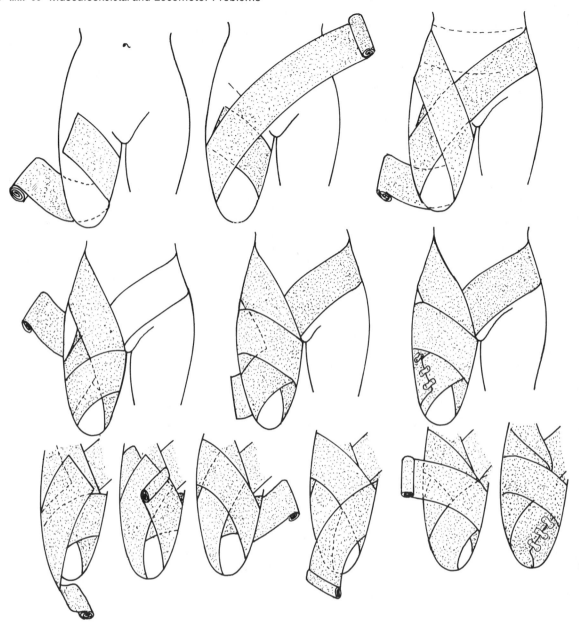

Figure 36.16 Wrapping above-knee residual limb. Bandaging reduces oedema and shapes the residual limb in a firm conical form for the prosthesis. (Brunner, L. S. and Suddarth, D. S. (1986) *The Lippincott Manual of Nursing Practice* (4th edition), J. B. Lippincott, Philadelphia.)

and resources. Talking with those who have successfully dealt with a similar problem may help the patient develop a satisfactory solution.

► *Evaluation*
► **Expected Outcomes**

1. Patient experiences less pain.
   a. Appears relaxed.
   b. Feels comfortable.

Uses measures to reduce discomfort.
   d. Participates in self-care and rehabilitative activities.
2. Has intact skin.
   a. Achieves healed, nontender, nonadherent scar.
   b. Is free of signs and symptoms of infection.
   c. Repositions self to prevent pressure sores.
   d. Controls residual limb oedema.
   e. Demonstrates residual limb care.
   f. Reports skin problems that need to be treated.
3. Demonstrates improved self-concept.

a. Patient acknowledges change in body image.

b. Projects self as a whole person.

c. Participates in self-care activities.

d. Demonstrates increasing independence.

e. Resumes role-related responsibilities.

f. Re-establishes social contacts.

g. Demonstrates confidence in abilities.

4. Resolves grieving.

a. Expresses grief.

b. Uses family and friends to work through feelings.

c. Focuses on future activities and possibilities.

5. Achieves independent self-care.

a. Maintains balance when sitting and transferring.

b. Demonstrates safe transferring ability.

c. Uses aids and assistive devices to facilitate self-care.

d. Asks for assistance when needed.

e. Verbalizes satisfaction with abilities to perform activities of daily living.

6. Achieves maximum independent mobility.

a. Is free of systemic immobility problems.

b. Avoids positions contributing to contracture development.

c. Repositions self frequently.

d. Demonstrates full, active range of motion.

e. Uses wheelchair and ambulatory aid safely.

f. Achieves functional use of prosthesis.

g. Is free of pressure-related problems.

h. Increases strength and endurance.

i. Overcomes environmental barriers to mobility.

j. Uses community services and resources as required.

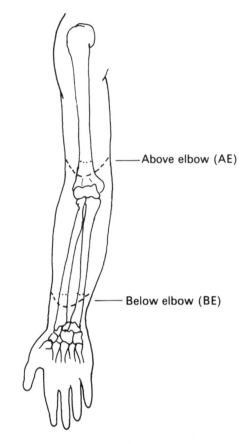

Figure 36.17 Levels of amputation of upper extremity.

Upper Extremity Amputations

The loss of an upper extremity can be a greater catastrophe than the loss of a lower extremity, because the upper extremity has such a highly specialized function. The major reasons for upper extremity amputation are severe trauma (acute injury, electrical burns, frostbite), malignant tumours, infection (gas gangrene, chronic osteomyelitis) and congenital malformations.

If time permits (and it usually does not with acute trauma), the patient is able to find out about the available prosthetic replacement and one-handed devices that aid independence. Regardless of what assistive devices are available, psychological support is essential to help the patient adapt to changes that will be made in lifestyle.

The objective of surgery is to conserve as much extremity length as possible, consistent with eradicating the disease process (Figure 36.17). Following surgery, a rigid plaster dressing with provision for the application of a temporary prosthesis or a compression bandage will be applied. Usually, suction drainage is used to eliminate haematoma and achieve better approximation of tissues. The residual limb may be elevated to control oedema.

Residual limb exercises (muscle-setting and joint-mobilizing exercises) are started as soon as tolerated to strengthen the muscles and mobilize the joints. These exercises are usually done under the supervision of the physiotherapist. The muscles of both shoulders are exercised, since an upper-extremity amputee uses both shoulders to operate the prosthesis. A patient with an above-the-elbow amputation or shoulder disarticulation is likely to develop a postural abnormality caused by loss of weight of the amputated extremity. Thus, postural exercises are helpful.

Usually, the wound is inspected and sutures are removed 7 to 10 days after surgery. If the patient is being treated with the rigid dressing, a new plaster socket with a temporary prosthetic device is applied. This type of management enables the patient to practise with the prosthesis and be fitted for a permanent device.

If a compression dressing (Figure 36.18) is used, the residual limb is rewrapped three to four times daily to maintain proper tension in the bandage in order to reduce the oedema and shape the residual limb so that a prosthesis may eventually be fitted. The residual limb is kept securely wrapped throughout the 24-hour period, except for periods of bathing and exercise.

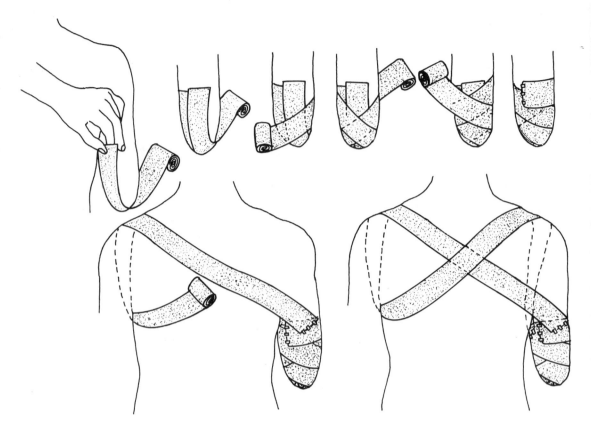

Figure 36.18 Wrapping above-elbow residual limb. A support bandage wrapping for an above-the-elbow residual limb minimizes oedema and shapes it for a prosthesis. The bandage may need to be secured by wrapping across the back and shoulders. (Brunner, L. S. and Suddarth, D. S. (1986) *The Lippincott Manual of Nursing Practice* (4th edition), J. B. Lippincott, Philadelphia.)

The fitting of the prosthesis depends on the level of the amputation, the patient's age and whether or not the joints proximal to the amputation site are weak or have limited range of motion.

Patient Education

The patient is advised about how to carry out the activities of daily living with one arm. The patient is started on one-handed self-care activities as soon as possible. The use of the temporary prosthesis is encouraged. The patient who learns to use the prosthesis soon after the amputation will rely less on one-handed self-care activities.

An upper-extremity amputee may wear a cotton T-shirt to prevent contact between the skin and shoulder harness and to promote absorption of perspiration. The prosthetist will advise about cleaning the washable portions of the harness. Periodically, the prosthesis needs to be checked for potential problems.

Complications

Skin problems occur from contact dermatitis that results from irritants in the prosthetic components and from lack of ventilation and poor skin hygiene. Residual limb contracture or residual limb contour problems may develop. Infection, necrosis of the skin edges and phantom sensations (feeling that the arm is still present) are other complications. Psychological problems (denial, withdrawal) may be influenced by the type of support the patient receives from the rehabilitation team and by how quickly one-handed activities and use of the prosthesis are taught and learned. Knowing the full options and capabilities available in the various prosthetic devices can give the patient a sense of control over the disability. The patient is not fully rehabilitated until a prosthesis has been fitted and the patient has learned how to use it. Training of this nature is best accomplished in a specialized rehabilitation unit or centre.

BIBLIOGRAPHY

Beckwith, N. (1985) Fluid resuscitation in trauma: an update, *Journal of European Nursing*, November/December, Vol. 11, No. 6, pp. 293–9.

Boore, J. (1978) *Prescription for Recovery*, Royal College of Nursing, London.

Brunner, L. S. and Suddarth, D. S. (1988) *Textbook of Medical-Surgical Nursing* (6th edition), Lippincott, Philadelphia.

Davies, P. (1985) *The Painful Process of Implementing Research* (unpublished), study undertaken at the Royal National Orthopaedic Hospital, Stanmore, Middlesex (copies held in the Nurse Education Library).

Hayward, J. (1975) *A Prescription Against Pain*, Series 2, No. 5, Royal College of Nursing, London.

Martinelli, A. M. (1987) Pain and ethnicity: How people of different cultures experience pain, *AORN J*, August, Vol. 46, No. 2, pp. 273–4, 276, 278.

Scales, J. T. (1982) Vaperm patient support system: A new general purpose hospital mattress, *Lancet*, 20 November, pp. 1150–2.

FURTHER READING

Books

Adams, J. C. (1987) *Outline of Fracture* (9th edition), Churchill Livingstone, Edinburgh.

Bradley, D. (1984) *Accident and Emergency Nursing* (2nd edition), Baillière Tindall, Eastbourne.

Campbell, W. C. and Crenshaw, A. H. (eds) (1987) *Campbell's Operative Orthopaedics* (7th edition), C. V. Mosby, St Louis.

Farrell, J. (1986) *Illustrated Guide to Orthopedic Nursing* (3rd edition), J. B. Lippincott, Philadelphia.

Gossling, H. R. and Pillsbury, S. L. (eds) (1984) *Complications of Fracture Management*, J. B. Lippincott, Philadelphia.

Green, S. A. (1981) *Complications of External Skeletal Fixation: Causes, Prevention, and Treatment*, Charles C. Thomas, Springfield, Illinois.

Kessler, R. M. and Hertling, D. (eds) (1983) *Management of Common Musculoskeletal Disorders*, Harper & Row, Philadelphia.

McRae, R. (1983) *Clinical Orthopaedic Examination* (2nd edition), Churchill Livingstone, Edinburgh.

McRae, R. (1989) *Practical Fracture Treatment* (2nd edition), Churchill Livingstone, Edinburgh.

Nelson, C. L. and Dwyer, A. P. (eds) (1984) *The Aging Musculoskeletal System*, The Collarmore Press, D. C. Heath & Co, Lexington.

Rockwood, C. A. and Green, D. P. (eds) (1984) *Fractures in Adults* (2nd edition), J. B. Lippincott, Philadelphia.

Royal College of Physicians (1989) *Fractured Neck of Femur: Prevention and Management. A Report*, Royal College of Physicians, London.

Turek, S. (1984) *Orthopaedics: Principles and Their Application* (4th edition), J. B. Lippincott, Philadelphia.

Wilson, F. C. (1983) *The Musculoskeletal System: Basic Processes and Disorders* (2nd edition), J. B. Lippincott, Philadelphia.

Articles

Musculoskeletal Trauma/Fracture

A plan of action for open pelvic fractures (1983) *Emergency Medicine*, 28 February, Vol. 15, No. 4, pp. 57, 60.

Barden, R. M. (1985) Osteonecrosis of the femoral head, *Orthopaedic Nursing*, July/August, Vol. 4, No. 4, pp. 45–51.

Barden, R. M. (1985) Case studies: Treatment of nonunions with electrical bone stimulator, *Orthopaedic Nursing*, March/April, Vol. 4, No. 2, p. 52.

Bassett, C. A. (1984) The development and application of pulsed electromagnetic fields (PEMFs) for ununited fractures and arthrodesis, *Orthopedic Clinics of North America*, June, Vol. 15, No. 1, pp. 61–88.

Bastiani, G. *et al.* (1984) The treatment of fractures with a dynamic axial fixator, *Journal of Bone and Joint Surgery*, August, Vol. 66B, No. 4, pp. 539–45.

Black, J. (1984) Tissue response to exogenous electromagnetic signals, *Orthopedic Clinics of North America*, January, Vol. 15, No. 1, pp. 15–22.

Brighton, C. T. (1984) The semi-invasive methods of treating nonunion with direct current, *Orthopedic Clinics of North America*, January, Vol. 15, No. 1, pp. 33–46.

Brocker, A. (1983) New techniques in fracture management, *Surgical Clinics of North America*, June, Vol. 63, No. 3, pp. 607–28.

Callahan, J. (1985) Compartment syndrome, *Orthop. Nurs.*, July/August, Vol. 4, No. 4, pp. 11–15.

Ceccio, C. M. (1984) Postoperative pain relief through relaxation in elderly patients with fractured hips, *Orthop. Nurs.*, May/June, Vol. 3, No. 3, pp. 11–19.

Celeste, S. M. *et al.* (1984) Identifying a standard for pin site care using the quality assurance approach, *Orthop. Nurs.*, July/August, Vol. 3, No. 4, pp. 17–24.

Connolly, J. F. (1984) Pathologic fracture, *Emergency Medicine*, 15 June, Vol. 6, No. 11, pp. 61–71.

Daniel, W. W. *et al.* (1983) Elbow injuries: Diagnosis and treatment, *Hospital Medicine*, September, Vol. 19, No. 9, pp. 211, 214, 217.

Duerksen, J. R. (1982) Hip fractures: Special considerations in the elderly, *Orthop. Nurs.*, January/February, Vol. 1, No. 1, pp. 11–19.

Evers, J. A. *et al.* (1984) Dealing with fractures, *RN*, November, Vol. 47, No. 11, pp. 53–5, 57.

Farrell, J. (1985) The trauma patient with multiple fractures, *RN*, June, Vol. 48, No. 6, pp. 22–5.

Geier, K. A. *et al.* (1985) Electrical bone stimulation for treatment of nonunions, *Orthop. Nurs.*, March/April, Vol. 4, No. 2, pp. 41–50.

Geier, K. A. *et al.* (1985) Case studies: Treatment of nonunions with electrical bone stimulation: The fully implantable, direct current stimulator, *Orthop. Nurs.*, March/April, Vol. 4, No. 2, p. 53.

Genge, M. (1986) Orthopaedic trauma: Pelvic fractures, *Orthop. Nurs.*, January/February, Vol. 5, No. 1, pp. 11–19.

Gill, K. P. and Laflamme, D. (1984) External fixation: The erector sets of orthopedic nursing, *Canadian Nursing*, May, Vol. 80, No. 5, pp. 29–30.

Gille, G. (1985) Patient care—not injury care . . . fracture and tissue injuries, *Emergency*, March, Vol. 17, No. 3, pp. 36–9.

Godina, E. (1981) Make or break, *Nursing Mirror*, 23 September, Vol. 153, No. 13, pp. 32–4.

Harper, A. (1985) Initial assessment and management of femoral neck fractures in the elderly, *Orthop. Nurs.*, May/June, Vol. 4, No. 3, pp. 55–8.

Heppenstall, B. R. (1984) The present role of bone graft surgery in treating nonunion, *Orthopedic Clinics of North America*, January, Vol. 15, No. 1, pp. 113–24.

Highfield, M. (1985) The Patrick splint: intertrochanteric fracture care, *Nursing Mirror*, 7 August, Vol. 161, No. 6, pp. 46–50.

Hughs, J. H. (1983) Diagnosis: Rib fractures and sequelae, *Hospital Medicine*, June, Vol. 19, No. 6, pp. 65–72.

Hull, R. D. and Raskob, G. E. (1986) Prophylaxis of venous thrombolic disease following hip and knee surgery, *Journal of Bone and Joint Surgery (America)*, January, Vol. 68-A, No. 1, pp. 146–50.

Keene, J. S. and Anderson, C. A. (1982) Hip fractures in the elderly: Discharge predictions with a functional rating scale, *Journal of the American Medical Association*, 6 August, Vol. 248, No. 5, pp. 564–7.

Kenzora, J. E. *et al.* (1984) Hip fracture mortality, *Clinical Orthopedics*, June, Vol. 186, pp. 45–56.

Kingman, S. (1989) Flexible clamp gives bones room to heal, *New Scientist*, Vol. 120, No. 1639, p. 35.

Laughlin, R. M. and Clancy, G. J. (1982) Musculoskeletal assessment: Neurovascular examination of the injured extremity, *Orthop. Nurs.*, January/February, Vol. 1, No. 1, pp. 43–8.

Lewis, A. F. (1981) Fracture of the neck of femur: prevention and changing incidence, *British Medical Journal*, 7 November, Vol. 283.

Miller, M. C. (1983) Nursing care of the patient with external fixation therapy, *Orthop. Nurs.*, January/February, Vol. 2, No. 1, pp. 11–15.

Mindell, E. R. (1985) Orthopedic surgery, *Journal of the American Medical Association*, 25 October, Vol. 254, No. 16, pp. 2313–15.

Montrey, J. S. *et al.* (1985) Thromboembolism following hip fracture, *J. Trauma*, June, Vol. 25, No. 6, pp. 534–7.

Mubarak, S. J. and Hargens, A. R. (1983) Acute compartment syndromes, *Surgical Clinics of North America*, June, Vol. 63, No. 3, pp. 539–66.

Nickens, H. W. *et al.* (1985) Toward a hip fracture prevention project...national hip fracture prevention demonstration program, *Orthop. Nurs.*, May/June, Vol. 4, No. 3, pp. 52–3.

Nideffer, R. (1983) The injured athlete—psychological factors in treatment, *Orthopedic Clinics of North America*, August, Vol. 14, No. 4, pp. 373–85.

Noon, S. (1984) Clinical Forum: Orthopaedic care, *Nursing Mirror*, 18 January, Vol. 158, No. 3, Supplement.

Parkinson, M. (1984) Repair of a comminuted fracture, *Nursing Mirror*, 18 April, Vol. 159, No. 16, pp. 23–6.

Paterson, D. (1984) Treatment of nonunion with a constant direct current: A totally implantable system, *Orthopedic Clinics of North America*, January, Vol. 15, No. 1, pp. 47–60.

Pina, M. *et al.* (1985) Dextran/aspirin versus heparin/dihydroergotamine in preventing thrombosis after hip fractures, *Journal of Bone and Joint Surgery (British)*, March, Vol. 67, No. 2, pp. 305–9.

Pradka, L. (1985) Use of the wick catheter for diagnosing and monitoring compartment syndrome, *Orthop. Nurs.*, July/August, Vol. 4, No. 4, pp. 17–18.

Preventing fat embolism after fracture ... a short course of corticosteroids (1984) *Emergency Medicine*, 15 March, Vol. 16, No. 5, pp. 142–4.

Robinson, J. E. *et al.* (1985) A nail-safe method ... intramedullary nailing of femoral fractures, *American Journal of Nursing*, February, Vol. 85, No. 2, pp. 158–61.

Rockett, C. P. (1985) Case studies: Treatment of nonunions with electrical bone stimulation. Nonunion of the humerus: Use of a semi-invasive technique of electrical bone stimulation, *Orthop. Nurs.*, March/April, Vol. 4, No. 2, pp. 53–4, 107.

Salmond, S. W. (1984) Trauma and fractures: Meeting your patient's nutritional needs, *Orthop. Nurs.*, July/August, Vol. 3, No. 4, pp. 27–33.

Sherman, M. (1985) Thrombophylaxis with antiembolism stockings, *Orthop. Nurs.*, July/August, Vol. 4, No. 4, pp. 33–7.

Simpson, E. F. (1983) Heat, cold, or both, *American Journal of Nursing*, February, Vol. 83, No. 2, pp. 271–3.

Smith, C. (1985) Trauma in the elderly, *Nursing Mirror*, 17 July, Vol. 161, No. 3, pp. 36–9.

Spickler, L. L. (1983) Knee injuries of the athlete, *Orthop. Nurs.*, September/October, Vol. 2, No. 5, pp. 11–19.

Sproles, K. J. (1985) Nursing care of skeletal pins: A closer look, *Orthop. Nurs.*, January/February, Vol. 4, No. 1, pp. 11–12, 15–20.

Stevenson, R. D. K. (1985) Take no chances with fat embolism...grave risk that follows bone fractures, *Nursing*, June, Vol. 15, No. 6, pp. 58–64.

Thygerson, A. L. (1982) Rib fracture, *Emergency*, November, Vol. 14, No. 1, pp. 48, 54.

Update on fractures. Fracture repair: Conflicts and consensus, Part 1 (1984) *Orthop. Nurs.*, Septemeber/October, Vol. 3, No. 5, pp. 25–9.

Update on fractures. Fracture repair: Conflicts and consensus, Part 2 (1984) *Orthop. Nurs.*, November/December, Vol. 3, No. 6, pp. 43–7.

Urbanski, P. A. (1984) The orthopedic patient: Identifying neurovascular injury, *Journal of American Operating Room Nurses*, November, Vol. 40, No. 5, pp. 707–11.

Wassel, A. C. (1984) Sports medicine: Acute and overuse injuries, *Orthop. Nurs.*, April/May, Vol. 3, No. 2, pp. 29–34.

Westaby, S. *et al.* (1983) Management of compound fractures, *Nursing Times*, 11 May, Vol. 79, No. 19, pp. 69–72.

White, L. *et al.* (1984) Who's at risk? Hip fracture epidemiology report, *J. Gerontol. Nurs.*, October, Vol. 10, No. 10, pp. 26–8.

Wittert, D. W. and Barden, R. M. (1985) Deep vein thrombosis, pulmonary emboli, and prophylaxis in the orthopaedic patient, *Orthop. Nurs.*, July/August, Vol. 4, No. 4, pp. 27–32.

Zarins, B. and Ciullo, J. (1983) Acute muscle and tendon injuries in athletes, *Clin. Sports Med.*, January, Vol. 2, No. 1, pp. 167–82.

Amputations

Bartlett, N. and Patman, D. (1989) Notes on the care of patients undergoing amputation: orthopaedics, *Nursing*, February, Vol. 3, No. 34, pp. 30–1.

Boren, A. H. (1985) Adolescent adjustment to amputation necessitated by bone cancer, *Orthop. Nurs.*, September/October, Vol. 4, No. 5, pp. 30–2.

Burgess, E. M. (1983) Amputations, *Surgical Clinics of North America*, June, Vol. 63, No. 3, pp. 749–70.

Crowther, H. (1982) New perspectives on nursing lower limb amputees, *Journal of Advanced Nursing*, September, Vol. 7, No. 5, pp. 453–60.

Dernham, P. (1986) Phantom limb pain, *Geriatric Nursing*, January/February, Vol. 7, No. 1, pp. 34–7.

Farrell, J. (1982) Helping the new amputee, *Orthop. Nurs.*, May/June, Vol. 1, No. 3, p. 18.

Hill, S. L. (1985) Interventions for the elderly amputee, *Rehab. Nurs.*, May/June, Vol. 10, No. 3, pp. 23–5.

Moye, C. E. (1982) Nursing care of the amputee: An overview, *Orthop. Nurs.*, May/June, Vol. 1, No. 3, pp. 11–13.

Rubin, G. and Fliess, D. (1983) Devices to enable persons with amputation to participate in sports, *Arch. Phys. Med. Rehabil.*, January, Vol. 64, No. 1, pp. 37–40.

Rutan, F. M. (1982) Preprosthetic program for the amputee, *Orthop. Nurs.*, May/June, Vol. 1, No. 3, pp. 14–17.

Smith, A. G. (1982) Common problems of lower extremity amputees, *Orthopedic Clinics of North America*, July, Vol. 13, No. 3, pp. 569–78.

Spross, J. A. and Hope, A. (1985) Alterations in comfort: Pain related to cancer, *Orthop. Nurs.*, September/October, Vol. 4, No. 5, pp. 48–52.

Stratmann, D. T. and Donnelly, L. T. (1984) Determination of ideal body weight and nutritional requirements post-amputation, *Orthop. Nurs.*, May/June, Vol. 3, No. 3, pp. 37–40.

chapter 37

ASSESSMENT AND CARE OF PATIENTS WITH MUSCULOSKELETAL DISORDERS

LOW BACK PAIN

Back pain is a major health problem. An estimated 80 per cent of the population will experience low back pain sometime during their lifetime. Impairments of the back and spine are the third leading cause of disability of people in their employment years. The limitations imposed by low back pain on the individual are severe. The economic cost, in terms of loss of productivity, is in the millions of pounds. The number of medical visits resulting from low back pain is second only to those for upper respiratory illnesses.

Low back pain may be caused by a large variety of conditions. Most low back pain is caused by musculoskeletal problems (e.g., acute lumbosacral strain, unstable lumbosacral ligaments and weak muscles, osteoarthritis of the spine, spinal stenosis, intervertebral disc problems, inequality of leg length). Older patients may have back pain associated with osteoporotic vertebral fractures or bone metastasis. Other causes include kidney disorders, pelvic problems, retroperitoneal tumours, abdominal aneurysms and psychosomatic problems. Most back pain due to musculoskeletal disturbances is aggravated by activity, whereas pain due to other considerations is not influenced by activity.

Obesity, stress and occasionally depression may contribute to low back pain.

Altered Physiology

The spinal column can be considered as an elastic rod constructed of rigid units (vertebrae) and flexible units (intervertebral discs) that are held together by complex facet joints, multiple ligaments and paravertebral muscles. The unique construction of the back allows for flexibility while providing maximum protection for the spinal cord. The spinal curves absorb vertical shocks from running and jumping. The trunk helps to stabilize the spine. The abdominal and thoracic muscles are important in lifting activities. Disuse weakens these supporting structures. Obesity, postural problems, structural problems or overstretching of the spinal supports may result in back pain.

The intervertebral discs change in character as the person ages. In the young, the disc is mainly fibrocartilage with a gelatinous matrix. It becomes dense, irregular fibrocartilage in the elderly. Disc degeneration is a common cause of back pain. Lower lumbar discs L4–L5 and L5–S1 are subject to the greatest mechanical stress and the greatest degenerative changes. Disc protrusion (herniated nucleus pulposa) or facet joint changes can cause pressure on nerve roots that leave the spinal canal and results in pain that radiates along a nerve pathway. Care of a patient with intervertebral disc disease is discussed in Chapter 33.

Clinical Features

The patient's history reveals a complaint of either acute pain (present less than three days) or chronic back pain and fatigue. During the initial assessment, the location of the pain and whether it radiates along a nerve root (sciatica) need to be identified. If the pain is of musculoskeletal origin, the patient will indicate that movement accentuates the pain.

Physical examination may reveal paravertebral muscle spasm (greatly increased muscle tone of the back postural muscles). There is a loss of the normal lumbar lordotic curve and possible spinal deformity. When the patient is examined in a prone position, these muscles relax and any deformity caused by the spasm disappears. The patient's gait, spinal mobility, reflexes, leg length, motor strength, sensory ability and leg movement (e.g., straight leg raises) are evaluated.

If the patient has some radiculopathy (nerve root problem) or chronic back pain, additional studies may be conducted.

Diagnosis

An X-ray of the spine reveals the presence of a fracture, a dislocation, an infection, osteoarthritis or scoliosis. An electromyogram (EMG) and nerve conduction studies are used to evaluate radiculopathies. A myelogram can indicate disc protrusions and nerve root compression, which could cause the pain. In situations that are difficult to diagnose, a discogram (in which a small amount of contrast medium in injected into the intervertebral disc) may be used to demonstrate degenerative or ruptured disc. Computed tomography (CT) is being used more frequently to identify precisely the underlying problem. Occult (obscure) soft-tissue lesions adjacent to the vertebral column and precise disc problems can be identified with current tomography techniques. Ultrasound may be used to help diagnose narrow spinal canals.

At times, an organic basis for the back pain cannot be identified. The pain becomes chronic (lasting more than two months without improvement) and may be due to a reaction to continuing emotional stresses or secondary gains associated with being incapacitated.

Patient Care

Physical Measures

Since most back pain improves with bedrest and inactivity, the patient is confined to bed on a firm, nonsagging mattress. Acute muscle spasms subside in three to seven days. The best position is a modified supine position with slight lumbar flexion (the head of the bed is elevated by 30 degrees and the patient's knees are slightly flexed; Figure 37.1) or a lateral position with knees and hips flexed and a pillow between the knees and legs. A prone position is avoided because it accentuates lordosis. Bathroom privileges may be permitted, but all other out-of-bed activities (e.g., answering the telephone, checking on the children, general activity due to restlessness) are to be avoided.

Frequently, the patient is unable to comply with a bedrest regime at home and is hospitalized for 'active conservative management'. Pelvic traction may be prescribed, promoting additional lumbar flexion (Figure 37.2). The patient feels something is being done to alleviate the back pain, and becomes an active participant in care by managing the traction. Bedrest with slight lumbar flexion is encouraged. Bedrest does have the associated side-effects of muscle disuse atrophy and circulatory

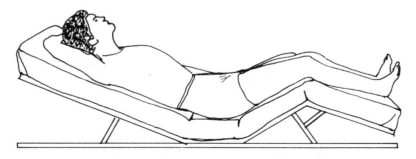

Figure 37.1 Positioning to provide lumbar flexion.

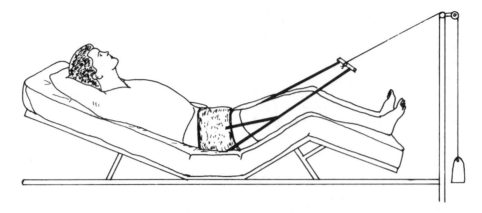

Figure 37.2 Pelvic traction with lumbar flexion to alleviate low back pain.

decompensation, for which the nurse needs to be alert when patient mobilization is begun.

Physiotherapy may be used to decrease pain and muscle spasm. Forms of therapy used are therapeutic cold, infrared radiant heat, hot moist packs, ultrasound, diathermy and the pool. If the patient has had previous episodes of back pain, the history of treatment that was successful previously is valuable for selecting the current approach. Patients with impaired circulation, diminished sensation and trauma may not be good candidates for hot packs. Pool therapy may be contraindicated for patients with cardiovascular problems. Ultrasound produces deep heat, which may increase discomfort due to swelling in the acute stages. Additionally, it is contraindicated if the patient has cancer or a haematological disorder. Gentle soft-tissue massage is useful to decrease muscle spasm and to increase circulation to the tissues.

Drug Therapy

Acute pain may need to be treated with medications. Narcotic analgesics are required initially to interrupt the muscle spasm pain cycle and to decrease paraspinal muscle spasm. Anti-inflammatory agents, including aspirin and other nonsteroidal anti-inflammatory drugs, are helpful in reducing the pain. Muscle relaxants and tranquillizers will relax the patient and muscles in spasm, thereby providing pain relief. Epidural steroid injections are used for pain relief as well as for diagnostic purposes. Infiltration of paraspinal muscles with local anaesthetics may result in relaxation and pain relief.

Trancutaneous Electrical Nerve Stimulation

Transcutaneous electrical nerve stimulation (TENS) is a portable, noninvasive pain-reduction device that allows the patient to participate in activities comfortably without medication. The unit is thought to afford pain relief by over-riding pain input (gate theory of pain control) and stimulating endorphins.

People working with the patient need to understand the device and accept its pain relief potential. Electrodes are attached to areas of the body where the patient is able to achieve maximum pain relief. The patient adjusts the stimulator's wavelength and intensity to achieve comfort (see also Chapter 2, Pain). Patients who use cardiac pacemakers should not use transcutaneous electrical nerve stimulation. Those who operate machinery need to be aware of the potential for accidental shocks. Generally, the patient uses the device for one to two months and gradually decreases its use as pain subsides and the back strengthens through graduated exercises.

Exercise Programme

As the patient achieves comfort at rest, activities can be resumed gradually and an exercise programme initiated. The goals are to increase mobility, muscle strength and flexibility. Hyperextension exercises strengthen the paravertebral muscles; flexion exercises increase back movement and strength; and isometric flexion exercises strengthen trunk muscles.

The exercise programme is carried out under the direction of the physiotherapist and is adapted to the individual patient. The exercise period begins with relaxation.

The nurse needs to encourage patient co-operation as erratic exercising is ineffective. For most exercise programmes, it is suggested that the person exercise twice a day, increasing the number of exercises gradually. After months of exercises, the patient may become bored with the routine. Recreational activities that the patient enjoys should be allowed. These activities should not cause excessive lumbar strain, twisting or discomfort. They may be increased gradually as tolerated.

Body Mechanics and Posture

The nurse observes how the patient moves and stands, and engages in patient teaching as required. However, good body mechanics and posture are essential to avoid recurrence of back pain. Providing the patient with a list of suggestions will help in making these long-term changes. If the patient wears high heels, low heels are suggested.

When sitting, the knees and hips should be flexed, and

the knees should be level with the hips or higher to minimize lordosis. The feet should be on the floor. The back needs to be supported. Bending forward for long periods is to be avoided.

If long periods of standing are necessary, the patient should shift the body weight frequently and should rest one foot on a low stool, which decreases lumbar lordosis. The patient can check the posture by looking in a mirror to see if the chest is up and the stomach is tucked in. Locking the knees when standing is to be avoided. The patient needs to know the correct way to lift objects—using the strong quadriceps muscles of the thighs and minimal use of weak back muscles. The object should be held as close to the body as possible.

The patient should sleep on one side with knees and hips flexed, or supine with knees supported in a flexed position.

It takes about six months for a person to readjust postural habits. Practising these protective and defensive postures, positions and body mechanics results in natural strengthening of the back and diminishes the chance of a recurrence of back pain.

Additional Therapies

At times, a patient with low back pain will need to lose weight. Decreasing the body weight will decrease the stresses on the low back. Incorporating weight reduction into the overall supervised plan is important.

Low back supports and braces may be prescribed to limit spinal motion, to correct posture, and to diminish stress on the lower lumbar spine. Long-term use of these devices is discouraged, since they may have the negative effects of promoting disuse muscle atrophy and weakness and decreased muscle elasticity. People with jobs that require heavy lifting may wear wide leather belts (trochanter belts) to decrease the strain on their backs. An individual exercise programme is essential so that eventually the needed back support can be supplied by the muscles.

Psychological Considerations

Sometimes low back pain can be a psychosomatic illness or a reaction to environmental and life stresses. Emotional problems resulting from anxiety and stress can evoke muscle spasm, which produces a cycle of anxiety, tension, more spasm and pain. In some persons, mental conflicts are manifested in physical symptoms. There are psychological components in all illnesses, and chronic pain has an emotional impact. In trying to help the patient, insight into personal relationships, environmental variables and work problems is needed. If the back problem stems from a recent accident, the possibility of compensation may be a factor. Psychiatric intervention may be necessary for the patient with chronic depression and low back syndrome.

If the patient has a prolonged recovery and has developed secondary gains associated with the low back disability, counselling may be required to assist the person in resuming a full, productive life.

► NURSING PROCESS
► THE PATIENT WITH LOW BACK PAIN

► *Assessment*

The patient with low back pain is encouraged to describe the discomfort. The onset may have been associated with a specific action (e.g., opening a garage door) or with an activity in which weak muscles were overused (e.g., weekend gardening). Information about previous successful pain control helps to plan current patient care. Descriptions of how this problem occurred and how the patient has dealt with it will suggest areas for patient teaching. Additionally, the patient may indicate how this acute or chronic recurring back problem is affecting lifestyle. Information on job and recreational activities will identify areas that need to be modified for back health.

During the assessment, the nurse observes the patient's posture, position changes and gait. Generally, the patient guards all movements, keeping the back as still as possible, and selects a chair for support with arms and a standard seat height. The patient may sit and stand in an unusual position, leaning away from the most painful side, and may ask for assistance when undressing because back movements are uncomfortable.

Note if the patient is overweight, as this could contribute to low back pain. A nutritional assessment is appropriate.

► *Patient's Problems*

Based on the assessment, the patient's major problems may include the following:

- Alteration in comfort—pain in lower back related to musculoskeletal problems.
- Impaired physical mobility related to pain, muscle spasms and decreased flexibility.
- Disturbance in self-concept, role performance related to immobility.
- Lack of knowledge about body mechanics and back conservation techniques.
- Alteration in nutrition—potential for more than body requirements.

► *Planning and Implementation*
► Expected Outcomes

The major outcomes for the patient may include relief of pain, resumption of activities, assumption of usual responsibilities, demonstration of back-conserving body mechanics and reduction of excess body weight.

Nursing Care

Relieving Pain

The patient's description of the acute low back pain and previous pain management techniques assist in planning care. As was indicated earlier, activities and stress must be limited; at times hospitalization is necessary to achieve rest and relaxation. The patient is encouraged to decrease stress on the back by resting in bed. A nonsagging mattress and bedboard are advised. The patient should lie on one side in a curled position or on the back with the head on a pillow and the legs elevated on a pillow to reduce lordosis. If the patient is hospitalized, the bed can be adjusted to achieve this position (see Figure 37.1), and intermittent pelvic traction may be applied (Figure 37.2). The patient is positioned to increase lumbar flexion, which reduces compression of the lumbar nerve roots. The head of the bed is elevated as well as the knees.

Analgesic, anti-inflammatory and anti-spasmodic drugs all play a part in the reduction of pain. The nurse should assess the patient's response to each drug. As the acute pain subsides, medications are reduced as prescribed to decrease dependence on habituating drugs.

Patients can be taught to control and modify the perceived pain through behaviour therapies that reduce muscular and psychological stress. Diaphragmatic breathing and relaxation will help reduce muscle tension contributing to low back pain. Diversion of attention from the pain to another activity (e.g., reading, conversation, watching television) is a well tried method of reducing pain perception. A sophisticated example of diversion is guided imagery, in which the relaxed patient learns to focus on a very pleasant event and thus block the perception of pain.

Resumption of Activities

As the back pain subsides, self-care activities are resumed to minimize strain on the injured structures. Position changes should be made slowly and carried out with assistance as required. The patient should learn to get out of bed with the least possible amount of discomfort. Twisting and jarring motions are avoided. Activities are gradually increased. The patient is encouraged to alternate lying, sitting and walking activities and is advised to avoid sitting, standing and walking for long periods. Planning for recumbent rest periods several times throughout the day is important in minimizing stress on the back.

Coping Strategies

As recovery from an episode of acute low back pain and immobility progresses, the patient may resume former role-related responsibilities. However, if these activities contributed to the development of low back pain, it may be difficult to resume such responsibilities without risking chronic low back pain syndrome with associated disability and depression. The patient may need help in coping with specific stressors and in learning how to control stressful situations. Once people deal successfully with stress, they learn to give themselves positive reinforcement for their success and develop confidence in their abilities to manage other stressful situations.

Dependency is another problem associated with low back pain. Because of the immobility associated with low back pain, the patient will need to depend on others to do various tasks. Dependency may continue beyond physiological needs and become a way to fulfil psychosocial needs. Assisting both patient and support people in recognizing extended dependency needs helps the patient to identify and cope with the real reason for continued dependency.

Referral to a back clinic or a pain clinic may be necessary. These clinics use multidisciplinary approaches to help the patient with the pain and with resumption of role-related responsibilities.

Proper Body Mechanics

Prevention of recurrence of acute low back pain is a major component of nursing care. The patient must be taught how to stand, sit, lie and lift properly. Prescribed exercises are designed to strengthen abdominal and trunk muscles, to reduce lordosis and to reduce strain on the back. Long-term co-operation with an exercise programme is difficult. Improvement of posture and regular use of good body mechanics, along with regular enjoyable exercise activities such as walking, bike riding or swimming, help to maintain a healthy back.

Patient Education

Standing

- Avoid prolonged standing and walking.
- When standing for any length of time, rest one foot on a small stool or box to relieve lumbar lordosis.
- Avoid forward-flexion work positions.

Sitting

Stress on the back may be greater in the sitting position than in the standing position.

- Avoid sitting for prolonged periods.
- Sit in a straight-back chair with back well supported. Use a foot stool to position knees higher than hips if necessary.
- Avoid knee and hip extension. When driving a car, have the seat pushed forward as far as possible for comfort.
- Maintain back support.
- Guard against extension strains—reaching, pushing, sitting with legs straight out.
- Alternate periods of sitting with walking.

Lying

- Rest at intervals, because fatigue contributes to spasm of the back muscle.
- Place a firm bedboard under the mattress.
- Avoid sleeping in a prone position.

- When lying on the side, place a pillow under the head and one between the legs, which should be flexed at the hips and knees.
- When supine, use a pillow under the knees to decrease lordosis.

Lifting

- When lifting, keep the back straight and hold the load as close to the body as possible. Lift with the large leg muscles, not the back muscles.
- Squat down while keeping the back straight when it is necessary to pick something off the floor.
- Avoid twisting the trunk of the body, lifting above waist level, and reaching up for any length of time.

Exercise

- Daily exercise is important in the prevention of back problems.
- Walking outdoors with progression in distance and pace is recommended.
- Do prescribed back exercises twice daily, increasing exercises gradually.
- Avoid jumping.

Weight Control

Obesity contributes to back strain by stressing the relatively weak back muscles. Exercises are less effective and more difficult to perform. Weight reduction is based on a sound nutritional plan that includes a change in eating habits to maintain desirable weight. Monitoring weight reduction, noting achievement and continuing encouragement facilitate co-operation. Frequently, the back problems resolve as a normal weight is achieved.

▶ *Evaluation*
▶ **Expected Outcomes**

1. Patient experiences relief of pain.
   a. Rests comfortably.
   b. Changes positions comfortably.
   c. Obtains relief through use of physical and psychological coping techniques and medications.
   d. Avoids drug dependency.
2. Demonstrates resumption of self-care activities.
   a. Resumes activities gradually.
   b. Avoids positions that cause discomfort and muscle spasm.
   c. Demonstrates decreased dependence on others for self-care.
3. Assumes role-related responsibilities.
   a. Uses coping techniques to deal with stressful situations.
   b. Resumes occupation as low back pain resolves.
   c. Resumes full, productive lifestyle.
4. Demonstrates back-conserving body mechanics.

a. Improves posture.
b. Positions self to minimize stress on the back.
c. Demonstrates use of good body mechanics.
d. Participates in exercise programme.
5. Achieves desired weight.
   a. Identifies need to lose weight.
   b. Sets realistic goals.
   c. Participates in development of weight reduction plan.
   d. Complies with weight reduction regime.

OSTEOPOROSIS

Osteoporosis is a disorder in which there is a reduction of total bone mass. There is a change in the normal homeostatic bone turnover; the rate of bone resorption is greater than the rate of bone formation, resulting in a reduced total bone mass. The bones become progressively porous, brittle and fragile. They fracture easily under stresses that would not break normal bone. Osteoporosis frequently results in compression fractures (Figure 37.3) of the thoracic and lumbar spine, fractures of the neck and intertrochanteric region of the femur and Colles's fractures of the wrist. Loss of bone mass is a universal phenomenon associated with ageing. Women develop osteoporosis more frequently, earlier, and more extensively than do men. Small-framed, nonobese women are at greatest risk, however. More than half of all women over the age of 45 show evidence of osteoporosis on X-ray.

Considerations For the Elderly

The prevalence of osteoporosis in women over the age of 75 is 90 per cent. The average 75-year-old woman has lost 25 per cent of her cortical bone and 40 per cent of her trabecular bone. With the ageing of the population, the incidence of fractures (1.3 million per year), pain and disability associated with osteoporosis is rising.

Aetiology and Pathogenesis

Normal bone remodelling in the adult results in increased bone mass until about the age of 35. Genetics, nutrition, lifestyle choices and physical activity influence the peak bone mass. Age-related loss begins soon after the peak is achieved. The withdrawal of oestrogens at menopause and with oophorectomy causes an accelerated bone resorption that continues during the postmenopause years. Men do not experience sudden hormonal changes. In addition, the peak bone mass is greater in men, which contributes to their lower incidence of osteoporosis.

Endogenous (produced by the body) and exogenous (from an external source) catabolic agents can cause osteoporosis. Excessive corticosteroids, Cushing's syndrome, hyperthyroidism and hyperparathyroidism contribute to

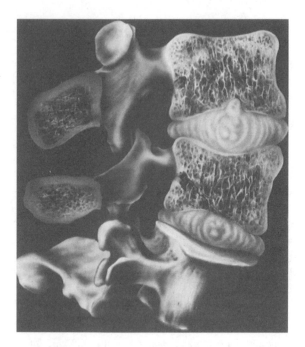

Figure 37.3 Artist's conception of progressive osteoporotic bone loss and compression fractures. (Printed with permission of Ayerst Laboratories, New York, New York.)

bone loss. The degree of osteoporosis is related to the length of glucocorticoid therapy. When the therapy is discontinued or the metabolic problem is corrected, the progression of osteoporosis is stopped, but restoration of lost bone mass usually does not occur.

Immobility contributes to the development of osteoporosis. Bone formation is enhanced by the stress of weight and muscle activity. When immobilized by casts, paralysis or general inactivity, the bone is resorbed faster than it is formed, and osteoporosis occurs.

Nutritional factors contribute to the development of osteoporosis. Dietary calcium and vitamin D must be adequate to maintain bone remodelling and body functions. Vitamin D is necessary for calcium absorption and for normal bone mineralization. Inadequate intake of calcium or vitamin D over a period of years results in decreased bone mass and development of osteoporosis. The best source of both calcium and vitamin D is fortified milk.

Coexisting medical conditions (e.g., malabsorption syndromes, alcohol abuse, renal failure, liver failure, endocrine disorders) contribute to the development of osteoporosis. Medications (e.g., heparin, tetracycline, anticonvulsants, corticosteroids and thyroid supplements) affect calcium utilization and metabolism.

A gradual collapse of a vertebra over a period of time may be asymptomatic and be observed as progressive kyphosis. With the development of kyphosis ('dowager's hump'), there is an associated loss of height (Figure

37.4). Some postmenopausal women may lose 2.5 to 15 cm in height from vertebral collapse. The postural changes result in relaxation of the abdominal muscles and hence a protruding stomach. The deformity may also produce pulmonary insufficiency. Many patients complain of fatigue.

Diagnosis

Laboratory studies (e.g., serum calcium, serum phosphate, alkaline phosphatase, urine calcium excretion, urinary hydroxyproline excretion, haematocrit, erythrocyte sedimentation rate) and X-ray films may be conducted to exclude other possible medical diagnoses (e.g., multiple myeloma, osteomalacia, hyperparathyroidism, malignancy) that contribute to bone loss.

Single photon absorptiometry is used to monitor bone mass of the cortical bone in the wrist. Computed tomography provides information on bone mass at the spine and hip. These are useful in identifying osteoporotic bone and assessing response to therapy. Osteoporosis can be identified on routine X-ray when there has been a 25 to 40 per cent demineralization.

Management

Management goals are to prevent osteoporosis, arrest or slow the process and relieve the symptoms. Prevention begins with the identification and education of those people at risk. Adequate dietary and/or supplemental cal-

A. 10 years postmenopause
B. 15 years postmenopause
   Height loss 4 cm
C. 25 years postmenopause
   Height loss 9 cm

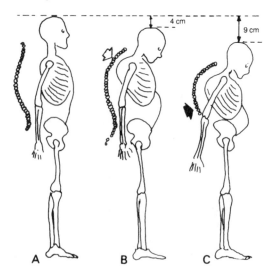

Figure 37.4 Typical loss of height associated with osteoporosis and ageing. (Courtesy of Wilson Research Foundation.)

cium, regular weight-bearing exercise and modification of lifestyle help to maintain bone mass. Exercise and physical activity are the primary keys to developing high-density bones that are resistant to becoming osteoporotic. An adequate, balanced dietary intake rich in calcium and vitamin D throughout life, with an increased calcium intake beginning in the middle years, protects against skeletal demineralization. Outdoor activities are encouraged to enhance the body's ability to use sunlight to aid in the production of vitamin D. Elderly people continue to need sufficient calcium, vitamin D, sunshine and exercise to minimize the osteoporotic process.

At menopause, oestrogen/progesterone replacement therapy may be given to retard bone loss and prevent occurrence of additional fractures. A woman who has had a hysterectomy or has undergone a premature menopause may develop osteoporosis at a fairly young age. Oestrogen replacement is also considered for this patient. Oestrogens decrease bone resorption but do not increase bone mass. Oestrogens are not able to diminish the rate of bone loss indefinitely, and are of little value in long-term care. Oestrogen therapy has been associated with a slightly increased incidence of breast and endometrial cancer. Therefore, during oestrogen therapy, the patient must examine her breasts monthly and have a pelvic examination once or twice a year.

Symptoms of osteoporosis are treated as they occur. Fractures of the wrist and hip are immobilized until healing occurs. Fractures of the vertebrae are treated with bedrest, analgesics and antispasmodics for days to weeks. Sometimes lumbosacral corsets are used for support. Physiotherapy, including intermittent local heat and paraspinous muscle massage, is used for muscle relaxation.

► NURSING PROCESS
► THE PATIENT WITH A SPONTANEOUS VERTEBRAL FRACTURE RELATED TO OSTEOPOROSIS

► Assessment

Health promotion, identification of people at risk for developing osteoporosis and recognition of problems associated with osteoporosis form the basis for nursing assessment. The initial assessment includes questions concerning the occurrence of osteoporosis in the family, previous fractures, exercise patterns, onset of menopause and use of steroids. Any symptoms the patient is experiencing such as back pain, constipation or altered body image are identified.

Physical examination may reveal a fracture, kyphosis of the thoracic spine or shortened stature. Occasionally, problems in mobility and breathing may exist as a result of changes in posture and weakened muscles. Constipation may be present due to inactivity.

► Patient's Problems

Based on the assessment, the major problems for the patient who experiences spontaneous vertebral fracture related to osteoporosis may include the following:

● Alteration in comfort—pain related to fracture and muscle spasm.
● Alteration in bowel elimination—constipation related to immobility and/or development of ileus.
● Potential for injury—additional fractures related to osteoporotic bone.

► Planning and Implementation
► Expected Outcomes

The major outcomes for the patient may include relief of pain, improved bowel elimination and absence of additional fractures.

Nursing Care

Relief of Pain

Relief of back pain may be accomplished by resting in bed in a supine or side-lying position for several days to a week. The mattress should be firm and nonsagging. Knee flexion increases comfort by relaxing muscles. Intermittent local heat and back rubs afford muscle relaxation. The patient is encouraged to move the trunk as a unit, and to avoid twisting. Good posture is encouraged, and body mechanics are taught. When the patient is helped out of bed, a lumbosacral corset may be worn for temporary support and immobilization, although such a device is frequently uncomfortable and poorly tolerated by elderly people. As the patient spends more time out of bed, encourage daily intermittent recumbent rest periods to relieve discomfort and the stress of abnormal posture on weakened muscles.

Oral narcotic analgesics may be needed for the first few days following the onset of back pain. After a few days, non-narcotic analgesics afford relief.

Improved Bowel Elimination

Constipation is a problem related to immobility, medications and age. Early institution of a high-fibre diet, increased fluids and the use of stool softeners help to prevent or minimize constipation. If the vertebral collapse involves a T10–L2 vertebra, the patient may develop an ileus. The nurse should therefore monitor the patient's intake, bowel sounds and bowel activity.

Avoiding Additional Fractures

Physical activity is essential to strengthen muscles, prevent disuse atrophy and retard progressive bone demineralization. Daily activity, preferably outdoors in the sunshine, is necessary. Isometric exercises can be used to strengthen trunk muscles. Walking, good body mechanics and good posture are encouraged. Sudden bending, jarring and strenuous lifting are to be avoided.

A balanced diet with adequate calcium, protein and vitamin D is generally prescribed to slow the rate of bone loss. A calcium preparation (calcium carbonate) may be given to add sufficient calcium to the diet, as many older people frequently suffer from a deficiency in dietary calcium.

When the menopause occurs, replacement hormonal therapy slows the development of osteoporosis. Adequate supervision of the woman on hormonal therapy is necessary.

Considerations For the Elderly

Elderly people are more at risk of falls as a result of environmental hazards, neuromuscular disorders, diminished senses and cardiovascular responses and responses to drugs. Hazards must be identified and eliminated. Supervision and assistance should be readily available.

The patient, family and other informal carers need to be included in planning for continued care and preventive management regimes. The home environment is assessed for potential hazards and a safe environment is created by using the occupational therapist's skills.

▶ *Evaluation*
▶ **Expected Outcomes**

1. Patient achieves a reduction in pain.
   a. Experiences pain relief at rest.
   b. Experiences minimal discomfort during activities of daily living.
   c. Demonstrates diminished tenderness at fracture site.
2. Maintains normal bowel elimination.
   a. Has active bowel sounds.
   b. Has regular bowel movements.
3. Experiences no new fractures.
   a. Maintains good posture.
   b. Uses good body mechanics.
   c. Consumes balanced diet high in calcium and vitamin D.
   d. Engages in weight-bearing exercises (walks daily).
   e. Rests by lying down a couple of times a day.
   f. Participates in outside activities.
   g. Creates a safe home environment.
   h. Accepts assistance and supervision as needed.

OSTEOMALACIA

Osteomalacia is a metabolic bone disease characterized by inadequate mineralization of bone. (A similar condition in children is called rickets.) In these patients, a large amount of osteoid or remoulded bone does not calcify. It is thought that the primary defect is a defective supply of calcium and phosphate from the extracellular fluid to the calcification sites in the bones. As a result of this faulty mineralization, there is softening and weakening of the skeleton, causing pain, tenderness to the touch and bowing of the bones. In adults, the condition is chronic, and skeletal deformities are not as severe as in children because skeletal growth has been completed.

Altered Physiology

There are a variety of causes of osteomalacia resulting from a generalized disturbance in mineral metabolism. Risk factors for the development of osteomalacia include dietary deficiencies, malabsorption problems, gastrectomy, chronic renal failure, prolonged anticonvulsant therapy (e.g., phenytoin) and insufficient vitamin D (dietary, sunlight).

Osteomalacia may occur as a result of inadequate dietary intake of calcium or phosphate ions, failure of these ions to be absorbed or excessive loss of these materials from the body.

The malnutrition type (deficiency in vitamin D often associated with poor intake of calcium) is due mainly to a lack of finance, but food faddism and lack of nutritional knowledge may also be factors. It occurs in parts of the world where vitamin D is not added to food and where dietary deficiencies exist and sunlight is scarce.

Gastrointestinal disorders in which fats are inadequately absorbed are likely to produce osteomalacia through loss of vitamin D (along with other fat-soluble vitamins) and calcium, the latter being excreted in the faeces in combination with fatty acids. Such disorders include coeliac disease, chronic biliary tract obstruction, chronic pancreatitis and small bowel resections or operative shunts (gastrectomy) that involve the small intestine.

Severe renal insufficiency results in acidosis. The available calcium is used to combat the acidosis, and the parathyroid hormone continues to cause a release of skeletal calcium in an attempt to re-establish a physiological pH. During this continual drain of skeletal calcium, bony fibrosis occurs and bony cysts form. Chronic glomerulonephritis, obstructive uropathies and heavy metal poisoning result in a reduced serum phosphate level and demineralization of bone.

In addition, liver and kidney diseases can produce a lack of vitamin D, as these are the organs that convert vitamin D to its active form. Finally, hyperparathyroidism leads to skeletal decalcification, and thus to osteomalacia, through the promotion of phosphate excretion in the urine.

Considerations For Elderly Patients

Special attention to a nutritious diet is important. Adequate intake of calcium and vitamin D needs to be assured. Since sunlight is necessary, older people should be encouraged to spend some time in the sun.

Prevention, identification and management of osteomalacia in elderly people are essential to reduce the incidence of fractures. When osteomalacia is combined with osteoporosis, the incidence of fracture in the elderly increases.

Clinical Features

The most common and distressing symptoms of osteomalacia are bone pain and tenderness. As a result of calcium deficiency, there is usually muscle weakness. The patient develops a waddling or limping gait. In the more advanced disease, the legs become bowed (due to body weight and muscle pull). The softened vertebrae become compressed, thus shortening the patient's trunk and deforming the thorax (kyphosis). The sacrum is forced down and forwards, and the pelvis is compressed laterally. These two deformities explain the characteristic shape of the pelvis that often necessitates caesarean section in pregnant women affected with this disease. Weakness and unsteadiness present a danger of falls and fractures.

Diagnosis

Generalized demineralization of bone is evident by X-ray. Studies of the vertebrae may reveal compression fracture with indistinct vertebral end plates. Laboratory studies reveal low serum calcium and phosphorus levels and a moderately elevated alkaline phosphatase level. Urine calcium and creatinine excretion is low.

Management

Osteomalacia can be treated with gratifying results on an individualized basis. The underlying cause is corrected as far as possible. Calcium intake is increased. Adequate dietary protein is provided.

Vitamin D is given in the treatment of many forms of osteomalacia. Its various therapeutic actions combine to raise the concentrations of calcium and phosphorus in the extracellular fluid. If osteomalacia is dietary in origin, a normal diet plus vitamin D is given. If vitamin D deficiency is due to malabsorption, larger doses of vitamin D are required in addition to supplementary doses of calcium. High doses of vitamin D are toxic and enhance the risk of hypercalcaemia. Therefore, the patient's serum calcium is monitored.

With malabsorption, the patient may also be treated with ultraviolet irradiation. The patient is encouraged to expose the skin to sunlight, as the ultraviolet portion of sunlight is necessary to transform a cholesterol substance present in the skin into vitamin D.

Frequently, skeletal problems associated with osteo-malacia resolve themselves when the underlying disease or nutritional deficiency is adequately treated. Some persistent orthopaedic deformities may need to be treated with braces or surgery (osteotomy for long bone deformity).

► NURSING PROCESS
► THE PATIENT WITH OSTEOMALACIA

► *Assessment*

Patients with osteomalacia usually complain of generalized bone pain in the low back and extremities, with an associated tenderness. The description of the discomfort may be vague. The patient may present with a fracture. During the assessment, information concerning coexisting diseases (e.g., malabsorption syndrome) and dietary habits is obtained.

On physical examination, skeletal deformities are noted. Spinal deformities and bending deformities of the long bones may give patients an unusual appearance and a waddling gait. Muscular weakness may be present. These patients may be unhappy about their appearance.

► *Patient's Problems*

Based on the assessment, the patient's major identified problems may include the following:

● Alteration in comfort—pain related to bone tenderness and potential fracture.
● Disturbance in self-concept—body image related to bowing legs and waddling gait.
● Potential nonadherence to therapeutic regime related to lack of information and understanding.

► *Planning and Implementation*
► Expected Outcomes
The major outcomes of the patient with osteomalacia may include relief of pain, acceptance of body image and adherence to the therapeutic regime.

Nursing Care

Relieving Pain
Physical, psychological and pharmaceutical measures are used to help the patient reduce discomfort. Since the patient has both skeletal pain and tenderness, gentle assistance needs to be provided when changing positions. Frequent position changes will decrease the discomforts from immobility. A convoluted foam mattress and soft pillows will support the body and conform to existing deformities. Diversional activities and focusing attention on conversation, television and other such distractions will decrease the patient's perception of pain. At times, analgesics will

be needed as prescribed to decrease the discomfort. The patient's response to the medications is monitored.

As the condition responds to therapy, the skeletal discomforts will diminish.

Body Image Adjustment

In an established, trusting relationship, the patient is encouraged to discuss any change in body image and methods for coping with the changes. The nurse accepts the patient's self-concept, but helps the patient to recognize and use existing strengths. The patient is included in the planning of care. Being an active participant promotes self-control and improves feelings of self-worth. Interactions with family and friends are encouraged. Social interactions help provide a feeling of being accepted regardless of physical changes.

Patient Education

Patient education focuses on the cause of osteomalacia and approaches to controlling it. Dietary sources of calcium and vitamin D are taught. Safe use of supplements is reviewed. The need for monitoring of serum calcium levels for therapeutic response is stressed. Measures to prevent injury are discussed with the patient. Long-term monitoring of the patient is appropriate to ensure stabilization or reversal of the osteomalacia process.

▶ *Evaluation*
▶ **Expected Outcomes**

1. Relief of pain and tenderness.
   a. Patient reports feeling comfortable.
   b. Experiences no tenderness.
   c. Does not experience fracture.
2. Shows improved self-concept.
   a. Participates in activities of daily living.
   b. Demonstrates confidence in abilities.
3. Adheres to therapeutic regime.
   a. Consumes therapeutic amount of calcium and vitamin D.
   b. Exposes self to sunlight.
   c. Has serum calcium level monitored throughout therapy.
   d. Keeps follow-up health care appointments.

MUSCULOSKELETAL INFECTIONS

Osteomyelitis

Osteomyelitis is an infection of the bone. This infection is more difficult to cure than a soft-tissue infection because of the limited blood supply. Osteomyelitis may be a chronic problem affecting quality of life and/or loss of an extremity.

The infection may be due to haematogenous (blood-borne) spread from other foci of infection (e.g., infected tonsils, boils, infected teeth, upper respiratory infections), erosion of adjacent soft tissue infection (e.g., middle ear infection, infected decubitus or vascular ulcers) or direct bone contamination (e.g., open fracture, gunshot wound, bone surgery). Acute osteomyelitis due to haematogenous spread is seen more frequently in children than in adults. Chronic osteomyelitis is seen more frequently in adults. *Staphylococcus aureus* causes 80 to 90 per cent of bone infections. Other pathogenic organisms frequently found in osteomyelitis include *Proteus*, *Pseudomonas* and *Escherichia coli*. There has been an increasing incidence of penicillin-resistant, nosocomial, gram-negative and anaerobic infections.

Altered Physiology

Osteomyelitis due to haematogenous spread occurs in a bone area where there is lowered resistance, possibly due to subclinical (nonapparent) trauma. It often develops in the long bones of children and vertebrae of adults. Regardless of the source of the infective microbe, the initial response is one of inflammation, increased vascularity and oedema. After two or three days, thrombosis of the blood vessels occurs in the area and results in ischaemia with bone necrosis due to increasing tissue and medullary pressure. The infection extends into the medullary cavity and under the periosteum. Infective pus may spread the infection into adjacent soft tissues and joints. Unless the infective process is controlled early, bone abscess forms.

In the natural course of events, the abscess may point and drain but, more often, incision and drainage are undertaken by the surgeon. The resulting abscess cavity has in its walls areas of dead tissue, as in any abscess cavity; however, dead bone tissue (the sequestrum) does not easily liquefy and drain. The cavity cannot collapse and heal as occurs in soft-tissue abscesses. A bone sheath (the involucrum) forms and surrounds the sequestrum. Thus, although healing appears to take place, a chronically-infected sequestrum remains that is prone to producing recurring abscesses throughout the life of the individual. This is the so-called chronic type of osteomyelitis.

Osteomyelitis may be associated with extension of soft-tissue infection or direct bone contamination. Identification of patients who are at risk is essential. These include poorly nourished, obese or diabetic patients, and patients who have rheumatoid arthritis, have been hospitalized for a long time, have required long-term corticosteroid therapy, have had surgery on a joint previously operated on or have a concurrent sepsis. Other patients at risk are those who have undergone lengthy orthopaedic surgery, have prolonged wound drainage, have marginal incisional necrosis or wound dehiscence or require evacuation of postoperative haematomas.

The onset of an osteomyelitis following orthopaedic surgery may occur during the first three months (acute fulminating—stage 1) and is frequently associated with haematoma drainage or superficial infection. Delayed onset (stage 2) infections are seen between 4 and 24 months after surgery. Late onset (stage 3) osteomyelitis is generally due to haematogenous spread and occurs two or more years after surgery.

Clinical Features

When the infection is carried by the blood, the onset is usually sudden, occurring often with the symptomatology of septicaemia (e.g., chills, high fever, rapid pulse and general malaise). In children, in whom the disease usually begins as an acute infection of the bone epiphysis (epiphysitis), the constitutional symptoms at first may overshadow the local signs completely. As the infection extends from the marrow cavity through the cortex of the bone, it involves the periosteum and the soft tissues, with the extremity becoming painful, swollen and extremely tender. The patient may describe a constant, pulsating pain that intensifies with movement and is due to the pressure of the collecting pus.

When osteomyelitis occurs from spread of adjacent infection or direct contamination, there is no septicaemia symptomatology. The area is swollen, warm, painful and tender to touch.

Diagnosis

With acute osteomyelitis, early X-rays will show only soft-tissue swelling. In about two weeks, areas of irregular decalcification, periosteal elevation and new bone formation will be evident. Serum studies will show elevated leucocytes and an elevated sedimentation rate. Blood cultures and cultures of the abscess are needed for proper antibiotic therapy.

The patient with a chronic osteomyelitis presents with a continuously draining sinus or experiences recurrent periods of pain, inflammation, swelling and drainage. The low-grade infection thrives in the scar tissue with its reduced blood supply. On X-ray, large, irregular cavities, sequestra or dense bone formations are seen.

Prevention

Prevention of osteomyelitis is the goal. Treatment of focal infections diminishes haematogenous spread. Management of soft-tissue infections controls erosion of the bone. Careful patient selection and attention to the surgical environment and technique can reduce the incidence of postoperative osteomyelitis.

Prophylactic antibiotics, administered to achieve adequate tissue levels at the time of surgery and for 24 to 48 hours after surgery, are helpful. Aseptic postoperative wound care techniques reduce the incidence of superficial infections and the potential development of an associated osteomyelitis.

Management

The initial goal of therapy is to control and arrest the infective process. Blood cultures and abscess cultures are carried out to identify the organism and select the best antibiotic. Frequently, the infection is caused by more than one pathogen.

Drug Therapy

Cultures of other loci of infection may be carried out if haematogenous spread is suspected. Antibiotic therapy is begun immediately, assuming a *Staphylococcus* infection is present that is sensitive to a semisynthetic penicillin. A sustained high therapeutic blood level of the antibiotic is important. Around-the-clock dosage administration is necessary for four to six weeks. The aim is to control the infection before the blood supply to the infection diminishes as a result of thrombosis. If necessary, when culture results are obtained, the antibiotic can be replaced by one to which the organism is more sensitive. When the infection appears to be controlled, the antibiotic can be administered orally and so continued for up to three months. To enhance absorption of oral antibiotics, these medications should not be administered with food. Suspected regions of pus may be evacuated by needle aspiration.

Surgery

If the patient does not respond to treatment, surgery is carried out whereby the involved bone is exposed, the purulent and necrotic material removed and the area irrigated directly with sterile, normal saline solution. A high blood level of antibiotic is maintained.

In chronic osteomyelitis, antibiotics control the infection. Generally, it is an adjunctive therapy to surgical débridement. All dead, infected bone and cartilage must be removed before permanent healing takes place. This operation, which is called a sequestrectomy, consists of the removal of enough involucrum to enable the surgeon to remove the sequestrum. Often, sufficient bone is removed to convert a deep cavity into a shallow saucer (saucerization).

Saucerization weakens the bone, which then may need stabilization or support from internal or external fixation devices. The débrided cavity may be packed with cancellous bone graft to stimulate healing. During the postoperative period, measures are taken to ensure adequate circulation (wound suction to prevent fluid accumulation, elevation of the area to promote venous drainage, avoidance of pressure on grafted area), to maintain needed immobility and to comply with weight-bearing restrictions.

▶ *Assessment*

The patient presents with an acute onset of symptoms (e.g., localized pain, swelling, erythema, fever) or recurrent draining of an infected sinus with associated pain, swelling and low-grade fever. The patient is assessed for risk factors (e.g., older age, diabetes or long-term steroid therapy) and for previous injury, infection or orthopaedic surgery. The patient will avoid pressure on the area and guard movement. In acute osteomyelitis, the patient will have generalized weakness due to the systemic reaction to the infection.

Physical examination reveals an inflamed, markedly swollen, warm area that is tender. Purulent drainage may be noted. The patient will have an elevated temperature. With chronic osteomyelitis, the temperature elevation may be only minimal, occurring in the afternoon or evening.

Laboratory studies will show an elevated white blood cell count and usually an elevated erythrocyte sedimentation rate. Blood and drainage cultures may be positive. Wound cultures will indicate the causative organisms and sensitivity to various antibiotics. X-rays may be negative until destruction, bone necrosis and elevation of the periosteum occur.

▶ *Patient's Problems*

Based on the nursing assessment, the main problems for the patient with osteomyelitis may include the following:

● Alteration in comfort—pain related to inflammation and swelling.
● Impaired physical mobility associated with positioning, immobilization devices, and weight-bearing limitations.
● Lack of knowledge about appropriate health education.

▶ *Planning and Implementation*
▶ Expected Outcomes

The outcomes for the patient may include relief of pain, adaptation to mobility limitations and adherence to a home health care programme.

Nursing Care

Relieving Pain

The wounds themselves are frequently very painful and must be handled with great care and gentleness. The joints above and below the affected part should be supported and the extremity moved in a smooth manner. The affec-

ted part may be immobilized with a splint until the wound has healed. Immobilization decreases pain and muscle spasm.

Elevation reduces swelling and associated discomfort. The neurovascular status of the affected extremity is monitored. Techniques for reducing pain perception and pain-relief medications may be useful.

Adapting to Mobility Limitations

Treatment regimes tend to be very restrictive. The patient needs to be taught the rationale for the various therapies and activity restrictions. Full participation within physical limitations is encouraged to promote general wellbeing.

Patient Education

Management of osteomyelitis frequently requires wound care and intravenous antibiotic therapy to continue at home. It is important that the patient and caregivers understand the antibiotic protocol. Proper education before discharge from the hospital and adequate supervision and support systems are important for successful home management of osteomyelitis. The patient must be medically stable and motivated, and the family and other informal carers must be supportive. The home environment needs to be conducive to promotion of health and co-operation with the therapeutic regime.

These patients need to be monitored carefully for the development of additional painful areas or sudden rises in temperature. The patient is taught to observe for drainage, odour and increased inflammation. These signs may indicate the extension of the infection or a secondary infection. The wound should be redressed.

The general health and nutrition of the patient are monitored and enhanced. Fluids and a balanced diet high in protein, vitamin C and vitamin D are desired to ensure a positive nitrogen balance and to promote healing.

▶ *Evaluation*
▶ Expected Outcomes

1. Patient experiences relief of pain.
   a. Does not complain of pain.
   b. Experiences no tenderness in area of previous infection.
   c. Experiences no discomfort with movement.
2. Functions within prescribed mobility limitations.
   a. Participates in self-care activities.
   b. Maintains full function of unimpaired extremities.
   c. Demonstrates safe use of adaptive and immobility devices.
3. Conveys an understanding of the health care programme.
   a. Takes medications as prescribed.
   b. Demonstrates proper wound care.
   c. Reports problems promptly.
   d. Eats a balanced diet.

e. Keeps follow-up health appointments.

f. Reports increased strength.

g. Reports no elevation of temperature or recurrence of pain, swelling or other symptoms at the site.

Septic (Infectious) Arthritis

Joints can become infected by spread of infection from other parts of the body (haematogenous spread) or directly by trauma or surgical instruments. Previous trauma to joints, coexisting arthritis and diminished host resistance contribute to the development of an infected joint. Gonococci and staphylococci cause most adult joint infections. Prompt recognition and treatment of an infected joint are important because accumulating pus results in chondrolysis (destruction of hyaline cartilage), which heals poorly.

Clinical Features

The patient with an acute septic arthritis usually presents with a warm, painful, swollen joint with decreased range of motion. Systemic chills and fever may be present. Assessment for a primary focus of infection (e.g., a carbuncle) should be done. Elderly patients and people taking corticosteroids or immunosuppressive drugs demonstrate decreased reaction to the infection.

Diagnosis

Diagnostic studies include aspiration, examination and culture of the synovial fluid. Arthrograms may reveal damage to the joint lining. Radioisotope scanning is useful in localizing the process and distinguishing between a joint infection and an overlying cellulitis.

Management

Prompt treatment is essential. Antibiotics, such as cephalosporin or gentamicin, should be started promptly by intravenous infusion. Penicillin G is used for gonococcal septic arthritis. The parenteral antibiotics are continued until symptoms disappear. Additionally, the synovial fluid is monitored for sterility and decrease in white blood cells.

In addition to prescribing antibiotics, the surgeon will drain the excessive joint fluid by needle aspiration to remove fluid, exudate and debris. Occasionally, arthrotomy or arthroscopy is used to drain the joint and to remove dead tissue. The inflamed joint should be supported and put at rest. A splint to immobilize the joint increases the patient's comfort. Codeine may be used to control pain. Nonsteroidal anti-inflammatory drugs may be prescribed after the infection has responded to the antibiotic. Range-of-motion and active exercises are started gradually when the infection subsides. The patient's fluids and nutrition are monitored to promote healing. If septic joints are treated early, recovery of normal function should occur.

The patient is assessed periodically for a recurrence of the problems. If the articular cartilage was damaged during the inflammatory reaction, joint fibrosis and diminished function may develop.

BONE TUMOURS

Neoplasms of the musculoskeletal system are of a variety of types. They include osteogenic, chondrogenic, fibrogenic and marrow (reticulum) cell tumours as well as nerve, vascular and fatty cell tumours. They may be primary or metastatic carcinomas from primary cancers elsewhere in the body (e.g., breast, lung, prostate, kidney). Metastatic bone tumours occur more frequently in older patients.

Benign primary neoplasms of the musculoskeletal system include osteoma, aneurysmal bone cyst, osteoid osteoma, chondroma, osteochondroma and fibroma. Malignant primary musculoskeletal tumours include osteosarcoma, fibrosarcoma, chondrosarcoma, Ewing's sarcoma and multiple myeloma. Giant cell tumour (osteoclastoma) is benign for long periods of time; it may invade local tissue, but distant metastasis is not common. Sarcomas originate in connective and supportive tissue.

The presence of a tumour in the bone causes the normal bone tissue to react by osteolytic response (bone destruction) or by osteoblastic response (bone formation). Some of the bone tumours are common and some are exceedingly rare. Some present no problem, while others rapidly become life-threatening. Some benign tumours have the potential of undergoing malignant transformation.

Clinical Features

Patients with a bone tumour present with a wide range of associated problems. They may be asymptomatic or may have pain (mild and occasional to constant and severe); varying degrees of disability; and, at times, obvious bone growth. Weight loss, malaise and fever may be present. The tumour may be diagnosed incidentally following pathological fracture.

Differential diagnosis is based on the history, physical examination, X-rays (including tomograms, bone scans and arteriography), biochemical assays of the blood and urine (alkaline phosphatase is frequently elevated) and, finally, surgical biopsy for histological identification (Figure 37.5). Extreme care is taken during biopsy to prevent seeding and recurrence following excision of the tumour. Radiological studies of the chest are done to determine the presence of lung metastasis. Staging is based on tumour size, grade and location as well as on metastasis. The treatment regime is based on findings. The nurse provides support during this diagnostic period.

Management

Management of bone tumours includes surgical excision (ranging from local excision to massive replacement,

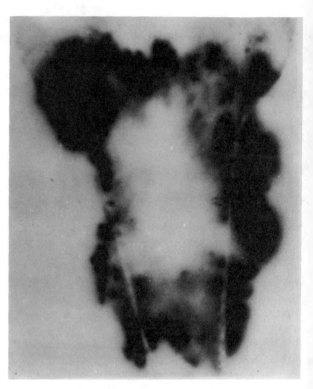

Figure 37.5 Bone scan of a patient with osteosarcoma. (Left) X-ray showing osteosarcoma at the proximal end of the tibia. Note the destruction of the normal anatomy of the bone. (Right) Contact autoradiograph of the same patient. The patient had received a radioisotope intravenously for bone scanning. Note the high uptake (black areas) in the peripheral growing margin and the relative lack of uptake centrally. (Armed Forces Institute of Pathology. Negative numbers 67-4-8, 67-4-9.)

amputation and disarticulation), radiation when the tumour is radiosensitive and chemotherapy. Major gains are being made in using wide block excision with restorative grafting technique and chemotherapeutics (preoperative, postoperative and adjunctive for possible micrometastasis). Survival and quality of life are important considerations in procedures that attempt to save the involved extremity.

Benign Bone Tumours

Benign bone tumours generally are slow-growing and well-circumscribed, present few symptoms and are not a cause of death.

Osteochondroma is the most common benign bone tumour, and usually occurs as a large projection of bone at the end of long bones (at the knee or shoulder). It develops during growth and then becomes a static bony mass. The cartilage cap of the osteochondroma may undergo malignant transformation following trauma, and a chondrosarcoma may develop.

Enchondroma is a common tumour of the hyaline cartilage that develops during the growing years in the hand, ribs, femur, tibia, humerus or pelvis. Generally, the only symptom is a mild ache. Pathological fractures may occur.

A painful tumour that occurs in children and young adults is the osteoid osteoma. The neoplastic tissue is surrounded by reactive bone formation that assists in its radiological identification.

Bone cysts are expanding lesions within the bone. Aneurysmal bone cysts are seen in young adults, and present with a painful, palpable mass of the long bones, vertebrae or flat bones. Unicameral bone cysts occur in children and cause mild discomfort and possible pathological fractures of the upper humerus and femur. These may heal spontaneously.

Management

The general therapeutic approach to benign bone tumours is to excise completely the tumour tissue and restore the bone continuity with bone grafts. The excised area may be packed with ilium chips to stimulate healing.

Nursing Care

The nursing care of a patient who has undergone excision

of a bone tumour is similar in many aspects to that for other patients who have skeletal surgery. The operative part should be elevated to control swelling; the neurovascular status of the extremity should be assessed. Generally, the area is immobilized by splints, casts or support bandages until the bone heals. The fluid and electrolyte balance of the patient is monitored. A diet high in protein, with adequate vitamins (especially vitamins C and D) and calcium, is encouraged.

Pain is present both at the surgical and the graft donor sites. Narcotics are prescribed during the early postoperative period. Later, oral, non-narcotic analgesics are adequate to control discomfort.

Postexcision complications include those associated with immobility, blood loss and infection. Osteomyelitis is a concern. Prophylactic antibiotics and strict aseptic dressing techniques are used to diminish the occurrence of this. During healing, other infections (e.g., colds) need to be avoided so that haematogenous spread does not result in an osteomyelitis.

Depending on the site of excision, the use of ambulatory aids may be required. An exercise programme is designed to restore function. Active participation in exercises and other rehabilitative activities is encouraged.

As the patient prepares to leave the hospital, the nurse provides education concerning continuing care and the medication and exercise regimes. The nurse also encourages needed follow-up medical visits.

Malignant Bone Tumours

Primary malignant bone tumours arise from bone tissue cells (sarcomas) or bone marrow elements (myelomas). Bone metastasis to the lungs is common. Secondary bone tumours (carcinomas) are due to metastasis from breast, prostate, kidney, thyroid or lung cancers.

Osteogenic Sarcoma

Osteogenic sarcoma (osteosarcoma) is the most common and most often fatal primary malignant bone tumour. It is characterized by early haematogenous metastasis to the lungs. The tumour carries a high mortality rate because the sarcoma often has spread to the lungs by the time the patient seeks help.

Osteogenic sarcoma appears most frequently in males in the age group between 10 and 25 years. It is manifested by pain, swelling, limitation of motion and weight loss (which is considered an ominous finding). The bony mass may be palpable, tender and fixed, with an increase in skin temperature over the mass and venous distension. The primary lesion may involve any bone; the most common sites are the distal femur, the proximal tibia and the proximal humerus.

Chondrosarcoma

Malignant tumours of the hyaline cartilage are called chondrosarcomas and are the second most common primary malignant bone tumour. They are large, bulky, slow-growing tumours that affect adults (men more frequently than women). The usual tumour sites include the pelvis, ribs, femur, humerus, spine, scapula and tibia. Metastasis to the lungs occurs in fewer than half the patients. If these tumours are well differentiated, large block excision or amputation of the affected extremity results in a good survival rate. These tumours may recur.

Giant cell tumours are benign for long periods of time but may invade local tissue and cause destruction. They occur in young adults and are soft and haemorrhagic. Eventually giant cell tumours become malignant and metastasize.

Management

The goal of management is to destroy or remove malignant tissue by the most effective method possible. This requires a multidisciplinary approach.

Surgical removal of the tumour frequently requires amputation of the affected extremity, with the line of amputation extending through the bone or joint above the bone tumour in order to achieve local control of the primary lesion. (See nursing care of the patient following an amputation, p. 1134.)

Limb-sparing (salvage) procedures remove the tumour and adjacent tissue. The resected portion is replaced by a custom prosthesis, total joint arthroplasty or bone tissue from the patient or cadaver donor. Soft tissue and blood vessels may need grafting because of the extent of the excision. Complications that may develop include infection, loosening or dislocation of the prosthesis, allograft nonunion, fracture, devitalization of the skin and soft tissues, joint fibrosis and recurrence of the tumour. Function and rehabilitation following limb salvage depend on reducing the risk of complications and positive encouragement.

Because of the real danger of metastasis with these tumours, combined chemotherapy is started before and continued after surgery in an effort to eradicate micrometastatic lesions. The hope is that combined chemotherapy will have a greater effect at a lower toxicity rate, while reducing resistance to the drugs. There is an improved long-term survival rate when a localized osteosarcoma is removed and chemotherapy is initiated.

Soft-tissue sarcomas are treated with radiation, limb-sparing excision and adjuvant chemotherapy.

▶ NURSING PROCESS
▶ THE PATIENT WITH A PRIMARY MALIGNANT BONE TUMOUR

▶ *Assessment*

The patient is encouraged to discuss the problem, and the onset and course of symptoms. During the interview, the nurse notes how the patient and loved ones have been coping and how the patient has managed the pain. Support during diagnostic studies and therapy is a major nursing concern.

On physical examination, the nurse needs to check any mass gently, noting size and associated soft-tissue swelling, pain and tenderness. Assessment of the neurovascular status and range of motion of the extremity provides baseline data for future comparisons. The patient's mobility and ability to perform activities of daily living are evaluated.

► Patient's Problems

Based on the nursing assessment, the main problems for the patient with a primary malignant bone tumour may include the following:

● Alteration in comfort—pain related to tumour.
● Potential for injury—pathological fracture related to tumour and complications of therapy.
● Lack of knowledge about the therapeutic regime.
● Potential ineffective coping related to perception of disease process and impact on lifestyle.
● Disturbance in self-concept related to loss of body part or role performance.
● Potential impaired home management related to alteration in functional abilities and treatment regime.

► Planning and Implementation
► Expected Outcomes

The patient's anticipated outcomes may include relief of pain, avoidance of injury from fracture or complication of therapy (surgery, chemotherapy, radiation therapy), active participation in the therapeutic regime, demonstration of effective coping, improvement of self-concept and demonstration of effective health care at home.

Nursing Care

Relieving Pain

Psychological, pharmaceutical and environmental pain management techniques are useful. The nurse needs to work with the patient in designing the most effective pain management regime, thereby increasing the patient's control over the pain. The nurse prepares the patient and gives support during painful procedures.

Avoiding Complications

Assistance is given with position changes and ambulation to prevent stress on the weakened bones. The patient is taught how to use aids safely and how to strengthen unaffected extremities.

The patient is informed of the possible side-effects of any chemotherapeutic drugs. Antiemetics and relaxation techniques reduce the gastrointestinal reaction. Stomatitis is controlled with anaesthetic and antifungal mouthwashes. Alopecia is temporary, and hair growth usually resumes after chemotherapy is discontinued. The patient is taught to avoid people with colds and infections when the patient's white blood cell count is low. Adequate hydration is essential. With nephrotoxic drugs, diuretics may be prescribed to increase excretion. Specific drugs may be toxic to specific organs (e.g., kidneys, heart, lungs, ears). Laboratory values are monitored to detect abnormalities that may necessitate a change in the treatment regime. The functioning of the organs potentially affected is monitored.

Additionally, vital signs are watched and other observations are made to assess for the development of complications: thrombophlebitis, pulmonary emboli, infection, contracture and disuse atrophy.

Patient Education

Education of the patient and family or friends is essential. They will want to know about the disease process and its diagnostic and management regimes. Co-operation and adherence are based on this understanding. The nurse can most effectively reinforce and clarify information provided by the surgeon by being present during these doctor–patient discussions. Explanation of diagnostic tests, treatments (e.g., wound care) and expected results (e.g., decreased range of motion, numbness, change in body contours) helps the patient deal with the procedures and changes that occur. Include the patient in an assessment of responses to the treatment regime and scheduling of care. This will increase the patient's understanding of the care.

Preparation for and co-ordination of continuing health care are begun early as a multidisciplinary effort. Patient education is directed at medication, dressing and treatment regimes, as well as physiotherapy and occupational therapy programmes. The safe use of special equipment is taught. The patient, family and other informal carers learn the signs and symptoms of possible complications. The patient is advised to have the telephone numbers of people to contact readily available in case problems arise. Frequently, arrangements are made for home care supervision. Follow-up appointments are scheduled. The need for long-term health supervision to ensure cure or to detect tumour recurrence or metastasis is emphasized.

Effective Coping

The patient and other carers must be encouraged to express their feelings honestly. They need to be supported and feel accepted as they come to grips with the impact of the malignant bone tumour. Feelings of shock, despair and grief are expected. The use of an independent counsellor may be appropriate.

Improved Self-Concept

Independence versus dependence is an issue with the patient who has a malignancy. Lifestyle is dramatically changed, at least temporarily. The family and other informal carers are supported in working through the adjustments that must be made. Changes in body image due to surgery and possibly amputation need to be recognized. The importance of achieving tumour cure, even if it involves a change in body image, is stressed. Nurses need to be realistically reassuring about the future and about resumption of role-related activities. Self-care and socialization are encouraged. The patient should help plan daily activities. Involvement of the patient, family and other informal carers throughout the treatment process promotes confidence, restoration of self-concept and a sense of control over decisions affecting lifestyle.

► *Evaluation*
► **Expected Outcomes**

1. Patient achieves relief of pain.
   a. Experiences no pain at rest, during activities or at surgical sites.
   b. Participates comfortably in activities of daily living.
2. Experiences no pathological fracture or injury from therapies.
   a. Avoids stress to weakened bones.
   b. Manages side-effects of therapies.
   c. Reports symptoms of drug toxicity or complications of surgery.
   d. Avoids contact with people with colds and infections when white blood cell count is suppressed.
3. Demonstrates an understanding of the treatment regime.
   a. Describes problem and management plan.
   b. Seeks clarification of information.
   c. Participates in self-care activities.
4. Demonstrates effective coping.
   a. Talks about feelings.
   b. Identifies strengths and abilities.
   c. Makes decisions.
5. Demonstrates positive self-concept.
   a. Performs self-care activities.
   b. Assumes responsibilities.
   c. Exhibits confidence in own abilities.
6. Demonstrates effective health care at home.
   a. Takes prescribed medications.
   b. Demonstrates dressing and treatment regimes.
   c. Continues physiotherapy and occupational therapy programmes.
   d. Reports occurrence of symptoms of complications.
   e. Uses special equipment safely.
   f. Schedules follow-up health care appointments.
   g. Acknowledges need for long-term health supervision.

Metastatic Bone Cancer

Metastatic bone cancer is more common than any primary malignant bone tumour. Tumours arising from tissues other than the bone may invade the bone and produce localized bone destruction, with results that are clinically quite similar to those occurring in primary bone tumours. Tumours that metastasize to bone most frequently include carcinomas of the kidney, the prostate, the lung, the breast, the ovary and the thyroid. Metastatic tumours most frequently attack the skull, spine, pelvis, femur and humerus. Bone scans are useful in confirming a diagnosis.

A sign of diagnostic importance in patients with metastatic carcinoma of the prostate is an elevation of the serum acid phosphatase. The first indication of disease in such cases may be a pathological bone fracture; in later stages, the peripheral blood may show evidence of bone marrow interference.

The treatment of metastatic bone cancer is palliative, and the therapeutic goal is to relieve the patient's discomfort as much as possible. Internal fixation of pathological fractures minimizes associated disability and pain. At times, large bone metastatic lesions are strengthened by prophylactic internal fixation. The patient is encouraged to be as independent as possible and function as long as possible. Surgery may be indicated in long bone fractures.

COMMON PROBLEMS OF THE UPPER EXTREMITY

Painful Shoulder Syndrome

The structures in and about the shoulder are frequently the sites of painful syndromes. With ageing, degenerative alterations occur in all joints, including the articulations that make up the shoulder joint (glenohumeral, sternoclavicular and acromioclavicular). Pain may arise from the shoulder, with the resultant inflammation spreading to the tendon sheaths (tenosynovitis), and the bursa, capsule, synovium, cartilage, bone and surrounding muscles. These syndromes are managed by rest, drug therapy and physiotherapy.

Patient Education. The nurse provides guidelines for general care and shows the patient how to carry out measures that will promote healing. This involves teaching the patient to do the following:

1. Rest the joint in a position that minimizes stress on the joint structures during the acute phase to prevent further damage and the development of adhesions.
2. Support the affected arm on pillows while sleeping, to keep from rolling over on the shoulder.
3. At first, apply cold intermittently, and then apply heat intermittently, to reduce discomfort and facilitate mobilization. Cold applications help reduce swelling, and heat promotes circulation.
4. Gradually resume motion and use of the joint. Assistance with dressing and other activities of daily living may be needed.

5. Avoid working and lifting above shoulder level or pushing an object against a 'locked' shoulder.
6. Do the prescribed daily range-of-motion exercises to strengthen the shoulder girdle and glenohumeral muscle.

'Tennis Elbow'

'Tennis elbow' is a chronic painful condition that is due to excessive pronation and supination activities of the forearm (e.g., tennis, sculling, using a screwdriver). The pain characteristically radiates down the extensor (dorsal) surface of the forearm. The patient has a weakened grasp. Most often, relief is obtained by resting the arm in a moulded splint, applying moist heat and taking analgesics. In some instances, local injection of a corticosteroid is prescribed. Gentle daily exercises help to prevent elbow stiffness.

Ganglion

A ganglion is a round, firm, cystic swelling, usually near the wrist. It is a collection of gelatinous material near the tendon sheaths and joints. Ganglions develop through defects in the tendon sheath or capsule. Ganglions occur most frequently in women under the age of 50. The ganglion is tender and may cause an aching pain. When a tendon sheath is involved, weakness of the finger occurs.

Carpal Tunnel Syndrome

Carpal tunnel syndrome is an entrapment neuropathy that occurs when the median nerve at the wrist is compressed by a thickened flexor tendon sheath, skeletal encroachment or soft-tissue mass on the median nerve at the wrist. The patient experiences pain, numbness, paraesthesia and possibly weakness along the median nerve (thumb, first and second fingers). Night pain is common. Rest splints, avoidance of work that requires flexion of the wrist and cortisone injections may relieve the symptoms. Surgical release may be necessary.

Dupuytren's Contracture

Dupuytren's deformity is a slowly progressive contracture of the palmar fascia that causes flexion of the little finger, the ring finger, and frequently the middle fingers, which renders them more or less useless (Figure 37.6). It is a fairly common abnormality, occurring most frequently in men over age 50 who are of North-Western European origin. It may be caused by an inherited autosomal dominant trait. It starts as a tender nodule of the palmar fascia. The tenderness resolves, and the nodule may not change, or it may progress where the fibrous thickening extends to involve the skin in the distal palm and produces a contracture of the fingers. This condition always starts in one hand, but eventually both become deformed symmetrically. Surgery consists of limited palmar and digital fasciectomies that improve function. The recurrence and extension rate is 45 to 80 per cent.

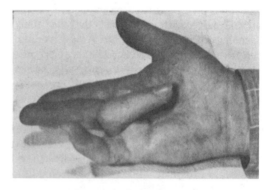

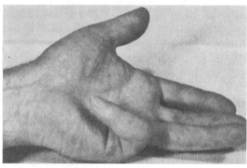

Figure 37.6 Dupuytren's contracture. (Boyes, J. H., *Bunnell's Surgery of the Hand* (5th edition), J. B. Lippincott, Philadelphia, p. 228.)

► NURSING PROCESS
► THE PATIENT UNDERGOING SURGERY OF THE HAND OR WRIST

► *Assessment*

Surgery of the hand and wrist is generally an ambulatory surgery procedure. Before surgery, the nurse assesses the patient's level and type of discomfort and limitations in function caused by the ganglion, carpal tunnel syndrome, Dupuytren's contracture or other condition of the hand. Following surgery, the nurse assesses the patient for swelling, neurovascular status, pain and function. Pain may be related to oedema, restrictive bandages, haematoma formation or surgery.

► *Patient's Problems*

Based on the assessment, the main problems for the patient with surgery of the hand or wrist may include the following:

● Alteration in comfort—pain related to inflammation and swelling.
● Inability to care for self related to bandaged hands.
● Potential for infection.

► *Planning and Implementation*
► **Expected Outcomes**

The outcomes for the patient may include relief of pain, improved self-care and absence of infection.

Nursing Care

Relieving Pain

To control swelling, the hand is elevated above heart level with pillows or with an elevating sling , which is attached to an intravenous pole or overhead frame when high elevation is prescribed. If the patient is ambulatory, the arm is elevated in a conventional sling. Active extension and flexion of the fingers promote circulation and are encouraged, even though movement is limited by the bulky dressing.

Neurovascular checks of the exposed fingers every hour for the first 24 hours are essential for monitoring function of the nerves and perfusion of the hand. Ask the patient to describe the sensations in the hands and to demonstrate finger movement ability. The patient's nerve function is observed carefully preoperatively because this information is needed for interpreting function after surgery. Compromised neurovascular functioning can contribute to pain.

Generally, the discomfort can be controlled by oral analgesics. The nurse evaluates the patient's response to the pain medications and to other pain-control measures. Patient education concerning the analgesics is carried out by the nurse.

Improving Self-Care

During the first few days following surgery, the patient will need assistance with activities of daily living because one hand is bandaged and function is impaired. The patient may need to arrange for assistance with feeding, bathing/hygiene, dressing, grooming and toileting. Within a few days, the patient is able to function with minimal assistance. The pain and swelling are controlled, functional abilities are returning and the patient has developed skills in one-handed activities of daily living. As rehabilitation progresses, the patient will resume use of the injured hand. Adherence to the therapeutic regime is emphasized.

Absence of Infection

As with all surgery, there is a potential for infection. The patient is taught to monitor temperature and pulse for elevations that may indicate a possible infection. The patient is shown how to keep the dressing clean and dry. Any drainage, foul odour associated with the dressing or increased pain and swelling should be reported. Patient education concerning aseptic wound care may be appropriate. The patient may be taking prophylactic antibiotics and need education in relation to these.

► *Evaluation*
► **Expected Outcomes**

1. Relief of pain.
   a. Patient reports increased comfort.
   b. Controls oedema through elevation of hand.
   c. Experiences no discomfort with movement.
2. Improved self-care.
   a. Patient secures assistance with activities of daily living during first few days postoperatively.
   b. Adapts to one-handed activities of daily living.
   c. Uses injured hand functionally.
3. Develops no infection.
   a. Has temperature and pulse within normal limits.
   b. Has no purulent drainage or wound inflammation.

COMMON FOOT PROBLEMS

Disabilities of the human foot not only develop from poorly fitting shoes but may be the result of hereditary influence. Probably the foot would cause little pain or disability on its own account if it were not for modern civilization, which disregards the physiology of the foot. Fashion, vanity and eye appeal, rather than function, are for the most part the determining factors in the design of footwear. The restriction of ill-fitting shoes distorts normal anatomy while inducing deformity and pain.

The discomfort of foot strain can be treated by rest, elevation, physiotherapy, supportive strappings and orthotic devices. Foot exercises in which active motion occurs will benefit the circulation and help strengthen the feet. Walking in properly fitting shoes is considered the best form of exercise.

Common Foot Ailments

A corn is an area of hyperkeratosis (overgrowth of a horny layer of epidermis) produced by pressure from within (the underlying bone is prominent due to congenital or acquired abnormality, commonly arthritis) or by pressure from without (shoes).

The usual sites are the lesser toes, mainly the fifth toe, but all toes may be involved.

Corns are treated by soaking and scraping off the horny layer with an instrument, by applying a protective shield or pads, or by surgical removal of the underlying offending osseous structure.

Soft corns are located between the toes and are kept soft by moisture and maceration. Treatment consists of drying the affected web spaces and separating the affected toes.

A callus is a discretely thickened area of the skin that has been exposed to persistent pressure or friction. Faulty foot mechanics usually precede the formation of a callus. Treatment consists of eliminating the underlying causes and having the callus pared if it is painful. A keratolytic ointment may be applied and a thin plastic cup worn over the heel if the callus is on this area. Felt padding with adhesive backing is also used to prevent and relieve pressure. Orthotic devices can be made to remove the pressure from the bony protuberance. The protuberance may be excised.

An ingrown toenail (onychocryptosis) is a condition in which the free edge of a nail plate has penetrated the surrounding skin, either laterally or anteriorly. It may be accompanied by secondary infection or granulation tissue. This painful condition is caused by improper self-treatment, external pressure (tight shoes or stockings), internal pressure (deformed toes; growth under the nail), trauma and infection. Trimming the nails properly can prevent this problem. Active treatment consists of relieving the pain by decreasing the pressure on the surrounding soft tissue by the nail plate. Warm, wet soaks help to drain an infection. A toenail may have to be excised if there is severe infection.

Common Deformities of the Foot

Flatfoot

Flatfoot (pes planus) is a common disorder in which the longitudinal arch of the foot is diminished. It may be due to congenital abnormalities or associated with bone or ligament injury, muscle and posture imbalances, excessive weight, muscle fatigue, poorly-fitting shoes or arthritis. Symptoms include burning sensation, fatigue, clumsy gait, oedema and pain.

Exercises to strengthen the muscles and to improve posture and walking habits are helpful. A number of foot devices are available to give the foot additional support. Severe flatfoot problems are usually treated by an orthopaedic surgeon.

Hammer Toe

Hammer toe is a flexion deformity of the interphalangeal joint and may involve several toes (Figure 37.7). The condition is usually an acquired deformity. Tight socks or

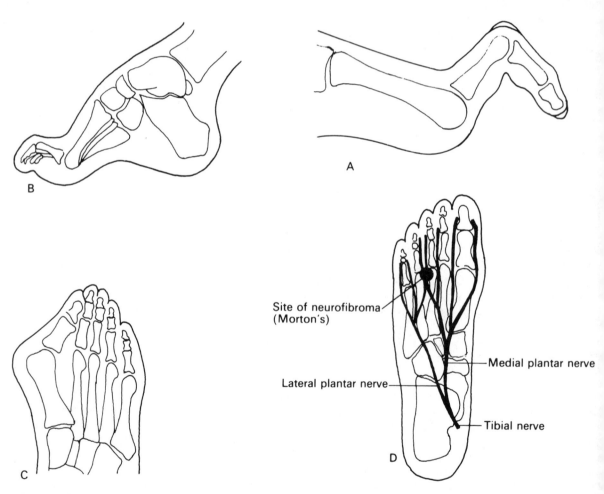

Figure 37.7 Common foot deformities. (A) Hammer toe. (B) Clawfoot (pes cavus). (C) Hallux valgus. (D) Site for Morton's neuroma.

shoes may push an overlying toe back into the line of the other toes. The toes usually are pulled upward, forcing the metatarsal joints (ball of foot) downward. Corns develop on top of the toes, and tender calluses develop under the metatarsal area. The treatment consists of conservative measures: carrying out manipulative exercises, wearing open-toed sandals or shoes that conform to the shape of the foot and protecting the protruding joints with pads. Surgical correction is necessary for an established deformity.

Hallux Valgus

Hallux valgus (bunion) is a progressive deformity in which the great toe deviates laterally (Figure 37.7).

Associated with this is a marked prominence of the medial aspect of the first metatarsal–phalangeal joint, over which a bursa may form (secondary to pressure and inflammation). Acute bursitis symptoms include a reddened area, oedema and tenderness. Aetiological factors include heredity, narrow shoes, arthritis and flatfoot.

Treatment depends on the patient's age, the degree of deformity and the severity of symptoms. If a bunion deformity is uncomplicated, wearing a shoe that conforms to the shape of the foot or one that is moulded to the foot to prevent pressure on the protruding portions may be all the treatment that is needed. If not, surgical removal of the bunion and realignment of the toe may be required.

Postoperatively, the patient may have intense throbbing pain at the operative site, requiring rather liberal doses of analgesic medication. The operated food is elevated above the level of the heart to decrease oedema and pain. The neurovascular status of the toes is assessed. The duration of immobility and initiation of ambulation depend upon the procedure used. Following surgery, exercises are initiated to flex and extend the toes, since toe flexion is essential in walking. Shoes that do not stress the foot are recommended.

Clawfoot

Clawfoot (pes cavus) refers to a foot with an abnormally high arch (Figure 37.7). This causes shortening of the foot and increased pressure that produces calluses on the metatarsal area and on the dorsum (bottom) of the foot. Exercises are prescribed to manipulate the forefoot into dorsiflexion and relax the toes. In severe cases, osteotomies are done to reshape the feet.

Morton's Neuroma

Morton's neuroma (plantar digital neuroma; neurofibroma) is a swelling of the third (lateral) branch of the median plantar nerve (Figure 37.7).

The result is a throbbing, burning pain in the foot that is usually relieved when the patient rests. Pain sometimes radiates up the leg. Conservative treatment consists of inserting innersoles, metatarsal bars and pads designed to spread the metatarsal heads and balance the foot posture.

Local injections of hydrocortisone and a local anaesthetic may give relief. If these fail, surgical excision of the neuroma is necessary. Pain relief is immediate and permanent.

Other Foot Problems

Several systemic diseases affect the feet. In the case of rheumatoid arthritis, deformities result. People with diabetes are prone to develop corns and peripheral neuropathies with diminishing sensation, leading to ulcers over pressure points of the foot. People with peripheral vascular disease and arteriosclerosis complain of burning and itching feet with attendant scratching and excoriations. Dermatolcogical problems commonly affect the feet in the form of fungal infections and plantar warts. The specifics of these problems and others can be found in the discussions of the various dysfunctions covered throughout the text.

▶ NURSING PROCESS
▶ THE PATIENT UNDERGOING FOOT SURGERY

▶ *Assessment*

Surgery on the foot may be necessary because of a variety of conditions, including neuromas and foot deformities (bunion, hammertoe, clawfoot). Generally, foot surgery is performed on an outpatient basis. The nurse assesses the patient's ambulatory ability and balance and the neurovascular status of the foot before surgery. Additionally, assessment of the availability of assistance at home following surgery and the structural characteristics of the home may help in planning for care during the first few days after surgery. These data, in addition to knowledge of the usual management of the problem, are used by the nurse in formulating appropriate patient care. Following surgery, the nurse assesses the patient for swelling, neurovascular function, pain, wound status and mobility.

▶ *Patient's Problems*

Based on the assessment, the main problems for the patient undergoing foot surgery may include the following:

● Alteration in comfort—pain related to inflammation and swelling.
● Impaired physical mobility related to the foot immobilizing device.
● Potential for infection.

▶ *Planning and Implementation*
▶ Expected Outcomes

The goals of the patient may include relief of pain, improved mobility and absence of infection.

Nursing Care

Relieving Pain

Pain experienced by patients who have had foot surgery is related to inflammation and oedema. Formation of a haematoma may contribute to the discomfort. To control the swelling, the foot should be elevated on several pillows when the patient is sitting or lying. Ice packs applied intermittently during the first 24 to 48 hours after surgery help to control swelling and provide some pain relief. As activity increases, the patient will find that the dependent positioning of the foot will be uncomfortable. Simply elevating the foot relieves the discomfort. Additionally, oral analgesics may be used to control the pain. The nurse provides the patient with information on the use of these medications.

Neuromuscular checks of the exposed toes every one to two hours for the first 24 hours are essential to monitor the function of the nerves and the perfusion of the tissues. If the surgery is done on an ambulatory basis, the patient and caregivers need to be taught how to assess for swelling and neurovascular status. Compromised neurovascular function can contribute to the pain experienced.

Improving Mobility

Following surgery, the patient will have a bulky dressing on the foot, protected by a light cast or a special protective boot. Weight-bearing on the foot will be prescribed by the surgeon; it varies according to the procedure and the preference of the surgeon. Some patients are allowed to walk on the heel and progress to weight-bearing as tolerated; others are to be non-weight-bearing. An ambulatory aid may be needed to assist the patient. Choice of the aid depends on the patient's general condition and balance and on the weight-bearing prescription. Safe use of the ambulatory aid must be ensured through adequate patient education and practice before discharge. Preoperative advice and practice with the ambulatory aid are desirable. Problems of moving around the house safely while using the ambulatory aid are discussed with the patient. As healing progresses, the patient will resume ambulation at the previous or an improved level. Adherence to the therapeutic regime is emphasized.

Absence of Infection

As with all surgery, there is a potential for infection. Since the foot is on or near the floor, care must be taken to protect it from soiling, dirt and moisture. When bathing, the patient can protect the dressing with a plastic bag secured around it. Additionally, patient advice concerning aseptic wound care may be appropriate. The patient is taught to monitor temperature and pulse for elevations that could indicate a possible infection. Any such elevations as well as any drainage on the dressing, foul odour or increased pain and swelling, should be reported. If the patient will be taking prescribed prophylactic antibiotics, education related to these will be needed.

▶ *Evaluation*
▶ Expected Outcome

1. Relief of pain.
   a. Patient controls oedema by elevating foot.
   b. Reports increased comfort.
2. Has improved mobility.
   a. Uses ambulatory aids safely.
   b. Resumes weight-bearing gradually as prescribed.
   c. Exhibits diminished disability associated with preoperative condition.
3. Develops no infection.
   a. Has temperature and pulse within normal limits.
   b. Has no purulent drainage or wound inflammation.
   c. Keeps dressing clean and dry.

FURTHER READING

Books

Bond, M. (1979) *Pain: Its Nature, Analysis and Treatment*, Churchill Livingstone, Edinburgh.

Coombs, R. and Friedlander, G. (eds) (1987) *Bone Tumour Management*, Butterworths, London.

Farrell, J. (1986) *Illustrated Guide to Orthopedic Nursing* (3rd edition), J. B. Lippincott, Philadelphia.

Finneson, B. (1980) *Low Back Pain* (2nd edition), J. B. Lippincott, Philadelphia.

Holbrook, T. L. *et al.* (1984) *The Frequency of Occurrence, Impact, and Cost of Selected Musculoskeletal Conditions in the United States*, American Academy of Orthopaedic Surgeons, Chicago.

Lipton, S. (1984) *Conquering Pain*, Martin Dunitz, London.

National Dairy Council (1984) *Calcium: A Summary of Current Research for the Health Professional*, National Dairy Council, Rosemont, Illinois.

Parsons, V. (1980) *A Colour Atlas of Bone Disease*, Wolfe Medical, London.

Pellino, T. *et al.* (eds) (1986) Anthony J. Jannetti in *National Association of Orthopaedic Nurses: Core Curriculum for Orthopedic Nursing*, Pitman, New Jersey.

Rosse, C. and Clawson, D. K. (1981) *The Musculoskeletal System in Health and Disease*, Harper & Row, Hagerstown, Maryland.

Sculco, T. P. (1985) *Orthopedic Care of the Geriatric Patient*, C. V. Mosby, St Louis.

Sjolund, B. and Eriksson, M. (1985) *Relief of Pain by TENS*, John Wiley, Chichester.

Turek, S. L. (ed) (1984) *Orthopedics: Principles and Their Application* (4th edition), J. B. Lippincott, Philadelphia.

Wilson, F. C. (1983) *The Musculoskeletal System: Basic Processes and Disorders* (2nd edition), J. B. Lippincott, Philadelphia.

Articles

Low Back Pain

Frampton, V. (1982) Pain control with the aid of TENS, *Physiotherapy*, Vol. 68, No. 3, pp. 77–81.

Lehmann, T. R. and Brand, R. A. (1982) Disability in the patient with low back pain, *Orthopedic Clinics of North America*, July, Vol. 13, No. 3, pp. 559–68.

Lucas, P. R. (1983) Low back pain, *Surgical Clinics of North America*, June, Vol. 63, No. 3, pp. 515–28.

McCarthy, R. E. (1984) Coping with low back pain through behavioral change, *Orthop. Nurs.*, May/June, Vol. 3, No. 3, pp. 30–5.

Selby, D. (1983) Conservative care of nonspecific low back pain, *Orthopedic Clinics of North America*, July, Vol. 13, No. 3, pp. 427–38.

Taylor, S. L. (1983) Musculoskeletal assessment: Low back pain assessment, part 1—history taking, *Orthop. Nurs.*, July/August, Vol. 2, No. 4, pp. 11–16.

Taylor, S. L. (1983) Musculoskeletal assessment: Low back pain assessment, part 2—defining range of motion and terminology, *Orthop. Nurs.*, September/October, Vol. 2, No. 5, pp. 39–44.

Taylor, S. L. (1983) Musculoskeletal assessment: Low back pain assessment, part 3—the physical examination, *Orthop. Nurs.*, November/December, Vol. 2, No. 6, pp. 21–7.

Problems of the Upper and Lower Extremities

Bartell, L. (1985) Bunionectomies, *Orthop. Nurs.*, January/February, Vol. 4, No. 1, pp. 21–8.

Berger, M. R. (1984) Bunions: An overview, *Orthop. Nurs.*, September/October, Vol. 3, No. 5, pp. 17–22.

Berger, M. R. (1982) Painful tendon problems of the hand: Trigger thumb, trigger finger, and de Quervain's syndrome, *Orthop. Nurs.*, September/October, Vol. 1, No. 5, pp. 20–23.

Berger, M. R. (1982) Morton's neuroma, *Orthop. Nurs.*, January/February, Vol. 1, No. 1, pp. 31–2.

Hill NA. Dupuytren's contracture: Current concepts review. J Bone Joint Surg [Am] 1985 Dec; 67-A(9):1439–1443.

Osteoporosis

Aloia, J. F. (1982) Oestrogen and exercise in prevention and treatment of osteoporosis, *Geraitrics*, June, Vol. 37, No. 6, pp. 81–5.

Armann, S. A. and Wells, C. L. (1985) A study of bone loss in ballerinas, *Nutr. News*, December, Vol. 49, No. 4, pp. 16–17.

Beauchamp, P. J. and Held, B. (1984) Oestrogen replacement therapy: Universal remedy for the post-menopausal woman? *Postgraduate Medicine*, May, Vol. 75, No. 7, pp. 42–9.

Chase, J. A. (1985) Spine fractures associated with osteoporosis, *Orthop. Nurs.*, May/June, Vol. 4, No. 3, pp. 31–3.

Chestnut, C. H. III (1984) An appraisal of the role of estrogens in the treatment of postmenopausal osteoporosis, *Journal of the American Geriatric Society*, August, Vol. 32, No. 8, pp. 604–8.

Gleit, C. J. and Graham, B. A. (1985) The role of calcium and estrogen in osteoporosis, *Orthop. Nurs.*, May/June, Vol. 4, No. 3, pp. 13–18.

Graham, B. A. and Gliet, C. J. (1984) Osteoporosis: A major health problem in postmenopausal women, *Orthop. Nurs.*, December, Vol. 3, No. 6, pp. 19–26.

Gray-Vickrey, M. (1984) Education to prevent falls, *Geriatric Nursing*, May/June, Vol. 5, No. 3, pp. 179–83.

Hallal, J. C. (1985) Osteoporotic fractures exact a toll, *Journal of Gerontology Nursing*, August, Vol. 11, No. 8, pp. 13–18.

Judd, H. L. *et al.* (1983) Estrogen replacement therapy: Indications and complications, *Annals of International Medicine*, February, Vol. 98, No. 2, pp. 195–205.

Lane, J. and Vigorita, V. (1984) Osteoporosis, *Orthopedic Clinics of North America*, October, Vol. 15, No. 4, pp. 711–21.

Liddel, D. B. (1985) An in-depth look at osteoporosis, *Orthop. Nurs.*, May/June, Vol. 4, No. 3, pp. 23–7.

Mindell, E. R. (1985) Orthopedic surgery, *Journal of the American Medical Association*, 25 October, Vol. 254, No. 6, pp. 2313–15.

Parfitt, A. (1983) Dietary risk factors for age-related bone loss and fractures, *Lancet*, 19 November, Vol. 2, No. 8360, pp. 1181–5.

Peck, W. A. (1985) Warding off osteoporosis, *Patient Care*, 15 January, Vol. 19, No. 11, pp. 20–49.

Ray, R. (1984) Symposium: Osteoporosis revisited, *Contemporary Orthopedics*, January, Vol. 8, No. 1, pp. 127–64.

The role of calcium in health (1984) *National Dairy Council Digest*, Vol. 55, No. 1, pp. 1–8.

Todd, B. (1985) Can osteoporosis be treated? *Geriatric Nursing*, November/December, Vol. 6, No. 6, pp. 359–60.

Torrance, C. (1985) Boning up on exercise, *Nursing Times*, 23 October, Vol. 81, No. 43, p. 38.

Veninga, K. S. (1984) Osteoporosis: Implications for community health nursing, *Journal of Community Health Nursing*, Vol. 1, No. 4, pp. 227–33.

Woolf, A. D. and Dixon, A. StJ. (1984) Osteoporosis: An update on management, *Drugs*, Vol. 28, pp. 565–76.

Osteomalacia/Paget's Disease

Doppelt, S. H. (1984) Vitamin D: Rickets and osteomalacia, *Orthopedic Clinics of North America*, October, Vol. 15, No. 4, pp. 671–96.

Lane, J. M. (ed.) (1984) Symposium on metabolic bone disease, *Orthopedic Clinics of North America*, October, Vol. 15, No. 4, pp. 567–820.

Nordin, C. (1978) Osteoporosis and osteomalacia, *Medicine (3rd Series)*, Vol. 10, pp. 491–500.

Nugent, C. A., Gall, E. P. and Pitt, M. J. (1984) Osteoporosis, osteomalacia, rickets, and Paget's disease, *Primary Care*, June, Vol. 11, No. 2, pp. 353–68.

Stacy-Spencer, E. (1984) Diagnostic overview: Osteomalacia, *Orthop. Nurs.*, July/August, Vol. 3, No. 4, p. 47.

Bone and Joint Infections

Arthritis (1983) *American Journal of Nursing*, February, Vol. 83, No. 2, pp. 253–62.

Bergers, R. M., Martin, R.N. and Streckfuss, B. L. (1985) A home IV antibiotic program, *NITA*, May/June, Vol. 8, No. 3, pp. 238–9.

Fitzgerald, R. H. and Kelley, P. J. (eds) (1984) Musculoskeletal sepsis, *Orthopedic Clinics of North America*, July, Vol. 15, No. 3, pp. 399–554.

Ho, G. Jr and Su, E. Y. (1982) Therapy for septic arthritis, *Journal of the American Medical Association*, 12 February, Vol. 247, No. 6, pp. 797–800.

Sheehan, K. and Gildea, J. (1985) Home antibiotic therapy, *NITA*, March/April, Vol. 8, No. 2, pp. 157–9.

Smith, D. L. (1983) Infectious arthritis, *Topics in Emergency Medicine*, July, Vol. 5, No. 2, pp. 40–5.

Bone Tumours

Berrettoni, B. A. and Carter, J. R. (1986) Mechanisms of cancer metastasis to bone, *American Journal of Bone and Joint Surgery*, February, Vol. 68-A, No. 2, pp. 308–11.

Chalmers, J. *et al.* (1988) A mini-symposium on tumours of the musculoskeletal system, *Current Orthopaedics*, Vol. 2, pp. 135–57.

Consensus Conference: Limb-sparing treatment of adult soft-tissue sarcomas and osteosarcomas (1985) *Journal of the American Medical Association*, 4 October, Vol. 254, No. 13, pp. 1791–4.

Eilber, F. R. *et al.* (1984) Limb salvage for skeletal and soft-tissue sarcomas, *Cancer*, 15 June, Vol. 53, No. 12, pp. 2579–84.

Fedora, N. L. (1985) Fighting for my leg...and my life, *Orthop. Nurs.*, September/October, Vol. 4, No. 5, pp. 39–42.

Fountain, M. J. (1985) Psychological support for the person experiencing cancer, *Orthop. Nurs.*, September/October, Vol. 4, No. 5, pp. 33–5.

Gregorcic, N. J. (1985) Functional abilities following limb-salvage procedures, *Orthop. Nurs.*, September/October, Vol. 4, No. 5, pp. 24–8.

Kerns, L. L. and Simon, M. A. (1983) Surgical theory, staging, definition, and treatment of musculoskeletal sarcomas, *Surgical Clinics of North America*, June, Vol. 63, No. 3, pp. 671–96.

Lambert, M. H. *et al.* (1984) Soft-tissue sarcoma: Functional outcome after wide local excision and radiation therapy, *Arch. Phys. Med. Rehabil.*, August, Vol. 65, No. 8, pp. 477–80.

Lamphier, P. C. (1985) Primary bone tumors, *Orthop. Nurs.*, September/October, Vol. 4, No. 5, pp. 17–23.

Matzke, K. A. *et al.* (1985) Case study: Nursing care of a patient with osteogenic sarcoma, *Orthop. Nurs.*, September/October, Vol. 4, No. 5, pp. 44–7, 69.

Moore, T. M. *et al.* (1984) Symposium: Soft-tissue sarcomas, *Contemporary Orthopedics*, April, Vol. 8, No. 4, pp. 89–126.

Nirenberg, A. (1985) The adolescent with osteogenic sarcoma, *Orthop. Nurs.*, September/October, Vol. 4, No. 5, pp. 11–15.

Piasecki, P. A. and Rodts, M. F. (1985) Bone banking: Its role in skeletal tumor resection, *Orthop. Nurs.*, September/October, Vol. 4, No. 5, pp. 56–60.

Sweetnam, R. (1982) Osteosarcoma, *British Journal of Hospital Medicine*, August, Vol. 28, No. 2, pp. 112, 116–21.

chapter **38**

ASSESSMENT AND CARE OF PATIENTS WITH INFECTIOUS DISEASES

THE CHALLENGE OF INFECTIOUS DISEASES

An infectious disease is any disease caused by the growth of pathogenic organisms in the body. It may or may not be communicable.

Infectious diseases are still the major health problem of the vast majority of people inhabiting the earth. In the developing countries, the principal causes of death are infectious diseases. The major tropical diseases endemic in many areas are actually increasing in number. New and fearful infectious diseases arising from the tropics in recent years include Lassa, Marburg and Ebola fevers. The increase in foreign travel has contributed to a resurgence of interest in tropical diseases. The conquering of these diseases is necessary for economic self-sufficiency and national development.

In the industrialized countries, the mortality from infectious diseases has declined dramatically, but these diseases represent the problems most frequently requiring professional attention, accounting for a large proportion of the cost of health care. Even in highly developed countries where many diseases have been eliminated, 'new' diseases are being introduced by invasive diagnostic techniques, immunosuppressive therapies, changing cultural behaviour and sexual patterns, and by the creation of high-risk environments such as intensive care units. The 'new' sexually transmitted diseases (infection caused by *Chlamydia trachomatis*, genital papillomaviruses and so on) have caused epidemics throughout the world; the most awesome problem is the global spread of acquired immune deficiency syndrome (AIDS). People whose normal host defences have been compromised are also susceptible to organisms that are considered minimally pathogenic. Included in this group are the elderly.

Advances in modern medicine have led to the development of more antimicrobial drugs, antiviral chemotherapy and the ability to cultivate viruses in tissue cultures, as well as an increased knowledge about immunity.

However, there has also been an increase in the number of organisms that have developed resistance to a variety of antimicrobials. Table 38.1 provides an overview of the current important infectious diseases.

GENERAL MANAGEMENT

The key to the management of any infection is identifying the specific organism responsible and instituting specific therapy if it is available. The drug of choice is usually the most active drug against the pathogenic organism or the least toxic alternative. Supportive therapy includes monitoring the patient's response to therapy; ensuring hydration, fluid balance and oxygenation; and maintaining constant watchfulness for complications.

Many early symptoms of infectious diseases are nonspecific. The illness may begin with malaise and all its attendant sequelae–listlessness, lightheadedness, headache, anorexia and arthralgia. As the disease progresses there is usually fever, although elderly people in general do not have as vigorous a febrile response as younger people, nor do patients who have previously received antibiotics or who are taking immunosuppressive drugs.

Other clinical features suggestive of infection include chills, myalgia, photophobia, pharyngitis, acute lymphadenopathy, nausea and vomiting. Since the signs and symptoms associated with infection are a result of the host's inflammatory response as well as the direct response to the pathogen, they can be nonspecific. (See chapters on specific organs or systems for signs and symptoms that suggest infection of a particular organ).

Careful medical assessment is vital in diagnosing infectious diseases and will usually aim to answer the following questions:

- History of fever? Chills? (Abrupt onset of fever is associated with chills.)
- Night sweats? (Associated with intermittent fever.)
- Back pain? General myalgias? Arthralgias? Headache? (All are commonly associated with fever.)
- Sore throat?
- Diarrhoea? (Does anyone in the household have diarrhoea?) Vomiting? Abdominal pain?
- Dysuria? Purulent discharge?
- Evidence of local infection: Redness? Heat? Swelling? Pain?
- Contact with an ill person, or that person's secretions/excretions?
- Insect bite? Animal bite? Cat scratch? Exposure to rodents or birds?
- Illness that compromises the body's defences?
- Medications, especially antibiotics, being taken? Alcohol intake?
- History of sexual practices?
- Travel to or from a developing country?

Table 38.1 *Epidemiology, therapy and control of communicable infections*

	Infective organism	Infectious sources	Entry site	Method of spread	Incubation period	Chemotherapy*	Prophylaxis
Amoebiasis	*Entamoeba histolytica*	Contaminated water and food	Gastrointestinal tract	Patients and carriers; faecal–oral route; oral and sexual contact	Variable	Metronidazole; diloxanide furoate	Detection of carriers and their removal from food handling; plumbing safeguards
Bacillary dysentery (shigellosis)	*Shigella* group	Contaminated water and food	Gastrointestinal tract	Patients and carriers; faecal–oral route	24–48 hours	Amoxycillin; trimethoprim; ciprofloxacin	Detection and control of carriers; inspection of food handlers; decontamination of water supplies
Brucellosis	*Brucella melitensis* and related organisms	Milk, meat, tissues, blood and absorbed fetuses and placentas from infected cattle, goats, horses and pigs	Gastrointestinal tract	Ingestion of or contact with infective material	5–30 days (variable)	Tetracycline and streptomycin	Milk pasteurization; control of infection in animals
Chancroid	*Haemophilus ducreyi*	Human cases and carriers	Genitalia	Direct sexual contact	3–5 days	Tetracycline	Effective case-finding and treatment of infection
Chickenpox (Varicella)	Varicella-zoster (V-Z) virus	Human cases	Probably nasopharynx	Probably respiratory droplets	13–17 days	Acyclovir (?)	Varicella-zoster immune globulin primarily for immunocompromised children and certain neonates exposed *in utero*
Diphtheria	*Corynebacterium diphtheriae*	Human cases and carriers; fomites; raw milk	Nasopharynx	Nasal and oral secretions; respiratory droplets	2–5 days	Diphtheria anti-toxin; penicillin; erythromycin	Active immunization with diphtheria toxoid

Disease	Organism	Reservoir	Portal of entry	Transmission	Incubation period	Treatment	Control/Prevention
Encephalitis, epidemic (Eastern and Western Equine)	Viruses	Chicken and wild-bird mites; horses	Skin	Mosquitoes	Variable	None	Destroy larvae; eliminate breeding of mosquitoes. Eastern equine encephalitis vaccine for those under continued and intensive exposure
Gonorrhoea	*Neisseria gonorrhoeae*	Urethral and vaginal secretions	Urethral or vaginal mucosa; pharynx; rectum	sexual activity	2–7 days	Amoxycillin with probenecid (or spectinomycin or ciprofloxacin if allergic to penicillin)	Examination culture; treatment of sexual partners
Infectious mononucleosis	Epstein-Barr virus	Human cases and carriers	Mouth	Probably oral-pharyngeal route; via blood transfusion in susceptible recipients	2–6 days	None	None
Influenza	Virus	Human cases	Respiratory tract	Respiratory	24–72 hours	Amantadine; rimantadine	Influenza virus vaccine
Lymphogranuloma venereum	*Chlamydia trachomatis*	Human cases	External genitalia; urethral or vaginal mucosa	Sexual intercourse; indirect contact with contaminated articles/clothing	5–21 days	Tetracyclines	Case-finding and treatment of infection
Malaria	*Plasmodium vivax, P. falciparum, P. malariae, and P. ovale*	Human cases	Skin	Mosquitoes (*Anopheles*)	Variable, depending on strain	Chloroquine; primaquine; amodiaquine; quinine	Co-ordinated measures for wide-scale mosquito control; prompt detection and effective treatment of cases; suppressive drugs in malarious areas
Measles	Virus	Human cases	Respiratory mucosa	Nasopharyngeal secretions	8–13 days	None	Measles vaccine

Table 38.1 *Continued*

	Infective organism	Infectious sources	Entry site	Method of spread	Incubation period	Chemotherapy*	Prophylaxis
Meningococcal meningitis	*Neisseria meningitidis*	Human cases and carriers	Nasopharynx; tonsils	Respiratory droplets	2–10 days	Benzyl penicillin	Meningococcal polysaccharide vaccine for people at risk; rifampin/ sulphadimidine for carriers or contacts
Mumps	Virus	Human cases (early)	Upper respiratory tract	Respiratory droplets	2–3 weeks (average 18 days)	None	Live mumps vaccine
Paratyphoid fever	*Salmonella paratyphi* A, B and C, and related organisms	Contaminated food, milk, water	Gastrointestinal tract	Infected faeces or rarely urine	7–21 days	Chloramphenicol; cotrimoxazole or ciprofloxacin	Control of public water sources, food vendors, food handlers; treatment of carriers
Pneumococcal pneumonia	*Streptococcus pneumoniae*	Human carriers; patient's own pharynx	Respiratory mucosa	Respiratory droplets	Variable	Penicillin G; erythromycin	Polyvalent pneumococcal vaccine; control of upper respiratory infections; avoidance of alcoholic intoxication
Poliomyelitis	Polioviruses (types I, II, III)	Human cases and carriers	Gastrointestinal tract	Pharyngeal secretions; faecal–oral	7–14 days	None	Oral polio vaccine, the live attenuated vaccine containing all three strains of poliovirus—produces long-lasting immunity in most recipients
Rubella (German measles)	Virus	Human cases	Respiratory mucosa	Nasopharyngeal secretions	14–23 days	None	Rubella virus vaccine; immune globulin (human) given to contacts of rubella; rubella in early stages of pregnancy legally recognized as an indication for abortion

Disease	Causative organism	Reservoir/Source	Portal of entry	Mode of transmission	Incubation period	Treatment	Control measures
Syphilis	*Treponema pallidum*	Infected exudates, body fluids, and secretions (saliva, semen, blood, vaginal secretions)	External genitalia; cervix; mucosal surfaces; placenta	Sexual activity; contact with open lesions; blood transfusion; transplacental inoculation	10–70 days	Penicillin; tetracycline	Case-finding by means of routine serological testing and other methods; adequate treatment of infected individuals
Tetanus	*Clostridium tetani*	Contaminated soil	Penetrating and crush wounds	Horse and cattle	4–21 days (average 10 days)	Tetanus immune globulin (human—TIG) and tetanus toxoid; penicillin	Wound debridement; toxoid booster injections for patients previously immunized; tetanus toxoid and tetanus immune globulin (separate sites and separate syringes) for nonimmune people
Tuberculosis	*Mycobacterium tuberculosis*	Sputum from human cases; milk from infected cows (rare in UK)	Respiratory mucosa	Sputum; respiratory droplets	Variable	Isoniazid; ethambutol; rifampin; streptomycin; pyrazinamide	Early discovery and adequate treatment of active cases; milk pasteurization
Typhoid fever	*Salmonella typhi*	Contaminated food and water	Gastrointestinal tract	Infected urine and faeces	1–3 days	Chloramphenicol; ciprofloxacin; cotrimoxazole	Decontamination of water sources; milk pasteurization; individual vaccination of high-risk people; control of carriers
Typhus, endemic	*Rickettsia typhi (mooseri)*	Infected rodents	Skin	Flea bites	1–2 days	Tetracyclines; chloramphenicol	Delousing procedures; case quarantine
Whooping cough (pertussis)	*Bordetella pertussis*	Human cases	Respiratory tract	Infected bronchial secretions	Commonly 7 days	Erythromycin; ampicillin	Active immunization with vaccine; case isolation

* Research developments produce changes in drug therapy. The reader is referred to drug brochures and digests to keep abreast of changing dosages and uses.

● Place of work?
● Vaccination history?

It is also important to examine the patient for breaks in the skin, skin rashes, skin and mucous membrane lesions, productive cough, breathing difficulties, purulent drainage from any site, lymph node enlargement, and to evaluate the patient's nutritional status.

► NURSING PROCESS
► THE PATIENT WITH AN INFECTIOUS DISEASE

► Assessment

When a patient is diagnosed as having an infection or where there is a strong suspicion of this, a nursing assessment must be made to calculate the degree of risk the patient may pose to others, i.e. is there a communicable or contagious aspect to the infection? In order to plan appropriate and individualized care, the assessment should consider four aspects (Caddow, 1989):

1. The site of infection.
2. The organism involved.
3. The additional risk related to symptoms, treatments and the mental ability of the patient.
4. The type of unit or clinical area in which the patient is being nursed.

Some patients may be assessed as immunocompromised and at increased risk of acquiring infection; this must also be taken into account when planning nursing care.

Considerations For the Elderly
Many elderly people with infections develop the typical signs and symptoms. However, infection in those who do not develop these signs and symptoms may come to the attention of the health care provider as a result of other health problems that appear in any illness of the elderly such as incontinence, confusion, immobility or falling. Diagnosis of infection and appropriate therapy are essential so that the underlying infectious condition can be managed along with the presenting problem.

► Patient's Problems

Ineffective Breathing Patterns
An altered breathing pattern in the patient with an infectious disease may result from the disease itself or occur when the normal respiratory defence mechanisms have become impaired or overwhelmed by microbial assault. Also, patients with impaired cell-mediated immunity are susceptible to bacterial, viral and fungal pneumonias.

Alteration in Body Temperature
Fever is a common symptom of illness. It may occur as a result of specific infection or a nosocomial infection related to invasive devices used to monitor and support the patient, or it may be of unknown origin.

Potential Fluid Volume Deficit
Fluid volume deficits in infectious illnesses can result from excessive fever, sweating and watery diarrhoea. Inability to ingest fluids is another cause and can lead to serious dehydration.

Alteration in Integrity of Oral Mucous Membranes
The oral tissues are bathed by the patient's own microbial flora and by other organisms that enter the mouth by way of food, water and other substances. The normal flow of saliva and the motion of the lips, cheeks and tongue help maintain the integrity of the oral mucosa. The combination of fever, dyspnoea and the inability to ingest fluids and food can cause dryness and cracking of the mucous membranes. Viral infections may affect the oral mucosa, beginning with vesicles which rapidly develop into ulcers. The patient receiving chemotherapy may have painful mouth ulcers from the toxic effect of the drug or may be increasingly susceptible to infection. Fungal infection involving the oral mucosa is also found in patients receiving chemotherapy. The treatment of the cause of the oral lesion is individualized, but the problem encountered by the patient, such as oral discomfort, can be relieved by appropriate nursing care.

Alteration in Bowel Elimination (Diarrhoea)
Normal bowel flora plays an important protective role. Diarrhoea may ensue whenever the bowel flora is altered (e.g., by taking broad-spectrum antibiotics). The normal flora of the bowel can be overcome by large numbers of virulent organisms such as occurs in salmonellosis. Diarrhoea is a common illness in travellers. Acute-onset diarrhoea is caused by a variety of bacterial, parasitic and viral agents, which will be discussed under the appropriate headings below.

Alteration in Nutrition
A severe and prolonged infection may result in muscle wasting and weight loss, because protein is being catabolized for energy. Patients who have been acutely ill and who have been without protein for several days, or who were malnourished at the onset of their illness, will require extra nutritional support.

Lack of Knowledge
One major expected outcome in the health education of everyone is to instil a sense of responsibility for one's own health care and the need to avoid injury to others. Additionally, the person with an infectious disease is taught about the specific disease and the therapeutic regime, and in some instances advised about personal hygiene and the maintenance of the home environment for infection prevention.

Potential For Infection (Spread to Others)

When caring for those with an infectious disease, all health care personnel must prevent the spread of infection to others. The type of infection control precautions which are used are based on the ways in which the disease is transmitted (see Chapter 2).

Potential for Social Isolation

Patients in isolation will often feel lonely and afraid. Such feelings can be exacerbated unless adequate reasons are given to explain the necessary isolation measures.

► *Planning and Implementation*
► Expected Outcomes

The main expected outcomes for the patient may include attainment of normal breathing pattern and normal body temperature, and achievement of fluid balance, intact healthy oral mucous membranes, attainment of normal bowel elimination, improvement of nutritional status, acquisition of knowledge about the condition, prevention of the spread of infection and achievement of social participation.

Nursing Care

Attaining a Normal Breathing Pattern

Health care personnel must be aware of those patients who are at risk of pulmonary infection and subsequent ineffective breathing patterns. Patients with pre-existing illness (immunosuppression, alcoholism, drug overdose) tend to have impaired lung clearance. Viral infections and haematological malignancies depress the cellular defences of the lungs. Pulmonary compliance is decreased in ageing patients. Pulmonary infection also occurs as a result of mechanical disruption of pulmonary defences, as seen in the patient with endotracheal intubation.

The nurse monitors these high-risk patients for cough, shortness of breath, change in colour and altered chest movements. Respiratory rate, depth and pattern are assessed. The patient's chest is auscultated for breath sounds.

Turning and changing the position of the patient help to drain secretions and thus reduce the potential for retention of secretions and infection. Yawning, taking deep breaths and coughing help to expand alveolar sacs. The use of suction may be indicated if the patient is unable to raise secretions effectively. A high fluid intake (within the limits of the patient's cardiac reserve) is encouraged because adequate hydration thins mucus and serves as an effective expectorant. The air may be humidified to loosen secretions and improve ventilation. As soon as the patient's condition permits, ambulation should be encouraged because it helps to mobilize secretions and expand the lungs.

If the patient shows signs of respiratory insufficiency, arterial blood gas values are obtained and recorded on a flow sheet so that comparisons can be made over time.

Attaining Normal Body Temperature

The patient's temperature, pulse and respiration are taken at regular intervals to determine the type of fever (continuous, remittent or intermittent). These checks also help to monitor the severity and duration of the infectious process and the patient's response to therapy. Since not all infected patients have a febrile response, the patient is assessed for signs and symptoms of infection: headache, joint pain, muscle aches, backache, cough, diarrhoea and enlarged lymph nodes.

An increased fluid intake is encouraged because adequate fluid is important to replace fluid losses due to fever, diaphoresis, dehydration and dyspnoea. Nursing care to combat the generalized discomfort that accompanies fever include helping the patient to change position, massaging the back, providing intermittent cool compresses for headache and encouraging rest to lower metabolic activity. Oral hygiene promotes comfort and may help to prevent oral complications, since many bacterial, mycotic and viral infections affect the oral cavity.

Although fever occurring during infection may be beneficial and may enhance host defences, there are times when fever may be deleterious; high fever can permanently damage body tissues. Tepid water sponging of the entire body, which cools the body through evaporation of water, may be carried out when medically indicated.

The ageing patient with fever requires special nursing surveillance. Fever increases the heart rate, decreases diastolic filling time and reduces stroke output. Decreased cardiac output in the elderly may cause reductions in perfusion and in the delivery of oxygen to the brain and kidneys. Many older patients, however, may have serious infections with minimal or no rise in temperature.

Attaining Fluid Balance

The patient is assessed for signs of dehydration: thirst, dryness of the mucous membranes, loss of skin turgor, muscle cramping, reduced peripheral pulses and decreasing urine output. Skin turgor is evaluated by pinching the skin over the sternum, the inner aspect of the thighs or the forehead. If the patient has a fluid volume deficit, the skin flattens more slowly after the pinch is released. The patient's oral cavity is inspected for dryness, and the tongue is examined for longitudinal furrows. The patient's weight is monitored because changes in weight may indicate fluid volume changes. A rapid loss of weight occurs when the total fluid intake is less than the total fluid output. Serum electrolyte values are noted because dehydration leads to an electrolyte imbalance. The nurse also keeps an intake and output record and monitors urine specific gravity. Concentrated scanty urine indicates a lack of fluids. Urinary specific gravity increases when oliguria (low urine output in relation to fluid intake) is present.

Oral administration of fluids is preferable to intravenous administration. Varying the type and temperature of oral fluids is helpful. Intravenous fluids may be prescribed if the patient is critically ill or vomiting. Nursing care includes informing the patient about the procedure, regulating and maintaining the proper rate of infusion flow, ensuring patient comfort and monitoring the patient for untoward side-effects of intravenous therapy.

Mouth Care

Infectious diseases may be accompanied by changes in lesions of the oral cavity. The nurse should inspect the patient's oral cavity for colour, signs of infection, bleeding and the presence of lesions, cracks or coatings.

The patient is taught the importance of oral hygiene and assisted when necessary. Warm normal saline or warm water rinsing of the mouth removes most debris and helps to keep the oral mucosa clean and moist. Gentle brushing with a toothbrush has been shown to be more effective than using strong mouthwashes and antiseptic gargles (Howarth, 1977). Petroleum jelly, water soluble jelly or mineral oil may be applied to cracked, dry lips to keep them soft and moist. Frequent toothbrushing and flossing remove plaque and help to prevent gingivitis.

A high-calorie, liquid diet is given when ingestion of solid foods is difficult because of painful oral lesions. If oral discomfort persists, a topical anaesthetic may be prescribed. Chewing is important for oral health, and the patient is encouraged to eat as soon as possible.

Attaining Normal Bowel Elimination

Most of the diarrhoeal illnesses that occur are mild and self-limiting. They may be antibiotic colitis, traveller's diarrhoea, food or water-borne diarrhoea, or the type of diarrhoea seen in immunosuppressed people.

The patient should be asked about the number, colour and form of their stools, and whether blood and mucus are present. The existence of other clinical features such as nausea, vomiting, fever and abdominal pain, is elicited. The number of stools in 24 hours will give a clue in determining how disabling the patient's diarrhoea is. In addition, the patient is assessed for signs of dehydration. The patient's intake, output and weight are monitored and recorded.

An important nursing function is the collection of faecal specimens. Enteric precautions are required, since there is a range of viral, bacterial and parasitic causes of diarrhoea. (Negative cultures do not rule out an infectious aetiology.)

Giving fluids and electrolytes represents the essential therapy. Oral fluids (oral glucose and electrolyte-containing rehydration solution) are given when the patient is able to tolerate them. Parenteral fluid replacement is necessary if severe dehydration is present.

The patient is asked to cleanse the perianal area with mild soap and water and blot the area dry after each bowel movement. This promotes comfort and prevents skin excoriation. The perianal area is inspected for signs of skin breakdown.

Enteric precautions are used in the hospitalized patient with infectious diarrhoea. Proper handwashing and the practice of good personal hygiene are emphasized. Other nursing care includes promoting patient comfort and advising rest for the patient who is having frequent bouts of diarrhoea.

Improving Nutritional Status

An assessment is made of what the patient is actually eating, because the generalized malaise, discomfort and anorexia that accompany infections may cause a lack of interest in food. Additionally, the patient with fever has increased catabolism and loss of nutrients. The patient's weight is monitored.

A high-protein diet is necessary for patients with fever to replenish energy used by increased metabolism and restlessness. Increased protein is needed to counteract the loss of nitrogen. Increased fluids are necessary to replenish losses due to perspiration and increased respiratory rate.

A referral may be made to the dietician so that a diet plan can be tailored to the patient's condition and food preferences. The importance of optimum nutrition during and beyond convalescence should be stressed.

Patient Education

Brief explanations can be made focussing on the organism and how it is spread, how the illness is treated, the importance of personal hygiene and environmental cleanliness, and the importance of seeking health care promptly in the event of an infectious disease. Knowledge of their specific illnesses and treatment imparts a sense of control to patients and helps them become active participants in their care. Nurses should encourage patients to ask questions because they serve as a guide to topics that need further clarification.

Health care personnel serve as educators in the prevention of infectious diseases. The programme of advice includes teaching about how infectious diseases are spread, methods of avoiding spread, the importance and availability of immunizations, the role of nutrition in health maintenance and the control of environmental contaminants, insects, rodents and other animal vectors and reservoirs of human infections.

Preventing the Spread of Infection

By using the information gained during the assessment, specific infection control precautions can be planned to prevent cross-infection. The answers to the following questions can help the nurse to plan individualized care:

1. What is infected?
2. How does it spread?

3. What can be contaminated?
4. How can contamination be prevented?

Specific precautions can then be planned using the general principles outlined in Chapter 2 and the relevant local hospital policy.

Promoting Social Participation
Patients with infectious diseases may experience heightened states of anxiety, fear and depression, which can reduce their ability to cope. An assessment is made of how the patient is reacting to the illness. The patient's family or friends may have a valuable stress-reducing effect on the patient, and they are encouraged to visit.

► *Evaluation*
► **Expected Outcomes**

1. Patient attains normal breathing pattern.
2. Demonstrates absence of elevated body temperature.
3. Attains fluid balance.
4. Attains/maintains healthy and intact oral mucous membranes.
5. Attains normal defecation pattern.
6. Achieves improved nutritional status.
7. Acquires some understanding of spread of infection.
8. Shows no evidence of spread of infection.
9. Achieves reduction of stress imposed by social isolation.

SPECIFIC BACTERIAL INFECTIONS

Gram-Negative Bacteraemia and Septic Shock

Gram-negative bacteraemia (invasion of the bloodstream by a variety of bacterial species) may cause a life-threatening state of inadequate tissue perfusion called septic shock (the terms septic shock, gram negative-shock, and endotoxic shock are used interchangeably.) Most cases occur when the body's normal protective barriers are disrupted or when the person's defences against infection are impaired. The organisms most frequently associated with gram-negative bacteraemia and septic shock are *Escherichia coli*, *Klebsiella*, *Enterobacter*, *Serratia* species, *Pseudomonas aeruginosa*, *Proteus* species, *Neisseria meningitidis* and *Bacteroides fragilis*. Gram-positive bacteria (*Staphylococcus aureus*, *Streptococcus pneumoniae*) have also been incriminated in septic shock.

Altered Physiology

The altered physiology of septic shock is complex and poorly understood. It is thought that when new organisms invade the bloodstream, shock results as a reaction to an endotoxin that initiates a number of events: cell injury, extracellular release of lysosomal enzymes from leucocytes, changes and interactions among the coagulation and fibrinolytic systems, and metabolic injury due to tissue anoxia.

Septic shock produces arteriolar and venous spasm leading to pooling of blood in the pulmonary, splanchnic, renal and peripheral tissues, resulting in anoxia and acidosis of these tissues. The intense vasoconstriction increases peripheral resistance, decreases cardiac output and diminishes blood flow to major organs.

Gram-negative bacilli or their endotoxins can activate Hageman factor (Factor XII) of the intrinsic coagulation, fibrinolysis and shock.

Clinical Features

The onset of septic shock may be abrupt, with a shaking chill and rapid rise in temperature. (Temperature elevation may be blunted in the elderly or those receiving corticosteroids.) The patient has warm, dry skin. Respirations are increased secondary to anoxia and increased lactic acid (respiratory alkalosis). Hypotension is present.

As the blood pressure falls, tissues and organs are inadequately perfused with oxygenated blood. When shock develops, the patient experiences tachypnoea, tachycardia, profound hypotension, cool extremities, mental obtundation (depression of cerebral function) and oliguria. Various abnormalities of intravenous coagulation (thrombocytopenia) are frequently observed. A variety of skin lesions may be encountered.

Considerations For the Elderly
In the elderly patient, septic shock may be manifest in atypical or confusing clinical signs. Septic shock should be suspected in any elderly person who develops an unexplained acute confused state, tachypnoea or hypotension.

Diagnosis

The patient is examined to identify the source of sepsis. The aetiological agent is isolated and identified through blood cultures. Other smears and cultures are taken from any possible site of infection. Urinalysis is done to detect the presence of pyuria, haematuria, casts and bacteria.

Management

Usually, the patient is too ill to await the result of culture and sensitivity tests. Therapy is started immediately with agents effective against a broad spectrum of bacteria and with consideration given to the prevalence of resistant strains of bacteria within the hospital. Antibiotics are usually given intravenously to provide high levels of the drug in the blood, tissue and body cavity fluids. Serum levels of antibiotics are monitored to assure adequate doses and to prevent toxicity.

Any possible source of infection such as an intravenous or urinary catheter is removed. Surgical drainage of localized infection (abscess) and debridement of necrotic tissues may be undertaken.

Aggressive fluid volume replacement with intravenous fluids is a priority to ensure perfusion of vital organs and to correct fluid and electrolyte disturbances. Shock is treated by fluid replacement and vasoactive drugs (to alter the capacity of the vessels to overcome abnormalities of blood flow). Oxygen is administered to keep arterial PO_2 at the desired level, although additional respiratory support with intubation and assisted ventilation may be necessary when arterial hypoxaemia complicates shock. Sodium bicarbonate may be given for severe acidosis. Heart failure is treated with pharmacological agents, such as dopamine, digitalis and diuretics.

▶ NURSING PROCESS
▶ THE PATIENT WITH SEPTIC SHOCK

▶ *Assessment*

The patient's nursing history may indicate risk factors for the current problem (previous use of urinary catheter, cytotoxic therapy or immunotherapy and so on). In addition to almost constant blood pressure monitoring, the nurse observes the patient for hyperventilation, apprehension, prostration, vomiting and diarrhoea. Reduced blood flow to cerebral vessels impairs mental status and causes the patient to be confused. The skin may be dry and warm or moist and pale, depending on the type of circulatory derangement. The urinary output is monitored; oliguria is evidence of circulatory insufficiency. Haemodynamic monitoring (pulmonary wedge pressure or central venous pressure, cardiac output) is part of assessment because respiratory failure and cardiac failure are important causes of septic shock.

▶ *Patient's Problems*

The patient's main problems may include the following: alteration in tissue perfusion (cerebral, renal, peripheral) related to vasoconstriction from septic shock, ineffective breathing pattern (tachypnoea, hyperpnoea) related to pulmonary complications and alteration in urinary elimination (oliguria) related to decrease in circulating blood volume.

Potential complications include disseminated intravascular coagulation, respiratory failure, cardiac failure, renal failure and metabolic acidosis.

▶ *Planning and Implementation*
▶ Expected Outcomes

The main expected outcomes for the patient may include

achievement of tissue perfusion, normal breathing, attainment of adequate urinary output, avoidance/management of complications and reduction of fever.

Nursing Care

Enhancing Tissue Perfusion

The nurse monitors those parameters that relate to tissue perfusion: state of responsiveness, skin temperature, moisture, colour and turgor, appearance of mucous membranes and nails, respiratory rate, pulse and blood pressure, heart and lung sounds, peripheral pulses, intake and urinary output. The assessment focuses on trends and patterns of change.

The intravenous catheter sites are monitored. Central venous pressure measurements provide a gauge for the rate and amount of volume replacement. The Swan-Ganz catheter measures pulmonary wedge pressure, which is an estimate of left ventricular–end diastolic pressure. The nurse should keep in mind that fluid deficit also occurs from fever, vomiting and diarrhoea, and should use appropriate care.

The lung fields are auscultated when fluid is being administered to detect inspiratory and expiratory wheezes, moist fine crackles and rhonchi, which may indicate impending pulmonary oedema.

Promoting Adequate Breathing Patterns

Blood gas and pH measurements are monitored to determine if the patient needs assisted ventilation, because inadequate respiratory exchange is a frequent cause of death. (Severe shock and metabolic acidosis require correction with bicarbonate because severe hypoxaemia does not respond too well to oxygen administration.) These measures represent a collaborative function with the doctor. Nursing care for the patient requiring assisted ventilation is found in Chapter 3.

The patient is requested to cough frequently and may need to be suctioned when a productive cough is present. Turning and changing the patient's position reduce the potential for retention of secretions and infection.

Assuring Adequate Urinary Output

Urinary output is monitored because kidney function deteriorates with septic shock. The specific gravity of urine is measured at prescribed intervals. Urinary specific gravity increases when oliguria is present. An increase in urine output (greater than 30 ml/hr) usually indicates that tissue perfusion and hence renal perfusion are improving.

Managing Complications

When shock occurs in the course of bacteraemia, there is an immediate threat to life, with a 30 to 60 per cent mortality rate in the elderly. Nursing support requires continuing patient assessment and strict adherence to handwashing and aseptic techniques. The nursing care for disseminated intravascular coagulation, respiratory failure, cardiac failure and renal failure are found in the appropriate sections of this book.

▶ *Evaluation*
▶ **Expected Outcomes**

1. Patient shows adequate tissue perfusion.
   a. Shows progressive increase in blood pressure to normal range.
   b. Reveals warm skin, normal skin colour.
   c. Has normal mentation.
   d. Responds to volume replacement by increasing urinary output.
2. Has normal breathing pattern.
   a. Shows no evidence of tachypnoea after infection has improved.
   b. Has respiratory rates within normal limits.
3. Attains adequate urinary output (greater than 30 ml/hr).
4. Absence of complications.
   a. No evidence of shock.
   b. Vital signs within normal range.
5. Attains normal body temperature.
   a. Shows progressive decline in fever.
   b. Has negative blood cultures.

Staphylococcal Infections

Staphylococci are widely distributed in nature, with humans serving as the predominant reservoir. Coagulase-negative *Staphylococci* are present as part of the normal skin flora and rarely cause infections, although they may cause serious problems at the sites of prostheses and central lines.

Staphylococcus aureus is found in the nose of 10 to 30 per cent of normal people, but only occasionally on healthy skin. It is a common cause of infection in the community and in hospital. Transmission is by contact with a person who is an asymptomatic carrier or who has a draining lesion. Food may become contaminated by an infected food handler. Staphylococci are also transmitted through the air (thereby contaminating a wound during dressing changes), by way of contaminated needles and through animal sources.

When the continuity of the skin has been disrupted or bypassed (abrasions, wounds, surgical incisions, burns, cutaneous viral infections), the patient is susceptible to infection by *Staphylococcus aureus*.

The organism is responsible for most human skin infections. The furuncle, or common boil, is almost always a staphylococcal abscess, and the carbuncle on the back of the neck represents a coalition of staphylococcal abscesses. Most staphylococcal abscesses are located in superficial subcutaneous tissues and do not extend beyond

the original site. Eventually, their purulent contents, under mounting pressure, perforate the overlying skin and are evacuated externally, leaving the empty cavities to fill in with granulation tissue, close over and heal.

Systemic Staphylococcal Infections

If the peripheral defences are unable to contain the staphylococci, the infection may spread or invade the bloodstream, attended by profound toxaemia. Invasion of the lymphatics may result in axillary, cervical, mediastinal, retroperitoneal or subdiaphragmatic abscesses. Bloodstream invasion may produce acute bacterial endocarditis, staphylococcal pneumonia, empyema, perinephric arthritis, meningitis, osteomyelitis or generalized sepsis. Constitutional symptoms are severe.

Irrespective of location, staphylococcal lesions possess many characteristics in common, including varying degrees of necrosis, a tendency to localize and a tendency to persist, despite intensive chemotherapy, until all the exudate finds an escape route or is evacuated.

Its resistance to therapy is explained in part by the extraordinary ability of the staphylococcus to adapt itself to an unfavourable environment. Resistance to the commonly used antibiotics is frequently observed in strains of staphylococci (Ayliffe, Collins and Taylor, 1989). Thus, responsiveness to antibiotic chemotherapy, however gratifying at the onset, may diminish to the point of true refractoriness.

Management

Control Measures and Prevention

The major means by which staphylococci are transmitted within the hospital is by person-to-person transmission. The prevention of hospital staphylococcosis requires an effective infection control policy, excellent handwashing and aseptic techniques and immediate isolation measures as soon as a staphylococcal infection is suspected (see Chapter 2, Infection Control).

Treatment

Treatment for severe staphylococcal infection is an antistaphylococcal antibiotic (penicillinase-resistant penicillin). An alternative antimicrobial agent (e.g., cephalosporin) is considered if the patient has a penicillin allergy. Intravenous administration is the route usually selected when large doses are required. Serious staphylococcal infection may require prolonged treatment to prevent infection of the heart valves.

Nursing Care

The nurse monitors the patient's response to the prescribed therapy. If the patient experiences continuing or recurring fever, the cause may be drug resistance, drug allergy or superinfection (infection with a second organism resistant to the antibiotic in use).

Careful observations are made of the patient because fatal complications may develop during the early period of antimicrobial therapy.

Streptococcal Infections

There are many strains of streptococci. Of particular significance are the beta-haemolytic streptococci, which account for a number of pathogenic infections in humans. Included in this group are the Lancefield Group A streptococci, which gain entrance to the body primarily through the upper respiratory tract from people with streptococcal infections or those who are asymptomatic carriers. Possible resultant infections include streptococcal pharyngitis, scarlet fever, sinusitis, otitis media, peritonsillar abscesses, pericarditis, pneumonia, empyema and various wound and skin infections—impetigo, puerperal infections and erysipelas. Rheumatic fever and acute glomerulonephritis may occur as a sequel to group A streptococci infection.

Streptococcal Pharyngitis

Streptococcal pharyngitis (strep throat) is caused by Group A streptococcus. Transmission occurs by way of droplets from respiratory secretions of infected people or from healthy carriers.

Clinical Features
The organism establishes itself in the lymphoid tissues and produces abrupt onset of illness, with sore throat, fever, chills and headache. The patient may complain of throat pain that is aggravated by swallowing or even turning the head.

Upon inspection, the pharynx shows varying degrees of redness and oedema and may be covered with an exudate. The presence of tender anterior cervical lymph nodes is a significant finding. Although these are the usual symptoms associated with streptococcal pharyngitis, most patients have some but not all symptoms.

In a few people, a rash appears, starting over the neck and chest and spreading over the skin of the abdomen and extremities. If the rash becomes pronounced, the patient has scarlet fever. This presentation is uncommon today.

Diagnosis
The presence of exudate suggests streptococcal pharyngitis. A throat culture is taken to confirm the presence of the streptococcus.

Management

Penicillin, in a variety of forms, is the drug of choice for treating streptococcal infections (except for enterococcal group D infections). If the patient is sensitive to penicillin, a course of erythromycin may be used. Therapy is continued for at least 10 days to eliminate the organisms, prevent relapses, reduce the frequency of suppurative complications and prevent the majority of cases of rheumatic fever. Unfortunately, the risk of developing acute glomerulonephritis has not been shown to be altered by treatment of the initial infection.

Patient Education

The patient must understand the importance of completing the course of antibiotic treatment in order to prevent the development of complications.

During the course of febrile illness, the patient is encouraged to rest at home and will be noncontagious to others 24 to 48 hours after treatment is started. A liberal fluid intake is important, especially if the patient has fever. Oral hygiene will help to prevent the development of fissures of the lips. Warm saline gargles may relieve some of the throat soreness. Patients are advised to monitor their temperature and familiarize themselves with the symptoms of possible complications.

Prevention
Ongoing health education programmes are needed to emphasize the relationship of streptococcal infections to heart disease and glomerulonephritis. People with these conditions, especially rheumatic heart disease, are at risk and may require long-term prophylaxis with penicillin. Hospitalized patients who are at risk, including the obstetric patient, must be protected from personnel or visitors with respiratory or skin infections.

Pulmonary Tuberculosis

Tuberculosis is an infectious disease caused by Microbacterium tuberculosis ('human type') and more rarely by Mycobacterium bovis ('bovine type'). Opportunistic mycobacteria may also cause mycobacterial disease in man. It usually involves the lungs, but it may spread to almost any part of the body, including the meninges, kidneys, bones and lymph nodes. Mycobacterium are classified as acid-fast aerobic organisms (Ziehl-Neelsen or other acid-fast stains are required for staining these organisms, which have cells walls containing abundant lipids).

Incidence

The incidence of tuberculosis in western Europe and North America has declined considerably in recent years due to improvements in housing, nutrition and specific preventive measures. In Britain today between 5,000 and 7,000 new cases are diagnosed each year, mostly among elderly men and young or middle-aged Asian immigrants. Pulmonary tuberculosis is the most common form accounting for two-thirds of patients with clinical tuberculosis.

Altered Physiology

The natural history of the disease is closely related to age. Characteristically, 'primary' tuberculosis occurs in childhood, consisting of a subpleural Ghon's focus of infection, with associated regional infected lymph nodes on the mediastinum. Primary infection is usually accompanied by mild or no symptoms, and is followed by spontaneous resolution. Complications of primary infection include:

1. Haematogenous spread leading to miliary tuberculosis, which may involve numerous body sites. (Such disseminated tuberculosis is rare today and is most often diagnosed in immunosuppressed patients, the elderly and immigrants.)
2. Direct spread causing tuberculosis bronchopneumonia.

Primary infection usually occurs after inhalation of infected droplet nuclei but can also occur after ingestion of unpasteurized milk containing tubercle bacilli. In the latter instance, the disease acquired is usually bovine tuberculosis and it is the intestine that is primarily affected. Following primary infection, the individual develops immunity to tubercle bacilli. Characteristically, there is a relatively insusceptible period to tuberculosis between the ages of 5 and 15 years.

'Post-primary' tuberculosis occurs in late adolescence and in adults following reactivation of a primary focus of infection or possibly repeat exposure to exogenous tubercle bacilli.

Primary Infection

Once inhaled by a susceptible host, the tuberculosis bacilli, in the form of droplet nuclei, pass through the airways and are deposited on the alveolar surface, where they begin to multiply. Swept along by the lymph and bloodstream, they lodge in susceptible tissues in small clumps, or tubercles. The neighbouring tissue cells quickly accumulate around each of these clumps, forming a protective wall that checks their further spread. If immunity is successful, the bacteria die after a considerable time, and the tubercle becomes transformed into a tiny mass of fibrous tissue. If unsuccessful, the tissue of the tubercle may become necrotic and transformed into a cheese-like mass, a process known as caseation. If this occurs, the germs are liberated and lymph sweeps them into the surrounding tissues, which respond by enclosing the freed bacteria in new tubercles. In this way the original miliary (like millet seeds) tubercles grow into larger and larger irregular masses.

The fate of the patient depends on which of these two processes prevails. If the tissue barriers survive, the imprisoned tubercle bacilli cease to multiply and may die.

However, if the germs survive and are freed from the tubercle, they multiply and are swept along by the lymph stream into neighbouring tissue, and by the bloodstream into other organs, where they lodge and repeat the same process.

'Post-primary' infection

In contrast with the relatively bland, silent, primary type of pulmonary tuberculosis, the course of the reinfection is complicated by necrosis, with resulting ulceration of the infected lung tissue. Clusters of tubercles form at once around the nest of organisms, but due to the sensitivity of the tissues, these clusters now become surrounded by zones of inflammatory reaction. The alveoli in the area become filled with exudate, and a tuberculosis bronchopneumonia develops. The tuberculosis tissue in this area becomes caseous and ulcerates into a bronchus, causing a cavity. At the same time, considerable scar tissue forms locally as the ulcerations heal, especially around the cavities. The pleura over the infected lobe (more often an upper lobe) becomes inflamed, then thickened and retracted by scar tissue.

This cycle of inflammatory bronchopneumonia proceeds to ulceration with cavitation, followed by scarring. Unless the process can be arrested, it spreads slowly downwards, towards the hilum and later into adjacent lobes. The activity of the process may be prolonged and characterized by long remissions, when the disease may appear to be arrested, only to be followed by periods of renewed activity.

When the cavitating lesions in the lungs communicate with the bronchial tree, tubercle bacilli are expectorated in the sputum and become contained in respiratory droplet nuclei, which are expelled during coughing. The patient has then developed 'open' tuberculosis, and contacts may become infected by inhaling the tubercle bacilli contained in the droplet nuclei.

Predisposing factors to the development of pulmonary tuberculosis include malnutrition, alcoholism, old age, immunodeficiency (including acquired immune deficiency syndrome), immunosuppression and exposure to dust and silica, as occurs in miners.

Clinical Features

Chronic pulmonary tuberculosis is insidious in its onset and course. The majority of patients present with fever, loss of strength, cough productive of mucopurulent sputum and weight loss. If the patient does not seek treatment until late in the disease, constitutional symptoms are marked—daily recurring fever with chills, weight loss, anaemia, haemoptysis and large numbers of bacilli in the sputum.

Considerations For the Elderly Patient

Tuberculosis may have atypical features in the elderly,

such as changes in behaviour or mentation, organ dysfunction or fever, anorexia and weight loss.

Diagnosis

The initial diagnosis includes a tuberculin skin test, examination of a sputum sample (smear and culture) and an X-ray evaluation of the chest.

Skin Testing For Tuberculin Hypersensitivity

Skin tests are used to find evidence of a 'delayed hypersensitivity' type of reaction to mycobacteria. In the Mantoux test, 0.1 ml of a standardized concentration of either 'old tuberculin' or 'purified protein derivative' is injected intradermally into the forearm using a 1.0 ml syringe and needle. The usual dilution of standardized antigen is 1/1,000, but when tuberculosis is strongly suspected, a start should be made with a 1/10,000 dilution, as patients who have tuberculosis may react strongly to the skin test and develop an inflamed indurated lesion that might ulcerate.

The Heaf test is more convenient than the Mantoux test when screening large numbers of people. In the Heaf test, a standardized suspension of purified protein derivative is applied undiluted over the skin surface and a metal Heaf gun is used to make multiple punctures at the skin site. Careful decontamination of the gun between patients is required, and many authorities now use a disposable applicator (the Tine test). The results of both the Mantoux or Heaf test are best read at about three days.

A positive Mantoux test is characterized by an area of induration greater than 5 mm in diameter over a 72-hour period, and a positive Heaf test by the appearance at three days of at least four papules at the multiple puncture sites.

Interpretation of Skin Test Interpretation of the results of tuberculin skin tests depends on the incidence of mycobacterial infections in the geographical area in which the patient is living, the age of the patient and general factors affecting the immunity of the patient. Today, a positive result in a young British person who has not had previous BCG (Bacille Calmette-Guérin) immunization is often suggestive of tuberculous infection. A positive Mantoux test in a child aged five years or younger is particularly suspicious of active tuberculosis, even if this is the only positive specific finding in the child. Chemoprophylaxis with an anti-tuberculous drug such as isoniazid is usually indicated. In an older person, conversion from a previously known negative to a positive result, without intervening immunization, is also strongly suggestive of tuberculous infection.

A negative reaction may occur if the disease has been present for less than six weeks, or if the patient has overwhelming tuberculosis.

Sputum Testing

Diagnosis is also confirmed by finding the acid-fast bacilli in smears of sputum. Sputum can be coughed up directly or induced by inhaling aerosols, which irritate the trachea and produce coughing. Bronchoscopic aspiration using a fibreoptic bronchoscope or transtracheal aspiration are other possible means of obtaining a sputum specimen. An early morning specimen has pooled overnight secretions and is therefore the best specimen to be examined. If the patient is unable to expectorate but has swallowed sputum, then a gastric specimen may be obtained by means of a nasogastric tube to permit study of swallowed sputum. Tubercle bacilli may also be cultured from ascitic fluid, pleural fluid, cerebrospinal fluid, urine and pus that has been aspirated or drained from abscesses. Tissue such as liver, bone marrow and lymph nodes may also be cultured.

Chest X-ray

Tuberculosis is a possibility in anyone with an abnormal chest X-ray. Certain patterns, such as patchy infiltrates, are suggestive of tuberculosis.

Management

The expected outcomes of nursing are: (1) to relieve pulmonary and systematic symptoms by eliminating all viable tubercle bacilli; (2) to return the patient to health, work and family and friends as quickly as possible; and (3) to prevent transmission of the infection.

Active tuberculosis is a notifiable infection, i.e. reportable to the Medical Officer for Environmental Health or Director of Public Health. This ensures that contacts are followed up and treated where necessary.

Chemotherapy

Active tuberculosis is usually treated with simultaneous administration of a combination of drugs to which the organisms are susceptible. Such therapy is carried out until the disease is brought under control. Multiple drug regimes are used to destroy as many viable organisms as quickly as possible and to minimize the emergence of organism resistance to the various antimicrobial drugs. Although the tubercle bacillus is susceptible to several drugs, there are no drugs to which it cannot develop resistance. Such resistance results from genetic manipulations of the organisms. The variety of drugs available enables one agent to destroy mutants resistant to the initial drug.

Today, standard triple therapy consists of 600 mg rifampicin, 300 mg isoniazid and 25 mg/kg ethambutol daily given orally for the first two months of treatment. Continuation therapy with the two drugs rifampicin and isoniazid is usually given for a further seven months, so that a total of nine months of anti-tuberculosis therapy is given. Pyrazinamide or streptomycin are sometimes used in place of ethambutol (see Table 38.2 for further information on anti-tuberculous drugs).

Examination of the sputum for acid-fast bacilli in smears and cultures is indicated each month until the smears are negative, then every few months.

Table 38.2 *Treatment of mycobacterial disease in adults and children*

Commonly used agents	Most common side-effects*	Drug interactions†	Remarks*
Isoniazid	Peripheral neuritis, hepatitis, hypersensitivity	Antiepileptics-synergistic	Bactericidal to both extracellular and intracellular organisms. Pyridoxine 10 mg as prophylaxis for neuritis; 50 to 100 mg as treatment
Rifampin	Hepatitis, febrile reaction, purpura (rare)	Rifampin inhibits the effect of oral contraceptives, quinidine, corticosteroids, Coumarin drugs and methadone, digoxin, oral hypoglycaemics; PAS may interfere with absorption of rifampin	Bactericidal to all populations of organisms. Orange urine and other body secretions. Disclouring of contact lens
Streptomycin	8th nerve damage, nephrotoxicity	Neuromuscular blocking agents—may be potentiated to cause prolonged paralysis	Bactericidal to extracellular organisms. Use with caution in older patients or those with renal disease
Pyrazinamide	Hyperuricaemia, hepatotoxicity		Bactericidal to intracellular organisms. Combination with an aminoglycoside is bactericidal
Ethambutol	Optic neuritis (reversible with discontinuation of drug; very rare at 15 mg/kg), skin rash		Bacteriostatic to both intracellular and extracellular organisms, primarily used to inhibit development of resistant mutants. Use with caution with renal disease or when eye testing is not feasible

* Check product labelling for detailed information on dose, contraindications, drug interaction, adverse reactions and monitoring.
† Reference should be made to current literature, particularly on rifampin, because it induces hepatic microenzymes and therefore interacts with many drugs.
(Modified from American Thoracic Society (1983). Treatment of tuberculosis and other mycobacterial diseases, Am. Rev. Respir. Dis., June, Vol. 127, No. 6, p. 791. Used with permission.)

Preventive Treatment

Eradicating tuberculosis depends on prevention, detection, health education and improved standards of living. Most cases of tuberculosis occur in people known to be significant tuberculin reactors. These patients are the reservoir from which more than 90 per cent of active disease develops. Infected people must be identified, and preventive therapy (isoniazid prophylaxis) given to those at risk of developing disease and becoming transmitters. Isoniazid for preventive therapy is given in a single daily dose for one year. The most significant adverse reaction is hepatitis; this risk is increased if the person drinks alcohol on a daily basis. All people taking isoniazid for preventive therapy should be seen in a health clinic on a regular basis to allow for detection of reactions to the medication, and to provide health personnel with an opportunity to encourage co-operation with medication.

BCG Vaccine

Another means of prevention is the BCG vaccine (Bacille Calmette-Guérin), which is used in areas of high tuberculosis in the United KIngdom. This vaccine does not prevent initial infection with *M. tuberculosis*, but it does alter the host defence mechanisms if such an infection occurs. Its use is restricted to people who have negative reactions to the tuberculin skin test, because it does not benefit those already infected. Also, BCG vaccinations will convert a negative tuberculin reactor to a positive one, which makes subsequent skin tests difficult to interpret.

In the developing countries, where limited resources must be concentrated on the detection and treatment of patients with sputum-positive disease, it has been found that BCG vaccine gives substantial protection against tuberculosis. BCG vaccination has been a major tool of the World Health Organization's efforts to control tuberculosis in those countries with high rates of transmission.

▶ NURSING PROCESS
▶ THE PATIENT WITH TUBERCULOSIS

▶ *Assessment*

The nursing history and nursing observation focus on the patient's fatigue, cough, sputum expectoration, weight loss, chills and fever. It is important to determine if the patient has experienced haemoptysis. The patient's educational level, emotional readiness to learn, and perceptions and understanding of tuberculosis are evaluated. Since therapy may be prolonged, the patient's social support system is assessed.

The results of the physical and laboratory evaluations are reviewed.

▶ *Patient's Problems*

Based on the assessment, the patient's main problems may include the following:

- Lack of knowledge about disease, medications and self-care techniques.
- Potential for cross-infection.
- Nonco-operation with treatment regime related to possible disorganized lifestyle, alcoholism or distrust of authority.

▶ *Planning and Implementation*
▶ Expected Outcomes
The main expected outcomes for the patient may include acquisition of knowledge and understanding of the disease and its treatment, prevention of infection to others and co-operation with the treatment regime.

Nursing Care

Prevention and Patient Education
There is evidence that patients probably forget at least 50 per cent of what they are told, especially when anxiety levels are high. The role of the nurse is pivotal in building a trusting relationship so that the patient education will be an ongoing process and behavioural changes will be made.

Although tuberculosis is a communicable disease, effective chemotherapy is the most effective means of preventing transmission. This fact bears frequent repetition.

- A major reason for treatment failure is that patients do not take their medications regularly, and for the period of time prescribed.

The patient is usually treated at home except in rare instances where social circumstances or drug-resistant organisms pose a threat to the community. In the home-treated patient, respiratory isolation is not usually necessary since the hazard to household members occurred before the disease was diagnosed (Joint Tuberculosis Committee, 1990). The patient is requested to cover the mouth and nose with tissues when coughing or sneezing; these can then be discarded into a paper bag and burned. Handwashing is demonstrated and stressed.

The patient and household members should be advised carefully about possible complications, including haemorrhage and pleurisy. Usually, patients can return to their former employment unless this involves exposure to silicone, as the dust may be harmful to the lungs.

In the hospitalized patient, respiratory isolation is used if the sputum smear is positive (See Chapter 2).

▶ *Evaluation*
▶ Expected Outcomes

1. Patient acquires knowledge and understanding of tuberculosis.
   a. Answers correctly questions about tuberculosis.
   b. Knows the names of medications and the timetable for taking them.
   c. Can name side-effects of medications.
2. Prevents spread of infection to others.
   a. Remains on drug therapy.
   b. Uses tissues correctly when coughing, sneezing and so on.
   c. Reports for sputum monitoring.
   d. Encourages people who are close contacts to report for examination.
3. Complies with treatment regime.
   a. Keeps appointments.
   b. Takes medications exactly as prescribed.

Atypical Mycobacteria

It is now recognized that some bacteria which give a staining reaction similar to that of *M. tuberculosis*, but which have distinctly different growth and culture characteristics, may produce pulmonary disease clinically similar to tuberculosis. When tuberculosis was a more common disease than at present, and when more sophisticated bacteriological techniques were not used, these infections were overlooked or the organisms disregarded as contaminants. Today, these strains of mycobacteria are classified more precisely. They are transmitted from the environment to humans by mechanisms not well understood. *Mycobacterium kansasii* and *Mycobacterium avium-intracellulare* are thought to cause the majority of pulmonary infections. Most of these species are found in a variety of environmental sources, including house dust, tap water, fresh and coastal waters, soil and milk. They have become more prominent since tuberculosis has declined. There is no evidence of person-to-person transmission.

These mycobacteria are usually partially or totally resistant to anti-tuberculosis drugs. Therapy usually involves the use of multiple drugs (four to five drug regimes). Surgical resection of the diseased lung tissue may be carried out.

The nursing care is similar to that of the patient with tuberculosis, except that respiratory isolation is not required.

Legionnaires' Disease

Legionnaires' disease is an acute respiratory infection from a gram-negative bacterium, *Legionella pneumophila*. It is named after an outbreak of the disease that occurred in Philadelphia, in 1976, among people attending the state convention of the American Legion.

Epidemiological evidence indicates that Legionnaires' disease is transmitted by inhalation of organisms in an aerosol form of infected water from environmental sources. Legionellae are ubiquitous in water, and the organisms have been found in plumbing fixtures, drinking water and air conditioning systems in hotels and hospitals (Harper, 1988).

It is proposed that one way in which the aerobic gram-negative bacillus finds its way into humans is through the cooling towers and evaporative condensers of large air conditioners, where the bacteria multiply and are discharged as infectious aerosols through fans and exhaust vents (Bartlett, Macrae and Macfarlane, 1986). People at risk are middle-aged and older men, especially those who smoke, consume alcohol, work in or near construction sites or are immunosuppressed from disease or medications that affect cellular immunity.

Altered Physiology
Autopsy specimens from lung tissue of patients with Legionnaires' disease have shown different amounts of lung consolidation in varying distributions. The histological pattern has been one of an acute lobar pneumonia. An exudate containing neutrophils, macrophages and fibrin is found in the alveolar spaces.

Clinical Features
The target organ appears to be the lungs. The earliest symptoms are profound malaise, myalgias, mild headache and a dry cough. Within a day, the patient experiences a rapidly rising fever and chills. The fever remains high and unremitting (39° to 41°C), until specific therapy is started. Occasionally, diarrhoea precedes other symptoms. Associated features include pleuritic pain, confusion and impaired renal function. A chest X-ray will document evidence of pneumonia. Tachypnoea and dyspnoea may reflect the extent of the pneumonic process. There may be clinical and laboratory evidence of abnormalities of the gastrointestinal, musculoskeletal, hepatic, renal and central nervous systems. The diagnosis is made on the basis of an increase in specific serum antibodies and by culture of the organisms on appropriate culture media.

Management
Erythromycin (administered early) is the drug of choice. These patients may be seriously ill, and death may occur from intractable shock and haemodynamic collapse.

Nursing Care
The nursing care is that described for pneumonia (see Chapter 5). There is no evidence of person-to-person spread of Legionnaires' disease (Lowbury, Ayliffe, Geddes, *et al.*, 1981), and secretory precautions rather than respiratory isolation are now recommended (see Chapter 2).

Salmonella Infections (Salmonellosis)

Salmonellosis is an infection caused by bacteria of the genus *Salmonella*. Clinically, salmonellosis is seen in four forms: gastroenteritis (the most common form), enteric fever (such as typhoid and paratyphoid disease), bacteraemia with or without focal extraintestinal infection and asymptomatic carrier state. Infection caused by *Salmonella typhi* (typhoid fever) is discussed on page 1189. Although approximately 2,000 serotypes are known, *Salmonella typhimurium* is the most commonly reported in the United Kingdom (Communicable Disease Report, 1988).

Salmonella organisms may penetrate the epithelial cells of the small intestine and colon, producing an inflammatory response. The patient is infected by ingesting the organism in food contaminated by human or animal faeces, in whole eggs and egg products, in meat and meat products and in poultry (especially turkey). It has been proposed that large numbers of eggs and chickens are contaminated by salmonella micro-organisms. Common foods causing salmonella infections include commercially processed meat pies, poultry, sausages, foods containing eggs or egg products, unpasteurized milk and other dairy products.

Clinical Features

Symptoms usually develop within 8 to 48 hours after ingestion of contaminated food. The patient experiences headache, abdominal discomfort, low-grade fever and watery diarrhoea that may contain blood and mucus. Some patients have only a headache and occasional loose stools. The infectious agent may localize and cause necrosis in any body tissue, producing abscesses, cholecystitis, arthritis, endocarditis, meningitis, pericarditis, pneumonia and pyelonephritis. Petechiae, splenomegaly and leucopenia may also be manifested. Salmonella infection complicated by bacteraemia is seen in the very old who have other underlying disease.

Diagnosis of salmonella infection is made by finding the organisms in faeces and blood. Later, after the acute infection subsides, serological agglutination tests are useful in establishing the diagnosis.

Management

Rehydration of the patient with fluids and essential salts is the foundation of treatment. Oral intake of fluids is sufficient in the majority of patients. Fruit juices and soft drinks are effective even in severe diarrhoea. (Glucose is absorbed in the small intestine.) The patient should avoid beverages with caffeine, which cause increased intestinal mobility.

Antispasmodic drugs (anticholinergics) may be counterproductive, since a slowed peristaltic activity may extend the period of infection by interfering with an effective clearing mechanism.

Patients with moderate to severe illness (those requiring hospitalization) may be treated with co-trimoxazole or chloramphenicol. Enteric precautions are indicated.

Prevention and Patient Education

There is no active or passive immunization against salmonella. Raw eggs or egg drinks should not be eaten, nor should dirty or cracked eggs be used, since salmonella can penetrate cracked eggs. All foods from animal sources, especially poultry, egg products and meat should be *thoroughly cooked*. Food service workers should be advised about food-borne illnesses and given guidelines on avoiding food contamination, storing and preparing food, cleaning food preparation and service areas (contaminated countertops can serve as a means of transmission) and practising good personal hygiene (DHSS, 1987). Foods should be refrigerated during storage and protected against insects and rodents.

Patients should wash their hands after going to the toilet, particularly during illness and carrier state to prevent transmission of infection to others.

Shigellosis (Bacillary Dysentery)

Shigellosis is an acute bacterial disease of the intestinal tract. There are approximately 40 serotypes of shigellae,

divided into four groups or species: *Shigella sonnei*, the most common serotype isolated in industrialized countries, *Shigella dysenteriae*, *Shigella flexneri* and *Shigella boydi*. The source of infection is faeces from an infected person, with the route of spread being faecal–oral. Shigellosis is readily transmissible and may be passed through toilet paper onto the fingers. The bacilli have also been removed from milk, eggs, cheese and shrimps.

While encountered in all countries, bacillary dysentery is endemic in the tropics, where serious epidemics are frequent.

Altered Physiology

The pathology of shigellosis, in severe cases, consists of organisms reaching the small intestine where they multiply and release a toxin that initiates secretion of water and electrolytes from the jejunal area. The shigella are thought to invade the distal epithelial cells, multiply, spread to adjacent cells and destroy them. The invading pathogens are capable of initiating an intense inflammatory response in the mucosa, followed by small patches of ulceration, which may coalesce to form large ulcers.

Clinical Features

Initially there is fever, cramping and abdominal pain. Watery diarrhoea soon appears, often followed by frank dysentery, with the passage of varying amounts of blood, mucus and pus. There may be high fever. At the height of the active infection, the symptoms are severe and the prostration is quite profound. The patient has a desire to defaecate, and the straining is severe during the attempts. The infection is usually self-limiting in healthy adults, and improvement is noted in about one week. Some cases last two or three weeks, and chronic cases last several months or even years, unless adequately treated. In severe cases, shock, volume depletion and electrolyte imbalance may supervene.

Management

The objectives of treatment are to maintain fluid and electrolyte balance and to eliminate the spread of shigellosis to the patient's contacts (e.g., eliminate the carrier state). Dysentery is a notifiable infection.

The organism may be recovered from the stool; sensitivity tests are carried out in order to determine the appropriate antibiotic, since the organism may be resistant to certain drugs. Treatment of shigellosis with antibiotics is important in shortening the period of faecal excretion and in stopping the course of illness. Antibiotics that are absorbed from the intestinal tract and to which the shigellae are sensitive (amoxycillin, trimethoprim, ciprofloxacin) may shorten the clinical course and decrease the period of intestinal shedding of the organisms, thus decreasing the period of communicability. The use of antispasmodic drugs (for example, diphenoxylate) to control diarrhoea prolong the symptoms and the presence of the organism in the intestines, and is therefore not recommended.

Intravenous fluids are administered to maintain the electrolyte balance and prevent profound dehydration due to an excessively large loss of water and electrolytes in the stool. The patient may require supplementary potassium.

Nursing Care

The patient is assessed for weight loss, skin turgor and dryness of mucous membranes; vital signs and urinary volume are monitored. Clear fluids are offered by mouth during the acute stage.

Prevention and Patient Education

Dysentery bacilli are spread by drinking water polluted by infected human excreta, by sexual transmission and by food handled carelessly by shigella carriers, some of whom have the active disease, others being entirely asymptomatic. Thus, the same precautions must be observed, and the same control of water sources and food handling enforced, in the prevention of shigellosis as of typhoid fever (see below). This includes proper hand washing, effective sanitation, adequate sewage disposal, a programme of fly control and the detection of carriers. Untreated sexual partners, particularly those of homosexual men, may reinfect the patient.

Typhoid Fever

Typhoid fever is an acute systemic bacterial disease resulting from infection with *Salmonella typhi*. The organism gains access to the body through ingestion of food or water that has been contaminated by infected faeces or urine. Since it is eliminated in the stools or urine of patients, the organism can find its way into food and water through sewage, flies and the hands of carriers handling raw fruits, vegetables and other food. Another source of infection is the ingestion of oysters and shellfish harvested from polluted waters. Typhoid fever, although rare in the United Kingdom, is a serious health problem in regions of the world where there is neither a safe water supply nor adequate sewage disposal.

Altered Physiology

The organism enters the body by way of the mouth and invades the walls of the gastrointestinal tract. There, multiplying rapidly, it gives rise to a massive bacteraemia that continues for about 10 days. The chief localization of the organism is in the mesenteric lymph nodes and the masses of lymphatic tissue in the mucous membrane of the intestinal wall, called Peyer's patches, and in small solitary lymph follicles, numerous in the ileum and the colon. The blood vessels of the Peyer's patches become thrombosed, and the swollen mass of lymphatic tissue dies and sloughs away, leaving clean ulcers in the mucous membrane, the floor of which may be the muscu-

laris or even the peritoneum, where they may cause peritonitis, if they perforate.

Clinical Features

The onset of typhoid fever is gradual, with headache, fever, malaise, somnolence and abdominal pain. The patient may not seek health care at this time since these are nonspecific symptoms. At the end of the first week, rose spots (a cluster of pink lesions that initially blanch with pressure) may be found on the chest and abdomen. Without therapy, the temperature rises steadily, reaching its highest level, usually 40° to 41°C, in three to seven days. During this period of rising temperature, most patients suffer with severe headache and a nonproductive cough. During the second week, if the patient is not treated, the temperature remains consistently high. During the third week, however, it becomes more and more remittent, a little lower each morning and not quite so elevated each afternoon. The pulse rate may be relatively slow in spite of high fever. Other clinical features are an enlarged liver and spleen, delirium and intestinal bleeding.

Diagnosis

The diagnosis is made by recovery of the causative agent from blood samples, bone marrow aspirate, rose spot aspirate or stool.

Management

Chloramphenicol, co-trimoxazole or ciprofloxacin are used in the treatment of typhoid fever. The fever usually subsides in about three to five days following initiation of antibiotic therapy. However, bacteriological cure is not achieved in all patients. Relapses have occurred and positive stool cultures have been obtained after one course, and even repeated courses, of antibiotic therapy. Thus, while chloramphenicol has reduced the fatality rate of typhoid fever significantly and has curtailed the excretion of typhoid bacilli during convalescence, it has not reduced the incidence of chronic carrier state following typhoid fever.

Nursing Care

The expected outcomes of nursing care are to give supportive care and to monitor for complications.

Delirium is common in the severe form of the disease, and patients will require special support during this period. Patients may be drowsy, indifferent to their surroundings and incontinent of urine and faeces. Enteric precautions are used while patients are ill, and they should be awakened for administration of medications, fluids and nourishment, and for position changes.

Tepid water fever sponges may be requested by medical staff for temperatures over 40°C. A high fluid intake is encouraged to prevent dehydration from fluid losses due to fever, perspiration and poor oral intake.

The nurse should observe for bladder distension, since patients may lose the urge to void during the toxic state. Retention of faeces may also pose a problem. Enemas, if indicated, are given *under low pressure* to diminish the chance of intestinal perforation.

Monitoring for Complications

Many structures may become infected in the course of typhoid fever, including the lungs, the pleura, the pericardium, the heart, the kidneys and the bones. However, the most common of the dangerous complications are intestinal haemorrhage and perforation of the bowel, with resultant peritonitis.

Intestinal haemorrhages, secondary to bacterial invasion of Peyer's patches, which leads to necrosis, ulceration and erosion of blood vessels, occur in 4 to 7 per cent of patients, usually during the third week. Signs of haemorrhage include apprehension, sweating, pallor, weak, rapid pulse, hypotension and bloody or tarry stools. Haemorrhage is generally managed by supportive measures, including blood transfusions. Operative intervention (bowel resection) is sometimes necessary.

Intestinal perforation, the most serious complication, may happen at any time, but most often occurs during the third week. The perforation usually takes place in the lower ileum. It occurs when the ulcer causing the slough involves the entire thickness of the bowel wall. The intestinal contents pour into the abdominal cavity at once causing peritonitis. Patients usually experience acute abdominal pain. There is associated abdominal tenderness and a rigidity and a silent abdomen. However, the pain may only last a few seconds and then stop, with patients falling sound asleep within a few minutes. If such signs occur, a nasogastric tube is passed and intravenous fluids started to correct fluid and electrolyte imbalance. Surgical closure of perforation is usually carried out.

Other complications of typhoid fever may occur when the typhoid bacilli localize in specific tissues, causing hepatitis, meningitis, cholecystitis, pneumonia and pericarditis. During the course of the disease, the gallbladder and bile ducts are routinely infected.

Patient Education

Since typhoid fever is a very serious disease, the process of recovery may be slow. Once patients have recovered, stools must be checked to see if they have become carriers, because approximately 3 per cent of treated typhoid patients become chronic carriers. Carriers harbour the organism and excrete it in their urine and stools. The presence of virulence-agglutinins (vi-agglutinins) in the blood of suspected carriers has strong predictive value for the carrier state. A positive stool or urine culture for a year or more indicates a carrier state. Carriers may be given ampicillin or amoxycillin with probenecid in an attempt to abolish the carrier state.

Typhoid is a notifiable disease and environmental health departments maintain surveillance of carriers, who must not become food or milk handlers until clear of the carriage state.

Prevention

There is no substitute for good sanitation. The eradication of typhoid fever depends upon the availability of safe water and sewer systems. The detection of carriers and restrictions of their occupations is also essential. Typhoid fever patients, convalescents and carriers must wash their hands after defaecation. All those handling food should use proper hand washing techniques. Flies must be controlled by screening and spraying, and their breeding controlled by adequate collection and disposal of refuse. Shellfish should be obtained from an approved source. Scrupulous cleanliness in the preparation and storage of food is vital.

Typhoid vaccination is recommended for those living with chronic carriers and is considered for people travelling to countries where typhoid is common. On the basis of the above recommendation, adults may be given typhoid vaccine subcutaneously on two occasions separated by four or more weeks.

Meningococcal Meningitis (Bacterial Meningitis)

Meningitis is an inflammation of the membranes surrounding the brain and spinal cord and is caused by a variety of bacteria, viruses, protozoa or fungi. The most important form is bacterial meningitis.

The bacteria most frequently encountered in acute bacterial meningitis are *Neisseria meningitidis, Streptococcus pneumoniae* (in adults) and *Haemophilus influenzae* (in children and young adults). The mode of transmission is by direct contact, including droplets and discharges from the nose and throat of carriers (most often) or infected people. Of those exposed to it, the great majority do not develop the infection but become carriers. There has been an increased incidence of meningitis caused by gram-negative bacteria in people over the age of 60 as well as those who are immunocompromised.

Meningococcal disease is endemic in the United Kingdom and throughout the world, and occurs most frequently in the winter and spring months. Epidemics usually occur in people who live in crowded conditions, notably in cities, crowded institutions, military institutions or prisons, but the disease can also occur in rural areas.

Bacterial meningitis starts as an infection of the oropharynx and is followed by meningococcal septicaemia, which extends to the meninges of the brain and upper region of the spinal cord. There are several distinct immunological strains of the meningococcus, but groups A, B, C and Y cause the majority of cases of bacterial meningitis (Communicable Disease Report, 1987). It can be one of the most fulminant of all diseases (i.e., coming on suddenly with severity).

Altered Physiology

Predisposing factors include upper respiratory tract infection, otitis media, mastoiditis, sickle cell anaemia, recent neurosurgical procedures, head trauma and immunological defects. The venous channels serving the posterior nasopharynx, middle ear and mastoid drain towards the brain and are near the veins draining the meninges; these channels favour bacterial proliferation.

The meningococci enter the bloodstream and cause an inflammatory reaction in the meninges and underlying cortex, which may result in vasculitis with thromboses and reduced cerebral blood flow. The cerebral tissue is metabolically impaired by the presence of meningeal exudate, vasculitis and underperfusion, and cerebral oedema. A purulent exudate may spread over the base of the brain and spinal cord. The inflammation spreads also to the membrane lining the cerebral ventricles. Bacterial meningitis is associated with profound alterations in intracranial physiology, including increased permeability of the blood brain barrier, cerebral oedema and raised cranial pressure.

In acute infections, however, the patient dies from the toxin of the bacteria before the meningitis develops. In these patients, meningococcaemia is overwhelming, with adrenal damage, circulatory collapse and associated widespread haemorrhages (Waterhouse-Friderichsen syndrome) occurring as a result of endothelial damage and vascular necrosis caused by the meningococci.

Clinical Features

The symptoms of meningitis result from infection and increased intracranial pressure. Usually, the patient experiences a sudden onset of severe headache, myalgia, back pain, photophobia, fever and neck pain and stiffness (from spasm of the extensor muscles due to meningeal irritation). Frequently, aggressive and almost maniacal behaviour is displayed. Another striking feature is a rash ranging from petechiae (small red spots) to a combination of petechiae and ecchymoses (large bruise-like areas) occurring in about two thirds of patients with meningococcal disease.

Upon physical examination there is resistance to neck flexion. Other signs of meningeal irritation include:

● Positive Kernig's sign: when the patient is lying with the thigh flexed on the abdomen, the leg cannot be completely extended.
● Positive Brudzinski's sign: when the patient's neck is flexed, flexion of the knees and hips is produced; when passive flexion of the lower extremity of one side is made, a similar movement is seen for the opposite extremity.

In approximately 10 per cent of patients a fulminating infection occurs with signs of overwhelming septicaemia: an abrupt onset of high fever, extensive purpuric lesions (over face and extremities), shock and signs of intravascular coagulation. Death may occur within a few hours after onset.

The infecting organisms can usually be identified through a smear and culture of cerebrospinal fluid and blood. Counter immunoelectrophoresis is widely used to detect bacterial antigens in body fluids, particularly cerebrospinal fluid and urine.

Management

Successful management depends on the administration of an antibiotic that crosses the blood–brain barrier into the subarachnoid space in sufficient concentration to halt the multiplication of bacteria. Antimicrobial therapy is started immediately when the cerebrospinal fluid and blood cultures are obtained. Penicillin, ampicillin or chloramphenicol, or one of the cephalosporins, may be used. Other antibiotics may be used if resistant strains of bacteria are identified. The patient is maintained on large intravenous doses of the appropriate antibiotic.

Dehydration or shock is treated with fluid volume expanders. Seizures, which may occur in the early course of the disease, are controlled with diazepam, while mannitol may be used to treat cerebral oedema.

Nursing Care

The outcome will depend on the supportive care given. The patient is very ill, and the combination of fever, dehydration, alkalosis and cerebral oedema may predispose to seizures. Airway obstruction, respiratory arrest or cardiac arrhythmias may follow.

In meningitis of all causes, the patient's clinical status and vital signs are assessed constantly, since altered consciousness may lead to airway obstruction. Arterial blood gas determinations, insertion of a cuffed endotracheal tube (or tracheostomy) and mechanical ventilation may be prescribed. Oxygen may be given to maintain the arterial PO_2 at desired levels.

The central venous pressure may be monitored to assess for incipient shock, which precedes cardiac or respiratory failure. Generalized vasoconstriction, circumoral cyanosis and cold extremities may be noted. The high fever must be reduced to decrease the load on the heart and the brain's oxygen demand.

Rapid intravenous fluid replacement may be prescribed, but care is taken not to overhydrate the patient because of the risk of cerebral oedema.

The body weight, serum electrolytes, urine volume and specific gravity, and osmolarity of urine are closely monitored, especially if inappropriate antidiuretic hormone secretion is suspected.

Continuing nursing care requires ongoing assessment of the patient's clinical status, attention to skin and oral hydration, promotion of comfort and protection during seizures and while comatose.

Discharges from the nose and mouth are considered infectious. Respiratory isolation is advised for the first 24 hours after the start of antibiotic therapy.

Prevention and Patient Education

People having close contact with the patient should be considered candidates for antimicrobial prophylaxis (rifampicin). Close contacts are observed and examined immediately if fever or other signs and symptoms of meningitis develop.

Vaccine may be of benefit against some strains of *Neisseria meningitidis* and *Haemophilus influenzae* for some travellers visiting countries that are experiencing meningococcal disease.

Tetanus (Lockjaw)

Tetanus is an acute disease caused by the tetanus bacillus, *Clostridium tetani*, whose spores are introduced into the body when an injury is contaminated with soil, street dust or animal and human faeces. The bacillus is an anaerobe (it cannot live in the presence of oxygen). It is found most commonly in wounds with small external openings, and is also seen in drug abusers. Not infrequently, the wound entrance is so insignificant that it cannot be found. Any wound such as scratches, bee stings, lacerations, frostbite, animal injuries, abortions, circumcision, surgery and dental and orofacial trauma may provide a portal of entry.

In developing countries, tetanus is a common and serious disease. The majority of cases are caused by contamination of a wound, of a newborn's umbilical stump or of the puerperal uterus.

Altered Physiology

Tissues with low oxygen tension (due to infection or foreign material, or damaged blood supply) provide conditions in which spores become vegetative, multiply and produce toxins. These neurotoxins are absorbed by the peripheral nerves and carried to the spinal cord, where they produce a reaction that amounts to a stimulation of the nervous tissue. The sensory nerves become sensitive to the slightest stimuli, and the hypersensitive motor nerves carry impulses that produce spasms of the muscles that they supply.

Clinical Features

Early symptoms include irritability, restlessness, headache, low-grade fever and muscle rigidity. The jaw muscles are the first group affected, making it difficult to open the mouth because of spasms of the masticatory muscles (trismus). This characteristic syndrome has given the disease the common name 'lockjaw'. The spasms of the facial muscles produce a distorted grin (risus sardonicus), which is quite characteristic of the disease and persists during convalescence.

The spasm rapidly involves other groups of muscles until the whole body is affected, with tightness of the chest and rigidity of the abdominal wall, back and extremities. The spasm is continuous, but the least stimulus—a door banging or a loud voice—may cause a generalized convulsion, with every muscle in violent contraction. In fact, fractures of the vertebral bodies can occur during severe spasms. Because the extensor muscles are stronger than the flexors, the head is retracted, the feet are extended fully and the back is arched, so that during a convulsion the whole body may be supported on the back of the head and the feet. The condition is called opisthotonos. The patient is alert and in pain from muscle spasms. Death may occur from asphyxia, due to spasms of the respiratory muscles, and from pneumonia.

Management

The aims of management are to provide an airway to prevent respiratory and cardiovascular complications and to neutralize the residual circulating toxins.

The patient with established tetanus is immediately given tetanus immune globulin one to two hours before wound debridement so that the neurotoxin released into the circulation during the debridement cannot attach to nerve endings. Active immunization with tetanus toxoid is also started at the beginning of the treatment since even severe tetanus produces no immunity. When tetanus toxoid and tetanus immune globulin are given concurrently, separate syringes and sites should be used.

The wound is debrided because necrotic tissue favours the growth of tetanus bacillus. The wound is irrigated copiously to wash out tissue fragments and foreign bodies; it may be left open and drainage instituted.

Immune globulin may also be infiltrated into the wound site. Usually penicillin G (or an alternative antibiotic) is given intravenously or intramuscularly in high doses to eradicate persisting *C. tetani* and other pathogens from the wound.

Diazepam is used to reduce restlessness and apprehension (which can induce spasm), for its amnesic effect and to provide muscle relaxation to treat spasm. Neuromuscular blocking agents are given for treatment of severe tetanus.

The overactivity of the sympathetic nervous system may lead to 'sympathetic crisis' and death. Isolated tachycardia, temporary hypertension, premature ventricular contractions and sweating require aggressive physiological monitoring and pharmacological treatment. Propranolol may be given to control hypertensive episodes.

Nursing Care

In severe tetanus infection, one of the most important nursing objectives and priorities is constant supportive care of the patient to assure respiratory function. Convulsive paroxysms, especially those involving the respiratory muscles, impair gas exchange by preventing normal swallowing and by obstructing the airway. Tetanic spasms of the larynx, pharynx and respiratory muscles usually occur during convulsions and can lead to asphyxiation and death. Rigidity and spasm of the trunk muscles also contribute to ventilatory failure. Ventilation ceases during a tetanus convulsion.

The patient requires expert respiratory management in an intensive care unit, with early endotracheal intubation and mechanical ventilation. Oral secretions are usually constant and profuse, requiring frequent use of suction. The nursing care of the patient with convulsions is discussed in Chapter 33, See Chapter 3 for the management of the patient requiring respiratory intensive care.

Objectivity of the sympathetic nervous system, as manifested by tachycardia, arrhythmias, labile blood pressure, hyperpyrexia and excessive sweating and salivation, may eventually lead to circulatory failure and death. A significant increase in the heart rate and mean arterial blood pressure may indicate a need for an adrenergic blocking agent (propanolol) to lessen the possibility of catecholamine-induced myocardial damage. Therefore, cardiac monitoring is essential.

Since the slightest stimulation may trigger paroxysmal spasm, sudden stimuli and light must be avoided. The patient is placed in a quiet, semidark environment to avoid stimulating reflex spasms. Nursing activities are carried out during the periods when sedation has its maximum effect so that the patient is disturbed as little as possible, since tactile stimulation often provokes spasms. Usually a vein is kept open for emergency situations, such as cardiac or respiratory arrest, and for infusions to maintain careful fluid and electrolyte balance. Insensible fluid losses in the form of sweat and saliva are high and result in dehydration, which, in the presence of impaired cardiovascular control and overactivity of the sympathetic nervous system, can predispose to deep vein thrombosis and pulmonary embolism. Parenteral nutrition may be required, since aspiration pneumonia during oral food intake is a hazard.

Constant attention is given to the eyes, mouth, skin, bladder and bowels. The patient is monitored for signs of infection (skin, urinary tract, aspiration pneumonia).

The nurse should observe the patient for signs of urinary retention, which occurs when perineal muscles are affected. Pressure sores and contractures can be the outcome of prolonged immobility; therefore, preventive nursing care is necessary (see Chapter 2). The reported mortality rate of tetanus varies from 0 to 60 per cent;

higher mortality rates tend to occur in centres with limited experience of treating the disease.

Prevention and Patient Education

Tetanus can be prevented through proper immunization programmes; immunization establishes basal immunity before exposure to the risk of tetanus. For primary immunization of adults, three doses of adult-type tetanus and diphtheria toxoids are given, followed by a booster dose every 10 years to maintain adequate immunity.

The most important step in the prevention of tetanus is the thorough washing and cleaning of the wound, with removal of all devitalized tissue. This helps to eliminate tetanus bacilli from wounds and removes the material that forms a focus in which the tetanus spores can develop.

Every break in the skin must be considered a potential portal of entry of *C. tetani*.

Following injury, the immunization status of the patient will determine whether or not to provide active immunization with tetanus toxoid and passive immunization with tetanus immune globulin. The nature of the wound, the conditions under which it was incurred and the treatment are considered on an individual basis. All patients should be encouraged to keep an up-to-date record of their immunization status.

Gas Gangrene

Gas gangrene is a severe infection of skeletal muscle caused by several species of gram-positive clostridia that may complicate trauma, compound fractures, contusions or lacerated wounds by producing exotoxins that destroy tissue. These organisms (*Clostridium perfringens*, *Clostridium novyi*, *Clostridium septicum* and others) may produce gas gangrene. They are anaerobes and spore-formers, and are found normally in the intestinal tract of humans and in the soil. Their growth occurs primarily in deep wounds where the oxygen supply is reduced, a situation enhanced by the presence of foreign bodies or necrotic tissue, which leads to further reduction of oxygen tension in wounds.

In contaminated wounds in which the vascular supply may be impaired, the environment is suited for the growth of spores and the production of exotoxins that adversely affect the blood and cause vessel thrombosis and damage to the myocardium, liver and kidneys.

Spores formed by anaerobic bacilli are highly resistant to heat, cold, sunlight, drying and many chemical agents. Because the clostridial bacillus is an inhabitant of the human intestinal tract, it is likely to be the infecting organism in thigh wounds following amputations, especially if the patient is incontinent. Patients with chronic arterial disease and diabetes mellitus are at risk of developing gas gangrene following amputation of the leg because these conditions favour the development of local tissue anoxia necessary for the development of gas gangrene.

Clinical Features

The onset of gas gangrene is usually attended by sudden, severe pain at the site of injury, which is caused by gas and oedema in the tissues, usually occurring one to four days following the injury. The wound is very tender. The surrounding skin initially appears normal, or white and tense, but later becomes bronzed, brown or even black in colour. Vesicles filled with red, watery fluid appear, and crepitus (cracking) produced by gas in the tissue may be felt. Frothy fluid with a foul, sweetish odour may escape from the wound. The gas and oedema fluid increase local pressure and impair the blood supply and drainage. The involved muscles become black or reddish purple (necrotic). Amputation of an affected extremity is sometimes necessary. The infection may spread quickly, resulting in systemic toxicity.

The patient is usually pale, prostrated and apprehensive, but usually quite alert. Pulse and respirations are rapid, but the temperature usually does not exceed 38°C. Anorexia, diarrhoea, vomiting and vascular collapse may occur. Death from toxaemia can occur.

Management

Prevention

Gas gangrene may be prevented if all devitalized and infected tissue is excised and debrided, using wide incisions made to render the wound unsuitable for the growth of clostridium.

Treatment

Treatment usually involves surgery, antibiotics and sometimes hyperbaric oxygen. Once infection has developed, extensive incisions in the affected part allow air to inhibit the growth of anaerobic organisms. Antibiotic therapy is combined with prompt surgical debridement of the wound.

Hyperbaric oxygen (oxygen administered under pressure greater than atmospheric) has proven extremely effective in treating gas gangrene. This increases the dissolved oxygen in the arterial system by increasing the partial pressure of oxygen breathed by the patient. With hyperbaric oxygen therapy, it may not be necessary to amputate the extremity.

Nursing Care

The nursing functions are collaborative with the surgeon. The patient is very ill, since the infection produces an intense toxaemia. The pulmonary capillary wedge pressures, central venous pressures and urinary output are closely monitored. Intravenous fluids are administered as prescribed to support the cardiovascular system and to maintain fluid and electrolyte balance. Transfusions may be necessary and are prescribed to maintain adequate haematocrit levels. Haemolysis and tissue destruction can lead to hyperkalaemia; thus, potassium levels are also evaluated. Enteral nutrition is critical in establishing nutritional balance.

Botulism

Botulism is a type of food poisoning, rarely encountered in the United Kingdom, that affects the central nervous system. It is caused by eating food in which the bacterium *Clostridium botulinum* has grown and produced toxins. These toxins are extremely potent and are rapidly absorbed by the gastrointestinal tract, becoming bound to neural tissue and producing a neuroparalytic syndrome. Toxic effects usually follow ingestion of contaminated foods: home-canned, dried or smoked foods or poorly processed foods.

Ornithosis (Psittacosis)

Ornithosis is an infectious and atypical form of pneumonia or systemic febrile illness transmitted to humans by infected birds. The agents responsible for ornithosis belong to the genus *Chlamydia* (intracellular organisms that were formerly considered viruses but are now classed as bacteria). The chlamydiae cause trachoma, lymphogranuloma venereum and ornithosis; they are found in nasal secretions and in the feathers, faeces and blood of sick birds. The organisms, *Chlamydia psittaci*, are transmitted to humans by inhaling the aetiological agent from dried droppings of infected birds, or directly from infected birds (i.e., workers in food processing plants), or rarely from person to person. Birds of the parrot family (parakeets, parrots, cockatoos, budgerigars), as well as many other species of birds (canaries, sparrows, pigeons, turkeys), may become infected.

Clinical Features

The illness may appear as a transient influenza-like illness or a severe pneumonia, or it may be asymptomatic. After an incubation period lasting 4 to 15 days (it may be as long as 6 weeks in humans, 6 months in parrots), the disease begins abruptly, with malaise, headache, photophobia and chills. Its course is characterized by high fever, great weakness, marked depression and delirium, with surprisingly slow pulse and respiration. Cough is a prominent symptom. The lungs become involved, with oedema, mononuclear cells and lymphocytes appearing in the alveoli and interstitial areas. Chest X-ray may reveal an interstitial pneumonitis. Convalescence is generally prolonged.

Management

Ornithosis responds to the tetracyclines. Supportive therapy includes bedrest, oxygen (when necessary) and measures to reduce the fever. Relapses are common.

Prevention

People at risk are those who work in pet shops or around poultry and pigeons, bird fanciers, workers who may handle infected birds in the food processing and marketing business, and vets. Care should be taken to avoid dust from feathers and bird cage contents. Infected birds should be treated or destroyed. No protective vaccination is available.

Spirochaetal Infections

Syphilis

See page 1206.

VIRAL INFECTIONS

Influenza

Influenza is an acute infectious disease caused by an RNA-containing myxovirus. It is characterized by respiratory and constitutional symptoms. It sweeps through the entire world approximately every 20 years, attacking as many as 40 per cent of the people in affected areas. The striking features of these epidemics have been the speed with which the disease has spread and an extremely high attack rate.

Typical epidemics of influenza have been characterized by three successive waves, separated by brief intermissions. The first wave lasts from three to six weeks and is explosive in outbreak, widespread and mild in form in most cases, with few complications. The second wave is also widespread, but lasts longer; the cases are more severe, and the complications are serious. The third wave lasts still longer (from 8 to 10 weeks) and involves fewer people, but the complications are quite severe. During the years succeeding a major epidemic, there follow scattered local waves of decreasing severity, with sporadic cases of influenza occurring during the intervals.

Aetiology

The primary factor in the aetiology of influenza is a filterable virus, of which three main strains have been isolated, designated as types A, B and C. Types A and B have been associated with epidemics. The numerous variants within a given type are called subtypes.

It is difficult to control influenza because the surface antigens of the virus have the capacity to change. Major changes in these viruses and new influenza strains arise from time to time. Therefore, previously acquired antibodies against earlier influenza strains may not be effective against the newly emerging strain, depending on the extent of the surface change. It has been observed that when a new influenza virus strain becomes prevalent throughout the country, the old virus strain disappears.

Transmission is by close contact or by droplets from the respiratory tract of an infected person. The virus is airborne and multiplies in the upper respiratory tract, invading the nasal, tracheal and bronchial mucosal cells.

Clinical Features

In the majority of patients, influenza begins after a short incubation period (24 to 72 hours) with an abrupt onset of chills, fever, headache, backache and malaise. Respiratory features include a dry cough, sore throat and nasal obstruction and discharge. Other patients start with acute sinusitis, bronchitis, pleurisy or bronchopneumonia. These symptoms are always abrupt in onset. In still another group, there are gastrointestinal symptoms of nausea, vomiting, abdominal pain and diarrhoea, and, finally, in each epidemic, cases develop without local symptoms but with chills or continuous fever. The patient usually recovers within a week if there are no complications.

Complications

People at risk of developing the complications of influenza are those over the age of 65, people with chronic pulmonary or cardiac disease (especially rheumatic valve disease) and those with diabetes or other chronic metabolic disorders or chronic renal disease. The influenza virus damages the ciliated epithelium of the tracheobronchial tree, rendering the patient vulnerable to the development of secondary invaders such as pneumonococci or staphylococci, *H. influenzae*, various streptococci and other organisms.

Dyspnoea early in the course of the disease points to bronchopneumonia, which is potentially life-threatening. This pneumonia may be viral, mixed viral or bacterial in origin. Significant mortality occurs not only as a result of pneumonia, but also from cardiopulmonary or other chronic diseases that are exacerbated during influenza infection. Other complications include myocarditis, myositis and meningoencephalitis.

Management

The aims of management are to relieve symptoms and to prevent and treat complications.

The troublesome symptom of cough is treated with an expectorant–linctus combination. The patient may be advised to take aspirin for headache and myalgias. (Children and young adults are not given aspirin because of its association with Reye's syndrome.) Antiviral therapy (amantadine hydrochloride), if given early, can shorten the course of the illness and reduce the titre of virus excreted.

The patient is encouraged to rest at home, not only to relieve malaise but also to reduce spread of the infection. Transmission of infection to others usually occurs early in the illness.

A liberal fluid intake (water, juices) is advised to thin secretions and help reduce fever. The patient is advised to avoid respiratory irritants, particularly smoking, since smoke interferes with clearance of secretions by impairing ciliary function. Alcoholic beverages are discouraged since they can increase viscosity of secretions.

If aspirin is prescribed, the patient is advised to take it regularly to avoid marked swings of temperature with sweating and chills, which can lead to dehydration and exhaustion.

Prevention and Patient Education

Annual influenza vaccination is recommended for adults with chronic cardiovascular and pulmonary disorders that are severe enough to require regular medical follow-up or that have required hospitalization during the previous year. In addition, residents of nursing homes and other chronic care facilities, as well as health care personnel who have extensive contact with high-risk patients (e.g., staff of intensive care units), are encouraged to have annual influenza vaccinations. The composition of the vaccine is changed yearly to match any new variation of the virus. It is recommended that influenza vaccine be administered in October or November.

The risk of developing influenza is related to crowding and close contact of groups of individuals. Therefore, visiting within health care facilities should be restricted during epidemics to minimize any chance of introducing influenza. Elective admissions and surgery are avoided as much as possible during an influenza outbreak.

Amantadine, an antiviral drug, can prevent clinical infection with influenza A virus. (It blocks an early step in the replication of this virus.) It is given only to certain high-risk patients, since most patients exposed to influenza require no prophylaxis. Amantadine does not protect against endemic influenza or influenza B. The drug is also given for the treatment of symptomatic influenza A infection, and may shorten and diminish the severity of illness. Adverse effects, occurring mainly in the elderly, include central nervous system toxicity, confusion, dizziness, slurred speech, headache, sleep disturbances and visual hallucinations. To be effective, amantadine should be given before, and for the duration of, exposure to type A influenza virus.

Infectious Mononucleosis

Infectious mononucleosis (glandular fever) is an acute infectious disease of the lymphatic system caused by the Epstein-Barr virus, a DNA virus of the herpesvirus group. Another virus, cytomegalovirus, can cause virtually identical symptoms. A third infecting organism, *Toxoplasma* (a protozoan), can also produce a similar clinical picture.

The basic pathology is an intense proliferative response of the lymphoid tissue and organs (lymph nodes, spleen, tonsils), but all organs can be affected. Infectious mononucleosis is usually self-limited, but in rare instances complications and even death do occur.

Epidemiology

Infectious mononucleosis is encountered most frequently in the 15 to 25 age group. It has been shown that when natural primary infection with Epstein-Barr virus develops in childhood, a mild and nonspecific or unapparent illness occurs, and the child has immunity for many years. Infectious mononucleosis occurs in individuals without immunity to Epstein-Barr virus. If natural infection does not take place in childhood and a susceptible person (adolescent/young adult) acquires the infection, this event will lead to clinical manifestation of infectious mononucleosis in about 50 per cent of patients. Thus infectious mononucleosis is more frequently encountered in countries with a high standard of living; in developing countries or among deprived socioeconomic groups, primary infection usually occurs in early childhood, so that the disease is virtually unknown in adults.

Transmission of infectious mononucleosis is by oral contact. The virus may persist in the pharynx for weeks or months. This suggests that a large number of young adults are probably convalescent carriers of the disease. The virus can also be spread by blood transfusion. The incubation period ranges from 30 to 50 days.

Clinical Features

The early clinical features are usually vague and masquerade as those of streptococcal sore throat, leukaemia and hepatitis. The triad of fever, sore throat and cervical lymph node enlargement suggests infectious mononucleosis. A typical attack begins with fever and chills, anorexia, sore throat and myalgia. Headache and diarrhoea are often seen. On the second or third day, the lymph nodes begin to swell and become tender, usually the posterior cervical group first, and then the anterior groups. This causes pain in the neck. Generalized lymphadenopathy may occur. Early in the course of the disease, supraorbital oedema occurs and the spleen enlarges in the majority of patients. Although hepatomegaly occurs in less than 25 per cent of patients, the majority of patients have abnormal liver function tests. A faint erythematous or maculopapular eruption may appear on the trunk and proximal extremities in the early stage of the disease.

There is evidence that the clinical syndrome of chronic Epstein-Barr virus infection does occur. These patients complain of chronic fatigue, recurrent sore throat and nonspecific symptoms (swollen glands, musculoskeletal pains, headaches, difficulty with concentration).

Diagnosis

The diagnosis is made on the basis of the typical picture of clinical illness, as well as such laboratory findings as lymphocytosis with many atypical lymphocytes, detection of heterophile antibodies and positive Epstein-Barr-virus-specific antibody test results. The slide agglutination 'spot test' is widely used to screen for heterophile antibodies. A few drops of the patient's blood are added to a specially prepared slide on which there are preserved red blood cells from horses. If the heterophile antibodies are present, agglutination (clumping) of the animal cells will occur. This test requires just a few minutes to perform and can generally be done in the doctor's surgery. Spot tests are generally accurate, but they can give false-positive or false-negative results.

Management
The treatment is symptomatic and supportive. The patient is encouraged to remain in bed while the fever lasts, and to rest at intervals during recovery. Aspirin or paracetemol is given for headache and muscle pains. Constipation (which leads to straining and sudden increase in portal venous pressure, which in turn can contribute to splenic rupture) is to be avoided. Steroids may be used when severe or life-threatening complications develop, such as marked hepatic dysfunction, neurological features, thrombocytopenia, haemologic anaemia and airway obstruction. Most patients recover in one to three weeks, although illness may be prolonged in some, with complaints of fatigue, poor exercise tolerance, and depression predominating for as long as a year.

Patient Education
The patient is advised of the need for additional rest and sleep for a period of time. Strenuous physical activity and competitive sports are discouraged until recovery is completed because the enlarged spleen of the patient with infectious mononucleosis is vulnerable to injury and may rupture if subjected to relatively mild trauma. For the athlete, this may mean up to six months. However, the exact length of time is uncertain, since the spleen may rupture even after clinical, haematological and serological evidence reveals recovery.

Rabies

This is an almost uniformly fatal encephalomyelitis, which is readily transmitted by inoculation of saliva from an infected animal. Carnivores, especially wolves and dogs, suffer a 'furious' form of the disease and can readily transmit it by biting. Other animals have 'dumb' rabies and may be listless and paralysed. Humans most often develop the excitable form.

Because the inoculated virus enters the peripheral nerves and invades the central nervous system by retrograde spread, the incubation period varies from 10 days to a year or more, depending on whether the bite or scratch was proximal or distal to the central nervous system. Eventually, pain and paraesthesia at the inoculation site

are followed by excitability and severe, painful pharyngeal and laryngeal spasms, producing apparent fear of water (hydrophobia), and later by paralysis and death. If exposure to rabies is considered likely the following regime is recommended:

1. The wound should be washed with soap and water.
2. A course of human diploid cell rabies vaccine should be given.
3. Human anti-rabies globulin should be instilled in and around the wound as soon as possible, to destroy viruses in the tissues and bloodstream.

If the animal concerned is well two weeks after the incident, it was almost certainly not infectious at the initial encounter. No cases of rabies originating in England and Wales have been reported since 1902, although a small number of imported cases are still seen. Rabies remains an important problem across the rest of Europe, and many European owners now have their pets immunized and possess certificates of vaccination.

PROTOZOAN INFECTIONS

Malaria

Malaria is an acute infectious disease caused by protozoa, which are transmitted by way of an intermediate host, the bite of an infective female *Anopheles* mosquito. Malaria has also been transmitted through blood transfusions and from needles and syringes shared by drug abusers.

Incidence
Malaria affects an estimated 300 million people in the world annually. It is claimed that in Africa, one fourth of all adults suffer from malaria at one time or another. It causes more disability and a heavier economic burden than any other parasitic disease. International travel and immigration have been responsible for the importation of cases of malaria into many nontropical countries. In addition, more than 20 species of anopheline mosquitoes have become resistant to commonly used insecticides.

Types of Malaria
There are four species of malarial parasites, grouped under the generic name *Plasmodium*, each causing a different type of malaria: *Plasmodium falciparum* (which poses the greatest danger), *Plasmodium vivax, Plasmodium malariae* and *Plasmodium ovale*. Each malarial parasite lives within a red blood corpuscle, using the haemoglobin as food. When fully grown, it divides (segments) into 10 to 20 small young parasites, called hyalines (segments), which burst the cell; this bursting of cells causes chills in the patient. The majority of these hyalines die, but a few find their way into new red cells, and the process is repeated.

Clinical Features

The majority of patients present with paroxysms of chills, fever and sweating. Nausea, fatigue and dizziness are present, along with intense headache and muscle pain. Paroxysms of chill and fever may last about 12 hours, after which the cycle may be repeated daily, every other day or every third day.

Complications occur most frequently with *P. falciparum*. Patients with severe malaria of any form may become comatose and die (pernicious malaria); they may develop renal failure (due to the precipitation of free haemoglobin in the kidney tubule), a serious gastrointestinal disturbance or cerebral symptoms (due to an accumulation of the parasites in the blood vessels of an affected organ).

Diagnosis

The patient should be asked about travel outside the United Kingdom. Travel or residence in an area where malaria is endemic is an important diagnostic clue. The diagnosis is confirmed by finding the parasites in stained peripheral blood smears. The blood should be examined as soon as the patient seeks treatment. More than one blood examination may be required, since the diagnosis can be missed on a routine smear.

Management

The aim of treatment is to destroy the blood trophozoites and schizonts of *Plasmodium* that cause the clinical features and the pathological effects that characterize the disease.

The use of antimalarial drugs depends on the stage of the life cycle of the parasite. The species of parasite infecting the patient is determined by means of a blood smear.

Chloroquine alone is adequate for *P. malariae* but is combined with a course of primaquine for *P. vivax* and *P. ovale* to eliminate the hepatic form of the species. Quinine is recommended to treat patients with malaria in areas known to be resistant to chloroquine or for malaria due to *P. falciparum* strains.

Cerebral malaria, which occurs in about 2 per cent of patients with an acute falciparum malaria, is the most feared complication. It produces changes in consciousness, behavioural changes, seizures and cerebral oedema. Patients with acute *P. falciparum* malaria are critically ill and must be hospitalized because the infection can be so overwhelming. Intravenous quinine is administered intermittently. Because neurological toxicity can occur from the quinine infusion, the patient is monitored for twitching, delirium, confusion, convulsions and coma. Oxygen is administered to counter tissue anoxia. The patient may have jaundice as a result of the density of malarial parasites in the blood and abnormalities in hepatic functions. The degree of anaemia present is related to the severity of the infection. Abnormal bleeding (nosebleeds, oozing of blood from venipuncture sites, passage of blood in the stool) may occur as a result of either decreased production of clotting factors by a damaged liver or disseminated intravascular coagulation.

Blood precautions are used during the patient's hospitalization.

Prevention and Patient Education

The essence of malaria control is the eradication of malaria as an endemic disease. In several areas of the world, this goal has been achieved. To escape malaria, one must avoid *Anopheles* mosquitoes that have fed on the blood of patients with malaria about three weeks previously. This includes remaining in well-screened areas, using mosquito nets and wearing clothes that cover most of the body. The application of mosquito repellent to exposed skin decreases the chance of being bitten. Travellers should be asked to reduce contact with mosquitoes between dusk and dawn since malarial transmission occurs primarily in these hours due to nocturnal feeding habits.

People planning to visit endemic malarious areas are advised to seek the most recent prophylactic recommendations, usually chloroquine and proguanil, which is taken before entry into the area and continued for a specific time after returning home. Recommendations and guidelines for those travelling abroad vary each year are given in appropriate leaflets produced by the Department of Health, available from local offices and health centres. Immigrants to Britain from endemic areas may lose their natural immunity and can develop severe malaria on re-entering the area unless effective prophylactic treatment has been taken.

The traveller is also advised that, regardless of the prophylactic regime used, it is still possible to contract malaria. The onset of fever, chills and headache should not be attributed to 'flu', and medical advice should be sought *promptly*. Travellers to malarious areas should not donate blood for up to three years.

Giardiasis

Giardiasis is a protozoan infection of the small intestine caused by the flagellate *Giardia lamblia*. This waterborne parasite is found in two forms: cysts and trophozoites. Transmission depends on the ingestion of cysts excreted in the faeces of a human or animal host. It is transmitted to humans by inadequately treated water, animal excretion into water and person-to-person spread.

Giardiasis is one of the causes of traveller's diarrhoea in many countries, both in underdeveloped and modern, usually associated with inadequately treated drinking water. Person-to-person transmission occurs by hand-to-mouth transfer of cysts from the faeces of an infected person, and is responsible for outbreaks in day care centres, nursing homes and other institutions. The incidence is high among homosexual men, particularly those practising oral–anal sexual activity.

Clinical Features

Patients with a mild infection report only a constant bloated feeling or abdominal pain without diarrhoea. Other patients have a persistent diarrhoea with loose, watery, foul-smelling stools, abdominal cramping and weight loss. Malabsorption of fats and fat-soluble vitamins may occur. The disease is usually self-limiting, lasting two to six weeks, but may recur intermittently and persist for months or even years.

Giardiasis is diagnosed by finding *Giardia lamblia* in faeces.

Management

The treatment of giardiasis for adults is either mepacrine or metronidazole.

Prevention and Patient Education. Raw, unpeeled fruits and vegetables should not be eaten in areas where giardiasis is endemic, and untreated water should be boiled. Control of person-to-person transmission requires personal cleanliness, careful hand washing and sanitary disposal of faeces.

Amoebiasis (Amoebic Dysentery)

Amoebae are protozoa, larger than leucocytes, that move by amoeboid action. Only a few amoeba infect humans. One of the most important of these is *Entamoeba histolytica*, the cause of amoebic dysentery. These amoebae survive outside the human body in resistant encysted forms.

Amoebiasis is a worldwide parasite of the large intestine. It is acquired through the ingestion of the cyst stage of *E. histolytica* in food or water contaminated by infected food handlers, who may be symptomless or convalescent carriers. The infection may also be transmitted through oral–anal or oral–genital sexual contact (both heterosexual and homosexual).

It is estimated that 10 per cent of the world's population is infected and in some tropical countries the infection rate may exceed 30 per cent. People at risk in this country are immigrants and visitors from developing countries, travellers returning from these areas and sexually active male homosexuals.

Altered Physiology

The amoebae burrow their way into the intestinal mucosa, where they feed mainly on bacteria. Pus pockets may form, with only a small orifice opening into the bowel from which numerous burrows extend for considerable distances in all directions under the mucous membrane. Here the amoebae live. Abscesses form in the mucous membrane, and eventually slough off, exposing an underlying ulcer that may enlarge to sizes of 1 to 2 cm in diameter. The large bowel may be so covered by such ulcers

that very little normal mucous membrane is left. Usually, the floor of these ulcers is the muscle wall of the bowel, but they may perforate its entire wall and cause fatal peritonitis.

In the small intestine, the organism may erode intestinal mucosa, invade the bloodstream and gain access to the liver through the portal vein.

Clinical Features and Course

The majority of infected individuals are asymptomatic. The clinical features depend on the site of the involvement. Amoebiasis may present as an intestinal or extraintestinal disease. When the amoebae become invasive in the intestines, the chief symptom is diarrhoea, with abdominal cramping and pain. Diarrhoea may be mild, with loose stools, or there may be severe dysentery, with stools containing considerable amounts of blood, exudate and mucus, the latter swarming with amoebae. People with chronic disease usually have associated weight loss and anaemia. Amoebiasis may mimic irritable bowel syndrome. The illness may present as appendicitis, abdominal mass or partial intestinal obstruction.

The two important features of this disease are its chronicity (one attack of acute dysentery following another, separated by periods of constipation that last for months) and the tendency of the infection to cause liver abscess, as a result of dissemination to the liver by way of the portal vein. Complications include peritonitis, abscess formation, haemorrhage and extraintestinal disease.

Diagnosis

The diagnosis is made by finding trophozoites or cysts in a freshly purged stool specimen, in a nonpurged, warm stool specimen or in proctosigmoidoscopic material or abscess contents. (Moving trophozoites disintegrate at room temperature, and false-negative tests can occur.) There are serological tests (indirect haemagglutination test and indirect fluorescent antibody test) to diagnose amoebiasis.

Management

The objectives of treatment are to eradicate the organism, to give symptomatic relief, to prevent spread of amoebae to other tissues and to replace fluid and electrolytes.

There is uncertainty about what constitutes the best treatment, and a significant number of patients require multiple courses of therapy. Usually two drugs are used: one to rid the intestines of the trophozoites and the other to dispose of the cysts. Metronidazole followed by diloxanide fluorate (active against the cyst form) is a standard form of treatment. Alternative therapies are available. Excretion precautions are observed.

To support the patient's general condition, intravenous infusions are given as required to correct fluid and electrolyte imbalance resulting from severe diarrhoea. If diarrhoea is acute, the patient remains on bedrest and is offered low-residue, bland foods. Follow-up study of the stools are necessary, since relapses are common.

Control and Patient Education

Transmission of *E. histolytica* is principally by ingestion of contaminated food or water. Methods of control include sanitary disposal of human faeces, protection of the public water supply, raising and preparing food free of contamination and an ongoing programme of health education, including emphasis on meticulous handwashing after defecation and before preparing and eating food. In areas of high prevalence, fresh fruits and vegetables that cannot be peeled may be a source of contamination. Contacts of recently diagnosed patients should be examined. Patients should abstain from oroanal and orogenital sexual practices while they are under treatment. Sexual partners of infected patients should have a stool examination.

Amoebic Liver Abscess

Amoebic liver abscess represents the most common extraintestinal complication of amoebiasis. It occurs when the amoebae invade the liver tissue and form abscesses that increase in size, progressively damaging the liver.

In most patients, the right lobe of the liver is involved, and the abscess may be single or multiple. The major complaints are pain in the right upper abdomen (caused by the liver's rapid enlargement and stretching of its capsule), right upper chest pain (due to the liver's enlarging in an upward direction), fever, anorexia and loss of weight. Physical examination reveals enlarged, tender liver (due to hepatic abscess) and auscultatory abnormalities of the right lung field (from direct extension or rupture of a contiguous liver abscess). If the abscess is on the left lobe of the liver, a tender epigastric pain is noted. There is also sweating, weight loss and pallor. A computerized tomographic scan of the liver suggests the diagnosis and is useful in identifying the site, size and number of lesions as well as in following the resolution of the abscess. Ultrasonography is used. Immunological techniques, mainly serological methods, are also used in diagnosis. One point to be emphasized is that not infrequently the abscesses are found unexpectedly in patients who have had few or no symptoms suggesting amoebiasis.

Usually, the patient responds promptly to amoebicidal therapy. Metronidazole has generally been successful, and it may be combined with other drugs. Needle drainage of the abscess may also be necessary if there is concern that the abscess may rupture and cause peritonitis, or after rupture to reduce spread of infection, or when clinical illness persists after adequate drug therapy. The supportive treatment is that outlined for amoebiasis.

SYSTEMIC MYCOTIC INFECTIONS (FUNGAL INFECTIONS)

Fungi are primitive organisms that take their nourishment from living plants and animals and decaying organic material. Fungi have the ability to exist as yeasts or as moulds, and may alternate between the yeast and mould form. The fungi present difficult problems in control because they are so widespread in nature—in soil, decaying vegetation and bird excreta. Although there are thousands of known species of fungi, 100 or more species are generally recognized as being pathogenic to humans. The three main types of mycoses (fungal infections), as determined by the tissue level at which the fungus settles, are as follows:

1. Systemic or deep mycoses involving primarily internal orgnas, with a primary focus in the lungs.
2. Subcutaneous mycoses that involve the skin, subcutaneous tissue and sometimes the bone.
3. Superficial or cutaneous mycoses that grow in the outer layer of skin (epidermis), the hair and the nails.

Systemic infections are usually acquired by accidental inhalation (spores carried on wind currents), occasionally by traumatic implantation (from contaminated soil or plant materials) or by the pathological takeover of a normal inhabitant when the resistance of the host is lowered. The responsible fungi commonly spread to other organs by either the haematogenous or, less frequently, the lymphatic route. These infections are not transmitted from person to person.

People at Risk

The systemic mycoses are occurring more frequently, since they are more common in patients with impaired immunological resistance and in some patients receiving immunosuppressive agents (steroids, chemotherapy for cancer). Many patients who are receiving such treatment, or who are debilitated or severely ill and have reduced defences, become prey to invasion by fungi that they could ordinarily withstand.

In addition to those receiving immunosuppressive agents, patients at risk for invasive fungal infections are those with certain immunological deficiencies, those with advanced malignancies, kidney or other organ-transplant patients, open heart surgery patients, severely burned patients, patients receiving prolonged intravenous feeds and those with renal failure and diabetes.

Histoplasmosis

Histoplasmosis is a chronic systemic fungus infection caused by a spore-bearing mould, *Histoplasma capsulatum*. This highly infectious mycosis is transmitted by airbone dust that contains *H. capsulatum* spores. Partially decayed droppings of pigeons, chickens, bats and birds offer an excellent medium for the growth of this fungus.

Clinical Features

The patient may have no detectable illness or may have signs and symptoms of a mild respiratory disease: fever, malaise, headache, myalgias and anorexia. If the illness is more severe, signs and symptoms will resemble those of pulmonary tuberculosis; fever, cough, dyspnoea, anorexia and loss of weight and strength. Fungal infections mimic symptoms of other diseases, and the patient may present findings of malignant lymphoma, including anaemia, thrombocytopenia, splenomegaly and hepatomegaly.

Management

Most patients do not require treatment, since a mild self-limiting course is the rule. Patients are followed clinically and radiologically to determine the course of the disease. Traditionally, amphotericin B has been the mainstay of treatment for disseminated or acute pulmonary disease, since it has a wide spectrum of activity against fungal infections. It is given intravenously and is reserved for serious infections, because this agent has significant toxicity. Severe toxic reactions include nausea, vomiting, chills, fever, diarrhoea, hypokalaemia and phlebitis.

Ketaconazole is an antifungal agent that is absorbed orally and is effective against the aetiological agents of systemic mycoses. It has been associated with hepatic toxicity, requiring close patient monitoring.

Patient Education

The patient should avoid stirring up dust by raking and sweeping around bird roosting sites. Exposure to dust in a contained, enclosed environment (chicken coop) should be minimized. The patient should be advised that spraying the area with water will reduce dust.

HELMINTHIC INFESTATIONS

Major helminthic (worms) infections are among the most prevalent of the human infectious diseases. They are global in distribution, and have a profound effect on the nutritional status of humans and animals, and on the physical and mental development of children. There are three major groups of helminths that are intestinal parasites in humans: the nematodes (roundworms), the cestodes (tapeworms) and the trematodes (flukes).

Ascariasis (Roundworm Infestation)

Ascariasis is an infection by the nematode *Ascaris lumbricoides* (intestinal roundworm). This is the most common worm parasitizing the human intestine, with an estimated one billion infestations worldwide. The disease is usually found in overcrowded areas with poor sanitation. Contamination of soil by human faeces is a factor in its spread. Indiscriminate defaecation in the fields, streets and doorways provide a major source of infective eggs. Humans are infected by ingestion of the eggs in contaminated raw vegetables and drinking water.

Geographical Distribution

Ascariasis is endemic in many regions of South East Europe, Africa, Asia and Central and South America, but it may occur in any country, either in the indigenous population or in travellers.

Life Cycle and Clinical Features

The eggs are swallowed and pass into the intestine, where they hatch as larvae. The larvae enter the bloodstream and pass through the pulmonary circulation, migrate through the lungs and return to the gastrointestinal tract, where they grow, mature and mate. Large numbers of worms migrate into various organs of the body and cause obstruction to the trachea, bronchi, bile duct, appendix and pancreatic duct. Masses of worms in the intestine cause gastrointestinal discomfort, severe abdominal pain and vomiting. Fever, chills, dyspnoea, cough and pneumonia may develop from invasion of the lungs by large numbers of larvae. Adult worms may migrate into the ampullae of Vater and then to the pancreatic or biliary ducts, causing acute and agonizing pain.

Ascariasis is diagnosed by detecting ova or worms in the faeces.

Management

Mebendazole given twice daily for three days is currently the drug of choice. Piperazine and pyrantel are also effective drugs. No isolation or precautions are required.

Prevention

Preventive measures include providing adequate toilet facilities and teaching the importance of personal hygiene. All patients with the infestation should be treated.

Hookworm Infection

Hookworm infection is the result of infestation of the small intestine by one or two quite similar roundworms about 1.2 cm long. Two species are parasitic in the human intestinal tract: *Necator americanus* and *Ancylostoma duodenale*. The infection is usually acquired by walking barefoot, whereby infected larvae of the worms penetrate the skin. Approximately 700 to 900 million people are infected with hookworm.

Geographical Distribution

It is found mainly in tropical and subtropical regions, notably Asia, the Mediterranean area, South America, Africa and in most of the western hemisphere.

Life Cycle and Clinical Features

The embryos of this worm, hatched from eggs passed in human faeces onto the ground, live in dirt, sand and clay, and easily infest humans. They enter the mouth when food is eaten with dirty hands, or they bore through the skin of bare feet, causing itching and burning followed by vesicular eruption (ground itch). Having gained access to the blood of lymph vessels, they are carried by the bloodstream to the lungs, and migrate from the pulmonary capillaries into alveolar sacs. The larvae migrate up the bronchi and trachea, pass over the epiglottis and down the oesophagus, and into the bowel. The worms attach themselves to the intestinal mucosa and suck the blood of the host. The effect of the blood-sucking and haemorrhages at the attachment sites is iron-deficiency anaemia.

A patient with a heavy infection and with inadequate dietary iron may develop profound anaemia and will present with lassitude, dyspnoea, anorexia and pedal oedema. Severe anaemia may cause cardiac symptoms. Maturation of the worms in the intestine may cause diarrhoea and gastrointestinal symptoms. A dry cough and dyspnoea develop when the larvae rupture through the capillary bed and are spread to the bronchial tree.

Management

Mebendazole or pyrantel are both effective for hookworm disease. The patient should be placed on a nutritious diet, since the hookworm disease occurs in people suffering from malnutrition. Protein and iron supplementation is administered to aid in the correction of anaemia.

Prevention

The prevention of hookworm disease depends on sanitary disposal of human excreta, proper handwashing and the wearing of shoes. Human excrement and sewage effluent should not be used for fertilizer.

Taeniasis (Tapeworm Infestation)

Taeniasis is caused by the beef tapeworm *Taenia saginata*, or by the pork tapeworm, *Taenia solium*. Asymptomatic infestation is common, although infestation by *Taenia solium* is potentially far more serious than that by *Taenia saginata*, because of the possible complication of human cysticercosis.

Geographical Distribution

Taenia saginata is widespread in most cattle-breeding countries but especially in Africa and the middle East. *Taenia solium* occurs in areas of Latin America, Southern Africa, India, South East Asia and Eastern Europe where sanitation is inadequate, pigs have access to human faeces and pork is eaten uncooked. *Taenia solium* is virtually never acquired in Britain.

Life Cycle and Clinical Features

Taenia saginata—Humans, the definitive hosts of the worm, eat undercooked beef containing the cysticerus (larval stage). An adult worm develops in the person's intestine and the sexual phase of the life cycle is completed there; ova in the faeces of humans are swallowed by the cow, which is the worm's intermediate host. The asexual multiplication phase of the life cycle is completed in the cow and cysticerus is found in its flesh.

Taenia solium—Humans become infected by eating undercooked pork containing the cysticerus stage. The life cycle is usually divided between the human as the definitive host, with the adult worm in the intestine, and the pig as the intermediate host. Patients with taeniasis may be asymptomatic, or have mild abdominal discomfort, diarrhoea or vomiting. The passing of a mature, wriggling segment through the anus into the toilet may be the main complaint. A complication of infection by *Taenia solium* is that the cysticercosis stage can develop in humans. Human cysticercosis can result in cysts in the brain, causing epilepsy or fatal encephalopathy, and cysts in muscle, eye, liver, lung or other sites.

Management

Treatment consists of niclosamide, administered with a glass of water after a light breakfast. Thirty minutes later 15 ml magnesium sulphate mixture is given as a purge.

Prevention

Inspection of pork and beef and adequate cooking.

SEXUALLY TRANSMITTED DISEASES

Sexually transmitted diseases (STDs) are diseases acquired through sexual activity with an infected person. These diseases include the traditional 'venereal diseases' (gonorrhoea, syphilis, chancroid, lymphogranuloma inguinale and lymphogranuloma venereum) and a complex array of infections and clinical syndromes that make up a new generation of sexually transmitted diseases, including the acquired immunodeficiency syndrome (AIDS). Because of its importance, AIDS is discussed separately in Chapter 26.

The term sexually transmitted disease has replaced venereal disease as the term of choice. Sexually transmitted diseases are endemic in most parts of the world. Portals of entry of sexually transmitted disease microorganisms and sites of infection include the skin and mucosal linings of the urethra, cervix, vagina, rectum and oropharynx. The most important sexually transmitted diseases are listed in Table 38.3. Those at high risk for acquiring sexually transmitted diseases are homosexual or bisexual men, sexual partners of infected people and those with multiple sex partners. In the developing coun-

Table 38.3 *Most important sexually transmitted pathogens and the diseases they cause*

Pathogens	Disease or syndrome
Bacterial agents	
Neisseria gonorrhoeae	Urethritis, epididymitis, cervicitis, proctitis, pharyngitis, conjunctivitis, endometritis, perihepatitis, bartholinitis, amniotic infection syndrome, disseminated gonococcal infection, premature delivery and premature rupture of membranes, salpingitis and related sequelae (infertility, ectopic pregnancy, recurrent salpingitis)
Chlamydia trachomatis	Urethritis, epididymitis, cervicitis, proctitis, salpingitis, inclusion conjunctivitis, infant pneumonia, otitis media, trachoma, lymphogranuloma venereum, perihepatitis, bartholinitis, Reiter's disease, fetal and neonatal mortality
Mycoplasma hominis	Postpartum fever, salpingitis
Ureaplasma urealyticum	Urethritis, chorioamniotis, low birth-weight
Treponema pallidum	Syphilis
Gardnerella haemophilus vaginalis	Vaginitis
Haemophilus ducreyi	Chancroid
Calymmatobacterium granulomatis	Donovanosis (granuloma inguinale)
Shigella, Campylobacter sp.	Enterocolitis (among homosexual men)
Group B ß-haemolytic streptococcus	Neonatal sepsis, neonatal meningitis
Viral agents	
Herpes simplex virus	Primary and recurrent genital herpes, aseptic meningitis, neonatal herpes with associated mortality or neurological sequelae, carcinoma of the uterine cervix, spontaneous abortion and premature delivery
Hepatitis B virus	Acute, chronic and fulminant hepatitis, with associated immune complex phenomena
Cytomegalovirus	Congenital infection: gross birth defects and infant mortality, cognitive impairment (e.g. mental retardation, sensorineural deafness), heterophile-negative infectious mononucleosis, cervicitis, protean manifestations in the immunosuppressed host
Genital wart (papilloma) virus	Condyloma acuminata, laryngeal papilloma in infants, cervical dysplasia
Molluscum contagiosum viruses	Genital molluscum contagiosum
Human T-lymphotropic viruses	Acquired immunodeficiency syndrome (AIDS)
Protozoan agents	
Trichomonas vaginalis	Vaginitis, urethritis, balanitis
Entamoeba histolytica	Amoebiasis (sexually transmitted especially among homosexual men)
Giardia lamblia	Giardiasis (sexually transmitted especially among homosexual men)
Fungal agents	
Candida albicans	Vulvovaginitis, balanitis
Ectoparasites	
Phthirus pubis	Pubic louse infestation ('crabs')
Sarcoptes scabiei	Scabies

(Reproduced with permission from the Annual Review of Public Health, *Vol. 6 (1985). Copyright by Annual Reviews, Inc.)*

tries, prostitution is the major reservoir for syphilis, chancroid and gonorrhoea.

Problems and Risk Factors

The problems and complications of sexually transmitted diseases are challenging. They frequently exist without causing symptoms (particularly among women). A high incidence of co-infection places individuals with one sexually transmitted disease at risk for concurrent infection (e.g., gonorrhoea together with chlamydial infection). Although some of the organisms that cause sexually transmitted diseases are sensitive to antimicrobial therapy, other pathogens demonstrate resistance to treatment. Another problem is that certain drugs used in treatment predispose the patient to superinfection. Diseases that occur in the genital mucosal areas may also occur in nongenital mucosal areas that are used for sexual activity (e.g., the pharynx).

Management of Sexually Transmitted Diseases

Primary prevention is the most important aspect of managing sexually transmitted diseases because some of these diseases are not readily cured by antibiotics. Infected people must be promptly identified and given effective available treatment.

Since no antimicrobial regime is 100 per cent effective, all patients require re-examination and retesting after treatment. Follow-up times vary with the disease.

At present, hepatitis B is the only sexually transmitted disease for which an effective vaccine is available.

Preventing the Spread of Sexually Transmitted Diseases

Arrangements for attending local genito-urinary clinics should be well advertised both within and outside the hospital, and patients encouraged to use the expertise and confidentiality this service provides. Most patients require counselling about the transmission and features of these diseases as well as advice about treatment, follow-up, and the importance of referring sexual contacts for treatment. For this reason, ideally, patients should be seen in a genito-urinary clinic, however, emergency departments, outpatients clinics, college health services and women's health facilities should be equipped to diagnose and treat sexually transmitted diseases in order to reduce their spread.

Women

Women need to be informed that untreated male partners and multiple sex partners increase their risk of developing these infections. The risk of infertility is greater with each subsequent recurrence of pelvic inflammatory disease.

The use of barrier methods of contraception (condom, diaphragm with spermicide) reduces the risk of acquiring certain infections.

Homosexual Men

Anal and oral intercourse and other sexual practices that involve direct contact with faeces increase the risk of sexual transmission of enteric infections. The decision of some male homosexuals to conceal their sexual preference has made it difficult to interpret transmission of disease by tracing and treating sexual contacts. Some male homosexuals do not seek health care because of anxiety and societal attitudes. However, since the AIDS crisis, the male homosexual community is showing a growing awareness of these problems and is promoting health education and disease detection to reduce the risk of infection.

Adolescents

Adolescents are not always aware of the cause-and-effect relationship between sexual intercourse and sexually transmitted diseases. In addition, denial and risk-taking behaviours are often characteristic of adolescents. Therefore, health care personnel should make efforts to reinforce and expand the knowledge of adolescents. Programmes designed to help teenagers deal with social and peer pressures may be an alternative approach to prevention of sexually transmitted diseases.

Controlling the spread of a sexually transmitted disease requires considerable patient involvement, education and co-operation. The following are important points to stress:

1. A sexually transmitted disease is acquired by sexual contact (vaginal sexual intercourse, anal intercourse, oral intercourse) and by close and direct contact with an infected person.
2. Anyone who thinks that they may have a sexually transmitted disease or who has been infected should have a regular checkup. Immediate treatment should be sought if symptoms develop.
3. Anyone who is sexually active with a number of sexual partners should have regular checkups.
4. Washing the sex organs (before and after sexual contact) and the use of a condom may give limited protection.
5. Birth control pills and intrauterine devices give no protection against sexually transmitted diseases.
6. Gonorrhoea and syphilis are different diseases, caused by different bacteria; they attack the body in different ways but are spread in the same manner. A person may have both gonorrhoea and syphilis as well as other sexually transmitted diseases at the same time.
7. There appears to be no natural or acquired immunity to gonorrhoea or syphilis. A person can get gonorrhoea and syphilis again and again.

8. A pregnant woman with syphilis may pass the infection to her unborn child. A pregnant woman with gonorrhoea may pass it to her baby during birth.
9. Bacteria from gonorrhoea may enter the bloodstream and affect joints, joint linings, heart valves and so on.

BACTERIAL SEXUALLY TRANSMITTED DISEASES

Gonorrhoea

Gonorrhoea is an infection involving the mucosal surface of the genitourinary tract, rectum and pharynx. It is caused by the gonococcus *Neisseria gonorrhoeae* and is an infectious disease transmitted sexually (the exception being gonococcal ophthalmia of the newborn). It may be acquired through sexual intercourse and by orogenital or anogenital contacts between members of the opposite sex as well as members of the same sex.

The highest rate of gonorrhoea occurs among people between the ages of 15 and 24.

Altered Physiology

The gonococcus causes a surface infection, ascending, in almost all cases, by way of the lower genital tract. The primary infection takes place in or near the urethra in males, and in the cervix, urethra or rectum in females. If drainage is good, the infection subsides spontaneously and clears in the course of a few days or weeks. However, infection of the prostatic urethra in the male and also of the female urethral and vaginal glands predisposes to chronic infection, and occasionally very serious sequelae. Females are apt to contract secondarily a mixed infection of the endometrium and, thereafter, of the uterine tubes, constituting pelvic infection, with resultant pelvic peritonitis. The upward spread of the infection into the reproductive tract is precipitated by such factors as menstruation, douches and the trauma associated with sexual intercourse or instrumentation.

Clinical Features and Complications

After an incubation period of two to seven days, most men develop dysuria or a urethral discharge, which may be a scanty, clear fluid or a purulent, copious drainage. The infection may extend to the prostrate, seminal vesicles and epididymis, causing prostatitis, inguinal lymphadenitis, pelvic pain and fever. Postgonococcal urethritis develops in one fourth to one third of men treated for gonorrhoea. Many cases of nongonococcal urethritis are secondary to chlamydial infections. A particularly serious problem is men with asymptomatic infection ('silent clap') who are carriers of gonorrhoea. These are often not discovered by the usual gonorrhoea control measures.

They remain infected, untreated and asymptomatic, and can infect their sexual partners.

In females, the infection is very frequently silent, so that a large percentage of women are asymptomatic and unaware that they are infected. A small number have vaginal discharge, urinary frequency and dysuria. The sites most frequently involved are the urethra and cervix. As the endocervical gonococcal infection spreads upwards into the reproductive tract, it causes pelvic infection (pelvic inflammatory disease), with endometritis, salpingitis or pelvic peritonitis. An estimated 10 to 15 per cent of women infected with the gonococcus develop pelvic infection, as evidenced by abdominal pain, fever and vaginal discharge. There is marked pelvic tenderness on movement of the cervix and uterus during bimanual pelvic examination. Pelvic infection causes adhesions about the pelvic organs and rectum. This is a major direct cause of infertility. It also leads to ectopic pregnancy and chronic pelvic inflammation, the sequelae of which require surgical intervention.

Other Features of Gonorrhoea

Anal features consist of anal itching and irritation (from erythema and oedema of the anal crypts), a sensation of rectal fullness, rectal bleeding or diarrhoea, mucus in the stools and painful defaecation. Oral features may be the result of direct contact of the infecting organisms with the pharynx, or of their transmission to the oral cavity from infection elsewhere in the body. Although the majority of pharyngeal infections are asymptomatic, the following oral features are seen: sore throat; painful, ulcerated inflammation of the lips; reddened, spongy and tender gingivae; reddened, dry tongue; and redness and oedema of the soft palate and uvula. The oropharynx may be covered in vesicles.

Systemic features may become apparent, since secondary foci of infection develop in any organ system, causing disseminated gonococcal infection (gonococcal bacteraemia). Disseminated gonococcal infection occurs when the gonococci invade the bloodstream from one of the primary sites of infection. The patient presents with tenosynovitis of the small joints and haemorrhagic skin rash. Two or three weeks later, untreated patients will develop septic arthritis, exhibiting hot, red and swollen joints.

Diagnosis

There are a variety of ways of identifying gonorrhoea through laboratory diagnosis. The gram-negative intracellular diplococci may be found in smears or through direct fluorescent antibody tests, or may be cultured on selective media. The pharyngeal and anal sites should be cultured in people who engage in oral or rectal sex; these cultures should be inoculated onto separate plates. In the male, specimens may be obtained from the urethra, anal canal and pharynx depending on the patient's sexual history and orientation. In the female, cultures are collected from the endocervix and anal canal and are inoculated onto separate plates. Disposable gloves should be worn when obtaining these cultures. As a rule, lubricating jellies are not used for the vaginal examination because they may contain substances that inhibit growth or kill some pathogens. Water is used as a lubricant instead.

The *Neisseria* gonococci are very susceptible to environmental changes, and the local laboratory policy for collection and transportation of these specimens must be followed strictly. Direct culture onto gonococcal-selective medium gives the best results. An alternative is to use charcoal-impregnated swabs broken off into Stuarts transport medium.

Treatment

Penicillin is active against the majority of gonococci seen in Britain, and most uncomplicated infections can be treated by a single intramuscular injection of procaine penicillin when given in conjunction with oral probenecid to delay excretion of the drug. A number of regimes are available to treat penicillin-resistant strains, or more severe forms of the infection. It is imperative that follow-up cultures are obtained from infected sites three to seven days after the treatment is completed since no therapy is completely effective.

Nursing Care

Infected discharge from a patient with gonorrhoea can be spread to the eyes from contaminated fingers. When examining a patient or coming into contact with vaginal or urethral discharge, the nurse should wear gloves, avoid touching the face and practise careful handwashing.

Syphilis

Syphilis is an acute and chronic multisystem disease caused by *Treponema pallidum* (a spirochaete). It is acquired through sexual contact or may be congenital in origin.

T. pallidum is a threadlike, actively motile spirochete 6 to 20 μm long that always produces it effects locally—never at a distance, as through toxins. It is killed quickly by a few minutes' exposure to drying, heat or air.

A chancre (primary sore) in syphilis appears at the site (or sites) where the organisms entered the body. Because these open, untreated lesions contain spirochaetes, the disease can be transmitted though contact with the lesions. In the pregnant woman, the fetus is infected from the mother by way of the placenta. The vast majority of cases are contracted through sexual activity; the danger of transmission is greatest in the early stage of syphilis.

Epidemiology

People known to have syphilis are interviewed and asked to identify their sexual contacts so that these contacts can be examined and treated within a minimum time period.

Each person with syphilis is a potential source for a small outbreak. Studies indicate that each infected individual has an average of three different sexual contacts who are at risk of contracting syphilis. Case reporting of early infectious syphilis is required.

Clinical Features

Primary Stage

The incubation period is 10 to 90 days, with an average of 21 days. During the primary (early) stage, which is also the most infectious stage, the chancre (primary sore) appears at the site or sites where organisms entered the body: genitalia, anus, rectum, lips, oral cavity, breasts or fingers (Figure 38.1). The sites are generally related to the pattern of sexual activity. The typical chancre is an indurated, painless nodule that breaks down, forming a shallow ulcer. The lymph nodes draining the ulcer become enlarged, firm and nontender. Untreated, the primary lesions heal in a few weeks.

Secondary Stage (Stage of Systemic Involvement)

Within a few weeks or months, the organisms have begun to spread throughout the body and a variable systemic illness develops, characterized by low-grade fever, malaise, sore throat, headache, lymphadenopathy, arthralgia and skin or mucosal rash.

The skin manifestations, which prompt many patients to seek health care, may stimulate practically every known skin disease. Typically, the rash is macular (non-elevated discolouration) or maculopapular (elevated lesions), but can become pustular. It can be anywhere on the body, but often the palms and the soles are involved. If untreated, the rash gradually fades. At the same time the hair may drop out, sometimes in patches, giving the scalp a moth-eaten appearance.

The lesions that appear on the mucous membrane of the mouth and tongue are glistening, slightly elevated, flat, circumscribed patches that are usually covered with a yellowish exudate. These so-called mucous patches contain large numbers of spirochaetes. The lesions that develop where the skin presses up against itself (about the vagina and anus) take the form of flat, wartlike plaques (condylomata); these plaques contain large numbers of spirochaetes and are therefore capable of transmitting infection.

Late Syphilis

After the second stage, there is a period of latency in which the patient shows no signs or symptoms of syphilis. This stage may last for months or years, and many patients have no further trouble, with or without treatment. Late

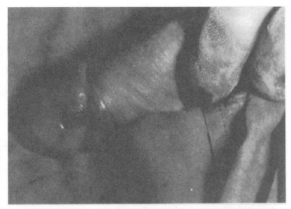

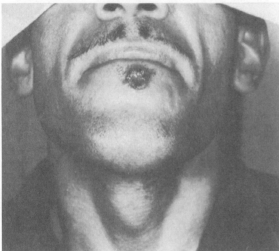

Figure 38.1 (Top) Syphilitic chancre on the external surface of the prepuce. (Bottom) Primary syphilis: typical Hunterian chancre on lower lip. (Top: Elliott, H. and Rhyz, K. *Venereal Diseases: Treatment and Nursing*, Ballière Tindall, Eastbourne. Bottom: *Syphilis—A Synopsis*, US Department of Health, Education and Welfare, Public Health Service.)

syphilis is a slowly progressive inflammatory disease that may involve almost any organ. In cardiovascular syphilis, the inflammatory reaction may involve the heart and great vessels, with lesions occurring in the aorta, pulmonary artery or great vessels arising from the aorta, resulting in aeortitis and aneurysms. In neurosyphilis, disabling lesions occur in the central nervous system, giving rise to a variety of neurological symptoms. Destructive noninfectious granulomatous lesions of the skin, viscera, bone and mucosal surfaces can occur, which may impair health and shorten life.

Diagnosis

Since syphilis is an imitator of many diseases, the clinical history and laboratory evaluation are very important. A number of serological tests are used in the diagnosis and management of syphilis; three are nontreponemal and two are treponemal.

- Nontreponemal or reagin tests measure antibodies formed in response to products of tissue destruction (called reagin) in the serum of infected patients. The most widely used are the Venereal Disease Research Laboratory (VDRL) slide flocculation test, the rapid plasma reagin circle card test (RPR-CT) and the automated reagin test (ART). These tests are reliable, simple to perform and inexpensive.
- Treponemal tests are tests to measure the specific antibodies to *T. pallidum*. These tests are recommended for patients who have negative reagin tests and atypical signs of primary or secondary syphilis and for diagnosis of late syphilis. The treponemal tests are the fluorescent treponemal antibody absorption test (FTA-ABS) and the microhaemagglutination test (MHA-TP).

Management

Recommendations for treatment are updated on a regular basis. The current treatment of all stages of syphilis is administration of antibiotics. Procaine penicillin, 6,000,000 units intramuscularly daily for 10 days, is currently the drug of choice. If penicillin allergy is present, tetracycline or erythromycin can be given instead, 500 mg six-hourly orally for two weeks.

Although therapy is recommended for established cardiovascular syphilis, antibiotics may not reverse the pathology (loss of elastic tissue in aortic wall) associated with this disease.

The Jarisch-Herxheimer reaction is a reaction appearing within hours after therapy is initiated for syphilis, particularly in the secondary stage. It consists of transient fever and influenza-like symptoms of malaise, chills, headache and myalgia that subside within 24 hours. The reaction is thought to be due to the sudden release of large amounts of treponemal antigen with subsequent antigen–antibody reaction in the patient. It is managed with bedrest, aspirin and reassurance.

Nursing Care

Chancres contain large numbers of spirochaetes and are contagious through direct contact. Body discharge precautions should be employed. The patient treated with penicillin is monitored for 30 minutes after the injection to watch for a possible reaction. The following are important preventive and patient education factors:

- Patients exposed to infectious syphilis within the preceding three months should be treated as for early syphilis.

- All patients with early syphilis should return for repeat follow-up testing. Follow-up should include evaluation and treatment of sexual partners. Patients with syphilis of more than one year's duration should, in addition, have a serological test 24 months after treatment.
- The nurse should assure the patient infected with primary syphilis that, with proper treatment and follow-up, the chancre will disappear (within a week or two), and blood tests should (but not always) become nonreactive within a year. Those with secondary syphilis will see the rapid disappearance of their rash, and blood tests will become nonreactive within two years.
- The nurse should advise the patient to refrain from sexual contact with previous partners not undergoing treatment.
- A programme of sex education and epidemiological screening should be ongoing. Mass screening of special groups with a known high incidence of sexually transmitted diseases should be conducted.

Chlamydial Infections

Genital chlamydial infections caused by *Chlamydia trachomatis* are now recognized as the most prevalent of all sexually transmitted diseases seen in the United Kingdom. These infections cause inflammation of the urethra and epididymis in men, and inflammation of the cervix with a mucopurulent discharge and an alarming increase in pelvic infections in women. These complications contribute significantly to the increase in the number of women who experience ectopic pregnancies. Chlamydial infections have been linked to infertility in both sexes and have been associated with many other health care problems.

VIRAL SEXUALLY TRANSMITTED DISEASES

Genital Herpes Infections

Genital herpes is among the most common and psychologically distressing of the sexually transmitted diseases. Genital herpes is significant because it can be transmitted to the newborn and because of its possible link to genital cancer.

BIBLIOGRAPHY

Ayliffe, G. A. J., Collins, B. J. and Taylor, L. J. (1989) *Hospital Acquired Infection: Principles and Prevention* (2nd edition), John Wright, Bristol.

Bartlett, C. L. R., Macrae, A. D. and Macfarlane, J. D. (1986) *Legionella Infections*, Edward Arnold, London.

Caddow, P. (ed.) (1989) *Applied Microbiology*, Scutari Press, Oxford.

Communicable Disease Report (1987) Acute meningococcal infections, *Communicable Diseases Report*, Vol. 87/50, p. 1.

Communicable Disease Report (1988) Salmonella enteritidis surveillance, *Communicable Disease Report*, Vol. 88/34, p. 1.

DHSS (1987) *Health Service Catering Hygiene*, HMSO, London.

Harper, D. (1988) Legionnaire's disease outbreaks—the engineering implications, *Journal of Hospital Infection*, Vol. 11 (suppl. A), pp. 201–8.

Howarth, H. (1977) Mouth care procedures for the very ill, *Nursing Times*, Vol. 73, pp. 354–5.

Joint Tuberculosis Committee of British Thoracic Society (1990) Control and Prevention of tuberculosis in Britain: an updated code of practice, *British Medical Journal*, Vol. 300, pp. 995–9.

Lowbury, E. J. L., Ayliffe, G. A. J., Geddes, A. M. *et al.* (1981) *Control of Hospital Infection: A Practical Handbook* (2nd edition), Edward Arnold, London.

FURTHER READING

Acheson, D. (1988) The microbiological contamination of food, *Health Trends*, Vol. 20, pp. 6–9.

Acheson, R. M. and Hagard, S. (1984) *Health, Society and Medicine* (3rd edition), Blackwell Scientific, Oxford.

Adler, M. W. (1984) ABC of sexually transmitted diseases. Urethral discharge: management, *British Medical Journal*, Vol. 287, pp. 1452–3.

Ayton, M. (1982) Microbiolocial investigations, *Nursing*, Vol. 2, No. 8, pp. 226–30.

Bannister, B. (1983) *Infectious Diseases*, Ballière Tindall, Eastbourne.

Blackwell, C. and Weir, D. M. (1981) *Principles of Infection and Immunity in Patient Care*, Churchill Livingstone, Edinburgh.

Bell, D. R. (1985) *Lecture Notes on Tropical Medicine* (2nd edition), Blackwell Scientific, Oxford.

Bell, D. H. and Manson-Bahr, P. E. (1987) *Manson's Tropical Diseases* (19th edition), Ballière Tindall, Eastbourne.

Benenson, A. S. (ed.) (1985) *Control of Communicable Disease in Man* (14th edition), American Public Health Association, New York.

Buxton, P. K. (1988) Bacterial infection, ABC of dermatology, *British Medical Journal*, Vol. 296, pp. 189–92.

Christie, A. B. (1987) *Infectious Diseases: Epidemiology and Clinical Practice* (4th edition), Churchill Livingstone, Edinburgh.

Cole, R. B. (1985) Modern management of pulmonary tuberculosis, *Prescribers Journal*, Vol. 25, pp. 110–18.

Cruickshank, J. G. (1984) The investigation of salmonella outbreaks in hospitals, *Journal of Hospital Infection*, Vol. 5, No. 3, pp. 241–3.

Douglas-Sleigh, J. and Timbury, M. C. (1981) *Notes on Medical Bacteriology*, Churchill Livingstone, London.

Edmundson, R. J. (1980) Tetanus, *British Journal of Hospital Medicine*, Vol. 23, pp. 596–602.

Edelstein, P. H. (1988) Nosocomial Legionnaires' disease: a global perspective, *Journal of Hospital Infection*, Vol. 11 (suppl. A), pp. 182–8.

Editorial (1984) Chlamydia in women: a case for more action? *Lancet*, Vol. i, pp. 892–4.

Emond, R. T. D. (1974) *A Colour Atlas of Infectious Diseases*, Wolfe Medical Books, London.

Galbraith, N. S. and Barrett, N. J. (1987) Changing patterns of communicable disease, *Health and Hygiene*, Vol. 8, pp. 102–17.

Galbraith, N. S., Forbes, P. and Mayton-White, R. T. (1980) Changing patterns of communicable disease in England and Wales, *British Medical Journal*, Vol. 281, pp. 427–30, 489–92, 546–9.

Gorbach, S. L. (1987) Bacterial diarrhoea and its treatment, *Lancet*, Vol. ii, pp. 1378–82.

Hare, M. J. (1986) Pelvic inflammatory disease, *British Medical Journal*, Vol. 293, pp. 1225–8.

Hobbs, B. C. and Roberts, D. (1987) *Food Poisoning and Food Hygiene* (5th edn), Edward Arnold, London.

Leading Article (1980) Isolation of patients with pulmonary tuberculosis, *British Medical Journal*, Vol. 281, p. 962.

Leading Article (1980) BCG in Britain, *British Medical Journal*, Vol. 281, p. 825.

Mandel, B. and Mayon-White, R. T. (1984) *Lecture Notes on Infectious Diseases* (4th edition), Blackwell Scientific, Oxford.

Maunder, J. W. (1981) Parasitology, *Nursing*, Vol. 1, No. 29, pp. 1290–1.

Pembroke, A. and Howard, A. (1978) Fungal infections, *Medicine* (3rd series), Vol. 5, p. 219.

Phillips, R. E. (1988) Malaria treatment and prophylaxis, *Prescribers Journal*, Vol. 28, pp. 72–7.

Phillips, R. E. and Gilles, H. M. (1988) Malaria, *Medicine International*, Vol. 54, pp. 2220–5.

Pilsworth, R. (1990) *The Smallest Enemy*, Grey Seal, London.

Report of Combined Working Party of the Hospital Infection Society of Antimicrobial Chemotherapy (1986) Guidelines for the control of epidemic methicillin-resistant *Staphylococcus aureus*, *Journal of Hospital Infection*, Vol. 7, p. 193.

Report from the PHLS Communicable Disease Surveillance Centre (1987) Botulism, *British Medical Journal*, Vol. 295, pp. 1545–6.

Shanson, D.C. (1989) *Microbiology in Clinical Practice* (2nd edition), John Wright, Bristol.

Smith, A. (ed.) (1985) Infectious disease and human travel, N. S. Galbraith in, *Recent Advances in Community Medicine*, Churchill Livingstone, Edinburgh.

Timbury, M. (1986) *Notes on Medical Virology* (6th edition), Churchill Livingstone, Edinburgh.

Thornbury, G. (1985) TB or not TB, *Nursing Times*, Vol. 81, No. 32, pp. 43–4.

Velimirovic, B. (1984) *Infectious Diseases in Europe*, World Health Organisation, Copenhagen.

Warrell, D. A. (1981) Tetanus, *Medicine International*, Vol. 1, pp. 118–22.

Wisdom, A. (1973) *A Colour Atlas of Venerology*, Wolfe Medical, London.

Worsley, M. (ed.) (1990) *Infection Control—Guidelines for Nursing Care, Infection Control Nurses Association Publication (available from Surgikos Ltd)*.

chapter 39

ASSESSMENT AND CARE OF PATIENTS REQUIRING EMERGENCY NURSING

NURSING IN EMERGENCY CONDITIONS

The term 'emergency management' has traditionally referred to the care given to patients with urgent and critical needs. However, hospital emergency departments and emergency clinics are increasingly being used for non-urgent problems, and the philosophy of emergency care has broadened to include the concept that an emergency is whatever the patient or the patient's family or close friends considers it to be. The staff have an obligation to treat the patient with understanding and to respect the anxiety that undoubtedly is felt.

The Nursing Process in the Emergency Department

The nursing process provides a logical framework for problem solving in the time-limited and pressured environment of the emergency department. The nurse in the emergency department, through specialized education, training and experience, has expertise in assessing and identifying patients' health care problems in crisis situations, establishing priorities, monitoring acutely ill and injured patients, supporting and attending to families, supervising allied health personnel, and teaching patients and their families or friends. The patient's condition may change from minute to minute, and nursing assessment is continuous. Thus the patient's problems change just as rapidly.

PSYCHOLOGICAL MANAGEMENT OF PATIENTS AND FAMILIES IN EMERGENCIES AND CRISIS SITUATIONS

Approach to the Patient

An assessment of the patient's psychological functioning

includes evaluation of emotional expression, degree of anxiety and cognitive functioning (oriented to time, place, person). In addition, a rapid physical examination, focusing on the clinical problem that caused the patient to seek help, is carried out. The patient's problems may include anxiety related to fears about the uncertainty of what is going to happen and feeling unable to cope with the situation. The first major goal is reduction of anxiety, which is a prerequisite to recovering the ability to cope.

Nursing Care

Patients experiencing sudden injury or illness are often overwhelmed by anxiety, because they have not had time to mobilize their resources to adapt to the crisis. They experience real and terrifying fear—of death, mutilation, immobilization and other assaults on their personal identity and body integrity. Those caring for the patient should act confidently and competently to help relieve this excessive anxiety. In addition, explanations should be given on a level that the patient can grasp; an informed patient is able to cope more positively with psychological and physical stress. Frequent human contact helps reduce the panic of the severely injured person, and reassuring words aid in dispelling fear of the unknown. Unconscious patients should be treated as if they were conscious: by touching them, calling them by name and explaining every procedure that is being done.

Approach to the Family/Other Informal Carers

In the admitting area, the family or close friend should be told where the patient is and that expert care is being given. When crises of trauma, severe disfigurement and sudden death are confronted, the other carers may go through several stages, beginning with 'unbearable anxiety' and progressing through denial, remorse, grief, anger and reconciliation.

They, too, need help recognize and talk about their feelings of anxiety. The nursing approach is to tune into their thinking and to deal with reality as gently and as quickly as possible. Prolonged denial should not be encouraged or supported, because they must be prepared for the reality of what has happened (and not for what they wish it could be) and for what may come.

Expressions of remorse and guilt are frequently heard, with the family or informal carers accusing themselves (or each other) of negligence or minor omissions. The nursing approach is to allow expressions of remorse, over and over if need be, until the family members realize that there was probably little that they could have done to prevent the accident or illness.

Expressions of anger are common in crisis situations; they are a way of handling the anxiety. The anger is fre-quently directed at the patient, but it is also often expressed towards the doctor and nurse.

In the event of sudden death in the emergency department, the following guidelines may help the family and the informal carers to cope:

- Take them to a private place.
- Talk to them together, so that they can mourn together.
- Assure them that everything possible was done; inform them of the treatment rendered.
- Allow them to talk about the deceased.
- Encourage them to support each other and to express emotions freely (grief, loss, anger, helplessness, tears, disbelief).
- Encourage them to view the body if they wish to do so.

PRIORITIES OF EMERGENCY MANAGEMENT

When care is being given to a patient in an emergency, many crucial decisions must be made. Such decisions require sound judgement based on an understanding of the condition that produced the emergency and its effect on the person.

The major goals of emergency medical treatment are: (1) to preserve life; (2) to prevent deterioration before more definitive treatment can be given; and (3) to restore the patient to useful living. When the patient is first received into the emergency department, the goal is to determine the extent of injury or illness and to establish priorities for the initiation of treatment.

EMERGENCY RESUSCITATION

The first priority in the treatment of any emergency condition is the establishment of the airway. Complete airway obstruction is readily recognized: the patient suddenly stops breathing, becomes cyanosed and falls unconscious for no apparent reason. Partial airway obstruction which interferes with air flow will produce an apprehensive look, inspiratory and expiratory stridor, laboured use of accessory muscles, flaring nostrils and progressive anxiety, restlessness and confusion. Partial obstruction of the airway can produce progressive hypoxia and hyper-capnoea and can lead to respiratory and cardiac arrest. Endotracheal intubation may be required.

Emergency Endotracheal Intubation

The purpose of endotracheal intubation is to establish and maintain the airway in patients with respiratory insuffi-ciency or hypoxia. Endotracheal intubation is indicated for the following reasons: (1) to establish an airway for patients who cannot be adequately ventilated with an oropharyngeal airway; (2) to bypass an upper airway obstruction; (3) to prevent aspiration; (4) to permit connection of the patient to a resuscitation bag or mechanical ventilator; and (5) to facilitate the removal of tracheobronchial secretions.

Because the procedure requires skill, endotracheal intubation should be done only by those who have had intensive training in which they have practised the technique on a mannequin. It should be done under expert clinical supervision.

Figure 39.1 shows how endotracheal intubation is carried out.

CONTROL OF HAEMORRHAGE

One of the primary causes of shock is the reduction in circulating blood volume. Only a few conditions, such as obstructed airway or a sucking wound of the chest, take precedence over the immediate control of hemorrhage. 'Stop the bleeding' is fundamental to the care and the survival of patients in an emergency or a disaster situation. The nurse should assess the patient for cool, moist skin (resulting from poor peripheral perfusion), falling blood pressure, increasing heart rate and decreasing urine volume. The goals of emergency management are to control the bleeding, maintain an adequately circulating blood volume for tissue oxygenation and prevent shock. Nursing care is carried out interdependently with other members of the health care team.

Management

The nurse should identify the area of haemorrhage, and carry out a rapid physical assessment. Direct, firm pressure should be applied over the bleeding area or the artery involved. Almost all bleeding can be stopped by direct pressure (except when a major artery has been severed). The nurse should apply a firm pressure dressing. The injured part should be elevated to stop venous and capillary bleeding. An injured extremity should be immobilized to control blood loss.

CONTROL OF HYPOVOLAEMIC SHOCK

Shock is a condition in which there is loss of effective circulating blood volume. Inadequate organ and tissue perfusion result, ultimately causing cellular metabolic derangements. In any emergency, it is wise to anticipate shock before it develops. Any injured person should be assessed immediately to determine the presence of shock. Its underlying cause must be discovered (hypovolaemic, cardiogenic, neurogenic or septic shock).

Hypovolaemia is the most common cause of shock. The nurse should look for the following signs and

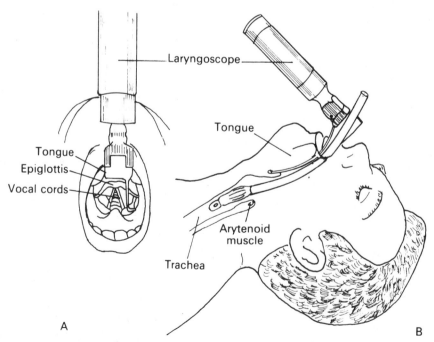

Figure 39.1 Endotracheal intubation. (A) The primary glottic landmarks for tracheal intubation as visualized with proper placement of the laryngoscope. (B) Positioning of the endotube. (Brunner, L. S. and Suddarth, D. S. (1986) *The Lippincott Manual of Nursing Practice* (4th edition), J. B. Lippincott, Philadelphia.)

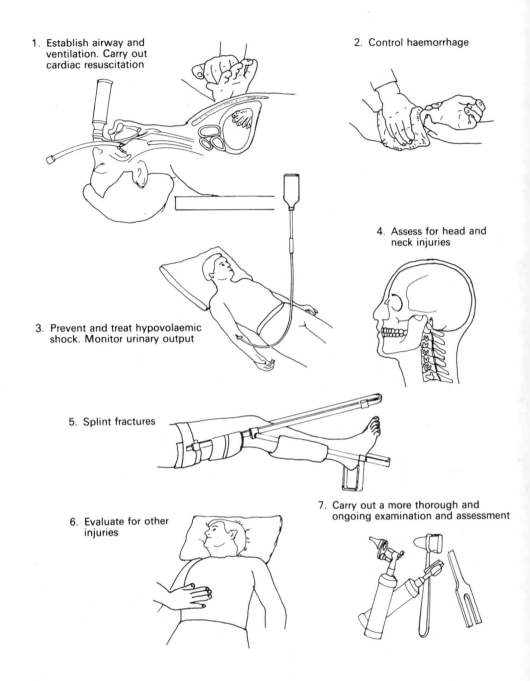

1. Establish airway and ventilation. Carry out cardiac resuscitation

2. Control haemorrhage

3. Prevent and treat hypovolaemic shock. Monitor urinary output

4. Assess for head and neck injuries

5. Splint fractures

6. Evaluate for other injuries

7. Carry out a more thorough and ongoing examination and assessment

Figure 39.2 Management of the patient with multiple injuries.

- Respiratory signs include nasal congestion, itching, sneezing, coughing, possible respiratory distress and tightness of the chest.
- Skin manifestations appear in the form of flushing with a sense of warmth and diffuse erythema. Generalized itching over the entire body indicates that a general systemic reaction is developing. Urticaria may also appear. Cardiovascular manifestations include tachycardia or bradycardia and peripheral vascular collapse as indicated by pallor, falling blood pressure and circulatory failure, leading to coma and death.
- Gastrointestinal discomforts, such as nausea and vomiting, may occur.

POISONING

A poison is any substance which, when ingested, inhaled, absorbed, applied to the skin or produced within the body in relatively small amounts, causes injury to the body by its chemical action. Poisoning from inhalation and ingestion of toxic materials, both accidental and by design, constitutes a major health hazard. The goals of emergency treatment are: (1) to remove or inactivate the poison before it is absorbed; (2) to give supportive care to maintain vital organ systems; (3) to use the specific antidote to neutralize the poison; and (4) to give treatment to hasten the elimination of the absorbed poison.

DRUG ABUSE

Drug abuse is the use of drugs for other than legitimate medical purposes. The clinical features may vary with the drug used, but the underlying principles of management are essentially the same. Drug users tend to take a variety of drugs simultaneously (e.g., alcohol, barbiturates, narcotics and tranquillizers) which may have additive effects. Intravenous drug abusers are at increased risk from acquired immunodeficiency syndrome and infectious hepatitis. The treatment goals for a patient suffering from drug intoxication are to support the respiratory and cardiovascular functions and to enhance the clearance of the agent.

Acute Alcohol Intoxication

Alcohol is a psychotropic drug affecting mood, judgement, behaviour, concentration and consciousness. There is a high prevalence of alcoholism in emergency patients. Because alcoholic patients return frequently to the emergency department, they are often exasperating, taxing the endurance of the health professionals caring for them. Thus, their management requires patience as well as thoughtful and correct treatment. The patient should be assessed for head injury, hypoglycaemia (which mimics intoxication) and other health problems. The patient's problems may include the potential for violence (self-directed or directed at others) related to severe intoxication from alcohol.

Delirium Tremens (Alcoholic Hallucinosis)

Delirium tremens is an acute toxic state which follows a prolonged bout of steady drinking or sudden withdrawal from prolonged intake of alcohol. It may be precipitated by acute injury or infection (pneumonia, pancreatitis, hepatitis).

Patients suspected of delirium tremens will show signs of anxiety, uncontrollable fear, tremor, irritability,

agitation, insomnia and incontinence. They will be talkative and preoccupied, and will experience visual, tactile, olfactory and auditory hallucinations which are frequently terrifying. Usually, all vital signs are elevated in the alcoholic toxic state.

Delirium tremens is life-threatening and carries a high mortality rate. The goals of management are to give proper sedation and support to enable the patient to rest and recover without injury or peripheral vascular collapse.

PSYCHIATRIC EMERGENCIES

A psychiatric emergency is an urgent, serious disturbance of behaviour, affect or thought that makes a person unable to cope with life situations and interpersonal relationships. A patient presenting with a psychiatric emergency may be (1) overactive or violent, (2) underactive or depressed, or (3) suicidal.

The most important concern for the emergency department staff is whether the patient is likely to cause personal harm and/or injury to self or to others. In general, the aim is to try to maintain the patient's self-esteem (and life, if necessary) while carrying out assessment and management. The nurse should determine from the family or another reliable source the events that led up to the crisis; whether the patient has had past mental illness, hospitalizations, injuries or serious illnesses; uses alcohol or drugs; or has experienced crises in interpersonal relationships or intrapsychic conflicts. It should be remembered that abnormal thought and behaviour may be a manifestation of an underlying physical disorder, such as hypoglycaemia, stroke, epilepsy or drug toxicity, including alcohol toxicity.

The nurse should approach the patient with a calm, confident and firm manner; this attitude is therapeutic and should have a calming effect. A psychotropic agent for emergency management of functional psychosis may be prescribed when appropriate. Chlorpromazine or haloperidol act specifically against psychotic symptoms. Usually the patient is admitted to a psychiatric unit or psychiatric outpatient treatment is arranged.

Violent Patients

Violent and aggressive behaviour is usually episodic and is a means of expressing feelings of anger, fear or hopelessness about a situation. The patient may have a history of outbursts of rage, temper tantrums or generally impulsive behaviour. People with a tendency to violence frequently lose control when intoxicated with alcohol or drugs. Family members are the most frequent victims of their aggression. Patients with a propensity for violence include those intoxicated by drugs or alcohol; those going through drug or alcohol withdrawal; and those with acute paranoid schizophrenic state, a paranoid character or an antisocial personality.

A specially designated room with at least two exits should be used for the interview. No objects that could be used as weapons should be in sight. Security staff, a family member or another health care worker should be asked to remain in case additional help is needed.

Suicidal Patients

Suicide is an act that stems from depression (e.g., because of the loss of a loved one, the loss of body integrity or status, poor self-image) and can be viewed as a cry for help and intervention. Those at risk include the following: older people; males; young adults; people who are enduring unusual loss or stress; those who are unemployed, divorced, widowed or living alone; those who are showing significant depression (evidenced by weight loss, sleep disturbances, somatic complaints, suicidal preoccupation); and those who have a history of previous suicidal attempt or completed suicide(s) in the family, or who have a psychiatric illness.

SEXUAL ASSAULT (RAPE)

Legally, rape is defined as carnal knowledge of a female by force or the threat of force against her will. It is one of the fastest growing crimes of violence. The manner in which the victim is received and treated in the emergency department is important to her future psychological well-being. She should be seen immediately upon entry into the emergency department. Most hospitals have a written protocol that reflects consideration for the victim's physical and emotional needs as well as concern for meeting requirements for subsequent legal proceedings.

The patient's reaction to rape has been termed the 'rape trauma syndrome' and is an acute stress reaction to a life-threatening situation. A rape trauma victim should be cared for by staff of the same sex. The nurse performing the assessment should be aware that the patient may go through several phases of psychological reactions:

1. An acute disorganization phase which may be manifested in two ways:
   a. Expressed state, in which shock, disbelief, fear, guilt, humiliation, anger, etc., are encountered.
   b. Controlled state, in which feelings are masked or hidden and the victim appears composed.
2. A phase of denial and unwillingness to talk about the incident, followed by a phase of heightened anxiety, fear, flashbacks, sleep disturbances, hyper-alertness and psychosomatic reactions.
3. A phase of reorganization, in which the incident is put into perspective. Some victims never fully recover and develop chronic stress disorders and phobias.

MANAGEMENT OF PATIENTS WITH BURN INJURY

Altered Physiology of Burns

Burns are caused by a transfer of energy from a heat source to the body. Heat may be transferred through conduction or electromagnetic radiation. Burns can be categorized as thermal, radiation, electrical or chemical. Tissue destruction results from coagulation, protein denaturation or ionization of cellular contents. The skin and the mucosa of the upper airways are the most common sites of tissue destruction. Deep tissues, including the viscera, can be damaged by electrical burns or through prolonged contact with the burning agent.

The first effect of a burn is to produce a dilatation of the capillaries and small vessels in the area of the burn, thus increasing capillary permeability. Plasma seeps out into the surrounding tissues, producing blisters and oedema. The type, the duration and the intensity of the burn affect the amount and duration of the fluid loss.

One of the first steps in the management of burns is to replace the plasma, proteins and electrolytes which are lost from the vascular compartment and move to the interstitial compartment.

The fluid loss following a burn results in reduced fluid volume in the vascular system and a fall in blood pressure and cardiac output. Prompt fluid resuscitation maintains the blood pressure in the low normal range.

Extent of Burns and Local Response

Burn Depth

Burns are classified according to the depth of tissue destruction, and are identified as superficial partial-thickness injuries, deep partial-thickness injuries or full-thickness injuries. Corresponding descriptive terms are first-degree, second-degree and third-degree.

- In a superficial partial-thickness (first-degree) injury, the epidermis is destroyed or injured and a portion of the dermis may be injured. The wound may be painful and may appear red and dry, as in the case of sunburn, or it may be blistered.
- A deep partial-thickness (second-degree) injury involves destruction of the epidermis and upper layers of the dermis, and injury to deeper portions of the dermis. The wound is painful, appears red and weeps fluid. Blanching of the burned tissue is followed by capillary refill; hair follicles remain intact.
- A full-thickness (third-degree) injury involves total destruction of epidermis and dermis and, in some cases, underlying tissues as well. The colour of the wound varies widely. The burn is painless, due to

destruction of nerve fibres, and has a leathery appearance.

Extent of Surface Area Burned

Rule of Nines

An estimation of the total body surface area involved as a result of a burn is simplified by using the 'Rule of Nines' (Figure 39.3). The Rule of Nines measures the percentage of the body burned by dividing the body into multiples of nine. The initial evaluation is made upon arrival at the hospital and revised on the second and third postburn days, because the demarcation usually is not clear until then.

Berkow Method

A more reliable method of estimating the extent of burned surface area is provided by use of the Berkow method. By dividing the body into very small areas and providing an estimate of the proportion of body surface area accounted for by such body parts, it is possible to obtain a very reliable estimate of total surface area involved. This is helpful in estimating fluid requirements and determining prognosis and surgical intervention.

Survival Prediction

The best survival rate occurs in children and young adults, aged 5 to 40 years. In this group, burns of about 60 per cent of the body result in a mortality rate of 50 per cent. A burn of more than 20 per cent of the body endangers life. Prognosis depends on the depth and extent of the burn, as well as on the condition and age of the patient.

Management

Although the local effects of a burn are the most evident, the systemic effects pose a greater threat to life. Therefore, it is important for the nurse to remember the 'ABC' of all trauma care during the early postburn period:

- Airway.
- Breathing.
- Circulation.

Breathing must be assessed and a patent airway established immediately during the initial minutes of emergency care. Many burn victims sustain some degree of concomitant pulmonary dysfunction, as previously described.

- Immediate therapy is directed toward establishing an airway, possibly through oropharyngeal aspiration followed by the administration of 100 per cent oxygen. If such a high concentration of oxygen is not available under emergency conditions, oxygen by mask or nasal prongs is given initially.

In mild cases, inspired air is humidified and the patient is

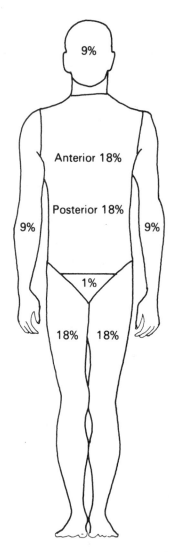

Figure 39.3 The 'Rule of Nines' for estimating the percentage of body burns in the adult.

encouraged to cough so that secretions can be aspirated. For more severe situations, it is necessary to remove secretions by bronchial aspiration and to administer bronchial dilators and mucolytic agents.

- When oedema of the airway is present, it may be necessary to intubate the patient. Continuous positive airway pressure and mechanical ventilation may also be required.

Prevention of shock in a person with a major burn is imperative. Therefore, intravenous fluid therapy should be initiated promptly. Nothing should be given by mouth, and the patient should be placed in a position which will prevent aspiration of vomitus, because nausea and vomiting often occur as a result of paralytic ileus resulting from the stress of injury. Assessment of the extent of body

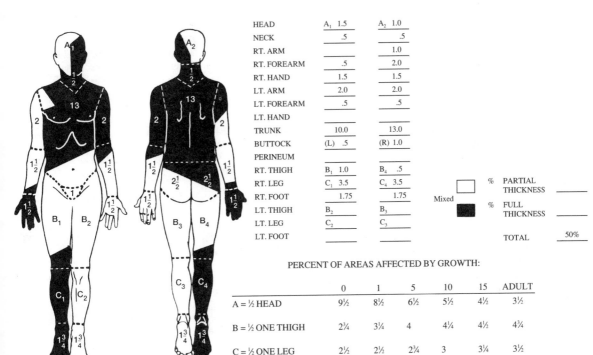

	A₁	A₂
HEAD	A_1 1.5	A_2 1.0
NECK	.5	.5
RT. ARM		1.0
RT. FOREARM	.5	2.0
RT. HAND	1.5	1.5
LT. ARM	2.0	2.0
LT. FOREARM	.5	.5
LT. HAND		
TRUNK	10.0	13.0
BUTTOCK	(L) .5	(R) 1.0
PERINEUM		
RT. THIGH	B_1 1.0	B_4 .5
RT. LEG	C_1 3.5	C_4 3.5
RT. FOOT	1.75	1.75
LT. THIGH	B_2	B_3
LT. LEG	C_2	C_3
LT. FOOT		

Mixed

	% PARTIAL THICKNESS	
	% FULL THICKNESS	
	TOTAL	50%

PERCENT OF AREAS AFFECTED BY GROWTH:

	0	1	5	10	15	ADULT
A = ½ HEAD	9½	8½	6½	5½	4½	3½
B = ½ ONE THIGH	2¾	3¼	4	4¼	4½	4¾
C = ½ ONE LEG	2½	2½	2¾	3	3¼	3½

Figure 39.4 Burn evaluation chart—estimation of percentage body burns. (Courtesy of Crozer-Chester Medical Center.)

surface area burned and the depth of the burn is carried out by the doctor and nurse. Full- and partial-thickness burns should be noted and documented on burn assessment diagrams (Figure 39.4). These assessments should beperformed after soot and debris have been gently cleansed from the burn wound. Assessment should be repeated frequently during the course of burn wound care.

FURTHER READING

Books

Abel, E. L. (1984) *A Dictionary of Drug Abuse Terms and Terminology*, Greenwood Press, Westport.

Abels, L. (1986) *Critical Care Nursing*, C. V. Mosby, St Louis.

Aguilera, D. C. and Messick, J. M. (1986) *Crisis Intervention*, C. V. Mosby, St Louis.

Bassuk, E. L. and Birk, A. W. (1984) *Emergency Psychiatry*, Plenum Press, New York.

Bayley, E. W. and Martin, M. T. (eds) (1985) *A Curriculum for Basic Burn Nursing Practice* (4th edition), University of Texas Medical Branch and Shriners Burns Institute for the American Burn Association, Galveston, Texas.

Bernstein, N. R. and Robson, M. C. (1983) *Comprehensive Approaches to the Burned Person*, Medical Examination Publishing Co, New Hyde Park.

Cain, H. D. (ed.) (1985) *Flint's Emergency Treatment and Management* (7th edition) W. B. Saunders, Philadelphia.

Cosgriff, J. H. Jr and Anderson, D. L. (1984) *The Practice of Emergency Care* (2nd editiion) J. B. Lippincott, Philadelphia.

DiGregorio, V. R. (ed.) (1984) *Rehabilitation of the Burn Patient*, Churchill Livingstone, New York.

Edlich, R. F., Spyker, D. A. and Haury, B. B. (1985) *Current Emergency Therapy '85*, Aspen Systems, Rockville, Maryland.

Etheredge, E. E. (1986) *Management Techniques in Surgery*, John Wiley, New York.

Eubanks, D. H. and Bone, R. C. (1985) *Comprehensive Respiratory Care*, C. V. Mosby, St Louis.

Figley, C. R. (ed.) *Trauma and Its Wake*, Brunner/Mazel, New York.

Fisher, S. V. and Helm, P. (1984) *Comprehensive Rehabilitation of Burns*, Williams & Wilkins, Baltimore.

Foley, T. S. and Davies, M. A. (1983) *Rape: Nursing Care of Victims*, C. V. Mosby, St Louis.

Fought, S. G. and Throwe, A. N. (1984) *Psychosocial Nursing Care of the Emergency Patient*, John Wiley, New York.

Gardner, L. B. (1986) *Textbook of Acute Internal Medicine*, Medical Examination Publishing, New Hyde Park, New York.

Goldfrank, L. R. *et al.* (1986) *Goldfrank's Toxicologic Emergencies* (3rd edition) Appleton-Century-Crofts, East Norwalk, Connecticut.

Harmon, A. R. (1985) *Nursing Care of the Adult Trauma Patient*, John Wiley, New York.

Heimbach, D. and Engrav, L. H. (1985) *Surgical Management of the Burn Wound*, Karger, New York.

Hoffer, H. P. (ed.) (1985) *Emergency Problems in the Elderly*, Medical Economics Books, Oradell, New Jersey.

Holloway, N. M. (1984) *Nursing the Critically Ill Adult*, Addison-Wesley, Menlo Park, California.

Hyman, S. E. (1984) *Manual of Psychiatric Emergencies*, Little, Brown & Co, Boston.

Johanson, B. C. *et al.* (1985) *Standards for Critical Care* (2nd edition), C. V. Mosby, St Louis.

Kreis, D. J. Jr and Baue, A. E. (1984) *Clinical Management of Shock*, University Park Press, Baltimore.

Krueger, D. W. (1984) *Emotional Rehabilitation of Physical Trauma and Disability*, SP Medical & Scientific Books, New York.

Mannon, J. M. (1985) *Caring for the Burned*, Charles C. Thomas, Springfield, Illinois.

May, H. L. (ed.) (1984) *Emergency Medicine*, John Wiley & Sons, New York.

Mills, J. *et al.* (1985) *Current Emergency Diagnosis and Treatment* (2nd edition) Lange Medical Publications, Los Altos, California.

Moore, E. E., Eiseman, B. and Van Way C. W. (1984) *Critical Decisions in Trauma*, C. V. Mosby, St Louis.

Nurse's Reference Library (1985) *Emergencies*, Springhouse Corp., Springhouse, Pennsylvania.

O'Boyle, C. M. *et al.* (1985) *Emergency Care: The First 24 Hours*, Appleton-Century-Crofts, Norwalk, Connecticut.

Parker, J. G. (1984) *Emergency Nursing*, John Wiley & Sons, New York.

Rippe, J. M. *et al.* (eds) (1985) *Intensive Care Medicine*, Little, Brown & Co, Boston.

Roberts, J. R. and Hedges, J. R. (1985) *Clinical Procedures in Emergency Medicine*, W. B. Saunders, Philadelphia.

Roberts, S. L. (1985) *Physiological Concepts and the Critically Ill Patient*, Prentice Hall, Englewood Cliffs, New Jersey.

Salisbury, R. E., Newman, N. M. and Dingaldein, G. P. (1983) *Manual of Burn Therapeutics*, Little, Brown & Co, Boston.

Wachtel, T. L., Kahn, V. and Frank, H. A. (eds) (1983) *Current Topics in Burn Care*, Aspen Systems, Rockville, Maryland.

Walsh, M. (1985) *A & E Nursing: A New Approach*, William Heinemann, Oxford.

Zander, H. and Stehling, L. (1984) *The Burn Patient: Anesthetic Management and Immediate Care*, Year Book Medical Publishers, Chicago.

USEFUL ADDRESSES

Chapter 2

Issues and Concepts in Medical–Surgical Nursing

INFECTION CONTROL

Division of Hospital Infection
Central Public Health Laboratory
61 Colindale Avenue
London
NW9 5HT

Communicable Disease Surveillance
Centre
61 Colindale Avenue
London
NW9 5HT

Hospital Infection Research Laboratory
Dudley Road Hospital
Birmingham
B18 7QH

Communicable Diseases (Scotland) Unit
Ruchill Hospital
Glasgow
G20 9NB

CANCER

BACUP (British Association of Cancer
United Patients)
121–3 Charterhouse Street
London
EC1M 6AA
(tel: 071-608 1661/1785; Freeline 0800
181199 for callers outside the 071 area)

Breast Care and Mastectomy
Association of Great Britain
26a Harrison Street
London
WC1H 8JG
(tel: 071-837 0908)

Cancer Relief Macmillan Fund
Anchor House
15–19 Britten Street
London
SW3 3TY
(tel: 071-351 7811)

CancerLink
17 Britannia Street
London
WC1X 9JN
(tel: 071-833 2451)

Line-Sainsbury Foundation
8–10 Crown Hill
Croydon
Surrey
CR0 1RY
(tel: 081-686 8808)

Marie Curie Memorial Foundation
28 Belgrave Square
London
SW1X 8QG
(tel: 071-235 3325)

Women's National Cancer Control
Campaign
1 South Audley Street
London
W1Y 5DQ
(tel: 071-499 7532)

PAIN

British Holistic Medical Association
179 Gloucester Place
London
NW1 6DX
(tel: 071-262 5299)

Council for Complementary and
Alternative Medicine
Suite 1
19a Cavendish Square
London
W1M 9AD
(tel: 071-409 1440)

Intractable Pain Society of Great Britain
and Northern Ireland
c/o Association of Anaesthetics of Great
Britain and Ireland
9 Bedford Square
London
WC1B 3RA
(tel: 071-631 1650)

TERMINAL ILLNESS

Cancer Relief Macmillan Fund
Anchor House
15–19 Britten Street
London
SW3 3TY
(tel: 071-351 7811)

CancerLink
17 Britannia Street
London
WC1X 9JN
(tel: 071-833 2451)

Compassionate Friends
6 Denmark Street
Bristol
BS1 5DQ
(tel: 0272 292778)

Cruse—Bereavement Care
Cruse House
126 Sheen Road
Richmond
Surrey
TW9 1UR
(tel: 081-940 4818)

Hospice Information Service
St Christopher's Hospice
51–9 Lawrie Park Road
Sydenham
London
SE26 6DZ
(tel: 081-778 9252)

Line-Sainsbury Foundation
8–10 Crown Hill
Croydon
Surrey
CR0 1RY
(tel: 081-686 8808)

Marie Curie Memorial Foundation
28 Belgrave Square
London
SW1X 8QG
(tel: 071-235 3325)

Terrence Higgins Trust
52–4 Gray's Inn Road
London
WC1X 8JU
(tel: Helpline (3 pm to 10 pm every
day)—071-242 1010; legal line (Weds
7 pm to 10 pm)—071-405 2381;
administration (weekdays, 10 am to
5 pm)—071-831 0330)

Chapter 7

Assessment and Care of Patients With Cardiac Disorders

British Heart Foundation
102 Gloucester Place
London
W1H 4DH
(tel: 071-935 0185)

International Studies of Infarct Survival
(ISIS)
Radcliffe Infirmary
Oxford
OX2 6HE

The Flora Project for Heart Disease
Prevention
25 North Row
London
W1R 2BY

Chest, Heart and Stroke Association
Tavistock House North
Tavistock Square
London
WC1H 9JE
(tel: 071-387 3012)

Chapter 9

Assessment and Care of Patients With Vascular and Peripheral Circulatory Disorders

Action on Smoking and Health (ASH)
5–11 Mortimer Street
London
WIN 7RH
(tel: 071-637 9843/6)

British Heart Foundation
102 Gloucester Place
London
W1H 4DH
(tel: 071-935 0185)

Raynaud's Association
112 Crewe Road
Alsager
Cheshire
ST7 2JA
(tel: 0270 872776)

The Society of Chiropodists
53 Welbeck Street
London
W1M 7HE

Chapter 10

Assessment and Care of Patients with Haematological Disorders

BACUP (British Association of Cancer
United Patients)
121–3 Charterhouse Street
London
EC1 6AA
(tel: 071-608 1661; Freephone 0800
181199 for callers outside the
071 area)

Cancer Aftercare and Rehabilitation
Society (CARE)
21 Zetland Road
Bristol
BS6 7AH
(tel: 0272 427419/232302)

CancerLink
17 Britannia Street
London
WC1X 9JN
(tel: 071-833 2451)

Hodgkin's Disease Association (also
caters for non-Hodgkin's lymphoma
sufferers)
PO Box 275
Haddenham
Aylesbury
Buckinghamshire
HP17 8JJ
(tel: 0844 291500 - 8.30 pm to 10 pm)

Leukaemia Care Society
PO Box 82
Exeter
Devon
EX2 5DP
(tel: 0392 64848)

Leukaemia Research Fund
43 Great Ormond Street
London
WC1N 3JJ
(tel: 071-405 0101)

Organization for Sickle Cell Anaemia
Research (OSCAR)
22 Pellatt Grove
Wood Green
London
N22 5PL
(tel: 081-889 3300)

Sickle Cell Society
54 Station Road
Harlesden
London
NW10 4BU
(tel: 081-961 7795)

UK Thalassaemia Society
107 Nightingale Lane
London
N8 7QY
(tel: 081-348 0437)

In addition to these organizations, all the national groups that provide the following: telephone helpline or information services; financial or practical help; emotional support or counselling; self-help or support groups (or help to set them up); hospice or domiciliary nursing to cancer patients, will generally do the same for patients with haematological malignancies.

Chapter 11

Assessment of Digestive and Gastrointestinal Function

KeyMed
Keymed House
Stock Road
Southend-on-Sea
Essex
SS2 5QH
(Publish information leaflets for patients: *Having an Upper GI Endoscopy*, *Having a Colonoscopy*, *Having an Oesophageal Dilatation*, *Looking After Your Oesophageal Tube*.)

Chapter 12

Assessment and Care of Patients With Upper Gastrointestinal Tract Disorders

British Association of Plastic Surgery
Nurses
Secretary, Mrs S. Briggs
11 Birds Close
Ransden Heath
Billericay
Essex

Chapter 13

Gastrointestinal Intubation and Special Nutritional Support

National Nutrition Nurses Group
Royal College of Nursing
Cavendish Square
London
W1

PINNT (Self-support group for those on home total parenteral nutrition)
c/o Carolyn Wheatley
76 Stirling Close
Raynham
Essex

Chapter 15

Assessment and Care of Patients With Intestinal Disorders

British Colostomy Association (BCA)
(formerly Colostomy Welfare Group)
13–15 Station Road
Reading
Berkshire
RG1 1LG
(tel: 0734 391537)

Colostomy Advisory Service
40 Craven Road
London
W2

Ileostomy Association of Great Britain and Ireland
David Eades
Amblehurst House
Black Scotch Lane
Mansfield
Nottinghamshire
NG18 4PF
(tel: 0623 28099)

Chapter 16

Assessment and Care of Patients With Hepatic and Biliary Disorders

Alcoholics Anonymous (AA)
General Service Office
PO Box 1
Stonebow House
Stonebow
York
YO1 2NJ
(tel: 0904 644026 admin.; Greater London 071-352 3001 (helpline), 10 am to 10 pm)

Al-Anon Family Groups
61 Great Dover Street
London
SE1 4YF
(tel:071-403 0888)

Alcohol Concern
305 Gray's Inn Road
London
WC1X 8QF
(tel: 071-833 3471)

Chapter 17

Assessment and Care of Patients With Diabetes Mellitus

British Diabetic Society
10 Queen Anne Street
London
W1M 0BD
(tel: 071-323 1531)

Chapter 22

Assessment and Care of Female Patients With Disorders Relating to the Reproductive Cycle

Abortion Counselling Service Phone-In
Monday to Friday, 7 to 9 pm
tel: 071-350 2229

Maternity Alliance
15 Britannia Street
London
WC1X 9JP
(tel: 071-837 1265)

Miscarriage Association
PO Box 24
Ossett
West Yorkshire
WF5 9XG
(tel: 0924 830515)

National Association for the Childless
Birmingham Settlement
318 Summer Lane
Birmingham
B19 3RL
(tel: 021-359 4887)

National Association for Premenstrual
Syndrome (NAPS)
PO Box 72
Sevenoaks
Kent
TN13 1QX
(tel: 0732 459378/(helpline) 0227
763133)

National Childbirth Trust (NCT)
(support for women who have
miscarried)
Alexandra House
Oldham Terrace
London
W3 6NH
(tel: 081-992 8637)

SAFTA, c/o Association for Spina
Bifida and Hydrocephalus
22 Upper Woburn Place
London
WC1 OPE
(tel: 071-388 1382: in cases of
termination for fetal abnormality only)

Women's Reproductive Rights
Information Centre
52–54 Featherstone Street
London
EC1

Chapter 23

Assessment and Care of Patients With Gynaecological Disorders

Endometriosis Self-Help Group
65 Holmdene Avenue
Herne Hill
London
SE2X 9LD
(tel: 071-737 4764)

Herpes Association
41 North Road
London
N7 9DP
(tel: 071-609 9061)

Hysterectomy Support Group (HSG)
The Venture
Green Lane
Upton
Huntingdon
Cambs
PE17 5YE
(tel: 081-690 5987)

Chapter 24

Assessment and Care of Patients With Breast Disorders

Booklets on breast self-examination
may be obtained from the following
organizations:

The Breast Care and Mastectomy
Association of Great Britain
26a Harrison Street
London
WC1H 8JG
(tel: 071-837 0908)

Health Education Council
78 New Oxford Street
London
WC1

Marie Curie Memorial Foundation Fund
28 Belgrave Square
London
SW1X 8QG
(tel: 071-235 3325)

Women's National Cancer Control
Campaign
1 South Audley Street
London
W17 5DQ
(tel: 071-499 7532)

Chapter 25

Assessment and Care of Male Patients With Disorders Relating to the Reproductive System

Patient information booklets available
from:

British Association for Cancer United
Patients (BACUP)
121–123 Charterhouse Street
London
EC1M 6AA
(tel: 071-608 1661; freephone 0800
181199 for callers outside the 071 area)

Chapter 26

The Immune System, Immunopathology and Immunodeficiency

Body Positive
51b Philbeach Gardens
London
SW5 9EB
(tel: 071-373 9124)

Department Of Health
AIDS Unit, Room 231
Friars House
157-68 Blackfriars Road
London
SE1 8EU
(tel: 071-972 2000)

Health Education Authority
Mabledon Place
London
WC1
(tel: 071-383 3833)

Landmark
47a Tulse Hill
Brixton
London
SW2 2TN
(tel: 081-678 6686)

National AIDS Helpline
(tel: 0800 567 123)

Red Admiral Project
51a Philbeach Gardens
London
SW5 9EB
(tel: 071-835 1495)

Terrence Higgins Trust
52-4 Gray's Inn Road
London
WC1X 8JU
(tel: Helpline (3 pm to 10 pm every
day)—071-242 1010; legal line (Weds
7 pm to 10 pm)—071-405 2381;
administration (weekdays, 10 am to
5 pm)—071-831 0330)

Chapter 27

Assessment and Care of Patients With Rheumatic Disorders

Arthritis Care
5 Grosvenor Crescent
London
SW1X 7ER
(tel: 071-235 0902/5)

Arthritis and Rheumatism Council for Research
41 Eagle Street
London
WC1R 4AR
(tel: 071-405 8572)

Back Pain Association
31–3 Park Road
Teddington
Middlesex
TW11 OAB
(tel: 081-977 5474)

British League Against Rheumatism
c/o Arthritis and Rheumatism Council
41 Eagle Street
London
WC1R 4AR
(tel: 071-405 8572)

British Red Cross Society
9 Grosvenor Crescent
London
SW1X 7EJ
(tel: 071-235 5454)

British Society of Motoring Disability
Training Centre
102 Sydney Street
London
SW3
(tel: 071-351 2377)

Disabled Drivers' Association
Drake House
18 Creekside
London
SE8 3DZ
(tel: 081-692 7141)

Disabled Living Foundation
380–4 Harrow Road
London
W9 2HU
(tel: 071-289 6111)

Motability
Gate House
West Gate
Harlow
Essex
CM20 1HR
(tel: 0279 635666)

Royal Association for Disability and Rehabilitation (RADAR)
25 Mortimer Street
London
W1N 8AB
(tel: 071-637 5400)

Royal College of Nursing
Rheumatology Nursing Forum
Chairman
Miss Jan Maycock
c/o 11 Orford Road
Walthamstow
London
E17 9LP
(tel: 081-520 8971)

SPOD (Association to Aid the Sexual and Personal Relationships of People With a Disability)
286 Camden Road
London
N7 0BJ
(tel: 071-607 8851)

Chapter 28

Assessment and Care of Patients With Skin Disorders

British Red Cross Society
Beauty Care and Cosmetic Camouflage
(contact local branches)

Dystrophic Epidermolysis Bullosa
Research Association
7 Sandhurst Lodge
Wokingham Road
Crowthorne
Berkshire
RG11 7QD

National Eczema Society
Tavistock House East
Tavistock Square
London
WC1H 9SR
(tel: 071-388 4097)

Psoriasis Association
7 Milton Street
Northampton
NN2 7BJ
(tel: 0604 711129)

Society of Skin Camouflage
Wester Pitmenzies
Auchtermuchty
Fife

Chapter 29

Assessment and Care of Patients With Visual Disturbances and Eye Disorders

Association of Blind Asians
14 Stranraer Way
Freeling Street
Off Caledonian Road
London
N1 0DR

British Retinitis Pigmentosa Society
c/o Greens Norton Court
Greens Norton
Towcester
Northamptonshire
NN12 8BS
(tel: 0327 53276)

British Wireless For the Blind Fund
22b Great Portland Street
London
W1N 6AA

Eye Care Information Bureau
4 Ching Court
Shelton Street
London
WC2H 9DG

Forfar Training Centre
Dundee Road
Forfar
Tayside
(tel: 0307 63531)

Guide Dogs for the Blind Association
Alexandra House
9–11 Park Street
Windsor
Berkshire
SL4 1JR
(tel: 0753 855711)

International Glaucoma Association
c/o Mrs Wright
King's College Hospital
Denmark Hill
London
SE5 9RS
(tel: 071-737 3265)

Jewish Blind Society
221 Golders Green Road
London
NW11

Macular Disease Society
c/o 1 Herbert Road
Hornchurch
Essex
RM11 3LA

National Library for the Blind
Cromwell Road
Bredbury
Stockport
SK6 2SG
(tel: 061-494 0217)

Optical Information Council
Temple Chambers
Temple Avenue
London
EC4 0DT

Partially Sighted Society
Registered Office
Queen's Road
Doncaster
DN1 2NX
(tel: 0302 323132)

Royal National Institute for the Blind
224 Great Portland Street
London
W1A 6AA
(tel: 071-388 1266)

Scottish National Federation for the
Welfare of the Blind
8 St Leonards Bank
Perth
PH2 8EB

SENSE (The National Deaf-Blind and
Rubella Association)
311 Gray's Inn Road
London
WC1X 8PT
(tel: 071-278 1005)

Wales Council for the Blind
Oak House
12 The Bulwark
Brecon
Powys
LD3 7AD

Chapter 30

Assessment and Care of Patients With Hearing Disturbances and Ear Disorders

Cochlear Implant Programme
Royal Ear Hospital
Gower Street
London
WC1

Hearing Research Trust
330-2 Gray's Inn Road
London
WC1X 8EE
(tel: 071-833 1733)

Menière's Society
98 Maybury Road
Woking
Surrey
GU21 5HX
(tel: 0483 740597)

Noise Abatement Society
PO Box 8
Bromley
Kent
BR2 0UH
(tel: 081-460 3146)

Royal National Institute for the Deaf
(includes British Tinnitus Association)
105 Gower Street
London
WC1E 6AH
(tel: 071-387 8033)

Chapter 32

Assessment and Care of Patients With Neurological Dysfunction

Action for Research into Multiple
Sclerosis (ARMS)
4a Chapel Hill
Stanstead
Essex
CM24 8AG
(tel: 0279 81553 (admin.);
071-222 3123 (counselling service))

British Epilepsy Association
Anstey House
40 Hanover Square
Leeds
LS3 1BE
(tel: 0532 439393 (information centre);
0345 089599 (helpline))

Headway (National Head Injuries
Association)
200 Mansfield Road
Nottingham
NG1 3HX
(tel: 0602 622382)

Multiple Sclerosis Society of Great
Britain and Northern Ireland
25 Effie Road
London
SW6 1EE
(tel: 071-736 6267)

Muscular Dystrophy Group of Great
Britain and N. Ireland
Nattrass House
35 Macauley Road
London
SW4 0QP
(tel: 071-720 8055)

Parkinson's Disease Society
36 Portland Place
London
W1N 3DG
(tel: 071-255 2432)

SPOD (Association to Aid the Sexual
and Personal Relationships of People
With a Disability)
286 Camden Road
London
N7 0BJ
(tel: 071-607 8851)

Chapter 33

Assessment and Care of Patients With Neurological Disorders

Action for Research into Multiple Sclerosis (ARMS)
4a Chapel Hill
Stanstead
Essex
CM24 8AG
(tel: 0279 81553 (admin.); 071-222 3123 (counselling service))

BACUP (British Association of Cancer United Patients)
121–3 Charterhouse Street
London
EC1M 6AA
(tel: 071-608 1661; Freeline 0800 181199 for callers outside the 071 area)

British Epilepsy Association
Anstey House
40 Hanover Square
Leeds
LS3 1BE
(tel: 0532 439393 (information centre); 0345 089599 (helpline))

CancerLink
17 Britannia Street
London
WC1X 9JN
(tel: 071-833 2451)

Headway (National Head Injuries Association)
200 Mansfield Road
Nottingham
NG1 3HX
(tel: 0602 622382)

Multiple Sclerosis Society of Great Britain and Northern Ireland
25 Effie Road
London
SW6 1EE
(tel: 071-736 6267)

Muscular Dystrophy Group of Great Britain and N. Ireland
Nattrass House
35 Macauley Road
London
SW4 0QP
(tel: 071-720 8055)

Parkinson's Disease Society
36 Portland Place
London
W1N 3DG
(tel: 071-255 2432)

SPOD (Association to Aid the Sexual and Personal Relationships of People With a Disability)
286 Camden Road
London
N7 0BJ
(tel: 071-607 8851)

Tak Tent Office
132 Hill Street
Glasgow
G3 6UD

Chapter 34

Assessment of Musculoskeletal Function

Arthritis and Rheumatism Council for Research
41 Eagle Street
London
WC1R 4AR
(tel: 071-405 8572)

National Osteoporosis Society
Barton Meade House
PO Box 10
Radstock
Bath
Avon
BA3 3YB
(tel: 0761 32472)

Chapter 35

Assessment and Care of Patients With Musculoskeletal Dysfunction

Arthritis and Rheumatism Council for Research
41 Eagle Street
London
WC1R 4AR
(tel: 071-405 8572)

Scoliosis Society (Arise)
c/o The Scoliosis Unit
Royal National Orthopaedic Hospital
Brockley Hill
Stanmore
Middlesex
HA7 4LP

Scoliosis Association
380–4 Harrow Road
London
W9 2HU
(tel: 071-289 5652)

Chapter 36

Assessment and Care of Patients With Musculoskeletal Trauma

British Sports Association for the Disabled
Mary Glen Haig Suite
34 Osnaburgh Street
London
NW1 3ND
(tel: 071-383 7277)

Disabled Living Foundation
380–4 Harrow Road
London
W9 2HU
(tel: 071-289 6111)

Royal Association for Disability and Rehabilitation (RADAR)
25 Mortimer Street
London
W1N 8AB
(tel: 071-637 5400)

Chapter 37

Assessment and Care of Patients With Musculoskeletal Disorders

BACUP (British Association of Cancer United Patients)
121–3 Charterhouse Street
London
EC1 6AA
(tel: 071-608 1661; Freephone 0800 181199 for callers outside the 071 area)

Health Education Authority
Hamilton House
Mabledon Place
London
WC1H 9T

National Osteoporosis Society
Barton Meade House
PO Box 10
Radstock
Bath
Avon
BA3 3YB
(tel: 0761 32472)

Appendix

Appendix ▰

DIAGNOSTIC STUDIES AND THEIR MEANING

ABBREVIATIONS

kg	=	kilogram
g	=	gram
mg	=	milligram
µg	=	microgram
µµg	=	micromicrogram
ng	=	nanogram
pg	=	picogram
dl	=	100 millilitres
ml	=	millilitre
cu mm	=	cubic millimetre
fL	=	femtolitre
mM	=	millimole
nM	=	nanomole
mOsm	=	milliosmole
mm	=	millimetre
µ	=	micron or micrometre
mm Hg	=	millimetres of mercury
U	=	unit
mU	=	milliunit
µU	=	microunit
mEq	=	milliequivalent
IU	=	International Unit
mIU	=	milliInternational Unit

SI Units

g	=	gram
l	=	litre
d	=	day
h	=	hour
mol	=	mole
mmol	=	millimole
µmol	=	micromole
nmol	=	nanomole
pmol	=	picomole

Reference Ranges—Haematology*

Determination	Reference range Conventional units	SI Units	Clinical significance
A₂ haemoglobin	1.5%–3.5% of total haemoglobin	Mass fraction: 0.015–0.035 of total haemoglobin	Increased in certain types of thalassaemia
Bleeding time	2–8 min	2–8 min	Prolonged in thrombocytopenia, defective platelet function and aspirin therapy
Factor V assay (proaccelerin factor)	60%–140%		
Factor VII assay (antihaemophiliac factor)	50%–200%		Deficient in classical haemophilia
Factor IX assay (plasma thromboplastin component)	75%–125%		Deficient in Christmas disease (pseudohaemophilia)
Factor X (Stuart factor)	60%–140%		Deficient in Stuart clotting defect
Fibrinogen	200–400 mg/dl	2.0–4.0 g/l	Increased in pregnancy, in infections accompanied by leucocytosis and in nephrosis Decreased in severe liver disease and abruptio placentae
Fibrin split products	Less than 10 mg/litre	Less than 10 mg/l	Increased in disseminated intravascular coagulation
Fibrinolysins (whole blood clot lysis time)	No lysis in 24 hr		Increased activity associated with massive haemorrhage, extensive surgery and transfusion reactions
Partial thromboplastin time (activated)	28–40 sec		Prolonged in deficiency of fibrinogen and of factors II, V, VIII, IX, X, XI and XII, and in heparin therapy
Prothrombin consumption	Over 20 sec		Impaired in deficiency of factors VIII, IX, and X
Prothrombin time (PT)	12–16 sec		Prolonged by deficiency of factors I, II, V, VII, and X, fat malabsorption, severe liver disease, and coumarin-anticoagulant therapy
Thrombin time (TT)	8–15 sec		
Erythrocyte count (RBC)	Males: 4,600,000– 6,200,000/cu mm	$4.6-6.2 \times 10^{12}$/l	Increased in severe diarrhoea and dehydration, polycythaemia, acute poisoning, and pulmonary fibrosis
	Females: 4,200,000– 5,400,000/cu mm	$4.2-5.4 \times 10^{12}$/l	Decreased in all anaemias, in leukaemia, and after haemorrhage, when blood volume has been restored
Erythrocyte indices Mean corpuscular volume (MCV)	80–94 (cu μ)	78–97 fl	Increased in macrocytic anaemias, decreased in microcytic anaemia
Mean corpuscular haemoglobin (MCH)	27–32 μμg/cell	27–32 pg	Increased in macrocytic anaemias, decreased in microcytic anaemia
Mean corpuscular haemoglobin concentration (MCHC)	33%–35 %	Concentration fraction: 32–35 g/dl	Decreased in severe hypochromic anaemia

(continued)

Reference Ranges—Haematology* (continued)

Determination	Reference range Conventional units	SI Units	Clinical significance
Reticulocytes	0.2%–2.0% of red cells		Increased with any condition stimulating increase in bone marrow activity (i.e., infection, blood loss [acute and chronic]); following iron therapy in iron deficiency anaemia, polycythaemia rubra vera Decreased with any condition depressing bone marrow activity, acute leukaemia, late stage of severe anaemias
Erythrocyte sedimentation rate (ESR)—Westergren method	Males under 50 yr: <10 mm/hr Males over 50 yr: <20 mm/hr	<15 mm/hr <20 mm/hr	Increased in tissue destruction, whether inflammatory or degenerative; during menstruation and pregnancy; and in acute febrile diseases
	Females under 50 yr: <15 mm/hr Females over 50 yr: <30 mm/hr	<20 mm/hr <30 mm/hr	
Erythrocyte sedimentation ratio—Zeta centrifuge	41%–54% in both sexes	Fraction: 0.41–0.54	Significance similar to ESR
Haematocrit	Males: 40%–54%	Volume fraction: 0.40–0.54	Decreased in severe anaemias, anaemia of pregnancy, acute massive blood loss
	Females: 38%–47%	Volume fraction: 0.38–0.47	Increased in erythrocytosis of any cause, and in dehydration or haemoconcentration associated with shock
Haemoglobin	Males: 13–18 g/dl Females: 12–16 g/dl	2.02–2.79 mmol/l 1.86–2.48 mmol/l	Decreased in various anaemias, pregnancy, severe or prolonged haemorrhage and with excessive fluid intake Increased in polycythaemia, chronic obstructive pulmonary diseases, failure of oxygenation because of congestive heart failure, and normally in people living at high altitudes
Haemoglobin F	Less than 1% of total haemoglobin		Increased in infants and children, and in thalassemia and many anaemias
Leucocyte alkaline phosphatase	Score of 15–100		Increased in polycythaemia vera, myelofibrosis and infections; decreased in chronic granulocytic leukaemia, paroxysmal nocturnal haemoglobinuria, hypoplastic marrow and viral infections, particularly infectious mononucleosis

(continued)

Reference Ranges—Haematology* (continued)

Determination	Reference range Conventional units	SI Units	Clinical significance
Leucocyte count	Total: 4,000–11,000/cu mm	$5\text{–}10 \times 10^9/l$	Elevated in acute infectious diseases, predominantly in the neutrophilic fraction with bacterial diseases, and in the lymphocytic and monocytic fractions in viral diseases
Neutrophils	40%–75%	Number fraction: 0.6–0.7	
Eosinophils	1%–6%	Number fraction: 0.01–0.04	
Basophils	<1%	Number fraction: 0.00–0.05	Elevated in acute leukaemia, following menstruation and following surgery or trauma
Lymphocytes	20%–45%	Number fraction: 0.2–0.3	Depressed in aplastic anaemia, agranulocytosis and by toxic agents, such as chaemotherapeutic agents used in treating malignancy
Monocytes	2%–10%	Number fraction: 0.02–0.06	Eosinophils elevated in collagen diseases, allergy, intestinal parasitosis
Osmotic fragility of red cells	Increased if haemolysis occurs in over 0.5% NaCl Decreased if haemolysis is incomplete in 0.3% NaCl		Increased in congenital spherocytosis, idiopathic acquired haemolytic anaemia, isoimmune haemolytic disease, ABO haemolytic disease of newborn Decreased in sickle cell anaemia, thalassaemia
Platelet count	100,000–400,000/cu mm	$0.1\text{–}0.4 \times 10^{12}/l$	Increased in malignancy, myeloproliferative disease, rheumatoid arthritis and postoperatively; about 50% of patients with unexpected increase of platelet count will be found to have a malignancy Decreased in thrombocytopenic purpura, acute leukaemic aplastic anaemia, and during cancer chemotherapy, infections and drug reactions

*By radioimmunoassay
(Laboratory values vary according to the techniques used in different laboratories.)

Reference ranges—serum, plasma, whole blood chemistries

Determination	Normal adult reference range Conventional units	SI Units	Clinical significance Increased	Decreased
Acetoacetate	0.2–1.0 mg/dl	20–98 µmol/l	Diabetic acidosis Fasting	
Acetone	0.3–2.0 mg/dl	52–344 µmol/l	Toxaemia of pregnancy Carbohydrate-free diet High-fat diet	

(continued)

Reference ranges—serum, plasma, whole blood chemistries (continued)

Determination	Normal adult reference range Conventional units	SI Units	Clinical significance Increased	Decreased
Adrenocorticotropic hormone (ACTH)—plasma, RIA*	Less than 50 pg/ml	Less than 50 ng/l	Pituitary-dependent Cushing's syndrome Ectopic ACTH syndrome Primary adrenal atrophy	Adrenocortical tumour Adrenal insufficiency secondary to hypopituitarism
Aldolase	3–8 Sibley-Lehninger U/dl at 37°C	22–59 mU/l at 37°C	Hepatic necrosis Granulocytic leukaemia Myocardial infarction Skeletal muscle disease	
Aldosterone—plasma, RIA	Supine: 3–10 ng/dl Upright: 5–30 ng/dl Adrenal vein: 200–800 ng/dl	0.08–0.30 nmol/l 0.14–0.90 nmol/l 5.54–22.16 nmol/l	Primary aldosteronism (Conn's syndrome) Secondary aldosteronism	Addison's disease
Alpha-1-antitrypsin	200–400 mg/dl	2–4 g/l		Certain forms of chronic lung and liver disease in young adults
Alpha-1-fetoprotein	None detected		Hepatocarcinoma Metastatic carcinoma of liver Germinal cell carcinoma of the testis or ovary Premature fetal neural tube defects due to elevation in maternal serum	
Alpha-hydroxy-butyric dehydrogenase	Up to 140 U/ml	Up to 140 U/l	Myocardial infarction Granulocytic leukaemia Haemolytic anaemias Muscular dystrophy	
Ammonia (plasma)	40–80 μg/dl (enzymatic method); varies considerably with method	22.2–44.3 μmol/l	Severe liver disease Hepatic decompensation	
Amylase	60–160 Somogyi U/dl	111–296 U/l	Acute pancreatitis Mumps Duodenal ulcer Carcinoma of head of pancreas Prolonged elevation with pseudocyst of pancreas	Chronic pancreatitis Pancreatic fibrosis and atrophy Cirrhosis of liver Pregnancy (second and third trimesters)

(continued)

Reference ranges—serum, plasma, whole blood chemistries (continued)

Determination	Normal adult reference range Conventional units	SI Units	Clinical significance Increased	Decreased
			Increased by drugs that constrict pancreatic duct sphincters: morphine, codeine, cholinergics	
Arsenic	6–20 µg/dl; if 50 µg/dl, suspect toxicity	0.78–2.6 µmol/l	Accidental or intentional poisoning Excessive occupational exposure	
Ascorbic acid (vitamin C)	0.4–1.5 mg/dl	23–85 µmol/l	Large doses of ascorbic acid as a prophylactic against the common cold	
Bilirubin	Total: 0.1–1.2 mg/dl	1.7–20.5 µmol/l	Haemolytic anaemia (indirect)	
Biliary obstruction and disease	Direct: 0.1–0.2 mg/dl Indirect: 0.1–1 mg/dl	1.7–3.4 µmol/l		
	1.7–17.1 µmol/l	Hepatocellular damage (hepatitis) Pernicious anaemia Haemolytic disease of newborn		
Blood gases Oxygen, arterial (whole blood):				Anaemia
Cardiac obstruction Partial pressure (PaO_2) Saturation (SaO_2)	95–100 mm Hg 94%–100%	12.64–13.30 kPa Volume fraction: 0.94–1	Polycythemia Anhydremia	Chronic Anemia
Cardiac obstruction Chronic obstructive pulmonary disease Carbon dioxide, arterial (whole blood): partial pressure ($PaCO_2$)	35–45 mm Hg	4.66–5.99 kPA	Respiratory acidosis Metabolic alkalosis	Respiratory alkalosis Metabolic acidosis
pH (whole blood, arterial)	7.35–7.45	7.35–7.45	Vomiting Hyperpnea Fever Intestinal obstruction	Uremia Diabetic acidosis Haemorrhage Nephritis Calcitonin

(continued)

Reference ranges—serum, plasma, whole blood chemistries (continued)

Determination	Normal adult reference range Conventional units	SI Units	Clinical significance Increased	Decreased
	Basal: Nondetectable 400 pg/ml	400 ng/l	Medullary carcinoma of the thyroid Some nonthyroid tumors Zollinger-Ellison syndrome	
Calcium	8.5–10.5 mg/dl	2.125–2.625 mmol/l	Tumor or hyperplasia of parathyroid Hypervitaminosis D Multiple myeloma Nephritis with uremia Malignant tumors Sarcoidosis Hyperthyroidism Skeletal immobilization Excess calcium intake: milk-alkali syndrome	Hypoparathyroidism Diarrhea Celiac disease Vitamin D deficiency Acute pancreatitis Nephrosis After parathyroidectomy
CO_2	Adults: 24–32 mEq/l Infants: 18–24 mEq/l (venous)	24–32 mmol/l 18–24 mmol/l	Tetany Respiratory disease Intestinal obstruction Vomiting	Acidosis Nephritis Eclampsia Diarrhea Anesthesia
Carcinoembryonic antigen (CEA) RIA	0–2.5 ng/ml	0–2.5 μg/l	The repeatedly high incidence of this antigen in cancers of the colon, rectum, pancreas, and stomach suggest that CEA levels may be a useful adjunct in the diagnosis of these conditions and therapeutic monitoring.	
Catecholamines— plasma, RIA	Epinephrine, random up to 90 pg/ml Norepinephrine, random 100–550 pg/ml Dopamine, random up to 130 pg/ml	Up to 490 pmol/l 590–3,250 pmol/l Up to 850 pmol/l	Pheochromocytoma	
Ceruloplasmin	30–80 mg/dl	300–800 mg/l		Wilson's disease (hepatolenticular degeneration)
Chloride	95–105 mEq/l	95–105 mmol/l	Nephrosis Nephritis Urinary obstruction Cardiac decompensation Anaemia	Diabetes Diarrhoea Vomiting Pneumonia Heavy metal poisoning

(continued)

Reference ranges—serum, plasma, whole blood chemistries (continued)

Determination	Normal adult reference range Conventional units	SI Units	Clinical significance Increased	Decreased
				Cushing's syndrome Burns Intestinal obstruction Febrile conditions
Cholesterol	150–250 mg/dl	3.9–6.5 mmol/l	Lipemia Obstructive jaundice Diabetes Hypothyroidism	Pernicious anaemia Haemolytic anaemia Hyperthyroidism Severe infection Terminal states of debilitating disease
Cholinesterase	Serum: 0.6–1.6 delta pH Red cells: 0.6–1 delta pH	0.6–1.6 U 0.6–1 U	Nephrosis Exercise	Nerve gas intoxication (greater effect on red cell activity) Insecticides, organic phosphates (greater effect on plasma activity)
Chorionic gonadotropin, beta subunit—RIA	0–5 IU/l	0–5 IU/l	Pregnancy Hydatidiform mole Choriocarcinoma	
Complement, human C_3	Males: 88–252 mg/dl Females: 88–206 mg/dl	880–2,520 mg/l	Some inflammatory diseases	Acute glomerulonephritis Disseminated lupus erythematosus with renal involvement
Complement C_4	14–51 mg/dl	140–510 mg/l	Some inflammatory diseases	Often decreased in immunological disease, especially with active SLE Hereditary angioneurotic oedema
Complement total (haemolytic)	90%–94% complement		Some inflammatory diseases	Acute glomerulonephritis Epidemic meningitis Subacute bacterial endocarditis
Copper	70–165 µg/dl	11–25.9 µmol/l	Cirrhosis of liver Pregnancy	Wilson's disease
Cortisol—RIA	8 AM: 7–25 µg/dl 4 PM: 2–9 µg/dl	193–690 nmol/l 55–248 nmol/l	Stress: infectious disease, surgery, burns, etc. Pregnancy Cushing's syndrome	Addison's disease Anterior pituitary hypofunction

(continued)

Reference ranges—serum, plasma, whole blood chemistries (continued)

Determination	Normal adult reference range Conventional units	SI Units	Clinical significance Increased	Decreased
			Pancreatitis Eclampsia	
C-peptide reactivity	1.5–10 ng/ml	1.5–10 µg/l	Insulinoma	Diabetes
Creatine	0.2–0.8 mg/dl	15.3–61 µmol/l	Pregnancy Skeletal muscle necrosis or atrophy Starvation Hyperthyroidism	
Creatine phosphokinase (CPK)	Males: 50–325 mU/ml Females: 50–250 mU/ml	50–325 U/l 50–250 U/l	Myocardial infarction Skeletal muscle diseases Intramuscular injections Crush syndrome Hypothyroidism Delirium tremens Alcoholic myopathy Cerebrovascular disease	
Creatine phosphokinase isoenzymes	MM band present (skeletal muscle); MB band absent (heart muscle)		MB band increased in myocardial infarction, ischaemia	
Creatinine	0.7–1.4 mg/dl	62–124 µmol/l	Nephritis Chronic renal disease	Kidney diseases
Creatinine clearance	100–150 ml of blood cleared of creatinine per minute	1.67–2.5 ml/s		
Cryoglobulins, qualitative	Negative		Multiple myeloma Chronic lymphocytic leukaemia Lymphosarcoma Systemic lupus erythematosus Rheumatoid arthritis Subacute bacterial endocarditis Some malignancies Scleroderma	
11-Deoxycortisol	1 µg/dl	<0.029 µmol/l	Hypertensive form of virilizing adrenal hyperplasia due to an 11-ß-hydroxylase defect	
Dibucaine number	Normal: 70%–85% inhibition Heterozygote: 50%–65% inhibition			Important in detecting carriers of abnormal cholinesterase activity who are

(continued)

Reference ranges—serum, plasma, whole blood chemistries (continued)

Determination	Normal adult reference range Conventional units	SI Units	Clinical significance Increased	Decreased
	Homozygote: 16%–25% inhibition			susceptible to succinyldicholine anasthetic shock
Dihydrotestosterone	Males: 50–210 ng/dl Females: None detectable	1.72–7.22 nmol/l		Testicular feminization syndrome
Oestradiol—RIA	Females: Follicular: 10–90 pg/ml Midcycle: 100–500 pg/ml Luteal: 50–240 pg/ml Follicular phase: 2–20 ng/dl Midcycle: 12–40 ng/dl Luteal phase: 10–30 ng/dl Postmenopausal: 1–5 ng/dl Males: 0.5–5 ng/dl	37–370 pmol/l 367–1835 pmol/l 184–881 pmol/l	Pregnancy	Depressed or failure to peak: ovarian failure
Oestriol—RIA	Nonpregnant females: <0.5 ng/ml Pregnant females: 1st trimester: up to 1 ng/ml 2nd trimester: 0.8–7 ng/ml 3rd trimester: 5–25 ng/ml	<1.75 nmol/l Up to 3.5 nmol/l 2.8–24.3 nmol/l 17.4–86.8 nmol/l	Pregnancy	Depressed or failure to peak: ovarian failure
Oestrogens, total—RIA	Females cycle days: Day 1–10: 61–394 pg/ml Day 11–20: 122–437 pg/ml Day 21–30: 156–350 pg/ml Males: 40–115 pg/ml	61–394 ng/l 122–437 ng/l 156–350 ng/l 40–115 ng/l	Pregnancy Measured on a daily basis, can be used to evaluate response of hypogonadotrophic, hypo-oestrogenic women to human menopausal or pituitary gonadotropin	Fetal distress Ovarian failure
Oestrone—RIA	Females: Day 1–10: 4.3–18 ng/dl Day 11–20: 7.5–19.6 ng/dl Day 21–30: 13–20 ng/dl Males: 2.5–7.5 ng/dl	15.9–66.6 pmol/l 27.8–72.5 pmol/l 48.1–74 pmol/l 9.3–27.8 pmol/l	Pregnancy	Depressed or failure to peak: ovarian failure

(continued)

Reference ranges—serum, plasma, whole blood chemistries (continued)

Determination	Normal adult reference range Conventional units	SI Units	Clinical significance Increased	Decreased
Ferritin—RIA	Males: 10–270 ng/ml Females: 5–100 ng/ml	10–270 µg/l 5–100 µg/l	Nephritis Haemochromatosis Certain neoplastic diseases Acute myelogenous leukaemia Multiple myeloma	Iron deficiency
Folic acid—RIA	4–16 ng/ml	9.1–36.3 nmol/l		Megaloblastic anaemias of infancy and pregnancy Inadequate diet Liver disease Malabsorption syndrome Severe haemolytic anaemia
Follicle stimulating hormone (FSH)— RIA	Females: Follicular phase: 5–20 mIU/ml Peak of middle cycle: 12–30 mIU/ml Luteinic phase: 5–15 mIU/ml Menopausal females: 40–200 mIU/ml	5–20 IU/l 12–30 IU/l 5–15 IU/l 40–200 IU/l	Menopause and primary ovarian failure	Pituitary failure
Galactose	<5 mg/dl	<0.28 mmol/l		Galactosaemia
Gamma glutamyl transpeptidase	Males: <45 IU/l Females: <30 IU/l	45 U/l 30 U/l	Hepatobiliary disease Anicteric alcoholics Drug therapy damage Myocardial infarction Renal infarction	
Gastrin—RIA	Fasting: 50–155 pg/ml Postprandial: 80–170 pg/ml Zollinger-Ellison syndrome: 200– over 2,000 pg/ml Pernicious anaemia: 130–2,260 pg/ml (mean 912)	50–155 ng/l 80–170 ng/l 200-over 2,000 ng/l 130–2,260 ng/l (mean 912)	Zollinger-Ellison syndrome Peptic ulceration of the duodenum Pernicious anaemia	
Glucose	Fasting: 60–110 mg/dl Postprandial (2 hr): 65–140 mg/dl	3.3–6.05 mmol/l 3.58–7.7 mmol/l	Diabetes Nephritis Hyperthyroidism Early hyperpituitarism Cerebral lesions	Hyperinsulinism Hypothyroidism Late hyperpituitarism Pernicious vomiting Addison's disease

(continued)

Reference ranges—serum, plasma, whole blood chemistries (continued)

Determination	Normal adult reference range Conventional units	SI Units	Clinical significance Increased	Decreased
			Infections Pregnancy Uraemia	Extensive hepatic damage
Glucose tolerance (oral)	Features of a normal response: 1. Normal fasting between 60–110 mg/dl 2. No sugar in urine 3. Upper limits of normal are: Fasting–125 1 hour–190 2 hours–140 3 hours–125	3.3–6.05 mmol/l 6.88 mmol/l 10.45 mmol/l 7.70 mmol/l 6.88 mmol/l	(Flat or inverted curve) Hyperinsulinism Adrenal cortical insufficiency (Addison's disease) Anterior pituitary hypofunction Hypothyroidism Sprue and coeliac diseases	(High or prolonged curve) Diabetes Hyperthyroidism Primary adrenal cortical tumour or hyperplasia Severe anaemia Certain central nervous system disorders
Glucose-6-phosphate dehydrogenase (red cells)	Screening: Decolourization in 20–100 min Quantitative: 1.86–2.5 IU/ml RBC	1,860–2,500 U/l RBC		Drug-induced haemolytic anaemia Haemolytic disease of newborn
Glycoprotein (alpha-1 acid)	40–110 mg/dl	400–1,100 mg/l	Neoplasm Tuberculosis Diabetes complicated by degenerative vascular disease Pregnancy Rheumatoid arthritis Rheumatic fever Infectious liver disease Lupus erythematosus	
Growth hormone—RIA	<10 ng/ml	<10 µg/l	Acromegaly	Failure to stimulate with argrine or insulin—hypopituitarism
Haptoglobin	50–250 mg/dl	500–2,500 mg/l	Pregnancy Oestrogen therapy Chronic infections Various inflammatory conditions	Haemolytic anaemia Haemolytic blood transfusion reaction
Haemoglobin (plasma)	0.5–5 mg/dl	0.08–0.78 µmol/l	Transfusion reactions Paroxysmal nocturnal haemoglobinuria Intravascular haemolysis	

(continued)

Reference ranges—serum, plasma, whole blood chemistries (continued)

Determination	Normal adult reference range Conventional units	SI Units	Clinical significance Increased	Decreased
Hexosaminidase, total	Controls: 333–375 nM/ml/hr Heterozygotes: 288–644 nM/ml/hr Tay-Sachs disease: 284–1,232 nM/ml/hr Diabetics: 567–3,560 nM/ml/hr	333–375 μmol/l/h 288–644 μmol/l/h 284–1,232 μmol/l/h 567–3,560 μmol/l/h	Diabetes Tay-Sachs disease	
Hexosaminidase A	Controls: 49%–68% of total Heterozygotes: 26%–45% of total Tay-Sachs disease: 0%–4% of total Diabetics: 39%–59% of total	Fraction of total: 0.49–0.68 0.26–0.45 0–0.04 0.39–0.59		Tay-Sachs disease and heterozygotes

High-density lipoprotein cholesterol (HDL cholesterol)

Age (yr)	Males (mg/dl)	Females (mg/dl)	Males (mmol/l)	Females (mmol/l)
0–19	30–65	30–70	0.78–1.68	0.78–1.81
20–29	35–70	35–75	0.91–1.81	0.91–1.94
30–39	30–65	35–80	0.78–1.68	0.91–2.07
40–49	30–65	40–85	0.78–1.68	1.04–2.2
50–59	30–65	35–85	0.78–1.68	0.91–2.2
60–69	30–65	35–85	0.78–1.68	0.91–2.2

Decreased: It has been claimed that HDL cholesterol is lower in patients with increased risk for coronary heart disease; this, however, has not been universally accepted

Determination	Conventional units	SI Units	Increased	Decreased
17-Hydroxy-progesterone—RIA	Males: 0.4–4 ng/ml Females: 0.1–3.3 ng/ml Children: 0.1–0.5 ng/ml	1.2–12 nmol/l 0.3–10 nmol/l 0.3–1.5 nmol/l	Congenital adrenal hyperplasia Pregnancy Some cases of adrenal or ovarian adenomas	
Immunoglobulin A	Adults: 50–300 mg/dl (in children the normals are lower and vary with age)	0.5–3 g/l	Gamma A myeloma Wiskott-Aldrich syndrome Autoimmune disease Hepatic cirrhosis	Ataxia telangiectasis Agammaglobulinaemia Hypogamma-globulinaemia, transient Dysgamma-globulinaemia Protein-losing enteropathies
Immunoglobulin D	0–30 mg/dl	0–300 mg/l	IgD multiple myeloma Some patients with chronic infectious diseases	
Immunoglobulin E	20–740 ng/ml	20–740 μg/l	Allergic patients and those with parasitic infestations	

(continued)

Reference ranges—serum, plasma, whole blood chemistries (continued)

| Determination | Normal adult reference range | | Clinical significance | |
	Conventional units	SI Units	Increased	Decreased

Immunoglobulin G	Adults:
	635–1,400 mg/dl
		6.35–14 g/l	IgG myeloma
			Following
			  hyperimmunization
			Autoimmune disease
			  states
			Chronic infections
				Congenital and
				  acquired
				  hypogamma-
				  globulinaemia
				IgA myelomas,
				  Waldenstrom's
				  (IgM) macro-
				  globulinaemia
				Some
				  malabsorption
				  syndromes
				Extensive protein
				  loss

Immunoglobulin M	Adults: 40–280 mg/dl	40–2,800 mg/l	Waldenstrom's
			  macro-
			  globulinaemia
			Parasitic infections
			Hepatitis
				Agamma-
				  globulinaemias
				Some IgG and IgA
				  myelomas
				Chronic lymphatic
				  leukaemia

Insulin—RIA	5–25 µU/ml	5–25 mU/l	Insulinoma Acromegaly	Diabetes mellitus
Iodine, butanol extractable	3.5–6.5 mg/dl	0.28–0.51 µmol/l	Hyperthyroidism	Hypothyroidism
Iodine, protein- bound	4–8 µg/dl	0.32–0.63 µmol/l	Hyperthyroidism	Hypothyroidism
Iron	65–170 µg/dl	11.6–30.4 µmol/l	Pernicious anaemia Aplastic anaemia Haemolytic anaemia Hepatitis Haemochromatosis	Iron deficiency anaemia

Iron-binding capacity	IBC: 150–235 µg/dl
	TIBC: 250–420 µg/dl
	% Saturation: 20–50
		26.9–42.1 µmol/l
		44.8–75.2 µmol/l
		Fraction of total
		  iron-binding
		  capacity:
		  0.2–0.5
			Iron deficiency
			  anaemia
			Acute and chronic
			  blood loss
			Hepatitis
				Chronic infectious
				  diseases
				Cirrhosis

Isocitric
  dehydrogenase
	50–180 U	0.83–3 U/l	Hepatitis: cirrhosis
			Obstructive jaundice
			Metastatic carcinoma of
			  the liver
			Megaloblastic
			  anaemia	

Lactic acid (whole
  blood)
	Venous: 5–20 mg/dl
	Arterial: 3–7 mg/dl
		0.6–2.2 mmol/l
		0.3–0.8 mmol/l
			Increased muscular
			  activity
			Congestive heart
			  failure
			Haemorrhage
			Shock
			Some varieties of
			  metabolic acidosis
			Some febrile
			  infections	

(continued)

Reference ranges—serum, plasma, whole blood chemistries (continued)

| Determination | Normal adult reference range | | Clinical significance | |
	Conventional units	SI Units	Increased	Decreased
			May be increased in severe liver disease	
Lactic dehydrogenase (LDH)	100–225 mU/ml	100–225 U/l	Untreated pernicious anaemia Myocardial infarction Pulmonary infarction Liver disease	
Lactic dehydrogenase isoenzymes Total lactic dehydrogenase LDH-1 LDH-2 LDH-3 LDH-4 LDH-5	100–225 mU/ml 20%–35% 25–40% 20–30% 0–20% 0–25%	100–225 U/l Fraction of total LDH: 0.2–0.35 0.25–0.4 0.2–0.3 0–0.2 0–0.25	LDH-1 and LDH-2 are increased in myocardial infarction, megaloblastic anaemia and haemolytic anaemia LDH-4 and LDH-5 are increased in pulmonary infarction, congestive heart failure, and liver disease	
Lead (whole blood)	Up to 40 µg/dl	Up to 2 µmol/l	Lead poisoning	
Leucine aminopeptidase	80–200 U/ml	19.2–48 U/l	Liver or biliary tract diseases Pancreatic disease Metastatic carcinoma of liver and pancreas Biliary obstruction	
Lipase	0.2–1.5 U/ml	55–417 U/l	Acute and chronic pancreatitis Biliary obstruction Cirrhosis Hepatitis Peptic ulcer	
Lipids, total	400–1,000 mg/dl	4–10 g/l	Hypothyroidism Diabetes Nephrosis Glomerulonephritis Hyperlipo-proteinemias	Hyperthyroidism
Lipoprotein phenotype (*see Summary of Findings on p 1246*)				

*By radioimmunoassay

Summary of Findings in the Primary Hyperlipoproteinaemias

Type	Frequency	Appearance	Triglyceride	Cholesterol	Lipoprotein staining				Secondary Causes
					Beta	Pre-Beta	Alpha	Chylomicrons	
Normal		Clear	Normal	Normal	Moderate	Zero to moderate	Moderate	Weak	
I	Very rare	Creamy	Markedly increased	Normal to moderately increased	Weak	Weak	Weak	Markedly increased	Dysglobulinaemia
II	Common	Clear	Normal to slightly increased	Slightly to markedly increased	Strong	Zero to strong	Moderate	Weak	Hypothyroidism, myeloma, hepatic syndrome, macroglobulinaemia and high dietary cholesterol
III	Uncommon	Clear, cloudy, or milky	Increased	Increased	Broad intense band	Extends into beta	Moderate	Weak	
IV	Very common	Clear, cloudy, or milky	Slightly to markedly increased	Normal to slightly increased	Weak to moderate	Moderate to strong	Weak to Moderate	Weak	Hypothyroidism, diabetes mellitus, pancreatitis, glycogen storage diseases, nephrotic syndrome, myeloma, pregnancy and oral contraceptives
V	Rare	Cloudy to creamy	Markedly increased	Increased	Weak	Moderate	Weak	Strong	Diabetes mellitus, pancreatitis and alcoholism

Types I and II are fat induced: types III and IV are carbohydrate induced; type V is fat and carbohydrate induced

Reference ranges—serum, plasma, whole blood chemistries (continued)

Determination	Normal adult reference range Conventional units	SI Units	Clinical significance Increased	Decreased
Lithium	Usual maintenance level:			
	0.5–1 mEq/l	0.5–1 mmol/l		
Low-density lipoprotein cholesterol (LDL cholesterol)	Age (yr) mg/dl 0–19 50–170 20–29 60–170 30–39 70–190 40–49 80–190 50–59 80–210	mmol/l 1.30–4.40 1.55–4.40 1.80–4.92 2.07–4.92 2.07–5.44	LDL cholesterol is claimed to be higher in patients with increased risk for coronary heart disease. This claim, however, is not universally accepted	

Luteinizing hormone—RIA	Males: 6–30 mIU/ml
	Females:
	  Follicular phase:
	    2–3 mIU/ml
	  Ovulatory peak:
	    40–200 mIU/ml
	  Luteal phase:
	    0–20 mIU/ml
	  Postmenopausal:
	    35–120 mIU/ml
		1.4–6.9 mg/l
		
		0.5–6.9 mg/l
		
		9.2–46 mg/l
		
		0–5 mg/l
		
		8–27.5 mg/l
			Pituitary tumour
			Ovarian failure
				Depressed or failure to peak—pituitary failure

Lysozyme (muramidase)	2.8–8 µg/ml	2.8–8 mg	Certain types of leukaemia (acute monocytic leukaemia) Inflammatory states and infections	Acute lymphocytic leukaemia
Magnesium	1.3–2.4 mEq/l	0.7–1.2 mmol/l	Excess ingestion of magnesium-containing antacids	Chronic alcoholism Severe renal disease, diarrhoea Defective growth
Manganese	0.04–1.4 µg/dl	72.9–255 nmol/l		
Mercury	Up to 10 µg/dl	Up to 0.5 µmol/l	Mercury poisoning	
Myoglobin—RIA	Up to 85 ng/ml	Up to 85 µg/ml	Myocardial infarction Muscle necrosis	
Nonprotein nitrogen	20–35 mg/dl	14.3–25 mmol/l	Acute nephritis Polycystic kidneys Obstructive uropathy Peritonitis Congestive heart failure Pregnancy	
5' Nucleotidase	3.2–11.6 IU/l	3.2–11.6 U/l	Hepatobiliary disease	
Osmolality	280–300 mOsm/kg	280–300 mmol/l	Useful in the study of electrolyte and water balance	Inappropriate secretion of antidiuretic hormone
Parathyroid hormone	160–350 pg/ml	160–350 ng/l	Hyperparathyroidism	

(continued)

Reference ranges—serum, plasma, whole blood chemistries (continued)

Determination	Normal adult reference range		Clinical significance	
	Conventional units	SI Units	Increased	Decreased
Phenylalanine	1.2–3.5 mg/dl 1st week	0.07–0.21 mmol/l	Phenylketonuria	
	0.7–3.5 mg/dl thereafter	0.04–0.21 mmol/l		
Phosphatase, acid, total	0–11 IU/l	0–11 U/l	Carcinoma of prostate Advanced Paget's disease Hyperparathyroidism Gaucher's disease	
Phosphatase, acid, prostatic—RIA	0–10 ng/ml Borderline: 2.5–3.3 IU/l	0–3.3 U/l	Carcinoma of prostate	
Phosphatase, alkaline	Adults: 30–115 mU/ml	30–115 U/l	Conditions reflecting increased osteoblastic activity of bone Rickets Hyperparathyroidism Liver disease	
Phosphatase, alkaline, thermostable fraction	Thermostable fraction greater than 35%: hepatic disease and combined disease with predominant hepatic component Thermostable fraction between 25% and 35%: combined hepatic and skeletal disease Thermostable fraction <25%: skeletal disease with increased osteoblastic activity		Hepatic disease	
Phosphohexose isomerase	20–90 IU/l	20–90 U/l	Malignancy Disease of heart, liver, and skeletal muscles	
Phospholipids	125–300 mg/dl	1.25–3 g/l	Diabetes Nephritis	
Phosphorus, inorganic	2.5–4.5 mg/dl	0.8–1.45 mmol/l	Chronic nephritis Hypoparathyroidism	Hyperpara-thyroidism Vitamin D deficiency
Potassium	3.8–5 mEq/l	3.8–5 mmol/l	Addison's disease Oliguria Anuria Tissue breakdown or haemolysis	Diabetic acidosis Diarrhoea Vomiting

(continued)

Reference ranges—serum, plasma, whole blood chemistries (continued)

Determination	Normal adult reference range Conventional units	SI Units	Clinical significance Increased	Decreased
Progesterone—RIA	Follicular phase: up to 0.8 ng/ml Luteal phase: 10–20 ng/ml End of cycle: <ng/ml Pregnant: up to 50 ng/ml in 20th week	2.5 nmol/l 31.8–63.6 nmol/l <3 nmol/l Up to 160 nmol/l	Useful in evaluation of menstrual disorders and infertility and in the evaluation of placental function during pregnancies complicated by toxaemia, diabetes mellitus or threatened miscarriage	
Prolactin—RIA	6–24 ng/ml	6–24 µg/l	Pregnancy Functional or structural disorders of the hypothalamus Pituitary stalk section Pituitary tumours	
Protein, total Albumin Globulin	6–8 g/dl 3.5–5 g/dl 1.5–3 g/dl	60–80 g/l 35–50 g/l 15–30 g/l	Haemoconcentration Shock Multiple myeloma (globulin fraction) Chronic infections (globulin fraction) Liver disease (globulin)	Malnutrition Haemorrhage Loss of plasma from burns Proteinuria
Electrophoresis (cellulose acetate) Albumin Alpha-1 globulin Alpha-2 globulin Beta globulin Gamma globulin	3.5–5 g/dl 0.2–0.4 g/dl 0.6–1 g/dl 0.6–1.2 g/dl 0.7–1.5 g/dl	35–50 g/l 2–4 g/l 6–10 g/l 6–12 g/l 7–15 g/l		
Protoporphyrin erythrocyte (RBC)	15–100 µg/dl	0.27–1.80 µmol/l	Lead toxicity Erythropoietic porphyria	
Pyridoxine	3.6–18 ng/ml			A wide spectrum of clinical conditions such as mental depression, peripheral neuropathy, anaemia, neonatal seizures and reactions to certain drug therapies
Pyruvic acid (whole blood)	0.3–0.7 mg/dl	0.03–0.08 mmol/l	Diabetes Severe thiamine deficiency Acute phase of some infections, possibly secondary to increased glycogenolysis and glycolysis	

(continued)

Reference ranges—serum, plasma, whole blood chemistries (continued)

Determination	Normal adult reference range Conventional units	SI Units	Clinical significance Increased	Decreased
Renin (plasma)— RIA	Normal diet: Supine: 0.3–1.9 ng/ml/hr Upright: 0.6–3.6 ng/ml/hr Low salt diet: Supine: 0.9–4.5 ng/ml/hr Upright: 4.1–9.1 ng/ml/hr	0.3–1.9 µg/h/l-1-1 0.6–3.6 µg/h/1l-1 0.9–4.5 µg/l-1l 4.1–9.1 µg/l-1.l-1	Renovascular hypertension Malignant hypertension Untreated Addison's disease Primary salt-losing nephropathy Low-salt diet Diuretic therapy Haemorrhage	Frank primary aldosteronism Increased salt intake Salt-retaining steroid therapy Antidiuretic hormone therapy Blood transfusion
Sodium	135–145 mEq/l	135–145 mmol/l	Haemoconcentration Nephritis Pyloric obstruction	Alkali deficit Addison's disease Myxoedema
Sulphate (inorganic)	0.5–1.5 mg/dl	0.05–0.15 mmol/l	Nephritis Nitrogen retention	
Testosterone—RIA	Females: 25–100 ng/dl Males: 300–800 ng/dl	0.9–3.5 nmol/l 10.5–28 nmol/l	Females: Polycystic ovary Virilizing tumours	Males: Orchidectomy for neoplastic disease of the prostate or breast Oestrogen therapy Klinefelter's syndrome Hypopituitarism Hypogonadism Hepatic cirrhosis
T_3 (tri-tiodothyronine) uptake	25%–35%	Relative uptake fraction: 0.25–0.35	Hyperthyroidism TBG deficiency Androgens and anabolic steroids	Hypothyroidism Pregnancy TBG excess Oestrogens and antiovulatory drugs
T_3, total circulating— RIA	75–200 ng/dl	1.15–3.1 nmol/l	Pregnancy Hyperthyroidism	Hypothyroidism
T_4 (thyroxine)—RIA	4.5–11.5 µg/dl	58.5–150 nmol/l	Hyperthyroidism Thyroiditis Elevated thyroxine-binding proteins caused by oral contraceptives Pregnancy	Primary and pituitary hypothyroidism Idiopathic involvement Cases of diminished thyroxine-binding proteins caused by androgenic and anabolic steroids Hypoproteinaemia Nephrotic syndrome

(continued)

Reference ranges—serum, plasma, whole blood chemistries (continued)

Determination	Normal adult reference range Conventional units	SI Units	Clinical significance Increased	Decreased
T_4, free	1–2.2 ng/dl	13–30 pmol/l	Euthyroid patients with normal free thyroxine levels may have abnormal T_3 and T_4 levels caused by drug preparations	
Thyroid stimulating hormone (TSH)—RIA	0–10 µIU/ml	0-10-3 IU/l	Primary hypothyroidism	
Thyroid-binding globulin	10–26 µg/dl	6–16 mg/l	Hypothyroidism Pregnancy Oestrogen therapy Oral contraceptives Genetic and idiopathic	Androgens and anabolic steroids Nephrotic syndrome Marked hypoproteinaemia Hepatic disease
Transaminase, serum glutamic-oxaloacetate (SGOT, aspartate aminotransferase)	7–40 U/ml	4–20 U/l	Myocardial infarction Skeletal muscle disease Liver disease	
Transaminase, serum glutamic-oxaloacetate (SGPT, alanine aminotransferase)	10–40 U/ml	5–20 U/l	Same conditions as SGOT, but increase is more marked in liver disease than SGOT	
Transferrin	230–320 mg/dl	2.3–3.2 g/l	Pregnancy Iron-deficiency anaemia due to haemorrhaging Acute hepatitis Polycythaemia Oral contraceptives	Pernicious anaemia in relapse Thalassaemic and sickle cell anaemia Chromatosis Neoplastic and hepatic diseases
Triglycerides	10–150 mg/dl	0.10–1.65 mmol/l	See lipoprotein phenotype	
Tryptophan	1.4–3 mg/dl	68.6–147 nmol/l		Tryptophan-specific malabsorption syndrome
Tyrosine	0.5–4 mg/dl	27.6–220.8 mmol/l	Tyrosinosis	
Urea nitrogen (BUN)	10–20 mg/dl	3.6–7.2 mmol urea/l	Acute glomerulonephritis Obstructive uropathy Mercury poisoning Nephrotic syndrome	Severe hepatic failure Pregnancy

(continued)

Reference ranges—serum, plasma, whole blood chemistries (continued)

Determination	Normal adult reference range Conventional units	SI Units	Clinical significance Increased	Decreased
Uric acid	2.5–8 mg/dl	0.15–0.5 mmol/l	Gouty arthritis Acute leukaemia Lymphomas treated by chemotherapy Toxaemia of pregnancy	Xanthinuria Defective tubular reabsorption
Viscosity	1.4–1.8 relative to water at 37°C		Patients with marked increase of the gamma globulins	
Vitamin A	50–220 µg/dl	1.75–7.7 µmol/l	Hypervitaminosis A	Vitamin A deficiency Coeliac disease Sprue Obstructive jaundice Giardiasis Parenchymal hepatic disease
Vitamin B_1 (thiamine)	1.6–4 µg/dl	47.4–135.7 nmol/l		Anorexia Beriberi Polyneuropathy Cardiomyopathies
Vitamin B_6 (pyridoxal phosphate)	3.6–18 ng/ml	14.6–72.8 nmol/l		Chronic alcoholism Malnutrition Uraemia Neonatal seizures Malabsorption, such as coeliac syndrome
Vitamin B_{12}—RIA	130–785 pg/ml	100–580 pmol/l	Hepatic cell damage and in association with the myeloproliferative disorders (the highest levels are encountered in myeloid leukaemia)	Strict vegetarianism Alcoholism Pernicious anaemia Total or partial gastrectomy Ileal resection Sprue and coeliac disease Fish tapeworm infestation
Vitamin E	0.5–2 mg/dl	11.6–46.4 µmol/l		Vitamin E deficiency
Xylose absorption test	2 hr, 30–50 mg/dl	2.0–3.3 mmol/l		Malabsorption syndrome
Zinc	55–150 µg/dl	7.65–22.95 µmol/l	Zinc is essential for the growth and propagation of cell cultures and the functioning of several enzymes	

(continued)

Reference ranges—urine chemistry

Determination	Normal adult reference range Conventional units	SI Units	Clinical significance Increased	Decreased
Acetone and acetoacetate	Zero		Uncontrolled diabetes Starvation	
Acid mucopoly-saccharides	Negative		Hurler's syndrome Marfan's syndrome Morquio-Ulrich disease	
Aldosterone	Normal salt: Normal: 4–20 µg/24 hr Renovascular: 10–40 µg/24 hr Tumour: 20–100 µg/24 hr	11.1–55.5 nmol/d 27.7–111 nmol/d 55.4–277 nmol/d	Primary aldosteronism (adrenocortical tumour) Secondary aldosteronism Salt depletion Potassium loading ACTH in large doses Cardiac failure Cirrhosis with ascites formation Nephrosis Pregnancy	
Alpha amino nitrogen	50–200 mg/24 hr	3.6–14.3 mmol/d	Leukaemia Diabetes Phenylketonuria Other metabolic diseases	
Amylase	35–260 units excreted per hour	6.5–48.1 U/hr	Acute pancreatitis	
Arylsulfatase A	Greater than 2.4 U/ml			Metachromatic leucodystrophy
Bence-Jones protein	None detected		Myeloma	
Calcium	<150 mg/24 hr	<3.75 mmol/d	Hyperparathyroidism Vitamin D intoxication Fanconi syndrome	Hypoparathyroidism Vitamin D deficiency
Catecholamines	Total: 0–275 µg/24 hr Epinephrine: 10%–40% Norepinephrine: 60%–90%	0–275 µg/d Fraction total: 0.10–8.4 Fraction total: 0.60–0.90	Pheochromocytoma Neuroblastoma	
Chorionic gonadotrophin, qualitative (pregnancy test)	Negative		Pregnancy Chorionepithelioma Hydatidiform mole	
Copper	20–70 µg/24 hr	0.32–1.12 µmol/d	Wilson's disease Cirrhosis Nephrosis	
Coproporphyrin	50–300 µg/24 hr	75–450 nmol/d	Poliomyelitis Lead poisoning Porphyria hepatica Porphyria erythropoietica Porphyria cutanea tarda	

(continued)

Reference ranges—urine chemistry (continued)

Determination	Normal adult reference range Conventional units	SI Units	Clinical significance Increased	Decreased
Cortisol, free	20–90 µg/24 hr	55.2–248.4 nmol/d	Cushing's syndrome	
Creatine	0–200 mg/24 hr	0–1.52 mmol/d	Muscular dystrophy Fever Carcinoma of liver Pregnancy Hyperthyroidism Myositis	
Creatinine	0.8–2 gm/24 hr	7–17.6 mmol/d	Typhoid fever Salmonella infections Tetanus	Muscular atrophy Anaemia Advanced degeneration of kidneys Leukaemia
Creatinine clearance	100–150 ml. of blood cleared of creatinine per minute	1.67–2.50 ml/s		Measures glomerular filtration rate Renal diseases
Cystine and cysteine	10–100 mg/24 hr	82–825 µmol/d	Cystinuria	
Delta aminolevulinic acid	0–0.54 mg/dl	0–40 µmol/l	Lead poisoning Porphyria hepatica Hepatitis Hepatic carcinoma	
11-Desoxycortisol	20–100 µg/24 hr	0.6–2.9 µmol/d	Hypertensive form of virilizing adrenal hyperplasia due to an 11-beta hydroxylase defect	
Oestriol (placental)	Weeks of pregnancy µm/24 hr 12 < 1 16 2–7 20 4–9 24 6–13 28 8–22 32 12–43 36 14–45 40 19–46	<3.5 nmol/d 7–24.5 nmol/d 14–32 nmol/d 21–45.5 nmol/d 28–77 nmol/d 42–150 nmol/d 49–158 nmol/d 66.5–160 nmol/d		Decreased values occur with fetal distress of many conditions, including pre-eclampsia, placental insufficiency and poorly controlled diabetes mellitus
Oestrogens, total (fluorometric)	Females: Onset of menstruation: 4–25 µg/24 hr Ovulation peak: 28 µg/24 hr Luteal peak: 22–105 µg/24 hr Menopausal: 1.4–19.6 µg/24 hr Males: 5–18 µg/24 hr	4–25 µg/d 28 µg/d 22–105 µg/d 1.4–19.6 µg/d 5–18 µg/d	Hyperoestrogenism due to gonadal or adrenal neoplasm	Primary or secondary amenorrhoea
Etiocholanolone	Males: 1.9–6 mg/24 hr Females: 0.5–4 mg/24 hr	6.5–20.6 µmol/d 1.7–13.8 µmol/d	Adrenogenital syndrome Idiopathic hirsutism	

(continued)

Reference ranges—urine chemistry (continued)

| Determination | Normal adult reference range | | Clinical significance | |
	Conventional units	SI Units	Increased	Decreased

Follicle-stimulating hormone—RIA	Females:
	  Follicular:
	    5–20 IU/24 hr
	  Luteal:
	    5–15 IU/24 hr
	  Midcycle:
	    15–60 IU/24 hr
	  Menopausal:
	    50–100 IU/24 hr
	Males: 5–25 IU/24 hr
		5–20 IU/d
		
		5–15 IU/d
		
		15–60 IU/d
		
		50–100 IU/d
		5–25 IU/d
			Menopause and primary ovarian failure	Pituitary failure

Glucose	Negative		Diabetes mellitus Pituitary disorders Intracranial pressure Lesion in floor of 4th ventricle	
Haemoglobin and myoglobin	Negative		Extensive burns Transfusion of incompatible blood Myoglobin increased in severe crushing injuries to muscles	
Homogentisic acid, qualitative	Negative		Alkaptonuria Ochronosis	
Homovanillic acid	Up to 15 mg/24 hr	Up to 82 μmol/d	Neuroblastoma	
17-hydroxycorti-costeroids	2–10 mg/24 hr	5.5–27.5 μmol/d	Cushing's disease	Addison's disease Anterior pituitary hypofunction
5-Hydroxyin-doleacetic acid, qualitative	Negative		Malignant carcinoid tumours	
Hydroxyproline	15–43 mg/24 hr	0.11–0.33 μmol/d	Paget's disease Fibrous dysplasia Osteomalacia Neoplastic bone disease Hyperparathyroidism	

17-ketosteroids, total	Males:
	  10–22 mg/24 hr
	Females:
	  6–16 mg/24 hr
		35–76 μmol/d
		
		21–55 μmol/d
			Interstitial cell tumour of testes
			Simple hirsutism, occasionally
			Adrenal hyperplasia
			Cushing's syndrome
			Adrenal cancer, virilism
			Arrhenoblastoma
				Thyrotoxicosis
				Female hypogonadism
				Diabetes mellitus
				Hypertension
				Debilitating disease of mild to moderate severity
				Eunuchoidism
				Addison's disease
				Panhypopituitarism
				Myxedema
				Nephrosis

Lead	Up to 150 μg/24 hr	Up to 60 μmol/d	Lead poisoning	

(continued)

Reference ranges—urine chemistry (continued)

Determination	Normal adult reference range Conventional units	SI Units	Clinical significance Increased	Decreased
Luteinizing hormone	Males: 5–18 IU/24 hr Females: Follicular phase: 2–25 IU/24 hr Ovulatory peak: 30–95 IU/24 hr Luteal phase: 2–20 IU/24 hr Postmenopausal: 40–110 IU/24 hr	 2–25 IU/d 30–95 IU/d 2–20 IU/d 40–110 IU/d	Pituitary tumour Ovarian failure	Depressed or failure to peak— pituitary failure
Metanephrines, total	Less than 1.3 mg/24 hr	Less than 6.5 μmol/d	Pheochromocytoma; a few patients with pheochromocytoma may have elevated urinary metanephrines but normal catecholamines and VMA	
Osmolality	Males: 390–1,090 mM/kg Females: 300–1,090 mM/kg	390–1,090 μOsmol/kg 300–1,090 mmol/kg	Useful in the study of electrolyte and water balance	
Oxalate	Up to 40 mg/24 hr	Up to 456 μmol/d	Primary hyperoxaluria	
Phenylpyruvic acid qualitative	Negative		Phenylketonuria	
Phosphorus, inorganic	0.8–1.3 gm/24 hr	26–42 mmol/d	Hyperparathyroidism Vitamin D intoxication Paget's disease Metastatic neoplasm to bone	Hypopara- thyroidism Vitamin D deficiency
Porphobilinogen, qualitative	Negative		Chronic lead poisoning Acute porphyria Liver disease	
Porphobilinogen, quantitative	0–1 mg/24 hr	0–4.4 μmol/d	Acute porphyria Liver disease	
Porphyrins, qualitative	Negative		See porphyrins, quantitative	
Porphyrins, quantitative (coproporphyrin and uroporphyrin)	Coproporphyrin: 50–160 μg/24 hr Uroporphyrin: up to 50 μg/24 hr	75–240 nmol/d 60 nmol/d	Porphyria hepatica Porphyria erythropoietica Porphyria cutanea tarda Lead poisoning (only coproporphyrin increased)	
Potassium	40–65 mEq/24 hr	40–65 mmol/d	Haemolysis	

(continued)

Reference ranges—urine chemistry (continued)

Determination	Normal adult reference range Conventional units	SI Units	Clinical significance Increased	Decreased

Pregnanediol	Females:
	  Proliferative phase:
	    0.5–1.5 mg/24 hr
	  Luteal phase:
	    2–7 mg/24 hr
	  Menopause:
	    0.2–1 mg/24 hr
	  Pregnancy:
	  Weeks of
	  gestation *mg/24 hr*
	  10–12 5–15
	  12–18 5–25
	  18–24 15–33
	  24–28 20–42
	  28–32 27–47
	
	  Males: 0.1–2
		
		1.6–4.8 µmol/d
		
		6–22 µmol/d
		
		0.6–3.1 µmol/d
		
		15.6–47 µmol/d
		15.6–78.0 µmol/d
		47.0–103.0 µmol/d
		62.4–131.0 µmol/d
		84.2–146.6 µmol/d
		
		0.3–6.2 µmol/d
			Corpus luteum cysts
			When placental
			  tissue remains in
			  the uterus following
			  parturition
			Some cases of
			  adrenocortical
			  tumours
				Placental
				  dysfunction
				Threatened
				  abortion
				Intrauterine death

Pregnanetriol	0.4–2.4 mg/24 hr	1.2–7.1 µmol/d	Congenital adrenal
			  androgenic
			  hyperplasia	

Protein	Up to 100 mg/24 hr	Up to 100 mg/d	Nephritis Cardiac failure Mercury poisoning Bence-Jones protein in multiple myeloma Febrile states Haematuria	

Sodium	130–200 mEq/24 hr	130–200 mmol/d	Useful in detecting
			  gross changes in
			  water and salt
			  balance	

Titratable acidity	20–40 mEq/24 hr	20–40 mmol/d	Metabolic acidosis	Metabolic alkalosis

Urea nitrogen	9–16 gm/24 hr	150–267 mmol
		  urea/d
			Excessive protein
			  catabolism
				Impaired kidney
				  function

Uric acid	250–750 mg/24 hr	1.48–4.43 mmol/d	Gout	Nephritis

Urobilinogen	Random urine:
	  <0.25 mg/dl
	24-hour urine: up to
	  4 mg/24 hr
		
		<4.2 µmol/d
		Up to 6.76 µmol/d
			Liver and biliary tract
			  disease
			Haemolytic
			  anaemias
				Complete or nearly
				  complete biliary
				  obstruction
				Diarrhoea
				Renal insufficiency

Uroporphyrins	Up to 50 µg/24 hr	Up to 0.06 µmol/d	Porphyria	

Vanillylmandelic acid
  (VMA)
	0.7–6.8 mg/24 hr	3.5–34.3 µmol/d	Pheochromocytoma
			Neuroblastoma
			Coffee, tea, aspirin,
			  bananas and
			  several different
			  drugs	

Xylose absorption
  test (5 hour)
	16%–33% of
	  ingested xylose
		Fraction absorbed:
		  0.16–0.33
				Malabsorption
				  syndromes

Zinc	0.15–1.2 mg/24 hr	2.3–18.4 µmol/d	Zinc is an essential nutritional element	

continued

Reference ranges—cerebrospinal fluid

Determination	Normal adult reference range		Clinical significance	
	Conventional units	SI Units	Increased	Decreased
Albumin	15–30 mg/dl	150–300 mg/l	Certain neurological disorders Lesion in the choroid plexus or blockage of the flow of CSF Damage to the blood–CNS barrier	
Cell count	0–5 mononuclear cells per cu/mm	$0–5 \times 10^6$/l	Bacterial meningitis Neurosyphilis Anterior poliomyelitis Encephalitis lethargica	
Chloride	100–130 mEq/l	100–130 mmol/l	Uraemia	Acute generalized meningitis Tuberculous meningitis
Glucose	50–75 mg/dl	2.75–4.13 mmol/l	Diabetes mellitus Diabetic coma Epidemic encephalitis Uraemia	Acute meningitides Tuberculous meningitis Insulin shock
Glutamine	6–15 mg/dl	0.41–1 mmol/l	Hepatic encephalopathies, including Reye's syndrome Hepatic coma Cirrhosis	
IgG	0–6.6 mg/dl	0–66 mg/l	Damage to the blood–CNS barrier Multiple sclerosis Neurosyphilis Subacute sclerosing panencephalitis Chronic phases of CNS infections	
Lactic acid	Less than 24 mg/dl	Less than 2.7 mmol/l	Bacterial meningitis Hypocapnia Hydrocephalus Brain abscesses Cerebral ischaemia	
Lactic dehydrogenase	One-tenth that of serum	Activity fraction: 0.1 of serum	CNS disease	
Protein: Lumbar Cisternal Ventricular	 15–45 mg/dl 15–25 mg/dl 5–15 mg/dl	 150–450 mg/l 150–250 mg/l 50–150 mg/l	Acute meningitides Tubercular meningitis Neurosyphilis Poliomyelitis Guillain-Barré syndrome	

(continued)

Reference ranges—cerebrospinal fluid (continued)

Determination	Normal adult reference range Conventional units	SI Units	Clinical significance Increased	Decreased
Protein electrophoresis (cellulose acetate)	% of total	Fraction:	An increase in the level of albumin alone can be the result of a lesion in the choroid plexus or a blockage of the flow of CSF. An elevated gamma globulin value with a normal albumin level has been reported in multiple sclerosis, neurosyphilis, subacute sclerosing panencephalitis and the chronic phase of CNS infections. If the blood–CNS barrier has been severely damaged during the course of these diseases, the CSF albumin level may also be elevated.	
Prealbumin	3–7	0.03–0.07		
Albumin	56–74	0.56–0.74		
Alpha$_1$ globulin	2–6.5	0.02–0.065		
Alpha$_2$ globulin	3–12	0.03–0.12		
Beta globulin	8–18.5	0.08–0.185		
Gamma globulin	4–14	0.04–0.14		

Miscellaneous values

Determinations	Normal Value	Clinical significance (Conventional units)	SI Units
Acetaminophen	Zero	Therapeutic level = 10–20 µg/ml	66–132 µmol/l
Aminophylline (theophylline)	Zero	Therapeutic level = 10–20 µg/ml	55–111 µmol/l
Bromide	Zero	Therapeutic level = 5–50 mg/dl	6.3–62.5 mmol/l
Carbon monoxide	0%–2%	Symptoms with over 20% saturation	Fraction >0.20
Chlordiazepoxide	Zero	Therapeutic level = 1–3 µg/ml	3.3–9.9 µmol/l
Diazepam	Zero	Therapeutic level = 0.5–2.5 µg/dl	0.18–0.88 µmol/l
Digitoxin	Zero	Therapeutic level = 5–30 ng/ml	6.6–39.3 nmol/l
Digoxin	Zero	Therapeutic level = 0.5–2 ng/ml	0.64–2.56 nmol/l
Ethanol	0%–0.01%	Legal intoxication level = 0.10% or above	2.2 mmol/l
		0.3%–0.4% = marked intoxication	6.5–8.7 mmol/l
		0.4%–0.5% = alcoholic stupor	8.7–10.9 mmol/l
Gentamicin	Zero	Therapeutic level = 4–10 µg/ml	8.4–16.7 µmol/l
Methanol	Zero	May be fatal in concentration as low as 10 mg/dl	3.1 mmol/l
Phenobarbital	Zero	Therapeutic level = 15–40 µg/ml	65–172 µmol/l

(continued)

Miscellaneous values (continued)

Determinations	Normal Value	Clinical significance (Conventional units)	SI Units
Phenytoin	Zero	Therapeutic level = 10–20 µg/ml	40–79 µmol/l
Primidone	Zero	Therapeutic level = 5–12 µg/ml	23–55 µmol/l
Quinidine	Zero	Therapeutic level = 0.2–0.5 mg/dl	6–15 µmol/l
Salicylate	Zero	Therapeutic level = 2–25 mg/dl Toxic level = over 30 mg/dl	145–1,810 µmol/l 2,172 µmol/l
Sulphonamide	Zero	Therapeutic levels: Sulphadiazine 8–15 mg/dl Sulphaguanidine 3–5 mg/dl Sulphamerazine 10–15 mg/dl Sulphanilamide 10–15 mg/dl	 80–150 mg/l 30–50 mg/l 100–150 mg/l 100–150 mg/l

Gastric analysis

Determination	Normal adult reference range Conventional units	SI Units	Clinical significance Increased	Decreased
pH	<2	<2		Pernicious anaemia
Basal acid output	0–6 mEq/hr	0–6 mmol/h	Peptic ulcer	Gastric carcinoma
Maximum acid	5–40 mEq/hr	5–40 mmol/h	Zollinger-Ellison syndrome	Chronic atrophic gastritis Decreased normally with age

GLOSSARY

Accommodation—adjustment of the eye for seeing at different distances, accomplished by changing the shape of the lens through the action of the ciliary muscles, thus focusing a clear image on the retina

Acidosis—an acid–base disturbance characterized by increased hydrogen ion concentration (decreased pH); may be due to increased production of acids or loss of base

Adenocarcinoma—malignant lesion of glandular tissue

Agranulocytosis—acute disease in which the white blood cell count decreases to extremely low levels and neutropenia is pronounced

Akinesia—inability to initiate a muscular movement

Alkalosis—an acid-base disturbance characterized by decreased hydrogen ion concentration (increased pH); may be due to loss of acids or increased production of base

Anaesthesia—inability to appreciate touch

Analgesia—inability to feel pain

Aneurysm—a dilation or swelling of an artery

Anterior horn—portion of spinal grey matter containing motor nerve cells

Anticoagulants—drugs that prevent the coagulation of blood (e.g., heparin, warfarin)

Anticonvulsants—medications used to control epileptic fits

Aortic incompetence—incomplete closure of the aortic valve cusps during ventricular diastole

Aortic stenosis—narrowing of the valve orifice between the left ventricle and the aorta

Aphakia—absence of the lens

Aphasia—inability to speak

Aplasia—failure of an organ or tissue to develop normally

Applanation tonometry—method of measuring intraocular pressure

Arteriogram/arteriography—a radio-opaque dye is injected into an artery and a series of X-rays is taken to show the path of the dye in the arteries

Astereogenesis—inability to recognize objects by size and shape

Ataxia—unsteady gait

Atherosclerosis—a generalized disease of the arteries in which plaques of yellow fatty (cholesterol) material called atheroma are deposited in the wall of the artery, resulting in narrowing and irregularity of the vessel

Band cell—immature granulocyte

Basal cell carcinoma (rodent ulcer)—cancer of the skin, which very rarely metastasizes; instead it spreads locally, following tissue planes

Basophil—a granular leucocyte

Blepharitis—inflammation of the lid margins

Bruit—murmur, noise heard with the aid of a stethoscope, that is due to turbulent blood flow within cardiovascular system

Bulbar—relating to, or affecting, the medulla oblongata

Burr hole—a hole drilled in the skull

Capsule—membrane around a tumour or abscess

Cardiopulmonary bypass procedure—mechanical means of circulating and oxygenating the blood while diverting it from the heart and lungs

Cataract—lens opacity

Chalazion—inflammation of a meibomian gland

Cheilitis—inflammation of the lip

Chiasma—X-shaped structure formed by the crossing of the two optic nerves

Cisterns—reservoir for cerebrospinal fluid, e.g. cisterna magna, lying beneath the cerebellum and behind the medulla oblongata

Concave lens—minus lens to correct myopia

Convex lens—plus lens to correct hypermetropia

Claudication (intermittent)—pain in the leg, usually calf but can be in the thigh, experienced on walking; pain is relieved by resting leg, but reappears on resumption of walking

Collateral circulation—alternative blood vessels that develop as a natural attempt to overcome an arterial occlusion

Dacron—artificial fibre used for making sutures and artificial arteries for grafting

Demyelination—Loss of myelin around neurone

Diabetes insipidus—deficiency of antidiuretic hormone leading to passage of large quantities of urine

Diadochokinesis—inability to perform quick alternating movements

Diffusion—passive movement of particles from an area of high concentration to one of lower concentration

Dioptre—unit of measurement of strength or refractive power of lenses

(a 1 dioptre lens brings parallel light rays to a focus at 1 metre from the lens)

Diplopia—seeing one object as two ('double vision')

Distal—furthest away

Dominant hemisphere—the cerebral hemisphere that controls speech

Dorsiflexion—bending backwards (wrist or ankle)

Dys—(prefix) difficulty, e.g. dysphasia—in expressing thoughts, dysarthria—in clear pronunciation

Ecchymosis—a blue/black discolouration that results from seepage of blood into skin or mucous membrane

Ectropion—turning-out (eversion) of the eyelid

Edentulous—without teeth

Electroencephalography (EEG)—electrical activity of the brain

Electromyography (EMG)—electrical activity of muscle

Embolectomy—an operation at which an embolus is removed

Embolus—a body, usually a blood clot, that travels in the bloodstream and causes obstruction to the circulation at the point where its progress is arrested

Endarterectomy—an operation in which an atherosclerotic plaque occlusion is removed

Endophthalmitis—extensive intraocular infection

Entropion—turning-in of the eyelid

Eosinophil—a granular leucocyte

Epiphora—watering eyes usually due to a fault in the lacrimal drainage channels

Erythrocyte—red blood cell

Erythroplakia—a red patch

Erythropoiesis—the formation of red blood cells

Erythropoietin—hormone that regulates red blood cell production

Esophoria—tendency for one eye to turn inwards

Exophoria—tendency for one eye to turn outwards

Extracranial—outwith the skull

Extradural—between the dura and the skull

Field of vision—the entire area that can be seen without shifting the gaze

Flaccid—loss of muscle tone (flabby, floppy)

Flexor spasm—painful contractions of spastic limb muscles

Focal—limited to, arising from one area

Focal epilepsy—a fit arising from one part of the brain, affecting one area of the body

Foramen—an opening

Functional—disturbance occurring to the working of some part and not to the actual structure

Ganglia—collection of nerve cells

Gangrene—the death of tissue with infection and putrefaction

Generalized fits—convulsions affecting all parts of the body

Glaucoma—abnormally raised intra-ocular pressure

Glioma—tumours growing from the supporting cells, glial cells

Glossitis—inflammation of the tongue

Grand mal—epilepsy characterized by major generalized fits

Granulocyte—granular leucocyte: polymorphonuclear leucocyte (neutrophil, basophil or eosinophil)

Granulocytopenia—abnormal reduction of granulocytes in the blood

Haematocrit—fraction of the blood occupied by erythrocytes

Haematopoiesis—production and development of blood cells

Haemopoietic—blood-producing

Haemoglobin—iron-containing pigment of red blood cells

Haemolysis—destruction of red blood cells with liberation of haemoglobin into the surrounding fluid

Hemianopia—blindness of one half of the field of vision of one or both eyes

Hemiplegia(-paresis)—paralysis (weakness) of one half of the body

Histiocyte—cell of loose connective tissue that shows phagocytic activity

Hydrostatic pressure—force exerted by a fluid against the walls of the container (in the body, the pressure of fluid against the walls of the blood vessels results from the weight of the fluid itself and the force resulting from cardiac contraction)

Hyperaemia—an increase in blood supply to an area

Hypermetropia—far-sightedness

Hyperplasia—excessive proliferation of normal cells in normal tissue

Hypertonic solution—one with more dissolved particles than another solution (i.e., more than the number of particles in normal body fluids)

Hypochromia—blood possessing less than normal colour and haemoglobin content

Hypotonic solution—one with fewer dissolved particles than another solution (i.e., fewer than the number of particles in normal body fluids)

Idiopathic—unknown cause

Infarct—small, localized area of dead tissue

Intracranial—within the skull

Involuntary movement—movement not under patient's control

Ischaemia—a reduction in the blood supply

Isotonic solution—solution in which the number of dissolved particles is equal to the number of particles dissolved in normal body fluids

Jacksonian fits—convulsion originating at one point of the body (e.g., the angle of the mouth, the thumb or great toe) and spreading to involve wider areas

Kernig's sign—inability to straighten knees when thighs are held at a right-angle to body, without causing severe pain from meningeal irritation

Lacrimation—excessive production of tears

Leucocyte—white blood cell

Leucopenia—abnormal decrease of white blood cells

Leucoplakia—white patch or plaque that cannot be classified clinically or pathologically as a disease, and is not derived from the use of any physical or chemical agent, except tobacco

Local/localize—one point affected/determination of the exact point affected

Lymphocyte—a mononuclear leucocyte

Lysis—disintegration or dissolution of cells

Macrocyte—a large-sized red blood cell

Macrophage—cells of the reticuloendothelial system that have the ability to phagocytose particulate matter

Megaloblast—abnormally large red blood cells

Meninges—three membranes surrounding the brain and cord

Meningitis—inflammation of the meninges

Microcyte—a small-sized red blood cell

Mitral incompetence—infectious process caused by rheumatic or bacterial endocarditis, which causes fibrotic and calcific changes that thicken, shorten and deform the valve cusps so that they do not completely close

Mitral stenosis—progressive thickening and contracture of valve cusps, with narrowing of the orifice and progressive obstruction to blood

Monocyte—a mononuclear leucocyte

Mononuclear leucocyte—agranulocyte (lymphocyte, monocyte)

Myasthenia—weakness of muscle

Myelography—X-ray of vertebral canal using radio-opaque contrast

Myopia—near-sightedness

Necrosis—death of tissue

Neuralgia—nerve pain

Neuromuscular junction—area where a motor nerve fibre meets the muscle fibre that it supplies

Neutrophil—a granular leucocyte

Normochromic—normal colour of cells

Normocytic—normal size of cells

Oculomotor—in relation to eye movement

Osmolality—number of dissolved particles contained in a specific unit or volume of fluid (i.e., 1 litre)

Osmosis—movement of fluid through a semipermeable membrane from an area of low concentration to an area of high concentration of particles to equalize the concentration on both sides of the membrane

Otorrhoea—any ear discharge

Oxyhaemoglobin—haemoglobin combined with oxygen

Pancytopenia—reduction in all cellular elements of the blood

Papilloedema—swelling of the optic disc

Paraesthesia—abnormal sensations

Paraplegia (paresis)—paralysis (weakness) of lower limbs

Parkinsonism—rigidity and tremor associated with Parkinson's disease

Percutaneous transluminal coronary angioplasty—technique of inserting a balloon-tipped catheter into the affected coronary artery and reducing the stenosis by inflating the balloon

Petit mal—minor epilepsy

Petechiae—small red or purple haemorrhagic spots on the skin

Phagocytosis—the process of ingestion and digestion of bacteria and particles

Photophobia—abnormal sensitivity to light

Plasma—liquid part of the blood

Platelet—thrombocyte; cell fragment found in the blood that plays an important role in coagulation, haemostasis and thrombus formation

Polymethylmethacrylate—synthetic used in intraocular lenses and hard contact lenses

Postpericardiotomy syndrome—group of abnormal behaviours that occur in varying intensity and duration; including fever, malaise and pleural effusion

Presbyopia—lessening of power of accommodation due to the ageing process

Proprioception—ability to know where each part of the body is in space

Ptosis—drooping of the upper eyelid

Quadraplegia/tetraplegia (paresis)—paralysis (weakness) of all four limbs

Reflex heating—electric heat pad is placed on the body trunk; warmed blood stimulates the vasomotor centre in the brain, causing vasodilation of the vessels in the affected limb

Reticulocyte—immature red blood cell

Reticuloendothelial system—cells scattered throughout the body that have the ability to phagocytose particulate matter (bacteria, colloidal particles)

Retinal detachment—separation of the retina from the choroid

Scotoma—a blind or partially blind area in the field of vision

Serum—the watery portion of the blood that remains after coagulation

Slit lamp—a combination light and microscope for examination of the eye, particularly the anterior segment

Squamous cell carcinoma (epithelioma)—a cancer arising in nonglandular, epithelial tissue (e.g., skin)

Spasticity—increased muscular tone

Spherocyte—an erythrocyte that assumes a spheroid shape

Spondylosis—degenerative changes in discs and vertebrae in spine

Status epilepticus—one fit rapidly following another

Stomatitis—inflammation of the mouth

Stomatitis nicotina—a characteristic form of leucoplakia of the palate, seen in pipe-smokers of long standing

Subarachnoid—between arachnoid and pia

Subdural—between dura and arachnoid

Sympathectomy—selective removal of sympathetic nerves to a limb

Sympathetic ophthalmitis—inflammation in one eye following severe trauma to the other eye

Thrombocyte—platelet

Thrombocytopenia—abnormal decrease in number of platelets

Tic—recurrent spasm, tic douloureux

Tone—tension present in a muscle when at rest

Tricuspid incompetence—allows the regurgitation of blood from the right ventricle into the right atrium during ventricular systole

Tricuspid stenosis—fibrotic and calcific changes of the valve that result in a narrowing of the orifice, which impedes the flow of blood from the right atrium to the right ventricle

Varicose veins— dilated, tortuous and lengthened superficial veins (varices); once the veins are dilated the valves become incompetent as they do not reach across the dilated vein; this increases the pressure in the vein, gradually causing the varicosities to increase

Visual acuity—detailed central vision

Xanthochronic—yellow coloured

INDEX